Colonial Massachusetts
Silversmiths and Jewelers

PATRICIA E. KANE

Colonial Massachusetts Silversmiths and Jewelers

*A biographical dictionary based on the notes
of Francis Hill Bigelow & John Marshall Phillips*

with contributions by JEANNINE J. FALINO

DEBORAH A. FEDERHEN

PATRICIA E. KANE

BARBARA MCLEAN WARD

GERALD W. R. WARD

and the assistance of Karen L. Wight & Edgard Moreno

Yale University Art Gallery

Distributed by University Press of New England, Hanover and London

The research for this publication was made possible by a grant from
THE NATIONAL ENDOWMENT FOR THE HUMANITIES,
a Federal agency, and the ongoing support of
THE FRIENDS OF AMERICAN ARTS AT YALE.

Publication costs were underwritten by
THE GARVAN PUBLICATION FUND,
THE VIRGINIA AND LEONARD MARX PUBLICATION FUND, *and*
JOSEPHINE SETZE.

Distributed for Yale University Art Gallery
by University Press of New England, Hanover and London.

Library of Congress Cataloging-in-Publication Data:

Kane, Patricia E.

Colonial Massachusetts silversmiths and jewelers : a biographical dictionary based on
the notes of Francis Hill Bigelow & John Marshall Phillips / Patricia E. Kane ; with
contributions by Jeannine J. Falino . . . [et al.] and the assistance of Karen L. Wight &
Edgard Moreno.

     p.   cm.

Includes bibliographical references and index.

ISBN 0-89467-077-8

  1. Silversmiths—Massachusetts—Biography—Dictionaries.

  2. Jewelers—Massachusetts—Biography—Dictionaries.

  3. Silverwork, Colonial—Massachusetts.

  I. Bigelow, Francis Hill, 1859–1933.

  II. Phillips, John Marshall, 1905–1953.

  III. Falino, Jeannine J.

  IV. Title

    NK7112.K35   1998

    739.2'3'722—dc21

    [B]

                  97-29813

                  CIP

Dedicated to the memory of

JOSEPHINE SETZE, 1902–82

Museum Assistant, 1930–40

Registrar, 1940–45

Assistant Curator of American Art, 1945–59

Curator of the Intra-University Loan Collection, 1959–67

Consultant to the American Silver Collection, 1967–82

at the Yale University Art Gallery

Contents

Foreword

SINCE 1930, when Francis P. Garvan donated the Mabel Brady Garvan Collection to Yale University, the Yale University Art Gallery has been one of the primary centers for the study and display of early American silver. The Art Gallery's collection of early American silver is acknowledged to be the finest in the nation, as silver was Garvan's favorite medium of American art. The presence of this great collection inspired many scholarly efforts in the field of American silver, one of which has culminated in this book.

When his collection was about to come to Yale, Garvan arranged for the University to hire as Assistant Curator John Marshall Phillips (1905–53), whose field of expertise was early American silver. From the age of seventeen, Phillips had been studying the subject, and his passion and knowledge of it enabled him to form a fast bond with Francis Hill Bigelow (1859–1933), the preeminent early scholar of the field. In the last years of his life, Bigelow was working on a biographical study of American silversmiths. After his death Bigelow's research notes passed to Phillips, who worked on the completion of the publication for twenty years until his own untimely death.

The saga of the Bigelow-Phillips papers affirms the Yale Art Gallery's commitment to research on the part of successive generations of Art Gallery curators. Phillips's colleague Josephine Setze cared for the papers and provided financial support for their publication after Phillips's death. A still younger generation of Art Gallery scholars, Jeannine J. Falino, Deborah A. Federhen, Barbara McLean Ward, and Gerald W. R. Ward have contributed to this project. Patricia E. Kane, Curator of American Decorative Arts, assumed leadership of this publication project in 1981 and carried it to completion. She oversaw the research and developed the drafts she received into this meticulously edited book. Without her constant attention and her belief in the importance of the drawers and boxes of files she inherited, these notes would never have become this exemplary permanent reference. Future generations of scholars will be indebted to her.

The long-awaited publication of this research would not have been possible without significant financial support from many sources in addition to the fund established by Josephine Setze. Grants from the National Museum Act brought Jeannine J. Falino and Deborah A. Federhen to the Art Gallery for year-long internships during which they began their contributions to this project. The Rose Herrick Jackson Memorial Fund and the Marcia Brady Tucker Fund provide stipends for Yale graduate students who participate in projects in the American Arts Office. The students who contributed to the preparation of this publication and were supported by these funds as well as the Woodrill Foundation include: Martin A. Berger, Elspeth Brown, Gretchen Townsend Buggeln, Lisa Koenigsberg, Joshua Lane, Jane Levey, Maurie McInnis, Marina Moskowitz, Kathleen B. O'Connor, James Sexton, Nancy Spiegel, Esther Thyssen, Veronica Tomasic, Elizabeth A. Valeika, Elizabeth A. White, Karen L. Wight, and Beryl Wright. A grant from the National Endowment for the Humanities covered the costs of the final manuscript preparation including travel, photography, and editing. The Virginia and Leonard Marx Publication Fund covered a large portion of the printing costs. The curatorial staff of the American Arts Office would not have been able to devote time to this project over the last sixteen years without the Friends of American Arts at Yale, whose annual support provided the clerical help, research materials, and travel funds so vital to the completion of this scholarly publication.

We thank these organizations and individuals for their financial support toward this publication which is a monument in the field of American decorative arts scholarship.

HELEN A. COOPER
Acting Director and The Holcombe T. Green Curator of American Paintings and Sculpture, Yale University Art Gallery

Preface

THE HISTORY of this research project goes back to the dawn of scholarship on early American silver in the first decade of the twentieth century. From June to November 1906 the Museum of Fine Arts, Boston, had on view "American Silver," a landmark exhibition that was accompanied by a handsome illustrated catalogue. "American Silver" was the first exhibition of American decorative arts held at a major art museum, and the catalogue was the first attempt at a comprehensive survey of early American silversmiths and their marks. Both the exhibition and the catalogue were organized by Francis Hill Bigelow. He was born in Cambridge, Massachusetts, in 1859, and, after graduating from high school, held a position with the firm of Howe and Goodwin, Boston merchants who traded in India. During his career with this Boston firm, Bigelow collected American furniture, silver, glass, and ceramics. When he retired from business in 1906, the year of the Boston show, he began his career as a silver scholar. Word of the exhibition reached England where it enticed the silver expert E. Alfred Jones to journey to Boston to view it. Jones was deeply impressed with what he saw, and sensing the importance of silver owned by American churches in identifying the marks and establishing the work of American silversmiths, he urged Bigelow to undertake a systematic search for silver among the churches in Massachusetts. Bigelow took up this challenge. Five years later the result was "American Church Silver," an exhibition at the Museum of Fine Arts, Boston, in 1911. His efforts for that show contributed significantly to Jones's subsequent publication in 1913, *The Old Silver of American Churches*, an encyclopedic tome that records the early silver owned by churches in the original thirteen colonies and that remains one of the most lavish publications ever produced in the field of American decorative arts. Late in life, in one of the drafts of the foreword for his proposed final book, Bigelow reflected on his contributions to *The Old Silver of American Churches*,

"Mr. Jones appreciated the amount of work I had done and suggested that my name should appear as colaborator [*sic*] but I declined the offer which I have sometimes since regretted." Following his contributions to ground-breaking publications in the history of American silver scholarship, Bigelow went on to write the first comprehensive survey of early American silver, *Historic Silver of the Colonies and Its Makers* (1917). At the same time he was active as a private dealer and was very instrumental in forming two of the era's most important private collections, that of Judge A. T. Clearwater which was lent to the Metropolitan Museum of Art where it was given in 1933 and that of Francis P. Garvan which began to be given to Yale in 1930. Bigelow's dealing activities, particularly the practice of wresting pieces of silver from old families, gained him the reputation of being something of a scoundrel with some of his contemporaries. However, it was hard to detract from his reputation as a preeminent scholar of American silver.

Following the publication of his survey, Bigelow set to work on what was to be the capstone of his scholarly career, a biographical dictionary of American silversmiths who worked between 1650 and 1775. In one draft of the foreword to the book, Bigelow dedicated the work to his friend the late John Ware Willard, the author of the biography of his great-grandfather, *Simon Willard and His Clocks* (1911), stating "for it is to him that all those interested in the subject of American silver are deeply indebted for the genealogical researches regarding the craftsmen who worked in that metal in Boston & the vicinity; at the writer's suggestion he undertook this during the first exhibition held in 1906 at the Museum of Fine Arts, Boston." Bigelow goes on to say that his friend the late George Munson Curtis, author of *Early Silver of Connecticut and Its Makers* (1913), was inspired by Willard's example and undertook the same kind of research for Connecticut. After Willard's death in 1914, Bigelow carried on the research, amplified it, added hitherto unknown silversmiths, and eliminated other individuals who proved not to be silversmiths. This research included endless hours of work in note-taking from the Suffolk County Registry of Deeds, the Registry of Probate, and from court records preserved in the Suffolk County Courthouse. To gather material for silversmiths trained abroad or for those who moved to other colonies, Bigelow generated a large correspondence that included silver scholars Frederick Bradbury, author of *The History of Old Sheffield Plate*, Walter Prideaux, then the Librarian of the Worshipful Company of Goldsmiths, London, and J. Hall Pleasants and Howard Sill, authors of *Maryland Silversmiths, 1715–1830* (1930). In particular these individuals helped find documents for Bigelow in their respective research areas.

According to another draft of the introduction to the biographical dictionary, Bigelow evidently planned to publish his findings in two stages. A first volume would cover the silversmiths who worked in the seventeenth century, or perhaps to 1710, with a second volume to follow.

One paper amongst the drafts of the introductory material for the dictionary bears the title "American Silverware and the Men Who Made It." In a letter to Bigelow in January 1933 Jones suggested that a better title would be "A Century of New England Silversmiths, working between 16.. & 17.." and urged Bigelow to make the closing date 1750 so that several prominent silversmiths could be included.

At the time of Bigelow's death in 1933 his research included some two-thousand pages of notes. The biographical work was yet unpublished, but in the last years of his life Bigelow had met the young silver scholar John Marshall Phillips (1905–53). Bigelow found in Phillips a

John Marshall Phillips, 1905–53.

dedication and knowledge of American silver that led him to entrust his scholarly legacy to him. The letter of application that John Marshall Phillips made to Francis P. Garvan in 1930 for a position with the collection that Garvan was about to give to Yale University sums up Phillips's early training. Writing from "The Woodlands" in Kennett Square, Pennsylvania, on 5 June 1930, Phillips stated that he had obtained a B.A. in 1927 from the University of Pennsylvania, where he had been elected to Phi Beta Kappa in 1926. After a year at the University's Law School he entered the Graduate School of English where he earned an M.A. in June 1929. He also stated that he had commenced the study of American silver in 1922, and that during his undergraduate years he paid many of his bills by buying and selling early silver. Moreover he regarded the recently completed catalogue of the early Philadelphia silver collected by Maurice Brix as his first creative work. For references he provided the names of Mrs. Maurice Brix, the wife of the collector;

Dr. Cornelius Weygandt, a Professor of English Literature at the University of Pennsylvania and a collector; John A. Mitchell, of the Department of English at the University of Pennsylvania, also a collector; and Samuel Yellin, the blacksmith, whom Phillips described simply as "artist." Phillips was hired for the Yale position and assumed his duties in September 1930 with the title of Assistant Curator of Silver.

Soon after he came to Yale, Phillips engaged in regular visits and correspondence with Bigelow. Phillips obliged Bigelow's requests for research help for his biographical study when he could. Bigelow wrote to Phillips on 30 November 1932, "I am still busy on my book and think I will try to get out 1600–1700 in the spring but it is slow work." A few months later on 8 January 1933 he wrote, "I want to bring out my book in the fall [illegible] born prior to 1700 or perhaps 1710 and another one subsequently but there is much still [to] be done in looking up *suspected* silversmiths. But I am endeavoring to finish up the earlier ones. . . . I sometimes think that my life may be too short to finish all I have to do! In which case it will be well for you to bear in mind the fact that I possess all this information and get in touch with my nieces to whom I have given them [*sic*]."

Following Bigelow's death Phillips sent a letter to Bigelow's executor, Charles H. Davis, on 27 November 1933. Phillips cited the letter that Bigelow had written to him on 8 January 1933 and stated further, "Many of the sketches I have already read as I spent a summer in Boston two years ago and spent many of my evenings discussing the work with Mr. Bigelow. I am very busy here with my duties but it would be a pleasure to find time to finish and edit the notes and the usual work attending the publication." On 1 December Mr. Davis agreed to turn over the notes to Phillips with the stipulation that he was to "take them and use them in any way you see fit and have them published with such alterations, extensions, changes, etc. as you deem desirable, said publication to cover on its face the fact that the book is based on Mr. Bigelow's work." On 8 January 1934 Phillips sent a letter of thanks to Mr. Davis in which he enumerated the material he had received: "1. Rough draft of the Introduction to the book; 2. Source references; 3. Photographs for his Historic Silver of the Colonies; 4. Biographical sketches, some unfinished, of the silversmiths born after 1700 which will constitute the second half of the book; 5. Letters pertaining to the above." Phillips expressed his concern about the material that seemed to be lacking "for the early men who were born in the seventeenth century." By 22 March 1934 those notes already had been found when Phillips wrote to George Francis Dow of the Society for the Preservation of New England Antiquities, "I can scarcely wait for summer to come when I can give my undivided attention to their arrangement and editing."

Bigelow's papers now at the Yale University Art Gallery include: references to silversmiths, jewelers, watchmakers, and other workers in metal that John M. Fitzgerald, an employee of the Suffolk County Courthouse, compiled for Bigelow from the Court of Common Pleas Records from 1699 to 1756; 175 negatives of silver objects that Bigelow and Jones put together for a proposed book on domestic plate that the First World War interrupted; Bigelow's annotated copies of books on silver; all of the research and final production material for *The Old Silver of American Churches* comprising a photographic file assembled at the time of the 1906 and 1911 exhibitions through the help of Mrs. Florence Paull Berger, then in charge of the Department of Western Art at the Museum of Fine Arts, Boston, of marks and rubbings of marks, which was used to create the dies for illustrations of the marks in the Jones volume as well as photographs of the engraving and the dies for illustrations of the engraving, and the glass plate negatives and the original prints from them; and the research notes of early American silver scholars including John H. Buck, an Englishman who wrote the first book that included a survey of early American silver (*Old Plate . . .* [1888]), John Ware Willard, George Munson Curtis, and Dr. Theodore S. Woolsey, whose article in *Harper's* in 1896 first encouraged Americans to collect and study the silver of their own country.

Phillips took seriously the trust Mr. Davis had placed in him. In 1934 when Hermann F. Clarke, the author of *John Coney, Silversmith 1655–1722*, was researching his book on Jeremiah Dummer, he wrote to Phillips asking if he could obtain a copy of Bigelow's notes on Dummer. Phillips replied "I do not feel that in my capacity as custodian or guardian of it [the Bigelow material] as it were until I find the time to annotate and finish it for publication that I can send it out of my possession." With Clarke, as with other researchers who sought information from the notes, Phillips confirmed what they knew and offered additional information from the notes, but did not allow first-hand inspection of them.

From 1932 to 1953 Phillips routinely offered a course on the arts and crafts in America that his students fondly dubbed "Pots and Pans." The teaching load in addition to his curatorial activities left little time for work on the Bigelow manuscript. Phillips spent the summers of 1937, 1938, 1940, and 1941 compiling biographies of silversmiths active in Massachusetts between 1630 and 1776. He made forays to Boston and Salem to consult additional court files, to acquire photostats of original documents, and to complete research on Bigelow's "suspected" silversmiths. He also corresponded regularly with Jones who conducted research for Phillips in England on the background of the silversmiths known to have been born or trained there. In addition, he used student help to compile references to the silversmiths in colonial Boston newspapers. These efforts came to a halt when Phillips served in the military between 1943 and 1945. When he returned to Yale after the war he was made Assistant Director, Associate Director, Acting Director (1945–48), and in 1948, Director of the Art Gallery, a post he held until his death in 1953. With his untimely death at age forty-eight of a heart attack on a train traveling from New York City to New Haven on 7 May 1953, Phillips's work on Bigelow's notes came to an end.

Phillips's colleague, Josephine Setze, who came to the Gallery a few months in advance of Phillips and who held the positions of Museum Assistant, Registrar (1940–45), Assistant Curator of American Art (1945–59), Curator of the Intra–University Loan Collection (1959–67), and Consultant on American Silver (1967–82), then took responsibility for caring for the notes. She organized Bigelow's biographical sketches and Phillips's research additions to them chronologically by the birth-dates of the silversmiths ranging from 1601 to 1752. She placed the papers in fourteen two-ring notebooks and numbered each piece of paper filed therein. This arrangement seems to have reflected Bigelow's original plan to organize the biographical sketches chronologically. Setze shared the material information with her good friend Kathryn C. Buhler, Assistant Curator at the Museum of Fine Arts, Boston, and a leading authority on early American silver. Buhler helped Setze with some of the unanswered questions and provided guidance as Setze sought to put the material into publishable form. Her plan was to publish Bigelow's sketches with appendages of the additional materials that Phillips had found. Toward this end Setze gave the University $30,000 in 1968, and at about the same time she employed Marion Sandquist, then an editorial typist at the Art Gallery, to make a type-script of the papers. For more than two decades Setze was a jealous guardian of the material and only in the mid 1970s permitted scholars access to it. As she reached retirement Setze relaxed her grip and allowed members of the staff of the American Arts Office at the Art Gallery to use the files. Charles F. Montgomery, Curator of the Garvan Collection and Professor of the History of Art, used the papers in the research phases of the traveling exhibition, "Silver in American Life." Subsequent users included myself, then Associate Curator of the Garvan and Related Collections; Gerald W. R. Ward, then Assistant Curator of the Garvan and Related Collections; and Barbara McLean Ward, Curatorial Assistant, as we prepared dissertations on early Massachusetts silversmiths.

In 1981 as the tour of "Silver in American Life" was approaching its end, the Wards and I agreed that the time had come to carry out the intentions of Josephine Setze to make the Bigelow-Phillips legacy available to a wider audience. The entries were divided along the lines of our dissertation research. I assumed responsibility for Hull and Sanderson and their contemporaries; Barbara Ward covered the Boston silversmiths who began working between 1690 and 1730; Gerald Ward was responsible for the Essex County silversmiths. Two National Museum Act interns at the Art Gallery, Deborah A. Federhen (1982–83) and Jeannine J. Falino (1984–85), were assigned additional biographies as their publication projects.

    Decisions about the form of the dictionary and the editorial process
also began to be made in 1981. Instead of publishing Bigelow's biographies with Phillips's discoveries appended—the form conceived by
Setze—the policy was to use their research as the basis for newly
drafted entries. For easier reference, the biographies were organized
alphabetically by silversmith as opposed to chronologically by date of
birth. Although the Bigelow-Phillips notes extended into the nineteenth century, the notebooks as organized by Setze stopped with
silversmiths born by 1752, reflecting Bigelow's and Phillips's intentions
to concentrate on the early makers. Because the Revolution set in
motion some fundamental changes in the lives and careers of most
Massachusetts artisans, silversmiths who were born in or before 1754
and who were therefore active by 1775, before the upheaval of the
Revolution, were included. The final list also included numerous silversmiths identified since Phillips's death. The editorial team also verified
the references to manuscripts and secondary sources cited in the Bigelow-Phillips notes. To supplement the research of George Francis
Dow (*The Arts and Crafts in New England 1704–1775: Gleanings from
Boston Newspapers*, 1927), Kathleen B. O'Connor, who held Marcia
Brady Tucker, Rose Herrick Jackson, and Woodrill Foundation fellow-
ships in the American Arts Office between 1986 and 1988, searched all
Massachusetts newspapers for the period 1775 to 1800 for additional
references to silversmiths. Many individuals contributed to the compiling of lists of surviving work for each silversmith from major collection
catalogues and archives, but this enormous task was completed through
the efforts of Karen L. Wight, a Marcia Brady Tucker and Rose Herrick
Jackson Fellow between 1991 and 1994. To serve scholars in a broad
variety of disciplines, the following information systematically was
sought for each silversmith: the names and occupations of his maternal
and paternal grandparents; the names and occupations of his parents;
his wife/wives' name(s), lifedates, parents, parents' dates and father's
occupation; his master; the apprentices the silversmith trained; his public
offices and military service; his land holdings, including shop, residence,
mortgages, and other real estate transactions; his religious affiliation;
his estate value and contents; and his court appearances.

    A grant from the National Endowment for the Humanities in 1989
provided the funds that were invaluable for covering the costs of manuscript preparation, particularly for obtaining the mark and other photographs with which the entries and essays are illustrated. Many graduate
students in American Studies and History of Art have contributed to
the research on this volume over the course of the last fifteen years.
Their contributions and those of many other individuals at Yale and
elsewhere are enumerated in the Acknowledgments.

    The most important contribution of Bigelow and Phillips was their
extensive research in manuscript and record repositories and the large
number of primary documents pertaining to silversmiths that they

discovered. The contributors have augmented this material with additional research in other archives. As a synthesis of all this research, the dictionary makes available for the first time vast amounts of primary data that are otherwise only accessible in widely-scattered archives. The data the dictionary provides should be useful for art historians, social historians, and other interpreters of such aspects of colonial culture as artisanal work, labor practices, tools, apprenticeship, merchandizing, patronage, and demographics. This publication puts into print research that started more than seventy years ago, but as Bigelow acknowledged with resignation in one of his draft forewords, "No list of silversmiths can be regarded as a finality, for unrecorded names or initials are constantly turning up on silver objects and many references are still likely to be found in genealogies, deeds, etc."

PATRICIA E. KANE
Friends of American Arts Curator of American Decorative Arts,
Yale University Art Gallery

Acknowledgments

MANY individuals have played a part in the completion of this volume. I am indebted to Barbara McLean Ward and Gerald W. R. Ward for their excellent essays and the many entries they also contributed. Jeannine J. Falino and Deborah A. Federhen have been conscientious contributors of entries as well. All the contributors have shared information generously with one another. In addition, Edgard Moreno provided his knowledge of silversmithing tools and processes in compiling the Glossary. Many more omissions would have occurred in the lists of surviving objects had it not been for the dedication of Karen L. Wight. Our colleagues Robert Barker and Janine E. Skerry faced the task of reading the manuscript with remarkable stoicism. The manuscript benefited from the editing skills of Lawrence Kenney and the sharp-eyed proofreading of Jenya Weinreb and Elise K. Kenney. James Anthony and Ike Showalter of Monotype Composition Company guided the manuscript through its demanding typesetting. Laura Moss Gottlieb generated a thorough index. It is always a pleasure to work with Roland Hoover, University Printer (now retired), who has provided his usual elegant typography. I am grateful to each of these individuals for their contributions to this project.

In the last sixteen years Yale University has committed considerable resources and staff time to the completion of this volume. The work began under Alan Shestack, The Henry J. Heinz II Director of the Art Gallery (1971–85), and continued under his successors, Anne Coffin Hanson, Acting Director (1985–86), Mary Gardner Neill (1987–94), Jules D. Prown, Interim Director (1994), and Susan Vogel (1995–97), who have all offered encouragement and support. Other Art Gallery staff members who have assisted along the way include Michael Agee, William Cuffe, Louisa Cunningham, Edward Douglas, Howard S. el-Yasin, Richard S. Field, Susan Frankenbach, Carl Kaufman, Joseph Szaszfai, and Suzanne Warner.

The brunt of this project has fallen on the staff of the American Arts Office. Lisa B. Newman, Administrative Assistant, has played a significant role in preparing the manuscript for the typesetter by ably keeping the materials, photo orders, and photographs organized, and by bringing her expertise with computers and her knowledge of graphic design to bear upon the numerous drafts that passed through her hands. David L. Barquist, Associate Curator of American Decorative Arts, contributed insightful readings of the manuscript at many different stages and always was generous in his willingness to offer assistance. Florence M. Montgomery, a Research Associate, devoted many hours to completing research at the library, as well as other tasks associated with compiling information for the book. The two file cases in which Josephine Setze housed the folders for this project have now grown to five, and the files in their drawers have been stuffed to overflowing by numerous bursary students and volunteers who do clerical tasks in the American Arts Office, including Christopher Barnard, Deborah Burness, David Castillo, Hwashing Cheng, John Choi, Jeffrey Collins, Marguerite French, Audrey Hing, Younhie Lee, Fred Murphy, Anthony Nygren, Horling Wong, and Patrice Yang. The task of measuring marks to determine the relative size for reproduction was ably assisted by Betsy Pitts. Ashley Vietor checked footnotes for two-thirds of the book and assisted with proofreading the transcriptions. All the researchers are grateful to Marion Sandquist, Administrative Assistant, for the typed transcription of the Bigelow-Phillips notes she prepared for Josephine Setze around 1970.

Every project in the American Arts Office is completed with the assistance of graduate students who have stipends through the Marcia Brady Tucker Fund or the Rose Herrick Jackson Memorial Fund. Numerous students have been diligent in carrying out research tasks for this book, including Martin A. Berger, R. Tripp Evans, Joshua Lane, Maurie McInnis, Marina Moskowitz, James Sexton, Nancy Spiegel, Esther Thyssen, Veronica Tomasic, Elizabeth A. Valeika, Elizabeth A. White, and Beryl Wright. Some students accepted assignments that required unusual commitment to the project: Elspeth Brown and Lisa Koenigsberg spent many hours in Massachusetts record repositories verifying deeds, probate records, and other primary sources; Jane Levey edited and proofread for many hours; Kathleen B. O'Connor read microfilm of early Federal newspapers for advertisements pertaining to silversmiths; John Stauffer photographed hundreds of silversmiths' marks; and Gretchen Townsend Buggeln organized all the initial orders for photographs of silversmiths' marks.

The staffs of the University libraries have contributed significant assistance to this project over the years. At Sterling Memorial Library in particular we acknowledge the help of Judith A. Schiff, Chief Research Archivist, and those who assisted readers in Manuscripts and Archives, Kevin E. Pacelli in the Newspaper and Microtext Reading Room,

Frederick W. Musto, Curator of the Map Collection, and John P. Burnham, Curator of the Numismatic Collection. In addition, Vincent André Giroud, Curator of Modern Books and Manuscripts, Beinecke Rare Book and Manuscript Library, and the Department of Prints, Drawings, and Rare Books at the Yale Center for British Art facilitated access to research materials in their care.

I echo Helen Cooper's thanks to those who provided financial support for this publication and the study of silver at Yale. The annual contributions of the Friends of American Arts at Yale enable the American Arts Office to carry on scholarly research projects, and that support is deeply appreciated. The National Endowment for the Humanities filled a critical void by funding many of the costs of manuscript preparation. In particular, the contributions steadfastly provided by Virginia and Leonard Marx for publishing books in the American Arts Office have played a significant role in the final production of this volume. The collections donated by Carl R. Kossack, and his sons Frederick, Alan, and Philip, have enhanced this publication by making many more marks and works of colonial Massachusetts silversmiths accessible for study.

Collectors and colleagues in other institutions provided opportunities to study and photograph examples of Massachusetts silver and related materials in their collections that yielded essential information for this undertaking. In particular we are grateful to Georgia B. Barnhill, American Antiquarian Society, Worcester, Massachusetts; Wendy A. Cooper, The Baltimore Museum of Art; Sarah Blank, Boston Public Library; David Wood, Concord Museum, Massachusetts; Elizabeth Pratt Fox, Connecticut Historical Society, Hartford; Gail F. Serfaty, Diplomatic Reception Rooms, United States Department of State, Washington, D. C.; Kevin Faughman; Donald L. Stover, The Fine Arts Museums of San Francisco, California; Ada Trecartin, First Congregational Church, Guilford, Connecticut; John H. Hinrichs, Jr., The Mrs. John Emerson Marble Collection of Early American Silver; Janine E. Skerry, Historic Deerfield, Inc., Massachusetts; Frances Gruber Safford, The Metropolitan Museum of Art, New York; Louis Migliorini; Michael A. Jehle, Nantucket Historical Association; Ulysses G. Dietz, The Newark Museum, New Jersey; Ruth Nutt; Dean Lahikainen, Peabody Essex Museum, Salem, Massachusetts; Thomas Michie, Museum of Art, Rhode Island School of Design, Providence; Hope Spencer and Cherie Summers, Santa Barbara Museum of Art, California; Iris and Seymour Schwartz; Anne C. Golovin, Smithsonian Institution, Washington, D. C.; Beth Carver Wees, Sterling and Francine Clark Art Institute, Williamstown, Massachusetts; Nancy and Richard Stiner; William N. Hosley, Jr., Wadsworth Atheneum, Hartford, Connecticut; and Mr. and Mrs. Erving Wolf. We are also indebted to Bert Denker of the Decorative Arts Photographic Collection, The Henry Francis du Pont Winterthur Museum, Delaware, for the endless research requests he responded to so promptly. This resource, as well as the Ineson-Bissell Collection at Winterthur, were critical tools in the preparation of this work. Another tool that provided vital assistance is the index to auction records that Michael Weller of Argentum, San Francisco, made available. David Thomas of Gebelein, also shared information from the archives of that firm. Henry L. P. Beckwith took the time to examine photographs of silver with engraved heraldic arms and crests recorded in this study and aided us in the identification of many of the arms.

Other colleagues, friends, and institutions provided useful assistance, information, and support, including Susan Faxon, Addison Gallery of American Art, Andover, Massachusetts; Dr. Judith A. Barter, Anka Matijevich, Anndora Morginson, and Lieschen A. Potuznik, The Art Institute of Chicago; The Ashmolean Museum, Oxford, England; Barbara R. Dailey, Baker Library, Harvard University; Jane Connell, Bank of Boston Corporation; Michael K. Brown, The Bayou Bend Collection, Houston, Texas; Stephen Nonack, Boston Athenaeum; Mattie Kelley and Henrietta M. Tye, Bowdoin College Museum of Art, Maine; The British Museum, London; Kevin Stayton, The Brooklyn Museum; Phillip M. Johnston and Rachel E. C. Layton, The Carnegie Museum of Art, Pittsburgh; Jeanne V. Sloane, Christie's, New York; Irene Roughton, The Chrysler Museum, Norfolk, Virginia; Anita Ellis, Cincinnati Art Museum, Ohio; Kelly Bahmer-Brouse, Henry H. Hawley and Emily Rosen, The Cleveland Museum of Art, Ohio; Carol Haines, Concord Museum, Massachusetts; Gail Nessell Colglazier, Connecticut Valley Historical Museum, Springfield, Massachusetts; Christine M. Guertin, The Currier Gallery of Art, Manchester, New Hampshire; Roxanne M. Stanulis, The Detroit Institute of Arts, Michigan; William Core Duffy; Elizabeth Gombosi and Timothy Anglin Burgard, Fogg Art Museum, Harvard University Museums, Cambridge, Massachusetts; Franklin D. Roosevelt Library-Museum, Hyde Park, New York; Sandra Gindlay, Harvard University Portrait Collection, Cambridge, Massachusetts; Haverhill Historical Society, Massachusetts; Donald L. Fennimore and W. N. Steltzer, Jr., The Henry Francis du Pont Winterthur Museum, Inc., Delaware; Dawn D. Johnston and Kathleen Latendresse, Henry Ford Museum and Greenfield Village, Dearborn, Michigan; Ian M. G. Quimby, Historical Society of Pennsylvania; Kathleen O'Malley, Hood Museum of Art, Dartmouth College, Hanover, New Hampshire; Barry L. Shifman and Rose M. Wood, Indianapolis Museum of Art, Indiana; Leslie Greene Bowman, Los Angeles County Museum of Art, California; Nicole Senecal Pelto, Lyman Allyn Art Museum, New London, Connecticut; Nan Cumming, Maine Historical Society, Portland; Edwin Churchill, Maine State Museum, Augusta; Anne Bentley, Edward W. Hanson, and Virginia Smith, Massachusetts Historical Society, Boston; Massachusetts State Archives; Linda Delone Best and Sarah Dwyer, Mead Art Museum, Amherst College, Massachusetts; Doreen Bolger and Peter M. Kenny, The Metropolitan Museum of Art, New York; Kristine Anderson and Melissa Moore, Minneapolis

Institute of Arts, Minnesota; Anna T. D'Ambrosio, Munson-Williams-Proctor Institute Museum of Art, Utica, New York; Karen L. Otis, Museum of Fine Arts, Boston; Deborah Chotner, The National Gallery of Art, Washington, D. C.; Oscar P. Fitzgerald, The Navy Museum, Washington, D. C.; Judith N. Lund, New Bedford Whaling Museum, Massachusetts; Donna-Belle Garvin, New Hampshire Historical Society, Concord; Eric P. Newman; Margaret K. Hofer, The New-York Historical Society; Nova Scotia Public Records; Mimika Nusrala; Donna K. Baron and Marguerite E. Haley, Old Sturbridge Village, Massachusetts; Cynthia A. Young, Old York Historical Society, Maine; Joyce M. Levitre, Paul Revere Insurance Group, Worcester, Massachusetts; MaryAnn T. Campbell, Nancy Heywood, Jane E. Ward, Robert K. Weis, and A. Paul Winfisky, Peabody Essex Museum, Salem, Massachusetts; Beatrice B. Garvan, Philadelphia Museum of Art; Stephen O'Neill, Pilgrim Hall Museum, Plymouth, Massachusetts; Grace M. Pittman; Suzanne L. Flynt, Pocumtuck Valley Memorial Association, Deerfield, Massachusetts; Princeton University Art Museum, New Jersey; Esther and Christopher Pullman; Jerry M. Bloomer, The R. W. Norton Art Gallery, Shreveport, Louisiana; Margaret C. Fay, St. Matthews United Church, Halifax, Nova Scotia; George R. Schoedinger III; James McConnaughy, S. J. Shrubsole Corp., New York; Elizabeth C. Leuthner and Carol Potter, The Society for the Preservation of New England Antiquities; Kevin Tierney and Ian Irving, Sotheby's, New York; Robert Keene, Town of Southampton, New York; Martha Asher, Sterling and Francine Clark Art Institute, Williamstown, Massachusetts; Strawbery Banke, Inc., Portsmouth, New Hampshire; Harry Kels Swan, Swan Historical Foundation, South Bound Brook, New Jersey; Jonathan Trace; Victoria and Albert Museum, London; Caroline D. Smith, Virginia Museum of Fine Arts, Richmond; Karen Blanchfield, Cynthia Roman, Mark Zurolo, Wadsworth Atheneum, Hartford, Connecticut; William R. Johnston, Walters Art Gallery, Baltimore; Kit J. Nichols and Gregory C. Schwarz, Woodstock Historical Society, Vermont; Susan E. Strickler, Worcester Art Museum, Massachusetts; David Beasley and Susan Hare, The Worshipful Company of Goldsmiths, London; and Edward S. Cooke, Jr., Yale University.

My parents, James and Alice Kane, have always been committed to my endeavors and offered unstinting support in the completion of this project. Finally, I convey my deepest thanks to my husband, W. Scott Braznell, for his many sacrifices that enabled me to oversee the editing of this volume. The last word is reserved for Josephine Setze whose conviction and financial support were critical factors in having this research completed. This volume is dedicated to her memory.

P. E. K.

Essays

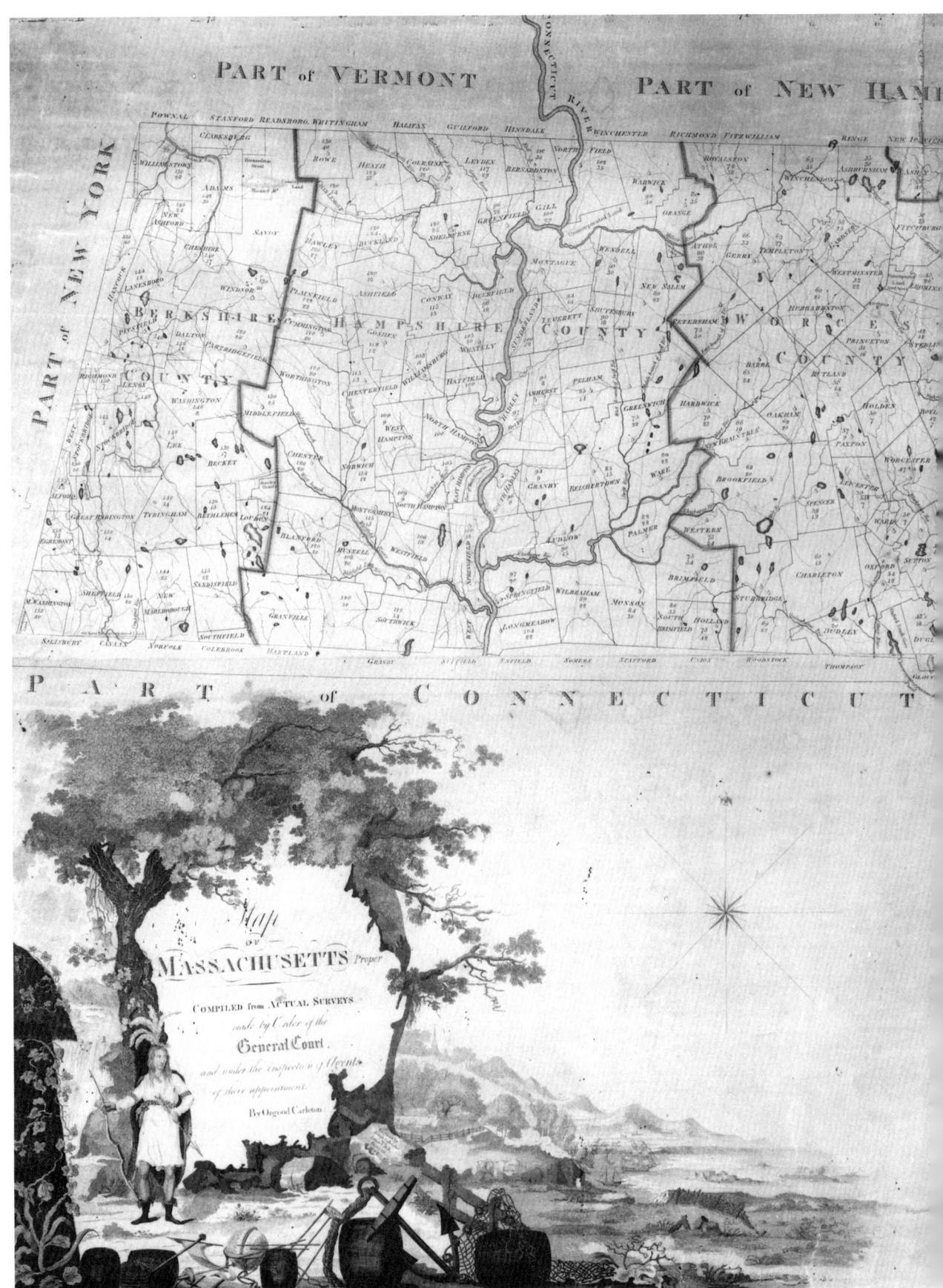

Samuel Hill, Jr., and Joseph Callender, after Osgood Carleton, Map of Massachusetts Proper *(detail), 1801, line engraving. Map Collection, Sterling Memorial Library, Yale University.*

MASSACHUSETTS

BAY.

CAPE COD BAY

BARNSTABLE BAY

MIDDLESEX

NORFOLK
COUNTY

PLYMOUTH
COUNTY

BRISTOL
COUNTY

BARNSTABLE
COUNTY

PART of
RHODE ISLAND

BUZZARDS BAY

ELIZABETH ISLANDS

MARTHAS VINEYARD

NANTUCKET

SUFFOLK COUNTY is composed of the
Town of Boston, Chelsea, Hingham, and Hull.

EXPLANATION.

State and Town lines except where bounded by water roads
County line
Road
Academy
Meeting House
Court House
River
Small Stream
Mountain
Pond
Island
Rock above water
Rock under water
Shoal
Falls
Bridge
Iron Ore
per number in each Town is the distance from BOSTON.
r the distance from the SHIRE TOWN.

SCALE OF MILES 4 to an Inch.

1. Frontispiece from William Badcock, A New Touchstone for Gold and Silver Wares *(London, 1679). Beinecke Rare Book and Manuscript Library, Yale University. This image of the goldsmith or silversmith's shop shows a retail shop (above) and a workshop (below). At the center of the retail shop is the figure of St. Dunstan (detail 1), patron saint of the silversmith. To the right, a goldsmith weighs a tankard on a balance scale. On the left, workers, with leather aprons to catch silver filings tied around their waists, perform fine finish work with the aid of natural light streaming in from a large window. Below, workers perform the more strenuous tasks of forging and raising, in close proximity to the large forge where silver was melted and refined. A smaller furnace to the rear (detail 13) is used for annealing. Notice the large tools distinctive to the trade illustrated above the forge.*

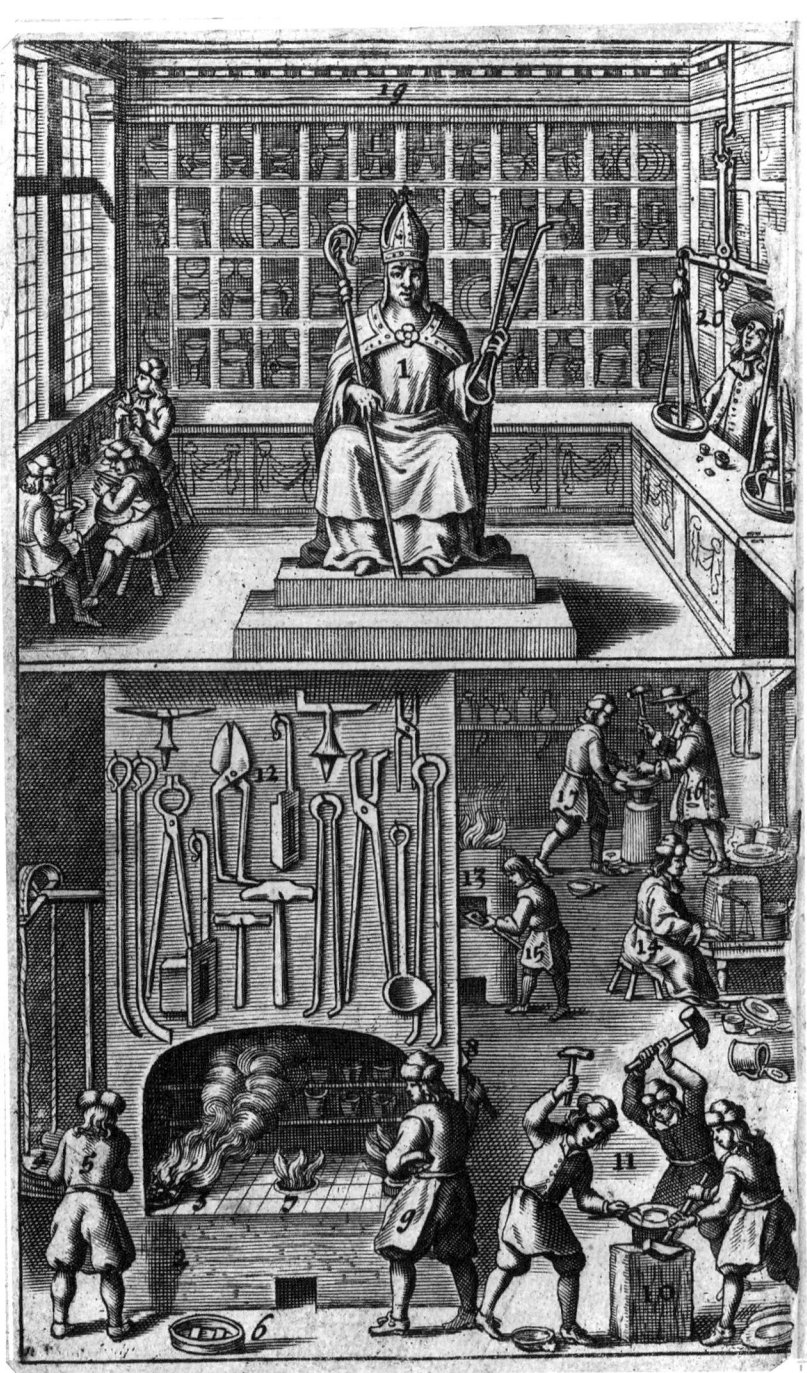

Barbara McLean Ward

Forging the Artisan's Identity: Tools and the Goldsmithing Trade in Colonial Massachusetts

Further information and illustrations of tools appear in Appendix C.

IN THE SUMMER OF 1703, Francis Richardson of Philadelphia traveled to Boston to buy goldsmithing tools. With about twenty working goldsmiths in 1703, Boston was clearly the center of the trade in British North America, and Richardson expected to find a plentiful supply of tools for sale there. In a letter home, he complained that although there was "such a dule [dull] time with the Goldsmith," he did not think he would be able to "prevaile with any of them" to part with the tools he needed for less than "a hundred or a hundred and fifty pounds." He was not inclined "to be in hast to give such an Extravegen[t] prises for Twoles" since he reckoned he could obtain the same tools in England for one-third the price. Nonetheless, he wrote that he could not go to London in the spring, and would be glad to get some tools "on reasonable terms" in Boston. In November 1704 he wrote to his mother from Boston telling her that he had acquired "a small parsell of tules and other Nessesary belonging to my Traid" and was on his way back home.[1]

For the silversmiths and goldsmiths who began their careers before the Revolution, tools represented a link to a tradition of skill and training and established their place within the hierarchy of a complex craft (1). This essay examines the documentary evidence for tool ownership, shop arrangement, and shop practices of the goldsmiths and silversmiths of Massachusetts who began their careers before the Revolution.[2] This analysis allows us to reconstruct, at least to some degree, the distinctions that existed between the workers in the craft. It also allows us to understand the nature of the relationships among master artisans working as largeworkers, smallworkers, and jewelers, and the relationships between these master artisans and their journeymen, jobbers, and apprentices. Master artisans faced the problems of obtaining raw materials—gold, silver, and jewels—and of performing, supervising, or subcontracting the fabrication of the items their patrons ordered. In their daily routine, these master artisans actively traded services with

5

one another, each large firm seeking to minimize its own overhead by drawing on the strengths of others. Independent master goldsmiths had significant capital invested in the tools of their trade, tools that defined the scope of their businesses and the ease with which they could complete certain tasks. Masters, in turn, sent out some work to individual jobbers, hired journeymen to work alongside them in their shops on a daily basis, and trained a handful of apprentices. Specialist jobbers and journeymen also owned tools that suited their talents and working methods. Even apprentices developed specialties and began collecting their own boxes of tools during the period of their training.

The laboring craftsmen who owned their own boxes of tools were proud to be identified with others in the craft and believed that their training would provide them and their families with economic security. Tools further assured artisans of a livelihood; they were a tangible expression of their skills and the means by which they exercised those skills. English common law recognized the critical connection between tools and livelihood; it decreed that tools were the last of a person's belongings that could be seized for debt.[3] Thus, Boston jeweler Daniel Légaré, who was imprisoned for debt probably late in 1722, still retained the tools of his trade after his incarceration. In 1722/23 Légaré petitioned for release from jail on the grounds of poverty, and court-appointed appraisers Edward Winslow and Nathaniel Morse, both Boston goldsmiths, found his tools to be "much less than is absolutely necessary for him to carry on his trade withall and that they would not (if they were to be sold) be worth more than ten or twelve pounds [£4.16 sterling]."[4] When a sheriff impounded an individual's tools, the county could be assured that the defendant would appear in court. The attachment of a "Vise which was in the Defendents Shop" from Boston goldsmith Benjamin Hiller was probably not critical to the continuation of his craft, but the court's decision to impound a box of tools and a chest owned by John LeRoux, a journeyman sojourning in Boston, was certainly calculated to make sure that the New York native did not leave town.[5]

For any young man who had finished his apprenticeship and hoped to become a master craftsman, a variety of different tools was absolutely essential to the practice of his trade.[6] Evidence for a strong association between an artisan and his tools can be drawn from the fact that many craftsmen bequeathed their tools to children or special apprentices. Richard Conyers, who died in Boston in 1708/09, bequeathed "all my Working Tools that Shall remain in my Shop, and I shall be possessed of at my decease" to his thirteen-year-old son James Conyers, who was living in London. "In Case of the Death of my s[d] Son . . . before his Receipt of the s[d] Working Tools Then I Give y[e] Same unto John House of London Goldsmith." Conyers also stipulated that "Thomas Miller of Boston afores[d] Goldsmith Shall have the Use and Improvem[t] of all my Working Tools upon his Giveing Security to return ye Same when demanded."[7] In 1777, Nathaniel Hurd, a noted Boston goldsmith and engraver, bequeathed his "large printing press & some tools in consideration for the love I bear to him, & the genius he discovers for the same business . . . to which I intended to have brought him up to" to his nephew John Mason Furnass.[8]

Levels of the Craft of Goldsmiths and Their Tools

Different types of goldsmiths owned different types of tools, and the quantities of tools they kept in their shops depended also on the numbers of people they had working for them at any one time. In *The London Tradesman* (1747), R. Campbell described many levels of London craftsmen working under the general designation of goldsmith in London and made a distinction between the goldsmith, who was employed in making "large Works," and the jeweler, who was employed in making "Toys and Jewels." He also commented that there were "almost as many" specialists in London "as there are different Articles" in the goldsmith's shop and that because these specialists were "so constantly employed in one Thing," they were able to carry out their work with a degree of perfection that was not possible in "many Foreign Nations . . . [where master goldsmiths were] obliged to employ the same Hands in every Branch of the Trade."[9] In France, Denis Diderot described the craft as being divided into three branches: *Orfèvre Grossier*, common goldsmiths or largeworkers (2), who made tureens, coffeepots, plates, and spoons; *Orfèvre Bijoutier*, goldsmith jewelers (3), who made snuffboxes, sword hilts, and rings; and *Orfèvre Jouaillier, Metteur en Oeuvre*, goldsmith smallworkers and stonesetters (4), who made pendants, rings, buckles, bracelets, stomachers, and hair ornaments, many of them set with stones.[10]

Most Massachusetts goldsmiths of the seventeenth and eighteenth centuries fell into categories similar to those described by Diderot. A Massachusetts advertisement of 1759 for an "Apprentice to a *large* and *small* Work, Goldsmith" indicates that these terms were in use in the colony, as were the terms *plateworker* and *chaser*, which were used to describe the skills of a journeyman largeworker in court documents of 1702.[11] Jewelers clearly identified themselves as such in their advertisements and in legal documents, and surviving inventories suggest that many of these individuals specialized in the setting of stones. Nonetheless, in Massachusetts these designations tended to be broadly applied, and we do not find the proliferation of narrow specialties that Campbell described for London.

Analysis of the tools, supplies, and finished goods owned by the Massachusetts goldsmiths who began their careers before the Revolution demonstrates that for the most part, these individuals developed

2. Largeworker's workshop, detail from Plate I, "Orfèvre Grossier," in Denis Diderot, Encyclopédie; Recueil de Planches, *vol. 8.*

3. Smallworker's workshop, detail from Plate I, "Orfèvre Bijoutier," in Denis Diderot, Encyclopédie; Recueil de Planches, *vol. 8.*

4. Jeweler's workshop, detail from Plate I, "Orfèvre Jouaillier, Metteur en Oeuvre," in Denis Diderot, Encyclopédie; Recueil de Planches, *vol. 8.*

an informal system of working relationships in which artisans defined
themselves as largeworkers, smallworkers, or jewelers. In Massachusetts,
however, these divisions were by no means rigid, because few artisans
could afford to turn away work of any kind. In the eighteenth century,
artisan-client networks were defined largely by interlocking credit obligations. In order to balance their books, artisans needed to find ways
in which they could serve the individuals from whom they themselves
sought goods and services. In order to service their customers fully,
artisans often accepted work that they knew they could not perform
within their own shops, jobbing away the work to colleagues in the
craft. Silversmiths also diversified into other business ventures and into
bi-occupations such as innkeeping and gravedigging, in order to keep
themselves financially solvent.[12]

Among the general working categories that we *can* identify, *largeworkers* were those goldsmiths who produced holloware. The biggest production firms—firms I have referred to elsewhere as those of merchant
artisans—were owned and directly managed by a trained largeworker
who employed a number of apprentices and journeymen and jobbed
out work to independents.[13] These merchant artisans produced not only
holloware, but rings, buckles, and other assorted items of jewelry. Some
largeworkers appear to have eschewed the role of retailer and worked
as jobbers for these large firms. Other silversmiths set up shop either
as *smallworkers*, concentrating on making spoons, ladles, rings, boxes,
and buckles, or as *jewelers*, specializing in enameling and the setting
of stones. Although smallworkers, particularly in Massachusetts towns
outside Boston, often retailed larger-size wares as well as producing
small items, shop inventories for people falling within this category
suggest that many conducted only limited retail business or worked as
jobbers for other goldsmiths. And among those Boston artisans who
referred to themselves as jewelers, several had major retail businesses.
Specialties such as chasing and engraving were generally performed by
individuals working within the firms of largeworkers, and a few notable
individuals—Jeremiah Dummer, John Coney, Nathaniel Morse, Nathaniel Hurd, and Paul Revere, Jr.—made a significant income from
copperplate engraving in addition to silversmithing.

Although the range of work performed by these various individual
artisans differed, many of the tasks associated with the craft of the
goldsmith or silversmith were common to everyone in the craft. The
following overview of the basic skills involved in making items out of
gold and silver is meant to provide a background for a discussion of
shop sizes, shop arrangement, and the significance of the tools listed
in estate inventories and other documents related to the work of Massachusetts goldsmiths and jewelers.[14]

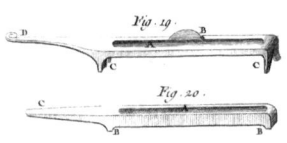

5. *Ingot molds, detail from Plate XV, "Orfèvre Grossier," in Denis Diderot,* Encyclopédie; Recueil de Planches, *vol. 8.*

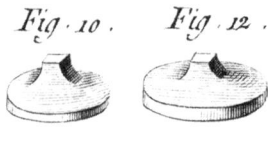

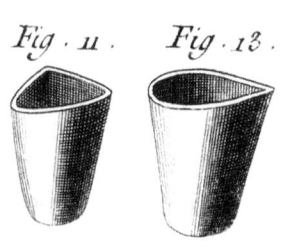

6. *Crucibles and covers, detail from Plate XV, "Orfèvre Grossier," in Denis Diderot,* Encyclopédie; Recueil de Planches, *vol. 8.*

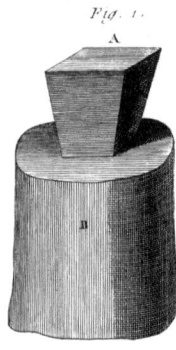

7. *Mounted forging anvil, detail from Plate X, "Orfèvre Grossier," in Denis Diderot,* Encyclopédie; Recueil de Planches, *vol. 8.*

The Largeworker

The largeworker was a multitalented individual with a full knowledge of all aspects of his craft. Campbell makes particular mention of the master goldsmith's talent as a moldmaker and his need to understand the proper method of refining silver and of mixing silver alloys and solders:

> The Goldsmith makes all his own Moulds, and for that Reason ought to be a good Designer, and have a good Taste in Sculpture. He must be conversant in Alchemy; that is, in all the Properties of Metals: He must know the proper Menstruums for their Solution, the various Methods of extracting and refining them from their Dross and Impurity; the Secret of mixing them with their proper Alloy: He must know the various ways of Essaying Metals, and distinguishing the real from the fictitious.
>
> From hence it must be conjectured that he ought to be possessed of a solid Judgment as well as a mechanical Hand and Head.[15]

Although in Massachusetts largeworkers often made rings, buckles, and other small items in anticipation of future sales, most of the wares made by largeworkers were bespoke, or custom-made, goods.

Largeworkers made these bespoke goods, usually substantial pieces of holloware—tankards, beakers, covered cups, bowls, and so forth—using the basic skills of forging and raising. Objects were decorated through the processes of chasing, embossing, and engraving, and the application of cut-card, cast, and molded ornaments. To begin the work, the goldsmith started with an ingot, which he made by melting old silver objects, coins, and refined or "burnt" silver in a crucible and pouring the molten metal into a round or rectangular iron ingot mold (2, detail a; 5). During the melting, the silversmith put some flux—usually borax—into the crucible to keep the metal from oxidizing. Crucibles were of primarily two types: less expensive ones of ceramic material called fire clay and more expensive ones of graphite (referred to as black pots or blue pots), each type being used for various purposes (6).[16] The goldsmith then flattened the ingot by hammering it down against a forging anvil with large hammers. Large forging anvils, weighing more than one hundred pounds, were among the most costly tools in a goldsmith's shop, and even the major producers of holloware in Massachusetts usually had only one (7; see also 1, detail 11; 2, detail e). Campbell observed that by the mid-eighteenth century in England, a new invention, the flatting mill (8), had begun to make this portion of the goldsmith's job easier: "Their Business required much more Time and Labour formerly than at present; they were obliged to beat their Metal from the Ingot into what Thinness they wanted; but now there are invented Flatting-Mills, which reduce their Metal to what Thinness they require, at a very small Expence."[17] In America, however, this

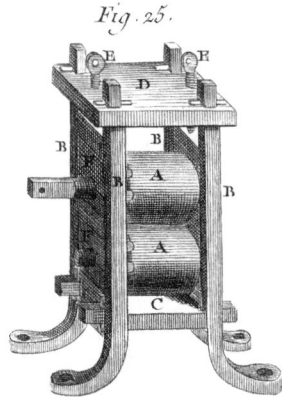

8. *Flatting mill, detail from Plate VI, "Orfèvre Bijoutier," in Denis Diderot,* Encyclopédie; Recueil de Planches, *vol. 8.*

technological improvement seems to have had little impact until after the Revolution. Even then, we only have evidence of a small number of Massachusetts artisans who owned these labor-saving flatting mills by the end of the eighteenth century.[18]

When the goldsmith determined that the sheet he had forged was thin enough, he cut the sheet of silver with shears to make the edges even and marked the center of the mass with a small pointed punch. Using this punch as his center point, the artisan scribed concentric circles—which would serve as guides to him in working the vessel—on the sheet with a compass. Beginning at the center of the sheet, he then hammered down on it with smaller hammers (9, 10) onto the end of a large tree trunk, stretching the silver into a dish-like form.

Once the object had been formed as far as possible through the forging process, in which the goldsmith stretched the metal by hammering it directly from above, he then turned the piece of silver over and began the process of raising (2, detail b). Working now on what would eventually be the outside of the object, with his raising hammer at a slight angle to the silver, the goldsmith hammered down against specially shaped raising anvils, "gathering up" the silver into the desired shape. Raising anvils were made in a great variety of shapes, such as the "beaker Anvill" owned by the Boston goldsmith Joseph Sanderson (1666) and the porringer anvil owned by another Boston goldsmith, Samuel Edwards

9. *Hammers, detail from Plate XII, "Orfèvre Grossier," in Denis Diderot,* Encyclopédie; Recueil de Planches, *vol. 8.*

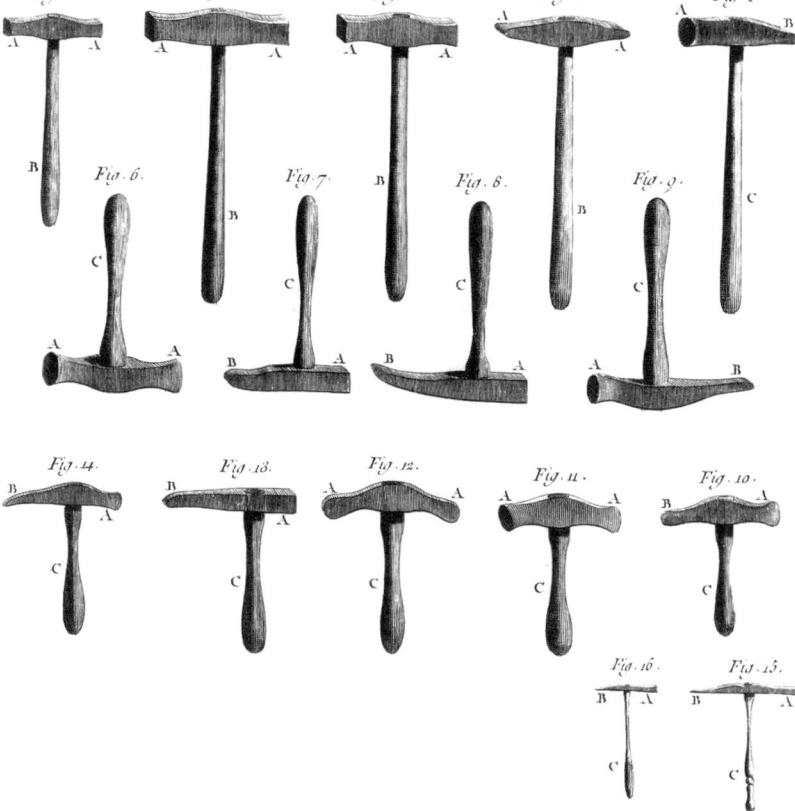

10. Silversmith's hammers, ca. 1900. Strawbery Banke Museum.

11. Anvils, stakes, and swages, detail from Plate XI, "Orfèvre Grossier," in Denis Diderot, Encyclopédie; Recueil de Planches, *vol. 8.*

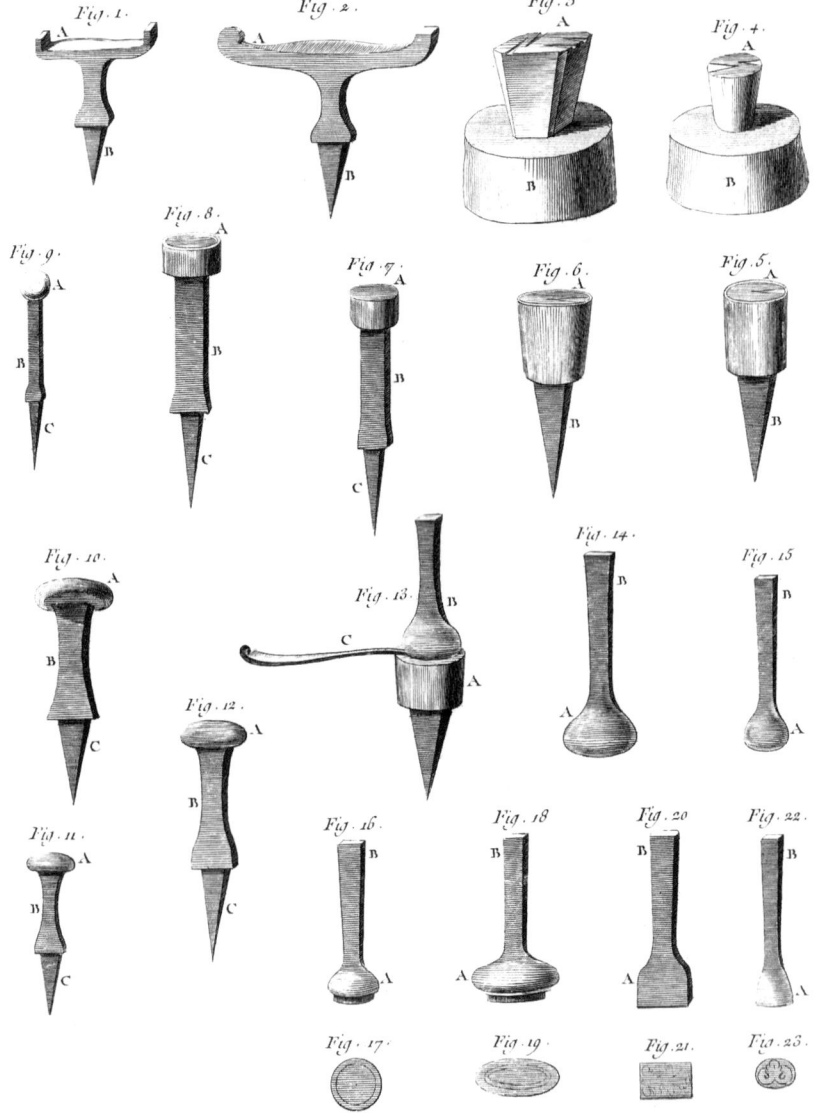

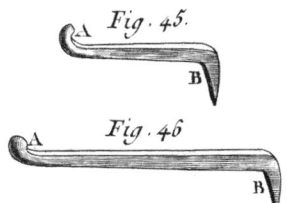

12. Snarling irons, detail from Plate XIV, "Orfèvre Grossier," in Denis Diderot, Encyclopédie; Recueil de Planches, *vol. 8.*

13. Snarling iron and its mode of application for raising, from George E. Gee, The Goldsmith's Handbook, *3rd edition, London, 1886. Yale University Library.*

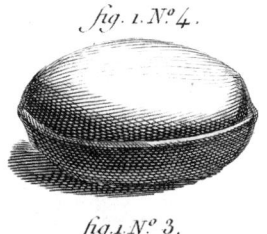

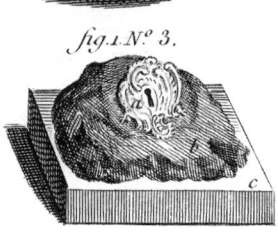

14. Sand cushion and cement block, detail from Plate I, "Argenteur," in Denis Diderot, Encyclopédie; Recueil de Planches, *vol. 8.*

(1762).[19] The raising process also involved working the object over a number of different stakes or teasts secured in bench vises or tree trunks (11) until the vessel achieved its final form. These stakes and teasts came in a variety of shapes, such as the "2 Tests with plaine and flower'd Spoon Swages" owned by the Boston goldsmith Edward Webb in 1718 and the "Round Teast" and "Locket d°" that appear in the inventory of the Boston goldsmith John Coney in 1722.[20] Objects with flat bottoms were completed using bottoming stakes and punches to square-off the base. After the vessel was raised, the goldsmith hammered the piece all over with a broad, flat planishing hammer in order to smooth the surface and remove the marks made by the raising hammers. Most large pieces of holloware were made in this manner, although later in

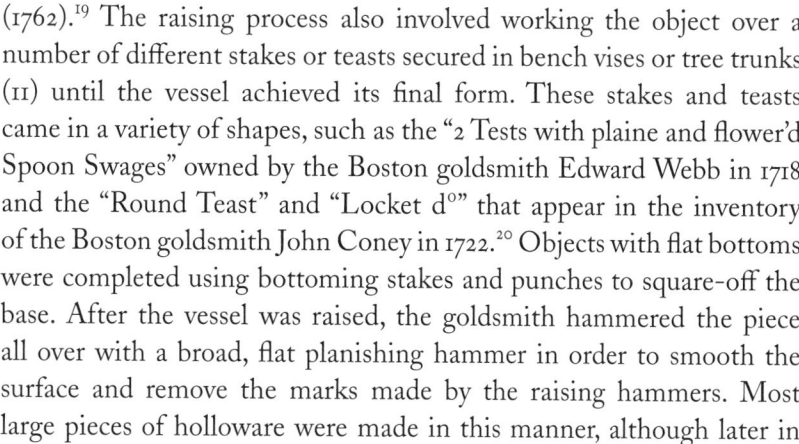

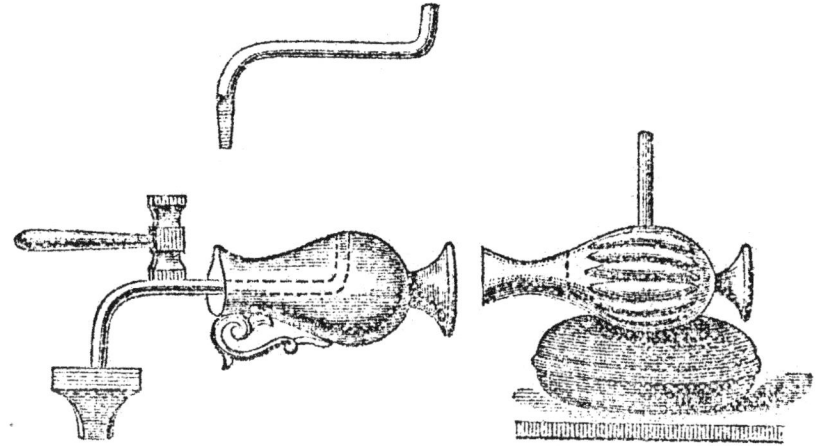

the eighteenth century, and in the early nineteenth century, some were made from sheet silver by cutting and seaming.

If objects were to be embellished with chasing and embossing, it was done at this point in the process. The snarling iron (12) was a specialized stake used for creating raised designs on the surface of a finished vessel. The goldsmith secured the curved iron in a vise and placed the body of the object to be decorated over the projecting arm of the iron. The silversmith then hammered the neck of the iron, which caused the pointed end to rebound against the silver vessel, creating a raised design on its surface (13, left). As George Gee noted in England in the late nineteenth century, "designs [were] only roughly raised in this manner, the perfecting of them being performed by the application of various kinds of chasing tools."[21] In order to prepare it for chasing, the body of the vessel was filled with pitch, or a mixture of pitch, resin, and brick dust referred to as cement, to prevent it from being damaged during chasing. The silversmith steadied the vessel on the bench by placing it on a sand-filled leather bag (13, right; 14, upper).[22] If the object to be chased was very small and did not need to be tipped or rotated while it was being worked, the goldsmith might choose to secure the entire object in a flat block of cement (14, lower).

During raising and all other hammering processes, the metal gradually hardened as its crystalline structure was altered and stretched. The silversmith had to anneal the silver in the forge many times (1, detail 13), heating it to between 1100 and 1200° F., so that the metal's crystalline structure could re-form, thus restoring its malleability.[23] The silver was then rapidly cooled by quenching it in water before working.

Seventeenth- and eighteenth-century silversmiths cast much of the small ornament on the objects they made, and some even cast fairly substantial parts of objects, such as caster bases and porringer handles. The method used was sand-casting, which employed special fine-grained molding sand that could retain even the most intricate details. The goldsmith pressed metal patterns into wet molding sand packed tight into special frames or flasks (15). Once a flask was filled, the two

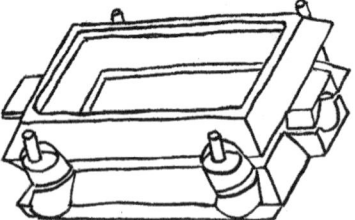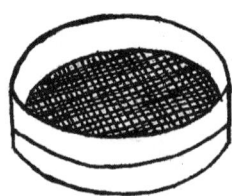

15. Sand casting flask, screen for sifting sand, and wooden sand rammer. Drawings by Geoffrey W. R. Ward.

halves were separated, the pattern removed, and the flask fastened together again. Molten metal was then poured into the mold, and when the castings cooled, the sand was brushed away. Although the mold was destroyed in the process of casting, many molds could be made using the same metal patterns, and many castings could be produced easily once the workshop was set up for the operation.

Although all goldsmiths cast metal, largeworkers may have been the primary fabricators of casting patterns. Samuel Edwards had hundreds of patterns in his inventory in 1762, and at least one porringer exists with his mark cast rather than struck into the handle and then later overstruck with his nephew's mark (16). This suggests that Samuel Edwards marked his casting patterns so that castings made from them would be identifiable as coming from his designs. Most goldsmiths' inventories list casting flasks, but only a few inventories—those of David Jesse, Edward Webb, John Coney, John Burt, and Daniel Henchman—list more than two.[24] Not all surviving inventories are detailed enough to include items of this type, but these listings suggest that most goldsmiths made a few simple castings and that only the larger firms had a reason to cast a wide variety of patterns at the same time. The survival of cast parts with marks in the castings suggests that some individuals occasionally may have sold pre-cast parts to other silversmiths and that some goldsmiths used parts of objects made by other artisans as patterns when making their molds.[25] Nearly all detailed Massachusetts goldsmiths' inventories include patterns and molds of one sort or another.

16. Detail of silver porringer handle bearing the mark of Joseph Edwards, Jr., struck over the mark of Samuel Edwards. Samuel Edwards's mark is actually part of the casting of the handle. Courtesy of Gebelein Silversmiths, photograph by George M. Cushing.

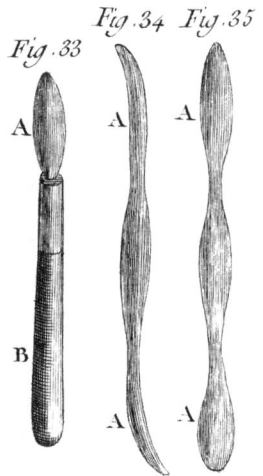

17. *Burnishers, detail from Plate XIV, "Orfèvre Grossier," in Denis Diderot,* Encyclopédie; Recueil de Planches, *vol. 8.*

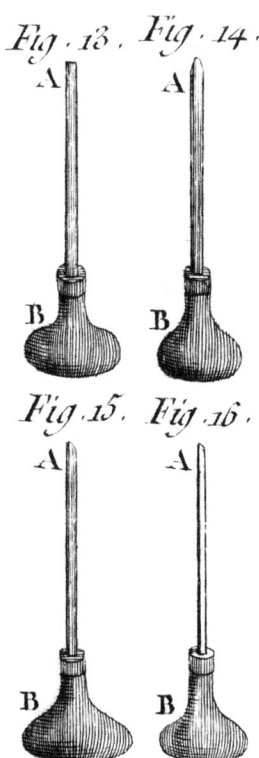

18. *Gravers, detail from Plate XIV, "Orfèvre Grossier," in Denis Diderot,* Encyclopédie; Recueil de Planches, *vol. 8.*

While being worked, the silver remained white and lusterless; dipping the object in various solutions, polishing it with rottenstone, emery, rouge, and other abrasives, and burnishing it with steel and stone burnishers brought out the shine of the silver (17). After polishing, the silversmith used gravers (18) to add any engraving that had been ordered by the client.

The masthead of an invitation issued by Goldsmiths' Hall, London, about 1707 (19) is a composite view of the many operations carried on in a goldsmith's shop. As such, it does not show the interior of a single shop but illustrates many of the tasks peculiar to goldsmithing. Forging and raising are depicted in the lower right-hand corner; the artisans at the bench are chasing and engraving with the aid of bench vises and sand-filled leather cushions—referred to as "Chasing Skins"—for holding objects steady. Soldering of small parts could be done over a table with a blowpipe and lamp (3, detail e; 4, detail a), but when parts to be attached were relatively large, objects were soldered in the forge. Much in evidence in the Goldsmiths' Hall masthead is the drawing bench (19 center, see also 20), used in making thin wire and long strips of decorative molding. At the upper left a workman uses a lathe for polishing and finishing.

Because of the size of their shops, their large assortment of tools, and the significant numbers of apprentices and journeymen they employed, largeworkers often carried out specialized functions. The Boston goldsmith Jacob Hurd, for instance, turned bodies of tankards for other silversmiths, smoothing them on a large metalworker's lathe (19, upper left), skimming off excess solder, and incising them with the lines that gave them a finished edge.[26] Hurd's lathe may be the one mentioned in the inventory of his son Benjamin's estate (1781) as "1 Turning Lathe, Wheel Blocks &c."[27] Gilding and refining shop sweepings (or lemel) may also have been generally limited to the shops of the biggest goldsmithing and jewelry firms. This may have been particularly true in the eighteenth century because touchstones for determining the quality of silver and gold wares only appear in inventories taken before 1750.[28] In addition, mercury, or quicksilver, which was used in making amalgams for gilding and silvering metals (and also in refining), appears in records of only three goldsmiths' shops—John Hull, Jeremiah Dummer, and John Coney—and it does not appear in lists of items available from the major retailers of goldsmiths' supplies in Boston, such as John Welsh, Daniel Parker, and Zachariah Brigden.[29]

A comparison between the shop and tools of John Coney and those of John Dixwell, and of George Hanners, Sr., makes clear the contrast between the largest goldsmithing establishments and the shops of more average largeworkers. John Coney (d. 1722), John Dixwell (d. 1725), and George Hanners (d. 1740) seem to have been engaged in similar work, and we know from extant objects that they produced similar forms.

19. Masthead, ca. 1707, Goldsmiths' Hall Invitation. The Worshipful Company of Goldsmiths, London.

20. Drawing bench, detail from Plate VIII, "Orfèvre Grossier," in Denis Diderot, Encyclopédie; Recueil de Planches, *vol. 8.*

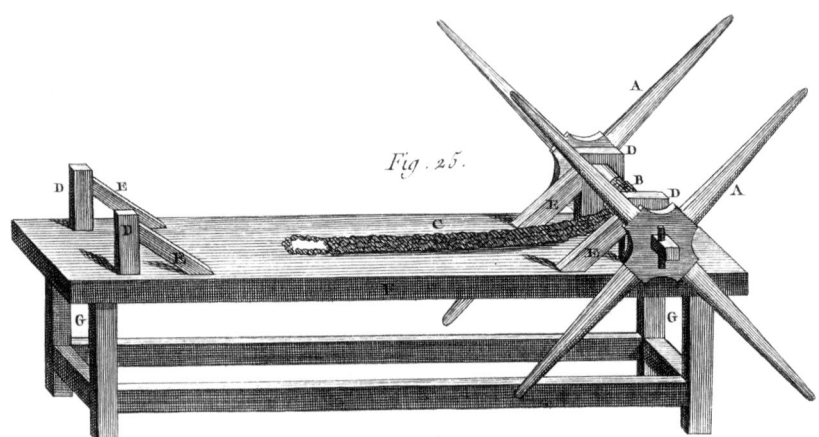

An analysis of the tools in their detailed estate inventories, which have been transcribed in full in their individual biographies in this volume, enables us to ascertain how the work done in each shop differed.[30]

John Dixwell owned tools and supplies worth £53.9.7 Massachusetts currency (£17.16 sterling) when he died in 1725. Forty percent of the money that Dixwell invested in his working shop was in large anvils and stakes, and he had only an additional £2.10.9 (£1 sterling), including his drawing bench, in smaller specialized shaping tools. George Hanners, who owned working tools worth £93.1 (£17.14 sterling), had most of his capital invested in "1 forge Anvil 3 Raising D°.," a "Belly Pott" anvil, and specialized stakes and stamps—one for shaping forks, and others for shaping spoons (see 11, fig. 13)—valued at £60.19.6 (£11.12 sterling), or 65 percent of the total value of his working tools. Both of these men made fairly plain objects, with little or no raised ornament, and both received modest public commissions. John Coney, the largest single producer of holloware in Boston before 1725, had the same heavy

Fig. 8.

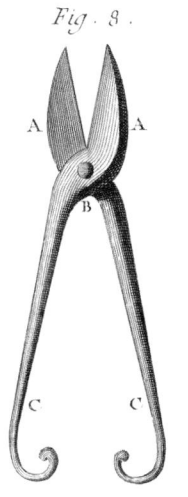

21. *Shears, detail from Plate XIII, "Orfèvre Grossier," in Denis Diderot,* Encyclopédie; Recueil de Planches, *vol. 8.*

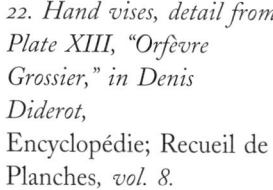

22. *Hand vises, detail from Plate XIII, "Orfèvre Grossier," in Denis Diderot,* Encyclopédie; Recueil de Planches, *vol. 8.*

anvils owned by Dixwell and Hanners, but they accounted for only £52.14.2 ¹/₂ (£21 sterling), or 29 percent, of his total inventory of shop tools and goldsmithing supplies valued at £183.3.¹/₂ (£73 sterling). He had another £48.3.9 (£19.4 sterling, 26 percent of the total) in specialized shaping tools, including "An Engine for Coining." Binding wire (for binding parts together during soldering), borax, saltpeter, sandover (fluxes for use when melting metal in a crucible and during soldering), and mercury were worth £25.13.7 (£10.5 sterling), or 14 percent of the total value of his tools and supplies. Coney also had a substantial amount of money tied up in crucibles, shears (21), bench and other vises (22), tongs (23), and hammers.

The numbers of tools Coney owned far exceeded those owned by Dixwell and Hanners. Dixwell owned 32 hammers and Coney owned 112; Hanners's stock of hammers was valued along with his drawing irons and files and, based on comparison with other inventories, probably numbered between 20 and 25.[31] Dixwell owned 1 forging anvil and 11 other anvils, 2 of which are described as bellypot anvils, while Coney owned 2 forging anvils, 24 anvils "of various sorts," and 1 tobacco box anvil. Dixwell had 2 teasts, 7 stakes, 4 "Ring & other Swages," 2 salt stamps, and 16 cutting and dapping punches (24, 25). Coney owned teasts (not specifically described) weighing 98 pounds, as well as a spoon teast, a round teast, and a locket teast, 46 different stakes, a cannister punch, 2 pepper box punches, 9 caster punches, 15 cutting punches, 6 dapping punches, and caster, salt, and spangle stamps. Coney owned 2 drawing benches, Dixwell owned 1, and Hanners owned drawing irons but no drawing bench, possibly because he used a drawing block similar to the ones illustrated in Diderot (26, 27).[32]

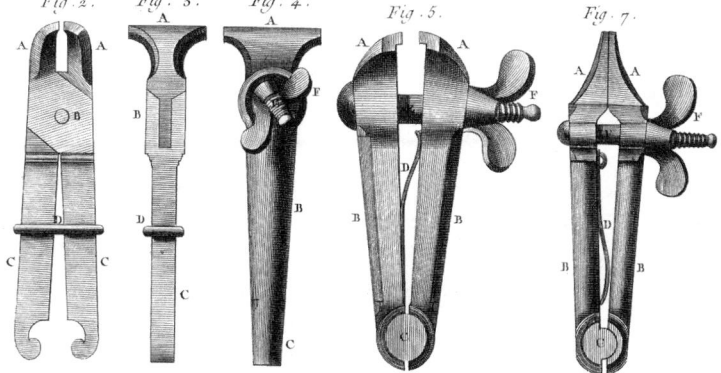

Coney's shop differed from the other two, then, in that he owned a large variety of stakes and teasts designed for the production of specific items. These tools allowed Coney's shop to produce some objects more quickly and economically than they could be produced in other shops. Dixwell and Hanners made objects that were generally very simple, with decorative castings and some engraved decoration, but rarely with any raised or chased ornament. Although all three shops were capable

23. Tongs and forge tools, detail from Plate XV, "Orfèvre Grossier," in Denis Diderot, Encyclopédie; Recueil de Planches, vol. 8.

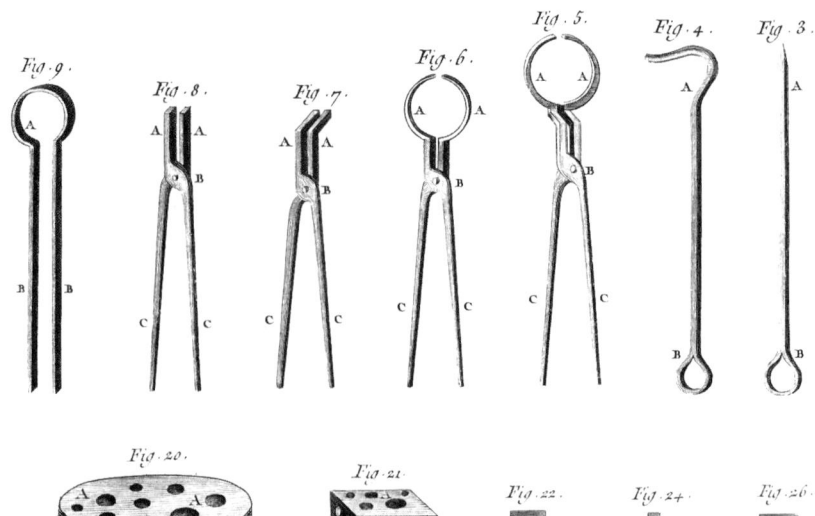

24. Dapping blocks (figs. 20–21), snuffbox punches (figs. 22–33), first, second, and third operations in making a small plate or dish (figs. 34–36), a brush (fig. 37), detail from Plate XII, "Orfèvre Grossier," in Denis Diderot, Encyclopédie; Recueil de Planches, vol. 8.

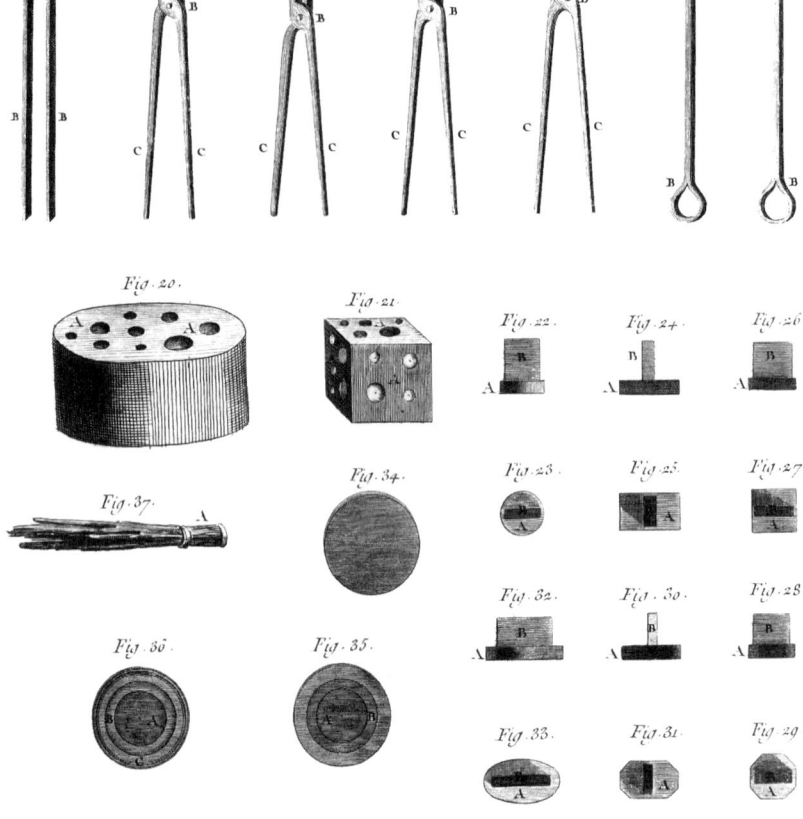

25. Chisels, punches, and scrapers, ca. 1900. Strawbery Banke Museum.

of making a wide variety of objects, Coney's specialized tools enabled him to produce them more efficiently.[33]

The appearance of glass showcases and scales and weights in all three inventories shows that all three men had retail sections in their shops

26. Drawing blocks and draw plates, detail from Plate IX, "Orfèvre Grossier," in Denis Diderot, Encyclopédie; Recueil de Planches, *vol 8.*

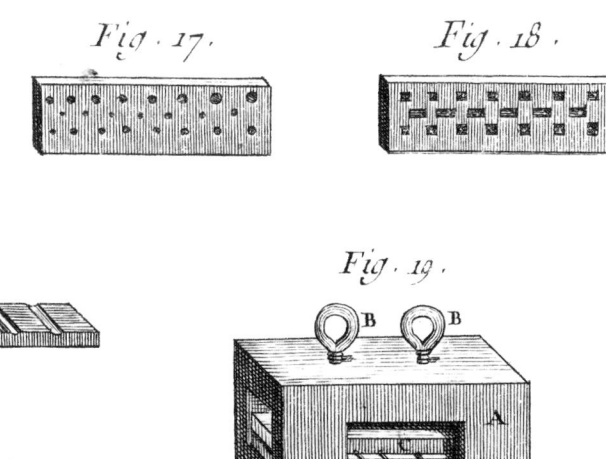

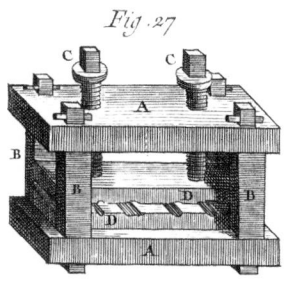

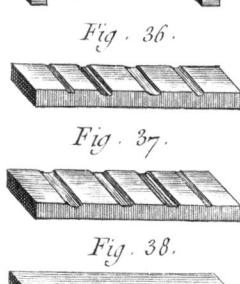

27. Drawing blocks and draw plates, detail from Plate IX, "Orfèvre Grossier," in Denis Diderot, Encyclopédie; Recueil de Planches, *vol. 8.*

(see 1, upper half; 3, detail f). Hanners, who worked at a time when metal was becoming increasingly scarce, owned unwrought and wrought silver and gold and jewelry that was worth less than his working tools (£87.17.2 Massachusetts currency, or £16.14 sterling). Dixwell, with tools worth only slightly more than Hanners's, and Coney, with tools worth four times more than either Dixwell's or Hanners's, were both able to keep large amounts of metal and wrought silver on hand, probably because both died before inflation increased substantially in Massachusetts. Dixwell had stock and metal worth £449.15.4 (£149 sterling), which was eight times more than the value of his tools, and Coney had stock and metal worth £579.4.2 (£230.16 sterling), or three times the value of his tools.[34]

The Smallworker

How did the shop of a smallworker, who concentrated on making such items as spoons, boxes, buckles, buttons, and rings and on doing repairs, differ from the shop of the average largeworker? On this point, the documents are often unclear. We have only a few inventories of such workers that appear to be complete, but even in those we sometimes encounter contradictory evidence.[35] What seems clear is that the artisan who chose to do primarily smallwork would not need to own the largest forging anvils, which weighed in excess of one hundred pounds, or specialized raising anvils needed for making the largest pieces of holloware. Instead, smallworkers owned lighter and therefore less expensive stakes, teasts, and swages that allowed them to make a few forms in a wide variety of designs. Nonetheless, artisans working outside of Boston who primarily made smallwares, in some cases also may have been called upon to make large objects. Like all goldsmiths they spent a significant amount of their time doing repairs on a variety of wares.

They also acted as agents for customers who wanted to order items from urban silversmiths.[36]

When John Hathorne of Salem, who was a smallworker, abandoned the craft to become a full-time merchant in 1787, he loaned his tools to twenty-one-year-old Ebenezer Bowditch (1766–1830), who was evidently just becoming established in business. This modest group of tools (see the transcription in Hathorne's biography) would have equipped Bowditch to function as a smallworker, and he is only known to have produced spoons.[37] To make a spoon or other piece of flatware, the silversmith cut out a narrow blank from a thick piece of sheet silver. He then hammered the thin edge to build up the thickness of the handle and hammered the width of the sheet to begin forming the bowl of a spoon or the end of a fork. The final shaping was done by hammering the spoon or fork end on an appropriate stake (11). In 1780, the silversmith Daniel Burnap of Connecticut noted directions for making spoons that place primary emphasis on judging the weight, thickness, and length of the proper blank for a particular size of spoon: "Larg Table Spoons are made in the following manner, first they are Cutt out at 2^{oz} & Draw^{ed}, to this Length [line approximately three inches long] then the boles & handles hammerd outt & neald & boild & Scowerd & half & hole hollowd & filed up & Scrapd & Neald & Boild & Scowerd & Burnished."[38]

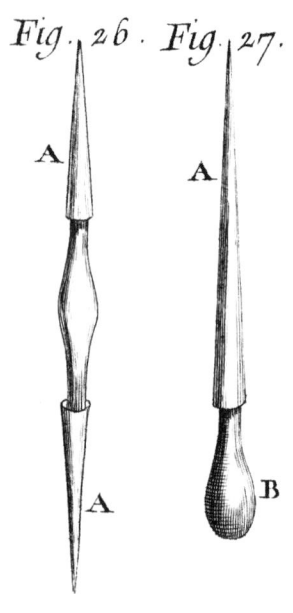

Fig. 26. Fig. 27.

28. Two types of triblets, detail from Plate V, "Orfèvre Bijoutier," in Denis Diderot, Encyclopédie; Recueil de Planches, *vol. 8.*

Bowditch had all of the tools needed to complete these operations, including one large anvil, a "hollering" (hollowing) stamp for fashioning the bowls of spoons, and burnishers for polishing. He made items such as rings, bracelets, and boxes using his pointed triblet (28) and his double-pronged sparhawk or sparrow hawk anvil (29).[39] Brass flasks for casting, pliers for cutting, and hand and bench vises for holding smallwork were other useful tools for the smallworker. Bowditch used blowpipes for soldering (3, detail e), copper boiling pans for preparing solutions, and burnishers for polishing. The pan to file gold in and the leming (or lemel) box indicate that Bowditch intended to gather up the silver and gold bits lost during working and have them refined for reuse.[40] The listing of fire tongs indicates that his shop had a forge. Nonetheless, the list is hardly complete. The whetstone suggests that Bowditch had cutting tools to sharpen that are not mentioned, and he would have had to purchase crucibles for melting silver and solder in the forge.

James Hill, a smallworker of Charlestown, claimed losses of tools resulting from the British bombardment of Charlestown in 1775 (see Hill's biography for a transcription).[41] Although it is possible that Hill owned more tools, the list is sufficiently detailed to demonstrate that Hill had a small retail area in his shop and that he had two workbenches with "skins." He also owned enough hammers and tongs for one workman, and a blowpipe and lamp for soldering, and he could make castings

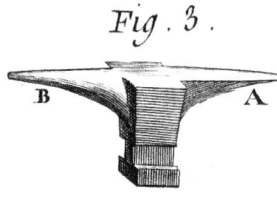

29. Small two-pronged anvil, detail from Plate V, "Orfèvre Bijoutier," in Denis Diderot, Encyclopédie; Recueil de Planches, *vol. 8.*

with his pair of flasks and molding box. These tools, although few in number, would have equipped Hill to carry on a modest business doing repairs and making such small items as buckles and boxes. He did not have the specialized tools needed to make holloware on a large scale, but his one anvil, weighing forty-nine pounds—an average weight for a raising anvil—may have enabled him to make a few small holloware items, or it may have been a small forging anvil on which he made flat sheet that he then cut with his shears ("serves" in the inventory), creased, and soldered into boxes and other small items.

The inventory (1781) of the Boston goldsmith Thomas Clark provides a full picture of a goldsmith's shop fitted for a smallworker.[42] (See the transcription of the inventory in his biography.) He owned "small" shop bellows, which indicates that his forge was not large, and his largest anvil weighed only fifty pounds. All of his specialized tools—spoon teasts and a ring swage—were designed for making small objects, and even his other anvil—a sparrow hawk—is pictured in Diderot as one type of anvil commonly owned by smallworkers and jewelers (29). He could do castings, and he had a pan for catching gold and silver filings. Although some authorities believe that some rings were cast, the frequent appearance of ring swages—hollow patterns into which the metal could be hammered to take on the design of the swage—suggests that ring blanks were hammered into a swage, shaped around a triblet, and then soldered together. It is clear that Clark made and sold only smallwork and jewelry because he owned only small weights—probably sufficient to weigh objects and metal of between ten and twenty ounces (3, detail f). The finished items in Clark's shop inventory further demonstrate that he specialized in making spoons, tongs, ladles, sugar shovels, rings, earrings, buckles, and an assortment of other small items.

The Jeweler

Jewelers made many of the same items made by smallworkers but were primarily differentiated from their colleagues by their knowledge of gemstones and their ability to set jewels. Campbell described the London jeweler:

> The Jeweller must be a Judge of all manner of precious Stones, their Beauties, common Blemishes, and their intrinsic Value: He must not only know real Stones, but fictitious Gems, and the manner of preparing them; his Business is to set them in Rings, Necklaces, Pendants, Ear-Rings, Buckles of all sorts, and in Watches and whatever Toys else are adorned with precious Stones. He makes his own Moulds, and forges all the Metal Part of his Work. Their Moulds are generally cut in burnt Bone, into which their Metal is cast. He ought to be an elegant Designer, and have a quick Invention for new Patterns, not only to range the Stones in such manner as to give Lustre to one another, but to create Trade; for a new Fashion

takes as much with the Ladies in Jewels as in any thing else: He that can furnish them oftenest with the newest Whim has the best Chance for their Custom.

A Jeweller then ought to have a good Eye, to observe the Flaws and Deceits in Jewels; a nice Taste in those kind of valuable Trifles, and a mechanical Hand and Head to execute his Designs. His Education may be merely *English*; I mean, he has no Occasion for any more than that Language: The Sciences are foreign to his Business.[43]

Fig.9.

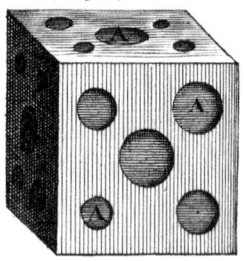

30. Dapping block, detail from Plate V, "Orfèvre Bijoutier," in Denis Diderot, Encyclopédie; Recueil de Planches, *vol. 8.*

Campbell commented that a master jeweler needed significant capital to set up a business, particularly if he intended to "furnish a Shop," but that "he that intends to work only for the Shopkeepers, and employ Apprentices and Journeymen, may begin with very little, and must be contented with less Profit than if he sold to the Wearer. These kind of Piece-Masters are paid according to the Work."[44]

The shop inventories of colonial Massachusetts jewelers demonstrate that they generally had few anvils, but owned large numbers of files, hand vises, and stones of all descriptions. Jewelers appear to have had some specialized tools, which many other workers in gold and silver also had. These included dapping blocks and punches for making beads and triblets for making rings (28, 30).[45] It was the large stock of gems and gemstones that made the jeweler's inventory distinctive. The Boston jeweler James Boyer, for instance, owned finished work and gold, silver, and stones worth £164.6.6, of which £117.13.6 was in stones and gems of various types; his working tools were valued at £71.11.6 (see Boyer's biography for a transcription of his inventory).[46] Stones were set in a variety of ways, but the appearance of foil in jewelers' inventories and advertisements suggests that colonial jewelers used metallic foils under stone settings in order to enhance the brilliancy of the stones. This is usually listed only as "foile," although an advertisement of 1771 lists "white and red foyle."[47] Another method of setting stones described by George Gee in *The Goldsmith's Handbook*, published in London in 1886, consisted of "drilling holes for the gems, and then with the scorper hollowing away a portion of the metal around the holes to fit the stones, and also in the direction the gems are to extend," while "bringing up of four little beads or caps . . . which act as claws, and form an efficient security for each gem."[48] A tool that seems to be distinctive to jewelers' work—whether within a shop where largework was also done or in a shop devoted solely to jewelry—was the drill stock and drill used in drilling and piercing (31). James Boyer owned three upright drills, and scorpers, too, appear in many inventories. Some settings also required bezels that the jeweler applied with solder; he then burnished the stone into place. Such delicate operations could not be done in the forge; jewelers also invariably owned lamps and blowpipes for soldering at the bench. Other common jewelers' tools and supplies include a large selection of files, several sparhawk or sparrow hawk anvils, saltpeter

31. Drills, drill stock, and bow, detail from Plate X, "Orfèvre Jouaillier, Metteur en Oeuvre," in Denis Diderot, Encyclopédie; Recueil de Planches, *vol. 8.*

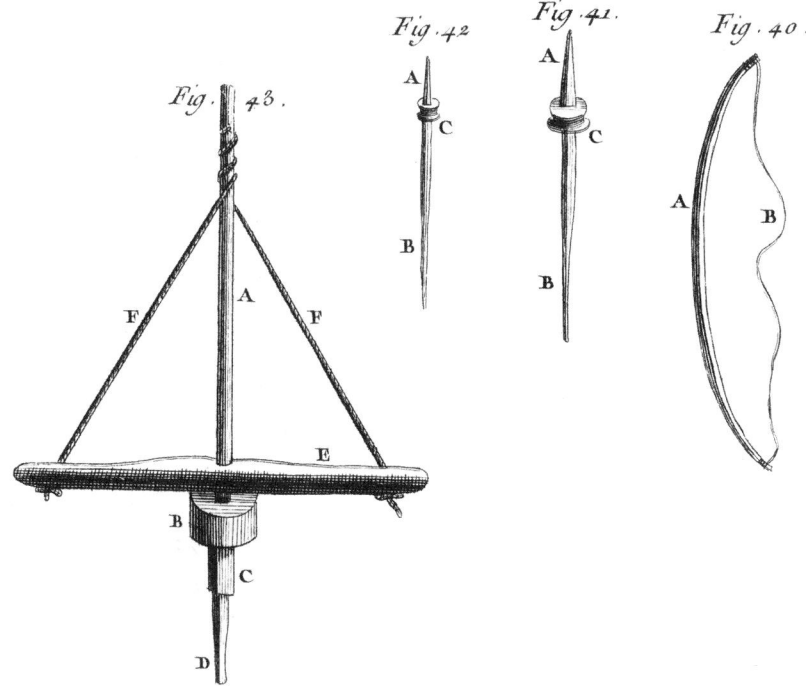

and borax for fluxes and for making enamel, dapping blocks and punches for making beads, and such items of especial use in the craft as "Ring Sizes" and the "pᵣ Diamond Scales" owned by James Boyer.[49]

Another technique practiced by the jeweler was the art of enameling. George Gee described enamels as "vitreous or glassy substances" that "must preserve a hard glassy appearance after fusion" and "adhere very firmly to the gold." Beginning with "transparent colourless bases, called fritz, or flux," the jeweler added color by mixing in metallic oxides. Once these were prepared, they were melted, cooled, and ground into a fine powder.[50] Then Gee describes how the item to be enameled (in Massachusetts, usually a mourning ring with white or black enamel) was prepared: "The pattern desired is first drawn on the work by the graver; the groundwork or part to receive the enamel is cut down very evenly, and this helps to heighten the effect. . . . After the work has been well cleaned by washing in a hot solution of soda, soap, and water, and dried, the enamel is applied . . . the work is then fired, and the enamel is laid on again as many times as required."[51] Enameling demanded an exact knowledge of the best temperatures for firing enamel as well as a knowledge of how to combine fluxes and oxides to obtain the desired color. Joseph Loring of Boston was reputed to have "excelled in enam-ellery."[52]

Massachusetts jewelers appear to have maintained large stocks of gold and gemstones, but there was a fair amount of variety within the trade. Some goldsmiths, such as Benjamin Greene of Boston, specialized in making beads and rings that were then set with stones by jewelers such as James Boyer.[53] Joseph Candish, who worked in Boston from about 1738 until the 1780s, made his living primarily by producing bezel wire, the thin piece of metal used to form the rim around a stone setting. Candish made the wire on a special wire-drawing apparatus that was apparently the "only one in town" at the time.[54] Other jewelers were known for their particular skill in one branch of the trade.

Journeymen and Their Tools

Upon finishing his apprenticeship, a young goldsmith usually worked for several years as a journeyman in a master's shop. Although he used the larger and more costly tools owned by his master, a journeyman was also expected to own his own chest of tools and to carry them with him as he went from shop to shop. In many cases the nature of the tools in an artisan's personal box, such as the one John LeRoux carried from New York to Boston, insured that he would find appropriate work.[55] The ownership of such a box of tools also gave journeymen goldsmiths the wherewithal to carry on some operations independently and to obtain work directly from patrons even during periods when they principally worked for master artisans on day wages.

Although Joseph Sanderson of Boston was nearly twenty-four years old when he died in 1666, the inventory of his tools—the earliest surviving inventory of a Boston goldsmith—suggests that he was probably still working for his father, Robert Sanderson, Sr., and his father's partner, John Hull. Joseph's collection of tools, therefore, reflects his special interests and expertise and shows that he was slowly accumulating the tools he would need to carry on the trade independently. Valued at just under £11 (£9.3 sterling), this modest assortment of tools (transcribed in Sanderson's biography) tells us much about Joseph Sanderson's abilities as a silversmith.[56] Although he did not own any large forging anvils, which would have been available to him in his father's shop, he did own several significant items: raising anvils, a beaker anvil, a snarling iron, chasing tools, a graver, a "Chasing bag & a New Skinne," triblets, swages, and patterns and sand-molding equipment. The earliest dated objects made in the Hull and Sanderson shops are beakers, and Joseph Sanderson's investment in a specialized anvil for making beakers demonstrates the demand for vessels of this shape for both domestic and church use during the early decades of Massachusetts settlement.

Sanderson's inventory lists a snarling iron—a specialized tool for embossing the surface of holloware—from which we can ascertain that he probably was skilled as an embosser and chaser. He also owned a "Chasing bag," a sand-filled bag used to support work during the chasing process, and a "New Skinne," probably a new leather bag that had yet to be filled with sand. Because he owned patterns, flasks, and sand—all used in sand casting—we know that he was able to make his own castings; the triblets and swages in the inventory suggest that he made small items that could be shaped on a triblet and that he used swages to form the ornament on some of his products. His graver and whetstone suggest that he was familiar with the art of engraving. These tools and the skills required to use them made Sanderson a valuable journeyman to a goldsmith looking for an embosser and chaser.

Sources of Tools

To fill their shops, Boston's earliest silversmiths had to obtain their tools in England. Men like Robert Sanderson, Sr., who arrived in New England from London about 1639, undoubtedly brought some of their tools with them. Sanderson and his partner, the Boston goldsmith John Hull, maintained close ties with London merchants, including Hull's cousin Edward, who purchased tools for Hull from Robert Jerrald of London in 1672.[57] Hull also supplied other Boston silversmiths with tools, including his former apprentice Jeremiah Dummer.[58] In 1674, Hull sent to England for a box of tools for his apprentice and relative Daniel Quincy. Quincy was approximately twenty-three years old at the time, so these may have been basic tools meant to help establish him in the trade.[59] No probate records survive for Hull's estate, but probably most of his tools remained with the business, which continued after his death under Sanderson and Sanderson's son Robert, Jr. After the death of Sanderson, Sr., in 1693, the younger Sanderson appears to have abandoned the trade, and the firm's stock of tools undoubtedly was purchased by other Boston artisans. John Coney's tools were sold, probably at auction, after his death in 1722, and in 1761, Hannah Simpson and Rebecca Cowell advertised the sale of goldsmiths' tools from the estate of William Cowell, Jr.[60] Sales such as these were major sources of tools and of specialized and sometimes unusual goldsmithing apparatus, such as John Coney's engine for making coins.[61]

   To create objects in the latest styles, goldsmiths were always anxious to obtain new swages, stamps, and stakes from England, and they needed quantities of files and crucibles and supplies such as borax and saltpeter on a regular basis. There were several men in Boston with significant mercantile connections in England who could have served as the source of many of these tools and supplies. Jeremiah Dummer, in particular, was a well-connected merchant who owned part interest in several shipping vessels and was actively involved in transatlantic trade. There is no evidence, however, that he was involved in selling tools. Instead, it appears that a less well established immigrant goldsmith, Richard Conyers, who emigrated from London about 1697, became a major source of tools for his fellow goldsmiths in early eighteenth-century Boston. Seeing that craftsmen found it difficult to obtain the tools they needed, Conyers attempted to exploit his English connections to serve this ready market. Unfortunately, his efforts were not as successful as he had hoped, or perhaps he merely spread his available resources too thin, for court records show that he was unable to pay off his English creditors. In 1700, Charles Groome, Conyers's former apprentice, a merchant from Middlesex County, England, sued Conyers for money owed him for a large assortment of goldsmiths' tools ordered in the year before, including molding sand and pumice as well as pots, flasks, files, and a hammer.[62] In 1701, Conyers was imprisoned because of his failure to pay a debt to a London gentleman for £135.15.4, some of which may well have been for tools.[63] From another suit brought to court in 1702, we know that Conyers's colleague David Jesse purchased £40 worth of tools from the Boston and New York merchant Joseph Mallinson, for whom Jesse had provided a number of different services, including clipping coins.[64]

Goldsmiths' anvils and supplies also could be obtained from other sources. In 1716/17, Samuel Bissell, an English anvilsmith living in Newport, Rhode Island, advertised in the *Boston News-Letter* that he made "all sorts of Black-smiths and Gold-smith's anvils, Brick-irons and stakes and new Faces [for] old ones." In 1713, the merchants Andrew and Jonathan Belcher advertised that they sold "Smiths Anvils" and other ironware made by "Sir *Ambrose Crowley* Knight and Alderman of the City of London" at their Boston warehouse.[65] In 1741, Richard Clarke, proprietor of an iron foundry, advertised that he could provide "Forge Hammers, anvils, or Plates, Smiths' Anvils . . . or any other Cast Iron Ware" to persons "giving speedy Notice (of the Sizes and Quantity they want)" to him "at his Furnace in the Gore" or at the warehouse of Oliver, Clarke, and Lee in King Street, Boston.[66] Supplies such as alum, saltpeter, and beeswax could be obtained from grocers and apothecaries, and copper boiling pans and other general metalware could be obtained from braziers and hardware merchants.[67] Scales and weights were also available in Boston from at least two instrument makers: Caleb Ray, who called himself "Chief Skale-maker of New England" in 1708; and Jonathan Dakin, a mathematical balancemaker who advertised between 1745 and 1753.[68] By 1741, Boston even had a specialized bellowsmaker, Joseph Clough, who maintained a shop near the Charlestown Ferry where he made and mended "all sorts of Bellows for Furnaces, Refiners, Blacksmiths, Braziers and Goldsmiths."[69]

By the middle of the eighteenth century, the revaluation and stabilization of the Massachusetts currency made it easier for American merchants to buy goods in England and made access to tools of all kinds less difficult. Several Boston goldsmiths diversified their businesses to include the importation and sale of all kinds of metalwares, including a full range of tools.[70] Perhaps the best known marketers of tools and goldsmithing supplies were Samuel Edwards, his former apprentice Daniel Parker, and Parker's brother-in-law John Welsh. Samuel Edwards's inventory of 1762 lists a huge assortment of tools for artisans in a variety of trades, indicating that he was a major retailer of tools of all sorts. After the listing of tools in the shop, the inventory goes on to list additional tools standard to the goldsmithing trade in small quantities, as well as larger quantities of smaller tools, including 30 pairs of hand vises of varying quality, 31 pairs of pliers, 30 pair of watch pliers, 10 pair of sliding tongs, 9 pair of screw compasses, 11 dozen engraving tools, 2 dozen "Freezing Punches," 6 pairs of nippers, 8 pairs of burnishers, 19 pairs of shears of various sizes, 36 dozen files, 30 dozen clockmakers' files, more than 5 gross of smaller files, sandpaper, sieves, molding sand, and whetstones. This inventory also includes hundreds of blue pots and crucibles, 2 chests of drawers filled with casting patterns, and dozens of scales of various sizes as well as 35 sets of weights, 50 sets of penny weights, and 156 sets of grain weights, with dozens of scales of various sizes.[71] Daniel Parker bought tools from Edwards's estate to add to his stock and throughout the 1760s continued to advertise that he had a large assortment of tools, supplies, and stones for goldsmiths, jewelers, and watchmakers. In addition to Parker and Welsh, Zachariah Brigden and Daniel Boyer supplied a similar assortment of tools to craftsmen in various trades during the years leading up to the Revolution, including silversmiths working outside of Boston. The Salem silversmiths John Touzell and John Hathorne bought tools from Boyer and Parker, even though Salem was the second most active port in New England at the time of the transactions.[72] Boston suppliers dealt in all kinds of tools, from the largest anvils to the smallest files and nippers.[73] Welsh advertised a large assortment of imported tools as well as "Borax, Salt Petre, Pummice Stone, Flour of ditto, Rotton Stone, Sandever, Emery, Putty, and sundry other Articles."[74]

Some goldsmiths fashioned their own tools or had specialized tools made for them by other artisans. The estate inventory of John Dixwell includes, among the listing of tools, several iron bars that may have been used in this way.[75] Goldsmiths may also have ordered patterns and stamps from local braziers and diecutters.

After the Revolution documents reveal that there was a slight change in the range and type of tools required by silversmiths. Flatting mills (8) begin to appear, and the specialized teasts and stakes formerly common in the goldsmith's stock of tools are listed in smaller numbers. The preference for rectilinearity and geometric forms that came with the new neoclassical style made it possible for goldsmiths to make many vessels by shaping sheet silver around simple wooden blocks, rather than raising them from forged sheet. From extant objects we know that sheet silver must have been readily available—perhaps from such local Boston artisans as the goldsmith Caleb Beal, who owned a "plating mill," and the jeweler John Codner, who owned a "flatting mill."[76] This availability of sheet silver made it easier for an artisan to set up shop as a holloware maker because the craft no longer required expensive forging and raising anvils. The resulting decrease in the basic cost of setting up shop may account, at least in part, for the increasing numbers of individuals who entered the trade after 1800.

Sources and Prices of Silver

During the seventeenth and eighteenth centuries silversmiths obtained most of the silver and gold they used in their work by melting down old objects and coins. As late as 1808, all European coins were accepted as legal tender in America, but the coin most common in the colonies at the time of independence was the Spanish dollar.[77] Although goldsmiths often made rings, buckles, and other small items in anticipation of future sales, most of the large objects made in the goldsmith's shop were bespoke, or custom-made, goods, for which the customer usually provided the goldsmith with some portion of the metal needed to make the object or objects ordered. Seventeenth-century silversmiths had less difficulty acquiring silver than their later counterparts because constant immigration during the early years of settlement meant that there was a steady influx of specie from the mother country. Nonetheless, Massachusetts, in an effort to stem the outflow of hard money to England, set up its own mint for coining shilling, sixpence, and three-pence coins. The Massachusetts Mint, under mintmasters John Hull and Robert Sanderson, Sr., struck flat coins whose face value was worth nearly twice their melt value. This had the effect of encouraging colonists to spend these pine tree, willow tree, and oak tree coins at home.[78]

In spite of these efforts, the outflow of specie continued as the balance of trade tipped in favor of England. In 1697, the colonial legislature declared that because of the scarcity of circulating coins all "wrought Plate, Bullion and Silver of Sterling Alloy . . . shall pass and be accepted in all payments at the rate of seven Shillings P ounce Troy weight."[79] The table on the facing page shows that, after the turn of the century, the problem became even more acute. Massachusetts suffered from high war debts incurred during King William's War and Queen Anne's War, and by 1720, Boston artisans and merchants were feeling the pinch of inflation coupled with the shortage of specie.[80] This probably explains why John Edwards added a 7.5 percent surcharge on his customers' bills unless they provided him with enough metal (in old, worn-out objects or in coin) to make the new wares they had ordered.[81] As the rate of inflation escalated, the cost of obtaining metal sometimes became prohibitive. Jacob Hurd probably went bankrupt because he was forced to pay as much as 30 percent interest to his suppliers when he purchased raw silver for his workshop on credit.[82] Benjamin Greene and goldsmiths who branched out into merchant activities seem to have fared far better. Through his trading connections Greene was able to obtain large amounts of metal, purchases he seems to have financed by buying and selling various colonial currencies.[83]

The Price of Silver, 1700–50
Shillings per ounce, Troy weight

Year	Price	Year	Price
1700	7		
1701	7	1726	16
1702	7	1727	16
1703	7	1728	16/6, 17, 18
1704	8	1729	19, 19/6, 20, 21, 22
1705	8	1730	21, 20, 19
1706	8	1731	18/6, 19
1707	8	1732	19/6, 20, 20/6
1708	8	1733	21, 21/6, 22, 22/6, 23
1709	8	1734	24, 25, 26, 26/6, 27
1710	8	1735	27/6
1711	8/4	1736	27, 26/6
1712	8/6	1737	26/6, 27
1713	8/6	1738	27/6, 28
1714	9	1739	29, 29/6, 29
1715	9	1740	28/6, 29, 28, 29
1716	10	1741	28/6, 28
1717	10	1742	28, 27/6, 28/6, 29
1718	11	1743	30, 32
1719	12	1944	32, 33, 34
1720	12/4	1745	35, 36, 37
1721	12/6, 13, 13/6	1746	37, 38, 40, 45, 48, 50
1722	14, 14/6	1747	53, 55, 58, 60, 58
1723	14/6, 15, 15/6	1748	58, 56, 55, 57, 55, 56, 58, 56
1724	16, 16/6	1749	56, 58, 60, 58
1725	16, 15	1750	56, +55

Source: "An Acco^t of ye Price of Silver from ye year 1700," *Zachariah Brigden Papers, Beinecke Rare Book and Manuscript Library, Yale University.*

Setting Up as a Master Artisan

Although some goldsmiths started their careers by renting space in another goldsmith's shop—Timothy Dwight, for example, paid £6 for the use of space in Hull and Sanderson's shop in 1677—for most, the first step in becoming a master goldsmith was to establish a working space or shop of their own.[84] The independent artisan's shop was usually located in a small building adjacent to his home or in one room of his living quarters, although some goldsmiths rented shops several blocks away from their homes. No contemporary view of the interior of an American goldsmith's shop exists, but several English and European prints provide information on the size and arrangement of goldsmiths' shops. Written descriptions and shop inventories also provide information that allows us to reconstruct the physical appearance of a Boston goldsmith's shop of the seventeenth and eighteenth centuries. The physical setting where the goldsmith worked varied considerably from the tiny workshop of the lone artisan to the large, bustling business establishments of such prolific goldsmiths as John Coney and Jacob Hurd.

Only a few documents that provide precise dimensions of shops survive. The Massachusetts Mint operated by John Hull and Robert Sanderson, Sr., was housed in a sixteen-by-sixteen-foot building (256 square feet) that may also have housed the partners' general goldsmithing operation.[85] The earliest and most prominent goldsmiths in town, Hull and Sanderson commanded the bulk of silversmithing commissions in Boston and the surrounding area between 1660 and 1680. The shops of William Pollard of Boston and Seth Ring of Salem are probably more representative of the shops of modest artisans. In 1711 Thomas Powell received permission from the town of Boston "to Erect a Timber building for a Goldsmith Shop for his son [stepson William Pollard] of 15 foot long, 12 foot wide, and 9 foot stud with a Flatt Roof" (180 square feet).[86] In 1778, the goldsmith Seth Ring purchased a shop in Salem that measured sixteen feet by fourteen feet from Edward Smith (224 square feet).[87]

The most prominent Boston goldsmiths at midcentury probably had larger shops comparable to the one operated by Hull and Sanderson. Samuel Edwards's shop occupied at least two first-floor rooms of his house in Hanover Street in Boston (and possibly an outbuilding). Although the exact dimensions of the house are not mentioned in any records, deeds indicate that the lot was only $22^{1}/_{2}$ feet wide, and therefore the house was probably no more than sixteen feet deep. The house was two-and-a-half stories high and had three rooms on each floor; there was a warehouse, a shop, and another building on the same property. From the estate inventory, it appears that the separate shop was used to store general shop goods, and that the goldsmithing shop was divided between the working shop and a retail section, each in a different lower room of the house. Edwards sold a huge assortment of imported metalwares in addition to silver holloware and flatware, and thus a separate retail area would have been essential to his business. The two rooms in the house that were devoted to the shop were probably sixteen-by-sixteen feet and sixteen-by-twenty feet, for a total of 576 square feet.[88]

Benjamin Walker's description of "ye finest Sight of silver plate belonging to Gouernour Charles Knowles" at Jacob Hurd's shop in Cornhill suggests that Hurd's shop also had a separate retail area suitable for displaying wares.[89] Hurd's land fronted on Cornhill Street, at which point the lot was thirty-nine feet wide. The house had been divided between two owners before Hurd purchased both halves of the house in 1742, and deeds indicate that the house had a central entryway that was used in common by the former owners. This and the width of the lot suggest that Hurd's house had two rooms and a central hall facing the street, at least one of which was used as a retail space.[90] Daniel Parker probably also had separate working and retail spaces. In 1758 he advertised that he had goods for sale at two locations in Boston—"his Shop near the Golden-Ball, or at his House next Door to Deacon Grant's in Union Street."[91]

Other references to shops and shop spaces offer a variety of information about goldsmiths and their business practices. Except for a few shop spaces rented by individuals in the center of Boston around Dock Square, most silversmiths' shops in Boston appear to have been located in or adjacent to their homes on Marlborough Street, Newbury Street, Cornhill Street, Hanover Street, Union Street, and Ann Street (32). Two very successful Boston silversmiths, Benjamin Burt and Joseph Foster (1760–1839), had shops on Fish Street, a little further from the town center but opposite the waterfront in a busy commercial area of town.[92] Although many of these shops were in goldsmiths' houses, some were rented. Joseph Coolidge, a tenant of Widow Norten, operated an extensive retail shop "opposite Mr. William Greenleaf's, Foot of Cornhill," in 1771.[93] In smaller towns, goldsmiths also seem to have preferred locations along main thoroughfares or near large public buildings, such as Thomas Hunt's shop in Springfield, which was located "a few Rods north" of the Court House. John Jackson operated a shop in the midst of the Nantucket waterfront, on Straight Wharf, in 1772.[94]

Sometimes shops were separate buildings built on a silversmith's house lot or were actual additions built onto an individual's dwelling. In 1797, at the age of sixty-two, Samuel Barrett of Nantucket sold his house and land to his son, "reserving only for my selfe the Liberty & privilege of my Goldsmiths Shop to Stand and abide on the Front of said Land. so long as my self shall want s'd Shop to work in."[95] In 1761, John Ball purchased a 6½ acre lot in Concord, Massachusetts, from his father that already had two dwelling houses and a brick shop on it, and records suggest that he built another shop on the lot within a few years.[96] In 1767, Thomas Grant of Marblehead, Massachusetts, owned a large lot with a small goldsmith's shop on the corner facing south on the Cart Road and east on the Highway.[97] In 1770 Andrew Croswell purchased a dwelling house on Market Street in Plymouth, Massachusetts, to which he added a goldsmithing shop on the south side; and in 1771 John Coverly owned "a house and shop adjoining" in Boston.[98]

Once the shop building or space had been set aside, the goldsmith began to furnish it with tools. A few documents survive to give us some idea of what tools an aspiring young largeworker would seek to acquire and how much such a stock of tools would cost him. Rufus Greene of Boston began his business on 7 October 1728, shortly after his mother, Ann Greene, a successful shopkeeper, died. The inventory

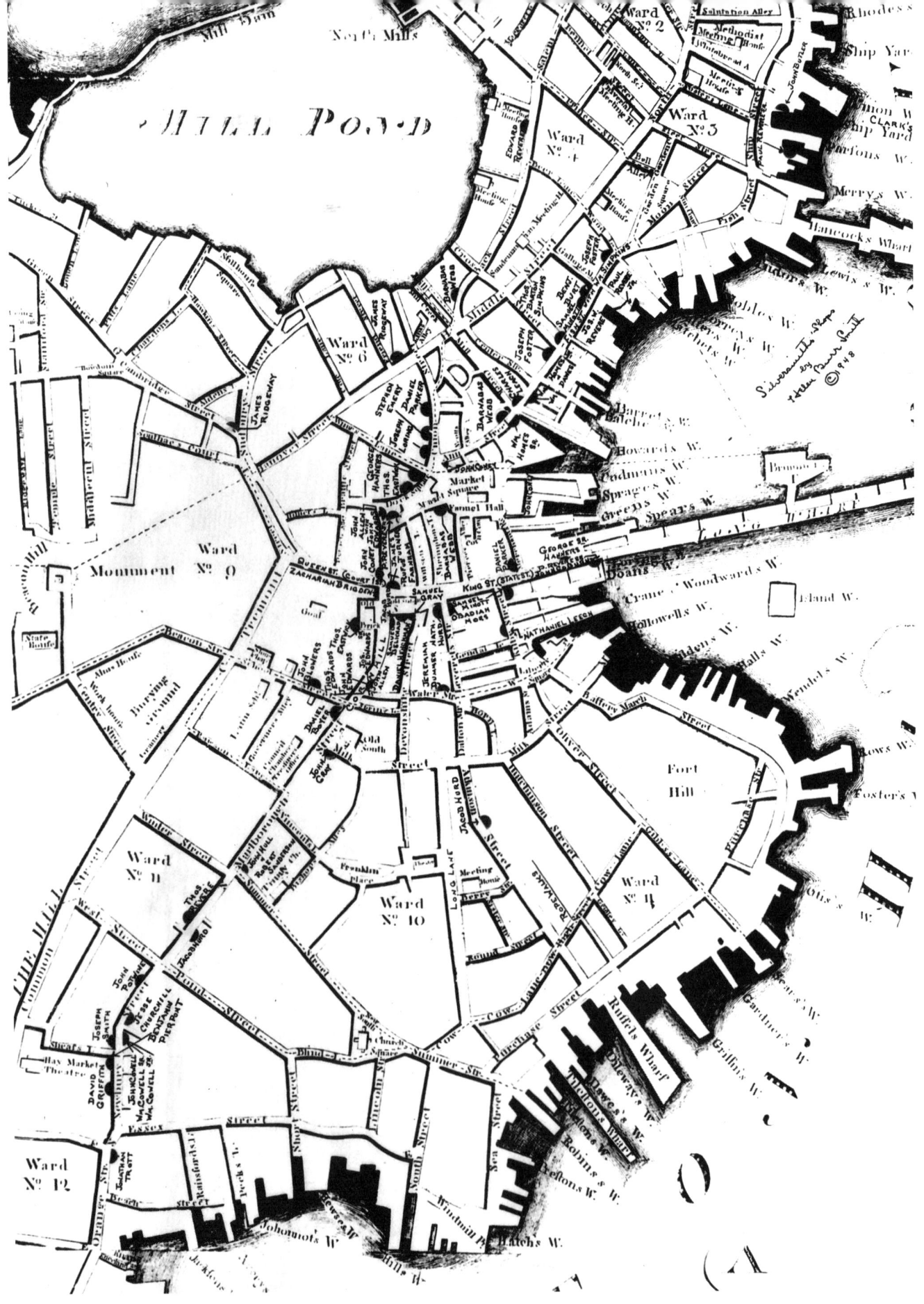

32. *The location of silversmiths' shops in Boston, 1650–1800. Compiled by Helen Burr Smith. Yale University Art Gallery, gift of Stephen G. C. Ensko.*

of her estate, dated 27 February 1727/28, lists a collection of goldsmithing tools that she had undoubtedly purchased to help her son establish his business.[99] The group of tools, though not large, gives us a good indication of what tools were considered essential to establish a young man in business as a largeworker in the third decade of the eighteenth century.

1 fforging Anvil w^{tlb} 1..3.0	@ 5^d	4. 1. 8
1 Raising ditto 51	@ 8^d	1. 14. —
3 Hammers Sorted	@	3.
1 Spoon Tast with Swages & Bolles 30^{lb}1/2	@ 8^d	2. 7. 4
1 Scillet w^t 20^{lb}		16. 3
3 Flasks Sorted		6. 9
6 p^r of Plyars		4. 3
1 Copper Pan for Boyling		12. 7
1 ffine Scratch Brush		1 —
1 brass Stamp 4^{lb}		8 —
4 Graving Irons Sorted		10 —
2 Spoon Punches		6. 2
2 Stakes for Cup & Tankard		8. 4
1 Thimble Stamp		1. 15. 6
4 doz: of Peircing files		8 —

Although the value of the tools is small (£14.2.10 in Massachusetts currency and only £4.14 in sterling), many of the items in this group of tools—forging and raising anvils, hammers, and stakes for cups and tankards—indicate that Greene planned to become a largeworker. Other items, such as piercing files and the spoon punches, spoon "tast" with swages, and thimble stamp, were more common and suggest that he intended to combine largework and smallwork in his shop. The inclusion of the graving "irons" was more unusual and probably indicates that he had received training as an engraver. The scratch brush, used to prepare surfaces for gilding and polishing; the skillet and flasks for casting; and the pliers for a variety of uses added to his supplies. The list of tools overall was not sufficient to get Greene started in business. Before opening his shop he would have had to obtain at least a scale and weights for weighing quantities of silver, a hand vise, a ladle, shears, tongs, burnishers, and bellows. Throughout his career he undoubtedly acquired other hammers, anvils (especially raising anvils), and stakes. Noticeably absent from the list are tools for embossing and repoussé work and variously shaped triblets (often referred to in inventories as tribs) for making rings and shaping other small objects. The list also does not include a drawing bench and irons.

Largeworkers had to spend a considerable amount of money setting up their shops. The costliest tools in a silversmith's inventory were his anvils. Valued by weight, the large forging and raising anvils needed by producers of holloware often cost ten times more than the small anvils that sufficed for a jeweler or smallworker. The average number and variety of shop tools needed by a largeworker cost approximately

£25 sterling, or roughly the amount of money a journeyman could expect to earn in cash in one year if he was employed for 250 days.[100] If the expenditure for raw materials is added to this figure, then the cost of establishing a goldsmith's shop becomes appreciably larger, particularly during the third and fourth decades of the eighteenth century, when inflation drove metal prices to all-time highs and interest rates followed suit. Although we do not know the full value of all his tools when he set up business in 1728, Rufus Greene recorded in 1737, at a time when he had at least one full-time journeyman (William Homes, Sr.) working in his shop, that his shop tools were worth £150 Massachusetts currency (£30 sterling). Two years later, when he closed the silversmithing side of his business, Greene had already disposed of some of his tools, for he lists tools worth only £100 (£20 sterling).[101] After he turned to full-time shopkeeping and general merchant activities Greene probably sold the rest of his tools to others in the trade, perhaps through his younger brother, Benjamin.[102]

Arrangement of the Shop

When John Edwards opened a new shop in his house in Cornhill Street in Boston in 1738, Benjamin Walker, his next-door neighbor, commented in his diary that "Mʳ Edwards open'd his Shop next door to me South & made a Show with his Glasse Cases & goods."[103] Edwards was creating a retail space within his shop that he hoped would make a favorable impression upon both former and potential customers. In his *Encyclopédie*, Denis Diderot included a view of the retail area of a smallworker's shop (3, detail f) that probably approximates the kind of display area found in most American goldsmiths' and jewelers' shops. David Jesse's shop (1706), for example, had "1 Press & 1 Glass case."[104] James Boyer's inventory (1741) includes "a Show Glass" and "2 Boards & a Counter Shop Windoˢ platform & Bar of Iron" (probably a countertop case for jewelry with a simple locking mechanism involving a sliding iron bar), as well as "a Jewelling Box & 2 Ring Cases."[105] The Boston jeweler Stephen Winter owned "3 Shop Windows," a "Jeweller's Sign," and "a Shop Sign," and the 1815 inventory of Joseph Loring's estate lists "1 Large hanging Case," "1 Small Dᵒ," "2 Outside show cases," and "1 Counter Case."[106]

The arrangement of the work area of most Massachusetts goldsmiths' shops in the eighteenth century was probably very much like that shown in Etienne Delaune's two engravings of the interior of a German goldsmith's shop of 1576 (33, 34).[107] Large anvils and small anvils were secured in large wooden blocks—usually tree trunks—and teasts, stakes, and swages were kept nearby for use in the formation of holloware by the raising process. With floor space at a premium, goldsmiths no doubt used the walls of their shops for the orderly storage of hammers, chisels,

punches, brushes, gravers, and burnishers, but several Massachusetts inventories also indicate that many silversmiths kept these items in chests of drawers. There are several cases of "draws" in Samuel Edwards's shop inventory that were used to hold patterns and small items, as well as a desk and bookcase filled with "Flukes & Tongues for Buckles," knee and shoe buckles, sets of weights, a hand vise, watch pliers, and other similar supplies.[108] James Boyer also stored small items in a similar way—"a Case of Drawers with Patterns & Enamel" appears in the inventory of his Boston shop.[109] John Coney's shop furniture included "1 Chest," "a Case of drawers," and also a desk, and John Codner's inventory specifically mentions "1 Writing Desk" and "4 Setting

Stools."¹¹⁰ The appearance of desks in some inventories suggests perhaps a small amount of floor space in large shops was given over to keeping business accounts, even though the example of Samuel Edwards's desk and bookcase demonstrates that artisans may not have used these pieces of furniture in the same way we would today.

If it faced the street or a sunny rear yard, the south end of an artisan's shop was fitted with large windows to take advantage of the best sunlight. Although Jonathan Reed of Boston did not own any real property, his inventory (1742) nonetheless lists "72 Squares of Glass to Sashes of the Shop and Door" as part of his personal estate. Reed probably purchased these panes of glass with his own money, using them to modify a rented building so that he would have the large windows that he required for his work.¹¹¹ When he died, the glass was valued as his property, and may well have been used again for the same purpose by another artisan. In the Delaune engravings (33, 34), the workmen's benches are shown running across and at right angles to the large windows. In the frontispiece to *A New Touchstone for Gold and Silver Wares* (1, upper left), workers in leather aprons perform fine finish work with the aid of natural light streaming in from a large window. Massachusetts inventories occasionally mention work stools and benches similar to those shown in these prints.¹¹²

Each work space at the bench was defined by the presence of a leather apron attached to the underside of the table (35). When the master or one of his workers sat down at the bench, he tied one of the aprons around his waist. The pouch thus formed served to catch any silver or gold filings produced during the course of his work. In addition,

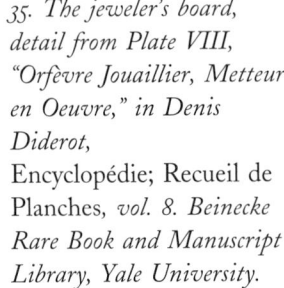

35. The jeweler's board, detail from Plate VIII, "Orfèvre Jouaillier, Metteur en Oeuvre," in Denis Diderot, Encyclopédie; Recueil de Planches, *vol. 8. Beinecke Rare Book and Manuscript Library, Yale University.*

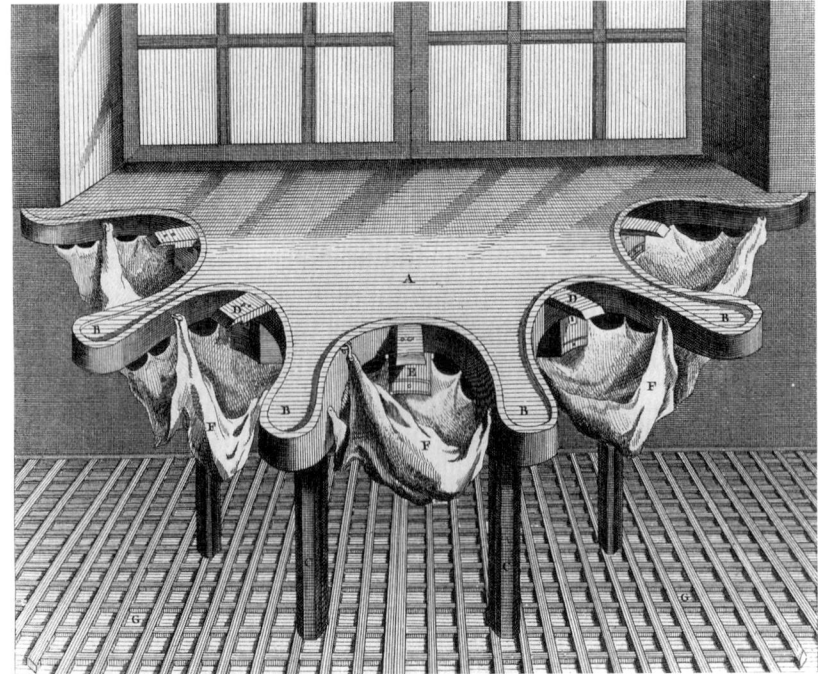

the floorboards of the shop were taken up and burned periodically to recover any tiny filing that had not collected in the aprons or been swept up at the end of each day. (Note in 3, 4, and 35 the open lattice flooring designed to keep workers from carrying away filings on their shoes. The filings were caught in the subfloor that could be taken up and burned periodically.) These sweepings and filings were carefully collected and refined. The lengthy, detailed inventory of John Coney's shop includes "2 Limmil boxes 2/."[113] An even more practical arrangement for catching gold and silver filings is shown in Diderot's *Encyclopédie* (3, detail a; 35) and also described by George Gee in *The Goldsmith's Handbook*:

> The jeweller's board commonly provides sittings for four workmen, the outline of which is nearly half-circular; holes are sawn or scooped out from the semicircular side to form places for the requisite number of men, and these hollowed places, with their appendages, form what is technically termed the "jeweller's skin." This "skin" consists of a piece of leather fastened securely underneath the two arms of the board, and round the semicircle, so as to form a receptacle into which the filings or articles accidentally dropped by the workmen may fall; and also to serve as a convenient place for tools.[114]

Some brief mention of a similar arrangement appears in at least three Massachusetts documents: in 1747 the estate of Stephen Winter included "a Bench & Skin," Samuel Edwards's inventory includes "1 Skin & frame," and in 1775 James Hill's shop in Charlestown included two shop boards and skins.[115] The largest shops had both a workbench, principally for largework, and a jeweler's board, principally for smallwork and jewelry, as well as areas in the shop set aside for forging, for raising, and for the placement of the drawing bench.

In describing the talents, training, education, and financial needs of prospective goldsmiths and jewelers in London, R. Campbell observed that both the goldsmith and the jeweler required "a large stock" to begin a business, meaning that it took a significant financial outlay to become a master silversmith in the eighteenth century.[116] Not every young artisan could aspire to a business of his own. Nonetheless, tools, whether basic or specialized, were part of the craftsman's sense of self. They were the objects that were with him every day and made the work of a day go faster. When a special tool was passed on, it meant that the new owner would be reminded of the giver every time he used the tool. And through such bequeathed tools, a loving father or doting master would be able to continue to help and teach the next generation.

We can learn a great deal about the type of work that artisans did, and their places within their craft, by looking closely at the combination of tools, supplies, and finished work that these artisans had in their shops. Although artisans within a particular trade felt a certain bond with one another because of common skills and training, they recognized that each craft had its own internal structure, and that master artisans occupied the upper echelons of the hierarchy.[117] Nonetheless, they also knew that these same master artisans relied upon and respected the specialists and jobbers who played a critical part in the daily production of goods. Pride of skill and reliance on hard work and diligence came from the fact that each artisan believed that this structure was essential and lasting. Few could foresee the world that would emerge with industrialization and the devaluing of their skills by the large manufactories. And yet, the Massachusetts goldsmiths and jewelers who came of age and began working in the craft before the Revolution were the last generation of fully trained artisans in their trade. These individuals were the last, we may say, of a dying breed. Although many experienced the changing relationships between masters and journeymen that characterized the period between 1780 and 1820, they remained tied through custom and training to the traditional ways of an ancient craft. Manual skills would continue to legitimize the roles that some would assume as proprietors and managers of large firms, and manual skills would be important to the few specialists who continued to practice their trade either independently or in conjunction with the large production houses that would emerge into the first manufactories. Tools, as material manifestations of these skills, were part and parcel of an artisan's identity.

Page 5

1. Francis Richardson to his mother, 15 August 1703; 6 November 1704; Richardson Papers, Downs Manuscript Library, WM. Fales 1974, 5–6. In his letter of 15 August, Richardson indicates that his mother was actively involved in decisions regarding his purchase of tools, and may well have been financing the purchase: "I take notis as to what my sister wrights of what thy mind is consarning supling my selfe with what is Nessesarey for my Trade."

2. Several authorities have also attempted to reconstruct tool ownership, shop arrangement, and shop practices for early American goldsmiths. The most notable examples are Avery 1920, Buhler 1950, and Fales 1973. Fales 1974, on the Richardsons of Philadelphia, is probably the most detailed study of American shop practices. In New England extensive work has been done on the workshop of Paul Revere, Jr.; see especially Federhen 1985, 1988. Spang 1962 deals with the early nineteenth-century Parker-Russell shop in Deerfield, Massachusetts.

    Much more is known of European than American practices. Hayward 1976 has been especially helpful to me in analyzing American practices. Elaine Barr's *George Wickes, 1698–1761: Royal Goldsmith* (New York: Rizzoli, 1980), includes helpful information on shop practices and shop hierarchy in eighteenth-century England.

    Similar efforts have been made to understand the dynamics of artisan interaction and to reconstruct shop floor practices in other trades. Edward S. Cooke, Jr.'s book, *Making Furniture in Preindustrial America: The Social Economy of Newtown and Woodbury, Connecticut*, (Baltimore: Johns Hopkins University Press, 1996), in particular has focused on working techniques as evidence of artisan interactions. Edward Cooke inspired me to undertake this study and urged me to learn how tools themselves communicate technical knowledge. Patricia Kane assisted in bringing together the material for this essay.

Page 6

3. Gaynor/Hagedorn 1994, 34.

4. SCCR, files 16479, 16553.

5. Hiller (SCCR, file 14226); LeRoux (SCCR, file 18500). Chairs were the most common items "attached" to assure that a defendant would appear in court.

6. I have taken the liberty of referring to the Massachusetts goldsmiths I am dealing with as male. In our research we encountered only one female artisan—the jeweler Mary Ann Boyer—and she seems to have entered the trade only as manager of her husband's shop after his death.

1Page 7*

7. SCPR 16:515–16, docket 3139.

8. SCPR 77:12–13. Other goldsmiths who bequeathed tools include René Grignon, who left all his goldsmith's tools to his apprentice Daniel Deshon in 1714/15 (New London Probate District, file 2317); Samuel Haugh, who left his "Working Tooles belonging to the Goldsmiths Trade" to his young son Edward "if he lives to be Twenty one Years old, and Inclines to work att the Goldsmiths Trade" (SCPR 20:11–13, docket 3851); and Francis Légaré, who left all the tools of his trade "both Jewelling & Glazing" and "all Jewelling stone both Chrystal & other" to his son Daniel (SCPR 17:373–74, docket 3376).

9. Campbell (1747) 1969, 142–43.

10. Diderot 1751–65, vol. 8, sections on "Orfèvre Grossier," "Orfèvre Bijoutier," and "Orfèvre Jouailler, Metteur en Oeuvre."

11. Dow 1927, 64; SCCR, file 5565a.

Page 9

12. Services were, in effect, traded. This meant that in addition to trying to serve those to whom they owed money, individuals were often compelled, in order to receive the money due to them, to patronize the businesses of their customers. Thus, if Patron A, a shopkeeper, sold coffee and chocolate to Silversmith A, Patron A might receive payment for those goods by purchasing a watch from Silversmith A. Silversmith A did not make watches, so he purchased a watch from Watchmaker A in order to suit the needs of Patron A. Pre-revolutionary account book evidence (see, especially, Benjamin Greene Ledger, 1734–56, MHS) shows that in transactions of this type the silversmith did not mark up the price of the watch in selling it to the patron.

13. Ward 1990, 129–47.

14. The information in the following discussion is drawn from: Badcock 1677; Cuzner 1965; De Matteo 1956; Diderot 1751–65; Fales 1973, 189–226; Gee 1885; Gee 1886; Hayward 1976, 19–72; Hawthorne/Smith 1979; Hazen (1837) 1970; Heal (1935) 1972; Kauffman 1969; Loyen 1980; *Silversmith of Williamsburg*, Color, 44 min., Colonial Williamsburg Foundation, 1971, videocassette; Untracht 1975; and the author's own very limited experience working with silver. Edgard Moreno provided comments and suggestions on this portion of the essay, particularly observations on the setting of stones.

Page 10

15. Campbell (1747) 1969, 142.

16. George Gee has this to say about crucibles: "There are various kinds of crucibles manufactured for the use of the precious metal workers. . . . They are calculated to bear very high temperatures and consist of English, Hessian, Cornish, Black lead, and Plumbago [graphite]. The last two are by far the best; the plumbago, however, being the hardest, and capable of standing the highest temperatures, is to be preferred before all others. It will also stand more frequent meltings than any of the rest. Such crucibles have been known to withstand the heat of the furnace for upwards of fifty times without giving way. The wear of them is very strong and resisting, as they only *gradually* become reduced in thickness, so that it is easy to distinguish their unfitness for use" (1885:95–96).

Gee also describes the process of refining lemel using a fire-clay crucible in which the goldsmith recovers the metal when the operation has been completed, by breaking the crucible at its base (1885:104–05). The inventory of Samuel Edwards lists both "Blue potts," which are apparently graphite crucibles, and "crucibles," apparently of clay. Because of the way they are enumerated—blue pots by size by the dozen, and crucibles by the "nest," it is difficult to make price comparisons. However, the entries "14 D° (large Crucibles) 2 in a Nest" at 8^d, and "32 Single Crucibles large" at 4^d, compared with "3 Blue potts, N° 8" at 10^d and the listing of blue pots of various sizes at between 4 and 8 shillings per dozen, suggests that graphite crucibles were considerably more expensive than those made of fire-clay (Inventory and accounts of the estate of Samuel Edwards, June 1762–78; Smith-Carter Papers, MHS).

17. Campbell (1747) 1969, 141–42.

Page 11

18. Boston jeweler John Codner owned a forging anvil worth £2 and a flatting mill worth £6 when he died in 1782 (SCPR, docket 17742).

Page 13

19. Sanderson (SCPR, docket 440); Edwards (Inventory and accounts of the estate of Samuel Edwards, June 1762–78; Smith-Carter Papers, MHS).

20. Webb (SCPR 21:261, docket 4086); Coney (SCPR 22:813–16, docket 4641).

21. Gee 1885, 121.

22. The composition of this "cement" is described in Gee 1885, 121. Another type of "cement," made up of a mixture of burgundy pitch, plaster-of-Paris, resin, and beeswax, was used by engravers (Gee 1886, 129–30). Gee describes its use as: "In common engraving a portion of

this cement is fixed upon various-sized blocks of wood, to which it strongly adheres by heat. The article to be manipulated upon is affixed to one of these, and embodied in the cement; and when properly set, the block is fastened in the vise, and the engraver performs the task allotted to him" (Gee 1886, 130). Diderot shows cement affixed to sticks of this type in the section "Orfèvre Jouaillier, Metteur en Oeuvre," plate X, figs. 35–36; see Plate 15, figs. 35–36. See also "Glossary of Silversmiths' and Jewelers' Tools, Supplies, and Processes" in this volume. Several Massachusetts goldsmiths' inventories include "Simmet" or "Cement" blocks used for this purpose. See, for instance, John Coney inventory, SCPR 22:813–16 ("2 Cement blocks"); Inventory and accounts of the estate of Samuel Edwards, June 1762–78; Smith-Carter Papers, MHS ("Simmet Bullet," "a Simel block," and "10 Simmet blocks"); Stephen Winter, SCPR 41:233–35 ("2 Draws of Cement Sticks"); and Benjamin Hurd, SCPR 80:314–19 ("1 Simmet Bullet").

Page 14
23. For further discussion of the chemical and physical properties of silver, see William A. Lanford, "'A Mineral of that Excellent Nature': The Qualities of Silver as a Metal," in Ward/Ward 1979, 3–9.

24. David Jesse (SCPR 16:99–100, docket 2960) owned six; Edward Webb (SCPR 21:261, docket 4086) owned eight; John Coney (SCPR 22:813–16, docket 4641) owned ten; John Burt (SCPR 39:160) owned six; and Daniel Henchman (SCPR 74:297–99) owned five.

25. Cooper 1978, 107–09.

Page 15
26. Benjamin Greene Ledger, 1734–56, 47, MHS.

27. SCPR 80:314–19. Turning tools are also mentioned in the inventories of John Coney, SCPR 22:813–16, docket 4641 ("2 Wheel blocks & turning tools"); Caleb Beal, SCPR, docket 21581 ("1 Lathe and Tools"); and Samuel Edwards, Inventory and accounts of the estate of Samuel Edwards, June 1762–78; Smith-Carter Papers, MHS ("4 Small Laths").

28. Edward Webb (SCPR 21:261, docket 4086), Richard Conyers (SCPR new series, docket 3139), John Dixwell (SCPR 25:275), John Burt (SCPR 39:160), all largeworkers, and James Boyer (SCPR 35:200–01), one of Boston's most prominent jewelers.

29. John Hull Ledger, vol. 1, fol. 133v, NEHGS; Samuel Sewall Journal 1685–89, n.p., Baker Library, HU; Coney inventory (SCPR 22:813–16). For listings of items sold by Welsh, Parker, and Brigden, see individual biographies in this volume. Examples of advertisements include *Boston Evening-Post*, 11 December 1752; *Boston Gazette and Country Journal*, 4, 11, 25 July 1763. Other information on these types of supplies can be found in English-Touzel-Hathorne Papers, PEM, and Zachariah Brigden Daybook, 1766–ca. 1775, fols. 6v, 11v, 32v, Brigden Papers, YU. Mercury, however, was available from Boston apothecaries.

Page 16
30. The information in the following discussion is based on the estate inventories of the three goldsmiths: Coney (SCPR 22:813–16); Dixwell (SCPR 25:274–80); Hanners (SCPR 35:89–90).

Page 17
31. The most direct comparison that can be made is with the inventory of Joseph Kneeland, which was also taken in 1740. Kneeland owned 28 hammers worth £5.12 and 30 files worth £1.10 (SCPR 35:137). Hanners's hammers, files, and drawing irons were valued together at £4.2.

32. This was not unusual; many goldsmiths owned drawing irons and tongs but no drawing bench, among them Daniel Henchman (SCPR 74:297–99), Benjamin Hurd (SCPR 80:314–19), Jonathan Reed (SCPR 36:240–41), John Codner (SCPR, docket 17742), Isaac Perkins (MCPR, docket 17145), and George Hanners, Jr. (SCPR 69:240–41). The latest mention of a drawing bench in an inventory is in Samuel Edwards's listing (1762), in which there is one drawing bench valued at 12 shillings (Inventory and accounts of the estate of Samuel Edwards, June 1762–78; Smith-Carter Papers, MHS).

Page 18
33. Gaynor/Hagedorn 1994 makes a similar point about the working tools owned by eighteenth-century cabinetmakers and joiners.

Page 19
34. William Jones of Marblehead, who died in Marblehead in 1730, had tools and shop goods that seem remarkably similar to those owned by Dixwell, although the tools were not specifically enumerated. The inventory included £60 worth of tools and "Utensels of the Shop" (£17.14 sterling) and £657.19.9 (£187.18 sterling) worth of wrought and unwrought silver, wrought gold, and jewelry (ECPR, docket 15237).

35. Knight Leverett, for instance, is known to have made and repaired sword hilts; see Benjamin Walker, Jr., Diaries, vol. 3, 29 April 1747, MHS. From a prominent Boston family, Leverett had the connections and the financial resources to establish himself as a master largeworker. However, Leverett sold much of the land he inherited to pay off debts during the 1720s and 1730s and may also have sold his more expensive tools. In any case, by the time he died, at age fifty, he owned only unenumerated goldsmith's tools valued at 26 shillings, 8 pence (new tenor); see SCD 47:251; 74:56; 75:203; SCPR, docket 10505.

Page 20

36. For extended treatment of the business dealings of these silversmiths see Ward 1984a and Gerald W. R. Ward's essay, pages 111–38.

37. Ward 1984a, 274–78. Hathorne Family Manuscripts, vol. 4, fol. 42, PEM.

38. From a facsimile of the original document illustrated in Fales 1973, 201.

39. See Gee 1885, esp. 119–20.

40. Pans also appear in other Massachusetts silversmiths' inventories: John Parkman, SCPR 42:148–50 ("1 Tinn pan"); Thomas Clark, SCPR 80:587–90 ("A Filing Pan"); and Benjamin Hurd, SCPR 80:314–19 ("1 Tin Linsmel pan") (misspelling of lemel). These may have taken the form described by George Gee in *The Goldsmith's Handbook* 1886, p. 81: "Many master-jewellers have now substituted iron pans or trays for these leather skins, which, in many cases, are better, as the lemel can be easily separated from the scrap. This is done by means of a small movable box provided in the bottom of the pan, with a perforated top, through which the lemel can at any time be swept by the workman; the lemel, to a considerable extent, where these trays are in use, being prevented from getting too much upon the tools. . . . No contrivance of this kind is attached to the ordinary leather skin, and the lemel continually accumulating upon the handles, and in the crevices, of the tools (which are sometimes rendered moist through constant handling) is a source of inconvenience to the workman and a loss to the employer."

41. Charlestown Fire Claims, box 3, BPL.

Page 21

42. SCPR 80:587–90.

Page 22

43. Campbell (1747) 1969, 143.

44. Campbell (1747) 1969, 143–44.

45. These tools include dapping punches and blocks (John Coney, SCPR 22:813–16, docket 4641; Richard Conyers, SCPR, new series docket 3139; John Dixwell, SCPR 25:274–80; David Jesse, SCPR 16:143–45); "bead punches" (Inventory and accounts of the estate of Samuel Edwards, June 1762–78; Smith-Carter Papers, MHS); lockets (locket teast, John Coney, SCPR 22:813–16; locket stamp, George Hanners, Jr., SCD 69:240–41); rings ("Heart & hand ring Swage," "Deaths Head Swage," Inventory and accounts of the estate of Samuel Edwards, June 1762–78; "Deaths head Stamp," George Hanners, Sr., SCPR 35:89–90); and button mold (Joseph Kneeland, SCPR 35:137).

46. SCPR 35:200–01.

47. Dow 1927, 70. According to the *Shorter Oxford English Dictionary*, foil was "A thin leaf of metal placed under a precious stone to increase its brilliancy or under some transparent substance to make it appear to be a precious stone."

48. Gee 1886, 90.

Page 23

49. These references come from the inventories of James Boyer (SCPR 35:200–01) and Stephen Winter (SCPR 41:233–35).

50. Gee 1886, 115–19.

51. Gee 1886, 120.

52. Steinway 1960, 8.

Page 24

53. Benjamin Greene Ledger, 1734–56, 1, 64, MHS.

54. Steinway 1960, 8.

55. SCCR, file 18500.

56. SCPR, docket 440.

Page 25

57. Hull Letter Book, fol. 96, AAS.

58. John Hull Ledger, vol. 1, fol. 31r, NEHGS.

59. John Hull Ledger, vol. 1, fol. 73v, NEHGS.

60. SCPR 22:813–16; Dow 1927, 43.

61. Fales 1973a, 186–87. For the images of the 1722 fractional currency, see Davis 1901, vol. 7, pl. 7. Coney probably obtained his "engine for coining" after the closing of the Massachusets Mint following John Hull's death. In buying or "inheriting" this piece of apparatus, Coney may have anticipated the eventual reopening of the Mint.

Page 26

62. SCCR, Court of Common Pleas Record Book 1699–1701, 72v, 73r.

63. SCCR, Court of Common Pleas Record Book 1699–1701, 136v, 137r.

64. SCCR, file 5559.

65. Dow 1927, 224.

66. Dow 1927, 265–66.

67. Dow 1927, 264, 293.

68. Dow 1927, 271, 279.

69. Dow 1927, 256.

70. This was one of the most common ways in which the wealthiest goldsmiths diversified their businesses. Inventories demonstrate that many goldsmiths engaged in a variety of supplementary occupations; some even turned goldsmithing into a mere adjunct to substantial mercantile activities, while others retained goldsmithing as their principal occupation even though they also engaged in service occupations such as innkeeping, gravedigging, serving as the town watchman, and other similar occupations that offered a steady income during lean times. See Ward 1983, Ward 1984, and Ward 1990.

Page 27

71. Inventory and accounts of the estate of Samuel Edwards, June 1762–78; Smith-Carter Papers, MHS.

72. English-Touzel-Hathorne Papers, box 6, folder 12, PEM.

73. Daniel Parker, for example: *Boston Evening-Post,* 11 December 1752; *Boston Gazette and Country Journal,* 4 July, 11 July, and 25 July 1763; English-Touzel-Hathorne Papers, PEM; Zachariah Brigden: *Boston Gazette,* 19 November 1764; Zachariah Brigden Daybook, 1766–ca. 1775, fols. 6v, 11v, 32v, Brigden Papers, YU; Daniel Boyer: *Massachusetts Gazette,* 30 October 1766; English-Touzel-Hathorne Papers, box 6, folder 12, PEM.

74. *Boston Gazette,* 21 May and 4 June 1764.

75. SCPR 25:274–80. Other goldsmiths who owned scrap and bar iron include David Jesse (SCPR 16:99–100, docket 2960), Edward Webb (SCPR 21:261, docket 4086), and John Coney (SCPR 22:813–16, docket 4641). Bernard Cuzner, in the second chapter of his *Silversmith's Manual,* recommends that silversmiths keep cast steel rods on hand for "tool making" (Cuzner 1965, 15).

76. Beal (SCPR, docket 21581); Codner (SCPR, docket 17742, 82:537).

Page 28

77. For a discussion of the various coins circulating in the colonies, see McCusker 1978, 3–8, 120–23, and John P. Burnham, " 'You Shall Not Crucify Man on a Cross of Gold': Silver and Money in America," in Ward/Ward 1979, 10–14.

78. Crosby 1875; Noe 1943; Noe 1947; Noe 1952.

79. An Act of the Province of the Massachusetts Bay, Ms. M. 3.2, BPL.

80. See Ward 1983, 64–65; Nash 1979, 59–60, 103–04.

81. John Edwards to George Curwin, 25 February 1713/14, Curwen Papers, PEM.

82. SCCR, file 62302; Ward 1989, 72–76.

Page 29

83. Benjamin Greene Ledger, 1734–56, MHS. These accounts appear throughout, particularly in Greene's dealings with London merchants, e.g., Benjamin Greene Ledger, 1734–56, 52, 65, 67, 119. For additional information on colonial exchange brokers, see McCusker 1978, 122.

84. Samuel Sewall Diary and Commonplace Book, 1675–1721, 22v, 23r, MHS.

Page 30

85. Samuel Sewall to William Vaughan, Portsmouth, N.H., 5 January 1712/13; *Sewall Letter Book* 2:9–10.

86. RC 29:204.

87. ECD 123:284.

88. The most common room dimensions in houses of this period were sixteen feet by sixteen feet and sixteen feet by twenty feet; the size of Edwards's lot, however, suggests that the rooms in his house were certainly no more than sixteen feet deep. Inventory and accounts of the estate of Samuel Edwards, June 1762–78; Smith-Carter Papers, MHS; SCD 45:210–11; SCPR 38:515–18.

89. Benjamin Walker, Jr., Diaries, vol. 3, entry for 7 October 1747, MHS.

Page 31

90. SCD 63:198–200; 64:195–97.

91. *Boston Gazette,* 30 October 1758.

92. Benjamin Burt, *Boston Directory* 1789, 11; 1798, 27; RC 22:189; Joseph Foster, *Boston Directory* 1800, 45.

93. Pruitt 1978, 32–33; *Boston News-Letter,* 9 May 1771.

94. For Hunt see *Hampshire Herald,* 1 February 1785, repeated 8, 15, 22 February; for Jackson see NCD 8:169.

95. NCD 15:88.

96. MCD 59:170–71; 62:174–75; *Boston News-Letter,* 17 March 1763.

97. ECD 124:268–69; ECPR, docket 11525.

98. Croswell (PCD 55:108; Davis 1883, 234); Coverly (Pruitt 1978, 44–45).

Page 33
Page 34

99. Rufus Greene Account Book, 1728–48, Karolik-Codman Papers, MHS; SCPR 26:406.

100. See Ward 1983, 82–88, for figures on journeymen's wages and the practice of paying journeymen for some services in-kind. See also Ward 1989, 74.

101. Rufus Greene Account Book, 1728–48, Karolik-Codman Papers, MHS.

102. Although Benjamin Greene's accounts list only that he sold "sundries" to John Potwine of Hartford, Connecticut, and Charles Simpson of North Carolina, both of whom had previ-

ously worked as goldsmiths in Boston, these sundries may have included some supplies related to the craft. In May 1738, approximately one year after he left Boston for Hartford, Potwine purchased "2 Pair of Earings," "1 pair of 3 Dropt Ditto," and "6 P Eairings" from Greene. Greene also sent Potwine "Sundrys P day book" and various types of cloth. The accounts with Simpson and his sometime partner, the brazier James Calf (also formerly of Boston), to whom Greene sent "Sundry Silver Things P daybook" in September of 1740, are even more extensive. See Benjamin Greene Ledger, 1734–56, (for Potwine) 5, 20, 164; (for Simpson) 49, 85, 104, 130, MHS.

103. Benjamin Walker, Jr., Diaries, vol. 2, entry for 4 May 1738, MHS.

104. SCPR 16:143–45.

105. SCPR 35:200–01.

106. Winter (SCPR 41:233–35); Loring (SCPR 113:564–67, docket 24763).

107. For a discussion of these prints, see Hayward 1976, 337.

Page 35

108. Inventory and accounts of the estate of Samuel Edwards, June 1762–78; Smith-Carter Papers, MHS.

109. SCPR 35:200–01.

Page 36

110. Coney (SCPR 22:813–16); Codner (SCPR, docket 17742).

111. SCPR 36:240–41, docket 7831.

112. The following craftsmen owned such equipment: Nathaniel Austin (Charlestown Town Records, MS/Bos/XC:23D, Rare Book Room, BPL); John Codner (SCPR, docket 17742); Joseph Kneeland (SCPR 35:120–21); and Joseph Sanderson (SCPR, docket 440).

Page 37

113. SCPR 22:813–16.

114. Gee 1886, 80–81.

115. Winter (SCPR 41:233–35); Edwards (Inventory and accounts of the estate of Samuel Edwards, June 1762–78; Smith-Carter Papers, MHS); Hill (Charlestown Fire Claims, box 3, BPL).

116. Campbell (1747) 1969, 142–43.

Page 38

117. For a further discussion of the hierarchy in the Boston goldsmithing trade see Ward 1983 and Ward 1990.

Advertisement of John Welsh, *Boston Gazette*, 21 May 1764. Beinecke Rare Book and Manuscript Library, Yale University.

Advertisement of Daniel Henchman, *Boston Evening-Post*, 28 December 1772. Beinecke Rare Book and Manuscript Library, Yale University.

Advertisement of Zechariah Brigden, *Boston Gazette*, 3 December 1764. Beinecke Rare Book and Manuscript Library, Yale University.

Bill from Joseph Edwards, Jr., to Joshua Green, 13 May 1765. Museum of Fine Arts, Boston, 12.1440.

Patricia E. Kane

Artistry in Boston Silver of the Colonial Period

BOSTON was the first center of goldsmithing and jewelrymaking in British North America, and for nearly one hundred years it had the colonies' largest concentration of craftsmen in these fields. More than 163 goldsmiths and 38 jewelers worked in Boston from the mid-seventeenth century to the time of the American Revolution.[1] The majority of these artisans were Boston-born, although as the regional center of silversmithing the town attracted youths from throughout New England who came to Boston to train. In the seventeenth and early eighteenth centuries a significant number of foreign-trained goldsmiths, jewelers, and engravers migrated to Boston, a trend that declined in the later colonial period. These immigrant craftsmen often had specialized skills that enabled local goldsmiths and jewelers to produce objects for their mercantile clientele that closely followed English fashions in domestic wares and jewelry. Local goldsmiths also made significant amounts of communion plate for New England's nonconformist churches that replicated and adapted domestic forms. The material brought together for this publication documents the lives of these goldsmiths and jewelers and those of allied craftsmen. The legacy of these artisans comprises some of the most impressive examples of craftsmanship dating from the colonial period.

The Era of Contrasts, 1635–70

John Hull and Robert Sanderson, Sr., were the first goldsmiths to have lasting and productive careers in Boston. They were preceded by John Mansfield, a ne'er-do-well who came to Boston in 1635 but failed to find employment as a goldsmith, and Richard Storer, who arrived in Boston in 1639 after completing his London apprenticeship. Storer returned to England after a brief stay, but before leaving he trained his fourteen-year-old half-brother John Hull, who had immigrated with

1. John Hull, beaker, ca. 1650. First and Second Church in Boston. Photograph, courtesy, Museum of Fine Arts, Boston.

his parents earlier. Using these skills, Hull began working about 1647 and made a beaker (1) about 1650, which is the earliest surviving piece of Boston silver. In 1652 he was appointed by the General Court of the Massachusetts Bay Colony to establish and operate a mint in Boston and asked his friend, the London-trained goldsmith Robert Sanderson, Sr., to be his partner. Hull and Sanderson established the craft of goldsmithing in Boston and over the next thirty years they made coins, flatware, and holloware and trained the first generation of native-born craftsmen at their shop in Boston's South End.

The enormous challenge posed by the establishment of the mint illuminates the problems faced by silversmiths working in a remote colonial setting. Although well trained, Hull and Sanderson lacked the specialized skills needed to mint coins. The partners either had to learn new skills or import specialized craftsmen from abroad. Hull and Sanderson seem to have taken the former path, adapting to the demands of their new undertaking: fabricating large numbers of uniform blanks, manufacturing dies, and developing a method of striking coins.

Both partners had enough engraving skill to be able to refine their abilities in the related field of diesinking, cutting designs in steel or other hard materials. The chronology of the mint's coins shows a steady improvement from crude and bungling early work to a credible product later on. In the life of the mint more than ninety dies were cut to make the New England coins of 1652 (2, left), the willow tree coins from 1652 to about 1659/60 (2, second), the oak tree coins from 1660 to 1667 (2, third), the large diameter pine tree series (2, right) introduced in 1667, and the small diameter pine tree coins of 1675.[2] When the later coins

2. John Hull and Robert Sanderson, Sr., (left) New England shilling, 1652, (second) willow tree shilling, 1652–59/60, (third) oak tree sixpence, 1660–67, (right) pine tree shilling, 1667–75. Yale University Art Gallery, Mabel Brady Garvan Collection, 1930.1356, .1357, .1361, .1364. Photograph by E. Irving Blomstrann.

were made more than two hands were cutting dies, which suggests that Hull and Sanderson expanded their operation. Among the craftsmen the partners may have employed were those in allied professions: Richard Taylor, a clockmaker in Boston from circa 1657 to 1673; John Hatton, a watchmaker there about 1663; Thomas Matson, a gunsmith (and grandfather of George Hanners, Sr.), who kept the town clock and was in Boston from 1654 to 1690; John Odlin, an armorer in Boston from 1635 to 1685; and Robert Punt, watchmaker at work about 1670. The fabrication of more than ninety dies for the mint demonstrates that diesinking flourished in Boston before the end of the seventeenth century.

Furthermore, Hull and Sanderson's career shows that as early as the seventeenth century specialized roles existed within Boston goldsmith shops. A letter written in 1712/13 by Hull's son-in-law Samuel Sewall to William Vaughan describes the operation of the shop more than three decades before: "The Business of the Mint was managed by it self, and the Account kept distinct. . . . The chief part of the Shop's Business went through Mr. Daniel Quinsey's hands; He was a very honest carefull Man. Mr. Saunderson and all that wrought in the Shop under him, used to be very diligent in paying for the Silver taken in."[3] In an earlier letter to Vaughan, Sewall wrote, "Had this been spoken of in Mr. Quinsey's Lifetime, probably, he might without any difficulty have cleared it up; he being used to keep the account in the Shop."[4] Sewall's letters imply that Quincy administered the business records whereas Sanderson supervised the workmen in the shop, which fit his greater experience as a goldsmith.

The careers of Hull and Sanderson reveal that their financial success as goldsmiths depended on ancillary activities. Sanderson was able to spend his life in the shop supervising production because the mint sustained and subsidized the Hull and Sanderson operation. Hull used his knowledge of goldsmithing as a cornerstone for a career that extended beyond the shop into the worlds of mercantile trade and government office. Many subsequent colonial goldsmiths and jewelers followed second trades to supplement their incomes.

Hull and Sanderson also laid the foundation for goldsmithing in Boston by training apprentices, the means whereby crafts skills were passed on from one generation to the next. Within the first eighteen years of their partnership, Hull and Sanderson trained Sanderson's sons John, Joseph, Benjamin, and Robert, Jr.; Hull's nephew Daniel Quincy; and Samuel Paddy, Jeremiah Dummer, Timothy Dwight, Samuel Clarke, and possibly John Hall. Dwight has been identified as a Hull and Sanderson apprentice because of the deeds he witnessed for Hull's many real estate transactions. This common practice of having apprentices witness legal documents offers circumstantial evidence for identifying many master-apprentice relationships in colonial Boston's goldsmithing and allied craft community.[5] A standard apprenticeship began at age fourteen and continued until age twenty-one, although documented apprenticeships in Boston show broader variations in starting age and term length.[6]

Following English fashions in silverware of the period of England's civil war and Commonwealth government, the wares from the Hull and Sanderson shop were embellished with flat-chasing, pouncing, or floral engraving and modest pricked or engraved monograms.[7] Both the holloware and flatware display pronounced visual contrasts and juxtapositions. For instance, on a dram cup (3) the compartments formed by the plain chased lines and bands of round punches manifest control of the abstract floral ornament, while the fragile link of the handles to

the rim implies the risk of impending failure. Opposition of light and dark repeat throughout the vessel. The dark lines on the exterior read as light on the interior, and the twists in the wire handles make bright ridges and dark crevices. On a beaker (4) engraved strapwork contains and interlocks abstract floral forms in a manner similar to the compartments on the dram cup. Hull and Sanderson's footed vessels also display the juxtaposition of plain and complex elements. The smooth expanse of the foot and bowl of a wine cup (5) contrasts with the fragmented surfaces of the cast stem. The cup's design is top-heavy, the rim being wider than the base and the mass of the baluster stem being inverted. On spoons of the Puritan era, such as the example by Hull and Sanderson (6), pendulous fig-shaped bowls and thin, narrow handles emphasize the disparity of the form's elements. Moreover, the spindly rod-like handle and broad, shallow bowl compromise the comfort of the grasp and the spoon's overall balance. These objects, therefore, exhibit dual concerns for control on the one hand and instability on the other. These qualities must have appealed to Hull and Sanderson's clientele, who were predominantly first-generation merchants or others sympathetic to the Puritan separatist cause.

The Restoration of Richness, 1670–90

A new era began in Boston silversmithing in 1670 when Hull and Sanderson's apprentice Jeremiah Dummer, British North America's first native-born goldsmith, opened his shop in Boston. Additional goldsmiths, both native born and foreign trained, and the first jewelers soon began practicing their trades there, a sign of the growth in New England's population and economy. From 1670 to 1690 the shops of three men dominated the goldsmithing trade: Jeremiah Dummer, John Coney, and the immigrant William Rouse. They patterned their silver after that of Restoration England. Embossed or engraved realistic flowers and surfaces worked in high relief replaced the linear, flat-chased decoration and abstract floral decoration of the earlier era. Rouse and other foreign-trained craftsmen provided the skills to make wares with richly wrought surfaces emulating London styles. The clientele for

5. *John Hull and Robert Sanderson, Sr., wine cup, ca. 1670. Yale University Art Gallery, Mabel Brady Garvan Collection, 1936.137. Photograph by E. Irving Blomstrann.*

6. *John Hull and Robert Sanderson, Sr., tablespoon, ca. 1670. Yale University Art Gallery, Mabel Brady Garvan Collection, 1948.100. Photograph by E. Irving Blomstrann.*

this silver included a new group of merchants, many of them recent immigrants who coalesced in New England in the last quarter of the seventeenth century. They favored this new style and commissioned holloware with large, showy coats of arms, emblematic of their desires to link their interests and tastes with those of the British establishment.

The pool of craftsmen working as goldsmiths and in allied crafts more than quadrupled during this period and underscored the era's expansion. Jeremiah Dummer established his own shop by 1670, and eight other Boston-trained craftsmen began to work in the following years.[8] Samuel Phillips and Eleazer Russell, youths from rural Massachusetts towns, came to Boston to be trained and finished their apprenticeships before 1690.[9] But it was the foreign-trained craftsmen drawn by the growing economy who figured most importantly in the design of silver during this period. Nearly a third of the twenty-one goldsmiths working in Boston during the period 1670–90 were foreign trained. One of them, William Rouse, who was in Boston by 1675, opened a workshop of his own. Most foreign-trained craftsmen, however, probably served as journeymen.[10]

Boston's first jewelers (as opposed to goldsmiths) were the émigré Huguenots Francis Légaré and René Grignon, both of whom arrived about 1687. At that time, the basic difference between the trade of goldsmith and of jeweler was much as it was described more than a half-century later by R. Campbell in *The London Tradesman* (1747): "He [the goldsmith] employs, besides those in his Shop, many Hands without; as first, the Jeweller, a Branch frequently connected with that of the Goldsmith; who differs only in this, that the one is employed in large Works, and the other only in Toys and Jewels." Describing the

jeweler's specialized skills, Campbell observed, "The Jeweller must be a Judge of all manner of precious Stones, their Beauties, common Blemishes, and their intrinsic Value: He must not only know real Stones, but fictitious Gems, and the manner of preparing them; his Business is to set them in Rings, Necklaces, Pendants, Ear-Rings, Buckles of all sorts, and in Watches and whatever Toys else are adorned with precious Stones."[11] (For further discussion of the jeweler's trade see the essay by Barbara McLean Ward.)

Both Légaré and Grignon were at times identified as goldsmiths as well as jewelers, and this ambiguous nomenclature for jewelers persisted throughout the colonial period. In Boston, jewelers combined jewelrymaking with retailing goldsmiths' work. Their craft skills, however, involved stone setting, enameling, hairwork, and small-scale glazing, as the supplies and tools in the estate administrations of these two early jewelers bear out (see their biographies). Documents show that a substantial amount of jewelry set with stones was made in Boston. Yet little Boston-made jewelry can be identified, especially that set with precious or semiprecious stones. Two factors help explain the lack of surviving jewelry: its small scale and complexity make it difficult to mark and the high intrinsic value of its materials makes it vulnerable to being converted to a newer style or smelted for the value of the gold.

As Campbell's description of the jeweler's craft indicated, a close working relationship existed between goldsmiths and jewelers. Jewelers probably procured most of the holloware and flatware they retailed from goldsmiths. The earliest example of this practice in Boston is the porringer that bears both Jeremiah Dummer's and René Grignon's marks.[12] Similarly, goldsmiths customarily procured the jewelry they retailed from jewelers, especially objects ornamented with stones or enamel.

The goldsmiths and jewelers working in Boston at this time were joined by allied craftsmen in the watchmaker's and clockmaker's trade. These included David Johnson, who was perhaps from London and settled in Boston in 1681; William Davis, who immigrated in 1683; and James Allen in 1684. Boston goldsmiths and jewelers may have called upon the specialized metalworking skills of these craftsmen for engraving, diesinking, and enameling.

The Boston silver of this period that is closest to current London styles also has the most technical skill and artistic ambition. Among these pieces were the monumental pair of columnar candlesticks (7) made about 1685 by Jeremiah Dummer. The candlesticks, which resemble English ones made between 1663 and 1683, bear the arms of the Lidgett family.[13] With these candlesticks, which stand more than ten inches high, Dummer brought a level of grandeur and opulence to this form in Boston unmatched throughout the colonial period. The Lidgett arms with ostrich-plume mantling (8), originally the only arms on the sticks, are an early instance of heraldic engraving on Boston silver. This custom quickly spread among second-generation and newly arrived merchants in Boston in the late seventeenth century. Following the Restoration of the Stuart monarchy to the throne in 1660, the English government began to integrate the New England colonies into the structure of the English empire. Merchants who wished to engage in transatlantic trade had to cooperate with English business and governmental leaders rather than maintain the isolation of the earlier generation's Bible Commonwealth. Consequently, merchants wishing to exhibit a new sympathy toward royalist and English causes ordered coats

7. Jeremiah Dummer, pair of candlesticks, ca. 1685. Yale University Art Gallery, Mabel Brady Garvan Collection, 1935.234, 1953.22.1.

8. Detail of the Lidgett arms on one of a pair of candlesticks by Jeremiah Dummer, ca. 1685. Yale University Art Gallery, Mabel Brady Garvan Collection.

of arms for their silver. Boston goldsmiths and engravers who utilized heraldic engraving in their work probably relied upon John Guillim's *Display of Heraldry* (1610), a systematic approach to the subject that had been published in three editions before 1650.

The finest examples of silver with large, showy coats of arms came from the shop of William Rouse. Although Rouse's surviving body of work is small, the engraving exhibits an elegant consistency that suggests Rouse himself had well-developed skills with the graver. A skillet (9)

9. William Rouse, skillet, ca. 1685. Yale University Art Gallery, gift of Mr. and Mrs. Donald W. Henry, 1976.127. Photograph by E. Irving Blomstrann.

10. William Rouse, tankard with unidentified arms, 1692. Los Angeles County Museum of Art, gift of Florence Alden Stoddard and Katharine Alden Stoddard, M. 86.24.

11. John Coney, covered caudle cup, ca. 1685. Yale University Art Gallery, Mabel Brady Garvan Collection, 1932.46. Photograph by E. Irving Blomstrann.

12. John Coney, plate, ca. 1685. The Minneapolis Institute of Arts, gift of James F. and Louise H. Bell, 34.6.

made for John Foster, a merchant who was a newcomer to New England from Aylesbury in Buckinghamshire, England, and his wife, Lydia Turell, bears an elaborate rendering of their arms. Delicate, multiple parallel strokes along the sides of the skillet's engraved shield make it float in front of the mantling. Multiple parallel strokes also define the richly textured form of the scrolled, splayed leaves. A related cartouche, bearing unidentified arms, appears on a Rouse tankard (10).

John Coney, another Boston craftsman who obliged patrons' demands to have large engraved coats of arms, had difficulty matching the quality of Rouse's work. Coney's imposing covered caudle cup (11), made for Isaac Addington with a legacy from his uncle Gov. John Leverett (d. 1679), has arms in which the mantling and shield are disembodied and the leafage is stiff and two-dimensional. A plate (12, 13) also bearing Coney's earliest mark, made for John Eyre, a second-generation merchant and his wife, Katherine, has a more integrated shield and mantling and illusionistic leaves rendered with multiple short arcs, closer to the rich textural finish of Rouse's work. Only the engraving on a third example of Coney's early work, a tankard also made for the Eyres (14), equals the quality of Rouse's work. The shading executed with clusters

of strokes near the edges of the leaves evokes Rouse's style. This piece shows that Coney had refined his own skills or found a specialist engraver to work for him.

The skills the Coney shop sometimes may have lacked in engraving it made up for by its achievements in chasing, as demonstrated by two

13. *Detail of the Eyre arms on a plate by John Coney, ca. 1685. The Minneapolis Institute of Arts, gift of James F. and Louise H. Bell, 34.6.*

14. *John Coney, tankard, ca. 1685. The Metropolitan Museum of Art, gift of Justine B. Trowbridge and Carolyn P. Pruyn, 1986, 1986.452.*

15. *John Coney, sugar box, ca. 1685. The Currier Gallery of Art, gift of Mrs. H. Ellis Straw in memory of her husband, 1955.1. Photograph by Cathy Carver.*

sugar boxes, one at the Currier Gallery (15) and the other at the Museum of Fine Arts, Boston.[14] The boxes, probably made in the early 1680s, are similar in design and are comparable to London boxes dating between 1675 and 1679.[15] In all likelihood Coney employed a London-trained craftsman to produce these objects, either the Englishman Nathaniel Gay or possibly the New England–born but London-trained Thomas Higginson. With his greater working experience in London, Gay is the more probable craftsman. Modeled on English examples, Coney's boxes have scroll feet, bulbous oval bodies divided into egg-shaped lobes, and lids with a ring of additional lobes framing a textured ground with leafage and a pointed ellipse topped by a twisted serpent handle. The tactile, bulging surfaces mitigate stark contrasts of light and dark, rough and smooth. Here the emphasis is on complexity, multiple shadings, and numerous nuances of surface texture. These splendid examples of the chaser's art revel in materiality and opulence.

In the 1680s another tradition of chased decoration also flourished in Boston, a style of naturalistic floral ornament that first emerged in Germany about 1650. From Germany this tradition spread to the Netherlands and then to England. Engravings of realistically rendered flowers predate the style in goldsmiths' work by only a few years. The earliest group of engraved floral designs for jewelry, cutlery handles, and other work common to goldsmiths was dated 1650 by the Nürnberg goldsmith Johann Paullus Hauer (b. ca. 1629).[16] Somewhat later Johann Conrad Reuttimann (w. ca. 1676–81) of Augsburg and Christoph Schmidt (b. 1632) produced sheets with flowers (16) that are counterparts to those engraved on New England silver.[17] Other examples of this genre from France, the Lowlands, and Germany abound, and the same floral motifs were taken up by such English engravers as John Smith.[18] The importation of French and German engravings and the return of

continental craftsmen to London at the close of the English civil war
generated the resurgence of the embossed floral style in English silver
between about 1658 and 1685.[19]

Three Boston caudle cups echo this European naturalistic floral
tradition. Jeremiah Dummer made one (17), engraved H/RM for an
unidentified couple, and John Coney made two, one (18) with a Holyoke
family history possibly made for Elizur Holyoke (d. 1711/12), and a
nearly identical example engraved M/IM for John and Mary Mico, who
were married in 1689. The differences between the Dummer and Coney
cups suggest that each goldsmith employed a different chaser.[20] The
work on the Dummer cup is facile; leaves and petals textured randomly
and accented at the edges by bold dots float amid ethereal curlicues
and strings of graduated punchwork. On the Coney cups the leaves
and petals are striated regularly and accented at the edges with neat,
subtle, indeed almost imperceptible punchwork that gives the chasing
a tighter and crisper appearance. These cups indicate that Boston was
able to support two chasers whose ability to rival London quality could
only have been learned abroad. By contrast, the more abstract portrayal
of the birds on the embossed cup (19) by Robert Sanderson, Sr. and
Jr., and the flowers on Dummer's bowl (20) reveal less proficiency than
that displayed by the work of foreign-trained specialists.

The craftsman who chased the Coney cups probably also engraved
the decoration and initials R/CE on a Coney plate (21), which possibly
was made for Caleb and Elizabeth Rawlins. In both the chased and
engraved work the cherubs have similar full cheeks and pointy chins,
v-shaped leaves close over the granular centers of open blossoms, and
the carnation petals fan out, displaying their sawtooth edges. The similarity of the carnations on the Coney plate with those on the tankard
(22) and snuffbox (23) by William Rouse suggests that Rouse was
responsible for the ornamentation of all these objects. Because Rouse
came from the Rhine valley, the area of Europe in which this tradition
of naturalistic floral ornament developed, it is logical that he was trained
in it and was employed by fellow goldsmiths in Boston to ornament
pieces in this style.

17. Jeremiah Dummer,
caudle cup, ca. 1685.
Museum of Fine Arts,
Boston, Philip Leffingwell
Spalding Collection. Given
in his memory by Katherine
Ames Spalding and Philip
Spalding, Oakes Ames
Spalding, Hobart Ames
Spalding, 42.229.

18. John Coney, caudle cup,
ca. 1690. Gift of Miss
Charlotte Hedge to
Harvard University, 1903.
878.1927.

19. Robert Sanderson, Sr.
and Jr., caudle cup, ca.
1685. Courtesy, The Henry
Francis du Pont
Winterthur Museum,
61.504.

20. Jeremiah Dummer, two-handled bowl, 1692. Yale University Art Gallery, Mabel Brady Garvan Collection, 1940.55. Photograph by E. Irving Blomstrann.

21. John Coney, plate, ca. 1690. Museum of Fine Arts, Boston, gift of Mr. and Mrs. Dudley Leavitt Pickman, 31.226.

22. Detail, top of a tankard by William Rouse, 1692. Los Angeles County Museum of Art, gift of Florence Alden Stoddard and Katharine Alden Stoddard, M. 86.24.

23. William Rouse, snuffbox, ca. 1690. Yale

Indeed, Rouse had a profound impact on the ornamentation of silver made in Boston. An intriguing similarity exists between the Coney cups and plate and the Rouse tankard and box and another group of objects—a tankard by Coney (24–26), a salver (27) and tankard by Timothy Dwight, and a tankard (28) by Jeremiah Dummer. Many of the design elements of these pieces correspond to the work attributed to Rouse: the pose, full cheeks, and pointy chins of the cherubs; the

24. John Coney, tankard, ca. 1690. Courtesy, The Henry Francis du Pont Winterthur Museum, 65.0033.

25. Detail of engraving on a tankard lid by John Coney, ca. 1690. Courtesy, The Henry Francis du Pont Winterthur Museum, 65.0033.

26. Detail of engraved arms on a tankard by John Coney, ca. 1690. Courtesy, The Henry Francis du Pont Winterthur Museum, 65.0033.

pattern of the cartouche surrounding the monogram on the plate and the Coney tankard; the shape and details of the carnations; the folded-over leaf tips; and the use of paired incised lines near leaf and petal edges to give definition to form. The engraving here attributed to Rouse features deep, strong cuts of the burin and long, multiple radiating lines that create the illusion of light and shadow. The engraving on the Coney and Dummer tankards and on the Dwight tankard and salver, however, has cuts that are lighter, fewer, and less incisive. The engravers of the latter pieces lacked the authority of Rouse but were imitating

his work and may have had access to his patterns. Furthermore, the cartouche with palm leaves and mask that first appeared on the Rawlins plate (21) continued to be used for at least three decades.[21] The similarity between these two groups of objects underscores the dependence of colonial craftsmen on new ideas and skills from abroad.

Nevertheless there were limits to the extent that London styles influenced colonial silversmiths. A tankard (29) by Jeremiah Dummer is the only surviving piece of silver that shows a Boston silversmith employing the chinoiserie style fashionable in London silver of the 1680s. Dummer may well have had in hand an example of English work that served as his model for the piece's strange birds and exotic trees and flowers. Or one of the immigrant craftsmen who came to

27. Timothy Dwight, salver, ca. 1690. Museum of Fine Arts, Boston, gift of Mr. and Mrs. Dudley Leavitt Pickman, 31.227.

28. Jeremiah Dummer, tankard, ca. 1690. The Saint Louis Art Museum, lent anonymously, 1977.481.

29. Jeremiah Dummer, tankard, ca. 1690. Private collection.

Boston in the 1690s may have been familiar with this decorative tradition and may have been responsible for the work.

In addition to chasing and engraving skills, immigrant craftsmen also brought new tools that affected the look of Boston-made silver. This can be demonstrated with spoons. Although spoons lack the range and degree of goldsmithing skills of elaborate holloware, they nevertheless illustrate the change in imported London styles that took place in Boston silver before and after 1670. Spoons of the Puritan era (6) emphasized the disparity between their thin, narrow handles and

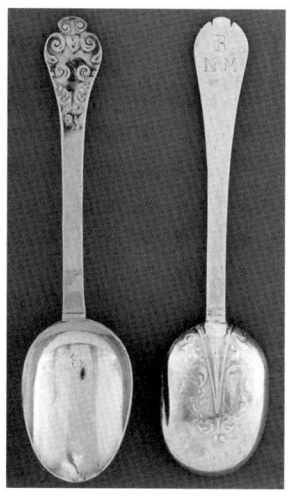

30. Jeremiah Dummer, tablespoons, ca. 1685. Yale University Art Gallery, Mabel Brady Garvan Collection, 1930.3346, 1934.346. Photograph by Carl Kaufman.

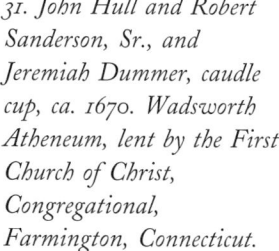

31. John Hull and Robert Sanderson, Sr., and Jeremiah Dummer, caudle cup, ca. 1670. Wadsworth Atheneum, lent by the First Church of Christ, Congregational, Farmington, Connecticut.

broad, shallow bowls. The London spoonmaker Matthew Mabely, who arrived in Boston early in 1683/84, probably brought swages with him for making the more practical spoons introduced in Boston in the 1680s. These spoons (30) had an egg-shaped bowl, a flatter and wider handle broadening at the tip, and an ornamented junction of handle and bowl. A more homogenous melding of form and ornament on spoons first made in the 1680s replaced the abrupt juxtaposition of shapes emphasized on spoons made from the 1650s through the 1670s.

As the discussion of engraving and chasing in the 1680s has shown, Boston's small goldsmithing community of the 1670s to 1690s quickly shared skills, resources, and ideas. This cross-fertilization coincided with the advent of multiple goldsmiths' and jewelers' shops in Boston. The plain caudle cup (31) now owned by the Farmington, Connecticut, church provides other evidence of interdependence among craftsmen. It bears Hull and Sanderson's marks overstruck by Dummer's, revealing the practice of a craftsman-retailer striking his own mark on the work of contemporary Boston silversmiths, a practice that would continue throughout the colonial period.[22] The benefits of this arrangement are unclear. Hull and Sanderson may have been indebted to Dummer for the value of the cup, which Dummer accepted as fulfillment of the obligation, marked it, and sold it to the church. Nevertheless the sharing of molds for casting thumbpieces on tankards underscores the interdependence of the two shops.[23]

Great differences exist between silver made before and after 1670. The taut surfaces of the flat-chased vessels of the earlier period and their modest monograms stand in sharp contrast to the undulating

forms and the coats of arms on silver made in the shops that opened after 1670. Flowers as realistic as botanical illustrations replace the abstract representations of tulips on earlier objects. Wind-tossed flowers, swirling leaves, and curling petals delight in motion as much as the designs of the previous era sought stasis and containment. With their prominent display of large coats of arms, these pieces also exalted rank and wealth and signaled a connection to the order of the English establishment that the earlier work eschewed. A half century after the first goldsmith arrived in Boston, the town had a craft community of almost two dozen workers with the skills to produce works in styles that were up-to-date in terms of London fashions.

The Era of Opulence, 1690–1710

Echoing the robust fluted and gadrooned classical London mode, Boston's most artistic and accomplished silver of the colonial period was produced between 1690 and 1710. This high point in the goldsmith's art coincided with the arrival of a new royal governor and charter in Boston in 1692, which made the government of the Massachusetts Bay Colony dependent on the Crown. As a result of a dramatic increase in the number of native-born goldsmiths and a continuation of the influx of foreign-trained craftsmen, the goldsmiths' community underwent rapid expansion in Boston beginning in 1690. The London-trained craftsmen who arrived in Boston in the 1690s brought a familiarity with the new London styles and the technical skills to execute their chased classical ornamentation. The pool of superior engraving skills also increased. Nevertheless American-born and -trained Jeremiah Dummer and John Coney continued to dominate the craft. The commissions they received for official seals and engraved copperplates for printing colonial currency, as well as for communion plate for New England's nonconformist churches, attest to their leadership in the trade. Among the younger goldsmiths Edward Winslow and John Edwards emerged as figures of importance during this period.

The size of the goldsmithing community increased by a third during the 1690–1710 period. Six of the established goldsmiths continued to run shops or served as journeymen in them after 1690.[24] Fourteen Boston youths trained as goldsmiths began practicing their trade, and as many as eight youths from elsewhere in New England came to Boston to train as goldsmiths, and four whose terms ended before 1710 remained there.[25] Eight foreign-trained goldsmiths also arrived in Boston, the same number that had arrived in the 1670 to 1690 period.[26] While Boston continued to attract immigrant craftsmen, some of Boston's goldsmiths and jewelers chose to leave Boston and settle elsewhere.[27] In spite of these losses to migration, a total of thirty-one goldsmiths worked in Boston between 1690 and 1710, as opposed to twenty-one in the preceding era.

Although the goldsmithing trade flourished in Boston at this time, the jeweler's trade languished. The goldsmith-jeweler Francis Légaré relocated to Hingham and then Braintree, probably about 1689. His son Francis Solomon Légaré went to South Carolina about 1696. Thomas Earthy and Joseph Soames were apprenticed to the goldsmith and jeweler René Grignon, but Earthy disappeared from the records and Soames died in 1705 soon after finishing his apprenticeship. Grignon moved to Norwich, Connecticut, about 1704, so Boston then lacked a trained specialist jeweler.

In addition to the craftsmen who worked as goldsmiths and jewelers, others began working in allied trades, including three with specialist engraver's skills.[28] In this period skills of the goldsmiths once again emerged as critical to the Colony's efforts to regulate its currency and mediums of exchange. The first authorized public paper currency issued in the Western world was the Colony, or Old Charter, bills authorized on 10 December 1690, with another issue authorized on 5 February 1690/91 (32). In all likelihood the General Court turned to Jeremiah Dummer, the more senior of the two leading native-born goldsmiths, to engrave the plates for these issues.[29] The major official commissions that came to the Coney shop illustrate his ability to provide superior engraving and diesinking skills. In 1693 Harvard College paid Coney £2.2.6 for "a seal for the use of the Colledge," and in 1702 the committee for colonial currency selected him to engrave new plates (33).[30] Unlike the earlier bills issued in 1690, these plates were engraved with the English arms, three lions passant, a change instituted now that Massa-

32. Attributed to Jeremiah Dummer, Massachusetts Bay Colony five shilling bill of credit, 1690. Peabody Essex Museum, 133,500.

33. Attributed to John Coney, Province of the Massachusetts Bay forty shilling bill of credit, 1702. Photograph, courtesy of Eric Newman.

*34. Edward Winslow, salt,
ca. 1690. Museum of Fine
Arts, Boston, Philip
Leffingwell Spalding
Collection, gift of Philip L.
Spalding, 38.64.*

chusetts had a royal governor. Coney altered these plates for the Massachusetts Bay Colony in 1708. The Connecticut Colony engaged Dummer to provide engraved plates for their currency in 1709.[31]

The fashionable silver made in Boston during this period was ornamented with chased gadrooned and fluted decoration. This vogue for
classical ornament came by way of London, where it had been brought
by refugee Huguenot goldsmiths from France. New England merchants
were eager to have works made for them in this new mode. The
immigrant craftsmen who came to New England played an important
role in executing this skilled and time-consuming work for the native-
trained goldsmiths.

Edward Winslow's shop may have been the first to produce silver
with this gadrooned decoration. A standing salt with gadrooned base
(34) bearing the Edes crest and the initials E/IM for John and Mary
Edes probably was made between 1690, when Winslow began to work,
and 1692, when John Edes died. Although Winslow may have used an
imported work as a model, he could also have called upon the services
of the recent immigrant William Cross, who would have had first-
hand experience with this type of ornament in London, where he
trained. He immigrated to Boston sometime before April 1691, when
he was sued in the Suffolk County Court of Common Pleas. On the
Edes salt, the flutes of the gadrooning are large scale and curved. Other
Boston pieces with similar large-scale gadrooning exist, including two
examples by John Allen and John Edwards, who were partners between
about 1696 and 1702.[32] The history of the Winslow salt, which places
it early in the period, and of the Allen and Edwards pieces suggests
that this large-scale and curved gadrooning was the first type executed
in Boston; some of it may have been Cross's work.

Richard Conyers was another London-trained goldsmith who arrived
in Boston in late 1696 or early 1697 and who could have executed some
of the chased ornament found on Boston silver in this period. The two
pieces with his mark have gadrooned decoration dissimilar from one
another. Straight gadrooning adorns the lid of a pint-sized tankard (35)
and narrow, curved gadrooning appears on a salt (36). Whether Conyers
chased either piece remains uncertain, especially since he brought a
journeyman (probably Thomas Milner) with him and later employed
an indentured servant, Henry Hurst, a Swedish-born chaser and engraver. The salt's narrow, curved gadrooning differs from the work on
a tankard (37, 38), Hurst's one marked piece with embossed decoration,
and more likely came from Conyers's or Milner's hand. The chaser of
the Conyers salt probably also executed similar gadrooning on a few
other Boston pieces that have long teardrop shapes open at one end
and curved at the other.[33]

The embossed foliage and fruits on the handle and flat-chasing and
straight gadrooning on the lid of Hurst's tankard provide a basis for

35. Richard Conyers, tankard, ca. 1700. Museum of Fine Arts, Boston, gift of Stuart Alan Goldman and Marion E. Davis Fund, 1980.278.

36. Richard Conyers, salt, ca. 1700. Photograph, courtesy Christie's, New York.

attributing other embossed work on Boston silver to Hurst. Hurst signed an agreement in London in October 1699 to come to Boston to work for Conyers for two years as a "plateworker or worker in silver Imboster, Graver." A lawsuit in Suffolk County courts against Hurst brought by the London goldsmith John House, who had arranged for Hurst's indenture, shows that Hurst left Conyers in June 1701, before his term was over. Edward Winslow may then have employed Hurst

37. Henry Hurst, tankard, ca. 1704. Museum of Fine Arts, Boston, gift of Mr. and Mrs. Dudley Leavitt Pickman, 31.228.

38. Detail of tankard lid by Henry Hurst, ca. 1704. Museum of Fine Arts, Boston, gift of Mr. and Mrs. Dudley Leavitt Pickman, 31.228.

as a journeyman, for he and James Barnes, Jr., posted a surety bond for Hurst at the time of the suit in 1702.[34] Some of the most splendid chased work found on colonial American silver adorns Winslow's sugar boxes. Because two are dated 1702 it has been speculated that Hurst contributed to their design and production.[35]

Subtle differences in the chased details of the Winslow boxes, how-ever, reveal that Winslow drew on the skills of different chasers in producing them. Hurst's chasing, as seen on his tankard (37, 38), resem-bles that on a box at Winterthur (39, 40), a box by Winslow at the

39. Edward Winslow, sugar box, 1702. Courtesy, The Henry Francis du Pont Winterthur Museum, 59.3363.

40. Detail of the top of a sugar box by Edward Winslow, 1702. Courtesy, The Henry Francis du Pont Winterthur Museum, 59.3363.

Museum of Fine Arts, Boston, and a salver by Winslow at Historic Deerfield. These objects share broad leaves, punchwork sprays (at the base of the handle on the tankard and above the band of decoration on the body of the box) that diminish gradually, and neat straight gadrooning.[36] The craftsman who ornamented the lids of the boxes at Yale (41, 42) and in Mrs. Edsel Ford's collection used smaller-scale leaves, punchwork sprays that diminish rapidly, and incised lines between each lobe of gadrooning. In addition to the foreign-trained craftsmen already mentioned, David Jesse, another London-trained craftsman who settled

41. Edward Winslow, sugar box, ca. 1702. Yale University Art Gallery, Mabel Brady Garvan Collection, 1935.152. Photograph by E. Irving Blomstrann.

42. Detail of the top of a sugar box by Edward Winslow, ca. 1702. Yale University Art Gallery, Mabel Brady Garvan Collection, 1935.152. Photograph by E. Irving Blomstrann.

in Boston by the mid-1690s, and Moses Prevereau, a Huguenot probably from the Continent who was working in Boston circa 1701, may have had the potential to execute such high-quality work.

Other Boston craftsmen besides Winslow had access to superior chasing skills, since objects from the shop of John Coney equal and perhaps surpass Winslow's. The majestic monteith by Coney (43) transcends in accomplishment the work of any craft produced in Boston

43. John Coney, monteith, ca. 1705. Yale University Art Gallery, Mabel Brady Garvan Collection, 1948.148. Photograph by E. Irving Blomstrann.

during the period. The spectacular chased ornament on its rim, a fleshy band with irregular edges that overlie a textured ground, suggests that an additional expert chaser worked in Boston at this time. In 1701 Coney's shop made another ambitious commission, a large grace cup (44) that William Stoughton presented to Harvard College. The chased decoration on this cup represents yet another variation of this ornamental tradition in Boston wherein the straight and regular fluting gives the whole form an imposing, if somewhat rigid, presence. The fluting on a salver with the Dudley arms by Coney echoes this stiffness. More than two dozen other pieces of Boston silver by various makers share this aesthetic.[37]

Simpler, less ambitious pieces of silver received the decorative treatment of flutes and gadroons, and examples with well-documented dates of manufacture help trace the chronology of the gadroon style in Boston. The Dummer shop filled commissions in 1700 (45) and 1701 for cups with gadrooned bowls and feet. Although the foot of the 1700 cup has narrow swirled chasing and the feet of the 1701 examples have large-scale swirled chasing, the similar punchwork between the top of each flute, a device employed to lay out as well as to decorate the fluting, appears on both vessels. This method of working found on other Boston

44. John Coney, grace cup, 1701. Gift of the Honorable William Stoughton, 1701, to Harvard College, 877.1927.

45. Jeremiah Dummer, wine cup, 1700. Museum of Fine Arts, Boston, anonymous gift, 37.1172.

pieces identifies a chasing style associated with the Dummer shop.[38] Either swirled or straight gadrooning without the punchwork indicates yet another chasing style and includes cups and beakers by Dummer, caudle cups and cups by Coney, and caudle cups and a cup by William Cowell, Sr. (46).[39] About 1704 an additional London-trained craftsman, Edward Webb, arrived in Boston. One chocolate pot in the gadrooned

46. William Cowell, Sr., caudle cup, ca. 1710. Yale University Art Gallery, Mabel Brady Garvan Collection, 1944.72. Photograph by E. Irving Blomstrann.

style bears his mark, and he may have been responsible for some of the embossed work executed in Boston after that date.[40]

Although engraving assumes a secondary role to chased decoration in this period, the diverse and superb quality of heraldic engraving on Boston silver from 1690 to 1710 suggests the wider availability of superior engraving skills. Rouse may have engraved acanthus cartouches for other Boston goldsmiths, notably Jeremiah Dummer. The cartouches on several Dummer objects—the caudle cup with the Brown arms (47),

47. Jeremiah Dummer, caudle cup, with arms possibly engraved by William Rouse, ca. 1690. The Minneapolis Institute of Arts, gift of James F. and Louise H. Bell, 32.21.2.

48. Edward Winslow, chocolate pot, ca. 1705. Yale University Art Gallery, Mabel Brady Garvan Collection, 1944.71. Photograph by E. Irving Blomstrann.

the tankard with the Saltonstall arms, and the cup with the Stoughton arms made for the Dorchester church—bear close comparison with the cartouches on Rouse's skillet and tankard (9, 10).[41] The heraldic engraving on Winslow's silver during this period is consistent in design and execution. For example, the cartouche on a chocolate pot (48, 49) has distinctive comma-shaped accents on the leaves, swirled knotlike background, leafage outlining the back of the knight's helmet, and an oval at the visor hinge-point, occasionally ornamented with a mask. Winslow may have employed a single engraver or perhaps did the engraving himself.[42] In contrast, Coney employed more than one engraver. The engraver who worked for him in about 1701 and 1702 used deeply cut double and sometimes triple parallel lines on the leaves and backgrounds of cartouches, and ornamented the mask at the knight's visor hinge-point with encircling petals (50).[43] Coney and John Edwards employed another skillful engraver, probably in the period about 1705.[44] The engravers who worked for Coney used a new cartouche style featuring interlocking scrolls framing an oval. The old acanthus cartouches continued, but the new style appears on arms on two Coney pieces made in the decade 1700–10—the Colman arms on the monteith

49. *Detail of the Auchmuty arms on a chocolate pot by Edward Winslow, ca. 1705. Yale University Art Gallery, Mabel Brady Garvan Collection, 1944.71. Photograph by E. Irving Blomstrann.*

50. *Detail of the Norton arms on a tankard by John Coney, ca. 1700. Worcester Art Museum, gift of Albert W. Rice, 1960.31.*

51. *John Coney, salver, ca. 1705. Hood Museum of Art, Dartmouth College, gift of Louise C. and Frank L. Harrington, Class of 1924, M.971.23.*

and the Checkley arms on a salver (51).[45] Specialist engravers who might have been responsible for some of this work include Joseph Allen, a limner, engraver, and watchmaker working in Boston by 1691, and Thomas Emmes, an engraver said to have been working in Boston about 1701.

Specialists probably also engraved the inscriptions and monograms on Boston silver, although many goldsmiths had the skill to do this work themselves. The lettering on Boston silver of this period evokes the aesthetics of the baroque style in its use of energetic finishing accents. For example, the inscription on the cup by Jeremiah Dummer (45) contains *d*'s and *h*'s with curling tops as well as an *m* with a looping end on the word *Eastham*. The engraver of this inscription probably trained with one of the many mid- to late seventeenth-century writing masters' copybooks, for example, Edward Cocker's *England's Pen-man* published in London in 1678 (52). The serifs on many monograms found on Boston silver of the late seventeenth century exhibit similar flourishes.

Engravers also probably fabricated the steel swages that Boston silversmiths began to use during the period 1690 to 1710 on the backs of spoon bowls for more streamlined ribbed or beaded v-shaped drops, often referred to as rattails. Diesinking was a highly developed skill in Boston by the third quarter of the seventeenth century, although immigrating craftsmen probably carried swages in the newer styles with them to Boston from abroad. For instance, the immigrant Edward Webb, who made spoons with the older style of foliate decoration on the bowl backs, also made spoons with a beaded rattail (53, left) from steel swages that he may have brought with him from England. Local goldsmiths probably also imported these specialized tools from England. Spoons with wavy ends also began to be made before 1710 (53, right).

The silver made in Boston between 1690 and 1710 reveals much about the aspirations of the merchant class that dominated Boston society. During this period, Boston, as the governmental center of the Massachusetts Bay Colony, completed its transition from being a Puritan oligarchy to being an integrated component of the English empire.

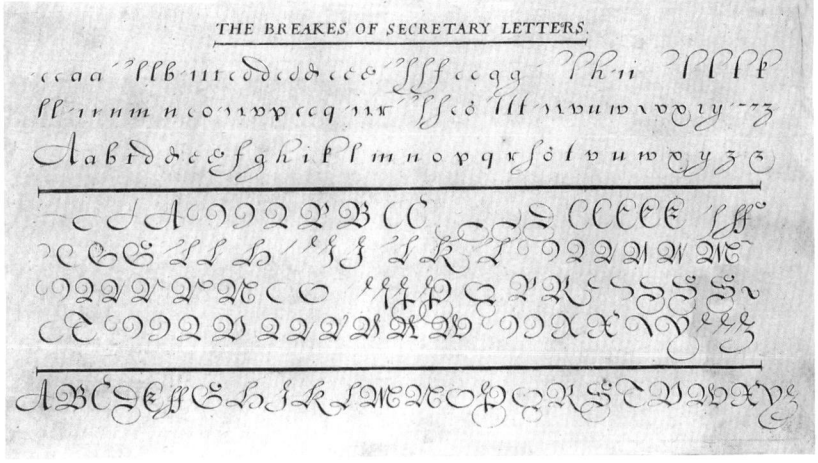

52. Edward Cocker, a page showing the breaks of Secretary letters from England's Pen-man, London, 1678. By permission of the Houghton Library, Harvard University.

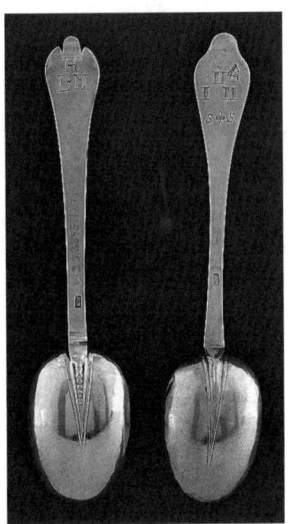

53. Left, Edward Webb, tablespoon, ca. 1710. Mabel Brady Garvan Collection, 1930.3345. Right, William Cowell, Sr., tablespoon, ca. 1710. Gift of Carl R. Kossack, B.S. 1931, M.A. 1933, 1988.93.7, Yale University Art Gallery. Photograph by Carl Kaufman.

Evidence of this change can be found on products of the goldsmith's trade, such as the replacement of the Indian seal on the currency issue of 1690 with a shield with the English arms on the issue of 1702 (32, 33). Mantling similar to that on the currency appears on the silver communion set made by the London goldsmith Francis Garthorne in 1694/95 and presented by the monarchs William and Mary to King's Chapel in 1694. The use of engraved arms gained wider acceptance, signifying New Englanders' desires to be part of the hierarchic, aristocratic social order of the English establishment. For domestic silver London styles were taken up quickly, and a sufficient demand supported the specially skilled craftsmen who fabricated them. Both the iconography of the Winslow sugar boxes (39, 41) and the formal vocabulary of the Winslow chocolate pots (48) offer evidence that Bostonians expended significant funds having silver ornamented with imagery that expressed their appreciation of the cosmopolitan world and the classical tradition that it embraced. The tradition of classical literature that informed the iconography of the sugar boxes has been chronicled eloquently elsewhere.[46] The domed lid of the Winslow pot recalls the dome of St. Paul's, a symbol of the cosmopolitanism of rebuilt London after the devastating fire of 1666. At the dawn of the new century, Boston silver, as exemplified by the Winslow chocolate pot, conveyed to its users a tangible link to the seat of English government.

Contained Formalism, 1710–22

Following Jeremiah Dummer's withdrawal from active business about 1710, John Coney emerged as Boston's leading producer of silver until his death in 1722. The increase in the number of goldsmiths working in Boston leveled off during this period. Boston attracted fewer apprentices and immigrant goldsmiths, although the jeweler's craft was revitalized. Following English fashion, Boston goldsmiths created silver ob-

54. John Coney, caudle cup, 1714. Courtesy, First Parish Church, Concord, Massachusetts. Photograph by David Bohl.

55. John Edwards, beaker, 1721. Yale University Art Gallery, Mabel Brady Garvan Collection, 1930.1244.

56. John Dixwell, two-handled cup, 1717. Yale University Art Gallery, Mabel Brady Garvan Collection, 1930.1295. Photograph by E. Irving Blomstrann.

jects in a severe, formal style that shunned chasing and emphasized volumes articulated with broad planes. This decreased need for chasing and engraving skills would account for the decline in émigré goldsmiths, whereas large-scale casting and other demanding techniques required by the new style were developed locally.

Fifteen goldsmiths who worked in the previous era continued to work in Boston at this time.[47] This pool was expanded by eleven younger goldsmiths who completed local apprenticeships.[48] Only four foreign-trained craftsmen immigrated to Boston in this period, all of whom lacked the wherewithal to open their own shops and probably worked as journeymen.[49] Some of these goldsmiths ultimately emigrated from Boston, but during this period the town supported a total of thirty-two goldsmiths, about the same number that had worked in the previous era.[50] Youths who came to Boston from elsewhere to learn their trade included Apollos Rivoire (later anglicized to Paul Revere, Sr.), who left the island of Guernsey to apprentice with John Coney in 1716, and Daniel Russell, who came from Branford, Connecticut, to train with John Dixwell about 1712.

By contrast, the number of jewelers working in Boston increased. The apparent vacuum in the trade after René Grignon's move to Norwich about 1704 was filled when Daniel Légaré relocated from Braintree about 1714. One and possibly two foreign-trained jewelers came to Boston in the next decade. Peter Boutett, who may have been from London, was in Boston about 1715. The arrival of the London-trained jeweler James Boyer about 1721 heralded the beginning of a family tradition in the craft that lasted throughout the colonial period. Moreover, immigrant craftsmen in trades allied to goldsmithing and jewelery-making came to Boston during this period. Francis Dewing, an engraver from London, worked in Boston between 1716 and 1725. Seven immigrant clockmakers and watchmakers, some of whom were from London, also arrived.[51]

Ecclesiastical vessels continued to be a mainstay of the goldsmith's craft at this time. The majority of surviving pieces made for nonconformist churches perpetuated traditional forms from the seventeenth century, such as the caudle cups Coney made for Concord (54) and the beaker (55) made by John Edwards for the Ipswich church in 1721. Goldsmiths adapted domestic forms to ritual use for other churches; John Dixwell applied handles to a beaker for the church in Charlestown in 1717 (56). Goldsmiths also made pieces that emulated the service presented to King's Chapel in 1694 by the Crown. Examples include the four flagons made for the Brattle Street Church by Nathaniel Morse, Peter Oliver (57), John Noyes, and Edward Winslow between 1711 and 1713. The broad concave and convex moldings of the flagons' bases, plain tapering bodies, and simple convex moldings of the lids are similar to Francis Garthorne's flagons for King's Chapel.

57. Peter Oliver, flagon, 1711. Courtesy, The Henry Francis du Pont Winterthur Museum, 66.1052.

By 1710 the art of geometry was inspiring goldsmiths to craft forms with broad modulated planes in place of gadrooned and fluted ornamental bands. The most important examples of this new aesthetic occurred in domestic plate. An inkstand (58) made by Coney for the Belcher family is a tour de force of Boston goldsmithing of this era.[52] It makes a rich visual and mental play on the number three and symbols of strength. Three lions couchant support a triangular platform that holds a trio of vessels for wax, sand, and ink. The iconography alluded to the official arms of the Province of Massachusetts Bay, the English arms whose design comprised three lions passant. As bearers of this essential implement of business and communication, the lions subtly linked the stand's user to official acts and powers. A trefoil-shaped salver (59) made about 1715 by Edward Winslow also plays with the number three. This form required technical competence, and the unusual shape suggests that it may have been made for supporting something that came in threes, such as a caster set. The design underscores the geometrical composition, with surface ornament of its unicorn crest playing a subsidiary role.

The style of silver that came into fashion in the second decade of the eighteenth century in Boston required goldsmiths to perfect other skills. Among the silver forms in which geometry inspired subtle surface contours, candlesticks needed goldsmiths to master the task of casting on a large scale. Coney's shop was among those to do such work, and his estate inventory of 1722 included two candlestick molds. One of these may have been used for a pair of candlesticks (60) made in 1716

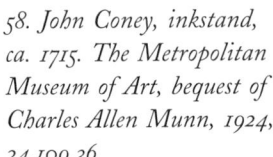

58. John Coney, inkstand, ca. 1715. The Metropolitan Museum of Art, bequest of Charles Allen Munn, 1924, 24.109.36.

59. Edward Winslow, trefoil salver, ca. 1715. The Art Institute of Chicago, gift of the Antiquarian Society, 1948.107. Photograph by Terry Schank.

60. John Coney, pair of candlesticks, 1716. Historic Deerfield, Inc., 62–43. Photograph by Taylor and Dull.

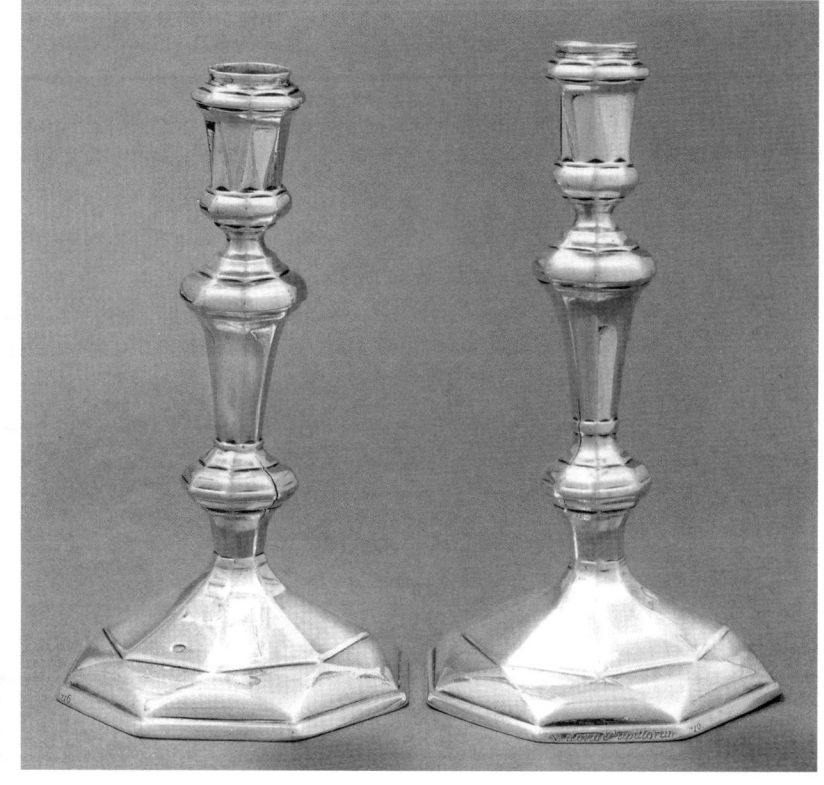

61. Benjamin Hiller, caster, ca. 1715. Yale University Art Gallery, Mabel Brady Garvan Collection, 1930.1224. Photograph by E. Irving Blomstrann.

as a tutorial gift for the Harvard tutor Henry Flynt. The prismatic play of light generated by their complex, geometric arrangement of planes distinguishes their lively and attractive design.

Another form of ornament rooted in geometry is the multipaneled body, a shape that necessitated extra steps to complete. The caster with the Dudley crest (61) by Benjamin Hiller is an exceptional example. The octagonal body of the caster first had to be raised so it could then be hammered over a stake to define the eight panels. The pepper box (62), a related and more common form, often took an octagonal shape in this period. The bodies of these vessels usually had seamed construc-

62. John Coney, pepper box, ca. 1715. Museum of Fine Arts, Boston, gift of Mrs. D. Edward Beede, 42.88.

tion, and their fitted covers and complex moldings were time-consuming to fabricate.

Many vessels made at this time have austere, plain surfaces that stand in striking contrast to the chased, fluted, and gadrooned pieces of previous decades. The earliest surviving New England teapot, which bears the Mascarene arms and was made by John Coney between 1710 and 1720 (63), has a stark pear-shaped body adorned with an engraved oval cartouche and controlled, intertwined mantling. Another major commission from the Coney shop, the grace cup (64) made as a tutorial gift for Henry Flynt in 1718, evokes a similar sense of containment with its smooth surfaces and compact cartouche. The rounded letter forms of the engraved inscription on the reverse (65) depart from the flourishes that dominated earlier engraved inscriptions (45) and mark this piece as "modern." The engraver undoubtedly was familiar with the new style of script, the round hand, that was becoming the norm for business and other types of written communication in England. Writing masters' copybooks, such as *The Art of Writing* published in 1711 by Charles Snell, provided instruction for this clear, flowing form of lettering (66). The cup's recipient, Tutor Henry Flynt of Harvard College, the colony's foremost educational institution, probably wanted the inscription to be in the most up-to-date form of script.

Coney's imposing monteith (67) for the wealthy New York landowner Robert Livingston (1654–1728) and his wife, Alida, has three major

63. John Coney, teapot, ca. 1710. The Metropolitan Museum of Art, bequest of A. T. Clearwater, 1933, 33.120.526.

64. John Coney, grace cup, 1718. Courtesy, The R. W. Norton Art Gallery. Photograph by Thurman C. Smith.

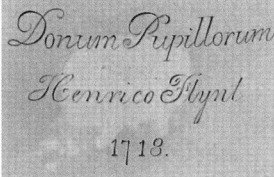

65. Detail of the engraved inscription on a grace cup by John Coney, 1718. Courtesy, The R. W. Norton Art Gallery. Photograph by Thurman C. Smith.

66. Charles Snell, The Art of Writing, *London, 1711, plate 22 in George Bickham, Jr.,* Penmanship in Its Utmost Beauty and Extent, *London, 1731. Yale Center for British Art, Paul Mellon Collection.*

elements emphasized by large rhythmic curves: the rim with wavy edge, the hemispherical bowl, and the foot with opposed convex and concave moldings. The bowl displays an oval cartouche with the Livingston arms set off by strapwork, leafage, and garland mantling; centered above, on the rim, is a cipher of the owners' initials. Few other pieces of this era exhibit such flamboyant and superb engraving. For this important commission Coney perhaps used the skills of the recent English immigrant Francis Dewing. The cipher on the monteith bears a close resemblance to the brilliantly engraved cipher CNH on the New Hampshire

67. John Coney, monteith, ca. 1720. Franklin D. Roosevelt Library–Museum.

68. John Coney, New Hampshire four pound bill of credit, 1722, obverse. Photograph, courtesy of Eric Newman.

69. Jeremiah Marlow, cipher for KR, A Book of Cyphers, London, 1683. Yale Center for British Art, Paul Mellon Collection.

bills of credit of 1722, for which the Coney shop charged for engraving the plates (68). Coney may also have relied on Dewing's services in filling this commission, since Dewing still resided in Boston in 1722.[53] Dewing and other Boston engravers relied upon cipher books for these designs. The cipher on the monteith and the New Hampshire bill bears a close relationship to a cipher in Jeremiah Marlow, *A Book of Cyphers* (London, 1683) (69). The *New Book of Cyphers* (ca. 1695) by Benjamin Rhodes was reissued in 1723, and Samuel Sympson's *A New Book of Cyphers* would appear in 1726.[54]

Goldsmiths continued to employ the steel swages they adopted in the previous period to make spoons with ribbed and beaded rattails. These spoons typically had wide, flat handles with splayed tips either cut with notches to form a trifid outline or shaped to be a large rhythmic curve (53, right). At the end of the period goldsmiths began to produce spoons (70) with plain rattails, more elongated bowls, and forward-bent handles with rounded, sculptural shafts culminating in bold central ribs, details in keeping with the more contained and controlled designs of the era.[55]

The dramatic shift in taste that took place in Boston silver between the first and second decades of the eighteenth century is evident in several of Coney's commissions for important forms, the grace cups of circa 1701 (44) and 1718 (64) and the monteiths of circa 1705 (43) and circa 1720 (67). The exuberant celebration of materiality of the earlier vessels is replaced by sleek, contained surfaces, which probably were

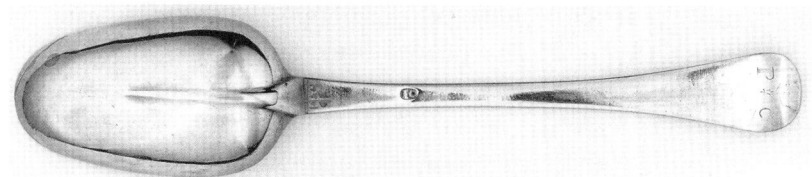

70. John Coney, tablespoon, ca. 1720. Mead Art Museum, Amherst College.

cheaper to fabricate, and whose restraint exudes geometrical discipline and a sense of formality and reserve. Objects made in this era, for example the inkstand (58) and candlesticks (60), have more intellectual appeal than tactile allure. Boston silver of the second decade of the eighteenth century is simple, but nonetheless powerful through its subtle use of iconography, as on the inkstand, and its overt employment of geometry as the foundation of its design.

Whimsical Embellishment, 1722–45

Following the death of John Coney in 1722, John Burt and particularly Jacob Hurd emerged as Boston's leading goldsmiths, while John Edwards commanded the market for ecclesiastical commissions. In this new era changes occured in the size of the goldsmithing community, the way it did business, and the style of the silver it produced. An increase in Boston youths who acquired goldsmithing skills caused the town's goldsmith population to more than double. The number of jewelers rose as well. The available talent among Boston goldsmiths was greater than the market demanded and led more than a dozen goldsmiths to relocate. Other goldsmiths responded to the heightened competition by initiating aggressive retailing techniques, such as introducing the use of surname marks. With the maturation of the late baroque style, they introduced playful engraved ornament that often combined human and animal imagery with otherwise austere shapes. This decoration, and a more ostentatious style of engraved armorials (following the styles prevalent in London), became integral to the design and artistic expression found in the era's silver. Some of the engravers who created this ornament can be identified.

Sixty-six goldsmiths worked in Boston from 1722 to 1745. Fifteen of these were already established, forty-three were Boston natives who completed apprenticeships and joined the trade, three were youths from outlying towns who stayed in Boston after training there, and five were craftsmen who trained in other colonies or abroad.[56] Five other youths from outlying towns completed training with Boston goldsmiths before 1745.[57] Eight native-born and foreign-trained craftsmen in the watchmaker's and clockmaker's trade also began to work during this period.[58] The glut of craftsmen caused twelve silversmiths to leave Boston and establish themselves in trade elsewhere and probably discouraged British silversmiths from immigrating to Massachusetts.[59] The migration of

71. Attributed to John Burt, gold sleeve buttons, ca. 1725. Yale University Art Gallery, Mabel Brady Garvan Collection, 1947.194. Photograph by E. Irving Blomstrann.

craftsmen to Boston was negligible with only John Jagger returning to his native Boston from Marblehead about 1735.

The number of jewelers in Boston also increased significantly: between 1722 and 1745 eleven jewelers were working there.[60] Accounts between the goldsmith Benjamin Greene and the jeweler James Boyer from 1735 until Boyer's death in 1741 offer insights into how the period's goldsmiths and jewelers interacted. Boyer bought small items of holloware and some jewelry from Greene and also supplied him with jewelry set with stones, perhaps even putting stones in settings that the goldsmith provided. Gold sleeve buttons marked IB (71) have sometimes been attributed to Boyer, although the recent scholarship attributes them to John Burt.[61] They number among the few pieces of surviving eighteenth-century Boston jewelry.

A revolutionary phenomenon took place in Boston goldsmithing at this time, when goldsmiths adopted the use of marks that spelled out their surnames. This innovation, which was at odds with the traditional London practice of marking silver with only the maker's initials, may have been a response to increased competition within the craft in Boston. Indeed, at least another generation passed before goldsmiths in New York and Philadelphia followed their Boston counterparts' example. Having punches that spelled out a surname came at a premium because such punches were more complex and time-consuming to make. Yet investing in a more expensive tool must have been deemed worthwhile; compared with a monogram, it promoted greater name recognition of the retailing goldsmith to the consumer.

The goldsmiths who introduced surname marks were the most aggressive silver retailers during this period. John Burt appears to have been the first to do so; the two-handled cup he made for the Hatfield church dated 1724 bears his I.BURT in a shaped cartouche (72). Goldsmiths who adopted the practice by 1730 included George Hanners, Sr., Jacob Hurd, William Cowell, Sr., Joseph Kneeland, Andrew Tyler, and John Potwine.[62] The oldest goldsmiths who worked then, namely, Edward Winslow (b. 1669), John Edwards (b. ca. 1671), and John Noyes (b. 1674), never used surname punches. Younger goldsmiths who refained from the practice were Joseph Goldthwait, Benjamin Hiller, and Samuel Edwards. These goldsmiths and those who were late to adopt the use of surname marks probably had a more traditional outlook.[63]

John Burt and Jacob Hurd used surname marks more frequently before 1730 than any other Boston goldsmiths, and eventually these two craftsmen also marked pieces with their full name. Although Hurd's biographer, Hollis French, claimed that Hurd used his full name in a shaped cartouche from 1724, this assertion cannot be documented.[64] The evidence suggests that Burt initiated the bold practice of identifying his products with his full-name mark JOHN/BURT in an oval, which appears on the grace cup (73) made with the bequest to Harvard College

72. John Burt, two-handled cup, 1724. Yale University Art Gallery, Mabel Brady Garvan Collection, 1930.1337b. Photograph by E. Irving Blomstrann.

73. John Burt, grace cup, ca. 1731. The Harvard University Art Museums, 882.1927.

74. Jacob Hurd, seal, ca. 1750. Yale University Art Gallery, Mabel Brady Garvan Collection, 1939.676.

of Samuel Browne, who died in 1731. The apprentices of these two craftsmen were the only other goldsmiths who followed this practice in colonial Massachusetts. Hurd's apprentice John Ball had a full-name touch as did two of Burt's sons, Samuel and Benjamin.

Engravers played an important role in the goldsmith's trade during this period. In addition to the engraver-goldsmith Nathaniel Morse, who had been practicing his craft since 1709, four more engravers began to work in Boston. Foreign-trained engravers included William Burgis, who was in Boston circa 1722, and Peter Pelham, who trained with John Simon in London and came to Boston around 1727. Burgis may have trained the native-born engraver Thomas Johnston, who was working in Boston by 1727. The engraver Thomas White of unknown origins was working in Boston by 1733, as was Nathaniel Morse's son, Obadiah. An additional native-born engraver, James Turner, would have finished his training about 1743.

The diesinking skills of engravers aided goldsmiths in a number of ways. Local engravers undoubtedly made the punches that goldsmiths used to strike their marks. Indeed, many Boston marks share specific traits, for example, the linked script letters in the initials and surname marks that Knight Leverett and John Potwine used by about 1730 (see the mark illustrations in the biographies), which suggest that the same diesinker/engraver cut the punches for these silversmiths. Seals were other objects produced by diesinkers/engravers, for example, the seal with the Phips arms by Jacob Hurd (74). Engravers may also have fashioned the steel swages for the spoon designs that prevailed at this time. Spoons with plain rattails and forward-bent handles with dominant midribs were the typical style throughout the period as on the examples by John Burt and William Cowell, Sr. (75, left and center). Spoons with double drops were made by such silversmiths as John Edwards (75, right). A shell design in the baroque aesthetic appeared by the end of this period on a spoon dated 1744 by Jacob Hurd (76). The similarity of the shell to those on English spoons suggests that Hurd and later Boston silversmiths may have imported these swages from abroad.[65] Spoons with Hurd's mark also exhibit unusual bellflower drops and occasionally swaged forward-bent tips.[66]

The engraver's role in ornamenting silver assumed new importance, particularly beginning in the 1730s. The engraved arms on Burt's cup for Harvard College (73) of circa 1731 ushered in a new style of armorial engraving. A shield-shaped cartouche with mantling of outward turning leaves and scrolls replaced the oval cartouche with its conforming mantling of interlocking scrolls and garlands. The engraver whom Burt employed to put the arms on the Harvard cup may also have been employed by Hurd to engrave a teapot for the Reverend Nathaniel Henchman in 1737 (77, 78), as well as other objects.[67] Subtle differences exist in the handling of the mantling on the cup and the teapot, but

75. *Left, John Burt, tablespoon, ca. 1735, Mabel Brady Garvan Collection, 1930.1298. Center, William Cowell, Sr., tablespoon, ca. 1735, Mabel Brady Garvan Collection, 1930.1476b. Right, John Edwards, tablespoon, ca. 1740, Mabel Brady Garvan Collection, 1935.605. Yale University Art Gallery.*

76. *Jacob Hurd, teaspoon, 1744. Courtesy, The Henry Francis du Pont Winterthur Museum, Ineson-Bissell Silver Collection, 62.0240.344.*

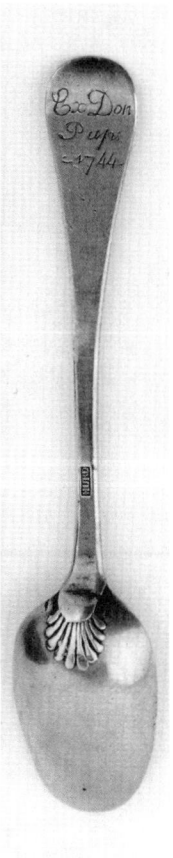

77. *Jacob Hurd, teapot, 1737. Museum of Fine Arts, Boston, Philip Leffingwell Spalding Collection. Given in his memory by Katherine Ames Spalding and Philip Spalding, Oakes Ames Spalding, Hobart Ames Spalding, 42.243.*

many details reveal distinctive similarities. For example, the large leaves that frame the shield are made up of small clusters of leaves linked by a curving central rib; often a teardrop-shaped opening creates the illusion of overlap between the clusters; and short, comma-shaped strokes define the edges of the leaves. A comparison of the armorials on the Burt cup, the Henchman teapot, and the province bills that Nathaniel Morse engraved for the Connecticut Colony in 1733 suggests that all this work can be attributed to the Morse shop. On the five pound bill (79), the central stem appears on the leafage framing the text, and short, comma-shaped strokes define the edges of bluntly pointed leaves.[68]

Although Thomas Johnston's work for goldsmiths is undocumented, a comparison of his copperplate prints with armorials on silver suggests that he may have engraved silver. A bank bill (80) attributed to Johnston, issued in the name of James Eveleth in 1741, exhibits key elements of Johnston's work: sharp contrasts of light and shadow, flowing robust leafage, and leaf tips that have sharply hooked ends. These features repeat on the Rhode Island New Tenor bills of credit of 1743/44 that bear Johnston's monogram. The Pepperrell arms on a teapot by Jacob Hurd (81, 82) exhibit related elements. Like the bank bill, the Pepperrell arms have strong contrasts of light and shadow and muscular, three-dimensional terminals on the scrolls framing the mantling and the

78. Engraved arms, attributed to Nathaniel Morse, on a teapot by Jacob Hurd, 1737. Museum of Fine Arts, Boston, Philip Leffingwell Spalding Collection.

79. Nathaniel Morse, Connecticut five pound bill of credit, 1733, reissued 1740. Photograph, courtesy of Eric Newman.

80. Thomas Johnston, bank bill, 1741. Peabody Essex Museum, 132,574.

81. Jacob Hurd, teapot, ca. 1740. Yale University Art Gallery, Mabel Brady Garvan Collection, 1930.350. Photograph by E. Irving Blomstrann.

shield. Strokes of the burin extending beyond the leaf tips form leaves that are sharp and menacing.

A number of other distinct styles have been identified that eventually may be linked to other engravers. An engraver who worked for the Burt shop in the 1740s and for William Simpkins had a style identified by jagged leaves and hurried strokes that often extend beyond the confines of the design, for example on the tankard with the Moulton arms made in 1745 (83).[69] Another expert engraver worked for Thomas Edwards and Jacob Hurd; his more fluid style can be seen in the Clarke arms on the salver (84) by Hurd.[70] The Clarke salver's engraver utilized

82. Engraved arms, attributed to Thomas Johnston, on a teapot by Jacob Hurd in Fig. 81.

83. John Burt, tankard, 1745. Yale University Art Gallery, Mabel Brady Garvan Collection, 1930.1195. Photograph by E. Irving Blomstrann.

84. Jacob Hurd, salver, ca. 1745. Yale University Art Gallery, Mabel Brady Garvan Collection, 1940.125. Photograph by E. Irving Blomstrann.

complex leafage delineated with feathery strokes and intermittent dark highlights that give noteworthy textural variation to all the elements. The shell often found at the base of his armorials has outlines that undulate softly and continue below the shell to mingle with the leafage. Since Edwards only returned to Boston from New York in 1744, the engraver of the Clarke salver, like the engraver who worked for Burt and Simpkins, also worked late in the period.

Exceptional isolated examples of the engraver's art occur on Boston silver of the 1730s and 1740s. An exceedingly rare tobacco box (85) made by Joseph Goldthwait for the Reverend William Welsteed combines the goldsmith's and engraver's skills. The tortoiseshell lid forms a background for a pierced overlay of silver framing the Welsteed arms with a structure of moldings and leafage inhabited by rabbits and squirrels, all engraved in crisp detail. The incorporation of architectural framework with leafage and animals points to the engraver's awareness of a tradition introduced in late seventeenth-century London by the French Huguenot goldsmith Simon Gribelin. A tankard made by John Potwine (86) for the Bromfield family displays armorials engraved in the same tradition. The facial expressions of the lions and herms and the spontaneous drawing accented by deep incisions of the burin lend the engraving uncommon liveliness.

The integration of form and engraved decoration on ambitious Boston pieces in this period gives them a more animated appearance than the formality and reserve of work of the previous era. This aspect of

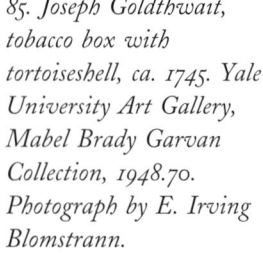

85. Joseph Goldthwait, tobacco box with tortoiseshell, ca. 1745. Yale University Art Gallery, Mabel Brady Garvan Collection, 1948.70. Photograph by E. Irving Blomstrann.

the style is particularly evident on the shoulders of globular-shaped teapots and the inner edges of salvers, where the engraved ornament rests on the forms like lace. These pieces present an engaging dialogue between strong structure and elegant, whimsical decoration, in contrast to the earlier era's tenor of staidness and restraint.

The Age of Aristocratic Refinement, 1745–75

The final three decades of goldsmithing in colonial Boston were marked by another period of stagnation in the growth of the trade. Paul Revere, Jr., and Benjamin Burt emerged as the major retailers following the deaths of John Edwards and John Burt in 1746 and the retirement of Jacob Hurd in the mid-1750s. In response to the oversupply of the previous era, the number of youths from Boston or outlying towns who finished apprenticeships and entered the trade remained stable, and foreign-trained immigrant goldsmiths ceased coming to Boston. On the other hand, the number of jewelers in Boston increased by half.

At the beginning of the period, the English rococo style was adopted in Boston ahead of other colonies. The chasing seen in Boston's rococo-style silver indicates that local goldsmiths were able to develop skills that the new style demanded independent of new talent from abroad. Some of this chased silver incorporates scenes of leisure activities that were evocations of aristocratic European life, an important element of the international rococo style. Engraving also played an integral part in interpreting the rococo aesthetic, and the previous era's pool of specialist engravers doubled.

Compared with the profusion of goldsmiths in Boston during the second quarter of the eighteenth century, the total number of goldsmiths working in Boston stabilized in the late colonial period. Thirty goldsmiths who had practiced in Boston in the previous era worked after 1745.[71] Thirty-six Boston natives completed apprenticeships and entered the goldsmith's trade, about the same number as in the previous era.[72] Eight of the thirteen youths from outlying towns who learned the goldsmith's trade in Boston between 1745 and 1775 remained there to work, and one youth who trained in an outlying town worked briefly in Boston.[73] Thus, a total of seventy-five goldsmiths worked in Boston in the late colonial period. On the other hand, the jeweler's trade increased 50 percent, twenty-five individuals identifying themselves as jewelers in Boston.[74] In spite of the number of Boston jewelers, few examples of their work can be identified. A ring bears a mark attributed to the jeweler Andrew Oliver (87, left). Several mourning rings also survive, and some incorporate enamel decoration (87, center and right).

87. Left, Andrew Oliver, ring, gold, base metal, and glass, ca. 1770, Mabel Brady Garvan Collection, 1936.173. Center, Zachariah Brigden, mourning ring, gold, 1766, Mabel Brady Garvan Collection, 1935.246. Right, unmarked mourning ring, gold, enamel, and glass, 1776, gift of Edward A. Harriman and Julie L. Andrews, 1941.316. Yale University Art Gallery. Photograph by Carl Kaufman.

The number of migrating goldsmiths and jewelers trained outside the colony or abroad shrank to nearly zero at this time, which suggests that these trades satisfied market demand through training local talent.[75] Moreover, the Boston market was unable to absorb all these craftsmen in the goldsmithing and jewelrymaking trades because more than a dozen craftsmen moved to other locales before the Revolution.[76] Emigration in the late colonial period involved relocations to smaller Massachusetts towns or towns to the north, rather than to distant locales on the Atlantic coastline or in the southern colonies, as had happened previously.

Within this community of craftsmen who worked in precious metals, the leading retailers of Boston-made holloware and flatware were Paul Revere, Jr., Jacob Hurd, and Benjamin Burt. Although Burt's father was a prominent silversmith in the previous era, Revere's father was not. The younger Revere's rise in the craft hierarchy in the next quarter century indicates that its structure was fluid.

In addition to Revere, Hurd, and Burt, other goldsmiths and jewelers retailed significant amounts of silver. Following Hurd's retirement about

1755, Burt and Revere's principal competitor was Samuel Minott, a native of Concord who remained in Boston after training there. A more expansive retailer than Burt and Revere during the colonial period, Minott identified himself as both a goldsmith and a jeweler, and his frequent newspaper advertisements announced a variety of wares besides silver. Although kinship bonds may have facilitated business, Minott's career demonstrates that personal initiative remained important to a silversmith's success. John Coburn, who trained in Samuel Edwards's shop, was another producer for whom more than 125 pieces survive. The middle level of the market (retailers for whom fifty to one hundred pieces survive) was shared by Samuel Edwards and an heir to the Hurd shop tradition, Daniel Henchman, as well as by Zachariah Brigden, the shop of William Homes, Sr. and Jr., Daniel Parker, and the jeweler Daniel Boyer.

Evidence of jewelers purchasing flatware and holloware from goldsmiths for resale burgeons between 1745 and 1775. For instance, the jeweler Daniel Boyer was among the era's major retailers; he was the only one, however, whose output was less than 50 percent holloware. The daybook of Zachariah Brigden documents transactions for many spoons and some holloware he furnished to Boyer. Possibly Boyer placed his own mark on the pieces Brigden made for him. That Boyer sold more flatware than holloware may have been typical of the jeweler's trade in general. Boyer's son-in-law, the jeweler Joseph Coolidge, Jr., also purchased flatware from Brigden. The jeweler Jonathan Trott procured the six tankards that he supplied to Jedodiah Foster for the Brookfield church from Paul Revere, Jr., in 1768 (88), and these pieces bear Revere's, not Trott's, mark. Following the Revolution, Trott's brother George Trott also purchased flatware and holloware to resell from Revere. Similarly, a great deal of the silver sold by the goldsmith-jeweler Samuel Minott was produced by other goldsmiths. The Revere daybooks show that Minott bought pieces requiring technical expertise from Revere and resold them. Moreover, Minott's mark occurs on prerevolutionary silver in conjunction with the marks of Revere, William Simpkins, and Josiah Austin.

Some silver retailed in Boston was produced in outlying towns. Accounts between the Salem silversmith Edward Lang and the Boston-based Stephen Emery during the Revolution indicate that Lang supplied Emery with buckles, strings of gold beads, and thimbles, which Emery probably retailed in Boston.[77] A similar phenomenon may have existed with Samuel Minott and Josiah Austin. Austin worked in Charlestown and made such silver as the tankard for the church in Newton, Massachusetts (89). The tankard bears his and Minott's marks, which suggests that Austin may have produced work for Boston silversmiths to retail. Conversely, silversmiths in outlying towns also purchased silver from Boston silversmiths that they then resold. The tankard

by Benjamin Burt on which the Charlestown goldsmith John Hancock overstruck Burt's mark with his own (90) provides evidence of this practice.

The late colonial period saw increased specialization within the trade. The goldsmith Joseph Candish, who began to work about 1738, apparently was the sole supplier to Boston goldsmiths and jewelers of bezel wire for stone setting. According to the memoirs of Samuel Davis (1765–1829), who trained in Boston during the Revolution, "A tool which he [Candish] possessed, being the only one in town, gave him employment."[78] Although from the seventeenth century onward Boston goldsmiths and jewelers supplemented their incomes by importing tools and supplies for resale to fellow craftsmen, documents and accounts reveal that from 1750 some craftsmen specialized in this activity. The most aggressive of these retailers soon began to advertise in newspapers. Among them were the goldsmiths Daniel Parker, his nephew John Symmes, and Zachariah Brigden; the jewelers John Welsh, his nephew

89. Josiah Austin, tankard,
1768, retailed by Samuel
Minott. Museum of Fine
Arts, Boston, gift of the
First Church in Newton,
1973.18.

John Dexter, Daniel Boyer, and his son-in-law Joseph Coolidge, Jr.;
and the goldsmith-jeweler Samuel Minott.[79] The extraordinarily detailed estate inventory of Samuel Edwards in 1762 shows that a large
part of his trade also was selling tools and supplies to other goldsmiths.[80]
Accounts and correspondence with John Touzell and other Salem goldsmiths and the memoir of Samuel Davis together offer evidence that
by the time of the Revolution, John Welsh was able to sell goldsmiths'
and jewelers' tools and supplies as his sole business.[81]

Other goldsmiths probably specialized in raising holloware. The
major producers of holloware in Boston at this time include those
makers who marked the most examples, and those makers whose work
is rare, although a high percentage of it is holloware.[82] Many members
of the second group may have been jobbers of holloware for the major
retailers. Evidence shows that two craftsmen in that group sometimes
made only the raised parts of vessels for retailing goldsmiths. For
example, an account between Thomas Townsend and Thomas Edwards

indicates that in 1748 and 1749 Townsend made more than thirty pieces for Edwards, including a cann body and two tankard bodies. In another case, Thomas Dane was credited by Thomas Edwards for making a milk pot body in 1752.[83] And in the postrevolutionary period, Zachariah Brigden made butter boat bodies for Benjamin Burt.[84]

Engraving also continued to be an important source of decoration in this period, and the supply of skilled engravers that retailing goldsmiths drew upon increased dramatically. Nathaniel Morse, Thomas Johnston, and James Turner all carried on their trade after 1745. From 1745 to 1752 the London-trained engraver Francis Garden also worked in Boston. Craftsmen who began their careers in this period include the engraver-silversmiths Nathaniel Hurd (1751) and Paul Revere, Jr. (1756); and the jeweler-engraver Josiah Flagg, Jr. (1760). Joseph Callender, an apprentice of Nathaniel Hurd's, would have begun his career just before the Revolution. It is probable that artists in Boston who made engraved prints may have turned their hands on occasion to engraving silver for silversmiths.[85] Silversmiths who specialized in engraving had superior drawing skills compared to their peers. Boston silversmiths may have used drawings on a regular basis to record design ideas and to convey them to clients, but few drawings survive and those that do reveal only rudimentary skill. An example is the account book Zachariah Brigden reused for drawings (91).

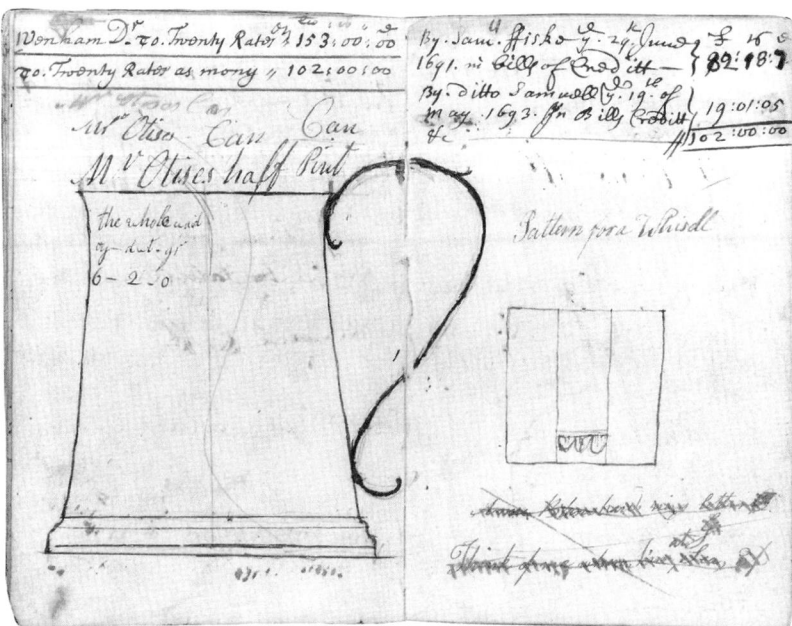

91. Zachariah Brigden, leaf from an account book with a drawing for a cann, ca. 1770. Beinecke Rare Book and Manuscript Library, Yale University.

Boston goldsmiths continued to use Thomas Johnston to engrave some of their most important commissions in this period. Johnston's style, which combined sharply pointed leaves, deliberate textural details, and dramatic contrasts of light and shade, appears in an engraved bookplate he made for Joseph Tyler (92). Armorials that share these characteristics and that can be attributed to him appear on three pieces of silver: two flagons by Samuel Burt for the Marblehead church in 1749 and a grace cup by William Swan presented to Benjamin Pickman in 1749 (93).[86] The shells at the base of the mantling on the flagon and the grace cup have base scrolls that unfurl and form the outer lobed perimeter of the shell. The close correspondences between the engraving on the silver and the bookplate include the way the upper scrolled corners of the shield overlap the molding on the mantling. Leaf tips engraved on these commissions reproduce the same sharply hooked ends with a menacing craggy quality seen on privately issued bank bills in 1741 (80). Other instances of Johnston's distinctive style and perhaps engraved by him are the shoulder decoration on a teapot by Daniel Henchman and two rococo-style armorials, one for a flagon by Benjamin

92. Thomas Johnston, bookplate for Joseph Tyler, ca. 1750. American Antiquarian Society.

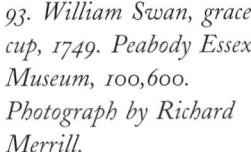

93. William Swan, grace cup, 1749. Peabody Essex Museum, 100,600. Photograph by Richard Merrill.

94. James Turner, bookplate of John Franklin, ca. 1745. American Antiquarian Society.

Burt made for the Marblehead church and one for a communion dish by Samuel Minott for the Brattle Street Church.[87]

Samuel Burt and other Boston goldsmiths also patronized the engraver James Turner. Turner's hand on Boston silver of this period can be identified through the bookplate he engraved for John Franklin about 1745 (94) and his engraving on a tankard sold in 1746 by Turner to Richard Derby (95). The similarity of these engravings to the Tyler bookplate as well as the armorials attributed to Thomas Johnston above suggests that Turner learned his craft in the Johnston shop. Yet Turner handled details of the Johnston style in subtly different ways. On the Derby tankard the upper corners of the shield touch, but do not overlap, the molding that supports the mantling; the shell lacks scrolls and a clearly outlined perimeter; and the ends of the leaves, while sharp, hook more gently. Similar armorials on another group of pieces may also have been cut by Turner, although Nathaniel Hurd also engraved bookplates with mantling in this style.[88]

Boston holloware began to echo the international rococo style in engraved ornament about 1745. Recent scholarship ascribes the first signs of the rococo style in English silver to a candelabra and kettle

95. James Turner, tankard, 1746. Courtesy, Peabody Essex Museum, 131,587.

stand made by Paul de Lamerie in 1731.[89] The vigorous designs that developed in English silver in the next two decades drew inspiration from the grotesque and fantastic interpretations of the Continent's seventeenth-century auricular style. Water imagery, sea creatures, and intimate scenes of bucolic life can be found in the ornament of English rococo silver.

The new style's fractured lines and sense of movement were novelties that Boston goldsmiths introduced to American silver. The well-established goldsmith's trade in Boston probably accounts for the alacrity with which its patrons and craftsmen embraced the new style. The earliest engraved asymmetrical cartouche in Boston is on the apple-shaped teapot by Jacob Hurd, bearing the inscription "The Gift/OF Edw[d] Tyng Esq[r]/to/H. Fayerweather/Dec[r] 9/1745" (96). The earliest instance in American rococo silver of the double-bellied, or inverted pear, shape, a benchmark of the rococo style, occurs on the sugar bowl made by the Boston goldsmith Thomas Dane and inscribed "Mary

96. Jacob Hurd, teapot, 1745. Hood Museum of Art, Dartmouth College, gift of Louise C. and Frank L. Harrington, Class of 1924, M.967.42.

Loring/the Gift of her Father/John Gyles Esq.ʳ/1748" (97). If the chasing on the shoulders of a teapot by the Boston goldsmith John Burt is original, then the teapot is the earliest documented example of rococo-style chasing on American silver because it would have been made prior to Burt's death in early 1746 (98).

With the rococo style, chasing reemerged as a decorative technique essential to creating rich, intricate ornamental effects. Because Boston was the oldest silversmithing center in the colonies, it had the residual pool of skilled chasers necessary to produce silver in the new aesthetic.

97. Thomas Dane, sugar bowl, 1748. Private Collection.

*98. John Burt, teapot, ca.
1745. Joyce and Erving
Wolf Collection.*

John Burt may have done the chasing on the teapot (98) himself, using techniques he learned early in life. He may have trained with Henry Hurst, a craftsman brought to Boston in 1699 because of his chasing skills, and who may have taught Burt the principles of this decorative technique. Edward Winslow's shop, which had made splendid chased pieces at the beginning of the eighteenth century, was still in operation early in the 1745–75 period and was another potential source of chasing skills. Because the chased decoration on Boston rococo silver was limited to the abilities of its indigenous craftsmen, it lacks the finesse of the best rococo-style chasing on New York, Philadelphia, and Baltimore silver, which probably was executed by chasers trained abroad.[90] As in the earlier period 1690–1710, when this style of surface decoration was last in vogue, this specialized and time-consuming ornament added substantial cost to making a piece of silver.

Boston goldsmiths were the only ones in the North American colonies who ornamented chased pieces with rococo-style scenes of leisure activities. The subject matter of many pieces corresponds with the tent-stitch pictures of scenic views peopled with animals and human figures made in Boston at this time. The strong tradition of such imagery in embroidered pictures may have informed the silver designs. The individuals who drew designs for embroidery could have provided those for the silver. The snuffbox by Thomas Dane (99), inscribed "Mary Loring/1752," depicts a pastoral scene—a solitary woman in a landscape accompanied by an animal, possibly a dog, chasing birds—framed with diapering and a raffle shell. Jacob Hurd produced four creampots in a similar rococo aesthetic (100), all incorporating chased cartouches outlined by c-scrolls framing narrative scenes. Perhaps these scenes were personalized for the individuals for whom the creampots were made. Although somewhat unschooled, the low relief, emphatic use of dots to outline shapes, and naive drawing give the chasing charming freshness.[91] If

these pots were made after 1750, they may well have been the work of Hurd's son Nathaniel, whose drawing skills advanced his career as an engraver. William Simpkins made the most ambitious example of chased Boston rococo silver with scenic illustration. His teapot (101) of circa 1755 shows on one side a man with his hounds in close pursuit shooting a stag with a bow and arrow, and on the other side a seated dog attends a seated woman and standing man who are sharing some activity— possibly spinning or yarnwinding. Like the embroidery, these silver pieces affirmed their owners' status by linking them with the refined figures rendered in silver, who had the leisure to gambol in idyllic landscapes.[92]

More typical chased designs on Boston silver employed c-scroll and floral decoration. An early example is the teapot (102) that Thomas Edwards retailed sometime before his death in 1755. The pattern of the decoration on this pot—horizontal broken c-scrolls with flowers above flanking a c-scroll with raffle leaf and three flowers below—also appears on teapots Benjamin Burt made in 1762 and 1763 for the sisters Sarah and Anna Brown of Providence. Three other pots with this pattern by Burt are known.[93] The chaser of the Edwards and Burt pots may be the same craftsman, because all the pots have the same pattern and the excessive use of round punchwork as opposed to more subtle and varied manipulations of the metal found, for example, on London chased silver of the period. On the other hand, the similarities between the chasing on the Edwards and Burt pieces may simply indicate the shared motifs of a regional style.

Other examples of chased Boston silver thought to be made in the 1750s and 1760s by Samuel Edwards, Benjamin Burt, and Paul Revere, Jr., incorporate elaborate embossed armorial cartouches and floral decoration.[94] Examples that can be dated with some certainty include a sugar bowl and creampot (103) made for the marriage of Lucretia

*101. William Simpkins,
teapot, ca. 1755. Courtesy,
Sterling and Francine
Clark Art Institute.*

*102. Thomas Edwards,
teapot, ca. 1755. Museum of
Fine Arts, Boston, gift of
Mrs. F. Carrington
Weems, 1970.508.*

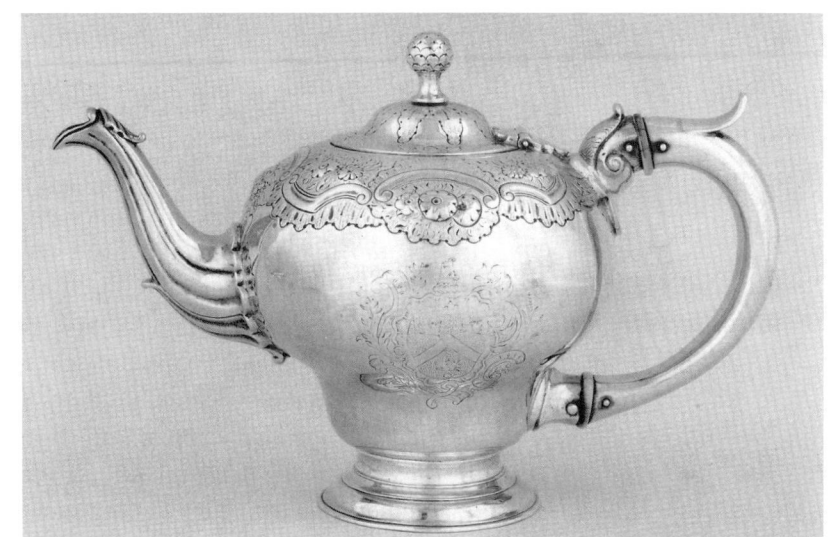

*103. Paul Revere, Jr.,
creampot and sugar bowl,
1761. Museum of Fine Arts,
Boston, Pauline Revere
Thayer Collection, 35.1781–
82.*

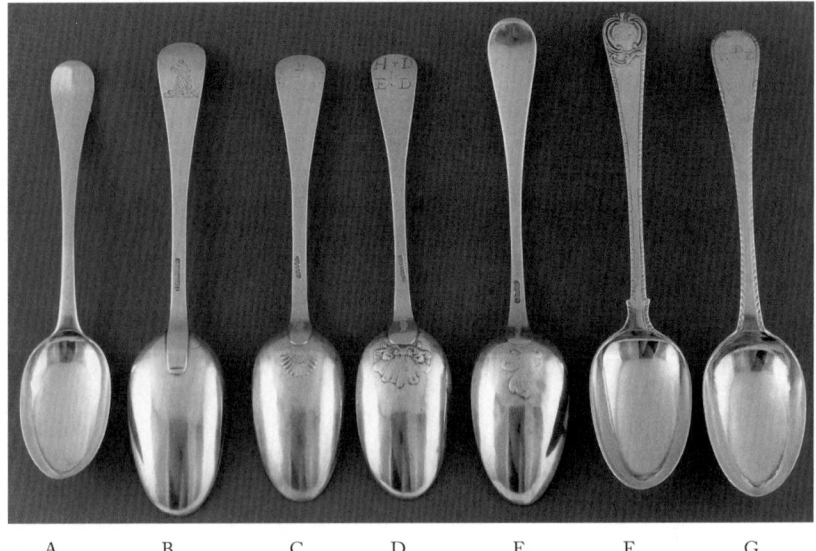

A   B   C   D   E   F   G

104. Tablespoons, 1750–75, (A) William Swan, Gift of Carl R. Kossack, B.S. 1931, M.A. 1933, 1988.93.23.1; (B) Daniel Henchman, Mabel Brady Garvan Collection, 1936.418a; (C) Joseph Loring, gift of Frederick C. Kossack, 1985.86.305; (D) Daniel Parker, gift of Frederick C. Kossack, 1985.86.352; (E) Stephen Emery, Mabel Brady Garvan Collection, 1936.259b; (F) Paul Revere, Jr., Mabel Brady Garvan Collection, 1936.216; (G) Stephen Emery, gift of Frederick C. Kossack, 1985.86.182. Yale University Art Gallery. Photograph by Carl Kaufman.

Chandler in 1761. The chasing on these vessels exhibits the staccato rhythm that typifies New England's abundant use of round punch-work.[95] Most of this chased decoration probably was executed by a specialist employed by the Revere shop because Revere supplied chased work to other Boston goldsmiths. Benjamin Hurd may also have made chased silver, since he owned chasing tools and a chased teapot bears his mark.[96]

Goldsmiths continued to make spoons with forward-bent handles with midribs and shell and double drops. They also introduced new designs for the drops and handles of spoons in this period. The full midrib gave way to a partial one (104A), and the double drop gave way to a slashed drop (104B). Many of the new designs were influenced by the rococo aesthetic, although two of them continued the late baroque style, a cockleshell (104C) and a webbed shell with pendant foliage (104D). Examples of drops in the new rococo style included the asymmetrical beaded scroll (104E). The details of these shell and asymmetrical scroll drops have counterparts in English examples, which suggests that Boston silversmiths continued to import steel dies.[97] The shop of Paul Revere, Jr., produced an even more flamboyant rococo design on spoons whose backward-bent handles bear asymmetrical cartouches (104F). More delicate than the forward-bent and midrib handles of the previous period, the backward-bent handles with gadrooning, or feathering, along the edges (104G) probably were introduced close to the time of the Revolution.

Either in response to a taste for more delicate forms of the rococo or as a means of achieving the style at lower cost, many goldsmiths in the 1760s made wares on which rococo ornament was engraved rather than chased. The diverse styles of armorial engraving found on both silver holloware marked by Nathaniel Hurd and prints signed by Hurd

105. Nathaniel Hurd, cann, ca. 1765. Historic Deerfield, Inc. Photograph by Amanda Merullo.

suggest that different workmen carried out his commissions.[98] Instances of this variation include the large-scale and relaxed Lloyd arms engraved on a cann of about 1765 (105) and the small-scale and delicate Howard arms on a teapot dated 1766 (106). Silver that William Paine ordered from Paul Revere, Jr., in 1773 also reflects several engravers' hands: haste is evident in the acanthus leafage descending at the right side of the cartouche on a teapot (107), particularly when compared with the careful definition of the acanthus on a coffeepot (108) and the precise cross-hatching in the crevices of the leafage on the canns and a tankard (109). The fashion in Boston silver of the late 1760s and early 1770s shifted away from a three-dimensional rococo to a more linear interpretation

106. Nathaniel Hurd, teapot, 1766. Courtesy, The Henry Francis du Pont Winterthur Museum, 60.1045.

107. Paul Revere, Jr., teapot, 1773. Worcester Art Museum, gift of Richard K. Thorndike, 1967.57.

of the style. Nonetheless, the gadrooned moldings on many of these pieces, such as the Paine service (107–09), continue to enhance the scattered effects of light, a key element of rococo design.

Beginning with the early colonial period and continuing throughout the century prior to the Revolution, Boston was a vital center of gold-smithing and jewelrymaking. During the first half-century of English settlement, immigrant craftsmen provided important specialized skills for the emerging Boston tradition, but as the number of native-born craftsmen increased, the migration of foreigners declined until it virtually ceased in the late colonial period. As the center of New England silversmithing, Boston always attracted youths from outlying towns in search of training, and silversmiths who apprenticed in Boston immi-

*109. Paul Revere, Jr.,
tankard, 1773. Worcester
Art Museum, gift of
Frances Thomas and Eliza
Sturgis Paine, in memory
of Frederick William Paine,
1937.55.*

grated to smaller regional towns, particularly in the era just before the
revolutionary war. Overall, the growth rate of the trade fluctuated
throughout the era and encountered periods of expansion, oversupply,
and stagnation.

The business documents and a close examination of the work of
these craftsmen provide ample evidence that those in the trade shared
services and skills with each other. Marks found on Boston silver identify
its retailer, but not necessarily its maker. From the time of Hull and
Sanderson's partnership, Boston shops were rarely without a number
of workmen of varying types and skill levels. Retailing silversmiths

relied on other independent working silversmiths to make objects or parts of objects for them. Goldsmiths probably obtained most of the jewelry they sold from jewelers, and jewelers probably acquired most of the holloware and flatware they retailed from goldsmiths. The small body of marked jewelry that survives today gives a skewed view of what the trade produced, because jewelry—in particular jewelry set with stones—is known to have been made in large quantities. Many of the almost forty jewelers who worked in Boston in the colonial period lack mark attributions. Goldsmiths without identifiable marks probably worked as journeymen or jobbers for retailing goldsmiths.

Fashions in Boston silver followed English models, with new styles taken up soon after they were introduced abroad. The stark, erratic creations of the Puritan goldsmiths quickly gave way to the tactile materiality of the Restoration era, the robust classicism of the turn of the eighteenth century, the austere formalism of its second and third decades, the whimsy and playful ornament of the 1730s, and the celebration of aristocratic refinement that marked the prerevolutionary period. During this whole period Boston attracted craftsmen with special skills, and these specialists made objects of enduring beauty in concert with American-born and -trained craftsmen. For when Boston goldsmiths had access to specialized skills, they created work whose artistry and technique rivaled that of their English counterparts.

Page 45

1. For details on the craftsmen discussed in this essay, see the biographical entries and the appendixes. Life dates are given for craftsmen excluded from this volume. Previous studies have addressed the development of the silversmith's trade and stylistic change in Boston silver. These include monographic studies on the major figures: John Hull and Robert Sanderson, Sr., (Clarke 1940, Roe/Trent 1982, Kane 1987); Jeremiah Dummer (Clarke/Foote 1935); John Coney (Clarke 1932); William Rouse (Hood 1968); John Edwards (Buhler 1951, Ward 1989): John Burt (Ormsbee 1940); Jacob Hurd (French 1939); Paul Revere, Jr. (Skerry 1988, Federhen 1988). For an analysis of the silversmithing trade in Boston between 1690 and 1730 see Ward 1983, 1984, and 1990. Stylistic development in colonial silver is addressed by Philips 1949, Buhler 1956, Hood 1971, and Fales 1973. For a discussion of heraldic engraving and Boston silver see Fales 1973a.

Page 46

2. Through careful study of surviving examples the numismatic historian Sydney Noe determined the number of dies used for the coins, and as additional coins have come to light new punches have been identified. See Noe 1943; Noe 1947; Noe 1952; Kane 1987, 51–52, 55–56; Michael Hodder, letter to the author, 2 February 1987.

Page 47

3. Letter from Samuel Sewall to William Vaughan at Portsmouth, 5 January 1712/13, *Sewall Letter Book* 2:9–10.

4. *Sewall Letter Book* 1:260–61.

5. Although this kind of evidence is questionable compared with an indenture or other document, this study has assumed that individuals who became goldsmiths or jewelers but who were under twenty-one when they witnessed deeds for goldsmiths or jewelers were apprentices in the craftsman's household. The custom was to use older apprentices (above sixteen years of age) as witnesses.

6. Some youths started at age twelve and a common term was eight years. The documented apprenticeships include those of Hull's apprentices Jeremiah Dummer and Samuel Paddy. In his diary Hull recorded the date, 1 July 1659, on which he took these youths into his household. Both boys were fourteen years of age and the term was for eight years. The same was true for Hull's last apprentice, Samuel Clarke, whose term began in November

Page 47, continued
1673. Samuel Haugh was fourteen years old when he was apprenticed to Thomas Savage, Sr., and the term of his apprenticeship, which began on 7 October 1690, was seven years and six months. Daniel Gookin was twelve and a half years old when he was apprenticed to Jeremiah Dummer for a term of eight years that began on 10 March 1695/96. Edmund Mountfort was just over twelve years old when John Burt was appointed his guardian on 4 August 1729. Benjamin Goodwin was fourteen years old when he was apprenticed to John Parkman for a term of seven years on 14 January 1745.

7. Kane 1987, Appendix B-6.

Page 49
8. Benjamin Sanderson ca. 1670, Robert Sanderson, Jr., ca. 1673, Timothy Dwight ca. 1675, John Coney ca. 1677, Thomas Wyllys ca. 1680, Samuel Clarke ca. 1681, Jonathan Belcher ca. 1682, and Thomas Savage, Sr., ca. 1685.

9. Jeremiah Dummer probably trained Samuel Phillips, who came from Rowley and completed his apprenticeship about 1679, and Eleazer Russell, who came from Hadley and completed his about 1684. Phillips relocated in Salem by 1687, and Russell continued to serve in Dummer's shop until his death in 1691.

10. These included Richard Nevill, a goldsmith whose origins are obscure, but who may have been foreign-trained and may have worked for Robert Sanderson, Sr., about 1674; Thomas Higginson, a New England native who trained with the London goldsmith Joseph Ash and may have worked with John Coney beginning in 1679 before returning to the town of Salem about 1687; Nathaniel Gay, who apprenticed with the London goldsmith William Gay and worked with John Coney beginning in 1679; Matthew Mabely, a spoonmaker who probably trained with the London goldsmith Isaac Corbett and migrated in 1683/84; John Cole, who probably trained with the London goldsmith John Gray and came to Boston probably in 1684; John Bingham, a London-trained goldsmith who was in Boston in 1678; and Benjamin Grignon, a Huguenot who was in Boston in 1685; Bingham and Grignon were denied permission to stay.

11. Campbell (1747) 1969, 143.

Page 50
12. Buhler/Hood 1970, no. 20.

13. For comparable English candlesticks, see Jackson (1911) 1969, 1:239–40, 457–58; Oman 1970, pl. 60A; Sotheby's, London, 12 December 1974, lot 202; Victoria and Albert Museum Silver Archive A1094; Clayton 1971, 39, no. 69; *Antique Collector* (June 1956): 93. The Dummer candlesticks may have been commissioned by the wealthy Boston merchant Col. Peter Lidgett before his death in 1676. Because they bear the Dummer mark struck after the stamp cracked, they were not made in the first decade of his career. The arms of the Clarke, Usher, and Jeffries families were added by later generations.

Page 53
14. Buhler 1972, no. 33.

15. Christie's, London, 24 November 1976, lot 174; Sotheby's, London, 22 January 1959, lot 144; Burlington (1901), 37, case D, no. 35, pl. CIX, fig. 1; Christie's, London, 1 May 1929, lot 53; Clayton 1971, 290, no. 585; Christie's, London, 16 June 1931.

16. Victoria and Albert Museum, London, 25418.1–4, along with a second group, 25419.1–4. Freer renderings of flowers are in Guillaume Toulouze (w. ca. 1650), *Livre de Fleurs, Feuilles et Oyzeaus* published in Montpelier in 1656 (Victoria and Albert Museum, London, E 1705–1734–1913). Another early example of a series of designs for jewelry, *Livre de Feuilles et le Fleurs Utile aux Orfèvres et Autres Arts*, was published in Paris in 1661 by Francois Le Februe (w. ca. 1635–57) (Victoria and Albert Museum, London, 28779 B14063 [EO.115]).

17. For Reuttiman, see Victoria and Albert Museum, London, E52–90; for Schmidt, see Victoria and Albert Museum, London, E46.1929.

18. In addition to the engravings cited above, other work in this tradition is Jean Vauquer (1621–86) of Blois, *Livres de Fleurs Propre pour Orfèvres et Graveurs*, Victoria and Albert Museum, London, 22761–3, 4, 11, 20; 14213; 16946; E91 B–1891; HL monogram, Victoria and Albert Museum, London, E452–1922 (EO.22); Heinrich Raab, working at Nürnberg from 1640 to 1650, Victoria and Albert Museum, London, E84 a, b, c–1891 and E1633–1923; Johann Heller (w. ca. 1650), *Schneidbüchlein*, Victoria and Albert Museum, London, E 3931–1910; Johann Wilhelm Heel (1637–1709), Augsburg and Nürnberg, *Goldschmidts Büchlein*, Victoria and Albert Museum, London, E13–18–1929; Johannes Thünkel (1642–83), Victoria and Albert Museum, London, 13781. English engravings in this tradition were also published by Edward Pierce (w. ca. 1660), *Friezes*, Victoria and Albert Museum, London, EO91; Simon Gribelin (1661 or 62–1733); and anonymously, *A Book of Flowers, Fruits, Beasts, Birds, and Flies Exactly Drawn* (London, 1661), Rare Book Room, Yale Center for British Art.

Page 54
19. See Kane 1987, Appendix B–10, for a list of more than eighty surviving examples.

Page 54, continued
20. Clarke 1932, no. 22; Buhler 1972, nos. 10, 34.

Page 57
21. It appears on a salver made by John Allen and John Edwards about 1700 (Bigelow 1917, 240); a tankard by John Noyes for the Brattle Street Church dated 1704 (Warren/Howe/ Brown 1987, fig. 19); a tankard by Andrew Tyler for the Brattle Street Church dated 1732 (on loan to the SFCAI); and a cup by John Edwards for the Brattle Street Church dated 1732 (Buhler 1972, no. 87).

Page 59
22. Another early example of this is a porringer, probably made about 1700, that has both Jeremiah Dummer's and René Grignon's marks (Buhler/Hood 1970, no. 20).

23. Robert Sanderson, Sr. and Jr., tankard (Buhler 1972, no. 1); Jeremiah Dummer tankard (YUAG loan).

Page 60
24. These included Jeremiah Dummer, Thomas Savage, John Coney, Thomas Wyllys, Jonathan Belcher, and William Rouse.

25. The craftsmen from Boston included Edward Winslow (with Jeremiah Dummer, w. ca. 1690); John Edwards (w. ca. 1692); John Allen (w. ca. 1692); Benjamin Coney (with John Coney, w. ca. 1694); John Noyes (with Jeremiah Dummer, w. ca. 1695); Samuel Haugh (with Thomas Savage, w. ca. 1696); Samuel Foster (w. ca. 1697); Job Prince (w. ca. 1699); James Barnes, Jr. (possibly with Edward Winslow, w. ca. 1701); Peter Oliver (with John Coney, w. ca. 1703); William Cowell, Sr. (w. ca. 1704); Samuel Gray (w. ca. 1705); Michael Rouse (with his father and possibly with Henry Hurst, w. ca. 1708); and Benjamin Hiller (with John Coney, w. ca. 1709). The youths from outlying towns were John Dixwell, who came from New Haven, Connecticut, about 1694 to learn his trade with Jeremiah Dummer; Daniel Gookin, son of the minister in Sherborn, Massachusetts, who was apprenticed to Dummer in 1695/96; Daniel Greenough from Rowley, Massachusetts, who possibly may have trained in Boston beginning about 1700; Shubael Dummer, who came from Newbury to train with his uncle Jeremiah Dummer about 1701; Nathaniel Morse, whose birthplace is unknown, but who was probably born outside Boston and trained with John Coney, about 1702 to 1709; Isaac Anthony, who probably came from Rhode Island about 1704 for an apprenticeship in Boston with Edward Winslow; Moody Russell, who came from Barnstable, Massachusetts, to train with Edward Winslow about 1708; William Jones, who came from New Haven, Connecticut, probably about 1708 to be apprenticed to John Dixwell.

26. By 1690, the London-trained goldsmith William Cross was probably at work. By late 1696 or early 1697 Richard Conyers had immigrated, perhaps accompanied by an apprentice, Thomas Milner. David Jesse had arrived by the mid-1690s. Conyers probably found the demand for specialized skills in Boston to be great enough that in 1699 he arranged to have Henry Hurst work in Boston as an indentured servant. Moses Prevereau, probably a continental craftsman, was in Boston by 1701. By about 1704, another London-trained goldsmith, Edward Webb, was also working in Boston. Thomas Mullins, whose birthplace is unknown, but who may have been trained abroad, first appears in Boston in 1708.

Page 61
27. Benjamin Coney relocated in Stratford, Connecticut, perhaps soon after completing his apprenticeship in 1694. Job Prince settled in Milford, Connecticut, about 1699. Thomas Savage, Sr., went to Bermuda in 1706 and worked there until 1714. Samuel Gray was in New London, Connecticut, by 1707. Daniel Greenough moved to New Hampshire when his apprenticeship finished about 1708.

28. Joseph Allen, a limner, engraver and watchmaker, was working in Boston by 1691, and Thomas Emmes, an engraver, is said to have been working in Boston about 1701. The watchmakers and clockmakers who began to work in Boston included Robert Williams, who was employed by 1689/90, Isaac Webb, who arrived by 1705, and James Batterson, who arrived in 1707. By about 1708 the clockmaker and engraver William Claggett, Jr., is said to have been working in Boston.

29. Davis 1898, 410–12.

30. *Mass. Historical Society Proceedings.* vol 6 (1862–63): 341.

Page 62
31. Newman 1967, 51.

32. The Allen and Edwards pieces include a salt (Safford 1983, 23) and a salver in a private collection. The others are two salvers and a candlestick by John Coney (see Clarke 1932, nos. 11 and 50, pls. VI and XX, and Flynt/Fales 1968, 114–15); two tankards by Jeremiah Dummer (Clarke/Foote 1935, nos. 92–93); a salver by Edward Winslow (Jones 1913, 97); and two salvers by Thomas Savage, Sr. (Buhler/Hood 1970, no. 41, and *Antiques* [August 1942]: 66).

33. A salt and a small bowl by John Coney (Buhler 1972, no. 45, and Buhler/Hood 1970, no. 29); possibly also a tankard by John Noyes (Safford 1983, 30).

Page 64
34. SCCR, file 5565a, Judical Archives, Mass. Archives.
35. Five boxes by Winslow are known. The dated examples by Winslow are the box at WM and the collection of Mrs. Edsel Ford (see Nygren 1971, 41). The other examples are at YUAG (Buhler/Hood 1970, no. 51), PMA, and at the MFAB (Buhler 1972, no. 69). See Ward 1984, 144, for a discussion of Hurst as the chaser for the Winslow boxes.

Page 65
36. A relationship exists between the chased lid of the box at WM and the chased border on the salver by Winslow at HD (Flynt/Fales 1968, 115–16). Both have a similar arrangement of overlapping leaves in which the voids between the bases of the leaves are round and regular and the parallel strokes texturing the leaves are coarse and broad.

Page 66
37. Other pieces by Coney include a sugar box (Buhler 1972, no. 48), three salvers (Buhler 1972, nos. 49 and 51, and Buhler 1965, 23–27), six tankards (Buhler 1979, no. 3; Buhler 1972, no. 52; Clarke 1932, nos. 97, 98, 99), and two cups (Buhler 1972, nos. 39 and 40). A salver by John Edwards is known (Buhler/Hood 1970, no. 61). A salver and salt by Dummer survive (Buhler 1972, nos. 20–21). Two pairs of candlesticks by John Noyes exist (Buhler 1972, no. 90, and AIC). Two chocolate pots, a tankard, a two-handled cup, and a cup bear Winslow's mark (Buhler/Hood 1970, nos. 49 and 57; Safford 1983, 22–23; Puig et al. 1989, no. 179; Buhler 1956, no. 145). Peter Oliver also made a chocolate pot in this tradition (Buhler 1956, no. 111).

Page 67
38. Other pieces employing this device are two beakers by Dummer that were Isaac Plaisted's gift to the First Church in South Berwick, Maine, in 1702 (Clarke/Foote 1935, no. 15); two beakers by Dummer at the Dedham, Massachusetts, church (Buhler 1956, no. 54); two beakers by Dummer for the Marblehead, Massachusetts, church (Clarke/Foote 1935, no. 12); a wine cup by Dummer at Old South Church, Boston (Clarke/Foote 1935, no. 47); a wine cup by Dummer, the gift of James Everill to the First Church, Boston, in 1705 (Clarke/Foote 1935, no. 48); three wine cups by Dummer, the gift of Joseph Bridgham to the First Church, Boston (Clarke/Foote 1935, nos. 39–41); caudle cup by Dummer for John and Lydia Fiske (Clarke/Foote 1935, no. 17); caudle cup by Dummer inscribed "Benjamin Coffin/to/ RC" (Clarke/Foote 1935, no. 18); and a caudle cup by William Cowell, Sr. (MMA).
39. Works in this tradition include a beaker by Dummer for the Brattle Street Church, Boston (Buhler 1972, no. 24); three wine cups by Dummer that his wife presented to the First Baptist Church, Boston, the First Church, Boston, and the Stratford, Connecticut, church fulfilling the obligations of her father's will (Clarke/Foote 1935, nos. 44–46); four caudle cups by William Cowell, Sr. (Buhler/Hood 1970, no. 88; Puig et al. 1989, no. 183; Jones 1913, 150, 178); a cup by Cowell (Buhler 1972, no. 98); caudle cups by Coney (Sotheby's, 30 January–1 February 1986, lots 402–03; 30 January–2 February 1991, lot 151; Flynt/Fales 1968, 84); and cups by Coney (DAPC 79.3079; Buhler 1972, nos. 39–40).

Page 68
40. The chocolate pot is in the collection of the MFAB.
41. For the Stoughton cup, see Clarke/Foote 1935, no. 42, and for the Saltonstall tankard, see Clarke/Foote 1935, no. 92.
42. See the tankard with the Pickering arms (Fales 1983, 10–11); tankards with the Chester arms (Quimby 1995, nos. 136–37); baptismal basin with the Winthrop arms (Jones 1913, 40–41); chocolate pot with the Hutchinson arms (Safford 1983, 22); chocolate pot with the Auchmuty arms (Buhler/Hood 1970, no. 49).
43. See tankard with the Norton arms (Buhler 1979, no. 3); tankard with the Foster arms (Clarke 1932, no. 97); tankard with the Holyoke arms (Clarke 1932, no. 104); tobacco box with the Jeffries arms (Buhler/Hood 1970, no. 30); grace cup with the Stoughton arms (Clarke 1932, no. 30); salver with the Dudley arms (Puig et al. 1989, no. 175).
44. See the engraving on a salver (Buhler/Hood 1970, no. 61) and tankard (*Witness to America's Past*, 108) by Edwards and on tankards by Coney (*Silver Supplement* 1973, no. 24; Buhler/ Hood 1970, no. 26; Buhler 1972, no. 43).

Page 69
45. Buhler/Hood 1970, no. 31; Buhler 1965, 24–27.
Page 70
46. Nygren 1971.
Page 71
47. They were John Coney, John Edwards, John Noyes, Edward Winslow, Samuel Haugh, William Cowell, Sr., Benjamin Hiller, John Dixwell, Nathaniel Morse, Thomas Milner, Henry Hurst, Thomas Mullins, Michael Rouse, and Edward Webb. Thomas Savage, Sr., returned from Bermuda in 1714. John Allen probably gave up goldsmithing about 1710, and James Barnes, Jr., did so shortly thereafter.
48. These included Isaac Anthony (probably with Edward Winslow, w. ca. 1711); William Pollard (w. ca. 1711); John Gray (w. ca. 1713); Andrew Tyler (w. ca. 1714); John Burt (w. ca. 1714); John Banks (w. ca. 1717); George Hanners, Sr. (w. ca. 1717); Bartholomew Green (w. ca.

Page 71, continued

1718); Thomas Bradford (with John Coney, w. ca. 1718); John Potwine (probably with William Cowell, Sr., w. ca. 1719); and Joseph Kneeland (with John Dixwell, w. ca. 1721).

49. They included Peter Denman, who came from England in 1710 and for whom Isaac Anthony became surety. Denman probably worked for Anthony. In 1716 two goldsmiths arrived on the ship *Globe* from Dublin: Abraham Barnes, a "Silver & Gold cup maker," and Daniel Gibbs. Just at the end of the period, about 1722, Matthew Delaney or Delaway, a goldsmith of undisclosed origin, appeared in Boston.

50. Michael Rouse may have gone to Maryland about 1711. John Gray relocated to New London, Connecticut, about 1714. Daniel Russell left Boston for Newport, Rhode Island, probably by 1722.

51. These included John Brand, who was in Boston between 1711 and 1715, and his German servant named John Copler; Joseph Essex and Thomas Badley, who worked together beginning about 1712 and who married sisters of Mary Bill, the wife of the goldsmith Henry Hurst; an unidentified watchmaker who came in 1712; Benjamin Bagnall, Sr., who immigrated about 1713; and John Hall, who came in 1716.

Page 72

52. The inkstand was made for either Andrew Belcher, a member of the Governor's Council, or Jonathan Belcher, who would later become governor of the colony.

Page 76

53. Fales 1973a, 191–92.

54. Later Boston pieces ornamented with ciphers include a grace cup by Jacob Hurd (Safford 1983, 37), teapots by Jacob Hurd (Sotheby Parke Bernet, 21 June 1989, lot 135; *Antiques* 116 [September 1979]:419), and a porringer by Jacob Hurd (French 1939, no. 153).

55. For another example of a spoon of this kind by Coney, see Parke-Bernet, 9 October 1954, lot 26.

Page 77

56. The older craftsmen included Isaac Anthony, John Edwards, Andrew Tyler, John Burt, George Hanners, Sr., Bartholomew Green, John Potwine, Joseph Kneeland, Edward Winslow, John Noyes, John Dixwell, Thomas Milner, William Cowell, Sr., Nathaniel Morse, and Benjamin Hiller. The Boston natives who joined the trade were John Edwards's sons Thomas (w. ca. 1723) and Samuel (w. ca. 1726); apprentices of the Andrew Tyler shop, including Knight Leverett (w. ca. 1724), Samuel Burrill (w. ca. 1725), and possibly Theophilus Burrill (w. ca. 1721); John Burt's apprentices, including John Blowers (w. ca. 1732), Samuel Gray (w. ca. 1732), John Parkman (w. ca. 1737), Joshua Doane (w. ca. 1738), Edmund Mountfort (w. ca. 1738), and John Doane (w. ca. 1741); apprentices of William Cowell, Sr., including Rufus Greene (w. 1728), John Cowell (w. ca. 1728), William Cowell, Jr. (w. ca. 1734), Benjamin Greene (w. ca. 1734), and Charles Simpson (w. ca. 1732). Other established silversmiths who probably trained their sons included Nathaniel Morse, whose son Obadiah began to work ca. 1733, and George Hanners, Sr., whose son George began to work ca. 1742. Paul Revere, Sr.'s apprenticeship with John Coney and Joseph Goldthwait's with John Dixwell must have been completed with other goldsmiths since both masters were dead before their apprentices' terms would have expired about 1725 and 1727, respectively. The apprentices of some of the younger goldsmiths are also known. Thomas Edwards trained Thomas Coverly (w. ca. 1729), Jacob Hurd trained Isaac Perkins (w. ca. 1731), and Rufus Greene trained William Homes, Sr. (w. ca. 1738). Goldsmiths who completed their training in Boston during this time but whose masters have not been identified included William Simpkins (w. ca. 1725), Thomas Townsend (w. ca. 1725), Jeremiah Snow, Jr. (w. ca. 1730), Jaspar Starr (w. ca. 1731), James Nash, Jr. (w. ca. 1732), Basil Dixwell (w. ca. 1732), John Pitts (w. ca. 1734), Joseph Pitts (w. ca. 1734), Thomas Skinner (w. ca. 1734), James Butler (w. ca. 1735), John Coverly (w. ca. 1735), John Whittemore (w. ca. 1735), Joseph Clark, Jr. (w. ca. 1737), Edward Foster (w. ca. 1738), William Breed (w. ca. 1740), Timothy Parrott (w. ca. 1741), John Bridge (w. ca. 1744), Luke Greenough Pierce (w. ca. 1744), Ebenezer Balch (w. ca. 1744), and Stephen Callas (w. ca. 1745). The youths who came from outside Boston and stayed there were Jacob Hurd, who came from Charlestown, Massachusetts, and was working ca. 1724; William Swan, who came from Charlestown about 1736; and possibly James Turner, who came from Marblehead, Massachusetts, about 1743. The immigrants included John LeRoux, who came from New York City and worked as a journeyman for Thomas Edwards in 1724 and 1725; William Caddow, who came from Dublin, Ireland, about 1726; Peter Feurt, who came from New York City in 1727; Thomas McCullough, who first appears in Boston in 1730 and worked as a journeyman for Edward Winslow; as well as Jonathan Reed, who first turns up in Boston records in 1724 and may have been an immigrant.

57. They included William Whittemore, who came from Kittery, Maine, to train with his uncle Andrew Tyler about 1724; Josiah Austin, who came from Charlestown, Massachusetts, and

Page 77, continued

apprenticed between about 1734 and 1741; Daniel Parker, who came from Charlestown to train with Samuel Edwards about 1740; Barnabas Webb, who came from Eastham, Massachusetts, about 1743, probably to train with William Homes, Sr.; and Daniel Henchman, who came from Lynn, Massachusetts, to train with Jacob Hurd probably beginning about 1744.

58. The watchmaker Elijah Collins, who probably was born in Lynn, Massachusetts, was in Boston by 1727. The watch and clockmaker Benjamin Bagnall, Sr., trained his sons, Benjamin, Jr., who began to work about 1736, and Samuel, who began to work about 1739. The English watchmaker Robert Peasley was in Boston by about 1735, and the watchmaker Moses Peck, who may have been foreign born, was in Boston by 1743. John Avery, Richard Avery, and William Ridgill were working about 1726.

59. Isaac Anthony returned to his native Rhode Island by 1725. Jaspar Starr was working in New London, Connecticut, by 1731 and ultimately gave up goldsmithing to become a mariner. Thomas Edwards worked in New York City between 1730 and 1744. Theophilus Burrill relocated to New London, Connecticut, about 1735. John Potwine moved to Hartford, Connecticut, by 1737, where he carried on goldsmithing in conjunction with other mercantile activities. Thomas Skinner moved to Marblehead, Massachusetts, by 1737. William Pollard resided in Newport, Rhode Island, briefly about 1730 and by 1738 had relocated to Charleston, South Carolina. Joshua Doane and Basil Dixwell relocated to Providence, Rhode Island, and Obadiah Morse went to Middletown, Rhode Island, about 1740. By 1740 Charles Simpson was in North Carolina. Ebenezer Balch settled in Hartford, Connecticut, upon completing his training in 1744.

Page 78

60. At the beginning of this period Daniel Légaré was jailed for debt and died soon after, leaving James Boyer the only jeweler carrying on the trade in Boston. Asahel Mason, another London-trained jeweler, immigrated to Boston, arriving there before 1745. Other jewelers who may have been trained abroad were William Cario, Sr., who first appears in Boston in 1735, and Josiah Flagg, Sr., who first appears there in 1737. No birth record exists for either of them in New England. Thomas Eastwick was working as a jeweler by 1738. Other jewelers who finished apprenticeships in this period include Stephen Winter (w. ca. 1736), Edward Whittemore (w. ca. 1739), Joshua Eames (w. ca. 1740), Joseph Hiller, Sr. (w. ca. 1742), and Andrew Oliver, who came from Nova Scotia to train with James Boyer about 1738. John Welsh came from Charlestown, Massachusetts, to begin his training about 1744.

61. For the attribution of these buttons to Burt, see Buhler/Hood 1970, nos. 107–08.

62. George Hanners, Sr., made pieces in 1726 marked with an initial and surname stamp, such as the two-handled cup for the Woburn church marked G·HANNERS (Jones 1913, 502). Jacob Hurd made an alms dish dated 1727 for the Marblehead church marked IHURD (French 1939, no. 1). William Cowell, Sr., made a tankard in 1727 for the First Church, Newton, Massachusetts, marked WCowell (Jones 1913, 322). Joseph Kneeland used his surname mark on two tankards with the Vassall arms made for Harvard College in 1729 (Fogg 1972, no. 174). A tankard by Andrew Tyler with an initial and surname mark bears the date 1729 (CGA *Bulletin* 1 [1971], fig. 4). John Potwine's baptismal basin, made for the New South Church, Boston, in 1730, is marked I:POTWINE (Buhler 1972, no. 136).

63. John Edwards continued to use his initials crowned in a shield for the next two decades, as on his cann made for John and Elizabeth (Smith) Dummer (Buhler/Hood 1970, no. 73), and his son Samuel never adopted a surname mark. Edwards's other son, Thomas, finally did adopt an initial and surname mark but continued to use an initials mark on holloware pieces until the end of his career. Winslow, whose retailing activities declined as his work as a public servant expanded, never used a surname mark, nor did Joseph Goldthwait, an apprentice of John Dixwell. Josiah Austin, who would have finished his apprenticeship about 1741, frequently used an initials mark.

64. The earliest piece with Hurd's full-name mark may be the beaker that was Samuel Stent's bequest to the North Branford, Connecticut, church in 1736 (French 1939, no. 22).

Page 80

65. Oman 1962, pl. XXII, no. 74.

66. For a spoon with the bellflower drop, see Buhler/Hood 1970, no. 155. For a spoon with a swaged tip, see Buhler 1972, 1:563.

67. A number of other pieces by Hurd have related engraving, including two canns, the gift of Jonathan Williams to the First Church, Boston, about 1737 (French 1939, nos. 64–65); a coffeepot with unidentified arms erased (YUAG files); a tankard with the Pickman arms at PEM; and a tankard with the Danforth arms about 1735 (French 1939, no. 242).

Page 81

68. Other works that exhibit an awareness of this tradition include a salver with the arms of

Page 81, continued

Bulfinch and Colman by Jacob Hurd (Flynt/Fales 1968, 85–86) and engraving around the shoulders and lid of a teakettle on stand with the Lowell arms by Hurd (Buhler 1972, no. 543). In particular, the pendant, tuliplike flowers on the teakettle bear close comparison to the tulips flanking the crown on the Connecticut notes of 1733.

Page 83

69. Other Burt silver engraved by this craftsman includes a teapot made for Mary Loring in 1748 (Puig et al. 1989, no. 194), another with the Dudley arms (Buhler/Hood 1970, no. 112), and a bowl with the arms of six Boston merchants (Phillips 1949, 75–76). The engraver also cut the Vaughan arms on a mug by William Simpkins (YUAG files).

70. The Jacob Hurd pieces include salvers (Buhler 1972, no. 184; Backlin-Landman 1969, 370) and a grace cup (Buhler 1972, no. 187). A Thomas Edwards salver also belongs in this group (Quimby 1995, no. 64).

Page 86

71. These included Jacob Hurd, Thomas Edwards, Samuel Edwards, Edward Winslow, Thomas Milner, Knight Leverett, John Blowers, John Parkman, Edmund Mountfort, Rufus Greene, William Cowell, Jr., Benjamin Greene, George Hanners, Jr., Paul Revere, Sr., Joseph Goldthwait, Thomas Coverly, William Homes, Sr., William Simpkins, Thomas Townsend, James Butler, John Coverly, John Whittemore, Jeremiah Snow, Jr., Joseph Clark, Jr., Edward Foster, William Breed, Timothy Parrott, Stephen Callas, John Bridge, and Luke Greenough Pierce.

72. Samuel Burt, William Burt, and Benjamin Burt were probably trained in their father's shop and would have been old enough to practice their trades in 1745, 1747, and 1750, respectively. Thomas Barton Simpkins probably began working with his father, William Simpkins, about 1749. Nathaniel Hurd probably began to work about 1751. Paul Revere, Jr., probably took over his father's shop on the death of his father in 1754. Benjamin Edwards, Jr., probably was trained in the Thomas Edwards shop, finishing his apprenticeship in 1752. Samuel Edwards probably trained his nephew Joseph Edwards, Jr. (w. ca. 1758). Jeremiah Snow, Jr., may have trained his son Jeremiah Snow III between about 1749 and 1756. Benjamin Hurd probably joined the trade about 1760. William Homes, Jr., probably trained in his father's shop and is said to have assumed running it upon finishing his apprenticeship in 1763. Some established goldsmiths also turned out apprentices who were not family members: Jacob Hurd, who trained John Ball (w. ca. 1745), Daniel Henchman (w. ca. 1751), Benjamin Goodwin (whose training began with John Parkman, 1752), and Houghton Perkins (w. ca. 1756); William Homes, Sr., who trained Barnabas Webb (w. ca. 1750) and Benjamin Tappan, Jr. (w. ca. 1768); Samuel Edwards, who trained Daniel Parker (w. ca. 1747); and Thomas Edwards, who trained Zachariah Brigden (w. ca. 1755). The goldsmiths who began to work after 1745 also produced apprentices who were working in the colonial period. Samuel Burt trained Caleb Parker (w. ca. 1752); and Paul Revere, Jr., trained David Moseley (w. ca. 1773). Daniel Henchman probably trained Benjamin Callender (w. ca. 1770). Benjamin Burt trained Edward Dane (w. ca. 1771). Daniel Parker probably trained John Symmes (w. ca. 1761). Thomas Dane trained his brother James Dane (w. ca. 1756). John Coburn trained Seth Storer Coburn (w. ca. 1765). The masters of a number of goldsmiths who trained in Boston and entered the trade at this time remain unknown. These include Thomas Clark (w. ca. 1746), Thomas Dane (w. ca. 1747), Samuel Barrett (w. ca. 1756), Andrew Croswell (w. ca. 1758), William Delarue (w. ca. 1761), Jonathan Crosby (w. ca. 1766), James Sherman (w. ca. 1768), I. or T. Tyler (w. ca. 1770), James Austin (w. ca. 1771), and Samuel Belknap (w. ca. 1772).

73. These included the York, Maine, native John Coburn (w. ca. 1745), who came to Boston to train with his uncle Samuel Edwards; Benjamin Loring, who came from Hull about 1745; Samuel Minott, who probably came to Boston from Concord to train about 1746; Ebenezer Austin, who came from Charlestown to train with his uncle Samuel Edwards in 1746; Daniel Rogers, who probably came from Ipswich to train with William Simpkins about 1749; David Greenleaf, Sr., who may have come from Lancaster to train with John Coburn about 1751; John Symmes, who came from Charlestown to train with his uncle Daniel Parker about 1754; Joseph Loring, who came to Boston possibly to train with his cousin Benjamin Loring about 1757; Samuel Pedrick, who came from Marblehead to train with Benjamin Burt about 1760; Benjamin Tappan, Jr., who may have come from Newbury to train with William Homes, Sr., about 1761; John Andrew from Salem, who was apprenticed to Benjamin Burt about 1761; Stephen Emery from Exeter, New Hampshire, who trained with Daniel Parker beginning about 1763; and Caleb Swan, who came from Charlestown to train with Benjamin Burt beginning in 1768. John Butler probably trained in Newbury, but worked in Boston from 1755 to 1761.

74. The individuals who identified themselves as jewelers included William Cario, Sr., Joseph

Page 86, continued

Hiller, Sr., and Joshua Eames, who continued to work in this period; Daniel Boyer, who was trained in his family's shop and assumed running it on his mother's death in 1747; Andrew Oliver, Boyer's brother-in-law, who would have finished his apprenticeship about 1745; George Foster, who was variously identified as a jeweler and a brewer and who worked in Boston in the late 1740s; John Welsh and Jonathan Trott, who probably began to work about 1751; John Dexter, who may have been trained by John Welsh and began to work about 1756; Josiah Flagg, Jr., who began to work about 1760; William Cario, Jr., who was probably trained by his father and would have finished about 1757; Joseph Coolidge, Jr., Andrew Oliver's nephew, who probably finished training with Daniel Boyer about 1768 and became his son-in-law; George Trott, the younger brother of Jonathan Trott, who finished his training about 1762; Isaac Parker from Charlestown, who trained with John Welsh beginning about 1763; John Raymond, who worked for John Touzell in Salem in the late 1760s and came to Boston sometime before 1775, the year of his death there; and John Codner and Nathaniel Croswell, who began working about 1775. A number of other individuals variously identified themselves as goldsmiths or jewelers, including Benjamin Loring, Joseph Loring, William Homes, Jr., Samuel Hichborn, Samuel Minott, Caleb Beal, Benjamin Pierpont, and James Ridgway. Of these individuals, Minott and Homes were among the major retailers of the period. They may have wanted to offer their clientele an expansive and diverse range of wares and services, as did the goldsmith Thomas Edwards, who had the jeweler William Cario, Sr., in his employ as a journeyman.

75. John Jackson may have immigrated to Boston from New York before moving on to Nantucket about 1753. Alexander Crouckshanks, a goldsmith and jeweler from Glasgow, came about 1768.

76. James Butler relocated to Nova Scotia between 1750 and 1767. Benjamin Edwards, Jr., moved to Woburn, Massachusetts, soon after finishing his apprenticeship in 1752. John Ball returned to Concord, Massachusetts, about 1752. James Turner left Boston for Philadelphia sometime between 1752 and 1756. William Swan moved to Marlborough, Massachusetts, by 1754 and then to Worcester, Massachusetts, in 1756. After finishing his apprenticeship about 1756, James Dane moved to Hartford, Connecticut, then New York City, and then Falmouth, Maine. Jeremiah Snow III moved to Springfield, Massachusetts, by 1759. Ebenezer Austin went to Hartford, Connecticut, by about 1760. John Butler, who probably trained in Newbury, Massachusetts, worked in Boston between 1758 and 1761 before relocating to Falmouth, Maine. William Cario, Jr., relocated to Portsmouth, New Hampshire, soon after his marriage in 1759. Samuel Barrett moved to Nantucket, and Andrew Croswell moved to Plymouth, Massachusetts, by 1763. Between about 1763 and the early 1770s John Coverly was in Framingham, Massachusetts. John Dexter relocated to Marlborough, Massachusetts, by 1765. Benjamin Tappan moved to Northampton, Massachusetts, in 1768. Houghton Perkins relocated to Taunton, Massachusetts, by 1772. Seth Storer Coburn was in Springfield, Massachusetts, by 1775.

Page 87
77. See the Emery biography for a transcription.

Page 88
78. Steinway 1960, 12.

Page 89
79. For transcriptions of the advertisements and dates of publication, see the biographies of these craftsmen.

80. Inventory and accounts of the estate of Samuel Edwards, June 1762–78; Smith-Carter Papers, MHS.

81. English-Touzel-Hathorne Papers, PEM; Steinway 1960, 8–9.

82. During the period 1745 to 1775, the first group, most of whom were major retailers, includes Jacob Hurd, Benjamin Burt, Paul Revere, Jr., Samuel Minott, John Coburn, Samuel Edwards, Daniel Henchman, Zachariah Brigden, Daniel Parker, William Homes, Sr. and/or Jr., and William Simpkins. The second group, many of whose members may have been jobbers for the major retailers, includes John Doane, Paul Revere, Sr., Thomas Dane, Joseph Goldthwait, George Hanners, Jr., Thomas Coverly, Thomas Townsend, William Breed, Samuel Burt, Knight Leverett, and William Burt.

Page 90
83. See the Townsend and Dane biographies for transcriptions of these accounts.

84. Bill from Burt to the Brigden estate, 18 April 1787, Brigden Papers, YU.

Page 91
85. These individuals include: Peter Pelham, his son, Henry, and his step-son, John Singleton Copley; Richard Jennys, Jr.; John Greenwood; see Appendix A.

86. Fales 1973a, 207–10, posits that these pieces probably were engraved by Turner, but here it is argued that the Johnston and Turner styles are closely related and that the details on this engraving correspond more with Johnston's work.

Page 92
87. Jones 1913, 262–63; *Antiques* 122 (July 1982): 43; Buhler 1972, no. 321.

Page 92, continued

88. The pieces with similar engraving include a teapot with the Foster arms by Paul Revere, Sr. (Buhler 1972, no. 149), a cann possibly with the Hutchinson arms by Benjamin Burt (*Antiques* 89 [April 1966]: 476), a cann with the arms of Ward impaling Burrill by Samuel Burt (*Antiques* 41 [January 1942]: back cover), and a pair of canns with the Jackson arms by Paul Revere, Jr. (Buhler/Hood 1970, no. 239). Two additional armorial engravings are closely related to those here ascribed to Turner, but are somewhat cruder: the Jacob Hurd teapot made for Thomas Clap in 1745 (French 1939, no. 266), and the Josiah Austin teapot with the Dudley arms (DAPC 72.1190). Cruder still are the engraved arms on a cann by Thomas Edwards (PEM loan TR 508/80). The bookplates by Nathaniel Hurd include Joshua Spooner's (Allen 1894, 110), Robert Jenkins, Sr.'s (French 1939, 124), and Andrew Tyler's (French 1939, 131, pl. XXVII).

Page 93
89. Snodin 1990, 16.

Page 95
90. For examples from the other colonies see Heckscher/Bowman 1992, 70–131.

91. An apple-shaped teapot by Jacob Hurd engraved with the Fleet coat of arms has shoulders with repoussé and chased flowers, c-scrolls, and scaled decoration in which dots are used emphatically throughout the design, suggesting that the workman who ornamented the creampots did the teapot (Buhler 1972, no. 194).

Page 96
92. Two other examples of chased rococo silver with scenic views are creampots in the collection of the CMA by Thomas Edwards and William Simpkins (Johnston 1994, 46, 144). The attribution of the Edwards piece and the date of the chasing have been questioned. Details of the work, however, especially the punchwork dots at the edges of the flowers, are comparable to other Boston chasing, for example, the teapots by Benjamin Burt (Emlen 1984, 40–41).

93. Emlen 1984, 40–41; Parke-Bernet, 4 January 1940, lot 153; teapot, YUAG files; teapot, SFCAI loan. A teapot with a different pattern by Burt has been in the marketplace; see Sotheby Parke Bernet, 19–22 November 1980, lot 182.

94. Benjamin Burt creampot (SFCAI loan); Samuel Edwards teapot (SFCAI loan); Paul Revere, Jr., teapot (Buhler 1972, no. 346).

Page 98
95. A few atypical examples are known—a teapot by Samuel Edwards dated 1757 (Quimby 1995, no. 57), a coffeepot by Benjamin Burt (*Antiques* 126 [December 1984]: 1371), and an unmarked example of chased work assumed to have been made in New England, the coffeepot for Elizabeth Crowninshield Derby dated 1769 (Flynt/Fales 1968, 123–24).

96. Buhler 1956, no. 84.

97. Davis 1976, 177.

Page 99
98. In Hurd's engravings on paper compare for instance the fluid style of the advertisement *Sperma-ceti Candles* engraved for Joseph Palmer before 1754 (Fales 1973a, 212) with the bookplate engraved for Robert Hale (Allen 1894, 107).

Gerald W. R. Ward

Micropolitan and Rural Silversmiths in Eighteenth-Century Massachusetts

THE WORLD OF SILVERSMITHING in colonial Massachusetts—indeed, in colonial New England—was dominated by Boston makers. Their shops produced the most goods, received the best commissions, employed the most men, and served as the source of supply for customers throughout the region. In the face of this hegemony, silversmiths outside of Boston practiced the craft in a different manner. This essay looks at the careers of some of these silversmiths, focusing on the makers in Salem, the principal town outside Boston, but also considering the craftsmen of Newburyport, Marblehead, Ipswich, Worcester, Concord, Deerfield, Plymouth, Barnstable, Nantucket, and elsewhere.[1]

Silversmithing started later in these communities than it did in Boston. The arrival of the first silversmith in a New England community other than Boston generally occurred about fifty years, or even later, after initial settlement, and indeed the number of new shops established in outlying towns and colonies did not increase significantly until the 1750s. The first silversmith in Connecticut, for example, was Job Prince (1680–1703/04), who arrived in Milford from Boston about 1699. Samuel Gray (1684–1713), again from Boston, arrived in New London, Connecticut (founded 1646), in 1707 and was the first member of the craft there. Even in Newbury, Massachusetts (founded 1635), destined to be a small center of silversmithing in the late eighteenth and early nineteenth centuries, the first silversmith was not active until after 1750.[2]

In the colonial period, Salem had the most silversmiths of any of these outlying towns, with fifteen craftsmen active before the Revolution and several more whose working lives encompassed the late eighteenth century. Only seven other Massachusetts towns had more than two silversmiths (although not necessarily simultaneously) in the colonial period: Charlestown (eleven), Marblehead (eight), Barnstable (six), Newburyport (six), Nantucket (four), Braintree (four), and Northampton (three). At an even lower level, several towns supported only one or two silversmiths: Concord, Gloucester, Ipswich, Lancaster, Marlborough, Newbury, Plymouth, Springfield, Taunton, Worcester, Hingham, and Cambridge. In those towns with two silversmiths, they usually worked consecutively, with perhaps a brief period of overlap between the two. These craftsmen faced limited opportunities and were forced to diversify. A number of them practiced clockmaking as well, and many of them may have been principally retailers, since little or no work marked by them is known.[3]

A general migration and fanning out of Boston goldsmiths occurred at the end of the seventeenth and beginning of the eighteenth centuries, a migration prompted by competition within the craft in Boston and a growing prosperity in the towns and villages outside of New England's commercial center. The entry of these silversmiths into specific towns can be seen as an index of each community's arrival at a certain stage of maturation, at a certain level of economic well-being and social sophistication that is difficult to define yet readily discernible. The presence of a silversmith in a community serves as a useful indicator of the first stages of something approaching urban life, an indicator that can be used to supplement more traditionally applied yardsticks.[4]

Prior to 1730 six outlying towns were able to support silversmiths and jewelers, including Salem, Hingham, Braintree, Charlestown, Barnstable, and Marblehead, of which Salem was the first. Samuel Phillips began to practice in Salem in the late 1680s, having come there from Boston. It is not surprising that Salem, on the verge of becoming more of a town than a village in the 1670s and 1680s, was selected as Phillips's choice. In 1683 the General Court of Massachusetts declared Boston and Salem the only legal ports of entry for foreign goods in the colony. Salem shipping between 1697 and 1714, although modest by English standards, thus ranked second only to Boston in Massachusetts.[5] As Benno M. Forman found to be true in the case of the furniture trades, Salem remained in a very different class from Boston, and in the realm of the decorative arts retained a distinctly nonurban character well into the eighteenth century.[6] A single statistic establishes Salem's subordinate role. Whereas some eighty-two goldsmiths found work in Boston between 1690 and 1730, with as many as forty-three being active during a single decade, Salem could support only Samuel Phillips during that time span.[7]

The other five towns where silversmiths and jewelers worked before 1730, although smaller and less important than Salem, supported additional practitioners of those crafts. The jeweler Francis Légaré settled in the south shore town of Hingham before locating in the inland community of Braintree. There, first he and then his son Daniel followed the jeweler's trade until about 1714, when Daniel moved to Boston. Braintree did not support a silversmith throughout the rest of the colonial period except for Peter Etter, a watchmaker known to have retailed jewelry and silver, who worked in the late colonial period before fleeing to Halifax at the time of the Revolution. Charlestown, situated across the Charles River from Boston, was where the French Huguenot silversmith Francis Bassett lived from about 1703 until 1715. Charlestown native Jeremiah Snow, Jr., may also have worked there briefly in the late 1720s before settling in Boston. A long tradition of silversmithing in Barnstable, on Cape Cod, began when Moody Russell returned to the town of his birth after completing his apprenticeship with the Boston silversmith Edward Winslow about 1716. Russell probably trained his brother Joseph, who worked in Barnstable from about 1723 to 1733 before moving to Bristol, Rhode Island. Salem's neighboring town of Marblehead, largely a fishing village, also supported two silversmiths before 1730. William Jones, a New Haven, Connecticut, native who probably trained in Boston with a former New Havener, John Dixwell, was working in Marblehead by 1722. Joseph Watkins was identified as a Marblehead goldsmith when he was tried for counterfeiting in 1727.

While Phillips and other craftsmen migrated within Massachusetts, other young craftsmen left the province. Job Prince and Samuel Gray, as mentioned, went to Connecticut, as did Thomas Higginson and René Grignon; Thomas Savage, Sr., went to Bermuda, Thomas Wyllys to Jamaica, and Francis Solomon Légaré to South Carolina. As the eighteenth century progressed, the migration of silversmiths from eastern Massachusetts to the Connecticut River Valley was notable. In the 1730s, for example, John Potwine left Boston for Hartford; other men would follow later. Jeremiah Snow III and Seth Storer Coburn relocated to Springfield, Benjamin Tappan, Jr., to Northampton, Isaac Parker to Deerfield, and Nathaniel Barstow to Sunderland.[8]

What was the nature of the craft of silversmiths and jewelers in outlying towns in the late seventeenth and early eighteenth centuries? How did their careers relate to those of their Boston colleagues? It is somewhat difficult to arrive at answers to these questions, for the documentary record on most of the silversmiths in outlying towns, as revealed by the biographies in this volume, is far from ample. The small number of objects that survive for most of these craftsmen indicates that they were not major merchant-producer goldsmiths of their generation. The tankards marked by William Jones (1) and Moody Russell (2), assuming that they made them, show that they were competent craftsmen who could make, if required, complex objects. But, in all likelihood, silversmiths in the outlying towns spent much of their time making repairs and fashioning small objects such as spoons and cups.

Silversmiths and jewelers in the outlying towns may have made objects that Boston craftsmen retailed. Some evidence of this practice is provided by an account that shows that Daniel Légaré made a gold ring with a stone, a gold hair ring, and a gold collar for the Boston

watchmaker Joseph Essex when Légaré was still living in Braintree.[9] It is possible that some of these craftsmen found their niche as middlemen or local contacts for Boston silversmiths, with whom they were acquainted as part of a craft network that may have been more active than we realize. A goodly number of silver objects flowed from Boston to Salem during the years spanned by Phillips's career, for example, and he may have served as a conduit for that traffic. There is some evidence that Salem silversmiths operated in this fashion later in the

eighteenth century, and Phillips may have pioneered the relationship.

The overwhelming weight of evidence suggests that the outlying towns where silversmiths and jewelers worked were able to support only one at a time, if that. Daniel Légaré abandoned Braintree for Boston by 1714. No silversmith was active in Charlestown between Bassett's death in 1715 and the late 1720s. The apprentices of Moody Russell—Joseph Russell and Ephraim Cobb—settled outside Barnstable. Phillips found enough business in Salem to remain active in his craft until the end of his life. He was able to own his dwelling and to work at silversmithing as a full-time occupation. Significantly, however, Phillips chose not to steer either of his sons into his profession. One son, Samuel (b. 1690), entered the ministry, while John (b. 1701) was apprenticed to the stationer's business with Daniel Henchman of Boston, perhaps evidence of another link in the chain uniting Phillips with the world of the Boston artisan. But it is equally significant that Phillips was able to provide his sons with enough education and support to enable them to enter professions with high, or at least middling, status. Although Phillips remained and was comfortable if not prosperous, the community failed to attract another silversmith until the 1730s.

Silversmiths in the seventeenth century generally were regarded as being at the top of the hierarchy of craftsmen. But the experience of those silversmiths working outside Boston in the early eighteenth century and even later casts considerable doubt on the validity of this generalization when applied outside of a truly urban setting. Moody Russell gained enough respect ultimately to become a deacon in his church. There is some evidence that Phillips was reasonably well regarded by his fellow citizens, although no more so than any other artisan and certainly less so than a member of the merchant community. He held, for example, several minor town offices, but he did not rise to the high social and official positions attained by his probable master, Jeremiah Dummer.[10] Nor was Phillips able to "move-up" from being an artisan to being a merchant, like Salem's shipwright-merchant Bartholomew Gedney, who became a leading figure in town affairs.[11] Daniel Légaré ended up in a debtor's prison toward the end of his life. Nothing is known about Watkins other than his run-ins with the law. There is no evidence as to the size of Phillips's or Bassett's estates in the probate records, but Jones's estate was valued at more than £1,100, a substantial sum. However, from what little we do know of these craftsmen, they clearly were more of a "middling sort," rather than in William Badcock's 1697 phrase "the most genteel of any in the Mechanic Way."

During the period between 1730 and 1760 the population of silversmiths increased in some of those towns where silversmiths had worked previously, and silversmiths began to work in towns where none had worked before. The population of silversmiths increased most dramatically in Salem. Phillips's death in 1722 brought to a close the first tentative beginnings of silversmithing in Salem. Nearly another decade would pass before Jeffrey Lang would arrive from Portsmouth, New Hampshire, and David Northey would come to Salem from Boston via Marblehead. They would renew the craft in the 1730s at a slightly more ambitious and higher level. Both Lang and Northey were probably established in business in town by the time each married a Salem woman in 1732. Lang had arrived as a fully trained and experienced silversmith from Portsmouth, and Northey probably came to Salem shortly after the completion of his apprenticeship. Each man was followed in the craft by his sons, and members of the Lang and Northey families were to remain active as Salem silversmiths for the remainder of the century and well into the next. In the 1740s, Jeffrey Lang and David Northey were joined by Joseph Gardner and John Touzell (3).

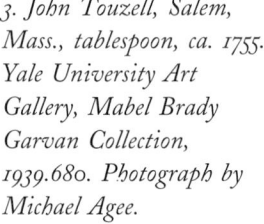

3. John Touzell, Salem, Mass., tablespoon, ca. 1755. Yale University Art Gallery, Mabel Brady Garvan Collection, 1939.680. Photograph by Michael Agee.

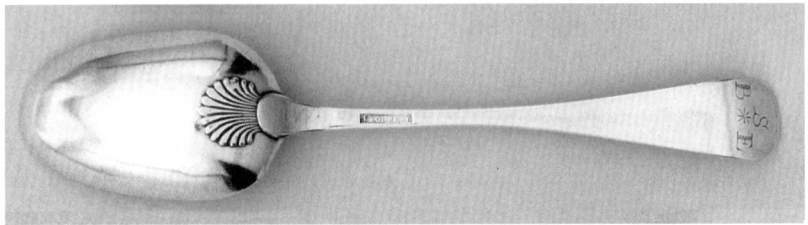

This group of four was augmented in the 1750s by Jeffrey Lang's sons
Richard and Nathaniel and by David Northey's son William.

In addition to Salem, the largest towns that had silversmiths working
prior to 1730—Charlestown and Marblehead—supported more silversmiths between 1730 and 1760. Next to Salem, neighboring Marblehead
had the largest number. John Jagger worked in Marblehead briefly
in the mid-1730s before moving to Boston, and the Boston-trained
silversmith Thomas Skinner settled in Marblehead by 1737. Skinner
was joined by Samuel Glover and Thomas Grant in the early 1750s.
Silversmithing in Charlestown was revived when Josiah Austin began
working there in the early 1740s. A second silversmith, John Hancock,
may have begun to practice there when he finished his training about
1753, and Josiah Austin's cousin Nathaniel Austin began to work there
about 1755.

During the period from 1730 to 1760 other Massachusetts towns had
grown large enough to support their own silversmiths. These included
the south shore town of Plymouth, where Ephraim Cobb, who perhaps
trained in his native Barnstable with Moody Russell, settled about
1730. Cobb worked in Plymouth until about 1755, when he returned to
Barnstable. Plymouth was without a silversmith for a few years until
the Boston-trained craftsman Andrew Croswell went there about 1763.
Beginning in 1742 William Moulton worked in the north shore seaport
of Newburyport. In Milton on the Neponset River southwest of Boston,
Samuel Davenport began working in the early 1740s. Nathaniel Barstow
settled about 1745 in the northern Connecticut River Valley town of
Sunderland. Benjamin Edwards, Jr., a relative of the Boston silversmith
Thomas Edwards, settled in the Middlesex County farming community
of Woburn about 1753. In the mid-1750s Joseph Moulton (1724–95) began
to work in Newbury; the Boston silversmith William Swan relocated
briefly to Marlborough and then moved further west to Worcester;
Daniel Steward began working in the remote Middlesex County town of
Lunenberg; John Jackson of Boston settled on Nantucket; the Concord
native John Ball returned to Concord from Boston; and Daniel Rogers
returned to Ipswich after an apprenticeship in Boston.

In the fifteen years prior to the American Revolution an accelerated
increase took place in the number of silversmiths working in outlying
towns and in the number of outlying towns that acquired silversmiths
for the first time. By the 1760s, the Salem silversmiths Joseph Gardner,
John Touzell, the surviving Lang family members (Jeffrey had died in
1758), and the Northey men were joined by John Andrew, perhaps the
most accomplished Salem silversmith of the eighteenth century. John
and Joseph Hathorne began working in the 1770s. In the 1770s and
1780s, several minor figures joined this existing establishment, swelling
the number of active silversmiths in each decade to thirteen, or nearly
one silversmith for every six hundred people in town.

The other more populous towns in which silversmithing had existed for some time acquired additional members of the craft in the 1760s and 1770s. In Charlestown, Richard Trumbull, Thomas Lynde, H. P. Sweetser, James Austin, and Eleazer Wyer began to work. Following the deaths of Samuel Glover and Thomas Skinner, Marblehead's only silversmith was Thomas Grant before William Bubier and Samuel Pedrick opened shops in the 1760s. Moody Russell's apprentices Abraham Higgins and Elpalet Loring, as well as Elisah Gray, carried on silversmithing in Barnstable. In Newburyport William Moulton's nephew Joseph Moulton (1744–1816) became active, as did William Coffin Little and Elias Davis. On Nantucket, John Jackson soon had competition in the form of Samuel and Nathaniel Barrett. Benjamin Bunker also began to work there just before the Revolution. Israel Bartlett opened a shop in Newbury and Ebenezer Staniford opened one in Ipswich.

There seems to have been a pattern of younger family members going (or being sent) from the Boston area to outlying towns, a pattern that created links between eastern and western Massachusetts and strengthened the retailing branch of the older family businesses. For example, the Boston jeweler John Welsh, the leading retailer of goldsmiths' and jewelers' supplies in the late colonial period, had three different relatives or apprentices settle in the outlying towns: his cousin Jeremiah Snow III went to Springfield in 1759; an apprentice, John Dexter, was in Marlborough by 1765; and another apprentice, Isaac Parker, was in Deerfield by 1776. (A similar pattern existed for some of Boston's merchant-producer goldsmiths. For example, Samuel Edwards's nephew Ebenezer Austin was in Hartford by 1761; Benjamin Tappan, Jr., the son-in-law of William Homes, Sr., went to Northampton in 1768; and John Coburn's nephew Seth Storer Coburn was in Springfield by 1775.)

After 1760 some Massachusetts towns acquired resident silversmiths for the first time. Several of these were long-established towns such as Taunton (founded 1639), where the Boston-trained silversmith Houghton Perkins settled in the 1770s; Gloucester (founded 1642), where the Newbury native Stephen Morse settled in the late 1760s and Edward Northey, son of the Salem silversmith David Northey, settled about 1770; and Medford (founded 1630), where the Charlestown native William Gowen located about 1770. Silversmiths also settled in Lancaster, Andover, and Northampton for the first time.

Practitioners of the craft also set up shop in the newer towns, such as Stoughton (founded 1726), where Lemuel Davenport, son of Samuel Davenport of neighboring Milton, opened a shop in the early 1760s; Danvers (founded 1752), where the native Henry Buxton began to work in the early 1760s; Leicester (founded 1714), where the native Reuben Earle began to work in the late 1760s; Sutton (founded 1714), where the native Timothy Sibley started to practice on the eve of the Revolution; and Upton (founded 1735), where the native Seth Sadler began to practice in the early 1770s. About half of the silversmiths who began to work in towns where no silversmiths had worked previously were natives to those towns, indicating that they trained elsewhere and then returned to the towns of their birth to begin silversmithing traditions there; one such was David Greenleaf, Sr., of Lancaster, who probably trained in Boston.

The obviously modest scale of silversmithing in towns outside of Boston in the eighteenth century again can be demonstrated by a comparison with the size of the craft in truly urban centers. There were at least two hundred silversmiths who worked in Boston between 1730 and 1800, and about five hundred silversmiths and artisans are known to have been active in New York City between 1690 and 1820. The scale of operations in Salem and other small towns was more akin to that of small towns in other colonies, such as New London, Connecticut, where only thirty-six silversmiths were active between 1690 and 1820. Similar figures for the same time span are available for Annapolis, Maryland (27), Lancaster, Pennsylvania (33), and Portsmouth, New Hampshire (47).[12]

On the basis of numbers alone, silversmiths in other small Massachusetts communities that leaned toward the urban but retained much of the rural were operating on a different level from that occupied by their brethren in Boston, New York, and Philadelphia. The differences were so great that one might argue that there was a difference in kind rather than degree between the truly metropolitan silversmiths, such as the leaders of the craft in Boston, and what might be called (to borrow a term from Kenneth Clark) the "micropolitan" silversmiths, such as the Salem practitioners.[13] These micropolitan communities did not have the entire upper level of the goldsmith's craft in which large shops, employing several journeymen and training several apprentices simultaneously, operated. These shops received important public and private commissions for lavish presentation objects or church silver, made and sold many objects, a good percentage of which have survived, and employed specialists in different facets of the craft. The master of such a shop served as an arbiter of quality control, leaving much of the labor to others, while he may have branched out into shipping, on his way to becoming a wealthy merchant. This upper end of the craft was dominated by men whom Barbara McLean Ward has termed the leading merchant-producer goldsmiths of a given generation.[14] This aspect of the craft simply did not exist anywhere in Massachusetts outside of Boston.

Silversmiths in outlying towns remained subordinate to their Boston colleagues throughout the eighteenth century, and their story needs to be told and understood in light of this domination. It may be useful to think of these silversmiths as the inhabitants of small satellite planets falling within the strong gravitational pull of Boston. In this craft, as in so many other respects, Boston was indeed the hub of New England. Some of the larger towns, such as Salem, in turn, eventually stood in something of an intermediary position and may have exerted something of their own influence on smaller Essex County and New Hampshire communities.

It is abundantly clear that the New England patrons conceived of the situation in something like these terms and were thus primarily responsible for creating it. From their point of view, any major commission was reserved for a Boston silversmith or, on a more exalted level, for a London goldsmith. This attitude had a great impact on the nature of the small-town silversmith's trade, an impact probably greater than that of any other single factor. Many patrons living outside of Boston were far from poor; they merely chose to spend their wealth elsewhere, when silver was in question.

This limited the silversmiths in outlying towns to a narrow range of production. The attitudes and choices of their patrons confined these craftsmen to the production of spoons (4), ladles (5), canns (6), jewelry (7), buckles (8), and other small items, with few exceptions. No eigh-

4. Isaac Parker, Deerfield, Mass., tablespoon, ca. 1755. Yale University Art Gallery, Mabel Brady Garvan Collection, 1930.1263.

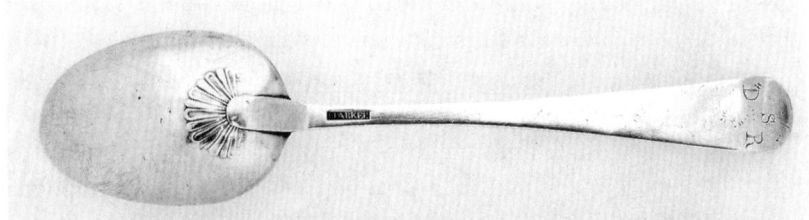

5. John Andrew, Salem, Mass., ladle, ca. 1775. Yale University Art Gallery, gift of Carl R. Kossack, B.S. 1931, M.A. 1933, 1986.103.29. Photograph by Michael Agee.

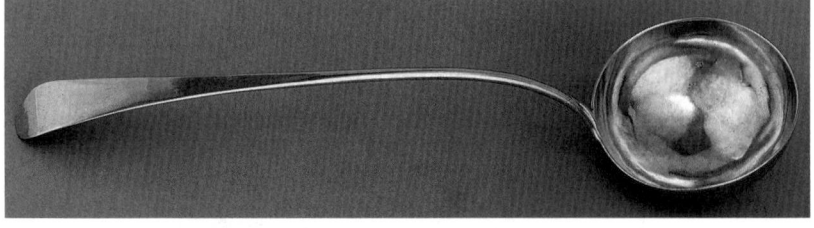

teenth-century Massachusetts silversmith outside of Boston, as far as we know, was ever asked to make an object of the complexity and stature of John Coney's monteith bowl (Kane essay, 43), Edward Winslow's sugar boxes (Kane essay, 40, 42), or Jacob Hurd's series of large, two-handled, or grace, cups. Such masterpieces were rare in American silver and permitted their makers to display the full range of skills they or other members of their shops possessed.

In contrast, the work produced by Massachusetts silversmiths outside of Boston was of a nearly uniform routine nature. Although men such as Coney, Winslow, and Hurd spent much, if not most, of their time engaged in routine tasks and in producing the simple objects that were the staple of their trade, they were fortunate in being able occasionally

6. Jeffrey Lang, Salem, Mass., cann, ca. 1740. The Metropolitan Museum of Art, bequest of A. T. Clearwater, 33.120.271.

7. Jeffrey Lang, Salem, Mass., gold mourning ring, 1736. Yale University Art Gallery, Mabel Brady Garvan Collection, 1934.344. Photograph by E. Irving Blomstrann.

8. Jeffrey Lang, Salem, Mass., knee buckles, ca. 1745. Yale University Art Gallery, Mabel Brady Garvan Collection, 1948.222a–b. Photograph by Michael Agee.

9. David Northey, Salem, Mass., trencher salt, ca. 1735. Yale University Art Gallery, Mabel Brady Garvan Collection, 1948.218. Photograph by E. Irving Blomstrann.

to escape this type of work; fortunate in economic terms, and perhaps in artistic and psychological ways as well. The makers in outlying towns were not able to do so. Eighteenth-century silver from the smaller Massachusetts towns does not exist in sufficient quantity, and the few surviving objects do not exhibit enough ornament or variety to permit any sort of meaningful analysis of local styles. Three examples by Salem's David Northey are typical of this simple silver: his small trencher salt (9), child's cup (10), and porringer (11). There is nothing crude about these objects from the standpoint of design or fabrication, but they are not distinguished. Nothing except their maker's mark and provenance links them to Salem. They could have been made by anyone anywhere in Massachusetts, including most shops in Boston.

The term *simple city silver*, borrowed from the Winterthur conference "Country Cabinetwork and Simple City Furniture" (1969), might appropriately characterize the output of shops in outlying Massachusetts towns.[15] As presented here, the term embraces a body of objects defined by workmanlike standards, equal or nearly equal in quality of construction to more complex objects, and not necessarily retardataire stylistically by American standards. It was a kind of work produced in urban areas, but it was the *only* kind of work, with rare exceptions, produced in

10. David Northey, Salem, Mass., cup, ca. 1734. Yale University Art Gallery, Mabel Brady Garvan Collection, 1930.1317. Photograph by Michael Agee.

11. David Northey, Salem, Mass., porringer, ca. 1760. The Metropolitan Museum of Art, bequest of A. T. Clearwater, 33.120.351.

micropolitan areas like Salem and in even smaller towns in Massachusetts, including Worcester (12), Concord (13), and Newburyport (14). A few rare exceptions, for example, the tankards discussed earlier made by William Jones of Marblehead (1) and Moody Russell of Barnstable (2), or a salver fashioned by Ephraim Cobb of Plymouth (15), serve only to prove the rule.

Again, this small output of simple city silver stemmed from a lack of patronage and did not necessarily mean that these silversmiths were incompetent or inferior craftsmen. Those few objects that survive bearing the maker's mark of John Andrew of Salem can be compared on a nearly equal footing with Boston work of the same era. Only in a

12. William Swan, Worcester, Mass., cann, 1755–60. Museum of Fine Arts, Boston, M. and M. Karolik Collection, 39.187.

slight awkwardness in the placement of the handle on his canns (16) and in the rather pinched outlines of their pear-shaped bodies can Andrew's nonurban origins be discerned. Andrew's most important commission, received from the First Church of Salem in 1769, was to copy an English flagon made in London by W. and J. Priest in 1767–68. Andrew's replica demonstrates that he was capable of producing objects of quality if required, yet he was never asked to do so again. Whether his patrons imposed this decision to copy rather than create or whether Andrew made the decision, it is an indication of the narrow range of options available to the small-town silversmiths either in fact or in their own perceptions. Limitations imposed by their patrons, rather than any inherent provincialism or rusticism within the craft itself, thus should be seen as the determining factor in the production of simple city silver. Society's attitudes toward silver shaped the craftsman's work in more ways than one. Only occasionally does work by makers in the towns outside of Boston—for example, the tablespoon by Isaac Parker of Deerfield (4) or the pepper box (17) by John Jackson of Nantucket—seem awkward when compared with its Boston counterparts.

*13. Samuel Bartlett,
Concord, Mass., creampot,
ca. 1775. Concord Museum.*

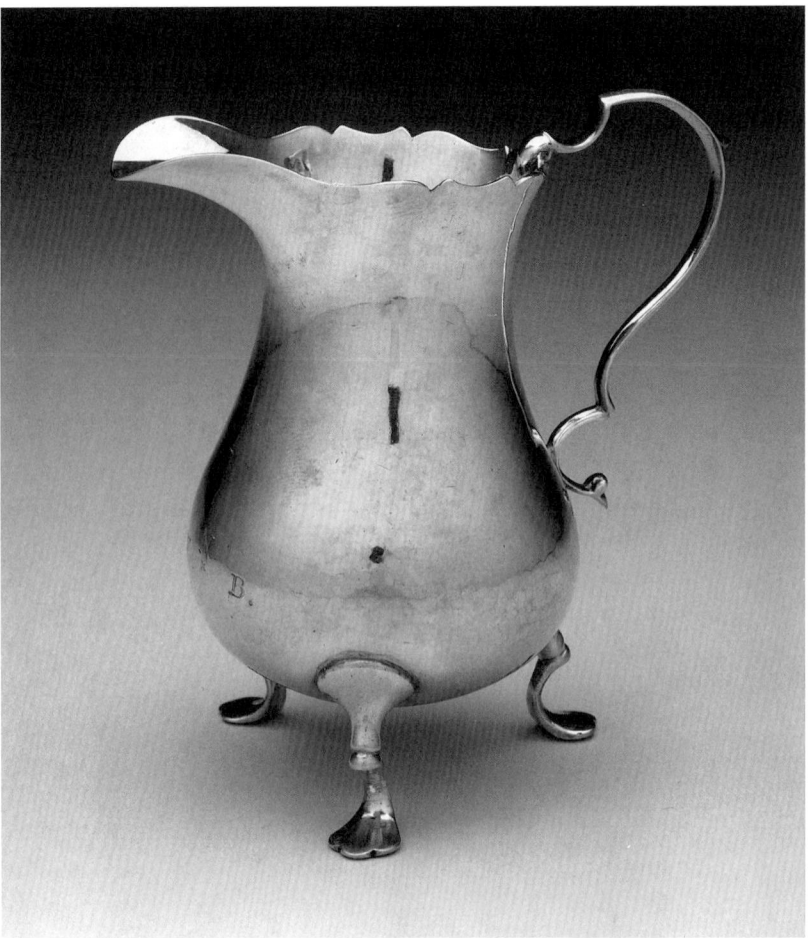

The account book of Edward Lang provides ample evidence of the limitations under which a silversmith in a small town outside Boston was forced to work. Lang was presumably well placed to have a successful career. His father, Jeffrey, was one of the early and most prolific silversmiths in Salem, active from about 1732 to 1758. Jeffrey was the leading Salem silversmith of his generation and is known to have made tankards, salvers, porringers, and other larger forms in addition to gold jewelry, spoons, and other small objects. Edward's brothers Richard and Nathaniel and his nephew Nathaniel (1757–1824) were also Salem silversmiths. Yet an analysis of Edward's account book spanning the years 1763 to 1786 reveals a modest, not to say humdrum, practice at best, one that probably never matched the levels attained by his father.[16]

The Lang account book lists his dealings with 160 individuals, 145 of whom were from Salem, 4 from Beverly, 3 from Topsfield, and 1 each from Danvers, Manchester, Amherst, Stoneham, Reading, Middleton, Wenham, and Boston. Lang transacted varying amounts of business with at least 7 other silversmiths and allied artisans, including Richard Lang, Samuel Webb (1762–1839), John Andrew, David Ropes (1763–1812), Edward Northey, Henry Buxton, and Stephen Emery. Many other

14. Joseph Moulton (1744–1816), Newburyport, Mass., cann, 1798. Yale University Art Gallery, Mabel Brady Garvan Collection, 1936.163. Photograph by E. Irving Blomstrann.

local craftsmen were among his customers, and merchants and sea captains such as Elias Hasket Derby, George Crowninshield, Jacob Crowninshield, and others were also valued customers.

About 1,929 separate transactions are recorded on the pages of the ledger. Of these, 677 (or 35 percent) involved the sale by Lang of various forms of gold and silver jewelry or jewelry of other materials, including buttons, buckles, chapes, hooks and eyes, necklaces, earrings, rings, clasps, gold beads, stones, broaches, and lockets. Mending, repairing, polishing, and other forms of maintenance work accounted for 492 entries, roughly 26 percent of his business. Spoons (18) of various sizes

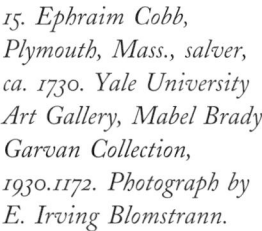

15. Ephraim Cobb, Plymouth, Mass., salver, ca. 1730. Yale University Art Gallery, Mabel Brady Garvan Collection, 1930.1172. Photograph by E. Irving Blomstrann.

16. John Andrew, Salem, Mass., cann, 1779. Peabody Essex Museum, 134,623. Photograph by Mark Sexton.

17. John Jackson, Nantucket, Mass., pepper box, ca. 1760. Yale University Art Gallery, gift of Dorothy Rea Macgregor in memory of her mother Marian Goddard Hussey Rea, 1990.55.1. Photograph by Michael Agee.

18. Edward Lang, Salem, Mass., tablespoon, ca. 1770. Peabody Essex Museum, 103,004. Photograph by Fredrik D. Bodin

and tongs are listed only 95 times, thus forming about 5 percent of his trade in terms of volume. Cash was involved in 11 percent and foodstuffs in 3 percent of the transactions. Generally, Lang received payment in goods and services and occasionally in old gold or silver or in cash.

Even though repair work constituted nearly one-quarter of Lang's transactions, the sums involved in each repair job were small. He charged, for example, 1 shilling for mending a sword in 1775; 8 pence for mending a coffeepot in 1766; 8 pence for repairing a silver cann in 1767; 2 pence for "Pollishing Gun-barril & Bayonett and cleaning the Lock" in 1775; 1 shilling and 6 pence for repairing silver porringers in 1776; 2 shillings for "cleansing & burnishing Silvr Teapot" in 1784; and so forth.[17] Thus, during a given year, such as 1773, there might be many entries for repairs, but the money received from them amounted to only 3 percent of his gross income for that year. In 1775, repairs constituted 5 percent of his gross income, while the relatively infrequent sale of spoons and tongs amounted to 12 percent of his annual gross income. However, there was little overhead and little or no material involved in most repair jobs, so Lang's profit on them was considerably higher. Although the exact figures are difficult to determine, it would seem that repair work brought Lang a small steady income that helped tide him over the long stretches between large sales of spoons and jewelry.

The occasional sales of gold jewelry and sets of spoons involved considerably more money and brought Lang a larger portion of his annual gross income. For example, in 1777, he charged Elias Hasket Derby £4.8.0 "To making 2 large spoons, 12 Tea Do. & a pair Tea Tongs," and in 1770 he sold Capt. Joseph Hodges "6 Large Spoons, 6 Tea Do., & a pair sugar Tongs" worth £6.7.0, while a "gold Necklace" sold to William Gray in 1767 brought £4.9.0.[18] Some transactions involving the sale of objects were, on the other hand, quite small. A mustard ladle sold for only 5 shillings, and a child's silver spoon was only worth 6 shillings and 8 pence. A "death head ring" was 14 shillings, and silver clasps were 2 shillings and 6 pence.[19]

Several of Lang's sales involved unusual objects. Beginning in 1773, an occasional charge is entered for "pointing an Electrical Spire with Silver."[20] In 1772, Lang made a "Silver Pipe for a sucking bottle" for Elias Hasket Derby, and ten years later he made a "Silver Call, for Ship Astrea" for Derby and "two Silver Calls for Ship. Gen. Green" and a "silver probe" (a medical instrument) for the same ship on the

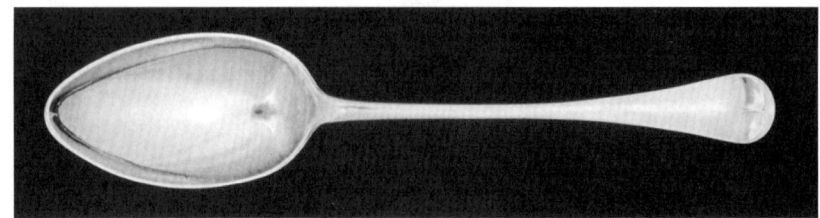

order of Samuel Page.[21] The next year Page purchased a silver call for the brig *Lively*.[22]

A year-by-year summary of Lang's annual gross sales indicates that Lang's fortunes moved along a fairly even keel for about ten years, from 1765 to 1775. In his more successful years during this period, Lang did business with thirty to forty customers annually. The war years were obviously difficult ones for Lang, and in 1775 his gross income dropped by half.[23] Preparations for the war years are evident in the work he performed in 1775 and 1776, as he cleaned and repaired guns, provided brass parts for bayonets, and helped arm his countrymen in other ways. Toward the end of 1776 Lang began his dealings with the Boston silversmith Stephen Emery, and their interaction would provide Lang with one of his few sources of income during the next three years. The patronage of Elias Hasket Derby also was important at this difficult time, but even with Derby's support, Lang's income hit rock bottom in 1779, when his gross income, as far as we know, amounted to only £15. His wife may have had to supplement their income by taking in sewing or performing other services, and it cannot have been a comfortable time for the Langs. By 1781, Lang had made a slight recovery, and his income improved slowly over the next few years, perhaps owing to inflation. By 1783, it had reached £41, the highest it had been since 1774, as indicated below:

Annual Gross Income of Edward Lang, 1765–83

Year	Amount	Year	Amount	Year	Amount	Year	Amount
1765	45	1770	55	1775	22	1780	23
1766	39	1771	62	1776	29	1781	35
1767	36	1772	40	1777	38	1782	36
1768	45	1773	69	1778	39	1783	41
1769	49	1774	44	1779	15		

Source: Edward Lang Account Book, PEM. Figures rounded to the nearest pound.

Lang must have found it difficult to support his large family on such a meager income. By December of 1784, entries in the account book indicate that he had joined his half-brother William in the auction and brokerage business. He pursued this line of work in 1785, before he was persuaded to accept the position of master of the East School in March of 1786. There are a few small transactions involving him with silver and jewelry as late as 1787, but his silversmithing career can be said to have stopped in 1784.

Lang's interaction with his fellow silversmiths is detailed in his account book. In these transactions, Edward is revealed as a specialist in jewelry who jobbed out his spoon work a good deal of the time. His brother Richard, for example, was credited between 1764 and 1766 for his purchases of jewelry with "forging" quantities of spoons in various sizes.[24] Samuel Webb, possibly a journeyman, was credited in 1787 for

"Making 37 Tea Spoons, and 2 large do. at sundry times," and for "a pair of Silver Clasps."[25] (These transactions with Webb probably took place earlier than they were recorded in the account book, in all likelihood before 1784.) Lang also must have been skilled as an engraver, for John Andrew paid him to engrave gold rings, gold and silver buttons, and to perform other services between 1773 and 1783.[26]

Lang's most extensive accounts with another silversmith were those with Stephen Emery of Boston from 1776 to 1779. Emery was credited with making sixty-nine teaspoons and twenty-nine tablespoons, along with supplying knee chapes, goldsmiths' tools and materials, and other articles. In exchange, Lang made twenty-four pairs of knee buckles, forty-eight pairs of silver buttons, a dozen stock buckles, twenty-two steel-top thimbles, two strings of gold beads, necklaces, and other articles as well. In essence, Lang the jewelry maker and Emery the spoonmaker were exchanging their specialties.[27]

The picture of Lang that emerges from his account book is one of a small-time jeweler, who survived (barely) on a steady diet of repair work and who made and sold a few spoons and a few other small objects each year. Edward Lang may have been merely an incompetent silversmith or an unpleasant person, or both, for the pattern of his life reveals a succession of difficulties and tribulations in many endeavors. Yet there is evidence that his career as a silversmith is not entirely atypical. An account between the Plymouth silversmith Ephraim Cobb and Capt. John Winslow from 1737 to 1739 shows that Cobb supplied Winslow with buttons, a seal, and shoe buckle and mended buttons, instruments, a ring, and needles.[28] Late in life Cobb began identifying himself as a yeoman and probably had begun to engage in farming to supplement his income as a craftsman. The account book of the Salem silversmith John Hathorne presents a similarly bleak picture.[29] Hathorne's accounts are extant from 1770 to about 1785, when he too gave up silversmithing, in his case in favor of the dry-goods business. And there is no reason to believe that the more successful practitioners in Salem, such as John Andrew or David Northey, or artisans in other small towns pursued careers that differed significantly. By buying, selling, and trading a wide variety of goods, some men, such as John Hathorne and Abijah Northey, eventually abandoned silversmithing altogether to become shopkeepers and traders in what must be considered horizontal, rather than vertical, movements on the socioeconomic ladder. Others, including John Andrew, sold "English goods" (textiles) while maintaining their silver practice. In order to make a living, the silversmiths in outlying towns had to diversify their business, rely a great deal on repair work for income, and develop connections with Boston silversmiths.

The Reverend William Bentley made the observation that in Salem the woodworking trades were "much confounded together," with crafts-

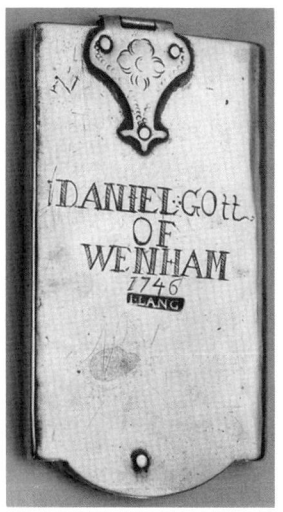

19. Jeffrey Lang, Salem, Mass., memorandum book with brass covers, 1746. Courtesy, The Henry Francis du Pont Winterthur Museum, 52.0127A.

men practicing more than one specialty.[30] This was equally true of the metalworking trades in the eighteenth century. Silversmiths supplemented their income by working in other metals, particularly tin, pewter, and brass. The tools in inventories of members of the Northey family indicate that they repaired and mended pewter and may have made it as well. As Bentley noted in a telling observation, William Northey "was educated in the occupation of his Father as a Goldsmith, tho' he wrought in all the common work of metals, as a Tinman, pewterer, as original ingenuity would suggest in a trade, of which a single branch could promise a very insufficient support."[31] Jeffrey Lang worked in brass and marked a small memorandum book with brass covers (19). Throughout his career, Daniel Greenough—who was born in Rowley, Massachusetts, went to New Castle, New Hampshire, and moved late in life to Bradford, Massachusetts—practiced simultaneously as a goldsmith and blacksmith. The account book of the Danvers bucklemaker Henry Buxton shows that he produced brass fittings for clocks and furniture and brass fireplace equipment. The practice of working in metals that are customarily cast, such as pewter and brass, must have been more common for silversmiths in the satellite towns than in Boston, where divisions between the crafts were more distinct.

Likewise, in Boston, the trades of goldsmiths and clockmakers and watchmakers were quite separate. Many silversmiths in smaller Massachusetts towns, however, counted watch- and clockmaking and repairing as part of their business. In like fashion, many craftsmen who were primarily watch- and clockmakers also made or marked silver objects, usually spoons. It is often possible to determine if a man was a silversmith or primarily a watchmaker, but there was a great commingling of the two. In the smaller towns, craftsmen often pursued clockmaking and silversmithing simultaneously. Some of those whose biographies are included in this study are Silas Rice of Lancaster, Reuben Earle of Leicester, Timothy Sibley of Sutton, Daniel Steward of Lunenberg, and Elijah Yeomans of Hadley.

Another means of diversification or alternative strategy for coping with their position was the linkages craftsmen developed with their Boston counterparts. By the late eighteenth century there is ample proof that the silversmiths in outlying towns drew on Boston silversmiths as a resource for tools, parts, and finished objects. These dealings indicate that there was indeed interchange between silversmiths in New England, amounting to a communications and sales network of at least modest dimensions as early as 1750. For instance, David Greenleaf, Sr., of Lancaster purchased six nests of crucibles from Zachariah Brigden in 1772.[32] The career of John Touzell of Salem is even more instructive in this regard. When Touzell came of age in 1749, he purchased his first set of tools from Samuel Edwards of Boston, a well-known goldsmith. These supplies included pliers, tongs, and shears, polishing mate-

rials such as pumice, rottenstone, and emery, scales and weights, crucibles, and other necessities of the goldsmith's trade amounting to a total
of £29.9.10. Touzell's master is not known, although it is tempting to
speculate that he was apprenticed to Edwards. But such a relationship
is not necessarily indicated, for the stock detailed in Edwards's inventory
indicates that he was widely known as a supplier of tools to the trade.
In the 1750s and 1760s, Touzell made regular purchases of jewelry from
John Welsh, Daniel Parker, and Benjamin Pierpont, all of Boston. In
some instances, the objects transferred were imported English jewelry
that found its way to Salem via Boston. A leading Boston jeweler,
Welsh wrote to Touzell concerning a shipment of "Cypher Button
Stones" in 1773: "I sent the Largest I have but Expect Some Larger if
they can be got by the Next Ship from London."[33] David Northey also
drew on Welsh as a source of watch parts, and John Hathorne (Touzell's
former apprentice) continued to buy jewelry from Welsh in the 1770s.[34]
Both Welsh and Parker seemed to have strong relations with Salem,
each advertising in its newspapers. Parker is said to have removed to
Salem for a brief time around 1775, although confirmation of this assertion is lacking.

Communication between outlying Massachusetts towns and Boston
was frequent, and thus the shipment of goods was not a logistical
problem, particularly for small objects such as silver, jewelry, and
watches. Richard Cranch, an English watchmaker who worked in Salem
before moving to Boston, placed a notice in the *Boston Evening-Post*
of 23 November 1767 informing "the Gentlemen of *Salem, Marblehead*,
and the neighbouring Towns, who favour'd him with their Custom
before he remov'd, that they may have their Watches bro't to him, and
carried back again to *Salem*, free of any Charge for Carriage, by applying
to Mr. *Boardman*, who goes regularly three Times a Week in the Stage-
Chaise between *Salem* and *Boston*." Silversmiths might well have taken
advantage of the same transportation system.

Touzell also served as a "collection agency" for Welsh in at least one
instance. In December of 1768, Welsh solicited Touzell's aid in settling
an overdue account of about £12 from a Captain Lemmont.[35] Touzell's
aid, if repeated on a wide enough scale, must have been an important
service in an era when obtaining payment from a client was a time-
consuming and difficult task, especially over any distance. There is
evidence that other Salem silversmiths acted in a similar capacity. Benjamin Burt's apprentice John Andrew served as Burt's representative in
Salem. In 1766 John Andrew received payment from Elias Hasket Derby
on behalf of Burt for two pairs of casters and two pairs of salts that
Derby had purchased from Burt.[36] Two years later, in 1768, Andrew again
received payment from Derby on behalf of Burt for three porringers.[37]
Andrew also bought from Paul Revere, Jr., in 1772 two very heavy
coffeepots priced at £5 and £5.6.8, respectively, and it is more than likely

that Andrew purchased them specifically on behalf of Salem customers, although given Andrew's speculative nature this may not have been the case.[38] In a similar vein, the Edward Lang account book details the relationship between Lang and Stephen Emery of Boston, and Lang may have served as Emery's local agent.

The communications network among silversmiths is given vivid life by a joint letter written to John Touzell in 1768 by silversmiths from Nantucket, John Jackson and Samuel Barrett.[39] A man named John Jones applied to Touzell for work as a journeyman, and Touzell wrote to Jackson and Barrett for their estimation of the man's abilities and character, inasmuch as Jones had come to Salem from Nantucket. It is significant that Touzell knew who the silversmiths on Nantucket were. One cannot imagine Jones supplying their names as references, as Jackson's reply makes clear: "In anshur to your Leter Respeecting the Careture of John Jons we Cannot say that he was convicted of Theft hear but Strongly Suspected being of a Low blackgard mak and was very burthensum to the Inhabentance of the Island and was orderd of[f] by the authority and when they had got him off would Not bring him again which is all we Say at prasent." Barrett's answer was more specific and even less encouraging about Jones's character: "I wold further informe you of Said Jones that he Came to Nantuckett about the first of December 1766 and wose in my Shop Servel times and on the 10 of said month my Shop wose Broken open and the things wich he wonted of me Befor wose taken away wich wose Boxes files &c for he Pretended to Be a tinker hear and tole me that he Sarved is time with a Copper-Smith and Sir I shuld be wary. Glad if you wold lett me hear how you make out with this Bad man." Unfortunately, we do not know how the story turned out, but the correspondence serves to illustrate the fact that silversmiths were not necessarily isolated creatures out of touch with one another and unaware of the goings-on around them. Other evidence of this phenomenon is the advertisement about a theft in 1767 that the Gloucester, Massachusetts, silversmith Stephen Morse placed in the *Boston Gazette* advising that if the thief was apprehended near Boston that the information be given to Daniel Parker. The advertisement implies that Morse and Parker had business associations or at least were acquainted.[40]

In addition to their contacts with the outside world, the eighteenth-century silversmiths in those towns where more than one silversmith worked also were well aware of one another and interacted frequently. As was true in other crafts and in other large cities, family connections and relationships were important linkages in the craft structure. Two of the later silversmiths in Barnstable, Abraham Higgins and Elpalet Loring, were associated either through apprenticeship or marriage with Moody Russell, the founding member of the craft there. In Newburyport, William Moulton's nephew Joseph Moulton (1744–1816) also practiced the craft. Thomas Grant and William Bubier of Marblehead were brothers-in-law.

Among the Salem silversmiths, there was a high degree of intergenerational occupational stability, or, in other words, it was not uncommon for a silversmith to have sons or grandsons who were also silversmiths. Of the nineteen active craftsmen before 1800, eight (more than 40 percent) belonged to either the Lang or the Northey families. Other silversmiths were also related by blood or through marriage, although in a town of Salem's size, the incidence of such relationships among the population as a whole was very high.

In Salem silversmiths were also united by a high degree of shared backgrounds and career experiences. Many of them lived and worked their whole lives in close proximity. Although Jeffrey Lang was born in Portsmouth and David Northey in Boston, the other seventeen silversmiths were all born in Salem (with one possible exception). And, of the entire group of nineteen, only John Andrew (who died in Maine) and William Northey (who retired to nearby Lynn shortly before his death) did not die in Salem. Clearly, the opportunities in the craft were not so great as to attract outsiders, yet business was at least prosperous enough to allow everyone except the ambitious and restless (and probably manic-depressive) John Andrew to remain in Salem. Only three members of the group of nineteen dropped silversmithing for other careers: Edward Lang became a schoolteacher, and Abijah Northey and John Hathorne became shopkeepers.

Another bond providing cohesion within the craft structure was similar family backgrounds. The father's occupation is known for many of the silversmiths working in outlying towns of Massachusetts. A few were the sons of silversmiths. The majority were the sons of other types of craftsmen or yeoman. John Touzell, whose father was a well-to-do merchant, and Andrew Croswell, whose father was a minister, were the only known exceptions to this pattern of solidly middle-class origins. The backgrounds of the eighteenth-century silversmiths working in outlying towns thus stand in marked contrast to the relatively high social standing of Samuel Phillips, Moody Russell, and Thomas Higginson, early silversmiths who worked outside of Boston, each of whom was the son of a prominent minister.

Ties within the craft were also strengthened by master-apprentice relationships, as was also true in large towns like Boston. Documentation of master-apprentice bonds for the men in the late colonial period is sparse. One might assume that Jeffrey Lang's and David Northey's sons were apprenticed to their fathers, with the documented exception of Edward Lang, who after his father's death was apprenticed to his relative David Griffeth (1735–79) of Portsmouth. What other little evidence exists also points in the direction of cohesion within the craft. John Hathorne completed his apprenticeship to John Touzell in 1770, and in 1774 accepted Stephen Baker of Salem as his own apprentice for six years. At the end of Baker's training, Hathorne accepted Ebenezer Bowditch (1766–1830) as an apprentice, Bowditch earning his freedom in 1787. Of the Salem silversmiths working in the late colonial period only John Andrew is known to have trained in Boston. A number of the other centers occasionally did have youths who went to Boston for their training, including Moody Russell of Barnstable, John Ball of Concord, Samuel Pedrick of Marblehead, and Daniel Rogers (20) of Ipswich. For these craftsmen the relationships forged during the years spent in Boston must have served them well later in their careers. As was discussed earlier, in the later colonial period a pattern exists of relatives or apprentices of Boston silversmiths settling in outlying towns, another natural vehicle for communication between silversmiths in those towns and in Boston.

The existence of a network based on religious lines has been seen as an important influence in the life of several New England craft groups. For example, the potters in the nearby South Danvers–Peabody area were linked by the Quaker faith, as were the Goddard-Townsend cabinetmaking families of Newport, Rhode Island. There is a trace of this kind of association in Salem, in that members of the Northey family were Quakers, but as yet no evidence has been found that would

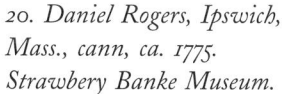

20. Daniel Rogers, Ipswich, Mass., cann, ca. 1775. Strawbery Banke Museum.

link the Northeys to other craftsmen either within or outside of Salem on religious grounds alone.

Although probate and tax data are sketchy and not available for everyone, it does not appear as if the silversmiths working outside of Boston were able to improve very much on their relatively humble beginnings, with perhaps one or two exceptions. Those silversmiths included in the Massachusetts tax list of 1771 tended to have modest holdings in real estate and merchandise. For colonial silversmiths in outlying towns who died before 1800, silversmithing offered at most a chance of a middle-class estate, with the very real possibility of economic failure. David Northey, who died in 1778, left a large estate valued at more than £1,600. In contrast, the elder Nathaniel Lang, who died at a very young age in 1764, had an estate valued at only £71, while Joseph Hathorne (d. 1786) had an estate of £264 overmatched by debts of £372. A middle range was achieved by Jeffrey Lang (d. 1758, £504) and Joseph Gardner (d. 1779, £586). For the members of the group who died after 1800, a similar pattern emerges. William Northey (d. 1804), with an estate of $15,000, and Joseph Moulton (d. 1816), with an estate of $22,000, were the most prosperous of their generation.[41]

The data for those silversmiths who died before 1800 would indicate that many silversmiths fit comfortably within the range of what Jackson Turner Main termed the middle class in revolutionary America.[42] Main defines this group as consisting of small property holders who were self-employed and the majority of whom had estates of about £400 or £500. Although David Northey came close, no silversmith for whom data are available was able to reach the minimum figure of £2,000 that Main sets as the bottom line of the upper economic group.[43] The monetary changes make direct comparison difficult, but a closely similar pattern is revealed by the estate values of those who died after 1800 but were active before that year, suggesting that again perhaps two-thirds of the members of the craft were in the middle class in economic terms, with one or two members falling toward the bottom. Only William Northey and Joseph Moulton were close to the threshold of the upper economic brackets.

There was thus nothing inherent in the craft of silversmithing that would provide economic success or create economic disaster. The contrasting experiences of the two main silversmithing families in Salem—the Langs and the Northeys—bear this out. Each family began silversmithing at the same time, in the 1730s, and the founder of each tradition seems to have done quite well. Jeffrey Lang died at the age of fifty-one with an estate of about £400, while David Northey's estate was more than four times greater when he died at the age of sixty-nine (silver in each estate was valued at virtually the same rate, suggesting that inflation was not an important factor). Longevity and a greater willingness to diversify were the keys to Northey's greater relative success. In succeeding generations, the disparity between the two family fortunes widened. Jeffrey Lang's sons did not fare as well as their father; Richard and Nathaniel were at the bottom end of the scale, and although no probate data are available for Edward, it is clear that he was not a financial success. The silversmithing Lang of the third generation, Richard's son Nathaniel, continued the downward spiral, leaving an estate only two-thirds as large as that of his poor father.

Meanwhile, David Northey's sons did rather better. William was near the top of the silversmiths of his generation financially and achieved a good social standing in the town. Although no estate data are available for Abijah Northey, other documents indicate that he was a successful trader of at least modest wealth. A third son, Edward, was trained as a goldsmith and worked in Gloucester and Manchester, Massachusetts, and later in New Hampshire, but no probate data for him have been located.

It is difficult to determine how silversmiths were regarded by their fellow citizens, or if they were at all active as a craft group in the town's politics and society. Silversmiths, because of their work in precious metals, had to be men of honesty and good social standing in the town. Their word and reputation were the only guarantee that the wares they sold were of high quality, for no assay office system existed in America until the nineteenth century. It was common for silversmiths to hold minor offices in town government. In Salem, Samuel Phillips did so in the early eighteenth century, and among the later group, only Joseph Gardner held similar posts, all at a level lower than selectman. Ephraim Cobb held a number of town offices in Plymouth. William Swan was clerk of the market and scaler of weights and measures in Worcester. Samuel Davenport was a selectman in Milton. This suggests that silversmiths in towns smaller than Salem may have had a better chance of holding higher public office.

In the 1770s and 1780s, silversmiths seem to have taken a more active political role, evidence of the growing politicization of the artisan that has been noted among urban craftsmen of this period.[44] In 1770, David Northey was one of nine members of a committee of Inspection and Correspondence, a nonimportation organization formed in Salem, the first time a Salem silversmith took so open a political stand.[45] A few years later, in 1774, William Northey was elected a selectman, the first member of his craft in Salem to be so honored, although far from the first craftsman. In that same year, William and David Northey were joined by six other silversmiths as signers of an open letter to Governor Thomas Gage protesting the closing of the port of Boston and "repudiating" any idea of Salem's benefiting by this measure against Boston. A number of silversmiths served in the colonial army during the Revolution, including Benjamin Bunker of Nantucket, Reuben Earle of Leicester, and William Northey, who was chastised by his fellow Quakers for this military service.

Thus, the eighteenth-century silversmiths in the outlying towns of Massachusetts were a relatively small group with shared backgrounds and life experiences. Some men were more successful than others; a few were abject failures; but most seemed to operate at a comfortable middle-class level. A combination of working with various metals, mending, and general merchandising formed the alloy of their work. Although their own production of objects was limited to simple city silver and jewelry, they served an important function as local representatives for Boston silversmiths. This aspect of their craft foreshadows the role of the local silversmith-jewelers in the nineteenth century who functioned primarily as retail outlets for the large silver and silverplating factories.

This survey of Massachusetts silversmiths outside of Boston suggests that the nature of the "colonial craftsman" is tied closely to time and place. The structure of a single craft such as silversmithing contained many internal layers and divisions, and men who nominally practiced the same craft experienced a great richness and variety of experience. Although techniques of raising, forging, casting, and soldering might remain the same from place to place, the day-to-day life of the individual might be substantially different depending on the size of the community. As workers in metal, Boston, Salem, and more rural silversmiths might have shared the same tools and techniques, but as businessmen, the large merchant-producer goldsmiths of Boston worked at a vastly different scale.

Perhaps because silver was a luxury rather than a necessity and because silver objects are small and easily transportable, the craft of silversmithing maintained a centralized focus in Boston, to which the silversmiths in outlying towns retained many important connections. The economic and technological links between the various levels of silversmiths within Massachusetts were significant. The craft system possessed an interconnective quality, and each level needs to be understood by evaluating its place within the entire craft hierarchy and by examining the ties as well as the divisions between each level.

Page 111

1. This essay is based largely on chapters 5 and 6 of Ward 1984a, and on the biographies in this volume, in each of which, unless otherwise noted here, documentation is provided. Patricia E. Kane provided detailed information on many silversmiths from outlying towns and provided editorial guidance and help in shaping this essay. Her contributions throughout the essay have been substantial. Barbara McLean Ward also commented on an early draft of this essay.

2. In colonial New York, a similar pattern can be discerned. Albany, founded in 1624, did not have its first silversmith until the 1680s, when Kiliaen van Rensselaer may have practiced there. See Rice 1964, 1–3.

Page 112

3. A few silversmiths also worked in Maine (which was a part of Massachusetts) in the colonial period, including John Butler, James Dane, and Paul Little in Falmouth and William Whittemore in Kittery. Patricia E. Kane provided the data on the number of silversmiths in each town as derived from the biographies in this volume.

4. The presence of luxury craftsmen has been cited recently as an indicator of urban growth in provincial England; see Borsay 1977, 586–87.

5. For a discussion of the economic growth of Salem in this period, see Phillips 1933, 171ff; Bailyn/Bailyn 1959; Jonas 1960; Davisson 1967a; Davisson 1967b; Koch 1969; Davisson/Dugan 1971; Boyer/Nissenbaum 1974, 86–89; and Gildrie 1975, chapter 10. For information on other crafts in Salem, including woodworking and upholstery, see Forman 1970, 17; Trent 1980, 39, 40; Tapley 1927, 165–69.

6. Forman 1970, 3 and passim.

7. Ward 1983, appendixes A and B, and other unpublished charts compiled by B. Ward.

Page 113

8. Patricia E. Kane summarized data on migrating craftsmen from this book.

Page 114

9. SCCR, file 9870.

Page 116

10. Clarke/Foote 1935, 31–35.

11. Goldenberg 1976, 22; Phillips 1933, 327.

Page 119

12. The approximate figure for Boston is based on this book, Fredyma 1975, and the Bigelow-Phillips files. For New York, see Von Khrum 1978; for New London, Goldsborough 1969; for Annapolis, Pleasants/Sill 1930; for Lancaster, Gerstell 1972; for Portsmouth, Parsons 1983.

13. Clark 1981, 57ff.

14. Ward 1983, 70–91.

Page 121

15. Morse 1970.

Page 124

16. The history and contents of this important document, now in the PEM, have been discussed in Tapley 1930.

Page 126

17. Edward Lang Account Book, fols. 12 (sword), 16 (coffeepot), 24 (cann), 57 (gun barrel), 58 (porringers), and 67 (teapot), PEM.

18. Edward Lang Account Book, fols. 59 (Derby), 24 (Hodges), and 9 (Gray), PEM.

19. Edward Lang Account Book, fols. 43 (ladle), 14 (child's spoon), 54 (ring), and 57 (clasps), PEM.

20. Edward Lang Account Book, fol. 43; see also fol. 53, PEM.

Page 127

21. Edward Lang Account Book, fols. 21 (pipe), 67 (*Astrea*), and 69 (*Gen. Green*), PEM.

22. Edward Lang Account Book, fol. 69, PEM.

23. A number of silversmiths changed their working location during the war, including Peter Etter, a loyalist, who left Braintree for Canada in 1776; Nathaniel Austin, who moved to Cambridge from Charlestown following the British bombardment and stayed in Cambridge until 1781; Barnabas Webb, who moved from Boston to Norton; Jonathan Crosby, who moved from Boston to Watertown. Henry Phillips Sweetser of Charlestown also made a claim for the loss of his shop and tools, although he does not seem to have relocated.

24. Edward Lang Account Book, fols. 4, 26, 30, 47, PEM. Zachariah Brigden and Daniel Boyer had a similar working relationship; Brigden made spoons and Boyer in turn made jewelry. In this regard, Salem and Boston craftsmen ran their businesses in a similar manner.

Page 128

25. Edward Lang Account Book, fol. 86, PEM.

26. Edward Lang Account Book, fol. 48, PEM.

27. Edward Lang Account Book, fols. 61–62, PEM.

28. Ephraim Cobb bill to John Winslow, 1737–39, Winslow Papers, MHS.

29. John Hathorne Account Book, PEM.

Page 129

30. Bentley 1905–62, 2:414.

31. Bentley 1905–62, 3:93.

32. Brigden Daybook, 1766–ca. 1775, fol. 32, Brigden Papers, YU.

Page 130

33. English-Touzel-Hathorne Papers, box 4, folder 1, PEM.

34. Northey Family Papers and John Hathorne Account Book, PEM.

35. English-Touzel-Hathorne Papers, box 4, folder 1, PEM.

36. Derby Family Papers, vol. 1, PEM.

37. Derby Family Papers, PEM; printed in *EIHC* 77, no. 1 (January 1941): 67.

Page 131

38. 20 January, 15 April, 1772, Paul Revere, Jr., Waste and Memoranda Book, vol. 1, 1761–83, 40, Revere Family Papers, MHS.

39. English-Touzel-Hathorne Papers, box 4, folder 1, PEM.

40. Brock Jobe has documented similar contacts between Boston craftsmen and men from outlying regions in the furniture industry in the eighteenth century, while focusing on the Boston artisans rather than the men from the smaller communities. The papers and accounts

Page 131, continued
of Nathaniel Holmes (1703–74) reveal his lively interchange of parts, supplies, and finished objects with ten cabinetmakers or joiners, six of whom lived outside of Boston, as well as with other woodworking craftsmen. Holmes manipulated this system so well that he was able to become a wealthy merchant. Yet the system also benefited the joiners in the satellite towns. This whole relationship between the metropolitan craftsman and the micropolitan artisan has been demonstrated in this study, by Jobe's work, and by others, yet its ramifications are as yet little realized. Certainly this symbiotic relationship was important in the transmission of style and of methods of construction. Its existence argues against the frequently encountered assertion that techniques and practices, for example, were rigidly established in a given shop tradition and passed down from generation to generation without outside influence. See Jobe 1974, 13–24.

Page 134
41. Patricia E. Kane provided tax and probate information on many outlying craftsmen.
42. Main 1965, 273–75.
43. Main 1965, 275–77.

Page 135
44. See Walsh 1959; Olton 1975; Foner 1976; Rock 1979; and Nash 1979.
45. Phillips 1937a, 306–12.

The Dictionary

Explanatory Notes Concerning Tabulated Data

Objects   Surviving objects are listed alphabetically by form. Objects within a given form are listed alphabetically by mark for silversmiths with more than one mark. An object will be listed under the general term (such as bowl), unless the form is known commonly by a more specific name within that category (such as sugar bowl or waste bowl). In general, spoons are divided into tablespoons (six inches to nine inches in length) and teaspoons (under six inches), although specialized spoons (e.g., salt spoons) are listed alphabetically as well. Individual objects in larger services, such as a teapot from a tea service, are listed alphabetically by form, with a note indicating that they belong to a larger assemblage. Objects that have been altered are listed under the form they were originally with a note indicating their current form. For instance, a creampot altered to a mustard pot appears under creampot. Coins and engraved printing plates are not listed.

Marks   The letter designations refer to the mark(s) illustrated for an individual silversmith. A slash between letters indicates that a piece bears more than one mark. The number of times a particular mark has been struck on a piece has not been recorded. An asterisk indicates that a clear representation of a given mark has been published or exists as a photograph or rubbing in the YUAG research files. A dagger indicates that the mark is illustrated in this volume. Letter designations without asterisks have been assigned on the basis of written descriptions, drawings, or poor quality illustrations and therefore may not be accurate.

Inscriptions   Inscriptions have been recorded both from first-hand observation and transcription recorded by others, and therfore may not be faithful to the original. Later inscriptions are recorded only partially and bear the indicator (later) or (+). Illegible portions of inscriptions are indicated by [illeg.]. The term "erased" indicates the inscription has been completely removed; "partially erased" indicated the inscription has been removed, but is partially legible.

The phrases "unidentified initials," "unidentified crest," and "unidentified arms" mean that engraving is present, but no image or description is available. A question mark indicates that it is not clear whether engraving is present. If an image of the heraldic engraving is available, the description of the devices is provided. Crests or arms modified by a family name, but with no description, indicate that the reference identified the arms, but provided no description or illustration.

Patrons This information is interpreted broadly as referring to individuals or institutions that commissioned, owned, or were memorialized by silver. Where possible the information indicates the individual, group, or institution that commissioned the work. In cases of presentation silver where clear documentation is lacking, the term and/or indicates that it is unclear as to whether the donor or donee commissioned the work from the silversmith. If silver bears heraldic arms or crests the name of the family is given in the column if more specific information is lacking. If the work was commissioned for or by a church, the name of the church is recorded as it appears in the standard reference, E. Alfred Jones, *Old Silver of American Churches* (e.g. Jones 1913), or if the church was not included in Jones, by the church's current name.

Dates Ca. (circa) indicates that an object could have been made approximately five years on either side of the date given.

References If an object is known to have been published, one reference is given for it. In general, monographs supersede other publications and collection catalogues supersede monographs.

Owners Information is provided for those objects owned by public institutions.

Other Notes

Extracts The type size of certain extracts (the inventory on pages 209–10, for example) has been reduced so that the transcription follows the original line for line.

Mark illustrations Marks have been reproduced approximately two-and-a-half times actual size with the exception of Samuel Bartlett (A), Benjamin Goodwin (A), William Gowen (B), David Greenleaf, Sr. (A), William Homes, Jr. (O), Joseph Kneeland (A), Knight Leverett (A), David Colson Moseley (B, C), Joseph Moulton (1724–95) (A), Joseph Moulton (1744–1816) (A), John Potwine (B), Paul Revere, Sr. (D, E, F), William Simpkins (C), and William Whittemore (A), which have been reproduced approximately twice actual size.

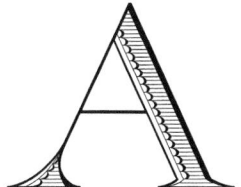

John Allen
1671/72–1760

A

B

John Allen was the son of the Reverend James Allen (1632–1710) and his second wife, Elizabeth (Houchin) Endicott (d. 1673), and was baptized in Boston in 1671/72.[1] James Allen arrived in Boston in 1662 and became teacher, or assistant minister, of Boston's First Church in 1668, serving in that capacity until his death in 1710. He was very wealthy and owned nearly all of what would later be known as Boston's West End as well as a large parcel of land in Salem near the Lynn town line. His house, the first stone house in Boston, stood on the corner of what are now Beacon and Somerset streets.[2] Reverend Allen had three sons: James (1670–before 1698) (Harvard College 1689), who served as minister to the church in Northampton; John, the subject of this biography; and Jeremiah (1673–1741/42), a merchant and later treasurer of the province of the Massachusetts Bay (1714).[3] He also had a daughter, Hannah (bap. 1669), by his first wife, Hannah Dummer (d. 1668), sister of the silversmith Jeremiah Dummer (q.v.); and two children, Thomas (bap. 1675) and Sarah (bap. 1679), by his third wife, Sarah (Hawkins) Beck, who predeceased him.[4]

Because Jeremiah Dummer was his step uncle, it has been assumed that Allen served his apprenticeship in Dummer's shop, probably together with his future partner and brother-in-law, John Edwards (q.v.). Three plain beakers made for the Ipswich church, marked IA (A) in an inverted heart and dated June 1693, may be Allen's work and, if so, suggest that Allen worked alone for a few years after he completed his apprenticeship in 1692.[5] His first documented connection with Edwards appears in a mortgage deed of 28 September 1696 between the Reverend Samuel Willard and the merchant Hezekiah Usher. The pertinent section of the deed reads, "That is to say All the s[d] Garden or parcel of Land with the Brick buildings thereon Standing, containing three Shop Tenements, and the Cellars under the Same, and all the Roomes and Apartments in the s[d] Tenements, being situate neer unto the Town house in Boston afores[d] Fronting unto the Broad Street in which the s[d] Town house standeth and are in the present Tenure and occupation of John Edwards and John Allen Goldsmiths and William Lackey Taylor."[6] In 1697 the partners sued the Boston goldsmith Jonathan Belcher (q.v.) for money lent to him and clothing provided to him "on account."[7] Belcher probably served the partners as a journeyman. During Allen's years in partnership with Edwards, his mark was IA in a quatrefoil (B). The partners made a wine cup for the First Baptist Church in Boston, which was purchased with a legacy left by Roger Kilcup, whose will, dated 4 December 1701, was witnessed by both Allen and Edwards.[8] This suggests that the two men remained in partnership until at least 1702. By 1709 John Allen had signed a petition against the freedom of servants and children to enlist in the army without their master's or parents' permission. His name appears between those of Michael Willis and Thomas Holland.[9]

In 1697 Allen married Elizabeth Edwards (d. 1749), sister of his partner, John Edwards. He had five children by her: James (b. 1698, d. 1698); Jeremiah (1699–1760), who later became a feltmaker and married Rebecca Kilby in 1722; Elizabeth (b. 1702), who married Hezekiah Blanchard, a baker; James (b. 1706/07–36), who became a tanner; and Susannah (b. 1711), who married as her first husband Ebenezer Welch (d. before 1736) in 1732 and as her second husband Francis Welles (d. before 1768) in 1738.[10]

In 1706, John's father, James, divided his Boston property on the north side of Cambridge Street among his three children, reserving his life right to the land. When the Reverend James Allen died in 1710, he bequeathed to his son John "all that my Farm (so called) or Lands in Boston, in his present Tenure and Occupation being, w:ch were Devised to me by my Uncle Penn deced Containing by Estimation Eighteen Acres, w:th all the Ediffices—Buildings, Members & Appur:ces. As Also Two Acres of my Meadow Ground lying next Adjoining to the afores:d Lands, being p:t of that I purchased of John Dassett. I Likewise Give unto my s:d Son John Allen, my Negro man Richard now living w:th him, who Cost me Fifty pounds." He also bequeathed John half of his books and one-third of his personal estate.[11] The next time John Allen appears in the recorded deeds (20 October 1710), he is listed as a grazier.[12] Evidently he decided to make his living from raising livestock after receiving his bequest of land, but by 28 August 1711, when he and his brother Jeremiah and sister Hannah collected one hundred pounds on a mortgage extended by Rev. James Allen to the goldsmith William Cowell, Sr., he is listed again as a goldsmith.[13] However, when he mortgaged the farm he inherited from his father for the sum of three hundred pounds, he again referred to himself as "grazier."[14] The mortgage was not discharged until 1729, perhaps by selling a number of parcels of land. Between 1710 and 1752 Allen was involved in no fewer than thirty real estate transactions.[15] His earliest transactions involved the sale of land to his brother Jeremiah and to his brother-in-law John Edwards. However, between April 1729 and September 1734 his rapid disposal of fourteen parcels of land seems to suggest declining fortunes. He sold six more parcels of land between 1736 and 1744. After 1746 the transactions consisted of the sale of land to his children.

The name John Allen appears frequently in the town records. However, because the name was a common one and occupations were not listed in the records, it is difficult to determine which John Allen was elected to numerous minor town offices. Because of his wealth and prominence, it is likely that the silversmith served in a number of capacities, including scavenger (1705/06), tithingman (1707–08), constable (1718), and clerk of the market (1730). He was also mentioned when the town selectmen voted on 9 February 1730 to extend the street running between Allen's land and a warehouse owned by Dr. Clarke. In 1733 Allen requested and was granted permission to build a timber dwelling on a parcel of land fronting southerly on Rawson's Lane, formerly belonging to Judge Samuel Sewall.[16]

Allen appears three times in the records of the Court of Common Pleas.

In 1728 he sued James Gardner, a Boston ropemaker, for default on a bond of one hundred pounds issued the year before. In 1744 and 1752 he sued the ropemaker James Barton of Boston.[17]

Allen wrote his will on 8 December 1736. He left his dwelling house and the small parcel that remained of his original eighteen-acre plot of land (82 feet on the street and at the rear and 138 feet deep) to his son Jeremiah, reserving half of the house for his widow, Elizabeth. He also bequeathed sums of money to his grandchildren. All of his personal estate was to go to his wife, who was to be the sole executor.[18] Elizabeth died before her husband, and on 24 July 1749 Benjamin Walker recorded her burial in his diary.[19]

Although it is not clear whether John Allen was a productive goldsmith between 1716 and 1756, there are a number of surviving objects marked IA with a pellet between in a rectangle that date between 1730 and 1745. Kathryn Buhler attributed this mark to John Allen, although other scholars attributed it to Josiah Austin (q.v.).[20] In this study those pieces are tentatively attributed to Austin. Nonetheless, John Allen referred to himself as a goldsmith in deeds and in court documents until 1756. On 10 September 1756, William Fairfield, a Boston bricklayer, was named guardian of John Allen, who was judged by the selectmen to be a person non compos.[21] Allen's estate was probated on 8 January 1760.[22] BMW

SURVIVING OBJECTS

	Mark	Inscription	Patron	Date	Reference	Owner
Beaker	A†	M.ʳ John Wain-wrights Gift to yᵉ Church of Ipswich June: 93	John Wainwright and/ or First Congregational Church, Ipswich, Mass.	1693	Buhler/Hood 1970, no. 74	YUAG
Beaker	A*	M.ʳ. William Stew-arts Gift to yᵉ Church of Ipswich June: 93	William Stewart and/or First Congregational Church, Ipswich, Mass.	1693	Buhler/Hood 1970, no. 75	YUAG
Beaker	A	M.ʳ John Appletons Gift to yᵉ Church of Ipswich June: 93	John Appleton and/or First Congregational Church, Ipswich, Mass.	1693	Jones 1913, 223	
Two beakers (with mark of John Edwards)	B*	IC; John Cates Legacy to The Church In Windham	John Cates (Kates, Keats) and/or Congregational Church, Windham, Conn.	ca. 1697	Jones 1913, 500	
Beaker (with mark of John Edwards)	B	S.R.; her gift to Taunton Church (later)	Sarah Richmond	ca. 1695	Jones 1913, 469	
Two beakers (with mark of John Edwards)	B*	The Gift of the Owners of the/Ship Adventure of Lon-don/1699	Messrs. Pickett and Christophers and/or First Congregational Church, New London, Conn.	1699	Jones 1913, 311–12	
Caudle cup (with mark of John Edwards)	B*	PH		ca. 1700	Antiques 27 (April 1935): 122	DIA
Mug (with mark of John Edwards)	B*	AC; The Gift of/Mʳˢ Sarah Jeffers . . . (later)		ca. 1700	Jones 1913, 45	

	Mark	Inscription	Patron	Date	Reference	Owner
Mug (with mark of John Edwards)	B*	Southack crest, a dexter arm embowed and cuffed holding a bleeding heart; AS to MC (later)	Southack family	ca. 1700	*Antiques* 41 (June 1942): 378	
Porringer (with mark of John Edwards)	B	G/NE		ca. 1700	Avery 1920, no. 17	MMA
Porringer (with mark of John Edwards)	B	G/EH	Gridley family (?)	ca. 1700	MFA 1911, no. 7	
Porringer (with mark of John Edwards)	B	unidentified initials (later) (+)		ca. 1700	*Antiques* 85 (June 1964): 623	
Salt (with mark of John Edwards)	B*	S/SE	Rev. Solomon and Esther (Warham) (Mather) Stoddard	ca. 1696	Safford 1983, 23	MMA
Salver (with mark of John Edwards)	B*	Coffin arms, 3 bezants or between 9 crosses crosslet, and crest, a demi-griffin segreant (+)	Coffin family	ca. 1705	MFA 1911, no. 6	
Spout cup (with mark of John Edwards)	B*	unidentified arms, a tyger rampant collared and chained; D/CM (later)		ca. 1700	Buhler 1960, no. 52	DIA
Tablespoon (with mark of John Edwards)	B*	S/SE	Rev. Solomon and Esther (Warham) (Mather) Stoddard	ca. 1700		HD
Tablespoon (with mark of John Edwards)	B†	MB		ca. 1695	Quimby 1995, no. 56	WM
Tablespoon (with mark of John Edwards)	B*	M/SA	Samuel and Ann (Adkins) Marshall	ca. 1705	Buhler/Hood 1970, no. 76	YUAG
Tankard (with mark of John Edwards)	B*	IE		ca. 1700	DAPC 75.4890	
Tankard (with mark of John Edwards)	B*	L(E?)/IS		ca. 1705	*Maine Antique Digest* (January 1985): 22–C	
Tankard (with mark of John Edwards)	?	B/AM		ca. 1705	*Antiques* 39 (April 1941): 204	
Wine cup (with mark of John Edwards)	B	Ex dono RK	Roger Kilcup and/or First Baptist Church, Boston	ca. 1702	Jones 1913, 44–45	

1. Mass. Archives 16:293; 40:49–52, 54, 64–65, 68, 69; RC 9:118, 125; Jones 1913, 21.
2. Roberts 1895, 1:201–02. Francis Hill Bigelow noted in his draft biography of John Allen that Rev. James Allen had owned "a larger part of the territory of Boston than was ever owned by one individual unless William Blackstone is an exception."
3. RC 9:113, 117, 118, 130; Roberts 1895, 1:302; *Sibley's Harvard Graduates* 3:405–06.
4. RC 9:113, 137, 147.
5. Buhler/Hood 1970, 1:75–76; Jones 1913, 222–23.
6. SCD 17:313–15.
7. SCCR, file 98567.

8. Jones 1913, 44–45.

9. Mass. Archives 71:542.

10. Thwing; RC 9:239, 244–46, 253.

11. SCD 23:8; SCPR 17:101–03, docket 3272, dated 12 March 1705/06, proved 1710.

12. SCD 25:135–36.

13. SCD 26:54.

14. SCD 31:68.

15. Thwing; SCD 25:135–36; 32:62–63; 40:9; 43:159–60, 172, 179, 282; 44:29–30, 147–48; 45:13; 46:14, 167, 290, 304–05; 48:299; 49:138; 50:52; 51:260; 54:96, 163; 55:24–25; 58:178; 68:227; 80:197–98, 200; 81:64–65; 85:18.

16. RC 8:35–37, 41–43, 45–48, 127–30; RC 12:18–20; RC 13:204, 206, 231.

17. SCCR, files 21781 and 21787, and Court of Common Pleas Record Book 1727–28, 489; 1743–44, 157; 1751–52, 215; Superior Court of Judicature Record Book 1752–53, 156.

18. SCPR 55:293–95, docket 12211, dated 8 December 1736, probated 8 January 1760.

19. Benjamin Walker, Jr., Diaries, vol. 3 (1743–49), MHS.

20. Buhler 1972, nos. 75–76; MFA 1911, 4; Bigelow 1917, 336–37. Louise Belden suggests that the mark ALLEN in a rectangle might have been used by John Allen; see Belden 1980, 30, and Charles Allen (q.v. Appendix B).

21. SCPR 51:590–91.

22. SCPR 51:293–95.

John Andrew
1747–91

A

John Andrew was Salem's most prominent silversmith during the second half of the eighteenth century. He was born in Salem on 27 September 1747, the son of Nathaniel Andrew (1705–62), a mariner who later became a merchant, and his first wife, Mary (Higginson) Andrew (1709–47). His paternal grandparents were Joseph (d. 1732) and Abigail (Walk) Andrew; his mother was the daughter of Nathaniel and Hannah (Gerrish) Higginson. Andrew's mother died shortly after childbirth, and he was raised by his father's second wife, Abigail Peele, who married Nathaniel on 20 May 1748. On 19 October 1769, John Andrew married Elizabeth Watson (1738–1830), daughter of the prominent Salem cabinetmaker Abraham Watson (1712–90). John and Elizabeth had a large family, and one of their grandchildren, John Albion Andrew (1818–68), was the governor of Massachusetts during the Civil War.[1]

It is likely that Andrew was apprenticed to Benjamin Burt (q.v.), the well-known Boston silversmith. He witnessed deeds for Burt on 24 October 1764 and 2 July 1766.[2] The first record of Andrew's career is in May and June of 1766, when he received payment from Elias Hasket Derby (1739–99) on behalf of Burt for two pairs of casters and salts.[3] On 19 August 1768, Andrew again received payment from Derby on behalf of Burt, this time for three porringers.[4] Andrew may have acted on Burt's behalf while visiting Salem during breaks in his training.

Andrew was the first silversmith to advertise in Salem's newspaper, the *Essex Gazette*, founded in 1768. His notice appeared in issue number 43 of the first volume, for the week of 16–23 May 1769, and read, "John Andrew, *Goldsmith* and *Jeweller*, AT the Sign of the *Gold Cup*, in *SALEM*, near the *Long-Wharf-Lane*, (so called) begs Leave to inform the Public, that he makes all Sorts of Goldsmith's and Jewellery Ware.—Those Persons who will favour him with their Custom, may depend on Dispatch and Fidelity." Andrew's position as the leading silversmith in town, even at the young age of twenty-two, was confirmed in 1769, when the First Church commissioned him to make a copy of an English flagon of 1767/68 in their possession. This superb object, as

Buhler has noted, is Andrew's "most ambitious published piece" and also enjoys the distinction of being the finest extant example of Salem silver known to date.[5]

Andrew's newspaper advertisements in the following years provide an indication of his growing business and of the speculative side of his nature, a weakness that eventually was to be his undoing. In 1771 he gave notice that he had just imported and was offering for sale at the sign of the Gold Cup, "An Assortment of Goldsmiths and Jewelry Articles, viz. Button and Earing Christal of all Kinds, Shoe and Knee Chapes, Crucibles, blue melting Pots, Files of all Kinds, Borax, Sandever, Salt Petre, Emory, Pumistone, and many other Articles, where Goldsmiths may be supplied at a low Advance."[6] Andrew thus may have been an important source of supply for the silversmiths of the rest of Essex County and northern New England. Later that same year he expanded his retail business to include imported "ENGLISH GOODS, Suitable for the Season, viz. MIddling & low-priced broad-Cloths, scarlet, claret and many other Colours; Ratteens, German Serges, Devonshire Kersies, Coatings, Baizes, Velverets, Shalloon, Tammies, Durants, Calamancoes of all Colours, yard-wide Poplins, half-yard Crapes, Cambleteens, Camblet for Ridinghoods, Dorseteens, Drawboys, Irish Linens of all Widths and Prices, Dowlas, check Linens, capuchin Silk, and many other Articles, too tedious to mention." He also noted that he "continues to make and sell Goldsmith and Jewellery Ware as usual," but it is significant that he began to diversify his business at such an early stage in his career.[7]

By 1775, Andrew had branched out to open an additional shop in Cambridge, Massachusetts, "Nearly opposite the Sign of the Anchor," where he made and sold "all Sorts of Goldsmiths Work, cheap for Cash." His advertisement in the *New-England Chronicle, or the Essex Gazette* (12–19 October 1775), which itself had moved its place of publication from Salem to Cambridge, indicated that his shop in Salem was still in operation.

During the 1770s and 1780s Andrew's outside business interests led him into deeper and deeper financial trouble and eventually into ruin. Andrew's difficulties are best related by the Reverend William Bentley:

Mr. A. never loved work, & by keeping a Shop of English Goods he soon reduced his estate to an humble maintenance, but was full of speculations in various ways, & having a large family, having left 10 children, he was obliged to think of putting his visionary schemes into execution, which his natural inclinations would otherwise have suffered to die in thought. He first planned a Tan yard, now improved & employed by Gardner and Chever, & originally the property of his Brother Andrew. He removed his Barn on the spot, & planned his labour. The work was left to hired men, & he commenced another scheme of speculation in the paper Bills of credit. To answer his ends, & his first great success, he changed all his old habit, from the plain man, became the Gentleman. For the first time began to powder his hair, drink his glass of wine after dinner, receive his company, ride the country, & mix with the best company on change. His cards were soon distributed, & besides the common conversation, which was very free on the subject, his cards stuck up J. A. Broker, were altered J. A. Broke. He rejected with disdain all such insinuations, but in about 10 months, the Town Tax in his hands was prudently taken out by his friends, John shut his doors, left his whole estate, & lay under an enormous weight of debt. Redeemed at last from this forlorn condition by his Wife's Father & Brother, he arose to entertain some new projects. In his prosperity he was evidently giddy; in his adversity he experienced an almost unexampled depression, & from this time was subject to the most sudden & extreme emotions.[8]

Abraham Watson and John Watson, in 1784, had bailed out Andrew to the amount of six thousand dollars, accepting a lien on his house and personal property as security. The personal estate mortgaged by Andrew gives some indication of his silversmithing activities; it included "Four hundred ounces of wrought silver plate . . . goldsmith's tools . . . three hundred pounds weight of wrought pewter . . . one large Copper boilling Kettle . . . one hundred and fifty pounds weight of wrought brass . . . Two watches silver cased."[9] This would seem to indicate that Andrew was retailing base as well as precious metals, and it is possible that he was working them himself, although no base-metal-working tools were mentioned.

By 15 April 1789, Andrew had moved with his family to Windham, Maine.[10] His father-in-law provided him with land in the "Township of Cumberland, 12 miles back of Portland, & furnished him with all the implements of a Farmer." Bentley continues the sad tale:

> He was soon wild in his repairs & buildings. The Farm was abandoned to his young sons, while he was sure of success in Trade and Business. At his last visit he was with me assuring of his purposes to explore a road to Dartmouth College, from his own town, first called New Marblehead, from the residence of the principal proprietors, & now Windham. He begged me to come down & go with him. He was determined to settle & trade at the lower part of Sebago Pond, about 12 miles above him. Upon his return he found his crop had failed. That his Cash he had expended on useless Looms, & Dairies, without any supplies of Stock, & that an hard winter was approaching. Blasted in his expectations, his old benefactor gone, the estate reduced, he gave himself up to the most distressing apprehensions. From our friends who lately visited him we were informed of his gloomy habit. His Brother had generously provided 20 bushels of grain for his family, but before he proceeded, John rushed from life.[11]

It is said that Andrew's death on 3 August 1791 was caused "by the discharge of his gun in his own hands," and given the bleak picture of his mental condition painted by Bentley, it is possible that his death was a suicide rather than an accident.[12]

Surviving silver objects by Andrew include canns, creampots, and porringers, in addition to the First Church flagon and assorted examples of flatware. A surviving document reveals that Andrew made at least one other form as well:

> Joseph Bowditch Esq. to John Andrew D[r].
> 1771
> Nov[r]. 19th For 1 Silver Spout Cup w[t]. 7 Oz[s].   2. 8.6
>   Making Ditto   1.13.4
>   4. 1. 10
>   Rec'[d]. Cash for the above
>   John Andrew[13]

Andrew's charge for making this spout cup for the elderly Mr. Bowditch was only about 40 percent of the cost of the metal, suggesting that it was a relatively simple example of the form.

In all likelihood, most of Andrew's silver can be dated from the late 1760s through the 1770s. We know that he was active in the field, if only as an apprentice, as early as 1766, and his first documented object can be dated to 1769. A cann and spoon (both owned by PEM) can be dated by inscription to 1779.[14] Andrew interacted with his fellow Salem silversmith Edward Lang (q.v.) between January 1773 and November 1783.[15] Bentley's narrative indicates that Andrew was involved in activities other than silversmithing long before he left town in 1789. His advertisements as a stockbroker appeared in 1784, and he had been speculating in other adventures prior to that time.[16]

The recorded pieces by Andrew are marked I·ANDREW in a rectangle (A). Belden cited J.ANDREW in a rectangle mark, but no example has been located.[17] GWRW

SURVIVING OBJECTS

	Mark	Inscription	Patron	Date	Reference	Owner
Cann	A	unidentified arms		ca. 1775	Parke-Bernet, 27 January 1945, lot 165	
Cann	A	A/Gift From/TB/ to/IB/June 16/1779/ Born Ap.ʳ 4 1760		1779	Fales 1983, no. 10	PEM
Cann	A*	H/IM		ca. 1775	Shepard 1978, 221	MAM
Cann	A	ES	Elisha Story	ca. 1775	MFA 1911, no. 14	
Cann	A*	H/BE	Benjamin and Elizabeth (Furness) Hartshorn	ca. 1775	YUAG files	
Cann	A	LD	Lydia Dodge	ca. 1775	YUAG files	
Cann	A	CS		ca. 1770	Johnston 1994, 4	CMA
Creampot	A	MP		ca. 1770		RISD
Creampot	A	none		ca. 1775		HD
Creampot	A	CW		ca. 1775	YUAG files	
Flagon	A*	This Flaggon be- longs to the first/ Church of Christ in SALEM/1769	First Congregational Society, Salem, Mass.	1769	Jones 1913, 421–22	
Ladle	A†	none		ca. 1775		YUAG
Porringer	A*	1784/IE (later)		ca. 1775	Christie's, 23 June 1993, lot 59	
Porringer	A	Kate,/three years old,/August 25ᵗʰ 1853 (later)		ca. 1775	*Maine An- tique Digest* 22 (April 1994): 21D	
Porringer spoon	A	SP	Sarah (Orne) Pickman	ca. 1770	Buhler 1972, no. 447	MFAB
Salt	A	none		ca. 1770	Johnston 1994, 4	CMA
Tablespoon	A	Edward Eells/born 26 Feby/1779	Edward Eells	1779		PEM
Tablespoon	A	R/IK		ca. 1775	DAPC 75.2783	WM
Tablespoon	A*	MA		ca. 1775		PEM
Tablespoon	A	H/TM		ca. 1775		VMFA
Tablespoon	A	MR; RR MP/1773 (later)		ca. 1770	YUAG files	

1. *Salem VR* 3:51, 496; 4:427; 5:47; Flynt/Fales 1968, 145; Pearson 1904, 1:1–2.

2. SCD 102:216–17; 110:203.

3. Derby Family Papers, vol. 1, PEM.

4. *EIHC* 77, no. 1 (January 1941): 67. Andrew himself made shoe buckles and performed other small services for Derby between 1769 and 1771; see Elias Hasket Derby Account Books, vol. 1, fol. 60, PEM.

5. The Massachusetts tax list of 1771 indicates Andrew's success. He owned two-thirds of a house and an adjoining shop with £450 of merchandise; see Pruitt 1978, 138–39; Buhler 1972, 2:498.

6. *Essex Gazette*, 10–17 September 1771.

7. *Essex Gazette*, 5–12 November 1771.

8. Bentley 1905–62, 1:298–99.

9. ECD 143:1.

10. Bentley 1905–62, 1:121.

11. Bentley 1905–62, 1:299.

12. Bentley 1905–62, 1:298; Pearson 1904, 1:2. Edwin F. Churchill of the Maine State Museum, who has been engaged in a lengthy research project on Maine silversmiths, indicates that the Cumberland County probate records were destroyed by fire in 1791. His files contain no references to Andrew, and he suspects that he never made any silver while in Maine.

13. MFAB, manuscript, no. 31.238.

14. The tablespoon (119,597) bears the inscription "Edward Eels, born 26 Feby 1779." This is probably for the son born to Robert L. and Ruth Eells in Hanover, Plymouth County, Massachusetts; see *Hanover VR*, 44.

15. Edward Lang Account Book, fol. 48, PEM.

16. Andrew advertised that he "BUYS, sells, and negotiates, at his House in the Main Street, near the Common, in SALEM, State Notes—Continental Securities—the Loan Officers' certificates which are receivable in the Continental Tax—the Treasurer's Orders on Collectors—New Emission Money—and every other kind of Publick Securities" in the *Salem Gazette* for 28 September 1784 and later issues.

17. Belden 1980, 31.

Isaac Anthony
1690–1773

A

B

Isaac Anthony was born in Portsmouth, Rhode Island, on 10 April 1690, the twelfth son of Abraham (1650–1727) and Alice (Woodell) Anthony (1650–1734) of Newport, who married in 1671. Abraham Anthony was the son of John (ca. 1607–75) and Susanna (Potter) Anthony. Alice (Woodell) Anthony was the daughter of William (d. ca. 1693) and Mary (d. 1676) Woodell of Newport.[1] Isaac Anthony was apprenticed in Boston and established his own business there about 1711. Wendy Cooper has speculated that Anthony may have apprenticed or worked with Edward Winslow (q.v.) because a porringer by Anthony has a handle cast from a mold with an impression of an English mark that was also used by Winslow.[2] Anthony appears in several Boston court documents. One of these is a suit brought by Roland Dyke, a Boston barber, in an effort to recover a debt of thirty-three pounds from Anthony for sundries delivered by a servant on 25 August 1712. The documents in the case mention debts incurred by "Your journeyman Deblin," probably the man elsewhere recorded as Peter Denman (q.v.).[3] Anthony was identified as a goldsmith in the ledger of the Boston stationer Daniel Henchman, from whom he purchased miscellaneous goods in 1715.[4]

Anthony's marriage is recorded in the Quaker Monthly Meeting: "Marcy Chamberlain of Boston, d. William of Hull, deceased, and Isaac Anthony of Boston, goldsmith, s. Abraham of Rhode Island, husbandman, at Boston, Sept. 16, 1714."[5] His wife was the daughter of William Chamberlain and his wife, Eunice. Marcy Chamberlain was born on 18 November 1686.[6] Isaac and Marcy Anthony had at least one daughter while they resided in Boston.[7]

Isaac Anthony returned to Rhode Island before September 1725, when he is referred to as being a goldsmith of Newport in a deed dated the twentieth of that month.[8] He purchased an additional piece of land in 1725 and bought and sold land in Newport in 1728 and 1729.[9] The witnesses to these deeds included John Casey, John Hammett, John Rhodes, Samuel Easton, Joshua Coggeshall, William Coddington, John Proud, and John Coddington (q.v.). Isaac's father, Abraham Anthony, died in 1727 and bequeathed to his son Isaac a great coat, a riding horse, a third of his wearing apparel, and two hundred pounds. He also bequeathed land to Isaac's daughter Mercy.

In addition to his regular retail goldsmithing business, Anthony ran several lotteries. In 1732 he advertised a lottery in the *Newport Mercury* with a first prize of a two-story house with adjoining shop in King Street. Other prizes included an eight-day clock with "a good Japann'd Case in Imitation of Tortoise-Shell and Gold" and goldsmith's wares.[10] His ventures must not have been uniformly successful, however, for he was sued by Henry Sabin, a gunsmith, for nonperformance in lotteries.[11]

Isaac Anthony died in Newport on 5 November 1773. His wife, Mary [*sic*], still a widow, died at the age of eighty-eight in 1775.[12]

Most of Anthony's surviving work dates from his years in Newport. Two marks, IA in an oval (A) and I:Anthony in a rectangle (B), have been attributed to him.[13]   BMW

SURVIVING OBJECTS

	Mark	Inscription	Patron	Date	Reference	Owner
Caudle cup	A	PC; ICP		ca. 1720	Sotheby's, 28–30 January 1988, lot 1059	
Cup	A*	SW/PP		ca. 1725	Carpenter 1954, 169	
Cup	?	Mary Boss	Mary Boss	ca. 1735		RISD
Patch box	A	CP		ca. 1750	*Moore Collection* 1980, no. 17	
Patch box	A	AS		ca. 1750	*Moore Collection* 1980, no. 18	
Porringer (with English mark WR; part of a service)	A	HH		ca. 1715	Cooper 1978, 107–09	
Porringer	A/B	E/NH		ca. 1750	*Moore Collection* 1980, no. 19	
Porringer spoon (part of a service)	A	HH		ca. 1715	Cooper 1978, 107–09	
Tablespoon	A	W/IC		ca. 1735	*Moore Collection* 1980, no. 20	
Tablespoon	A†	W/IC		ca. 1725	Buhler/Hood 1970, no. 460	YUAG
Tablespoon	A*	erased		ca. 1725		YUAG

	Mark	Inscription	Patron	Date	Reference	Owner
Tablespoon	A*	M/AA		ca. 1720	Carpenter 1955, 48	
Tablespoon	A	R/BA	Benjamin and Abigail (Howland) Russell	ca. 1715	Buhler 1972, appendix no. 91	MFAB
Tablespoon	B†	SW/to/MH		ca. 1725		SI
Tablespoon	B*	T/EE		ca. 1730	Carpenter 1955, 48	
Tablespoon	?	G/WK		ca. 1735		RISD
Tankard	A	R/TH (+)		ca. 1720	Gourley 1965, no. 221	RISD
Tankard	A*/B	Arnold arms, 3 escal-lops, in fess point a mullet, and crest, a mullet; BE; March/ ye 25th/1727	Arnold family	ca. 1727	Warren 1975, no. 286	BBC
Tankard	?	Newdigate arms	Newdigate family	ca. 1730	*Antiques* 113 (April 1978): 688	

1. Arnold 1911, 4:5, 53; Savage 1860–62, 1:59; *Anthony Family*, 63–64.
2. Cooper 1978, 107–09.
3. SCCR, file 10844.
4. Daniel Henchman Ledger, 1712–ca. 1735, fol. 111, NEHGS.
5. *Lynn VR* 2:87.
6. *Hull VR*, 14.
7. A daughter, Marcy or Mercy, was born to the couple in Boston on 4 November 1715; RC 24:103. Her death is recorded in a notice printed in the *Boston Gazette* for 21–28 March 1737; Dow 1927, 41.
8. Colonial Town Records, Land Evidence 2:113–14, Newport Historical Society.
9. Colonial Town Records, Land Evidence 2:81, 113, 114, 127, 301, 319, 320; 8:57, 58; 9:115, 116, Newport Historical Society.
10. *Newport Historical Magazine* 2 (1881–82): 250–51.
11. Flynt/Fales 1968, 145.
12. Arnold 1911, 12:38.
13. IA in an oval (A) also has been attributed to Josiah Austin (q.v.); see Kovel 1961, 17.

Ebenezer Austin
1733–1802 +

A

B

Related by marriage to the Edwards family of silversmiths, Ebenezer Austin was born in Charlestown, Massachusetts, on 9 November 1733 to Ebenezer Austin (1703/04–45), a merchant, and Mary Smith (1710–1800), who married in Charlestown on 30 November 1732.[1] His paternal grandparents were Ebenezer Austin (1662–1722/23), a saddler, and his second wife, Rebecca Sprague (1675–1769).[2] His maternal grandparents were William Smith (1667–1730) and Abigail Fowle (1679–1760).[3] Austin's maternal grandmother married John Edwards (q.v.) as her second husband in 1740.[4]

Following the death of his father, twelve-year-old Ebenezer Austin became the ward of his uncle by marriage, Samuel Edwards (q.v.), in March 1746, and presumably trained with him.[5] Austin would have completed his apprenticeship about 1754. He may have worked in Boston or Charlestown for a few years before moving to Hartford, Connecticut. He was called a goldsmith of Hartford in a deed of 23 June 1761, when he sold Charlestown land inherited from his father.[6] He began advertising in the Hartford *Connecticut Courant* in 1765 and continued to do so fairly regularly until the Revolution.[7] Offering tools and materials for goldsmiths and jewelers, his advertisements state that his shop was located near the courthouse on the west side of Main Street, a few doors below Pearl Street.[8] In a deed of 1772 he again was identified as a goldsmith of Hartford when he and other relatives sold a dwelling house in Charlestown.[9]

Austin presumably served in the revolutionary war, because his advertising in the *Courant* ceased between 1774 and 1780. His advertisement of December 1780 was reminiscent of those appearing before the war.[10] In July 1781, however, he advertised silk handkerchiefs and jewelry, appealing directly to consumers rather than to tradesmen for the first time.[11] Another of his postrevolutionary advertisements indicates that he continued to emphasize selling his wares to consumers. It lists

> Large Table Spoons, newest fashion; large and small Tea do various fashions ready for sale, Shoe and Knee Buckles different fashions, Stock Buckles wrought and plain, Gold Necklaces ready made, cyphered and white stone Ear-Rings set in gold, cyphered and white stone Tops do. Silver Thimbles plain and engraved with steel and silver tops. Said articles sold made and mended as cheap as before the late war.[12]

In 1782 Austin advertised that "the whole APPARATUS of a Gold-Smith's and Jeweller's TOOLS" was for sale.[13] Perhaps the void left in Charlestown by the death about 1780 of his cousin, the silversmith Josiah Austin (q.v.), encouraged him to contemplate returning there. Apparently he found no immediate buyers, for five years later, in December 1787, he ran a similar advertisement.[14] By May 1789 he had relocated his shop "Near the Square" in Charlestown.[15] He was also identified as a goldsmith from Charlestown when he joined with the heirs of his grandparents William and Abigail Smith in selling the house occupied by his mother, the widow Mary Austin, to his brother Nathaniel Austin, "pewterer of Charlestown."[16] The survey of Charlestown conducted in 1802 suggests that he then lived in a house on the corner of Main and Water streets, a block below the square.[17] How long Ebenezer Austin remained there is not known. Previous scholarship has consistently identified him with the Ebenezer Austin who was granted a pension for revolutionary war service in 1818; that Ebenezer Austin, however, was a blacksmith, born ca. 1759, then living in New York State.[18] No record of the silversmith's death has been found.

About two dozen pieces of silver by Austin survive; all are flatware or related serving pieces. The key object for attributing marks to this silversmith is a punch strainer made for the Hartford merchant Capt. John Chenevard, bearing a surname mark (A) and an initials mark (B).[19] Kathryn Buhler has suggested that the full name mark may also have been used by Nathaniel Austin (q.v.), but that assertion cannot be substantiated.[20] PEK

SURVIVING OBJECTS

	Mark	Inscription	Patron	Date	Reference	Owner
Ladle	A	DB		ca. 1785	Hammerslough/ Feigenbaum 1958–73, 3:112–13	
Two salt spoons	B†	RL		ca. 1800		YUAG

	Mark	Inscription	Patron	Date	Reference	Owner
Strainer	A*/B*	JC	John Chenevard	ca. 1785	Bohan/Hammerslough 1970, 90–91	WA
Two tablespoons	A*	RC		ca. 1790		YUAG
Tablespoon	A*	I(or J)MF		ca. 1790	DAPC 72.3463	WM
Tablespoon	A*	IG		ca. 1770	DAPC 72.3460	WM
Tablespoon	A*	NRG; MBV (later)	Nathaniel and Rebecca (Call) Gorham	ca. 1790	Buhler 1972, no. 325 (as Nathaniel or Ebenezer Austin)	MFAB
Tablespoon	A*	PK (partially erased); RKR (later)		ca. 1790		YUAG
Tablespoon	A	AE		ca. 1765		CHS
Tablespoon	A	JL	John Lawrence	ca. 1775		CHS
Teaspoon	A†	TB		ca. 1785	Buhler/Hood 1970, no. 364	YUAG
Two teaspoons	A*	HA		ca. 1770		HD
Teaspoon	A*	erased		ca. 1785		YUAG
Teaspoon	A	AR		ca. 1765		CHS
Four teaspoons	A	MT		ca. 1765		CHS
Teaspoon	A*	H/JG		ca. 1770		PEM
Teaspoon	B*	B/IH		ca. 1770	YUAG files	

1. *Charlestown VR* 1:199, 315, 323; *NEHGR* 30:182; *Index of Obituaries, 1784–1840*, 1:146; Griffen 1952, 7; Wyman 1879, 1:30; MCPR, docket 528.
2. *Charlestown VR* 1:40, 151, 273; Wyman 1879, 1:28–29; MCPR, docket 526.
3. *Charlestown VR* 1:58, 107, 305; Wyman 1879, 2:874; MCPR, docket 20780.
4. RC 28:214.
5. MCPR, docket 529.
6. MCD 107:370–72.
7. The advertisements appear 24 June, 1, 6 July 1765; 13, 20, 27 October 1766; 15, 22, 29 June, 13, 20, 27 July, 3, 10 August 1767; 16, 23, 30 May 1768; 30 October, 6, 20, 27 November 1769; 28 May, 4, 11, 18, 25 June, 2, 9 July 1771; 20, 27 April, 4, 18, 25 May, 1, 8, 15, 22, 29 June, 6, 13 July 1773; 24 May, 7, 21, 28 June, and 12 July 1774.
8. Barber 1838, 48.
9. MCD 76:179–80.
10. See the issues of 19, 26 December 1780 and 2 January 1781.
11. See issues of 24, 31 July 1781.
12. See issues of 31 October and 7, 14 November 1785.
13. See issues of 2, 9, 16 July 1782.
14. See issues of 24 December 1787 and 7 January 1788.
15. *Massachusetts Centinel*, 20, 27 May 1789.
16. MCPR 123:351.
17. RC 3:247, 249.
18. Revolutionary War Pension and Bounty-Land Application Files, National Archives and Records Administration, no. W20642, microfilm M-804, reel 91.
19. Kovel 1961, 17, also shows the marks EJ AUSTIN and AUSTIN, both in rectangles, but examples of these marks have not been located.
20. Buhler 1972, 1:370–71.

James Austin
1750–85+

James Austin, the brother of Nathaniel Austin (q.v.) and nephew of Josiah Austin (q.v.), was born in Charlestown, Massachusetts, on 9 August 1750. He was the son of Thomas Austin (1706–49), a barber, who died shortly before his birth, and Ruth Frothingham (1712–95), who had married in Charlestown on 7 January 1730/31.[1] His maternal grandparents were Nathaniel Frothingham (1671–1730) and Hannah Rand (1672–1760).[2] His paternal grandparents were James Austin (1679–1741) and Mary Tufts (1681–1745).[3] James Austin was apprenticed about 1764 probably to either his brother or his uncle, completing his training about 1770.

After finishing his apprenticeship, Austin apparently moved to Boston, because on 21 March 1771 he was notified by the selectmen that he had been there six months.[4] However, the Massachusetts tax list for 1771 includes a James Austin in Charlestown, and on 2 May 1772, when he sold land in Charlestown, he was identified as a "goldsmith of Charlestown."[5] The Boston tax list for 1780 refers to him as a goldsmith and notes that he had moved to Watertown, Massachusetts, where he was probably residing as early as 1775, because a James Austin served as a private from Watertown in the alarm of 19 April 1775 and again for six months in 1778.[6] At a Watertown town meeting of 5 September 1785, James Austin's taxes were abated.[7] Austin probably died sometime between this date and 1797, since he is not among the heirs who sold land from his mother's estate that year.[8]

No silver by him is known. PEK

1. *Charlestown VR* 1:212, 235, 308, 406; Griffen 1952, 8; Wyman 1879, 1:37.
2. *Charlestown VR* 1:306; *NEHGR* 26:53; 29:72; Griffen 1952, 46; Wyman 1879, 1:383.
3. *Charlestown VR* 1:107; Griffen 1952, 7; MCPR, docket 545.
4. Wyman 1879, 1:39.
5. MCD 73:468–69; Pruitt 1978, 180–81.
6. "Assessors' 'Taking-Books,'" 49; *Mass. Soldiers and Sailors* 1:357.
7. *Watertown Records* 1894, 5–6:333.
8. MCD 133:108–10.

Josiah Austin
1719/20–ca. 1780

A

B

C

The most productive member of the Austin family of silversmiths, Josiah Austin was baptized in Charlestown, Massachusetts, on 24 January 1719/20, the son of James Austin (1679–1741), an innholder, and Mary Tufts (1681–1745), who were married about 1705.[1] His paternal grandparents were Richard Austin (ca. 1632–1703) and Abigail Bachelder (1637–93);[2] his maternal grandparents were Peter Tufts (1648–1721) and Elizabeth Lynde (1650–84) of Malden, Massachusetts.[3] He was a cousin of Ebenezer Austin (q.v.).

Josiah Austin would have begun his apprenticeship about 1734, possibly with his cousin Jacob Hurd (q.v.), and completed it about 1741. On 25 August 1743 Austin married Mary Phillips (1724–82+) of Charlestown, the daughter of Eleazer Phillips (1682–1763), a bookseller, and Lydia Waite (1689–1737).[4] Austin may have trained a number of apprentices: his nephew Nathaniel Austin (q.v.) from about 1748 to 1755; Thomas Lynde (q.v.) between 1759 and 1766; another nephew, James Austin (q.v.), from about 1764 to 1770; and Eleazer Wyer, Sr. (q.v.), from about 1766 to 1773. The latter married Austin's daughter Lydia.

Josiah Austin is identified as a goldsmith in Middlesex County deeds a number of times. In 1744 he bought two acres of land from John Asbury; on 13 May 1748 he and his brothers Thomas and John sold land in Charlestown

D

E

F

inherited from their father; and in 1757 Josiah and his wife, Mary, mortgaged two acres of upland to Richard Boylston.[5] This mortgage was paid off in 1768, whereupon the land was sold to Thomas Frothingham, Jr.[6] On 12 March 1764 Austin, Mary, and Mary's sister Lydia Hood mortgaged to Isaac Rand part of a dwelling house inherited from Mary and Lydia's father. The deed implies that Austin was then living in the house.[7] A Josiah Austin appears in the Massachusetts tax list for 1771 in Charlestown with two polls and a quarter of a house with a shop adjoining.[8] Austin is said to have died in 1780, but no record of his death has been found. His wife resided with the couple's son James in Haverhill, Massachusetts, for a forty-three-week period ending 1 February 1782 for which the state allowed James 4 shillings a week, or £8.12, for her support, "she being one of the Poor of Charlestown."[9] Presumably, Josiah was dead before she moved to Haverhill.

Austin may not have been economically successful, but he was productive. On 20 March 1749/50 Austin tendered a bill for a spectacle case to Mrs. Faith Russell.

March	M^d Russell to Josiah Austin D^r	
20	to a Spectacle Cais 1^{oz}.2^{dt}.0 @ 52/	£2:17: 4
1749/50	making 50/ Graving 10/	3. 0. 0
	a tagg	0. 9. 0
		£6: 6: 4[10]

Later that year an advertisement in the *Boston Gazette* of 14 August indicated that a pint silver cann marked Austin on the bottom had been stolen from a Cambridge, Massachusetts, house. Austin also submitted a bill on 21 April 1774 to the town of Charlestown for gold rings for Rev. Hull Abbott's funeral, which the selectmen agreed to pay on 6 June 1774.[11]

More than three dozen pieces of holloware and flatware with marks attributed to Austin survive. Key to the attributing of his marks is a sugar bowl that belonged to the Russell family that bears an initial and surname mark (A) as well as an initials mark (B). Other initials marks, with a pellet (C, D), have sometimes been attributed to Austin and sometimes to John Allen (q.v.), but are more likely to belong to the former, because Allen seems to have given up silversmithing after his partnership with John Edwards (q.v.) ended about 1702.[12] A stylistically related initials mark (E) may also be Austin's. Another initials mark with pellet has sometimes been attributed to Austin, but the character of the mark and the engraving on the pieces with this mark are quite different from the other Austin work; thus it is doubtful that the mark belongs to him.[13] A second initial and surname mark (F) continued to be used after Austin's death by his nephew Nathaniel Austin. Some scholars claim that Austin worked in partnership with Daniel Boyer (q.v.), but no evidence of this has been found.[14] Two tankards with Austin's initials mark also bear the surname mark of Samuel Minott (q.v.), which suggests that Austin made pieces for Minott to resell. PEK

SURVIVING OBJECTS

	Mark	Inscription	Patron	Date	Reference	Owner
Beaker	B†	Belonging to the first Church of Christ in Woburn 1769	First Congregational Church, Woburn, Mass.	1769	Jones 1913, 504	

	Mark	Inscription	Patron	Date	Reference	Owner
Bowl	A	Dudley crest	Dudley family	ca. 1750	Phillips 1939, no. 6	
Bowl	A *or* F	Tilghman crest, a demi-lion crowned	Tilghman family	ca. 1760	Christie's, 10 October 1987, lot 86	
Cann	B	the Gift of/Jonas Dix Jun'/to his Sis-ter Mary Dix/1772	Jonas Dix and/or Mary Dix	1772	Christie's, 26 January 1985, lot 94	
Cann	B, C, *or* D	unidentified initials		ca. 1765	Parke-Bernet, 4 January 1940, lot 57	
Cann	F (?)	unidentified crest; ECC to ILA to FLRA		ca. 1750	Parke-Bernet, 4 January 1940, lot 60	
Cann	F*	This cup belonged to Isaac Appleton of Ipswich . . . (later)	Isaac and Elizabeth (Sawyer) Appleton	ca. 1760	DAPC 82.3352	
Cann	?	1749		1749	*Antiques* 51 (January 1947): 74	
Cann	?	Green (?) crest, a stag's head erased; G/IK	Green family (?)	ca. 1750	American Art Associa-tion–Ander-son Galler-ies, 12 March 1938, lot 39	
Creampot	A	MB		ca. 1745	*Antiques* 105 (January 1974): 112	
Creampot	c†	H/MB/1878 (later?)		ca. 1740	Buhler 1972, no. 75 (as John Allen)	MFAB
Creampot	F	L/IM; ASDLD (later)		ca. 1745		MFAB
Cup	C	Ruth Wyer (later)		ca. 1745	*Silver Supple-ment* 1973, no. 1 (as John Allen)	
Ladle	B*	none		ca. 1760	DAPC 74.2162	NM
Mourning ring (gold)	C, D, *or* E	P. Bowman Ob 20 Decem' 1751 AE' 78	Phoebe Bowman	1751	Phillips 1939, no. 206	
Papboat	A*	S.R. 1750/I.D.R. 1836 (later)		ca. 1750	Buhler 1972, no. 232	MFAB
Pipe tongs (steel)	F	none		ca. 1750	Sander 1982, no. 24	SPNEA
Porringer	A*	N/AA	Abijah and Abigail Northey	ca. 1760	Anderson Galleries, 7–12 January 1924, lot 856	
Porringer	A*	F/RM		ca. 1760	*Antiques* 90 (August 1966): 151	

	Mark	Inscription	Patron	Date	Reference	Owner
Porringer	F*	GE/SG/1776		1776	*MMA Bulletin* 18 (April 1922): 93	MMA
Porringer spoon	B	P/NI/1748		ca. 1748	MFA 1911, no. 25	
Two salts	E†	E/PE	Philip and Emily Endicott	ca. 1760	Avery 1920, nos. 59–60	MMA
Salver	F*	Temple arms, argent two bars or each with three martlets	Temple family	ca. 1760	MFA 1911, no. 22	
Strainer	C	R/CM		ca. 1760	Buhler 1972, no. 76 (as John Allen)	MFAB
Strainer	F†	R/IK		ca. 1760	Buhler/Hood 1970, no. 189	YUAG
Sugar bowl	A	Bradstreet crest, a mailed arm embowed grasping a scimitar	Bradstreet family	ca. 1750	Bigelow 1917, 402–03	
Sugar bowl	A*/B*	Russell (?) crest, a lion rampant holding a staff	Russell family (?)	ca. 1770	Phillips, 24 January 1984, lot 270	
Tablespoon	A	MC		ca. 1760	Quimby 1995, no. 5	WM
Two tablespoons	A*	initials erased		ca. 1770		YUAG
Tablespoon	A†	H/SE		ca. 1750	Buhler/Hood 1970, no. 191	YUAG
Tablespoon	F*	SE/to/SB		ca. 1750	Buhler/Hood 1970, no. 190	YUAG
Tablespoon	F	KG		ca. 1770	YUAG files	
Tankard (with mark of Samuel Minott)	B, C, or D	Watertown Church (later; defaced)		ca. 1770	Jones 1913, 482	
Tankard (with mark of Samuel Minott)	B, C, or D	The Gift of/Deacon John Stone to the/Church of Christ in Newton/1768	John Stone and/or First Church, Newton, Mass.	1768	Jones 1913, 323	MFAB
Tankard	B, C, or D	?		ca. 1775	Christie's, 17–18 January 1992, lot 168	
Tankard (mate below)	F*	CC/1763 (+)	First Parish Church, Charlestown, Mass.	1763	Quimby 1995, no. 3	WM
Tankard (mate above)	F*	CC/1763	First Parish Church, Charlestown, Mass.	1763	Quimby 1995, no. 4	WM
Tankard	F	WW [WILLIAM WINTHROP], Esq.ʳ/ of Sᵀ. MARYS CHURCH/in/ NEWTON	William Winthrop (?) for St. Mary's Church, Newton Lower Falls, Mass.	ca. 1770	Jones 1913, 325–26	
Tankard	?	?		ca. 1765	*Antiques* 68 (October 1955): 327	

	Mark	Inscription	Patron	Date	Reference	Owner
Teapot	D†	Dudley arms, a lion rampant, and crest, a lion's head erased	Dudley family	ca. 1740	Quimby 1995, no. 2 (as John Allen)	WM
Teapot	F*	Bradstreet arms, sable 3 crescents gules on a fess argent above a greyhound passant argent, and crest, an armored arm embowed grasping a scimitar	Bradstreet family	ca. 1750	Buhler/Hood 1970, no. 188	YUAG
Teapot	F	Ware arms, 2 lions passant contourné within a bordure with 8 escallops, and crest, a griffin's head pierced with an arrow; S/RE	Ware family	ca. 1760	Safford 1983, 45	MMA
Teaspoon	B, C, D, *or* E	?		ca. 1760		CHM
Teaspoon	C	E/WR	Ellery family	ca. 1765	*MHS Proceedings* 20:534	MHS
Two-handled cup	A*	The gift of M.ʳ Thomas Brooks to the Church of Medford/1759	Thomas Brooks and/or First Parish, Medford, Mass.	1759	Jones 1913, 274	

1. *NEHGR* 31:326; *Charlestown VR* 1:107; Griffen 1952, 7; Wyman 1879, 1:28, 37; 2:958; MCPR, docket 545.
2. Griffen 1952, 7–8; *Charlestown VR* 1:38; *NEHGR* 25:149.
3. Wyman 1879, 2:958; *Charlestown VR* 1:77; *Malden VR*, 51, 382.
4. *Charlestown VR* 1:107, 114, 284; Wyman 1879, 2:744; *NEHGR* 27:278; Griffen 1952, 89.
5. Wyman 1879, 1:39; MCD 45:125; 49:352; 56:60.
6. MCD 67:420–21.
7. MCD 62:211–12. Rand foreclosed the mortgage on the house on 21 February 1784.
8. Pruitt 1978, 182–83.
9. Mass. Archives 141:589.
10. Josiah Austin bill to Faith Russell, 20 March 1749/50, Lemuel Shaw Papers, MHS.
11. Charlestown Town Records 8:262, microfilm, BPL.
12. The teapot at WM with this mark was published with a tentative attribution to Austin in MFA 1911, no. 28, and Bigelow 1917, 336–37, but more recently has been given to John Allen. See Buhler 1956, no. 1. A creampot and strainer with the same mark have also been attributed to Allen; see Buhler 1972, nos. 75 and 76.
13. See Belden 1980, 36 (mark b), on WM spoon 62.0240.870; Johnston 1994, 5, for a teaspoon at CMA; and a spoon in the Berger photograph collection, YUAG files. Kovel 1961, 17, also shows IA in an oval, but this is probably the mark that belongs to Isaac Anthony (q.v.).
14. See, for instance, Kovel 1961, 17; Flynt/Fales 1968, 147.

Nathaniel Austin
1734–1818

Nathaniel Austin, the older brother of the goldsmith James Austin (q.v.), was born in Charlestown, Massachusetts, on 17 July 1734.[1] (See the entry on James Austin for biographical information on his parents and grandparents.) He probably began his apprenticeship about 1748, in all likelihood with his uncle Josiah Austin (q.v.), although Francis Hill Bigelow suggests that he might

A

B

C

D

E

F

have been apprenticed to Samuel Edwards (q.v.) because Austin's aunt Sarah (Smith) was married to Edwards.[2] Austin probably began practicing his trade about 1755 and may have trained his brother James beginning about 1764.

On 24 May 1759 Austin married Anna Kent (1740–97), born in Charlestown on 3 August 1740 to Ebenezer Kent (1699–1776), a mariner, and Anna Smith (1708–81).[3] Nathaniel and Anna had six children: Anna (bap. 1760, d. 1760); Nathaniel (b. 1761); Anna (1764–87); Sarah (1765–89); Thomas (b. 1771); and Ebenezer (d. 1800).[4] The Nathaniel Austin included in the Massachusetts tax list for 1771 with one poll, half a house, an additional building, £11.5 annual value of real estate, £66.18 in merchandise, three horses, cattle, and some acreage was probably the goldsmith.[5] Austin and his wife lost "harlf a house, barn and woodhouse" during the British bombardment of 1775, claiming a loss of £343.0.4, comfortably above the average of £263, though it is unclear where in Charlestown this real estate was located.[6] On the list of possessions that Austin claimed losses on were

To 2 Glass cases	2. 8. 0
To 2 Benches	0. 16. 0
To a Molden Box	1. 0. 0

No other silversmith's tools were included.[7]

After 1776 the Austins ceased living in Charlestown. On the bond of 26 August 1777 for his father-in-law's estate, Austin is identified as "goldsmith of Cambridge."[8] The Nathaniel Austin who marched from Cambridge to Boston in 1778 during the Revolution may have been the goldsmith.[9] By 1781 Austin was described as being of Boston when he purchased property on Back Street, and in that year he also was licensed to sell tea there.[10] In 1783 he sold land inherited from his father in Charlestown, and in 1787, together with Thomas Welch and Samuel Cooper, he appraised the silver in the estate of the Boston merchant Isaac Smith.[11]

Little silver bearing Austin's mark survives. An initials mark (A) that appears on a coffeepot made for John and Abigail Adams has been attributed to him. Three other initials marks also have been attributed to him (B–D). Nathaniel Austin also used a surname mark (E) as well as the initial and surname mark (F) of his uncle Josiah Austin after the latter's death around 1780.[12] A bill of sale of 1787 from Nathaniel Austin to William Smith documents this. It reads as follows:

Mr. William Smith   Boston June 28 1787
Bo[t] of Nath[l.] Austin

To 12 Shell bowl Tea Spoons w[t] 6 [oz.] 13	
To Making @ 3/4	2..0..0
To 12 Silver Tea Spoons w[t] 6..5	
To Making @ 3/	1..16..0
To a pair Sugar Tongs w[t] 1..5	
To Making	0.. 8..0
To Engraving 25 Cyphers @ 6[d]	0..12..6
To a pair Silver Canns w[t] 28..1	
To Making	4..16..0
To Engraving	0..16. 0
To 3 Large Spoons w[t] 6..7	
To Making 13/6 Engraving 6/	0 .19. 6

To a Silver Tea Pot w^t 5..2
To Making 33/ Engraving 8/ 53..13   2..1..0
To 53..13 oz—Silver at 6/8   17..17..10
                                          £ 31..6..10 ¹³

The pieces surviving from this order bear Josiah Austin's mark (F) and include the teapot and six of the shell teaspoons. On the teapot and stand the J·AUSTIN mark overstrikes that of Paul Revere, Jr. (q.v.), indicating that Austin retailed work produced by another shop at least once. These wares that Austin sold to Smith correspond exactly with the silver described in Paul Revere's charges to Austin recorded on 9 June 1787 and 29 June 1787, with the exception of the teapot, which does not appear. On the earlier date the Revere daybook shows the following:

Mr Nathl Austin   D^r
To 12 Scolop^d Tea Spoons w^t 6^{oz} 13–
To Making @ 3/4   2 —
To 12 Silver Tea Spoons w^t 6-5-
To Making @ 3/   1 16
To 1 p^r Silvr Sugar tong 1 ..5-
To Making   8
To Engraving 25 Cypers @ 6^d   12 6

On the later date, the account shows

Mr Nathl Austin   D^r
To p^r Silv^r Cann Weight 28^{oz} 1 –
Making   4 16 –
Engrav^g   – 16 –
To 3 large Spoons w^t 6-7-
To Making 4/6   – 13 6
To Engraving 6 Cyphers   1/   – 6 –
To one Silver cream pot w^t 5^{oz} 2-
To Making   1 13 –
To Engrav^g   – 8 – ¹⁴

A curious feature of these accounts is that Austin did not mark up the price of the goods when he sold them to Smith. Austin may have been acting as an agent for Revere, rather than as a middle man, and may have been remunerated by Revere.

In 1790 the Revere daybook shows that Austin purchased additional silver from Revere. On 24 March 1790 the account notes

Mr Nathl Austin D^r
To a Silv^r Tea pot w^t 18^{oz} 15
To making   4 16 –
To Engrav^g   1 16 –
To a wooden handle & knob   6 ¹⁵

A few years later a bill dated 30 August 1797 documents another of Smith's silver purchases from Austin:

To Harlf a dozen of Tea Spoons Silver aded   0. 6.8
To macking and Cyphers   0. 19.0
                                          £ 1. 5.8.
                          Rec^d pay Nathl Austin¹⁶

The following year, on 22 October 1798, Smith paid Austin forty dollars for a coffeepot costing eighty-one dollars, leaving a balance due of forty-one dollars.[17]

Beginning in 1789 Austin is listed in Boston directories as a goldsmith living on Back Street, in Boston's fourth ward.[18] In that same year he and his siblings, acting on their mother's behalf, sold real estate in Charlestown that she had inherited from her husband.[19] In 1792 he served on the town visiting committee and on a smallpox committee.[20] By 1795 Austin had paid off the mortgage on his Back Street property.[21] Later that year his mother died, and in 1797 Austin's wife, who had sold her dower share of real estate in Charlestown in 1794, died.[22] Austin sold additional land in Charlestown in 1797, 1800, 1803, and 1808.[23] Along with Joseph Callender (q.v.), he was involved in the estate administration of Caleb Beal (q.v.), who died in 1801.[24] Austin died in Boston on 14 October 1818.[25] His will, dated 18 August 1818, mentions only his sisters and a granddaughter; his inventory amounted to $17,058 and included a pew in the New North Church and real estate at 36 Back Street and in Charlestown.[26] PEK

SURVIVING OBJECTS

	Mark	Inscription	Patron	Date	Reference	Owner
Cann (made by Paul Revere, Jr.)	E	HC	William Smith for Hannah Carter	1787	Thomas 1988, 16–17	
Caster	?	MC (?)		ca. 1760	Parke-Bernet, 27 January 1967, lot 29	
Coffeepot	A*	JAA	John and Abigail (Smith) Adams	ca. 1800	Conger/ Rollins 1991, no. 220	USDS
Creampot (made by Paul Revere, Jr.)	none	HC; 1787	William Smith for Hannah Carter	1787		MFAB
Creampot	?	unidentified crest; IBA		ca. 1770	Parke-Bernet, 14–15 May 1948, lot 177	
Two spoons	B, C, or D	S/IE		ca. 1770	MFA 1911, no. 30	
Tablespoon	A†	SP		ca. 1765	DAPC 72.3173	WM
Tablespoon	B†	EN		ca. 1790	DAPC 72.3182	WM
Tablespoon	B*	P/CS		ca. 1770		HD
Teapot	E†	MC		ca. 1790		CM
Teapot (with mark of Paul Revere, Jr.)	F	HC; 1787 (later)	William Smith for Hannah Carter	1787	Buhler 1972, no. 381	MFAB
Teapot stand (with mark of Paul Revere, Jr.)	none	HC; 1787 (later)	William Smith for Hannah Carter	1787	Buhler 1972, no. 381	MFAB
Two teaspoons	A*	LA		ca. 1770	YUAG files	
Teaspoon	C†	LS		ca. 1760		HD
Teaspoon	D†	MB		ca. 1760		CM
Teaspoon	D*	MC		ca. 1760		HD
Six teaspoons (made by Paul Revere, Jr.)	F†	HC	William Smith for Hannah Carter	1787	Buhler/Hood 1970, no. 248	YUAG
Teaspoon	?	MF		ca. 1770	YUAG files	

1. Wyman 1879, 1:37–38; *Charlestown VR* 1:323.
2. Bigelow-Phillips files, 1476.
3. *Charlestown VR* 1:315, 349, 477; *Index of Obituaries, 1784–1840,* 1:143; Griffen 1952, 66.
4. Thwing.
5. Pruitt 1978, 182–83.
6. Hunnewell 1888, 121, 166. Stephen Ensko stated that James Hill (q.v.) claimed the loss of Austin's house in 1775, but Ensko misread Thomas Wyman's entry on Hill; see Ensko 1927, 49; Ensko 1948, 70; Wyman 1879, 1:500.
7. Charlestown Town Records, MS/Bos/XC: 23D, Rare Book Room, BPL.
8. MCPR, docket 13138.
9. *Mass. Soldiers and Sailors* 1:360.
10. SCD 132:220–21; 133:187–89; RC 25:177.
11. Inventory of household furniture of Isaac Smith, 1787, Smith-Carter Papers, MHS; MCD 112:203–04.
12. Kathryn Buhler has suggested that Nathaniel Austin also used the full name mark, Austin in a rectangle, used by Ebenezer Austin (q.v.), but that assertion cannot be substantiated; see Buhler 1972, 1:370–71.
13. Nathaniel Austin bill to William Smith, 28 June 1787, Smith-Carter Papers, MHS.
14. 9, 29 June 1787, vol. 2, Waste Book, 1783–97, 57–58, Revere Family Papers, MHS. The teapot in Austin's bill to Smith probably is an error. Its weight corresponds to the creampot in the Revere daybook.
15. 24 March 1790, vol. 2, Waste Book, 1783–97, [87], Revere Family Papers, MHS.
16. Nathaniel Austin bill to William Smith, 30 August 1797, Smith-Carter Papers, MHS.
17. Nathaniel Austin receipt to William Smith for payment, 22 October 1798, Smith-Carter Papers, MHS.
18. *Boston Directory* 1789, 6; 1796, 14; 1798, 14; 1800, 12; 1803, 13; 1805, 13; 1806, 13; 1807, 29; 1809, 17; 1810, 18; 1813, 55; 1816, 55.
19. MCD 81:766.
20. RC 31:306.
21. SCD 132:221.
22. MCD 122:280–81.
23. MCD 133:108–10; 139:41–43; 152:417–18; 176:326–27.
24. SCPR, docket 21581.
25. *Index of Obituaries, 1784–1840,* 1:146.
26. SCPR 116:582–83; 117:2–3, 42.

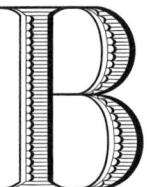

Loring Bailey
1740–ca. 1814

A

Loring Bailey was born on 1 May 1740 in Hull, Massachusetts, the sixth of seven children born to Thomas Bailey, Jr. (b. 1699/1700), originally of Gloucester, Massachusetts, and Anna Loring (b. 1706) of Hull, who married on 29 June 1726 in Hull.[1] His paternal grandparents were Thomas, Sr., and Mary Bailey.[2] His maternal grandparents were Benjamin Loring (ca. 1671–1732) and Anna Vickery (ca. 1676–1723).[3]

Loring Bailey may have apprenticed with his cousin Benjamin Loring (q.v.) in Boston, because the latter would have finished his apprenticeship there when Bailey was about to begin his around 1754. As an apprentice or fellow silversmith, he probably also knew Caleb Beal (q.v.), six years his junior, who was born in nearby Hingham and had moved to Boston by 1771. In 1782, Beal sold land in Hingham in a transaction witnessed by Loring Bailey.[4] Where Bailey worked during the period between the end of his training and his move to Hingham around 1780 is not known. Although he is not listed in the Massachusetts tax valuation list of 1771, he did serve in the Revolution as a private in Capt. Peter Cushing's third company of Hingham in Col. Solomon Lovell's regiment, doing duty for one day, from 15 March to 16 March 1776.[5]

According to George Lincoln's *History of the Town of Hingham*, Bailey maintained a shop there, near Broad Bridge, with Caleb Gill (1774–1855), Leavitt Gill (1789–1854), and Samuel Norton (w. 1790) working as his apprentices.[6] As late as 1800, at age sixty, Bailey identified himself as a silversmith in two Suffolk County deeds.[7] These documents record Bailey's purchase of land for $40 from several of his nieces and nephews in January 1800, and sale of it the following August, a transaction in which he made a profit of $360, which he apparently shared with his spinster sister, Anna. Bailey appeared in the federal census of 1810.[8] According to Lincoln, he died, unmarried, on 3 January 1814, but his death was not formally recorded.[9]

Bailey probably made the dozen or so pieces of flatware marked L·B in a rectangle (A). This mark has been attributed erroneously to the New Haven, Connecticut, silversmith Luther Bradley (1772–1830).[10] A baptismal spoon bearing this mark and a date of 1779 indicates that this mark was in use before Bradley would have been working. An LB in a rectangle without a pellet has also been attributed to him.[11] JJF

SURVIVING OBJECTS

	Mark	Inscription	Patron	Date	Reference	Owner
Sugar tongs	A*	KC		ca. 1780	Cutten 1946, 113	NM
Tablespoon	A*	W/SB		ca. 1780	DAPC 71.1578 (as Luther Bradley)	WM
Tablespoon	A	LC		ca. 1785	Avery 1920, no. 195	MMA
Tablespoon	A*	O/IM		ca. 1810		YUAG
Tablespoon	A†	L/TJ	Thomas and Joanna (Quincy) (Thaxter) Loring	ca. 1800	Buhler 1972, appendix no. 1	MFAB
Tablespoon	A	ET	Eliza Thaxter	ca. 1795	Buhler 1972, appendix no. 2	MFAB
Tablespoon	A*	B/PM		ca. 1800		YUAG
Tablespoon	A*	BE/born April 8/1779		ca. 1779	DAPC 68.2304	SI
Tablespoon	A	MC/to/Eli.ᵈ C; C/WM (later)		ca. 1785		RISD
Tablespoon	A*	JHL		ca. 1800		YUAG
Tablespoon	A	MS; Lina (later)		ca. 1800	YUAG files	
Teaspoon	A*	C/CE		ca. 1805	Buhler/Hood 1970, no. 417 (as Luther Bradley)	YUAG
Teaspoon	A*	FS		ca. 1780		PEM

1. *Gloucester VR* 1:87; *Hull VR*, 9, 26, 41; *Weymouth VR* 1:16; *Hull Church Registry 1725–1766*, copied by S. E. Pond while the book was at the State House for repairs, ca. 1930, handwritten, NEHGS Library, p. 4 of copy, p. 47 of original registry.
2. The names of the paternal grandparents were drawn from the birth record of their son Thomas. No marriage record in Gloucester was found for them.
3. *Hull VR*, 51, 69.
4. SCD 182:235–36.
5. *Mass. Soldiers and Sailors* 1:458.
6. Lincoln (1893) 1982, 1, part 2, 177.
7. SCD 195:59–60, 208–09.
8. Third Census of the United States.
9. Lincoln (1893) 1982, 1, part 2, 177; 2:17.
10. Buhler/Hood 1970, no. 417; Belden 1980, 71.
11. See French (1917) 1967, 8, and Kovel 1961, 19. No example of this mark that could be attributed to Bailey with certainty has been found. A teapot marked LB in a rectangle (Buhler 1965, 108, 110), now at HMA, is no longer attributed to him. A cowrie shell box with LB in a cut-corner rectangle at AIC has been attributed to him, but the skillful craftsmanship of the box suggests it was not made by the same person who made the pieces with the L·B mark.

Ebenezer Balch 1723–1808

Ebenezer Balch, described in his family's genealogy as both a goldsmith and a clockmaker, was born in Boston on 14 May 1723.[1] Balch was the son of Joseph Balch (d. 1733), a mariner, and Mary Osgood (1689/90–1752), who were married in Boston on 23 October 1712.[2] Balch's paternal grandparents were Samuel (ca. 1651–1723) and Martha (Newmarsh) Balch (ca. 1653–1720); his maternal

A

grandparents were Timothy (1659–1748) and Deborah (Poor) Osgood (1664–1724) of Andover, Massachusetts.[3] Balch probably trained in the town of his birth.

The silversmith is said to have settled in Hartford, Connecticut, upon reaching his majority in 1744.[4] On 28 June 1750, he married Sarah Belden (1727–56), daughter of Capt. Jonathan Belden (1695–1768) and Martha James of Wethersfield, Connecticut, in a ceremony performed by Rev. James Lockwood in Wethersfield.[5] Balch's marriage into the Belden family added considerably to his social standing and provided him with a large familial network of potential patrons. His father-in-law was a justice of the peace and town treasurer of Wethersfield for many years.[6] Balch's diary records the birth of two of the couple's three children, Mary on 17 November 1752 and Jonathan "Belding" on 14 November 1754.[7]

In 1752, Balch traveled to Boston to administer his mother's estate following her death on 22 October of that year.[8] In February 1753 Balch bought his three sisters' portions of the house and land on Prince Street in Boston that their mother, Mary (Osgood) Balch, had left her children.[9] He sold the property six days later to his brother Timothy, a tailor living in Newport, Rhode Island.[10] The deeds for these transactions describe Balch as a goldsmith residing in Hartford.

Sarah Balch died in Hartford on 3 April 1756 at the age of twenty-nine, "after a Long & tedious and Distressing Sickness of aboutt 4 months Confinement."[11] The silversmith married Lois Belden (1737–93), a cousin of his first wife, on 29 November 1756.[12] Her parents, Ezra Belden (b. 1699) and Elizabeth Belden (Belding) (b. 1698), were also cousins, part of the extensive Belden family of Wethersfield.[13] Balch had seven children by Lois, including Joseph (1760–1855), a goldsmith, watchmaker, and clockmaker who was probably trained by his father.[14] Joseph Balch worked in Hartford and Wethersfield, Connecticut, Williamstown, Massachusetts, and Johnstown, New York, where he died.[15] Ebenezer Balch also trained his son Ebenezer (1766–1846) as a silversmith and clockmaker, but the younger son did not pursue a career in either of these trades.[16]

Balch sold some Hartford property, including land and buildings near Great Bridge, to James Codwell on 19 November 1755 for three thousand pounds old tenor.[17] He moved to Wethersfield in April 1756—a move probably related to the death of his first wife and to his remarriage—but eventually returned to Hartford, where he died on 28 April 1808.[18] No evidence exists that he ever worked as a silversmith outside Connecticut, except during his apprenticeship.

Very few objects by Balch survive. A tablespoon in the collection of the Yale University Art Gallery bears the mark E·BALCH in a rectangle (A). In *Early Silver of Connecticut and Its Makers*, George Munson Curtis mentions that he located a number of spoons with this mark.[19] DAF

SURVIVING OBJECTS

	Mark	Inscription	Patron	Date	Reference	Owner
Tablespoon	A*	ML		ca. 1755	Buhler/Hood 1970, no. 346	YUAG
Three tablespoons	A	T/MM		ca. 1755		CHS
Tablespoon	A†	IS		ca. 1755		CHS

	Mark	Inscription	Patron	Date	Reference	Owner
Tablespoon	A	MC		ca. 1755		CHS
Teaspoon	A*	MS		ca. 1750	YUAG files	

1. RC 24:158; Balch 1897, 23–24, 40; *Balch Leaflets* 1896, 47.

2. *Beverly VR* 1:34; RC 28:38; SCPR 30:32–33; 47:23–24; *Andover VR* 1:286.

3. *Andover VR* 1:288, 311; 2:258, 513, 516; *Balch Leaflets* 1896, 47; Balch 1897, 23–24; *Beverly VR* 2:28, 371; *Ipswich VR* 2:38. The name of Samuel Balch's wife has been variously given as Martha Newmarsh, Martha Newmarth, and Martha Newmarch.

4. Curtis 1913, 84.

5. Balch 1897, 23, 40; *Balch Leaflets* 1896, 48; *Early Conn. Marriages* 3:8; Stiles 1904, 80; Hinman 1861–62, 295.

6. Stiles 1904, 80.

7. *Balch Leaflets* 1896, 48; Hinman 1861–62, 135–36.

8. *Balch Leaflets* 1896, 47; SCPR 47:23–24.

9. SCD 81:262–63.

10. SCD 81:263–64.

11. *Balch Leaflets* 1896, 48.

12. Stiles 1904, 80; Balch 1897, 40.

13. Stiles 1904, 78, 80; Hinman 1861–62, 246, 296.

14. Hinman 1861–62, 135–36.

15. Balch 1897, 60–61.

16. Balch 1897, 63–64.

17. Hartford, Connecticut, Deeds 9:46.

18. Curtis 1913, 84; Balch 1897, 40–41; *Balch Leaflets* 1896, 47.

19. Curtis 1913, 84; Kovel 1961, 20, also records E.BALCH in a rectangle.

John Ball
1723/24–81+

A

B

C

John Ball was born in Concord, Massachusetts, on 8 February 1723/24, the son of Jonathan Ball (b. 1691), a yeoman, and Hannah Clark (b. 1691), who married on 24 April 1713.[1] His paternal grandparents were John Ball (1660–1703) and Hannah Rugge (Ruggles).[2] His maternal grandparents were Samuel (ca. 1647–1729/30) and Rachel (1654–1722) Clark.[3]

Ball would have begun his apprenticeship about 1737, possibly with Jacob Hurd (q.v.), as he witnessed a deed for Hurd on 11 December 1745.[4] He would have completed his training about 1745. In March 1745 he was identified as being "of Boston, Goldsmith" when purchasing "Sundry Tools" for more than £190 from another Boston goldsmith, Benjamin Greene (q.v.), in all likelihood to set up a shop.[5] Ball was again described as being of Boston when on 20 November 1746 he married Sarah Brooks (1723/24–80), daughter of Benjamin Brooks (b. 1698) and Sarah Hayward (b. 1700/01) of Concord.[6] The John Ball who served as a Boston constable in ward 9 from 1745 to 1747 may have been this goldsmith, or he may have been another John Ball, a scrivener by trade.[7] A daughter, Sarah, and a son, John, were born in Boston in 1747 and 1748, respectively.[8] Ball had moved to Concord by 1752, where the birth of a daughter, Elizabeth, is recorded.[9]

In 1759 John Ball's father mortgaged 6½ acres of Concord land, including a dwelling house, to William Homes, Sr. (q.v.).[10] The fact that Homes lent Ball's father money suggests that Ball worked in association with Homes, although no evidence confirms this. In 1761 John Ball bought this land from his father; by then it had two dwelling houses and a brick shop, along with the 6½ acres.[11] Ball advertised the land with the dwelling house in the *Boston*

News-Letter of 17 March 1763, selling it with the westerly part of a house and goldsmith's shop later that year. The deed recording this transaction suggests that Ball's parents moved into the easterly part of the new house; that Ball was living in the old house; and that a second shop had been built on the land. It states that the boundaries came within four feet "of an old House of my own then moving westerly excluding said House and a brick shop . . . Reserving the Easterly half part of the House during the Natural Lives of my Honour'd Parents."[12] In 1763, Ball also sold the two remaining lots he had bought from his father in 1761.[13]

Since Ball advertised the public vendue of six acres with a brick shop, barn, and corn barn as being for sale again in the *Boston Gazette and Country Journal* between May and July 1766, the earlier transaction probably was more like a mortgage than a sale.[14] Ball advertised another public vendue of this land to be held on 6 May 1767, and a few weeks later he, Simon Hunt, and Thomas Barrett, who had bought the property in 1763, mortgaged it to Jacob Cummens of Roxbury, Massachusetts.[15] By 1769 Ball had paid back enough of his debt so that he could again mortgage the westerly end of the house. The deed indicates that the land surrounding the house was still owned by Jacob Cummens and makes clear that John Ball was now living there. It reads, "westerly End of a dwelling house where I said John Ball now dwell" and describes how the house was divided "thro the kitchen to a Jog in the Jamb of the Chimney thro the House to the Middle of the foor door with the Privilege of improving the South Door the Chamber Stairs & Garrett Stairs for passing and repassing without any Molestation."[16] In March 1773 this property was again sold, this time by Joseph Butler to Thomas Cordis.[17] Whether the property left John Ball's hands permanently because of his inability to pay his debts is not clear, but the Massachusetts tax list for 1771 places Ball in Concord with two polls, two houses, a shop adjoining, £2 annual worth of real estate, and £13.6.8 of merchandise.[18]

Ball's daughter Elizabeth married Amos Flint in 1779, and his son Jonathan married Abigail Child in 1780, the year his wife, Sarah, died.[19] The last reference to Ball appears on a deed he witnessed for the Concord silversmith Samuel Bartlett (q.v.) on 1 September 1781.[20] The date of Ball's death is not known.

Only about two dozen pieces of silver by Ball have been identified. These include five beakers bearing the date 1761 in the First Congregational Church at Lincoln, Massachusetts, and another, bearing the date 1762, in the First Congregational Church at Northborough, Massachusetts. Three marks (A–C) are identified for Ball, including one with both first and surnames. Because tankards at Yale and Historic Deerfield each bear all three marks, the attributions of the initial and surname mark (A) and the surname mark (C) are quite certain. PEK

SURVIVING OBJECTS

	Mark	Inscription	Patron	Date	Reference	Owner
Beaker	A*/B*	The Gift of Mr Joseph Brooks to the Church of Christ in Lincoln 1761	First Congregational Church, Lincoln, Mass., for Joseph Brooks	1761	Jones 1913, 250	

	Mark	Inscription	Patron	Date	Reference	Owner
Four beakers	B	The Gift of Mͬ Joseph Brooks to the Church of Christ in Lincoln 1761	First Congregational Church, Lincoln, Mass., for Joseph Brooks	1761	Jones 1913, 250–51	
Beaker	B	The gift of Capͭ James Eager & Leiuͭ Willͫ Holloway/to the 2ͩ Cͪͪ in Westborough 1762	First Congregational Church and Society, Northborough, Mass., for James Eager and William Holloway	1762	Jones 1913, 350	
Cann	A*/B*	none		ca. 1765		SI
Cann	A/B	MF; OI/to/MI		ca. 1765	MFA 1906, no. 5	
Porringer	B*	S Little (later)		ca. 1765		PMA
Porringer	B	W/WR	William and Rebecca Winthrop	ca. 1760	Hammerslough/ Feigenbaum 1958–73, 1:31	
Ring (gold)	c†	Let virtue be a guide to thee		ca. 1770	Buhler/Hood 1970, no. 299	YUAG
Strainer spoon	A*	MT		ca. 1760	Johnston 1994, 6 (as unknown maker)	CMA
Sugar tongs	c*	none		ca. 1755	Buhler 1972, no. 243	MFAB
Sugar tongs	c	MS		ca. 1755	Christie's, 22–23 January 1993, lot 236	
Tablespoon	A*	F/EB		ca. 1760	YUAG files	
Tablespoon	A*	B/IM		ca. 1760		CM
Tablespoon	A*	AM		ca. 1760		CM
Tablespoon	A*	P/HF		ca. 1770		PEM
Tankard	A*/ B*/c*	M/WM	William and Mary (Nickels) Miller	ca. 1760		HD
Tankard	A†/ B†/ c*	B/WE		ca. 1770	Buhler/Hood 1970, no. 298	YUAG
Teaspoon	c*	DH		ca. 1770	YUAG files	
Teaspoon	c	PB		ca. 1760	DAPC 74.1151	WM
Teaspoon	c*	LA		ca. 1765	Johnston 1994, 6	CMA
Teaspoon	c*	SJ		ca. 1765		CM
Teaspoon	c*	WW		ca. 1770		SFCAI

1. *Concord VR*, 35, 83, 109.
2. *Concord VR*, 9, 34, 60.
3. *Concord VR*, 121.
4. SCD 71:80.
5. Benjamin Greene Ledger, 1734–56, 63, MHS.
6. *Concord VR*, 45, 50, 101, 111, 166, 417.

7. RC 14:81; 17:153. John Ball the scrivener died in 1768.

8. RC 24:262, 265.

9. The births of five children to John and Sarah Ball are recorded in Concord: Elizabeth, 1752; Jonathan, 1755; Marcy, 1757; Thomas Brooks, 1760; and Briggs, 1762. See *Concord VR*, 186, 189, 196, 207, 213.

10. MCD 56:634–35.

11. MCD 59:170–71.

12. MCD 62:174–75.

13. MCD 61:196; 71:215–16.

14. *Boston Gazette and Country Journal*, 26 May, 2, 9, 16, 26, 30 June, and 7, 14, 21, 28 July 1766.

15. MCD 67:467–70. *Boston Gazette and Country Journal*, 20, 27 April, 4 May 1767.

16. MCD 69:337–38.

17. MCD 74:208–09.

18. Pruitt 1978, 196–97.

19. *Concord VR*, 242, 252, 417.

20. MCD 84:56–57.

John Banks
ca. 1696–1737 [+]

The vital records indicate that there were at least two men named John Banks living in Boston during the first half of the eighteenth century. It is unclear whether both worked as goldsmiths. John Banks, son of John Banks, a cooper (d. 1698), and Mehitable Mattocks (b. 1672), daughter of Samuel and Constance (Fairbanks) Mattocks, probably was born about 1696.[1] His father died in 1698, and his mother was made administrator of the estate on 22 June 1698. She married Thomas Webber in 1704 and had four other children.[2]

Mehitable (Mattocks) Banks Webber apprenticed her oldest son to Nathaniel Morse (q.v.) about 1710 but apparently was unhappy with the training he received. In 1712 she brought her grievance to court. Because Mehitable Webber's petition does not survive, the nature of the problem remains unknown. The court, "Upon Reading the Petition of Mehetable Webber in behalf of her Son John Banks an Apprentice to Nathaniel Morse, and his Wife and hearing the whole matter,—Ordered that [t]he said Apprentice Return to the Service of his Mistress in Order to his [*sic*] Instruction in his Trade of a Goldsmith, there to Continue until the Court in January next, a further Direction then to be given, if need be."[3] The matter does not appear again in the court record.

The same John Banks may have completed his apprenticeship with Edward Winslow (q.v.). In 1716 he and Thomas Mullins (Moulin) (q.v.), who was working as a journeyman, witnessed a deed for Winslow.[4] It can be established that it was this John Banks who married Sarah Gwin, daughter of Thomas (b. 1661) and Sarah Gwin, in 1719/20 because the couple, as was the prevailing custom, named their second daughter (1723) after her grandmother. The couple was married by Peter Thacher of the New North Church, which they apparently attended. New North, which split from the Second, or North, Church in 1714, was known as the artisans' church and was distinguished by its retention of traditional Puritan doctrine at a time when most of Boston's churches were liberalizing the requirements for church membership, baptism, and admittance to the Lord's Supper. They had five children between 1721 and 1731, including a son, John, born in 1722.[5] The John Banks who witnessed the bond for the estate administration of John Coney (q.v.) in 1722 may have been the goldsmith.[6]

Evidence from the Boston records strongly suggests that John Banks worked as both a goldsmith and a distiller. It is unclear when Banks started his distilling business. In 1724 he appears as a witness, this time for a deed and a mortgage between the goldsmith Andrew Tyler (q.v.) and the distiller James Gooch. Francis Hill Bigelow posited that Banks was working for Tyler at this time, although it seems possible that he served as a witness because he was Gooch's neighbor.[7] In a deed of 1726, in which Banks mortgaged his house to Gooch, it is stated that his lot in the North End of Boston, on Green Lane, bordered Gooch's land on the north and east. At this point, and in deeds recorded in 1726, 1729, and 1739, Banks appears in the deeds as a distiller. However, the same parcels of land are mentioned in a deed of 1736 in which John Banks identified himself as a goldsmith.[8] One of these lots of land was adjacent to land owned by Knight Leverett (q.v.). Banks was also referred to as a goldsmith when he was sued by the shopkeeper Ephraim Baker in 1732 and by the shopkeeper William Williams in 1735, and as a distiller in a suit dated 1735.[9]

Change in occupation was common in urban areas, particularly for a man of limited means like Banks, who may have practiced more than one trade according to where he could find work. Living close to the distiller Gooch, Banks may have decided to enter what was at that time a lucrative calling and may actually have carried on the two businesses simultaneously, identifying himself in the public record according to which profession seemed the most important at any one time.

The date of John Banks's death is unknown. Bigelow did not find him in the Boston death records, and his estate was not probated.[10] He may have died about 1740. A Sarah Banks, either his widow or his daughter, married Thomas Foster, Jr., on 8 January 1740.[11] It is also possible that, like many other Boston artisans, Banks left town to ply his trade elsewhere. However, although the name appears frequently in Connecticut as well as in other Massachusetts towns, no other John Banks appears who is listed as a goldsmith.

No objects made by John Banks are known. BMW

1. RC 9:124, 217.
2. RC 28:17; SCPR 14:11, docket 2459.
3. SCCR, Court of General Sessions of the Peace Record Book, vol. 3 (1712–19), 5.
4. SCD 33:154, dated 28 March 1716, witnessed 28 July 1716.
5. RC 28:80; RC 24:142, 153, 159, 191, 201.
6. Another John Banks, who resided in Boston and married Elizabeth Gill in 1719, may have been the witness for the Coney estate administration; see RC 28:80.
7. Bigelow-Phillips files, 798.
8. SCD 38:49; 40:35, 206–07; 43:38; 44:135–36; 58:203–04; 54:113.
9. SCCR, Court of Common Pleas Record Book 1732, 255, session of 27 July 1732; SCCR, Court of Common Pleas Record Book 1735, 32; SCCR, Court of Common Pleas, session of October 1735, file papers. He was identified as a goldsmith in two additional suits: with the baker Jonathan Furnall in 1735 and the mariner Samuel Butler in 1736. See SCCR, Court of Common Pleas Record Book 1735–36, 546, and 1736–37, 127. John M. Fitzgerald to Francis Hill Bigelow, List of Boston Court Record References to Silversmiths, Bigelow-Phillips files.
10. Bigelow-Phillips files, 798–99.
11. RC 28:245.

Abraham Barnes
w. ca. 1716

Abraham Barnes is listed as a silver and gold cupmaker in the list of arrivals to the city of Boston aboard the ship *Globe* from Ireland in June of 1716.[1] There is no record of his apprenticeship in the Goldsmiths' Companies of either London or Dublin, and he does not appear in the Suffolk County court or probate records. BMW

1. RC 29:236.

James Barnes, Jr.
1680–1721?

James Barnes, Jr., apparently had a very short career as a goldsmith. Two key documents identify him as a member of the craft, but other facts of his life are ambiguous. A document that links him to Edward Winslow (q.v.) suggests that he was the son of a prominent and wealthy man. He was probably the son of James Barnes, Sr. (d. 1711), merchant and baker, and his second wife, Temperance.[1] The elder James served as a selectman and assessor of Boston several times between 1696 and 1709. He also served as representative in 1700, 1708, 1709, and 1710.[2] He was part owner of eight ships, including the *Unity*, in which Jeremiah Dummer (q.v.) owned a share. He was also full owner of two ships, the *Endeavor* and the *Swan*, on which his son Thomas served as master.[3] The elder James's partnership with Dummer suggests that he may have apprenticed his son James to him, perhaps as much to learn the trade of merchant as that of goldsmith.

When James achieved his majority in 1701, his father must have provided him with enough capital to establish his own business, for in December 1702 James Barnes, Jr., and Edward Winslow, goldsmiths, appeared as sureties for Henry Hurst (q.v.), for the sum of two hundred pounds, in a suit before the Supreme Judicial Court of Suffolk County.[4] It is possible that Barnes and Winslow had entered into a brief partnership at this time. The following year, James Barnes, merchant, and James Barnes, Jr., goldsmith, were found by the Court of General Sessions not guilty of the charge of "making and stamping with the French Kings Armes Sundry Peices of Mettal & emitting the same at the value of a penny each."[5]

In 1708 James married Mary Tay (d. before 1727), daughter of Isaiah Tay (1650–1730), a shopkeeper of Boston who served several times with James Barnes, Sr., as a selectman. They had six children: Huldah (b. 1710), who married Benjamin Edes, a mariner; James (b. 1711/12), who became a tobacconist; Isaiah (b. 1714/15), who appears listed as a laborer; John (b. 1716/17–d. before 1727); Benjamin (b. 1718–d. before 1727); and Peter (b. 1719/20–d. before 1727).[6]

The estate of the elder James Barnes was probated on 13 August 1711. In his will he divided his estate among his sons James, John, Benjamin, Peter, and the children of his deceased son Thomas.[7] By his father's will James evidently inherited a substantial estate and presumably ceased working as a goldsmith. Thereafter, he is listed first as a baker and later as a wharfinger.[8] In 1719, he began renting a wharf from the town, and in 1720, John Coney (q.v.), owner of the adjacent wharf, petitioned the town, arguing that it had no right to let the wharf to Barnes.[9] The following year Barnes appears in the town records again, this time in a petition for a license to sell liquor at a house near Bull Wharf.[10]

No record of James Barnes's death exists, and from documentary evidence two possible scenarios can be developed for him in the 1720s. Barnes may have died in 1721, for in 1722 a Mary Barnes began petitioning the town for a license to sell liquor.[11] On the other hand, Barnes's wife may have died, and the James Barnes who married Mary Gross in 1724/25 could have been the wharfinger and former goldsmith, and the father of the Mary Barnes born in 1725/26.[12] In March 1727/28, when Isaiah Tay wrote his will, he mentioned his daughter Mary as being deceased and bequeathed her portion of the estate to her surviving children, Huldah Edes, James, Jr., and Isaiah.[13] The designation of James as junior suggests either that his father was still living or that he had other relatives by that name who were still living in Boston.[14] The legatees of the will of Isaiah Tay conveyed land to the merchant Peter Thomas and the goldsmith Andrew Tyler (q.v.), overseers of the will, on 25 April 1735.[15] The will also mentions that Thomas Savage, Sr. (q.v.), was Isaiah Tay's tenant.

No objects marked by James Barnes have been identified. BMW

1. RC 9:151.
2. RC 7:225, 229, 243; RC 8:22–25, 37–39, 41–43, 45–48, 54–55, 58–60, 61–62, 64–69, 72–76; RC 11:56, 57, 88, 93, 100, 104.
3. Mass. Archives 7:87, 95, 118, 140, 141, 144, 162, 212, 250, 280, 310.
4. SCCR, file 5565ᵃ.
5. SCCR, Court of General Sessions of the Peace Record Book 1702–12, 14.
6. Savage 1860–62, 4:258; RC 28:18; RC 24:66, 74, 96, 112, 128, 135.
7. SCPR 17:287, docket 3335. There is no inventory of the estate.
8. In 1712, James Barnes, identified as a baker, bought land from William Lackey (SCD 31:74), and from John, Peter, and Benjamin Barnes, his brothers (SCD 28:176). By 1720, after he leased the wharf from the town, James Barnes is listed as a wharfinger in a deed of the legatees of the estate of the merchant James Barnes to the cooper John Marshall (see Thwing).
9. RC 13:50, 67, 74.
10. RC 13:84.
11. RC 13:98–99, 139.
12. RC 24:168; RC 28:118.
13. SCPR 28:71–74.
14. It is also possible that the James Barnes who married Mary Gross was James, son of Thomas and Lydia, who was born in 1703 (RC 24:19). The latter would have been about ten years older than the James Barnes, Jr., mentioned in reference to the estate of Isaiah Tay.
15. The overseers in turn conveyed the land to the widow Sarah Jones, one of the legatees. The deeds give occupations of all legatees, including the children of Mary Tay and James Barnes; SCD 50:210–12.

Nathaniel Barrett
1748–1827

Little is known about the early life and career of Nathaniel Barrett, a hitherto unknown silversmith. According to Nantucket vital records, he was born on 22 December 1748, but since no parentage appears for him there, he may actually have been born on the New England mainland and later migrated to Nantucket.[1] The Nantucket silversmith Samuel Barrett (q.v.), or more likely John Jackson (q.v.), may have been his master, if Nathaniel was on the island by 1762, the year he would have begun an apprenticeship.

Barrett married Eunice Gardner (1750–78) of Nantucket on 12 May 1774.[2] She was the daughter of Grafton Gardner (1707–89) and Abigail Coffin (ca. 1712–96) of Edgartown, Martha's Vineyard, who were married on 22 September 1730 in Edgartown.[3] Nathaniel and Eunice Barrett had two children before her death in 1778.[4]

Barrett married his second wife, Margaret (Brock) Coffin (1752–1837), the widow of Jethro Coffin of Nantucket, on 3 June 1779, and the couple had six children.[5] Margaret was the daughter of John Brock (1728–1816) and Anna Bunker (1728–64), both of Nantucket, who married on 13 March 1746;[6] her maternal grandparents were Caleb Bunker (1699–1777) and Priscilla (Bunker) Coffin (1703–95) of Nantucket.[7] Caleb and Priscilla Bunker were also the paternal grandparents of the Nantucket silversmith Benjamin Bunker (q.v.), making him and Margaret first cousins. Nathaniel and Margaret's marriage brought the two silversmiths, who may have trained with the same master, into the same family.

Benjamin Bunker, Nathaniel Barrett, and Margaret Brock Barrett's relationships are revealed in the deeds documenting land transactions related to Margaret's inheritance of property from her grandfather Caleb Bunker. Five deeds dated between 1787 and 1817 specifically named Bunker and Barrett, three listing Bunker's trade and two listing Barrett's.[8] Indeed, the numerous deeds transacted by Nathaniel Barrett were nearly all related to the sale of property inherited through his two wives.[9] His only known purchase of land occurred in 1802, when Barrett purchased a homestead in Nantucket for $600.[10]

Probate records for Barrett at his death in 1827 list his trade as silversmith, but no tools or objects appear in the inventory to prove that he was still practicing his craft at the end of his life. His modest estate included a small amount of furniture, some crockery, woodenware, a Bible, and one silver watch valued at $10; the homestead he had purchased for $600 was devalued in his estate to $350.[11]

No familial relationship has been established between Nathaniel and the Nantucket silversmith Samuel Barrett, and no silver can be attributed with any certainty to Nathaniel Barrett's hand. jjf

1. *Nantucket VR* 1:98.
2. *Nantucket VR* 2:34; 3:86; 5:57; NCCR, Court of General Sessions of the Peace, 1:18.
3. *Nantucket VR* 2:40, 5:301; *Edgartown VR*, 20, 107.
4. *Nantucket VR* 1:96, 98.
5. *Nantucket VR* 1:123; 3:278; 5:57; NCCR, Court of General Sessions of the Peace, 1:23. Children of Nathaniel and Margaret: Margaret, b. 1780; John, b. 1782; Priscilla, b. 1784; Jethro, b. 1786; Peter, b. 1789; Samuel, b. 1793. *Nantucket VR* 1:97–98.
6. *Nantucket VR* 1:122, 137; 3:133; 5:71.
7. *Nantucket VR* 1:139, 158; 5:82, 92.
8. NCD 13:277–78; 14:199; 15:121; 19:5–6; 24:323–24.
9. NCD 9:534; 13:277–78; 15:121; 19:5–6, 55–56, 95–96, 99–100, 103–04, 107–08, 262–64; 20:126–27, 280; 21:131, 301–02; 22:340; 24:323–24, 327–28.
10. NCD 16:519.
11. NCPR 12:247–48, 252.

Samuel Barrett
ca. 1735–1815

A

Samuel Barrett probably was baptized in Cambridge, Massachusetts, on 3 August 1735 and most likely was the son of William Barrett (b. 1696/97) of Cambridge and Mary Church of Watertown, Massachusetts, who were married on 28 December 1727.[1] His paternal grandfather may have been William Barrett (b. 1665) of Cambridge; his maternal grandparents are unknown.[2]

Assuming a birth date of 1735, Barrett would have begun his apprenticeship about 1749 and completed it about 1756, but his master is unknown. Barrett may have worked as a journeyman on the mainland in these early years, which could explain his absence from the public record until his move to Nantucket.

Barrett married Sarah Manning (1737–97) of Cambridge on 26 August 1762 at Christ Church, Boston.[3] She may have been the daughter of William Manning (b. 1700) of Cambridge and Mary White (1702/03–74) of Charlestown, Massachusetts, who married in Charlestown.[4]

Shortly after the birth of their first son, Samuel, on 7 March 1763, Barrett moved his family to the island of Nantucket in the hope of establishing himself there as a silversmith.[5] This plan was thwarted in May of that year; the Nantucket court records for that month state that "one Samuel Barrot [*sic*] of Boston in the County of Suffolk Goldsmith came from Boston about one week past with a Design to settle and live in this town and as we are not in want of any such tradesmen in this town it may be a bad consequence to this town you are therefore required to warn the sd Samuel Barrot that he depart from this town as soon as may be or he will be proceeded against."[6] If the Nantucket silversmith John Jackson (q.v.) initiated this formal warning, he and Barrett nevertheless must have subsequently achieved a relatively amicable relationship. The two joined in 1768 to provide a character reference for John Jones, as recorded in a joint letter to the Salem silversmith John Touzell (q.v.):

M[r] Touzel   Nantuckett June 8

                                                      1768

        Sir In anshur to your Leter

        Respeecting the Careture of John Jons we Cannot Say
        that he was convicted of Theft hear but Strongly
        Suspected being of a Low blackgard mak and was
        very burthensum to the Inhabentance of the Island
        and was orderd of [f] by the authority and when
        they had got him off would Not bring him a
        gain. which is all we Say at prasent yours to
        Sarve
                        John Jackson

        Mr Touzel Sir I wold further informe
        you of Said Jones that he Came to Nantuckett
        about the first of December 1766 and wose in my
        Shop Servel times and on the 10 of Said month my
        Shop wose Broken open and the things wich he
        wonted of me Befor wose taken away wich wose Boxes files
        &c for he Pretended to Be a tinker hear and tole me
        that he Sarved [h]is time with a Copper-Smith
        and Sir I Shuld Be wary Glad if you wold lett me
        hear how you make out with this Bad man
                Yours to Sarve   Sam[l] Barrett[7]

Although records of apprenticeship do not survive, Barrett may have trained Nathaniel Barrett (q.v.) and Benjamin Bunker (q.v.).

By 1774, more than ten years after his arrival on Nantucket, Barrett became sufficiently well established to purchase the dwelling house and land that he had occupied and presumably used as a shop.[8] Barrett also had joined the Union Lodge of Nantucket by then and became fourth master from 1774 until 1798.[9] Five additional children, Francis, John, Sarah, George, and Elizabeth, were born to Samuel and Sarah between 1768 and 1775.[10]

Sarah (Manning) Barrett died on 7 January 1797. In October of that year, at the age of sixty-two, Barrett sold his dwelling house, land, and goldsmith shop to his son Francis for $327.50, while retaining access to the shop: "hereby Reserving only for my self the Liberty & priviledge of my Goldsmiths Shop to Stand and abide on the Front of said Land. so long as my self shall want s'd Shop to work in."[11] Several months later, on 21 November 1797, Barrett married his second wife, Sally (Tilden) Wendell Gardner (1743–1821).

The nine known deeds transacted by Barrett all refer to him as a goldsmith of Sherburne, known as the town of Nantucket after 1795.[12] In spite of this consistency and the length of his tenure as a self-described craftsman on the island, only spoons survive as testimony of his activities. His mark is S·BARRETT within a rectangle (A). The mark is also recorded with a period and with star pseudo-hallmarks; however, examples of these marks were not located.[13]

Although no probate papers survive for Barrett, the will of his second wife, Sally, mentions a gift of one silver porringer to her natural daughter Sally (Wendell) Macy, wife of Peleg, and a spoon, engraved "JW to RW," to her deceased husband's granddaughter Rebecca (Barrett) Gardner. Sally Barrett's inventory included a porringer and spoon (probably those mentioned in her will), seven tablespoons, six teaspoons, one pair of silver tongs, and one pepper caster. Although no holloware by Barrett is known today, it is possible that this silver was made by his hand.[14] JJF

SURVIVING OBJECTS

	Mark	Inscription	Patron	Date	Reference	Owner
Tablespoon	A	Solomon Gardner	Solomon Gardner	ca. 1765	Bigelow 1917, 268–69	
Tablespoon	A†	G/GR		ca. 1765	DAPC 70.1227	WM
Tablespoon (part of a service)	A*	AG	Anna (Gardner) Smith	ca. 1790		YUAG
Tablespoon	A*	TRB/NB (later)		ca. 1765	DAPC 72.3408	WM
Tablespoon	A*	I Bunk/born Decr./ 19 17 [illeg.]	I. Bunk	ca. 1775		YUAG
Tablespoon	A*	WC		ca. 1765		YUAG
Three tablespoons	A	FWC/1872 (later)		ca. 1785		CHS
Teaspoon	A*	WLB		ca. 1790	Flynt/Fales 1968, 153 (mark only)	HD
Five teaspoons	A	SI		ca. 1790		NHA
Teaspoon	A	EB		ca. 1765	Avery 1920, no. 196	MMA
Teaspoon	A*	JRF	John and Rebecca (Barrett) Fitch	ca. 1795		YUAG
Teaspoon (part of a service)	A*	AG	Anna (Gardner) Smith	ca. 1790		YUAG
Teaspoon	A*	P/BI		ca. 1770		YUAG
Teaspoon	A	RM		ca. 1805	DAPC 75.3057	WM
Teaspoon	A*	C/MC (altered to C/ MA)		ca. 1770	DAPC 74.1216	WM
Teaspoon	A	RC	Richard Coffin	ca. 1770		NHA

1. *Cambridge VR* 1:43 notes a "Samuel son of William" who was baptized on 3 August 1735 in the First Congregational Church of that town; *Nantucket VR* 5:58. A birth record of 22 April 1740 for Samuel Barrett listed in *Nantucket VR* 1:98 probably is inaccurate, or it may document the birth of another individual. *Cambridge VR* 2:26.
2. *Cambridge VR* 1:42.
3. *Cambridge VR* 1:462; *Nantucket VR* 5:58; RC 30:333.
4. *Cambridge VR* 1:462; 2:255, 649; *Charlestown VR* 1:197, 282.
5. *Nantucket VR* 1:98: "Samuel, son of Samuel of Boston and Sarah Manning." Samuel's birth does not appear in mainland records and was probably entered in Nantucket at a later date.
6. NCCR as cited in Carpenter/Carpenter 1987, 128.
7. English-Touzel-Hathorne Papers, box 4, folder 1, PEM.
8. NCD 9:83.

9. Flynt/Fales 1968, 153.
10. *Nantucket VR* 1:96–99, which cites church record, First Methodist Episcopal Church.
11. NCD 15:88.
12. NCD 9:83, 560; 11:548; 14:85; 15:88–89; 16:27, 376; 17:26, 255.
13. Ensko 1948, 231; Thorn 1949, 19; Kovel 1961, 24.
14. NCPR 6:222, 347–48; *Nantucket VR* 1:98; 3:86.

Nathaniel Barstow
1717–ca. 1788

Nathaniel Barstow (Bestow) was baptized in the Second Church of Scituate, Massachusetts, on 11 August 1717.[1] His parents were Benjamin Barstow (1690–1751) and Mercy Randall (1684/85–1728), both of Scituate, who were married there on 20 December 1709. Benjamin Barstow was a shipwright who operated a shipyard established by his family on the North River.[2] Nathaniel's paternal grandparents were William (b. 1652) and Sarah Barstow of Scituate.[3] Nathaniel's maternal grandparents were Joseph Randall (1645–1723) of Scituate and Hannah Maycumber (b. 1652) of Marshfield, Massachusetts.[4]

Barstow's master is unknown, but he may have apprenticed with Ephraim Cobb (q.v.) of Plymouth, about twenty miles down the coast from Scituate. Cobb would have just finished his apprenticeship and begun working on his own in Plymouth in 1730, when Barstow would have been thirteen years of age. Sometime after finishing his apprenticeship, Barstow moved to Sunderland, Massachusetts, in the Connecticut River Valley.

The first record of Barstow's life in Sunderland is his marriage there on 28 May 1745 to Martha Hovey (1724–1803) of Hatfield, the daughter of Thomas Hovey, Jr. (1680–1728), of Hadley, Massachusetts, and his second wife, Hannah Dickenson (1689–1758) of Amherst, Massachusetts.[5] Martha Hovey cared for her mentally unstable widowed mother Hannah from the age of eighteen through the early years of her marriage to Barstow until Hannah's death in 1758. In 1759, Hannah Hovey's guardian, Jonathan Russell, compensated the Barstows for their years of service, awarding Nathaniel Barstow £228.4.11. This money may have allowed the silversmith to make the first of his land purchases, because the same document records Barstow's purchase of three lots of land formerly in Hannah Hovey's possession.[6]

Of the ten land transactions known to have been made by Barstow between 1759 and 1787, only in one, dated 1781, is he identified as a goldsmith.[7] In the history of his wife's family written by Daniel Hovey, Barstow is called a farmer and buckle maker.[8] He is listed in the Massachusetts tax list of 1771 with two polls, two houses and shops adjoining, real estate worth twenty pounds annually, and considerable livestock and land, which would bear out the description of him as a farmer.[9] In his will, written in Sunderland on 29 June 1787, when he was seventy years of age, Barstow identified himself as a yeoman. There he named his wife, Martha, as the beneficiary of his entire personal estate during her lifetime. The will was administered in March 1789, suggesting that Barstow died between late 1788 and early 1789.[10]

No silver from Barstow's hand has been found. JJF

1. *Scituate VR* 1:34.
2. *Scituate VR* 1:33, 307; 2:245; Radasch 1966, 12; PCPR, docket 1148.
3. *Scituate VR* 1:32.
4. *Scituate VR* 1:307; 2:245, 436.
5. Sunderland VR, n.p., Corbin Ms. Coll., NEHGS, reel 82–36; Wells/Wells 1910, 428; Sunderland

Marriages 1720–1843, 77, Corbin Ms. Coll., NEHGS, reel 82–36; Sunderland Cemetery, grave-
stone no. 425 and Sunderland Deaths 1721–1893, n.p., Corbin Ms. Coll., NEHGS, reel 82–36;
Hovey 1913, 60, 62; Hatfield Marriages, 119, Corbin Ms. Coll., NEHGS, Reel 82–36. Hannah
Hovey's death date has been established from her estate administration, which records that
Nathaniel Barstow was reimbursed for her care until 5 November 1758; HaCPR, box 74, file 26.

6. HaCPR, box 74, file 26.

7. FCD 2:27–28. In other deeds he is identified as a yeoman or husbandman; HCD 23:171; FCD
1:92, 100; 2:249–50. Other deeds list no occupation: FCD, Hampshire Abstracts, 2:440; 4:114;
HCD 12:86; 23:468–69.

8. Hovey 1913, 62.

9. Pruitt 1978, 462–63.

10. HaCPR, box 10, file 34.

N. Bartlet
w. ca. 1765–1810

A

B

The identity of N. Bartlet remains a mystery. Ensko was the first scholar to
publish N. Bartlet's location as Concord, Massachusetts, and since 1927 the
standard literature has repeated that information. Upon no apparent basis,
Nathaniel has been identified as the name represented by the initial N.[1] Spoons
marked N·BARTLET (A) and N·B (B) have seven-lobed shells reminiscent of
those found on Massachusetts examples, which suggests that their maker
worked in the colony. A few of the spoons have intricate floral drops.[2] However,
no evidence has been found to confirm that a silversmith named N. Bartlet
worked in Concord. A search through Massachusetts vital records suggests
that N. Bartlet was more likely to have worked in Essex or Plymouth counties
because the name turns up in those locations frequently.[3] Thus far, however,
no concrete proof has been found to document the presence of a silversmith
named N. Bartlet in either county. PEK

SURVIVING OBJECTS

	Mark	Inscription	Patron	Date	Reference	Owner
Tablespoon	A	EL		ca. 1760	Avery 1920, no. 67	MMA
Tablespoon	A*	S (over earlier initials)		ca. 1765		PEM
Tablespoon	A†	DC/1783 (later)		ca. 1760	DAPC 75.5285	WM
Tablespoon	A*	C/SS		ca. 1760	Hammerslough/ Feigenbaum 1958–73, 3:122–23	
Two Tablespoons	A	DT		ca. 1810	YUAG files	
Teaspoon	B†	SB		ca. 1760	Buhler/Hood 1970, no. 292	YUAG
Teaspoon	B*	HG		ca. 1760	Buhler/Hood 1970, no. 293	YUAG
Teaspoon	B*	JS		ca. 1760	DAPC 74.1337	WM
Teaspoon	B*	SS		ca. 1810	DAPC 74.1430	WM
Teaspoon	B*	S/IM		ca. 1770		YUAG
Teaspoon	B*	IS/to/HC		ca. 1770		HD
Teaspoon	B*	S/EH		ca. 1770		CM
Four teaspoons	B	DB		ca. 1810	YUAG files	

1. French (1917) 1967, 11; Ensko 1927, 62; Graham 1936, 6; Okie 1936, 242; Ensko 1937, 59; Ensko 1948, 19; Thorn 1949, 20 (all show N.BARTLETT in a rectangle); Kovel 1961, 24 (shows N BARTLETT in a rectangle); Flynt/Fales 1968, 154; Belden 1980, 50.

2. Hammerslough/Feigenbaum 1958–73, 3:122.

3. For instance, the Massachusetts tax list of 1771 includes two Nathaniel Bartlets in Plymouth. See Pruitt 1978, 658–59.

Israel Bartlett
1748–1838

Unknown artist. Israel Bartlett, *ca. 1820, silhouette. Reproduced from George Wingate Chase,* The History of Haverhill *(1861), opposite page 620.*

A

B

Israel Bartlett was born in Newbury, Massachusetts, on 8 May 1748, the son of Israel (1712–54) and Love Bartlett. He was the grandson of Thomas (1681–1744) and Sarah (Webster) Bartlett (1685–1726/27). When his father died in 1754, tradition records that young Israel went to live with his uncle at Bartlett's Cove, until he was apprenticed, possibly to Joseph Moulton (1724–95) (q.v.) in Newbury. (Moulton was related to Israel through the Websters.) At the completion of his apprenticeship, probably about 1769, he is said to have worked in Newbury. He married Tabitha Walker (1751–1824) in Haverhill, Massachusetts, on 8 June 1775, and they had nine children. About 1800, he moved to Haverhill, where he remained for the rest of his long life.[1]

Although never an important silversmith, Bartlett was involved in the military and in politics and was an esteemed citizen of Haverhill. He entertained George Washington at his house on the northeast corner of Water and Kent streets. The house was valued at $950 in 1798. He was remembered in an early town history in the following manner:

> Though his early education was limited, Mr. Bartlett made such good use of his odd hours, that he became well versed in ancient and modern history, and familiar with the standard literature of his day. He enjoyed, deservedly, the respect and attachment of all who knew him. In his earlier years, he was active in the service of his country; he was present at the surrender of Burgoyne, and has left a brief account of that expedition. In 1810 and 11, also from 1816 to 21, he served the Commonwealth as a member of the State Senate. He sustained various offices in the town, and always discharged his duties with great fidelity. Shortly before his death, at the advanced age of 90, he received a renewal of his appointment, as a justice of the Peace.
>
> For very many years he was an honored and consistent member of the First Church in this town, and, at the ripe age of 90 years, he went down to his grave strong in the hope of a glorious immortality.[2]

Bartlett died on 21 April 1838, and his estate was appraised by Caleb Hersey, Chauncey Hastings, and William Caldwell on 9 June. The value of his estate was $4,274.31, including his "Dwelling House & Garden" ($2,500), land on Kent Street ($1,000), and his "Shop & Land [on] Merrimack Street" ($450). His personal estate, which is enumerated in detail, included 78 oz. 10 dwt. of silver plate ($78.50). The "Articles in Shop on Merrimack St." included

1 Glass Case	.75
1 Rolling Mill	15.00
1 Anvil	1.00
1 Lot of old Iron	1.00
Scales & Beam	1.00
1 more Anvill	2.50
Lot of old Tools	5.00
Money scales & Waitt	1.00
another Anvill	2.00
1 Desk	1.00
1 Show Case	1.50

These goods were valued at $31.75. In the settlement of the estate, which dragged on into the 1850s, the shop was sold for $448.49.[3]

Although he seems to have been in business for nearly seventy years, few objects by Bartlett are known. His mark is usually given as I·BARTLET in a serrated rectangle (A).[4] An initials mark IB (B), sometimes attributed to John Bedford of Fishkill, New York, may have been used by Bartlett because it is found on a spoon with a Bartlett family history.[5] A few additional spoons with this mark and distinctive drops of roulette work have been recorded. A silhouette of Bartlett has been published (illus.).[6] GWRW

SURVIVING OBJECTS

	Mark	Inscription	Patron	Date	Reference	Owner
Tablespoon	A†	EB		ca. 1815	DAPC 75.2843	WM
Tablespoon	A	?		?		RISD
Tablespoon	B†	RL (later)		ca. 1805	Buhler/Hood 1970, no. 720 (as John Bedford)	YUAG
Tablespoon	B*	TB (+)	Bartlett family	ca. 1805	DAPC 75.3689	
Tablespoon	B*	SW		ca. 1805	DAPC 86.2017	
Two tablespoons	B*	HS (+)		ca. 1800	DAPC 86.2619	
Teaspoon	A*	DK		ca. 1805		YUAG

1. *Newbury VR* 1:40, 44, 536, 537; 2:36, 545; *Bradford VR*, 162; *Haverhill VR* 2:27, 356; *Index of Obituaries, 1784–1840*, 1:279; ECPR 334:164, docket 1881. Some sources indicate that he was born in Nottingham, New Hampshire; see Chase 1861, 621; see also pp. 428, 447, 466, 661. Another such source indicates that he was the son of Samuel Bartlett; see Cogswell (1878) 1972, 167.
2. Chase 1861, 621.
3. ECPR, docket 1883. Bartlett's death is also recorded in *Haverhill VR* 2:355; *Index of Obituaries, 1784–1840*, 1:273.
4. Currier 1938, 11; Ensko 1989, 14, 278; Flynt/Fales 1968, 154; Belden 1980, 50.
5. DAPC 75.3689.
6. Chase 1861, facing p. 620.

Samuel Bartlett
1752–1821

A

B

C

Samuel Bartlett probably was born in Boston on 17 November 1752, the son of Roger Bartlett (1725/26–1805), a sea captain from Branscombe, Devonshire, England, and Anna Hurd (1723/24–91), who married in Charlestown, Massachusetts, on 10 October 1749.[1] His paternal grandparents were Roger Bartlett (b. 1695) and Mary Norket (b. 1702 or 1711).[2] His maternal grandparents were Benjamin Hurd (1678–1750) and Elizabeth Barlow (b. 1686) of Charlestown.[3]

According to a biographical sketch written in 1858, Bartlett had been studying for a professional career when he was deafened by gunfire during the Boston Massacre in 1770 and therefore had to relinquish his studies. He was then apprenticed to Samuel Minott (q.v.), but about the time he finished his training the Revolution broke out, and he moved to Woburn, Massachusetts, with his family.[4] Before leaving Boston, Bartlett married Polly Barrett (1752–1823) on 29 September 1776.[5] She was the daughter of Isaiah Barrett (1715–81), a Boston merchant, and Elizabeth Wadsworth (1720–56).[6] By year's end, Bartlett and his wife had moved to Concord, Massachusetts.

Soon after arriving in Concord, Bartlett acquired a parcel of land in the southern part of town.[7] In 1781 he bought some land near the meetinghouse but sold a portion.[8] John Ball (q.v.) witnessed the deed for the latter transaction.[9] It was on this land near the meetinghouse that Bartlett may have had his shop. In 1789 Bartlett sold that land, which now included a shop, when he bought a house near the burying ground, where he perhaps incorporated his shop.[10] During this period Bartlett gained social prominence in Concord, becoming a member of the town's Social Circle, a club that met regularly to discuss events of civil, political, and religious interest.[11]

In 1794 Bartlett was elected registrar of deeds for Middlesex County, a position with administrative responsibilities that may have eclipsed his silversmithing career.[12] He moved to Cambridge, Massachusetts, shortly after his election as registrar, selling his land and house in Concord.[13] In 1811 Bartlett and his wife transferred their membership from the Concord to the Cambridge church.[14] He held the office of registrar of deeds until his death in 1821.[15] His estate amounted to $4,765.84.[16]

More than four dozen pieces of holloware and flatware by Samuel Bartlett are known. The key objects for identifying his work are a pair of flagons made for the First Parish, Concord, each bearing his initial and surname mark (A) as well as a script initials mark (B). A variation of the script initials mark (C) appears on a miniature teapot at Yale. Another initials mark sometimes has been attributed to him.[17] Three canns, two ladles, and two porringers also bear the mark of Joseph Loring (q.v.), and a strainer in the Concord Museum also bears the mark of Samuel Minott. These pieces suggest that Bartlett may have retailed the work of Boston makers in Concord or that he supplied pieces to Minott and Loring to retail in Boston. PEK

SURVIVING OBJECTS

	Mark	Inscription	Patron	Date	Reference	Owner
Cann	A	HHEW to TEW		ca. 1785	American Art Association–Anderson Galleries, 22–23 January 1937, lot 290	
Cann	A*	II; unidentified arms (later)		ca. 1780		CM
Cann	A	H(or IC)M		ca. 1785	YUAG files	
Cann (altered to milk pot; with mark of Joseph Loring)	B*	H?; BL (later)		ca. 1775	DAPC 77.3001	
Cann	B*	W/JH		ca. 1775	Johnston 1994, 7	CMA
Cann (with mark of Joseph Loring)	B or C	C/EM		ca. 1785	Antiques 68 (July 1955): 26	
Cann (with mark of Joseph Loring)	B or C	TEP	Theophilus and Elizabeth (Greenleaf) Parsons	ca. 1785	Buhler 1965, 113–15	HMA

	Mark	Inscription	Patron	Date	Reference	Owner
Cann	?	unidentified initials		ca. 1780	Parke-Bernet, 26–27 January 1945, lot 168	
Creampot	B†	none		ca. 1785	Buhler/Hood 1970, no. 289	YUAG
Creampot	B*	none		ca. 1780	*Silver Supplement* 1973, no. 79	CM
Creampot	B*	N/WB		ca. 1775	Parke-Bernet, 17–20 May 1944, lot 642	CM
Flagon	A†	The Gift/of/Deacon Thomas Waite/ to/The First Church of Christ/ in/Boston/May 15th, 1775	First Church, Boston, for Thomas Waite	1775	Jones 1913, 31–32	
Two flagons	A*/B*	The gift/of/John Cuming Esq:/to the Church/in Concord	First Parish, Concord, Mass., for John Cuming	1793	Jones 1913, 135	
Ladle (with mark of Joseph Loring)	B or C	OAC		ca. 1785	*Antiques* 68 (July 1955): 26	
Ladle (with mark of Joseph Loring)	?	?		ca. 1785		CHM
Porringer	A	H/TA		ca. 1785	YUAG files	
Porringer	A	Charles James Ellis/ from/Harriet Lewis (later)		ca. 1780	YUAG files	
Porringer	A*	LH	Lucy (Hubbard) Rice	ca. 1785		CM
Porringer	A*	AF		ca. 1780		CM
Porringer (with mark of Joseph Loring; mate below)	A	L/IM; 1765 (later)	Joseph and Mary (Atkins) Loring	ca. 1780	*Antiques* 92 (August 1967): 139	
Porringer (with mark of Joseph Loring; mate above)	A*	L/IM	Joseph and Mary (Atkins) Loring	ca. 1780		CM
Two salts	B*	MB		ca. 1785		CM
Salt	B or C	A/DS; TP (later)		ca. 1780	Hammerslough/ Feigenbaum 1958–73, 4:77	
Two shoe buckles	A*	?		ca. 1780	*Silver* 23 (July–August 1990): 19–20	
Two shoe buckles	A*	none		ca. 1780		CM
Spoon	B*	?		ca. 1780	YUAG files	
Strainer (with mark of Samuel Minott)	B*	none		ca. 1790	*Silver Supplement* 1973, no. 80	CM
Tablespoon	A*	H/SM		ca. 1780		CM

	Mark	Inscription	Patron	Date	Reference	Owner
Tablespoon	B*	PH		ca. 1790		CM
Tankard	A	The Gift/of/Isaac Biglow A.M./To the Church of Christ/ in/WESTON/1777	Executors of Isaac Bigelow's estate for First Parish, Weston, Mass.	ca. 1785	Jones 1913, 486	
Teapot (miniature)	C†	T(or J)LB		ca. 1780	Buhler/Hood 1970, no. 288	YUAG
Teaspoon	B*	RW		ca. 1780	Eitner 1976, no. 88	
Teaspoon	B	PW		ca. 1775	DAPC 74.1416	WM
Teaspoon	B*	RB	Ruth Brooks	ca. 1780	DAPC 75.2473	WM
Four teaspoons	B*	IC		ca. 1775	YUAG files	
Teaspoon	B or C	?		ca. 1780	YUAG files	
Teaspoon	B or C	SL		ca. 1780	YUAG files	
Teaspoon	B or C	EB/to/AB		ca. 1790	Buhler 1979, no. 71	WAM
Four wine cups	B	The gift/of/John Cuming Esq:/to the Church/in Concord	First Parish, Concord, Mass., for John Cuming	ca. 1793	Jones 1913, 134	
Wine cup	B	The property/of the Church/in Concord	First Parish, Concord, Mass.	ca. 1793	Jones 1913, 135	
Wine cup	B*	The gift of/Richard Kates/to the Church/in Concord	First Parish, Concord, Mass., for Richard Kates	ca. 1793	Jones 1913, 134	
Two wine cups	B	The Widow/Mary Sartell/to the/Church of Christ/in Groton/1792	First Parish, Groton, Mass., for Mary Sartell	ca. 1792	Jones 1913, 192	

1. No record of Samuel Bartlett's birth has been found. *Index of Obituaries, 1784–1840*, 1:278; RC 28:292; *Charlestown VR* 1:284, 373; *Index of Obituaries, 1704–1800*, 2:62.
2. *Register of the Parish of Branscombe*, 14, 75, 87.
3. *Charlestown VR* 1:103, 132, 213; Griffen 1952, 62.
4. *Social Circle in Concord* 1882, 68–69.
5. RC 30:373; *Cambridge VR* 2:463.
6. RC 24:110, 148; RC 28:210; MCPR, docket 1187; Otto 1992, 28.
7. MCD 82:311.
8. MCD 82:312–13.
9. MCD 84:56–57.
10. MCD 100:170–73.
11. *Social Circle in Concord* 1882, 60.
12. *Social Circle in Concord* 1882, 72–73.
13. MCD 121:311–12; 126:268–71.
14. Sharples 1906, 460.
15. *Index of Obituaries, 1784–1840*, 1:278.
16. MCPR, docket 1360.
17. Four spoons with this mark, which has a distinctive drooping knob on the upper serif of the B, have been found. Tablespoons at YUAG (1985.86.65) and at RISD (1989.045.12.113) are monogrammed MW and have bright-cut pendants similar to New York engraving. Teaspoons at YUAG (1985.87.226) and CM, monogrammed RC, have bird-on-a-branch drops. Kovel 1961, 24, also shows SB in a rectangle, but no example has been found.

Francis Bassett
ca. 1678–1715

Possibly a Huguenot, Francis Bassett may have been one of the children of the "Docter Basset" who is included on a list, dated 1 February 1691, of "persons of the French nation" admitted into the Massachusetts Bay Colony with Gabriel Bernon and Francis Légaré (q.v.).[1] Francis Bassett married Mary Goose (1677–1743), daughter of John Goose (b. 1644) of Salem, Massachusetts, and his second wife, Sarah (Trerice) Goose (d. 1686), on 22 April 1703. Mary (Goose) Bassett signed the covenant in the Charlestown, Massachusetts, church on 25 March 1703 and was admitted as a full member on 30 August 1713.[2] On 4 March 1704, Francis "Bassit," "Goldsmith," and his wife, Mary, sold 2 ½ acres of land in Charlestown granted to Daniel Gould, for £1.4.[3] Bassett and his wife had seven children: Mary, born 23 April 1704, who married James Brintnall; Sarah, born 8 May 1706; Ann, born 13 February 1707/08; Peter, born 1 March 1709/10; Rebecca, born 18 July 1712; John, born 2 October 1713; and Frances, born 13 November 1715, who married John Farnham of Boston on 28 April 1740.[4]

Francis Bassett died intestate in Boston on 20 July 1715, aged thirty-seven years. His wife, Mary, died on 12 October 1743 in "the 66th year of her age." She was buried in Copp's Hill Burying Ground; another stone, inscribed only "Bassett," may mark Francis's grave.[5]

No silver by Francis Bassett is known. BMW

1. RC 10:62.
2. Wyman 1879, 1:67, 423; Boston Deaths, 1700–1800. Wyman gives the name as Bassnet or Bassuet. *Charlestown VR* 1:23, 205; *NEHGR* 26:158; Whitmore 1878, 74, no. 1377.
3. MCD 13:692.
4. Wyman 1879, 1:67; RC 28:215; *Charlestown VR* 1:200, 210, 215, 223, 234, 254.
5. Boston Deaths, 1700–1800; Bridgman 1851, 145, 175. There are no probate records for the estate of Francis Bassett.

Caleb Beal
ca. 1746–1801

A

B

C

Caleb Beal's origins cannot be traced with certainty. He probably came from Hingham, Massachusetts, where many residents named Beal lived and where the goldsmith owned land, possibly property he had inherited.[1] He may have been the Caleb Beal born in Hingham to Joshua Beal on 11 May 1746, which corresponds to his age at death, fifty-five.[2]

Beal probably began his apprenticeship about 1760 and completed it about 1767. His training may have taken place in Boston, where he possibly trained with Benjamin Loring (q.v.), who had relocated to Boston earlier from Hull, a neighboring town of Hingham. The Massachusetts tax valuation list for 1771 registered Caleb Beal in Boston with one poll; real estate worth five pounds; seventy pounds' worth of merchandise; and a tanhouse, a term assessors used to describe a building for a variety of businesses, among them those of blacksmiths, coopers, joiners, weavers, gunsmiths, tailors, saddlers, and, undoubtedly, gold-smiths. The tanhouse in the 1771 tax list may be the same shop Beal owned at the time of his death.[3] Beal also was married in Boston, on 8 October 1772, to Mercy Harris (d. 1813).[4] No record of children from this union can be found.

Beal is listed as a goldsmith, silversmith, and jeweler in nine real estate transactions that took place in Boston between 1781 and 1792. He and his wife bought a house for four hundred pounds on the corner of Ann and North streets from Thomas Greenough in October 1781, financed in part with the assistance of a two-hundred-pound mortgage from the seller.[5] The next July,

Beal is called "Jeweller" when he sold his Hingham land; the deed was witnessed by Loring Bailey (Bayley) (q.v.), a silversmith known to have been working in Hingham after 1780.[6] In July 1785 Beal and his wife purchased additional land adjacent to their property on North Street from the merchant Gideon Batty, who ran a shop on Ann Street.[7] In 1786 Beal sold the housewright Joshua Hurd a house and lot facing Salutation Alley, at the back of his residence.[8] In September 1790 Beal bought another house and land, both adjacent to the house he was then living in, from the estate of his neighbor John Hinkley. The deeds, which were transacted on the same day, are confusing: one conveys the property to Hinkley's widow Abigail, and the other conveys the property back to Beal. These transactions may have constituted a mortgage arrangement or perhaps a simple conveyance and reconveyance to establish Abigail Hinkley's clear title to the property following her husband's death.[9] In December 1792 Beal and his wife sold to the merchant Joseph Howard the Ann Street house they had purchased in 1781.[10] However, Beal evidently retained ownership of the goldsmith shop there: the Boston directories of 1796, 1798, and 1800 list him as a goldsmith on Ann Street, with a house on North Street, although by 1800 he is called a jeweler.[11]

Beal died on 10 December 1801 and is buried on Copp's Hill.[12] On 22 December 1801, his widow was appointed administrator of his estate. The engraver Joseph Callender (q.v.) was one of the signers of the bond, and Nathaniel Austin (q.v.) one of the inventory's compilers.

Beal's estate was valued $1,523.86, a relatively substantial amount. Although the shop, appraised at $50, is the only real estate listed, he owned substantial shares of three sloops valued at $900, and a "Pew in the Rev.d John Elliot's meetinghouse No. 100" is noted. His household furnishings included some luxury items, for example, carpets and looking glasses. The shop contained most of his tools, along with stock of plate and jewelry listed separately. Beal owned a plating mill valued at twelve dollars. The term *plating mill* may have been an alternate name for a flatting mill, a tool silversmiths used to produce mechanically flattened sheets of silver. The tool Beal possessed, however, also could have enabled him to do small-scale fusion plating. He did have plated buckles in his inventory.

1 Plating mill 12. 1 Teaste 8,	20 —
1 Vice & 1 Anvil	16 50
Sundry Tools in the Goldsmiths line exclusive } of the ones already mentioned	35 —
. . .	
155 oz. 5 pwts Plate @ 1.10	170.77
1 " 10 " Gold	26 66
2 " 11 " 18 d.º necklaces	45 90
13 Fancy Rings 6 p.r Stone Sleeve buttons	8 87
16 p.r Ear drops & 1 p.r Pendals	26 66
1 String Carol & Gold beads	1 25
8 Seals, plated buckles, pin cushen chain } & Ring & Watch chains	5 25
1 Box fancy Articles & Ingot	4 —
Box & 9 gold beads & Stones	1 —
1 Shop	50 —
1 Lathe & Tools	40 —

A draw bench, plates, irons, scales, weights, and other tools, valued at four dollars, and three "Screws & Beam," valued at five dollars, were listed as being in the cellar, although it is not clear whether this cellar was located in the shop or at his abode. The estate's administration between 1801 and 1803 included payments to Loring Bailey, Joseph Callender, Joseph Loring (q.v.), and J. Balch, Jr. The latter may have been the silversmith Joseph Balch's son and the grandson of Ebenezer Balch (q.v.). A payment of forty dollars was also made to the judge of probate for "services as guardian of J. Coleman," perhaps one of Beal's young apprentices. The number of tools and working supplies and the disbursements to other silversmiths suggest that Beal was an active silversmith until his death.[13]

Although for at least thirty years Beal maintained a separate building that he worked in and that was stocked with ample tools and goldsmiths' and jewelers' supplies, only about three dozen pieces of silver by him are known to survive. Beal may therefore have been a craftsman who fabricated pieces that were retailed by other individuals, although in 1787 he purchased a creampot from Paul Revere, Jr., which he in turn may have sold.[14] The majority of his marked pieces are spoons with handles that often feature distinctive bright-cut ovals and swags. One initial and surname mark (A) and a surname mark (B) are known. An initials mark (C) has been attributed to Beal based on the similarity of the spoons with this mark to those with the surname mark.[15] DAF and PEK

SURVIVING OBJECTS

	Mark	Inscription	Patron	Date	Reference	Owner
Two creampots (attrib.)	none	C/BS		ca. 1780	*Antiques* 124 (September 1983): 553	
Salt	B	C/BS		ca. 1780	*Antiques* 124 (September 1983): 553	
Sugar tongs	C	Pell		ca. 1790		MFAB
Tablespoon	A†	SH		ca. 1775		YUAG
Two tablespoons	A	MC		ca. 1785		CHS
Tablespoon	B	RC		ca. 1800	YUAG files	
Tablespoon	B*	W/EM		ca. 1780	Flynt/Fales 1968, 155 (mark only)	HD
Tablespoon	B*	AB		ca. 1780	YUAG files	
Tablespoon (with pseudomarks of two pine trees)	B	TE		ca. 1795	DAPC 81.3641	
Tablespoon (with pseudomark of a tree in a rectangle)	B	EW		ca. 1785	YUAG files	
Tablespoon	B*	HAB		ca. 1795	Johnston 1994, 8	CMA
Tablespoon	B†	none		ca. 1795	DAPC 75.5270	WM
Tablespoon	B	IC/to/IHL		ca. 1795		SPNEA
Four teaspoons	C	WT		ca. 1785	YUAG files	
Teaspoon	C	CG		ca. 1800	YUAG files	

	Mark	Inscription	Patron	Date	Reference	Owner
Teaspoon	C	H/IA		ca. 1770	YUAG files	
Teaspoon	C	SO	Sally Otis	ca. 1785		SPNEA
Teaspoon	C	SL		ca. 1790		YUAG
Teaspoon	C	I(or J)H		ca. 1790	DAPC 74.2107	WM
Teaspoon	C	W/JN		ca. 1795	DAPC 74.2076	WM
Teaspoon	C	WT	William Tidmarsh	ca. 1790	Buhler 1972, appendix no. 3	MFAB
Teaspoon	C*	R/IE		ca. 1785	Buhler 1972, appendix no. 4	MFAB
Teaspoon	C	RF		ca. 1795	DAPC 82.3145	
Teaspoon	C*	KR		ca. 1775		YUAG
Teaspoon	C†	AMH		ca. 1785	Buhler/Hood 1970, no. 282	YUAG
Two teaspoons	C*	H		ca. 1795	Gourley 1965, no. 20	RISD
Four teaspoons	C*	F/NS		ca. 1775		PEM

1. Beal sold land there in 1782; see SCD 182:235–36.
2. Whitmore 1878, 38, no. 722. The parentage of his father and identity of his mother have not been traced. Two different Joshua Beals lived in Hingham at this time and wed in 1744: one married Elizabeth Leavitt, the other wed Priscilla Paine. Lincoln's history of the town of Hingham also records the marriage of a Joshua Beal to Elizabeth Stodder; this couple had a son named Caleb, but he died at an early age; see Lincoln (1893) 1982, 2:62, 64.
3. Pruitt 1978, 34–35.
4. RC 30:69; *Index of Obituaries, 1784–1840*, 1:319.
5. SCD 133:142–44.
6. SCD 182:235–36.
7. SCD 174:209–10.
8. SCD 168:202.
9. SCD 168:173–74.
10. SCD 174:210–12.
11. RC 10:226; *Boston Directory* 1798, 19; 1800, 17.
12. Whitmore 1878, 38, no. 722.
13. SCPR, docket 21581.
14. 4 September 1787, vol. 2, Waste Book, 1783–97, 62, Revere Family Papers, MHS.
15. Kovel 1961, 26, also shows BEAL in a plain rectangle and CB in a rectangle without a pellet, but examples have not been located.

Jonathan Belcher 1661–99+

Jonathan Belcher was born in Boston on 1 September 1661, the fourth child of Josiah (1631–83) and Ranis (Rainsford) Belcher (b. 1638). He was baptized in the First Church in 1664, as were his elder brothers Josiah and John and his younger sister, Elizabeth.[1] His father, Josiah Belcher, was the son of Gregory (d. 1675) and Catherine Belcher (d. 1680). Ranis Rainsford was the daughter of Edward (ca. 1611–80) and Elizabeth Rainsford (ca. 1607–88) and sister of Anna (Rainsford) Haugh, whose son Samuel Haugh (q.v.) was also a Boston goldsmith.[2]

Jonathan Belcher is identified as a goldsmith in the division of his father's estate in September 1693 and again in November of 1693, when he deeded a portion of his share of the estate to his brother Edward.[3] Belcher appears again in court records in a suit brought against him in 1697 by John Allen and John Edwards (q.q.v.), "for not paying to ye p^{lts} the sum of two pound nine shillings and ten pence in money due by Booke for Severals he hath had & rec'^{d} of y^e p^{lts} in y^e yeare 1697." The attached account is as follows:

Jonathan Belcher D^r to
John Edwards & John Allen
August 26th 1697

	£	s	d
To money due upon y^e acc^t: of a Coat	00	08	0
To a p^r Shoes	00	06	6
To money lent him at Se=verall times	00	15	4
To money due upon y^e acc^t of a hatt	00	09	0
To 4 neckcloaths & 4 hand-kerchers	00	11	0
£	02	09	10[4]

Allen and Edwards charged that Belcher refused to pay the amount that he owed them. The fact that the items in question were clothing suggests that Belcher, who was then thirty-six years old, had worked as a journeyman for Allen and Edwards and considered the items due to him as part of his agreement with them. The goldsmith John Noyes (q.v.) signed as surety for Belcher, indicating that he may have been Belcher's employer at the time of the suit.

There is no other record of the goldsmith Jonathan Belcher in Boston. He may have changed professions after 1697, but this is difficult to determine because of the confusion with others of the same name. No silver by him has been identified. BMW

1. RC 9:6, 51, 60, 69, 78, 87, 94; Codman 1918, 34.
2. Bridgman 1853, 37–38.
3. The estate division, which took place ten years after Josiah Belcher's death, is dated 20 September 1693, but it was not entered until 20 July 1699; SCD 19:158–60; SCPR, docket 1994. John Allen, perhaps the goldsmith, was one of the witnesses to the deed between Jonathan and Edward Belcher; SCD 16:220–21.
4. SCCR, file 98567.

Samuel Belknap
1751–1821

Samuel Belknap was born on 28 May 1751 in Boston to Mary Rand (1718–95) and Jeremiah Belknap (1720–96), who were married by Rev. Joseph Sewall of Boston's Old South Church on 30 June 1748.[1] Belknap's maternal grandparents were Capt. Samuel Rand (1679–1748), a tailor and shopkeeper, and Sarah Paine (d. 1762); his paternal grandparents were Jeremiah Belknap (1686/87–1751), a leather breeches maker and leatherdresser, and Sarah Fosdick (1693–1754).[2] Mary (Rand) Belknap was named as a legatee in her father's will; she received a sixth of the total estate, less "such Sum or sums I have advanced or shall hereafter be advanced to her to Set her off in Marriage."[3]

No marriage record exists for Samuel Belknap in Boston. He may have been a member of Old South Church because his father, brother, and several of his sisters were members of this congregation.[4] The Belknap family association with this church began in 1669 with the silversmith's great-great-grand-father, Joseph Belknap, who was one of the church's founders.[5] Belknap joined the Ancient and Honorable Artillery Company in 1773 and is listed as being present at a meeting in 1782.[6] In 1819, he and William Homes, Jr. (q.v.), were among those honored by the company for their services during the Revolution.[7]

Following his apprenticeship, Belknap would have been ready to practice his trade about 1772. At the time of his induction into the Ancient and Honorable Artillery Company, Belknap was described as being a shopkeeper.[8] In addition to his silversmithing activities, he probably followed the common practice of retailing imported household goods in his shop. In the tax list of 1780 the Boston assessors rated Samuel Belknap, goldsmith, of ward 8, with real estate worth an annual rent of forty pounds.[9] His father, Jeremiah, and a maternal relative, Abigail Rand, were listed as living next door to him. In 1781, Belknap, "Goldsmith, of Boston," bought a house on Greenhill for which he paid "750 good Spanish milled Dollars."[10] He bought additional land on Cornhill in April of the following year at a cost of "800 Spanish Dollars."[11] The Boston directories for 1789, 1796, and 1798 list Samuel Belknap as either a goldsmith or silversmith located at 30 Cornhill.[12] This property was described in the United States Direct Tax of 1798 as a brick dwelling: "Land, 1,407 square feet; house, 630 square feet; 3 stories, 13 windows; Value, $6,000."[13] Samuel A. Belknap, jeweler, is recorded as occupying 30 Cornhill in the 1820s. The relationship between these two silversmiths, perhaps uncle and nephew, has not yet been determined.[14]

Belknap's success as a silversmith was facilitated by his familial and professional relationships. Belknap's cousin was the silversmith Joseph Edwards (q.v.), the son of his aunt Sarah (Belknap) Edwards. Through more remote family ties, Belknap was related to Joseph Sanderson, Knight Leverett, and Samuel Phillips (q.q.v.).[15] In 1803, the heirs of Jeremiah Belknap, including Samuel, sold land in west Boston to Polly Hurd, who was married to the son of the goldsmith Benjamin Hurd (q.v.).[16] Samuel Belknap also served as one of the appraisers of the estate of Samuel Minott (q.v.), the inventory for which was presented to Suffolk County Probate Court on 17 October 1803.[17]

By the time he had reached the age of sixty-seven, Belknap had achieved sufficient financial success and social status to call himself a gentleman. "Samuel Belknap, Gentleman," purchased the mortgage on John Fox's property for four thousand dollars on 18 June 1818.[18]

Samuel Belknap died intestate at age seventy on 30 June 1821. The administration of his estate was granted to his brother Jeremiah on 9 July of that year, at which time Jeremiah Belknap, merchant, Mary Belknap, single woman, and Joseph Head, Esq., posted bond for twenty thousand dollars to administer Belknap's estate.[19] Belknap was buried in the Belknap family tomb in the Granary Burying Ground.[20]

Belknap was mentioned in the memoirs of the Plymouth silversmith and jeweler Samuel Davis (1765–1829) as a silversmith who showed "Professional Merit" and a respectable character.[21] No mark has yet been associated with him. DAF

1. RC 24:131, 143, 276; RC 28:238; *Index of Obituaries, 1784–1840*, 1:346; *Index of Obituaries, 1704–1800*, 1:24.
2. Wyman 1879, 2:783, 792; RC 9:168; RC 28:14, 22; *NEHGR* 16:130; 28:121; Warren 1859, 17–18; SCPR 42:203–05; 45:124–29; 49:562–63; *Charlestown VR* 1:106.
3. SCPR 42:203–05.

4. *Old South Church* 1883, 42, 46, 49, 53, 130.

5. Roberts 1895, 1:185.

6. Roberts 1895, 2:175, 191, 220.

7. Roberts 1895, 2:417.

8. Roberts 1895, 2:175.

9. "Assessors' 'Taking-Books,'" 36.

10. SCD 132:271–72.

11. SCD 134:155–56.

12. RC 10:176, 226; *Boston Directory* 1789, 9; 1796, 18; 1798, 19.

13. RC 22:287.

14. Roberts 1895, 2:419.

15. Bigelow-Phillips files, 1698.

16. SCD 207:157–58.

17. SCPR 101:577–79.

18. SCD 259:16.

19. SCPR 171:105; 206:183.

20. Codman 1918, 35.

21. Steinway 1960, 7.

John Bingham
ca. 1650–78 +

The Boston records for 28 October 1678 list those people who were to be excluded from the town; among them was the goldsmith John Bingham.[1] Bingham may have been the John Binham (or Benham), son of the yeoman John Benham of the City of Westminster, whose eight-year apprenticeship to Anthony Ricketts, a London goldsmith, was recorded on 8 October 1664. He was made a freeman of the Goldsmiths' Company on 29 November 1672.[2] No record of John Bingham's birth has been found, and because he was not admitted into the Massachusetts Bay Colony, his stay in Boston was probably brief. No silver by him is known. PEK

1. RC 10:57.

2. Apprentice Book 2, fol. 145v; Court Book 6, fol. 311r, Worshipful Company of Goldsmiths, London. Robert B. Barker letter to the author, 9 February 1993.

John Blowers
1710/11–48

A

John Blowers was born in Beverly, Massachusetts, on 1 January 1710/11, the fourth child of the Reverend Thomas (1677–1729) and Emma (Eliot) (Woodberry) Blowers (b. 1681), daughter of Andrew Eliot (ca. 1651–88) and Mercy (Shattuck) Eliot (b. 1655) of Beverly.[1] Rev. Thomas Blowers was born in Cambridge, Massachusetts, the son of Pyam (ca. 1638–1709) and Elizabeth (Belcher) Blowers (1640–1709).[2] Thomas graduated from Harvard College in 1695 and served pastor of the First Church in Beverly, Massachusetts, from 1701 until his death.[3]

John Blowers served his apprenticeship in Boston with John Burt between about 1724 and 1732. In 1730, "John Blower of Boston in the County of Suffolk Apprentice to M.r John Burt [q.v.] of Boston afores.d Goldsmith" was "accused by Sarah Parker of Needham Single woman of being the Father of a Bastard Child born of her Body in March last, appeared and pleaded not Guilty." Blowers was acquitted by the court.[4] Blowers witnessed a deed for Burt along with Samuel Gray (1710/11–48) (q.v.) in 1728/29.[5] Blowers witnessed a second deed for Burt in 1730.[6]

Blowers married Sarah Salter (b. 1715/16), daughter of the Boston brewer Sampson Salter (1692–1778) and Martha (Robinson) Salter (b. 1695/96) on 27

November 1735 in the New Brick Church, Boston.[7] John and Sarah Blowers had five children: Sarah (b. 1736), Martha (b. 1738), Emma (b. 1740), Sampson Salter (b. 1741), and Martha (b. 1744).[8]

John Blowers went to court several times to recover debts. In 1736 and 1737, John Blowers appeared in two suits against the goldsmith Thomas Townsend (q.v.) for money Townsend owed him. The defendant defaulted, and Blowers was awarded the full amount of the suit plus costs of court.[9] The file papers in the case do not survive to explain the nature of the account between the two men, but the suit suggests that they had a working relationship. Blowers also evidently traded goods and services with Mary Ann Boyer, widow of the jeweler James Boyer (qq.v.), for £3.2.4 owed to him on account. The account among the file papers for the case indicates that Mary Ann Boyer gave Blowers 1 oz. 6 dwt. of silver worth £1.17.8 on 19 August 1741, and that on 1 September 1741, Blowers charged Boyer £5 "To making a Snuf Box & Silver for d°," leaving a balance of £3.2.4.[10] In 1737, Blowers sued Peter Cade, a merchant, and in 1738, he sued William Bennett, a mariner.[11]

Blowers's father, Thomas, died in 1729, and in his will he bequeathed to his son Pyam the "plate I have mark^d with ye two first Letters of his name"; to his daughters Emma Charnock and Elizabeth Blowers, each a silver tankard; to his son Thomas, "my silver cup marked with ye two first letters of his name"; and to his sons John and Andrew, each a silver porringer. He also bequeathed five pounds to the First Church in Beverly to be "laid out in a piece of plate for ye Communion Table."[12] The church now owns a mug engraved "The Legacy of the Rev^nd Mr Tho: Blowers/ To the First Church in Beverly/ dec^d: June the 17th 1729." The mug is unmarked and has been presumed to be the work of young John. Although John Blowers was only eighteen at the time his father died, Thomas's will stipulated that the money bequeathed to the church was to be paid by his executor one year from the time of his decease.[13] The mug, therefore, was made no earlier than 1730 and, like many pieces of church silver, may actually have been made even later. It is certainly possible that it is John Blowers's work.

When Sarah (Salter) Blowers's grandfather George Robinson, a carver, died in 1737, he bequeathed his "Mantletree Sett of Carv'd Work and Sconces" to her and his "Silver Spouted Cup" and "Robert Robinson's Daughter's Picture" to her mother. Robinson also directed that ten rings be made for his funeral, six for the pallbearers and one each for Reverend Gee, Reverend Mather, Reverend Welsteed, and Doctor Pemberton.[14] These rings may well have been made by John Blowers. In April 1745, John and his wife, Sarah, sold their portion of the land bequeathed to them by Robinson to Sarah's father, who is identified in the record as Sampson Salter, gentleman.[15]

John Blowers was commissioned lieutenant in the Ninth Regiment of the militia, Joseph Dwight, Esq., colonel, on 5 July 1745. He served with the troops occupying Louisbourg and died of camp sickness in July 1748 soon after his return.[16]

John Blowers's surviving silver suggests that he was not only an accomplished silversmith, but an accomplished engraver as well. George Francis Dow records two notices of lost or stolen silver marked "I Blowers," a gold thimble (*Boston Gazette*, 13/20 March 1738) and a silver spoon (*Boston Gazette*, 23 December 1746), but no work with this mark is known to survive.[17] During his brief career Blowers also made tankards, a porringer, a cann, pepper boxes, a strainer, and salts marked with his surname mark (A).[18] The most ambitious of Blowers's surviving works is a large cylindrical coffeepot with a tapered body and a domed cover with a bell finial made for John Jones and Mary Anne Faneuil, who were married about 1732. It is engraved with the Jones family coat of arms surrounded by handsome baroque mantling. The same design appears on a footed salver made for the Quincy family. BMW

SURVIVING OBJECTS

	Mark	Inscription	Patron	Date	Reference	Owner
Cann	A	IT		ca. 1740	MFA 1911, no. 49	
Coffeepot	A	Jones (?) arms, gules a stag statant, and a crest, a stag's head erased; impaling unidentified arms, with quarters 1 and 4 per pale or and azure, quarters 2 and 3 azure a bend or	Jones (?) family	ca. 1735	Sotheby Parke Bernet, 30 June–1 July 1983, lot 96	
Ladle	A	Byfield crest	Nathaniel Byfield (?)	ca. 1732	Sotheby's, 30 June–1 July 1982, lot 230	
Mug (attrib.)	none	The Legacy of the Rev.nd Mr Tho: Blowers/To the First Church in Beverly/ dec.^{d} June the 17th 1729	First Parish Church, Beverly, Mass., for Rev. Thomas Blowers	ca. 1730	Jones 1913, 16–17	
Pepper box	A	S/EM; G/BS	E. and M. Smith	ca. 1740	Gourley 1965, no. 21	MWPI
Pepper box	A	Given to D. Russell/in Remembrance of her/ Nephew Sam:^{ll}/Eliot/Who Died upon the/Coast of Africa 1st Jan^y/1741 AE 24.	D. Russell; in memory of Samuel Eliot	1741	Stillinger 1990, 75, 155	
Porringer	A	EB/to/EW		ca. 1740	MFA 1911, no. 48	
Two salts	A	B//JM		ca. 1740	Hammerslough/ Feigenbaum 1958–73, 1:46	
Salver	A*	Quincy arms, gules 7 mascles, 3, 3, 1; AQ	Anna (Quincy) Thaxter	ca. 1740	Buhler/Hood 1970, no. 177	YUAG
Strainer	A	none		ca. 1740	Silver Supplement 1973, no. 4	
Tankard	A†	EF	Edmund Fowle (?)	ca. 1740	Buhler 1972, no. 223	MFAB
Tankard	?	?	Second Church, North Beverly, Mass.	?	YUAG files	
Teaspoon	A*	none		ca. 1740	DAPC 71.2455	WM

1. *Beverly VR* 1:47, 124; 2:38, 107, 380; *Cambridge VR* 1:69; *Salem VR* 2:277; Savage 1860–62, 2:108; Upham 1905, 97.
2. *Cambridge VR* 2:40, 473; *Sudbury VR*, 15.
3. Stone 1843, 222–30; *Sibley's Harvard Graduates* 4:225–28.
4. SCCR, Court of General Sessions Record Book 1725–32, 281.
5. *York Deeds* 14:196–97.
6. YCD 20:158–59.
7. RC 24:119; RC 9:202, 223; RC 28:60, 190; SCPR, docket 16549; Roberts 1895, 1:437–38.
8. RC 24:224, 232, 239, 242, 251.
9. SCCR, Court of Common Pleas Record Book 1735–36, 616; 1736–37, 498. John M. Fitzgerald to Francis Hill Bigelow, List of Boston Court Record References to Silversmiths, Bigelow-Phillips files. The Record Book for 1735–36 is now missing.
10. SCCR, Court of Common Pleas Record Book 1741, 271; SCCR, file 54815, vol. 351, Judicial Archives, Mass. Archives.
11. The Record Book for 1738 is now missing. The reference to Blowers vs. Bennett is in the Bigelow-Phillips files: Fitzgerald List of Boston Court Record References to Silversmiths, Court of Common Pleas Record Book 1738, 62. The reference to Blowers vs. Cade is in the Bigelow-Phillips files: Fitzgerald List of Boston Court Record References to Silversmiths. SCCR, Court of Common Pleas Record Book 1737, 52.
12. ECPR 319:160–62.
13. Jones 1913, 16–17, pl. VI.
14. SCPR 33:271–73.
15. SCD 70:174–75.
16. Hudson 1871, 24:375; 25:264; *Sibley's Harvard Graduates* 15:359; *Beverly VR* 2:380.
17. Dow 1927, 41.
18. IBLOWERS and BLOWERS in a rectangle have also been published; see Kovel 1961, 35.

Peter Boutett
ca. 1685–1715 +

A Pierre Bourtet is listed as a goldsmith in St. Giles's, London, in 1708, by Sir Ambrose Heal.[1] He may be the same individual whose name appears in Boston as Peter Boutett in a suit brought against him by Isaiah Tay, in which he is referred to as "Goldsmith or Jeweller," on 5 July 1715. The case, which was eventually heard before the Superior Court, involved Boutett in the receipt of stolen goods. He was found guilty and ordered to pay the injured parties, including Tay, double the value of the goods stolen.[2] There is no other record of Boutett in Massachusetts, and no silver or jewelry by him is known. BMW

1. Heal (1935) 1972, 111.
2. SCCR, Court of Common Pleas Record Book 1714–15, 296–97; Superior Court of Judicature Record Book 1715–21, 69.

James Bowtell
w. ca. 1782–92

The *Massachusetts Spy* of 5 December 1782 published the following advertisement:

JAMES BOWTELL,

GOLDSMITH, from CHARLESTOWN, No. IV.
Carries on the Gold and Silversmith's
business in LANCASTER. All sorts
of Gold, Silver and Jewelry ware made in
the neatest manner. Likewise Engraving.
December 4th, 1782.

Henry Flynt and Martha Gandy Fales used this advertisement to document the fact that Bowtell came from the Connecticut River town of Charlestown, New Hampshire, to work in Lancaster, Massachusetts. "Charlestown, No. IV" referred to a designation for land grants from Massachusetts before a boundary existed for New Hampshire.[1] Prior to Flynt and Fales, scholars claimed that Bowtell worked in Worcester, Massachusetts, in either 1783 or 1787, although no evidence supports that contention.[2]

Flynt and Fales also assigned life dates to this maker, stating that he was the James Bowtell who was born on 18 March 1754 in Framingham, Massachusetts, to Ebenezer and Ann Bowtell and who died in Leominster, Massachusetts, in 1822. But the estate papers of that James Bowtell clearly demonstrate that he was a yeoman, and the absence of silversmith's tools or supplies in his estate inventory raises serious doubts as to whether he ever was a working silversmith.[3] Flynt and Fales also state that a James Bowtell was listed in the census of 1790 in Charlestown and was a taxpayer there in 1792. The more likely scenario, therefore, is that the goldsmith who advertised in Lancaster in 1782–83 returned to his native Charlestown. Nothing more of him is known, and his parentage has not been determined. No silver by him has been identified. JJF and PEK

1. Flynt/Fales 1968, 161.
2. French (1917) 1967, 15; Ensko 1927, 63; Okie 1936, 244; Thorn 1949, 30; Kovel 1961, 38.
3. WCPR, docket 6368.

Daniel Boyer
1725–79

A

B

C

D

E

F

Daniel Boyer, the son of James Boyer (q.v.) and Mary Ann Boyer (q.v.), was born in Boston on 25 June 1725 and was probably baptized in the French Church.[1] Boyer would have begun his apprenticeship in the jeweler's trade about 1739, probably with his father. Because his father died in 1741, Boyer's training most likely was completed in the family shop, which Boyer's mother continued to run following her husband's death, probably with the help of journeymen. Andrew Oliver (q.v.), who would marry Boyer's sister Susannah, may have trained in the shop at about the same time. Boyer could have begun working as early as 1746 and probably carried on the business following his mother's death in 1747.

Boyer published his intentions to marry Elizabeth Bulfinch (ca. 1726–95) on 18 January 1749.[2] Elizabeth was the daughter of John Bulfinch and Elizabeth Bumstead (1706–37).[3] Boyer had been a member of the Brattle Street Church since 1742, and the couple's daughters Elizabeth and Katherine were baptized there in 1753 and 1755.[4] In 1753 Boyer purchased from his brother Peter and sister Susannah and her husband Andrew Oliver their quarter interests in the real estate left to them by their grandfather Daniel Johonnot.[5] In 1757 he purchased the remaining quarter from his brother and sister Abraham and Mary Boyer.[6] William Homes, Sr., and Samuel Minott (qq.v.) witnessed the deed for the purchase from the Olivers.

During this same period Boyer became involved in civic activities. He was chosen constable in 1754 but was excused.[7] He served the town as clerk of the market in 1754, 1755, 1757, and 1758, but he declined to serve in that post in 1763.[8] Boyer also joined the Ancient and Honorable Artillery Company in 1756 and was made a fourth sergeant in 1762.[9]

Probably about 1761 Boyer took Joseph Coolidge (q.v.) as an apprentice. Coolidge later became Boyer's son-in-law. Boyer joined the Old South Church in 1770.[10] The Massachusetts tax list for 1771 includes Boyer in Boston with two polls, one house, £26.13.4 of annual worth of real estate, one servant for life, and £180 of merchandise.[11] Andrew Oliver's name appears immediately before Boyer's, which suggests that they lived and may have worked in close proximity.

Boyer conducted business from his shop on Cornhill, not far from Thomas Edwards and his successor Zachariah Brigden (qq.v.). He sold imported goldsmiths' and jewelers' supplies, made jewelry that he supplied to other silversmiths and jewelers and sold retail, and merchandized silver made by others. An advertisement in the *Massachusetts Gazette* of 30 October 1766 indicates Boyer's place of business and the goods he carried:

IMPORTED *from* LONDON *in the* Hannah, *Capt.*
Jarvis, *and to be sold by*
Daniel Boyer,
Jeweller, at his shop opposite the Governor's, in

BOSTON:

Brilliant and cypher	* coral Beads, and paste
earing and Button	* for Whistles
Stones	* Shoe and Knee Chapes
brilliant and cypher ring	* binding Wier
Stones	* rough and smooth Files
ring and buckle Sparks	* Crucibles and black Pots
diamond Sparks	* Borax, saltpetre
Garnets, Amethysts and	* Pomice and rotten Stone
Topazes	* Shears, Plyers, Blowpipes
locket Stones and Cyphers	* moulding Sand, Sand
ruby and white Foyle	* Paper, etc.

Also at said Shop may be had, a handsome Pair
Cluster Earings with three Drops; with most
Sorts of Jewellers and Goldsmiths Work, cheap
for Cash.

Similar advertisements appeared in the *Boston News-Letter* of 22 October 1767 and the issues of 14 and 21 March and 29 August 1771. Among the craftsmen to whom Boyer sold these supplies and tools was John Hathorne (q.v.) of Salem. An account in 1770 reveals the nature of this trade:

M^r: John Hathorn Bou^t⎫   Boston Novr. 1. 1770
  of Daniel Boyer   ⎭

1 Doz Shoe Chapes 70/ 1 Doz Knee D^o. 45/	5:15—
1 p^r. Spring plyers 30/ 1 p^r. Watch plyers 18/	2: 8—
6 Buckle Brushes 25/ 6 oz Borax 33/9	2:18:9
1 Blowpipe 9/ 2 hanks Wire 10/3	19: 3
Sundry Files 48/6 1/2 lb Rotten Stone 6/	2:14:6
1 p^r. Small Scales 40/ 1 p^r. Cutting Nippers 30/	3:10—
	£18 ″5 ″6

Rec^d. the above in full p^r. Daniel Boyer

Boyer also sold supplies to Hathorne in 1776.[12] In 1777 Boyer sold Brigden tools and supplies.[13] Boyer also bought supplies from fellow craftsmen. For example, in 1769 he purchased nineteen quarts of molding sand from Brigden.[14]

Although Boyer may have made small silver objects, the chief production of his shop was jewelry. A receipt indicates that from July through September 1770 Boyer sold thirty-one rings to Brigden.[15] On 16 July 1761 the Boston silversmith Rufus Greene (q.v.) paid Boyer £3.12 for two rings.[16] Boyer also sold rings to Thomas Amory, as a bill dated 24 May 1770 from Daniel Boyer indicates that Amory was debtor for "2 Split shank motto Rings with an amethiste & 2 Dimonds in each £6."[17]

Many of the pieces of flatware and holloware that Boyer sold may have been made for him by his neighbor Brigden. Brigden's papers show that beginning as early as 1767, and especially from 1770 to 1775, Brigden routinely made flatware and holloware for Boyer and did repair work for him. In these transactions Boyer generally supplied the silver.[18] Other craftsmen with whom Boyer may have done business were William Cowell, Jr., and Daniel Henchman (qq.v.). When Cowell died in 1761, Boyer owed the estate £3.12.4½.[19] Boyer appraised the estate of Daniel Henchman with Brigden in 1775.[20] Some scholars claim that Boyer worked in partnership with Josiah Austin (q.v.), but no evidence of this has been found.[21]

About seventy pieces of jewelry, holloware, and flatware with Boyer's marks survive. They span thirty-one years: a beaker once owned by the church in Rehoboth, Massachusetts (now at Yale), bears the date 1748, and a mourning ring commemorating Mrs. T. Gordon, at the Museum of Fine Arts, Boston, is dated 1779. He used three initials marks (A, B, c) and three surname marks (D, E, F). One of his initials marks has been confused with a mark of Daniel Russell (q.v.).[22]

In 1776, Boyer, at the age of fifty-one, was among those in ward 10 who were drafted, to serve in the conflict with Great Britain.[23] Three years later, on 26 August 1779, being sick and weak, he made his will, naming his brother Peter Boyer and son-in-law Joseph Coolidge as executors; they executed the will on 3 September 1779.[24] PEK

SURVIVING OBJECTS

	Mark	Inscription	Patron	Date	Reference	Owner
Beaker	D*	The Gift of Deacon/Samuel Newman/to the Church in/Rehoboth/1748	Newman Congregational Church, East Providence, R.I., for Samuel Newman	1748	Buhler/Hood 1970, no. 198	YUAG
Cann	D	none		ca. 1760	Silver Supplement 1973, no. 5	
Three canns (mates below)	D	Symmes arms, ermine 3 increscents gules, and crest, a sun in splendor; The Gift of Edwd Kitchen Esqr . . . (later)	Edward Kitchen	ca. 1750	Jones 1913, 437	
Three canns (mates above)	D*	Symmes arms; The Gift of Edwd. Kitchen Esqr. . . . (later)	Edward Kitchen	ca. 1750	Jones 1913, 429–30	
Cann	D	F/HD; SF (later)		ca. 1765	The Antiquarian 13 (November 1929): 94	

	Mark	Inscription	Patron	Date	Reference	Owner
Cann	E *or* F	ST		ca. 1760	Buhler 1965, 73–74	HMA
Cann	E *or* F	SF to AF; ISR (or IFR) (later)		ca. 1770	Avery 1920, no. 68	MMA
Cream pail	A*	EH		ca. 1765	DAPC 79.3303 (as Daniel Parker)	
Creampot	B	?		ca. 1765	MFA 1906, no. 9	
Ladle	A	unidentified crest, a demi-lion holding a sword; IS		ca. 1770	Eitner 1976, no. 54	
Mourning ring (gold)	A	Mʳˢ. T. Gordon. ob. 21 April 1779 AE 48.	T. Gordon	1779	Buhler 1972, no. 291	MFAB
Porringer	A	The Gift of/Samu-ell/Barnard Esq/To Mʳˢ/Mary Williams	Mary (Porter) Williams in memory of Samuel Barnard	1762	Flynt/Fales 1968, 52–53	HD
Porringer	A†	L/DI	Daniel and Jerusha (Tal-cott) Lathrop	ca. 1760	Buhler/Hood 1970, no. 197	YUAG
Porringer	D	W/IB		ca. 1760	Sotheby's, 23–25 January 1992, lot 185	
Porringer	?	EB (later)		ca. 1775	YUAG files	
Porringer	?	IC (later)		ca. 1760	Parke-Bernet, 10 November 1970, lot 65	
Serving spoon	E*	unidentified crest, a scallop shell; AM/to/CM (later)		ca. 1760	Buhler 1972, no. 290	MFAB
Two sleeve buttons (gold)	B†	E; T	Elizue Talcott	ca. 1770	Ham-merslough/Feigenbaum 1958–73, 3:146	
Spoon	C†	?		ca. 1775	YUAG files	
Strainer	A*	W/RR		ca. 1750	Buhler 1979, no. 31	WAM
Strainer	A	B/IA		ca. 1765	YUAG files	
Tablespoon	D, E, *or* F	unidentified initials		ca. 1770	*Antiques* 17 (June 1930): 505	
Tablespoon	E†	AT		ca. 1770	DAPC 72.3397	WM
Tablespoon	E*	MH		ca. 1770		YUAG
Tablespoon	E*	ES (later)		ca. 1770	Buhler 1979, no. 33	WAM
Tablespoon	E*	DW		ca. 1770	YUAG files	
Tablespoon	E*	SP		ca. 1750	YUAG files	
Tablespoon	E*	AB		ca. 1770	YUAG files	
Tablespoon	E *or* F	?		ca. 1770	*Antiques* 17 (June 1930): 505	

	Mark	Inscription	Patron	Date	Reference	Owner
Tablespoon	E or F	?		ca. 1770	*Antiques* 17 (June 1930): 505	
Tablespoon	E or F	?		ca. 1770	*Antiques* 17 (June 1930): 505	
Two tablespoons	E or F	LB		ca. 1760	Buhler 1972, appendix no. 5	MFAB
Tablespoon	F†	D/TA		ca. 1750		YUAG
Three tablespoons	F*	S/WA		ca. 1770		YUAG
Two tablespoons (mate below)	F*	IP		ca. 1770	YUAG files	
Tablespoon (mates above)	F*	IP		ca. 1770	YUAG files	
Two tablespoons	?	C/AT		ca. 1760	Sotheby Parke Bernet, 22–23 May 1980, lot 580	
Tablespoon	?	EH/to/EP		ca. 1765	YUAG files	
Tablespoon	?	?		ca. 1770	*Antiques* 17 (June 1930): 505	
Tankard	E	Dwight arms; H/EA	Dwight family	ca. 1770	Gourley 1965, no. 23	
Two tankards	E*	The first/Church of Christ/*IN*/FALMOUTH	First Parish in Falmouth, Portland, Maine	ca. 1770	Jones 1913, 377	
Tankard	E	B/GE		ca. 1770	Gourley 1965, no. 22	
Tankard	E or F	PLW; 1775		ca. 1775	MFA 1906, no. 8	
Teaspoon	C	DH		ca. 1770		HD
Teaspoon	C	B/IE/1733	Jonathan and Elizabeth Bowman	ca. 1750	MFA 1911, no. 62	
Teaspoon	C	?		ca. 1760	Buhler 1972, appendix no. 7	MFAB
Two teaspoons	C	SW		ca. 1760	Buhler 1972, appendix no. 8	MFAB
Teaspoon	D*	unidentified initials		ca. 1750		HD
Teaspoon	D*	SW		ca. 1765	Eitner 1976, no. 55	
Teaspoon	D*	RR		ca. 1760	Johnston 1994, 9	CMA
Teaspoon	D*	H/RS		ca. 1760	Johnston 1994, 9	CMA
Three teaspoons	D	MS	Martha (Saunders) Salisbury	ca. 1760	Buhler 1979, no. 32	WAM
Teaspoon	D*	B/DE		ca. 1755	Buhler/Hood 1970, no. 199	YUAG

	Mark	Inscription	Patron	Date	Reference	Owner
Teaspoon	D†	MS/to/HS		ca. 1750		YUAG
Teaspoon	D *or* E	EL		ca. 1770		CHM
Teaspoon	E*	DA		ca. 1755	Buhler/Hood 1970, no. 200	YUAG
Two teaspoons	E *or* F	TG		ca. 1770	Buhler 1972, appendix no. 6	MFAB

1. RC 24:195.
2. RC 28:293; *Index of Obituaries, 1784–1840*, 1:526.
3. Boston Deaths, 1700–1800; RC 24:40; RC 28:131.
4. *Church in Brattle Square*, 101, 174, 176.
5. SCD 82:52–53, 122–23.
6. SCD 90:255–56.
7. RC 14:245.
8. RC 14:248, 270, 294; RC 16:2, 82.
9. Roberts 1895, 2:80, III.
10. *Old South Church* 1883, 143.
11. Pruitt 1978, 40–41.
12. English-Touzel-Hathorne Papers, box 6, folder 12, PEM.
13. Bill from Boyer to Brigden from 6 August to 4 September 1777, Brigden Papers, YU.
14. Zachariah Brigden Daybook, 1766–ca. 1775, fol. IIv, Brigden Papers, YU.
15. Bill from Boyer to Brigden for rings, settled 22 November 1770, Brigden Papers, YU.
16. Rufus Greene Account Book, 1748–74, n.p., MHS.
17. Daniel Boyer bill to Thomas Amory, 24 May 1770, Amory Papers, MHS.
18. Zachariah Brigden Daybook, 1766–ca. 1775, fols. 19v, 20r, 25v, 26r, 26v, 27r, 27v, 28r, 28v, 29r, 37v, 38r, 38v, 39r, 39v, 40r. See also loose receipts. Brigden Papers, YU.
19. SCPR, docket 12763.
20. SCPR 74:297–99.
21. See, for instance, Kovel 1961, 17; Flynt/Fales 1968, 147.
22. Belden 1980, 70, illustrates an initials mark for Boyer that is actually the mark of Daniel Russell of Newport, Rhode Island. See, for example, Buhler/Hood 1970, 1:331, for the mark on Russell pieces nos. 465–66.
23. RC 25:23.
24. SCPR 78:416–18; also docket 17051.

James Boyer
ca. 1700–1741

James Boyer, son of Peter Boyer, a Huguenot distiller of St. Giles-in-the-Fields, London, served his apprenticeship with James Papavoine, jeweler, of St. James's, Westminster, for seven years beginning on 30 June 1712.[1] Boyer immigrated to Boston about 1721, and on 31 December and 7 January 1722/23, the following advertisement appeared in the *New-England Courant:*

> This is to inform the Publick, That Mr. *James Boyer*, Jeweller, from London, living at Mr. Eustone's, a Dancing Master in King Street, Boston, setts all manner of Stones in Rings, &c. and performes every thing belonging to that Trade. N.B. *The said Mr. Boyer is lately recovered of a Fit of Sickness.*

In 1724, Boyer married Marian or Mary Ann Johonnot (q.v.).[2] The couple had six children: Daniel (1725–79) (q.v.); Peter (1726–before 1731); Susannah (b. 1727), who married the jeweler Andrew Oliver (q.v.) in 1747; James (b. 1729); Peter (b. 1731); and Mary (dates unknown).[3]

The Harvard tutor Henry Flynt was a customer of Boyer's, and on 28 September 1725 he recorded that

Boyer the Jeweller told mee That 24 graines of gold made a peny weight & 20 peny weight was an Ounce a grain of gold is 5$\frac{d_1}{2}$ of OE money a peny weight 11^{sh} an ounce is 11^{lb} 2 smal ring I shewed him weighed 3^{dwt} 17 gr another smal ring I commonly wear 2$^{d\,wt}$ a great ring 5^{dwt} whereof twould take 3^{dwt} to make my Stone ring The setting of the Stone would cost 20 shillings.[4]

On 4 October 1725 he wrote,

Mem—That the Stone of my ring cost 7^{sh} Sterling the Cutting my coat of arms in it 21 sh Sterling for wch I paid Coz Esther Flynt by Mr Boylestones Order a 5^{lb} Bill. The Jeweller Mr Boyer tells mee the Stone weighs 10 graines The Gold of the ring is 2 p^{wt} 21 graines. The making came to 20 Shil[5]

On 6 December 1725 Flynt again went to Boyer, this time to have a pair of gold buttons weighed.

Mem. That Mr Taylor tells mee from Boyer the Jeweller That my gold buttons 5 p$^{w.}$ 2 gr. 1 p^{wt} is 11^{sh} 1 gr. is 5$\frac{d_1}{2}$ an ounce of gold is 11^{lb} a half penny weight more of gold wil make mee a pair flat buttons & a pair of Studds with Stones[6]

Flynt apparently decided to have the work done, for on 4 February 1726, he noted,

Mem. That Mr Boyer askt 9^{sh} for the Stones 6^{sh} for the Silver & making a pair of ristband buttons & 5^{sh} for Stones 10^{sh} for Silver & making a pair of Studds or more or less in proportion to the goodness & clearness of the Stones & nicety of the work. I gave him 30^{sh} for a pair of buttons with Christal Stones.[7]

James Boyer also received £22.14.6 from Nathaniel Cunningham for supplying sixteen rings for the estate of John Panton and £21 for supplying six mourning rings for the estate of Ann Penelope Parker.[8] James Boyer "jeweller" was on the bond for the estate of Bartholomew Feurt in 1733/34 and was paid £1.19.6 from the estate of Isaac Perkins (q.v.).[9] Boyer appeared in cases before the Court of Common Pleas several times between 1730 and 1739, including one case against Charles Sanders, a mariner, who owed Boyer £3.10 for a pair of stone buttons.[10]

The ledger of Benjamin Greene (q.v.) contains accounts with Boyer beginning in 1735 and continuing until after Boyer's death, when his business was managed by his wife, Mary Ann. According to these accounts, Greene sold Boyer such items as strainers, casters, buckles, buttons, thimbles, earrings, snuffboxes, teaspoons, spectacle frames, pipe stoppers, sugar tongs, and silver hilts for swords. He paid Boyer for stay hooks, mourning rings, and studs; for rings, buttons, earrings, and buckles set with stones, including cipher stone buttons; for mending rings and buttons; and for mending and "Changeing" earrings. On occasion, Greene also colored gold chains for Boyer, and after Boyer died Greene made gold beads for Mary Ann Boyer, a function that he had not performed while James Boyer was alive. The accounts further suggest that Boyer set stones in mounts for rings, earrings, buttons, and buckles that Greene provided.[11] Boyer and his apprentices made all of the gold beads that they needed in their own shop until James's death in 1741, after which time some of this work was also done by other goldsmiths. Among the apprentices in Boyer's shop were his son Daniel and possibly Andrew Oliver.

James Boyer died intestate, the administration of his estate being granted to his father-in-law, Daniel Johonnot, a distiller, on 5 May 1741. The estate, which was appraised by Stephen Boutineau, Jeffrey Bedgood, and Jacob Hurd (q.v.), included £71.11.6 (Massachusetts currency) in tools and £164.6.6 (Massachusetts currency) in shop goods and stones:

In the Shop

1 p.ʳ Organ Bellows &c 30/ 2 Ingots 20/	£ 2 .10.—
1 p.ʳ kneelen Tongs 5/ 1 Lamp & 2 blow Pipes 10/	— .15.—
2 Candles.ᵏˢ & Snuffers 2/ fire shovel & Melting Iron 3/6	— . 5. 6
3 Tinpans 10/ 3 Sparrhawks 12/	1. 2.—
a Case of Drawers with Pattens & Enamel	4.10.—
3 upright Drills 60/ a frame Saw 15/	3.15.—
Sundry old Files & a Rasp & Scorper & Gravers	— . 5.—
a Ring Sizes 15/ 3 brass Stamps 70/ 2 Oyle Stones 60/	7 . 5.—
2 p.ʳ Sliding Tongs 4/ 11 p.ʳ Plyers & 2 p.ʳ Screw Compasses & } 3 p.ʳ Corning Tongs 40/ 5 Drawing Irons 35/ 2 Wooden vices 3/ }	4. 2.—
2 borax Boxes 10/ 7 p.ʳ Shares 30/	2.—.—
1 p.ʳ Scissars & Semitsticks 2/ 2 board Vices 80/	4. 2.—
2 Copp.ʳ Boyling pans 16/ a Touchstone 5/	1. 1.—
2 Lead Cisterns 60/ a Drawing Bench & 2 Draw.ᵍ Tongs 50/	5.10.—
2 Ring Swages 12/ 7 Hamers 20/ Sundry punches Comon 20/	2.12.—
Sundry wrought punches 60/ a Drawing press 60/	6.—.—
Flask & Screws 20/ a Box moulding Sand 5/ Pewt.ʳ & Lead 5/	1.10.—
2 Lemell Boxes 7/ a Show Glass 40/ 3 Stakes 60/	5. 7.—
Sundry melting Potts & Cast Iron 10/ a Gun Sword & Cartouch box	6.10.—
2 Boards & a Counter Shop Wind.ᵒˢ platform & Bar of Iron	8.—.—
4 pr. Scales & weights 70/ a p.ʳ Diamond Scales 20/	4.10.—
7 Snuff Boxes 70/ 2 Shell boxes D.ᵒ 40/ 3 oz. wro.ᵗ Silv.ʳ £ 5.	10.10.—
a Garnet Ring 70/ a p.ʳ Cypher Buttons 30/	5.—.—
a Sma: Buckle 20/ 3 D.ᵒ 60/ Sundry Stone Buttons Hooks } & Earings 60/ Sundry Refuse Stones in a Drawer 60/ }	10.—.—
Sundry Polishing Stones &c.ᵃ in a Drawer	—.15.—
Gold & Silver Dust in a Drawer	2.—.—
Salt Petre & Borrax in a Drawer 8/ 4 Sma:Rose Diamonds 20/	1. 8.—
45 Sheets Foile@6/ £13.10/ 1 Box Cyphers & Lett.ʳˢ 70/	17.—.—
1 Paper of Garnetts 70/ 1 Ditto Emeralds 10/	4.—.—
1 Paper Emathist 60/ 2 Stones mock topaz 20/	4.—.—
1 Paper Coffin Stones &c 80/ 1 Pap.ʳ Buckle Sparks 35/	£ 5.15.—
11 Bristol Stones 12/ Deaths Head & Cyphers 40/ Gold Powd.ʳ 15/	3. 7.—
a Box with Sundry Stones	64. 7. 6
a Box with Sundry Stones &c	24.—.—
a Jewelling Box & 2 Ring Cases 25/ Sundry Stones £9.15/	11.—.—
Ditto Stones	1. 4.—[12]

Boyer's personal estate amounted to £680.12.3 (Massachusetts currency); he owned no real estate. The inventory of the estate was taken room by room and indicated that the house Boyer and his family lived in was three stories in height and probably one room deep with a shop fronting on the street. The rooms listed are the shop, kitchen, low room, front chamber, back chamber, front upper chamber, and back upper chamber.[13]

Boyer's estate was declared insolvent, and Boutineau, Bedgood, and Hurd, along with Rowland Houghton, were named commissioners to examine the claims of creditors.[14] The list of claims against the estate included £25.7.5 owed to Benjamin Greene, £50.3.10 owed to Jacob Hurd, £1 owed to Samuel Gray (1710/11–48) (q.v.), £29.6 owed to Joseph Goldthwait (q.v.), £2.11.9 owed to the estate of George Hanners, Sr. (q.v.), £63.11.7 owed to Rufus Greene (q.v.), and 15 shillings and 10 pence owed to John Burt (q.v.).[15]

James Boyer was buried in the Granary Burying Ground. His tombstone is inscribed, "HERE LYES BURIED | THE BODY OF | Mᵣ JAMES BOYER | AGED 41 YEARS | Decᵈ April yᵉ 26ᵗʰ 1741."[16]

No silver or jewelry by James Boyer has been identified. BMW

1. Robert B. Barker provided this information from the London Public Record Office, Inland Revenue Records, first series, Tax Roll on Apprenticeships, IR 1, vol. 1, fol. 123.
2. RC 28:160.
3. RC 24:174, 180, 190, 195, 201; SCPR 78:416–18.
4. Henry Flynt Memorandum Book, HU.
5. Henry Flynt Memorandum Book, HU.
6. Henry Flynt Memorandum Book, HU.
7. Henry Flynt Memorandum Book, HU.
8. SCPR 26:25–27; 31:510. The latter estate administration was presented in 1733.
9. SCPR, docket 6543; MCPR 24:184.
10. SCCR, Court of Common Pleas Record Book 1730, 470; 1733–34, 358; 1735, 67; 1738, 204; 1739, 27; SCCR, files 17175, 30618.
11. Benjamin Greene Ledger, 1734–56, 1, 64, 93, 99, MHS.
12. SCPR 35:400–01.
13. SCPR 35:400–02.
14. SCPR 35:429–30; 36:310–11.
15. SCPR 37:136–38.
16. Bridgman 1856, 181, annotated copy, YUAG, and photograph of tombstone in the Bigelow-Phillips files with all but the date of death readable.

Mary Ann (Johonnot) Boyer 1706–47

Mary Ann (Johonnot) Boyer was born in Boston on 17 August 1706, the daughter of Daniel (ca. 1668–1748) and Susan (Sigourney) Johnson Johonnot.[1] Daniel Johonnot was from La Rochelle in France and was one of the Huguenot settlers who established the town of Oxford, Massachusetts. He was living in Oxford in 1686 with his uncle Andrew Sigourney (ca. 1638–1727), and in 1696 he saved his cousin, Susan (Sigourney) Johnson, during the Indian attack in which her husband, John Johnson, and her three children were killed.[2]

Mary Ann married the jeweler James Boyer (q.v.) in 1724.[3] The couple had six children, five of whom survived to adulthood, and one of whom, Daniel (q.v.), became a jeweler.[4] James Boyer died in 1741, and Mary Ann Boyer assumed management of his business. According to the administration account on her husband's estate, one hundred pounds in "Necessary Implements of Household [were] allowd yᵉ Widow for the Support of herself & five children." Mary Ann Boyer also received twenty pounds for "Housekeeping" and ten pounds for mourning. She must have taken a large part of her share of the estate in tools and stock, as she continued her husband's jewelry business.[5]

Accounts with Benjamin Greene (q.v.) between June 1741 and April 1744 indicate that Mary Ann Boyer kept the business active. There is only one significant difference in the accounts between Benjamin Greene and James Boyer and between Benjamin Greene and Mary Ann Boyer. Greene sold only ten beads to James Boyer. However, after James died Greene made large numbers of gold beads for Mary Ann.[6] In 1742 John Blowers (q.v.) sued Mary Ann Boyer for payment on an account. According to the bill filed with the court, Blowers made a snuffbox worth £5 for Boyer and was still due £3.2.4.[7]

Mary Ann Boyer died on 22 May 1747 at age forty-one.[8] In his will (written in May 1748) Daniel Johonnot mentions his deceased daughter Mary Ann Boyer.[9] Johonnot left her portion of his estate to her five living children. In 1753 Daniel Boyer purchased the portion of his grandfather's estate inherited by his sister Susannah (Boyer) Oliver, wife of Andrew Oliver (q.v.), a jeweler who may have trained in the Boyer shop.[10]

No jewelry has been identified as Mary Ann Boyer's work. BMW

1. RC 24:42.
2. Savage 1860–62, 2:559–60; RC 28:1; SCPR 41:288–90, docket 9036; Sigourney 1857, 8.
3. RC 28:160.
4. RC 24:174, 180, 190, 195, 201.
5. SCPR 37:138–39. The court ordered that there was £468.14.5 left in the estate after the "Subduction of Funeral Expences Necessary Implements of Household allow'd the Widow and Charges of Adminacon &c." The estate was declared insolvent, and the administrator was ordered to pay the creditors "Three Shillings and nine pence half penny on the Pound of the Debts to them respectively owing."
6. Benjamin Greene Ledger, 1734–56, 1, 64, 93, 99, MHS.
7. SCCR, Court of Common Pleas Record Book 1741, 271; SCCR, file 54815.
8. Codman 1918, 43.
9. SCPR 41:288–90.
10. SCD 82:52.

Thomas Bradford
1697–1743 +

Thomas Bradford was born in Boston on 24 December 1697, the second son of Moses Bradford (1670–1729/30?) and Elizabeth Allen (d. before 1731), who were married by Rev. James Allen of the First Church, Boston, in 1692.[1] Moses was the son of Moses Bradford (1644–92) and his wife, Elizabeth.

Thomas appears as a witness to a deed of John Coney (q.v.) in 1716, when he would have been nineteen years old.[2] It is therefore likely that he served his apprenticeship under Coney. In 1721, he and several other artisans occupied a house on Marlborough Street that had belonged to Samuel Haugh (q.v.) before his death.[3] Bradford apparently rented a shop from Haugh, and it is possible that Bradford purchased tools from Haugh's estate in 1717. In 1721, Bradford married Abigail Dyer (b. 1695), daughter of Benjamin (1653–1718), a shopkeeper, and Hannah (Odlin) Dyer (1666–1730), and the couple had seven children: Thomas (b. 1723), John (b. 1724), Abigail (b. 1726), Thomas (b. 1728), Mary (bap. 1729), Elizabeth (bap. 1729), and Abigail (bap. 1732).[4]

Bradford inherited substantial wealth from his parents. Although the estate of Moses Bradford was not probated, he apparently left his children a sizable estate, including several parcels of land mentioned in deeds dated between 1725 and 1740. The main parcel was situated near the Town Dock. When part of that land was sold in 1725, the deed was witnessed by Thomas Mullins (q.v.).[5] Another parcel sold jointly by Thomas and his siblings in Wing's Lane in 1731 had been given to their mother, Elizabeth, by their grandmother Allen.[6] In these deeds Bradford is identified as a goldsmith.

Bradford was involved in suits in the Court of Common Pleas in 1721, 1736, and 1737.[7] He was living in Newbury Street when he applied for a license as a retailer of liquor in July 1731 (petition disallowed) and in Essex Street when he applied for a similar license in 1732 (license granted).[8] In 1734–35 and 1741–56 the town of Boston paid Thomas Bradford, probably the silversmith, as a watchman and constable of the South Watch. His son Thomas, a wharfinger, succeeded him as watchman, serving from 1768 to 1773.[9]

In the 1730s Bradford was one of several Boston goldsmiths who received payments for services rendered to a group of merchants who attempted to create a private bank in Boston. This silver- and gold-based Merchants' Bank took commodities and coins on account and issued bank notes on the strength of these assets. The bank issued its notes in November of 1733; these notes were redeemable in silver and gold in three installments over a period of several years. In connection with the bank, Joshua Winslow, one of the principal "Subscribers to the Scheme for emitting Notes of hand" made payments of £2.10, £3 (twice), £5 and £8 (twice) to Bradford on behalf of Nathaniel Morse (q.v.) in 1733, and direct payments to "Millner & Bradford" that totaled more than £100 in 1733 and 1736. These payments suggest that Thomas Milner (q.v.) and Bradford working in partnership with one another, were brought into the "scheme" through the efforts of Nathaniel Morse, who was specifically paid for "ingraving and printing the plates."[10] It is possible that Milner and Bradford assisted Morse in these efforts, but it is also possible that they assisted in weighing and appraising silver objects and coins (as the "lad" employed by John Burt [q.v.] did in 1734), or that they kept objects and coins for safekeeping. They may also have been engaged to melt down old objects and determine their value as specie. This appears to have been the beginning of an ongoing relationship because between 1736 and 1738 Bradford worked in conjunction with Milner and Morse on several reissues of the Massachusetts Province bills of credit.[11]

The goldsmith Thomas Bradford does not appear in the Suffolk probate records, and the date of his death is unknown.[12] His son Thomas is referred to as Jr. in 1761, which suggests that the father was still alive at that time.[13] The last documentary reference to "Thomas Bradford, goldsmith," however, is in 1743.[14]

No silver by him has been identified. BMW

1. RC 9:113, 203, 232; *Index of Obituaries, 1704–1800*, 1:36. Elizabeth Allen was probably the daughter either of Edward and Lydia Allen, born 21 March 1672 (RC 9:122), or of Hope and Hannah Allen, born also in 1672 (RC 9:122). However, it is also possible that she was the daughter of Bozoon and Rachel Allen, born 17 July 1678 (RC 9:144).
2. Although Bigelow gives the source for the deed as SCPR 18:41, the information does not appear there and has not been located elsewhere.
3. SCCR, Court of Common Pleas Record Book 1721–22, 47.
4. RC 9:101, 198, 221; RC 24:158, 163, 174, 185, 191; Pierce 1961, 368, 391, 393, 395, 397, 398, 399, 401; Bridgman 1853, 156; Roberts 1895, 1:284; RC 28:99.
5. SCD 46:152–53. The land was adjacent to land owned by George Hanners, Sr. (q.v.).
6. SCD 46:117, 200–01; 50:187; 65:250–51.
7. SCCR, Court of Common Pleas Record Book 1721–22, 47; 1735–36, 310; 1736–37, 438; John M. Fitzgerald to Francis Hill Bigelow, List of Boston Court Record References to Silversmiths, Bigelow-Phillips files. Fitzgerald notes a case in the Court of Common Pleas Record Book for 1735–36. That book is now missing.
8. RC 13:209, 219–20.
9. Seybolt 1939, 196*n*.
10. Joshua Winslow Account Book and Case Book, n.p., NEHGS. For information on the Merchants' Bank and other banking schemes of the 1730s and 1740s, see Warden 1970 and Brooke 1989, 57.
11. Mass. Archives, 101, docs. 525, 528, 571; 245, docs. 610, 611, 689.
12. It is unlikely that he is the mariner Thomas Bradford of Portsmouth, New Hampshire, whose will was probated in Boston in 1762; SCPR 61:125.
13. SCD 97:88–90.
14. SCD 65:250–51.

William Breed
1719–61 or 62

William Breed was born on 20 May 1719 and was baptized in the Second Church, Boston.[1] He was the second son of Nathaniel Breed (1685–1761) and Sarah Davis (1685–1739/40), who were married on 31 March 1709 by the Reverend Cotton Mather in the Second Church.[2] William Breed's paternal grandparents were Allen Breed (1660–1730) and Elizabeth Ballard (d. 1743) of

A

B

C

Lynn, Massachusetts; his maternal grandparents were William and Martha Davis.[3]

On 20 October 1743, William Breed married Susanna Barrington (b. 1721), daughter of Sarah (Robinson) and Richard Barrington (d. by 1744), a perukemaker from Ireland. Rev. Joseph Sewall performed the ceremony in Boston's Old South Church.[4] A daughter, Susanna, was born to the goldsmith and his wife in 1744.[5]

It is not known with whom Breed was apprenticed, but he would have been ready to practice his trade about 1740. "William Breed of Boston, Goldsmith," appeared as the plaintiff in the Suffolk County Court of Common Pleas on 3 April 1744 for a writ dated 18 June 1743 against Samuel Scollay, a baker living in Medford.[6] William was awarded "£5.7 shillings lawful money or £5.9 shillings, 9 pence in Bills of the last tenor Damage" and costs of £1.14 by the court. He was a beneficiary of his father's will, written in November 1760 and presented for probate on 2 October 1761.[7] The estate, which included over eighty-seven ounces of silver valued at £29, was appraised on 30 October 1761 by Samuel Edwards (q.v.), John Pimm, and Thomas Coverly (q.v.).[8] Breed was to receive an equal quarter of the estate, deducting the sum of £65.5 that he had been advanced between 1744 and 1750, money probably intended to help him establish himself as a silversmith and support his new wife and young family.[9] His sister, Elizabeth, received similar parental support of £79.11.9 in 1749, the year she married Richard Richardson, possibly the silversmith (q.v.).[10]

William Breed probably died in late 1761 or early in 1762 because on 29 January 1762, the brewer Sampson Salter of Boston was appointed to be the guardian of "William Breed a minor under fourteen years of age Son of William Breed late of Boston afores'd Goldsmith, deceased."[11] This may be the same Sampson Salter who was the father-in-law of John Blowers (q.v.), suggesting that a close relationship existed between Breed and Blowers. The younger William is listed in the tax assessor's list of 1780 and in the *Boston Directory* for 1789 as a baker located on Temple Street.[12]

During his twenty-one-year silversmithing career, Breed produced a wide variety of holloware and flatware forms. Three marks have been identified as his. The earliest may be the initial and surname mark (A) that appears on a punch strainer owned by the Massachusetts Historical Society. The strainer is an elegant, accomplished example of Breed's craftsmanship: the bowl is elaborately pierced with a pattern of crosses, dots, and stars; the handles are extensively engraved with a memorial inscription to Jonathan Vryling, who died on 25 November 1744. Another initial and surname mark (B) occurs with the initial mark (C) on a pair of porringers.[13] The use of these marks together establishes the attribution of the initial mark (C) to Breed with certainty. DAF

SURVIVING OBJECTS

Mark	Inscription	Patron	Date	Reference	Owner
Cann A or B	?		ca. 1755	*Antiques* 98 (December 1970): 878	
Cann B*	K/BE		ca. 1750	*Silver Supplement* 1973, nos. 6a–b	

	Mark	Inscription	Patron	Date	Reference	Owner
Cann	B*	AED (cipher)		ca. 1750	*Silver Supplement* 1973, nos. 6a–b	
Cann	B*	none		ca. 1755	Puig et al. 1989, no. 208	MIA
Cann	B	P/WA	William and Abigail (Bromfield) Phillips	ca. 1750	YUAG files	
Ladle	?	SB		ca. 1750	Parke-Bernet, 17 June 1969, lot 21	
Pepper box	A†	IEC (cipher)		ca. 1755	DAPC 68.3438	MMA
Pepper box	A	P/PM	Philip and Mehitable Pollard	ca. 1750	Hammerslough/ Feigenbaum 1958–73, 1:54	
Pepper box	?	?		?	Buhler 1972, 1:291	
Porringer	B	P/WA		ca. 1750	YUAG files	
Porringer	B	unidentified		ca. 1750	Buhler 1972, 1:291	
Porringer (mate below)	B†/ c†	I/AE		ca. 1745	Buhler 1972, no. 244	MFAB
Porringer (mate above)	B*/c*	I/AE		ca. 1745	Quimby 1995, no. 8	WM
Two salts	B*	Codman crest, a bird with a sprig in its beak; IC to IG	Codman family	ca. 1745	Buhler/Hood 1970, no. 192	YUAG
Strainer	A*	Tyng crest, a martlet; (engraved on one handle) Apud Cartagenam in Hispania Nova Obsessam Die Dominica Aprilis 12th 1741 Spolia inter Alia Argentum ew quo Factus sum accept *JOANNES VRYLING*; (on the back) In memoriam Jnº Vryling qui ex hoc vita decessit 25 Novembris 1744 Haerides ad Jonª Tyng cognatum & Amicum delectum donaverunt; (on the other handle) Meminisse Iuvabit; (on the back) Isq: morens Johanni Loring	The Heirs of Jonathan Vryling	1744	English-Speaking Union 1960, no. 57	MHS
Strainer	?	IS		ca. 1750	YUAG files	

	Mark	Inscription	Patron	Date	Reference	Owner
Two tablespoons	B*	F/SM		ca. 1750	Christie's, 26 January 1985, lot 86	YUAG
Teapot	B*	none		ca. 1750	Wenham 1931, 32	AG
Teaspoon	C	MM		ca. 1750		CHS
Whistle with coral and bells	A or B	AW/1750; SW/1752 (later); IW/1766 (later)		ca. 1750	Buhler 1972, 291	

1. RC 24:134; Robbins 1852, 232, records the baptismal date as 10 May 1719.
2. RC 9:165; RC 28:22; *Lynn VR* 1:61; SCPR 59:286–88; Whitmore 1878, 44, nos. 823–24.
3. *Lynn VR* 1:61; 2:55, 433, 439; RC 9:165.
4. RC 28:38, 237; Robbins 1852, 229; SCPR 37:133–34.
5. RC 24:252.
6. SCCR, Court of Common Pleas Record Book 1743–44, 244.
7. SCPR 59:286–88.
8. SCPR 59:347–49.
9. SCPR 61:383–84.
10. SCPR 61:383–84; RC 28:261.
11. SCPR 60:61. Breed was also identified as deceased when real estate from his father's estate was divided in 1765; SCPR 64:421.
12. "Assessors' 'Taking-Books,'" 34; *Boston Directory* 1789, 9.
13. One porringer of the pair is in the WM, the other in the MFAB. Kovel 1961, 41, also records WB in a heart. No example was found to verify this attribution.

John Bridge
1723–55 +

A

B

C

John Bridge, the son of Ebenezer Bridge (1687–1747), a blacksmith, and Mary Roberts (b. 1690), who were married on 11 May 1710, was born in Boston on 21 July 1723 and was baptized the same day in the New Brick Church.[1] His paternal grandparents were Samuel (1647?–1717), a house carpenter, and his first wife, Hannah Bridge (ca. 1651–90); his maternal grandparents were John and Experience Roberts.[2] John Bridge's mother died sometime before 19 March 1729/30, the date his father married Mary Greenough (b. 1696), the widow of Thaddeus Maccarty.[3]

Bridge was probably apprenticed about 1737 and would have begun practicing his trade about 1744. He received a commission as an ensign in the ninth company, First Massachusetts Regiment, on 5 February 1744/45 and participated in the Cape Breton expedition under Sir William Pepperrell.[4] His name appears on a list, dated 13 September 1745, of those who wished to receive their plunder following the attack on Louisbourg.[5] Bridge is first called a goldsmith in Suffolk Deeds on 16 September 1749, when his stepmother quitclaimed her interest in her husband Ebenezer's estate.[6]

Sometime between 11 March 1750/51 and 1 April 1751, Nathan Greenwood, John Greenough, and John Baker, the executors of the estate of Mrs. Mary Hunnewell, paid £18.10 for 55½ ounces of silver at 6 shillings and 8 pence an ounce to make a flagon and £7.17¾ "To John Bridge for making the Flaggon and Ingraving," and £11.14.8 "To John Bridge for making Seventeen Gold Rings."[7] That flagon, made for the New North Church, Boston, another at the Second Church in Boston, and a punch strainer are the only pieces by Bridge known to survive. The punch strainer bears an initial and surname mark (A). The flagon made for the New North Church bears both a surname mark (B) and an initial and surname mark (C) in cartouches.

Little more is known of John Bridge's life. In 1751 he joined the Ancient and Honorable Artillery Company, and William Simpkins (q.v.) was surety for him. The next year Bridge was a fourth sergeant.[8] He served as a constable in Boston from 1752 to 1755.[9] No record of a marriage exists; he probably lived with his stepmother, who married Ebenezer Dorr in 1749.[10] An account for the estate of Ebenezer Bridge indicates that John paid fourteen pounds' rent from 11 July 1751 to 22 September 1753.[11] In the documents pertaining to the sale of the property from his father's estate on 21 September 1753, John Bridge describes himself as a gentleman.[12] Since there are no subsequent references to John Bridge in Boston records, it seems likely that Bridge died shortly after this time. Contrary to what some scholars have suggested, the John Bridge found in Suffolk Deeds in the 1790s is probably not the goldsmith.[13] PEK

SURVIVING OBJECTS

	Mark	Inscription	Patron	Date	Reference	Owner
Flagon	B	Welstone arms, azure a bend chequey argent and gules; The Rev.d Mr. Welsteed Pastor of this/Church order'd on his Death bed this flaggon/to be given as a token of the Tender affection/he bears towards us 1753	Rev. William Welsteed and/or Second Church, Boston	ca. 1753	Jones 1913, 40	
Flagon	B†/ C†	The Gift/OF/Mrs Mary Hunewell/ Decd to the New/ North Church/Bos- ton/1751. (+)	Executors of Mary Hunnewell's estate for New North Church, Boston	1751	Jones 1913, 62–63	
Strainer	A†	H (later)		ca. 1750	Buhler 1972, no. 236	MFAB

1. Roberts 1895, 1:397; RC 9:172, 191; RC 24:158; RC 28:26.
2. Roberts 1895, 1:252; *Charlestown VR* 1:10; Codman 1918, 46; SCPR, docket 3899.
3. RC 28:65, 148.
4. *NEHGR* 24:369.
5. *NEHGR* 25:252, 255.
6. SCD 77:137–38.
7. SCPR 64:186–88.
8. Roberts 1895, 2:59–60.
9. RC 14:207, 229, 233, 245; RC 19:3, 20.
10. RC 28:243.
11. SCPR 48:402–04.
12. SCD 83:52–54.
13. SCD 178:128; 185:281; 190:44.

Zachariah Brigden
1734–87

A

B

C

D

E

Zachariah Brigden was born in Charlestown, Massachusetts, on 21 December 1734 to Michael Brigden (1698–1767), a blacksmith, and Winifred Sprague (1699–1739), who were married in 1720.[1] Zachariah Brigden's paternal grandparents were Michael Brigden (1664–1709) and Joanna Wilson (1667–1735).[2] His maternal grandparents were Samuel (1662–1739) and Sarah Sprague (d. 1744).[3] Following Brigden's mother's death in 1739, his father married Elizabeth Gill (b. 1707), widow of Capt. John Gill, in 1740.[4]

Brigden probably began his apprenticeship in 1748, in all likelihood with Thomas Edwards (q.v.). The twenty-one-year-old Brigden witnessed a mortgage between Benjamin Edwards, Jr. (q.v.), and Thomas Edwards on 1 April 1755.[5] Thomas Edwards died in 1755, and the marriage intentions of Brigden and Edwards's daughter, Sarah (1724–68), were published on 9 December 1756.[6] She was ten years Brigden's senior. The couple continued to live in her father's Cornhill house, where, in 1765, they were assessed by the town for repair of a pump.[7] Strong familial bonds existed between Brigden and the Edwards family goldsmiths. In 1758, when Brigden and his wife sold property in Cambridge, Massachusetts, Samuel Edwards (q.v.) witnessed the deed along with Joseph Edwards, possibly his nephew the silversmith (q.v.).[8] Brigden also bought goldsmiths' tools and supplies from the estate of Samuel Edwards in 1762.[9]

From his surviving business and personal papers and advertisements, much is known about how Brigden ran his business.[10] Brigden probably employed the jeweler William Cario, Sr. (q.v.), as a journeyman, because his name turns up frequently in Brigden's papers. Cario witnessed deeds for Brigden when he sold land in Cambridge in 1758 and 1759.[11] Brigden paid for wood delivered to Cario between 1761 and 1763.[12] Brigden also sold tools and other supplies to Cario in 1764.[13] When Zachariah and Sarah Brigden were settling part of her father's estate in 1767, Joseph Edwards and William Cario again witnessed a deed.[14] In 1767 Brigden also paid for a pair of gravestones for Cario's daughter-in-law, Abigail, wife of the silversmith, William Cario, Jr. (q.v.).[15]

Brigden was one of the Boston goldsmiths who specialized in selling supplies to other craftsmen. In the *Boston Gazette* for 19 November 1764 Brigden advertised,

> Just Imported from LONDON,
> And to be Sold by
> Zechariah Brigden,
> Goldsmith;
> *At his Shop opposite the West Door of the Town-House.*
> CORAL Beeds, and Stick Coral
> for Children's Whistles; Money Scales and
> Weights; neat Watch Plyers; Sliding Tongs; Shears
> and Hand Vices; coarse and fine Iron Binding Wire;
> Brass Hollow Stamps and Blow Pipes; an Assortment
> of Files for the Goldsmith's Use; Gravers; Scorpers;
> Dividers; Sand Paper; Sandever; Black Lead Pots;
> large and small Crucibles; Wood and Bone Polishing
> Brushes; Borax; Salt Petre; Rotton and Pummice
> Stone; Moulding Sand by Cask or Retail.
>   ALSO, Shoe, Knee and Stock Stone Buckles;
> Buttons; Christial and Cornelian Seals; Neat Stone
> Bosom Broaches; Garnet; Hoop Rings. A few

Pair of neat Stone Earings sett in Clusters, in Shagreen Cases, cheap for Cash.[16]

Brigden's daybook documents his sale of silver to Seth Coburn (q.v.), molding sand to Daniel Boyer (q.v.), and crucibles to David Greenleaf (q.v.).[17] Brigden is also known to have purchased supplies from Joseph Loring (q.v.).[18]

When he needed particular skills, Brigden turned to other craftsmen. After the death of the jeweler William Cario, Sr., he tended to purchase enameled jewelry, and jewelry set with stones, from others rather than have it made in his shop. In three instances he bought rings from Boston jewelers. There are receipts for rings from Josiah Flagg, Jr. (q.v.), in December 1766, Benjamin Pierpont (q.v.) in January 1767, and Daniel Boyer from July to September 1770.[19] Brigden also patronized Boston engravers. Receipts survive from Joseph Callender (q.v.) to Brigden for engraving in 1785 and 1787.[20]

Brigden's shop had the capacity to make significant amounts of flatware and holloware. The daybook that survives for the period 1767 to ca. 1775 contains evidence on the range of wares he made for retail customers, jewelers, and other goldsmiths. The jeweler Daniel Boyer was a principal customer. Brigden, using silver Boyer provided, produced a steady stream of work for him between 1770 and 1775. Brigden also did a considerable amount of repair work for Boyer and other jewelers and goldsmiths. With Boyer, Brigden appraised the estate of Daniel Henchman in 1775.[21] Brigden also witnessed Nathaniel Hurd's (q.v.) will in 1777.[22] Among the other jewelers Brigden served was Joseph Coolidge (q.v.), Boyer's son-in-law.[23] Brigden also made raised parts of objects for Benjamin Burt (q.v.). A receipt from Burt to Brigden's estate shows that Burt gave Brigden credit for "making 4 Butter Boat Bodys" valued at £4.[24] Their relationship was a long-standing one. When Brigden sold silver to Seth Storer Coburn in 1767, Brigden acknowledged part payment as "cash Rec^d of Burt," probably Benjamin Burt.[25] In 1781 Brigden and Burt appraised the estate of Benjamin Hurd (q.v.), and that same year Brigden and Caleb Swan (q.v.) signed the bond when Burt became the administrator of the estate of his brother-in-law Joseph Glidden.[26]

After Brigden's first wife died in 1768, he married Elizabeth Gillam (1734–93) in 1774.[27] Just prior to this marriage Brigden mortgaged the Cornhill property.[28] In 1772 he was chosen a warden at a Boston town meeting.[29] In 1777 and 1782 he also sold land he had inherited in Charlestown.[30] In 1781 and 1782 he was chosen a juror for the maritime court.[31] In March and May 1782 he borrowed ninety-five pounds from Benjamin Burt, and in June he paid off a mortgage on a house and land held by the estate of William Maycock.[32] In 1784 Brigden and his wife sold property on Summer Street in Boston.[33]

Brigden died in Boston on 10 March 1787.[34] The administration of the estate was granted to his widow on 19 March 1787.[35] The inventory of the estate was taken by Benjamin Burt, Moses Grant, and Jacob Cooper. It is of interest because it lists the contents of the goldsmith's glass display cases:

In the Shop brass beam & Scales 24/ 2 p^r Scales 12/ Goldsmiths tools £30	31. 16.0
67 & ¹⁄₂ Ounces of Family plate @ 6/	20. 5.0
3 p^r plated buckles 6/ Pewter Rings 2/	0. 8.0
In the Glass Cases, Shoe buckles, knee, Can, Spoons Salts &c &c w^t 96 ^{oz} @ 6/	28. 16.0
Limmen Box 7 ^{oz} @ 6/ 42/	2. 2.0
11 p^r Earing Tops set in Gold 88/ 3 p^r Earings with drops 36/	6. 4.0
p^r three drop Garnet Earings 18/ 5 p^r Stone buttons 20/	1. 18.0
11 Stone Rings set in Gold 49/6 5 p^r Earings 4 Rings p^r buttons Gold 12 ^{dwt}12^{gr} 4/50/	4. 19.6

Stone Stock buckle & other odd Stone buckles 16/   0. 16.0
2 p.ʳ Stone Earings 6/ 3 Stone pins 4/6 3 Glass Cases 30/   2. 0.6[36]

In April 1787 his widow petitioned the Suffolk Court of Common Pleas to
grant her the authority to sell real estate "where it can be best spared" to cover
Brigden's debts.[37] In December 1787 Brigden's estate was sued by the estate of
Nathaniel Sparhawk of Portsmouth, New Hampshire, for notes amounting
to £83.0.5 that Brigden had signed in 1783 and 1784.[38] By the spring of 1788
his widow had sold his share in the Charlestown Bridge for £150, forty-four
ounces of the family plate for £13.4, and £28.16 worth of the wares in the shop.
The tools and other goods were still unsold, "it being impossible to sell them
for any Sum near their value."[39] Later that summer she sold land in Charlestown
to Benjamin Burt and Moses Gill.[40] Some silver scholars have said that
Benjamin Burt bought Brigden's tools, but no evidence has been found.[41]
Brigden's widow may have continued to live in the "mansion house & land in
Cornhill," which was valued in the estate at £1,200. This property was sold
in 1792, and his widow died in Charlestown in 1793.[42]

   More than 120 pieces by Brigden are known to survive, including a number
of communion vessels in New England churches. Brigden's work is identified
by an initial and surname mark (A) and four initials marks. One of the initials
marks (B) is found on pieces with the surname mark. Two initials marks (C,
E) have pellets; mark (D) has no pellet. A spurious initials mark is known.[43]
Through a typographical error for Z. Brigden, the maker C. Brigdens (q.v.
Appendix B) has been included in lists of American silversmiths. PEK

SURVIVING OBJECTS

	Mark	Inscription	Patron	Date	Reference	Owner
Three beakers	A	The Gift of/Cap.ᵗ Joshua Loring/to the Church of Christ/in/DUXBURY	First Congregational Church, Duxbury, Mass., for Joshua Loring	ca. 1781	Jones 1913, 157	
Beaker	?	JW		ca. 1780	Hobbies (June 1938): 109	
Bowl	A	Bradstreet (later)		ca. 1775	Buhler 1960, no. 1	MFAB
Cann	A	unidentified crest, a wyvern; R (later)		ca. 1765	Antiques 94 (July 1968): 14	HMA
Cann	A	H/RM		ca. 1770	Silver Supplement 1973, no. 7	
Cann	A	Grey arms, argent a lion rampant within bordure or engrailed, and crest, a unicorn passant collared and chained	Grey family	ca. 1770	MFA 1911, no. 68	
Cann (mate below)	A*	Cunningham crest, a unicorn's head (+)	Cunningham family	ca. 1780	Hammerslough/ Feigenbaum 1958–73, 1:2	WA
Cann (mate above)	A	Cunningham crest, a unicorn's head	Cunningham family	ca. 1780	Buhler 1965, 97–99	HMA

	Mark	Inscription	Patron	Date	Reference	Owner
Cann (mate below)	A	Murray arms, a hunting horn, in chief a crescent above 3 stars, and crest, a demi-man nude, blowing a horn	Murray family	ca. 1770	MFA 1906, no. 16	
Cann (mate above)	A	Murray arms, a hunting horn, in chief a crescent above 3 stars, and crest, a demi-man nude, blowing a horn	Murray family	ca. 1770	YUAG files	
Two canns	A	The Gift/of Josiah Dwight Esq'/to the first Church/of Christ in/Spring-field/1761	Josiah Dwight and/or First Church of Christ, Springfield, Mass.	1761	Jones 1913, 456–57	
Cann (mate below)	A*	BFG; 1778		1778	Johnston 1994, 10	CMA
Cann (mate above)	A*	BFG; 1778 (+)		1778	DAPC 76.2964	
Cann	A*	AC (+)		ca. 1785	YUAG files	
Cann	A	Sayward crest	Jonathan Sayward	ca. 1775		SPNEA
Cann	A	MC		ca. 1770	MFA 1906, no. 15	
Cann	A/C or E	P/BL (+)		ca. 1780	*Moore Collection* 1980, no. 155	
Cann	B	none		ca. 1780	DAPC 68.3780A	
Caster	B*	none		ca. 1765	YUAG files	
Caster	B*	A/IS		ca. 1765	YUAG files	
Caster	B*	D; MS (later)		ca. 1775	Puig et al. 1989, no. 211	MIA
Caster	B	MN		ca. 1780	*Silver Supplement* 1973, no. 67	
Caster	B*	A/WP (+)		ca. 1775	Quimby 1995, no. 10	WM
Caster	B	?		ca. 1760	Skinner, 15 June 1991, lot 164F	
Caster	B	MD		ca. 1780	*Antiques* 108 (November 1975): 908	
Caster	B	C/RE		ca. 1760	YUAG files	
Two casters	C or E	?		ca. 1770	MFA 1911, nos. 79–80	
Caster	D	FCA		ca. 1785	Hammerslough/Feigenbaum 1958–73, 3:55	

	Mark	Inscription	Patron	Date	Reference	Owner
Caster	?	AC		ca. 1780	YUAG files	
Chocolate pot	A*	unidentified arms, or a lion rampant, and crest, a lion rampant crowned, impaling De(e)ring, gules 3 roebucks' heads	De(e)ring family	ca. 1760	Flynt/Fales 1968, 100–01	HD
Chocolate pot	A/B†	Storer arms, 3 quatrefoils on a chevron engrailed gules between 3 mullets, and crest, a talbot's head erased	Ebenezer and Mary (Edwards) Storer	ca. 1760	Buhler 1972, no. 326	MFAB
Creampot	B	EH		ca. 1775	Silver Supplement 1973, no. 9	
Creampot	B*	MW		ca. 1785	Flynt/Fales 1968, 101–02	HD
Creampot	B*	I/TM		ca. 1775	YUAG files	
Creampot	B*	MH (+)		ca. 1765	YUAG files	
Creampot	B*	Sayward arms, gules on a fess 3 leopards' faces argent between 2 chevrons ermine, and crest, a leopard's face; AURUM NON OPTO	Sayward family	ca. 1770	YUAG files	
Creampot	B*	M/LT		ca. 1775	YUAG files	
Creampot	B*	OB to MB	Moses Brown (?)	ca. 1770	Hammerslough/ Feigenbaum 1958–73, 3:79	HD
Creampot	B*	JW		ca. 1785	Johnston 1994, 10	CMA
Creampot	B	P/NE		ca. 1775	YUAG files	
Creampot	B	IM to IS		ca. 1785	YUAG files	
Creampot	C or E	?		ca. 1770	MFA 1911, no. 81	
Creampot	C or E	W/IE		ca. 1785		MFAB
Creampot	D	SF		ca. 1775	Hammerslough/ Feigenbaum 1958–73, 3:78	
Creampot	?	none		ca. 1775	Antiques 95 (June 1969): 773	
Creampot	?	unidentified initials		ca. 1780	Parke-Bernet, 1–3 December 1960, lot 618	

	Mark	Inscription	Patron	Date	Reference	Owner
Cup	B	M/WS; Mary Ann Stearns (later)		ca. 1760	Johnston 1994, 11 (as unknown maker)	CMA
Ladle	A	A	John and Katharine (Willard) Amory, Jr.	ca. 1785	Buhler 1972, no. 330	MFAB
Ladle	A/B	JS		ca. 1785	Sotheby's, 23–24 June 1994, lot 104	
Mourning ring (gold)	B*	Mad<u>m</u> Deb.^h Prince = ob 1 June 1766 AE 67	Deborah Prince	1766	Buhler/Hood 1970, no. 236	YUAG
Mug	A	Third Church in Salem	South Church, Salem, Mass.	ca. 1770	Jones 1913, 437	MFAB
Mug	B*	S/DD		ca. 1760	Johnston 1994, 11	CMA
Porringer	A	H/TA		ca. 1770	American Art Association–Anderson Galleries, 22–23 January 1937, lot 298	
Porringer	A	T/IR		ca. 1770	Buhler 1972, no. 329	MFAB
Porringer	A*	F/BM (+)		ca. 1770	YUAG files	
Porringer	A	MH	Mary (Whipple) Holyoke	ca. 1765	Avery 1920, no. 71	MMA
Porringer	A/B	R/CJ	Chandler and J. Robbins	ca. 1785	YUAG files	
Porringer	C	SB/to/LH		ca. 1775	Avery 1920, no. 200	MMA
Porringer	?	MW		ca. 1760	*Antiques* 108 (December 1975): 1036	
Porringer	?	?		ca. 1760	*Antiques* 66 (October 1954): 259	
Porringer spoon	A	LH	Lucy Hall	ca. 1775	YUAG files	
Salt	B*	AM		ca. 1760	Johnston 1994, 14 (as unknown maker)	CMA
Two salts	B	Bliss crest, a garb or	Jonathan Bliss	ca. 1770	Buhler 1972, no. 328	MFAB
Two sauceboats	A	Winthrop crest, a hare courant	Winthrop family	ca. 1760	Buhler 1972, no. 327	MFAB
Two sauceboats	A	Sayward arms, gules on a fess 3 leopards'	Sayward family	ca. 1760	Sotheby Parke Bernet,	

	Mark	Inscription	Patron	Date	Reference	Owner
		faces between 2 chevrons ermine, and crest, a leopard's face; AURUM NON OPTO			15–17 November 1973, lot 697	
Two shoe buckles	B	LW		ca. 1780	Avery 1920, nos. 201–02	MMA
Two pairs of sleeve buttons (gold)	B*	none		ca. 1760	Buhler/Hood 1970, no. 235	YUAG
Snuffbox	B	CW		ca. 1780	DAPC 70.3591	
Spoon	E*	?		ca. 1775	YUAG files	
Stock buckle	B	none		ca. 1775	Mazur/ Daniels 1969, 22–23	
Sugar bowl	A	?		ca. 1770	*Antiques* 119 (June 1981): 1342	
Sugar bowl	A†/ B*	Grey arms, argent a lion rampant within bordure or engrailed, and crest, a unicorn passant, impaling Lewis arms, a chevron between 3 trefoils slipped	Grey and Lewis families	ca. 1770	Buhler/Hood 1970, no. 234	YUAG
Sugar tongs	B*	E Lefebure	E. Lefebure	ca. 1765	Buhler 1972, no. 550	MFAB
Sugar tongs	B or C	LT		ca. 1775	*Hobbies* (June 1938): 109	
Sugar tongs	C*	T?L (+)		ca. 1785	YUAG files	
Sugar tongs	?	NML		ca. 1770	Christie's, 2 October 1982, lot 55	
Tablespoon	A*	ARB		ca. 1770	Quimby 1995, no. 12b	WM
Tablespoon	A*	ICH		ca. 1770	DAPC 76.2092	WM
Tablespoon	A*	D/JM		ca. 1760	Quimby 1995, no. 12a	WM
Tablespoon	A	ABB		ca. 1785	*Moore Collection* 1980, no. 157	
Tablespoon	A*	LD		ca. 1760		YUAG
Tablespoon	A	C/EZ		ca. 1760	*Moore Collection* 1980, no. 156	
Tablespoon	A*	SR		ca. 1770		YUAG
Tablespoon	A*	AE		ca. 1770		RISD
Tablespoon	A*	Alice Hussey/to/ Alice Alley	Alice Hussey and/or Alice Alley	ca. 1770		PEM
Tablespoon	A*	MW/to/IW		ca. 1775	YUAG files	
Tablespoon	A	E/EM		ca. 1770	YUAG files	

	Mark	Inscription	Patron	Date	Reference	Owner
Two tablespoons	A	RD		ca. 1775	MFA 1906, nos. 13–14	
Tablespoon (mate below)	C*	MC		ca. 1780		YUAG
Tablespoon (mate above)	C†	MC		ca. 1780	Quimby 1995, no. 11a	WM
Tablespoon	C	SS		ca. 1775	Quimby 1995, no. 11b	WM
Tankard	A*	Edwards arms, ermine a lion rampant, on a canton gules a double-headed eagle displayed, and crest, a demi-lion rampant holding a tower; SE	Sarah (Edwards) Brigden	ca. 1762		NHCHS
Tankard	A	The Gift of/Deacon Mathies:Rice/& Anna His Wife/ To the Church of Christ/in North-brough	Anna (Bigelow) Rice and/or First Congregational Church, Northborough, Mass.	ca. 1764	Jones 1913, 351–52	
Tankard	A	EL to ELE (later?) (+)		ca. 1770	Green/ Holland 1973, no. 1	
Teapot	A	MC		ca. 1780	English-Speaking Union 1960, no. 67	
Teapot	A	depiction of the Charles River Bridge; Presented to/Cap! David Wood,/by the Proprietors of/ CHARLES RIVER BRIDGE,/in Testimony of their entire Approbation/of his faithful Services,/as a special Director of that Work,/begun A.D. 1785,/and Perfected/A.D. 1786.	Proprietors of the Charles River Bridge, Boston, for David Wood	1786	Buhler 1972, no. 331	MFAB
Teapot	A	Sargent arms, a chevron sable between 3 dolphins embowed, impaling Winthrop arms, 3 chevrons embattled gules, overall a lion rampant; The.Gift. of.Col!: Epes.Sergeant.to.his./ daughter.Mary.	Epes Sargent and/or Mary Sargent	1760	Buhler 1972, no. 549	MFAB

	Mark	Inscription	Patron	Date	Reference	Owner
Two teaspoons	A	none		ca. 1760		MFAB
Three teaspoons	A	?		ca. 1775		MFAB
Teaspoon	B*	none		ca. 1775	YUAG files	
Teaspoon	B*	SD (+)		ca. 1785		YUAG
Teaspoon	B*	B/IR		ca. 1775		YUAG
Six teaspoons	B*	HC		ca. 1785		YUAG
Two teaspoons	B*	MM		ca. 1775		SI
Teaspoon	B*	RA		ca. 1770	YUAG files	
Teaspoon	B	O/IM		ca. 1770	YUAG files	
Teaspoon	B*	R/IA		ca. 1775		SFCAI
Teaspoon	C	AW		ca. 1780		WHS
Teaspoon	C*	SS		ca. 1770	DAPC 74.1403	WM
Teaspoon	C *or* E	EC	Elizabeth Cheever	ca. 1775	MFA 1911, no. 82	
Teaspoon	C *or* E	none		ca. 1785		BBC
Teaspoon	D†	LF		ca. 1775		YUAG
Teaspoon	E†	M/AS		ca. 1785	Eitner 1976, no. 61	
Two-handled cup	A	The Gift of/C/HE/ to the first Church of Christ/in Hadley		ca. 1770	YUAG files	
Two-handled cup	A	The Gift of/Mr Abraham Gould/to the/Church of Christ/in/ Stoneham/1786	Abraham Gould and/or First Congregational Church, Stoneham, Mass.	1786	Jones 1913, 461–62	
Two-handled cup	A	Belonging/to the/ Church of Christ/ in/Stoneham/1786	First Congregational Church, Stoneham, Mass.	1786	Jones 1913, 461–62	
Two-handled cup	A/C *or* D	This piece of/plate is presented to ye/ first Church in/Kit-tery by an/Un-known/Hand	Lady Pepperrell and/or First Congregational Church, Kittery, Maine	ca. 1770	Jones 1913, 237	
Two wine cups	A/B *or* C	The Gift of/Col John Pitkin/to the Church of the/3rd Sociy Hartford	John Pitkin and/or Con-gregational Church, East Hartford, Conn.	ca. 1785	Jones 1913, 157–58	
Two wine cups	A/B *or* C	The Gift of the/ Honbl Wm Pitkin Esqr/to the Church of the 3rd Sociy Hartford	William Pitkin and/or Congregational Church, East Hartford, Conn.	ca. 1785	Jones 1913, 158	
Wine cup	B	The Gift of/Elizth (Adams) Richard-son/To the Church of Christ/in/Med-field	Elizabeth (Adams) Richardson and/or First Parish Unitarian Church, Medfield, Mass.	ca. 1770		MFAB
Wine cup	B	The Gift of/Eleazer Bullard/To the	Eleazer Bullard and/or First Parish Unitarian	ca. 1770		MFAB

	Mark	Inscription	Patron	Date	Reference	Owner
		Church of Christ/ in/Medfield	Church, Medfield, Mass.			
Wine funnel	C or E	TB		ca. 1780	Hammerslough/ Feigenbaum 1958–73, 4:129	

1. *Charlestown VR* 1:177, 263, 339; Wyman 1879, 1:128; Griffen 1952, 17; *Malden VR*, 81.
2. *Charlestown VR* 1:27, 47, 58; Griffen 1952, 17.
3. Wyman 1879, 2:890; *Malden VR*, 80, 378.
4. Wyman 1879, 1:409. Moses Gill was their son.
5. SCD 86:256–57.
6. RC 30:22; RC 24:165.
7. RC 20:143.
8. MCD 64:312–13.
9. Invoice from the executors of Samuel Edwards to Brigden, 9 November 1762, Brigden Papers, YU.
10. The Brigden Papers are the property of the Beinecke Rare Book and Manuscript Library, YU. They document the lives of Zachariah Brigden and other members of the Brigden and Edwards families. The papers span the dates 1691–1798, but the bulk of the material covers the period 1748–87. They include daybooks, bills and receipts with customers, papers pertaining to household affairs, and estate administration.
11. MCD 56:354–56; 59:367–68.
12. Bills from Benjamin Phillips to Brigden, 17 September to 17 November 1761, 11 June 1764, Brigden Papers, YU.
13. Bill from Brigden to William Cario, Brigden Papers, YU.
14. SCD 115:39.
15. Bill from John Homer to Brigden, Brigden Papers, YU.
16. Advertisement repeated 26 November, 3 December 1764.
17. Zachariah Brigden Daybook, 1766–ca. 1775, fols. 6v, 7r, 11v, 32v, Brigden Papers, YU.
18. See the Loring entry for a transcription of an undated receipt from Loring to Brigden in the Brigden Papers, YU.
19. Brigden Papers, YU.
20. Bills from Joseph Callender to Brigden, March 1785 and 25 January 1787, Brigden Papers, YU. See the Callender entry for transcriptions.
21. SCPR 74:297–98.
22. SCPR 77:12–13.
23. Zachariah Brigden Daybook, 1766–ca. 1775, fols. 17v, 18v, 19r, 30v, 32v, 33r, 33v, Brigden Papers, YU.
24. Bill from Burt to Brigden estate, 18 April 1787, Brigden Papers, YU.
25. Zachariah Brigden Daybook, 1766–ca. 1775, fol. 7r, Brigden Papers, YU.
26. SCPR 80:314–19, 199.
27. RC 30:402; RC 24:216.
28. SCD 124:162–63.
29. RC 18:77.
30. MCD 78:143–44; 84:555.
31. RC 25:157, 185.
32. SCD 135:149–50. This deed does not say where this property is. It refers to vol. 114, p. 67, but that volume has been lost. That mortgage was dated 27 January 1769.
33. SCD 142:221–22.
34. *Index of Obituaries, 1784–1840*, 1:587.
35. SCPR 86:137.
36. Inventory, Brigden estate, Brigden Papers, YU; see also SCPR, docket 18844.
37. SCCR, Court of Common Pleas Record Book 1787, 110.
38. SCCR, Court of Common Pleas Record Book 1788, 164.
39. SCPR 87:236.
40. MCD 98:60–61; 100:142–44.

41. Flynt/Fales 1968, 166.
42. SCD 174:34; *Index of Obituaries, 1784–1840*, 1:586.
43. Puig et al. 1989, no. 242, for a basket at MIA and a sauceboat at MMA.

Daniel Brown, Jr.
w. ca. 1777

On 30 January 1777, Boston's *Independent Chronicle* published a notice that Mr. Daniel Brown, a goldsmith, had been married at Ipswich Hamlet to Miss Sofireree Dane.[1] The marriage record for the couple in the South Church, Ipswich, Massachusetts, indicates that Daniel Brown, Jr., and Zerviah Dane were married on 5 January 1777.[2] This is probably the Daniel Brown from Ipswich Hamlet who served as a corporal in Capt. Elisha Whitney's company of minutemen, which marched on the alarm of 19 April 1775, and who also served in Capt. Richard Dodge's company in 1777.[3] No records for the births of Daniel Brown or Zerviah Dane have been found in Ipswich vital records. An Essex County deed of 1795 mentions Daniel Brown and Zerviah Brown as heirs of Israel Dane of Ipswich, a housewright.[4] Nothing more is known about this goldsmith and his working career, and no silver by him has been identified. PEK

1. *Independent Chronicle*, 30 January 1777.
2. *Ipswich VR* 2:58.
3. *Mass. Soldiers and Sailors* 2:608.
4. ECD 164:218–19.

Jonas Bruce
1753–ca. 1820

Jonas Bruce, the son of Samuel Bruce, Jr. (b. 1730), of Woburn, Massachusetts, and his wife, Marcy, was born in Bolton, Massachusetts, on 6 October 1753.[1] His parents probably married by 1752, the year before Bruce's birth. His paternal grandparents were Samuel Bruce (b. 1701) and Rebecca Winn, both of Woburn.[2] His master remains unknown, but if Bruce served a typical apprenticeship, he would have begun working on his own by 1773. Within three years, however, Bruce began his service in the revolutionary war, enlisting on four occasions between 1776 and 1780.[3]

Bruce married Lucy Taylor of Berlin, Massachusetts, on 14 June 1781.[4] Their six children were born in Bolton, Berlin, and Winchendon, Massachusetts, during the first twelve years of their marriage; these changes of residence suggest that the family may have suffered a peripatetic existence owing to Jonas Bruce's lack of steady employment.[5] Esther Whitcomb's *History of Bolton* refers to Bruce as a silversmith who purchased "the Godding place" in 1783, paying one hundred pounds for the property, yet selling it at a loss within a year. She speculated that "evidently there was not enough demand for silver articles in Bolton to induce a silversmith to make his permanent residence here."[6]

Jonas Bruce probably practiced silversmithing as his primary occupation between 1782 and 1786. In the documents recording the six land transactions conducted by Bruce during these years, he identified himself as either a silversmith or goldsmith from Bolton.[7] All deeds immediately preceding and following these years list him as a laborer or yeoman, which suggests that he worked primarily as a farmer who occasionally supplemented his income with metalwork.[8] Sometime between 1801 and 1820, Jonas Bruce and his wife, Lucy, moved to Winchester, New Hampshire, after which nothing is known of him.[9]

No silver by Bruce has been identified. JJF

1. *Bolton VR*, 17; *Woburn VR* 1:32.
2. *Woburn VR* 1:31, 36, 277.
3. Whitcomb/Mayo 1985, 13; *Mass. Soldiers and Sailors* 2:712–13.
4. *Marlborough VR*, 235, 315.
5. *Winchendon VR*, 20, 188.
6. Whitcomb 1938, 246.
7. WCD 99:590; 91:552, 574; 95:8; 101:256–57.
8. WCD 86:257; 98:562; 123:173; 146:34–35; 148:331–32.
9. FCD 45:39–40; 49:216–18; Cheshire County, N.H., deeds 84:176. Grace M. Pittman letter to the author, 12 July 1989.

William Bubier
1746–92

A minor Marblehead, Massachusetts, goldsmith, William Bubier (also spelled Boobyer and in a variety of other ways) was born in Marblehead and baptized there on 30 March 1746. He was the son of the yeoman Christopher Bubier (1706–89) and his wife, Margaret Bubier (1709–82), who were married in 1726. His paternal grandparents were Christopher Bubier (ca. 1675–1706), a mariner or fisherman who died in Surinam, and his wife, Margaret (Palmer) Bubier, who were married in 1700. His mother's father was Peter LeVallier, who moved from Marblehead to Rhode Island and died there.[1]

William would have begun working about 1767. He married Deborah Howard (1747–1808), the daughter of Joseph and Elizabeth (Pitts) Howard, in Marblehead on 19 June 1770, and they had two daughters, Elizabeth (1770–1837) and Deborah (1772–1857). William's sister Margaret was married to the silversmith Thomas Grant (q.v.), and both Bubier and Grant served in Col. John Glover's Marblehead regiment during the Revolution, as a first lieutenant and a captain, respectively. The Massachusetts tax list of 1771 includes a poll tax for Bubier and indicates he had ten pounds worth of merchandise in his shop.[2] In 1772, Bubier served as surety for the estate of his fellow Marblehead goldsmith Samuel Pedrick (q.v.), which suggests a working relationship between the two craftsmen.

According to a family genealogy, Bubier was on board the ship *Hancock* in 1792 when he was captured and taken to Halifax, Nova Scotia, as a prisoner. He is said to have become ill during his captivity and to have died a few days after his return to his home in Marblehead.[3]

On 4 September 1792, administration of all the goods and estate of William Bubier, "late of Marblehead ... Goldsmith ... deceased," was granted to Deborah Bubier.[4] Although Deborah gave bond with Edward Bowen and Philip Besom as sureties to exhibit an inventory within three months, no inventory has survived. No objects by Bubier are known today. GWRW

1. *Marblehead VR* 1:54 (under Boobyer); see also Bubier 1959, 34, 39–41, 53–54; and the estate papers, 1789, of Christopher Bubier in ECPR 360:238–39. Some sources suggest that William was the son of Joseph and Mary Bubier and give his date of birth as 1737; see Flynt/Fales 1968, 169; Lord/Gamage 1972, 291.
2. *Marblehead VR* 2:65; *Mass. Soldiers and Sailors* 2:742; Knight 1976, 48; Lord/Gamage 1972, 291; Pruitt 1978, 100–01.
3. Bubier 1959, 53–54. The same source also indicates that Bubier purchased land in 1775 in Windham, Maine.
4. ECPR, docket 3929.

Benjamin Bunker
1751–1842

A

B

Probably Nantucket's most prolific silversmith, Benjamin Bunker was born on 18 March 1751 in Nantucket, Massachusetts, the son of William Bunker (1726–68) and Mary Russell (1724–98) of Nantucket, who were married on the island on 20 February 1745/46.[1] His paternal grandparents were Caleb Bunker (1699–1777) and Priscilla (Bunker) Coffin (1703–95).[2] Caleb Bunker was also the grandfather of Margaret Brock, the wife of the Nantucket silversmith Nathaniel Barrett (q.v.). Bunker's maternal grandparents were Samuel Russell (d. 1780) and Huldah Odar (1706–40).[3]

By 1764, when Bunker was thirteen years of age, he may have been apprenticed to Samuel Barrett (q.v.), who, at age twenty-five, would have been in the early phase of his career. Equally likely is that Bunker served his apprenticeship with John Jackson (q.v.). Moreover, Nathaniel Barrett, three years Bunker's senior, undoubtedly knew of the young silversmith or shared workshop space with him. Their relationship as fellow craftsmen may have had some bearing on Barrett's marriage to Bunker's first cousin, Margaret Brock.

Evidence of Bunker's work as a silversmith dates from the period immediately following his apprenticeship. A porringer engraved "C/EL" was made by Bunker for Edward and Lydia (Hussey) Carey, who were married in Nantucket on 12 November 1770.[4] A ladle presented to the Nantucket Union Lodge by Bunker and Jethro Hussey in 1774 provides the first indication of Bunker's long affiliation with the Masonic Order.[5] Shortly after his marriage to Rebecca Folger (1758–1839), the daughter of George Folger (1730–1813) and Sarah Coleman (1734–78) of Nantucket, on 2 September 1775, Bunker made an additional gift of ritual paraphernalia to the lodge.[6] On 15 December 1775 the members "Voted that the Thanks of this Lodge be given to Bro. Benjamin Bunker for the presents Given to the Lodge viz. too Complet Ivory Tipt Rolls and one Ivory mallet."[7]

Bunker served in the revolutionary war as an armorer aboard the privateer brigantine *Hazard* from July to September of 1779 and was taken prisoner by the British and imprisoned on the vessel *Jersey* in New York. Bunker was brought to Portsmouth, New Hampshire, for exchange with British prisoners.[8]

Bunker's thirty known deeds indicate that he, like Nathaniel Barrett, inherited a large quantity of land from Caleb Bunker, his grandfather.[9] Bunker and Barrett appear together in five deeds, three listing Bunker's trade and two listing Barrett's.[10] Nine deeds between 1786 and 1821 describe Bunker as either a goldsmith or silversmith, but a deed from 1835, transacted when Bunker was eighty-four years old, shows that he had changed his trade to that of a watchmaker and clockmaker.[11] Perhaps because clock parts could be obtained from other sources and assembled at the bench, Bunker chose to work in this related trade, which was less physically demanding than silversmithing.

In spite of these numerous deeds, the public record is silent on the location of Bunker's shop. In 1820 he purchased from his brother George Bunker all "rights derived from their mother Mary," which included her dwelling house, where Benjamin had lived for many years—but whether this property was also the site of his silversmith shop is unknown. Although no probate records survive for Bunker or his wife, Rebecca, an abundance of works are known from Bunker's hand. His mark appears as BB within a rectangular punch (A), occasionally bracketed by an abstract symbol unique to Bunker (B). Bunker died on 14 April 1842.[12] JJF

SURVIVING OBJECTS

	Mark	Inscription	Patron	Date	Reference	Owner
Cann	A*	SPE		ca. 1790	Flynt/Fales 1968, 122–23	HD
Cann	A	MP/to/EMP		ca. 1790		NHA
Porringer	A*	P/IM		ca. 1780	Warren 1975, no. 299	BBC
Porringer	A	D/AE		ca. 1780	*American Art of the Colonies and Early Republic*, no. 110	
Porringer	A	PMC		ca. 1780		MFAB
Porringer	A (?)	F/WR/LF		ca. 1780	Crosby 1953, 191	
Porringer	A	EN	Eunice (Gardner) Norris	ca. 1793	Crosby 1953, 191	
Porringer	A	C/EL	Edward and Lydia (Hussey) Carey	ca. 1772	Carpenter/ Carpenter 1987, 130	
Porringer	A*	RF/to/SBP		ca. 1780		RISD
Porringer	A	H/IM		ca. 1780		NHA
Porringer	A*/B*	MP; Mary Perry	Mary Perry	ca. 1790	Christie's, 23 June 1993, lot 60	
Porringer	A/B	S/GH		ca. 1780	YUAG files	
Serving spoon	A/B	LM		ca. 1800		NHA
Sugar tongs	A*	DLB		ca. 1805		YUAG
Sugar tongs	A/B	AB		ca. 1810		NHA
Tablespoon	A	AM/to/HM	Anna Marshall	ca. 1780		NHA
Tablespoon	A	AM/to/RF		ca. 1780		NHA
Tablespoon	A	Peter Folger/to/Peter Ewer/born 15 March/1800	Peter Folger for Peter Ewer	1800	DAPC 72.3270	AIC
Tablespoon	A	S/TM		ca. 1780		NHA
Tablespoon	A	PB		ca. 1775	DAPC 80.3938	WM
Tablespoon	A/B	Margaret/Hussey/ born 4mo—/22nd 1815	Margaret Hussey	ca. 1815	Carpenter/ Carpenter 1987, 132	
Tablespoon	A†/ B†	JMM		ca. 1795		YUAG
Two teaspoons	A	MC		ca. 1780		NHA
Teaspoon	A	PC		ca. 1780		NHA
Teaspoon	A	AB		ca. 1790		NHA
Teaspoon	A	H/RM		ca. 1800		NHA
Teaspoon	A*	SR		ca. 1780	Johnston 1994, 12	CMA
Teaspoon	A	LB		ca. 1780	DAPC 80.3942	
Teaspoon	A	RC; GCS (later)		ca. 1780	DAPC 80.3470	
Six teaspoons	A	EMB		ca. 1810	Carpenter/ Carpenter 1987, 131	NHA

	Mark	Inscription	Patron	Date	Reference	Owner
Six teaspoons	A/B	MS/(L?)		ca. 1810		NHA
Teaspoon	A/B	RB/RC		ca. 1790		NHA
Teaspoon	A/B	JF	Folger family	ca. 1810	YUAG files	

1. *Nantucket VR* 1:139, 164; 2:450; 3:160; 5:89, 95.
2. *Nantucket VR* 1:139, 158; 3:135; 5:82, 92.
3. *Nantucket VR* 2:345; 4:351; 5:520, 523.
4. *Nantucket VR* 3:182.
5. Carpenter/Carpenter 1987, 130–31. The ladle, which does not survive, may have been made by Bunker.
6. Conversation with John Hamilton, curator of the Museum of Our National Heritage, May 1991; *Nantucket VR* 1:377, 480, 500; 3:135, 350; 5:92, 263, 277.
7. Carpenter/Carpenter 1987, 130, fig. 107.
8. *Mass. Soldiers and Sailors* 2:808; *Historic Nantucket* (July 1963): 7; Revolutionary War Pension and Bounty-Land Application Files, National Archives and Records Administration, no. S19575, microfilm M-804, reel 405.
9. NCD 2:265, 371–72, 375–76; 6:388–89; 11:371; 13:277–78; 14:199; 15:285, 294–95; 19:5–6; 21:129, 331–32; 24:323–24; 25:357–58; 26:471–73; 27:121; 28:303–04; 30:210; 31:27–28, 160–61, 382–83; 34:291–92, 464, 493; 37:81–82; 39:102–03, 255–56, 261–62; 40:94–95.
10. NCD 13:277–78; 14:199; 15:121; 19:5–6; 24:323–24.
11. NCD 34:464.
12. *Nantucket VR* 5:81.

Samuel Burrill
1704–ca. 1740

A

B

Samuel Burrill was born in Boston on 17 April 1704 and baptized in the Second Church on 23 April 1704. He was the son of Samuel Burrill (1656/57–1740/41), a sailmaker, and his wife, Martha (ca. 1664–1742). His father was the son of George Burrill (d. 1698) and Deborah (Simpkins) Burrill.[1] There is no record of Samuel Burrill's marriage or of the birth of any children; presumably he never married. He does not appear in the deed records and probably lived in one of the houses his father owned at Fish and North streets.[2] Theophilus Burrill (q.v.) was his first cousin.

When he was eighteen years old, Samuel Burrill witnessed (with Knight Leverett [q.v.]) a deed for the goldsmith Andrew Tyler (q.v.), which suggests that Burrill served his apprenticeship with Tyler.[3] Two years later, on 17 May 1724, he witnessed a second deed for Tyler along with Theophilus Burrill.[4] There are two documentary references to silver by Burrill. A spoon bearing his mark, "S.Burril.at length," was advertised as being lost or stolen in 1733, and an advertisement of 1742 lists a porringer by Burrill as being lost or stolen. These references and a small group of objects marked by Burrill suggest that he had an independent shop, although he may have worked primarily as a jobber for other artisans. An ambiguous announcement in the *Boston News-Letter* of 15 April to 6 May 1731 notes that Joseph Goldthwait, goldsmith (q.v.), had just removed from "Mr. Burrel's Shop."[5] Goldthwait was married to Samuel Burrill's niece, Martha Lewis, and may have worked with Burrill briefly. The flagon Burrill made for the Second Church, Boston, bears his initial and surname mark (A) and the mark SB within a rectangle (B). He also made a tankard with his initial and surname mark for the First Church in Watertown. The mark SB above fleur-de-lis in a heart, found on two porringers, has been attributed to Burrill.[6]

Samuel Burrill appeared in court at least three times: in 1727, 1728, and 1737. John Brewster, a cordwainer, recovered judgment against Burrill for £2.17.7 in damages, and Joseph Walker, a staymaker, recovered judgment against Burrill for £5, the cost of a silver snuffbox that Walker had sold to Burrill. The record of the suit brought against Burrill by George Colesworthy, a barber, in 1737, has not survived.[7]

Apparently the goldsmith died before October 1740, when his father wrote his will, because only daughters Martha Lewis, Deborah Prince, and Katharine Barton are mentioned as heirs in either the will or the subsequent estate division.[8] BMW

SURVIVING OBJECTS

	Mark	Inscription	Patron	Date	Reference	Owner
Two chafing dishes	B*	S. Pease; M (later)	Samuel Pease	ca. 1730	Flynt/Fales 1968, 104–05	HD
Creampot	A	AJC/1823 (later)(+)		ca. 1735	Quimby 1995, no. 13	WM
Flagon	A†/ B†	This Flagon/is the Gift of M^{rs}/Dor^y Frizell to the/ Second Church of/ Christ in Boston/ Decm.^{r} 1733	Second Church, Boston, for Dorothy Frizell	1733	Jones 1913, 39–40	
Porringer	A/B*	C/IM (+)		ca. 1735	Puig et al. 1989, no. 192	MIA
Tablespoon	A/B*	none		ca. 1730	Quimby 1995, no. 14	WM
Tankard	A	The G[ift of Mr. Jon]athan Stone/to the first C[hurch of Chr]ist In Watertown	Jonathan Stone and/ or First Parish, Watertown, Mass.	ca. 1735	Jones 1913, 481–82	

1. RC 24:26. Martha's maiden name is unknown. The couple was married before 1685 and eventually had twelve children; see RC 9:168, 173, 178, 189, 213, 221, 231, 246; RC 24:5, 33; Thwing. RC 9:55, 245; Codman 1918, 51; Savage 1860–62, 1:309.
2. At least two brick and three wooden houses at Fish and North streets, along with a wharf and flats, are mentioned in the division of the estate of Samuel Burrill, Sr., in September of 1741; SCD 62:19–21.
3. SCD 37:1.
4. SCD 38:49.
5. Dow 1927, 42, 46.
6. *Pennsylvania Museum Bulletin* 68 (June 1921): 10; Bigelow-Phillips files, 984–86. The Bigelow-Phillips files indicate that one porringer was in a Massachusetts collection and that the other, engraved "RS" for Rebecca Sprague and "LA" for Lydia Austin, descended in a Massachusetts family. SB in a cartouche has sometimes been attributed to this maker; see Kovel 1961, 49.
7. John M. Fitzgerald to Francis Hill Bigelow, List of Boston Court Record References to Silversmiths, Bigelow-Phillips files; SCCR, Court of Common Pleas Record Book 1727–28, 165, 208; 1736–37, 337; SCCR, files 21239, 21240.
8. SCPR 35:334; SCD 62:19–21.

Theophilus Burrill
ca. 1700–39

Although authorities differ, Francis Hill Bigelow and John Marshall Phillips believed that the goldsmith Theophilus Burrill was the son of George Burrill (1653/54–1719), a tailor, and his wife, Mary.[1] His paternal grandparents were George (d. 1698) and Deborah (Simpkins) Burrill.[2] Samuel Burrill (q.v.) was his first cousin. Theophilus's birth is not recorded in Boston, but he was baptized in the Second Church in 1710 along with his brothers John, James, and George and his sister Elizabeth just one week after his mother, Mary, was admitted as a member.[3]

Theophilus Burrill appears as a witness to two deeds of Andrew Tyler (q.v.) dated 17 May 1724 and 10 February 1727; the first deed was also witnessed by Samuel Burrill.[4] Theophilus also witnessed a deed for John Burt (q.v.) dated 15 January 1731/32.[5] Burrill married Mary Partridge (b. 1715), daughter of William, a mariner (d. 1717), and Rachel (Goff) Partridge (b. 1694) on 14 December 1732.[6] He apparently moved to New London, Connecticut, soon after this, for on 1 January 1738/39, Joshua Hempstead of New London made the following entry in his diary: "I was at the Town meeting and ye Choice of Taverners & Theophilus Burrell a Goldsmith aged about [ ] Died with Convulsion fitts. he belonged to Boston but hath Sojourned in Town 2 or 3 years." Hempstead also recorded that Burrill was buried on 3 January.[7] There is no record of his estate in the Connecticut or Boston probate records. No silver by him has been identified. BMW

1. Bigelow-Phillips files, 1076–77; RC 9:41; SCPR 21:549.
2. RC 9:245.
3. Robbins 1852, 234.
4. *York Deeds* 12:331; SCD 38:49.
5. SCD 46:161.
6. RC 28:36, 175; RC 24:107; SCPR, docket 3884; RC 9:214.
7. Curtis 1913, 90; *Diary of Joshua Hempstead*, 344.

Benjamin Burt
1729–1805

A

B

C

Benjamin Burt was born in Boston, the fifth son of the silversmith John Burt (q.v.) and his wife, Abigail Cheever (1691–1778).[1] John Burt recorded his son's birth in the family bible as "Benjamin Burt a Twin Borne y[e] 29 Decem[r] . . . 1729," but Benjamin's twin was not entered and probably had died at birth.[2] Benjamin Burt married Joan Hooton (1731–85) on 10 October 1754.[3] The bride was the daughter of the oarmaker John Hooton (d. 1760) of "Great Brittain" and Sarah Wye, who were married in 1719.[4] Joan Burt died on 31 October 1785 at the age of fifty-four and was buried in the Granary Burying Ground.[5] The couple's only child, John, was born in 1757 and died at the age of forty-one in 1798.[6]

Burt was born into a prominent family of silversmiths that included his brothers Samuel and William (qq.v.). Benjamin and his brothers probably apprenticed with their father until his death in 1745/46. Burt's selection of his mother to act as his guardian in December 1748 indicates that he remained with his family, rather than seeking an apprenticeship with another silversmith after his father died. It is likely that Benjamin Burt finished his training with one or both of his brothers, since Samuel Burt had completed his apprenticeship by 1745 and William by 1747.

Burt would have completed his apprenticeship in 1750. The earliest identification of him as a goldsmith occurs in a deed dated 31 December 1751, when he sold his portion of his father's landholdings in York County, Maine, to his brother-in-law, Francis Shaw, for £13.6.8.[7] He continued to be called either goldsmith or silversmith on official documents throughout his life. The Massachusetts tax valuation of 1771 assessed him with two polls, a house and shop with an annual worth of £16, and £80 of merchandise.[8] In 1780, Burt continued to receive an assessment of two polls, but showed an increase in the value of his real estate holding to an annual rent of £60.[9]

Eight of Burt's apprentices can be identified. Several apprentices witnessed deeds for Burt during the 1760s. Samuel Pedrick (q.v.) witnessed three documents in April and May 1763.[10] John Andrew (q.v.) signed deeds on 24 October 1764 and 2 July 1766.[11] In 1766 and 1768, Andrew delivered silver objects made by Burt to Elias Hasket Derby, a customer in Salem, possibly while visiting his own family.[12] Edward Dane (q.v.), who was bound as an apprentice to Burt in 1759, appears on deeds on 7 July 1766 and 29 August 1768.[13] Caleb Swan (q.v.) also trained with Burt and continued close ties with Burt in his subsequent career, having married Burt's niece Sarah Semple in 1777. Nineteen-year-old Joseph Foster (1760–1839) witnessed two deeds for Burt in 1779. His presence in the Burt household during his training from 1774 to 1781 made him a convenient witness.[14] Another apprentice, Edward Revere (1768–1820), a nephew of the silversmith Paul Revere, Jr. (q.v.), witnessed seven deeds for Burt from February 1787 until November 1790, one of which was also witnessed by James Sherman (q.v.), who may have worked as a journeyman for Burt.[15] On 5 April 1792, Burt financed a two-hundred-pound mortgage on Edward Revere's house on Ship Street.[16] Revere repaid his former master in installments, one hundred dollars on 25 May 1796 and two hundred on 7 July 1796.[17] When this debt was resolved on 5 November 1798, Burt arranged another two-hundred-dollar mortgage loan for Revere.[18] A deed between Burt and Revere on 5 April 1792 was witnessed by another apprentice, Samuel B. Waters.[19] Waters performed this function again in 1799 and 1800, when he witnessed deeds between Burt and Caleb Swan.[20] Waters and Stephen Emery (q.v.) witnessed a deed in 1801 when Burt sold property in Charlestown to Sarah Swan.[21] Burt left "all his Goldsmiths working Tools now in my shop" to Waters in his will, written on 18 April 1804.[22] According to the census report, the Burt household included only three members in 1790, the silversmith, one female, and a boy, presumably Waters.[23] Joseph Veazie (1788–1863), a jeweler and silversmith working in Boston and Providence, Rhode Island, may also have trained with Burt.[24] Burt's will included a bequest to Veazie of "silver shoe buckles that I have in wear, two pair Silver knee buckles, Stone Stock buckle and Ten Dollars."[25] Since Veazie was only sixteen years old when Burt wrote his will, an apprenticeship is the most likely relationship between the two craftsmen.

The silversmith maintained relationships with several other colleagues. William Simpkins (q.v.) served as an appraiser of Burt's father's estate, and thirty-five years later, Burt served as an appraiser of Simpkin's estate.[26] Burt and Simpkins probably were neighbors. Burt and Zachariah Brigden (q.v.) appraised the estate of Benjamin Hurd (q.v.) in 1781.[27] Burt and another silversmith, Joseph Loring (q.v.), served as the appraisers for the estate of John Codner (q.v.) in 1782.[28] When Seth Storer Coburn (q.v.) purchased two ounces of silver from Zachariah Brigden in February 1767, he used "cash Rec'd of Burt" as partial payment.[29] Burt retailed objects made by his colleague Zachariah Brigden. He credits Brigden's estate with four pounds for "making 4 Butter Boat Bodys" in an account dated 18 April 1787.[30] He served as an appraiser of Brigden's estate in 1787; the following year he bought 4½ acres of pastureland from the estate.[31] Burt also made a tankard that John Hancock (q.v.) retailed. Burt purchased finished objects from Paul Revere, Jr., and utilized Revere's skills as an engraver to decorate some of his own work.

Burt participated in town affairs, serving in a variety of offices and committee appointments. He was chosen a scavenger in 1764, and in 1776 he was appointed to represent ward 2 on a committee to collect an "Account of the Damages sustained since the Boston Port Bill."[32] The following year, he was selected by the inhabitants of Boston to serve on the Committee of Correspondence, Inspection, and Safety.[33] He led the goldsmiths and jewelers in the procession honoring the visit of George Washington to Boston in 1789, and he was selected by his colleagues to lead the contingent of goldsmiths in the memorial procession honoring the death of Washington in 1800.[34] Samuel Davis remembered him in his memoirs (1811) as one of the "eldest of the trade."[35]

Burt's three appearances before the Suffolk County Court of Common Pleas testify to his position as a respected community leader. On 11 November 1780, the silversmith was appointed with Francis Shaw, Esq., and the cabinetmaker George Bright to referee a dispute between the mariner Thomas Sheridan and the cabinetmaker David Underwood.[36] In April of the following year he appeared in court as the administrator of the estate of his brother-in-law Joseph Glidden, a Boston shipwright, to obtain authorization to sell the deceased's house and land for payment of debts against the estate.[37] Zachariah Brigden and Caleb Swan signed the bond of that estate administration.[38] Burt and his brother-in-law, the oarmaker John Hooton, serving as executors of Lydia Dyer's will in October 1785, successfully prosecuted John White of Billerica for outstanding debts of £92.16.8.[39]

Although numerous deeds exist relating to Burt's real estate transactions, he appears to have lived in only two locations. In September and October 1760, he purchased a house and land on Ship Street from seven other heirs of John Hooton.[40] Three years later he purchased an additional strip of land "on which a part of the Kitchen of the said Benjamin stands" from his sister-in-law, Sarah Semple, for twenty shillings.[41] On 30 May 1763, Burt sold the Ship Street property to the feltmaker Ezra Collins for three hundred pounds; he repurchased it the following day for the same price.[42] The second transaction may have been a mortgage or it could have been a means of establishing clear title to the property. Burt's mother, Abigail, died in August 1778 at the age of ninety. Benjamin was listed as a beneficiary in her will, written on 1 December 1758 and presented for probate on 11 September 1778.[43] Burt was chosen to replace his mother as administrator of his father's estate on 23 April 1779, with Andrew Symmes, Jr., and Alex Edwards serving as bondsmen.[44] A week later, he presented an appraisal of John Burt's property on Fore Street, valued at more than one thousand pounds.[45] Burt purchased his father's house on Fish Street from the other heirs in July and November 1779 at a cost of more than five hundred pounds.[46] He lived in this house until his death in 1805. The Boston directories for 1789 and 1798 list Burt as a silversmith on Fish Street.[47] The United States Direct Tax of 1798 described the house as a two-story brick and wooden structure of 1,260 square feet with seventeen windows, valued at fifteen hundred dollars.[48]

Some of the silversmith's real estate transactions appear to have been speculative ventures. The silversmith acquired a piece of land in North Street from the Hooton estate on 2 July 1766 for £16, which he sold to the carver Simeon Skillin in 1790 for £25.[49] In 1787 Burt purchased a lot in north Boston, adjoining the Hooton property, for £50 and sold it the following year to Thomas Stoddard for a modest profit of £2.[50] He arranged a much more lucrative transaction in 1789 with Arthur Noble, the administrator of the estate of James Noble, who sold a house and barn on Hanover Street to Burt for £450 on 16 October that year and bought it back the following day for £500.[51] His final real estate venture involved the purchase of two houses, a wharf, cart way, and several plots of waterfront land from the mariner Silas Atkins on 19 March 1793 for £1,172.12.1.[52] Atkins paid £1,187.6.8 to reacquire the properties on 26 March 1795.[53]

Burt occasionally made loans to his neighbors and relatives in the form of mortgages. The shipwright Joseph Glidden borrowed more than £46 from the silversmith in May 1760, using his house on Fish Street as collateral.[54] Glidden borrowed an additional £20 four years later.[55] In August 1768, Burt lent £10 to Joseph Mountfort, a carter whose shop was located on Fish Street.[56] Another Fish Street resident, the wharfinger John Ballard, received a loan of £80 on 11 August 1781.[57] The baker Peter Hunt used property on North and Ship streets to obtain £260 from Burt in 1786 and 1787.[58] Burt's last loan, made in 1788, was to William and Mary Harris, who borrowed £200 from him, using their Chelsea residence as security.[59]

Benjamin Burt died on 9 October 1805 after an apparently protracted illness.[60] The executor's accounts record the following payments: $2.73 for "Watch lights &c in the last Sickness," $17.00 for "Abigail Jeffs for nursing," $46.25 for "Doctor Rands Bill," and $9.50 for "Doct[r]. John Brooks attend[ce] at Malden."[61] His tombstone in the Copp's Hill cemetery erroneously gives the year of his death as 1803 but correctly states his age as seventy-five.[62] The silversmith's will, written on 18 April 1804, was presented for probate on 28 October 1805 by his executor and former apprentice, the goldsmith Joseph Foster. Burt left his house on Fish Street to the twelve children and grandchildren of his sisters, Sarah Shaw and Abigail Howland. In addition to many monetary bequests, Burt designated recipients for some of his most treasured possessions. His niece Susannah Howland received his folio Bible and "two sconces of quill work and a needle worked picture that were wrought by her aunt Susanna Burt." The heirs of Burt's deceased nephew William Shaw received "two silver Tumblers with my name engraven thereon, also my largest china Punch bowl which his brother Samuel Shaw sent me from Canton." Another nephew, Benjamin, was given the largest silver punch bowl and a smaller china punch bowl. Benjamin Burt Swan, son of the silversmith Caleb Swan, received a "large Silver Tankard having a Coat of Arms engraven thereon." After making other specific bequests he left the remainder of his estate to Sarah Swan, wife of the silversmith, "for her own comfort and at her own disposal without any hindrance disturbance or molestation from any person whomsoever."[63]

The silversmith Ebenezer Moulton (1768–1824) was among the appraisers who evaluated Burt's estate in November 1805.

Inventory of the Real and Personal Estate of Benjamin Burt late of Boston Goldsmith as taken and appraised by us the Subscribers

1 Bible 3. Sundry Books 2.	5.—
1 Bedstead 2 Beds and Bedding	33.—
1 Silk quilt	7.—
Trunk and wearing Apparel	15.—
207 oz. 15 pwt of Silver @ 110 Cents pr oz.	228.52
A house and land in Fish Street at the north }	4500.—
part of Boston }	$4788.52

1 Loan office certificate 3 per Cent Stock
1 D.°   "   6 "D°.   "
1 Share in Charles River Bridge
2 Certificates Union Bank Stock.
>   November 1805
>   Jacob Holland }
>   Eben. Moulton } appraisers
>   Jedidiah Parker }[64]

In *Reminiscences and Traditions of Boston* (1827), Hannah Mather Crocker described Burt as "a respectable goldsmith and a very large man [who] weighed three hundred and eighty pounds. He lived and died in the house [on Fish Street], well respected and beloved."[65]

A significant body of work survives with Benjamin Burt's marks, including a full-name mark (A) and two variations of an initial and surname mark (B,C). Spurious examples of mark (A) are known.[66] Burt excelled as both a craftsman and an engraver. His silver is well constructed, elegantly proportioned, and tastefully embellished. Many of his objects feature elaborate, beautifully rendered engraved crests and arms. Repoussé work encircles the lids of several teapots. Burt was a conservative rather than an innovative craftsman. He produced a full range of traditional forms, including beakers, canns, casters, tankards, tea- and coffeepots, porringers, sauceboats, teaspoons and tablespoons. Burt's patrons were among the leading citizens of Boston and surrounding towns, such as Salem, Danvers, and Worcester, including Isaac Royall, Moses Brown, John Hancock, the Derby family, Harvard students, and the Proprietors of the Charles River Bridge. Burt was a leading producer of church silver, furnishing baptismal basins, beakers, canns, cups, flagons, and tankards for at least seventeen churches in Massachusetts. One bill from Burt to a client survives:

D.ͬ Cap.ᵗ John D Wolf To Benj.ᵃ Burt   C.ͬ
1793 To Silver Takard and porringers w.ᵗ 51.ᵒᶻ18 @ 7/p.ͬ oz   £18– 3–4
July 1ˢᵗ   Making Tankard   4–10
>   Making porringers   2
>   Engraving Tankard   8
>   _____
>   25– 1–4
To Cash paid M.ͬ Mumford, the Balance   8–8
>   _____
>   £25–10–0
C.ͬ By Six oz Gold Dust @ £4–5 p.ͬ oz   £25–10–[67]

One of the pieces mentioned in the bill, a tankard engraved "JDW," has been published.[68] DAF

SURVIVING OBJECTS

	Mark	Inscription	Patron	Date	Reference	Owner
Baptismal basin	B or C	The Legacy of the Hon.ᵇˡᵉ ISAAC ROYALL ESQ. TO the CHURCH OF CHRIST in Medford 1781	Simon Tufts, Isaac Royall's agent, for First Parish, Medford, Mass.	1781	Jones 1913, 277	AIC

	Mark	Inscription	Patron	Date	Reference	Owner
Beaker	A	The Gift of M.ͬ Palatiah Rice/and Thaddeus Fay to the Church/of Christ in North-borough 1797	First Congregational Church and Society, Northborough, Mass., for Palatiah Rice and Thaddeus Fay	1797	Jones 1913, 350–51	
Beaker	A	The Gift of/M.ͬ Isaac Stone;/to the first Church of Christ,/in Woburn. 1771	Isaac Stone and/or First Congregational Church, Woburn, Mass.	1771	Jones 1913, 504	
Beaker	A	The Gift of M.ͬ Kendal Goodwin/ to the 1ˢᵗ Church in Reading	First Congregational Church, Wakefield, Mass., for Kendal Goodwin	ca. 1755	Jones 1913, 475–76	
Beaker	A	The Gift of Deacon Jonathan Temple/to the first Church of Christ in Reading/ 1758	Jonathan Temple and/ or First Congregational Church, Wakefield, Mass.	1758	Jones 1913, 476	
Beaker	A	The Legacy of M.ͬ Jabez Baker/Ruling Elder of the 5ᵗʰ Church/in Gloces-ter 1758	First Congregational Church, Rockport, Mass., for Jabez Baker	1758	Jones 1913, 404–05	
Beaker	A	The Gift of M.ͬ Rich.ͩ Arms/to the Church of Christ in/Lexington 1763	First Congregational Society, Lexington, Mass., for Richard Arms	1763	Jones 1913, 245	
Beaker	A	The Legacy of Mr Israel Tisdale/to the Church of Christ in Berkley	Executor of Israel Tis-dale and/or First Church of Christ, Berkeley, Mass.	ca. 1769	Jones 1913, 12–13	
Beaker	B	IADW	DeWolfe family	ca. 1785	Avery 1920, no. 73	MMA
Six beakers	B	Property/of the Church of Christ in/Chelsea./1798	First Unitarian Society, Revere, Mass.	1798	Buhler 1972, no. 313	MFAB
Beaker (mates below)	B	BRAY/1797; AAB (later)	John Bray	1797	Buhler 1965, 81, 84–85	HMA
Beaker (mates above and below)	B	BRAY/1797; ACB (later)	John Bray	1797	Buhler 1965, 82, 84–85	HMA
Beaker (mates above)	B (?)	BRAY/1797; Presented by Miss Laura Bray to John Story Bullard May 10, 1840 (later)	John Bray	1797	Buhler 1965, 85	
Beaker	?	?		ca. 1790	Parke-Bernet, 30 Novem-ber 1946, lot 135	
Bowl	A	G. Leonard 1767	George Leonard	1767	*Antiques* 129 (May 1986): 1024	

	Mark	Inscription	Patron	Date	Reference	Owner
Cann	A*	A/IS		ca. 1765	YUAG files	
Cann	A	B (later)		ca. 1765	DAPC 79.3106	CaMA
Cann	A	none		ca. 1765	Buhler 1972, no. 305	MFAB
Cann	A	R/HL; IHR (later)		ca. 1750	*Moore Collection* 1980, no. 140	
Cann	A	R/TI (+)		ca. 1780	Sotheby's, 27 January 1989, lot 910	
Cann	A	SL to EL		ca. 1760	Sotheby's, 26 and 28 January 1984, lot 393a	
Cann	A	TIMOTHEO HILLI-ARD/Harvardinates/ Anno Domini MDCCLXIX con-scripti/Bienno sub ejus Tutela fere per-acto,/In gratum Rei memoriam,/HUNC CALICEM/Dono dant	Timothy Hilliard and/ or the Harvard College class of 1769	1769	*Silver Supplement* 1973, no. 10	
Cann	A*	Leonard arms, on a fess gules 3 fleur-de-lis, and crest, a ti-ger's head emerging from a ducal crown; L/GE/1779 (+)	George and Experience (White) Leonard	1779	Flynt/Fales 1968, 97–98	HD
Cann	A	AMT		ca. 1790	Hammerslough/ Feigenbaum 1958–73, 3 (supplement):5	
Two canns	A	JB/to/JT; Presented by the Hon John Treadwell Esq/to the Tabernacle Church in Salem/ 1808 (later)	John Treadwell (?)	ca. 1800	Jones 1913, 430–31	
Cann (with cover)	A	Greenwood crest; I/ DM	Greenwood family	ca. 1775	MFA 1911, no. 106	
Cann	A	Saltonstall crest (+)	Saltonstall family	ca. 1775	YUAG files	
Cann	A	The Gift of the Pro-prietors of Point Shirley to Mrs. Mary Pratt 1752.	Proprietors of Point Shirley for Mary Pratt	1752	MFA 1911, no. 102	
Three canns	A*	The Gift of Saml-Epes Esqr to the South Church/of Christ in Ipswich	South Church, Ipswich, Mass., for Samuel Epes	ca. 1761	Buhler/Hood 1970, no. 210	YUAG
Two canns	A*	K/TH		ca. 1770		SI

	Mark	Inscription	Patron	Date	Reference	Owner
Cann	A*	G/OE		ca. 1770	DAPC 65.1962	
Cann	A	WWP		ca. 1770	Anderson Galleries, 7–12 January 1924, lot 874	
Cann	A	unidentified arms; McC/DA		ca. 1770	MFA 1906, no. 32	
Two canns	A*	Fuller or Bradstreet crest, arm in armor embowed grasping a sword	Fuller or Bradstreet family	ca. 1770		HD
Cann (part of a service)	A	FMB	Boardman family	ca. 1790	Northeast Auctions, 3–4 August 1991, lot 434	
Cann	A	Moss crest, a griffin's head emerging from a coronet; II; R/IA (later)	John Jones	ca. 1760	*Antiques* 128 (July 1985): 46	DMA
Cann	A/B	Hodges arms, or 3 crescents, on a canton a ducal coronet, and crest, a crescent rising from the clouds; H/IE	Hodges family	ca. 1760	McFadden/Clark 1989, no. 31	CHM
Cann	A	unidentified arms; AD COELUM SPIRO		ca. 1765	DAPC 78.3264	
Cann	A/C	L/IE; HEW/to/IW (or TW)		ca. 1760	Buhler 1972, no. 299	MFAB
Two canns	A†/C*	Moore arms, gules a swan standing within a bordure engrailed or, and crest, a swan's head	Moore family	ca. 1765	Buhler/Hood 1970, no. 218	YUAG
Cann (mate below)	A/C	unidentified arms, azure a fess wavy between 3 estoiles, and Fayerweather crest, a beaver passant with a fish in its mouth; Ex Dono T·F	Thomas Fayerweather	ca. 1760	Buhler 1972, no. 304	MFAB
Cann (mate above)	A/C	unidentified arms, azure a fess wavy between 3 estoiles, and Fayerweather crest, a beaver passant with a fish in its mouth; Ex Dono T·F	Thomas Fayerweather	ca. 1760	Gourley 1965, no. 27	SPNEA
Cann (see also unmarked mate)	B	RES	Russell and Elizabeth (Perkins) Sturgis	ca. 1773	Buhler 1979, no. 41	WAM
Cann	B	unidentified arms (later)		ca. 1765		AIC

	Mark	Inscription	Patron	Date	Reference	Owner
Cann	B*	none		ca. 1765	Johnston 1994, 14 (as unknown maker)	CMA
Cann	B *or* C	OMC		ca. 1790	Hammerslough/ Feigenbaum 1958–73, 2:7	
Cann	B *or* C	The Legacy of Mr Wil^m Cogswell/to the 4th Church in Ipswich	Congregational Church, Essex, Mass., for William Cogswell	ca. 1750	Jones 1913, 169–70	
Cann	B *or* C	IM		ca. 1770	Parke-Bernet, 9 November 1946, lot 54	
Cann	B *or* C	none		ca. 1765		AG
Cann	?	unidentified initials		ca. 1770	Sotheby Parke Bernet, 16–18 November 1972, lot 107	
Cann	?	Hutchinson (?) arms, a lion rampant on a field of crosses crosslet, and unidentified crest, a lion's head erased; NG (later)	Giddings family	ca. 1760	*Antiques* 89 (April 1966): 476	
Cann	?	?		ca. 1770	Parke-Bernet, 14–15 October 1955, lot 285	
Cann	?	?		ca. 1770	*Antiques* 73 (June 1958): 530	
Cann	?	?		ca. 1770	*Antiques* 86 (October 1964): 365	
Cann	?	?		ca. 1770	Parke-Bernet, 3–4 February 1956, lot 265	
Cann	?	IMM (+)		ca. 1770	Parke-Bernet, 14–15 October 1955, lot 284	
Cann	?	EAP (later?)		ca. 1785	Parke-Bernet, 11 February 1970, lot 195	
Cann	?	Family Plate from M.E.A. 1893 (later)		ca. 1770	Parke-Bernet, 10 November 1970, lot 64	
Cann	?	Once owned by Increase Sumner, Gov.	Increase Sumner	ca. 1780	YUAG files	

	Mark	Inscription	Patron	Date	Reference	Owner
		of Mass., 1797–1799 (later)				
Cann	?	unidentified initials (+)		ca. 1770	Parke-Bernet, 10 November 1970, lot 68	
Cann	?	Ex Dono/Pu-pillorum/[illeg.] & duorum/[illeg.] ad-missi/Anno/MDCCLXXI	Andrew Eliot and/or the Harvard College class of 1771	1771	YUAG files	
Cann	?	unidentified initials		ca. 1785	Anderson Galleries, 20–21 January 1928, lot 238	
Cann	?	S/IS		ca. 1775	YUAG files	
Two canns	?	P(?)F		ca. 1785	*Antiques* 142 (October 1992): 498	
Cann	?	M (later)		ca. 1770	Christie's, 26 January 1985, lot 75	
Cann (attrib.; see also mate with mark B)	none	RES	Russell and Elizabeth (Perkins) Sturgis	ca. 1773	Buhler 1979, no. 42	WAM
Caster	B	Atkins crest, 2 hounds' heads en-dorsed, collar dove-tailed per pale gold and azure counter-changed erased gules	Atkins family	ca. 1760	*Moore Collec-tion* 1980, no. 138	
Caster	B	AR		ca. 1775	Sotheby's, 23–24 June 1994, lot 106	
Two casters	B	B/IA	Brown family (?)	ca. 1765	Quimby 1995, no. 15a, b	WM
Caster	B or C	KB		ca. 1770	MFA 1911, no. 121	
Two casters	C	AGM		ca. 1770	*Bulletin DIA* 18 (May 1939): 6	DIA
Caster	C	?		ca. 1775	YUAG files	
Caster	C*	unidentified crest, a griffin passant		ca. 1780	*Silver Supple-ment* 1973, no. 11	USDS
Caster	C	D/RM	Richard and Mary (Hodges) Derby	ca. 1750	Buhler 1972, no. 298	MFAB
Caster	?	W/TA		ca. 1775		CHM
Caster	?	none		ca. 1760	Christie's, 26 January 1991, lot 61	

	Mark	Inscription	Patron	Date	Reference	Owner
Coffeepot	A	IT (+)	Israel Thorndike	ca. 1775	*Antiques* 126 (December 1984): 1371	
Coffeepot	A	RBW (later)		ca. 1765	*Silver Supplement* 1973, no. 12	
Coffeepot	A	N/CM; 1745 (later) (+)		ca. 1770	Norman-Wilcox 1962, no. 8	
Coffeepot	B*	Williams arms, azure a lion rampant, and crest, a moorcock	Williams family	ca. 1775	Puig et al. 1989, no. 214	MIA
Coffeepot	B	L (later)		ca. 1780	Sotheby's, 24–27 January 1990, lot 161	
Creampot	B	MPE		ca. 1765	McFadden/Clark 1989, no. 63	CHM
Creampot	B	B/IE		ca. 1770	Sotheby Parke Bernet, 6–8 November 1975, lot 604	
Creampot (part of a service)	C*	Brown arms, a chevron azure between 3 lions' gambs within a bordure, on a chief an eagle displayed, and crest, a griffin's head couped; OB to AB	Moses Brown for Anna Brown	1763	Safford 1983, 46	MMA
Creampot	C*	HD		ca. 1765	Avery 1920, no. 74	MMA
Creampot	C	unidentified initials		ca. 1765	*Antiques* 110 (July 1976): 36	
Creampot	C	MM/to/EB (later)		ca. 1765	Sotheby Parke Bernet, 20–23 June 1979, lot 133	
Creampot	C*	D/SH		ca. 1765	DAPC 86.2631	
Creampot (part of a service; attrib.)	none	none	Joanna (Sigourney) (Doane) Bond	ca. 1795	Buhler 1972, no. 311	MFAB
Cup	A	The Legacy of Mr Saml Jenks,/to the third Church of Christ/in Lynn. 1774	Third Church of Christ, Lynn, Mass., for Samuel Jenks	1774	Sotheby's, 26 and 28 January 1984, lot 411	
Two cups	A	The Property/of the third Church of Christ/in Lynn./1774	Third Church of Christ, Lynn, Mass.	1774	Shelley 1958, 174	HFM
Flagon	A	Swett arms, gules 2 chevrons between 2 mullets in chief and	First Congregational Church, Marblehead, Mass., for Joseph Swett	1759	Jones 1913, 262–63	

	Mark	Inscription	Patron	Date	Reference	Owner
		in base argent seeded; Hoc Legatum Josephi Sweett Ar.ᶦ una cum/Additamento ejus Hoeredum Dᶦ S Sweett Dᵒᵉ/R. Hooper Dᵒᵉ M. Lee et Di J. Lemmon ad/Usum Sacrosantae Coenae in primâ Christi/Ecclesiâ apud Marblehead consecratum/ Maii, 7, 1759				
Flagon	A	Hoec Lagena argentea, ad Usum/Sacrosanctoe Coenoe, in primâ Christi Ecclesiâ/apud Marblehead, ex ejus Thesauro,/consecrata: Maii, 7, 1759	First Congregational Church, Marblehead, Mass.	1759	Jones 1913, 263	
Flagon	?	Cheever arms	Cheever family	ca. 1750	YUAG files	
Ladle	A	WM		ca. 1750	DAPC 68.3537	
Ladle	A	ISW; 1830 (later)		ca. 1780	YUAG files	
Ladle	A	M/DA	Daniel and Ann (Fudge) Malcom	ca. 1750	Buhler 1972, no. 297	MFAB
Ladle	A	The Gift of Cap.ᵗ Will.ᵐ Noble to M.ʳˢ Eliz·Service	William Noble and/or Elizabeth Service	ca. 1765	Gourley 1965, no. 28	HMA
Ladle	B	H/CE		ca. 1780	Skinner, 15 June 1991, lot 181A	
Ladle	B	B; Edmund Baker 1811 (later)	Baker family	ca. 1785	MFA 1911, no. 123	
Ladle (bowl only)	c*	H/CE		ca. 1775	Johnston 1994, 13	CMA
Ladle	?	ENE		ca. 1785	Green/ Holland 1973, no. 4	
Porringer	A*	ND	Nathaniel Dodge	ca. 1785	Buhler 1965, 80, 84	HMA
Porringer	A	R/IM		ca. 1765	Sotheby's, 27 January 1989, lot 918	
Porringer	A*	AD	Antiss (Derby) Pickman	ca. 1785	Buhler/Hood 1970, no. 214	YUAG
Porringer	A*	HR		ca. 1760	Buhler/Hood 1970, no. 212	YUAG
Porringer	A*	L/GE; G Leonard Iunʳ 1761	George and Experience (White) Leonard	ca. 1760	Buhler 1979, no. 35	WAM
Two porringers	A	RES (+)	Russell and Elizabeth (Perkins) Sturgis	ca. 1773	Buhler 1979, no. 39	WAM

	Mark	Inscription	Patron	Date	Reference	Owner
Porringer	A*	B. Crowninshield to M. Crowninshield (+)		ca. 1760	DAPC 78.3251	
Porringer	A*	TC		ca. 1760	DAPC 88.3457	
Porringer (mate below)	A	RES	Russell and Elizabeth (Perkins) Sturgis	ca. 1773	Buhler 1979, no. 40	WAM
Porringer (mate above)	A*	RES; E.O.P.S. (later) (+)	Russell and Elizabeth (Perkins) Sturgis	ca. 1773		PEM
Porringer	A*	IC/1790		1790	Buhler/Hood 1970, no. 213	YUAG
Porringer	A	AH		ca. 1785	Christie's, 19 October 1990, lot 84	
Porringer (part of a service)	A	Brown crest, a griffin's head couped; OB to AB	Moses Brown for Anna Brown	1763	*American Silver* 1967, no. 12	RWNAG
Porringer (part of a service)	A*	Brown crest, a griffin's head couped; OB to AB	Moses Brown for Anna Brown	1763	Safford 1983, 42	MMA
Porringer (part of a service)	A*	Brown crest, a griffin's head couped; OB to AB	Moses Brown for Anna Brown	1763	*Antiques* 116 (October 1979): 738	
Two porringers (part of a service)	A*	B/FM	Boardman family	ca. 1770	Shepard 1978, 223	MAM
Porringer	A	L/EM		ca. 1760	Avery 1920, no. 77	MMA
Porringer	A	GD		ca. 1770	Sotheby Parke Bernet, 26–29 January 1977, lot 328	
Porringer	A	JC		ca. 1770	Sotheby Parke Bernet, 27–30 January 1982, lot 205	
Porringer	A*	C/ZE		ca. 1770	*Antiques* 90 (August 1966): 141	
Porringer	A*	B/IE	Isaac and Elizabeth Brown	ca. 1760	Parke-Bernet, 10 November 1970, lot 57	
Porringer	A*	M/NE		ca. 1760		SI
Porringer	A*	WM^c/to/FH; EBH (later) (+)	William MacKay	ca. 1775	Christie's, 17–18 January 1992, lot 159	
Porringer	A	H/NE	Hichborn family	ca. 1775	*Antiques* 103 (February 1973): 242	
Porringer	A/B or C	H	Holland family	ca. 1775	Parke-Bernet, 4–5 October 1963, lot 325	
Two porringers	A/C*	W/TE (+)		ca. 1775	Buhler 1972, no. 306	MFAB
Porringer	B*	Elizh Fellows (later) (+)	Elizabeth Fellows (?)	ca. 1775	Warren 1975, no. 297	BBC

	Mark	Inscription	Patron	Date	Reference	Owner
Porringer	B*	W/CM		ca. 1770	Johnston 1994, 13	CMA
Two porringers	B	MM		ca. 1770	*Antiques* 67 (February 1955): 128	
Porringer	B*	A. MᶜK	A. MacKay (?)	ca. 1770	MFA 1911, no. 122	
Porringer	B	none		ca. 1770	Christie's, 1 October 1988, lot 75	
Porringer	B *or* C	P/DB (+)	Pearce family (?)	ca. 1770		CF
Porringer	B *or* C	W. Mackay	William MacKay	ca. 1775	MFA 1911, no. 119	
Porringer	B *or* C	The Gift of/James Brown Thornton . . . (later)	James Brown Thornton	ca. 1775	*CGA Bulletin*, no. 1 (1971): fig. 12	CGA
Porringer	B *or* C	WM to EB		ca. 1770	Christie's, 26 January 1991, lot 60	
Porringer	B *or* C	WH		ca. 1775	YUAG files	
Porringer	B *or* C	RLW		ca. 1775	YUAG files	
Porringer	B *or* C	E/EM		ca. 1765	Green/Holland 1973, no. 3	
Porringer	B *or* C	?		ca. 1775	Parke-Bernet, 1–4 February 1978, lot 674	
Porringer	B *or* C	?		ca. 1775	*Antiques* 119 (April 1981): 815	
Salt	A*	none		ca. 1765	Buhler/Hood 1970, no. 215	YUAG
Salt	A	H/SA (S over earlier initial)	Hastings family	ca. 1760	Buhler 1972, no. 303	MFAB
Two salts	B *or* C	RW to SS (+)	Warren or Sumner families	ca. 1775	MFA 1911, no. 120 (one only)	MFAB
Two salt spoons	B*	D/FE	Francis and Elizabeth (Ellery) Dana	ca. 1773	*YUAG Bulletin* 35 (Summer 1974): 86	YUAG
Sauceboat	A	?		ca. 1760	MFA 1911, no. 91	
Sauceboat (mate below)	A	D/RM/1735 (+)	Richard and Mary (Hodges) Derby	ca. 1760	Buhler 1972, no. 302	MFAB
Sauceboat (mate above)	A	D/RM (+)	Richard and Mary (Hodges) Derby	ca. 1760	Buhler 1972, no. 301	MFAB
Sauceboat (mate below)	B	C	Curtis family	ca. 1790	Buhler 1972, no. 308	MFAB
Sauceboat (mate above)	B	C	Curtis family	ca. 1790	Buhler 1972, 1:350	

	Mark	Inscription	Patron	Date	Reference	Owner
Sauceboat	B*	NRP	Nathan and Rebecca Pierce	ca. 1790	Buhler/Hood 1970, no. 219	YUAG
Sauceboat	B*	JSB		ca. 1790		SI
Sauceboat	B*	OEG		ca. 1800	Gourley 1965, no. 29	RISD
Two serving spoons	B	LN/12		ca. 1800		RISD
Serving spoon	?	M/DA		ca. 1755	Bigelow 1917, 276–77	
Strainer	B	AB		ca. 1775	YUAG files	
Strainer	B	GAP		ca. 1760	*Moore Collection* 1980, no. 139	
Strainer	B*	CT; GHA (later)		ca. 1765	Anderson Galleries, 20–21 January 1928, lot 236	
Strainer	C*	SG		ca. 1772		MMA
Strainer	C	C/ES		ca. 1755	Buhler 1972, no. 300	MFAB
Strainer	C*	M/WF		ca. 1755	Johnston 1994, 15 (as unknown maker)	CMA
Strainer	C†	none		ca. 1765	Buhler/Hood 1970, no. 216	YUAG
Strainer	C*	R (later)		ca. 1770	Conger/Rollins 1991, no. 200	USDS
Sugar bowl (part of a service)	A*	LW	Lois (Walker) Snelling (?)	ca. 1785	Hammerslough/Feigenbaum 1958–73, 4:25	WA
Sugar bowl (part of a service)	A*	FMB	Boardman family	ca. 1765	Shepard 1978, 222	MAM
Sugar bowl	B	D/CM	Caleb and Martha Davis	ca. 1775	YUAG files	
Sugar bowl	B	F		ca. 1795		MAM
Sugar bowl (part of a service; attrib.)	none	none	Joanna (Sigourney) (Doane) Bond	ca. 1795	Buhler 1972, no. 312	MFAB
Sword	?	?		ca. 1765	Medicus 1944, 342	
Sword	?	?		ca. 1760	*Antiques* 38 (October 1940): 148	
Tablespoon	A*	T/IM		ca. 1760	Quimby 1995, no. 19a	WM
Tablespoon	A	H/IS		ca. 1760	Quimby 1995, no. 19b	WM
Tablespoon	A*	SB		ca. 1770		YUAG

	Mark	Inscription	Patron	Date	Reference	Owner
Two tablespoons	B	B		ca. 1800	Buhler 1972, appendix no. 11	MFAB
Six tablespoons	B†	C/BS	Benejah and Susannah (Tracey) Collins	ca. 1775	Flynt/Fales 1968, 112	HD
Tablespoon	B	S/SH		ca. 1790	YUAG files	
Tablespoon	B	T/PH		ca. 1765	YUAG files	
Tablespoon	B*	D/EA		ca. 1765	DAPC 88.3568	
Tablespoon	B	PD		ca. 1785		CHS
Two tablespoons	B	BMG		ca. 1790	Buhler 1972, appendix no. 10	MFAB
Tablespoon	B*	MW		ca. 1790		SI
Tablespoon	B	L		ca. 1780	Buhler 1972, appendix no. 9	MFAB
Tablespoon	B	W/JM	Joseph and Mary (Sheafe) Willard	ca. 1775	Sander 1982, no. 29	SPNEA
Tablespoon	B *or* C	SBA	Sarah Burt Atkins	ca. 1795	Norman-Wilcox 1962, no. 9	LACMA
Six tablespoons	B *or* C	MF		ca. 1785	Green/Holland 1973, no. 10	
Two tablespoons	C	PD		ca. 1785	YUAG files	
Four tablespoons	?	SRG		ca. 1785	Parke-Bernet, 9 November 1946, lot 5	
Tablespoon	il-legible	L/GE	George and Experience (White) Leonard	ca. 1760	Buhler 1979, no. 37	WAM
Tankard	A*	Winthrop arms, 3 chevrons gules over all a lion rampant, and crest, a hare courant	Winthrop family	ca. 1760	YUAG files	
Tankard	A*	NM		ca. 1760	*Silver Supplement* 1973, no. 13	
Tankard (part of a service)	A	Brown arms, argent a chevron azure between 3 lions' gambs a bordure or, on a chief an eagle displayed, and crest, a griffin's head couped; OB to AB	Moses Brown for Anna Brown	1763	*Silver Supplement* 1973, no. 14	
Tankard	A	The GIFT of/the EPISCOPAL CHURCH/to the/ SECOND PRESBYTERIAN CHURCH/in/ NEWBURY PORT/as a token of their grat-	Episcopal Church, Newburyport, Mass.	1800	American Art Association–Anderson Galleries, 8 February 1936, lot 40	HFM

	Mark	Inscription	Patron	Date	Reference	Owner
		itude for the/use of the Meeting House in Harris Street,/ while S.ᵗ Paul's Church was Re-building/A.D. 1800.				
Tankard	A	Watertown Church (defaced)	First Parish, Water-town, Mass.	ca. 1775	Jones 1913, 482	
Tankard	A	The Gift of/M.ʳˢ Su-sanna Dobel./to the Second Church of Christ in/BRAIN-TREE/1773	Susanna Dobel and/or Second Church, Brain-tree, Mass.	1773	YUAG files	
Tankard (with mark of John Hancock)	A*	1766/Benjᵐ Wyman	Benjamin Wyman	1766	Avery 1920, no. 111	MMA
Tankard	A*	The Gift of the Honᵇ/John Choate Esqʳ to the/South Church	South Church, Ipswich, Mass., for John Choate	ca. 1766	Buhler/Hood 1970, no. 211	YUAG
Tankard	A	unidentified arms, azure a chevron be-tween 3 estoiles and a heart, and crest, an estoile; AD COE-LUM SPIRO; ship within cartouche		ca. 1778	Sotheby Parke Bernet, 16–18 November 1978, lot 408	
Tankard	A	The gift of/Lois Wiswell/ . . . (later)	Lois Wiswell (?)	ca. 1800	Jones 1913, 148–49	
Tankard	A*	D/IE	Isaac and Elizabeth (Day) Dodge	ca. 1760	Buhler 1965, 79, 83	HMA
Tankard	A*	W/BM; L (later)	DeWolfe family	ca. 1765	Davis 1972, 198–99	
Tankard	A	H/DE (+)	William Hyslop for David and E. Hyslop	ca. 1769	McFadden/Clark 1989, no. 33	CHM
Tankard	A	unidentified initials (+)		ca. 1770	Sotheby's, 21 June 1989, lot 132	
Tankard	A	BSC	Benejah and Susannah (Tracey) Collins	ca. 1785	Antiques 96 (October 1969): 458	
Tankard	A*	IS		ca. 1770	Antiques 119 (January 1981): 142	
Tankard	A	?	Fox family	ca. 1780	Antiques 83 (May 1963): 521	
Tankard	A*	North arms, azure a lion statant between 3 fleur-de-lis, and crest, a griffin's head erased, impaling Pit-son (?) arms, a chev-ron ermine between	John North for Elizabeth North	1756	Buhler/Hood 1970, no. 209	YUAG

	Mark	Inscription	Patron	Date	Reference	Owner
		3 cocks' heads; The Gift of John North/ to his Wife, Eliza-beth/1756				
Tankard	A*	none		ca. 1770	Puig et al. 1989, no. 213	MIA
Tankard	A	IGM; HJG Denny (later)		ca. 1775	YUAG files	
Tankard	A	H Lee 1782 (later)		ca. 1775	YUAG files	
Tankard	A	Rogers arms, a chev-ron between 3 stags trippant, and crest, a stag trippant; HLR	Rogers family	ca. 1770	YUAG files	
Tankard	A*	W/PS		ca. 1770	American Art Associa-tion–Ander-son Galler-ies, 8 February 1936, lot 41	
Tankard	A*	Charles River Bridge in ellipse; D/RE; Presented to/ Richard Devens, Esq.ʳ/by the Proprie-tors of/CHARLES RIVER BRIDGE,/in Testimony of their entire Approbation/ of his faithful Ser-vices,/as a special Director of that Work/begun A.D. 1785,/and perfected/ A.D. 1786.	Proprietors of Charles River Bridge for Rich-ard Devens	1786	Buhler 1972, no. 307	MFAB
Tankard	A	?		ca. 1775	YUAG files	
Tankard	A	BS		ca. 1760	Sotheby Parke Bernet, 20–23 June 1979, lot 145	
Tankard	A	TIMOTHEO HILLI-ARD/Harvardinates/ Anno Domini MDCCLXIX con-scripti/Bienno sub eius Tutelâ fere per-acto,/In gratum Rei Memoriam,/Hunc Calicem/Dono dant	Timothy Hilliard and/ or the Harvard College class of 1769	1769	Buhler 1960, no. 5	HFM
Tankard	A*	Rich.ᵈ Derby/to/ John Derby/Jan.ʸ 1/ 1763	Richard Derby for John Derby	1763	Downs 1948, 79	MMA
Tankard	A*	Stone arms, per pale or and sable a lion rampant counter-	Stone family	ca. 1765	Safford 1983, 40–41	MMA

	Mark	Inscription	Patron	Date	Reference	Owner
		changed, and crest, a lion's head erased; ES				
Tankard	A*	Phillips arms, or a lion rampant gorged and chained, and crest, a lion sejant gorged and chained; GHP (later)	Phillips family	ca. 1770		SI
Tankard	A	G. Leonard Iunr. 1761	George Leonard, Jr.	1761	DAPC 88.3457	
Tankard	A	Leonard arms, on a fess gules 3 fleur-de-lis, and crest, a tiger's head emerging from a ducal crown; L/GE (+)	George and Experience (White) Leonard	ca. 1760	Sotheby's, 28–31 January 1993, lot 122	
Tankard *(see also unmarked mate)*	A	S/IS	Jonathan and Sarah (Mitchell) Sayward	ca. 1770	Sprague 1987, no. 44	OYHS
Tankard	B	John Bray Goodwin/1799	John Bray Goodwin	1799	MFA 1911, no. 124	
Tankard	?	Lowell quartering Leversedge arms (later) (+)	Lowell or Leversedge family	ca. 1775	Sotheby Parke Bernet, 1–4 February 1978, no. 666	
Tankard	?	JDW	John DeWolfe	1793	Ormsbee 1940, 6	
Tankard	?	MSP	Pomeroy family (?)	ca. 1785	*American Collector* 9 (August 1940): 2	
Tankard	?	C + H.B.L./to/J.B.L./ + M.W. (later?)		ca. 1775	YUAG files	
Tankard *(see also mate with mark A)*	none	S/IS	Jonathan and Sarah (Mitchell) Sayward	ca. 1770	Sander 1982, no. 25	SPNEA
Teapot (part of a service)	A	LW	Lois (Walker) Snelling (?)	ca. 1785	Hammerslough/ Feigenbaum 1958–73, 4:24	WA
Teapot	A	unidentified initials		ca. 1770	Sotheby Parke Bernet, 29 April–1 May 1981, lot 392	
Teapot (part of a service)	A*	FMB	Boardman family	ca. 1765	Shepard 1978, 222	MAM
Teapot	A	ECS		ca. 1770	*Antiques* 30 (November 1936): 197	
Teapot	A	?		ca. 1765	YUAG files	
Teapot	A	MR; M.E.P. (later)		ca. 1755	Buhler 1976, 4–5, 7	VMFA
Teapot	A	Unidentified arms, a bird flying, and crest, a double-	Obadiah Brown or Jabez Bowen for Sarah Brown	1762	Emlen 1984, 40–41	MFAB

	Mark	Inscription	Patron	Date	Reference	Owner
		headed eagle; OB to SB				
Teapot (part of a service)	A	Brown arms, argent a chevron azure between 3 lions' gambs a bordure or, on a chief an eagle displayed, and crest, a griffin's head couped; Brown crest; OB to AB	Moses Brown for Anna Brown	1763	Emlen 1984, 42	MFAB
Teapot	A	T/IM		ca. 1765	Parke-Bernet, 1–2 June 1950, lot 330	
Teapot	A*	none		ca. 1765	Parke-Bernet, 28 October 1969, lot 133	
Teapot	A	R/HL		ca. 1770		AIC
Teapot (part of a service)	B*	none	Joanna (Sigourney) (Doane) Bond	ca. 1795	Buhler 1972, no. 309	MFAB
Teapot	B*	S/PE; 1765; A.A. Lord (later)	Peter Thacher and Elizabeth (Wendell) Smith	ca. 1785	Buhler/Hood 1970, no. 220	YUAG
Teapot	B or C	Hancock arms, gules a dexter hand argent couped, on a chief argent 3 cocks, and crest, a demi-griffin (+)	Gov. John Hancock	ca. 1765	English-Speaking Union 1960, no. 63	
Teapot	?	M:ʸ DERBY	Mary Derby	ca. 1755	Fales 1970, 23–24	
Teapot	?	none		ca. 1765	Jones 1936, 84–85	
Teapot (attrib.)	none	G/NS; GEL/1770 (later)		ca. 1765	Buhler 1979, no. 36	WAM
Teapot stand (part of a service; attrib.)	none	none	Joanna (Sigourney) (Doane) Bond	ca. 1795	Buhler 1972, no. 310	MFAB
Teaspoon	B	BC		ca. 1760	Avery 1920, no. 78	MMA
Teaspoon	B	IM		ca. 1775	Quimby 1995, no. 18a	WM
Teaspoon	B*	H/IS		ca. 1775	DAPC 82.3141	
Teaspoon	B	DS		ca. 1760	Buhler 1979, no. 38	WAM
Teaspoon	B	D/IS		ca. 1785	Quimby 1995, no. 18b	WM
Teaspoon	B	WT		ca. 1780	Quimby 1995, no. 16b	WM
Teaspoon	B	LP (?)		ca. 1790	YUAG files	
Teaspoon	B	WH		ca. 1765	YUAG files	
Two teaspoons	B*	HS		ca. 1790	Eitner 1976, nos. 56–57	
Six teaspoons	B	N (?) C		ca. 1800	Buhler 1965, 85	HMA

	Mark	Inscription	Patron	Date	Reference	Owner
Teaspoon	B	K/IS		ca. 1775		WHS
Teaspoon	B*	IT		ca. 1780	Quimby 1995, no. 16a	WM
Teaspoon	B*	AS		ca. 1795	DAPC 82.3143	
Three teaspoons	B*	B/WM		ca. 1795		YUAG
Teaspoon	B*	W/JE		ca. 1795		YUAG
Two teaspoons	B*	S/SH		ca. 1795		YUAG
Teaspoon	B *or* C	WH		ca. 1795	DAPC 79.3423	
Teaspoon	C	Brown crest, a griffin's head couped; OB/to/AB	Moses Brown for Anna Brown (?)	ca. 1763		HD
Teaspoon	C*	AB		ca. 1755	Buhler/Hood 1970, no. 217	YUAG
Teaspoon	C*	MP		ca. 1775	Quimby 1995, no. 17	WM
Teaspoon	C*	ST		ca. 1760	DAPC 68.3987	
Teaspoon	?	S/IH	Jacob and Hannah (Seavey) Sheafe	ca. 1760	Decatur 1941, 7	SPNEA
Two-handled cup (mate below)	A*	The gift of Jos.h Allen esq.r and Wife/To the 4th Church in Glocester 1751	Joshua Allen and wife and/or Fourth Church, Gloucester, Mass.	1751	Norman-Wilcox 1962, no. 7	
Two-handled cup (mate above)	A*	The gift of Jos Allen esq and Wife/To the 4th Church in Glocester 1751	Joshua Allen and wife and/or Fourth Church, Gloucester, Mass.	1751	Johnston 1994, 15 (as unknown maker)	CMA
Two wine cups	C	The Gift of/William Hyslop Esq.r/to the Church of Christ;/in BROOK-LYN:/of which, Joseph Jackson, A.M. is Pastor/1792	William Hyslop and/or First Parish, Brookline, Mass.	1792	Jones 1913, 101–02	

1. RC 24:190.
2. Burt Family Bible, HD.
3. RC 30:354; RC 24:203.
4. RC 28:98; SCPR 57:102–03.
5. Codman 1918, 51.
6. Bigelow-Phillips files, 1388; Boston Deaths, 1700–1800.
7. YCD 29:269.
8. Pruitt 1978, 4–5.
9. "Assessors' 'Taking-Books,'" 17.
10. SCD 100:23–24; 156:231–33.
11. SCD 102:216–17; 110:203.
12. Derby Family Papers, PEM.
13. SCD 110:203; 113:99.
14. SCD 131:34–35, 43–44. Burt's relationship with Foster continued throughout his life. Foster operated a shop on Fish Street near his former master. Burt's will appointed his "trusty friend Joseph Foster of Boston Goldsmith" as the sole executor of his estate and left him a bequest of one hundred dollars, SCPR 103:497–500.
15. SCD 159:199–200; 163:196, 215–17; 166:267–68; 172:101; MCD 101:10–11. Edward Revere married Eliza Potter (d. 1804) on 9 November 1800 and Elizabeth Allen on 17 May 1807. When he

died on 18 January 1820, he was described as "formerly of Reading, now of Boston." Bigelow-Phillips files.

16. SCD 172:249–50.

17. SCD 183:122–23, 224.

18. SCD 172:249–50; 190:234.

19. SCD 183:122–23. Very little is known about Waters. He appears in the Boston directories for 1803–05 as a goldsmith on Fifth Street. A creampot by him is at CHM (see McFadden/Clark 1989, no. 67), and a tankard by him is at the Church of Christ in Billerica, Massachusetts (MFAB loan 138.50).

20. MCD 134:233–34, 487–89.

21. MCD 190:197–98.

22. SCPR 103:498–500.

23. RC 22:452.

24. Flynt/Fales 1968, 346.

25. SCPR 103:498–500.

26. SCPR 39:160–61; 79:286–89.

27. SCPR 80:314–19, docket 17461.

28. SCPR, docket 17442.

29. Zachariah Brigden Daybook, 1766–ca. 1775, fol. 6v, Brigden Papers, YU.

30. Benjamin Burt to Brigden estate, 18 April 1787, Brigden Papers, YU.

31. MCD 98:60–61; SCPR, docket 18844. Flynt/Fales 1968, 166, state that Burt bought tools from Brigden's widow in 1787, however, the widow still retained possession of the tools in 1788.

32. RC 16:110; RC 18:253.

33. RC 18:270.

34. *Pennsylvania Gazette*, 4 November 1789; *Independent Chronicle*, 9–13 January 1800.

35. Steinway 1960, 7.

36. SCCR, Court of Common Pleas Extended Record Book 1780–81, 132.

37. SCCR, Court of Common Pleas Extended Record Book 1780–81, 132.

38. SCPR 80:199.

39. SCCR, Court of Common Pleas Extended Record Book 1785, 107.

40. SCD 95:85–86; 97:236–37; 110:202–03.

41. SCD 100:23–24.

42. SCD 156:231–33.

43. SCPR 77:226–28, 496–97.

44. SCPR 78:578.

45. SCPR, docket 8435.

46. SCD 131:34–35, 43–44.

47. *Boston Directory* 1789, 11; 1798, 27.

48. RC 22:189.

49. SCD 110:203; 172:101.

50. SCD 161:277–78; 163:196.

51. SCD 166:267–68.

52. SCD 175:109–13.

53. SCD 180:145–50.

54. SCD 94:198–99. Although scheduled to be repaid by May 1761, Glidden's debt was not resolved until August 1781.

55. SCD 102:216–17. This debt was repaid in August 1781.

56. SCD 113:99.

57. SCD 133:23–25. The loan was repaid on 25 April 1797.

58. SCD 156:233–35; 159:199–200.

59. SCD 163:215–17. Harris repaid his loan in December 1794.

60. Burt Family Bible, HD.

61. SCPR 105:289.

62. Whitmore 1878, 28, no. 533.

63. SCPR 103:497–500.

64. SCPR 103:522. The inventory was presented for probate on 11 November 1805.

65. Crocker 1827, 12.

66. See a ladle at CMA (Johnston 1994, 14) and a covered butter dish at YUAG (1930.3380).

67. Bigelow-Phillips files.

68. *American Collector* 9 (August 1940): 6.

John Burt
1692/93–1745/46

A

B

C

D

E

F

G

John Burt was the founding member of a renowned Boston family of gold-smiths that included his sons Samuel, William, and Benjamin (qq.v.). Born in Boston on 5 January 1692/93 to Elizabeth (Wood?) and William Burt (ca. 1653–93), he was baptized in the Old South Church.[1] William and Elizabeth Burt had three children in addition to John: Susanna (b. 1686), Benjamin (b. 1688), and Samuel (b. 1690).[2] William Burt died on 10 November 1693, when his son John was less than two years old. Because his father's tombstone also bears the epitaph of James Wood of London, who died at age thirty-four in 1681/82, Francis Hill Bigelow speculated that Burt's mother's maiden name might have been Wood.[3] Elizabeth did not remarry until 1708, taking as her second husband the mariner Thomas Lawler (1682–1743).[4] For most of his youth, then, Burt was raised by his mother.

Burt would have been ready to begin an apprenticeship about 1707, and his training would have been completed about 1714. On 3 June of that year he married Abigail Cheever (1691–1778), the daughter of Rev. Thomas Cheever (1658–1749) of Chelsea and Sarah Bill (1659–1704/05).[5] Although other authori-ties believe Burt probably served his apprenticeship under John Coney (q.v.), Bigelow speculated that Burt was apprenticed to Henry Hurst (q.v.), because Burt's wife's cousin Mary Bill was married to Hurst.[6] Other cousins of Abigail Burt were married to craftsmen in allied trades: Hannah Bill was the wife of the watchmaker Joseph Essex; Abigail Bill, the wife of the watchmaker Thomas Badley; and Mehitable Bill would become the wife of the engraver William Burgis (q.q.v. Appendix A). In this manner Burt established kinship ties by marriage with a sizable group of craftsmen. The first evidence of Burt's practice of his trade is the suit brought by him in 1718 against the weaver Samuel Cranston. Burt claimed he had never been paid for a gold locket and two gold rings sold and delivered to Cranston in Boston.[7] Surviving objects also reveal that beginning in 1724 Burt received a number of commissions from the Harvard tutor Nicholas Sever and in 1727 made £8.10 worth of rings for the funeral of the widow Hannah Sharp.[8]

Burt was involved in a few cases in the Court of Common Pleas, both as defendant and plaintiff. He was the defendant in suits filed on 7 October 1718, on 2 January 1727/28 (with Knight Leverett [q.v.] as plaintiff), and on 6 July 1736. He was a plaintiff on 6 January 1719 and 6 July 1736.[9]

Unlike other prominent craftsmen, Burt participated only modestly in Bos-ton's civic affairs. He was made a clerk of the market in 1718/19, tithingman in 1721/22, and constable in 1725/26, although he refused to serve in the office of constable.[10]

In 1719 Burt's stepfather Thomas Lawler received three hundred pounds from the owners of the brigantine *Dove* and their heirs, in a deed witnessed by John Burt.[11] The profits from the sale of the brigantine and her cargo were meant to compensate Lawler for his years of imprisonment in France, where he was sent as a hostage when John Patterson, master of the *Dove*, ransomed the vessel. This windfall must have provided Burt and his family with a measure of financial security. In 1720 Thomas Hutchinson, one of the owners of the *Dove*, also sold Burt and his wife part of a house in the north part of Boston for £320.[12]

Burt must have been reasonably successful from the outset of his career because slightly more than a decade after he began to work he started specu-lating in real estate. In 1728 Burt paid £160 for a tract of land west of the Sheepscut River in the province of Maine, the first of many such transactions by him in the next dozen years involving Maine real estate.[13] Over the next eight years he sold parcels of this land: a quarter in 1729; a sixty-fourth part in 1730; and three-eighths in 1736. He received a total of £150 for these transactions, while retaining ownership of more than a third of his acreage.[14] In 1729 he spent £78 to purchase a one-fifth part of the real estate of Nathaniel Draper, also on the Sheepscut River.[15] Subsequently Burt and other individuals subdivided a tract of more than ten thousand acres.[16] In addition to his Maine transactions, Burt speculated in Boston. In 1731 he mortgaged his Fish Street property. He sold that property in 1736 for £850 to Deacon John Tudor, whose diary under the date 26 April 1737 reads, "I went into my house which I bought of Mr. John Burt goldsmith."[17]

The deeds for these transactions provide valuable information regarding the identities of Burt's apprentices and silversmithing associates. Numbered among his apprentices were Samuel Gray (1710/11–48) and John Blowers (qq.v.), who would both have been eighteen years old when they witnessed a deed for Burt in 1728/29 and probably apprenticed with Burt from 1724 to about 1732.[18] In 1730 Gray acknowledged payment on an account "for my Master John Burt" for six funeral rings sold to the estate of William Smith.[19] Blowers was identified as an apprentice of Burt's in a court case of 1730.[20] Although Samuel Gray does not appear again as a witness, Blowers witnessed another deed for Burt in 1730.[21] John Parkman (q.v.) was probably another of Burt's apprentices because he would have been only twenty years old when he witnessed a deed for him in 1736.[22] Parkman probably trained in Burt's shop from 1730 to 1737. His contemporary Edmund Mountfort (q.v.) was also a Burt apprentice since Burt was appointed his guardian in 1729. The twenty-year-old Mountfort witnessed a deed for Burt with William Simpkins (q.v.) in 1737.[23] Another likely Burt apprentice was John Doane (q.v.), who would have been twenty years old when he witnessed deeds in 1739.[24] Doane's brother Joshua (q.v.) may also have trained with Burt. In addition to these craftsmen, Burt presumably trained his son Samuel and began training his sons William and Benjamin, who were minors when their father died. Kathryn Buhler speculated that Jacob Hurd might have been apprenticed to Burt.[25]

Craftsmen who may have worked for Burt as journeymen or otherwise had business associations with him include Theophilus Burrill, Bartholomew Green, George Hanners, Sr. (qq.v.), and William Simpkins. Burrill witnessed a mortgage for Burt in 1731/32.[26] Burt witnessed a deed for Green in 1734.[27] When the Boston brazier Jonathan Jackson (1672–1736) died, Burt owed his estate £60.5 and was one of three silversmiths who owed the brazier money, the others being Samuel Haley (q.v.) and George Hanners, Sr.[28] When George Hanners, Sr., died in 1740, his estate owed Burt 60 shillings.[29] Simpkins witnessed the 1737 deed discussed above and was one of the appraisers of Burt's estate in 1745/46.[30]

Burt's income in the 1730s may have been boosted by his involvement with a project for emitting bank notes organized by a group of Boston merchants. In his account book between 1734 and 1736, Joshua Winslow recorded that the "Subscribers to the Scheme" were debtors to Burt for his service in weighing silver and gold:

1734
Nov. 29. pᵈ Mʳ Burts Lad for
Attendᶜ. wᵗʰ Scales & Waits }   .10:_____

. . .
dec^e.
24. p^d.　　　Jno Burt for attend^c. of his Lad wth. Sca:&c　　　　1.10 ⎯⎯⎯

. . .
1735
Jan　　　　allowd Mr Burt for his Servants
　　　　　attendance 9 days　　　　pd Feb. 3　　2:10
. . .　　　allw'd s^d Servant for himself　　　　　10　　　　3 – – ⎯⎯⎯
1736
Feb.8.　　　Cash p^d Mr Burt for his Man's attend^a. }
　　　　　wth Scales & Weights 23 days 8/　　　　}
　　　　　　　　　　　　　　　　　　　　　　　　[£]9.4[31]

Burt's familiarity with the value of specie in relation to the bills is underscored by his testimony before the Superior Court at Cambridge in 1734:

> John Burt: Goold Smith of Lawfull Age Testifieth
> And Saith: That haveing Searched in his Book of
> Accomp^{ts}: found that in [illeg. insert] ye year 1714 that Silver was
> Eight & Ten pence an oz which makes In Every
> Twenty Shillings About five and Eight pence
> Difference between silver att Seventeen [illeg.] eight & province
> Bills: And in ye year 1718: y^e: Difference between
> Silver att: 17 [illeg.] & province Bills was About Ten
> & Six pence : on: ye pound.[32]

Harvard tutor Henry Flynt also noted Burt's expertise concerning the value of silver, entering in his memorandum book on 9 July 1739: "to be determined by Mr Burt as to the price of Silver between the 18th of April & 9th July."[33]

　　Burt died intestate on 23 January 1745/46 and was buried in the Granary Burying Ground.[34] His estate administration was granted to his widow, Abigail, and son Samuel Burt on 11 February 1745/46.[35] The inventory, presented on 27 August 1746, amounted to £6,460.4.6, which included his mansion (£1,350), a negro woman (£90), farms at Woburn (£2,870), land along the Sheepscut River, two thousand acres at Sunderland, and one thousand acres at Bedford. The tools included:

316^{oz}.4^{dwt} of Silver @ 36/℔ oz £569.3 Gold 18^{oz}:11^{dwt}: @ £27 ℔ oz £500.17	£1070
cash £100 33^{oz}: of Correll @ 20/ ℔ oz £33	133
5 pair of Stone Earings & 3 Sett of Stone buttons £30.. a parcell of old Stones £7	37
a parcell of Christals for Buttons & Earings	82
a parcell of Old stone work	5
2 Show Glasses £5..0/53 pair of Chapes & tongs £10.2	15.2
11 Files 33/ a pair of large and small bellows 40/	3.13
a large Forgin Anvil 120^{lb} @ 2/6 ℔ lb £15 1 small d^o. £9	24
9 Raising Anvils 217^{lb} @ 3/6 ℔ lb £37.19.6 2 planishing Teastes 39.^{lb} @3/6 ℔ lb 6.16.6	44.16
2 Spoon Teastes £26– 2 planishing ditto 25/ 3 bench vises £12	39.5
9 small vises 45/ 2 beak Irons 20/ 47 hammers @ 8/ ℔ ham^r. 18.16.10	22.1
2 Melting Skillets £5–37 Bottom Stakes & punches 155^{lb} @ 4/ £31	36
a Drawing bench & tongs 40/ 11 Drawing Irons £11 10 pair of Shears £6	19
2 brass Hollowin Stamps £5 a pair of brass Salt punches 30/	6.10
1 Thimble Stamp £4.10/ 6 p^r. of flasks for Casting £4.10/	9
15 pair of Tongs & plyers @ 5/ a p^r. 75/ a pair of large Scales & Weights £8	11.15
4 pair of small Scales & weights 40/ pewter & lead Moulds 85^{lb} @ 1/6 6.7.6	8.7.6
36 old Files 18/ 12 Strainers 12/ 1 Oyl Stone 25/ 3 Small Saws 25/	4

4 boreax boxes 5/ 3 burnishers 20/ 1 Triblet 10/ 2 boiling pans 60/   4.15
a parcell of Punches £5 1 Touch Stone 5/   5.5
. . .
2 Ingotts 1 large Iron Kittle 1 p.^{r} of Screws & a Brass plate 90/   4.10^{36}

The estate was not divided immediately. On 21 December 1748 the widow petitioned the General Court for permission to sell the Woburn farm.[37] Abigail Burt wrote her will on 1 December 1758, and it was probated on 11 September 1778.[38] In 1779 Benjamin Burt was appointed executor of his father's estate and presented the final accounting in 1780.[39]

More than 180 pieces survive with marks attributed to John Burt. Among them are a cup owned by Abijah Northey (q.v.) and a pepper box later owned by William Northey (q.v.). Burt's marks include IB crowned in a shaped shield (A), I.BURT in a shaped rectangle (B), BURT in a rectangle (C), JOHN/BURT in an oval (D), J:BURT in an oval (E), and IB in a rectangle (F, G). Burt probably was the earliest Boston goldsmith to use surname and full-name marks. Spurious examples of marks (A), (D), and (E) are known.[40] A large amount of Burt's surviving silver is holloware, including commissions from Harvard College and communion plate for New England churches. PEK

SURVIVING OBJECTS

	Mark	Inscription	Patron	Date	Reference	Owner
Baptismal basin	B*	Hocce Lavacrum Ecclesiae Charlestonensi Nov-Anglia in Baptismi Usum dedicat Henricus Phillips I mo Maii. 1726.	Henry Phillips and/or First Parish Church, Charlestown, Mass.	1726	Buhler/Hood 1970, no. 110	YUAG
Three beakers	B	The Gift of Mr James Partridg to the/Church of Christ in Duxborough A.D./1731	James Partridge and/or First Congregational Church, Duxbury, Mass.	1731	Jones 1913, 156–57	
Beaker	D	The Gift of Messrs Mathew Bridge:/ and Thomas Meriam: to the Church./In Lexington:/1738	First Congregational Society, Lexington, Mass., for Matthew Bridge and Thomas Merriam	1738	Jones 1913, 243–44	
Beaker	D	The Gift of Mrs Sarah Seawell/To the Church of Christ in Exeter/ 1738	Sarah Seawell and/or First Congregational Church, Exeter, N.H.	1738	Jones 1913, 172	
Beaker	D	The Gift of Wm Sumner Son of Deacon/Roger Sumner to ye Church of/ Christ in Milton. 1739	First Congregational Parish, Milton, Mass., for William Sumner	1739	Jones 1913, 290	
Beaker	D	The gift of Mr Roland Cotton to the first Church of Christ in Woburn 1741	Roland Cotton and/or First Congregational Church, Woburn, Mass.	1741	Jones 1913, 503	

	Mark	Inscription	Patron	Date	Reference	Owner
Bowl	D	Gowen arms, fess argent between 3 gowans, and crest, a lion's head erased; Grant arms, argent 3 lions rampant, a chief azure, and crest, a lion rampant; Greenleaf arms, a chevron between 3 leaves, and crest, a bird with a sprig in its beak; Martain (?) arms, azure on a bend 3 fleur-de-lis, in chief or 3 eagles displayed, and crest, an eagle displayed; Mountfort arms, bendy of 10 or and purpure, and crest, a lion's head erased; and Winslow arms, on a bend 6 lozenges conjoined gules, and crest, a tree trunk with new branches	Lemuel Gowen, Joseph Grant, Jr., John Greenleaf, Samuel Martain, Jonathan Mountfort, Jr., and Kenelm Winslow	ca. 1740	Phillips 1949, 74–76	
Candlesnuffer and tray (set with candlesticks)	D*	W/DS	Daniel and Sarah (Hill) Warner	ca. 1730	Quimby 1995, no. 21a, b	WM
Two candlesticks	A*	Donum/ Pupillorum/1724	Nicholas Sever and/or the Harvard College class of 1724	1724	Hood 1971, 93, 95–96	HU
Two candlesticks (set with candlesnuffer and tray)	E*	W/DS	Daniel and Sarah (Hill) Warner	ca. 1730	Quimby 1995, no. 20a, b	WM
Cann	A	W/M^c/S; MH (partially erased)		ca. 1725	Buhler 1972, no. 118	MFAB
Cann	A	?		ca. 1730	*Antiques* 104 (December 1973): 977	
Cann	B	ON (later)		ca. 1730	DAPC 79.3398	
Cann	B*	Ex Dono Pupillorum 1728 (+)	Nicholas Sever and/or the Harvard College class of 1728	1728	Hale 1931, n.p.	HU
Cann	D*	Second/Presbyterian Church Newburyport	Second Presbyterian Church, Newburyport, Mass.	ca. 1735		SI
Cann	D	MW; Polley Wallingford's (later)	Margaret (Clements) Wallingford	ca. 1745	Christie's, 3 June 1989, lot 307	
Cann	D	unidentified arms, per chevron 3 leaves slipped, impaling on a chevron between 3 leopards' heads 3 fleur-de-lis		ca. 1740	American Art Association–Anderson Galleries, 2–3 April 1937, lot 284	

	Mark	Inscription	Patron	Date	Reference	Owner
Cann	D*	S/?I; T(?)/WE (+)		ca. 1740	Puig et al. 1989, no. 195	MIA
Cann	D	B/TH (later)		ca. 1735		AG
Cann	D	A/IM; MA		ca. 1740	McFadden/ Clark 1989, no. 29	CHM
Cann	D*	AB; AAW 1851 (later)		ca. 1735		RISD
Cann	D	unidentified arms		ca. 1740	Skinner, 15 June 1991, lot 164B	
Cann	?	Willet arms (?)	Willet family	ca. 1735	YUAG files	
Cann	?	unidentified arms; illegible initials		ca. 1745	*Silver Supplement* 1973, no. 16	
Caster	D	AG		ca. 1740	*Moore Collection* 1980, no. 104	
Caster	D†	G/TI M	Thomas James and Mary (Dumaresq) Grouchy (?)	ca. 1740	Buhler/Hood 1970, no. 113	YUAG
Caster	E*	RM		ca. 1740	DAPC 70.2200	MMA
Two caudle cups	B*	M. Church Plate 1728	First Church, Malden, Mass.	1728	Jones 1913, 257	MFAB
Two chafing dishes	A	NS; Donum Pupillorum 1724 (+)	Nicholas Sever and/or the Harvard College class of 1724	1724	Gourley 1965, no. 36	
Chafing dish (mate below)	B	original initials erased; M/JM (later)		ca. 1730		CF
Chafing dish (mate above)	B	original initials erased; M/JM (later)		ca. 1730	Hanks 1970, 420	AIC
Chafing dish	D	P/SA		ca. 1740	Avery 1920, no. 18	MMA
Coffeepot	B, D, *or* E	unidentified crest, a unicorn's head; DMG (later)		ca. 1740	*Bulletin DIA* 18 (May 1939): 4–7	DIA
Creampot	D	?		ca. 1740	DAPC 68.2305	
Creampot	?	MB		ca. 1745	Christie's, 17–18 January 1992, lot 160	
Cup	B	The Gift of Mʳ- Wᵐ- Whipple to the/First Church of Christ In Kittery- 1728	William Whipple and/ or First Congregational Church, Kittery, Maine	1728	Jones 1913, 237–38	
Cup	B	AN	Abijah Northey	ca. 1741	*Old-Time New England* 63 (January– March 1973): iv	
Cup	D*	Ionᵃ Mountfort Tert:ˢ/Ex Dono IG Terts/May 18ᵗʰ 1747	Jonathan Mountfort III	ca. 1745	Buhler/Hood 1970, no. 115	YUAG

	Mark	Inscription	Patron	Date	Reference	Owner
Cup	?	W/SR		ca. 1725	*Antiques* 106 (November 1974): 761	
Flagon	A*	Frizell arms, quarts 1 and 4 argent 3 antique crowns, 2 and 3, 3 fraises argent, and crest, a stag's head between 2 battle axes addorsed; JESU EST PRET; The Legacy of/M.r- John Frizell/Who died April y.e 10.th. 1723/to the/Second Church of Christ/In Boston	Second Church, Boston, for John Frizell	ca. 1723	Jones 1913, 39	
Two flagons	A	Belonging/to that Church/of Christ in Marblehead/of which the Rev.d M.r/ Edward Holyoke is/ Pastor/1722.	Second Congregational Society, Marblehead, Mass.	1722	Jones 1913, 267	MFAB
Flagon	E	The Gift of M.rs/Rebecca Waters to the/New North Church in/Boston of which the/Rev.d M.r Webb and/y.e Rev.d M.r Eliot/are Pastors/1745	New North Church, Boston, for Rebecca Waters	1745	Jones 1913, 62	
Grace cup	E	Browne arms, argent on a bend sable double cotised 3 eagles displayed, and crest, an eagle	Harvard College for Samuel Browne	1731	Buhler 1956, no. 12	HU
Mug	D	Andrews arms; R/CE	Andrews family	ca. 1725		MFAB
Two pepper boxes	B*	Mary Cutt	Mary Cutt	ca. 1725	*Antiques* 112 (November 1977): 897	
Pepper box	B	unidentified crest, a unicorn and a crown; M/IE		ca. 1730	YUAG files	
Pepper box	B	EH; 1732	Elizabeth Henchman	1732	Bigelow 1917, 320	
Pepper box	B	AL		ca. 1730	*Moore Collection* 1980, no. 103	
Pepper box	B	N/WR/1768 (later)	David Northey	ca. 1735	Fales 1983, 16–17	PEM
Pepper box	B, D, or E	E.C. to S.C. (later?)		ca. 1735	Parke-Bernet, 30 April–1 May 1954, lot 230	
Pepper box	D*	AT (altered to HW?)		ca. 1730	DAPC 73.3436	

	Mark	Inscription	Patron	Date	Reference	Owner
Pepper box	E	O/IH		ca. 1735	Buhler 1956, no. 14	
Pepper box	E*	MB; Iohn Basset	John Basset (?)	ca. 1735	Johnston 1994, 16	CMA
Pepper box	?	EM		ca. 1735	*Silver Supplement* 1973, no. 17	
Pepper box	?	unidentified initials; 1720		1720	*Antiques* 100 (December 1971): 852	
Porringer	A	T/RE (+)	Thaxter family	ca. 1735	YUAG files	
Porringer	A	AC/to/RC		ca. 1725	*American Art of the Colonies and Early Republic*, no. 98	
Porringer	A*	FI/to/CI (+)		ca. 1720		YUAG
Porringer	A	B/SM		ca. 1725	Sotheby's, 24 October 1987, lot 388	
Porringer	A	Appleton crest, a pineapple; MA; H Gibbs/to/MA	Henry Gibbs for Margaret Appleton	ca. 1720		MFAB
Porringer	B	C/IS		ca. 1730	Buhler 1972, no. 122	MFAB
Porringer	B	ASR		ca. 1735	*Bulletin DIA* 12 (March 1931): 70–72	DIA
Two porringers	B*	AO		ca. 1735	Puig et al. 1989, no. 193	MIA
Porringer	C	?		ca. 1735	Buhler 1972, 1:151	
Porringer	D	L/RI		ca. 1740	*American Art of the Colonies and Early Republic*, no. 99	
Porringer	D	W/RE		ca. 1740	Christie's, 19 October 1990, lot 83	
Porringer	D (?)	QRT (later)		ca. 1740	Parke-Bernet, 25–26 October 1949, lot 368	
Porringer	D*	I/EB		ca. 1735	YUAG files	
Porringer	D	SW (+)		ca. 1740	DAPC 68.3434	MMA
Porringer	D*	R/WR (altered to P/IM)		ca. 1740	Buhler 1972, no. 125	MFAB
Porringer	D	initials erased; Carroll (later)		ca. 1740	Buhler 1972, no. 126	MFAB
Porringer (mate below)	D*	S/NS; J.W.S. (later)	Nicholas and Sarah (Warren) (Little) Sever	ca. 1740	Skerry 1984, 853	WA
Porringer (mate above)	D*	S/NS; N.S. 1680–1764 . . . (later)	Nicholas and Sarah (Warren) (Little) Sever	ca. 1740	Hale 1931, n.p.	

	Mark	Inscription	Patron	Date	Reference	Owner
Porringer	D	MH	Hubbard family	ca. 1740	Gourley 1965, no. 37	SPNEA
Porringer	D*	SB		ca. 1740	Warren 1975, no. 295	BBC
Porringer	D*	SB		ca. 1740		RISD
Porringer	D	SB		ca. 1740	*Antiques* 99 (January 1971): 58	
Porringer	D*	T/BP		ca. 1735	Bartlett 1984, 9	SLAM
Porringer	D	G/PM	Peter and Mary Gilman	ca. 1735	YUAG files	
Porringer	D	H/WH		ca. 1740	*Antiques* 81 (May 1962): 462	
Porringer	E	S/HN		ca. 1740	*Antiques* 100 (September 1971): 334	DAI
Porringer	?	Mary Traill Spence/ Lowell		ca. 1740	Norman-Wilcox 1962, no. 6	
Porringer	?	?		ca. 1730	Sotheby Park Bernet, 12–16 November 1974, lot 1023	
Porringer	?	unidentified engraving		ca. 1740	*Antiques* 87 (April 1965): 404	
Porringer	?	IF		ca. 1740	Christie's, 5–6 June 1987, lot 528	
Two salts	A	none	Nicholas Sever	ca. 1725	Hale 1931, n.p.	
Salver	A	Donum Pupillorum/ 1724	Nicholas Sever and/or the Harvard College class of 1724	1724	Hale 1931, n.p.	
Salver	B	none	Nathaniel and Elizabeth (Dennis) Day	ca. 1728	Buhler 1965, 41–43	HMA
Salver (attrib.)	none	Ex Dono Pupillorum 1728	Nicholas Sever and/or the Harvard College class of 1728	1728	Hale 1931, n.p.	
Two sauceboats	D*	Simpson arms, on a chief vert 3 crescents, and crest, a bird rising; AS (+)	Ann (Simpson) Glover	ca. 1740	Bigelow 1917, 415–16	HD
Two pairs sleeve buttons (gold)	F†	HANNAH CARTER	Hannah (Gookin) Carter	ca. 1725	Buhler/Hood 1970, no. 107	YUAG
One pair sleeve buttons (gold)	G†	none		ca. 1730	Buhler/Hood 1970, no. 108	YUAG
Spout cup	B*	Shaw/FS (later)		ca. 1730	Warren 1975, no. 303	BBC
Strainer spoon	C†	MS		ca. 1735	Buhler 1972, no. 123	MFAB

	Mark	Inscription	Patron	Date	Reference	Owner
Strainer spoon	E*	IS		ca. 1735	DAPC 80.3956	
Sugar bowl	D	T/EL; EBH (later)	Rev. Ebenezer and Lucy (Davenport) Turell	ca. 1740	Buhler 1972, no. 124	MFAB
Sword	B*	Henry Allyn/1729	Henry Allyn	1729	YUAG files	
Tablespoon	A†	T/IH		ca. 1715	Quimby 1995, no. 25	WM
Tablespoon	B*	E. Watkins (later)		ca. 1735	DAPC 72.3323	WM
Tablespoon	B*	MB		ca. 1725		NM
Tablespoon	B†	CC		ca. 1720	Quimby 1995, no. 22	WM
Tablespoon (mate? below)	B	AL		ca. 1740		MFAB
Tablespoon (mate? above)	B	AL		ca. 1740	YUAG files	
Tablespoon	B	AB		ca. 1730	YUAG files	
Tablespoon	D*	IR		ca. 1735	Buhler/Hood 1970, no. 111	YUAG
Tablespoon	D*	MW		ca. 1745	Quimby 1995, no. 24	WM
Tablespoon	D*	EM		ca. 1725	Johnston 1994, 16	CMA
Tankard	A*	Martyn arms, 2 bars wavy gules, and crest, an estoile; The gift of Mrs. Sarah Martyn . . . (later)	Edward and Sarah (White) Martyn	ca. 1715	MFA 1911, no. 166	
Tankard	A*	P/DA		ca. 1725	Johnston 1994, 17	CMA
Tankard	A	HW		ca. 1725	Avery 1920, no. 20	MMA
Tankard	A	L/FH	Lamb family	ca. 1720	YUAG files	
Tankard	A	Belonging to the Church of Christ In Cambridge 1724	First Parish, Cambridge, Mass.	1724	Jones 1913, 107–08	
Tankard	A	The Gift of/M.ʳˢ Dorothy Frizell/To the Church of Christ/In Boston of which/the Reverend Mʳ/William Waldron/Is the Pastor 1724.	Dorothy Frizell and/or Second Church, Boston	1724	Jones 1913, 37	
Tankard	A	F/SA		ca. 1720	Buhler 1965, 38–41	HMA
Two tankards	B	For the use of the first Church/of Christ in Andover. 1728	North Parish of North Andover, North Andover, Mass.	1728	Jones 1913, 345	
Tankard	B	For the use of the first Church of/Christ in Andover. 1728	North Parish of North Andover, North Andover, Mass.	1728	Jones 1913, 345	

	Mark	Inscription	Patron	Date	Reference	Owner
Tankard	B	For the use of the first Church/of Christ in Andover 1729	North Parish of North Andover, North Andover, Mass.	1729	Jones 1913, 345–46	
Tankard	B*	W^m & Frances Mackay/1775 (later) (+)		ca. 1730	Buhler 1972, no. 121	MFAB
Tankard	B	The Gift of Benj^a Stevens Esqr/to the first Church of Christ in Andover 1728.	Benjamin Stevens and/ or North Parish of North Andover, North Andover, Mass.	1728	Jones 1913, 344–45	
Tankard (missing cover)	B*	DH		ca. 1740		RISD
Tankard	B	MR; The.Gift.of.Mary. RichardSon/ . . . (later)	Mary Richardson	ca. 1730	Jones 1913, 298	
Tankard	B*	J. Harrod 1729 (+)	John Harrod and/or New North Church, Boston	1729	Jones 1913, 66	AIC
Tankard	B	Cowell arms (later)		ca. 1740	*American Silver* 1967, no. 6	RWNAG
Tankard	B*	M/CE		ca. 1740	Parke-Bernet, 25–29 January 1972, lot 119	
Tankard	B (?)	unidentified arms; B/??		ca. 1740	Sotheby Parke Bernet, 29 January 1975, lot 83	
Tankard	B	?		1740	*Antiques* 100 (October 1971): 533	
Tankard	B	L/IM		ca. 1730	YUAG files	
Tankard	B *or* E	S/ET		ca. 1740	YUAG files	
Tankard	D*	Porter arms, 3 bells, and crest, a bird on a steeple	Porter family	ca. 1740	*Sack Collection* 4, 932	
Tankard	D	unidentified arms; S/DK		ca. 1740	Parke-Bernet, 14–15 October 1955, lot 289	
Tankard	D	WN/and/AB (later)		ca. 1730		MFAB
Tankard	D*	initials erased		ca. 1735		WA
Tankard	D*	Moulton arms, 3 bars gules between 8 escallops sable (3, 2, 2, 1), and crest on a pellet a falcon rising; M/IH	Sir William Pepperrell for Jeremiah and Hannah Moulton	1745	Buhler/Hood 1970, no. 114	YUAG
Tankard	D*	B/IE; unidentified arms (later)		ca. 1730	*Antiques* 110 (October 1976): 642	

	Mark	Inscription	Patron	Date	Reference	Owner
Tankard	D*	I/IS		ca. 1740	Flynt/Fales 1968, 96–97	HD
Tankard	D*	M/GI		ca. 1740	YUAG files	
Tankard	D	AN; Alice Norwood	Alice Norwood	ca. 1740	MFA 1911, no. 136	
Tankard	D	The Gift of Mr. Ebe-nezer/Osgood to the first Church of/ Christ in An-dover:1745	Ebenezer Osgood and/ or North Parish of North Andover, North Andover, Mass.	1745	Jones 1913, 347	
Tankard	D*	Frye arms, 3 horses courant; F/IS (+)	James Frye	ca. 1740	DAPC 81.3771	
Tankard	D	SW; P (later)		ca. 1740	YUAG files	
Tankard	D*	AT		ca. 1740	DAPC 65.4306	Rosen-bach Foun-dation
Tankard	D	SECOND/ PRESBYTERIAN CHURCH/ NEWBURYPORT (later)		ca. 1740	Ham-merslough/ Feigenbaum 1958–73, 2:2–3	
Tankard	D	The half of this Ves-sel was given to/the first Church of Christ in Beverly/by Capt I·Herrick and his two Sons/and the other half by Deacon I·Wood/and his two Sons/ H·H·I·H. 1747 I·W·I·W	Joseph, Henry, and Joshua Herrick and Is-rael, Sr., Israel, Jr., and Joseph Wood and/or First Parish Church, Beverly, Mass.	1747	Jones 1913, 14–15	
Tankard	D	G/PM/1724; G/JT/ 1828 (later) (+)	Peter and Mary Gilman	1724		MFAB
Tankard	D*	H/JS		ca. 1740	YUAG files	
Tankard	F	P/MB	Pickman family	ca. 1740	YUAG files	
Tankard	?	Flynt arms (+)	Henry Flynt and/or the Harvard College class of 1726	1726	*American Col-lector* 9 (August 1940): back cover	
Tankard	?	B/IH		ca. 1735	YUAG files	
Tankard	?	unidentified arms, a chevron azure be-tween 3 trees, and crest, a dexter arm couped grasping flowering sprigs		ca. 1735	*Antiques* 138 (September 1990): 473	
Tankard	?	?		ca. 1740	Norman-Wilcox 1962, no. 5	

	Mark	Inscription	Patron	Date	Reference	Owner
Tankard	?	unidentified arms; R		ca. 1725	Parke-Bernet, 17–20 May 1944, lot 663	
Tankard	?	JB (later)		ca. 1740	*Antiques* 103 (February 1973): 266	
Tankard	?	ED		ca. 1740	Parke-Bernet, 23–26 April 1947, lot 638	
Tankard	?	C/IA (+)	Crowninshield family	ca. 1740	Christie's, 12 December 1980, lot 432	
Tankard (attrib.)	none	A/SM (later) (+)	Abigail (Burt) Howland	ca. 1720	*Antiques* 102 (September 1972): 394	
Teapot	D	Tasker arms (later)		ca. 1745	Christie's, 2 June 1990, lot 79	
Teapot	D*	Dudley arms, or a lion rampant, and crest, a lion's head erased	Dudley family	ca. 1730	Buhler/Hood 1970, no. 112	YUAG
Teapot	D*	Giles arms, per chevron argent and azure a lion rampant counterchanged, and crest, a lion's gamb erect and erased holding a fruited branch; Mary Loring/the gift of her father/John Gyles, Esqr/1748	John Gyles and/or Mary (Gyles) Loring	1748	Puig et al. 1989, no. 194	MIA
Teapot (attrib.)	none	Ex dono Pupillorum 1728	Nicholas Sever and/or the Harvard College class of 1728	1728	Hale 1931, n.p.	
Teaspoon	B*	RW		ca. 1735		YUAG
Teaspoon	E*	ZT		ca. 1740	DAPC 80.3954	
Teaspoon	E†	RS/to/IC		ca. 1720	Quimby 1995, no. 23	WM
Thimble (attrib.)	none	I·BVRT·		ca. 1740	DAPC 68.6266	Historical Society of York County, Pennsylvania
Two-handled cup	A	The Gift of Mr J. Floyd to the/Chur^h of Christ in Rumney Mayrsh/1724	First Unitarian Society, Revere, Mass., for John Floyd	1724	Buhler 1972, no. 119	MFAB
Two-handled cup	B	The Gift of De:^{n} John Tuttle to the/Church of Christ in Rumneymarsh	First Unitarian Society, Revere, Mass., for John Tuttle	ca. 1725	Buhler 1972, no. 120	MFAB

	Mark	Inscription	Patron	Date	Reference	Owner
Two-handled cup	B	Belonging to the Church of/Christ in Medford 1725 (+)	Thomas Willis and/or First Parish, Medford, Mass.	1725	Jones 1913, 273	
Two two-handled cups	B*	The Gift of M.ʳ Jos. Kellogg to the/ Church of Christ in Hatfield 1724	First Congregational Church, Hatfield, Mass., for Joseph Kellogg	1724	Buhler/Hood 1970, no. 109	YUAG
Two two-handled cups	B	For the Use of the first/Church In Bradford 1730	Bradford Congregational Church, Haverhill, Mass.	1730	Jones 1913, 213	
Two-handled cup	B	The gift of Samel. Barrett to the New North Church of Christ in Boston May 4th, 1728	Samuel Barrett and/or New North Church, Boston	1728	Jones 1913, 66	MFAB
Two-handled cup	B	Ex dono SW to the Church of/Christ in Medford 1725; Gift of/Mrs. Sarah Ward (later)	First Parish, Medford, Mass., for Sarah Ward	1725	Jones 1913, 273	
Two-handled cup	B	The Gift of Mʳˢ Mary Wolcot/to the First Church In Salem 1728	Mary Wolcott and/or First Congregational Society, Salem, Mass.	1728	Jones 1913, 419–20	
Two two-handled cups	B	Ipswich Second Church 1728	Congregational Church, Essex, Mass.	1728	Jones 1913, 169	
Two two-handled cups	D	Ipswich Second Church/1732	Congregational Church, Essex, Mass.	1732	Jones 1913, 169	

1. RC 9:200; Burt Family Bible, HD.
2. RC 9:168, 178, 189.
3. Bridgman 1856, 337, annotated copy, YUAG; Bigelow-Phillips files, 729.
4. RC 28:19; Whitmore 1878, 56, no. 1046.
5. RC 9:69, 195; RC 28:49; *Ipswich VR* 1:85; SCPR 43:314–18; 77:226–28, 496–97; *Sibley's Harvard Graduates* 2:501–06.
6. Bigelow-Phillips files, 731.
7. SCCR, file 12784.
8. Hale 1931, n.p.; SCPR 26:49.
9. SCCR, Court of Common Pleas Record Book 1718, 46, 138; 1727–28, 121, 223; 1735–36, 401–02.
10. Seybolt 1939, 150, 158, 168.
11. SCPR 21:420.
12. SCD 35:163–64.
13. YCD 27:268–69.
14. *York Deeds* 14:196–97; 18:223–24; YCD 20:158–59; 27:268–69.
15. *York Deeds* 18:616–17.
16. *York Deeds* 18:617–22; YCD 19:232; 21:49–52; 23:214–15. The management of this property involved one court case to eject an illegal resident. See YCCR, Court of Common Pleas, box 84, file 40.
17. Tudor 1896, 1; SCD 46:161.
18. *York Deeds* 14:196–97.
19. John Burt bill to William Smith estate, 6 June 1730, with receipt acknowledged by Samuel Gray, 2 July 1730, Smith-Townsend II Papers, MHS.
20. SCCR, Court of General Sessions Record Book 1725–32, 281.
21. YCD 20:158–59.
22. *York Deeds* 18:223–24.
23. YCD 19:232.

24. YCD 19:172; 23:214–15.
25. Buhler 1956, 40–41.
26. SCD 46:161.
27. SCD 50:36–38.
28. SCPR, docket 6861.
29. SCPR 35:457.
30. SCPR 39:160–61.
31. Joshua Winslow Account Book and Case Book, n.p., NEHGS.
32. SCCR, file 37652.
33. Henry Flynt Memorandum Book, n.p., HU.
34. Burt Family Bible, HD.
35. SCPR 38:375–76.
36. SCPR 39:160–61.
37. Mass. Archives 18:412.
38. SCPR 77:226–28, 496–97.
39. SCPR 78:247, 578, 641; 79:232–33.
40. Spurious mark (A) is on a porringer in a private collection (YUAG files). Spurious mark (D) is on a serving spoon (383480), bell (383481), and strainer (383479) at SI, two casters at BBC (Warren 1975, no. 305), a bell, candle snuffer and tray, and cann at CMA (Johnston 1994, 18–20), a beaker (1932.82) at YUAG, and a teapot (DAPC 85.2145). Spurious mark (E) is on a teaspoon at CMA (Johnston 1994, 20).

Samuel Burt
1724–54

A

B

Samuel Burt, the son of John Burt (q.v.) and Abigail (Cheever) Burt (1691–1778), was born in Boston on 4 September 1724. He would have begun his apprenticeship about 1738, perhaps with his father, and completed it about 1745.[1] He probably took over the shop following his father's death in 1745/46. The administration of his father's estate was granted to Samuel and his mother on 11 February 1745/46.[2] Samuel's brothers William and Benjamin (qq.v.) likely completed their training with him. Burt may also have trained Caleb Parker (q.v.) between 1745 and 1752 because Parker witnessed a deed for Burt in 1753 shortly after his apprenticeship would have ended.[3]

Burt was married on 7 January 1747 to Elizabeth White (1728–ca. 1748), the daughter of Samuel White (d. 1733), a merchant, and Elizabeth Greenwood (b. 1698) of Boston. Rev. William Welsteed of the New Brick Church married them.[4] In March 1748 Burt was identified as a goldsmith when he and his wife purchased part of a brick house on Ship Street in the north end of Boston from his wife's mother and her second husband, Benjamin Edwards, Sr., father of Benjamin Edwards, Jr. (q.v.), paying £350 for it.[5] The deed for this transaction was witnessed by Joseph Hiller, Sr., and Luke Greenough Pierce (qq.v.), who may have worked in association with Burt.

Burt was married for a second time on 7 December 1749, on this occasion by Rev. John Lowell, to Elizabeth Kent (1726–1804), the daughter of Lt. Col. Richard Kent (1672–1740) and Hannah (Gookin) Carter (d. 1758) of Newbury, Massachusetts.[6] Hannah Kent's will was witnessed in 1754 by the goldsmiths William and Joseph Moulton (1724–95) (qq.v.).[7] On 12 February 1750 Burt and his wife sold the house on Ship Street to Francis White, a brother of Burt's first wife.[8] In 1753, he and his second wife sold property in Newbury that she had inherited.[9] During this period Burt was excused twice from serving in the town office of constable, in 1752 and 1754.[10] His will, dated 19 September 1754, gave all his estate to his wife, who was appointed to administer it on 4 October 1754.[11] Burt is buried in the Copp's Hill Burying Ground.[12]

More than three dozen pieces of holloware and flatware by Burt have been recorded. Burt used an initial and surname mark (A) and a full-name mark (B).[13] PEK

SURVIVING OBJECTS

	Mark	Inscription	Patron	Date	Reference	Owner
Cann	B	W/DR/1733 (+)	David and Ruth (Hopkins) Wood	ca. 1750	Buhler 1972, no. 242	MFAB
Cann	B*	Ward arms, azure a cross flory, and crest, a wolf's head erased, impaling Burrill arms, or a saltire gules, on a chief azure a crescent between 2 stars of 6 points or (+)	Joshua and Lydia (Burrill) (Hawkes) Ward	ca. 1750	Antiques 41 (January 1942): back cover	PEM
Cann	B*	? A (+)		ca. 1750	YUAG files	
Cann	B*	unidentified crest, a sinister wing; HW (later)		ca. 1750	Antiques 110 (September 1976): 412	
Cann	B*	unidentified initials		ca. 1750	National Art Galleries, 3–5 December 1931, lot 436	
Cann	B	HB; ALP (later)		ca. 1750	YUAG files	
Caster	A*	LA		ca. 1750	Buhler 1972, no. 240	MFAB
Caster	B*	IE/Larrabee; MTRF (later)		ca. 1750		HD
Caster	B*	?		ca. 1750	Antiques 131 (January 1987): 139	
Chafing dish	B	none		ca. 1745	Buhler 1972, no. 237	MFAB
Creampot	B*	C/NM/1742	Nathaniel and Mary (Beck) Carter	1742	Puig et al. 1989, no. 203	MIA
Creampot	B	L/EE; SL (later)	Enoch and Elizabeth Little	ca. 1750	Hammerslough/ Feigenbaum 1958–73, 2:54	
Creampot	B	R/IR	Isaac and Ruth Reddington	ca. 1750	Ormsbee 1940, 14	
Flagon	B*	Hooper arms, on a fess vert between 3 boars passant 3 annulets or, and crest, a boar's head erased; Robertus Huperus Arm: hanc Crateram, ad Usum Sacrosanctae in Ecclesia Christi prima, apud Marblehead, dedicavit, Jan. 1, 1748/9	Robert Hooper and/or First Congregational Church, Marblehead, Mass.	1749	Jones 1913, 261–62	

	Mark	Inscription	Patron	Date	Reference	Owner
Flagon	B*	Barnard arms, argent a bear rampant [sable] muzzled [or], and crest, a demi-bear couped [sable] and muzzled [or]; FOEDERE NON VI; Johannis Barnardus, Pastor Secundus primae Ecclesiae Christi apud Marblehead, hanc Crateram, ad Usum, Sacrosanctae Coenae, in Ecclesia dicta, dedicavit. Jan:1, 1748/9	Rev. John Barnard and/or First Congregational Church, Marblehead, Mass.	1749	Jones 1913, 262	
Porringer	B*	C/ZE		ca. 1750		PEM
Porringer	B	?		ca. 1750	*Antiques* 96 (August 1969): 141	
Porringer	B*	MA		ca. 1750		CM
Porringer	B*	CP		ca. 1750	Johnston 1994, 21	CMA
Porringer	B	PR		ca. 1750	MFA 1906, no. 50	
Porringer	B	none		ca. 1750	YUAG files	
Salt	B	LA	Lucy Allen	ca. 1750		DAR Museum
Two salts	B	W/DR	David and Ruth (Hopkins) Wood	ca. 1750	Buhler 1972, no. 241	MFAB
Sauceboat (mate below)	B	M/NC	Nathaniel and Mary (Beck) Carter	ca. 1750	Buhler 1972, no. 239	MFAB
Sauceboat (mate above)	B	C/NM	Nathaniel and Mary (Beck) Carter	ca. 1750	Buhler 1972, no. 238	MFAB
Sauceboat	B	none		ca. 1750	*Antiques* 139 (May 1991): 916	
Strainer	A	?		ca. 1750	YUAG files	
Strainer	A†	none		ca. 1750		HD
Strainer	B*	none		ca. 1750	Parke-Bernet, 25 March 1969, lot 80	
Strainer	B	none		ca. 1750	DAPC 77.2239	
Tablespoon (mate below)	B*	C/WM		ca. 1750	DAPC 72.3334	WM
Tablespoon (mate above)	B*	C/WM		ca. 1750	Johnston 1994, 21	CMA
Tablespoon	B*	SM/to/MH		ca. 1750	DAPC 72.3331	WM
Tablespoon	B*	IHM/RA		ca. 1750		SI
Tablespoon	?	unidentified initials		ca. 1750	Skinner, 11 January 1992, lot 55A	

	Mark	Inscription	Patron	Date	Reference	Owner
Tankard	B	S/FS; B (later) (+)		ca. 1745	*American Silver* 1967, no. 8	RWNAG
Tankard	B*	L/NE; The Gift of Samuel Cookson Esq[r]/to the Second Church of Christ/in Roxbury/1806 (later)		ca. 1750	Jones 1913, 490–91	
Tankard	B	none		ca. 1750	DAPC 79.4063	
Teapot	B†	unidentified arms		ca. 1750		MFAB
Teapot	B	EF (+)		ca. 1750		MFAB
Teaspoon	A*	C/IM		ca. 1750	DAPC 74.1209	WM
Teaspoon	?	?	?	?		BM

1. RC 24:163.
2. SCPR 38:375–76.
3. ECD 98:101.
4. RC 9:240; RC 24:190; RC 28:158, 236; SCPR 31:290.
5. SCD 75:117. Benjamin Edwards, Sr., and Elizabeth White married in 1740, RC 28:214.
6. RC 28:293; *Newbury VR* 1:258, 260; 2:270–71, 632–33.
7. ECPR 335:241.
8. SCD 79:124.
9. ECD 98:101.
10. RC 14:211, 245.
11. SCPR 49:592–93.
12. Whitmore 1878, 28, no. 533.
13. Kovel 1961, 50, also shows SB in an oval, but an example of this mark has not been found.

William Burt
1726–52

A

William Burt was born in Boston on 6 September 1726, the fourth son of John (q.v.) and Abigail (Cheever) Burt (1691–1778).[1] Burt's twin sister, Sarah (1726–99), married Francis Shaw (1721–84).[2] Two of his brothers, Samuel and Benjamin (qq.v.), were also silversmiths. William Burt married Mary Glidden (1728–1804) on 27 April 1749 in a ceremony performed by Rev. Andrew Eliot of the New North Church.[3] The bride was the daughter of the shipwright Joseph (1697–1772) and Mary (Hood) Glidden (1704/05–46).[4] Burt and his wife sold the portion of the Glidden property on Middle Street that they had inherited to Ephraim Bosworth, a yeoman of Hull, Massachusetts, on 3 September 1750 for eighty-five pounds Old Tenor.[5]

William died intestate in February 1752 at the age of twenty-six. He was buried in the Copp's Hill Burying Ground on the nineteenth of that month.[6] Rev. Andrew Eliot noted in his annotated copy of *Poor Job's Almanack* for 1752 that he received two gloves at Burt's funeral.[7]

Very little silver by William Burt has survived because his career was so brief, and only one mark can be attributed to him: (A) W.BURT with conjoined serifs in a rectangle.[8] The pieces bearing this mark suggest that Burt was a craftsman of superior technical and design skills. Spurious examples of Burt's mark are known.[9]

Burt's young widow probably remarried. Boston church records indicate that women named Mary Burt married Charles Giles in October 1752 and Richard Brackett of Braintree, Massachusetts, in February 1755.[10] However, it is possible that the "Mrs. Mary Burt" who died in Newburyport, Massachusetts, on 28 April 1804 was the silversmith's widow. She may have been living with the widow of Samuel Burt, Elizabeth Burt, who died in Newburyport on the same date.[11] DAF

SURVIVING OBJECTS

	Mark	Inscription	Patron	Date	Reference	Owner
Cann	A*	FW; Bishop arms (later) (+)		ca. 1750	YUAG files	
Caster	A	DA		ca. 1750	American Art Association–Anderson Galleries, 8 February 1936, lot 36	
Flagon	A†	Cunningham arms, [argent] a pall azure, and crest, a unicorn's head; YOURE YOURE; The Gift of/Nathaniel CUNNINGHAM Esq.!/to the South Church in/Boston Sep.! 18ᵗʰ/ 1748	Old South Church, Boston, for Nathaniel Cunningham	1748	Jones 1913, 55	
Ladle	A*	MW		ca. 1750	Hammerslough/ Feigenbaum 1958–73, 3:110–11	WA
Porringer	A*	MM		ca. 1750	Quimby 1995, no. 26	WM
Strainer	A*	T/IT		ca. 1750	Sotheby's, 30 January–2 February 1991, lot 135	
Strainer	?	?		ca. 1750	Ormsbee 1940, 14	
Tablespoon	A*	T/SM		ca. 1750	YUAG files	
Teaspoon	A	IN		ca. 1750	YUAG files	

1. RC 24:174.
2. RC 28:263; Whitmore 1878, 28, no. 532. Francis and Sarah (Burt) Shaw were married by Rev. Andrew Eliot on 22 September 1747.
3. RC 28:239.
4. RC 9:232; RC 24:32, 187; RC 28:113; Whitmore 1878, 8, no. 157; *Index of Obituaries, 1704–1800*, 2:430; SCPR 73:685–86. Benjamin Burt was the administrator of Joseph Glidden's estate.
5. SCD 95:31.
6. Whitmore 1878, 28, no. 533.
7. *Poor Job's Almanack* (1752), annotated by Rev. Andrew Eliot, MHS.
8. Two additional marks, W BURT in a rectangle and oval, have been recorded in the literature, but examples have not been found for illustration; see Kovel 1961, 50; Okie 1936, 247.
9. The spurious examples of mark (A) are on a strainer (383484) and tankard (383483) at SI and on a caster (YUAG files).
10. RC 30:324, 368.
11. *Newburyport VR*, 2:572.

James Butler
1713–76

A

James Butler was born in Boston on 4 December 1713 to James Butler (1688–1715), a ropemaker, and Abigail Eustis (1690–1713), who were married by Rev. Ebenezer Pemberton of the Old South Church on 6 April 1710.[1] The goldsmith's paternal grandparents were James Butler (1665–89), a vintner, and Grace Newcomb (1664–1713).[2] Grace married her second husband, the mariner Andrew Rankin, in 1692.[3] The goldsmith's maternal grandparents were John Eustis (1659–1722), a housewright, and his first wife, Elizabeth Morse (1660–1714).[4] The goldsmith's father married his second wife, Mary Bowditch (b. 1689) of Salem, Massachusetts, on 17 August 1715.[5] When James, Sr., died in 1715, his fathers-in-law, William Bowditch and John Eustis, were appointed to administer his estate. In 1727, when William Bowditch died, Suffolk Probate Court appointed the distiller Thomas Jackson, the shipwright William Lee, and the tallow chandler Daniel Parker as guardians for "James Butler a minor about 14, son of the late James Butler, ropemaker, of Boston."[6] It is not known with whom James the goldsmith trained, but he probably began his training about this time. In a quitclaim of February 1734/35 releasing Thomas Jackson from guardianship, James Butler is identified as a goldsmith of Boston and probably by that time had begun to practice his trade.[7]

In 1735 James Butler was again identified as a goldsmith when he purchased the shares of his elder sisters Abigail and Elizabeth in real estate on Middle Street, Boston.[8] The next year in the Suffolk Court of Common Pleas he sued Joseph Wiley, John Clark, and James Boyd, all yeomen of Worcester County, for £150. The jury found for the plaintiff, who was to recover the sum of £79.13.9, but the defendants appealed to the Superior Court of Judicature.[9] James Butler was again plaintiff on 2 January 1738/39, when he sued Edward Ellis, physician, for £23.9.9, rendered in the following account:

1736	Doct.ʳ Edwᵈ Ellis Dʳ to James Butler	
May 10th	To mending a pare of Silver buckels	£0 .3
Jun 12th	To making a Staple for a bosam bottle	.4
	To Cash	1 .6 .3
1737		
Sepʳ 12th	To 11 funerall Rings	21 .12 .4
1738		
Apʳ 18th	To A Silver Thimble	4 .2
		£23 ..9..9

Errors Excepted

pʳ James: Butler
Boston Decbʳ 18: 1738.[10]

The case continued in the Superior Court of Judicature and finally was settled in Butler's favor on 29 May 1740.[11] Butler was also paid 9 shillings in 1737 by the estate of Isaac Perkins (q.v.).[12]

When James Butler joined the Ancient and Honorable Artillery Company in 1739, Bartholomew Gedney and Thomas Simpkins were surety for him.[13] That same year Butler married Elizabeth Davie, who was born in Boston on 6 March 1715/16, the daughter of Humphrey Davie (1673–1718), a brazier, and Margaret Gedney (b. 1694).[14] Elizabeth died on 15 February 1739/40.[15] The following year James Butler mortgaged a third part of a dwelling house on Back Street inherited from his maternal grandfather, John Eustis.[16] In 1742/43 Butler was elected constable, but declined to serve and paid the fine.[17] His second marriage, to Sarah Wakefield (1722–82), took place on 29 November 1744.[18] She was the daughter of John Wakefield (b. 1682) and his wife, Sarah Russell (b. 1695).[19] Butler and his new wife probably lived in a house owned by the silversmith William Homes, Sr. (q.v.), and described in a mortgage of 1746 as containing a "cellar Shop Low Room Chamber & Garrett."[20] Because the goldsmiths William Simpkins and John Doane (qq.v.) were witnesses to real estate transactions of Butler's in 1745 and 1747, Butler may have been associated with them in business.[21] Butler also witnessed a deed for Simpkins in 1744, along with Edmund Mountfort (q.v.).[22] The close ties that Simpkins, Doane, and Mountfort had to John Burt (q.v.) suggest that Butler may have had ties to him as well. Eunice Cravath, the guardian of Butler's sister Elizabeth's children, who was living in Middletown, Connecticut, granted him power of attorney in 1747.[23]

In 1748 Butler was appointed captain of the militia.[24] By 1750, however, he seems to have made the decision to try his fortune in Nova Scotia.[25] That year he and his wife appointed Thomas Jackson, Jr., of Boston as their attorney. Shortly thereafter, in a deed of 31 July 1751 recording the sale of the Middle Street property, they are described as being of Halifax in the Province of Nova Scotia.[26] An account of 1750 and 1751 rendered by Thomas Edwards (q.v.) to Jackson mentions "M.r James Butler Note & Ballance of Acc.t" which suggests that Butler may have been trading with him at this time.[27] Butler may have trained Jackson's son, also Thomas Jackson, Jr. (q.v.), when he was in Canada. According to a genealogy of the Butler family, Butler's enterprise in Halifax proved to be unsuccessful, and he ultimately returned to Boston.[28] Nehemia Somes's sloop *Betsey* arrived at Boston from Halifax on 31 March 1767 with James Butler of Boston listed among the passengers.[29] Butler afterward lived awhile in Sutton, Massachusetts.[30] He appears in the Massachusetts tax list of 1771 as residing in Boston with two polls, real estate worth twenty pounds annually (including a house, shop, and another building lumped under the category of tanner house), and thirty-six pounds' worth of merchandise.[31] He died in Boston in 1776 at the age of sixty-three and was interred at the Granary Burying Ground.[32] Sarah died on 17 October 1782.[33]

Few pieces of silver bear Butler's initial and surname mark (A). Initials marks have been attributed to this silversmith, but there is not sufficient evidence to support such attributions.[34] PEK

SURVIVING OBJECTS

	Mark	Inscription	Patron	Date	Reference	Owner
Beaker	A (?)	IB/A/Gift to y.e first/Church/in Say-brook (+)	First Congregational Church, Saybrook, Conn., for Joseph Blague	ca. 1742	Jones 1913, 443	
Tablespoon	A	Anna Way 1756	Anna Way	ca. 1750	MFA 1911, no. 179	
Tablespoon	A†	C/SE; 1660 (later)		ca. 1750	Puig et al. 1989, no. 206	MIA
Tablespoon	A	T/IL		ca. 1735	DAPC 71.1807	WM
Tablespoon	A*	HB (+)		ca. 1735		YUAG
Tablespoon	A*	IP		ca. 1750	YUAG files	

	Mark	Inscription	Patron	Date	Reference	Owner
Tankard	A*	IW		ca. 1750	Skinner, 27 March 1993, lot 188	

1. RC 9:178, 189; SCPR 18:511–12; RC 24:89; RC 28:26.
2. Savage 1860–62, 3:270; RC 9:93, 95.
3. Thwing; SCPR 18:153–54; SCPR docket 1692.
4. *NEHGR* 32:205; Thwing; RC 9:69, 74; Bridgman 1853, 171; Roberts 1895, 1:374; SCPR, docket 4570.
5. RC 28:94; *Salem VR* 1:104.
6. SCPR 18:511–12.
7. SCPR 30:492–93, docket 5573.
8. SCD 51:26–27. Butler finalized the purchase from his sister Abigail in 1746; see SCD 74:74.
9. SCCR, Court of Common Pleas Record Book 1737, 39–40.
10. SCCR, Court of Common Pleas Record Book 1738, 88.
11. SCCR, Superior Court of Judicature, files 51134 (vol. 331, 88) and 51660 (vol. 334, 81), Judicial Archives, Mass. Archives.
12. MCPR 24:184.
13. Roberts 1895, 2:8.
14. RC 9:127; Thwing; SCD 25:168; SCPR, docket 4119; RC 24:113; RC 28:93, 210; *Salem VR* 1:352.
15. Boston Deaths, 1700–1800.
16. SCD 61:196–97.
17. Seybolt 1939, 229.
18. RC 24:158; RC 28:236.
19. RC 9:159, 223; RC 28:48.
20. SCD 72:137–39.
21. SCD 71:146–47; 73:161–62.
22. SCD 68:137–38.
23. SCD 74:73–74.
24. Roberts 1895, 2:8.
25. Langdon 1966, 54.
26. SCD 80:36–37.
27. For a transcription of the account from the Brigden Papers, see the Thomas Edwards entry.
28. Bridgman 1856, 268.
29. RC 29:291.
30. *NEHGR* 1:169.
31. Pruitt 1978, 4–5.
32. Codman 1918, 52; Bridgman 1856, 268.
33. *Index of Obituaries, 1704–1800*, 1:50.
34. Fales 1958, no. 65; Buhler/Hood 1970, no. 183.

John Butler
1734–1827

A

John Butler was born in Newbury, Massachusetts, on 9 May 1734 to Phillip Butler and Mary Tucker (1709–73). His paternal grandparents were the shipwright Matthew Butler and Susanna (Gallup) Butler.[1] Butler probably served his apprenticeship in Newbury between 1748 and 1755. His intention to marry Mary "Morgaridge" (1738–before 1763), daughter of John and Elizabeth (Osgood) "Morgridge" of Salisbury, Massachusetts, was published on 20 August 1757.[2] "Molly Mugridg" and Butler were married the following October in Salisbury.[3] Their two children were born in Newbury: John on 23 October 1758 and Philip on 30 December 1760.[4]

Shortly after his marriage, Butler was working in Boston; given that his paternal grandparents lived on Fish Street in Boston, Butler may have been living with his relatives while contemplating a career relocation.[5] The *Boston News-Letter* of 16 and 30 November 1758 reported that

WHEREAS the Shop of John Butler, *Goldsmith at the Corner of* Clark's *Ship-Yard, was broke open on the 6th of this Instant* November, *at Night and stolen from thence 7 Stone Rings, 6 of them with Cyphers: 2 grape Gold Rings, 2 Heart and Hand Rings, 7 plain Gold Rings, 6 or 7 Pair of Stone Buttons, 1 Pair of Stone Ear-Rings set in Gold, 3 ditto in silver, 1 ditto with Cyphers, 2 Pair of large plain wide-rimm'd Silver Buckles with Silver Flukes and Tongues, a cross'd Pair with ditto, 6 Pair of open-work'd Buckles, 1 Pair of Neck-Clasps, and several other Articles.*

By 1761, Butler had relocated to Falmouth, Maine, where he formed a partnership with another Newbury native, Paul Little (q.v.), that was to last four years.[6] Butler may have trained Little, because they became partners in 1761, the year Little would have completed his apprenticeship. The date of Mary Butler's death is unknown, but Butler married his second wife, Ann Codman (1732–83), daughter of the saddler and sea captain John Codman (1696–1755) and Parnel Foster (1696–1752) of Charlestown, Massachusetts, on 8 July 1763 in Falmouth.[7] On 15 July of that year "John Butler of Falmouth, County of Cumberland, Goldsmith and Ann his wife" and two of Susanna Butler's other grandchildren sold their interest in their grandmother's buildings and wharf on Fish Street, Boston, to the merchant Nathaniel Loring for £51.11.3.[8] Three years later, Butler and several of his cousins purchased a brick house on Brattle Street in Boston from Benjamin Dolbeare for £500.[9]

In July 1767 Butler purchased his first property in Falmouth, a three-quarter share of two parcels of land, one on King Street and the other along the river, for £50 from William and Edward Tyng of Boston.[10] John Tyng of Dunstable, who owned the remaining share, agreed that Butler would occupy the portion of the plot fronting on King Street, while he would retain the back half of the plot.[11] These deeds identify Butler as a Falmouth goldsmith. In April 1772, "John Butler, Goldsmith," paid £35.6.8 to Jabez Bradbury for additional land on King Street.[12] Butler's appointment as power of attorney from 1772 until 1775 for Mrs. Tufton, widow of Capt. Thomas Tufton, indicates the respected position he had achieved in the community.[13] Butler suffered considerable property damage when the British fleet burned Falmouth in October 1775. The silversmith was assessed £1,523 in damages, one of the largest amounts recorded.[14]

Butler probably moved to Gorham, Maine, in 1778, when he purchased fifty acres of land there for £240 from Thomas and Elizabeth Russell of Boston in a deed that identified him as "John Butler Yeoman."[15] Butler's second wife, Ann, died in 1783.[16] Butler had remarried by 1788, when a deed for the sale of his property in Falmouth identifies his wife as Jane. Falmouth included Portland until 1786, when Portland was established as a separate town. Described as a merchant living in Gorham, Butler sold part of his land on King Street and Clay Cove to John Tyng, Esq., of Dunstable for "49½ Spanis[h] Milled Dollars."[17] He sold the remainder of this property to the Portland cordwainer Moses Plummer, Jr., for £165 on 26 March 1795.[18]

Butler lived in Gorham until November 1793, when "John Butler, Gentleman" and his wife, Jane, sold 47 acres of their property to the Portland merchant Josiah Cox for £230.[19] Three weeks later Butler bought a house and shop at Stroudwater in Falmouth, Maine, from Cox at a cost of £110.[20] The silversmith lived in Stroudwater for seven years, selling the house and shop to Joseph

Holt Ingraham, a Portland merchant, for $500 on 1 July 1800.[21] Butler's third wife, Jane, is not mentioned in any deed after 1800, so she may have been deceased by this time. The silversmith relocated to North Yarmouth, Maine, on 20 January 1801, when he paid $525 to the Portland housewright Nathaniel Gordon for a house and 43½ acres in North Yarmouth; he arranged a mortgage of $191.67 with Gordon to purchase the property.[22] He was still living in North Yarmouth in 1813.[23]

In addition to buying and selling real estate relating to his changes of residence, Butler appears to have speculated in land. He purchased two plots in Pearson Town in January 1769, selling one in February 1769 to Stephen Longfellow, an early patron of his, and the other to Jonathan Philbrook in June 1780.[24] In November 1770 Butler bought land in Falmouth from James Swain and sold it to George Tate, a Falmouth merchant.[25] Butler sold land in Standish, Maine, sporadically to Israel Thorn, Samuel Thombes, and Lathrop Lewis from 1790 until 1813.[26]

Butler's interest in pursuing a mercantile career is evident as early as 1770, when he is described as a merchant in the deeds relating to the purchase and resale of land in Falmouth.[27] In his *History of Portland*, William Willis described Butler as "originally a jeweller, but afterwards engaged in trade," recording the silversmith as operating a store on King [India] Street from the time of the Revolution until at least 1785.[28] He is called a merchant again in deeds dated June 1784 and September 1788.[29] By 1785, Butler had begun to dismantle his silver shop. He advertised in the Boston *Independent Chronicle* on 10 March 1785, "To be sold at Falmouth, Casco-Bay, A House-Lot . . . LIKEWISE a compleat sett of Goldsmith's Tools, suitable for large work." However, Butler was consistently described as a goldsmith on official documents until 1801.

Cumberland County deeds also refer to his status as a landowner. In deeds for 1778 and 1813, Butler was described as being a yeoman, probably in reference to his ownership of fairly large tracts of land.[30] In 1793 and 1800, he was referred to as a gentleman.[31] The census for 1790 records a John Butler living in Waterborough Town in York County and describes him as the head of a household composed of two adult males and one woman.[32] In 1800, he and his wife, Jane, were living alone in York County.[33] Butler does not appear in the census lists for 1810 or 1820.

The silversmith may have suffered from mental illness toward the end of his life. The Reverend Thomas Smith observed in his journal, "John Butler, . . . a Silversmith by trade, and a very respectable merchant before the Revolution, but better known in modern times as Crazy Butler."[34] The Portland historian Willis ascribed his illness to "his misfortunes by losses of property and children, [which] unthroned reason from her seat" and recorded that Butler died in Westbrook, Maine, in December 1827, having been supported by the town for several years.[35]

Butler's earliest documented objects were commissioned by another Newbury native, the Falmouth schoolmaster Stephen Longfellow. Longfellow received a bequest from his father's will in 1764 and used his legacy to order some silver, including a tankard and a porringer.[36] The tankard's domed top, midrib, and cast corkscrew finial are stylistically very similar to Boston forms. The porringer has a pierced keyhole handle engraved "S * L / Ex Dono / Patris." The mark on these objects is J.BUTLER in a rectangle (A).[37] The mark J. BUTLER in a shaped cartouche has also been recorded.[38] DAF

SURVIVING OBJECTS

	Mark	Inscription	Patron	Date	Reference	Owner
Porringer	A†	SL/Ex Dono/Patris	Stephen Longfellow	ca. 1765	*YUAG Bulletin* 1991, 89, 107 (as James Butler)	YUAG
Porringer	A*	S/TL		ca. 1765	MFA 1911, no. 178	
Tablespoon	A*	M/IS		ca. 1765	DAPC 75.4937 (as James Butler)	
Tankard	A	SL/Ex Dono/Patris	Stephen Longfellow	ca. 1765	Fales 1985, 339	MEHS

1. SCD 28:21; 100:102; 152:12; *Newbury VR* 1:77; 2:76; *Newburyport VR* 2:572; Flynt/Fales 1968, 175.
2. *Newbury VR* 2:75; *Salisbury VR*, 178, 424.
3. *Salisbury VR*, 437.
4. *Newbury VR* 1:77, 78.
5. SCD 100:102.
6. Fales 1985, 338.
7. Wyman 1879, 1:161, 224; *NEHGR* 32:287; Whitmore 1878, 29, no. 545; *Charlestown VR* 1:170–71, 337. Parnel Foster was the daughter of Capt. Richard Foster (1663–1745) and his wife, Parnel Winslow (d. 1751), both of Charlestown.
8. SCD 100:102.
9. SCD 117:134–35. In November 1773, June 1784, and October 1785, Butler was involved in several more Boston real estate transactions, primarily concerned with the sale of property inherited from his paternal grandparents. These deeds list him as a goldsmith residing in Falmouth or Gorham. SCD 125:40–41; 152:12–15; 185:76–77.
10. CCD 6:56–58, 58–59.
11. CCD 6:68–70.
12. CCD 5:451.
13. CCD 36:167–68.
14. Willis 1865, 900–01. The total amount of damages recorded for the town was £54,527.13. Butler's house and store near the foot of King Street was one of only two or three structures in Falmouth constructed with brick ends, an expensive treatment that would explain the high assessment value. Willis lists the location of Butler's house as India Street; another house with brick ends was owned by John Greenwoods in Middle Street; Willis 1865, 467. A comparison of Portland maps drawn in 1831 and 1852 shows that King Street was renamed India Street, probably as a prosperous trade with the West Indies developed in the mid-nineteenth century. The maps are reproduced in *Portland* (Portland, Me.: Greater Portland Landmarks, Incorporated, 1972), 40, 50.
15. CCD 11:124.
16. Whitmore 1878, 29, no. 545.
17. CCD 16:265.
18. CCD 22:312–13.
19. CCD 20:470–71.
20. CCD 20:497–98.
21. CCD 33:167–68.
22. CCD 35:60–61, 61–62.
23. CCD 96:304.
24. CCD 6:321–23, 403–04; 10:485–86.
25. CCD 11:137, 145.
26. CCD 18:119–20; 27:79; 33:136–37; 96:304.
27. CCD 11:137, 145.
28. Willis 1831–33, 2:179, 291.
29. SCD 185:76–77; CCD 16:265.
30. CCD 11:124; 96:304.
31. CCD 20:470–71, 497–98; 33:167–68.

32. Dept. of Commerce 1908, 69.

33. Maine census, 1800, York County, 956.

34. Smith 1849, 191, 207; Flynt/Fales 1968, 175.

35. Willis 1831–33, 2:291.

36. Fales 1985, 339.

37. Kovel 1961, 51, also records ıв in an oval for Butler, but the attribution of such a mark remains to be confirmed.

38. Gebelein Silversmiths own a lead impression of this mark from a tablespoon monogrammed "м/dн" (yuag files).

Henry Buxton
1740–1827

Henry Buxton, the "Buckle Maker," was the subject of a lengthy article by Bessie Raymond Buxton, a descendant, published in 1955. The author analyzed two surviving daybooks by Buxton, detailing his career from 1761 to 1773 and 1784 to 1800 as a maker of buckles and other small pieces of jewelry.[1]

Henry, the son of John (b. 1695), a tanner, and Elizabeth (Buffum) Buxton, was born in Danvers, Massachusetts, in 1740. His grandparents were Joseph (b. 1678) and Esther Buxton and Joshua and Elizabeth (Beck) Buffum. Henry married Elinor Osborn (1746–1817) on 17 October 1765, in a Quaker ceremony for which the certificate survived. They lived in a house at the corner of Central and Warren streets in Danvers, and Buxton's shop stood on the north side of the house, near the back door, until it was torn down in 1911. The Massachusetts tax list of 1771 assessed Buxton for one-half of a house, an adjacent outbuilding, and a considerable amount of livestock and grain, suggesting that Buxton supported himself, at least in part, by farming.[2]

Buxton seems to have worked primarily in brass, but he also made and sold silver shoe and knee buckles. John Touzell, Nathaniel Lang, and John Hathorne (qq.v.) were among his customers, who came from Salem, Ipswich, and elsewhere as well as from Danvers. As a specialist, Buxton filled a niche in the local craft organization. Entries for large, "middlen," and small buckles, sleeve buttons, boot hasps, harness furniture, brass fittings for clocks and furniture, and brass fireplace equipment appear in his account books, along with the customary entries for mending and repair work. After the Revolution, he seems to have fallen on hard times and to have produced harness work and engaged in a variety of tasks.

No objects by Buxton are now known, although in 1955, Bessie Raymond Buxton stated that she owned "a few of the things which he made, [including] shoe and knee buckles, sleeve buttons, brass buttons for men's clothing and candlesticks."[3] GWRW

1. Buxton 1955, 80–91. The account books are in the J. D. Phillips Library, pem (F.Ms.B9912).

2. *Danvers VR* 1:58; 2:48, 345; *Salem VR* 1:135, 148; 2:127; 3:161, 177; 5:124; *Index of Obituaries, 1784–1840*, 1:750; Buxton 1955, 80; Pruitt 1978, 46–47.

3. Buxton 1955, 80–82.

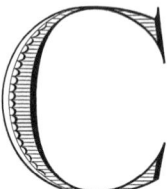

C

William Caddow
1691–ca. 1745

According to the records of the Goldsmiths' Company of Dublin, Ireland, a William Caddow enrolled as an apprentice to Benjamin Pemberton in 1706. This William Caddow was born in Dublin on 15 September 1691 to John, a shoemaker, and Mary Caddow. William appears on the list of quarter brothers of the Goldsmiths' Company of Dublin in 1715–16 but does not appear on any later lists of the company, including the list of freemen.[1] It is very likely that he is the same William Caddow who arrived in Boston in the 1720s.

William Caddow was in Boston sometime before 6 December 1726, when he appraised the estate of Richard Jenkins, a hatter, and on 4 April 1727 he married Jenkins's widow Mary (Plinkinton) Jenkins in Christ Church.[2] He is identified as a goldsmith on a bond of 22 December 1726.[3] Caddow's occupation is also listed as goldsmith or silversmith in several court documents. On 26 April 1729, he and his wife sued Robert Mattlin of Newbury, Massachusetts, a baker, for a debt of £23.18.2 owed to Mary Caddow as administrator of her late husband's estate. A year later, Caddow accused Henry Sweeting, a mariner, of breaking "with force & arms" into Caddow's "Chest & Case of Bottles." Caddow charged that Sweeting took a sugar loaf worth 30 shillings from the chest and a "Quantity of Rum & Cordial Liquers" worth 20 shillings from the case of bottles. It is not clear from the records whether or not Sweeting was found guilty. Two years later Caddow was accused of selling strong liquor without a license, and in January 1733, Caddow sued Jabez [Jacob?] Clark, a Boston feltmaker, for nonpayment of a debt. Caddow also was plaintiff in a suit against Edward Ellis, a physician, in January 1737/38.[4] In 1739 Caddow was fined five pounds for firing a gun loaded with powder at his wife and wounding her in the face.[5]

In 1744 William Caddow, identified as a sentinel, appears on the roll of a company in his majesty's service mustered under the command of Ammi Ruhamah Cutter at Saco Fort, Maine, on 20 August. He is listed as having served ten weeks and three days prior to the time of his muster.[6] Caddow evidently died in 1745 during the campaign against Louisbourg, as Mary Caddow, widow of Boston, married John Whitley on 23 April 1746.[7]

No silver by Caddow is known. BMW

1. Berry 1909, 303; Jackson (1921) 1964, 644, 658.
2. RC 28:23, 131.

3. SCPR 25:155; docket 5359.
4. SCCR, files 23060, 31912, 33498; Court of Common Pleas Record Book 1731, 204; 1733, 245; John M. Fitzgerald to Francis Hill Bigelow, List of Boston Court Record References to Silversmiths, Bigelow-Phillips files, mentions a suit recorded in the Court of Common Pleas Record Book 1737, 153; the book is now missing.
5. SCCR, Court of General Sessions of the Peace Minute Book, October 1737–October 1739, 9 October 1739, Judicial Archives, Mass. Archives.
6. Muster rolls, vol. 92:27, Mass. Archives.
7. RC 28:267.

Stephen Callas
ca. 1720–47 +

Only scanty evidence of Stephen Callas's family life and training exists. His intention to marry Eunice Rea was published on 20 September 1746.[1] He appeared as a plaintiff during the Court of Common Pleas session held on 7 October 1746, at which "Stephen Callas, Boston, goldsmith" was sued by another goldsmith, Thomas Edwards (q.v.). Callas defaulted and Edwards was awarded £8.15 plus court costs of 26 shillings 6 pence.[2] Edwards evidently had difficulty recovering his debt, for the court issued execution orders to collect the debt on 11 November 1746, 6 February 1747, and 17 April 1747.

No objects have been attributed to Callas. DAF

1. RC 28:284.
2. SCCR, Court of Common Pleas Record Book 1744–46, 371.

Benjamin Callender
ca. 1749–1811

Benjamin Callender probably was born in Boston about 1749, the son of Joseph Callender (1712–67), a baker, and Elizabeth/Lydia Savell (b. 1717/18), who were married in 1735.[1] His paternal grandparents were Joseph Callender (ca. 1676–after 1755) and Lydia Pierce (b. 1676).[2] His maternal grandparents were John (ca. 1680–1756), a hatter, and Priscilla Savell (d. before 1747).[3] Priscilla was dead by 1747, when John Savell married Jane Bryant, who survived him.[4] Joseph Callender (q.v.) was a second cousin, and John and Joshua Doane (qq.v.) were distant cousins.

Benjamin would have begun his training about 1763, possibly with Daniel Henchman (q.v.). A receipt of 1767 from Henchman to Thomas Amory is signed by Benjamin Callender, perhaps the silversmith. Callender would have completed his apprenticeship about 1770.[5] The Massachusetts tax list of 1771 includes Benjamin Callender, a lodger with William Sherlock, with a poll of one.[6]

On 27 May 1773 Callender married Elizabeth Hall (ca. 1749–1810), who probably was the daughter of Stephen and Sarah Hall of Medford, Massachusetts, and sometime after his marriage Callender moved to Medfield or Medford.[7] The birth of the couple's daughter Abigail is recorded in Medfield in 1777, as was that of their daughter Hepsabeth in 1780.[8] The Benjamin Callender of Medfield who was drafted to march to Bristol, Rhode Island, in 1777 and who hired Timothy Smith to serve in his stead may have been the goldsmith.[9] A deed of 21 September 1781, recording Callender's purchase of a parcel of land and a dwelling house in Medfield from William Peters, identifies him as a "goldsmith, of Medford."[10] The following year Callender sold this parcel of land and house in Medford and may have returned to Boston. A deed of 1784 identifies him as a silversmith of Boston.[11] The Benjamin Callender who was approved as a "Retailer of Spirits" at his shop in Boston's Temple Street in 1791 may have been the silversmith.[12] Callender died in Boston in November 1811.[13] No silver by Callender is known to survive. PEK

1. No record of his birth has been found. His birth date is calculated from his age at the time of death; see *Index of Obituaries, 1784–1840*, 1:768; RC 24:87, 124; RC 28:190; *Boston Gazette*, 27 November 1767; Thwing; Woodworth-Barnes 1990–91, 208–10.
2. RC 9:139; RC 28:3; Woodworth-Barnes 1990–91, 201–02.
3. SCPR, docket 11226; Codman 1918, 208.
4. RC 28:263.
5. Receipt from Daniel Henchman to Thomas Amory, 17 June 1767, Amory Papers, MHS.
6. Pruitt 1978, 38–39.
7. RC 30:72.
8. *Medfield VR*, 28.
9. *Mass. Soldiers and Sailors* 3:29.
10. SCD 167:195.
11. SCD 163:147–48; 159:50–52.
12. RC 27:140.
13. *Index of Obituaries, 1784–1840*, 1:768.

Joseph Callender
1751–1821

A

Joseph Callender was born in Boston on 6 May 1751 to Eleazer Callender (1709–90) and Susanna (Hiller) Bound (b. 1719), the daughter of Benjamin Hiller (q.v.).[1] Susanna Bound, the widow of James Bound, whom she had married in April 1737, was married to Eleazer Callender on 24 June 1740 in a ceremony performed in Boston by Rev. Jeremiah Condy.[2] Joseph Callender's paternal grandparents were John Callender (1674–after 1742), a clothier, shopkeeper, and tobacconist who worked in Swansea and Boston, and his first wife, Priscilla Ballard (1680–ca. 1716), of Lynn, Massachusetts.[3]

Joseph Callender's marriage to Elizabeth Laughton (ca. 1753–93?), who may have been the daughter of William and Abigail (Edwards) Laughton, was announced in the *Massachusetts Centinel* on 1 August 1789.[4] The Boston census of 1790 recorded three Joseph Callenders, the silversmith/engraver and two of his cousins, the ship chandler Joseph Callender (1736–1802) and the grocer Joseph Callender (1763–1823).[5] The entry for the silversmith/engraver reflects the small size of his family. In addition to Callender, his wife, and his infant daughter, Sarah (ca. 1790–1859), the household included a man and a woman over the age of sixteen, whose roles in the extended family were probably that of apprentice, servant, or elderly relative. The couple had four daughters, Sarah, Mary (ca. 1792–1880), Helen (ca. 1800–56), and Elizabeth (ca. 1805–73), all of whom died unmarried.[6]

Several other members of Callender's family were active silversmiths and engravers, including his uncle Joseph Hiller, Sr. (q.v.), and his cousin Joseph Hiller, Jr. (q.v. Appendix A). Joseph Callender may have trained his nephew, Benjamin Callender (1773–1856), who worked as an engraver and merchant in Northfield, Massachusetts, because the younger man married Sally Laughton, a relative of his aunt, Elizabeth (Laughton) Callender.[7] Benjamin Callender (q.v.) was Callender's second cousin, the son of his father's cousin Joseph Callender (1712–67).[8] John and Joshua Doane (qq.v.) were his distant cousins.

The memoirs of the silversmith Samuel Davis, written in 1811, state that Joseph Callender "was a pupil of [Nathaniel] Hurd's [q.v.] and is respectable in the same line—Engraving."[9] By 1774, Callender was an active engraver and was probably a journeyman for his neighbor on Cornhill, Paul Revere, Jr. (q.v.).

In conjunction with Revere, Callender engraved some plates for the *Royal American Magazine*, founded in 1774 by Isaiah Thomas; they included "The Hill Tops, A New Hunting Song," "The Fortune Hunter," and "The Night Scene."[10]

Callender was employed as a diesinker by the Massachusetts Mint, and in 1784, he cut the seal of the Massachusetts Bank.[11] On 23 September 1784, Callender advertised in the *Independent Chronicle* that he had moved from "Cornhill, to the Shop formerly improved by Mr N. Hurd, Engraver, Half-Square, back of Mr. Shimmin's School, State-Street—where he carries on the Engraving, Seal Cutting and Copper-Plate Printing, in all its Branches."[12] Callender engraved a variety of silver objects for Zachariah Brigden (q.v.) in 1785:

M^r. Zach^y. Brigden to Joseph Callender D^r.

1785			
March	To Engra^g Arms on Tankard	£0..12	[torn]
	To Engra^g Teapot	1..10	[torn]
	To Engra^g Cypher on 12 Tea Spoons	..	[torn]
	Rec^d payment	£2..	[torn]
	Joseph Callender[13]		

He engraved several teapots for Brigden two years later:

M^r. Zac^h. Brigden   Boston Jany 25.th 1787
                                        to Joseph Callender D^r.

	To Engra^g Tea pot	£2– 8–
Feby 26th	To Engra^g Teapot	2– 8–
		4–16–
	Supra C^r By Cash	3–12–
	Ball^n due	£1– 4–
	Rec^d payment	
	Benj Callender[14]	

Callender also may have had a close working relationship with the silversmith Caleb Beal (q.v.) because Callender signed Beal's estate administration bond in 1801.[15] The Boston directories for 1789, 1796, and 1798 record Callender as being an engraver in State Street.[16] The property tax list of 1798 described him as a tenant in a brick and wooden building owned by John McLane on State Street.[17] He continued to be listed in the city directories until 1805.[18]

In February, October, and November 1816, Joseph Callender, his wife, Elizabeth, and other members of the Laughton family sold property on Fleet Street that they had inherited; the buyer, Redford Webster, paid two thousand dollars for it.[19] Callender died on 10 November 1821, at the age of seventy, and was buried in the Granary Burying Ground.[20] An inscription on a tomb for "Joseph, fam. Joseph, Nov. 10, 1821 ae 71 y" probably refers to the silversmith despite the erroneous paternal reference.[21]

An initials mark in a shaped cartouche (A) on a seal of the Massachusetts Bank has been attributed to Callender.[22] The unmarked *Columbia-Washington Medal* also has been attributed to him.[23] However, most of the objects that can be documented as his—bookplates, billheads, and prints—are examples of his work as an engraver. Callender engraved bookplates for patrons in Massachusetts, New Hampshire, and Maine; business cards for the Danvers and Beverly Iron Works Company and for Samuel Emery, son of the silversmith

Stephen Emery (q.v.); and membership certificates for the Boston Marine Society and the Amicable Fire Society.[24] He also engraved "New Zealand War Canoe" for Bickerstaff's *Almanac*, a "Plan of Boston" for West's Boston directory, and, in 1801, in collaboration with Samuel Hill, Jr. (q.v. Appendix B), the *Map of Massachusetts Proper* (illus. pp. 2–3).[25]   DAF

SURVIVING OBJECTS

	Mark	Inscription	Patron	Date	Reference	Owner
Seal	A†	SEAL OF THE MASSACHUSETTS BANK.; 1784 (+)	Massachusetts Bank	1784		Bank of Boston Corporation

1. Woodworth-Barnes 1990–91, 207, 329; *Swansea VR*, 59; Flynt/Fales 1968, 175; Stauffer 1907, 1:40; RC 24:141.
2. RC 28:200, 214; Woodworth-Barnes 1990–91, 207.
3. RC 9:132; *Lynn VR* 2:84; Woodworth-Barnes 1990–91, 200.
4. *Brookline VR*, 44, 132–33, 213–14; Woodworth-Barnes 1990–91, 330; *Massachusetts Centinel*, 1 August 1789; Stauffer 1907, 1:40; *Columbian Centinel*, 27 March 1793; *Index to Obituaries, 1784–1840*, 1:768. A Callender genealogist, Esther Littleford Woodworth-Barnes, has postulated a second marriage for Callender to an unidentified Elizabeth shortly before 1800; see Woodworth-Barnes 1990–91, 330. However, it is likely that the Elizabeth Callender who died in 1793 was another member of this large family and not the silversmith's wife.
5. RC 22:468, 481, 508.
6. Woodworth-Barnes 1990–91, 330.
7. Benjamin Callender was the eldest son of the silversmith's brother, Benjamin Callender (1745–1828), and Abigail Belcher (1751–85). Woodworth-Barnes 1990–91, 323–24; RC 30:238; Temple/Sheldon 1875, 417.
8. Woodworth-Barnes 1990–91, 208–09, 42.
9. Steinway 1960, 8.
10. Stauffer 1907, 1:40; 2:51; Flynt/Fales 1968, 175; Federhen 1985, 25.
11. Flynt/Fales 1968, 175.
12. *Independent Chronicle*, 23 September 1784.
13. Brigden Papers, YU.
14. Brigden Papers, YU.
15. SCPR, docket 21581.
16. *Boston Directory* 1789, 13; 1796, 25; 1798, 28. There are three Joseph Callenders listed in the directories, the engraver, a merchant, and a ship chandler.
17. RC 22:314.
18. Lichtenstein 1886a, 204.
19. SCD 252:22; 254:89–92.
20. Codman 1918, 54; Flynt/Fales 1968, 175; Woodworth-Barnes 1990–91, 329.
21. A tomb in the Copp's Hill Burying Ground inscribed "Joseph Callender 1823" is the burial spot of Joseph Callender (1763–1823), son of Joseph Callender (1736–1802), another cousin of the silversmith. Whitmore 1878, 77, no. 1425; Bridgman 1851, 151; Woodworth-Barnes 1990–91, 33–35.
22. Flynt/Fales 1968, 175.
23. *Witness to America's Past*, no. 99.
24. Lichtenstein 1886b, 298–99; Lichtenstein 1887, 297; Fielding 1917, 74, no. 226; Stauffer 1907, 2:51.
25. Stauffer 1907, 2:51.

Joseph Candish
b. 1717

Joseph Candish was born in Boston on 12 May 1717, the son of Joseph Candish and Susannah Trunde, who were married in 1714 in Newbury, Massachusetts.[1] The younger Joseph Candish probably began his apprenticeship about 1731 and would have completed it about 1738. The name of his master remains unknown. On 23 October 1740 Candish married Abigail Mallard (1717–before 1752), daughter of William Mallard and Abigail Dawson (b. 1685) of Boston.[2] The couple's first child, Rebecca, was baptized on 9 August 1741 at the New Brick Church, and Joseph was admitted to membership the same day. The baptisms of two other daughters at the same church—Susannah on 25 November 1744 and Elizabeth on 15 March 1747—followed.[3]

Joseph Candish is first called a goldsmith in Suffolk Deeds in 1749, when he and Makepiece Horton, acting as executors for the estate of Sarah Corser, sold land on Middle Street in the North End.[4] Sometime before 1752 Candish's first wife died, for on 15 November that year he married Katherine (Haley) Lord (b. 1710/11), widow of Robert Lord and daughter of the shipwright William (ca. 1674–1760) and Sarah Haley (ca. 1675–1752).[5] In 1753, the Boston selectmen licensed Candish as a retailer of strong drink on Fleet Street.[6] Retailing strong drink is an activity that Candish may have engaged in continuously to supplement his income, for the Boston selectmen later licensed Candish as a retailer "Adjoining Mʳ Elliots Church" in 1766.[7] He declined to serve as constable in 1753 but did serve in the town offices of hogreeve and scavenger between 1754 and 1759.[8] His personal property loss was £5.4 in the devastating fire of 1760.[9]

In the period 1766–69 Suffolk Deeds record a number of real estate transactions of Candish and his wife.[10] He appears in the Massachusetts tax list of 1771 with one poll as a lodger with Josiah Nottage.[11] In all likelihood Candish made his living as a goldsmith who supplied other craftsmen with parts, specifically bezel wire. The memoirs of Samuel Davis (1765–1829) recall his years as an apprentice to the silversmith's trade in Boston just after the Revolution and reveal this portrait of Candish:

> There was an old man, Candish by name, at the north end, a bissell wire drawer (this wire is flat-bisected by a raised ridge and forms the rim in stone setting) to the Silversmiths. A tool which he possessed, being the only one in the town, gave him employment—he was very poor and this tool was his dependence. It was my lot to visit his humble habitation often and these visits early taught me to pity ingenious men, who frequently live in obscurity and poverty.[12]

No record of Candish's death has been found, and no silver by this maker has been identified. PEK

1. RC 24:127; *Newbury VR* 2:78.
2. RC 28:13, 214; RC 24:123; RC 9:165.
3. *NEHGR* 18:337.
4. SCD 77:75–76, 269–70.
5. RC 24:68; RC 30:367; Whitmore 1878, 50, no. 932; Thwing.
6. RC 17:298.
7. RC 20:221. This was the New North Church where Andrew Eliot was the minister.
8. RC 14:233, 247, 285; RC 16:18.
9. RC 29:91.
10. SCD 108:247–49, 256–57; 115:15–16.
11. Pruitt 1978, 8–9.
12. Steinway 1960, 8.

William Cario, Jr.
ca. 1736–1809

Cario was born to the silversmith William Cario, Sr. (q.v.), and his wife, Mary Ann Pollard, probably shortly after their marriage in 1735.[1] Little is known about his training, but presumably he acquired his professional skills from his father. Cario's intention to wed Abigail Peavey (1725/26–67), the daughter of

A

William Peavey (Peevey), a mariner of Portsmouth, New Hampshire, was published in Boston on 5 July 1759.[2]

Cario relocated to Portsmouth after his marriage on 31 October 1759. He became an active participant in community affairs and signed several petitions to the governor and Council of New Hampshire, including the "Protest against Theatrical Performances" on 13 January 1773.[3] On 31 October 1765, William Peavey's heirs, including "William Cario Goldsmith Abigail his Wife in her Right," sold their shares in his property on Portsmouth's Narrow and Main streets to their brother John Peavey, a carpenter.[4] Abigail Cario died in 1767 and was buried in the Point of Graves Cemetery with an epitaph reading, "Here lies buried the body of Mrs Abigail Cario wife of Mr. William Cario who separated this Life September 17th 1767 in the 41st Year of her Age."[5] Her gravestones were procured in Boston by family friend Zachariah Brigden (q.v.), who purchased a "pr grave stone for Mrs Cario" from John Homer on 12 October 1767.[6] The following year, Cario married Lydia Croxcroft (Croxford) (d. 1831), daughter of William and Mary Croxcroft (Croxford) of Portsmouth, in a ceremony performed at South Church in Portsmouth on 16 April 1768.[7] Four of the couple's children were baptized in this church between 1769 and 1774; two appear to have survived infancy: Samuel, baptized on 12 July 1772, and Daniel, baptized on 19 June 1774.[8]

Cario moved fifteen miles inland to Newmarket, New Hampshire, sometime before the Revolution. He was living there when he signed the "association test" on 12 July 1776 pledging to "oppose the Hostile Proceedings of the British Fleets, and Armies, against the United American Colonies."[9] On 4 February 1785, "William Cario of Newmarket, Silversmith" purchased land and buildings in Newmarket on "the highway leading to Newfields landing place" for eighty-four pounds at a public auction of the estate of Daniel Warner.[10] He arranged a two-year mortgage with Jonathan Warner, the estate's administrator, which was repaid in 1794.[11] Cario bought additional land adjoining his property on Newfields Landing Road for thirty-six shillings from the Portsmouth tailor Stephen Hardy on 14 April 1790.[12] Hardy was the father of the silversmith Stephen Hardy (1781–1843), who worked in Boston and Portsmouth.[13] Cario expanded his property holdings further by buying land for three pounds from James Hill in July 1791 and for four dollars from Henry Wiggen in March 1798.[14] The silversmith's house was still standing in 1941, when Stephen Decatur published his study of Cario in the *American Collector,* in which he suggested that Cario maintained his shop in the ell of his home.[15] The New Hampshire census of 1790 records Cario as the head of a family of two men and two women, all over sixteen years of age, although only Cario and his wife occupied his house in 1800, when the second national census was conducted.[16]

Cario may have tried to expand his business into mercantile pursuits in the early nineteenth century. "William Cario, Trader" mortgaged his house to James Sheafe of Portsmouth for $163.20 on 16 September 1808, perhaps to obtain funds to finance his activities as a trader.[17] Whatever venture he was planning was short-lived, however, as Cario died on 20 July 1809.[18] The *New-Hampshire Gazette* reported his death on 1 August of that year:

> At Newmarket, on Thursday the 20th of July, very suddenly, Mr. WILLIAM CARRIO, formerly of Portsmouth, aged 75, leaving a wife and one child to bemoan the loss.
>
> To highly paint the character of a deceased friend appears superfluous; suffice it to say, Mr. Carrio has been the kind husband, indulgent parent, and the

affectionate friend to his numerous acquaintance:—which with many other pleasing traits in his character rendered him worthy of imitation.

Because Cario died intestate, his widow approved the appointment of William Blasdell, a Portsmouth bricklayer, as the administrator of the goldsmith's estate on 29 July 1809. William Blasdell, Abner Blasdell, a Portsmouth merchant, and Putnam Safford, an Exeter baker, put up a bond of $4,000 on 1 August 1809, and the estate was appraised two days later at a total value of $623.16.[19] Cario's household furnishings indicate that he enjoyed a comfortable life. Among his belongings were such luxury items as thirty-eight ounces of silver, a gold ring, a looking glass, framed pictures, a silver watch, silver stock and knee buckles, and a large service of blue and white ceramics. The inventory, including the contents of Cario's silver shop as part of the house, supports Decatur's contention that the shop was located in the ell of his house. His shop was large and well stocked with anvils, vises, hammers, files, pliers, shears, tongs, and bellows in addition to other unspecified tools. Cario kept small silver objects in three glass display cases: a variety of buckles and buttons are included in the inventory. Although some early accounts speculated that Cario worked in pewter, no evidence supports this contention, since the pewter, brass, copper, lead, and iron objects listed in the inventory appear in the context of other kitchenware and dinnerware. His tools included

pr. large Scales 1.25 pr. D$^{\underline{o}}$. .42	1.67
pr. small D$^{\underline{o}}$ 20 pr. steel yards 1^D	1.20
3 pewter measures 1^D sett Tin D^o & tunnels 1.25	2.25
sett of wooden measures	.75
(Goldsmiths Tools [vertically in margin])	
1 large Anvil 96 lbs @12^{cts}	11.52
1 small D$^{\underline{o}}$. 24 lbs @ 16^{cts}	3.84
large Vise $3. 2 hand D^o .60^{cts}	3.60
18 large & small hammers	6.00
38 large & small files	4.50
lot of old D^o .50^{cts} 8 pr. plyers 2^D	2.50
3 pr shears 1.50 3 pr. Tongs 1.25	2.75
pr. bellows 1$^{\underline{D}}$ remainder of Goldsmiths	
tools of all kinds..........10^D 2 pr. dividers 1.75	11.75
Remnants of Goods in Shop	3.—
1 shop bell .25 Slate .17^{cts} Case & bottles 2^D	2.42
3 glass Cases 3^D 8 pr. plated Shoe buckels 2.50	5.50
2 silver stock buckels & one hat D$^{\underline{o}}$.	1.00
2 pr. knee D^o. & pins 1$^{\underline{D}}$. 2 pr sleave buttons .42	1.42
. . .	
21 lbs old Copper & brass	4.20
50 lbs D Lead & pewter	4.—
50 lbs D$^{\underline{o}}$. Iron	2.—[20]

On 3 October 1809 the *New-Hampshire Gazette* reported the sale of the goldsmith's estate:

To be sold at Auction, on the 16 of October inst. at the dwelling house of the late WILLIAM CARIO of Newmarket, deceased, a quantity of Household Furniture and other articles, belonging to the estate of said deceased.

The same newspaper also included the additional advertisement:

> NOTICE is hereby given that the subscriber has been duly appointed Administrator of the estate of WILLIAM CARIO, late of Newmarket, Goldsmith, deceased, and has taken upon him that trust by giving bonds as the law directs—. . . .
> WILLIAM BLASDEL, Administrator.
> Portsmouth, Oct. 2 1809.

In spite of the sale, the estate was declared insolvent on 19 June 1811, and the administrator was directed to sell the house and land in Newmarket, excluding the widow's portion, to pay the outstanding debts.

No gravestone has been found for Cario in Portsmouth, Exeter, or Newmarket. Since Newfields's laws prohibited burial markers for those who died insolvent, he was probably buried without a marker in the Newfields Burial Ground. Lydia (Croxcroft) Cario died in November 1831 in Newfields.[21]

Although several initials marks have been attributed to Cario, none can be substantiated yet.[22] Only one mark, initial and surname in a serrated rectangle (A), can be associated with Cario with certainty. Few objects made by him have been located, although several are very well documented and indicate his proficiency as a silversmith and engraver. In 1769, the silversmith made a snuffbox for his new bride, Lydia Croxcroft, skillfully utilizing several different materials: a tortoiseshell top, silver sides and bottom, and a pierced silver overlay riveted to mother-of-pearl accents. The box is inscribed "The property of Lydia Cario, 1769." Cario fashioned a communion beaker with flared sides and a molded foot rim for the Newmarket church. The beaker is inscribed "The Gift of/Deacon Joseph Judkins, to the/Church in Newmarkett/by his Last Will/1770." Judkins's will, proved on 28 March 1770, provided for the commission of this beaker: "I give and bequeath unto the Church of Our Lord Jesus Christ in Newmarket, whereof my ancient, Cordial and faithful friend the Reverend Mr. John Moody is now Pastor, a handsome Silver Communion Cup at the descretion of my Executors in convenient time after my decease."[23] Cario's skills as an engraver were employed by Gov. Theodore Atkinson in 1771, when he ornamented an English salver with a tablet containing the names, ages, and dates of death of forty-eight people who died between 1740 and 1771, most of whom were related to the Wentworth family by marriage.[24] Stephen Decatur and Kathryn Buhler suggest that Atkinson may have served as a pallbearer for his relatives and purchased the tray with the gold mourning rings he had received.[25] Other marks, including W.Cario in a stepped rectangle, W.CARIO in an oblong, W.CARIO in a plain rectangle, and W CARIO in a serrated rectangle have been published, but no examples of these variations could be found for illustration.[26] DAF

SURVIVING OBJECTS

	Mark	Inscription	Patron	Date	Reference	Owner
Beaker	A	The Gift of/Deacon Joseph Judkins, to the/Church in New- markett/by his Last Will/1770	Executors of Joseph Judkins's estate for the church in Newmarket, N.H.	1770	NHHS 1973, no. 119	NHHS
Snuffbox	A	The property of Lydia Cario, 1769	William Cario, Jr., for Lydia Cario	1769		SI
Tablespoon	A†	S/SS		ca. 1765	Buhler/Hood 1970, no. 270	YUAG

	Mark	Inscription	Patron	Date	Reference	Owner
Three tablespoons	A*	Rogers (later)	Daniel Rindge and Hannah (Cutter) Rogers	ca. 1770	Smith 1939, 6	
Three tablespoons	A*	S/IH	Jacob and Hannah (Seavey) Sheafe	ca. 1770	Decatur 1965, 81–82	SPNEA

1. *Newbury VR* 2:78.
2. Decatur 1941, 6; RC 30:32; RCD 9:335–36. Although some earlier studies have suggested that Abigail Peavey was married to William Cario, Sr., the documentary evidence does not support this assertion. In fact, the elder Cario was still in Boston in August 1767, two years after "William Cario Goldsmith and Abigail his wife . . . of Portsmouth" were recorded in a Rockingham County deed; see RCD 91:417–19.
3. Smith 1939, 6; Decatur 1941, 6.
4. RCD 91:417–19.
5. *New Hampshire Genealogical Record* 1:15.
6. John Homer to Zachariah Brigden, 12 October 1767, Brigden Papers, YU.
7. Gooding 1927–30, 82:284; Decatur 1941, 6; Smith 1939, 6. The South Church records give her name as Croxford.
8. Gooding 1927–30, 82:32.
9. Batchellor 1910, 100; Smith 1939, 6.
10. RCD 119:225–26.
11. RCD 119:214–15.
12. RCD 127:138.
13. Flynt/Fales 1968, 242.
14. RCD 129:307; 160:270.
15. Decatur 1941, 7.
16. Jackson/Teeples/Schaefermeyer 1974, 15; Dept. of Commerce 1908, 73.
17. RCD 183:265.
18. Decatur 1941, 20; Smith 1939, 6; *New-Hampshire Gazette*, 1 August 1809.
19. RCPR, docket 8139, old ser.
20. RCPR, docket 8139, old ser.
21. Smith 1939, 6.
22. Flynt/Fales 1968, 176–77; Belden 1980, 98; Parsons 1983, 87.
23. Smith 1939, 6; NHHS 1973, 51.
24. Decatur 1941, 20.
25. Decatur 1941, 20; Buhler 1957a, n.p.
26. Kovel 1961, 54; Ensko 1948, 244; Graham 1936, 14; Okie 1936, 248; Thorn 1949, 46; French (1917) 1967, 24.

William Cario, Sr.
ca. 1714–before 1771

Very little is known of the jeweler William Cario's early life. Some silver scholars suggest that he was the brother of the jeweler Michael Cario, an Englishman who served his apprenticeship in London, was made a freeman in New York in 1728, and later settled in Philadelphia, but no proof of this connection exists beyond the unusual name of Cario.[1] William Cario was born by 1714 at the latest because he would have been at least twenty-one in 1735, when he and Mary Ann Pollard, both described as being from Boston, married in Queen Anne's Chapel on 5 September.[2] The couple had a son William, who became a silversmith (q.v.).

Nothing is known of William Cario's apprenticeship or training. The earliest professional reference to Cario dates to the year following his marriage. "William Cario, Jeweller" appeared in the Suffolk County Court of Common Pleas in 1736 to resolve a suit against John Bradley, a Boston rope drawer.[3] Cario's case, initially filed on 14 June 1736, stated that Bradley had "fourth Day of

Aprill Last Seduced & Enticed away the Pltfs Negro Servant named Lambeth & kept him concealed from his s.^d Master [words crossed out] from that Time untill the fourth Day of this Instant." Cario was awarded damages of £3.11 and costs.[4]

In March 1737, Cario advertised in the *Boston Gazette* that, "Whereas a Silver Spoon was taken up in the Street about three Weeks ago, and has not been observ'd to be advertis'd; This is to give Notice that the Owner of the said Spoon by applying to Mr. Cario, Jeweller, or the Publisher hereof, and describing the Mark, may have it return'd."[5] An advertisement placed in the *Boston Gazette* on 6 and 13 March 1738 announced, "Lost about six Weeks past, a Pair of Sleeve Buttons with Christials sat in Gold, a solid Link of the same. The Person that has found them is desired to bring them to Mr. Cario Jeweller near Dr. Colman's Meeting House, and they shall be by him Rewarded for their Trouble." That same year, the silversmith placed another advertisement in the *Boston Gazette*: "NOTICE is hereby given, that *William Cario is removed from his late Dwelling near the Rev. Dr.* Colman's *Meeting House, to the south End of the Town over against the White Swan, where all sorts of Jewellers Work is made & sold after the best and newest Manner, likewise fine Sword Blades, and Canes Sold and mounted there.*"[6] Cario appeared in court in July 1741 as the defendant in a suit of debt brought by the Boston retailer William Randall and was ordered to pay his debt of £5.11.1 and court costs of £2.16.[7]

After working independently, Cario appears to have worked as a journeyman in the shop operated by Thomas Edwards and subsequently by Zachariah Brigden (qq.v.). He witnessed a receipt for Edwards in April 1753.[8] On 7 August 1758 and 26 April 1759, Cario served as a witness to deeds for Zachariah Brigden.[9] Brigden's accounts with the wood merchant Benjamin Phillips record a number of shipments of cordwood purchased for Cario between November 1761 and December 1763.[10] A lengthy account between the two from September 1764 to April 1765 records Cario's purchase of numerous shop supplies from Brigden. In addition, Cario was billed for rent paid on his behalf to Mr. Belknap.

Mr Willm Cario To Zech Brigden		D.^r
1764	To Cash paid Mr Belknap for Rent	£1: 13: 4
Sep.^r	To Ditto for 1/2 doz Salters & 2 doz Primers	0.12 + 0
	To Ditto for 1^{lb} of Pot Ash	0. 1. 2
	To Ditto for 19^{lb} of Candles	0:12 + 0
	To Ditto for 2 Sett of Cypher Button Stones	0: 5: 4
	To Ditto for 1 Sett of Top Stones	0. 0. 9¹/₂
Nov.^r	To 1/4^{lb} of Borax	0. 4. 0
	To 1 doz of blew pots	0: 7: 0
	To 1 doz Nest of Crucibles	0:7 + : 2¹/₂
	To 6 Sheets of Sand paper	0: 0: 9¹/₂
	To 1 Brass Hallowing Stamp	1: 4: 0
	To Cash for 20^{lb} of Candles	0: 12 + 0
	To Ditto for 6^{lb} of Ginger	0: 3: 2¹/₂
	To 6^{lb} of Rotten Stone	0: 4. 0
Jan.^r	To Cash for 20^{lb} of Candles	0: 12: 8
	To Ditto for 2^{lb} of Chocolate	0:3 + ..0
	To Ditto for 5 p.^r of Steel Chapes	0: 4. 6¹/₂
	To Ditto for 2 Cards of buttons	0: 1: 4

	To Ditto for 3 Ring Stones	0:	1:	$6^{1}/_{2}$
	To 1 Doz of Sparks	0:	2:	11
	To 1 Doz of Screw Boxes	0:	0:	$9^{1}/_{2}$
	To 1^{lb} of Salt Petre	0:	2:	8
	To 1^{lb} of Sandiver	0:	0:	$9^{1}/_{2}$
	To 3 hanks of binding wier	0:	2:	0
	To 6 Bone brushes	0:	3:	7
	To 6 Ditto of wood	0:3 +	:	7
	To Cash for one of Pilgrim Progress	0:	3:	7
1765	To 2 Sett of Cypher Earing Stones	0:	5:	4
April 10	To 1 Nest of Large Crucibles	0:	1:	0
		£8:	16:	2 [11]

Cario and a colleague, Joseph Edwards (q.v.), witnessed a deed for Brigden on 18 August 1767, while Brigden was serving as executor to the will of Thomas Edwards.[12]

Stephen Decatur has suggested that Cario died before 1769, the year his son William stopped denoting himself as Jr.[13] Although previous scholars have stated that Cario moved to Portsmouth, New Hampshire, and have attributed silver made for Portsmouth patrons to him, no documentary evidence supports this claim. Cario probably died in Boston before 1771 because he does not appear in the tax valuation list for that year.

The mark W·CARIO in a shaped rectangle probably was used by the son and not by the elder Cario. A number of initials marks have been assigned variously to William Cario, William Cowell, and William Cleveland but have not yet been successfully differentiated. Swords also have been attributed to Cario.[14] One example made for the Peirce family is marked with W.C. in a clipped rectangle, however, the ornate embellishment of the sword hilt and the character of the mark are both indicative of English manufacture.[15] DAF

1. Decatur 1941, 6.
2. *Newbury VR* 2:78, 405.
3. SCCR, Court of Common Pleas Record Book 1736–37, 10.
4. SCCR, file 41984, Judicial Archives, Mass. Archives.
5. *Boston Gazette*, 7–14 March 1737.
6. *Boston Gazette*, 23–30 October 1738.
7. SCCR, Court of Common Pleas Record Book 1741, 142–43.
8. Thomas Edwards, receipt, 4 April 1753, Brigden Papers, YU.
9. MCD 59:367–68; 56:354–56.
10. Benjamin Phillips to Zachariah Brigden, 17 September–17 November 1761; Benjamin Phillips to Zachariah Brigden, 14 August 1761–17 March 1764, Brigden Papers, YU.
11. Zachariah Brigden to William Cario, Account, September 1764–10 April 1765, Brigden Papers, YU.
12. SCD 115:39.
13. Decatur 1941, 7.
14. Peterson (1954) 1991, no. 4.
15. The Peirce sword is illustrated in Decatur 1941, 7.

Joshua Cheever
w. ca. 1780

Samuel Davis (1765–1829), in his memoirs of his years as an apprentice in Boston in the late eighteenth century, included the name Cheever in a list of "The eldest of the trade whom I now recollect."[1] The man Davis identified may have been the Joshua Cheever who appears in the Boston tax list of 1780 as Joshua Cheever "Goldsmith" in ward 4.[2] In spite of this evidence, the identity of this goldsmith, who may have been a descendant of the Reverend Thomas Cheever of Malden, Massachusetts, remains elusive. PEK

1. Steinway 1960, 7.
2. "Assessors' 'Taking-Books,'" 23.

Joseph Clark(e), Jr.
1716–83

A

Joseph Clark, Jr., the nephew of the silversmith Samuel Clarke (1659–1705) (q.v.), was born in Boston on 19 August 1716 to Joseph Clark (1679–1760) and Margaret Jarvis (1692–1761), who married in 1713.[1] His paternal grandparents were Jonas Clarke (ca. 1621–1699/1700) and his third wife, Elizabeth Cook, of Cambridge, Massachusetts.[2] His maternal grandparents were Elias (1663/64–95), a mariner, and Margaret Jarvis.[3] His maternal grandmother married Samuel Burrill of Lynn, Massachusetts, in 1697.[4]

Clark's master is not known, but he would have begun his training about 1730 and completed it about 1737. Soon thereafter he made two wine cups and two beakers for the Third Church in Lynn, paid for from the bequest of Theophilus Burrill (1669–1737), who was perhaps related to Samuel Burrill, Clark's grandmother's second husband.

In 1740 Clark married Prudence Hill (1721–89), daughter of Abraham Hill (1697–1754), a bricklayer, and Prudence Hancock (1696–1780) of Cambridge.[5] A son Joseph was born to the couple in 1742; a daughter Prudence was born in 1746; and a daughter Mary in 1748.[6]

Through kinship Clark was related to other craftsmen in the goldsmithing and jewelrymaking trades. In 1747 Clark's sister, Margaret, married the jeweler Joshua Eames (q.v.). Eames's first wife was the sister of the silversmith John Parkman (q.v.), and Eames's sister Elizabeth was married to Parkman. Clark was one of the appraisers of Parkman's estate in 1748.[7] Clark may also have trained his nephew by marriage, the jeweler John Codner (q.v.), the son of his wife's sister Mary, beginning about 1768.

At least two other individuals named Joseph Clark lived in Boston in the mid-eighteenth century, and therefore it is difficult to establish the goldsmith's activities with certainty.[8] The goldsmith may have been the Joseph Clark who was chosen as a sealer of leather in Boston from 1771 to 1774.[9] No individuals named Joseph Clark were included in the Massachusetts tax list of 1771 in Boston. The goldsmith Joseph Clark died on 16 October 1783 and was buried in the Copp's Hill Burying Ground. No Suffolk County probate record for him survives.[10]

In addition to the church silver discussed above, Clark is known to have charged the estate of Seth Parker £6.16.6½ for mourning rings in 1750.[11] About two dozen other pieces of Clark's work have been identified by his initial and surname mark (A). An initials mark has been attributed to him, but the grounds for the attribution are extremely tentative.[12] Moreover, Joseph Clark's mark has been confused with those of Thomas Clark (q.v.) and Jonathan Clark of Newport and Providence, Rhode Island.[13] PEK

SURVIVING OBJECTS

	Mark	Inscription	Patron	Date	Reference	Owner
Beaker	A	The Gift of Thomas Bartlet to the first Church in Plimouth	First Parish, Plymouth, Mass., for Thomas Bartlet	ca. 1765	Jones 1913, 374–75	PS

	Mark	Inscription	Patron	Date	Reference	Owner
Beaker	A	S/IM; The Gift of, M.ʳ Jonathan Merritt to/The first Church of Christ in Situate/1757 (later)	Jonathan Merritt	ca. 1750	Jones 1913, 444	
Two beakers	A*	The Gift of/The Honr,ᵇˡᵉ/THEOPHILUS, BURRILL, Esq.ʳ to the/Third Church of Christ in Lynn	First Parish Church, Saugus, Mass. (successor to Third Church, Lynn), for Theophilus Burrill	ca. 1737	Buhler/Hood 1970, no. 269	YUAG
Cann (mate below)	A*	IC/CT		ca. 1750		SI
Cann (mate above)	A	IC/CT		ca. 1750	YUAG files	
Cann	A (?)	M/IM; WPM (later) (+)	Matchett family	ca. 1755	National Art Galleries, 3–5 December 1931, lot 422 (as Jonathan Clark)	
Porringer	A	unidentified crest, an eagle		ca. 1750	YUAG files	
Porringer	A	F/IS		ca. 1755	Avery 1920, no. 87	MMA
Porringer	?	M/IM; WPM (later) (+)	Matchett family	ca. 1755	National Art Galleries, 3–5 December 1931, lot 429	
Two salts	A	RM		ca. 1760	Christie's, 17–18 January 1992, lot 165	
Sword	A	none		ca. 1775	Hammerslough/Feigenbaum 1958–73, 2:87	
Tablespoon	A	?		ca. 1750	YUAG files	
Two tablespoons	A†	P/HW (+)		ca. 1750	DAPC 72.2718 and 72.3041	WM
Tankard	A	A Gift to The first Church/In Andover the Desire of/Timothy Osgood Full filled by his/Grandson Peter Osgood 1754	North Parish of North Andover, North Andover, Mass., for Peter Osgood	1754	Jones 1913, 347–48	
Tankard	A	The Gift of the Widow Elizebeth, Abbot to the/First Church of Christ in Andover. 1756	North Parish of North Andover, North Andover, Mass., for Elizabeth Abbot	1756	Jones 1913, 348	
Tankard	A	unidentified initials	Matchett family	ca. 1755	National Art Galleries, 3–5 December 1931, lot 430	
Teaspoon	A*	LA		ca. 1760		SFCAI

	Mark	Inscription	Patron	Date	Reference	Owner
Teaspoon	A	P/IM		ca. 1750		CHS
Teaspoon	A*	WE	Mary Wood and Thomas Edes	ca. 1740	Buhler 1972, no. 233	MFAB
Teaspoon	A*	GK/A		ca. 1750		YUAG
Teaspoon	A*	R/MD		ca. 1730		RISD
Two wine cups	A	The Gift of/the Honourable/ THEOPHILUS/ BURRILL Esqʳ/To the third/Church of Christ/In Lynn	First Parish Church Saugus, Mass. (successor to Third Church, Lynn), for Theophilus Burrill	ca. 1737	Jones 1913, 441	

1. *Cambridge VR* 1:142; Whitmore 1878, 10, nos. 198–99; RC 9:201; RC 24:112; RC 28:43.
2. *Cambridge VR* 2:78.
3. RC 9:88; SCPR, docket 2233.
4. RC 9:235.
5. RC 28:235; *Cambridge VR* 1:323, 352, 355; 2:196, 601; *Index of Obituaries, 1784–1840,* 1:941; MCPR, docket 11401; MCD 39:658.
6. RC 24:245, 259, 266.
7. SCPR 42:148.
8. An innholder named Joseph Clark and his wife, Mary, appear in many Suffolk deeds; see SCD 129:54; 144:93; 161:122; and 167:148. This Joseph Clark probably is the Joseph Clark who is in the Boston tax list of 1780 with the occupation "lodgers." See "Assessors' 'Taking-Books,'" 54. There also was a shipwright named Joseph Clarke who was chosen as a member of the Committee of Five for ward 2 in 1776; see RC 18:253 and "Assessors' 'Taking-Books,'" 17.
9. RC 18:42, 67, 113, 154. See also a note from Thwing that he held town office 26 May 1740, RC 15:240.
10. Whitmore 1878, 10, no. 200.
11. SCPR, docket 9512.
12. Belden 1980, 109 (c); Ensko 1948, 191.
13. The teapot at RISD that Buhler alludes to is actually by Jonathan Clark of Newport and Providence. The mark Buhler illustrates as (b) for Joseph Clark belongs to Thomas Clark, see Buhler 1972, 1:279. See also Flynt/Fales 1968, 182–83; Belden 1980, 109 (b); Graham 1936, 15.

Samuel Clarke
1659–1705

The son of Jonas Clarke (ca. 1621–1699/1700) and his second wife, Elizabeth Clarke (d. 1673), Samuel Clarke was baptized in the First Church of Cambridge, Massachusetts, on 6 November 1659.[1] His father, an elder of the church and a prominent citizen of the town, began his career as a shipmaster and navigator. When Jonas died on 11 January 1699/1700, Samuel Sewall noted in his diary that he was "a good man in a good old Age, and one of my first and best Cambridge friends."[2] Jonas Clarke had two other sons by his second wife, Thomas (1653–1704), Harvard College 1670, who served as minister of the church in Chelmsford, Massachusetts, from 1678 until his death, and Timothy (1657–1737), a mariner and lieutenant in the Artillery Company.[3]

Samuel Clarke served his apprenticeship under John Hull (q.v.) of Boston. In a diary entry for 1673, Hull recorded accepting Clarke as an apprentice for eight years. Aside from a notation that Clarke had smallpox in 1678, Hull made no further mention of Clarke. Samuel Sewall's diary reveals that Clarke resided in the Hull-Sewall household for more than ten years.[4] Clarke witnessed deeds for John Hull's estate, for Judith Hull, and for Samuel Sewall in 1683 and 1684.[5]

Clarke apparently worked as a goldsmith for only a few years. Sewall mentions Clarke several times prior to his entry of 20 September 1685, when he recorded that "Sam. Clark keeps on Board his Brother's Ship, intending a Voyage to Sea, having no work in the Shop."[6] On the list of Boston inhabitants of 1695 he is included as a mariner in division 1.[7]

On 1 October 1696 Clarke purchased a brick house in the south end of Boston, along the road to Roxbury, from John Squire, a yeoman, for two hundred pounds, and in 1698 he married Hannah (Paine) (Eliot) Fairweather (1662–1717). She was the daughter of John (ca. 1632–74) and Sarah (Parker) Paine of Boston, and widow of Asaph Eliot and Thomas Fairweather.[8] Hannah already had at least two children by her second husband, Thomas Fairweather— Hannah and Thomas—when she married Samuel Clarke.[9] The Clarkes had three children of their own, Samuel (b. 1699), Sarah (b. 1701), and John (b. 1703), but only Samuel survived his father.[10] On 9 September 1702 Samuel and Hannah sold land in Sherborn, Massachusetts, that she had inherited from her grandfather Richard Parker.[11]

When Clarke's father died in 1700, Samuel received a bequest of twenty acres of land, to be divided with his sister Dorcas Green, and a legacy of three pounds. His legacy was smaller than that given to the other children, which suggests that his father had already given him a substantial portion of his share of the estate. Although the other children each received several pieces of plate, Samuel did not receive any of his father's sizable collection of silver.[12]

Samuel Clarke died at sea in 1705. On 25 November of that year Sewall wrote in his diary, "This day hear of Capt. Samuel Clark's death very suddenly at Sea, about 3 weeks ago: Sail'd from St. Thomas 2 or 3 days before. Was a good man, liv'd in our house more than Ten years, left one Son."[13]

A mark, SC in a heart, has been attributed to Clarke. Because this mark is found only on trifid-end spoons with foliate decoration on the bowls, which if made in New England would postdate 1685 when Clarke supposedly ceased silversmithing, it is more likely that the mark belongs to an English silversmith who specialized in making spoons.[14] BMW

1. *Cambridge VR* 1:143; 2:78, 505–06; Savage 1860–62, 1:397–98.
2. *Sewall Diary* 1:420.
3. *Sibley's Harvard Graduates* 2:320–23; Roberts 1895, 1:335–36.
4. "Hull Diaries," 162–63; *Sewall Diary* 1:532.
5. *Suffolk Deeds* 13:62, 131–32.
6. *Sewall Diary* 1:77. An entry in Sewall's letter book, "Place £5. laid out for Sam. Clark, to my account," is dated 24 February 1690/91 and suggests that Sewall may have taken care of some of Clarke's financial transactions for him while he was at sea; *Sewall Letter Book* 1:116.
7. RC 1:160.
8. SCD 18:243–46; RC 9:85, 243; MCD 18:543; Thwing; Savage 1860–62, 3:333, 337–38; Roberts 1895, 1:208.
9. RC 9:189, 201.
10. RC 9:246; RC 24:6, 20; Thwing; will of Hannah Clarke, SCPR 19:278–80.
11. MCD 18:43–44.
12. MCPR 10:97–100.
13. *Sewall Diary* 1:532.
14. The mark on the example at MMA is illustrated in Flynt/Fales 1968, 184; two additional examples in private collections are recorded in the YUAG files.

Samuel Clarke
b. 1663

The Apprentice Register of the Goldsmiths' Company of London contains the following entry dated 10 September 1679: "I Samuell Clarke the sonn of Daniell Clarke of Topsfield in New England Carpenter doe put my selfe Apprentice unto Thomas Price Citizen and Goldsmith of London for the terme of seaven years." Samuel had been born in Topsfield on 5 December 1663 to Daniel Clarke.[1]

The records at Goldsmiths' Hall indicate that Samuel Clarke never received the freedom of the Goldsmiths' Company, which would have been necessary had he planned on staying and working in London as a principal. Thus we do not know if he completed his training.[2]

The will of Samuel's father, Daniel (d. 1690), dated 10 January 1688, suggests that Samuel stayed on in England after his apprenticeship: "Item I give and bequeath to my Son Samuell Clarke in England ten shillings in silver."[3] Samuel's brothers John and Humphrey are mentioned in the will, and a fourth brother, Daniel, was bequeathed a silver cup.

Although the Clarke family figures often in the early town records of Topsfield, no other information about Samuel Clarke has been found. Like Thomas Higginson (q.v.) of Salem, whose London training was coming to a close just as Clarke's was beginning, Samuel Clarke is an unusual instance of an individual from Massachusetts who received his training in England but who apparently never practiced his craft on this side of the Atlantic. GWRW

1. Apprentice Book 3, fol. 87r, Worshipful Company of Goldsmiths, London. Clarke's apprenticeship was first noticed by Patricia E. Kane, and a copy of the document was provided by Susan M. Hare, librarian of Goldsmiths' Hall. *Topsfield VR*, 25.
2. Letters to the author from Susan M. Hare, 6 and 25 August 1981.
3. ECPR, docket 5415.

Thomas Clark(e)
1725–81

A

B

Thomas Clark(e) has sometimes been confused with an immigrant clockmaker and watchmaker from London with the same name who arrived in Boston in 1764 (q.v. Appendix A). The goldsmith Thomas Clark was born in Marblehead, Massachusetts, on 19 July 1725 to Thomas Clark, a tailor, and Mary Merritt, who married there on 14 November 1722.[1] The goldsmith's paternal grandfather was Thomas Clark (1671–1729), a tailor of Ipswich, Massachusetts.[2]

Clark probably began his apprenticeship about 1739 and would have completed it about 1746. This training probably took place in Boston because he married there soon after finishing and is described in documents as being a Boston resident. The goldsmith published his intention to marry Mary Tyley (1726–85), the daughter of Thomas (b. 1691) and Catherine Tyley, at Boston on 12 October 1749.[3] Deeds from 1754, in which Clark quitclaimed interest to property in Marblehead, identify him as a Boston goldsmith.[4] Clark and his wife had a number of children, one of whom, a six-year-old son, was drowned in 1766 when he fell from a wharf in the south part of town, according to a notice in the *Boston News-Letter* of 25 July.

In the early 1760s Clark may have worked in association with Benjamin Pierpont (q.v.), another goldsmith who was established in the south part of Boston. Clark received payment on behalf of Pierpont for jewelry he sold to the Salem, Massachusetts, silversmith John Touzell (q.v.) on 12 April and on 24 and 25 September 1762, and on 14 August 1764. The latter receipt was witnessed by Benjamin Loring, possibly the silversmith (q.v.).[5]

Francis Hill Bigelow's notes state that Clark's shop was on the site of the Lamb Tavern but do not cite a source.[6] On 3 June 1779 Clark purchased from Daniel Parks of Boston a piece of land in Marlborough Street "with a Shop standing thereon."[7] The Boston tax list of 1780 includes Thomas Clark, "Goold Smith," in ward 12 with a poll of one.[8] Clark conducted his business at this shop until he himself drowned in Boston harbor on 24 August 1781. The notice of his death, which appeared in the *Boston Gazette*, related that four people had been fishing and in returning to town their canoe overturned. The account mistakenly gives Clark's name as John.[9] The shop and land were valued at £93 in his inventory, taken on 10 September 1781. The detailed enumeration of his tools and wares is exceptional:

Shop Tools as follows Viz.ᵗ			
Small pᵣ Shop Bellows	1.	16	—
Molding Box	0.	9	—
Large Anvill Wᵗ 50ˡᵇ	3.	12	—
Small Spoon Teast	1.	8	—
5 Hammers	0.	12	—
Small Shop Vice	—	12	—
Hand Vice & Sparhawk	—	6	—
3 pᵣ Plyers. 1 pᵣ Shares. 1 pᵣ Screw Cumpasˢᵉˢ } & a Brass Blow Pipe	—	6	—
An old Spoon Teast	—	9	—
A Ring swage	—	4	—
A Large Skillet for Silver	—	18	—
2 pᵣ Goldsmiths Tongs	—	4	—
Hollowing Stamp	—	12	—
pᵣ Casting Flasks & Screws	—	8	—
A Filing Pan	—	4	—
2 pᵣ Old Scales & Small waits	—	12	—
Old Files, Punches, Charges &c	—	8	—
Spoon Punches, Chissells &c	1.	4	—
18ˡᵇ Old Pewter & Lead	—	12	—
Boiling Pan, 2 Malletts, Copper mold } Borax Box	—	9	—
An old Glass Case	—	6	—
Goldsmiths Ware Viz.ᵗ			
1 Tareen Ladel 7 1/2 Ounces	3.	8.	0
13 Large Spoons Chased 25 ounces	10.	5.	8
17 Plain dᵒ 32 1/2 ounces	12.	10.	8
61 Tea Spoons 21 ounces 16 penneyweight	10.	6.	4
Gold Beeds 1 ounce 7 penney weight	8.	12.	9
Pᵣ Silver Spurs 3 Ounces	1.	12	—
1 Silver Salt 3 ounces 16 penneyweight	1.	5.	4
1 Silver Whistel 2 ounces 12 penneyweight	1.	4	—
2 Desert Spoons 1 3/4 Ounces	—	17	—
1 pᵣ Sugar Tongues 1 ounce 6 penneyweight	—	16	—
1 pᵣ Sugar Tongues & 2 shovels. 1 oz. 9 Pw.	—	16	—
4 Gold Rings 4 pen:ʸ Wᵗ 13 Grains	1.	8.	—
2 pᵣ Gold Buttons 6 pennʸ wᵗ 15 Grains	2.	0	4¹/₂
Gold Earings & Wyers 4 penney wᵗ 15 grains	1.	9.	5
Garnet Ring	—	12	—
1 pᵣ Silver Buckels	1.	4	—
1 pᵣ dᵒ 18/ 1 pᵣ dᵒ 15/ 1 pᵣ dᵒ 13/ 1 pᵣ dᵒ 12/	2.	18	—
1 pᵣ dᵒ with Silver Flukes & Tongues	—	18	—
3 pᵣ Knee Buckells	—	15	—

6 Broaches	— 12 —
3 Thimbles	— 6 —
7 p.ʳ Silver Buttons	— 14 —
2 Hair Pins & 2 Stay Hooks	— 8 —
1 p.ʳ Shoe Clasps	3. 6
4 Gold Broaches unfinished	1. 3. 4
8 p.ʳ Buckells without Hitches & Tongues	4. 12 —
Old Gold	2. 2 —
Old Silver Fillings &c 65 1/2 Ounces	21. 0. 9

Benjamin Pierpont and Joseph Loring (q.v.) appraised the estate.[10]

Thomas Clark, probably the goldsmith's son, was the executor of the estate, and he advertised in the *Independent Chronicle* on 13 September 1781, "All Persons indebted to, or that have any just demands against the estate of Mr. Thomas Clarke, late of Boston goldsmith, deceased, are desired to settle the same with Thomas Clarke, administrator, who has for sale a number of valuable articles in the goldsmith way, goldsmith's tools, &c., Roxbury. September 13, 1781." The number of spoons, pieces of jewelry, and other small wares listed in his glass display case leads to the conclusion that Clark ran a productive shop, yet only about ten pieces of his silver have been identified. A spoon in the Ineson-Bissell Collection bears an initial and surname mark in a shaped rectangle (A). An initials mark (B) has been attributed to him because it is found on a spoon with engraving and shell drop similar to those on spoons with the initial and surname mark. His mark has sometimes been confused with that of Joseph Clark, Jr. (q.v.).

The *Massachusetts Centinel* of 21 September 1785 had the following notice: "Died Mrs. Mary Clarke, widow of the late Mr. Thomas Clarke of this town, Goldsmith. Her funeral is to be to-morrow afternoon, precisely at 5 o'clock, from her House near Wheeler's point, at which time her relatives and friends are requested to attend." The goldsmith is thought to have had a son Joseph who followed his father's trade, although no record of his birth has been found.[11] PEK

SURVIVING OBJECTS

	Mark	Inscription	Patron	Date	Reference	Owner
Tablespoon	A*	A8H		ca. 1775	YUAG files	
Tablespoon	A†	EB (later) (+)		ca. 1765	DAPC 70.1261	WM
Tablespoon	A*	EL		ca. 1770	Buhler 1972, no. 234 (as Joseph Clark)	MFAB
Tablespoon	A	AH		ca. 1760		OYHS
Teaspoon	A*	AV		ca. 1755		YUAG
Teaspoon	A*	MB		ca. 1750		YUAG
Teaspoon	A*	A/CS		ca. 1755		YUAG
Teaspoon	A*	RB		ca. 1770	Eitner 1976, no. 51	
Teaspoon	A*	RA/to/SB		ca. 1770		HD
Teaspoon	B†	OP		ca. 1780	DAPC 74.1361	WM

1. Flynt/Fales 1968, 184; Belden 1980, 111; RC 29:261; *Marblehead VR* 1:104; ECD 100:86–87; *Marblehead VR* 2:290.

2. ECPR, docket 5528; ECD 56:195–96.

3. RC 28:292; *Church in Brattle Square*, 147; *Index of Obituaries, 1784–1840*, 1:951; RC 9:197.

4. ECD 100:87–88.

5. English-Touzel-Hathorne Papers, box 4, folder 5, PEM.

6. Bigelow-Phillips files, 1321.

7. SCD 130:164–65.

8. "Assessors' 'Taking-Books,'" 59.

9. *Boston Gazette*, 27 August 1781.

10. SCPR 80:587–90.

11. Flynt/Fales 1968, 183.

Ephraim Cobb
1708–75

A

Ephraim Cobb was born in Barnstable, Massachusetts, on 8 December 1708, the son of John Cobb (1677–1754) and Hannah Lothrop (1682–1747), who were both of Barnstable and who married there.[1] His paternal grandparents were James Cobb (1634–95) of Plymouth, Massachusetts, and Sarah Lewes or Lewis (1643–1735) of Barnstable.[2] His maternal grandparents were John Lothrop (b. 1659) of Plymouth and Mary Cole (b. 1658) of Eastham, Massachusetts.[3]

Ephraim Cobb would have begun his apprenticeship about 1722 and completed his term of service by 1729. Moody Russell (q.v.) of Barnstable, fourteen years his senior, may have been his master. The same year in which Cobb may have completed his apprenticeship he wed Margaret Gardner (ca. 1713–96) of Brookline and later Yarmouth, Massachusetts, on 7 January 1729/30 in Yarmouth.[4]

Shortly after his marriage, Cobb left his family enclave in Barnstable (and the likely competition from Moody Russell) to establish himself in Plymouth. His first child, Susanna, was born in Plymouth in 1730/31.[5] He may also have taken Nathaniel Barstow (q.v.) from the nearby town of Scituate as an apprentice at about that time. In thirteen deeds transacted by Cobb between 1733/34 and 1773, he named himself goldsmith or silversmith.[6] In 1733/34 Cobb purchased land and a house in Plymouth from James Shurtleff but mortgaged the property twice, in 1735 and 1738 (in one instance to his father).[7]

Between 1737 and 1739, Cobb performed a variety of services for Capt. John Winslow. These modest tasks included mending buttons, needles, locks, and instruments. Cobb also repaired a gold ring and provided shoe buckles for Winslow:

November 1737 Capt[n] John Winslo Jr.

1737:	to balance an old Acount 2/6 two Silver Butons 9/9	0–	12	–3
Decmb[r]:	to mending a buton & Lock 4/6 Cash 10/	0–	14:	6
1738	to mending Instrumints /6 to Cash 40/ Dito 30/	3–	10	=6
	to a ferel 3/ mending Instrumants 2/6	0–	5–	6
febery	to 3[d] and a half, worck at your Cd 35/ 7 days Dito 91/	6–	6–	0
1738/9	to mending 2 gold Rings 3/ Cea & butons 6/6	0	9	6
1739	to 2 od Shu buckels 64/pipe 1/ mending butons & neadels 8/6	3	13	6
		£15–	11–	9

C[r] gold   2/6[8]

In 1738 the thirty-one-year-old goldsmith quarreled violently with Thomas Jackson, a mariner, and was charged with disturbing the peace.[9] This episode may have marked a turning point in Cobb's life, for thereafter he became a model citizen of Plymouth, taking on a variety of public roles, including that of hogreeve, juror, surveyor of highways, warden, and tithingman.[10]

Within a few months of the death of his father in 1754, Ephraim Cobb sold his house and land on Main Street in Plymouth and returned to Barnstable, where he continued his public service in many of the same offices between 1758 and 1763.[11] In 1764 he served as the administrator of the estate of Joseph Sylvester.[12] Three deeds he transacted between 1756 and 1773 identify him as a yeoman and suggest that he also engaged in agriculture. His mark for livestock, "a crop on the left ear and two holes in the same ear," recorded in 1762, substantiates this activity.[13] Yet the Massachusetts tax valuation of 1771 showed Cobb to have no cattle of any kind but twenty pounds' worth of merchandise, possibly silver.[14]

Cobb wrote his will on 30 August 1775 and in it left "To my Beloved Wife Margaret the Use & Improvement of my Estate Real & Personal as Long as She Lives." The estate was to be divided equally among their daughters at Margaret's death. Following Cobb's death on 6 September 1775, Margaret was appointed executor of the estate on 4 December 1775. No inventory or valuation of the estate at the time of Cobb's death survives. Margaret petitioned the court in 1791 to sell a portion of the estate in order to maintain her property; following her death in 1796, the remainder of the estate was appraised at $933.33.[15]

Cobb's only known touchmark is ECobb in a rectangle (A). The initial and surname marks E.Cobb and E COBB in rectangles have also been recorded, but examples have not been located.[16] A spurious mark E. Cobb is known.[17] The variety and number of forms that have survived demonstrate Cobb's skill as well as the relative wealth of the Cape Cod population that enabled him to make such ambitious pieces. The history of ownership of a spout cup in the Lothrop family and Anna Palmer's gift of a tankard to the Plymouth First Parish suggest some family and church patronage as well. Moreover, it is tempting to speculate that the pair of gold buttons reported lost in the *Boston Evening-Post* of 22 December 1746—buttons engraved with the letters "R.G." and having a maker's mark E.C.— may have been Cobb's work. An EC in a rectangle has sometimes been attributed to him but is more consistently considered Ebenezer Chittenden's of Guilford and New Haven, Connecticut.[18] JJF

SURVIVING OBJECTS

	Mark	Inscription	Patron	Date	Reference	Owner
Porringer	A	B/IE; EL to PL (later)	Jonathan and Elizabeth Barnes	ca. 1740	Sotheby's, 27 January 1989, lot 917	
Salver	A†	Anna Leonard	Anna (Tisdale) Leonard	ca. 1730	Buhler/Hood 1970, no. 174	YUAG
Spout cup	A	L/IE; PLB/to/PLH (later)	Isaac and Elizabeth Lothrop	ca. 1740		PS
Sword	A*	none		ca. 1760	Northeast Auctions, 14–15 March 1992, lot 416	WM
Sword	A	crest, a lion rampant; NT; Thomas	N. Thomas	ca. 1760		Navy Museum
Tablespoon	A	A/FK		ca. 1750	YUAG files	
Tablespoon	A	EB		ca. 1750	DAPC 77.2779	
Tablespoon	A*	EF to ST		ca. 1750	DAPC 72.2704	WM

	Mark	Inscription	Patron	Date	Reference	Owner
Tankard	A*	AL; Anna Leonard	Anna (Tisdale) Leonard	ca. 1730	Johnston 1994, 27	CMA
Tankard	A	The.gift.of.Mʳˢ. Anna.Palmer.to. the.Church.In. Plymouth.1737.	Anna Palmer and/or First Parish, Plymouth, Mass.	1737	Jones 1913, 375–76	
Tankard	A	E/HD (+)		ca. 1750	MFA 1906, no. 53	HU

1. *Mayflower Descendant* 3:73; 6:238; 14:225; 32:149; *Plymouth Church Records* 1:404; Kingman 1892, 46; Swift 1888, 1:173.
2. Swift 1888, 1:172; *Mayflower Descendant* 3:73.
3. *Mayflower Descendant* 18:68; 6:238.
4. *Brookline VR*, 29; Kingman 1892, 75, no. 683, reports that at her death she was "aged 85 years," which would place her birth at 1711, as opposed to the year 1713 recorded in *Brookline VR*.
5. *Mayflower Descendant* 15:39.
6. PCD 28:169–70; 31:171; 32:6; 38:186–87, 198; 41:47; 45:31; 48:154; 49:172.
7. PCD 28:169–70; 31:171; 32:6.
8. Ephraim Cobb bill to John Winslow, 1737–39, Winslow Papers, MHS.
9. BCCR, Massachusetts Superior Court of Judicature, Plymouth, Massachusetts, 17 April 1739, fols. 8–9, microfilm, Judicial Archives, Mass. Archives.
10. Plymouth Town Records, 30, 34, 51–52, 54–55, 147, Town Hall, Plymouth, Massachusetts.
11. Barnstable Town Records 2:207, 219, 227, 242, 259, Town Hall, Hyannis, Massachusetts.
12. PCPR, dockets 19992 and 19993.
13. PCD 43:263; 46:7; 57:88; Barnstable Town Records 2:259, Town Hall, Hyannis, Massachusetts.
14. Pruitt 1978, 650–51.
15. PCPR, docket 4510; 24:44–46; 33:5; 34:340; 36:480–81; Kingman 1892, 46, no. 438. Although some scholars suggest that Cobb's death date may be incorrect because he served on committees in 1776, no proof of such activity has been found; see Flynt/Fales 1968, 185.
16. Ensko 1927, 181; Okie 1936, 250; Graham 1936, 16; Ensko 1937, 32.
17. A beaker (383495) at SI.
18. The EC mark appears in French (1917) 1967, 28; Ensko 1927, 181; Ensko 1937, 32; Ensko 1948, 172; Graham 1936, 16; Okie 1936, 250; Thorn 1949, 52; Belden 1980, 106; Buhler/Hood 1970, no. 351; Flynt/Fales 1968, 181. There is a pair of spoons marked EC in a rectangle at MMA and a related spoon at the Webb-Deane-Stevens Museum in Wethersfield, Connecticut, all engraved "HG/to/MT." Stylistically these relate to spoons marked EC at CMA (40.174) and at YUAG (1985.84.406 and .407 and 1985.86.125–27). None of the spoons has a provenance that relates them to either Cobb or Chittenden, and none corresponds stylistically to either silversmith's other known work.

John Coburn
1724–1803

A

B

John Coburn was born in York, Maine, on 25 May 1724 to the tailor Ebenezer (1675/76–1749) and Sarah (Storer) Coburn (1682–1770).[1] His paternal grandparents were Robert Coburn (Colburn) (1646–1701) of Ipswich, Massachusetts, and Mary Bishop of Chelmsford, Massachusetts.[2] His mother's parents were Joseph (d. 1729/30) and Hannah (Hill) Storer (b. 1664) of Wells, Maine.[3] Coburn was in Boston by 7 February 1750, when he published his intention to marry Susanna Greenleaf (1722–82), daughter of Rev. Daniel (1679/80–1763) and Elizabeth (Gookin) Greenleaf (1681–1762).[4] Daniel Greenleaf, a graduate of Harvard College (1699), worked as: a physician in Cambridge, Massachusetts, from 1699 to 1701 and 1703 to 1705; a schoolteacher in Portsmouth, New Hampshire, from 1701 to 1703; a minister of the Congregational Church in Yarmouth, Massachusetts, from 1707 to 1728; and proprietor of an apothecary shop in Boston from 1728 until his death.[5] John and Susanna Coburn had

C

D

no children. Following the death of Susanna on 26 February 1782, Coburn married Catharine Vance (ca. 1739–1807) on 16 August 1784 in a ceremony performed by Rev. Joseph Eckley at Old South Church.[6] The bride was the daughter of the Scottish emigrant Hugh Vance and Mary (Clark) Pemberton (b. 1703) of Boston.[7] Coburn attended the Brattle Street Church; family reminiscences state that Rev. Peter Thacher made many visits to the Coburn home between 1785 and 1802 when he was pastor of the Brattle Street Church.[8]

Coburn was related to several prominent Boston silversmiths through the Storer family. His uncle, Rev. Seth Storer, married Mary Coney, daughter of John Coney (q.v.).[9] Coburn's second wife, Catharine (Vance) Coburn, provided another tie to the Coney family as the granddaughter of John Coney's second wife, Mary (Atwater) Clark. Another uncle, Ebenezer Storer, married Mary Edwards, daughter of John Edwards (q.v.).[10] Coburn was also related to the Boston silversmiths Thomas Edwards (q.v.) and Joseph Edwards, Jr. (q.v.), through his aunt, Mary Edwards Storer. Coburn probably served his apprenticeship with Samuel Edwards (q.v.), his aunt's brother. He joined Daniel Parker (q.v.) as a witness to a deed for Edwards on 13 September 1746.[11] Both Parker and Edwards witnessed the bond for the estate administration of Coburn's uncle, Seth Coburn, in 1752.[12] Coburn also served as an appraiser of Edwards's estate in June 1762, with Joseph Bradford and William Simpkins (q.v.).[13] Coburn, in turn, may have trained his nephews David Greenleaf and Seth Storer Coburn (qq.v.) and James Ridgway (q.v.), who married in succession two of Coburn's nieces.

Coburn served the town of Boston in a number of positions between 1751 and 1776. He joined the Artillery Company on 2 April 1751, with Capt. John Phillips and Lt. Thomas Stoddard as sureties. He was promoted to third sergeant of the company the following year. Coburn was selected as a Boston constable in 1753, but declined to serve and paid a fine. He served as a warden in 1772 and a census taker in 1776.[14] Coburn was named in the December 1776 draft ordered by the Massachusetts General Court to select reinforcements for the Continental Army, but he paid the ten-pound fine in lieu of service.[15]

The first professional reference to Coburn appeared in the *Boston News-Letter* on 2 November 1750, when "John Coburn Goldsmith, at the Head of the Town-Dock," advertised that he had received a stolen silver spoon.[16] In April 1755 John and Susanna Coburn purchased a house on Middle Street from the estate of the Boston merchant William Bant for £220. On 1 July of the following year, Coburn arranged a mortgage of £146.13.4 with Ezekiel Goldthwait, executor of the Bant estate, using the Middle Street property as collateral.[17] The mortgage was not paid off until 1768. Coburn's outstanding debt may have influenced his 1756 suit against James Cutler of Cambridge for debts totaling £12.1.8.[18] He had moved to Fish Street by 1764 when his family was among the residents of this street affected by a smallpox epidemic.[19] The Massachusetts tax valuation of 1771 assessed Coburn with one ratable poll and a building valued at an annual rate of £40.[20] In addition, he was credited with one "servant for life" and £60 of merchandise. The silversmith moved to King Street adjoining the Bunch of Grapes Tavern in 1773, when he purchased a large brick house and outbuildings for £1,100 from the Boston merchant John Hunt on 23 July.[21] Coburn paid for this property by borrowing £300 from Ezekiel Goldthwait and £500 from Thomas Bulfinch the following day, loans he repaid in 1786.[22]

Coburn moved out of Boston shortly after the move to King Street. However, he had returned to the city by August 1776, when he advertised in the *New-England Chronicle:*

> JOHN COBURN
> HEREBY informs his Customers and others
> that he has removed into Boston again
> and carries on the Goldsmith's Business at his
> Shop in King-Street, opposite to the American
> Coffee-House; where they may be supplied
> with any Articles in the Goldsmith or Jewellery
> Way, upon the most reasonable Terms — He
> likewise continues to take Gentlemen and
> Ladies, to Board, as usual.
>   N.B. Cash given for old Gold and Silver
> or Gold and Silver-Lace.[23]

Coburn had retained his Middle Street house as a rental property. In October 1782 he sued his tenant Merlino de St. Pry, a Boston merchant, for back rent.[24] Coburn borrowed money against his property in 1784 and 1786, including £300 from the Boston merchant William Phillips, Jr., executor for the estate of Josiah Quincy, Jr., £200 from the Overseers of the Poor, and £100 from Mary Rand.[25] Presumably this money was needed to purchase a brick house in State Street. Coburn advertised his change in residence in the *Massachusetts Gazette* on 24 July 1786:

> John Coburn, of Boston,
> GOLDSMITH,
> INFORMS his friends and customers in
> town and country, that they may be sup-
> plied with every article in the *Goldsmith's Busi-
> ness*, upon the most reasonable terms, at his
> House in State-street; where he has again re-
> moved, — and takes Boarders as usual, and shall
> be extremely obliged to them for their custom.[26]

The Boston directory for 1789 lists Coburn with the occupation of "gentlemen boarders" on State Street, and the directory for 1796 lists him with the identification "gentleman" on State Street.[27] The silversmith sold his rental property on Middle Street in June 1796 to the Boston merchant Nathan Webb for $4,000.[28] On 12 September 1797, he bought a house on Federal Street from the Boston merchant James Magee for $8,200.[29] Six days later he sold the State Street house to the Boston merchant David Sears for $10,666.66.[30] His new residence at 29 Federal Street was valued at $6,000 in the Federal Direct Tax of 1798 and was described as a three-story brick and wooden dwelling comprising 2,770 square feet and forty-seven windows on 7,980 square feet of land.[31] Rev. Amos Smith's memoirs describe the property as a large wooden house with an ell and a cupola "which in those days commanded a view of the harbor" as well as a barn and an extensive garden.[32]

Coburn appeared in the records of the Suffolk County Court of Common Pleas six additional times during the 1780s and 1790s. In July 1783 Coburn initiated a case against Isaac Sears, Pascal Nelson, and Smith and James Jarvis for failure to deliver a chest of tea from Amsterdam.[33] Although the court ruled in favor of the defendants, Coburn filed an appeal. In January 1785, he was the defendant in a case filed by John Hurd of Boston and Joseph Cordis of Charleston [Charlestown?]; Coburn failed to appear in court and was ordered to pay twelve pounds and court costs.[34] Three years later he sued Amos Windship, a Boston physician and apothecary, recovering debts of more than ten pounds and court costs.[35] Windship's countersuit was unsuccessful.[36] The silversmith appeared in two cases in April 1798 to recover debts from William Alline, a Boston gentleman, and Benjamin Alline, an auctioneer.[37]

Since Coburn never had any children, he and his second wife, Catharine (Vance) Coburn, brought her niece Catharine Langdon (b. 1774) of Wiscasset, Maine, into their home to raise, although there was never any formal adoption because her parents were still living. The seven-year-old girl arrived in 1781 and remained with her aunt and uncle throughout their lives.[38] According to Rev. Amos Smith's memoirs, "The domestic, social, educational, and religious advantages which she there enjoyed were of the very best which Boston could supply."[39] The census of 1790 lists Coburn as the head of a household composed of two men over the age of sixteen, four women, and one additional "Free Person," probably a free black or Indian servant.[40] Reverend Smith's memoirs describe Coburn as "a man of the strictest integrity—and uprightness,— conscientious in the highest degree. He was very conservative in his ideas; old fashioned in his tastes; of most exact method, system and regularity in all the conducting of his affairs; a diligent reader of pious books, remarkably careful and cautious as to all he did or said, in temper and disposition uniformly placid, even, kind and considerate—; and everywhere known as a sympathetic, benevolent, hospitable, friendly and good man."[41]

Coburn died on 21 January 1803 at the age of seventy-eight.[42] His will, written on 1 May 1800, was presented for probate on 14 February 1803.[43] "John Coburn of Boston . . . Goldsmith being in good health of Body and through the goodness of God of sound disposing mind and memory" left his "household furniture and Plate of every kind and sort" to his wife, Catharine, along with a life interest in the income from his estate, his portrait, a portrait of his first wife, a portrait taken for Susanna Coburn Ingraham, the "Coat of Arms in Philligree" and two "Cases of Work" made by Susanna Coburn. Coburn specified residual legacies to be paid following his wife's death, including legacies to his wife's sisters, Mary Mason and Sarah Langdon; to the children of William Vance and Sarah Langdon; to Susanna Draper and Sarah Warden, daughters of the silversmith's brother Ebenezer Coburn; to Joseph Coburn and his three children, Ebenezer Coburn, Sarah Ridgway, and Esther Ridgway; to Priscilla Smerdon of Charleston, South Carolina, and Seth Storer Coburn, respectively, the granddaughter and son of Seth Coburn, deceased; to Elizabeth Courtney, wife of James Courtney of Charleston, South Carolina; and to the silversmith's sisters Mary Simpson of York, Maine, widow of Daniel Simpson, and Hannah Hammond of Kittery, Maine, widow of George Hammond. His kinswoman Susanna Coburn Ingraham, daughter of Duncan Ingraham, received the portraits, coat of arms, and needlework after Catharine Coburn's death. Coburn appointed his wife Catharine and friend Gen. John Winslow as executors. An inventory of the estate valued the silversmith's possessions at $14,699.59 and listed goldsmith's tools valued at $5 and plate worth $162.25.[44]

Catharine Coburn continued to live in Federal Street until her death on 14 July 1807, at the age of sixty-eight.[45] The following August, John Winslow, the remaining executor of Coburn's will, sold the house on Federal Street at public auction, where it was purchased for $9,150 by Margaret Magee, a

Roxbury widow.[46] The executor's account for 18 January 1808 assessed Coburn's total estate at $12,338.40, including the sale of the real estate.[47]

The estate administration of Spencer Phips of Cambridge, Massachusetts, shows that in 1760 Coburn was paid twelve pounds for funeral rings.[48] Three years later, Coburn produced an unspecified quantity of silver plate for Nathaniel Ropes at a cost of more than £33 as two receipts record:

Boston Feb^{ry}: 2^d 1763
Received of Nath^{ll} Ropes Esqr twenty four pounds
twelve Shillings Lawfull Money toward Some
Plate which I am to Make for him as p^r memo^{randum}
£24:12:0
Law^{ll} M^o P^r Jno: Coburn

Boston Feb^{ry}: 15th 1763
Received of the Honr^{ble}: Nath^{ll}: Ropes Esqr
Nine pounds Eighteen Shillings Law^{ll} Money
on Acc^t of Some plate wh^{ch} I am to Make
for him   P^r Jno: Coburn
£9 = 18 = 0[49]

Coburn's transactions with Paul Revere, Jr. (q.v.), span more than a decade, from November 1762 until August 1774. While he commissioned a selection of specialized forms from Revere, including a pair of chased creampots, a pair of snuffboxes, and a sword guard, Coburn primarily utilized Revere's skills as an engraver. Coburn paid his colleague to add crests, arms, and initials to a variety of silver forms, including spoons, teapots, coffeepots, and dishes. Revere's daybook records the following transaction with Coburn on 19 November 1762:

Mr John Couborn   D^r
To two Silver Chased Cream Pots   w$^{t\ oz}$ 9:5

To The Making   2 13 4
Mr John Couborn   C^r
                                            oz
By Silver Receiv^d }   4..17
                    }   3..18
                    oz 8..15[50]

The first of the transactions in which Coburn paid Revere for engraving occurred four years later on 10 June 1766:

Mr John Cobourn   D^r
To Making two Snuff Boxes at 13^s/4 Each   1 6 8
To the Silver   Weigh^t 3^{oz}:5 =
To Engraving a Tea Pot   0 9 4
Mr John Couborn   C^r
By Silver Receiv^d 3^{oz}:13^{dt}
By Cash   1 6 8[51]

Further transactions for engraving followed on 5 August 1772.

Mr John Coburn   D^r
To Engraving Arms on Coffee pot   0 14 8
To Dito On Tea pot   0 10 0
To Engraving 8 Crests at 8^d 5 4[52]

On 1 December that year Revere credited Coburn for twenty ounces and five pennyweights of silver.[53] In the winter of 1773 Coburn apparently had a commission for a teakettle and called on Revere's services for the teakettle's frame and burner and its engraving. On 11 February 1773 Revere recorded,

M[r] John Couborn D[r]
To a Silver Frame & lamp [oz]20
To the Making[54]

Slightly more than a month later on 18 March 1773 the daybook shows:

M[r] John Couborn D[r]
To Engraving Arms on tea kittle   0 16 0
To Dito on Tank[d]   10[55]

Later that spring on 10 May 1773, Coburn had Revere engrave crests on spoons:

M[r] John Coburn   D[r]
To 6 Crests on Large Spoons at 8[d]   4   8
To 6 Dito on Tea Spoons   3

A similar order for large spoons, teaspoons, and sugar tongs appears in the daybook on 15 June 1773.[56] Later that year on 16 October 1773, Revere's daybook records that Coburn owed £3.7.7 for cash received.[57] The final transaction between Coburn and Revere recorded in the daybook occurred on 25 August 1774.

M[r] John Couborn   D[r]
To Engravin Crests & two letters on 42 Dishes }
                          & plates at 5/[d] }   17   6
To Engraving 24 Crest on Spoons at 6[d]   12   0
To making a Guard to Swoard Silver added 16/[tw] 6   8
                                                  5   4[58]

The diverse assortment of holloware and flatware forms that Coburn produced vividly demonstrates his versatility and skill. A large number of his silver objects as well as a few small gold items survive. Four marks are associated with this silversmith, J.COBURN in a rectangle (A); I COBURN in a rectangle (B); and two initials marks (C, D). Mark (A) is by far the most prevalent and appears to have been used throughout his career. In addition to making silver objects for several churches in Connecticut, Maine, and Massachusetts, Coburn served a distinguished New England clientele, including members of the Hancock, Salisbury, and Welles families as well as Storer relatives. DAF

SURVIVING OBJECTS

	Mark	Inscription	Patron	Date	Reference	Owner
Baptismal basin	A	The Gift of M[r] Comfort Starr March[t]/In Danbury Connecticutt N:E/ to the Church of Christ in/Said Town Aug[t] 25, 1753	Comfort Starr and/or First Congregational Church, Danbury, Conn.	1753	Jones 1913, 135–36	
Beaker	A	The Gift of Jona-than Nicholls Jun[r]/	Jonathan Nicholls, Sr., for First Congrega-	1763	Jones 1913, 476	

	Mark	Inscription	Patron	Date	Reference	Owner
		to the First Church of Christ/in Reading Feb.^{ry} 10th/1763	tional Church, Wakefield, Mass.			
Cann	A	FP		ca. 1760	Buhler 1965, 70–71	HMA
Cann	A†	ES	Elizabeth (Storer) Smith	ca. 1755	Buhler 1972, no. 264	MFAB
Cann	A	Barrett arms impaling Gerrish arms; IAG; The Gift of the Honble Jos. Gerrish Esqr to Samuel Barrett 1761	Joseph Gerrish and/or Samuel Barrett	1761	Buhler 1956, no. 20	
Cann (altered to milk pot)	A*	C		ca. 1780		YUAG
Cann (mate below)	A	Gardner arms, gules a chevron or between 3 griffins' heads erased argent, a chief embattled or, and crest, a griffin's head erased	Samuel and Elizabeth (Clarke) (Winslow) Gardner	ca. 1760	Buhler 1972, no. 265	MFAB
Cann (mate above)	A	Gardner arms, gules a chevron or between 3 griffins' heads erased argent, a chief embattled or, and crest, a griffin's head erased; G/SE	Samuel and Elizabeth (Clarke) (Winslow) Gardner	ca. 1760	Sotheby Parke Bernet, 30 April–3 May 1980, lot 185	
Cann	A	Ex Dono/Juvenum Aliquorum/Rev^{DO}: Samueli Deane/Pastori Fidelissi/Mo. 1775 (+)	twenty-one young men of First Parish, Falmouth, Maine	1775	Jones 1913, 377–78	
Two canns	A	The Gift of/Edwd Pynchon Esqr/To the first Church/of CHRIST in/SPRINGFIELD	First Church of Christ, Springfield, Mass., for Edward Pynchon	ca. 1770	Jones 1913, 456	
Cann	A	Barrett arms, ermine 3 lions rampant on a fess azure, and crest, a lion passant	Barrett family	ca. 1765	Quimby 1995, no. 35	WM
Cann	A	TW	Thomas Welles	ca. 1760		CHS
Cann	A	?		ca. 1760	*Antiques* 132 (July 1987): 98	
Cann	A or B	?		ca. 1765	Parke-Bernet, 20 October 1957, lot 30	
Cann	A or B	Orne arms, a chevron sable between 3 hunting horns sable, and crest, a unicorn; RO	Rebecca Orne	ca. 1765	Christie's, 31 May 1986, lot 58	

	Mark	Inscription	Patron	Date	Reference	Owner
Cann	A *or* B	Orne arms, a chevron sable between 3 hunting horns sable, and crest, a unicorn; EOP	Orne family	ca. 1765	Christie's, 31 May 1986, lot 58	
Cann	A *or* B	S/IA		ca. 1770	Christie's, 16 June 1984, lot 69	
Cann	A *or* B	F/EM	Enoch and Mary (Wright) Freeman	ca. 1750	YUAG files	
Cann	A *or* B	MT		ca. 1760	YUAG files	
Cann	?	unidentified engraving (later)	Anne Shelton	ca. 1749	YUAG files	
Caster	A	Salisbury crest, a bird; SS	Stephen Salisbury	ca. 1765	Buhler 1979, no. 28	WAM
Two casters	A	MT	Mary (Toppan) Pickman	ca. 1762	Buhler 1972, no. 269	MFAB
Two casters	A	MB		ca. 1760	Christie's, 22 June 1994, lot 69	
Caster (part of Welles service 1)	A*	TW	Thomas Welles	ca. 1755	Flynt/Fales 1968, 136–38	HD
Caster (part of Welles service 2)	A	TW	Thomas Welles	ca. 1755	Hammerslough/ Feigenbaum 1958–73, 2:86b	WA
Caster	C	none	John Coburn (?)	ca. 1750	Buhler 1972, no. 260	MFAB
Coffeepot	A*	Barrett arms, ermine 3 lions rampant on a fess azure, and crest, a lion passant	John and Sarah (Gerrish) Barrett	ca. 1765	*Antiques* 92 (September 1967): 335	SFCAI
Coffeepot	A	Symmes arms, ermine 3 increscents gules, and crest, a sun in splendor; O (later)	Symmes family	ca. 1755	Buhler 1972, no. 263	MFAB
Communion dish (mates below)	A	Hancock arms, gules a dexter hand couped, on a chief or 3 cocks, and crest, a demi-griffin; The Gift of the Hon[ble] THOMAS HANCOCK ESQ[R]/to the CHURCH in Brattle Street Boston 1764	Brattle Street Church, Boston, for Thomas Hancock	1764	Buhler 1972, no. 272	MFAB
Communion dish (mates above and below)	A	Hancock arms, gules a dexter hand couped, on a chief or 3 cocks, and crest, a demi-griffin; The Gift of the Hon[ble]	Brattle Street Church, Boston, for Thomas Hancock	1764	Buhler 1972, 1:316	SI

	Mark	Inscription	Patron	Date	Reference	Owner
		THOMAS HANCOCK ESQ^R/to the CHURCH in Brattle Street Boston 1764				
Communion dish (mates above)	A	Hancock arms, gules a dexter hand couped, on a chief or 3 cocks, and crest, a demi-griffin; The Gift of the Honble THOMAS HANCOCK ESQ^R/to the CHURCH in Brattle Street Boston 1764	Brattle Street Church, Boston, for Thomas Hancock	1764	Buhler 1972, 1:316	
Creampot (part of Welles service 1)	A	TW	Thomas Welles	ca. 1755	Flynt/Fales 1968, 136–38	HD
Creampot (part of Welles service 2)	A*	TW	Thomas Welles	ca. 1755	Hammerslough/ Feigenbaum 1958–73, 2:86b	WA
Creampot	A	SB	Sarah Barrett	ca. 1765	YUAG files	
Creampot	A*	MG		ca. 1765	YUAG files	
Creampot	A*	W/AE	Aaron and Elizabeth (Hall) Wait	ca. 1780	Johnston 1994, 28	CMA
Creampot	A*	none		ca. 1755	Johnston 1994, 27	CMA
Creampot (altered to mustard pot)	A*	EB (later)		ca. 1770	Eitner 1976, no. 52	
Creampot	A or B	W/WR	William and Rebecca White	ca. 1760	YUAG files	
Creampot	?	HG		ca. 1760	*Silver Supplement* 1973, no. 20	
Cup	A	unidentified crest, a stag's head; RR (later)		ca. 1760	YUAG files	
Ladle	A*	unidentified crest, a swan rising; ECy to SCy		ca. 1760		YUAG
Ladle	C	JMC		ca. 1785		BM
Marrow scoop	A*	W changed to S/EM		ca. 1770	Johnston 1994, 28	CMA
Mourning ring (gold, attrib.)	none	T:BARTON:/ ESQ.OB·APR/ 28:1751·AE 71	Thomas Barton	1751	Buhler 1972, no. 276	MFAB
Mourning ring (gold, attrib.)	none	HON. B/PICKMAN/ OB.20 AUG/1773·AE 66	Benjamin Pickman	1773	Buhler 1972, no. 277	MFAB
Nutmeg grater	A	Greenleaf crest, a bird with a sprig in its beak; SG	Susannah (Greenleaf) Coburn	ca. 1750	Buhler 1972, no. 261	MFAB

	Mark	Inscription	Patron	Date	Reference	Owner
Porringer	A	D/GL		ca. 1765	*Antiques* 98 (August 1970): 288	
Porringer	A	CW	Catherine [Katharine] (Chandler) Willard	ca. 1760	Buhler 1972, no. 266	MFAB
Porringer	A*	M/EP		ca. 1770		PEM
Porringer	A	M/TA		ca. 1750	*Moore Collection* 1980, no. 133	
Two porringers	?	MG		ca. 1760	Sotheby Parke Bernet, 6–8 November 1975, lot 612	
Two salts (mates below)	A*	P/BM	Benjamin and Mary (Toppan) Pickman	ca. 1762	Hammerslough/ Feigenbaum 1958–73, 1:47	WA
Two salts (mates above)	A	P/BM	Benjamin and Mary (Toppan) Pickman	ca. 1762	Buhler 1972, no. 268	MFAB
Two salts	A*	unidentified crest, a bird rising from a ducal coronet		ca. 1770		HD
Two salts	A	W/AE		ca. 1765	DAPC 72.2314	DIA
Two salt spoons	A/B (?)	?		ca. 1755	Buhler 1972, appendix no. 12	MFAB
Salt spoon	D†	MT		ca. 1760	DAPC 73.1167	WM
Two salt spoons (attrib.)	none	BP	Benjamin Pickman	ca. 1762	Buhler 1972, no. 270	MFAB
Salver	A	Barrett arms, ermine 3 lions rampant on a fess azure, and crest, a lion passant; DH to SB	Dorothy Hancock and/ or Sarah Barrett	ca. 1765	Buhler 1956, no. 19	
Salver	A	Storer arms, 3 quatrefoils on a chevron engrailed gules between 3 mullets, and crest, a talbot's head	Ebenezer Storer	ca. 1750	Buhler 1972, no. 258	MFAB
Two sauceboats	A	SH on one	Woodbury family (?)	ca. 1750	Christie's, 21–22 January 1994, lot 115	
Sauceboat	A	none		ca. 1760	*Moore Collection* 1980, no. 134	
Sauceboat	A or B	MB to MT		ca. 1760	YUAG files	
Saucepan	A	The Gift/of/Mary Storer/to/Isaac Smith Junr/May 7th 1749 (+)	Mary Storer for Isaac Smith, Jr.	1749	Buhler 1960, no. 19	MFAB

	Mark	Inscription	Patron	Date	Reference	Owner
Spout cup	A*	W/WR	William and Rebecca Winthrop	ca. 1750	Hammerslough/ Feigenbaum 1958–73, 1:42	WA
Stock buckle (gold)	C *or* D	none		ca. 1770	Hammerslough/ Feigenbaum 1958–73, 2:96	
Strainer	A	none		ca. 1765	Avery 1920, no. 93	MMA
Strainer	A	EOP	Esther (Orne) Paine	ca. 1775		MFAB
Strainer	A	MCB		ca. 1775	*Bulletin DIA* 24 (1944): 21	DIA
Strainer	B	none		ca. 1770	Jones 1974, 478	HMA
Sugar bowl	A	S/IE	Isaac and Elizabeth (Storer) Smith	ca. 1746	Buhler 1972, no. 257	MFAB
Sugar bowl	A*	B/TA (?; erased); AP (later)		ca. 1755	Buhler/Hood 1970, no. 201	YUAG
Sugar bowl	A	Orne arms, a chevron sable between 3 hunting horns sable, and crest, a unicorn; RO	Rebecca (Orne) Cabot	ca. 1765	Buhler 1972, no. 273	MFAB
Sugar tongs	C†	LCS (later)		ca. 1765	Buhler 1972, no. 274	MFAB
Sugar tongs	C	none		ca. 1775	YUAG files	
Sugar tongs (attrib.)	none	F/EM	Enoch and Mary (Wright) Freeman	ca. 1750	Warren 1975, no. 319	BBC
Sugar tongs (attrib.)	none	none	Benjamin Pickman	ca. 1762	Buhler 1972, no. 271	MFAB
Tablespoon	A*	TW/WC		ca. 1770		SI
Tablespoon	A	MT		ca. 1765	Quimby 1995, no. 36a	WM
Tablespoon	A	CB/to/SL		ca. 1765	Quimby 1995, no. 36b	WM
Eleven tablespoons	A	Codman crest, a dove with an olive branch	Codman family	ca. 1770	YUAG files	
Tablespoon	A	P/IM		ca. 1760	YUAG files	
Two tablespoons	B†	Chandler crest, a pelican in her piety	Chandler family	ca. 1760	Johnston 1994, 29	CMA
Tankard	A*	Y/IR; Street (later)		ca. 1760	Buhler/Hood 1970, no. 202	YUAG
Tankard	A	unidentified engraving (later)		ca. 1760	Sotheby Parke Bernet, 17 November 1981, lot 180	
Tankard	A	MSC		ca. 1785	Sotheby's, 27 and 29 January 1983, lot 127	

	Mark	Inscription	Patron	Date	Reference	Owner
Tankard	A	?		ca. 1760	Sotheby Parke Bernet, 17 November 1981, lot 181	
Tankard	A*	IM/to/MD; SCD, TD (later)		ca. 1750	*Moore Collection* 1980, no. 132	
Tankard	A	G/ES; BG (later)		ca. 1765	Buhler 1972, no. 275	MFAB
Tankard	A	HW (+)		ca. 1760	Sotheby's, 27–28 June 1985, lot 50	
Tankard	?	?		ca. 1765	*Antiques* 69 (May 1956): back cover	
Teapot	A	unidentified arms, ermine a saltire (gules?); H. Lewis (later)		ca. 1750	Davidson 1971, 840	CAM
Teapot	A*	Gardner arms, gules a chevron or between 3 griffins' heads erased argent, a chief embattled argent, and crest, a griffin's head erased (+)	Samuel and Margaret (Gardner) Barton	ca. 1764	Flynt/Fales 1968, 134–36	HD
Teapot (part of Welles service 1)	A	Welles arms, a bend gules between 3 fleur-de-lis, and crest, a hound's head; TW	Thomas Welles	ca. 1755	Flynt/Fales 1968, 136–38	HD
Teapot (part of Welles service 2)	A	Welles arms, a bend gules between 3 fleur-de-lis, and crest, a hound's head; TW	Thomas Welles	ca. 1755	Hammerslough/ Feigenbaum 1958–73, 1:74	WA
Teapot	A*	erased		ca. 1752	*Bulletin DIA* 14 (May 1935):109–11	DIA
Teapot	A*	GHLD (later)		ca. 1755	Warren 1975, no. 309	BBC
Teapot	A	Gardner arms, a chevron vert between 3 griffins' heads erased, and crest, a griffin's head erased; SG	Samuel Gardner	ca. 1750	Buhler 1972, no. 262	MFAB
Teapot	A*	Orne arms, a chevron gules between 3 hunting horns, and crest, a unicorn's head; O/TR	Timothy and Rebecca (Taylor) Orne	ca. 1750	Conger/ Rollins 1991, no. 191 (as mark B)	USDS
Teapot	A	Pickman arms, 2 battle-axes in saltire be-	Love (Rawlins) Pickman	ca. 1762	Buhler 1972, no. 267	MFAB

	Mark	Inscription	Patron	Date	Reference	Owner
		tween 4 martlets; LP to MP (+)				
Teapot	A *or* B (with London hall-marks)	TD/to/ET	Thomas Dwyer	ca. 1746	YUAG files	
Two teaspoons	A*	Storer crest, a talbot's head	Ebenezer and Mary (Edwards) Storer	ca. 1750	Buhler 1972, no. 259	MFAB
Two teaspoons	A*	G/IS		ca. 1775	Eitner 1976, no. 53	
Four teaspoons	A	TW	Thomas Welles	ca. 1760	YUAG files	
Teaspoon	C*	CB		ca. 1755		YUAG
Teaspoon	C*	SH		ca. 1765	YUAG files	
Two teaspoons	D*	HF		ca. 1770		HD
Two-handled cup	A*	The Gift of the Hon.rble Thomas Welles Esqr./To the First Church of Christ/in Glassen-bury/May 11/1762	Thomas Welles and/or Congregational Church, Glastonbury, Conn.	1762	Jones 1913, 185	
Two-handled cup	A	This belongs to the first Church of/Christ in Glastenbury	Congregational Church, Glastonbury, Conn.	ca. 1765	Jones 1913, 185	

1. Gordon/Coburn 1913, 31; *York VR*, 19, 601; *Beverly VR* 1:79; Sargent 1887, 619–21; *York Deeds* 9:253–54.
2. Gordon/Coburn 1913, 16–17; *Concord VR*, 58.
3. Sargent 1887, 305–08.
4. RC 28:296; Greenleaf 1854, 69; *Cambridge VR* 1:297; 2:167, 172; *Newbury VR* 1:195; *Index of Obituaries, 1704–1800*, 1:136.
5. Greenleaf 1854, 52; *Sibley's Harvard Graduates* 4:472–76.
6. RC 30:161.
7. RC 28:135; RC 24:23; *Index of Obituaries, 1784–1840*, 1:979.
8. Rev. Amos Smith letter to Catharine Langdon Rogers, 1882, Bigelow-Phillips files, 1311.
9. RC 28:188.
10. RC 28:116.
11. John Edwards deed to Samuel Edwards, 13 September 1746, Smith-Carter Papers, MHS.
12. SCPR, docket 10043.
13. SCPR 63:37.
14. Roberts 1895, 2:59–60; RC 18:64; Seybolt 1939, 267, 344.
15. Roberts 1895, 2:187.
16. *Boston News-Letter*, 2 November 1750.
17. SCD 89:11–13.
18. SCCR, Court of Common Pleas Extended Record Book 1755–56, 312.
19. Roberts 1895, 2:121.
20. Pruitt 1978, 38–39.
21. SCD 123:188.
22. SCD 124:109–10, 171–72.
23. *New-England Chronicle*, 2 August 1776.
24. SCCR, Court of Common Pleas Extended Record Book, October 1782, 221.
25. SCD 141:102–04; 156:81–83; 158:138–40.
26. *Massachusetts Gazette*, 24 July 1786; repeated 31 July, 7 August 1786.

27. RC 10:181, 235.

28. SCD 183:194–95. On 21 June 1796, Coburn extended a mortgage of three thousand dollars to Webb, which was repaid in 1801. SCD 183:195–97.

29. SCD 188:80–81.

30. SCD 188:66–67.

31. RC 22:326.

32. Rev. Amos Smith letter to Catharine Langdon Rogers, 1882, Bigelow-Phillips files, 1310. According to Reverend Smith the house was destroyed in "the great fire of Nov. 9th, & 10th, 1872." Reverend Smith was the son of Catharine Langdon and Amos Smith, Sr.

33. SCCR, Court of Common Pleas Extended Record Book, July 1783, 214.

34. SCCR, Court of Common Pleas Extended Record Book, 1784, 215.

35. SCCR, Court of Common Pleas Extended Record Book, January 1788, 4.

36. SCCR, Court of Common Pleas Extended Record Book, January 1788, 9–10.

37. SCCR, Court of Common Pleas Extended Record Book, April 1798, 60, 61.

38. Rev. Amos Smith letter to Catharine Langdon Rogers, 1882, Bigelow-Phillips files, 1309–10.

39. Rev. Amos Smith letter to Catharine Langdon Rogers, 1882, Bigelow-Phillips files, 1310. Catharine Langdon was married to Amos Smith, Sr., by Rev. William Ellery Channing of the Federal Street Church in 1808. Reverend Channing had lived in the Coburn house as a boarder in 1803–04.

40. RC 22:509.

41. Rev. Amos Smith letter to Catharine Langdon Rogers, 1882, Bigelow-Phillips files, 1312.

42. Roberts 1895, 2:59. Reverend Smith gives 20 January as the date of Coburn's death; see Rev. Amos Smith letter to Catharine Langdon Rogers, 1882, Bigelow-Phillips files, 1311.

43. SCPR 101:99–105, 137.

44. The Bigelow-Phillips files contain a brief summary of the inventory, but there is no record of this document at the Suffolk County Probate Registry.

45. *Index of Obituaries, 1784–1840*, 1:979.

46. SCD 222:291–92.

47. SCPR 106:17–19.

48. MCPR, docket 17400. The notes of John Marshall Phillips from the Phipps probate papers record the payment to Coburn for mourning rings, but the account is no longer in the docket; see Bigelow-Phillips files, 1316.

49. Ropes Family Papers, box 1, folder F, PEM.

50. 19 November 1762, vol. 1, Waste and Memoranda Book, 1761–83, [13], Revere Family Papers, MHS.

51. 10 June 1766, vol. 1, Waste and Memoranda Book, 1761–83, [30], Revere Family Papers, MHS.

52. 5 August 1772, vol. 1, Waste and Memoranda Book, 1761–83, [41], Revere Family Papers, MHS.

53. 1 December 1772, vol. 1, Waste and Memoranda Book, 1761–83, [42], Revere Family Papers, MHS. The silver is recorded as "18^{oz}" and an additional amount. The second figure is unclear.

54. 11 February 1773, vol. 1, Waste and Memoranda Book, 1761–83, [43], Revere Family Papers, MHS.

55. 18 March 1773, vol. 1, Waste and Memoranda Book, 1761–83, [44], Revere Family Papers, MHS.

56. 10 May, 15 June 1773, vol. 1, Waste and Memoranda Book, 1761–83, [44–45], Revere Family Papers, MHS.

57. 16 October 1773, vol. 1, Waste and Memoranda Book, 1761–83, [48], Revere Family Papers, MHS.

58. 25 August 1774, vol. 1, Waste and Memoranda Book, 1761–83, [51], Revere Family Papers, MHS.

Seth Storer Coburn
1744–after 1796

A

Seth Storer Coburn, descended from a prominent family of Boston silversmiths, was born on 29 December 1744, the son of Seth Coburn (1718–ca. 1752), a shopkeeper, and Elizabeth Scott (b. 1725), both of whom were from Boston and married there on 27 July 1742.[1] Coburn's paternal grandparents were Ebenezer Coburn (1675/76–1749) of Beverly, Massachusetts, and Sarah Storer (1682–1770) of York, Maine.[2] His maternal grandparents were Joseph Scott (1694–1751), a brazier, and Mehitabel Webber of Boston.[3]

Coburn may have apprenticed with his uncle, John Coburn (q.v.), beginning his training about 1758 and completing it about 1765. His familial relationships to the silversmithing trade were extensive: his great-uncle Seth Coburn married

Mary Coney, the daughter of John Coney (q.v.), Boston's preeminent early-eighteenth-century silversmith. His great-uncle Ebenezer Coburn married Mary Edwards, sister of Samuel and Thomas Edwards (qq.v.) and the daughter of John Edwards (q.v.); these men were members of perhaps the most important family of Boston silversmiths working at the time. His first cousins Sarah (b. 1743) and Esther Coburn (b. 1757) married James Ridgway (q.v.) in 1774 and 1780, respectively. Further testimony to the number of silversmiths with whom Seth had connections were Samuel Edwards, Benjamin Greene (q.v.), and Daniel Parker (q.v.), witnesses to the administration of Seth Coburn's estate, and David Greenleaf (q.v.), whose aunt Susanna Greenleaf married John Coburn.[4] Greenleaf and Seth Storer Coburn may have served together as apprentices to John Coburn. Coburn's connections to these silversmiths might have provided contacts from which he could have profited.

Several entries in the daybook of the Boston silversmith Zachariah Brigden (q.v.) suggest that Coburn worked in Boston for a short time after his apprenticeship. One, dated February 1767, records Coburn's purchase of two ounces of silver from Brigden, paid for in part by "cash Rec^d of Burt," possibly the silversmith Benjamin Burt (q.v.).[5] Another, recording Coburn's debt to Brigden of 7 shillings and 6 pence "To a pr of brass Chaps," is dated February 1767.[6]

By 1775, however, Coburn was settled in Springfield, Massachusetts. He served as a private of that town and marched to Lexington in April of that year.[7] He advertised in the 16 August 1775 issue of the *Connecticut Journal* that he had lost a china-faced silver watch engraved "Moses Peck, Boston" and entreated whoever found it to return it to him in Springfield.[8] Another advertisement in the *Connecticut Courant* for 15 July 1776 records that a china-faced watch was stolen from his shop and suggests that Coburn sold or repaired such wares.[9]

Coburn married Elisabeth Day (1735/36–95) of West Springfield on 12 November 1775.[10] Day was forty years old at the time of her marriage, nine years Coburn's senior. She was the daughter of Josiah Day (1701–70) and Elisabeth Bliss (1703/04–39) of Springfield, who wed there on 25 February 1730.[11]

Elisabeth Day inherited a substantial amount of land from her uncle, Dr. Jonathan Bliss (1699–1761).[12] Over a ten-year period, beginning in 1786, the Coburns sold off the property in a series of small parcels, ultimately selling their home lot in 1796.[13] Coburn apparently lived on his wife's dower, suggesting they may have led a marginal existence. Since Coburn purchased almost no land in his lifetime and probably made little silver, the income derived from the sale of land must have eased the craftsman's burden of supporting his household. Coburn's poor financial situation is reflected in a suit successfully brought against him in 1789 by Joel Marble, apothecary of Greenfield, Massachusetts. Coburn was briefly jailed for his inability to pay a fine of £10.16.14 levied against him.[14] In spite of his precarious finances, however, Coburn may have had an apprentice, the silversmith Nathan Storrs (1768–1839) of Northampton, Massachusetts. Storrs was eighteen years old when he witnessed a deed for Coburn in 1786.

Coburn produced a cylindrical nutmeg grater engraved "Mary / Storer / 1770" for one of his two great-aunts, either Mary (Coney) Storer (1699–after 1774) or Mary (Edwards) Storer (1700–71). Its unusual form and Coburn's choice of a cylindrical shape connect the grater with a similar one made circa 1750 by his uncle John Coburn.[15] The only other silver known to be from the younger Coburn's hand is a spoon. In both cases, his mark (A), S·S·C appears in Roman capitals in a rectangle.

Seth Storer Coburn appeared as a Springfield resident in the census of 1790.[16] Elisabeth Coburn died in 1795; the last recorded activity by her husband took place in 1796, when he sold his home lot in Springfield; nothing further is known of him. JJF

SURVIVING OBJECTS

	Mark	Inscription	Patron	Date	Reference	Owner
Nutmeg grater	A†	Mary/Storer/1770	Mary (Coney) Storer or Mary (Edwards) Storer	1770	Buhler 1987, 8–9	MFAB
Spoon	A	?		ca. 1775	DAPC 75.2258	

1. RC 24:173, 252; Gordon/Coburn 1913, 31; Benjamin Greene Ledger, 1734–56, 112, 139, 150, 163, MHS; SCPR, docket 10043; RC 28:240.
2. Gordon/Coburn 1913, 17; *Beverly VR* 1:79; Noyes/Libby/Davis (1928–39) 1976, 153, 665.
3. RC 9:216; RC 28:85.
4. SCPR, docket 10043. Benjamin Greene and Elizabeth Storer were administrators of Seth Coburn's estate. Samuel Edwards and Daniel Parker witnessed the bond.
5. Zachariah Brigden Daybook, 1766–ca. 1775, fol. 6v, Brigden Papers, YU.
6. Zachariah Brigden Daybook, 1766–ca. 1775, fol. 7r, Brigden Papers, YU.
7. *Mass. Soldiers and Sailors* 2:694.
8. The advertisement was repeated on 6 September 1775. Flynt/Fales 1968, 186, incorrectly states that the advertisement appeared in the *Connecticut Courant*.
9. The advertisement was repeated in the issue of 22 July 1776.
10. *Index of Obituaries, 1784–1840*, 1:979; *Descendants of Robert Day* 1848, 16.
11. *Descendants of Robert Day* 1848, 13; Warren 1934–35, 1:235.
12. HaCPR, Box 16, no. 24.
13. HCD 28:566–67; 29:380, 621, 627; 30:159; 31:677–78; 32:670; 33:408–09; 35:443.
14. HCD, Book B, 534–35.
15. For John Coburn's nutmeg grater, see Buhler 1972, no. 261. The fact that Seth Storer Coburn's nutmeg grater carries a history of family ownership may supply further evidence for Seth Storer Coburn's possible apprenticeship with John Coburn; see Buhler 1987, 8–9.
16. Massachusetts Census of 1790, 125.

John Coddington
ca. 1690–1743

A

B

In 1709 John Coddington acted as a witness on a deed for Edward Winslow (q.v.), and presumably this man is the John Coddington who later became a goldsmith in Newport, Rhode Island.[1] In 1709 he would have been about nineteen years old, having been born in Newport about 1690. He was baptized in Bristol on 6 June 1697.[2] Coddington was the son of Nathaniel Coddington (1653–1724) and Susanna Hutchinson (b. 1649), Winslow's aunt.[3] Coddington's paternal grandparents were William Coddington (b. 1601) and Anne Brinley.[4] His maternal grandparents were Edward Hutchinson (1613–75) and Catherine Hamby (d. ca. 1650).[5]

Coddington would have completed his apprenticeship about 1711 and probably returned to Newport. In the account book of the Boston stationer Daniel Henchman, Coddington is identified as being "of Rhode Island" beginning in 1714. From Henchman Coddington purchased the following stationery and watchmaking supplies:

1714 John Coddington of Rhode Island D^r
       1 French Grammer sent him
Septr To Commiss for Selling ye Gold   £ 1. 10. 6
Oct 4   To 2 Crystals for Watch 5/
         To 5 Watch Glasses & 6 Watch keys   1. 7. 6
Feby 28 To 1 French Bible sent p Post   — 9. 6
1714 Contra   £31   .2
Septr 27 By 5 oz & 9 pw^t of Gold sold to Cummins at   £30. 13 .4

    By Cash in full   8 .8
                                 £31   .2

Coddington is said to have married Nancy Wanton (d. before 1720) in Newport on 23 May 1715.[6] The next year he accepted Peter Vewness as an apprentice to the goldsmith's trade. On 14 April 1716 they signed the following indenture:

> Paul Vewness, with consent of his father, Paul Vewness, Doth Put himself apprentice unto John Coddington in Newport on Rhode Island, Silver Smith, to learn his Art with him after the manner of an apprentice to serve from the Day and Date hereof to the full End and Term of Nine years from thence next ensuing; sd apprentice shall ever keep his master's commands Gladly, Do no damage to his master nor see it done by others, shall neither buy or sell without his master's consent, nor marry. Said master in consideration of sd service shall teach the sd apprentice in the Art or Mistory of a Silversmith which he now useth and shall teach and Instruct or cause to be taught and instructed the best way and manner he can and furnish sd apprentice with sufficient meat, drink, apparel, washing, Lodging and all the necessaries during sd term and at the expiration of sd term to find sd apprentice one suitable apparel or suit for him.[7]

As his second wife Coddington married, on 25 August 1720, Elizabeth Rogers (1705–45). On 20 July 1721 Coddington received land "on the Harbour" from his father.[8] A few weeks later on 8 August 1721 Coddington was identified as a goldsmith when he and his wife mortgaged land on Thames Street to the Colony.[9] He was identified as "Esquire" in a deed of 5 May 1725 when he and his wife sold Joseph Whipple land "bounded westerly upon ye Sea or Bay."[10] Coddington and his wife executed a number of deeds in the subsequent decade.[11] The couple had one child, who died young. Coddington was a justice of the peace in 1722, member of the House of Deputies in 1721, 1722, 1723, 1726, 1727, and 1729, and was sheriff of Newport County from 1733 to 1735.[12] He witnessed a deed for fellow Newport silversmith Isaac Anthony (q.v.) in 1728/29.[13]

Coddington, being sick and weak, wrote his will on 15 June 1736, and it was proved on 24 October 1743.[14] The inventory of his estate, appraised by Jonathan Clarke and Josiah Clarke on 29 September 1743, amounted to £639.19.6. The inventory included "1 Large Anvil, 1 Smal D^o. 1 Small Raising Anvill 5 Hammers 1 Pr Drawing Tongs 1 old Iron Skillet 1 Drawing Bench part of a nest of weights 1 p^r of Round Plyers" valued at £20.[15] His widow, Elizabeth, was appointed administrator on 7 November 1743 and presented her account on 4 December 1744. His widow died the next year and on 8 October 1745, Elnathan Hammond, as nearest of kin, was appointed administrator of the estate of Elizabeth Coddington, widow of Col. John Coddington.[16]

Only a small number of pieces by Coddington survive. They are marked

with an IC within a shaped cartouche (A). Another initials mark within conjoined circles (B) also has been attributed to him tentatively. PEK

SURVIVING OBJECTS

	Mark	Inscription	Patron	Date	Reference	Owner
Three cups	A*	MD		ca. 1740	*Moore Collection* 1980, no. 16	
Cup	A	IC; AC	John and Anne Crawford	ca. 1715	Gourley 1965, no. 256	RISD
Salver	A	St G.T. AD 1762 (later)		ca. 1715	Jones 1913, 459	
Tablespoon	B†	Eun.^c Starbuck	Eunice Starbuck	ca. 1715	Buhler/Hood 1970, no. 461	YUAG
Tankard	A†	unidentified arms, a fess gules between 3 lions' heads erased; R/IC		ca. 1725	Buhler/Hood 1970, no. 462	YUAG
Tankard	A	none		ca. 1730	Gourley 1965, no. 258	RISD
Tankard	A	IV		ca. 1720	Sotheby's, 30 January–2 February 1991, lot 143	

1. SCD 24:218.
2. *Genealogies of Rhode Island Families* 2:373. No record of Coddington's birth has been found, although it has been said to be 23 March 1690; see Austin 1887, 279.
3. Arnold 1911, 7:51; RC 9:30; Savage 1860–62, 2:509.
4. Savage 1860–62, 2:513.
5. Savage 1860–62, 2:509.
6. Flynt/Fales 1968, 186.
7. Annie B. Minsenberger letter to Francis Hill Bigelow, 20 December 1932, citing Colonial Town Records, Land Evidence 1:184, Newport Historical Society, Newport, Rhode Island.
8. Annie B. Minsenberger letter to Francis Hill Bigelow, 20 December 1932, citing Colonial Town Records, Land Evidence 2:11, Newport Historical Society, Newport, Rhode Island; Arnold 1911, 10:442.
9. Annie B. Minsenberger letter to Francis Hill Bigelow, 20 December 1932, citing Colonial Town Records, Land Evidence, 5:58–60, Newport Historical Society, Newport, Rhode Island.
10. Annie B. Minsenberger letter to Francis Hill Bigelow, 20 December 1932, citing Colonial Town Records, Land Evidence, 6:575, Newport Historical Society, Newport, Rhode Island.
11. Annie B. Minsenberger letter to Francis Hill Bigelow, 20 December 1932, citing Colonial Town Records, Land Evidence, 3:68; 9:63, 69, 166; 10:40, 119, 206, Newport Historical Society, Newport, Rhode Island.
12. *Records of the Colony of Rhode Island* 4:292, 319, 324, 383, 385, 419, 481, 497, 508.
13. Colonial Town Records, Land Evidence 2:319–20, Newport Historical Society, Newport, Rhode Island.
14. A transcription of Coddington's will is in the Bigelow-Phillips files, YUAG. Flynt/Fales 1968, 186; Carpenter 1954, 156–57.
15. Annie B. Minsenberger letter to Francis Hill Bigelow, 20 December 1932, citing Town Council 10:26, 27, 45, Newport Historical Society, Newport, Rhode Island.
16. Colonial Town Records, Abstracts of Wills, Newport Historical Society, Newport, Rhode Island.

John Codner
ca. 1754–82

John Codner was born probably in Boston about 1754 to William Codner (1709–69), a Boston stonecutter, and Mary Hill (1722–1800) of Cambridge, Massachusetts, who were married in Boston in 1745.[1] His paternal grandparents were James Codner (ca. 1676–1715), a cooper, and Mary Gordon (b. 1683).[2] His maternal grandparents were Abraham Hill (1697–1754), a bricklayer, and Prudence Hancock (1696–1780) of Cambridge.[3]

John Codner would have begun his training about 1768. His master may have been his uncle by marriage, Joseph Clark, Jr., or William Simpkins (qq.v.), a neighbor to whom Codner's parents mortgaged a third part of a house and land in 1766. However, because these craftsmen were goldsmiths and Codner was a jeweler, it is more probable that he trained with a Boston jeweler.[4] The Massachusetts tax list of 1771 includes a William Codner, possibly the jeweler's brother, as having a Widow Codner and son as lodgers, the latter possibly being the jeweler.[5] Codner would have completed his training about 1775. In 1776 he was among those drafted from ward 5 in Boston to serve with the continental forces.[6] The Boston tax records of 1780 indicate that Codner had 2 polls and rents valued at twenty–five pounds, noting that he had gone to Holland.[7] By 1782 Codner had returned from Europe, for in the first half of that year he lent money to the Boston merchant Edmund Dunkin.[8] Codner probably died late in June or early in July of 1782, for an advertisement in the Boston *Independent Chronicle* for 11 July 1782 states, "John Codner of Boston, Jeweller, died at New London where he lately arrived from Europe, at 28 years."[9] On 1 August of that year the same paper carried a notice stating, "All persons indebted to or have demands on estate of John Codner, late of Boston, Jeweller" settle accounts with Mrs. Mary Codner. His mother was appointed administrator of the estate on 12 July 1783, and on behalf of the estate she sued Edmund Dunkin for debt in 1783 and Henry Clinton for debt in 1784.[10] Codner's probate papers list a large assortment of gold, silver, and pewter, numerous tools, and pieces of jewelry, including

78 p.^{r} Shoe Buckles w.^{t} 124^{oz}:16^{dwt}-@ 6/8	£41: 12:	0
78 D.^{o} Chapes for D.^{o} @ 1/	3: 18:	0
Makeing D.^{o} 6/ p.^{r}	23: 8:	0
40 p.^{r} Knee Buckles @ 5/ p.^{r}	10: 0:	0
17 Stock D.^{o} @ 5/ Each	4: 5:	0
22 p.^{r} Stone-Buttons @ 7/6 p.^{r}	8: 5:	0
10 Stone Rings @ 10/	5: 0:	0
7 p.^{r} Stone nubs set in Gold @ 10/	3: 10:	0
7 p.^{r} D.^{o} D.^{o} in Silver @ 5/	1: 15:	0
6 Doz.^{n} & 2 Tea-spoons w.^{t} 17^{oz}: @ 6/8	5: 13:	4
Makeing D.^{o} @ 8/ p.^{r} Doz.^{n}	2: 9:	4
6 Large Spoons w.^{t} 10:^{oz}4:^{dwt} @ 6/8	3: 8:	0
Makeing D.^{o} @ 8/	0: 8:	0
1 Silver Ladle w.^{t} 7:^{oz}13^{dwt}: @ 6/8	2: 11:	0
Makeing D.^{o} 6/	0: 6:	0
1 p.^{r} Pepper Castors w.^{t} 6:^{oz} @ 6/8	2: 0:	0
4 Silver Calls w.^{t} 4^{oz}1/2 @ 6/8	1: 10:	0
Makeing D.^{o} 6/ p.^{s}	1: 4:	0
4 p.^{r} Sugar Tongs w.^{t} 4:^{oz}16^{dwt} @ 6/8	1: 12:	0
Makeing D.^{o} 5/ p.^{r}	1: 0:	0

113 Thimbles @ 1/6	8: 9: 6
4 Free-Masons Medles @ 4/p.s	0: 16: 0
21 Large Broaches @ 2/	2: 2: 0
13 Small D.o @ 1/	0: 13: 0
55 p.r Silver Buttons @ 1/6	4: 2: 6
56 o.z Old Silver @ 6/5	17: 19: 4
1 Sissars Chain 10/	0: 10: 0
Carried up	£ 158: 7: 0
Bro't up	158: 7: 0
4^{oz}1/4 Burnt Silver @ 6/	1: 5: 6
12 Gold Necklaces w.t 13:^{oz}8 }	17: 0: 0
@ £5:p.r Ou	
Makeing D.o 6/ p.s	3: 12: 0
7 p.r Gold Sleve Buttons 14 1/2^{dwt} }	3: 12: 6
at 5/^{dwt}	
Makeing D.o 6/ p.r	2: 2: 0
25 plain Gold Rings w.t 1:^{oz}2^{dwt} }	5: 10: 0
@ £ 5:p.r oz	
Makeing D.o 20/	1: 0: 0
10 p.r plain Gold nubs w.t 6^{dwt}	1: 10: 0
Makeing D.o 10/	0: 10: 0
5 p.r Gold wires 2/ p.r	0: 10: 0
2 Gold Broach's @ 6/	0: 12: 0
2 Gold Lockets w.t 2 1/2^{dwt}	0: 12: 6
Makeing D.o 6/	0: 6: 0
1:^{oz}3^{dwt}. Old Gold @ £4:12	5: 5: 9
Old Stone Earings 20/	1: 0: 0
^{oz}1/2 Gold filings £2:6	2: 6: 0
3 y.ds Silver Lace @ 3/	0: 9: 0
1 Large forging Anvil & Block	2: 0: 0
1 Small peecking Iron 1/	0: 1: 0
1 Large Sledge Hammer 1/	0: 1: 0
1 Large forgeing D.o 1/6	0: 1: 6
3 Small Bench D.o 2/	0: 2: 0
1 p.r Drawing wire Tongs 6/	0: 6: 0
sum Carried over	208: 1: 9
Sum Bro't Over	208: 1: 9
1 p.r forgeing Tongs	£0: 0: 4
1 p.r Large Spring fire D.o	0: 4: 0
1 Small Bench Vice	0: 6: 0
2 p.r Cutting Shears	0: 1: 0
1 p.r Cutting Nippers	0: 0: 6
1 Brass Hollowing Stamp	0: 10: 0
1 p.r Spring plyers	0: 1: 6
1 p.r flat D.o	0: 1: 0
1 p.r Small D.o	0: 1: 0
1 p.r D.o Round D.o	0: 1: 0
1 p.r Screw Comp.s	0: 2: 0
1 Small Spring Saw	0: 2: 0
1 Drilling Stock	0: 6: 0
1 p.r Large Brass flasks	0: 6: 0

5 p^r Small D^o	1:	10:	0
1 p^r Wooden Screws	0:	3:	0
1 Large & 1 Small Copper boil^{ng} pann	0:	10:	0
1 Copper large spoon mould	0:	2:	0
1 Large Iron spoon punch	0:	3:	0
1 Box of Scales & Weights Large	1:	16:	0
1 Small D^o Money D^o	0:	6:	0
1 p^r Small Scales	0:	2:	0
1 Blowing pipe	0:	1:	0
1 Tinn Lamp & 1 Soldring Iron	0:	2:	0
1/2 Doz^n Rough files	0:	1:	0
3 Smooth D^o	0:	2:	0
1 Broken sett Cutting tools	0:	3:	0
1 p^r forge Bellows	0:	12:	0
1 Baskett	0:	0:	1
1 Pail & 1 Iron Kettle	0:	1:	0
4 Setting Stools	0:	4:	0
2 Brushes	0:	1:	0
2 Large & 1 Small Glass Cases	1:	16:	0
a number Pewter patterns 1/^{lb} 1^1/$_2$^{lb}	0:	1:	6
Sum Carried up	218:	0:	8
Sum bro't up	£ 218:	0:	8
1 Tinn pann & 1 Limmy Box	0:	3:	0
1 Wooden Moulding Box	0:	1:	0
2 Iron Balls & 2 Bench's	0:	6:	0
1 Writing Desk	0:	6:	0
1/2 Doz^n 8 Inch 1/2 Round files	0:	6:	0
7 flatt D^o 8 Inch	0:	7:	0
2 1/2 Round Smooth D^o	0:	3:	0
3 Doz^n & 2 6 Inch flat D^o	0:	19:	0
4 peircing 1/2 Round D^o	0:	1:	6
3 Doz^n p^r Square Shoe Chapes	2:	5:	0
8 p^r Small Round D^o	0:	8:	0
4 1/2 Doz^n p^r Best Knee D^o @ 10/	2:	5:	0
3 1/3 D^o D^o 10/	1:	13:	4
2 1/3 D^o Large Shoe D^o 12/	1:	8:	0
15 p^r Small D^o 4/Doz^n	0:	5:	0
18 p^r Smallest D^o 4/ D^o	0:	6:	0
18 p^r Coarse Knee D^o 6/	0:	9:	0
1 Doz^n p^r Brass Shoe D^o	0:	6:	0
7 p^r Knee D^o D^o	0:	1:	9
a number odd D^o	0:	2:	0
10 p^r Brass Shoe Buckles	0:	10:	0
4 Doz^n & 9 Earring top stones 10/Doz^n	2:	7:	6
7 Sheets foyl	0	4:	0
10 Gravers	0:	10:	0
185 Nests Small Crucibles @ 1/nes^t	9:	5:	0
65 D^o Large D^o 1/6	4:	17:	6
9 Doz^n Earring tops @ 10/Doz^n	4:	10:	0
4 D^o Garnetts @ 4/ D^o	0:	16:	0
Sundry Odd Stones & Chapes	0:	9:	0

The inventory also included a flatting mill valued at £6. The only other items in the inventory were clothing, a few books, personal jewelry, and some lace and other textiles. The total value of the inventory, compiled in 1782 by Benjamin Burt and Joseph Loring (qq.v.), was £326.14.3.[11]

In his memoirs of the Boston silversmith's trade in the period just after the Revolution, Samuel Davis (1765–1829) recalls Codner as one of the trade.[12] Codner's probate records indicate that he had a productive shop with large stocks of jewelry and flatware that jewelers specialized in. No work marked by this craftsman has been identified yet. PEK

1. John Codner's birth is not known to be recorded: the date of birth is estimated from his obituary notice. RC 24:60; Whitmore 1878, 47, no. 880; Thwing; RC 28:281; *Index of Obituaries, 1784–1840,* 1:984; *Cambridge VR* 1:354; SCPR 68:325, 395.
2. Whitmore 1878, 47, no. 873; RC 28:3; RC 9:160.
3. *Cambridge VR* 1:323, 352; 2:196, 601; MCPR, docket 11401.
4. SCD 111:163–66.
5. Pruitt 1978, 18–19.
6. Thwing.
7. "Assessors' 'Taking-Books,'" 29.
8. SCCR, Court of Common Pleas Record Book 1783, 222.
9. *Index of Obituaries, 1704–1800,* 2:226.
10. SCPR 82:537; SCCR, Court of Common Pleas Record Book 1783, 222; 1784, 33.
11. SCPR, docket 17742.
12. Steinway 1960, 7.

John Cole
w. ca. 1686

John Cole, a "Goldsmith, at James Smiths," was among a group of individuals not admitted to be citizens of Boston in August 1686 and may be the same man for whom Solomon Rainsford acted as surety in 1684.[1] In 1689 John Cole and Edward Winslow (q.v.) witnessed a deed for Jeremiah Dummer (q.v.), which suggests that Cole stayed in Boston and worked as one of Dummer's journeymen.[2] The New England goldsmith may also be the son of the late John Cole, a fellmonger in Northampton, England, who was apprenticed to the London goldsmith John Gray. That John Cole was made a freeman of the Goldsmiths' Company in 1669.[3] Because at least two other individuals named John Cole—one a mariner, the other a schoolmaster—lived in Boston at this time, it is difficult to ascertain whether references in the records are to the silversmith.

No silver by this craftsman has been identified. PEK

1. RC 10:61, 75.
2. SCD 15:148.
3. Apprentice Book 2, fol. 120r; Court Book 6, fol. 57v, Worshipful Company of Goldsmiths, London. Robert B. Barker letter to the author, 9 February 1993.

Benjamin Coney
1673–1721

The youngest son of John and Elizabeth Nash Coney, Benjamin Coney, born in Boston on 16 October 1673, probably served his apprenticeship with his brother John Coney (q.v.), who was seventeen years his senior. (See the entry on John Coney for biographical information on Benjamin's parents and grandparents.) In 1694, at the age of twenty-one, Benjamin witnessed a mortgage deed between Jane Kind, widow, and John Foster for the house occupied by William Rouse (q.v.).[1] This suggests that he may have been serving as a journeyman for Rouse at the time.

Benjamin Coney does not appear in the record again until 1721, when his will and inventory were filed in Stratford, Connecticut. In his will he bequeathed ten shillings each to his brothers John and Nathaniel Coney (b. 1677) and to his sister Elizabeth Booth (b. 1672). He left the remainder of his estate to his wife, Mehitable, who also was to serve as sole executor.[2]

The inventory of Benjamin Coney's estate was appraised by Josiah Curtis and John Beardslee and amounted to £338.2.3, including a house worth £100 and shop goods and tools as follows:

Silver small work unfinished-18^s-4^d-	00. 18. 04
thirty two ounces & a half of silver at-8^s-p ounce—13^1	13. 00. 00
Silver sorder —10^s	00. 10. 00
. . . .	
All ye Goldsmith tules	25. 00. 00
Six ounces of hare	00. 15. 00

The "hare" may have been hair used for jewelry, as it is listed immediately after the goldsmith's tools. The inventory indicates that Benjamin's house was modest but comfortable. Although the appraisers did not inventory the house room by room, it seems probable that his six turkeywork chairs, great chair, and looking glass were in the parlor. He also had a chest of drawers, an oval table, and twenty-six additional chairs. No featherbeds are listed, only a "last" bedstead, a couch bedstead, and a silk grass bed, but each had bolsters and coverlids. Most of his kitchenware was of pewter, iron, and wood, with only a small amount of brass, including one brass candlestick. He owned a fair quantity of clothes as well and evidently attempted to cut a gentlemanly figure, for he owned a sword and two wigs. The inventory does not include any silver objects for the family's personal use.[3]

The Coney family evidently had strong ties to the town of Stratford. Benjamin's brother John's first wife was born in Stratford, and his second wife's father, Joshua Atwater, bequeathed silver to several New England churches, including the Stratford church. John Coney made two caudle cups for the Stratford church, and his sister Elizabeth Booth probably also resided in Stratford.[4]

No silver by Benjamin Coney is known. BMW

1. RC 9:127; SCD 16:408.
2. Edward S. Cooke, Jr., provided information on Coney from the Fairfield County, Connecticut, Probate District, file 1707, dated 25 December 1716, entered 29 March 1721, CSL.
3. Fairfield County, Connecticut Probate District, file 1707.
4. RC 9:217; Jones 1913, 463.

John Coney
1655/56–1722

John Coney was the leading Boston silversmith of his time, and he remains renowned for his craftsmanship today. Coney was the first American silversmith to be the subject of a major exhibition and monograph. The exhibition was held in 1932 at the Museum of Fine Arts, Boston, the same year that Hermann Clarke published his biography.[1] Coney's parents were married in Boston on 24 June 1654. His father, the Boston blacksmith John Coney (1628–90), was the son of John (d. 1630) and Elizabeth (Hawkredd) Coney. The silversmith's

A

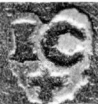

B

C

D

E

F

mother, Elizabeth Nash (ca. 1635–87), was the daughter of Robert (d. 1661), a butcher, and Sarah Nash.[2] Coney was born on 5 January 1655/56.[3] He would have been fourteen years of age on 5 January 1669/70 and was apprenticed to Jeremiah Dummer (q.v.) about that time. Although no indenture survives, circumstantial evidence documents this relationship. The Boston tax lists of 1674 record Dummer as the sole goldsmith in division 5, with Coney included in a separate section of the division 5 list entitled "servants."[4] Coney also witnessed a deed for Dummer in 1676.[5]

Coney married shortly after becoming of age in 1677, wedding Sarah Blakeman (1658–94), daughter of James Blakeman (d. 1689) of Stratford, Connecticut.[6] Sarah was a cousin of Anna Atwater, Jeremiah Dummer's wife, further evidence of a relationship between Coney and Dummer. Coney took the oath of allegiance to the Massachusetts Bay Colony on 11 November 1678.[7] On 31 October 1680 he joined the Old South Church, where the couple's nine children were baptized.[8] Sarah Coney died on 17 April 1694.[9] Even though he was a member of the Old South Church, he subscribed a guinea toward the erection of King's Chapel, the first Anglican church in Boston, in July 1689.[10] Unlike his contemporaries Dummer and Edward Winslow (q.v.), Coney served in only a few civic offices, notably constable in 1688 and tithingman in 1693.[11]

Coney probably lived in his father's house until its sale in 1691, when he acquired a house on Cotton Hill.[12] He was living there in 1698 when a new schoolhouse was to be built near his land.[13] On 12 April 1699, Coney and his second wife, Jeremiah Dummer's sister-in-law Mary Atwater Clark (1659/60–1726), whom he had married in 1694, sold the property for £275.[14] Coney maintained a close relationship with Dummer. The two were administrators of the estate of their mother-in-law, Mary Higginson, in 1708/09 and were sued by Col. John Higginson concerning the estate.[15] Coney and Dummer also signed the bond for the administration of Mary Clark's estate in 1691.[16] Coney's wife, Mary, was admitted to the First Church on 22 September 1695 and the couple's six children were baptized there.[17] On 11 January 1700 Coney bought a brick tenement on Ann Street and land near the entrance to the town dock for £780 from John Nelson.[18] He expanded this property by buying adjoining properties—a brick warehouse in 1704 for £370 and property on Conduit Street in 1717 for £845.[19] James Barnes (q.v.) rented a wharf, erected by the Boston selectmen, next to Coney beginning in 1719.[20] Coney petitioned the selectmen in 1720 complaining that Barnes kept the wharf covered with wood blocking access to his own wharf.[21]

More than 225 pieces of silver by Coney survive and testify to his familiarity with the mannerist and early and late baroque styles. His artfully wrought forms are noteworthy for their beauty, complexity, and variety. Coney made more ambitious and unusual objects than any other Boston silversmith of the time, including an inkstand and monteiths. The earliest pieces are marked IC in a shaped shield (A); he used a similar mark with a less complexly outlined shield (B) later. About 1710 Coney began to use IC crowned with a rabbit below (C), a rebus for his last name. A small mark, IC in a rectangle (D), is sometimes found in conjunction with (B) or (C) and a few times by itself. Another IC in a rectangle (E) has been attributed to him. IC in an oval (F) sometimes is found in conjunction with mark (C) and was probably used late in his career. Spurious examples of mark (C) are known, and marks have been misattributed to him.[22]

Prominent citizens numbered among his clients, including Edward Holyoke, Isaac Addington, Henry Flynt, Nathaniel and Margaret Appleton, and Samuel

Sewall. Sewall was one of Coney's early patrons and bought a considerable number of pieces from him throughout his career. Among Sewall's first purchases were a pair of shoe buckles bought on 25 August 1688 for seven shillings and nine pence.[23] Coney also purchased large amounts of bullion from Sewall, as this account between them reveals:

1695   Mr. John Conney Aurifaber Dr.

Sept 3   To Bullion 294 $1/4$ ounces fine
               sow-Plate at 7^s.1^d per o 104.04.3
9^r Oct^o To Ditto 211 Ounces at ditto prise 74.14.7
1696 July 6   To Ditto 285 $1/2$ at 7.1 101 = 2.3
               contra
1710.7^r.27   To Bills of Credit £12[24]

The accounts show that Coney paid for this material in large part by making cash payments to other individuals, namely, Major Walley, Simon Stoddard, and William Hubbard.[25] In 1710 Sewall acted as an agent for Samuel Gerrish in purchasing three pieces of plate, a tankard, a salver, and a spout cup.[26] Sewall also bought a tankard from Coney in 1701; his ledger for 7 May reads, "To Mr. Jno Coney per Wm Hubbard in full for Betty's Tankard £16.6." On 4 December the same year he noted that he had paid "Mr. Coñey for the Massachusetts Spear £3," probably an emblematic pike carried by a pikeman in the spring and fall parades of the Ancient and Honorable Artillery Company.[27] The following year he paid Coney £14 for a chain and £2 for a silver cup.[28] In purchasing the spear and the cup Sewall was acting as agent for the Artillery Company, for elsewhere in the ledger he notes that the company owed him for these goods:

Artillery Comp^a- of ye Massachusetts D^r

1701
Octob^r- To cash p^d Mr Jno Coñey for ye Spear
    or Half Pike £3 To Joseph Hill varnishing 5^s 3–5–

1702
May 14 To a Silver Cup for a Prize-wch En John Noyes [q.v.] won 2– –[29]

On 10 April 1707 Sewall paid Coney £1.19.2 for a silver cup marked on the bottom with the date "March, 5. 706/7."[30] In subsequent years he purchased a silver spoon (1713), a gold thimble (1713), and a spur clasp (1716).[31] A bill survives for a mug with a hollow handle Coney made for Rev. Joseph Baxter in 1713:

May 11th: 713: The Reverend Mr Baxter   Dr
    To a Silver mug wth a holow handle w^t 9^{oz}:14^{dwt} at 8^s ℞ oz ⎫
    & ye advance   ⎬ £4: 1: 5
    To fasho of D^o 1: 1: 0
                                                                     ——————
                                                                      5: 2: 5

        ℞ Contra   Cr
    By cash recd   £1: 3: 0
    By balanc due   3: 19: 5
                                                    ——————
            ℞ Jno Coney.   5:02: 5 [32]

Colonial silversmiths were often called upon to make mourning rings for funerals, and John Coney was no exception. In 1684 Peter Sargent paid for thirty rings from Coney in three different weights for the funeral of John Curwin. The bill was rendered as follows:

Mr Peter: Sergeant Dr

	£	s	d
Jan:5th:84. To 10 gold Rings w^t ^{3}/$_4$^{ous} & 1^{dwt} at 5$^£$ ℔ oz is	04:	00:	00
To fasho of Ditto	01:	00:	00
To 10 rings w^t ^{1}/$_2$^{ou} & 2^{dwt}	03:	00:	00
To fasho	01:	00:	00
To 10 rings more w^t ^{1}/$_2$^{ou} & 3 granes	02:	10:	07 ^{1}/$_2$
To fasho of Dittoe	01:	00:	00
	12:	10:	07 ^{1}/$_2$

Jno Coney, Jun.[33]

In 1711 Coney made rings for the funeral of Francis Wainwright. These cost more than Sargent's rings because of a £1.0.6 increase in the price of gold and a 6 pence price increase imposed by Coney for making them:

1711   The Estate of Fra = Wainwright Esqr Dr

Augst 6:	To 12 gold Rings for funerall w^t 1^{ou} = 6^{dwt} = 8gr⎫ at six pounds 5^s ℔ oz is ⎭	£8: 4: 6
	To fasho & waste of Do at 2^s/6^d ℔ ps is	1: 10: 0
		£9: 14: 6

John Coney.

Three years later, when Coney made forty-eight gold rings for Wainwright's widow's funeral at a total cost of £37.10.6, the charge for the gold increased again, by five shillings.[34] But since each ring for Mrs. Wainwright's funeral weighed slightly less than each of her husband's, each ring cost less. Coney also made rings for the funeral of John Baker in 1697; the account of the estate's executor filed in 1699 shows that Coney was paid £25 for the rings.[35] The estate of Grove Hirst (d. 1717) paid Coney £10.5.8 for rings, and £1.5 for a "Ring for C. Addams," and the estate of Richard Kates (d. 1718) of Concord paid him £15.7 for rings and a silver cup.[36]

A letter to Coney in 1700 from John Chester of Wethersfield, Connecticut, shows that when clients were at a distance, silversmiths had some latitude in determining how orders would be filled. The letter indicates that orders sometimes were not filled to the customer's satisfaction and that pieces could leave a shop unmarked. The dissatisfied Mr. Chester wrote,

I have received the Letter & bill of loading & contents
℔ Mr Jonas Clark & have paid Your Mony to him
said for the Solver & shod not have returnd
that, but my wife & Children had rather have the
value of it in other plate. I must say that I recon
you charge me more than Ever I gave to you in
Boston & provided I had been there with you I shoud
not have Given so much by a Considerable Matter
but I am unwilling Now I am at so great a Distance
to frustrate your Expectation. I have found you an
Ingenious Gent & doubt not of it for the future, the
plate is larger than I intended, a salt seller of 4^{lb} had been

big Enough & other things proportionable, & one
thing that troubles me I gave you my Coat of arms
to sett upon the Tankard which you have omitted, &
also omitted ye marking of all but ye tankard, which
will give me the trouble of bringing y to Boston, to
gett them Done, or I must keep them as they are, w^{ch}
will bee against my mind. The tankard I bought of you in June
weighs: 6^{ou} 14^{dwt} & I gave 8^{lb} 8^s for it, that wch I bought near
7 years since, weighs 10^{ou}:14^d: & I gave 11^{lb};18^s for that
& these things are Equivalent in prise to the tankard
made in June Last: I have paid Mr Clark a peice of 8^t
for fraight but as I remember, you was to Deliver the plate, & take
the mony here free of Charge to me, & I think the
bringing of it by Land, would not have cost me, more
then what I have paid If soe much/verse
I Delivered to m^r Clark 145 pieces of 8^t by weight
Equivalent to forty five pounds five shillings & 8^d: and
it is the best parcell of mony I Ever was Master
of, some of the peices weighing above 18 weight
and have his Receipt of the same.
Sr I shall not Enlarge at present but desire a line from you
when you have oppertunity to send, of yor Receiving ye mony
& to set me in some way about marking of ye plate if
it may be done here, wch with hearty respects to yor
Self & Madam Coney is the Needfull at present
I am yor Ready friend & very/humble servt/John Chester[37]

Other documents also offer ample evidence about Coney's business. Like many silversmiths, Coney's shop was robbed on at least one occasion. In 1688 James Herbert was tried for stealing a silver tumbler valued at twelve shillings, a silver rivet valued at fourteen pence, and molds for buckles.[38] The watchmaker David Johnson (q.v. Appendix A) served as a juror in the trial. Coney also had transactions with his fellow craftsmen, appraising the tools in the estate of William Rouse (q.v.) and being owed twenty-three shillings by the estate of David Jesse (q.v.). Along with Edward Winslow and John Noyes (q.v.), Coney was asked by the justices of the Superior Court in 1706 to inspect a parcel of money to determine if any of the coins had been clipped.[39]

Coney's reputation as a goldsmith was such that important public commissions came his way, as for example the aforementioned spear for the Artillery Company. He also made a seal for Harvard College in 1693 at the cost of £2.2.6.[40] It is possible that Coney was responsible for having the plates engraved for the bills of credit issued by the Massachusetts Province from the time they were introduced in 1702 until his death in 1722.[41] He was paid £10.15 in 1711 for "new engraving the plates."[42] The Colony of New Hampshire paid him £15.10 for engraving the plates for its bills of credit in 1722.[43] His name also had enough recognition value to be mentioned in newspaper advertisements for stolen plate. The *Boston News-Letter* of 3 November 1712 listed "a Silver Tankard that holds about a Quart, made by Mr. *Coney*, mark'd M.W. on the Handle" and the *New-England Weekly Journal* of 10 November 1729 publicized the loss of a "*Fashionable Silver Spoon of Mr.* Coney's *make, Crest with a Talbotts (or Dogs) head erased.*"

Coney trained a number of apprentices and employed many journeymen in his shop. His first journeyman may have been Thomas Higginson (q.v.), a New England native whose London training ended in 1677. Higginson may have been recommended to Coney by Coney's former master, Jeremiah Dummer, whose mother-in-law, Mary Atwater, married Higginson's father in 1676. A Thomas Higginson took the oath of allegiance in Boston in 1679 and was included in the tax list of 1681 in the same area of town as Coney.[44] In 1679 Coney signed a bond so that the London-trained goldsmith Nathaniel Gay (q.v.) could remain in Boston, presumably to work for Coney, but how long Gay remained with Coney is not known. Coney is also thought to have trained Benjamin Hiller and Nathaniel Morse (qq.v.), both of whom witnessed a deed for Coney in 1709, and possibly Andrew Tyler (q.v.), who was one of the appraisers of Coney's estate.[45] Since Coney became the guardian of Peter Oliver (q.v.) in 1699, presumably he trained Oliver as well.[46] He may also have trained Thomas Bradford (q.v.) because the nineteen-year-old Bradford witnessed a deed in 1716, and some authorities believe that Coney trained Samuel Gray (1684–1713) (q.v.), although no documentary evidence exists.[47] Coney may also have trained his brother Benjamin and Thomas Savage (qq.v.). John Banks (q.v.) may have worked for Coney as a journeyman since he witnessed the bond for the administration of Coney's estate in 1722.[48] The apprenticeship of Paul Revere, Sr. (q.v.), was not completed when Coney died on 20 August 1722. The value of the remainder of that indenture, about three and a half years, was appraised at £30 in the estate inventory and was sold for £10 more than that amount.

The estate inventory, compiled by Jonathan Williams, Jonathan Jackson, and Andrew Tyler, is remarkable for its detailed description of a fully equipped silversmith's shop. Following his death, Coney's tools were sold at auction. The advertisement read, "This Evening the remaining part of the Tools of the late Mr. Coney are to be Sold. About 5 a Clock."[49] The tools included

Gold 8 oz.12dw.t 9gr. at 10£. ℔ oz. £86.3.9. Peices of eight 28 ¾ oz. at 13/ £18.13.9   104. 17. 6
Wrought Plate &c. 515 Oz. 12 dw.t ½ at 12/. £309.7.6 Province Bills £142.—.6   451. 8
1 Stone Ring £3. 1 Ditto 30/. 1 pr. Gold Earrings w.th glass drops,
 25/.2 Gold drops, & Gold Soder 6/   6. 1.—
1 Box of Pearl 40/. Coral Beads 35/. A small shagareen Trunk w.th stones
 30/. 14 ½ oz Silver Lace 40/   7. 5.—
1 Snuffbox 15/. 1 Toothpick case 20/. 1 Pr. Forceps 6/. Burnt Silver & Ingot silver 5/   2. 6.—
1 Gripe for a Sword 10/. Gold Limmel 6/. 1 ¼ oz Joint wire 15/. 1 pr
 Silver Compasses 10/   2. 1.—
Refin'd Silver 8 oz. 2dw.t ½ at 13/. ℔ oz   5. 5. 8
1 Forging Anvil weighing 161 lb at 12d £12.8.—.1 Ditto w.t 98 lb at 8d £3.5.4   11. 6. 4
11 Anvils of various sorts w.t 48 ½ lb at 12d £12.8.6. 3 Ditto w.t 126 ½ lb. at 10d £5.5.5.   17. 13. 11
8 Ditto w.t 313 ½ lb. at 8d £10.9. 2 small raising D.o 5/ 1 Tobacco box anvil 3/   10. 17.—
2 Teasts w.t 60 ½ lb. 15d £3.15.7 ½ D.o 32 ½ lb. 12d. £1.12.6. 1 Spoon Teast 39 ½ lb. £3.9.6 @ 4d   8. 17. 7½
1 Round Teast w.t 10 lb. at 8d 6/8. 1 Locket d.o 6 lb. 6/. 1 Broken Anvil 20 lb.@ 4d. 6/8   19. 4
20 Stakes w.t 74 lb. 12d £3.14.— 3 D.o w.t 34 ½ lb. at 8d 23/. 23 small ditto 23/   6. —
9 Spoon punches 21/11. 1 Canister punch 4/. 2 Pepper box punches 10/   1. 15. 11
6 Caster punches 14/6. 4 Cutting punches 12 lb. 12/. 6 Smaller ditto 6/   1. 12. 6
6 Dapping punches 11 lb. at 6d. 5/6. 3 Boxes of Chasing punches &c 45/   2. 10. 6
7 Boxes of punches, chizells &c £3 5 Cutting punches 5/6. Old
Punches & swages 5/   3. 10. 6
1 Block of Steel, w.th 5 boxes of seal punches £7. 1 Cold Chizell 1/. 13 Triblets 4/4   7. 5. 4
2 Ring swages 10/6. 7 Swages w.t 18 lb. 20/. 6 Sparrowhawks at 2/6. 15/   2. 5. 6
1 Brass Stamper 20/. 15 Strainers 7/6. 1 Brass Salt Stamp w.t 11 ½ lb. 12/   1. 19. 6
4 Brass Caster Stamps w.t 19 lb. 19. 2 Spangle Stamps 5/. 1 Brass Sodering pan 10/   1. 14.—
1 Brass Cullender 10/. 1 Morter w.t 7 lb. 7/. 1 Iron d.o w.t. 134 lb. at 3d £1.13.8   2. 10. 8
1 Standing Vice 20/. 1 Board d.o 18/. 6 Hand d.o 13/ 2 Drill d.o 6/. 1 Turn d.o 15/   3. 12.—
1 Large Skillet w.t 47 lb. 8d 31/4. 2 D.o w.t 66 lb. 4d 22/. 1 D.o broken w.t. 18 lb. 3d. 4/6   2. 17. 10
2 Ingots 4/. 9 Iron Flasque 25/. 1 Brass d.o 2/6. 1 Pr. Flasque screws 8/   1. 19. 6

1 Pr. Casting tongs 1/. 4 pr. Forging d.º 6/. 4 pr. Nealing d.º 6/	—. 13.—
1 Pr. Bellows 30/. 50 Blew Crucibles of several sizes £6.13.6	8. 3. 6
127 Nests of white Crucibles of several sizes £4.14.4. 1 Iron Ladle 1/6	4. 15. 10
3 Two-hand Hammers w.ᵗ. 3 lb. at 12.ᵈ £1.16.—. 1 D.º w.ᵗ. 9 lb. at 8.ᵈ. 6/	2. 2
112 Hammers for Raising, Pilking, Swelling, Hollowing, Creasing, Planishing &c	8.—.—
3 Pr. Stock Shears 25/6. 4 pr. hand shears 6/. 4 Screw plates & Taps. 12/	2. 3. 6
Files 33/8. 13 pr. Compasses 19/6. 16 pr. Plyers 25/. 1 Pr. Vice clamps 1/6	3. 19. 8
4 Frame saws 12/6 1 Drill Iron 6.ᵈ 1 BeckIron w.ᵗ 6 ½ lb. at 6.ᵈ. 3/3. 2 Gaugers 2/	—. 18. 3
2 Drawing benches Leath.ʳ. & Tongs 16/. 9 Drawing Irons 25/. 1 Swage Drawer 20/	3. 1.—
2 Wheels blocks & turning tools £4 10/. Gravers 5/10. 3 Borax boxes 3/. 2 Cement blocks 1/	4. 19. 10
2 Oile Stones 3/. 2 Oile things 2/. 2 Loam pots 2/. 1 Puttee box 6.ᵈ. 2 Limmel boxes 2/	9. 6
2 Scratch brushes 6/. 2 Blowpipes 1/. 1 Square 1/. 1 Copper measure 1/. 3 Gluepot 1/4	10. 4
1 Sand Cushion 2/. 2 Small Copper plates 5/. 3 Copper boiling pans w.ᵗ 13 lb. at 2/. 26/	1. 13.—
7 Stone Burnishers 15/. 1 Touchstone 2/. 1 Loadstone 10/. 1 Ditto set in Silver 22/	2. 9.—
1 Fine large Beam & Scales 18/. 4 Pile of weights q.ᵗ. in all 520 Oz £3.2	4.—.—
5 Pr. Smaller scales & weights 17/ 15 small Rasps 17.ᵈ 1 Sugar hatchet 1/. 2 Mallets 1/	1.—. 5
2 Candlestick moulds 3/3. Patterns £4.18.6 12 Watch keys & the body of a watch 5/	5. 6. 9
1 Glass case 10/. 1 Desk 10/. Chest 40/. A Case of Draws 6/	3. 6.—
130 ½ lb of Binding Wire at 2/. £13.1 14 ¾ lb of Borax at 12/. £8.17	21. 18.—
7 ½ lb Saltpetre 2/3 ℔ lb 16/11. 100 lb Sandover at 2.ᵈ. 16/8. 2 lb Mercury 42/	3. 15. 7

. . .

1 Small Iron Stove 30/. 1 Old Iron Candlestick 3/. Charcole 40/. 1 Gun barrel 2/.	3. 15.—
535 lb Old wrought Iron at 3.ᵈ. £6.13.9. 38 lb. of Cast Iron at 1.ᵈ. 3/2	6. 16. 11
An Engine for Coining with all Utensils belonging thereto	10. 10.—
7 ¼ lb Old Brass at 10.ᵈ. 6/6. 36 lb Lead. at 3.ᵈ. 9/	15. 6
123 lb Old Iron at 4d. £2.1.— 1 Iron Weight of ½ lb 15/	2. 16.—[50]

Among the cash payments received by the estate were 25 shillings from Nathaniel Morse, £15.10 from the Massachusetts Bay Province, probably for Coney's work engraving the plates for Province bills, and 18 shillings 6 pence for "a Muffring Soder, & Coral Necklace." The total value of the inventory was more than £3,700.

Coney's son-in-law Rev. Thomas Foxcroft preached his funeral sermon noting that his father-in-law was "excellently talented for the Employment assign'd Him, and took a peculiar Delight therein."[51] At a meeting of the Boston selectmen on 24 September 1722 permission was granted for a tomb to be built in the Granary Burying Ground.[52] Coney is interred there along with his wife who died on 12 April 1726.[53] PEK

SURVIVING OBJECTS

	Mark	Inscription	Patron	Date	Reference	Owner
Baptismal basin	B*	Clarke arms, 3 swords erect in pale, points up, the middle sword bears on an inscutcheon a sinister hand, and crest, an armed dexter arm embowed (+)	William and Mary (Withington) Clarke	ca. 1700	Clarke 1932, no. 1	
Baptismal basin	C*	Dom.ˢ Johannes Legg Arm.ᵍ Ecclesiam J. Christi apud Marblehead/eujus Rev.ᵈˢ D. Edv.ᵈˢ Holyoke est Pastor, hoc pietatis testimonia religiose donavit/ Anno 1718	Second Congregational Society, Marblehead, Mass., for John Legg	ca. 1718	Clarke 1932, no. 2	MFAB

	Mark	Inscription	Patron	Date	Reference	Owner
Beaker (with later handle)	A	HNR (later)		ca. 1695	Buhler 1972, no. 38	MFAB
Beaker	A*	Thomas Knowlton	First Congregational Church, Ipswich, Mass., for Thomas Knowlton	ca. 1692	Buhler/Hood 1970, no. 27	YUAG
Two beakers	A *or* B	The gift of Nathaniell Byfeild/To the Church in Bristol./1693	Nathaniel Byfield and/or First Congregational Church, Bristol, R.I.	1693	Clarke 1932, no. 3	
Five beakers (altered to two-handled cups)	A *or* B	Ex dono Wm Browne sen^r, Esqu^r.	First Congregational Society, Salem, Mass., for William Browne	ca. 1687	Clarke 1932, no. 6	
Beaker	B*	P/AE (+); THE GIFT OF ELIZABETH POTTER TO THE CHURCH OF IPSWICH, 1699 (later)	Anthony and Elizabeth (Stone) Potter	ca. 1690	Buhler/Hood 1970, no. 28	YUAG
Beaker	C	The gift of Jonath^n Wade & Wife to ye 3^d Church in Ipswich	Jonathan and Jane Wade and/or Congregational Church, Hamilton, Mass.	ca. 1715	Clarke 1932, no. 33	
Eight beakers	C	Hamp^{tn}: Old Chh 1713	Congregational Church, Hampton, N.H.	1713	Clarke 1932, no. 8	
Two beakers	C	LC	First Church of Christ, Lynn, Mass.	ca. 1715	Clarke 1932, no. 9	
Two beakers	C	E: Brattle to Mr Holyokes Church	Edward Brattle and/or Second Congregational Society, Marblehead, Mass.	ca. 1716	Clarke 1932, no. 35	MFAB
Two beakers	C	A Gift to Mr Holyoks Church/Marblehead/1716	Second Congregational Society, Marblehead, Mass.	ca. 1716	Clarke 1932, no. 34	MFAB
Beaker	C	Ex dono M/WP to South Church	William and Phebe (Brook) Manley and/or Old South Church, Boston	ca. 1715	Clarke 1932, no. 36	
Beaker	C	SC (+)	Old South Church, Boston	ca. 1715	Clarke 1932, no. 7	
Bowl	C	Riddell arms, a chevron between 3 pine trees; HOPE TO SHARE	Walter Riddell (?)	ca. 1710	MFA 1991, no. 50	MFAB
Two candlesticks	C*	none	Thomas and Mary (Willoughby) Barton	ca. 1710	Buhler 1972, no. 57	MFAB
Candlestick	D	RA	Angier family (?)	ca. 1695	Buhler 1972, no. 44	MFAB
Two candlesticks	F*	Ex dono Pupillorum 1716	Henry Flynt and/or the Harvard College class of 1716	1716	Flynt/Fales 1968, 56–58	HD
Cann	C*	Stoddard crest, a demi-horse issuing from a ducal coronet; W/IE	Stoddard family	ca. 1720	Buhler 1972, no. 63	MFAB

	Mark	Inscription	Patron	Date	Reference	Owner
Caster	A	G/TB		ca. 1700	Buhler 1972, no. 539	MFAB
Caster	B*	S/SS		ca. 1700	Buhler 1960, no. 30	NM
Caster	C*	F/ID (+)		ca. 1710	Buhler 1972, no. 53	MFAB
Caster	C*	G/IL		ca. 1715	Ward 1980, 1301	YUAG
Two casters	C*	none	Gibb family (?)	ca. 1710	Buhler 1972, no. 55	MFAB
Caster (mate below)	C	Charnock arms, on a bend 3 crosses crosslet	John and Hannah (Holyoke) Charnock	ca. 1715	Buhler 1972, no. 62	MFAB
Caster (mate above)	C*	Charnock arms, on a bend 3 crosses crosslet	John and Hannah (Holyoke) Charnock	ca. 1715	Christie's, 22 January 1983, lot 425	
Caster	C	P/WE (later)		ca. 1710	Buhler 1972, no. 56	MFAB
Two casters	C	Hutchinson arms, per pale a lion rampant over a field of nine crosses crosslet	William Hutchinson	ca. 1715	Phillips 1939, no. 31	
Caudle cup (see also mates with mark B)	A*	II (later altered to IRDP)		ca. 1700	Sotheby's, 30 January–2 February 1991, lot 151	
Caudle cup (with cover)	A*	Addington arms, per pale ermine and ermines on a chevron between 3 fleur-de-lis 4 lozenges all counterchanged; crest, a cat-a-mount passant guard bezantée; Ex Dono IL (+)	Isaac Addington	ca. 1685	Buhler/Hood 1970, no. 22	YUAG
Caudle cup	A*	C/DS; M/DT; M.P (later)		ca. 1680	Clarke 1932, no. 20	
Caudle cup	A*	M/IM (+)	John and Mary (Brattle) Mico	ca. 1690	Buhler 1972, no. 34	MFAB
Caudle cup	A*	Holyoke arms (later)	Elizur and/or Rev. Edward Holyoke	ca. 1690	Clarke 1932, no. 22	HU
Caudle cup	A*	The Gift of m^rs Margaret Bridges of/finglas in Ireland to ye Church of/ Concord Apr:6:1676	First Parish, Concord, Mass., for Margaret Bridges	1676	Clarke 1932, no. 23	
Caudle cup	A*	The Gift (cheifly) of Tho:/Browne Senr a member of y^e/Church of Concord to y^e/Said Church 82	Thomas Brown, Sr., and/or First Parish, Concord, Mass.	1682	Clarke 1932, no. 24	

	Mark	Inscription	Patron	Date	Reference	Owner
Two caudle cups	A*	M:Church plate	First Church, Malden, Mass.	ca. 1690	Clarke 1932, no. 26	MFAB
Two caudle cups	A*	M:C:Plate	First Church, Malden, Mass.	ca. 1690	Clarke 1932, no. 27	MFAB
Two caudle cups	A*	SC	Congregational Church, Stratford, Conn.	ca. 1690	Clarke 1932, no. 28	
Caudle cup	A or B	S/TM (+)	Thomas and Mary Savage	ca. 1680	Clarke 1932, no. 25	
Caudle cup	B*	SH	Sarah (Savage) Higginson (?)	ca. 1700	Flynt/Fales 1968, 84–85	HD
Caudle cup (see also mate with mark A and mate below)	B	II (later altered to IRDP)		ca. 1700	Sotheby's, 30 January–1 February 1986, lot 402	
Caudle cup (see also mate with mark A and mate above)	B*	II (later altered to IRDP)		ca. 1700	*Antiques* 129 (April 1986): 781	
Four caudle cups	C*	Concord Church Treasure 1714.	First Parish, Concord, Mass.	1714	Clarke 1932, no. 29	
Chafing dish	C	none		ca. 1715	Clarke 1932, no. 16	MFAB
Chafing dish	C	F/IS	John and Sarah (Lynde) Foye	ca. 1710	Buhler 1972, no. 58	MFAB
Two chafing dishes	C*	P/WE (later)		ca. 1710	Buhler 1972, no. 60	MFAB
Chafing dish	C*	none	Mehitable (Coney) Foxcroft	ca. 1715	Buhler/Hood 1970, no. 36	YUAG
Chafing dish	C*	W/IH (later altered)		ca. 1715		BMA
Chafing dish	C	A/NM (+)	Nathaniel and Margaret (Gibbs) Appleton	ca. 1715	DAPC 68.3407	MMA
Two chafing dishes	C*	Hutchinson crest, a wyvern couped	Thomas Hutchinson	ca. 1715	Sotheby's, 28–30 January 1988, lot 1061	
Chocolate pot	B*/D	The gift of Wm Stoughton Esquire/ To Mrs Sarah Tailer: 701	William Stoughton and/or Sarah (Byfield) Tailer	1701	Buhler 1972, no. 50	MFAB
Chocolate pot	C†	C/WD E (later)		ca. 1715	MFA 1991, no. 51	MFAB
Cup	B (?)*	EB; AE/IB (+)		ca. 1705	YUAG files	
Cup	B*	B/BS (+)		ca. 1700	*MMA Bulletin* (November 1941): 233–35	MMA
Cup	B*	MC		ca. 1700	DAPC 79.3079	
Cup	B	MW; SPL (later)	Mary (Willoughby) Barton	ca. 1700	Buhler 1972, no. 39	MFAB
Cup	B	MW; MP/to/FWP (later)	Mary (Willoughby) Barton	ca. 1700	Buhler 1972, no. 40	MFAB

	Mark	Inscription	Patron	Date	Reference	Owner
Cup	B*	?		ca. 1700	*Antiques* 76 (August 1959): 90	
Cup	B*	S. Russell (+)	Samuel Russell	ca. 1710	Clarke 1932, no. 46	
Cup	B*	C/TP; WA (later) (+)		ca. 1700	Sotheby's, 23–24 June 1993, lot 91	
Cup	C*	C/IH		ca. 1722	Eitner 1976, no. 35	
Cup (with mark of Rufus Greene)	C	Capt ID; Lucy Smith Aged 10 Yrs 9 Mos. 15 Days — Mary E. Comstock (later)		ca. 1715	Parke-Bernet, 14–15 May 1948, lot 195	
Cup	C*	none		ca. 1715	Johnston 1994, 30	CMA
Cup	C*	IR (+)	Samuel Robinson	1717	Buhler/Hood 1970, no. 37	YUAG
Cup	C	The Gift of Robt Brisco 1718.	Robert Brisco and/or First Parish Church, Beverly, Mass.	1718	Clarke 1932, no. 38	
Cup	C*	EB (later) (+)		ca. 1715	Buhler 1965, 23–24, 27–29	HMA
Cup	C	Ex dono: Elias Parkman to ye New N^h/ Church (+)	New North Church, Boston, for Elias Parkman	ca. 1715	Clarke 1932, no. 37	
Cup	?	?		ca. 1700	*Antiques* 30 (November 1936): 197	
Cup	?	unidentified arms; DE		ca. 1700	Parke-Bernet, 10–12 March 1949, lot 545	
Dram cup	A*	MB		ca. 1680	Fales 1970, 41	
Dram cup	A*	S/RS	Robert and Sarah Stone (?)	ca. 1680	Safford 1983, 5, 8–9	MMA
Fork (miniature)	D	MW	Mary (Willoughby) Barton	ca. 1700	Buhler 1972, no. 46	MFAB
Grace cup	A or B	Stoughton arms, on a saltire gules between 4 door staples an escallop, and crest, a demi-lion holding an escallop in its paws (+)	William Stoughton	1701	Clarke 1932, no. 30	HU
Grace cup	C	Flynt arms, 3 flint stones; Donum Pupillorum/Henrico Flynt/1718.	Henry Flynt and/or the Harvard College class of 1718	1718	*American Silver* 1967, no. 5	RWNAG
Inkstand	C*/F	Belcher crest, a greyhound's head erased and collared	Jonathan Belcher	ca. 1715	Safford 1983, 32	MMA

	Mark	Inscription	Patron	Date	Reference	Owner
Monteith	B*	Colman arms, on a pale rayonée a lion rampant (+)	John Colman	ca. 1705	Buhler/Hood 1970, no. 31	YUAG
Monteith	C	RAL (cipher)	Robert and Alida (Schuyler) Livingston	ca. 1715	Clarke 1932, no. 41	Franklin D. Roosevelt Library–Museum
Mourning ring (gold)	D†	SC: obt: 17: Ap^{rll}: 94 AEt: 36	Sarah Coney	1694	Fales 1983, 10–11	PEM
Mug	B*	H/WS; EW (later)		ca. 1705	DAPC 84.3187	
Mug	B*	Ex Dono: E.L. ad E:G		ca. 1700	*Silver Supplement* 1973, no. 22	
Mug	C*	unidentified crest, a lion rampant holding a curving battle-ax		ca. 1715	Buhler/Hood 1970, no. 38	YUAG
Mug	C*	I/SR (over earlier initials?)		ca. 1710	Buhler 1972, no. 59	MFAB
Mug	C*	TH; SP (later)	Thomas Holland	ca. 1715	*Bulletin DIA* 26 (1947): 22	DIA
Mug	C	SB		ca. 1715		AIC
Mug	?	EV		ca. 1710		MFAB
Patch box	D	P/NI		ca. 1715	*Antiques* 105 (January 1974): 62	
Pepper box	C	none		ca. 1715	Clarke 1932, no. 58	
Pepper box	C	Appleton crest, a pineapple; PA; MA	Priscilla (Appleton) Ward	ca. 1715	Buhler 1972, no. 61	MFAB
Pepper box	C*	?		ca. 1710	*Antiques* 114 (October 1978): 751	
Pepper box	F*	MH		ca. 1710	Parke-Bernet, 17 December 1968, lot 42	
Pepper box	F*	?		ca. 1710	Clarke 1932, no. 57	
Plate	A*	R/CE (+)	Caleb and Elizabeth Rawlins	ca. 1690	Buhler 1972, no. 36	MFAB
Plate	A*	Eyre arms, argent a chevron ermines between 3 escallops, and crest, a lion rampant	John and Katherine Eyre	ca. 1685	Puig et al. 1989, no. 173	MIA
Plate	A	SE	Sarah Eliot	ca. 1705	*Antiques* 51 (May 1947): 338	
Porringer	A or B	E/IM	Joseph and Mary (Willys) Eliot	ca. 1700	Clarke 1932, no. 62	

	Mark	Inscription	Patron	Date	Reference	Owner
Porringer	A *or* B	B/IS		ca. 1700	Clarke 1932, no. 63	
Porringer	A *or* B	SDS (later)		ca. 1700	Clarke 1932, no. 64	
Porringer	A *or* B	C/WCD E (later)		ca. 1700	Clarke 1932, no. 65	
Porringer	B*	HB		ca. 1705	Buhler/Hood 1970, no. 33	YUAG
Porringer	C	ST (later)		ca. 1715	Clarke 1932, no. 71	
Porringer	C	B/TM	Thomas and Mary (Willoughby) Barton	ca. 1710	Buhler 1972, no. 54	MFAB
Porringer	C*	initials erased; MS (later)		ca. 1715	Buhler/Hood 1970, no. 34	YUAG
Porringer	C*	D/TM		ca. 1715	Buhler/Hood 1970, no. 35	YUAG
Porringer	C	EH	Rev. Edward Holyoke	ca. 1715	Clarke 1932, no. 70	
Porringer	C	MJLP (later?)		ca. 1715	Clarke 1932, no. 67	
Porringer	C	P/BR		ca. 1715	Clarke 1932, no. 66	
Porringer	C*	HR (later)		ca. 1710	*Antiques* 107 (June 1975): 1044	VMFA
Porringer	C	H/NM		ca. 1710	Sotheby's, 27–28 June 1985, lot 60	
Porringer	C	LDL (+)		ca. 1710		HMA
Porringer	C*	AO (later)		ca. 1690		PEM
Porringer	C	S/TS		ca. 1715	YUAG files	
Porringer	D	PU	Phineas Upham	ca. 1700	MFA 1906, no. 60	
Porringer	F*	P/FR; JD to/MS		ca. 1710	Phillips 1939, no. 44	
Porringer	?	Gilman (later)		ca. 1700	Parke-Bernet, 1, 2, 4 April 1953, lot 431	
Porringer	?	HP		ca. 1705	*Antiques* 113 (May 1978): 930	
Porringer	?	unidentified initials (later)		ca. 1700	*Antiques* 61 (April 1952): 308	
Porringer	?	M/DE	David and Elizabeth Mason	ca. 1700	YUAG files	
Porringer	?	from SH to SHH 1840 (later)		ca. 1700	YUAG files	
Salt	A	SM	Sarah (Winslow) (Standish) (Payne) Middlecott	ca. 1695	Buhler 1972, no. 45	MFAB

	Mark	Inscription	Patron	Date	Reference	Owner
Two salts	C	A/TH; W (later)		ca. 1720		MFAB
Salver	B*	Dudley arms, a lion rampant, and crest, a lion's head erased; NEC GLADIO NEC ARCV	Joseph Dudley	ca. 1705	Puig et al. 1989, no. 175	MIA
Salver	B	SW (+)	Willoughby family (?)	ca. 1700	Buhler 1972, no. 49	MFAB
Salver	B*	Lowell arms (later)		ca. 1700	Clarke 1932, no. 50	MMA
Salver	B*	Checkley arms, a chevron between 3 mullets; initials erased (+)	Checkley family	ca. 1705	Buhler 1965, 23–27	HMA
Salver	B	R/KD (?, erased); T/IA (later)		ca. 1700	Flynt/Fales 1968, 114–15	HD
Salver	C	W/IK		ca. 1710	Clarke 1932, no. 55	
Salver	C	MW (+)	Mary (Willoughby) Barton	ca. 1710	Buhler 1972, no. 51	MFAB
Saucepan	C	Dummer crest (+)	Dummer family	ca. 1715	Clarke 1932, no. 72	
Snuffbox	E†	Wentworth arms, sable a chevron or between 3 leopards' faces, and crest, a griffin passant; EN DIEU EST TOUT	Wentworth family	ca. 1705	Buhler/Hood 1970, no. 30	YUAG
Spoon (miniature)	D	MW	Mary (Willoughby) Barton	ca. 1700	Buhler 1972, no. 46	MFAB
Spout cup	B*	Apthorp crest, a mullet	Apthorp family	ca. 1695	Puig et al. 1989, no. 174	MIA
Spout cup	B*	unidentified arms; SP (?)		ca. 1710	Flynt/Fales 1968, 109	HD
Spout cup	C*/D	Willm. Parsons 1825 (later)(+)		ca. 1715	Shepard 1978, 225	MAM
Spout cup	C*/F†	B/WM (+)	William and Mary Bowditch	ca. 1715	Clarke 1932, no. 83	MFAB
Sucket fork	D	ES		ca. 1700	YUAG files	
Sugar box	A	SG	Samuel Gardner	ca. 1700	Buhler 1972, no. 48	MFAB
Sugar box	B*	The gift of Grandmother Norton to Anna Quincy born 1719 (later) (+)	John and Mary (Mason) Norton (?)	ca. 1685	Buhler 1972, no. 33	MFAB
Sugar box	B	none		ca. 1685	Gourley 1965, no. 51	CGA
Sugar box	B*	L/IE		ca. 1700	*Antiques* 79 (March 1961): 227	CW

	Mark	Inscription	Patron	Date	Reference	Owner
Sword (attrib.)	F (?)	SB	Samuel Barton (?)	ca. 1720	Buhler/Hood 1970, no. 39	YUAG
Tablespoon	A†	S/RS	Robert and Sarah Stone	ca. 1680	Buhler/Hood 1970, no. 23	YUAG
Tablespoon	A	G/IE		ca. 1700	*Silver Supplement* 1973, no. 23	
Tablespoon	A*	W/IE (later)(+)		ca. 1690	Buhler 1972, no. 35	MFAB
Two tablespoons (mates below)	A*	KP (+)	Katharine (Brackenburg) Phips (?)	ca. 1680	Buhler 1972, no. 32	MFAB
Tablespoon (mates above and below)	A*	KP (+)	Katharine (Brackenburg) Phips	ca. 1680	DAPC 68.3207	MMA
Tablespoon (mates above)	A*	KP (+)	Katharine (Brackenburg) Phips	ca. 1680	Buhler/Hood 1970, no. 24	YUAG
Tablespoon (mates below)	A*	MS; H/IE (later)	Mary Shrimpton	ca. 1690	*Antiques* 112 (July 1977): 22	
Tablespoon (mates above and below)	A*	MS; H/IE (later)	Mary Shrimpton	ca. 1690	Buhler/Hood 1970, no. 25	YUAG
Tablespoon (mates above)	A*	MS; H/IE (later)	Mary Shrimpton	ca. 1690		MFAB
Tablespoon	B	MW	Mary (Willoughby) Barton	ca. 1710	Buhler 1972, no. 47	MFAB
Tablespoon	C	DI	David Jeffries (?)	ca. 1710	DAPC 91.3261	
Tablespoon	C	IC (later altered)		ca. 1710	Quimby 1995, no. 38	WM
Tablespoon	F	PC		ca. 1720	Shepard 1978, 225	MAM
Tablespoon	?	IGD		ca. 1700	Freeman, 26–28 April 1982, lot 173	
Tablespoon	?	EGD		ca. 1700	Freeman, 26–28 April 1982, lot 173	
Tablespoon	?	RN	Richard Norman	ca. 1710	YUAG files	
Tankard	A*	unidentified arms, 3 crescents, a crest, an increscent; TP		ca. 1690	*Silver Supplement* 1973, no. 24	USDS
Tankard	A*	Shrimpton arms, on a cross 5 escallops, an annulet for difference, and crest, a demi-lion holding an escallop; MS; Mary Shrimpton (+)	Mary Shrimpton	ca. 1690	Buhler/Hood 1970, no. 26	YUAG
Tankard	A*	B/MS		ca. 1690	Quimby 1995, no. 37	WM

	Mark	Inscription	Patron	Date	Reference	Owner
Tankard	A*	Eyre arms, argent a chevron ermines between 3 escallops, and crest, a lion rampant; E/IK	John and Katherine Eyre	ca. 1685	Safford 1983, 10–11	MMA
Tankard	A*	Allen arms, per bend rompu argent and azure 6 martlets counterchanged, and crest, a bird; MA	Allen family	ca. 1695	Buhler 1972, no. 41	MFAB
Tankard	A	Norton arms, a fret, a bend varié vert and or cotised sable, and crest, a griffin	Rev. John Norton	ca. 1700	Buhler 1979, no. 3	WAM
Tankard	A	Love Rawlins Pickman./to her great niece./Martha Pickman Codman./1864. (later)	John and Love (Prout) (English) Rawlins	ca. 1695	Buhler 1972, no. 42	MFAB
Tankard	A*	Browne arms [argent] on a bend [sable] double cotised 3 eagles displayed, and crest, an eagle displayed; MB	Mary (Browne) Lynde	ca. 1695	Buhler 1972, no. 43	MFAB
Tankard	A*	S/RS (altered to H/RS); unidentified arms (later)	Robert and Sarah Stone (?)	ca. 1690	*Antiques* 68 (November 1955): 461	
Tankard	A*	W/DM		ca. 1690	*Antiques* 31 (April 1937): 163	
Tankard	A*	W/WR		ca. 1690	Bartlett 1984, 4–5	SLAM
Tankard	A or B	W/WE (+)	William and Elizabeth (Dering) Welsteed	ca. 1710	Clarke 1932, no. 91	
Tankard	A or B	C/IS		ca. 1690	Clarke 1932, no. 88	
Tankard	A or B	MS; The Gift of/ Miss Mary Allin/to the Church/in/ Brooklin/1750 (later)	Mehitable or Mary Shepard	ca. 1690	Clarke 1932, no. 89	
Tankard	A or B	AF	Arthur Fenner	ca. 1700	Phillips 1939, no. 52	
Tankard	A or B	Fowle arms, a leopard and 3 roses	Fowle family	ca. 1700	YUAG files	
Tankard	A or B	Belonging to yᵉ Church of Christ in Cambridge	First Parish, Cambridge, Mass.	ca. 1700	Clarke 1932, no. 99	
Tankard	A or B	A/NM (+)		ca. 1700	Sotheby Parke Bernet, 6–8 November 1975, lot 607	

	Mark	Inscription	Patron	Date	Reference	Owner
Tankard	A or B	Clarke arms, 3 swords erect in pale, points up, the middle sword bears on an inscutcheon a sinister hand, and crest, an armed dexter arm embowed (+)	William and Elizabeth Clarke (?)	ca. 1700	Clarke 1932, no. 101	
Two tankards	A or B	The Gift of Mʳ-William Wilcocks to the/Church of Christ in Cambridge N. E./Anno Dom 1654	First Parish, Cambridge, Mass., for William Wilcocks	1705	Clarke 1932, no. 98	
Tankard	B	Foster arms, a chevron between 3 hunting horns, and crest, a dexter arm, armed and embowed, holding a broken tilting spear (+)	John Foster	ca. 1700	Clarke 1932, no. 97	BBC
Tankard	B	?M (later)		ca. 1700	Parke-Bernet, 15–16 April 1955, lot 239	
Tankard	C	Cranston arms, gules 3 cranes within a bordure, embattled argent, and crest, a crane passant; DUM VIGILO CURO; C/IM	James and Mary Cranston	ca. 1722	Clarke 1932, no. 94	MFAB
Tankard	C*	MW (+)	Mary (Willoughby) Barton	ca. 1710	Buhler 1972, no. 52	MFAB
Tankard	C*	Hannah Wadsworth; EMM (later)	Hannah Wadsworth	ca. 1720	Puig et al. 1989, no. 176	MIA
Tankard	C*	L/RA	Richard and Abigail (Warren) Lord	ca. 1715	Clarke 1932, no. 95	WA
Tankard	C	Sargent arms; S/EE (+)	Sargent family	ca. 1715	Clarke 1932, no. 109	
Tankard	C	DP		ca. 1715	Clarke 1932, no. 103	
Tankard	C*	II	John Jones	ca. 1715	Clarke 1932, no. 110	
Tankard	C	unidentified initials (later)		ca. 1715	YUAG files	
Tankard	C	H/NM	Nathaniel and Mary (Green) Hunting	ca. 1715	*Silver Supplement* 1973, no. 25	
Tankard	C	M/IS	MacDonald or Morse family (?)	1715–22	Buhler 1979, no. 4	WAM
Tankard	C*	MR; HAH (later)		ca. 1710	DAPC 82.3053	

	Mark	Inscription	Patron	Date	Reference	Owner
Tankard	c*	H/NS		ca. 1710	Flynt/Fales 1968, 114	HD
Tankard	c*	T/SH (?) (+)	Samuel and Hannah (Gridley) Thaxter	ca. 1710	Sotheby's, 24 October 1987, lot 395	
Tankard	c	?		ca. 1720	Norman-Wilcox 1962, no. 12	
Tankard	c	A/IE (+)		ca. 1720	YUAG files	
Tankard	c/D	Ex dono S: More	Samuel More	ca. 1716	Clarke 1932, no. 105	
Tankard	c*/D	RK (+)		ca. 1720	Puig et al. 1989, no. 177	MIA
Tankard	c*/D*	S/NM		ca. 1720	Sotheby's, 24–27 January 1990, lot 177	
Tankard	c/D	EI: I/BA		ca. 1715	Clarke 1932, no. 107	CGA
Tankard	c/D	G/RH		ca. 1715	Hanks 1970, 419	AIC
Tankard	c*/D	Holyoke arms, azure a chevron argent cotised or between 3 crescents, and crest, a crescent; EH (later)		ca. 1715	Clarke 1932, no. 104	MMA
Two tankards	c/F	A Gift to M.ͬ Holyokes [holyoaks] Church/Marble=head/1716	Second Congregational Society, Marblehead, Mass.	1716	Clarke 1932, no. 106	MFAB
Tankard	c/F*	unidentified crest, a lion rampant; D/TP		ca. 1715	Clarke 1932, no. 108	
Tankard	?	none		ca. 1695	DAPC 69.8220	
Tankard	?	unidentified arms		ca. 1700	Parke-Bernet, 27 January 1967, lot 2	
Teapot	c/F	Mascarene arms, a lion rampant in chief 3 mullets	Jean Paul and Elizabeth (Perry) Mascarene	ca. 1710	Safford 1983, 32–33	MMA
Teaspoon	F	R (later)		ca. 1715		RISD
Tipstaff	none	Agmen Massachusettense/est in tutelam Sponsae/AGNI Uxoris/1701./Ex dono Honorabalis/SAMUELIS SEWALL Armigeri	Samuel Sewall	1701	YUAG files	
Tobacco box	B†	Jeffries arms, a lion rampant between 3 scaling ladders, and crest, a tower embattled; Donum RG 1701	Jeffries family	1701	Buhler/Hood 1970, no. 32	YUAG

	Mark	Inscription	Patron	Date	Reference	Owner
Tripod bowl	A*	unidentified crest, a greyhound's head collared and erased; The gift of the Honble Judge Davenport and formerly belonging to the Honble Mr Secretary Addington Octo^br 18/1731 (later)	Isaac Addington	ca. 1705	Buhler/Hood 1970, no. 29	YUAG

1. Clarke 1932.
2. RC 9:48, 193; Savage 1860–62, 3:262; Codman 1918, 66.
3. RC 9:51.
4. RC 1:50, 55.
5. *Suffolk Deeds* 9:58–59.
6. RC 9:219; Stratford VR, LRI, 54; Fairfield County, Connecticut Probate District, docket 835, CSL.
7. RC 29:164.
8. *Old South Church* 1883, 197; John (1678), Robert (1679), Sarah (1684), James (1685), Mary (1687), John (1689), Sarah (1691); see RC 9:145, 148, 165, 173, 183, 195.
9. *Old South Church* 1883, 219.
10. Foote 1882, 1:89.
11. Seybolt 1939, 75, 86.
12. SCD 15:145; no recorded deed exists for the purchase of the house on Cotton Hill.
13. RC 7:232.
14. SCD 19:53; RC 9:217.
15. ECPR, dockets 13243, 13248.
16. SCPR, docket 1900.
17. RC 9:225. The children of this marriage were: Mary (born 7 November 1695); Anna (born 23 January 1696/97); Mehitable (baptized 16 January 1698); Mary (born 11 November 1699); Abigail (born 5 January 1701); and Mehitable (born 27 February 1703); see RC 9:221, 226, 238, 245, 246; RC 24:2.
18. SCD 19:248.
19. SCD 22:195; 34:79. A portion of this property was sold by his heirs; SCD 37:182–83.
20. RC 13:67.
21. SCCR, file 14367, Judicial Archives, Mass. Archives.
22. Spoons with spurious marks are at YUAG (1930.3349) and BM. A mark related to mark (A) has been attributed to Coney, but probably is not his. See a porringer at RIHS, Davidson 1971, 345.
23. Samuel Sewall Account Book, 1688–92, MHS.
24. Samuel Sewall Account Book and Ledger, NEHGS.
25. Samuel Sewall Account Book and Ledger, NEHGS.
26. Samuel Sewall Account Book and Ledger, fol. 128v, NEHGS.
27. Samuel Sewall Account Book and Ledger, fol. 198r, NEHGS; Roberts 1895, 1:4.
28. Samuel Sewall Account Book and Ledger, fol. 197v, NEHGS.
29. Samuel Sewall Account Book and Ledger, NEHGS.
30. Samuel Sewall Account Book and Ledger, fol. 196r, NEHGS.
31. Samuel Sewall Account Book and Ledger, fols. 192r, 193v, NEHGS.
32. Photostat in the Bigelow-Phillips files, YUAG.
33. Photostat in the Bigelow-Phillips files, YUAG.
34. ECPR, docket 28673.
35. SCPR, docket 2350.
36. MCPR, docket 12979; SCPR, docket 3875.
37. John Chester to John Coney, 21 October 1700, F.L. Gay Papers, MHS.
38. SCCR, file 2487, Judicial Archives, Mass. Archives.
39. Mass. Archives 40:847, 856–57.
40. *MHS Proceedings* 6 (1862–63): 341.

41. Newman 1967, 126–28.
42. Mass. Archives 101:409.
43. *Boston Prints and Printmakers*, 192.
44. RC 29:169; RC 1:72–73.
45. SCD 24:171.
46. SCPR 14:42, docket 2518.
47. Bigelow's notes state that Bradford witnessed a deed for Coney in 1716, but no such deed has been found. Flynt/Fales 1968, 233, and Bohan/Hammerslough 1970, 236, suggest Gray was Coney's apprentice.
48. Document reproduced in Clarke 1932, 13.
49. *Boston Gazette*, 5–12 November 1722.
50. SCPR 22:813–16, docket 4641.
51. *A Funeral Sermon Occasion'd by Several Mournful Deaths and Preach'd on the Decease of Mr. John Coney*, 63.
52. RC 13:103.
53. Boston Deaths, 1700–1800.

Richard Conyers
ca. 1666–1708/09

A

The records of the Worshipful Company of Goldsmiths, London, reveal that on 28 July 1682 "Richard Conyers the sonn of Robert Conyers of Helmesly, in the County of York Sadler doe put my self Apprentice unto Roger Graing Cittizen & Goldsmith of London for the Terme of Seaven yeares from this p^{r}sent day."[1] Baptized at Helmsley on 31 October 1666, he was sixteen years old at his apprenticeship.[2] On 16 August 1689 he was admitted to the freedom of the company and was elected to the Livery in 1694.[3] Conyers took three apprentices in London: on 26 August 1690 Jonathan Lambe, son of John Lambe of Raynes (illegible), Essex, clerk, was apprenticed for seven years; on 14 July 1693 John Cooke, son of Joseph Cooke, citizen and joiner of London, was apprenticed for seven years; and on 9 March 1693/94 Charles Groome, son of Thorp Groome of Hammersmith, Middlesex, cordwainer, was apprenticed for seven years.[4] A marriage record exists for Richard Conyers and Mary James on 31 December 1693 in London's Saint Mary Abchurch. Their only son, named James, perhaps after his mother's maiden name, was baptized at St. Mary's Woolnoth in April 1696.[5]

The first of Conyers's apprentices gained the freedom of the Goldsmiths' Company on 1 July 1697. The record states, "At this Court Jonathan Lambe Appr Richd Conyers & his service testified by Geo: Hawson . . . sworne & made free by service & paid as of Custome." The record suggests that since Hawson testified on Lambe's behalf, Conyers was unable to attend the court on the day of his apprentice's application for freedom and had probably left London by that time.[6] By August 1698 he appears with a servant, possibly Thomas Milner (q.v.), on a list of Boston inhabitants.[7] He was there the following year when he attended a meeting of the congregation of the Church of England in Boston on Easter Monday, 10 April 1699.[8]

As a recent immigrant Conyers may have had difficulty establishing himself in Boston. But his knowledge of the London goldsmiths' trade and his personal contacts there probably helped him stay abreast of the latest fashions and acquire silversmiths' supplies that he could resell in New England. He may not have found as ready a market for these supplies in the New World as he had hoped. By April 1700 he was being sued by his former apprentice, the Middlesex County, England, merchant Charles Groome. The court papers show that Conyers owed Groome money for a large assortment of goldsmith's tools:

Richard Conyers D.^r to Charles Groome

Aprill ye 1:1700	
To a p.^r of Scales & box	£o- 14- 6
To 3 files	0- 1- 0
To 2 .^{lb} of Limon	0- 1- 6
To Moulding Sand 1 peck ¹/₂	0- 5- 0
To 18 Nest of pots at 4^d ℔ nest	0- 6- 0
To 24 Nest of pots at 5^d ℔ nest	0- 10- 0
To 12 Nest of Large pots at 8^d	0- 8- 0
To 6 blew pots	0- 5- 6
To 2 p.^r of flask	0- 7- 0
To a hamer w.^t 5^{lb} at	0- 4- 6
To 6 .^{lb} of pumis	0- 4- 0
To 2 Swords with steel hilts	4- 0- 0
May ye 30 To Silver w.^t 28^{oz}:6^d agred }	
for ye 6/6 ℔ oz In all agred }	9- 4- 0
Due	16- 11- 0
Due to Mr Conyers In mony	1- 0- 0
Due for 18 Silver buttons w.^t	
1^{oz}:11.^{wt} fashon & silver agred for	0- 14- 0
Due to Conyers	1- 14- 0
Due to me on	
Ballance	£14- 17- 0

Conyers contested Groome's claims but agreed to pay Charles Groome when requested.[9] In 1701 Conyers was imprisoned as the result of a suit brought by John Symons of St. Giles-in-the-Fields for a debt of £135.15.4. Conyers petitioned for release from prison on the grounds that he was insolvent stating that he was "not being worth Tenn pounds in the world."[10] In spite of the suits and imprisonment, Conyers commanded the respect of some individuals, for in 1700 the Boston merchant George Baker granted Conyers his power of attorney.[11]

Another suit involving Conyers in the Suffolk County Court of Common Pleas suggests that Conyers used his London contacts to procure a chaser, a specialized craftsman whose skills were necessary to create the swirled, gadrooned ornament then in fashion. According to the writ served on 19 December 1702, in 1699 Henry Hurst (q.v.) made an agreement with the London goldsmith John House that Hurst would work for Conyers for two years, but Hurst left Conyers's establishment without warning before the two years of his agreement were up.[12] The plaintiff in the suit was actually House, which suggests that House, probably at Conyers's request, found a chaser willing to migrate to Boston and arranged for his passage. The relationship between House and Conyers probably was well established, because House, described by George Vertue as an "Engraver. living oposit to Pontack's abchurch lane, London," came from the same parish in which Conyers was married. House also would be remembered in Conyers's will. House probably belonged to the decorative branch of the trade because he had been apprenticed in 1679 to Launder Smith, who in turn had been apprenticed to Thomas Simon, a known mint engraver or diesinker. House therefore would have been a reliable source to judge the skills of a migrant chaser.[13] In 1702 Conyers's taxes were abated by 11 shillings, perhaps because he originally was levied for having a journeyman, probably Hurst, who subsequently left his shop.[14]

On 23 December 1708 Conyers, "being sick & weak," made out his will, which was probated on 6 January 1708/09.[15] He appointed his friends John Oulton and Henry Franklin as his executors, "Desiring their Speedy care to send Word to my afores.[d] wife & son." This statement suggests that Conyers's wife and son did not accompany him to New England. He left his working tools to his son with the stipulation that if his son died before receiving them, they were to go to the aforementioned London goldsmith John House. (No record exists of any children of Richard Conyers either apprenticed through the Goldsmiths' Company or having been made free of that company by patrimony.)[16] Thomas Milner was to have use of the tools upon his giving security to return them when demanded. The inventory, appraised 4 April 1709 by Jeremiah Dummer and Edward Webb (qq.v.), contained a detailed listing of an extensive assortment of tools:

Item	Weight/Price	£	s	d
1 Large forging Anvill	268[lb] at 110[s] ℔ lb	11..	3..	8
9 Raising Anvills	172 at 10 1 Broke	7..	3..	4
1 Large planishing Teast	58 ½ Do	2..	8..	9
1 Spoon Teast	29 at 12	1..	9..	—
4 Spoon Punsons	15 ¼ at 10	—..	12..	8
7 Stakes	27 at D[o]	1..	2..	6
1 Skillet 1 Ingott	29 ½ at D[o]	1..	4..	7
1 Large Vice	22 at 9s	—..	16..	6
3 Forging handers		—..	7..	6
25 Small hamers		1..	5..	—
1 Ring swage		—..	3..	6
1 Clasp Stamp		—..	4..	—
1 Tankard & Swage		—..	1..	—
12 Cuting punsons		—..	10..	—
6 Dapping punsons		—..	3..	—
p[r] Flasks		—..	10..	—
3 p.[r] Sheers		—..	3..	—
4 p.[r] hand Vices		—..	5..	—
5 p.[r] plyers		—..	5..	—
2 p.[r] Nurling Tongs		—..	2..	—
2 p.[r] holding Tongs		—..	2..	—
1 p.[r] Casting Tongs		—..	2..	—
1 p[r] Drawing Tongs		—..	2..	—
1 Drawing Bench		—..	5..	—
1 p.[r] Large Bellows		1..	10..	—
1 p.[r] hand Bellows		—..	2..	—
1 p.[r] Screw plates		—..	5..	—
2 Engines for Swages		—..	10..	—
3 p.[r] Compasses		—..	4..	—
2 Iron Triblets		—..	1..	6
Old files 4[lb]		—..	2..	—
2 Gravers		—..	—..	4
1 Cuting Chissell		—..	1..	—
1 Nurling Iron		—..	1..	—
3 Old Brass pans	26[lb] at /12	1..	6..	—

Item	Weight/Qty	Rate	£	s	d
2 Copper pans	6 3/4 at 2 8/		—	13	6
Old Brass patterns	17 1/2 /10		—	14	7
3 p.r Scales			—	12	—
			£36	13	11
3 p.r Brass Weights	12 lb at		—	15	—
1 pile of Weights	48 oz		—	5	—
1 Sett of Small Weights			—	1	—
1 Button Stamp	W 11 lb		1	—	—
9 training Weights			—	3	—
Glass Case			—	10	—
2 Burnishing stons			—	2	—

The Tools &c.a aforementioned
are in Thomas Millners hands
In the hands of Henry Franklin
as follows Viz.t

Item	Weight/Qty	Rate	£	s	d
Old Cast Brass	W.t 60 lb 1/2	at /6	1	10	3
3 Bell weights	480 oz		1	—	—
1 pile old Weights	256		—	10	—
5 Anvils W.t	100	at /10	4	3	4
2 Ditto W.t	13	D.o	—	10	10
4 Small Teasts 5 Swages	54 lb	/6	1	7	—
6 Spoon punsons 4 Stakes	39 lb	/8	1	6	
17 Cuting punsons	at 8	p.r p.r	[torn]		
27 Dapping punsons	45 lb/	8 s	[torn]		
1 p.r of Large Stock Sheers	28 1/2	8	—	19	—
3 p.r hand Sheers			—	3	—
12 forging hamers	87	at 7 s	2	10	9
25 Small hamers			—	18	—
3 Drawing Irons			—	3	—
3 Nurling Irons				2	—
1 pestle, 1 Ingott, 1 Ladle	55	at /3	—	6	3
1 p.r Small Screw plates			—	3	—
1 Small Ingott			—	1	—
1 p.r board Vice			—	2	—
1 p.r Large holding Tongs			—	2	—
2 Sawes			—	2	—
1 Screw Box			—	5	—
1 p.r of Large Scales			—	12	—
2 p.r Small Scales			—	5	—
1 p.r Nealing Tongs			—	1	—
1 Iron			—	2	—
1 p.r Brass Flasks 5 lb 1/2			—	6	—
1 Glew pott			—	1	—
1 p.r hand Bellows			—	2	—
2 Box's Chassing punsons			—	6	—
15 Canes			1	4	—
15 Sword Blades			—	15	—
			61	9	8
1 Glass Case			—	2	6
1 Large Raising Anvill	73 lb at /6		1	16	6

1 Large Skillet	42 at 9	1.. 11.. 6
9 Rings with Stones and pearls	at 10/ p^r p^s	4.. 10.. –
3 Ditto wth Large stons	at 16	2.. 8.. –
1 p^r Gold Earrings with pearl Drops		–.. 12.. –
1 Large Stone Ring		1.. 5.. –
1 p^r Stone Earrings Sett in Silver		–.. 1.. 6
1 Gold Ring wth Six Small Stons		–.. 12.. –
2 p^r Stone buckles		–.. 6.. –
2 Stone Girdle buckles		–.. 10.. –
1 Olde hatt buckle		–.. 1.. –
6 p^r Stone buttons		–.. 4.. –
3 p^r Ditto		–.. 3.. –
10 Cornelions 1 Chrystall		–.. 5.. 6
10 Glass Necklaces		–.. 5.. –
5 Ivory Boxes		–.. 2.. 6
Enamell		–.. 2.. 6
parcell Small pearle		–.. 4.. –
Large pearle		–.. 9.. –
[torn] pearle		.. 5.. –
1 Lead Stone		1.. 0.. –
2 Bone heads for Canes		–.. 4.. –
4 Ditto		–.. 1.. –
1 Knife handle		–.. 1.. –
1 Watch		2.. –.. –
1 Silver Tankard 1 Tobacco Box wth 36^{oz} 10^{dw} at 8/		14.. 12.. –
Seventy Seven Ounces of Silver in Sundry old & New things in the hands of Thomas Milner at 8/ p^r oz		30.. 16.. –
		126.. –.. 2^{17}

Only a small body of work, marked with an RC crowned (A), has been attributed to this silversmith. Conyers, who was equipped with a great assortment of tools and who maintained a journeyman and had available at one time the services of an expert chaser, therefore probably produced silver that other members of the trade sold to retail customers and that may bear the retailers' marks. No doubt his personal contacts with the London goldsmith's trade enhanced the reputation of his goods and services. PEK

SURVIVING OBJECTS

	Mark	Inscription	Patron	Date	Reference	Owner
Two mugs	A	R/CM		ca. 1700	Buhler 1956, no. 44	
Porringer	A*	EB (+)	Bass family (?)	ca. 1703	Buhler/Hood 1970, no. 47	YUAG
Salt	A	?		ca. 1700	Christie's, 17–18 January 1992, lot 170	
Tankard	A*	R/TI	Thomas and Jane Redmond	ca. 1700		MFAB
Tankard	A†	EB (later)	Francis Brinley	ca. 1700	Quimby 1995, no. 39	WM

	Mark	Inscription	Patron	Date	Reference	Owner
Tankard	A*	F/IM (+)	Jacob and Mary (Bacon) Fuller	ca. 1700	Buhler 1965, 20–23	HMA

1. Apprentice Book 3, fol. 119r, Worshipful Company of Goldsmiths, London. Robert B. Barker letter to Patricia E. Kane, 9 September 1993. For additional discussion of Conyers's career, see Ward 1983, 46–47, 160, 350.
2. E. Alfred Jones letter to John Marshall Phillips.
3. Court Book 10, fols. 26v, 89v, Worshipful Company of Goldsmiths, London. Robert B. Barker letter to Patricia E. Kane, 9 September 1993.
4. Apprentice Book 3, fol. 193r; Apprentice Book 4, fols. 32v, 37v, Worshipful Company of Goldsmiths, London. Robert B. Barker letter to Patricia E. Kane, 9 September 1993.
5. Brooke/Hallen 1886, 81.
6. Court Book 10, fol. 151v, Worshipful Company of Goldsmiths, London. Robert B. Barker letter to Patricia E. Kane, 9 September 1993.
7. RC 10:88.
8. Foote 1882, 1:133.
9. SCCR, file 4825, Judicial Archives, Mass. Archives.
10. SCCR, files 5177, 5222, Judicial Archives, Mass. Archives. Barbara M. Ward brought these files to my attention.
11. SCCR, file 4800, Judicial Archives, Mass. Archives.
12. SCCR, file 5565, Judicial Archives, Mass. Archives. For further discussion of this case, see Ward 1984, 142–44.
13. Robert B. Barker letter to Patricia E. Kane, 9 September 1993; see also *George Vertue, "Notebooks"* 1:89, 123–24.
14. RC 11:25.
15. SCPR 16:515.
16. Robert B. Barker letter to Patricia E. Kane, 9 September 1993.
17. SCPR 4 new series, 421–25.

Joseph Coolidge, Jr.
ca. 1747–1821

Gilbert Stuart, Joseph Coolidge, *1820, oil on canvas. National Gallery of Art, Washington, Andrew W. Mellon Collection.*

Joseph Coolidge, Jr., the son of Joseph Coolidge (1718/19–71), a gunsmith, and Margaret (Marguerite) Oliver (ca. 1726–1816), had familial connections to other members of the Boston jewelers' trade both through his mother's family and through marriage.[1] His mother was the sister of Andrew Oliver (q.v.). Coolidge married first Elizabeth Boyer (1753–86) in 1771 and second Katherine Boyer (1755–1829) in 1788, the daughters of Daniel Boyer (q.v.), who presumably was Coolidge's master.[2] Coolidge's paternal grandparents were John Coolidge (b. 1691) and Hannah Ingraham (b. 1693).[3]

Coolidge would have finished his training about 1768 and soon thereafter began retailing silver holloware and jewelry. Like his master, he purchased wares from Zachariah Brigden (q.v.) that he in turn probably retailed. Brigden's daybook shows sales of silver to Coolidge beginning in 1770. "Coolige goldsmith," probably Joseph Coolidge, bought in September and October 1770, respectively, a pair of silver buckles for £7.10 and a silver spoon for £4. Sometime in 1771—the entry does not specify the month—Joseph Coolidge was charged £7 for a soup ladle. That year he also purchased other goods at various times: in March he bought a neck buckle for £2.15 and in October six teaspoons (£2), a clasp (£2.4.6), a child's spoon (12 shillings), and another spoon (£1.6.8). In 1772 Brigden "refit" a cann for him and made a half-pint porringer, a child's spoon, and three other spoons. In some of these transactions, Coolidge paid with silver.[4]

An advertisement in the *Boston News-Letter* of 9 May 1771 indicates that Coolidge's shop was at the foot of Cornhill:

Joseph Coolidge, jun'r.
Has just IMPORTED from LONDON, and has to sell
at his Shop opposite Mr. William Greenleaf's, Foot
of Cornhill,
A Variety of Jewellry, among which are Paste shoe-buckles, knee and stock
ditto, paste, rose and star earings. garnet ditto, paste, marqueset and garnet
sprigs and pins, paste combs, plain tortoise-shell ditto, stay-hooks, broaches,
watch-seals, cornelian and moco buttons; also, plated buckles and spurs, watch-
chains, keys and hooks, steel-top thimbles, coral beeds, teeth brushes, moneyscales, sets of pennyweights and grains, pinchbeck buckles and buttons, and
many other articles, with all kinds of Goldsmiths and Jewellers Work.

Goldsmiths and Jewellers may be supplied with all sorts of christal, garnet,
white and red foyle, shoe and knee chapes, large black lead pots, crucibles,
moulding sand, buckle brushes, sand paper, iron and brass bar wire, binding
wire, borax, pumace stones, gravers, knife tools, scorpers, frezing punches, sandover, files, flour of emery, &c.

The accounts with Brigden and this newspaper advertisement suggest that Coolidge functioned more as an active retailer than as a working silversmith. The Massachusetts tax list for 1771 underscores this supposition; he is listed as a tenant of Widow Norten with a poll tax of one and merchandise valued at £240.[5] The surname mark Coolidge, italic in a cartouche, said to be on a strainer and spoon, has been attributed to him, but these pieces could not be located for illustration.[6]

Following the Revolution, deeds and court records consistently identify Coolidge as a merchant. The number of Court of Common Pleas suits in which he was involved, mostly as plaintiff, but sometimes as defendant, with other merchants and traders indicates his widespread business interests.[7] Coolidge also executed many real estate transactions between 1785 and the time of his death.[8] His portrait was painted twice by Gilbert Stuart (see illus.).[9] He died on 6 October 1821 and left bequests totaling more than one hundred thousand dollars.[10] DAF and PEK

1. RC 24:134; RC 28:241; SCPR 70:506; 71:57; Bridgman 1851, 189.
2. Church in Brattle Square, 174, 176; RC 30:161, 431; Index of Obituaries, 1784–1840, 2:1059, 1060.
3. Watertown Records 1894, "Births, Deaths, and Marriages," 1:63; RC 9:212; RC 28:44.
4. Zachariah Brigden Daybook 1766–ca. 1775, fols. 17v, 18v, 19r, 30v, 31r, 32v, 33v and r, Brigden Papers, YU.
5. Pruitt 1978, 32–33.
6. French (1917) 1967, 31; Ensko 1937, 28; Graham 1936, 18; Thorn 1949, 57.
7. SCCR, Court of Common Pleas Record Books 1783, 10–11, 152–53, 237; 1784, 215, 268; 1785, 244; 1787, 129, 141; 1789, 230–31; 1797, 10, 84; 1798, 76.
8. SCD 151:35–36, 189–90; 170:16; 171:137–38; 172:140–41; 176:224–25; 177:196; 179:192–93; 180:209; 182:90–91, 135–36; 183:222–23; 192:182, 272, 281; 193:68–69, 71, 94, 159; 194:71–72, 96, 208, 227; 196:1, 51; 197:251–53; 202:22; 206:3; 212:86–88; 222:49–51; 226:46; 231:271; 232:225–26, 280–81; 290–91; 242:69; 245:76, 225; 272:105; 274:165; 276:209–13; 280:70.
9. Park 1926, 1:237–38.
10. SCPR 118²:37–40; Bridgman 1851, 190.

John Coverly
1713–83

John Coverly was the younger brother of Thomas Coverly (q.v.). He was born in Boston on 29 December 1713, the son of the mariner Thomas Coverly (ca. 1684–1747) and his wife, Mary Wells. He was baptized in the Second Church, Boston, on 3 January 1713/14.[1]

A

B

In 1735 Coverly married Elizabeth Pierce (1715/16–68), the daughter of Isaac and Grace (Tucker) Pierce. They had six children: John (bap. 1736), Wells (bap. 1737/38), Thomas (bap. 1739/40), Elizabeth (bap. 1741), Rowel (bap. 1738), and Elizabeth (bap. 1739).[2]

There is no record of his ownership of land, and the records of his father's estate do not survive. John was the plaintiff in a case before the Court of Common Pleas in 1741, when he sued John Colson, a shinglemaker, for the sum of £6.6.6 owed to him on account. In 1763 he is referred to in a court document as John Coverly of Framingham, Middlesex County, goldsmith. In 1766 he was still living outside Boston when a notice in the *Boston News-Letter*, describing him as "late of *Boston*, Goldsmith, an insolvent Debtor," advised creditors to present claims at the house of Edward Procter on 19 December.[3] However, he must have returned to Boston by 1771 because the Massachusetts tax list of that year includes Coverly with one poll, a house and shop adjoining, and £4 annual worth of real estate.[4] He was buried in the Granary Burying Ground, and his epitaph reads, "Mr. John Coverly died 6 October 1783 in the 71 year of his age."[5]

Only a few pieces of silver by Coverly survive, and they are marked with two variations of an initial and surname mark (A, B). Because of the small number of objects known, it is likely he worked primarily as a jobber for other goldsmiths. BMW

SURVIVING OBJECTS

	Mark	Inscription	Patron	Date	Reference	Owner
Cann	B†	none		ca. 1755	Avery 1920, no. 94 (as Thomas Coverly)	MMA
Tankard	A†	P/IH		ca. 1770	Johnston 1994, 33	CMA
Teaspoon	A*	B/IA		ca. 1760	DAPC 74.1230	WM

1. RC 28:9; RC 24:89; Robbins 1852, 239; Codman 1918, 68.
2. RC 28:20, 190; Robbins 1852, 239; Codman 1918, 68; RC 24:108.
3. *Boston News-Letter*, 11 December 1766.
4. Pruitt 1978, 44–45.
5. SCCR, Court of Common Pleas Record Book 1741, 193; Superior Court of Judicature, 25 January 1763; Codman 1918, 68; the transcription of the epitaph is in the Bigelow-Phillips files and is similar, but not identical, to the epitaph in an annotated copy of Bridgman 1856, 11, at YUAG.

Thomas Coverly
1708–78

A

Previous authorities have confused Thomas Coverly (1708–78) with his nephew Thomas, who was born in 1740.[1] The goldsmith Thomas Coverly was the son of Thomas Coverly (ca. 1684–1747), a mariner, and his wife, Mary Wells. He was born on 30 May 1708 and was baptized in the Second Church, Boston, a week later.[2] The Thomas Coverly who became a member of the Second Church in 1728 could have been either the father or the son.[3] In 1727 the younger Thomas Coverly witnessed deeds of the goldsmith Thomas Edwards (q.v.), suggesting that he was working as an apprentice to Edwards at the time.[4] John Coverly (q.v.), his younger brother, also became a goldsmith.

B

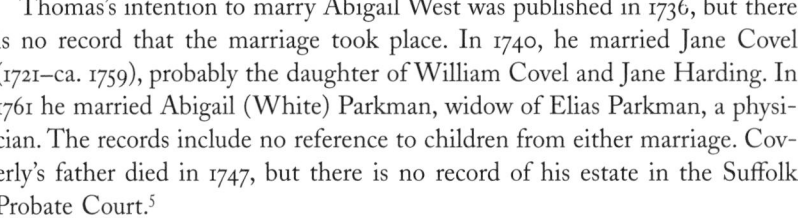

C

D

Thomas's intention to marry Abigail West was published in 1736, but there is no record that the marriage took place. In 1740, he married Jane Covel (1721–ca. 1759), probably the daughter of William Covel and Jane Harding. In 1761 he married Abigail (White) Parkman, widow of Elias Parkman, a physician. The records include no reference to children from either marriage. Coverly's father died in 1747, but there is no record of his estate in the Suffolk Probate Court.[5]

Thomas Coverly, identified as a goldsmith of Boston, appears in court documents once as a plaintiff and four times as a defendant between 1735 and 1752.[6] In 1761 he was one of the appraisers of the estate of William Breed's (q.v.) father.[7] Coverly bought a watch case from Paul Revere, Jr., in February 1762 and paid Revere £1.4 for it the following June.[8] In 1764, Coverly and his wife, Abigail, petitioned the Superior Court for permission to sell a piece of land that was part of her former husband's estate, in order to pay debts due from the estate. The petition further explained that the Coverlys were unable to expend the money necessary to repair the building that stood on the land.[9] The Massachusetts tax list of 1771 includes Coverly with a poll of one as a tenant of Elias Parkman, possibly his wife's son.[10]

Thomas Coverly died in 1778 and was buried in Copp's Hill Burying Ground. His tombstone is inscribed, "Mr. Thomas Coverly Died Jan[r]y 29[th], 1778 Aged 69 years 8 months."[11]

The small number of objects Thomas Coverly marked over a career of almost forty years suggests that he did not work as an independent goldsmith during much of his career, but primarily as a jobber for other silversmiths. However, he did receive some measure of success in the eyes of his peers because he was identified as "Mr. Thomas Coverly" in 1744 when the Boston town meeting chose him to serve as constable, a position he declined.[12] Although his surviving works are few, three different initial and surname marks (A–C) and one initials mark (D) used by Coverly are known. BMW

SURVIVING OBJECTS

	Mark	Inscription	Patron	Date	Reference	Owner
Cann	A	LA		ca. 1750	MFA 1911, no. 280	
Cann	A	H/CM		ca. 1770	Moore Collection 1980, no. 63	
Cann	A*	B/TA		ca. 1770	Gourley 1965, no. 260	RISD
Cann	A*	The Gift/of M.[r] James Pittee/to the first Church of/Christ in Weymouth/A.D. 1764	James Pittee and/or First Church of Christ, Weymouth, Mass.	ca. 1764	Jones 1913, 493	
Cann	A (?)	?		ca. 1740	Bulletin DIA 55 (1977): 111–12	DIA
Cann	A	none	Jonathan Sayward	ca. 1770	Sander 1986, 597	SPNEA
Cann	?	?		ca. 1760	Antiques 98 (September 1970): 321	

	Mark	Inscription	Patron	Date	Reference	Owner
Cup	A*	erased		ca. 1740	Gourley 1965, no. 261	RISD
Cup	?	MG to EE (later)		ca. 1740	Christie's, 24 January 1987, lot 61	
Pepper box	A	B/TA		ca. 1760	Norman-Wilcox 1944, 80–81	
Pepper box	B†	IP/1760		1760	YUAG files	
Porringer	A	I Barr	I. Barr	ca. 1760	MFA 1906, no. 66	
Porringer	A†/ D†	LH (+)	Lydia Hutchinson (?)	ca. 1775	*Antiques* 117 (February 1980): 368	HMA
Porringer spoon	A	EH/GH		ca. 1770	DAPC 86.2453	
Strainer	?	?		ca. 1770	Parke-Bernet, 10 November 1970, lot 60	
Tablespoon	A* (?)	TC		ca. 1740		PEM
Tablespoon	C†	DM		ca. 1770		YUAG

1. Flynt/Fales 1968, 191.
2. RC 28:9; RC 24:59.
3. Robbins 1852, 239.
4. SCD 41:176–77, 205–06.
5. RC 24:150; RC 28:69, 214, 225; SCCR, file 100301; Thwing; Bridgman 1856, 11, annotated copy, YUAG.
6. SCCR, Court of Common Pleas Record Book 1735, 188; 1742–43, 45, 245; 1744–46, 83; 1751–52, 213: John M. Fitzgerald to Francis Hill Bigelow, List of Boston Court Record References to Silversmiths, Bigelow-Phillips files.
7. SCPR 59:347–49.
8. 18 February, 1 June 1762, vol. 1, Waste and Memoranda Book, 1761–83, [5, 10], Revere Family Papers, MHS.
9. SCCR, file 100301, Judicial Archives, Mass. Archives.
10. Pruitt 1978, 6–7.
11. Whitmore 1878, 13, no. 256.
12. RC 14:30.

John Cowell
1707–31 +

A

John Cowell was the son of William Cowell, Sr. (q.v.), and Elizabeth Cowell. He was born in Boston on 1 July 1707 and was baptized in the Brattle Street Church a few days later.[1]

Cowell never married, and he died before the second inventory of his father's estate was taken in 1745. The earliest reference to his activity as a goldsmith is an advertisement for the "Choice good Coffee" for sale by "John Cowell, *Goldsmith, at the South End*" in 1728.[2] Cowell owed 16 shillings and 8 pence to the estate of Ann Greene, mother of Rufus and Benjamin Greene (qq.v.), in 1728.[3] He may have worked as a journeyman for Rufus because a John Cowell, along with a Joseph Cowell, witnessed a deed for Greene in 1729.[4] Masters commonly had their apprentices and journeymen witness deeds for them, although in this case Cowell apparently was already working independently, and the John and Joseph Cowell who witnessed this deed may also have been the heirs of Joseph Cowell, who owned a piece of property adjacent to the land that Greene was selling. In 1731 John Cowell, goldsmith, appeared in the Suffolk County Court of Common Pleas as plaintiff in a suit against Collin Frasier, a trader, for nonpayment of a debt.[5] There is no further documentary evidence concerning Cowell, and the date or place of his death is not recorded. Only one piece with his mark (A) is known to survive. BMW

SURVIVING OBJECTS

	Mark	Inscription	Patron	Date	Reference	Owner
Cann	A†	unidentified device (over earlier initials?); I/TM		ca. 1730	Flynt/Fales 1968, 119–20	HD

1. RC 24:47.
2. *Boston News-Letter*, 11–18 July 1728.
3. SCPR 26:413.
4. SCD 43:127–28.
5. SCCR, Court of Common Pleas Record Book 1731, 421–22.

William Cowell, Jr.
1713–61

A

B

William Cowell, Jr., the son of William Cowell, Sr. (q.v.), and his wife, Elizabeth Kilby, was born in Boston on 19 July 1713 and baptized in the Brattle Street Church the month following.[1] He probably was trained by his father and worked with him upon reaching his majority about 1734. Following his father's death in 1736, William Cowell, Jr., continued to use marks used by his father: W:Cowell in a shaped rectangle (A) (his father's mark [C]) and WC in a rectangle (B) (his father's mark [D]); hence it can be difficult to establish whether pieces bearing these marks are the work of the father or the son.[2] The younger Cowell was identified as a goldsmith when he was appointed administrator of his mother's and father's estates in 1745.[3]

Cowell interacted with other craftsmen in the south end of Boston. With Rufus Greene (q.v.) and Jacob Hurd (q.v.) he served as arbiter in a suit between Thomas Townsend (q.v.) and Thomas Edwards (q.v.).[4] Charles Simpson (q.v.) was his brother-in-law, and Cowell signed the bonds for Simpson's father's estate and Simpson's estate administration in 1738 and 1749, respectively.[5]

Cowell was active in Boston affairs in the ensuing decades. He served in a number of town offices: clerk of the market in 1740, constable in 1741 (for which he was excused) and again in 1742 (for which he was not), scavenger in 1749, and hogreeve in 1753.[6] He was the plaintiff in a suit in January 1739/40, but no details of the case exist.[7] In the *Boston News-Letter* of 24–30 April 1741 he advertised, "*STop'd by* William Cowell *Goldsmith at the South End of* Boston, *sometime ago, the Handle of an old Fashion'd Silver Spoon, and Two Pieces of a Silver Cup, which looks like the top Part of a Dram Cup, and likewise a large Plain Silver Buckel, about a Month ago. If the Owners will give the Marks, he will inform them of the Persons they were stop'd from they paying Charge.*" Cowell's father had trained Rufus Greene (q.v.), and the ties between the Cowell and Greene family goldsmiths remained strong in the ensuing decades. For instance, Rufus Greene paid the younger Cowell £7.12.8 for eleven gold rings on 22 October 1760.[8]

William Cowell died unmarried in 1761. In August 1761 his sisters Hannah

Simpson and Rebecca Cowell were appointed to administer the estate for which Rufus Greene signed the bond.[9] Cowell's estate papers reveal that he maintained an active shop. As a practicing goldsmith Cowell left an estate of £155.13.3 once all the expenses had been paid. Goods and tools related to his trade appear near the end of his inventory, which was compiled by Samuel Edwards (q.v.), John Smith, and William Simpkins (q.v.):

Sundry Goldsmiths tools		45..16.. 7
. . .		
Sundry's of Chapes & tongs, Swords, Cane heads & ferrills	{	12.. 17.. 8
360 Ounces, 13 penny Weight of Silver 6/8		120.. 4.. 4
a Quantity Lead, Bulletts & Shott		9.. 6.. 3
Bees wax 22/.Writing desk & Sundry odd Things in the Shop 12/	{	1..14.. 0
4 Dozen Razors. 6 doz: Cowskin Whips Iron kettle, 2 Glass Cases Shod Shovells & 1 Iron & 1 Bell Mettle Morter	{	3.. 13.. 0
Sundry Tools		3.. 9.. 0
Sundrys of Stock		16.. 6.. 4
Gold 5 Ounces.5 pennyweights 21 Grains @ £5..1..4.		26..16.. 4 3/4
188[lb] old Iron		.. 15.. 8
1 Silver Watch		4.. 0.. 0
5 yards Kerseys	6/8	1.. 13.. 4
4 p[r] tooth Drawers		.. 6.. 0
Silver Ladle w[t] 5[oz]3[dwt s].	@ 6/8	1.. 14.. 4 [10]

The accounts of his administrators Hannah Simpson and Rebecca Cowell reveal additional information about Cowell's business. Their advertisement in the *Boston Gazette* on 14 September 1761 likewise confirms that Cowell ran an active shop:

All Persons having Demands on the Estate of *William Cowell*, late of *Boston*, Goldsmith, deceas'd, and those who have accounts open with said Estate, are hereby desired, without Delay, to send such Demands and Accounts to *Hannah Simpson* or *Rebecca Cowell*, of said *Boston*, Administratrixes on said Estate—To be sold by said Administratrixes, a very good Assortment of Goldsmith's Tools; a good Silver Watch; a Quantity of Lead, Bullets and Shot; old Iron, Brass, and Bell-Metal. Those Persons who have left any Work to be done are desired to call for it.[11]

The estate was paid £3.12.4 1/2 by Daniel Boyer (q.v.) and £4.19.1 by Rufus Greene and made payments to Benjamin Greene ([q.v.], £1.19.4), William Simpkins (£1.5), Paul Revere, Jr. ([q.v.], £11.14.10), and Samuel Haley ([q.v.], £2.16), indicating that Cowell had dealings with a number of other Boston goldsmiths. The considerable size of Cowell's debt to Paul Revere may indicate that he purchased finished silver goods from him. Among the items the administrators sold in addition to most of the silver, the gold, and the silversmith's tools were "sandpaper and buckles patrens 2/," "5pr. Pinch beck buttons 3/4," "Tortes shell Rings 5/4," "Wier 3/," "Stone Earings 22/8," "Coral Beads 60/," and "old Stones 3/4." They still had left to sell "Old box of Stones 52/ -5 old Stone Rings & for the Neck 20/-pastey buttins 4/" in addition to "a Stone Stock buckle 24/-Stone Seal5/-Earin 20/."[12] These accounts suggest that a good part of Cowell's trade was in small jewelry items. At least one gold locket marked by him is known. Like other goldsmiths of his era, Cowell also seems to have handled large amounts of base metals. PEK

SURVIVING OBJECTS

	Mark	Inscription	Patron	Date	Reference	Owner
Beaker	A*	The Gift of/Richard Abbe Esqr/to the First Church/of Christ in/Windham	Congregational Church, Windham, Conn., for Richard Abbe	ca. 1737	Jones 1913, 501–02	
Cann	A	P/IH		ca. 1750	Washington 1925, no. 27	
Cann	A*	none		ca. 1760	*Antiques* 109 (February 1976): 274	
Cann	A*	I/FM/1752		ca. 1752	Bartlett 1984, 14	SLAM
Cann	A	Morris arms (?); I/FM	Morris family (?)	ca. 1750	Parke-Bernet, 3 December 1938, lot 13	AIC
Cann	A	HR to TC		ca. 1740	American Art Association–Anderson Galleries, 2–3 April 1937, lot 283	
Cann	A	AC		ca. 1745	YUAG files	
Caster	B	I/IA		ca. 1745	MFA 1906, no. 77	
Flagon	A	Dummer arms, azure 3 fleur-de-lis or on a chief or a demi-lion issuant sable, and crest, a demi-lion holding in his dexter paw a fleur-de-lis; This/Humbly Dedicated by William Dummer/To the Church of Christ in Hollis Street/for the Communion Table/1753	William Dummer and/or Hollis Street Church, Boston	1753	Jones 1913, 81–82	
Locket (gold)	B*	none		ca. 1740	YUAG files	
Mug §	A*	AC		ca. 1740	MFA 1911, no. 297	
Pepper box §	A*	HS		ca. 1740	*Moore Collection* 1980, no. 101	
Porringer	A	Gelston (later)		ca. 1750		MFAB
Porringer §	A†	A/WE		ca. 1740	Buhler/Hood 1970, no. 92	YUAG
Porringer	A*	S/RS/MG/1760		1760	American Art Association–Ander-	

	Mark	Inscription	Patron	Date	Reference	Owner
					son Galleries, 2–3 April 1937, lot 256	
Porringer	A	C/IM		ca. 1735	*American Art of the Colonies and Early Republic*, no. 106	
Porringer	A*/B*	C/IK		ca. 1750	DAPC 68.2309	SI
Serving spoon	A	I/FM/1754	Francis and Mary Johonnot	ca. 1754	MFA 1911, no. 299	
Spout cup	A*/ B†	EL		ca. 1740	Buhler/Hood 1970, no. 181	YUAG
Sugar tongs	B	FC		ca. 1750	MFA 1906, no. 78	
Sugar tongs	?	?		ca. 1750	National Art Galleries, 3–5 December 1931, lot 415 (as I. Clark)	
Sword	A*	none		ca. 1745	Buhler/Hood 1970, no. 179	YUAG
Sword	A	none		ca. 1750	Peterson (1955) 1991, no. 11	HFM
Tablespoon	A*	P/EE		ca. 1750	DAPC 72.2734	WM
Tablespoon	A*	H/IM		ca. 1740	DAPC 68.3204	MMA
Tablespoon	A*	M/TS		ca. 1740	DAPC 72.2736	WM
Tablespoon	A*	The Gift/of/Faith Cookson/to/Eliz Cookson	Faith Cookson	ca. 1745	American Art Association–Anderson Galleries, 3–5 December 1936, lot 404	
Tablespoon §	A*	AB; 1736 (later)		ca. 1735		YUAG
Tablespoon	A*	none		ca. 1750		HD
Tablespoon	A*	M/NA		ca. 1750	Avery 1920, no. 95	MMA
Tankard §	A	W/SM		ca. 1740	Christie's, 22 January 1993, lot 118	
Tankard §	A	Boardman arms, ermine 3 stringed bows erect 2 and 1, and crest, an armored arm embowed holding three arrows; VINCIT AMOR PATRIAE; DEB (later)	Boardman family	ca. 1740	YUAG files	
Tankard	A*	A/ES (+)		ca. 1750	Eitner 1976, no. 48	

	Mark	Inscription	Patron	Date	Reference	Owner
Tankard	A*	By a Subscription/ of a Number of the Brethren/& Sisters of the first Church in Beverly, procured & collected/by John Thorndike jun.'/one of the Church A.D. 1754	First Parish Church, Beverly, Mass.	1754	Jones 1913, 15–16	
Tankard	A*	Purchased/with Six pounds of ye stock/ of the first Church in Beverly & a Sub- scription of ye Breth- ren/& Sisters, pro- cured & collected by John Thorndike jun.'/one of ye Church/A.D. 1754	First Parish Church, Beverly, Mass.	1754	Jones 1913, 15–16	
Tankard	A	?		ca. 1760	*Antiques* 99 (June 1971): 778 (as Wil- liam Cowell, Sr.)	
Tankard	A	B/EA		ca. 1750	DAPC 77.2475	
Teaspoon	B*	MS		ca. 1750	Buhler/Hood 1970, no. 182	YUAG
Teaspoon	B*	AW/1747		ca. 1747	Buhler 1972, appendix no. 13	MFAB
Teaspoon	B (?)	TA (later)		ca. 1740	DAPC 87.3119	
Teaspoon	B*	RR		ca. 1750	Johnston 1994, 35	CMA
Two-handled cup	A	The Gift-/of the Hon^{eble};/ Samuel Par- tridge Esqre:/to the CHURCH of CHRIST/ IN/HATFIELD/1745	First Congregational Church, Hatfield, Mass., for Samuel Par- tridge	1745	Buhler/Hood 1970, no. 180	YUAG

§ Possibly made by William Cowell, Sr.

1. RC 24:89; *Church in Brattle Square*, 133.
2. Some authorities, namely, French 1917, 32, Ensko 1948, 244, and Belden 1980, 124, have also attributed WC in an oval to the son. The pieces bearing this mark are too early to be his work. A variation on the initial and surname mark, W. COWELL in a shaped rectangle, was first published by Ensko 1927, 196, and has been reproduced by subsequent authors, but no example was found to illustrate.
3. SCPR 37:512–14.
4. SCCR, Court of Common Pleas Record Book 1749–51, 220–21; Court of Common Pleas session 1 January 1750/51, file 128.
5. SCPR, dockets 7126, 9239.
6. Seybolt 1939, 218, 220, 229, 254, 268.
7. SCCR, Court of Common Pleas Record Book 1739, 125.
8. Rufus Greene Account Book, 1748–74, under the date 5 February 1762, Karolik-Codman Papers, MHS.
9. SCPR 59:213.
10. SCPR 59:263, docket 12763.
11. His administrators advertised again in the *Boston News-Letter* on 10 June 1762.
12. SCPR 59:451–53.

William Cowell, Sr.
1682/83–1736

A

B

C

D

E

William Cowell, Sr., was born in Boston on 25 January 1682/83 to John Cowell (1644–93), a blacksmith, and Hannah Hurd (1640–1713), the daughter of John Hurd.[1] His paternal grandparents were Edward Cowell (ca. 1616–91), a yeoman, and his wife, Margaret (d. by 1668). The goldsmith's father died when Cowell was only ten years old. The estate administration shows that the house and land were mortgaged to Rev. James Allen, father of the silversmith John Allen (q.v.), to whom Francis Hill Bigelow speculated Cowell may have been apprenticed.[2] His training would have begun about 1697, when Allen was working in partnership with John Edwards (q.v.).

Cowell could have been working on his own by 1704. In 1706 he married Elizabeth Kilby (1686–1745), daughter of John Kilby (ca. 1664–1722) and Elizabeth Simpkins.[3] On 7 August 1715 Elizabeth Cowell became a communicant of the Brattle Street Church, the church where all the couple's children born after 1707 had been baptized.[4] Certainly Cowell was operating his own shop by 1707, when Samuel Sewall, a close family friend, recorded the theft of silver from there: "Billy Cowell's shop is entered by the Chimney, and a considerable quantity of Plate stolen. I gave him a Warrant to the Constable, they find James Hews hid in the Hay in Cabal's Barn, on the Back side of the Common; while they was seising of him under the Hay, he strip'd off his Pocket, which was quickly after found, and Cowell's silver in it."[5] On 1 October 1707 Cowell petitioned the Court of General Sessions to have the stolen goods returned to him from Constable Salter, noting that the thief, named Richard [*sic*] Hughes, had absconded.[6]

Cowell always lived and worked in the South End of Boston in the house on Newbury Street mentioned in his father's estate administration. In 1711 Cowell paid the heirs of James Allen to cancel the mortgage. The following year his three sisters relinquished their shares to him in consideration of his advancing £100 to free their father's estate from incumbrance and his caretaking of their mother for the remainder of her life.[7] (Hannah Cowell was a nurse whom Sewall mentions many times in his diary.)[8]

Throughout his career Cowell worked actively as a silversmith, but his income was supplemented by his wife's and his activities as innholders.[9] Sewall patronized Cowell often over the years. In 1711 he paid Cowell 13 shillings and 9 pence for "clasping 2 Psalters."[10] In 1719 he recorded the purchase of

> To 90 Gold Beads 9. P. w.t 10 grains, £4-4-9 Fashion 45.ˢ
>
> Gold Locket 2 P. wt 3 grains 19.ˢ Fashion 10.ˢ   }
>   of Mr. William Cowell Goldsmith[11]   7.18.9

Sewall's account for his wife Abigail's funeral shows that he purchased sixteen rings from Cowell at a cost of £19.2.3.[12] He also bought two silver spoons in 1725/26 for £2.15 and a chain for his wife's scissors in 1726.[13] Peter Sargent's estate also paid Cowell £9.12.6 for funeral rings in 1713/14, and Mary White purchased £10.7.5 worth of rings for her husband Benjamin's funeral in 1726.[14] Cowell may also have made communion plate for King's Chapel, for that church's records show that on 7 May 1728 the church "pᵈ Wᵐ-Cowell for Mʳ Wat'ˢ plate £25.5.10."[15]

Cowell had ties to other Boston goldsmiths, both through kinship and through his training of a number of younger craftsmen. Andrew Tyler (q.v.) was the son of Cowell's mother-in-law's sister. Margaret Cowell, a child of Cowell's grandfather and his second wife, married Samuel Haugh (q.v.). Two of Cowell's sons, William, Jr., and John (qq.v.), probably trained in his shop, and John Potwine (q.v.) was probably also a Cowell apprentice. Cowell had particularly close ties to the family of Rufus and Benjamin Greene (qq.v.). He witnessed the will of their father, Nathaniel, in 1714 and was paid £20.17.6 for making rings for the funeral of their mother, Ann.[16] Rufus Greene became his apprentice about 1721, and Benjamin may also have been trained by Cowell. Cowell may also have trained Jacob Hurd (q.v.), William Simpkins (q.v.), who was Cowell's cousin, and Charles Simpson (q.v.), who became his son-in-law.

Cowell was the plaintiff in suits filed in Boston on 1 April and 7 October 1718 against the estate of John Latimer of Eastham, Massachusetts.[17] Cowell and the mariner Thomas Ruck sued the innholder Richard Avery in 1731.[18] When Daniel Légaré (q.v.) was sued for debt in 1723, Cowell was listed as a debtor who owed five shillings.[19]

Cowell held a number of civic offices. He was elected constable in 1717/18 and clerk of the market in 1725/26, but refused to serve in both offices. He did serve as a tithingman in 1721/22, a scavenger in 1723/24, and as an engineman both in 1733 and 1735/36.[20]

The *Boston News-Letter* for 29 July–5 August 1736 announced William Cowell's death on 3 August 1736 at the age of fifty-three. His widow was appointed to administer the estate on 10 September following, and the inventory, taken on 27 September, was appraised by John Endicott, William Cunningham, and Jacob Hurd and valued at £3,309.19.4.[21] Cowell's estate had considerable value in tools and wrought and unwrought silver.

Sundry Tools in the Shop	145. 1. 3
152 oz. 14 dwt. Silver as Stock at 27/℔ oz.	206. 2. 9
a plcell of coarse Silver 60/Workmanship of some of y℮ above Silver £5	8. –. –
57 ½ oz. wro.t Plate in the Family's Use @ 27/	77. 12. 6
Gold Wro.t & unwro.t as Stock at £20.10/℔ oz.	52. 5. 4
21 ¼ oz burnt Silver as Stock at £23/℔ oz. £24.8/9 Shop Sweepings £10	34. 8. 9

When Elizabeth Cowell died in 1745, William Cowell, Jr., was called upon to finish the administration of his father's estate. Rufus and Benjamin Greene were appraisers of the inventory compiled at that time.[22]

The mark WC in an oval (A), sometimes given to William Cross (q.v.), is probably the earliest mark that William Cowell used. Also attributed to him is WC in a shaped cartouche with star and pellets above and pellet below (B). The initial and surname mark W:COWELL (script) in a rectangle with a shaped top (C) and the initials mark WC in a rectangle (D) continued to be used by his son, William Cowell, Jr., who took over the shop upon his father's death. A fourth initials mark, W•C in a rectangle (E), tentatively is attributed to Cowell. A spurious version of mark (C) is known.[23] A fairly sizable body of work survives for this maker. PEK

SURVIVING OBJECTS

	Mark	Inscription	Patron	Date	Reference	Owner
Baptismal basin	A	The gift of Mr Benj.m Edmond, late of London, Marchant, to/the Church in Brattle Street, Boston N.E./1716	Benjamin Edmond and/or Brattle Street Church, Boston	1716	Buhler 1972, no. 100	MFAB

	Mark	Inscription	Patron	Date	Reference	Owner
Beaker	A	John Cates Legacy to the Church In Windham	Congregational Church, Windham, Conn., for John Cates (Kates, Keats)	ca. 1705	Jones 1913, 500	
Two beakers	B	Belonging to the first/Church of Christ/att New Lon-don/1724	First Congregational Church, New London, Conn.	1724	Gourley 1965, no. 54	
Beaker	B*	none	Brattle Street Church, Boston	1718	Buhler 1972, no. 101	MFAB
Cann	C*	C/RM (over earlier initials)		ca. 1735	Buhler 1972, no. 105	MFAB
Caudle cup	A	The Gift of Deacon Thº Wells to the/first Church of Christ in Stratford	Thomas Wells and/or Congregational Church, Stratford, Conn.	ca. 1710	Jones 1913, 463–64	
Caudle cup (miniature)	A	EG	Gilman family	ca. 1710	Sotheby's, 26–27 June 1991, lot 118	
Caudle cup	A	Ebenezer With-ington (+)	Ebenezer Withington	ca. 1710	Jones 1913, 150	
Caudle cup	A*	CR/W (erased)	Wolcott family (?)	ca. 1710	Puig et al. 1989, no. 183	MIA
Caudle cup	A*	HW	Henry Wolcott	ca. 1710	Buhler/Hood 1970, no. 88	YUAG
Caudle cup	A*	EA	Elizabeth Atherton (?)	ca. 1710	Andrus 1955, no. 14	MMA
Caudle cup	B*	FC	First Church of Christ, Congregational, Farmington, Conn.	ca. 1715	Jones 1913, 178	
Cup	A*	DS		ca. 1715	Gourley 1965, no. 57 (as William Cross)	RISD
Cup	A*	IS		ca. 1715	Johnston 1994, 34	CMA
Cup	A*	F/TW		ca. 1705	Buhler 1972, no. 98	MFAB
Cup	B*	B/EE (+)	Edward and Experience Battles	ca. 1715	Buhler/Hood 1970, no. 93	YUAG
Cup	B*	The gift of Mat-thew Loring/to ye Church of Crist in hull/1724	Methodist Episcopal Church, Hull, Mass., for Matthew Loring	1724	Bartlett 1984, 8	SLAM
Cup	C*	B/TM (+)		ca. 1730	YUAG files	
Cup	D	A/IM	James and Mary Avery	ca. 1710	American Art Associa-tion–Ander-son Galler-ies, 3–5 December 1936, lot 442	
Dram cup	D†	none		ca. 1705	Flynt/Fales 1968, 74–76	HD

	Mark	Inscription	Patron	Date	Reference	Owner
Mug	B*	Ex dono AW to The first/Church of Christ/In Hartford/ 1727 (later) (+)	Abigail (Warren) (Lord) Woodbridge	ca. 1710	Jones 1913, 207–08	
Mug	B*/C*	D/SC; HM		ca. 1730	Warren 1975, no. 281	BBC
Mug §	C*	AC		ca. 1735	MFA 1911, no. 297	
Nutmeg grater	A	SE		ca. 1705	Avery 1920, no. 25	MMA
Patch box	A	Hannah Bray 1712	Hannah Bray	1712	Doty 1979, no. 97	CGA
Patch box	E†	Mary Mendum/M Mendum/anno 1722	Mary Mendum	1722	Avery 1920, no. 26	MMA
Pepper box	A	N/IM	Rev. John and Mary Norton (?)	ca. 1710	Bigelow 1917, 319–20	
Pepper box	B	R Wyer (+)	R. Wyer	ca. 1720		AIC
Pepper box	B*	EC		ca. 1730	Buhler 1972, no. 104	MFAB
Pepper box	C	C/EL	Coit family	ca. 1735	Buhler 1965, 35–38	HMA
Pepper box §	C	HS		ca. 1730	*Moore Collection* 1980, no. 101	
Pepper box	C*	W/TG	Thomas and Grace (Waite) Wallis (?)	ca. 1730	Buhler/Hood 1970, no. 91	YUAG
Porringer	A	MD	Mary Dudley	ca. 1710	MFA 1911, no. 289	
Porringer	A*	B/RH	Butler family (?)	ca. 1710	Warren 1975, no. 291	BBC
Porringer	A	H/SL		ca. 1710	Christie's, 17 June 1992, lot 53	
Porringer	A	AE ES (later) (+)	Abigail Edwards	ca. 1720	Davidson 1941, 233–35	MMA
Porringer	B	W M^c/S		ca. 1720	Buhler 1972, no. 103	MFAB
Porringer	B	M/WM		ca. 1730	YUAG files	
Porringer	B†	S/IS; AI/ST		ca. 1720	Buhler/Hood 1970, no. 89	YUAG
Porringer	B/C	EC		ca. 1730	YUAG files	
Porringer	B/C	P/GH	George and Hope Phillips	ca. 1730	*Silver Supplement* 1973, no. 26	
Porringer	B/C	?		ca. 1730	*Antiques* 58 (October 1950): 312	
Porringer	B*/ C†	F/TW		ca. 1730	Buhler/Hood 1970, no. 90	YUAG
Porringer	B*/C*	E/AR	Andrew and Ruth (Symonds) Eliot (?)	ca. 1730	Flynt/Fales 1968, 74–75	HD

	Mark	Inscription	Patron	Date	Reference	Owner
Porringer	C*	I/WE; AS; The Gift of Thomas Gray Esqr. to Ann Williams, Dec 13 1770 (later)		ca. 1735	*Moore Collection* 1980, no. 100	
Porringer §	C*	A/WE		ca. 1730	Buhler/Hood 1970, no. 92	YUAG
Porringer	C	ES		ca. 1730	Sotheby Parke Bernet, 16–18 November 1972, lot 113	
Porringer	C	O(?)/PK		ca. 1730	Christie's, 19 September 1981, lot 92	
Porringer	C	Spooner (later)		ca. 1730	YUAG files	
Porringer	C	L/SM		ca. 1730	Avery 1920, no. 27	MMA
Porringer	D	P/DM		ca. 1730	*Antiques* 122 (October 1982): 652	
Salver	C*	PDI/M		ca. 1730	Buhler 1972, no. 102	MFAB
Spout cup	A*	?		ca. 1705	*Silver Supplement* 1973, no. 27	
Strainer spoon	E	none		ca. 1730	YUAG files	
Tablespoon	A*	DL		ca. 1720		HD
Tablespoon	A†	I/DD; EW		ca. 1715	DAPC 72.3035	WM
Tablespoon	A*	IW		ca. 1715		YUAG
Tablespoon	A*	I/SM		ca. 1710	Buhler/Hood 1970, no. 86	YUAG
Tablespoon	A*	BW	Bathsheba (Walker) Godfrey	before 1709	Buhler 1972, no. 99	MFAB
Tablespoon	A	W/WM		ca. 1715	*Moore Collection* 1980, no. 102	SLAM
Tablespoon	A*	H/IM		ca. 1710		YUAG
Two tablespoons	B*	PC	Prudence Chester (?)	ca. 1735	Buhler/Hood 1970, no. 94	YUAG
Tablespoon	B*	R/IE		ca. 1710	YUAG files	
Tablespoon	C	T/WK; AT (later)		ca. 1730	Johnston 1994, 34	CMA
Tablespoon §	C*	AB; 1736 (later)		ca. 1735		YUAG
Two tablespoons	C*	S/NS		ca. 1735		YUAG
Tablespoon	C	M/SH to RD		ca. 1730	MFA 1906, no. 70	
Tablespoon	C	PP		ca. 1730	MFA 1906, no. 71	
Tablespoon	?	WEB		ca. 1720	Christie's, 26 January 1991, lot 64	

	Mark	Inscription	Patron	Date	Reference	Owner
Tablespoon	?	SA		ca. 1710	Parke-Bernet, 30 November 1946, lot 109	
Tankard	A	Jeffries crest; LI (+)		ca. 1710	YUAG files	
Tankard	A	This belongs to the Church in Brattle street 1705		1705	YUAG files	
Tankard	A*	M/IA		ca. 1710	Buhler/Hood 1970, no. 87	YUAG
Tankard	A	Delabere arms, azure a bend or cotised between 6 martlets, and crest, 5 ostrich plumes emerging from a ducal crown; D/IS (+)	Delabere family	ca. 1720	Sotheby Parke Bernet, 15 July 1980, lot 287	
Tankard	B*	W/BF (+)	Benjamin Woods	ca. 1720	*American Silver* 1967, no. 2	RWNAG
Tankard	B	H/DS	Daniel and Sarah Humphreys	ca. 1720	YUAG files	
Tankard	B*	B/IH (+)	John and Hannah (Lee) Griswold	ca. 1720	Sotheby Parke Bernet, 30 April–3 May 1980, lot 192	
Tankard	B*	H/IM	John and Mary (Collins) Hamlin	ca. 1720	National Art Galleries, 3–5 December 1931, lot 435	
Tankard	B	unidentified arms, quarter 1 azure a cross crosslet ermine, quarter 2 azure 6 annulets 3, 2, 1, quarter 3 a lion rampant, quarter 4 azure 2 bands gules in chief 3 fleur-de-lis, and a crest, a wyvern holding a sword erect; P/CS	Page family	ca. 1735	*Silver Supplement* 1973, no. 28	
Tankard	B*	W/TG to EW		ca. 1720	YUAG files	
Tankard	B	unidentified arms, per fess 3 fleur-de-lis; E/R (P or R)		ca. 1725	Washington 1925, no. 28	MMA
Tankard	B	M/SH		ca. 1715	Christie's, 22 June 1994, lot 65	
Tankard (mate below)	B (?)	A/SR	Armington family (?)	ca. 1725	Flynt/Fales 1968, 45, 50	Deerfield Academy
Tankard (mate above)	B	A/SR	Armington family (?)	ca. 1725		CAM

	Mark	Inscription	Patron	Date	Reference	Owner
Tankard	B/C	unidentified initials		ca. 1730	*Antiques* 119 (May 1981): 1008	
Tankard	B/C	Wolcott arms, between a chevron ermine 3 chess rooks; W/RS	Gov. Roger and Sarah (Drake) Wolcott	ca. 1730	Sotheby Parke Bernet, 17 November 1981, lot 184	
Tankard	B/C	The Gift of/Mr John Staples/TO THE Church of Christ/IN/Newtown May 28th/1727	John Staples and/or First Church, Newton, Mass.	1727	Jones 1913, 322	MFAB
Tankard	C	I/WE	William and Elizabeth (Allen) Ireland	ca. 1730	Jones 1913, 54	
Tankard§	C	Boardman arms, ermine 3 stringed bows erect 2 and 1, and crest, an armored arm embowed holding three arrows; VINCIT AMOR PATRIAE; DEB (later)	Boardman family	ca. 1735	YUAG files	
Tankard§	C	W/SM		ca. 1730	Christie's, 22 January 1993, lot 118	
Tankard	?	Lyon crest	Lyon family	ca. 1730	YUAG files	

§ Possibly made by William Cowell, Jr.

1. RC 9:10, 157; Codman 1918, 68–69; SCPR 13:402.
2. Codman 1918, 69; SCPR 8:74–75; 11:164–66, 382–83; 14:32, 168–69; Bigelow-Phillips files, 586–87.
3. RC 28:9; RC 9:170; Codman 1918, 144, 69.
4. *Church in Brattle Square*, 104, 128–29, 131, 133, 136, 138, 141, 143, 147–48, 151.
5. *Sewall Diary* 1:568.
6. SCCR, Court of General Sessions, file 162807.
7. SCD 27:160–62.
8. *Sewall Diary* 1:327, 363–64, 460, 462; 2:734. Sewall includes a description of her funeral on 9 December 1713: "Nurse Hannah Cowell buried, Bearers, Mr. Odlin, Tho. Walker; Deacons Maryon, Hobart; Brother Wheeler, Foreland. Was a very pious Woman, and a true Lover of the first Ways of New England."
9. RC 13:177, 233, 287.
10. Samuel Sewall Account Book and Ledger, fol. 194v, NEHGS.
11. Samuel Sewall Account Book and Ledger, fol. 94v, NEHGS.
12. Mass. Archives 17:379.
13. Samuel Sewall Account Book and Ledger, fols. 187v and r, NEHGS.
14. SCPR 18:248; 22:328.
15. Foote 1882, 1:355.
16. SCPR 18:354–55 (will); docket 5574.
17. John M. Fitzgerald Notes on Suffolk Court of Common Pleas Record Books to Francis Hill Bigelow, SCCR, Court of Common Pleas Record Book 1715–18, 311; 1718, 97–98; SCCR, file 12542, vol. 116, Judicial Archives, Mass. Archives.
18. John M. Fitzgerald Notes on Suffolk Court of Common Pleas Record Books to Francis Hill Bigelow, SCCR, Court of Common Pleas Record Book 1731, 218.
19. SCCR, file 16553, Judicial Archives, Mass. Archives.
20. Seybolt 1939, 146, 158, 163, 169, 189, 200.
21. SCPR 32:495; 33:66–67.
22. SCPR 37:512; 38:162–63.
23. Johnston 1994, 35.

Jonathan Crosby
ca. 1746–97

A

Jonathan Crosby was born probably about 1746 to Jonathan Crosby (1722–60), a mariner, and Sarah Skilling (d. ca. 1779), who were married on 19 April 1744 by Rev. John Webb of Boston's New North Church.[1] His paternal grandparents were Thomas Crosby (1688/89–ca. 1759) of Braintree, Massachusetts, and Mary Worth (1692–after 1760).[2] Jonathan probably began his training about 1759 and would have completed it about 1766; his master is not known. On 26 May 1768 Rev. Andrew Eliot of the New North Church married the goldsmith to Susannah Brown (b. 1751), possibly the daughter of Jonathan and Elizabeth Brown of Reading, Massachusetts.[3] Later that year, on 10 December 1768, Crosby was identified as a Boston goldsmith when he signed an indenture for Susanna Smith, "a poor child" of Boston who was to remain with him until 11 September 1779, when she would be eighteen years of age, and who was to be taught "to Knit & Sew & all other Branches of good Housewifry. Also to Read & Write."[4] The Massachusetts tax list of 1771 included Jonathan Crosby, a lodger with Thomas Loring, with one poll.[5] He and his wife quitclaimed land in Charter Street to Elizabeth Brown, widow, on 27 January 1772.[6]

Crosby was living in Watertown, Massachusetts, by 1778, when he enlisted to serve as a guard at the powder house during the War of Independence.[7] He was also identified as living in Watertown when he signed the bond for administering the estate of his mother in 1779, which Benjamin Loring (q.v.) of Braintree signed with him.[8] That same year Jonathan and his siblings sold the house in Ship Street that had belonged to their father.[9] His taxes were abated in Watertown in 1782 and 1785.[10] Sometime thereafter he returned to Boston, for the *Boston Directory* of 1796 lists him as a goldsmith on Fish Street.[11] His obituary, which appeared in the *Boston Gazette* for 3 April 1797, also indicates this change in residence, stating, "Died in this Town on Friday Evening, Mr. Jonathan Crosby, goldsmith, formerly of Watertown at 52." The *Columbian Centinel* of 5 April 1797 gives his date of death as 31 March 1797.[12]

An initials mark in conjoined circles (A), found on a cann and on a teaspoon with a ruffled shell, has tentatively been attributed to him. PEK

SURVIVING OBJECTS

	Mark	Inscription	Patron	Date	Reference	Owner
Cann	A†	D/CM	Caleb and Mary Davis	ca. 1785	YUAG files	
Teaspoon	A*	AW		ca. 1770	YUAG files	
Two teaspoons (mate below)	A	LW		ca. 1770		CHS
Teaspoon (attrib.; mates above)	none	LW		ca. 1770		CHS

1. *Braintree VR*, 712; Thwing; RC 28:241. No record of the goldsmith's birth has been found; his birth date has been calculated from his age at death.
2. *Braintree VR*, 665; SCPR 54:106–07; RC 9:203. In his will (1760) Jonathan Crosby, Sr., mentions that his mother, Mary, is living in his house; SCPR, docket 12531.
3. RC 30:46.
4. Boston Indentures 3 (1763–69): 169, Rare Book Room, BPL.
5. Pruitt 1978, 10–11.
6. SCD 120:217.
7. *Mass. Soldiers and Sailors* 4:152.
8. SCPR, docket 17078.
9. SCD 174:43–44.
10. *Watertown Records* 1894, 6:281, 334.

11. RC 10:237.

12. *Index of Obituaries, 1784–1840*, 2:1128.

William Cross
1658–1715 +

William Cross probably was born in Hinton Parva, Wiltshire, England, on 12 August 1658 to Francis and Mary Cross. His father was minister of the church in Littlehinton, Wiltshire. In 1673 William became the apprentice of Abraham Hind, goldsmith, whose shop was located in Fenchurch Street, London, at the sign of the Golden Ball. William became a freeman of the Goldsmiths' Company in 1681 and probably immigrated to New England about 1690.[1] Peter Barbour sued William Cross, of Boston, goldsmith, for a debt of £2.14 in the Suffolk Court of Common Pleas session of 28 April 1691.[2] In a list of country rates of 1692 his name appears with Bozoon Allen, Capt. John Wing, and Francis Légaré (q.v.).[3] Cross was taxed 10 shillings for country rates in 1692 in division 5, and he was on the list of inhabitants in 1695 in the same division.[4] He served on a jury of inquest on 6 July 1693 for a body that washed up in Boston harbor.[5]

William Cross was the defendant in a court case in 1692, when the goldsmith Thomas Wyllys (q.v.) of Boston brought suit against him for a debt of £1.14.3 still due to Wyllys from the account between them. The total account originally had amounted to £14.7.1, indicating that the two goldsmiths must have done considerable business with one another.[6]

In 1695 the records of King's Chapel indicate that the church "p^d Cross for makeing 2 p^s plate £3.00.00." Unfortunately the King's Chapel plate does not survive, and without that documentation it is impossible to be certain whether or not the WC in an oval mark sometimes attributed to him, but more frequently attributed to William Cowell, Sr. (q.v.), could in fact have been his mark.[7]

Because no objects marked by Cross can be identified and his stay in Boston was brief, it is doubtful that he was ever able to achieve enough success in his craft to act as an independent producer and retailer. Most of his work probably was done for other silversmiths. Cross may have returned to England after only a short time in Boston. In 1715, a William Cross, pawnbroker, is listed with a shop in Grub Street, London.[8] BMW

1. Apprentice Book 3, fol. 33v; Court Book 8, fol. 234v, Worshipful Company of Goldsmiths, London. E. Alfred Jones, letter to John Marshall Phillips, 23 August 1935; Register of Baptisms of the Parish of Hinton Parva for the year 1658.

2. SCCR 1940, 70.

3. SCCR, file 2658, Judicial Archives, Mass. Archives.

4. RC 10:132; RC 1:160.

5. SCCR, file 2776, vol. 32, p. 130, Judicial Archives, Mass. Archives.

6. SCCR, Court of Common Pleas Record Book 1692–98, 8.

7. See mark A, William Cowell, Sr.; Foote 1882, 1:115.

8. Heal (1935) 1972, 134.

Andrew Croswell, Jr.
1737–96

Andrew Croswell, Jr., was born in Ledyard or Groton, Connecticut, on 3 August 1737.[1] He was the eldest son of the Reverend Andrew Croswell (1708/09–85) and Rebecca Holmes or Harlow (1720–79), both from Plymouth, Massachusetts, who were married by Rev. Nathaniel Leonard in Plymouth on 6 May 1736.[2] His paternal grandparents were Caleb (1677/78–1713) and Abigail

(Stimpson) Croswell (1679–ca. 1738).[3] A graduate of Harvard College (1728), the Reverend Croswell was ordained in the Second Church in Groton on 14 October 1736 and presided over a parish in Ledyard, Connecticut, until at least 1743.[4] He was installed as minister of the Eleventh Congregational Church in Boston on 6 October 1748 and resided on Cold Lane in Boston until his death in April 1785 at the age of seventy-seven.[5] His will, written on 23 March 1785 and presented for probate on 8 November 1785, included bequests to his five surviving children. Andrew Croswell received one-eighth of his father's estate, valued at £41.6.11, after specific bequests to his sister Sarah and brothers William, Nathaniel (q.v.), and Joseph. The will mentioned a £100 loan made to Croswell by his father and stipulated repayment of this sum to the estate within one and a half years.[6]

Although his master's identity is unknown, Croswell probably served his apprenticeship in Boston. He would have been fully trained by 1758 but does not appear to have practiced his trade there very long. He established himself in Plymouth shortly after completing his training, probably at the time of his marriage. A purpose of marriage between Andrew Croswell of Boston and Mary Clark (1744–73) of Plymouth, the daughter of Thomas Clark (d. before 1763) of Plymouth, was published in April 1763.[7] They were married in Plymouth on 9 June 1763 by Rev. Jacob Bacon.[8] The couple had one child, Rebeckah, who died on 2 February 1767, five days after her birth.[9] In the Massachusetts tax valuation of 1771, Croswell was credited with two ratable polls and real estate comprising two buildings and forty-two acres of land, valued at an annual rent of £25.[10] His assets, twenty tons of vessels, £10 of merchandise, one horse, two oxen, six cattle, twenty-five goats and sheep, and two swine, suggest that the silversmith was successful and prosperous with diverse mercantile interests. Mary (Clark) Croswell died on 30 August 1773 at the age of twenty-nine. Both mother and daughter were buried on Plymouth's Burial Hill.[11]

Two years after his first wife's death, on 30 September 1775, Croswell published his intention to marry Sarah Palmer (1737–96) of Falmouth, Massachusetts.[12] Nine children were born to this marriage: Andrew, baptized on 11 August 1776 and died 23 September 1777; Andrew, born on 9 April 1778, graduated from Harvard College in 1798, became a physician, and died in Mercer, Maine, in 1858; a son Samuel, baptized on 16 January 1780; Sarah, born on 24 September 1781 and died on 28 September 1782; Sarah, baptized on 11 March 1787; Abigail, baptized on 1 March 1789; Thomas, baptized on 17 April 1791; Elizabeth, baptized on 24 March 1793; and Anna, baptized on 6 September 1795.[13] Most of the Croswell children were baptized in the Plymouth church; several were buried on Burial Hill.

Croswell appears frequently in the Plymouth County deed records. On 23 April 1764 Andrew Croswell, Boston goldsmith, purchased one-half of the "Clark homestead" and a total of eight acres from his sister-in-law Elizabeth (Clark) Finney and her husband, the Bristol, Rhode Island, cooper Thomas Finney, property that the Clark sisters had inherited from their father, Thomas Clark.[14] Croswell paid £268.13.4 for half of the house, a field called Beach Field, a flat adjacent to the beach, and a woodlot. In June 1765 Croswell, identified as a Plymouth goldsmith in the deed, purchased additional property in Plymouth from the housewright Abiel Shurtleff for £26.13.4.[15] Shurtleff sold the Croswells a "garden spot and dwelling house" on Market Street for £133.6.8 in 1770.[16] Croswell extended the house by constructing a shop on its south side. Although he sold the northern edge of the Market Street property to Robert Brown in 1782, Croswell continued to occupy the dwelling house and shop until his death.[17] The remainder of his real estate transactions appear to have been investments or speculations. The silversmith was involved in five real estate transactions with Daniel Dinar between 1766 and 1781. He sold part of the Clark estate to Dinar in December 1766 and repurchased it for £260 in January 1767.[18] Croswell bought a lot in Cedar Swamp in Plimpton from Dinar for £3 two years later.[19] Another deed, dated 8 January 1781, records Croswell's payment of "£60 silver money" to Dinar for land in Plymouth.[20] Benjamin Croswell and Joseph Croswell, perhaps relatives serving apprenticeships with Croswell, served as witnesses for some of the deeds. In October 1783 the silversmith bought land at the foot of Fort Hill from Mercy Russell for £10.4.[21] His brother-in-law Thomas Finney sold him a house, lot, and garden in April 1784 for £13.14.7.[22] Finally, Croswell acquired additional property in Plymouth from the widow Abigail Churchill in June 1792 for £31 and from the physician James Thatcher for £20 in January 1794.[23]

Croswell also appears in Plymouth and Boston court records. He was mentioned as a legatee in the will of James Doten, probated on 22 September 1785; payment was made by the administrator, Stephen Doten, on 9 April 1788.[24] The goldsmith was appointed administrator of the estate of a Plymouth single woman, Mercy Barnes, on 7 March 1786.[25] He appeared once in the Suffolk County Court of Common Pleas, as a plaintiff with David Nye of Wareham, Massachusetts, Gentleman, in a suit of debt against the Boston merchant Joseph Green, heard at the session of January 1790.[26]

Croswell died on 10 September 1796 at the age of fifty-nine and was buried on Burial Hill in Plymouth.[27]

No mark has been identified for this silversmith. DAF

1. Kingman 1892, 76, no. 690; Davis 1883, Part II:75.
2. *Charlestown VR* 1:217; *Mayflower Descendant* 14:156; 17:137; SCPR 84:653; Davis 1883, Part II:75; *Index of Obituaries, 1704–1800*, 1:77. Weis (1936) 1977 gives Holmes as the maiden name of Rebecca Croswell; Davis records her name as Harlow.
3. Weis (1936) 1977, 64–65; *Charlestown VR* 1:102, 108, 186.
4. Weis (1936) 1977, 64–65.
5. Weis (1936) 1977, 65; *Index of Obituaries, 1704–1800*, 1:77.
6. SCPR 84:653.
7. PCD 57:96; *Mayflower Descendant* 26:42.
8. RC 30:312.
9. Kingman 1892, 39, no. 364.
10. Pruitt 1978, 650–51.
11. Kingman 1892, 39, no. 364, 44, no. 418.
12. Davis 1883, Part II:75; *Mayflower Descendant* 27:177.
13. *Plymouth Church Records* 2:462–63, 467, 478, 479, 483; *NEHGR* 12:363; Kingman 1892, 48, no. 459, 55, no. 510; *Boston Transcript*, 20 September 1915, 4914.
14. PCD 49:56–57.
15. PCD 54:129.
16. PCD 55:108.
17. Davis 1883, Part I:234.
18. PCD 57:96.
19. PCD 54:248.
20. PCD 60:108.
21. PCD 64:23.
22. PCD 62:183.
23. PCD 78:41; 84:194.

24. *Mayflower Descendant* 19:180.
25. *Mayflower Descendant* 34:15.
26. SCCR, Court of Common Pleas Record Book 1789, 137.
27. Kingman 1892, 76, no. 690.

Nathaniel Croswell
ca. 1754–98⁺

Nathaniel Croswell was a younger brother of Andrew Croswell (q.v.). No birth record has been found for Nathaniel, but he is mentioned as one of the legatees in his father's will, probated on 8 November 1785, in which he received part of his father's wearing apparel and two-eighths of the residual estate after specific bequests.[1] Nathaniel Croswell first appears in the Boston records with his intention of marriage to Polly (Mary) Whitman, daughter of Frances Whitman (ca. 1716–93), published on 11 September 1776.[2] The *Independent Chronicle* announced the wedding of "Nathaniel Croswell, goldsmith," and Polly Whitman on 14 November 1776.

Croswell appears in the Boston tax list of 1780 as a resident of ward 5 and was assessed "rents" at £60.[3] In January 1781, Nathaniel Croswell represented William Croswell, an unidentified minor relative, in a trespassing suit filed against the Boston buttonmaker John Clark. William Croswell was awarded "£500 Old currency equal to £12,10 shillings New Emission Damages & Costs of Suit."[4] The census for 1790 records an entry for "_____ Croswell [*sic*]" heading a household of one adult man and four women.[5] This entry's placement, immediately following that of Frances Whitman, suggests that Nathaniel Croswell was living on Prince Street next to his mother-in-law and that he may have had one or more daughters.[6] On 10 January 1798, the heirs of Frances Whitman, including Nathaniel Croswell, goldsmith, and wife, Mary (Whitman); Thomas Hunstable, bricklayer, and wife, Sarah (Whitman); Elizabeth Kessick, widow; and Aaron Clap, yeoman, and wife, Abigail (Whitman), all of Boston, were paid $300 by another heir, Thomas Whitman, also of Boston, for their right to property on Prince Street.[7]

No objects by Nathaniel Croswell have been identified. DAF

1. SCPR 84:653.
2. RC 30:437; *Index of Obituaries, 1704–1800,* 1:324.
3. "Assessors' 'Taking-Books,'" 28.
4. SCCR, Court of Common Pleas Record Book 1780, 102–03.
5. RC 22:468.
6. The *Independent Chronicle* reported the death of Francis (*sic*) Whitman on 16 October 1793 at the house of her son Thomas in Prince Street. *Index of Obituaries, 1704–1800,* 1:324.
7. SCD 189:117–18.

Alexander Crouckshanks
w. ca. 1768

The jeweler and goldsmith Alexander Crouckshanks arrived in Boston on 29 August 1768 aboard Hugh Morris's vessel *Catherine*, bound from Glasgow.[1] He may have been the Alexander Cruckshanks apprenticed to Colin Allen of Aberdeen, Scotland, in 1755 for a term of seven years.[2] In the *Boston Chronicle* for 19–26 December 1768 he placed the following advertisement:

A

Alexander Cruckshanks
JEWELLER *and* GOLD-SMITH,
Lately from London, hath just opened Shop

*in Marlborough-street, near School-house-
lane, and nearly opposite Dr. Sewall's
Meeting-House.*
MAKES and sells all
Sorts of Jewellery and Gold-
Smith's Work in the newest and neatest
fashion; likewise mends all Jewellers
Work in the neatest manner.—Those
Ladies or Gentlemen who please to fa-
vour him with their custom, may depend
on being as well and cheap served as by
any in Town.
   N.B. Cash for old Gold and Silver
Lace, and old Jewels.—Commissions from
the Country will be strictly attended to.

The same advertisement with minor variations was repeated in the issue of
26 December–2 January. The Massachusetts tax list of 1771 includes him in
Boston with a poll of one, one work building, and real estate valued at six
pounds annually.[3] Crouckshanks probably either died or left Boston by 1780
because he does not appear on that year's tax list or any thereafter.

Three pieces of silver with an initials mark (A) have been attributed to him,
with the attributions based on a punch strainer in the Museum of Fine Arts,
Boston, collection that has a history of Massachusetts ownership. PEK

SURVIVING OBJECTS

	Mark	Inscription	Patron	Date	Reference	Owner
Creampot	A	SH		ca. 1770	YUAG files	
Strainer	A†	P/TH E	Thomas Handasyd and Elizabeth Peck	ca. 1770	Buhler 1972, no. 332	MFAB
Tablespoon	A*	JF		ca. 1770		YUAG

1. RC 29:307.
2. London Public Record Office, IR 1, vol. 52, fol. 120.
3. Pruitt 1978, 40–41.

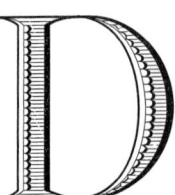

D

Edward Dane
1750–72 +

Edward Dane (Dean), the eldest son of Thomas Dane (q.v.), was baptized in Boston's New Brick Church on 8 July 1750.[1] He was referred to as the son of Abigail, probably following his father's death, when his apprenticeship, whose term was twelve years and four months, was arranged with Benjamin Burt (q.v.) on 18 March 1759.[2] An additional document of 1 July 1761, in which the overseers of the poor bound out Dane to Burt, states that the apprenticeship was to last until 18 July 1771, when Dane would have been twenty-one.[3] He witnessed deeds for Burt in 1766 and 1768, the former with John Andrew (q.v.).[4] An Edward Dane, probably the goldsmith, was made a member of the New Brick Church on 1 March 1772, but nothing further has been found on Edward Dane in the Boston records, and no work by him is known.[5] PEK

1. Wyman 1864–65, 18:338.
2. Boston Indentures 2 (1752–62): 122, Rare Book Room, BPL.
3. Boston Indentures 2 (1752–62): 168, Rare Book Room, BPL.
4. SCD 110:203; 113:99.
5. Wyman 1864–65, 18:339; SCD indexes do not list Edward Dane.

James Dane
1735–62 +

James Dane (Dean) was baptized in Ipswich, Massachusetts, on 20 July 1735, the son of Philemon Dane (1695–1748), a hatter, and Antise Manning, who were married in 1716.[1] His paternal grandparents were Philemon Dane (d. 1716), an Ipswich physician, and his second wife, Ruth Converse (d. 1735).[2] His maternal grandparents were Thomas Manning (d. 1737), an Ipswich gunsmith, and his wife, Mary.[3] The clockmaker Richard Manning (q.v. Appendix A) was James's uncle. Both Dane's father and paternal grandfather helped found the Second Church of Ipswich in 1747.[4] His father died when James was young, and he was a legatee in his father's will of December 1748, receiving a third of the estate, exclusive of specific legacies to his mother and brother Thomas (q.v.).[5]

Dane's apprenticeship began about 1749, possibly with his brother Thomas, who was working in Boston as a silversmith by the time the younger man was old enough to begin his training. The fact that James witnessed two Suffolk County deeds for his older brother on 23 February 1754/55 lends support to this possibility.[6] Dane would have completed his apprenticeship about 1756.

Dane probably went to Hartford, Connecticut, upon completing his training, for on 25 September 1758 he is described as being of Hartford when he sold land in Ipswich inherited from his father.[7] The next year, however, he was in New York; on 21 March 1759 at age twenty-three a "James Deane . . . born Epswich Boston, trade-Silver Smith" enlisted in Capt. James Smith's company of the Queens County militia.[8] He presumably was still residing in New York when he married Agnes Caldwell (Choulwell) there on 14 February 1760.[9] He was in Falmouth, Cumberland County, Maine, by 17 November 1762, when he sold a quarter interest in a house, garden, barn, and outhouse in Ipswich to another Falmouth goldsmith, Paul Little (q.v.).[10] At a session of the Inferior Court of Common Pleas held at Falmouth on 14 October 1763 in reference to the sale, James Dane is described as "now removed out of the Province." Where he settled after leaving Falmouth is not known, but the James Dean listed as a private on the muster of Capt. Daniel Cozen's company on Long Island on 27 January 1778 may be the silversmith or perhaps his son.[11] The date and location of Dane's death have not been determined. The surname mark DANE generally is attributed to his brother Thomas (see Thomas Dane mark [B]), although it is possible that this mark was used by James.   DAF and PEK

1. *Ipswich VR* 2:130; ECD 50:90; ECPR 328:303–06, 354; 330:92; Hammatt 1850, 13.
2. *Ipswich VR* 2:123, 536; *Woburn VR* 1:57; Hammatt 1850, 13.
3. ECPR, docket 17574.
4. Waters 1917, 127, 133, 135, 471.
5. ECPR 330:92.
6. SCD 84:135–36, 257–58.
7. ECD 116:121.
8. *New-York Historical Society Collections* (1891) 24:150–51.
9. *New York Marriages*, 97.
10. ECD 113:168; 116:123.
11. Robbins 1921, 257.

Thomas Dane
1726–59

A

B

Thomas Dane (Dean), baptized in Ipswich, Massachusetts, on 5 June 1726, was the older brother of the goldsmith James Dane (q.v.).[1] (See the entry on James Dane for biographical information on his parents and grandparents.) Little information about Dane's early life or training exists, but both brothers were mentioned in their father's will, written on 5 December 1748; Thomas received as part of his third of the estate a silver tankard and a "great brass kettle."[2] The clockmaker Richard Manning (q.v. Appendix A) was his uncle.

Dane probably began his apprenticeship about 1740 and would have completed it about 1747. This training may have taken place in Boston. He was married in Boston, by the Reverend Ellis Gray of the New Brick Church, on 3 August 1749 to Abigail Fernald (Furnell), probably the daughter of William and Elizabeth Fernald born in 1726.[3]

On 16 March 1749/50 Thomas Dane sold land in Ipswich that he had inherited from his father; he sold off additional land there on 15 November 1751.[4] The previous month, on 1 October 1751, "Thomas Deane, goldsmith," was cited as a defendant in the Suffolk County Court of Common Pleas. Charged with trespass by Katharine Bulfinch, a single woman of Boston, Dane defaulted on the damages assessed against him.[5] On 22 February 1754/55 Dane bought land with a dwelling house on Middle Street in Boston, purchasing two-thirds of the parcel from Thomas Hutchinson of Milton, Massachusetts, and the remaining third from Elizabeth Pecker. He signed mortgages with

Hutchinson and Pecker for the property the next day, in transactions that were witnessed by Dane's brother James, who was probably apprenticed to him at the time.[6]

Dane did business with the Boston silversmith Thomas Edwards (q.v.): Edwards's daybook indicates that he sold Dane fifteen pennyweights and nine grains of gold on 15 June 1749 and a card of stone buttons on 17 January 1752. Dane may also have been making pieces for Edwards, as a transaction dated 13 December 1752 shows that he was Edwards's debtor for silver, presumably for use as raw material, and that he made Edwards a milk pot body, probably to pay that debt.

"To Silv.r taken of the milk pott
w.t
Ditto C.r By the fashion of }
of a milk pott body   }   2..5..[7]

Dane also made gold rings for the funerals of James Varney and his wife of Boston as John Tudor recorded in a leger on 13 May 1752:

To Cash paid M.r Dane for Makeing ten Rings
& finding Gold for five for Father & Mothers Funer.l   27.4.8[8]

Although twentieth-century silver scholars have contended that Thomas Dane lived until the late eighteenth century, clear evidence exists that he died sometime before the last Tuesday of March 1759, when he was referred to as "lately deceased" in testimony before the Essex County Inferior Court of Common Pleas.[9] Moreover, on 8 March 1759, when his son Edward Dane (q.v.) was apprenticed to Benjamin Burt (q.v.), the younger Dane was referred to as "the son of Abigail," indicating that Dane had died by then.[10] His wife may have been the "Dean, Abigail, widow" listed in the *Boston Directory* of 1796 as residing on Wilson's Lane and the Abigail Dean who died in 1799 at age sixty-nine.[11]

Dane's silversmithing career therefore lasted just slightly longer than a decade, and only about a dozen pieces marked by him survive. These bear an initial and surname mark (A) or a surname mark (B). Though few in number, the quality and diversity of form and ornament of these holloware objects testify to Dane's skills as a silversmith. He crafted a set of four candlesticks, now at Historic Deerfield, with elaborate foliate and beaded decoration. Another pair of candlesticks that bear English marks suggest Dane sold imported silver. A chafing dish in the Hood Museum of Art at Dartmouth College is pierced intricately with hearts, scrolls, and checkerboard patterns. A brass cylinder with a piece of flint mounted on one end and engraved "T DANE," "TD," and "1755" may have been owned by the silversmith and used as a practice surface for engraving on silver.[12] The cylinder is covered with initials, including "BW," "HB," "R," "I," and "H," and shows experimentation with different types of lettering and engraving techniques, such as cross-hatching and shading. The Maine Historical Society owns a tankard by Dane elaborately engraved with scrolls, foliage, arms, and a commemorative inscription, commissioned by the officers of the Second

Battalion on 20 April 1757 to present to their commander, Joseph Frye, Esq. DAF and PEK

SURVIVING OBJECTS

	Mark	Inscription	Patron	Date	Reference	Owner
Two candlesticks (with English marks)	?	G/RA		1741/42	Bigelow 1917, 289–90	
Four candlesticks	A*	none	Benjamin Hallowell	ca. 1750	Fales 1968, 521	HD
Cann	A*	The Gift of Mᵣ Benjⁿ- Crocker/to the South Church of Christ/in Ipswich 1748.	South Church, Ipswich, Mass., for Benjamin Crocker	1748	Buhler/Hood 1970, no. 204	YUAG
Cann	B*	D/WR		ca. 1750	*Moore Collection* 1980, no. 153	
Chafing dish	A	none		ca. 1750	Buhler 1965, 74–77	HMA
Chafing dish	A	(?)		ca. 1750	YUAG files	
Cream pail	A†	I: Tudor	John or Jane Tudor	ca. 1750	Buhler/Hood 1970, no. 205	YUAG
Creampot	A	MWF/Margaret Whitwell to M.W. Foster (later)		ca. 1755	Sotheby's, 23–24 June 1994, lot 108	
Porringer	A*	unidentified crest, a [erased] or emerging from a ducal coronet		ca. 1755	YUAG files	
Snuffbox	A*	Mary Loring/1752	Mary (Gyles) Loring	1752		AIC
Sugar bowl	A	Giles crest, a lion's gamb erect and erased holding a fruited branch; Mary Loring/the Gift of her Father/Iohn Gyles Esqʳ./1748	John Gyles for Mary (Gyles) Loring	1748	Phillips 1939, no. 60	
Tankard	B†	To JOSEPH FRYE Esq = /Colonel and Commander in Chief of the Forces in the Service of the Province of the Massᵃ Bay and late Major of the 2ᵈ Battalion of General Shirleys Provincial Regiment . . .	Officers of the 2ᵈ Battalion of General William Shirley's Provincial Regiment for Joseph Frye	1757		MeHS

1. *Ipswich VR* 1:114.
2. ECPR 328:303–06, 354; 330:92, docket 7126.
3. RC 28:243; Gooding 1927–30, 81:425.
4. ECD 104:284; 120:196.

5. SCCR, Court of Common Pleas Record Book 1751–52, 96.

6. SCD 84:135–36, 241–43, 257–58.

7. Thomas Edwards Account Book 1749–53, Brigden Papers, YU.

8. John Tutor II Collection, vol. 1, 155, Baker Library, HU.

9. ECD 104:284.

10. Boston Indentures 2 (1752–62): 122, Rare Book Room, BPL.

11. *Boston Directory* 1796, 36; *Index of Obituaries, 1784–1840*, 2:1271. Francis Hill Bigelow thought that Dane married Abigail Fernald (b. 1726). The Abigail Dean who died in 1799 would have been born about 1730, therefore the ancestry of Dane's wife is somewhat uncertain.

12. The cylinder is owned by YIM. It is also struck four times with an illegible shield-shaped mark.

Lemuel Davenport
1742–1802

A

Lemuel Davenport, the son of the goldsmith Samuel Davenport (q.v.) and his wife, Sarah Whiten, was born in Milton, Massachusetts, on 10 March 1742, the eldest of seven children.[1] He was baptized in the First Church of Milton by Rev. John Taylor four days later.[2] An intention of marriage between Lemuel Davenport of Milton and Patience Stone of Stoughton, Massachusetts, was published on 5 September 1764, and the couple was married by the Reverend Samuel Dunbar on 4 October 1764.[3] Patience Stone, the eldest child of the Stoughton innholder Henry Stone (1721–84) and Lydia Wadsworth (1726–97), was born on 23 March 1743/44; her father and his partner, Edward Wentworth, established the first chocolate mill in the colonies.[4]

Lemuel Davenport probably served his apprenticeship from 1756 until 1761 with his father and appears to have worked in Milton and Stoughton at various times during his career. All of his eight children were born in Stoughton between 1764 and 1787, with the possible exception of his first child, Sarah, whose birth in December 1764 is listed in both the Milton and Stoughton vital records.[5] Davenport was listed in the Massachusetts tax valuation of 1771 as a landowner in Stoughton, with holdings that included a house and 11 1/2 acres valued at an annual rent of £3.8.[6] The tax list also assessed the silversmith with two ratable polls, one horse, three cattle, ten goats and sheep, and two swine. However, in the interval between 1771 and the birth of his son Samuel in 1777, Davenport appears to have resided in Milton at the foot of Blue Hill; he was appointed the Milton town coroner on 10 February 1774.[7]

In July 1783, Lemuel Davenport, goldsmith of Stoughton, brought suit against Charles Fenno, a Stoughton tanner, in the Suffolk County Court of Common Pleas. Davenport recovered damages of £14.5.3 and court costs of £1.10.10.[8]

Although none of his children appears to have become a silversmith, Davenport did train his grandson, Rufus Davenport Dunbar, son of his daughter Sarah and Samuel Dunbar.[9] Rufus Dunbar established a silver shop in Worcester, Massachusetts.

The census for 1800 listed Davenport in Norfolk County as the head of a family composed of himself and his wife, both over forty-six years of age, two boys and one girl between the ages of ten and sixteen, one boy and one girl between sixteen and twenty-six, and two women between twenty-six and forty-six.[10] Davenport died in Canton, Massachusetts, in July 1802.[11] Patience Davenport died in Milton in 1819 at the age of seventy-five.[12]

An initial mark (A) in a serrated rectangle can be attributed to Lemuel Davenport. It appears on spoons in private collections. Another mark, an incuse L. D., has been associated with Davenport but was probably not used by him because this type of mark was not in common use by American silversmiths until the 1820s.[13] DAF

SURVIVING OBJECTS

	Mark	Inscription	Patron	Date	Reference	Owner
Spoon	A	?		?	DAPC 75.2362	
Teaspoon	A†	AE		ca. 1790	DAPC 84.3521	

1. *Milton VR*, 21.
2. Trask 1869, 450.
3. *Milton VR*, 111; *Stoughton VR*, 179–80.
4. Stone 1882, 367; *Stoughton VR*, 17, 19; SCPR 83:622–23, 658–61.
5. *Milton VR*, 21; *Stoughton VR*, 89, 96, 97, 120.
6. Pruitt 1978, 514–15.
7. Flynt/Fales 1968, 197.
8. SCCR, Court of Common Pleas Extended Record Book 1783, 274.
9. Flynt/Fales 1968, 197.
10. Massachusetts Census, 1800, Norfolk County, 130.
11. *Index of Obituaries, 1784–1840*, 2:1229.
12. *Milton VR*, 217.
13. The incised mark is found on a privately owned teaspoon in DAPC.

Samuel Davenport, Jr. 1720–93

Samuel Davenport, Jr., was born in Roxbury, Massachusetts, on 1 September 1720, the eldest son of the housewright Samuel Davenport (1697–1773) and Rebecca Holbrook (1699–1777) of Milton, Massachusetts.[1] His paternal grandparents were John Davenport (1664–1725), a husbandman of Dorchester and Milton, and Naomi Foster (1668–1739); his maternal grandparents were Daniel and Abigail (Craft) Holbrook.[2] When the younger Samuel came of age in 1741, his father gave him the family estate in Milton and moved to Mendon, Massachusetts.[3] Davenport was married on 4 June of that year to Sarah Whiten (d. 1764) of Dedham, Massachusetts.[4] Their son Lemuel (q.v.) was born on 10 March 1742.[5] Six more children were born to Samuel and Sarah Davenport between 1744 and 1759.[6] Milton documents record the death of "Sarah, wife of Lt. Samuel Davenport," on 11 June 1764.[7] Davenport married Sarah Tucker (d. 1795) of Milton, the widow of Nathaniel Tucker, on 24 September 1769.[8]

Samuel Davenport was active in Milton town government. Appearing on the tax lists of 1750 as a taxpayer living in the west end of town, Davenport served as moderator for the town meeting in 1765 and as a selectman in 1764–67 and 1772–74.[9] In both 1766 and 1767, he was listed as a lieutenant and in 1774 as a captain in the town militia. "Samuel Davenport, Silversmith," was chosen in November 1770 to serve as a member of the jury that tried Captain Preston in the Boston Massacre case.[10]

In 1774, Samuel Davenport and six other Milton residents drafted a letter commending the departing Massachusetts Bay governor Thomas Hutchinson. Criticized for this action at a town meeting on 21 September 1774, the men were required to sign a public retraction and apology.[11]

Capt. Samuel Davenport died in Milton on 6 December 1793 at the age of seventy-three.[12] His obituary appeared in the *New-England Chronicle* for 16 December 1793.[13]

Although a tablespoon in the Worcester Art Museum marked Davenport in a rectangle ([A]; too worn to illustrate) has been attributed to Lemuel Davenport, it is more likely the work of Samuel Davenport. The feather-edged handle and the raised shell on the bowl differ from the ornamentation found on the spoons made by Lemuel. The engraved initials "SD to SD" may indicate that the spoon was a gift from Samuel Davenport to his second wife, Sarah Tucker Davenport.[14]   DAF

SURVIVING OBJECTS

	Mark	Inscription	Patron	Date	Reference	Owner
Tablespoon	A	SD/to/SD	Sarah Davenport	ca. 1769	Buhler 1979, no. 65	WAM

1. Davenport 1879, 28, 33; SCD 55:98–99; *Roxbury VR* 1:90.
2. Adams 1910, 1656; Davenport 1879, 28, 132; *Milton VR*, 217; *Cambridge VR* 1:192; RC 21:11; *Roxbury VR* 1:183; 2:209; SCPR 24:32–34.
3. Teele 1887, 563.
4. Davenport 1879, 33.
5. Teele 1887, 563; *Milton VR*, 21.
6. *Milton VR*, 21.
7. *Milton VR*, 217; Davenport 1879, 33.
8. Robbins 1862, 52; *Milton VR*, 111; Davenport 1879, 33.
9. Teele 1887, 217, 224, 229.
10. Teele 1887, 430, 563; Roberts 1895, 2:203.
11. Teele 1887, 421–23.
12. Teele 1887, 563; *Milton VR*, 217.
13. *Index of Obituaries, 1704–1800*, 2:285.
14. Buhler 1979, 51.

Elias Davis
ca. 1746–83

A

B

C

Elias Davis of Newburyport, Massachusetts, remains an elusive figure, mentioned in only a few documents. It is commonly thought that Elias Davis and E. Davis, usually referred to as Edward Davis (q.v. Appendix B), were both silversmiths in Newburyport active in the 1770s and early 1780s. However, it is suggested here that they are one and the same man and that the proper first name is Elias.

Elias Davis probably was born in Newburyport about 1746 and died there on 15 September 1783, aged thirty-seven. He was termed a captain at the time of his death.[1] In a deed dated 21 July 1778, Elias Davis of Newburyport, goldsmith, purchased a house and land in Newburyport from Samuel Plumer of Epping, New Hampshire, a cordwainer.[2] A document from 1797 in the Essex County probate records refers to the "guardianship of Elias Davis a minor aged fifteen years & Catherine Smith Davis a minor aged thirteen years both Children of Elias Davis late of Newburyport in said county Goldsmith deceased."[3] An earlier, related document, dated 27 September 1790, mentions four other minor children but refers to Elias as "gentleman."[4] (The son Elias mentioned in each document was probably Elias Davis [1782–1856], who became a silversmith and worked in Newburyport, Boston, and Gardiner, Maine.)[5]

Elias probably married Phoebe (or Phebe) Woodman on 28 December 1769. The Massachusetts tax list of 1771 lists Davis as having one-half of a house with one-half of a shop adjoining and gives the value of his merchandise as

£10.[6] Elias Davis (occupation not specified) was one of the appraisers of the estate of Benjamin Greenleaf III (q.v. Appendix B) in Newburyport in March 1781.[7]

Elias may have made the spoon marked E. Davis that was stolen in 1775 and announced as recovered by William (Coffin) Little (q.v.) in the Newburyport *Essex Journal* of 18 August. A large spoon made for the First Church of Newburyport is attributed to him; it is engraved "The Gift of Josiah Titcomb to the I Church N P" and was purchased with funds bequeathed to the church by Titcomb in 1770.[8] A porringer engraved "N.M.W.," a cann engraved "M.S.M. to M.S.R.," a second cann engraved "MMR," and a creampot are among the holloware forms attributed to E. Davis that have been published. Three marks (A–C) are here attributed to Elias Davis. His lion pseudo-hallmark (C) is unusual for a Massachusetts silversmith of his period. Other variations recorded are EDAVIS and E.DAVIS in rectangles and EDAVIS in an oval, but examples could not be located for illustration here.[9]

It is always stated that Davis left his business to his young apprentice, Jacob Perkins (1766–1849), who was only seventeen years old in 1783. Perkins went on to become famous as a silversmith, engraver, and inventor of machinery.[10] GWRW

SURVIVING OBJECTS

	Mark	Inscription	Patron	Date	Reference	Owner
Cann	A	F M PARDEE (later)		ca. 1775	American Art Association–Anderson Galleries, 3–5 December 1936, lot 459	
Cann	A	MMR		ca. 1775	Gourley 1965, no. 60 (as Edward Davis)	
Cann	A/C	M.S.M. to M.S.R.		ca. 1775	*Newburyport Maritime Society Antiques Show* 1981, 2 (as Edward Davis)	
Cann	B†/ C*	PAA		ca. 1775	Bigelow 1917, 185	
Creampot	A	AS/ES		ca. 1775		SI
Creampot	A	IBA		ca. 1775	National Art Galleries, 3–5 December 1931, lot 226	
Creampot	A/C	IB/ob.ͭ N'yok/Ap.ͬ 14 1782/AE17		ca. 1782	Avery 1920, no. 214	MMA
Porringer	A/C	N.M.W.		ca. 1775	*Newburyport Maritime Society Antiques Show* 1981, 2 (as Edward Davis)	

	Mark	Inscription	Patron	Date	Reference	Owner
Salt	?	?		ca. 1775	*Antiques* 93 (April 1968): 425 (as Edward Davis)	
Two salts	A	YBEG Todd (?)		ca. 1775		MFAB
Spoon	A*	?		ca. 1775	YUAG files	
Strainer	A/C†	C/WI	William and I. (Wheelwright) Codman	ca. 1775	*Antiques* 107 (February 1975): 276 (as Edward Davis)	
Tablespoon	A	The Gift of Josiah Titcomb to the I Church NP	Heirs of Josiah Titcomb	ca. 1780	Jones 1913, 300–01	
Teaspoon	A*	EH		ca. 1780	Johnston 1994, 42 (as Edward Davis)	CMA
Teaspoon	A*	AL/E		ca. 1775		HD
Teaspoon	A*	PP		ca. 1765	Johnston 1994, 42 (as Edward Davis)	CMA
Teaspoon	A	PT	Patrick Tracy	ca. 1775	YUAG files	
Teaspoon	A*	AT		ca. 1775	DAPC 74.1460	WM
Teaspoon	A†	EP		ca. 1775		HD
Teaspoon	A*	AC		ca. 1775	DAPC 74.1514	WM
Teaspoon	A*	MC		ca. 1775	DAPC 74.1331	WM
Teaspoon	A*	SC		ca. 1775	DAPC 74.1334	WM

1. *Newburyport VR* 2:609.
2. ECD 138:18.
3. ECPR 365:415.
4. ECPR, docket 7314.
5. Flynt/Fales 1968, 198.
6. *Newburyport VR* 2:129; Pruitt 1978, 114–15.
7. ECPR 355:286–88.
8. Jones 1913, 301.
9. Gourley 1965, no. 60, describes the mark on a cann owned by Towle Silversmiths as E.D in a rectangle, but a photograph was not available. Ensko 1927, 60; Ensko 1937, 33; Ensko 1948, 45; Graham 1936, 20; Thorn 1949, 63; and Kovel 1961, 78.
10. *DAB*, s.v. "Perkins, Jacob."

Matthew Delaney
w. ca. 1722

The only records that identify Matthew Delaney of Boston as a goldsmith relate to the suit he brought in 1722 against the Boston pewterer Daniel Darninger in the Suffolk County Court of Common Pleas.[1] The file papers for this case and Darninger's appeal contain information regarding the relationship between the two men and shed light on how business was conducted between craftsmen during this period. At the time of the appeal, in November of 1723, Jonathan Jackson testified that "on the 26.th of October 1722 I sold To Mr Daniel Durninger 71lb 3/4 of Pewter @ 17 pence p pound, being thick ash mettall and unfitt to cast into any Small Ware, which mettall I bought of M[r] Thomas Francis."[2] The deposition of Benjamin Pollard indicates that Darninger's journeyman, Matthew Delaney, then took the metal to have it weighed by him:

> Benjamin Pollard of full age Declareth and Saieth That Some time in the Month of Septem[br] last Mathew Delaney who was a Journeyman with Daniel Daurninger of Boston Pewterer came to this Depon[ts] Shop and Desired that he might have liberty to Weigh a quantity of Mettal which was in a Lump and accordingly weighed the Same the whole weight being Sixty nine pounds which this Depon[t] took to be thick Mettal The Said Delany told this depon[t] that his Master was not at home and that he should borrow the money of M[rs] Button to pay for the s[d] Mettal for his masters use.[3]

A receipt filed as part of the case indicates that Delaney did just as he said he would and borrowed money from Mrs. Sarah Button to pay for the metal. The receipt, which acknowledges Delaney's repayment of the money borrowed, is dated 10 December 1722: "Reseaved of Mathew Dallany fower pounds & six pence which he borroed of me for y[e] use of m[r] Dannil Duringer to pay for sixty nine waite of puter."[4] Delaney had come to court to sue Darninger for the £4.6 borrowed and paid out on his behalf. Darninger, in his countersuit, insisted that he owed Delaney nothing; in both cases the court ruled in Delaney's favor.[5]

Several interesting facts emerge from this case. The first of these is that Delaney, a goldsmith, was working as a journeyman for a pewterer. Also, Delaney was acting independently of his master in the purchase of raw pewter, and the pewter came from a merchant. Delaney was able to take the metal "on approval" as it were and have it weighed in another shop—in other words, to obtain a second weighing of the metal. Knowing that his master wanted the metal and that it might not be available if he waited any longer, Delaney took the liberty of borrowing the money necessary to purchase the metal. That he borrowed it from a woman is significant. Boston court records often show women acting as landlords and as moneylenders, presumably because these were acceptable functions for women that did not involve them in competitive labor.

No objects bearing Delaney's mark have survived, suggesting that he worked as a journeyman to other craftsmen throughout his career.

Matthew Delaney (recorded as Delaway) and Elizabeth Gavit were married by the Reverend Peter Thacher of New North Church on 28 May 1723.[6] The marriage evidently did not last, however, because on 29 July 1723, Elizabeth Delaney petitioned the Court of General Sessions of the Peace, "praying that her Husband Mathew Delaney might be obliged to give sufficient Security that her person maybe in Safty & She have a reasonable maintenance."[7] The petition was read and then dismissed. Why it was filed is unclear, but presumably the couple was living apart by this time. The Boston birth records include no references to any children of Matthew and Elizabeth Delaney. Neither Matthew's nor Elizabeth's estate was probated in Massachusetts, and the dates of their deaths are unknown. BMW

1. SCCR, Court of Common Pleas Record Book 1722, 236.
2. SCCR, file 17386, Judicial Archives, Mass. Archives.
3. SCCR, file 16987, Judicial Archives, Mass. Archives.
4. SCCR, file 16987, Judicial Archives, Mass. Archives.
5. SCCR, files 16987, 17386, Judicial Archives, Mass. Archives.
6. RC 28:112.
7. SCCR, Court of General Sessions of the Peace Record Book, 1719/20–25, 218.

William Delarue
ca. 1740–before 1778

William Delarue was born probably in Boston about 1740 to Elias Delarue (d. 1755), a mariner, and Elizabeth Nowell (ca. 1714–47), the daughter of Philip Nowell (d. 1752), a laborer, and Ann Mulbery (1677–ca. 1746).[1] After Elizabeth's death Elias Delarue published his intention to marry Sarah Parker in 1747; she died, and he married another Sarah.[2] Elias was appointed his son's guardian in 1752.[3] Before beginning his apprenticeship about 1754, Delarue attended public school in Boston, for his name appears among the eighty-six scholars of writing and arithmetic in Boston in 1753.[4]

When Elias Delarue died in 1755 he left his son "a silver punch ladle two silver spoons a pair of gold buttons a set of silver buckles which I got made for him, a pair of gold buttons and the one quarter part of all my wearing apparel."[5] Thomas Kirk, probably William Delarue's uncle by marriage, became his guardian, overseeing his upbringing until Delarue completed his training about 1761.[6] The identity of his master is unknown. On 20 June 1765 Delarue is said to be "of Boston" and a goldsmith when he sold Kirk one-quarter of a house in Brattle Street, probably the house mentioned in his father's will.[7] On 7 July 1765 Delarue married Katharine Bryant (b. 1742), possibly the daughter of Timothy Bryant of Wakefield and Reading, Massachusetts.[8] Twins, William and Elizabeth, were born to the couple on 26 May 1766.[9]

Misfortune plagued Delarue's life. He may have abandoned his wife and young children: the Suffolk County Court files show that Katharine Delarue was warned out of Boston in August 1767. Described as being "last from Stoton" (Stoughton?) and as having twin children, Elizabeth and William, she came to Boston on 8 July 1767 and was living in the South End.[10] In October 1770 Kirk sued Delarue for debt in the Suffolk County Inferior Court of Common Pleas and won a judgment against him. Kirk was allowed to possess one-quarter of Delarue's real estate in Cole Lane to satisfy some of the debt, and Delarue was to be jailed until the rest of the debt was paid.[11] Delarue died before 3 April 1778, when William Boyes was made the guardian of Delarue's son William.[12]

No silver by this maker has been identified. PEK

1. SCPR, docket 11038; RC 28:13, 196, 225; Codman 1918, 79, 176; SCPR, docket 10046; RC 9:142.
2. RC 28:287; Codman 1918, 79.
3. SCPR 46:411.
4. RC 29:243.
5. SCPR, docket 11038.
6. Elias Delarue's estate papers show that Kirk was the guardian, and the name Sarah Nowell is changed to Sarah Kirk. Sarah Nowell may have been Delarue's mother's sister. Thomas Kirk and Sarah Nowell married in 1754; see RC 30:12.
7. SCD 104:220–21.
8. RC 30:361; *Wakefield VR*, 25; MCPR dockets 3331 and 3332 contain guardianship papers in 1749 for Katharine, daughter of Timothy and Suzannah.
9. RC 24:312.
10. SCCR, file 87907, vol. 510, Judicial Archives, Mass. Archives.
11. SCD 118:138–39.
12. SCPR, docket 16510.

Peter Denman
w. ca. 1710–12

The Boston selectmen's records for 27 November 1710 include the following notation: "Peter Denman Silversmith being present Sayes he came from Engl^d into this Town wth Capt Wentworth in May Last, the Sel. m do warn him to depart ye Town unless he find Surtie to ye value of forty pounds, by the Last monday in Decr next."[1] This is probably the same man who appears in an account filed in a court case in 1712 as the journeyman of Isaac Anthony (q.v.).[2] Denman apparently did not remain in Boston for very long because he does not appear in town records again. BMW

1. RC 11:122.
2. SCCR, file 10844.

Daniel Deshon
ca. 1698–1781

Daniel Deshon was born about 1698. Some scholars have speculated that he was born in Norwich, Connecticut, to a Huguenot family whose name may have been Deschamps, because an individual named Deschamps and René Grignon (q.v.), the jeweler who would become Daniel Deshon's master, appear among the settlers at "Frenchtown" near East Greenwich, Rhode Island, in the 1690s.[1] Deshon may also have been descended from the Moses Deshen who with René Grignon presented a deposition from the French Church to the governor of Massachusetts in February 1691/92.[2]

Daniel Deshon became the apprentice of René Grignon in Norwich, Connecticut, about 1712. In his will, written 20 March 1714/15, and proved 12 April 1715, Grignon states "I Give and bequeath unto Daniel Dishon all my Gooldsmith Tools, and Desire he may by my Execut^{es} be bound out to some sutable person in Boston till he arrive att the age of Twenty one Years, to Learn the Trade of a Goldsmith, and I also give unto him ten pounds money to be paid . . . when the s^d Daniel comes of Age."[3] Deshon finished his apprenticeship with John Gray (q.v.) of Boston and New London. When Gray's widow presented Gray's estate administration on 21 February 1720/21 it included charges for "⁴/₅ parts of 8$^£$.6^s for a Coat Jacket briches Shirt hatt and Shoes to Dan^{ll} Dishon when his time was out [£] 06.12.09" and "3 shirts, a p^r of shoes, a p^r of lether briches & 2 Neck Cloths . . . that were his masters [£] 02.00.00."[4] Because Gray spent part of the period from 1715 to 1720 in Boston, Deshon probably received some of his training there.

On 7 October 1724 Deshon married in New London, Ruth Christopher (1705–75), the daughter of Christopher Christopher of New London. Daniel and Ruth had three sons, one of whom, John (1727–94), married Sarah Starr (1731–92), a sister of the silversmith Jasper Starr (q.v.).[5] Deshon wrote his will on 11 February 1772, leaving to his wife the use of his dwelling house and land during her life as well as his Negro woman, Dinah. His wife and son John were to be the executors.[6] Ruth Deshon died in New London on 6 January 1775, and the silversmith died there in November 1781.[7] His will, which was proved on 6 February 1782, directed the residue of the estate be divided among their children.

John Marshall Phillips attributed a conjoined script initials mark to Deshon.[8] The absence of additional pieces with this mark that have Connecticut histories of ownership makes the attribution dubious. No other marks or silver by Deshon have been identified. PEK

1. Goldsborough 1969, 15; Daniels 1892, 23–24; Freeland 1894, 160–61.
2. SCCR, file 288.
3. New London Probate District, docket 2317, CSL.
4. New London County Probate District, docket 2274, CSL.
5. *Starr Family*, 240, no. 354.

6. Copy of the original from the New London County, Connecticut, Probate Records is in the Bigelow-Phillips files, Connecticut Silversmiths, YUAG.

7. *Ye Ancient Buriall Place of New London, Conn.*

8. Phillips 1935, no. 60; Buhler/Hood 1970, no. 336.

John Dexter
1735–1800

John Dexter was born in Dedham, Massachusetts, on 12 August 1735, the son of the Reverend Samuel Dexter (1700–55), the minister at Dedham, and Catherine Mears (1701–97), who were married in Boston on 9 July 1724.[1] His paternal grandparents were John Dexter (1671–1722) and Winifred Sprague (ca. 1673–1752) of Malden, Massachusetts.[2] His maternal grandparents were Samuel Mears (1671–1727) and Maria Catherine Smith (1680–1706) of Boston.[3]

Dexter would have begun his apprenticeship about 1749 and would have completed it about 1756. He probably was trained in Boston because he advertised having a shop there in the *Boston Gazette* of 7 November 1757. His advertisement read,

> JOHN DEXTER Jeweller, has opened Shop in
> *Fish-Street*, a little to the Northward of *Cross-*
> *Street*, near Mr. *Pigeon's;* where he makes and sells,
> and likewise mends, all Sorts of *plain* and *Stone* Rings,
> Earings, Buttons, and every other Kind of Stone-
> Work, at the cheapest Rates—Has also to sell Stones,
> Foil, &c. &c. and expects soon a larger Assortment.
>   Goldsmiths in Town or Country may be sup-
> plied with the above-mentioned Articles.—N.B. Choice
> *Kippen's* Snuff, Indigo, and several Sorts of Cutlary Goods.

Dexter may have been trained by John Welsh (q.v.) for on 24 September 1757 he and Benjamin Loring (q.v.), probably the Boston silversmith, witnessed a receipt from John Welsh to Zachariah Symmes, father of the goldsmith John Symmes (q.v.), involving the settlement of Isaac and Grace Parker's estate.[4] Perhaps Dexter represented Parker's and Welsh's retailing interests when he moved from Boston to Marlborough, Massachusetts. Dexter probably had left Boston by the time he married Mary Howe (1746–1822) in Marlborough on 14 October 1765.[5] She was the daughter of Josiah Howe (b. 1720), a yeoman, and Mary Goodale (b. 1719).[6] The Massachusetts tax list of 1771 includes John Dexter in Marlborough with a poll of one, a house, and another building, possibly a shop. The annual worth of the real estate was calculated at two pounds; Dexter also had two cattle.[7] A number of John Dexters of Marlborough served in the War of Independence, and the jeweler may have been one of them.[8] Dexter died in Marlborough on 7 February 1800.[9] As is often the case with jewelers, no mark for Dexter has been identified. PEK

1. *Dedham VR* 1:63; RC 24:8; RC 28:119; *Malden VR*, 21.

2. Winifred Sprague's birth date was calculated from her age at death; see *Malden VR*, 340.

3. RC 9:119, 151, 236; Boston Deaths, 1700–1800.

4. MCPR, docket 16584.

5. *Marlborough VR*, 104, 270, 356.

6. *Marlborough VR*, 81, 101, 269; WCD 45:280.

7. Pruitt 1978, 240–41.

8. *Mass. Soldiers and Sailors* 4:722–23.

9. *Marlborough VR*, 356.

Basil Dixwell
ca. 1711–45

Basil Dixwell, the son of John Dixwell (q.v.) and his wife, Mary Prout, is said to have been born in Boston on 7 July 1711 and named for his father's cousin Sir Basil Dixwell.[1] Basil's father died on 2 April 1725, and on the following 3 August John Prout was made guardian of his nephews and niece: Basil, aged fourteen years; Elizabeth, nine years; and John, seven years.[2] On 6 November 1725 Prout, acting as the children's guardian, granted a mortgage to Hannah Wormall for a brick tenement in Wood Lane.[3] Basil probably began training with his father, but since Basil was only fourteen at the time of his father's death, his training would have been completed with another silversmith whose identity is not known. The administration of his father's estate shows a payment of 11 shillings and 4 pence made for "1 p.r Shoes & Buttons for Bassil."[4] On 30 September 1732, Basil Dixwell of Boston, goldsmith, released John Prout from his guardianship of the estate left him by his father.[5] That year Dixwell witnessed a deed with William Simpkins (q.v.) for Samuel Gray (1710/11–48) (q.v.).[6] Dixwell and Gray may have been working as journeymen for Simpkins, who was slightly older.

Sometime after finishing his apprenticeship, Dixwell went to Providence, Rhode Island. A deed of 17 September 1741 in which he and his two siblings sold land in Wood Lane, Boston, identifies him as "silversmith" of Providence, Rhode Island.[7] He must have remained in Providence for only a short time because he served in the Louisbourg campaign in the company of the Boston goldsmith Joseph Goldthwait (q.v.), his father's former apprentice. Goldthwait, a captain in his majesty's service at Cape Breton, petitioned Governor Phips that "his Lieutenant Bazil Dixwell in the year 1745 proceeded with your Petitioner and his Company to Louisbourg in the Service where he was taken sick and died—That your Petitioner was at the charge of his sickness and Funeral and for Nurses, medicines & expended one hundred pounds old Tenor of his own money. That the said Bazil Dixwell left no Estate to reimburse or pay your Petitioner saving the wages due to him from the Province."[8] The court granted Goldthwait's petition in 1749. No silver by Basil Dixwell is known to survive. PEK

1. Savage 1860–62, 2:55. No record of Dixwell's birth has been found in vital records.
2. SCPR 24:151.
3. SCD 39:220–21.
4. SCPR 25:295–97.
5. SCPR 31:123–24.
6. SCD 47:14–15.
7. SCD 62:4–6.
8. Drake 1870, 232; Mass. Archives 73:625–26.

John Dixwell
1680/81–1725

A

John Dixwell was the son of John Dixwell (ca. 1607–89), who, as a member of the English High Court of Justice, tried and condemned King Charles I. After the restoration of the monarchy, the elder Dixwell fled to the colonies and lived in seclusion for the rest of his life, first in Hadley, Massachusetts, with the Reverend John Russell, the father of Eleazer Russell (q.v.), and finally in New Haven, Connecticut, under the alias James Davids. Late in life he married as his second wife Bathsheba How (1644–1729), the daughter of Jeremiah How (d. 1690).[1] Their son, the goldsmith, was born as John Davids in New Haven on 6 March 1680/81.[2] After James Davids died of dropsy on

B

C

D

E

18 March 1689, the family resumed the name Dixwell. The silversmith is thought to have been trained by Jeremiah Dummer (q.v.) because he and Daniel Gookin (q.v.) witnessed a deed on 17 December 1698 before Dummer in Dummer's capacity as justice of the peace.[3] Dixwell along with Shubael Dummer (q.v.) witnessed another deed for Dummer on 31 August 1704, which suggests that he may have worked for Dummer as a journeyman after completing his training.[4]

Soon after he came of age Dixwell attempted to reclaim his father's English land, which his father had conveyed to Dixwell and his mother through indentures executed on 20 October 1682 and filed in 1691. Upon leaving England the elder Dixwell had deeded these estates, with power of revocation, to his nephew Sir Basil Dixwell (ca. 1650–89), then a minor, and provided £2,500 for their upkeep. The Reverend James Pierpont of New Haven sent a letter on 4 May 1708 to the son of the nephew, also Sir Basil Dixwell, identifying John Dixwell as the son and heir of his father. In 1710 the goldsmith went to England to recover his father's estates for himself and his mother. He carried a letter of introduction from Rev. Cotton Mather dated 13 November 1710 that gives an idea of the high regard that the people of Boston had for the young goldsmith:

> He is one of Ingenuity. He has a Genius elevated above the common Level of the countrey, where he had his Birth and Breeding. There is in him, a Modest but yet a Sprightly Soul; Thoughtful and Cautious enough too; And a Natural good Sense agreeable to the stock of which he comes. A Little cultivation which the place of his Nativity afforded him not, would have made him Extraordinary. . . . Yes, I will venture to say this of him, though he has lived for near twice seven years in my neighborhood, I never heard, that he did one ill or Base Thing in his Life. . . . People of the best fashion here, have advised him to intermit his Other Business for half a year, and wait upon his kinsman and see.—Tis in Obedience to their Advice that he does what he does.[5]

However, the powers of revocation in the original deeds were not valid because the government had changed, and Dixwell gained nothing from this trip except a promise that if he named a son Basil, he would inherit the estates. Dixwell and his wife, Mary Prout (1686–1721), daughter of Capt. John (b. 1649) and Mary (Rutherford) (Hall) Prout (b. 1649) of New Haven, whom he married on 1 September 1708, named a son Basil (q.v.); however, his English cousin apparently never deeded the estates to him.[6]

Dixwell would have begun working about 1702. An entry in Samuel Sewall's diary for 11 September 1705 reveals that Dixwell was actively practicing his trade by then. Sewall wrote, "Her Majesties Letter of the Third of May 1705. from St James's, is read at the Board, wherein a new seal is order'd, and the old one to be defac'd: John Dixwell, the Goldsmith, being sent for, cut it in two in the middle, with a Chisel."[7] The administrator's account for the estate of Jane Kind, mother-in-law of William Rouse (q.v.), submitted in 1710, shows that John Dixwell was paid £13.1.6 for the rings specified in the deceased's will.[8] Identifying himself as "*Mr.* John Dixwell *in Union Street*," he advertised in 1713 the sale of an Indian man aged about twenty years who spoke good English.[9]

Dixwell's connections to New Haven, his birthplace, remained strong and some of his patronage came from there. Francis Browne, captain of the sloop *Speedwell*, which sailed between New Haven and Boston, made payments to Dixwell between 1707 and 1713 on behalf of Yale College and a number of

New Haven residents: James Pierpont, John Prout, Mr. Atwater, George Pardy, John Miles, and Samuel Smith. Some of the payments may have been for silver made by Dixwell.[10] In 1715 the New Haven town meeting voted to have Dixwell convey a letter from the New Haven church to several ministers in Boston. According to a letter written in 1715, on at least one occasion Dixwell acted as an agent for Stephen Alling and Capt. Joseph Whiteing, both of New Haven, shipping iron and nails to them, and selling their rum in Boston.[11]

Dixwell trained a number of apprentices. From about 1708 to 1715 he probably trained William Jones (q.v.), for Jones's family was also from New Haven. Dixwell's father and Jones's grandparents, William (d. 1706) and Hannah Jones (d. 1707), were close friends because in his will the elder Dixwell named the Joneses the guardians of his children in the event of his wife's death and until friends in England could send for them.[12] The goldsmith William Jones also named his eldest child Basil, a Dixwell family name. Daniel Russell (q.v.) is known to have been Dixwell's apprentice and probably trained between about 1712 and 1718. On 3 December 1723 twenty-three-year-old Joseph Kneeland (q.v.) and seventeen-year-old Joseph Goldthwait (q.v.) witnessed a deed for Dixwell.[13] Their ages suggest that they were a journeyman and an apprentice, respectively. Goldthwait also witnessed a bond for Dixwell on 26 March 1723 when Dixwell was acting as power of attorney for Mary Pierpont of New Haven.[14] Kneeland also may have been Dixwell's apprentice. In the settlement of Dixwell's estate, Kneeland was paid £3.15, further evidence of his journeyman status.[15] Dixwell also probably began to train his son Basil.

Dixwell twice assisted in settling the estates of his fellow craftsmen. In 1717/18 with Thomas Milner (q.v.), he appraised the tools and plate in the estate of Henry Hurst (q.v.), and in the same year he appraised the estate of Edward Webb (q.v.) with John Edwards (q.v.).[16] The ledger book of the Boston stationer Daniel Henchman reveals how some of Dixwell's trade was conducted. Between 1721 and 1724 Dixwell purchased books and other stationery supplies from Henchman which amounted to £20.15. This account was settled by a silver tankard valued at £18.12 with the balance paid in cash.[17]

Dixwell's name turns up in the Suffolk County Court records a number of times. He sued the mariner Cornelius Clince in 1712 for Clince's failure to pay rent on a dwelling.[18] Dixwell was a defendant in a suit at Boston on 2 July 1717 brought by Matthew Tindale of London and was the plaintiff in suits in 1720 and 1723.[19] Dixwell and his wife sold their share of a house and land in Long Lane to the blacksmith John Manning of Boston in 1723. Dixwell also owned a house and land in Wood Lane in Boston's North End and a farm in Roxbury, both of which he rented on a regular basis.[20]

Seventeen mechanics, including Dixwell, founded the New North Church in 1714, "unassisted by the more wealthy part of the community except by their prayers and good wishes." In 1717 Dixwell was chosen deacon and on 7 September 1720 became ruling elder.[21] He presented a beaker to the church in 1717 and made several other objects for that church between 1714 and 1722. Dixwell's first wife died in 1721, and on 26 April 1722 he married Martha (Remington) Bowes, who died the following October.[22] On 18 April 1723 he married Abigail (Walker) Bridgham (1683–1740).[23] Dixwell died from a smallpox inoculation on 2 April 1725 and was buried in the Copp's Hill Burying Ground.[24] The following 24 May his widow Abigail was made administrator of the estate, and the inventory, amounting to £952.11.5, was appraised on 9 June by John Edwards, Jonathan Loring, and William Tyler. The equipment and silver in the shop show that Dixwell was active at his trade:

7 p.^r Scales 1 pile of w.^{ts} Troy & avoirdupoire   £3.. 15.. —

1 Leather Chair 2/. 8^{lb} Saltpeter 24/   1.. 6.. —

1 ^{lb} of Borax   15.. —

1 Touch Stone 1/. 1 Scrath brush 2/6   3.. 6—

24 Nests of Crucibles 25/ 36 black potts 36/.   3.. 1.. —

2 old Iron beams 15/ 7 Draw Irons 20/   1.. 15.. —

16 Cutting & Dapping punches 8/ 5 Spoon }

         punches 25/ }   1.. 13.. — 12.. 8.. 6

1 Spoon Ring & Pewter 6/ 12 smalest 6/   12.. —

2 Brass Salt Stamps 5/. 1 Iron Ladle 1/   6.. —

Chisells 5/ 5 p.^r Tongs 5/ 2 Ingotts 7/   17.. —

4 Burnishers 18/. 1 Old brass Stamp }

     10 Strainges with frames 25/ }   2.. 3.. —

1 borax box 2 blow pipes 4/ 6 p.^r Shears 10/.   14.. —

3 p.^r hand vices 5/. 6 p.^r plyers & flat Tongs   14.. —

1 p.^r Sliding Tongs 1 p.^r Compasses 1 p.^r Dividers   3.. 6

1 Square Trib 1 Small bekern 1 p.^r bellows   7.. 6

1 p.^r Large bellows 40/ 1 board Vice 18/   2.. 18.. —

1 forging anvile 5 Raising anvills 2 belly

pott anvills, 3 bekern anvills, 2 Tasts 7 Stakes }   21.. 9.. 4—

1 Large Chisell all w.^t 322^{lb} neat at 16^d ℔ lb }

4 Ring Swages & other Swages w.^t 15^{lb} at 15.^d   18.. 9—

1 Small Skillet w.^t 10^{lb} at 15.^d   12.. 6—

32 hammers 40/. 3 boiling pans w.^t 11 ½^{lb} 34/6   3.. 14.. 6—

1 Drawing bench Tongs & Ring   1.. —.. —

Moulding sand 12/. 2 brass panns 16   1.. 8.. — 37. 18. 1

· · ·

397.^{oz} 5.^{dwt} Silver at 15/6   307.. 12.. 4

   1 19   S   at 10/.   19.. 6

   3 15   Soder at 10/   1.. 17.. 6

  10 6   Gold   at £11   113.. 6.. —

· · ·

34^{oz} 7/8 Course Silver taken out of }

the Ashes at 10/ ℔ oz. }   17.. 8.. 9

17.^{dwts} 3.^{gr} gold at £10 ℔ oz: }

     being Course }   8.. 11.. 3²⁵

The administrator's account approved by the probate court on 10 April 1727 shows that the total value of the estate was £1,211.8.11 less £868.9.12 for expenses, and £519.8.1 of outstanding debts.[26]

A significant number of Dixwell's surviving pieces are in New England nonconformist churches, which suggests that his close familial ties with the English Puritan Revolution stood him in good stead with traditional congregations. An advertisement for stolen silver in the *Boston News-Letter* of 20 April 1713 reads in part, "Silver Tankard containing better than a Beer Pint, made by Mr. *John Dixwell*, Mark'd only with his mark ID." Five variations of ID in an oval have been attributed to him (A–E).[27] A spurious example of his mark is known. PEK

SURVIVING OBJECTS

	Mark	Inscription	Patron	Date	Reference	Owner
Baptismal basin	A	The Gift of Mr David Farnum/to the New North Chh/In Boston N:E:/1722	New North Church, Boston, for David Farnum	1722	Jones 1913, 65	
Beaker (mate below)	A†	Harwich: Chh:/ Cup:	First Parish, Brewster, Mass. (formerly North Parish, Harwich, Mass.)	ca. 1715	Buhler 1972, no. 94	MFAB
Beaker (mate above)	A	Harwich: Chh:/ Cup:	First Parish, Brewster, Mass. (formerly North Parish, Harwich, Mass.)	ca. 1715	Buhler 1972, 117	
Beaker	A	Ex: dono: David Lawrence:/To the Church of Exceter-/ April:25:1710:	First Congregational Church, Exeter, N.H., for David Lawrence	1710	Jones 1913, 170–71	
Beaker (with later handle)	A	Ex dono: N: Lor- ing/to the New N: Church/1716 (+)	Nathaniel Loring	1716	Jones 1913, 63	
Beaker (mate below)	B	Harwich Chh Cup	First Parish, Brewster, Mass. (formerly North Parish, Harwich, Mass.)	ca. 1715	Buhler 1972, 118	
Beaker (mate above)	B†	Harwich Chh Cup	First Parish, Brewster, Mass. (formerly North Parish, Harwich, Mass.)	ca. 1715	Buhler 1972, no. 95	MFAB
Two beakers	B	C	Theophilus Cotton (?)	ca. 1720	Jones 1913, 203	NHHS
Beaker	B	The Gift of Henery Yatts/to y̧ Church of Guilford	First Congregational Church, Guilford, Conn., for Henry Yates	ca. 1705	Jones 1913, 193	
Cann	?	MS (+)		ca. 1715	Sotheby's, 29 April–1 May 1981, lot 396	
Caudle cup	A	A/IR (+)	Jonathan and Ruth (Peck) Atwater	ca. 1705	Jones 1913, 307	
Caudle cup	A	R/HS; The Gift of Mrs Mary Prout . . . (later)	Mary (Rutherford) (Hall) Prout	ca. 1705	Jones 1913, 302–03	
Caudle cup	A	Given by m^r Jno Pot- ter to N: Hav: Chh.	First Church of Christ, New Haven, Conn., for John Potter	ca. 1707	Jones 1913, 303	
Caudle cup	A	RT		ca. 1710	Quimby 1995, no. 40	WM
Caudle cup	B	The Gift of M^rs Ab- igail Davenport	Abigail (Pierson) Dav- enport	ca. 1718	Jones 1913, 303	
Caudle cup	?	?		ca. 1710	Antiques 114 (December 1978): 1116	
Cup	A	RA (+)		ca. 1715	Avery 1920, no. 28	MMA
Cup	A*	P/IA (+)		ca. 1715	Buhler/Hood 1970, no. 80	YUAG

	Mark	Inscription	Patron	Date	Reference	Owner
Cup	A*	P/WE (+)		ca. 1715	Buhler/Hood 1970, no. 81	YUAG
Cup	?	M. C. Chew. from her Grandfather. (later)		ca. 1715	Sotheby's, 17 November 1981, lot 187	
Cup	B*	K/SS		ca. 1715		PEM
Cup	B*	AW		ca. 1715	MFA 1911, no. 336	
Cup	B*	DH; The Gift of Mʳ Daniel harris to the first/Church in Middeltown/1735 (later)	Daniel Harris	ca. 1720	Jones 1913, 283	
Cup	B (?)	?		ca. 1710	*Antiques* 118 (September 1980): 378	
Patch box	A	Abigail Taylor	Abigail Taylor	ca. 1720	Naeve/ Roberts 1986, no. 54	AIC
Patch box	E	S. Pierpont	Sarah (Pierpont) Edwards	ca. 1720	Ward/Hosley 1985, no. 164	YUAG
Porringer	A*	S/WM		ca. 1720		YUAG
Porringer	A*	W/IM	Williams family (?)	1720–25	Warren 1975, no. 294	BBC
Porringer	D*	R/??; H/IG (worn)		ca. 1720	DAPC 77.2427	
Porringer	D	B/RS		ca. 1720	Naeve/ Roberts 1986, no. 52	AIC
Porringer	?	SG		ca. 1725	*Moore Collection* 1980, no. 99	
Porringer	?	P/IE (+)		ca. 1720	Levy 5:32	
Porringer	?	A/IR		ca. 1720	Sotheby Parke Bernet, 6–8 November 1975, lot 608	
Porringer	?	AP		ca. 1720	Sotheby's, 30 June–1 July 1982, lot 233	
Porringer	?	L/OS	Lloyd family (?)	ca. 1720	*Antiques* 118 (July 1980): 91	
Porringer	?	EC		ca. 1720	Kroening 1982, no. 7	
Porringer	?	G/DM	Greenleaf family	ca. 1725		MFAB
Ring (gold)	E†	Be.true.in.heart		ca. 1720	Buhler/Hood 1970, no. 84	YUAG
Salver	A*	B/ND; ES		ca. 1715	Johnston 1994, 43	CMA
Snuffbox	D†	WB		ca. 1715	Buhler/Hood 1970, no. 78	YUAG

	Mark	Inscription	Patron	Date	Reference	Owner
Spout cup	B*	C/NS	Noah and Sarah (Turell) Champney (?)	ca. 1710	Quimby 1995, no. 41	WM
Spout cup	C†	A/MB		ca. 1710	Puig et al. 1989, no. 182	MIA
Tablespoon (mate? below)	A*	B/IR		ca. 1710	Quimby 1995, no. 42	WM
Tablespoon (mate? above)	A*	B/IR		ca. 1710	DAPC 85.2193	
Tablespoon	B	erased		ca. 1720		SI
Tankard	A	Given by John Baker/to the new NC/1714 (+)	John Baker and/or New North Church, Boston	1714	Jones 1913, 62	
Tankard	A	New NC, Octor. 21, 1714	New North Church, Boston	1714	MFA 1911, no. 314	
Tankard	A*	D/WE	William and Elizabeth (Davenport) Dudley	ca. 1720	Buhler/Hood 1970, no. 83	YUAG
Tankard	A	This belongs to the/ New North Church (+)	New North Church, Boston	1714	Jones 1913, 61–62	
Tankard	A*	Bernard arms (later) (+)	Bernard family	ca. 1720	Sotheby Parke Bernet, 16–18 November 1978, lot 402	YUAG
Tankard	D	IS		ca. 1720	DAPC 77.3078	MAM
Tankard	E*	Grosvenor arms, a garb, and crest, a garb; T (altered to P) G (+)	Thomas Grosvenor (?)	ca. 1715	Buhler/Hood 1970, no. 79	YUAG
Tankard (altered)	?	New N.C. Octr. 20, 1714	New North Church, Boston	1714	MFA 1911, no. 337	
Two-handled cup	A	Ex dono: C. lyman/to yᵉ New NC/Octoʳ: 20 1714	Caleb Lyman and/or New North Church, Boston	ca. 1714	Jones 1913, 59–60	
Two-handled cup	A	Ex dono Alice Buckingham/to the Church of Christ/In Milford	Alice Buckingham and/ or First Congregational Church, Milford, Conn.	ca. 1715	Jones 1913, 286–87	
Two-handled cup	A	New Noᵗʰ Church Cup/1717 (+)	New North Church, Boston	1717	Jones 1913, 60–61	
Two-handled cup	A	Ex: dono I.D.; This belongs to the/New North Church (+)	John Dixwell	1717	Jones 1913, 60	
Two two-handled cups	A	This Cup belongs to the Church of medford, Annod: 1719	First Parish, Medford, Mass.	1719	Jones 1913, 273	CW
Two-handled cup	A	Given by Mr Samˡˡ Stone/to the Chh of Christ/in Milford/1714	First Congregational Church, Milford, Conn., for Samuel Stone	1714	Jones 1913, 286	
Two-handled cup	A	none	First Congregational Church, Milford, Conn.	ca. 1720	Jones 1913, 287	

	Mark	Inscription	Patron	Date	Reference	Owner
Two-handled cup	A*	Ex Dono Mrs Elis.^{a} Smith/to the Church of Charles-town/april: 12 1717	First Parish Church, Charlestown, Mass., for Elisabeth (Wadland) Smith	1717	Buhler/Hood 1970, no. 82	YUAG
Two-handled cup	B	The gift of Sarah Knight to the/Chh of Christ in Nor-wich/Ap^{r} 20: 1722	Sarah Knight and/or First Congregational Church, Norwich, Conn.	1722	Buhler 1972, no. 96	MFAB
Two-handled cup	B	The gift of Samuel Barret to the New North Church, 1723	Samuel Barrett and/or New North Church, Boston	1723	Jones 1913, 66	
Two-handled cup	C*	Deerfield Chh	First Congregational Church, Deerfield, Mass.	ca. 1720	Jones 1913, 138	

1. *New Haven VR* 1:47, 70, 79.
2. *New Haven VR* 1:51.
3. SCD 19:33–34. The deed involved Thomas Savage (q.v.) and his wife Mehitable (Phillips) Savage, which raises the possibility that Dixwell and Gookin could have worked with Savage.
4. SCD 75:171.
5. The Reverend James Pierpont to Sir Basil Dixwell, Bigelow-Phillips files, 562a; the Reverend Cotton Mather to Sir Basil Dixwell, Mss 8, Box 1, folder G, John Dixwell papers, NHCHS.
6. Stiles 1794, 125–67; RC 9:29; *New Haven VR* 1:2, 48, 59; Whitmore 1878, 19, no. 358.
7. *Sewell Diary* 1:528.
8. SCPR 17:179, docket 3242.
9. *Boston News-Letter*, 18 May 1713.
10. Francis Browne Account Book, n.p., Manuscripts and Archives, Sterling Memorial Library, YU.
11. *New Haven Town Records*, 368–69; Dixwell to Captain Joseph Whiteing, 19 November 1715 (with bill), Ezra Stiles Papers, Box 1, folder K, NHCHS.
12. Bigelow-Phillips files, 558.
13. SCD 37:177–78.
14. SCCR, file 16988.
15. SCPR 25:295.
16. SCPR 21:261–62, dockets 3956, 4086.
17. Daniel Henchman Ledger, fol. 133, NEHGS.
18. SCCR, Court of Common Pleas Record Book 1710–13, 225.
19. SCCR, Court of Common Pleas Record Book 1715–18, 188; 1720, 50; 1722, 222.
20. SCD 37:117–78; SCCR, files 13930, 16988; Court of Common Pleas Record Book 1710–13, 225–26; 1720–21, 50.
21. Winsor 1880–81, 2:220–21; Drake 1856, 544.
22. RC 28:106; Whitmore 1878, 19, no. 357.
23. RC 9:161; RC 28:112; Abigail subsequently married William Stacey of Marblehead, Massachusetts, and John Clough of Boston; see RC 28:140, 201. She left her estate to the children of her deceased brothers and sisters; see SCPR 35:223.
24. Boston Deaths, 1700–1800.
25. SCPR 24:66–67; 25:274–80.
26. SCPR 25:295–97.
27. The mark is on a tablespoon at YUAG; see Buhler/Hood 1970, no. 85.

John Doane
1719–67

Born in Boston on 1 September 1719, John Doane was the son of John Doane (d. 1723), a mariner, and Abiah Callender (b. 1690), who were married on 23 June 1714 by the Reverend Cotton Mather.[1] Doane's maternal grandparents were the Reverend Ellis (ca. 1639 to 41–1728) and Mary Callender (d. by 1719)

A

of Boston.[2] Rev. Ellis Callender, a merchant by trade, was one of the founders of the First Baptist Church in Boston and the minister there from 1708 until 1726.[3] Doane's paternal grandparents were John Doane, Esq. (1664–1755), a distiller, and his first wife, Mehitabel Scudder, who were married on 30 June 1686.[4] Doane's grandfather may be the John Doane who was the guardian of the children of Samuel Haugh (q.v.). Doane's brother Joshua (q.v.) was a silversmith who worked in Providence, Rhode Island, and his distant cousins Benjamin and Joseph Callender (qq.v.) were engravers and silversmiths in Boston. His uncle John Doane (q.v. Appendix A), who was a clockmaker and watchmaker, has been frequently confused with the silversmith.

John Doane would have begun his apprenticeship as a silversmith in 1733 and been ready to practice his trade about 1741. He probably trained with John Burt (q.v.) because he would have been twenty years old when he witnessed deeds for Burt in 1739.[5] He may have worked with William Simpkins (q.v.) because he appears with Simpkins on a deed dated 28 January 1745 that the two men witnessed for James Butler (q.v.).[6] Doane and Simpkins witnessed another deed for Butler on 15 April 1747.[7] Doane may have trained Gideon Myrick (q.v.), whose stepfather was Edmund Doane, possibly the silversmith's relative.

John Doane had a distinguished career of public service to the town of Boston. He was selected to serve as a constable on 11 March 1750. At the same town meeting, Doane was also chosen to "collect, seal and keep until next Quarter sessions the votes of the Town for a new County Treasurer," an indication of his respected position in the community.[8] In 1752 the Boston selectmen appointed Doane the constable for ward 4.[9]

John Doane, Esq., grandfather of the silversmith, died in December 1755. In his will, written 17 November 1755, he left only twenty shillings apiece to each of his grandchildren, Mehitabel Cowley, John Doane, and Elisha Doane, "because of their ill wild Carriage to me, & mine, for these many years past, & still continue in it."[10]

The *Boston News-Letter* for 13 August 1767 reported the death of "John Doane, formerly of this Town, Goldsmith, but for some years past resident at the Island of Barbados," a statement supported by the Doane family genealogy.[11]

Very few objects that can be associated with this silversmith survive. A tankard with a cast lion mask in the Yale University Art Gallery and a porringer with a keyhole handle at Historic Deerfield, both engraved "I^Es," are marked I·DOANE in a rectangle (A). The form of the tankard is very typical of Boston tankards; the cast mask terminal is similar to one used by Doane's colleagues Paul Revere, Jr. (q.v.), and William Simpkins. Although the mark on the tankard has been attributed to Joshua Doane, it is probably John Doane's. The keyhole handle of the porringer with this mark is cast from a different mold than those documented to Joshua Doane. A cann by John Doane bears the same mark. DAF

SURVIVING OBJECTS

	Mark	Inscription	Patron	Date	Reference	Owner
Cann	A*	WW to TLJ (later) (+)		ca. 1750	DAPC 90.3187	MFAB

	Mark	Inscription	Patron	Date	Reference	Owner
Porringer	A*	E/IS		ca. 1745	Flynt/Fales 1968, 99 (as Joshua Doane)	HD
Tankard	A†	E/IS		ca. 1745	Buhler/Hood 1970, no. 492 (as Joshua Doane)	YUAG

1. RC 24:136; Doane 1902, 63; RC 28:50; RC 9:189; SCPR, docket 4774.
2. Savage 1860–62, 1:330.
3. Woodworth-Barnes 1990–91, 195–99; Doane 1902, 63; Thwing; *NEHGR* 48:444; SCPR 26:289–90.
4. Doane 1902, 34–35; SCPR 50:702–05; Hamblin 1852, 44.
5. YCD 19:172; 23:214–15.
6. SCD 71:146–47.
7. SCD 73:161–62.
8. RC 14:188–89.
9. RC 17:273.
10. SCPR 50:702–05.
11. *Index of Obituaries, 1704–1800*, 2:311; Doane 1902, 64.

Joshua Doane
1717–53

A

Joshua Doane, born in Boston on 22 September 1717 to John Doane (d. 1723) and Abiah Callender (b. 1690), was the elder brother of John Doane (q.v.).[1] (See the entry on John Doane for biographical information on his parents and grandparents.) He would have served his apprenticeship between 1731 and 1738, possibly with John Burt (q.v.), who trained his brother. The silversmiths Benjamin and Joseph Callender (qq.v.) were Doane's distant cousins.

Doane probably moved to Providence, Rhode Island, shortly after attaining his freedom. The silversmith was married to Mary Cooke (b. 1720/21) in Providence on 22 February 1752/53 by Justice of the Peace Richard Waterman.[2] She was the daughter of Daniel Cooke and Mary Power, who were married on 4 February 1713/14.[3] Doane died on 16 July 1753, shortly after his marriage, leaving a small personal estate to his widow.[4]

Past publications have confused the work of Joshua Doane with that of his brother John Doane. However, a surname mark in a shaped cartouche (A) can be assigned to Joshua Doane with some certainty. A beaker made for St. John's Church, Providence, bears this mark and the inscription, "An Oblation/from Nathaniel Kay a/Publican for the use of the/blessed Sacrament in the/Church of England/in Providence/1734."[5] Nathaniel Kay's will, proved on 28 April 1734, two weeks after his death, provided one hundred pounds to each of the "four churches of England in Newport Bristol, Providence and Kingstown Narraganset . . . to furnish each of them with a peice of plate for the holy Communion."[6] Because the beaker would have been ordered shortly after the distribution of the estate, this object is certainly one of Doane's earliest commissions.[7] Nathaniel Kay, an innkeeper and the collector of royal customs for Newport, made similar bequests to all the Church of England congregations in Rhode Island.[8] The porringer made by Joshua Doane has a keyhole handle cast from a mold that is noticeably different from the one used by John Doane. DAF

SURVIVING OBJECTS

	Mark	Inscription	Patron	Date	Reference	Owner
Beaker	A	An Oblation/from Nathaniel Kay a/ Publican for the use of the/blessed Sacrament in the/Church of England/in Providence/1734	St. John's Church, Providence, R.I., for Nathaniel Kay	ca. 1738	Gourley 1965, no. 262	
Porringer	A	MT; AC/to/ST		ca. 1745	*Antiques* 89 (February 1966): 210	
Tablespoon	A†	R/TA		ca. 1738	Gourley 1965, no. 263	RISD
Tablespoon	A	1747		1747	National Art Galleries, 3–5 December 1931, lot 216	

1. Doane 1902, 64, 492; RC 24:121.
2. Arnold 1911, 2:60, 218; Doane 1902, 492.
3. Arnold 1911, 2:47.
4. Arnold 1911, 2:265; Doane 1902, 492.
5. Jones 1913, 386.
6. Jones 1913, 97.
7. Jones 1913, 97, 385–86; Gourley 1965, nos. 206, 262.
8. Jones 1913, 97; Casey 1940, 56.

Daniel Doler
w. 1765

The port records for Boston indicate that on 8 October 1765 Daniel Doler, a goldsmith, arrived in Boston on Timothy Parker's sloop *Three Friends* from Philadelphia.[1] No further evidence of Doler exists in the Boston public records, so it is unlikely that Doler settled there. No silver by him is known. PEK

1. RC 29:271.

Jeremiah Dummer
1645–1718

A

B

Jeremiah Dummer, the first native-born New England goldsmith and the subject of a monograph by Hermann Clarke and Henry Foote, was born in Newbury, Massachusetts, on 14 September 1645.[1] His father, Richard (ca. 1599–1678), emigrated from Bishopstoke, Hertfordshire, England, to Boston in 1632 and settled in Roxbury, Massachusetts, where he built a mill in 1633. He then moved to Boston, where his wife, Mary, died. After her death he settled in Newbury. In 1644 he married Frances (ca. 1612–82), widow of Rev. Jonathan Burr of Dorchester, Massachusetts.[2] In addition to Jeremiah, this couple's other children were Hannah (b. 1647), who married Rev. James Allen, the father of John Allen (q.v.), and Richard (b. 1649), the father of Shubael Dummer (q.v.).[3]

Dummer was an apprentice of John Hull (q.v.) and learned his trade alongside his contemporary Samuel Paddy (q.v.) in the shop Hull ran with his business partner, Robert Sanderson, Sr. (q.v.). Hull's diary entry for 1 July

1659 says: "I received into my house Jeremie Dummer and Samuel Paddy to serve me as apprentices eight years. The Lord make me faithful in discharge of this new trust committed to me and let this blessing be to me and them."[4] Dummer witnessed several deeds for Hull between 1666 and 1670. Dummer also contracted smallpox during his apprenticeship.[5] He probably did not leave Hull's shop upon completing his apprenticeship, but in the summer of 1667 his status may have changed to that of a journeyman. However, a suit that took place in the Suffolk County Court on 4 March 1670/71 wherein Robert Punt (q.v. Appendix A) was sued by Freegrace Bendall suggests that Dummer was operating his own shop by then. Bendall's watch, which had been purchased from John Hull, was to have been fixed by Punt, and the watch was delivered to him at "Mr. Dummers shop," presumably some months prior to this court date.[6] Even after Dummer left the Hull and Sanderson shop he continued to purchase supplies from them, buying two papers of files from John Hull on 21 December 1671 for £1.1 and slightly more than forty-nine ounces of mercury from Hull's son-in-law Samuel Sewall on 16 July 1687 for £11.16.[7]

Upon setting up his own shop, Jeremiah Dummer undoubtedly took the first of a number of apprentices. John Coney (q.v.) would have been fourteen years of age on 5 January 1669/70 and probably became Dummer's apprentice about then. Dummer may have trained Samuel Phillips (q.v.) between 1672 and 1679.[8] Eleazer Russell (q.v.) probably became Dummer's apprentice late in 1677. Before Eleazer Russell's term was up, Dummer took on another apprentice, the nineteen-year-old Kiliaen van Rensselaer (q.v.), son of Jeremias and Maria van Rensselaer of New York, who stayed only briefly. In the late 1680s and 1690s Dummer's name appears in Boston tax lists and lists of inhabitants, usually along with servants or additional men, which could have included apprentices.[9] Edward Winslow (q.v.) would have trained between 1683 and 1690 and witnessed a deed for Dummer in 1688/89.[10] Dummer presumably also trained his nephew John Allen between 1686 and 1693 and Allen's future partner, John Edwards (q.v.), although no proof of these relationships exists. John Noyes (q.v.) would have been a Dummer apprentice between 1688 and 1695, and when Samuel Sewall recorded selling borax to Dummer on 16 April 1691, he noted that he delivered it to "Jnº Noyes."[11] Some scholars have thought that between 1694 and 1701 Dummer trained James Barnes, Jr. (q.v.), whose father and Dummer had business dealings. John Dixwell (q.v.) probably was an apprentice between about 1695 and 1702, and Daniel Gookin (q.v.) would have been one between 1696 and 1704. Samuel Sewall had arranged for Gookin's apprenticeship, and Gookin and Dixwell witnessed a deed for Dummer in 1698.[12] Dixwell may have worked for Dummer as a journeyman after finishing his training because he witnessed a deed for Dummer in 1704.[13] A list of inhabitants of 1698 shows that Dummer had two servants, or apprentices, in that year.[14] Francis Hill Bigelow believed that Samuel Gray (1684–1713) (q.v.) apprenticed with Dummer.[15] Such training would have taken place about 1698 to 1705. Dummer's nephew Shubael probably also trained and worked in his shop, because he witnessed deeds for Dummer in 1704, 1707, and 1709.[16] John Cole (q.v.) may have worked for Dummer as a journeyman, for a John Cole witnessed a deed for Dummer with Winslow in 1689.[17]

Dummer worked and lived in the central part of Boston. On 3 September 1672 the merchant Joshua Atwater (d. 1676) and his wife, Mary (Blakeman) Atwater (ca. 1637–1708/09), deeded Dummer a dwelling house and land on High Street near the courthouse just before his marriage to their daughter

Anna (1652–1715).[18] Dummer resided there for the rest of his life. Dummer's wife was born in New Haven, Connecticut, where her father settled in 1638 before moving to Boston in 1659. Dummer became a member of the Old South Church in 1675, but in 1679 he switched to the First Church.[19]

Dummer maintained a close, lifelong relationship with his first apprentice, John Coney. Following Joshua Atwater's death in 1676, Mary, his widow, married Rev. John Higginson and became the stepmother of Thomas Higginson (q.v.). When Anna's sister Mary became the second wife of John Coney in 1694, Dummer and Coney became brothers-in-law. They were joint executors of their mother-in-law Mary Higginson's estate in 1708/09, and both were accused in 1713 by Col. John Higginson of not accounting for "Sundry Sums of Money . . . comitted to . . . [their] Trust and Custody." Dummer insisted that all items from the estate had been accounted for except for one sheet used to wrap the deceased to prepare her for burial.[20] Dummer and Coney also signed the bond for the administration of Mary Clarke's estate in 1691.[21]

Documentary evidence amplifies Dummer's wide-ranging silversmithing career. In Suffolk County Court on 25 January 1675 Dummer, with Robert Sanderson, Sr., provided expert testimony on the value of a French crown as compared to New England money.[22] In 1684/85 the estate of Capt. George Corwin of Salem owed Dummer £30.2.6 for thirty mourning rings.[23] Dummer was also paid £6.4 for rings by the estate of the Boston mariner John Blowers in 1706/07 and £11.9 for rings in 1707 by the estate of Elizabeth Rouse, daughter of the silversmith William Rouse (q.v.) and sister of Michael Rouse (q.v.).[24] Samuel Sewall was also a patron. In August 1707 Sewall paid Dummer £3.14.8 for five silver spoons weighing eight ounces and eight pennyweight.[25] In a running list of expenses for 1710 Sewall noted,

[May] 13 To C^z Jer. Dumer in full for self 4-10-0

For Sam's Porringers 21^s. Whistle 3^s. 1- 4-0[26]   5- 14—

Sewall also made payments to Dummer for unspecified services in 1695 and 1701. In 1705 he paid Dummer for "half the prize of ye Bell given to the Parish of Byfield." In 1708/09 he sold Dummer 28 ½ ounces of silver plate, including "4 spoons, 3 Dram-Cups, 1 Copper's Taster, 1 Bason, 1 Spanish Fruit-dish," on behalf of Elizabeth Wallie.[27]

Also among Dummer's patrons was Capt. James Grant, who advertised in the *Boston News-Letter* of 20 April 1713 that silver had been stolen out of his house, including "One Silver Cup containing a Wine Pint, made by *Mr. Dummer* mark'd at the bottom I^{G}F ex dono II." Other documents reveal that Dummer sometimes had difficulties getting paid, as the following account in the estate papers of Francis Wainwright shows:

Col: Fra. Wainwright is D^r left to pay of his Ladys
funerall Rings, march:18th. 1709/10. given him ye Note of
thirteen shillings six pence, & he promised payment but
never did, or came to Boston after, but throw a mistake
in casting was 12^d more, which is now Justly due to
to me 14^s.6^d. this day.   00-14-6
June:11th. 1712.   Jer:Dummer,
Boston, June, 11. 1712. Then Rec^d the Contents
above mentioned p^r mee   Jer. Dummer.
of m^r. John Whiple of Ipwich.[28]

Like many silversmiths, Dummer probably often had quantities of precious metal on hand to use either for fabricating objects or as specie for mercantile ventures. Jonathan Corwin (1640–1718) wrote in his account book in 1686 that Dummer was debtor to him for gold valued at £35.14.[29] The estate papers of Thomas Downes, a mariner, dated 1709, show that he had left "4 Baggs NE money 115 oz 5 dw.[t] @ 5[d]/10s £461.15" in the hands of Jeremiah Dummer.[30] And in his will the Boston merchant Daniel Westfield designated that his bequest to Thomas Pemberton, a minor, be "put into the hands" of Dummer "to be put out at interest." Dummer also engaged in merchant ventures owning shares in at least eleven different ships.[31]

Dummer may have also been responsible for engraving the plates used to print the Massachusetts currency of 10 December 1690, the first authorized paper currency in the Western world, and the subsequent issue of 3 February 1690/91. By order of the General Court on 2 July 1692, all bills were to be endorsed on the back by Jeremiah Dummer or Francis Burroughs. These bills were reissued from time to time until a new issue was introduced in 1702 produced with plates engraved by John Coney. Dummer was also responsible for the engraving and printing of the New Hampshire bills of credit of 1709. In the same year he engraved plates for the colony of Connecticut and in 1711/12 received payment from the Connecticut Council for printing 6,550 sheets of bills.[32]

Dummer twice appraised tools in the estates of his fellow craftsmen. In 1667, with Samuel Paddy, he appraised the estate of Joseph Sanderson (q.v.), and in 1709, with Edward Webb (q.v.), he appraised the tools of Richard Conyers (q.v.).[33]

Dummer served in many civic capacities during his life. He became a member of the Ancient and Honorable Artillery Company in 1671; was a member of the jury for trials in 1674; served as a Boston constable in 1675–76 and as a tithingman in 1680 and 1684; took the oath of allegiance in 1679; and was made a freeman in 1680.[34] He was one of the Council of Safety in 1689; "prizer" of wheat in 1690; Boston selectman in 1690–92; commissioner in 1691; justice of the peace from 1693 to 1718; town auditor and treasurer of the county in 1701; and an overseer of the poor in 1701/02.[35] The payment of £10.6.8 that Dummer received from Suffolk County on 7 October 1698 probably concerned his civic activities.[36]

As a consequence of holding these important offices and of his declining health during the first decade of the eighteenth century, Dummer probably spent less time at the bench. Writing a letter of condolence to John Higginson, Jr., upon the death of his mother in 1708/09, Coney says, "I am afraid Bro[th] Dumer can not come to y[e] funerall, he is so weak & [torn] he can scarce go about, & such a numness [torn] hands y[t] he could not wright."[37] Because his shop still was providing gold and silver wares to customers at that time, Dummer probably employed journeymen to keep his enterprise going.

The *Boston News-Letter* of 2 June 1718 published a death notice that stated Dummer had died on 25 May "after a long retirement, under great infirmaties of age and sickness." Dummer's will, written on 17 March 1715/16, was proved on 18 June 1718.[38] In it are mentioned his son William, who became lieutenant governor of Massachusetts in 1716 and who, at his death in 1761, bequeathed his dwelling house, farm, and all his real estate in Newbury for a grammar school, now known as Dummer Academy; his son Jeremiah, who settled in London, became agent for the colonies of Massachusetts and Connecticut, and who was responsible for soliciting the benefactions from Elihu Yale for the Collegiate School, which became Yale College; his son Samuel, who was sheriff of Middlesex County from 1719 to 1731; and his daughter Anna, who married John Powell, a merchant from Wales.

A significant body of work survives bearing either of the two marks (A, B) that Dummer used. A caudle cup bearing his mark over those of John Hull and Robert Sanderson, Sr., and a porringer made and marked by Dummer bearing the mark of the jeweler René Grignon (q.v.) suggest that early in the history of silversmithing in Massachusetts goldsmiths both marked work by others that they retailed and produced work for others to retail. Dummer made communion silver for churches throughout New England and made tutorial plate for the Harvard tutor William Brattle. Prominent merchant families numbered among his patrons, for example, the Lidgetts for whom he made an impressive pair of candlesticks. In their monograph Clarke and Foote discussed portraits with Dummer's signature that came to light in 1921 and raised the possibility that Dummer's talents included portrait painting. More recent scholarship has concluded that the signatures are fraudulent.[39]   PEK

SURVIVING OBJECTS

	Mark	Inscription	Patron	Date	Reference	Owner
Basin	A	none	Gurdon Saltonstall	ca. 1700	YUAG files	
Basin	A*	Brattle arms, a chevron engrailed between 3 battle-axes erect; Ex dono Pupillorum 1695 (+)	William Brattle and/or the Harvard College class of 1695	1695	Clarke/Foote 1935, no. 1	
Beaker	A*	Ex dono James Babcock/to the Church in Wrentham/1699	James Babcock and/or Congregational Church, Wrentham, Mass.	ca. 1699	Clarke/Foote 1935, no. 7	
Beaker	A*	The Gift of Henery Yats:/to the Church of Guilford:	First Congregational Church, Guilford, Conn., for Henry Yates	ca. 1711	Clarke/Foote 1935, no. 4	
Beaker	A*	The Gift: of H: Yats: to the/Church: of: Guilford/1711	First Congregational Church, Guilford, Conn., for Henry Yates	1711	Clarke/Foote 1935, no. 3	
Beaker	A*	Ex Dono. Capt: Simon Stacy/to the Church of Ipswich/1697	Simon Stacy and/or First Congregational Church, Ipswich, Mass.	1697	Buhler/Hood 1970, no. 14	YUAG
Beaker	A*	D/AI; The: gift: of: The: Rev^{d}.: Theophelus: Cotten . . . (later)	Andrew and I. Diamond	ca. 1700	Clarke/Foote 1935, no. 8	
Two beakers	A*	Church of Dedham	First Church, Dedham, Mass.	ca. 1705	Buhler 1956, no. 54	
Beaker	A*	the: gifft/of/·E·B·	Edward Brattle (?) and/or Brattle Street Church, Boston	ca. 1700	Buhler 1972, no. 24	MFAB
Two beakers	A	Ex. dono. I.$^{a}_{c}$ Plaisted/1702	Ichabod Plaisted and/or First Congregational Church, South Berwick, Maine	1702	Clarke/Foote 1935, no. 15	

	Mark	Inscription	Patron	Date	Reference	Owner
Four beakers	A*	The Church of Pourtm.ª/1705	North Church (First Church of Christ, Congregational), Portsmouth, N.H.	1705	Clarke/Foote 1935, no. 14	
Two beakers	A	MHC	First Congregational Church, Marblehead, Mass.	ca. 1705	Clarke/Foote 1935, no. 12	
Two beakers	A	MC	First Congregational Church, Marblehead, Mass.	ca. 1705	Clarke/Foote 1935, no. 13	
Beaker	A*	MC	First Congregational Church, Marblehead, Mass.	ca. 1700	Clarke/Foote 1935, no. 5	
Two candlesticks	A*	Lidgett arms, a fess wavy or between 3 estoiles; Clarke, Usher, and Jeffries arms (later)	Peter Lidgett (?)	ca. 1685	Buhler/Hood 1970, no. 9	YUAG
Caudle cup	A*	E/IM		ca. 1690	Buhler/Hood 1970, no. 8	YUAG
Caudle cup	A	E/WM		ca. 1690	Clarke/Foote 1935, no. 36	
Caudle cup	A*	W/IS (+)		ca. 1675	Clarke/Foote 1935, no. 22	
Caudle cup (with marks of John Hull and Robert Sanderson, Sr.)	A*	FC	First Church of Christ, Farmington, Conn.	ca. 1670	Clarke/Foote 1935, no. 19	
Caudle cup	A*	FC	First Church of Christ, Farmington, Conn.	ca. 1690	Clarke/Foote 1935, no. 20	
Caudle cup	A*	FC	First Church of Christ, Farmington, Conn.	ca. 1690	Clarke/Foote 1935, no. 21	
Caudle cup	A	Ab.ʳ/&/Han/ Broadley	Abraham and Hannah (Thompson) Bradley	ca. 1685	Clarke/Foote 1935, no. 25	
Caudle cup	A	The Gift of M.ʳ Jn.º Hodson/to N-Hav Chh/1690	First Church of Christ, New Haven, Conn., for John Hudson	1690	Clarke/Foote 1935, no. 26	
Caudle cup	A*	F/IL; CC (later)	John and Lydia (Fletcher) Fiske	ca. 1690	Clarke/Foote 1935, no. 17	
Caudle cup	A*	MH	Mary (Hollingsworth) English	ca. 1675	Clarke/Foote 1935, no. 35	HFM
Caudle cup	A*	H/RM (over earlier initials?)		ca. 1685	Buhler 1972, no. 10	MFAB
Caudle cup	A*	Ex dono Deacon Thomas Metcalfe to the Church of Dedham	Church of Dedham, Dedham, Mass.	ca. 1690	Buhler 1956, no. 52	
Caudle cup	A*	Lambert Chinnory Ex dono to the Church of Dedham	Church of Dedham, Dedham, Mass.	ca. 1690	Buhler 1956, no. 53	
Caudle cup	A*	W/IE (+)	Joseph and Elizabeth (Watson) Williams	ca. 1685		OCHS
Caudle cup	A*	for the Church/MT (+)	Margaret (Webb) (Sheaffe) Thacher	ca. 1685	Clarke/Foote 1935, no. 28	

	Mark	Inscription	Patron	Date	Reference	Owner
Caudle cup	A*	Justin Patten. her/ gift. 84 (+)	First Church, Dorchester, Mass., for Justin Patten	1684	Clarke/Foote 1935, no. 27	
Caudle cup	A	T/PM (+)	Peter and Mary (Cotton) Tufts	ca. 1690	Clarke/Foote 1935, no. 29	
Caudle cup	A*	G/IA	Joseph and Ann (Waldron) Gerrish (?)	ca. 1700	Flynt/Fales 1968, 83–84	HD
Two caudle cups	A	The gift of H & E Glouer/to y̆ Chh in N. Hav:	Henry and Ellen Glover and/or First Church of Christ, New Haven, Conn.	ca. 1700	Clarke/Foote 1935, nos. 23–24	
Caudle cup	A*	O/TD		ca. 1695	Buhler 1972, no. 15	MFAB
Caudle cup	A*	MI/to/HFA (later)		ca. 1690	Clarke/Foote 1935, no. 32	AIC
Caudle cup	A*	H/WS (erased)	William and Sarah (Crisp) Harris	ca. 1695	*Silver Supplement* 1973, no. 29	
Caudle cup	A*	G/BS		ca. 1695	Buhler 1972, no. 11	MFAB
Caudle cup	A*	S/NM		ca. 1690	Skinner, 31 October 1992, lot 248	
Caudle cup	A*	Benjamin Coffin to RG	Benjamin Coffin	ca. 1692	Quimby 1995, no. 46	WM
Caudle cup	A*/ B*	Brown(e) arms, a two-headed eagle displayed, and crest, a demi two-headed eagle couped	Brown(e) family	ca. 1690	Puig et al. 1989, no. 172	MIA
Caudle cup	A*; B†	The gift of MC; B/ IH	Mary (Clapp) Bird (?)	ca. 1690	Quimby 1995, no. 47	WM
Caudle cup	?	?		?		BBC
Cup	A	DANIEL HUSEY GAVE THOMAS HOWES 1710	Daniel Husey for Thomas Howes	1710	*Antiques* 89 (January 1966): 15	
Cup	A†	F/IE	John and Elizabeth Forland	ca. 1705	Clarke/Foote 1935, no. 53	
Cup	A*	B/WM; H/IS (later)	William and Mary (Gardner) Bowditch	ca. 1690	Buhler 1956, no. 50	
Dram cup	A	C/EE	Ezekiel and Ellen (Lothrop) Cheever	ca. 1675	Buhler 1965, 11–17	HMA
Dram cup	A*	IL		ca. 1680	Buhler 1972, no. 9	MFAB
Dram cup	A*	SB (+)	Silence Baker (?)	ca. 1700	Buhler/Hood 1970, no. 15	YUAG
Dram cup	B*	S/RS	Robert and Sarah Stone (?)	ca. 1680	Clarke/Foote 1935, no. 37	MMA
Mourning ring (gold)	B*	Iames Lloyd. Obyt. 21. Aug^t.. 1693	James Lloyd	1693	Quimby 1995, no. 50	WM

	Mark	Inscription	Patron	Date	Reference	Owner
Mug	A*	Clarke crest; C/IS (+)	John and Sarah (Shrimpton) Clarke	ca. 1710	*Silver Supplement* 1973, no. 30	
Patch box	B*	AW		ca. 1705	*Moore Collection* 1980, no. 90	
Plate	A*	C/IS	John and Sarah (Shrimpton) Clarke (?)	ca. 1691	Buhler 1972, no. 19	MFAB
Porringer	A*	C/EE	Ezekiel and Ellen (Lothrop) Cheever (?)	ca. 1690	Clarke/Foote 1935, no. 58	AG
Porringer	A*	NG (+)	Abigail ("Nabby") Gardner	ca. 1685	Buhler 1972, no. 8	MFAB
Porringer	A	P/EA		ca. 1690	Buhler 1979, no. 1	WAM
Porringer	A	MS		ca. 1690	Buhler 1956, no. 55	MFAB
Porringer (with mark of René Grignon)	A*	R/IE	James and Elizabeth (Andrews) Rayner (?)	ca. 1695	Buhler/Hood 1970, no. 20	YUAG
Porringer	A	WB; A Pupil 1695 (+)	William Brattle (?) and/or a Harvard College student, class of 1695	1695	Clarke/Foote 1935, no. 55	
Porringer	A	S/TR (+)	Thomas and Rebecca (Glover) Smith	ca. 1700	Clarke/Foote 1935, no. 57	
Porringer	A*	B/BP (erased) (+)		ca. 1700	Buhler/Hood 1970, no. 16	YUAG
Porringer	A*	MD	Dudley family	ca. 1700	*Antiques* 72 (September 1957): 258	AIHA
Porringer	A*	S/EP	Erasmus and Persis (Bridge) Stevens (?)	ca. 1710	Buhler 1972, no. 18	MFAB
Porringer	A*	V/NM/1641 (later?)	Nathaniel and Mary (Belcher) Vose (?)	ca. 1700	Flynt/Fales 1968, 74–75	HD
Porringer	A	D/SI		ca. 1700	Warren 1975, no. 290	BBC
Porringer	A*	AP (later)		ca. 1700	Buhler 1972, no. 17	MFAB
Porringer	A*	W/IM		ca. 1700	Clarke/Foote 1935, no. 62	AG
Porringer (attrib.)	none	SB	Sarah (Bowditch) Hathorne	ca. 1700	Buhler/Hood 1970, no. 19	YUAG
Porringer	?	Ex dono Pupillorum 1695	William Brattle and/or the Harvard College class of 1695	1695	Buhler 1955, 53	
Porringer	?	P/MM (?)		ca. 1700	*Antiques* 81 (January 1962): 60	
Salt	A*	R^{ebe} . . . ; RR; R;ussell	Rebecca Russell (?)	ca. 1700	Buhler 1972, no. 20	MFAB
Salver	A	C/NE (+)	Nathaniel and Elizabeth Cary	ca. 1690	Clarke/Foote 1935, no. 54	

	Mark	Inscription	Patron	Date	Reference	Owner
Salver	A	B/WM (+)	William and Mary (Gardner) Bowditch	ca. 1700	Buhler 1972, no. 21	MFAB
Spout cup	A*	C/SE (+)	Stephen and Elizabeth (Randall) Codman	ca. 1680	Buhler 1972, no. 12	MFAB
Spout cup	A*	H/DE (later)		ca. 1680	Buhler 1972, no. 16	MFAB
Tablespoon	A	L (?)		ca. 1695	Clarke/Foote 1935, no. 75	
Tablespoon	A	M/SN	Mott family	ca. 1695		CHS
Tablespoon	A	P/I(?)S (+)		ca. 1705	*Antiques* 51 (January 1947): 49	New York Society Library
Tablespoon	A*	F/TI		ca. 1695		HD
Tablespoon	A*	A/AA (+)	Abraham and Abigail Adams	ca. 1690	Fairbanks/ Trent 1982, no. 289	MFAB
Tablespoon	A	RB/RS/1685 (+)		1685	Buhler 1972, no. 13	MFAB
Tablespoon	A*	RB/RS/1685		1685	Minor 1946, 238	
Tablespoon	A*	MV	Mary Vergoose	ca. 1675	Buhler/Hood 1970, no. 7	YUAG
Tablespoon	A*	IH		ca. 1675	Buhler 1972, no. 7	MFAB
Tablespoon	A	B/HI/1682		1682	Clarke/Foote 1935, no. 72	
Tablespoon	A*	unidentified crest, a sword in a stone; IB (+)		1696	Johnston 1994, 45	CMA
Tablespoon	A	IB; B/ID . . .		1696	*Silver Supplement* 1973, no. 31	
Tablespoon	A*	R/NM	Rev. Noadiah and Mary (Hamlin) Russell	ca. 1685	Buhler/Hood 1970, no. 12	YUAG
Tablespoon	A*	R/NM	Rev. Noadiah and Mary (Hamlin) Russell	ca. 1685	Buhler/Hood 1970, 21	WA
Tablespoon	A	AH	Abigail Hancock	ca. 1695	Clarke/Foote 1935, no. 66	
Tablespoon	A	FP		ca. 1695	Clarke/Foote 1935, no. 67	
Tablespoon	A*	T/TS		ca. 1685	Buhler/Hood 1970, no. 13	YUAG
Tablespoon	A	SC		ca. 1695	Clarke/Foote 1935, no. 71	BBC
Tablespoon	A	MA	Appleton family	ca. 1695	YUAG files	
Tablespoon	A*	EB	Eleazer Bellows	ca. 1695	Quimby 1995, no. 48	WM
Tablespoon	A*	C/IM		ca. 1695	Quimby 1995, no. 49	WM
Tablespoon	A	MH/MP		ca. 1705	Buhler/Hood 1970, no. 17	YUAG

	Mark	Inscription	Patron	Date	Reference	Owner
Tablespoon	A*	C/TI		ca. 1695	DAPC 68.2629	HMA
Tablespoon	A*	C/II		ca. 1695	Safford 1983, 18	MMA
Tablespoon	A*	MW		ca. 1700	Buhler 1972, no. 25	MFAB
Tablespoon	A	I/LM		ca. 1700	Skinner, 16 June 1990, lot 49	
Tablespoon	A*	A/IE/1709		1709	Kroening 1982, no. 4	
Tablespoon	A	C/IS		ca. 1710	Sotheby's, 23–24 June 1994, lot 101	
Tankard	A*	none		ca. 1685	Buhler 1972, no. 14	MFAB
Tankard	A*	RR/to/CC	First Parish Church, Charlestown, Mass., for Richard Russell	ca. 1676	Quimby 1995, no. 43	WM
Tankard	A*	CC	First Parish Church, Charlestown, Mass.	ca. 1670	Quimby 1995, no. 44	WM
Tankard	A*	C/NE (+)	Nathaniel and Elizabeth Cary	ca. 1680	Clarke/Foote 1935, no. 81	
Tankard	A*	unidentifiable initials		ca. 1680	YUAG files	
Tankard	A*	B/WH; B/WH	William and Hannah Browne (?)	ca. 1675	DAPC 68.3362	MMA
Tankard	A*	B/RI	Robert and Joanna (Mason) Breck	ca. 1685	Clarke/Foote 1935, no. 87	
Tankard	A	?		ca. 1700	Clarke/Foote 1935, no. 80	
Tankard	A	Foxcroft arms	William Foxcroft	ca. 1690	Fales 1970, 50–51	
Tankard	A*	C/IR		ca. 1700	Buhler 1972, no. 22	MFAB
Tankard	A*	MA/1692		1692	Clarke/Foote 1935, no. 83	Dummer Academy
Tankard	A	W/BS (+)	Benedict and Sarah Webber	ca. 1680	Clarke/Foote 1935, no. 82	
Tankard	A*	G/WE		ca. 1690	Clarke/Foote 1935, no. 84	HFM
Tankard	A*	Claypoole arms; P/WH	Claypoole family	ca. 1690	Clarke/Foote 1935, no. 86	
Tankard	A*	WS/ED (later)	John Gorham	ca. 1700	Buhler/Hood 1970, no. 11	YUAG
Tankard	A*	R/DS (+)	Daniel and Sarah (Appleton) Rogers	ca. 1700	Quimby 1995, no. 45	WM
Tankard	A*	R/CM (+)	Ridgway family	ca. 1700	Safford 1983, 31	MMA
Tankard	A*	P/FH		ca. 1700	Clarke/Foote 1935, no. 91	AG

	Mark	Inscription	Patron	Date	Reference	Owner
Tankard	A	Saltonstall arms, a bend between 2 eagles displayed, and crest, out of a ducal coronet a pelican vulning her breast; C/RE (+)	Rowland and Elizabeth (Saltonstall) Cotton	ca. 1705	Clarke/Foote 1935, no. 92	
Tankard	A*	I/RM		ca. 1690	YUAG files	
Tankard	A*	S/WS (+)	William and Susannah (Lothrop) Shurtleff	ca. 1705	Clarke/Foote 1935, no. 93	
Tankard	A*	Trowbridge arms, an arched and embattled wall	Trowbridge family	ca. 1710	Buhler/Hood 1970, no. 18	YUAG
Tankard	A	MC/to/TW . . .	Gregory Cook (?)	ca. 1700	Flynt/Fales 1968, 51–52	HD
Tankard	A*	RB/I (+)		ca. 1705	Gourley 1965, no. 66	
Tankard	A*	RR (+)	Rebecca Russell	ca. 1710	Buhler 1965, 11–15, 17–20	HMA
Tankard	A*	F/DS (+)		ca. 1700	*Antiques* 90 (July 1966): 80–81	
Tankard	A*	S/IE (+)	John and Experience (Folger) Swain	ca. 1700	Warren 1975, no. 284	BBC
Tankard	A	241/LE (later)		ca. 1700	*Antiques* 99 (April 1971): 460	
Tankard	A	B/IE		ca. 1705	Naeve/ Roberts 1986, no. 51	AIC
Tankard	A*/B	Davenport arms, a chevron gules between 3 crosses crosslet fitchée, and crest, a griffin's head erased; D/IM (+)	Rev. John and Martha (Gold) (Sellick) Davenport	ca. 1690	Clarke/Foote 1935, no. 88	
Two-handled bowl	A	P/RI; 1692 (+)	Richard and Jane Pateshall (?)	1692	Buhler/Hood 1970, no. 10	YUAG
Two-handled cup	A	Elizabeth Browne gave this/for the Churches use/1686 (+)	Elizabeth Browne and/ or South Church, Salem, Mass.	1686	Jones 1913, 436–37	
Two-handled cup	A	The gift of/Francis Skerry/to the Church/in Salem	First Congregational Society, Salem, Mass., for Francis Skerry	ca. 1684	Clarke/Foote 1935, no. 2	
Wine cup	A*	The gift of a friend W:D	Old South Church, Boston	ca. 1676	Clarke/Foote 1935, no. 49	
Wine cup	A	Ex dono/Mʳ. Joshua &/Mʳˢ Hanna/ Bangs To The Church of Eastham/1700	Joshua and Hannah Bangs and/or Church of Eastham, Mass.	1700	Buhler 1972, no. 23	MFAB

	Mark	Inscription	Patron	Date	Reference	Owner
Wine cup	A	Ex dono AD Se: Test.ᵐ IA	Anna (Atwater) Dummer for First Church, Boston	ca. 1700	Clarke/Foote 1935, no. 45	
Wine cup	A	EX DONO AD/Se: Testᵐ/Ex petito per IA	Anna (Atwater) Dummer for First Baptist Church, Boston	ca. 1700	Clarke/Foote 1935, no. 44	
Wine cup	A	ExDono AD/Sec Testᵐ IA	Anna (Atwater) Dummer for Congregational Church, Stratford, Conn.	ca. 1700	Clarke/Foote 1935, no. 46	
Wine cup	A	The Gift of James Everill/to the first Church in Boston/1705	First Church, Boston, for James Everill	1705	Clarke/Foote 1935, no. 48	
Wine cup	A*	Property of the OLD SOUTH CHURCH (later)	Old South Church, Boston	ca. 1705	Clarke/Foote 1935, no. 47	
Wine cup	A	The Gift of the Hon.ᵇˡᵉ/Wᵐ Stoughton Esqʳ . . .	William Stoughton and/or First Congregational Parish, Milton, Mass.	1701	Clarke/Foote 1935, no. 43	
Three wine cups	A	The Gift of Elder Joseph Bridgham/to the first Church in Boston/1708	First Church, Boston, for Joseph Bridgham	1708	Clarke/Foote 1935, nos. 39–41	
Two wine cups	A	Stoughton arms, on a saltire or between 4 door staples an escallop; Ex dono Honᵇˡˢ Guliel: Stoughton Armigʳⁱˢ Anno 1701 (+)	William Stoughton and/or First Church, Dorchester, Mass.	1701	Clarke/Foote 1935, no. 42	
Two wine cups	A*	Made from a large cup/Gift of Capt John Silliman/1752 (later)	Congregational Church, Fairfield, Conn.	ca. 1710	Clarke/Foote 1935, no. 50	
Wine cup	A	CC/1712	Congregational Church (formerly Chebacco Church), Essex, Mass.	1712	Clarke/Foote 1935, no. 51	

1. Clarke/Foote 1935; *Newbury VR* 1:153.
2. *Newbury VR* 2:586; Savage 1860–62, 2:79.
3. *Newbury VR* 1:152–53.
4. "Hull Diaries," 150.
5. *Suffolk Deeds* 6:225–26, 230–32, 235–37; 7:97; 10:4, 14–15, 18–19, 24–25; "Hull Diaries," 157.
6. SCCR, file 1043. Dummer actually testified that "the watch which Mr. Bendall gave about 15 gallons of madera wine for is now by the want of the first wheele and Ballance judged not worth 10s and further saith not . . . this addition that it is the same watch that he bought of Mr. Hull."
7. John Hull Ledger, vol. 1, fol. 31, NEHGS (Mss Cb.110, vol. 1); Samuel Sewall Journal 1685–89, n.p., Baker Library, HU.
8. Phillips witnessed a deed with Dummer in 1678, see *Suffolk Deeds* 11:104.
9. RC 1:117, the 1687 tax list shows Dummer was taxed 9 shillings 10 pence for two heads, twenty acres, one cow, and estates and trade forty; the 1688 tax list shows "Jerimyah Dumer & man," RC 1:142; neither the published tax list of 1691 nor the list of inhabitants in 1691

gives specifics, RC 1:154, 161; a list of males above sixteen years of age in 1698 contains Jeremiah Dummer and two servants, RC 10:88.

10. SCD 15:148.
11. Samuel Sewall Account Book, 1688–92, MHS.
12. SCD 19:33–34.
13. SCD 75:171.
14. RC 10:88.
15. Bigelow-Phillips files, 605.
16. SCD 23:151–52; 24:265; 75:171.
17. SCD 15:148.
18. *Suffolk Deeds* 9:58; 10:118–19; *Salem VR* 5:327; *New Haven VR* 1:2.
19. *Old South Church* 1883, 199; Pierce 1961, 77.
20. ECPR, dockets 13243, 13248.
21. SCPR, docket 1900.
22. SCCR, file 1430.11.
23. ECPR, docket 6944.
24. SCPR, dockets 3018, 3057.
25. Samuel Sewall Account Book and Ledger, fol. 196r, NEHGS.
26. Samuel Sewall Account Book and Ledger, fol. 194v, NEHGS.
27. Samuel Sewall Account Book and Ledger, fols. 200r, 198v, 196v, 102r, NEHGS.
28. ECPR, docket 28672.
29. Jonathan Corwin Account Book, n.p., AAS.
30. SCPR 17:35.
31. SCPR 13:502–03; Clarke/Foote 1935, 28.
32. Newman 1967, 51, 124–26, 157; Fales 1973a, 186.
33. SCPR, docket 440; new series 4:421.
34. RC 29:169; Roberts 1895, 1:217; Shurtleff 1853, 5:539; Seybolt 1939, 48, 59, 68; Colonial Society 1933, 29:457.
35. Seybolt 1939, 80, 81, 83–84, 101–02; Whitmore 1969, 31, 126; Clarke/Foote 1935, 31–35.
36. A photostat of the original document from Mass. Archives is in the Bigelow-Phillips files.
37. John Coney and Jeremiah Dummer letter, 11 March 1708/09, to John Higginson, Jr., AAS.
38. SCPR, docket 4055.
39. Clarke/Foote 1935, 101–27; Fairbanks 1985, 19–26.

Shubael Dummer
1686/87–1711 +

Shubael Dummer was the son of Capt. Richard (1649–89) and Elizabeth (Appleton) Dummer of Newbury, Massachusetts, and the nephew of Jeremiah Dummer (q.v.), with whom he probably trained. Elizabeth (Appleton) Dummer was the daughter of John Appleton (ca. 1612–82) and Priscilla Glover (ca. 1634–97/98).[1] Shubael's paternal grandparents were Richard (ca. 1599–1678) and Frances (Burr) Dummer (ca. 1612–82).[2] Shubael is mentioned in his father's will of 1689 and was to receive one hundred pounds from his brothers when he reached the age of twenty-one.[3]

Although Shubael is not listed in any records as a goldsmith or silversmith, he appears in Boston as witness to deeds of Jeremiah Dummer in 1704, 1707, and 1709, and he signed a receipt when he received payment for twelve rings made for the estate of Francis Wainwright in 1711:

The Estate of Francis Wainwright Esq.ʳ decᵈ　　　　Dʳ
To 12 Rings weighing 1 oz. & 2ᵈʷᵗ at £6 5/ ℔ oz　　　£6. 17.　6
　fashioning ditto at 2/6ᵈ.　　℔ ps　　　　　　　　 1. 10. —
　　　　　　　　　　　　　　　　　　　　　　　　£8.　7.　6
　　　　　　　　　　　　　　　　　　　　Shubael Dummer[4]

John Marshall Phillips recorded a snuffbox marked SD and engraved "Ann Drier" or "Dumer" with the date "July 12, 1711," which he believed may have been made by Shubael Dummer, but the whereabouts of this object are unknown.[5] There are no further records of Shubael in Boston. He may have returned to Newbury, where his father was a prominent landowner. BMW

1. *Newbury VR* 1:152, 153; 2:154, 586.
2. *Newbury VR* 2:586.
3. ECPR, docket 8360.
4. SCD 23:151–52; 24:265; 75:171; ECPR, docket 28673.
5. Bigelow-Phillips files, 636, 638.

Timothy Dwight
1654–91/92

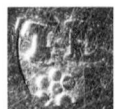

A

Timothy Dwight was born in Dedham, Massachusetts, on 26 November 1654, the son of Capt. Timothy Dwight (ca. 1631–1717/18) of Dedham and his second wife, Sarah Powell (1632–64), who were married in 1653.[1] His paternal grandparents were John (d. 1661) and Hannah Dwight (d. 1656).[2] His maternal grandparents were Michael (ca. 1606–72) and Abigail Powell (d. 1677).[3]

Dwight would have begun his apprenticeship about 1668, training in Boston with John Hull (q.v.), who worked in partnership with Robert Sanderson, Sr. (q.v.). Between 1672 and 1674 Dwight witnessed a number of deeds and a bill of sale for Hull, and although his apprenticeship was completed by 1675, his association with Hull continued.[4] On 5 May 1676 Dwight was appointed coronet of the Boston Horse Troop, and during King Philip's War Hull cites numerous instances in his account book of Dwight's being paid for military service.[5]

Dwight remained closely linked to the Hull and Sanderson shop and continued to live in Hull's household. Samuel Sewall, Hull's son-in-law, recorded in his diary an account of a fit Dwight suffered on 12 August 1676:

> just as prayer ended Tim. Dwight sank down in a Swoun, and for a good space was as if he perceived not what was done to him: after, kicked and sprawled, knocking his hands and feet upon the floor like a distracted man. Was carried pick-pack to bed by John Alcock, there his cloaths pulled off. In the night it seems he talked of ships, his master, father, and uncle Eliot. The Sabbath following Father went to him, spake to him to know what ailed him, asked if he would be prayed for, and for what he would desire his friends to pray. He answered, for more sight of sin, and God's healing grace. I asked him, being alone with him, whether his troubles were from some outward cause or spiritual. He answered, spiritual. I asked him why then he could not tell it [to] his master, as well as any other, since it is the honour of any man to see sin and be sorry for it. He gave no answer, as I remember. Asked him if he would goe to meeting. He said, 'twas in vain for him; his day was out. I asked, what day: he answered, of Grace. I told him 'twas sin for any one to conclude themselves Reprobate, that this was all one. He said he would speak more, but could not, &c. Notwithstanding all this semblance (and much more than is written) of compunction for Sin, 'tis to be feared that his trouble arose from a maid whom he passionately loved: for that when Mr. Dwight and his master had agreed to let him goe to her, he eftsoons grew well.[6]

The maid may have been Elizabeth Alcock, the woman Dwight would marry. A few months later Sewall recorded in his diary that on a March evening in 1676/77 "going into the kitchin, [i] fell into discourse with Tim about Mettals."[7] On 10 July 1677, Sewall entered in his ledger that Dwight owed ten pounds for money loaned him and six pounds for use of the shop, sums that Dwight repaid the next month.[8] Hull paid Dr. William Avery for attending Dwight in December 1677 and noted that Dwight contracted smallpox in October

1678.[9] Dwight may also have had a close relationship with Benjamin Sanderson (q.v.). Sanderson was one of the appraisers of Dwight's grandmother's estate in April 1677.[10] In 1686 Dwight appraised the estate of John Viall, probably the John Viall who had been Sanderson's father-in-law.[11] Dwight lived on his own from about 1680 on, but he continued to have business dealings with Sewall. Dwight paid Sewall five shillings on 8 August 1688 for use of a mill, probably the powder mill on the Neponset River.[12]

The date of Dwight's marriage to Elizabeth Alcock (1659–1710/11), daughter of John Alcock (1627–67), a physician, and Sarah Palsgrave (d. 1665) of Roxbury, Massachusetts, is not recorded, but he may have been married by 13 August 1681, when he bought land in the South End of Boston on the new highway to Roxbury.[13] In a deposition to the Court of Assistants in Boston, Dwight reported that on 21 August 1681 George Fairfax broke into his house and stole money and goods. These were enumerated in the account as follows:

To Spanish money	£16..00.. 00
To french money	02.. 10.. 00
To 2 duz of buttons 15^d p^{er} payr	01.. 10.. 00
To old English money	01.. 12.. 00
To new English money	00.. 19.. 00
To 6 gold rings at 10^s p^{er} ring	03..00.. 00
	25.. 11.. 00

In September the court granted Dwight's request to indenture Fairfax in some other plantation so that he could recover some of his losses.[14] The tax list for 1681 records Dwight as being a member of division number 8, Capt. John Hull's Company, and his name reappears on the lists for 1687, 1688, and 1691.[15] By 10 October 1683 he was made a lieutenant in the Boston Horse Troop and two years later was elected a tithingman in Boston.[16] In 1686 he sued Nicholas Moorey for debt, a case that went unresolved until after his death in 1691/92.[17]

Dwight made out his will on 9 December 1691, appointing his wife, Elizabeth, executor.[18] He died on 2 January 1691/92, presumably of the "sore and languishing sickness" mentioned in his will. Samuel Sewall recorded the events of Dwight's burial day, 4 January: "Cousin Dummer, Capt. Jn° Walley, Capt. Wing, Rowse, Tho. Savage Goldsmith, Robt Saunderson, Bearers. Mr. Joyliff and I went next the Relations; by the Dock-head Mr. Willard struck in: no Minister before; buried at the new burying place; somthing troublesom going, by reason of the great Snow fell yesterday. 38 years old."[19]

Dwight's inventory, taken on 27 January 1691/92 by William Rouse (q.v.), Thomas Savage, Sr. (q.v.), and Nicholas Cock, included "several goldsmith tooles of all sorts" valued at £20.10.[20]

Only two pieces of silver by Dwight have been identified, a tankard and a salver, and these are marked with an initials mark (A). A spurious example of his mark is known.[21] PEK

SURVIVING OBJECTS

	Mark	Inscription	Patron	Date	Reference	Owner
Salver	A†	T (+)		ca. 1690	Buhler 1972, no. 26	MFAB
Tankard	A*	C/WD E (later)		ca. 1690	Buhler 1956, no. 56	

1. *Dedham VR* 1:6, 9, 44, 127.
2. Savage 1860–62, 2:85–87.
3. SCPR, dockets 642, 886; Boston Deaths, 1630–1699.
4. *Suffolk Deeds* 8:2; 10:8–10, 21; 12:174–75. The bill of sale of 26 November 1672 is in the Hull Letter Book.
5. Shurtleff 1853, 5:87; John Hull Ledger, vol. 2, fols. 330–31, 345, 397, 401, 413, 458, NEHGS.
6. *Sewall Diary* 1:19.
7. *Sewall Diary* 1:38.
8. Samuel Sewall, Diary and Commonplace Book, 1675–1721, 22v, 23r, MHS.
9. John Hull Ledger, vol. 1, fols. 135–36, NEHGS. "Hull Diaries," 163.
10. SCPR 14:146–48, docket 886.
11. SCPR, docket 1566.
12. Samuel Sewall Account Book, 1688–92, MHS.
13. *Sibley's Harvard Graduates* 1:124–26; RC 6:122, 203, 205; Savage 1860–62, 1:21–22; SCD 15:184. After Dwight's death Elizabeth married Joseph Gallop (see *Sewall Diary* 2:654).
14. SCCR, Court of Assistants, file 2026.
15. RC 1:75, 104, 138, 151.
16. Shurtleff 1853, 5:418; RC 7:176.
17. Samuel Snow and Timothy Dwight letter to Nicholas Moorey, 26 March 1686; deposition of Thomas Mussey and John Sanders, 5 November 1687, James Otis, Sr., Papers, MHS.
18. SCPR 8:60.
19. *Sewall Diary* 1:286; Codman 1918, 87.
20. SCPR 8:228.
21. The mark is on a spoon (DAPC 86.2381).

Joshua Eames
1719–72

Joshua Eames (Emmes) was identified as a jeweler in his obituary in the *Boston Gazette* for 10 August 1772.[1] He was born in Boston on 17 November 1719 to Nathaniel (ca. 1690–1750) and Hannah (Grafton) Eames (1691–ca. 1758). His grandparents on his father's side were Henry (ca. 1649–1724/25) and Elizabeth Eames (ca. 1650–1715).[2] His mother, who was born in Salem, Massachusetts, was the daughter of the mariner Joshua Grafton (1660–99) and Hannah Gedney (b. 1667) of that town.[3] Eames was related through marriage to two Boston goldsmiths. His first wife, Martha Parkman (1724–46/47), whom he married on 9 August 1743, was the sister of John Parkman (q.v.); his second wife, Margaret Clark (1723–78), whom he married on 11 November 1747, was the sister of Joseph Clark, Jr. (q.v.).[4] Eames's sister Elizabeth was married to Parkman, further strengthening that bond. The Massachusetts tax list of 1771 includes Eames with only one poll.[5] No estate papers were filed for Eames; his remains are in the Copp's Hill Burying Ground, where the gravestone records his death on 6 August 1772.[6] No silver or jewelry by him is known. PEK

1. *Index of Obituaries, 1704–1800*, 2:336.
2. Savage 1860–62, 2:90; Whitmore 1878, 19, nos. 353–54.
3. *Salem VR* 1:352, 377; 2:438; ECPR, docket 11478.
4. RC 24:159, 166; RC 28:244; Whitmore 1878, 19, nos. 350, 352.
5. Pruitt 1978, 12–13.
6. Whitmore 1878, 19, no. 355.

Reuben Earle
1747–1825

Reuben Earle was born in Leicester, Massachusetts, on 8 May 1747, the son of William Earle, Jr. (1713–1805), and Mary Cuting (1717–1808), who were married in Leicester on 31 January 1740.[1] William Earle, Jr., a farmer, had inherited much of his land from his father, William, Sr. (1690–1769), who had moved to Leicester as a young man and purchased a large amount of land from the town's original proprietors. Reuben Earle's paternal grandmother was Anna Howard of Tiverton, Rhode Island.[2] His maternal grandparents were Hezekiah Cuting (b. 1688) of Sudbury, Massachusetts, and Mary Hagar (b. 1697) of Watertown, Massachusetts.[3] Reuben Earle married Mary Harrington (b. 1751) of Worcester, Massachusetts, on 3 January 1770 in Leicester.[4] Her parents were Josiah Harrington (1709–ca. 1786) and Dinah Flagg Harrington

(1709–after 1779).[5] They were born in Watertown, married there on 29 May 1730, and settled first in Waltham and then in Worcester in 1754.[6]

Where Reuben Earle acquired his skills is uncertain, but he could have obtained his metalworking experience from his father's first cousin, Thomas, a gunsmith who was ten years his senior.[7] By the time of the revolutionary war, Earle was recorded as being a private from Leicester and "reported [as] an armorer."[8] In a deed of 1783 Earle identified himself as an armorer, and in deeds from 1785 and 1786, he called himself a silversmith.[9] No silver by him is known.

Between 1778 and 1783 Earle purchased three lots of land in Brimfield and South Brimfield, towns near his birthplace in Leicester. In 1785 and 1786, Earle sold this property and left Massachusetts for Herkimer County, New York, probably having received one of the land grants that became available to veterans following the revolutionary war.[10] The census of 1790 provides the earliest record of Earle's move to Caunawaga, New York; in 1791 he purchased land there, identifying himself as a gunsmith. Between 1796 and 1824, Earle bought additional parcels in nearby German Flatts, which he later sold off in small lots; these later deeds do not record his trade. Earle continued to appear in the census as a resident of German Flatts, New York, from 1800 to 1820. He died there on 21 February 1825.[11] JJF

1. *Freetown VR*, 3; *Leicester VR*, 140, 253, 254; *Sudbury VR*, 36; for genealogy of the family of Reuben Earle, see Earle 1888, 38–39, 52–53, 84.
2. *Freetown VR*, 2; *Leicester VR*, 254; Earle 1888, 38–39, 52.
3. Bond 1860, 194, 264.
4. Bond 1860, 276; Weis 1958, 26, cites that Mary Harrington was baptized in Waltham on 15 September 1751. According to Leicester vital records, Mary Harrington was residing in Worcester at the time of her marriage; see *Leicester VR*, 147, 161.
5. *Watertown Records* 1894, vol. 2, "Births, Deaths, Marriages," 39, 46; WCPR, dockets 27303 and 27304. Dinah Flagg Harrington was alive at the time Josiah Harrington made his will in 1779, but her name does not appear when his estate was probated in 1787.
6. *Watertown Records* 1894, vol. 2, "Births, Deaths, Marriages," 86; Weis 1958, 25.
7. Earle 1888, 52–53, 57, 59.
8. *Mass. Soldiers and Sailors* 5:150.
9. HCD 25:223; 28:203–05. Two earlier deeds are known to have been transacted by Earle in Brimfield: HCD 15:679, in which he is called a yeoman, and HCD 27:580, in which no occupation is given.
10. Earle 1888, 84.
11. Herkimer, New York, County Deeds: 1:561–62; 3:524–25; 5:489–90, 486–87; 8:142–43; 12:5–7; 13:187; 15:304–06; 16:479–80; 30:32–33. New York census of 1790, Caunawaga, Montgomery County; New York census of 1800, 1810, and 1820 in German Flatts, Herkimer County, New York; Herkimer County, New York, Probate Records, 28 February 1825, Book B of Wills, 189, File Folder 02242.

Thomas Earthy
ca. 1680–96 +

Thomas Earthy was the son of John Earthy, who was accepted into the town of Boston in 1686 after John Wilson, a merchant, posted bond for him.[1] The following year John and Mary Earthy appear in the birth records as parents of a daughter, Abigail, born on 23 December.[2] Thomas was apprenticed to the goldsmith and jeweler René Grignon (q.v.), who became his guardian when John Earthy died in 1696. The letter of guardianship reads as follows: "Know all men by these presents That I Thomas Earthy Son of John Earthy late of Boston in the County of Suffolke in New England Mariner dece.[d] (being a Minor of about Sixteen yeares of age) Have nominated and appointed And Do hereby make choice of nominate depute and appoint my Hono^ed Master Rene Grignon of Boston aforesaid Goldsmith to be my Guardian."[3] This is the last record of Earthy in Boston. Grignon had belonged to a group of Huguenots who attempted to settle the town of Oxford, Massachusetts, beginning in 1685 but were forced back to Boston in 1696 because of raids on the settlement by the local Indians.[4] John Earthy's appearance in Boston in the late 1680s suggests that he may have been a Huguenot fleeing France following the revocation of the Edict of Nantes in 1685, but there is no indication that he was involved in the Oxford venture. BMW

1. John Earthy [Earthie] bond posted by John Wilson, 25 October 1686, Boston. Strangers Records, MHS.
2. RC 9:173.
3. SCPR 11:176–77; dated 22 June 1696.
4. Daniels 1892, 23–24; Freeland 1894, 160–61.

Thomas Eastwick
w. ca. 1738–55

Thomas Eastwick's birth is not recorded in the Boston records, but he was possibly the son of John Eastwick and Grizzel Lloyd (ca. 1678–1723), who were married in Boston on 9 September 1703 and then moved to Jamaica before returning to Boston about 1716.[1] His maternal grandparents would have been James Lloyd (ca. 1650–93) and Griselda (or Grizzel) Sylvester (d. by 1691).[2]

Thomas Eastwick was working in Boston by 1738, when he was identified as a jeweler in a suit with John McKenzie, a perukemaker, in the Suffolk Court of Common Pleas.[3] The identity of his master is unknown. On 31 January 1742 Eastwick was among the creditors of the estate of Samuel Weeks and was owed £5.4.4, which suggests that he continued to work as a craftsman.[4] In December of that year, along with Nathaniel Morse (q.v.) and Samuel Haley (q.v.), he appraised the estate of the Boston goldsmith Jonathan Reed (q.v.).[5] Eastwick's life was plagued by financial difficulties. In 1744 Eastwick was sued by the tinplate worker Aaron Boardman for failing to pay Boardman for board and lodging from August 1741 to June 1744.[6] In March 1745/46 the merchant John Smith sued Eastwick for failure to pay rent of £5 lawful money annually for a shop from November 1742 to February 1745/46.[7]

On 17 November 1748 Eastwick married Mary Hall.[8] The marriage took place in Boston. Eastwick was a defendant once again in the Suffolk Court of Common Pleas in 1754/55, when he was sued by John Grainger, a wigmaker.[9] This is the last reference to him found in the Boston records. No silver or jewelry by him is known. PEK

1. RC 28:9; Wright 1966, 18.
2. NEHGR 49:504; SCPR, docket 2071.
3. SCCR, Court of Common Pleas Record Book 1737–38, 223.
4. SCPR 36:395–97.
5. SCPR 36:191, 240.
6. SCCR, Court of Common Pleas, file 58653.
7. SCCR, Court of Common Pleas Record Book 1744–46, 288; file 62857, vol. 392, Judicial Archives, Mass. Archives.
8. RC 28:244.
9. SCCR, Court of Common Pleas Record Book 1753–54, 174.

Benjamin Edwards, Jr.
1731/32–1803

Benjamin Edwards, Jr., was born on 22 February 1731/32 and was baptized on 28 February in Boston's New Brick Church.[1] He was the son of Benjamin Edwards (d. 1751), a merchant, and Bathsheba Evans (1701–d. before 1740), who married in Boston on 14 March 1730.[2] The maternal grandparents of Benjamin Edwards, Jr., were Jonathan (b. 1663) and Mary Evans.[3] Edwards's father married a second time, on 7 May 1740, to Elizabeth White (1698–1753), widow of the merchant Samuel White (d. 1733) and daughter of Samuel Greenwood (d. 1721) and Elizabeth (d. by 1738).[4] Edwards's stepmother's daughter, Elizabeth, married Samuel Burt (q.v.) in 1747.

Benjamin Edwards would have begun his apprenticeship about 1745 and would have completed it by 1752. He was probably apprenticed to Thomas Edwards (q.v.), probably a relative, although the relationship has not been established. Thomas Edwards lent Benjamin money in the years that would have immediately followed his training. Benjamin Edwards had moved to Woburn, Massachusetts, by 7 August 1753, when he, Nathaniel Greenwood, and Thomas Edwards were bound to William Hyslop, William Hall, William Moor, and Samuel Sloan, executors of the estate of Robert Duncan, in order to pay for a house costing £267 on Back Street, Boston, a dwelling that had belonged to Benjamin Edwards's father.[5] This document identifies Edwards as a shopkeeper of Woburn. In a mortgage of 1 April 1755 witnessed by Zachariah Brigden (q.v.), Edwards, identified as a goldsmith of Woburn, acknowledged indebtedness of £32.15.4 to his probable master, Thomas Edwards. He secured this debt by transferring to Edwards his portion of the Back Street property, in which as eldest son he had received a two-sevenths interest.[6]

Edwards was called a goldsmith and also a shopkeeper of Woburn when he sued Lot Brewster, a Woburn physician, a suit that continued in the courts from 1753 to 1758.[7] The suit probably involved the west half of a dwelling house and fourteen acres of land that the two jointly purchased in Woburn in February 1753.[8] Edwards arranged a mortgage for this real estate that was to be paid by February 1754.[9] Edwards sold additional acreage to Brewster, transactions that may have been mortgages.[10] In the 1750s Edwards arranged mortgages for some of this real estate and purchased other real estate in Woburn.[11]

By 1760, however, Edwards may have retired from business because deeds from 1760 to 1762 call him yeoman, "Esq[r].," and "Gentleman."[12] For the next decade or more he continued to buy and sell acreage and real estate in Woburn and surrounding towns.[13] The Massachusetts tax list of 1771 places him in Woburn as a "Captain" with a poll of one, one house, and nine pounds' annual worth of real estate.[14]

Edwards was living in Framingham, Massachusetts, by 1774 when a deed recording his purchase of ninety acres of land in Framingham identified him as a gentleman from there.[15] Edwards married Mary Bent (1743–1824), the daughter of Thomas Bent (1706–75), a yeoman, and Mary Stone (1717–75) of Sudbury, Massachusetts, in Framingham on 20 February 1777.[16] For the next ten years Edwards continued to trade actively in real estate.[17] Edwards's real estate trading involved him in a number of legal suits. In October 1783 Jonathan Amory, a Boston merchant, sued Edwards and some of his associates for failure to pay a promissory note. The court upheld the defendants, but the plaintiff appealed.[18] In January 1790 Rufus Greene Amory sued Edwards for nonpayment of six pounds and Edwards defaulted.[19] In March 1790 Edwards signed a mortgage with Jonathan Amory that was paid off by 1797.[20] In January

1798 Edwards was sued for debt by Winthrop Smith of Newmarket, New Hampshire, but the court found for Edwards.[21]

Edwards died in March 1803 at the age of seventy-one.[22] Edwards had numerous debts at the time of his death, and his estate was declared insolvent.[23] No silver bearing his mark is known to survive. Early in his career he probably was a retailer of silversmiths' work rather than a practitioner of the craft, especially since he was referred to alternately as a goldsmith and shopkeeper. Later in life he shifted his focus to real estate. PEK

1. RC 24:197.
2. SCPR 45:374; 48:316; RC 24:7; RC 28:154.
3. RC 9:88.
4. RC 9:240; RC 28:214; SCPR 48:86–88; 22:211–14; SCD 76:248–49.
5. SCD 83:96–97.
6. SCD 86:256; SCPR 48:316.
7. Superior Court of Judicature Record Book 1753–54, 136, 298; MCCR, Inferior Court of Common Pleas Record Book May 1754–December 1758, 273, Judicial Archives, Mass. Archives.
8. MCD 52:16, 56.
9. MCD 52:23.
10. MCD 52:25, 27.
11. MCD 51:166; 52:26, 57; 53:352; 54:641, 644, 645; 55:108; 56:205, 342, 347.
12. SCD 106:34; WCD 52:181; 76:124–25; MCD 57:407; 58:68; 60:359.
13. MCD 63:167, 596; 66:257, 302, 594; 69:175, 292; 70:47, 53, 334, 438; 73:291, 489, 529; 75:145, 152.
14. Pruitt 1978, 300–03.
15. MCD 67:520.
16. *Sudbury VR*, 17, 18, 138, 169, 273; *Framingham VR*, 427; *Wayland VR*, 130; MCD 42:221.
17. SCD 129:25; MCD 75:146; 76:387, 582; 77:2–3; 78:208; 80:138, 473; 83:387, 442; 85:190; 87:273; 89:324–25; 91:381–83; 92:366.
18. SCCR, Court of Common Pleas Record Book 1783, 108.
19. SCCR, Court of Common Pleas Record Book 1789, 268.
20. SCD 79:102.
21. SCCR, Court of Common Pleas Record Book 1797, 261.
22. *Framingham VR*, 427.
23. MCPR, docket 6884.

John Edwards
ca. 1671–1746

A

B

John Edwards's place of birth is unknown.[1] He probably arrived in Charlestown, Massachusetts, sometime between 1679 and 1685. His family included his father, John (d. 1690/91), a ship's surgeon from Lymehouse, Stepney, Middlesex, who may have traveled to Massachusetts several times before settling permanently in the colonies; his mother, Elizabeth (Walker?) Edwards (d. 1694); his two sisters, Elizabeth and Anne; and his widowed grandmother, Elizabeth (Palsgrave) Edwards (ca. 1627–1707).[2] Dr. John Edwards counted several influential Bostonians among his acquaintances and served as surgeon on the ship *America* in late 1689, caring for Samuel Sewall and his fellow passenger Thomas Brattle on their return trip from England. Sewall mentions Dr. Edwards in his diary for the last time on 27 January 1689/90; Edwards's estate was probated in Charlestown on 13 February 1690/91.[3] His widow, Elizabeth Edwards, died in Charlestown in 1694, and administration of her estate was granted to her brother, the pewterer Benjamin Walker.[4]

In 1694 the younger John Edwards married Sybil Newman (1670–1739),

C

D

daughter of the minister of the church in Wenham, Massachusetts, Antipas Newman (d. 1672) and his wife, Elizabeth Winthrop (b. 1636). Elizabeth (Winthrop) Newman was the daughter of John Winthrop, Jr. After Newman's death she married Zerubbabel Endicott, son of Gov. John Endicott.[5] John and Sybil Edwards had nine children: John (1695/96–1725), a bookseller and printer; Elizabeth (b. ca. 1697), who married Bartholomew Cheever in 1733; Antipas (1698–before 1744); Mary (b. 1700), who married Ebenezer Storer, a merchant from York, Maine, in 1723; Thomas (q.v.); Ann (b. 1703), who married William Baker, a tobacconist, in 1748; Samuel (q.v.); Joseph (b. 1707), a stationer, who married Sarah Belknap in 1734 and whose son, Joseph, became a silversmith (q.v.); and Richard (1712–before 1744).[6]

All available evidence suggests that Edwards was apprenticed to Jeremiah Dummer (q.v.) about 1685.[7] His uncle, Benjamin Walker, may have helped John to select his trade, and John was lucky that he secured a favorable apprenticeship before his father died in 1690/91. Edwards achieved his freedom about 1692 and probably worked as a journeyman for two or three years. He began practicing his trade in partnership with John Allen (q.v.). Allen married Edwards's sister Elizabeth in 1697, and Allen and Edwards may have served together as Dummer's apprentices. The partners first appear in the records in 1696, when they are mentioned as the tenants of a shop in a tenement near Boston's Town Dock. In October 1697, Allen and Edwards sued Jonathan Belcher (q.v.) for a debt of £2.9.10, for a hat, neckcloths, and handkerchiefs, suggesting that Belcher may have worked as a journeyman in their shop.[8] John Edwards and John Allen made a number of objects in the early baroque style, including one of the three known American standing salts. While working in partnership with Allen, Edwards used an initial mark, IE, in a quatrefoil (A). Although in October 1699 only John Edwards is mentioned as occupying the shop in Dock Square formerly mentioned as being occupied by both Edwards and Allen, the two men may have remained in partnership until at least 1702. They marked a wine cup made for the First Baptist Church in Boston with a legacy from Roger Kilcup, whose will was probated in 1702.[9]

Edwards's silver demonstrates that he had the ability to expand on design ideas he encountered, and that he attracted clients from throughout New England. Although his work was essentially conservative, Edwards made his mark as perhaps the most talented mold designer among goldsmiths working in Boston in the 1710s and 1720s. His silver demonstrates the greatest diversity of castings of any silversmith working in Boston during this time, and several designs are unique to him.[10] During the years when he worked alone, Edwards used four different marks: the IE in quatrefoil (A) that he began using while in partnership with Allen, IE in a notched quatrefoil (B), IE crowned over a device (probably meant to be a fleur-de-lis) (C), and IE in a rectangle (D). A spurious example of mark (B) is known.[11]

Several bills in John Edwards's elegant handwriting survive. These demonstrate that he made a wide variety of forms in silver, including candlesticks, and that his shop was equipped to provide heraldic engraving, small objects such as thimbles and rings, and objects set with stones. Surviving bills and accounts also demonstrate that, like most working silversmiths, much of his business involved mending or altering objects. He occasionally worked in gold, but the vast majority of his work was in silver. In 1711 Edwards billed Gov. Joseph Dudley:

1711
Aug.ᵗ 17ᵗʰ. To 2 Silv.ʳ Thimbles   £0 = 4 = 4
    22ᵈ.   To 2 Silv.ʳ Candlesticks wᵗ 18ᵒᶻ = 17ᵈʷᵗ   7 = 10 = 10
          To fashion & Wast   3 = 10 = 0
                                                               £11 = 5 = 2 [12]

And in 1712, he billed Dudley again:

1712
June 26ᵗʰ To a new Screw to a Silv.ʳ Chafingdish & ⎫
          mending yᵉ bottom   ⎬   £0 = 5 = 0
          To a pʳ Silv.ʳ Taggs 1/6 Setting a Stone in Silv.ʳ 2/   0 = 3 = 6
July 8ᵗʰ   To 6 Silv.ʳ Tea Spoones a Strainer & tongs   2 = 18 = 8
Aug.ᵗ 18ᵗʰ To 3 gold Rings   1 = 12 = 6
Octo.ʳ 9ᵗʰ To a pʳ Stone pendants   0 = 12 = 0
Dec.ʳ 10.ᵗʰ To yᵉ Exchange of a Silv.ʳ Spoone   0 = 10 = 6
1712/13   To altering yᵉ Chaines of 2 pʳ gold buttons   0 = 0 = 9
Jan.ʳy 5ᵗʰ To a Silv.ʳ Tea pott wᵗ 19ᵒᶻ: 13ᵈʷᵗ 1/2   12 = 2 = 3
                                                               £18 = 5 = 2

                              Contra   Cʳ

1712
Octoʳ 9ᵗʰ By gold Rec.ᵈ   £0 = 7 = 6
    23.ᵈ   To y money Rec.ᵈ   5 = 0 = 0
                                                               £5 = 7 = 6
          Errors Excepted   due to Ballance £12 = 17 = 8 [13]

John Edwards also made forty-eight gold rings for the funeral of Wait Winthrop in 1717, twenty-three gold rings for the funeral of Bridget Usher in 1723,
eighteen gold rings costing £29.6.2 for the funeral of Hannah Sewall in 1724,
rings for the funeral of Thomas Clarke in 1732, and rings for the funeral of
William Dudley in 1743.[14] Bridget Usher's estate also paid Edwards for silver
spoons, for silver buckles, and for three additional rings between 1716 and
1725.[15] Samuel Sewall patronized Edwards regularly. In 1724 he purchased a
silver porringer from Edwards for £7.16 and sent a tankard to him for mending.[16]

  In addition to these bills and accounts, a letter and bill regarding silver that
Edwards made for George Curwin of Salem provide us with an unusual insight
into the manner in which an individual silversmith conducted his business
and dealt with his clients. Curwin apparently saw some of Edwards's work in
the home of his friend Mrs. Gibbs and asked if she would inquire for him
about the cost of having a porringer made. Apparently Curwin wanted to find
out what Edwards's terms were. The reply that Edwards wrote to Curwin
shows that the silversmith must have kept meticulous business records.

                                     Boston February 25.ᵗʰ 1713/14

Mr. George Curwin

  Sʳ this comes in answer to yours to Mʳˢ Gibbs of
  yᵉ 22ᵈ Instant concerning yᵉ Silvʳ porringer I made for her which
  weighed 10ᵒᶻ: 7ᵈʷᵗ: at 8/ ℔ oz is   £ 4: 2: 9 ½
  yᵉ advance at 7 & ½ ℔ C wᵗ is   0: 6: 2 ³/₄
  yᵉ fashion at 13ᵈ ℔ oz is   0: 11 2
                                           £ 5: 0: 2 ¹/₄

if you send y^e weight in good Silv^r you will Save
y^e advance which is 6/ 2 ^{3}/$_4$, so that y^e porrenger
will stand but in £4:13:11 ^{1}/$_2$. [with (crossed out)] to take the
porrenger againe will be a damage to me there
being none of that plaine fashion now made
this with due Respects is what offers at present from

> Your humble Servt
> John Edwards[17]

From Edwards's letter it appears that Curwin wanted to know how much credit he would receive toward a new piece of silver if he sold Edwards an old porringer. Edwards was inclined to give Curwin only the value of the weight of the silver in the old porringer because it was out of fashion, and he doubted that he would be able to sell it as a wrought object. Although bills and accounts with Boston clients do not include this provision, this letter and Edwards's subsequent bill indicate that Edwards expected Curwin to pay him an advance equal to 7 ^{1}/$_2$ percent of the value of the silver needed for the object unless Curwin could provide him with the full weight in used or unwrought silver. This provision may have been a safeguard applied only to out-of-town customers, but it also suggests that by 1714 Edwards was paying 7 ^{1}/$_2$ or 8 percent interest to buy unwrought silver on credit.[18] A surviving bill demonstrates that Curwin regarded Edwards's terms as reasonable and that he bought several objects from the silversmith during the years 1715 and 1716:

1715
Octo^r. 20th. To a Silv^r pepper box w^t 3^{oz}:1^{dwt} £ 1 = 8 = 1
        To y^e fashion   0 = 10 = 0

1716
June 7th.   To a Silv^r whistle w^t 1^{oz} = 4^{dwt} 0 = 11 = 1
        To y^e fashion. 7/6 y^e Corrall 6/   0 = 13 = 6
        To a porrenger w^t– 4^{oz}. = 4^{dwt} 1 = 18 = 8
        To y^e fashion   0 = 8 = 0
July 19th.   To a Salvor. w^t 12^{oz} = 18^{dwt} 5 = 18 = 9
        To y^e fashion. 24/. Engraveing y^e Armes 8/   1 = 12 = 0
28th.   To a Spout Cup wth a Cover w^t 7^{oz} = 6^{dwt} 2 = 19 = 2
        To y^e fashion 20/. Engraveing y^e Crest 8^d 1 = 0 = 8
        £ 16 = 19 = 11

1715/16

Jany. 11th Ditto C^r By Silv^r Rec^d of Henry Gibbs   £ 1 = 15 = 8
        due to Ballance   £ 15 = 4 = 3
Errors Excepted
John Edwards

The Silv^r is chargd at 8/. ℔ oz & 15 ℔ Cent adv^{19}

In 1707 John Edwards inherited his grandmother Edwards's house and land in "Broad Street, at ye loer End of Anckorhoape Aley . . . in stepny parish" in England. He evidently sold this land because he did not mention it in his will.[20] The sale of such a piece of property could have provided Edwards with a means of obtaining credit in England. Edwards's land purchases in Boston show a steady rise in his means. In 1720, John Edwards bought land from his brother-in-law and former partner, John Allen, in the west end of Boston, bounded on the west, north, and east by Allen, for £100.[21] He was still renting shop space, however, for in 1729 he signed a seven-year lease with the town on a shop in Dock Square.[22] In 1731, he purchased a brick house and land in Hanover Street from the widow Rachel Proctor for £600. The house must have been set gable end to the street because according to the deed the lot was only 22 feet in width "throughout the whole length" and 380 feet in depth.[23] In 1737, Edwards purchased a house and land in Cornhill Street next to the heirs of Benjamin Walker from William Speakman, a Boston baker, for £1,760.[24] On Monday 10 April 1738, Benjamin Walker, Jr., who had inherited his father's house, wrote the following in his diary:

> M[r] Jn[o] Edwards Goldsmith some months agoe (y[e] 19, January last by Pulic Vendue[)], bo[tt] per his Son In Law Barth[l] Cheevers, John Checklys house adjoying Southward to me said Edwards is now Staing on his Side the fence between us.[25]

and on 3 May

> M[r] Edwards wife & family cum in [illegible] Inhabit this afternoon.[26]

and on 4 May

> M[r] Edwards open'd his Shop next door to me South & made a Show with his Glasse Cases & goods.[27]

Beginning in 1738, then, the house in Cornhill was the site of Edwards's shop as well as of his home. Edwards's land acquisitions indicate that he hoped to provide for each of his children after his death, and he owned several houses in Boston at the time he wrote his will in 1744. Although there is evidence that he began investing in shipping after 1740, during most of his career Edwards put his profits back into his silversmithing business.[28]

John Edwards's contemporaries admired his diligence: he was elected to the most prestigious town offices. Edwards was elected tithingman in 1698/99, 1699/1700, 1708/09, and 1711/12; constable in 1715 (refused to serve); and served in one of the town's most highly regarded offices—tax assessor—from 1720 to 1727. He became a member of the Artillery Company in 1699 and was a member of the Boston militia. He was elected fourth sergeant of the Artillery Company in 1704. He was a member of the Brattle Street Church.[29] He acted as an executor of the estate of the mariner John Edwards in 1716/17.[30] He appears only once as a defendant in the records of the Court of Common Pleas, when, in 1735, Robert Browne, a Boston distiller, sued John Edwards and Oxenbridge Thatcher, identified as a gentleman, for retaining household goods that belonged to Browne. Edwards and Thatcher were ordered to return the goods and apparently did so.[31]

Edwards was sometimes called upon to appraise silver in estates and to participate in settling disputes. In May 1700 Edwards and the glazier Nathaniel Douse appraised two tankards, one beaker, three porringers, six spoons, one "Belly Cup," one "Cup with a Cover," one plate, and one sugar box weighing 163 1/4 troy ounces from the estate of Randell Nichols, a Charlestown biscuit baker, at 6 shillings and 8 pence per ounce, for a total of £54.8.4. In 1705 he and Benjamin Dyer appraised the estate of Elizabeth Dowell of Boston, which included seventy-two ounces of plate, three ounces, twelve pennyweight, and twenty-three grains of gold, and a gold and pearl pendant.[32] He was an appraiser of the estate of Richard Draper in 1728/29, and with George Minott, Timothy

Prout, and Edward Winslow (q.v.) he was a trustee of the estate of Stephen Minott (d. 1732).[33] In 1708 he was a member of a committee to measure the town's part of new pavement in Newbury Street, and in 1722 he was chosen to serve with the town selectmen as a member of a committee to inspect the writing school. Sewall records that a Mr. Henchman (possibly Daniel Henchman, the bookseller) chose John Edwards to act as arbitrator for him in a dispute with Madam Bridget Usher in 1726. He and John Dixwell (q.v.) were also appraisers of the estate of Edward Webb (q.v.) in 1718.[34]

Benjamin Walker recorded the death of Sybil (Newman) Edwards "of a Coma or Lethargy" on 17 November 1739. In 1740, Edwards married Abigail (Fowle) Smith (b. 1679), the mother of Sarah (Smith) Edwards, who married John's son Samuel in 1733. Abigail was the widow of William Smith (d. 1730) and the daughter of Isaac Fowle and Beriah (Bright) Fowle. Another of Abigail's daughters, Mary (Smith) Austin, was the mother of the silversmith Ebenezer Austin (q.v.).[35] Through his first marriage, Edwards had formed a strong link with one of New England's most important minister-magistrate families; through his second marriage, he solidified his family's alliance with one of Boston's most prominent merchant families. In 1735, Abigail Smith's dower portion of her husband William Smith's estate amounted to £115.14.6, including a slave named Caesar, a silver tankard, two silver porringers, one silver spoon, a brass kettle, a tin pan, tin colander, and tin sauce pan, a funnel, a pepper box, and a brass chafing dish and ladle. Many of these items are also listed in the division of Abigail Edwards's estate in May 1760.[36] When John Edwards wrote his will on 17 January 1743/44 he bequeathed "Fifty pounds old Tenor over and above what she will have by Virtue of my Contract made on her behalf before Mariage" to his wife Abigail.[37]

In a series of lengthy provisions, John Edwards bequeathed his three houses in Boston to his sons, Thomas, Samuel, and Joseph, and made monetary bequests to his daughters, Elizabeth Cheever, Mary Storer, and Ann Edwards. He named his sons Samuel and Joseph and his sons-in-law Bartholomew Cheever and Ebenezer Storer executors of the estate.[38]

On Tuesday, 8 April 1746, Benjamin Walker recorded the death of his neighbor and kinsman in his diary:

> M.r John Edwards Sen.r about or Between Eleven & Twelve of th Cloc: Dyed mostly I believe of age an old man 74 years & 9 months old my Next Neighbour (Tho to me my self not fryendly[)] he was a Gold smith by Trade & had a good character from y.e Generall & Sober man but I think very much Conceited & fresh colour'd fair man allway a blush on Cheeks [illeg.] lay out of order a few days abo.tt 6, or 7, days[39]

The *Boston Evening-Post* remembered him as "a Gentleman of a very fair Character" who was "well respected by all that knew him."[40]

John Edwards's estate was appraised by Jacob Hurd (q.v.), Samuel Grant, and Thomas Baxter. The inventory filed with the court is cursory and gives only aggregate values for each category of objects in inflated Old Tenor.[41] The tools were not enumerated; their value was placed at £336.5.9. Goods in the shop were valued at £1,042.10.5. There is also a listing for silver and gold worth £2,305.6.4, which may have included household silver and gold as well as unwrought metal in the shop. Two "Negromen" are also listed in the inventory, one of whom may have been the slave whom Abigail Smith owned at the time of her marriage to Edwards. The inventory, which does not include most of Edwards's real estate, gives the value of his estate as £4,840.8 Old Tenor.[42]

If this amount is combined with an estimate of the value of his three major parcels of land in Boston, his total worth in 1746 can be estimated at over £1,800 sterling—an amount large enough to put him in the wealthiest 10 percent of Boston decedents.[43] BMW

SURVIVING OBJECTS

	Mark	Inscription	Patron	Date	Reference	Owner
Baptismal basin	B	This belongs to yᵉ Church of Portsᵐᵒ 1714	North Church (First Church of Christ, Congregational), Portsmouth, N.H.	1714	Jones 1913, 379	
Two beakers (with mark of John Allen)	A*	IC; John Cates Legacy to the Church In Windham	John Cates (Kates, Keats) and/or Congregational Church, Windham, Conn.	ca. 1697	Jones 1913, 500	
Beaker (with mark of John Allen)	A	S.R.; her gift to Taunton church (later)	Sarah Richmond	ca. 1695	Jones 1913, 469	
Two beakers (with mark of John Allen)	A*	The Gift of the Owners of the/Ship Adventure of London/1699	Messrs. Pickett and Christophers and/or First Congregational Church, New London, Conn.	1699	Jones 1913, 311–12	
Beaker	A	II; The Gift of/Isaac Jones/to the/Church in Dorchester/1699 (later)	Isaac Jones	ca. 1695	Jones 1913, 144	
Beaker	A†	AD's/EB's/Gift ᵗᵒ the Church of Ipswich	First Congregational Church, Ipswich, Mass., for Andrew Diamond and Edward Bragg	1708	Buhler/Hood 1970, no. 64	YUAG
Two beakers	C	L.C.	Follen Church, Lexington (East), Mass.	ca. 1715	Jones 1913, 248	
Three beakers	C	T/OC	First Church, Boston	ca. 1715	Jones 1913, 28	
Beaker	C*	The Gift of Joseph Quilter to the First Church in Ipswich 1724	First Congregational Church, Ipswich, Mass., for Joseph Quilter	1724	Buhler/Hood 1970, no. 72	YUAG
Beaker	C*	The Gift of Samuel Bernard to the Church in Deerfeild. 1723	Samuel Barnard and/or First Congregational Church, Deerfield, Mass.	1723	Flynt/Fales 1968, 45–47	
Beaker	C	The gift of Deacon Sam Stone to Lexington Church 1715	Samuel Stone and/or Follen Church, Lexington (East), Mass.	1715	Jones 1913, 248	
Beaker	C	The gift of Barnstable Church, 1716	Congregational Church, Canterbury, Mass.	1716	Jones 1913, 112	
Two beakers	C	This belongs to the Church in Truro/ 1717	First Congregational Church, Truro, Mass.	1717	Jones 1913, 471	
Beaker	C	The Gift of M Nich Boone Bookseller, to the Church on Church Green in Boston. 1720.	Nicholas Boone and/or New South Church, Boston	1720	Buhler 1972, no. 85	MFAB

	Mark	Inscription	Patron	Date	Reference	Owner
Beaker	c	The gift of Giles Rickard to Plimouth Church	First Parish, Plymouth, Mass., for Giles Rickard	ca. 1710	Jones 1913, 374	PS
Beaker	c	The gift of Hannah Ware to the Church in Dedham 1722	Hannah Ware and/or First Church, Dedham, Mass.	1722	Winchester 1956, 552	
Beaker	c†	The Gift of Doct.ʳ John Bridgham to the Church of Christ in Ipswich. 1721.	First Congregational Church, Ipswich, Mass., for John Bridgham	1721	Buhler/Hood 1970, no. 71	YUAG
Beaker	c	The gift of/Thomas Hale ESQ.ᴿ	Thomas Hale and/or First Congregational Church, Rowley, Mass.	ca. 1730	Jones 1913, 406	
Beaker	c	The Gift of M.ʳ John Clough to the Church of Christ in/Summer Street of which the Rev.ᵈ M.ʳ Samuel Checkley is Pastor/ 1744.	John Clough and/or New South Church, Boston	1744	Buhler 1972, no. 89	MFAB
Beaker	c	The Gift of Nath.ˡ Gilman Esqʳ in his Last will and/Testament to the first Church of Christ in Exeter May 1740	First Congregational Church, Exeter, N.H., for Nathaniel Gilman	1740	Jones 1913, 172	
Beaker	c	Ex dono Elizabeth Gaskill to the Church/of Christ in Easthaven in Newhaven/1736	Elizabeth Gaskill and/ or Congregational Church, East Haven, Conn.	1736	Jones 1913, 159–60	
Two beakers	c	The Gift of Elder Nathan Lord/to the Church of Christ in Berwick 1734	First Congregational Church, South Berwick, Maine, for Nathan Lord	1734	Jones 1913, 453	
Beaker	c	The Gift of Mr: Sam.ˡ Haugh to Lexington Church. 1727	Follen Church, Lexington (East), Mass., for Samuel Haugh	1727	Jones 1913, 248	
Beaker	c	The Gift of Kinsley Hall Esqʳ and his two Sons, to the Church of Christ at Exeter. December 1.ˢᵗ 1726	Kinsley, Josiah, and Paul Hall and/or First Congregational Church, Exeter, N.H.	1726	Jones 1913, 171	
Three beakers	c	Exeter Church December 1st 1726	First Congregational Church, Exeter, N.H.	1726	Jones 1913, 171	
Beaker	c	The Gift of M.ʳ James Dudley, and M.ʳˢ Elizabeth Dudley, to the Church of Christ at Exeter, December 1.ˢᵗ 1726.	James and Elizabeth Dudley and/or First Congregational Church, Exeter, N.H.	1726	Jones 1913, 172	

	Mark	Inscription	Patron	Date	Reference	Owner
Cann	c*	Dummer crest, a demi-lion holding a fleur-de-lis in his dexter paw; D/IE (+)	John and Elizabeth (Smith) Dummer	ca. 1730	Buhler/Hood 1970, no. 73	YUAG
Cann (mate below)	c	Whipple arms, sable on a chevron between 3 swans' heads erased 3 crescents, and crest, a swan's head; W/WM	William and Mary (Cutt) Whipple	ca. 1730	Kernan 1961, 106–07	
Cann (mate above, attrib.)	none	Whipple arms, sable on a chevron between 3 swans' heads erased 3 crescents, and crest, a swan's head; W/WM; Whipple (later)	William and Mary (Cutt) Whipple	ca. 1730	Kernan 1961, 106–07	MWPI
Cann	?	?	First Church in Wenham, Congregational, Wenham, Mass.	?	YUAG files	
Caster	c*	?		ca. 1740	*Antiques* 134 (July 1988): 41	
Caster	?	?		ca. 1715	*Antiques* 103 (June 1973): 1075	
Caudle cup (with mark of John Allen)	A*	PH		ca. 1700	*Antiques* 27 (April 1935): 122	DIA
Caudle cup	A*	P/IS		ca. 1700	Fales 1970, 41	PEM
Chafing dish	c	Wyllys arms, a chevron sable between 3 mullets gules, a falcon with wings expanded (+)	George Wyllys (?)	ca. 1735	DAPC 71.1681	
Creampot	c*	none		ca. 1735	Buhler 1956, no. 61	
Cup	A*	M/SS (?); Belonged to Mrs. Markland, who was aunt to Mrs. Ames, who was great-grandmother to Susette V.S. Reed (later)		ca. 1700	American Art Association–Anderson Galleries, 2–3 April 1937, lot 276	
Cup	A (?)	L/IE		ca. 1700	YUAG files	
Cup	A	P/IE		ca. 1700	*Antiques* 99 (May 1971): 632	
Cup	A *or* B	AKC/to/ABC/1860 (later)		ca. 1720	Sotheby Parke Bernet, 30 June–1 July 1983, lot 95	

	Mark	Inscription	Patron	Date	Reference	Owner
Cup	B	S Lindall 1708/ Love Rawlins Pickman/1788 (later) (+)	Sarah Lindall	ca. 1715	Buhler 1972, no. 80	MFAB
Cup	C	Payne crest; F/II	John and Jerusha (Groce) Fayerweather	ca. 1715	Gourley 1965, no. 70	SPNEA
Cup	C	ED	Elizabeth (Dennis) Day	ca. 1715	Buhler 1965, 34–35	HMA
Cup (with mark of Samuel Gray, 1684–1713)	C	M/TZ to EM		ca. 1710	*Moore Collection* 1980, no. 98	
Cup	?	?		ca. 1710	*Antiques* 134 (July 1988): 41	
Flagon	B*	This belongs to/the Church in/Brattle Street/1712	Brattle Street Church, Boston	1712	Buhler 1972, no. 82	MFAB
Flagon	C	Dummer crest, a demi-lion holding a fleur-de-lis in his dexter paw; The Gift of the Honble William Dummer Esqr/to the first Church in Boston 1726	William Dummer and/ or First Church, Boston	ca. 1726	Jones 1913, 31	
Mourning ring (gold)	D*	M Berry Ob. 25 Aug.ᵗ 1727 AEt. 33.	M. Berry	1727	YUAG files	
Mug (with mark of John Allen)	A	AC; The Gift of/Mʳˢ Sarah Jeffers . . . (later)		ca. 1700	Jones 1913, 45	
Mug (with mark of John Allen)	A	Southack crest, a dexter arm embowed and cuffed holding a bleeding heart; AS to MC (later)		ca. 1700	*Antiques* 41 (June 1942): 378	
Mug	A*	original initials erased; S Russell (later)		ca. 1700	Buhler 1972, no. 79	MFAB
Mug	B	B/GM (?)		ca. 1710	*Antiques* 86 (November 1964): 531	
Mug	B*	S/IP		ca. 1710	Flynt/Fales 1968, 96–97	HD
Mug	B	G/FR		ca. 1720	Sotheby's, 30 January–2 February 1991, lot 145	
Mug	C*	Tuthill arms, on a bend double cotised or a lion passant; TH (+)	Tuthill family	ca. 1715	Hammerslough/ Feigenbaum 1958–73, 3:21	WA

	Mark	Inscription	Patron	Date	Reference	Owner
Mug	c	unidentified initials		ca. 1735	Sotheby Parke Bernet, Los Angeles, 2–5 June 1980, lot 630	
Mug	c	Dudley crest, a lion's head; (+)	Dudley family	ca. 1715	*Silver Supplement* 1973, no. 32	
Mug	c*	W/IS	Jacob and Sarah (Oliver) Wendell	ca. 1720	Buhler 1972, no. 86	MFAB
Patch box	c*	MD	Marion Danforth	ca. 1720	DAPC 68.3860	
Patch box	D*	LH/1721/2		ca. 1722	Hammerslough/ Feigenbaum 1958–73, 2:39	WA
Pepper box	A*	B/HA		ca. 1705	Buhler/Hood 1970, no. 62	YUAG
Pepper box	c*	W/IR	Joseph and Rebecca Williams	ca. 1715	*Moore Collection* 1980, no. 92	
Pepper box	c*	C/EE (+)		ca. 1715	Johnston 1994, 47	CMA
Pepper box	c/D†	L/CS	Charles and Sarah (Warren) Little	ca. 1720	Buhler 1979, no. 10	WAM
Porringer	A*	Storer crest, a tal-bot's head; M: Storer	Ebenezer and Mary (Edwards) Storer (?)	ca. 1705	Buhler/Hood 1970, no. 63	YUAG
Porringer	A*	AT		ca. 1705		SFCAI
Porringer (with mark of John Allen)	A	G/NE		ca. 1700	Avery 1920, no. 17	MMA
Porringer (with mark of John Allen)	A	G/EH		ca. 1700	MFA 1911, no. 7	
Porringer	A	T/RE	Thaxter family (?)	ca. 1715	*Antiques* 106 (July 1974): 26	
Porringer	B	C/BP	Benjamin and Priscilla Collins	ca. 1705	Buhler 1972, no. 81	MFAB
Porringer	B	SB to B/IT		ca. 1713	*Moore Collection* 1980, no. 93	
Porringer	c*	O/TL		ca. 1725	DAPC 68.378	SI
Porringer	c*	AL		ca. 1715	Buhler/Hood 1970, no. 66	YUAG
Porringer	c	W/IS		ca. 1720	Quimby 1995, no. 52	WM
Porringer	c	B/TM	Thomas and Mary (Willoughby) Barton	ca. 1720	Buhler 1972, no. 84	MFAB
Porringer	c	E/NH		ca. 1730	Sotheby's, 21 June 1989, lot 128	
Porringer	c	R/DR		ca. 1735	Avery 1920, no. 29	MMA

	Mark	Inscription	Patron	Date	Reference	Owner
Porringer	c*	Palmes arms, 3 fleur-de-lis, a chief chequey, a crescent in fess point (+)	Palmes family	ca. 1735	Avery 1920, no. 30	MMA
Porringer	c	LBS (later)		ca. 1730	Quimby 1995, no. 53	WM
Porringer	c	ML		ca. 1740		CHS
Porringer	c*	B/IS		ca. 1730	Warren 1975, no. 293	BBC
Porringer	c	T/IM (+)		ca. 1730	DAPC 70.3134	
Porringer	c	SF; 1745 (later)	S. Franklin	ca. 1720	*Antiques* 59 (April 1951): 289	
Porringer	c	I/IK		ca. 1730	Norman-Wilcox 1962, no. 18	DIA
Porringer	c	?		ca. 1730	Parke-Bernet, 4 January 1940, lot 66	
Porringer (with mark of John Allen)	?	unidentified initials (later) (+)		ca. 1700	*Antiques* 85 (June 1964): 623	
Porringer	?	unidentified initials	Ruth Cheever (?)	ca. 1705	YUAG files	
Ring (gold)	D*	April 13th, 1718	Francis and Deborah (Lynde) Brinley	1718	Bohan 1963, no. 110	
Salt (with mark of John Allen)	A*	S/SE	Rev. Solomon and Esther (Warham) (Mather) Stoddard	ca. 1696	Safford 1983, 23	MMA
Salver (with mark of John Allen)	A	Coffin arms, 3 bezants or between 9 crosses crosslet, and crest, a demi-griffin segreant (+)	Coffin family	ca. 1705	Bigelow 1917, 240	
Salver	A*	Walker arms, between a chevron 3 crescents and in a canton a bird with a sprig in its beak	Walker family	ca. 1705	Buhler/Hood 1970, no. 61	YUAG
Salver	B	C/IA	John and Anna (Orne) Cabot	ca. 1710	Buhler 1972, no. 83	MFAB
Salver	c	A/HM		ca. 1715	*Moore Collection* 1980, no. 91	
Salver	c	ES; S/EM (+)	Ebenezer and Mary (Waters) Stedman	ca. 1715	Jones 1913, 325	
Serving spoon	c	W/IA		ca. 1725	English-Speaking Union 1960, no. 27	MFAB
Serving spoon	c	?		ca. 1725	YUAG files	

	Mark	Inscription	Patron	Date	Reference	Owner
Spout cup *(with mark of John Allen)*	A	unidentified arms, a tyger rampant collared and chained; D/CM (later)		ca. 1700	Buhler 1960, no. 52	DIA
Spout cup	A*	C/BI; Ex dono/D^m Iohannis George/ 1706 (+)	John George for Rev. Benjamin and Jane (Clark) Colman	1706	Buhler 1979, no. 9	WAM
Spout cup	A*	EP; In memoria Lovet Sanders/Obijt 26 March 1708.	Lovet Sanders	1708	Flynt/Fales 1968, 108–09	HD
Spout cup	C*	SM (+)	Sarah (Webb) Marshall	ca. 1715	Quimby 1995, no. 51	WM
Spout cup	C*	EG; Elizabeth Greenleaf	Elizabeth Greenleaf	ca. 1712	DAPC 68.3345	MMA
Spout cup	C*	L/CS	Charles and Sarah (Warren) Little	ca. 1720		MFAB
Spout cup (lacks cover)	C	R/IM		ca. 1720		MFAB
Sword	?	TD		ca. 1740	Peterson (1955) 1991, no. 5	
Tablespoon	A*	G/IM		ca. 1700	Quimby 1995, no. 54	WM
Tablespoon	A*	C/IA	John and Anna (Orne) Cabot	ca. 1705	Fales 1983, 8–9	PEM
Tablespoon *(with mark of John Allen)*	A*	MB		ca. 1695	Quimby 1995, no. 56	WM
Tablespoon	A*	[illeg.]ath Turner/ Bathshua Stockbridge	Bathshua Stockbridge	1707	*Antiques* 103 (April 1973): 631	
Tablespoon	A*	MP		ca. 1700	Buhler 1972, no. 78	MFAB
Two tablespoons	A*	T/OC	First Church, Boston	ca. 1705	Jones 1913, 35	
Tablespoon *(with mark of John Allen)*	A*	S/SE	Rev. Solomon and Esther (Warham) (Mather) Stoddard	ca. 1700		HD
Tablespoon *(with mark of John Allen)*	A	EM		ca. 1700	YUAG files	
Tablespoon *(with mark of John Allen)*	A*	M/SA	Samuel and Ann (Adkins) Marshall	ca. 1705	Buhler/Hood 1970, no. 76	YUAG
Tablespoon	B*	A/IS (altered to D/IS)		ca. 1710	Johnston 1994, 47	CMA
Tablespoon	C*	MY		ca. 1729	Johnston 1994, 48	CMA
Tablespoon	C*	MY/June 16/1729		1729	Johnston 1994, 48	CMA
Tablespoon	C*	G/GE (+)		ca. 1700	Quimby 1995, no. 55	WM
Tablespoon	C*	AF (?)		ca. 1715	*Antiques* 106 (September 1974): 386	HMA

	Mark	Inscription	Patron	Date	Reference	Owner
Tablespoon	c	Dudley crest; H Sewall/given by/his uncle/P Dudley	P. Dudley for H. Sewall	ca. 1720	*Silver Supplement* 1973, no. 33	
Tablespoon	c	F/TM		ca. 1730	Parke-Bernet, 15–16 April 1955, lot 210	
Tablespoon (mates below)	c*	MC (+)		ca. 1715	*Silver Supplement* 1973, no. 34a	
Tablespoon (mates above and below)	c*	MC (+)		ca. 1715	*Silver Supplement* 1973, no. 34b	
Tablespoon (mates above and below)	c*	MC (+)		ca. 1715	Sotheby's, 17 November 1981, lot 186	
Tablespoon (mates above)	c*	MC (+)		ca. 1715	Sotheby's, 30 June–1 July 1982, lot 228	
Tablespoon	c*	MI/MW		ca. 1710	Avery 1920, no. 31	MMA
Tablespoon	c*	IW		ca. 1715		HD
Tablespoon	c	L/NR/ML		ca. 1715	*Moore Collection* 1980, no. 97	
Tablespoon	c*	S/TM		ca. 1725	Buhler/Hood 1970, no. 69	YUAG
Tablespoon	c*	SS (+)		ca. 1730	*Antiques* 56 (November 1949): 372, 375	
Tablespoon	c*	MP	Margaret Pilfrey	ca. 1740	Buhler/Hood 1970, no. 70	YUAG
Tablespoon (mate? below)	c	MP		ca. 1730		HD
Tablespoon (mate? above)	c	MP	Mary (Prentice) Cushing	ca. 1730	Skinner, 11 January 1992, lot 55	
Tablespoon	c*	M/EB/HW		ca. 1730		HD
Tablespoon	c	MC/MB (+)		ca. 1710	*Moore Collection* 1980, no. 96	
Tablespoon	?	CH		ca. 1705	*Antiques* 87 (January 1965): 13	
Tankard (with mark of John Allen)	A*	IE		ca. 1700	DAPC 75.4890	
Tankard (with mark of John Allen)	A	L(E?)/IS		ca. 1705	*Maine Antique Digest* (January 1985): 22–C	
Tankard	B (?)	?		ca. 1710	*Antiques* 115 (June 1979): 1112	
Tankard	c	B/NH (+)	Nathaniel and Hannah (Hirst) Balston	1725	Jones 1913, 30–31	

	Mark	Inscription	Patron	Date	Reference	Owner
Tankard	c	Parks arms, gules on a pale argent 3 bucks' heads ca-bossed	Parks family	ca. 1725	*Moore Collection* 1980, no. 95	
Tankard	c	This belongs to/the Church in/Brattle-Street/1728 (+)	Brattle Street Church, Boston	1728	Jones 1913, 272–73	
Tankard	c	The Gift of Man-assah Tucker Jun.ʳ to the Church/of Christ in Milton 1729	Manassah Tucker, Jr., and/or First Congregational Parish, Milton, Mass.	1729	Jones 1913, 291–92	
Tankard	c	Sewall arms, a chevron between 3 bees, and crest, a bee in a wreath; Given to the South-Church/1730	Sewall family and/or Old South Church, Boston	1730	Jones 1913, 53–54	
Tankard	c	Titcomb arms, a fess between 3 grey-hounds' heads erased and gorged, and crest, a grey-hound's head; The Gift of Benaiah & William/Titcomb to the third Church in/Newberry/1731	First Religious Society, Newburyport, Mass., for Benaiah and William Titcomb	1731	Jones 1913, 295–96	
Tankard	c	T/BM; The Gift of M.ʳ Benaiah Tit-comb/To:The.. Third.Church/In Newbury../1742 (later)	Benaiah and M. Titcomb	ca. 1725	Jones 1913, 296–97	
Tankard	c	The Gift of Priscilla Faunce/to the Church of Plymouth	Priscilla Faunce and/or First Parish, Plymouth, Mass.	ca. 1730	Jones 1913, 376	PS
Tankard	c*	G/GE		ca. 1730	*Moore Collection* 1980, no. 94	HMA
Tankard	c	The Gift of Ebe-nezer Stone Sen.ʳ/to the Church of Christ in Newtown/1730	Ebenezer Stone and/or First Church, Newton, Mass.	1730	Jones 1913, 323	MFAB
Tankard	c	C/WH		ca. 1735	Sotheby Parke Bernet, 19–22 November 1980, lot 193	
Tankard	c	The Gift of the Rev.ᵈ H: Gibbs to Watertown Church 1723	First Parish, Watertown, Mass., for Rev. Henry Gibbs	1723	Jones 1913, 480–81	

	Mark	Inscription	Patron	Date	Reference	Owner
Tankard	c	The Gift of M:B to Watertown Church 1677	First Parish, Watertown, Mass., for Michael Barstow	ca. 1723	Jones 1913, 480–81	
Tankard	c*	B/SC; SB to RA		ca. 1720	Johnston 1994, 49	CMA
Tankard	c	MH (+)		ca. 1715	Buhler/Hood 1970, no. 68	YUAG
Tankard	c	C/PE	Coffin family (?)	ca. 1725	Wardwell 1966, 81	
Tankard	c*	S/BM (+)		ca. 1715	Buhler/Hood 1970, no. 67	YUAG
Tankard	c	Norton arms, a fret, a bend varié azure and argent, and crest, a wyvern sergeant; EQ /To/LT	Elizabeth (Norton) Quincy	ca. 1720	Jones 1913, 395–96	
Tankard	c*	Norton arms, a fret, a bend varié azure and argent, and crest, a wyvern sergeant; This tankard was John Quincy's . . . (later)	Rev. John Norton	ca. 1715	*Witness to America's Past*, 108	MHS
Tankard	c	Parker arms (?)		ca. 1720	YUAG files	
Tankard	c	T/IG		ca. 1730		SPNEA
Tankard	c	The Gift of I:K and M:B to Watertown Church 1677	First Parish, Watertown, Mass., for John Knowles and Michael Barstow	ca. 1723	Jones 1913, 480–81	
Tankard	?	M/BH		ca. 1730		VMFA
Tankard	?	?		ca. 1725	American Art Association–Anderson Galleries, 29–30 November 1935, lot 72	
Tankard (with mark of John Allen)	?	B/AM		ca. 1705	*Antiques* 39 (April 1941): 204	
Teaspoon	D	D/IM		ca. 1730	DAPC 74.1484	WM
Two-handled cup	B†	The Gift of Lieut: Daniel White/to the Church of Hatfield	First Congregational Church, Hatfield, Mass., for Daniel White	ca. 1713	Buhler/Hood 1970, no. 65	YUAG
Wine cup (with mark of John Allen)	A	Ex dono RK	Roger Kilcup and/or First Baptist Church, Boston	ca. 1702	Jones 1913, 44–45	
Wine cup	A	none	Christ Church Parish, South Carolina	ca. 1705	Jones 1913, 128	
Wine cup (with paten cover)	c	The Gift of Capt. Thomas Tudar to Christ Church in Boston 1724	Christ Church, Boston, for Thomas Tudor	ca. 1724	Jones 1913, 74	

	Mark	Inscription	Patron	Date	Reference	Owner
Wine cup	C	Hall arms, over a semée of crosses crosslet 3 talbots' heads erased 2 and 1 langued, and crest, a talbot's head erased; A Gift/To the Church/in Lynde Street/Boston	Hugh (?) Hall and/or West Church, Lynde Street, Boston	ca. 1737	Buhler 1972, no. 88	MFAB
Wine cup (mate below)	C	The Legacy/of/Stephen Minott, Esqʳ to the Church/in Brattle-street./1732	Brattle Street Church, Boston, for Stephen Minott	1732	Buhler 1972, no. 87	MFAB
Wine cup (mate above)	C	The Legacy/of/ Stephen Minott, Esqʳ to the Church/ in Brattle-street./ 1732	Brattle Street Church, Boston, for Stephen Minott	1732	Buhler 1979, no. 11	WAM
Two wine cups	C	Dummer crest; Dedicated/By Wᵐ Dummer Esqʳ/to the Church of Newbury Falls/for the Communion Table/1729	William Dummer and/ or Byfield Parish Church of Newbury, Mass.	1729	Buhler 1956, no. 63	

1. According to the diary of Benjamin Walker, John Edwards's aunt Palsgrave (Edwards) Walker (Benjamin Walker's mother) was born in Watertown, Massachusetts, about 1652. See Benjamin Walker, Jr., Diaries, MHS. We know that Palsgrave Edwards married Benjamin Walker, pewterer of London, in Stepney in 1671/72; see *NEHGR* 67:297–98. This would suggest that the Edwardses traveled frequently between New England and Old England, and that John Edwards's great grandfather was Richard Palsgrave. It is unclear whether the goldsmith, John Edwards, had a mother whose maiden name was Walker; *NEHGR* 67:297–98.
2. MCPR, docket 3069.
3. *Sewall Diary* 1:235, 239–41, 243–44, 250; MCPR 7:201–03, docket 6889. John Edwards, surgeon, wrote his will on 11 August 1676 and renewed it 9 October 1688. The will mentions only his wife, Elizabeth, to whom he bequeathed everything.
4. MCPR 8:463–64, docket 6888.
5. RC 9:4, 217; Savage 1860–62, 3:274; *Wenham VR*, 63, 149, 213. John Edwards served as his mother-in-law's attorney in a suit brought against her by Anne Endicott at the Superior Court in Ipswich in 1702 (SCCR, file 5523). On the basis of his wife's relationship to Governor Endicott, John Edwards petitioned the Boston selectmen in 1722 for permission to improve the tomb of the late governor and make use of it for his own family.
6. RC 9:226, 240; RC 24:2, 12, 21, 34, 48, 82; RC 28:116, 182, 183, 238; SCPR 38:515–18.
7. Kathryn Buhler considered Edwards to be one of Dummer's apprentices, based on the similarity of objects produced in the two shops and on the fact that Jeremiah Dummer's son, Governor William, patronized Edwards. It seems likely that John Allen and John Edwards became partners after training in the same shop. Dummer was Allen's step-uncle and therefore might have taken Allen as an apprentice. For Buhler's reasons for believing that Edwards was one of Dummer's apprentices, see Buhler 1951, 288; Buhler 1956, 27–29; Buhler 1965, 32–34; and Buhler 1972, 1:95.
8. RC 9:235; SCD 17:313–15; SCCR, file 98567.
9. SCCR, Court of Common Pleas Record Book 1699–1701, 57. The shop was located in a building owned by Hezekiah Usher that was involved in a long dispute between Usher's estate and his divorced wife, Bridget.
10. Ward 1989, 70–71, 77–83.
11. Johnston 1994, 50.

12. Bill of John Edwards to Joseph Dudley, photostat, Bigelow-Phillips files.

13. Bill of John Edwards to Joseph Dudley, 1712, Document no. 737, Bostonian Society, Boston, Mass.

14. *Massachusetts Historical Society Collections* 5 (series 6): 358; "Expended in the Funeral of my Dater Mrs. Hannah Sewall who died August 16th 1724," Samuel Sewall Account Book and Ledger, fol. 176v, NEHGS; SCPR 30:308.

15. "Accounts of the Estate of Madam Bridget Usher," Sewall Account Book and Ledger, NEHGS.

16. Samuel Sewall Account Book and Ledger, fols. 174v, 175r, NEHGS. In the same ledger Sewall received £1.3.6 from Edwards for two pair of silver shoe buckles in 1719 (fol. 191r). Sewall records the purchase of three rings in 1716 and 1717 (fol. 192r), twenty-three gold rings in 1723 (fol. 173r), and a silver spoon for his wife in 1725/26 (fol. 187v).

17. Curwen Papers, PEM.

18. This may be one reason Edwards enjoyed so much economic success. His younger contemporary Jacob Hurd went into bankruptcy because of the high interest rates he had to pay to buy silver bullion on credit.

19. Curwen Papers, PEM.

20. SCPR 16:358–60; 38:515–18.

21. SCD 43:172–73.

22. RC 13:193.

23. Rachel Proctor deed to John Edwards, 15 April 1731, Smith-Carter Papers, MHS; SCD 45:210–11.

24. SCD 55:225–26.

25. Benjamin Walker, Jr., Diaries, vol. 2, MHS.

26. Benjamin Walker, Jr., Diaries, vol. 2, MHS.

27. Benjamin Walker, Jr., Diaries, vol. 2, MHS.

28. Isaac Smith Account Book, 1741–44, Smith-Carter Papers, MHS.

29. Seybolt 1939, 97, 99, 121, 130, 139, 153, 154, 157, 159, 163, 165, 168, 171; Roberts 1895, 1:318.

30. SCPR, docket 3811.

31. SCCR, Court of Common Pleas Record Book 1735, 96. The court record makes no mention of how "Seven Sattin Chairs and an easy Chair covered with Sattin a Bed wrought Viz^t Curtains & Valens Curtain rods & bows Window Curtains & Valens a Feather Bed & Bolster a Sattin Quilt & Bedstead & two large looking Glasses all of the Value of a hundred & fifty pounds" "came into the hands of" Edwards and Thatcher.

32. SCCR, file 4767; SCPR 16:1–2.

33. SCPR 27:129–30; SCD 50:93–97; 81:266–68.

34. RC 11:80; Roberts 1895, 1:318; *Sewall Letter Book* 2:205; SCPR 21:261–62.

35. Benjamin Walker, Jr., Diaries, vol. 2, MHS; RC 28:214, 221; Wyman 1879, 1:331, 370; 2:874; *Charlestown VR* 1:305. Joseph Badger painted Abigail Edwards's portrait about 1750–60. The painting is now owned by the MFAB.

36. Administrators' accounting of the division of the estate of William Smith, 1735; estate inventory of Abigail Edwards in the receipt book of Isaac Smith and Samuel Edwards, 1760–61. Both estate divisions are in the Smith-Carter Papers, MHS.

37. SCPR 38:515.

38. SCPR 38:515–18. It is unusual that Thomas, the eldest son and principal heir, is not named as one of the executors of the estate. Other evidence suggests that Thomas was residing in New York in 1744, and this may be the reason his father did not make him one of the executors.

39. Benjamin Walker, Jr., Diaries, vol. 2, MHS.

40. Dow 1927, 44.

41. At this date silver was valued at approximately thirty-eight shillings per ounce.

42. SCPR 39:77.

43. For figures on decile rankings of Boston decedents, see Nash 1979, 400.

Joseph Edwards, Jr.
1737–83

A

Joseph Edwards, Jr., was born in Boston on 11 November 1737 and was baptized in the Brattle Street Church two days later.[1] He was the son of Joseph Edwards (1707–77), a bookseller and stationer, and his first wife, Sarah Belknap (1713–before 1763), the daughter of Jeremiah Belknap (1687–1751), a leather dresser, and Sarah Fosdick (1685–1754).[2] The couple married on 16 May 1734, in a ceremony performed by Rev. Joseph Sewall of the Old South Church.[3]

Joseph Edwards, Jr., belonged to a family of successful Boston goldsmiths:

his father's brothers were Thomas Edwards (q.v.) and Samuel Edwards (q.v.). His grandfather, John Edwards (q.v.), left Joseph, Sr., two hundred pounds, a share in his pew in the Brattle Street Church, and a house on Staniford Street in the westerly part of Boston (which Joseph and Sarah Edwards sold on 28 September 1748 to purchase a house in Cornhill).[4] Kathryn Buhler believed that the younger Joseph trained with his uncle Samuel Edwards, in an apprenticeship that would have begun about 1751 and been completed about 1758, although he may also have trained with his uncle Thomas Edwards.[5] Joseph Edwards and Samuel Belknap (q.v.) were first cousins. He may be the Joseph Edwards who witnessed deeds for Zachariah Brigden (q.v.) with Samuel Edwards in 1758.[6]

On 27 January 1762 an indenture was made between the stationers Joseph and John Edwards, the goldsmith Joseph Edwards, Jr., and the spinster Sarah Edwards in which they sold one quarter of a Cornhill dwelling house to the spinsters Mary and Sarah Belknap.[7] That same year Edwards purchased several items from the estate of his uncle Samuel Edwards, including household goods, a hat and waistcoat, a coat of arms, and six silver spoons.[8] With William Cario, Sr. (q.v.), Joseph, Jr., witnessed a deed for Zachariah Brigden in 1767 in conjunction with the estate of his uncle Thomas Edwards.[9]

On 21 March 1765 Edwards advertised in the *Boston News-Letter* that his shop had been broken into the night previously and offered twenty dollars' reward for the discovery of the thief. The stolen inventory was extensive:

> 34 pair of wrought Silver Shoe Buckels.—20 pair of ditto, Knee ditto.—6 pair plain Shoe ditto.
> —2 Silver Snuff-Boxes.—1 ditto Tortoise Shell Top.—2 Silver Pepper Castors, stamp'd I. E.—12 Tea Spoons, same stamp.—2 large ditto, Name at length; 9 stock Buckles; 3 gold Necklaces; 5 gold Rings; 1 Cream pot, stamp'd I. E. ; 1 Punch-ladle, same stamp; several pair Stone Buttons; 3 pair briliant Stone Earings, set in Gold; 5 pair Cypher ditto; several ditto set in Silver; several stone Rings; a Box with gold Beads; 3 pair Tea Tongs; gold Earings; 2 pair small Buckles, R.; 1 pair old Tea-Tongs I.M. 1 old Spoon; 3 Child's Whistles; 1 pair small Scales and Weights; 1 pair gold Buttons; 1 silver Pipe.

The matter seems to have been resolved, for on 25 November the *News-Letter* stated, "Friday last Joseph Pomroy was severely whipt 40 Stripes at the public Whipping-Post for Stealing a large Quantity of Plate, &c. out of the shop of Mr. Joseph Edwards of this Town, Goldsmith."

One of Edwards's bills of sale survives; made out to Joshua Green in 1765, it includes a pair of canns, one of which is now in the Museum of Fine Arts, Boston:

M.ʳ Joshua Green to Joseph Edwards Jun.ʳ D.ʳ		
April 22, To pʳ Pocket Book Clasps	£0: 7ˢ:	2ᵈ
1765		
May 11, To pʳ Tea Tongs	0: 18 :	8
18, To 2 Silver Canns	11: 18:	10
To 1 Silver Porrenger	3: 11 :	1½

June 3,	To 2 Silver Castors	4 : 1 : 7 1/4
7,	To 6 D.º Tea Spoons	1 : 5 : 8
17,	To 6 D.º Table Spoons	5 : 9 : 8
21,	To 1 D.º Punch Strainer	2 : 5 : 6
July 5	To 2 D.º Gravey Spoons	3 : 6 : 1 1/2
6	To 1 D.º Marrow Spoon	0 : 11 : 8
	To Engraving 12 Crests	0 : 8 : —
	To D.º 2 coats of Arms	0 : 18 : 8

£35 : 2 : 8 1/4 [10]

At a Boston town meeting on 9 March 1767, Edwards was chosen a clerk of the market for the ensuing year.[11] The Massachusetts tax list of 1771 places him in Boston with a poll of one, and merchandise worth £63.19.4.[12] In a list drawn up 24 April 1775 he is among those inhabitants lodging their firearms with the Boston selectmen.[13] The name Joseph Edwards appears there twice: one is probably the father, the other the son. In the Boston Assessors' "Taking-Books" of 1780, Edwards is listed in ward 8 with a poll of one and rents valued at one hundred pounds.[14]

Joseph Edwards died in Boston on 25 April 1783, aged forty-five years. He did not marry, and his sister Sarah Hammett was appointed on 29 April to administer the estate.[15] Approximately fifty pieces of silver by Edwards survive. He used two marks, an initials and surname mark (A) and an initials mark (B). The punch for mark (A) may have been recut from his uncle Thomas Edwards's punch for mark (B). Another initials mark, J·E, has been recorded, but no example was located. An additional I·E mark found on a spoon has been attributed to him; however, the spoon's ornamentation does not relate to his other work, and the spoon has no history to tie it to Massachusetts.[16] PEK

SURVIVING OBJECTS

	Mark	Inscription	Patron	Date	Reference	Owner
Baptismal basin	A	The Gift of BENJA-MIN PICKMAN EsQ.ʳ/ to the North Church in Salem/ 1772	Benjamin Pickman and/or North Church, Salem, Mass.	1772	Jones 1913, 435	
Beaker (mates below)	A	The Gift of Deacon Joseph Stockbridge to the Church of Christ in Hanover. 1768	Joseph Stockbridge and/or First Congregational Church, Hanover, Mass.	1768	Avery 1920, no. 99	MMA
Beaker (mates above and below)	A	The gift of Deacon Joseph Stockbridge to the Church of Christ in Hanover. 1768	Joseph Stockbridge and/or First Congregational Church, Hanover, Mass.	1768	Buhler 1972, no. 426	MFAB
Beaker (mates above and below)	A	The Gift of Deacon Joseph Stockbridge to the Church of Christ in Hanover. 1768	Joseph Stockbridge and/or First Congregational Church, Hanover, Mass.	1768	Washington 1925, no. 43	
Beaker (mates above)	A	The Gift of Deacon Joseph Stockbridge	Joseph Stockbridge and/or First Congrega-	1768	Jones 1913, 206	

	Mark	Inscription	Patron	Date	Reference	Owner
		to the Church of Christ in Hanover. 1768	tional Church, Hanover, Mass.			
Six camp cups	?	NG; N Greene	Nathaniel Greene	ca. 1780	Hammerslough/ Feigenbaum 1958–73, 3:35	
Cann	A*	MS		ca. 1770		PEM
Cann	A*	CK (+)		ca. 1775	Eitner 1976, no. 66	
Cann	A	B		ca. 1770	*Moore Collection* 1980, no. 158	
Cann	A	Green arms, on a fess or a dragon between 2 escallops; 3 lions' heads erased in circles, and crest, a woodpecker pecking at a tree stump; G/IH	Joshua and Hannah (Storer) Green	1765	Buhler 1972, no. 424	MFAB
Cann	A	M/TA		ca. 1770		MFAB
Cann	A*	none		ca. 1770	Bartlett 1984, 14	SLAM
Cann	A	AS (+)	Anthony Sherman	ca. 1770	Skinner, 24 May 1985, lot 181	
Cann	?	?		ca. 1770	*Antiques* 89 (June 1966): 779	
Cann	?	crest, a talbot's head erased; (+)		ca. 1780	Christie's, 12 June 1982, lot 36	
Cann	?	?		ca. 1775	*Antiques* 72 (December 1957): 504	
Caster	B	Gov.ʳ Pitkin/to/PW	Gov. William Pitkin	1766–69	American Art Association–Anderson Galleries, 3 April 1937, lot 248	
Two casters	B*	Green crest, a woodpecker pecking at a tree stump; G/IH	Joshua and Hannah (Storer) Green	1765	Buhler/Hood 1970, no. 272	YUAG
Caster	B	Dana crest, a fox	Dana family	ca. 1765	YUAG files	
Caster	?	AK		ca. 1770	Parke-Bernet, 17 May 1968, lot 166	
Creampot	A*	Storer crest, a talbot's head		ca. 1770	DAPC 68.3206	MMA
Creampot	B†	G/WM; E.B.D./to E.A.P. (later)		ca. 1775	Johnston 1994, 50	CMA

	Mark	Inscription	Patron	Date	Reference	Owner
Creampot	B*	L/GE (+)		ca. 1775	Eitner 1976, no. 47	
Ladle	A	Dudley crest; MC	Dudley family	ca. 1765	MFA 1911, no. 432	
Porringer	A*	SW (cipher)	Sarah Wheat	ca. 1775		LAM
Porringer (with mark of Samuel Edwards)	A	H/SL		ca. 1760	*Antiques* 100 (August 1971): 162	
Porringer	A	W/IS		ca. 1760	MFA 1911, no. 431	
Porringer	A	(unidentified later engraving)		ca. 1775	Anderson Galleries, 7–12 January 1924, lot 854	
Two salts	B	WP		ca. 1770		BBC
Salt spoon	B*	MR		ca. 1780	Belden 1980, 152 (mark	WM
Snuffbox and trowel	B	Mary Smith (later)		ca. 1765	Sander 1982, no. 7 (as John Edwards)	SPNEA
Spout cup	A	R. Leonard/1782	R. Leonard	1782	DAPC 68.3359	MMA
Strainer	A	?		ca. 1770	MFA 1911, no. 433	
Sugar bowl (missing cover)	A	TW		ca. 1765	*Moore Collection* 1980, no. 159	
Two tablespoons	A†	Q/IA	Josiah and Ann Quincy	ca. 1770	Buhler 1972, appendix no. 20	MFAB
Tablespoon	A*	H/JJ		ca. 1780		YUAG
Tablespoon	A*	Church/in/Brattle/Street.	Brattle Street Church, Boston	ca. 1765	Buhler 1972, no. 425	MFAB
Six tablespoons	A	IW		ca. 1770	Buhler 1972, appendix no. 19	MFAB
Tablespoon	B*	HW (?; partially erased)		ca. 1770		YUAG
Tankard	A*	Jackson arms, quarterly 4 escallops, and crest, an escallop; SH	Jackson family	ca. 1770	Puig et al. 1989, no. 215	MIA
Tankard	A*	Porter arms, sable 3 bells, and crest, a bird with a sprig in its beak; MP	Mary (Porter) Edwards	ca. 1770	Buhler/Hood 1970, no. 271	YUAG
Tankard	A	The Gift of [Jo]nathan Buterfield to the Second Church [of Chr]ist in Cambridge 1769. (partially obliterated)	Jonathan Butterfield and/or First Congregational Parish, Arlington, Mass.	1769	Jones 1913, 7–8	
Teapot	A	HC		ca. 1770	MFA 1911, no. 435	

	Mark	Inscription	Patron	Date	Reference	Owner
Teapot	A*	ED (+)		ca. 1770	Avery 1920, no. 100	MMA
Teaspoon	B*	RA		ca. 1780	Flynt/Fales 1968, 212 (mark only)	HD
Two teaspoons	B	MG		ca. 1775	DAPC 68.3209	MMA
Teaspoon	B*	JAC		ca. 1780	Johnston 1994, 51	CMA
Two teaspoons	B	MW		ca. 1775		HD
Teaspoon	B	DD		ca. 1780		YUAG
Teaspoon	?	F		ca. 1775	Green/ Holland 1973, no. 22	

1. RC 24:229; *Church in Brattle Square*, 160.
2. SCPR 49:562–63, docket 10842; 77:9–10, 44; 79:1; docket 9809; RC 9:162, 168; RC 24:48, 88; RC 28:22, 183; Roberts 1895, 1:373–74.
3. This was to be the elder Edwards's first marriage: he was wed again on 19 May 1763 to Hepzibah Small, in a ceremony performed by Rev. Charles Chauncy of Boston's First Church; see RC 30:48.
4. SCD 76:151–52.
5. Buhler 1951, 292.
6. MCD 64:312–13.
7. SCD 97:122–23.
8. SCPR, docket 12962.
9. SCD 115:39.
10. Buhler 1972, no. 424.
11. RC 16:199.
12. Pruitt 1978, 32–33.
13. RC 29:323, 327.
14. "Assessors' 'Taking-Books,'" 36.
15. SCPR 82:365–66.
16. Eitner 1976, no. 67.

Samuel Edwards
1705–62

A

B

Samuel Edwards was born on 21 June 1705, the fourth son of John Edwards (q.v.) and Sybil (Newman) Edwards (1670–1739) and younger brother of Thomas Edwards (q.v.). Samuel probably trained in his father's shop and began working about 1726. He married Sarah Smith (1704–75), daughter of William (1666/67–1730), a merchant, and Abigail (Fowle) Smith (1679–1760) of Charlestown, Massachusetts, on 4 October 1733. The couple had no children.[1]

Samuel Edwards's name is notably absent from the recorded Boston deeds. His father evidently provided him with a brick house in Hanover Street that was later bequeathed to him.[2] The initial deed described a three-story brick house with its gable end on the street. The lot was only 22 feet in width and 380 feet deep, and the house had three rooms on each floor.[3] Two of the rooms on the first floor evidently were used for the shop, as only one "lower" room, used as a parlor, is mentioned in Samuel Edwards's inventory. Edwards also had a warehouse, and the executor's account of his estate mentions a "Shop in friend Street," "the Store at yᵉ Lower End of the Ground," and "a building at yᵉ lower End of yᵉ Ground."

Samuel Edwards's inventory indicates that he had a vast array of goods

C

D

E

F

G

available in the shop, including whistles and toys and a large stock of wrought silver and tools.[4] The large number of toys and the large inventory of goldsmiths' supplies that Edwards had in his possession at the time of his death suggest that the sale of these items made up a major portion of his business. In 1749 he sold pliers, tongs, a draw iron, a black pot, crucibles, wire, sandpaper, pumice, and other tools and goldsmiths' supplies to John Touzell (q.v.) of Salem, Massachusetts, for £26.9.10.[5] Edwards appears several times in the accounts kept by his merchant brother-in-law Isaac Smith, but these transactions suggest only that they did business together, not that Edwards was involved in broader mercantile activities.[6]

Edwards kept a framed rendering of the goldsmiths' arms in his parlor and consistently identified himself as a goldsmith throughout his life.[7] His extant silver is conservative in form and decoration, but some objects bear elegant rococo engraving that may have been done in his shop. In spite of the evidence that Edwards had a large silversmithing business, only a few bills survive from his shop. In 1746 he sold a silver hilted sword to Isaac Smith for £22.15, and a number of surviving objects by Edwards were made for Smith, who was a major patron.[8] In 1739 Edwards advertised that he had in his possession a large silver spoon that was stolen.[9] Samuel Edwards used several marks on his silver, including four variations on his initials, SE, crowned, over a device in shield (A–D) as well as three simpler marks: SE in a rectangle (E), SE in an ellipse (F), and S·E in an ellipse (G).[10] Immediate family members numbered among his clients, including his mother-in-law Abigail (Fowle) (Smith) Edwards. Some of his relatives were his best customers, for example, Joshua and Hannah (Storer) Green and Ebenezer Storer.

Edwards interacted with a number of other goldsmiths. Between 1746 and 1752 Edwards trained his ward Ebenezer Austin (q.v.), and between 1751 and 1758 he trained his nephew Joseph Edwards, Jr. (q.v.). He may also have trained John Coburn (q.v.), his nephew by marriage, and Daniel Parker (q.v.), both of whom witnessed a deed for him on 13 September 1746.[11] Parker also witnessed the will of Seth Coburn with Edwards in 1752 and bought tools from Edwards's estate.[12] Francis Hill Bigelow suggested that Edwards might have trained his nephew by marriage, Nathaniel Austin (q.v.).[13] In 1748 Edwards was one of the appraisers of the estate of Nathaniel Morse (q.v.), which owed him £1.19. Edwards also appraised the estates of William Cowell, Jr., and William Breed's (qq.v.) father in 1761.[14] The watchmaker Richard Cranch (q.v. Appendix A) also purchased goods from Edwards's estate. Edwards also had a close relationship with his nephew by marriage Zachariah Brigden (q.v.) and witnessed a deed for him in 1758.[15] Samuel Edwards was very active in town affairs. He served as one of the clerks of the market between 1748 and 1751. In 1752 he was elected an assessor, and he served in that capacity until his death in 1762.[16] He became a member of the Brattle Street Church in 1736, where he and his brother Joseph inherited their father's pew in 1746.[17]

After her husband's Charlestown house was sold in 1735, Sarah Edwards's mother, Abigail (Fowle) Smith, evidently resided for a time with her daughter and son-in-law. The papers in the estate of William Smith indicate that Samuel Edwards received the portions of the estate that were allocated to his wife and to his mother-in-law. Edwards also managed some of his mother-in-law's rents and loans for her and collected wages for hiring out her slave Caesar.[18] Edwards and other heirs of Smith sold a Charlestown wharf in 1733 and a house in 1742.[19] Abigail (Fowle) Smith married Samuel Edwards's father,

John, in 1740. John Edwards died in 1746, and Abigail (Smith) Edwards may have gone back to live with her daughter and son-in-law for the remaining years of her life.[20] The couple undoubtedly took special care of her, for Abigail Edwards's will, dated 11 June 1755, included the following bequest:

> I Give to my daughter Sarah Edwards my double dark silk damask gown, my black suit of bambazeen, my cloth riding hood, a chest of Drawers and table, six [c]ain chairs a small feather bed two glass sconces & a silver porringer. I also give to my son in law Samuel Edwards & his wife my said daughter Sarah Edwards the Sum of thirteen pounds Six shillings & eight pense lawfull Money in token of my remembrance of their Kindness to me.—[21]

Samuel Edwards and Isaac Smith were named as the executors of Abigail Edwards's estate. James Clark billed them on 15 January 1760 for funeral expenses for "their Mothers funeral."[22] On 13 September 1761 the estate paid Samuel Edwards £93.15.10 ½ for making ten gold rings and for providing seven pair of gloves for the mourners.[23] Sarah Edwards and her sister Mary Austin, mother of Ebenezer Austin, also received portions when their mother's widow's portion of the real estate of their father, William Smith, was divided in 1760.[24]

Samuel Edwards appears in the court records only three times. He was the plaintiff in a suit against the tailor George McEwen in 1735; and defendant, with several others, in two suits also filed in 1735, one filed by the yeoman Ichabod Paddock and the other by the housewright Everil Wakum.[25] He does not appear often in other court records, but he may have been peripherally involved in a court case in 1749.[26]

On 19 April 1762 the *Boston Gazette* recorded Edwards's death on 14 April:

> Last Wednesday Night died here after a few Days Illness of a violent Fever, in the 57th Year of his
> Age, Mr. SAMUEL EDWARDS, Goldsmith; who,
> for several Years has been one of the Assessors of the
> Town; and esteemed as a Man of Integrity; exact
> and faithful in all his Transactions: His Death is la-
> mented as a publick Loss.[27]

Edwards's incredibly detailed shop inventory is perhaps the most complete surviving inventory for any eighteenth-century craftsman and includes not only at least three benches' worth of silversmiths' tools, but also an inventory of the contents of his desk and bookcase and a complete listing of the books in his possession. Recorded among the books, which were valued at £28.7.11, were "1 New Touchstone for Silv^r," "1 Comp^t. Tradesman 2 vol," "1 Quarles's Emblems," and "a flower book."

According to the inventory in the estate papers, the appraisers of the estate were Thomas Simpkins, possibly Thomas Barton Simpkins (q.v.), Joseph Bradford, and John Coburn; however, the inventory recorded in the probate court record book lists the appraisers as William Simpkins (q.v.), Joseph Bradford, and John Coburn. The inventory reads as follows:

The Appriment of the Estate of Samuel
Edwards Late of Boston Goldsmith Dec^d
Taken in June 1762 ℞ Messrs Thos Simpkins
Joseph Bradford & John Coburn Apprizers

Viz.^t

1 Great forging Anvil — w.^d 120.^{lb} — @ 10^d £.	5.	0.	0
1 Pair Large Bellows	1.	0.	0
1 Large Melting Skillet	1.	4.	0
1 Bench Vise	1.	0.	0
1 Brass Hollowing Stamp	0.	13.	4
1 Mould for a Spoon tin	0.	8.	0
3 Pair Brass flasks	2.	5.	0
1 Simmet Bullet	0.	2.	6
1 Pr Drawing tongs	0.	6.	0
3 Flat bottom Stakes @4/	0.	12.	0
5 Round bottom D^o & a Gibbet D^o	1.	0.	0
3 Castor punches	0.	18.	0
1 Large Spoon punch & tea spoon D^o	0.	6.	0
2 Ingots & 2 p.^r tongs	0.	10.	0
7 Small Anvils & a Sparhawk	1.	10.	0
1 Heart & hand ring Swage & 3 D^o	1.	0.	0
2 Shells & Handle for tea Spoons, 2 Salt Shovels & 3 Punches }	0.	9.	4
4 Hollowing punches 1 Bell D^o & 1 Cutting punch }	0.	4.	0
3 Bead punches & 3 hollowing D.^o	0.	6.	0
1 Small Sparhawk & Chisell	0.	6.	0
3 pair round plyers	0.	4.	0
2 p.^r Watch plyers, 2 p.^r flat tongs & 1 p.^r smal tongs	0.	4.	0
2 p.^r Charg^g. tongs, 1 p.^r Spring D^o & 1 p.^r Sm.^{ll} Forg^g. D^o	0.	4.	0
4 Square Tribblets	0.	6.	0
3 Burnishers 4/. 2 Hand vises 3/. 1 Drawing Iron 4/	0.	11.	0
1 Framd Saw 3/ 3 p.^r Shears 3/4 4 p.^r Compasses 2/8^d	0.	9.	0
1 Wooden Screw & woods 1/4 1 Shrinker & Strainers 8/	0.	9.	4
22 Buckle Punches, 2 Sm.^{ll} Chissels & 6 Engravers	1.	0.	0
20 Files 2/8^d. 2 Borax boxes, Wood Vise, 1 Simel block 3/	0.	5.	8
2 Boiling pans w.^d 15.^{lb} @ 1/4^d	1.	0.	0
3 Raising Anvils, 1 Teast & Large hammers weighed 121.^{lb} @ 1/. }	6.	1.	0
3 Hollowing Hammars	0.	7.	0
5 Forging D^o 8/. 22 Hammars 32/.	2.	0.	0
4 Spoon tins w.^d 14.^{lb} & ½ @ 6^d	0.	7.	3
A parcel pewter patterns	0.	18.	0
	£ 33.	6.	5
1 Glass Case 20/. 2 Raising Anvils & 1 Teast.w.^d 70^{lb}: 70/	4.	10.	0
1 p.^r Flasks 20/. 2 Bottom Stakes 6/	1.	6.	0
1 Large Drawing Iron 6/8 1–8 Square Tribblet 3/	0.	9.	8
1 p.^r Shears 2/. 11 Hammars 14/8^d	0.	16.	8
4 Cutting punches 5/4 5 Brushes 3/4	0.	8.	8
3 Nests Large Crucibles @ 1/2 ½	0.	3.	[illeg.]
Sold to Mr Loring 7.14.7 ½	41.		[illeg.]
Sum bro.^t over	£41.	1.	0 ½
1 Large Boiling pan @ 1/4^{lb}			
1 small raising anvil 8/ 1 p.^r Draw^g. tongs 4/	0.	12.	0

3 Bottom Stakes 10/ 3 Spoon punches 12/	1.	2.	0
1 Olive Oyl Stone 1/ 1 Large Iron Ladle 2/	0.	3.	0
1 p.^r Drawing Iron 1/ 1 p.^r Nealing Tongs 1/	0.	2.	0
1 Sodering Iron & Copper 1/4.^d	0.	1.	4
4 Hammers 9/. 1 p.^r Round plyers 8.^d	0.	9.	8
3 Chissells 3/. 1 Ring Swage 6/. 1 Tankard D^o 3/	0.	12.	0
1 Small Teast 6/ 2 Blowpipes 1 p^r Shears,	0.	14.	0
2 p.^r Charger 1 Sm.^{ll} Vise, 2 brushes & 1 p.^r Nippers 8/ }			
1 Iron Ladle & 1 p.^r Nealing tongs	0.	3.	0
2 Hammers 4/ 1 Shovel 1/4.^d 1 Skin & frame 3/	0.	8.	4
1 Large Ingot 4/ 1 Block & 3 Stools 5/	0.	9.	0

$$31^{lb}. 1/4$$

2 Raising Anvils & Porringer Anvil @ 12^{d lb}.	1.	11.	3
1 Eight Square Tribblet & top for a pepper box	0.	8.	10
1 Beam Compass 4/. 3 Hammers 6/.	0.	10.	0
1 Round tribblet 1/4.^d 3 Drawing Irons 8/	0.	9.	4
1 Round bottom Stake, Cutting punch & hollowing } punch 2/8^d	0.	2.	8
1 Small Screw plate & fram'd Saw	0.	4.	0
2 Crooked files & Sieve 1/4.^d 1 Burnisher 3/. Oil stone 4/.	0.	8.	4
1 Bilbow & stock 1 Simmel Bullet	0.	3.	0
1 Large forging anvil w.^d 144^{lb} – – – @ 10^{d lb}.	5.	10.	0
2 Iron Rings for a forge	0.	2.	0
1 Soldering Kettle @ 10.^{d lb} w.^t	0.	3.	0
1 Old Brass Kettle – – @ 10.^{d lb} w.^t	0.	3.	0
1 p.^r Brass flasks 20/ 2 p.^r Large Iron D^o 8/	1.	8.	0
3 p.^r Iron D^o	0.	4.	0
1 Lead Glue pot – @6.^{d lb}	0.	3.	0
2 Tin Limmel pans 6/. 1 Large Ingot 6/	0.	12.	0
1 Large Iron Ladle 2/. 1 D^o. 1/4.^d 1 p.^r Iron screws 8/.	0.	11.	4
5 p.^r forging tongs 6/8.^d 5 p.^r D^o. Smaller 5/.	0.	11.	8
1 p.^r Casting tongs 1/. 1 p.^r nealing D^o. 1/.	0.	2.	0
1 p.^r Small Iron Screws	0.	6.	0
1 Large Hammer – @ 8.^{d lb}	0.	2.	0
4 Large planishing D^o. @3/	0.	12.	0
2 Forging D^o 4/. 3 Raising D^o 3/	0.	7.	0
4 Hollowing D^o. 12/ 1 Large Swage 3/	0.	15.	0
11 Swages @ 1/4.^d 14/8 12 Small Hammers 12/.	1.	6.	8
22 Hammers 29/4 12 Old D^o. 12/.	2.	1.	4
1 Brass D^o. 1/4.^d 1 Drawing bench 12/	0.	13.	4
1 Large Spoon Teast w.th Long Swages w.^t @ 12.^{d lb}	0.	15.	0
2 D^o Smaller @ 12.^{d lb}	1.	0.	0
3 Wooden bowls 1/4.^d 1 Brass w.^t 2/.2 p^r L:Shears 2/.	0.	5.	4
a parcel old files 3/.2 Mugs w.th Cov.^r 8.^d 1 Ring Swage 3/		6.	8
6 Raising Anvils – @ 1/.^{d lb}	1.	16.	0
3 Belly pot D^o. @1/.^{lb}	1.	0.	0
[torn] Sparhawks @1/4.^d	0.	18.	
Sum Carried forward	71.	8.	3 [torn]
Sum bro.^t forward	£71.	8.	3¹/₂
4 Snarling Irons – @ 2/	0.	8.	0
1 Stake to planish a cann 4/ 1 D^o 2/	0.	6.	0

	£	s	d
3 D.° for a Milk 4/ 2 Small Bole Stakes 2/8^d	o.	6.	8
1 [illeg.] Gibbet Stake 3/. 1 D.° 2/	o.	5.	o
1 Large flat bottom Stake	o.	4.	o
2 D.° Smaller 6/. 4 D.° Smaller 4/.	o.	10.	o
1 Large Soop Spoon punch	o.	6.	o
7 Large Spoon punches @ 2/8	o.	18.	8
2 Childs D.° 4/. 10 Tea Spoon D.° 13/4^d	o.	17.	4
2 Salt D.° 2/8.^d 2 Eight Square Castor D.° 4/.	o.	6.	8
5 D.° Smaller 5/. 2 Bottom punches for Castors & 2 tops 4/.	o.	9.	o
1 Punch for a Punch Ladle	o.	4.	o
1 Sand bag & brush 4.^d 18 Hollowing punches 9/	o.	9.	4
21 Cutting punches 21/.	1.	1.	o
3 Pricket punches & 2 Earing D° 1/4^d	o.	1.	4
6 Chissells in a tin Box	o.	2.	o
2 Iron Kettles 3/. 1 Hang.^g Candlestick & Trammel 4/	o.	7.	o
1 Drill Stock 8.^d Gimblets & 1/. 1 Lamp 1/4.^d	o.	3.	o
4 Small Laths 5/4 1 fram'd Saw 1/4^d	o.	6.	8
2 Iron Mortars & pestles @ 2.^{d lb} w^t	o.	6.	o
1 Brass Stamp for Castor tops	o.	4.	o
1 Large Pile of weights	o.	6.	o
1 Smaller D.° 2/. 1 Out Side w.^t 2/.	o.	4.	o
1 p.^r Brass Scales 1/4.^d 1 p.^r Smaller D.° & w.^{ts} 2/	o.	3.	4
62 Punches 4/ 6 clasp punches 6/. 3 button D.° 3/.	o.	13.	o
1 Punch for Whistle 1/4 1 Small Spoon Teast 3/	o.	4.	4
1 Small Spoon Swage 1/ 1 Cannister Square ^{top} Punch 2/	o.	3.	o
3 Marrow Spoon punches	o.	3.	o
10 Bole Stakes 6/8.^d 10 Swages 6/8^d	o.	13.	4
8 Small Bottom Stakes 4/.	o.	4.	o
1 Spangle Stamp 2/. 1 Deaths Head Swage 2/.	o.	4.	o
3 Box Vises 3/. 11 Drawing irons 13/4	o.	16.	4
5 pair Compasses 5/. 4 p.^r Nippers 3/.	o.	8.	o
11 Money Stamps 1/. 10 Simmet blocks 3/2	o.	4.	2
1 Box of Punches 6/8.^d 1 D.° 1/. D.° 2/.	o.	9.	8
2 D.° 1/. 1 D.° 2/. 1 Sett D.° 2/. 1 Box D.° 2/. 1 D.° 1/.	o.	8.	o
2 – 8 Square tribblets & a broken one	o.	1.	o
1 Draw w.th Chasing punches	o.	12.	o
1 Screw plate 1/4 50 files 6/8^d	o.	8.	o
21 Engravers 2/8.^d 5 p.^r flat Tongs 2/8^d	o.	5.	4
4 Pair Screw Compasses 3/.	o.	3.	o
6 p.^r Round plyers 4/. 2 p.^r Spring D.° 2/	o.	6.	o
4 p.^r Watch plyers & 1 p^r Nippers 3/.	o.	3.	o
4 p.^r Old Shears 1/4.^d 9 Vises 8/	o.	9.	4
Brass patterns of Spoons & 1/4.^d 2 Oyl Stands 1/.	o.	2.	4
1 Drill bow & Stock 1/4 13 Strainers 1/6.^d	o.	2.	10
1 Wooden thing for Sand 1/. 7 Tribblets 2/8.^d	o.	3.	8
Sum Carried Over	£ 87	[torn]	
Sum bro.^t over	87.	10.	7^{1/2}
1 Drill Stock 2/. 1 Load Stone 1/.	o.	3.	o
1 Small Vise 6/. 1 D.° 10/. 5 Mallets 6.^d	o.	16.	6

8 Old Hammers 8/.3 D.º 9/. 1 Stand.ᵍ Vise 2/		0. 19.	0
1 Brass Spoon Tin 4/. 1 D.º Crackt 2/		0. 6.	0
2 Wooden Screws 2/8.ᵈ		0. 2.	8
1 Raising Anvill @ 8.ᵈ ˡᵇ w.ᵗ 60ˡᵇ		2. 0.	0
1 Iron bolt for a Window 2/ 1 Old Hatchet 8ᵈ		0. 2.	8
1 Brass Mortar & pestle 2/6		0. 2.	6
3 Boiling pans & 1 Copper pot @ 1/4ˡᵇ		0. 4.	0
Pewter & Lead mixt @6.ᵈ ˡᵇ		0. 4.	0
1 Brass rule 2/. 2 Brass Candle Sticks ⎫		0. 5.	0
1 w.ᵗ & 2 p.ʳ Scissors ⎭ 3/			
1 Draw w.ᵗʰ a flower book &c		0. 1.	4
8 Burnishers in a Draw & 2 pollish.ᵍ Stones 7/		0. 7.	0
1 Case of Draws where the patterns are		0. 4.	0
The Patterns in it @ 1/..ˡᵇ		0. 3.	0
1 Case of Draws 1/4 The patterns in it @8.ᵈ ˡᵇ		0. 3.	0
1 Block 1/4 3 Stools 2/. 1 Case w.ᵗʰ 9 draws 2/.		5.	4
14 Hanger blades & 2 Sword D.º @ 2/.		1. 12.	0
1 Case Draws w.ᵗʰ a door 4/.		0. 4.	0
1 Moulding box w.ᵗʰ draws		0. 1.	4
Patterns in the Moulding box @ 8.ᵈ ˡᵇ		0. 8.	
2 Bolts 3/. 3 Boxes 1/. 1 Bird Cage 2/.		0. 6.	0
1 Tobacco Knife 1/ 1 Lath 6/. 1 D.º Largr 12/		0. 19.	0
1 Grind Stone 1/. 2 Setts Draws 2/		0. 3.	0
Patterns in the Draws @ 1/4.ᵈ ˡᵇ		0. 1.	4
1 Screw plate 2/. 1 Drill Stock 1/		0. 3.	0
1 Small Iron Lath 1/4.ᵈ 3 Crooked files 1/		0. 2.	4
1 Box Vise 8/. 1 Drawing Swage & Swages 2/		0. 10.	0
1 Augur 1/. 1 Small Screw plate 1/4.ᵈ		0. 2.	4
1 Saw & Gimblet		0. 1.	0
		98. 12.	7¹/₂

In the Press — in the Room

7 Doz. Babes	@ 1/Doz.		0. 7.	0
3 D.º Trunks	@ 1/Doz.		0. 3.	0
1 Doz. Swords (wooden)	1/ doz.		0. 12.	0
22 [illeg.] Doz.&⁸ Paper back pictures	0/8ᵈ doz.		0. 15.	1
5 Doz. Looking Glasses	0/8 doz.		0. 3.	4
7 Doz.&² Small pictures	0/4 doz. 2/5		0. 2.	5
5 Doz. Trumpetts Tin & wood	1/0 doz.		0. 5.	0
21 Doz: Screw boxes Sorted	10ᵈ doz.		0. 17.	6
1 Doz. Boxes Nine pins	8ᵈ box		0. 8.	0
44 Single boxes of Different Toys	2ᵈ box		0. 7.	4
39 Single Glass Watches	3.ᵈ piece		0. 9.	9
52 Doz Lead Toys	4.ᵈ Doz		0. 17.	4
7 Doz Box Wood Combs	4/doz.		1. 8.	0
45 Bags of Hair buttons	4/bagg		9. 0.	0
16 Gross of Black horn Buttons G&Sm.ˡˡ	3/ᵍʳᵒˢˢ		2. 8.	0
2 Doz Pocket Glasses	6/doz		0. 12.	0
7 Doz Wood Toys viz.ᵗ Birds & Babes	.1/dz		0. 7.	0
2 Doz Boxes Sorted	3/dz		0. 6.	0
3 & ¹/₂ Doz Tops	2/dz		0. 7.	0

Item	Rate	£	s	d
4 Gross & 9 Doz Cotton & Thread Laces	6/gross	1	8	6
1 & ½ Doz Silk Ditto	8ᵈ doz	0	1	0
[illeg.] Doz & ½ Toys Sorted in a great Box	4ᵈ doz.	0	1	6
3 Doz Whistles	8ᵈ doz	0	2	0
3 Doz Tin Ditto	8ᵈ doz	0	2	0
10 Doz Bird Calls	2ᵈ doz.	0	1	8
10 Doz Lead Watches	6ᵈ doz	0	5	0
3 Doz Tin Toys	6ᵈ doz	0	1	6
6 Doz Pewter Ditto	2/dz	0	12	0
7 Doz Porringers & Dishes	2ᵈ dz	0	1	2
22 Coaches &c	@8ᵈ pʳ	0	14	8
15 Pair Hand Vises	1/8 pʳ	1	5	0
5 pʳ Dᵒ Better	4/ pʳ	1	0	0
10 Pair Dᵒ not so good	1/3 pʳ	0	12	6
1 Doz Plyers	12/Dz.	0	12	0
13 Ditto	1/.pʳ	0	13	0
6 pʳ Ditto	1/ pʳ	0	6	0
1 Doz. pʳ Watch Plyers	14/ doz	0	14	0
14 pair Ditto better	1/ pʳ	0	14	0
4 pʳ Dᵒ best Sort	2/ pʳ	0	8	0
10 pʳ Sliding Tongs	2/ pʳ	1	0	0
9 pʳ Screw Compasses	1/6 pʳ	0	13	6
11 Doz Engravers	1/4 dz.	0	14	8
2 Doz Freezing Punches	8/ dz.	0	16	0
3 Pair Nippers 2/pʳ 3 Dᵒ better	3/6 pʳ	0	16	6
6 Burnishers 8ᵈ pᶜ 2 Dᵒ	3/ pᶜ	0	10	0
5 Pair Shears	@ 2/0 pʳ	0	10	0
6 Pair Dᵒ Larger			16	
3 Pair Dᵒ Small 1/pʳ Dᵒ 1/pʳ		0	4	0
Sum Carried Over		35	[torn]	
Sum broᵗ Over		35	11	11
4 Pair Shears	1/4 pʳ	0	5	4
5 Drawing Irons	@5/ 3 pʳ dᵒ 2/pʳ	1	11	0
1 Screw Plate	6/	0	6	0
1 Drawing Iron	3/	0	3	0
5 Sparhawks	16/	4	0	0
15 Hammers	3/	1	10	0
6 Hollowing Stamps	at 8/pᶜ	2	8	0
1 Thimble Stamp	40/	2	0	0
8 Setts Weights	2/sett	0	16	0
2 Nests Dᵒ 16.ᵒᶻ	6/nest	0	12	0
6 Ditto . 8.ᵒᶻ	4/	1	4	0
11 Ditto 4.ᵒᶻ	3/nest	1	13	0
8 Ditto . 2.ᵒᶻ	2/	0	16	0
1 Ring Swage	2/	0	2	0
6 Doz Needle files	1/4ᵈᶻ	0	8	0
4 Doz Ink Cases	8ᵈ dᶻ	0	2	8
14 Boxwood Comb Brushes	1/4ᵈᶻ	0	18	8
12 Doz Large Files	6/dᶻ	3	12	0

12 Doz Ditto	2/6^{dz}	1.	10.	0
12 Doz Small Ditto	2/^{dz}	1.	4.	0
16 Doz Clockmakers files	2/d^z	1.	12.	0
12 Doz & 5 doz. d^o. Small Ditto	2/d^z	1.	14.	0
12 Doz Small Ditto	1/6d^z	0.	18.	0
4 gross & 1 Doz: Sm^{ll} files	8/gross	1.	12.	8
2 Doz & 9 Ditto	3/d^z	0.	8.	3
3 Doz Ditto Flemish	4^{d}dz	0.	1.	0
10 Doz & 8 Smooth Files	8/dz	4.	5.	4
1 Scratch Brush	1/4	0.	1.	4
7 Doz & 10 Snuff Boxes	2/doz	0.	15.	8
4 Doz & 5 D^o. Larger	2/d^z	0.	8.	10
1 Doz & 10 D^o.	2/d^z	0.	3.	8
3 Doz & 4 Flower'd D^o.	2/4d^z	0.	7.	9
3 Doz & 5 Larger	2/6	0.	8.	6
3 Blow Pipes	8^d peice	0.	2.	0
41 Dish Matts	6^d peice	1.	0.	6
3 Dress'd Babes & 1 Negro	1/peice	0.	3.	0
5 Boxes Scales at 6/8	at 6/8	1.	13.	4
6 Ditto Smaller	at 4/	1.	4.	0
5 Ditto Smaller	at 4/	1.	0.	0
2 Spoon Teasts w^d 45^{lb}	at 1/^{lb}	2.	5.	0
1 Ingotts	2/	0.	2.	0
2 Skilletts	at 20/p^c	2.	0.	0
1 p^r Tongs				
10 & [illeg.] ^{lb} fine Wier	1/8^{lb}	0.	16.	8
10 & [illeg.] ^{lb} D^o. Larger	1/	0.	10.	0
15^{lb} Large D^o.	8^d	0.	10.	0
12^{lb} & 1/4 Brass D^o.	2/4	1.	8.	7
Pepper	at 1/4	0.	6.	9
9 ^{lb} Alspice	8^d	0.	6.	0
Powder blue 60^{lb}	1/^{lb}	3.	0.	0
		82.	13.	8

In the Press next the Shop		82.	13.	8
20 Peices none so pretty	at 6^d p^c	0.	10.	0
60 p^s Tape Sorted	at 12^d	3.	0.	0
35 p^s Stay tape	3^d	0.	8.	9
38 p^s Bobbin	2^d p^c	0.	6.	4
16 Skains Silk Cord	1/4	1.	1.	4
5 peices Diaper tapes	10^d	0.	4.	2
16 peices Coarse D^o.	8^d	0.	10.	8
30 D^o. fine Narrow tapes	8^d	1.	0.	0
8 peices D^o. wider	10^d	0.	6.	8
3 peices D^o. finer	12^d p^c	0.	3.	0
3 peices white braid	1/4	0.	4.	0
38 peices worsted cord	1/4	2.	10.	8
8 peice Coarse Narrow tape	12^d	0.	8.	0
13 peice Coarse tape	2/p^c	1.	6.	0
1 p^c Ditto wider	2/2	0.	2.	2
5 Bags Cherryderry buttons	at 1/bagg	0.	5.	0

		£	s	d
16 Gross Stay Buckles	1/gross	0.	16.	0
1 Gross Stay hooks	12/gross	0.	12.	0
29 pair Stay buckles	1^d		2.	5
93 Cards Metal Sleeve buttons	3^d Card	1.	3.	3
55 Cards Glass Ditto	2^d	0.	9.	2
91 & ½ Doz Rings	at 2/Doz.	9.	3.	0
18 p^r Scissors best Sort	8^d	0.	12.	0
18 p^r D^o not so good	6^d	0.	9.	0
10 p^r D^o	8^d	0.	0.	8
2 Doz. D^o	6^d p^r		12.	0
4 Doz D^o Ordinary	1/4 d^z		5.	4
1 Doz Needle Cases	2/	0.	2.	0
10 Pewter Rattles	4^d	0.	3.	4
3 Gross Black Hooks & Eyes	2^d gross	0.	0.	6
52 p^r bone Knives & forks	1^d p^r	0.	4.	4
3 Doz Iron Jews Harps	8^d doz.	0.	2.	0
33 Doz & 9 pewter Tea Spoons	1/doz.	1.	13.	9
7 Hard Metal Spoons	2^d p^c	0.	1.	2
19 Tea Strainers	2^d	0.	3.	2
50 Setts Penny weights	3^d	0.	12.	6
156 Setts grain weights	5^d	3.	5.	0
48 Setts Apothecary D^o	3^d	0.	12.	0
6 Doz Rowels for spurs	8^d doz.	0.	4.	0
16.^{lb} Coll^d Threads	2/2^{lb}	1.	14.	8
3 & ½ ^{lb} Coarse white D^o	3/^{lb}	0.	10.	6.
3 & ½ ^{lb} Spanish Silk	40^{lb}/	7.	0.	0
2 .^{lb} 15 ^{oz} Bellandine D^o	50/	7.	6.10$^{1/2}$	
9 Doz & 5 pair Metal bow'd Spectacles	2/6^{doz}	1.	3.	6
14 Pair Joynted D^o	6^d	0.	7.	0
6 Pair Leather D^o	4^d	0.	2.	0
23 Pair Tin & horn D^o	2/6 doz	0.	4.9$^{1/2}$	
Sum Carried forward		£135.	0 [torn]	
Sum brought forward		135.	0.	4
7 Doz & 5 p^r Scissors	at 6/d^z	2.	4.	0
4 Gross Shirt Buttons	1/gross	0.	4.	0
4 & ½ Gross Waiscot D^o	1/6 gross	0.	6.	9
8 Gross Shirt buttons in a draw	1/	0.	8.	0
13 Doz Bath Thimbles	1/0 doz	0.	13.	0
2 Gross & [illeg.] Doz & 9 Brass D^o	8^d d^z	0.	18.	0
20 Doz. Taylors D^o	8^d doz	0.	13.	4
3 Doz. & 8 D^o Brass	8^d doz	0.	3.	4
19 Bath Thimbles in a draw	1/6 doz	0.	3.	0
52 Letter Cases	1^d peice	0.	4.	2
6 .^{lb} Putty	2/^{lb}	0.	12.	0
8 Doz Pins N° 4	12/doz	4.	16.	0
3 .^{lb} Pins N° 11	10/	1.	10.	0
1 ½.^{lb} D^o N° 12	10/8 doz	0.	16.	0
14000 Pins	10^d tho	0.	11.	8
10000 Mimikin D^o	1/tho	0.	10.	0
28000 Pins	1/tho	1.	8.	0

79 Papers Small Caulkers brass	3^d paper	o.	19.	3
8 Papers D?. Large d?. _____	3^d	o.	2.	o
18 pair Brass Buckles	10^d	o.	15.	o
3 Doz Pewter D?.	12^d doz	o.	3.	o
5 Doz Large D?.	1/4 doz	o.	6.	8
4 Doz Small D?.	4/doz	o.	16.	o
2 Doz Knee D?.___	1/4 doz	o.	2.	8
34 p^r heal Spurrs	4^d. p^r	o.	11.	4
3 Scail Boxes	at 8^d	o.	2.	o
1 Bottle Snuff	1/	£154.	19.	6
In the Shop		154.	19.	6
138 Pair Buckles N?. 1.	at 6^d p^r	3.	4.	o
272 D?._____ N?. 2.	3^d	3.	8.	o
115 D?._____ N?. 3	6^d	2.	17.	6
152 D?._____ N?. 4	4^d	2.	10.	6
193 D?._____ N?. 5	3^d	2.	8.	3
56 D?._____ N?. 6	6^d	1.	8.	o
12 Doz Knives Sorted	4/doz	2.	8.	o
2 Doz & 4 Razors	6/doz	o.	14.	o
4 Pair Spectacles & Cases	3/pr	o.	12.	o
5 Pair D?.	2/6 pr	o.	12.	6
5 Spect: Cases	@ 1/	o.	5.	o
3 Doz Horn Combs & Cases	4/ doz	o.	12.	o
28 Pair Scissars Sorted	3^d p^r	o.	7.	o
3 Doz & 4 Horn Combs Sorted	1/4 doz	o.	4.	5
6 Doz & 8 Ivory Ditto	6/ doz	2.	0.	o
11 Acomey Spoons	2^d p^c	o.	1.	10
4 Doz & 1/2 Tea Spoons	1/ doz	o.	4.	6
4 Pair Tongs	4^d p^r	o.	1.	4
4 Doz. & 7 Cork Screws	2/ doz	o.	9.	2
6 Reading Glasses	8^d p^c	o.	4.	o
5 D?. in a Box	1/2 p^c	o.	5.	10
22 pair Snuffers	2^d p^r	o.	3.	8
2 Doz Graters in Cases	2/ doz	o.	4.	o
6 Buckle Brushes	1/p^c	o.	6.	o
11 D?. not so good	6^d p^c	o.	5.	6
1 Doz pewter Spoons	2/doz	o.	2.	o
7 Hard Mettal	2^d p^c	o.	1.	2
33 Fans	8^d. p^c	1.	2.	o
3 & 1/2 ^{lb}. Knitting Needles	1/^{lb}	o.	3.	6
4 Fishing lines	4^d p^c	o.	1.	4
4 Pencil [illeg.] Steel Cases	6^d. p^c	1.	4.	o
10 Tweezers	2^d p^c	o.	1.	8
1 Doz. Tooth Brushes	2/ doz	o.	2.	o
4 Penknife Cases	1^d. p^c	o.	0.	4
9 Ink potts w.th Penknives	6^d. p^c	o.	4.	6
7 Horse Phlems	8^d. p^c	o.	4.	8
30 Knives & forks Different Sorts	N? 1:2^d p^c	o.	5.	o
37 D?._____ N?. 2	at 1^d. p^c	o.	3.	1
18 D?._____ N?. 3	4^d. p^c	o.	6.	o

21 Locks Scutcheons & Handles	3/	3.
2 Doz. Razors [crossed out]		
9 .^{lb} Cruels	6/^{lb}	2. 14. 0
5 .^{lb} 11 .^{oz} Silk & Hair	4/^{lb}	1. 2. 0
14 .^{oz} Twist	@ 8/^{lb}	0. 6. 6
17 .^{oz} Coarse Hair		4.
5 Pair Shapes	1/p^r	0. 5. 0.
17 p^s Button hole Bind^g	2/p^c	1. 14.
5 & ¼.^{lb} Black beads	4/^{lb}	1. 1. 0
8 & ½.^{lb} D^o.	2/^{lb}	0. 17. 0
Sum Carried forward		193. 10. [torn]
Sum Bro^t. forward		193. 10. 3
3 Pair Hose	at 3/p^r.	0. 9. 0
4 y^{ds}. & ¾ Blue Shalloon	1/4 y^d	0. 6. 4
4 y^{ds}. & ½ D^o.	1/4	0. 6. 0
5 y^{ds}. Coarser	1/	0. 5. 0
13 y^{ds}. & ½ Red Stuff	1/	0. 13. 6
7 y^{ds}. & ½ White D^o.	1/	0. 7. 6
8 y^{ds}. & ½ Speckled D^o.	1/	0. 8. 6
21 y^{ds}. & ¼ fustian	1/6	1. 11. 6
23 y^{ds}. D^o. better	2/ yds	2. 6. 0
2 Worsted Waiscoats	8/ p^c	0. 16. 0
3 Breeches	6/ p^r	0. 18. 0
6 y^{ds}. & ½ Glaz'd Linnen	1/4 y^{ds}	0. 8. 8
16 y^{ds}. Baze	1/4	1. 1. 4
12 y^{ds}. & ¾ White Fustian	1/4	0. 17. 0
13 y^{ds}. & ¾ plain D^o.	1/	0. 13. 9
12 y^{ds}. Coarse Diaper	8^d	0. 8. 0
19 y^{ds}. Linnens	1/4	1. 5. 4
7 y^{ds}. & ¼ D^o.	1/8	0. 12. 1
10 y^{ds}. D^o.	1/	0. 10. 0
27 y^{ds}. D^o.	1/4	1. 16. 0
7 y^{ds}. D^o.	1/4	0. 9. 4
10 & ¾ y^{ds}. D^o.	1/2	0. 12.6½
8 y^{ds}. & ¼ D^o.	1/4	0. 11. 0
3 y^{ds}. & ½ D^o.	1/2	0. 4. 1
5 y^{ds}. D^o.	1/8	0. 8. 4
13 y^{ds}. & ¼ D^o.	1/8	1. 2. 1
2 y^{ds}. & ½ D^o.	1/2	0. 2. 11
13 y^{ds}. & ¾ D^o. Corse	1/	0. 13. 3
16 y^{ds}. & ¾ D^o.	1/	0. 16. 9
7 y^{ds}. & ¾ D^o.	1/	0. 7. 9
86 & ½ y^{ds}. Crocus	1/y^{ds}	4. 16. 6
4 Silk Handkerchiefs	3/p^c	0. 12. 0
14 Silk Muslin D^o.	10^d p^c	0. 11. 8
9 Linnen D^o.	2/	0. 18. 0
9 D^o.	1/	0. 9. 0
6 D^o.	1/4	0. 8. 0
4 D^o.	8^d	0. 2. 8
4 D^o. stampt	1/	0. 4. 0

36 Cotton Handkerchiefs	1/p^c	1. 16. 0
9 y.^{d} & [illeg.] Checkt Linnen	1/4 yds	0. 12. 0
14 y.^{ds} D.^{o}	1/	0. 14. 0
15 y.^{ds} & 1/4 D.^{o}	1/2	0. 17.9$^{1/2}$
8 y.^{ds} D.^{o}	1/6	0. 12. 0
12 & 1/2 y.^{ds}. D.^{o}	1/	0. 12. 6
11 & 1/4 y.^{d} D.^{o}	1/6 y^d	0. 16.10$^{1/2}$
Sum Carried Forward		219. 0.9$^{1/2}$
Sum bro.^{t} forward		£219. 0.9$^{1/2}$
4 y.^{ds} & 1/4 Striped Holland	at 1/4 y^{ds}	0. 5. 8
3/4 50 y.^{ds} & 1/4 Oznabriggs	8^d	1. 13. 6
24 y.^{ds} D.^{o}	8^d y^{ds}	0. 16. 0
383 Doz. Buttons	2^d doz	3. 3. 10
109 D.^{o} & 6 buttons	2^d doz	0. 18. 2
1136 Doz. Coat Buttons	2^d doz	9. 9. 4
929 Doz. Waistcoat D.^{o}	1^d doz	3. 17. 5
704 Doz. & 1/2 Metall D.^{o}	2.^{d} doz	5. 17. 5
69 Doz. Ditto Gilt	4.^{d} doz	1. 3. 0
15 Doz. Coat Double Wash'd	8^d doz	0. 10. 0
34 Doz. Waiscoat D.^{o} D.^{o}	4^d doz	0. 11. 4
20 Tin peper Boxes	2^d p^c	0. 3. 4
11 Key Rings	2^d p^c	0. 1. 10
5 Hearth Brushes	8^d p^c	0. 3. 4
4 Boxes w.th hooks & Eyes	1/6 box	0. 6. 0
27 Sail Needles	[illeg.]	0. 2. 10
11 Awl Blades	1.^{d} p^c.	0. 0. 11
3 Parcells Needles	8^d	8
a Parcel of fish hooks D^o	8^d	8
11 Spectacle Cases	1^d p^c	0. 0. 11
9 Shoemakers Stamps	2^d	0. 1. 2
4 Peices Quality 18 y.^{ds} each	1/4 p^c	0. 5. 4
19 Parts of p.^{s} Quality	8^d p^c	0. 12. 8
4 parts of p.^{s} boot Straping	1 p^c	0. 4. 0
4 Oyl Stones	8^d p^c	0. 2. 8
14 Polishing D.^{o}	3.^{d} p.^{c}	0. 3. 6
45 Gimblets	1.^{d} p.^{c}	0. 3. 9
3 Tap Borers	3.^{d} p.^{c}	0. 0. 9
18 Perch Lines	3.^{d} p.^{c}	0. 4. 6
14 Lines	1.^{d} p.^{c}	0. 1. 2
2 & 1/2 Peices Gray Silk ferritts	3/p.^{c}	0. 7. 6
5 Coll.^{o} D.^{o} Ordinary	2/p.^{c}	0. 10. 0
11 p.^{ts}. 8 p.^{s} Silk Quality	3/p.^{c}	1. 4. 0
8 peices remn.^{ts} of ferritts & Galloons	2/p^c	0. 16. 0
17 p.^{c} Remn.^{ts} of Silk ferritts	3/2 p^c	2. 13. 10
85 y.^{ds} Remnants of Ribbons	6^d y^{ds}	2. 2. 6
1 p.^{c} Wide Black D.^{o}	18/p^c	0. 18. 0
110 y.^{ds} Narrow Ribbons	4.^{d} y^{ds}	1. 16. 8
138 y.^{ds} Ditto	2.^{d} y^{ds}	1. 3. 0
3 p.^{c} Pink & Cherry Ribbon	@ 6/	0. 18. 0
4 doz. Cotton & Silk ribbons	3/p^c	0. 12. 0

70 y.^{ds} figured ribbon remn.^{ts}	4^d y^{ds}	1.	3.	4
132 y.^{ds} Padusoy D.^{o}	6^d y^{ds}	3.	6.	0
3 Doz. Silk Girdles	1/6 doz	0.	4.	6
9 Parcel p.^{c} fine worsted Quality	1/3 p.^{c}	0.	11.	3
15 parts p.^{c} Shoe Bindings	7^d p^c	0.	8.	9
15 p.^{c} & p.^{t} of p.^{c} Garter [illeg.]	2/p^c	1.	10.	0
13 p.^{c} Narrow Silk ferretts	2/p^c	1.	6.	0
2 pair Shears	8^d p^r	0.	1.	4
Sum Caried forw.^{d}		£271.	0.	[torn]
In the Ware house		271.	9.	3$^{1/2}$
24 Doz Babes	at 1/ doz	1.	4.	0
4 Doz Trumpets	1/ doz	0.	4.	0
15 Doz Pewter Toys	4.^{d} doz	0.	5.	0
6 & ½ Doz Trunks	1/ doz	0.	6.	6
4 Doz Small Babes	1/ doz	0.	4.	0
20 & ½ Gross Lead Toys	3/gross	3.	1.	6
16 & ½ Doz Wood Rattles	3/gross	0.	4.	1$^{1/2}$
8 Doz D.^{o} Whistles	8^d doz	0.	1.	4
69 Doz Screw Boxes Sorted	10.^{d} doz	2.	17.	6
2 & ½ Doz. Birds	8^d doz	0.	1.	8
14 Doz. Trumpets	1/ doz	0.	14.	0
17 Doz Straw Rattles	1/ doz	0.	17.	0
3 & ½ Doz Basket D.^{o}	1/ doz	0.	3.	6
12 Single Bags Buttons	3/ bag	1.	16.	0
11 Brushes w.th Handles	4^d pc.^{s}	0.	3.	6
9 Ditto Smaller	4^d	0.	3.	0
7 D.^{o} painted backs	1.^{d}	0.	0.	7
5 D.^{o} plush backs	1.^{d}	0.	0.	5
4 Shoe brushes	2^d	0.	0.	8
8 Pails	6^d peice	0.	4.	0
fine Wier 9^{lb}	1/^{lb}	0.	9.	0
20 Quier Sand paper	at 2/	2.	0.	0
[illeg.] Sieves	@ 6^d	0.	1.	0
1–2 q.^{t} Measure	4/	0.	4.	0
1–1 q.^{t} Ditto	2/	0.	2.	0
1 New Teast w.^{t} 26.^{lb}	1/^{lb}	1.	6.	0
1 Small Anvill w.^{t} w.^{d}26^{lb}	1/^{lb}	1.	6.	0
17 & ½ Doz Blue potts N.º 1	4/ doz	3.	10.	0
29 Doz D.^{o}_____ N.º 2	5/ doz	7.	5.	0
3 Doz D.^{o}_____ N.º 3	6/ doz	0.	18.	0
2 Doz. & 10 D.^{o} N.º 4	7/ doz	0.	14.	0
3 Doz & 2 D.^{o} N.º 6	8/6 doz	1.	5.	4
2 Nests Small Crucibles	@ 4^d	0.	0.	8
17 D.^{o} Larger	8^d	0.	11.	4
14 D.^{o} 2 in a Nest	8^d	0.	9.	4
32 Single Crucibles large	4^d	0.	10.	8
3 Blue potts N.º 8	10^d	0.	2.	6
1 Bundle Wading	1/	0.	1.	0
19 p.^{r} Cards	1/8 p^r	1.	11.	8
1 p.^{r} Large Scales & weights	50/	2.	10.	0

Pumice Stone 210^{lb}	3.^{d} lb	2. 12. 6
Rotton Stone 58^{lb}	4^d lb	0. 19. 4
47 Quils	2^d	7. 10
4 Casks merchandise lost £16:18: 6 ^{Sterling} }		29. 6. 8
advance £12 pc^t 203: 2: 0 }		
£220. 0. 6 }		
1 glass Case		12
		342. 13. 5
		342. 13. 5
1 Scillit	21/4	1. 1. 4
2 Boxes with Nailes		8
1 old Brass Kettle 27^{lb}	@ 8$^{d\ lb}$	18. 0
		345. 0. 9

In the Shop Continued

a parcel of Rub Stones –at		3
4 m^d. 200 Small Nails	1/4 tho	0. 5. 7
3 m^d. D^o. Rusty	1/	0. 3. 0
5 m^d. Small Tacks	6^d	0. 2. 6
4 m^d. Small Brads ½ Tack	6^d	0. 2. 0
6 m^d. 2.^{d} D^o.	6^d	0. 3. 0
1000 3.^{d} D^o.	6^d	0. 0. 6
1800 4.^{d} D^o.	8^d tho	0. 1. 3
200 5.^{d} D^o.	3^d	0. 0. 6
391 & ½		
29 Doz Wire Shirt Ditto		
A Parcel Loose Buttons		
30 Doz Cotton Shirt D^o.		
3 Gross Shoemakers Awls	3/ gross	0. 9. 0
21 Shoemakers peggs	1½^d p^c	0. 2.7½
9 Sticks Sealing wax	2^d	0. 1. 6
A Box w.th TP nails ab.^{t} 2m^d.	6^d tho	0. 1. 0
About 4 m^d. Shingle nails	3/ tho	0. 1. 0
2 .^{lb} Starch	4^d lb	0. 0. 8
Sandiver 42.^{lb}	4.^{d} lb	0. 14. 0
Sum Carried forward_____		2 [torn]
Sum bro.^{t} forward_____		2. 10. 5½
A Parcel Glass Buttons 1/4		1. 4
6 & ½ Doz. Small Screws		1. 4
2 Doz & 5 Rowells for Spurrs		4
Tripoly		8
3 Girdle Buckles 1 p.^{r} Spurrs }		1
Buttons &c }		
8 Doz & 8 Glass rings		1
A Parcel Horn Rings & Sleeve buttons		2
250 Shoe makers tacks	2/ tho	0. 6
19.^{lb} Corn Emery_____	6.^{d} lb	9. 6
8 m^d. Clasp Hobbs Long	1/4 tho	10. 8
8 m^d. Long Hobbs	1/4 tho	10. 8
2 m^d. Batts	1/ tho	0. 2. 0

6 m.^d Tax	2/ tho	o.	12.	o
14 .^{lb}& 10 ^{oz} Bees wax	1/2 ^{lb}	o.	17.	1
A Draw w.th w.^{ts} &c putty	1/4	o.	1.	4
1 Large Box w.th Scales & w.^{ts}.	20/	1.	o.	o
1 D.^o w.th 3 p.^r Scales & w.^{ts}	20/	1.	o	
1 Smaller D.^o	4/	o.	4.	o
1 Box w.th a p.^r Scales old	1/4	o.	1.	4
1 Small D.^o w.th Scales w.^{ts}	2/	o.	2.	o
1 D.^o Old	2/	o.	2.	o
1 Box for Stone work	1/	o.	1.	o
1 Box w.th Baggs	4/	o.	4.	o
1 Book frame	1/	o.	1.	o
4 Canes	4/ ye wole	o.	4.	o
2 p.^c Cat Gutt	1/	o.	1.	o
Old Gimblets, tools &c	1/	o.	1.	o
2 Pr Still y.^{ds}	2/6 p.^r	o.	5.	o
5 Swords	at 3/ p.^c	o.	15.	o
1 Brass Kettle	3/	o.	3.	o
1 p.^r Scales	2/	o.	2.	o
1 p.^r Large Scale Beams ^{Scailes}. & w.^{ts}	20/	1.	o.	o
2 Casks w.th Allum — 140 ^{lb} at	3.^d lb	1.	15.	o
3 pair Mittens	2.^d p.^r	o.	o.	6
2 p.^r yarn Hose	1/ p.^r	o.	2.	o
1 p.^r worsted D.^o	1/4	o.	1.	4
A parcell Laces & Tape	1/	o.	1.	o
2 Sieve Bottoms	1/	o.	1.	o
A Box w.th Sandiver w.^d 15.^{lb}	4.^d lb	o.	5.	o
6 Whet Stones	8.^d p.^c	o.	4.	o
Moulding Sand	6.^d Quart			
A Box w.th Coll.^d Tapes	6/	o.	6.	o
1 D.^o w.th Cord & Braids	6/	o.	6.	o
A Box w.th Loose Buttons	3/	o.	3.	o
23 Papers w.th threads 4 & 1/2.^{lb}	4/^{lb}	o.	18.	o
Sum Carried forward		15.	14.	8 1/2
Sum bro.^t forward_____		15.	14.	8 1/2
6 Black Gauze fans	at 6.^d p.^c	o.	3.	o
14 Small Padlocks	2.^d p.^c	o.	2.	4
Home spun Thread				3
1 p.^c Buckram		1.	10	
3 doz. 9 p.^r Hinges	@ 12^d doz	o.	3.	o
6 Handles [illeg.]dles	@ 2^d	o.	1.	o
1 box w.th Brass pins [illeg.] joyners			1	
1 draw with Col.^d therds			1	
1 box w.th threds white		1		
4 boxes mixt Buttons about 30 doz	@1 1/2		4	
3 doz. Specktakles Cases . . .	8.^d doz	o.	2.	o
1/2 Ream paper			6	
1 Glass Case & toys			12	
5 Drawing irons	@ 1/p.^c	o.	5.	o
Mill to Clean Silver Durt	8/	o.	8.	o

1 p.^r Large wood Screws	6/	0. 6. 0	
2 Shod Shovels	@ 1/p.^c	0. 2. 0	
1 Box & 2 p.^r Scailes		4	

$\begin{array}{rr} £21. & 8.0^{1/2} \end{array}$

Bro.^t from y.^e other side

345. 0. 9

366. 8.9^{1/2}

In the Desk & Book Case —

12 p.^r Brass Sleave buttons	0. 6. 0	
Cork Screws &c in a Draw	0. 4. 0	
Case of Instruments, rule & 3 Compasses	1. 0. 0	
Prospect Glass, rule, Knife &c	0. 6. 0	
129 pair Flukes & Tongues for Buckles & ⎱ @ 6.^d p.^r ⎰	3. 4. 6	
3 Doz. p.^r Rowels	0. 1. 0	
Old flukes loose & Wier in the Draw	0. 2. 0	
3 pair Knee & 3 p.^r Shoe Buckles	0. 3. 0	
1 Sett of weights	0. 1. 4	
1 Hand Vise 2/. 3 p.^r watch plyers 3/	0. 5. 0	
1 p.^r Hand Shears 1/4 Scratch Brush 1/4	0. 2. 8	
2 Brushes 8^d 1 Brass rule 1/4	0. 2. 0	
Tobacco Boxes &c in a Draw	0. 6. 0	

£ 6. 3. 6

3 ⎱ Silver Tankards w.^t 69 ½ .^{oz} at 6/8.^{oz}			23. 3. 4	
⎰ fashion of .^{sd} tankards 68/			3. 8. 0	
2 Cans w.^t	.28.^{oz}.19.^{pt} at	6/8.^{oz}	fashion 26/8	10. 19. 8
5 porringers	30.10 – at	6/8	fashion 28/	11. 11. 4
8 Cream potts	27.5 – at	6/8 . . .	d^o ..64/	12. 6. 8
1 Sugar Dish	11·8 ——	6/8 ..	d^o ..13/4	4. 9. 4
2 Salvers. . .	13.5. . . .	6/8. . .	d^o..30/ 17.5.0	6. 1. 8
13 peper Casters	38.15. . .	6/8. . .	d^o. 86/8	17. 5. 0
1 Spout Cup	7.3 . .	6/8	d^o 13/4	3. 0. 0
3 peper boxes	6.15..	6/8. . .	d^o.18/	3. 3. 0
4 punch Strainers	16.12..	6/8. . .	d^o.32/	7. 2. 8
3 round Salts..	5.10. . .	6/8. . .	D^o.12/	2. 8. 8
3 punch Ladles	5.3..	6/8. . .	d^o..18/	2. 12. 4
3 Whistles with Corals				1. 10
17 Silver boxes	15.0.^{oz}	at 8/.^{oz}		6. 0. 0
1 Large Spoon	2.13	at 7/4.^{oz}		0. 19. 7
52 Spoons – – –	81.0 –	at 7/4		29. 14. 0
6 Snuff Boxes mother perl & Turtil Shell				3. 10. 4
5 Cupps. . .	18.^{oz}–8.^{pt}. . . .	at 7/6..^{oz}		7. 6. 0
4 Strait cans.	31.10. . .	at 7/. . .		6. 0. 6
1 Tancord. . .	23..8. . .	at 7/		8. 3. 10
2 candlesticks.	21.4. . .	6/8. 7.1.4		7. 1. 4
2 tee potts. . .	33.5 . . .	6/8		11. 1. 8
4 Salts .	9.5 . . .	6/8		3. 1. 8
105 tee Spoons	25.15 . . .	8/8 . . .		11. 1. 8
6 Childs spoons .	3.12 . . .	8/		1. 8.9^{1/2}
11 tee tongues ⎱ 3 Salt Shovels ⎰	11 ..0	8/. . . .		4. 8. 0

21 Bells . . .	1..12.....	8/	0. 12. 9¹/₂
1 porringer 2 tancords 1 Can..part of sword			5. 3. 3
w.ᵗ 14ᵒᶻ.15ᵈˢ at 7/oz..			
N.º 1—1 Box buckles – 64ᵒᶻ..o . . . .at 7/ᵒᶻ			22. 8. 0
2—1 d.º Buckles . 53..0. . .at 7/ᵒᶻ			18. 11. 0
3 41 Stock dº .....16.4......8/			6. 9. 6
4 55 p.ʳ Buckles .. 48.10.....8/			19. 08. 0
5 44 p.ʳ nee dº.....11..0.....9/			4. 19. 0

6 1 ⎰ Box Buttons w.ᵗʰ Specktakle frames—
    ⎱ 14 p.ʳ Specktakle frames ⎰ w.ᵗ 7ᵒᶻ 10ᵖᵗ. 0ᵒᶻ at 12/ᵒᶻ
      56 Sett Buttons   ⎱   4. 10. 0

7 Box Clasps &c	31 ᵒᶻ. . . .	at 7/ᵒᶻ	5. 17. 0
8 Box Buckles	30.5.0 . at	8/ᵒᶻ	12. 2. 0

9 ⎰ 10 Stock Buckles ⎱
  ⎰ 2 p.ʳ nee dº   ⎱ 16. 0. 0   9/ᵒᶻ   7. 4. 0
  ⎱ 8 Thimbles   ⎱
    2 plates & work 104ᵒᶻ.10.0   6/8   34. 16. 8

10 Box gold beads .	3ᵒᶻ.18ᵈʷᵗ.0ᵍ	at £6.8/ ℔ oz.	24. 19. 3
11 Box old beads .	5. 2 .0	£5. oz	25. 10. 0
12 Box old beads ..	2 .2. .0	£5. oz	10. 10. 0
13 Box old gold ..	18. 12 .0	£4.16/oz	89. 5. 7
14 Box New gold work	12 .7 .8	£5 10/oz	68. 0. 4
15 Box gold buttons .	1 .7 .0	£6 8/oz	8. 13. 0
16 Box 19 p.ʳ Earings	0. 15 .0	6 8/oz	4. 16. 0
			591. [torn]
			591. 3. 3

N.º 17 ⎱ 6 p.ʳ Stone Earings Sett in gold @ 18/ p.ʳ   5. 8. 0
  17 ⎰ 5 p.ʳ ditto Sett in Silver w.ᵗʰ gold wiers 8/   2. 0. 0
  18 ⎰ 3 p.ʳ Stone d.º in gold & 6 drop   3. 12

6 Stone Rings . . . . at		6/8 pᶜ	2. 0. 0
2 Splits Shank ditto . . .		20/pᶜ	2. 0. 0

Shagreen ⎰ 4 garnetts .. ditto . . .   10/pᶜ   2. 0. 0
Box   ⎰ 2 old Rings 5/4 pᶜ   0. 10. 9
N.º 18 ⎰ 1 Stone Shirt Buckle – –   8/   0. 8. 0
      ⎰ 3 p.ʳ 7 Stone Earings 12/p.ʳ   1. 16. 0
      ⎰ 10 Old Stone Rings   1. 10
      ⎱ 1 p.ʳ Stone Top Earings 6/   0. 6

Box Sundrys of old work in gold .		60/	3. 0. 0

N.º 19 ⎰ 9 Sett Stone buttons . . . . at   6/ p.ʳ   2. 14. 0
      ⎰ 1 p.ʳ Studs 5/   0. 5. 0
      ⎱ 2 p.ʳ Buttons no Chaines to yᵐ. . .   at 5/   0. 10. 0

Box   ⎰ 5 p.ʳ Black buttons Sett in silver @   2/p.ʳ   0. 10. 0
N.º 20 ⎰ 3 p.ʳ Black Studds   dº   1/p.ʳ   0. 1. 0
      ⎰ 1 p.ʳ Blew Earings   4/   0. 4. 0
      ⎰ 4 Stone Stays Hooks   1/pᶜ   0. 4. 0
      ⎰ 1 Stone Seal   3/   0. 3. 0
      ⎰ 1 p.ʳ Stone Buckles   18/   0. 18. 0
      ⎱ 1 Stone girdle dº   9/   0. 9. 0

12 Stone Buttons in Card		@ 1/pᶜ	0. 12. 0
Box } Sundrys of old Stones &c—		8/	0. 8. 0

N°.21}

22 Box Stones & Cyphers ——	10/	0. 10. 0	
23 Box Stones	8/	0. 8. 0	
24 Box d°	8/	0. 8. 0	
25 Box ditto	1/	0. 1. 0	
26 Box ditto	2/	0. 2. 0	
27 Box ditto	2/	0. 2. 0	

Box N°. 28 6 p.ˢ Corall — at 10/pᶜ — 3. 0. 0

15 oz Corale beads — at 9/4 oz — 7. 0. 0

3 gold & Corale Necklases : @ — 1. 6

Box

N°. 29   7 Thimbles, Steel Tops .. — @ 2/4 — 0. 16. 4

30   2 Rings·old Earings — 10

Box N°. 31 with 18.ᵒᶻ ¼ Silver Coines — @ 6/8 — 6. 1. 8

Bagg. Silver 19:15.0 Cobbs ...... — 6/8 — 6. 11. 8

2 Turtoile Shell Boxes in paper ... — 4/ — 4

1 Box Corale Beads ...... — 6/ — 0. 6. 0

{ Burnt Silver in Box 10ᵒᶻ ... — 6/oz: — 3. 0. 0

Silver Lace & Thread — 6

2 Shagerene Cases ...... — at 1/ — 0. 2. 0

1 Silver Hilted Sword — 60/ — 3. 0. 0

3 Sword Blades ...... — 1

N°. 32.   Box Silver Earings &c 18ᵖᵗ ... — 8/ᵒᶻ — 0. 7.2½

in Box N°. 1 Box perl Necklace & ... — 6/8 — 0. 6. 8

Silver in the Box 290ᵒᶻ. 10ᵖ @ — 6/8 — 96. 16. 8

10 Jackett Buttons — 1/ — 0. 1. 0

Twezers Cases & Snuff Boxes 6ᵒᶻ. @ 6/8 oz. — 2. 0. 0

Lymull Box Silver 10:ᵒᶻ ¾ @ — 6/8 — 3. 6. 8

Box wᵗʰ Tortoile Shell buttons & seal — 6

Box with gold ...   2 .ᵒᶻ 9 .ᵈᵗ. at 96/oz — 11. 15. ½

[illegible] Box with gold .. 0.15 – at 96/oz — 3. 11.10½

2ᵒᶻ 3ᵈ 12ᵍ of yᵉ 290. 10ᵈ – waste in Iron Flukes & tongues

775.03.3½ [28]

The inventory demonstrates that Edwards was involved in the production and sale of a wide variety of metalwares from small toys to elegant jewelry and holloware. The executors ran several notices of the sale of items from his estate, including one in the *Boston Gazette* on 17 June 1765, which mentions silver snuffboxes, salts, porringers, canns, tankards, creampots, sugar dishes, teapots, salvers, punch strainers, punch ladles, large and small teaspoons, shoe and knee and neck buckles, thimbles, and gold beads, buckles, and buttons.[29] Perhaps at a later sale, Zachariah Brigden bought goldsmiths' tools and supplies that included chisels, a swage for a tankard, a teast, hammers, blowpipes, brushes, nippers, an iron ladle and annealing tongs, a shovel, "1 Skinn & frame," a large ingot mold, and a block and three stools.[30] The executors' accounts also show that Daniel Parker bought tools and supplies. Most of these were the new goldsmiths' tools that Edwards had on hand to sell, which he stored in the press in the shop. Parker, a major purveyor of goldsmiths' tools, bought the tools at prices discounted by as much as a third of the value assigned to them in the estate inventory. Presumably, Parker bought the tools and supplies for stock. Joseph Edwards, Jr., purchased several miscellaneous items from the estate, including household goods, a hat and a waistcoat, the goldsmiths' coat of arms, and six silver spoons.[31]

Because Edwards left his entire estate to his widow with instructions as to how the estate should be divided after her decease, the estate was not completely settled for many years. On 31 March 1780, Isaac Smith, the surviving executor, filed the final account with the probate court. This account indicates that Edwards had owed a small amount of money to the estate of William Cowell, Jr., that "P. Adams of N. London," probably the New London, Connecticut, goldsmith Pygan Adams (1712–76), owed Edwards's estate £3.10, and that his executors paid £1.4.5 to "M^r. Russell for Commissions for Plate sold at Vendue."[32] The estate paid the firm of Russell and Clap £10 for selling the house.[33] BMW

SURVIVING OBJECTS

	Mark	Inscription	Patron	Date	Reference	Owner
Baptismal basin	C*	The Bequest of M^r– John Willis to the Church of Christ in Medford 1755.	First Parish, Medford, Mass., for John Willis	ca. 1755	Jones 1913, 276	AIC
Two beakers	A, B, C, or D	The Gift of Deacon Abiah Whitman to the First Church of Christ in Weymouth 1760	Abiah Whitman and/or First Church of Christ, Weymouth, Mass.	1760	Jones 1913, 493	
Three beakers	A, B, C, or D	The Gift of Josiah Waterman to the First Church of Christ in Weymouth/1753	Josiah Waterman and/or First Church of Christ, Weymouth, Mass.	1753	Jones 1913, 493	
Beaker	A, B, C, or D	The Gift of Deacon Joseph Brown 1759	Joseph Brown and/or Church of Christ, Lexington, Mass.	1759	Jones 1913, 248–49	
Three beakers	A, B, C, or D	The Gift of Deacon Thomas White to the First Church of Christ in Weymouth/1753	First Church of Christ, Weymouth, Mass., for Thomas White	1753	Jones 1913, 492–93	
Two beakers	A, B, C, or D	The Gift of M^{rs}— Jane Smith to the Church of Christ in Waltham June 18, 1754	Jane Smith and/or First Parish, Waltham, Mass.	1754	Jones 1913, 478	
Beaker	A, B, C, or D	The Gift of Madam Mary Hill to the Church of Christ in Berwick 1753	First Congregational Church, Berwick, Maine, for Mary Hill	1753	Jones 1913, 453–54	
Beaker	A, B, C, or D	The.Gift.of.M. George.Farrer.to.the. Church.of.Christ. in.Lincoln.1757	George Farrer and/or First Congregational Church, Lincoln, Mass.	1757	Jones 1913, 250	
Three beakers	A, B, C, or D	The.Gift.of.M. Edward.Flint.to. the.Church.of.Christ. in.Lincoln. 1757.	First Congregational Church, Lincoln, Mass., for Edward Flint	1757	Jones 1913, 249–50	

	Mark	Inscription	Patron	Date	Reference	Owner
Beaker	A, B, C, *or* D	The Gift of M^r- Nathaniel Whittemore to the Church of Christ in Lexington 1756	First Congregational Society, Lexington, Mass., for Nathaniel Whittemore	1756	Jones 1913, 245–46	
Cann	A, B, C, *or* D	H/SM (+)	Stephen and Mary Hall	ca. 1740	Jones 1913, 274	
Two canns	A, B, C, *or* D	T/CS	Charles and Sarah Tilden	ca. 1745	Christie's, 23 May 1985, lot 52	
Cann	B*	Williams arms, gules a stag trippant; This Cann Is Presented to Mrs Anna Williams/By her Uncle and Aunt Hinsdale – / –1754–	Ebenezer and Mrs. Hinsdale for Anna Williams	1754	*Silver Supplement* 1973, no. 35	HD
Cann	B*	EQ		ca. 1740	*Antiques* 110 (August 1976): 219	
Cann	B*	AB.E/to/S/IE	Abigail (Fowle) (Smith) Edwards	ca. 1746	Puig et al. 1989, no. 205	MIA
Cann (mate below)	C	N/IE (+)	John and Elizabeth North	ca. 1750	YUAG files	
Cann (mate above)	C*	N/IE (+)	John and Elizabeth North	ca. 1750		SI
Cann	?	Traill arms, azure a chevron between 2 mascles in chief and a trefoil slipped in the base, and crest, a column; DISCRIMINE SALUS; T/RM	Robert and Mary Traill	ca. 1750	MFA 1911, no. 467	
Cann	?	?		ca. 1740	*Antiques* 91 (January 1967): 11	
Caster	A, B, C, *or* D	E/IM		ca. 1740	*Silver Supplement* 1973, no. 36	
Caster	A, B, C, *or* D	B/SS		ca. 1740	*Moore Collection* 1980, no. 127	
Caster	A, B, C, *or* D	none		ca. 1740	*Moore Collection* 1980, no. 127	
Caster	A, B, C, *or* D	Pemberton (?) crest, a dragon's head; P/DR	Pemberton family (?)	ca. 1745	*Antiques* 106 (August 1974): 174	
Three casters	A, B, C, *or* D	E/IA		ca. 1750	Sotheby's, 26–27 June 1991, lot 113	

	Mark	Inscription	Patron	Date	Reference	Owner
Caster	A, B, C, or D	LL (+)		ca. 1760	*Moore Collection* 1980, no. 128	
Caster	A, B, C, or D	HS		ca. 1750	Sotheby's, 28–31 January 1993, lot 112	
Caster	B*	C/BP		ca. 1740	Eitner 1976, no. 44	
Caster	B*	S/IE	Isaac and Elizabeth (Storer) Smith	ca. 1745	American Art Association–Anderson Galleries, 3 April 1937, lot 249	
Caster	B*	C/HT (?; erased) (+)		ca. 1755	Buhler/Hood 1970, no. 166	YUAG
Caster	F*	L/DP		ca. 1750	DAPC 76.2759	
Caster	F*	P/NM; B (later)		ca. 1750	Avery 1920, no. 228 (as Stephen Emery)	MMA
Caster	G	LQ; ESF (later)		ca. 1750	MFA 1911, no. 487 (as Stephen Emery)	
Caster	?	AB; M (later)		ca. 1750	DAPC 70.3571	
Caster	?	MS		ca. 1750	Parke-Bernet, 14–15 May 1948, lot 201	
Caster	?	unidentified initials		ca. 1750	Parke-Bernet, 15–16 April 1955, lot 226	
Coffeepot	C	ES (later)	Elizabeth (Storer) Smith	ca. 1755	Safford 1983, 48	MMA
Cup	A, B, C, or D	DH		ca. 1735	American Art Association–Anderson Galleries, 8 February 1936, lot 38	
Cup	B*	KD		ca. 1740	Johnston 1994, 51	CMA
Cup	?	T/SL		ca. 1735	*Silver Supplement* 1973, no. 37	
Ladle	B*	S/IE (+)	Isaac and Elizabeth (Storer) Smith	ca. 1755	Safford 1983, 47	MMA
Ladle	E	Storer crest, a talbot's head	Ebenezer Storer, Jr.	ca. 1750	Buhler 1972, no. 204	MFAB
Ladle	F	none		ca. 1755	Quimby 1995, no. 58	WM

	Mark	Inscription	Patron	Date	Reference	Owner
Ladle	?	?		ca. 1750	Skinner, 15 June 1991, lot 181	
Mourning ring (gold; attrib.)	none	MRS. ABᵗ/EDWARDS/OB.9.JAN/1760.AE.81	Abigail Edwards	1760	Buhler 1972, no. 208	MFAB
Mourning ring (gold)	F	I·QUINCY Ob. 16 May. 1754. AE 18.	I. Quincy	1754	Buhler 1972, no. 205	MFAB
Mug	A†	Storer arms, 3 quatrefoils on a chevron engrailed gules between 3 mullets, and crest, a talbot's head; The Gift of Mary Storer./to/Mary Smith./1758	Mary (Edwards) Storer and/or Mary Smith	1758	Buhler 1972, no. 207	MFAB
Mug	A	Storer arms, 3 quatrefoils on a chevron engrailed gules between 3 mullets, and crest, a talbot's head; The gift of Mary Storer/to/Mary Storer Junʳ/1758	Mary (Edwards) Storer and/or Mary Storer, Jr.	1758	Buhler 1972, 1:246	
Mug	A, B, C, *or* D	SW (+)		ca. 1740	Skinner, 26–27 October 1984, session 3, lot 17	
Mug	B*	Traill arms, azure a chevron between 2 mascles in chief and a trefoil slipped in the base, and crest, a column; DISCRIMINE SALUS; T/IM	Traill family	ca. 1735	Eitner 1976, no. 43	
Mug	C*	GMB (cipher)	Barrell family (?)	ca. 1735	*Moore Collection* 1980, no. 126	
Mug	?	unidentified cipher		ca. 1740	Sotheby Parke Bernet, 12–16 November 1974, lot 999	
Patch box	G	Mary Storer 1759	Mary (Edwards) Storer	1759	Buhler 1956, no. 66	MFAB
Pepper box	A, B, C, *or* D	G/BM		ca. 1750	MFA 1911, no. 464	
Pepper box	B*	C/IC; 1732 (later)		ca. 1735	Eitner 1976, no. 42	
Pepper box	C*/F*	B/NA (erased); MR 1744 (later)		ca. 1745	Sotheby Parke Bernet, 25–26 April 1978, lot 637	
Pepper box	E, F *or* G	MH	Mary Hale	ca. 1750	YUAG files	

	Mark	Inscription	Patron	Date	Reference	Owner
Two pepper boxes	?	?		ca. 1740	Norman-Wilcox 1962, nos. 20–21	
Plate (mate below)	B	Jackson arms, quarterly 4 escallops, and crest, an escallop; E. Jackson (later)	Edward Jackson	ca. 1740	Buhler 1972, no. 199	MFAB
Plate (mate above)	B	Jackson arms and crest; E. Jackson (later)	Edward Jackson	ca. 1740	Buhler 1972, 1:240	
Porringer	A, B, C, *or* D	RI (later)		ca. 1730	National Art Galleries, 3–5 December 1931, lot 419	
Porringer	A, B, C, *or* D	SG/1747 (+)	Stephen Gorham	1747	*American Art of the Colonies and Early Republic*, no. 109	
Porringer	A, B, C, *or* D	P/IS		ca. 1740	American Art Association–Anderson Galleries, 28–29 February 1936, lot 265	
Porringer	A, B, C, *or* D	E/SS	Samuel and Sarah (Smith) Edwards	ca. 1745	*Moore Collection* 1980, no. 129	
Porringer	A, B, C, *or* D	LD	Lucy Dudley	ca. 1745	MFA 1911, no. 442	
Porringer	A, B, C, *or* D	AK		ca. 1740	Anderson Galleries, 7–12 January 1924, lot 855	
Porringer	A, B, C, *or* D	B/SC		ca. 1750	Parke-Bernet, 17–20 May 1944, lot 659	
Porringer	B*	B/WC		ca. 1740	Buhler/Hood 1970, no. 167	YUAG
Porringer (with mark of Joseph Edwards)	B*	H/SL		ca. 1760	*Antiques* 100 (August 1971): 162	
Porringer	B*	P/IM		ca. 1740		LAM
Porringer	B*	S/IE	Isaac and Elizabeth (Storer) Smith (?)	ca. 1750	Watkins 1957, 144	SI
Porringer (with mark of Jacob Hurd cast in handle)	C*	none	Mary (Whipple) Holyoke (?)	ca. 1735	Avery 1920, no. 101	MMA
Porringer	C	Green crest, a woodpecker pecking at a tree stump; G/IH	Joshua and Hannah (Storer) Green	1762	Buhler 1972, no. 209	MFAB

	Mark	Inscription	Patron	Date	Reference	Owner
Salt	A, B, C, *or* D	AE to CT		ca. 1750	YUAG files	
Two salts	F*	EW (+)		ca. 1745	*Antiques* 110 (September 1976): 391	
Salver	A, B, C, *or* D	T/PH	Patrick and Hannah Tracy	ca. 1750	Buhler 1956, no. 67	
Salver	A, B, C, *or* D	W/WR	William and Rebecca White	ca. 1750		MFAB
Salver	B*	SE		ca. 1745	*Moore Collection* 1980, no. 124	
Two sauceboats	A, B, C, *or* D	none		ca. 1740		HMA
Saucepan	A, B, C, *or* D	The Gift of Mrs. Eliz^a Peirce to Eb. Storer Tertius Augt 10th 1752	Elizabeth Pierce for Ebenezer Storer III	1752	Buhler 1956, no. 65	MFAB
Snuffbox	G*	John Holland	John Holland	ca. 1740	Buhler/Hood 1970, no. 165	YUAG
Spout cup	A*	T/SL		ca. 1740	YUAG files	
Spout cup	A, B, C, *or* D	E/SS (+)	Samuel and Sarah (Smith) Edwards	ca. 1735	*CGA Bulletin* 1971, no. 1, fig. 10	CGA
Spout cup	?	?		ca. 1750	*Antiques* 51 (April 1947): 272	
Strainer	B†	S/IE (+)	Isaac and Elizabeth (Storer) Smith	ca. 1746	Buhler 1972, no. 202	MFAB
Strainer	C	T/PH (+)	Patrick and Hannah Tracy	ca. 1750	Buhler 1972, no. 201	MFAB
Strainer (with mark of Thomas Edwards)	E *or* F	none		ca. 1750	Quimby 1995, no. 62	WM
Sugar tongs	F*	MH		ca. 1750	Quimby 1995, no. 59	WM
Tablespoon	A, B, C, *or* D	S/IE	Isaac and Elizabeth (Storer) Smith (?)	ca. 1750	Quimby 1995, no. 60a	WM
Tablespoon (mate below)	A, B, C, *or* D	Green crest, a woodpecker pecking at a tree stump; G/EM	Edward and Mary (Storer) Green	ca. 1750	*Antiques* 103 (April 1973): 631	
Tablespoon (mate above)	A, B, C, *or* D	Green crest, a woodpecker pecking at a tree stump; G/EM (+)	Edward and Mary (Storer) Green	ca. 1750	Quimby 1995, no. 60d	WM
Tablespoon	A, B, C, *or* D	EH		ca. 1730	*Antiques* 103 (April 1973): 631	

	Mark	Inscription	Patron	Date	Reference	Owner
Tablespoon (mate? below)	A, B, C, *or* D	MH		ca. 1750	Quimby 1995, no. 60e	WM
Tablespoon (mate? above)	A, B, C, *or* D	MH		ca. 1750	*Moore Collection* 1980, no. 130	
Tablespoon	A, B, C, *or* D	S/IH		ca. 1750	Quimby 1995, no. 60b	WM
Tablespoon	A, B, C, *or* D	MP		ca. 1750	Quimby 1995, no. 60c	WM
Tablespoon	B*	LD		ca. 1755	Watkins 1957, 144	SI
Tablespoon	B*	MT		ca. 1735		PEM
Tablespoon	C*	LR		ca. 1745		AIC
Tablespoon	C*	SD		ca. 1755	*Silver Supplement* 1973, no. 38	
Two tablespoons	C*	MS	Mary Smith	ca. 1755		PEM
Tablespoon	C†	W/IP		ca. 1755	Buhler/Hood 1970, no. 168	YUAG
Tablespoon	D†	The Gift of H. Storer/to H. Storer	Hannah (Hill) Storer (?) and/or Hannah Storer	ca. 1748	Buhler 1972, no. 203	MFAB
Tablespoon	D*	AD		ca. 1730	YUAG files	
Tablespoon	?	?		ca. 1760		MFAB
Tankard	A, B, C, *or* D	HF		ca. 1740	*Moore Collection* 1980, no. 125	
Tankard	A, B, C, *or* D	The Gift of Cap.ᵗ Benjamin Payson,/to the Second Church of Christ in Roxbury/1761	Benjamin Payson and/or First Parish, West Roxbury, Mass.	1761	Jones 1913, 489	
Tankard	A, B, C, *or* D	N/DM	David and Mary Newell	ca. 1755	YUAG files	
Tankard	A, B, C, *or* D	M/CM/1759		1759	Parke-Bernet, 10 November 1970, lot 67	
Tankard	A, B, C, *or* D	T/SA; Turell Tufts Medford 1835 (later)	Tufts family	ca. 1740	*Antiques* 132 (August 1987): 208	
Tankard	A, B, C, *or* D	MB; SB; Trowbridge arms (later)	Samuel and Mary (Boutwell) Brooks	ca. 1735	Brooks 1932, 17–18	
Tankard	B*	W/IB; W/EM (later)	John Williams	ca. 1750		HD
Tankard	C*	The Gift of M.ʳ Ebenezer Wells to the Church of Deerfield An.ᵒ 1758	Ebenezer Wells and/or First Congregational Church, Deerfield, Mass.	1758	Flynt/Fales 1968, 45, 47–48	

	Mark	Inscription	Patron	Date	Reference	Owner
Tankard	D*	C/EH	Cottle family (?)	ca. 1740	*Antiques* 106 (August 1974): 174	
Tankard (miniature)	F	M Storer/to/Mary Smith	Mary (Edwards) Storer and/or Mary Smith	ca. 1757	Sander 1982, no. 26	SPNEA
Tankard	?	KG/1738	Katherine Graves	1738		LACMA
Teapot	A*	LD to ER/1757 (+)	Lucy Dudley	1757	Quimby 1995, no. 57	WM
Teapot	C*	Allen arms, per bend rompu argent and azure 6 martlets counterchanged, impaling Warren, gules a lion rampant a chief chequy argent and azure; C/OM	Obadiah and Martha Curtis	ca. 1760	*Antiques* 118 (July 1980): 32	
Teaspoon	D	?		ca. 1750	Buhler 1972, appendix no. 21	MFAB
Teaspoon (see mate with mark F)	E†	Green crest, a woodpecker pecking at a tree stump; G/EM	Edward and Mary (Storer) Green	ca. 1757	Buhler 1972, no. 206	MFAB
Teaspoon	E or F	S/IE	Isaac and Elizabeth (Storer) Smith (?)	ca. 1750		SI
Teaspoon (see mate with mark E)	F	Green crest, a woodpecker pecking at a tree stump; G/EM	Edward and Mary (Storer) Green	ca. 1757	Buhler 1972, no. 206	MFAB
Teaspoon	F†	TL/to/R/EH		ca. 1755	Flynt/Fales 1968, 213 (mark only)	YUAG
Teaspoon	F*	HA		ca. 1755		HD
Teaspoon	G	HS		ca. 1755	Quimby 1995, no. 61a	WM
Teaspoon	G†	RW		ca. 1745	Quimby 1995, no. 61b	WM
Wine cup	B	Belongs/To the Church/in Lynde Street/Boston	West Church, Lynde Street, Boston	ca. 1740	Buhler 1972, no. 200	MFAB
Wine cup	D*	Belongs/To the Church/in Lynde Street/Boston	West Church, Lynde Street, Boston	ca. 1740	Safford 1983, 34	MMA

1. RC 9:217; RC 24:34; RC 28:221; Savage 1860–62, 3:274; Wyman 1879, 2:874; Boston Deaths, 1700–1800; SCPR 74:301–02; *Charlestown VR* 1:58, 107, 199, 305, 316.
2. SCPR 38:515–18. The house was appraised at £550 in 1762; SCPR 63:37.
3. SCD 45:210–11.
4. Inventory and accounts of the estate of Samuel Edwards, June 1762–78, Smith-Carter Papers, MHS.
5. English-Touzel-Hathorne Papers, PEM.
6. Isaac Smith Account Book 1744–48, Smith-Carter Papers, MHS.
7. Inventory and accounts of the estate of Samuel Edwards, June 1762–78, Smith-Carter Papers, MHS.
8. Isaac Smith Account Book 1744–48, Smith-Carter Papers, MHS.

9. Dow 1927, 45; *New-England Journal*, 6 November 1739.
10. Marks (F) and (G) have sometimes been confused with those of Stephen Emery (q.v.).
11. John Edwards deed to Samuel Edwards, 13 September 1746, Smith-Carter Papers, MHS.
12. SCPR, docket 10043; Inventory and accounts of the estate of Samuel Edwards, June 1762–78, Smith-Carter Papers, MHS.
13. Bigelow-Phillips files, 1476.
14. SCPR 59:347–49, docket 12763.
15. MCD 64:312–13.
16. Seybolt 1939, 255, 258, 262, 266, 268, 271, 274, 278, 281, 285, 289, 291, 295, 299, 301.
17. SCPR 38:515–18.
18. Papers relating to the estate of William Smith, 1735 (including the division of the estate); see also MCD 36:436–38. Abigail Smith's Account Book, 1734–39; bond of Hezekiah Blanchard to Abigail Smith, Smith-Carter Papers, MHS.
19. MCD 34:514–15; 43:160–61.
20. RC 28:214; SCPR 38:515–18.
21. Will of Abigail Edwards, dated 11 June 1755, probated 18 January 1760, Smith-Carter Papers, MHS. See also division of the estate of Abigail Edwards, 25 August 1760, Smith-Carter Papers, MHS.
22. James Clark bill to Samuel Edwards and Isaac Smith, 15 January 1760, Smith-Carter Papers, MHS.
23. Receipt book of Isaac Smith and Samuel Edwards, 1760–61, Smith-Carter Papers, MHS.
24. MCPR, docket 20780.
25. John M. Fitzgerald to F. H. Bigelow, Boston Court Record References to Silversmiths, Bigelow-Phillips files, Court of Common Pleas Record Book 1735, 118–19, 425–28, 431–35.
26. The court case involved a Rhode Island £3 note that Thomas Goddard testified he had gotten from "mr Edwards, the Goldsmith." The court took the bill to Mr. Edwards who said, "he paid him or gave to his Daughter to pay him a £3 bill" but that he could not be certain that it was the same one. The reference may be either to Samuel Edwards or to his brother Thomas. Mass. Archives 43:21.
27. Dow 1927, 45.
28. Inventory and accounts of the estate of Samuel Edwards, June 1762–78, Smith-Carter Papers, MHS; SCPR 63:37.
29. Dow 1927, 45.
30. Receipt signed by Joseph Edwards, Brigden Papers, YU.
31. Inventory and accounts of the estate of Samuel Edwards, June 1762–78, Smith-Carter Papers, MHS.
32. Inventory and accounts of the estate of Samuel Edwards, June 1762–78, Smith-Carter Papers, MHS.
33. SCPR, docket 12962.

Thomas Edwards
1701/02–55

A

B

C

Thomas Edwards was born on 14 January 1701/02, the third son of John Edwards (q.v.) and Sybil (Newman) Edwards (1670–1739).[1] He and his younger brother Samuel (q.v.) probably received their training in their father's shop. Thomas Edwards married Sarah Burr (1701–29), daughter of Samuel Burr (1679–1719) of Cambridge and Charlestown, Massachusetts, and his first wife, Dorothy (Thompson-Shove) Burr (ca. 1671–1701), on 20 November 1723.[2] In his will, probated in 1719, Sarah's father left her his bed and its hangings, a silver tankard, and a staff, which was her great-grandfather Steadman's, as well as twenty pounds to be paid at the time of her marriage.[3] After her marriage to Thomas Edwards, the couple sued her stepmother for failing to pay for Sarah's clothing between the time of her father's death and her marriage.[4] Thomas and Sarah Edwards had two daughters: Sarah (1724–68), who married Zachariah Brigden (q.v.) in 1756; and Elizabeth (b. 1729), who married William Downs Cheever, sugar baker and merchant, in 1749. Both daughters were baptized in the Brattle Street Church.[5]

Thomas Edwards's career is intriguing. Following the completion of his

D

apprenticeship and his marriage, he was active in Boston affairs. He became a member of the Artillery Company in 1724 and served as third sergeant in 1729; he was also elected to the influential town office of clerk of the market in 1729.[6] During his early years in Boston, Edwards was in court as a plaintiff several times. The most notable of these suits was one Edwards filed against John LeRoux (q.v.) for room and board and sundries totaling £8.6.9 on 6 July 1725. The accounts accompanying the case indicate that Edwards employed LeRoux, son of Bartholomew LeRoux and brother of Charles LeRoux, two of New York City's most respected goldsmiths, as a journeyman during the years 1724–25.[7] The only other record we have of Edwards's business dealings during these early years is a lengthy account in which Edwards is a debtor to the watchmaker and clockmaker Benjamin Bagnall, Sr. (q.v. Appendix A):

1725				£	s	d
December	26	To mending a Silver watch		5	0	0
	31	to 37^{lb} pounds of Cheese att 9^d/		1	7	9
1728						
Novemb	14	to Cash paid James Shead on his Account		1		
1729 August	26	to a new christal 4/6 removeing a Clock 3^s/		0	7	6
		to a file, a Watch key, & two Christals		0	13	6
	27	to Cleaning his Clock & Silvering the Sircels[?]		1	12	—
		By Cash fiveteen pounds		15		
		to Sundryes 3/8 to Ditto 1/4			5	
February	4	to the rent of two Acres of Marsh		1	10	—
		By Cash 40/ to 15^{dwt} penny Weight of silver		2	15	—
		To the rent of a Stable two Years from 1728				
		to 1730 att £2.10 p^r Annum		5	0	0
1730		to 6 feet of joyce 1^s/ to repairing a Watch 7/6		0	8	6
June	26	to Cleaning and Sundry repair to a Watch		1	11	—
		to Sundryes p^r Shop Book		3	7	4
1731 January	5	to Cleaning a Clock 12^s/ A packing Case for D^o 12/		1	4	—
		to two Gilt Balls 5/ to a Glass 16/		1	1	—
1732 Decemb^r		to Truckage		0	2	6
	4	to 24^{lb} 1/2 pounds of Allom att 5/6		5	15	—
		to a Christal to a watch		0	6	
		to mending a Watch as p^r Agreement		8	—	—
1733 Nov^r	13	to Sundry repairs to a Watch		2	—	—
				£ 58	6	1
		Cash paid this Day to John Hunt for Interest on y^r Bond		4	10	—
		to two months Interest			4	—
1734 July	27	By Cash paid on Account of y^r Bond		9	15	—
		to Interest to July 1735 to D^o 1736 & 1737		3	14	—
		to Interest 1738 to D^o 1739		2	11	5
1739 Decemb^r 1		To Cash paid John Hunt towards the princ: of s^d Bond		30	9	—
		to Interest one year to 1740 Ditto to 1741		6	4	2
		to Ditto 1742 to 1743		6	19	6
		to 1744 £3.16 to 1745 £4.0.4		7	16	4
		to Interest one year & half to 1747		6	7	9
		To 18 Years Interest from 1747 to 1765 att 6/7 [illeg]		78	11	2
				84	0	3
				162	11	5

On the credit side the only listings are

1728 April 28	By Cash Ten pounds in part of the fiveteen pounds Borrowed	10	0	0
	By Sundryes Out of the Shop	4	6	0[8]

Most interesting is the large amount of money that Edwards borrowed from Bagnall, for which Bagnall evidently calculated the interest over the life of the loan and charged Edwards for the interest in advance. The inclusion of "truckage" and a "packing case" for clocks repaired in 1731 suggests that some items were shipped a significant distance, perhaps to New York, where Edwards resided during the 1730s. Edwards may also have had business transactions with Nathaniel Morse (q.v.) because the two signed a fifty-pound bond when they borrowed twenty-five pounds from the pewterer Samuel Carter in 1727.[9]

During the 1720s Thomas Edwards lived in the house on Union Street that he bought for six hundred pounds from the Boston "Cloathier" George Skinner on 23 October 1727. On 7 March 1727/28 Thomas Edwards was granted permission "to take up the Pavement and Ground to Carry His Drain from his Celler in union Street into the Comon Shore there provided he forthwith make good the Ground & Pavement to the Satisfaction of the Select men & from time keep it in Repair."[10] On 10 May 1728 Edwards and his wife sold a strip of land eighteen feet wide by twenty-one feet long immediately adjacent to their property on Union Street, and on 29 June 1730 they sold the house and land to Thomas's brother-in-law, Ebenezer Storer, for twenty-four hundred pounds even though the three-hundred-pound mortgage on the property was not paid until 14 February 1731.[11] Edwards purchased several small pieces of property from Samuel Atkinson, a feltmaker of Newbury, Massachusetts, on 28 November 1727 and sold them to the mason John Blower on 18 August 1730.[12] He is then noticeably absent from Boston records until 1744.

Edwards apparently sold his land in Boston because he intended to go to New York. The economic situation in Boston was steadily worsening, and he may have felt that he would do better elsewhere. He may have believed that he was too much in competition with his father, John Edwards, or his brother, Samuel Edwards, or there may have been a rift in the family. It is equally possible that Thomas was dispatched to New York to open up a branch of the family business there. His move may have been precipitated by his wife's death in 1729. Edwards became a freeman of New York in 1731, and apparently it was there that he married his second wife, Eleanor.[13] We know nothing else of his time in New York except that, when he returned to Boston, he was sued for unpaid rent by his former New York landlords Jane Gilbert (1743/44 and 1750) and Thomas Darcy (1750).[14]

Edwards probably returned to Boston sometime between January 1743/44, when his father wrote his will, and August 1744, when Benjamin Walker mentioned in his diary that Thomas Edwards and his wife, sister, and daughter had gone down to watch a brigantine owned by his neighbor Grigs leave port for the West Indies.[15] At this time Edwards may have been living in his father's house in Cornhill and operating his father's shop. There is no other mention of Thomas in the records until 1746, when he inherited his father's house and shop in Cornhill and many of his tools.[16] On 8 May 1746, in an advertisement regarding the settlement of the estate of John Edwards, it was noted that "the Goldsmith's Business is carried on at the Shop of the deceased, as usual, by his Son, Thomas Edwards."[17] On 21 June 1746, just three months after John Edwards's death, Benjamin Walker recorded in his diary, "Mr Thomas Edwards, Gold Smith my Next butting Neighbour in my rear is pulling down his back Shed or Shop he workt in (is now pulling down my fence that was built by my father October 1711 []) & ware his Shop Stood is now goeing to raise a fram^d Wood for a workin Shop."

Walker noted in the margin that W. Reeks, carpenter, raised the "new Work shop," which was twenty feet in height.[18]

Edwards resumed active membership in the Artillery Company and was elected ensign in 1747, lieutenant of the Artillery Company in 1750, and captain in 1753, and occasionally entertained the company on training days. He was again elected clerk of the market in 1747.[19]

After he returned to Boston, Edwards continued to file suits against his fellow craftsmen. In 1746 he sued the goldsmith Stephen Callas (q.v.) for £8.15, and in 1749/50 he sued the goldsmith Daniel Parker (q.v.) for £24.14 for "Sundries to Ballance" the account between them.[20] He also frequently appeared in court as a defendant. On 19 November 1747, Edwards advertised in the *Boston News-Letter* that he had in his possession "A Large Silver Spoon, sundry Tea Spoons, and a silver Spur, lately offer'd to Sale, suspected to be stolen."[21] In spite of his demonstrated honesty, Edwards was accused of receiving stolen goods and arrested on 21 December 1747. The warrant accusing Edwards reads, "buying & privately receiving on the 5th of August last at Boston afores[d] of one Joseph Smith of said Boston Labourer a parcel of Silver Lace, a pair of silver Tea Tongs, two silver Spoons, a silver Girdle, a White Metal Teapot all together of the value of four pounds lawful money, the goods & property of Joseph St. Lawrence of s[d] Boston Gent[n] from whom the said Joseph Smith had lately stolen the same."[22] Edwards was found not guilty of the charges in the Superior Court.[23] It is highly unusual for someone of Edwards's stature in the community to be accused of such a severe crime. It is possible that this court case refers to another goldsmith named Thomas Edwards, although evidence of another goldsmith with this name in Boston is lacking.

In 1750, Thomas Townsend (q.v.), whom Edwards had employed as a jobber to make tankard bodies and other pieces of holloware that Edwards then assembled and retailed, brought suit against Edwards for unpaid work. The dispute apparently hinged on the value of money owed to Townsend in the new tenor, and the case had to be settled with the assistance of three arbiters: Rufus Greene (q.v.), Jacob Hurd (q.v.), and William Cowell, Jr. (q.v.).[24] This account demonstrates that Edwards, like most master artisans, paid journeymen only one-half to one-third of their wages in cash, and the rest in goods. Edwards also purchased parts of objects from Thomas Dane (q.v.). In addition to jobbing out work to day laborers like Townsend, Edwards dealt with many other independent craftsmen. He purchased jewelry supplies from Asahel Mason (q.v.) in 1747/48.[25]

Like the work of his father, extant silver by Thomas Edwards is essentially simple in design. However, in their creations both father and son expanded upon designs they had seen in existing objects.[26] Edwards counted a number of family members among his patrons, including Ebenezer and Mary (Edwards) Storer. A strainer bears the marks of both Thomas Edwards and his brother Samuel. The two may have worked together early in their careers, but there is no evidence of a working relationship between them after 1730. Thomas Edwards used at least four different marks during his career: T·E crowned in a shield (A); T·Edwards in a rectangle (B); T·EDWARDS in a rectangle (C); and TE in a rectangle (D). Spurious examples of mark (B) exist.[27] Thomas Edwards devoted most of his energy to his business activities and is known to have trained at least two craftsmen, Thomas Coverly (q.v.) and Zachariah Brigden. He may also have trained his nephew Joseph Edwards, Jr. (q.v.), and Benjamin

Edwards, Jr. (q.v.), who probably was also a relation.[28] Edwards employed the jeweler William Cario, Sr. (q.v.), as a journeyman.

Thomas Edwards amassed a sizable fortune in the silversmithing trade and was one of the three most productive silversmiths of his generation.[29] Several extant bills from his later years of activity in Boston suggest the extent of his business. The estate administration of Anthony Stoddard filed in 1749 shows that Thomas Edwards was paid £201.11.8 for rings.[30] Edwards appears in the ledger of Timothy Orne of Salem in 1749 with the following account:

Tho[s] Edwards of Boston Silversmith

1 June 1749	To 24 oz of silver @ 60/ £72	
8 Sept. 1749	To Twenty Six Pounds old Ten[r] 26 98	
Contra		
8 Sept. 1749	By 2 Silver Cans w[t] 24 oz @ 60/ £72	
	By make[g] D[o] £20 By Engrave[g] D[o] £6 26 98[31]	

A receipt from June of that year shows that Orne also bought jewelry from Edwards:

M[r] Orne Bo[t] }
of Thom[s] Edwards }   June 10.th 1749

1 Sett of Stone button Sett in gold	£ 7. 10.
1 Stone Ring Ditto	10.
	£17. 10.

Rec[d] the Contents in full
℔ Tho[s] Edwards[32]

A number of accounts survive for debts due to and from Edwards's estate, which was administered by Thomas's daughter, Sarah (Edwards) Brigden. One of these, Edwards's account with the distiller Thomas Jackson, demonstrates that Edwards, like most Boston silversmiths, did a great deal of repair work in his shop:

1750/1

Feb[y] 28th	To mending a Spoone	£ : 3: —
March 15th	To a Silver Spoone more then an old one	10: —
1751	To 6 tea Spoones	8: 6: —
Octo[r] 5th	To mending a fan	: 10 —
1752		
May 29th	To 6 p[r] hook & Eyes	1: 18 —
July 7th	To 2 p[r] Gold buttons & Mend[g] 2 p[r]	7: 15 —
Aug[st] 4th	To mending A Straner & Spoone	1:—: —
	To making Silv[r] wires for 3 p[r] of pendents	: 15: —
	To m[r] James Butler Note & Ballance of Acc[t]	16: 12: —
		£ 37: 9: —
	Reduc[d] to lawfull money	4: 19: 10
	Ballance due to T. Jackson	: 13: 8
		£ 5: 13: 6

1751

Sep.ᵗ 16   To mending an Earrings   2:   2

On the other side of the account, Edwards purchased molasses from Jackson, and Jackson provided Edwards with gold and silver worth £21.15.[33] The James Butler mentioned in the account is probably the goldsmith (q.v.) for whom Jackson was acting as a power of attorney. Another account, between Edwards and Thomas Josselyn, consists almost entirely of jewelry:

1749

Octo.ʳ 12ᵗʰ   To 6 Silv.ʳ tea Spoones   £   8: 17: —

              To the Exchange of a ⎫
              gold Ring   ⎭   1: 13: —

1750

Sep.ᵗ 22ⁿᵈ   To 6 large Silvor Spoones   37: 7: —
Nov.ʳ 1ˢᵗ   To a p.ʳ Chaips   : 10 —
10ᵗʰ   To 2 p.ʳ mettle buckles   1: 8 —
13ᵗʰ   To a p.ʳ Earrings   4: 10: —
              To Sundrys to your wife   : 18 —
22ᵈ   To Sundrys to Ditto   : 12 —
              To a p.ʳ gold wires   2: 14 —
1750/1   To a p.ʳ Chaips   : 10 —
Jan.ʸ 3ᵈ   To the Exchange of a Sett ⎫
              of gold buttons   ⎭   6: 3 —
Feb.ʸ 6   To a p.ʳ buckles   : 14: —
26ᵗʰ   To mending a p.ʳ Ditto   : 4 —

1751/1

June 7ᵗʰ   To a p.ʳ of Silv.ʳ buckles   5: 1: 6
              To 1 p.ʳ Steal Ditto   : 14: —
              To a Sett of Silv.ʳ buttons   : 15 —
              To 2 ¹/₂ £ Leather   8: 15: —
              To 8 ³/₄ Ditto @d.ᵈ Sometime
              ago   30: 12: 6
Aug.ˢᵗ 6ᵗʰ   To 6 tea Spoones   7: 6 —
Sep.ᵗ 28ᵗʰ   To 6 Large Spoones   32: 19 —
              To 1 Sett of gold buttons   7: 11 —
              To 1 p.ʳ tea tongs & buckles   11: 9 —
Octo.ʳ 12   To mend.ᵍ a p.ʳ Earrings⎫
              & 2 Rings   ⎭   1: 6 —
Nov.ʳ 18ᵗʰ   To Sett of gold buttons   7: 10 —
Dec.ʳ 6ᵗʰ   To 9ˡᵇ: 10ᵒᶻ of Leather   34: 13: 9
                                                  £214: 12: 9

Josselyn paid Edwards by orders on the firm of Boiso and Phillips, an order on Phillips alone, and in cash. The balance due to Edwards, when "Reduc.ᵈ to lawfull Money," was £12.1. An additional expense, incurred on 18 March 1752 for two sets of gold buttons, brought the total to £14.3.10 ¹/₂.[34] A similar account exists to document Thomas Edwards's dealings with Edward Bromfield:

1750

May 3.   To mending 2 Fans   0: 1: 7¹/₄
Aug.ᵗ 31.   To making 2 Stone Hooks more than an ⎫
              old one received   ⎭   0: 5: 4

Novr 25.	To a Silver Porringer more than an old one	o: 19: 2$^{1}/_{2}$
1751	To mending a Spoon	o: o: 4$^{3}/_{4}$
May 6.	To mending 1 pair Earings more than } Gold received	o: 1: 8$^{3}/_{4}$
Novr 10.	To mending a pair Buckles	o: 1: 7$^{1}/_{4}$
1753		
April 12.	To the Exchange of a pair Buttons	o: 1: 4$^{3}/_{4}$
Novr 6.	To the Exchange of 2 Setts Ditto	1: 8: 3
1754		
May 22.	To a Silver Thimble	o: 2: 4
July 27.	To mending 2 Fans	o: 1: o$^{3}/_{4}$
Septr 28.	To mending a pair Wires	o: o: 4$^{3}/_{4}$
Decr 9.	To mend^g 2 Fans	o: 1: 4
1755		
Janu.^a 28.	To a pair Spectacles	o: 2: o$^{1}/_{4}$
July 26.	To mending a Silver Button	o: o: 2$^{1}/_{2}$
	To a Stone Ring dd y^r Dau^r more than } Gold received omitted June 18th 1753	o: 10: 10$^{1}/_{4}$
		3: 17: 8$^{3}/_{4}$

Bromfield was credited with giving Edwards £2.9. $^{3}/_{4}$ in old gold, and a box worth £0.10.08.[35] The accounts also demonstrate that Edwards bought shoes and gloves from Rebecca Amory; bread, milk, and flour from Belhazer Bayard; bread from John Soren; candles from Thomas Clark; household tools from Moses Harrington; wine from Seth Chipman; and upholstery from William Downe.[36] He had other business dealings with Joseph Rude, Abijah Adams, Joseph Webb, and James Blin, and he borrowed money from James Bowdoin.[37] There is an interesting bill of lading in the Brigden Papers for 103 pounds of deerskins that Thomas Edwards sent on board the ship *Good Friend* from New York to Boston on 19 October 1744.[38] This, along with the leather mentioned in the Thomas Josselyn account, suggests that Edwards had an ongoing business dealing in leather.

On 14 September 1755 Ebenezer Storer recorded Thomas Edwards's death in his diary: "I have this Day had another awful warning to prepare for Eternity in ye sudden & surprising Death of my Uncle Thos Edwards, who was this morning to all appearance in good Health & before noon was a pale & lifeless Corpse.—O what a sudden Change doth Death make."[39]

Thomas Edwards wrote his will on 23 October 1753. He left the bulk of his estate, including his house and land in Boston, a house and land in Cambridge, and a house and land in Plymouth, to his widow, Eleanor, and to his daughter Sarah Edwards. He left ten pounds to his daughter Elizabeth Cheever; ten pounds to his nephew John Edwards, son of his deceased brother John; ten pounds each to his nephews Joseph and John, sons of his brother Joseph; ten pounds to his cousin Ebenezer Storer; and "a handsome gold Motto Ring" to his brother Samuel. He named his wife, Eleanor, and his daughter Sarah executors of his estate. The will was witnessed by Jacob Griggs, Robert Jenkins, Jr., and Dudson Kilcup.[40] The inventory, which was appraised by David Cutler, Nathaniel Thayer, and Joseph Hiller, Sr. (q.v.), included

Sundry Goods in the Shop	106: 14: 10
a parcell of Buttons & Buckles	6: 8: 9

Knives & Scissars	4: 13:	10
Tapes & Threads	10: 11:	6
Stone Buttons, Buckles & Earings	102: 18:	4
Snuff Boxes & Stay Hooks	15: 5:	—
532 ^{oz}: 9^{dwt}: 16^{gr} Wrought Silver @ 7/4	195: 4:	10
365:13:12 unwrought & Houshold plate 6/8	121: 17:	10
11– 2:18 Wrought & unwrought Gold	62: 2:	6
Burnt Silver, Bullion, Lace, & Fringe	20: 6:	6
Scales & Weights	16: 4:	6
Black Lead potts & Crucibles	14:	5
a parcell of Stones of Different Sorts	43: 16:	9
a parcell of Goldsmiths Tools	52: 11:	2
. . .		
A Negro Man named Caesar	6: —	—
A Negro Man named Jersey	6: —	—
122 Books of Gold Leaf	11:	1 —[41]

The total value of Edwards's inventory was £1,780.12.4. At his death Edwards was among the top 10 percent of Boston's wealthiest citizens. BMW

SURVIVING OBJECTS

	Mark	Inscription	Patron	Date	Reference	Owner
Baptismal basin	B	Royall arms, azure 3 garbs, and crest, a demi-lion rampant with a garb in his paws; PECTORE PURO; THE GIFT of Isaac Royall Esqr to St Michaels/Church in BRISTOL 1747	Isaac Royall and/or St. Michael's Church, Bristol, R.I.	1747	Jones 1913, 97–98	
Beaker	B	The gift of M^r. Eben^r. Tucker to the Church in Milton 1728	Ebenezer Tucker and/or First Congregational Parish, Milton, Mass.	1728	Jones 1913, 290	
Beaker	B	The.Gift/of:Joseph: Bowman: Esqr/to: the: Church: of Christ/in: Lexington: 1755:	Joseph Bowman and/or First Congregational Society, Lexington, Mass.	1755	Jones 1913, 245	
Two buckles	?	?		ca. 1730		CW
Cann	B*	Unidentified arms, in fess point a crescent or on a chief azure 2 cinquefoils, and crest, an estoile		ca. 1745	YUAG files	
Cann	B*	CLS		ca. 1750	YUAG files	
Caster	D†	AQ (+)	Anna Quincy	ca. 1735	Buhler 1972, no. 140	MFAB
Caster	D	AG		ca. 1735	YUAG files	
Caster	D	IF	Israel Forrester	ca. 1750	Hammerslough/ Feigenbaum 1958–73, 3:53	

	Mark	Inscription	Patron	Date	Reference	Owner
Caster	D	M/SE (+)		ca. 1750	*Moore Collection* 1980, no. 113	HMA
Two casters	?	?		ca. 1745	*Antiques* 128 (July 1985): 84	
Two chafing dishes	B†	Storer arms, 3 quatrefoils on a chevron engrailed gules between 3 mullets, and crest, a talbot's head; S/EM (+)	Ebenezer and Mary (Edwards) Storer	ca. 1740	Buhler 1972, no. 141	MFAB
Creampot	D	?		ca. 1750	YUAG files	
Creampot	D	?	Sybil Farnham (?)	ca. 1750	*Antiques* 105 (February 1974): 249	
Creampot	D*	Speakman arms, or a chevron between 3 boars' heads couped	Speakman family	ca. 1755	Johnston 1994, 46 (as TE unidentified)	CMA
Creampot	?	?		ca. 1750	Parke-Bernet, 11–14 October 1944, lot 665	
Cup	A	S/EM (+)	Ebenezer and Mary (Edwards) Storer	ca. 1725	Buhler 1972, no. 137	MFAB
Cup	A*/D	S/EM (+)	Ebenezer and Mary (Edwards) Storer	ca. 1725	Buhler 1972, no. 138	MFAB
Ladle	B	none		ca. 1750	Sotheby's, 23–24 June 1994, lot 100	
Mourning ring (gold)	D	E. PAINE. Ob. 17. Oct.ʳ 1747: AE. 42	E. Paine	1747		MHS
Papboat	B	Cunningham crest, a unicorn's head	Cunningham family	ca. 1750	*American Silver* 1967, no. 7	RWNAG
Pepper box	D*	T/MM	Matthew and Mary Talcott	ca. 1750	Hammerslough/ Feigenbaum 1958–73, 1:53	WA
Porringer	A†	AE/ES		ca. 1730	*Antiques* 128 (September 1985): 456	
Porringer	A*	D/IS		ca. 1735	Buhler/Hood 1970, no. 128	YUAG
Porringer	A or D	H/IS (?)		ca. 1750	Anderson Galleries, 20–21 January 1928, lot 251	
Porringer	B*	SW		ca. 1730	Conger/ Rollins 1991, no. 188	USDS

	Mark	Inscription	Patron	Date	Reference	Owner
Porringer	B*	The/Gift/of M.^{rs}/ Rachel Barnard/to/ M.^{rs}/Rachel Ward/ 1736 (+)	Rachel Barnard and/or Rachel Ward	1736	Fales 1983, 13	PEM
Porringer	B/D*	AW	Abigail West	ca. 1735	MFA 1911, no. 472	
Porringer (with mark of Knight Leverett)	D	MWE (later)		ca. 1740	Washington 1925, no. 65	
Porringer	D	ES/to/IS	Elizabeth (Storer) Smith	ca. 1749	Buhler 1972, no. 142	MFAB
Porringer	?	Ex Dono Pupillorum 1749	John Wyeth (?) and/or the Harvard College class of 1749	1749	Buhler 1955, 56–57	
Porringer	?	EWS		ca. 1730	YUAG files	
Porringer	?	unidentified initials		ca. 1740	*Antiques* 89 (February 1966): 210	
Porringer	?	IP		ca. 1750	*Antiques* 16 (October 1929): 341	
Two salts	B	H/IM (+)		ca. 1740	YUAG files	
Salver	B*	Gibbs arms, 3 battle-axes in fess, and crest, a dexter mailed arm embowed grasping a battle-axe (+)	Robert Gibbs	ca. 1750	Hammerslough/ Feigenbaum 1958–73, 1:93	WA
Salver	B*	BP/to/SH		ca. 1745	Quimby 1995, no. 63	WM
Salver	B*	Allen arms, per chevron [gules] and ermine, in chief 2 lions' heads erased [or]; unidentified crest, a lion's head erased; impaling Parker arms, a chevron between 3 leopards' faces or	Allen and Parker families	ca. 1750	Quimby 1995, no. 64	WM
Sauceboat	B	?		ca. 1750	YUAG files	
Serving spoon	B*	Spooner (?) crest, a boar's head couped	Spooner family (?)	ca. 1745	Buhler/Hood 1970, no. 130	YUAG
Strainer (with mark of Samuel Edwards)	D	none		ca. 1735	Hammerslough/ Feigenbaum 1958–73, 1:102	
Sugar tongs	D	BR		ca. 1750	*Moore Collection* 1980, no. 112	
Tablespoon	B	AC		ca. 1750	MFA 1906, no. 111	
Tablespoon	B*	Storer crest, a talbot's head; Mary Storer/Jany 1 1755	Mary (Storer) Green	1755	Buhler 1972, no. 143	MFAB

	Mark	Inscription	Patron	Date	Reference	Owner
Tablespoon (mate below)	B*	Gibbs crest, 3 broken tilting spears, 2 in saltire and one in pale, ensigned with a wreath argent and azure; Eliz^h Gibbs	Elizabeth Gibbs	ca. 1755	Gourley 1965, no. 81	RISD
Tablespoon (mate above)	B*	Gibbs crest, 3 broken tilting spears, 2 in saltire and one in pale, ensigned with a wreath argent and azure; Eliz^h. Gibbs/ 1752	Elizabeth Gibbs	1752		RIHS
Tablespoon	B*	N/IH		ca. 1750		HD
Tablespoon	B	EH		ca. 1725	*Moore Collection* 1980, no. 114	
Tablespoon	B*	D/EM		ca. 1730		YUAG
Tablespoon	B*	Hannah Stor[illeg.]/ Jan 1 1755	Hannah Storer (?)	ca. 1755	Quimby 1995, no. 65	WM
Tablespoon	B*	W/SP		ca. 1750	Buhler/Hood 1970, no. 131	YUAG
Four tablespoons	B *or* C	unidentified crest; RT		ca. 1750	Christie's, 4 June 1988, lot 68	
Tablespoon	C*	I/DS		ca. 1750		RISD
Three tablespoons	?	?		ca. 1750	*Antiques* 99 (March 1971): 333	
Tankard	B *or* C	Minor arms, gules a fess argent between 3 plates; M/RM	Minor family	ca. 1740	Sotheby's, 27–29 January 1983, lot 132	
Teapot	A	Speakman arms, or a chevron between 3 boars' heads, and crest, a boar's head erect	Speakman family	ca. 1750	Buhler 1972, no. 542	MFAB
Teapot	B*	Lockwood arms (later; erased); LA (+)	Lockwood family	ca. 1735	Buhler/Hood 1970, no. 129	YUAG
Teapot	B	Alden (?) arms	Alden family (?)	ca. 1750	Washington 1925, no. 46	
Teapot	B	William Greenleaf/ Mary Brown/ June 1747	William Greenleaf and/ or Mary Brown	1747	MFA 1906, no. 112	
Teaspoon	B*	IC		ca. 1750		YUAG
Teaspoon	C†	none		ca. 1750	Quimby 1995, no. 66	WM
Teaspoon	C*	MS		ca. 1750		YUAG
Teaspoon	D	SA		ca. 1750		CHS
Two teaspoons	D*	S/EM	Ebenezer and Mary (Edwards) Storer	ca. 1750	Buhler 1972, no. 139	MFAB

	Mark	Inscription	Patron	Date	Reference	Owner
Teaspoon	D*	SA (over earlier initials)		ca. 1750		HD
Teaspoon	D*	DS		ca. 1750		YUAG
Two teaspoons	D	C/IH		ca. 1750	MFA 1906, nos. 113–14	
Whistle with coral and bells	D	Fayerweather crest, a beaver with a fish in its mouth; IF	Fayerweather family	ca. 1730	Whitehill et al. 1975, no. 109	AIC

1. RC 24:12.
2. Wyman 1879, 1:157; *Cambridge VR* 1:108; 2:61; RC 28:160; RC 9:120; Fairfield VR, vol. LR-A2, 681. Sarah's half-sister, Elizabeth Shove, married the Boston clockmaker Benjamin Bagnall, Sr.
3. MCPR, docket 3634. The tankard Samuel Burr bequeathed to his daughter may also have belonged to her great-grandfather John Steadman and may have been the tankard with embossed acanthus leaves on the body and floral engraving on the cover that was made by Timothy Dwight (q.v.) and that Steadman owned. Still in private hands, it has been published several times, most notably in Bigelow 1917 (131–33) and in Buhler 1956 (p. 58, fig. 19). Samuel Burr married Elizabeth Jennor (d. 1756) as his second wife in 1707. In her will, Elizabeth (Jennor) Burr bequeathed land to her step-granddaughters, daughters of Thomas Edwards, Elizabeth (Edwards) Cheever and Sarah Edwards.
4. SCCR, Court of Common Pleas Record Book 1725, 274; and SCCR, files 17540, 19521.
5. RC 24:165, 192; RC 28:242; RC 30:22; *Church in Brattle Square*, 146, 152; Dow 1927, 41 (notice of death of Sarah [Edwards] Brigden).
6. Roberts 1895, 1:416; Seybolt 1939, 176.
7. SCCR, Court of Common Pleas Record Book 1725, 75; and SCCR file, 18500. For a full account of the case, see John LeRoux biography.
8. Thomas Edwards Accounts, Brigden Papers, YU.
9. SCCR, file 29204.
10. SCD 41:175–76; RC 13:173.
11. SCCR, file 21468. The house was mortgaged to Skinner on 27 October 1727; SCD 41:176–77.
12. SCD 41:205–06; 44:235.
13. There is no record of guardianship papers being filed for his daughters, and Edwards may have taken them to New York with him.
14. SCCR, Court of Common Pleas Record Book 1744–46, 46; 1749–51, 73, 205.
15. Benjamin Walker, Jr., Diaries, vol. 3, entry for 7 August 1744, MHS.
16. SCPR 38:515–16. Although John Edwards left the largest share of his estate to Thomas, his oldest surviving son, he did not name him as one of the executors of the estate, probably because Thomas was residing in New York at the time John Edwards wrote his will.
17. Dow 1927, 44; advertisement repeated 15 and 22 May.
18. Benjamin Walker, Jr., Diaries, vol. 3, MHS.
19. Roberts 1895, 1:416; Seybolt 1939, 247. Thomas Edwards invited his neighbors Benjamin and John Walker to attend an entertainment for the Artillery Company at his house on 5 October 1747 (Benjamin Walker, Jr., Diaries, vol. 3, MHS), and an account in his estate papers indicates that he incurred expenses for an Artillery Company dinner in 1754 (Thomas Edwards Accounts, Brigden Papers, YU).
20. SCCR, Court of Common Pleas Record Book 1744–46, 371; 1749–51, 56.
21. Dow 1927, 46; the advertisement was repeated on 27 November and 10 December.
22. SCCR, file 170003.
23. SCCR, Superior Court of Judicature Record Book 1747–50, 85.
24. SCCR, Court of Common Pleas Record Book 1749–51, 220–21; file papers of the Court of Common Pleas, Court held 1 January 1750/51, no. 128. For a full account, see Thomas Townsend biography.
25. Thomas Edwards Accounts, Brigden Papers, YU. For a full account, see Asahel Mason biography.
26. Ward 1989, 66–76; and Ward 1983, 64–91, 119–20, 153–54, 183–84.
27. The mark is on mugs (DAPC 77.2471 and 90.3021).

28. Roberts 1895, 1:416; Buhler 1972, 1:171. In 1727, when he was nineteen years old, Thomas Coverly witnessed two deeds for Edwards (SCD 41:176–77, 205–06).

29. The other two were Edwards's brother Samuel and Jacob Hurd.

30. SCPR, docket 8959.

31. Timothy Orne Ledger 1738–58, fol. 24, PEM.

32. Photostat in the Bigelow-Phillips files.

33. Thomas Edwards Accounts, Brigden Papers, YU.

34. Thomas Edwards Accounts, Brigden Papers, YU.

35. Thomas Edwards Accounts, Brigden Papers, YU.

36. Thomas Edwards Accounts, Brigden Papers, YU.

37. The occupations of these individuals are not known because the receipts are for cash. Thomas Edwards Accounts, Brigden Papers, YU.

38. Thomas Edwards Accounts, Brigden Papers, YU.

39. Ebenezer Storer Diary 1749–64, fol. 53, NEHGS.

40. SCPR 50:544.

41. SCPR 51:52.

Stephen Emery
1749–1801

A

B

C

D

E

F

Stephen Emery was born on 23 March 1749 in Exeter, New Hampshire.[1] His father, Rev. Stephen Emery (1707–82), the son of Rev. Samuel Emery (1670–1724) and Tabitha Littlefield (d. 1724), had married his mother, Hannah Allen (d. 1799) of Falmouth, Maine, the daughter of Rev. Benjamin Allen (1680–1754) and Elizabeth Crocker (b. 1692), on 8 October 1742.[2] The Emery family was well respected among Boston's educated elite: the silversmith's father, paternal grandfather, and brother Samuel were all graduates of Harvard College.[3] Emery was related by marriage to a silversmith: his sister Hannah married the Exeter, New Hampshire, silversmith John Ward Gilman on 3 December 1767.[4] Stephen Emery married Mary Ann Knox (1755–1801), the daughter of Thomas Knox (ca. 1732–1805), a cooper, and Mary (Howard) Knox (1736–1800), in Boston's New North Church on 20 March 1777.[5]

Stephen Emery probably was apprenticed to Daniel Parker (q.v.). Emery would have completed his training by 1770, but there is evidence that he remained in Parker's shop as a journeyman or partner after his apprenticeship: he witnessed Daniel Parker's will, which was written on 18 June 1772 and presented for probate in 1786.[6] He also witnessed a deed of Parker's on 16 September 1772, and a presentation spoon made for the Eliot family bears the marks of both Emery and Parker.[7] Emery maintained a close relationship with Parker, appearing as a creditor against the Parker estate for £1.18.5 in 1789.[8]

By August 1776, Emery had established his own shop and professional ties with colleagues like Edward Lang of Salem (q.v.). Between that date and November 1777 Emery purchased a considerable number of small wares from Lang as shown by the following account:

1776. M^r. Stephen Emery of/Boston/D^r.

August 23^d.	To ball,^{ce} at Settlement this day	1.	4.	9
Octob^r. 5th	To 18 dollars, w^t 15^{oz}.12^{pt}.0^{grs} at 6/8	5.	4.	—
Nov^r– 6.	⎧ To 24 pair knee buckles w$_—^t$ 6^{oz}.19^{pt}.0^{gr} @ 6/8	2.	6.	4
	⎨ To making d^o at 2^s/8^d	3.	4.	—
	⎩ To 3^{pwt}.12^{gr} Silver Left of Coll^l. Pickering spoon	.	1.	2
1777 Jany. 8.	To 10 dollars w^t. 8^{oz}.13^{pt}.0^{grs} at 6/8	2.	17.	8
Feby 21st	To 1 doz^n Stock buckles, w^t. 3^{oz}.10^{dwt}.0^{gr}	1.	3.	4
	To making d^o at 4^s/	2.	8.	0
	⎰ To two Strings gold beeds w^t. ⎱			
	⎱ .11^{dwt}.12^{grs} at £5.1^s.4^d p^r. oz ⎰	2.	18.	3

	To making d.º at 20ˢ/. a string	2. —.	—
	To 11 dollars w.ᵗ 9ᵒᶻ.11ᵈᵗ.12ᵍʳˢ	3. 3.	10
Septem.ʳ 26	To 2 Gold necklaces wt:11ᵈᵗ.16ᵍʳˢ	2. 19.	1
	To making d.º	—. 16.	—
Octob.ʳ	To making 22 Steel Top thimb.ˢ	1. 2.	—
	To Silver for d.º 2.ᵒᶻ	13.	4
	To a Necklace w.ᵗ 0.ᵒᶻ.6.ᵈᵗ.3ᵍˢ	1. 11.	0¹/₂
Nov.ʳ	To making d.º	. 8.	—
		£34. 0.	9¹/₂

		oz dwᵗ grs
The whole Stock above Charg'd		
Reckoning the gold as Silver at 6/8 is		68. 14. 2
The whole Stock Creditted }		
on the other Leaf is } carried		66. 15. 0
Ball.ᶜᵉ in Stock due to EL to new acc.ᵗ		1. 19. 2
Settled the above Acc.ᵗ Jan.ʸ the 9ᵗʰ 1778		

In exchange Emery supplied Lang with flatware and shop supplies.

	Supra	C.ʳ
1776		
Septem.ʳ 2.ⁿᵈ	By Sundries as p.ʳ Bill	1. 19. 2
Octob.ʳ	By 9 Dollars w.ᵗ 7.ᵒᶻ 16ᵖᵗ 0ᵍʳˢ at 6ˢ/8ᵈ	2. 12. —
	By 2 Small button Stones	.8
28ᵗʰ	By 1 doz.ⁿ Tea Spoons w.ᵗ 4.ᵒᶻ 6.ᵈ 0	
	By 6 Large d.º w.ᵗ 10.15.0	
	15. 1. 0 @ 6/8	5. —. 4
	By making 18 Tea Spoons at 2/8	1. 10. —
	By making 6 Large d.º at 3ˢ/4ᵈ	1. —. —
Nov.ʳ 26	By 6 pair knee Chapes	. 6. —
	By a pair Large Shears	. 8. —
1777 Jan.ʸ 8ᵗʰ	By 4 pr large Spoons & three } Tea d.º w.ᵗ 8.ᵒᶻ 10.ᵖᵗ 0ᵍʳˢ at 6/8	2. 16. 8
	By making d.º	. 18. 4
Feb.ʸ 14	By Four large Silver Spoons } w.ᵗ 7.ᵒᶻ 3.ᵈʷᵗ 0ᵍʳˢ at 6/8 }	2. 7. 8
	By making d.º at 6ˢ/.	1. 4. 0
April	By 1 doz.ⁿ Tea Spoons w.ᵗ 5.ᵒᶻ 6.ᵈᵗ.0ᵍʳˢ	1. 15. 4
	By making d.º	2. —. —
	By Six Large Spoons w.ᵗ 10.ᵒᶻ 18.ᵈᵗ 0ᵍʳˢ } at 6/8 }	3. 12. 8
	By making d.º at 6/	1. 16. —
Aug.ˢᵗ 13.ᵗʰ	By 13 Small files, 2 black Pots } 4 Crucibles, & 2 lb Sandiver }	1. 5. 4
Septemb.ʳ	By 2 Large Spoons & 6 Tea } d.º w.ᵗ 7.ᵒᶻ 3.ᵈᵗ 0ᵍʳˢ at 6/8 }	2. 7. 8
	By making d.º	. 6. 8
Nov.ʳ 6ᵗʰ	By three large Spoons } w.ᵗ 4.ᵒᶻ 18.ᵈᵗ 0ᵍʳˢ at 6/8 }	1. 12. 8
	By making d.º	. 4. —
		£35. 3. 2

The whole of the above Credit,
Exclusive of the Stock is 12. 18. 2
The whole Charge on the other
leaf, Exclusive of the Stock is 11. 2. 9

£ 1. 15. 5

Ball.^{ce} due to S.E. Carry'd to new Acc.^{t}
Settled the above Acc.^{t} Jany the 9.th 1778.
Carried over to 62^9

The Boston Assessors' list of 1780 recorded "Stephen Emmery" as a resident of ward 6 occupying property worth an annual rent of £120.[10] Emery also began training apprentices: in his diary, Rev. William Bentley stated that both his brother Thomas (1764–1804) and his brother-in-law Robert Dawes (b. 1767) were apprenticed to Stephen Emery, "a jeweller, or Silversmith, who was then in high reputation."[11] Emery also may have trained his son Thomas Knox Emery (1781–1815), who followed him into the trade.[12]

Stephen Emery, silversmith, purchased land in Gorham and Scarborough, Cumberland County, Maine, from William Wescot, a Falmouth innholder, for £74.6 on 20 July 1786, but he seems never to have lived there.[13] On 11 March 1785, "Stephen Emery, Goldsmith, of Boston" bought a brick house and land on Union Street, Boston, next door to his former master, Parker, for £1,260.13.4 from the upholsterer Moses Grant.[14] He arranged a mortgage with Grant of 500 Spanish milled dollars at an interest of 6 shillings each.[15] In August 1787, Emery and his wife, Mary Ann, used this property, described in the deed as their residence, as collateral for a loan of £1,600 from the merchants Isaiah and Elisha Doane, of Boston, and David Greenough, of Roxbury.[16] Emery's shop was also located at this address, for he advertised in the *Massachusetts Centinel* in 1789 that he carried on "The GOLDSMITH'S BUSINESS, *in all its branches*," at 5 Union Street.[17] *The Boston Directory* of 1789 lists Stephen Emery at 5 Union Street, next door to the shop of Joseph Loring (q.v.) at 3 Union Street.[18] A year earlier the two men had served as bondsmen for "Mr. Procter's" application for an auctioneer's license.[19]

On 18 December 1790, Stephen and Mary Ann Emery sold their house on Union Street for £750 and paid off their earlier mortgages.[20] In March 1791, Emery's address was described as "the House lately improved by Mr. JONATHAN STODDAR[D], in *Ann-street*, at the bottom of *Cross-street*—where the SILVERSMITH'S BUSINESS is carried on in all its branches, as *Cheap*, as at any Shop in town."[21] On 3 November 1792, the silversmith's advertisement in the *Columbian Centinel* gave the location of his shop as "No. 1, Fish-Street, *Boston*, Bottom of Cross-Street," the same location recorded for him in the Boston directories of 1796 and 1798.[22] The United States Direct Tax for 1798 described this property as being owned by Susannah Stoddard and occupied by Stoddard and Emery: "wooden dwelling; S. W. on Cross Street; N. W. on Fish Street, making the Corner. Land, 2,432 square feet; house, 1,460 square feet; 3 stories, 35 windows; Value, $3,000."[23]

Emery appears in the daybook of Paul Revere, Jr. (q.v.), seven times between 1785 and 1789.[24] He commissioned from Revere a variety of holloware items, including two teapots with matching stands, a tankard, a punch bowl, a small porringer, and a creampot. Emery probably sold these in his shop, perhaps purchasing them to fulfill large orders he was unable to meet on his own. On 25 April 1785, Revere recorded,

Mr Stephen Emmery   D^r
To a Silver Tea pot w^t }   oz p
To a Silver Salver w^t }   22:13
Mak^g Tea pot   3 15 —
Mak^g Salver   1 — —

On 30 January 1787 Emery was debited:

Mr Stephen Emmery D^r
To a Silver punch bowl w 13:10
Making   1 16—

Mr Step^n Emmery   C^r
By Silver   8^{oz}— 9 —
By Silver   5— 1

On 3 April 1787 the ledger shows:

Mr Stephen Emery   D^r
To making a small porringer   — 15 —

A few months later on 4 August, Revere noted,

Mr Stephen Emmery   D^r
To making Silver Tankard   4 10 —

On 5 September 1788, Revere recorded the following transaction:

Mr Stephen Emery   D^r
To a Silv^r Teapot w^t 17:10
Making $^£$ 4—16 Engrav 26/   6 12 —
Wooden handle   4 —
To a Silver Stand for do w^t 7^{oz}
Making & Engraving   1 10 —

On 17 October 1788, the following charge was recorded:

M^r S Emery   D^r
To Making Cream pot   1 2 —

Finally, on 7 September 1789, Revere recorded:

Mr Step^n Emery   D^r
To engrav^g a cream jug   12
To a graver   8

Emery advertised extensively in Boston newspapers; at least forty-six advertisements documenting his activities as a silversmith and retailer were published between 1785 and 1793. The first appeared in the *Independent Ledger* of 12 December 1785 and was repeated on 19 and 26 December. In it Emery announced "A large Assortment of GOLDSMITH and JEWELLER'S WARE, TO BE SOLD, *Cheap for Cash*, At Stephen Emery's SHOP, No. 5, UNION-STREET" in addition to teas, coffee, chocolate, and spices. Emery was willing to give "CASH, or any of the above Articles for old Gold and Silver, Pewter, Lead, Brass, or Copper." Twenty notices placed by Emery in the *Independent Chronicle* and the *Herald of Freedom* between August 1787 and June 1789 advertised a comprehensive list of goldsmithing services and supplies. The one that appeared in the *Herald of Freedom* in May and June 1789 is representative:

ENGLISH and AMERICAN
Plated Buckles.
MEN's, women's and children's warranted PLATED SHOE BUCKLES, made
and sold, by

STEPHEN EMERY,
At his SHOP, No. 5, UNION STREET.
Also, to be sold very cheap, an assort-
ment of Articles, in the GOLDSMITH, JEWEL-
LERY and FOUNDERY ways, viz.
Best English Blew Pots, of all sizes,
Crucibles, by the dozen or single Nest,
Files of all sorts,
Brass and Tin Wire;
Fine Binding Wire,
Cast Steel,
Grain Tin,
Watch Glasses and Main Springs;
An affortment of Watch Files,
Borax, Salt Petre and Sandifer;
Pumice Stone,
Moulding Sand,
Steel Shoe Chapes, and other Articles.
The GOLDSMITH's BUSINESS, *in all its
branches, carried on as usual.*
Pewter, Brass and Copper, will be
taken in payment for any of the above articles.
Cash, and the highest price given for
OLD SILVER.
Wanted, a good second-hand TAN-
KARD, one ditto CAN.
Boston, May 15, 1789.[25]

Emery's repeated requests for base metals suggest that he may have cast pewter, brass, and copper objects, an unusually extensive range of materials for an eighteenth-century silversmith. Emery issued condensed versions of this advertisement thirteen times in the *Massachusetts Centinel* and the *Independent Chronicle* between April 1789 and March 1790.

Anticipating the sale of his shop on Union Street, Emery advertised in the *Massachusetts Centinel* of 17 March 1790 that "his whole stock, consisting of an assortment of articles in the Goldsmith's, Jeweller's and Founder's Way" was for purchase. Specifically identifying ready-made wares, buckles, cleaning powders, and pumice stones for purchase, he also included his customary plea for old gold, silver, pewter, brass, and copper.[26]

In addition to managing his growing business, Emery presided over a large domestic establishment. The census of 1790 listed him as the head of a household composed of three adult men, three boys under the age of sixteen, and six women, an indication that he housed four apprentices, journeymen, or servants as well as his wife and six children.[27]

Emery's advertisement of 30 March 1791 announcing his move to Ann Street included a request for "A quantity of Old Silver—Also, *Two* second-hand TANKARDS one pair of CANS, and one pair of PORRINGERS, for which the *Cash* will be given."[28] These recurring requests for specific forms of silver objects are an unusual feature of Emery's numerous advertisements. He may have intended these objects for his own use or may have planned to refurbish them to fill specific commissions. A similar notice published on 1 April 1791 ended with a request for an apprentice.[29] The following year Emery promised cash for old metal objects and expressed his willingness to accept "English or West-India Goods" as payment for his services.[30] He also reiterated his need for a second-hand tankard. In July 1793, the silversmith announced the following: "*Wanted*, A second-hand silver TANKARD, and one pair CANS, for which cash will be given. Apply to STEPHEN EMERY, at his shop, bottom of Cross-Street; where is carried on as usual, the Silver Smith's business, in its various branches."[31] Emery's final advertisement appeared in the *Independent Chronicle* on 28 November 1793.[32] By then, after eight years of aggressive advertising, Emery had probably developed a large enough client base to reduce his search for new customers.

In addition to his many Boston patrons, Emery had customers in outlying areas. Elisabeth Boyles's will, written on 30 September 1777 and probated on 2 September 1782, states, "I do hereby give to the Church of Christ in the first Parrish in said Beverly one silver Tankard to be purchased at the discretion of my executor as soon as may be after my decease."[33] Her executor, Thomas Stephens, recorded a payment of £11.10 to Stephen Emery for a tankard to be given to this church, and the First Church in Beverly, Massachusetts, currently owns an unmarked tankard that can be attributed to Emery based on this evidence. The engraved inscription establishes it as "The / Gift of Mrs. Elisabeth Boyles / To / The First Church / in Beverly / 1785." Emery also made a porringer and a pair of sauceboats for Thomas and Elizabeth Cutts of Portsmouth, New Hampshire, and a baptismal basin for Trinity Church, Newport, Rhode Island.

Emery was selected as one of eight petit jurors for the Circuit Court in 1794, which indicates the respect and esteem he was accorded by neighbors and colleagues.[34] Seven years later Emery died intestate; the *Columbian Centinel* reported his death on 18 November 1801.[35] His daughter Mary was appointed an administrator of his estate on 24 November, along with Edward Proctor, Esq., and the apothecary Bradford Webster.[36] Emery's estate was inventoried on 7 December 1801.[37] Valuing $147.55, it included a mahogany desk, tables, and stand, a "Rittenhouse" stove and a shop stove, and household furnishings, many described as old. The description of his tools was brief. The lot of shop tools and utensils was the second most expensive entry in the inventory, and the large value placed on the tools shows that Emery remained active in his trade throughout his life.

Emery was a competent and prolific silversmith, producing all the standard flatware and holloware forms. Five marks are associated with him: S·EMERY in a cartouche (A); the same mark with the first initial broken off (B); initials separated by a pellet in a rectangle (C and D); and initials in a rectangle (E and F). The SE in an oval mark occasionally attributed to him is the mark of Samuel Edwards (q.v.).[38] Mark (A) is most common and appears on the majority of holloware pieces. It was in use until at least 1789, when Emery made a pair of porringers for David and Hannah West, who married that year. By 1793, the die for this mark had been broken; Emery reshaped the cartouche to

compensate for the missing initial and continued to use it in modified form
(B). A creampot shaped like a Liverpool jug, inscribed "I[ohn] Allen to M[ary]
Eaton 1793," bears this mark. The initial marks (C) and (D) appear primarily
on flatware. Emery made spoons with a variety of bowl decorations, including
single drops, seven- and eleven-lobed scallop shells, a bird on a branch, and
an acanthus leaf with a beaded center vein. Many of the spoons have engraved
"ruffle" edges and feature Emery's characteristic engraved design of adjoining
bright-cut ovals enclosing a monogram above pendant bellflowers.

A comparison of Emery's marked objects suggests that he occasionally
retailed silver made by his contemporaries, a practice also suggested by Emery's
public requests for specific silver items. Although probably quite common
during the eighteenth century, specific retailed objects are difficult to document.
However, several objects associated with Emery offer evidence of this practice.
A caster sold by Christie's in May 1986 is marked SE (mark E or F) on the
base, but also bears an unidentified mark IB on the inside. A porringer in a
private collection bearing mark (A) features a keyhole handle that differs from
other Emery porringers but resembles many produced by Paul Revere. In
addition, this porringer's diminutive size suggests that it was the "small porringer" Emery ordered from Revere in April 1787. Similarly, the cast elements,
moldings, proportions, and shape of a tankard marked by Emery in the Yale
University Art Gallery collection resemble Revere's work more than Emery's,
which suggests that this could be the tankard commissioned from Revere in
August 1787.

Similarities in the spoons made by Emery and by his neighbor Joseph
Loring suggest that they also may have had a professional relationship. Spoons
marked by Loring generally feature one of three different decorative patterns
on the bowl, two variations of an intricate beaded-stem acanthus leaf design
and an eleven-lobed, three-tiered shell. A number of Emery's spoons appear
to have been made with the same swages Loring used, which suggests an
exchange of goods or equipment between the two shops. The eleven-lobed
shell that appears on the bowls of the Loring spoons made for the Eells family
is similar to the one on the bowl of the Emery spoon engraved "WCW," mark
(A).[39] The bowl decoration on a pair of teaspoons engraved "H/ES" in the
Ineson-Bissell collection, mark (C), is the same acanthus leaf design that
appears on a Loring spoon in a private collection.[40] A more intricate acanthus
leaf design used on two Emery tablespoons, mark (A), also appears on a pair
of Loring spoons made for Hannah Breed.[41]   DAF

SURVIVING OBJECTS

	Mark	Inscription	Patron	Date	Reference	Owner
Cann	A*	Motey Deering	Motey Deering	ca. 1785		MMA
Two canns (mate below)	A	G/JA		ca. 1775	YUAG files	
Cann (mates above)	A	G/JA		ca. 1775	YUAG files	
Caster	E or F	V/FI		ca. 1770	Silver Supple- ment 1973, no. 39	
Caster	E or F	S/DI		ca. 1780	Christie's, 31 May 1986, lot 50	
Creampot	B†	IALLEN/TO/ MEATON/1793 (+)	John Allen and/or Mary Eaton	1793	Buhler 1972, no. 450	MFAB

	Mark	Inscription	Patron	Date	Reference	Owner
Creampot	C or D	LB		ca. 1770	*Moore Collection* 1980, no. 150	
Creampot	?	?		ca. 1780	Parke-Bernet, 14–15 May 1948, lot 186	
Ladle	B*	JJJCC		ca. 1790		SI
Ladle	B*	AL/to/ALB		ca. 1790	Buhler 1979, no. 70	WAM
Ladle	C or D	?		ca. 1770	MFA 1911, no. 486	
Ladle	?	R		ca. 1785	*Antiques* 69 (January 1956): 18	
Paten	A	Donum D./Johannes Mulderi et D. Guilielmi Bright/in usum Ecclesiae Anglicanae/in Novo Porto in Insula/De Rhode Island	Trinity Church, Newport, R.I., for John Muldery and William Bright	ca. 1770	Jones 1913, 318 (as a baptismal basin)	
Porringer	A	S/IE	Jonathan and Elizabeth (Plummer) Sayward	ca. 1785	Sander 1982, no. 32	SPNEA
Porringer	A*	S/WT		ca. 1775	*Antiques* 71 (May 1957): 394	
Porringer	A	?		ca. 1775	MFA 1911, no. 483	
Porringer	A	R/BA		ca. 1770	Sotheby's, 27 January 1989, lot 919	
Porringer	A	unidentified initials		ca. 1785	*Antiques* 103 (February 1973): 242	
Porringer (mate below)	A*	W/DH	David and Hannah (Watts) West	ca. 1790	Buhler 1972, no. 449	MFAB
Porringer (mate above)	A*	W/DH	David and Hannah (Watts) West	ca. 1790	Eitner 1976, no. 89	
Porringer	A*	JL; RR/JL/June 1801 (later) (+)		ca. 1785		PEM
Porringer	A*	B/SM		ca. 1775	YUAG files	
Porringer (see also mate with mark B)	A*	C/TE (+)	Thomas and Elizabeth Cutts	ca. 1775	*Moore Collection* 1980, no. 152	
Porringer	A	E or F	E. Phelps to S.D. Phelps (later?)	ca. 1775	MFA 1911, no. 483	
Porringer (see also mate with mark A)	B	C/TE	Thomas and Elizabeth Cutts	ca. 1775	Hammerslough/ Feigenbaum 1958–73, 3:41	
Porringer	?	unidentified arms; unidentified initials		ca. 1775	Parke-Bernet, 27 January 1967, lot 3	

	Mark	Inscription	Patron	Date	Reference	Owner
Porringer	?	IWG		ca. 1775	*Antiques* 90 (September 1966): 288	
Porringer	?	?		ca. 1775		ChM
Two salt spoons	C, D, or E	H	Moses Michael and Rachel (Myers) Hays	ca. 1790	Christie's, 17–18 January 1992, lot 180	
Two salt spoons	C	A		ca. 1790	DAPC 72.3638	WM
Salt spoon	E*	W/WM		ca. 1775		YUAG
Salt spoon	F†	ED	Elizabeth Derby	ca. 1790	Buhler 1972, appendix no. 25	MFAB
Two sauceboats	A	TEC (+)	Thomas and Elizabeth Cutts	ca. 1775	*Moore Collection* 1980, no. 151	
Tablespoon	A	The/Property/of the third/Church in/ Reading	Third Church of Christ, Reading, Mass.	ca. 1775	YUAG files	
Tablespoon	A*	RB		ca. 1790		HD
Tablespoon (mate below)	A*	SPT		ca. 1785		SI
Tablespoon (mate above)	A*	SPT		ca. 1785		YUAG
Two tablespoons	A*	AB		ca. 1790	Eitner 1976, nos. 90–91	
Tablespoon	A*	S IENKS (+)	S. Jenks	ca. 1785		YUAG
Tablespoon	A*	IF		ca. 1785		MMA
Tablespoon	A*	A/IS		ca. 1770	YUAG files	
Tablespoon	A*	B/WE		ca. 1775		YUAG
Tablespoon	A†	MB		ca. 1770	YUAG files	
Tablespoon	A*	SM		ca. 1775		YUAG
Tablespoon	A*	SAH		ca. 1785	Buhler/Hood 1970, no. 284	YUAG
Tablespoon (mate below)	A	Appleton (?) crest, a pineapple	Appleton family (?)	ca. 1785	DAPC 75.5116	WM
Tablespoon (mate above)	A*	Appleton (?) crest, a pineapple	Appleton family (?)	ca. 1785	Buhler/Hood 1970, no. 284	YUAG
Tablespoon	A	EV/1785	Elizabeth Vose	ca. 1785	MFA 1911, no. 482	
Tablespoon	A*	SB; JHB	Barrell family	ca. 1780	Sander 1982, no. 31	SPNEA
Tablespoon	A*	TEC	Thomas and Elizabeth Cutts	ca. 1785	DAPC 72.1930	WM
Tablespoon	A	MC		ca. 1785	DAPC 72.1932	WM
Tablespoon	A	WCW		ca. 1790	DAPC 72.2215	WM
Tablespoon	A	IC/to/LW		ca. 1790	DAPC 86.2006	
Two tablespoons	A*	W	Wood family	ca. 1790	Buhler 1972, appendix no. 23	MFAB
Tablespoon	B	SE		ca. 1795	DAPC 75.4256	WM
Tablespoon	B	AME		ca. 1785		RISD

	Mark	Inscription	Patron	Date	Reference	Owner
Two tablespoons	D	W	Wood family	ca. 1790	Buhler 1972, appendix no. 22	MFAB
Twelve tablespoons (with mark of Daniel Parker)	?	Ex Dono Pupillorum [illeg.] XXI [illeg.]	Andrew Eliot and/or the Harvard College class of 1771	ca. 1771	YUAG files	
Tankard	A*	P/LM		ca. 1785	Buhler/Hood 1970, no. 283	YUAG
Tankard	A	L/EA		ca. 1780	YUAG files	
Tankard	A	Everett		ca. 1785	DAPC 77.2112	
Tankard (attrib.)	none	The/Gift of/Mrs Elisabeth Boyles/ To/The First Church/in Beverly/ 1785	Thomas Stephens, executor of Elisabeth Boyles's estate, for First Parish Church, Beverly, Mass.	1785	Jones 1913, 16	
Two teaspoons	C*	H/ES		ca. 1785	DAPC 74.1122; and 74.1487	WM
Teaspoon	C*	K/RA		ca. 1775		YUAG
Teaspoon	C*	unidentified crest, a lion rampant holding a halberd		ca. 1780		YUAG
Teaspoon	C†	H/AE		ca. 1775		YUAG
Two teaspoons	C*	N/DD		ca. 1775		YUAG
Teaspoon	C or D	B/BM		ca. 1775	DAPC 74.1312	WM
Four teaspoons	C or D	II		ca. 1775	Sotheby's, 27 January 1989, lot 908	
Two teaspoons	C or D	EV/1785	Elizabeth Vose	ca. 1785	MFA 1911, no. 484	
Two teaspoons	D*	M/MR		ca. 1785		SFCAI
Teaspoon	D†	Greenleaf crest, a bird with a sprig in its beak; MS	Mary Storer	ca. 1775	Buhler 1972, no. 448	MFAB
Teaspoon	D	F/EI		ca. 1780	Eitner 1976, no. 92	
Teaspoon	D*	none		ca. 1790	Buhler 1972, appendix no. 24	MFAB
Teaspoon	E†	Y/JD		ca. 1775	DAPC 74.1496	WM
Teaspoon (mates below)	E*	C		ca. 1790	YUAG files	
Two teaspoons (mate above)	E*	C		ca. 1790		PEM
Teaspoon	F*	TC/to/DC		ca. 1790		HD
Three teaspoons	?	B		ca. 1785	YUAG files	
Twelve teaspoons	?	WMW		ca. 1790	Christie's, 24 January 1987, lot 53	
Teaspoon	?	SM		ca. 1775		YIM

	Mark	Inscription	Patron	Date	Reference	Owner
Two-handled cup	C *or* D	The/Gift of/deacon Timothy Pratt/To the Third Church/ of Christ/in/ Reading	Timothy Pratt and/or First Congregational Church, Reading, Mass.	ca. 1775	YUAG files	
Two-handled cup	C *or* D	Part/of this Cup/is the Gift of the/ Rev$^{\underline{nd}}$ Timothy Dickinson/To the third Church/of Christ in/ Reading	Rev. Timothy Dickin-son and/or Third Church of Christ, Read-ing, Mass.	ca. 1775	YUAG files	

1. Emery 1890, 20.
2. Emery 1890, 6, 20; Dexter 1885, 74–76; *Newbury VR* 1:161; *Barnstable and Sandwich VR*, 19, 50; *Index of Obituaries, 1704–1800*, 2:11.
3. *Sibley's Harvard Graduates* 4:99–100; 8:707–10.
4. Emery 1890, 39.
5. RC 30:373; Emery 1890, 39; RC 24:225, 287; RC 30:13; *Index of Obituaries, 1784–1840*, 3:2679–80.
6. SCPR 85:43–44, docket 18604.
7. SCD 122:48. The spoon is recorded in the Emery files, YUAG, but its location is unknown.
8. SCPR 88:172.
9. Edward Lang Account Book, fols. 60v, 61r, PEM.
10. "Assessors' 'Taking-Books,'" 30.
11. Bentley 1905–62, 2:121; 3:126.
12. Another of Emery's sons, Samuel (1787–1882), who was not trained by him, pursued the related profession of making mathematical instruments. SCPR 105:40.
13. William Wescot to Stephen Emery, 20 July 1786; D.S. Greenough Papers, MHS.
14. SCD 147:216–18.
15. SCD 147:218–20.
16. SCD 160:276–77.
17. *Massachusetts Centinel*, 22, 29 April, 6 May 1789.
18. RC 10:183, 190; *Boston Directory* 1789, 18.
19. RC 27:70.
20. SCD 168:268–69; 160:276–77; 147:218–20.
21. *Columbian Centinel*, 30 March 1791, repeated 6, 13, 20 April.
22. *Columbian Centinel*, 3 November 1792, repeated 10 and 14 November; RC 10:243; *Boston Directory* 1796, 40; *Boston Directory* 1798, 45. During the 1790s, North Street was known as Ann Street from Union Street to Cross Street and as Fish Street from Cross Street to Scarlett's Wharf (Thwing 1920, 34). Since Emery's shop was located at the Cross Street junction, the address change reflects an ambiguity about the division between Ann and Fish streets.
23. RC 22:226.
24. 25 April 1785; 30 January, 3 April, 4 August 1787; 5 September, 17 October 1788; 7 September 1789, vol. 2, Waste Book, 1783–97, 28, 50, 54, 61, [70], [72], [81], Revere Family Papers, MHS.
25. *Herald of Freedom*, 15, 19, 22, 29 May, 5/6, 12 June 1789.
26. *Independent Chronicle*, 8 and 22 July 1790.
27. RC 22:446.
28. *Columbian Centinel*, 30 March, 6, 13, 20 April 1791.
29. *Independent Chronicle*, 1 April 1791.
30. *Columbian Centinel*, 3 November 1792.
31. *Columbian Centinel*, 13 July 1793.
32. *Independent Chronicle*, 28 November 1793.
33. Jones 1913, 16.
34. RC 27:238.
35. Boston Deaths, 1800–1810; *Index of Obituaries, 1784–1840*, 2:1504.
36. SCPR 99:610.

37. SCPR 99:634–35.

38. French (1917) 1967, 42; Avery 1920, no. 228; Kovel 1961, 92.

39. All three spoons are in the Ineson-Bissell collection, WM: Emery (62.240.1140), Loring (62.240.1261, 62.240.1263). Another Loring tablespoon with this shell is in the Ineson-Bissell collection, WM (62.240.1270).

40. The WM spoons are 62.240.222 and 62.240.224; the Loring spoon is DAPC 89.3141.

41. The Loring spoons are in the MFAB (31.19,20); the Emery spoons are in WM (62.240.1091) and a private collection (DAPC 86.2006). Another Emery spoon in a private collection (DAPC 86.2006) has an intricate acanthus leaf bowl decoration that incorporates a linear C-scroll into the right-hand foliage, a design not yet found on any Loring spoons.

F

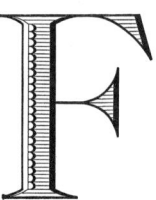

A

In the spring of 1727, the Boston selectmen granted "Liberty . . . to Peter furt, Gold Smith from New York to Reside in this Town to open A Shop and Exercise his Calling Having given to the Satisfaction of the Select men to Indemnifie the Town in £100."[1] The son of Bartholomew and Madelaine (Peiret) Feurt, Peter was baptized in the French Church, New York, on 19 December 1703. His godparents are listed as Pierre Peiret and Susanne Lambert.[2]

On 23 April 1728, Feurt married Susanna Gray (b. 1703), one of the daughters of the baker Samuel (ca. 1660–1707/08) and Susanna (Langdon) Gray (d. after 1721), in Christ Church. Susanna was the youngest sister of the goldsmiths Samuel (1684–1713) and John Gray (qq.v.).[3] Just after her marriage, she deeded her portion of a dwelling house on Marlborough Street to her brother Joseph, the father of the silversmith Samuel Gray (q.v.) (1710/11–48).[4] There are no children of Peter and Susanna Feurt recorded in Boston.

In a plea of trespass filed in the Suffolk County Court of Common Pleas in 1727, Feurt is described as the occupant of a house in Cornhill and may have had a shop there.[5] He was elected in 1730 to serve as one of Boston's constables.[6] In 1733 he was the defendant in a suit by the joiner Jacob Hurd. Sarah Tailer, widow, sued Feurt in January 1736 for three years' back rent on a shop in Marlborough Street.[7]

At this time Feurt was probably strapped financially because of his involvement in a scheme to develop an iron mine and build an iron foundry on land in Bellingham, Massachusetts. His entrance into partnership in February 1734 with at least eight other venturers put him in debt to Andrew LeMercier, pastor of the French Church in Boston, for one thousand pounds. As recorded in the deed,

> Peter Feurt is now actually intituled to one Eighth part of a Mine purchased of Robert Staples of Bellingham and John Bartlett of Attleborough wherein is contained an Iron Mine which he with the rest of the proprietors have mutually agreed to build a Furnace for the Smelting of the same And the above named Andrew Lemercier hath agreed with the said Peter Feurt to Disburse all the Money that the said Proprietors shall Vote and agree for the Carrying on the same.[8]

In return for the loan from LeMercier, Feurt agreed to give the pastor two-thirds of any profit he realized from the mine. In July 1735 Feurt borrowed twenty-five pounds from the elders of the French Church as a mortgage on his portion of the mine.[9] This probably helped him to stay in business, although Sarah Tailer's suit indicates that he had been unable to pay the annual rent of thirteen pounds on his shop. Finally, in 1735/36 Feurt and three of the partners in the Bellingham iron mine—Andrew LeMercier, a Boston clerk; John Metcalf, Esq., of Dedham; and Eleazar Metcalf, an Attleborough yeoman—sold their portions of the mine to William Clarke, a Boston physician, for the sum of £5,700, of which Feurt's share was £2,375. Twelve days later, Feurt paid off his mortgage and, presumably, his debts to LeMercier and to his landlady.[10] By this time, however, Feurt was caught in a cycle of debt from which even the sale of his portion in the mine could not extricate him. In January 1736/37, the ropemaker Hugh McDaniel sued him for an outstanding debt of twenty pounds, and when Feurt died in August 1737, Charles Butcher, a Boston farrier, had a suit pending against him for more than eighty-five pounds.[11]

Feurt died intestate, and the court appointed Andrew LeMercier as administrator. No widow is mentioned in the probate records, so Susanna must have predeceased her husband. There is no inventory on record for Feurt, but in 1742 the court declared his estate insolvent and insufficient to pay his debts, appointing Ebenezer Fisher, William Salter, and James Hill to act as commissioners for the estate to examine the claims of Feurt's creditors.[12]

Feurt's mark, PF crowned, lozenge below, in a shaped shield (A), appears on fewer than a half-dozen objects. One of these is a sophisticated grace cup inscribed "Ex Dono Henricus Hope Armiger." It is mentioned in the will of Edward Mills, Jr., of Placentia, Newfoundland, "now residing at Charlestown," as his bequest to Henry Hope. The will is dated 24 May 1732 and was probated on 1 June 1733. Presumably the bequest was in the form of money, and Hope commissioned Feurt to make the cup. The cup was later purchased by Charles Apthorp and descended to Sarah Apthorp Morton.[13] Although little of his work survives, this grace cup shows that Feurt was well trained and aware of the latest London styles. BMW

SURVIVING OBJECTS

	Mark	Inscription	Patron	Date	Reference	Owner
Cann	A	unidentified crest, a couchant lion holding a British flag (+)		ca. 1730	Buhler 1956, no. 72	
Grace cup	A†	Hope arms, quarters 1 and 4, azure a chevron argent and cotised between 3 bezants, and crest, a rainbow issuing from 2 clouds, impaling Hicks, quarters 2 and 3, gules a castle between 3 battleaxes; AT SPES IN FRACTA; DUM SPIRO SPERO; Mills arms, ermine a mill-rind, and crest, a lion	Henry Hope and/or Edward Mills, Jr.	ca. 1727	Buhler/Hood 1970, no. 136	YUAG

	Mark	Inscription	Patron	Date	Reference	Owner
		rampant; NEMO SINE CRIMINE VIVIT; Ex dono Henricus Hope Armiger (+)				
Serving spoon	A*	Winslow arms, on a bend gules 5 lozenges conjoined, and crest, a tree trunk with new branches	Winslow family	ca. 1730		HD
Serving spoon	A	Atkins crest, a bird vulning itself	Atkins family	ca. 1730	YUAG files	

1. RC 13:164.
2. Wittmeyer 1886, 98.
3. Raymond 1887, 142–43; genealogical notes in Theodore Gray to Francis Hill Bigelow, 21 July 1931, Bigelow-Phillips files, 611–14; Thwing; RC 24:21; SCPR 18:343–44; RC 28:143.
4. SCD 42:94.
5. SCCR, Court of Common Pleas Record Book 1727–28, 222.
6. RC 12:15.
7. John M. Fitzgerald to Francis Hill Bigelow, Boston Court Record References to Silversmiths, Bigelow-Phillips files; SCCR, Court of Common Pleas Record Book 1733–34, 142; 1735–36, 141.
8. SCD 49:223.
9. SCD 51:120–21.
10. SCD 55:34–35; 51:121.
11. SCCR, Court of Common Pleas Record Book 1736–37, 261; Superior Court of Judicature Record Book 1739–40, 204; Fitzgerald to Bigelow, Boston Court Record References to Silversmiths, Bigelow-Phillips files.
12. SCPR 33:252–53; 36:186.
13. SCPR 31:412–14; Buhler/Hood 1970, I:119.

Josiah Flagg, Jr.
1738–95

Josiah Flagg, Jr., was born in Boston on 28 March 1738 to Josiah (q.v.) and Mary (Willis) Flagg. He was baptized in the Church in Brattle Square on 5 November 1738.[1] After the deaths of his father in 1741 and his mother in 1751, the twelve-year-old Flagg was committed to the guardianship of his grandmother, Martha Willis (d. 1752/53).[2] When his grandmother died two years later, Flagg selected the Boston cooper Nathan Spear as his guardian.[3] Spear, who also served as the executor of Martha Willis's estate, maintained an account of his administration of the Flagg estate from 20 February 1752 to 16 May 1760.[4] Payments were disbursed for clothing, shoes, and repairs to the house; income was received from the rental of the shop and the kitchen to Samuel Tollman, Howen & Collyer, and Spear. However, there is no evidence to indicate the identity of Flagg's master. The intention of marriage between Flagg and seventeen-year-old Elizabeth Hawkes (ca. 1741–1816), daughter of Capt. Samuel Hawkes, was published on 13 March 1760.[5] The marriage was performed on 7 April 1760 in the New North Church.[6]

Flagg was active in his profession by 1761; he was called a "Jeweller" in a deed dated 24 October 1761 for the sale of one-third of a house near the Mill Creek in Boston to the bricklayer Thomas Parker for £103.6.8. This property had originally belonged to his grandfather Thomas Willis.[7] In the Massachusetts tax valuation of 1771, Flagg was assessed for two adult males, one house and shop, £40 of real estate, and £20 of merchandise. "Widow Greer" was listed as a lodger with Flagg.[8] He appears in the census of 1790 as the head of a household consisting of three adult males and five females.[9] "Josiah Flagg, Esq. otherwise Jeweller," appeared in the Suffolk County Court of Common Pleas in January 1790 as the defendant in a suit with Peregrine Foster of Worcester, Massachusetts. Flagg owed £6 on a note dated 9 February 1785 and was ordered by the court to pay Foster £7.15.11 and court costs of £1.19.6.[10]

Flagg provided a number of services to his patrons: small metalwork, gilding, hair jewelry, china repairs, and engraving. A receipt of 1766 in the Zachariah Brigden papers indicates that Flagg made rings for Brigden (q.v.):

> Boston Dec.[r] 22[d] 1766
> D[r] M[r] Zed[h] Brigden to Josiah Flagg
> To three Enamield Splitshank rings
> at 1[p]·10·8[ps]   4· 12·   0
> By [illegible] Gould [?] Sup[r] C[r]   2· 5· 10
>   9·1[gr]   2· 6·   2
> Rec[d] the Within Josiah Flagg

The bill suggests that Brigden supplied Flagg with 9 pennyweights and 1 grain of gold for making the rings. One of the latest references to Flagg is an advertisement in the *Independent Chronicle* of 1 July 1790, in which he announced,

> Josiah Flagg, senior, BEGS leave to acquaint the public, that he gilds in all the various colours and branches of gilding, Goblets, Cans, Urns, Cups, Watch-cases, Caneheads, Gorgets, Buckles, &c. &c. mends China by drilling, rivetting, hooping or otherwise. Makes enamelled Rings—Also executes, Copperplate Printing with unchangeable inks—Jewelry made and repaired perfectly neat—Hair devices elegantly finished for lockets &c. &c.—watch, locket and cane Strings, and Tassels wove with hair, equally to those imported &c. &c. *Just published, and to be sold at the Post-Offices in all the New-England States, and at the several Watch and Mathematical Instrument-Makers in this town, and by the Engraver,* J. FLAGG, A curious ALMANACK, calculated for a watch case, contained in quarterly circles, with the explanation, &c.

A devotee of music throughout his career, Flagg founded a guild of bell ringers at Christ Church in 1750 with six other young men, including Paul Revere, Jr. (q.v.).[11] During the 1760s Flagg collaborated with Revere on several songbooks for which Flagg produced the musical scores, Revere engraved the pictorial plates, and both split the three-hundred-pound production costs.[12] Flagg received permission from the selectmen to "make use of Faneuil Hall one Evening, for a Concert of Vocal & Instrumental Musick."[13]

An active patriot, Flagg was a member of the Sons of Liberty, as were Revere and John Welsh (q.v.).[14] He reached the rank of colonel in the Rhode Island Line.[15] The *Columbian Centinel* reported the death of "Josiah Flagg Esq" in Boston on 3 January 1795 in an obituary that underestimated his age by two years as fifty-five.[16]

Josiah and Elizabeth Flagg had eight children. Their son Josiah, Jr., born on 24 July 1763, was a dentist, surgeon, and musician in Boston and appeared in the city directories from 1796 until 1849/50.[17] His advertisement appeared in the *Independent Chronicle* (Boston) on 1 July 1790 immediately below that of his father. Josiah, Jr., and his son, Josiah Foster Flagg (1788–1853), patented a design for an "elastic lamp reflector" on 17 May 1810, possibly inspired by the special lighting needs of dentistry, a profession practiced by both men.[18]

There are several unascribed I F marks, but none has been firmly documented to Josiah Flagg, Jr. DAF

1. *Church in Brattle Square*, 161.
2. SCPR 45:38–39, 672–73.
3. SCPR 48:278–79.
4. SCPR 35:463–65.
5. RC 30:35; *Index of Obituaries, 1784–1840*, 2:1624.
6. RC 30:371; *Boston Transcript*, 5 February 1908, 9747; *Boston Transcript*, 19 February 1908, 9747.
7. SCD 99:101–03.
8. Pruitt 1978, 32–33.
9. RC 22:507.
10. SCCR, Court of Common Pleas Record Book 1789, 220–21.
11. Babcock 1947, 192–93.
12. Federhen 1985, 29.
13. RC 23:194.
14. Federhen 1985, 34.
15. *Boston Transcript*, 5 February 1908, 9747; *Boston Transcript*, 31 May 1910, 1290.
16. *Index of Obituaries, 1704–1800*, 1:110.
17. *Boston Directory*, 1796–1849/50.
18. Flagg 1907, 156; *Index of Obituaries, 1704–1800*, 1:110; Hubbard 1935, n.p. Josiah Foster Flagg was listed in the Providence directories from 1828 until 1841/42 and in the Philadelphia directories from 1844 to 1849: see the *Providence Directory*, 1828, 45; 1831, 69; 1832, 61; 1836, 49; 1838, 55; 1841/42, 70; *McElroy's Philadelphia Directory*, 1844, 101; 1845, 116; 1846, 114; 1847, 111; 1849, 120.

Josiah Flagg, Sr.
d. 1741

Little is known of the life or career of the Boston jeweler Josiah Flagg, Sr. He married Mary Willis (d. 1751), daughter of Thomas and Martha Willis (d. 1752/53), on 29 September 1737 in a ceremony performed by the Reverend William Cooper.[1] Their son Josiah (q.v.) was born in 1738, the eldest of two sons.[2]

The next mention of Flagg appears in the appointment of his widow, Mary Flagg, as the administrator of his estate on 4 August 1741.[3] He was called "Gentleman" there, indicating that he had achieved financial success and professional respect during his brief career. Although the inventory of his estate does not include any jeweler's tools, his occupation is confirmed in the guardianship papers for his son filed in 1753, in which he is described as "Josiah Flagg, late of Boston . . . Jeweller."[4] The jeweler's possessions also reflect his prosperity; he owned many luxury items, such as a clock, two bird cages, one looking glass worth ten pounds, six pictures, and a variety of household textiles, including bed curtains, counterpanes, quilts, and bed rugs.

Mary Flagg operated a retail shop in Back Street in September 1741, possibly the site of Flagg's jewelry-making activities.[5] By the following year, she had moved to Ann Street, where she lived until her death in 1751.[6]

No objects by Josiah Flagg, Sr., have been identified.[7]   DAF

1. RC 28:201; *Boston Transcript*, 31 May 1910, 1290; SCD 99:101–03; SCPR 45:38–39, 672–73.
2. Thwing.
3. SCPR 35:452.
4. SCPR 35:452–53; 48:278–79.
5. RC 15:308.
6. RC 15:360; SCPR 35:463–65. The income reported in the guardianship accounts from "Rent for the Shop" presumably refers to the Ann Street property.
7. Kovel 1961, 100, and Thorn 1949, 82, show a J.F in a rectangle mark for this maker; however, objects that bear this mark appear to have been made after 1741.

Edward Foster
1717–52

Edward Foster was born in Boston on 16 November 1717, the son of Thomas Foster (1686–1752), a housewright, and Ann Bossinger (d. 1746), who were married in Boston in 1711.[1] His paternal grandparents were Timothy Foster (1638–88) and Relief Holland Dowse (1650–1743) of Dorchester, Massachusetts.[2] Edward Foster was a cousin of William Swan (q.v.) and would have trained at about the same time as Swan, who was slightly older.

Edward Foster's apprenticeship would have begun about 1731 and been completed about 1738; the identity of his master is unknown. On 11 October 1739 the goldsmith married Abigail Wolcott (1722–before 1744), daughter of Benjamin Wolcott (d. 1745), a blacksmith, and Abigail Walters.[3] The estate of Foster's father-in-law, Wolcott, shows that Foster owed him £250 and that Abigail's share of her father's personal estate was £198.14.8 ½.[4] Abigail apparently died before 7 March 1744, when the goldsmith married Martha Henderson (b. 1723), the daughter of Heman (d. 1729), a mariner, and Mary Henderson.[5]

In 1746 Foster was chosen and excused as constable.[6] Apparently Foster died late in 1752 and was identified as a "goldsmith" when his estate's administration was granted to his brother Thomas, a brazier, on 5 January 1753.[7] In the *Boston News-Letter* of 25 January 1753 the following notice appeared: "All Persons Indebted to the Estate of *Edward Foster*, late of *Boston*, Goldsmith deceased, are desired to pay the same to *Thomas Foster*, Administrator on said Estate: And those who have any Demands thereon, are likewise desired to bring their Accounts to said Administrator." The silver included in the estate inventory, filed on 19 January 1753, was one pair of old silver knee buckles valued at three shillings.[8] Foster's three daughters, Abigail, Ann, and Zibiah, were placed under the guardianship of Hopestill Foster, "gentleman," in June 1753.[9]

No silver by Foster has been identified. PEK

1. RC 21:32; RC 24:121; RC 28:34; SCPR 46:118; 48:546–49.
2. RC 21:24, 121, 139; Savage 1860–62, 2:186, 191.
3. RC 28:103, 211; RC 24:158; SCPR 39:341–43.
4. SCPR 43:396.
5. RC 24:160; RC 28:245; SCPR 27:147, 243; Thwing.
6. RC 14:107.
7. SCPR 47:289.
8. SCPR 47:346–47.
9. SCPR 48:187–89.

George Foster
w. ca. 1749

The Suffolk County Court of Common Pleas session of 3 April 1750 reveals that "George Foster late of Boston aforesaid Brewer but now residing in Providence . . . Jeweller" sued the Boston watchmaker James Atkinson (q.v. Appendix A) for one dozen pinchbeck seals that he had delivered to Atkinson the previous 12 September, but for which Atkinson refused to pay. The jury ruled in favor of the plaintiff, but the case was appealed by the defendant to the next Superior Court of Judicature.[1] Although Foster was probably known as a brewer when living in Boston, this evidence suggests that he was also dealing in jeweler's wares. Beyond this, the Massachusetts and Rhode Island vital records for this period contain no evidence about Foster. No work by him is known. PEK

1. SCCR, Court of Common Pleas Record Book 1749–51, 119–20; file 67002, vol. 416, Judicial Archives, Mass. Archives.

Samuel Foster
1676–1701/02

Samuel Foster was born in Boston on 27 December 1676, the youngest child of Hopestill Foster (1644/45–78), a soapboiler originally of Dorchester, Massachusetts, and Elizabeth (Payson) Foster (b. 1645) of Roxbury, Massachusetts. Hopestill Foster was the son of Hopestill Foster (ca. 1621–76) and Mary (Bates) Foster (ca. 1620–1703). The elder Hopestill was a brewer by trade, immigrated to the colony as a young boy, and became prominent in Dorchester town affairs. Elizabeth Payson was the daughter of Giles Payson (ca. 1609–88/89) and Elizabeth (Dowes) Payson (d. 1677). About 1698 Samuel Foster married Rebecca Brisco (b. 1679), daughter of Joseph Brisco (b. 1658), a loaf-bread baker, and his wife, Rebecca, and had two children, Rebecca (b. 1699), who married John Best in 1721, and Samuel (b. 1701), who married Rachel Kneeland in 1722.[1]

Samuel is first mentioned as a goldsmith in a deed of 1698 wherein he sold his portion of his uncle Samuel Payson's estate—a house, orchard, and acre plot in Roxbury—to Stephen Minott, a Boston tailor, for £70.[2] The following year Samuel and his wife sold additional land in Roxbury to Richard Hall, a Roxbury tanner, for £16.11.10.[3]

In 1699/1700, Samuel Foster entered into an unusual agreement with his father-in-law, Joseph Brisco, whereby Brisco would hold housing, tenements, gardens, orchards, marshes, and other lands in Boston, Roxbury, and Dorchester from the estates of Hopestill Foster and Samuel Foster's uncle, Samuel Payson, in trust for Foster's wife Rebecca and their daughter Rebecca "in case she survives me and for the better setling and Establishing of my Property right." The agreement is dated 9 March 1699/1700 but was not entered in the registry of deeds until 2 January 1701/02, just two months before Samuel Foster's death.[4] Perhaps Foster entrusted Brisco with his property because he was planning a long voyage or because he was ill and unable to carry out his normal obligations. Such an arrangement gave Joseph Brisco the right to use the property for the benefit of the family and protected the property in the event of Rebecca Foster's remarriage.[5]

Henry Flynt and Martha Gandy Fales record one unmarked spoon in a private collection "supposedly" made by Foster.[6] No other objects he made have come to light. BMW

1. RC 9:65, 138, 148, 247; RC 21:29, 125; RC 24:7; RC 28:99, 106; *Roxbury VR* 2:152, 311, 609; Roberts 1895, 1:121, 223, 292–93; SCPR, docket 843, 1038.
2. SCD 18:282–83; 19:41–42.
3. SCD 19:178–79.
4. SCD 21:150–52; Boston Deaths, 1700–1800, indicate that Foster died on 10 March and was buried on 11 March.
5. According to the English laws of the period, any property that belonged to a woman became her husband's property when she married.
6. Flynt/Fales 1968, 221.

Joseph Gardner
1718–79

Although not known by any surviving works, Joseph Gardner appears to have been a silversmith of at least modest importance in Salem, Massachusetts, during the middle years of the eighteenth century. Baptized on 28 September 1718, the youngest son of the husbandman Abell (1673–1739) and Sarah Gardner, Joseph was the grandson of Samuel (ca. 1629–89) and Mary (White) Gardner (d. 1675). He married Mehittable Pope (b. 1719) on 29 September 1741.[1] They first lived in a house inherited from his father in what is now Peabody but in 1747 moved to what is now Cambridge Street in Salem.[2] In 1760, they moved again, this time to High Street, where Joseph remained until his death. Joseph and Mehittable had seven children, and Joseph served as constable and fence-viewer in 1744 and performed other services for the town into the mid-1760s. Two Joseph Gardners, one with only one-third of a house and the other with no assets, are included in the Massachusetts tax list of 1771; one of them may be the silversmith.[3]

Only a few documents shed light on Gardner's career, and nothing in those documents suggests that he made anything other than jewelry and spoons. Between November 1745 and October 1765, Gardner supplied the well-known Salem merchant Timothy Orne with gold buttons, silver buckles, silver tea-spoons, and other small articles in exchange for salt, corn, rum, sugar, cloth, and old silver.[4] These accounts, totaling £8.16.3/4, indicate that Gardner made at least some of the spoons, buckles, and buttons; performed frequent repairs on similar items; and refined gold and cast lead for cod and sounding lines. Gardner purchased spoons and jewelry from his fellow silversmith John Touzell (q.v.) in 1749.[5]

Joseph Gardner died intestate in early 1779. The inventory of his estate suggests that although he still owned some of his silversmithing tools, he may have retired before his death. His tools included "Goldsmith's Vice £6—small Anvil 20/ ditto 10/. Tongs 12/. sundry old Tools & old Iron 30/. 9.12.0." His total estate value of £586.5, which included his house and twelve poles of land valued at £400, placed him firmly in the middle economic class of the period.[6] GWRW

1. *Salem VR* 1:338, 341; 2:186; 3:402; 5:272; ECPR 324:15–17. See also Gardner 1907, 159–62, and Savage 1860–62, 2:230.
2. ECD 80:52, 63; 91:108.

3. *Salem VR* 1:341; Gardner 1907, 159–62; Pruitt 1978, 138–39, 150–51.

4. Timothy Orne Ledger, fol. 50, PEM.

5. English-Touzel-Hathorne Papers, two receipts Joseph Gardner to John Touzell, Dʳ 1749, box 4, folder 3, PEM.

6. No papers are on file in Gardner's docket no. 10646 in the ECPR. Copies can be found in the bound volumes (353:364, 439), and these have been relied on here.

Nathaniel Gay
ca. 1641–79 +

Nathaniel Gay was probably one of the first journeymen employed by John Coney (q.v.), because the Boston town records for 2 February 1679 establish that "I, John Coney junʳ doe binde myselfe to Thomas Brattle Treasʳ for the Towne of Boston in the Sum of forty pounds yᵗ Nathanell Gay, Gouldsmith Shall not be Chargeable to the Towne."[1] This individual also may have been the Nathaniel Gay who was born about 1641 probably in Nettlecombe, Somersetshire, England, to Robert Gay (1602–72), a minister and clerk there, and his wife, Martha.[2]

The records of the Goldsmiths' Company, London, contain the following entry: "18th day of January 1655. . . . Nathaniel Gay the sonne of Robert Gay of Nettlecombe in ye County of Somersett Clerke doe put my selfe apprentize unto William Gay Cittizen & goldsmith of London for ye terme of nyne yeares from ye First day of this instant January."[3] Nathaniel Gay was made a freeman of the company on 10 February 1664/65.[4] He probably immigrated to America sometime after this date, but since no references to him appear in the Boston records after 1679, Gay may have returned to London.[5] No silver by him is known. PEK

1. RC 10:64.

2. The approximate date is arrived at on the basis of the beginning date of his apprenticeship. Parish records at Nettlecombe list the births of other children to Robert and Martha Gay, but not of Nathaniel.

3. Apprentice Book 2, fol. 76r, Worshipful Company of Goldsmiths, London. Robert B. Barker letter to the author, 9 February 1993.

4. Court Book 4, fol. 199v, Worshipful Company of Goldsmiths, London. Robert B. Barker letter to the author, 9 February 1993.

5. Shurtleff 1853, 5:536–37. Two other Nathaniel Gays were in the Massachusetts Bay Colony at this time, but neither one appears to be the goldsmith.

Daniel Gibbs
ca. 1691–1716 +

Daniel Gibbs, identified as a silversmith, was one of the passengers who arrived in Boston in 1716 aboard the ship *Globe* from Ireland. There is no record of his apprenticeship at the Goldsmiths' Company, Dublin.[1] The following advertisement appeared in the *Boston News-Letter* for 18–25 June 1716:

> Arrived from Ireland per the Globe Capt *Nicholas Oursell* Commander, and to be disposed of by him, the following Protestant Servants & Merchandizes, *viz.* Men, Anchor & Ship Smith, House Carpenters, Ship Joyners and Carver, Cooper, Shoe-makers, and Pattoun Maker, Naylors, Lock-Smiths, Currier, Taylor, Book Printer, Silver & Gold Lace Weaver, Silver Smith. And Women, Milliners, Ribband & Lace Weavers, Button Maker, Earthen Ware Potter Maker, House Keepers, Washer Women and Cooks.[2]

Henry Flynt and Martha Gandy Fales speculated that this silversmith may have been the same Daniel Gibbs, merchant, who died in Gloucester in 1762, at the age of fifty-nine.[3] This seems unlikely because he would have been only thirteen in 1716, hardly old enough to have been referred to as a "man" or as a trained silversmith. BMW

1. RC 29:236; West and Son, Diamond Merchants, Dublin, to Francis Hill Bigelow 18 July 1931, Bigelow-Phillips files, 797a.
2. Dow 1927, 280.
3. Flynt/Fales 1968, 226. This Daniel Gibbs's will is filed in ECPR, docket 10807.

Samuel Glover
1731–62

Samuel Glover was baptized in the First Church in Salem, Massachusetts, on 4 July 1731, the son of Jonathan Glover, Jr. (b. 1702), and his wife, Tabitha (Bacon) (b. 1712), who had been married in 1727. He was the grandson of Jonathan (b. 1677) and Abigail (Henderson) Glover (b. 1676), who were married in 1699, and of John (b. 1680) and Hannah (King) Bacon (b. 1681), who were married in 1701.[1]

Samuel Glover married Mary Andrews in Marblehead, Massachusetts, on 20 August 1751, and four children were born to them in that town between 1754 and 1760.[2] Glover seems to have served as a captain in a Marblehead regiment during the French and Indian War. Administration of his estate was granted to his widow, Mary, on 4 December 1762, when the guardianship of his children Samuel and Daniel was given to Jonathan Glover, Jr.[3]

An account of the Marblehead regiment of Gen. John Glover notes that Samuel Glover was "a goldsmith by trade." To date, this is the only reference linking Samuel Glover to the craft.[4] GWRW

1. *Salem VR* 1:60, 61, 359, 360, 435, 492; 3:69, 421; *Marblehead VR* 1:15. A later source gives his date of birth as 13 June 1731, and other particulars; see Sanborn 1903.
2. *Marblehead VR* 2:171; 1:207–08.
3. ECPR, docket 11045.
4. Sanborn 1903.

Joseph Goldthwait
1706–1780

A

Joseph Goldthwait was born in Boston on 11 November 1706. His parents were John Goldthwait (1677–1766), a brick mason, son of Samuel (b. 1637) and Elizabeth (Cheever) Goldthwait (b. 1645); and Sarah (Hopkins) Goldthwait (d. 1715), daughter of Charles and Margaret (Henchman) Hopkins. After his first wife's death when the young Joseph was only nine years old, John Goldthwait married Jane (Tawley) Halsey, widow of John Halsey and daughter of Thomas and Mary Tawley.[1]

On 8 February 1727/28, Joseph Goldthwait married Martha Lewis (1708–83), daughter of Phillip (d. 1732), a mariner, and Martha (Burrill) (Hender) Lewis (ca. 1684–1744).[2] Joseph and Martha Goldthwait had at least seven children: Joseph (1730–79), who married Hannah Bridgham; John (b. 1731), who married Mehitabel Pratt; Phillip (b. 1733), who married first May Jordan, and second Abigail Dyer; Samuel (b. 1735), who married Amy [surname unknown]; Benjamin (b. 1737), who married Sarah (White) Dawes; Martha (b. 1739), who married the physician Joseph Gowen, the brother of the goldsmith William Gowen (q.v.); Michael Burrill (b. 1740), who married first Sarah [surname unknown], and second Abigail Langdon; and Sarah, who married Richard Montsure, a London merchant.[3]

Joseph Goldthwait appears in the court records only once, when, in 1728, he sued Moses Markham, scrivener or merchant, for failure to pay rent on half a house in Union Street.[4] In 1751 Joseph and his wife mortgaged their house and land in Fish Street, which was theirs by right of inheritance from her grandfather Samuel Burrill, to Jacob Holyoke, a Boston merchant. They sold the house and land to John White, a Boston baker, in 1757, and White assumed the mortgage with Holyoke as well as an additional mortgage to Joseph's brother, Ezekiel Goldthwait.[5] Joseph Goldthwait held minor town offices: he was elected constable in 1734/35 (and served with Bartholomew Green [q.v.]), scavenger in 1743, and sealer of cordwood from 1756 until 1773, when the selectmen's minutes record that he had "removed out of Town."[6]

Goldthwait probably served his apprenticeship with John Dixwell (q.v.) because he and Joseph Kneeland (q.v.) appear as witnesses to a deed between Dixwell and the blacksmith John Manning on 3 December 1723, when Goldthwait was seventeen years old.[7] Goldthwait also witnessed a bond for Dixwell in March 1723.[8] Dixwell would have been a close associate of Joseph's father, John Goldthwait, because Dixwell and John Goldthwait were among the seventeen founding members of the New North Church in 1714.

In 1731 Joseph Goldthwait advertised,

> Joseph Goldthwait *Goldsmith is removed from Mr.* Burrel's *Shop, to the House adjoining to the Sign of the Red Lyon, where any Gentlemen or Women may be supplied with any sort of Pocket Instrument Cases at a very reasonable Rate.*[9]

Mr. Burrill may have been Samuel Burrill (q.v.) who, although he was only four years older, was Joseph Goldthwait's wife's uncle. The estate of the jeweler James Boyer (q.v.) owed Goldthwait £29.6 in 1741.[10] Only one mark, I·G crowned, with a cross below, in a shield (A), is attributed to Goldthwait.[11] Another mark, IG crowned in a shield, which has been attributed to Goldthwait, probably belongs to Jean Gruchy, who worked on Jersey in the Channel Islands.[12]

In addition to his goldsmithing business, Goldthwait, like his father, was licensed as a retailer of strong drink in 1737 at his shop in Marlborough Street; his license was renewed in 1742.[13] He lived in Fish Street in 1744, and in deeds recorded between 1744 and 1757 he referred to himself as a "gentleman," which suggests that he had given up the goldsmithing trade by this time.[14] In 1754 he petitioned the General Court for a license to operate a house of public entertainment.[15] In 1767 he was an innholder in Back Street. He joined the New Brick Church before 1730, and all of his children were baptized there.[16]

Joseph Goldthwait joined the Ancient and Honorable Artillery Company in 1732 and was elected first sergeant in 1738.[17] He served as a captain and adjutant of Sir William Pepperrell's regiment at the siege of Louisbourg in 1745. His master's son, Basil Dixwell (q.v.), was under his command in this campaign, and Goldthwait looked after him in his final sickness and covered his funeral expenses.[18] Goldthwait retired to a mansion house and ten-acre farm in Weston, Massachusetts, that he purchased in 1773. The family were loyalists and were scattered by the events of the Revolution.[19]

Goldthwait died in Weston on 1 March 1780; in his will he refers to himself as "Esquire."[20] He left one thousand pounds (sterling) to his daughter Sarah Williams, bequeathed two hundred pounds (sterling) per year to his widow, Martha, and one hundred pounds (sterling) apiece to his grandchildren Elizabeth Goldthwait, Frances Montsure, and Anna Langdon Goldthwait. He left the residue of his estate to his children Phillip, Samuel, Benjamin, and Martha. The will mentions his son Joseph, deceased. On 3 April 1782 Goldthwait's son-in-law, Joseph Gowen, was appointed administrator of the estate, and William Gowen signed the bond. The inventory, which was made by Isaac Jones, Edward Brinley, and Estis How, does not include any goldsmith's tools, and very little household silver is listed. Goldthwait did own a silver-"headed" sword, a gold watch, and four silver teaspoons, but otherwise his personal estate shows that he maintained a modest lifestyle in spite of his wealth. The total value of the inventoried estate in Weston was £372.16.8, with additional land in Boston valued at £1,500. The executors' accounts demonstrate that in 1780 Goldthwait was in the process of settling the estate of his son Joseph, who died in New York. It is possible that the inventory filed with the Middlesex County Probate court does not represent the elder Goldthwait's entire estate.[21] BMW

SURVIVING OBJECTS

	Mark	Inscription	Patron	Date	Reference	Owner
Cann	A	unidentified arms		ca. 1735	Silver Supplement 1973, no. 43	
Caudle cup	A	DLF (over earlier initials)		ca. 1740	DAPC 68.3205	MMA
Six cups	A	The Gift of yᵉ Honourable Coll/Burrill, Esqʳ to yᵉ Second Church in Lynn	First Church, Lynnfield, Mass. (formerly the Second Church of Lynn), for Theophilus Burrill	ca. 1735	Jones 1913, 257	
Ladle	A	H/CM		ca. 1735	Hammerslough/ Feigenbaum 1958–73, 1:106	
Pepper box	A	B/EM		ca. 1735	YUAG files	
Porringer	A	ER/to/AB		ca. 1740	Silver Supplement 1973, no. 44	
Porringer	A*	H (?) B		ca. 1750	Silver 22 (March–April 1989): 2	
Tablespoon	A	CDLP		ca. 1735	YUAG files	
Tankard	A†	C/NH		ca. 1750	Buhler 1972, no. 210	MFAB
Tankard	A*	Bell arms, a fess ermine between 3 bells, and crest, a falcon	Bell family	ca. 1740	DAPC 71.1039	YUAG
Tobacco box	A*	Welsteed arms, per pale sable and azure a bend chequey argent and gules; WW	Rev. William Welsteed	ca. 1745	Buhler/Hood 1970, no. 169	YUAG
Two-handled cup	A	Goodridge arms, a fess in chief 3 crosses crosslet fitchée, and crest, a bird; A Friends Gift to the/North Brick Church/1730	Walter Goodridge, Jr., and/or Second Church, Boston	1730	Jones 1913, 35–36	

	Mark	Inscription	Patron	Date	Reference	Owner
Two-handled cup	A	crest, a cock; 1731	James Halsey and/or Second Church, Boston	1731	Jones 1913, 36	

1. RC 24:41; Roberts 1895, 1:375; RC 28:4, 95; SCPR 18:421, 19:175.
2. RC 28:12, 138; *Weston VR*, 316. Martha (Burrill) Lewis (b. ca. 1684) was the eldest child of Samuel Burrill, Sr. (1656/57–1740/41), a sailmaker, and the silversmith Samuel Burrill was her younger brother by nineteen years. Joseph Goldthwait and his wife inherited a portion of her grandfather Samuel Burrill, Sr.'s estate, which consisted of houses and land in Fish and Back streets. The estate division named Martha (Burrill) (Hender) Lewis as one of the children of the deceased; SCD 62:19–21.
3. RC 24:197, 202, 212, 221, 229, 237, 240; MCPR 59:470–71, docket 9299.
4. SCCR, file 21775.
5. SCD 62:19–21; 75:170; 80:253–54; 90:269–70.
6. Roberts 1895, 1:450; Seybolt 1939, 197, 235, 279, 300n, 353n.
7. SCD 37:177.
8. SCCR, file 16988.
9. *Boston News-Letter*, 15–22, 22–29 April, 29 April–6 May 1731.
10. SCPR 37:137.
11. It is possible that John Gray (q.v.) used this mark.
12. Flynt/Fales 1968, 228; Mayne 1969, 35, pl. 23; for two forks with the mark see *DIA Bulletin* 34 (1954–55): 19.
13. Roberts 1895, 1:450.
14. SCD 75:170; 80:253–54; 90:269–70.
15. Mass. Archives 3:288.
16. Bigelow-Phillips files, 1029b.
17. Roberts 1895, 1:405.
18. Petition to the General Court, Mass. Archives 73:625–26, and cited in Drake 1870, 232; for a fuller discussion, see Basil Dixwell.
19. Jones 1930, 146–47.
20. *Weston VR*, 314.
21. MCPR, docket 9299; 59:470–71; 64:4, 183–87.

Benjamin Goodwin
ca. 1731–92

A

Benjamin Goodwin probably was born on 2 February 1731 to John Goodwin (1699–ca. 1745) and Mercy Robie (1704–62), who were married in Boston on 18 September 1722.[1] Goodwin's paternal grandparents were Nathaniel (b. 1672) and Elisabeth (Emes) Goodwin (d. before 1708); his maternal grandparents were the Boston wharfinger and merchant William Robie (1648–1718) and his wife, Elizabeth Greenough.[2]

The silversmith's father, John Goodwin, served in the military during King George's War and was authorized to return home from Louisbourg in July 1745. No further mention of him can be found after this date, however.[3] The Boston Overseers of the Poor apprenticed Benjamin, described as "a poor Child," to his cousin John Parkman (q.v.) on 14 January 1745.[4] This arrangement, intended to teach him "the Art & Mistery of a Gold Smith Also to Read Write & Cypher," was to have lasted for seven years, until Goodwin's twenty-first birthday.[5] However, Parkman died in 1748, and Goodwin completed his apprenticeship with Jacob Hurd (q.v.), as a deed witnessed by Goodwin and another apprentice, Daniel Henchman (q.v.), for Hurd on 6 October 1750 reveals.[6] Goodwin would have been fully trained by 1752. He was practicing his trade by 1756, when "Benjamin Goodwin, Goldsmith, of Boston," and his three brothers sold the brick house on Cornhill that they had inherited from their father to the Boston physician John Greenleaf.[7] In June 1762, Benjamin

Goodwin, goldsmith, was appointed administrator for the estate of his deceased mother, Mercy Goodwin.[8] Daniel Parker (q.v.) served as a bondsman for Goodwin, which suggests that there may have been a professional relationship between the two silversmiths.

The marriage intentions of Benjamin Goodwin and Hannah LeBarron (1733–75), daughter of Lazarus LeBarron (1698–1773), a Plymouth, Massachusetts, physician, and Lydia (Bartlett) LeBarron (1697/98–1742), were published on 30 August 1757.[9] The couple married on 17 November of that year in Plymouth.[10] "Hannah Goodwin, the wife of Benjamin Goodwin of Boston," was mentioned in her father's will, written 24 September 1772, in which she received one-fifth of the medicines in his shop.[11]

On 3 March 1765, "Benjamin Goodwin, Merchant," purchased a brick house on Fleet Street in Boston from Ezekiel Goldthwait, Esq., and the merchant Robert Gould for £633.6.8; a £333.6.8 mortgage for this property arranged with Goldthwait on 24 April 1765 was repaid by 27 August 1771.[12] This transaction marks the first time that Goodwin designated himself a merchant. In May 1765, "Benjamin Goodwin of Boston, Goldsmith," brought suit against Jeremiah Snow III (q.v.) of Springfield, Massachusetts.[13] Goodwin was awarded £59.2.2 in damages and costs of £2.16.10, for which an execution order was issued on 14 June 1765. The record of a robbery of his storehouse in September 1766 confirms Goodwin's activities as both a silversmith and a retail merchant. The report of the theft presented at the General Quarter Session Court on 7 October 1766 enumerates the stock of ready-made articles that Goodwin kept on hand for sale, including a variety of small silver items. The court records reported that John Hood, a mariner, and Lucy Lewfield, a spinster, both of Boston, had broken into Goodwin's storehouse on 4 September 1766

> & did from thence with force & Arms then & there feloniously Steal take & carry away five pair of wrought silver shoe buckles of the Value of twenty Shillings each, nine pair of wrought Silver Knee buckles of the value of Six Shillings each, one plain silver stock buckle of the value of seven shillings, fourteen pair of Stone Ear-rings set in silver of the value of fourteen shillings each, one pair of Stone Ear-rings set in Gold of the value of twenty Shillings, twenty-five pair of Stone sleeve buttons of the value of eight shillings each, nineteen pair of cyphered Sleeve buttons of the value of nine shillings each, nine stone rings of the value of fourteen shillings each, three stone stayhooks of the value of six shillings each, three silver tea spoons of the value of three shillings each.[14]

They also took such household goods as spices and textiles. Goodwin's use of a storehouse and the quantity and value of the objects stored there attest to his financial success as a silversmith and merchant, success that his family connections were undoubtedly helpful in achieving, in spite of his childhood status as one of Boston's poor. His uncle, Thomas Goodwin (1705–52), a graduate of Harvard College in 1725, was a shopkeeper in Boston and Wethersfield, Connecticut, and part owner of two sloops and a schooner.[15] His grandfather Nathaniel, a bricklayer and later a shopkeeper, was a member of the Ancient and Honorable Artillery Company and served the town of Boston in several minor civic posts, including hogreeve and tithingman.[16] His sister-in-law, Mary LeBarron, was married to William Bradford (1728–1808), a deputy governor and senator of Rhode Island.[17] Goodwin's wife, Hannah LeBarron, was the great-granddaughter of Richard Warren, who had immigrated to Massachusetts on the *Mayflower* in 1620.[18]

In 1768, Benjamin and Hannah Goodwin purchased several lots of land valued at £1,020, containing buildings, wharves, and warehouses on Charter and Lynn streets near the Charlestown ferry site.[19] Subsequent deeds describe the mortgage arranged for the purchase and the couple's sale of the Fleet Street property in 1771, probably to pay off the mortgage.[20] The Boston tax valuation list compiled in 1771 credits "Benjamin Gooding" with ownership of real estate valued at an annual worth of £64, including a house and shop, 2,010 feet of wharf, and a "still house."[21] Goodwin also owned a bakehouse and blacksmith shop; he lived opposite his wharf on the corner of Charter Street.[22] The Boston tax valuation list of 1780 listed Goodwin as a merchant in ward 8 with property valued at an annual rent of £150 and a grown son, Benjamin, Jr., recorded as living with his father.[23] Two relatives, Joseph and Henry Goodwin, both traders, were listed next by the assessors. The absence of a property valuation in their entries suggests that they were occupying Goodwin's house as well. He and the other landowners along Ferry Street were paid 5 shillings apiece in May 1786 for land they gave the town of Boston so that the street could be widened and a sea wall constructed alongside it.[24]

Goodwin, a reputable member of the community, actively participated in the community's civic affairs. At the Boston town meeting on 13 March 1769, "Benjamin Gooding" was elected as a warden for that year.[25] He held another town office in 1770 and in May 1774 was invited by the selectmen to join a committee to examine the Boston public schools.[26]

Benjamin Goodwin, merchant, appeared as the plaintiff in several cases tried before the Suffolk County Court of Common Pleas between 1781 and 1783.[27] Goodwin was seeking to recover various sums from Moses Roach, a Dorchester, Massachusetts, merchant, in April 1781 and October 1783 and from John Noyes, a Watertown, Massachusetts, trader, in July 1783 and was awarded the amount requested and court costs in every case. However, in a case of 1786 against the wheelwright William Rogers he is identified as a "Gentleman" rather than a merchant, indicating that he had attained a prosperous and respected position in the community.[28]

Hannah Goodwin died on 25 October 1775, four days after the death of her infant daughter Nancy Weatherston Goodwin. Mother and daughter are buried in the Copp's Hill Burying Ground.[29] Goodwin purchased land in Easton, Massachusetts, in 1783 and 1784 and was identified as being of Easton when he bought additional land there in 1789 and 1790.[30] He was also identified as being of Easton in court documents from 1790.[31] The census taken that year listed the silversmith in Easton as the head of a family composed of three men over the age of sixteen and two women.[32] Goodwin made out his will on 26 November and died in Easton on 30 November 1792.[33] His obituary, which appeared in the *Columbian Centinel* on 15 December 1792, suggests another aspect of Goodwin's mercantile pursuits by describing him as "formerly a distiller in Boston, at Easton, a 60 y."[34] His inventory amounted to £2,134.18.8.[35] Administration of the estate took four years.[36] Goodwin is buried in the Copp's Hill Burying Ground with his wife and daughter.[37]

Goodwin trained his son, Joseph (1761–1821+), as a silversmith. Joseph Goodwin had left Boston by 1784, only two years after attaining his freedom, to reside with his wife, Susanna, in Lenox, Berkshire County, where he worked as a goldsmith and ironmonger.[38] In 1821, he was living in Hudson, New York, and probably died there.[39]

In view of Goodwin's financial success, the output of his silver shop must have been considerable, a supposition substantiated by the large quantity of silver objects stolen from his storehouse in 1766. However, very few objects marked by Goodwin have been located. An initial and surname mark (A) is associated with this silversmith. Later engraving on the base of a porringer with his mark records the marriages of four generations of owners; the earliest, "N · G · & L · L · B · Dec · 25 · 1746," corresponds with the contemporary engraving of "N ^{G} L 1746" on the handle and probably refers to Nathaniel Goodwin and Lydia LeBarron, the silversmith's brother and sister-in-law, who were married in 1745. The porringer must have been made considerably after this date, however, because Goodwin was only fifteen years old in 1746. DAF

SURVIVING OBJECTS

	Mark	Inscription	Patron	Date	Reference	Owner
Cann	A†	G/NL	Nathaniel and Lydia (LeBarron) Goodwin (?)	ca. 1760	MFA 1911, no. 521	MFAB
Porringer	A*	G/NL; 1746 (later) (+)	Nathaniel and Lydia (LeBarron) Goodwin (?)	ca. 1760	DAPC 78.3412	
Tablespoon	A*	W/IE		ca. 1760	Johnston 1994, 59	CMA
Tablespoon	A	?		?	YUAG files	
Tankard (attrib.)	none	Goodwin arms, lion passant on a chief or 3 mascles gules, and crest, a stag trippant; G/NL	Nathaniel and Lydia (LeBarron) Goodwin	ca. 1760	Christie's, 22 January 1993, lot III	

1. Whitmore 1878, 30, no. 562; Boston Indentures 1 (1734–51): 83, Rare Book Room, BPL; letter from Robert F. Seybolt to John Marshall Phillips, 26 August 1937, Bigelow-Phillips files, 1441; Savage 1860–62, 3:549; RC 24:30; RC 28:106, 349; SCD 17:38; SCPR 60:393. The record in Boston indentures states that he is to be apprenticed until 2 February 1752, when he would be twenty-one years of age. No other birth record has been found.
2. *Charlestown VR* 1:87; Wyman 1879, 1:415; SCPR 20:214–15.
3. Hudson 1871, 251.
4. Parkman's mother, Hannah, was the sister of Benjamin Goodwin's grandfather Nathaniel Goodwin. Bigelow-Phillips files, 1440; Wyman 1879, 1:415.
5. Boston Indentures 1 (1734–51): 83, Rare Book Room, BPL.
6. MCD 48:586.
7. SCD 90:62–63.
8. SCPR 60:393.
9. RC 30:25; Stockwell 1904, 16–17; Kingman 1892, 44; Goddard 1871, 181; *Plymouth Church Records* 1:402.
10. RC 30:311.
11. Stockwell 1904, 18–19.
12. SCD 104:99–100.
13. SCCR, Court of Common Pleas Docket Book 24:142.
14. SCCR, General Sessions of the Peace Docket Book 1766, October Term, 99–100, Judicial Archives, Mass. Archives.
15. *Sibley's Harvard Graduates* 7:517–18.
16. *Sibley's Harvard Graduates* 7:517.
17. Goddard 1871, 181; Fessenden 1850, 49–50.
18. Goddard 1871, 181.
19. SCD 113:72–74.
20. SCD 113:74–75; SCD 118:99.
21. Pruitt 1978, 2–3.

22. Thwing 1920, 76.

23. "Assessors' 'Taking-Books,'" 40.

24. SCD 157:187–89.

25. Drake 1856, 756; RC 16:265–66.

26. RC 18:167; Thwing.

27. SCCR, Court of Common Pleas Record Book 1780–81, 128; 1782–83, 182; 1783–84, 4.

28. SCCR, Court of Common Pleas Record Book 1786, 185.

29. Bridgman 1851, 58.

30. BrCD (Taunton) 61:432–33; 62:530; 68:240; 70:144.

31. SCCR, Court of Common Pleas Record Book 1789, 270.

32. *U.S. Census, Head of Families 1790, Massachusetts*, 44.

33. Bridgman 1851, 58; BrCPR 32:115–16.

34. *Index of Obituaries, 1704–1800*, 2:311.

35. BrCPR 32:246–49.

36. BrCPR 32:531–33; 33:73–76; 34:327–29.

37. Bridgman 1851, 58; Whitmore 1878, 30, no. 562.

38. SCCR, Court of Common Pleas Record Book 1783–84, 279; SCD 230:208.

39. SCD 273:109.

Daniel Gookin
1683–before 1706

Daniel Gookin was born in Sherborn, Massachusetts, on 7 July 1683, the son of the Reverend Daniel Gookin (1650–1717/18) and his wife, Elizabeth Quincy (d. 1690), sister of the goldsmith Daniel Quincy (q.v.).[1] In addition to preaching to the people of Sherborn, the Reverend Gookin gave weekly lectures to the Christian Indians at Natick from the time of his settlement there in 1685 until at least 1713.[2] Gookin's paternal grandfather, Maj.-Gen. Daniel Gookin, Sr. (ca. 1612–86/87), of Cambridge, Massachusetts, was a prominent citizen and active in raising and furnishing troops for King Philip's War in 1676. In his will, dated 13 August 1685, he bequeathed a number of specific items to his son Daniel, all of which were "in case of his Death before me" to go to "*his* wife & sonn Daniel three monthes after my Death." In addition, he bequeathed "a silver spoone" to his grandson Daniel.[3]

Gookin served his apprenticeship with Jeremiah Dummer (q.v.). On 6 January 1695/96, Samuel Sewall wrote the following notation in his diary: "Unkle Quinsey lodged here last night, having received a Letter from Mr. Gookin to desire him, agrees to bind Daniel Gookin to Cous. Dummer for 8 years from the 10th of March next. Not being able to stay, desires me to see it effected."[4] In 1698 Gookin and another apprentice, John Dixwell (q.v.), witnessed a quit-claim deed brought before Dummer between the heirs of Henry Phillips and Abigail Walter involving rights in a house and land near Peter Oliver's dock.[5]

The goldsmith Daniel Gookin probably died before 1706 because he is not mentioned in his father's will of that year.[6] There is no record of his marriage or of any children born to him. No silver by Gookin is known. BMW

1. *Sherborn VR*, 40, 203; *Cambridge VR* 1:297.

2. *Sibley's Harvard Graduates* 2:277–83.

3. Roberts 1895, 1:149–50; SCPR 11:75–79; *Cambridge VR* 2:575.

4. *Sewall Diary* 1:344.

5. SCD 19:33–34.

6. MCPR 15:81–83, dated 12 June 1706, probated 13 March 1718.

William Gowen
1749–1809

William Gowen was born in Charlestown, Massachusetts, on 13 September 1749, the son of Hammond Gowen (1728–62), a mariner and physician, and Mary Croswell (b. 1730), who were married in Charlestown on 19 May 1748.[1] Gowen's paternal grandparents were Joseph Gowen (d. 1752) and Elizabeth

A

B

Ford (b. ca. 1705).[2] His maternal grandparents were Thomas Croswell (b. 1707) and Mary Pitts (d. 1731).[3]

Following the death of Gowen's father in 1762, his mother married Nathan Sargent, who became William's guardian.[4] Gowen would have begun his apprenticeship about this time and would have completed it about 1770. The identity of his master is unknown. On 30 June 1770 Gowen received £100 from Nathan Sargent as part of the distribution of his father's estate, and the following year he received an additional £66.13.4.[5] Gowen probably moved to Medford, Massachusetts, immediately after finishing his training: he is called "goldsmith of Medford" in deeds dated 20 September and 22 October 1771, when he sold a Charlestown wharf and warehouse as well as land and a dwelling house inherited from his father.[6] The Massachusetts tax list of 1771 places him in Medford with a poll of one, half a shop, 10 shillings worth of real estate annually, £12 worth of merchandise, £20 money lent at interest, and a horse.[7] On 29 April 1772 he married Eleanor Cutter (1753–1826) of Medford, the daughter of Ebenezer Cutter (1726–58) and Elinor Floyd (b. 1731).[8]

In 1776, Gowen was drafted to fight in the War of Independence but did not serve.[9] That same year he leased a shop in Medford for forty shillings annually.[10] On 14 May 1777 he bought land in Grafton, Massachusetts, with the Medford watchmaker and clockmaker Ephraim Willard (b. 1755), with whom he may have been in partnership at the time.[11] Gowen was called "goldsmith of Medford" in a deed of 5 April 1783, when he sold his interest in lands in Malden, Massachusetts, inherited from his mother to his brother Joseph of Boston.[12] Later that year he sold half a dwelling house in Medford.[13] A bond of 18 May 1784 for the administration of the estate of Joseph Goldthwait (q.v.), his brother Joseph's father-in-law, identifies Gowen as a merchant of Medford, which indicates that he may have engaged in a broader range of mercantile activities than a goldsmith's business.[14] On 24 August 1786 he was again identified as "goldsmith of Medford" when he sold land, a dwelling house, and other buildings near Medford's marketplace.[15] But on 26 May 1789 he was identified as "merchant of Medford" when he and his wife, Eleanor, along with other heirs, executed their power of attorney in settling the estate of Sarah Cutter, Eleanor's father's widow.[16] Gowen, called a "trader of Medford," was the defendant in two suits brought to the Suffolk Court of Common Pleas in January 1790.[17] Later that year, when he sold his pew in the Medford meetinghouse, he was referred to as "gentleman," which suggests that he may have relinquished his goldsmithing and mercantile activities by this time, after more than twenty years in business.[18]

By 5 December 1794 Gowen was living in Boston when he again sold the pew in the Medford meetinghouse, and the *Boston Directory* of 1796 indicates that he ran a Brattle Street boarding house.[19] Between 1799 and 1803 he and his wife, Eleanor, executed a number of deeds disposing of land in Malden.[20] No record of Gowen's death has been found, although biographies of his daughter Maria Gowen Brooks, a noted poet, give his death date as 1809.[21] His widow died in Medford on 3 June 1826 at the age of seventy-two.[22]

Only about half a dozen pieces by Gowen are known to survive, and because they are all flatware they suggest he specialized in small wares. Among them is a strainer with a history of ownership in Medford that bears an initials mark (A). An initial and surname mark (B) is also known. A second initials mark has been attributed to Gowen, but because it is also found on a piece with ornament associated with Philadelphia, this attribution may be erroneous.[23] PEK

SURVIVING OBJECTS

	Mark	Inscription	Patron	Date	Reference	Owner
Strainer	A*	H/RL	Richard and Lucy (Jones) Hall	ca. 1790	Buhler/Hood 1970, no. 285	YUAG
Tablespoon	B	H/BH		ca. 1775	MFA 1911, no. 522	
Tablespoon	B†	A/IP		ca. 1775		YUAG
Tablespoon	B*	B/LM		ca. 1775	DAPC 84.3080	
Teaspoon	A†	EF		ca. 1780		YUAG

1. Wyman 1879, 1:430; *Charlestown VR* 1:295, 309, 388, 399; MCPR, docket 9601.
2. *Charlestown VR* 1:206, 298.
3. Wyman 1879, 1:250; *Charlestown VR* 1:215, 300, 311.
4. Wyman 1879, 1:430.
5. MCPR 55:172.
6. MCD 72:207; 73:375.
7. Pruitt 1978, 242–43.
8. *Cambridge VR* 1:177; *Medford VR*, 46, 209, 378; *Chelsea VR*, 112; MCPR, docket 5601.
9. *Mass. Soldiers and Sailors* 6:696.
10. Bigelow-Phillips files, 1686.
11. WCD 78:255; 80:130–31; 82:158–59.
12. MCD 84:551–52.
13. MCD 87:404–05.
14. SCPR 83:488.
15. MCD 94:193–94.
16. MCD 100:415–17.
17. SCCR, Court of Common Pleas Record Book 1789, 167, 271.
18. MCD 102:432–33.
19. MCD 116:424–25; RC 10:249.
20. MCD 139:16–18, 21–23; 141:275–78, 391–93; 150:88–91.
21. See for instance DAB.
22. *Medford VR*, 378.
23. The mark on a shoe buckle (Buhler/Hood 1970, no. 286) is identical to one on a pair of tongs (YUAG 1985.85.336) purchased in Philadelphia that have bright-cut decoration of the Philadelphia type. Therefore, this mark is no longer attributed to Gowen.

Thomas Grant
1731–1804

A

Although he was the most active goldsmith in Marblehead, Massachusetts, in the second half of the eighteenth century, Thomas Grant remains a shadowy figure. The son of the shoreman Thomas Grant (b. 1708) and his wife, Ann Stanford (1708–65), who were married in 1730, Thomas was born in Marblehead. His father's parents were Francis Grant, Jr. (b. 1673), and Priscilla (Hawkins) Grant (b. 1684/85); on his mother's side, he was descended from Thomas and Mary (Fluent) Stanford.[1] Through the Stanford branch of the family Grant may have been related to Ebenezer Staniford (q.v.), a goldsmith of Ipswich, Massachusetts.

Documentary evidence suggests that Grant knew and may have worked for the Salem, Massachusetts, silversmith John Touzell (q.v.), either as an apprentice or as a journeyman. In October 1752, about the time he would have finished an apprenticeship, Grant acknowledged receiving from Touzell sixteen shillings "in full of all accounts." Grant also was familiar with the tools in Touzell's shop. An undated order from Grant to Touzell reads, "please to Get maid a Large Cold Chissell the size of yours & a Tea Spoone punch of your Large Size & Charge to my accompt."[2] Grant also was an appraiser of the estate of his fellow Marblehead silversmith Thomas Skinner in 1761.[3]

Thomas Grant married Margaret Bubier (1742–89), sister of William Bubier (q.v.), in 1761, and they had eight children. Grant and his brother-in-law participated in the Revolution in Col. John Glover's regiment, and Grant was the owner of the seventy-two-ton schooner *Hancock*, one of the vessels used by Glover in the war.[4]

The inventory of his estate included a "Small Goldsmiths Shop" valued at $200, in addition to his "Mansion House & Garden" worth $750.[5] A deed of 1767 includes a diagram indicating that Grant's shop was located in a corner of a large lot owned by Grant and the shopkeeper Edward Weld; the corner lot was "S. 14 Feet upon Ye Cart Road of 15′ wide and E. 11′ upon Highway."[6] His shop equipment included

Curtain Rods. 50 C^{ts}. Shop Bellows. 50 C^{ts}	1 —
1 Old Lathe. 75 C^{ts}. 12 Hammers. $1	1. 75
1 Large Hammer 60C^{ts}.	60
1 hollowing Stamp brass Weights. &c	1 00
1 Vice. $1 a parcel of Old Tools $2	3 —

The only personal item of silver mentioned in the inventory was a spoon valued at $1.50.[7]

Grant is most well known for a pair of beakers and a tankard he made for the Second Congregational Church of Marblehead in 1772 and 1773, and for several casters, including a pair made for Capt. Thomas and Elizabeth Gerry of Marblehead.[8] He used an initial and surname mark (A). Grant trained Robert Wormsted (1755–82) from roughly 1769 to 1776.[9] Grant's sons, Thomas, Jr. (1761–1815), and William (1766–1809), followed their father in the craft but did not leave much of a mark on the record.[10] GWRW

SURVIVING OBJECTS

	Mark	Inscription	Patron	Date	Reference	Owner
Two beakers	A	The Gift of M^r. E. Stacey to yee Rev^d. M^r. Story's Church/ 1772	John Pedrick and/or Second Congregational Society, Marblehead, Mass.	1772	Jones 1913, 266–67	
Cann	A	G/TE	Thomas and Elizabeth Gerry	ca. 1755	Skinner, 15 June 1991, lot 164A	
Cann	A	The Gift of Benjamin Pickman to his grand Daughter Elizabeth Derby Pickman 1811 . . . (later)		ca. 1770	YUAG files	
Cann	A	P/IM	John and Mary Phillips	?	MFA 1911, no. 527	
Caster	A	MB		ca. 1755	Hammerslough/ Feigenbaum 1958–73, 4:41	

	Mark	Inscription	Patron	Date	Reference	Owner
Caster (mate below)	A	G/TE	Thomas and Elizabeth Gerry	ca. 1755	Flynt/Fales 1968, 131–33	HD
Caster (mate above)	A*	G/TE	Thomas and Elizabeth Gerry	ca. 1755		SPNEA
Creampot	A†	C/JM		ca. 1760	Buhler 1972, no. 318	MFAB
Porringer	A	The Gift of Mrs. Elizabeth Russell to her great grand-daughter, Eliz^h Russell Wendell, Novr 1 1766	Elizabeth Russell for Elizabeth Russell Wendell	ca. 1766	Lord/ Gamage 1972, 21	Lee Mansion, Marblehead, Mass.
Spoon	?	?		ca. 1765	Skerry 1983, n.p.	
Tablespoon	A	?		ca. 1780	Buhler 1972, appendix no. 32	MFAB
Tablespoon	A*	WMH		ca. 1790	YUAG files	
Tablespoon	A*	B/PA		ca. 1770		CM
Tankard	A	Belonging to y^t. Church in M Head/ where of ye Revd Mr Storey is Pastor/1773	Second Congregational Society, Marblehead, Mass.	1773	Jones 1913, 265–66	MFAB
Teaspoon	A*	SI		ca. 1760	MFA 1911, no. 529	
Teaspoon	A*	H/EW		ca. 1760	DAPC 73.3327	WM
Teaspoon	A*	S/IR		ca. 1770	*Silver* 24 (July–August 1991): 28	
Two teaspoons	A	IHB		ca. 1790	Buhler 1972, appendix no. 33	MFAB
Teaspoon	A	ML		ca. 1770		Lee Mansion, Marblehead, Mass.
Teaspoon	A	HB		ca. 1790		Lee Mansion, Marblehead, Mass.
Two teaspoons	A	EH		ca. 1785		PEM
Teaspoon	?	?		ca. 1785		ChM

1. *Marblehead VR* 1:217–18, 248; 2:179, 405, 562.
2. English-Touzel-Hathorne Papers, box 4, folder 5, and box 4, folder 3, PEM.
3. ECPR 338:106.

4. *Marblehead VR* 2:180; Knight 1976, 48–49.
5. ECPR, docket 11525.
6. ECD 124:268–69.
7. ECPR, docket 11525.
8. Jones 1913, 266–67; Flynt/Fales 1968, 132–33.
9. Although Wormsted finished his training, he joined the military at the beginning of the Revolution and then entered upon a seafaring career, in which he lost his life at a young age. Alastair Dickenson letter to the author, 4 May 1994.
10. Flynt/Fales 1968, 232.

Elisha Gray, Jr. 1744–ca. 1776

Elisha Gray, Jr., was born on 22 June 1744 in Barnstable, Massachusetts, the son of Elisha Gray, Sr. (1711–before 1766), of Harwich, Massachusetts, and "Mrs." Susannah Davis (d. after 1768), who married on 16 August 1739.[1] His paternal grandparents were John Gray (1671–1732), a wealthy owner of land and whaling vessels from Harwich, and Susanna Clark(e) (1674–1731) of Plymouth, Massachusetts.[2] His maternal grandparents are unknown.

Gray's master is also unknown, but he may have been acquainted with or possibly apprenticed alongside Elpalet Loring (q.v.) because Gray's mother's will was witnessed by an "Elpalit" and Elijah Loring.[3] Gray married Mary Crosby (1747–1837), the daughter of Moses Crosby and his wife, Abigail, of Harwich, and the couple had two children.[4]

In 1772 Gray, identified as a goldsmith in the court record detailing the incident, was the target of a prank that provoked him to violent behavior. On 2 November, while seated at a dance that followed husking, James Paine Freeman "tied the Button of the Sd. Gray's Coat to the Chair with a Large Twine [such that] . . . when Gray Jumped up to Dance the Chair follow'd Him." Gray waited until 12 November to whip and assault "sd. James with a Stick About as thick as one's thumb as the Witnesses Say and Beat him with Great Violence till the Stick Broak to Pieces."[5]

Elisha Gray, Jr., died intestate before 13 February 1776. In 1777 David Gorham, his executor, petitioned the Superior Court for permission to sell Gray's real estate because the estate lacked £110.7.8 to pay its debts and charges.[6] The inventory of his insolvent estate included "Shop Tools, viz Bellows, Anvils, Vice and Sundry other small tools, patterns, wts & all" valued at £15.16, and his administrator's account showed he had "part of a gold necklace, unfinished," some stones for buttons, and filings of silver and gold.[7] These documents suggest that Gray was a working goldsmith; however, no examples of his work have been located.

Mary (Crosby) Gray married her husband's nephew, David Loring (1756–1838), in 1782.[8] She appeared as "Mary Loring, as her Dower in the . . . Estate of her late husband Elisha Gray," in the probate records of her deceased son William in 1797.[9] JJF

1. *Mayflower Descendant* 4:209, 248; 23:127–28; 33:128, 167; *Harwich VR*, 9, 72.
2. Paine 1971, 114, 121; *Harwich VR*, 29; BCPR 5:163.
3. BCPR 13:397–98. In her will Susannah Gray bequeathed her "Punch ladle" and six teaspoons to her grandson Thomas Davis Freeman.
4. *Harwich VR*, 105; BCPR 28:342–43; Raymond 1887, 249.
5. Edmund Hawes to Robert Treat Paine, 23 February 1773 and 12 April 1773, Robert Treat Paine Papers, MHS.
6. Supreme Judicial Court, 961:128, file 144351, Mass. Archives.
7. BCPR 16:81; 17:342, 483–85.

8. Paine 1971, 121.
9. BCPR 28:342–43.

John Gray
1692–1719/20

A

John Gray was the third son of the baker Samuel (ca. 1660–1707/08) and Susanna (Langdon) Gray of Boston. He was born on 16 August 1692, making him eight years younger than his brother Samuel (1684–1713) (q.v.).[1] Given the difference in their ages, John may have served his apprenticeship with his older brother.

In 1713/14, Susanna Gray, widow and executor of the estate of her son Samuel Gray, late of New London, Connecticut, deeded her portion of her son's estate to her sons John and William (both of whom she referred to as merchants).[2] She empowered her son John to act as her attorney in the settlement of Samuel's estate, and John traveled to New London to take care of his brother's affairs. While there, on 21 October 1714, he married Mary Christophers (b. 1694), daughter of Richard (1662–1726) and Grace (Turner) Christophers (1668–1734).[3]

John was back in Boston by 1715/16, when he mortgaged his $4/_{11}$ths part of the brick house and land at the corner of Marlborough Street and Bishop's Lane formerly owned by his father, Samuel Gray, to Paul Dudley, Esq.[4] Only six days later, John Gray was summoned to "Answer unto Enoch Greenleafe of Marblehead . . . Sadler, In a plea of the Case for not paying to the pl^t the sume of five pounds & one penny money." According to a notation on the back of the writ, Ezekiel Cleasby, deputy sheriff, "attached one Chaier in the house of the within named John Gray" to assure his payment.[5]

In July 1717 John Gray, identified as a goldsmith, advertised in the *Boston News-Letter* that he had a house to sell or let near the Old South Church formerly belonging to his brother Samuel. The following month, his brother Ebenezer, merchant, sold his share in his father's real estate to John. John Gray appeared as defendant in a case before the Court of Common Pleas in October 1717 for failure to pay a debt of seven pounds due to the merchant Thomas Moffatt. In the record he is referred to as being a "Goldsmith or Baker," which suggests that he carried on his father's business.[6]

Things apparently did not go well for John and his mother because in December 1717 she finally declared bankruptcy and sold, along with the other remaining owners (all heirs of Samuel Gray, baker), the house and land in Marlborough Street from her husband's estate to the commissioners of her bankruptcy—William Dummer, Elisha Cooke, Jonathan Remington, and Henry Dering—for seven hundred pounds.[7]

Although the occupation of the writer is not given, it seems probable that John Gray wrote the following note to Sheriff Stephen Greenleaf during his imprisonment for debt: "Honored Sir I take pleasure to Return you my Humbly & hearty thanks for Great & undersved kindness to me During my Imprisonment & beg y^r Honour further Lenity as I have Petitioned the Honourable Court to forgive my fees Which Your Honour I pray if present to forward for the Reasons in Said Petition Sett forth & Ever Shall Remain as is Duty Bound y^r unworthy but Respectfull Humble Servant."[8]

John Gray evidently left his troubles behind him and returned to New London about 1718. He died in New London on 14 January 1719/20, intestate, and his estate was inventoried there.[9] His estate included

To sixteen oz. & 1ˢ wᵗ of Silver Buttons Buckels &c 9ˢ pʳ   07. 05. 00
To 4 oz 1ˢ wᵗ old plate 8ˢ pʳ   01. 13. 00
To 16 oz 1ˢ wᵗ in Coind plate 9ˢ pʳ   07. 05. 00
To 3 dollers 13ˢ/6ᵈ to 35 oz plate tanker Sarcruʳ & Spoons, 14ˡᵇ 14. 13. 06
To two Cane heads Silver   00. 15. 00
To half an ozᵉˢ wanting 1ˢ wᵗ of Gold Rings Jewels   03. 14. 00
To two ozᵉˢ Gold part fileings   12. 10. 00
To almost Nine ozᵉˢ of Silver   03. 19. 00
To Billes of Creditt 59ˢ/3ᵈ more 8ˢ   03. 07. 03
To two Chafing dishes   00. 06. 00
To a pair of Large Scales & weights wᵗʰ triangles   03. 10. 00

. . .

To a Gunn 30ˢ/ to Scales & weights for money. 12ˢ.   02. 02. 00
To the Gold Smiths Tooles vizᵗ bellows Anvel, ⎫
Hamers. files Implements of divers Sorts al be. ⎬
longing to sᵈ trade   ⎭   06. 10. 00
To an Indian or mustee boy Named Cuffee   16. 00. 00

. . .

a parcel of CharCoal. 3ˢ/¹⁰

The total value of Gray's inventoried estate was £220.6.1. He did not own a house or land. The estate was divided between his widow and his mother; the former received the utensils of the baking trade and the latter received the goldsmith tools. The nature of the tools and goldsmith's work that he had on hand indicates that he had the capability to make smaller pieces of holloware for his customers. Although he may not have made the tankard listed in his inventory, and the chafing dishes mentioned are of too little value to have been made of silver, the spoons, cane heads, and rings mentioned probably were made by Gray. Gray's estate administration reveals some of his activities as a goldsmith. The account of Jeremiah Chapman, Jr., shows that Gray received credit of £1.3.6 for a pair of silver buckles for services rendered by Chapman that included "work about your bake house." In January 1720/21 Gray's widow paid John Rogers 15 shillings for "a broken Gold Ring which I [Rogers] delivered to her sᵈ husband to be mended & Never had it of him againe." Gray also trained Daniel Deshon, who began his apprenticeship with René Grignon (qq.v.). The administrator's account of Gray's estate shows that when Deshon's apprenticeship was completed he received "⁴/₅ parts of 8ᶠ·6ˢ for a Coat Jacket briches Shirt hatt and Shoes" as well as "3 shirts & a pʳ of Shoes, a pʳ of lether briches & 2 Neck Cloths . . . that were his masters."[11]

No mark has ever been firmly attributed to John Gray; another man with the same initials, Joseph Goldthwait (q.v.), was also working in Boston at nearly the same time. Goldthwait did not begin working on his own until after 1727, however, and two objects, a pepper box in a private collection and a teaspoon at the Lyman Allyn Museum (both marked IG in a rectangle [A]) are of an early date and may be the work of John Gray. Sugar tongs marked I GRAY are of too late a date to be the work of this John Gray.[12]

The tradition of silversmithing continued in the Gray family: Gray's nephew Samuel Gray (1710/11–48) (q.v.) was apprenticed to John Burt (q.v.) about 1724, and Gray's sister married Peter Feurt (q.v.) in 1728. BMW

SURVIVING OBJECTS

	Mark	Inscription	Patron	Date	Reference	Owner
Pepper box	A	?		ca. 1720	YUAG files	
Teaspoon	A†	CL		ca. 1720		LAM

1. RC 9:201; Thwing; Raymond 1887, 142–43. Correspondence between Francis Hill Bigelow and Theodore Gray, 21 July 1931, 19 August 1931, Bigelow-Phillips files, 611–20. In these letters Theodore Gray quotes extensively from the family Bible kept by Ebenezer Gray, brother of John Gray and Samuel Gray.
2. SCD 28:40–41.
3. *Scituate VR* 1:374; New London VR 1:20, 22; 2:6, 8; Savage 1860–62, 1:383.
4. SCD 30:114. The original deed is dated 2 March 1715/16; the debt was canceled on 11 December 1717.
5. SCCR, file 11422.
6. *Boston Newsletter*, 15–22 July 1717; SCD 32:98; SCCR, Court of Common Pleas Record Book 1715–18, 258; SCCR, file 11848.
7. SCD 32:101–02. The commissioners sold the land to Col. John Alford in December 1720; see SCD 35:32.
8. SCCR, file 28365.
9. Bigelow-Phillips files, 720, records his epitaph.
10. New London County Probate District, docket 2274, CSL. The inventory was taken on 12 February 1719/20 and presented on 26 February 1719/20.
11. New London County Probate District, docket 2274, CSL.
12. Examples are at LAM and are recorded in *Antiques* 87 (April 1965): 383 and YUAG files.

Samuel Gray
1684–1713

A

Samuel Gray was the eldest son of Samuel (ca. 1660–1707/08), a baker, and his wife, Susanna (Langdon) Gray. His parents arrived in Boston in November 1684, and he was apparently born during their transatlantic crossing.[1] Although some authorities believe that he may have served his apprenticeship under John Coney (q.v.), there is no documentary evidence to support it, and Francis Hill Bigelow believed that he apprenticed with Jeremiah Dummer (q.v.).[2]

In June 1705, Gray asked the Suffolk County Court of Common Pleas to issue a writ of attachment on the bricklayer Thomas Adkins for failing to pay him the sum of £4.15 "for goods sold & delivered to [the] Def.". When Gray failed to take any further action in the case, Adkins instituted a countersuit and was awarded costs of court.[3] Oliver A. Roberts records that Gray became a member of the Ancient and Honorable Artillery Company in 1706, but the honor may have actually been bestowed upon his father, rather than upon the goldsmith.[4] The goldsmith Samuel Gray left Boston within the next year, and in April of 1707 married Lucy Palmes (ca. 1686–1737), daughter of Edward Palmes, in New London, Connecticut. He stayed in New London and set up a substantial goldsmithing business that he carried on until his death in 1713.[5] Joshua Hempstead of New London mentioned Gray's death in his diary and commented that he had been sick for a long time.[6] Gray died on 26 May 1713 and was buried in the Ancient Burial Place in New London.[7]

In his will, dated 5 June 1712, Samuel left everything to his mother, Susanna Gray, of Boston, and made her sole executor of his estate. His wife, Lucy, contested the estate, and eventually the court divided the estate between Susanna Gray and Lucy Gray. His brother, John Gray (q.v.), went to New London to represent his mother in the settlement. Samuel's estate lists the following shop items and tools:

To 99 ounces plate In 3 tankers 3 Cups one Spoon. 6 forks &c. at 7ˢ pʳ ounce	34. 13. 00
To more plate In buckels buttons 20 ounz ¹/₄	07. 01. 9
To 76 ounces Quind plate 8pʳ	30. 08. 00
To 2 ounces & half Quind Gold wanting 40 grains—att. 5–10s pʳ ounce	13. 05. 00
To one ounce & on Quarter & one pany wᵗ Gold plate—more Gold plate 6ˢ/	06. 08. 06
To 16 ounces half & half Quarter Silver plate 7ˢ pʳ ounce	05. 16. 4
To one Silver watch wᵗʰ a Chane	02. 17. 0
To two ditto damnified	01. 00. 0
. . .	
To an old Negro man Named Samson	01. 0. 0
To Gold Smiths tooles. & Implemᵗˢ with a parcel of Enemel. Some Gold and Silver filings. with other Smal Tools wᵗʰ a parcel of Char Coals	13. 0. 0⁸

In addition to the shop goods related to goldsmithing, Gray owned shop goods of a general nature including cloth, cutlery, locks, buttons, notions, tinware, spices, apothecary items, and nails. Although the list of his goldsmithing tools suggests that he could not produce large work on his own, the extent of his general shop goods and the total value of his estate are testimony to the success that he enjoyed in his business. The inventory amounted to £539.11.7, the debts were £405.9, leaving a balance of £134.2.7. His slave, Samson, is referred to as an "old man" in the inventory but may have been able to assist Gray either in his goldsmithing or in his general shopkeeping enterprises.

The mark SG in a heart (A) has been attributed to Samuel Gray, but only three objects that bear the mark are known. One of them is a cup also bearing the mark of John Edwards (q.v.) that Gray may have retailed or repaired. The marks of his nephew, Samuel Gray (1710/11–48) (q.v.), who worked in Boston later, sometimes have been incorrectly attributed to this silversmith.[9] BMW

SURVIVING OBJECTS

	Mark	Inscription	Patron	Date	Reference	Owner
Cup (with mark of John Edwards)	A	M/TZ to EM		ca. 1710	Moore Collection 1980, no. 98	
Fork	A	?		ca. 1710	YUAG files	
Porringer	A†	I/DS		ca. 1710	Buhler/Hood 1970, no. 332	YUAG

1. Bohan/Hammerslough 1970, 236; RC 10:76.
2. Flynt/Fales 1968, 233; Bohan/Hammerslough 1970, 236; Bigelow-Phillips files, 605.
3. SCCR, file 6500; SCCR, Court of Common Pleas Record Book 1701–06, 274.
4. Roberts 1895, 1:358; Roberts also lists him as a tithingman and a member of the militia in 1705. Although he was probably the same Samuel who served in the militia, it was probably his father, Samuel, the baker, who served in the prestigious office of tithingman, which was usually reserved for an older man.
5. Theodore Gray to Francis Hill Bigelow, 19 August 1931, Bigelow-Phillips files, 615–20.
6. *Diary of Joshua Hempstead*, 23.

7. *Ye Ancient Buriall Place of New London, Conn.*, 21.

8. New London Probate District, docket 2276, CSL. The inventory was taken on 3 October 1713 and presented on 13 October 1713; the will, dated 5 June 1712, was proved in Boston, 17 June 1713 (SCPR 18:116–17). In spite of the fact that Gray named his mother sole executor, the court in Connecticut appointed his wife, Lucy Gray, and his brother-in-law Andrew Palmes as administrators on 9 June 1713 (see New London Probate District, docket 2276). For further information about Lucy (Palmes) (Gray) Lynde, see Jones 1913, 443.

9. Kovel 1961, 121.

Samuel Gray
1710/11–48

A

B

C

Samuel Gray was the nephew of Samuel Gray (1684–1713) (q.v.) and John Gray (q.v.), and the nephew by marriage of Peter Feurt (q.v.). He was born in Boston on 19 January 1710/11 to Joseph Gray (1687–1716), a victualler, and Rebecca Sears (1686–1750), the daughter of Alexander (ca. 1664–1736), a shipwright, and Rebecca Sears (ca. 1664–1732).[1] Following his father's death in 1716, Samuel Gray was raised by his stepfather, Arthur Hill, a mariner, whom his mother married in 1719.[2] His paternal grandparents were Samuel (ca. 1660–1707/08), a baker, and Susanna (Langdon) Gray.

His career started about 1732 after an apprenticeship with John Burt (q.v.), which probably began about 1724. In 1728/29 with John Blowers (q.v.) he witnessed a deed for John Burt.[3] On 6 June 1730 the estate of William Smith was billed £10.69 by Burt for six funeral rings, and on 2 July Samuel Gray acknowledged payment of the account "for my Master John Burt."[4] One day after his twenty-first birthday on 20 January 1732, Gray sold his interest in a dwelling house inherited from his grandfather Samuel Gray to his brother Joseph. William Simpkins and Basil Dixwell (qq.v.) witnessed the deed.[5] This document, in which Gray is called a goldsmith, suggests that Gray and Dixwell, who were almost exact contemporaries, may have been working as journeymen for Simpkins, who was slightly older. The estate administration of Isaac Perkins (q.v.) shows that Gray was paid 4 shillings by the estate.

By 1737 Gray must have attained some financial stability because on 18 August of that year he married Sarah Williams.[6] Gray must have been one of the minor retailers of silver in Boston at midcentury because fewer than a dozen pieces of holloware bearing the marks GRAY in a rectangle (A), S:GRAY in a rectangle (B), or SG in a rectangle (C) survive. His mark has been confused with that of his uncle, Samuel Gray.[7] A case in the Court of Common Pleas, wherein Gray sued the Boston joiner William Hunt for failure to pay for some gold buttons he had bought in 1740, indicates that Gray also produced jewelry.[8] When the jeweler James Boyer (q.v.) died in 1741 his estate owed Gray one pound.[9] According to the epitaph in the Granary Burying Ground, Gray died on 1 May 1748 at age thirty-seven.[10] PEK

SURVIVING OBJECTS

	Mark	Inscription	Patron	Date	Reference	Owner
Cann	B	H/AT; 1750 (later)		ca. 1740	MFA 1911, no. 530	
Creampot	A†	LB; The Gift of/The Hon.be/J:Hancock, Esq.r/to/Lydia Bowes (later)		ca. 1745	Buhler 1972, no. 222	MFAB
Pepper box	A	A/SM	Silas and Mary (Gyles) Atkins	ca. 1742	Buhler 1972, no. 221	MFAB

	Mark	Inscription	Patron	Date	Reference	Owner
Porringer (mates below)	A	A/SM	Silas and Mary (Gyles) Atkins	ca. 1742	Norman-Wilcox 1962, no. 24	LACMA
Porringer (mates above and below)	A	A/SM	Silas and Mary (Gyles) Atkins	ca. 1742	Buhler 1972, no. 220	MFAB
Porringer (mates above)	A	A/SM	Silas and Mary (Gyles) Atkins	ca. 1742	Christie's, 26 January 1991, lot 66	
Porringer	B	EG		ca. 1740	*Antiques* 36 (October 1939): 167	
Snuffbox	A*	EW 1735; EH (later)		1735	MFA 1911, no. 531	
Tankard	A*/ c†	A/SM	Silas and Mary (Gyles) Atkins	ca. 1745	*Antiques* 145 (January 1994): 72	
Tankard	B†	P/WA		ca. 1740	Sotheby's, 21 June 1989, lot 136	

1. RC 9:171, 174; RC 24:68; Codman 1918, 113, 128, 210; RC 28:10; *Salem VR* 2:274; SCPR 32:399, 421–22; 21:299.
2. RC 28:82; SCPR 44:531.
3. *York Deeds* 14:196–97.
4. John Burt bill to William Smith estate, 6 June 1730, with receipt acknowledged by Samuel Gray, 2 July 1730, Smith-Townsend II Papers, MHS.
5. SCD 47:14–15.
6. RC 28:201.
7. Kovel 1961, 121.
8. SCCR, Court of Common Pleas Record Book 1741, 73.
9. SCPR 37:137.
10. Codman 1918, 113.

Bartholomew Green
1697–before 1746

A

Bartholomew Green was born on 12 July 1697 and was baptized six days later in the Second Church, Boston, where his maternal grandfather, Increase Mather, was pastor. He was the son of Bartholomew (1663/64–1713) and Maria or Mariah (Mather) Green (1664–1746), who were married in Boston in 1688.[1] His father, a mariner, was born in Charlestown, Massachusetts, to Jacob (ca. 1625–1701), a leading citizen and member of the Ancient and Honorable Artillery Company, and Mary (Bartholomew) (Whipple) Green (d. ca. 1713/14).[2] Bartholomew Green's mother, Maria, was one of the daughters of Increase Mather (1639–1723) and Maria Cotton (1641/42–1714). On 25 October 1696, Samuel Sewall recorded a fire in a house in Boston belonging to Peter Butler: "Mr. Green, who married Mr. Mathers daughter, is one of the Tenants: He and his family were at Charlestown, keeping Sabbath there."[3] Following her husband's death in 1713, Maria Green married Richard Fifield, also a mariner.[4]

Although in 1956 Kathryn C. Buhler stated that Bartholomew Green was a documented apprentice of Henry Hurst (q.v.), she failed to cite a source for this and omitted the information in her catalogue of 1972.[5] Evidence that Green apprenticed with Hurst still is lacking. In 1717 Bartholomew and his sister Maria Elliot and her husband, John Elliot, a mariner, and Green's mother, Maria Fifield, conveyed property to Capt. Ephraim Breed of Charlestown. A blank in the deed after Bartholomew's name suggests that he intended to marry, but his wife's name was never entered.[6] Several Bartholomew Greens resided in Boston at this time, and because no wife was named in a deed with Bartholomew Green and because his mother's will mentioned only her Elliot grandchildren, it is likely that he never married.

A deed dated 30 August 1725 records the sale of property to a man named Sartell by Bartholomew Green, his brother Mather Green, a mariner, and their mother.[7] In this deed Bartholomew is identified as a silversmith, but when he appeared in court in 1729, as defendant in a suit brought by the Boston tailors John and Richard Billings, he is referred to as a goldsmith.[8] Bartholomew Green appeared as a defendant in two other cases, one involving a debt due to John Flower, a Boston barber, in 1732, and one involving an unpaid promissory note that Green gave to Joseph Brandon, a Boston merchant, in 1733.[9] In 1733 he again joined with his mother and brother in the sale of a piece of property that was theirs by right of inheritance, and in 1734, Bartholomew Green and his mother bound themselves to the merchant James Smith of Boston for £240. This latter deed was witnessed by John Burt (q.v.).[10] Green was chosen as a Boston constable with Joseph Goldthwait (q.v.) in 1734/35.[11] Green died before 1746, as he is not mentioned in his mother's will of that year.[12]

At least three objects have been found to date that may be identified as the work of Bartholomew Green. Kathryn Buhler ascribed the B:GREEN in rectangle mark (A) to him on the basis of the fact that Benjamin Greene (q.v.) had a terminal "e" at the end of his name and Bartholomew Green did not. Furthermore, Benjamin Greene's surviving account book covering the years 1734–58 indicates that he was primarily a jeweler and a merchant. Bartholomew Green's surviving covered spout cup in the Museum of Fine Arts, Boston, demonstrates that he was a fine craftsman.[13] He also made some jewelry, for he was paid £37.5.8 for making rings for the estate of Capt. Daniel Brown, a mariner late of Kenton in Great Britain, in 1732.[14] BMW

SURVIVING OBJECTS

	Mark	Inscription	Patron	Date	Reference	Owner
Porringer	A	F/WE	William and Elizabeth (Campbell) Foye	ca. 1725	YUAG files	
Porringer	A	E/PE		ca. 1720	Skinner, 15 June 1991, lot 172	
Spout cup	A†	R/IK	James and Katherine (Graves) Russell	ca. 1738	Buhler 1972, no. 144	MFAB

1. RC 9:93, 233; *Charlestown VR* 1:46; Wyman 1879, 1:346, 437; SCPR 18:182–83, 340. There were three Bartholomew Greens born in Boston between 1697 and 1702, two recorded as sons of Bartholomew (the printer) and Mary Green and one recorded as the son of Bartholomew and Mariah Green (RC 9:233; RC 24:2, 7). Deeds between the legatees of the estate of the mariner Bartholomew Green make it clear that the goldsmith Bartholomew Green was the son of the mariner and his wife, Maria or Mariah Mather. Kathryn Buhler mistakenly recorded Bartholomew Green as the son of the printer; Buhler 1972, 1:179.

2. Roberts 1895, 1:169–70; Wyman 1879, 1:435–36.

3. *Sewall Diary* 1:358.

4. RC 9:12; RC 28:44. Proof that Maria (Green) Fifield was the daughter of Increase Mather is contained in a deed in which she joined with her sisters in selling land that was part of their father's estate; SCD 44:24.

5. Buhler 1956, 27.

6. MCD 21:12–13.

7. MCD 25:181–82.

8. SCCR, Court of Common Pleas Record Book 1728, 604.

9. SCCR, Court of Common Pleas Record Book 1732, 334; 1733, 316.

10. SCD 47:281; 50:36–38.

11. Seybolt 1939, 197.

12. It is possible that Green died, like so many other Boston men, in the last campaign against Louisbourg; however, his name is not to be found on the muster rolls in the state archives. SCPR 39:366–67.

13. Buhler 1972, 1:179–80.

14. SCPR 29:507–09. The payment was made to "Barth° Green Goldsmith for Rings."

Benjamin Greene
1712/13–76

A

Benjamin Greene, the younger brother of Rufus Greene (q.v.), was born in Boston on 11 January 1712/13 and like his brother may have been trained by William Cowell, Sr. (q.v.).[1] He could have been working as early as 1734 and was identified as a goldsmith in a deed of 10 April 1734 selling his interest in his parents' estate to his brother Thomas.[2] After completing his apprenticeship he boarded with his older brother, Rufus, and may have served him as a journeyman. An account book kept by Rufus shows that he charged Benjamin for board between 1733 and 1737 and that the board sometimes came to more than what Benjamin "has dun for me." In 1737 the board was calculated at twenty-five shillings a week.[3] The charges for board cease about the time of Benjamin's marriage.

The marriage intentions for Benjamin Greene and Mary Chandler (1717–56) of Worcester, Massachusetts, were published in Boston on 24 December 1736.[4] Born in Woodstock, Connecticut, on 9 September 1717, Mary Chandler was the daughter of the judge John Chandler, Jr. (1693–1762), of Worcester and Hannah Gardiner of New London, Connecticut.[5] Her uncle by marriage, Ebenezer Gray, was the brother of Samuel and John Gray (qq.v.).

Greene's name appears a few times in Boston records. He was the plaintiff in a suit against the woolcomber Samuel Foster for a debt of £52.12 brought before the Court of Common Pleas in 1741.[6] In 1743 he and his brothers were defendants in a successful suit brought by William Speakman, a Boston baker, over a piece of land.[7] With his brother Rufus, he was one of the appraisers of the estate of William Cowell, Sr., in 1745.[8] With Samuel Edwards and Daniel Parker (qq.v.) he witnessed Seth Storer Coburn's father's estate administration in 1752.[9]

A ledger kept by Greene shows that he supplied other silversmiths with finished wares that probably were fabricated in his shop, and that after 1740 he became heavily involved in merchant ventures to North Carolina, South Carolina, the West Indies, Surinam, and England. Beginning in 1735, he sold many small items and jewelry to James Boyer, Mary Ann Boyer, Charles Simpson, and Samuel Usher (qq.v.).[10] After Simpson moved from Boston to North Carolina, Greene sent him general merchandise as well as goldsmith's work, which indicates that his business combined dealing in various commodities with silversmithing. In 1747 Benjamin and his brothers, Rufus and Thomas, signed an agreement to build a ship. The ship was named the *Three Brothers* and the brothers used it for some of their joint trading ventures.[11] Mercantile activities provided Greene with a large estate. In the Massachusetts tax list of 1771 he was assessed one poll, a house, warehouse, £40 worth of real estate,

120 tons of vessels, and £600 worth of merchandise.[12] His worth exceeded that of any other silversmith on the list.

Greene relied on Jacob Hurd (q.v.) to do specialized work for him, such as finishing the feet of milk pots and lips of canns on a lathe.[13] Greene also sold goldsmiths' supplies to his fellow craftsmen. He sold a melting pot to Jeremiah Snow, Jr. (q.v.), in 1739.[14] Between 1738/39 and 1740 the watchmaker and clockmaker, Benjamin Bagnall, Jr. (q.v. Appendix A), purchased goods from Greene.[15] In January 1742/43 he sold a pair of shoe buckles for £3 to his brother Rufus for Rufus's wife.[16] John Ball (q.v.) purchased more than £190 worth of tools and supplies when setting up his shop in 1745.[17] Other craftsmen Greene did business with were William Cowell, Jr. (q.v.), whose estate paid Greene £1.19.4, and William Homes, Sr. (q.v.), his brother Rufus's former apprentice and journeyman.[18] A caster and creampot bearing Benjamin Greene's mark (A) are the sole objects that have been identified. The mark B:GREEN, which belongs to Bartholomew Green (q.v.), has sometimes been mistakenly attributed to Benjamin Greene.

Greene's wife, Mary, died on 28 February 1756, and he outlived her by twenty years, dying on 10 April 1776; both were buried in the Granary Burying Ground.[19] No probate is filed for him in Suffolk County, but on 30 November 1784 his children Hannah, Joseph, Lucretia, Sarah, and Gardiner sold their brother Benjamin their interest in a dwelling house in south Boston that had been deeded to their father.[20] PEK

SURVIVING OBJECTS

	Mark	Inscription	Patron	Date	Reference	Owner
Caster	A†	Eliott arms, azure a fess or; Given to H- Gale in Remem- brance/of her Brother-Saml Eliott who/died on the Coast of Affrica/1 Ian[y] 1741 Aged 24	H. Gale in memory of Samuel Eliot[t]	1741	Buhler/Hood 1970, no. 178	YUAG
Creampot	A	HR; DC; 1794 (?)		ca. 1750		MWPI

1. RC 24:83.
2. SCD 48:206.
3. Rufus Greene Account Book, 1728–48, n.p., Karolik–Codman Papers, MHS.
4. RC 28:226.
5. Woodstock VR, 1:22, 25, 27; New London VR, 1:22; Roberts 1895, 1:469– 70. John Chandler was one of the surveyors to run the line between Massachusetts and Connecticut in 1714 and in 1728 was coroner of Suffolk County. When courts were established in Worcester in 1731 he became clerk of all the courts there, an office he held until 1754 when he was appointed judge. He became chief justice in 1757 and held that post until his death in 1762.
6. SCCR, Court of Common Pleas Record Book 1741, 73; docket 254.
7. SCCR, Court of Common Pleas Record Book 1742–43, 220.
8. SCPR 38:162–63.
9. SCPR, docket 10043.
10. Benjamin Greene Ledger, 1734–56 1, 31, 49, 64, 85, 93, 99, 104, 130, MHS.
11. Document 347.4, Bostonian Society, Boston.
12. Pruitt 1978, 44–45.
13. Benjamin Greene Ledger, 1734–56, 47, MHS.
14. Benjamin Greene Ledger, 1734–56, 31, MHS.

15. Benjamin Greene Ledger, 1734–56, 18, MHS.
16. Rufus Greene Account Book, 1728–48, n.p., Karolik–Codman papers, MHS.
17. Benjamin Greene Ledger, 1734–56, 63, MHS.
18. Benjamin Greene Ledger, 1734–56, 78, MHS; SCPR, docket 12763.
19. Codman 1918, 114.
20. SCD 146:174–76.

Rufus Greene
1707–77

*John Singleton Copley,
Rufus Greene, 1758–61, oil on
canvas. Private collection.*

A

B

C

Born on 30 May 1707, Rufus Greene was the son of Nathaniel (1679–1714) of Warwick, Rhode Island, and Ann (Gould) Greene (d. 1727/28), shopkeepers of Boston. His father was the son of Thomas Greene (1630/31–1717) of Rhode Island and his wife, Elizabeth (Barton) Greene (1641–93). His mother was the daughter of Thomas Gould and Frances (Robinson) Gould of Boston.[1] When Rufus was only seven years old his father died. The will mentions sons Thomas (1705–63), Rufus, Nathaniel (b. 1709), William (b. 1711), and Benjamin (q.v.), all of whom were to receive legacies, and was witnessed by William Gold or Gould, William Cowell, Sr. (q.v.), and Robert Snow.[2] No guardians were named for the boys, and evidently Ann's father and brothers helped her to raise her young family. Ann continued in her husband's business, and her father may have helped her to send her oldest son, Thomas, to Yale College (class of 1727). Rufus became apprenticed to William Cowell, Sr., a close friend of his father, about 1721. Rufus became a loyalist when war broke out with England in 1776, and shortly after he died, his son William made the following record of the silversmith's life in his diary: "Perhaps no one has met with more trouble than my parent. He was born May 30, 1707 Old Stile. He served his time with Mr. Cowell, a silversmith in Boston. . . . Tarrying a while and settling a correspondence in England [he] returned to Boston, carried over with him many articles of the silversmiths' trade."[3]

Rufus Greene's mother, Ann Greene, still a widow, died in February 1727/28. William Cowell, Sr., Joseph Cowell, and Joseph Marion witnessed her will, which named her son Thomas as sole executor. Her estate, valued at £6,232, included a house on Newbury Street. John (a wheelwright), Joseph, William, Elizabeth, and John Cowell (q.v.), John Potwine (q.v.), and Jacob Hurd (q.v.) all appear in a list of people who owed money to the estate. William Cowell, Sr., was paid £20.17.6 for making mourning rings for the funeral. In addition to receiving a legacy from his mother, Rufus received a legacy from his grandmother, Frances Gold or Gould.[4]

The inventory of Ann Greene's estate included the following goldsmith's tools:

1 fforging Anvil w.t lb 1..3.0	@ 5d	4.	1.	8
1 Raising ditto 51	@ 8d	1.	14.	—
3 Hammers Sorted	@	3.		—
1 Spoon Tast with Swages & Bolles 30lb½ @ 8d		2.	7.	4
1 Scillet w.t 20lb			16.	3
3 Flasks Sorted			6.	9
6 prs of Plyars			4.	3
1 Copper Pan for Boyling			12.	7
1 ffine Scratch Brush			1	—
1 brass Stamp 4lb			8	—
4 Graving Irons Sorted			10	—
2 Spoon Punches			6.	2

2 Stakes for Cup & Tankard	8.	4
1 Thimble Stamp	1. 15.	6
4 doz: of Peircing files	8	—
	14. 2.	10
Advance at 175 ℔ 6s	24. 14.	11 £38. 17. 9½ [5]

Ann Greene may have acquired these tools to enable her son, Rufus, to establish his business. Eight months after his mother's death Rufus Greene began his goldsmith business as he recorded in his account book, "I Began or Sett up my Bisness October the 7:1728 and the Making of the things from that time to January the 1:1732 Came to £1624..6..0." [6] In the first few pages of that account book Greene recorded for the years 1732 to 1739 the value of the "making part" or labor of what he made in the shop as well as the value of the making part of what he merely sold in the shop. These figures indicate that the cost of the labor to make the objects was greater than the value that Greene received for the labor when the objects were sold. The more abbreviated entries for the year 1739 suggest that Greene shifted his business from running a goldsmith's shop to broader mercantile activities at that time.

In December 1728, Rufus Greene and Katharine Stanbridge (ca. 1708–68), daughter of Edward Stanbridge, one of the original pewholders in Christ Church, Boston, were married by the Reverend Henry Harris of King's Chapel, Boston. [7] The couple had ten children: Ann (b. 1729, d. young), Katharine (b. 1731, m. John Amory, merchant, in 1756), Rufus (b. 1733, d. before 1772), Mary (b. 1734, d. before 1772), Ann (b. 1736), Henry (b. 1738, d. before 1772), Elizabeth (b. 1739/40), William (b. 1741), Sarah (b. 1743, m. Thomas Hickling, 1764), and Martha (bap. 1748). All of the children probably were baptized in King's Chapel, where Rufus Greene served as a vestryman. [8]

There are several documentary references to silver by Rufus Greene but few surviving objects. A spoon marked "R. GREENE, *at length*" was reported lost or stolen in the *Boston News-Letter* of 26 July–2 August 1733. [9] The estate of Thomas Greene paid him £18.13.9 for rings for the funeral in 1731. [10] A receipt records his sale of four pieces of shalloons as well as a silver cann (£19.2.8), six teaspoons, tongs and strainer (£6.0.6), two silver hooks (£0.4.6) and six additional teaspoons, tongs and strainer (£7.4) to Mr. John Maverick in 1737 and 1738. [11] His known marks are R·GREENE in a shaped rectangle (A), R·G in a shaped rectangle (B), and R·G in a rectangle (C). Other variations of his mark have been published in the literature, including R·GREENE in stepped rectangle, R·G in conjoined circles, RG in a rectangle, and R·G in a stepped rectangle. [12]

Other evidence indicates that Greene had business dealings with a number of Boston goldsmiths. When James Boyer (q.v.) died in 1741, his estate owed Greene £63.11.7. [13] Greene was also a creditor of the estate of Nathaniel Morse (q.v.). [14] Greene's long-term association with the Cowells continued. John Cowell may have been a journeyman in Greene's shop. With his brother Benjamin, Greene was one of the appraisers of the estate of William Cowell, Sr., in 1745, and when William Cowell, Jr. (q.v.), died, Greene owed the estate £4.19.1. [15] In addition, in the 1730s Greene trained at least one apprentice, William Homes, Sr. (q.v.). [16] Rufus evidently employed his brother Benjamin in his shop because Benjamin received fifty-two weeks' board from his older brother in 1736 and in 1737 compensated Rufus for "my Absence 3 ½ weeks at 25/." Benjamin bought tools, knee chapes and tongs, cipher stones and buttons, chasing punches and saltpeter from his brother in 1740 and made rings for him in 1743; but otherwise most of their early transactions involved cloth and other dry goods. In 1748 Rufus Greene paid Paul Revere, Sr. (q.v.), £45 for twelve spoons.[17] In 1750/51, Rufus served with Jacob Hurd and William Cowell, Jr., as one of the arbiters in a dispute between Thomas Edwards and Thomas Townsend (qq.v.).[18] In 1761 Greene paid Daniel Boyer (q.v.) £3.12 for two rings and Gawen Brown (q.v. Appendix A) for cleaning a clock.[19]

After establishing his goldsmithing business Rufus Greene appears to have used his craft as a stepping-stone toward a career as a general merchant. Identified variously as a goldsmith and a silversmith, he was a plaintiff in court cases in 1735, 1738, 1740, 1741, and 1743.[20] In the surviving accounts between him and his brother Benjamin, Rufus is called a goldsmith in 1736, just "of Boston" in 1743 and 1745, and a merchant by 1752. In a deed of 1728/29 witnessed by Joseph and John Cowell, Rufus Greene was described as a goldsmith.[21] In 1743 he still was referred to as a goldsmith, but in a deed of 1749 he was called a merchant.[22]

Rufus Greene's numerous deeds indicate that he was engaged in land speculation. In 1729, Rufus sold a house and his share of land on Newbury Street from his parents' estate to his brother Thomas.[23] Ten years later he sold more land, this time in Orange Street, to his brother Thomas. The deed was witnessed by his brother Benjamin and by John Chandler, Jr.[24] Thomas, Rufus, and Benjamin along with their cousins Nathaniel Greene and John Greene, gentlemen of Milton, were involved in a quitclaim deed to the Boston baker William Speakman regarding land in Newbury Street in 1743.[25] In 1749 Rufus sold a house and land in Back Street to the Boston trader John Gwean.[26]

Beginning in 1743 Benjamin Greene's accounts indicate that he and Rufus were selling consignments of rum and sugar for one another. In 1747 Thomas, Rufus, and Benjamin Greene signed an agreement with the shipwrights Oliver Luckis, Jr., and John Richardson for the building of a sailing vessel "to be rigged a Ship." The agreement stipulates that the ship was to be built of "good substantial White Oak Timber" with some parts and strips of pine, and that it was to be seventy feet by the keel, twenty-five feet by the beam, eleven feet nine inches deep in the hold, and four feet six inches between the decks with a rise of twelve inches in the forecastle and fourteen inches in the quarterdeck. The brothers bound themselves for fifteen hundred pounds in payment for the ship, a cost calculated on the basis of twenty-seven pounds Old Tenor per ship ton. The ship was evidently named the *Three Brothers* because Benjamin's account book includes payments made by him and his brothers for voyages of the ship in 1752.[27]

All of these ventures brought Rufus Greene economic prosperity, and his family enjoyed a comfortable standard of living. In 1728, Rufus purchased leather chairs, bedsteads, ticking, and "1 Sute Blew ch.ª curtains, Vall.ˢ Insided ͦ headcloth & Tester full trim'd" from the upholsterer Samuel Grant.[28] Between 1758 and 1761, Rufus and Katharine Greene had their portraits painted by John Singleton Copley. Greene is shown wearing a simple wig and a plain waistcoat, a prosperous but modest man (illus.).[29] Greene's inventory submitted to the probate court in 1790 reveals that his was a well-appointed house, in spite of the reversals that, as a loyalist, he no doubt suffered during the early years of the Revolution. It also indicates that Rufus continued to own land in Newbury Street until his death, as well as a "Homestead and Store," "a House on the corner occupied by Mr Benjamin Pierpont," probably the silversmith (q.v.), and "a small house . . . occupied by Mr John Jones," all located on the "Street Leading to the Common," or Marlborough Street. Pierpont made rent payments to Greene's estate between 1787 and 1790. No silversmiths' tools or shop goods of any kind are listed in Greene's inventory, as he was no doubt retired by this time. All of the silver enumerated but not valued in the inventory was for his domestic use: one tankard, three porringers, two canns, one caster, one cup, six tablespoons and fifteen teaspoons, one pair of sugar tongs, one creampot, two knives, and one fork. The caster survives and is now in the Museum of Fine Arts, Boston. Although he was a long-time member of King's Chapel, at the time of his death he owned a pew in Trinity Church.[30] Both Rufus, who died on 31 December 1777, and Katharine Greene are buried in the Greene family tomb in the Granary Burying Ground.[31] BMW

SURVIVING OBJECTS

	Mark	Inscription	Patron	Date	Reference	Owner
Box	A	Auchmuty arms; The Gift of Hugh Hall Esqr to his Daughter/Sarah (+)	Hugh Hall and/or Sarah Hall	ca. 1740	YUAG files	
Box (with ivory cover)	B	II; (+)	James Ivers	ca. 1750	Buhler 1972, no. 218	MFAB
Cann	A*	EL (+)		ca. 1735	Johnston 1994, 60	CMA
Cann	A*	?		ca. 1735	MFA 1911, no. 533	
Cann	A (?)	unidentified initials		ca. 1740	Parke-Bernet, 26–27 January 1945, lot 170	
Cann	A/B	W/HA		ca. 1740	Buhler 1956, no. 74	
Cann	B	none		ca. 1760	Quimby 1995, no. 70	WM
Cann	B*	none		ca. 1735	YUAG files	
Cann	B	RL/to/EJT (later)		ca. 1740	*Antiques* 112 (July 1977): 52	
Two casters	B	I/SR (+)	Samuel and Ruth (Chapin) Jackson	ca. 1730	Buhler 1972, no. 217	MFAB
Caster	B*	FR	Faith (Robinson) Trumbull	ca. 1735	Buhler/Hood 1970, no. 171	YUAG
Caster	B*	EA		ca. 1735	Hammerslough/Feigenbaum 1958–73, 3:54	WA
Cup (with mark of John Coney)	B or C	Capt ID; Lucy Smith Aged 10 Yrs. 9 Mos. 15 Days-Mary E. Comstock (later)		ca. 1715	Parke-Bernet, 14–15 May 1948, lot 195	

	Mark	Inscription	Patron	Date	Reference	Owner
Cup	B *or* C	E.A. Brown (later)		ca. 1730	National Art Galleries, 3–5 December 1931, lot 428	
Two flagons	A/B*	Belonging to Christ Church/In Boston/ New England/A:D: 1729	Christ Church, Boston	1729	Jones 1913, 75	
Pepper box	A†/ B*	G/RK	Rufus and Katharine (Stanbridge) Greene	ca. 1730	Buhler 1972, no. 216	MFAB
Porringer	A*	L/WE		ca. 1730	*Antiques* 121 (May 1982): 987	
Porringer	A*	C/CS; MD (later)		ca. 1730	YUAG files	
Porringer	B†	G/TE	Thomas and Elizabeth (Gardiner) Greene	ca. 1735	Buhler/Hood 1970, no. 170	YUAG
Porringer	C	EB (+)	Elizabeth Bass	ca. 1735	American Art Association–Anderson Galleries, 2–4 January 1930, lot 386	
Two sauce dishes	?	?		ca. 1735	YUAG files	
Spoon	?	RG (?)		ca. 1735		WM
Tankard	A/B*	none		ca. 1740	YUAG files	
Teaspoon	C†	MW	Mary Wood	ca. 1750	Buhler 1972, appendix no. 34	MFAB

1. RC 24:48; Arnold 1911, 1:51, 169; RC 28:10; *Genealogies of Rhode Island Families*, 1:508–09.
2. SCPR 18:354–55.
3. As cited in Buhler 1956, 34; present location of diary unknown. The entry is dated 19 April 1778.
4. SCPR 26:146–47, 401–15; 28:443–46; 31:264. In addition to an extensive shop inventory and personal estate, the inventory of Ann Greene's estate includes "70[illegible] ounces of Silver Money bought for Rufus Greene @ 15/ 52.17..6."
5. SCPR 26:406.
6. Rufus Greene Account Book, 1728–48, n.p., Karolik–Codman Papers, MHS.
7. Prown 1966, 1:29, 107, 164–65, 217, figs. 61 and 62, gives Katharine Stanbridge's birth date as about 1706; her epitaph suggests she was born about 1708, see Codman 1918, 114; RC 28:143.
8. RC 24:192, 202, 212, 217, 225, 233, 237, 243, 249; RC 30:22, 398.
9. Dow 1927, 46.
10. SCPR 29:416.
11. Photostat in the Bigelow-Phillips files.
12. See Kovel 1961, 121. None of these could be located for illustration.
13. SCPR 37:137.
14. SCPR, docket 9040.
15. SCPR, docket 12763; 38:162–63.
16. Tappan 1834, 119–28.
17. Rufus Greene Account Book, 1748–74, n.p., under the date 18 November 1748, Karolik–Codman Papers, MHS.
18. Benjamin Greene Ledger, 1734–56, 37, 41, MHS; SCCR, Court of Common Pleas Record Book 1749–51, 220–21.
19. Rufus Greene Account Book, 1748–74, n.p., Karolik–Codman Papers, MHS.
20. SCCR, Court of Common Pleas Record Book 1735, 327; 1738, 15; 1740, 254, 267; 1741, 72; 1742–

43, 220; only one of these, the suit brought by Rufus Greene against the watchmaker Robert Peasely (q.v. Appendix A), appears to have involved any silversmiths' work, but the record mentions only a debt of fifteen pounds "for value received," so it is difficult to tell the nature of the business carried on between the two men.

21. SCD 43:127–28.

22. SCD 66:140; 77:2–3.

23. SCD 43:127–28.

24. SCD 58:137–38.

25. SCD 66:140.

26. SCD 77:2–4.

27. Benjamin Greene Ledger, 1734–56, 113, 145, 147, 153, 161, MHS; document 347.4, Bostonian Society, Boston, Mass.

28. Samuel Grant Account Book, MHS.

29. According to Prown 1966, 1:29, 217, the portraits were originally three-quarter length but were cut down after being damaged by fire. In his table of sitters, Prown records Rufus Greene as a moderate Tory of high income.

30. SCPR, docket 16447.

31. Jones 1930, 315; Codman 1918, 114.

David Greenleaf, Sr.
1737–1800

A

David Greenleaf, Sr., was born in Lancaster, Massachusetts, on 13 July 1737 and baptized there on 24 July 1737.[1] He was the son of Daniel Greenleaf (1701–95), who was born in Cambridge, Massachusetts, and became a physician.[2] Dr. Greenleaf was living in Boston when he married Silence (Nichols) Marsh (1702–62) of Hingham, Massachusetts, in that town on 18 July 1726.[3] The couple lived in Hingham, where their first three children were born, until at least 1732.[4] Greenleaf moved to Bolton, Massachusetts, by 1734, where the birth of his fourth child, Israel, is recorded.[5] David Greenleaf's paternal grandparents were Rev. Daniel Greenleaf (1679/80–1763) of Newbury, Yarmouth, and Boston, Massachusetts, a minister who was also a physician and apothecary, and Elizabeth Gookin (1681–1762) of Cambridge.[6] His maternal grandparents were Israel Nichols (1650–1733/34), a weaver of Hingham, and Mary Sumner (1665–1723/24), of Lancaster, Massachusetts.[7]

Where David Greenleaf acquired his skills as a silversmith is uncertain, but his apprenticeship probably began about 1751 and would have been completed around 1758. Because of his family contacts, Greenleaf's training probably took place in Boston, possibly with his uncle, John Coburn (q.v.), whom his aunt Susannah Greenleaf (1722–82) had married.[8] His father's brothers were notable Bostonians: the Honorable Stephen Greenleaf (1704–95) was sheriff of the king for Suffolk County, John (1717–78) was a physician, and the Honorable William Greenleaf (1725–1803) married Mary, daughter of Judge Robert Brown. His paternal grandparents were also then living in Boston.

By 1761 David Greenleaf had moved to Norwich, Connecticut, motivated perhaps by its being, unlike Lancaster, a growing town. As goldsmith of Norwich, he purchased land and built a house in the merchant/craftsman district known as Leffingwell Row.[9] George Munson Curtis suggests in *Early Silver of Connecticut* that Greenleaf studied with Thomas Harland (1735?–1807) in Norwich, but because Harland did not arrive in Norwich until 1773, Curtis may have meant Greenleaf's son, the silversmith David, Jr. (1765–1835).[10] David Greenleaf married Mary Johnson (1738–1814) of Norwich in that town on 2 June 1763.[11] Mary Johnson was the daughter of Ebenezer Johnson (1693/94–1779) of Norwich and Deborah Champion (1697–1778) of Lyme, Connecticut, who were married on 29 October 1717.[12] David and Mary's first child, Mary, was born in Norwich on 7 January 1764.[13]

Greenleaf moved several times while struggling to maintain financial stability. By 1767 he may have moved to Coventry, Connecticut, where his son Daniel was probably born.[14] Greenleaf sold the Norwich property to Jesse Williams in 1769 for three hundred pounds, two hundred pounds more than he had paid for it eight years previously. In 1769 he also paid fifty-six pounds for land in Lancaster, presumably moving back to the family enclave.[15] In Lancaster two more children were born: Annis, or Nancy, baptized in 1769/70, and Susannah, born in January 1772.[16] Greenleaf was included in the Massachusetts tax valuation list of 1771, but in January of 1772, within three years of returning to Lancaster, Greenleaf sold his land without profit to his younger brother Calvin Greenleaf.[17] David Greenleaf's trade was listed as goldsmith in both Lancaster deeds, and his continued work as a craftsman is evidenced by his debt of January 1772 to Zachariah Brigden (q.v.) for "6 nest of Crucibles."[18]

In 1772, Greenleaf repurchased the Leffingwell Row property from Jesse Williams for £330, but within two months he needed to obtain a mortgage loan from John Huntington, Jr., for £115.17.2, payable in two years.[19] In November of the same year, he received a loan of £54.17.2 from his brother Daniel, Jr., for the same property.[20] This loan was never repaid, as noted in the estate of Daniel, Jr., dated 29 November 1777.[21] In May 1773, Greenleaf mortgaged the property a final time for £20 to John Lamb, who may have actually taken possession of the land because no document survives proving that Greenleaf retained or sold the property.[22] Greenleaf's place of residence is listed on the deeds as "late of Norwich, now of Lancaster" or "Bolton," suggesting his return to Norwich was unsuccessful.

Greenleaf's activities are difficult to follow between 1773 and 1778. He may have taken part in the revolutionary war as a Massachusetts soldier because a Pvt. David Greenleaf is shown to have served on three occasions between 1777 and 1780.[23] An enlistment would prove he had returned to Massachusetts, even though he apparently no longer owned land there.

Greenleaf's return to Connecticut in 1778 is signaled by the purchase of land in Coventry and by the birth of his son William (b. 1778), who also became a silversmith.[24] Greenleaf remained in Coventry until his death on 11 December 1800 at age sixty-three, presumably living on the same land that he sold to his son David, Jr., a silversmith of Hartford, in 1791.[25]

Greenleaf used an initial and a surname mark, D·Greenleaf, script, in a rectangle (A). The marks D.Greenleaf in a rectangle and Greenleaf in a serrated rectangle have been attributed to him, but examples could not be found to illustrate. Greenleaf in a serrated rectangle has also been attributed to his son, David Greenleaf, Jr.[26] Aside from several spoons and a pair of sugar tongs, no other work by David Greenleaf, Sr., is known to survive. JJF

SURVIVING OBJECTS

	Mark	Inscription	Patron	Date	Reference	Owner
Sugar tongs	A*	EB		ca. 1780		YUAG
Tablespoon	A†	LK		ca. 1795	Belden 1980, 202 (mark only)	WM
Two tablespoons	A*	AR		ca. 1795	Eitner 1976, nos. 10–11	

	Mark	Inscription	Patron	Date	Reference	Owner
Tablespoon	A*	ER (+)		ca. 1795		YUAG

1. *Lancaster VR*, 286, notes the baptism of "David, son of Doctor Greenleaf" on 24 July 1737. The birth record for Greenleaf, on 13 July 1737, gives his mother's name erroneously as Elizabeth. *Lancaster VR*, 64.

2. *Bolton VR*, 203; buried in Old Cemetery, Bolton. For Greenleaf genealogy, see Greenleaf 1854 and Greenleaf 1896.

3. RC 28:162; *Bolton VR*, 204; buried in Old Cemetery, Bolton; Lincoln (1893) 1982, 85; Farber gravestone photograph no. 1357, YUAG.

4. David (died in infancy), Elizabeth, and Daniel Greenleaf were born in Hingham between 1728 and 1732; see Lincoln (1893) 1982, 279.

5. *Lancaster VR*, 61.

6. *Newbury VR* 1:195; *Index of Obituaries, 1704–1800*, 1:136; 2:458–59; *Cambridge VR* 1:297; 2:172; *Sibley's Harvard Graduates* 4:472–76.

7. Lincoln (1893) 1982, 84–85.

8. Greenleaf 1896, 89, 205–09.

9. Perkins 1895, 76–77; Norwich, Connecticut, Deeds 14:348.

10. Curtis 1913, 98; Flynt/Fales 1968, 242.

11. Norwich VR 2:354; *Connecticut Courant* 2 May 1814.

12. Norwich VR 1:51, 91, 283; Lyme VR, 34; *Lyme VR*, 225. A photograph of their tombstone is no. 4045 in the Farber collection, YUAG.

13. Norwich VR 1:429.

14. Greenleaf 1896, 288, cites the birth of Daniel in Coventry (19 January 1767). A record of this birth has not been found in Norwich or Coventry vital records.

15. Norwich, Connecticut, Deeds 18:67; WCD 67:100.

16. *Lancaster VR*, 307–08. Greenleaf 1896, 288, gives the birth of a daughter Sarah in 1769, but no record of this birth has been found.

17. WCD 67:100, 184.

18. Zachariah Brigden Daybook, 1766–ca. 1775, fol. 32v, Brigden Papers, YU.

19. Norwich, Connecticut, Deeds 20:24, 28.

20. Norwich, Connecticut, Deeds 19:527.

21. WCPR, docket 25710, "To David Greenleaf, note rendered / Def[?]rate 54–17–7." In the deed the sum was listed as £54.17.2.

22. Norwich, Connecticut, Deeds 21:114–15.

23. *Mass. Soldiers and Sailors* 6:848.

24. Coventry, Connecticut, Deeds 6:365. Baptism of William: First Church of Coventry in Coventry VR, 201.

25. Coventry VR, 231; *Connecticut Courant*, 29 December 1800; Coventry, Connecticut, Deeds 8:276.

26. Ensko 1948, 168, 181; Currier 1938, 64; Graham 1936, 33; Okie 1936, 261; Thorn 1949, 96.

Daniel Greenough
1685/86–1746

A

Although he was colonial New Hampshire's first and most important silversmith, Daniel Greenough was born and died in Massachusetts and thus is included in this volume. His life has been discussed at length in articles by Frank O. Spinney in 1942 and Kenneth Scott in 1960; these provide a detailed record of Greenough's career, which is only summarized here.[1]

Greenough was born in Rowley, Massachusetts, on 22 February 1685/86, the second son of Robert (d. 1718) and Martha (Epes) Greenough (1654–86 or 87), who were married in 1679. Robert was apparently born in England; he was the town recorder for Rowley in the early 1690s and was a prosperous individual. Daniel's mother, who died shortly after he was born, was the daughter of Daniel Epes II (d. 1693) and Elizabeth (Symonds) Epes (1624–85).[2]

Greenough must have been trained in Boston or Salem, Massachusetts, although no record of his apprenticeship is known. It is possible that he was trained in Salem by Samuel Phillips (q.v.), to whom Greenough was related; Greenough's stepmother, Sarah (Phillips) (Mighill) Greenough, was Phillips's sister and married Robert Greenough as his second wife in 1688. Phillips was in business in Salem about 1687, and it would have been natural for him to accept his sister's stepson as his apprentice beginning about 1700.[3]

Greenough had arrived in New Hampshire by 1708, when he married Abigail Eliot on 16 December; after her death in 1719, he took Elizabeth Hatch (ca. 1692–1765) as his second wife on 25 January 1721/22. He had a total of twelve children. His first wife was well connected by marriage to the most prosperous families in the Piscataqua region.[4]

Greenough worked as a goldsmith and as a blacksmith, apparently simultaneously, in New Castle from about 1708 until about 1738. Although he is often termed a goldsmith in the Rockingham and York county deeds between 1712 and 1741, on at least one occasion in 1719 he is referred to as a blacksmith and in a deed of 26 March 1726 he is identified as a "goldsmith alias blacksmith." As Scott indicates, Greenough also operated a store and sold a general line of merchandise, including "brass kettles, scales, weights, ladles, skimmers, chains, trivets, scythe tackling, fleshforks, iron racks, saws, Indian corn, black crepe, iron, anchors, deck nails, hinges, locks, spades, earthenware, fish, trammels, and molasses."[5]

By 1738, Greenough had moved to Bradford, Massachusetts, where he continued to be referred to as a silversmith, blacksmith, or gentleman. He remained in Bradford until his death on 20 April 1746. His will, dated 15 March 1745, divided his estate among his wife and children. Elizabeth was appointed executor of the estate and received "one half of my dwelling House in Bradford, as also of ye Land about it . . . as also all my houshold Goods & plate, & my negro servant maid, Violet, & all my personal Estate whatever" except for things reserved for his children. His son Nathaniel and his daughters, Sarah Robins and Abigail Colefax, received his "House at New Castle in New Hampshire in which I formerly lived & my pasture Lands there . . . to Each an Equal Division." Abigail also received "one Looking glass, one Oval Table, one bed & likewise one silver porringer & two silver Spoons, & one iron pott." His sons Symon and John were bequeathed "a dwelling House at New Castle in New Hampshire, wherein dwell at present one Sparks & Sparling, with my Land about said House . . . with all my Lands at Epsom in New Hampshire, to be equally divided." Another son, William, inherited "my Blacksmiths Shop & all my utensils belonging to said Trade, & also ye other half of my dwelling House in Bradford & of ye Land about it," after he paid his younger brothers Benjamin, Samuel, and James the sum of fifty pounds when they reached the age of majority.[6]

Greenough is known today by only two surviving objects, his superb sugar box, now in the collection of the Metropolitan Museum of Art, and a porringer in a private collection. Made for Robert and Sarah Eliot, Greenough's in-laws, and engraved with their initials, the sugar box is the only one of the ten known colonial American sugar boxes not made by John Coney (q.v.) or Edward Winslow (q.v.), both of whom were much older.[7] Documents indicate that Greenough also produced other forms and did repair work. The will of Samuel Winkley of Portsmouth, written 13 November 1726, for example, makes reference to a silver tankard and two silver spoons made by Greenough. Other sources indicate that he made such items as thimbles, rings, chains, bodkins, nipples, buttons, buckles, and cups and repaired a similar variety of objects.[8] Only one mark has been attributed to Greenough: DG in an irregular shield (A). GWRW

SURVIVING OBJECTS

	Mark	Inscription	Patron	Date	Reference	Owner
Porringer	A*	W/IA		ca. 1725	Sotheby's, 31 January, 1–2 February 1985, lot 91	
Sugar box	A†	E/RS (later) (+)	Robert and Sarah Eliot	ca. 1710	Safford 1983, 20–21	MMA

1. Spinney 1942; Scott 1960. See also Hennessy 1955 and Flynt/Fales 1968, 235.
2. *Rowley VR*, 82; Platt 1895, 5–8; Spinney 1942, 371–72.
3. Platt 1895, 8, and entry for Phillips.
4. Spinney 1942, 372.
5. RCD 11:224; 9:443–44; 15:305–06; 25:192–93; YCCR, box 12, file 19; RCD 18:344–45. Other deeds refer to him as "Capt." or "gentleman"; see, for example, RCD 11:315–16; 13:308–09; 19:231–32; 77:3–4; YCCR, box 75, file 83; box 77, file 39; and box 79, file 22. See also Scott 1960, 30.
6. Scott 1960, 27; ECPR, docket 11826.
7. For the sugar box, see Parsons 1983, 17; for the porringer, Sotheby's, 31 January–2 February 1985, lot 91.
8. New Hampshire Provincial Probate Records, docket 950, New Hampshire State Archives, Concord. Scott 1960, 30.

Benjamin Grignon
ca. 1660–85+

Only one record exists to document Benjamin Grignon's brief career in the colonies. In 1685 he is listed as a goldsmith and one of seven Frenchmen from the Carolinas seeking admittance to the town of Boston. Their petition was rejected by the selectmen, and there is no record of where they went.[1] Henry Flynt and Martha Gandy Fales suggested that they may have joined the Huguenot settlement at Oxford, Massachusetts, but Benjamin's name does not appear in any of the Oxford records.[2] E. A. Jones was not able to find any record of him at Goldsmiths' Hall, London, and E. Milby Burton was unable to find any record of him in South Carolina.[3] His relationship to René Grignon (q.v.) is unclear. BMW

1. RC 10:61.
2. Flynt/Fales 1968, 236–37; Benjamin does not appear in either Daniels 1892 or Freeland 1894.
3. E. A. Jones to J. M. Phillips, 23 August 1935, Bigelow-Phillips files; Burton/Ripley 1991, 42.

René Grignon
ca. 1652–1714/15

René Grignon may have immigrated to Boston by the mid-1680s. The Boston tax list of 1687 includes Rignall Gregnon with a poll of one, housing and mills valued at three pounds, and a tax of one shilling and eleven pence.[1] He appears on subsequent tax lists with various spellings: in 1689 as Reney Grignon; in 1691 as Rignall Grignall; and in 1695 as Regnale Grinian.[2] In a deposition made in February 1691/92 he stated his age as thirty-nine.[3] His relationship to Benjamin Grignon (q.v.), who was in Boston in 1685, is unclear.

It is not known where René was apprenticed; there is no record of his

A

training at Goldsmiths' Hall in London. He left England's capital with a group assembled by Gabriel Bernon, a successful Huguenot merchant, who had obtained a patent for 2,672 acres of land for the refugees to settle in Oxford, Massachusetts. Bernon and his followers intended to settle this frontier town near the Massachusetts-Connecticut border and preach the Gospel among the Indians. The Indians, however, were largely hostile to the group's attempts to Christianize them, and the settlement was always in peril. Grignon and a Deschamps (perhaps the father of his later apprentice) appear briefly among the settlers at "Frenchtown" near East Greenwich, Rhode Island, but they apparently returned to Oxford, where Grignon joined Bernon and Jean Papineau as a partner in a wash-leather mill to produce chamois cloth. In 1696 Oxford was again threatened, and Grignon was one of the signers of a petition that declared the breakup of the town.[4] Grignon moved to Boston shortly thereafter and appears as an elder of the French Church in a petition to the governor.[5] In the same year, Grignon's apprentice, Thomas Earthy (q.v.), chose Grignon, who is referred to as being "of Boston . . . Goldsmith," to be his legal guardian.[6]

René Grignon had returned to Oxford by early 1704 because on 3 February 1703/04 he is described as being "late of Boston now of Newoxford" in a suit brought to court by the goldsmith Joseph Soames (q.v.). According to the deposition "the s[d] Joseph Soames on the ffirst day of November Anno: Domini 1697 at Boston . . . of his own free will and accord as also withe the free Consent of his father Did put and Bind himself an apprentice unto the s[d] Rene Grignon to Lerne his arts and with him and Mary his wife after the maner of an apprintice to serve from the first day of November unto the full end and term of five years."[7] Soames charged that Grignon had failed to teach him the art of "Goldsmith and Jeweller" and thus had not fulfilled his end of the bargain. Grignon appeared in court in April to answer the charge, but since Soames did not appear to press his charges further, Grignon was awarded costs of court and the suit was dropped.[8]

After the Deerfield Massacre in 1704, the town of Oxford was abandoned completely, and Grignon appears in Norwich, Connecticut, as the master of a ship. He became a leading member of the community and established a successful business. From the inventory of his shop goods and the fact that land records refer to him as a merchant, we can determine that he was a general shopkeeper as well as a silversmith and jeweler.[9] The estate of David Jesse (q.v.) paid him five pounds following Jesse's death in 1706, which suggests that Grignon continued to do business with his Boston colleagues.[10] He continued to train apprentices in his craft, for he mentions Daniel Deshon (q.v.) (perhaps the son of the Deshamps who had been his fellow settler at Oxford or the Moses Deshen listed in the deposition of February 1691/92) in his will: "I Give and bequeath unto Daniel Dishon all my Gooldsmith Tools, and Desire he may by my Execut[es] be bound out to some sutable person in Boston till he arrive att the age of Twenty one Years, to Learn the Trade of a Goldsmith, and I also give unto him ten pounds money to be paid . . . when the s[d] Daniel comes of Age."[11] Deshon completed his training with John Gray (q.v.). Grignon's wife had predeceased him, and his will does not mention any children. He made small bequests to Capt. Richard Bushnell and to Jean Jearson and directed that his "man" James Barret be freed after his death. "All the Rest and Residue" of the estate went to his "Dear and well beloved friend Mary Urenne," which indicates that perhaps he had intended to remarry.[12]

The inventory of Grignon's estate provides a detailed listing of all of his shop goods as well as a dwelling house worth £400 and other land valued at £371, including a gristmill and a sawmill. In his will, Grignon refers to himself as a "Jueller," and the goods in his shop bear this out, although his tools were worth more than the average tools owned by someone engaging merely in smallwork. His inventory lists the following:

To plate & Bullion	041. 03. 06
To bullion	000. 19. 00
To Gold	009. 09. 06
To Gold dust	000. 07. 06
To fileings of silver	004. 04. 00
To rare juells of Gold	002. 00. 00
To silver twist	000. 02. 10
To 316 precious stones	010. 00. 00
To Perls & precious stones	010. 00. 00
To one Bagg of blood Stones & other stones	005. 00. 00
. . .	
To Scales & weights	005. 10. 00
To Goldsmiths Tools	050. 00. 00
To Soader 8ˢ	000. 08. 00[13]

Grignon's more general shop goods included a large number of brass and steel shoe buckles, surgeon's instruments, cutlery, cloth, spices, and apothecary goods, including ointments, elixirs, salves, and various drugs. His inventory also lists a handsaw and turner's tools. A long list of creditors indicates that his business stretched over a large area. His own debts were considerable, and the residue of the estate was probably less than expected. Shortly after his death, Mary Urenne, who had by then married Nathaniel Clarke of Saybrook, Connecticut, petitioned the General Court to recover debts due to the Grignon estate because "certain bonds and books of account [had] been lately burnt."[14]

René Grignon's mark, RG crowned in conforming punch (A), has been found on only two objects, both porringers, one of which Grignon may only have repaired or retailed, as it also bears the mark of Jeremiah Dummer (q.v.).[15] BMW

SURVIVING OBJECTS

	Mark	Inscription	Patron	Date	Reference	Owner
Porringer (with mark of Jeremiah Dummer)	A†	R/IE	James and Elizabeth (Andrews) Rayner	ca. 1700	Buhler/Hood 1970, no. 20	YUAG
Porringer	A	?		ca. 1700	Chase 1938, 26–27	

1. RC 1:96.
2. RC 1:138, 151, 162.
3. SCCR, vol. 37, 288.
4. E. A. Jones to J. M. Phillips, 23 August 1935, Bigelow-Phillips files; Chase 1938, 26–27; Curtis 1913, 98–99; Daniels 1892, 23–24; Freeland 1894, 160–61.
5. Mass. Archives 11:150.
6. SCPR 11:176–77, dated 22 June 1696, docket 2316.
7. SCCR, file 6035.
8. SCCR, file 6035; SCCR, Court of Common Pleas Record Book 1701–06, 170.
9. Chase 1938, 26–27.

10. SCPR 17:500.

11. New London Probate District, docket 2317, CSL; will dated 20 March 1714/15, proved 12 April 1715.

12. Chase 1938, 26–27; will, New London Probate District, docket 2317, CSL.

13. New London Probate District, docket 2317, CSL; inventory taken 28 March 1715, presented 12 April 1715.

14. New London Probate District, docket 2317, CSL. Petition as quoted in Chase 1938, 27.

15. Curtis also attributed a cup, marked RG crowned with a stag passant below within a shaped shield, as the work of Grignon (Curtis 1913, 47, pl. xv) and mentions that there was another extant object that bore the same mark. In a letter to Francis Hill Bigelow, Curtis wrote, "I lately located two pieces of silver in New London, made by Rene Grignon. Mark is like this [RG crowned over stag passant in shaped shield]. I think when we go to New London and Norwich, we will find a large lot of silver to look at"; Bigelow-Phillips files, 219. Ada R. Chase apparently examined the child's cup that Curtis published as Grignon's work and commented simply that "a cup formerly attributed to the master has been definitely eliminated." The implication is that she found the cup to be a fake; Chase 1938, 27. On the basis of this, and Chase's belief that the RG crowned over stag mark could not be attributed to Grignon, the number of authentic works ascribed to Grignon has been limited to two.

Isaac Guernsey
1741–67

Isaac Guernsey was born in Waterbury, Connecticut, on 11 December 1741, the son of Deacon Jonathan Guernsey (1704–72) and Abigail Northrup (1699–1756). His parents were born in Milford, Connecticut, and married there on 6 January 1724/25.[1] Guernsey's paternal grandparents were Joseph Guernsey (1674–1754) and Elisabeth Disbrow (b. 1676), both of Milford.[2] His maternal grandparents were Samuel Northrup (1658–ca. 1713/14) of Milford and his wife, Sarah.[3]

Guernsey's master is unknown. His motives in moving north to Massachusetts are also unclear; he may have hoped for a good livelihood in Northampton, which had no silversmith at that time. James R. Trumbull's *History of Northampton* states that Guernsey was "the first goldsmith in Northampton [who] established himself [t]here in 1765, or a little before."[4] Henry Flynt and Martha Gandy Fales note that he also worked in Hadley, circa 1765, but evidence of this has not been found.[5] Isaac Guernsey married Esther Pomeroy (1745–1822) of Northampton, Massachusetts, the daughter of Capt. Elisha Pomeroy (1721–62) and Esther (Wright) Pomeroy (b. 1721) of Northampton, on 11 September 1766.[6] Guernsey died in his adopted town on 16 February 1767, at the age of twenty-six.[7]

No silver by his hand is known to survive. JJF

1. Card 1979, 70, 351, 368; Milford VR 1:77, 117; Watertown VR, 351, 368; Waterbury VR 1:295.

2. Milford VR 1:78.

3. Milford VR 1:117. There is no record of Samuel Northrup's marriage. Death date drawn from probate records, dated 30 January 1713/14, New Haven County as cited in Abbott 1979, 487.

4. Trumbull 1898–1902, 2, part 1:202.

5. Flynt/Fales 1968, 237. This source incorrectly notes that Guernsey married Pomeroy Culver. Esther Pomeroy married Dr. Robert Cutler after the death of Isaac Guernsey. Pomeroy 1912, 286; Bridgman 1850, 171.

6. Pomeroy 1912, 192, 286; Bridgman 1850, 88; Trumbull 1898–1902, 2, part 1:521; First Church of Northampton, book 1, 162, Corbin Ms. Coll., NEHGS, reel 82–11; Boltwood 1862, 34.

7. First Church of Northampton, book 1, 27, Corbin Ms. Coll., NEHGS, reel 82–11; Bridgman 1850, 50.

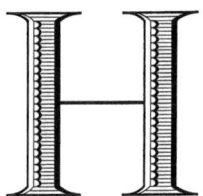

Samuel Haley or Healey
d. 1773

A

The *Boston News-Letter* of 18 November 1773 included the following notice: "Mr. ———— Healey, goldsmith, died in Boston about Nov. 15, 1773."[1] Although there is no other record of a goldsmith named Healey working in Boston, Henry Flynt and Martha Gandy Fales suggested that this Healey may have been Samuel Healey.[2] It is likely that the obituary notice refers to the Samuel Haley who, with Nathaniel Morse and Thomas Eastwick (qq.v.), appraised the estate of the goldsmith and jeweler Jonathan Reed (q.v.) in 1742.[3] On 30 November 1742, Haley signed a bond with Mary Reed, widow of Jonathan Reed, and the tailor William Hinckley in conjunction with the settlement of Reed's estate. There are no children recorded to Jonathan and Mary Reed, but this latter document suggests that the Mary Reed whom Samuel Haley had married on 30 April 1741 was Jonathan Reed's daughter, rather than his widow.[4] Samuel "Haly" was dismissed from Dr. Colman's church and was admitted to the New Brick Church in January 1739. Mary "Haly" was admitted a member in 1747.[5] Samuel Haley was one of three silversmiths who were debtors to the estate of the Boston brazier Jonathan Jackson (1672–1736), the others being John Burt (q.v.) and George Hanners, Sr. (q.v.). Haley owed £15.2.[6] Samuel Haley was paid £2.16 by the estate of William Cowell, Jr. (q.v.), in 1761, which suggests that Haley worked for Cowell as a journeyman.[7] Kathryn Buhler attributed a teaspoon of circa 1750 marked S·H in a rectangle (A) to Samuel Haley, but no other work by him has been identified. BMW

SURVIVING OBJECTS

	Mark	Inscription	Patron	Date	Reference	Owner
Teaspoon	A†	LF	Louis Foye	ca. 1750	Buhler 1972, no. 295	MFAB

1. Dow 1927, 47.
2. Flynt/Fales 1968, 244.
3. SCPR 36:240–41.
4. RC 28:248; SCPR docket, 7831.
5. Wyman 1864–65, 18:342.
6. SCPR, docket 6861.
7. SCPR, docket 12763.

John Hall
1641/42–91

Although he apparently never practiced in this country, John Hall may have been trained here as a silversmith prior to his departure for England in the early 1660s. At the time of his death in 1691, he called himself a goldsmith of London, and for that reason he, like Thomas Higginson and Samuel Clarke (qq.v.), is included in this volume.

John Hall was born in Salisbury, Massachusetts, on 18 March 1641/42, the son of John Hall and Rebecca (Swayne) Hall. Little is known about John's father. He was born in London, the second son of John Hall of London, merchant, and Sarah, the daughter of Sir Martyn Lumley, knight alderman of London. John Hall received land in Salisbury, Massachusetts, in 1641 and 1642, married the widow Rebecca on 3 April 1641, and died before 1647.[1]

John's mother's life is better documented. She was born in England in the early seventeenth century, the daughter of Bennett and Bridget Swayne of the city of New Sarum, Wiltshire. Bennett Swayne's will was proved on 27 January 1630; in it he bequeathed considerable amounts of money to the poor and articles of precious metal to his family. Rebecca received £150 and "one silver bowl."

On 21 January 1632, young Rebecca married Henry Byley (b. ca. 1612–d. ca. 1641) in St. Edmunds in Salisbury, England. Henry Byley came to New England in the *Bevis* from Southampton in May 1638, settling first in Newbury, Massachusetts, and, the next year, in Salisbury. Tradition records that Rebecca came over shortly after Henry. Henry was one of the first settlers of Salisbury, but he died within a few years of his arrival.

His widow, Rebecca, married John Hall in 1641 but was widowed again by 1647; on 18 November of that year she conveyed property in Salisbury left to her by John Hall to Henry Ambrose, a carpenter. Rebecca's third husband was the Reverend William Worcester, the first minister of Salisbury; they were married on 22 May 1650. After his death on 28 October 1662, Rebecca took as her fourth husband Deputy Governor Samuel Symonds of Ipswich, Massachusetts, joining him in marriage in 1663. She died on 21 July 1695, at age seventy-nine. John Hall arrived in England by 1663, at about age twenty-one. This strongly suggests that he was trained in a trade or craft in New England, as does the fact that he was from a well-connected family. If he was trained as a goldsmith, as he later styled himself in his will, he must have apprenticed with John Hull and Robert Sanderson, Sr. (qq.v.), in Boston in the late 1650s and early 1660s. No record of such an apprenticeship has been found.

In England, Hall married Elizabeth Lynne in 1669, and they had a daughter, Elizabeth (b. 1674), and a son (b. 1675/76), who apparently died young. Hall had Elizabeth's portrait painted in 1685 and sent to her grandmother Rebecca in Ipswich. (If it has survived, the portrait has not been identified.)[2]

Between 1663 and 1685 John Hall wrote regularly to his mother and stepfather in Ipswich; forty-eight letters from England from this correspondence have survived and are in the collection of the American Antiquarian Society in Worcester. These letters have been known and published by scholars for more than a century, but David Cressy recently called attention to them as key documents of the transatlantic links between England and New England.[3] Hall's mother's four marriages had created an extensive kinship network of relatives on both sides of the Atlantic, and in New England the family was firmly lodged in the upper echelons of colonial society.

While in England, Hall acted as a business agent for his relatives in New

England, and much of his correspondence deals with collecting rents and handling legal matters. The letters to his mother occasionally deal with more personal concerns, especially his state of health and religious development. Of greatest interest for students of material life are the letters dealing with fashion and taste, in which John kept his mother abreast of the latest London fashions in dress and jewelry. He occasionally would send over small articles, including some minor objects of silver, and books.

In his will, written on 13 April and proved on 6 May 1691, Hall referred to himself as a goldsmith of London and notes that he lived in the parish of Islington.[4] A will from 1665 written by his uncle James Hall of London refers to John Hall as a merchant; another will written by a relative in 1679 refers to Hall as a gentleman.[5] Research in the literature on English silver has yet to produce any evidence concerning John Hall's career as a goldsmith. Several IH marks in the 1663–91 period are listed by Sir Charles James Jackson, but none associated with the name John Hall. In all probability, Hall was a goldsmith/banker, rather than a working silversmith who produced objects. GWRW

1. Genealogical data on John Hall, his mother, and his family were taken from several sources, including Waters 1893, 136–40; Waters 1893a, 244–45; Waters 1893b, 507–09; Hammatt 1980, 129–31, 360–62; Hoyt 1981, 193–94, 754; *NEHGR* 52:44–45, 50; *NEHGR* 3:55.
2. Cressy 1987, 232.
3. Cressy 1987, 59–60, 181–82, 204–05, 214, 222, 225, 229–32, 234, 284–85, 289–90. The "Letters of John Hall, 1663–1685," AAS.
4. Waters 1893, 138–39, citing Vere, 81.
5. Waters 1893, 140; Waters 1893a, 244–45; Waters 1893b, 507–09.

John Hancock
1732–84

A

John Hancock was born in Charlestown, Massachusetts, on 10 October 1732, the son of John Hancock (1699–1776), a shoemaker, and Susannah Chickering (1700–63), who married in Charlestown on 25 April 1727.[1] His paternal grandparents were Samuel (1673–1735) and Dorothy Hancock (d. 1756).[2] His maternal grandparents were John Chickering (b. 1670) of Charlestown and Susannah Symmes (b. 1671) of Bradford, Massachusetts.[3]

John Hancock would have begun his apprenticeship about 1746 and would have completed it about 1753. The identity of his master is unknown. He was married in Cambridge, Massachusetts, on 20 November 1760 to Martha Sparhawk (1732–65), the daughter of Noah Sparhawk (1697–1749), a yeoman, and Priscilla Brown (1702–65) of Cambridge.[4] In 1763 Hancock bought a dwelling house in Charlestown from S. Sweetser.[5] On 28 May 1763 Hancock was identified as "of Charlestown . . . Goldsmith" when he mortgaged this house to Thomas Flucker.[6] In 1764 the house was mortgaged again, this time to Constant Freeman.[7] Hancock also made a silver cup for Peleg Stearns (1721–80) of Charlestown in 1764, as is documented by the following bill:

A silver cup w^t 9^{oz} 4^{dwt} 0 @ 52/ ℔ oz.   £23 = 18 =   0
Making   6 —5   —0
                                                     £30 3:   0 [8]

On 24 September 1765 Martha Hancock died, and on the following 29 October John Hancock, Sr. and Jr., signed a five-hundred-pound bond as guardians of the younger Hancock's children, John (b. 1762), Nathan Sparhawk (b. 1763), and Martha (b. 1765).[9] In 1767 Hancock was in Providence, Rhode Island, when he gave his father power of attorney for the Charlestown house.[10]

The father sold the house the next year, the mortgage held by Constant Freeman having been discharged in 1766.[11] When the elder Hancock died he left his son a token bequest of twenty shillings, noting that "what I have already done & paid for him & the charges I have been at in Boarding his Children shall be his full part & proportion in my Estate & he shall be excluded from any Demands to any part of what I have."[12]

John Hancock, Jr., ultimately settled in Maryland, where on 15 June 1774 he purchased an acre of land in Trappe, Oxford District, Talbot County, from William Martin for £15.[13] He evidently married again, for on 5 October 1784 the administration of his estate was granted to Mary Hancock.[14] The inventory, taken on 2 August 1785, amounted to £104.15.5 and included silversmith's tools valued at £30. The inventory asserted that Hancock had "no relations,"[15] but his children in Massachusetts pursued the estate. On 12 June 1788 Nathan Sparhawk Hancock and Phineas Brentnal, on behalf of his wife, Martha, both yeomen of Barre, Massachusetts, gave a power of attorney to their brother John Hancock of Malden, Massachusetts, so he could ascertain the extent of their father's estate.[16] Gov. John Hancock forwarded a certificate dated 10 October 1788 and signed by the selectmen of Charlestown (among whom was Caleb Swan [q.v.]) attesting to John Hancock's departure from Charlestown some years before and their belief that he had settled in Oxford.[17] The probate court apparently granted the children legal right to the property, for on 22 July 1789 John Hancock, "farmer, of Middlesex County Massachusetts, heir at law" of "John Hancock late of Talbot Co., deceased," sold the acreage in Trappe occupied by Mary Hancock for £50 to Charles Pickering, Jr.[18]

Fewer than six pieces of holloware by Hancock are known to survive, and they are marked with an initial and surname mark (A). An initials mark on a piece with a Massachusetts history has been attributed to him, but because its style postdates his departure from Massachusetts, the attribution is doubtful.[19] On at least one occasion Hancock retailed work made by another silversmith, because on a tankard his mark overstruck that of Benjamin Burt (q.v.). PEK

SURVIVING OBJECTS

	Mark	Inscription	Patron	Date	Reference	Owner
Porringer	A	JSH (later?)		ca. 1770	Christie's, 3 June 1989, lot 303	
Porringer	A	S/PE		ca. 1765	*Antiques* 98 (September 1970): 354	
Porringer	A*	B/WA		ca. 1765	MFA 1911, no. 538	
Tankard (with mark of Benjamin Burt)	A†	1766/Benj^m.. Wyman	Benjamin Wyman	1766	Avery 1920, no. 111	MMA

1. *Lexington VR*, 31; *Cambridge VR* 1:586; *Charlestown VR* 1:187, 298, 319; Wyman 1879, 1:463; Griffen 1952, 54.
2. Wyman 1879, 1:463; *Cambridge VR* 1:324; *Charlestown VR* 1:313; *NEHGR* 16:38.
3. Wyman 1879, 1:213; 2:928; *Charlestown VR* 1:76; *Bradford VR*, 149.
4. *Cambridge VR* 1:97, 657; 2:365, 743; MCPR 36:440, docket 20901; MCD 35:402.
5. MCD 60:528–29.
6. MCD 60:536–37.

7. MCD 62:405–06.

8. John Hancock, Jr., bill to Peleg Stearns, 1 August 1764, H. H. Edes Papers, MHS.

9. MCPR 36:440.

10. MCD 68:256–57.

11. MCD 62:405–06; 68:403.

12. MCPR 56:421–22, docket 10270.

13. Talbot County, Maryland, Deeds 20:408; J. Hall Pleasants to Francis Hill Bigelow, Bigelow-Phillips files, 1452.

14. No record of this marriage has been found.

15. Talbot County, Maryland, Administration vol. 1, fol. 43; J. Hall Pleasants to Francis Hill Bigelow, Bigelow-Phillips files, 1452.

16. Talbot County, Maryland, Administration vol. 1, fol. 43; J. Hall Pleasants to Francis Hill Bigelow, Bigelow-Phillips files, 1452.

17. Talbot County, Maryland, Deeds 23:497; J. Hall Pleasants to Francis Hill Bigelow, Bigelow-Phillips files, 1453–54.

18. Talbot County, Maryland, Deeds 23:544; J. Hall Pleasants to Francis Hill Bigelow, Bigelow-Phillips files, 1455.

19. Buhler 1972, no. 319. Buhler also attributes a spoon with this mark to Hancock; see Buhler 1972, appendix no. 35. Hammerslough/Feigenbaum 1958–73, 2:32, also attributes a caster with a script IH mark that was purchased in Maryland to Hancock. Kovel 1961, 128, also shows J.HANCOCK in an oblong and J.HANCOCK in serrated rectangle, but these variations could not be located.

George Hanners, Jr.
1721–60

A

B

George Hanners, Jr., the son of George Hanners, Sr. (q.v.), and his wife, Rebecca Pierson, was born in Boston on 2 September 1721.[1] He probably trained with his father and came of age just after the time of his father's death in 1740. He continued to use his father's stamp G·HANNERS (A) in a rectangle, and pieces bearing this mark may be the work of either father or son. He also used a variation on this initial and surname mark (B). Some authorities have attributed initials marks to him, although these attributions have not been proved.[2]

A few references in public records provide evidence of Hanners's activities in Boston during his relatively short career. With his mother, acting as guardian for her minor children, Hanners, identified as a goldsmith, mortgaged the family home on Wing's Lane to Joseph Ricks on 7 January 1742.[3] On 11 October 1742 he was identified as a goldsmith when he was appointed administrator of the estate of his aunt Elizabeth Chickering, wife of John Chickering, a Boston mariner.[4] In 1744 Hanners and his mother obtained a mortgage on the house in Wing's Lane from William Downe, her stepfather, and as part of the collateral Hanners put up his working tools, listed in one of the deeds as follows:

> a Forging Anvil three raising anvils, one porringer Ditto, one Teast four bottom Stakes one Fork stake one Thimble Stamp one Copper Boiling pan one pan Teast Eighteen Hammers five Drawing Irons half another two spoon Punches one Tea Ditto two small raising anvils one small flatt stake a brass Hallowing Stamp Death head stamp twelve Cutting punchers a Lockett Stamp two Skillets one about Eighteen or Twenty Ounces the other Smaller two pair of nealing Tongs one Ingot, a Vice a pair of Bellows a sett of Waits three pair of Scales.

By his will and testament William Downe forgave the debt, as was recorded on the deed on 13 February 1748.[5] The recording of the tools as collateral is remarkable for its specificity and suggests that Hanners could have made a variety of holloware and flatware in a well-equipped shop with tools probably inherited from his father.

Following forgiveness of this debt, Hanners may have felt financially secure enough to marry, for on 17 August 1749 he wed Sarah Foster (b. 1725). She was the daughter of Hopestill Foster (ca. 1701–72) and Sarah Allen (ca. 1702–72).[6] Following his marriage, Hanners seems to have continued to struggle financially; in 1750 he and his wife borrowed £95.10 from Asahel Mason (q.v.), and in 1751 he and his brother Benjamin, a Boston brazier, were sued in two separate actions by the merchant James Smith, who was to recover almost £130 and the costs of the suits.[7]

Hanners joined the local militia to take part in the French and Indian War. The *Boston Gazette* of 28 January 1760 reported that a vessel from Louisbourg brought news of the death of Capt. George Hanners of a provincial company belonging to Boston. His father-in-law, Hopestill Foster, was appointed administrator of his estate on 8 February 1760, and the inventory, presented on 24 October 1760, contained half a pew in the Reverend Pemberton's meetinghouse and amounted to only £12.8.6.[8] Among the individuals with claims on the estate was Edward Whittemore, possibly the silversmith (q.v.), who was owed 17 shillings 9 ¾ pence.[9] In 1762 Hanners's widow married Joshua Hersey of Hingham, Massachusetts.[10] PEK

SURVIVING OBJECTS

	Mark	Inscription	Patron	Date	Reference	Owner
Bowl §	A	K/IE		ca. 1740	Buhler 1972, no. 132	MFAB
Cann §	A*	G/TR/to/LH (+)		ca. 1740	DAPC 68.3213	MMA
Coffeepot §	A	Bulfinch arms, gules a chevron between 3 garbs argent, and crest, a dexter arm couped below the elbow, erect and grasping a baton	Bulfinch family	ca. 1745	MFA 1911, no. 547	
Mug §	A	unidentified initials		ca. 1740	Skinner, 15 June 1991, lot 164H	
Mug	B†	PF/RL/1750 (+)		1750	Avery 1920, no. 112	MMA
Pepper box §	A†	B/BL		ca. 1740	Buhler/Hood 1970, no. 124	YUAG
Porringer §	A	Y/SM	Samuel and Mary York	ca. 1740	MFA 1911, no. 540	
Porringer spoon §	A	WB/to/LB		ca. 1740	MFA 1911, no. 539	
Spout cup §	A*	P/PM	Phillip and Mehitable (Gardner) Pollard	ca. 1740	YUAG files	
Tablespoon §	A*	AB/to/MB		ca. 1740	Johnston 1994, 66	CMA
Tablespoon §	A*	B/IA		ca. 1740	DAPC 89.3087	
Tablespoon §	A*	HA		ca. 1740	Johnston 1994, 67	CMA

	Mark	Inscription	Patron	Date	Reference	Owner
Tablespoon §	A	W/TM		ca. 1740	National Art Galleries, 3–5 December 1931, lot 217	

§ Possibly made by George Hanners, Sr.
1. RC 24:151.
2. Graham 1936, 34, was the first to attribute initials marks to Hanners, and Thorn 1949, 102, followed suit, as did Kovel 1961, 129. Objects with marks resembling those illustrated cannot be verified as having been made by Hanners.
3. SCD 65:50–52.
4. SCPR 36:163.
5. SCD 68:131–32; 69:240–41. The latter deed records the tools as collateral.
6. RC 28:249; *Index of Obituaries, 1704–1800*, 1:113; 2:392.
7. SCCR, Court of Common Pleas Record Book 1751–52, 37; SCD 78:205–06.
8. SCPR 56:170; 57:285.
9. SCPR 59:190.
10. RC 30:51.

George Hanners, Sr. ca. 1696–1740

A

B

C

D

George Hanners, Sr., probably was born in Boston in 1696, although his birth record has not been found. His parents were Robert Hanners (Hannah) (d. before 1714), a joiner or housewright, and Hannah Matson (d. ca. 1732), who were married in 1695.[1] His maternal grandparents were the Boston gunsmith Thomas Matson (1633–90) (q.v. Appendix A) and Mary Read.[2]

Hanners would have begun his apprenticeship about 1710 and finished about 1717. He probably trained with Andrew Tyler (q.v.) because he witnessed the will of Tyler's mother in 1716/17, when he was still a minor.[3] On 28 July 1720 he married Rebecca Pierson, daughter of Rebecca (Emmons) Pierson (b. 1673).[4] Hanners probably worked and lived all his life at the same location, a house near the dock-head. An advertisement placed in the *Boston News-Letter* for 11–18 July 1720 reads, "George Hannah [*sic*], goldsmith, at his House at the Dock-Head, Boston, stopt a pocket book with some paper Bills in it." On 9 April 1725 Hanners signed an indenture for a house in Wing's Lane (near the dock-head) with Thomas Platts of Newport, Rhode Island.[5] This may be the same property mentioned in Hanners's mother's will, written in 1730 and probated in 1732.[6]

Hanners's name appears several times on legal documents in association with other craftsmen, indicating Hanners's possible working relationships with these men. Thomas Mullins (q.v.) witnessed Hannah Hanners's will in 1730, and George Hanners and Benjamin Hiller (q.v.) witnessed the will of the Boston brazier Jonathan Jackson in 1735. Hanners also owed Jackson's estate one shilling and six pence.[7]

Documentary evidence shows that Hanners made silver holloware and gold jewelry and sold supplies to other craftsmen. Very few spoons survive by him, which is unusual. In 1728 the estate of John Wilson of Braintree, Massachusetts, paid George Hanners £7.12.6 for rings.[8] The same year Bartholomew Gedney paid George Hanners £14.0.6 for eleven gold rings at 25 shillings 6 pence each for the funeral of William Bowditch of Marblehead, Massachusetts.[9] A suit brought by Hanners against Thomas Townsend (q.v.) in 1739 details the business relationship between the two craftsmen in an account preserved in the court files (see the Thomas Townsend biography for a transcription). Townsend bought a ring, a tankard, gold, several pounds of allum, and two nests of crucibles from Hanners and signed a promissory note for the amount in 1738. Hanners won the case and a writ was served against Townsend in 1739. Hanners died shortly thereafter, but as Townsend does not appear in the estate papers presumably the debt was paid.[10]

Administration of the estate of George Hanners was granted to his widow, Rebecca, on 31 May 1740. The inventory, dated 22 July 1740, was appraised by William Palfrey, John Simpson, and John Salter. It amounted to £2,667.11.11, which included the following items in the shop:

Shop. 1 forge Anvil 3 Raising D.º 1 Belly Pott D.º 1 Teast 2 bottom ⎫	44.	7.	6
Stakes 2 bottom & 1 fork Stake w.ᵗ 355ˡᵇ @ 2/6 ⎭		
1 Thimble Stamp & ½ D.º £7.10/ 1 Copp.ʳ Boyler 35/	9.	5.	—
1 Teast for Spoons £10. Hamm.ʳˢ Drawing Irons & files 82/	14.	2.	—
Spoon Punch 12/ 1 D.º 12/ 1 Sma: Raising Anvil 27/6	2.	11.	6
1 Sma: flat Stake 2/6 Tea Spoon punch 6/	—.	8.	6
Tobacco box handle 2/10 brass hole Ring Stamp 40/	2.	2.	10
Punches 19/ Deaths head Stamp 15/ Melting Pott 25/	2.	19.	—
25 ˡᵇ Allom 41/8 1 Skillet for Silver 60/ 3 p.ʳ Tongs & 1 Ingott 25	6.	6.	8
Vice & Bell.ˢ 60/ 1 Sett Weights & 3 p.ʳ Scales 90/	7.	10.	—
Sundry sma: Things 50/ Iron Kittle & Ladle 18/	3.	8.	—
Silv.ʳ w.ᵗ 14ᵒᶻ 1/4 @ 28/ D.º 13 3/4oz @ D.º D.º 4ᵒᶻ @ D.º	44.	16.	—
Silv.ʳ & Gold ware £14.3.2 Gold w.ᵗ 18ᵈʷᵗ £18.18/	33.	1.	2
1 p.ʳ Stone Buttons Set in Gold 80/ 24 Coral Necklaces @ 5/	10.	—.	—
2 Glass Cases	3.	—	11

The estate was owed £2.11.9 by the estate of James Boyer (q.v.).[12] Several craftsmen were among the creditors paid by the widow, including John Burt (q.v.), who was owed 60 shillings. Thomas Mullins was paid for providing the pall, the porters, and the ringing of the bells at Hanners's funeral.[13] On 7 January 1742 Hanners's widow, acting as guardian for her minor children, and his son George (q.v.) mortgaged the house in Wing's Lane to Joseph Ricks, and on 11 May 1744 Rebecca Hanners, widow of George Hanners, goldsmith, and her son George mortgaged the house and land in Wing's Lane to her stepfather, William Downe.[14]

Most of Hanners's surviving silver is simple in design, and only a few pieces have engraving other than block letters. Hanners used two variations of an initials mark GH crowned in a shaped shield (A, B) as well as an initial and surname mark G·HANNERS (italic) in a rectangle (c), and GH in a rectangle (D). Because his son, George assumed management of the shop on his death, it is often difficult to know with certainty whether works with the initial and surname mark (c) were made by the father or by the son. PEK

SURVIVING OBJECTS

	Mark	Inscription	Patron	Date	Reference	Owner
Two beakers (mates below)	c	none	Congregational Church, Greenland, N.H.	ca. 1730	Jones 1913, 187–88	
Beaker (mates above and below)	c	none	Congregational Church, Greenland, N.H.	ca. 1730	Buhler 1972, no. 131	MFAB
Beaker (mates above and below)	c	none	Congregational Church, Greenland, N.H.	ca. 1730	Avery 1920, no. 34	MMA

	Mark	Inscription	Patron	Date	Reference	Owner
Beaker (mates above)	c	none	Congregational Church, Greenland, N.H.	ca. 1730	Norman-Wilcox 1954, 48–49	LACMA
Beaker	c	The Gift of Lieu.ᵗ Sam.ˡˡ Stent to the first Church in Branford	Samuel Stent and/or Congregational Church, Branford, Conn.	ca. 1735	Jones 1913, 91	
Bowl §	c	K/IE		ca. 1730	Buhler 1972, no. 132	MFAB
Cann §	c*	G/TR/to/LH (+)		ca. 1735	DAPC 68.3213	MMA
Caudle cup	b*	Breck arms, gules on a chief per bend sinister indented or and argent 4 hurts 2 and 2; B/IS	Breck family	ca. 1720	Johnston 1994, 67	CMA
Coffeepot §	c	Bulfinch arms, gules a chevron between 3 garbs argent, and crest, a dexter arm couped below the elbow, erect and grasping a baton	Bulfinch family	ca. 1730	MFA 1911, no. 547	
Cup	b†	The gift of Thomas Colyer To the Church of hool 1720	Thomas Collier and/or Methodist Episcopal Church, Hull, Mass.	ca. 1720	Buhler/Hood 1970, no. 121	YUAG
Cup	b*	P/IS		ca. 1725	Fales 1970, 41	PEM
Mug	A or B	C/TS	Timothy and Sarah Clark	ca. 1725	Buhler 1979, no. 15	WAM
Mug	A or B	D/WR		ca. 1730	*American Silver* 1967, no. 4	RWNAG
Mug §	c	unidentified initials		ca. 1740	Skinner, 15 June 1991, lot 164H	
Pepper box §	c†	B/BL		ca. 1730	Buhler/Hood 1970, no. 124	YUAG
Porringer	A or B	EI(?) (+)		ca. 1725	Buhler/Hood 1970, no. 122	YUAG
Porringer	A or B	H/SH; RC		ca. 1730	Skinner, 15 June 1991, lot 171	
Porringer	A or B	SM; 1715 (later)		ca. 1720	Buhler 1960, no. 64	
Porringer	A or B	P/SH	Phillips family	ca. 1730		MFAB
Porringer §	c	Y/SM	Samuel and Mary York	ca. 1730	MFA 1911, no. 540	
Porringer	?	?	John and Mary Austin	ca. 1730	*Antiques* 72 (December 1957): 504	
Porringer spoon §	c	WB/to/LB		ca. 1730	MFA 1911, no. 539	

	Mark	Inscription	Patron	Date	Reference	Owner
Spout cup	B*	R/EE		ca. 1725		NM
Spout cup §	C*	P/PM	Philip and Mehitable (Gardner) Pollard	ca. 1725	YUAG files	
Tablespoon	A or B	?		ca. 1720		ChM
Tablespoon §	C*	AB/to/MB		ca. 1730	Johnston 1994, 66	CMA
Tablespoon §	C*	B/IA		ca. 1735	DAPC 89.3087	
Tablespoon §	C*	HA		ca. 1735	Johnston 1994, 67	CMA
Tablespoon §	C	W/TM		ca. 1730	National Art Galleries, 3–5 December 1931, lot 217	
Two tablespoons	C*	Susa Clark	Susa Clark	ca. 1730	Buhler/Hood 1970, no. 123	YUAG
Tablespoon	C	H/PI		ca. 1725	DAPC 72.3088	
Tankard	A†	W/FM; WW (later)	Wright family (?)	ca. 1725	Buhler 1972, no. 541	MFAB
Tankard	A or B	SH	Sarah Heywood	ca. 1725	Buhler 1965, 46–48	HMA
Tankard	A or B	unidentified arms; M/DL (?) (+)		ca. 1725	Skinner, 25 March 1989, lot 24	
Tankard	A or B/D	P/SH (+)	Phillips family	ca. 1730		MFAB
Tankard	C	B/EM		ca. 1730	YUAG files	
Tankard	C	P/PM; 1738	Philip and Mehitable Pollard	1738	Bigelow 1917, 136–37	
Two-handled cup	A*/D†	crest, a cock	Second Church, Boston	ca. 1725	Jones 1913, 36	
Two-handled cup	C	The Gift of Co^{ll} Eleazer Flegg/to the Church in Wooburn 1726	Eleazer Flagg and/or First Congregational Church, Woburn, Mass.	1726	Jones 1913, 502	

§ Possibly by George Hanners, Jr.

1. RC 9:224; SCPR 29:369–70.
2. RC 9:2, 76, 193; SCPR 8:156.
3. SCPR 29:387–88.
4. RC 28:44, 87; RC 9:127; Rebecca (Emmons) Pierson married William Downes as her second husband in 1713.
5. SCD 38:188–89.
6. SCPR 29:369–70.
7. SCPR 29:369–70, docket 6861.
8. SCPR 26:237.
9. ECPR, docket 2896. Apparently the rings were not suitable and had to be altered, requiring more gold, so that they cost an additional ten pounds. It is not clear whether Hanners was the craftsman who altered them.
10. SCCR, Court of Common Pleas Record Book 1738, 286, file 50260.
11. SCPR 35:89–90.
12. SCPR 37:137.
13. SCPR 35:27.
14. SCD 65:50–52; 68:131–32.

John Hathorne
1749–1834

Born in Salem, Massachusetts, on 29 May 1749, the son of John (1720–50) and Susannah (Touzell) Hathorne (ca. 1722–1802), John Hathorne married Susannah Herbert (1754–1834), the daughter of Benjamin (1709–51) and Elizabeth (Fowler) Herbert (1717–72) of Salem, on 18 October 1772.[1] A cousin of Joseph Hathorne (q.v.) and nephew of John Touzell (q.v.), he was Touzell's apprentice. In 1763, Touzell was named as one of the sureties for John Hathorne, a fatherless minor aged fourteen, and Hathorne's training presumably began about that time. On 29 May 1770, Hathorne billed Touzell £13.6.8 "to my freedom Cloths" and £18 "to my work from 29 May to 29 Nov., Six Months @ 60/."[2] Stephen Baker was to be Hathorne's apprentice for six years beginning in 1774.[3]

Although no silver by Hathorne is known today, his account book for the years 1770 to 1799 is preserved at the Peabody Essex Museum and gives a good indication of the nature of his trade.[4] The accounts reveal that Hathorne made and sold the usual forms of jewelry, thimbles, and other small items in addition to tongs and spoons of varying sizes. No entries for holloware are included, and even spoons were a small part of his business, but Hathorne seems to have done quite well at the jewelry trade. During the fifteen years that Hathorne practiced silversmithing, from 1770 until about 1785, when he opened a dry goods business, he sold a total of 105 spoons (33 tablespoons and 72 teaspoons) and 4 pairs of sugar tongs. This modest production of objects that might bear his mark no doubt accounts for the absence of any objects by him known today.

Hathorne often received payment in kind from his customers, particularly from his fellow craftsmen. For example, William Doak bought silver buckles, stone buttons, and a gold-and-coral necklace and paid for them with a "half Dozen burch Chairs."[5] William Lander, Jr., acquired silver shoe buckles, knee buckles, a stone locket, large silver spoons, brass buckles, and six yards of cloth in exchange for a dozen chairs,[6] and Huebestus Metoon, a blacksmith, paid for his jewelry with hardware.[7] John Beckett, Jr., exchanged sixty-three gallons of New England rum for his purchases,[8] and Thomas Porter of Topsfield, Massachusetts, was credited with lamb, mutton, and veal.[9] Most of Hathorne's clientele were from Salem, but occasionally he sold goods to people from Danvers, Beverly, Ipswich, Reading, and other nearby towns.

Some of the buckles sold by Hathorne, or parts of them, were acquired from Henry Buxton (q.v.), a bucklemaker from Danvers. In the 1780s, for example, Hathorne supplied Buxton with tea, coffee, salt, shoes, West India rum, and textiles in exchange for numerous pairs of hitches and tongs.[10] Like his uncle, Hathorne purchased jeweler's supplies from the Boston goldsmith John Welsh (q.v.). He purchased stones, foil, and other supplies from Welsh on 2 March, 9 August, and 2 November 1770, on 5 February and 10 August 1772, on 30 January 1773 as well as on 5 April and 28 June 1776.[11] He also purchased seven enameled rings from Welsh's nephew Isaac Parker (q.v.) in 1772.[12] He bought supplies from Daniel Boyer (q.v.) in 1770 and 1776.[13] Hathorne engaged in minor business transactions with the silversmiths John Touzell and John Andrew (q.v.) of Salem and Robert Swan (q.v.) of Andover, Massachusetts.[14]

The account book also reveals that Hathorne hired Joseph, Angier, and Samuel McIntire for carpentry work on his house and outbuildings in the 1770s and 1780s.[15]

By 1785, the entries in the account book reflect the change in Hathorne's stock in trade from that of a silversmith to that of a dry goods merchant. His newspaper advertisements also indicate that he was now a full-time merchant in his house and shop on Essex Street and had abandoned his original craft. For example, on 26 April 1785, Hathorne served notice in the *Salem Gazette* that "he has imported, in one of the last Ships from LONDON, A GOOD ASSORTMENT of the most useful SPRING & SUMMER GOODS, Which he is now selling at his Store, in PAVED-STREET, just above the Town-House.—He is determined to sell as cheap as at any Store in Town. HATS To be Sold at said Store." From this time forward until the end of his account book and possibly until his retirement, Hathorne was exclusively a dry goods merchant, apparently a well known and successful one. His conversion to his new career is attested to by his employment in 1793 of Joseph Rust, a Boston silversmith, to repair a silver tankard for him.[16]

When Hathorne decided to change careers, he lent his tools to a young Salem silversmith named Ebenezer Bowditch (1766–1830). Bowditch had just turned twenty-one when he signed the following agreement with Hathorne on August 31, 1787:

> Recv.d of John Hathorne the Following
> Articles Which I am to be Accountable
> to him for and Return to him when
> Called for Viz—one Large Anvil
> 1 Large planishing Stake 2 Copper Boiling
> panns 1 Large and one Small Scales & waits
> . . .
> 1 p.r Brass flasks one bench Vice one hand Vice
> one hollering Stamp, Liming Box, Sparhawk
> p.r Wooden Screws a pann to file Gold in
> p.r forgin Tongs p.r fire Tongs five hammers
> Summit Blocks busboard whet stone 2 blow
> pipes p.r Cutting plyers 2 p.r Round plyers 1 p.r Chargon
> Tongs 3 burnishers one Trivlet one Mallet
> p.r Shears one Large one Small Vise plates
> one Wooden Chair.

Hathorne apparently never asked for his tools back, and Bowditch went on to work in silver and other metals into the 1820s.[17]

It is difficult to assess the significance of Hathorne's change of career. It was probably not an instance of upward mobility; it was a horizontal, rather than vertical, transition. Hathorne died on 15 December 1834 at the age of eighty-five and was termed "Esq." in the probate records.[18] His estate was valued at slightly more than $4,000 but was about $5,600 in debt to various creditors. His principal asset was the house and shop on Essex Street, valued at $3,500. His personal estate included fifty-seven ounces of silver, valued at $1 per ounce, and consisting of twelve tablespoons, fifteen teaspoons, a sugar cup, a cream pitcher, a porringer, a cup, a pepper box, and a pair of tongs. GWRW

1. *Salem VR* 1:414, 424, 425; 3:380, 477; 5:317, 323; *Ipswich VR* 1:150; *Index of Obituaries, 1784–1840*, 3:2139.
2. ECPR 340:464–65; English-Touzel-Hathorne Papers, vol. 3, fol. 92, PEM.
3. English-Touzel-Hathorne Papers, vol. 3, fol. 103, PEM.
4. John Hathorne Account Book, PEM (FMs 3644). This document contains eighty-three pages of accounts and a two-page index detailing Hathorne's transactions with more than 220 people.

5. Hathorne Account Book, fol. 2.

6. Hathorne Account Book, fol. 2; see also fol. 4.

7. Hathorne Account Book, fol. 1.

8. Hathorne Account Book, fol. 1.

9. Hathorne Account Book, fol. 6.

10. Hathorne Account Book, fols. 7, 12, 20. John Touzell was also a customer of Buxton.

11. English-Touzel-Hathorne Papers, box 6, folder 12, PEM.

12. English-Touzel-Hathorne Papers, 17 November 1772 receipt, box 6, folder 12, PEM.

13. English-Touzel-Hathorne Papers, box 6, folder 12, PEM.

14. Hathorne Account Book, fols. 26, 37, 17, 67.

15. Hathorne Account Book, fols. 7, 8, 15, 30, 33, 39, 41.

16. English-Touzel-Hathorne Papers, vol. 4, fol. 103, PEM.

17. English-Touzel-Hathorne Papers, I, vol. 4, fol. 42, PEM. For Bowditch, see Ward 1984a, 274–75.

18. *Salem VR* 5:316; ECPR, docket 12873.

Joseph Hathorne
1745–86

Born in Salem, Massachusetts, on 5 September 1745, Joseph Hathorne was the son of William (1715/16–94) and Mary (Touzell) Hathorne (ca. 1724–1805). His mother's parents were John (d. 1738) and Susannah (English) Touzell (d. 1739); on his father's side, he was descended from Joseph and Sarah (Bowditch) Hathorne.[1] Joseph may have been apprenticed to his uncle John Touzell (q.v.), and he was a cousin of John Hathorne (q.v.). Joseph married Elizabeth Sanders (or Saunders) (1747–1836), the daughter of Philip and Mary (Elkins) Sanders (bap. 1710) of Salem, on 9 April 1769; they may have had as many as seven children.[2] He died of "decay" and was buried on 17 May 1786.[3]

Hathorne is referred to in the probate records as a goldsmith and silversmith, and the inventory of his estate, taken on 31 August 1786 by Abraham Watson, Benjamin Ward, Jr., and Miles Greenwood, indicated that he owned "A Shop Standing on Land belonging to M^{rs}. Mary Hathorne, situate in ye Main Street," valued at £27.[4] He also owned "Part of a House together with ten poles of land . . . situate in Church Street . . . in said Salem," valued at £160, and a pew-and-a-half in St. Peter's Church valued at £10. His total estate was worth £264, but he was more than £372 in debt, including a debt of more than £100 to John Touzell's estate. After the widow's dower of one-third was set aside and charges of administration subtracted, Hathorne's creditors received less than 20 percent on the pound.

The tools and stock listed in his personal estate suggest that he made primarily spoons and jewelry. His tools included two pairs of scales (10 shillings and 5 shillings), a bench vise (6 shillings), a hand vise (1 shilling and 6 pence), a pair of pliers (1 shilling), black lead pots (1 shilling), thirty-six small files (4 shillings and 6 pence), and four other files (4 shillings and 16 pence). He owned 43 ounces 13 pennyweight of wrought silver plate valued at 6 shillings per ounce, and an additional 10 ounces at 6 shillings and 8 pence per ounce, along with three gold rings, a pair of gold wires, eight pair of silver knee buckles, fifteen pair of silver shoe buckles, one pinchbeck watch, eight pair of knee chapes, and fifty-seven shoe chapes. He also owned eight muskets and three pistols. No objects by Hathorne have been identified. GWRW

1. *Salem VR* 1:414; 3:477; 5:316.

2. *Salem VR* 3:477; 1:275, 412; 6:208.

3. *Salem VR* 5:315.

4. ECPR, docket no. 12876. See also ECD 149:69.

Samuel Haugh
1675/76–1717

A

Samuel Haugh was the great-grandson of Atherton Haugh, mayor of Boston, England, in 1628, who came to Boston, New England, with John Cotton in 1643.[1] His grandfather Samuel Haugh (1621–62) was pastor of the church in Reading, Massachusetts, for many years; his grandmother was Sarah (Symmes) Haugh (d. 1681), who married the Reverend John Brock as her second husband. The silversmith's father, also Samuel Haugh (b. 1651), was a merchant. He died in 1679 when his son Samuel was only three years old. The silversmith's mother, Anna (Rainsford) Haugh (1651–89/90), was the daughter of Edward (ca. 1611–80) and Elizabeth Rainsford (ca. 1607–88); Jonathan Belcher (q.v.), whose mother was Ranis (Rainsford) Belcher, was his first cousin.[2] When Anna (Rainsford) Haugh wrote her will on 12 January (probably 1689/90), she was still a widow. She provided for her sons Samuel and Atherton, making a slightly larger bequest to Atherton because Samuel had been so well provided for in his grandfather's will.[3] She probably died in January or February 1689/90 because it was her older brother Solomon (bap. 1646) who asked Samuel Sewall to be her son's guardian. Solomon presented the will for probate on 11 April 1690.[4]

In March 1689/90, Samuel Sewall recorded that "Sam. Haugh, 14 years old last February, chuses me for his Guardian. Solomon Raynsford introducing of him with a pretty handsome Speech for my acceptance. Dept. Governour was by and told him he must now hearken to me and take me for his Father."[5] Although Sewall accepted and became Samuel's guardian, he made an entry in his diary two months later that suggests that he did not take Samuel into his home: "May 9. Friday 1690 . . . At Billinges heard Sam. Haugh was dead, which made me sad: but it proves not so."[6] As his guardian Sewall's major role was evidently to procure a good apprenticeship for Haugh. On 6 November 1690, he wrote, "At my House in Boston Samuel Haugh and Mr. Thomas Savage [q.v.] mutually sign'd, seal'd and deliver'd Indentures to each other; Sam. to serve him from 7th Octr last, Seven years and Six Moneths."[7] Nonetheless, Sewall continued to oversee Samuel Haugh's welfare and also seems to have become guardian for his younger brother Atherton Haugh. The two young men appear in the diary from time to time as guests in Sewall's home. On 1 February 1695/96, when Sam was just twenty years old, Sewall wrote one particularly interesting entry regarding Samuel's conduct:

> Sam. Haugh came to speak about Frank's burial: I sent Atherton away before and spake to Sam as to his Mistress' Maid being with child, and that she Laid it to him, and told him if she were with child by him, it concerned him seriously to consider what were best to be done; and that a Father was obliged to look after Mother and child. Christ would one day call him to an account and demand of him what was become of the child: and if [he] married not the woman, he would always keep at a distance from those whose temporal and spiritual good he was bound to promote to the uttermost of his power. Could not discern that any impression was made on him. I remark'd to him the unsuitableness of his frame under a business of so great and solemn Concern.[8]

It is not clear how the whole affair was resolved, as Sewall does not comment on it again, and Haugh did not marry until the next year. The Reverend Samuel Willard of the Third Church officiated at his marriage, on 30 September 1697, to Margaret (Cowell) Johnson (1673–1719), daughter of Edward and Sarah (Hobart) Cowell and widow of John Johnson.[9]

Samuel inherited two houses along the road to Roxbury (Marlborough

Street) from his grandfather, and legacies from his father, mother, and brother. His name appears in deeds and in court records several times during the next few years, usually in regard to the settlement of these or other estates. In 1697 he was defendant in a court case as the son and heir of Samuel Haugh, and in the same year he witnessed a deed for his guardian, Samuel Sewall.[10] The following year he and his wife, as administrators of her late husband's estate, sued William Johnson, a Charlestown shipwright, for the value of a bond he had taken out with John Johnson.[11] In 1698/99, articles of partition between Samuel and his brother Atherton, involving one of the houses in Marlborough Street, were entered in the registry of deeds. Immediately after this settlement, both Samuel and Atherton Haugh mortgaged their shares of the property to the widow Susanna Jacob of Boston: Samuel for £150 and Atherton for £100. Both brothers completed payment on their loans in March 1699/1700.[12] Atherton died in 1706, and Samuel was made administrator and sole legatee of his estate, which was small and encumbered with debts.[13] In all of these documents, Haugh is identified as a goldsmith.

Little evidence of Haugh's work survives. Three pieces marked SH in a rectangle (A) are known. In 1710 Samuel Sewall paid him £5.16.2 for making six rings for his daughter's funeral, and an account of 1713 survives for the "balance of a silver Sarver" worth £1.1 that Haugh made for Elizabeth Wainwright. In June of 1711, Haugh appraised gold and silver rings, silver thimbles, silver clasps, and parcels of gold and other money for the estate of the shopkeeper John Hayward of Roxbury, Massachusetts.[14] In addition to his work as a goldsmith, Haugh began selling strong drink as a retailer from his home in 1708, a venture that gave him added income.[15] In 1701 he served as a constable, and in 1704 he served on a petty jury for the Court of Common Pleas. He joined the Ancient and Honorable Artillery Company in 1711, and in 1716 he was elected scavenger for the Pond Ward.[16]

Samuel and his wife, Margaret, had five children: Edward (b. 1699), Margaret (b. 1701), Atherton (b. 1708; married Jane [Baxter] Doane, mother of the clockmaker John Doane [q.v. Appendix A]), Anna (b. 1710), and Sarah (b. 1713); in addition, Margaret had a son, John Johnson (b. 1694), by her first husband.[17] Samuel died and was buried on 9 June 1717, and his former guardian, Samuel Sewall, was a bearer at his funeral.[18] Haugh bequeathed his entire estate to his wife "for her to Possess and Injoy all the time of her widdowhood, for the Edication and bringing up of my Children, and to Injoy my said Estate no Longer then the time of her widowhood." If Margaret remarried she was to divide the estate equally among the five Haugh children. Samuel's eldest son, Edward, was to receive "all my Working Tooles belonging to the Goldsmiths Trade . . . if he lives to be Twenty one Years old, and Inclines to work att the Goldsmiths Trade. Provided he pay out of the tooles Twelve pounds in Money towards the bringing up of the rest of the Young Children."[19] Margaret Haugh became sole executor of the estate.

Margaret Haugh lived for only two more years, and at the time of her death her husband's estate still was not settled. By her will, dated 27 November 1719 and probated 7 December 1719, she bequeathed land to her son John Johnson that was hers from her first husband's estate and provided for the division of other lands in her possession to her other five children. She named her "good Friends" Nathaniel Williams and Peter Cutler as executors of the estate.[20] Following Margaret Haugh's death John Doane of Eastham in Barnstable County, Massachusetts, became the guardian of the three youngest Haugh children. John Johnson was already twenty-five years old and was working as a carpenter, and Edward, now twenty, probably was pursuing the trade of a mariner. Margaret, who was seventeen, is not mentioned in the guardianship documents.[21] In 1727 the mariner Edward Haugh sold his right in the house on the corner of Marlborough and School streets to John Doane of Eastham, Massachusetts.[22] None of the records indicate whether John Doane was a relative of either Samuel or Margaret Haugh, although it is possible that he was the John Doane who was the grandfather of John and Joshua Doane (qq.v.).

There is no inventory on file for Samuel's estate, although there is one for Margaret's. The administration accounts for both estates were filed in 1721 and reveal that the house and household goods were all sold. After funeral expenses were paid and the children provided with additional clothing, the total estate came to £188.11.3; no goldsmith's tools were listed in Margaret's inventory, although from Samuel's will it can be assumed that the tools were worth at least £20.[23] A court document of 4 July 1721 reveals that the Haugh estate would have been much larger if the Haughs had not mortgaged the house in Marlborough Street to Eliakim Hutchinson for £464. The loan, payable by 11 June 1716, was never discharged, and Hutchinson seized the house. However, the occupants refused to move, and in 1721 Hutchinson's estate brought them to court. Thomas Bradford (q.v.) was one of the inhabitants of the house at this time, which suggests that perhaps it was he who purchased Haugh's tools.[24] BMW

SURVIVING OBJECTS

	Mark	Inscription	Patron	Date	Reference	Owner
Cup	A*	E/IS (+)	John and Sybil (Newman) Edwards	ca. 1694	*Antiques* 128 (October 1985): 688	
Spout cup	A	TD; AS (later)		ca. 1710	Bigelow 1917, 386–87	
Tablespoon	A†	Mary Payn	Mary Payne	ca. 1710	Eitner 1976, no. 37	

1. Roberts 1895, 1:131.
2. RC 9:25, 33, 35, 136; *Reading VR*, 121, 363, 500, 530; Bridgman 1853, 38.
3. SCCR, miscellaneous file papers vol. 1, 1679–1789, papers relating to the estate of Samuel Haugh, merchant, d. 1679, and his wife, Anna Haugh. The papers include Samuel Haugh's inventory of 1679; Anna Haugh's will; articles of division between Samuel Haugh of Boston, goldsmith, and Atherton Haugh of Boston, tailor, of 1698; and a certificate regarding the estate of Atherton Haugh, 1706, of which Samuel Haugh, goldsmith, was executor. Haugh took the certificate to Jeremiah Dummer (q.v.), who in 1713 acknowledged it to be Haugh's "act and deed." See also SCPR 12:309, 345, for the elder Samuel Haugh's estate administration.
4. SCPR 11:135–36.
5. *Sewall Diary* 1:253.
6. *Sewall Diary* 1:258.
7. *Sewall Diary* 1:269.
8. *Sewall Diary* 1:346.
9. RC 9:127, 235.
10. SCCR, Court of Common Pleas Record Book 1692–98, 163; SCD 19:37–39.
11. SCCR, Court of Common Pleas Record Book 1692–98, 241.
12. SCD 19:49, 90–93.
13. SCPR 16:203–05, 254–56; miscellaneous papers, SCCR.
14. Samuel Sewall Account Book and Ledger, fol. 194v, NEHGS; ECPR, docket 28673; SCPR 17:257.
15. RC 11:74.

16. RC 10:146–47; SCCR Court of Common Pleas Record Book 1701–06, 171; RC 13:2; Roberts 1895, 1:376.

17. RC 9:215, 247; RC 24:12, 56, 68, 95.

18. *Sewall Diary* 2:855.

19. SCPR 20:11–13, docket 3851; will dated 4 March 1717, probated 22 July 1717.

20. SCPR 21:570–71.

21. SCPR 22:523–26.

22. SCD 41:204.

23. SCPR 21:682–83; SCPR 22:405–06.

24. SCCR, Court of Common Pleas Record Book 1721–22, 47.

Daniel Henchman
1730–75

A

B

Daniel Henchman was born in Lynn, Massachusetts, on 23 November 1730, the son of Nathaniel Henchman (1699–1761), a minister, and Deborah Wager (d. 1730), who were married in 1727.[1] Daniel Henchman's mother died a few days after his birth, and his father remarried on 3 December 1734; his new wife was Lydia Lewis, daughter of John and Mary Lewis of Lynn.[2] The goldsmith's paternal grandparents were Nathaniel Henchman (1655–1749), a bookbinder, and Hannah Green (ca. 1669–1706).[3] Henchman was apprenticed to the eminent Boston goldsmith Jacob Hurd (q.v.) at the same time as Benjamin Goodwin (q.v.) because they witnessed a deed for Hurd in 1750. Henchman married Hurd's daughter Elizabeth (b. 1730) on 20 March 1753; he was the brother-in-law of Nathaniel and Benjamin Hurd (qq.v.).[4]

Daniel and Elizabeth probably lived near Oliver's Dock because their house was one of those burned in the devastating fire there in 1760, for which he claimed a loss of £30.5.5.[5] In 1763 Henchman sold land in Chelsea, Massachusetts. This sale may have enabled him to buy a house on Milk Street that year, which he mortgaged a number of times between 1764 and 1767 to Thomas and John Fleet.[6] The deed of 1767 was witnessed by his brother-in-law Nathaniel Hurd (q.v.). The Massachusetts tax list of 1771 includes Henchman in Boston with one poll, one house, and £30 annual worth of real estate.[7]

Henchman was an active goldsmith who served both residents of Boston and individuals living elsewhere in New England. The Amory papers at the Massachusetts Historical Society include a bill from Henchman to Thomas Amory that reads as follows:

Mr Thomas Amory to Daniel Henchman Dr
June 17t— 1767 To 1 Silver punch Strainer wt 4.7.0 £10 [torn]

To fashg Ditto	£6
Old tenor	£17.(7?)
Benjamin Callender	

The Benjamin Callender who signed the bill may have been the goldsmith Benjamin Callender (q.v.), who was eighteen years old at the time and probably Henchman's apprentice. Another bill documents Henchman's sale of a silver tankard to Norton Quincy.[8] It reads,

Mr Norton Quincy to Danl Henchman Dr

To 1 Silver Tankard wt 24..2 0 @ 52/s	£62. 13. 6	
To fashg Ditto	20.. 0.. 0	
To engraving	1.. 16.. 0	
old tenor	£84. 9. 6	

Boston Septr 4th 1768
   Recd the Contents in full Danl Henchman

In the *Pennsylvania Journal* of 6 April 1774, Thaddeus Burr of Fairfield, Connecticut, advertised the theft of a large amount of silver made by Daniel Henchman, including a pair of chafing dishes, a pair of butter cups, a cann, two soupspoons, a pepper box, six tablespoons, six teaspoons, and a strainer.

Henchman complained against the unfair competition of imported silver in an advertisement appearing in the *Boston Evening-Post* during January 1773:

> Daniel Henchman
> Takes this Method to inform his Customers in Town & Country,
> That he still continues to carry on the
> GOLD and SILVERSMITHS Business at his Shop opposite the
> Old Brick Meeting House in Cornhill, where he makes with his
> own Hands all Kinds of large and small Plate Work, in the
> genteelest Taste and newest Fashion, and of the purest Silver;
> and as his Work has hitherto met with the Approbation of the
> most Curious, he flatters himself that he shall have the Preference
> by those who are Judges of Work, to those Strangers among us
> who import and sell English Plate, to the great Hurt and Preju-
> dice of the Townsmen who have been bred to the Business.—
> Said HENCHMAN therefore will engage to those Gentlemen
> and Ladies who shall please to employ him, that he will make
> any Kind of Plate they may want equal in goodness and cheaper
> than any they can import from London, with the greatest Dispatch.

Henchman died in Boston on 7 January 1775, and his estate administration was granted to his widow on 3 February 1775.[9] The inventory included shop tools, which were valued at £13.18.6:

5 p.ʳ brass casting Flasks, 1:10/– 2 p.ʳ iron d.º 2/	1:	12 —
30 Hammers of different sorts & sizes	1:	10 —
2 iron casting Ingotts, 1/6.ᵈ 2 p.ʳ forging Tongs 1/		2: 6
Car.ᵈ over	£3:	4: 6
Brot over	3:	4: 6
6 Stakes, 12/s 2 draw Plates 3/ 2 Anvils 10/8	1:	5: 8
1 Sparhawk 1/6 3 Swages 2/s 3 wood mallets 2.ᵈ		3: 8
2 Goose Neck Anvills 2/s 1 Large Spoon Punch 2/s		4 —
1 p.ʳ draw.ᵍ Tongs 3/s 3 p.ʳ fire Tongs 3/		6 —
2 p.ʳ Money Scales & w.ᵗˢ 6/s 1 brass hollow.ᵍ Stamp 4/		10 —
1 Lamp 1/s 2 glass Cases 8/s		9 —
1 Box, contain.ᵍ sund.ʸ old & broken Files, Nippers &.ᶜ &.ᶜ		9 —[10]

The estate was appraised by Daniel Boyer (q.v.), Zachariah Brigden (q.v.), and Joseph Russell, presumably not the silversmith.

More than seventy pieces of holloware and flatware by Henchman are known to survive. They bear the surname mark Henchman in upper- and lowercase Roman letters (A), or an initials mark D·H in a rectangle (B). Since a number of pieces bear both marks, the attribution of the initials mark is very sound.[11] Henchman and his brother-in-law Nathaniel Hurd are known to have worked together on some commissions, including the monteith for John Wentworth, the governor of New Hampshire. PEK

SURVIVING OBJECTS

	Mark	Inscription	Patron	Date	Reference	Owner
Beaker	A	GD; George Domett	George Domett	ca. 1770	YUAG files	

	Mark	Inscription	Patron	Date	Reference	Owner
Two beakers	?	?	United Parish of Upton, Mass.	ca. 1760	YUAG files	
Cann	A*	JBD . . . (later)		ca. 1770	DAPC 76.2974	USDS
Cann	A	JMR		ca. 1770	DAPC 72.2636	DIA
Cann	A	unidentified initials		ca. 1765	American Art Association–Anderson Galleries, 16–17 April 1937, lot 36	
Cann	A	Holyoke arms	Edward Holyoke	ca. 1760		MFAB
Cann	A*	F/BM		ca. 1770		NM
Cann	A*	D/BR		ca. 1765	Christie's, 23 June 1993, lot 55	
Cann (mate below)	A/B	Lloyd arms, gules a lion rampant within a bordure or engrailed, and crest, a pelican in her piety	Lloyd family	ca. 1770	*Antiques* 110 (September 1976): 414	
Cann (mate above)	A/B	Lloyd arms, gules a lion rampant within a bordure or engrailed, and crest, a pelican in her piety	Lloyd family	ca. 1770	Hammerslough/ Feigenbaum 1958–73, 1:3	
Two canns	A/B	The Gift of/Thaddeus Burr/Dec^d/to Eunice Winecoop/ 1755	Thaddeus Burr or Eunice Winecoop	ca. 1755	*Silver Supplement* 1973, no. 45	Fairfield Historical Society
Cann	A/B	Lawrence arms	Lawrence family	ca. 1760	Sotheby Parke Bernet, 17 November 1981, lot 183	
Cann (mate below)	A*/ B*	Walker arms, between a chevron sable 3 crescents sable in a canton sable a bird, and crest, a bird with a sprig in its beak	Walker family	ca. 1770	Buhler/Hood 1970, no. 223	YUAG
Cann (mate above)	A/B	Walker arms, between a chevron sable 3 crescents sable in a canton sable a bird, and crest, a bird with a sprig in its beak	Walker family	ca. 1770		Newport Preservation Society
Caster	B	SR		ca. 1755	Buhler 1972, no. 316	MFAB
Two casters	B	IS to SS		ca. 1760	Christie's, 23 January 1982, lot 89	

	Mark	Inscription	Patron	Date	Reference	Owner
Chafing dish	A*	none		ca. 1770	Puig et al. 1989, no. 212	MIA
Coffeepot	A	Codman crest, a bird with a sprig in its beak; AHC	Codman family	ca. 1775	Buhler 1976, 2–4	VMFA
Coffeepot	A	CCW (later) (+)		ca. 1775	*Antiques* 115 (February 1979): 220	MFAB
Coffeepot	A†/ B†	Winthrop arms, 3 chevrons gules over all a lion rampant, and crest, a hare courant; The Gift of T. Lindall Esq.ʳ/To mr.ˢ Jane Winthrop (+)	Timothy Lindall and/or Jane Winthrop	ca. 1760	Buhler/Hood 1970, no. 221	YUAG
Creampot	A	S/RR		ca. 1760	DAPC 67.2048	
Creampot	B*	O/HM		ca. 1760	Flynt/Fales 1968, 86	HD
Creampot (part of a service)	B*	W/DS	Dudley and Sarah (Sheldon) Woodbridge	ca. 1760	Buhler/Hood 1970, no. 222	YUAG
Ladle	A	ES		ca. 1770	Hammerslough/Feigenbaum 1958–73, 2:74–75	
Ladle	B*	RH		ca. 1760	DAPC 69.2551	
Monteith	A	His Excellency John Wentworth Esq.ʳ/Governor of the Province of New Hampshire,/And those Friends who accompanied him/To Dartmouth College the first Commencement 1771./In Testimony of their Gratitude and good Wishes/Present this to the/Revᵈ Eleazer Wheelock, D.D. President/And to his successors in that office	John Wentworth and friends	1771	Phillips 1949, 96	HMA
Mourning ring (gold)	B	N Henchman Esq.ʳ obᵗ 30 May 1767 AE:39	Rev. Nathaniel Henchman	1767	Buhler 1972, no. 317	MFAB
Porringer	A	E		ca. 1775	YUAG files	
Porringer	A	IP/to/HP		ca. 1760		MFAB
Sauceboat	A	none		ca. 1755	*Moore Collection* 1980, no. 111	
Sauceboat	A	none		ca. 1750		HMA

	Mark	Inscription	Patron	Date	Reference	Owner
Two sauceboats	A	Barrett arms (+)	Barrett family	ca. 1770	Buhler 1956, no. 76	MFAB
Strainer	?	?		ca. 1765	Davis 1991, 198–99	CW
Sugar bowl	?	P/TE		ca. 1770	Norman-Wilcox 1962, no. 28	
Sugar tongs	B*	EC		ca. 1760	DAPC 78.3339	
Tablespoon	A*	MD/to/IFI		ca. 1770	DAPC 73.3243	WM
Tablespoon	A	unidentified crest, a bird with a sprig in its beak		ca. 1765	Sotheby Parke Bernet, 27 January 1989, lot 909	
Two tablespoons (mates below)	A*	unidentified crest, a griffin's head erased		ca. 1770	Buhler/Hood 1970, no. 224	YUAG
Two tablespoons (mates above and below)	A	unidentified crest, a griffin's head erased		ca. 1770	Avery 1920, nos. 114–15	MMA
Six tablespoons (mates above and below)	A*	unidentified crest, a griffin's head erased		ca. 1770		HD
Tablespoon (mates above)	A*	unidentified crest, a griffin's head erased		ca. 1770	DAPC 72.1939	WM
Tankard	A*	Taylor crest, an eagle displayed with two heads grasping crosses crosslet in its beaks; The Gift of A· Tailer 1752; Jonathan French . . . (later)	A. Tailer	1752	Silver Supplement 1973, no. 46	USDS
Tankard	A	The Gift of the/Honll John Quincy Esq./to the First Church of/Christ in Braintree/1767	Norton Quincy, executor of John Quincy's estate, for First Congregational Society (Unitarian), Quincy, Mass.	ca. 1768	Jones 1913, 396–97	
Tankard	A	Wheelwright crest, a wolf's head erased; Wheelwright (later)	John Wheelwright	ca. 1765		MHS
Tankard	A	ND		ca. 1765		HMA
Tankard	A	C/GP		ca. 1761	American Silver 1967, no. 16	RWNAG
Tankard	A	IEH/To/Catherine Hurd	John Hurd	ca. 1760	Phillips 1939, no. 107	
Tankard	A	Presented/by/Mrs Abigail Prescott . . . (later)	William and Abigail (Hale) Prescott (?)	ca. 1765	Jones 1913, 362	
Tankard	A/B	Phillips arms, azure a lion rampant a chief ermine, and crest, a demi-lion rampant; The Gift	William White and/or Sarah Phillips	1759	Buhler 1960a, 84	AG

	Mark	Inscription	Patron	Date	Reference	Owner
		of Mr Wm White to/Sarah Phillips Jany 1759				
Tankard	A/B	Greene crest, a stag's head erased	Greene family	ca. 1765	Christie's, 17 June 1992, lot 68	
Teapot	A	unidentified arms, or a chevron gules between 2 roses and a mullet, and crest, a demi-lion rampant		ca. 1765	Antiques 115 (February 1979): 220	HMA
Teapot	A*	none	William Ellery	ca. 1760	Antiques 122 (July 1982): 43	DeYoung
Teapot	A*	Berry arms, gules 3 bands or	Berry family	ca. 1760	Flynt/Fales 1968, 86–87	HD
Teapot (part of a service)	A	Woodbridge arms, on a bend 3 chaplets, and crest, a chaplet; W/DS	Dudley and Sarah (Sheldon) Woodbridge	ca. 1760	American Silver 1967, no. 11	RWNAG
Teaspoon	A	unidentified crest, a unicorn's head erased, collared with a coronet and leashed		ca. 1770	YUAG files	
Teaspoon	B	SC		ca. 1755	Buhler 1965, 85–89	HMA
Teaspoon	B	LK		ca. 1765	Avery 1920, no. 113	MMA
Four teaspoons	B*	MS		ca. 1760		YUAG
Teaspoon	B*	TP		ca. 1770		YUAG
Teaspoon	B*	M (altered to H) A (+)		ca. 1765	DAPC 73.3057	WM
Teaspoon	B	none		ca. 1770		WHS
Two wine cups	B*	Hancock arms, a dexter hand couped, on a chief 3 cocks, and crest, a demi-griffin, impaling Henchman arms, a chevron between 3 hunting horns sable, on a chief 3 lioncelles; The Gift of/Mrs LYDIA HANCOCK/to the first Church/of Christ in/BOSTON/Sept. 4, 1773	Lydia Hancock and/or First Church, Boston	1773	Jones 1913, 26–27	

1. RC 9:247; Lynn VR 1:190; 2:180, 500.
2. Lynn VR 2:180.
3. RC 9:210; Whitmore 1878, 55, no. 1029.
4. RC 24:198; RC 30:5, 376; MCD 48:586. Bigelow wrote that Henchman was apprenticed to

Hurd at the age of thirteen because on 22 September 1743 Henchman witnessed a deed for Hurd; Bigelow-Phillips files, 1407; SCD 67:22. It is more than likely, however, that the Daniel Henchman who witnessed this deed was the Daniel Henchman (1689–1761) who was a justice of the peace in Suffolk County.

5. RC 29:93, 124.
6. SCD 102:208–09; 103:26, 36–37; 107:173–74; 110:172–74.
7. Pruitt 1978, 32–33.
8. MFA 1911, illus. opp. p. 64.
9. SCPR 74:298–99; *NEHGR* 85:5.
10. SCPR 74:297–99.
11. An initials mark in a serrated rectangle (Flynt/Fales 1968, 245) is certainly not Henchman's because it is on a coffin-end spoon made about 1810. Drawings of an initials mark with periods and a surname mark in script have been published; Kovel 1961, 135.

Samuel Hichborn
1752–1828

Samuel Hichborn was baptized in the New Brick Church in Boston on 2 August 1752, the son of Thomas Hichborn (1708–77), a boatbuilder, and Hannah Fadry (Fadree) (1712–1800), who were married in 1734/35.[1] The goldsmith's paternal grandparents were Thomas Hichborn (1673/74–1731), a joiner, and Frances Pateshall (ca. 1676–1749).[2] His maternal grandparents were Nathaniel Fadry and Susannah (Isanna) Pitman (ca. 1684–1732), who were married in 1704.[3]

Paul Revere, Sr., was Samuel's uncle by marriage, and Paul Revere, Jr., was his cousin (qq.v.). Samuel would have begun his apprenticeship about 1766, perhaps with the younger Revere. The apprenticeship would have been completed about 1773.

On 28 April 1777 Samuel Hichborn married Ann Williams (1758–83), the daughter of the shopkeeper Robert Williams, Jr. (1727–1807), of Boston, and Ann Boylston of Roxbury, Massachusetts.[4] Shortly after Samuel's marriage, his father died. On 19 April 1779 Samuel Hichborn, "jeweler," together with Hannah Hichborn, widow, and his sisters and brothers sold property "near the drawbridge," probably their inheritance, to Samuel's brother Thomas.[5] The following year on 5 January Samuel is identified as a goldsmith in a deed for property he bought on Ann Street from James Cary.[6] Ann Street was in ward 5, so the Samuel Hichborn listed in that ward on the Boston tax lists of 1780 as paying a poll tax of two and as having rents valued at forty pounds annually undoubtedly was the craftsman discussed here.[7] He is again identified as a goldsmith in a deed of 5 August 1782, when with his mother, brothers, and sisters he sold land to his brother Nathaniel.[8]

Following his second marriage on 13 February 1785 at Trinity Church to Ann Ramsey (1764–1828), Samuel Hichborn no longer called himself goldsmith or jeweler in his real estate transactions.[9] Whether he ceased to practice the trade of goldsmith or jeweler or both is difficult to ascertain. On 28 November 1787 Hichborn was called a gentleman when he granted a mortgage to Paul Revere and was variously termed shopkeeper and trader in a series of transactions that took place in 1793.[10] In the *Boston Directory* of 1796, he is called shopkeeper and in 1800, merchant. On 24 January 1803 he mortgaged land in Ann Street to Susannah Hatch and called himself merchant, discharging this obligation three years later.[11]

Samuel Hichborn's real estate dealings then ceased until the last years of his life; in 1824, 1826, and 1827, he granted mortgages to a number of people.[12] The *Columbian Centinel* for 6 August 1828 records the death of Samuel Hichborn, age seventy-six, in Dorchester, Massachusetts; his estate was valued at

$12,303.80.[13] Accounts of the administration were presented to the probate court on 14 September 1829.[14]

No mark is ascribed to this maker. Because he is identified as a jeweler as well as a goldsmith, he probably retailed small wares that he did not mark. PEK

1. *NEHGR* 18:343; RC 24:56, 82; RC 28:184; *Index of Obituaries, 1784–1840*, 3:2216; Codman 1918, 127.
2. RC 9:128; RC 28:10; Codman 1918, 126–27.
3. RC 28:10; Boston Deaths, 1700–1800.
4. RC 24:184, 295; RC 28:294; RC 30:84; *Church in Brattle Square*, 280; Thwing.
5. SCD 131:25.
6. SCD 131:28–29.
7. "Assessors' 'Taking-Books,'" 26.
8. SCD 175:165.
9. RC 30:412; Codman 1918, 126.
10. SCD 161:237–38; 175:166–67; 176:288–89; 177:159–61; 189:48–49; 200:101–02.
11. SCD 204:67–68.
12. SCD 288:41–42; 307:169–71; 323:271–72.
13. SCPR 126²:184–88, 191–92.
14. SCPR 127:226–27.

Abraham Higgins
1738–63

Abraham Higgins was born in Eastham, Massachusetts, on 10 October 1738, the son of Isaac Higgins, Jr. (1708–ca. 1760), of Eastham and Wellfleet and Abigail Freeman (b. 1715) of Eastham, who were married in Eastham on 5 July 1733.[1] His paternal grandparents were Isaac Higgins, Sr. (1672–ca. 1760), one of Eastham's early proprietors, and Lydia Collins (b. 1676).[2] His maternal grandparents were Capt. Samuel Freeman (ca. 1688–1742/43), another early proprietor of Eastham, and Bathsheba (Lothrop) Smith (b. 1671) of Barnstable, Massachusetts, the widow of Samuel Smith.[3]

Higgins's apprenticeship with Moody Russell (q.v.) of Barnstable is documented in Massachusetts muster rolls that record his service from April to October 1758, and April to November 1759, in the later stages of the French and Indian War.[4] A powder horn showing the city of Quebec on one side and a forest landscape of tents and deer on the other and inscribed "Abraham Higgins His Horn maid September 27th, 1759," commemorates his service.[5] The powder horn may have been inscribed by Higgins during the calm that followed the fall of Quebec to the British in 1759.[6]

Following his return from Quebec, Higgins may have worked briefly as a journeyman in Barnstable for his former master, Moody Russell. Higgins died in 1763, only a few years later, at the age of twenty-five. Although Russell had died in 1761, two years earlier, the relationship with his family was sufficiently strong that Russell's widow, Dinah (Sturgis) Russell, served as administrator of Higgins's estate.[7] Higgins was identified as a goldsmith in these probate documents; however, aside from the powder horn, no mark and no silver have been ascribed to his hand. JJF

1. *Mayflower Descendant* 6:202; 9:12; 17:80; 28:176; Higgins 1918, 118–19.
2. Higgins 1918, 54; *Mayflower Descendant* 3:230.
3. Capt. Samuel Freeman's birth date is arrived at from his age at the time of death as recorded on his gravestone; "in his 82nd yr," *Mayflower Descendant* 6:202. For Bathsheba Lothrop, see *Mayflower Descendant* 6:13, 238.
4. Higgins served the colonial forces on at least two occasions: 8 April–23 October 1758 and 28 April–12 November 1759. Mass. Archives, Muster Rolls 96:126, 434; 97:306. Moody Russell was named as his master.

5. The powder horn is in the collections of the Onondaga Historical Association, Syracuse, New York.

6. According to William H. Guthman, the carving does not fit into any of the groups of specialized carving, leaving open the possibility that Higgins, who probably had some training as an engraver, made the horn himself. William H. Guthman to Patricia E. Kane, 12 March 1994. For the work of specialized carvers, see Guthman 1993.

7. BCPR 10:143.

Thomas Higginson
ca. 1655–ca. 1696 +

Salem's first silversmith, Thomas Higginson, came from an important and successful family, but was himself something of a failure. Son of the Reverend John Higginson (1616–1708) and his wife, Sarah (Whitfield) (ca. 1620–75), Thomas was born about 1655, probably in Guilford, Connecticut.[1] He was sent to England to learn the goldsmith's trade, a career choice that indicates the high regard still held for silversmithing in the late seventeenth century. The records of the Worshipful Company of Goldsmiths in London contain the following entry under the date 13 April 1670: "That I Thomas Higginson the sonne of John Higginson of Salem in New England Clerke doe put my selfe Apprentize unto Joseph Ash Cittizen and Goldsmith of London for the Terme of Eight yeares from Xmas last past."[2]

Little is known about Joseph Ash. He was the son of a minister from the county of Dorset and was apprenticed in 1662 to William Harrison of London. Ash received his freedom in 1669, and Higginson was his first apprentice.[3]

Higginson's apprenticeship would have been over in December 1677, but his movements thereafter remain somewhat shrouded in mystery. A Thomas Higginson took the oath of allegiance in Boston in 1679 and was included in the tax list of 1681 in the same ward as John Coney (q.v.).[4] If this Higginson was the silversmith, he may have been working for Coney as a journeyman. Family tradition and other records report Higginson back in Salem from 1687 to 1689 and in Guilford from 1690 to 1694.[5] He witnessed a deed for the Salem silversmith Samuel Phillips (q.v.) in 1690.[6] By 1696, Higginson had left Salem, as his father noted, for "Arabia, whither he was gone with privateers, contrary to my mind and against his own promise."[7] The Reverend Mr. Higginson despaired of his son, although he left Thomas a legacy in his will should he still be alive. In a letter of 1693 to his other son, Nathaniel, Higginson wrote, "yr Brothr Thos is now 38 a Single man & yett nott in any settled way of Imployment haveing failed in yt he was in, I canott help him he is an object of pity." Thomas appears never to have returned from Arabia and was lost to history. His brother Nathaniel noted in 1699 that "the unhappy miscarriage of Thomas has much troubled me. I have never heard anything of him in India, though I have met with several who have been taken by pirates and returned or escaped." Almost a year later, on 29 August 1700, Nathaniel wrote another letter that serves as Thomas's epitaph: "I have not heard any thing of our brother Thomas, since he went away out of this country; do'nt doubt he is come to some untimely end."[8]

No silver by Higginson is known today, and no mark has been attributed to him. Because his stepmother was Mary Atwater, whose daughters married Jeremiah Dummer (q.v.) and John Coney, Francis Hill Bigelow believed that Higginson may have been associated in business with these two leading Boston silversmiths.[9] However, given his father's comments and the rest of the sparse documentary record, it does not seem reasonable to assign Thomas Higginson a significant place in the history of seventeenth-century American silver, although his English training would have given him the necessary background to play an important role. GWRW

1. The date of Thomas's birth is not known precisely. In a letter of 1693, his father refers to Thomas as being thirty-eight years old, which would indicate a birth date of ca. 1655.
2. Apprentice Book 2, fol. 186r, Worshipful Company of Goldsmiths, London, 13 September 1670; photocopy courtesy of Susan M. Hare, librarian, Goldsmiths' Hall, London. The tradition of Higginson's London apprenticeship is noted in Wheatland 1863, 35, and in Higginson 1910, 54.
3. Susan Hare, letter to author, 6 August 1981, citing documentation in the records of Goldsmiths' Hall.
4. RC 29:169; RC 1:72–73.
5. Higginson 1910, 7, for the family tradition. At a town meeting of 3 March 1689/90, Higginson was abated ten shillings as constable; see *Town Records of Salem* 3:213. Steiner 1897, in a section on the Guilford schools (397), states, "On July 4, 1690, Mr. Thomas Higginson of Salem, a son of the Rev. John Higginson, former pastor at Guilford, was invited to teach the school for half a year 'on tryall' and, he accepting, taught until 1694." John Higginson's letter of 18 July 1692 to Nathaniel Higginson states "Brother Thomas Lives at Guilford"; see *Collections of the Massachusetts Historical Society*, 3d ser. (Boston: Charles C. Little and James Brown, 1838), 7:198.
6. ECD 8:175.
7. Letter of John Higginson to his son Nathaniel, n.d., in *Collections of the Massachusetts Historical Society*, 3d ser. (Boston: Charles C. Little and James Brown, 1838), 7:198–99.
8. Letter of John Higginson to his son Nathaniel, printed in *EIHC* 43, no. 2 (April 1907): 183. Although this letter was published as having been written on 31 August 1698, internal evidence suggests that the proper date is 1693; see Phillips 1937a, 6, n. 1. Nathaniel's letters are in *Collections of the Massachusetts Historical Society*, 3d ser. (Boston: Charles C. Little and James Brown, 1838), 7:217, 221.
9. Bigelow-Phillips files, 243.

James Hill
1747–1809+

James Hill was born in April 1747 to Samuel Hill (1716/17–53) and Bethiah Webb (1720–95) of Charlestown, Massachusetts.[1] When Hill's mother remarried in 1761, Thomas Call (d. 1772), a joiner, became his stepfather.[2] All of Hill's grandparents were Charlestown natives: Samuel (1693–1729), a mariner, and Joanna Hill, and Samuel (1689–1739), a miller, and Abigail (Austin) Webb (1695–1747).[3] James Hill presumably would have begun his apprenticeship about 1761 and completed it about 1768. He may have trained with Daniel Parker (q.v.) because Hill signed a receipt on Parker's behalf in 1768.

References to James Hill appear in both Boston and Charlestown records from the 1770s through the 1790s, although it is unclear whether they are all to the same individual. James Hill paid taxes in Charlestown in 1773 and claimed a loss in 1775 as a result of the British bombardment of Charlestown. The estimate that Hill submitted included a shop valued at £20, as well as

Goldsmith Tool's

viz

1 Anvil 49/4 2 Boiling Pans 13/4 –	3. 2. 8
1 Ingot 6/8 2 Pair Tongs 6/ —	12. 8
1 Pair Serves 6/ 1 moulding Box 16/	1. 2. 0
2 Pair Scails + wts 24/1 Pair Flasks 6/	1.10. 0
1 Blow Pipe + Lamp	3 —
2 Shop Board + [illeg.] skins	16 —
6 Hammers 18/ 1 Tin Funnell 8/	1. 6. —

1 Glass Case 30/ Sundreys Files 8/   1. 18.

10:10:   4 [4]

However, a Franklin County deed of 6 January 1784 identifies him as James Hill, "[of] Boston, goldsmith."[5] The *Boston Directory* of 1796 includes a James Hill on Summer Street, and that of 1798 lists one at 48 Newbury Street, but their occupations are not given.[6] On 11 October 1798 "James Hill of Charlestown . . . Goldsmith" conveyed a house that formerly belonged to the estate of his stepfather, Thomas Call, to the Charlestown pewterer Nathaniel Austin, with the option to reclaim the house if he paid Austin $339 within a year. A note in the margin of the record book indicates that the obligation was canceled and settled by referees on 30 January 1801.[7]

An engraver named James Hill worked in Massachusetts in the first decade of the nineteenth century and may be the Hill earlier identified as a goldsmith. The goldsmith had a nephew Samuel Hill, Jr. (q.v. Appendix B), who was an engraver in Boston. James Hill published engraved Bible illustrations in Charlestown in 1803, and the *Boston Directory* of 1809 lists "Hill, James, engraver, 7 Marlboro Street."[8] The directory listing of 1809 is the last time James Hill appears in Massachusetts records. Some silver scholars have ascribed the mark J·HILL in either a rectangle or an oval to this silversmith, but no example of this mark could be found.[9] PEK

1. *Charlestown VR* 1:246, 249, 265, 365, 380; Wyman 1879, 1:169, 500–01; 2:1003; MCPR, docket 11509.
2. *Charlestown VR* 1:404; MCPR, docket 3894.
3. *Charlestown VR* 1:159, 164, 246, 466; *Braintree VR*, 666; Wyman 1879, 2:1003; MCPR, dockets 23980, 23978, 11507.
4. Wyman 1879, 1:500; Ensko went so far as to say that James Hill claimed the house of Nathaniel Austin (q.v.) for a loss in 1775; however, that is a misreading of Thomas Wyman's cryptic entry on James Hill; see Ensko 1927, 49, and Ensko 1948, 70. Hunnewell 1888, 171, states that Hill claimed a loss of £85.3.2. This figure is based on the Fire Loss book (vol. 59 of the Charlestown Archives, BPL). The estimate that Hill prepared, including the goldsmith's tools and shop, amounted to £108.9.10. See Charlestown Fire Claims, box 3, BPL.
5. Flynt/Fales 1968, 247. James Hill does not appear in the indexes to Franklin County deeds, and hence this reference has not been verified.
6. *Boston Directory* 1796, 255; 1798, 63.
7. MCD 137:275–76.
8. Fielding 1917, 169; *Boston Directory* 1809, 74.
9. See for instance Kovel 1961, 137.

Benjamin Hiller
1687/88–ca. 1745

A

Benjamin Hiller was born in Boston on 19 January 1687/88. He was the son of Joseph (ca. 1653–1721) and Susanna (Dennis) Hiller. His father, a tinplate worker, immigrated to New England from Watford, Hertfordshire. Joseph and Susanna were married in Boston on 20 October 1684 and were among the earliest members of the town's First Baptist Church. Joseph, his wife, and his children (Benjamin, Joseph [1685–1753], and Susanna [1686–1747]) each received a legacy of five pounds from the estate of Elizabeth Bellingham in 1697. Benjamin and his sister, who would later marry Jeremiah Condy, joined the First Baptist Church on 1 June 1708.[1]

In 1709, at the age of twenty-one, Benjamin Hiller, along with Nathaniel Morse (q.v.), witnessed a deed of mortgage between William Taylor, a Dorchester gentleman, and John Coney (q.v.). Because of this document scholars have supposed that Hiller served his apprenticeship with Coney and stayed on to work for him as a journeyman after completing his training.[2]

At this time Hiller could look forward to a promising future. In 1714 he became a member of the Ancient and Honorable Artillery Company, serving as its clerk in 1716 and 1717, and as its fourth sergeant in 1717.[3] On 10 February 1714 he married Elizabeth Russell (b. 1697), daughter of Joseph and Mary Russell (d. by 1715); Cotton Mather of Boston's Second Church officiated.[4] The couple's first child, Elizabeth, was born in 1717, followed by Susanna in 1719, Joseph (q.v.; father of Joseph Hiller, Jr., who also worked as a silversmith, but was primarily a clockmaker [q.v. Appendix A]) in 1721, and Benjamin in 1723.[5] Susanna later became the mother of Joseph Callender (q.v.). Hiller's mark, BH over addorsed crescents in a shaped shield (A), appears on a substantial number of well-crafted objects and attests to his initial success as a goldsmith. He may have trained his son Joseph, who followed the trade of jeweler. Hiller may have worked in association with George Hanners, Sr. (q.v.), because they witnessed the will of the brazier Jonathan Jackson in 1735.[6]

Hiller's accounts with the bookseller Daniel Henchman between 1713 and 1719 show that in addition to being a productive silversmith, Hiller was a serious student of religion. He purchased many books, including *Horneck's Law of Consideration*, Burrough's sermons, Moody's sermons, Tate's psalms, Watts on prayer, a Latin Bible, a tune book, and one book of interlined psalms as well as a *British Apollo, Salmon's Polygraphice*, the *Compleet Chimist*, three French books, and a number of others, some of which are identified by short-hand titles. He also bought pens, pencils, pasteboard, penknives, writing books, paper, and a wig and had several books bound. In return, Hiller made rings for Henchman's father and a porringer, five spoons, a belt buckle, gold beads, and a gold bead necklace for the bookseller. He also sold Henchman several parcels of old books.[7]

During these years Hiller and his family were active in the Baptist church. In 1714 and 1715, his wife's parents bequeathed mugs of his fashioning to the church. The deacons commissioned Hiller to make a similar mug in 1727 from the legacy of William Snell.[8] Benjamin's wife, Elizabeth Hiller, was baptized and received into the communion of the church in 1719. Earlier that year a Mr. Hiller was elected one of the deacons of the church. Although some authorities have supposed this was Benjamin, it may have been his father, Joseph, or his brother, Joseph, Jr., a shopkeeper.[9]

Hiller was either living in or had a shop in Middle Street by 1717, when he advertised, "A Very Likely Negro Boy about 12 or 13 years of age, has been above three years in the Country, to be Sold by Mr. *Benjamin Hiller* at his House in Middle-Street, Boston."[10] He also witnessed two deeds of mortgage in 1714 and 1716, and his wife received a small legacy from her mother's estate in 1715.[11]

Money problems began to plague the young craftsman beginning in 1719. In that year he was codefendant with his parents in a plea of trespass wherein Thomas Clark, a Boston merchant, attempted to repossess the Hillers' house in Cornhill after they failed to repay a mortgage bond of six hundred pounds. The record indicates that Benjamin, who is referred to as being a silversmith, was residing in the house with his parents at the time. Earlier in the same year, Hiller, identified as being a goldsmith, and his brother-in-law, the merchant Jeremiah Condy, were codefendants in a suit brought by Abigail Steenman, widow of the merchant Thomas Danforth of Surinam, for defaulting on a bond of one hundred pounds. It is interesting that the two were doing business with a West Indian merchant, but unfortunately no evidence exists to elucidate their relationship.[12] In 1720 Hiller was again in court, this time at the suit of the victualler Josiah Langdon of Boston. The writ of attachment in the case indicates that the undersheriff "attacht a Vise which was in the Defendents Shop and Leaft a Summons" to assure Hiller's appearance in court.[13] By 1721, Hiller was renting a house in Shrimpton's Lane. He was arrested and brought to court in September of that year for failing to pay a half-year's rent.[14] Sewall recorded the death of Benjamin's father in 1721, when he "Went to the Funeral of Mr. Hiller, AEtat 68, in the old burying place."[15] Although Joseph Hiller, Sr., had played a prominent role in local affairs, his estate was not probated, and Benjamin does not appear to have received a legacy large enough to help him out of his financial difficulties. Suits by William Stoddard in 1726, Benjamin Eddy in 1727, Ellis Callender and Josiah Boyles as executors of the will of Mary Greenhill in 1728, Sarah Kinsman as administrator of the estate of the shopkeeper Peletiah Kinsman in 1728, and the butcher Robert Taintin in 1734 bear testimony to Hiller's increasing difficulty in keeping up with his debts.[16]

Exactly what prompted the First Baptist Church to take action against Hiller in 1728 is unclear, but perhaps he had decided to temporarily drown his troubles in alcohol. The church record includes the following notation made at a meeting on 16 July 1728:

> Upon information & Complaint made to yᵉ Chur[ch]
> Relating to yᵉ Disorderly Carriage of our Brothr Benj
> Hillar It was voted:
>
> 1 first that in a tender Brotherly & Christian Manner
> he should be admonished for his Disorde[rliness]
> 2 That he be Informd yᵗ it is yᵉ mind & will [of] yᵉ
> Church That he withdraw from the Lords Ta[ble] till the
> Church shall inform him furth[er]
> 3 That Deacon Drowne & Brother Bound be [the] Persons
> to goe & Admonish him in yᵉ na[me] of ye Church: &
> Inform him

Deacon Shem Drowne and Brother James Bound found that Hiller had "Come to a Due Sense of his Eurror" and that he was "Desirous to be Resto[red]" in August of the following year, and he was restored to full membership on 7 September 1729. Apparently he was able to keep his promise, for there is no further mention of the problem in the church record.[17] Nonetheless, this incident and the fact that the problem existed for at least a year suggest that Hiller's business reversals took their toll on him.

The last mention of Hiller in the Boston records is in January 1738/39. That month he and Jacob Hurd (q.v.) witnessed a deed for the currier Samuel Torrey and the periwigmaker Joseph Webb, and Hiller witnessed the bond when Hurd was appointed guardian of Houghton Perkins (q.v.). These two documents suggest that Hiller may have been working for Hurd at the time.[18] According to family tradition Hiller died in 1745, but there is no record of his death, and his estate was not probated.[19] BMW

SURVIVING OBJECTS

	Mark	Inscription	Patron	Date	Reference	Owner
Bowl	A*	W/WS; MR (later)		ca. 1740	Antiques 68 (July 1955): 13	
Caster (mate below)	A*	Dudley crest, a lion's head erased; EJ (later)	William and Elizabeth (Davenport) Dudley	ca. 1715	Buhler/Hood 1970, no. 103	YUAG
Caster (mate above)	A	Dudley crest, a lion's head erased; EJ (later)	William and Elizabeth (Davenport) Dudley	ca. 1715		MFAB
Cup	A†	M/IK		ca. 1720	Buhler/Hood 1970, no. 102	YUAG
Cup	A	?		ca. 1720	YUAG files	
Cup	A	F/FD		ca. 1720	CGA Bulletin, no. 1 (1971): fig. 8	CGA
Cup	A	P/IH; HE		ca. 1720	Quimby 1995, no. 75	WM
Mug	A*	The Gift of Wm Snell/to ye Baptist Church/in Boston/ 1727.	William Snell and/or First Baptist Church, Boston	ca. 1727	Jones 1913, 46	
Mug	A	Ex dono of I & M/ Russell to the Church/1714	Joseph and Mary Russell and/or First Baptist Church, Boston	1714	Jones 1913, 45–46	
Mug	A	Ex dono Mary Russel/to ye Church	Mary Russell and/or First Baptist Church, Boston	ca. 1715	Jones 1913, 46	
Porringer	A*	P/IH (+)	James and Hannah Pitson	ca. 1715	Buhler/Hood 1970, no. 99	YUAG
Porringer	A	W/EH		ca. 1735	DAPC 81.3778	
Porringer spoon	A*	MR		ca. 1720	Buhler 1972, no. 108	MFAB
Spout cup	A*	R/IL	Joseph and Love (Macy) Rotch	ca. 1735	Buhler/Hood 1970, no. 101	YUAG
Tablespoon	A	I/DK	David and Katherine Jeffries	ca. 1720	MFA 1911, no. 558	
Tankard	A*	The gift of Sam^ll More to the first Church/in Boston	Samuel More and/or First Church, Boston	ca. 1715	Jones 1913, 29	
Tankard	A	EI/to/AEC		ca. 1720	Quimby 1995, no. 74	WM
Tankard	A	P/N?		ca. 1715	Buhler 1972, no. 109	MFAB
Tankard	A*	B/RA		ca. 1715	Buhler/Hood 1970, no. 100	YUAG
Tankard	A	Donum Pupillorum/ 1717; Thomas Robie (later)		ca. 1717	Antiques 131 (April 1987): 782	
Tankard	A	IMF; Sarah Fuller to WW Fuller (later?)	Fuller family	ca. 1720		MFAB

1. *Sewall Diary* 2:971; RC 9:169, 174; RC 28:9; SCPR 8:283; Record Book, First Baptist Church, Boston, n.p., microfilm copy, BPL.
2. SCD 24:171.
3. Roberts 1895, 1:389.
4. RC 9:234; RC 28:52.
5. RC 24:122, 141, 151, 160.
6. SCPR 32:444–45, docket 6861.
7. Daniel Henchman Ledger, 1712–ca. 1735, fols. 57, 146, NEHGS.
8. Jones 1913, 45–46. Snell also made a small bequest to Benjamin Hiller.
9. Record Book, First Baptist Church, Boston, n.p., microfilm copy, BPL.
10. *Boston News-Letter*, 26 August–2 September 1717.
11. SCD 28:213–14; 30:127–28; SCPR 18:455; 20:203.
12. SCCR, Court of Common Pleas Record Book 1718–19, 390, 157.
13. SCCR, Court of Common Pleas Record Book 1720, 108; SCCR, file 14226.
14. SCCR, Court of Common Pleas Record Book 1721, 105; SCCR, file 15501.
15. *Sewall Diary* 2:971.
16. SCCR, Court of Common Pleas Record Book 1725, 421; SCCR, file 20743; file 21345; file 21317; Court of Common Pleas Record Book 1734, 730.
17. Record Book, First Baptist Church, Boston, n.p., microfilm copy, BPL.
18. SCD 57:148–49; MCPR, docket 17154.
19. A. Regina Foster to Francis Hill Bigelow, Bigelow-Phillips files, n.p.

Joseph Hiller, Sr.
1721–58

Joseph Hiller, Sr., was born in Boston on 1 June 1721, the son of Benjamin Hiller (q.v.).[1] Hiller was the third generation of his family to pursue a trade in metalwork; his paternal grandfather, Joseph Hiller, was a tinplate worker.[2] The younger Joseph's intention of marriage to Hannah Welsh (1720–74), a sister of John Welsh (q.v.) of Charlestown, Massachusetts, was published on 13 December 1744, and they married in Charlestown on 24 January 1744/45.[3] One of their children, Joseph, Jr. (q.v. Appendix A), followed the allied trade of clockmaker, watchmaker, and engraver. Joseph Sr.'s nephew Joseph Callender (q.v.) also became an engraver. Hiller's two youngest children were baptized in the New North Church, Benjamin in March 1753 and Mary in February 1758, indicating the silversmith's affiliation with this church by 1753.[4]

Joseph Hiller may have served his apprenticeship with his father; however, because his father was a goldsmith and Joseph became a jeweler, it is more likely that he trained with a jeweler. Joseph Hiller appears in the Suffolk County Probate records in 1741 as a witness to the will of Jeremiah Condy, his uncle by marriage.[5] The twenty-year-old Hiller may have been boarding with his uncle and aunt, Susanna (Hiller) Condy, at this time, which suggests that his father may have died before 1741. Hiller would have been fully trained by about 1742. Hiller may have trained his wife's brother John Welsh, beginning about 1744. On Wednesday, 4 February 1746/47, Hiller moved to property owned by Benjamin Walker. Walker's diary for that year mentions "Mr. Joseph Hiller, Jeweler, my Tennant Wed Feb 4."[6] Hiller, along with Greenough Pierce (q.v.), witnessed a deed for Samuel Burt (q.v.) in 1748, evidence that may indicate that Hiller worked as a journeyman for Burt.[7] Hiller was one of the appraisers of the estate of Thomas Edwards (q.v.) in 1755.[8] On 29 October 1757 he signed a receipt for having accepted three pounds from James Peirse on behalf of John Touzell (q.v.), which suggests he may have had a business relationship with Touzell.[9]

Joseph Hiller was interested in exploring the scientific applications of silver in the development of electrical power. He advertised in the *Boston Gazette* on 5 March 1754 that he would exhibit "Electrical Experiments" near the Old

North Meeting House. The advertisement further stated, "N. B. *Said* Hiller *also does all Sorts of Jeweller's Work, in a neat Manner.*" He advertised again in the *Boston Gazette* for 9 January 1758: "JOSEPH HILLER, Jeweller, at his House near Concert-Hall," announced that "Electrical Experiments, with Methodical Lectures," are again exhibited by him, beginning "at Six-o'Clock in the Evening, one Pistereen each Lecture."

Joseph Hiller died on 20 July 1758 and was buried in the King's Chapel cemetery, as was his wife, who died in December 1774.[10]

No mark has been identified for Hiller, probably because most of the jewelry he made was unmarked. DAF

1. RC 24:151.
2. SCCR, Court of Common Pleas Record Book 1699–1701, 85.
3. RC 28:279; Wyman 1879, 1:504; 2:1006; *Charlestown VR* 1:264; Bridgman 1853, 93.
4. Record Book, New North Church, 147, 156 microfilm, BPL.
5. SCPR 35:441.
6. Benjamin Walker, Jr., Diaries, 1743–49, MHS.
7. SCD 75:117.
8. SCPR 51:52–53.
9. English-Touzel-Hathorne Papers, box 4, folder 5, PEM.
10. Wyman 1879, 1:504; Bridgman 1853, 93; *Boston News-Letter*, 29 December 1774.

William Homes, Jr.
1742–1825

A

B

C

D

E

F

G

William Homes, Jr., was born on 7 May 1742 to the Boston silversmith William Homes, Sr. (q.v.), and his wife, Rebecca Dawes.[1] A family genealogy compiled by Homes's sister Sarah Tappan in 1834 described him as an "exemplary Christian."[2] He joined the Old South Church on 17 November 1765 and remained an active member until his death.[3] Homes married three times: he wed Elizabeth Whitwell, daughter of William (b. 1714) and Rebecca (Keen) Whitwell (b. 1715), on 1 November 1764; Anna Darracutt on 23 January 1777; and finally, Mary Greenough (d. 1831), daughter of the Boston sailmaker Newman (1708–before 1794) and Elizabeth Greenough, on 14 January 1794.[4] Homes had eight children: William (b. 1765), Henry, Robert, John, Nathaniel B., Sally Whitwell (b. 1773), Rebecca, and Elizabeth.[5] One of his sons, Robert Homes (d. before 1882), pursued a career as a brass founder at 33 Union Street. In April 1804, Homes financed a mortgage on his son's Union Street store for $6,500, a loan not repaid until 1823.[6] The silversmiths Barnabas Webb and Benjamin Tappan, Jr. (qq.v.), were Homes's brothers-in-law.

Homes was trained by his father, and, according to Sarah Tappan's memoirs, he took over his father's shop on Ann Street in 1763, when he reached the age of twenty-one. He worked and lived there for the rest of his life.[7] The Boston tax valuation for 1771 assessed Homes with two polls, a house and shop valued at £20 annually, and merchandise worth £140.9.2.[8] In April 1784 William and Anna Homes sold a house on Love Street to Samuel Ridgway for £180, a transaction that, on 1 June 1784, enabled the silversmith to pay off a mortgage of £600 held by Mary Bartlett on a row house, formerly owned by his father, opposite the younger Homes's residence on Ann Street.[9] This property is described in the deed as "divided by partition from top to bottom from the messuage now in the occupation of Mr. Joseph Brown and owned by Mr. William Lambert, containing a Cellar shop parlour & Kitchen also all the Chambers above and garret." The United States census of 1790 recorded "William Homes" as the head of a household of three adult males, three boys under the age of sixteen, and three females.[10] Homes's large family occupied

The Silversmith's Shop of William Homes, Jr., unknown artist, oil on canvas, Yale University Art Gallery, gift of Josephine Setze, 1973.128

H

I

J

K

L

a wooden house on Ann Street, described in the tax list of 1798 as "Land, 1,139 square feet; house, 1,019 square feet; 3 stories, 12 windows; Value, $1,800."[11] He also owned a two-story brick commercial building on the opposite side of Ann Street valued at $800, which he rented to Norton Brailsford, as well as land on Charter Street that his wife, Mary, inherited from her father and that the couple sold in 1794.[12] The Boston directories list William Homes, goldsmith and jeweler, on Ann Street in 1789, 1796, and 1798, and he appeared in the Boston census records for 1810 and 1820.[13] Between 1816 and 1825, Homes shared his shop at 63 Ann Street with his son John Homes, who was listed in the *Boston Directory* of 1816 as a hardware merchant. A small oil painting in the Yale University Art Gallery (illus.) depicts the exterior of the Homes shop with a variety of ready-made wares displayed in the bow windows to entice customers, including flatware, jewelry, and teapots, probably a combination of imported objects and silver goods made by Homes.

Three cases appearing before the Suffolk County Court of Common Pleas during 1783 and 1785 demonstrate the geographic diversity of Homes's clients and illustrate the difficulties faced by a craftsman attempting to recover unpaid

M

N

O

debts. Homes sued to recover £107.5 from Timothy Stone of Ashley, Massachusetts, £3.2.4 from Hooker Osgood of Ashby, Massachusetts, and £13.5.16 from the mariner Jeremiah Leighton of Gloucester, Massachusetts.[14] The silversmith Samuel Davis (1765–1829) remembered Homes in his memoirs (1811) as a silversmith of "respectable character as well as professional merit."[15] Homes participated actively in the political and economic life of North Boston, and Homes's apprentices took part in the Boston Tea Party.[16] His first wife's uncle, the merchant Samuel Whitwell, kept a hardware store at the corner of Ann and Union streets. Like Whitwell, Homes was also an active member of the Ancient and Honorable Artillery Company, joining in 1766 and being elected sergeant in 1771. At age sixty-eight, Lieutenant Homes and Samuel Belknap (q.v.) were honored by the Artillery Company for their service in the Revolution.[17]

His fellow Artillery Company member Zachariah Whitman described William Homes, Jr., as "a man of small stature, pious, amiable and much beloved" and speculated that the eighty-three-year-old silversmith contracted his final illness by venturing out on an extremely cold day to be a witness before the Massachusetts Supreme Court in the "Price will" controversy between Trinity Church and King's Chapel.[18] Homes's obituary appeared in the *Columbian Centinel* on 19 February 1825, and his will, written on 18 November 1822, was presented for probate on 21 February 1825.[19] His widow, Mary Homes, received a lifetime interest in all his property, with his children Henry, John, Rebecca, Elizabeth Scott, and Nathaniel B. Homes as residual beneficiaries. His daughter-in-law Sara Persis Homes and eleven grandchildren inherited bequests of $1 each. Homes appointed the Boston merchant John Tappan, his nephew, executor of his estate. Following Mary Homes's death in 1831, the Ann Street property was auctioned for $2,945.15, and the estate was divided among the surviving heirs.[20]

The silversmith's household furnishings, stocks, and real estate were appraised in March 1825.[21] Homes owned many luxury items, including forty-six books valued at $10.95, an eight-day clock valued at $12, pictures, looking glasses, and a variety of household textiles, including counterpanes, coverlids, bedding, table linens, window curtains, and carpets. Silversmithing tools worth $10, unspecified except for a bellows, and some unfinished teaspoons indicate that he was active as a craftsman until his death:

30 oz 15 dwt.ˢ Tea Spoons		7/	35. 87
Making 14 Setts Tea Spoons	@	3/9	8. 75
24 ¹/₂ oz other ware	@	7/6	30. 63
16 ³/₄ oz Old Silver	@	6/8	18. 61
¹/₂ Doz Thimbles	@	24/	6. 00
¹/₂ Doz Dᵒ	@	18/	1. 50
Lot Goldsmiths Tools including Bellows		60/	10. 00
Old Gold & Stones		12/	2. 00
Sett New Gold Beads & Coral Dᵒ		30/	5. 00
Lot of Ear Drops &		36/	6. 00

Homes's dwelling house in Ann Street was valued at $7,000, and the total estate inventory came to $9,238.34.

Homes probably used the same marks (A–I) as his father, William Homes, Sr., and, because their careers overlapped, it can be difficult to separate the work of the father and the son. Additional initials marks (J–N) and a surname mark (o) found on pieces made about 1800 were probably used by the son alone. The younger Homes also appears to have used marks (B) and (I) more frequently than his father. Homes, Jr., made a fairly limited range of holloware forms. In addition to a large number of spoons, also attributed to him are beakers, canns, creampots, porringers, and a snuffbox. A strainer also bears the mark of Samuel Minott (q.v.). Homes advertised for apprentices in September 1784 and June 1792; he also requested a journeyman trained in "plating Buckles with hard solder" in June and July 1792.[22] His inventory indicates that he made flatware and small items like jewelry and thimbles, in addition to unspecified "other ware."[23] Homes purchased 915 strings of gold beads from the Ipswich silversmith Daniel Rogers (q.v.) between 1796 and 1800, paying for them with a combination of cash and gold.[24] DAF

SURVIVING OBJECTS

	Mark	Inscription	Patron	Date	Reference	Owner
Beaker	I or J	PRESENTED/TO/PARK-STREET CHURCH/BY/WILLIAM LADD/1809.	William Ladd and/or Park Street Church, Boston	1809	Jones 1913, 89	
Beaker	I or J	PRESENTED/TO/PARK-STREET CHURCH/BY/Josiah Bumstead 1809.	Josiah Bumstead and/or Park Street Church, Boston	1809	Jones 1913, 89	
Beaker	I or J	PRESENTED/TO/PARK-STREET CHURCH/BY/George J. Homer 1809.	George J. Homer and/or Park Street Church, Boston	1809	Jones 1913, 89	
Beaker	I or J	PRESENTED/TO/PARK-STREET CHURCH/BY/William Thurston 1809.	William Thurston and/or Park Street Church, Boston	1809	Jones 1913, 89	
Beaker	I or J	PRESENTED/TO/PARK-STREET CHURCH/BY/Daniel Baxter 1809.	Daniel Baxter and/or Park Street Church, Boston	1809	Jones 1913, 89	
Beaker	I or J	PRESENTED/TO/PARK-STREET CHURCH/BY/John E. Tyler 1809.	John E. Tyler and/or Park Street Church, Boston	1809	Jones 1913, 89	
Two beakers	?	?		ca. 1793	Antiques 79 (May 1961): 431	
Cann	G, H, I, J, K, L, M, or N	INB		ca. 1775	MFA 1911, no. 569	
Cann	?	R	Edward Hutchinson Robbins (?)	ca. 1785	Antiques 88 (August 1965): 139	
Creampot	A*	none		ca. 1810	DAPC 68.855	SI

	Mark	Inscription	Patron	Date	Reference	Owner
Creampot	A	?		ca. 1790	American Art Association–Anderson Galleries, 28–29 February 1936, lot 263	
Creampot	G, H, I, J, K, L, M, *or* N	CSC		ca. 1795	Sotheby Parke Bernet, 14 July 1981, 490	
Creampot	G, H, I, J, K, L, M, *or* N	TH		ca. 1770	DAPC 70.2551	AIC
Ladle	J†	none		ca. 1800	Eitner 1976, no. 69	
Ladle	O†	none		ca. 1770	Buhler/Hood 1970, no. 274	YUAG
Porringer §	E†	MC/to/DS		ca. 1785	Buhler 1972, no. 230 (as William Homes, Sr.)	MFAB
Porringer	G, H, I, J, K, L, M, *or* N	B		ca. 1790	YUAG files	
Porringer §	I†	M/IK		ca. 1765		WA
Porringer	?	Sam'l Whit'll	Samuel Whitwell (?)	ca. 1775	DAPC 68.5829	
Snuffbox	G, H, I, J, K, L, M, *or* N	?		ca. 1790	American Art Association–Anderson Galleries, 2–3 April 1937, lot 241	
Strainer § (*with mark of Samuel Minott*)	G, H, I, J, K, L, M, *or* N	none		ca. 1770	Hammerslough/Feigenbaum 1958–73, 3:92–93	
Tablespoon §	A*/G†	TC		ca. 1765	DAPC 72.1959	WM
Tablespoon §	B*	IB/to/IB/Dec.ʳ 2/1769 (+)	Belknap family	1769	YUAG files	
Tablespoon	B*	P/ER/to/LN		ca. 1790		HD
Tablespoon	B†	C/TH		ca. 1765	DAPC 72.1961	WM
Tablespoon §	D†	D/HE		ca. 1765		YUAG
Two tablespoons	G, H, I, *or* J	EB		ca. 1775	Bigelow 1917, 272–73	

	Mark	Inscription	Patron	Date	Reference	Owner
Two tablespoons	G, H, I, J, K, L, M, *or* N	WB		ca. 1790	YUAG files	
Tablespoon	L	LD		ca. 1810	DAPC 90.3042	
Tablespoon	O	IW; altered to IW/S/N		ca. 1775	DAPC 72.1957	WM
Teaspoon §	A†	IK		ca. 1770	YUAG files	
Teaspoon §	C†	IL		ca. 1765		YUAG
Six teaspoons	E*	RT		ca. 1795		YUAG
Teaspoon	F*	ML		ca. 1795		YUAG
Teaspoon	F*	MS		ca. 1795		HD
Two teaspoons	F*	P/WT		ca. 1795	Eitner 1976, nos. 75–76	
Teaspoon	F†	AJ		ca. 1795		HD
Teaspoon	G, H, I, J, K, L, M, *or* N	PC; 1777		1777	YUAG files	
Two teaspoons	G, H, I, J, K, L, M, *or* N	B		ca. 1790	YUAG files	
Teaspoon	H*	SC		ca. 1785		YUAG
Two teaspoons §	H†	W/IL		ca. 1765		YUAG
Teaspoon	J*	RB		ca. 1770	DAPC 85.2201	
Teaspoon	K*	H/BA		ca. 1800		HD
Two teaspoons	K*	SD		ca. 1810	Buhler 1972, appendix no. 39	MFAB
Two teaspoons	K†	PV		ca. 1795		YUAG
Teaspoon	K*	SDL; 1794 (later)		1810		LAM
Teaspoon	K	BB		ca. 1800	DAPC 86.2353	
Teaspoon	K*	EG		ca. 1795	DAPC 86.2350	
Two teaspoons	K	H/BA		ca. 1800	DAPC 68.4507–08	
Teaspoon	L*	IG		ca. 1770	DAPC 85.2198	
Teaspoon	L*	SG		ca. 1775	Eitner 1976, no. 70	
Two teaspoons	L†	SG		ca. 1775	Buhler/Hood 1970, no. 187 (as William Homes, Sr.)	YUAG
Teaspoon	L (?)	SG		ca. 1775	DAPC 85.2198	
Two teaspoons	M†	TSE		ca. 1815	Eitner 1976, nos. 71–72	
Teaspoon (mate below)	N†	AD; 2		ca. 1800	Eitner 1976, no. 73	

	Mark	Inscription	Patron	Date	Reference	Owner
Teaspoon (mate above)	N	AD; 5		ca. 1800	Eitner 1976, no. 74	
Teaspoon	?	?		?		CHS
Two-handled cup	C, D, E, *or* F	1769 (later)	First Congregational Church, Norwich, Conn.	ca. 1769	Jones 1913, 360	
Two-handled cup (attrib.)	none	1769 (later)	First Congregational Church, Norwich, Conn.	ca. 1769	Jones 1913, 360	
Two-handled cup (attrib.)	none	1769 (later)	First Congregational Church, Norwich, Conn.	ca. 1769	Jones 1913, 360	

§ Possibly made by William Homes, Sr.

1. RC 24:246; Roberts 1895, 2:139–40.
2. Tappan 1834, 119–28.
3. *Old South Church* 1883, 49; Roberts 1895, 2:139–40.
4. RC 30:51, 130, 438; RC 24:55, 102, 111.
5. SCPR 123:210–12; Thwing.
6. SCD 208:122–23.
7. Tappan 1834, 119–28.
8. Pruitt 1978, 20–21.
9. SCD 146:125–26.
10. RC 22:447.
11. RC 22:217.
12. RC 22:18; SCD 179:66–67. The other heirs of Newman Greenough included the housewright William Craft and the prominent Boston merchants Samuel and Nathaniel Greenough.
13. *Boston Directory* 1789, 24; 1796, 58; 1798, 65; Jackson/Teeples/Schaefermeyer 1976, *1810*, 176, 207, 213; *1820*, 77.
14. SCCR, Court of Common Pleas Extended Record Book, July 1783, 218; October 1783, 35; July 1785, 66.
15. Steinway 1960, 7.
16. Roberts 1895, 2:100.
17. Roberts 1895, 2:139–40, 165, 417.
18. Whitman 1842, 316.
19. SCPR 123:210–12.
20. SCPR 129:622–23; SCPR 129, part 2:318–19.
21. SCPR 123:344–46.
22. *Boston Gazette & Country Journal*, 13 September 1784; *Columbian Centinel*, 30 June, 7, 14 July 1792.
23. SCPR 123:346.
24. Daniel Rogers Account Book as cited in Ward 1984a, 200–01.

William Homes, Sr. 1716/17–85

A

B

William Homes, Sr., was the son of the mariner Robert Homes (1694–1727) and Mary (Franklin) Homes (b. 1694), who were married on 3 April 1716 by Rev. Ebenezer Pemberton.[1] Robert Homes was the master of a ship that traded between Boston and Philadelphia. Mary Franklin was the sister of the celebrated author, inventor, and patriot Benjamin Franklin. The silversmith's paternal grandfather was the Reverend William Homes (1663–1746), an Irish Presbyterian minister who emigrated to Chilmark, Martha's Vineyard, with his wife, Katherine Craghead (ca. 1672–1754), of Londonderry and his nine children in 1715.[2] The silversmith's maternal grandparents were Josiah (1655–1744) and Abiah (Folger) Franklin (1667–1752) of Boston.[3] Homes was born on 10 January 1716/17 and was baptized on 13 January 1716/17 in the Second

C

D

E

F

G

H

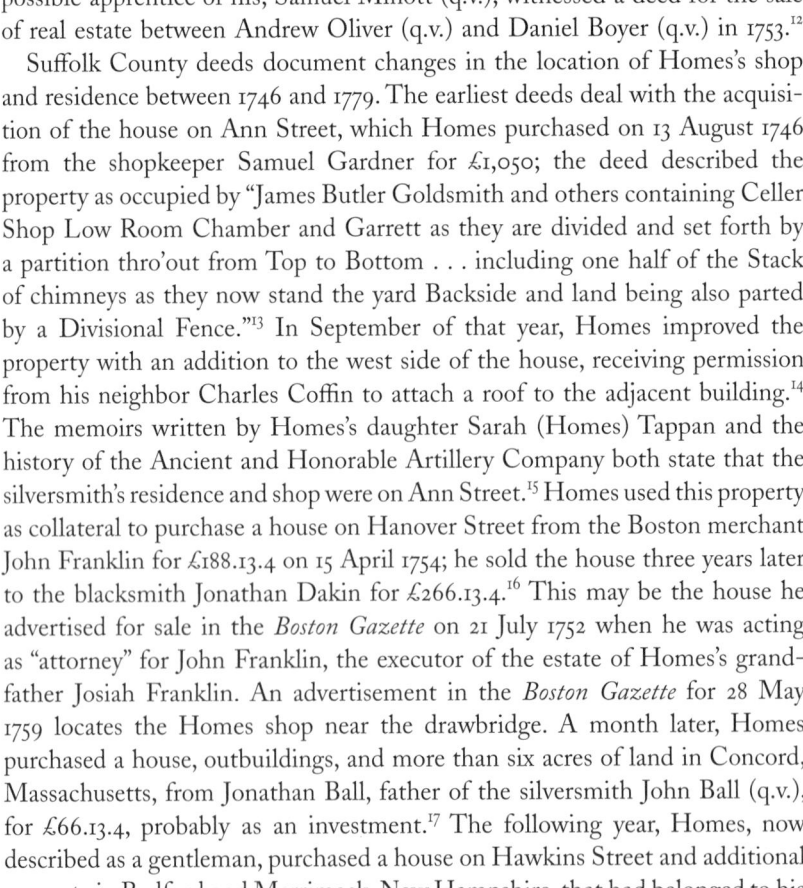

I

Church, Boston, the church he attended until 29 January 1748, when he joined the Old South Church.[4]

According to family genealogy, Homes apprenticed with Rufus Greene (q.v.) in his shop on Newbury Street.[5] He would have been fully trained by 1738. Homes apparently worked for Greene as a journeyman for about two years once his apprenticeship was completed. Greene recorded paying Homes £82.16.9 for work done in the year 1738. In 1739 he paid Homes £107.3.[6] In January 1739, "William Homes of Boston Goldsmith" ordered "Sundrys p day book" from the Boston silversmith Benjamin Greene (q.v.), Rufus Greene's brother.[7] He paid for his order on 9 May 1740 with a cash payment of £4.13.6. In October of the following year "William Homes, Goldsmith," appeared in the Suffolk County Court of Common Pleas to recover a debt of £9.15 from the mariner John Thomas.[8]

Homes married Rebecca Dawes (1717/18–87), daughter of Thomas (1680–1749/50), a mason, and Sarah (Storey) Dawes, on 24 April 1740 in a ceremony performed by Rev. Joseph Sewall.[9] The couple had fifteen children, many of whom died in infancy. Homes's extended family included several important Boston silversmiths. Two of his apprentices, Barnabas Webb (q.v.) and Benjamin Tappan (q.v.), married his daughters Mary (1740/41–1833) and Sarah (1748–1826), respectively.[10] Homes also trained his son, William Homes, Jr. (q.v.), as a silversmith. In addition, James Butler (q.v.) was a tenant in the house Homes purchased in 1746, and Daniel Henchman (q.v.) lived adjacent to property on Hawkins Street that Homes purchased in 1760.[11] Homes, along with another possible apprentice of his, Samuel Minott (q.v.), witnessed a deed for the sale of real estate between Andrew Oliver (q.v.) and Daniel Boyer (q.v.) in 1753.[12]

Suffolk County deeds document changes in the location of Homes's shop and residence between 1746 and 1779. The earliest deeds deal with the acquisition of the house on Ann Street, which Homes purchased on 13 August 1746 from the shopkeeper Samuel Gardner for £1,050; the deed described the property as occupied by "James Butler Goldsmith and others containing Celler Shop Low Room Chamber and Garret as they are divided and set forth by a partition thro'out from Top to Bottom . . . including one half of the Stack of chimneys as they now stand the yard Backside and land being also parted by a Divisional Fence."[13] In September of that year, Homes improved the property with an addition to the west side of the house, receiving permission from his neighbor Charles Coffin to attach a roof to the adjacent building.[14] The memoirs written by Homes's daughter Sarah (Homes) Tappan and the history of the Ancient and Honorable Artillery Company both state that the silversmith's residence and shop were on Ann Street.[15] Homes used this property as collateral to purchase a house on Hanover Street from the Boston merchant John Franklin for £188.13.4 on 15 April 1754; he sold the house three years later to the blacksmith Jonathan Dakin for £266.13.4.[16] This may be the house he advertised for sale in the Boston Gazette on 21 July 1752 when he was acting as "attorney" for John Franklin, the executor of the estate of Homes's grandfather Josiah Franklin. An advertisement in the Boston Gazette for 28 May 1759 locates the Homes shop near the drawbridge. A month later, Homes purchased a house, outbuildings, and more than six acres of land in Concord, Massachusetts, from Jonathan Ball, father of the silversmith John Ball (q.v.), for £66.13.4, probably as an investment.[17] The following year, Homes, now described as a gentleman, purchased a house on Hawkins Street and additional property in Bedford and Merrimack, New Hampshire, that had belonged to his wife's father. Because this property had been inherited by seventeen children, grandchildren, and great-grandchildren of Dawes, ten deeds between January 1760 and November 1761 were required before the silversmith and his wife gained title.[18]

Sarah (Homes) Tappan stated that her father pursued a career as a merchant and turned over responsibility for the silver shop to his son, William Homes, Jr., in 1763, when the younger man had completed his training.[19] William Homes, Sr., purchased property in nine transactions between 1764 and 1768 to serve his expanded mercantile ventures, including a brick house and land on Eliot Street, land in Williams's Court, and a warehouse and wharf near the town dock.[20] He sold the house, barn, outbuildings, and land in Williams's Court for £533 on 3 April 1770 to the Boston merchants Jonathan and John Amory.[21] That same year, the silversmith and his wife received £400 from Nathaniel Davenport of Milton, Massachusetts, for a house and barn on seventy-five acres in West Milton.[22] Seven years later, in May 1777, the silversmith sold the house in Hawkins Street to the merchant Joshua Loring for £300 just prior to his move to Norton, Massachusetts, in Bristol County.[23] Two years later, "William Homes, Esq.," of Norton mortgaged the warehouse site and the house on Ann Street, containing "Cellar, Shop, 2 lower rooms, 3 chambers and garretts," to Gideon Batty of Eastham for £3,033.6.8.[24]

Homes was prosperous and held a responsible position in the community. He served as an attorney for the estate of his grandfather, Josiah Franklin, following the death of his grandmother in 1752.[25] On 28 October 1756, "William Homes, Gentleman," served as the attorney for his uncle Wilmot Wass of Chilmark, Dukes County, in the sale of Wass's property in South Boston.[26] Homes loaned money to several neighbors: £157.14.6 in June 1757 to the blacksmith Jonathan Dakin, who lived on the corner of Union and Hanover streets, and £186 in January 1768 to the housewright Jacob Thayer of Williams Court.[27]

Homes was very active in the civic and military affairs of Boston. He joined the Ancient and Honorable Artillery Company on 5 September 1747 with Ebenezer Storer and Thomas Stoddard as sureties.[28] Homes was elected first sergeant in 1752, fourth sergeant in 1754, lieutenant in 1761, and captain in 1765.[29] He held many public offices, serving Boston as clerk of the market in 1753, 1754, and 1763, warden in 1764, purchaser of grain from 1766 through 1770, surveyor of the highways from 1767 through 1769, fire-ward from 1764 through 1770; he was also a member of various committees in 1762, 1764, 1765, 1766, 1768, 1769, and 1770 to boycott the purchase of lamb in compliance with various nonimportation agreements, inspect the town and the public schools, and settle land disputes involving eminent domain.[30] Homes served as a justice of the peace before the Revolution.[31] He paid a fine in lieu of military service during the draft of 1776, a decision probably influenced by his age.[32]

Homes died of dysentery in June 1785 while on a visit to Boston, where he had been staying as a guest in the Newbury Street house of his son-in-law, Barnabas Webb.[33] His widow, Rebecca Homes, returned to Boston to live with her son, William Homes, Jr., until her death in 1787.[34] William and Rebecca Homes are buried in the Chapel Burying Ground on Tremont Street.[35]

Homes used a surname mark (A) as well as an initial and surname mark (B) on his work. Initials marks with pellets (C, D, E, F) and without pellets (G, H, I) are also attributed to him.[36] Because William Homes's working dates overlap those of his son William Homes, Jr., pieces bearing these marks might be the work of the son if their style indicates they date from his working period. A considerable number of works survive that are marked Homes (A) and that date on the basis of style to the 1740s and 1750s. These can be attributed to Homes, Sr., with some certainty and include predominantly spoons, canns, tankards, and porringers. A gold mourning ring made for the funeral of Sarah Holt in 1743 and a beaker presented to the First Parish Church of Milton in 1747 are the earliest dated objects by this silversmith. The presence of a Homes mark over that of Andrew Tyler (q.v.) on a porringer in the Cleveland Museum of Art may indicate that Homes made repairs to the Tyler porringer or retailed the porringer in his shop. Tyler died in 1741, so a partnership with Homes is unlikely. However, a strainer marked by both Homes and his colleague Samuel Minott suggests a collaboration between these two silversmiths. In addition to a diverse clientele within Boston, Homes produced silver for churches in Lexington and Andover, Massachusetts, and Fairfield, Connecticut. DAF

SURVIVING OBJECTS

	Mark	Inscription	Patron	Date	Reference	Owner
Beaker	G, H, *or* I	The Gift/of the Wido Eliz^a Wadsworth/Relict of Deac^n/ John Wadsworth/TO/THE/ CHURCH OF CHRIST/IN/ MILTON/1747	Elizabeth (Vose) Wadsworth and/or First Congregational Parish, Milton, Mass.	1747	Jones 1913, 291	
Cann	A	?		ca. 1755	Parke-Bernet, 4 January 1940, lot 58	
Cann	A*	I/TK		ca. 1750		RISD
Cann	B*	none		ca. 1765	DAPC 90.3026	
Cann	B	initials erased		ca. 1750	Christie's, 17–18 January 1992, lot 164	
Cann	B*/I*	JAD		ca. 1750	DAPC 89.3033	
Cann	C, D, E, *or* F	D/WM	William and Martha (Crocker) Davis (?)	ca. 1755	YUAG files	
Cann	C, D, E, *or* F	unidentified arms		ca. 1760	Washington 1925, no. 53	
Cann	G*	unidentified arms, a fess gules indented between 3 lions' faces crowned, and crest, a demi-griffin holding a sword, impaling Winslow arms, on a bend gules 6 lozenges or		ca. 1760	Buhler/Hood 1970, no. 185	YUAG
Cann	G*	P/WK; depiction of a cannon and the British flag; Louisbourg./June, 17./ 1745.		ca. 1745		PEM

	Mark	*Inscription*	*Patron*	*Date*	*Reference*	*Owner*
Cann	?	unidentified initials		ca. 1755	Parke-Bernet, 5–7 November 1959, lot 466	
Cann	?	?		ca. 1765	Christie's, 26 January 1985, lot 73	
Cann	?	?		ca. 1740	*Antiques* 58 (August 1950): 84	
Caster	A	B/LL	Bradford family (?)	ca. 1760		MFAB
Caster	G, H, *or* I	CE/T		ca. 1760	YUAG files	
Caster	?	?		1739	*Antiques* 91 (May 1967): 579	
Caster	?	C/HA; TH (later)		ca. 1765	Christie's, 13 October 1983, lot 57	
Creampot	G, H, *or* I	SB		ca. 1760	YUAG files	
Ladle	G	?		ca. 1760	Levy 4:33	
Milk pot	I*	S/WK		ca. 1750	DAPC 68.6154	MMA
Mourning ring (gold)	F†	Sarah/Holt/Ob:/24 Sep:/1743/Aet:/29	Sarah Holt	1743	Eitner 1976, no. 50	
Porringer	A	IQ/to/HQ	Josiah Quincy and/or Hannah Quincy	ca. 1760	Buhler 1972, no. 545	MFAB
Porringer	B	KW/1760	Katherine Whitwell	ca. 1760	MFA 1911, no. 564	
Porringer *(with mark of Andrew Tyler?)*	B*/ G*(?)	D/WL		ca. 1740	Johnston 1994, 73	CMA
Porringer	C, D, E, *or* F	PR		ca. 1765	American Art Association–Anderson Galleries, 22–23 January 1937, lot 291	
Porringer §	E†	MC/to/DS		ca. 1750	Buhler 1972, no. 230	MFAB
Porringer	G, H, *or* I	HP	Paine family	ca. 1775	MFA 1911, no. 577	
Porringer	G, H, *or* I	WER		ca. 1760	YUAG files	
Porringer §	I†	M/IK		ca. 1750		WA
Porringer	I	S/DS; W/IA		ca. 1760	Sotheby's, 23–24 June 1994, lot 95	
Porringer	I*	?		ca. 1750	DAPC 72.2094	
Porringer spoon	C	G/IH (+)	Joshua and Hannah (Storer) Green	ca. 1765	Buhler 1972, appendix no. 36	MFAB

	Mark	Inscription	Patron	Date	Reference	Owner
Punch bowl	A*/C*	Dawes arms, argent on a bend azure cotised gules between 6 battle-axes erect 3 swans, and crest, a halberd erect on the point a flying dragon without legs, tail nowed bezantée vulned; The Gift/of the Field Officers and/Captains of the Regiment/of the Town of BOSTON to/THOMAS DAWES Esq.r/for his past Services as Ad/jutant to said Re/giment Sep.t 14/1763	Officers and Captains of the Boston Regiment for Thomas Dawes	1763	Buhler 1972, no. 231	MFAB
Salt	?	?		ca. 1750	*Antiques* 114 (October 1978): 827	
Serving spoon	A	unidentified crest, a talbot's head collared and erased		ca. 1745	Hammerslough/Feigenbaum 1958–73, 4:107	
Serving spoon	C	B/IH		ca. 1750	Buhler 1972, appendix no. 38	MFAB
Strainer§ *(with mark of Samuel Minott)*	G, H, or I	none		ca. 1770	Hammerslough/Feigenbaum 1958–73, 3:92–93	
Sugar bowl	A	J·Tyler	J. Tyler	ca. 1760	Gourley 1965, no. 98	CGA
Sugar tongs	G*	AI to/MM		ca. 1760	Buhler/Hood 1970, no. 186	YUAG
Two tablespoons	A*	EP/1757		1757	Johnston 1994, 72	CMA
Tablespoon§	A*/ G†	TC		ca. 1765	DAPC 72.1959	WM
Tablespoon§	B*	IB/to/IB/Dec.r: 2/ 1769 (+)	Belknap family	1769	YUAG files	
Tablespoon	B*	SW		ca. 1750	Johnston 1994, 72	CMA
Tablespoon	B*	C/IR		ca. 1740	Johnston 1994, 74 (as unknown maker)	CMA
Tablespoon	B†	C/TH		ca. 1765	DAPC 72.1961	WM
Tablespoon§	D†	D/HE		ca. 1755		YUAG
Tablespoon	H*	W/BM (+)		ca. 1745		YUAG

	Mark	Inscription	Patron	Date	Reference	Owner
Tankard	A	Ex Dono/Sturgis Lewis/1753	Lothrop Lewis, executor of Sturgis Lewis's estate, for Congregational Church, Fairfield, Conn.	ca. 1753	Jones 1913, 174	
Tankard	A	This is a gift of Thomas/Hill Esqʳ to the Church of/Christ in the First Society/in Fairfield/1757	Thomas Hill and/or Congregational Church, Fairfield, Conn.	ca. 1757	Jones 1913, 174	
Tankard	A	The Gift of/Capᵗ. Timʸ Johnson/to the First Church/of Christ in Andover/Janʸ 1761	Timothy Johnson and/or North Parish of North Andover, North Andover, Mass.	1761	Jones 1913, 348	
Tankard	A	THD		ca. 1760	*Silver Supplement* 1973, no. 47	
Tankard	A	PRESENTED/by/Deacon Willᵐ Tompson Esqʳ/to the/CHURCH OF CHRIST/in/BILLERICA	William Tompson and/or First Parish Church, Billerica, Mass.	ca. 1760	YUAG files	
Tankard	A*	none		ca. 1750	Bartlett 1984, 12–13	SLAM
Tankard	C, D, E, *or* F	The Gift of/Rachel Buterfield/to the Church of Christ/in Lexington	Rachel Butterfield and/or First Congregational Society, Lexington, Mass.	ca. 1750	Jones 1913, 246–47	
Tankard	D*	W/ES		ca. 1760	Buhler/Hood 1970, no. 184	YUAG
Tankard	G *or* I	Belknap arms, azure 3 eagles displayed on a bend cortised, and crest, a hound passant; D,W/WC	Belknap family	ca. 1750	*Antiques* 110 (July 1976): 36	
Tankard	G, H, *or* I	P/TL		ca. 1760	YUAG files	
Tankard	?	?		ca. 1745	Parke-Bernet, 27 January 1967, lot 30	
Teaspoon	A*	ED		ca. 1760		YUAG
Teaspoon §	A†	IK		ca. 1765	YUAG files	
Teaspoon §	C†	IL		ca. 1755		YUAG
Teaspoon	E	D/WM (+)	William and Mehitable Dawes	ca. 1770	Buhler 1972, appendix no. 37	MFAB
Teaspoon	G*	RT		ca. 1770		HD
Teaspoon	H*	IP		ca. 1765		YUAG

	Mark	Inscription	Patron	Date	Reference	Owner
Two teaspoons §	H†	W/IL		ca. 1755		YUAG
Teaspoon	?	?		ca. 1760	*Antiques* 38 (October 1940): 148	

§ Possibly made by William Homes, Jr.

1. Roberts 1895, 2:45; RC 28:64; "Diary of Rev. William Homes," *NEHGR* 48:446–48; 50:161.
2. *NEHGR* 14:186; Tappan 1834, 119–28; "Diary of Rev. William Homes," *NEHGR* 48:446–47; *Chilmark VR*, 87.
3. Codman 1918, 102; *Nantucket VR* 1:465; 3:439, 481.
4. Robbins 1852, 254; *Old South Church* 1883, 38, 44; RC 24:114. Rebecca Dawes joined Old South Church on 8 February 1735.
5. Tappan 1834, 119–28.
6. Rufus Greene Account Book, 1728–48, n.p., Karolik–Codman Papers, MHS.
7. Benjamin Greene Ledger, 1734–56, 78, MHS.
8. SCCR, Court of Common Pleas Extended Record Book, October 1741, 209.
9. RC 28:3, 215; RC 24:126; *Index of Obituaries, 1784–1840*, 3:2290; *Index of Obituaries, 1704–1800*, 1:88; SCPR 43:455–59; RC 9:151; Boston Deaths, 1700–1800.
10. RC 24:240.
11. SCD 72:137–39; 73:22–23; 97:13.
12. SCD 82:52–53.
13. SCD 73:22–23; 72:137–39.
14. SCD 72:140.
15. Tappan 1834, 119–28; Roberts 1895, 2:46.
16. SCD 85:63–65. Homes arranged a mortgage on the Ann Street property house with the Boston baker John White for £133.6.8 on 12 May 1755. SCD 87:39; 90:111–12, 118–19.
17. MCD 56:634–35.
18. SCD 93:201–02; 97:12–16, 67–68.
19. Tappan 1834, 119–28.
20. SCD 101:173–74; 104:175–76; 110:36; 111:221–22, 222–23, 249–50; 113:268–69; 206:168–69.
21. SCD 116:233–34.
22. SCD 116:234–35.
23. SCD 127:267–68.
24. SCD 131:199–201.
25. *Boston Gazette*, 21 July 1752.
26. SCD 89:139–40.
27. SCD 111:250–51.
28. Roberts 1895, 2:45–46.
29. Roberts 1895, 2:60, 64, 104, 124.
30. RC 16:105, 163, 168, 199, 204, 233, 235, 266, 270, 285, 290; RC 18:6, 11, 13, 47; Roberts 1895, 2:45–46; Drake 1856, 756.
31. Tappan 1834, 119–28.
32. Roberts 1895, 2:187–88.
33. Tappan 1834, 119–28; *Index of Obituaries, 1704–1800*, 1:160.
34. Tappan 1834, 119–28; *Index of Obituaries, 1784–1840*, 3:2290.
35. Tappan 1834, 119–28.
36. A miniature salver at HD marked W·H has been attributed to him, but the attribution is doubtful because the form is atypical for Boston and the mark does not correspond with others given to Homes; see Flynt/Fales 1968, 108.

John Hull
1624–83

A

B

C

The earliest surviving piece of New England silver was made by John Hull. For that reason and because he was appointed mintmaster of the Massachusetts Bay Colony in 1652, he has received considerable attention in the literature.[1] Hermann F. Clarke's important monograph *John Hull: A Builder of the Bay Colony* (1940) drew upon the unusually rich archival material, including diaries, account books, and letter books, that documents the events of Hull's life.[2]

Hull was born in Market Hareborough, Leicestershire, England, about 18 December 1624.[3] He came to Boston in New England in 1635 with his father, Robert Hull (1593–1666), a blacksmith, and mother, Elizabeth Storer (d. 1646), widow of Paul Storer.[4] According to his own account, Hull was trained as a goldsmith by his half-brother, Richard Storer (q.v.), probably between 1639, when Storer arrived in New England, and about 1646, when he probably had returned home.

During the years between his majority in 1645 and his partnership with Robert Sanderson, Sr. (q.v.), in 1652, Hull laid the groundwork for a successful life in Boston. In 1647 he married Judith Quincy (1626–95), the daughter of his recently remarried stepmother, Judith (Pares) Quincy (d. 1654), and Edmund Quincy (1602–35), a founder of Braintree, Massachusetts. Hull's wife was also a stepdaughter of Moses Paine (d. 1643).[5] The next year Hull became a member of Boston's First Church, a central event in the life of a seventeenth-century Puritan because it acknowledged being one of God's elect.[6] Within a short time Hull was a corporal in the military company of Maj. Edward Gibbons and was made a freeman of Massachusetts Bay.[7] By 1650 he engaged in trading in the transatlantic import-export business, an activity he was to continue throughout his life.[8]

On 26/27 May 1652 the General Court of the Massachusetts Bay Colony established a mint for coining silver money to ensure that the colony had a reliable medium of exchange. John Hull persuaded the court to make Robert Sanderson his partner. The partners were appointed on 10 June 1652 and were sworn as mintmasters the following day.[9] The partners ran this lucrative venture until their last contract expired in 1682. The coins the two produced, generally referred to as pine tree shillings, have been analyzed by Sydney Noe.[10] The sixteen-foot-square building that housed the mint was built on land owned by John Hull, and the partners probably also did their silversmithing there. As Hull's son-in-law Samuel Sewall later wrote in 1712/13, however, "the Business of the Mint was managed by itself, and the Account kept distinct."[11]

Hull trained a number of apprentices to be goldsmiths, one of whom was John Sanderson (q.v.), one of his partner's sons. When Hull wrote in his diary of John's death in the fall of 1658, he identified him as, "My boy, John Sanderson."[12] Hull's partner's other sons, Joseph, Benjamin, and Robert, Jr. (qq.v.), probably also trained in the shop. On 1 July 1659, Hull accepted Jeremiah Dummer and Samuel Paddy (qq.v.) as apprentices, noting, "I received into my house Jeremie Dummer & Samuel Paddy to Serve me as Apprentices eight years." About 1664, when Hull's nephew Daniel Quincy (q.v.) was fourteen years of age, he too may have begun an apprenticeship in the shop Hull ran with his partner, Robert Sanderson, Sr., although Quincy had been living in the Hull household before then. About 1668 Timothy Dwight (q.v.) began his training in the Hull and Sanderson shop, followed by Samuel Clarke (q.v.) in 1673. He may also have trained John Hall, Thomas Savage, Sr., and Samuel Phillips (qq.v.), although no evidence of these apprenticeships exists.

Hull's day-to-day participation in the shop was limited by his burgeoning mercantile activities and civic responsibilities. In addition to preparing shipments of goods to London each fall, Hull was elected annually as one of Boston's selectmen for ten years beginning in March 1656/57 (except in 1661/62, when he traveled to England to help negotiate the renewal of the Massachusetts Bay Charter). Beginning in 1658, Hull's fellow selectmen also elected him town treasurer.[13]

Hull bought vast amounts of real estate as well as investing capital in the yearly shipment of goods to London.[14] His most ambitious acquisition was the Pettiquamscut Purchase, a tract, which roughly corresponded with what is today South Kingston, Rhode Island, including Boston and Point Judith necks, that several influential men banded together to buy from Rhode Island's Narragansett Indians beginning in 1656/57.[15] In 1660 he became a member of the Ancient and Honorable Artillery Company, an organization that included almost all the Bay area's merchants.[16] Not only did Hull increasingly associate with merchants, but he also frequently began to be called one, instead of goldsmith, in legal documents.[17]

A schism within Boston's First Church led to the founding of the Third Church in 1669. The necessity of finding a minister for the new church sent Hull back to England that year, a trip that probably helped him cement relations with the London merchants so vital to his participation in transatlantic trade. In addition to textiles, Hull imported ironware, some in the form of silversmiths' tools. In 1671 he imported goldsmiths' files, some of which he charged the shop for and some of which he sold to Jeremiah Dummer. In 1675 he charged the shop £5.0.6 for "12 iron potts 3 lbs small wyer"; in 1677 he charged the shop for 21 pounds of quicksilver at 5 shillings an ounce.[18]

His transatlantic trips also kept Hull in touch with the London goldsmiths' trade. In 1671 he wrote to his London cousin Edward Hull that he was sending three pieces of gold "to bestow in Corrall for Childrens whissells not of the largest but of a midle sort," advising him to go to "Mr. Dixson" (perhaps the goldsmith George Dixon to whom Robert Sanderson had much earlier consigned his apprentice William Rawlings upon leaving London in 1638).[19] A year later Hull directed his cousin to Robert Jerrald in London's Foster Lane to buy goldsmiths' tools.[20]

Hull rarely referred to the sale of objects from the shop in his business papers, although he did record selling a ring to Richard Smith in 1671, a silver whistle to William Brenton in 1672, a dram cup to Thomas Temple the next year, gold rings and a bodkin to Joseph Eliot in 1674, and sixteen gold rings for the funeral of Samuel Symonds in 1678.[21] These scattered references suggest that the shop produced many small wares, such as rings and whistles, although most of the surviving work is larger pieces of holloware.

Another aspect of Hull's business was buying old pieces of silver and gold, some of which he may have resold, but most of which apparently were melted down. A court case of 1674 reveals that Andrew Edmunds and Joseph Waters stole a porringer from Benjamin Gibbs and that "part whereof was sold at Mr. Hull's shop valued at twelve shillings."[22] Hull also often bought large quantities of plate or silver for coinage at the mint, purchasing them from New Englanders and others engaged in the Caribbean trade.[23] In addition to producing silverware and coins and conducting mercantile activities, Hull entered an agreement with several others in 1673 to build a gunpowder mill in Neponset.[24]

Beginning in 1671 Hull advanced to high levels of the colony's government. He was elected a member of the General Court and served on the committee for King Philip's War, eventually becoming the war's treasurer.[25] In 1676 he was made treasurer of the colony, a post he held until he was made an assistant of the General Court in 1680. He died intestate on 30 September 1683.

Only one piece of silver bearing Hull's mark (A) alone survives, the beaker he made before entering his partnership with Sanderson. The rest of his surviving work was made in cooperation with Sanderson and bears either mark (A) or one of Hull's other two marks (B, C). The wealth of manuscript material that survives for Hull provides unusual insight into the workings of a seventeenth-century colonial silver shop, and the number of native-born craftsmen trained in his shop attests to his importance as a founder of goldsmithing in Massachusetts. PEK

SURVIVING OBJECTS

	Mark	Inscription	Patron	Date	Reference	Owner
Beaker	A†	T/BC		ca. 1650	Clarke 1940, no. 1	
Beaker (with mark of Robert Sanderson, Sr.)	B*	WR/TR/1670; Richards arms (later)	Welthian Richards	ca. 1660	Parke-Bernet, 10 November 1970, lot 135	
Beaker (with mark of Robert Sanderson, Sr.)	B*	Belonging to the First/Church of Christ in/Marblehead 1728 (later)		ca. 1665	Clarke 1940, no. 6	
Beaker (with mark of Robert Sanderson, Sr.)	B†	T/BC; 1659	First Church, Boston	1659	Clarke 1940, no. 2	
Beaker (with mark of Robert Sanderson, Sr.)	C†	IP; The Gift of/Mʳ Daniel Perren . . . (later) (+)		ca. 1675	Buhler/Hood 1970, no. 4	YUAG
Beaker (with mark of Robert Sanderson, Sr.)	C*	Property/of the/OLD SOUTH CHURCH (later)		ca. 1675	Clarke 1940, no. 4	
Two beakers (with mark of Robert Sanderson, Sr.)	C*	The Gift of L/TA (+)	Henry Leadbetter, executor of Thomas Lake's estate, for First Church, Dorchester, Mass.	ca. 1679	Clarke 1940, no. 3	
Beaker (with mark of Robert Sanderson, Sr.)	?	?		ca. 1660	YUAG files	
Caudle cup (with mark of Robert Sanderson, Sr.)	B*	EC; PM (+)		ca. 1660	Safford 1983, 6–7	
Caudle cup (with mark of Robert Sanderson, Sr.)	B*	C/AE (+)	Augustine and Elizabeth Clement	ca. 1665	Clarke 1940, no. 8	
Caudle cup (with marks of Robert Sanderson, Sr., and Jeremiah Dummer)	C*	FC	First Church of Christ, Congregational, Farmington, Conn.	ca. 1670	Clarke 1940, no. 7	

	Mark	Inscription	Patron	Date	Reference	Owner
Caudle cup (with mark of Robert Sanderson, Sr.)	c*	The gift of Eliezer Moody to the Church in Dedham, 1720 (later)	Eliezer Moody	ca. 1675	Buhler 1956, no. 83	
Caudle cup (with mark of Robert Sanderson, Sr.)	c*	ED; BB (+)	Beriah Bright	ca. 1671	Buhler 1972, no. 4	MFAB
Caudle cup (with mark of Robert Sanderson, Sr.)	c*	T/WD; Dorothea 1891 (later)		ca. 1675	Buhler 1972, no. 5	MFAB
Dram cup (with mark of Robert Sanderson, Sr.)	B*	D/DP	Daniel and Patience Dennison	ca. 1660	Parks 1958, no. 1	
Dram cup (with mark of Robert Sanderson, Sr.)	B*	RB (later)		ca. 1670	Buhler/Hood 1970, no. 1	YUAG
Dram cup (with mark of Robert Sanderson, Sr.)	c*	C/IE; H/IM (later)		ca. 1675	Buhler 1972, no. 3	MFAB
Dram cup (with mark of Robert Sanderson, Sr.)	c*	G/IA	Rev. Joseph and Ann (Waldron) Gerrish	ca. 1675	Buhler 1972, no. 6	MFAB
Porringer (with mark of Robert Sanderson, Sr.)	B*	M/AI; M. B. LEM. (later) (+)	Arthur and Johannah (Parker) Mason	ca. 1670	Buhler 1972, no. 2	MFAB
Porringer (with mark of Robert Sanderson, Sr.)	c*	V/IM; WF (later)	Isaac and Mary (Balston) Vergoose	ca. 1675	Quimby 1995, no. 76	WM
Tablespoon (with mark of Robert Sanderson, Sr.)	A*	P/BM		ca. 1655	Quimby 1995, no. 77	WM
Tablespoon (with mark of Robert Sanderson, Sr.)	B*	1667/RB (+)		1667	Johnston 1994, 77	CMA
Tablespoon (with mark of Robert Sanderson, Sr.)	B*	H/EA	Edward and Abigail (Button) Hutchinson	ca. 1670	Buhler/Hood 1970, no. 3	YUAG
Tablespoon (with mark of Robert Sanderson, Sr.)	B*	B/WH	William and Hannah (Corwin) Browne	ca. 1670	Fales 1983, 8–9	PEM
Tablespoon (with mark of Robert Sanderson, Sr.)	c*	F/CM		ca. 1675	YUAG files	
Tablespoon (with mark of Robert Sanderson, Sr.)	c*	MY		ca. 1675		MFAB
Tankard (with mark of Robert Sanderson, Sr.)	B*	BL (later) (+)	Simon Lynde (?)	ca. 1665	Clarke 1940, no. 26	
Wine cup (with mark of Robert Sanderson, Sr.)	B*	T/BC; 1661; The Gift of A Fri^{c}nd: RH	Robert Hull	ca. 1660	Clarke 1940, no. 14	

	Mark	Inscription	Patron	Date	Reference	Owner
Wine cup (with mark of Robert Sanderson, Sr.)	B*	Property/of the/OLD SOUTH CHURCH (later)		ca. 1660	Clarke 1940, no. 19	
Wine cup (with mark of Robert Sanderson, Sr.)	B*	F/RE; H/GH (later)	Richard and Elizabeth Fairbanks	ca. 1660	Clarke 1940, no. 16	
Wine cup (with mark of Robert Sanderson, Sr.)	B*	B/RA	Richard and Alice Brackett	ca. 1660	Clarke 1940, no. 20	
Wine cup (with mark of Robert Sanderson, Sr.)	B*	The Gift of william Needham to Brantry Church 1688 (later)	William Needham	ca. 1660	Clarke 1940, no. 21	
Wine cup (with mark of Robert Sanderson, Sr.)	B*	TC (altered to The Gift of a Friende TC); T/BC (later)	Thomas Clarke	ca. 1660	Clarke 1940, no. 15	
Wine cup (with mark of Robert Sanderson, Sr.)	B*	Cap.ᵗ Willets' donation to,/yᵉ Ch: of Rehᵒboth, 1674, (later)	Thomas Willet	ca. 1670	Buhler/Hood 1970, no. 2	YUAG
Three wine cups (with mark of Robert Sanderson, Sr.)	C*	The Gift of Jnᵒ Oxenbridg	First Church, Boston, for Rev. John Oxenbridge	ca. 1675	Clarke 1940, no. 17	

1. Fairbanks/Trent 1982, 2:144.
2. One diary is the so-called Private Diary, which Hull began about 1654 and entitled "Some Passages of God's Providence about Myself and in Relation to Myself; Penned down that I May be more mindful of, and Thankful for, All God's Dispensations Towards Me"; the second is the so-called Public Diary, begun about 1649 and entitled "Some Observable Passages of Providence Toward the Country"; now at AAS. A letter book of Hull's pertaining to business transactions covers the period 4 August 1671 to 18 August 1683 (AAS). Four volumes of account books or ledgers cover the period from 1671 to 1680, with a fifth volume that is an index (NEHGS). A ledger that belonged to Samuel Sewall contains twelve leaves not sewn in pertaining to John Hull (NEHGS). Notes by Hull on Boston sermons delivered between 1671 and 1679 are at MHS.
3. John Hull, Private Diary, fol. 2r, AAS.
4. Savage 1860–62, 2:494–95.
5. "Hull Diaries," 143; Savage 1860–62, 3:333–34, 500; RC 9:225.
6. Pierce 1961, 39, 50.
7. "Hull Diaries," 145; Shurtleff 1853, 2:295.
8. Indications of Hull's mercantile activities occur as early as 17 April 1650, when the London merchant John Parris drew a bill of exchange for twenty pounds to be paid to John Hull, who in turn assigned it to Daniel Hoare; see RC 32:336.
9. Mass. Archives 100:40a.
10. See Noe 1943, Noe 1947, and Noe 1952.
11. Letter from Samuel Sewall to William Vaughan at Portsmouth, 5 January 1712/13, *Sewall Letter Book* 2:9–10.
12. "Hull Diaries," 148.
13. RC 2:134, 143, 144, 150, 154, 155; RC 7:1, 5, 14, 15, 20, 21, 24, 25, 30, 34.
14. His purchases included a 280-acre farm in Braintree in 1657, *Suffolk Deeds* 3:71–72; 1,000 acres of land in Massachusetts in 1658/59, *Suffolk Deeds* 3:202–03; a 300-acre farm in Medfield, perhaps also acquired in 1659, "Hull Diaries," 149; a warehouse in Boston in 1659/60, *Suffolk Deeds* 11:55–57; more land in June 1661, *Suffolk Deeds* 10:22–24; a tract between Boston and Braintree in June 1663, *Suffolk Deeds* 10:25–26; 12:173–74; 200 acres in Braintree in October 1663, *Suffolk Deeds* 4:155–56; and another 200 acres in Braintree the following December, *Suffolk Deeds* 4:165–66.

15. Clark 1940, 87–88; Potter 1835, 275–99. On 20 January 1656/57 Hull and Samuel Wilbor, John Porter, Samuel Wilson, and Thomas Mumford made initial purchase of a tract of land from the Narragansett Indians in Rhode Island called Pettequamscut. Subsequent purchases were made on 29 January 1657, 20 March 1657, 24 June 1660, and 25 February 1661. The group of partners ultimately included William Brenton and Benedict Arnold. In his diary Hull records accounts of two extended trips dealing with this land, one of about nine days in July 1659 and another of four days in August 1661; "Hull Diaries," 150–53.

16. Roberts 1895, 1:193–94.

17. *Suffolk Deeds* 4:155, 165.

18. John Hull Ledger, vol. 1, fols. 26v, 31r, 133v, NEHGS.

19. Hull Letter Book, 16 October 1671.

20. Hull Letter Book, 96.

21. Hull Letter Book 1:18; John Hull Ledger, vol. 1, fols. 13v, 37v, 74r, 85v, 134r, NEHGS.

22. Colonial Society 1933, 29:486.

23. For a standard order, see Hull to William Pulford, Hull Letter Book, 25 June 1672.

24. *NEHGR* 31:272–76.

25. Shurtleff 1853, 5:44.

Thomas Hunt
1753–1812

Thomas Hunt was born in Northampton, Massachusetts, on 25 March 1753, the son of Capt. John Hunt (1712–85) and Esther Wells (ca. 1720–87) of Northampton, who were married there about 1743.[1] Hunt's paternal grandparents were Jonathan Hunt, Jr. (1665/66–1738), of Northampton and Martha Williams (1671–1751) of Pomfret, Connecticut; his maternal grandparents are unknown.[2] Because Hunt would have been in his early twenties at the start of the revolutionary war, he may have been the private Thomas Hunt from the Hampshire County militia who served in the war during 1777.[3]

Although his master remains unknown, Thomas Hunt was the first of several men in his family to become silversmiths. Hunt would have been old enough to train the younger members of his family in the craft, including his brother Jared (1760–1812), who became a silversmith in Northampton and died insolvent.[4] Moreover, Jared's two sons-in-law were the silversmiths Nathan Storrs (1768–1839) and Nathaniel Fowle, Jr. (w. 1815–33), and Thomas Hunt's cousin was Joseph Hunt Breck (1766–1801), whose inventory at his death recorded many silversmithing tools.[5]

In 1779, at the age of twenty-six, Hunt left Northampton to purchase four acres of land in Springfield, Massachusetts, identifying himself as a goldsmith of that town. Three years later, he married Sarah Gray (1753–88) of Stockbridge, Massachusetts, daughter of Rev. James Gray (d. 1782) and Sarah Spring (1736/37–1809) of Stockbridge.[6]

Hunt may have practiced as a silversmith for about six years, dating from his first land purchase in 1779 until 1785. Shortly after the death of his father, John Hunt, on 9 January 1785, Hunt may have decided to end his years of silversmithing in Springfield. An advertisement placed on 1 February 1785 by the Springfield silversmith Alexander Ely (1763–1848) in the *Hampshire Herald* announced that Ely had taken over Hunt's shop "a few Rods north of the Court House" in Springfield.[7] Thomas Hunt proceeded to sell off his inheritance of land in Northampton in four transactions, in which he called himself merchant, trader, and last, yeoman of Springfield.[8] If Hunt was trying to generate capital for a silversmith or mercantile business by selling his inheritance, he may have failed. By 1786, Hunt sold the original land that he had purchased in Springfield and removed to Stockbridge, his wife's place of birth.[9]

Hunt lived in Stockbridge from 1786 to at least 1795, during which time his occupation changed from goldsmith/merchant to that of goldsmith/yeoman. A Thomas Hunt of Stockbridge recorded in the Massachusetts census of 1790 maintained at least one male over sixteen years of age other than himself and three males younger than sixteen. If this was the silversmith, some individuals in his household may have been apprentices in his shop. During his Stockbridge years, Hunt called himself a goldsmith only once, in a deed of 1786.[10] The remaining nine deeds transacted by Hunt identify him as a yeoman or gentleman and suggest that he had given up his attempt at a mercantile trade.[11]

Hunt's wife, Sarah Gray, died in 1788, and on 27 October 1789 Hunt married Mary Patten (or Pattin) (b. ca. 1759–after 1792) of Roxbury, Massachusetts, the daughter of Nathaniel Patten of the same town. Nathaniel, their child, named for his maternal grandfather, was born in 1793.[12] Hunt was married to Mary Soren, his third wife, on 9 February 1800.[13] Their three children, Thomas, Sarah Gray, and Mary S., were born in Malden, Massachusetts, between 1801 and 1805.[14] Little is known of Hunt's activities during this time. He died in Malden on 6 or 9 May 1812, and his estate papers identify him as a yeoman.[15]

No silver by Hunt has been identified. JJF

1. Wyman 1862–63, 176, 179; Trumbull 1898–1902, "Northampton Genealogies," 226, 229. Trumbull gives Thomas Hunt's birth year as 1751. Esther Wells's birth date was extrapolated from her death date as cited in Trumbull, "January 9, 1787, in her sixty-fifth year." Marriage date estimated, as first child, John, was born in 1744; see Wyman 1862–63, 179.
2. Trumbull 1898–1902, "Northampton Genealogies," 226; Wyman 1862–63, 177.
3. *Mass. Soldiers and Sailors* 8:542.
4. HaCPR, box 76–9; Flynt/Fales 1968, 253.
5. Flynt/Fales 1968, 164, 221, 332; HaCPR, box 19–26.
6. HCD 15:467; Spies 1931, 8, 31.
7. *Hampshire Herald*, 1 February 1785, repeated February 8, 15, 22. Alexander Ely, cited in Flynt/Fales 1968, 214.
8. HCD 25:573; 26:142–43; 27:351; HaCPR, box 76–13. Scholars suggest that Hunt worked in the lumber business in Hartford, Connecticut, about 1785, but this has not been proven; Flynt/Fales 1968, 254.
9. HCD 29:225.
10. BerkCD 29:190.
11. BerkCD 27:237–38; 30:116–17, 171; 31:9–10; 33:481–82; 34:25–26, 163–64; 35:399.
12. *Roxbury VR* 2:217, 312, "Mary Pattin and Thomas Hunt of Stockbridge." Mary Patten died sometime after being recorded in a deed of 4 June 1792; see BerkCD 31:9–10; Wyman 1862–63, 184.
13. Wyman 1862–63, 184.
14. Wyman 1862–63, 184; *Malden VR*, 45.
15. *Malden VR*, 355; MCPR, docket 12301.

Benjamin Hurd
1739–81

A

B

Benjamin Hurd, part of an important kin network of silversmiths, was the son of the goldsmith Jacob Hurd (q.v.) and Elizabeth Mason and was baptized in Boston's New South Church on 12 August 1739.[1] Hurd married Priscilla Craft(s) (1743–1811), daughter of Jonathan (1708–95) and Susanna (Gore) Craft(s) (1712–1803), on 15 September 1774 in Roxbury, Massachusetts.[2] Hurd's relatives in the silversmithing trade included his father, his brother Nathaniel (q.v.), and his brother-in-law Daniel Henchman (q.v.).[3] In addition, William Cowell, Sr. (q.v.), was distantly related.[4]

Hurd probably was trained by his father. Following Jacob Hurd's death, the nineteen-year-old Benjamin selected his brother John to be his guardian, an appointment formalized on 9 March 1759.[5] The silver scholar Hollis French

C

suggests, however, that Hurd continued his training with another brother, Nathaniel.[6] The silversmith inherited thirty pounds' worth of tools, clothes, and money from Nathaniel, whose will, dated 8 December 1777, was probated on 13 January 1778.[7]

Hurd was relatively prominent in Boston town affairs. In November 1774, he served on a nine-person committee that sought to ensure compliance with the resolves of "the Grand American Congress and of the Provincial Congress" within Boston.[8] He was the town's treasurer from 1772 to 1776.[9]

Hurd died in Roxbury on 2 June 1781 and was buried in Boston's Granary Burying Ground.[10] In the absence of a will, his widow, Priscilla, was appointed estate administrator, with John Hurd and Nathaniel Crafts, Esq., posting the bond.[11] Four of the silversmith's colleagues and relatives appraised "the Estate of Benj.ᵃ Hurd of Roxbury Goldsmith" in August 1781; John Hurd and Thomas Clarke appraised the household furniture, and Benjamin Burt (q.v.) and Zachariah Brigden (q.v.) appraised the shop tools and furniture. Hurd's ownership of many luxury items, for example, porcelain bowls and cups and saucers, reflects the comfortable life-style of an active, successful silversmith. Approximately half of the inventory is devoted to the tools and supplies from Hurd's well-equipped workshop:

Sundry Shop Tools & furniture

1 Grind Stone, Trough & Iron Crank		1. 16
1 Iron Mortar & pestle		. 12
1 pair Large Shop Bellows		2. 8. 0
1 pair Small dᵒ		1. 4
1 small Teast for Tea Spoons		1. 10
1 forging Anvil wᵗ 49ˡᵇ	@ 1/4	3. 5. 4
1 Smaller ditto wᵗ 15ˡᵇ	dᵒ	1. 10
1 Large Spoon Teast		4.
1 Thimble Stamp		1. 10
1 ditto dᵒ		1. 4
1 Large Spoon punch		0. 6
1 ditto dᵒ		0. 4
1 Childs spoon punch		0. 3
4 Tea Spoon punch		0. 8
1 Bench Vise		1. 10
1 Large Standing		2. 8
2 Ring Swages 6/. 4/		0.10.
1 Spoon swage, or Stake		0. 3
1 smaller ditto		0. 1. 6
2 small stakes 4/. 1 ditto 1/6		0. 5. 6
1 plain small round Stake 2/. 1 Dᵒ 3/		0. 5. 0
1 Beck Iron 6/ 1 Cross Stamp 1/		0. 7
1 Castor punch 4/. 1 drawing Tongs 8/		0. 12
1 pair Casting Tongs 6. 1 pʳ forging 2/		0. 8
2 pair Neeling Tongs	@ 3/	0. 6
1 pair Stock Sheers 6/. 2 pʳ small Dᵒ 2/		0. 8
1 Salt Stake 3/. 4 Short Stakes 4/		0. 7
2 Cutting punches 2/. 1 Bead punch 1/		£0. 3
1 small Chizell 1/ 8 punches 3/		0. 4
1 Button punch 2/. 1 s[c]rew plate 3/		0. 5

2 large drawing plates 9/. 2 small 9/		o. 18
2 small Saw frams	@ 6/	o. 12
2 small Ingots 4/. 1 small Casting Skillet 12/		o. 16
2 Upright drill Stocks	@ 6/	o. 12
1 p.^r round & 1 p.^r flat plyers	@ 2/	o. 4
2 Large forging Hammers	@ 3/	o. 6
2 planishing Ditto	@ 4/	o. 8
6 Old Hammers 6/ 1 old sledge 3/		o. 9
4 hollowing Hammers	@ 3/	o. 12
3 small board Hammers	1/	o. 3. o
1 small Beam Compass		o. 6
1 small Steel D.^o 1/. 1 s[c]rew D^o 2/		o. 3
1 Brass hollowing Stamp		o. 15
1 p.^r Brass Caster Stamps		o. 4
1 p.^r Large brass Casting flasks 8/.2 p.^r Small D.^o 5/		o. 13
18 Old files 6/ sand bag 1/		o. 7
1 Box old Chaps, patterns &c		o. 3
1 Simmet Bullet & 2 Rings		o. 3
1 Brass Linsmel Box 4/		o. 4
1 Borax box 1/ 1 blowing pipe 1/		o. 2
2 plain Stakes 2/ 3 soldering Irons 1/		o. 3
1 Stone Burnishers & 1 small D.^o without handle		o. 3
1 p.^r Box Beams brass Scales		o. 12
1 p.^r Scales & Beam smaller		o. 6
1 Sett Brass Weights from 64^{ozs} down		o. 12
5 Large odd Ditto		o. 6
1 small New hand Vise		o. 6
1 small oyl Stone		o. 3
1 Tin Linsmel pan 2/. 2 small round stakes 2/		o. 4
1 pair large hand Sheers		o. 3
3 Cutting punches 3/ 2 Little Stakes 1/		o. 4
1 small boras Box & 1 p.^r Old plyers		o. 1
1 Turning Lathe, Wheel Blocks &c		2. 10
1 Iron forge Ring w.^t 5 1/2^{lb} @ 6^d		o. 2. 9
1 Old Carving knife 2/. 1 french Cutteaw 1/		o. 3
1 Brass box cont^g a Set chasing Tools		o. 12
2 p.^r Steel Chapes & Tongs 3/. 1 Old Broach 1/		o. 4
1 p.^r Smallest Gold Scales & Old W.^{ts}		o. 3
1 p.^r Silver knee buckels unfinished		o. 6
1 Old Silver Watch		1.
1 paper cont^g some odd Christials button ⎫ Stones, foils &c ⎭		o. 6
a Rasor Box with Strop		o. 3
a Brass Cullender ⎫ forclesning		o. 6
a Copper pan wth handle ⎭ Shop Sweep		o. 12
a Large Stand^g Bench Vise		2. 2 ¹²

Furnished with anvils and bellows in two sizes, the shop also contained an assortment of hammers, stakes, tongs, shears, punches, and stamps. Hurd owned many specialized tools for the production of specific forms, including teasts, swages, stamps and punches for salts, casters, beads, thimbles, buttons, rings, and several kinds of spoons. The inventory included patterns, but they were not described.

Hurd's versatility and expertise are demonstrated by the few objects by him that have been located. Three marks can be associated with Hurd—an initials mark (A) and two initial and surname marks: mark (B), B·Hurd in an oval; and mark (C), B·HURD in a rectangle. The literature describes two additional marks, B·HURD in a cartouche and B:HURD in a rectangle, but no examples were located for illustration.[13] Initial mark (A), the most common, is featured on several teaspoons with a seven-lobed shell with each concave lobe separated by webbing. Other decorative bowl motifs used by Hurd include an acanthus leaf and a double drop. A double-bellied teapot with repoussé floral and scroll ornamentation is the most elaborate of Hurd's extant works.

In addition to domestic objects, Hurd also made church plate. On 7 August 1769, Hurd returned to Boston from Halifax on the schooner *Massachusetts Ninety Two*, probably following a visit to his brother Jacob, who had relocated to Canada.[14] Contacts made on this trip undoubtedly resulted in Hurd's commission on 25 October 1769 from Francis White for a baptismal basin for the First Protestant Dissenting Church in Halifax.[15] In 1774, the silversmith made a broad-rimmed baptismal basin for the Second Church of Christ in Roxbury, the site of his marriage in September 1774 to Priscilla Craft, a church member since 1769.[16]

Hurd augmented his silversmithing business with copperplate engraving and printing. The Grand Lodge of Masons in Massachusetts owns certificates that Hurd printed for his lodge that were still being used in 1796 and 1797.[17] He was also an accomplished heraldic painter; his watercolor coat of arms commemorating the marriage of Isaac Baldwin and Eunice Jenison in 1761 is in the Museum of Fine Arts, Boston.[18] DAF

SURVIVING OBJECTS

	Mark	Inscription	Patron	Date	Reference	Owner
Baptismal basin	A*	The Gift of/Mr John Mory/To the Second Church of Christ in/Roxbury:/1774.	John Morey and/or First Parish, West Roxbury, Mass.	ca. 1774	French 1939, no. 323	
Baptismal basin	C†	The Gift of Francis/White Esqr to the First/Protestant Dissenting/Church in Halifax/October 25th 1769.	Francis White and/or First Protestant Dissenting Church, Halifax, N.S.	1769	French 1939, no. 322	
Creampot	A	CYI (later)		ca. 1765	French 1939, no. 324	MFAB
Ladle	B	IP		ca. 1770	Hammerslough/Feigenbaum 1958–73, 2:68–69	
Tablespoon	A†	M/JS		ca. 1780		YUAG
Tablespoon	A*	SH (later?)		ca. 1765	Buhler 1972, no. 428	MFAB
Tablespoon	A*	AW		ca. 1775	French 1939, no. 330	

	Mark	Inscription	Patron	Date	Reference	Owner
Tablespoon	A*	T/DS		ca. 1775	YUAG files	
Tablespoon (mates below)	B*	SZ		ca. 1770	Johnston 1994, 78	CMA
Tablespoon (mates above and below)	B	SZ		ca. 1770	French 1939, nos. 325–28	
Two tablespoons (mates above)	B†	SZ		ca. 1770	French 1939, nos. 325–28	YUAG
Tankard	A	unidentified arms (defaced)		ca. 1760	Skinner, 27–28 October 1989, lot 61	
Teapot	A	G/SM		ca. 1765	Buhler 1956, no. 84	
Six teaspoons	A	SR to SB		ca. 1775	Sotheby's, 27 January 1989, lot 907	
Teaspoon	A*	SC		ca. 1780		SI
Teaspoon (mates below)	A*	RA		ca. 1770	Johnston 1994, 78	CMA
Four teaspoons (mate above)	A	RA		ca. 1770	French 1939, nos. 332–35	
Teaspoon (mate? below)	A	PG		ca. 1775	French 1939, no. 336	
Teaspoon (mate? above)	A	PG		ca. 1775		MFAB
Teaspoon	A	SB		ca. 1770	DAPC 73.3034	WM
Teaspoon	A	erased		ca. 1775	French 1941, no. 337	

1. *NEHGR* 19:123–24.
2. *Roxbury VR* 1:78, 151; 2:92, 174, 496; Crafts/Crafts 1893, 86–88; *Index of Obituaries, 1784–1840,* 2:1099; 3:2420. Priscilla Hurd's maiden name appears as both Craft and Crafts in contemporary records. Benjamin and Priscilla Hurd had at least three children: Benjamin, Jr. (1778–1818), a bookbinder and merchant; Sarah (Hurd) Rhoades (1779–1870); and Charlotte (Hurd) Brown; French 1939, 143; SCPR 207:157. The existence of another son who died before 1818 is suggested by the will of Benjamin Hurd, Jr., which included a bequest to "my sister Sarah Benjamin Hurd"; SCPR 207:157.
3. See French 1939.
4. William Cowell's father, John Cowell, married Hannah Hurd, daughter of John Hurd, the great-great-great-grandfather of Benjamin Hurd.
5. SCPR 54:176.
6. French 1939, 143.
7. SCPR 77:14.
8. French 1939, 145.
9. Winsor 1880–81, 2:330.
10. French 1939, 145; Codman 1918, 136; *Roxbury VR* 2:560.
11. SCPR 80:295.
12. SCPR 80:314–19, docket 17461.
13. The mark composed of an initial and surname separated by a colon in a rectangle was described in Buhler 1972, 2:476; B.HURD in a cartouche is recorded in Hammerslough/Feigenbaum 1958–73, 2:68.
14. RC 29:317. Jacob Hurd was described as being "now of Halifax" in Nathaniel Hurd's will, dated 8 December 1777; SCPR 77:12–15.
15. The basin and mark were described in detail in a letter from R. M. Hattie, clerk of the Kirk-Session, St. Matthew's Church, Halifax, to Francis Hill Bigelow, 23 February 1932.
16. RC 6:110.
17. French 1939, 146; Buhler 1956, 62.
18. *Heraldic Journal* 4:192; Buhler 1972, no. 427.

Jacob Hurd
1702/03–58

A

B

C

D

E

F

G

Jacob Hurd was the most talented and prolific of all Boston silversmiths who made silver objects in the late baroque style. He made more than 50 percent of the surviving silver produced by Boston silversmiths of his generation, and he and his sons were the subject of a monograph by Hollis French, *Jacob Hurd and His Sons Nathaniel and Benjamin, Silversmiths* in 1939.[1] Born in Charlestown, Massachusetts, on 12 February 1702/03, Jacob was the son of Jacob Hurd (1676–1749), a joiner, and his wife, Elizabeth Tufts (1673–1721). His father was the son of Jacob Hurd (1653–94), a tailor, and Anna Wilson (1655–1728).[2] Elizabeth (Tufts) Hurd was the daughter of Capt. Peter Tufts (1648–1721) and Elizabeth (Lynde) Tufts (1650–84) of Medford, Massachusetts, and must have inherited some wealth from her family because after she died, guardianship papers were filed in 1723 with the Middlesex County Probate Court for her children "Jacob of 20 years . . . Mary of 18 . . . Rebecca of 16 . . . [and] John of 14 years" making their father, Jacob Hurd, "Hatter alas [alias] ferryman," guardian.[3] Jacob Hurd the elder is referred to as a joiner of Charlestown when he and his children, including Jacob the goldsmith, received bequests from the estate of his wife's father, Peter Tufts, in 1729 and again in 1746 when he sold land to his son, the goldsmith Jacob Hurd.[4]

On 20 May 1725, Jacob Hurd married Elizabeth Mason (1705–64), daughter of John and Prudence (Balston) Mason, who had come to Boston from Kingston, Jamaica.[5] Jacob and Elizabeth Hurd had fourteen children: Jacob (1726–77+), who became a trader in Nova Scotia and married Margaret Brown in 1760; John (b. 1727), who married (i) Elizabeth Foster (1731–79), (ii) Mary (Russell) Foster, and (iii) Rebecca Leppington; Nathaniel (1729/30–77) (q.v.); Elizabeth (b. 1730), who married (i) Daniel Henchman (q.v.) and (ii) D. Rae; Prudence (died at birth); Prudence (1733–36); Ann (1735–after 1777), who married John Furnass; Prudence (1736–37); Sarah (b. 1738), who married Thomas Walley; Benjamin (1739–81) (q.v.), who married Priscilla Crafts; Mary (b. 1740, died in infancy); Mary (1742–before 1777), who married Samuel Hall; Joseph (1744/45–47/48); and Prudence (b. 1749, died in infancy). Two of their sons, Nathaniel and Benjamin, were trained in their father's shop.[6]

Hurd devoted most of his attention to his silversmithing business and therefore was not very active in town affairs. He was elected tithingman in 1727, and clerk of the market (with Knight Leverett [q.v.]) in 1727/28.[7] He was chosen to be one of the town's constables in 1731 and again in 1736 but declined to serve. In 1743 Hurd was elected a member of the Ancient and Honorable Artillery Company; in 1745 he became first sergeant and eventually rose to the rank of captain.[8] Hurd made several appearances in court as an expert witness in cases involving the value of silver in certain years, indicating that he must have kept detailed business records.[9] In 1750/51 he served as one of the referees, along with Rufus Greene and William Cowell, Jr. (qq.v.), in a dispute involving Thomas Edwards and Thomas Townsend (qq.v.). He appeared several times in court—six times as plaintiff and five times as defendant. He was never sued by anyone who worked for him or by any of his fellow goldsmiths.[10] He joined the New South Church on 5 November 1721.[11]

There has been much speculation concerning the identity of Jacob Hurd's master. Because of his proficiency as an engraver, Kathryn Buhler believed that Hurd must have trained with either John Edwards or John Burt (qq.v.), but William Cowell, Sr. (q.v.), was his father's cousin, and it is possible that

Hurd trained with him. Hurd's designs, construction techniques, and business practices, however, most strongly suggest an apprenticeship with John Burt.[12]

It is not clear where Hurd received the money that he needed to establish himself in business. He inherited some land from his mother, and his father may have been able to provide him with a small amount of capital. He may not have worked as a journeyman because he was already working on his own by June 1725 and was honored with the title "Mr." when Samuel Sewall bought a spoon for presentation to his infant grandson, Samuel Clark, noting in his diary that "Mr Hurd engraved on the back side of it as in the Margin. S C March 28, April 4, 1725." In August 1725 Sewall bought another spoon for £1.8 from Hurd and noted in his ledger that it was meant for "Fr. Pickard," an individual whose identity remains unknown.[13] The Harvard tutor Henry Flynt also patronized Hurd, recording in his memorandum book on 12 December 1725, "Mr Hurd below Henchmans makes my Spoons for 52sh."[14] Although these purchases were small, they indicate that even as he began his business, Hurd was able to attract the patronage of important customers who had previously done business primarily with other leading Boston goldsmiths. Sewall and Flynt both patronized John Coney (q.v.), who had died in 1722; Sewall also was a good customer of John Burt and John Edwards.[15]

In 1729/30, Jacob Hurd and his wife sold their share in a house at the corner of Pudding Lane and Water Street that she had inherited from her grandfather Thomas Ofield.[16] However, Hurd still had a shop on Pudding Lane, near the south side of the Town House in 1732, which was mentioned in an advertisement for the return of a stolen string of gold beads.[17] He probably resided in the same building because in 1733 the town granted him "liberty . . . to take up the Pauement and to digg up the Ground in Pudding Lane to Carry His Drain from His House to the comon Shore there."[18] Whether this house was rented or was another piece of property that Elizabeth (Mason) Hurd had inherited from her grandfather is not clear. However, the Hurds did not sell this property—Hurd may have continued to keep his shop there—before purchasing a piece of land and the "buildings thereon" on Atkinson Street, near Fort Hill, from Abigail Penhallow of Portsmouth, New Hampshire, in 1734/35.[19] A year later Hurd mortgaged half the value of the house to the merchant James Smith, perhaps to help finance his growing business.[20] In 1738, Hurd's "large new House in *Atkinson's Street* . . . was struck by the Lightning, and considerably damag'd, but the Lives of all in the Family, were mercifully preserved."[21] Hurd apparently repaired the house and continued to inhabit it for a few more years before he purchased a brick dwelling house and land in Cornhill in 1742.[22] His shop evidently was in or near his house, for on 7 October 1747 Benjamin Walker records seeing the plate owned by Governor Charles Knowles of Nova Scotia on display at Hurd's shop: "At mr Hurds Gold Smith in Cornhill Street in Boston I see ye finest Sight of silver plate belonging to Gouernour Charles Knowles [of] Lewisburg on Cape Briton some part of his Sideboard, such fine Craft work & Variety I can't Enumerate & It's sd he has much more."[23] Knowles, who was trying to impress Bostonians with his wealth and power—his impressment gangs soon caused such anger among the town's inhabitants that they took to the streets in protest—chose to have his silver displayed in the most prominent goldsmith's shop in Boston, where artisans and shopkeepers like Walker would be sure to see it. Hurd sold his house in Cornhill to the stationer John Leverett for £640, lawful money, in May 1755. In the deed he is referred to as "Jacob Hurd, late of Boston, but now of Roxbury, Goldsmith."[24]

Hurd trained a number of apprentices—his sons Nathaniel and Benjamin, his nephew and ward Houghton Perkins (q.v.), son of his good friend Isaac Perkins (q.v.), who died in 1737, and Daniel Henchman, who later became his son-in-law.[25] He also trained Benjamin Goodwin (q.v.) after Goodwin's master, John Parkman (q.v.), died, because Goodwin and Henchman witnessed a deed for Hurd in 1750.[26] He may also have trained his cousin Josiah Austin as well as John Ball (qq.v.).[27] A clause in the will of Edward Winslow (q.v.) suggests that Hurd occasionally employed Thomas McCullough (q.v.) as a journeyman, and after Hurd's death, the administration accounts indicate that he owed £26.7 to the estate of Edward Winslow, probably for McCullough's services.[28]

Hurd had working relationships with other Massachusetts silversmiths and jewelers. When the Marblehead silversmith William Jones (q.v.) died in 1734 his estate owed "Jacob Heard" £54.8. Hurd was an appraiser of the estates of William Cowell, Sr. (q.v.), in 1736, of James Boyer (q.v.) in 1741, and of John Edwards in 1746.[29] With Benjamin Hiller (q.v.) Hurd witnessed a deed for Samuel Torrey and Joseph Webb in 1738/39.[30] At about the same time, when Hurd became the guardian of Houghton Perkins, Hiller witnessed the bond, which suggests that he was then working with Hurd.[31] Jacob Hurd's shop must have been an extremely busy establishment, and there were undoubtedly more journeymen employed there than can be documented. More than five hundred objects bearing one or more of Hurd's six marks survive—Jacob Hurd in shaped shield (A), used between 1721 and 1755; I HURD in cartouche (B), used between 1727 and 1747; Hurd in script in an oval (C), used between 1729 and 1740; HURD in a rectangle (D), used between 1750 and 1756; a larger version of the HURD in rectangle mark (E), used ca. 1750; Hurd in a cartouche (F), used from 1740 to 1750; and I·H in conforming surround (G).[32] Spurious examples of marks (B), (C), and (D) exist.[33]

There is abundant physical evidence that many specialist engravers contributed to the appearance of objects made in the Hurd shop. The engraving on Hurd's earliest silver has a tentative quality that points to the young silversmith as the engraver of his own products. Later objects from his shop display a wide variety of engraving styles, indicating that he employed specialist engravers either as journeymen or on a piecework basis. His son Nathaniel was a very talented engraver and presumably did the engraving on a significant number of objects that bear his father's mark.[34]

Larger shops like Hurd's must have found it necessary to perform a wide variety of specialized tasks—including refining, gilding, turning, burnishing, and engraving—in order to ensure that they could meet the demands of their customers. Accounts between Jacob Hurd and fellow silversmith Benjamin Greene (q.v.) reveal the variety of work that went on in Hurd's shop and demonstrate that many Boston goldsmiths may have relied on Hurd for work involving specialized tools or specialized skills that they could not maintain in their smaller establishments. Between 1738 and 1740, Jacob Hurd "turned," or finished on a lathe, the feet of milk pots and the feet and lips of canns, turned a salver, and burnished porringers for Greene:

1738
Septe[r] 16.	By Turning a Milk Pot foot	£0: 2: 6
April 18.	By Turning 2 Can feet	0: 6: —

1739

May 8.	By Turning a Salver	0:	3: —
Dec[r] 24:	By Burnishing p [??] Porringers	0:	3: —

1740

April 29.	By a Silver Tankard w[t] 37[oz]18[pw] @ 9/		54: 19: —	
	By fashon of Ditto		10: 0: —	
			65: 13: 6	
	By Turning fott & Lipps Canns Des[?] a4[?]		0: 10: —	
			£66: 3: 6	
Febu[r]y 7.	By 1 Silver Milk Pott		£7: 2: —	
	By Turning 2 feet & 2 lips of Cans		0: 10: —	
	By mending a Box		0: 12: —	
	By turning a foot for a Milk Pott		0: 2:	
May 3				
1741.	By 1 Sword Blade & 1 p[r] Chapes & Tungs		2: 5:	
Dece[r]	By 1 p[r] Tobacco Tongs		1: 10: —	
			£12: 1: 0	
	By Sundrys Omited Giveing C[r] for		4: 06: 6	
Jan[y]. 29.	Ballance due to B. Greene		38: 0: 6	
			£54: 8: 0	
Jan[ry]. 30	By Turning 2 feet for Peper Boxe		£0: 5: —	
Feb[ry]. 17.	By Chapes & Tungs		1: 7: —	
April 3:1742.	By 2 hh[ds][?] Mollases 194 Gall[o] @ 7/		67: 18: —	
June 26.	By 6 p[r] knee Chapes & Tungs		1: 1: —	
Nove[r].	30 By 2 p[r] Chapes & Tungs		0: 10: 0	
Jan[y] 1743			£71: 1: 0	
Jan[ry] 12.	By Sundrys omited ℔ his acco[t]		4: 3: 8	
			£75: 4: 8	

In return for these services, Greene paid Hurd in cash, and in goods—corks, chapes and tongues, cloth, rum, butter, silver, pipe stoppers, and silver earrings. On one occasion Greene made a string of gold beads for Hurd.[35]

Hurd received many of the most important commissions for public presentation objects and was the favored artisan among Boston's elite. He made a silver oar for the head of the great mace carried by the judge of the Admiralty Court, and in 1744 he was commissioned by leaders of Boston's merchant community to make ceremonial cups for two ship captains—Capt. Edward Tyng of the snow *Prince of Orange* and Capt. Richard Spry of the *Comet-Bomb*—who were responsible for capturing French privateers off the coast of Massachusetts during King George's War. He also made communion silver for more than twenty-five churches throughout Massachusetts, Connecticut, and New Hampshire and filled hundreds of private commissions. Surviving bills indicate, however, that not all of his shop's time was devoted to the production of large holloware items. Like every other Boston silversmith of the time, Hurd seems to have spent much of his time in making small repairs and even in selling secondhand silver. On 9 August 1748 Benjamin Walker wrote in his diary, "m[r] Hurd Goldsmith fixt & ga[ve?] me a pair of floocks to my silver Buckles my old ones y[e] points y[tt] hold in y[e] Strap worn out. I askt him w[ht] I owed him he s[d] nothing I gave him Thanks for them & s[d] am oblidg."[36] An account between Hurd and Rebecca Townsend includes the following services for which Townsend is listed as debtor:

1740
June 5   To 1 Sett Stone Buttons   2: —: —
1741
May 4   To 1 p^r Buckles   3: 10: —
June 19   To mending a Bosom Bottle   3: 6
1742
Sepr 14   To mending a Snuff Box   4: —
1744
March 7   To mending a Fan   : 6: –
1746
Novr 3   To 6 tea spoons & tongs 2^{oz}..18^{dw}..10^{gr} @ 50/   7: 5: —
                fashioning   5: 0: 0
March 21   To 6 large Spoons 11^{oz}..17^{dw} @ 50/   29: 12: 6
                fashioning   6: —: —

1747
May 1   To a p^r Casters 7^{oz}..11^{dw} 50/   18: 17: 6
                fashioning   12: —: —
                to 1 pare of Shew Buckels   5: 0: 0
                                                                               £89. 18: 6

                To her part of one Silver Salver
                made for & given to Deacon John
                Phillips for Discharging his Trust of
                ye Executorship on ye Estate of J. Townsend   26: 13: 4
                                                                              116: 11: 10

On the creditor side, Townsend is credited with £24.15 "by Old Buckles" and "By Silver."[37]

A bill from Hurd to Thomas Hancock for goods and services rendered between 1750 and 1752 shows that Hurd may have worked in other metals because he supplied a brass ferrel and mended a harness iron:

Thomas Hancock Esq to Jacob Hurd D^r

1750
May 15   To a Silver Frame w^t 1^{oz} 3^{dw} £ 3. 2
                To fashioning   2.
                To Sperits of Wine   6
Augst 21   To mending Silver Buttons   8
                To a Stone Stud   1. 5
Septr 21   To a Ring for Mr Glover   15.
Oct 16   To a Tea pott Handle   1. 5
Jany 2   To a Sett Gold Buttons   7. 15
Feby 26   To a p^r Knee Buckles   2. 10
1751
Nov 26   To a Brass Ferrell   . 8
Novr 6   To a p^r Stone Buttons   for Mr Glover   4.
1752
Mar.^{h} 7   To 6 Large Spoons w^t 17^{oz}..13..12 }   27. 15
                To fashioning   } Mr Bowman   6.
                To mending a Harnes Iron   . 7
                                              Carried over   £72. 1

                Supra   C^r

1749
Feb^y7   By his former Acco:^{tt} for Ball^{ce} Old Ten^{or}   £38. 12
1750/ 1 Feby By Old Knee Buckles   1.   5
        26   Carried over   £39. 17[38]

The stationer Daniel Henchman also patronized Hurd, purchasing among other things a pair of chafing dishes from him in 1738.[39]

The Harvard tutor Henry Flynt records additional dealings with Hurd in his diary. On 21 February 1733/34, he paid Hurd 8 shillings for a silver strainer, and on 22 October 1736 he records purchasing a "christal ristband" from Hurd that cost 2 shillings, 6 pence. In a memorandum in the diary dated 19 September 1740, Flynt recorded, "Nov. 22 Mr Hurd told me he parted with a Second hand Tea Tongues and might in a Month have another to dispose of. They consist he says of an Ounce of Silver *at 29 Shillings* and If now he has *20s* for the fashion If second hand ones *10s* and when he had again such a pair he would Let mee know it or Leave them for mee at Sister Flynts. The cost 39 Shillings."[40] The probate records also include numerous accounts of payments to Hurd for gold mourning rings.[41]

Unlike other silversmiths of his generation, Hurd did not diversify his business but devoted all of his energies to silversmithing. Jacob Hurd's huge family and substantial business created great expenses. The large volume of his business and the runaway inflation that plagued Boston in the 1740s eventually caused his financial ruin. Forced to borrow money in order to buy the metal he needed for his business, Hurd sometimes paid interest rates of 30 percent and higher to such individuals as Benjamin Bourne. Bourne sued Hurd for nonpayment of a debt, and one of the depositions filed in the case indicates that in 1745, Hurd had borrowed "Gold Dust and Silver and Paper" from Bourne at 30 percent interest. However, when Bourne came to collect, Hurd calculated that he was being charged 34 percent interest. Bourne, aware of the high rate of inflation, had tied his interest rate to the price cost of molasses so that it would keep up with rising costs. Hurd protested that he could not pay Bourne right away and could pay only the "Least Note which was for 476:18:0 old Tenor," because if he paid both notes he would not be able to pay for "a Large Quantity of Silver which he had bargained for." Hurd was therefore forced to sign a new note, again at the rate of 34 percent interest.[42]

The case between Hurd and Bourne was so infamous at the time that Benjamin Walker mentioned it in his diary on 29 August 1746, noting that the "Verdict [was] for Hurd p^r Bourn Extortionable Usury."[43] Bourne argued that he was not charging exorbitant interest but rather tying the value of the silver to the value of molasses because, as a creditor, he did not want to lose money during a time of rapid inflation. Public opinion and the courts, however, were on Hurd's side.

Jacob Hurd went bankrupt in 1755 and moved from Boston to Roxbury. Had he continued to work until the time of his death, it is likely that his shop inventory would be nearly as elaborate as the one that survives for his colleague Samuel Edwards (q.v.). By the time Hurd moved to Roxbury in 1755 his financial situation had so deteriorated that he was asked to give security to the Roxbury town selectmen in order to ensure that he would not become a public charge.[44]

Jacob Hurd died in Boston in 1758, probably of a stroke, while visiting a relative, perhaps one of his children. Short notices of his death appeared in both of Boston's newspapers. The *Boston News-Letter* recorded that Hurd "being in Town [Boston] at a Relation's House, was seiz'd with an Apoplexy, in which he continued speechless till Friday Evening, when he departed this Life." The *Boston Gazette* had carried nearly the same story a few days earlier, adding that he died "much lamented."[45] Hurd abandoned the goldsmithing trade before his death, possibly when he left Boston for Roxbury in 1755. His estate, which was declared insolvent, was valued at only £72.13; his debts exceeded £700 including £447 sterling to William Sitwell and Company.[46] Samuel Edwards and William Simpkins (qq.v.) were two of the appraisers of the estate.[47]

In spite of his financial difficulties, Hurd stands as the most important Boston silversmith of his generation. Not only did his shop turn out the town's most sophisticated silver objects, but its accomplished specialists, including engravers, chasers, burnishers, and turners, performed work for other firms as well. Hurd's work thus affected the look of all Boston silver made during this period. BMW

SURVIVING OBJECTS

	Mark	Inscription	Patron	Date	Reference	Owner
Admiralty oar	D	Arms of Great Britain; Admiralty anchor	Boston Vice-Admiralty Court	ca. 1740	Fales 1970a, 96	MHS
Alms dish	B	Belonging to that Church of Christ in/Marblehead of wch the Rev^d M^r. Edwd Holyoke/is the Pastor	Second Congregational Society, Marblehead, Mass.	1728	French 1939, no. 2	MFAB
Alms dish	B	Skinner arms, sable on a chevron or between 3 griffins' heads erased a crescent, and crest, a griffin's head erased holding in its beak a dexter hand couped; Dom^s Richardus Skinner, Ecclesiae-isti Jesu/Christi apud Marblehead, cujus nuper Diaco-nus/suit Primarius, hoc Donum Testa-mentarium/Legavit Anno 1727	Second Congregational Society, Marblehead, Mass.	1727	French 1939, no. 1	
Baptismal basin	B	Savage arms, 6 lioncelles 3, 2, 1, sable, and crest, a lion's gamb; The Gift of/ Arthur–Savage Esqr/to Christ= Church in/BOSTON/ 1732	Arthur Savage and/or Christ Church, Boston	1732	French 1939, no. 5	
Baptismal basin	B	Byfield arms, sable 5 bezants in saltire, a	First Church, Boston, for Nathaniel Byfield	1733	French 1939, no. 3	

	Mark	Inscription	Patron	Date	Reference	Owner
		chief or, and crest, a demi-lion holding a bezant				
Baptismal basin	C	Burrill arms, or a saltire gules, on a chief azure a crescent between 2 pierced stars of 6 points or; The Gift of Theo: Burrill Esq/ to the first Church of Christ in/Lynn	Executor of the estate of Theophilus Burrill and pastor of First Church of Christ, Lynn, Mass.	1737	French 1939, no. 4	
Baptismal basin	D	The Gift of Mr John Harris to the/ first Church of Christ in Middletown,/of Which he is a Member	John Harris and/or First Church of Christ, Middletown, Conn.	ca. 1750	French 1939, no. 6	
Beaker	A	The gift of/Mr Ebenezer Clap/to the Church of Milton	Ebenezer Clapp and/or First Congregational Parish, Milton, Mass.	ca. 1735	French 1939, no. 33	
Beaker	A*/D	The Gift/OF Mrs MARY WALKER/ Dec^d to the First/ Church of Christ In Rehoboth, 1747	Newman Congregational Church, East Providence, R.I., for Mary (Abell) Walker	1747	Buhler/Hood 1970, no. 160	YUAG
Beaker	A*/F	The Gift of Lieutenant Samuell Stent to the 2^d Church of Christ In/Branford	Congregational Church, North Branford, Conn., for Samuel Stent	1736	French 1939, no. 22	
Two beakers	B	Byfield arms	Congregational Church, South Byfield, Mass., for Nathaniel Byfield	ca. 1735	French 1941, no. 23a	
Beaker	B	The Gift of/N = Saltonstall and R = Cotton/to the first Church of Christ in Wobourn	Nathaniel Saltonstall and Roland Cotton and/or First Congregational Church, Woburn, Mass.	ca. 1740	French 1939, no. 11	
Beaker	B	The Gift of/Mr William Clap/To The First Church/ OF Christ/In Dorchester/1745	First Church, Dorchester, Mass., for William Clapp	1745	French 1939, no. 24	
Beaker	C	The Gift of ye Honble Edmund Quincy Esqr- to ye First Church in Braintree Feby 23^d 1737/8	First Congregational Society (Unitarian), Quincy, Mass., for Edmund Quincy	1738	French 1939, no. 28	
Four beakers	C*	The Gift of Dea^n:/ John Jacobs/to the 2^d Church/of Christ in/Hingham/1728	John Jacobs and/or First Congregational Society, Cohasset, Mass.	1728	French 1939, no. 12–15	
Two beakers	C	Burrill arms, or a saltire gules, on a chief azure a crescent	Executor of the estate of Theophilus Burrill and pastor of First	1737	French 1939, nos. 30–31	

	Mark	Inscription	Patron	Date	Reference	Owner
		between 2 pierced stars of 6 points or; The Gift of Theo: Burrill Esqr/ to the first Church of Christ in/Lynn	Church of Christ, Lynn, Mass.			
Beaker	C	The Gift of/Dea^n Nathl Meriam/to the Church of Christ/in BEDFORD/ with a legacy of £5/ from E. Taylor/1738	Nathaniel Meriam and/ or First Parish Church, Bedford, Mass.	1738	French 1961, 1	
Beaker (altered to cup)	D	S/DM		ca. 1745	French 1941, no. 35a	
Beaker	D	The Gift of/Lieu^t Eben Curtis/To the first Church/of Christ in/Stratford/ 1752	Congregational Church, Stratford, Conn., for Ebenezer Curtis	1752	French 1939, no. 26	
Beaker	D	The Gift of the Honble: /Isaac Lothrop Esqr/to the Third Church of/ Christ in Plymouth/ Sepr ye 7 1743	Isaac Lothrop and/or First Parish, Plymouth, Mass.	1743	French 1939, no. 27	PS
Beaker	D*	The Gift of/Mr Peter Smith to/The First CHURCH/ IN/Shrewsbury/ AD; 1748	Congregational Church, Shrewsbury, Mass., for Peter Smith	1748	French 1939, no. 34	
Beaker	D	The Gift of Mr Peter Emerson To/ The first Church/of Christ in/Reading/ 1750	First Congregational Church, Wakefield, Mass., for Peter Emerson	1750	French 1939, no. 16	
Beaker	D	The Gift/of Mr John Pratt/To the first Church/In Reading/1746	First Congregational Church, Wakefield, Mass., for John Pratt	1746	French 1939, no. 17	
Beaker	D	This Cup/was given to/The First Church/In Stratford By/Leu^t Jos^h Beach/ 1746	Josiah Beach and/or Congregational Church, Stratford, Conn.	1746	French 1939, no. 20	
Beaker	E	The Gift/of the Rev^d/Mr Eb^{nr} Hancock/to the Church of/Christ in/LEX- INGTON	Rev. Ebenezer Hancock and/or First Congrega- tional Society, Lexing- ton, Mass.	ca. 1740	French 1939, no. 23	
Two beakers	F	The Gift of Capt Thos Pool/to ye 1st Church in READING	First Congregational Church, Wakefield, Mass., for Thomas Pool	ca. 1740	French 1939, nos. 18–19	
Beaker	F	The Gift of Mrs Mehetabel Fisher/to	First Congregational Society (Unitarian),	1741	French 1939, no. 21	

	Mark	Inscription	Patron	Date	Reference	Owner
		the first Church of Christ in/BRAIN-TREE/1741	Quincy, Mass., for Mehitable (Vesey) Fisher			
Beaker	F	The Gift of/Mrs Hannah How To the Church of Christ/On Church Green/BOSTON/ In memory of her Husband/Mr Abr^m How. Dec^d/Feb 12th 1740	Hannah (Wheeler) How in memory of Abraham How for New South Church, Boston	1740	Buhler 1972, no. 183	MFAB
Beaker	F	The Gift of/Mr Brice and Mrs Ann Blair/For the Use of the presbytieria/ Church in Long-Lane, where of/The Revd Mr John Moorhead is/Pastor/in Gratitude to God for/His Goodness/ to them and theirs in a Strange/land/ BOSTON: May 1:1744/Set Deo Maxima Laus	Brice and Ann Blair for Long Lane or Federal Street, now Arlington Street, Church, Boston	1744	French 1939, no. 25	
Four beakers	F	Hampton Old Church/1744	Congregational Church, Hampton, N.H.	1744	French 1939, nos. 7–10	
Beaker	F	The Gift of/Deacon William Trow-bridge/ to/The Church of Christ/in/ Newtown/1744	First Church, Newton, Mass., for William Trowbridge	1744	French 1939, no. 29	MFAB
Beaker	F	The Gift of/Mr. John & Mrs. Deborah Heartwell To The/Church of Christ/in BEDFORD/ 1742	First Parish Church, Bedford, Mass.	1742	French 1961, 1	
Beaker	F*	unidentified crest, a stag tripping		ca. 1745	French 1939, no. 122 (as a cup)	
Bowl	C	Dummer crest, a demi-lion holding a fleur-de-lis in his dexter paw	Dummer family	ca. 1740	French 1939, no. 38	
Bowl	C	Deborah Fraser/1738	Deborah Fraser	1738	French 1939, no. 39	
Bowl	D	E/IL		ca. 1740	French 1939, no. 37	MFAB
Bowl	F	MW; E B Curtis (later)		ca. 1750	French 1939, no. 40	DIA

	Mark	Inscription	Patron	Date	Reference	Owner
Bowl	?	The Gift of Mr Jonas Rowlandson to Mr Thos. Woodbridge 1740	Jonas Rowlandson and/or Thomas Woodbridge	1740	French 1939, no. 36	
Two candlebranches	C*	none	Elizabeth (Hunt) (Wendell) Smith	ca. 1735	Quimby 1995, no. 81a, b	WM
Cann (mate below)	A*/C*	Pierce arms, a fess humettée between 3 ravens rising, and crest, a raven rising with 3 sprigs in its beak; DEVS MIHI SOL	Pierce family	ca. 1740	Warren 1975, no. 283	BBC
Cann (mate above)	A/C	Pierce arms, a fess humettée between 3 ravens rising, and crest, a raven rising with 3 sprigs in its beak; DEVS MIHI SOL	Pierce family	ca. 1740	French 1939, no. 60	DIA
Cann	B	R/IL	Joseph and Love (Macy) Rotch	ca. 1740	Gustafson 1982, 436	ODHS
Cann	B*	JG (later)		ca. 1735	*Antiques* 95 (May 1969): 587	
Cann	B	unidentified arms		ca. 1735	*Silver Supplement* 1973, no. 48	
Cann	B	unidentified crest, a griffin		ca. 1735	French 1939, no. 69	
Cann	B*	Simpson arms, on a chief vert 3 crescents, and crest, a bird rising; MS	Mary Simpson	ca. 1745	Fales 1983, 18–19	PEM
Cann	B	?		ca. 1735	French 1941, no. 87b	
Cann	B	I/IS		ca. 1735	French 1939, no. 77	
Cann	B/D	B/II		ca. 1740	French 1961, 1	
Cann	C	M to TC		ca. 1735	French 1939, no. 78	
Cann	C*	B/ND/to/M/TM; The Gift of/Mary Ingraham/to the Church in/Concord (later)	Nathan and D. Bond to Tilly and Mary Merrick	ca. 1735	French 1939, no. 66	
Cann	C	EW		ca. 1735	Quimby 1995, no. 86	WM
Cann	C*	P/MM; SECOND PRESBYTERIAN CHURCH/NEWBURYPORT (later)		ca. 1735	Hammerslough/ Feigenbaum 1958–73, 2:6	WA
Cann	C	Sarah Bishop	Sarah Bishop	ca. 1735	French 1939, no. 74	
Cann (mate below)	C	Mason arms impaling Williams arms; M/TE	Thaddeus and Elizabeth (Sewall) Mason	ca. 1736	*Silver Supplement* 1973, no. 49	

	Mark	Inscription	Patron	Date	Reference	Owner
Cann (mate above)	C	Mason arms and crest, a lion's head couped, impaling Williams arms; M/TE	Thaddeus and Elizabeth (Sewall) Mason	ca. 1736	French 1939, nos. 62–63	
Cann	C	Welles arms, or a lion rampant, and crest, a demi-lion rampant; ESW (later)	Welles family	ca. 1735	French 1941, no. 70a	
Cann	C	unidentified arms; IH		ca. 1735	French 1939, no. 70	
Cann	C	Green arms, on a fess azure a dragon passant between 2 escallops; 2 lions' heads in chief on sable roundles, and crest, a woodpecker pecking at a tree stump (+)	John Green	ca. 1735	Warren 1975, no. 282	BBC
Cann	C	Catherine Amelia from her Father June 1st 1835 (later)		ca. 1735	French 1961, 1	
Two canns	C	Williams arms, sable a lion rampant, and crest, a moorcock; The Gift of Deacon Ionathan Williams/To the first Church in Boston/at his decease/ March 27 1737	Jonathan Williams	ca. 1735	French 1939, nos. 64–65	
Cann	C	JED/from/SOB		ca. 1740	YUAG files	
Cann	C	SO		ca. 1740	YUAG files	
Cann	D	Quincy arms	Quincy family	ca. 1745	French 1939, no. 88	
Cann	D*	R/HS		ca. 1735	French 1941, no. 78a	LAM
Cann	D	unidentified arms (later)		ca. 1735	*Moore Collection* 1980, no. 118	
Cann	D*	A GIFT/From some of The/PRINCIPALL/ Officers in the regiment/of BOSTON to/ M.r Adjutant/HUNT/ 1747. (+)	Officers of the Boston regiment for Jabez Hunt	1747	Johnston 1994, 79	CMA
Cann	D	TW; NH (later) (+)		ca. 1750	*Moore Collection* 1980, no. 117	
Cann	D	unidentified crest, a lion's head crowned and erased; W/DH (later)	West family (?)	ca. 1740	Buhler 1972, no. 185	MFAB

	Mark	Inscription	Patron	Date	Reference	Owner
Cann	D	S/JT		ca. 1745	*American Silver* 1967, no. 10	RWNAG
Cann	D	IB		ca. 1735	DAPC 73.2250	
Cann	D	EH		ca. 1745	French 1941, no. 78b	
Cann	D	Prescott arms	Prescott family	ca. 1745	French 1939, no. 79	
Two canns	D	Vassall arms, in chief a sun in splendor, in base a chalice, and crest, a full-rigged ship, sails furled; Edmund Baker/1811 (later)	Vassall family	ca. 1745	French 1939, nos. 81–82	
Cann	D	unidentified arms, vert a lion rampant, and crest, a lion statant; LL		ca. 1745	French 1939, no. 85	
Cann	D	Chauncy arms, a cross crosslet, on a chief a lion passant, and crest, a demi-griffin emerging from a ducal crown	Chauncy family	ca. 1750	French 1939, no. 86	
Cann	D	unidentified crest		ca. 1745	French 1941, no. 87a	
Cann	D	A/GH	Gibbs and Hannah Atkins	ca. 1745	French 1961, 1	
Cann	D	A/FK (+)		ca. 1745	French 1961, 1	
Cann	D	Weaver arms (+)	Weaver family	1744	French 1961, 1	
Cann	E	Quincy and Conant arms impaled; I/DS	Quincy and Conant families	ca. 1750	French 1939, no. 73	
Cann	E*	R/IH; RL (later)	John and Hannah (Speakman) Rowe	ca. 1735	*Antiques* 100 (September 1971): 320	
Cann	E	M/DE/1746; The Gift/of/Elizabeth Brooks/to the/First Church of Christ/in/Malden	Daniel and Elizabeth (Sweetser) (Tufts) Mansfield	1746	French 1939, no. 87	MFAB
Cann	F	MC		ca. 1745	Sotheby Parke Bernet, 31 January–3 February 1979, lot 107	
Cann	F	Gardner arms, a chevron gules between 3 bugle horns, and crest, a dexter armed arm grasping a staff; G/SA (+)	Gardner family	ca. 1745	French 1939, no. 75	MMA
Cann	F	Person or Barrett arms; P/EH (+)	Person or Barrett family (?)	ca. 1745	Buhler 1972, no. 186	MFAB

	Mark	Inscription	Patron	Date	Reference	Owner
Cann	F	Lynde arms, gules in chief or 3 mallets, and crest, a griffin holding a mallet	Benjamin Lynde	ca. 1745	Buhler 1972, no. 190	MFAB
Cann	F	W/AS; SRS		ca. 1745	French 1939, no. 68	
Cann	?	Quincy arms; I/DS	Quincy family	?	French 1939, no. 71	
Cann	?	Walker crest	Walker family	ca. 1740	Northeast Auctions, 14–15 March 1992, lot 411	
Cann	?	JN (cipher; later)		ca. 1750	Sotheby Parke Bernet, 1–4 February 1978, lot 667	
Cann	?	Rogers arms; Ex dono Pupillorum	Rev. Daniel Rogers	ca. 1740	YUAG files	
Caster	A	EA; AP		ca. 1740		CHS
Caster	C	EP (over erased initials); Stevenson/ 1750–1868 (later)		ca. 1735	Sotheby Parke Bernet, 31 January–3 February 1979, lot 108	
Caster	D*	EP	Elizabeth Pepperrell	ca. 1745	Buhler/Hood 1970, no. 148	YUAG
Two casters	D*	RT	Rebecca Townsend	1747	Hammerslough/ Feigenbaum 1958–73, 1:59	WA
Caster	D	B/SM		ca. 1745	Hammerslough/ Feigenbaum 1958–73, 4:38	
Caster	D	SH		ca. 1745	French 1939, no. 104	MMA
Caster	D	none		ca. 1750		CaMA
Two casters	D	D:HEWES	D. Hewes	ca. 1745	French 1939, nos. 100–01	
Caster	D	none	Gov. Joseph Talcott	ca. 1740		CHS
Caster	D	S/II; I/IS		ca. 1745	French 1939, no. 105	
Caster	D	none		ca. 1750	French 1939, no. 108	SPNEA
Caster	D	?		ca. 1745	French 1961, 1	
Caster	D	unidentified crest, a bird		ca. 1745	French 1961, 1	
Caster	D	S/RM	Richard and Mary (Cooke) Saltonstall	ca. 1745	Skinner, 15 June 1991, lot 164D	
Caster	D	R/ER		ca. 1740	Johnston 1994, 84	CMA

	Mark	Inscription	Patron	Date	Reference	Owner
Caster	F*	EC		ca. 1735		AIC
Caster	?	SC from SEL (+)		ca. 1745	Christie's, 26 January 1991, lot 63	
Two casters	?	Jackson crest, an escallop; MI	Mary Jackson	ca. 1740	*Antiques* 135 (June 1989): 1395	AIC
Caster	?	?		ca. 1740	Parke-Bernet, 17 May 1968, lot 197	
Caster	?	unidentified crest, a sinister hand		?	French 1961, 1	
Caster (attrib.)	none	H/AS	Harris family	ca. 1735		HD
Caudle cup	D	The Gift/OF/Capᵗ Joseph Burnap/to yᵉ First Church in/ Reading	First Congregational Church, Wakefield, Mass., for Joseph Burnap	ca. 1745	French 1939, no. 121	
Chafing dish	B*	Henchman arms, a chevron between 3 hunting horns, on a chief 3 lioncelles rampant, and crest, a cubit arm vested, holding 2 spears; LH	Lydia (Henchman) Hancock	ca. 1730	Buhler/Hood 1970, no. 142	YUAG
Chafing dish (mate below)	B*	Henchman arms, a chevron between 3 hunting horns, on a chief 3 lioncelles rampant, and crest, a cubit arm vested, holding 2 spears	Lydia (Henchman) Hancock	ca. 1730	Buhler/Hood 1970, no. 143	YUAG
Chafing dish (mate above)	B*	Henchman arms, a chevron between 3 hunting horns, on a chief 3 lioncelles rampant, and crest, a cubit arm vested, holding 2 spears	Lydia (Henchman) Hancock	ca. 1730	Bartlett 1984, 10–11	SLAM
Two chafing dishes	B*	Henchman arms, a chevron between 3 hunting horns, on a chief 3 lioncelles rampant, and crest, a cubit arm vested, holding 2 spears	Daniel Henchman	ca. 1730	Buhler/Hood 1970, no. 141	YUAG
Chafing dish	B	Walker arms (+)	Walker family	ca. 1735	French 1939, no. 53	
Chafing dish	B	Cotton or Gardner arms, a chevron between 3 griffins' heads, and crest, a griffin's head erased, impaling unidentified arms, a chevron	Cotton or Gardner families	ca. 1735	French 1939, no. 54	

	Mark	Inscription	Patron	Date	Reference	Owner
		between 3 eagles displayed				
Chafing dish	C	unidentified crest, a hound's head collared		ca. 1735	French 1939, no. 55	
Chafing dish	C	Lynde crest; L/BM	Benjamin and Mary (Bowles) Lynde	ca. 1735	French 1939, no. 56	
Chafing dish	D	none		ca. 1745	Buhler 1972, no. 189	MFAB
Chafing dish	F	Phillips arms, azure a lion rampant a chief ermine, and crest, a demi-lion rampant; The Gift/ of M.ʳ W.ᵐ Blair Townsend Merc:/to/ Cap.ᵗ John Phillips i/ in Boston 1745	William Blair Townsend and/or John Phillips	1745	Buhler 1972, no. 188	MFAB
Chafing dish	?	?		ca. 1735	Parke-Bernet, 17–18 May 1946, lot 298	
Coffeepot	B*	unidentified arms (erased); From a Friend/to the Reverend Doctor/Sam.ᵗ Stillman (later)		ca. 1735	YUAG files	
Coffeepot	C*	Traill arms, a chevron or between 2 mascles in chief and a trefoil slipped in the base, and crest, a column on a rock, impaling Gale arms, argent a griffin segreant or within a bordure gobony argent and azure; DISCRIMINE SALUS (+)	Traill family	ca. 1735	*Antiques* 102 (December 1972): 972	
Coffeepot	D	Clarke arms, 3 swords erect in pale hilts up, and crest, a sword hilt up	Clarke family	ca. 1745	Quimby 1995, no. 79	WM
Coffeepot	D	Alleyne arms, per chevron gules and ermine, in chief 2 lions' heads erased, and crest, a unicorn's head ducally gorged	Alleyne family	ca. 1745	French 1939, no. 112	
Creampot	C*	none		ca. 1740	DAPC 69.1775	MMA
Creampot	C*	Traill crest, a column; WEH (later)	Traill family	ca. 1735	Johnston 1994, 86 (as unknown maker)	CMA

	Mark	Inscription	Patron	Date	Reference	Owner
Creampot	C	B/PE		ca. 1735	French 1939, no. 117	
Creampot	D	TMP (later)		ca. 1745	French 1939, no. 120	
Creampot	D	unidentified crest, a mailed arm embowed; S Holland	S. Holland	ca. 1745	French 1941, no. 120a	
Creampot	D	?		ca. 1740	*Antiques* 103 (April 1973): 825	
Creampot	D*	Vassall arms, in chief a sun in splendor, in base a chalice, and crest, a full-rigged ship, sails furled; ECP (later)	Vassall family	ca. 1745	Johnston 1994, 80	CMA
Creampot	D*	Johnson (?) arms, argent 3 and a half bands gules, and crest, a lion's head erased emerging from a ducal crown; I/IS (partially erased) (+)	Johnson family (?)	ca. 1750	Buhler/Hood 1970, no. 149	YUAG
Creampot	D*	ME (+)		ca. 1750	Buhler/Hood 1970, no. 150	YUAG
Creampot	D	IOL		ca. 1750	Sotheby's, 26–27 June 1991, lot 112	
Creampot	D	C/WM (+)	William and Mary Cory	ca. 1735	DAPC 72.3243	BBC
Creampot (with later cover)	F†	L/NM; L		ca. 1745	Johnston 1994, 85 (as unknown maker)	CMA
Creampot	?	The Gift/G Russell to/his grand daughter/Eliz: Trivet/1749	G. Russell for Elizabeth Trivet	1749	French 1939, no. 116	
Creampot	?	?		ca. 1740	*Antiques* 128 (August 1985): 201	
Creampot	?	unidentified crest, a bird with a sprig in its beak; B/JR		ca. 1750	*Antiques* 120 (December 1981): 1378	
Cup	B	Phoebe Collman	Phoebe (Coleman) Folger	ca. 1725	Buhler 1972, no. 163	MFAB
Cup	C	?		ca. 1735	French 1939, no. 124	
Cup	C	?		ca. 1735	French 1961, 2	
Cup (with cover)	D	Hooper arms	Hooper family	ca. 1745	French 1939, no. 123	
Cup	?	?		?	French 1961, 2	

	Mark	Inscription	Patron	Date	Reference	Owner
Grace cup	A/C	WC (cipher); Cave impaling Petit arms (later)	William Cave (?)	ca. 1735	Safford 1983, 37	MMA
Grace cup	A†/ D*	To/EDWARD TYNG Esqʳ./Commander of ye SNOW/Prince of Orange/As an Ac-knowledgement of/his good Service done the/TRADE in Taking yᵉ First/French Privateer/on this Coast the 24ᵗʰ of June/1744 This Plate is presented/BY Several of yᵉ Merch.ᵗˢ/in Boston New/England	several Boston merchants for Edward Tyng	1744	Buhler/Hood 1970, no. 157	YUAG
Grace cup	A/D	TO/Richard Spry Esqᶠ./Commander of yᵉ COMET BOMB/For his gallant Be-haviour/& Singular Service Done/yᵉ TRADE in taking a/french Privateer This/Piece of Plate Is Pre/sented By Several/of yᵉ Mer-chants/in Boston NEngᵈ/Decʳ 21, 1744	several Boston merchants for Richard Spry	1744	Warren/ Howe/ Brown 1987, no. 57	
Grace cup	B/G	Rowe arms, 3 pas-chal lambs with staves and banners, and crest, a paschal lamb	John Rowe	ca. 1740	Buhler 1972, no. 187	MFAB
Ladle	D	none		ca. 1745	Ham-merslough/ Feigenbaum 1958–73, 1:107	
Ladle	D	HE	Edes family	ca. 1745	Buhler 1972, no. 191	MFAB
Ladle	D*	none		ca. 1740	Flynt/Fales 1968, 116–17	HD
Ladle	D	N/IM		ca. 1745	French 1939, no. 134	MFAB
Ladle	D*	Winthrop crest, a hare courant; EX DONO/IH to IW/1747	Winthrop family	1747	French 1961, 2	
Ladle	?	RTS		ca. 1740	YUAG files	
Miniature case (gold)	C	none		1734	Saunders/ Miles 1987, no. 18	
Mourning ring (gold)	C*	ED Obt 13″ Sept. 1740 AE 36		1740	French 1939, no. 173	PEM

	Mark	Inscription	Patron	Date	Reference	Owner
Mourning ring (gold)	D*	Revd. Mr. I·Ro-gers. Ob 28 Dec: 1745 AE: 80	Rev. John Rogers	1745	Buhler/Hood 1970, no. 156	YUAG
Mourning ring (gold; attrib.)	none	HON: MRˢ.K/ DUMMER/OB: 13 JAN/1752 AE 62.	Katherine (Dudley) Dummer	1752	Buhler 1972, no. 195	MFAB
Mug	A/B	S/FH		ca. 1735	French 1941, no. 143a	
Two mugs	B	Samuel Whitney/ Castine (later?) (+)		ca. 1730	French 1939, nos. 139–40	
Mug	B	G/IL		ca. 1730	French 1939, no. 142	HMA
Mug	C	P/CM	Caleb and Mary (Adams) Parker	ca. 1730	Buhler 1972, no. 165	MFAB
Papboat	D	C/IM/to/MC	John and Mary Channing	ca. 1746	French 1939, no. 144	
Patch box	B*	Greenleaf crest, a bird with a sprig in its beak	Greenleaf family	ca. 1735	Buhler/Hood 1970, no. 137	YUAG
Patch box	C*	EB		ca. 1735	DAPC 83.2228	
Pepper box	A	none		ca. 1735	*Silver Supple-ment* 1973, no. 54	
Pepper box	A	L/TL		ca. 1735	French 1939, no. 97	
Pepper box	A	EA		ca. 1735	DAPC 76.2359	CHS
Pepper box	B*	?	Warren family	ca. 1730	*Sack Collec-tion* 3:627	
Pepper box	B	W/IC	Comfort Weeks	ca. 1735	French 1939, no. 99	
Pepper box	B	C/AM		ca. 1735	Buhler 1972, no. 176	MFAB
Pepper box	B	K/ID	Kendall family	ca. 1735	*CGA Bulletin*, no. 1 (1971): fig. 11	CGA
Pepper box	B*	HP		ca. 1735	YUAG files	
Pepper box	B*	unidentified crest, a demi-lion rampant; CALEB &/MARTHA/ EDDY/1747; M; C	Caleb and Martha Eddy	1747	French 1939, no. 96	SFCAI
Pepper box	B/C	K/ID	Kendall family	ca. 1735	Buhler 1965, 56–57	
Pepper box	C*	M/EB (altered to EP)		ca. 1740	Flynt/Fales 1968, 116–17	HD
Pepper box	C	ET		ca. 1735	Shelley 1958, 175	HFM
Pepper box	C	none		ca. 1735	French 1939, no. 95	
Pepper box	C	B/ME	Matthias and Elizabeth Burnett	ca. 1735	French 1941, no. 98a	
Pepper box	D*	L/DI	Lane family	ca. 1740	Quimby 1995, no. 83	WM

	Mark	Inscription	Patron	Date	Reference	Owner
Pepper box	D	none		ca. 1735	*Moore Collection* 1980, no. 116	
Pepper box	D	BEH		ca. 1740		DIA
Pepper box	E	?		ca. 1750	French 1939, no. 98	
Pepper box	F*	The Gift of/M^{rs} J· Ross/to H·T/1743 (+)	Mrs. J. Ross	1743	Johnston 1994, 79	CMA
Pepper box	?	B/TM	Thomas and Mary (Mix) Belden	ca. 1730	Sotheby Parke Bernet, 17 October 1972, lot 112	
Pepper box	?	Hancock crest, a demi-griffin; LH	Lydia (Henchman) Hancock	ca. 1730	French 1939, no. 91	Bostonian Society
Pepper box	?	?		ca. 1735	Parke-Bernet, 26–27 January 1945, lot 164	
Porringer	A	B/TM	Thomas and Margaret Binney	ca. 1740	French 1939, no. 156	
Porringer	A*	S/AM		ca. 1740	YUAG files	
Porringer	A	Flynt crest; The Gift of/Henry Flynt . . . (later)	Henry Flynt and/or the Harvard College class of ca. 1735	ca. 1735	Buhler 1972, no. 177	MFAB
Porringer	A	P	Phillips family	ca. 1740	French 1941, no. 167b	
Porringer	A	IR	Rotch family	ca. 1740	French 1961, 2	
Porringer	A	JL to MEL		ca. 1740	French 1939, no. 158	
Porringer	A	D/WS	William and Sarah Diadoti	ca. 1740	French 1961, 2	
Porringer	A/B	SH		ca. 1735	French 1939, no. 165	
Porringer	A/C	EW		ca. 1735		MFAB
Porringer	A/C	?		ca. 1740	Parke-Bernet, 4 January 1940, lot 67	
Porringer	A/C	?		ca. 1735	French 1961, 2	
Porringer	A/C	PC	Prudence (Chester) Stoddard	ca. 1735	Stillinger 1990, 70–71	
Porringer	B	B/SD		ca. 1735	French 1939, no. 157	
Porringer	B*	unidentified crest, a griffin rampant holding a lance		ca. 1735	*Sack Collection* 3:662	
Porringer	B	CNC/1790 (later)		ca. 1740	*CGA Bulletin*, no. 1 (1971): fig. 12	CGA
Porringer	B	C/MM		ca. 1735	French 1939, no. 148	

	Mark	Inscription	Patron	Date	Reference	Owner
Porringer	B*	TC (+)	Thomas Clapp	ca. 1740	French 1939, no. 150	MMA
Porringer	B	B	Baker family	ca. 1740	French 1939, no. 163	
Porringer	B	AB		ca. 1735	French 1939, no. 155	
Porringer	B*	IH (later)		ca. 1740	French 1961, 2	
Porringer	B	B/ME		ca. 1740	YUAG files	
Porringer	B/C	DF (+)		ca. 1735	Buhler 1972, no. 178	MFAB
Porringer	C*	HH		ca. 1735	Buhler/Hood 1970, no. 146	YUAG
Porringer	D	PL		ca. 1740	*American Art of the Colonies and Early Republic*, no. 105	
Porringer	D	unidentified crest, wings and twisted rope		ca. 1740	Washington 1925, no. 62	
Porringer	D	WR	William Rotch, Sr.	ca. 1735	Gustafson 1982, 436	ODHS
Porringer	D	unidentified crest, a mailed arm grasping a stag's antler (+)	Bowditch family (?)	ca. 1745	French 1939, no. 147	
Porringer	D*	MP/to/RP	Mercy (Gibbs) Prescott	ca. 1745	Buhler/Hood 1970, no. 154	YUAG
Porringer	D*	unidentified crest, a lion rampant; W/TA		ca. 1740	French 1939, no. 164	HD
Porringer	D	CJM (cipher) (+)	John and Mary Channing	ca. 1740	French 1939, no. 153	
Porringer	D*	P/IS (+)		ca. 1745	Eitner 1976, no. 39	
Porringer	D	ES 1771 (later) (+)	Salisbury family (?)	ca. 1745	French 1939, no. 162	
Porringer	D/F	The Gift of M:rs Elizabeth Russel/To Her Grand Daughter/Eliz:h Trivet	Elizabeth Russell for Elizabeth Trivet	ca. 1744	*American Silver* 1967, no. 9	RWNAG
Porringer	D/F	DA; SM (later) (+)	Daniel Ayrault	ca. 1740	Biddle 1963, no. 101	
Porringer	F	SB		ca. 1740	*Antiques* 112 (August 1977): 290	
Porringer	F*	E/IS		ca. 1745	Conger/ Rollins 1991, no. 190	USDS
Porringer	F*	H/IM/SS (+)	Jabez and M. Hamlin	ca. 1740	DAPC 78.3795	
Porringer	F	W/BE		ca. 1745	French 1961, 2	
Porringer	F	HSF (later)		ca. 1745	French 1939, no. 152	
Porringer	F	C/ST/to/RL	Rachel Leonard	ca. 1745	French 1939, no. 160	

	Mark	Inscription	Patron	Date	Reference	Owner
Porringer	?	Lynde crest, a griffin holding a mallet	Benjamin Lynde	ca. 1745	Christie's, 17 June 1992, lot 53A	
Porringer	?	?		ca. 1730		ChM
Porringer	?	RL	Rachel Leonard	?	YUAG files	
Porringer	?	LM		ca. 1740	Ellesin 1971, 538	
Porringer	?	?		?	French 1939, no. 149	
Porringer	?	R/SM		?	French 1939, no. 166	
Porringer	?	?		?	French 1939, no. 167	
Porringer	?	AB; IN GREENE (later)		?	French 1961, 2	
Two salts	D	unidentified crest, a deer; D:HEWES	D. Hewes	ca. 1745	French 1939, nos. 176–77	
Two salts	D	IG; B (later)		ca. 1745	French 1941, no. 177a–b	
Salt	D	?		ca. 1745	French 1939, no. 178	
Two salts	D	C/IS		ca. 1745	Buhler 1972, no. 544	MFAB
Salt	D	Belcher crest, a talbot's head gorged and erased; AB/to/AA	Belcher family	ca. 1735	DAPC 69.1766	MMA
Two salts	D	none	William and Mehitable Bradley	ca. 1740	Johnston 1994, 88 (as unknown maker)	CMA
Two salt spoons	D	CI/to/TEW		ca. 1745	French 1939, nos. 233–34	MFAB
Salver	B*	Browne arms, argent on a bend sable double cotised 3 eagles displayed, and crest, an eagle	Browne family	ca. 1745	French 1939, no. 293	SI
Salver	B*	Bulfinch arms, 3 thistles, and crest, a bird, impaling Colman arms, azure upon a pale rayonée or a lion rampant	Thomas and Judith (Colman) Bulfinch	ca. 1730	Flynt/Fales 1968, 85–86	HD
Salver	B	Bromfield arms, on a chevron 3 broom sprigs, on a canton a spear's head embrued, in chief point a mullet, and crest, a demi-tyger holding a broken sword (+)	Bromfield family	ca. 1730	DAPC 81.3871	

	Mark	Inscription	Patron	Date	Reference	Owner
Salver	c	H/WL		ca. 1745	*Silver Supplement* 1973, no. 50	
Salver	c	unidentified inscription (later)	Greenleaf and/or Moseley family (?)	ca. 1735	Christie's, 23 January 1982, lot 93	
Salver	c	Oliver arms, an arm from a cloud at the sinister side fessways grasping a dexter hand couped at the wrist, and crest, a bird with a sprig in its beak	Oliver family	ca. 1735	Buhler 1972, no. 171	MFAB
Salver	c*	Oliver arms, an arm from a cloud at the sinister side fessways grasping a dexter hand couped at the wrist, and crest, a bird with a sprig in its beak	Oliver family	ca. 1740	DAPC 78.4226	
Salver	c	O/IS; John and Sarah Osborn (later)	John and Sarah Osborn	ca. 1740	Sotheby's, 28–31 January 1993, lot 135A	
Salver	d	IT		ca. 1740	*Bulletin DIA* 33 (1953–54): 95	DIA
Salver	d	Hubbard arms, gules 3 lions passant on a bend or, and crest, a lion's head erased on a wreath ermine	Hubbard family	ca. 1745	Quimby 1995, no. 82	WM
Salver	d*	arms erased		ca. 1750	Puig et al. 1989, no. 197	MIA
Two salvers	d*	Hastings arms, a manche, and unidentified crest, a stag statant; H/AT/1750	A. and T. Hastings	1750	Johnston 1994, 81	CMA
Salver	d	Colman arms (erased)	Sarah or Benjamin Colman	ca. 1740	Buhler 1972, no. 184	MFAB
Salver	d*	Gorham arms, gules 3 fetterlocks conjoined in fess, and unidentified crest, a lion rampant; H.F.I. to A.G.W. (later) (+)	Gorham family	ca. 1745	YUAG files	
Salver	d	AM/to/SM (later)	Abigail May (?)	ca. 1745	Buhler 1972, no. 193	MFAB
Salver	d	C/IS	Chauncy family	ca. 1745	French 1941, no. 296a	
Salver	d*	Clarke arms, 3 swords erect in pale,	William Clarke	ca. 1745	Buhler/Hood 1970, no. 151	YUAG

	Mark	Inscription	Patron	Date	Reference	Owner
		points up, and crest, an armed dexter arm embowed				
Salver	D*	Smith arms, 3 broken lances erect in fess, a chief chequey or and gules, and crest, a sea lion; DEUS NOBIS HAEC OTIA FECIT	William Peartree Smith	ca. 1740	Backlin-Landman 1969, 370	Princeton University
Salver	E	Greene arms	Gov. William Greene (?)	ca. 1745		MFAB
Salver	F	J.Q. 1742	J. Quincy (?)	ca. 1742	French 1939, no. 295	
Salver	?	Jackson arms, quarterly 4 escallops, and crest, an escallop; MI	Mary Jackson	ca. 1740	*Antiques* 135 (June 1989): 1395	
Salver	?	R/GE		?	French 1939, no. 294	
Salver	?	AT		?	French 1961, 2	
Sauceboat (mate below)	D*	unidentified crest, a lion's head crowned	Pickering family (?)	ca. 1745	Buhler/Hood 1970, no. 152	YUAG
Sauceboat (mate above)	D*	unidentified crest, a lion's head crowned	Pickering family (?)	ca. 1745	Buhler/Hood 1970, 131	
Sauceboat	D	unidentified arms, a griffin rampant, and crest, a unicorn's head couped; TH (later)	Harris family	ca. 1745	*Silver Supplement* 1973, no. 52	
Sauceboat	D	P/TS		ca. 1745	French 1939, no. 179	
Sauceboat	D	Walter arms, azure a fess dancettée or between 3 eagles displayed, and crest, an eagle's head couped	Walter family	ca. 1745	Quimby 1995, no. 84	WM
Sauceboat	D	unidentified crest		ca. 1745	French 1941, no. 181a	
Sauceboat (mate below)	D	Andrews crest, a saracen's head wreathed with a ribbon couped at the shoulders	Andrews family	ca. 1745	French 1961, 2	CF
Sauceboat (mate above)	D	Andrews crest, a saracen's head wreathed with a ribbon couped at the shoulders	Andrews family	ca. 1745	Hanks 1970, 420	AIC
Sauceboat	E*	M/IM; LB (later)		ca. 1750	*Silver Supplement* 1973, no. 53	
Two sauceboats	F*	unidentified crest, a demi-lion rampant collared and chained on an eagle's wing		ca. 1745	*Silver Supplement* 1973, nos. 51a–b	

	Mark	Inscription	Patron	Date	Reference	Owner
Saucepan	A/C	PD		ca. 1735	Buhler 1972, no. 175	MFAB
Seal	D*	Phips arms, or a trefoil slipped between 8 mullets, and crest, a lion's gamb holding a trefoil	Spencer Phips	ca. 1750	Buhler/Hood 1970, no. 153	YUAG
Serving spoon	A*	Spooner (?) crest, a boar's head pierced by an arrow; EH	Edmund Hobart (?)	ca. 1745	Eitner 1976, no. 40	
Serving spoon	B*	A Small Token/of Gratitude/to one of the Best/of/Guardian's		ca. 1740	DAPC 86.2573	
Serving spoon	B	Mascarene crest	Mascarene family	ca. 1735	French 1939, no. 189	
Serving spoon	B	unidentified crest, a griffin passant		ca. 1735	French 1939, no. 190	MFAB
Serving spoon	C	unidentified crest, a bird rising; S/WK		ca. 1735	French 1939, no. 187	MMA
Two pairs of sleeve buttons (gold)	B	none		ca. 1735	French 1939, nos. 136–37	WA
Snuffbox	B*	Joseph Burbeen/1729	Joseph Burbeen	1729	Buhler/Hood 1970, no. 138	YUAG
Snuffbox (gold)	C	Dummer arms, azure 3 fleur-de-lis or, on a chief or a demi-lion issuant sable, and crest, a demi-lion holding a fleur-de-lis in his dexter paw	William Dummer	ca. 1735	Buhler 1972, no. 173	MFAB
Snuffbox	D	Hurd	Hurd family	ca. 1745	Hammerslough/Feigenbaum 1958–73, 4:93	
Snuffbox	D	unidentified crest; GL		ca. 1745	French 1939, no. 185	
Spoon	B	Elizabeth Rotch/was born the 28/of the 4 mo 1749	Elizabeth Rotch	1749	French 1961, 2	
Spoon	D	P/SA	Samuel and Anna Porter	ca. 1745	French 1961, 2	
Strainer	D*	C/PM		ca. 1750	Flynt/Fales 1968, 116–17	HD
Strainer	D*	none		ca. 1750	Puig et al. 1989, no. 198	MIA
Strainer	D*	none		ca. 1755		AIC
Strainer	D	?		ca. 1745	French 1939, no. 235	
Strainer	D	?		ca. 1745	French 1939, no. 236	

	Mark	Inscription	Patron	Date	Reference	Owner
Strainer	D	?		ca. 1745	French 1961, 2	
Strainer	D	?		ca. 1745	French 1961, 2	
Strainer	D*	Tyng	Edward Tyng	ca. 1745	*Sack Collection* 2:480	
Strainer	F	none		ca. 1750	Sotheby's, 30 January–2 February 1991, lot 134	
Strainer spoon	B*	W/KA (+)	Kenelm and Ann (Taylor) Winslow (?)	ca. 1730	Buhler 1972, no. 170	MFAB
Strainer spoon	C*	none		ca. 1735	Buhler/Hood 1970, no. 144	YUAG
Strainer spoon	D*	ER		ca. 1745	YUAG files	
Sugar bowl	B	FI		ca. 1735	Buhler 1965, 53–56, 60–61	HMA
Sugar bowl	B	unidentified crest, a griffin's head erased; C		ca. 1735	Buhler 1972, no. 172	MFAB
Sugar bowl	C*	Howard arms, gules a bend argent between 6 crosses crosslet, and crest, a lion passant guardant	Howard family	ca. 1735	Puig et al. 1989, no. 196	MIA
Sugar bowl	C	Henchman arms, a chevron between 3 hunting horns, on a chief 3 lioncelles rampant, and crest, a cubit arm vested, holding 2 spears	Lydia (Henchman) Hancock	ca. 1730	Buhler 1972, no. 179	MFAB
Sugar bowl	D*	Henchman arms, or between a chevron azure 3 hunting horns, on a chief gules 3 lioncelles rampant, and crest, a dexter arm quartered or and vert grasping an antler	Henchman family	ca. 1740	Safford 1983, 38–39	
Sugar bowl (part of a service)	F	Henchman arms, or a chevron sable between 3 hunting horns, on a chief gules 3 lioncelles rampant, and crest, a dexter arm quartered or and vert grasping an antler; VULNERAT ET VINCIT	Rev. Nathaniel Henchman	1737	Buhler 1972, no. 180	MFAB
Sugar bowl	F*	Traill arms, azure a chevron or between 2 mascles or in chief	Traill family (?)	1745	French 1939, no. 43	YUAG

	Mark	Inscription	Patron	Date	Reference	Owner
		and a trefoil slipped in the base, and crest, a column on a rock, impaling Gale arms, sable a griffin segreant or within a bordure gobony or and azure; DISCRIM-INE SALUS (+)				
Sugar bowl	?	Wendell arms; AW	Ann Wendell	ca. 1740	French 1939, no. 46	SPNEA
Sugar bowl	?	Hooper arms, or on a fess between 3 boars passant 3 annulets, and crest, a boar's head erased; H/RR	Robert and Ruth Hooper	?	French 1939, no. 41	
Sugar tongs	D	B/IF (+)		ca. 1745	Hammerslough/Feigenbaum 1958–73, 4:124–25	
Sugar tongs	D*	PM (over earlier initials)		ca. 1745	Flynt/Fales 1968, 116–17	HD
Sugar tongs	D*	unidentified crest, a lion's head erased		ca. 1750	Johnston 1994, 87 (as unknown maker)	CMA
Sugar tongs	D*	NL		ca. 1750	Johnston 1994, 82	CMA
Sugar tongs	D*	none		ca. 1750		SI
Sugar tongs	D	?		ca. 1745	French 1939, no. 237	
Sugar tongs	D	V/AD		ca. 1745	French 1939, no. 240	
Sugar tongs	?	R		ca. 1745	Christie's, 12 June 1982, lot 39A	
Sugar tongs	?	LM		ca. 1745	Christie's, 26 January 1985, lot 69	
Sword	A	Lieut. Samuel Clarke 1752	Samuel Clarke	1752	French 1939, no. 170	
Sword	B	The Sword of-/Col. William Prescott . . . (later)	William Prescott	ca. 1750	*Witness to America's Past*, 87	MHS
Sword	B*	none		ca. 1740	Quimby 1995, no. 85	WM
Sword	C	RH; R Hazen of/Haverhill A:D/1735; Cost £13-15-9	Richard Hazen	1735	*Silver Supplement* 1973, no. 56	MFAB
Sword	C	?		ca. 1735	Norman-Wilcox 1954, 49	

	Mark	Inscription	Patron	Date	Reference	Owner
Sword	c	?	Thomas Noyes	ca. 1730	French 1941, no. 172a	
Sword	D	none	John Winslow	ca. 1745	French 1939, no. 171	PS
Sword	D	I.L. BRACKET.	I. L. Bracket	ca. 1745	French 1939, no. 172	PHS
Sword	F	EL	Enoch Little	ca. 1740	Buhler 1972, no. 174	MFAB
Sword	?	Sam Lord		ca. 1745	Peterson (1955) 1991, no. 8	
Tablespoon	B*	PC		ca. 1735	Quimby 1995, no. 87a	WM
Tablespoon	B	K/EL		ca. 1730	Avery 1920, no. 116	MMA
Tablespoon	B	AW		ca. 1730	*Silver Supplement* 1973, no. 55	
Tablespoon	B	DG/to/RC	First Congregational Church, Wakefield, Mass.	ca. 1735	French 1939, no. 196	
Tablespoon	B*	Q/IH	Josiah and Hannah (Sturgis) Quincy	ca. 1733	Buhler 1972, no. 169	MFAB
Six tablespoons	B*	none		ca. 1735		HD
Tablespoon	B*	ES		ca. 1735		HD
Tablespoon	B*	Green crest, a woodpecker pecking a tree stump; Joshua/Green	Joshua Green	ca. 1731	Buhler 1972, no. 166	MFAB
Tablespoon	B*	NSC	New South Church, Boston	ca. 1730	Buhler 1972, no. 164	MFAB
Tablespoon	B*	S/DI		ca. 1735	Buhler/Hood 1970, no. 139	YUAG
Tablespoon	B	MB; MS (later)		ca. 1735	French 1939, no. 192	
Tablespoon	B	SH		ca. 1735	French 1939, no. 193	
Tablespoon	B	unidentified crest, a demi-griffin; MI born 1774 (later)		ca. 1735	*Moore Collection* 1980, no. 120	
Tablespoon	B	T/EE		ca. 1735	French 1939, no. 198	
Six tablespoons	B	N/IM		ca. 1735	French 1939, nos. 199–204	
Four tablespoons	B*	B/ID		ca. 1735	French 1939, nos. 205–08	
Tablespoon	B	BW to DW	Rev. Benjamin Wadsworth	ca. 1735	French 1939, no. 216	HU
Tablespoon (mate? below)	B	K/BD		ca. 1740	Buhler 1972, appendix no. 41	MFAB

	Mark	Inscription	Patron	Date	Reference	Owner
Tablespoon (mate? above)	B	K/BD		ca. 1740	French 1939, no. 217	
Tablespoon	B	Ex Dono SC Pupilli 1743	Harvard College class of 1743	1743	French 1961, 2	
Tablespoon	B*	B/IH (+)		ca. 1735	YUAG files	
Tablespoon	B	SH		ca. 1735	French 1939, no. 213	
Tablespoon	B	D.T/to/D. Webb/ born Feb 26/1735/6	D. Webb	1736	French 1939, no. 214	
Tablespoon	B*	AC		ca. 1735	Quimby 1995, no. 87b	WM
Tablespoon (mate below)	E*	Ware crest, a griffin's head pierced by an arrow	Ware family	ca. 1750	Johnston 1994, 87 (as unknown maker)	CMA
Tablespoon (mate above)	E	Ware crest, a griffin's head pierced by an arrow	Ware family	ca. 1750	French 1941, no. 216a	
Tablespoon	F	W/IM		ca. 1745	French 1939, no. 209	
Tablespoon	G*	D/IH; EAT (later)		ca. 1745	*Moore Collection* 1980, no. 119	
Tablespoon	G*	SC	Chipman family	ca. 1745	YUAG files	
Tablespoon	G*	RW		ca. 1745	*Moore Collection* 1980, no. 119	
Tablespoon	G†	HS		ca. 1735	Buhler/Hood 1970, no. 161	YUAG
Tablespoon	G	H/IS	John and Susannah (Touzell) Hathorne	ca. 1746	Buhler 1972, no. 192	MFAB
Tablespoon	?	IF		ca. 1735	*Antiques* 88 (December 1965): 749	
Tankard	A/B/ C	IT; Trumbull arms (later) (+)	Gov. Jonathan Trumbull	ca. 1740		CHS
Tankard	A/C	Belonging to the C<u>hh</u> of Christ/in NEWTOWN/1740	First Church, Newton, Mass.	1740	French 1939, no. 244	MFAB
Two tankards	A/C	The Gift of/Lie^{nt} Jonaⁿ Lawranc/to the Church of/ Christ in Groton/ Ob^t Sep^{tmbr} 19th/ 1729	First Parish, Groton, Mass., for Jonathan Lawrence	ca. 1734	French 1939, nos. 246–47	
Tankard	B	Dwight arms, er-mine a lion passant, in base a cross cross-let fitchée, on a chief gules a cres-cent, and crest, a demi-lion rampant; D/TE	Timothy and Experi-ence Dwight	ca. 1735	French 1939, no. 254	

	Mark	Inscription	Patron	Date	Reference	Owner
Tankard	B	The Gift of/Captn Iohn Breed/ Deceas'd to the first/Church in Lynn/Decemb[r], ye 14th, 1728	First Church of Christ, Lynn, Mass., for John Breed	1728	French 1939, no. 248	
Tankard	B*	none		ca. 1735	*Silver Supplement* 1973, no. 57	
Tankard	B*	B/DI; ES to IS		ca. 1730	*Antiques* 54 (November 1948): 355	
Tankard	B	G/EA	E. Grant (?)	ca. 1735	French 1939, no. 258	
Tankard	B	WW to P/EM		ca. 1735	Sotheby Parke Bernet, 30 January–1 February 1986, lot 398	
Tankard	B	unidentified initials		ca. 1735	Sotheby Parke Bernet, 28 March 1973, lot 141a	
Tankard	B*	Worthington arms, 3 dung forks sable, and crest, a goat passant with an oak branch in its mouth(+)	Rev. William and Temperance Worthington	ca. 1735	Hammerslough/ Feigenbaum 1958–73, 1:14–15	WA
Tankard	B*	unidentified arms, a chevron azure between a heart gules and a band gules above 2 quartrefoils, on a chief 3 mullets, and crest, a ducal coronet, impaling unidentified arms, a tree; MC (later)		ca. 1750	Buhler/Hood 1970, no. 158	YUAG
Tankard	B	TM to AM (+)	Thaddeus Mason for Anne Mason	ca. 1735	French 1939, no. 251	
Tankard	B	B/IL		ca. 1735	French 1939, no. 257	
Tankard	B	S/RS; The Gift of/ M[rs] Susanna Sharp/ to the Church in/ Brooklin/1770 (later)	Robert and Susannah (White) Sharp	ca. 1735	French 1939, no. 252	
Tankard	B	Whipple arms	Whipple family	ca. 1735	French 1939, no. 262	
Tankard	B*	Winslow arms, on a bend 6 lozenges conjoined sable, and crest, a tree trunk with new branches, a strap and buckle; W/IS	Isaac and Sarah Winslow	ca. 1730	French 1939, no. 264	

	Mark	Inscription	Patron	Date	Reference	Owner
Tankard	B	B/EM		ca. 1735	French 1939, no. 265, and French 1961	
Tankard	B	W/NL; 1731		1731	*Antiques* 93 (June 1968): 722	
Tankard	B	The Gift/of Mr. Ebenezer Metcalf/ to the First Church/in Lebanon	Ebenezer Metcalf and/or First Church, Lebanon, Conn.	ca. 1735	French 1941, no. 265a	
Tankard	B*	MG		ca. 1735	Shepard 1978, 227	MAM
Tankard	B	L/ID		ca. 1730	*Antiques* 86 (August 1964): 131	
Tankard	B*	Pickman arms, gules 2 battle-axes in sal-tire between 4 mart-lets; WF/to/AR (?; erased) (+)		ca. 1745		PEM
Tankard (missing cover)	B	Dudley arms, lion rampant, and crest, a lion's head	Dudley family	ca. 1735	French 1939, no. 141 (as a mug)	
Tankard	B/C	Checkley arms; C/SE	Rev. Samuel and Eliza-beth (Rolfe) Checkley	ca. 1735	Gourley 1965, no. 109	
Tankard	B*/C*	IP		ca. 1750	Conger/ Rollins 1991, no. 189	USDS
Tankard	B*/D	W/SS		ca. 1740	French 1939, no. 260	
Tankard	C	Burrill arms, or a sal-tire gules, on a chief azure a crescent be-tween 2 pierced stars of 6 points or; The Gift of Theo: Burrill Esqʳ/ to the first Church of Christ in/Lynn	Executor of the estate of Theophilus Burrill and Rev. Nathaniel Henchman for First Church of Christ, Lynn, Mass.	1737	French 1939, no. 249	
Tankard	C†	Danforth arms, in chief an eye in base a lozenge; The Gift of Elijah Danforth Esqʳ/to the Church in Dorchester/Anno Domini 1736	Elijah Danforth	ca. 1730	French 1939, no. 241	
Tankard	D	Rogers arms, per chevron between 3 bucks trippant, and crest, a buck's head; The Gift of Dea-con/Hopestill Clap to the Church/of christ in Dorches-ter/1748	Hopestill Clap and/or First Church, Dorches-ter, Mass.	1748	French 1939, no. 242	

	Mark	Inscription	Patron	Date	Reference	Owner
Tankard	D	The Gift/OF/Nath.^{ll} Thomas Esqr/to the FIRST/Church of Christ/IN/ PLYMOUTH/1745	First Parish, Plymouth, Mass., for Nathaniel Thomas	1745	French 1939, no. 245	PS
Tankard	D	unidentified arms; IHOB (later) (+)		ca. 1745	French 1941, no. 243a	
Tankard	D	S/IS (+)	James and Sarah (Smith) Sproat	ca. 1745	Jones 1913, 370–71	
Tankard	D	Sherburne arms	Sherburne family	ca. 1740	French 1961, 3	SPNEA
Tankard	D/F	The Gift of/Mrs. Sarah Phelps/to the first Church/in Leb- anon/1746	Sarah Phelps and/or First Church, Lebanon, Conn.	1746	French 1941, no. 265b	
Tankard	E	C/NE/1770	Nathaniel and Eliza- beth Curtis (?)	ca. 1750	French 1939, no. 253	
Tankard	E†	The Gift/OF/ THO^s WELLS Esq./ Dec^d to the Church of/Christ in/DEAR- FIELD/1750	First Congregational Church, Deerfield, Mass., for Thomas Wells	1750	French 1939, no. 256	
Tankard	F	R/MA		ca. 1745	French 1939, no. 250	
Tankard	?	H; bison in cartouche		ca. 1750	Wardwell 1966, 81	
Tankard	?	Saltonstall arms (+)	Saltonstall family	?	French 1939, no. 259	
Tankard	?	unidentified cipher; 1751	William Lithgow	1751	French 1939, no. 261	
Tankard	?	?	Joseph Talcott	?	French 1961, 3	
Tankard (missing cover)	?	?		?	French 1961, 3	
Tankard	?	unidentified arms, a chevron gules be- tween 3 fleur-de-lis, and crest, a fleur- de-lis (+)		ca. 1745	*Antiques* 112 (October 1982): 726	
Teakettle on stand	B/C	Lowell arms, quar- ters 1 and 4, sable a hand couped at the wrist grasping 3 darts, one in pale, and crest, a stag's head cabossed, im- paling Leversedge arms, quarters 2 and 3, sable a chevron or between 3 dolphins; OCCAIONEM COCNOSCE	John Lowell	ca. 1735	Buhler 1972, no. 543	MFAB
Teapot	A*	none		ca. 1735	French 1961, 3	RISD
Teapot	A	Clarke arms, 3 swords erect in pale, points up, the mid- dle sword bears on	Clarke family	ca. 1745	French 1939, no. 280	

	Mark	Inscription	Patron	Date	Reference	Owner
		an inscutcheon a sinister hand, and crest, an armed dexter arm embowed				
Teapot	A/C	Sturgis arms (+)	Josiah and Hannah (Sturgis) Quincy	ca. 1730	Buhler 1972, no. 167	MFAB
Teapot	B†	Pepperrell arms, a chevron gules between 3 pineapples; RB	William Pepperrell	ca. 1735	Buhler/Hood 1970, no. 140	YUAG
Teapot	B*	Coffin arms, 3 bezants or between 9 crosses crosslet, and crest, a demi-griffin segreant	Coffin family	ca. 1730	Comstock 1958, 530	HD
Teapot	B	Storer arms, 3 quatrefoils on a chevron engrailed gules between 3 mullets, and crest, a talbot's head; SSM (cipher); S/SM	Rev. Seth and Mary (Coney) Storer	ca. 1735	Buhler 1972, no. 168	MFAB
Teapot	B	G/FR; W McK		ca. 1735	French 1939, no. 283	
Teapot	B	inscription erased		ca. 1735	French 1939, no. 285	
Teapot	B*	none		ca. 1745	*Historic Deerfield Quarterly* 29, n.p.	HD
Teapot	B*	G/DR (+)		ca. 1735	Quimby 1995, no. 80	WM
Teapot	B*/C*	CIM (cipher); CIM	John and Mary Channing	ca. 1735	Sotheby's, 21 June 1989, lot 135	
Teapot (part of a service)	C	Henchman arms, or between a chevron sable 3 hunting horns, on a chief gules 3 lioncelles rampant, and crest, a dexter arm grasping an antler; VULNERAT ET VINCIT; The Gift of/Theo: Burrill Esq.̲/to the Rev.ᵈ Mr.̲/Nath: Henchman/Pastor of yᵉ̲ first/Church in Lynn/July 5.̲ᵗʰ 1737	Rev. Nathaniel Henchman from Theophilus Burrill	1737	Buhler 1972, no. 181	MFAB
Teapot	C*	Townsend arms, a chevron ermine between 3 escallops, and crest, a stag statant; The Gift of Jamˢ̲ Townsend to Reb. Mason./1738	James Townsend and/or Rebecca (Townsend) Mason	1738	Buhler/Hood 1970, no. 147	YUAG

	Mark	Inscription	Patron	Date	Reference	Owner
Teapot	c	Flynt arms, 3 flintstones, and crest, a lion rampant; Ex dono Pupillorum/1738 (+)	Henry Flynt and/or the Harvard College class of 1738	1738	Buhler 1972, no. 182	MFAB
Teapot	c*	Eliot arms, argent a fess gules between 4 cotises wavy sable, and crest, an elephant's head	Jared Eliot (?)	ca. 1735	Flynt/Fales 1968, 76–77	HD
Teapot	c	unidentified arms, 3 griffins' heads erased		ca. 1735	French 1939, no. 269	DIA
Teapot	c	Gibbs arms; 1735 (+)	Gibbs family	ca. 1735	French 1939, no. 276	
Teapot	c	Holyoke arms, azure a chevron argent cotised or between 3 crescents, and crest, a crescent	Rev. Edward and Margaret (Appleton) Holyoke	ca. 1735	French 1939, no. 272	
Teapot	d*	Whipple arms, sable on a chevron between 3 swans' heads erased 3 crescents, and crest, a swan's head	Whipple family	ca. 1740	Johnston 1994, 83	CMA
Teapot	d	Fleet (?) arms, 2 dolphins embowed on a bend or 3 escallops, and unidentified crest, an erect arm grasping a dolphin (+)	Thomas and Elizabeth (Vergoose) Fleet (?)	ca. 1750	Buhler 1972, no. 194	MFAB
Teapot	d	unidentified arms (obliterated); c/MW		ca. 1745	French 1939, no. 284	
Teapot	d*	unidentified arms, a chevron with 3 trefoils over a fleur-de-lis; EX DONO PUPILLORUM 1745	Rev. Thomas Clapp and/or the Yale College class of 1745	1745	French 1939, no. 266	YUAG
Teapot	d	unidentified arms, a bend raguly between 6 roses; The Gift/ OF Edwd Tyng Esqr/to/H. Fayerweather/Decr 9/1745	Edward Tyng and/or Hannah Fayerweather	1745	Buhler 1965, 57–60	HMA
Teapot	e*	Sherburne arms, quarters 1 and 4, a lion rampant, quarters 2 and 3, azure an eagle displayed, and crest, a unicorn's head erased	Sherburne family	ca. 1750	French 1939, no. 286	WA

	Mark	Inscription	Patron	Date	Reference	Owner
Teapot	F*	T/CS	Christopher and Sarah Tilden	ca. 1740	French 1939 and 1961, no. 278	AIC
Teapot	F	Symmes arms, ermine 3 increscents, and crest, a sun in splendor, impaling Wolcott arms, a chevron ermine between 3 chess rooks; W/IA	Wolcott or Symmes family	ca. 1745	French 1939, no. 282	
Teapot	?	LS (cipher)	L. Seymour	ca. 1735	*Antiques* 116 (September 1979): 419	
Teaspoon	B	PM		ca. 1735	French 1939, no. 231	
Teaspoon	C*	ST		ca. 1735	Quimby 1995, no. 90	WM
Teaspoon	C	EB		ca. 1730	Buhler 1972, appendix no. 40	MFAB
Three teaspoons (mate below)	C	none		ca. 1750	French 1939, no. 226	MHS
Teaspoon (mates above)	C	none		ca. 1750	Buhler 1972, appendix no. 43	MFAB
Teaspoon	C*	PT (+)		ca. 1735	Johnston 1994, 84	CMA
Teaspoon	C	RW; 1758 (later)		ca. 1735	French 1941, no. 220a	
Teaspoon	D*	AS		ca. 1745	Buhler/Hood 1970, no. 155	YUAG
Teaspoon	D	AT		ca. 1745	French 1941, no. 220b	RISD
Teaspoon	D	HE		ca. 1745	French 1939, no. 221	
Teaspoon	D*	HE (over earlier initials)		ca. 1745	YUAG files	
Teaspoon	D	ML/1756		ca. 1756	French 1939, no. 222	PS
Two teaspoons	D	I/IM		ca. 1745	French 1939, nos. 227–28	
Teaspoon	D	EP		ca. 1745	French 1939, no. 229	
Teaspoon	D	MY		ca. 1745	French 1939, no. 230	
Teaspoon (see also unmarked mate)	D	K/BD		ca. 1740	Buhler 1972, appendix no. 42	MFAB
Teaspoon	D	unidentified crest; EP		ca. 1745	French 1941, no. 231b	MFAB
Teaspoon	D†	Ex Don/ Pup:/1744		1744	Quimby 1995, no. 88a	WM

	Mark	Inscription	Patron	Date	Reference	Owner
Teaspoon	D*	MM		ca. 1750	Quimby 1995, no. 88b	WM
Teaspoon	D*	MB		ca. 1750	Quimby 1995, no. 88c	WM
Teaspoon	D*	EH		ca. 1750	Quimby 1995, no. 88d	WM
Two teaspoons	F	unidentified crest, a ship		ca. 1745	French 1939, nos. 223–24	
Two teaspoons	F	Wendell crest (+)	Wendell family	ca. 1745	Buhler 1956, no. 88	MFAB
Teaspoon	F	SI		ca. 1745	Quimby 1995, no. 89	WM
Teaspoon	G	HB		ca. 1745		HD
Teaspoon	G	EL		ca. 1740		RISD
Teaspoon (see also mate with mark D)	none	K/BD		ca. 1740	Buhler 1972, appendix no. 42	MFAB
Teaspoon	?	PW		ca. 1740	Parke-Bernet, 11 February 1970, lot 189	
Teaspoon	?	OL		ca. 1740	Parke-Bernet, 11 February 1970, lot 189	
Thimble (gold)	C*	Elizh Gooch; 1714 (later)	Elizabeth Gooch	ca. 1735	Buhler/Hood 1970, no. 145	YUAG
Two-handled cup	B*	The Gift/of M.ʳ Ichabod Alis/to the Church In/HAT-FIELD/1747	First Congregational Church, Hatfield, Mass., for Ichabod Allis	1747	Buhler/Hood 1970, no. 159	YUAG
Two-handled cup	F	none	Second Church, Boston	ca. 1745	French 1939, no. 125	
Two two-handled cups	F	The Gift of M.ʳ Francis Leath to the Ch.ʰ/of Christ in Medford 1742	First Parish, Medford, Mass., for Francis Leath	1742	French 1939, nos. 126–27	
Wine cup	B	A Gift to the/PRIS-BITERIAN Church/in Long Lane/BOSTON MARCH yᵉ I./1731	Long Lane or Federal Street, now Arlington Street, Church, Boston	1731	French 1939, no. 109	

1. For further information on Jacob Hurd, see French 1939, 3–15. For further analysis of the impact of Hurd's work on Boston goldsmithing, see Ward 1983 and Ward 1990.
2. French 1939, 5–7.
3. Wyman 1879, 1:530–31; MCPR 16:495; *Charlestown VR* 1:17, 77, 92, 98, 126; *Malden VR*, 51, 382. The guardianship reference is very clearly to the silversmith's father, and therefore raises some doubt as to what his real trade was. The guardianship could not have been granted to their grandfather Jacob, the tailor, because he died in 1694.
4. SCD 45:252–53 enumerates all of the heirs of Peter Tufts and names their spouses or late spouses. In the case of Elizabeth (Tufts) Hurd, deceased, the deed names her husband and all of her children, including Jacob Hurd, goldsmith; Wyman 1879, 1:530–31.
5. RC 28:12, 126.
6. French 1939, 6–8, provides full information on all of Hurd's children, with some additional notes on his sons Nathaniel and Jacob and his daughter Sarah. Other sections of the book are devoted to biographies of Nathaniel and Benjamin; French 1939, 57–146.

7. Seybolt 1939, 175, 184; French 1939, 9.

8. French 1939, 9; Roberts 1895, 2:26.

9. SCCR, file 67316, also includes a Hurd signature.

10. SCCR, Court of Common Pleas Record Book 1729, 308; 1734, 41; 1739, 258; 1742–43, 198; 1744–46, 286, 335; 1748–49, 206, 207; 1749–51, 179; 1753–54, 171, 176; 1755–56, 25. References to books that are now missing are from John M. Fitzgerald to Francis Hill Bigelow, List of Boston Court Record References to Silversmiths, Bigelow-Phillips files.

11. Records of the New South Church, Boston, vol. 1, BPL.

12. Buhler 1956, 40–41, presents an argument in favor of all of these possibilities and Edward Winslow as well. For a detailed comparison of the designs and construction techniques of Boston's leading silversmiths during this period, see Ward 1983, 100–56, 245–335.

13. *Sewall Diary*, 2:1034; Samuel Sewall Account Book and Ledger, fol. 187v, NEHGS.

14. Henry Flynt Memorandum Book, HU.

15. For an analysis of Sewall's patronage of silversmiths, see Ward 1984, 130–32.

16. SCD 45:29–30.

17. *Boston News-Letter*, 21–28 September 1732.

18. RC 13:236. In 1734, the selectmen granted Hurd and his neighbors permission to open up the ground again; RC 13:255.

19. SCD 50:66–67. The purchase price was £300 in Massachusetts bills.

20. SCD 53:6–8.

21. *Boston Gazette*, 15–22 May 1738.

22. SCD 63:198–200; 64:195–97. Hurd purchased the house by two deeds between him and the heirs of Abraham Blish. He purchased one-half of the house for £1,100 Old Tenor and the other half of the house for £250 New Tenor. He mortgaged his new house twice, once on 20 October 1749 to Mary Traill, a Boston widow, for £300; SCD 78:110–11; and once on 9 February 1754/55 to his son John Hurd for £140; SCD 84:261–62.

23. Benjamin Walker, Jr., Diaries, vol. 3, MHS.

24. SCD 87:63–64.

25. Buhler 1956, 42. Buhler here suggests that Samuel Casey (ca. 1724–ca. 1770) was also apprenticed to Hurd; however, no evidence has been found that this was the case. Casey witnessed no deeds for Hurd during the period when he would have been an apprentice to him and does not appear in any records as a resident of Boston during those years. The guardianship of Houghton Perkins was not effected immediately after his father's death but is dated 14 January 1738/39; MCPR 22:345. Perkins witnessed deeds for Hurd in 1749 (SCD 78:110–11), in 1754 (SCD 84:261–62), and in 1755 (SCD 87:63–64). Henchman may have witnessed a deed for Hurd in 1743, but it is more likely that Daniel Henchman (1689–1761), who was then a justice of the peace in Suffolk County, was the witness; SCD 67:22.

26. MCD 48:586.

27. Ball witnessed a deed for Hurd in 1745; see SCD 71:80–81.

28. French 1939, 12.

29. SCPR 33:66; 35:400–02; 39:77.

30. SCD 57:148–49.

31. MCPR, docket 17154.

32. French 1939, 29. Kathryn Buhler (1972, 1:201) suggests a slightly different chronology, as does Patricia Kane (see p. 78).

33. See French 1939, nos. 89, 90, 111, 131; Johnston 1994, 86.

34. See Ward 1983, 245–335.

35. Benjamin Greene Ledger, 1734–56, 47, MHS.

36. Benjamin Walker, Jr., Diaries, vol. 3, MHS.

37. Jacob Hurd bill to Mrs. Rebecca Townsend, 1740–47, C. E. French Collection, MHS.

38. Jacob Hurd receipt to Thomas Hancock, 26 May 1752. Photostat in the Bigelow-Phillips files; whereabouts of the original are unknown.

39. Daniel Henchman Ledger, 1729–ca. 1755, fol. 187v, NEHGS. The other silver items included a necklace, stone rings, cutting of three dozen plates, part payment of a pepper box, and mending of a porringer and tea tongs. In 1742 Hurd was credited with six spoons (fol. 312v). Other accounts with Hurd appear in the ledger; see fols. 120v, 164r, 248r, and 343r. Henchman's and Hurd's business dealings date back to 1727; see Daniel Henchman Ledger 1712–ca. 1735, fol. 40, NEHGS.

40. Henry Flynt Memorandum Book, HU.

41. Hurd was paid £70.18.4 on 7 August 1738 for rings for the funeral of Capt. William Browne,

Jr.; Mass. Archives 18:158. On 23 October 1732 the estate of John Danforth recorded that it paid Hurd £2.11.6 for rings; SCPR, docket 5962. John Guttridge's estate administration submitted in 1750 shows payments to Hurd of £99.4.5 for rings; SCPR, docket 8744. The estate of Col. John Wainwright paid Hurd £27.8 for eleven gold rings in 1739; ECPR, docket 28680.

42. Ward 1989, 72–76; SCCR, file 62302.
43. Benjamin Walker, Jr., Diaries, vol. 3, MHS.
44. SCCR, file 75062.
45. *Boston Gazette*, 20 February 1758; *Boston News-Letter*, 23 February 1758.
46. French 1939, 12.
47. SCPR 53:581; 54:58.

Nathaniel Hurd
1729/30–77

John Singleton Copley,
Nathaniel Hurd, *ca. 1765,*
oil on canvas. The
Cleveland Museum of Art,
gift of the John Huntington
Art and Polytechnic
Trust, 15.534.

A

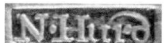

B

The third child of the silversmith Jacob Hurd (q.v.), Nathaniel Hurd was born in Boston on 13 February 1729/30.[1] He attended Boston Latin School in 1738 and served his apprenticeship with his father until about 1751.[2] It is not clear where he learned his skills as an engraver.

He first appears in Boston records as a silversmith in April 1756, when he purchased a third part of a house on Marlborough Street from his older brother John Hurd for one hundred pounds. Hurd sold the property back to his brother one month later.[3] The silver scholar Hollis French suggested that Hurd continued his father's business and completed the training of his younger brother Benjamin (q.v.) following their father's death in 1758.[4] In April 1758 "Nathaniel Hurd, engraver," appeared before the Superior Court judge to give evidence against James Appleby for producing "counterfeit publick bills of Credit of ye province of North Carolina."[5] The *Boston Gazette* for 14 April 1760 announced,

> Nathaniel Hurd
> *INFORMS his Customers he has remov'd his Shop*
> *from* Maccarty's *Corner, on the Exchange, to the*
> *back Part of the opposite Brick Building, where Mr.*
> Ezekiel Price *kept his Office, where he continues to do*
> *all sorts of Goldsmith's Work; likewise engraves in*
> *Gold, Silver, Copper, Brass, and Steel, in the neatest*
> *Manner, and at a reasonable Rate.*[6]

On 3 July 1760, the silversmith bought a house adjoining the MacCarty property behind Half Square Court for £233.6.8 from Thomas Waite. He arranged a mortgage of £160 with Waite to be repaid in one year.[7] The Massachusetts tax valuation of 1771 assessed Hurd with one poll, annual real estate rents of £20, a house, and a "tanhouse," or workshop.[8]

The silversmith Daniel Henchman (q.v.) served as the witness on all these deeds. Hurd and Henchman shared familial as well as professional ties: an apprentice of Jacob Hurd, Henchman married Nathaniel Hurd's sister Elizabeth in 1753. The two silversmiths may have been partners. They collaborated on a monteith that was commissioned by Gov. John Wentworth and others for presentation to the president of Dartmouth College; Henchman fashioned the bowl and Hurd engraved the lengthy inscription. Hurd also witnessed a deed for Henchman and served as an appraiser for his estate in 1775.[9]

The daybooks of Paul Revere, Jr. (q.v.), contain several entries for Hurd, who was ordering difficult-to-make or unusual forms of silver from the younger man in 1762 and 1763. On 16 April 1762, Hurd commissioned Revere to make two "small Scolopᵈ Salvers" weighing twenty-three ounces and eleven pennyweights at a total cost of £12.9.2.[10] Hurd supplied twenty-four ounces of silver for which he was credited £8.8. Hurd made additional purchases the following month, including one on 3 May 1762:

Mr Nathl Hurd	D^r
To Making a Silver Chafing Dish W^t 19^oz:15	6. 18. 3
To The Making	3. 0. 0
	9. 18. 3[11]

He paid for the chafing dish with twenty-two ounces of silver and £6.5.5 in cash. Additional accounts were recorded on 19 May 1762:

Mr Nathl Hurd	D^r
To a Pair of Silver Canns W^t 26:0	
To The Making	2. 13. 4
Mr Nathl Hurd C^r	
By Silver Recev^d 25^oz:0	

The payment for these was recorded on 23 May 1762:

Mr. Nathl Hurd	C^r
By Cash Recev^d	2. 13. 4
By one Ounce of Silver	

He ordered several unusual silver forms on 1 October 1762:

To a Silver frame for a Picture	1. 8. 0
To a Silver Indian Pipe W^t 9:5:0	
To The Making	0. 14. 8[12]

On 22 June the following year, Hurd paid sixteen shillings for a snuffbox and eight shillings for mending a picture frame.[13]

Hurd was active in community affairs. In 1759, he was sworn in as the fire-ward.[14] He was chosen as a clerk of the market in 1759, 1760, and 1761, as was Daniel Henchman.[15] Hurd also acted as an examiner for the accounts of the Boston lotteries in 1760.[16] In 1768 and 1769, he was a scavenger for ward 9.[17] He served on the jury at the inquest of Michael Johnson, also known as Crispus Attucks, who was killed in the Boston Massacre.[18]

Hurd died unmarried on 17 December 1777 at the age of forty-eight and was buried in the Granary Burying Ground.[19] His will, written on 8 December 1777, was presented for probate on 13 January 1778.[20] The Boston silversmith Zachariah Brigden (q.v.) was one of the witnesses. Hurd "Goldsmith & Engraver, being Sick & weak in body but of perfect mind & memory," left twenty pounds apiece for "silver spoons or other piece of plate" to his brothers Jacob Hurd of Halifax and John Hurd and to his sisters Sarah Walley and Mary Hall. He also stipulated the following bequests: to Benjamin Hurd thirty pounds in tools, clothes, and money and remission of his debt; to his sister Elizabeth Henchman, widow of Daniel Henchman, sixty pounds in furniture and money and a miniature of Nathaniel Hurd; to his sister Ann Furnass thirty pounds in furniture and money; to his nephew Nathaniel Hurd Furnass thirteen pounds "as a legacy for bearing my name"; to Polly Sweetser fifteen pounds "for her kindness & tenderness to me in my sickness"; to his nephew John Mason Furnass "my large printing press & some tools in consideration for the love I bear to him, & the genius he discovers for the same business which I have followed & to which I intended to have brought him up to."[21] Hurd's silver watch with "Brown, Boston" on the face was designated for the Boston printer Thomas Fleet, who also served as a witness to the will.[22] The remainder of his estate was divided equally between Benjamin Hurd, Elizabeth Henchman, and Ann Furnass. Hurd appointed Elizabeth Henchman and his brother-in-law Jonathan Furnass as executors. No inventory was taken of Hurd's estate. The executors placed a notice in the *Boston Gazette and Country Herald* on 19 January 1778 notifying creditors to apply to the executors for settlement of any outstanding debts.

Hurd is perhaps best known for his work as an engraver. His talent was evident early in his career. A bookplate for Thomas Dering dated 1749 was made while he was still an apprentice.[23] His impressive technical and artistic skills are displayed brilliantly in the elaborate heraldic bookplates that he made for more than fifty-five notable Bostonians and institutions, including the Apthorp, Dana, Greene, Hooper, and Wentworth families, Harvard College, and Phillips Academy.[24] At least twenty-eight of the arms shown on these bookplates were illustrated in John Guillim's *A Display of Heraldry*. Hurd was painted about 1765 by John Singleton Copley seated at a table on which lies a copy of this book (illus.).[25]

Hurd also engraved a variety of other documents. He made trade cards for the tallow chandler Joseph Palmer in 1754, for the apothecary Philip Godfrid Kast in 1774, and for the upholsterer Ziphon Thayer.[26] A Massachusetts bill of exchange dated 21 January 1761 and signed "Nathl Hurd sculp" is in the collection of the Massachusetts Historical Society.[27] He also engraved loan certificates (1762) and provincial currency for the Massachusetts provincial government.[28] The presence of a variety of provincial currency as well as foreign specie in eighteenth-century Boston complicated business transactions for tradesmen and craftsmen. Hurd printed a table of foreign coins in circulation with comparisons of the weights and value in Old Tenor and New Tenor.[29] In the *Boston Evening Post* for 27 December 1762, Hurd advertised the sale of several prints "engraved and sold by Nath Hurd, a striking likeness of his Majesty King George the Third, Mr. Pitt and General Wolfe fit for a picture or for Gentlemen and Ladies to put in their watches."[30] Hurd created several political caricatures, a popular form of public communication during the eighteenth century. In 1762, he ridiculed the counterfeiter Dr. Seth Hudson and, in 1765, criticized the Stamp Act and the tariff collectors, a print that was described in detail in the 7 November edition of the *Boston Gazette*. An undated caricature depicts "Courtship and Marriage."[31] Hurd engraved summons forms for his Masonic lodge and commission forms for the Massachusetts government.[32] In addition to his own engravings, Hurd advertised imported prints in 1765 and 1766, including a caricature of the Liberty Tree by Wilkinson and a mezzotint of the Reverend Jonathan Mayhew by Richard Jennys, Jr. (q.v. Appendix A).[33]

In his memoirs (1811), the Boston and Plymouth silversmith Samuel Davis (1765–1829) remembered Hurd as "an original genius . . . in the manner of Hogarth, whom he resembled in genius. In Seal Cutting and Die sinking he would be unrivalled even now, in New England, if not in the U States." Davis's memoirs also reveal that Hurd trained Joseph Callender (q.v.).[34]

Hurd's engraving can also be found on silver produced by other silversmiths. On 12 October 1770, the executor of Mary Ireland's estate paid Hurd 12 shillings for engraving an inscription on a tankard made by William Cowell, Jr. (q.v.),

that was bequeathed to the Old South Church.[35] He billed Thomas Fayerweather £4.13 on 16 June 1773 for removing the engraving on salts and a
coffeepot and for engraving new crests on these objects and on a large saucepan.

Although his production of silver was secondary to his career as an engraver,
about fifty examples of Hurd's silver marked with initial and surname marks
(A, B) survive.[36] In his monograph on the Hurd family of silversmiths, Hollis
French records an initial and surname mark in a stepped rectangle (C) and an
initials mark (D), but the whereabouts of the objects are unknown, and therefore
the marks could not be illustrated.[37] Hurd also worked in gold. William Palfrey
paid £1.16 for a gold medal on 26 July 1765.[38] DAF

SURVIVING OBJECTS

	Mark	Inscription	Patron	Date	Reference	Owner
Two beakers	B	Hancock arms, gules a dexter hand cou-ped, on a chief 3 cocks, and crest, a demi-griffin; Gift of the Honourable THOMAS HANCOCK Esq to the Church of CHRIST in LEX-INGTON/1764	The First Congrega-tional Society, Lexing-ton, Mass., for Thomas Hancock	ca. 1764	French 1939, nos. 298–99	
Cann	A	L/LS (+)		ca. 1760	French 1941, no. 301a	
Cann	A*	Dumaresq (?) arms, 3 bows and arrows, and crest, a bull pas-sant; W/WP/1750 (+)	Dumaresq family (?)	ca. 1765	YUAG files	
Cann	A*	Sturgis arms, azure a chevron argent be-tween 3 crosses cross-let fitchée, and crest, a lion's head erased	Sturgis family	ca. 1765	YUAG files	
Cann	B	unidentified arms, quartered: 3 hearts; a crosslet; 3 nails; a bugle horn		ca. 1760	French 1941, no. 301b	
Cann	B*	Lloyd arms, azure 3 scaling ladders a spear head in fess point, on a chief gules a castle, and crest, a lion rampant	Lloyd family	ca. 1765	Flynt/Fales 1968, 97–98	HD
Cann	B*	Howard arms, a bend gules between 6 crosses crosslet, and crest, a lion pas-sant guardant	Howard family	ca. 1765	Eitner 1976, no. 58	
Cann	B	unidentified arms, a chevron between 3 fleur-de-lis (+)	Brook Watson for John Huston (?)	ca. 1765	Christie's, 20–21 January 1989, lot 298	
Coffeepot	A	Chauncy arms, a cross crosslet, on a	Rev. Charles and Mary (Stoddard) Chauncy	ca. 1765	French 1939, no. 302	HU

	Mark	Inscription	Patron	Date	Reference	Owner
		chief a lion passant, and crest, a demi-griffin emerging from a ducal crown, impaling Stoddard, argent 3 mullets bordure or				
Coffeepot	B*	Mayor (?) arms, an anchor erect on a chief or 3 cinquefoils, and crest, a sheep's head	Mayor family (?)	ca. 1755	Warren 1975, no. 311	BBC
Cream pail	B	RS (+)	Rebecca (Salisbury) Waldo	ca. 1755	Buhler 1979, no. 43	WAM
Creampot	A	L/DI; C/DE (+)		ca. 1755	Quimby 1995, no. 92	WM
Creampot	A*	Hickling arms, bands or and vert, on a chief vert 3 lions' heads erased, and crest, a greyhound running; S. Hickling (+)	Susannah (Hickling) Cox (?)	ca. 1765	Buhler/Hood 1970, no. 225	YUAG
Creampot	C	Howard arms; 1766	Howard family	1766	French 1939, no. 304	
Grace cup	A *or* B	Whitechurch arms; Maddock crest	Whitechurch family	ca. 1760	French 1939, no. 305	
Grace cup	A	unidentified arms (+)		ca. 1750	*Silver Supplement* 1973, no. 59	
Marrow spoon	A	none		ca. 1765	*Silver Supplement* 1973, no. 60	MFAB
Milk pot	A	Bromfield arms, sable on a chevron 3 broom sprigs, on a canton or a spear's head embrued, in chief point a mullet, and crest, a demi-tyger holding a broken sword erect, impaling Lidgett arms, a fess wavy between 3 estoiles; B/HM (+)		ca. 1770	Hammerslough/ Feigenbaum 1958–73, 4:49	
Mourning ring (gold)	B	Alex: Ross Esq\ᵣ: Ob: 24 Nov. 1768 AEt. 51	Alex Ross	ca. 1768	Gourley 1965, no. 118	
Porringer	B	SS/to/CW		ca. 1750	Sotheby's, 23–25 January 1992, lot 181A	
Two salvers (with mark of Paul Revere, Jr.)	B	Franklin arms, on a bend between 2 lions' heads erased gules, a dolphin em-	Franklin family	1762	Buhler 1976, 7	

	Mark	Inscription	Patron	Date	Reference	Owner
		bowed between 2 martlets, and crest, a dolphin's head between 2 branches				
Sauceboat	A	SW	Sarah Warren (?)	ca. 1765	French 1939, no. 307	
Sauceboat	B	Prentice crest, a hound seated on a ducal coronet	John Prentice	ca. 1765	Hammerslough/ Feigenbaum 1958–73, 2:57	
Seal	A	Mather arms	Mather family	ca. 1765	French 1939, no. 308	
Seal	A *or* B	?	Provincial Grand Lodge of Masons, Boston	1752	French 1939, no. 310	
Seal	B	Boston Marine Society arms	Boston Marine Society	1754	French 1939, no. 309	
Skewer	A	none		ca. 1765	Buhler 1972, no. 315	MFAB
Sugar tongs	B	unidentified crest, an eagle		ca. 1760	French 1941, no. 318a	DIA
Three tablespoons	A	unidentified crest, a lion rampant		ca. 1760	Quimby 1995, no. 93a–c	WM
Tablespoon	B	Stoddard crest, a demi-horse issuing from a ducal coronet	Stoddard family	ca. 1755	*Silver Supplement* 1973, no. 61a	BBC
Two tablespoons	B (?)	Stoddard crest, a demi-horse issuing from a ducal coronet	Stoddard family	ca. 1755	*Antiques* 102 (September 1972): 368	
Tablespoon	B	M/IM		ca. 1765	French 1939, no. 313	
Six tablespoons	B*	Dumaresq crest, a bull passant	Dumaresq family	ca. 1770	Flynt/Fales 1968, 111–12	HD
Tablespoon	B†	Holyoke (?) crest, a cubit arm grasping an oak branch	Holyoke family (?)	ca. 1765	Quimby 1995, no. 94	WM
Tankard	A	unidentified arms, quartered 1 and 4, vert a chevron argent between 3 griffins' heads erased; 2 and 3, or a chevron vert between 3 eagles displayed; femme: or a chevron gules between 3 eagles displayed; crest, none; replaced by a basket of fruit		ca. 1760	French 1941, no. 318b	
Tankard	B	Stoddard arms, argent 3 mullets gules	Prudence Stoddard	ca. 1760		WA

	Mark	Inscription	Patron	Date	Reference	Owner
		bordure or, and crest, a demi-horse issuing from a ducal coronet				
Teapot	A†	Stoddard arms, argent 3 mullets bordure or, and crest, a demi-horse emerging from a ducal coronet; 1731 (later)	Prudence (Chester) Stoddard for Prudence (Stoddard) Williams	ca. 1755	Buhler 1972, no. 314	MFAB
Teapot	A*	Gibbs arms, 3 battle-axes in fess, and crest, 3 broken tilting spears, 2 in saltire and one in pale, ensigned with a wreath argent and azure	Gibbs family	ca. 1755	Johnston 1994, 89	CMA
Teapot	B	Howard arms, a bend between 6 crosses crosslet, and crest, a lion passant guardant; 1766	Samuel and Sarah (Lithgow) Howard	1766	Quimby 1995, no. 91	WM
Two teaspoons	A	Hutchinson crest	Hutchinson family	ca. 1775	French 1939, nos. 316–17	
Teaspoon	B	Hubbard crest, a lion's head erased on a wreath ermine	Hubbard family	ca. 1760	YUAG files	
Teaspoon	B	Stoddard crest	Stoddard family	ca. 1755	*Silver Supplement* 1973, no. 61b	BBC
Teaspoon	B*	?		ca. 1760	French 1939, no. 315	
Teaspoon	D	S/DI		ca. 1765	French 1939, no. 314	
Teaspoon	D	?		ca. 1775	French 1939, no. 318	

1. RC 24:193.
2. French 1939, 57.
3. SCD 89:67. Daniel Henchman witnessed the deeds.
4. French 1939, 143.
5. SCCR, Superior Court, file 78721.
6. The advertisement was repeated on 21 and 28 April.
7. SCD 94:229–31. Daniel Henchman witnessed the deeds.
8. Pruitt 1978, 38–39.
9. SCPR 74:287; SCD 107:173–74.
10. 16 April 1765, vol. 1, Waste and Memoranda Book, 1761–83, [8], Revere Family Papers, MHS.
11. 3 May 1762, vol. 1, Waste and Memoranda Book, 1761–83, [8], Revere Family Papers, MHS.
12. 19, 23 May, 1 October 1762, vol. 1, Waste and Memoranda Book, 1761–83, [9, 12], Revere Family Papers, MHS.
13. 22 June 1763, vol. 1, Waste and Memoranda Book, 1761–83, [18], Revere Family Papers, MHS.
14. French 1939, 58.
15. RC 16:18, 34, 49.
16. French 1939, 59.

17. RC 16:236, 270.

18. French 1939, 59.

19. Codman 1918, 136; Bridgman 1856, 320.

20. SCPR 77:12–13.

21. Samuel Davis's memoirs (1811) noted that "John M. Furness, a nephew of Hurd's was a young man of genius and excelled in drawing, Miniature Painting, Seal Cutting and Engraving. I believe he became deranged and died young"; Steinway 1960, 7–8. French notes that John Mason Furnass was an engraver and portrait painter who was born on 11 November 1762 and died of epilepsy in Dedham, Massachusetts, on 22 June 1804; French 1939, 60.

22. The watch was probably made by the Boston clockmaker Gawen Brown (q.v. Appendix A).

23. Described in French 1939, 103. The only other dated bookplate was made for the Boston merchant Benjamin Greene in 1757; French 1939, 107.

24. French 1939, 92–137, describes 110 of Hurd's bookplates and illustrates a number of them.

25. Other likenesses of Hurd include two copies of the portrait at CMA, an unfinished sketch for the portrait, and a miniature painted in oil on copper; see Prown 1966, 1:220.

26. French 1939, 72–73, 77, 80; Dow 1927, illus. p. 258.

27. French 1939, 73.

28. French 1939, 74, 80.

29. French 1939, 78–79; Fales 1970, fig. 195. Examples of this print survive at AAS; Memorial Library, Deerfield, Mass.; YIM; and YUAG.

30. French 1939, 63.

31. French 1939, 78.

32. French 1939, 77, 79.

33. *Boston Gazette*, 11 November 1765; *Boston News-Letter*, 17 July 1766.

34. Steinway 1960, 7–8.

35. SCPR 69:309.

36. Kovel 1961, 147, also shows N.HURD in rectangle. An example of this mark has not been located.

37. French 1939, 66.

38. William Palfrey receipts, 20 April–26 July 1765; Photostat Collection, MHS.

Henry Hurst
ca. 1666–1717/18

A

In recent scholarship this silversmith's name has been anglicized to Henry Hurst, but in the eighteenth-century Boston records he is referred to in a variety of ways. By the time he wrote his will he spelled his name Henry Hirst, but prior to that he most commonly signed his name Hindrich Husst.[1] According to a court record of about 1715, Hurst was a "Sweed by birth."[2] The similarity of the tankard made by him (now at the Museum of Fine Arts, Boston) to Swedish work suggests that he was trained in Stockholm between 1680 and 1687. Sometime thereafter he traveled to London, where he worked as a journeyman for John House, citizen and goldsmith of London.

By October 1699, Hurst "was willing & desirous by Gods permission suddenly to undertake a voyage to Boston in New England in order to serve Richard Conyers [q.v.] of Boston afores[d] after the manner of a plateworker or worker in silver Imboster, Graver . . . for & during the full Term of Two years." Hurst "did Covenant promise & agree to & with sd John Howse [citizen and goldsmith of London] . . . that he the sd Hinderich Huss should & would diligently carefully & faithfully give his due attendance to the sd Rich[d] Conyers during the space of two whole years from the time of Entrance into his sd Masters service in Boston in New England aforesd & should work in plate Ingrave Imbost or hammer silver at all reasonable & convenient times & seasons that his sd Master Rich[d] Conyers should think fit to appoint & desire him & for no other person or persons whatsoev[e]."[3] Hurst was sued for failing to live up to the terms of the agreement when he left Conyers's employ without warning on 6 June 1701. The wages due to Hurst under his contract were lower than prevailing Boston rates, and it is likely that Hurst was enticed to leave Conyers by an offer of higher wages.

Hurst may have had other than economic reasons for seeking a different employer, however. Shortly after leaving Conyers's shop, Hurst testified in court that while having a pot of beer with the saddler Winsor Goulding of Boston at the Half Moon Tavern, his companion told him of a misfortune that had befallen his mother-in-law, Mrs. Smith. A Mr. Taylor, who had lodged with Mrs. Smith for some time, paid his debt to her in 550 Dog or Lion dollars that she in turn sent to Pennsylvania, where they were discovered to be counterfeit. Hurst apparently believed that Conyers was the source of the counterfeit coins, for he testified that this Mr. Taylor "and m.^r Conyers of Boston SilverSmith were acquainted" during the time Hurst "wrought with said Conyers" and that Conyers "went several times to s.^d Taylor at his Lodgeing in the s.^d widow Smiths house."[4]

When Conyers sued Hurst for breach of contract in 1702, the goldsmiths Edward Winslow and James Barnes, Jr. (qq.v.), came forward as sureties and posted a bond of two hundred pounds on Hurst's behalf. The bond is dated 21 December 1702, the same year that two of Winslow's most elaborate sugar boxes were produced.[5] It is likely that Hurst was working as a journeyman in Winslow's shop during 1701 and 1702 and that Hurst made the intricately chased sugar boxes that are so unlike any of Winslow's other work.[6]

Henry Hurst married Mary Bill (1682–1717) on 31 August 1704, and in the list of Boston inhabitants for 1707 he is listed as a tenant of his father-in-law, James Bill (1651–1717/18), to whom he paid sixteen pounds' rent.[7] Hurst and his wife had three children, two of whom survived infancy: Mary (b. 1705) and Mehitable (b. 1709).[8] Mary married her mother's cousin, Josiah Bill, on 26 December 1720.[9] Mehitable apparently predeceased her father because she is not mentioned in his will or in her grandfather's will.

Hurst witnessed a deed for William Rouse, Jr., the son of the deceased silversmith William Rouse, Sr. (q.v.), in 1707 and may have been training another of Rouse's sons, Michael (q.v.), at that time. Francis Hill Bigelow speculated that John Burt (q.v.) was apprenticed to Hurst because Burt married Abigail Cheever, Hurst's wife's cousin, but the connection seems distant.[10] In 1709 Hurst accused one Joseph Perrin, a minor and servant to the cooper Samuel Burrill, of stealing goods from his shop, which indicates that he was operating his own business by that time.[11] In 1715 Hurst was brought before the Superior Court of Judicature on two counts of receiving stolen goods. He was found guilty and sentenced to pay the owners of the silver objects twice their value in money.[12] Hurst filed the following petition to the court in reference to this case: "That your Poor Pet.^r is a Sweed by birth, not well acquainted with the English tongue; nor can he distinctly speak it, so as to be understood: In Consideration whereof he humbly Intreats yor hon.^rs to assign him an attorney to make his defence as in such Cases is usual in the Law. That he may be enabled to acquit himselfe of the Crime of Receiving Stolen goods—whereof he Stands Endicted, & after wch he is not (he thanks God) in the least guilty, or Concern'd."[13]

Hurst continued to ply his trade in Boston and died on 30 January 1717/18 with a small estate. He left a will in which he bequeathed all of his estate, real and personal, to his daughter Mary. He directed his executors to sell all of his goods and estate and to put the "money so made to Interest for ye bringing up my Said Daughter." If she died before marrying, John Comer and Mary Watson, grandchildren of the pewterer John Comer, one of Hurst's executors, were to receive twenty-five pounds apiece, and the Old North and New North churches were each to receive a silver flagon worth thirty pounds. Hurst directed that the remainder of his estate be divided between the executors, John Comer and the tailor Samuel Gardner, both of Boston.[14]

Hurst's estate was appraised by Alexander Sears, Nathaniel Coney, and Erasmus Stevens; Thomas Milner and John Dixwell (qq.v.) signed as evaluators "for the Plate & Tools." The items in the inventory related to the goldsmithing trade are as follows:

165^{oz} of Plate	at 10/6	£86. 12. 6
Liming and Soder		18. 1
A Helt of a Sword		4. 4. —
$4.^{oz}$ $12.^{dwt}$ 16^{grs} of Gold at £8 ℔ oz	37. 1. 4	£128. 15. 11
Shop Tooles$^{£23}$ & a Look.^{g} Glass$^{£5.2.6}$		28. 2. 6
. . .		
A Forge, & an old Window		1. 2. —
A p.^{r} Spectacles & burnisher		7. —

The total value of the inventory was £239.17.9. Hurst owned no real estate, but he did have "A Negro boy" who was valued at £15.[15] In the administration accounts payments to "Miller the Goldsmith" of 12 shillings and 6 pence and to John Dixwell of 2 shillings are listed along with the cost of a buckle (6 shillings and 8 pence) and two rings made for the executors (£2.14).[16] In 1722, Mary (Hurst) Bill signed a quitclaim deed transferring all of her interest in her father's estate to Samuel Gardner.[17]

Only a very small number of silver objects by Hurst have survived. He is known by only one mark: two H's conjoined in a conforming rectangle (A). It is likely that Hurst worked as either a journeyman or jobber during most of his career. References to his ability as an embosser and engraver indicate that he may have specialized in these branches of the trade. Although he worked for Conyers he may have been responsible for a tankard described in an advertisement of 1706 as having the workman's mark R.C. and a handle "wrought with Chas'd work." The tankard described probably was very similar to the Swedish-style chasing on Hurst's tankard at the Museum of Fine Arts, Boston.[18] BMW

SURVIVING OBJECTS

	Mark	Inscription	Patron	Date	Reference	Owner
Porringer	A*	RR; Rebecca Russell	Rebecca Russell	ca. 1705	*Antiques* 101 (March 1972): 494	Fairfield Heritage Association, Lancaster, Ohio
Tankard	A†	AL (+)	Abigail Lindall	ca. 1704	Buhler 1972, no. 64	MFAB
Tankard	A*	P/IM (+)	John and Mary Parker	ca. 1710	Jones 1913, 272	HMA

1. The spelling of his name as Henry Hurst by silver scholars goes back as far as MFA 1911, 80. Some of the variations in early documents are Hendrick Huss, Henrick Huss, and Hendrick Hurst.
2. SCCR, file 173884.
3. SCCR, file 5565ᵃ. Prior to this case, in July 1701, Hurst sued Conyers for £7.9; Conyers countersued Hurst in the same court session. Hurst won his case; Conyers was unable to produce the documentation necessary to support his case, and it was dismissed.
4. The Rijksdaalder, minted in Utrecht, was commonly referred to as a Dog or Lion dollar in the seventeenth and eighteenth centuries. These and all other European and South American coins were legal tender in the colonies and circulated along with English and American coins. The court case is recorded in Mass. Archives 8:118.
5. SCCR, file 5565.
6. Ward 1984, 142–45. It is also conceivable that Hurst had enough money by this time to set up a small shop for himself in which he could do outwork for other goldsmiths.
7. RC 28:10; RC 10:119; RC 9:157; Whitmore 1878, 45, no. 847; SCPR 20:269–71, docket 3960. Three of Mary Bill's sisters married immigrant craftsmen in related metalworking fields. Mehitable (b. in the mid 1670s) married as her second husband the engraver William Burgis (q.v. Appendix A). Hannah (b. 1687) married the watchmaker and clockmaker Joseph Essex (q.v. Appendix A). Finally, Abigail (b. 1691) married the clockmaker Thomas Badley (q.v. Appendix A). Although Burgis arrived in Boston after Hurst's death, Hurst probably knew the other two craftsmen, who would have been his contemporaries.
8. RC 24:35, 49, 61.
9. RC 28:86.
10. Bigelow-Phillips files, 731.
11. SCCR, Court of General Sessions of the Peace Record Book, 4 October 1709.
12. SCCR, Superior Court of Judicature Record Book 1715–21, 69.
13. SCCR, file 173884.
14. SCPR 20:252–54, docket 3956, dated 25 January 1717/18; probated 24 February 1717/18; Whitmore 1878, 45, no. 846.
15. SCPR 21:276–77, docket 3956, dated 3 February 1717/18.
16. SCPR 21:277–78, docket 3956, dated 9 February 1717/18.
17. SCPR 22:541, docket 3956, dated 23 March 1721/22.
18. As quoted in Buhler 1965, 22. See also Buhler 1972, 1:76–78.

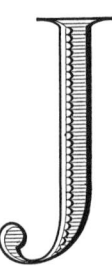

John Jackson
d. 1772

A

The birthplace and training of Nantucket's first silversmith, John Jackson, have intrigued scholars ever since examples of his work were first recognized in the 1920s.[1] Efforts to discover his New England roots have not borne fruit; although research has uncovered a number of eighteenth-century men born in the region who bear both Jackson's name and likely birth dates, none has proven conclusively to be the silversmith.

That Jackson came to Nantucket from Boston is clear from land transactions made at the time of Jackson's marriage in 1753 to Abigail Fitch (ca. 1730–ca. 1789–93), the illegitimate child of Jerusha Coffin (ca. 1710–62) and Peter Fitch.[2] Jerusha Coffin later married John Matthews of Boston on 17 October 1731 and shortly afterward had another daughter, whom she named Catherine. Jackson's future mother-in-law, Jerusha (Coffin) Matthews, must have favored the marriage of her young daughter, Abigail, to Jackson; prior to the wedding, perhaps as a gift or dowry, she gave eight rods of land to her "well respected Friend John Jackson of Boston in the County of Suffolk . . . goldsmith."[3] (Jackson returned the favor in 1759 when, as "goldsmith," he made her a gift of two square rods of land).[4] An additional deed of 13 February 1761 formalizes a division of land among Jerusha Matthews, her two daughters, and their husbands.[5] On his land Jackson built a house and barn that he sold to his brother-in-law, Joseph Heath, on 16 April 1761.[6]

Although a "John Jackson, goldsmith," appeared on a list of New York freemen dated 6 April 1731, it is unclear whether he was the same Jackson who was described as being "of Boston" in Nantucket records in 1753.[7] To have been considered a freeman John Jackson would have to have been at least twenty-one at the time, which would place his birth around 1710 or before. If he was the same goldsmith who migrated to Nantucket and married there in 1753, he would have been in his mid-forties at the time, somewhat older than the norm for such a move.

On 1 March 1763, John Jackson, "goldsmith of Sherborn," as the town of Nantucket was then known, appeared before the Inferior Court of Common Pleas as a defendant against David Gardner, merchant of the same town. Gardner contended that Jackson owed him £7.4.8 for sundry goods delivered on 14 February 1763 to Judith Coffin.[8] The court found Jackson guilty and ordered him to pay Gardner the full sum plus £2.1.8 for legal expenses, but Jackson appealed to the Superior Court of Judicature that met in August 1763.

In February 1763 and the following October, Jackson, his wife Abigail, her half-sister Catherine, and Catherine's husband, Joseph Heath, sold two parcels of land, one containing a rod and a quarter and the other two acres, that they inherited from Jerhusa Matthews.[9] Furthermore, in October, Jackson, as "goldsmith," also sold his dwelling house in Sherburne, probably in preparation for the new home he was building in the "Seventh Fish Lot Share."[10] Toward that end in 1765, he purchased two contiguous pieces of land there.[11] Written evidence of Jackson next appears in 1766, when the Nantucket blacksmith Stephen Hussey recorded the sale of various tools and hardware to Jackson in his account book, presumably to be used in the construction of the goldsmith's house.[12] Jackson purchased additional land in the "Seventh Fish Lot Share" in 1767.[13]

Although these activities suggest that Jackson was a well-established Nantucket goldsmith, two incidents hint at his sensitivity to encroachment by other craftsmen working in his trade. In one, Samuel Barrett (q.v.) was warned out of Nantucket in 1763 but managed to remain on the island and work as a silversmith. Whether Jackson had a hand in the warning issued against Barrett is unknown; but in a second incident five years later, he and Barrett wrote a joint letter to the Salem silversmith John Touzell (q.v.), warning him of John Jones, a supposed craftsman whom Barrett accused of stealing items from his shop and whom Jackson alleged was ordered to leave Nantucket by island authorities (for a transcription see the Samuel Barrett biography).[14] Jackson may have trained Nathaniel Barrett and Benjamin Bunker (qq.v.).

In March 1771 and February 1772, Jackson acquired two more parcels of land adjoining his new home, for a total of about 14 1/4 square rods of land.[15] With that extension of his property, Jackson seemed to have achieved a measure of prosperity. His prosperity proved to be short-lived, however, because two weeks after the second purchase, on 22 February 1772, Jackson died, leaving his entire estate to his wife, Abigail.[16] Evidence that he worked as a silversmith until his death emerges in a deed of 1772, in which Huldah Daggett sold land to William Rotch "near the Wharf [Straight Wharf] & on which the Goldsmiths Shop late belonging to John Jackson Deceased now stands."[17]

Artifactual evidence adds to the confusion about this silversmith and his working dates. A spoon engraved "Deborah Macy/Born 17th 4 mo/1726," thought to have been made for Deborah Macy of Nantucket, bears the mark associated with Jackson.[18] Though the inscription was dated "1726," it was probably of a commemorative nature, rather than one that indicates the spoon's date of manufacture. This piece was probably made after 1753, when Jackson can be placed on the island with certainty. Jackson is also said to have made another early piece, a pepper box, engraved "A * C" for a Nantucket resident, Abigail Coffin, about 1730, the date of her marriage to Grafton Gardner.[19] However, this attribution probably is erroneous: the box more likely was made about 1760, closer to the time that Jackson is known to have been on Nantucket, for a second, nearly identical pepper box attributed to Jackson exists, this one engraved "John Way/To/Anna Joy 1761." Jackson's silver is identifiable by a single mark that he consistently used: IACKSON in a rectangle (A). JJF

SURVIVING OBJECTS

	Mark	Inscription	Patron	Date	Reference	Owner
Marrow spoon	A*	SB/to/ER		ca. 1740	Buhler/Hood 1970, no. 684	YUAG

	Mark	Inscription	Patron	Date	Reference	Owner
Pepper box	A*	AC	Abigail Coffin	ca. 1760	Merriman 1976, 24	YUAG
Pepper box	A	John Way/To/Anna Joy 1761	John Way and/or Anna Joy	1761	Buhler 1972, no. 502	MFAB
Porringer	A	C/RR	Richard and Ruth (Bunker) Coffin	ca. 1760	Merriman 1976, 28	NHA
Tablespoon	A	DM; M/IC (later)	Macy family	ca. 1765	Johnston 1994, 93	CMA
Tablespoon	A	AF; MCW (later)	Abigail Folger	ca. 1765	Merriman 1976, 26–27	NHA
Tablespoon	A*	S/IE	John and Experience (Folger) Swain	ca. 1750	Merriman 1976, 25	NHA
Tablespoon (mate below)	A*	S/TR	Thomas and Rachel (Allen) Starbuck	ca. 1750	Merriman 1976, 25	NHA
Tablespoon (mate above)	A	S/TR	Thomas and Rachel (Allen) Starbuck	ca. 1750	Buhler 1972, no. 501	MFAB
Tablespoon	A*	Sarah Fish/1767	Sarah Fish	ca. 1767	DAPC 72.1281	WM
Tablespoon	A†	LM; SG (later) (+)	Lydia Macy	ca. 1760	Belden 1980, 247	WM
Tablespoon	A*	DM		ca. 1730	Buhler/Hood 1970, no. 682	YUAG
Tablespoon	A*	Deborah Macy/Born 17th 4 mo/1726	Deborah Macy	ca. 1730	Buhler/Hood 1970, no. 683	YUAG
Tablespoon	A	P/IM; FC (later)		ca. 1760	DAPC 77.2107	YUAG
Tablespoon	A*	MM	Macy family	ca. 1760	Merriman 1976, 28–29	
Tablespoon	A*	David Hussey/Bo^{n} 22^{m}/1757	David Hussey	1757	Merriman 1976, 29	NHA
Two tablespoons	A	MB	Mary Bunker (?)	ca. 1760	Merriman 1976, 30	
Tablespoon	A*	DG	Deborah (Gardner) Gardner (?)	ca. 1760	Merriman 1976, 30	
Tablespoon	A	DC	Deborah Coffin	ca. 1760	Merriman 1976, 30–31	N.Y. State History Coll., Albany, N.Y.
Tablespoon	A*	none		ca. 1770	DAPC 74.3290	WM
Tablespoon	A	H/SA	Silvanus and Alice (Gray) Hussey	ca. 1760	Merriman 1976, 32	
Tablespoon	A*	F/SP	Seth and Phoebe Folger	ca. 1760	DAPC 77.2874	NHA
Tablespoon	A	Elisabeth/Freeborn/Born June 8/1770	Elisabeth Freeborn	1770		NHA

1. For a detailed discussion of Jackson's likely origins, see Merriman 1976.
2. For information on the illegitimacy of Abigail Fitch, see NCCR, Court of the General Sessions of the Peace 1721–85, 62, 67. "Births, Marriages and Deaths on Nantucket 1662–1827," MS, NHA, 1:27. NCCR, Court of General Session of the Peace, Book 1, 188. *Nantucket VR* 3:432; 5:254, 442.
3. NCD 5:319; Merriman 1976, 40.
4. NCD 6:165.

5. NCD 6:306.

6. NCD 9:245.

7. *The New-York Historical Society Collections* (New York, 1885), 17, cited in Merriman 1976, n. 7.

8. NCCR, Court of Common Pleas 1:213–14. According to the court records, Judith Coffin was the daughter of Peleg Coffin.

9. NCD 6:478, 533; NCPR 3:7–8.

10. NCD 6:515.

11. NCD 7:88, 93.

12. Stephen Hussey Account Book, 1759–69, NHA, cited in Merriman 1976, 17–18.

13. NCD 7:181.

14. John Jackson to John Touzell and Samuel Barrett to John Touzell, 8 June 1768, English-Touzel-Hathorne Papers, box 4, folder 1, PEM.

15. NCD 7:420; 8:5.

16. NCPR 3:173–74; *Nantucket VR* 5:377. John Jackson identified himself as a goldsmith in his will, written on 1 December 1766. The will was witnessed by Seth and Phoebe Folger, who owned at least one spoon by Jackson. Administration papers were filed on 4 April 1772; the inventory of the estate is missing.

17. NCD 8:169.

18. A Deborah Macy was born on this date to Thomas and Deborah Macy of Nantucket; *Nantucket VR* 2:269.

19. Merriman 1976, 24.

Thomas Jackson, Jr.
1740–80 +

The Boston tax list of 1780 includes a Thomas Jackson, Jr., goldsmith, assessed with a poll tax of one and real estate valued at thirty pounds.[1] The goldsmith may have been the son of Thomas Jackson (b. 1709), also designated as Jr. in the record, and his wife, Anne Davis (b. 1713).[2] The goldsmith's paternal grandfather was probably Thomas Jackson, a distiller who was appointed, with William Lee and Daniel Parker, the guardian of James Butler (q.v.) in 1728 and who had married Butler's aunt, Grace Butler (b. 1685).[3] When James Butler moved to Nova Scotia in 1750, he gave the elder Thomas Jackson, Jr., the distiller's son, his power of attorney.

Considering the strong family ties between the Jackson family and James Butler, the elder Thomas Jackson, Jr., may have sent his son to Nova Scotia to apprentice with his cousin James Butler around 1754, when he was about fourteen.[4] This possibility is supported by the arrival in Boston in 1766 of a craftsman from Canada named Thomas Jackson, who went to work for the Boston clockmaker and watchmaker Gawen Brown (q.v. Appendix A). The minutes of the Boston selectmen's meeting of 22 October 1766 reported that "Mr. Gowen Brown appeared and informed the Selectmen that he had received into his House as a Workman, one Lawrence Ash & Thomas Jackson, they came to Town about fourteen days since, the last from Cannada [*sic*]the former from Philadelphia."[5] The timing of this Thomas Jackson's appearance in Boston correlates to events in James Butler's life, happening as it does six months before Butler's return to Boston in March 1767 following the unsuccessful conclusion of his venture in Nova Scotia.[6]

Thomas Jackson, Jr., does not appear in the Massachusetts tax list of 1771. If the history conjectured for him above is accurate, the goldsmith may have been living in Gawen Brown's household, even though Brown appears on the tax list with a poll of one (indicating he was the only male over sixteen in the household). Alternatively, Jackson may have been residing with his relative and former master James Butler, who appeared in the same tax list with a poll of two.[7] Aside from the Boston tax list for 1780, no references to Thomas

Jackson, Jr., as a goldsmith have been found, and no death records for the goldsmith Thomas Jackson, Jr., have been uncovered.

No silver by him has been identified. PEK

1. "Assessors' 'Taking-Books,'" 37.
2. RC 24:62, 89; RC 28:185.
3. SCPR 18:511–12, docket 3685; docket 5573; RC 28:11; RC 9:164.
4. Thomas Jackson, Jr., was born on 5 October 1740; see RC 24:242.
5. RC 20:234.
6. RC 29:291.
7. Pruitt 1978, 4–5, 34–35.

John Jagger
1713–40⁺

A

John Jagger was born in Boston on 28 December 1713, the son of John Jagger and Mary (Feathergill) Tyhurst (b. 1682/83), who were married in Boston in 1711.[1] His paternal grandfather possibly was Francis Jagger, an inhabitant of Barbados.[2] His maternal grandparents probably were Robert and Elizabeth Feathergill of Boston.[3]

Jagger would have begun his apprenticeship about 1727, possibly with William Jones (q.v.) of Marblehead because on 22 July 1735 Jagger married Jones's widow, Sabella (Burrington) Jones (1697–1764), in Marblehead.[4] Jagger moved back to Boston sometime after this because he was identified as being a goldsmith "of Boston" at a court session held on 1 April 1740. He and his wife were plaintiffs in an action against James Barry, who was charged with entering their dwelling in Boston on 1 September 1738 and assaulting "Isabella" with a horsewhip and fists. The suit was settled in favor of the plaintiffs for ten shillings and costs.[5]

A tankard with the initials "B/SM" for Rev. Simon and Mary Bradstreet, who were married in Marblehead on 16 November 1738, is marked with an initial and surname mark (A). Little else is known of Jagger, who died sometime before 24 December 1764, when Sabella Jagger, identified as "widow of John," died in Lynn.[6] PEK

SURVIVING OBJECTS

	Mark	Inscription	Patron	Date	Reference	Owner
Tankard	A†	B/SM	Simon and Mary (Strahan) (Hills) Bradstreet	ca. 1740	Buhler 1972, no. 225	MFAB

1. RC 9:157; RC 24:91; RC 28:35.
2. *NEHGR* 39:136.
3. Bigelow-Phillips files, 1154.
4. RC 9:232; *Marblehead VR* 2:237; *Lynn VR* 2:511.
5. SCCR, Court of Common Pleas Record Book 1739, 251.
6. *Lynn VR* 2:511.

David Jesse
ca. 1669–1705/06

Most authorities have speculated that David Jesse was born in Hartford, Connecticut, because he married Mary Wilson, who was born in Dublin, Ireland, and immigrated to Hartford with her parents, Phineas (d. 1692) and Mary (Sanford) Wilson.[1] Francis Hill Bigelow, however, was aware that in Goldsmiths' Hall, London, there is the following record: "March yᵉ 7th 1682

A

... David Jesse sonn of John Jesse Cittizen & Joyner of London doe put my selfe Apprentice unto Alexander Roode Cittizen & Goldsmith of London for the terme of Eight yeares."[2] Jesse became a freeman of the company on 1 April 1691.[3] He probably immigrated to New England soon after that date. Although Jesse's future wife lived in Hartford, he probably met her in Boston, where her father frequently traveled on business. When he wrote his will in May 1691, Phineas Wilson described himself as "merchant of Hartford, presently sojourning in Boston." In his will Wilson referred to his daughters Hannah and Mary Wilson and named several friends, including Benjamin Montfort of Boston (who became the sole administrator), as overseers and guardians of his children "to take care of their Education and Estate." Phineas Wilson died on 11 July 1692, and Mary and her sister evidently remained in Boston with their guardian.[4]

Mary Wilson married David Jesse sometime before 1698, when she and her husband acknowledged receipt of her legacy of £955.12 from the portion of her father's estate administered by her mother, Mary Wilson, in Hartford.[5] In 1703, she received an additional £258 from the portion of the estate entrusted to Benjamin Montfort in Boston.[6] Jesse won the respect of his fellows and in 1700 was elected a member of the Ancient and Honorable Artillery Company.[7]

His wife's inheritances undoubtedly made it easy for David Jesse to establish a substantial business. In addition to being named a goldsmith in the receipt of her legacy, bills dated 1696 and 1703 in the Suffolk County Court files indicate that Jesse combined his craft with general shopkeeping.[8] Although Jesse did not specialize in jewelrymaking, most of the written accounts of his works refer to jewelry that he made, sold, or repaired. In 1702 Jesse sued Hopestill Capen, a Dorchester husbandman, for £6.2, "owing for sundry goods," including a "Gold Chaine & Locket," "a Stone ring," and "three Gold Rings."[9] Jesse was paid £8.19.3 in 1705 for making eight rings for the funeral of James Gray.[10] Although no jewelry with his mark survives, there are several extant pieces of his holloware that bear his mark, DI below a pellet within an oval (A), including a tankard in the Winterthur Museum and a child's cup in the Harrington Collection at the Hood Museum of Art.[11]

Other documents indicate that Jesse lent money by bond frequently, witnessed bonds for other merchants, and, like most goldsmiths, was called upon to weigh hard currency. In 1701 he weighed some of the pieces of eight contained in three bags of money bound for the island of Nevis.[12] He sued the trader Arthur Jeffryes of Boston for nonpayment of a bond of £35 in 1701/02, and his widow, acting for the estate in 1707, sued Margaret Partree, a Boston widow, for £19.13.9 "by cash lent and Sundries."[13] Throughout the year 1703, Jesse was involved in a suit and countersuit with the Boston merchant Joseph Mallinson of Boston and New York. The accounts and depositions filed in the case reveal that Jesse bought £40.2 worth of goldsmiths' tools from Mallinson, ruined a watch that Mallinson had to have repaired elsewhere, and paid Mallinson a commission for buying lace and "for Sales." The controversy arose over "Nine hundred forty Eight peices of Eight delivered to s[d] Jesse p M[r] Malinson & w[ch] M[r] Mallinson saith he was to hand Cutt to twelve penny weight & is willing to allow two pence per pieice for the Cutting, but M[r] Jesse saith he will give his oath he was to have five shillings for Each peice of Eight when Cutt as afores[d]." Apparently Jesse's action was legal, and the price he expected to be paid was not excessive, for the court eventually ruled in his favor.[14]

Jesse and his wife, Mary, had five children: David (b. 1700), Mary (b. 1701), Phineas (b. 1702), Elizabeth (b. 1704), and Susanna (b. 1705), three of whom were still living when their father died on 13 January 1705/06.[15] Mary Jesse was made administrator of her husband's intestate estate. The inventory, taken on 7 February 1705/06, lists household goods and tools worth £264.09.02. The "Working Tools in the Shop & Cellar" indicate that Jesse had a substantial goldsmithing business:

9 Anvells Con.ᵗ 273.ˡᵇ at 5ᵈ ℔ˡᵇ	5: 13: 9
3 Teasts 70ˡᵇ at 5ᵈ ℔ˡᵇ	1: 09: 2
75.ˡᵇ of Hammers at 5.ᵈ ℔ˡᵇ	1. 11. 3
10 Ditto 40.ˡᵇ at 5ᵈ ℔ˡᵇ	0: 16: 8
20 Ditto at	0: 15: 0
2 Sheares & 1 Skellet 9ᵗ 52.ˡᵇ at 5ᵈ ℔ˡᵇ	1: 08: 8
5 p.ʳ of Kneeling Tongs at 16ᵈ ℔ p.ʳ	0: 06: 8
1 Clasp Stamp at	0: 06: 0
2 Drawing Doggs, 2 Swages 9.ᵗ 23.ˡᵇ at 6ᵈ ℔ˡᵇ	0: 11: 6
4 paire of Tongs at 18.ᵈ ℔ p.ʳ	0: 6: 0
4 p.ʳ of Sheares at 2/℔ p.ʳ	0: 08: 0
4 Drawing Irons at	0: 12: 0
1 Brass Stamp at	0: 08: 0
8 Cutting punches at 9ᵈ ℔ pᶜ	0: 06: 0
10 Dabbing punches at 6ᵈ ℔ pᶜ	0: 05: 0
1 hand saw at	0: 03: 0
2 Salt Stamps at	0: 06: 0
3 p.ʳ of Scales and weights at	1: 10: 0
1 Screw plate & tapps at	0: 02: 0
12 old hangers at 2/℔ pᶜ	1: 04: 0
8 Canes at	0: 12: 0
6 flasks & 1 Inglett at	0: 08: 0
3 hand Vices at 12.ᵈ ℔ pᶜ	0: 03: 0
6 flat Tongs & files at	0: 06: 0
5 small brass skelletts at	1: 10: 0
1 Anvell at	2: 10: 0
1 p.ʳ of Bellows at	2: 00: 0
1 old board Vice at	0: 06: 0
4 Burnishers & punches & Crusibles	2. 10. 0
1 Press & 1 glasscase at	1: 06: 0
Some old Iron &ᶜ	0: 06: 0[16]

In spite of his extensive collection of tools, there were no finished objects in Jesse's shop when he died. The total estate was not large and there is no real estate listed, but Mary Jesse's first administration account mentions "Cash since received" amounting to £228.14.7, for a total estate of £493.3.9. Of this amount she used £394.2.7 to pay outstanding debts, including 38 shillings to a Mr. Edwards (possibly John Edwards [q.v.]), 23 shillings to Mr. Coney (possibly John Coney [q.v.]), and £5 to René Grignon (q.v.).[17] As guardian for her children, she was obliged to account for the remainder of the estate, and in her final account of administration filed in 1716 she asked for an allowance of £50 "To bringing up her husbands Three Children one of Them being but Three weeks old, the Second Child but 19 months old and the Eldest but four years of age when their Father dyed" as well as "for bedding, Utensills and Implements of Household necessary for the upholding of Life for her and her ffamilys use according to the direction of the laws."[18] It seems sadly ironic that a woman who brought so much wealth to her husband should be held accountable for every penny that she spent in support of her family. BMW

SURVIVING OBJECTS

	Mark	Inscription	Patron	Date	Reference	Owner
Beaker	A	W/PT; The Gift of/ Mrs. Thatcher of Boston/to the/ Church in Dorchester/1672 (later)	Philip and Thankful (Pond) Withington	ca. 1700	Jones 1913, 143–44	
Caudle cup	A*	A/AM	Alexander and Mary (Grant) Allen (?)	ca. 1700	Jones 1913, 178	
Cup	A*	K		ca. 1700	Buhler 1965, 31	HMA
Porringer	A	EF		ca. 1700		MFAB
Porringer	A	AG		ca. 1700	YUAG files	
Tankard	A†	G/RK (later)		ca. 1700	Buhler 1972, no. 74	MFAB
Tankard	A	L/IE (+)	Isaac and Elizabeth (Barnes) Lothrop	ca. 1700	Quimby 1995, no. 95	WM
Tumbler	A	TF	Thomas Fenner	ca. 1700	Buhler 1956, no. 104	RIHS

1. Savage 1860–62, 2:547; 4:587; Flynt/Fales 1968, 258; Buhler 1972, 1:90.
2. Apprentice Book 3, fol. 125v, Worshipful Company of Goldsmiths, London. Bigelow included the information that Jesse was apprenticed in London and made a freeman of the Goldsmiths' Company in his draft biography of Jesse; see Bigelow-Phillips files, 357. Phillips received partial confirmation of this in a letter dated 29 April 1935 from G.R. Hughes of the Goldsmiths' Company. Robert B. Barker provided the citations from the Goldsmiths' Company's records; see Robert B. Barker letter to Patricia E. Kane, 9 February 1993.
3. Court Book 10, fol. 48v, Worshipful Company of Goldsmiths, London. Robert B. Barker letter to Patricia E. Kane, 9 February 1993.
4. SCPR 13:37–39.
5. Manwaring 1904, 1:522–23.
6. SCPR 15:120–21.
7. Roberts 1895, 1:325.
8. Manwaring 1904, 1:522–23; SCCR, files 3475, 5555.
9. SCCR, file 5554.
10. Receipt from David Jesse to Paul Dudley, Esq., 11 July 1705. Photostat in the Bigelow-Phillips files; whereabouts of the original are unknown.
11. A drawing of a related mark, namely, initials in an oval with a period, has been published, but no actual example has been found; see Kovel 1961, 151. A D·I mark has been misattributed to him (Johnston 1994, 90). A keyhole-handle porringer with his mark at SI (383534) seems too late in style to be Jesse's work.
12. SCCR, file 5178; Mass. Archives 40:751.
13. SCCR, Court of Common Pleas Record Book 1701–06, 25; SCCR, file 5335; SCCR, Court of Common Pleas Record Book 1706–10, 65–66.
14. SCCR, Court of Common Pleas Record Book 1701–06, 55–56, 100–02; SCCR, files 5559, 5920.

15. RC 24:2, 11, 15, 29, 35. Notice of David Jesse's death was printed in the *Boston News-Letter* of 7–14 January 1706.

16. SCPR 16:99–100, 143–45, docket 2960.

17. SCPR 17:500.

18. SCPR 19:153–54. By this time Mary had gone to live in Hartford (SCPR 19:154–55). She was discharged from "further Accts. & Reckonings" regarding the estate on 20 November 1716 (SCPR 19:218–19).

William Jones
1694/95–1730

A

B

C

Marblehead, Massachusetts's, first and probably most successful goldsmith, William Jones, was descended from a distinguished Connecticut family. He was the namesake and grandson of William Jones (d. 1706), deputy governor of Connecticut in the seventeenth century, whose wife, Hannah (Eaton) Jones (d. 1707), was the daughter of Gov. Theophilus Eaton, a prominent merchant and one of the original settlers of New Haven. His parents were the clothier Isaac (b. 1671) and Deborah (Clark) Jones (1672–1735), who were married in 1692 in Stratford. William Jones was born in New Haven on 20 January 1694/95.[1]

Jones married Sabella [Isabella] Burrington (1697–1764), the daughter of Thomas (d. 1702) and Lydia Burrington of Boston, in 1720.[2] He may have been in Boston serving his apprenticeship, possibly with John Dixwell (q.v.); John Marshall Phillips theorized a relationship between Jones and Dixwell because of their common background in New Haven and because Jones named one of his children Basil, a Dixwell family name. Jones was probably in Marblehead by the time he made a book clasp dated 1722 for Mercy English (b. 1704) of Salem. His other known patrons—Samuel and Elizabeth Russell and Humphrey and Abigail (Burrill) Devereaux—were residents of Marblehead.

Kathryn C. Buhler pointed out that Jones's death in 1730 was caused by smallpox because the charges against his estate included fees for 3 "nurses in Small Pox" at 20 shillings a week for six weeks.[3] Jones died on 17 October 1730.[4] He was survived by his widow, Sabella, and three young children. His widow was instructed to leave "a small silver cup to ye Communion Table" of the Congregational church, probably, as Buhler notes, of his own making. (This was subsequently melted down in 1772.) Within five years of his death, Sabella Jones married John Jagger (q.v.).[5]

Jones's total estate was valued at £1,142.19; his debts amounted to £416.0.3. A detailed, room-by-room inventory of his estate taken on 1 March 1730/31 by Richard Trevit, Jr., Joseph Swett, and William Goodwin enumerates the furnishings of the "Garrett," "Great Chamber," "Little Chamber," "Lower Room," "Kitchen," and "worke Shops." The shop goods included

To a Cross Cutt Saw	1:	0:	0
To 140^{Oz} 15^{dwt} of wrought Silver at 21/℔ oz:	153:	0:	9
To 417^{Oz} 10^{dwt} of unwrought Silver at 18/℔ oz:	375:	15:	0
To 8^{oz} 5^{dwt} of wrought &c Gold at £15 ℔ oz:	123:	15:	0
To a pair of Stone Earrings & pendles	2:	10:	0
To a Stone Lockett 16/ To a Stone Ring 25/	2:	1	=0
To 3 Strings of Corral beeds at 6/℔	0:	18:	0
To the working tools, weights & scails Glass cases & the Utensels of the Shop	60:	0:	0
To Province Bills of Creditt	167:	0:	0

Listed in the Great Chamber was 91 oz. 2 dwt of "plate for houshold use" valued at 18 shillings an ounce. Buhler suggested that the values for silver given in the inventory—both 18 shillings and 21 shillings per ounce—may have indicated that the silver appraised at the higher value was of a higher standard of metal, namely, the Britannia standard required in London from 1697 to 1720. As she acknowledges, however, the difference may have been attributable to differences in the degree of workmanship involved or to the age of the articles involved. The administration of Jones's estate included payment of £54.8 to "Jacob Heard," possibly Jacob Hurd (q.v.) of Boston.[6]

Given his short career, a surprisingly large and diverse body of objects is associated with Jones, including porringers, mugs, a pepper box, the aforementioned unusual book clasp, and a tankard. Phillips also made reference to a snuffbox by Jones engraved "My love is fixt: wil not Range/I like my choyce too well to change."[7] Jones's prestigious ancestors and family connections, both of which would have given him status in colonial society, may help to account for the success he had during his brief life. There are three marks attributed to Jones (A–C).[8] GWRW

SURVIVING OBJECTS

	Mark	Inscription	Patron	Date	Reference	Owner
Book clasp	c†	Mercy English/1722	Mercy (English) Beadle	ca. 1722	Buhler/Hood 1970, no. 116	YUAG
Mug	A*	R/SE	Samuel and Elizabeth Russell	ca. 1725	Buhler 1965, 44–45	HMA
Mug	A (?)	K/WM		ca. 1720	Parke-Bernet, 25–29 January 1972, lot 117	
Pepper box	A	D/HA (+)	Humphrey and Abigail (Burrill) Devereaux	ca. 1725	DAPC 69.1593	MMA
Porringer	A*	GN		ca. 1725	Buhler 1972, no. 129	MFAB
Porringer	A†	N/AA (altered to N/AW)		ca. 1725	Buhler 1972, no. 130	MFAB
Porringer	A*	D/HA	Humphrey and Abigail (Burrill) Devereaux	ca. 1730	Johnston 1994, 94	CMA
Porringer	A*	HN/HD		ca. 1720	DAPC 73.2624	AMB
Porringer	A*	erased		ca. 1725		SI
Porringer spoon	A*	G/MR		ca. 1730	DAPC 72.3110	
Tablespoon	B†	KK; KB		ca. 1720		YUAG
Tablespoon	B*	B/WS		ca. 1725		PEM
Tankard	A*	MB; B/FE		ca. 1725	Christie's, 19 October 1990, lot 102	
Teaspoon (mate below)	A	EB		ca. 1725		CHS
Teaspoon (mate above)	A	EB; 1752 (later)		ca. 1725		CHS
Teaspoon	B*	HCA		ca. 1730	DAPC 73.2395	WM

1. The key document in linking Jones to New Haven is a court order dated 26 February 1739/40 in which Bassil Jones (b. 1725), the minor son of William Jones late of Marblehead, asked the New Haven court to appoint his grandfather, Isaac Jones of New Haven, as his guardian; see New Haven Probate Records 6:293. For Jones's ancestry, see New Haven

Probate Records 3:92, 111–12; *New Haven VR*, 34, 65, 74, 203, 256. See also Savage 1860–62, 1:393–94; 2:561, 567–68; *Marblehead VR* 1:296–97; Stratford VR, vol. LR1, 45. Patricia E. Kane and Barbara M. Ward provided information for determining Jones's Connecticut background; see Ward 1983, 364.

2. RC 28:88; RC 9:232; *Lynn VR* 2:511.
3. ECPR, docket 15237; Buhler 1972, 1:158.
4. *Marblehead VR* 2:513.
5. Buhler 1965, 44–45; Flynt/Fales 1968, 260; and Buhler 1972, 1:158, are the best secondary accounts. See also Buhler 1972, 1:267.
6. ECPR, docket 15237; see also ECPR 319:82–83 for the inventory; Buhler 1965, 44–45.
7. Phillips 1949, 85.
8. As Buhler 1972, 1:158, suggested, the marks she illustrated are different impressions of the same mark. WI in a serrated rectangle sometimes has been attributed to Jones, but because this mark is on a spoon with a shell drop at HD, which is too late stylistically for Jones, this mark was not used by him; see Johnston 1994, 92.

K

Joseph Kneeland
1700–40

A

Joseph Kneeland's life dates have been given consistently in the literature as 1698–1760, although in fact he was born in 1700 and died in 1740.[1] The confusion over his birth date has arisen because scholars have assumed that the goldsmith was the Joseph Kneeland born to John and Mary Kneeland in 1698.[2] The goldsmith was actually the Joseph born to Solomon Kneeland, a leatherdresser (1670/71–1743), and Mary (Pollard) Kneeland (1673–ca. 1742), daughter of Samuel (ca. 1645/46–78), a tailor, and Mary Pollard of Boston, on 14 December 1700.[3] Evidence from deeds and probate records confirms this relationship. Joseph, the goldsmith, appears in several deeds with the leatherdresser Solomon Kneeland (either his father or his brother). His father's will, dated 4 September 1741 and proved on 10 January 1743/44, mentions bequests to "the four Children of my Son Joseph Kneeland, namely Joseph [b. 1729/30], Mary [b. 1731/32], John [b. 1736], and Sarah [b. 1740]."[4] Joseph Kneeland had predeceased his father; administration on the estate of the goldsmith was granted on 9 September 1740 to the mastmaker Nathaniel Greenwood of Boston.[5] Joseph's paternal grandparents were the laborer John Kneeland (ca. 1632–91), a Scottish immigrant and one of the founders of the Scots Charitable Society of Boston, and his wife, Mary (Hawkins) Kneeland.[6] Kneeland was a cousin of William Pollard (q.v.).

Solomon Kneeland may have apprenticed his son to John Dixwell (q.v.) because of their mutual interest in the New North Church; Joseph's father was one of the founders of New North Church and later of the New Brick Church. It is likely that Joseph Kneeland at least worked as a journeyman for Dixwell, for he appears, along with Joseph Goldthwait (q.v.), as witness to a deed between John Dixwell and the blacksmith John Manning of Boston in 1723.[7]

In 1726/27 Kneeland purchased the "Northerly part of a Certain House and Land Situate in Marshalls Street in Boston" from Nathaniel Newdigate of Newport, Rhode Island, for £250. According to the deed, this side of the house was already "in the Present Tenure and Occupation of the sd Joseph Kneeland." Kneeland immediately mortgaged the property to Katherine Menzies, wife of John Menzies of Leicester, Middlesex County, for £150.[8] In 1731, he made some improvements to the house in order to prevent water from falling onto his roof from the adjoining house.[9] One of the abutters was Capt. John

637

Ballentine, the grandfather of Kneeland's wife, Mary Wharton (b. 1701), daughter of the merchant John (d. ca. 1712/13) and Sarah (Ballentine) Wharton. Joseph and Mary married on 6 February 1728/29; the Reverend Thomas Foxcroft of the First Church performed the ceremony.[10] A Joseph Kneeland, perhaps the silversmith, served as a constable in 1737–38. A court record of 1739 names "Joseph Kneeland, of Boston Goldsmith . . . an Under Sheriff of said County [Suffolk]" as defendant.[11]

Kneeland's early years as a silversmith apparently were very successful because he was commissioned to make silver for churches outside of Boston. He made a beaker for the First Church in Middletown, Connecticut, in 1726, a baptismal basin for the First Church of Christ in New Haven, Connecticut, in 1735, and a beaker for the First Church in Dedham, Massachusetts.[12] The commissions from the Connecticut churches may have come to Kneeland because of his apprenticeship with John Dixwell, a New Haven–born goldsmith who made many pieces for Connecticut churches during his career. Leonard Vassall commissioned Kneeland to make a pair of tankards for his sons John and William, who were admitted as fellow commoners in 1729, to present to Harvard College. The tankards are engraved with coats of arms with baroque mantling in a style reminiscent of the work of John and Thomas Edwards (qq.v.).[13] All of the known objects by Kneeland are marked I:Kneeland in a conforming rectangle (A).

In addition to his work as a goldsmith, Kneeland was evidently involved in some mercantile activities because on 7 September 1729 he sued Roger Paxton, a Boston mariner, "In a plea of the Case for that whereas the pl.[t] on the 6.th day of Jan.[ry] last past at Boston afores.[d] shipt on board the Ship Kezia whereof the Def.[t] was then Mast.[r] three barrells of Cranberrys . . . of the value of Three pounds Ten Shillings to be deliv[d] . . . at Antegoa . . . unto Doctor Jackson, or his Assignes . . . that he has not deliv[d] the Same, at port afores[d] accord[g] to his promise."[14] Kneeland may have begun to run into financial difficulties about 1734, when he again mortgaged his house, this time to Lydia Draper, as collateral on a bond of £200 that Kneeland held jointly with the leatherdresser Solomon Kneeland (either his father or his brother) and the mariner George Beard. In subsequent deeds he further mortgaged the same land for £400 to Solomon Kneeland and George Beard, and for £75 to the shipwright Nathaniel Greenwood and the brazier David Cutler. Kneeland's debt to Draper, Greenwood, and Cutler was still unpaid at the time of his death.[15]

Joseph Kneeland died intestate, and administration on his estate was granted on 9 September 1740.[16] Jabez Hunt, David Cutler, and Joseph Bradford appraised the estate and filed the inventory with the court on 16 September 1740. The total value of Kneeland's estate, including the house and land appraised at £500, was £659.5. In addition to a small number of household goods that included three beds and bedsteads, a chest of drawers, four tables, a desk, six leather chairs and one leather armchair, seven other chairs, nineteen pictures, two maps, a looking glass, and cooking and serving utensils, the inventory lists the following:

The Tools. The Draw Bench & Drawing Irons	4.	10.	—
2 Burnishers 20/ 1 large Vice 80/ 3 sma: D.[o] 7/	5.	7.	—
1 Thimble Stamp 60/ 3 Anvils w.[t] 91[lb] @ 2/6 £10.17.6	13.	17.	6
2 Chizzels 2 Swages 10 bottom Stakes & Anvels w.[t] @ 2/6	9.	2.	6
28 Hamers £5.12/ 30 Files 30/ 5 p.[r] Pliers 10/	7.	12	—

Sundry Sma: Tools 53/ 3 p.^{r} Scales & w.^{ts} 97/   7. 10. —
1 Sett Ring Strainers 25/ brass Button Mould 40/ 2 boxes 4/   3. 9 —
2 Sett of Salt Stamps 24/ a p.^{r}cell Patterns 30/   2. 14 —
2 p.^{r} Flasks & 1 p.^{r} Skrews 26/ 3 Stools two Moulds 16/6   2. –. 6
1 Beak Iron 8/ 3 p.^{r} Tongs 25/ 1 Skillet 30/ 1 Inget 2/   3. 5 —
1 Boiling pan 20/ 1 p.^{r} Bellows 50/ 2 blow Pipes 2/   3. 12 —[17]

The estate was declared insolvent, and the court appointed Kenelm Winslow, Richard Abbot, and William White as commissioners to distribute the estate among the deceased's heirs and debtors.[18] BMW

SURVIVING OBJECTS

	Mark	Inscription	Patron	Date	Reference	Owner
Baptismal basin	A	The Gift of Mr Jeremiah Atwater/ to the first Church of Christ in Newhaven,/A.D. 1735	First Church of Christ, New Haven, Conn., for Jeremiah Atwater	1735	Jones 1913, 305	
Beaker	A	The Gift/of/Mr Thomas Metcalf to y.^{e}/first Church in/ Dedham	Thomas Metcalf and/or First Church, Dedham, Mass.	ca. 1730	Winchester 1956, 552	
Beaker	A*	Given by M.^{r}- Andrew Warner/to the first Ch:h: in Middle town 1726	First Church of Christ, Middletown, Conn.	ca. 1726	Jones 1913, 281	WA
Chafing dish	A	?		ca. 1730	Silver Supplement 1973, no. 63	
Nutmeg grater	A†	RW		ca. 1730	Buhler 1972, no. 134	MFAB
Tankard	A	Vassall arms, in chief a sun in splen- dor, in base a chal- ice, and crest, a full- rigged ship, sails furled; Donum/ Joannis Vassale/ Comm[en]salis/ A.D.: 1729	John Vassall and/or Harvard College	1729	Fogg 1972, no. 174	HU
Tankard	A	Vassall arms, in chief a sun in splen- dor, in base a chal- ice, and crest, a full- rigged ship, sails furled; Donum/ Guilielmi Vassale/ Commensalis/A.D.: 1729	William Vassall and/or Harvard College	1729	Fogg 1972, no. 174	HU

1. Buck 1903, 108; French (1917) 1967, 72; Ensko 1927, 51; Graham 1936, 43; Ensko 1937, 45; Currier 1938, 84; Ensko 1948, 83; Thorn 1949, 124; Kovel 1961, 160; Flynt/Fales 1968, 263 (correctly identifies death date as 1740).
2. RC 9:241.
3. RC 24:4; RC 9:20, 115, 129; RC 28:349; SCPR 12:29, 361.

4. SCD 49:100–01; 50:205–07; SCPR 36:514–15; RC 24:193, 203, 213, 226, 240. Joseph and Mary Kneeland had two daughters named Sarah; the first, born in 1733/34, evidently died young. Buhler indicates that she felt some confusion over Joseph Kneeland's marriage; 1972, 1:166. However, it is clear that the goldsmith Joseph Kneeland was married to a woman named Mary because the two appeared as husband and wife in SCD 49:100–01 and 50:205–07. His son Joseph Kneeland married Lydia.

5. SCPR 35:120–21, 137, 168. Kneeland had mortgaged property to Greenwood, and Greenwood sued Kneeland for failing to pay off the bond. The court ruled in favor of Greenwood on 3 April 1739, and at the time of his death Kneeland still had not paid Greenwood; SCCR, Court of Common Pleas Record Book 1738, 182–83.

6. *Roxbury VR* 2:569; SCPR 1:6; SCD 26:10; 25:112.

7. SCD 37:177–78.

8. SCD 40:301–02.

9. SCD 48:142.

10. RC 9:244; RC 24:11; RC 28:144; SCPR 18:60–61, 392–93.

11. Seybolt 1939, 206; SCCR, Court of Common Pleas Record Book 1738, 182–83.

12. Jones 1913, 281, 305; Buhler 1956, 65.

13. Fogg 1972, no. 174; Ward 1983, 246–57. Similar engraving also appears on canns by Knight Leverett (q.v.) in the Bortman-Larus collection published in *Silver Supplement* 1973, 37.

14. SCCR, Court of Common Pleas Record Book 1729, 259; file 24007.

15. SCD 49:100–01; 50:205–07; SCCR, Court of Common Pleas Record Book 1738, 182–83.

16. SCPR 35:120–21.

17. SCPR 35:137.

18. SCPR 35:168.

L

Edward Lang
1742–1830

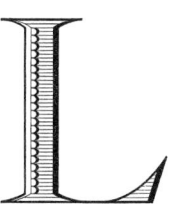

A

B

Son of the silversmith Jeffrey Lang (q.v.) and his wife, Hannah, Edward was the younger brother of Richard and Nathaniel (qq.v.) Lang, and the uncle of the silversmith Nathaniel Lang (1757–1824). (See the entry on Jeffrey Lang for biographical information on Edward's parents and grandparents). Edward's long life, dogged with difficulties, is as well documented as one could expect for a minor craftsman of his period. The artifactual record is not as rich, for there are few objects by him known today.

Edward was born on 3 September 1742 and baptized by his parents at the First Church in Salem.[1] Although it is usually assumed that he was apprenticed to his father, Jeffrey died in 1758, before Edward began his training. He was placed in the care of his older brother Richard and Benjamin Goodhue, who elected to send Edward to Portsmouth, New Hampshire (Edward's father's home town), to serve his time with his kinsman David Griffeth (1735–79).[2] Edward's guardians apparently were not pleased with the treatment he received from Griffeth, prompting Griffeth to defend himself in a rambling but impassioned letter to Goodhue, written from Portsmouth on 30 April 1761:

> I am informed you hear a bad character of me, and that I dont use Edward Lang well; I should be glad to see you here, more Especially, as you hear that he is not Like to live long, and as I purpose to use him as I always have, when you come then you can see how he has been used, and how he now lives. I am sorry you have heard such a pack of Lyes of me, as you will find them Reports to be false, and without any foundation, moreover If I dont use him as I ought to, you can take him from me, we have the same Laws here, In general, that there Is in your province, you are misinformed as to his health, he has had the Jaundice but Is a great deal better, as you are his Guardian I should be very glad, and think it is your Duty, to see that he is well used, by me, as you bound him to me, and I am very sorry he does not know when he is well of[f], his Brother Intimates as tho he would not Serve out half his time, and I think his Brother advises him to Run away . . . I should be glad you would give Such advice as you think proper, when you have seen into the right of the matter.

He closed with a postscript: "It would surprize you, to See the letter I had from Rich[d] Lang By the post, Such a parcel of Lyes I never saw put together, against a Person, except they had some Reason for so doing, I know myself Innocent."[3] In spite of all the contretemps, Edward survived his apprenticeship and returned to Salem to pursue his career beginning in 1764 or perhaps

641

slightly earlier. Edward married Rachel Ward (b. 1746) on 3 April 1768, and they had eight children. Rachel was the daughter of Ebenezer (1710–91) and Rachel (Pickman) Ward (1717–89).[4]

Lang's twenty-year career as a silversmith is amply documented in his account book, preserved at the Peabody Essex Museum.[5] Among those he did business with was the Boston silversmith Stephen Emery (q.v.). As Lang's ledger reveals (and as is discussed in the essay in this volume on silversmiths who worked outside of Boston), he achieved only moderate success until severe economic hardship, first encountered at the beginning of the Revolution, forced him to change careers.

Silversmithing for Edward Lang thus was not a stepping-stone to success. He never achieved, for example, the one hundred pounds required annually "to live in some comfort" in revolutionary America.[6] In fact, his annual income, unless supplemented in some unrecorded fashion, would place Lang and his family at the subsistence level.[7] It is no wonder that he accepted a teaching position at the East School, which brought him an income of about ninety-six pounds. Even then, the standard of living for teachers "was, on the whole, not only below that of other professional men, but less than that of many artisans."[8]

On 19 March 1786, the Reverend William Bentley recorded in his diary that "on Wednesday morning Mr. Lang the School Master took the School, and I attended with him."[9] Lang would remain in charge of this new East Writing School for nearly a quarter of a century, until he was ousted in 1810. During these years, personal misfortune seems to have plagued Lang. Bentley noted on 22 December 1795 that "Master Lang has lost another daughter. He buried one last Sunday evening. This makes the third daughter, & the fourth child, including a son who foundered at Sea, which have been lost to him within two years."[10]

Bentley and Lang were well acquainted, even friends, and frequent references to meals, travels, and visits together can be found in Bentley's diary.[11] Lang also appears in the records of the Essex Lodge of Masons, to which he was admitted in 1781 and "filled successively its offices, being master in 1808."[12]

As time passed, Bentley's comments on Lang's performance as a teacher became increasingly critical. As early as 1793, trouble seemed to be brewing. Bentley noted that Lang, although "a most worthy man," did "not succeed to the public wishes" in the operation of the school.[13] By 1797, things seemed to be improving,[14] but Bentley continued to record frequent observations of Lang's deteriorating work.[15] Things finally came to a head in 1810, when Lang was forced to resign.

Although Lang seems to have been an incompetent teacher, if we can believe Bentley, his dismissal had political overtones. Lang, a Federalist, was under attack from a Republican faction, and Bentley was a well-known rabid Republican. Lang's own account of his troubles clearly indicates that he felt he was fired for no substantial reason and that his former friend Bentley had betrayed him.[16] His letter of resignation to Bentley is a poignant statement of his feelings of persecution and misplaced friendship.[17] Bentley, naturally, had a somewhat different view of the matter, claiming that he "did not dismiss him in old age without emotion"[18] and that the school had for "twenty years [been] without any proper Instructor or discipline."[19] The scandal eventually found its way into the newspapers, and although Bentley continued to maintain that he had dismissed Lang because he was incompetent, others saw "political motives" involved and placed "a great share of the blame" on Bentley.[20] The controversy simmered for awhile but eventually died down.[21]

After his removal from the school, Lang found a job as a clerk in the Essex Bank, "till the time of its collapse from empty vaults and depleted cash boxes."[22] No doubt thoroughly discouraged and more than a little disappointed in men of the cloth, Lang died on 26 January 1830 at the age of eighty-seven.[23]

Two marks have been attributed to Edward Lang: E·LANG in a rectangle (A) and EL in a rectangle (B).[24] His surviving work seems to consist of spoons, although a miniature tea service by him has been published.[25] GWRW

SURVIVING OBJECTS

	Mark	Inscription	Patron	Date	Reference	Owner
Tablespoon	A*	H⸴ Crowninshield.	Hannah Crowninshield	ca. 1770	Fales 1983, 8–9	PEM
Tablespoon	A†	M/TE		ca. 1780		YUAG
Tablespoon	A*	HW; Russell (later)		ca. 1770	DAPC 75.3220	WM
Tablespoon	B*	ML		ca. 1770		PEM
Tea set (miniature)	?	?		?	Kernan 1961b, 568–69	
Teaspoon	B†	MA		ca. 1770	DAPC 73.2370	WM

1. *Salem VR* 1:509; Pierce 1974, 306.
2. Edward Lang Account Book, fol. 95, PEM. Goodhue (1707–83) was a Salem blacksmith. For Griffeth (or Griffith), see Flynt/Fales 1968, 235–36.
3. Benjamin Goodhue Manuscripts, box 4, folder 6, PEM.
4. *Salem VR* 3:586. For Rachel's parents, see *Salem VR* 2:389; 6:304; 2:175; 6:307.
5. Edward Lang Account Book, PEM.
6. Main 1965, 118. The Massachusetts tax list for 1771 indicates that Lang owned one-half of a house with a shop adjoining, and that the annual worth of his real estate was six pounds; see Pruitt 1978, 134–35.
7. See Main 1965, 115–63, for a discussion of the standards and styles of living in this period.
8. Main 1965, 144. Lang's salary as a schoolteacher is derived from a receipt dated 1791 and published in *EIHC* 76, no. 1 (January 1940): 55.
9. Bentley 1905–62, 1:32.
10. Bentley 1905–62, 2:168.
11. Bentley 1905–62, 2:37, 66, 96, 102, 210, 228, 452.
12. Leavitt 1861, 127–28. See also Hadley 1979, 58 and 87, for a portrait of Lang.
13. Bentley 1905–62, 2:31.
14. Bentley 1905–62, 2:219.
15. Bentley 1905–62, 3:39, 278, 315, 329, 417, 499.
16. Edward Lang Account Book, fol. 95, PEM.
17. Edward Lang Account Book, fols. 94–95, PEM.
18. Bentley 1905–62, 3:533.
19. Bentley 1905–62, 3:533.
20. Bentley 1905–62, 3:533.
21. Bentley 1905–62, 3:533–34; see also Browne 1913, 195.
22. Bentley 1905–62, 4:594; Browne 1913, 195.
23. *Salem VR* 5:390.
24. LANG in a rectangle has been recorded, but no example bearing this mark has been located; see Belden 1980, 264.
25. A bowl published in *American and English Silver*, 59, no. 345 (recorded in DAPC 71.1068) cannot, on the basis of style, be considered Lang's work.

Jeffrey Lang
1707–58

A

B

C

Jeffrey Lang was Salem's first silversmith of any stature and the town's most important silversmith during the first half of the eighteenth century. A native of Portsmouth, New Hampshire, Lang was the patriarch of a family of Salem silversmiths that spanned three generations. His sons Richard, Nathaniel, and Edward (qq.v.) and his grandson Nathaniel (1757–1824) all worked as silversmiths in Salem, although none with the distinction their forebear achieved.

Lang was born in Portsmouth on 16 January 1707, the son of Nathaniel and Elizabeth Lang.[1] His father was a fisherman by trade and a deacon of the church.[2] Lang's master is not known. He probably was trained when he arrived in Salem, sometime before his marriage to Hannah Symmes (1707–48), the daughter of Richard and Hannah (Hasket) Symmes (or Sims) (b. 1675), on 24 August 1732.[3] Jeffrey and Hannah had nine children in Salem before her death at the age of forty-one.[4] Jeffrey then married the widow Esther Ruck, by whom he had two more children.[5] Lang was admitted to membership in the First Church on 6 March 1737.[6] He lived and worked in a house that he built in 1740 on the upper end of Essex Street.[7]

On 27 May 1745, Lang placed the following notice in a Boston newspaper:

"*RUN away from his Master* Jeffery Lang, *Goldsmith of* Salem, *some time in the Month of* April *last, a Man Servant named* Nathaniel White, *between nineteen and twenty Years of Age, of a Middle Stature and of a dark Complexion. He had on when he went away a dark colour'd Drugget Coat and Jacket, Leather Breeches and a Castor Hat. This is to forewarn all Persons of entertaining, harbouring, trusting, or trading with said Servant upon peril of the Law in that Case made and provided. It is thought he is gone towards* Piscataqua. *If any Person will give Intelligence to his said Master where he is, they shall be Rewarded for their Trouble.*"[8]

It is not known if White had a craft relationship with Lang.

Lang died on 14 May 1758, at the age of fifty-one.[9] His total estate of £504 included his house and land, valued at £373. John Touzell (q.v.), who may have been trained by Lang, was one of the appraisers of his estate. His goods "In the Shop" included

Sundry working Tools am.º in the Whole to	£21. 17. 5
a p.ʳ of Stillyards 6/8 a p.ʳ D.º 2/ 17 p.ʳ Chapes & Tongues 6/9	15. 5
a p.ˢ large brass Wire 8ᵈ some Iron Wire 1/	1. 8
30 p.ʳ brass Buttons /10ᵈ ℔ 24ˡᵇ old Iron 4/9 a brass Cock 1/	1. 10. 9
7ˡᵇ Brass /8ᵈ ℔ 1ˡᵇ Sandiver/4.ᵈ 5 Hanks of Wire 2/8	7. 8
13 z.º Silver workt into Buckles &c 8/℔	5. 4. 0
2.ᵒᶻ 4ᵖ 12ᵍ Silver @ 6/8 ℔ 18.ᴾʷᵗ12ᴳʳ Solder 4/ 10 1ᵈʷ Gold D.º 4/	1. 4. –
a Gold Necklace with some other Gold	3. 6. 8
2ᵒᶻ1/2 Silver Filings 16/8 Some Stones for Button 3/	. 19. 8
12 Grains Gold Filings 2/6 Some Salt Peter 8ᵈ	3. 2

The room-by-room inventory goes on to enumerate the articles in the great room, best room, chamber over the best room, hall chamber, shop chamber, garret, and kitchen. His personal silver, stored in the kitchen, consisted of a porringer, a cup, and five spoons worth a total of £4.16.8. Pictures, maps, books, and a violin were among his many household possessions.[10] Lang's estate owed £43.3 to the Boston silversmith Benjamin Pierpont (q.v.), which suggests the two had business transactions.

Lang's work for local patrons can be documented in a few bills and receipts and in a relatively large body of surviving objects. His marks were I·LANG in a rectangle (A), and IL in a rectangle (B, C). A second surname mark also has been attributed to him, although no example could be located to illustrate.[11]

In a bill dated 11 June 1739, Lang received payment of £3.8 from Timothy Pickering "for Makeing Eight Rings for Mrs Touzels funerall & Weighing a Parcell of Gold & Silver."[12] These rings may have resembled the one Lang made about 1736 for the funeral of the young son of Edward and Freke Kitchen of Salem. At least one other example of Lang's jewelry, a pair of knee buckles, has also survived.

Five objects—two salvers, a porringer spoon, a strainer spoon, and another spoon—were made by Lang for members of the Barton-Toppan-Pickman family of Salem, and they descended through that family until given to the Museum of Fine Arts, Boston. The salvers (one is unmarked) are an unusually ambitious form for a Salem silversmith. Another large object, possibly made by Lang, was a silver tankard sold and delivered by Lang to Richard Derby on 27 June 1746.[13] This tankard is not known today, so we do not know if Lang was its maker or if he was acting solely as a retailer. A simple cann by Lang has survived, suggesting that he made at least some drinking vessels. At least three keyhole-handled porringers by Lang are known as well. Other forms by Lang include an oval box engraved "Christian Crowning-shield" and a memorandum book with ivory leaves and a brass cover engraved DANIEL GOtt/OF/WENHAM/1746. GWRW

SURVIVING OBJECTS

	Mark	Inscription	Patron	Date	Reference	Owner
Cann	A*	H/IM/RM		ca. 1740	Ward 1984a, fig. 18	MMA
Clasp	C*	ID; C (later?)		ca. 1755	DAPC 72.2972	
Two knee buckles	C†	KM (+)		ca. 1745	Buhler/Hood 1970, no. 173	YUAG
Memorandum book (brass)	A	DANIEL GOtt/OF/WENHAM/1746	Daniel Gott	1746	Schiffer 1978, 294	WM
Mourning ring (gold)	B†	E. Kitchen. obt 25. Octr. 1736. AE 3	Edward Kitchen	1736	Buhler/Hood 1970, no. 172	YUAG
Porringer	A*	LO	Lois (Orne) Lee	ca. 1750	Fales 1983, 12–13	PEM
Porringer	A*/C*	G/AF; 1794 (later)		ca. 1750	Fales 1983a, 1193	PEM
Porringer	A*/C*	T/RS		ca. 1750	Fales 1983a, 1193	PEM
Porringer spoon	A	WT	Willoughby Toppan	ca. 1735	Buhler 1972, no. 214	MFAB
Salver (attrib.)	none	none	Barton or Toppan family (?)	ca. 1730	Buhler 1972, no. 212	MFAB
Salver	A	MB (+)	Mary (Barton) Toppan	ca. 1730	Buhler 1972, no. 211	MFAB
Snuffbox	A*	Christian Crowning-shield	Christian Crowninshield	ca. 1740	Fales 1983a, 1193	PEM
Strainer spoon	B or C	none	Mary (Willoughby) Barton	ca. 1740	Buhler 1972, no. 215	MFAB

	Mark	Inscription	Patron	Date	Reference	Owner
Tablespoon	A*	MV		ca. 1730		PEM
Tablespoon	A	G/SM		ca. 1753	Avery 1920, no. 117	MMA
Tablespoon	A†	B/TM	Thomas and Mary (Willoughby) Barton	ca. 1730	Buhler 1972, no. 213	MFAB
Tablespoon	A*	O/IS		ca. 1740		SI
Teaspoon	A*	GM (over earlier initials?)		ca. 1740	DAPC 73.2355	WM

1. "Materials for a Genealogy of the Lang Family," 257, quoting memoranda from the Bible kept by Jeffrey Lang, gives his date of birth. The Salem First Church records state that Lang "was baptised in Portsmouth in Piscataqua"; see Pierce 1974, 335; see also Moore 1935, 42–44, 66. Most sources give Salem as Lang's birthplace.
2. Moore 1935, 42–44.
3. *Salem VR* 3:587; see also 2:292, 411; 3:475.
4. *Salem VR* 1:509–10; 5:390.
5. Moore 1935, 66, gives 5 December 1751 as the marriage date for Jeffrey and Esther. This is surely a mistake because their first child, William, was born on 5 January 1750; *Salem VR* 1:510. Their marriage is not recorded in the *Salem VR*.
6. Pierce 1974, 335. Lang's children were baptized at the First Church; see pp. 76, 78, 79, 81, 82, 304, 306.
7. Jeffrey noted in his Bible that "I Rais'd my House ye 9 day of June 1740 and I moved into it on the 10th day of December following"; quoted in "Materials for a Genealogy of the Lang Family," 257. See also ECD 133:180 and Thayer 1884, 220.
8. *Boston Evening-Post*, 27 May 1745; repeated 3 and 10 June 1745.
9. "Materials for a Genealogy of the Lang Family," 257.
10. ECPR, docket 16357.
11. Belden 1980, 265.
12. John Touzell Miscellaneous Papers, PEM; ECPR, docket 27953.
13. Richard Derby Account Books, vol. 1 (receipts), PEM.

Nathaniel Lang 1736–64

A

Previously confused with his younger nephew Nathaniel Lang (1757–1824), the son of his brother Richard Lang (q.v.), this Nathaniel Lang "was born the 17 of October 1736 of a Sabbath day at ten of the Clock in the morning," the third child and second son of Jeffrey (q.v.) and Hannah Lang.[1] His father, brothers Richard and Edward (q.v.), and nephew were all Salem silversmiths. He may have been apprenticed to his father. (See the entry on Jeffrey Lang for biographical information on Nathaniel's parents and grandparents.)

Nathaniel never married, and he died intestate in 1764 at the age of twenty-eight. His undivided real estate was not appraised, and his personal goods were worth slightly more than £71. His older brother Richard was the administrator of his estate, and John Touzell (q.v.) was one of the compilers of the inventory. His shop goods included "sundry Goldsmith's Tooles" valued at £2.13.4, "silver Sodder" (2 shillings), and "Some Tinn pans" (8 pence). Stock in trade consisted of five large silver spoons, a porringer, half a dozen teaspoons, a cup, two pairs of large buckles, a stock buckle, a silver medal, and a pair of stone buttons and "some Beads & Locket." Among his personal items were nine pictures, a mahogany desk (£6), "Sundry Books," and a "Box w.th 2 wigs" (9 shillings and 4 pence).[2]

The mark NL in a rectangle (A) found on objects that can be dated, on the basis of style, to before ca. 1765 (such as a teaspoon at Yale) conceivably could be by the older Nathaniel.[3] GWRW

SURVIVING OBJECTS

	Mark	Inscription	Patron	Date	Reference	Owner
Tablespoon	A*	M/IP		ca. 1760	DAPC 72.1097	WM
Teaspoon	A†	E/IP		ca. 1760		YUAG

1. "Materials for a Genealogy of the Lang Family," 257, being memoranda from the Lang family Bible owned by Jeffrey Lang. See also *Salem VR* 1:509. Most secondary sources list a single Nathaniel Lang with the life dates of 1736 to 1824, thus combining the birth date of this man with the death date of his nephew. See, for example, Flynt/Fales 1968, 264, and Belden 1980, 265. For the younger Nathaniel, see Ward 1984a, 320–21.
2. ECPR, docket 16359.
3. Some scholars have attributed N·LANG in a rectangle to the older Nathaniel Lang; see Belden 1980, 265. Probably this mark was used by the younger Nathaniel Lang, whose working career spanned roughly 1778 to 1824, rather than by the elder Nathaniel Lang, whose brief career dates only between 1757 and 1764. Those objects, such as a tablespoon (PEM, 113,382), which can be dated on the basis of style to after the Revolution, can safely be attributed to the younger Nathaniel. The younger Nathaniel Lang may also have used NL in a rectangle.

Richard Lang
1733–1820

A

B

The oldest son of the silversmith Jeffrey Lang (q.v.), Richard Lang "was born December ye 23 1733 of a Sabbath day morning at five of the Clock."[1] His brothers Nathaniel and Edward (qq.v.) and his son Nathaniel (1757–1824) were all Salem silversmiths. It is usually stated that Richard was apprenticed to his father, although as yet there is no documentation confirming this relationship. (For biographical information on Richard's parents and grandparents, see the entry on Jeffrey Lang.)[2] A receipt of 14 March 1755 indicates that he was paid six shillings by the Salem silversmith John Touzell (q.v.), for whom he may have been working.[3]

Richard married Catherine (or Katherine) Cox (1735–88) on 16 March 1755, and they had eleven children, five of whom died in infancy.[4] In 1771, Lang owned only one-half a house and real estate valued at four pounds annually, modest assets that confirm his economic status.[5] Richard died in Salem at the age of eighty-seven of "old age" on 8 September 1820.[6] He was still identified as a goldsmith in the probate records, although he may have retired some years before his death, perhaps in 1809, when he wrote his will.[7]

His modest estate was valued at $906.64, and the inventory, taken on 13 October 1820 by Elijah Sanderson, Joseph Ross, and Daniel Bancroft, indicates that he was living in reduced circumstances. He owned "part of a dwelling house and land" worth $650 and had a personal estate of $256.64. He still owned "1 Lot hammers, plyers, files, pr tongs & other Goldsmith tools" valued at $1. His household furniture included his bed and bedding valued at $20, and "8 Chairs—1 Desk—chest drawers—3 tables—1 Stand & fire board," worth a total of only $3.75. His daughter Hannah Boyce was the principal beneficiary, although his other surviving children received part of the estate.

Two marks are assigned to Richard Lang: R·LANG in a rectangle (A) and RL in a square (B).[8] A rattail spoon by Lang is engraved "1760," and a gold mourning ring made by Lang for the funeral of the Reverend Dudley Leavitt in 1762 has been published. Other tablespoons and teaspoons by Lang are known, and a porringer with a keyhole handle by Lang also has been published, making him one of only five Salem silversmiths of the eighteenth century by whom any surviving holloware is known. GWRW

SURVIVING OBJECTS

	Mark	Inscription	Patron	Date	Reference	Owner
Mourning ring (gold)	B	Rvᵈ D. Leavit: ob. 7. Febʳ 1762. AE 41.	Rev. Dudley Leavitt	1762	Phillips 1939, no. 217	
Porringer	A	FC		ca. 1770	*Antiques* 107 (February 1975): 276	
Tablespoon	A	MC		ca. 1760		MFAB
Two tablespoons	A*	ML		ca. 1770		PEM
Tablespoon	A†	SR/1760		ca. 1760	DAPC 72.1267	WM
Teaspoon	B†	SH		ca. 1770	DAPC 73.2347	WM
Teaspoon	B (?)	MF		ca. 1770	YUAG files	

1. "Materials for a Genealogy of the Lang Family," 257, being memoranda copied from the Lang family Bible owned by Jeffrey Lang. See also *Salem VR* 1:509.
2. Belden 1980, 265.
3. English-Touzel-Hathorne Papers, box 4, folder 5, PEM.
4. *Salem VR* 3:587; 1:508–10; see also Moore 1935.
5. Pruitt 1978, 144–45.
6. *Salem VR* 5:391.
7. ECPR, docket 16361.
8. Belden 1980, 265. R.LANG in a rectangle has also been published; see Kovel 1961, 163.

Daniel Légaré 1689–1724/25

Daniel Légaré was born in Hingham, Massachusetts, on 4 April 1689.[1] He was the son of Francis Légaré (q.v.) and undoubtedly trained with his father. Daniel married Ruth Bass sometime before 3 October 1709, when their son John was born in Braintree, Massachusetts.[2] He followed his trade in that town, probably working in his father's shop. When Francis Légaré died in 1711, his will confirmed his previous gift of one-half of his house, barns, and stock in Braintree and all the tools of his trade "both Jewelling & Glazing" and "all Jewelling stone both Chrystal & other" to his son Daniel. The remainder of the estate he bequeathed to his widow, Ann.[3] Two more of Daniel Légaré's children were born in Braintree: Francis (b. 1711) and Mary (bap. 1713), who later married the painter Benjamin Blythe of Salem, Massachusetts.

Daniel remained in Braintree for three more years. On 3 March 1711/12 he was elected a field driver at the Braintree town meeting.[4] By September of 1713 he had evidently made up his mind to move to Boston, because on 1 September 1713 he and his wife sold farmland, orchard, and meadow with two dwelling houses and two barns, forty-six acres of woodland, two shares in the little common, a share in the cedar swamp, thirteen acres of pasture, and twelve acres of upland and swamp to William Rawson of Braintree for £580, and on 22 September they sold seven acres of salt marsh, fresh meadow near the beach, and upland to Joseph Marsh for £80. On 14 June 1714, Daniel Légaré quitclaimed all of his rights in his father's personal estate to Ann Légaré, widow, in return for title to his father's dwelling house in Braintree. As part of the agreement, Daniel was to pay Ann an additional £10 a year for the rest of her life. When Légaré sold additional land in Braintree on 9 October 1714 he was identified as being "of Boston Jeweller." His third son, Daniel, was born in Boston on 14 December 1714. Three more children—a daughter Ann (b. ca. 1717), who later married Joseph Johnson, a child who died at birth

(d. 1717), and a son Josiah (bap. 1720/21)—were born in Boston; the youngest was baptized in the Old South Church.[5]

In 1714 Légaré sued the watchmaker Joseph Essex (q.v. Appendix A) of Boston for the sum of £2.15.6. The record of the suit indicates that Légaré was doing business with Essex before he decided to move to Boston. Although Légaré dropped the suit by failing to appear in court, an account submitted in the case reveals something about the type of work that Légaré did as a jeweler:

1712/13 Brantrey Joseph Essex to Daniel Légaré is D[r]

To a Ring ye Gold ye Stone & fashioning	} 01. 7. 0
To a hair Ring the gold & fashioning	00. 15. 0
To a gold Coller with ye Stone & fashion	00. 16. —
Jan. 1714	
To a pair of Ear Rings red Stones with gold & fashion	} 01. 13. 6
Feb	
To Gilding a Copper Case of a watch with finding gold	} 00. 16. —
To [illeg.] gold [illeg.] enemeld	00. 13. 6
	6: 00: 6

In the credit column the following was recorded:

1713	
By a watch as ℔ agreement	3. 00. 00
By a brown glas & cleaning	0. 5
	3. 5. 0
Balla.	2: 15: 6

Due to.
> Daniel Légaré
> [signature][6]

This account suggests that Légaré was a goldworker, gilder, and enameler. With the extensive capital that he was able to raise from the sale of land in Braintree, and at least one established client in Boston, Légaré's prospects would have appeared to have been very good.

In June 1715 Légaré mortgaged a tenement and land that he had purchased from John and Joseph Breed of Lynn to George Whitehorne of Boston for £250.[7] Légaré further mortgaged this property as well as his working tools and household inventory to John Breed for £550 on 6 December 1715.[8] The house and land were located next to Barton's Ropewalk on the lane leading from the Ropewalk to Forthill Lane. According to the agreement with Whitehorne, if Légaré paid his mother the £10 per year previously agreed to (which Whitehorne supposed would total approximately £250), then the obligation to Whitehorne was to be void. Whitehorne discharged the obligation on 14 April 1721, saying that he had received full satisfaction.[9]

For some unknown reason Daniel Légaré entered into a business agreement with the Boston miller Caleb Thomas in 1716, and the two bound themselves for the sum of £300 to the mariner Thomas Pinell of Gloucester and the housewright Benjamin Purrington of Boston. Pinell and Purrington sued Légaré and Thomas for defaulting on the bond and recovered judgment of £56 and costs of court. A writ filed on 30 January 1716/17 charged Légaré and

Thomas with failing to pay the £58.14; Légaré immediately paid £8.10 to the plaintiffs, but Thomas was jailed for debt.[10] This case marks the beginning of Légaré's money problems. In 1720 Ann Légaré sued both Daniel Légaré and George Whitehorne, saying that the two acknowledged owing her £250. She asked only damages of £20, and the judgment in the case was against Whitehorne only, who was asked to pay £15.10 "being the Chancery of the Bond."[11] In 1722 the mariner John Jenkins sued Daniel Légaré "at present residing at Scituate within the County of Plymouth, Jeweller," for £65 on a bond issued to Légaré and Caleb Thomas, now deceased, in 1716.

Daniel Légaré was unable to pay the amount granted to Jenkins by the court, and he was imprisoned for debt.[12] On 28 January 1722/23 Légaré petitioned for release from prison:

> The Petition of Daniel Legare now a Prisoner within His Majesties Goal in Boston for Debt Most Humbly Sheweth That your Petition[r] upon ye 7th Day of November Last past had a Writt of Execution served upon him at the suit of John Jenkins of Boston Mariner for the sum of forty Eight Pounds, Which your Petition[r] not being Able by any Possible means to satisfy yet Willing[ly] was Imprisoned and altho the Debt was not more properly his Own than By (very Unadvisedly) becoming Bound with & for another man which failed him, your Petition[r] further Shews that he Hath by Sundry Disappointm[ts] and Casualties which hath Attended him in the Carrying on of His Outward affairs, Been so Very Considerably Reduced as to an absolute Inabillity at the Present of Answering his s[d] Creditors Demands, and he being so Obstinately Averse to the allowing your Petition[r] Reasonable time for the satisfying of him which was the only thing your Petition[r] Desired as hath Laid your Petition[r] under an indispensible Necessity for his Relief to Have Recourse to the Law of this province in that Act Entituled an Act for the Relief and Release of Poor Prisoners for Debt—Accordingly your Petition[r] Hath Hitherto Attended the Directions in s[d] Act Required, And taken the Preliminary Oath therein mentioned . . . in Order to His Receiving the Benifit of the said Act.[13]

On 23 March 1723 Légaré's assets were appraised, and his debtors and creditors listed. Among the people who owed Légaré money were Joseph Essex, William Cowell, Sr. (q.v.), and "[?] Boddily late of Boston Watchmaker Run Away," possibly a son of the watchmaker Thomas Badley (q.v. Appendix A).[14] Edward Winslow and Nathaniel Morse (qq.v.) were appointed by the court to appraise Légaré's tools, and they submitted the following statement: "We the Subscribers having view'd the Tools belonging to m[r] Daniel Leggery, shew us, as the whole he has for his use; do declare it as our Opinion, That as for the quantity it's much less than is absolutely necessary for him to carry on his trade withall and that they would not (if they were to be sold) be worth more than ten or twelve pounds."[15] Légaré's release was granted pending opposition from his creditor.

Légaré's wife, Ruth, died sometime between 1715 and 1723, and he married Elizabeth Williamson on 5 March 1723/24. He died in Boston on 20 January 1724/25.[16] No silver or jewelry by Daniel Légaré is known to have survived. BMW

1. Winifred Lovering Holman, "Genealogical Notes—Légaré," 56, NEHGS. Lincoln (1893) 1982, 2:439, gives Daniel's mother's name as Elizabeth, which is probably an error.
2. *Braintree VR*, 688.
3. Holman, "Genealogical Notes—Légaré," 59; SCPR 17:373–74, docket 3376. The glazing tools may have been for small-scale glazing, such as setting crystals on watches.
4. *Braintree VR*, 77.
5. SCD 27:307–09; 29:197–98; 32:242; RC 24:99; Holman, "Genealogical Notes—Légaré."

6. SCCR, file 9870; Court of Common Pleas Record Book 1714–15, 129.
7. SCD 29:198–99.
8. SCD 35:135.
9. SCD 29:198–99.
10. SCCR, files 11294, 11388; Court of Common Pleas Record Book 1715–18, 100.
11. SCCR, Court of Common Pleas Record Book 1720–21, 226.
12. SCCR, Court of Common Pleas Record Book 1721–22, 315, 378.
13. SCCR, file 16479, vol. 146, Judicial Archives, Mass. Archives.
14. SCCR, file 16553. No values were assigned to the household goods—which included a bed, bedstead and bedding, two tables, an old chest of drawers, a chest, a small looking glass, and cooking utensils and plates, all of which were put up as collateral on a loan from John Breed. The inventory also mentions "a smal Box Cont[a] parcel of Cut [Cristal?] stone value about twelve or fifteen shillings."
15. SCCR, file 16533.
16. RC 28:114; Codman 1918, 150.

Francis Légaré
ca. 1636–1711

Francis L'égaré (later simplified to Légaré), a jeweler and Huguenot refugee, along with his wife, Ann, and three children—Francis Solomon (q.v.), Daniel James, and Stephen John—was naturalized in England in March 1682.[1] He first appears in the Boston tax list in 1687 and is in those of 1688, 1691, and 1692, as well as the list of inhabitants of 1695.[2] Légaré is also named in a "List of persons of the french nation admitted into the Colony by the Govern[t] & Councill," dated Boston, 1 February 1691, with only two sons. Gabriel Bernon, organizer of the French Huguenot settlement at Oxford, Massachusetts, appears on the same list as does "Docter [Francis] Basset," probably the father of the silversmith Francis Bassett (q.v.). On 10 June 1691, the merchant John Nelson became surety for "Franicis Legarr, Goldsmith."[3]

Légaré may have had interests in the Huguenot colony at Greenwich, Rhode Island, but there is no record of him there.[4] The *Report of a French Protestant Refugee in Boston, 1687*, contains the following account of his house and lands to the south of Boston: "M. Légaré a French merchant Goldsmith, has bought one [estate] twelve Miles from here toward the South on the Seashore, where he has a very pretty House and ten Acres and a half of Land for eighty Pistoles, of [ten] Livres of France each. He has also his Share in the Commons where he can send his Cattle to Pasture and cut Wood for his Needs, and for selling here, it being conveniently sent by Sea."[5] This may refer to a house in Hingham, Massachusetts, where Légaré was living in 1689 when his son Daniel (q.v.), the second of the name, was born.[6] In 1688 Légaré had petitioned Gov. Edmund Andros to be granted sixty acres of land in Hingham.[7] However, in 1693, he was identified as a goldsmith of Boston when he purchased a house, barn, and twenty-nine acres of land in Braintree, Massachusetts, for £210.[8] He was granted license to "sell strong Liquors by Retail" after a petition of the Braintree selectmen, dated 1 January 1702/03, stated that they were "sensable that there is not that Provision here—allready that is necessary & needfull."[9]

Légaré's name appears in Suffolk County court records on a few occasions. He was involved in a suit for £3.10 with John Smith on 25 February 1689/90.[10] His name also appears in a court file in 1692 with Bozoon Allen, Capt. John Wing, and William Cross (q.v.).[11] In July 1700 Légaré witnessed a power of attorney from John Mariette to Mouns. George Chabot.[12]

The diary of John Marshall records that "Mr Frances Legaree dyed on the Sabbath day december 30th 1711 Aged about 75 years."[13]

Légaré died in Braintree, and by his will written on 3 February 1710/11 and probated 26 January 1711/12, he bequeathed only 20 shillings to his son Francis Solomon, "now at Carrolina," because Solomon had deserted him during his training "before he was of age" and married against his will. He confirmed his previous gift of one-half of his house, barns, and stock in Braintree to his son Daniel and bequeathed the other half to his widow, Ann, along with "all my Plate, and Cash in Posesion, or due to me by Bonds; with all goods in the House; my Negro girle, and also my Colash all which I give to her for her Sole use and Improvement during her life, with full power to Sell and dispose (if her Necessity Shall so Require) of any part (or all) of the Lands goods, Moneys, or what ever els is herein & hereby Willed to her." He left all the tools of his trade, "both Jewelling & Glazing" and "all Jewelling stone both Chrystal & other," to his son Daniel.[14]

Francis Légaré's inventory is not very detailed but does list

Negro Girl, Shop goods, books and plate	073 .16
Cash & Due by Bond	114 .00
the stock for the Trade both of gold & silver	061 .10
Tools, Materials for the Trade and [torn] things	30 .00

These listings indicate that Légaré was doing a substantial business in jewelry and possibly some small holloware items. They also suggest that he dealt in shop goods of a more general nature and that he made some loans.[15] The latter is further confirmed by deeds recording mortgages of land to Légaré by the husbandman Samuel Penniman of Braintree and the weaver Thomas Wells of Braintree, both in 1707.[16] Légaré's inventory also lists husbandry tools and tackling, and he undoubtedly combined his trade of jeweler and glazer with seasonal farm work.

No silver or jewelry by Francis Légaré has been identified. BMW

1. Authorities differ on where the naturalization took place—Bristol or London. Francis Légaré advertised in London in 1682; Heal 1935, 193. Winifred Lovering Holman, "Genealogical Notes—Légaré," NEHGS; Baird 1885, 2:111–12; Agnew 1871, 1:42.
2. Holman, "Genealogical Notes—Légaré"; RC 1:117, 141, 153, 165; RC 10:133.
3. RC 10:62, 80.
4. Baird 1885, 2:111.
5. Fisher 1868, 35.
6. Lincoln (1893) 1982, 2:439, gives Daniel's mother's name as Elizabeth, which is probably an error. In his will Francis identifies his wife as Ann and calls her Daniel's mother; SCPR, docket 3376.
7. Mass. Archives 128:260.
8. SCD 16:263–64.
9. SCCR, file 5591, vol. 56, Judicial Archives, Mass. Archives.
10. SCCR 1940, 64.
11. SCCR, file 2658.
12. SCCR, file 4750.
13. John Marshall Diary, MHS.
14. SCPR 17:373–74. Ann Légaré apparently left Massachusetts and went to live in Charleston, South Carolina, with her son Solomon because a tomb in the Circular Church graveyard is believed to be hers; Mrs. A. G. Rose to Francis Hill Bigelow, 6 October 1928, Bigelow-Phillips files, 497a. The glazing tools mentioned in the will may have been used for small-scale glazing such as putting crystals on watches.
15. SCPR, docket 3376. Inventory dated 11 January 1711/12 presented for probate on 26 January 1711/12.
16. SCD 24:87–88; 26:23–24, 90.

Francis Solomon Légaré
ca. 1674–1760

Known as Solomon throughout his adult life, Francis Solomon Légaré was born in France and immigrated as a child with his parents, Francis Légaré (q.v.) and his wife, Ann, and two brothers to England, where they were naturalized.[1] He was admitted to the Massachusetts Colony with his family on 1 February 1691.[2] He apparently trained in his father's shop after the family arrived in Boston, but about 1693 married Sarah (surname unknown) against his father's wishes. His father's will, dated 3 February 1710/11, includes the following: "My will is That my Son Solomon, Now at Carrolina shall have Twenty Shillings paid to him out of my Estate, wch I give to him, to cutt him off from any further part or portion thereof, and that for this Reason viz His deserting my Service and going wholly from me, contrary to my minde Some years before he was of age, and Marrying utterly against my Will & consent."[3] Francis Solomon and his wife, Sarah, had two children while in Boston: Solomon, born 17 September 1693, and Sarah, born 18 July 1695. Solomon, Sr., joined the Second Church, Boston, 28 July 1695.[4]

Solomon Légaré left Boston for South Carolina about 1696; his third child, Mary, was born there about 1697. His wife, Sarah, died about 1702, and he married as his second wife Keltie Carter, widow of Zebulon Carter, who became the mother of Solomon (1703–74), Daniel (1711–91), Mary (d. by 1797), and Hannah (d. 1751). By his third wife, Ann Jones, widow of Thomas Jones, whom he married about 1714, Solomon had two more sons, Thomas (1714 or 1715–78) and John.[5]

In 1700, Solomon Légaré petitioned, with others, for permission to exploit silver mines in the western part of the Carolina colony. In documents concerning the mining venture he is referred to as being both a silversmith and a goldsmith. Although his silver mines never amounted to anything, Légaré nonetheless became a prosperous citizen of Charleston and a member and officer of the Circular Congregational Church. He died in Charleston on 8 May 1760, in his eighty-seventh year. His inventory lists 68 oz. 16 dwt. of old silver and gold. His total estate amounted to more than £18,000.[6]

No silver made by Légaré is known to survive. BMW

1. Baird 1885, 2:111–12.
2. RC 10:62.
3. SCPR, docket 3376.
4. RC 9:207, 222; Winifred Lovering Holman, "Genealogical Notes—Légaré," 57, NEHGS.
5. Holman, "Genealogical Notes—Légaré," 62.
6. Burton/Ripley 1991, 57–58; *South-Carolina Gazette*, 17–24 May 1760.

John LeRoux
1695–1725+

John LeRoux was born in New York City and baptized in the Dutch Church in 1695. His parents were the celebrated goldsmith Bartholomew LeRoux (1663–1713) and Gertrude (Van Rollegom) LeRoux; Charles LeRoux (1689–1745), his elder brother, was also a goldsmith.[1] John undoubtedly trained in his father's shop. He was made a freeman of the city on 8 January 1722/23. Most authorities believe that he worked first in New York and then in Albany.[2] However, he appears in a court record in July 1725 that indicates he was working in Boston as a journeyman for Thomas Edwards (q.v.) during the years 1724 and 1725.

Thomas Edwards, goldsmith, was plaintiff against John LeRoux of Boston, goldsmith, for money due to him by his account. The account was filed with the court and reads,

Boston March 20 1724/5
M.ʳ John Le Roux D.ʳ to Tho.ˢ Edwards

1725 To yᵉ ballance of acc.ᵗ made up this day	£7. 14. —
April 3ᵗʰ To bourd 8/ To Cash & 1 p.ʳ of buckles £2:11.2	2. 19. 2
To Cash 1/3 Ditto 3/ To Silv.ᵉ 1/3	. 5. 6
	£10. 18. 8
Ditto C.ʳ By 5 Days work	£1. . 10
April 3 By 2 ditto 8/4 By 2 1/2 D° 10/3 4 D° 12/6	1. 11. 1
	£2. 11. 11
Errors Excepted due to ballance	8. 6. 9³

The writ of attachment filed with the case indicates that the sheriff, when he served LeRoux his summons to appear in court, attached the following goods from LeRoux's "estate":

In a box
1 Forging Hanvile
1 Raising D°
10 Hammars
1 Chist the Contents unnone⁴

According to the accounts filed as part of the case, John LeRoux worked by the day for Edwards and also paid Edwards rent. LeRoux's tools suggest two possible working arrangements between Edwards and LeRoux. LeRoux may have worked by the day in Edwards's shop, bringing with him a small chest of tools filled with hammers, punches, and chisels. Or he may have worked as a jobber, hammering out pieces of holloware in his own workroom to Edwards's specifications. It is particularly significant that John LeRoux owned two anvils. Forging anvils, necessary only for goldsmiths who intended to produce large pieces of holloware, usually weighed between 100 and 150 pounds and were valued at approximately 8 shillings per pound at this time. The acquisition of anvils—particularly a forging anvil—marked the goldsmith's first steps toward setting up his own independent shop. LeRoux's anvils were "In a box." Perhaps LeRoux brought the anvils with him from New York in expectation of setting up an independent shop and his hopes were never realized, or perhaps LeRoux had already packed up his things and was ready to move on to another town by the time the writ was served. If LeRoux had even partially succeeded in establishing his own shop by this time, he probably did work for more than one Boston goldsmith.

John LeRoux's later career has been something of an enigma to scholars. He may have returned to New York or he may have gone on to Albany.⁵ An initials mark with a barred "I" once attributed to John LeRoux has more recently been attributed to Jacob Gerritse Lansing (1681–1767).⁶ BMW

1. Purple 1890, 2:205, 195.
2. Von Khrum 1978, 79.
3. SCCR, Court of Common Pleas Record Book 1725, 75; SCCR, file 18500.
4. SCCR, file 18500.
5. McKinsey 1984, 45.
6. Ensko 1948, 194, attributed this mark to John LeRoux, but Norman Rice reassessed the IL initials marks used by Albany silversmiths and suggested that the barred IL mark, of which there are four variations, was used by Jacob Gerritse Lansing; see Rice 1964, 23; Kernan

1961a, 60. Among the pieces bearing the barred IL mark are a tankard (MMA, 33.75.73), a teapot (Buhler/Hood 1970, no. 584), a salt dish (Rice 1964, fig. 23, center), a mug (Rice 1964, fig. 25, center), a porringer (Rice 1964, fig. 25, right), a serving spoon (Rice 1964, fig. 26, center), a tablespoon (Rice 1964, fig. 26, bottom), a tankard (Rice 1964, fig. 28, left), and a teapot (Rice 1964, fig. 28, right). Other IL marks have also been attributed to John LeRoux in the past; see Puig et al. 1989, no. 210.

Knight Leverett
1702/03–53

A

KL

B

Knight Leverett was born in Boston on 1 January 1702/03. His father, Thomas Hudson Leverett (1674–1706), a barber, was the son of Hudson Leverett (1640–1694) and his first wife, Sarah (Payton) Leverett (d. 1679), and the grandson of Gov. John Leverett (1616–79).[1] Knight Leverett's mother was Rebecca (Winsor) Leverett, daughter of Joshua and Sarah Winsor (ca. 1650–1717) of Boston; when his father died, his mother and his grandfather Joshua Winsor were appointed guardians of him and of his brother Joshua and sister Rebecca, all of whom were minors.[2]

Knight Leverett married Abigail Buttolph (1704–74), daughter of Nicholas (1668–1736/37) and Mary (Goodridge) Buttolph (ca. 1677–1728) on 1 February 1725/26.[3] He and his wife had four children: John (b. 1726/27), a merchant who later settled in Middletown, Connecticut; Rebecca (b. 1728), who married the printer John Green in 1759; Thomas (b. 1730), who became a bookbinder and shopkeeper; and Abigail (b. 1731/32).[4]

Like his father and grandfather before him, Knight Leverett was elected to the Ancient and Honorable Artillery Company, in 1729. He also served in numerous town offices, being elected hogreeve in 1726/27 and serving as clerk of the market with Jacob Hurd (q.v.) in 1727–28. When he was elected to be one of the town's constables in 1728/29, however, he declined to serve and paid the fine. Leverett also served as town scavenger in 1742, 1745, and 1748 and was elected third sergeant of the Artillery Company in 1736.[5]

Knight Leverett was involved in several lawsuits regarding land he inherited from his grandfather. Between 1725 and 1727, as his grandfather's only surviving male heir, he and his first cousins—the gentlewoman Sarah Leverett of Cambridge, Massachusetts, and the widow Mary Denison of Ipswich, Massachusetts, daughters of his father's brother, Harvard president John Leverett (1662–1724)—sued the ropemaker James Barton and his tenants for rent on land leased to Barton by John Leverett's heirs in 1678. The Leverett heirs eventually received a judgment in their favor, and Sarah Leverett and Mary Denison deeded their rights in the land to Knight Leverett. The occupants still failed to vacate the land, and a writ of attachment was served on the tenants in December 1727 for five hundred pounds in damages and costs of court.[6]

Knight Leverett probably served his apprenticeship with Andrew Tyler (q.v.) because on 30 July 1722, when he was nineteen years old, he and Samuel Burrill (q.v.), then eighteen, witnessed a deed for Tyler.[7] Shortly after obtaining his freedom, Leverett apparently had business dealings with John Burt (q.v.): on 2 January 1727/28 Leverett sued Burt but did not appear in court, resulting in a nonsuit. Apparently Burt bore Leverett no ill will because he did not ask Leverett to pay the costs of court. The reason for this suit is not known, and no monetary value is mentioned in the record.[8] Leverett and Thomas Townsend (q.v.) were codefendants in a case brought before the Inferior Court of Common Pleas in 1735/36 by the brewer Sampson Salter on a debt of £139.8 due on 7 March 1733. Leverett and Townsend defaulted, and Salter was awarded £74.8.8.[9] As early as 1734, Knight Leverett began to engage in general shopkeeping, and he is referred to, seemingly interchangeably, as both a shopkeeper and a goldsmith throughout his career. At the time of his death he was described as being a goldsmith.[10] He was related to many prominent residents of Boston and Cambridge and would have been able to attract wealthy patrons. Very little Leverett silver survives, however, perhaps because he was so heavily engaged in general shopkeeping. Several receipts for funeral rings made by Leverett survive in the Suffolk Probate Records, and in 1738 a porringer bearing his mark was reported stolen in the *Boston News-Letter*.[11] Leverett used at least three marks: K Leverett in script in a conforming rectangle (A), KL in a rectangle (B), and KL in a cartouche (C, not illustrated), an example of which survives only as a rubbing.[12] One porringer bears the marks of both Leverett and Thomas Edwards (q.v.), which suggests that the two may have bought silver from one another. Another link between Knight Leverett and Thomas Edwards is a pair of canns marked by Leverett that are engraved with a coat of arms reminiscent of engraving on objects by John (q.v.) and Thomas Edwards.[13] Thomas Townsend made objects for Thomas Edwards, and the fact that Townsend and Leverett were codefendents in a lawsuit suggests that Townsend may have made objects for Leverett as well.

Evidence from several lawsuits in the Suffolk County Court Records suggests that Leverett's business began to falter in 1734. Prior to that date, the lawsuits that involved Leverett were for small sums of money, but in 1734 the records include two suits, one involving a bond of £700 from the shopkeeper Charles Coffin and one involving a bond of £168 from the shopkeeper Edward Emerson, both of which Leverett was unable to pay.[14] Bonds between shopkeepers, like short-term loans today, allowed small businessmen to acquire substantial amounts of merchandise. The bonds were usually paid off quickly, when merchandise was sold, but an unsuccessful shopkeeper could experience serious cash flow problems. These large debts, along with Leverett's mortgage in 1733 for £300 (Old Tenor) of a parcel of property he had inherited, suggest that Leverett needed to raise cash in order to stay in business.[15] A brief entry in the diary of Benjamin Walker for 20 November 1734, although partially illegible—"Knight Leveret Shop [illegible]ed up again"—suggests that Leverett's problems may have been caused by troubles beyond his control, perhaps one or more fires in his shop during 1734.[16] One fire would have caused him enough trouble—and may explain why he appealed the judgment in the suits brought against him by Coffin and Emerson in July 1734—but two could have been devastating, particularly because Boston's economic outlook was bleak at that time.

Leverett continued in business, however, and evidently recovered somewhat. On 29 April 1747 Benjamin Walker recorded in his diary that "M[r] Knight Levert bro[tt] y[e] sword Into my Shop, to Show me & brother y[tt] Gouvernour Charles Knowles . . . bo[tt] of Salmon y[e] Truckman to make a present it cost 60£ old Tenor." Apparently Leverett was either cleaning or repairing the sword so that Knowles could present it to Capt. Phineas Stevens, commander of a fort forty miles north of Northfield, Massachusetts. Walker again mentions Leverett on 13 May 1747, when the two took a walk together down Queen Street to the Common and Frazier's tanyard, passing through Pleasant Street and Winter Street.[17]

Knight Leverett died intestate on 11 July 1753, and his widow, Abigail, was made administrator of the estate. Jacob Hurd, Samuel Hewes, and David Cutler appraised the estate, which was valued at £27.1, evidently New Tenor, and included unenumerated goldsmith's tools worth only 26 shillings and 8 pence. The widow's administration account added the value of three-quarters of a pew in the Old Brick Meeting House—£7.10—to the total, but Leverett's tiny estate was still insufficient to pay debts of £162.0.9 ³/₄.[18] Fortunately, his children had been provided for by bequests from their great-grandfather Joshua Winsor.[19] There is no real estate listed in Leverett's inventory. Evidently he sold all of the many parcels of land he inherited; perhaps his widow was able to retain some as her dower right.[20] The estate was finally settled when the order for the creditors to be paid was issued in November 1755.[21] Knight Leverett was buried in the tomb of Nicholas Buttolph, his father-in-law, in the Granary Burying Ground.[22] BMW

SURVIVING OBJECTS

	Mark	Inscription	Patron	Date	Reference	Owner
Beaker	B	The Gift of the Rev:ᵈ Mr John Sparhawk/to the Church of Christ in Bristol 1718	Rev. John Sparhawk and/or First Congregational Church, Bristol, R.I.	ca. 1730	Jones 1913, 95–96	
Two candlebranches	A*	RR (cipher)/1720	Ruth Read	ca. 1735	Quimby 1995, no. 97a, b	WM
Two canns	A	Bulfinch arms, gules a chevron between 3 garbs argent	Thomas Bulfinch (?)	ca. 1745	Silver Supplement 1973, nos. 65a–b	
Cann	A	W/ID		ca. 1740	Buhler 1972, no. 156	MFAB
Caster	A†/ B†	Hall crest, a talbot's head erased (+)	Hugh and Elizabeth (Pitts) Hall	ca. 1735	Safford 1983, 6, 36	MMA
Pepper box	B	WF; E.Storer to M.A.S.H. (later)		ca. 1735	Silver Supplement 1973, no. 64	
Porringer	A*	P/SK (+)	Samuel and Katharine Phips	ca. 1740	Buhler/Hood 1970, no. 162	YUAG
Porringer (with mark of Thomas Edwards)	A	MWE (later)		ca. 1740	Washington 1925, no. 65	
Porringer	A	D (later)		ca. 1740	Johnston 1994, 99	CMA
Porringer (mate? below)	A	D/SH		ca. 1745		HMA
Porringer (mate? above)	A	D/SH		ca. 1745	Sotheby's, 28–31 January 1993, lot 113	
Porringer	A	Presented/by/Isaac H. Cary (later)		ca. 1740	DAPC 76.2750	
Porringer	A*/ B*	none		ca. 1745		RISD
Strainer spoon	B	none		ca. 1740		MWPI
Sword	B*	none		ca. 1740		DeYoung
Tablespoon	A*	L/CL		ca. 1740		SI

	Mark	Inscription	Patron	Date	Reference	Owner
Tablespoon	A*	C/IA		ca. 1735	Buhler/Hood 1970, no. 163	YUAG
Tablespoon	A*	T/TD		ca. 1740	DAPC 64.2223	
Tankard	A	I/WM (+)	William and Martha (Pierce) Johnson (?)	ca. 1735	Buhler 1972, no. 155	MFAB
Tankard	B/C*	?		ca. 1740	MFA 1911, no. 707	
Tankard	?	Solly arms, a chevron between 3 sole fishes, and crest, a sole fish; T/AM	Samuel Solly (?)	ca. 1745	Wardwell 1966, 82–83	
Teaspoon	B	CA	Content Ally	ca. 1750	Buhler 1972, appendix no. 44	MFAB

1. RC 9:9, 15; RC 24:16; RC 28:4; Roberts 1895, 1:186–87, 437; Bridgman 1853, 34.
2. SCPR 16:178; RC 9:26; Bridgman 1853, 102.
3. RC 9:107, 250; RC 28:127; RC 24:26; Boston Deaths, 1700–1800; SCPR 20:105, 274–75; Codman 1918, 52; *Index of Obituaries, 1704–1800*, 3:60.
4. RC 24:177, 187, 198, 203; RC 30:325; SCD 159:8–10.
5. Roberts 1895, 1:437; Seybolt 1939, 172, 175, 177, 225, 239, 251.
6. SCCR, Court of Common Pleas Record Book 1725–26, 223, file nos. 18990, 19082, 21206, 27845.
7. SCD 37:1.
8. SCCR, Court of Common Pleas Record Book 1727–28, 121.
9. SCCR, Court of Common Pleas Record Book 1735–36, 340.
10. As shopkeeper: SCCR, Court of Common Pleas Record Book 1732, 179; 1734, 48; SCD 47:251–52; 75:203. As goldsmith: SCCR, Court of Common Pleas Record Book 1733, 19; 1733–34, 509; 1734, 133; 1736–37, 336; SCD 74:56.
11. Buhler 1972, 192; SCPR, docket 6975; *Boston News-Letter*, 26 October–2 November and 2–9 November 1738.
12. The KL in cartouche mark is recorded in MFA 1911, no. 707. The whereabouts of the tankard on which the mark appeared (in combination with the KL in rectangle) are unknown, so the mark cannot be illustrated here. A rubbing of it is in the Berger file, American Arts Office, YUAG. Kovel 1961, 168, also records drawings of K LEVERETT in a rectangle and K LEVERETT in a rectangle, but actual examples have not been found.
13. Washington 1925, 70, no. 65; Ward 1983, 246–57.
14. SCCR, Court of Common Pleas Record Book 1732, 179; 1733, 19; 1733/34, 509; 1734, 48, 133.
15. SCD 47:251–52.
16. Benjamin Walker, Jr., Diaries, vol. 1, MHS.
17. Benjamin Walker, Jr., Diaries, vol. 3, MHS.
18. SCPR, docket 10505.
19. SCD 159:8–10.
20. In 1747 Leverett sold a parcel of land on Summer Street for £700 and a parcel of land on Spring Street for £140 (both Old Tenor); see SCD 74:56; 75:203.
21. SCPR, docket 10505.
22. Codman 1918, 151.

Paul Little
1740–1818

Paul Little was born on 1 April 1740 in Newbury, Massachusetts, the son of Moses Little (1691–1780), a farmer, and Sarah Jacques (1697–1763), who married there on 12 February 1716.[1] His paternal grandparents were Moses Little (1657–91) and Lydia Coffin (1662–94/95) of Newbury. Lydia Coffin Little married John Pike following Moses Little's death.[2] Paul Little's maternal grandparents were Stephen Jacques (1661–1744) and Deborah Plumer (b. 1664/65), also of

A

B

Newbury.[3] Paul Little was the uncle of the Newburyport silversmith William Coffin Little (q.v.), who was five years his junior.

Paul Little would have begun his apprenticeship about 1754 and would have completed it about 1761. He may have trained with John Butler (q.v.) because together with Butler he settled in Falmouth (now Portland), Maine, on 3 September 1761, as the Reverend Thomas Smith noted.[4] Little was also said to be "of Falmouth" when he married Hannah Emery (1743/44–71) of Newbury on 20 May 1762.[5] She was the daughter of Stephen Emery and Hannah Rolfe. In November 1762 Little was identified as a "goldsmith of Falmouth" in a deed recording his purchase from James Dane (q.v.) of a quarter part of a house, garden, barn, and outhouse in Ipswich, Massachusetts.[6] Little sold this real estate to Joseph Manning of Ipswich in July 1764, the same month he bought a lot on the neck in Falmouth.[7] Between 1768 and 1775 Little purchased additional land in Falmouth and granted two mortgages.[8]

On 30 August 1772, following the death of his first wife, Little married Sarah (Norton) Souther (1743–97), the daughter of Thomas and Mary Norton (d. 1753) of Ipswich.[9] In 1775 Little began acquiring land in Windham, Maine, purchasing 33 acres in 1775 and 50 acres in 1776.[10] During the Revolution Little's house on King Street in Falmouth suffered damages amounting to £683 in the British bombardment of 1776.[11] Little was living in Windham by October 1776, when he was identified in a deed as a Windham merchant.[12] Between 1778 and 1787 he acquired more than 175 acres of land in Windham from the town's tax collectors by paying outstanding back taxes.[13] In all these deeds he was identified as being a Windham goldsmith. He also purchased more than 100 acres in Windham from private individuals in 1779, 1788, and 1789.[14] In the deed transacted in 1789 he was identified as "Esquire." Other real estate transactions in these years probably were mortgages he granted.[15]

After 1790, Little consistently was identified as "Esquire" in deeds, which indicates that he had given up the goldsmith's trade by then. Beginning in 1790, Little began selling his real estate holdings in Falmouth, sales that continued until 1812.[16] He also sold some of his landholdings in Windham and granted mortgages on other tracts in that town.[17] Little gave a 100-acre lot in Windham to his son Timothy in 1798.[18] In the Court of Common Pleas in 1812 Little recovered judgment against another son, Paul, Jr., whose farm was mortgaged to Josiah and David Little of Newbury. The elder Little sold this farm in 1814.[19] Other real estate transactions of Little involved his acting as trustee for the ministerial fund of Windham and sales of land in Poland, Buxton, and Raymond, Maine.[20] In addition to his activities in acquiring and selling real estate, Little is said to have engaged in farming and in 1800 served on a committee concerned with constructing a new bridge.[21] He married for a third time, Sarah Emerson (1760–1817), widow of Samuel Emerson of Haverhill, Massachusetts, and daughter of Abraham Redington (b. 1729), a housewright of Boxford, Massachusetts, and Sarah (Kimball).[22] Paul Little died on 11 February 1818.[23] In writing about Portland's early history, William Willis, citing Rev. Thomas Smith's journal, noted that Little was a goldsmith by trade but pursued commercial business.[24]

Two marks have traditionally been attributed to Little, P·L in a shaped rectangle (A) and PL in a plain rectangle (B).[25] Only spoons, bearing one or the other of these marks, are known. PEK

SURVIVING OBJECTS

	Mark	Inscription	Patron	Date	Reference	Owner
Tablespoon	B†	SW		ca. 1765		WM
Teaspoon	A†	IB		ca. 1765	Eitner 1976, no. 30	
Teaspoon	A	ML		ca. 1765	Eitner 1976, no. 31	

1. *Newbury VR* 1:248, 283; 2:293, 644.
2. *Newbury VR* 1:112, 283; 2:293.
3. *Newbury VR* 1:249, 415; 2:258; ECPR, docket 14783.
4. Willis 1849, 191; Willis 1865, 699, 778.
5. *Newbury VR* 1:159; 2:294; *NEHGR* 16:320.
6. ECD 113:168.
7. ECD 116:123; CCD 4:255–56.
8. CCD 5:444; 7:300–01; 8:250, 275. A mortgage to Timothy Cutler was discharged in 1772; CCD 4:490. The land Little bought from Thomas Porter in Raymond Town in 1775 and then sold back to Porter in 1777 probably was also a mortgage; CCD 10:390; 11:1.
9. *Ipswich VR* 1:277.
10. CCD 11:388–89.
11. Little 1882, 47–48.
12. CCD 12:74.
13. CCD 12:75–76; 18:339–43, 346–47.
14. CCD 18:344–46; 12:74–75.
15. CCD 14:201, 486; 19:481–83.
16. CCD 17:285–86; 22:469–70; 23:293–94; 36:247–51; 38:517; 39:380–81; 42:469, 545; 51:224–25; 65:230.
17. CCD 55:321–22; 67:230–32; 69:370; 72:290; 80:175. The mortgages are recorded in CCD 48:366–67. A transaction with Joseph Allen in 1810 may have pertained to an earlier mortgage; CCD 81:365.
18. CCD 35:593–94.
19. CCD 65:43–44; 69:305–06.
20. CCD 54:287; 58:475; 62:385; 70:95–96; 73:548; 75:281.
21. Fobes 1894, 381.
22. *Boxford VR*, 79–80, 193; ECD 108:87–88; 114:257.
23. Little 1882, 48.
24. Willis 1849, 191.
25. Kovel 1961, 170, also shows a drawing of a mark P.L. in a rectangle with notched ends, but no example of this mark has been found.

William Coffin Little
1745–1816

A

B

C

A family genealogy indicates that William Coffin Little was the son of John (1721–99), a teamster of Newburyport, Massachusetts, and his wife, Temperance (Ripp) Little (1725–62). He was the grandson of Moses Little (1691–1780) of Turkey Hill Farm, and his wife, Sarah (Jacques) Little (1697–1763), and of William and Abigail Ripp. He was the nephew of Paul Little (q.v.) of Newbury.[1]

William Coffin Little was born on 17 November 1745, one of seven children. He married Mary (1745–1840), the daughter of Thomas (ca. 1703–90) and Abigail (Stevens) Rowell (ca. 1706–86) of Amesbury, Massachusetts, in January 1769.[2] William Coffin and Mary would have eight children between 1769 and 1790. One of their sons, William (1771–1836), became a silversmith and practiced in Philadelphia.[3] He probably learned his trade with his father, who may have started using his middle initial when his son began approaching maturity.

William Coffin Little first appears in print in a notice in the Newburyport *Essex Journal* of 18 August 1775:

D

TAKEN, supposed to be Stolen, two
large SILVER SPOONS, the owners name
scratched out; the makers name on one, E Davis, on
the other, J. Moulton, they were offered for sale by a
man who calls himself William Stewart, the owner
by applying to WILLIAM LITTLE, Goldsmith, and
proving them to be his property, may have them again
paying the charges. Newbury Port, Aug. 17, 1775.[4]

Little may have had business transactions with Simon Greenleaf (q.v. Appendix B) because he was one of Greenleaf's creditors in 1776.[5] A "Stop Thief!" notice in the Newburyport *Essex Journal* for 20 February 1788 reads,

ON Thursday evening last, was
Stolen from the Shop of the
Subscriber, a large Goldsmith's Case,
containing Silver Shoe and Knee
buckles, Tea-spoons, Stock-buc-
kles, Broaches, small white Stone
Sleeve-buttons—Plated Shoe and
Knee-buckles, &c. &c. . . . William C. Little.

Little also advertised "ENGLISH and WEST-INDIA GOODS—Cheap for CASH."[6]

Family history indicates that William Coffin Little moved to Amesbury about 1790 and remained there for some ten years. He was identified as a yeoman of Amesbury in two deeds in 1795, when he sold land in New Hampshire.[7] He was living there in 1793 when his son ran into trouble with the law over charges of counterfeiting. In December 1793, the sheriff of Essex County was commanded to arrest John Burrough(s) of Newbury and William Little of Newburyport, goldsmiths, for

having in their Custody and Possession two dies
for stamping and Counterfeiting Spanish milled
Dollars with an Intent to use and improve the same
for that Purpose, Also for having and keeping in their
Possession one plate for forging and counterfeiting Notes
in Imitation of those issued by the Union Bank and one
other plate for counterfeiting Notes issued by the Massachusetts
Bank with an intent to use them for counterfeiting the Notes
issued by said Banks as is more fully set forth in s[d] Indctmt.

Although Burrough(s) could not be found, the younger Little was committed to the commonwealth jail in Newburyport in June 1794. At the June session of the court at Ipswich, Massachusetts, William Little pleaded not guilty and was found not guilty. Another court document, of 16 June 1794, refers to father and son: William C. Little of Amesbury, goldsmith, and George J. Osborn, printer, of Newburyport, place bond for William Little, Newburyport, goldsmith, "for counterfeiting the money or Coin of said State, & for having in his Possession Implements for counterfeiting said coin."[8]

In 1801, William Coffin Little moved to Salisbury, New Hampshire, north of Concord, where he engaged in farming until his death on 16 December 1816. In his will, probated 11 January 1817, Little left his wife "all my household and kitchen furniture (except one bed), two cows, four sheep, four swine, one half of the Pew in the Meetinghouse, ten cords of wood annually during her natural life to be delivered as she may want the same cut and prepared for the fire." He also made modest bequests to his children and grandchildren, and his sons Francis and Thomas R. were to divide his property in Salisbury and his "stock, farming utensils and tools" between them.[9]

A number of spoons and other small objects have been attributed to a William Little, working ca. 1725 to ca. 1775 (q.v. Appendix B). Because there is no documentary evidence so far identifying a William Little as a Massachusetts goldsmith before 1765, it is suggested here that this earlier William Little did not exist. Spoons marked W·L (A), which date stylistically from about 1765 and later, are probably by William Coffin Little. They are ornamented with shell drops frequently found on New England spoons. No holloware can be attributed to William Coffin Little.[10] A number of pieces marked WL in capitals in a rectangle (B, C) and W.L in a rectangle (D) dating from 1800 to 1810 may also be the work of William Coffin Little or his son. GWRW

SURVIVING OBJECTS

	Mark	Inscription	Patron	Date	Reference	Owner
Saltspoon	D†	JD		ca. 1800		HD
Sword (attrib.)	none			ca. 1770	Peterson (1955) 1991, no. 3	
Tablespoon	A†	N/SS		ca. 1775	DAPC 70.3012	WM
Tablespoon	B *or* C	H/BM	Benjamin and Mary Harrod	ca. 1775	Benes 1986, no. 53	
Tablespoon	B *or* C	?		ca. 1775	Benes 1986, no. 53	
Teaspoon	A*	EH		ca. 1790		PEM
Teaspoon	A*	IW		ca. 1770		YUAG
Teaspoon	A*	ML		ca. 1765	DAPC 86.2442	
Teaspoon	A	MP		ca. 1770		CHS
Teaspoon	B*	TP		ca. 1805	DAPC 73.1953	WM
Teaspoon	B*	MM (?)		ca. 1800	DAPC 70.2686	
Teaspoon	B†	MT		ca. 1800	DAPC 73.2398	WM
Teaspoon	C†	CEJ		ca. 1810	DAPC 70.2332	WM
Teaspoon	?	?		ca. 1775		ChM

1. *Newbury VR* 1:280, 283, 285, 439; 2:292, 293, 643, 644, 645; Little 1882, 19–20, 40, 107. See also Dearborn 1890, 652–53; see also 210, 221.
2. *Newburyport VR* 2:283; *Amesbury VR*, 209, 463, 580, 581.
3. Flynt/Fales 1968, 267. See also Parsons 1983, 113.
4. The advertisement was repeated on 25 August and 5 September 1775.
5. ECPR, docket 11803.
6. The advertisement was repeated on 27 February 1788.
7. RCD 141:171–73.
8. SCCR, Supreme Judicial Court, files 134608, 134596.
9. Little 1882, 107; Hillsborough County Probate Court, Nashua, New Hampshire, docket 05934.
10. A neoclassical sugar bowl marked W·L formerly attributed to Little is now thought to be by a New York maker; see Hammerslough/Feigenbaum 1958–73, 2:50–51. Janine E. Skerry letter to G. W. R. Ward, 9 March 1994.

Benjamin Loring
1731–98

Benjamin Loring, born in Hull, Massachusetts, on 16 July 1731, was the son of Benjamin Loring (1704–68), a yeoman, and Elizabeth Gould (b. 1704), both of Hull.[1] His paternal grandparents were Benjamin Loring (ca. 1671–1732) and Anna Vickery (ca. 1676–1723), of Hull, and his maternal grandparents were John Gould (1672–1762) and Lydia Jacobs (1681–1741/42), also of Hull.[2] Loring's apprenticeship would have begun about 1745 and been completed about 1752. The identity of his master is unknown; he probably trained in Boston because his intention to marry Rachel Wilson was published there on 27 November 1755.[3] On 24 September 1757 Loring and John Dexter (q.v.) witnessed a receipt for the jeweler John Welsh (q.v.) and Zachariah Symmes, father of the silversmith John Symmes (q.v.), involving the settlement of Isaac and Grace Parker's estate.[4] This document indicates that Loring was well acquainted with Dexter, Welsh, and probably Welsh's brother-in-law Daniel Parker (q.v.), the son of Isaac and Grace Parker, and suggests that he may have trained with Welsh. Loring in turn may have trained his cousins from Hull, Loring Bailey, who began his apprenticeship about 1754, and Joseph Loring (qq.v.), who began his apprenticeship about 1757.

Benjamin Loring was identified as a jeweler when his house at the upper end of Wilbauer Street in Boston burned in 1762, and he was identified as a goldsmith on the bond for the administration of his father's estate in 1768.[5] He was identified as a Boston jeweler, and once as a goldsmith, in deeds recording his sales and purchases of land in Hull and Hingham in 1767, 1769, and 1770.[6] The jeweler may have been the Benjamin Loring who witnessed a receipt for jewelry that Thomas Clark sold to John Touzell on behalf of Benjamin Pierpont (qq.v.) on 14 August 1764.[7] During the Revolution he may have still been in Boston because a Benjamin Loring served as a guard of stores in Boston.[8] Loring may also have been associated in business with Jonathan Crosby (q.v.) because he signed the bond for the administration of Crosby's mother's estate in 1779.[9]

On 7 January 1779 Loring married Eunice (Curtis) Soper (1736–85), the widow of Edmund Soper of Braintree, Massachusetts.[10] Loring may have moved to Braintree before this second marriage. He was identified as a resident of the town when he was sued for debt in 1780 by Ebenezer Davenport of Dorchester, Massachusetts.[11] In 1781, however, he and his wife, Eunice, were said to be of Boston when they were sued by Oliver Wendell, judge of probate for Suffolk County, over the estate of Eunice's deceased husband.[12] In August 1789 Loring still was living in Boston when Mehitable Soper, a Braintree spinster, was named guardian of Eunice Soper (b. 1776) and Fanny Loring, daughter of Benjamin Loring "of Boston."[13]

Benjamin Loring's funeral was in Boston in the house of his son-in-law William Turnbull, a ropemaker, on Elliott Street on 6 March 1798.[14] His obituary gave his age as sixty-five, although at the time it was actually sixty-six.

No work by this maker has been identified. PEK

1. *Hull VR*, 18, 26, 47; SCPR, docket 14233.
2. *Hull VR*, 19, 66, 69.
3. RC 30:17.
4. MCPR, docket 16584.
5. Bigelow-Phillips files, 1628a; SCPR, docket 14233.
6. SCD III:168–69; 115:65–66, 139–40, 214; 117:251–52.
7. English-Touzel-Hathorne Papers, box 4, folder 5, PEM.

8. *Mass. Soldiers and Sailors* 9:963.

9. SCPR, docket 17078.

10. RC 30:406; SCPR 87:277–79.

11. SCCR, Court of Common Pleas Record Book 1780, 24.

12. SCCR, Court of Common Pleas Record Book 1780–81, 203–04. Guardianship papers show that Mrs. Loring provided board, clothing, and schooling for a minor named Eunice Soper from April 1781 to April 1785; SCPR 89:111–13. Following Loring's wife's death, John Vinton became administrator of her estate; SCPR 87:277–79. Loring was also sued for debt in 1783 and 1785 and defaulted both times; SCCR, Court of Common Pleas Record Book 1783, 231, and 1785, 145.

13. SCPR 88:348; *Braintree VR*, 839.

14. *Index of Obituaries, 1704–1800*, 1:195. The name in the *Independent Chronicle* actually reads Trumbull, and no first name is given. The *Boston Directory* of 1796 lists William Turnbull on Elliott Street. William Turnbull and Deborah Whitemarsh were married in 1795; see RC 30:154. Deborah Loring married Nehemiah Whitemarsh in 1787; see RC 30:112. There is no record of Deborah's birth in Boston.

Elpalet Loring, Sr.
1740–ca. 1768

A

Elpalet Loring, Sr., was born in Barnstable, Massachusetts, on 4 September 1740, the sixth son of David Loring, Jr. (b. 1704), of Hingham and Barnstable, and Sarah Beal (b. 1709) of Hingham, who were married on 10 April 1729.[1] His paternal grandparents were David Loring, Sr. (1671–1752), of Hull, Massachusetts, and Elizabeth (Otis) Allyn (ca. 1671–1748) of Scituate, Massachusetts, and his maternal grandparents were Joshua Beal (1680–1723/24) of Hingham and Susanna Nichols (1681–1748) of Scituate.[2]

Loring probably began his apprenticeship in 1754, completing it about 1761. Moody Russell (q.v.) may have been his master, as Russell's granddaughter Abigail Gilman (after 1746–ca. 1767) married Loring on 15 November 1764.[3] She was the daughter of Nathaniel Gilman of Exeter, New Hampshire, and Abigail Russell (1725?–ca. 1748) of Barnstable, who were married in Barnstable on 25 December 1746.[4] Moody Russell's will, dated 8 April 1761, allowed for the support of his granddaughter Abigail.[5] Loring was probably also acquainted with fellow Barnstable silversmith Elisha Gray, Jr. (q.v.), because he witnessed Gray's mother's will in 1766.[6]

Elpalet Loring and Abigail Gilman had two children: Elpalet, Jr., also a silversmith, who was born on 15 September 1765;[7] and Gilman, who may have been born in 1767 and died young.[8] Abigail Gilman apparently died in childbirth with her second son or shortly thereafter. Barnstable probate records indicate that Elpalet Loring, goldsmith, was appointed his son Gilman's guardian on 12 May 1767, which suggests that Abigail had died.[9] Elpalet Loring, Sr., planned to marry a second time, as his intention to wed Elizabeth Taylor was published in late 1767 or early 1768. But since no record of the union has been found, the marriage may not have taken place, possibly because Loring died in early 1768 at the age of twenty-eight.[10] Loring was practicing his craft until his untimely death. His inventory, dated 20 May 1768, included "shop tools & Wrought silver" valued at £54.19.6 and "shop goods" worth £24.18.1, nearly half the full value of his estate.[11] Even after Loring's death, Moody Russell's widow, Dinah (Sturgis) Russell, continued to provide for his family. In her will, dated 8 February 1773, she left a bequest to her great-grandson, Loring's son Elpalet, Jr.[12]

Silver by Elpalet Loring, Sr., has long been misattributed to his brothers Eliphalet and Elijah, who, although they shared his first initial, were not goldsmiths (qq.v. Appendix B). E·Loring, script, in a cartouche (A) has been recorded as the mark of Elpalet Loring, Sr. JJF

SURVIVING OBJECTS

	Mark	Inscription	Patron	Date	Reference	Owner
Two canns	A†	none	Congregational Church, West Parish of Barnstable, West Barnstable, Mass.	ca. 1765	Jones 1913, 483	
Porringer	A	MR/TO/RW		ca. 1765	Hammerslough/ Feigenbaum 1958–73, 3:45	

1. Lincoln (1893) 1982, 3:31, 58; Pope 1917, 40; *Mayflower Descendant* 32:58.
2. Lincoln (1893) 1982, 3:28–29, 58; Elizabeth (Otis) Allyn married first Thomas Allyn, 9 October 1688, who died ca. 1696, *Mayflower Descendant* 2:212; marriage of David Loring and Elizabeth Allyn, widow, in *Mayflower Descendant* 11:96. Hingham Town Records 1635–1830, 27, microfilm, Corbin Collection, NEHGS.
3. Barnstable Town Records 2:253, 266, Hyannis Town Hall, Hyannis, Massachusetts.
4. Barnstable Town Records 3:48 as recorded in Bigelow-Phillips files, 775. According to the same files, n.p., Nathaniel Gilman was uncle to John Ward Gilman, silversmith, of Exeter, New Hampshire.
5. BCPR 12:162–63.
6. BCPR 13:397–98.
7. A pair of salt spoons survive that may be by Elpalet, Jr.; WM, DAPC 75.2976. For a general discussion, see McCulloch/Beale 1963, 72–74.
8. *Mayflower Descendant* 32:58; Barnstable Town Records 2:359, Hyannis Town Hall, Hyannis, Massachusetts.
9. BCPR 14:189.
10. Marriage intentions for 1767 are recorded by Pope 1917, 69, and in *Mayflower Descendant* 19:126.
11. BCPR 13:366. Following the goldsmith's death, his young son Elpalet Loring, Jr., appeared in several guardianship papers; BCPR 11:4; 14:8, 216; 18:83.
12. BCPR 17:69.

Joseph Loring 1743–1815

A

B

C

D

Joseph Loring was born in Hull, Massachusetts, on 21 July 1743 to Caleb Loring (1688/89–1756) and his third wife, Rebecca Lobdell (1701–66), who were married on 6 January 1732.[1] The silversmith's paternal grandparents were John Loring and his second wife, Rachel Buckland; his maternal grandparents were Joseph (d. 1725) and Elizabeth Lobdell.[2] Following his father's death, Loring's brother Caleb, a Boston feltmaker, became his guardian in 1758.[3]

Loring probably trained in Boston with a cousin, Benjamin Loring (q.v.). He would have finished his apprenticeship about 1764. By 21 August 1766, he published his intention to marry Mary Atkins (1745–1831), the daughter of Joshua and Rebecca (Atwood) Atkins.[4] Joseph and Mary Loring had four children: Joseph (1767–1838), Joshua (b. 1769), Mary (1770–1833), and Henry (1773–93).[5]

Loring was identified as "Joseph Loring, Goldsmith," when he and seven other heirs of Caleb Loring disposed of their father's property on 14 May 1767.[6] Within several years, Loring had established himself successfully. The Massachusetts tax list of 1771 records him as the owner of a house and "tanhouse," or workshop. His real estate was valued at £17.6.8, and his personal property included £140 of merchandise and £1,404 in notes of credit.[7] On 9 October 1782, "Joseph Loring, goldsmith," purchased a house on Court Street

E

F

G

H

I

J

from the estate of Benjamin Pemberton for £940. "Joseph Loring, jeweller," sold a strip of the land to a neighbor, the brazier John Andrews, for £85 later that month.[8] Loring and his family lived on Court Street for many years; the Boston directories for 1796 and 1798 continued to list this house as his residence.[9] The U.S. Direct Tax of 1798 described Loring's home as occupying 2,255 square feet of land with a brick dwelling house "840 square feet, 2 stories, 17 windows; Kitchen, 360 square feet; 1 story; wood; wood house, 432 square feet; Value, $3,500."[10] Loring's shop was located at 3 Union Street in the city directories of 1789, 1796, and 1798.[11] The silversmith also owned property on Queen Street; he successfully sued Mary and Elizabeth Minott in 1783 for £75 in back rent due.[12] In the 1790 census, Loring was the head of a family composed of four men above the age of sixteen, one younger boy, and three females.[13] He appears in the Massachusetts census for 1810.[14]

Loring served in the military and as an official for the town of Boston between 1773 and 1791.[15] In March 1773, he was chosen a "Scavinger" for ward 6, a position he also held in 1774.[16] He served as a juror for maritime courts held in September 1776 and July 1777.[17] The silversmith joined the Ancient and Honorable Artillery Company in 1788.[18] He returned to civic duty in 1791 as a "Searcher and packer of barrel'd Beef Pork and Fish for the Town."[19]

"Joseph Loring, Jeweller," wrote his will on 1 November 1808; he had died by 23 October 1815, when his will was presented for probate. He bequeathed $20 to his son Joseph, one-eighth of the income from his real and personal estate to his daughter, Mary, and seven-eighths of the income to his wife, Mary. Following the death of his wife, his real and personal estate was to be divided equally among his three children, Joseph, Joshua, and Mary. All four heirs were named as executors. Joseph Peirce and the Boston silversmiths Henry Loring (1773–1818) and Jesse Churchill (1773–1819) appraised Loring's estate on 11 December 1815. He had $497.40 of household goods, including $63.75 of silver. At the time of his death, he was a prosperous craftsman who had been able to furnish his home with a variety of luxury items. The detailed inventory of his shop goods and equipment reveals the nature of Loring's silversmithing business as well as his financial success:

		One Trunk Containing Viz.tt			
N°	1.	52 pair Buttons Stones Chrystal	@ 17ct.	$8..84	
	2.	157 Pair Earring D° D°	@ 20.	31..40	
	3.	26 Pair D°. D°. D°	@ 17.	4..42	
	4.	33 Pair D°. D°. D°	@ 12.	3..96	
	5.	A Lot of old Christal Stones 100		1..00	
	6.	A Lot of Garnit D°		..50	
	7.	35 Stones for Rings	@ 10.	3..50	53..62
	8.	16 Pair Stone Earrings set in Gold }			
		3 D° D° D° D°			22..00
	9.	9½ Pair Gold Wires with Joints }			
		12½ Pair D° D° D°			10..00
	10.	7 Pair Fancy Gold Earrings			4..00
		Trunk Jewellery Continued			$587..02
N°.	11.	15 Fancy Gold Rings			7..00
	12.	2 Stone Rings set in Gold			2..00
	13.	4 Gold Rings, 3 Silver & Stone D°			6..00
	14.	4 Gold Hallfe [?] Pins with Stones. 8 D° D° D°			6..00

15.	7 Gold Rings set with Chrystals	18..00
16.	1 Miniature Setting 1 D° D° with White Enamel	10..00
17.	6 ¹/₂ Pair Stone Buttons set in Silver	4..00
18.	9 Pair Hooks & Eyes 5 Pair Silver Buttons	
	2 Stone Seals Set in Silver 4 Lockets D° D°	
	1 Pair Silver Clasps 2 Stay Hooks	
	4 Silver Thimbles 1 Silver Clasp	6..00
	1 Box Containing to wit	
N°. 19.	12 Doz Minature Glasses @ 40ᶜᵗ each	57..60
20.	2 Doz large size D° @ 40 "	9..60
	¹¹/₁₂ D° D° D° @ 40 "	4..40
21.	3 ¹/₄ Doz Glasses for pins @ 40. "	15..60
22.	5 Parcels Beta Skin (Gold) Containing 9 ¹/₃ Doz Skins	2..00
23.	1 D° D° in ¹/₄ sheets	1..00
24.	1 Box containing quantity black Enamel	1..00
25.	1 D° D° D° white D°	
26.	1 D° D° 8 ³/₄ Doz Foil	26..00
27.	1 Pestle & Mortar to grind Enamel	4..00
	1 Patent Sheet Iron Stove with 47 lb Funnell	10..00
	1 Pair Large Bellows $4. 1 Pair Small D° 20ᶜ	4..20
	1 Writing Desk $1. 3 Small Chairs 60ᶜ	1..60
		$783..02

1 Anvil $5. 1 Standing Vise $4	9..00
1 Large hanging Case $8. 1 Small D° $2.	10..00
2 Outside show cases $3. 1 Counter Case $4.	7..00
1 Iron Kettle 50ᶜ 1 Pair tongs 50.	1..00
1 Pair Large Elegant Scales & Weights Complete	12..00
1 Pair midling Size D° & 1 Pair Small D°	2..00
9 Pair Brass Flasks & Screws for D°	5..50
1 Small Teste $2. Lot Shop Tools $41.	43..00
12 Pair Silver Kneebuckles $8. ¹/₂ Box plate Powder 50ᶜᵗ }	8..50
1 Lot Plated Buckles $5. 7 Breast Pins @ 25ᶜ $1.75.	6..75
3 Doz Glasses $6. 7 Papers Cyphers $12.	18..00
1 Box Containing 13 Cases $2..25 A Basket with small Empty	
Boxes $1 ea }	3..25[20]

Loring seems to have specialized in making jewelry and other small enameled works. In his memoirs (1811), the Plymouth silversmith Samuel Davis (1765–1829) noted that "Loring in Market square (now living) excelled in enamellery."[21] Loring's possession of five display cases indicates an extensive trade in such ready-made items as the jewelry, buckles, buttons, and thimbles enumerated in the inventory. He sold a variety of buckle chapes and shop supplies to Zachariah Brigden (q.v.), probably goods imported from England:

Mʳ Zachariah Brigden		Bo't of Joseph Loring			
			£		
2 dozⁿ. Knee Chaps	at 18ˢ/		1	..	16
1 dozⁿ ditto	at 14ˢ/4ᵈ			14	.. 4
1 dozⁿ Shoe ditto	at 27ˢ/		1	..	7
1 dozⁿ. ditto	at 28/		1	..	8

6 Files	at 1ˢ/6		9	
1 Pair flat Plyars	7/6		7 .. 6	
			£6 .. 1 .. 10²²	

Loring had professional relationships with several other Massachusetts silversmiths. He was a witness of his neighbor Daniel Parker's (q.v.) will in June 1772.²³ On 3 April 1787, Loring hired his colleague Paul Revere, Jr. (q.v.), to mend and burnish a tankard, a service for which he was charged 12 shillings.²⁴ In September 1788, Loring and Stephen Emery (q.v.) provided a bond for a Mr. Procter's application for an auctioneer's license.²⁵ Loring's shop at 3 Union Street was next door to Emery at 5 Union Street. Loring was an appraiser of Thomas Clark's estate along with Benjamin Pierpont in 1781 and of John Codner's estate along with Benjamin Burt (qq.v.) in 1782.²⁶ The account book of the Ipswich silversmith Daniel Rogers (q.v.) indicates that Loring purchased gold beads from Rogers between 1796 and 1800.²⁷ The estate of Caleb Beal (q.v.) made a payment of $7.36 to Loring between 1801 and 1803.²⁸ In addition to serving as an appraiser for Loring's estate, Jesse Churchill and his firm, Churchill and Treadwell, were paid £11.9.5 by Loring's executors in December 1815 and $34.13 in November 1817.²⁹

Although few pieces of jewelry bearing Joseph Loring's mark survive, two variations of his initials and surname mark (A, B) and eight variations of his initials mark (C–J) appear on numerous pieces of holloware and flatware. Many of the objects made during the 1780s and 1790s feature elaborate medallions, bowknots, and border designs that incorporate punch details and roulette work. Loring also retailed silver made by several of his colleagues, including the Concord silversmith Samuel Bartlett (q.v.), the Newburyport and Boston silversmith Ebenezer Moulton (1768–1824), Jesse Churchill, and Paul Revere, Jr.³⁰ DAF

SURVIVING OBJECTS

	Mark	Inscription	Patron	Date	Reference	Owner
Baptismal basin	A	The Gift of DEA. RICHARD HALL, to the CHURCH OF CHRIST in Medford 1814	Richard Hall and/or First Parish, Medford, Mass.	1814	Jones 1913, 276–77	
Beaker	A*	IB; ARB		ca. 1800	Buhler/Hood 1970, no. 278	YUAG
Two beakers	A or B (?)	?		ca. 1785	Washington 1925, no. 67	
Beaker	A or B	The Gift of Mrs. Susanna Dean/in part to the Church of Christ in/ BEDFORD	Susanna Dean and/or First Parish, Bedford, Mass.	1806	YUAG files	
Bowl	A	C	William Cunningham	ca. 1795	Moore Collection 1980, no. 160	
Bowl	A*	AB		ca. 1790	Christie's, 23 June 1993, lot 54	

	Mark	Inscription	Patron	Date	Reference	Owner
Cann *(with mark of Samuel Bartlett)*	D	TEP	Theophilus and Elizabeth (Greenleaf) Parsons	ca. 1785	Buhler 1965, 112–15	HMA
Cann	D†	Martin (?) arms, vert a chevron ermine between 3 martlets, and crest, a sun in splendor above a Masonic emblem; M/IL; JACOB MARTIN	Jacob Martin	ca. 1775	Buhler/Hood 1970, no. 279	YUAG
Cann *(with mark of Samuel Bartlett)*	I	C/EM		ca. 1785	*Antiques* 68 (July 1955): 26	
Cann *(with mark of Samuel Bartlett)*	I	H?; BL (later)		ca. 1780	DAPC 77.3001	
Cann	?	unidentified crest		ca. 1775	Parke-Bernet, 14–15 October 1955, lot 283	
Cann	?	The Gift of/Madam Sarah Abbot/TO/ Miss Abigail French/ANDOVER	Sarah Abbot and/or Abigail French	ca. 1795	*Antiques* 93 (January 1968): 6	
Creampot	A*	HV		ca. 1800	YUAG files	
Creampot	A or B	unidentified initials		ca. 1800	Sotheby's, 29 April–1 May 1981, lot 381	
Creampot	A or B	B		ca. 1795	McFadden/ Clark 1989, no. 66	ChM
Creampot	?	EB (?)		ca. 1800	*Antiques* 38 (November 1940): 200	
Creampot	?	?		ca. 1800		ChM
Creampot (part of a set; attrib.)	none	SH (+)	Loring family (?)	ca. 1797	Warren 1975, no. 327	BBC
Creampot (part of a set; attrib.)	none	ML (+)	Mary (Atkins) Loring (?)	ca. 1797	Warren 1975, no. 325	BBC
Creampot (attrib.)	none	A	John and Katharine (Willard) Amory, Jr.	ca. 1795	Buhler 1972, no. 437	MFAB
Cup	A	PP/to/SPN		ca. 1770		AIC
Two cups	A or B	D		ca. 1785	Washington 1925, no. 66	
Dessert spoon	A*	SL/to HHL	Loring family	ca. 1797	Warren 1975, no. 345	BBC
Ladle	A*	Avery	Avery family	ca. 1800		YUAG
Ladle	A	A	John and Katharine (Willard) Amory, Jr.	ca. 1795	Buhler 1972, no. 438	MFAB
Ladle	A or B	ARA		ca. 1790	MFA 1911, no. 716	
Ladle	C	MC		ca. 1780	DAPC 75.5119	WM

	Mark	Inscription	Patron	Date	Reference	Owner
Ladle *(with mark of Samuel Bartlett)*	I (?)	OAC		ca. 1785	*Antiques* 68 (July 1955): 26	
Ladle *(with mark of Samuel Bartlett)*	?	?		ca. 1780		ChM
Ladle	?	?		ca. 1785		ChM
Two mustard spoons	J	A	Amory family	ca. 1790	Buhler 1972, appendix no. 54	MFAB
Pitcher (with mark of IC*)*	A	EG/June 14.th 1811.	Elizabeth (Chapman) Goodwin	1811	Ham- merslough/ Feigenbaum 1958–73, 4:30–31	
Pitcher (with mark of IC*)*	A*	EG/March 10, 1810 (+)	Elizabeth (Chapman) Goodwin (?)	1810	*Antiques* 101 (May 1972): 756	
Porringer	A	N.Coll,/to N. Coll Stearns/June 10.th 1804	N. Coll and/or N. Coll Stearns	1804	DAPC 77.2417	
Porringer	A	A/JR	John and Ruth (Skillins) Adams or John and Ruthy (Vinal) Adams	ca. 1780	Buhler 1972, no. 432	MFAB
Porringer (mate below)	A	ET		ca. 1790	*American Sil- ver* 1967, no. 20	RWNAG
Porringer (mate above)	A (?)	ET; May 19th 1808 (later)		ca. 1790	Christie's, 17– 18 January 1992, lot 155	
Porringer	A (?)	unidentified crest; MA		ca. 1790	*CGA Bulletin*, no. 1 (1971): fig. 12	CGA
Porringer	A	C/JE		ca. 1800	Sotheby's, 23–24 June 1994, lot 88	
Porringer	A	C/JE; unidentified later initials (+)		ca. 1800	Sotheby's, 23–24 June 1994, lot 88	
Porringer	A or B	?		ca. 1780	American Art Association– Anderson Galleries, 22–23 January 1937, lot 297	
Porringer *(with mark of Samuel Bartlett;* *mate below)*	I†	L/IM	Joseph and Mary (Atkins) Loring	ca. 1780		CM
Porringer *(with mark of Samuel Bartlett;* *mate above)*	?	L/IM; 1765 (later)	Joseph and Mary (Atkins) Loring	ca. 1780	*Antiques* 92 (August 1967): 139	
Porringer	?	SW; 1792 (later)		ca. 1790	Christie's, 11 April 1981, lot 239	

	Mark	Inscription	Patron	Date	Reference	Owner
Porringer	?	TPM		ca. 1785	*Antiques* 94 (July 1968): 13	
Salt spoon	H†	I or J		ca. 1810		YUAG
Salt spoon	J*	S		ca. 1795		YUAG
Shoe buckle	J*	none		ca. 1785		YUAG
Spoon (miniature)	G†	none		ca. 1800		YUAG
Strainer	A	A	John and Katharine (Willard) Amory, Jr.	ca. 1795	Buhler 1972, no. 434	MFAB
Sugar bowl	A*	MTC; HTQ		ca. 1800	Eitner 1976, no. 77	
Sugar bowl	B†	MI		ca. 1810	Buhler 1972, no. 440	MFAB
Two sugar bowls (with mark of Ebenezer Moulton)	B	A	Amory family	ca. 1800	Parke-Bernet, 28 October 1969, lot 64	
Sugar bowl (part of a set; attrib.)	none	ML (+)	Mary (Atkins) Loring (?)	ca. 1797	Warren 1975, no. 326	BBC
Sugar bowl (attrib.)	none	A	John and Katharine (Willard) Amory, Jr.	ca. 1795	Buhler 1972, no. 436	MFAB
Sugar tongs (attrib.)	none	A	John and Katharine (Willard) Amory, Jr.	ca. 1795	Buhler 1972, no. 436	MFAB
Two tablespoons	A	C		ca. 1795	Avery 1920, nos. 262–63	MMA
Tablespoon	A	L/MR		ca. 1775	DAPC 75.3238	WM
Tablespoon	A	PAC; ACM (later?)		ca. 1780	DAPC 72.1247	WM
Tablespoon	A	LW		ca. 1770	DAPC 75.3223	WM
Tablespoon	A	MS	?		DAPC 72.1239	WM
Tablespoon	A	Betsey Eells/Born Oct.r/30.1760.	Betsey Eells	ca. 1770	DAPC 72.1249	WM
Tablespoon	A	Nabby Eells/Born. Nov./29.1767	Nabby Eells	1767	DAPC 72.1245	WM
Tablespoon	A	JT to JTO		ca. 1775	DAPC 72.1251	WM
Tablespoon	A	H/WC		ca. 1770	DAPC 68.4523	
Tablespoon	A	MB		ca. 1780	DAPC 75.2973	WM
Tablespoon	A†	B		ca. 1800	Buhler/Hood 1970, no. 277	YUAG
Tablespoon	A*	B/IM		ca. 1770		YUAG
Tablespoon	A*	AA		ca. 1785		PEM
Tablespoon	A*	G		ca. 1810		SI
Two tablespoons	A*	EF; ELSB (later)		ca. 1785		BM
Tablespoon (see also mate with mark F)	A	HB	Hannah (Breed) Osgood	ca. 1780	Buhler 1972, no. 431	MFAB
Two tablespoons	A/F	A	John and Katharine (Willard) Amory, Jr.	ca. 1795	Buhler 1972, no. 439	MFAB
Tablespoon	A or B	S/ ? E		ca. 1770		RISD

	Mark	Inscription	Patron	Date	Reference	Owner
Two tablespoons	A *or* B	unidentified initials		ca. 1790	YUAG files	
Two tablespoons	A *or* B	TEP	Theophillus and Eliza-beth (Greenleaf) Parsons	ca. 1785	Bigelow 1917, 272–74	
Tablespoon	B	IB/to/SB		ca. 1770	Eitner 1976, no. 82	
Tablespoon	B	HD	Hannah Dawes	ca. 1800	Buhler 1972, appendix no. 55	MFAB
Tablespoon	C	D; Davis	Davis family	ca. 1790		RISD
Tablespoon	C	W/JS		ca. 1780		RISD
Two tablespoons	C*	SC	Sally (Cross) Preble	ca. 1790	Eitner 1976, nos. 80–81	
Tablespoon	C*	SW		ca. 1780	Eitner 1976, no. 79	
Tablespoon (altered to feeding spoon)	C†	SB		ca. 1795	Buhler/Hood 1970, no. 276	YUAG
Tablespoon	E*	SH/1797 (+)	Loring family	ca. 1797	Warren 1975, no. 344	BBC
Tablespoon	E†	AF		ca. 1780		YUAG
Tablespoon (see also mate with mark A)	F†	HB	Hannah (Breed) Osgood	ca. 1780	Buhler 1972, no. 431	MFAB
Two tablespoons	G	SB		ca. 1780	DAPC 72.1095 and 72.1504	WM
Tablespoon	J†	J/CE		ca. 1770		WM
Tablespoon	J	B/NH		ca. 1770	Buhler 1972, appendix no. 45	MFAB
Tankard	A*	A Donation/from L! Elijah/Arms to the/Church in Deer-/field 1802.	Elijah Arms and/or First Congregational Church, Deerfield, Mass.	ca. 1802	Flynt/Fales 1968, 45, 49	
Tankard	A*	FIELDS FOUNTAIN SOCIETY/TO/ DEACON JOHN FIELD	Field's Fountain Soci-ety, Providence, R.I., and/or John Field	ca. 1770	Hammerslough/ Feigenbaum 1958–73, 1:16–17	WA
Teapot	A *or* B	HTQ; MH	Harriet (Tufts) Quincy	ca. 1810		MFAB
Teapot (part of a set; attrib.)	none	H/SL/1797 (later)	Loring family	ca. 1797	Warren 1975, no. 324	BBC
Teapot (probably made by Paul Revere, Jr.)	none	A	John and Katharine (Willard) Amory, Jr.	ca. 1795	Buhler 1972, no. 435	MFAB
Teapot stand (probably made by Paul Revere, Jr.)	A	A	John and Katharine (Willard) Amory, Jr.	ca. 1795	Buhler 1972, no. 435	MFAB
Teaspoon	C	RD		ca. 1790		RISD
Teaspoon	C	E?A		ca. 1790		RISD
Six teaspoons	C	P		ca. 1810	Buhler 1979, no. 68	WAM

	Mark	Inscription	Patron	Date	Reference	Owner
Two teaspoons	C	ET	Elizabeth (Tuckerman) Salisbury	ca. 1795	Buhler 1979, no. 67	WAM
Teaspoon	C	Foxcroft crest, a fox's head	Mehitable (Coney) Foxcroft (?)	ca. 1775	Buhler 1979, no. 66	WAM
Teaspoon	C*	SL		ca. 1790		PEM
Teaspoon	C*	B/IE		ca. 1785		SFCAI
Teaspoon	C	BW (altered to PW)		ca. 1775	DAPC 74.1469	WM
Teaspoon	C	FS		ca. 1775	DAPC 75.5102	WM
Teaspoon	C*	B		ca. 1790		HD
Eleven teaspoons	C*	AR		ca. 1795		YUAG
Four teaspoons	C*	SC	Sally (Cross) Preble	ca. 1790	Eitner 1976, nos. 83–86	
Teaspoon	C*	S/IH		ca. 1780	Eitner 1976, no. 87	
Teaspoon	E *or* J	LH		ca. 1785	Curtis 1913, pl. iv	
Teaspoon	F	AW		ca. 1810	DAPC 72.1668	
Teaspoon	F*	PJ		ca. 1810		HD
Two teaspoons	F	HD	Hannah Dawes	ca. 1800		MHS
Two teaspoons	F	M/JP		ca. 1805		YUAG
Teaspoon	G	FS (partially erased)		ca. 1790	DAPC 73.2383	WM
Teaspoon	G	JHS		ca. 1780	DAPC 89.3141	
Teaspoon	J*	HL		ca. 1800		HD
Teaspoon	J*	B		ca. 1800		HD
Teaspoon	J	MB (+)		ca. 1770	Buhler 1972, appendix no. 46	MFAB
Two teaspoons	J	SS		ca. 1790	Buhler 1972, appendix no. 47	MFAB
Teaspoon	J	B/WE		ca. 1790	Buhler 1972, appendix no. 48	MFAB
Teaspoon	J	MW		ca. 1780	Buhler 1972, appendix no. 49	MFAB
Two teaspoons	J	HES	Henry and Elizabeth (Quarles) Smith	ca. 1795	Buhler 1972, appendix no. 50	MFAB
Teaspoon	J	CS		ca. 1800	Buhler 1972, appendix no. 51	MFAB
Teaspoon	J	ES		ca. 1800	Buhler 1972, appendix no. 52	MFAB
Teaspoon	J	A	Amory family	ca. 1795	Buhler 1972, appendix no. 53	MFAB

	Mark	Inscription	Patron	Date	Reference	Owner
Two two-handled cups *(with cover; mate below)*	A*	PROPERTY/OF/ BRATTLE STREET CHURCH/BOSTON.	Brattle Street Church, Boston	ca. 1790	Buhler/Hood 1970, no. 275	YUAG
Two-handled cup *(with cover; mates above)*	A	PROPERTY/OF/ BRATTLE STREET CHURCH/BOSTON.	Brattle Street Church, Boston	ca. 1790	Avery 1920, no. 261	MMA
Two-handled cup (with cover)	A	The GIFT of/M.ʳ William Johnston/ TO/BRATTLE STREET CHURCH/ BOSTON/1707	Brattle Street Church, Boston, for William Johnston	ca. 1790	Buhler 1972, no. 433	MFAB
Wine cup	A	Rowe arms, gules 3 paschal lambs with staves and banners, and crest, a stag's head erased; INNOCBNS NON TIMIDUS; Presented to Trinity Church/ by M.ʳˢ Hannah Rowe/November 1790	Hannah (Speakman) Rowe and/or Trinity Church, Boston	1790	Jones 1913, 86	

1. Lincoln (1893) 1982, 3:30–31; Bridgman 1853, 48; *Hull VR*, 25–27, 51, 69; SCPR 51:644–45; 52:475–77.
2. *Hull VR*, 52; SCPR 24:88–89; Bridgman 1851, 222.
3. SCPR 53:19.
4. RC 30:425; *Truro VR*, 21, 39; *Index of Obituaries, 1784–1840*, 3:2859.
5. A silversmith named Henry Loring who worked in Boston and Concord and died in 1818 has been identified as the son of Joseph Loring in the literature. However, the son born to Joseph and Mary Loring in 1772 or 1773 died in 1793 at the age of twenty-one. Henry Loring served as an appraiser for Joseph Loring's estate in 1815, which suggests that they were related.
6. The house in Hull was sold to the silversmith's brother, the Boston hatter Caleb Loring, for £18, and a tract of land comprising over eighteen acres at Hemples Hill, Hull, was sold to the Hingham yeoman Jeremiah Stodder for £254.14.3; SCD 110:211–12; SCD 168:164–65.
7. Pruitt 1978, 24–25.
8. SCD 136:52–55.
9. *Boston Directory*, 1796, 69; 1798, 76.
10. RC 22:312.
11. *Boston Directory*, 1789, 28; 1796, 69; 1798, 76.
12. SCCR, Court of Common Pleas Extended Record Book 1783, 228–29.
13. RC 22:483.
14. Massachusetts census, Suffolk County, 1800, 196.
15. There are two Joseph Lorings listed in the Boston Assessors' "Taking Books" of 1780, one credited with two polls and real estate rents valued at £70, another credited with one poll and real estate rents of £120; "Assessors' 'Taking-Books,'" 30–31. It has not been possible to identify which entry refers to the silversmith; similarly, it is possible that the Loring who appears in the Boston town minutes is not the silversmith.
16. RC 18:117, 155.
17. RC 18:243, 289.
18. Roberts 1895, 2:233. Roberts states that Loring served as a lieutenant during the Revolution and was captured by the British on Long Island in November 1776. However, this appears to have been another Loring and not the silversmith.
19. RC 27:146.

20. SCPR, docket 24763.

21. Steinway 1960, 8.

22. Joseph Loring to Zachariah Brigden, undated, Brigden Papers, YU.

23. SCPR, docket 18604.

24. 3 April 1787, vol. 2, Waste Book, 1783–97, 54, Revere Family Papers, MHS.

25. RC 27:70.

26. SCPR 80:587–90, docket 17442.

27. Daniel Rogers Account Book, PEM.

28. SCPR, docket 21581.

29. SCPR, docket 24763.

30. There are three canns, two porringers, and two ladles that feature the marks of both Loring and Samuel Bartlett. Two pitchers attributed to Jesse Churchill also have Loring's mark, and two sugar bowls have Loring's mark struck over an incised mark of Ebenezer Moulton. A fluted teapot and stand, now at MFAB, have been attributed to Paul Revere on the basis of style, construction, and engraving; the stand bears a Loring mark; see Skerry 1988, 53–55.

Thomas Lynde
1745–1811

A

B

Thomas Lynde was baptized in Charlestown, Massachusetts, on 31 March 1745, the son of Joseph Lynde (b. 1702/03), a merchant, and Mary Lemmon (1717–98), who were married in Charlestown on 24 February 1737.[1] His paternal grandparents were Nicholas Lynde (1672–1703) of Charlestown and Dorothy Stanton (b. 1682) of Stonington, Connecticut; his maternal grandparents were Joseph Lemmon (1692–1750) and Elizabeth Phillips (1692–1775+).[2]

Thomas Lynde would have begun his apprenticeship about 1759, possibly with the Charlestown silversmith Josiah Austin (q.v.), and would have completed his training about 1766. He probably married shortly before the Revolution and moved to Worcester, Massachusetts, where his sister Dorothy Dix was living.[3] Lynde's wife was Sarah Greenleaf (b. 1744), the daughter of Jonathan Greenleaf (1716–58), an upholsterer, and Mary Cunningham (1717/18–83).[4] Seven children were born to Sarah and Thomas Lynde in Worcester between 1777 and 1788.[5] Thomas and Sarah Lynde sold the dwelling house where they lived and an acre of land in Worcester on 1 November 1783.[6] Since they continued to live in Worcester, the transaction may have been a mortgage. The Thomas Lynde who served in Colonel Crafts's Company in 1775 may have been the goldsmith.[7]

In 1788 Lynde advertised for sale a house in Worcester (probably his own), but he did not leave the town immediately. He still was identified as being a goldsmith "of Worcester" in 1790 when he and his wife sold land in Boston that she had inherited from her father and when he sold a small parcel of land with a canal on it on his houselot in Worcester.[8] About 1792 Lynde moved to Leicester, Massachusetts, because he was identified as being "of Leicester, jeweller," when he and his wife sold additional land that year.[9]

Lynde was lost in a violent snowstorm in Leicester on 24 December 1811; his body was not found until the following spring.[10] On 30 May 1812 Sarah Lynde was appointed to administer her husband's estate. The inventory, which amounted to $251.72, included goldsmith's tools valued at fifty cents and a brooch valued at $1.50. The estate proved to be insolvent.[11] Only half a dozen pieces by Lynde are known, marked with an initial and surname mark either with a pellet (A) or without a pellet (B).[12] PEK

SURVIVING OBJECTS

	Mark	Inscription	Patron	Date	Reference	Owner
Beaker	A	TW		ca. 1775	Avery 1920, no. 267	MMA

	Mark	Inscription	Patron	Date	Reference	Owner
Porringer	A *or* B	P/CM		ca. 1770	DAPC 68.2630	
Sugar bowl	A†	none		ca. 1770	Johnston 1994, 102	CMA
Tablespoon	B†	L/RE		ca. 1770	Buhler 1979, no. 69	WAM
Tankard	A	The Gift of Nathaniel Carter Esq.ʳ/to the/First Church in Newbury Port./1768 (later)	Nathaniel Carter	ca. 1768	Jones 1913, 299	
Tankard	A	The Legacy of Mʳ William Titcomb/to the third Church in Newbury	First Religious Society, Newburyport, Mass., for William Titcomb	ca. 1770	Jones 1913, 297–98	

1. Flynt/Fales 1968, 271, incorrectly states that Lynde was born in Malden, Massachusetts, on 19 April 1748 to Mary and Jacob Lynde. *Charlestown VR* 1:330, 375, 462; *NEHGR* 31:216; Wyman 1879, 2:639; Stonington VR 1:87.
2. *Charlestown VR* 1:84, 155, 186, 236; Wyman 1879, 2:615–16, 639, 743; Stanton 1891, 81–82.
3. *Charlestown VR* 1:422.
4. No record of the marriage has been found. RC 24:114, 120, 253 (recorded as Mary); RC 28:206; SCD 167:162–63, 223–24; SCCR, Court of Common Pleas Record Book 1783, 185–86; SCPR 54:47–48, 180–81; Boston Deaths, 1700–1800.
5. *Worcester VR*, 170.
6. WCD 91:182.
7. *Mass. Soldiers and Sailors* 10:81.
8. *Massachusetts Spy*, 31 July, 7, 14, 21 August, and 4, 11 September 1788; SCD 167:162–63, 223–24, 233–34; WCD 109:154.
9. SCD 173:280–81.
10. Denny 1894, 372–73.
11. WCPR 44:403; 45:17–18; 130:52; 172:6; 280:112; 468:417.
12. Kovel 1961, 174, shows a drawing of T LYNDE in an oval, but an example of this mark has not been found.

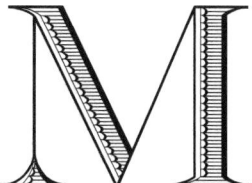

Matthew Mabely
ca. 1650–87+

On 28 January 1683/84 James Butler and William Paine gave surety to the town of Boston for Matthew Mabely, a "spoonmaker," and his family.[1] Some London goldsmiths specialized in making flatware, which apparently was Mabely's specialty. This individual may have been the Matthew Mabely who was born ca. 1650 in Hanslope, Buckinghamshire, England, son of Matthew Mabely, a yeoman, and who was apprenticed on 4 November 1664 to Isaac Corbett, a London goldsmith, for a term of eight years.[2] This Mabely was made a freeman of the Goldsmiths' Company on 10 July 1674, and on 5 January 1676 he took Nathaniel Markham as an apprentice.[3] A Matthew Maberley, who also may have been the goldsmith, and his wife, Mary, had a daughter Elizabeth, baptized on 8 February 1678, and a son Henry, baptized on 20 November 1682, at Saint Botolph Bishopsgate.[4] Possibly following Henry's birth, Mabely immigrated to New England, arriving there in early 1683/84. Mabely was listed on the Boston tax list of 1687 as owing one shilling and ten pence, but nothing more about him appears in the Boston records.[5] No silver by him is known. PEK

1. RC 10:74.
2. Apprentice Book 2, fol. 146v, Worshipful Company of Goldsmiths, London. Robert B. Barker letter to the author, 9 February 1993.
3. Court Book 7, fol. 60v; Apprentice Book 3, fol. 63r, Worshipful Company of Goldsmiths, London. Robert B. Barker letter to the author, 9 February 1993.
4. Hallen 1889–95, 3:273, 305.
5. RC 1:127.

John Mansfield
ca. 1601–74

John Mansfield, who had a checkered career as a goldsmith, was born in Henly, Buckinghamshire, England, about 1601 to John (d. 1601) and Elizabeth Mansfield (d. 1634). Mansfield's father made his will on 13 July 1601, and it was proved on 31 July. In it he mentions his wife, Elizabeth, daughter Elizabeth, daughter Ann, and David Waterhouse of the Inner Temple, who was to oversee the upbringing of the elder Mansfield's son John.[1]

He is probably the John Mansfield, age thirty-four, who left London in April 1635 on the *Susan and Ellen* bound for New England, where his sister Elizabeth's husband, the Reverend John Wilson, had been installed as pastor of Boston's First Church in 1630.[2] Mansfield's sister Ann, the wife of the merchant Robert Keayne, also came to Boston that year.[3] When Mansfield was given a house plot in Boston in 1638, his service to his brother-in-law Mr. Robert Keayne was noted on the deed.[4] Mansfield also witnessed documents in Boston in 1639 and 1640 and was made a freeman in 1643.[5] He left Boston for Charlestown, Massachusetts, about 1648, when he married Mary Gove, the widow of John Gove (d. 1647/48), of Charlestown.[6]

Robert Keayne gave a rather unflattering assessment of Mansfield in his will of 1653. Leaving money to Mansfield's children but not to Mansfield directly, Keayne justifies his actions by noting that Mansfield

> hath proved an unworthy & unthankfull brother to me, though I have done very much for him in England divers times, in releasing him out of Prisons, in paying his debts for him, in furnishing him with a stocke to set up his trade, when he had spent all his owne, in takeing up many quarrelsome bussinesses, which he in his distempered fitts, had plunged himselfe into of dangerous consequence, yet I compounded them for him, & at his sisters my wifes intreatie, with some other friends of hirs I sent him over into New England when his life was in some hazard, I payd his passage & some of his debts for him in England & lent him money to furnish himselfe with clothes & other necessaryes for his voyage, for many years I found him dyet & clothes gratis, till for his distempered carriages & unworthy behavio[r] I was fayne to putt him out of my house, all the worke that ever he did for me, not being worth his cloathes, yet was he never quiet from disturbing my whole family & pursueing me with continuall complaynts to our Eld[rs] & others seekeing to pull a maintenance out of my estate whilst himselfe lived idlie & spent what he gott in drinke & company keeping & so spitefull & envious he was to me, notwithstanding all my former care over him in seeking & endeavouring his good, that he would have cutt my throate with his false accusations if it had lyen in his power.[7]

That John Mansfield was a contentious ne'er-do-well is reinforced by other evidence. In 1649 Mansfield had a dispute with Maj. Robert Sedgwick that had to be settled in court and for which Mansfield may have been jailed.[8] In the account book of Richard Russell, treasurer of the Massachusetts Bay Colony, a reference to Mansfield suggests he was in prison in April 1650, for his bill of five shillings and six pence is listed under "Charges of Prisoners is Dr to the Treasurer."[9] Later that year Mansfield's wife, Mary, petitioned the General Court to grant her husband liberty to sue certain debtors.[10] In 1651 Samuel Adams, Joshua Tidd, and Faithful Rouse testified that Mansfield verbally abused Major Sedgwick while in the stocks.[11]

In a petition of 1654 to the General Court of the Massachusetts Bay Colony in which he asked to be appointed an assistant to John Hull and Robert Sanderson, Sr. (qq.v.), for coining money, Mansfield claimed to have been apprenticed to the goldsmith's trade for eleven and a half years in London and also to be a freeman.[12] However, no record of John Mansfield's apprenticeship at the Goldsmiths' Company exists. The picture of his life the petition describes is a pathetic one:

> Our howse do take fire manny times because it wants mendings, is like to fall uppon our headds before we be awarr, & wee are not able to mend it: but is in great want of foode & other nessessaries both for ourselues & Children, my selfe broaken bellied, my Wife much troubled in hir Mind because of som Wrongs & to see how hard it is with us and how wee run our selues in debt

& all for the belly, and No worke stirring; nor are wee respected heare because we are soe poore & cannot haue imployment in our callings.

The General Court did not see fit to grant his request.[13] Thomas Duton, John Wrightman, and Abel Benjamin testified on 25 December 1655 that they had observed John Mansfield drunk while they were on their night watch.[14]

Perhaps because of his destitute condition, in 1656 Mansfield and his wife were forced to part with their twin children, who were then eight years old. John was placed with his widowed aunt, Ann Keayne, and Mary went to live with the Reverend Samuel Whiting of Billerica, Massachusetts.[15]

In 1659 Mansfield submitted the first of his petitions to the court requesting permission to sue his sister Ann for his share of his mother's estate, and he submitted similar ones in 1661 and 1663.[16] In 1661 Mansfield and his wife petitioned the town for help in fixing their house, a request that the town granted.[17] Similar petitions pleading for repairs to their dwelling or for a better place to live followed in 1664, 1665, 1667, 1668, 1670, and 1671.[18] Barnabus Davis, Jr., and William Redland were called upon to testify in court on 7 April 1662 for the breach of the peace charges lodged against John Mansfield on 16 January 1662.[19] Then in 1665 Mansfield accused Thomas Watts of being alone with his wife in his house and of possibly committing adultery with her on 17 March of that year.[20]

Mansfield and his wife's joint will, dated 21 August 1665, mentions "lands left me in Yorke in Old England, my dwelling house in Charlestown, my ground at Boston one acre or more, with fourteen acres at the Mount which some calls Braintree."[21] In 1672 Mansfield was sued by his stepson Edward Gove, who claimed he had not received his share of his father's estate.[22] Mansfield died on 26 June 1674, and his estate's inventory amounted to £8.9.6 and included an anvil and a vise valued at £1.3 and his working tools valued at £1.5.[23] His own statements testifying to his difficulty finding work suggest that he made little silver in New England. The mark IM on a sweetmeat dish, once thought possibly to be by him, is identical to the mark on another dish with the London dateletter for 1639. Because Mansfield was already in New England by this time, this IM mark must belong to a London maker.[24] PEK

1. Waters 1901, 1:594–95.
2. Hotten 1874, 59.
3. Hotten 1874, 107.
4. RC 2:33.
5. *NEHGR* 2:261; 3:179; Shurtleff 1853, 2:293.
6. Wyman 1879, 1:429; Savage 1860–62, 2:288.
7. RC 10:25–26.
8. MCCR, 29 October 1649, sworn statement by Mansfield that the troubles between him and Major Sedgwick had ended.
9. Richard Russell Account Book, fols. 8, 78, NEHGS.
10. Shurtleff 1853, 3:213.
11. MCCR 1:18–19, file 332.
12. Mass. Archives 105:4.
13. Mass. Archives 105:4.
14. MCCR, file 561.
15. MCCR, 30 December 1656.
16. MCCR 1:196, files 1283, 1145, 1664, 1665, 2372, 2373.
17. MCCR 1:118, file 1721.
18. MCCR 1:282, file 2496; 3:15.

19. MCCR, file 2182.
20. MCCR, 3 April 1666.
21. MCPR 4:179.
22. MCCR 3:46.
23. MCPR, docket 14620.
24. Buhler/Hood 1970, no. 516; Nightingale 1891, 208–09.

Asahel Mason
d. 1751

Asahel Mason was born in England, the son of John Mason (d. before 1725), a London ironmonger. In 1725, he obtained his freedom of the city of London and attached himself to the Waxchandlers' Company in order to establish a business in the city. On 22 June that year he purchased his freedom by redemption, the most expensive method.[1] Mason's use of redemption suggests that he did not complete a regular London apprenticeship. He was admitted to the Waxchandlers' Company on 23 June 1725 as a jeweler working at the Crowne & Pearle on Little Lombard Street in London.[2] The expense of setting himself up in business seems to have placed a financial strain on the jeweler, and he declared bankruptcy in 1726.[3] The records of the Waxchandlers' Company document that Mason continued his business enterprises in London for some time following his bankruptcy and show that he did not leave London for Boston shortly after his financial difficulties as the English silver scholar E. Alfred Jones has claimed.[4] A reference of 31 December 1751 in the probate records of Suffolk County relating to the administration of the estate of "Asahel Mason, formerly of London, in Great Britain, but last of Boston aforesaid Jeweller" confirms that Asahel Mason of London and the Boston jeweler were the same man.[5]

Mason appears twice in Boston court records. In July 1746, Asahel Mason, jeweler, was sued by Benjamin Kent, a Boston lawyer.[6] Kent claimed that he had been retained by Mason for a libel case and demanded five pounds as payment for preparing Mason's defense. The court upheld Mason's denial of the charges and awarded him the costs of the suit. Mason appeared again in the Court of Common Pleas on 7 July 1747.[7] William Blair Townsend, a Boston merchant, and John Winthrop, a Cambridge gentleman, and his wife, Rebecca, had initiated a writ of ejectment against Mason on 18 June 1746. The case was dropped, however, when the plaintiffs did not appear in court.

A bill of 1747/48 records an exchange of goods and services between Asahel Mason and Thomas Edwards (q.v.). Edwards received from Mason

			£ s d
1747/8	Jan.ʸ 12	To a sheet of Red Foyle	1
		To a Bril.ᵗ for a Midle stone	10
	Feb 8	To a pʳ of Bril.ᵗ Earrings	8.10
		To 3 Coff. Ch.ˡˢ wᵗʰ Deaths	2. 5
	19	To 2 Bril.ᵗˢ for midle stones	1
	Mar. 9	To 1 sheet of red Foyle	1
	26	To 1 p.ˢ of Correll	3
	Ap.ˡ 19	To 3 sets of Lassange Bril.ᵗˢ for 3 Drop Earrings	6. 12
		To Bottle of Bitters	12
			24: 9:

Edwards paid for these supplies as follows:

1747/8	By Fashion of 3 ⎤	
Mar 10	Large Spoons ⎦	2. 10
	By a Button Christial	10
	By mending a Locket	1. 4
Ap!.	By silver wyer 16 1/[?]	3. 5
		£7. 9
May 3.d	Balance paid	17
		£24. 9

Rec.d y.e Contents   Asahel Mason[8]

Mason was a creditor of the estate of Nathaniel Morse (q.v.) in 1748.[9] George Hanners, Jr. (q.v.), and his wife, Sarah, borrowed £95.10 from Mason on 11 August 1750, using their property on Union Street as collateral.[10]

Asahel Mason died intestate at sea on 24 December 1751, while returning from a visit to London.[11] The jeweler's remains were buried in Boston. During January, February, and March of 1752, Nathaniel Oliver, Samuel Whittemore, and Ebenezer Hough traveled to Chelsea, Massachusetts, to conduct an inventory of "Sundry Goods & Cloathing being the apparent Estate of Mr. Asahel Mason, deced."[12] Mason did not own any real estate, and his personal property was appraised at £735.1.11 Old Tenor. An entry in the inventory for "Sund.y Cloath.g Chamber Utensils &c" valued at £122.10.6 probably covered all of Mason's household goods. The remainder of the inventory appears to be items from his shop, including £55 of "Sund.y Silver Smith's Tools." Mason's inventory indicates that he was selling hard metal, an expensive form of imported pewter, in his shop.[13] His estate contained a large variety of hard metal objects:

6 hard metal Dishes weig'd 20.lb @ 11/	£11. –
3 doz: d.o plates @ £7. .10/p doz	22. 10
3 doz: common d.o @ £5.10/	16. 10
3 doz: smaller d.o @ 4.15/	14. 5
12 small handbasons @ 11/each	6. 12
6 milk pots @12/each	3. 12
12 midling porrengers @ 7/each	4. 4
12 smaller d.o @ 6/each	3. 12
9.lb & 14.oz candlemoulds	6. 10
12 doz: hard mett!. spoons @ 18/	10. 16
6 doz: tea spoons @ 8/	2. 8
14 common dishes w.t 35.lb 8.oz at 8/6	15. 1. 9
12 Com.n quart potts @ 15/	9. –
12 Pint d.o @ 10/. 120/. 18 large porrengers 8/£7.4/	13. 4
4 Quart Breakfast Basons 23/	4. 12
4 pint d.o 12/. 48/. 4 ½ pint d.o. 8/4. 1.13.4	. 1. 4
6 Quart hardmett.l Mugs @ 2/3/6	7. 1
pint d.o 15/ £4.10/. 4 pint & ½ Tea Pots 25/ £5	9. 10
4 pint d.o 20/. 80/. 4 ¾ pint d.o 18/. £3.12/	7. 12
4 ½ pint 16/. 64/. 34 Guinea Basons w.t 49.lb 8/.£19.12/	22. 16

Mason's inventory also included a notable number of waiters in brass as well as in silver, which suggests that he specialized in making flat objects and worked in both these metals:

two waiters brass Rim'd @ 20/ 40/.	8.
2 Square hopper Coffee Mills @ 1.12/	3. 4
2 Waiters brass rim'd @ 16/	1. 12
4 d.º plain @ 11/	2. 4
3 d.º @ 10/ is 30/. 2 d.º @ 7/6 is 15/.	2. 5
6 d.º @ 7/. 42/. 2 d.º Silver fashion'd @ 30/	5. 2
2 d.º lesser @ 25/	2.10
6 bottle stands brass rim'd @ 12/	3. 12
6 d.º plain @ 9/ £2.14/1 doz: Varnished d.º @ 8/. 4.16/	7.10
1 Elegearant Tea Chest	7.10
1 d.º Mahogany & Walnut	3.10
18 high top Pepper Boxes @ 4/	3. 12
19 low top d.º @ 3/	2. 17
6 doz: Boxwood tops @ 9/ ℔ doz:	2. 14
4 doz: fine hair Bottoms @ 40/ ℔ doz:	8. –
4 doz: Coarse d.º @ 35/	7. –
18 black hair hatts @ 35/£31.10 1 blew d 60/5 gray d.º	
@ 50/12.10/	47. –
7 Doz: Table Matts @ 12/ ℔ doz:	4. 4
Sund.ʸ Cloath.ᵍ Chamber ℔ utensils &c	122.10. 6
Sund.ʸ Silver Smiths' Tools	55. –
1 Silver Watch exclusive of Repairs	21. –
1 Bible & Watts's leric poems	2. –
5 Stone Girdle Buckles	55. –
Chelsea March 4 1752 Old Tenor	£735. 1. 11

On 19 December 1752, the Reverend William McClenachan of Chelsea and Deacon Henry Prentice of Cambridge, Massachusetts, administrators of the estate of "Mr. Asahel Mason, late of London, Jeweller," placed a notice in the *Boston Gazette* reporting the silversmith's estate as insolvent and requesting creditors to present their claims at the next meeting of the administrators in January 1753. More of Mason's belongings were located aboard the ship *Bumber*; Rev. McClenachan paid the captain's boy for informing him where the sailors had concealed Mason's clothes. The administrators' account was presented on 29 March 1754.[14] After the charges for Mason's funeral and for the administration of his estate were deducted, only £62.10.4 remained, an amount insufficient to meet the demands of his creditors, which totaled £93.5.2.[15] A subsequent account was presented in 1755.[16]

On 26 May 1755, Jemima Mason of the parish of St. Buttolph, Bishopsgate, London, "the only surviving Sister and Heir at Law of Asahel Mason, late of the Province of Massachusetts Bay in New England Jeweller," petitioned the court through Rev. McClenachan to recover the money and property of her brother.[17] No wife or children were mentioned in any of the documents disposing of Mason's estate.

No objects have been attributed to this jeweler. DAF

1. Corporation of London Record Office, City Freedom Papers CF 1/450, June 1725. Robert B. Barker letter to Patricia E. Kane, 9 February 1993.
2. Waxchandlers' Company admissions, MS 9487, Guildhall Library, London. The silver scholar Robert Barker notes that the selection of this company may have been made owing to convenience or cost.
3. Heal (1935) 1972, 202; Grimwade 1976, 593. A goldsmith, Thomas Mason, at the Golden Key on Lombard Street in 1706, may be related to Asahel Mason.

4. E. Alfred Jones in a letter to John Marshall Phillips, 10 September 1938, speculated that Mason left London soon after his bankruptcy, but records of the Waxchandlers' Company suggest this was not the case; Robert B. Barker letter to Patricia E. Kane, 9 February 1993.

5. SCPR 45:641–42.

6. SCCR, Court of Common Pleas Record Book 1744–46, 329–30.

7. SCCR, Court of Common Pleas Record Book 1746–48, 106.

8. Asahel Mason to Thomas Edwards, Bill, January 1747/48–May 1748, Brigden Papers, YU.

9. SCPR, docket 9040.

10. SCD 78:205–06.

11. SCPR 49:224–27.

12. SCPR 47:509–11.

13. Hatcher/Barker 1974, 227–28.

14. SCPR 49:224–27.

15. SCPR 49:225.

16. SCPR 49:943–44.

17. SCPR 53:116–17.

Thomas McCullough
w. ca. 1730–53 +

Little is known about Thomas McCullough, who is referred to variously as Maccollo, Maccello, and Cully. He first appears in the Boston records in 1730 when he married Mary Rose (ca. 1705–39) on 29 July 1730.[1] In 1731/32 he and his wife had a daughter whom they named Margaret. Their second child, Thomas, is recorded in 1733.[2] However, the records of the Brattle Street Church, where Mary and Thomas were members, include references to baptisms for a Thomas on 22 November 1730, Margaret on 2 January 1731/32, another Thomas on 20 January 1733/34, and James on 16 November 1735.[3]

McCullough probably worked throughout his career as a journeyman for Edward Winslow (q.v.). He witnessed a deed for Winslow on 23 May 1734.[4] On Friday, 4 February 1743, Benjamin Walker, a Boston shopkeeper, noted the following in his diary: "In ye Afternoon I was in Mr. Sherif Winslow Shop Tom Cully his Journyman th [torn] Mr. Isaac Winslow came into ye. Shop & askt Tom for a Tub."[5] Edward Winslow's will clearly indicates that McCullough was still working for him in 1748:

> furthermore if my Dear Wife is willing to continue her care of my Granchild Rebecca Winslow I give her the Waiges of Thos Maccollo toward her Support. She my Dear Wife paying sd Maccollo twenty shillings a weke wekely that is to say fifteen shillings by her self and five shillings by Mr Hurd or any other that may imploy him. Allso to pay said Maccollo's House Rent three pounds every quarter of a year and Tenn pounds toward his Wood all in old Tenor Bills or equivalant, and cloath him as there may be occation, and Support him in case of Sickness, all out of sd Maccollos wages or ernings.[6]

This puzzling passage suggests that McCullough was a long-term employee of Winslow, and that sometimes Winslow may have hired McCullough out to work for other goldsmiths, such as Jacob Hurd (q.v.). Winslow apparently expected McCullough to continue to work for his wife, in return for relatively small wages, rent, and the security of knowing that he would be cared for if he became sick. Clearly McCullough's earnings were considerably larger than what Mrs. Winslow was expected to pay him; otherwise his income would not have assisted her in caring for her husband's grandchild. One cannot help wondering why McCullough did not work directly for other silversmiths or for himself when other silversmiths were earning higher wages.

The evidence suggests that McCullough had been left in charge of Winslow's shop for some years, when the duties of the office of sheriff of Suffolk County made it impossible for Winslow to carry on his trade. Evidently, Winslow intended for McCullough to keep the shop going, taking in work from other silversmiths, in order to supplement the work of the shop. Thus, McCullough would continue to keep the shop, and the shop would earn a small profit, even after Winslow's death. The fact that Winslow's will was not changed between 1748 and his death in 1753 suggests that McCullough continued to work for him throughout that period. Whether the arrangement with Mrs. Winslow ever materialized is a matter of conjecture.

No silver marked by Thomas McCullough is known. The possibility exists that the initial marks attributed here to Thomas Milner (q.v.) may have been used by McCullough. BMW

1. RC 28:55.
2. RC 24:204, 213; Whitmore 1878, 80, no. 1490.
3. *Church in Brattle Square*, 153, 154, 156, 158.
4. SCD 48:231–32.
5. Benjamin Walker, Jr., Diaries, miscellaneous leaves 1743, MHS.
6. SCPR, docket 10609.

William Mills
w. ca. 1780

The Boston tax list of 1780 includes a William Mills, goldsmith, in ward 12, but nothing more about this silversmith's identity can be established.[1] Although no one named William Mills was listed in Boston on the Massachusetts tax list of 1771, three men from Boston with this name served in the revolutionary war.[2] According to the Boston city directory of 1796, a William Mills did live on Frog Lane in ward 12, but he was a brass-founder. Since this William Mills worked in a metalsmithing trade allied to goldsmithing, he may have been the goldsmith or perhaps his relative. PEK

1. "Assessors' 'Taking-Books,'" 53.
2. *Mass. Soldiers and Sailors* 10:805.

Thomas Milner or Miller
ca. 1682–1745+

A

B

C

Thomas Milner is mentioned in the will of Richard Conyers (q.v.) in 1708 and was probably the servant above the age of sixteen listed for Conyers in the tax records for 1698.[1] According to Conyers's will, his working tools were to go to his son James in England, if he desired to follow the goldsmithing trade. Until such time as his son needed the tools, however, "Thomas Miller of Boston afores^d Goldsmith" was to have "the Use and improvem^t of all my Working Tools upon his Giveing Security to return ye Same when demanded."[2] Milner, along with John Dixwell (q.v.), was one of the appraisers of the estate of the immigrant goldsmith Henry Hurst (q.v.), and another London-trained silversmith who worked in Boston, Edward Webb (q.v.), left twenty pounds to his "kind friend Thomas Miller" in 1718. These connections led John Marshall Phillips to speculate that Milner, too, came from London. Unfortunately, there is no evidence of his apprenticeship at Goldsmiths' Hall.[3]

In 1703, Thomas Milner was married by the Reverend James Allen of the First Church to Mary Thwing (1686–before 1715), daughter of William (d. 1707/08) and Mary Thwing (d. 1716).[4] The couple had a daughter Mary who died on 19 December 1706.[5] As his second wife, Milner married Mary Reed (b. 1684), daughter of the housewright Obadiah (ca. 1640–1721/22) and Elizabeth (Broughton) Reed (ca. 1640–1712/13) on 20 May 1715; the Reverend Cotton Mather of the Second Church officiated.[6] In 1722, Mary (Reed) Milner inherited a portion of the land owned by her father in Black Horse Lane as well as the shop "her husband now works in" and the house adjoining it.[7] Thomas and Mary had five children: Thomas (b. 11 June 1716); Jane (b. 1 April 1718); Thomas (b. 28 March 1721); Elizabeth (b. 28 December 1722); and Elizabeth (b. 16 July 1725).[8]

Milner joined the New North Church in 1724 and continued to operate his business from his shop on Black Horse Lane in the North End.[9] His house and shop became a matter of controversy in the 1730s when his brothers-in-law tried to sue him and his wife for rental costs. Apparently the portion of Obadiah Reed's estate that he bequeathed to his sons Obadiah and Thomas was under a deed of mortgage at the time of his death, and the brothers were responsible for repaying the loan. Because they were unable to pay right away, the holder of the mortgage, Samuel Turrell, forced them to pay rent on their property. They charged that Milner was responsible for a portion of this rent. However, in court Milner and his wife were able to prove that they had also paid rent to Turrell and that nothing more was due from them. The jury decided in the Milners' favor and awarded them damages.[10] Ultimately, Milner himself had to mortgage the property in 1736 to the shopkeeper Samuel Gardner for £100 and to the schoolmaster Owen Harris for £100 in 1745.[11] Although the mortgage deed between Milner and Harris includes the notation that it was paid off in 1762, there is no indication of whether it was paid by Milner or by his estate.[12] There is no record other than this after 1745 concerning Milner, and no record of his death in Boston.

Milner may have worked in association with Nathaniel Morse and Thomas Bradford (qq.v.) in engraving and printing various bills of credit. In the 1730s Milner was one of several Boston goldsmiths who rendered services to a group of merchants who issued bank notes as part of a private banking scheme. The bank issued its notes in November of 1733; these notes were redeemable in silver and gold in three installments over a period of several years. In connection with the bank, Joshua Winslow, one of the principal "Subscribers to the Scheme for emitting Notes of hand" made a payment of two pounds to Milner on behalf of Nathaniel Morse in 1733. In connection with the printing of the notes, Winslow recorded payments to "Millner & Bradford" in 1733 and 1736 that totaled more than one hundred pounds. It is possible that Milner and Bradford assisted Morse in engraving and printing the plates, but it is also possible that they assisted in weighing and appraising silver objects and coins (as John Burt's [q.v.] "lad" did in 1734), or that they kept objects and coins for safekeeping for the merchants' bank.[13] Milner also worked in association with Morse and Bradford on reissues of the 1713 and 1714 Massachusetts Province bills of credit, and on the new bills issued by the province in 1736/37 and 1737. The committee for bills of credit paid £39.18 to "Milner & Bradford" in May 1735 and £67.4.$^{1}/_{3}$ in July 1738.[14]

Several objects bearing TM marks (a–c) may have been made either by Milner or by his fellow Boston silversmiths Thomas Mullins or Thomas McCullough (qq.v.).[15] Because Mullins seems to have devoted most of his time to attending at funerals and McCullough worked principally as a journeyman for Edward Winslow and other silversmiths with large clienteles, it has been assumed that these objects were made by Milner. Milner's second wife's ancestry in Chelmsford lends credence to the attribution of mark (c) to Milner because it is on a tankard made for the minister of Chelmsford Church, Samson Stoddard. BMW

SURVIVING OBJECTS

	Mark	Inscription	Patron	Date	Reference	Owner
Cup	A*	H/MM (+)	Mathias and Mary Hutchinson (?)	ca. 1720	Buhler/Hood 1970, no. 98	YUAG
Mug	A†	A.P./1808 (later) (+)		ca. 1730	*YUAG Bulletin* 38 (Winter 1982):67	YUAG
Porringer	A*	S/ID		ca. 1730		HMA
Tankard	B†	Eyles (?) arms, on a fess gules a crescent, on a chief 3 fleur-de-lis	Eyles family (?)	ca. 1740	Avery 1920, no. 37	MMA
Tankard	C†	The Gift/of/The late Rev$^{d}_{,,}$/Mr Samson Stoddard . . . (later)	Samson Stoddard	ca. 1715	Jones 1913, 125–26	

1. RC 10:88.
2. SCPR 16:515–16.
3. SCPR 21:141–42, 276–78; Bigelow-Phillips files.
4. RC 28:12; RC 9:171; SCPR 16:383–84, 415; 19:252, 311–13.
5. Boston Deaths, 1700–1800.
6. RC 28:59; RC 9:163; Whitmore 1878, 4, no. 70; 86, no. 1617; Savage 1860–62, 3:515.
7. SCPR 22:480–85; SCCR, Court of Common Pleas Record Book 1725–26, 401.
8. RC 24:115, 130, 151, 156, 171.
9. Records of the New North Church, BPL.
10. SCCR, Court of Common Pleas Record Book 1721, 434; 1725–26, 401; 1726–27, 176, 226; Mass. Archives 17:359–61; SCCR, file 20126.
11. SCD 54:143–44; 71:27–28.
12. SCD 71:28.
13. Joshua Winslow Account Book and Case Book, n.p., NEHGS; Newman 1967, 135.
14. Mass. Archives 101:528, 571.
15. An additional TM rectangle mark found on a beaker (YUAG files), on a cann (MAM), and on a two-handled cup (WM; Quimby 1995, no. 98) has sometimes been attributed to Milner. The style of the engraving (three initials in a row) and the forms of the vessels do not conform to New England practice, however, and therefore the attribution of these pieces to this maker is doubtful.

Samuel Minott
1732–1803

A

B

C

Samuel Minott was born in Concord, Massachusetts, on 23 December 1732, the son of Samuel Minott (1706–66) and Sarah Prescott (d. 1737), who were married in 1731/32.[1] The goldsmith's paternal grandparents were James Minott (1653–1735) and Rebecca Jones (ca. 1666–1734).[2] His maternal grandparents were Jonas Prescott (1678–1750) of Groton, Massachusetts, and Thankful Wheeler (1682–1716) of Concord.[3]

Samuel Minott would have begun his apprenticeship about 1746, probably in Boston. He may have trained with Edward Winslow (q.v.), as Minott obtained three goldsmith's tools from Winslow's estate for four shillings and eight pence in 1753, the year he would have completed his training, and in 1762 he married Winslow's granddaughter, Elizabeth Davis (1738–1823).[4] She was the daughter of William Davis (1686–1746), a physician, and Hannah Winslow (1697/98–1775).[5] It is also possible that Minott trained with William Homes, Sr. In 1753 he witnessed a deed with William Homes, Sr. (q.v.), for the sale of land from Andrew Oliver (q.v.) and his wife, Susannah, to her

D

E

F

brother Daniel Boyer (q.v.).[6] William Simpkins (q.v.) has been suggested as his master, as well, and their marks appear together on a number of pieces. Samuel Minott was working on his own by 1755, when he charged William Brattle, Esq., for silver in a bill, a copy of which is in the Bigelow-Phillips papers:

Boston William Brattle Esq[r] to Samuel Minot D[r]

1755 Octo[r] 21	to a pair of flow[d] Silver knee Buckels		£0 =	8–0	
Novemb[r] 14	to a Silver Strainer w[t] four ounces one pennywight		1 =	7–0	
	to makeing Ditto		0 =	14–8	
	to two Large Silver Spoons w[t] four ounces five penny & a half		1 =	8–6	
	to makeing Ditto		0 =	5 = 4	
decem 2	to a Silver punch Bole w[t] fifteen ounces six grains		5 =	0 = 1	
	to makeing Ditto		0 =	18–0	
			10 =	1 = 7	
	C[r] By 2 Spoons a Silver Cup & a peppercaster		7 =	17 = 2	
	Ballance Due		2 =	4 = 5[7]	

Accounts between Minott and Paul Revere, Jr. (q.v.), suggest that Minott sometimes chose to purchase technically difficult pieces from Revere. On 16 August 1762 Minott bought "two Silver Waiters Chasd" which weighed 22 ounces 18 pennyweights. Revere charged £6 for them, which Minott paid in August by delivering the silver for the salvers, plus cash.[8] On 5 October Minott purchased a "Silver Chased Sugar Dish" weighing 12 ounces 10 pennyweights for £5 and again supplied the silver and cash.[9] Later that month he purchased a "Large Silver Salver."[10]

In a mortgage Minott granted to the widow Miriam Tyler, possibly the relict of Andrew Tyler (q.v.), in 1762 Minott was identified as being a "goldsmith . . . of Boston."[11] The deed was witnessed by Thomas Townsend (q.v.). The Massachusetts tax list of 1771 includes Minott in Boston with three polls, a house and additional building, £22 annual worth of real estate, a servant for life, £308 worth of merchandise, and £6.13.4 money lent at interest.[12] About this time Samuel Bartlett (q.v.) became his apprentice. In 1772 Samuel Minott advertised in the *Boston News-Letter* that he had tea, spices, and groceries for sale as well as silver-mounted swords, coral beads, plate, and jewelry at a shop located opposite William's Court, Cornhill; the advertisement continued, "He carries on the Goldsmiths Business in all its Branches as usual, at his other Shop, Northward of the Draw-Bridge, near the Drum-Maker's."[13]

Minott was a Tory at the time of the Revolution, and the Massachusetts Council ordered his arrest in April 1776.[14] He probably remained in Boston during the war, however, and is listed on the city's tax list of 1780 as being in ward 7 with a poll of one and rents valued at one hundred and fifty pounds.[15] Samuel Davis (1765–1829) recalled Minott as being among the members of the trade during Davis's Boston apprenticeship, which began in 1779.[16]

Following the Revolution, Minott did not advertise again in the Boston newspapers until 1786, but from that year until 1795 he did so annually. The types of wares he advertised during this period varied only slightly from those appearing in his initial advertisement in the *Independent Chronicle* of 8 June 1786:

Samuel Minot,
Has for Sale, at his Shop Northward of the Draw-Bridge,

PLATED, pinchbeck, black & metal
Buckles,
Paste Shoe, knee, stock and breeches Buckles,
Paste and garnet Earings, Rings, Breast-Pins, Broaches
    and Sliders,
Paste Sprigs and Hat Pins,
Lockets, Seals, Watch Keys, steal and gilt Chains,
Cypher'd, gilt and common Sleeve Buttons,
Steel-Top Thimbles, cypher Button-Stones, Ruby Foil,
Miniature Crystals, Tooth-Pick and Pencil Cases,
Coral and Bells, Coral Beads, Temple Spectacles,
Cork Screws, Penknives, Rasors, Scissars,
Paintings on Glass, and a Variety of Trinkets Also,
An Assortment of silver & gold Ware.[17]

Whereas Minott probably imported most of the paste jewelry and other small items from England, the additional gold- and silverware was probably of his own manufacture or was purchased from local silversmiths for resale. For instance, between 1796 and 1800 Minott purchased gold beads from the Ipswich silversmith Daniel Rogers (q.v.).[18]

Minott's activities as both an importer and a goldsmith are suggested further by his purchase in 1786 of 232 ounces 5 pennyweights of old plate from the estate of David Jeffries at the cost of 6 shillings per ounce and in 1787 of another 67 ounces 15 pennyweights from the same source.[19] In 1786 he again had Paul Revere, Jr., make silver for him, for Revere's account books show that Minott was credited on 2 March for 32 ounces 17 pennyweights of silver to make a tankard.[20] In the *Boston Directory* of 1789 Minott is listed as a "goldsmith and importer of plated and jewelery-ware Ann-street."[21] The directory of 1796 lists him as a goldsmith on Ann-street, but with a house on Court Street, and similar listings appear in the directories for 1798, 1800, and 1803.[22]

Administration of the estate of Samuel Minott, "late of Boston, jeweller," was granted on 10 October 1803 to his widow, Elizabeth. The inventory, amounting to $837.10, was appraised by Samuel Belknap (q.v.), Stephen Howe, and Azor G. Archbold and included extensive stock and goldsmith's tools:

1 lot buckles	$20.
1 " Spoons &c	15
1 " Sundries	15
2 small boxes of sundries	4.
1 " trinkets	4.
1 box files &c.	5.
1 " trinkets	2.
1 trunk Spectacles &c	15
1 small box knee buckles &c	3.
1 lot seales &c	3.
1 " Kneebuckles &c	10
3 waiters	2.
1 small box	5.
1 trunk lockets &c	75
1 small trunk do.	10
1 Do kneebuckles.	30
1 Chest sundries	8.

2 lot gold rings	40
1 " silver trinkets	10
1 Gold Necklaces &c	12.
2 pair sugar tongs	4
10 large Spoons	20.
24 tea do	16
1 caryol and bells	3.
1 Silver Watch	10.
1 lot crucibleys	20.
7 " scales & weights	8
1 " goldsmiths tools	75.
5 Glass cases	3.
Pew Nº 17 in Brattle Street Meeting-house	120 [23]

Minott's marks are found on pieces that also bear the marks of Josiah Austin, Samuel Bartlett, Paul Revere, Jr., William Homes, Jr., and Thomas Townsend, in addition to those of William Simpkins (qq.v.), which indicates that Minott routinely retailed silver made by others. Approximately 170 pieces by Minott survive, making him one of the principal retailers of silver in Boston in the late colonial period along with Paul Revere, Jr., and Benjamin Burt (q.v.). Minott used a single initial mark (A) usually in conjunction with his surname mark (B). Four initials marks (C–F) can also be attributed to him. Mark (D) appears on pieces made earlier in his career. As Belden has noted, silver bearing his mark (C) has been incorrectly attributed to Silas Merriman of Cheshire and New Haven, Connecticut.[24] Spurious examples of the initials marks exist.[25] PEK

SURVIVING OBJECTS

	Mark	Inscription	Patron	Date	Reference	Owner
Baptismal basin	B	Pepperrell arms, a chevron gules between 3 pineapples, on a canton a fleur-de-lis, on an escutcheon a dexter hand; The Gift of the Honᵇˡᵉ Sir WILLIAM PEPPERRELL Baronet, Lieuᵗ General of his Majesty's Forces, & of the Province of the Massachusetts, &c. &c. to the first Church in KITTERY.	First Congregational Church, Kittery, Maine, for William Pepperrell	ca. 1759	Jones 1913, 236–37	
Beaker	A/B	Given for the/Service of the/Holy Communion/To Christ Church in Braintree/By Caesar/Servᵗ to E. Miller Esqʳ/A.D./1770	Caesar, servant to Ebenezer Miller, and/or Christ Church, Quincy, Mass.	ca. 1770	Jones 1913, 399	

	Mark	Inscription	Patron	Date	Reference	Owner
Beaker (with mark of William Simpkins)	B	The Gift of Mrs. Susannah Dean/to the Church of Christ in Bedford	Susanna Dean and/or First Parish, Bedford, Mass.	ca. 1770	YUAG files	
Beaker	B	The Gift of Capt./ Samuel Bucking-ham/to the 2.ᵈ Church/In Leba-non/1756	Congregational Church, Columbia, Conn., for Samuel Buckingham	1756	Jones 1913, 132	
Six beakers (part of a service)	C	D/DH/Gift	David and Hannah Day	ca. 1770	Jones 1913, 484–85	CHS
Beaker	D*	The Gift of Miss Abigail Parker/to the Church of Christ in Newton/ 1768	First Church, Newton, Mass., for Abigail Parker	1768	Jones 1913, 324	MFAB
Cann	A*/ B*	RH (+)		ca. 1760	Buhler/Hood 1970, no. 231	YUAG
Cann	A/B	H/EE		ca. 1760	YUAG files	
Cann	A/B	M. Thompson (later)		ca. 1765	Avery 1920, no. 123	MMA
Cann (mate below)	A/B	HARVARDINATIBUS/ Anno Domini MDCCLXX initiatis/ Tertium sub ejus tu-tela annum agenti-bus, Hoc poculum acceptum/Refert JOSEPHUS WILLARD.	Joseph Willard and/or the Harvard College class of 1770	1770	Buhler 1972, no. 323	MFAB
Cann (mate above)	A*/ B*	HARVARDINATIBUS/ Anno Domini MDCCLXX initiatis/ Tertium sub ejus tu-tela annum agenti-bus, Hoc poculum acceptum/Refert JOSEPHUS WILLARD.	Joseph Willard and/or the Harvard College class of 1770	1770	Buhler/Hood 1970, no. 232	YUAG
Cann	A/B	unidentified initials		ca. 1770	Sotheby Parke Bernet, 20–23 June 1979, lot 143A	
Cann	B	ES/1755		1755	*Antiques* 90 (October 1966): 423	
Cann	B*	ED; E DAY (+)	Elizabeth (Day) Dodge (?)	ca. 1755	Buhler 1965, 90–92	HMA
Cann	B	JO/to/W/JM	James Otis	ca. 1754	*Sack Collection* 2: no. 1328	
Cann	B	Ex Dono Pu-pillorum, qui/Ad-missi Sunt/Anno Domini/1758	William Kneeland and/ or the Harvard College class of 1758	1758	*Silver Supple-ment* 1973, no. 66	

	Mark	Inscription	Patron	Date	Reference	Owner
Cann	B*	B/IA; unidentified arms (later) (+)		ca. 1770	DAPC 69.1771	MMA
Cann	B*	later engraving erased		ca. 1760	Johnston 1994, 109	CMA
Cann	B*	LW		ca. 1770	YUAG files	
Cann	B*	EM		ca. 1770	DAPC 89.3036	
Cann	B*	EW		ca. 1765		LAM
Cann	B*	Williams arms, a lion rampant, and crest, a moorcock; EW to EW	E. Williams (?)	ca. 1765	Flynt/Fales 1968, 54	HD
Cann	B	The Gift of/The Honble: Thomas Berry Esqr./to ye South Church in Ipswich	South Church, Ipswich, Mass., for Thomas Berry	ca. 1756	Jones 1913, 229	
Cann	B	Revd. E. Turrell to T. Tufts	Rev. Ebenezer Turell	ca. 1765	Parke-Bernet, 14–15 May 1948, lot 187	
Cann	B*	The Gift of John Appleton/to/the South Church in Ipswich	South Church, Ipswich, Mass., for John Appleton	after 1767	Buhler/Hood 1970, no. 230	
Cann	B	T/IF	Jonathan and Faith (Robinson) Trumbull	ca. 1770		CHS
Caster	A	H/SL		ca. 1760	*Silver Supplement* 1973, no. 68	
Caster	A	?		ca. 1770	National Art Galleries, 3–5 December, lot 211	
Caster	A/B	C/DM		ca. 1765	Christie's, 22–23 January 1993, lot 218	
Caster	A/B	K/WM		ca. 1766	YUAG files	
Caster	B	PG Esqr/to/DT		ca. 1770	Buhler 1972, no. 547	MFAB
Caster	B*	SP/to/ISP (+)		ca. 1790		MMA
Caster	C	B/IP		ca. 1760	Washington 1925, no. 69	MWPI
Caster	C, D, or E	H/BH		ca. 1770	MFA 1911, no. 737	
Caster	D*	DV/RV	Daniel and Rachel Vose	ca. 1765	DAPC 75.3124	
Caster	F	PM		ca. 1770	Parke-Bernet, 11 February 1970, lot 179	
Caster	?	IF/LF		ca. 1765	Norman-Wilcox 1962, no. 33	
Caster	?	WDB (later)		ca. 1770	Christie's, 26 January 1985, lot 81	

	Mark	Inscription	Patron	Date	Reference	Owner
Coffeepot	A†/ B†	IF		ca. 1765	Buhler/Hood 1970, no. 233	YUAG
Communion dish (mates below)	B	Hancock arms, gules a dexter hand couped, on a chief argent 3 cocks, and crest, a demi-griffin; The Gift of the Honble; THOMAS HANCOCK ESQ^R; to the CHURCH in Brattle Street Boston 1764	Brattle Street Church, Boston, for Thomas Hancock	1764	Safford 1983, 46	MMA
Communion dish (mates above and below)	B	Hancock arms, gules a dexter hand couped, on a chief argent 3 cocks, and crest, a demi-griffin; The Gift of the Honble; THOMAS HANCOCK ESQ^R; to the CHURCH in Brattle Street Boston 1764	Brattle Street Church, Boston, for Thomas Hancock	1764	Buhler 1979, no. 47	WAM
Communion dish (mates above)	B	Hancock arms, gules a dexter hand couped, on a chief argent 3 cocks, and crest, a demi-griffin; The Gift of the Honble; THOMAS HANCOCK ESQ^R; to the CHURCH in Brattle Street Boston 1764	Brattle Street Church, Boston, for Thomas Hancock	1764	Buhler 1972, no. 321	MFAB
Creampot	A/B	R/WS		ca. 1770	National Art Galleries, 3–5 December 1931, lot 224	
Creampot	B	B/IA		ca. 1770	*Antiques* 107 (March 1975): 418	
Creampot	B	BMH; EH/to/EHH		ca. 1755	*Moore Collection* 1980, no. 154	
Creampot	B	GPH		ca. 1760	Christie's, 18 October 1986, lot 84	
Creampot	B*	IH/to/MH; Born may 24th/1789		1789	Buhler 1965, 89–90, 92–95	HMA
Two flagons (part of a service)	A/B	The Gift of/David & Hannah Day/to the 2.^d Church of Christ/IN/COLCHESTER	David and Hannah Day and/or Congregational Church, Westchester Parish, Colchester, Conn.	ca. 1770	Jones 1913, 484	CHS

	Mark	Inscription	Patron	Date	Reference	Owner
Flagon	B	Simpson arms, on a chief vert 3 crescents, and crest, a bird rising; The Gift/of Mr John Simpson of/Boston Merchant, to the South Church/in said Town; who died at sea July 12th:/1764 on his Return to his native land	Old South Church, Boston, for John Simpson	ca. 1764	Jones 1913, 56	
Flagon	B	The Gift of/Mr Benjamin Barker/ to the first Church of/Christ in/Andover/1765	Benjamin Barker for North Parish of North Andover, North Andover, Mass.	1765	Jones 1913, 346	
Two flagons	B	The gift/of the late/ Thos. Wibird Esqr/ to the First Church of Christ/Portsmouth New Hampshire/of which he was a pious and worthy member/ who departed this life/12 of November/1765/in the 59 year of his age/The making paid by the church/Decr 1770	North Church (First Church of Christ, Congregational), Portsmouth, N.H., for Thomas Wibird	1770	Jones 1913, 379	
Mourning ring (gold)	D	F. Brattle.ob 10.July.1754. 11 years	F. Brattle	1754	Buhler 1972, no. 320	MFAB
Mug	B	The gift of Mr/Edward Richardson/to the baptist/Church/ in/boston.	Baptist Church, Boston, for Edward Richardson	ca. 1760	Jones 1913, 46	
Porringer	A/B	ED/to/RD (E over earlier R?)	Elizabeth (Day) Dodge (?)	ca. 1770	Buhler 1965, 95–96	HMA
Porringer	B*	M/IA		ca. 1765	Sotheby's, 27 January 1989, lot 912	
Two porringers (mate below)	B	unidentified crest, a wyvern with an arrow in its beak; I/DI	Jennings family (?)	ca. 1770	YUAG files	
Porringer (mates above)	B*	unidentified crest, a wyvern with an arrow in its beak; I/DI	Jennings family (?)	ca. 1770	Warren 1975, no. 298	BBC
Porringer	B*	WL/A/HP		ca. 1770	Eitner 1976, no. 59	
Porringer	B*	W/TE (altered to H/WM)		ca. 1770	Flynt/Fales 1968, 99	HD

	Mark	Inscription	Patron	Date	Reference	Owner
Porringer	B	S/MS		ca. 1775	*Antiques* 120 (July 1981): 92	
Porringer (with mark of William Simpkins)	B	IP/to/PC		ca. 1765	DAPC 65.4298	Rosenbach Foundation
Porringer (with mark of Thomas Townsend)	B	The gift of/Jotham Gay/to/Mary Gay	Jotham Gay and/or Mary Gay	ca. 1730	Buhler 1965, 49–51	
Porringer	?	HC (?)		ca. 1785	*Antiques* 37 (June 1940): 269	
Porringer	?	P/AA; JP (later)		ca. 1770	Christie's, 26 January 1985, lot 77	
Salt	B	SS	Sarah (Smith) Brown	ca. 1760	Gourley 1965, no. 136	
Two salts	B*	I/SS	Samuel and Susannah (Hawthorne) Ingersoll	ca. 1772	Flynt/Fales 1968, 132–34	HD
Two salts	B	Ex Dono Pupillorum qui/Admissi Sunt Anno Domini/1758	William Kneeland and/ or the Harvard College class of 1758	1758	*Silver Supplement* 1973, nos. 67a–b	
Two salts	B	WCR (+)		ca. 1770	Jones 1936, 87, 89	
Salt spoon	B*	unidentified crest, a bird rising		ca. 1775		YUAG
Strainer (with mark of William Homes, Sr.)	B	none		ca. 1770	Hammerslough/ Feigenbaum 1958–73, 3:92–93	
Strainer	B/E	none		ca. 1775	National Art Galleries, 3–5 December 1931, lot 238	AMB
Strainer (with mark of Samuel Bartlett)	D*	none		ca. 1790	*Silver Supplement* 1973, no. 80	CM
Sugar tongs	C, D, or E	E Day	Elizabeth (Day) Dodge (?)	ca. 1775	Buhler 1965, 92–93	HMA
Four tablespoons	B*	I/DF		ca. 1760		YUAG
Tablespoon	B*	MW		ca. 1765	DAPC 72.1301	WM
Four tablespoons	C*	RW	Rebecca (Woolsey) Hillhouse	ca. 1782	Buhler/Hood 1970, no. 365 (as Silas Merriman)	YUAG
Tablespoon	C*	F/IE		ca. 1770	DAPC 75.3227	WM
Five tablespoons	C*	Simpson crest, a bird rising	Simpson family	ca. 1785		YUAG

	Mark	Inscription	Patron	Date	Reference	Owner
Two tablespoons	c*	B/IA		ca. 1785	Buhler/Hood 1970, no. 366 (as Silas Merriman)	YUAG
Tablespoon	c*	B/NA		ca. 1785		YUAG
Four tablespoons	c†	ED/to/IB		ca. 1785	Buhler/Hood 1970, no. 366 (as Silas Merriman)	YUAG
Tablespoon	c, d, or e	Chandler crest	Chandler family	ca. 1770	MFA 1911, no. 741	
Tablespoon	d*	PSCC		ca. 1790	DAPC 71.3408	WM
Tablespoon	f†	DW		ca. 1765	DAPC 71.3414	WM
Tablespoon	?	?		ca. 1775		ChM
Tankard	a*/b*	The Gift/of/Deacon SAMUEL SEABURY/to the Church of Christ/in/DUXBOROUGH	Samuel Seabury and/or First Congregational Church, Duxbury, Mass.	ca. 1762	Jones 1913, 156	
Tankard	a/b	1769 (+)	Edward Augustus Holyoke	1769	Jones 1913, 434–35	
Tankard	a*/b*	MB; C.G.W. (later)		ca. 1770	YUAG files	
Tankard	a/b	HARVARDINATIBUS/Anno Domini MDCCLXX initiatis/Tertium sub ejus tutela annum agentibus, Hoc poculum acceptum/Refert Josephus WILLARD.; (on the bottom) Josephus Willard/Coll: Harv: tutor/Cal: Septembris electus fuit/Anno MDCCLXVI.	Joseph Willard and/or the Harvard College class of 1770	1770	Buhler 1972, no. 322	MFAB
Tankard	a*/b*	Tuckerman arms, vert on a bend engrailed between 3 arrows 3 hearts vert, and crest, a heart gules issuing from a ducal coronet, impaling unidentified arms, gules 3 crescents	Edward Tuckerman	ca. 1775	Flynt/Fales 1968, 134–35	HD
Tankard	b	Cary and Solly arms	Cary and Solly families	ca. 1770	YUAG files	
Tankard	b	WB/1772		1772	*Antiques* 117 (January 1980): 114	
Tankard	b	AH		ca. 1770	YUAG files	

	Mark	Inscription	Patron	Date	Reference	Owner
Tankard (with mark of Josiah Austin)	B	The Gift of/Deacon John Stone to the/ Church of Christ in Newton/1768	John Stone and/or First Church, Newton, Mass.	1768	Jones 1913, 323	MFAB
Tankard	B	The Gift of/ M^r:Edward Devotion/to the church in Brooklin/1744	First Parish, Brookline, Mass., for Edward Devotion	ca. 1765	Jones 1913, 100–01	
Tankard (with mark of William Simpkins)	B	The Gift of/Mrs Sarah Adams; (Relict/of Mr Edward Adams late of/Milton) to the first Church in/Braintree	Sarah (Brackett) Adams and/or First Congregational Society (Unitarian), Quincy, Mass.	ca. 1760	Jones 1913, 397	
Tankard	B	SA/SA (+)	Samuel and Sarah Abbot	ca. 1790	*Silver Supplement* 1973, no. 69	
Tankard	B*	EHD; Richard: Derby to E:S Haskit Derby/1763 (+)	Richard Derby	1763	Watkins 1957, 144	SI
Two tankards (with mark of William Simpkins)	B	This Tankard is the Property/of the Church of Christ in Milton/and was purchased with part/of its Stock February 15th 1770	First Congregational Parish, Milton, Mass.	1770	Jones 1913, 292	
Tankard (with mark of Josiah Austin)	B	Watertown Church (later; defaced)		ca. 1770	Jones 1913, 482	
Tankard	B*	Bulkley arms, sable a chevron or between 3 bulls' heads cabossed, and crest, a bull's head rising from a ducal crown; Hubbard/IR	Bulkley or Hubbard family	ca. 1770	Puig et al. 1989, no. 218	MIA
Tankard	B*	R/AR		ca. 1770	*Antiques* 97 (January 1970): 6	
Tankard	B	Moulton arms, 3 bars between 8 escallops sable, 3, 2, 2, 1, and crest, on a pellet a falcon rising	Moulton family	ca. 1770		MHS
Tankard	B*	?		ca. 1775	*Antiques* 92 (December 1967): 759	
Tankard	B	H/TM		ca. 1760	Wardwell 1966, 82–83	
Tankard (with mark of Paul Revere, Jr.)	B*	JCY		ca. 1785		LAM
Tankard	B	SWG (later?)		ca. 1785	Skinner, 31 May–1 June 1984, lot 534	

	Mark	Inscription	Patron	Date	Reference	Owner
Tankard	B*/ D†	PH; EB/to/PH		ca. 1760	Gourley 1965, no. 137	RISD
Tankard	?	Smith arms; BS to SS	Benjamin Smith for Sarah (Smith) Brown	ca. 1760	*Antiques* 104 (December 1973): 998	RIHS
Tankard	?	AP; LWG		ca. 1764	Skinner, 12 January 1991, lot 172	
Tankard	?	S/NL	Nathaniel and Lydia (Merriam) Sherman	ca. 1765	YUAG files	
Tankard	?	?	Second Church, North Beverly, Mass.	?	YUAG files	
Teapot	B	Smith (?) arms, a rampant lion crowned over 5 bars ermine, and crest, a unicorn's head erased; SS	Sarah (Smith) Brown (?)	ca. 1760	YUAG files	
Teapot	B	A decem Gratis/ Suum accepit Fides/ 1763	William Kneeland and/ or the Harvard College class of 1763	1763	Buhler 1955, 57	HU
Teapot	B	Hancock arms; Ex Dono Hon. di Dom. ni homas Hancock Armigeri		ca. 1760		MFAB
Teaspoon	C	AN		ca. 1770	DAPC 73.2432	WM
Teaspoon	C*	BF		ca. 1770	DAPC 88.3485	
Teaspoon (see also unmarked mate?)	C*	MW		ca. 1775		SI
Teaspoon	C	unidentified crest, a stag's head erased		ca. 1775		NHCHS
Two teaspoons	C	Simpson crest, a bird rising		ca. 1795	*New Haven Silversmiths*, no. 46 (as Silas Merriman)	NHCHS
Teaspoon	C	?C (partially erased)		ca. 1765	DAPC 74.2011	WM
Teaspoon	C*	SEM		ca. 1785		HD
Teaspoon	C*	WS		ca. 1760		SFCAI
Two teaspoons	C	?		ca. 1775		MWPI
Two teaspoons	C, D, E, or F	DCL		ca. 1775	MFA 1911, no. 739	
Teaspoon	C, D, E, or F	Leverett crest	Leverett family	ca. 1770	MFA 1911, no. 740	
Nine teaspoons	C, D, or E	ESH		ca. 1775	Christie's, 22 January 1993, lot 102 (as Silas Merriman)	

	Mark	Inscription	Patron	Date	Reference	Owner
Two teaspoons	D*	MP		ca. 1760		YUAG
Teaspoon	D*	SM		ca. 1765	Eitner 1976, no. 60	
Teaspoon	D*	MS		ca. 1770	YUAG files	
Teaspoon	D	MH		ca. 1760	Buhler 1972, appendix no. 56	MFAB
Teaspoon	E†	EC		ca. 1760		HD
Teaspoon	E*	IC		ca. 1760		HD
Teaspoon	F*	IG		ca. 1775	DAPC 73.2429	WM
Three teaspoons	F	S	Salisbury family	ca. 1775	DAPC 74.2182	WAM
Four teaspoons	F*	O/IA		ca. 1765		PEM
Teaspoon	?	DP		ca. 1775		SCFAI
Teaspoon (*see also mate? with mark* C; *attrib.*)	none	MW		ca. 1775		SI
Two-handled cup	B	The gift/of Isaac Stone/to ye church of/Christ in/Lexing-ton/1763.	Isaac Stone and/or First Congregational Society, Lexington, Mass.	ca. 1763	Jones 1913, 248	
Two-handled cup	C	The Bequest/of Mʳˢ JANE TURELL/to the first Church of/Christ in/KITTERY.	First Congregational Church, Kittery, Maine, for Jane Turell	ca. 1765	Jones 1913, 238	

1. *Concord VR*, 65, 124, 133, 433. Following his wife's death Samuel Minott, Sr., married her sister Dorcas, who died in 1803.
2. James and Rebecca Minott's birth dates were calculated from their ages at the time of death. *Concord VR*, 27, 128, 432.
3. *Groton VR* 1:139, 191; 2:257; *Concord VR*, 25, 50.
4. SCPR, docket 10609, executor's account.
5. RC 9:168, 234; RC 28:57; RC 30:327; *Church in Brattle Square*, 251, 288; Benjamin Walker, Jr., Diaries, MHS; *Index of Obituaries, 1704–1800*, 2:288.
6. SCD 82:52–53.
7. A copy of the bill is in the Bigelow-Phillips files with the notation "Boston Antique Shop." The present whereabouts of the bill are unknown.
8. 16 August 1762, vol. 1, Waste and Memoranda Book, 1761–83, [11], Revere Family Papers, MHS.
9. 5 October 1762, vol. 1, Waste and Memoranda Book, 1761–83, [12], Revere Family Papers, MHS.
10. 29 October 1762, vol. 1, Waste and Memoranda Book, 1761–83, [13], Revere Family Papers, MHS.
11. SCD 98:39–40.
12. Pruitt 1978, 20–21.
13. *Boston News-Letter*, 1, 8, 15 October 1772.
14. Sabine 1864, 2:84; Jones 1930, 316.
15. "Assessors' 'Taking-Books,'" 32.
16. Steinway 1960, 7.
17. The subsequent advertisements appeared in the *Independent Chronicle*, 11, 18, 25 January 1787; 26 July and 2, 16 August 1787; 3, 10, 17 July 1788; 4, 11, 18 December 1788; 2, 9, 30 July 1789; 19, 29 November, 3 December 1789; 6, 13, 20 May 1790; 7, 14, 21 October 1790; 2, 9, 16 December 1790; 27 October, 3, 10 November 1791; 31 May, 7, 14 June 1792; 15, 22 November, 6, 13 December 1792; 31 October, 8, 21, 25, 28 November 1793; 19, 26 October, 2 November 1795; *Columbian Centinel* 10, 24 December 1794.
18. Daniel Rogers Account Book, PEM.

19. SCPR 88:100.

20. 2 March 1786, vol. 2, Waste Book, 1783–97, 38, Revere Family Papers, MHS.

21. RC 10:193.

22. RC 10:269; *Boston Directory* 1798, 83; 1800, 78; 1803, 89.

23. SCPR 101:569, 577–79.

24. Belden 1980, 298–99; see, for instance, Buhler/Hood 1970, nos. 365–66.

25. See a spoon at CMA (Johnston 1994, 104). Related marks are on a tankard at RISD (21.256) and a pepper pot at MFAB (Buhler 1972, no. 483, as Silas Merriman).

Jacob Morse
1751–1819

Jacob Morse was born in Hampstead, New Hampshire, on 31 March 1751, the son of Lt. Edmund Morse (1726–1816) of Newbury, Massachusetts, and Rachel Rowell (1725/26–63) of Amesbury, Massachusetts, who were married on 26 April 1750.[1] His paternal grandparents were Peter Morse (b. 1701) and Thomasine Hale (b. 1700), who were both born in Newbury but settled in Hampstead, New Hampshire, sometime after the birth of Edmund.[2] Jacob's maternal grandparents were Philip Rowell (b. ca. 1682) and Sarah Davis (b. 1685), both of Newbury.[3]

The Morse family's strong connections to Newbury suggest that Jacob Morse was apprenticed in his family's ancestral town to one of the many silversmiths active there in the mid-1760s. He may also have trained with William Moulton (q.v.) who purchased land in Hampstead in 1762. Morse's apprenticeship would have been completed by 1772. Where he lived then or in 1776, when, at the age of twenty-five, he probably served in the Revolution, is unknown.[4] He was in Westfield, Massachusetts, by November 1779, when his intentions to marry Naomi Sikes (1759–1802) of Springfield, Massachusetts, were published; they were married in Springfield on 9 December 1779.[5] She was the daughter of Capt. James Sikes (1719–95) of Springfield and Dinah Hitchcock (ca. 1719–61), possibly of Colchester, Connecticut, who were married in Springfield on 24 April 1752.[6] Ten children were born in Westfield to Jacob and Naomi Morse.[7] Their son James (1784–1828) was later a silversmith in Westfield.[8] James's son, James Harvey, who was born in 1829, may be the same man cited as being an engraver of Westfield.[9]

Jacob Morse first purchased land in Westfield in 1781. In all eight deeds transacted by Morse between 1781 and 1804 he was listed as a goldsmith of Westfield.[10] During these years, Morse accumulated small lots of land around Westfield's town green, land that appreciated in value over time and was sold by him later in life.[11]

Morse's second wife was Mehitable Williams (1761–1850) of Wethersfield, Connecticut, whom he married on 26 February 1805.[12] She was the daughter of Deacon and Capt. Elisha Williams (1718–84), a representative to the Connecticut General Assembly, and Mehitable Burnham (1720–1809), who were both of Wethersfield and married there on 24 August 1749.[13]

At his death in Westfield on 6 December 1819 at the age of sixty-eight, Jacob Morse possessed a comfortable estate.[14] His inventory of 1819 reveals scattered possessions of silver, including spoons, sugar tongs, and "old silver." Morse also owned farming tools and a number of books on geography, grammar, religion, and history. Four French watches, watch trinkets, one old clock case, and one clock and case along with a clock "enjoin," or engine, a mechanism for fashioning clock gears, prove that Morse was making clocks and possibly watches near the end of his life, if not earlier. Because no silversmithing tools were found in his inventory, it is likely that sometime before his death Morse had handed them down to his son James. His real estate included seventeen acres of land, on which stood his dwelling house, shed, shop, and barn.[15]

No mark has been identified for Jacob Morse. The J·MORSE mark, often attributed to Jacob Morse's grandson James Harvey Morse, was probably used by Jacob's son James Morse.[16] JJF

1. *Newbury VR* 1:342; "Hampstead VR," 58, 105, 183; *Amesbury VR*, 207; RCPR, docket 9419, old series.
2. *Newbury VR* 1:212, 345; 2:219, 345.
3. *Newbury VR* 1:317; *Amesbury VR*, 334, 464.
4. Jacob Morses of Douglas, Uxbridge, and Princeton are listed in *Mass. Soldiers and Sailors* 11:94–95, 127, which could suggest Morse's westward movement. See also Hammond 1887, 2:634, 649, 731; 3:16, 25, 102, 186, 211, 221, 278, 503, 617. Hammond 1887, 3:503, 617, notes the presence of a Jacob Morse in Deerfield, New Hampshire, home ca. 1800 to Newbury-born Stephen Morse (q.v.).
5. Warren 1934–35, 2:497; Lewis 1938, 13, 65; Morse/Leavitt 1903, 263–64.
6. Lewis 1938, 45, 54; Warren 1934–35, 1:347, 606, 608.
7. Clarissa (1782), James (1784), Betsey (1786), Harvey (1788), Henry (1790), Edmund (1792), Edmund (1794), Theodore (1796), Theodore (1797), Mary (1799); see "Public Records of the Church of Christ at Westfield," n.p., n.d., typescript, 239, NEHGS.
8. Flynt/Fales 1968, 279.
9. "Public Records of the Church of Christ at Westfield," n.p., n.d., typescript, 239, NEHGS; Flynt/Fales 1968, 279; Groce/Wallace 1957, 456.
10. HCD 18:302–03; 22:349; 25:76; 34:66; 36:89; 42:261; 44:175.
11. HCD 57:288; 59:632; 60:180; 65:36. Morse was also listed as a Westfield resident in the Massachusetts censuses of 1790, 1800, and 1810.
12. Wethersfield VR, 299; Tillotson 1899, 94.
13. Stiles 1904, 2:806.
14. "Westfield Deaths," 392.
15. HCPR, docket 8021.
16. Flynt/Fales 1968, 279; Buhler/Hood 1970, nos. 313–18.

Nathaniel Morse
ca. 1688–1748

A

B

C

D

The absence of a birth record for the silversmith Nathaniel Morse in Massachusetts leaves his parentage unknown. Because he cowitnessed a deed with Benjamin Hiller for John Coney (qq.v.) in 1709, he probably trained in Coney's shop.[1] On 9 March 1709/10 he married Sarah Draper (1690–1775), the daughter of Sarah Kilby and Richard Draper (d. 1728).[2] Through his mother-in-law Morse was linked by kinship to a number of Boston goldsmiths, including John Allen, William Cowell, Sr., William Simpkins, and Andrew Tyler (qq.v.).[3] Morse worshiped and had his children baptized at the Brattle Street Church, for which he made one of his earliest works, a flagon dated 1711.[4] Morse began training John Banks (q.v.) starting about 1710, but Banks's mother was unhappy with the training and brought a grievance to court in 1712. Although the court ordered Banks to return to his master, Banks may have completed his training with Edward Winslow (q.v.).[5] Between 1722 and 1744 Nathaniel Morse was the defendant in more than thirty suits in the Suffolk County Court of Common Pleas, many involving his failure to pay debts for rent, supplies, food, and clothing. These cases suggest that Morse struggled to make a living throughout most of his career. In 1722 the Boston merchant Samuel Banister sued him for a debt of £88.14. Morse defaulted, and Bannister was allowed to recover £18.10.[6] Another Boston merchant, John Marshall, brought suit in 1724 for Morse's failure to pay a debt of £11.[7] The Boston shopkeepers Thomas Boylston and Bryan Toole sued him in 1725 for the £16 and the £2.11.1 that Morse respectively owed them.[8] That year Morse was also sued for failing to

E

F

G

pay rent on a brick tenement in King Street for a two-year period beginning 1 January 1723.[9] The Boston tailor John Matthews sued him in 1725 for failure to pay for his wife's clothes.[10] Eliezer Moody's action to retrieve a debt of £7.10 was dismissed in 1725 because Moody was deceased.[11] Additional suits for nonpayment of debts followed between 1733 and 1744.[12]

A few of the suits involved Morse's professional shortcomings as a silversmith, such as his inability to fill clients' orders and pay his suppliers. In 1724 the Boston mariner Thomas Taylor sued Morse for the silversmith's failure to make a pair of silver canns from a silver salver and to return the salver to Taylor.[13] In March 1724 Morse received five ounces and fourteen pennyweights of silver to make a tankard lid, and more than a year later he acknowledged that he had not yet made it.[14] The Dedham husbandman Eliphalet Chickering sued Morse for not paying for a load of charcoal, which Morse would have used in his forge.[15] In 1737 Morse was sued by John Potwine (q.v.), who was then living in Hartford, Connecticut.[16]

Some of the cases reveal how Morse exchanged products from his shop for goods and services. The account that brought him to court with Thomas Moffatt in 1735 is one example:

D^r M [torn] Nath: Mors		C^r	
1724	1727		
To his N^t of hand	27.. 10..—	by 2 poringers made	2.. 4.. –
To had out of goods I			
p^d. for	1.. 16.. 8	by mending a Sword	0. 5..
To 2^{oz} Silver	2.. 15.. –	By a p^r Gold Studs	2. 16. 3
	32.. 1.. 8	by an Issue Plate	. 16. –
	10.. 14.. 3	By a p^r Ear Rings	4. —. –
Ball^n due to Plt	21.. 7.. 5	by a p^r. Silver Hookes	7. –
Boston Jan^{ey}.6..1735		by mending Stone Ring	6. –
			10. 14. 3

Errors Excepted Thos Moffatt[17]

In another case, Morse and Thomas Edwards (q.v.) were sued jointly by the pewterer Samuel Carter in 1729 for not paying £25 each on a bond in 1727. The sheriff attached Thomas Edwards's house and a table in Morse's dwelling.[18] But in at least one of Morse's appearances in court he was not a defendant. With Edward Winslow he testified in 1723 that the tools of Daniel Légaré (q.v.) were not sufficient for him to practice his trade.[19]

Morse did not serve in public office. In 1720, however, he did act as one of the commissioners appointed to oversee the insolvent estate of the watchmaker Thomas Badley (q.v. Appendix A).[20] In 1742, he appraised the estate inventory of his fellow craftsman Jonathan Reed with Thomas Eastwick and Samuel Haley (qq.v.).[21] Morse probably had other apprentices besides John Banks, but none have been identified; presumably he trained his son Obadiah (q.v.). Some prominent citizens were among Morse's clients. Samuel Sewall paid him £1.13 in 1723 for "Madam Grove's Ring," which weighed two pennyweights and eighteen grains.[22]

Morse's silversmithing talents were overshadowed by his skills as an engraver. He is known to have engraved copperplates for bills of credit issued in Connecticut in 1733.[23] Morse was responsible for redating and printing many of the plates of the Massachusetts bills of credit that were reissued periodically from the time they were first emitted in 1713/14 until 1740.[24] For example, the colony paid Morse £37.18.9 "for repairing the plate printing &c" on 26 May 1731 and £23.18.7 on 8 December 1731, probably for work on the "middle plate" for reissues in April and May of that year.[25] Thomas Bradford and Thomas Milner (qq.v.) assisted him with this work. In May 1735 the colony paid Morse £194.6.0¹/₂ and £39.18 for labor by Milner and Bradford.[26] In July 1735 Morse was paid again by the Province of Massachusetts Bay for engraving and printing with labor by Henry Crump & Winborn "in Bradford's absence."[27] The bills that were issued by Massachusetts Bay in 1736–37 also were engraved by Morse. The Province of Massachusetts Bay paid him £185.19.6¹/₃ for "Making & Perfecting Bills of New Tenor 22 July 1738" as well as paying £67.4.¹/₃ to Bradford and Milner.[28] A detailed bill for similar services in 1740 survives:

> Boston Aug[s] 25:[th] 1740
> The Com[t.] for the Province Bills D[r]
> To Dateing the Grate Plate   0 = 15– 0
> To Strikeing from y[e]   Same 17 40 ⎱
> Ditto from y[e] Midle   52–64 ⎰   72– 18– 4
>   paper   70 04 ⎰
> att 2:¹/₂ pr Sheete
> To Dateing the Midle plate   0– 15– 0
> To 1 Lode of Cole   4–00– 0
> To Linsede Oyle   2–00– 0
> To Red Inke for the Back   1–00– 0
> To Makeing 4 Pots of Varnish   4–00– 0
> To Whighting for y[e] Plats   1– 15– 0
> To 1 Prescloth   1– 16– 0
>   _____
>   £88– 19– 4
>
>   Error Excep[t]:
> [illeg.] Oc[b.] 31st:   p[r] Nat[hl] Mors
> Exam[d.] ⅌ RB
>   Red of [illeg.] Contenu
>   of the Above Account
> Sworne to ⅌ m[r] Jeffries   Nat[hl] Mors
> allowed ⅌ the Committee
>   E.H[29]

In the 1730s Nathaniel Morse was one of several Boston goldsmiths who received payments for services rendered to a group of merchants involved in creating a private bank in Boston. In 1733, Joshua Winslow, acting on behalf of the "Subscribers to the Scheme for emitting Notes of hand," paid Morse £286.18.5 for "ingraving and printing the plates" and for other unspecified services. In the same year Winslow also made payments on Morse's behalf to Thomas Milner and Thomas Bradford that suggests that Morse may have subcontracted some of the work to them. On 5 November 1736 Morse was paid £84.8 for engraving an additional plate and printing more bills for the merchants. Morse's son Obadiah assisted in these projects and is also named in the accounts. Morse probably employed at least one journeyman because Winslow records that he "gave y[e] Labourer at Mors's 10s."[30]

At his death in 1748 Morse was owed £423 from the committee appointed by the Massachusetts General Court for the signing of the province bills, which suggests that Morse was responsible for engraving the plates for the bills of 1741 (redated 1742) and 1744.[31] In addition to the notes and province bills, Morse's other documented engraving is his portrait of Matthew Henry, and Morse may have been responsible for engraving armorials on silver (see pp. 81–82).[32]

When Morse died on 17 June 1748, his obituary notice identified him as an "ingenious" engraver.[33] The estate administration account was presented by his widow on 14 April 1749. Among his creditors were Samuel Edwards (q.v.), who was also one of the appraisers, and Asahel Mason (q.v.). The widow's final accounting, presented on 24 April 1753, after she had married Thomas Dolbeare of Dorchester, Massachusetts, includes payments to Elias Dupee and Rufus Greene (q.v.), which suggests that they too were creditors.[34] The inventory included a house and land in possession of the widow, which probably was the house Morse bought on Back Street in 1746, the only evidence of his property ownership in Boston.[35] He also owned two old copybooks and "sundry small Tools" valued at £7.7. The books undoubtedly were writing masters' copybooks, from which Morse would have learned lettering. (For a discussion of these books, see pp. 69–70, 74–75.)

Only a modest body of silver by Morse survives, another indication that much of his skill was spent in engraving. Six initials marks (A–F) and an initial and surname mark (G) are attributed to this craftsman. William Northey's (q.v.) mark sometimes has been misattributed to Morse.[36] PEK

SURVIVING OBJECTS

	Mark	Inscription	Patron	Date	Reference	Owner
Two candlesticks	D	Faneuil arms, a heart in the center, 4 six-pointed stars in chief, 3 like stars below the dexter star, all in pale, and a cross within an annulet in the sinister base (+)		ca. 1730	Quimby 1995, no. 99a, b	WM
Candlestick	G†	none		ca. 1720	Flynt/Fales 1968, 81–82	HD
Caster	A*	H/PS (+)		ca. 1715	Buhler/Hood 1970, no. 95	YUAG
Chafing dish	A†	TLW (later); AWW (later)		ca. 1720	Buhler/Hood 1970, no. 96	YUAG
Creampot	E*	MB (later)		ca. 1745	*Antiques* 120 (August 1981): 211	
Cup	F†	T/CF		ca. 1730		HD
Flagon	A*	This belongs to/the Church in/Brattle Street/1711	Brattle Street Church, Boston	1711	Buhler 1972, no. 106	MFAB
Mug	B	C/WD E (later)		ca. 1720	MFA 1911, no. 751	
Paten	D	C/WD E (later)		ca. 1720	MFA 1911, no. 752	
Salver	?	unidentified arms		ca. 1740		RIHS

	Mark	Inscription	Patron	Date	Reference	Owner
Spout cup	D†	Leith crest/ TRUSTY·TO·THE·END (later)		ca. 1720	Buhler/Hood 1970, no. 97	YUAG
Tankard	A *or* B	C/TM		ca. 1715	Sotheby Parke Bernet, 16–18 November 1978, lot 406	
Tankard	A/G	IM		ca. 1730	Stillinger 1990, 75, 155	
Tankard	B†	A/IM (+)	John and Mary (Osgood) Aslebe	ca. 1720	Jones 1913, 347	
Teaspoon	C†	EP		ca. 1725	DAPC 75.5143	WM
Teaspoon	E†	HD		ca. 1745		HD

1. SCD 24:171.
2. RC 9:186, 189; RC 21:264; SCPR 27:42; RC 28:24.
3. Sarah Kilby's niece Rebecca, the daughter of Christopher Kilby, married John Allen; another niece Elizabeth, daughter of John Kilby, married William Cowell, Sr. Sarah's brothers, Christopher and John, were married to the daughters of Pilgrim Simpkins, grandfather of William Simpkins and Andrew Tyler.
4. *Church in Brattle Square*, 130, 131, 143, 144, 146, 149: Sarah (1710), Obadiah, Sarah, Anna, Nathaniel (all baptized 1721), Deborah (1722), Lydia (1725), and Mary (1727).
5. SCCR, Court of General Sessions of the Peace Record Book, vol. 3 (1712–19), 5.
6. SCCR, Court of Common Pleas Record Book 1722, 398.
7. SCCR, Court of Common Pleas Record Book 1724, 358. The same year Edward Eustone and Mary Siry also sued Morse but did not appear for the trial; see Court of Common Pleas Record Book 1724, 144.
8. SCCR, Court of Common Pleas Record Book 1725, 239, 251. The debt to Toole was primarily for foodstuffs.
9. SCCR, Court of Common Pleas Record Book 1725, 307.
10. SCCR, Court of Common Pleas Record Book 1725, 71.
11. SCCR, Court of Common Pleas Record Book 1725, 91.
12. SCCR, Court of Common Pleas Record Book 1733, 423; 1735, 358, 570; 1735–36, 205, 92, 45, 501; 1736–37, 93, 245; 1737, 105, 202, 179, 320, 321; 1738, 44, 324; 1739, 153, 173, 178; 1740, 56, 126; 1741, 147; 1743–44, 204.
13. SCCR, Court of Common Pleas Record Book 1724, 277.
14. SCCR, file 18498.
15. SCCR, file 31260.
16. SCCR, Court of Common Pleas Record Book 1737, 276.
17. SCCR, Superior Court file 220–1735, 673. Photostat in the Bigelow-Phillips files.
18. SCCR, file 29204.
19. SCCR, file 16553.
20. SCPR 21:710.
21. SCPR 36:240–41.
22. Samuel Sewall Account Book and Ledger, fol. 173r, NEHGS.
23. Newman 1967, 56.
24. Newman 1967, 131–34.
25. Mass. Archives 101:516–17; Newman 1990, 168.
26. Mass. Archives 101:528.
27. Mass. Archives 101:525.
28. Mass. Archives 102:83.
29. Mass. Archives 101:571; Newman 1990, 171.
30. Joshua Winslow Account Book and Case Book, n.p., NEHGS; Newman 1967, 135.
31. Newman 1967, 139, 141–42.
32. Fales 1973a, 187.

33. *Boston Gazette*, 21 June 1748.

34. SCPR, docket 9040.

35. SCD 72:215.

36. See Buhler 1972, 1:131, 133, for a teaspoon bearing the disputed mark. Buhler argues that Northey would have been too young to have made the spoon. Northey would have been working by ca. 1755, and much evidence supports dating spoons with this type of shell at least up to the American Revolution.

Obadiah Morse
1711/12–42+

A

Obadiah Morse, the son of Nathaniel Morse (q.v.), was born in Boston on 29 February 1711/12 and was baptized in the Brattle Street Church on 2 March.[1] Probably trained by his father, he would have finished his apprenticeship about 1733. The account book of the merchant Joshua Winslow shows that Nathaniel Morse's son, probably Obadiah, was paid £4 at the time the elder Morse was engraving plates for privately issued bills of credit in 1733.[2] The younger Morse opened a shop on King Street, and in the *Boston News-Letter* of 13–20 December 1733 he advertised the theft from his shop of twenty-three large silver coat buttons and eleven buttons for a jacket marked "Mors" on the backside of each.[3] Morse's tenuous start in the trade persisted, for he was the defendant in nine suits for debt incurred in 1734 and 1735 in the Suffolk County Court of Common Pleas, where he was generally identified as a goldsmith.[4] In one of the cases, however, he was described as a "goldsmith or painter" when he was sued by the Boston merchant John Merrett for painting supplies and gold leaf he had purchased.[5] In addition to being a silversmith and engraver—engraving being his father's specialty—Morse probably made a living as a decorative painter. In 1736, when Obadiah's father was engraving plates for privately issued bills of credit, Winslow paid £5.12 for sixteen days of Nathaniel Morse's son's labor at 7 shillings a day; these payments probably were made to Obadiah.[6]

On 9 January 1735 Obadiah Morse married Elizabeth Higginson (b. 1714) of Salem, Massachusetts, the daughter of Nathaniel Higginson (1680–1724), a merchant, and his wife, Hannah Gerrish (b. 1678).[7] Elizabeth's sister Mary would become the mother of the Salem silversmith John Andrew (q.v.). In October and November 1735, Elizabeth and Obadiah Morse sold land that she had inherited from her father.[8] The couple's daughter Hannah was born in Boston on 25 March 1737.[9] Later that year Obadiah and Elizabeth mortgaged land near the Merrimack River that she also had inherited from her father to Isaac Perkins (q.v.) in a deed witnessed by Jacob Hurd (q.v.).[10]

Obadiah Morse was still identified as being of Boston in 1738 in a deed transacted that year.[11] Sometime between that date and 1741, however, he relocated to Middletown, Rhode Island. That year Simeon Palmer and William Fairfield traveled from South Kingston, Rhode Island, to Middletown to engage Morse to engrave a plate for counterfeit bills. Morse was not home, but Fairfield made a second trip to Middletown and persuaded Morse to come to South Kingston. Morse's wife probably did not accompany him but returned to her family in Salem, for the baptism of the couple's son Nathaniel took place there on 8 November 1741.[12] Fairfield later testified that Morse had cut the counterfeiting plate by 17 July 1741. The mastermind of the counterfeiting scheme, John Potter, was building a new house in South Kingston and also employed Morse to do interior painting and to make silver for himself and his relations. In South Kingston Morse had a painter, William Heffernan, Jr., as an apprentice. In 1742 the counterfeiters were arrested, including Morse, who was possibly in Massachusetts by that time. After escaping from the Newport, Rhode Island, jail, Morse was recaptured and sentenced to stand in the pillory and have his ears cropped. He was sold into service for no more than five years because he lacked sufficient funds to pay the fine, and nothing is known of him after this date.[13]

Only one teaspoon bearing a surname mark (A) has been attributed to him. PEK

SURVIVING OBJECTS

	Mark	Inscription	Patron	Date	Reference	Owner
Teaspoon	A†	H/SS		ca. 1735		YUAG

1. RC 24:79; *Church in Brattle Square*, 131.
2. Joshua Winslow Account Book and Case Book, n.p., NEHGS.
3. The advertisement was repeated in the issue of 27 December 1733 to 3 January 1734.
4. SCCR, Court of Common Pleas Record Book 1735, 243, 313, 536, 539; 1735–36, 46, 114, 194, 328; 1736–37, 563.
5. A record of this suit is in SCCR, Court of Common Pleas Record Book 1735, 539. Notes on the account between the plaintiff and defendant are in the Bigelow-Phillips papers, 1131.
6. Joshua Winslow Account Book and Case Book, n.p., NEHGS.
7. RC 28:222; *Salem VR* 1:349, 429–30; 3:496; ECPR, docket 13250; ECD 30:67–68.
8. ECD 68:217, 249.
9. RC 24:230.
10. ECD 73:264–65.
11. ECD 131:60.
12. *Salem VR* 2:86.
13. Scott 1957, 106–24. In his account Scott assumes that the Middletown referred to in testimony is the town in Connecticut. It is more likely to be Middletown, Rhode Island. Superior Judicature Court of Assize and General Gaol Delivery, September 1741–September 1746, Newport County, volume C, 26, 27, 65, 80 and attendant file papers. State of Rhode Island Supreme Court Judicial Records Center, Pawtucket, Rhode Island.

Stephen Morse
1743/44–1800 +

Stephen Morse was born in Newbury, Massachusetts, on 23 January 1743/44, the son of Joshua Morse (1714–56), a joiner, and Prudence Ordway (b. 1723), who were married on 19 August 1741.[1] His paternal grandparents were Anthony Morse (1688–1729) and Judith Moodey (b. 1691).[2] His maternal grandparents were Stephen Ordway (b. 1697) and Abigail Merrick (b. 1698).[3]

Stephen Morse's apprenticeship probably began about 1758, and he would have completed his training about 1765. The identity of his master is uncertain. On 5 February 1759 Tristram Coffin was appointed Morse's guardian, Morse's father having died in 1756.[4] His first shop was in Gloucester, Massachusetts. The *Boston Gazette and Country Journal* for 11 and 18 January 1768 contained the following advertisement:

Gloucester, December 25, 1767

WHEREAS the Shop of the Subscriber was broke
open on Tuesday Night last, and the following
Articles stolen from thence, viz. 2 GoldNecklaces–1 Piece
of plated Gold, value 4 Dollars–1 Pair Stone Nubs–
1 Pair round plain Silver Shoe Buckles–1 pair square Silver
ditto, old–1 new square ditto, partly wrought– 1 open-
work ditto, newly mended–1 round Silver ditto, with
Silver Flukes and Tongs–1 large Silver Spoon–9 Silver

Thimble–2 Stay Hooks –1 Stone Ring, Gold–1 small
Box, containing sundry Articles old Stone Buttons, &c.
–1 Pair round Silver Shoe Buckles, mark'd T.S.-and
4 Silver Tea Spoons–Whoever shall discover the Thief or
Thieves, so that the Subscriber may obtain the above Articles again, shall have TWO GUINEAS Reward, and
all necessary Charges paid.

STEPHEN MORSS [*sic*]

N.B. If the Thief should be apprehended near *Boston*,
'tis desired that Information may be given to Mr. *Daniel
Parker*, Goldsmith, who will pay the above Reward.

Morse's acquaintance with the Boston goldsmith Daniel Parker (q.v.) suggests that Parker might have been his master.

By 1771 Morse had moved to Portsmouth, New Hampshire. An advertise-ment in the *New-Hampshire Gazette and Historical Chronicle* of 8 March 1771 stated, "Stephen Morss, At his shop in Portsmouth, opposite Dr. Langdon's Meeting House, on the Parade, Makes all sorts of Goldsmith's and Jewellery Work." The goldsmith may have been the same Stephen Morse who served as a delegate from Chester, New Hampshire, to the Fourth and Fifth Provincial Congresses in 1775. He may also have been the Stephen Morse who served in Stark's brigade and joined the Northern Continental Army at Bennington and Stillwater in 1777. A Stephen Morse also served as a private in Capt. Benjamin Scias's company of New Hampshire volunteers in the expedition to Rhode Island in 1778.[5]

Following the Revolution, Morse moved to Concord, New Hampshire, where he advertised in 1791:

Stephen Morse
Has opened a shop at the Clock Manufac-
tory of Messrs. Levi & Abel Hutchins,
a few rods south of the Printing Office in Concord—Where he carries on the Goldsmith and
Jewellers' business in its various branches—
Whoever are pleased to favour him with their
commands may depend on having them executed with fidelity & dispatch.
Concord Jan. 1, 1791 [6]

He is also identified as being "of Concord New Hampshire goldsmith" on 16 March 1791, when he quitclaimed to Joshua Morse of Hopkinton, New Hampshire, all right to the dower interest of his mother's estate.[7] He may have moved subsequently to Boston because the directory of 1796 lists a Stephen Morse, goldsmith, on Hanover Street.[8] Four years later he is described as "goldsmith of Deerfield" (New Hampshire) when he and his wife, Frances, sold land she had been deeded by Joseph Mills, Esquire, in Deerfield.[9] Nothing further is known of Morse. No probate records have been found for Morse in Rockingham County, and no silver by him has been identified. PEK

1. *Newbury VR* 1:338–39, 375; 2:341, 666; ECPR 336:39; ECD 79:201; 103:191–92.
2. *Newbury VR* 1:327, 342; 2:342, 668.
3. *Newbury VR* 1:323, 375; 2:367.
4. ECPR 336:39.
5. Scott 1958, 145.
6. *Concord Herald* 4, 12, 26 January, 2, 16 February, 2 March 1791.

7. ECD 161:202.

8. RC 10:269.

9. RCD 153:396; 157:254–55. Frances's maiden name and a record of the marriage have not been found.

David Colson Moseley
1752–1812

A

B

C

D

E

David Colson Moseley was born on 17 December 1752 to the Boston housewright Unite Moseley (1716–56) and his second wife, Elizabeth Colson (1716–before 1766), the daughter of David (1682–1757), a leatherdresser, and Hannah (Cowell) Colson (b. 1677/78), whose marriage intention was published on 19 December 1751.[1] Hannah Cowell was the sister of William Cowell, Sr. (q.v.). David Moseley's paternal grandparents were Thomas (1666/67–1749) and Rebecca (Mason) Moseley (d. before 1751).[2] Following the death of his parents, Moseley was left to the care of his uncle James Lourie, who arranged for his apprenticeship with Paul Revere, Jr. (q.v.). Moseley's service with Revere was terminated in unfortunate circumstances. On 12 October 1772, Revere filed suit against Lourie for removing Moseley from his duties and withholding him from his master.[3] Revere recovered £150 as compensation for the loss of his apprentice. Moseley's unsatisfactory behavior was the beginning of a career troubled by alcoholism and debt.

On 28 April 1775, Moseley received a generous bequest from his uncle David Colson, a Boston leatherdresser.[4] In addition to "the old Mansion house" on Frog Lane in south Boston, Colson gave his nephew all his "personal estate, Apparell and Household furniture." This property, on the corner of Frog Lane and Newbury Street, served as Moseley's residence throughout his lifetime. The city directories of 1796 and 1798 list his address as Frog Lane.[5] The United States Direct Tax of 1798 assessed Moseley as the owner and occupier of a wooden house on the corner of Frog Lane and Newbury Street described as "6,174 square feet; house, 800 square feet; 2 stories, 34 windows; Value, $3,600."[6] Shortly after receiving this windfall the silversmith was married on 29 May 1776 to Elizabeth Revere (ca. 1745–1811), sister of his former master, Paul Revere, Jr., and daughter of Paul Revere, Sr. (q.v.). In December 1778 the younger Revere paid more than £45 of Moseley's debts to John Preston.[7] The couple had at least two children: David C. Moseley, born in 1780, and Betsey, baptized in the Second Church on 24 May 1788.[8] Elizabeth (Revere) Moseley was admitted to covenant, or membership, in the Second Church on 23 March 1788, shortly before her infant daughter's baptism.[9]

The Boston assessors rated Moseley with one poll and rents of £20 in the tax list for 1780.[10] Revere sold his brother-in-law two lots of land, one on Main Street and one on Frog Lane, on 26 July 1784 for a token five shillings.[11] Moseley sold the plot on Frog Lane adjoining his own property to the Boston glazier William Cunningham for £160 a month later.[12] He sold another small piece of his Frog Lane property to Cunningham in June 1788.[13] In January of the following year, Moseley successfully sued the Springfield trader Simeon Ashley for recovery of a £3.15 debt.[14]

In spite of these transactions, Moseley continued to experience problems with debt. In January 1790 the Suffolk County Court of Common Pleas awarded Deidemia Stoddard of Stoughton, Massachusetts, recovery of Moseley's unpaid notes: £20.9.11 on 17 January 1787, £26.15.8 on 3 March 1788, and £14.3 on 12 December 1788.[15] When the debt remained unpaid in May of that year, the court awarded Stoddard the use and rents of Moseley's remaining Frog Lane property for three years. However, the census of 1790 lists Moseley as the head of a family in the same location, immediately following the listings for his tenants Israel Cook and Mrs. Sullivan.[16] His family comprised one male under the age of sixteen and five women, presumably his wife, ten-year-old son, and four daughters.

By the 1790s, Moseley's financial status had deteriorated considerably. Paul Revere's memoranda book records payments of cash to Moseley's wife in November 1796 and January 1797.[17] Revere purchased a parcel of land on Newbury Street from his brother-in-law for £5 on 26 April 1797.[18] He released it to Moseley the following day for £5.[19] Revere's son-in-law Thomas S. Eayres (1760–1813/14), a silversmith working in Boston and Worcester, witnessed the deed. On 14 November that year, Revere was "admitted Guardian to David Mosely of s^d Boston, a Person Waisting his Estate."[20] Amos Lincoln and Revere's son, the silversmith Paul Revere III (1760–1813), were bound with him to perform this task. Revere's duties commenced five days later with the payment of some of Moseley's bills and continued until 1808.[21] An inventory of Moseley's estate taken in December 1797 included a modest number of household goods valued at £12.11.6 and two houses and land valued at £2,000. Because there are no goldsmith's tools listed in the inventory, Moseley was probably working as a journeyman or living off the rents from his tenants. A statement of debts compiled on 20 February 1798 totaled $1,129 and included $39 to the silversmith David Tyler (1760–1804) and $700 to Revere.[22] Empowered by the court to sell some of Moseley's land to pay the debts, Revere auctioned some land and buildings on Frog Lane to the Boston truckman John Wales (Wiles) on 18 June 1798 for $1,170.[23]

Moseley was still considered "a Person wasting his Estate by Excessive drinking" in November 1808, when Revere petitioned for release from his duties as guardian, "being advanced in years and having had the trouble of said Guardianship for a long time past."[24] Revere's final accounting showed a balance of $621.80.[25] The silversmith's son, the Boston saddler David C. Moseley, was appointed guardian for his father.[26]

Moseley died of consumption on 15 June 1812 at the age of fifty-nine and was buried in the Granary Burying Ground.[27] His estate was appraised on 24 August 1812.[28] Moseley owned few possessions at his death; the extra beds, chairs, tables, and kitchenwares included in the inventory of 1797 undoubtedly had been given to his wife or children prior to his death.

Moseley's career as a silversmith is tied integrally to that of his master, Paul Revere. He received more than £163 of shop supplies without payment from Revere between November 1783 and June 1787. However, he was paid by Revere for making teaspoons in October 1796 and October 1797. Although there are few objects marked by Moseley, five marks are associated with him: (A) surname mark with pellets; (B) and (C) initial and surname marks; and (D) and (E) initials marks. A spurious example of mark (D) exists.[29] In spite of his difficult personal life, Moseley possessed considerable skills as a silversmith. He made canns, tankards, a porringer, a beaker, and flatware as well as an unusual holloware form, a hooped pitcher. DAF

SURVIVING OBJECTS

	Mark	Inscription	Patron	Date	Reference	Owner
Beaker	B†	AH		ca. 1780	Avery 1920, no. 271	MMA
Cann	A†	T/IR		ca. 1785	Buhler 1972, no. 451	MFAB
Cann	B (?)	AC		ca. 1800		OSV
Cann (mate below)	B or C	Joy arms, or on a chevron vert between 3 oak leaves 5 drops of water, and crest, a jay standing on a stump with 2 leaves sprouting	Joy family	ca. 1785	MFA 1911, no. 753	
Cann (mate above)	D	Joy arms	Joy family	ca. 1785	MFA 1911, no. 756	
Ladle	C†	none	James Bowdoin III (?)	ca. 1785		BCMA
Pitcher (with cover)	B*	Henry/Barney Smith	Henry Barney Smith	ca. 1810	Buhler/Hood 1970, no. 290	YUAG
Porringer	C	Joy	Joy family	ca. 1785	MFA 1911, no. 754	
Serving spoon	A*/ D†	DL		ca. 1780	YUAG files	
Spoon	E†	?		?	DAPC 69.7078	
Three tablespoons	D	WC		?	YUAG files	
Two tablespoons	D*	EM		ca. 1780	DAPC 91.3208	
Tankard	B or C	?	Joy family	ca. 1775	*Antiques* 70 (December 1956): 524	
Teaspoon	D	AC	Cowen family (?)	ca. 1775		MHS

1. RC 9:141; RC 24:119, 280; RC 28:8, 299; SCD 80:25; SCPR 51:579–80; RC 21:63; *Reading VR*, 54. Elizabeth (Colson) Moseley was still alive in 1760 because she received a legacy from her father's estate in that year; SCPR 52:782–87.

2. RC 21:10, 103, 247; SCPR 52:782–87.

3. SCCR, file 91313.

4. SCPR 74:421–22.

5. *Boston Directory* 1796, 75; 1798, 84.

6. RC 22:425.

7. 19 December 1778, vol. 2, Waste Book, 1761–83, [55], Revere Family Papers, MHS; *Medway VR*, 234; *Index of Obituaries, 1784–1840*, 4:3199.

8. Codman 1918, 171; also see this source for the death of David C. Moseley on 1 January 1848 at the age of sixty-eight. Five females were listed in Moseley's household in the census of 1790, which indicates the possible existence of three daughters in addition to Betsey; RC 22:488.

9. Bigelow-Phillips files, 1727, citing "Records of Admissions and Baptisms of the Second Church, Boston, 1741–1816," 39.

10. "Assessors' 'Taking-Books,'" 53.

11. SCD 144:155–56.

12. SCD 144:156–57.

13. SCD 163:56–57.

14. SCCR, Court of Common Pleas Extended Record Book 1788, 289.

15. SCCR, Court of Common Pleas Extended Record Book 1789, 159.

16. RC 22:488.

17. Vol. 51, Memoranda Book, 1796–98, Revere Family Papers, MHS.

18. SCD 186:46–47.

19. SCD 186:68–69.

711 JOSEPH MOULTON, 1724–95

20. SCPR 95:549. A second bond reaffirming this guardianship appointment appears in the court records on 10 April 1798; SCPR 96:152.
21. SCPR 96:105–06; 96:103, 414–16.
22. SCPR 96:103.
23. SCD 190:56–57. The mortgage for $670 that Revere arranged for Wales was paid back by 25 July 1798; SCD 190:51.
24. SCPR 106:600–01; 405:101.
25. SCPR 106:600.
26. SCPR 106:601.
27. Boston Deaths, 1810–1848.
28. SCPR 110:477–78.
29. The mark is on a tablespoon, YUAG 1930.1262; Washington 1925, no. 71.

Joseph Moulton
1724–95

A

B

C

D

Joseph Moulton, the younger brother of William (q.v.), was the son of the blacksmith Joseph (1694–1756; q.v. Appendix B) and Mary (Noyes) Moulton, and the grandson of William (1664–1732; q.v. Appendix B) and Abigail (Webster) Moulton (1661/62–1723). He was the uncle of his namesake Joseph (q.v.). Born in Newbury, Massachusetts, on 4 August 1724, Joseph married Anna Boardman.[1] The couple was childless. Joseph was identified as a goldsmith in a deed of 31 March 1753, when he and Edmund Greenleaf bought land in Newbury from Daniel and Mary March.[2] In 1754, Joseph Moulton, along with William Moulton and Parker Noyes, witnessed the will of Hannah Kent of Newbury, the mother-in-law of Samuel Burt (q.v.).[3]

Joseph Moulton was active in Newbury for nearly fifty years. He may have trained the Newbury native Israel Bartlett (q.v.) between about 1762 and 1769. A Suffolk County court record indicates that Joseph drowned in the Merrimack River in 1795, as testified to by Daniel Balch, Jr., Eben. Greenleaf, Jr., Moses Titcomb, William Stickney, and others.[4]

Identified as a goldsmith throughout his probate records, Joseph's estate included his "homestead containing about 100 acres of land & the buildings thereon" valued at $2,167. His personal estate, valued at a total of $620.90, included the following silver and tools:

Money on hand 14/27 Old Silver and Gould/ Gouldsmiths tools 2/ [$]16 27 Silver shoe buckels 3/ Silver Neabuckles/ 66 Silver Creempot 5/50   9 16 three silver Porrangers 28/ four silver spoons 6/ six teaspons 4/   38 Gouldsmith's Case/50

He also had a pew in Mr. Dana's Meeting House in Newburyport. John Atkinson, Edmund Chase, and Joseph Sawyer were the appraisers of the estate, which was valued at a total of slightly more than $3,000.[5]

Stephen Decatur attributed three marks to this Joseph Moulton: I·MOULTON in a rectangle (A); J·M in a rectangle (B); and J·M in a serrated rectangle (C).[6] Louise Belden suggests that the first two of these marks as well as a third mark consisting of J M with cross between in a rectangle (D) were shared by this Joseph and his nephew.[7] GWRW

SURVIVING OBJECTS

	Mark	Inscription	Patron	Date	Reference	Owner
Cann §	A	1750; MM		1750	Avery 1920, no. 124 (as Joseph Moulton, 1694–ca. 1756)	MMA

	Mark	Inscription	Patron	Date	Reference	Owner
Creampot §	D	EW		ca. 1790	Parke-Bernet, 28 October 1969, lot 129	
Porringer	A	D.P.A.		ca. 1790	*Newburyport Maritime Society Antiques Show* 1981, 1 (as Joseph Moulton, 1744–1816)	
Porringer §	?	ESP (?)		ca. 1790	*Antiques* 86 (July 1964): 11	
Two salt spoons §	A	SSS		ca. 1785	Buhler/Hood 1970, no 196	YUAG
Two salt spoons §	B	C		ca. 1780	*Newburyport Maritime Society Antiques Show* 1981, 1 (as Joseph Moulton, 1744–1816)	
Salt spoon §	D*	BB		ca. 1790		PEM
Two salt spoons §	D*	EG		ca. 1790		PEM
Serving spoon §	D	MWB (cipher)	Mary (White) Brown	ca. 1785	Benes 1986, no. 184 (as Joseph Moulton, 1744–1816)	
Tablespoon §	A	ES		ca. 1765	DAPC 75.3230	WM
Tablespoon	A	MC		ca. 1755	*Newburyport Maritime Society Antiques Show* 1981, 3	
Tablespoon	A	W/IA		ca. 1765	*Newburyport Maritime Society Antiques Show* 1981, 1	
Tablespoon §	B*	CM		ca. 1765	DAPC 75.3234	WM
Tablespoon §	B*	AM		ca. 1770		CM
Two tablespoons §	D	ME		ca. 1775	Avery 1920, nos. 273–74 (as Joseph Moulton, 1744–1816)	MMA
Tablespoon §	D	ES		ca. 1775	Avery 1920, no. 275 (as Joseph Moulton, 1744–1816)	MMA
Tablespoon §	D†	IS		ca. 1775	DAPC 71.3425 (as Joseph Moulton, 1744–1816)	WM

	Mark	Inscription	Patron	Date	Reference	Owner
Tablespoon	D	IB		ca. 1775		AIC
Tablespoon §	D*	MB		ca. 1795		YUAG
Tablespoon (attrib.)	none	EK		ca. 1760	*Newburyport Maritime Society Antiques Show* 1981, 1	
Teaspoon §	A	P		?	MFA 1911, no. 761	
Teaspoon §	A*	A/MM		ca. 1755		HD
Teaspoon §	A*	TL		ca. 1755		YUAG
Teaspoon §	A*	HN		ca. 1765	DAPC 88.3493	
Teaspoon §	A†	C/BM		ca. 1765	DAPC 73.3189	WM
Teaspoon §	A*	KP		ca. 1765	DAPC 73.3192	WM
Teaspoon §	B*	SS		ca. 1755		YUAG
Teaspoon §	B*	LE		ca. 1755		HD
Teaspoon §	B*	MT		ca. 1755		YUAG
Teaspoon §	B*	HB		ca. 1765	DAPC 73.2421	WM
Teaspoon §	B†	IB		ca. 1765	DAPC 73.2418	WM
Teaspoon §	B*	MB		ca. 1765		SFCAI
Teaspoon §	B, C, or D	BW		ca. 1790	*American Art of the Colonies and Early Republic*, no. 132	
Teaspoon	C*	MA		ca. 1780	Buhler/Hood 1970, no. 195	YUAG
Teaspoon	C*	S/SS		ca. 1760		PEM
Teaspoon	C*	none		ca. 1755		HD
Teaspoon	C†	RH/to/IH		ca. 1750	DAPC 88.3489	
Teaspoon §	C*	M/WI		ca. 1760		YUAG
Teaspoon	C	EI		?	MFA 1911, no. 757	
Teaspoon §	D*	SC		ca. 1765		SCFAI
Teaspoon §	D*	EC		ca. 1760	YUAG files	
Teaspoon §	D	AL		ca. 1785		YUAG
Teaspoon (mate below) §	D	HM	Hannah Moody	ca. 1775	MFA 1911, no. 758	
Teaspoon (mate above) §	D	HM (+)		ca. 1775		YUAG
Teaspoon §	D*	HD/1768		1768	DAPC 73.2424 (as Joseph Moulton, 1744–1816)	WM
Teaspoon §	D*	HH		ca. 1775	Johnston 1994, 112	CMA
Two teaspoons §	D*	EC		ca. 1790		YUAG
Teaspoon §	D*	MN		ca. 1755		YUAG
Teaspoon §	D*	MM		ca. 1790		HD
Teaspoon §	D	AW		ca. 1790	DAPC 73.2350 (as Joseph Moulton, 1744–1816)	WM

	Mark	Inscription	Patron	Date	Reference	Owner
Teaspoon §	D*	IP		ca. 1790		HD
Teaspoon §	D	L/SL/1786	Silas and Lucretia (Little) Little	1786	Benes 1986, no. 27 (as Joseph Moulton, 1744–1816)	
Teaspoon §	D*	none		ca. 1780	DAPC 73.2414 (as Joseph Moulton, 1744–1816)	WM
Teaspoon §	D	RE		ca. 1775		LACMA
Teaspoon §	D	?		ca. 1785	YUAG files	
Teaspoon §	D*	SWM		ca. 1795		YUAG
Teaspoon §	D*	HT		ca. 1790		HD
Teaspoon §	D	DC		ca. 1755		OYHS
Teaspoon	?	?		ca. 1757		ChM

§ Possibly made by Joseph Moulton (1744–1816).

1. *Newbury VR* 1:325, 347, 536; 2:347–48, 661; Moulton 1906, 270; Decatur 1941a, 15.
2. ECD 100:75.
3. ECPR 335:241.
4. SCCR, file 134737.
5. ECPR, docket 19034.
6. Decatur 1941a, 15.
7. Belden 1980, 305 (mark c).

Joseph Moulton
1744–1816

A

B

C

D

E

F

The son of William Moulton (q.v.) and his wife, Lydia (Greenleaf) Moulton, Joseph was born in Newburyport, Massachusetts, in 1744 and probably apprenticed with his father. His uncle Joseph (q.v.) was also a member of the craft, and it is possible that the younger Joseph may have trained with his uncle. It is often stated that Joseph was referred to as Joseph, Jr., until after his uncle's death in 1795.[1] The younger Joseph married Abigail (1744–1818), daughter of Daniel (1703–65) and Abigail (Toppan) Noyes (1707–87), on 24 October 1765. They had twelve children between 1766 and 1786, four of whom became silversmiths: Ebenezer (1768–1824), William (1772–1861), Enoch (1780–1820?), and Abel (1784–1840 +).[2]

Joseph worked in Newburyport for many years in a shop on State Street, and the town historian records that he made gold beads as well as silverware. The account book of the Ipswich silversmith Daniel Rogers (q.v.) shows that Moulton purchased gold beads from Rogers between 1796 and 1800.[3] In 1796 he formed a partnership with Theophilus Bradbury (1763–1803), under the name Moulton and Bradbury. Joseph died in Newbury on 12 March 1816; Abigail died on 8 September 1818, aged seventy-three.[4]

Joseph died intestate, and administration was granted to his son Ebenezer, a Boston goldsmith. His estate, nearly evenly divided between real estate and personal estate, was valued at a total of $22,063.28. His house was on High Street in Newbury, and he owned a floor pew in the Reverend W. Milton's Meetinghouse in Newburyport. His shop, materials, and tools included

Goldsmith's Shop Standing on Land of Israel
  Young with all the tools in Said Shop   [$]131. —
329 ^{oz} 5 ^{P} of wrought Silver at 133 $^{1}/_{3}$ Cents p^{er}. Ounce   439. —
42 ^{oz} 5 ^{P} of old Silver at 110 Cent p^r. ounce   46. 52
285^{oz}.18^P of old Silver at the house at 110 C^t.   314. 49
50 brest pins   25. —
79 pair of earings   59. 70
39 Finger Rings   14. 30
old earings & box   3. —
Plated ware   5. —
13 pair of knee buckels & 3 Stock Buckels   6. 10
Rings & Brooches   1. 10
Glass beeds & Sundrys in the Old Case   3. —
Earring and buttons Stones   5. —
48 ^{oz}. 1^P. 6^g of Gold beads @ 22..44 p^r. ounce   1078. 52
3 ^{oz}. 11 ^{P}. 12^g. of old Gold @ 5/p^r. penny w^t.   59. 58
104 Silver Thimbles   26. —

Notes from about thirty people were received, including Thomas P. Drowne (1782–1849), Theophilus Bradbury, and other silversmiths.[5] The "Old Case" mentioned in the inventory may have been one of the glass cases made by the cabinetmaker Jonathan Kettell in June 1782 for £1.4 for a Joseph Moulton (although Kettell's client could have been the older Joseph).[6]

Stephen Decatur attributed six marks to this Joseph Moulton in 1941; more recent research by Louise C. Belden attributes a total of eight, including three marks (her A, B, C) that she believes were shared by uncle and nephew.[7] Although conclusive evidence is lacking, Joseph Moulton probably used two initial and surname marks (A, B), a surname mark (C), and three initials marks (D, E, F).[8]

Joseph Moulton's masterpiece is an engraved cann presented by the Proprietors of the Locks and Canals on the Merrimack River to James Varnum in 1798 for "HIS / SPIRITED EXERTIONS FOR THE / PRESERVATION OF THEIR PROPERTY / AT THE PATUCKETT CANAL, / DURING A GREAT FRESHETT / IN THE MONTH OF / APRIL, 1798."[9] GWRW

SURVIVING OBJECTS

	Mark	Inscription	Patron	Date	Reference	Owner
Beaker	C	unidentified initials		ca. 1810	Parke-Bernet, 10 November 1970, lot 119	
Cann §	A	1750; MM		1750	Avery 1920, no. 124 (as Joseph Moulton, 1694–ca. 1756)	MMA
Cann	D*	PRESENTED/BY THE PROPRIETORS OF THE LOCKS AND CANALS/ON MERRIMACK RIVER, TO/James	Proprietors of the locks and canals on the Merrimack River	1798	Buhler/Hood 1970, no. 280	YUAG

	Mark	Inscription	Patron	Date	Reference	Owner
		Varnum, Esq.ʳ/ᴀs AN ACKNOWL-EDGEMENT ᴏғ ʜɪs/SPIRITED EXERTIONS ғᴏʀ ᴛʜᴇ/PRESERVA-TION ᴏғ ᴛʜᴇɪʀ PROPERTY/ᴀᴛ ᴛʜᴇ PATUCK-ETT CANAL,/ᴅᴜʀ-ɪɴɢ ᴀ ɢʀᴇᴀᴛ FRESHETT/ɪɴ ᴛʜᴇ ᴍᴏɴᴛʜ OF/APRIL,/1798				
Creampot	ʙ	AC		ca. 1805	Avery 1920, no. 272	MMA
Creampot §	ᴅ	EW		ca. 1790	Parke-Bernet, 28 October 1969, lot 129	
Creampot	ғ	G		ca. 1800	*Antiques* 86 (November 1964): 565	
Dessert spoon	ᴀ or ʙ	P.P.		ca. 1800	*Newburyport Maritime Society Antiques Show* 1981, 1	
Ladle	ғ (?)	ESK		ca. 1800	MFA 1911, no. 760	
Porringer	ᴄ	unidentified initials		ca. 1800	Christie's, 16 June 1984, lot 66	
Porringer	ᴄ	SP		ca. 1800	Parke-Bernet, 25 March 1969, lot 62	
Porringer	ᴄ (?)	JL/to/MWP		ca. 1775	Hammerslough/Feigenbaum 1958–73, 3:38	
Porringer	ᴅ	D.P.A.		ca. 1790	*Newburyport Maritime Society Antiques Show* 1981, 1	
Porringer §	?	ESP (?)		ca. 1790	*Antiques* 86 (July 1964): 11	
Porringer	?	AG		ca. 1775		SI
Two salt spoons §	ʙ†	SSS		ca. 1780	Buhler/Hood 1970, no. 196 (as Joseph Moulton, 1724–95)	YUAG

	Mark	Inscription	Patron	Date	Reference	Owner
Two salt spoons §	c	c		ca. 1780	*Newburyport Maritime Society Antiques Show* 1981, 1	
Two salt spoons §	D*	EG		ca. 1790		PEM
Salt spoon §	D*	BB		ca. 1790		PEM
Serving spoon §	D	MWB (cipher)	Mary (White) Brown	ca. 1785	Benes 1986, no. 184	
Strainer	F	none		ca. 1765	Kent/Levy 1909, no. 396	
Sugar bowl	c	DD/to/DH		ca. 1805	McFadden/ Clark 1989, no. 74 (as Joseph Moulton, 1724–95)	ChM
Sugar tongs	c	EM		ca. 1790		OYHS
Sugar tongs	D*	ES		ca. 1800		YUAG
Tablespoon §	A	ES		ca. 1765	DAPC 75.3230 (as Joseph Moulton, 1724–95)	WM
Tablespoon	A *or* B	P.L.M.		ca. 1800	*Newburyport Maritime Society Antiques Show* 1981, 1	
Tablespoon	A *or* B	DT		ca. 1805	DAPC 71.3367	WM
Tablespoon	B	IB		ca. 1775		AIC
Tablespoon	c†	TT/to/RF		ca. 1775	DAPC 72.1236	WM
Tablespoon	c*	H		ca. 1795		YUAG
Tablespoon §	D	ES		ca. 1775	Avery 1920, no. 275	MMA
Two tablespoons §	D	ME		ca. 1775	Avery 1920, nos. 273–74	MMA
Tablespoon §	D*	MB		ca. 1795		YUAG
Tablespoon (with mark of Ebenezer Moulton)	D	none		ca. 1800	DAPC 82.3584	
Tablespoon §	D†	IS		ca. 1775	DAPC 71.3425	WM
Tablespoon §	E*	AM		ca. 1770		CM
Tablespoon §	E	CM		ca. 1765	DAPC 75.3234 (as Joseph Moulton, 1724–95)	WM
Tablespoon	F†	CG		ca. 1800	Belden 1980, 306 (mark H)	WM
Teaspoon §	A*	A/MM		ca. 1770		HD
Teaspoon §	A*	TL		ca. 1770		YUAG

	Mark	Inscription	Patron	Date	Reference	Owner
Teaspoon §	A*	HN		ca. 1765	DAPC 88.3493 (as Joseph Moulton, 1724–95)	
Teaspoon §	A†	C/BM		ca. 1765	DAPC 73.3189 (as Joseph Moulton, 1724–95)	WM
Teaspoon §	A*	KP		ca. 1765	DAPC 73.3192 (as Joseph Moulton, 1724–95)	WM
Teaspoon §	A *or* B	P		?	MFA 1911, no. 761	
Teaspoon § *(mate ? below; see also mate with mark* D*)*	B (?)	HM	Hannah Moody	ca. 1805	MFA 1911, no. 762	
Teaspoon § *(mate above?; see also mate with mark* D*)*	B	HM (+)		ca. 1775		YUAG
Teaspoon	B*	RK		ca. 1805	Eitner 1976, no. 119 (as Joseph Moulton, 1724–95)	
Teaspoon §	B*	SC		ca. 1765		SFCAI
Teaspoon §	B	?		ca. 1785	YUAG files	
Teaspoon	B*	TCW		ca. 1805	Eitner 1976, no. 120 (as Joseph Moulton, 1724–95)	
Teaspoon	B*	IT		ca. 1800		HD
Teaspoon	B*	SC		ca. 1810		HD
Teaspoon	B*	PF		ca. 1805		YUAG
Teaspoon	B	EB		ca. 1810	DAPC 68.4552	
Six teaspoons	C	AH		ca. 1810	DAPC 68.2654	
Teaspoon	C*	KH		ca. 1795	DAPC 80.3893	WM
Two teaspoons	C	?		ca. 1800		RISD
Two teaspoons	C	B		ca. 1810		PEM
Teaspoon	C	RRP		ca. 1810		MFAB
Teaspoon	D	PM		ca. 1795		SB
Teaspoon §	D*	EC		ca. 1760	YUAG files	
Teaspoon §	D*	none		ca. 1780	DAPC 73.2414	WM
Teaspoon §	D*	AL		ca. 1785		YUAG
Teaspoon § *(see also mates ? with mark* B*)*	D	HM	Hannah Moody	ca. 1775	MFA 1911, no. 758	
Teaspoon §	D*	SWM		ca. 1795		YUAG
Teaspoon	D	I		ca. 1800	Buhler 1972, appendix no. 59	MFAB
Teaspoon §	D*	HD/1768		1768	DAPC 73.2424	WM

	Mark	Inscription	Patron	Date	Reference	Owner
Teaspoon §	D*	HH		ca. 1775		CMA
Two teaspoons §	D*	EC		ca. 1790		YUAG
Teaspoon §	D*	MN		ca. 1775		YUAG
Teaspoon §	D*	AW		ca. 1790	DAPC 73.2350	WM
Teaspoon §	D	L/SL/1786	Silas and Lucretia (Little) Little	1786	Benes 1986, no. 27	
Teaspoon	D*	LP		ca. 1800		RISD
Teaspoon §	D*	HT		ca. 1790		HD
Teaspoon §	D*	MM		ca. 1790		HD
Teaspoon §	D*	IP		ca. 1790		HD
Teaspoon §	D	DC		ca. 1770		OYHS
Teaspoon §	D	RE		ca. 1775		LACMA
Teaspoon	D or E	MT		ca. 1770		ChM
Teaspoon §	D or E	BW		ca. 1795	American Art of the Colonies and Early Republic, no. 132	
Teaspoon §	E*	M/WI		ca. 1760		YUAG
Teaspoon §	E	MB		ca. 1765		SFCAI
Teaspoon §	E*	SS		ca. 1755		YUAG
Teaspoon §	E*	LE		ca. 1755		HD
Teaspoon §	E*	MT		ca. 1755		YUAG
Teaspoon §	E*	HB		ca. 1765	DAPC 73.2421 (as Joseph Moulton, 1724–95)	WM
Teaspoon §	E†	IB		ca. 1765	DAPC 73.2418 (as Joseph Moulton, 1724–95)	WM
Teaspoon	E	?		ca. 1795		YUAG
Teaspoon	E	MAO		1810		YUAG

§ Possibly made by Joseph Moulton (1724–95).

1. Decatur 1941a, 15.
2. *Newburyport VR* 2:328; Moulton 1906, 280; Decatur 1941a, 15. For Abigail, see *Newbury VR* 1:356; 2:669; for her parents, *Newbury VR* 1:358, 503; 2:355, 673.
3. Daniel Rogers Account Book, PEM.
4. Currier (1909) 1978, 1:169; Flynt/Fales 1968, 282, 162; Moulton 1906, 280.
5. ECPR, docket 19036. An error in the arithmetic occurred in calculating the value of the 3 oz. 11 dwt. 12 gr. of gold.
6. Fales 1967a, 200. David Boynton, a Newburyport joiner or house carpenter, performed work for a Joseph Moulton from 1768 to 1774, as recorded in his account book (now in YUAG collection). Boynton made a "Buckle Case" for Moulton (fol. 13v) and also worked on Moulton's "office house" (account book unfolioed at this point). He submitted a charge for "tending masons" on several occasions, suggesting that they may have been building a forge (n.p.).
7. Decatur 1941a, 15; Belden 1980, 305–06; MOULTON in a rectangle, sometimes attributed to Joseph Moulton (see, for example, Eitner 1976, nos. 121–22), is assigned to William Moulton IV (1772–1861) by Belden.
8. Examples of all the marks illustrated by Decatur could not be found.
9. Buhler/Hood 1970, no. 280.

William Moulton
1720–ca. 1793

A

B

C

Although others in his family are said to have preceded him in the craft, William Moulton was the first Moulton to practice silversmithing in Newburyport, Massachusetts. He was born on 12 July 1720 in Newbury, the son of Joseph (1694–1756) and the grandson of William (1664–1732), both of whom have been cited occasionally as silversmiths (qq.v. Appendix B). His mother was Mary (Noyes) Moulton. His brother Joseph (q.v.), born four years later, would also enter the trade.[1] With his brother he witnessed the will of Hannah Kent, Samuel Burt's (q.v.) mother-in-law, in 1754.[2]

William married Lydia Greenleaf (b. 1723), who was possibly related to Benjamin or Simon Greenleaf (qq.v. Appendix B), on 16 September 1742 and moved to Newburyport. Lydia was the daughter of Edmund (ca. 1694–1759) and Lydia (Brown) Greenleaf (b. 1697). William and Lydia had seven children: Joseph (b. 1744 [q.v.]), William (b. 1749), Anna (b. 1750), Mary (b. 1754), Lydia (b. 1757), Edmond (or Enoch) (b. 1759), and Catherine (b. 1762).

William practiced as a silversmith in Newburyport, but then relocated to Hampstead, New Hampshire. He signed a petition for a parish on 1 January 1743/44, and in 1762 he purchased land there. During the next two decades he bought and sold land in Hampstead and Londonderry, New Hampshire. In two of these transactions he is identified as a goldsmith.[3] At the time he wrote his will on 23 November 1787, he was living in Hampstead, Rockingham County, New Hampshire, and referred to himself as a yeoman. He had already acquired land in the Ohio Company by that time, and he may have written his will in anticipation of the rigors of the journey west because by 1788 he and some members of his family had traveled to Marietta, Ohio, where they were part of the initial settlements there in April of that year. An early history of that area discusses the Moultons' evacuation of their house during "the time of the Indian troubles there in 1791":

> Next [leaving the house], old Mr. William Moulton from Newburyport, Mass., aged 70, with his leather apron full of old goldsmith's tools and tobacco. Close at his heels came his daughter, Anna, with the china teapot, cups and saucers. Lydia brought the great Bible. But when all were in, the mother was missing. Where was mother? She must be killed. "No," says Lydia, "mother said she would not leave the house looking *so*. She would put things away and a little more to rights, and then she would come." Directly mother came, bringing the looking-glasses, knives and forks, etc.

William Moulton died in Marietta, probably in 1793 during a smallpox epidemic. His will was probated on 16 May 1795 and his inventory taken on the same day. His estate, valued at a total of $508.22, included three silver tablespoons, six silver teaspoons, and blacksmith's bellows (valued at $2.50), a vise ($4), one stake, four hammers, and two pairs of tongs (at a total of $6.50). William was in debt to Joseph Moulton (1724–95) of Newbury for $935 and to Joseph Moulton (1744–1816) of Newburyport for $50.40.[4]

William's son Joseph became a silversmith, and some works, including two spoons at the Ohio Historical Society in Columbus, have been attributed to his daughter Lydia (d. 1823).[5] His grandsons Ebenezer (1768–1824), William (1772–1861), Enoch (1780–1820?), and Abel (1784–1840 +), all the children of Joseph, also became silversmiths.[6]

William's known work is largely limited to flatware, with the exception of several swords attributed to him by Harold L. Peterson, who suggested that "more swords bearing his mark have survived than those of any other of

the famous colonial silversmiths except perhaps John Bailey."[7] William used
W·Moulton in a rectangle with pellet between, italic capitals and script lowercase (A), and two initials marks W·M in a plain rectangle (B) and WM in serrated
rectangle (C) have been attributed to him. The mark (B) is found on silver
made about 1760 but is also found on pieces that date later than William's
working career. Hence, the mark may also have been used by his grandson
William Moulton (1772–1861).[8] The mark W·MOULTON has also been attributed
to the elder Moulton, but because no pieces bearing this mark date within his
working career, it is more likely that the mark belongs to his grandson.[9] GWRW

SURVIVING OBJECTS

	Mark	Inscription	Patron	Date	Reference	Owner
Spoon (miniature; attrib.)	none	none		ca. 1770	Newburyport Maritime Society Antiques Show 1981, 1	
Sword	?	?		?	Peterson 1955, no. 31	
Sword	?	?		ca. 1770	Peterson 1955, no. 30	
Sword (possibly same as one of the above; attrib.)	none	none		ca. 1770	Newburyport Maritime Society Antiques Show 1981, 1	
Tablespoon	A	J.A.M.ˢ–J.U.D./ M.O.R.S.S./1753		1753	Newburyport Maritime Society Antiques Show 1981, 1	
Tablespoon	A†	S/AS		ca. 1755	Buhler/Hood 1970, no. 194	YUAG
Tablespoon	A	DS		ca. 1750	DAPC 84.3083	
Tablespoon	C (?)	C.A.M.		ca. 1790	Newburyport Maritime Society Antiques Show 1981, 1	
Teaspoon	A	KG		ca. 1760	DAPC 73.3178	WM
Teaspoon	B	EG		ca. 1785		CHS
Teaspoon	B†	PT		ca. 1760	DAPC 79.4493	
Teaspoon	B	ISB		ca. 1755		OYHS
Unspecified number of teaspoons	B (?)	K/EM		ca. 1785	Newburyport Maritime Society Antiques Show 1981, 1	
Teaspoon	C†	A/NN		ca. 1755	Buhler/Hood 1970, no. 193	YUAG
Two teaspoons	C (?)	JB		ca. 1780	Newburyport Maritime Society Antiques Show 1981, 1	

1. *Newbury VR* 1:348; Moulton 1906, 270; Decatur 1941a, 14.
2. ECPR 335:241.

3. Moulton is identified as a goldsmith when he sold land in Hampstead to Benjamin Greenleaf of Newburyport in 1772 and in a deed where he bought land in 1782; see RCD 103:118; 119:117–18. Otherwise he is identified as a gentleman; see RCD 111:294, 545; 109:38, 481, 521–22; 106:39; 107:11–12; 147:327; Noyes 1903, 1:19–21, 155, 295–96, 372, 399.

4. *Newbury VR* 2:348. For Lydia, see *Newbury VR* 1:196; for her parents, see *Newbury VR* 1:74; 2:205, 603; Moulton 1906, 184; Decatur 1941a, 14, citing Julia P. Cutter, *The Founders of Ohio: Brief Sketches of the Forty-Eight Pioneers* (1888). For Moulton's estate, see Probate Court Records, Washington County, Marietta, Ohio, 1:15–16, 19. I am grateful to Kim McGrew of the Campus Martius Museum in Marietta for her assistance.

5. Decatur 1941a, 17; Flynt/Fales 1968, 282. Mrs. Edgar F. Whittaker, Jr., of Pigeon Cove, Massachusetts, continues to work on documenting Lydia's career as a silversmith.

6. Flynt/Fales 1968, 280–83.

7. Peterson 1954, 212–13; Peterson 1955, nos. 30–31. The sherry label and skewer attributed to Moulton (Gourley 1965, nos. 143–44) were unavailable for examination. American examples of these forms, especially at this early date, are rare, and the attribution of these pieces is doubtful. Moulton also made shoe and knee buckles, which he supplied as payment to the carpenter David Boynton in 1769 and 1770 in exchange for Boynton's "Casing a Looking Glass" (perhaps one of the very objects that Mrs. Moulton saved during the Indian alarm of 1791); see David Boynton Account Book, fols. 25v, 26r, YUAG.

8. See, for example, a teaspoon DAPC 70.2362.

9. This mark was one of four that Stephen Decatur attributed to the elder Moulton; see Decatur 1941a, 14. For examples of pieces with this mark, see DAPC 85.2161, 73.3181, and 73.3176.

Edmund Mountfort
1717–49 +

Edmund Mountfort was born in Boston on 20 May 1717, the son of John Mountfort (1670–1724), a cooper, and Mary Cock (b. 1679), who were married in 1693/94.[1] His paternal grandparents were the shopkeeper Edmund (ca. 1630–90) and Elizabeth Mountfort (ca. 1634–1703).[2] His maternal grandparents were Joseph Cock (d. 1678) and Susannah Upshall (b. 1639).[3]

On 4 August 1729 John Burt (q.v.) of Boston was appointed to be the guardian of Edmund Mountfort, "a minor aged about 12 yrs son of John Mountfort late of Boston aforesaid cooper dec." The one-thousand-pound bond was signed by John Burt, William Lee, shipwright, and William Warner, cooper of Boston.[4] Along with William Simpkins (q.v.), Mountfort witnessed a deed for Burt in 1737.[5] Edmund Mountfort would have finished his apprenticeship with Burt about 1738. Mountfort may have been a journeyman for William Simpkins because along with James Butler (q.v.) he witnessed a deed for Simpkins in 1744.[6] In 1742 and 1748 Edmund Mountfort was described as being a goldsmith of Boston in two deeds in which he sold real estate from his father's estate to his sister Hannah and her husband, William Warner.[7] No records of his marriage or death in Massachusetts exist, and no silver marked by him has survived. PEK

1. RC 9:115, 210; RC 24:123; SCPR 27:254.
2. Codman 1918, 172.
3. RC 9:72; SCPR 14:280–82; RC 21:4.
4. SCPR 27:254.
5. YCD 19:232.
6. SCD 68:137–38.
7. SCD 64:178–79; 76:37.

Thomas Mullins or Moulin
ca. 1680–1744 +

The date and place of Thomas Mullins's birth are unknown. He first appeared in the Boston records in 1708, when he was married by the Reverend Cotton Mather to Hannah Ballard.[1] He must have joined the Brattle Street Church in 1710/11, when his eldest son, Thomas, a year-old child, and his daughter Hannah, one week old, were baptized there.[2] Thomas and Hannah Mullins had four more children, all of whom were baptized in the Brattle Street Church: Elizabeth (b. 1712/13), John (b. 1714), Benjamin (b. 1716/17), and Charles (b. 1719).[3]

In 1709/10, Mullins witnessed a deed for Edward Winslow (q.v.), which suggests that he may have been employed in Winslow's shop as a journeyman.[4] Mullins's association with Winslow was a long one: he witnessed additional deeds for him in 1710/11 (with Moody Russell [q.v.]) and in 1716 (with John Banks [q.v.]).[5] He also witnessed a deed for Thomas Bradford (q.v.) in 1725.[6]

Mullins is named as a goldsmith in several documents during this same period. He is listed as "Thomas Mullin, Goldsmith," in accounts with the bookseller Daniel Henchman dated 1713. His purchases from Henchman included a Bible, a catechism, two dozen primers, and binding for a book.[7] When Peter Sargent died in 1713/14, Mullins, along with Winslow and William Cowell, Sr. (q.v.), all provided rings for which Mullins charged the estate £6.[8] In 1715, Mullins appears as plaintiff in a suit against the trader Robert Boyd of Boston, charging that Boyd had neglected to pay him £5.3.6 "due to balance accounts." Mullins had provided Boyd with small silver items detailed on the bill:

Mr. Robert Boyd Dr.					Contra Cr.			
1714		£	S	D	1715		£	S D
June 7th To 1 Pair Buckles		1.			Apr.ll 30.th By Silver			.12
Jan.ry 5 To 6 Thimbles & 6 buckles			.18		By 6oz 10dwt Ditto		2.	12
1715					By Cash			. 1
May 11 To one Wigg		1.	15		By ditto			. 5
14 To 1 pair Buckles		1.	1. 6		By ditto			1. 6
27 To 1 Snoffe box		2.	6				3.	11. 6
					Ballance due to			
					Thomas Mullins }		5.	3. 6
30 To 1 Ditto			.18				£8.	15.
July 12 To 1 pair Gloves			. 3					
13 To 1 Snoffe box			. 12					
To Cash lent			. 5					
15 To one Gold Ring		1.						
To one Seale			. 5					
To 1 Watch Cheane			. 15					
£8. 15. –					Sworne in Court			

Sworne in Court
New England Boston July 18th
[17??]
Except Errors
₧ Thomas Mullins[9]

Another bill dated 9 October 1715 to a Mr. Stoddard was for small items and a pair of chafing dishes:

october ye 9 1715   <u>M^r: Stoderd D^r</u>

November To one Silver houck	o – 2 – 6
ye 21	
To making one panakin	o – 18 – o
Decber	
y^e 27 To making one Spoune	o – 3 – o
To making one houck and nie	o – 2 – o
March	
y^e 12 To tiping a Sesas Case	o – 2 – o
28 To manding one bell	o – 1 – o
April	
y^e 26 To making Chafin dishes	6 – 5 – o
To 11^{oz} of Silver at 3^s to the pound	5 – 1 – o

$$12 = 14 = 6$$

Rec^d: one pound   1–oo

£11 = 14 :6

abat^{ed} 4 :6

£11:10:— [10]

Apparently Stoddard covered the bill by providing Mullins with a discount with the clockmaker Benjamin Bagnall, Sr. (q.v. Appendix A), and by making up the balance in cash. An interesting aspect of the bill with Stoddard is the inscription on the obverse:

Boston May ye 17.th 1716
Rec^d. in full of ye Bill Twelve
pounds tenn shill^g y^t is to
say ℔ dis^{ct} wth Benj^a Bagnall
Eight pounds & in mony four
pounds tenn shill^g
£ 8: –: –
£ 4:10: –
£12:10: – Thomas Mullins

While continuing to call himself a silversmith, Mullins appears to have built up a lucrative business attending at funerals. In 1738 he is referred to as "Thomas Moulin of Boston, Goldsmith," in a court case. The account attached indicates that the defendant, the boatbuilder Jonathan Burnell of Boston, owed Mullins for funeral services:

Sepr ye 8 Mr Jonathan Burnell To Thos Moulin D^r	
for his Mothers funerall	
1737 To carring the Corpes and attendance	£3. o. o
To the us of the Paul	o. 12. o
To opining the tumb and Bells	1. 2. o
	4. 14. o [11]

In 1734 and 1741, Mullins was appointed as one of three gravediggers for the town and assigned to the Old and South burying grounds.[12] In 1741 he received payment for "Pall Porters Ringing Bells &c." at the funeral of George Hanners, Sr. (q.v.), a fellow silversmith with whom he may have had a close relationship because in 1730 Mullins witnessed Hanners's mother's will. By the time of Hanners's funeral Mullins's business seems to have grown considerably, for the payment is listed as due to "Tho Moulin & Comp."[13] Similar accounts exist for funerals that he attended to in 1739, 1741, and 1743.[14] Mullins submitted bills for ringing the town bells from March 1733/34 to March 1743/44.[15] He sued the oarmaker William Harmon in 1733, but the details of the case are not clear.[16] He may also be the Thomas Mullins who served as a watchman for the town intermittently from 1721/22 to 1736.[17]

There is no record of Mullins's death in Boston, and no estate probated in Suffolk County. His son Thomas appears to have dropped the use of Jr. from his name about 1748.

No silver marked by Thomas Mullins is known to survive. The possibility exists that the TM mark attributed here to Thomas Milner (q.v.) may have been used by Mullins. BMW

1. RC 28:20.
2. *Church in Brattle Square*, 130.
3. *Church in Brattle Square*, 132, 134, 137, 140; RC 24:65, 73, 88, 102, 127, 141.
4. SCD 25:11–12.
5. SCD 26:173–74; 33:154.
6. SCD 46:152.
7. Daniel Henchman Ledger, 1712–ca. 1735, fol. 59, NEHGS.
8. SCPR 22:328.
9. SCCR, Court of Common Pleas Record Book 1714–15, 351; SCCR, file 10477.
10. D. Greenough papers, MHS. The value for silver given in the last line of the bill is too low. The figure is clearly 3^s to the pound, which does not add up to the figure at the right and was probably a clerk's error.
11. SCCR, Court of Common Pleas Record Book 1737, 277; file papers, writ dated 16 June 1738.
12. RC 15:286–88; Seybolt 1939, 195, 222.
13. SCPR 29:369–70; 35:457; 37:47–48.
14. SCCR, file 54772.
15. Seybolt 1939, 195–96.
16. SCCR, file 35402.
17. Seybolt 1939, 156, 159, 161, 176, 202.

Gideon Myrick
born between 1735 and 1741

A

Gideon Myrick was the second child born to Elizabeth Osborn (1715–98) and Capt. William Myrick (d. 1742), who were married in Eastham, Massachusetts, on 23 January 1733/34. Gideon's birth took place after William, their first child, was born on 26 October 1734, and before Elizabeth, their third child, was born in 1742, but his exact date of birth cannot be determined.[1] Myrick's father, William Myrick, was born in Harwich (now Brewster), Massachusetts, to Nathaniel and Alice (Freeman) Myrick and was lost at sea in 1742.[2] Gideon's mother, Elizabeth Osborn, was the daughter of the Reverend Samuel Osborn and Jedidah Smith (b. 1689) of Sandwich, Massachusetts. Following her husband's death in 1742, Elizabeth married William Paine, a merchant and representative in the Provincial Legislature who died at Cape Breton in 1746 while serving as a lieutenant in Capt. Elisha Doane's Company in the Louisbourg Expedition. Elizabeth remarried for the second time to Edmund Doane of Eastham and Barrington, Nova Scotia, on 10 November 1749, and she died in Barrington in 1798.[3]

As a result of William Myrick's and William Paine's early deaths, Edmund Doane became Gideon Myrick's stepfather in 1749, a role he would have assumed between Myrick's eighth and fourteenth year. Doane may have been related to the silversmiths John and Joshua Doane (qq.v.), and he may have arranged for his stepson's apprenticeship with John Doane in Boston.

The genealogy for the Doane family of Boston, Massachusetts, notes that Gideon Myrick "was a goldsmith by trade; went to sea, fell overboard in the night and was drowned," although the date of this accident is not recorded.[4]

No silver by Myrick's hand has been identified for certain. Spoons with a G:M mark (A) have been found and may be by Myrick. According to family history, the spoon in the Museum of Fine Arts, Boston, was handed down in the Shrimpton/Gibbs families of Salem, Massachusetts. JJF

SURVIVING OBJECTS

	Mark	Inscription	Patron	Date	Reference	Owner
Tablespoon	A†	IN/EB		ca. 1750		MFAB
Tablespoon	A	HT		ca. 1775	DAPC 84.3496	
Tablespoon	A	H/CR	Hastings family (?)	ca. 1760	DAPC 71.3427	WM
Tablespoon	A*	S/TR		ca. 1755	YUAG files	

1. Doane 1902, 75, 508–09.
2. Doane 1902, 508.
3. *Edgartown VR*, 160; *Sibley's Harvard Graduates* 9:551.
4. Doane 1902, 75, 509.

James Nash, Jr.
1711–37

James Nash, Jr., was born in Boston on 27 October 1711 to James Nash, a housewright, and Sarah Marion (d. before 1730), who were married on 7 December 1710 by the Presbyterian minister Rev. Thomas Bridge.[1] The silversmith's maternal grandparents were Samuel Marion (1655–1726), a tailor, and his second wife, Mary Wilson (1662–after 1726).[2] James Nash, Jr., goldsmith, married Margaret (Winter) Linaker on 29 April 1736, in a ceremony performed by Rev. Charles Chauncy.[3] Margaret Linaker was a sister of the jeweler Stephen Winter (q.v.).

James Nash, goldsmith, "being weak in Body but of sound & perfect mind & memory," wrote his will on 6 May 1737. It was presented for probate on 24 May that same year. Margaret, the executor of his estate, was also the sole beneficiary, designated to receive his "Household Goods, Plate &c."[4] No inventory was taken of the Nash estate; instead a five-hundred-pound bond was offered by his widow, her brother the blacksmith Edward Winter, and Stephen Winter.[5]

Nash's brief career as a silversmith lasted from about 1732, when he would have completed his apprenticeship, to his death in 1737. No surviving objects can be attributed to him. DAF

1. RC 24:77; RC 28:28; Thwing. James Nash, Sr., married his second wife, Anne Earle, in 1730; see SCD 96:146.
2. Thwing; Wyman 1879, 1:656, *NEHGR* 25:343; RC 9:51. The will of Samuel Marion included a legacy for his daughter Sarah Nash in August 1726; see SCPR 25:33.
3. RC 28:198.
4. SCPR 33:164–66.
5. SCPR 19:411–12, new ser.

Richard Nevill
w. ca. 1674–76

Richard Nevill is identified in the Boston records as a goldsmith when the town selectmen decided not to admit him as an inhabitant on 27 January 1674/75.[1] Two days earlier "Richard Nevill formerlie Aprentice to Robt Sand[rs] now serv[t] to John Whalie" had been ordered returned to the court, probably the Court of Common Pleas, upon the complaint of Richard Way and Thomas More.[2] It is tempting to think that "Robt. Sand[rs]" is an abbreviation for Robert Sanderson, Sr. (q.v.), and that Nevill was his apprentice.[3] Richard Nevill's birth records have not been found in England or in New England, and there is no record of an apprenticeship for him at Goldsmiths' Hall. In spite of the Boston selectmen's refusal to admit him as an inhabitant, Nevill served in King Philip's War a few months later and was paid £1.19.6 for his services on 20 August 1675.[4] No further evidence of him has been found in the Boston records, and no silver by him is known. PEK

1. RC 10:56.
2. RC 7:90.
3. Savage 1860–62, 4:22. A Robert Saunders also lived in the Boston area at the time and may also be the individual in the document.
4. John Hull Ledger, vol. 4, fol. 31, NEHGS.

Abijah Northey
1741–1816

A

B

A member of the Northey family of Salem, Massachusetts, silversmiths, Abijah Northey was born on 1 August 1741, the son of David (q.v.) and Miriam (Bassett) Northey and brother of William and Edward Northey (qq.v.).[1] Presumably he was trained by his father in silversmithing and other metalworking skills. He married Abigail Wood (1745–1814) of Charlestown, Massachusetts, the daughter of Thomas (1707/08–59) and Rebecca (Osborne) Wood (ca. 1718–1801), on 31 October 1765 in Charlestown.[2] They had three children, two sons and a daughter. By 1771, Northey owned a house with a shop adjoining in Salem and presumably was in business.[3]

Abijah combined numerous other enterprises with silversmithing, and by the late 1790s he seems to have abandoned silversmithing in favor of being a general trader. He advertised in 1789 that he had "moved from the Shop he lately occupied, to one on the opposite side of the street, two doors below the Post-Office; where he has for Sale, as usual, Hard-ware and Pewter; a good assortment of GOLDSMITH and JEWELEY WARE, and CROCKERY: all which he will sell at the lowest rates. He gives Cash for old Silver, Pewter, Brass, Copper and Lead."[4] Later advertisements, in 1791, list only an extensive assortment of base metals, making no mention of silver.[5]

Account books kept by Abijah and later by his son Abijah, Jr. (1774–1853), indicate that by 1797 Abijah was importing and purchasing large shipments of earthenware, crockery, and glass, some from England.[6] These accounts continue until his death in 1816, when he was identified as a trader in the probate records.[7]

Silversmithing was thus probably always something of a sideline for Abijah Northey. The first memoir of him merely notes that he "kept a store," and silver by him is rare.[8] His marks are AN in a rectangle (A, B), and two tablespoons made by him for his own use are at the Peabody Essex Museum.[9] A caster by Paul Revere, Jr. (q.v.), made ca. 1755–60, was given, according to tradition, by Revere to Northey, and a child's cup by John Burt (q.v.), also said to have been owned by Northey, has been published.[10] GWRW

SURVIVING OBJECTS

	Mark	Inscription	Patron	Date	Reference	Owner
Two tablespoons	B†	AN	Abijah Northey	ca. 1790	Fales 1983, 24–25	PEM
Teaspoon	A*	IT		ca. 1775		PEM
Two teaspoons	A*	MC		ca. 1775		HD

	Mark	Inscription	Patron	Date	Reference	Owner
Teaspoon	A*	SD		ca. 1775	MFA 1911, no. 795	
Teaspoon	A*	S/AM		ca. 1770	DAPC 73.2437	WM
Teaspoon	A†	IA		ca. 1770	DAPC 73.3345	WM
Teaspoon	A *or* B	SW		ca. 1775	DAPC 70.1226	WM

1. Manuscript Northey family genealogy, Northey Family Papers, box 1, folder 3, PEM.
2. *Salem VR* 4:129; Browne 1862, 80; *Salem VR* 6:94–95; *Charlestown VR* 1:376; Wyman 1879, 2:1045–46; *Index of Obituaries, 1784–1840*, 4:3305.
3. *Salem VR* 2:112–13; Pruitt 1978, 150–51.
4. *Salem Mercury*, 8 December 1789.
5. *Salem Gazette*, 29 November 1791.
6. Abijah Northey Account Books, two volumes, PEM.
7. ECPR, docket 19596.
8. Browne 1862, 80.
9. Belden 1980, 316.
10. Buhler 1972, no. 337; advertisement of Gebelein Silversmiths, Inc., in *Old-Time New England* 63, no. 3 (January–March 1973): iv.

David Northey
1709–78

A

B

C

Patriarch of the Northey family of Salem, Massachusetts, silversmiths, David Northey (or Northee, as it sometimes appears) was born in Boston on 30 March 1709, the son of John, a glazier, and Sarah (Hill) Northey.[1] His family moved to Marblehead, Massachusetts, sometime thereafter. Northey may have trained in Marblehead because in June 1729 he was tending his father's shop in Marblehead when he was assaulted in a robbery. The robbery was committed by Jacob Fowler who stole tools and supplies that Northey's father had bought from Joseph Watkins, probably the Marblehead goldsmith Joseph Watkins (q.v.) who was tried for counterfeiting two years earlier. The inventory of the tools presented in the court case suggests that Northey's father purchased the goldsmith's tools from Watkins to set his son up in business. The tools Watkins sold to John Northey in April 1729 included:

1 forgeing anvill prime cost	£7. 0. 0
1 Pair of Bellows Dº	3. 10. 0
1 Teast	1. 0. 0
1 pair of Large Scales & Weights	2. 0. 0
1 Big Iron 9/ 1 Small Dº 6/	0. 15. 0
1 Hollowing Stamp	1. 0. 0
1 Linhett 5/ one pair of forgeing Tongs 6/	0. 11. 0
1 Pair of Nealing Tongs and Poker	0. 6. 0
1 Slise 2/ 1 Lamp 3/ Small Bellows 6/6	0. 11. 6
1 pair Small Scales	0. 9. 0
1 Sett of Small weights	0. 3. 0
1 Straner £1:5: a Limitt Box 3/6	1. 8. 6
3 Tin Callisters 3/ 2 Tin Candlesticks 5/	0. 8. 0
2 Brass blow pipes 6/ Sundry Small punches	0. 16. 0
2 Simmett Blocks & two malletts	0. 4. 0
10 Large punches @ 2/6	1. 5. 0
1 flat Bottom Stake	0. 9. 0

5 Large Hammers @ [torn]	2. 0. 0
3 midlin Hammers 5/	0. 15. 0
12 Small Hammers @ 3/6	2. 2. 0
2 Small Vices	0. 14. 0
1 pair Spring plyers	0. 6. 0
4 pair of plyers 3/6	0. 14. 0
4 doz: of Files one with another	2. 8. 0
Borax & Sundry Small Things	0. 5. 0
9 Black Potts	0. 12. 0
12 Nests of Crucibles	0. 12. 0
Sand	0. 3.[0]
a Pair Skrew & flask	0. 6. 0
a boyling pan	0. 6. 0
a pair of Skrew Compasses	0. 5. 0
2 Iron Tribletts 2/6 Coles 18/	1. 0. 6
The Sashes (the Glass being Northeys own)	1. 14. 4
The Benches and Skyns	1. 5. 0
	37. 3.10[2]

The Lynn vital records state that David Northee of Salem, goldsmith, son of John of Marblehead, married Miriam Bassett (1712–92) on 25 July 1732.[3] Of their children, Abijah, Edward, and William (qq.v.) followed in their father's footsteps as silversmiths or, perhaps more accurately, metalsmiths.

Although David Northey consistently styled himself a goldsmith, there is considerable documentary evidence that he sold a general line of merchandise and that he repaired and worked in base metals as well. In the 1730s, 1740s, and 1750s Northey bought for resale such objects as pewter plates, soup dishes, brass candlesticks, warming pan covers and bottoms, spoons, horn knives and forks, tongs and shovels, and other types of hardware and metal goods from several Boston braziers, coppersmiths, and merchants, including Mary Jackson and Son, Jackson and Charles, and John Spooner. Court documents reveal that Northey engaged in shipping furniture to the West Indies as well.[4] He also repaired and may have made watches. He purchased watch-repairing supplies from John Welsh (q.v.) of Boston in 1769, and several accounts testify to his watchmaking and watch-repairing activities. Other bills and documents related to repair work and to the sale of pewter and hardware survive.[5]

The diverse nature of Northey's business is revealed in the inventory of his estate taken after his death in 1778.[6] Northey appears to have prospered at his trades. His total estate inventory was valued at £1,657.10.72, including his "Mansion House & its Dependencies in Salem" worth £350 and other real estate valued at £182. His household furnishings included walnut and mahogany furniture, prints, books, and £22 worth of silver plate.

The inventory included a long list of goods and tools found in Northey's shop. The list is important in establishing the diverse nature of his business:

33 lb Tobacco, 16 lb Indigo & 64 lb Flax all at	6	19	0
12 p.ʳ Wool Cards, 16 lb Bees Wax, 7 lb Baberry Tallow	3	1	3
80 Tea Pots, 44 pieces Sundrys in Bowls, Cups, Saucers	1	18	8
20 lb Currants 17 lb Raisins 1 ½ lb Nutmegs all	1	13	8
43 lb Sugar 68 lb Allem 8 lb Capperas all at	2	19	2
12 lb Tea 34 lb Coffee 8 lb Black Peppʳ at	3	12	—

Item	£	s	d
16 lb Snuff 2 lb Brimstone 20 lb Logwood all at	2	4	—
10 lb Starch 8 lb Sheeps Wool 3 lb Ginger all at	1	0	8
96 p^r Buckles 33 pair Yarn Mitts 7 lb Beads all at	4	15	0
40 Pair Mens Womens Boys & Girls Leather Shoes	5	14	4
Sundry Toys 40 Brass Thimbles 36 Pipes all at	1	17	6
12 Wooden Boxes & Buckets, 1 Piggin, Sundry Corks all at		11	6
3/4 lb Cinamon 2 lb All Spice 1 pair Candlesticks all	1	7	4
3 lb Sewing Silk 8 lb Sewing thread 5 Silk Handks all at	7	13	1½
34 hanks Twist, 15 ½ doz. hanks Worsted all at	1	5	4
8 pair Spectacles 7 ¼ Doz^n Ordinary Pocket Knives	1	5	9
13 Leather Pocket Books, 36 Pair brass sleeve Buttons	16	—	
29 Ivory Combs 34 Horn D^o 1 Brass Skillet all	2	0	6
10 Pieces Tape 10 Jackets & Trowsers 3 Razors	1	16	6
1 Doz^n Metal Tea Spoons 2 Ink Horns, Rheam Pap^r	13	—	
37 Pair Cloth Wom^s Shoes, 26 p^r Wom^s Leat^r D^o	8	16	—
9 Pair Yarn Hose 9 lb Stocking Yarn all at	1	10	—
1 Scale Beam & Scales 26 lb of Weights 2 Warming Pans	2	2	
28 y^{ds} White Linen 26 Printed Handks 5 y^{ds} Buckram	4	5	4
219 y^{ds} Stripe & Plain Cotton Linens 157 y^{ds} Tow Cloth	18	16	—
104 y^{ds} Woolen Cloth 15 ¼ y^{ds} Crape, Grizell &c all at	9	19	—
8 ¼ Doz^n Pewter Spoons 3 ½ Doz. Pint D^o Porringers	2	18	6
4 ¼ Doz^n D^o Cups 22 pewter Plates all at	2	1	—
7 Doz^n Pint D^o Basons 28 D^o Quart Pots all	6	14	—
30 Pewter large Basons Coffee Pot Dipp^r Drudg^r Box	3	2	6
8 y^{ds} Micklenburg 4 y^{ds} Shalloon 2 ½ Bundles Pins	2	5	0
144 lb Cotton Wool Sundry Needles all at	11	12	—
. . .			
Sundry Haberdashery, Silk Ribbons, Ferrits &c	4	11	9
5 Sheets Bonnet Board 2 p^s Gartering 9 Dolls &c	1	9	—
1 Gross Hitches & Tongues, Sundry Black & White Lace	4	—	—
Sundry Blacking Balls &c all at	2	—	
. . .			
Two Handsaws, Pair Fetters, a Bench Vice, Old Tools	1	12	—
. . .			
One Box Watchmakers Tools, Springs, Keys &c.	3	—	—
. . .			
3 Razors & Hone, A set of Cast Letters & a Bell		12	—
. . .			
1100 lb Old Pewter, 253 lb Lead, 30 lb Old Tools	40	6	7
1 Anvil 1 Pair Sheers & Tongs, A Copper Driping Pan	3	12	—
Lath, Wheels, Pewter Tools & Grind Stone all at	16	—	—
. . .			
1 pair Goldsmiths Bellows An Old Cradle all at	1	0	0

Northey thus sold clothing, foodstuffs, hardware, woodenware, pewter, brass, textiles, and many other goods and was equipped to perform pewter-working, watchmaking, and, it would seem, printing, in addition to whatever work he may have performed as a goldsmith. Northey's activities are strong evidence that, in some cases, there were no sharp dividing lines between the metal-working crafts.

Northey's estate included a house and about six acres of land in Ferry Lane in Salem as well as his mansion house and its dependencies in Salem, along with three common rights in the Great Pasture.[7] His household goods included 66 ounces of wrought plate, 2,200 Paper Dollars, and nearly £100 of gold and silver money. A plow, a wheelbarrow, sundry farming tools, 1½ tons of hay, a chaise, a cow, and salt listed in his inventory suggest that farming was another of Northey's part-time activities. Northey left his house and his slave girl Venus to his wife.[8]

Three marks have been assigned to David Northey: DN in a rectangle (A, B) and D·NORTHEE (C) in a rectangle.[9] Among the rare surviving silver objects bearing his mark are a gold mourning ring dated 1748, a trencher salt, a child's cup, a porringer, and a spoon. No pewter objects bearing his mark are known. A family descendant, William E. Northey, owned a swage, some molds for pewter spoons, and other tools that were owned by several generations of the Northey family.[10]   GWRW

SURVIVING OBJECTS

	Mark	Inscription	Patron	Date	Reference	Owner
Cup	C†	AN	Abijah or Anthony Northey (?)	ca. 1740	Buhler/Hood 1970, no. 176	YUAG
Mourning ring (gold)	A†	E · H · Ob · Aug.ᵗ · 19 · 1748 AE · 34		1748	Buhler 1972, no. 219	MFAB
Porringer	A*	EM/CC		ca. 1760	YUAG files	
Porringer	C	MO		ca. 1760	Avery 1920, no. 128	MMA
Salt	A*	CW (altered to CH)	Cynthia (Winslow) Northey (?)	ca. 1735	Buhler/Hood 1970, no. 175	YUAG
Tablespoon	C	1730		1730	Antiques 15 (June 1929): 472	
Tablespoon	C (?)	IM		ca. 1770		ChM
Tablespoon	C	G/ZE		ca. 1740	DAPC 88.3015	
Teaspoon	B†	ND/No 4		ca. 1760	Buhler 1972, appendix no. 62	MFAB
Teaspoon	B*	ST		ca. 1770		WHS

1. RC 24:63. Northey's mark spells the name as "Northee," although later generations spell the name "Northey."
2. Photostat in the Bigelow-Phillips files.
3. *Lynn VR* 2:279. See also *Salem VR* 4:129; 6:95. Northey is referred to as a goldsmith of Salem as early as 12 January 1732 in ECD 60:269.
4. Photostat in the Bigelow-Phillips files.
5. Numerous bills documenting Northey's business can be found in the Northey Family Papers, PEM. Other Northey transactions can be found in the Timothy Orne Ledger, fols. 72, 88, PEM; the Samuel Barton Account Books, for 1731–48, fol. 118, and for 1743–64, fol. 91, PEM; and the Derby Family Papers, vol. 28, fol. 17, PEM; SCCR, Court of Common Pleas Record Book 1739, 72. Laughlin [1940, 1970] 1981, 71–72, notes Northey's activities as a pewterer.
6. ECPR, docket 19597.
7. Northey acquired land butting southerly on Ferry Lane in 1751, including the "Windmill thereon and the Tackle and Geer thereof"; see ECD 96:132.
8. His will, written on 24 July 1773, is in the Northey Family Papers, PEM. The slave girl Venus may be the servant for life recorded for Northey in the Massachusetts tax list of 1771. The list shows that Northey had a house with shop adjoining and ten pounds' annual worth of real estate; see Pruitt 1978, 146–47.

9. Flynt/Fales 1968, 289; see also Buhler 1972, 1:259. Kovel 1961, 200, also records D.N. in a rectangle, D.NORTHEE, and D I NORTHEE, but examples of these marks have not been found.

10. The early eighteenth-century swage iron (PEM, 130,679) is illustrated in Fales 1983, 15, fig. 8. Two brass molds for pewter spoons (PEM, 130,687 and 130,688) were among the objects stolen from PEM in 1970.

Edward Northey
1737–1802 +

The middle son of the Salem, Massachusetts, silversmith David Northey (q.v.), Edward was born on 27 March 1737.[1] Like his brothers Abijah and William (qq.v.), he may have been trained by his father, and he may have worked in Salem from about 1758 to 1770, although no record of his work has yet been found. In 1770 he married Susanna Parsons (b. 1748), the daughter of Jonathan (b. 1713) and Susannah (Hadley) Parsons (b. 1709) of Gloucester, Massachusetts.[2]

Edward moved to Gloucester, where he practiced as a silversmith in a shop in the "harbour parish so called on the northerly side of the Middle Street."[3] The tax list of 1771 records Edward there, with a house and a shop and merchandise valued at forty pounds (assets that compare favorably with those of his father and brothers, suggesting his marriage may have been an advantageous one).[4] In 1773 Northey was identified as a Gloucester goldsmith when he successfully sued the Newburyport cabinetmaker Samuel Smith for a debt of £10.12.[5] By 1785 Northey is referred to as being "of Manchester [Massachusetts]" in the deeds, reflecting his purchase there of a large amount of land.[6] By 17 June 1797 he had moved to Hopkinton, New Hampshire, and he was living there as late as 1802.[7]

No silver by him is known today, although in 1895 it was said that "some of [his] workmanship is in the possession of a descendant" in Manchester.[8] GWRW

1. Manuscript Northey family genealogy, Northey Family Papers, box 1, folder 3, PEM.
2. *Gloucester VR* 1:313, 516, 525; 2:388, 407.
3. ECD 128:117–18; 130:38; 133:53, 60; 136:187; 139:180; 144:215.
4. Pruitt 1978, 58–59.
5. SCCR, file 132344.
6. ECD 144:57.
7. ECD 162:182.
8. Lamson 1895, 324.

William Northey
1735–1804

A

B

William Northey, like his father, David (q.v.), was a silversmith who also worked in pewter and other metals. Born in Salem, Massachusetts, on 13 March 1735, William was the older brother of Abijah and Edward Northey (qq.v.), who also were silversmiths.[1] Like them, he probably was trained by his father.

William Northey was active in Salem by about 1762, when his name appears in a list as one of the silversmiths working in Salem at that time.[2] He married Rebecca Collins (1739/40–1826) of Lynn, Massachusetts, on 25 January 1764. She was the daughter of Zaccheus (b. 1698) and Elizabeth (Sawyer) Collins (b. 1703).[3] A Quaker, Northey was active in town affairs, much more so than any other Salem silversmith, as well as being an enterprising businessman. The Massachusetts tax list of 1771 indicates that Northey owned a house and a shop, and he was rated for two polls, which suggests that he employed a journeyman. He was still accepting apprentices in 1803, when Edward Stacey of Marblehead, Massachusetts, placed his nine-year-old son as an apprentice to Northey for five years.[4]

After Northey's death on 13 June 1804, the Reverend William Bentley wrote the following lengthy biographical notes, which provide a good understanding of the character of this craftsman:

> Died after complaints of declining health, at last suddenly, William Northey, aet. 70. He was born in Salem, of the Society of Friends, & was educated in the occupation of his Father as a Goldsmith, tho' he wrought in all the common work of metals, as a Tinman, pewterer, as original ingenuity would suggest in a trade, of which a single branch could promise by a very insufficient support. In the old French war he fell in readily with the taste of the Seamen in their buttons, buckles, &c. & had a great run of business, & placed himself in easy circumstances. In the American war he was not so unyielding as the Sect of Friends & adventured among his fellow citizens in depredations in English Commerce & was therefore 'read out' by his sect to which he had no partiality, excepting in regard to simplicity of opinions. He still worshipped with the sect & died in their affections. He served the Town, faithful in every important trust, & was President of the board of Selectmen when Gen. Washington visited Salem in 1789, Oct. 29 & welcomed him in the language of a Friend. "Friend W. Welcome to Salem." A few years before his death he bought the Cherry Farm, Marblehead side, 3 miles from Salem on Lynn bounds . . . & there he spent his last days & died. He married a Collins of Lynn, of whom it may be said, she has not her superior among women in her character of life. . . . Friend Northey was always esteemed an honest, blunt, but hard dealer. In conversation he was ready but dry in his replies. Seized characters easily & entertained all men in their own way happily. He was hospitable & yet never imposed upon. He could get rid of men as inoffensively as he could entertain them. A fund of humour, a consistency of character, an equality of temper, when not suddenly provoked & then he easily recovered himself, & never scrupled to confess his fault in the most public manner. He was original in his manners & thoughts, & if he sometimes speculated freely, he acted honourably. In his retired life . . . he did not grasp his hours so prudently as might have been wished, but no excess deprived him of the confidence, esteem & preference he had secured in his active life. He was tormented by obstructions in the urinary passages & died without much notice, at the moment, tho' last week in town he said he should never go into it again. He was of fine proportions. Large but not corpulent. His large hat & wig gave him distinction as well as his flowing wit. He could assume the most grave manners & in his first humour never appeared to trifle. 40 Carriages were in his funeral procession & he was interred in the friends grounds in Lynn.

The next day, Bentley attended Northey's funeral and added the following comments:

> Persons of every character in life attended & he was with great respect carried to his grave. Among all the Friends in this vicinity no one could compare with him in strength of mind, comprehensive views of men & manners, & in established reputation for integrity of mind. He was much beyond human nature in form & mind & never failed to secure respect from all men. Few of our citizens appear to profit from leaving their native soil, especially in old age. From my heart I did respect & reverence Friend Northey.[5]

In Northey's will, written in 1803 and witnessed by the silversmith David Ropes (1763–1812), Addison Richardson, and John Daland, he left "all my Tools for the Goldsmith Pewterer & Tinmans Business" to his son Ezra (b. 1779).[6]

His total estate amounted to some $15,000, including his homestead in Lynn valued at $4,500 and other real estate in Salem, Danvers, and Lynn. His personal estate included large numbers of pewter basins, quart and pint pots, spoons, and porringers; iron candlesticks; bell-metal skillets; and other base-metal goods in stock. Northey's personal silver amounted to 75 ounces valued at $1.25 per ounce. The presence of his apprentice is indicated by "Bed & Bedding in the Boy's Chamber" valued at $8, while his son Ezra's bed and bedding were worth $23.[7]

Little silver by William Northey is known today. His marks are WN in a rectangle (A, B).[8] The Peabody Essex Museum has tablespoons by Northey engraved for his own use, and pewter attributed to him has been published.[9] A silver caster of ca. 1735 by John Burt (q.v.) of Boston, perhaps owned originally by David Northey, is engraved for William and Rebecca (Collins) Northey.[10] GWRW

SURVIVING OBJECTS

	Mark	Inscription	Patron	Date	Reference	Owner
Spoon	A*	?		ca. 1770	YUAG files	
Tablespoon	A	IM		ca. 1770	DAPC 71.3445	WM
Three tablespoons	A*	N/WR	William and Rebecca (Collins) Northey	ca. 1770		PEM
Two tablespoons	A†	N/WR	William and Rebecca (Collins) Northey	ca. 1770		PEM
Tablespoon	A*	N/WR	William and Rebecca (Collins) Northey	ca. 1770		PEM
Teaspoon	A*	LP	Love (Pickman) Frye	ca. 1770	Buhler 1972, no. 107 (as Nathaniel Morse)	MFAB
Teaspoon	A	BG		ca. 1770	DAPC 73.2017	WM
Teaspoon	B†	MP		ca. 1770		PEM

1. Manuscript Northey family genealogy, Northey Family Papers, box 1, folder 3, PEM.
2. Forman 1971, 64.
3. *Lynn VR* 1:118, 119; 2:279, 339; *Newbury VR* 1:463.
4. Pruitt 1978, 152–53; Northey Family Papers, box 1, folder 3, PEM.
5. Bentley 1905–62, 3:93–94; see also 2:434. Northey's greeting of Washington is one of the cherished bits of Salem folklore and is mentioned in numerous sources in slightly varying form. Northey also served as a selectman in 1774, the same year he served on the Salem Committee of Safety and Correspondence; see Phillips 1937a, 327, 334, 463.
6. ECPR, docket 19606.
7. Although not included in the probate records, a copy of Northey's inventory is in the Northey Family Papers, box 1, folder 3, PEM.
8. Belden 1980, 316. This mark, misread as NM, has sometimes been attributed to Nathaniel Morse (q.v.); see Buhler 1972, 1:131.
9. PEM acc. no. 130,506.1–.3. Pewter attributed to Northey is published in Hammond 1984, 95.
10. Fales 1983, 16–17, fig. 9 (left), PEM acc. no. 126,513.

John Noyes
1674–1749

A

B

John Noyes was born on 4 November 1674, the son of John (1645–78), a cooper, and Sarah (Oliver) Noyes (1643/44–1707/08) of Boston. His father was the son of the Reverend James Noyes (1608–56) of Newbury, who came to Massachusetts in 1635 from Choulderton, Wiltshire, and Sarah (Brown) Noyes (d. 1691). John Noyes, Sr., was one of the founding members of the Third, or Old South, Church in 1669. John Noyes's mother was the daughter of Capt. Peter (1618–70) and Sarah (Newgate) Oliver.[1] He was one of three children; he and his sister, Sarah (b. 1672), and his brother, Oliver (1676–1721), later a physician, were all very young when their father died in 1678, but no guardianship papers were filed with the probate court.[2] Oliver Noyes, evidently more of a scholar than his elder brother, went to study at Harvard College, graduating in the class of 1695. Sewall mentions the death of the senior Noyes in his diary and refers to Sarah (Oliver) Noyes as his "old cordial Christian dear friend" at the time of her death in 1707/08.[3]

John was apprenticed to Jeremiah Dummer (q.v.), as evidenced by an account book of Samuel Sewall, who sold borax to Dummer on 16 April 1691 and delivered it to "Jn°" Noyes.[4] Noyes was evidently working on his own by 1697, when Jonathan Belcher (q.v.) was being sued by John Allen and John Edwards (qq.v.), and Noyes signed as surety for Belcher, indicating that he may have been Belcher's employer at the time of the suit.[5]

Both John Noyes and his brother, Oliver, like their father and their grandfather Oliver, became members of the Ancient and Honorable Artillery Company, John joining in 1698 and Oliver in 1699. John was elected fourth sergeant of the company in 1699 and ensign in 1704.[6] On 4 May 1702, Samuel Sewall records in his diary that the Artillery Company held its training day, exercising in the Town House in the morning because of the rain, and then

> Went to Pollards to avoid the Rain. March'd out and shot at a Mark. Before they began, I told the Company that I had call'd them to shoot in October, and had not my self hit the Butt; I was willing to bring my self under a small Fine, such as a single Justice might set; and it should be to him who made the best Shott. Mr. Gerrish and Ensign John Noyes were the competitors, At Pollards, by a Brass Rule, Ens. Noyes's Shot was found to be two inches and a half nearer the centre, than Mr. John Gerrishes; His was on the right side of the Neck; Ensign Noyes's on the Bowels a little on the Left and but very little more than G. on the Right of the middle-Line. When I had heard what could be said on both sides, I Judg'd for Ensign Noyes, and gave him a Silver cup I had provided engraven
>
> May. 4. 1702.
> Euphratem Siccare potes.
>
> Telling him, it was a Token of the value I had for that virtue in others, which I my self could not attain to.[7]

According to Sewall's ledger, he purchased the cup from John Coney (q.v.) for two pounds.[8] In 1704 the town meeting elected Noyes to the office of constable, but he declined to serve and paid the fine.[9]

On 16 March 1699 the Reverend Samuel Willard of Old South Church presided at John Noyes's marriage to Susanna Edwards (1676–1725), daughter of David (ca. 1639–96) and Mary (Sweet) Edwards (1653/54–1722).[10] Susanna (Edwards) Noyes evidently had a considerable estate of her own because when she died John was appointed to act as administrator of her estate.[11] John and Susanna Noyes had five daughters: Sarah (1701–before 1712);

Mary (b. 1703), who married Richard Buckley; Susanna (b. 1705), who married the tailor Benjamin Ranken; and Sarah (b. 1712) and Abigail (b. 1716), both of whom were unmarried at the time of their father's death in 1749.[12]

No evidence exists to indicate that Noyes worked as a journeyman for any of his Boston colleagues during his early years. In 1698 he is mentioned in a deed as the occupant of a tenement at the head of the Town Dock owned by Benjamin Pemberton, and Noyes probably carried on an independent business from that location until at least 1710.[13] He established a good reputation among the members of his craft and was one of "three Skilfull Goldsmiths" (along with John Coney and Edward Winslow [q.v.]) asked by the justices of the Superior Court in 1706 to inspect a parcel of money to determine if any of the coins had been clipped.[14] He is known to have used two marks: IN in an oval (A) and IN above a cross-crosslet in a shield (B).[15] The relatively few surviving objects made by Noyes demonstrate that he was a fine craftsman. His hollow columnar candlesticks, now in the Museum of Fine Arts, Boston, show him to have been a clever artisan, one who was able to manipulate his materials to solve design problems. He also made an unusually constructed tankard, now in the Henry Ford Museum, engraved with the Oliver coat of arms and the initials of John Noyes's uncle Daniel Oliver (1664–1732) and his wife, Elizabeth Belcher (1678–1735), which has a seamed body and an inset bottom.[16] Noyes also fashioned a set of six silver beakers for the church in Newbury where his grandfather was teacher and a flagon for the Brattle Street Church, of which he was one of the founding members. He also made silver for the churches in Saybrook and Stratford, Connecticut. An advertisement for a stolen tankard engraved with a coat of arms "with three water pouches or buckets" bearing the maker's mark "IN" appeared in the *Boston News-Letter* in 1707/08.[17]

In spite of his success and seeming financial stability, Noyes's name appears several times as a debtor in the records of the Inferior Court of Common Pleas. In most cases he seems to have been able to satisfy his creditors before the cases came to court: most of the suits were dropped because the plaintiffs failed to appear in court. In one instance Noyes paid the money due his creditor to Edward Winslow, who, as sheriff, came to his house to serve the writ of execution in the case. Another case involved a bond held jointly by John Noyes and his brother, Oliver, and a third involved a bond held jointly by John Noyes and Elisha Cooke, Esq.[18] Cooke was for many years moderator of the Boston town meeting.

Noyes died intestate in 1749, and administration of his estate was granted to his daughter Abigail Noyes, a spinster.[19] Although an inventory was ordered to be taken before 15 November 1750, it was never filed with the court. On the day of Noyes's burial, 27 May 1749, the shopkeeper Benjamin Walker, who often mentioned talking with Noyes in his shop, made the following notation in his diary: "Buried John Noyes large Number follow'd y[e] Corps from Rankins house his son In Law . . . an aged man ab[tt] 75 years old born In y[t] Town (he dyed its Thot of an appolexy or Palsey[)] had bin ailling many years with Gout a good lookt man wore his own Gray hair (he dyed at his Son in Laws Rankins a Taylor[)] he livd In y[tt] was Lilly[s] house in Drawbridge allias Ann Street now."[20] BMW

SURVIVING OBJECTS

	Mark	Inscription	Patron	Date	Reference	Owner
Six beakers	A	none	Congregational Church, Newbury, Mass.	ca. 1705	Jones 1913, 294	
Beaker	B	S.C. Ex dono domini Mathai Griswoald (+)	Matthew Griswold and/or First Congregational Church, Saybrook, Conn.	ca. 1715	Jones 1913, 442	
Two candlesticks	A†	Bowdoin crest	Pierre Bowdoin	ca. 1700	Buhler 1972, no. 90	MFAB
Two caudle cups	B	S:C	Congregational Church, Stratford, Conn.	ca. 1715	Jones 1913, 463	
Caudle cup	A	SB; Ch:Bilerica	First Parish Church, Billerica, Mass.	ca. 1700	Buhler 1956, no. 109	
Dram cup	A*	NT/1697; GMT (later)		1697	Flynt/Fales 1968, 108	HD
Flagon	B†	This belongs to/the Church in/Brattle street/1711	Brattle Street Church, Boston	1711	Buhler 1972, no. 93	MFAB
Two forks (mate below)	A*	HA	Hannah (Arnold) Welles (?)	ca. 1710	Buhler 1972, no. 92	MFAB
Fork (mates above)	A*	HA	Hannah (Arnold) Welles (?)	ca. 1710		SFCAI
Locket (gold)	A*	RR	Rebecca (Russell) Greenleaf (?)	ca. 1710	Buhler/Hood 1970, no. 77	YUAG
Porringer	A*	none		ca. 1710	Avery 1920, no. 39	MMA
Salver	A*	Oliver arms, from a cloud at the sinister side fessways grasping a hand couped at the wrist, and crest, a bird with a sprig in its beak	Oliver family	ca. 1715	Biddle 1963, no. 98	
Tankard	A	David Parker/ Born . . . (later)		ca. 1705		MFAB
Tankard	A*	B/IS (later)	Brattle Street Church, Boston	ca. 1700	Buhler 1972, no. 91	MFAB
Tankard	A	S/WA	William and Abigail (Fowle) Smith	ca. 1705	Winchester 1956, 553	Adams National Historic Site
Tankard	A*	SL/1708; I/TM (later)		1708	Safford 1983, 30	MMA
Tankard	A*	P/IE	John and Elizabeth (Lindall) Pitts	ca. 1705	Phillips 1939, no. 145	
Tankard	A	G/IE	John and Elizabeth Gardner	ca. 1710	Gourley 1965, no. 148	
Tankard	A*	This belongs to/the Church in/Brattle-street/1704	Brattle Street Church, Boston	1704	Warren/ Howe/ Brown 1987, 33–36	

	Mark	Inscription	Patron	Date	Reference	Owner
Tankard	A	P/RE; AWW (+) (later)		ca. 1710	Shelley 1958, 175	HFM
Tankard	A	Oliver arms (later); O/DE	Daniel and Elizabeth Oliver	ca. 1710		HFM

1. RC 9:17, 133; Buhler 1972, 1:110; Roberts 1895, 1:132, 242; *Newbury VR* 2:674, 677; Codman 1918, 177; Boston Deaths, 1700–1800.
2. *Sibley's Harvard Graduates* 4:260–64; RC 9:124.
3. *Sewall Diary* 1:46, 591.
4. Samuel Sewall Account Book, 1688–92, MHS.
5. SCCR, file 98567.
6. Buhler 1972, 1:110; *Sibley's Harvard Graduates* 4:260–64; Roberts 1895, 1:314.
7. *Sewall Diary* 1:466–67. Translated, the inscription reads "Thou canst drain the river Euphrates."
8. Samuel Sewall Account Book and Ledger, under accounts headed Artillery Company of ye Massachusetts D^r, entry for 4 May 1702, NEHGS.
9. Seybolt 1939, 109.
10. RC 9:251, 138, 41; Whitmore 1878, 49, no. 924. Buhler (1972, 1:110) mistakenly assumed that Susanna Edwards was the daughter of John and Elizabeth Edwards and sister of John Edwards (q.v.). Susanna (Edwards) Noyes's mother, Mary Sweet Edwards, was the sister of Susanna Sweet Oliver, mother of Peter Oliver (q.v.). Susanna (Edwards) Noyes and her children are mentioned in her mother's will, probated in 1722; SCPR 22:649–51.
11. SCPR 24:211; 22:649–51.
12. RC 24:9, 22, 36, 85, 115; RC 28:141, 234.
13. SCD 19:9–10; in 1710, when Benjamin Pemberton's executors sold the "New Built Brick Messuage Containing Two Tenements," Noyes was described as the occupant of one tenement, and "John Glover, Habberdasher of Hatts," as the occupant of the other; SCD 25:99–102.
14. Mass. Archives 40:847, 856, 857.
15. Buhler (1972, 1:110) also mentions a small cartouche-shaped mark on a spoon in a private collection. The same mark and also an IN in a shaped shield are shown in Ensko 1989, 285. Ensko's note indicates that the small mark in a cartouche was found on a spoon at the MFAB in 1963, so he and Buhler were undoubtedly referring to a mark from the same object. Buhler's comment seems to indicate that she doubted the attribution to Noyes. Graham 1936, 53, and Thorn 1949, 154, also record an IN in an irregular outline. None of these marks were located for illustration.
16. In spite of this strange construction, which has not been found on other Noyes tankards, it appears to be a genuine piece. Although conceivably the tankard could have been taken apart when the spout was added, one would expect that the alteration would have marred the engraving, as the seam runs directly through the middle of the shield.
17. Dow 1927, 49.
18. SCCR, Court of Common Pleas Record Book 1718, 24, 118, 119; 1724, 405; 1726, 319; SCCR, files 12388, 12560, 12583, 18364, 19108, 20345.
19. SCPR 43:23–25.
20. Benjamin Walker, Jr., Diaries, vol. 3, MHS.

Andrew Oliver
1724–76

A

B

C

Andrew Oliver, a jeweler of Huguenot descent, was born in Annapolis Royal, Nova Scotia, on 20 September 1724, the son of Anthoine Olivier and Mary Sigourney, whose marriage intentions were published in Boston in 1711.[1] His parents moved to Nova Scotia about 1720.

Andrew Oliver would have begun his training about 1738 and probably came to Boston for his apprenticeship. He may have started his apprenticeship with fellow Huguenot James Boyer (q.v.), for on 9 July 1747 he married Boyer's daughter Susannah, who had been born in Boston on 16 March 1727.[2] Boyer died in 1741, which would have interrupted Oliver's training. It is not known with whom Oliver finished his apprenticeship, although he may have continued in the Boyer shop, which was run by Mary Ann Boyer (q.v.) following her husband's death.

On 20 February 1753 Andrew Oliver, "of Boston jeweller," and his wife sold to her brother Daniel Boyer (q.v.) all her right to the estate of her grandfather Daniel Johonnot, bequeathed to her in his will of 29 May 1748.[3] This deed was witnessed by William Homes, Sr., and Samuel Minott (qq.v.). In 1753 Andrew Oliver was elected clerk of the market in Boston and was chosen as a tithingman in 1770.[4] Oliver's nephew Joseph Coolidge (q.v.) married his wife's niece Elizabeth Boyer in 1771 and may have been associated in business with Oliver and Boyer. The Andrew Oliver included in the Massachusetts tax list of 1771 in Boston, with one poll, one house, and sixteen pounds' annual worth of real estate is probably the jeweler.[5] Daniel Boyer's name follows immediately in the list, which suggests that Oliver and his brother-in-law lived in close proximity. In an entry in his diary dated 17 February 1776, Ezekiel Price noted that he had "heard of the death of Mr. Andrew Oliver jeweller," though no formal death record for Oliver has been found.[6]

About a half-dozen pieces by Oliver have been identified, and these bear either an initial and surname mark (A) or initials marks (B, C). PEK

SURVIVING OBJECTS

	Mark	Inscription	Patron	Date	Reference	Owner
Pepper box	A	TC	Thomas Churchill	ca. 1745	Moore Collection 1980, no. 131	

740

	Mark	Inscription	Patron	Date	Reference	Owner
Ring (gold)	c†	A Friend's Gift		ca. 1760	Buhler/Hood 1970, no. 203	YUAG
Spoon	A*	?		?	YUAG files	
Two tablespoons	A†	P/PM (altered to P/TM)(+)		ca. 1765	DAPC 71.3376 and 71.3378	WM
Teaspoon	B†	DB		ca. 1750	Buhler 1972, no. 235	MFAB

1. RC 28:91; Olivier Bible, Boston Athenaeum.
2. RC 24:180; RC 28:257.
3. SCD 82:52–53.
4. RC 18:19; Seybolt 1939, 269.
5. Pruitt 1978, 40–41.
6. "Diary of Ezekiel Price," 237.

Peter Oliver
ca. 1682–1712

A

B

The son of John Oliver (1644–84), a merchant, and his wife, Susanna (Sweet) Oliver (1647–93), Peter Oliver was born in Boston. John Oliver was the son of John Oliver (ca. 1616–46) and Elizabeth (Newgate) Oliver (ca. 1616–1709). Susanna (Sweet) Oliver was the daughter of John Sweet (ca. 1603–85), a ship carpenter, and his wife, Susanna (ca. 1622–66). Peter Oliver probably was apprenticed to John Coney (q.v.) because when he was seventeen years old he chose Coney, his "trusty Friend," to be his guardian after his mother's death.[1]

In 1704 Peter and his brother, John, sold their share in the land in the North End of Boston left to them by their grandfather John Sweet to their mother's sister, Mary Edwards, for £150.[2] The property consisted of a dwelling house, warehousing, and a wharf with the adjoining "Ground & Flatts." One year later, Peter Oliver sold his interest in his father's land and house in the North End near the Charlestown ferry to his brother, John. John, in turn, sold Peter the front section of the house, which consisted of "one Low room, one Entry . . . the Cellars under the same[,] Two chambers over the Low room & Entry Two Garretts over the s[d] Chambers and a little closett adjoining to one of the s[d] chambers," as well as a "ffull halfe part of the Garden," the "right of ingress and egress," and the use of the well.[3] Oliver's shop was not in his house; by 1707 he was renting a shop from Benjamin Gallop for £5 per year.[4]

Peter Oliver married Jerusha Mather (ca. 1684–1710), daughter of the Reverend Increase Mather, in March 1709/10 and became a member of his father-in-law's church two months later.[5] The couple had one child, Jerusha. Jerusha (Mather) Oliver apparently died in childbirth, for she was listed as deceased at the time of the child's baptism on 31 December 1710.[6] The child evidently died before she reached maturity, for she is not mentioned in her father's will of 1712. Oliver married Hopestill Wensley, his second wife, in March 1711/12.[7]

Two marks have been identified as Peter Oliver's: PO in a heart (A) and PO in a rectangle (B). Although little silver by Oliver survives, what does survive is of exceptional quality. His chocolate pot with gadrooned ornament, although lacking cut-card decoration on the cover, is similar to the masterful examples by Edward Winslow (q.v.). Oliver probably made his chocolate pot for Beulah Jacquett, who later married Thomas Coates; it then descended to the couple's granddaughter, Beulah Paschall, and subsequently to six generations in the female line.[8] Samuel Sewall purchased ten gold mourning rings from Oliver and may well have been one of his regular customers.[9] Oliver also made a large flagon for his mother-in-law, Elizabeth Wensley, to present to the Second (or Old North) Church in 1711.

Peter Oliver died on 27 April 1712, just three days after writing his will. He left the bulk of his estate, including plate and shop furniture, to his wife, Hopestill, and made small bequests to Increase Mather (five pounds), to Cotton Mather (five pounds), and to his brother John Oliver (ten pounds). Hopestill Oliver was made sole executor of the estate; no inventory was ever filed with the court.[10] BMW

SURVIVING OBJECTS

	Mark	Inscription	Patron	Date	Reference	Owner
Chocolate pot	A	Beulah Paschall 1760 . . . (later)	Beulah (Jacquett) Coates (?)	ca. 1705	Buhler 1956, no. 111	
Flagon	A†	M.rs Elizabeth Wensley/to the Second Church/of Christ In/Boston/1711.	Elizabeth Wensley and/ or Second Church, Boston	1711	Quimby 1995, no. 102	WM
Mug	A*	Howard arms, a bend between 6 cross-crosslets; A/IM	Howard family	ca. 1710	Warren 1975, no. 280	BBC
Porringer	A*	B/TM	Thomas and Mary (Willoughby) Barton	ca. 1710	Buhler 1972, no. 97	MFAB
Porringer	A	unidentified crest, a talbot's head erased		ca. 1705	Quimby 1995, no. 103	WM
Tankard	A*	TS; OR/3I I4		ca. 1705	*Antiques* 28 (December 1935): 226	AG
Tankard (miniature)	B†	O/PI/to/PW	Peter and I. (Mather) Oliver (?)	ca. 1710	Buhler 1979, no. 12	WAM

1. RC 9:18, 25; Savage 1860–62, 3:310, 4:238; Whitmore 1878, 46, nos. 864, 865; "Hull Diaries," 172; *Sibley's Harvard Graduates* 1:102–06. Peter Oliver's birth is not included in RC 9, but, according to the guardianship papers filed after his mother's death, he was seventeen years old in 1699; SCPR 14:42. When his mother died, the remainder of his father's estate left unadministered by Susanna Oliver, widow, also deceased, was probated and inventoried. Included in the estate were household goods worth £68.7; a dwelling house worth £250; and half of a warehouse and lands that Susanna's father, John Sweet, a carpenter, left to her two sons, John and Peter; SCPR 13:249–50, docket 1356; SCD 21:526–29.
2. SCD 21:526–29.
3. SCD 21:529–32.
4. RC 10:125.
5. RC 28:24. Jerusha Mather's birth is not recorded in RC 9, but according to the records of the Second Church, a Jerusha Mather became a member in 1700, and in 1711, Cotton Mather, Jerusha's brother, named a daughter Jerusha, evidently in memory of his recently deceased sister, a naming practice common at the time; Robbins 1852, 263. Oliver's membership in the North Church is recorded on p. 267. Bigelow gives 20 April 1684 as the date of Jerusha Mather's baptism; see Bigelow-Phillips files, 575.
6. Robbins 1852, 267.
7. RC 28:36.
8. YUAG files; Buhler 1956, 65–66.
9. Samuel Sewall Account Book and Ledger, 21 October 1710, fol. 194v, NEHGS.
10. Whitmore 1878, 49, no. 911; SCPR 17:449–50.

Jonathan Otis
1723–91

A

B

C

D

E

Jonathan Otis, the son of Nathaniel Otis (1690–1739) and Abigail Russell (1687–1774), was born in Barnstable, Massachusetts, on 30 April 1723.[1] His mother, the daughter of the Reverend Jonathan Russell (1655–1710/11) and Martha Moody (1662–1729), was the sister of the Barnstable silversmiths Moody and Joseph Russell (qq.v.) and first cousin of the Newport, Rhode Island, silversmith Daniel Russell (q.v.).[2] Jonathan's paternal grandparents were John Otis (1657–1727) and Mercy Bacon (b. 1659/60).[3]

Jonathan Otis would have begun his apprenticeship about 1737. Some previous scholars have assumed that he trained in Barnstable with his uncle Moody Russell, and for that reason Jonathan is included in this volume.[4] It is also possible that Jonathan trained with his other uncle Joseph Russell, who was in Bristol (now Rhode Island) by 1734, or more likely with his cousin Daniel Russell in Newport. Soon after completing his training about 1744, Jonathan married Catherine Coggeshall in Newport, Rhode Island, in 1745. Births of their children in the next few years are recorded there (Abigail, 1746; Katherine, 1748; Mary, 1750; and Susanna, 1752).[5] In 1747 Otis purchased a shop standing on land of Jahleel Brenton from the Newport silversmith Daniel Vernon, and in 1753 Otis and his wife sold land in Newport.[6]

Jonathan Otis may have carried on business as a general merchant as well as a silversmith because an advertisement in the *Newport Mercury* on 13 May 1765 about a burglary at his shop states that he lost cloth as well as gold and silver.[7] He was a member of Ezra Stiles's congregation, and in his diary Stiles noted that Otis fled to Middletown, Connecticut, during the British occupation of Newport.[8] After the Revolution Otis sold land in Newport in 1787 and 1788.[9] Otis died in Middletown on 20 February 1791.[10] The administration of his estate was granted on 14 March 1791 to his son-in-law the Hartford silversmith Caleb Bull, Thompson Phillips, and Samuel Bull of Middletown.[11]

Otis was a prolific silversmith for whom numerous examples survive from his years in Rhode Island and Connecticut. He used three variations of a surname mark (A, B, C), an initial and surname mark (D), and an initials mark I:O (E). Other initials marks are attributed to him, but examples could not be found for illustration.[12]   PEK

SURVIVING OBJECTS

	Mark	Inscription	Patron	Date	Reference	Owner
Beaker *(see also mates with mark C)*	A	The Gift/of Dea-con/JONATHAN ALLEN/to the First/CHURCH of CHRIST/in/MIDDLETOWN/1784	First Church of Christ, Middletown, Conn., for Jonathan Allen	1784	Jones 1913, 282–83	
Beaker	A*/ c†	The Gift of/Deacon EZRA BALDWIN/to the Church of/ CHRIST IN DURHAM/1782	Congregational Church, Durham, Conn., for Ezra Baldwin	1782	Buhler/Hood 1970, no. 347	YUAG
Beaker	B†/ D†	The Gift of/Deacon EDWARD GLOVER/Dec.d: to the First/Church of Christ/In Reho-both, 1751	Executor of Edward Glover for Newman Congregational Church, East Providence, R.I.	1751	Buhler/Hood 1970, no. 478	YUAG

	Mark	Inscription	Patron	Date	Reference	Owner
Two beakers (see also mates with mark A)	C	The Gift/of Deacon/JONATHAN ALLEN/to the First/CHURCH of CHRIST/in/MIDDLETOWN/1784	First Church of Christ, Middletown, Conn., for Jonathan Allen	1784	Jones 1913, 282–83	
Three beakers	C	The First Church/of Christ in/Middletown/1785	First Church of Christ, Middletown, Conn.	1785	Jones 1913, 282	
Four beakers	C	The Gift of/MR WILL^M. KING/to the first/Church in SUFFIELD/1782	Congregational Church, Suffield, Conn., for William King	1782	Jones 1913, 465	
Cann	A*	unidentified initials		ca. 1765	Avery 1920, no. 131	MMA
Cann	A	none		ca. 1765	DAPC 76.2978	
Cann	D*	S/RK		ca. 1755	Carpenter 1954, no. 113	
Cann	?	I/AP		ca. 1760	Christie's, 16 June 1984, lot 92	
Caster	C	LA		ca. 1765	American Art Association–Anderson Galleries, 2–3 April 1937, lot 252	
Caster	C*	MO	Mary Otis	1778	Buhler/Hood 1970, no. 479	YUAG
Caster	D/E	AI/to/MH		ca. 1765	Avery 1920, no. 129	MMA
Caster	D	none		ca. 1770	Flynt/Fales 1968, 106	HD
Caster	E†	M/IH; IHM (later)		ca. 1765	Gourley 1965, no. 286	RISD
Caster	E	?		ca. 1765	Carpenter 1954, no. 104	
Caster	?	?		ca. 1760	*Antiques* 131 (January 1987): 139	
Creampot	A	DA; GMT (later)		ca. 1760	Avery 1920, no. 130	MMA
Creampot	C*	AB		ca. 1780	*Moore Collection* 1980, no. 47	
Cup	?	MB		ca. 1755	Parke-Bernet, 28 October 1969, lot 99	
Necklace and clasp (gold)	E	none	Tabitha (Lippitt) Brown	ca. 1770	Gourley 1965, no. 288	RISD

	Mark	Inscription	Patron	Date	Reference	Owner
Porringer	C	I/DC		ca. 1770	Parke-Bernet, 17–20 May 1944, lot 660	
Porringer	D	?		ca. 1770	Sotheby Parke Bernet, 18–20 November 1976, lot 604	
Porringer	D*	Carr/TM		ca. 1770	Buhler 1972, no. 489	MFAB
Porringer	D	L/DE		ca. 1765	*Moore Collection* 1980, no. 40	
Porringer	D	EA		ca. 1770	DAPC 67.2051	
Porringer	D	DM		ca. 1760	DAPC 77.2424	
Porringer	D	EH		ca. 1770	Sotheby's, 30 January–2 February 1991, lot 142	
Porringer	?	S/R AE (latter conjoined)		ca. 1760	*Antiques* 97 (June 1970): 823	
Porringer	?	DM		ca. 1760	*Moore Collection* 1980, no. 41	
Porringer	?	?		ca. 1770	Sotheby Parke Bernet, 17 October 1972, lot 102	
Sauceboat (mate below)	?	H (later)		ca. 1770	Christie's, 11 April 1981, lot 252	
Sauceboat (mate above)	?	H (later)		ca. 1770	Christie's, 22 January 1983, lot 423	
Strainer	D	?		ca. 1770	Gourley 1965, no. 289	RISD
Sugar tongs	D	MC		ca. 1760	*Moore Collection* 1980, no. 46	
Sugar tongs	E	none		ca. 1760	*Moore Collection* 1980, no. 42	
Sugar tongs	?	IVSH		ca. 1760	*Moore Collection* 1980, no. 44	
Sword	D	none		ca. 1770	Peterson (1955) 1991, no. 15	
Tablespoon	A	S/SR		ca. 1770	DAPC 71.3374	WM
Two tablespoons (part of a service)	A*	KTS	Kezia Taylor Stiles	1784	Buhler/Hood 1970, no. 349	YUAG

	Mark	Inscription	Patron	Date	Reference	Owner
Tablespoon	A	B/WI/PB		ca. 1765	Carpenter 1954, no. 133 (center)	
Tablespoon	A*	SD		ca. 1785		YUAG
Tablespoon	A†	MOB	Mary (Otis) Bull	ca. 1785	Buhler/Hood 1970, no. 348	YUAG
Tablespoon	D*	MB		ca. 1760		YUAG
Tankard (lacks cover)	A	JC 1783		1783	*Moore Collection* 1980, no. 39	
Tankard	D	P/ZM		ca. 1760	*Moore Collection* 1980, no. 38	
Teaspoon	A*	SO		ca. 1780		YUAG
Teaspoon	A*	E/EA		ca. 1760		YUAG
Teaspoon	C*	LB		ca. 1760		YUAG
Teaspoon (part of a service)	C	KTS	Kezia Taylor Stiles	1784	DAPC 73.2231	WM
Two-handled cup	D*	M/BM		ca. 1760	*Moore Collection* 1980, no. 43	

1. *Barnstable and Sandwich VR*, 42–44, 48; *Literary Diary of Ezra Stiles* 1:437–38.
2. *Barnstable and Sandwich VR*, 44; Cullity 1994, 160.
3. Savage 1860–62, 1:91; 3:323–24; *Barnstable and Sandwich VR*, 11, 42.
4. Buhler 1972, 2:560; Ward/Hosley 1985, 292.
5. Arnold 1911, 4:108.
6. Bigelow-Phillips files, notes on Rhode Island silversmiths and Newport Land Records 13:10–11.
7. Flynt/Fales 1968, 292. The advertisement does not appear in the *Newport Mercury* on that date and has not been verified.
8. *Literary Diary of Ezra Stiles* 1:83, 141, 143.
9. Bigelow-Phillips files, notes on Rhode Island silversmiths, Newport Land Records 4:84, 93, 218.
10. *Literary Diary of Ezra Stiles* 3:412.
11. Middletown Probate District, file 2476, CSL.
12. A JO script in a rectangle was recorded on a creampot; see *Moore Collection* 1980, no. 45. An IO in an oval is said to be on sugar tongs; see *Moore Collection* 1980, no. 44.

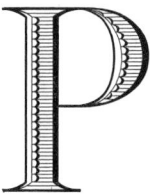

P

I. P.
w. ca. 1725

A

B

About a half-dozen pieces of silver dating from the third decade of the eighteenth century bear one or the other of two closely related initials marks, IP crowned (A, B). These pieces include a cup made for the church in Hull, Massachusetts, in 1724, a round pepper box, an octagonal pepper box, and three tablespoons. The silversmith who made these pieces probably worked in Massachusetts because the cup was made for a Massachusetts church and one of the tablespoons also has the mark of Paul Revere, Sr. (q.v.). In the past, these marks have been attributed to Isaac Perkins (q.v.).[1] The attribution of mark (A) to Perkins is doubtful because Perkins only was about fourteen years old, and therefore too young to be a practicing silversmith, when the cup for the church at Hull was made. Mark (A) may have been used by one of the two Massachusetts silversmiths with the initials IP who was working in 1724— John Pitts or John Potwine (qq.v.). Mark (B) could also have been used by Joseph Pitts (q.v.) or Isaac Perkins, who started working slightly later. Or these marks could belong to an as yet unidentified silversmith. PEK

SURVIVING OBJECTS

	Mark	Inscription	Patron	Date	Reference	Owner
Cup	A†	The gift of Mathew Loring to the Church in Hull/1724	Methodist Episcopal Church, Hull, Mass., for Matthew Loring	1724	Buhler/Hood 1970, no. 518	YUAG
Pepper box	A*	I/TA		ca. 1730	YUAG files (as John Pitts)	
Pepper box	A or B	W/IP		ca. 1730	Hammerslough/ Feigenbaum 1958–73, 1:54–55 (attributed to Isaac Perkins)	WA
Tablespoon	A*	EB		ca. 1730		HD
Tablespoon	A*	?		ca. 1720	YUAG files	
Tablespoon (with mark of Paul Revere, Sr.)	B†	MB		ca. 1730	DAPC 70.3022	WM

1. Flynt/Fales 1968, 297; Hammerslough/Feigenbaum 1958–73, 1:54–55.

747

Samuel Paddy
1645–86

Samuel Paddy was born in Plymouth, Massachusetts, about 1 August 1645, the son of William Paddy (d. 1658), a skinner who had emigrated from London to Boston in 1635 and then settled in Plymouth, where he married Alice Freeman (ca. 1618–51) on 24 November 1639.[1] His maternal grandfather was Edmund Freeman (ca. 1590–1682) of Lynn, Massachusetts.[2] Following the death of Alice Paddy on 24 April 1651, William moved to Boston, where he married Mary Greenough Payton on 3 February 1652.[3]

Paddy began his apprenticeship with John Hull (q.v.) shortly after his father's death and just before his fourteenth birthday. Hull noted in his diary that on 1 July 1659, "I received into my house Jeremie Dummer and Samuel Paddy to serve me as apprentices eight years."[4] While he was an apprentice in the shop Hull ran with his partner Robert Sanderson, Sr. (q.v.), Paddy witnessed deeds for his master on three occasions.[5] When Paddy came of age in 1666, he received sixty pounds from the division of his father's estate.[6] With Jeremiah Dummer (q.v.) he appraised the estate of Joseph Sanderson (q.v.) in 1666/67.[7] In January 1667, Paddy contracted smallpox. Hull noted in his diary that his apprentice "went to his mother's house; but there I provided for him. The Lord was pleased to restore him in three weeks' time."[8] On 20 October 1668 Paddy identified himself as being "of Boston Gold Smith" when he sold to Capt. William Davis his interests in the warehouses that had been apportioned to him from his father's estate.[9]

Some time after this Paddy left Boston for Jamaica. He was described as being "of Jamaica" in 1681 in an indenture for which his former master, John Hull, acted as his power of attorney.[10] Hull also wrote to Paddy in Jamaica that year, chastising the goldsmith that "had you abode here and followed your calling you might have been worth many hundred pounds of clear estate and you might have enjoyed many more helpes for your sole. Mr. Dummer lives in good fashion hath a wife and three children and a good estate is a member of the church and like to be very useful in his generation."[11] Paddy was known as a goldsmith in Jamaica but also engaged in other mercantile activities, some with his former master.[12] After Hull's death his son-in-law Samuel Sewall settled accounts with Paddy. Writing him in Jamaica on 22 August 1685, Sewall says,

> Sir, your brother Thomas coming to me with a letter from yourself, ordering him to receive into his own hand what was due to you from Capt John Hull, my late honored father-in-law, accordingly I looked at your account and found your debt to be thirteen pounds seven shillings and threepence in one article. Your credit was twenty-eight pounds. So I gave your brother Thomas fourteen pounds twelve shillings and ninepence, the balance, and delivered him a bond for three pounds one shilling dated Nov. 10, 1668, with some pewter, linen and earthenware,—all that was left by my father for you. Wherefore I desire that you write me by the next, expressing your approbation of what I have done in this kind on your behalf.[13]

Samuel Paddy died the next year. His will, dated 8 May 1686 and proved 27 May, identifies him as "Samuell Paddy of Port Royall, in the island aforesaid Gold Smith son of William Paddy of Boston, in New England deceased." He bequeathed everything to "my well beloved Friend Solomon Carter of Port Royall aforesaid Gold Smith," who was appointed sole executor. He also bequeathed five pounds sterling to William Hutchinson, a Port Royal merchant.[14] No silver by Paddy has been identified. PEK

1. According to Savage 1860–62, 2:203, Alice Freeman's age was given as seventeen when she left London with her father in 1635, which suggests that she was born about 1618. SCPR, docket 189; Roberts 1895, 1:174; *Mayflower Descendant* 13:85; 16:237; 17:184.

2. According to Savage 1860–62, 2:203, Edmund Freeman's age was given as forty-five in 1635, which suggests he was born about 1590.

3. RC 9:34.

4. "Hull Diaries," 150.

5. *Suffolk Deeds* 6:230–31; 10:19.

6. *Suffolk Deeds* 10:39–40.

7. SCPR, docket 440.

8. "Hull Diaries," 156–57.

9. *Suffolk Deeds* 10:286–88.

10. SCD 22:254–55; 23:217–18.

11. Hull Letterbook, fol. 359, AAS.

12. Barker 1986, 136.

13. "Hull Diaries," 150n.

14. Robert B. Barker letter to Patricia E. Kane, 21 June 1992, extracted from Jamaica, Island Record Office, Wills, Liber Old Series, 4:138.

Caleb Parker
1731–before 1767

Caleb Parker was born in Boston on 2 February 1731, the son of the blacksmith Caleb Parker (1693/94–1771) and Mary Adams, who were married on 6 June 1728 by Rev. John Webb in the New North Church, Boston.[1] Caleb Parker, Jr., and Mary Mellens published their marriage intentions on 2 November 1758.[2] Mary Mellens, the daughter of William Mellens (1707–55), a mariner, and Katherine Lamsdell (d. 1759), was born on 18 March 1735 in Boston.[3]

Caleb Parker would have served his apprenticeship between 1745 and 1752. Samuel Burt (q.v.) may have been his master because Parker witnessed a deed for Burt on 28 April 1753, shortly after his apprenticeship period would have ended.[4]

Mary Parker received a legacy of twenty shillings from her father's estate in April 1755.[5] In 1759, Caleb Parker, silversmith, joined with the Mellens heirs to sell a portion of Mellens's estate to Benjamin Hurd of Charlestown, Massachusetts.[6] The will further stipulated that the remainder of Mellens's estate, left to the widow during her lifetime, would be divided among Mary, her sister Katherine, and her brother Charles upon the death of their mother. The estate was settled on 21 July 1769; Mary "Baird," Parker's remarried widow, received the back portion of her father's house and a cash settlement.[7]

Parker died early in his career because Mary Parker was married to James Beard in December 1767.[8] The will of Caleb Parker's father, written in June 1771, left a portion of his estate to "my Two Grand Children Caleb Parker and Mary Parker the Children of my Eldest Son Caleb Parker deces'd & to my Daughter in Law formerly Mary Millings But now Mary Bird."[9]

No objects by this silversmith have been identified. Although traditionally ascribed to Parker, the mark found on a spoon owned by Historic Deerfield, C·PARKER in a rectangle, was not used by him. The style of the spoon indicates that it was made in the nineteenth century, long after Parker's death.[10] DAF

1. RC 24:204; RC 28:145; *Reading VR*, 167.

2. RC 30:30; Wyman 1879, 2:728.

3. RC 24:50, 222; Wyman 1879, 2:665; Thwing; RC 28:178; Whitmore 1878, 88, nos. 1643–44. The "40th" year in William Mellens's epitaph is probably a misreading of "48."

4. ECD 98:101.

5. SCPR 50:92.

6. Wyman 1879, 2:728.
7. SCPR 67:467.
8. RC 30:45.
9. SCPR 70:390–94.
10. Flynt/Fales 1968, 293.

Daniel Parker
1726–85

A

B

C

Daniel Parker was born in Charlestown, Massachusetts, on 20 November 1726, the son of Isaac Parker (1692–1742), a potter, and Grace Hall (1696–1754), who married in 1715.[1] His paternal grandparents were Daniel Parker (ca. 1667–94) and Anne Harrington (ca. 1669–1731).[2] His grandmother Parker married second John May and third Thomas Coping.[3] His maternal grandparents were Stephen Hall (ca. 1667–1749), a Charlestown weaver and painter, and Grace Willis (ca. 1664–1721).[4] Parker's grandfather Hall married second Martha Hill and third Ann Newell.[5]

Parker probably came to Boston from his native Charlestown for training, which began about 1740. Samuel Edwards (q.v.) very likely was his master because on 13 September 1746, when Parker was nineteen years old, he, along with John Coburn (q.v.), witnessed a deed for Edwards.[6] Parker maintained a close relationship with Edwards because on 22 May 1752 he and Edwards witnessed the estate administration of Seth Coburn, father of the silversmith Seth Storer Coburn (q.v.).[7] Parker probably was operating his own shop by January 1749/50, when the Boston silversmith Thomas Edwards (q.v.) sued him for defaulting on a debt on 27 June 1748 and for owing £24.14 for "sundries" (possibly for Parker's newly established business). The court upheld Parker's claim that the sheriff had served the writ against him incorrectly, and he was awarded the costs of the suit.[8] In February 1748/49 Parker joined in a suit with other relatives, among whom was his nephew John Symmes (q.v.), then a minor, over possession of land in York County in the province of Maine.[9]

On 3 October 1751 Parker married Margaret Jarvis (1729–1815), the daughter of Elias Jarvis (d. 1755), a mariner, and Mary Sunderland (b. 1693/94), both of Boston.[10] Margaret Parker was a legatee in her father's will, probated in July 1755.[11] Shortly thereafter, in 1756, the couple sold land on Boston's Beacon Hill along with other heirs of their relative William Willis, including Parker's sister Mary and her husband, the jeweler John Welsh (q.v.).[12]

Parker advertised frequently in the Boston newspapers between 1752 and 1767, detailing changes in his shop's location, the variety of objects he made, and the availability of imported goods. His earliest notice, in the *Boston-Evening Post* of 11 December 1752, reveals his move from one Boston location to another:

> Daniel Parker, *Goldsmith,*
> *Hereby informs his Customers and others in Town and*
> *Country, that he has removed from his Shop near the* BLUE BALL,
> *to a Shop in* MERCHANTS-ROW, *between the* Golden Ball *and the*
> *Sign of Admiral* Vernon, *where may be had good moulding Sand, black*
> *Lead Pots, and crucibles.*

Beginning with the *Boston Gazette* of 30 October 1758, Parker announced he sold wares in two locations, "at his Shop near the Golden-Ball, or at his House next Door to Deacon Grant's in Union Street." Starting in 1763, he advertised only his shop on Union Street, which suggests that he gave up his Golden-Ball location about then, possibly turning it over to his nephew and probable apprentice, John Symmes, who would have completed his apprenticeship at about that time and who advertised at that location in 1766.

Parker's advertisements in Boston newspapers imply that a large part of his trade was retailing imported supplies to goldsmiths, jewelers, clockmakers, and watchmakers in the tradition of his master, Samuel Edwards. The following announcement typifies the variety of his goods:

Imported from *LONDON*,
AND TO BE SOLD BY
Daniel Parker,
G O L D S M I T H;
At his Shop, next Door to Deacon *Samuel Grant's*,
In Union-Street, *Boston*:

A Variety of Goldsmith's, Jeweller's
and Watchmaker's Tools and Ware, *viz.*

Cypher'd Earing & Button Chris-
tials, with Cyphers for ditto; brilliant Earing Top
and Drop Christials; round and square brilliant Button
ditto; red and white Foyl; Amethist & Topaz Foyl;
cypher'd and brilliant Ring Stones; Garnets, Amethist, Topaz and Emerald ditto; Chrystial RingSparks;
Buckle Stones and Stone Buttons in Silver by the Card;
Stone Shoe, Knee and Stock Buckles; neat Stone Bosom Broaches; a Variety of the best fine round and
square Steel Shoe Chapes and Tongs, small Knee ditto;
an assortment of Files for the Goldsmith's Use; Coral
Beeds, and Stick Coral for Children's Whistle's;
Forging Anvils, raising Anvils for Tankards, Cans and
Cream-Pots; Planishing Hammers; Spoon Teats,
plain ditto; Hand Vices, Shears, Clock and Watch
Plyers, polish'd Spring ditto; polish'd Draw Plates;
best Ivory Buckle and Ring Brushes; Watch Chrystals,
Main Springs, and Silver Pendants; Scales and Weights,
small Money ditto for the Pocket, Penny Weights and
Grains; Piles of Brass Weights; Silver Thimbles
with Steel Ends; Brass hollowing Stamps; Steel Gra-
vers; Freezing Punches; Brass Rivet Wire; fine
Iron Binding Wire, Coarse ditto; Moulding Sand;
Borax, Salt-Petre—*a neat and valuable Diamond Ring*,
—with sundry other Articles cheap for Cash.[13]

When Samuel Edwards died in 1762, Parker paid the estate £93.8.11$^{1}/_{2}$ for goldsmiths' and jewelers' supplies.[14] The Salem silversmith John Touzell (q.v.) was one of Parker's customers for goldsmiths' supplies. A typical bill for one of their transactions reads,

M^r. John Towzell Bo^t Boston 14th Augst 1764
of Daniel Parker

1 Doz Large Round chapes & tung 12/	£0. 12.0
1 Doz Square Ditto 10/-0-$^1/_2$ Doz Round Ditto at 12/	0. 16.0
1 Doz Round Ditto 10/8 wire 1/4 1 Doz Knee Chaps 6/	0. 18–0
6 p^r. Round Ditto 6/ 1 Doz p^r Squar 12/	0. 18.0
2 Sheets Sandpaper 4^d 1^{lb} Sandover 1/	0. 1: 4
	3: 05: 4

1 Doz smallfiles 3/4		3.4
		3— 8—8
The old Ballance left In January last		14.4
	LM°	£4— 3:0

Rec^d. the Above In full p^r. Daniel Parker[15]

Parker's newspaper advertisements for silverware and goldsmiths' supplies ceased in 1767, perhaps because of the nonimportation agreements.

Parker's extensive familial ties within Boston provided him with an invaluable network of mercantile contacts and patrons essential to a successful career. Many of the imported items Parker sold in his shop in 1765 he obtained from Captain Jarvis, a relative of his wife's.[16] Some of his earliest objects, including a pair of sauceboats, a punch strainer, a porringer, and a tablespoon, were made for Benjamin and Hepzibah Hall, relations of Parker's mother's.

Equally important to Parker's economic success were his close ties to many other Boston goldsmiths and jewelers in addition to his brother-in-law John Welsh and nephew John Symmes. Benjamin Goodwin (q.v.) may have been a business associate because Parker signed the bond for the administration of Goodwin's mother's estate in June 1762.[17] Parker may have had some association with John Dexter and Benjamin Loring (qq.v.) because on 24 September 1757 they witnessed a receipt from John Welsh to Zachariah Symmes involving Parker's parents' estate.[18] The jeweler and silversmith Joseph Loring (q.v.) was Parker's neighbor, occupying 3 Union Street.[19] Parker probably also trained Stephen Emery (q.v.). Emery remained in Parker's shop following the completion of his training in 1770, probably to work as a journeyman. Both Loring and Emery witnessed Parker's will on 18 June 1772, and Emery witnessed a deed for him later that year as well.[20] Moreover, presentation spoons made for the Eliot family that bear both Parker's and Emery's marks testify to the pair's close working association, one that continued until Parker's death in 1785. In 1789, Emery filed a claim of £1.18.5 against Parker's estate, further evidence of their professional relationship.[21] Parker undoubtedly also knew Paul Revere, Jr. (q.v.), a fellow member of the Sons of Liberty. Parker was one of the fifteen in that group who commissioned Revere to make a bowl in 1768 honoring ninety-two members of the Massachusetts Bay House of Representatives who voted not to rescind the House's letter to the other colonies protesting Parliament's passage of the Townshend Acts. The bowl has come to be known as the Sons of Liberty Bowl.[22]

Parker also maintained relations with fellow goldsmiths outside of Boston. The Gloucester, Massachusetts, silversmith Stephen Morse (q.v.) knew Parker well enough to advise people in the Boston area to contact him should they apprehend goods stolen from Morse's shop.[23] Parker extended his mercantile contacts into the Connecticut River Valley with the migration of his nephew Isaac Parker (q.v.) to Deerfield, Massachusetts, about 1776. Parker's distant relative Jeremiah Snow III (q.v.), the cousin of his brother-in-law John Welsh, migrated to Springfield, Massachusetts, about 1759 and perhaps gave Parker a contact there. These contacts probably provided Parker with customers outside the Boston area. Christopher Toppan of Hampton, New Hampshire, was among Parker's clients who lived at a distance from Boston. A surviving bill documents a sale between them:

Mr Christopher Toppan

Boston 29 September 1768

Bo^t of Daniel Parker

1 Silver peper Castor	13.10.0
6 Silver Tea Spoons	7.16.6
6 Silver ditto	6.14.0
1 pair Tea Tongs	6.12.6

Old tenor   £34.13.0

Received the above In Full
For Daniel Parker pr James Hill[24]

The Charlestown silversmith James Hill (q.v.) probably is the individual who acknowledged payment of this receipt. He may have been Parker's apprentice, and in 1768 he would have been near the completion of his apprenticeship.

Parker was commercially successful immediately prior to the Revolution, as his assessment in the Massachusetts tax valuation list of 1771 attests: one poll, a house and shop, real estate valued at £26.13.4, a slave, 100 tons of vessels, and £350 of merchandise.[25] Of the Boston silversmiths on this list, only Benjamin Greene (q.v.) had real estate and merchandise valued higher. A number of real estate transactions reflect Parker's growing prosperity. In 1762 he bought land with a tanyard and dwelling house in the town of Brimfield.[26] His other transactions were with distillers, a sign that Parker may have ventured into this lucrative sector of the mercantile trade. In March 1772 he and his cousin Nathaniel Hall, a distiller, offered a distilling house near Boston's Mill Pond as collateral on a loan of £400 from Grace Gardner, which they repaid two years later.[27] On 7 September, the two men purchased a two-thirds share in land adjoining the property they owned jointly on Tattle Street from the widow of the distiller Thomas Jackson.[28] The next day, they sold land for £80 to another distiller, Thomas Ivers.[29] Finally, in December, Parker sold property on Salem Street in North Boston to the merchant Francis Creguie for £633.6.8, in a deed witnessed by his brother-in-law John Welsh.[30] The Boston tax list of 1780 included Parker in ward 4 as a distiller and assessed him at £450, further evidence that he was pursuing the distilling trade.[31]

During the revolutionary war, Parker served on a number of committees concerned with the conflict, including those that raised funds to fortify the harbor, solicited troops for the Continental Army, and strove to ensure the army adequate provisions.[32] Upon his appointment in 1782 as one of Boston's four collectors of taxes, Parker assumed the additional responsibility of finding the funds required to pay off the fledgling nation's huge war debt. Parker's involvement with the Boston town government began long before his stint as a tax collector. He was chosen a clerk of the market in 1759 and again in 1761 and 1762.[33] In 1766 and 1770 he was appointed a warden; in 1770, a tithingman; and in 1774, an assessor.[34] Parker's membership on a committee formed in 1774 to visit Boston's free schools along with the town's selectmen also signaled his rise in local government.

During the Revolution and immediately following, Parker continued pursuing mercantile activities in addition to distilling. A Daniel Parker advertised truck horses for sale in Salem in 1775, a notice possibly placed by the silversmith.[35] By 1779, Parker was calling himself a merchant in deeds, testimony to his increasing retailing activities.[36] His son Daniel Parker, Jr., who lived next door to his father, is described as a trader and was assessed at £30 in the tax list of 1780.[37] In 1781, father and son together petitioned the Boston selectmen for auctioneers' licenses, and in 1782 Parker sold Nathaniel Hall his half of the house, distillery, and equipment he and Hall had jointly purchased.[38] These actions suggest that Parker was cutting back not only on his goldsmithing, but on his distilling activities. During this period Parker was also investing in real estate. In April 1783, for example, he purchased a Salem Street tenement at auction for £75 and made a healthy profit by selling the building to Elias Robinson for £230 the following November.[39]

Although Parker is one of the men Samuel Davis recalled as being a goldsmith from Davis's apprenticeship in revolutionary and postrevolutionary Boston, Suffolk County deeds and court records between 1782 and 1785 do not record him as one.[40] Instead Parker is identified as a merchant and occasionally as a gentleman, lending more evidence of his evolution from silversmith to merchant.[41] In the Suffolk County Court of Common Pleas session of October 1785, Parker and Benjamin Guild, identified as Boston merchants, were named defendants in a suit initiated by Howard Carnes and Peter Penet, factors from Nantes, France. Carnes and Penet's occupation and residency suggest that Parker was importing merchandise from France as well as from England, underscoring the broad geographic reach of Parker's trading ventures.[42]

Parker died on 31 December 1785 at the age of fifty-nine.[43] The *Massachusetts Centinel* of 4 January 1786 noted that "his funeral which was to have been held yesterday, on account of the storm was deferred to this afternoon at 3 o'clock, when it will be from his house in Back-Street, where his relations and friends are desired to attend." A separate notice, appearing in the same issue, announced, "TO Let The north part of a large Brick House, with a shop, late occupied by Mr. Daniel Parker, in Back Street, being an exceeding good situation for a person in business."

Administration of Parker's estate was granted to his widow on 17 January 1786.[44] The inventory, presented on 24 January 1786, totaled £761.14.6 and included 150 ounces of plate and a house and land in Ann Street.[45] Missing from this listing are tools, shop supplies, and retail merchandise, but the suit the French factors Carnes and Penet filed against Parker shortly before his death, as well as a claim of £85.91 made against his estate by the Amsterdam firm of John Hodgdon & Sons, together suggest that Parker was actively retailing until his death.[46] A second inventory of his shop presumably was taken, but it has not survived.

When the estate was settled in 1788, Margaret Parker was awarded dower rights amounting to one-third of her husband's real estate, including

> the Shop, front room, front chamber, with the front of the Cellar, taking in the round of the arch under the chimney of the front room, with liberty to pass through the entry, in & out of doors back or front, & up & down stairway, a priviledge in the yard to hang Cloaths, & of the privy house, & Cistern for rain water; reserving to those who may occupy the other part of said house, a priviledge to pass through the front part of the Cellar, all which premises so assigned & set off, are part of dwelling house & Land situate in Ann Street & is in full for her dower or thirds of & in the real estate aforesaid, reserving as aforesaid.[47]

In spite of Parker's prosperity during his lifetime, his estate, after paying funeral charges, medical expenses, mourning clothes, and probate fees, could not pay his creditors, among whom were many relatives, including John Welsh, Edward Procter, Nathaniel Hall, and Edward Jarvis.[48] Moreover, Parker had not successfully collected all the taxes owed the Treasury for 1784, and upon his death in 1785 Boston's selectmen sought remuneration from his estate.[49] This action may have been related to the estate's payment of £970.6.11½ to Paul Dudley Sargent and Thomas Sherborn, two of Parker's bondsmen when he was a collector of taxes.[50]

Parker's widow subsequently sold her "house furniture and personal estate" in March 1788. Edward Parker, possibly the goldsmith's son, bought the house on Ann Street at auction that June, paying £200 for it.[51] Margaret Parker sold her dower rights in the house for £10 the following May to the Boston merchant Joseph Russell, Jr.[52]

An advertisement in the *Boston Gazette* for 28 May 1759 describes Parker's marks:

> *THIS is to inform the Publick, that the Subscriber*
> *has still missing a Variety of Articles that were*
> *stole from him the 8th Instant; at Night, viz. Three*
> *large Silver Spoons stamp'd* D. Parker, 12 *Tea Spoons,*
> *most of them stamp'd* D.P. 3 *pair Silver Tea Tongs,*
> *not stamp'd, one large Gold Locket, 4 pair Stone Ear-*
> *ings set in Silver, with Gold Wires, 3 pair round Stone*
> *Buttons in Silver, 14 pair large open-work'd Silver*
> *Shoe Buckles with Steel Chapes, several odd Shoe Buckles,*
> *sundry pair Silver Knee Buckles, and some odd ditto's.*[53]

Approximately seventy pieces of silver by Parker are known. They bear an initial and surname mark D·PARKER (A) or one of two initials marks D·P in a cartouche (B) and D:P in a rounded rectangle (C), but their letter forms and punctuation do not exactly match those the advertisement describes. Some sources cite a D:PARKER mark, but no example could be found.[54] Spoons by Parker also bear the mark of Stephen Emery. DAF and PEK

SURVIVING OBJECTS

	Mark	Inscription	Patron	Date	Reference	Owner
Cann	A	SBS (later?)		ca. 1770	*Antiques* 109 (March 1976): 470	
Cann	A	S/TE; 1762 (later) (+)		ca. 1770	*Antiques* 109 (March 1976): 470	
Cann	A	?		ca. 1760	*Moore Collection* 1980, no. 137	
Cann	A	none		ca. 1760		MFAB
Cann	A	C/FA; 1770 (later)	Foster and Ann (Breck) Cruff or Cruft	ca. 1760	Buhler 1972, no. 293	MFAB
Cann	A	LL		ca. 1760	YUAG files	
Cann	B*	The Gift/of Mrs. Allice/Tompson to the/Church in/Billerica	Alice Tompson and/or First Parish Church, Billerica, Mass.	ca. 1770	YUAG files	
Two casters	B	?		?	MFA 1911, no. 817	

	Mark	Inscription	Patron	Date	Reference	Owner
Caster	?	?	Christopher Toppan	1768	Northeast Auctions, 16–17 November 1991, lot 436	
Cream pail	B*	EH		ca. 1760	DAPC 79.3303	
Creampot	C*	H/IS	John and Susannah (Touzell) Hathorne	ca. 1750	Buhler 1972, no. 292	MFAB
Pepper box	A	LB		ca. 1740	Sotheby's, 30 January–2 February 1991, lot 113	
Porringer	A*	The Gift of Sarah Brown to her Dau.ʳ E. Thornton Jan.ʸ 1769 (+)	Sarah Brown and/or E. Thornton	1769	Flynt/Fales 1968, 131–32	HD
Porringer	A	H/BH	Benjamin and Hepzibah (Jones) Hall	ca. 1765	Hammerslough/ Feigenbaum 1958–73, 3:37	
Porringer	A*	IR to WR		ca. 1750	Moore Collection 1980, no. 136	
Porringer	A*	E/FM (+)		ca. 1760	YUAG files	
Two salts	A*	Edmund Baker/1807 (later)		ca. 1760	Bigelow 1917, 257	
Two sauceboats	A	Hall arms, a chevron sable between 3 columbines slipped; Dudley crest (?; later) (+)	Benjamin and Hepzibah (Jones) Hall	ca. 1765	Buhler 1972, no. 294	MFAB
Snuffbox	A*	Robert Calef/to/ Mary Calef (+)	Robert Calef and/or Mary Calef	ca. 1760	Buhler/Hood 1970, no. 206	YUAG
Strainer	B or C	?		ca. 1760	Davis 1991, 198–99	CW
Strainer	C*	R/DE		ca. 1765	Flynt/Fales 1968, 102–03	HD
Strainer	C†	PL/To/SW	Sarah (Leonard) White	ca. 1770	YUAG files	
Strainer	C*	H/BH	Benjamin and Hepzibah (Jones) Hall	ca. 1765	Johnston 1994, 117	CMA
Strainer	?	none		ca. 1770	Antiques 97 (November 1970): 739	
Strainer	?	EG		ca. 1765	Christie's, 19–20 January 1990, lot 277	
Tablespoon	A	P/AH; Abraham/&/ Hannah/ Pease/ Married/Nov. 24ᵗʰ/ .1763. (later)	Abraham and Hannah Pease (?)	ca. 1765	DAPC 79.3548	
Tablespoon	A	L/EM		ca. 1770	DAPC 82.3221	WM
Two tablespoons	A†	F/II		ca. 1755	Buhler/Hood 1970, no. 207	YUAG

	Mark	Inscription	Patron	Date	Reference	Owner
Tablespoon (mate below)	A	Deborah/Swain/ Bo$_r^n$ 30 Mar/–1739–	Deborah Swain	ca. 1750		DeYoung
Tablespoon (mate above)	A	Deborah/Swain/ Bo$_r^n$ 30 Mar/–1739–	Deborah Swain	ca. 1750	YUAG files	
Tablespoon	A	HD	Hezekiah Doane	ca. 1760	WAM 1913, no. 74	
Tablespoon	A	H/BH	Benjamin and Hepzibah (Jones) Hall	ca. 1765	MFA 1911, no. 815	
Tablespoon	A*	IA		ca. 1760	DAPC 75.3243	WM
Tablespoon	A	S/SA		ca. 1755	DAPC 75.3247	WM
Tablespoon	A*	HD to ED		ca. 1770		YUAG
Tablespoon	A	E/ML; 1774 (+)		1774		MFAB
Two tablespoons	A	IB to LB		ca. 1760		MFAB
Tablespoon	A*	NH	Nancy Hiller	ca. 1760		PEM
Tablespoon	A	T/EM		ca. 1770		YUAG
Tablespoon	C*	H/IE		ca. 1770	DAPC 73.2012	WM
Twelve tablespoons (with mark of Stephen Emery)	?	Ex Dono Pupillorum [illeg.] XXII [illeg.]	Andrew Eliot and/or the Harvard College class of 1771	ca. 1771	YUAG files	
Tankard	A*	D/EA	Elisha and Ann Doane	ca. 1770	Buhler 1979, no. 34	WAM
Tankard	A	R/IL; WER (later)		ca. 1760	Christie's, 20–21 January 1989, lot 296	
Tankard	A	Pickman arms, gules 2 battle-axes in saltire between 4 martlets, and crest, a martlet; The Gift/of Benjn Pickman Esqr to the/First Church in Salem 1759./ Transferred to the/ North Church SALEM/1772	Benjamin Pickman and/or North Church, Salem, Mass.	ca. 1759	Jones 1913, 433–34	
Tankard	A	The Gift of Samuel Griffin Dec^d/to the West Church in/ ROXBURY	First Parish, West Roxbury, Mass., for Samuel Griffen	ca. 1770	Jones 1913, 490	
Four tankards	A	Gift of Alex. Maxel to the 1st Church in York	Alexander Maxel and/ or First Congregational Church, York Village, Maine	ca. 1770	Jones 1913, 510	
Tankard	A*/ B*	H/IE (?); (altered to W/ME)		ca. 1765	DAPC 68.385	SI
Tankard	?	unidentified initials (later)		?	YUAG files	
Tankard	?	?		ca. 1770	*Antiques* 93 (June 1968): 713	
Teapot	A	L/PS; SL (later)	Peter and Sarah (Spaulding) Lanman	1764	DAPC 76.2358	CHS

	Mark	Inscription	Patron	Date	Reference	Owner
Two teaspoons	B†	M/CLOUGH	M. Clough	ca. 1770	Johnston 1994, 118	CMA
Teaspoon	C*	H/IE		ca. 1765	DAPC 73.2012	WM
Teaspoon	C	C/SC		ca. 1760		HD

1. *NEHGR* 28:121; Wyman 1879, 1:457; 2:727; *Charlestown VR* 1:238, 291; *Medford VR*, 72; MCPR, docket 16584.
2. Daniel and Anne Parker's dates of birth were calculated from their ages at time of death; Wyman 1879, 2:726; *Charlestown VR* 1:163; Whitmore 1878, 80, no. 1483.
3. Wyman 1879, 1:240; 2:726.
4. Stephen and Grace Hall's dates of birth were calculated from their age at time of death; Wyman 1879, 1:457; *Charlestown VR* 1:272.
5. Wyman 1879, 1:457; *Charlestown VR* 1:365.
6. John Edwards deed to Samuel Edwards, 13 September 1746, Smith-Carter Papers, MHS.
7. SCPR, docket 10043.
8. SCCR, Court of Common Pleas Record Book 1749–51, 56.
9. The relatives in the suit were Parker's brother John and sisters Sarah and Mary (minors represented by their mother) and his nephews Zachariah, William, John, and Isaac Symmes (children of his deceased sister Grace represented by their father Zachariah); YCCR, box 106, file 3.
10. SCPR 52:450; RC 9:208; RC 24:193; RC 28:58, 259; Whitmore 1878, 51, no. 954.
11. SCPR 52:450.
12. SCD 87:273–74.
13. *Boston Gazette and Country Journal*, 4, 11, 25 July 1763. Similar advertisements appeared in the issues of 30 October, 6 and 13 November 1758; 16, 23 February 1761; 5, 12, 19 October 1761; 28 November 1763; 5, 12 December 1763; 10, 17, 24 September 1764; 20, 27 May 1765; 28 October 1765; 4, 11 November 1765; 7 July 1766; 1, 8, 15 June 1767.
14. Inventory and accounts of the estate of Samuel Edwards, June 1762–78, Smith-Carter Papers, MHS.
15. Other accounts between Parker and Touzell in 1759 and 1764 also survive. See English-Touzel-Hathorne Papers, 10 December 1759–26 May 1760, 17 January 1764, and 14 August 1764, PEM.
16. *Boston Gazette*, 20, 27, May, 3 June 1765.
17. SCPR 60:393.
18. MCPR, docket 16584.
19. *Boston Directory* 1789, 28; 1796, 69; 1798, 76.
20. SCPR, docket 18604; SCD 122:48.
21. SCPR 88:172.
22. Buhler 1972, no. 356.
23. *Boston Gazette*, 18 January 1768.
24. The caster and the accompanying bill of sale sold at auction and are reproduced in the catalogue; see Northeast Auctions, 16–17 November 1991, lot 436.
25. Pruitt 1978, 10–11.
26. HCD 4:902–03; 31:256.
27. SCD 121:24–25.
28. SCD 122:45–46. They paid £173 for this land and assumed a mortgage made on the property in 1757 with Lois Lee of Salem.
29. SCD 122:48.
30. SCD 122:166.
31. "Assessors' 'Taking-Books,'" 25.
32. RC 18:293; RC 26:18, 36, 74, 162, 184–85, 190.
33. RC 16:17, 49, 69.
34. RC 16:163; RC 18:19, 40, 153.
35. *Essex Gazette*, 14–21 September 1775.
36. SCD 131:39–43, 45–49.
37. "Assessors' 'Taking-Books,'" 25.
38. RC 25:146; SCD 133:221–22.

39. SCD 143:196–98.

40. Steinway 1960, 7.

41. SCD 133:221; 143:196, 198; in April 1782 "Daniel Parker, Merchant," sued Isaac Hall, Ebenezer Toothaker, Abraham Toothaker, and William Willson of Harpswell, Cumberland County, and recovered damages of £149.15.10 and court costs of £7.6.2; SCCR, Court of Common Pleas Extended Record Book 1782, 84. In the session of July 1783 Parker recovered a debt from Joseph Brown of Boston; SCCR, Court of Common Pleas Extended Record Book 1783, 223. In April 1784 he recovered £9.14.3 from Gilharn Taylor of Dorchester; SCCR, Court of Common Pleas Extended Record Book 1783, 221. In October 1785 he was awarded £16 and costs from Peter Sigourney, a Boston founder; SCCR, Court of Common Pleas Extended Record Book 1785, 188.

42. SCCR, Court of Common Pleas Extended Record Book 1785, 123.

43. Boston Deaths, 1700–1800.

44. SCPR 85:148–49. The widow's name is erroneously given as Abigail.

45. SCPR 85:43–44.

46. SCPR 88:172.

47. SCPR 87:539–40.

48. SCPR 87:538–40; 88:171–72.

49. RC 25:184, 250–52, 276–77, 289–91, 299, 302; RC 26:264, 266, 269, 316; RC 31:9, 32, 58, 71, 73, 99, 108, 117, 149, 151, 172–73, 202.

50. SCPR 88:172.

51. SCD 166:45–46.

52. SCD 166:243–44.

53. This advertisement was repeated on 28 May, 4 and 11 June 1759. Dow 1927, 50, reported that a similar advertisement appeared in the *Boston Gazette* of 14 May 1761, but no such advertisement is in that issue of the newspaper.

54. Ensko 1948, 169; Kovel 1961, 206.

Isaac Parker
1749–1805

A

B

Isaac Parker was born in Charlestown, Massachusetts, on 6 July 1749.[1] His parents were John Parker (1725–65), a potter of Charlestown, and Abigail Goodwin Center (1725–89), widow of Samuel Center, who were married in 1748; Daniel Parker (q.v.) was his uncle.[2] His paternal grandparents were Isaac Parker (1692–1742), also a potter, and Grace Hall (1696–1754), both of Charlestown.[3] Parker's maternal grandparents were Timothy Goodwin (1686–1742), a joiner of Reading, Massachusetts, and Abigail Blunt (b. 1689).[4] John Symmes (q.v.) was a first cousin.

Parker would have begun his apprenticeship about 1763 and completed his service by 1770, very likely with his uncle by marriage John Welsh (q.v.). After finishing his apprenticeship, Parker may have worked in association with Welsh. A bill of 5 February 1772 wherein Parker acknowledged receipt of payment from the Salem, Massachusetts, silversmith John Hathorne (q.v.) on behalf of Welsh offers evidence of their relationship:

Boston Feby 5 1772

Mr John Hathorne }
Bot of John Welsh }

12 Dozen of Cyphord Button Stones @41^s/	£	24. 12
7 Sheets of Ruby Foyl		2. 8
1 Dozen of Buckel Bruches		2.
1 Bench Vice		4. 10
	£	33. 10

Received the above in full for John Welsh

Isaac Parker

Nine months later another receipt, dated 17 November, suggests that Parker was selling rings to Hathorne on his own account:

Boston Nov^{er} 17 1772

Received of Mr John Hathorne six pounds six shilling
for Seven Enamel'd rings by the hand of Ezra Burrill
in full

£ 6. 6. o   Isaac Parker[5]

Isaac Parker married Deborah Williams (1753–1838) of Roxbury, Massachusetts, in that town on 27 June 1776.[6] She was the daughter of Samuel Williams (1711–86), a yeoman, and Abigail May (ca. 1721–93), both of Roxbury.[7] Parker may have moved to Deerfield, Massachusetts, shortly after his marriage, for an Isaac Parker of Deerfield served twice in the Revolution, once under Colonel Williams and once under Col. Elisha Porter. This perhaps disproves Henry Flynt and Martha Gandy Fales's suggestion that Parker went to Deerfield in 1774 because he was a "peace-loving citizen, troubled by the Revolutionary events about Boston."[8] Parker may have moved to Deerfield because his wife had family in the area.[9] Their eldest child, Isaac, was born there in 1778.[10]

Evidence of Parker's work as a jeweler and as a maker and repairer of small silver goods lies in the account book of his Deerfield neighbor, the hatter Justin Hitchcock (1752–1822).[11] Between 1778 and 1785 the two sold each other a number of goods. Hitchcock's account book notes that Parker purchased "old Silver" from him for 3 shillings and 8 pence and "1 pr Old Buckles" for 9 shillings and 4 pence, indicating that Parker bought old buckles to sell or, more likely, to melt down. Hitchcock records these purchases of silver goods from Parker:

Jany 21 1778	By 1 pair of Shoe Buckles	£	1	2	o
	. . .				
Oct 7	By making 1 knee buckle		o	2	2
Jany 12 1779	By mending my Buckles		o	o	6
. . .					
Octr 14	By 1 Sett Tea Spoons		1	1	o
April 1780	. . .				
	By mending Earrings		o	1	o
Novr 17	By Cash Silver		o	4	o
Augst 16 1781	By 1 Pair Brass Sleeve Buttons		o	o	8
	. . .				
	By 1 Pair Shoe Buckles		1	5	o
	By 2 Hair pins		o	6	o
	By 1 pair kneebuckles		o	7	6
	. . .				
Augst 18 1785	By mending Sleeve button (price grouped with other objects)				

In addition, Hitchcock's six purchases of "WI" (West Indies) rum from Parker during 1785 suggests that Parker may have begun to trade goods brought from the Boston waterfront. Between 1783 and 1789, Parker conducted seven land transactions, one of which may have been to purchase land near Deerfield Academy said to hold his workshop.[12] In all but one of these transactions, Parker was listed as a jeweler.

Some scholars contend that the silversmith and clockmaker John Russell

(1767–1839) of Deerfield was Parker's apprentice.[13] Further research is required to prove this relationship, but one tantalizing record in Hitchcock's account book notes that on 26 December 1785 he paid Parker for "John to help me."

A Suffolk county deed of 1787 records the sale of Deborah Williams's share of her father's estate to the prosperous merchant Giles Alexander (1751–1816). That a child born to Deborah and Isaac in 1783 was christened Giles Alexander Parker underscores Parker's personal and mercantile ties to Boston through Alexander by this date.[14] Indeed, by 1789 Parker had returned to the city. A deed of that year identified him as a Boston trader, and the *Boston Directory* of 1789 listed him at No. 1, Long-wharf.[15] Parker's departure from Deerfield may be further inferred from the tasks performed in 1791 and 1796 by Hitchcock, presumably to maintain Parker's property. Hitchcock charged Parker "to 1900 shingle nails," "to ⅔ of a days work," "to work done at yr Barn," "to 7 posts," "to 12 rails," and "to ½ days setting fence."[16] Parker's return to Boston marked an end to his career as a jeweler. The Boston directories from 1798 to 1805 recorded his profession as merchant, with offices at No. 52 Long Wharf and a home on Hawkins Street.[17] Suffolk County probate records identify him as a merchant and bear out his change of profession. An August 1805 inventory of his personal effects in Suffolk County Probate Records reveals that Parker owned silver, glass, "pictures," carpeting, and furniture, but no silversmithing or jeweler's tools from his earlier career. The impressive size of his personal estate suggests that his career evolved into that of a successful merchant. The estate amounted to $6,191.49 after $4,952.98 in debts and fees were deducted from $11,144.47.[18]

In spite of his years as a jeweler in Deerfield, little evidence of Parker's craft survives. One mark (A) combines his first initial and surname, I·PARKER in a rectangle. A second touchmark of his initials, I·P in a rectangle (B), tentatively is attributed to Parker.[19] JJF

SURVIVING OBJECTS

	Mark	Inscription	Patron	Date	Reference	Owner
Tablespoon	A†	S/DR		ca. 1775	Buhler/Hood 1970, no. 287	YUAG
Tablespoon	B†	SC	Sarah Catlin (?)	ca. 1770		PVMA

1. *Charlestown VR* 1:390.
2. *Charlestown VR* 1:286, 399; "Memoirs of Prince's Subscribers," *NEHGR* 6:375; Wyman 1879, 2:727; *NEHGR* 32:64; Griffen 1952, 86.
3. MCPR, docket 16584; *NEHGR* 28:121; *Charlestown VR* 1:238; *Medford VR*, 72; Griffen 1952, 86.
4. RC 28:18; *Charlestown VR* 1:144.
5. English-Touzel-Hathorne Papers, box 6, folder 12, PEM.
6. *Roxbury VR* 1:377; 2:434, 606; *Index of Obituaries, 1784–1840*, 4:3412.
7. *Roxbury VR* 1:237, 383; 2:274, 437, 668, 672; *Index of Obituaries, 1704–1800*, 3:564; *Index of Obituaries, 1784–1840*, 5:4937, 4960.
8. *Mass. Soldiers and Sailors* 11:861; Flynt/Fales 1968, 293–94.
9. A Deerfield Williams family relationship to Deborah Williams has not yet been proven. According to Spang 1962, 639–40, Parker "married a woman who was related to the prominent Williams family." The relationship of Colonel Williams (under whom Parker may have served in the Revolution) to Deborah Williams is unknown. J. Peter Spang, letter to author, 14 November 1989.
10. *Deerfield VR*, 102. In addition to Isaac, the children of Isaac and Deborah Parker were John (b. 1781), Giles Alexander (b. 1783), and Samuel Williams (b. 1785).
11. Justin Hitchcock Account Book, fol. 3, PVMA.

12. HCD 21:159–61; 25:175; FCD 1:37, 68, 108, 452; Spang 1962, 640, suggests that Parker's shop was located on the south side of Albany Road near the present Deerfield Academy headmaster's house. Land described in the deeds makes this attribution difficult to prove. The land referred to may be that purchased from the Stebbins family; HCD 25:175.

13. Sheldon 1895–96, 2:276; Spang 1962, 640; Miss Lucia Russell to John Marshall Phillips, letter 2 August 1937.

14. SCD 162:34; *Deerfield VR*, 102.

15. FCD 1:452; RC 10:196.

16. Justin Hitchcock Account Book, fol. 3, PVMA.

17. RC 10:272; *Boston Directory* 1798, 83; 1800, 83; 1803, 95; 1805, 95.

18. SCPR 103:421, 441–42, 471–72, docket 22414.

19. A spoon bearing the initials mark is at PVMA. The spoon is engraved with the initials "SC" and was said to have belonged to Sarah Catlin (b. 1738; married Moses Smith, 1761) when given to the association by a descendant. Letter from Suzanne L. Flynt to the author. According to its history, the spoon predates Isaac Parker's arrival in Deerfield; however, the shell on the association's spoon bears a striking resemblance in its width and the technique of outlining the rays to the shell on the spoon with Parker's initial and surname mark at YUAG (Buhler/Hood 1970, no. 287). This similarity leaves open the possibility that the spoon with the initials mark may have been made by Parker.

John Parkman
1716–48

A

John Parkman was born in Boston on 19 November 1716, the son of William Parkman, Jr. (1685–1769), a joiner, and Hannah Goodwin (1687–1756), who were married in 1709.[1] His paternal grandparents were William Parkman (1658–1730), a shipwright, and Elizabeth Adams (1660–1746).[2] His maternal grandparents were John Goodwin (ca. 1647–1712) and Martha Lathrop (1652–1728), who were married in Charlestown, Massachusetts.[3] Parkman's grandmother Goodwin married John Pierson of Reading, Massachusetts, following the death of her husband.[4]

John Parkman would have begun his apprenticeship about 1730 and would have completed it about 1737. This training probably took place with John Burt (q.v.), because Parkman witnessed a deed for Burt in 1736 when he would have been twenty years old.[5] Shortly after completing his apprenticeship he was the plaintiff in a lawsuit with another goldsmith, Thomas Townsend (q.v.). The court record of 1739 reported that Parkman was to recover £16.4.10 for a note that Townsend failed to pay as well as £3.1.6 for the costs of court.[6] Parkman's only known apprentice was Benjamin Goodwin (q.v.), who signed an indenture on 14 January 1745.[7] After Parkman's death, Goodwin finished his apprenticeship with Jacob Hurd (q.v.).

On 1 May 1740 Parkman married Elizabeth Eames (Emmes) (1715–73), the daughter of Nathaniel Eames (ca. 1690–1750), a stonecutter, and Hannah Grafton (1691–ca. 1758), who were married in 1714.[8] Through this marriage Parkman became the brother-in-law of the jeweler Joshua Eames (q.v.). This kinship bond was strengthened further when Eames married Parkman's sister Martha in 1743.[9] The relationship between these two craftsmen was enlarged to include another of their contemporaries when Eames married second Margaret Clark, sister of the silversmith Joseph Clark, Jr. (q.v.), in 1747. Clark was one of the appraisers of Parkman's estate when the inventory was compiled on 15 December 1748, two days after administration was granted to Elizabeth Parkman.[10] The inventory contained a detailed listing of goldsmith's tools:

1 Forging Anvil, 1 Teast, 1 Large raising Anvil, 1 Thimble Stamp, 1 p.[r] Drawing Tongs, 1 small raising Anvil, 2 Spoon punches, 2 beek Irons w.[t] 262[lb] at 8/   } 104.. 16 —

11 doz.^{n} & 3 Wool Cards £78.15/. 9 pair Ditto £8	86.. 15 —
Files and Sundry small Tools £6—7 Hamers 100/ 1 old Saw 2/	11. 2 —
Sundry Punches & Chizells w.^{t} 14^{lb} at 10/	7.. —
Glass case 120/ 6 small Hammers 30/, 1 p.^{r} Sheers 25/ 1 p.^{r} Scales & w^{ts}: 85/	13.
2 p.^{r} small drawing Irons 30/ 5 p.^{r} brass buckles 60/ 1 bench w.th ⎫	
3 Irons 100/, 1 small Board Vice 30/ 1 Board Screw plate 50/ ⎭	13: 10 —
1 Tinn pan 7/ 1 Box Contain^{g} 1 p.^{r} Scales & 32 ^{oun} ^{wts}100/	5: 7 —
3 small p.^{r} Scales w.th weights 45/ 1 box punches &c 15/	3: : —
2 small Strainers 20/ Vise & Bench 60/ 1 Box file Handels 7/	4: 7 —
2 Iron flasks 20/ 2 p.^{r} Tongs belonging to the forge 15/	1: 15 —
48^{lb} Card wire at 12/ Tacks 60/ old Iron 33^{lb} ^{1}/$_{2}$ at 18^{d}	31: 6. 3
19^{lb} of mixt pewter & Lead at 4/ 12^{lb} Lead at 3/ 3 Cop.^{r} boiling pans 25/	6: 17 —
18 Card Screws 90/ 1 p.^{r} Forge Bellows 100/	9: 10 —
1 Screw w.th Iron Plate & Sundry small Tools 30/ 5 ^{lb} ^{1}/$_{2}$ old brass 35/	3: 5 —
19: ^{ouns} 16^{pwt}. of wrought plate, consisting of 6 large Spoons, 23 Tea Ditto ⎫	59: 8
1 p.^{r} Clasps, 1 p.^{r} flukes & Tongues, 2 Thimbles 1 Knee Buckle at 60/ ⎭	
for the fashion of y.^{e} aboves.^{d} plate	9: — —
21 ^{ouns}:^{3}/$_{4}$ of old plate at 56/, ^{3}/$_{4}$ ounce of silver made in Sawder 42/	61: 19 —
25.^{ouns}: 17$^{P.wt}$: of Wrought plate in y.^{e} Family Viz.^{t} 1 Can, 1 porring.^{r}: 2	
spoons at 60/	77: 11 —
1.^{ou}: 1$^{P.wt}$: 5.^{gra}: of Wrought Gold at £42 ℔ on: vizt 4 p.^{r} buttons, 1 Necklace	44: 10 —
fashioning y.^{e} aboves^{d} Gold	7:106 —
1.^{oun} 17 p$^{w.t}$ ^{1}/$_{2}$ of Gold viz: 9 p.^{r} of Buttons partly made at £42 ℔ ounce	79: 15 —
for the workmanship of s.^{d} Gold	3: 10 —

At the end of the inventory the following items were also listed:

11 p.^{r} of Steel Flooks & Tongues for Buckles at 6/	£3: 6 —
2 p.^{r} small plyers 12/, 3 small hammers 30/, 1 brass Stamp 30/	4: 2 —
10 ^{lb} ^{1}/$_{2}$ of small Punches 60/, 5 Broken Sheets of Foyle 30/	4: 10 —
1 small Teast w.^{t} 9^{lb} at 7/6,^{d} 1 Barr of Silver 2^{oun}: 3^{pwt} 9^{Gra}: at 56/	9: 8 —
1.^{oun} ^{1}/$_{2}$ of boreax 18/ Allum 5/ 1 large old Teast £7	8: 3 —

The total value of Parkman's estate was £2,135.5.3 Old Tenor.[11] Its substantial size, including such household goods as mezzotints, china, and a sconce with a gilt frame and such apparel as a wig valued at £5, suggests that Parkman was successful financially. He also owned a slave named Prince, who was valued at £400. The number and variety of the silversmith's tools in the estate indicate that at his death Parkman had the capability of making holloware and maintained an active shop in which spoons and gold and silver jewelry were being made. Surprisingly, only a few spoons bearing a surname mark in script (A) have been recorded from Parkman's decade-long career.[12] Parkman appears to have been a productive silversmith who probably chose to fabricate work for others to sell, rather than involving himself in the retail side of the business. In addition, Parkman's personal estate contained card boards, card wire, and a machine to prick cards, valued together at more than £60, which suggests that a substantial amount of material for carding wool was being made in

Parkman's household. Following Parkman's death his widow, Elizabeth, married Samuel Brown in 1754.[13] PEK

SURVIVING OBJECTS

	Mark	Inscription	Patron	Date	Reference	Owner
Tablespoon	A†	MS; RB (later)		ca. 1745		SI
Tablespoon	A*	none		ca. 1745	YUAG files	

1. Roberts 1895, 1:377; RC 9:166, 174; RC 24:116; RC 28:24.
2. *Salem VR* 2:139; Whitmore 1878, 14, no. 264, 19, no. 365; RC 9:73.
3. John Goodwin's birth date was calculated from his age at the time of death; see Whitmore 1878, 9, no. 161. *Charlestown VR* 1:18, 71.
4. RC 28:54.
5. *York Deeds* 18:223–24.
6. SCCR, Court of Common Pleas Record Book 1738, 261.
7. Boston Indentures 1 (1734–51): 83, Rare Book Room, BPL.
8. RC 28:51, 216; Nathaniel Eames's birth date was calculated from his age at the time of death; see Whitmore 1878, 19, no. 1712; SCPR 43:491–93; 72:601–02; *Salem VR* 1:377; Whitmore 1878, 91, no. 1717; RC 24:105.
9. RC 28:244.
10. SCPR 42:67–68.
11. SCPR 42:148–50.
12. Ensko also attributed a surname mark in Roman capitals to this silversmith, but that mark was probably used by the later Boston silversmith Charles Parkman; Belden 1980, 327.
13. RC 30:368; SCPR 72:601–03.

Timothy Parrott
1719/20–before 1757

A

Timothy Parrott was born in Boston on 1 March 1719/20 and was baptized in the Brattle Street Church five days later.[1] His parents were Bryant Parrott (1690–1754), son of Bryant and Hannah (Marshall) Parrott, and his second wife, Abigail Clarke (d. before 1724).[2] Abigail was the daughter of Capt. Timothy Clarke (ca. 1657–1737), a mariner, and Sarah Richardson.[3] Abigail (Clarke) Parrott was deceased by 1724, when Bryant Parrott married Ruth Wadsworth.[4] In a Suffolk County deed dated 3 September 1735, Bryant Parrott represented his children's interests as their sole guardian.[5]

Timothy Parrott was born into a prosperous family. His maternal grandfather had begun to denote himself Esq. by 1717. His father was a successful merchant who owned a brick "mansion house" and stable on Water Street, both of which were listed among the 295 buildings destroyed by fire in 1760.[6] At Bryant Parrott's death in 1754, his estate was valued at £2,177.4.2 and included 127 ounces of silver worth £42.13.[7]

Parrott apparently never married.[8] His date of death is not known; however, he probably was no longer alive on 13 May 1757, when his brother Benjamin was listed as the only son in the division of Bryant Parrott's estate.[9]

Although Parrott's master is unknown, his extended family included several Boston metalworkers. His mother, Abigail (Clarke) Parrott, was the niece of Samuel Clarke (1659–1705) (q.v.). Her sister Katherine married the coppersmith Shem Drowne (q.v. Appendix B), who was mentioned in Timothy Clarke's will dated 8 June 1737.[10] A more distant familial connection existed between Parrott and the Newport, Rhode Island, silversmith Samuel Vernon.[11]

No documents identifying Timothy Parrott as a silversmith survive. Three objects bearing an initial and surname mark (A) are the only evidence of Parrott's career. A description of a second mark, an initial and surname with pellet in a ribbon, has been published, but an example of this mark has not been located.[12] DAF

SURVIVING OBJECTS

	Mark	Inscription	Patron	Date	Reference	Owner
Porringer	A†	ORF/to/EAE		ca. 1745	MFA 1906, no. 212	
Porringer	A	T/CS		ca. 1745	*American Silver* 1967, no. 13	RWNAG
Spoon	A	?		ca. 1745	DAPC 69.724	

1. RC 24:141; *Church in Brattle Square*, 141.
2. RC 28:42; Bridgman 1853, 174, 197–98; *Church in Brattle Square*, 106, 232; Thwing; RC 9:190; Codman 1918, 182.
3. SCPR 33:228–29.
4. Bridgman 1853, 198.
5. SCD 53:180–81.
6. Bridgman 1856, 197–98.
7. SCPR 52:341–50.
8. Bridgman 1853, 198.
9. SCPR 52:341–50.
10. SCPR 33:228–29.
11. Bigelow-Phillips files, 1260.
12. Flynt/Fales 1968, 295.

Parsons
w. ca 1750

A

From 1937, when Stephen Ensko published the mark I·PARSONS in a rectangle and identified it as the mark of John Parsons from Boston, who worked about 1780, this name has been included in lists of American silversmiths; Ensko, however, offered no explanation of how the name John Parsons could be linked to the I·PARSONS mark.[1] In 1949, C. Jordan Thorn attributed that mark, as well as PARSONS in a rectangle, to John Parsons.[2] The latter mark (A), which appears on a teaspoon with an eleven-lobed shell drop, was first published in *American Church Silver*, the catalogue of the important silver exhibition held in 1911 at the Museum of Fine Arts, Boston. The shell's style suggests that the spoon was made in Massachusetts in the mid-eighteenth century.[3] Henry Flynt and Martha Gandy Fales further confused the issue by asserting that a candlestick illustrated by Francis Hill Bigelow in 1917 bore Parson's mark, even though Bigelow clearly stated that the candlestick was made in Sheffield, England, by John Powers & Co.[4]

The artifactual evidence substantiates the existence of a silversmith named Parsons who probably worked in Massachusetts in the mid-eighteenth century. But linking both marks to the same maker is much less certain because the objects on which they appear cannot be traced. And whether the "I" in the I·PARSONS mark stands for John has not been established. Although a number of John Parsons lived in Massachusetts during the period, none has yet proven to be a silversmith. PEK

SURVIVING OBJECTS

	Mark	Inscription	Patron	Date	Reference	Owner
Teaspoon	A†	EW		ca. 1750	MFA 1911, no. 820	

1. Ensko 1937, 46.
2. Thorn 1949, 159.
3. An overall photograph of the spoon is at the MFAB (1377.11). A photograph of the bowl back and mark is in the Berger file, YUAG. Notes on the card accompanying the photograph date the spoon ca. 1740 and ca. 1750; see also French 1917, 90; Okie 1936, 276; Graham 1936, 55.
4. Flynt/Fales 1968, 295; Bigelow 1917, 290–91.

Samuel Pedrick
d. 1772

Samuel Pedrick of Marblehead, Massachusetts, was identified as a goldsmith when the administration of his estate was granted to his widow, Sarah Pedrick, in June 1772. Another Essex County goldsmith, William Bubier (q.v.), served together with William Curtis III as surety, which suggests that Bubier and Pedrick may have maintained a working relationship.[1] Pedrick's personal estate inventory, filed at the same time and compiled by Isaac Mansfield, Thomas Lewis, and Samuel Reed, amounted to £38.5.10 and included "Sundry Gold-smiths Tools & Case £3.12" as well as "3 oz 3 dwt silver @ 6/8 £1.1," which indicates that Pedrick was a working silversmith with a shop and display case.[2] A year later William Curtis III was appointed guardian of Pedrick's four-year-old daughter Sarah, presumably because her mother had died; William Bubier again was involved, this time signing the bond.[3]

The goldsmith probably was the son of Joseph (d. 1770) and Sarah Pedrick (ca. 1705–88) and was born in Marblehead on 11 March 1743.[4] Pedrick probably trained with Benjamin Burt (q.v.) because he witnessed deeds for Burt in 1763.[5] The silversmith was working at least by 1767, when he married Sarah Stacey (b. 1750), the daughter of Ambrose Stacey (1729–53) and Mary Vickrey (b. 1730) of Marblehead.[6]

No silver by Pedrick has been identified. PEK

1. ECPR 347:515.
2. ECPR 347:529, docket 21109.
3. ECPR, docket 21110.
4. *Marblehead VR* 2:632. Another Samuel Pedrick was born in Marblehead to Samuel and Elizabeth Pedrick in 1733. Since the goldsmith is not mentioned in Joseph Pedrick's estate papers, it is possible that he is the son of Samuel and Elizabeth. ECPR for Joseph Pedrick 346:270; 369:531; 370:101, 359; 373:45.
5. SCD 100:23–24; 156:231–32; 156:232–33.
6. *Marblehead VR* 1:478, 482, 532; 2:400, 670.

Houghton Perkins
1735–78

A

Houghton Perkins, the son of Isaac Perkins (q.v.), was born in Boston on 10 February 1735.[1] His father died when he was only three years old, and his mother, Sarah (Hurd) Perkins, became his guardian. In 1739 at the time of Perkins's mother's second marriage, Perkins's uncle Jacob Hurd (q.v.) assumed the role of guardian.[2] In all likelihood Perkins trained with Hurd because Perkins witnessed deeds for him in 1749, 1754, and 1755.[3] His apprenticeship would have been completed about 1756.

B

Perkins was identified as being "of Boston goldsmith" when he sold land near the Merrimack River in 1758.[4] This land was purchased by his father from the Boston silversmith Obadiah Morse (q.v.). In 1760 and 1761 Perkins served as one of Boston's clerks of the market.[5] He may have married about 1764, but no record has been found. Two sons of a Mrs. Houghton Perkins were baptized in the West Church, Boston: William on 24 February 1765 and Houghton on 29 November 1767.[6] In 1770 Perkins and his wife, Elizabeth, bought a house and land in Boston from John Hurd, Esq., of Portsmouth, New Hampshire.[7] Within the next two years Perkins moved to Taunton, Massachusetts, for he was identified as being of Taunton and "late of Boston" when he mortgaged his house and land in Boston in 1772.[8] Perkins received pay for a day's services guarding prisoners at Taunton on 8 December 1776 during the Revolution. He evidently was taken prisoner of war, for an order of the Committee of Correspondence dated 24 December 1777 directed the commissary of prisoners to send John Brant and Peter Moore in the next cartel bound for Halifax: they were to be exchanged for David Greelay and Houghton Perkins, who were being held prisoners by the British at Halifax.[9] Perkins died, however, before he could be exchanged, and the *Boston Gazette* of 4 May 1778 carried a report of his death.[10] No probate papers exist for him in Suffolk or Bristol counties.

Only a few pieces of silver with Perkins's marks, an initial and surname mark (A) and an initials mark (B), are recorded. A second initials mark has been attributed to him, but the spoon that bears it seems too late stylistically to be by Perkins.[11] PEK

SURVIVING OBJECTS

	Mark	Inscription	Patron	Date	Reference	Owner
Caster	B	PEC		ca. 1775	Hammerslough/ Feigenbaum 1958–73, 2:31	
Mourning ring (gold)	B*	E. Quill, Ob + 1 July 1763 AE 22	Elizabeth (Harris) Quill	1763	DAPC 86.2358	BBC
Teaspoon	A*	RA		ca. 1770	YUAG files	
Teaspoon	A†	A/NE		ca. 1775	DAPC 73.2044	WM
Teaspoon	B†	AH	Ann (Hurd) Furnass	ca. 1765	Buhler 1972, no. 333	MFAB

1. RC 24:222.
2. MCPR 22:103, 345, docket 17154.
3. SCD 78:110–11; 84:261–62; 87:63–64.
4. ECD 119:34.
5. RC 16:34, 49.
6. Records of Baptisms in the West Church, Boston, 1737 to 1880, fols. 25, 30, Boston City Archives, City Hall.
7. SCD 117:91–92.
8. SCD 122:127, 211.
9. *Mass. Soldiers and Sailors* 12:154.
10. *Index of Obituaries, 1704–1800*, 3:230.
11. Belden 1980, 333. The engraving on the spoon is script with sprigs.

Isaac Perkins
ca. 1710–37

According to the Perkins family genealogy, Isaac Perkins was born in Boston in October 1710. His father, Isaac, a Boston shipmaster, was born in Ipswich, Massachusetts, on 23 May 1676 to the yeoman Isaac Perkins (1650–1726) and Hannah Knight.[1] The goldsmith's grandfather agreed to pay his son one hundred pounds in ten yearly installments if he would marry Mary Pike (or Pickett), a Boston widow then living in Ipswich, which he did on 3 June 1703.[2] In addition to the goldsmith, the births of other children to this couple are recorded in Boston: Isaac (b. 1703/04 [who must have died young]); Richard (b. 1705); Mary (b. 1706); and Hannah (b. 1708).[3] The death of the goldsmith's mother is not recorded but would have occurred before 10 October 1723, when his father was married a second time, to Lydia Key, widow of John Vivien, whom she had wed the previous 3 April.[4] The elder Perkins died on 14 June 1725, leaving his wife, Lydia, the £250 she had when she married him; his will mentions only two surviving children, Isaac and Hannah, who would both have been minors.[5]

Isaac Perkins would have begun his apprenticeship about 1724, possibly with Jacob Hurd (q.v.) because he married Hurd's sister Sarah (1712–before 1746) on 12 October 1732.[6] A record exists of the birth of one child, Houghton (q.v.), to this couple.[7] In 1737 Perkins bought land near the Merrimack River from Obadiah Morse (q.v.) and his wife Elizabeth.[8] Perkins's wealth can be explained by his inheritances, mentioned in his will, which he made out on 27 January 1736/37:

> Whereas my Hon.ᵈ uncle Richard Houghton late of yᵉ parish of Sᵗ pauls Shadwell in the County of Middlesex [England] marriner Decesᵈ by his Laste will & Testament baring date the Thirtyeth day of March one Thousand Seven Hundred & Thirty Six . . . Bequeath unto me . . . Five Hundred pounds of Lawfull money of Graite Britain & . . . & Interest both in Law & Equity which he then had of in & to a certain messuage or Tenemᵗ . . . in Boston in New England which was mortgaged to him . . . by his Father Mʳ James Smith & further . . . one Fifth part of yᵉ residue & Remainder of all . . . Ships, Stocks, Annuities, Dividends, Goods . . . Thomas Pennywell of yᵉ parish of Tunbridge in the County of Kent, Esqʳ & Mʳ William Harrison of London Gunfounder Exceutors of his sᵈ Last will . . .[9]

Perkins left one-third of his estate to his wife, Sarah, and two-thirds to his son Houghton. Administration was granted to his widow on 1 November 1737.[10] The inventory, compiled on 10 January 1737/38, identifies him as being of Charlestown, Massachusetts. The appraisers, Thomas Call, Joseph Phillips, and Steven Badger, valued his assets at £372.7.10, which included numerous tools:

> To one Doz: files 12/: Two pair Plyars 1/ 4: Riveting hammers 1/6   0. 14. 10
> To Small Screw Plate & Pin 5/ kneeling Tongs 4/   0. 9. 0
> To one skillet for melting 60/: to one Swage Test £9.7.6   12. 7. 6
> To one Planishing Dᵒ. 4ᴸ To one Can Anvil 3 = 15 = 0   7. 15. 0
> To one Square drawing Iron 12/: one Large Round Dᵒ, 15/   1. 7. 0
> To 3 Iron Flasks 20/ one Pair drawing Tongs 15/   1. 15. 0
> To one Flatt Stake 18/: one long Planishing Hammer 7/6   1. 5. 6
> To one Dᵒ large 10/: Gibbet Stake 7/6 Stock Shears [crossed out]   0. 17. 6
> To one pair Stock shears 50/:To one pair kneeling tongs 7/6   2. 17. 6
> To 3 brass stamps ᴸ8 = 0 = 0   8. .
> To one large Chissell with an Eye 7/6 Brass Kettle 30/   1. 17. 6

| To sundry Patterns 8/: Board Vice 40/ | 2. 8. 0 |
| 1 square Triblet 5/ | 0. 5. 0[11] |

The inventory also included a negro girl valued at £90 and "To one Ingate, tool" 10 shillings. The amount of the estate greatly increased with £1,011.6.2 cash received from Jacob Hurd, who became Houghton's guardian, and £1,787.10 from England. Among the payments made out of the estate were £1.19.6 to James Boyer (q.v.), 9 shillings to James Butler (q.v.), and 4 shillings to Samuel Gray (1711–48) (q.v.).[12] Perkins's widow married William Baker in 1739 and was probably dead when administration of the estate was committed to Baker on 31 May 1746.[13] Jacob Hurd witnessed that bond.

No silver by this maker has been positively identified. The marks IP crowned in a shaped shield, here identified as marks (A, B) of IP (q.v.), have sometimes been attributed to Perkins.[14] Because mark (A) was being used before Perkins was fully trained, it could not belong to him. Mark (B) might have been his.   PEK

1. *Ipswich VR* 1:287; ECPR 315:329–30.
2. Perkins 1889, 44; *Ipswich VR* 2:337.
3. RC 24:25, 36, 45, 57.
4. RC 28:110, 115.
5. SCPR 24:111–12.
6. *Charlestown VR* 1:237; RC 28:179.
7. RC 24:222.
8. ECD 73:264.
9. MCPR 20:426; the will is transcribed from docket 17154.
10. MCPR 20:487.
11. MCPR 20:459; the inventory is transcribed from docket 17154.
12. MCPR 24:184.
13. MCPR 24:184.
14. Ensko 1989, 285.

Samuel Phillips
1658–1722

Although he has been included in lists of American silversmiths for many years, little is known about Samuel Phillips, one of Salem's first silversmiths.[1] Like his contemporary Thomas Higginson (q.v.), Phillips was the son of a prominent and influential minister. He was born on 23 January 1658 in Rowley, Massachusetts, the son of the local clergyman, the Reverend Samuel Phillips (1625–96; Harvard College, 1650) and his wife, Sarah (ca. 1628–1714). His paternal grandfather was the Reverend George Phillips (1593–1644), the first minister of Watertown, Massachusetts; his maternal grandparents were Samuel (1586–1670) and Mary (Everhard) Appleton.[2]

It is likely that Phillips served his apprenticeship with Jeremiah Dummer (q.v.) of Boston.[3] His training would have been completed about 1679, and Phillips seems to have stayed in Boston for about eight years afterward. He was living there in 1685, perhaps working as a journeyman, when his father deeded half of the family farm in Bradford, Massachusetts, to him.[4]

By 1687, however, Phillips had moved on to Salem, where he would remain for the rest of his life. He was living there at the time of his first marriage to Mary Emerson (1664/65–1703) of Gloucester, Massachusetts, on 26 May 1687.[5] This marriage, which produced six children, united the families of two Essex County ministers: Mary was the daughter of the Reverend John (d. 1700) and Ruth (Symonds) Emerson of Gloucester.[6] The marriage was an advantageous one for Phillips. Prior to the wedding, the Reverend Mr. Emerson agreed to pay Samuel and Mary the sum of one hundred pounds within a reasonable amount of time and also to leave Mary an equal part of his estate after his decease.[7]

Mary Emerson Phillips died on 4 October 1703, and Phillips took as his second wife a widow, Sarah Mayfield, on 27 April 1704.[8] Samuel and Sarah had one child, Patience, born on 8 August 1706.[9]

Only scattered references to Phillips can be found in Salem documents of the time. His house and land were located near the meetinghouse, and he owned other property in town.[10] Thomas Higginson witnessed a deed for Phillips in 1690, which has prompted speculation about their relationship.[11] Phillips may have trained Daniel Greenough (q.v.) from about 1700 to 1707. Phillips served the town in several capacities, acting as tithingman, constable, sealer of weights and measures, and clerk of the market at various times.[12]

In his will, written on 3 May 1722, Phillips bequeathed his estate to various family members, with the following reservation: "That I do reserve & keep my Tools of what nature or kind soever which I have & use in my Trade as a Goldsmith to Sell or Dispose of if I should Live to want them for my reliefe & then if any of them remaining to be Sold & Equally Divided among my Children."[13] Phillips died on 13 October 1722; there is no inventory of his estate.[14]

No silver by Phillips is known, although he has been assigned the maker's mark SP in an oval or rectangle by several sources.[15] GWRW

1. MFA 1911, 151; French (1917) 1967, 92; Belknap 1927, 111; Flynt/Fales 1968, 299.
2. *Rowley VR*, 161; Savage 1860–62, 3:410, 414; 1:61; *Sibley's Harvard Graduates* 1:221–28.
3. Phillips witnessed several deeds in Boston in the 1670s and 1680s, including one also witnessed by Jeremiah Dummer in 1678; see *Suffolk Deeds* 10:340; 11:104 (Dummer), 213; 12:179, 216, 244, 274, 386; 13:331. If Phillips apprenticed in Boston and was not apprenticed to Dummer, he must have trained in the shop of John Hull and Robert Sanderson, Sr. (qq.v.).
4. ECD 8:176.
5. *Salem VR* 4:187.
6. *Salem VR* 2:163–64.
7. ECD 8:176. The Reverend Emerson took about eight years to fulfill his obligation; see ECD 11:68.
8. *Salem VR* 6:136; 4:187.
9. *Salem VR* 2:164.
10. ECD 8:175; 13:47; 15:131; 38:242.
11. ECD 8:175.
12. References to Phillips can be found in the Salem Town Records, box 2, pp. 139, 143, 174, 181, 190, 354, 490, 639, 641, PEM. See also *EIHC* 83, no. 3 (July 1947): 247.
13. The will, in the form of a deed of gift, is in the ECD 38:237.
14. Bigelow-Phillips files, 306.
15. Ensko 1948, 234; Thorn 1949, 163; Kovel 1961, 212–13. A teaspoon marked S.P in a rectangle was included in MFA 1906, p. 79, no. 220, but its present whereabouts are unknown. A creampot has also been published as his work, although it is clearly too late in style to be by Phillips; see *Colonial Furniture, Silver, & Decorations . . . The Collection of the Late Philip Flayderman*, American Art Association–Anderson Galleries, 2–4 January 1930, lot 378.

Luke Greenough Pierce
1723–48+

Luke Greenough Pierce was born in Boston on 16 March 1723, the son of the tailor Nathaniel Pierce (b. 1689) and Abigail Greenough (b. 1690), who were married in 1712.[1] His maternal grandparents were Luke Greenough (1667/68–ca. 1691) and Abigail Hammond (b. 1667).[2] Pierce's grandmother Hammond married James Whippo of Barnstable, Massachusetts, in 1692, following her husband's death.

Luke Greenough Pierce would have begun his apprenticeship about 1737 and would have completed his training about 1744, although the identity of his master is not known. Pierce is identified as a silversmith of Boston in the records of the Suffolk Court of Common Pleas for 1746–48 when he was sued for debt by Sanderson West, a merchant of Boston. The court found in favor of West, and Pierce appealed to a higher court.[3] Pierce witnessed a deed on 30 March 1748, along with Joseph Hiller, Sr. (q.v.), for the sale of land from Benjamin Edwards to Samuel Burt (q.v.), which suggests that Pierce may have worked as a journeyman for Burt.[4] No further references to Pierce have been found in the Boston records, and no silver by him is known. PEK

1. RC 24:161; RC 28:41; RC 9:190; Thwing.
2. RC 9:104; *Charlestown VR* 1:58, 150.
3. SCCR, Court of Common Pleas Record Book 1746–48, 77–78.
4. SCD 75:117.

Benjamin Pierpont
1730–97

Unknown artist, Benjamin Pierpont, *1774, oil on card. Collection of Ann and Herbert Berezin. Photograph, courtesy, Nathan Liverant & Son.*

A

B

C

Benjamin Pierpont was born in Roxbury, Massachusetts, on 22 November 1730 to Ebenezer (1694–1754/55) and Anne (Hilton) Pierpont (d. 1745).[1] He was baptized in Roxbury on 3 December of that year.[2] His paternal grandparents were Ebenezer (1661–96) and Mary (Ruggles) Pierpont (b. 1666), who were married in Roxbury on 20 October 1692.[3] The Pierponts were a large family of successful bakers, millers, and merchants in Roxbury. At the time of his death in February 1755, the jeweler's father owned a "mansion house," bake house, gristmills, more than eighteen ounces of silver, and a "library of books."[4]

On 29 March 1759 in the Brattle Street Church, Boston, Pierpont married Elizabeth Shepard (1739–before 1797), daughter of John (d. 1762) and Mary (Eddy) Shepard (1713–65).[5] Mary Eddy was the daughter of the shipwright/mariner Benjamin and Mary (Hallowell) Eddy.[6] Benjamin and Elizabeth Pierpont had five children: Benjamin, Elizabeth, Sally, William, and Mary.[7] The first two children were baptized in Roxbury on 10 February 1760 and 23 August 1761, respectively; the last two children were baptized in the Brattle Street Church, Boston, on 15 May 1763 and 30 August 1767, respectively.[8] Pierpont served as clerk of the market for Boston in 1766.[9]

Pierpont was involved in numerous legal transactions between 1767 and 1787 as an executor of the estate of his brother Ebenezer Pierpont (1725–67), a Roxbury merchant and baker.[10] During this period, the jeweler appeared in probate court seven times to present inventories and estate accounts, and he executed seven real estate transactions for the estate between October 1778 and May 1787.[11] He was appointed guardian to his nephew Ebenezer Pierpont on 7 April 1769.[12] Another brother, the Roxbury miller John Pierpont, acquired full ownership of a milling complex, waterways, house, and land in Roxbury by buying out his siblings. However, when John defaulted on his payment to the estate, Benjamin foreclosed on the property in July 1787 and sold it to the Boston merchant William Marshall the following September for £90.[13]

Pierpont would have finished his apprenticeship by 1751, but the identity of his master is not known. He was active in his profession by 16 September 1760, when "Benjamin Pierpont, Boston, Jeweler," paid £135.12 to Thomas and Lydia Emmons for a house on the lane leading to Sudbury Street.[14] He sold the house four years later to the Boston carpenter William Clough and his wife, Dorcas, for £165.[15] On 5 November 1764 "Benjamin Pierpont, Roxbury, Jeweler," bought one-half of a brick house next to Zachariah Brigden (q.v.) on Cornhill for £335 at the public auction of the shopkeeper Jacob Griggs's estate.[16] The following day, he sold the house to the innkeeper Robert Stone for £359.[17] Because Pierpont does not appear again in Suffolk deeds until 1780 or in the Massachusetts tax list of 1771, he was probably living in rented quarters and spending some time in Roxbury during these early years of his career.

The earliest indications of Pierpont's professional activities appear in Salem records. The settlement of the Salem silversmith Jeffrey Lang's (q.v.) estate in 1759 recorded a debt of £43.3 to Pierpont, indicating a possible professional relationship.[18] Ten receipts document the sale of jewelry from Pierpont to the Salem silversmith John Touzell (q.v.) between January 1762 and November 1764.[19] Thomas Clark (q.v.), a silversmith working in Boston and Roxbury, accepted payment on behalf of Pierpont in 1762 and 1764 and may have worked in association with him. Pierpont was an appraiser of Clark's estate in 1781. One of these receipts reads as follows:

M.[r] John Tusdel to Benj.[a] Pierpont		D.[r]
To four pair of white Stone Earrings		4 · 5 · 4
To one pair of Small Ditto		1 · 0 · 0
To one pair of Cypher Ditto		1 · 2 · 8
Boston Jan.[y] y.[e] 19 1762	£	6 · 8 · 0
Ap.[r] 12 To three Sett Stone buttons		1 · 5 · 0
		7 ·· 13 ·· 0

Recived Five Shillings four pence towards y.[e] bove
Thomas Clark[20]

Another of the receipts was witnessed by Benjamin Loring, possibly the silversmith (q.v.), which suggests that he may have worked in association with Pierpont and Clark:

Boston Aug.[t] 14 1764

Then Recd of M.[r] John Tusell the Sum
four Pounds Sixteen Lawfull money upon
acount of M.[r] Benj.[a] Pairpint
Rec.[d] By Me Thomas Clark
Tes.[t] Benj.[a] Loring[21]

Pierpont was also acquainted with the Springfield, Massachusetts, silversmith Jeremiah Snow III (q.v.). Snow mortgaged his property to Pierpont in 1765 in order to pay a debt to another Boston silversmith, Benjamin Goodwin (q.v.).[22]

In addition to dealing with silversmiths from outlying towns, Pierpont did business with the local craftsman Zachariah Brigden, who purchased three enamel rings from him on 2 January 1767 for £4.13.4.[23] Pierpont was respected by his contemporaries. Samuel Davis (1765–1829), who served an apprenticeship with George Tyler (q.v. Appendix B) between 1779 and 1785, remembers Pierpont in his memoirs (1811) as one of the "eldest of the trade."[24] Benjamin Pierpont had his portrait painted in 1774, compelling evidence that he was a prosperous, successful craftsman (illus.).[25]

The silversmith advertised the loss of some silver spoons in the *Boston News-Letter* on 31 October 1771: "LOST, Four Silver Table SPOONS, Two London made, marked Crest, a Spread Eagle; Two no Mark, Maker's Name, *B. Pierpont*; If offered for Sale, it is desired thay may be stopped."

On 20 June 1780, "Benjamin Pierpont, Boston, Goldsmith," purchased a brick house in Brattle Square from his brother Robert Pierpont for £533.6.8 lawful silver money.[26] The funeral of the silversmith's son Benjamin Pierpont, Jr., was held in this house, described as being on Frog Lane, on 6 April 1785.[27]

The jeweler was still living in Brattle Square in September 1786, when he mortgaged this property to his son-in-law the watchmaker Joseph Pope (q.v. Appendix A) for £350, a loan that he repaid by October 1790.[28]

Pierpont had moved out of the Brattle Square house by 1787, when he was renting a house on Newbury Street from the estate of Rufus Greene (q.v.) next to a shop and store occupied by Robert Pope. The administrators' accounts for Greene's estate record rent payments from Pierpont between 1787 and 1790.[29] The census of 1790 recorded Pierpont's household as two adult men and four women.[30] In the *Boston Directory* of 1796 he was listed as occupying 33 Newbury Street, the former residence of the watchmaker and silversmith John Deverell (1764–1813), who advertised from this address in 1785.[31] Pierpont sold the house in Brattle Square on 1 June 1796 to the watchmaker Isaac Townsend (1760–1812) for £905.[32]

The silversmith appeared before the Suffolk County Court of Common Pleas three times between October 1784 and April 1785. Pierpont, the plaintiff in each case, recovered £21.75 and court costs from the husbandman Edward Brinley of Weston, Massachusetts, £10.15 and court costs of £1.5.10 from the Boston printer John Gill, and £60.16 and court costs from the Boston shipjoiner John Ballard.[33]

Benjamin Pierpont died at his house on Newbury Street on 10 June 1797 at the age of sixty-six.[34] His will, written on 5 June 1797 and presented for probate eight days later, left legacies of $2,000 to his daughters Elizabeth Pope and Mary Pierpont and $750 to his grandsons William and Henry Taylor.[35] He specified that "all [his] silver plate in the house" be equally divided among his children William Pierpont, Elizabeth Pope, and Mary Pierpont. His executor, William Pierpont, received "the Residue of my Estate, including the House-hold furniture, stock, tools, cash, debts, &c wherever the same may be found." Joseph Pope and the merchant Pepperrell Tyler, brother of the silversmith George Tyler, witnessed the administration order.[36]

Pierpont used an initial and surname mark (A) as well as two initials marks (B, C). Although flatware comprises the majority of his surviving work, the silversmith made several forms of holloware, including a beaker for the First Church of Christ in Dorchester, Massachusetts, in 1773 and a set of four two-handled cups for the Church of Christ in Hatfield, Massachusetts, in 1788. Initials marks B·P in conjoined circles and in an oval as well as B.P in a rectangle have also been attributed to him. Published variations include an initial and surname mark B+PIERPONT, as well as B·PIERPONT, and the surname only in a cartouche, oval, and rectangle. None of these marks could be found to illustrate.[37]   DAF

SURVIVING OBJECTS

	Mark	Inscription	Patron	Date	Reference	Owner
Beaker	B*	The Gift of/M. EBENEZER MOSLEY/ to the first Church of Christ in/DOR-CHESTER/1773	First Church, Dorchester, Mass., for Ebenezer Moseley	ca. 1773	Jones 1913, 146	
Cann	A	CKT (later)		ca. 1775		N-YHS
Cann	A*	AG		ca. 1765	Johnston 1994, 120	CMA

	Mark	Inscription	Patron	Date	Reference	Owner
Cann	A	ILR (+)		ca. 1785	MFA 1906, no. 213	
Sauceboat	A*	EF		ca. 1790	*Antiques* 92 (December 1967): 767	
Strainer spoon	c†	AH		ca. 1765	Buhler/Hood 1970, no. 226	YUAG
Sugar bowl	A	?		ca. 1790	*Connoisseur* 156 (June 1964): 118–19	DIA
Tablespoon	A	RB		ca. 1765	DAPC 72.1965	WM
Tablespoon	A*	BC	First Parish, Brookline, Mass.	ca. 1770	Jones 1913, 103	
Tablespoon	A*	HB		ca. 1785		YUAG
Tablespoon	A†	E (?)		ca. 1785		YUAG
Tablespoon	A*	ET	Elizabeth (Tuckerman) Salisbury	ca. 1780	Buhler 1979, no. 44	WAM
Twelve tablespoons	A	ET	Elizabeth (Tuckerman) Salisbury (?)	ca. 1790	Buhler 1979, no. 46	WAM
Tablespoon	A*	S	Salisbury family	ca. 1790	Buhler 1979, no. 45	WAM
Tablespoon (mate below)	A*	AT		ca. 1755	Johnston 1994, 120	CMA
Tablespoon (mate above)	A	AT		ca. 1755	Buhler 1972, appendix no. 64	MFAB
Two tablespoons	A	EBT		ca. 1790	Buhler 1972, appendix no. 65	MFAB
Four tablespoons	A	SB		ca. 1790	YUAG files	
Tankard	A	Breck arms, per fess gules and on a chief per bend sinister indented or and azure 4 hurts 2 and 2, and crest, an arm couped grasping a dagger; B/RR	Rev. Robert and Eunice (Brewer) Breck	ca. 1765	Ward/Hosley 1985, no. 173	CVHM
Six teaspoons	B†	SP		ca. 1790	Flynt/Fales 1968, 112–13	HD
Two-handled cup (mates below)	A*	The Gift of/Deacon Obadiah Dickinson/ to/the Church of Christ in Hatfield/ 1788	Obadiah Dickinson and/or First Congregational Church, Hatfield, Mass.	ca. 1788	Buhler/Hood 1970, no. 227	YUAG
Two-handled cup (mates above and below)	A	The Gift of/Deacon Obadiah Dickinson/ to/the Church of Christ in Hatfield/ 1788	Obadiah Dickinson and/or First Congregational Church, Hatfield, Mass.	ca. 1788	Jones 1913, 212	AIC
Two two-handled cups (mates above)	A*	The Gift of/Deacon Obadiah Dickinson/	Obadiah Dickinson and/or First Congrega-	ca. 1788	Bartlett 1984, 22–23	SLAM

Mark	Inscription	Patron	Date	Reference	Owner
	to/the Church of Christ in Hatfield/ 1788	tional Church, Hatfield, Mass.			

1. *Roxbury VR* 1:280; 2:322, 615; Moffat 1913, 43. Ebenezer Pierpont married three times: (i) Anne Hilton (d. 1745) on 19 February 1722/23 in Roxbury, (ii) Hannah Wiswell (Witzel) (d. 1747) of Dorchester on 10 September 1746, and (iii) Sarah Cushing; Moffat 1913, 43; RC 28:317; *Roxbury VR* 2:322, 615; RC 21:223.
2. Moffat 1913, 57.
3. *Roxbury VR* 1:280, 301; 2:321, 348, 616; SCPR, docket 2354. Mary (Ruggles) Pierpont married Isaac Morris on 3 November 1702; Savage 1860–62, 3:432.
4. SCPR 49:925–27.
5. RC 30:326; *Church in Brattle Square*, 249; RC 24:238, 95; SCPR, dockets 13497, 17648. John and Mary (Eddy) Shepard were married by Rev. Elisha Callender on 24 May 1736; RC 28:198.
6. SCD 33:250. Benjamin Eddy and Mary Hallowell were married in 1712; Thwing.
7. Moffat 1913, 57.
8. *Church in Brattle Square*, 181, 184.
9. RC 16:172.
10. SCPR 66:206–08. Benjamin was named an executor of the estate in Ebenezer Pierpont's will, written on 3 September 1767 and presented for probate on 13 November that year.
11. SCPR 66:206–07, 440–42; 73:10; 80:809; 81:159; 82:795–96, 798; SCD 153:166–67; 160:21–25, 27–28.
12. SCPR 67:449.
13. SCD 161:238–39.
14. SCD 95:59–60.
15. SCD 101:130–31. Clough arranged a mortgage with Pierpont for £150 on the same day as the deed of sale, 28 January 1764, which he repaid in April 1767; SCD 101:131–32.
16. SCD 102:205–06.
17. SCD 102:217–18.
18. ECPR 336:421–22.
19. In addition to the two receipts transcribed, the others in the English-Touzel-Hathorne Papers are 24 September 1762, 25 September 1762, 4 May 1763, 19 May 1763, 4 August 1763, 12 November 1764, 23 October 1764, box 4, folder 5; also 4 August 1763, box 4, folder 3, PEM.
20. English-Touzel-Hathorne Papers, box 4, folder 5, PEM.
21. English-Touzel-Hathorne Papers, box 4, folder 5, PEM.
22. HCD 3:349; 12:824–25.
23. Benjamin Pierpont to Zachariah Brigden, 2 January 1767, Brigden Papers.
24. Steinway 1960, 7.
25. *Antiques* 76 (October 1959): 321.
26. SCD 131:216–17.
27. *Massachusetts Centinel*, 6 April 1785; *Index of Obituaries, 1704–1800*, 1:240.
28. SCD 159:157–58. Elizabeth Pierpont married Joseph Pope of Boston; Moffat 1913, 57.
29. SCPR 89:361–71, 702; 93:362.
30. RC 22:486.
31. *Boston Directory* 1796, 83; Flynt/Fales 1968, 201–02; *Massachusetts Centinel*, 3 September 1785.
32. SCD 183:138–39. Townsend arranged a £455 mortgage with Pierpont that was repaid by 31 August 1796; SCD 183:139–40.
33. SCCR, Court of Common Pleas Extended Record Book 1784, 131, 206, 238.
34. *Index of Obituaries, 1704–1800*, 1:240.
35. SCPR 95:276–78.
36. SCPR 95:262.
37. Kovel 1961, 213.

John Pitts
w. ca. 1734

In 1730 Paul Revere, Sr. (q.v.), advertised in the Boston *News-Letter* that he was "Removed from Capt. Pitts, at the Town Dock, to the North End over against Col. Hutchinson's."[1] This reference led Kathryn Buhler to speculate that Captain Pitts was a goldsmith.[2] Further evidence that this was the case is provided by a document, dated 2 April 1734:

A

Habijah Savage Esq.ʳ John Baker John Hunt Jacob Wendell & Andrew Tyler [q.v.] Genᵗˢ all of Boston in the County of Suffolk Trustees for the Town of Boston aforesᵈ—ec plᵗˢ vs. John Pitts of Boston aforesᵈ Goldsmith Defᵗ In a plea of Debt For that whereas the Defᵗ on the Sixteenth of April 1728 by his bond of that date bound himself in Two hundred pounds in good bills of Credit on this Province to be paid to the sᵈ Trustees on demand yet the Defᵗ has not paid the Same.³

Only a few months earlier one John Pitts, undoubtedly the same man, signed a receipt indicating that he had received payment of three pounds for gold buttons from the executors of the estate of John Langdon of Lynn.⁴ Court documents dated between 1731 and 1737 indicate that "Paul Revere Goldsmith Robert Pateshall Leatherdresser & Capᵗ John Pitts Mariner . . . bound themselves Joyntly and severally" to Elijah Collins, watchmaker (q.v. Appendix A), for the sum of one hundred pounds in February 1731/32, further strengthening the connection between John Pitts and Paul Revere, Sr.⁵

Although at least three men named John Pitts married and fathered children in Boston, between 1721 and 1725, it seems probable that the man known as Capt. John Pitts worked briefly as a goldsmith, but was principally a mariner. The goldsmith John Pitts may have been related to a John Pitts, mariner, who died in Boston in May 1714. He may also have been the man named John Pitts who arrived in Boston aboard the ship *John & Sarah* from Antigua.⁶ Or, the goldsmith may have been John Pitts, son of James Pitts and Elizabeth (Hough) Pitts and older brother of Joseph Pitts (q.v.).⁷ Ambrose Heal records a Captain Pitts, goldsmith, working in London in 1695 at a shop next door to the Cross Keys tavern in Holborn.⁸ It is also remotely possible that Captain Pitts of London came to Boston via Antigua and practiced his craft in Boston between 1714 and 1734.

The wording of the suit brought against John Pitts, the goldsmith, in 1734 suggests that he was being sued for not collecting taxes during his term as a town constable. There was a John Pitts elected to the position of town constable in 1723/24, and thus he was probably the goldsmith. One or more of the men named John Pitts were elected to several other town offices between 1712 and 1728: tithingman in 1712/13, 1715/16, 1716/17, 1721/22 (along with William Cowell, Sr. [q.v.], Thomas Townsend, Sr., and John Burt [q.v.]), and 1727/28; watchman for the dock watch in 1723; and clerk of the market in 1723/24 (refused).⁹

A spoon at the Winterthur Museum bears not only Paul Revere, Sr.'s mark but also the mark IP crowned. Some authorities have attributed this IP crowned mark to Pitts. Other authorities, however, have linked it with other goldsmiths with the initials IP (see I. P., mark B). The mark Pitts, script in a rounded rectangle (A), may have been used by John Pitts, although Joseph Pitts is another maker who could have used this mark. BMW

SURVIVING OBJECTS

	Mark	Inscription	Patron	Date	Reference	Owner
Porringer	A	EEB (later)		ca. 1730	American Art Association–Anderson Galleries, 8 February 1936, lot 35	

	Mark	Inscription	Patron	Date	Reference	Owner
Two tablespoons	A†	ES/to/IB		ca. 1730	DAPC 80.3958	

1. Dow 1927, 54.
2. Buhler 1972, 1:181.
3. SCCR, Court of Common Pleas Record Book 1733–34, court of 2 April 1734, 612.
4. Photostat in Bigelow-Phillips files from ECPR 32:271.
5. SCCR, Court of Common Pleas Record Book 1736–37, 592; SCCR, file 46500.
6. SCPR 18:315; RC 10:161; Thwing.
7. RC 9:198; RC 24:3; SCPR, dockets 4607, 5240.
8. Heal (1935) 1972, 224.
9. Seybolt 1939, 133, 142, 144, 158, 162, 163, 175. One or all of these references may also be to John Pitts, merchant, who died in 1731 (will of John Pitts of Boston, merchant, dated 10 October 1729, Bostonian Society, document 347.6, Boston).

Joseph Pitts
1712/13–34 +

Joseph Pitts was born in Boston on 6 March 1712/13, the son of James Pitts (ca. 1670–1722), a merchant, and Elizabeth Hough (ca. 1670–1726), who were married in Boston in 1691.[1] His maternal grandparents were William (ca. 1647–1714), a tallow chandler, and Lydia Hough (ca. 1645–83).[2] He had a brother John who may have been the goldsmith John Pitts (q.v.). Joseph Pitts would have begun his training about 1727 and would have completed it about 1734; his master is unknown. He is described as a goldsmith in 1734, when he sold his share in a house and land in Boston where his late father and mother lately dwelt to John Foye, who was named his guardian in 1732. The sale was for the benefit of Ebenezer, John, and Sarah Hough, the minor children of the late Ebenezer Hough, who was probably Pitts's uncle.[3] No further evidence of Joseph Pitts has been found in Boston records. The mark Pitts, script in a rounded rectangle, attributed to John Pitts, could have been used by Joseph. PEK

1. RC 24:92; SCPR 31:143, dockets 4607, 5240; RC 9:198.
2. William and Lydia Hough's birth dates were calculated from their ages at time of death; see Whitmore 1878, II, no. 208, and Wyman 1879, 1:520. SCPR, docket 3626.
3. SCD 48:175v–76r; SCPR 31:143; Wyman 1879, 1:520, records that William Hough had a son Ebenezer who married Hannah Foye in 1723.

William Pollard
1690–1740

A

William Pollard's father, also William (1652/53–1690/91), was the son of William (d. 1686), an innholder, and his wife, Ann (ca. 1622–1725), who was celebrated in her old age as the oldest living original settler of the Massachusetts Bay Colony.[1] An innholder himself, William Pollard, Jr., was a member of Old South Church, a member of the military company (1679), and served in King Philip's War. He married Margaret Payne (d. before 1715) sometime before 1687, when their first child, William, was born. Their first child evidently died young because the couple had another child named William, who became the silversmith, on 2 April 1690.[2] Margaret (Payne) Pollard was the granddaughter of Elder William Colborne (d. 1662), from whom she inherited land, and daughter of William Payne and Elizabeth (Colborne) Payne. William Pollard, Jr., died in January 1690/91, and Margaret (Payne) Pollard married the mariner Thomas Powell, who later became an innholder. Margaret and Thomas Powell had their first child, John (d. before 1715), on 25 August 1692.

They had two more children: Margaret (1693–before 1715) and Thomas (b. 1695), who became a mariner.[3]

It has long been assumed that the silversmith William Pollard trained with Edward Winslow (q.v.) because his father's brother, Jonathan Pollard, married Edward Winslow's sister Mary in 1693.[4] The day after William Pollard's twenty-first birthday, the town of Boston granted his stepfather, Thomas Powell, permission to

> Erect a Timber building for a Goldsmith Shop for his Son of 15 foot long 12 foot wide and 9 foot stud with a Flatt Roof on his Land Abutting on Newbury Street in Boston One End of the said building to Stand joyning to the Northerly End of your Petitioners Dwelling house and the other End thereof to stand about Thirty foot Distant from the Dwelling house of Mr. John Barrell On Condition that he Carry up the End next to Mr Barrells house with a Brick Wall to Extend in Heighth three foot above the Timber work thereof.[5]

Pollard's mother, Margaret Powell, evidently died in 1715 because in that year the goldsmith quitclaimed his interest in pastureland in Boston that his mother and stepfather had sold to the fellmonger John Clough for £90 in 1703, in consideration of the money his parents had "laid out for and towards [his] Education and for divers other good causes and Considerations."[6] In June 1715, Pollard's stepfather, Thomas Powell, deeded his tenement on Newbury Street and all of his household possessions to his sons William Pollard and Thomas Powell, Jr., in return for £200, money to pay his debts, and support during his lifetime. Thomas Powell, Jr., in turn, deeded his portion of the land and goods to William Pollard for £300 partly in consideration of the fact that Pollard had "taken upon him to pay . . . all the . . . debts due from my Honoured Father Thomas Powell."[7]

On 25 December 1712 William Pollard married Dorcas Marshall (1694–1770), daughter of Thomas (1656–1719), a cooper, and Dorcas Marshall of Boston; the ceremony was performed by the Reverend Ebenezer Pemberton of the Old South Church. Pollard and his wife had one child who lived to maturity, Dorcas (1721–71).[8] William Pollard was elected clerk of the market in 1716/17 and hogreeve in 1722/23; his cousin Benjamin Pollard (1696–1756) succeeded Edward Winslow as sheriff of Suffolk County.[9] William Pollard was plaintiff in one case and defendant in several cases brought before the Suffolk County Court of Common Pleas between 1715 and 1731.[10]

In 1715, when William Pollard assumed the care of his stepfather, as well as his debts, he was probably making a modest living through his craft. The house in Newbury Street may have included the shop that his stepfather built for him in 1711, which, although modest in size, was large enough for Pollard and two or three journeymen to work in. He was not the recipient of major church commissions, although he made a mug for the First Church, Boston, and a caudle cup that was eventually given to the First Church in Deerfield.[11] The mug in the First Church, Boston, was given to the church by the tobacconist John Forland (d. 1729) in 1717. His widow, Sarah, employed Pollard's aunt, Mary (Winslow) Pollard, as her housekeeper. Other forms Pollard produced include tankards, trencher salts, casters, canns, and spoons. He used one mark, w·p in an oval (A).[12]

After 1717, his sale of several properties suggests that Pollard was experiencing financial difficulties, perhaps as a result of paying off Thomas Powell's debts. In December 1717, Pollard sold his tenement in Newbury Street to the cooper Thomas Marshall of Boston, probably one of his wife's relatives, for £1,000;

and in 1722 he sold his interest in the Sign of the Horse Shoe, near the Common, to his uncle, Jonathan Pollard, for £50.[13] In 1724 the shopkeeper John Barrell of Boston successfully sued Pollard for one year's rent of £24 on a tenement in Newbury Street near the White Horse Tavern. According to the record of the case, Pollard had occupied the house since March 1722.[14]

Perhaps it was his financial difficulties that led him to try his luck as a craftsman in a town with a stronger economy. About 1730 Pollard resided, at least briefly, in Newport, Rhode Island. He was back in Boston by July of 1731, when he was sued by the carter John Partelow and the vintner James Davis of Newport in two separate cases, for debts incurred in Newport in October of 1730. In the suit with Davis he is referred to as "William Pollard now resident in Boston in the County of Suffolk Goldsmith otherwise called William Pollard of Newport . . . Goldsmith." This is the last record of Pollard in Boston.[15]

Finally giving up on Boston, Pollard moved to Charleston, South Carolina, before 1738, when he appears as number 29 on a list of members of the South Carolina Society. The register of St. Philip's Church records that "William Pollard, Silversmith," was buried on 1 December 1740. He apparently died intestate because Nicholas Haynes and Alexander Smith placed a notice in the *South-Carolina Gazette* of 1–8 January 1740/41 indicating that they intended to "administer on the estate of William Pollard late of Charles town, Silversmith deceased." There is no surviving inventory of his estate.[16] His widow returned to Boston and in 1747 married Henry Laughton (d. before 1762) in the New South Church. His daughter, Dorcas, also returned to Boston and married the mariner Francis Ingraham (d. 1763) in 1745.[17] BMW

SURVIVING OBJECTS

	Mark	Inscription	Patron	Date	Reference	Owner
Cann	A†	RH		ca. 1720	Buhler/Hood 1970, no. 104	YUAG
Cann	A*	The Gift of John Forland/to the first Church of Christ/in Boston for the Use of/the Table/1717.	John Forland and/or First Church, Boston	ca. 1717	Jones 1913, 32	
Caudle cup	A*	H BEAMON	Hannah Beamon and/or First Congregational Church, Deerfield, Mass.	ca. 1739	Flynt/Fales 1968, 45	
Cup	A*	MW		ca. 1730	DAPC 71.3482	
Pepper box	A*	LC		ca. 1725	DAPC 68.6153	MMA
Serving spoon	A*	none		ca. 1730	Buhler 1972, no. 110	MFAB
Tankard	A	S/ST		ca. 1735	Buhler 1972, no. 111	MFAB
Tankard	A	RH		ca. 1725	Buhler 1956, no. 114	
Tankard	A	AH (+)		ca. 1720	DAPC 77.2454	

1. RC 9:36, 194; Roberts 1895, 1:257; *Index of Obituaries, 1704–1800*, 1:241; *Witness to America's Past*, 56–58; SCPR 11:1.
2. RC 9:175, 190.

3. SCD 47:201–03; RC 9:208, 223. Margaret Payne Pollard married Thomas Powell sometime before their first child was born on 25 August 1692; RC 9:202.

4. RC 9:210.

5. RC 29:204. The existence of this document led Henry Flynt and Martha Gandy Fales (Flynt/Fales 1968, 302, 304) to conclude mistakenly that Thomas Powell was a goldsmith. There is no evidence that this was the case; Powell clearly built the shop for his stepson.

6. SCD 21:266; 29:215.

7. SCD 29:211–12; 30:201.

8. RC 9:54, 215; RC 28:42; Codman 1918, 163; SCPR 21:550–51; *Index of Obituaries, 1704–1800*, 3:43.

9. Seybolt 1939, 145, 160; Roberts 1895, 1:424.

10. SCCR, Court of Common Pleas Record Book 1715–18, 25; 1722, 408; 1724, 64; 1725, 59, 385; 1731, 247–48.

11. Jones 1913, 32, 138–39.

12. Other authorities have attributed marks to Pollard. These include W.P in an oval (Ensko 1948, 249; Currier 1938, 113); W·P in a rectangle (Thorn 1949, 166; Okie 1936, 278); and WP, device below, in a heart (Flynt/Fales 1968, 302).

13. SCD 32:146; 38:91–92.

14. SCCR, Court of Common Pleas Record Book 1724, 64–65.

15. SCCR, Court of Common Pleas Record Book 1731, 247–48.

16. Burton/Ripley 1991, 80.

17. RC 28:280, 286, 346.

John Potwine
ca. 1698–1792

A

B

C

D

John Potwine probably was born in Boston in 1698, although no record of his birth exists. His father, also John (d. 1700), a physician, was a Huguenot refugee said to have lived in London before settling in New England.[1] The elder Potwine was in Boston as early as January 1688, when he signed a bond with the yeoman Thomas Bannister.[2] According to the list of inhabitants of 1695, which includes him in ward 7, the elder Potwine lived in the south part of Boston.[3] He married Sarah Hill, a daughter of the cordwainer Edward (d. by 1727) and Deborah Hill (d. by 1688?), whose maiden name may have been Pentheon.[4] Following his father's death, the goldsmith's mother married Joseph Curtis in 1703 and then the mariner Robert Holiday in 1713.[5]

Potwine probably began his apprenticeship about 1712, possibly with William Cowell, Sr. (q.v.). Joseph Cowell, probably William Cowell's uncle, was one of the witnesses of Potwine's father's will.[6] A mortgage of 1724/25, discussed below, indicates that Potwine rented a house adjacent to Cowell's property, which suggests that Potwine lived in proximity to the Cowell family and that the elder Cowell might have been Potwine's master. Moreover, in 1715 the seventeen-year-old Potwine joined the Brattle Street Church, the church in which Cowell's children were baptized.[7]

Potwine probably began working about 1719. On 20 April 1721 he married Mary Jackson (1698–1766), a daughter of Thomas Jackson and Priscilla Grafton (b. 1670).[8] The births of seven of the couple's children were recorded in Boston.[9] In 1724/25 Edward Durant mortgaged two brick tenements in the "southerly part of Boston . . . Northerly by the land of William Cowell," one of which was described as being occupied by John Potwine, identified as a goldsmith.[10] Potwine's business probably involved selling general merchandise as well as goldsmith's work because he was buying large quantities of goods from Peter Faneuil in 1732, as in this account between the two:

P. Faneuil   Laus Deo Boston NE 20 Apr 1732
John Pottwine Dr.
To Invoice 212 for 3 p^s thread Sattins con^g 216 y^{ds} @ 5/4   57.12–

To Invoice 209 for 2 Dozen black Silk Gloves @ £7:15/   15.10

    D Henchman   £73.2—[II]

Potwine assumed some civil offices after refusing to serve as a Boston constable in 1727/28. He was a scavenger in 1732/33 and clerk of the market in 1734.[12] He also served as an executor of the estate of Elizabeth Grafton Hughes, widow of William Hughes, in 1734.[13]

Sometime after July 1735, when Benjamin Greene recorded Potwine in his ledger as a goldsmith in Boston, and before 1737, when Potwine's son Nathaniel was born in Hartford, Connecticut, Potwine relocated to Hartford. Between 1735 and 1739 Potwine purchased a sword blade and nine pairs of earrings from Greene.[14] In 1737 the records of the Suffolk County Court of Common Pleas identify Potwine as a goldsmith of Hartford, when he sued the Scituate, Massachusetts, housewright Ebenezer Steton and the Boston goldsmith Nathaniel Morse (q.v.).[15] The ledger of the Boston stationer Daniel Henchman identified Potwine as being of Hartford from 1738 through 1745.[16] Potwine sold jewels and gold necklaces in Hartford in 1752 and 1753.[17] About that time he moved to Coventry, Connecticut, where his wife died in 1766. After her death he moved to East Windsor, Connecticut, where his son Thomas (b. 1731) was a minister. In 1771 he married his second wife, Elizabeth Lyman Moseley (d. 1778), and continued to live in East Windsor until his death on 16 May 1792.[18]

The major part of Potwine's surviving work was probably made before he left Boston, although a few objects owned by Connecticut residents and churches were likely to have been made after he relocated there. Two marks are firmly attributed to this maker because they are found together on a porringer, I·P in a cartouche (A) and I:Potwine in a shaped rectangle (B). The attribution of two additional initials marks (C, D) is more tentative. Two marks, IP crowned, have also sometimes been assigned to this maker, but other Boston silversmiths, namely, John Pitts, Joseph Pitts, and Isaac Perkins (qq.v.), could also have used these marks. The body of work with this mark has only been identified here as the work of I. P. (q.v.). PEK

SURVIVING OBJECTS

	Mark	Inscription	Patron	Date	Reference	Owner
Baptismal basin	B*	The Gift of/Cap.ᵗ Eleazer Dorby to yᵉ New South = Chh of Christ/in BOS- TON 1730.	Eleazer Dorby (Derby) and/or New South Church, Boston	1730	Buhler 1972, no. 136	MFAB
Three beakers	B*	The Gift of Mʳ/ Wᵐ Thomas to the Church of Christ/in Durham 1740	Congregational Church, Durham, Conn., for William Thomas	1740	Buhler/Hood 1970, no. 337	YUAG
Two beakers	B	RW/1756	Gov. Roger Wolcott and/or Congregational Church, East Windsor, Conn.	1756	Jones 1913, 165	
Cann	B*	Storer arms; S/EM (+)	Ebenezer and Mary (Edwards) Storer	ca. 1725	Buhler 1972, no. 135	MFAB
Cann	B	Pynchon arms, per bend argent and	William Pynchon	ca. 1760	Ward/Hosley 1985, no. 170	CVHM

	Mark	Inscription	Patron	Date	Reference	Owner
		sable 3 roundels within a bordure engrailed all counterchanged, and crest, a talbot's head				
Cann	B*	unidentified crest, a peacock head; Mauran (later?)		ca. 1730	DAPC 78.3257	
Caster	A	H/TH		ca. 1730	Antiques 97 (May 1970): 657	CF
Chafing dish	B*	Symmes crest, a sun in splendor	Symmes family	ca. 1735	DAPC 84.3191	
Chafing dish (mate below)	B	none	Francis Brinley	ca. 1730	Quimby 1995, no. 106	WM
Chafing dish (mate above)	B*	none	Francis Brinley	ca. 1730	Johnston 1994, 123	CMA
Flagon	B*	Lemon arms, vert a fess argent between 3 dolphins embowed, and crest, a pelican in her piety; The Gift of Mrs Mary Lemon/TO THE/1st Church of Christ/IN/ Charlstown	Mary Lemon and/or First Parish Church, Charlestown, Mass.	ca. 1730	Buhler/Hood 1970, no. 125	YUAG
Mourning ring (gold)	D†	IT Esqr ob^t 20 Jan 1733/4 AE^t 67	Jared Talbot	1733/34	Flynt/Fales 1968, 82	HD
Mug	B	HP	Hannah Potwine	ca. 1730	Hammerslough/ Feigenbaum 1958–73, 1:10	
Patch box	A*	AP		ca. 1735		HD
Pepper box	A	CLL		ca. 1730	Potwine 1935, 109	
Pepper box	B	IW		ca. 1730	Norman-Wilcox 1944, 22	DIA
Porringer	A*	BTB (later)		ca. 1725	Eitner 1976, no. 38	
Porringer	A	I/IR; AC (later)	Jenckes family	ca. 1725	Moore Collection 1980, no. 108	HMA
Porringer	A	?		ca. 1725	National Art Galleries, 3–5 December 1931, lot 417	
Porringer	A	D/BH		ca. 1725	YUAG files	
Porringer	A*/ B*	G?N/ING (partially erased)		ca. 1730		YUAG
Porringer	B	H/TH	Thomas and Hannah Hill	ca. 1730	Buhler 1972, no. 540	MFAB

	Mark	Inscription	Patron	Date	Reference	Owner
Porringer	B	Bliss (?) crest, a garb; K/BE	Jonathan Bliss (?)	ca. 1735	*Antiques* 35 (May 1939): 250	
Porringer (attrib.)	?	GS to ST		ca. 1730	*Moore Collection* 1980, no. 109	
Porringer	?	S/DM		ca. 1735	Norman-Wilcox 1962, no. 37	LACMA
Porringer spoon	B	P/TA	Thomas and Abigail (Moseley) Potwine	ca. 1725	Potwine 1935, 108	
Salt	A	?		ca. 1725	DAPC 72.3553	
Salver	B*	Traill arms, a chevron or between 2 mascles in chief and a trefoil slipped in the base, and crest, a column, impaling Gale arms, argent a griffin segreant or within a bordure gobony argent and azure; DISCRIMINE SALUS		ca. 1735		PEM
Salver	B*	TC (cipher)		ca. 1730	DAPC 78.3967	RISD
Serving spoon	B	CW (later) (+)		ca. 1735	Buhler 1972, appendix no. 66	MFAB
Serving spoon	C*	IT to IH Tudor 1732	I. H. Tudor	1732	*Antiques* 106 (October 1974): 503	
Sword	C*	none	Gov. Roger Wolcott (?)	ca. 1735	MFA 1911, no. 844	
Tablespoon	A†	P/DE		ca. 1720	DAPC 71.3427	WM
Tablespoon	B*	MS		ca. 1730	Quimby 1995, no. 107	WM
Tablespoon	B	P/TA	Thomas and Abigail (Moseley) Potwine	ca. 1755	Phillips 1935, no. 133	
Tablespoon	C†	EC		ca. 1735	Buhler/Hood 1970, 338	YUAG
Tankard	B	Stoddard arms, argent 3 mullets gules bordure or, and crest, a demi-horse emerging from a ducal coronet; THT; THT/to/Weston Church	Thomas Hubbard Townsend and/or First Parish, Weston, Mass.	ca. 1730	Jones 1913, 486	
Tankard	B	Presented/to/Joseph Tolman/by his Father/1749 (+) later	Joseph Tolman	ca. 1730		MFAB
Tankard	B	unidentified cipher (+)	Sarah (Hutchinson) Welsteed (?)	ca. 1730	Jones 1913, 38	

	Mark	Inscription	Patron	Date	Reference	Owner
Tankard	B	AT	Trott family	ca. 1730	YUAG files	
Tankard	B*	Bromfield arms, on a chevron 3 broom sprigs, on a canton a spear's head embrued, in chief point a mullet, and crest, a demi-tyger holding a broken sword	Edward and Abigail (Coney) Bromfield	ca. 1730	Buhler/Hood 1970, no. 127	YUAG
Three tankard covers	B	none		ca. 1730	Phillips 1935, no. 131 (two only)	
Teapot	B†	Edwards (?) arms, a fess engrailed ermines between 3 martlets, and crest, a horse's head emerging from a ducal coronet on a chapeau; A DIEU JE DOIS TOUT(+)	Samuel Welles (?)	ca. 1740	Buhler/Hood 1970, no. 126	YUAG
Teaspoon (attrib.)	none	M/AE	Abner and Elizabeth Moseley	ca. 1750	Phillips 1935, no. 134	

1. SCPR 14:205.
2. SCCR, *County Court Record Books 1680–92*, vol. 1, part 2, 354, Judicial Archives, Massachusetts State Archives.
3. RC 1:167.
4. No death records have been found for Deborah and Edward Hill. The will of William Pentheon, written 18 December 1688, states that he brought Deborah, the wife of his cousin Edward Hill, from old England to make her his heir; he leaves bequests to her children and to Edward Hill, who was also the executor, which suggests that Deborah was dead by that time; see SCPR 10:458–59. Edward was dead by 1726/27, when his daughters and son-in-law sold land on the highway leading to Roxbury; see SCD 40:202.
5. RC 28:8, 52.
6. SCPR 14:205; Savage 1860–62, 1:466.
7. *Church in Brattle Square*, 96.
8. RC 9:241, 245; RC 28:102; *Salem VR* 1:378.
9. RC 24:157 (Mary, b. 1722), 166 (Sarah, b. 1724), 177 (Elizabeth, b. 1726), 188 (John, b. 1728), 194 (Ann, b. 1729), 204 (Thomas, b. 1731), 218 (Mary, b. 1734).
10. SCD 38:91.
11. As recorded in the Bigelow-Phillips files, 856; present whereabouts unknown.
12. Seybolt 1939, 173, 188, 194.
13. SCPR 30:235–36.
14. Benjamin Greene Ledger, 1734–56, 5, 20, 164, MHS. Greene and Potwine continued to trade in general merchandise until 1753.
15. SCCR, Court of Common Pleas Record Book 1737, 273, 276.
16. Daniel Henchman Ledger, 1729–ca. 1755, fol. 214, NEHGS. Potwine also appears in a Henchman daybook in 1748; see Daniel Henchman Daybook, 25 March 1745–31 March 1750, n.p., entries for 29 June and 17 October 1748, NEHGS.
17. Bigelow-Phillips files, 849–50. A daybook, whereabouts unknown, cited in Potwine 1935, 107.
18. Ward/Hosley 1985, 286–87; Potwine 1935, 108.

Moses Prevereau
w. ca. 1701

Moses Prevereau's work as a goldsmith is known from only one set of documents in the Massachusetts Archives. On 16 June 1701 Prevereau signed a deposition regarding goods allegedly stolen from William Hill and his wife by one Elizabeth Baker:

> The Deposition of Moses Prevereaux of
> full age, who testifieth and Saith, that
> Sometime in or about the month of December
> anno 1700, Elizabeth Baker wife of George
> Baker of Boston, delivered unto the Deponant
> one Silver Spoone markt with a French marke, and
> thirteen or fourteen Silver Coat buttons, which
> the s.^{d} Elizabeth Baker desired the Deponant
> to melt down for her, and therewith to make her a
> Silver chaine, and also desired the Deponant not to
> tell any body that she had delivered unto him the
> s.^{d} Spoone and buttons to melt down as aforesaid—
> But the Deponant not having melted down s^d things
> so soon as the s.^{d} Elizabeth Baker expected, she
> tooke them again from him, not being melted down
> and the Deponant further Saith That about the
> Same time that s.^{d} Eliz.^{a} Baker put into his
> hands the Silver Spoon & buttons as afores.^{d} she
> also told the Depon.^{t} that She had Silver thread
> buttons (both for Coats & Jackets) to sell, and
> offered to sell the Deponant some of s^d buttons for Jackets
> which Silver thread buttons she said she had of a Shopkeeper
> in Town—And further Saith that She said she
> bought the s.^{d} Spoon of a woman in Town for nine shillings
> And the Deponant saw the s.^{d} Baker try to run the s.^{d} buttons
> and had one of them in Melting pot over
> the Fire at m.^{rs} Mossets house and m.^{rs} Mosset
> helpt to blow the Coals, but they could not melt
> the Silver.[1]

A notation on the deposition reads, "The Depont Prevereau being bound to Sea was Sworn to the above written Evidence." Prevereau's testimony that the spoon bore French marks suggests that he may have had European or English training. His name is French, and Prevereau may have been a Huguenot. It would not have been prudent for Baker, a servant in the Hills' household, to take stolen goods to the shop of a prominent silversmith, and therefore it is likely that Prevereau briefly worked in the Boston area as an independent silversmith, possibly jobbing for other goldsmiths.[2] The reference to "Town" suggests that Prevereau's shop was not in Boston itself but perhaps in Charlestown or Cambridge. He probably decided to become a mariner because he met with little encouragement in his trade. BMW

1. Mass. Archives 8:112.
2. In her deposition the defendant, Elizabeth Baker, testified that she gave "to m^r Privroe Goldsmith to run down for her fourteen large plate buttons and a peice of one, and a Silver spoon which She saith She brought with her from England"; Mass. Archives 8:104–05.

Job Prince
1680–1703/04

Job Prince was born in Boston on 10 November 1680.[1] His father, Job Prince (1647–93), a mariner, was the son of John Prince (ca. 1610–76) of East Shefford in Berkshire, England, who settled in Hingham, Massachusetts, in 1635 and removed to Hull in 1638. The goldsmith's mother was Rebecca Phippeny (1657–1712), daughter of Gamiliel Phippeny (d. ca. 1672), a blockmaker, and Sarah (Purchase) Phippeny (d. 1683).[2] After her husband's death and sometime before October 1697, Rebecca (Phippeny) Prince married George Clarke of Milford, Connecticut.[3]

Job Prince may have served his apprenticeship in Boston. Although his father left a substantial estate, he was heavily in debt when he died intestate in 1693. The estate was divided between Job and his brothers and sisters Gamiliel, Sarah, Josiah, and Rebecca, all of whom were minors.[4] In 1701 they were all mentioned, along with their mother, in a deed involving the mortgage of property owned by their father near the drawbridge in Boston.[5] Job Prince moved to Milford, Connecticut, about 1699, presumably because he learned of opportunities there from his mother. The tailor Thomas Clarke of Milford recorded transactions with Job Prince in his account book between October 1699 and August 1703. During that period Prince sold a dozen silver buttons to Clarke and paid him for clothing with a gallon of rum and "buttons or mohair." Prince purchased three vests (one of silk), three pairs of britches (one specified as silk and one as broadcloth), and three coats from Clarke. The coat that Prince bought in November 1702 was a "wedding coat," indicating that he married in either late 1702 or early 1703.[6] In May 1703, when Prince sold the land in Boston that he had inherited from his father, his wife, Deborah Prince, signed the deed relinquishing her right of dower.[7]

Prince is identified as a goldsmith in two deeds, and at the time of his death he was referred to as a jeweler.[8] The mark IP in a rectangle that appears on a distinctive group of pepper boxes has been attributed to him, but the attribution is doubtful.[9] The inventory of Prince's estate is dated 24 January 1703/04 and lists silversmith's tools, a pair of small bellows, a pair of silver buckles, a tobacco box, a tankard, a porringer, and six spoons valued at £16.01 but no pepper boxes. His estate also included a Gunter's scale, a navigational instrument, and a book on practical navigation, both of which he may have inherited from his father. The total value of the estate as recorded in New Haven probate district was only £34.0.5 after debts were deducted. The estate probated in Boston consisted of part of a house worth £662 and numerous debts. His mother claimed one-third ownership in the house, which was part of her husband's estate, and ultimately the estate was declared insolvent.[10] In 1726 Deborah Judson, wife of the cordwainer Joshua Judson of Fairfield, relinquished all of her dower right in the estate of her late husband, Job Prince.[11] BMW

1. RC 9:152.
2. Savage 1860–62, 3:418, 487; RC 9:63; *Hull VR*, 72; SCPR 7:187–89; 9:146.
3. SCPR 11:348–49.
4. SCPR 11:348–49; 13:144; 14:404.
5. SCD 20:386–90.
6. Thomas Clarke account book, present whereabouts unknown, photocopies in the Bigelow-Phillips files.
7. SCD 21:322–24.

8. SCD 20:386–90; 21:322–24.

9. This attribution was made by John Marshall Phillips at the time of the Connecticut Tercentenary Exhibition (1935). Examples of the pepper boxes are at HD (Flynt/Fales 1968, 122), YUAG (Buhler/Hood 1970, no. 331), in the collection of Mrs. Edsel B. Ford, and others have been in the marketplace (see American Art Association–Anderson Galleries, 2–3 April 1937, lot 275, and *Antiques* 117 [June 1980]: 1265). The fact that the mark appears only on objects of one form suggests that it is the mark of a specialist working in an urban center. For illustrations of the mark, see Ensko 1937, 46 (I·P in an oval); Ensko 1948, 107 (IP in an oval); Graham 1936, 59 (I.P in a rectangle); Thorn 1949, 169 (I.P in a rectangle); Flynt/Fales 1968, 305 (I.P in a rectangle).

10. SCPR 16:375, 437; New Haven Probate District, file 8504.

11. SCD 40:150–51.

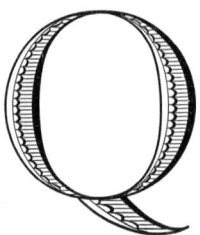

Daniel Quincy
1651–90

Daniel Quincy was born in Braintree, Massachusetts, on 7 February 1651, the son of the yeoman Edmund Quincy (1627/28–98) and Joanna Hoar (1635–80), who were married in 1648.[1] His maternal grandmother was Joanna Hoar (d. 1661).[2] His paternal grandparents were Edmund Quincy (1602–35) and Judith Pares (d. 1654). Judith married as her third husband Robert Hull, father of John Hull (q.v.).[3] Quincy was also related to John Hull through his aunt, Judith Quincy (1626–95), who wed Hull in 1647. Quincy lived with the Hulls from at least the age of seven.[4] He trained in the shop Hull ran with Robert Sanderson, Sr. (q.v.), probably between 1665 and 1673, during which time he witnessed many deeds for Hull.[5] Quincy's sister, Elizabeth, married the Reverend Daniel Gookin, and their son, Daniel (q.v.), became a silversmith.

Hull, who had no surviving male children of his own, treated Quincy as a son. In January 1674 Hull sent to London for a box of tools that he gave to Quincy.[6] Although Hull did not indicate whether these were goldsmith's tools, it is tempting to speculate that they were and hence that Quincy was being equipped to begin his career. Hull served as Quincy's surety in 1675, when he enrolled in the Ancient and Honorable Artillery Company.[7] Hull also continued to provide him board, helped him fund the building of his house in Boston, and wrote letters on his behalf when Quincy traveled to England in 1676.[8]

The year he spent in England broadened Quincy's experience in transatlantic trading. New Englanders like Hull sent furs, foodstuffs, and specie to England in exchange for textiles, hardware, and related merchandise to sell in the New World. Like his master, many of his contemporaries, and silversmiths who would follow, Quincy earned part of his livelihood through these trading activities.[9]

Samuel Sewall came into the Hull household in 1676 when he married Hull's only surviving child, Hannah. Quincy's friendship with him probably dates from this period, when they lived in Hull's house together. A letter written by Sewall to settle his father-in-law's affairs provides a glimpse of Quincy's role within the shop. Quincy "used to keep the account in the Shop. . . . The chief part of the shop's Business went through Mr. Daniel Quinsey's hands; He was a very honest carefull Man."[10] Although Quincy did receive a six-shilling credit in Hull's ledger for "mending M[r] Phillips watch" in 1677, his work probably was largely administrative.[11] He also continued to witness Hull's land transactions.[12] Quincy's name appears on the Boston tax list of 1681 in Hull's ward.[13]

Quincy continued to live in the Hull household until his marriage on 9 November 1682 to Anna Shepard (1663–1708), the daughter of Thomas Shepard (1635–77), teacher of the church at Charlestown, Massachusetts, and Hannah Tyng (1639/40–1709).[14] In his diary Sewall describes how the wedding celebration ended precipitously when Elizabeth Brattle, at whose home the wedding was taking place, took ill suddenly and died. The corpse was placed in the bridal bed, and the bride and groom went elsewhere, "going away like Persons put to flight in Battel."[15] Hull died the next year, and his administrators gave Quincy a gift of £167.10.5, which essentially balanced Quincy's and Hull's accounts.[16]

After Hull's death the shop continued to operate, and Quincy remained closely bound to it, to the Hull household, and to Samuel Sewall; he witnessed deeds for the Hull estate, for Robert Sanderson, Sr., and for Samuel and Hannah Sewall.[17] Quincy did night rounds with Sewall in 1685 and 1686 after being chosen a constable in 1684, and the two men combined their efforts in shipping goods to and from England.[18] Quincy and Sewall granted a mortgage to Hezekiah Usher in 1686.[19] After Quincy's death Sewall and Anna Quincy brought a suit to gain possession of the property.[20] On the Boston tax lists of 1687 and 1688 Quincy appears in ward 7.[21] He and his siblings received proceeds from the sale of land in Braintree in June 1687.[22]

In the summer of 1690 Quincy became ill; Sewall recorded the course of his illness.[23] Quincy died on 10 August 1690, and his will was probated on 18 September.[24] His widow and children moved back to Charlestown the following spring but kept in touch with Sewall.[25] In 1701 Quincy's widow married the Reverend Moses Fitch of Braintree.[26] PEK

1. No vital record to confirm the date traditionally given for the silversmith's birth has been found; SCPR 8:125; *Braintree VR*, 630; *Suffolk Deeds* 9:362–63; *NEHGR* 11:17.
2. *Braintree VR*, 638.
3. Savage 1860–62, 3:500.
4. Hull's diary describes Quincy's being taken ill in 1658; see "Hull Diaries," 148.
5. *Suffolk Deeds* 6:225–26, 237; 7:97; 10:4, 5, 14, 15, 16, 20, 24, 27; 12:174–75.
6. John Hull Ledger, vol. 1, fol. 73v, NEHGS.
7. Roberts 1895, 1:238–39; Bigelow-Phillips files, 204.
8. John Hull Ledger, vol. 1, fols. 73v, 74r, 94r, 119r, 123v, 124r, 161v, NEHGS; Hull Letterbook, typescript 1:293, 301, AAS.
9. Hull Letterbook, typescript 1:302, 308, 327; 2:358, 370, 389, AAS; John Hull Ledger, vol. 1, fol. 107v, NEHGS.
10. *Sewall Letter Book* 1:260–61.
11. John Hull Ledger, vol. 1, fols. 123v, 124r, NEHGS.
12. *Suffolk Deeds* 9:146; 10:4, 5, 6, 8, 10, 18, 20; 12:6–7, 22; 13:136.
13. RC 1:76.
14. *Charlestown VR* 1:20, 45, 100; *Braintree VR*, 696; RC 9:8; *Milton VR*, 242.
15. *Sewall Diary* 1:53.
16. John Hull Ledger, vol. 1, fols. 161v, 162r, NEHGS. The exception was a piece of land next to Quincy's garden that he still owed money to Hull for in April 1683. Judith Hull and Hannah and Samuel Sewall ultimately gave Quincy this land in 1688; SCD 15:138.
17. *Suffolk Deeds* 13:62, 92–94, 99, 308.
18. RC 7:165; *Sewall Diary* 1:86, 94, 103; Sewall Lading Book, 1686–98, 4, 26 June 1689, 1 July 1689, 29 August 1690, MHS.
19. *Suffolk Deeds* 14:164–66.

20. SCCR, file 3655.
21. RC 1:122, 142.
22. *Suffolk Deeds* 11:387–88; SCD 17:236–37.
23. *Sewall Diary* 1:261–64, 326.
24. SCPR 8:1–2.
25. *Sewall Diary* 1:276, 301.
26. *Braintree VR*, 696, 721.

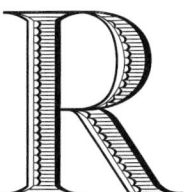

John Raymond
ca. 1746–75

A miscellaneous record of deaths in Boston indicates that John Raymond, jeweller, died in 1775 at the age of twenty-nine.[1] However, no record of his birth has been found in Massachusetts vital records, and no trace of a jeweler named John Raymond has surfaced in any Boston public records. He may be the John Raymond who made jewelry for the Salem, Massachusetts, silversmith John Touzell (q.v.) in 1767 and 1768. Their relationship is documented by two accounts. In October 1767, Raymond made twelve pairs of earrings as well as ciphered buttons for Touzell:

	Salem Octber 19 1767	
	Mr John Touzel to John Raymond	
Octbor the 7	to making 2 Pair of Earings	£ 4:00:0
Octbor the 12	to making 6 Pair of Earings	£12: 0.0
Octbor the 17	to making 4 Pair of Earings	£08. 0.0
Octbor the 19	to making 5 Pair of Cypherd butns	£04 10 0
	to mistak in old Acct. 15/8	£28:10.0
		15. 8
		£29: 5: 8
	Cr by his Acct : to this day	13– 4–0
	Balance due	£16–1–8 [2]

The obverse of the account shows that Raymond was paid in full on 20 October 1767. The second bill, rendered by Raymond on 16 July 1768, is for setting stones and cleaning jewelry:

	Salem July. ye 16.th 1768	
John Touzel To John Raymond Dr		
To setting 2 Pair Stone earings @ 36s/pr		3.. 12..0
To setting 12 Pair of Stone buttons @. 18/pr		10.. 16..0
To Cleansing 4 pair stone earing 10/		10..0
		£14.. 18..0
Cr. by one weeks. board @ 70/ pr		3..10..0
	balance due	£11.. 8..0

Part of Raymond's payment was credit for board, which suggests that he was living in Touzell's household.[3] No evidence of this John Raymond has been found in Essex County records, and no silver by him is known. PEK

1. "Boyle's Journal of Occurrences in Boston," *NEHGR* 85:5.
2. English-Touzel-Hathorne Papers, box 4, folder 3, PEM.
3. English-Touzel-Hathorne Papers, box 4, folder 3, PEM.

Jonathan Reed
ca. 1695–1742

A

B

Although very little is known about Jonathan Reed, his inventory suggests that he was at least moderately successful and that his business specialized in small wares and jewelry. Reed's wife, Mary, was probably Mary Wincoll (Winkel). According to Boston vital records, the Reverend Timothy Cutler of Christ Church married the couple on 21 January 1724.[1] No children are recorded, but on 30 April 1741 a Mary Reed, probably their daughter, married Samuel Haley (q.v.), one of the goldsmiths who appraised Reed's estate.[2] Haley also signed a bond with Mary Reed, widow of Jonathan Reed, and the tailor William Hinckley on 30 November 1742 in conjunction with the settlement of Reed's estate, suggesting that he was the deceased's son-in-law.[3]

Because of the many Reeds that appear in the Boston records during this period and the lack of any evidence linking the goldsmith to other Reeds in Boston, Jonathan Reed's parents cannot be identified. Likewise, Mary Wincoll's origins are obscure. The fact that Jonathan and Mary were married by an Anglican minister suggests that they may have been recent immigrants. Jonathan apparently later attended Boston's New Brick Church; his most notable works are the two cups engraved with a cockerel crest that he made for the church in 1723/24.[4] A John Reed who, when warned out of Boston in 1716, was referred to as a "Smith who lately came from Engld" is later identified in the record as a blacksmith.[5] Although not the goldsmith, this John Reed may have been related to him.

When Reed died in 1742 Nathaniel Morse, Thomas Eastwick (qq.v.), and Samuel Haley appraised his estate. His shop included

1 Large forgin Anvill w^t 110 lb		13. 15 —
1 Large Teest	48 lb	7. 4
1 Spoon Teest	35 lb	5. 5
1 small Raising Anvil	17 lb	17
1 pair forge bellows		1. 10
1 bench Vice		1. 15
1 small raising Anvill		7. 6
3 spoon Punches		12
1 Cutting Chissell 2 Swages large		12
4 forgeing hammers different Sizes		1. 5
4 planishing hammers		13
1 booge Hammer 3 small		8
1 pair drawing tongs		15
2 Ingotts 1 forge 1 nealing tongs		1. 5
2 Round 2 half Round Draw^g Irons		1. 0 —
1 large 9 small cuting punches		
16 dapping Punches		1. 12 —
7 Earring Punches		14

31 small Dittos	5
1 Brass Hollowing Stamp 12 Strainers	3. 0
1 Sett brass weights	1. 10
3 pair Scales with boxes	1. 10
40 O^z leaden Patterns	3.
1 Oil Stone	5
1 beeck Iron 2 hand vices 3 p^r Sheers	
2 p^r Spring Plyers 4 p^r flat plyers	3. 2. 6
1 Borax Box 1 Chargeing Tongs	
3 Burnishers 2 Stone 1 Steel	12. 0
2 Dozen fileing files - 1 p^r Clams	1. 2. 0
1 Iron Ladle 10/ 2 pr Flasks 10/	1. .
1 p^r Flask screws 5/ 1 Odd Drew finch	
1 Lamp 1 blow Pipe	. 10 —
25 Large Nest Melting potts $^£$5.10^s 63 Ditto 3.3	8. 13 —
51^{oz} 12 ^{Dwt} Silver wrought & unw^t: @ 26^{s}8^d p^r oz.	68. 16 —
20 . 8^{wt} Gold @ 19$£$12s	19.18. 6
22 black Melting Pots 1/6 Each	1. 13 —
72 Squares of Glass to Sashes of the Shop	
and Door 14$^£$8^s	16. 8. 0
2 p^r Wainscot Shutters of the parlour	
1 Large Glass Shew Case	3. 0. 0
	173.18. 6

Reed's personal estate, valued at £428.10.6 Old Tenor (£78.1 sterling), included a looking glass, a black walnut chest of drawers and table, six caned chairs, six black chairs with carved backs, a veneered walnut desk, and a square tea table with a japanned teaboard.[6]

Although Reed's estate did not include any real property, he sued the joiner Charles Hay of Boston for rent in 1726. The court record explains that Reed did not own the rooms he rented to Hay, but that "the Plan^t . . . by Lease parol demised to the Def^t a Chamber a Shop & a Cellar in the Dwelling house of Philip Bongarden of . . . Boston (which the Plan^t hired of one Isaac Boynton Tayler Tenant to the s^d. Bongarden) situate at the Bottom or lower End of King Street in Boston."[7] Three years later, Reed purchased and then immediately resold or mortgaged a "Wooden Dwelling house with the land . . . yard & Garden" in King Street from Thomas Dudding, a Boston mariner. Although the deed does not make clear the actual terms of the second sale, the fact that both sales took place on the same day strongly suggests that Reed mortgaged the property to Dudding. The terms of the agreement are not stated, however, and there is no debt discharge endorsed on the deed.[8] Reed may have eventually lost the property because he was unable to pay off the mortgage. In 1740, Reed was sued by the gentlewoman Jane Cooke in a plea of trespass. Like most suits of this type, the dispute probably arose when Cooke attempted to evict Reed for nonpayment of rent. Reed defaulted, and Cooke recovered her property.[9]

Objects bearing an IR crowned within a shield (A) overstruck by IR in a rectangle (B) have been attributed to Jonathan Reed, and the marks can be documented by an account signed by Jonathan Reed and dated 1723:[10]

Boston June the 2 [torn]

Mr Tosel   Dr

	oz pw d		
		To making	£1 12 0
To 2 poringers wate	15: 4: 0		
To 6 spons wate	10 18 1/2	To making	£1: 10:0
	26 2 1/2		
To Silver reced of } Rowland Houghton }	9: 16 1/2		
Remains	16 oz 6 pwt: at 14/		£11: 8: 3
			£14:10. 3

Boston ye 25th June
1723[11]

The spoons in the account are probably those engraved "T/IS" for John and Susanna Touzell, parents of John Touzell (q.v.), that survive in the collections of the Museum of Fine Arts, Boston, and the Metropolitan Museum of Art. The bill also shows that Reed charged different rates for fashioning according to the type of object involved. BMW

SURVIVING OBJECTS

	Mark	Inscription	Patron	Date	Reference	Owner
Pepper box	A*	W/IP		ca. 1720		WA
Porringer	A	FI/to/SI	Francis Johonnot	ca. 1730	Quimby 1995, no. 108	WM
Porringer	A	B/TA	Barrows family (?)	ca. 1735	*Antiques* 58 (October 1950): 289	
Tablespoon	A*	DR		ca. 1730	Buhler/Hood 1970, no. 228	YUAG
Two tablespoons (mates? below)	A*/ B*	T/IS	John and Susanna (English) Touzell	1723	Buhler 1972, no. 133	MFAB
Three tablespoons (mates? above)	A*/ B†	T/IS	John and Susanna (English) Touzell (?)	ca. 1725		MMA
Two-handled cup	A†	crest, a cock; Given By WL to the New Brick Church/1723/4	William Lee and/or New Brick Church, Boston	1723/24	Jones 1913, 37	
Two-handled cup	A*	crest, a cock; Given by Nathanel Loring/to the New Brick Church/1723/4	Nathaniel Loring and/ or New Brick Church, Boston	1723/24	Jones 1913, 36–37	

1. RC 28:122.
2. RC 28:248.
3. SCPR 36:191, docket 7831.
4. Jones 1913, 36–37; Buhler 1972, 1:164.
5. RC 13:9, 12.
6. SCPR 36:240–41.
7. SCCR, Court of Common Pleas Record Book 1725–26, 435, 5 July 1726.
8. SCD 43:302–04.
9. John M. Fitzgerald to Francis Hill Bigelow, Boston Court Record References to Silversmiths, Bigelow-Phillips files; SCCR, Court of Common Pleas Record Book 1740, 102.
10. Buhler 1972, 1:164.
11. Photostat in the Bigelow-Phillips files, from the English-Touzel-Hathorne Papers, PEM.

Paul Revere, Jr.
1734–1818

John Singleton Copley, Paul Revere, Jr., *1768, oil on canvas. Museum of Fine Arts, Boston, gift of Joseph W. Revere, William B. Revere, and Edward H. R. Revere.*

A

B

C

D

E

F

G

H

Paul Revere, Jr., was born in Boston on 21 December 1734 to the Huguenot silversmith Paul Revere, Sr. (q.v.), and his wife, Deborah (Hi[t]chborn) Revere (1703/04–77), and was baptized the following day by Rev. William Welsteed in New Brick Church.[1] Little is known of his youth but that he attended the North Writing School until 1741.[2] In 1750, a group of six boys including Revere and Josiah Flagg, Jr. (q.v.), formed a guild of bellringers and requested permission to ring the bells for two hours every week in "Dr. Cuttler's church," which was Christ Church, now often called Old North Church. Revere attended New Brick Church throughout his life.[3] Revere began his training with his father, probably around 1748. Since the elder Revere's death on 22 July 1754 occurred two years before his son would have finished his apprenticeship, the young Paul may have helped to maintain the family shop under his mother's name until he came of age in 1755. Revere described his training in a letter to his French cousin Mathias Rivoire on 6 October 1781: "My father was a goldsmith. He died in the year 1754. . . . I was the eldest son. I learned the Trade of him and have carried on the business ever since."[4]

On 4 August 1757, Revere published his intention to marry Sarah Orne (ca. 1736–73), and they were married thirteen days later.[5] The couple had eight children: Deborah (1758–97), Paul (1760–1813), Sarah (1762–91), Mary (1764–68), Frances (1766–99), Mary (1768–1853), Elizabeth (1770–1805), and Isanna (1772–73).[6] In November 1762 Revere established his family in a house on Fish Street that he rented from Dr. John Clark for £16 a year.[7] This house was near his childhood home on Hi[t]chborn's Wharf; many of Revere's early patrons were Hichborn relatives, neighbors, and members of Christ Church, where he was a bellringer.[8] Revere moved to a house on Clark's Square that he purchased on 16 February 1770 for £213.6.8 from John Irving.[9] Revere arranged a mortgage of £160 with Irving, which he repaid by 18 December 1798.[10]

After Sarah (Orne) Revere died in Boston on 3 May 1773, Revere married Rachel Walker (1745–1813) on 23 September 1773.[11] Rachel was the daughter of Richard Walker (d. 1777) and Rachel Carlisle (1705–82).[12] Paul and Rachel Revere had eight children: Joshua (1774–1801); John (10–27 June 1776); Joseph Warren (1777–1868); Lucy (15 May–9 July 1780); Harriet (1783–1860); John (1784–86); Maria (1785–1847); and John (1787–1847).[13] Many of Revere's children were still living at home in 1790 when the census listed him as the head of a large household composed of two adult men, three boys, six women and girls, and one free person.[14] The United States Direct Tax of 1798 described the property on Clark's Square as a lot of 4,730 square feet, containing a wooden dwelling of "630 square feet; 3 stories, 17 windows," and a 400-square-foot barn, with a total value of $2,000.[15] In June of the following year, Revere sold a strip of this parcel to the Boston cooper Manassah Marston for £17.13.4.[16] In August 1795 Revere began to buy land on Charter Street when he purchased a lot from Joseph Gardner for £78.[17] He increased his holdings there the following year with the acquisition of two additional parcels.[18] In April 1799 the silversmith moved his family a third time to a large brick house on Charter Street, which he purchased for $4,200 from the distiller Henry Hill.[19]

Revere was extremely active in a variety of civic, political, and military organizations. Political clubs offered the silversmith an outlet for his fervent revolutionary convictions as well as providing him with another source of potential patrons. Revere belonged to the Sons of Liberty, the Long Room Club, and the North End Caucus. Revere's patrons included many of his political associates: Joseph Warren, Benjamin Edes, and Thomas Hichborn belonged to the North End Caucus; Warren, Edes, Thomas Dawes, and Moses Gill attended the Long Room Club; and Warren, Gill, Josiah Flagg, Jr., Joshua Brackett, Josiah Quincy, Oliver Wendell, John Pulling, John Homer, William Mackay, Caleb Hopkins, John Welsh, Fortesque Vernon, and several members of the Hichborn family belonged to the Sons of Liberty. In addition to participating in the Boston Tea Party, the silversmith served as a courier for the Committees of Correspondence, delivering dispatches to New York, Philadelphia, and outlying Massachusetts towns. His most famous ride took place on 18 April 1775, when he and William Dawes (q.v. Appendix B) were sent to warn the residents of Lexington and Concord of the approach of British regulars. Revere described his adventure: "On Tuesday evening, the 18th, it was observed, that a number of Soldiers were marching towards the bottom of the Common. About 10 o'Clock, Dr. Warren Sent in great haste for me, and beged that I would imediately Set off for Lexington."[20] Revere's military career had actually begun years earlier, in February 1756, when he was stationed at Lake George, New York, as a lieutenant of artillery, and he resumed his military activities as an enthusiastic supporter of the American Revolution.[21] He was commissioned a major in the Massachusetts militia but transferred to the artillery by November 1776, when he was promoted to lieutenant colonel.[22] Revere's active military career ended shortly after he led a regiment of artillery on an unsuccessful expedition to capture a British fort on the Penobscot River in Maine in 1779.[23] In a letter to his French cousin Mathias Rivoire in October 1781, Revere explained why he ceased being a silversmith in 1775: "From that time till May 1780 I have been in the Government service as Lieut. Col. of an Artillery regiment."[24]

Revere participated in other organizations as well. He became a Freemason in 1760, when he joined St. Andrew's Lodge. His association with the Masonic order lasted for fifty years, during which time he held many offices in the organization, including that of grand master.[25] On 26 December 1777 Revere, John Symmes (q.v.), and three other men purchased a house and land to be held in trust for the lodge.[26] In February 1783, Revere was one of the plaintiffs who received a considerable monetary settlement in exchange for a quitclaim on "Free Mason's Hall."[27] The money was designated as a fund for "the relief of indigent and distressed Brethern." Many of the merchants, mariners, and artisans who belonged to Boston's Masonic lodges patronized Revere's shop, and, in fact, they comprised almost half of his clientele.[28] Revere was also elected the first president of the Massachusetts Charitable Mechanic Association in 1794. The following year, he was included among the dignitaries who assisted in laying the cornerstone of the State House on Beacon Hill.

Revere's combination of ambition, abilities, and social connections enabled him to achieve both financial stability and professional respect. In 1768 the fashionable portrait painter John Singleton Copley painted the silversmith seated at a polished mahogany table with some of the tools and products of his craft (illus.). A drawing of Revere by Saint-Memin of about 1800 and a portrait completed by Gilbert Stuart in 1813 show Revere late in life when he was a successful businessman.[29]

Revere's career as a silversmith is broken into two distinctly different periods, separated by his years of military service in the revolutionary war.[30] With the death of his father in 1754, Revere inherited a fully equipped silver shop, so that he was immediately able to begin practicing his trade. His earliest mark,

P·REVERE in a rectangle (A), is one his father also used. His other marks are ·REVERE (B), and later variations without the pellet (c, D). Marks (c) and (D) probably were struck with degraded states of the die used for mark (B). He also used three script initials marks (E, F, G) and PR in a rectangle (H), another mark used by his father. Spurious examples of marks B, C, D, and the script initials marks exist.[31]

Revere trained a number of apprentices in his shop. David Moseley (q.v.), who would become Revere's brother-in-law, probably began his apprenticeship with Revere about 1766.[32] It is possible that Samuel Hichborn (q.v.) trained with Revere between 1776 and 1773 because he was Revere's nephew by marriage.[33] In 1774, Revere received an anxious letter from Josiah Collins of Newport, Rhode Island, the father of another apprentice, who wrote expressing the hope that his inability to pay for his son's board would not interfere with the boy's training.[34] Revere's son Paul III and Revere's future son-in-law Thomas S. Eayres (1760–1813 or 14) probably began their training with him on the eve of the Revolution. Although Revere would have begun to train his son Paul only in 1774, however, the younger man was left in charge of the house and shop during the revolutionary war, an indication of Revere's confidence in his son's abilities.

Revere continued to train apprentices and employ the younger members of his family when he resumed his silversmithing activities after the revolutionary war. By 1782, Paul Revere III had completed both his military service and his unconventional apprenticeship. Father and son were working as partners in the silver shop by 1783 under the name Paul Revere & Son. The distribution of responsibility within the shop is partially explained in Revere's second daybook, when in June 1789 he provided a key for the sporadic notation of hatchmarks, naughts, and crosses recurring in the margins of the book next to orders for silver.[35] The mark that identifies objects made by Paul Revere, slanting hatchmarks, occurs most frequently during the 1780s but declines after 1791. The younger Revere's marks, horizontal hatchmarks or a cross, occur quite regularly throughout the book. The silversmith's nephew Thomas Revere (q.v. Appendix B) worked in his uncle's shop during the 1790s. The daybook records thirty cash payments to Thomas between November 1791 and January 1792 and between April 1795 and January 1797, indicating his status as a journeyman. Since Thomas Revere was a journeyman rather than a partner in the shop, his work is not indicated in the daybook with a specific notation. It can be identified, however, by comparison with silver objects that bear his own mark, for example, a creampot in the Museum of Fine Arts, Boston. Thomas Revere's distinctive feathery tassel and swag engraving appears on objects that he made for his uncle's shop.[36] A second nephew, Edward (1768–1820), probably apprenticed with Benjamin Burt (q.v.), but apparently produced silver for the Revere shop because one of Revere's memoranda books records a payment to Edward Revere for making spoons in August 1796.[37] Thomas Stevens Eayres married Revere's daughter Frances on 27 May 1788.[38] Revere supported Eayres's efforts to establish a business in Worcester, Massachusetts, recommending his services to Isaiah Thomas in a letter of 8 May 1791.[39] Unfortunately, Eayres suffered from mental illness and had to return to Boston. His condition had so deteriorated by 1802 that Revere was appointed to be his guardian, a position he filled until Eayres's death in 1813 or 1814.[40] Other apprentices of Revere's include David Ripley (1768–1836) of Hingham, Massachusetts. He boarded with Revere in October 1789 and received a cash payment, presumably for his professional services as well as 14½ ounces of silver and some chapes, suggesting that he was making buckles for Revere.[41] Henry Flynt and Martha Gandy Fales suggest that Stephen Hardy (1781–1843) of Portsmouth, New Hampshire, trained with Revere as well.[42]

Revere's silver shop was an extremely active one that changed locations frequently, offered a diverse assortment of goods and services, and engaged in international trade. The daybooks record the sale and barter of textiles, spices, and food products in the 1760s. During the Revolution, Revere continued to "trade some with Holland."[43] On 21 June 1781 the silversmith paid £5.2 to Capt. Mungo Mackay for "freight on some goods from France."[44] In his eagerness to receive supplies from England, the patriot anticipated the Treaty of Paris by several months by receiving six casks of imported hardware and flatware worth £444.17.2 from a London contact, Nathaniel Fellowes, a fellow Mason.[45] His Bristol agent, Frederick William Geyer, supplied him with imported goods in 1783 and 1784.[46] Revere paid for his purchases with a combination of coins, silver objects, and scrap silver. In 1783 he sent Geyer "three hundred & forty Spanish Mill'd dollars besides four Ingots of Silver. Nº 9 is a composition of mettals the sweep of a Goldsmith's shop. Nº 10 is English silver which had the Hall Stamp on it. Nº 11 of Gold Lace burned & melted. Nº 12 is silver Ditto. Which be kind enough to get assayed and write a particular account of the value of what each piece Fetched pʳ Ounce for I expect it will be in my power to make considerable remittances in such things."[47] Beginning in 1784, the silversmith ordered tools from the London jeweler John Sampson in spite of England's ban on exporting these objects to the former colonies.[48] Revere placed four different advertisements in the *Independent Chronicle*, the *American Herald*, and the *Massachusetts Centinel* eight times between January 1784 and December 1785 that give "Directly opposite Liberty-Pole, No. 2, Newbury-Street" as the address of Revere's silver and retail shops. Revere advertised a large quantity of household goods and hardware supplies for sale at his store. On 29 January 1784, he itemized a selection of imported silverplated wares:

Paul Revere,
Directly Opposite the LIBERTY POLE,
South end, Boston, has imported in
the Rosamond, Capt. Love and
Hope, Capt. Peirson (in addition to
his former Stock) a very elegant As-
sortment of PLATED WARE.
Consisting of
Tea-Pots, plain and chased,
Butter Boats,
3-Pint Vase Coffee Pots,
Cream Jugs, plain and chased
Goblets, inside-gilt,
Salts with Glasses,
Vase and streight Pepper Boxes,
Half and 1 Pint gilt inside Beakers,
Festoon, Castor and Soy Frames,
Soup Ladles, shell Bowls,
Sugar and Milk Basons,
Sugar Baskets,
Dish Cases with lamps,

Ink Stands,
Scuffer Pans,
Tea Caddy with Locks,
Candlesticks, &c.
With an Assortment of London Pew-
ter.[49]

Revere also stocked a variety of household iron, brass, fabric, and paper products in addition to metalsmithing supplies. An advertisement in the *Independent Chronicle* on 30 September and 7 October 1784 is representative of the diverse assortment sold by the silversmith:

Paul Revere,
Directly opposite LIBERTY POLE,
South-End, BOSTON.
Has Imported,
And will sell, at a very low Advance
for CASH.
Nails, Brads, Door Locks,
with Rings or Knobs, ditto Brass Cases
H-L and H Hinges,
Closet, Chest, Stock, Beaureau, Till and
Pad Locks,
Wood Screws, Coffee Mills, Steel, Knob
and Iron Latches,
Warming and Frying Pans, Flat Irons,
A very elegant Assortment of Princes Me-
tal Candlesticks highly finished in the
newest Taste,
Fire Shovels and Tongs, Shovel Pans,
Kitchen and other Bellows,
Brass Kettles, Iron Candlesticks,
House, Cloaths and Shoe Brushes,
Pewter,
Hard metal Tea Pots, quart and pint
Canns, Tankards, &c.
Paper Hangings,
An Assortment of Looking Glasses,
Moulding Sand, Pumice,
Borax, Salt Petre, Sand paper,
Ruby and White Foil,
Playing Cards,
A few Pieces of yard-wide Irish Linnen,
Ditto German Serges,
Ditto Coatings and Kersey Coatings,
Coat and Waistcoat Buttons,
Some very elegant plated Spurs,
Cutlery,
Plated, green, white, black, and sham-stag
handle Knives and Forks,
Green, ivory, tortoise-shell and buffalo
Penknives,
Cutlass, Rasers, Scissars, Snuffers,
Black Shoe and Knee Buckles,
Black Lead Melting Pots, from No. 1
to 30 Crucibles,

Binding Wire, and many other Articles
With an elegant Assortment of
Jewelry and plated Ware,
among which is Coffee Urns which hold
three Pints, gilt Gob ets, &c.
JAPAND WARE,
among which are, a few large elegant
patented TEA-TRAYS in Setts, Tea Urns,
&c, &c.
Willard's Patent CLOCK-JACKS,
Some of the above Goods will be sold
for the Costs and Charges

In May and June 1785 Revere reminded his customers that he carried on "the Gold and Silversmith's Business . . . in all its Branches, where may be had at a short Notice any Vessel from a Thimble to Tea-Urn made in the newest Taste and finished in the neatest Manner."[50] Revere announced a change in location in January 1786: "From the south part of the town, opposite Liberty Pole, to DOCK-SQUARE, in the Store adjoining Mr. Joseph Bush, near the MARKET."[51] On 6 June 1787, he moved from Dock Square to No. 50 Cornhill, "At which place the Gold and Silversmith's Business are carried on in all their branches By Revere and Son."[52] The *Boston Directory* for 1789 listed Revere as a goldsmith at this location; however, he had moved his shop to No. 8 Union Street by 30 May 1789.[53] The *Boston Directory* for 1796 indicates yet another relocation, listing "Paul and JW Revere" as silversmiths on Ann Street, where they remained for less than a year.[54] On 24 May 1797, the *Columbian Centinel* announced the final address change for the silver shop: "Revere *and* Son, Beg leave to acquaint their Friends and Customers, That they have Removed their Work Shop, six doors to the Northward of *Cross-street*, at the North corner of the entrance on *Goldsbury's* Wharf— where the GOLD and SILVERSMITH's Business is carried on in all its branches Cash and the highest price given for old Gold, Silver and Silver Lace."

Beginning in 1798, Revere was no longer described as a goldsmith in city directories. "Revere & Son, bell and cannon founders," consisting of Paul Revere and his son Joseph Warren Revere, were listed on Lynn Street, from 1798 to 1807, on Charter Street in 1809, on Water Street in 1816, and on Kilby Street in 1813 and 1818, but these address changes probably refer to the retail shop since it is unlikely that the foundry moved.[55] A license to "sell Retail merchandize other than wine & spirits" was granted to Paul Revere & Son for their store in Kilby Street on 3 March 1816.[56]

Revere frequently relied on other Boston craftsmen to furnish him with specialized objects, services, or shop supplies, and his special talents in turn were utilized by his colleagues. The turner Isaac Greenwood provided him with a variety of services from 1757 until 1774:

1757	Mr Paul Revear to Isaac Greenwood Dr	
Sept	to a Colloped Tebord	£4– 0–0
	to a Server	0–10–0
1758	to a handell for a Tepot	1– 5–0
Novem	to a pattron for a Wine Cup	0– 9–0
1759		
March	to a Nut for a Tepot	0– 3–0
June	to Turning a Coffee pot	2–10–0

Sep.^t	to a Punch Ladell handell	0– 9–0
Decm	to Turning a Tepot	0 = 9–0
1760	to a Pair of Casters	1–10–0
	to a Tepot handell	1 = 5–0
O^{ct}	to Turning a Caster	0–10–0
1761	to a Pair of Caster[?]	1–10–0
Aprill	to a Larg Tankard	1–10–0
	to a Can	0 = 10–0
	to a Pair of Cans	1– 0–0
May	to to a Rim & T[illeg.] for a Tepot	0–10–0
June	to a pair of Caster	1–10–0
O^{ct}	to 12 Turtell Shell Buttons	0–10–0
	to a Caster	0–15–0
	to a Can	0–10–0
	to a Tankard	1– 5–0
	to a Coffee pot handell	1 = 5–0
Novem	to a Tankard	1 = 5–0
or December	to the half of a Roiling Press	5 = 15–0

£30 = 15–0

L Money   £4 = 3–0[57]

Prior to the Revolution, Revere's accounts include transactions with eleven silversmiths and jewelers, including John Coburn, Thomas Coverly, Benjamin Greene, Samuel Hichborn, Nathaniel Hurd, John Jackson, Samuel Minott, Andrew Oliver, John Symmes, Jonathan Trott, and John Welsh (qq.v.). Revere received shop supplies, including crucibles, gravers, files, black pots, shoe chapes, wire, and "pichter glass," from Welsh between 1761 and 1765 in exchange for cash and services, particularly engraving.[58] The estate of William Cowell, Jr. (q.v.), owed Revere £11.14.10 in 1761.[59] Revere may have employed Joseph Callender (q.v.) as a journeyman by 1774.

Revere's ability to create such difficult forms as the flat surface of a tray and the complex texture of repoussé work was recognized by his colleagues. Samuel Minott paid Revere for three salvers and a "chased" sugar dish in August and October 1762.[60] John Coburn, Nathaniel Hurd, and John Symmes also ordered chased objects or salvers from Revere in 1762 and 1767.[61] Many of the objects that Revere made for other silversmiths were unusual or unique forms, evidence of the professional respect accorded his craftsmanship and design skills by his colleagues. He created an ostrich egg snuffbox for Andrew Oliver; two scalloped salvers, a chafing dish, a picture frame, an Indian pipe, and a snuffbox for Nathaniel Hurd; a watch case for Thomas Coverly; a set of six tankards for Jonathan Trott; a squirrel chain for John Welsh; and a pair of chased creampots, a silver lamp and frame, and a sword guard were among the many items he made for John Coburn.[62]

In the post-war period, Revere continued to exchange services with Boston craftsmen. His long-term relationship with Isaac Greenwood continued into the 1790s, as attested by a receipt dated 27 November 1783 for "five shillings in full of all accounts to this date."[63] Revere supplied shop equipment, raw materials, and finished products to many of his peers, including Nathaniel Austin, Caleb Beal, Benjamin Burt, Stephen Emery, Joseph Loring, Samuel Minott, and George Trott (qq.v.). His reputation as an engraver attracted patronage from his colleagues. Benjamin Burt commissioned Revere to engrave a dish, a cup, a pair of gold buttons, cyphers on eight spoons and a pair of tea tongs, and cyphers on eighteen teaspoons in May and October 1792.[64] Additionally, a fluted teapot, covered sugar urn, and creampot in the Museum of Fine Arts, Boston, marked by Burt feature engraving characteristic of the Revere shop and were probably decorated there.[65]

Revere supplemented his silversmithing work with other activities, including printing and dentistry. Revere studied dentistry with Dr. John Baker, a surgeon-dentist who practiced in Boston in 1767–68. Revere advertised his ability to make artificial teeth in the *Boston News-Letter* of 25 August 1768 and the *Boston Gazette* of 19 September 1768.[66] Copperplate engraving and printing developed into an important facet of Revere's business. In the 1760s Revere collaborated with Josiah Flagg, Jr., on several music books. The *Boston Gazette* announced on 4 February 1765, "Just Published and to be Sold by Josiah Flagg, and Paul Revere, in Fish-Street, at the North-End of Boston, A Collection of The best Psalm-Tunes, in two, three and four Parts, from the most celebrated Authors; fitted to all Measures, and approved of by the best Masters in Boston, New-England. To which are added, Some Hymns and Anthems; the greater Part of them never before Printed in America. Set in Score by Josiah Flagg, Engraved by Paul Revere." In December 1761, Revere paid Isaac Greenwood £5.15 for "half of a Roiling Press."[67] Orders for prints rose into the thousands after 1770. The silversmith supplied illustrations for the *Royal American Magazine* and political broadsides, many of which were derived from English sources. He also printed paper money for the Massachusetts provincial government.[68] Beginning in 1773, Revere began supplying hat bills to a number of Boston hatters, including William Boardman and William Williams.[69] By the close of the second daybook, he had produced more than seventeen thousand of these small printed advertising labels.[70]

After the Revolution, Revere continued to diversify his business interests. In addition, Revere stopped calling himself a goldsmith on official documents and began styling himself "Esquire." An advertisement of 1786 for the retail shop mentions the silver shop in an addendum.[71] Rather than being the sole focus of Revere's activities, the shop was now part of a larger business network and was often used to finance other speculative ventures. From 1783 until 1789 numerous entries in the daybook for cash taken out of the shop amount to hundreds of pounds. One of the earliest of these ventures was Revere's partnership with Simon Willard (q.v. Appendix A) to make clock jacks.[72] Begun in 1782, the business flourished for a few years but ended in 1785 at a loss for Revere.

Revere's next enterprise was an ambitious expansion into another branch of metalwork. In 1788, he opened a foundry for smelting iron and brass on Lynn Street. To supplement funds obtained from the silver shop, Revere received financial assistance from his Hichborn cousins, Samuel and Benjamin, who paid several bills relating to the foundry in 1787 and 1788.[73] He mortgaged his house on Clark's Square to the silversmith Samuel Hichborn for £200 on 8 November 1787.[74] Revere appears to have rented the foundry site from his nephew Benjamin Hichborn of Dorchester until 28 June 1792, when he purchased the land on Lynn Street "with the furnace Utensils & bldg thereon" for £300.[75] He acquired two additional pieces of land adjoining the furnace in May 1796, one from the cordwainer James Bruce (in trade for a piece of land on an alley from Charter Street) and another in March 1801 from the truckman James Perkins (in trade for land on Foster's Lane, near Charter Street).[76] The United States Direct Tax of 1798 listed Revere as the owner and occupier of "a lott of land on which there is a Foundry, 40 by 46" totalling 10,675 square feet on Lynn Street and valued at $750.[77] The silversmith purchased additional land on Lynn Street in December 1799 from the Henniker, New Hampshire, trader Edward Whitman for $600, and in April 1807 from Jacob Rhoades for $5.[78] Revere sold this property in May 1807 at an enormous profit to John Rice and William Savage for $8,800.[79] The city directories for 1796, 1798, and 1800 list Revere as a "bell and cannon founder" on Lynn Street.[80] The business was listed as Paul Revere & Son after 1803, when Joseph Warren Revere joined his father in the base metal trade.[81] The trade card for the foundry illustrates the product lines manufactured there, such as shipbuilding materials, cannons, and bells.[82] By 1800, Revere had almost completely granted control of the silver business to Paul Revere III and devoted himself to the establishment of a copper rolling mill in Canton, Massachusetts, and the exploration of new markets for his copper and brass products, particularly in the South.[83] Samuel Paine sold some of Revere's hardware goods in his Richmond store in June 1790.[84] Newspapers in Savannah, Charleston, Alexandria, Richmond, Norfolk, and Baltimore reported on his manufacture of copper and brass articles.[85]

Paul Revere died at his home on Charter Street on 10 May 1818 and was buried in the Granary Burying Ground.[86] His obituary in the *Boston Intelligencer* of 16 May 1818 describes him as a dedicated patriot and shrewd businessman, generous to friends and family alike:

> Such was Col. Revere. Cool in thought, ardent in
> action, he was well adapted to form plans and to carry
> them into successful execution,—both for the benefit
> of himself and the service of others. In the early scenes
> of our revolutionary drama, which were laid in this
> metropolis, as well as at a later period of its progress,
> his country found him one of her most zealous
> and active of her sons. His ample property, which his
> industry and perseverance had enabled him to amass, was
> always at the service of indigent worth, and open
> to the solicitations of friendship or the claims of
> more intimate connexions. His opinions upon the events
> and vicissitudes of life, were always sound, and founded
> upon an accurate observation of nature and an extensive
> experience. His advice was, therefore, as valuable as
> it was readily proffered to misfortune. A long life,
> free from the frequent afflictions of disease, was the
> consequence of constant bodily exercise and regular
> habits—and he has died in a good old age, and all which
> generally attend it.

Revere's will was written on 15 November 1816 and presented for probate on 18 May by his son John Revere, who was named sole executor.[87] He left monetary bequests of $4,000 each to his surviving children, Mary Lincoln, Joseph Warren Revere, John Revere, Harriet Revere, and Maria Balestier; $500 each to eighteen grandchildren; $1000 to his grandson Frederick Walker Lincoln, youngest son of his daughter Deborah; $250 to his grandson Joseph Eayres; and $1 to his grandson Frank Lincoln, who evidently annoyed his grandfather by changing his name to "Francis Lincoln." His unmarried daughter Harriet received all his household furniture. Joseph Warren Revere was named the guardian of the minor children of his sisters Deborah, Frances, and Elizabeth and received an option on all the estate concerned with the rolling mill in Canton:

> As I have at great pains and Expense with the assistance of
> my said Son Joseph Warren brought the Copper business to the
> State in which it now is, And in order to bring it to that
> perfection of which it is capable, I am desirous of giving
> it every encouragement in my Power consistently with my duty
> to my other children. It is my will that all my Real Estate
> in the Town of Canton and County of Norfolk whether lands,
> houses, Mills, Furnaces together with the Tools and
> instruments thereunto belonging with all my Stock
> Manufactured and unmanufactured in Canton Boston or
> Elsewhere which was employed by me in the Said Copper
> Manufactory shall be offered to my said Son Joseph Warren.

Joseph Warren Revere was authorized to mortgage the real estate in order to purchase the copper mill and was also designated as beneficiary of all the residual estate after the specific legacies had been paid. A codicil added on 14 March 1818 directed Joseph Warren Revere to establish a trust of $12,000 and to divide the interest on a quarterly basis equally among his three surviving sisters or their heirs.

Joseph Peirse, Robert Williams, and the silversmith Samuel Hichborn appraised Revere's estate on 18 June 1818. It included mahogany and upholstered furniture, as well as a large amount of silver for his personal use indicative of a comfortable standard of living. Revere's personal silver was listed as follows:

	oz
1 Silver Coffee Pot	42
1 Silver Tea Pot	19
1 Silver Sugar "	14
1 Silver Cream "	8
1 Silver Large Pitcher	23
1 Silver 2^d. Size D^o.	10
1 Silver 3^d. Size D^o.	12$^1/_2$
1 Silver Porringer	8
2 Silver Salts	6
1 Silver Ladle	4$^1/_4$
12 Silver Table Spoons	26$^1/_4$
22 Silver Teaspoons	12$^1/_2$
1 Silver Sugar Tongs	2
1 Silver Cup	2—189$^1/_2$ ^{oz} @ 112$^1/_2$^{cts} $113.19

The total value of the inventory was $20,222.94, including "about 10 Acres in Canton, where the mills and building are together with the Dwelling House Stable and out Houses rolling Mill[,] Mill Priviledge Trip Hammer & Priviledge the Furnace and Implements."[88] Revere had already given the silver shop to his son Paul Revere III, probably around 1800 when he opened the rolling mill, so it does not appear in either the will or the inventory.

Revere was the most prolific eighteenth-century Boston silversmith. His daybooks record more than 5,355 objects produced between 1761 and 1797.[89] The 1,145 objects recorded in Revere's early period of production from 1761 to 1775 are distinguished by the great variety of forms that he made. The ninety different types of objects included cups, canns and casters; buckles, buttons and butter boats; tea sets, trays, thimbles and tankards; and numerous flatware forms, as well as children's whistles, pistol grips, an Indian pipe, a set of surgeon's instruments, and a squirrel chain. Many of Revere's most unusual forms were commissioned during the earliest period of his shop operation, before a lull in production in 1769 and 1770. These items, many of them unique examples of a particular form, reveal Revere's impressive skill and versatility as both a designer and a craftsman. In the pre-revolutionary period 52.4 percent of his total production was comprised of objects for dining and drinking, sacremental vessels for ritual use by churches, and flatware. Spoons of varying sizes, sometimes specified as tea, table or salt spoons, were produced in increasing quantities during the 1760s and 1770s. The remaining 47.6 percent of Revere's pre-revolutionary production was comprised of miscellaneous unusual forms and small personal items. The 448 personal items (39.2 percent) constitute a significant category of his total work. Revere supplied his patrons with buckles for their shoes, coats, stocks, and breeches; as well as gold, silver, and stone buttons for their garments. His work in gold was confined to small objects: buttons, broaches, beads, bracelets, and rings. These unpretentious articles contributed substantially to the financial success of Revere's shop. However, very few of these items have survived.

During the second period of shop operation, between 1779 and 1797, Revere's output changed dramatically both in the number and type of objects produced. The daybooks record 4,210 objects made between 1779 and 1797, almost four times the number listed during the earlier period. Although the variety of forms remained the same, slightly fewer holloware forms were produced. Flatware forms, however, proliferated.[90] The objects made after 1779 are predominantly standard forms, a change that allowed Revere to establish patterns and procedures that his journeyman and apprentices could execute. Objects for drinking and dining continued to dominate his post-revolutionary silver production. Revere produced a wide variety of drinking vessels during the 1780s and 1790s, including canns, tankards, and cups. Wares for serving tea, including fifty-five teapots, constitute the largest group of silver holloware made by Revere's shop during this period. The bulk of Revere's production in the post-revolutionary period was comprised of small objects. Personal items, especially buckles and buttons, made up almost 15 percent of his output. In addition, he formed partnerships with four saddlers and harness makers and produced more than 1,000 harness fittings for them between 1787 and 1793. The wares from these business relationships constituted almost one-quarter of his total silver production. There are no extant examples of these smaller goods.

Advances in technology contributed to Revere's increased production in the post-revolutionary period. By November 1785 Revere acquired a plating mill, a tool that allowed him to produce sheet silver.[91] With this ability Revere was able to speed production and reduce his overhead costs on standardized forms such as teapots. He experimented with several techniques for seaming sheet silver. The majority of the teapots from the post-revolutionary period are constructed by overlapping the edges and using silver rivets or solder. This technique provided a stong joint that could be executed by a journeyman or apprentice without extensive training or experience. Variations in the width and direction of the overlap, the placement of the seams, and the quality of the soldering indicate that several craftsmen produced Revere's teapots. Standardization released Revere from direct involvement in the design of each object and enabled him to diversify his business interests, while still drastically increasing the output of his silver shop. The more than one thousand objects that survive with Revere's marks attest to his industry and skill as a silversmith. DAF

SURVIVING OBJECTS

	Mark	Inscription	Patron	Date	Reference	Owner
Baptismal basin	B	Lemon arms, or on a fess gules between 3 dolphins embowed an annulet, and crest, a pelican in her piety; The Donation of Doc.ʳ JOSEPH LEMMON: to the/ First Church of CHRIST, in MARBLEHEAD/ 1773	First Congregational Church, Marblehead, Mass., for Joseph Lemmon	1773	Jones 1913, 263–64	
Baptismal basin	B	The Gift of Epes Sargent Jun.ʳ Esqʳ/ To the first church in Glocester/June 16th:/1762	Epes Sargent for First Parish Unitarian Society, Gloucester, Mass.	1762	Jones 1913, 185	
Baptismal basin	B	Johonnot arms, on a chief a sun in splendor, and crest, a bird with a sprig in its beak; Presented to the Church of CHRIST in/Boston under the Pastoral care of the/ Rev.ᵈ MATHER BYLES, D.D./by ZACHARIAH JOHONNOT Esqʳ Decʳ 1761.	Zachariah Johonnot for Hollis Street Church, Boston	1761	Jones 1913, 83	
Baptismal basin	C	KING'S CHAPEL/ The Gift of/ Ebenezer Oliver Esq.ʳ/1798	Ebenezer Oliver and/or King's Chapel, Boston	1798	Jones 1913, 65	
Two beakers (see also unmarked mate)	B	Sargent crest, a dolphin embowed (+)	Sargent family	ca. 1790	Christie's, 22–23 January 1993, lot 227	
Three beakers	B	This Cup is/Generously Dedicated by the/Contributors for the sole use & benefit/of the Presbyterian Church and/ Congregation in Bury Street of/ which the Revᵈ Mʳ Moorhead is/Minis-	Contributors to the Arlington Street Church, Boston	1753	Jones 1913, 79	

	Mark	Inscription	Patron	Date	Reference	Owner
		ter N = England 8^{br} y^{c}/1753				
Two beakers	B	The Gift of Epes Sargent Esqr/to the first Church of Christ in Gloucester, 1765	Epes Sargent for First Parish Unitarian Society, Gloucester, Mass.	1765	Jones 1913, 186	
Beaker	B*	W.N. Boylston	Ward Nicholas Boylston	ca. 1790	*Antiques* 99 (April 1971): 502	
Beaker	B, C, or D	JCB		ca. 1800	Parke-Bernet, 29 November– 2 December 1950, lot 571	
Beaker	C*	Deac,^{n}/Jacob Mitchel/to the first Church/in N-Yarmouth/1795	Jacob Mitchell and/or Congregational Church, Yarmouth, Maine	1795	Buhler/Hood 1970, no. 255	YUAG
Two beakers (mates below)	C	none		1795 or 1797	*Paul Revere* 1988, nos. 62–63	MMA
Beaker (mates above and below)	C	none		1795 or 1797	Garrett 1985, 146	DAR Museum
Five beakers (mates above)	C	none		1795 or 1797	*Paul Revere* 1988, 158	
Beaker (mate below)	C	BSR	Benjamin and Sarah (Guest) Russell	ca. 1803	Bigelow 1917, 98–99	
Beaker (mate above)	C	BSR; GSR (later) (+)	Benjamin and Sarah (Guest) Russell	ca. 1803	Sotheby's, 28–30 January 1988, lot 1056	
Beaker (mate below)	C	JSS	Sanborn family	ca. 1800	*CGA Bulletin*, no. 1 (1971): fig. 16	CGA
Beaker (mate above)	C (?)	JSS	Sanborn family	ca. 1800	Christie's, 23 January 1982, lot 95	
Two beakers (altered to creampot and sugar bowl)	C or D	Sargent crest, a dolphin embowed; DS	Daniel Sargent	ca. 1780	Cullity 1989, no. 128	
Beaker	C or D	E; Masonic compass and squares; EHC		ca. 1800	YUAG files	
Two beakers (mates below)	D*	G	Ozias and Elizabeth (Chapman) Goodwin	ca. 1800	*Paul Revere* 1988, no. 45	RISD
Two beakers (mates above and below)	D*	G	Ozias and Elizabeth (Chapman) Goodwin	ca. 1800	Lippert 1982, 42–43	IMA
Two beakers (mates above)	D	G	Ozias and Elizabeth (Chapman) Goodwin	ca. 1800	Buhler 1972, no. 418	MFAB
Two beakers (mates below)	D*	T	Isaiah Thomas	ca. 1796	Buhler/Hood 1970, no. 260	YUAG
Beaker (mates above and below)	D (?)	T	Isaiah Thomas	ca. 1795	Buhler/Hood 1970, 1:200	
Beaker (mates above)	D	T	Isaiah Thomas	ca. 1795	Bortman 1954, 304	

	Mark	Inscription	Patron	Date	Reference	Owner
Beaker	D	Frances Loring/ Born 1783		1783	WAM 1965, no. 1	
Beaker	?	?		ca. 1800	Norman-Wilcox 1962, no. 44	
Beaker (attrib.; see also mates with mark B*)*	none	Sargent crest, a dolphin embowed (+)	Sargent family	ca. 1790	Christie's, 22–23 January 1993, lot 227	
Beaker (attrib.)	none	The Gift of Epes Sargent Esqr/To the first church in Glocester/1773	Epes Sargent, Jr., for First Parish Unitarian Society, Gloucester, Mass.	1773	Jones 1913, 186	
Bowl	B*	RH; Hays	Moses Michael and Rachel (Myers) Hays or Rebecca (Hays) Myers	ca. 1795	Conger/ Rollins 1991, no. 216	USDS
Bowl	B	EHD; 1789/to/JD/ 1799 (later) (+)	Elias Hasket Derby	1794	YUAG files	
Bowl	B*	B/RS (over earlier initials)		ca. 1770	Flynt/Fales 1968, 117–18	HD
Bowl	B	To the Memory of the glorious NINETY-TWO: Members/of the Hon^{bl},, House of Representatives of the Massachusetts-Bay,/who, undaunted by the insolent Menaces of Villains in Power,/ from a Strict Regard to Conscience, and the LIBERTIES/ of their Constituents, on the 30th of June 1768,/ Voted NOT TO RESCIND; (below the rim) Caleb Hopkins, Nathl Barber, John White, Willm Mackay, Danl Malcom, Benjn Goodwin, John Welsh, Fortescue Vernon, Danl Parker John Marston, Icabod Jones, John Homer, Willm Bowes, Peter Boyer, Benj^a Cobb (+)	Sons of Liberty	1768	Buhler 1972, no. 356	MFAB
Bowl	B*	none		ca. 1770	Sotheby's, 23–25 January 1992, lot 177	
Bowl	D	MD	Martha Derby	ca. 1800	YUAG files	
Bowl	?	TB		ca. 1795	*Antiques* 109	

	Mark	Inscription	Patron	Date	Reference	Owner
					(June 1976): 1165	
Two candlesticks	D*	none		ca. 1795	Buhler/Hood 1970, no. 262	YUAG
Cann §	A	M/IM		ca. 1760	MFA 1906, no. 227 (as Paul Revere, Sr.)	
Cann (mate below)	B	ME		ca. 1765	Buhler 1965, 100–02	HMA
Cann (mate above)	B	ME		ca. 1765	Sotheby's, 30 January– 2 February 1991, lot 146	
Cann	B	WPG/to/MLB		ca. 1785	*CGA Bulletin*, no. 1 (1971): fig. 15	CGA
Cann	B	Benjamin and Judith Bussey	Benjamin and Judith (Gay) Bussey	ca. 1785	Lippert 1982, 38–40	IMA
Two canns	B	Orne arms, a chev-ron gules between 3 hunting horns sable, and crest, a unicorn emerging from a du-cal coronet; LO	William Paine for Lois Orne	1773	Buhler 1979, no. 53	WAM
Two canns	B*	EHED; D/EHE		1783	*Paul Revere* 1988, no. 60	MMA
Cann	B	RW		ca. 1790	DAPC 68.6156	MMA
Cann	B	A/IM	Isaac and Mary (Adams) Appleton or Rev. Joseph and Mary (Hook) Appleton	ca. 1770	WAM 1965, no. 4	
Cann	B	I/ZE; EP (later)	Zachariah and Eliza-beth (Waldron) Johonnot	1766	Buhler 1972, no. 355	MFAB
Cann	B*	Hutchinson arms, azure a lion rampant over a field of crosses crosslet, and crest, a wyvern; For the/Rev^d= E^d= Bass (later) (+)	Hutchinson family	ca. 1775	Whitehill et al. 1975, no. 12	
Cann	B	unidentified arms, on a bend azure be-tween 3 unicorns' heads 3 rings, and crest, an arm couped pointing at a star	Dennie family	ca. 1775	*American Silver* 1967, no. 14	RWNAG
Cann	B*	RSH		ca. 1770	Flynt/Fales 1968, 98	HD
Cann	B	TIL	Thomas and Jane (Miller) Lee	1787	Buhler 1972, no. 380	MFAB
Two canns	B	HMB	Bowers family (?)	ca. 1765	Buhler 1972, no. 353	MFAB

	Mark	Inscription	Patron	Date	Reference	Owner
Two canns	B*	Jackson arms, gules 3 suns in splendor, on a chief ermine, and crest, a sun in splendor; HJ (later)	Jackson family	ca. 1765	Buhler/Hood 1970, no. 239	YUAG
Cann	B*	JSF		1783	Christie's, 19–20 January 1990, lot 275	USDS
Two canns	B	Stephano Scales,/HARVARDINATES/A.D. MDCCLXVIII/Conscripti,/Biennio sub ejus Tutela per-acto,/Hoc Poculum/Grati Animi Moni-mentum/DONANT.	Stephen Scales and/or the Harvard College class of 1768	1768	*American Silver* 1967, no. 17	RWNAG
Cann	B*	F/GS; EMM (later)		ca. 1770	Christie's, 23 June 1993, lot 61	
Cann	B*	?		ca. 1775	Christie's, 22–23 January 1993, lot 226	
Cann (mate? below)	B	EMH	Elizabeth (Moore) Hall (?)	ca. 1785	YUAG files	
Cann (mate? above)	B*	EMH	Elizabeth (Moore) Hall	ca. 1785	DAPC 70.3279	BMA
Cann	C	SDS	Stillman and Deborah (Ellis) Smith	ca. 1785	Gustafson 1979, 316	HP
Cann	C	OP		ca. 1785	Parke-Bernet, 9 November 1946, lot 38	
Two canns	C	The Gift of/Mʳˢ Mary Pickman/to the/NORTH CHURCH of Christ/in Salem/under the Pastoral Care of the/Revᵈ Thomas Barnard D.D./1802	Mary (Toppan) Pickman and/or North Church, Salem, Mass.	1802	Jones 1913, 435	
Cann	C	none		ca. 1775	Jones 1913, 33	
Cann	?	unidentified crests, an owl and a grey-hound		ca. 1790	*Bulletin DIA* 24 (1944): 21	DIA
Cann	?	unidentified crest, a rampant horse couped		ca. 1765	Norman-Wilcox 1962, no. 38	
Cann	?	Presented to/JOSHUA SWETT/by Citizens of New York for his exertion in saving Four Men from the . . . (later)		ca. 1770	*Antiques* 15 (February 1929): 89	
Two canns	?	?		?	Shelley 1958, 174–75	HFM

	Mark	Inscription	Patron	Date	Reference	Owner
Cann (attrib.)	none	SEB	Samuel Ebenezer Bradlee	ca. 1795	Avery 1920, no. 136	MMA
Caster§	A	G/ES; P/ZR	Zacharias and Rebecca Pool (?)	ca. 1760	Parke-Bernet, 16 March 1971, lot 126A	
Caster	A	unidentified initials (defaced); N/AA (later)		ca. 1755	Buhler 1972, no. 337	MFAB
Caster	B	A/EM		ca. 1760	Shelley 1958, 174–75	HFM
Caster	B	R/UM		ca. 1780	*Antiques* 96 (October 1969): 458	
Caster	B*	unidentified initials		ca. 1770	Sotheby Parke Bernet, 29 April– 1 May 1981, lot 396E	
Caster	B*	S/JJ		ca. 1775	*Antiques* 92 (September 1967): 334	SFCAI
Caster	B	G/JH		ca. 1760	Shelley 1958, 174–75	HFM
Caster	B	Hickling crest, a greyhound running	Hickling family	ca. 1795	Sotheby's, 27 January 1989, lot 921	
Caster	B	Coffin crest, a cross crosslet fitché; Trusty·to·the·End		ca. 1770	MFA 1906, no. 281	
Caster	C	EW to EW	Williams family	ca. 1790	Flynt/Fales 1968, 52–54	HD
Caster	E	B/RS	Rev. Robert and Sarah (Tyler) Breck (?)	ca. 1760	Buhler 1972, no. 348	MFAB
Two casters	E	RMS		ca. 1775	Baumann 1976, 37–47	University of Missouri– Co- lumbia
Caster (mate below)	E or F	Williams (?) crest, a cock; IW to LW (+)	Williams family?	ca. 1795	*Paul Revere* 1988, nos. 84–85	HU
Caster (mate above)	E or F	Williams (?) crest, a cock; EW to LW (+)	Williams family?	ca. 1795	*Paul Revere* 1988, nos. 84–85	HU
Caster§	H	C/DM; C/IM		ca. 1760	MFA 1911, no. 906	
Caster	H*	EDLR/S		ca. 1760	YUAG files	
Caster	?	?		ca. 1793	YUAG files	
Caster	?	B/SM		ca. 1779	Sotheby Parke Bernet, 17–19 Novem-	

	Mark	Inscription	Patron	Date	Reference	Owner
					ber 1977, lot 411	
Caster	?	?		ca. 1770	*Antiques* 121 (January 1982): 118	
Caster	?	?		1757	*Antiques* 85 (June 1964): 619	
Caster (attrib.)	none	WHS/1787 (+)	William and Hannah (Carter) Smith	1787		MFAB
Two casters (attrib.)	none	Paine crest, a wolf's head collared and erased	Robert Treat Paine	1772	YUAG files	
Coffeepot	B	M/WF; MC (later) (+)	William MacKay	1769	Shelley 1958, 174–75	HFM
Coffeepot	B	Warren arms, a lion rampant a chief chequy or and azure; IAW	John and Abigail (Collins) Warren	1791	Buhler 1972, no. 388	MFAB
Coffeepot	B	Sargent arms, a chevron sable between 3 dolphins embowed, and crest, a dolphin embowed	Paul Dudley and Lucy (Saunders) Sargent	1781	Buhler 1972, no. 367	MFAB
Coffeepot	B	Orne arms, a chevron gules between 3 hunting horns sable, and crest, a unicorn emerging from a ducal coronet; LO	William Paine for Lois Orne	1773	Buhler 1979, no. 50	WAM
Coffeepot	B	none		ca. 1760	Buhler 1972, no. 341	MFAB
Coffeepot	B	D/IE; FCS to FBT/ 1863 (later)	Richard Derby for Jonathan and Elizabeth Derby	1772	*Paul Revere* 1988, no. 68	
Coffeepot	B	none		ca. 1775	Snow 1962, 303	
Coffeepot	B/E	Flynt arms, 3 flintstones, and crest, a lion rampant	Dorothy (Quincy) Jackson	ca. 1760	Buhler 1972, no. 339	MFAB
Coffeepot	C	RMH	Robert and Mary (Ingalls) Hooper	1769	Warren 1973, 1046–49	BBC
Coffeepot	C or D	MSS		ca. 1775	Sotheby Parke Bernet, 30 April–3 May 1980, lot 184	
Coffeepot	D*	HCL (?)		ca. 1795	Buhler 1956, no. 123	MFAB
Coffeepot	D	EET	Edward and Elizabeth (Harris) Tuckerman	1792	Buhler 1979, no. 59	WAM

	Mark	Inscription	Patron	Date	Reference	Owner
Coffeepot	D	Greene arms, azure 3 bucks trippant, and crest, a buck's head; DG	David Greene	ca. 1790	*Antiques* 40 (October 1941): 208	
Coffeepot	?	unidentified arms, or 2 lions passant within bordure engrailed, and crest, a lion's head emerging from a ducal coronet; FRANGAS NON FLECTES		ca. 1775	Parke-Bernet, 9 November 1946, lot 58	
Coffeepot (attrib.)	none	ALS	Abiel and Lydia Smith	1795	Warren 1973, 1049	
Two communion dishes	C	The property of the first Church in Beverly./Purchased by the Pastor, Dea.ᶜⁿ Benj.ⁿ Cleaves, and Dea.ᶜⁿ Robert Roundy, 1801.	The pastor and deacons Benjamin Cleaves and Robert Roundy for First Parish Church, Beverly, Mass.	1801	Jones 1913, 18	
Four communion dishes	C	Given by SUVIAH THAYER in testimony of her/respect for the FIRST CHURCH of CHRIST in/*BOSTON* AD 1796	Suviah Thayer and/or First Church, Boston	1796	Jones 1913, 34	
Creampot §	A	The Gift/of/ME to MB	Maria Barber	ca. 1755	Christie's, 22–23 January 1993, lot 228	
Creampot §	A	M.S.L.	Mary Spence Lowell	ca. 1760		MFAB
Creampot §	A	SC		ca. 1760	YUAG files	
Creampot	B	PAA		ca. 1790	Buhler 1972, no. 391	MFAB
Creampot	B	MRH	Moses Michael and Rachel (Myers) Hays	1783	English-Speaking Union 1960, no. 73	
Creampot	B	none		ca. 1760	Buhler 1979, no. 48	WAM
Creampot (part of a service)	B	TO		ca. 1785	Buhler 1972, no. 553	MFAB
Creampot	B	ASR; JR/dedit/Nov.ʳ 30 1778.		1782–85	Buhler/Hood 1970, no. 243	YUAG
Creampot	B	SL	Samuel Lazell	ca. 1790	WAM 1965, no. 7	
Creampot	B	IDB		ca. 1790		MMA
Creampot	B	RO; HM (later)		ca. 1755	Buhler 1972, no. 338	MFAB
Creampot	B*	T/JM	John and Mehitable (Bacon) (Lawless) Templeman	1792	Puig et al. 1989, no. 221	MIA

	Mark	Inscription	Patron	Date	Reference	Owner
Creampot (with cover)	B	Swan crest, an arm holding a knight's helmet	James Swan	1784	YUAG files	
Creampot	B	HW (cipher)		ca. 1765	YUAG files	
Creampot	B*	IPB	John and Polly Bishop	ca. 1790	Spencer 1994, 21–23	
Creampot	B	ADW		ca. 1790	YUAG files	
Creampot	B	Dudley arms, a lion rampant, impaling Apthorp, per pale nebuly argent and azure 2 rowels counterchanged	Dudley and Apthorp families	ca. 1785	*Antiques* 78 (July 1960): 9	AIC
Creampot (part of a service)	B/E	Chandler arms, chequy argent and azure on a bend argent 3 lions passant	Benjamin Greene and/or Lucretia (Chandler) Murray	1761	Buhler 1972, no. 345	MFAB
Creampot	B/E	unidentified crest; RW to LW (+)		ca. 1795	*Paul Revere* 1988, no. 83	HU
Creampot	C	EOT		ca. 1785		MFAB
Creampot	C	Carter crest	Anna Sidney (Carter) Tappan	ca. 1760	*Antiques* 27 (April 1935): 131	
Creampot	C	CED		ca. 1785	*Moore Collection* 1980, no. 143	
Creampot (part of a service)	C	none		ca. 1795	Avery 1920, no. 300	MMA
Creampot	C	unidentified initials		ca. 1800	Parke-Bernet, 29 November–2 December 1950, lot 572	
Creampot	C*	MD; MH (later)		ca. 1790		CM
Creampot	C	HM; Agnes McKean (later)		ca. 1800	Christie's, 25 June 1991, lot 31	
Creampot	C or D	BEW		ca. 1800		MFAB
Creampot	C or D	C		ca. 1790	*Bulletin DIA* 14 (May 1935): 109–11	DIA
Creampot	C or D	JLH		ca. 1800	MFA 1906, no. 241	
Creampot	C or D	RM to EB		ca. 1800	YUAG files	
Creampot	D*	IR (+)	Joseph Ropes	ca. 1795	Fales 1983, 26–27	PEM

	Mark	Inscription	Patron	Date	Reference	Owner
Creampot	D	FAB (later)		ca. 1800	Buhler 1972, no. 417	MFAB
Creampot	D	FPI [or J] (+)		ca. 1795	Buhler 1972, no. 403	MFAB
Creampot	D	A		ca. 1800	Biddle 1963, no. 125	
Creampot (part of a service)	D	EH	Fellow Boston citizens for Edmund Hartt	1799	Buhler 1972, no. 416	MFAB
Creampot	D	TSW		ca. 1800	Buhler 1972, no. 410	MFAB
Creampot	D	SI		ca. 1800	Buhler 1972, no. 409	MFAB
Creampot	E	none?		ca. 1770	DAPC 68.590	
Creampot	G†	PH to PE (+)	Priscilla Holyoke	ca. 1770	Johnston 1994, 124	CMA
Creampot	?	SDS	Stillman and Deborah (Ellis) Smith	ca. 1770	Bigelow 1917, 410, 412	
Creampot	?	?	Nathaniel and Abigail (Odlin) Gilman	ca. 1790	YUAG files	
Creampot	?	?		ca. 1800	YUAG files	
Creampot	?	?	Thomas Greenleaf	1791	YUAG files	
Creampot	?	JC/to/BC		ca. 1795	*Antiques* 85 (May 1964): 482	
Creampot	?	JT (?)		ca. 1790	*Antiques* 119 (February 1981): 374	
Creampot	?	IP		ca. 1785	*Antiques* 39 (February 1941): 57	
Creampot	?	MS		ca. 1790	Green/ Holland 1973, no. 6	
Creampot	?	unidentified initials		ca. 1798	*Antiques* 110 (December 1976): 1237	
Creampot (attrib.)	none	JR (+)	Andrew Ritchie for Janet Ritchie	1798	Parke-Bernet, 12–16 November 1974, lot 1017	
Creampot (attrib.; retailed by Nathaniel Austin)	none	HC; 1787	William Smith for Hannah Carter	1787		MFAB
Creampot (part of a service; attrib.)	none	JAB	Joseph and Anna Blake	1793	Hammerslough/ Feigenbaum 1958–73, 1:68–69	
Cup	C	SS		ca. 1785	WAM 1965, no. 2	
Cup (mate below)	C	SSE	Sarah Sargent (Ellery) Sargent	ca. 1795	Buhler 1972, no. 404	MFAB

	Mark	Inscription	Patron	Date	Reference	Owner
Cup (mate above)	D	SSE	Sarah Sargent (Ellery) Sargent	ca. 1795	Buhler 1972, no. 404	MFAB
Cup	?	B.H. to B.H.G.	Benjamin Henderson	ca. 1800	Sotheby Parke Bernet, 28 March 1973, lot 162	
Flagon	B	Johonnot arms, ermine on a chief azure a sun in splendor, and crest, a bird with a sprig in its beak; Humbly Presented/to the Church of *CHRIST* in Hollis-Street/ under Pastoral Care of/the Revd *MATHER BYLES*, D. D./for the Communion Table/By *ZACHARIAH JOHONNOT* Esqr/ 1773	Zachariah Johonnot for Hollis Street Church, Boston	1773	Jones 1913, 82	
Flagon	C	The/Gift of/ Cap^T.Peter Osgood/To the first/Church of Christ in Andover/1801	Peter Osgood for North Parish of North Andover, North Andover, Mass.	ca. 1801	Jones 1913, 346–47	
Flagon	C	King's Chapel/ 1796	King's Chapel, Boston	ca. 1796	Jones 1913, 65	
Flagon	C	The property of the first Church in Beverly./Bought with the church's stock by a committee/consisting of the Pastor and Deacon/ Benjamin Cleaves, and Deacon Robt. Roundy/1798	The pastor and deacons Benjamin Cleaves and Robert Roundy for First Parish Church, Beverly, Mass.	1798	Jones 1913, 18	
Grace cup (altered to a pitcher)	B	Presented by the/ Society in Hollis street/*BOSTON.*/to M^r = Charles Bulfinch, as/a testimony of their grateful/ acknowledgment for the Ele-/gant Plan furnished them/for their Meeting-House,/and for his unwearied/attention in the exe-/ cution./1787	Hollis Street Church, Boston, for Charles Bulfinch	1787	Sotheby's, 27 January 1989, lot 913	

	Mark	Inscription	Patron	Date	Reference	Owner
Ladle	B	THD	Thomas and Hannah (Blake) Dawes	ca. 1780	Buhler 1972, no. 366	MFAB
Ladle	B	Swan	James Swan	ca. 1785	Buhler 1972, no. 375	MFAB
Ladle	B*	SMD	Mary (Quincy) Stedman-Donnison	ca. 1783	Puig et al. 1989, no. 220	MIA
Ladle	B	ESP		ca. 1785	WAM 1965, no. 8	
Ladle	B	Tyrian Lodge/No. I	Tyrian Lodge, Gloucester, Mass.	ca. 1773	Buhler 1972, no. 365	MFAB
Ladle	B	C		ca. 1790	Buhler 1972, no. 385	MFAB
Ladle	B	SH		ca. 1790		MFAB
Ladle	B	BAC	Burrell and Anne (Zeagers) Carnes	1793	Buhler 1972, no. 395	MFAB
Ladle (part of a service)	B	Hickling crest, a greyhound running	Hickling family	ca. 1785	Hammerslough/ Feigenbaum 1958–73, 1:114	
Ladle	B	none		ca. 1770	Sotheby's, 28–31 January 1994, lot 605	
Ladle	B	initials erased		ca. 1780	Sotheby's, 24 October 1987, lot 391	
Ladle	B	G		ca. 1785	YUAG files	
Ladle	B	UR		ca. 1785	*Campbell Museum Collection*, no. 145	Campbell Museum
Ladle	B	SM Howard	S. M. Howard	ca. 1790		MFAB
Ladle	B, C, or D	CVB (later)		ca. 1780	Christie's, 23 January 1988, lot 79	
Two ladles	C	Nº 2/The Gift of/Bʳ = Samˡ = Barrett to/Sᵗ Andrew's Lodge/Nº 82/1762	Samuel Barrett for St. Andrew's Lodge, Boston	1762	*Paul Revere 1988*, no. 208	
Ladle	C*	H		ca. 1780	Conger/ Rollins 1991, no. 204	USDS
Ladle	C*	TIB (?)		ca. 1800	*Antiques* 134 (July 1988): 104	
Ladle	C*	The Gift of/Brother John Soley	John Soley	1797	*Paul Revere 1988*, no. 218	
Two ladles	C or D	?	St. Paul Lodge	ca. 1770	YUAG files	
Ladle	C or D	WPCS	Smith family	ca. 1795	*Antiques* 134 (July 1988): 41	

	Mark	Inscription	Patron	Date	Reference	Owner
Ladle	C or D	AW		ca. 1790	MFA 1906, no. 269	
Ladle	C or D	Apthorp crest, a mullet; M/PS	Perez Morton for Sarah (Wentworth) Apthorp	1781	Buhler 1972, 2:413	MFAB
Ladle	D	NMLS	Nathaniel and Mary Lynde (Walter) Smith	ca. 1797	Buhler 1972, no. 408	MFAB
Ladle	D	P		ca. 1800	Buhler 1972, no. 421	MFAB
Ladle	D	AA		1796	*Paul Revere* 1988, no. 80	PRMA
Two ladles	D	SSP	Samuel and Sarah (Rogers) Parkman	ca. 1805	YUAG files	
Ladle	E, F, or G	?		ca. 1790	Sotheby's, 23–25 January 1992, lot 178	
Ladle	?	SW		ca. 1785	*Antiques* 109 (January 1976): 14	
Ladle (attrib.)	none	Rising States Lodge.	Rising States Lodge, Boston	1786	YUAG files	
Masonic jewel (attrib.)	none	Presented/by/King Hiram's Lodge/to Jon. Cook	Jonathan Cook for King Hiram's Lodge, Provincetown, Mass.	ca. 1805	*Paul Revere* 1988, no. 221	Museum of Our National Heritage
Twelve Masonic jewels (attrib.)	none	?	Washington Lodge, Roxbury, Mass.	1796	*Paul Revere* 1988, nos. 222–33	Washington Lodge, A.F. & A.M.
Memorial urn (gold; attrib.)	none	This URN incloses a Lock of HAIR/of the Immortal WASH-INGTON/PRESENTED JANUARY 27, 1800/to the Massachusetts GRAND LODGE/by HIS amiable WIDOW./Born Feb.y 11.th 1731/Ob.t Dec.r 14. 1799	Grand Lodge of Masons in Massachusetts, Boston	ca. 1800	*Paul Revere* 1988, no. 217	Grand Lodge of Masons in Massachusetts A.F. & A.M.
Miniature frame (gold; attrib.)	none	none	Paul and Rachel (Walker) Revere	ca. 1784	Buhler 1972, no. 373	MFAB
Mourning ring (gold; attrib.)	none	L. MURRAY/ OB.21.MAR/ 1768.AE.38	Lucretia (Chandler) Murray	1768	Buhler 1972, no. 357	MFAB
Mourning ring (gold; attrib.)	none	J. CROWNIN-SHIELD/OB. 25. MAY/ 1761. AE.65	J. Crowninshield	1761		MHS
Mug	B	SB; Blagge arms (later)	Samuel Blagge	1792	Buhler 1972, no. 389	MFAB
Mug	C	?		ca. 1800	Bigelow 1917, 179	

	Mark	Inscription	Patron	Date	Reference	Owner
Mug	C	WT	William Tuck	ca. 1785	NHHS 1973, no. 130	NHHS
Mug (attrib.; with mark of Nathaniel Austin)	none	HC	William Smith for Hannah Carter	1787	Thomas 1988, 16–17	
Mustard pot and spoon	C†/ F*	D	Elias Hasket Derby	ca. 1800	Buhler/Hood 1970, no. 263	YUAG
Papboat	B, C, or D	none		ca. 1775	YUAG files	
Pitcher	C	PRESENTED/to the/ Rev.d Joseph Mc Kean/by a number of his Friends/late Parishioners of/ MILTON,/as a testimonial of their affection/and to hold in remembrance how deeply/ they regret his separation/from them./ 1804	Parishioners of First Congregational Church, Milton, Mass., for Joseph McKean	1804	Quimby 1995, no. 112	WM
Pitcher	C*	AHS; Jany 1804	Alfred Sylvester (?)	1804	Buhler 1976, 9, 11–13	VMFA
Pitcher	C or D	TLC (?)		ca. 1805	Parke-Bernet, 23 March 1940, lot 32	
Pitcher (mate below)	D*	ILH	John and Lucy Howard	ca. 1805	Buhler/Hood 1970, no. 264	YUAG
Pitcher (mate above)	D*	ILH	John and Lucy Howard	ca. 1805	Lippert 1982, 42–44	IMA
Pitcher (mate below)	D	BRAY/1804	John Bray	1804	Buhler 1965, 105–07	HMA
Pitcher (mate above)	D	BRAY/1804; ACB (later)	John Bray	1804	YUAG files	
Pitcher (mate below)	D	R; Paul and Rachel Revere./Charter Street. (later)	Revere family	ca. 1800	Buhler 1972, no. 420	MFAB
Pitcher (mate above)	D*	R; Paul and Rachel Revere./Charter Street. (later)	Revere family	ca. 1800	*Antiques* 97 (April 1970): 444	
Pitcher	D	L		ca. 1805		MFAB
Pitcher	D	none		ca. 1805	*American Silver* 1967, no. 21	RWNAG
Pitcher	D*	R; 1802		1802	Buhler/Hood 1970, 1:201	
Pitcher	D	OH (later)		ca. 1800	DAPC 79.4124	
Pitcher	D	PRESENTED/by/The Government of the Mechanic Association,/TO/ Mr. SAMUEL GILBERT/	The Government of the Massachusetts Charitable Mechanic Association, Boston, for Samuel Gilbert	1806	Fales 1959, 476–77	

	Mark	Inscription	Patron	Date	Reference	Owner
		As compensation for his faithful/and extra services while their/SECRETARY./ Boston Jan.ʸ 1st 1806/Jona. Hunnewell. Presᵗ./Benjᵃ. Russell. Vice Presᵗ.				
Two porringers §	A*	unidentified crest, a wyvern's head	Tristram Dalton	ca. 1760	Christie's, 22 June 1994, lot 71	
Porringer	A	W/?H (partially erased); GLM (later)		ca. 1760	Buhler 1972, no. 336	MFAB
Porringer §	A*	unidentified arms, gules a saltire sable, and crest, a lion rampant; A/BH	Aspinwall family	ca. 1760	Avery 1920, no. 135 (as Paul Revere, Sr.)	MMA
Porringer §	A	PGK (+)	Philip Godfrid Kast	ca. 1755	Sotheby Parke Bernet, 29 April–1 May 1981, lot 395A	
Porringer §	A	SW		ca. 1760	Sotheby Parke Bernet, 16–18 November 1978, lot 413	
Porringer §	A	MP		ca. 1760	MFA 1906, no. 225	
Porringer	A	HAD (later)		ca. 1760	Christie's, 13 October 1984, lot 85	
Porringer	B*	YMB		ca. 1770		LAM
Porringer	B*	unidentified initials (erased)		ca. 1770	Conger/ Rollins 1991, no. 199	USDS
Porringer	B*	E/BT		ca. 1775	DAPC 68.6157	MMA
Porringer	B	P/DB; MP (later) (+)	David and Betiah (Ingersoll) Pearce	ca. 1770	WAM 1965, no. 11	
Porringer	B*	RGS/to/RGSW		ca. 1780	*Paul Revere* 1988, no. 42	SFCAI
Porringer	B	AG/to/ED		ca. 1760	Buhler 1972, no. 340	MFAB
Porringer (mate below)	B	Hickling crest, a greyhound running	Hickling family	ca. 1770	Buhler 1972, no. 361	MFAB
Porringer (mate above)	B	Hickling crest, a greyhound running	Hickling family	ca. 1770	YUAG files	
Porringer	B	P/TS	Thomas and Sarah (Sawyer) Parsons	1769	Buhler 1972, no. 358	MFAB
Porringer	B	none		ca. 1765	Eitner 1976, no. 62	
Porringer	B	M/PM		ca. 1765	Eitner 1976, no. 63	

	Mark	Inscription	Patron	Date	Reference	Owner
Porringer	B	LA; to/SM Jᴿ (later)	Aspinwall family (?)	ca. 1765	Buhler 1979, no. 49	WAM
Porringer	B*	SWK	Sarah W. (Knapp) Stickney	ca. 1790	Parke-Bernet, 10 November 1970, lot 139	
Porringer	B	D/EA; SHH (later)		ca. 1760	Parke-Bernet, 4 January 1940, lot 64	
Porringer	B*	Sally Inman Kast (later)		ca. 1770	*Antiques* 132 (December 1987): 1226	
Porringer	B	Jackson crest, a sun in splendor; I/JA	Jackson family	ca. 1770	Sotheby Parke Bernet, 15–17 November 1973, lot 699	
Porringer	B	EC; ECM/1791 (later) (+)		ca. 1790	Sotheby Parke Bernet, 16–18 November 1978, lot 412	
Porringer	B*	JW		ca. 1790	Christie's, 4 June 1988, lot 72	
Porringer	B	T/WB	William and Bethiah (Boss) Torry	1762	MFA 1906, no. 223	
Porringer	B*	ES		ca. 1765	MFA 1911, no. 858	
Porringer	B	FJH (cipher)		ca. 1770		MHS
Porringer	B	A/JR		ca. 1770	American Art Association– Anderson Galleries, 8–10 January 1931, lot 338	
Porringer	B *or* C	AS/C		ca. 1770	DAPC 67.1827	
Porringer	B, C, *or* D	RWH; Capt. Robert Wormsted/Aet 28/ was lost at sea in Oct./1782	Robert Wormsted	1782	Bonhams, 28 June 1994, lot 231	
Porringer	C*	D/IS (altered to AD/IS); Davis to Alice (later)		ca. 1785	Sotheby's, 23–24 June 1994, lot 96	
Porringer	C	MW		ca. 1775	Christie's, 26 January 1991, lot 58	
Porringer	C	NAG (+)	Nathaniel and Abigail (Odlin) Gilman	ca. 1775	Hammerslough/ Feigenbaum 1958–73, 1:35	
Porringer	C	IMD	Isaac and Mary May Davenport	ca. 1795	Parke-Bernet, 25–29 January 1972, lot 53	

	Mark	Inscription	Patron	Date	Reference	Owner
Porringer	C*	Apthorp crest, a mullet	Sarah (Apthorp) Morton (?)	ca. 1800	Buhler/Hood 1970, no. 257	YUAG
Porringer	C or D	MTT to MTS (+) (later)		ca. 1800	YUAG files	
Porringer	C or D	L/TF		ca. 1770	Sotheby Parke Bernet, 30 April–3 May 1980, lot 193	
Porringer	D	CT (or TC)		ca. 1800	YUAG files	
Porringer	D	HH	H. Hooper	ca. 1795	*American Silver* 1967, no. 22	RWNAG
Porringer	D*	?		ca. 1795	*Antiques* 101 (May 1972): 808	
Porringer (part of a service)	D	SS Junior	Salisbury family	ca. 1798	Buhler 1979, no. 61	WAM
Porringer	H	KW 1793 (+)		1793	MFA 1906, no. 230	
Porringer	?	P/IS	John and Sarah Pettingel	ca. 1770	Norman-Wilcox 1962, no. 39	
Porringer	?	unidentified initials		ca. 1770	Norman-Wilcox 1954, 49	
Porringer (attrib.)	none	Moreland crest, a falcon; Fides et Fortitudo (+)	Moreland family	ca. 1770		MFAB
Porringer (with cover; attrib.)	none	PRR	Paul and Rachel (Walker) Revere	ca. 1773	Buhler 1972, no. 364	MFAB
Porringer spoon (part of a service)	D	SS Junr	Salisbury family	ca. 1798	Buhler 1979, no. 61	WAM
Punch urn	D	depiction of the Boston Theatre; THE PROPRIETORS/OF THE/BOSTON THE- ATRE/TO/ Samuel Brown, Esqr./one of their TRUSTEES/ 1796.	Elisha Sigourney for the Proprietors of the Boston Theatre for Samuel Brown	1796	Warren/ Howe/ Brown 1987, no. 110	
Punch urn	D	depiction of the Boston Theatre; THE/ PROPRIETORS/OF THE/BOSTON THEATRE/TO/ GEN^l Henry Jack- son, Esqr/ONE OF THEIR TRUSTEES/ 1796.	Elisha Sigourney for the Proprietors of the Boston Theatre for Henry Jackson	1796	Buhler 1972, no. 406	MFAB
Ring (gold; attrib.)	none	none	Rachel (Walker) Revere	ca. 1773	Buhler 1972, no. 363	MFAB
Salt §	A	H/IM; WPM		ca. 1760	National Art Galleries, 3–5	

	Mark	Inscription	Patron	Date	Reference	Owner
					December 1931, lot 425	
Salt	A†	W/TA		ca. 1765	Buhler/Hood 1970, no. 242	YUAG
Salt	B, C, *or* D	?		ca. 1765	Parke-Bernet, 9 November 1946, lot 15	
Salt	E*	H/WE; The Illustri-ous NINETY-TWO		ca. 1769	Buhler/Hood 1970, no. 241	YUAG
Two salts §	H	E *or* G		ca. 1760		MFAB
Salt spoon	B	Apthorp crest, a mullet	Perez Morton for Sarah (Wentworth) Apthorp	1781	YUAG files	
Salt spoon	E	JMT	John and Mehitable (Bacon) (Lawless) Templeman	1792	Buhler 1972, no. 390	MFAB
Four salt spoons	E, F, *or* G	HEW	Williams family	ca. 1790	Avery 1920, nos. 305–08	MMA
Salt spoon	E, F, *or* G	B/AH	Alden and Hannah (Tyler) Bass	ca. 1775	Buhler 1965, 104–05	HMA
Four salt spoons	E, F *or* G	Swan crest, a long-necked bird stand-ing in grass	Swan family	ca. 1775		MFAB
Two salt spoons	E, F *or* G	SSE	Sarah (Sargent) Ellery (?)	ca. 1785	YUAG files	
Two salt spoons	E, F *or* G	D		ca. 1790		MFAB
Two salt spoons	E, F *or* G	WS		ca. 1785	Kroening 1982, no. 22	
Two salt spoons	E, F *or* G	T	John Templeman (?)	1792 (?)	*Antiques* 96 (December 1969): 935	
Two salt spoons	E, F, *or* G	AA		1796	*Paul Revere* 1988, nos. 81–82	PRMA
Three salt spoons	F	?		ca. 1790	Sotheby Parke Bernet, 16–18 November 1972, lot III	
Salt spoon	H	none		ca. 1800	DAPC 68.3892	
Salt spoon	?	D		ca. 1790	*Antiques* 93 (March 1968): 273	
Two salt spoons (attrib.)	none	HH	Hepzibah (Jones) Hall or Hepzibah (Hall) Fitch	ca. 1790	Buhler 1972, no. 386	MFAB
Salver	B	Chandler arms, chequy argent and azure on a bend argent 3 lions passant, and crest, a pelican in her piety; L. Chandler	Lucretia (Chandler) Murray	1761	Buhler 1972, no. 343	MFAB

	Mark	Inscription	Patron	Date	Reference	Owner
Salver	B	Tyng arms, on a bend cotised azure 3 martlets, and crest, a martlet; The Gift of James Tyng to his/ Sister Sarah Tyng 1761.	James Tyng and/or Sarah Tyng	1761	*Paul Revere* 1988, no. 67	HU
Two salvers (with mark of Nathaniel Hurd)	B	Franklin arms, on a bend between 2 lions' heads erased gules, a dolphin embowed between 2 martlets, and crest, a dolphin's head between 2 branches	Franklin family	1762	Buhler 1976, 7	
Salver	B*/E, F, *or* G	Phillips arms; The Gift/of William White to/William Phillips/1760	William White and/or William Phillips	1760	*Antiques* 101 (January 1972): 19	
Sauceboat (mate below)	A	M/MR	Mungo and Ruth (Coney) Mackay	ca. 1765	Safford 1983, 47	MMA
Sauceboat (mate above)	B	M/MR	Mungo and Ruth (Coney) Mackay	ca. 1765	Safford 1983, 47	MMA
Two sauceboats	B	I/ZE	Zachariah and Elizabeth (Waldron) Johonnot	ca. 1765	Buhler 1972, no. 354	MFAB
Two sauceboats	B	Orne arms, a chevron gules between 3 hunting horns sable, and crest, a unicorn emerging from a ducal coronet; LO	William Paine for Lois Orne	1773	Buhler 1979, no. 54	WAM
Two sauceboats	B	D/EH E (+)	Elias Hasket and Elizabeth (Crowninshield) Derby	1783	Buhler 1972, no. 371	MFAB
Two sauceboats	B	unidentified crest, a lion's head issuing from a crown; JES	Smith family (?)	ca. 1790	Buhler 1972, no. 387	MFAB
Two sauceboats	B	I/FM	Francis and Mary (Oliver) Johonnot	ca. 1765	Buhler 1972, 2:406	AG
Sauceboat	B	F		ca. 1775	WAM 1965, no. 13	
Sauceboat	B	EH	Haven family (?)	ca. 1765	WAM 1965, no. 12	
Two sauceboats	B	Sargent arms	Sargent family	ca. 1780	MFA 1906, nos. 270–71	
Two sauceboats	B	?	Frothingham family	ca. 1785	YUAG files	
Sauceboat	B, C, *or* D	crest, a long-tailed creature		ca. 1765	Parke-Bernet, 25–26 October 1949, lot 376	
Sauceboat	?	?		ca. 1770	*Antiques* 68 (November 1955): 425	

	Mark	Inscription	Patron	Date	Reference	Owner
Two sauceboats (mates below)	?	Hays	Moses Michael and Rachel (Myers) Hays	ca. 1790	Sotheby Parke Bernet, 28 March 1973, lot 161	
Sauceboat (mates above and below)	?	Hays	Moses Michael and Rachel (Myers) Hays	ca. 1790	Parke-Bernet, 17 October 1972, lot 117	
Sauceboat (mates above)	?	Hays	Moses Michael and Rachel (Myers) Hays	ca. 1790	Sotheby Parke Bernet, 28 March 1973, 32	
Saucepan	B, C, or D	Thomas Greene	Thomas Greene	ca. 1760	Parke-Bernet, 17–18 May 1946, lot 294	
Seal (gold; attrib.)	none	Greene arms, vert 3 bucks trippant, and crest, a buck's head; NG; DISCE/SCIRE/TE/IPSUM	Greene family	ca. 1790	Buhler/Hood 1970, no. 251	YUAG
Seal (attrib.)	none	BOSTON YE SEAL OF RISING STATES LODGE	Rising States Lodge, Boston	ca. 1784	*Paul Revere* 1988, no. 209	Grand Lodge of Masons in Massachusetts, A.F. & A.M.
Seal (attrib.)	none	SIGILL: SOC: MED: MASSACHUSETT: A.D. 1781/NATURA DUCE.	Massachusetts Medical Society	ca. 1782	*Paul Revere* 1988, no. 92	Massachusetts Medical Society
Seal (attrib.)	none	SIGIL. PHILLIP. ACAD./EINIS ORIGINE PENDEL/NON SIDI	Phillips Academy	ca. 1785	Fales 1970a, 97	AG
Two serving spoons	B	MRH	Moses Michael and Rachel (Myers) Hays	1786	Buhler 1960, no. 104	
Skewer	C	B; CHBC (later)		ca. 1790		BM
Skewer	D	B	Samuel Blagge	1796	Buhler 1972, no. 407	MFAB
Snuffbox	B	SH	Samuel Hollis	ca. 1775	Hammerslough/Feigenbaum 1958–73, 1:64	
Snuffbox (attrib.)	none	BR		ca. 1800	*Paul Revere* 1988, no. 203	Massachusetts Charitable Mechanic Association
Strainer	B*	none		ca. 1790	Buhler/Hood 1970, no. 252	YUAG

	Mark	Inscription	Patron	Date	Reference	Owner
Strainer	B*	none		ca. 1780		SFCAI
Strainer	B*	none		ca. 1760	Johnston 1994, 125	CMA
Strainer	B, C, or D	none		ca. 1780	Christie's, 17–18 January 1992, lot 181	
Strainer (attrib.)	none	T/JM	John and Mehitable (Bacon) (Lawless) Templeman	1792	Puig et al. 1989, no. 221	MIA
Sugar bowl	B	none		ca. 1765	Phillips 1939, no. 164	
Sugar bowl	B	MRH; Hays	Moses Michael and Rachel (Myers) Hays	1787	Buhler 1960, no. 119	USDS
Sugar bowl	B	ITL (later)		ca. 1765	*Silver Supplement* 1973, no. 73	
Sugar bowl	B*	MC/to/MTQH	Lucretia (Greene) Callahan or Mary (Chandler) Greene (?)	ca. 1765	Warren 1975, no. 317	BBC
Sugar bowl	B	unidentified arms, possibly Breck, gules a griffin rampant, on a chief per bend sinister indented or and argent 4 hurts 2 and 2; B/RS	Rev. Robert and Sarah (Tyler) Breck	ca. 1765	Buhler 1972, no. 551	MFAB
Sugar bowl (part of a service)	B	BAC	Burrell and Anne (Zeagers) Carnes	1793	Buhler 1972, no. 394	MFAB
Sugar bowl (part of a service)	B	JMT	John and Mehitable (Bacon) (Lawless) Templeman	1792	Puig et al. 1989, no. 221	MIA
Sugar bowl	B	G/TJ M; ABF (later)	Thomas James and Mary (Dumaresq) Grouchy	ca. 1756–60	Buhler/Hood 1970, no. 238	YUAG
Sugar bowl (part of a service)	B	TO	Timothy Orne (?)	ca. 1785	Buhler 1972, no. 554	MFAB
Sugar bowl	B	R/UM		ca. 1780	*Antiques* 96 (October 1969): 458	
Sugar bowl	B	JAW	John and Abigail (Collins) Warren	1785	Buhler 1972, 2:438	
Sugar bowl	B	ED (+)		ca. 1790	YUAG files	
Sugar bowl	B	CC		ca. 1800	DAPC 81.3785	
Sugar bowl	B/E	Chandler arms, chequy argent and azure on a bend argent 3 lions passant; B. Greene to L. Chandler	Benjamin Greene and/or Lucretia Chandler	1761	Buhler 1972, no. 344	MFAB

	Mark	Inscription	Patron	Date	Reference	Owner
Sugar bowl	B, C, *or* D	?	Coffin family	ca. 1770	American Art Association–Anderson Galleries, 18–19 January 1935, lot 92	
Sugar bowl	C	WPCS		ca. 1800	Doty 1979, fig. 18	CGA
Sugar bowl	C	HH		ca. 1790	WAM 1965, no. 15	
Sugar bowl	C *or* D	JED		ca. 1790	YUAG files	
Sugar bowl	C *or* D	RM to EB		ca. 1800	YUAG files	
Sugar bowl	C *or* D	MS; AMF; 1866 (later)		ca. 1790	*Bulletin DIA* 14 (May 1935): 109–11	DIA
Sugar bowl	C *or* D	unidentified arms; IS (or IL)		ca. 1790	Norman-Wilcox 1962, no. 42	
Sugar bowl (part of a service)	D	To/Edmund Hartt/ Constructor of the Frigate BOSTON/Presented by a number of his fellow citizens as a/Memorial of their sense of his Ability, Zeal, and Fidelity/in the completion of that Ornament/of the AMERICAN NAVY./ 1799	Fellow Boston citizens for Edmund Hartt	1799	Buhler 1972, no. 415	MFAB
Sugar bowl (part of a service)	D	H	Jonathan Hunnewell	1796	Avery 1920, no. 302	MMA
Sugar bowl	D	EC	Elizabeth Crowninshield (?)	ca. 1795	Buhler 1972, no. 401	MFAB
Sugar bowl	D	ET/to/EHT	Edward Tuckerman (?)	ca. 1798	Buhler 1972, no. 413	MFAB
Sugar bowl	D*	SSE	Sarah (Sargent) Ellery	ca. 1790	Buhler/Hood 1970, 1:197	SFCAI
Sugar bowl	D	OEG	Ozias and Elizabeth (Chapman) Goodwin	ca. 1795	Buhler 1972, no. 402	MFAB
Sugar bowl (part of a service)	D	none		ca. 1795	Avery 1920, no. 301	MMA
Sugar bowl	D	SEB		ca. 1792	Shepard 1978, 228	MAM
Sugar bowl	D*	DMA		ca. 1795	Bartlett 1984, 24–25	SLAM
Sugar bowl	?	?		ca. 1790	Norman-Wilcox 1962, no. 41	

	Mark	Inscription	Patron	Date	Reference	Owner
Sugar bowl	?	?	Nathaniel and Abigail (Odlin) Gilman	ca. 1790	YUAG files	
Sugar bowl (missing cover?)	?	?		ca. 1765	*Antiques* 65 (April 1954): 272	
Sugar bowl (attrib.)	none	none	Revere family	1790	Buhler 1972, no. 384	MFAB
Sugar tongs	B*	Madey crest	Madey family	1792	DAPC 68.212	SI
Sugar tongs	B	M/FC		ca. 1765	Buhler 1972, no. 349	MFAB
Sugar tongs	B*	D		ca. 1790	*Antiques* 106 (September 1974): 344	
Sugar tongs	B	IML		ca. 1800	Avery 1920, no. 325	MMA
Sugar tongs	B	none		ca. 1770	*Moore Collection* 1980, no. 141	
Sugar tongs	B	IMK		ca. 1790		MHS
Sugar tongs	B	G		ca. 1790	YUAG files	
Sugar tongs	B	SI		ca. 1790	YUAG files	
Sugar tongs	B	ML/TL		ca. 1790	DAPC 70.3558	
Sugar tongs	B	GW		ca. 1785		MHS
Sugar tongs (part of a service)	B	none	John and Mehitable (Bacon) (Lawless) Templeman (?)	ca. 1792	Puig et al. 1989, no. 221	MIA
Sugar tongs	B	none		ca. 1785	Buhler 1972, no. 370	MFAB
Sugar tongs	C	LJD		ca. 1775	*Moore Collection* 1980, no. 142	
Sugar tongs	C	GAD	Gilbert and Anna Densh	ca. 1790	Christie's, 26 January 1991, lot 57	
Sugar tongs	C	HQ	Hannah (Quincy) Hill	ca. 1780	Buhler 1972, no. 552	MFAB
Sugar tongs	C or D	MA		ca. 1800	Parke-Bernet, 14–15 May 1948, lot 175	
Sugar tongs	C or D	ISH		ca. 1795	*Silver Supplement* 1973, no. 72	
Sugar tongs	C or D	?		ca. 1795	Sotheby Parke Bernet, 1–4 February 1978, lot 685	
Sugar tongs	D	SSP	Samuel and Sarah (Rogers) Parkman	ca. 1785	WAM 1965, no. 14	
Sugar tongs	D	R		ca. 1785	Christie's, 22–23 January 1993, lot 229	

	Mark	Inscription	Patron	Date	Reference	Owner
Sugar tongs	D*	AF		ca. 1800	Cutten 1946, 113	NM
Sugar tongs	D	EML	Miss Legree (?)	ca. 1800	Buhler 1972, no. 411	MFAB
Sugar tongs	D	ISD	James and Sarah (Templeton) Dunbar	ca. 1795	Buhler 1972, no. 412	MFAB
Sugar tongs (part of a service)	E, F, or G	Orne crest, a unicorn emerging from a ducal coronet; LO	William Paine for Lois Orne	1773	Buhler 1979, no. 57	WAM
Sugar tongs	H†	I/DR		ca. 1760	Buhler/Hood 1970, no. 237	YUAG
Tablespoon	A*	O/IE		ca. 1765	YUAG files	
Tablespoon	B*	EC		ca. 1795	Buhler/Hood 1970, no. 247	YUAG
Tablespoon	B	EP to EN		ca. 1790	Quimby 1995, no. 115b	WM
Two tablespoons	B*	IGE		ca. 1785		PEM
Tablespoon	B	SW	Williams family	ca. 1775	Avery 1920, no. 309	MMA
Eleven tablespoons (part of a service)	B	Orne crest, a unicorn emerging from a ducal coronet	William Paine for Lois Orne	1773	Buhler 1979, no. 55	WAM
Tablespoon	B	ED		ca. 1775		MFAB
Tablespoon	B	S/SD to I/WD		ca. 1785		MFAB
Two tablespoons	B	MD		ca. 1790		MFAB
Tablespoon	B	ASP		ca. 1775	Sotheby's, 30 June–1 July 1983, lot 91	
Three tablespoons	B	MW (later)		ca. 1785	Sotheby's, 31 January–2 February 1985, lot 69	MFAB
Tablespoon	B	M/GR		ca. 1770	DAPC 74.1089	HSP
Tablespoon (mates below)	B*	Sargent crest, a dolphin embowed	Sargent family	ca. 1775	DAPC 68.6150	MMA
Tablespoon (mates above and below)	B	Sargent crest, a dolphin embowed	Sargent family	ca. 1775	Quimby 1995, no. 115a	WM
Tablespoon (mates above and below)	B*	Sargent crest, a dolphin embowed	Sargent family	ca. 1775	Buhler/Hood 1970, no. 245	YUAG
Tablespoon (mates above and below)	B	Sargent crest, a dolphin embowed	Sargent family	ca. 1775	YUAG files	
Two tablespoons (mates above)	B*	Sargent crest, a dolphin embowed	Sargent family	ca. 1775		USDS
Tablespoon (mate below)	B*	TAH; In memory of Eliz[h] M. Hill (later)	Thomas and Ann (McNeal) Hill in memory of Elizabeth M. Hill	1772	Fales 1983, 24–25	PEM
Tablespoon (mate above)	B	TAH; In memory of Eliz[h] M. Hill (later)	Thomas and Ann (McNeal) Hill in memory of Elizabeth M. Hill	1772	Buhler 1972, no. 360	MFAB

	Mark	Inscription	Patron	Date	Reference	Owner
Tablespoon	B*	ERL		ca. 1790	Lippert 1982, 39–40	IMA
Three tablespoons	B	EAO	Edward A. Oliver	ca. 1787	Avery 1920, nos. 312–14	MMA
Two tablespoons	B	C/IP		ca. 1785	Avery 1920, nos. 310–11	MMA
Tablespoon	B	V/IR		ca. 1785		MFAB
Tablespoon	B*	IHL (+)		ca. 1785	Eitner 1976, no. 65	
Tablespoon	B	HP; H. Pearce	Harriet Pearce	ca. 1795	Sotheby's, 30 January– 2 February 1991, lot 128	
Tablespoon	B	H/TH (+)		ca. 1770	Sotheby's, 30 January– 2 February 1991, lot 131	
Tablespoon	B	ISW		ca. 1795	Buhler 1972, appendix no. 69	MFAB
Tablespoon	B*	ISW		ca. 1785	DAPC 68.6148	MMA
Two tablespoons (mates below)	B	Spooner (?) crest, a boar's head pierced with an arrow	Spooner family (?)	ca. 1785	Buhler 1972, appendix no. 68	MFAB
Two tablespoons (mates above)	B	Spooner (?) crest, a boar's head pierced with an arrow	Spooner family (?)	ca. 1785	YUAG files	
Tablespoon	B	MAS		ca. 1785	Buhler 1965, 102–03	HMA
Two tablespoons	B	DET		ca. 1785	Sotheby's, 28–31 January 1994, lot 606	
Two tablespoons (see also mates with mark C*)*	B	IMK	Israel M. Keith (?)	ca. 1785	Buhler 1972, appendix no. 67	MFAB
Tablespoon	B	PCS	Peter Chardon Scott (?)	ca. 1795	WAM 1965, no. 21	
Five tablespoons	B	MRH	Moses Michael and Rachel (Myers) Hays	ca. 1790	Christie's, 17–18 January 1992, lot 179	
Ten tablespoons (part of a service)	B	Hickling crest, a greyhound running	Hickling family	ca. 1785	Hammerslough/ Feigenbaum 1958–73, 1:114	
Tablespoon	B	Jackson crest, a sun in splendor; HJ	Jackson family	ca. 1760	Buhler 1972, no. 342	MFAB
Two tablespoons	B*	MM		ca. 1785	Johnston 1994, 126	CMA
Two tablespoons	B	JEE		ca. 1780	Sotheby's, 27 January 1989, lot 894	

	Mark	Inscription	Patron	Date	Reference	Owner
Tablespoon	B*	GF		ca. 1785	Buhler/Hood 1970, no. 246	YUAG
Six tablespoons	B	OEG	Ozias and Elizabeth (Chapman) Goodwin	ca. 1784	Buhler 1972, no. 372	MFAB
Two tablespoons (mate below)	B	HH	Hepzibah (Hall) Fitch	ca. 1785	Buhler 1972, no. 377	MFAB
Tablespoon (mates above)	B	HH	Hepzibah (Hall) Fitch	ca. 1785	Sotheby's, 28–30 June 1984, lot 74	
Tablespoon (mates below)	B	OLE	Oliver and Lucy (Hill) Everett	ca. 1787		MFAB
Two tablespoons (mate above)	B	OLE	Oliver and Lucy (Hill) Everett	ca. 1787	Buhler 1972, no. 382	MFAB
Tablespoon	B	SBM		ca. 1795	Buhler 1972, no. 399	MFAB
Tablespoon	B	MB	Mary (Buckley) Hewes	ca. 1770	Parke-Bernet, 4 January 1940, lot 37	
Three tablespoons (mate below)	B	MB	Mary (Buckley) Hewes	ca. 1795	Buhler 1972, no. 398	MFAB
Tablespoon (mates above)	B	MB	Mary (Buckley) Hewes	ca. 1780	Sotheby's, 27–28 June 1990, lot 144	
Tablespoon	B*	CW		ca. 1790		SI
Tablespoon	B*	JK		ca. 1775	Tvrdik 1977, no. 180	AIC
Tablespoon	B*	D		ca. 1790	*Antiques* 107 (June 1975): 1046	
Three tablespoons (see also unmarked mate?)	B	BH	Benjamin Hall	ca. 1785	Buhler 1972, no. 376	MFAB
Tablespoon (mates below)	B	ESP; MBB/to JCB & MEP/1856 (later)		ca. 1790	Buhler 1965, 102–03	HMA
Two tablespoons (mates above and below)	B (?)	ESP (?)		ca. 1790	Buhler 1965, 102	MFAB
Tablespoon (mates above)	B	ESP; MBB/to JCB & MEP/1856 (later)		ca. 1790	WAM 1965, no. 22	
Tablespoon (mate? below)	B	SH; 1760 (later) (+)	Stephen Hunneman	ca. 1765	Avery 1920, no. 138	MMA
Tablespoon (mate? above)	B	SH	Stephen Hunneman (?)	ca. 1765	Christie's, 26 January 1985, lot 90	
Two tablespoons	B*	M/PM		ca. 1770		HD
Tablespoon (see also mates with marks c and d)	B*	unidentified crest, a dexter arm holding an estoile		ca. 1795	*Moore Collection* 1980, no. 144	
Two tablespoons	B	CD		ca. 1770	*Moore Collection* 1980, no. 145	

	Mark	Inscription	Patron	Date	Reference	Owner
Tablespoon	B*	ASW		ca. 1790	Sotheby Parke Bernet, 16–18 November 1972, lot 109	
Tablespoon	B*	unidentified initials		ca. 1775	Parke-Bernet, 12–16 November 1974, lot 1018	
Tablespoon	B, C *or* D	EH		ca. 1785	DAPC 69.2305	WM
Tablespoon	C	Apthorp crest, a mullet; SA	Sarah (Wentworth) Apthorp	ca. 1770		PEM
Tablespoon	C	KLC		ca. 1785	Avery 1920, no. 315	MMA
Three tablespoons	C	JVR		ca. 1790		MFAB
Tablespoon (mates? below)	C	L		ca. 1790	Quimby 1995, no. 114	WM
Two tablespoons (mate? above)	C (?)	L		ca. 1790	American Art Association– Anderson Galleries, 29–30 November 1935, lot 46	
Tablespoon	C	PV		ca. 1775		MFAB
Six tablespoons (see also mates with mark B)	C	IMK	Israel M. Keith (?)	ca. 1785	Avery 1920, nos. 316–21	MMA
Two tablespoons	C	EIG		ca. 1790		SI
Tablespoon	C	B/TM		ca. 1790	Sotheby Parke Bernet, 16–18 November 1972, lot 108	
Tablespoon	C	MB		ca. 1795	Buhler 1972, appendix no. 72	MFAB
Two tablespoons	C	MLW	Mary Lynde Walter	ca. 1790	Buhler 1972, appendix no. 71	MFAB
Tablespoon	C*	unidentified initials		ca. 1790	Parke-Bernet, 12–16 November 1974, lot 1019	
Six tablespoons	C*	C	William Cunningham	1796	*Moore Collection* 1980, no. 147	
Tablespoon	C (?)	NSR		ca. 1780	American Art Association– Anderson Galleries,	

	Mark	Inscription	Patron	Date	Reference	Owner
Tablespoon	c (?)	NSR (?)		ca. 1780	22–23 January 1937, lot 284 American Art Association– Anderson Galleries, 22–23 January 1937, lot 285	
Three tablespoons (mates? below)	c*	JMB		ca. 1790		USDS
Three tablespoons (mates? above)	c (?)	JMB		ca. 1790	*Antiques* 70 (September 1956): 178	
Tablespoon	c (?)	MPM; SEB; 1889 (later)		ca. 1780		DIA
Tablespoon (see also mates with mark b *and mark* d*)*	c*	unidentified crest, a dexter arm holding an estoile; HAH (later)		ca. 1795		CM
Tablespoon	C *or* D	W		ca. 1810		MFAB
Tablespoon	C *or* D	The Gift of Eliza^b Rogers to Benj^a Varney	Elizabeth Rogers and/ or Benjamin Varney	ca. 1785		MFAB
Two tablespoons	C *or* D	AH		ca. 1800	MFA 1906, nos. 266–67	
Tablespoon	C *or* D	Hawthorne crest	Hawthorne family	ca. 1800	MFA 1906, no. 265	
Two tablespoons	C *or* D	HLP 1793(+)		1793	MFA 1906, nos. 263–64	
Six tablespoons	C *or* D	SSE	Sarah (Sargent) Ellery	ca. 1785	Christie's, 3 June 1989, lot 302	
Six tablespoons	C *or* D	DMS	Daniel and Mary Sargent	ca. 1785	Christie's, 3 June 1989, lot 301	
Tablespoon (see also mates with mark b *and mark* c*)*	D	unidentified crest, a dexter arm holding an estoile; HAH (later)		ca. 1795	Sotheby's, 30 January– 2 February 1991, lot 129	
Tablespoon (mates below)	D*	unidentified crest, a dexter arm holding an estoile; AKL (later)		ca. 1795		USDS
Two tablespoons (mate above)	D	unidentified crest, a dexter arm holding an estoile; AKL (later)		ca. 1795		MFAB
Three tablespoons (mate below)	D*	SSP	Samuel and Sarah (Rogers) Parkman	1789	Christie's, 22 June 1994, lot 66	

	Mark	Inscription	Patron	Date	Reference	Owner
Tablespoon (mates above)	D	SSP	Samuel and Sarah (Rogers) Parkman	1789	Sotheby's, 28–31 January 1987, lot 288	
Tablespoon	D†	ESB		ca. 1795	Buhler/Hood 1970, no. 258	YUAG
Tablespoon (mate below)	D	F	Anne (Frances) Trott	ca. 1806	Hammerslough/Feigenbaum 1958–73, 1:113	
Tablespoon (mate above)	D*	F	Anne (Frances) Trott	ca. 1806	Lippert 1982, 39–41	IMA
Two tablespoons	D	JLH	John and Lucy Howard (?)	ca. 1775	Avery 1920, nos. 323–24	MMA
Two tablespoons	D	EDC		ca. 1805	Sotheby's, 30 January– 2 February 1991, lot 130	
Twelve tablespoons	D*	AA	Anna Amory	1796	*Antiques* 107 (April 1975): 630	
Tablespoon (mate below; see also unmarked mate)	D*	R		ca. 1785	Christie's, 22–23 January 1993, lot 230	
Tablespoon (mate above; see also unmarked mate)	D(?)	R		ca. 1785		MFAB
Six tablespoons	E	JSD		ca. 1785	WAM 1965, no. 24	
Tablespoon	F	AJK		ca. 1790	Quimby 1995, no. 113d	WM
Tablespoon	?	?		ca. 1760		ChM
Tablespoon	?	CS		ca. 1770	Norman-Wilcox 1962, no. 45	
Six tablespoons (mates below)	?	Russell crest	Russell family	ca. 1775	Buhler 1972, 2:413	
Tablespoon (mates above and below)	?	Russell crest	Russell family	ca. 1775	DAPC 88.3381	BBC
Tablespoon (mates above)	?	Russell crest	Russell family	ca. 1775	YUAG files	
Tablespoon (see also mates with mark B)	?	BH (altered to H/BH)	Benjamin and Hepzibah (Jones) Hall	ca. 1785	Buhler 1976, 6–7	VMFA
Tablespoon	?	?		ca. 1765		RISD
Six tablespoons	?	JMT	John and Mehitable (Bacon) (Lawless) Templeman	1792	Puig et al. 1989, 274	
Two tablespoons	?	EH		ca. 1805	Christie's, 16 June 1984, lot 86	
Tablespoon	?	JSD		?	*Antiques* 52 (December 1947): 398	
Tablespoon	?	EAH		ca. 1790	Christie's, 26 January 1985, lot 91	

	Mark	Inscription	Patron	Date	Reference	Owner
Tablespoon	?	GG	Gardiner Greene	ca. 1775	*Antiques* 86 (November 1964): 531	
Tablespoon (attrib.; see also mate with mark D)	none	R		ca. 1785	Christie's, 22–23 January 1993, lot 230	
Tankard§	A	unidentified arms, per pale gules and argent, a lion rampant, and crest, a dexter arm embowed holding a battle-axe, impaling unidentified arms, sable on a chevron or between 3 arrows in pale, points in chief, 3 roundles		ca. 1760		MMA
Tankard	B	ASD	Amasa and Sarah Davis	1793	Buhler 1960, no. 110	Bostonian Society
Tankard	B*	Henshaw arms, a chevron sable between 3 heronshaws, and crest, a falcon preying upon the wing of a bird; H/BH (+)	Benjamin and Huldah Henshaw	ca. 1770	Gourley 1965, no. 170	RISD
Tankard	B*	Jackson arms, gules 3 suns in splendor, on a chief ermine, and crest, a sun in splendor; J/JA (later)	Jackson family	ca. 1765	Gourley 1965, no. 169	RISD
Tankard	B	Pynchon arms (partially obliterated); MP; ML (later)	William Pynchon	ca. 1770	Kroening 1982, no. 16	
Tankard	B	unidentified arms, possibly Breck, gules a griffin rampant, on a chief per bend sinister indented or and argent 4 hurts 2 and 2, and crest, a griffin's head couped; The first owner of this Tankard was Col. William Raymond Lee . . . (later)	Joseph Breck (?)	ca. 1766	Parke-Bernet, 4 January 1940, lot 62	
Tankard	B	Breck arms; B/RS	Rev. Robert and Sarah (Tyler) Breck (?)	ca. 1765	Buhler 1972, no. 347	MFAB
Tankard	B*	The Gift of/Samuel Barnard Esq!/to the Church of Christ/in Deerfield/1763	Joseph Barnard for First Congregational Church, Deerfield, Mass.	1764	Jones 1913, 137	

	Mark	Inscription	Patron	Date	Reference	Owner
Tankard	B	Banks arms, 4 hurts on a cross or between 4 fleur-de-lis and crest, an armed arm embowed holding a sword; BEM 1765	Banks family	1765	MFA 1906, no. 278	
Six tankards (retailed by Jonathan Trott)	B†	The Gift of,/Mary Bartlett. Widow of Eph^m.. Bartlett,/to the third Church in Brookfeild./1768	Jedidiah Foster, executor of Mary Bartlett's estate, for First Congregational (Unitarian) Society, Brookfield, Mass.	1772	Quimby 1995, no. 111a–f	WM
Tankard	B	Skillings arms; S/NE	Nehemiah Skillings	1774	Phillips 1939, no. 167	
Tankard	B*	none		ca. 1765	*Antiques* 65 (January 1954): 36–37	DeYoung
Tankard	B	Orne arms, a chevron gules between 3 hunting horns sable, and crest, a unicorn emerging from a ducal coronet; LO	William Paine for Lois Orne	1773	Buhler 1979, no. 52	WAM
Tankard	B	unidentified initials (erased); John Prince to John Prince Jr. (later)	Alden and Hannah (Tyler) Bass (?)	ca. 1765	Buhler 1972, no. 352	MFAB
Tankard	B	unidentified crest, a stag's head; RG; G/DR		ca. 1770	MFA 1906, no. 275	
Tankard	B	?L (partially erased)	Sarah Lord	1765	Buhler 1972, no. 351	MFAB
Tankard	B	JLH		ca. 1795	DAPC 77.2492	
Tankard	B	unidentified arms, a chevron between 3 eagles displayed, and crest, a griffin's head erased		ca. 1765	YUAG files	
Tankard	B	Memento/obt: October 1777/Beulah Danielson/Sarah Danielson/Martha Danielson/lovely in Life/and in Death/not divided	Timothy Danielson	1777	*Antiques* 123 (April 1983): 675	
Tankard	B	Goodwin arms, a lion passant on a chief or 3 mascles gules; Joseph Goodwin	Joseph Goodwin	1769	Buhler 1972, 2:398	
Tankard	B	D/EA	Ebenezer Dorr	ca. 1770	Buhler 1972, 2:451	

	Mark	Inscription	Patron	Date	Reference	Owner
Tankard	B/C	initials possibly erased		ca. 1795	YUAG files	
Tankard	B*/ E†	Greene arms, azure 3 bucks trippant, and crest, a buck's head; TG/to/MG	Thomas Greene	1762	Buhler/Hood 1970, no. 240	YUAG
Tankard	C	SEB	Samuel Ebenezer Bradlee	1795	Avery 1920, no. 137	MMA
Tankard	C (?)	Stephano Scales,/ HARVARDINATES/ A.D. MDCCLXVIII. Conferipti,/Biennio fub ejus Tutelâ peracto,/Hoc Poculum,/Grati Animi Monimentum, DONANT.	Stephen Scales and/or the Harvard College class of 1768	1768	*Paul Revere* 1988, no. 94	MFAB
Tankard	C	WMT	William and Mary (Bemis) Todd	1795	Buhler 1972, no. 400	MFAB
Tankard	C or D	N/WM		ca. 1770	YUAG files	
Tankard	D	?		ca. 1775	*Antiques* 103 (March 1973): 473	
Tankard (with mark of Samuel Minott)	E*	JCY		ca. 1785		LAM
Tankard	?	?	Second Church, North Beverly, Mass.	?	YUAG files	
Tankard	?	?	Elizabeth Goodwill	ca. 1760	*Antiques* 60 (September 1951): 167	
Tea caddy (part of a service)	B	T/JM	John and Mehitable (Bacon) (Lawless) Templeman	1792	Puig et al. 1989, no. 221	MIA
Tea caddy key (attrib.; part of a service)	none	none	John and Mehitable (Bacon) (Lawless) Templeman	1792	Puig et al. 1989, no. 221	MIA
Tea caddy spoon (attrib.; part of a service)	none	JMT	John and Mehitable (Bacon) (Lawless) Templeman	1792	Puig et al. 1989, no. 221	MIA
Tea caddy stand (part of a service)	B	JMT	John and Mehitable (Bacon) (Lawless) Templeman	1793	Puig et al. 1989, no. 221	MIA
Teapot §	A	?		ca. 1760		MFAB
Teapot (see matching teapot stand inscribed MA +)	B	Nourse-Quincy-1906 . . . (later)		ca. 1790	Parke-Bernet, 12 January 1946, lot 49	
Teapot (part of a service)	B	T/JM	John and Mehitable (Bacon) (Lawless) Templeman	1792	Puig et al. 1989, no. 221	MIA
Teapot	B*	JSC		ca. 1785	Buhler/Hood 1970, no. 244	YUAG

	Mark	Inscription	Patron	Date	Reference	Owner
Teapot	B	SIB	Stephen and Isannah Bruce	1782	*Paul Revere* 1988, no. 44	MMA
Teapot	B	Parsons arms, 2 chevrons ermine between 3 eagles displayed; TSP/to/SP (later)	Jonathan Parsons	ca. 1770	Buhler 1972, no. 359	MFAB
Teapot	B*	BRI; WLA		ca. 1790	Kent/Levy 1909, no. 457	SFCAI
Teapot	B	MRH	Moses Michael and Rachel (Myers) Hays	1783	Bortman 1954, 304–05	
Teapot	B	Orne arms, a chevron gules between 3 hunting horns sable; LO	William Paine for Lois Orne	1773	Buhler 1979, no. 51	WAM
Teapot	B	none	Thomas Hichborn	1782	Buhler 1972, no. 368	MFAB
Teapot	B	MB	Moses Brown	1789	Buhler 1972, no. 383	MFAB
Teapot	B*	TCT/ET (later)		ca. 1790	Buhler/Hood 1970, no. 253	YUAG
Teapot *(see matching teapot stand)*	B	BAC	Burrell and Anne (Zeagers) Carnes	1793	Buhler 1972, no. 393	MFAB
Teapot *(with mark of Nathaniel Austin; see matching teapot stand)*	B	HC; 1787 (later)	William Smith for Hannah Carter	1787	Buhler 1972, no. 381	MFAB
Teapot *(see matching teapot stand)*	B	SMH	Samuel and Martha (Hunt) Henshaw	ca. 1790	WAM 1965, no. 17	
Teapot	B	Bigelow (?) arms, or 3 lozenges (or passion nails) 2 and 1	Call family	ca. 1765	Sotheby's, 24 October 1987, lot 390	
Teapot *(see matching teapot stand)*	B	none		ca. 1795	Sotheby's, 17 November 1981, lot 166	
Teapot	B	JR(?)L		ca. 1795	Christie's, 21–22 January 1994, lot 119	
Teapot *(see matching teapot stand)*	B	DD		ca. 1790	DAPC 75.2422	
Teapot	B/E	B/RS; Ross crest (later)		ca. 1765	Buhler 1972, no. 346	MFAB
Teapot	C	OEG	Ozias and Elizabeth (Chapman) Goodwin	ca. 1795	Buhler 1972, no. 555	MFAB
Teapot	C	SES	Stephen and Elizabeth (Tuckerman) Salisbury	ca. 1797	Buhler 1979, no. 60	WAM
Teapot (see matching teapot stand with mark D)	C	H; G (later)	Jonathan Hunnewell	1796	Buhler 1972, no. 405	MFAB
Teapot	C	RRG; SPG	Rebecca (Russell) Gardner	ca. 1797	Sotheby's, 23–24 June 1994, lot 97	
Teapot	C or D	Presented by the Proprietors/of	Proprietors of Boston Neck for William Dall	1797	*Paul Revere* 1988, no. 69	MFAB

	Mark	Inscription	Patron	Date	Reference	Owner
		BOSTON NECK to Mr WILLIAM DALL/for Services render'd them 1797				
Teapot	C or D	SA MO in 1782 (+)		1782	YUAG files	
Teapot	C or D	A McK	Agnes McKean	ca. 1790	Garrett 1985, 24	DAR Museum
Teapot (see matching teapot stand)	C or D	SH	Moses Michael Hays for Sally Hays	ca. 1796	Buhler 1976, 9–10	VMFA
Teapot	C or D	B. Sept. 5, 1736 William Coombs . . . (later)		ca. 1790	Bulletin DIA 18 (May 1939): 4–6	DIA
Teapot	C or D	unidentified crest, a hand holding a heart; JAW		ca. 1785	Shelley 1958, 174–75	HFM
Teapot	C or D	H/JS		ca. 1785		HFM
Teapot	C or D	RMH	Robert and Mary (Ingalls) Hooper	ca. 1790	American Silver 1967, no. 18	RWNAG
Teapot	D*	RP	Rebecca Partridge	ca. 1795	Buhler/Hood 1970, no. 256	YUAG
Teapot (see matching teapot stand)	D	JH	Moses Michael Hays for Judith Hays	ca. 1796	Buhler 1960, no. 115	USDS
Teapot	D	SB		1796	Avery 1920, no. 304	MMA
Teapot	D*	ET/to/EHT	Edward Tuckerman to Elizabeth (Harris) Tuckerman	ca. 1798	Silver Supplement 1973, no. 74	
Teapot (see matching teapot stand; part of a service)	D	EH; To/Edmund Hartt/Constructor of the Frigate BOSTON/Presented by a number of his fellow citizens as a/Memorial of their sense of his Ability, Zeal, and Fidelity/in the completion of that Ornament/of the AMERICAN NAVY./1799	Fellow Boston citizens for Edmund Hartt	1799	Buhler 1972, no. 414	MFAB
Teapot	?	?		ca. 1760	Norman-Wilcox 1962, no. 40	
Teapot	?	?		?	Buhler 1972, 2:420	
Teapot (see matching teapot stand)	?	PW	Leonard White for Peggy (White) Bartlett	1786	Norman-Wilcox 1954, 50	
Teapot	?	?		ca. 1785	Antiques 50 (October 1946): 198	

	Mark	Inscription	Patron	Date	Reference	Owner
Teapot (attrib.)	none	Warren arms; JAW	John and Abigail (Collins) Warren	1785	Buhler 1972, 2:438	
Teapot (attrib.)	none	A	John and Katharine (Willard) Amory, Jr.	ca. 1795	*Paul Revere* 1988, no. 52	MFAB
Teapot (attrib.; see matching teapot stand with mark C or D; part of a service)	none	JAB	Joseph and Anna Blake	1793	Hammerslough/ Feigenbaum 1958–73, 1:68–69	
Teapot stand (see matching teapot)	B	BAC	Burrell and Anne (Zeagers) Carnes	1793	Buhler 1972, no. 393	MFAB
Teapot stand (retailed by Nathaniel Austin; see matching teapot)	B	HC; 1787 (later)	William Smith for Hannah Carter	1787	Buhler 1972, no. 381	MFAB
Teapot stand (see matching teapot)	B	SMH	Samuel and Martha (Hunt) Henshaw	ca. 1790	WAM 1965, no. 17	
Teapot stand (part of a service)	B	JMT	John and Mehitable (Bacon) (Lawless) Templeman	1792	Puig et al. 1989, no. 221	MIA
Teapot stand (see matching teapot)	B	MA (+)		ca. 1790	Parke-Bernet, 12 January 1946, lot 49	
Teapot stand (see matching teapot)	B	none		ca. 1795	Sotheby's, 17 November 1981, lot 166	
Teapot stand (see matching teapot)	B	DD SH		ca. 1790	DAPC 75.2422	VMFA
Teapot stand (see matching teapot)	C or D		Moses Michael Hays for Sally Hays	ca. 1796	Buhler 1976, 9–10	
Teapot stand (see matching unmarked teapot; part of a service)	C or D	JAB	Joseph and Anna Blake	1793	Hammerslough/ Feigenbaum 1958–73, 1:68–69	
Teapot stand (see matching teapot; part of a service)	D	EH	Fellow Boston citizens for Edmund Hartt	1799	Buhler 1972, no. 414	MFAB
Teapot stand (see matching teapot)	D	JH	Moses Michael Hays for Judith Hays	ca. 1796	Buhler 1960, no. 115	USDS
Teapot stand (see matching teapot with mark C)	D	H	Jonathan Hunnewell	1796	Avery 1920, no. 303	MMA
Teapot stand (see matching teapot)	?	LW/to/PW	Leonard White for Peggy (White) Bartlett	1786	Norman-Wilcox 1954, 50	
Teapot stand (attrib.; marked and retailed by Joseph Loring; see matching teapot)	none	A	John and Katharine (Willard) Amory, Jr.	ca. 1795	*Paul Revere* 1988, no. 52	MFAB
Twelve teaspoons (mates? below)	B	SSP	Samuel and Sarah (Rogers) Parkman	1795	*American Silver* 1967, no. 23	RWNAG
Two teaspoons (mates? above and below)	B	SSP	Samuel and Sarah (Rogers) Parkman	1795	Buhler 1972, no. 397	MFAB

	Mark	Inscription	Patron	Date	Reference	Owner
Teaspoon *(mates? above)*	B (?)	SSP	Samuel and Sarah (Rogers) Parkman (?)	1795		ChM
Six teaspoons	B*	D/IB		ca. 1785	Hammerslough/ Feigenbaum 1958–73, 3:126–27	
Six teaspoons	B	EAD		ca. 1785		MFAB
Teaspoon (mates below)	B*	EB to EBC		ca. 1775	*Sack Collection* 3:716	
Two teaspoons (mate above)	B	EB to EBC		ca. 1775	YUAG files	
Two teaspoons	B	LD to/EB		ca. 1785	Buhler 1972, no. 378	MFAB
Teaspoon	B	M/IK		ca. 1780	YUAG files	
Teaspoon	B	JK		ca. 1785	DAPC 79.3676	CM
Four teaspoons *(see also mates with mark E)*	B	SP	Sarah (Chandler) Paine	ca. 1780	DAPC 73.2254	
Twelve teaspoons	C	MRH	Moses Michael and Rachel (Myers) Hays	ca. 1790	Christie's, 17–18 January 1992, 94	USDS
Two teaspoons	D	MP		ca. 1775	*Moore Collection* 1980, no. 146	
Teaspoon	D*	JSH		ca. 1790	YUAG files	
Two teaspoons (mates below)	E	F	Anne (Frances) Trott	ca. 1806	Buhler 1972, no. 422	MFAB
Two teaspoons *(mates above and below)*	E	F	Anne (Frances) Trott	ca. 1806	Buhler 1965, 108–09	HMA
Two teaspoons *(mates above and below)*	E	F	Anne (Frances) Trott	ca. 1806	Buhler 1979, no. 62	WAM
Six teaspoons (mates above)	E	F	Anne (Frances) Trott	ca. 1806	Hammerslough/ Feigenbaum 1958–73, 1:113	
Three teaspoons	E	SD		ca. 1790	Buhler 1972, appendix no. 70	MFAB
Six teaspoons *(see also mates with mark B)*	E	SP	Sarah (Chandler) Paine	ca. 1780	Buhler 1979, no. 58	WAM
Teaspoon	E	I/IS		ca. 1785	Avery 1920, no. 322	MMA
Teaspoon (mates below)	E	NAG	Nathaniel and Abigail (Odlin) Gilman	ca. 1785	Buhler 1972, no. 379	MFAB
Two teaspoons *(mates above and below)*	E	NAG	Nathaniel and Abigail (Odlin) Gilman	ca. 1785	WAM 1965, no. 20	
Teaspoon *(mates above and below)*	E (?)	NAG	Nathaniel and Abigail (Odlin) Gilman	ca. 1785	MFA 1906, no. 233 ¹/₂	
Two teaspoons *(mates above)*	E (?)	NAG (?)	Nathaniel and Abigail (Odlin) Gilman	ca. 1785	*Antiques* 72 (December 1957): 504	
Eleven teaspoons	E	AQ	Abigail (Phillips) Quincy	ca. 1790	Parke-Bernet, 17 October 1972, lot 116	

	Mark	Inscription	Patron	Date	Reference	Owner
Teaspoon	E	JW/to/RD		ca. 1785		MWPI
Two teaspoons (mates below)	E, F, or G	PM/to/EC	Philip Marrett	ca. 1775		CF
Teaspoon (mates above and below)	E, F, or G	PM/to/EC	Philip Marrett	ca. 1775	Parke-Bernet, 28 October 1969, lot 116	
Teaspoon (mates above)	E, F, or G	PM/to/EC	Philip Marrett	ca. 1775	MFA 1906, no. 235	
Teaspoon (see also unmarked mate)	E, F, or G	J(?)ML		ca. 1785		MFAB
Teaspoon	E, F, or G	L		ca. 1790	American Art Association–Anderson Galleries, 12 March 1938, lot 34	
Teaspoon	E, F, or G	AMC		ca. 1785		MFAB
Teaspoon	E, F, or G	unidentified crest, a lion's head crowned		ca. 1785		MFAB
Teaspoon	E, F, or G	erased		ca. 1785		MFAB
Two teaspoons	E, F, or G	SA		ca. 1790	MFA 1911, no. 904	
Teaspoon	E, F, or G	AJK		ca. 1785	DAPC 71.3049	WM
Teaspoon	E, F, or G	JSR		ca. 1785	DAPC 77.2856	
Teaspoon	E, F, or G	unidentified crest		ca. 1775	Shepard 1978, 228	MAM
Nine teaspoons	E, F, or G	ISH		ca. 1775	*Moore Collection* 1980, no. 148	
Ten teaspoons	E, F, or G	AA	Anna Amory	1796	*Paul Revere* 1988, nos. 70–79	PRMA
Six teaspoons	E, F, or G	JSD		ca. 1805	WAM 1965, no. 24	
Eleven teaspoons	E, F, or G	Orne crest, a unicorn emerging from a ducal coronet	William Paine for Lois Orne	1773	Buhler 1979, no. 56	WAM
Two teaspoons (mates below)	E, F, or G	NDG	Nathaniel and Dorothy (Folsom) Gilman	ca. 1800		BBC
Teaspoon (mates above and below)	E, F, or G	NDG	Nathaniel and Dorothy (Folsom) Gilman	ca. 1800	YUAG files	
Six teaspoons (mates above)	E, F, or G	NDG	Nathaniel and Dorothy (Folsom) Gilman	ca. 1800	YUAG files	
Teaspoon	F†	MLS		ca. 1785	Buhler/Hood 1970, no. 250	YUAG
Teaspoon	F*	D		ca. 1790		YUAG
Teaspoon	F*	Madey arms, azure	Madey family	1792	DAPC 68.2291	SI

	Mark	Inscription	Patron	Date	Reference	Owner
		a lion's head affrontée holding a bar in two paws, and crest, a crown				
Teaspoon (mates below)	F	Sargent crest, a dolphin embowed	Sargent family	ca. 1775	Quimby 1995, no. 113b	WM
Teaspoon (mates above and below)	F	Sargent crest, a dolphin embowed	Sargent family	ca. 1775	YUAG files	
Teaspoon (mates above)	F*	Sargent crest, a dolphin embowed	Sargent family	ca. 1775	Buhler 1976, 6–7	VMFA
Three teaspoons (mate below)	F	SSE	Sarah (Sargent) Ellery (?)	ca. 1785	WAM 1965, no. 23	
Teaspoon (mates above)	F	SSE	Sarah (Sargent) Ellery (?)	ca. 1785	Christie's, 18 October 1986, lot 82	
Two teaspoons	F	SG		ca. 1790	Parke-Bernet, 4 January 1940, lot 35	
Teaspoon (mate below)	F*	ID		ca. 1790		PEM
Teaspoon (mate above)	F (?)	ID		ca. 1790	Quimby 1995, no. 113c	WM
Teaspoon (mates below)	F	JMT	John and Mehitable (Bacon) (Lawless) Templeman	1792	Quimby 1995, 113a	WM
Two teaspoons (mates above and below)	F	JMT	John and Mehitable (Bacon) (Lawless) Templeman	1792	Puig et al. 1989, 274	
Teaspoon (mates above)	F	JMT	John and Mehitable (Bacon) (Lawless) Templeman	1792	Sotheby Parke Bernet, 15–17 November 1973, lot 698	
Teaspoon	F (?)	PW		ca. 1790	Parke-Bernet, 11 February 1970, lot 184	
Two teaspoons	G	ED		ca. 1810	Parke-Bernet, 16 March 1971, lot 138	
Two teaspoons	G*	MP		ca. 1790	YUAG files	
Teaspoon	G*	AB		ca. 1775		SI
Teaspoon	G	JRC		ca. 1785	Sotheby Parke Bernet, 16–18 November 1972, lot 110	
Teaspoon	H	MF		ca. 1775	Avery 1920, no. 139	MMA
Teaspoon	H	G/HK		ca. 1770	MFA 1906, no. 229	
Teaspoon	?	?		ca. 1760		ChM
Teaspoon	?	?		ca. 1795	Shelley 1958, 174–75	HFM
Two teaspoons	?	?		ca. 1770	Shelley 1958, 174–75	HFM

	Mark	Inscription	Patron	Date	Reference	Owner
Teaspoon	?	Belcher crest	Belcher family	ca. 1775		BBC
Three teaspoons	?	initials erased		ca. 1785	*Antiques* 87 (February 1965): 143	
Two teaspoons	?	B/JE		ca. 1785	*Antiques* 88 (July 1965): 15	
Teaspoon	?	I.S. to E.M.		ca. 1775	Parke-Bernet, 28 October 1969, lot 122	
Teaspoon (attrib.; see also mate marked E, F, *or* G)	none	J(?)ML		ca. 1785		MFAB
Six teaspoons (attrib.; with mark of Nathaniel Austin)	none	HC	William Smith for Hannah Carter	1787	Buhler/Hood 1970, no. 248	YUAG
Thimble (gold; attrib.)	none	Maria Revere Balestier (later)	Revere family	ca. 1805	Buhler 1972, no. 423	MFAB
Thimble (gold; attrib.)	none	LD (later)		ca. 1805	Christie's, 19–20 January 1990, lot 219	
Tongue depressor	C *or* D	none		ca. 1785	Gourley 1965, no. 173	
Tray	D*	EHD	Elias Hasket Derby	1797	Buhler/Hood 1970, no. 259	YUAG
Tray	D*	BJB; Benjamin and Judith Bussey	Benjamin and Judith (Gay) Bussey	ca. 1800	Buhler/Hood 1970, no. 261	YUAG
Two-handled cup	A	HC (+)		ca. 1775	DAPC 68.5298	
Urn	B	BAC	Burrell and Anne (Zeagers) Carnes	1793	Buhler 1972, no. 392	MFAB
Urn	B*	HR	Hannah (Speakman) Rowe	1791	*MMA Bulletin* (Fall 1991): 58–59	MMA
Urn	C *or* D	To/PERPETUATE/The Gallant defence/Made by/Capt GAMALIEL BRADFORD./in the Ship Industry on the 8th of July 1800/when Attacked by four French Privateers/in the Streights of Gibraltar./This URN is Presented to him/by/SAMUEL PARKMAN	Samuel Parkman for Gamaliel Bradford	ca. 1800	*Witness to America's Past*, no. 104	MHS
Waste bowl	B	TJL (+)	Thomas and Jane (Miller) Lee	ca. 1785	Buhler 1972, no. 374	MFAB
Waste bowl	D	SS	Sarah (Swan) Sullivan	ca. 1800	Buhler/Hood 1970, 1:197	
Waste bowl	D*	BMF		ca. 1795	Warren 1975, no. 318	BBC
Waste bowl	?	TB		ca. 1790	*Antiques* 109 (June 1976): 1165	

	Mark	Inscription	Patron	Date	Reference	Owner
Wedding ring (gold; attrib.)	none	[L]IVE Co[n]tented (defaced)	Paul Revere, Jr.	1773	Buhler 1972, no. 362	MFAB
Whistle with coral (missing coral)	D*	none		ca. 1800	Buhler 1972, no. 419	MFAB
Whistle with coral and bells	E, F, or G	none		ca. 1795	Buhler 1972, 2:469	
Wine cup	B	The Gift of the Revd Mr Thos. Prince to the/South Church in Boston/ who was ordained Pastor of said/ Church Oct:1th 1718 & died/Oct: 22. 1758 AE 72	Old South Church, Boston, for Rev. Thomas Prince	1758	Jones 1913, 50–51	
Four wine cups	B	MRH	Moses Michael and Rachel (Myers) Hays	1792	Buhler 1960, no. 107	
Two wine cups	B	NMT	Nathaniel and Mary (Lee) Tracy	1782	Buhler 1972, no. 369	MFAB
Wine cup (mates below)	C	AMC	Andrew and Mary (Lewis) Cunningham	ca. 1796	Shepard 1978, 228	MAM
Wine cup (mates above and below)	C	AMC	Andrew and Mary (Lewis) Cunningham	ca. 1796	*Antiques* 111 (May 1977):928	
Two wine cups (mates above and below)	C*	AMC	Andrew and Mary (Lewis) Cunningham	ca. 1796	Lippert 1982, 41–43	
Wine cup (mates above)	C (?)	AMC; CC to JL 1871 (later) (+)	Andrew and Mary (Lewis) Cunningham	ca. 1796	Lippert 1982, 44	
Two wine cups (attrib.)	none	The Gift.of his Honour. Moses Gill Esqr/to the Church of Christ.in Prince-Town./1796	Moses Gill and/or First Congregational Church, Princeton, Mass.	1796	Gourley 1965, no. 164	
Two wine cups (attrib.)	none	The Gift of the Honble Artemas Ward, Esqr/to the Church of Christ in Shrewsbury, 1796	Artemas Ward for Congregational Church, Shrewsbury, Mass.	1796	Jones 1913, 447–48	

§ Possibly made by Paul Revere, Sr.

1. RC 24:218; Wyman 1864–65, 19:235. For more in-depth information on Revere, see Federhen 1985 and *Paul Revere* 1988; Goss 1891, 11.

2. Forbes 1942, 27–28.

3. Babcock 1947, 192–93. The inventory of his estate taken in 1818 included a "Pew in the Brick Meeting House"; SCPR 116:315. Joseph Warren Revere purchased the Revere pew in Christ Church in 1808; Babcock 1947, 95.

4. Paul Revere to Mathias Rivoire, Letter, 6 October 1781, Revere Family Papers, MHS.

5. RC 30:25; Codman 1918, 198; *Index of Obituaries 1704–1800*, 1:252; Goss 1891, 25, 111. The Revere biographer Esther Forbes speculated that Sarah Orne was the daughter of John Orne and Martha Lackey; however, no birth record has been found. John Orne was a second cousin of Lois Orne of Salem, who married Dr. William Paine of Worcester in 1773. Paine commissioned Revere to make a large silver service for his bride, an important order that could have resulted from a family connection. The silver is in WAM. Forbes 1942, 485–86.

6. Forbes 1942, 486.

7. 2 November 1762, vol. 1, Waste and Memoranda Book, 1761–83, [13], Revere Family Papers, MHS.

8. Forbes 1942, 31–32.

9. SCD 116:128–29.

10. SCD 116:129–30.

11. Sarah Orne Revere was buried in the Granary Burying Ground; see Codman 1918, 197–98. RC 30:434.

12. Forbes 1942, 487; Walker Family Bible (from Bigelow-Phillips files, 1536). Richard Walker and Rachel Carlisle were married on 1 January 1742; RC 28:333. Rachel Walker Revere died on 26 June 1813 at the age of sixty-eight and was buried in the family tomb in the Granary Burying Ground; see Codman 1918, 197–98.

13. Codman 1918, 197–98; Forbes 1942, 487.

14. RC 22:452. The Revere family lived close to Benjamin Burt in North Square.

15. RC 22:201.

16. SCD 119:136–37.

17. SCD 181:155.

18. SCD 183:253–54; SCD 185:20–21.

19. SCD 191:225.

20. Revere Family Papers, MHS; *Paul Revere's Ride*, n.p.

21. Forbes 1942, 42–47.

22. Paul Revere to Mathias Rivoire, Letter, 6 October 1781, Revere Family Papers, MHS.

23. Leehey 1988, 29.

24. Revere was relieved of command in September 1779 as the result of the confusion surrounding this expedition. This decision was eventually reversed by a court–martial held in February 1782, and Revere was fully exonerated; Weisberger 1977, 35; Grant 1977, 5–11.

25. For a discussion of Revere's association with Freemasonry, see Steblecki 1988, 117–47.

26. SCD 128:180.

27. SCCR, Court of Common Pleas Extended Record Book 1784, 18–19.

28. Steblecki 1988, 122.

29. Whitehill et al. 1975, 18–19, 202, 204.

30. Fifty-six volumes of ledgers, daybooks, memoranda books, letter books, and accounts in the Revere Family Papers at MHS document his activities in the silver shop, foundry, hardware store, and rolling mill.

31. Fraudulent examples of Revere marks abound. For example, see: the pellet mark (B) on a skewer, spurs, and sugar basket at CMA (Johnston 1994, 128–129), on a snuffbox at YUAG (Buhler/Hood 1970, no. 254), and on a tankard at SI (383, 565); Revere in a rectangle (C) on a porringer and spoons at CMA (Johnston 1994, 127, 130), a creampot (1984.32.62), and a bowl (Buhler/Hood 1970, no. 249) at YUAG, and a creampot (26.025) at RISD; Revere in a clipped corner rectangle (D) on a tablespoon at CMA (Johnston 1994, 129); and PR script (E, F, or G) on teaspoons at CMA (Johnston 1994, 130–31).

32. SCCR, file 91313.

33. Flynt/Fales 1968, 248.

34. Josiah Collins to Paul Revere, Letter, 22 November 1774, Revere Family Papers, MHS.

35. Vol. 2, Waste Book, 1783–97, [77], Revere Family Papers, MHS.

36. Silver with Thomas Revere's unique engraving includes teapots made for Samuel Paine and Jonathan Hunnewell at MMA and two teapot stands and a sugar basket made for Jonathan Hunnewell at MFAB. For the creampot with Thomas Revere's mark, see Buhler 1972, no. 429. He is listed in the Boston directories as a silversmith from 1789 until 1803.

37. 13 August 1796, vol. 51, Memoranda, 1795–1803, Revere Family Papers, MHS. Edward Revere is listed in the Boston directories as a silversmith from 1796 until 1830.

38. Forbes 1942, 486.

39. Paul Revere to Isaiah Thomas, Letter, 8 May 1791, as cited in Buhler 1979, 56. Revere wrote, "Eayres . . . has a minde to carry on his business, which is a Gold Smith, in the Town of Worcester. . . . I can recommend him as an Industrious and Ingenious Tradesman, and of good morals, and I dare say, he will be an acquisition to the citizens of any town he may settle in, your Kind notice and advice to him will be received as done to myself."

40. According to Flynt/Fales 1968, 211, Eayres was able to operate a silver shop on Essex Street for a few years during the 1790s.

41. 31 October 1789, vol. 2, Waste Book 1783–97, [82], Revere Family Papers, MHS.

42. Flynt/Fales 1968, 242.

43. Paul Revere to Mathias Rivoire, Letter, 6 October 1781, Revere Family Papers, MHS.

44. 21 June 1781, vol. 1, Waste Book, 1761–83, [64], Revere Family Papers, MHS.
45. Account with Nathaniel Fellowes, July 1783, vol. 37, Invoices, 1783–91, Revere Family Papers, MHS.
46. Frederick William Geyer to Paul Revere, Shipping invoices, 22 August, 20 September 1783 and 12 February 1784, vol. 37, Invoices, 1783–91, Revere Family Papers, Letter Book, MHS.
47. Paul Revere to Frederick William Geyer, Letterbook, 3 November 1783, vol. 53, Revere Family Papers, MHS.
48. John Sampson to Paul Revere, Shipping invoices, 1784–86, vol. 37, Invoices, Revere Family Papers, MHS; John Sampson to Paul Revere, Letter, 2 February 1785, Revere Family Papers, MHS.
49. *Independent Chronicle*, 29 January 1784.
50. *American Herald*, 23, 30 May, 13 June 1785.
51. *American Herald*, 23, 30 January, 6, 13, February 1786; *Massachusetts Centinel*, 25, 28 January 1786; *Independent Chronicle*, 26 January, 2, 9 February 1786.
52. *Massachusetts Centinel*, 6, 13 June 1787.
53. *Boston Directory* 1789, 37; *Massachusetts Centinel*, 30 May, 6 June 1789.
54. *Boston Directory* 1796, 86.
55. *Boston Directory* 1798, 95; 1800, 91; 1803, 104; 1805, 104; 1806, 103; 1807, 126; 1809, 115; 1810, 163; 1813, 212; 1816, 179; 1818, 177.
56. Bigelow-Phillips files, 1535a.
57. Isaac Greenwood to Paul Revere, Account, 1757–61, loose manuscripts, Revere Family Papers, MHS.
58. Paul Revere to John Welsh, Account, 1761–65, Revere Family Papers, MHS.
59. SCPR, docket 12763.
60. 2 August, 5, 29 October 1762, vol. 1, Waste and Memoranda Book, 1761–83, [11], [12], [13], Revere Family Papers, MHS.
61. 16 April, 3 May, 19 November 1762 and 17 September 1767, vol. 1, Waste and Memoranda Book, 1761–83, [8], [13], [33], Revere Family Papers, MHS.
62. 18 February, 3, 19 May, 1 October, 19 November 1762, 22 June 1763, 14 September 1764, 10 June 1766, 9 January, 21 November, 1 December 1772, 11 February 1773, vol. 1, Waste and Memoranda Book, 1761–83, [5], [8], [9], [12], [13], [18], [23], [30], [39], [42], [43], Revere Family Papers, MHS.
63. Isaac Greenwood to Revere & Son, Receipt, 27 November 1793, Revere Family Papers, MHS.
64. May and 10 October 1792, vol. 51, Memoranda Book, 1788–95, Revere Family Papers, MHS.
65. Buhler 1972, nos. 309–12.
66. Dr. Baker advertised in the *Boston Gazette* on 22 January 1768 and again in April of that year, when he announced his imminent departure from Boston. In his advertisements Revere states that he learned to fix false teeth from John Baker; see Dow 1927, 55.
67. Isaac Greenwood to Paul Revere, Account, 1757–61, loose manuscripts, Revere Family Papers, MHS.
68. Newman 1967, 143–44.
69. 1 January 1773, vol. 1, Waste and Memoranda Book, [43]; 12 May 1787, 10 October, 2 December 1788, 15 November 1790, 21 May, 27 September, 5 December 1791, 13 March, 16 April, 24 June, 26 August, 8 November 1792, 5 March, 2 August, 18 December 1793, July, 12 October 1794, 24 October 1795, 10 February, 3 June, 16 July, 15 September, October 1796, 28 January, 9 February 1797, 7 February 1798, vol. 2, Waste Book, [57], [71], [73], [78], [83], [98], [106], [112], [114], [117–18], [122–23], [126], [128], [130], [132], [134], [140–41], [148], [151], [154–55], [157–58], [161–62], [165], Revere Family Papers, MHS.
70. For further information on Revere's activities as an engraver, see Brigham 1954.
71. *American Herald*, 23, 30 January, 6, 13, February 1786.
72. Simon Willard to Paul Revere, letters, 1782–86, Revere Family Papers, MHS; Bortman 1952.
73. Rising States Lodge Record Book, 5 December 1787; 12 August, 10 October 1788. Massachusetts Grand Lodge of Masons, Boston.
74. SCD 161:237–38.
75. SCD 175:144–45. A second deed for this transaction described the furnace as an "Air furnace"; SCD 175:145.
76. SCD 184:230–31, 236–37; SCD 197:77–78.
77. RC 22:4.
78. SCD 193:82–83; 222:22. Whitman unsuccessfully contested Revere's ownership of this property in December 1813; SCD 236:209.
79. SCD 222:17. He arranged a mortgage of $6,600 with the purchasers, to be repaid in three installments by 1810; SCD 222:23.

80. *Boston Directory* 1796, 86; 1798, 95; 1800, 91.

81. *Boston Directory* 1803, 104.

82. The trade card is illustrated in Moreno 1988, 100; Goss 1891, 557; Stickney/Stickney 1976, 6. Thirty-four Revere bells have been identified by the Stickneys, many still located in church steeples throughout New England.

83. For an in-depth analysis of Revere's copper rolling mill, see Moreno 1988, 95–115.

84. Samuel Paine to Paul Revere, 12 June 1790, Revere Family Papers, MHS.

85. *Gazette of the State of Georgia*, 11 May 1786.

86. Codman 1918, 197.

87. SCPR 116:246–50.

88. SCPR 116:315–17.

89. These numbers are tabulated from the daybooks. A detailed tabulation of all the objects listed in the daybooks can be found in Federhen 1988, 69. Revere also made other silver objects that do not appear in the daybooks.

90. Revere made fourteen types of spoons, including spoons for mustard, marrow, capers, ragout, dessert, and pap, as well as the more usual teaspoons, tablespoons, and salt spoons. In quantity, production of both holloware and flatware increased during the second period; however, holloware decreased significantly as a percentage of the total output from 16.6 percent to 8.9 percent, whereas flatware constituted more than 49 percent of the total, an increase of almost 14 percent.

91. On 17 November 1785 Revere was billed 8 shillings by Solomon Munro for "one day work a putting up plating mill" and 1 shilling and 8 pence for "16 feet joist" used to construct a frame for the mill, suggesting a mill of considerable size. Solomon Munro to Paul Revere, Bill, 17 November 1785, Revere Family Papers, MHS.

Paul Revere, Sr.
1702–54

A

B

C

D

E

F

Paul Revere, Sr., came from a Huguenot family in southwestern France. His grandparents Jean Rivoire and Magdeleine (Malapogne) Rivoire lived in Riocaud, a village near Ste.-Foye-la-Grande, a town about forty miles east of Bordeaux. The goldsmith's father, Isaac, married Serenne Lambert in 1694 and was relatively well-to-do. A private family record reveals that the goldsmith was born as Apollos Rivoire on 13 November 1702 and was baptized at Riocaud. At age thirteen he was sent by his parents to his uncle Simon Rivoire on the island of Guernsey, who arranged for his passage to Boston and his apprenticeship there. Apollos Rivoire arrived in Boston early in 1716 and was apprenticed to John Coney (q.v.).[1] In 1722 the inventory of Coney's estate included "Paul Rivoire's Time. about Three years and half as Indenture" valued at £30. The estate also received cash "for Pa' Rivoire's Time, more than it was prized at [£]10."[2] The Coney estate papers leave unclear who purchased Revere's time, but presumably he spent the next three and one-half years finishing his indenture with another Boston goldsmith.

On 19 June 1729 Revere married Deborah Hichborn (1703/04–77), a daughter of Thomas Hichborn (1673/74–1731), a joiner, and Frances Pateshall (ca. 1676–1749), who had been born in Boston on 25 January 1704.[3] In the 14–21 May 1730 issue of the *Boston News-Letter* a notice announced that "Paul Revere goldsmith is removed from Capt. Pitts at the Town Dock to the North end over against Col. Hutchinson's." Capt. Pitts perhaps was the silversmith John Pitts (q.v.). This new location may have been a property owned by his wife's parents because when his mother-in-law wrote her will on 10 September 1742 (proved 26 September 1749), she bequeathed her daughter Deborah Revere "¹/₂ years rent of the house she now lives in together with one fourth interest in the remainder of the property."[4] Revere and his wife were members of the New Brick Church, and their nine children were baptized there: Deborah (1731/32); Paul (1734) (q.v.); Frances (1736); Thomas (1738); Thomas again (1739/

G

40) (q.v. Appendix B); John (1741); Mary and Elizabeth (1743); and Elizabeth again (1744/45), who was to marry David Moseley (q.v.).[5]

Little written evidence documents Revere's silversmithing career. The Boston watchmaker Elijah Collins (q.v. Appendix A) sued Revere, Robert Pateshall, a leatherdresser, and John Pitts, a mariner, for a £100 debt due on a bond in 1737. The plaintiff was awarded £52.10 plus costs. The case was appealed and continued in the Supreme Judicial Court, where the defendants again lost.[6] On 18 November 1748 Rufus Greene (q.v.) paid Revere £45 for twelve silver spoons, noting "my silver being short."[7] A tablespoon marked by Revere also bears the mark IP (q.v., mark B). A tankard by Revere at Winterthur also has a cast terminal with the initials WS on the back, possibly for William Simpkins (q.v.), which suggests that Revere may have purchased component parts from Simpkins.[8] In 1753 Revere's wife and her sisters Mary Merritt and Frances Douglass sold three-fourth's interest in their father's estate to their brother Thomas Hichborn, father of the silversmith Samuel Hichborn (q.v.).

Paul Revere died intestate on 22 July 1754, and his epitaph in the Granary Burying Ground records his age as fifty-one years and eight months.[9] His widow appears to have lived with her son Paul from at least 1760 through 1764 because the latter charged her board in his accounts.[10] She died in 1777.[11]

Three initials marks have been attributed to this maker: PR in a shaped shield (A), found on a tankard dated 1726, and PR in a rectangle (B, C).[12] Four initial and full-name marks are also thought to be his: P·Revere script in a plain rectangle (D); P·Revere script in a shaped rectangle (E); P·REVERE in a scalloped rectangle (F); and P·REVERE in a plain rectangle (G). The latter mark may also have been used by his son Paul Revere, Jr. A fraudulent example of mark A exists.[13]   PEK

SURVIVING OBJECTS

	Mark	Inscription	Patron	Date	Reference	Owner
Cann	E*	C/WM/AG		ca. 1730	Buhler 1972, no. 147	MFAB
Cann	G	Edes	Thomas Edes (?)	ca. 1745	Buhler 1972, no. 154	MFAB
Cann§	G	M/IM		ca. 1750	MFA 1906, no. 227	
Caster	A	DT		ca. 1745	Buhler 1972, no. 151	MFAB
Caster§	C	D/CM; C/IM		ca. 1750	MFA 1911, no. 906 (as Paul Revere, Jr.)	
Caster	C†	EDLR/S		ca. 1740	YUAG files	
Caster§	G	G/ES; P/ZR	Zacharias and Rebecca Pool (?)	ca. 1750	Parke-Bernet, 16 March 1971, lot 126A	
Chafing dish	F†	G/TI M (altered to W/WR)	Thomas James and Mary (Dumaresq) Grouchy	ca. 1745	Buhler 1972, no. 152	MFAB
Creampot	B or C (?)	MH (+)	Mary Hitchbourn	ca. 1740	Buhler 1979, no. 18	WAM
Creampot	B or C	A/BH	Aspinwall family (?)	ca. 1750	CGA Bulletin no. 1 (1971): fig. 14	CGA

	Mark	Inscription	Patron	Date	Reference	Owner
Creampot	D*	none		ca. 1735	YUAG files	
Creampot	D*	E/BE		ca. 1740	Gourley 1965, no. 154	
Creampot §	F	The Gift/of/ME/to MB	Maria Barber	ca. 1750	Christie's, 22–23 January 1993, lot 228	
Creampot §	G	SC		ca. 1750	YUAG files	
Creampot §	G	M.S.L	Mary Spence Lowell	ca. 1750		MFAB
Milk pot (with cover)	A	none		ca. 1740	Buhler 1972, no. 150	MFAB
Pepper box	A	none		ca. 1730	Buhler 1979, no. 16	WAM
Pepper box	?	?		ca. 1725	Norman-Wilcox 1944, 22	
Porringer (child's)	A	DM; D Mason	D. Mason	ca. 1735	Buhler 1960, no. 101	
Porringer	A	S/AM; 1731	Andrew and Mary (Ronshon) Sigourney	1731	Buhler 1965, 52–53	
Porringer	A	M/BH	MacDonald family	ca. 1735	Buhler 1979, no. 17	WAM
Porringer	A	RC to EC AC (+)	Collins family	ca. 1735	YUAG files	
Porringer	D	Sallie Macintosh Tucker (later)		ca. 1740	Avery 1920, no. 134	MMA
Porringer	D *or* E	W Mᶜ./S		ca. 1750	*Antiques* III (April 1977): 660	
Porringer (mate? below)	E (?)	P/IM	John and M. Parsons	ca. 1745	*Antiques* 119 (February 1981): 275	
Porringer (mate? above)	E†	P/IM (altered to IP)	John and M. Parsons (?)	ca. 1745	Buhler/Hood 1970, no. 133	YUAG
Porringer §	G	SW		ca. 1750	Sotheby Parke Bernet, 16–18 November 1978, lot 413	
Two porringers §	G*	unidentified crest, a wyvern's head	Tristram Dalton	ca. 1750	Christie's, 22 June 1994, lot 71	
Porringer §	G	MP		ca. 1750	MFA 1906, no. 225	
Porringer §	G	unidentified arms, gules a saltire sable, and crest, a lion rampant; A/BH	Aspinwall family	ca. 1750	Avery 1920, no. 135	MMA
Porringer §	G	PGK (+)	Philip Godfrid Kast	ca. 1750	Sotheby Parke Bernet, 29 April–1 May 1981, lot 395A	
Porringer	G	AP		ca. 1745	Avery 1920, no. 133	MMA

	Mark	Inscription	Patron	Date	Reference	Owner
Porringer	?	MW		ca. 1740	*Antiques* 107 (January 1975): 55	
Two Salts §	C	E *or* G		ca. 1750		MFAB
Salt §	G	H/IM; WPM		ca. 1750	National Art Galleries, 3–5 December 1931, lot 425	
Saucepan	G	none		ca. 1745	Buhler 1972, no. 153	MFAB
Two pairs of sleeve buttons (gold)	B†	none		ca. 1730	Buhler/Hood 1970, no. 135	YUAG
Two strainer teaspoons	B *or* C	none	Second Church, Boston	ca. 1725	Bigelow 1917, 278	
Strainer	D	none		ca. 1750		MFAB
Strainer	G*	Simpson crest, a bird rising		ca. 1745	Buhler/Hood 1970, no. 134	YUAG
Sugar bowl	G*	none	Andrew Oliver, Jr.	ca. 1753	*Paul Revere* 1988, no. 5	HD
Tablespoon (mate below)	A	T/IS	John and Susanna (English) Touzell	ca. 1725	Buhler 1972, no. 146	MFAB
Tablespoon (mate above)	A*	T/IS	John and Susanna (English) Touzell	ca. 1725	MFA 1911, no. 853	
Tablespoon	A*	B/IE		ca. 1730		PEM
Tablespoon	A*	SB		ca. 1740	Quimby 1995, no. 110	WM
Tablespoon (with mark of IP*)*	A*	MB		ca. 1730	DAPC 70.3022	WM
Tablespoon (mate below)	G†	Sarah Dole	Sarah Dole	ca. 1740	Buhler 1972, no. 148	MFAB
Tablespoon (mate above)	G	Sarah Dole (+)	Sarah Dole	ca. 1740	Buhler 1972, 1:184	
Tablespoon §	G*	O/IE		ca. 1750	YUAG files	
Tablespoon	?	AF		ca. 1750	Christie's, 29–30 January 1980, lot 573	
Tankard	A*	W/IR; The gift of/ Cap.ͭ Henr.ʸ Love-bond/In building the/Ann Gally/1726	Henry Lovebond	1726	Warren/ Howe/ Brown 1987, 52	
Tankard	A	A Gift of Sarah Preston/To the Church in Dorches-ter/1805 (later)		ca. 1745	Jones 1913, 148	
Tankard	A*	C/JN		ca. 1745	Quimby 1995, no. 109	WM
Tankard	A†	R/EM (R later ?)		ca. 1740	Buhler/Hood 1970, no. 132	YUAG
Tankard	D	B/BM		ca. 1750	Christie's, 2 October 1982, lot 59	

	Mark	Inscription	Patron	Date	Reference	Owner
Tankard§	G	unidentified arms, per pale gules and argent, a lion rampant, and crest, a dexter arm embowed holding a battle-axe, impaling unidentified arms, sable on a chevron or between 3 arrows in pale, points in chief, 3 roundles		ca. 1750		MMA
Tankard	G	Rebecca Goodwill/ 1747; RG to LH (later)	Rebecca Goodwill	1747	Bigelow 1917, 338–40	
Tankard	?	C/EG; ship flying Royal Ensign		ca. 1750	*Silver Supplement* 1973, no. 71	
Teapot	A*	T/WB		ca. 1745	MFA 1911, no. 851	
Teapot	D†	Foster arms, a chevron or between 3 hunting horns, and crest, a dexter arm, armed and embowed, grasping a broken tilting spear; S.L. Robbins/1813 (later)	Lydia (Foster) Hutchinson or Lydia (Hutchinson) Rogers (?)	ca. 1740	Buhler 1972, no. 149	MFAB
Teapot	G*	none	John and Martha (Mountjoy) Pulling	ca. 1730	*Antiques* 120 (September 1981): 629	MFAB
Teapot§	G	?		ca. 1750		MFAB
Two-handled cup	F	Winslow crest, a tree trunk with new branches; WHW (later)	Winslow family	ca. 1750	*Antiques* 72 (August 1957): 102	

§ Possibly made by Paul Revere, Jr.
1. Leehey 1988, 16–20.
2. SCPR 22:813–16, docket 4641.
3. RC 24:22; RC 28:10, 151; SCPR 43:280; Codman 1918, 126–27; RC 9:128.
4. SCPR 43:280.
5. Wyman 1864–65, 19:235.
6. SCCR, Court of Common Pleas Record Book 1736–37, 592; Supreme Judicial Court file 46500.
7. Rufus Greene Account Book, 1748–74, n.p., entered under the date noted, Karolik-Codman Papers, MHS.
8. Skerry 1988, 45.
9. Codman 1918, 197.
10. 6 August 1761, 12 December 1762, 12 December 1764, 25 December 1764, vol. 1, Waste and Memoranda Book, 1761–83, fols. [5], [14], [21], [25], Revere Family Papers, MHS.
11. *Index of Obituaries, 1704–1800,* 1:252.
12. Buhler (1972, no. 145) attributed an additional initials mark, found on a miniature caudle cup, to Revere. The cup easily predates the beginning of Revere's career by seventy-five years and is unlikely to be his work.
13. The mark is found on candlesticks at SI (383.563).

Silas Rice
1749–1835

A

Silas Rice was born in Bolton, Massachusetts, on 6 August 1749, son of Abraham Rice, Jr. (b. 1725), a husbandman and gentleman of Framingham, Massachusetts, and Susanna Wilder (b. 1730) of Lancaster, Massachusetts, who married in Bolton on 18 December 1747.[1] His paternal grandparents were Abraham Rice, Sr. (1697–1777), of Sudbury, Massachusetts, and Patience Eames (1702–96). His maternal grandparents may have been Richard Wilds and his wife, Ruth, of Lancaster, Massachusetts.[2]

Where Silas Rice received his training is unknown. By the age of twenty-six, according to his enlistment and marriage records, Rice was living in Lancaster. Rice served at least three times in the revolutionary war; after answering the Lexington alarm in 1775, he saw duty twice in 1777.[3] Elisabeth Taft (b. 1750) of Uxbridge, Massachusetts, and Silas Rice's marriage intentions were published on 31 December 1775.[4] Elisabeth's parents were Gideon Taft (b. 1714/15), a "yeoman alias blacksmith," and his wife, Elisabeth, both of Uxbridge.[5] These events marked Rice's entry into adulthood, and the following year he made the first of many land transactions in which he identified himself as a goldsmith, alternately residing in Lancaster, Northborough, Worcester, and Shrewsbury, Massachusetts.[6] In 1783 he was identified as a goldsmith of Shrewsbury when he was sued for debt by Joseph Joseph, a weaver of Richmond, New Hampshire.[7]

Three of Rice's advertisements in the *Massachusetts Spy* between 1777 and 1803 reveal much about his silversmithing activities. In the first, he announced his business in Lancaster near the meetinghouse in the second parish, where he made and sold "SILVER SHOE and *Knee Buckles*; Silver Stock ditto, Broaches; Paste-Pins; Silver and Brass Sleeve Buttons, Copper and Brass SHOE and KNEE Buckles, Rings, Buttons and Earrings mended and cleaned at said Shop. Also, *Clock* and *Watches*. Many other articles done in the Gold and Silverway." Rice indicated that he would work "as cheap as he has done at any time within two years past," suggesting that he had opened his shop by 1775, if not earlier.[8]

A previously unknown silversmith from Sterling, Massachusetts, John Robbins (ca. 1756–1833), appears in deeds with Rice, which suggests some kind of relation between the two men. Robbins witnessed a deed in 1788 in which Rice purchased two lots of land in Lancaster with a "dwelling house and Barn and shop thereon"; two days later, Robbins purchased the same land from Rice.[9] Robbins may have been one of Rice's apprentices, and the purchase may have represented a mortgage arrangement between them.

In 1800, an advertisement announced Rice's move to Worcester, where he set up shop across from the courthouse. Rice stated that "he manufactures all sorts of Gold and Silversmith work and jewelry.—Watches repaired and cases gilt on the shortest notice. . . . Warranted Clocks made and sold at said shop."[10] After twenty-five years in Lancaster, Rice may have felt his business could benefit by a move to a prime location in the county seat. This advertisement also hints that by 1800 Rice may have been capable of making more than buckles and buttons for the more sophisticated and perhaps wealthier Worcester clientele. Rice's progression in his craft is also suggested by his announcement that he made his own clocks; in the earlier advertisement it was unclear whether he made them or repaired them.

A third advertisement in the *Massachusetts Spy*, which Rice placed in 1803, implied that the demand for his work was high enough to warrant additional help: "As he employs none but the most experienced workmen, he flatters himself shall give complete satisfaction to those who favor him with their custom."[11]

Given that these advertisements highlight a silversmithing career that spanned more than twenty-five years, silver by Rice is surprisingly difficult to identify. A spoon with the mark S RICE in a rectangle (A) may be the work of this maker. Two surname marks in scalloped cartouches have been attributed to this maker but now appear to be the work of the Baltimore silversmith Joseph T. Rice (1761–1808).[12] Perhaps the problem of identifiing silver by Rice's hand is better understood in light of a surviving invoice from the silversmith to the prosperous Worcester printer Isaiah Thomas. The bill describes various mending services performed by Rice from 1797 to 1806; the small amount of silver mentioned could have been made or retailed by him. The homely tasks detailed below contradict the bustling image of Rice's workshop imparted by his advertisements. Rather, the bill presents the reality of working life for even a successful silversmith in central Massachusetts.

1797	Mr Isaiah Thomas to Silas Rice	D^r
3 April	to 2 Silver thimbles 3/6 each	$ 1, 17
4 Nov.^{r}	to 3 Silver table Spoons	9,00
1798	3 Sept. to one water Hook	0,12, $^1/_2$
25	to mending Coffee pot	0,08
1800 Novr 1st	to mending Coffee pot	0,06
1801 May 16th	to clensing Jewells & mending ring	0, 34
19 June	to mending cullender	0, 25
5th Sept	to mending fan 9^d to mending Coffee pot 10^d	0, 19
22	to making canehead and finding Silver and Brass ferrel on the foot of the cane }	3,00
3 Oct^r	to repairing 3 Large Silver Spoons & polishing	0, 25
1803 March 31	to mending cream cup	0, 84
12 April	to mending teapot handle	0, 50
13	to making teapot handle	0, 67(?)
9 July	to making Brass boxes for pulley to Jack	0, 75
	to mending Gold Buttons	0, 58
2 August	to mending plated terret	0, 08
12	to mending teapot handle with Silver	0, 50
	to mending Coffee pot	0,12, $^1/_2$
26 Sept	to piecing Bolt to DoorLock Dld David Brown	0, 28
23 Dec.^{r}	to puting 2 Silver hoop on a tobacco Box	1,00
1804 15th May	to mending key	0, 12$^1/_2$
	to puting 2 Silver hoops on the Ivory of an umbrello	0, 25
1806 Jan 21.^{y}	to mending cream pitcher	0, 83
	deduct c.^{r} on backside	20.99 $^1/_2$
1806 April 2^d		6. 27

Rec^d payment in full of this acc.^{t} and all demands Silas Rice $14 72

On the reverse of the receipt:

1798	Mr Isaiah Thomas credit on the within account

Oct[r]   by 5 ounces and 14 penneyweight of old
                             Silver at one crown p[r] oz $ 6,27[13]

Silas Rice died in Millbury, Massachusetts, on 31 May 1835 and was buried
in the Old Burial Ground on the Worcester Common.[14] JJF

SURVIVING OBJECTS

	Mark	Inscription	Patron	Date	Reference	Owner
Teaspoon	A†	WMJG		ca. 1820	DAPC 70.1926	

1. *Framingham VR*, 167; Ward 1858, 86; WCD 37:61; 48:20; *Bolton VR*, 71, 164.
2. Ward 1858, 46; *Framingham VR*, 65, 362, 459, 461. The names of Susannah Wilder's parents
   were drawn from her birth record.
3. *Mass. Soldiers and Sailors* 13:182; *DAR Patriot Index* 1966, 1:567.
4. *Uxbridge VR*, 152, 297, 315; *Lancaster VR*, 136. The births of their five children are recorded
   in Ellis 1970, 229.
5. *Mendon VR*, 172; WCD 24:543.
6. WCD 75:348; 80:341–42; 84:23; 85:415; 90:107; 91:47; 93:41.
7. WCCR, Court of Common Pleas Record Book, vol. 11, 1782–84, 207.
8. *Massachusetts Spy*, 30 January 1777, repeated 6, 13 February 1777.
9. WCD 80:341–42; 84:23.
10. *Massachusetts Spy*, 6 August 1800, repeated 13, 20 August 1800.
11. *Massachusetts Spy*, 21 September 1803.
12. Goldsborough 1975, 194.
13. Invoice from Silas Rice to Isaiah Thomas, 2 April 1806, Isaiah Thomas Papers, AAS.
14. "Burial Grounds in Worcester," 109; Ward 1858, 86; *Index of Obituaries, 1784–1840*,
    4:3781.

Richard Richardson
1723–53[+]

Richard Richardson was identified as a goldsmith on a bond dated 12 October
1753 for the estate administration of William Millburn, a Boston mariner.[1] He
probably was the Richard Richardson born in Charlestown, Massachusetts,
on 24 January 1723 to Richard Richardson, a shipwright, and Ann Gretian.[2]
He may also have been the Richard Richardson who married Elizabeth Breed,
the sister of William Breed (q.v.), on 6 July 1749.[3] The estate of William
Breed's father mentions a daughter named Richardson.[4] It is probable therefore
that these two goldsmiths were brothers-in-law. Nothing further is known of
Richardson, and no silver by him has been identified. PEK

1. SCPR, docket 10578.
2. *NEHGR* 32:65; RC 28:115.
3. RC 28:261.
4. SCPR 59:286–88.

James Ridgway
ca. 1753–ca. 1800

James Ridgway probably was born in Boston about 1753 to James Ridgway
(1720?–63), a bricklayer of Boston, and Mary Brazer (1721–66 +) of Charlestown, Massachusetts, who wed in 1743/44. No record of Ridgway's birth exists
in Boston, but in guardianship papers pertaining to his father's estate in
1766 he is said to be under fourteen years of age.[1] The goldsmith's paternal
grandparents were John Ridgway (1693/94–1761) and Rebecca Knap (1696/97–
1736).[2] After Rebecca's death, his grandfather married Sarah Cowling in 1738.[3]

His maternal grandparents were Thomas Brazer (1691–ca. 1763) and Hannah Webb (b. 1694) of Charlestown.[4]

Ridgway may have been trained by John Coburn (q.v.), beginning his apprenticeship about 1767 and ending it about 1774. He apparently married two of Coburn's nieces from York, Maine: first, Sarah Coburn (1743–before 1779) in 1774, and second, Esther Coburn (1757–before 1791) in 1780.[5] Sarah Coburn was the daughter of Coburn's brother Joseph (b. 1714) and his first wife, Hepzibah Stone (1721–50); Esther Coburn was the daughter of Joseph and his second wife, Esther Rawlins.[6] No children are recorded from Ridgway's first marriage, but four are recorded from his second: Betsey in 1781, Sarah in 1783, James in 1786, and Esther in 1789.[7] The James Ridgway of Boston who served in the Revolution may have been the goldsmith.[8]

The Boston tax list of 1780 lists Ridgway in ward 5 with one poll and rents worth seventy pounds annually.[9] In 1784 he bought land near the Mill Pond in Boston, next to land he owned already.[10] In 1785 Thomas Barley sued Ridgway for debt, and Ridgway defaulted.[11] The James Ridgway listed in Boston town records as a fenceviewer in 1787 and 1788 may have been the goldsmith.[12] The *Boston Directory* of 1789 lists Ridgway as a goldsmith and jeweler on Friend Street.[13]

Ridgway's second wife must have died sometime between the birth of their fourth child, Esther, in 1789 and 27 January 1791, when Ridgway married Catherine Stimpson (b. 1758) of Reading, Massachusetts, the daughter of William Stimpson (1732–1808), a merchant, and his wife, Catherine.[14] Just prior to his marriage, Ridgway traded land with his sisters Mary and Hannah from their father's estate, mortgaged part to John Lathrop (paid off in 1796), and sold some to Thomas Whalley.[15] The piece sold to Whalley was described as having a shop, perhaps Ridgway's place of business. Ridgway may have left Boston to settle in Worcester, Massachusetts, shortly after his third marriage, for at a Boston town meeting on 26 September 1791, "Capt Nazro of Engine N°°. 6 proposes John Fessenden as an Engine Man in the room of James Ridgway who has left the Town."[16] The following advertisement appeared in the *Massachusetts Spy* for 15 August 1793:

JAMES RIDGEWAY
GOLDSMITH & JEWELLER, *from* BOSTON,
RESPECTFULLY informs his
friends and the publick, that he has removed
to the shop lately occupied by Mr. T. S. EAYRES,
nearly opposite the Court House, WORCESTER,
where he hopes to merit a continuance of their fa-
vours; and he assures them that every favour in
the line of his business, will be thankfully acknowledged.

The following November, when Ridgway purchased a tract of land near the courthouse through a mortgage, he is said to be "of Worcester."[17] However, when he and his wife, Catherine, sold land in Boston the next year, Ridgway is described as being "of Boston" again.[18] No record of his death has been found, but Ridgway probably was dead by 1800 because he is not mentioned in John Coburn's will, although his daughters Sarah and Esther Ridgway are.[19] The Catherine Ridgway who married Benjamin Smith of Boston on 1 November 1802 may have been Ridgway's widow.[20]

Although some authorities have claimed that the James Ridgway who married Faith Stowell, daughter of the clockmaker Abel Stowell, Sr. (q.v. Appendix A), in 1802 is the silversmith, that man was undoubtedly another James Ridgway (w. ca. 1809–25) who went on to work in Groton, Massachusetts, and Keene, New Hampshire.[21] The J·RIDGWAY mark sometimes attributed to the James Ridgway of Boston and Worcester probably was not used by him. The style of the mark suggests a nineteenth-century date. The James Ridgway who worked in Groton and Keene or the John Ridgway (1780–1851), possibly his brother, who worked in Boston in the nineteenth century are more likely to have used it. No silver by the earlier James Ridgway has been identified. PEK

1. SCPR 62:640; 63:85–86; 65:202–03, 320, 349; 66:438–40, 449; *Charlestown VR* 1:370; *NEHGR* 31:327.
2. *Charlestown VR* 1:160; Codman 1918, 199; RC 28:72; *Cambridge VR* 1:417; SCPR, docket 12851.
3. RC 28:228.
4. Wyman 1879, 1:117; *Charlestown VR* 1:257; *Braintree VR*, 663.
5. RC 30:435, 445; *York VR*, 63. Because Ridgway married a second time, in 1779, his first wife, Sarah, died before that date, although no record of her death has been found. Presumably, Ridgway's second wife, Esther, died before his marriage to Catherine Stimpson in 1791.
6. *York VR*, 15, 63, 127, 135, 372.
7. Bigelow-Phillips files.
8. *Mass. Soldiers and Sailors* 13:321.
9. "Assessors' 'Taking-Books,'" 27.
10. SCD 167:150–51.
11. SCCR, Court of Common Pleas Record Book 1785, 82.
12. RC 31:137, 163.
13. RC 10:197.
14. RC 30:313; *Reading VR*, 214–15, 435, 567; MCD 84:610–12.
15. SCD 169:32–34, 38–41.
16. RC 27:162.
17. WCD 118:504–05; 119:345.
18. SCD 179:106–07.
19. SCPR 101:99–105.
20. RC 30:204.
21. Flynt/Fales 1968, 311; Dresser 1935–36, 56. See *Worcester VR*, 414, for a record of the marriage. Parsons 1983, 121. The relationship of this James Ridgway to the silversmith from Boston and Worcester is unclear. It is unlikely to be the silversmith's son, who would have been only sixteen years old in 1802.

Seth Ring
d. 1792

A good deal of confusion exists surrounding the identity of this individual, but at least two possibilities appear credible.

There was a Seth Ring, identified as a goldsmith, who was buried in Salem, Massachusetts, on 29 March 1792. Although his birth is not recorded in the Salem vital records, he may have married Anne Paterson on 25 November 1770, and he may have been the father of the younger Seth Ring (discussed below).[1] (It is also possible that through an error in transcription, a man identified in a document from 1791 as Seth King might be this individual.)[2] The Massachusetts tax list of 1771 includes a listing for Seth Ring in Salem.[3] Seth Ring, "goldsmith," purchased a sixteen-by-fourteen-foot shop in Salem on 6 February 1778 from Edward Smith of Wheelersborough, Massachusetts, on land belonging to the blockmaker Joseph Chipman of Salem. Ring sold this shop on 26 April 1783 to Amos Hovey, a cordwainer from Boxford, Massachusetts.[4]

Henry Belknap identified Seth Ring (1773–1806) as a Salem jeweler.[5] However, several surviving bills and the probate records all indicate that although he was referred to as a brassfounder and occasionally as a goldsmith, he was a gunsmith by trade.[6] GWRW

1. *Salem VR* 6:187; 4:258; 2:238. An earlier child named Seth, baptized on 1 September 1771, presumably died as an infant, although his death is not recorded.
2. A Seth King, identified as a goldsmith from Portsmouth, New Hampshire, was one of 261 people "warned out" of Salem in 1791 by the Salem constables, acting under orders from the selectmen. The list of these individuals is printed in *EIHC* 43, no. 4 (October 1907): 345–52. The original document, said to be in the PEM collection, could not be found in 1982. King may have been a typographical error for Ring, although there was a John King, silversmith of Portsmouth, active in 1779 (see Flynt/Fales 1968, 262), and a King family of mathematical instrument makers was active in Salem (see Belknap 1927, 103).
3. Pruitt 1978, 140–41.
4. ECD 123:284; 137:216.
5. Belknap 1927, 113.
6. Seth Ring received payment from Ezekiel Hersey Derby in 1797 for twelve pounds of musket balls, and from Henry Price in 1798 for ten pounds of musket balls and four pounds of pistol balls; see Derby Family Papers, vol. 32, fols. 20, 28, PEM. He is consistently referred to as a gunsmith in the ECPR, docket 23778. The newspaper termed him a brassfounder and noted that he died suddenly; see *Salem VR* 6:187. He sometimes is referred to as a goldsmith in deed records (after the death of the other Seth Ring in 1792), an added source of confusion; see ECD 161:31; 177:112; 178:168; 179:133; 181:15, 21.

Daniel Rogers
1735–1816

A

B

C

D

E

F

G

For many years, American silver with the mark D·ROGERS with pellet in a rectangle was attributed to the silversmith Daniel Rogers (1753–92) of Newport, Rhode Island. In the 1960s, however, Martha Gandy Fales demonstrated that much, if not all, of this silver should properly be ascribed to a different silversmith with the same name, Daniel Rogers (1735–1816) of Ipswich, Massachusetts. Fales, beginning with a hunch based on the existence in the Essex Institute collection of church silver from Ipswich and Hamilton with the mark in question, established "first that there were two men named Daniel Rogers practicing the goldsmith's art at the same time, one in Newport and the other in Ipswich" and then discovered "an Ipswich history of ownership for silver bearing the mark D·ROGERS with pellet in rectangle." The results of her research were published in two articles in which she presented full particulars concerning the Ipswich Daniel Rogers. (She also identified a third Daniel Rogers working in New York City about 1835.)[1]

The first reference Fales found identifying a Daniel Rogers in Ipswich was a single sentence in the second volume of Thomas Franklin Waters's massive compendium *Ipswich in the Massachusetts Bay Colony*: "One goldsmith, Daniel Rogers, found room for his trade."[2] Fales subsequently discovered a large amount of primary material concerning Daniel Rogers, including a group of family papers in the collection of the Peabody Essex Museum. Her articles, which contain copious documentation, are only summarized here.

Rogers was born in Ipswich on 29 August 1735, the son of Richard (1703–42) and Mary (Crompton) Rogers (b. 1701/02). His first wife was Elizabeth Simpkins (1726/27–65), daughter of the Boston silversmith William Simpkins (q.v.), and Fales found it "impossible to resist speculation that Rogers might have served his apprenticeship to William Simpkins in Boston and married his master's daughter."[3] Daniel and Elizabeth were married on 23 October 1760 and had three daughters.[4] Simpkins's son Thomas Barton Simpkins (q.v.) was Rogers's brother-in-law.

H

I

J

After his first wife's death in 1765, Rogers married Elizabeth Rogers (1736–74), his cousin and daughter of the Reverend Nathaniel and Mary (Leverett) Rogers. They would have seven children, of whom only two survived. For his third wife, Rogers took Mary (Appleton) Leatherland (1745–1832), daughter of John Appleton of Ipswich, and they had five children born between 1776 and 1786.[5]

During most of his long working career, roughly from 1756 until the early years of the nineteenth century, Rogers was Ipswich's only goldsmith. Only from about 1771 to 1782 did he have any competition, in the person of Ebenezer Staniford (q.v.). At least two deeds refer to Rogers as a goldsmith, although he was also styled a merchant, gentleman, and esquire.[6] One of the earliest documents concerning his working life is a receipt dated 28 March 1760 and marked Newbury: "Receiv^d. of Mr Daniel Rogers of Ipswich twelve oz of Silver to make Nine large Spoons - - -p^r Jonathan Parsons Ju^r."[7] The diary of William Pynchon of Salem includes an entry dated 18 January 1781 that reads, "Sent to R. [mistake for *D*] Rogers, goldsmith, at Ipswich, a pattern for 6 teaspoons, and tea-tongs, by Mr. Dennis, the tongs to be 33 pwt."[8] The document suggests that Rogers was working during the Revolution, even though he served as a captain in the war. Fales notes several references to Rogers's active service as a member of the First Church of Ipswich, in which he owned two-thirds of a pew.[9]

Late in his career, Rogers seems to have specialized in the making of large quantities of gold beads for retail by a number of Boston and Essex County silversmiths. His account book detailing his activities in this regard from 1796 to 1800 is in the collection of the Peabody Essex Museum and indicates that he made an average of 354 strings of gold beads a year for his fellow craftsmen. William Homes, Jr. (q.v.), of Boston purchased a total of 915 strings and was Rogers's best customer, followed by Ebenezer Moulton (1768–1824), then of Boston, who accounted for 618 strings. Smaller amounts were purchased by Roger Evans (1768–1812), David Tyler (1760?–1804), Isaac Townsend (1760–1812), Joseph Loring (q.v.), and Samuel Minott (q.v.) of Boston, Samuel Davis (1765–1839) of Plymouth, and Joseph Moulton (1744–1816) (q.v.) and William Moulton (1772–1861) of Newburyport.[10]

Rogers died on 23 September 1816. His obituary was published in the *Salem Gazette* for 11 October 1816, noting his death in Ipswich at age eighty-one:

His surviving family mourn the departure of an affectionate husband and brother; society that of a valuable member; and religion of an ardent friend and a bright ornament. He loved the day, the house, the word, and the people of God. He was, more than half a century, a constant and devout attendant at the Lord's table. During his sickness and in his dying hour his faith in the Redeemer and his hope of immortality were his firm support. *He knew whom he believed and was persuaded that he was able to keep what he had committed to him till the decisive day.* His living and dying counsel, example, and prayers will be long remembered by his intimate friends, while they point out to them the path to heaven. *Blessed are the dead, who die in the Lord.*[11]

In his will, dated 6 May 1807, Rogers bequeathed to his sons Daniel and Richard "all my Shop Tools, except such of them as are calculated for Plate work, which I Order to be Sold." He also gave "To my Son Daniel . . . my Silver Tankard, To My Daughter Elizabeth Tallant [by his first wife] . . . the work'd Picture that was her Mothers, two Silver Spoons mark'd E.S. and also

6 work'd botom Chairs which were her mothers," and he made other bequests of money and real estate. His real estate included his dwelling house and outbuildings valued at one thousand dollars; his personal silver included two tablespoons, six teaspoons, and a pepper caster valued at a total of nine dollars.[12]

A reasonably large amount of silver bearing the ten marks (A-J) attributed to Daniel Rogers is known, much of it flatware. His holloware specialty seems to have been canns; five examples are in museum collections. A piece of gold by Rogers has been published, although no documented examples are known of the many gold beads that he made.[13] GWRW

SURVIVING OBJECTS

	Mark	Inscription	Patron	Date	Reference	Owner
Beaker	B*	The Gift/of/M^r. John & M^{rs}: Martha Thompson/to y^e-3^d./Church in Ipswich	David Thompson, executor of John Thompson's estate, for Congregational Church, Hamilton, Mass.	1781	Fales 1983, 32–33	PEM
Beaker (attrib.)	none	The gift of Capt Daniel Rindge/to the third Church in Ipswich	Daniel Rindge and/or Congregational Church, Hamilton, Mass.	ca. 1795	Fales 1983, 32–33	PEM
Cann	A, B, or C	unidentified arms (later)		ca. 1780	Silver Supplement 1973, no. 81	
Cann (mate below)	B*	F/IL; The Gift of/ Col. Robert Dodge/ and other members of the Church/in Hamilton (later)		ca. 1780	Fales 1983, 32–33	PEM
Cann (mate above)	B*	F/IL; The/Gift of the/Hon · Symond Epes . . .(later)		ca. 1780	Fales 1983, 32–33	PEM
Cann	B	unidentified crest, a unicorn; TML	Tobias and Mary (Stillson) Lear	ca. 1775	Ward/ Rowland 1992, 93	SB
Cann	B*	C/JE	Crowninshield or Derby family (?)	ca. 1790	Buhler 1972, no. 335	MFAB
Cann	B*	unidentified arms, on a bend sinister between 2 lions' heads erased 3 lozenges gules and argent, and crest a cross with a lozenge gules and argent; T/IM	John and Martha Thompson or John and Mehitable Treadwell (?)	ca. 1780	Gourley 1965, no. 174	RISD
Cann	?	unidentified initials		ca. 1775	Antiques 96 (September 1969): 317	
Creampot	E*	unidentified crest		ca. 1775	DAPC 76.2742	
Creampot	?	MH		ca. 1775	Christie's, 22 January 1993, lot 109	

	Mark	Inscription	Patron	Date	Reference	Owner
Ladle (pierced)	H*	MRD		ca. 1785	Buhler/Hood 1970, no. 268	YUAG
Locket (gold)	J†	RC		ca. 1760	Buhler 1972, no. 334	MFAB
Porringer	A *or* B	IH		ca. 1770		MFAB
Porringer (mate below; part of a service)	B*	K/ES	Kendall family (?)	ca. 1770	Johnston 1994, 132	CMA
Porringer (mate above; part of a service)	B*	K/ES	Kendall family (?)	ca. 1770	DAPC 73.3434	SFCAI
Porringer	E*	E. Lord/to/E. Slade (later)		ca. 1770	DAPC 76.2739	
Two porringer spoons (part of a service)	B	K/ES		ca. 1770	MFA 1911, no. 918	
Salt spoon	H†	R		ca. 1775	Fales 1967, 491, fig. 10	WM
Tablespoon	A*/B (?)	none		ca. 1775	Carpenter 1954, 191 (as Daniel Rogers, 1753–92)	
Two tablespoons	A/E	OR (+)		ca. 1775	DAPC 87.3049	
Tablespoon	A†/ E†	none		ca. 1775	DAPC 69.4198	WM
Tablespoon (mate below)	B*	D/BE	Barnabus and Elizabeth (Giddings) Dodge	ca. 1775	Fales 1965, 848	
Tablespoon (mate above)	B	D/BE	Barnabus and Elizabeth (Giddings) Dodge	ca. 1775	Fales 1967, 488	WM
Tablespoon	B	IP/to/LB/1779		1779	Fales 1967, 489, fig. 3	
Tablespoon	B	erased		ca. 1770	Fales 1967, 490, fig. 4	WM
Tablespoon	B	?		ca. 1775	Fales 1967, 490, fig. 6	WM
Tablespoon	B*	L/TR		ca. 1765	Buhler/Hood 1970, no. 265	YUAG
Tablespoon	B	Sam¹ Gidds/ob. 1777 AE 59/HG (altered to BG)	Samuel Giddings (?)	1805	Bigelow 1917, 274–75 (as Daniel Rogers, 1753–92)	WM
Tablespoon	B†	Joanna Good^he:/Ob. 1775 AE 52/HG (altered to BG)	Joanna Goodhue	1805	Bigelow 1917, 274–75 (as Daniel Rogers, 1753–92)	WM
Tablespoon	B	SW		ca. 1765	DAPC 68.2296	SI
Tablespoon	B	BA		ca. 1775	Fales 1967, 489, fig. 2	
Tablespoon	C	MP		ca. 1785	*Moore Collection* 1980, no. 78 (as Daniel Rogers, 1753–92)	

	Mark	Inscription	Patron	Date	Reference	Owner
Tablespoon	C	B/HM		ca. 1775	DAPC 69.4194	WM
Tablespoon	C†/ G†	S/HH		ca. 1775	Fales 1967, 490, fig. 7	WM
Tablespoon (mate below; part of a service)	C*/I* and K	EHC		ca. 1765	Buhler/Hood 1970, no. 266	YUAG
Tablespoon (mate above; part of a service)	C*/I*	EHC		ca. 1765		WM
Tablespoon	C*/I*	M/IR		ca. 1775	YUAG files	
Tablespoon	D†/ F†	JDH		ca. 1775	Fales 1967, 491, fig. 9	WM
Tablespoon	F, H, or J	LH; NJO (later?)		ca. 1785	*Moore Collection* 1980, no. 77 (as Daniel Rogers, 1753–92)	
Tablespoon	H	O (later)		ca. 1775	Fales 1967, 491, fig. 10	WM
Tablespoon	H*	?		ca. 1800	MFA 1911, no. 919	
Two tablespoons	J	ST	Sarah Thurston	ca. 1760	Buhler 1972, appendix no. 75	MFAB
Five tablespoons	?	?		ca. 1775	Christie's, 26 January 1985, lot 86	
Tankard	C (?)	DI	Dorothy (Jewett) Califf	ca. 1756	YUAG files	
Teaspoon	A, B, or C	?		ca. 1775	*Pennsylvania Museum Bulletin* 68 (June 1921), no. 226 (as Daniel Rogers, 1753–92)	
Teaspoon	B*	PW		ca. 1770	YUAG files	
Teaspoon	B	AD		ca. 1770	Fales 1967, 490, fig. 5	WM
Teaspoon	B*	PT		ca. 1765	DAPC 79.4497	
Teaspoon	E	AB; 4		ca. 1780		NM
Teaspoon	E*/I*	A/IA		ca. 1780	DAPC 73.1638	WM
Teaspoon	G*	C/RM		ca. 1775	DAPC 73.1632	WM
Two teaspoons	H*	MC	Mary (?) Cleaves	ca. 1800	DAPC 70.3163	
Teaspoon	H*	PG		ca. 1800	Eitner 1976, no. 384	
Teaspoon (mate below; part of a service)	I†	EHC (+)		ca. 1795	Buhler/Hood 1970, no. 267	YUAG
Teaspoon (mate above; part of a service)	I	EHC (+)		ca. 1795	DAPC 73.1640	WM

	Mark	Inscription	Patron	Date	Reference	Owner
Two teaspoons	J	ET	Thurston family	ca. 1760	Buhler 1972, appendix no. 76	MFAB

1. Fales 1965, 40–49, and Fales 1967, 487–91; quotation 487.
2. Waters 1917, 2:262.
3. *Ipswich VR* 1:315. Quotation from Fales 1965, 44.
4. *Ipswich VR* 2:372; 1:315–18; Fales 1965, 44.
5. Fales 1965, 44–45.
6. ECD 164:254; 166:240, cited in Fales 1965, 42.
7. Rogers Family Papers, PEM, cited in Fales 1965, 45.
8. *The Diary of William Pynchon of Salem,* ed. Fitch Edward Oliver (Boston: Houghton Mifflin, 1890), 84, cited in Fales 1967, 487.
9. Fales 1965, 43.
10. Daniel Rogers Account Book, PEM; Fales 1965, 44–45; Ward 1984a, 200–01. For an example of the kind of beads Rogers made, see Benes 1986, cat. 31.
11. *Ipswich VR* 2:661. Obituary quoted in Fales 1965, 43.
12. ECPR, docket 23975.
13. The Rogers marks are discussed in Fales 1967, passim, and in Belden 1980, 363–64.

Michael Rouse
1687–1711 +

Michael Rouse, son of the goldsmith William Rouse (q.v.) and Sarah (Kind) Rouse (1646–1705), was born in Boston on 12 October 1687 and baptized in the Second Church.[1] His father was an immigrant who apparently came to Boston from the town of Wesel, in Germany, and his mother was the daughter of Arthur and Jane Kind of Charlestown, Massachusetts.[2] The youngest of the Rouse children, Michael was eighteen when his parents died. Michael probably served the early part of his apprenticeship with his father prior to the latter's death in 1704/05. When his mother died in 1705, Michael chose David Farnum (b. 1662), a Boston merchant, as his guardian.[3] The connection between the Rouse and Farnum families is not clear, but David Farnum appraised William and Sarah Rouse's estates and was involved as a codefendant in a lawsuit with William Rouse, Jr., which suggests that he was a close family friend.[4] As Michael's guardian, Farnum would have helped the young man to find a master with whom to serve out his apprenticeship. He may have finished his training with Henry Hurst (q.v.), whose wife was the cousin of Michael's sister-in-law and who witnessed a deed between Michael's brother, the cooper William Rouse, and the mariner James Pitts in March 1706/07.[5]

Michael Rouse is mentioned in his mother's will, and according to the settlement of both parents' estates, as recorded in March 1706/07, he was to receive a share in the estate from his brother William (b. 1678).[6] Rouse's sister Elizabeth (1679–1706/07), a spinster, referred to her "Dear Brother Michael Rouse" in her will, dated 29 November 1706 and proved 22 January 1706/07.[7]

The last time Michael Rouse appears in Boston public records is in a deed of 8 September 1711, in which he is referred to as a goldsmith. By this deed, Michael Rouse, his sister Mary, and her husband, William Fasitt of Simpuxunt, Maryland, quitclaimed to their sister, Sarah Guille, widow of Noah Guille, their right in the real estate of their grandfather Arthur Kind.[8] Michael Rouse may have given up his right to his grandfather's estate because he was planning to leave Boston. Not yet married, he may have decided to move to Maryland with his sister and brother-in-law.

No silver by Michael Rouse is known to survive. BMW

1. RC 9:176.
2. Will of Sarah Rouse, SCPR 16:54–55. Sarah Rouse was born Sarah Kind and was married to William Tyer (d. 1667/68) and possibly to Robert Brickenton before she married William Rouse. The executors of her estate were: Sarah (Brickenton) Guille, her daughter by her second husband; Sarah's husband, Noah Guille; and Elizabeth Rouse, Sarah Rouse's daughter by William Rouse.
3. SCPR 16:210–11. The letter of guardianship is dated 26 November 1706.
4. SCPR 16:86–87, 88; SCCR, Court of Common Pleas Record Book 1706–10, 10, session for 7 January 1706/07.
5. SCD 23:126–27.
6. SCPR 16:54–55, 256–57.
7. SCPR 16:234–35.
8. SCD 26:53–54.

William Rouse
ca. 1640–1704/05

A

B

C

Jaspar Dankers, a Dutchman touring the American colonies in 1679 and 1680, wrote in his journal about visiting Boston: "We wanted to obtain a place where we could be at home, and especially to ascertain if there were no Dutchmen. They told us of a silversmith, who was a Dutchman, and at whose house the Dutch usually went to lodge. . . . His name was William Ross, from Wesel."[1] Rouse's tombstone records that he died on 20 January 1704/05 in his sixty-fifth year; presumably he was born about 1640, probably in Wesel, a town on the Rhine in the Duchy of Cleves adjacent to the United Netherlands.[2] He apparently learned his trade before coming to the New World. Rouse may have been in Boston as early as the late 1660s because he made a beaker for the Guilford, Connecticut, church from a legacy of Henry Kingsnorth, whose will was proved 4 November 1668.[3] The first evidence in public records of Rouse's presence in Boston is Richard Rogers's suit brought against him in 1676 for a debt of four pounds that Rogers claimed he was owed for two and three-quarters ounces of bad gold that he delivered to Rouse on 14 April 1676.[4]

Following his marriage to Sarah (Kind) Tyer (1646–1705), the daughter of Arthur Kind (ca. 1612–86/87), an innholder, and Jane Knaur (ca. 1624–1710) and widow of William Tyer (d. 1667/68), Rouse lived in the North End of Boston for the rest of his life.[5] No record of the marriage exists, but the couple's first child, Mary, was born on 29 December 1676.[6] The births of several subsequent children are also recorded in Boston: William (1678); Elizabeth (1679); and Michael (1687) (q.v.).[7] Rouse and his wife probably lived in one of the two adjoining dwelling houses near the meetinghouse in the North End that Sarah had purchased in 1667/68 following the death of her first husband.[8] According to a deposition given on 8 July 1704 by Rouse's neighbor Susannah Martin, Rouse's house burned at the time of the fire in the meetinghouse in the North End in 1676 and was subsequently rebuilt by him.[9] On 5 March 1676/77 Rouse, with the consent of his wife, Sarah, mortgaged a parcel of land in the North End—probably the land where the fire had occurred—to John Usher for seventy-five pounds; the mortgage was canceled in 1680.[10] Rouse may have mortgaged this property to his mother-in-law, Jane Kind, at some point because in 1694 she mortgaged "premises in the present tenure and occupation of William Rouse of Boston Goldsmith" in a deed witnessed by Benjamin Coney, possibly the silversmith and brother of John Coney (qq.v.).[11]

Rouse is listed on the Boston tax lists of 1681, 1687, and 1688, and on the list of inhabitants of 1695.[12] (The 1687 tax list shows him owing taxes of three shillings, five pence.) On behalf of residents of the north part of Boston, he and others petitioned the Suffolk County Court in 1694 about land in the estate of Thomas Clarke that they had contracted to buy in order to enlarge the meetinghouse.[13]

Dankers's comment that the Dutch usually lodged at Rouse's house is partly born out by Rouse's administration of the estate of Harmon Jonson, whose name suggests Dutch or Scandinavian ancestry. Jonson's will, in which he identifies himself as "now in Boston NE late an Inhabitant in Jamaica," was witnessed by Sebastian Baubience, possibly a Huguenot, and Frans Cornelijsen, probably also a Dutchman.[14] In the executor's account, presented by Rouse on 30 January 1678, he noted that Jonson owed nine weeks' board to him.[15]

Rouse was active in civic affairs. In the accounts John Hull (q.v.) kept for disbursements during King Philip's War, he paid Rouse on 24 August 1676, which suggests that Rouse participated in this military campaign.[16] He also took the oath of allegiance in 1678.[17] He was elected a Boston selectman in 1686, a surveyor in 1689, overseer of chimneys in 1690, and constable in 1691.[18] He signed three surety bonds, two of them for family members: for Simon Lebush in 1684; for Mary Salmons, a relative of his wife's, in 1686/87; and for Noah Guille in 1701, who married Rouse's stepdaughter Sarah.[19]

A number of lawsuits reveal Rouse's contentious and probably aggressive nature. The 1676 suit discussed earlier was concluded in favor of Rogers, the plaintiff. Rouse filed a suit in 1681 against Thomas Hanches for breaking the leg of Rouse's apprentice or journeyman, Thomas Wyllys (q.v.), and thus depriving Rouse of his servant's services.[20] Rouse sued Bernard Randolph in 1683/84, but the details of the case are not clear.[21] In 1686 William Thurloe sued Rouse for withholding £100 pounds, which his wife, Jane (Tyer) Thurloe (Rouse's stepdaughter), was to have received from her father's estate. The court ruled in favor of the plaintiff, and Rouse was to pay £59.17 plus costs of 52 shillings and 6 pence.[22] In his last years, Rouse was involved in two more suits. In the first Rouse sued the Boston mariner John Halsey, who was bound to Rouse for £500 and who was also the master of Rouse's son James. Rouse apparently sought James's share of bounty from privateering voyages and managed to recover £4.15. Rouse probably undertook the suit because James, who is not recorded in his mother's will of 1705, may have died in this venture.[23] In 1704 the heirs of Michael Martin sued Rouse for having encroached on Martin's land when Rouse rebuilt his house after it burned in the fire that destroyed the meetinghouse in the North End. According to Susannah Martin's deposition, Rouse told her that his house frame would extend an inch or so onto her land, but when the house was completed the Martins found it extended much more than that. They claimed that Rouse did nothing to compensate them for the incursion.[24]

Rouse died intestate, and his estate was appraised in October 1705, with the combined value of the real and personal property amounting to £575.11.6. John Coney appraised the tools in the shop at £12.5. Once debts and expenses were paid by his surviving executor, William Rouse, Jr., little was left of the personal estate, although the housing and land remained, valued at the substantial sum of £450.[25]

During his thirty-year career in Boston, Rouse produced some remarkable pieces of silver and was accepted by other members of the craft community in spite of being an immigrant whose native tongue was not English. In addition to possibly training Thomas Wyllys and Benjamin Coney (or employing them as journeymen), Rouse also must have been well acquainted with Timothy Dwight (q.v.) because he served as a bearer at Dwight's funeral in 1692 and appraised his estate. Rouse probably also trained his son Michael but died before Michael would have completed his apprenticeship. Graham Hood has observed that Rouse's small body of work is beautifully executed and attests to his skill with the graver.[26] Three marks have been attributed to this maker: WR in a circle (A); WR in a shaped cartouche (B); and WR in an oval (C). PEK

SURVIVING OBJECTS

	Mark	Inscription	Patron	Date	Reference	Owner
Beaker	A†	HK	First Congregational Church, Guilford, Conn., for Henry Kingsnorth	ca. 1680	Jones 1913, 192–93	
Beaker	B*	John Gengen; The Gift of/John Gengen . . . (later)	John Gengen and/or First Church, Dorchester, Mass.	ca. 1685	Jones 1913, 144–45	
Cup	B	LF	Lydia (Turell) Foster	ca. 1685	Buhler/Hood 1970, 1:11	
Cup	B*	T/IR		ca. 1690	Quimby 1995, no. 117	WM
Cup	B*	M/EE		ca. 1690	Buhler 1956, no. 127	DIA
Patch box	C†	LF	Lydia (Turell) Foster (?)	before 1689	Buhler/Hood 1970, no. 6	YUAG
Skillet	B†	Foster arms, a chevron or between 3 hunting horns	John and Lydia (Turell) Foster	ca. 1685	Hood 1968, 879–81	YUAG
Two sucket forks	C	F/IL	John and Lydia (Turell) Foster	ca. 1685	Cutten 1950, 441	MFAB
Tankard	B*	unidentified arms; May 8 1692; E/AR (later)		1692	*Antiques* 31 (April 1937): 175	LACMA
Tankard	B*	D/WE (later)	Joseph Dudley (?)	ca. 1685	Buhler/Hood 1970, no. 5	YUAG

1. *Memoirs of the Long Island Historical Society*, vol. 1, 1867, 378–79.
2. Whitmore 1878, 15, no. 282.
3. Jones 1913, 192–93.
4. Colonial Society 1933, 30:689.
5. Sarah and William Tyer had a daughter Jane; see SCPR 5:82. Sarah (Kind) Tyer may have been married a second time to Robert Brickenton before she married Rouse. Although the marriage is unrecorded, her daughter was identified as Sarah "Bricknidine" when she married Noah Guille in 1701; see RC 28:4. A Sarah was born to Robert and Mary [*sic*] Brickenton on 3 September 1669; see RC 9:110.
6. RC 9:23, 139; Whitmore 1878, 34, nos. 642–43.
7. RC 9:146, 149, 176. They may also have had other children whose births were not recorded because the Bigelow-Phillips files, 116, list the deaths of Rachel and James.
8. SCD 21:411–14.
9. Mass. Archives 8:158.

10. *Suffolk Deeds* 10:52–55.

11. SCD 16:408–10.

12. RC 1:69, 87, 137, 167.

13. SCCR, file 2737.

14. SCPR 6:414–15.

15. SCPR 12:260.

16. John Hull Ledger, vol. 2, fol. 442, NEHGS.

17. RC 29:167.

18. RC 7:189, 196, 197, 201, 205.

19. RC 11:1, 8; for Lebush and Salmons see Boston. Strangers, MHS; RC 10:80.

20. SCCR, Supreme Civil Court 1680–92, 49.

21. SCCR 1940, 46.

22. SCCR 1940, 60.

23. SCCR, file 6043; SCPR 16:54–55, docket 2942.

24. SCCR, Court of Common Pleas Record Book 1701–06, 168, 191; Mass. Archives 8:158.

25. SCPR 18:86–87, 236–37.

26. Hood 1968, 880.

Daniel Russell, Sr.
1698–ca. 1780

A

B

C

Previous silver scholars have failed to differentiate between the careers of Daniel Russell, Sr., and Daniel Russell, Jr. (ca. 1727–78), both of whom were silversmiths.[1] The father was the son of the Reverend Samuel Russell (1660–1731) and his wife, Abigail Whiting (1666–1733), of Branford, Connecticut. The fifth of seven children, Daniel was born on 19 June 1698.[2] According to Ezra Stiles, Daniel Russell served his apprenticeship with John Dixwell (q.v.) of Boston, son of the John Dixwell, alias Davids, who was one of the judges who condemned Charles I to death.[3] When the elder Dixwell first came to the colonies after the Stuart Restoration, he and two of the other regicides took refuge with the Reverend John Russell (ca. 1626–92) of Hadley, Daniel's grandfather.[4] His maternal grandfather, John Whiting (d. 1689), was also a minister in Hartford, Connecticut.[5] Moody Russell and Joseph Russell (qq.v.) were his first cousins, and Eleazer Russell (q.v.) was his uncle.

Daniel Russell may have worked as a journeyman for Dixwell or others in Boston for a while after he achieved his freedom about 1719. It also has been said that Russell went to Newport, Rhode Island, immediately after finishing his training because he is thought to have made a baptismal basin for the First Trinity Church of Newport in 1718; however, no evidence substantiates the date. The similarity of the engraving on that basin to that on another basin by Russell and on flagons by Benjamin Brenton (1710–66) made circa 1733 and 1734 suggests that all this silver was made at about the same time.[6] Russell also is said to have married Mary Rumrell (ca. 1703–45) in the First Trinity Church in Newport, in 1722, but no record of this marriage has been found.[7] The first evidence of him in Newport is the record of his having been made a freeman in 1732.[8] He may have trained his cousin Jonathan Otis (q.v.). Russell is identified as "of Newport, goldsmith," in a court document of 1745, when he sued the vendue master Benjamin Church of Boston for thirty-four pounds.[9] He was declared non compos mentis in 1750, and his son Daniel Russell, Jr., became his guardian.[10] It was probably the son, Daniel, who advertised in 1769 that he was selling his stock at low prices at his shop in Thames Street, next door to Peleg Thurston, because he intended to go out of business.[11]

Ezra Stiles mentions Daniel Russell, possibly the father, as one of his Newport parishioners whom he visited regularly during the 1770s.[12] On 9 May

1780 Stiles recorded the inventory of a Daniel Russell's estate in one of his diaries. It included the following list of items in the shop:

> Left in the Garret of DR^s House
> 12 large Silversmiths Tools
> Some Window Sashes Glaz'd, 1 Old Table
> and 2 Cider Tubbs
> In the Shop with S.R.
> 1 large Anvil
> 1 Teast & Block, 2 Swages
> 1 large Vice, 1 Beak Iron
> 1 Draw Bench & Tongs, 1 large Ladle
> 2 p forging Tongs, 2 p kneeling d^o
> 2 Ingotes, 1 Melting Ladle
> 1 Iron Poker 7 Ring Stakes & Stand
> 2 Limmel Stocks, Ring & Shaft
> 1 Borax Box, 6 Hammers
> Small Swage, Porringer Tool
> 1 Copp^r Pann, 4 Braz^g Irons
> 1 flask, 1 other Borax Box with
> Lamp & blow pipe[13]

Whether this inventory represents the estate of Daniel, Sr., or of Daniel, Jr., is unclear. The reference to S.R. is puzzling and may refer to the silversmith who inherited his tools.

Two initials marks (A, B) can be attributed to Russell with certainty. Mark (A) is found on Rhode Island church silver made in the 1730s and 1740s, and mark (B) is found in conjunction with mark (A) on a porringer at Yale.[14] A third initials mark (C) is on a gold locket. His son probably continued to use these marks. Clearly a number of these objects were made after 1750, when Daniel Russell, Sr., was declared non compos, and support the contention that Daniel Russell, Jr., carried on his father's business. BMW

SURVIVING OBJECTS

	Mark	Inscription	Patron	Date	Reference	Owner
Baptismal basin	A	Legatum. Nathanaelis. Kay/Armigeri, in usum Ecclesiae/ Anglicanae, in novo-portu, in/Insula De Rhode Island/Anno Salutis/1734	Trinity Church, Newport, R.I., for Nathaniel Kay	1734	Ballard 1981, 922, 924	
Baptismal basin	A	Donum D./Johannes Mulderi et D. Gullielmi Bright/in Usum Ecclesiae Anglicanae/in Novo Portu in Insula/De Rhode Island	Trinity Church, Newport, R.I., for John Muldery and William Bright	ca. 1734	Ballard 1981, 922, 924	
Three beakers	A	none	United Congregational Church, Newport, R. I.	ca. 1735	Jones 1913, 319	
Beaker	A	Given By/ Tho:^{s} Baley to y^e/Church of Christ/in Little Compton June ye first/1741	United Congregational Church, Little Compton, R.I., for Thomas Bailey	ca. 1741	Jones 1913, 251	

	Mark	Inscription	Patron	Date	Reference	Owner
Cann	A *or* B	C/NS		ca. 1740	Gourley 1965, no. 297	RISD
Creampot	B	?		ca. 1740	*Antiques* 117 (April 1980): 742	
Locket (gold)	B*	1742/IB/PA	John Barrington	1742	Buhler/Hood 1970, no. 466	YUAG
Locket (gold)	C†	H (over earlier initial) C		ca. 1740	Buhler 1972, no. 487	MFAB
Pepper box	A*	F/TE		ca. 1735	Buhler/Hood 1970, no. 464	YUAG
Pepper box	A *or* B	TH	Thomas Hornsby	ca. 1730	*Moore Collection* 1980, no. 22	
Two porringers	A†	D/IE (+)		ca. 1735	Buhler/Hood 1970, no. 463	YUAG
Porringer	A*	BBF		ca. 1740	DAPC 91.3265	
Porringer	A*/ B*	E/IM		ca. 1745	Buhler/Hood 1970, no. 465	YUAG
Porringer	A/B	W/GA	George and Abigail (Ellery) Wanton	ca. 1745	Sotheby Parke Bernet, 27–30 January 1982, lot 208	
Porringer	A *or* B	B/TA		ca. 1750	*Moore Collection* 1980, no. 23	
Porringer	?	FA		ca. 1740	*Antiques* 92 (July 1967): 13	
Porringer	?	SM (+)	Sally Mumford	ca. 1730	Sotheby's, 27–28 June 1985, lot 58	
Tablespoon	A*	H/GH		ca. 1735	Quimby 1995, no. 120	WM
Tablespoon	A*	IH		ca. 1720	DAPC 77.2781	
Tablespoon	A*	B/IS		ca. 1740	Johnston 1994, 134	CMA
Tankard	A	A/II		ca. 1735	*Moore Collection* 1980, no. 21	
Tankard	A	IHM (later)		ca. 1735	Quimby 1995, no. 118	WM
Tankard	A	?		ca. 1735	Anderson Galleries, 20–21 January 1928, lot 244	
Teaspoon	B*	EC		ca. 1730		HD
Teaspoon	B†	H/TE		ca. 1730	DAPC 73.1626 (as Daniel Boyer)	WM

1. Carpenter 1954, 157; Flynt/Fales 1968, 315; *Moore Collection* 1980, nos. 21–23; Beaman 1985, 345.
2. *Sibley's Harvard Graduates* 3:236–38; Branford VR 2:345.
3. Ezra Stiles Papers, Miscellaneous vol. 1, 325, Beinecke Library, YU.
4. *Sibley's Harvard Graduates* 3:236.
5. *Sibley's Harvard Graduates* 1:343–47.
6. Ballard 1981, 922–25; Ballard 1955, n.p.
7. Beaman 1985, 345; Buhler 1972, 2:557. Flynt/Fales 1968, 315, records his wife's name as Mary Mumford. No record of his marriage has been found in vital records. Daniel Russell, probably his son, married Mary Runiel in Newport in 1754/55; see Arnold 1911, 4:60; *Rhode Island Historical Magazine* 4 (1883): 10.
8. *Records of the Colony of Rhode Island* 4:466.
9. SCCR, Court of Common Pleas Record Book 1744–46, 140; court for 2 July 1745.
10. Ballard 1981, 922.
11. Flynt/Fales 1968, 315.
12. *Literary Diary of Ezra Stiles*, 1:84, 141, 328, 429, 505; 2:132.
13. Ezra Stiles Itineraries, vol. 3, 415, 9 May 1780, Ezra Stiles Papers, Beinecke Library, YU.
14. DR in oval (Belden 1980, 368; Kovel 1961, 236) probably was used by his son. Belden misattributes Russell mark B to Daniel Boyer; see Belden 1980, 70 (mark B).

Eleazer Russell
1663–91

Eleazer Russell was born in Hadley, Massachusetts, on 8 November 1663, the son of the Reverend John Russell (ca. 1626–92), the Hadley minister who concealed the regicides Edward Whalley and William Goffe in his house, and his second wife, Rebecca Newberry (ca. 1631–88).[1] The goldsmith descended from staunch Puritan stock: his maternal grandparents were Thomas Newberry (d. ca. 1636) and his wife, Jane, both early settlers of Dorchester, Massachusetts.[2] Before assuming the ministry in Hadley, Russell's father had been the minister at Wethersfield, Connecticut, where the silversmith's paternal grandfather, John Russell (ca. 1597–1680), settled about 1648 and the next year married his second wife, Dorothy, widow of the Reverend Henry Smith.[3]

Russell was sent to Boston to apprentice with Jeremiah Dummer (q.v.), probably about 1677, when he would have been fourteen years old. When Dummer purchased ten pounds' worth of Spanish reales and pilars from John Hull (q.v.) on 20 November 1679, the coins were handed over to Russell, whom Dummer presumably had sent to fetch them.[4] Dummer probably kept Russell in his employ after the younger man completed his term of service about 1684. The tax lists of 1687, 1688, and 1691 record that Dummer was taxable for two "heads," or males, over sixteen years of age; the second head may well have been Russell, who did not marry and may have continued to live in Dummer's household.[5] Russell was identified as being a goldsmith in a deed when he conveyed land to John Gardner and Priscilla Hunt in 1689.[6] He was the uncle of Daniel Russell (q.v.), the son of his brother the Reverend Samuel Russell, and the two Barnstable-area silversmiths Moody Russell and Joseph Russell (qq.v.), the sons of his brother the Reverend Jonathan Russell.

On 26 December 1690 Russell made out his will, which was witnessed by Dummer as well as by Eliezer Moody and Ann Kay.[7] He left property to his niece Rebecca Russell, his brother Jonathan's daughter. Samuel Sewall noted in his diary that Russell was buried on 2 January 1690/91.[8]

No silver by him is known. PEK

1. Savage 1860–62, 3:590–91; Bridgman 1850, 131–32; *Sibley's Harvard Graduates* 1:110–18.
2. Savage 1860–62, 3:269; SCPR, docket 1.
3. Savage 1860–62, 3:590–91.

4. John Hull Ledger, vol. 1, fol. 44v, NEHGS.

5. RC 1:117, 142, 154; the figures for the tax lists of 1688 and 1691 are not printed in the Record Commissioners' Reports but are found on the originals; Rare Book Room, BPL.

6. SCD 16:178.

7. SCPR, docket 1777.

8. *Sewall Diary* 1:274.

Joseph Russell
1702–80

A

Born in Barnstable, Massachusetts, on 11 October 1702, Joseph Russell and his twin brother, Benjamin (who died in infancy), were sons of the Reverend Jonathan Russell (1655–1710/11) and Martha (Moody) Russell (ca. 1662–1729), daughter of the Reverend Joshua Moody (1633–97) and Martha (Collins) Moody of Portsmouth, New Hampshire. Jonathan Russell was the son of the Reverend John Russell (ca. 1626–92) of Wethersfield, Connecticut, and Hadley, Massachusetts.[1] Joseph Russell's older brother, Moody (q.v.), was also a silversmith, and it has always been presumed that Moody, who finished his apprenticeship in Boston about 1716 and returned to Barnstable by 1718, was Joseph's master. Eleazer Russell (q.v.) was his uncle and Daniel Russell (q.v.) was his first cousin. He may have trained his nephew Jonathan Otis (q.v.).

Joseph Russell married Anne Vassall in Barnstable in 1728/29. Anne died in childbirth in 1729/30 together with the couple's infant son, Leonard.[2] Joseph Russell was living in Barnstable in 1733 when he married Sarah Paine (1706/07–64) of Bristol (now in Rhode Island), and he moved to Bristol soon thereafter.[3] He is identified as a goldsmith of Bristol in a deed transacted on 18 February 1734/35 when he bought a quarter of an acre with house and barn in Bristol.[4] Sarah (Paine) Russell was the daughter of Nathaniel Paine (1661–1723/24) and Dorothy (Rainsford) Paine (d. 1755).[5] Her sister, Elizabeth (Paine) Prince, married the Rhode Island silversmith Samuel Vernon (1683–1737).[6] Joseph and his second wife had five children: Anna (b. 1734), Sarah (b. 1735), Jonathan (b. 1736/37), Nathaniel (b. 1738), and Anna (b. 1747).[7] Joseph Russell continued to be identified as a goldsmith in a number of deeds between 1736 and 1739 when he bought and sold land in Bristol.[8] But beginning in 1739 he was referred to as a gentleman or as esquire, indicating that he must have achieved enough success in his business to allow him to live the life of a landed gentleman.[9]

Joseph Russell was appointed the administrator of the estate of his mother-in-law, Dorothy Paine, in 1755. In the division of his father-in-law Nathaniel Paine's real estate, recorded on 3 May 1758, Joseph and Sarah Russell received some land, a shop, and a crib, the latter two properties being described as those that "he now hath the improvement of."[10] Russell served as council clerk from 1749 to 1779. He was a representative to the General Assembly of Rhode Island in 1751, 1753–55, and also in 1758 and 1759. He was an associate justice of the Supreme Court of the Colony from 1751 to 1763 and chief justice in 1765, 1766, and 1768.[11] His death is recorded in Bristol on 31 July 1780.[12] No probate papers survive for him.

The mark IR in an oval (A) has been attributed to Joseph Russell on the basis of several objects surviving in areas where he worked, including a beaker in the church in Truro, Massachusetts, and a chalice and flagon dated 1734 in St. Michael's Church, Bristol.[13] BMW

SURVIVING OBJECTS

	Mark	Inscription	Patron	Date	Reference	Owner
Beaker	A†	This belongs to yᵉ Chh/of Christ in Truro/1730	First Congregational Church, Truro, Mass.	1730	Avery 1920, no. 40	MMA
Cup (altered to a pitcher)	A*	?		ca. 1730	McCulloch/ Beale 1963, 73	
Flagon	A	A Legacy/of Na-thaniel Kay Esqʳ/for the Use of the/ blessed Sacrament in the Church of England/in Bristol:1734/Lux Perpetua/ Credentibus Sola	St. Michael's Church, Bristol, R.I., for Nathaniel Kay	1734	Jones 1913, 98	
Tablespoon	A*	WB/to/SK		ca. 1740	Belden 1980, 368 (mark only)	WM
Wine cup	A	A Legacy of/ Nathaniel Kay Esqʳ/ for the Use of the/ Church of England/ in Bristol/1734	St. Michael's Church, Bristol, R.I., for Nathaniel Kay	1734	Jones 1913, 96–97	

1. *Barnstable and Sandwich VR*, 44, 97, 121; *Sibley's Harvard Graduates* 2:455–57; Jonathan Russell was the son of John Russell (1627–92) and either his first wife, Mary (Talcott) Russell, or his second wife, Rebecca (Newberry) Russell. "Diary of Rev. William Homes of Chilmark," *NEHGR* 50:163.
2. *Barnstable and Sandwich VR*, 106; "Diary of Rev. William Homes of Chilmark," *NEHGR* 50:163.
3. McCulloch/Beale 1963, 73; Arnold 1911, 6:47, 96, 161; *Barnstable and Sandwich VR*, 118.
4. BrCD (Taunton) 24:3.
5. Paine 1878, 7, 10.
6. Arnold 1911, 6:54.
7. Arnold 1911, 6:101.
8. Bristol Deeds 1:133–34, Town Hall, Bristol, Rhode Island; BrCD (Taunton) 25:114; 26:345, 354.
9. Bristol Deeds, 1:81–82, 228–29, 373–74; 2:257–58; 3:252–53, Town Hall, Bristol, Rhode Island; BrCD (Taunton) 26:242, 360, 495–96; 27:496.
10. Bristol Probate Records, Will Book 1, 258–63, 300–01, 317–18; Town Hall, Bristol, Rhode Island.
11. Cullity 1994, 160; *Records of the Colony of Rhode Island*, 5:327, 370, 382, 428; 6:144, 206, 433, 490, 544.
12. Arnold 1911, 6:161.
13. Jones 1913, 96, 471; McCulloch/Beale 1963, 73.

Moody Russell
1694–1761

A

Moody Russell was born in Barnstable, Massachusetts, on 30 August 1694. His father, Jonathan Russell (1655–1710/11), was born in Wethersfield, Connecticut, and grew up in Hadley, Massachusetts, where his father, John (ca. 1626–92), was minister. Jonathan graduated from Harvard College in 1675 and became minister of the Barnstable church in 1683. About 1680 he married Martha (ca. 1662–1729), daughter of the Reverend Joshua Moody (1633–97) and Martha (Collins) Moody of Portsmouth, New Hampshire. Moody Russell was the seventh of twelve children. His eldest brother, John (1685–1759), graduated

B

C

D

from Harvard College in 1704 and was a physician in Barnstable; his brother Jonathan (1689/90–1759), who graduated from Yale College in 1708, succeeded his father in the Barnstable pulpit; his younger brother Joseph (q.v.) became a silversmith.[1]

Jonathan and Martha Russell's decision to apprentice their fourth son to a silversmith may have been influenced by the fact that both the Reverend Russell's brother Eleazer (q.v.) and Martha Russell's brother-in-law Edward Winslow (q.v.) were silversmiths. Moody probably apprenticed with Winslow, as he witnessed deeds for Winslow in 1710/11 and 1712/13.[2] The earlier deed was also witnessed by Thomas Mullins (q.v.). Russell's Connecticut cousin, Daniel Russell (q.v.), was also in Boston training to be a silversmith at about this time but in the shop of John Dixwell (q.v.). Moody Russell returned to Barnstable after completing his apprenticeship; he witnessed the will of John Phinney in 1718, and in 1721 he weighed silver for the appraisers of the estate of Mary Freeman.[3]

Moody Russell and Dinah Sturgis (1700–73), daughter of Thomas (d. 1708) and Abigail (Lothrop) Sturgis (1660–1723), were married in Barnstable on 8 October 1724.[4] Moody became a deacon of the East Church of Barnstable on 28 May 1740.[5] Moody and Dinah Russell had one daughter who lived to maturity, Abigail (died ca. 1748); she married Nathaniel Gilman in 1746. Moody's granddaughter, Abigail Gilman, married Elpalet Loring (q.v.), who may have trained with Russell.[6]

Moody Russell wrote his will on 8 April 1761, noting that he was "very Sick and Weak in Body but of Perfect mind & memory." He left his entire estate to his widow, Dinah, asking only that she support their granddaughter, Abigail Gilman, out of the estate.[7] Dinah Russell died in 1773; her inventory includes several items that her husband may have made for her:

To Cash & purse 30/4 Gold Necklace	2. 11.8
To Sleeve buttons gold rings & shoe buckels	1. 8.0
To Stock buckel 2/ hooks & eyes 1/6 Silver porringer	2. 14.6
To Jewelry Cyphers a box and old buttons & some Stones for Dº	0. 1.4[8]

As a member of one of Barnstable's leading families, Moody would have had an enviable position as a craftsman. He made silver beakers for the East and West Barnstable churches and for the churches in Truro and Sandwich, and several fine examples of his work attest to his skill as a maker of holloware. He undoubtedly trained his younger brother Joseph. Russell may also have trained his nephew Jonathan Otis as well as Ephraim Cobb and Solomon Sturgis (qq.v.).[9] Abraham Higgins (q.v.) is documented as one of Moody Russell's apprentices. Moody Russell used several different marks, including two variations of MR in a rectangle (A, B) and two variations of MR in a shaped shield (C, D). BMW

SURVIVING OBJECTS

	Mark	Inscription	Patron	Date	Reference	Owner
Beaker (mate below)	A	This belongs to yᵉ Church of Christ in Truro	First Congregational Church, Truro, Mass.	ca. 1715	Avery 1920, no. 41	MMA
Beaker (mate above)	A*	This belongs to yᵉ Church of Christ in Truro	First Congregational Church, Truro, Mass.	ca. 1715	Johnston 1994, 134	CMA

	Mark	Inscription	Patron	Date	Reference	Owner
Beaker	A *or* B	The Gift of Josiah Crocker/to yᵉ West Cʰ: In Barnstable/ 1729	Congregational Church, West Parish of Barnstable, West Barnstable, Mass., for Josiah Crocker	1729	Jones 1913, 483	
Three beakers	A *or* B	C/EB	East Parish Congregational Church, East Barnstable, Mass.	ca. 1740	Jones 1913, 9	
Beaker	A *or* B	This belongs to the Church att Truro	First Congregational Church, Truro, Mass.	ca. 1715	Buhler 1972, no. 127	MFAB
Beaker (mate below)	B*	The gift of Shearjashub Bourn Esqᵣ./ to the Church ᵃᵗᵗ Sandwich 1719	First Parish Church, Sandwich, Mass., for Shearjashub Bourn	1719	Jones 1913, 439	MMA
Beaker (mate above)	B*	The gift of Shearjashub Bourn Esqᵣ./ to the Church att Sandwich 1719	First Parish Church, Sandwich, Mass., for Shearjashub Bourn	1719	Jones 1913, 439	MMA
Creampot	?	MA	Marie Appelby (?)	ca. 1760	Parke-Bernet, 19–20 October 1955, lot 198	
Cup	A	H/SK	Samuel and Keziah Hinkley	ca. 1720	*Silver Supplement* 1973, no. 82	
Cup	B*	SC	Coffin family	ca. 1740	Johnston 1994, 135	CMA
Cup	B	MG		ca. 1725	*Moore Collection* 1980, no. 106	HMA
Cup	?	unidentified initials		ca. 1730	Parke-Bernet, 26–27 January 1945, lot 162	
Pepper box	A*	EB/to DL (later)		ca. 1730	Buhler/Hood 1970, no. 118	YUAG
Pepper box	A*	SC	Coffin family	ca. 1730	Buhler/Hood 1970, no. 119	YUAG
Pepper box	A	C/TM		ca. 1730	Avery 1920, no. 42	MMA
Pepper box	A*	B/SM		ca. 1730		AIC
Pepper box	B*	MG; M (later)		ca. 1720	Johnston 1994, 135	CMA
Pepper box	?	?		ca. 1730	*Antiques* 131 (January 1987): 139	
Porringer	A*	W/ER		ca. 1740		RISD
Porringer	A *or* B	MO	Mercy Otis	ca. 1730	*Moore Collection* 1980, no. 107	
Porringer	A *or* B	SC		ca. 1715	Sotheby's, 27–28 June 1985, lot 55	

	Mark	Inscription	Patron	Date	Reference	Owner
Porringer	A *or* B	G/IH		ca. 1730	YUAG files	
Porringer	B*	A/PA		ca. 1725	Tvrdik 1977, no. 172	AIC
Porringer	D	R/TB		ca. 1740	YUAG files	
Porringer	D†	B/SM		ca. 1730	Buhler/Hood 1970, no. 117	YUAG
Porringer	?	?		ca. 1720		ChM
Spout cup	A	L/TE		ca. 1725	*CGA Bulletin*, no. 1 (1971): fig. 9	CGA
Spout cup	A *or* B	A/ER; HH		ca. 1730	Buhler 1972, no. 128	MFAB
Spout cup	B*	P/IR		ca. 1725	*Moore Collection* 1980, no. 105	
Spout cup	B*	F/IM; TRA/JDA (+) (later)	John and Mercy (Prence) Freeman	ca. 1725	Johnston 1994, 136	CMA
Tablespoon	A*	C/TM		ca. 1740	DAPC 68.2296	SI
Tablespoon	A†	L/CL		ca. 1730	DAPC 70.2049	WM
Tablespoon	A	H/IA		ca. 1730	DAPC 75.3017	WM
Tablespoon	A *or* B	WC		ca. 1730	National Art Galleries, 3–5 December 1931, lot 218	
Tablespoon	A *or* B	I; H/IH		ca. 1730		ChM
Tablespoon	A *or* B	?		ca. 1730		ChM
Tablespoon	B†	I/AM		ca. 1730	DAPC 76.2053	WM
Tankard	A*/ C†	Gorham arms, gules 3 fetterlocks con-joined in fess, and unidentified crest, a lion rampant; G/IE	John and Elizabeth (Allen) Gorham	ca. 1735	Buhler/Hood 1970, no. 120	YUAG
Tankard	C *or* D	R/EL; William Ingalls (later)	Remington family	ca. 1740	Sotheby's, 28–30 January 1988, lot 1058	
Tankard	C *or* D	T/IR (+)		ca. 1740	MFA 1906, no. 300	
Teaspoon	A*	EC/IL		ca. 1750		SFCAI

1. *Barnstable and Sandwich VR*, 44; *Sibley's Harvard Graduates* 2:455–57; 4:256–59; 1:367–80; Dexter 1885, 1:77–78; Bartlett 1879, 188; the Reverend Jonathan Russell was the son of the Reverend John Russell and either his first wife, Mary (Talcott) Russell, or his second wife, Rebecca (Newberry) Russell. "Diary of Rev. William Homes of Chilmark," *NEHGR* 50:163.
2. SCD 26:173–74; 27:55–57.
3. BCPR 5:50; 4:97.

4. *Barnstable and Sandwich VR*, 35, 97, 121; BCPR 3:55, 61; 4:237–40.
5. Worthley 1970, 30.
6. *Barnstable and Sandwich VR*, 56, 58; SCPR 62:348; McCulloch/Beale 1963, 72–74.
7. BCPR 12:162–63.
8. BCPR 17:69, 174.
9. Jones 1913, 9, 439, 471, 483.

Seth Sadler
1752–ca. 1820

Seth Sadler was born on 8 November 1752 in Upton, Massachusetts, the son of Abiel (b. 1720) and Esther Sadler.[1] His father was among a number of Rowley, Massachusetts, inhabitants who moved to Upton, where he became a prominent member of the community. Abiel Sadler's Upton tavern served as an ammunition storehouse for volunteers during the Revolution; Abiel was chosen as a committeeman to the Provincial Congress of Massachusetts and as a member of the local Upton committee for purchasing war materials and supplies.[2] Seth Sadler's paternal grandparents were John Sadler of Gloucester, Massachusetts, and Sarah Scot (b. 1690/91) of Rowley, Massachusetts; his maternal grandparents are unknown.[3]

Sadler's apprenticeship to an unknown silversmith may have brought him east to Dedham, Massachusetts. He married Olive Battelle (b. 1760) of Dedham on 25 October 1774.[4] She was the daughter of John (1718–1800) and Mehitable (Sherman) Battelle (b. 1718), who were married in Dedham on 26 April 1739.[5] Shortly after his marriage, Sadler responded to the Lexington alarm and later served in the revolutionary war in 1777 and 1780.[6] His three children, Anna, Esther, and Joel, were born in Upton between 1775 and 1781.[7]

Two Franklin County deeds reveal evidence of Sadler's trade as a goldsmith. Sadler, identifying himself as a goldsmith of Upton, purchased fifty acres of land in Conway, Massachusetts, in 1782. He probably moved there in 1782, as the census of 1790 records his family's presence in Conway.[8] Nine years later, Sadler, now goldsmith of Conway, sold the same acreage, and he may have moved to New York State, for the death of a Seth Sadler is recorded in Saratoga circa 1820.[9]

No silver by Sadler is known to survive. JJF

1. *Rowley VR*, 185; *Upton VR*, 48; Crane 1907, 3:395–96.
2. Johnson 1984, 76–77.
3. *Rowley VR*, 191, 389.
4. *Dedham VR*, 94; Battelle 1889, 8; *Upton VR*, 79.
5. *Dedham VR*, 45, 66, 94; Battelle 1889, 8; Sherman 1974, 129, 135.
6. *Mass. Soldiers and Sailors* 13:733–34.
7. *Upton VR*, 48–49. Anna Sadler, born on 15 September 1775; Esther Sadler, born on 25 December 1777; Joel Sadler, born on 29 March 1781.
8. *Census 1790*, 108.
9. FCD 5:60–61; *DAR Patriot Index* 1966, 1:589.

Benjamin
Sanderson
1649–78 or 79

A

Benjamin Sanderson, the son of Robert Sanderson, Sr. (q.v.), and Mary Cross, was baptized in Watertown, Massachusetts, on 29 July 1649.[1] His apprenticeship in the shop run by his father and John Hull (q.v.) probably began about 1663 and would have been completed about 1670. He witnessed a power of attorney for Edward and Margaret Cock in 1672, and around that time he married Mercy Viall (1649–before 1678), the daughter of the vintner John and Mary Viall.[2] The John Viall who died in Swansey, Massachusetts, in 1686 and some of whose estate was appraised by Timothy Dwight (q.v.) may have been his father-in-law.[3]

At the time of their marriage Sanderson and his wife probably settled in the North End of Boston, where the Vialls provided them with a house.[4] On the tax list of 1674 Sanderson is listed in ward 2 and owed a town tax of eight shillings and a country tax of four shillings.[5] The Robert Sanderson listed as a lodger in his house was probably his younger brother Robert Sanderson, Jr. (q.v.), who upon finishing his training with his older brother may have worked for him as a journeyman.[6] Between 1673 and 1678 Benjamin Sanderson bought goods from John Hull, including powder, shot, salt, oil, and cloth. The large quantities he bought on different occasions—22 yards of blue duffel, 73 1/2 yards of cotton, and 21 yards of ducape—suggest that Sanderson was buying the textiles for resale, thus supplementing his income from silversmithing.[7] Sanderson also appraised the estate of Timothy Dwight's mother in 1677.[8]

Sanderson died in late 1678 or early 1679, after practicing his trade for only six years. His wife and three children—Joseph, born 4 March 1673, Benjamin, born 25 May 1674, and Mary, born 29 November 1677—must have predeceased him because they are not mentioned in his will of 11 December 1678.[9] It is not clear whether Sanderson died late in 1678 or early in 1679. His will, which was probated on 30 January 1678/79, reads,

> Benjamin Sanderson being very sick & weake but of good understanding and memorie did declare this as his last will: That he did constitute his Hono[rd] & dear Father m[r] Robert Sanderson his sole Execut[or] and that hee did give unto the North Church ten pound. Also he did give to his beloved Sister Mary Sinderlin, five pound. And he desired the rest of his Estate might be for some honest poor persons and he thought there might be enough found amongst theire owne kindred. He desired that Elder Edward Rainsford & m[r] Jereme Dumer [q.v.] would Assist his father: All this the s[d] Benjamin expressed of his own accord the eleventh day of Decemb[r] 1678.[10]

The Mary Sinderlin referred to was his wife's sister, who had married John Sunderland on 26 January 1658.[11] It was Sunderland's father who gave the First Church of Boston the wine cup made by Benjamin Sanderson. In addition to that cup, three other pieces from Sanderson's short career are known, all bearing an initials mark (A). PEK

SURVIVING OBJECTS

	Mark	Inscription	Patron	Date	Reference	Owner
Caudle cup	A	initials erased	Prichard family (?)	ca. 1675	Buhler 1979, no. 2	WAM
Dram cup	A†	M.A. BOWDITCH (later; erased)		ca. 1675	Buhler/Hood 1970, no. 21	YUAG
Dram cup	A	P/SM		ca. 1675	Bigelow 1917, 250–51	

	Mark	Inscription	Patron	Date	Reference	Owner
Wine cup	A*	IS (+)	John Sunderland	ca. 1675	Jones 1913, 26	

1. *Watertown Records* 1894, vol. 1, "Records of Births, Deaths, and Marriages, First Book," 14.
2. *Suffolk Deeds* 8:4–5, 83; RC 9:29.
3. SCPR, docket 1566.
4. *Suffolk Deeds* 4:272.
5. RC 1:36.
6. RC 1:36, 38.
7. John Hull Ledger, vol. 1, fol. 73v, NEHGS.
8. SCPR, docket 886.
9. RC 9:129, 134, 143.
10. SCPR, docket 1046.
11. RC 9:67.

John Sanderson d. 1658

John Sanderson, whose birth is unrecorded, was a son of Robert Sanderson, Sr. (q.v.), and probably his wife, Lydia. He probably was born in Hampton, New Hampshire. John was apprenticed to John Hull (q.v.) and died before his training as a goldsmith was completed. Hull wrote in his diary in the fall of 1658, "My boy, John Sanderson, complained of his head aching, and took his bed. A strong fever set on him; and, after seventeen days' sore sickness, he departed this life."[1] When John's death was recorded in Boston records as taking place on 17 September 1658, he was identified as the son of Robert.[2] PEK

1. "Hull Diaries," 148.
2. RC 9:66.

Joseph Sanderson 1642/43–66

Joseph Sanderson, the son of Robert Sanderson, Sr. (q.v.), and Mary Cross, was born in Watertown, Massachusetts, on 1 January 1642/43.[1] His training, which took place in the shop his father ran with John Hull (q.v.), probably began about 1656 and would have been completed about 1663, the year he witnessed a deed for John Hull.[2] No record of Sanderson's marriage to his wife, Mary (ca. 1639–1711), has been found, but it must have taken place about this time. A daughter, Mary, was born on 6 July 1666.[3] A second daughter, Abiah, probably was born in 1667 after her father's death because according to the inventory of his estate Joseph Sanderson died on 24 December 1666.[4]

The inventory (prepared in the presence of Jeremiah Dummer and Samuel Paddy [qq.v.]), amounted to £40.9.0 and included in the shop a considerable lot of goldsmith's tools:

	£ s d
An inventory of the Estate of Joseph Sanderson: deceased ye 24th of ye 10 m° 1666	
In ye Shope	£ s d
1 Spowne test & oune hammer & skillet	: 1: 0:0
2 Raising Anvelles	: 1: 5:0
2 Stakes	: 0: 10:0
1 Square test & oune hand vise	: 0: 7:0
9 hamers & oune swage	: 1: 3:0
1 beaker Anvill & oune snarling Iron	: 0: 11:6
1 pr holding tongs & oune pair of Shares	: 0: 5:0
4 treblettes & a paire of fflasks	: 0: 8:0
Chasing towles & small towles in a box }	: 0: 11:0

a Chasing bag & a New Skinne	: 0: 3:0
4 Burnishing Irones & 3 paire of Compasses	: 0: 6:0
1 Box & weights burnishers pipe & tonges	: 0: 2:6
1 Swage a [illeg.] & a graver & oune hoane & a whetstoane	: 0: 10:0
2 Boyling panns	: 0: 5:0
1 punche & chisell & a frame & glass	: 0: 7:0
1 Chest two Stanvilles & tynne drust bookes & two paire of Stoles	:00: 15:0
oune Ladell & [illeg.] a drawer & [illeg.]	: 0: 8:0
pattarns Sandbox & sand	: 0: 7:0
1 Codline & Carpenters towles	: 0: 10:6
1 drawing benche & tonges	: 0: 15:0

The inventory then lists household furnishings and a few additional tools, ending with the statement "All accounts being made up and debts satisfied for money received to make plate for several there remained In hand £1.15.0."[5] The outstanding orders for silver at the time of Sanderson's death and the number of tools in the inventory indicate that he was an active goldsmith, although no silver by him is known to survive.

Joseph Sanderson's widow, Mary, became the fourth wife of Augustin Lindon but was divorced by order of the court on 15 October 1679; she and William Ardell then made a marriage agreement on 21 December 1681.[6] Two years later her father-in-law Robert Sanderson, Sr., deeded her and her two daughters land in Boston.[7] PEK

1. *NEHGR* 7:282.
2. *Suffolk Deeds* 10:26.
3. RC 9:101; Codman 1918, 25. Joseph's wife's birth date has been calculated from her epitaph, which records that she was seventy-two when she died on 20 October 1711.
4. SCCR, Supreme Civil Court 1680–92, 180, records that Abiah, daughter of____Sanderson, sometime of Boston, goldsmith, deceased, appearing in court chose William Gilbert of Boston, cordwainer, to be her guardian. The court approved Gilbert on April 29, 1684. This arrangement was probably made because her mother, Mary, was about to move to Exeter, New Hampshire, with her husband, William Ardell.
5. SCPR, docket 440.
6. Shurtleff 1853, 5:248–49.
7. *Suffolk Deeds* 13:99.

Robert Sanderson, Jr.
1652–1714

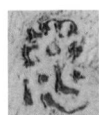

A

Robert Sanderson, Jr., the son of Robert Sanderson, Sr. (q.v.), and Mary Cross, was baptized in Watertown, Massachusetts, on 22 October 1652.[1] His apprenticeship in the shop his father ran with John Hull (q.v.) would have begun about 1666 and would have been completed about 1673. He may have finished his training with his older brother Benjamin Sanderson (q.v.) and then worked for him as a journeyman, for he was listed as a lodger in his house in 1674.[2] He may have remained in his brother's house until Benjamin Sanderson died in 1678/79. He had married by 10 October 1684, when a son Joseph was born to him and his wife, Elizabeth, but the date of the marriage and his wife's maiden name are not recorded.[3]

Objects made in the Hull and Sanderson shop following John Hull's death in 1683 are struck twice with the elder Sanderson's initials mark (Robert Sanderson, Sr., mark c). The second mark symbolized the work of the father and son together and can be identified as the younger Sanderson's mark (A). In those years the younger Robert Sanderson seems to have been very much a part of the Hull-Sewall-Sanderson households. He witnessed a deed for his father in 1685.[4] In his diary Sewall noted the death of Sanderson's young son Joseph in August 1685 and recorded Sanderson's presence as bearer at Henry Phillips's funeral in February 1685/86.[5] In January 1686/87, when Samuel Sewall needed to return belongings to John Alcock—Alcock had been living in the Hull-Sewall household but had moved out upon contracting smallpox—Robert Sanderson delivered them for him.[6] No evidence suggests that Robert Sanderson, Jr., made silver following his father's death in 1693.

Robert Sanderson, Jr., appeared on the tax lists of 1688 and 1691 in ward 8, which was in the same ward as the shop.[7] The elder Sanderson's will, made on 18 July 1693, confirms the deed of gift to his son of all lands belonging to his son's dwelling house in Boston as well as his dwelling house. The younger Sanderson's wife, Elizabeth, must have died shortly after that will was made. Sanderson married Sarah Crow (d. ca. 1694), on 21 December 1693, whom Robert Sanderson, Sr., called his trusty maid in his will.[8] But she could not have survived long because the following year the younger Robert Sanderson married Esther Woodward (1663–1715), the daughter of Thomas Woodward (d. 1685) and Esther of Muddy River.[9] Robert and Esther had several children: Sarah (1695–96); Robert (b. 1696/97); Joseph (b. 1698/99); Benjamin (b. 1700); Mary (b. 1703); and Anna (b. 1708).[10] Robert Sanderson and his wife sold property in Watertown on 11 March 1713.[11] He died on 11 April 1714, and his widow died on 5 October 1715. Thomas Woodward was appointed the administrator of his brother-in-law's estate on 27 October 1715. The inventory, taken on 28 June 1716, included a house and land valued at £100 and household goods worth £26.16.10. No goldsmith's tools were recorded.[12] A few years after Sanderson's death his sons, Robert, Joseph, and Benjamin, sold land in the southerly part of Boston that they had inherited from their father.[13] PEK

SURVIVING OBJECTS

	Mark	Inscription	Patron	Date	Reference	Owner
Caudle cup (with mark of Robert Sanderson, Sr.)	A*	9th Septr 81; IF/SB (+)	Silence (Baker) Eliot in memory of John Foster	ca. 1685	Clarke 1940, no. 28	
Caudle cup (with mark of Robert Sanderson, Sr.)	A†	S/TA		ca. 1685	Quimby 1995, no. 121	WM
Caudle cup (with mark of Robert Sanderson, Sr.)	A*	Joanna Yorke/1685/ BC	First Congregational Church (Unitarian), Quincy, Mass., for Joanna Yorke	1685	Clarke 1940, no. 29	
Tankard (with mark of Robert Sanderson, Sr.)	A*	V/IM	Isaac and Mary (Balston) Vergoose	ca. 1690	Buhler 1972, no. 1	MFAB
Two wine cups (with mark of Robert Sanderson, Sr.)	A*	The Gift of Richard Jackson CC (+)	First Church in Cambridge, Cambridge, Mass., for Richard Jackson	ca. 1692	Jones 1913, 108–09	

1. *Watertown Records* 1894, vol. 1, "Records of Births, Deaths, and Marriages, First Book," 16.
2. RC 1:36, 38.
3. RC 9:163.
4. *Suffolk Deeds* 13:351.
5. *Sewall Diary* 1:73, 95.
6. *Sewall Diary* 1:130.
7. RC 1:144, 157.
8. RC 9:210.
9. RC 9:89; RC 6:186.
10. RC 9:223, 228, 230, 242; RC 24:4, 25, 58.
11. MCD 16:509.
12. SCPR 18:512–13; 19:152; docket 3686.
13. SCD 33:211; 34:204; 36:213–14.

Robert Sanderson, Sr.
ca. 1608–93

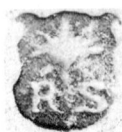

A

B

C

In a deposition given at an Essex County court in 1653, Robert Sanderson testified that he was in his forty-fifth year, which makes his birth date about 1608.[1] Little is known about his parentage or place of origin in England other than that he called himself the son of Sandersonne of Higham in 1623 when he was apprenticed to William Rawlings, "Citizen and Goldsmith of London."[2] Higham may have been the parish outside the city walls of Norwich, Norfolk, but no record exists there of Sanderson's birth.[3]

By 1632 Sanderson was a freeman of the Goldsmiths' Company, but he failed to maintain the standards of the assay office on at least one occasion.[4] For the next six years he practiced his trade in London, where he trained his master's son, William Rawlings, Jr.[5] Sanderson probably married during this period, although no marital records have been found, and his wife Lydia's maiden name is not known.[6] Sometime in 1638 Sanderson signed his apprentice, William Rawlings, Jr., over to the London goldsmith George Dixon in preparation for immigrating to New England.[7]

With his wife, Robert Sanderson settled at Hampton, in what is now New Hampshire, where he became a freeman in 1639.[8] That same year a daughter Mary was born, and Sanderson received eighty acres of land.[9] The following June he received an additional land grant in Hampton.[10] A son, John (q.v.), also may have been born to Robert and Lydia in Hampton. Sometime before 1642 Lydia died, and Sanderson married Mary Cross (ca. 1607–81), the widow of John Cross of Watertown, Massachusetts, the town where Sanderson's brother Edward lived.[11] The Watertown church recorded the baptisms of Robert and Mary's children: Joseph (q.v.) in 1642/43; Benjamin (q.v.) in 1649; Sarah in 1650/51; and Robert (q.v.) in 1652.[12] In 1645 Robert Sanderson purchased a dwelling house and lot in Watertown, and in 1650 he sold his Hampton land.[13]

After the General Court established a mint for coining money in Boston and appointed John Hull (q.v.) as mintmaster on 10 June 1652, Hull recommended Sanderson as his partner, and the General Court approved his appointment. This undertaking brought Sanderson to Boston, where he was admitted as an inhabitant on 30 May 1653.[14] In October of that year Sanderson bought additional land in Watertown adjoining land he owned already, and in December he purchased a house and land in Boston adjacent to Hull's property.[15] Presumably the two men's plateworking partnership dates from their work together as mintmasters. Of the two partners, Sanderson had the superior training and experience as a working goldsmith. Writing in

1712/13, Samuel Sewall, Hull's son-in-law, recalled "Mr. Saunderson and all that wrought in the Shop under him," an image that evokes an accomplished craftsman with a supervisory role over the shop's production.[16] Within these first years of settling in Boston Sanderson also formed a mining company.[17]

Sanderson probably trained many of the apprentices in the shop, whether they were formally Hull's apprentices or his. Sanderson's son John may have been apprenticed to Hull, who described him as "my boy" when recording John's death in his diary in 1658.[18] In the ensuing years Robert Sanderson trained his sons Joseph, Benjamin, and Robert as goldsmiths. The other apprentices he trained in the shop included: Jeremiah Dummer; Samuel Paddy; John Hall; Timothy Dwight; Daniel Quincy; Samuel Clarke; and possibly Thomas Savage (qq.v.). Sanderson may have had Richard Nevill (q.v.) working for him as a journeyman.

Sanderson actively participated in town affairs. He was chosen constable for a year in 1662/63.[19] He and his wife became members of the First Church in 1665, and he became a deacon in 1670, fulfilling those duties until his death.[20] In 1673 he entered into an agreement with others to build a powder mill on the Neponset River in Canton.[21] Sanderson joined Jeremiah Dummer in a court deposition in 1675 concerning the value of French crowns.[22]

Sanderson conducted a number of real estate transactions late in life, some of which he may have undertaken to benefit family members. In 1662 he bought land in Boston from Thomas Munt.[23] In June 1670 he purchased two pieces of land on the neck in Boston for "a peece of plat^e to ye value of five pounds."[24] In 1674 Sanderson's son-in-law, John Penniman, mortgaged his house and land in Boston to him, and Sanderson bought a shop in Boston that he sold six months later. In 1678 he bought another shop.[25] On the tax list of 1676 Sanderson is listed as having houses and wharves valued at thirty pounds, cows valued at two pounds, and estate valued at twenty pounds.[26] Following the death of his second wife on 21 June 1681, Sanderson married a third time. On 24 August 1681 he made a marriage agreement with Elizabeth Kingsmill, the widow of the Quaker William Kingsmill and a woman of some education. When writing his will in 1674, the Reverend John Oxenbridge advised his wife to consult Elizabeth Kingsmill for guidance because she was "more experienced and prudent to order affairs and write letters."[27]

Following Hull's death in 1683, the shop continued with Sanderson as its mainstay. Sanderson died a decade later on 7 October 1693.[28] His inventory, taken on 23 October 1693, amounted to £718.18 and included "old working Tooles £20" and real estate totaling £535.[29] His widow died in 1695.[30]

A tremendous number of objects made by Sanderson survive. Hundreds of coins from Hull and Sanderson's career as mintmasters are extant.[31] Six pieces survive from Sanderson's London career, approximately thirty-five from his partnership with Hull, and six from the period following Hull's death, probably when he was working in partnership with his son Robert Sanderson, Jr.[32] Sanderson always used an initials mark in a shaped shield, and three marks have been identified (A–C). The longer silver is in use, the greater the likelihood of its being melted down to be refashioned as coins, jewelry, or plate; therefore, the number of pieces surviving from Sanderson's career—although not great compared to later makers—attests to his productivity and success as a craftsman. PEK

SURVIVING OBJECTS

	Mark	Inscription	Patron	Date	Reference	Owner
Beaker (with mark of John Hull)	A*	WR/TR/1670; Richards arms (later)	Welthian Richards	ca. 1660	Parke-Bernet, 10 November 1970, lot 135	
Beaker (with mark of John Hull)	A†	T/BC; 1659	First Church, Boston	1659	Clarke 1940, no. 2	
Beaker (with mark of John Hull)	B*	Belonging to the First/Church of Christ in/Marblehead 1728 (later)		ca. 1665	Clarke 1940, no. 6	
Beaker (with mark of John Hull)	C*	IP; The Gift of/M.[r] Daniel Perren . . . (later) (+)		ca. 1675	Buhler/Hood 1970, no. 4	YUAG
Beaker (with mark of John Hull)	C*	Property/of the/OLD SOUTH CHURCH (later)		ca. 1675	Clarke 1940, no. 4	
Two beakers (with mark of John Hull)	C*	The Gift of L/TA (+)	Henry Leadbetter, executor of Thomas Lake's estate, for First Church, Dorchester, Mass.	ca. 1679	Clarke 1940, no. 3	
Beaker (with mark of John Hull)	?	?		ca. 1660	YUAG files	
Caudle cup (with mark of John Hull)	A*	EC; PM (+)		ca. 1660	Safford 1983, 6–7	
Caudle cup (with mark of John Hull)	B*	C/AE (+)	Augustine and Elizabeth Clement	ca. 1665	Clarke 1940, no. 8	
Caudle cup (with marks of John Hull and Jeremiah Dummer)	C*	FC	First Church of Christ, Congregational, Farmington, Conn.	ca. 1670	Clarke 1940, no. 7	
Caudle cup (with mark of John Hull)	C*	The gift of Eliezer Moody to the Church in Dedham, 1720 (later)	Eliezer Moody	ca. 1675	Buhler 1956, no. 83	
Caudle cup (with mark of John Hull)	C*	ED; BB (+)	Beriah Bright	ca. 1671	Buhler 1972, no. 4	MFAB
Caudle cup (with mark of John Hull)	C*	T/WD; Dorothea 1891 (later)		ca. 1675	Buhler 1972, no. 5	MFAB
Caudle cup (with mark of Robert Sanderson, Jr.)	C*	9th Sept[r] 81; IF/SB (+)	Silence (Baker) Eliot in memory of John Foster	ca. 1685	Clarke 1940, no. 28	
Caudle cup (with mark of Robert Sanderson, Jr.)	C*	S/TA		ca. 1685	Quimby 1995, no. 121	WM
Caudle cup (with mark of Robert Sanderson, Jr.)	C*	Joanna Yorke/1685/ BC	First Congregational Church (Unitarian), Quincy, Mass., for Joanna Yorke	1685	Clarke 1940, no. 29	
Communion cup	A*	none		1632/33	Evans 1906, 67	
Communion cup	A*	IHS	Thomas and Mary (Napier) Myddleton	1635/36	Flynt/Fales 1968, 72–73	HD

	Mark	Inscription	Patron	Date	Reference	Owner
Communion cup	A	none		ca. 1635	How 1971, 718–19	
Dram cup (with mark of John Hull)	A*	D/DP	Daniel and Patience Dennison	ca. 1660	Parks 1958, no. 1	
Dram cup (with mark of John Hull)	C*	RB (later)		ca. 1670	Buhler/Hood 1970, no. 1	YUAG
Dram cup (with mark of John Hull)	C*	C/IE; H/IM (later)		ca. 1675	Buhler 1972, no. 3	MFAB
Dram cup (with mark of John Hull)	C*	G/IA	Rev. Joseph and Ann (Waldron) Gerrish	ca. 1675	Buhler 1972, no. 6	MFAB
Paten	A	none		ca. 1635	How 1971, 718–19	
Paten	A*	Myddleton impaling Napier arms	Thomas and Mary (Napier) Myddleton	1635/36	Flynt/Fales 1968, 72–73	HD
Porringer (with mark of John Hull)	C†	M/AI; M. B. LeM. (later) (+)	Arthur and Johannah (Parker) Mason	ca. 1670	Buhler 1972, no. 2	MFAB
Porringer (with mark of John Hull)	C*	V/IM; WF (later)	Isaac and Mary (Balston) Vergoose	ca. 1675	Quimby 1995, no. 76	WM
Salver	A	?		1635/36	Jackson (1921) 1964, 119	
Tablespoon (with mark of John Hull)	A*	P/BM		ca. 1655	Quimby 1995, no. 77	WM
Tablespoon (with mark of John Hull)	B*	1667/RB (+)		1667	Johnston 1994, 77	CMA
Tablespoon (with mark of John Hull)	B*	H/EA	Edward and Abigail (Button) Hutchinson	ca. 1670	Buhler/Hood 1970, no. 3	YUAG
Tablespoon (with mark of John Hull)	C*	B/WH	William and Hannah (Corwin) Browne	ca. 1670	Fales 1983, 8–9	PEM
Tablespoon (with mark of John Hull)	C*	F/CM		ca. 1675	YUAG files	
Tablespoon (with mark of John Hull)	C*	MY		ca. 1675		MFAB
Tankard (with mark of John Hull)	B†	BL (later) (+)	Simon Lynde (?)	ca. 1665	Clarke 1940, no. 26	
Tankard (with mark of Robert Sanderson, Jr.)	C*	V/IM	Isaac and Mary (Balston) Vergoose	ca. 1690	Buhler 1972, no. 1	MFAB
Wine cup (with mark of John Hull)	A*	T/BC; 1661; The Gift of A Fri^{e}nd: RH	Robert Hull	ca. 1660	Clarke 1940, no. 14	
Wine cup (with mark of John Hull)	A*	Property/of the/ OLD SOUTH CHURCH (later)		ca. 1660	Clarke 1940, no. 19	
Wine cup (with mark of John Hull)	A*	F/RE; H/GH (later)	Richard and Elizabeth Fairbanks	ca. 1660	Clarke 1940, no. 16	
Wine cup (with mark of John Hull)	A*	B/RA	Richard and Alice Brackett	ca. 1660	Clarke 1940, no. 20	
Wine cup (with mark of John Hull)	A*	The Gift of william Needham to Brantry Church 1688 (later)	William Needham	ca. 1660	Clarke 1940, no. 21	

	Mark	Inscription	Patron	Date	Reference	Owner
Wine cup (with mark of John Hull)	A*	TC (altered to The Gift of a Friende TC); T/BC (later)	Thomas Clarke	ca. 1660	Clarke 1940, no. 15	
Wine cup (with mark of John Hull)	c*	Cap.ᵗ Willets' donation to,/yᵉ Ch: of Rehᵒboth, 1674, (later)	Thomas Willet	ca. 1670	Buhler/Hood 1970, no. 2	YUAG
Three wine cups (with mark of John Hull)	c*	The Gift of Jnᵒ Oxenbridg	First Church, Boston, for Rev. John Oxenbridge	ca. 1675	Clarke 1940, no. 17	
Two wine cups (with mark of Robert Sanderson, Jr.)	c*	The Gift of Richard Jackson CC (+)	First Church in Cambridge, Cambridge, Mass., for Richard Jackson	ca. 1692	Jones 1913, 108–09	

1. ECCR files 1:87.
2. Apprentice Book 1, fol. 261r, Worshipful Company of Goldsmiths, London.
3. Roe/Trent 1982, 483.
4. Court Book R, part 2, fols. 111, 214r, Worshipful Company of Goldsmiths, London.
5. Apprentice Book 1, fol. 326, Worshipful Company of Goldsmiths, London.
6. The records of London's parish of St. Mary Abchurch reveal that on 26 February 1632/33 Robert Sanderson and his wife, Lydia, christened a son Robert. They may also have had a daughter Lydia because in December 1654 Lydia Sanderson married Thomas Jones of Taunton, Massachusetts. Robert Sanderson acted as Jones's surety a few months later when his son-in-law became an inhabitant of Boston; see RC 2:123, 138.
7. Court Book W, fol. 20v, Worshipful Company of Goldsmiths, London.
8. Shurtleff 1853, 1:376.
9. Dow 1893, 2:961.
10. Dow 1893, 1:17–19.
11. Bond 1860, 2:416; Mary Sanderson's tombstone gives her age as seventy-four at the time of her death in 1681, from which her birth date is calculated. Codman 1918, 207.
12. *Watertown Records* 1894, vol. 1, "Births, Deaths, and Marriages, First Book," 10, 14, 16; *NEHGR* 7:282.
13. *Suffolk Deeds* 1:79, 119.
14. Shurtleff 1853, 3:261; RC 2:116.
15. Bond 1860, 2:416; *Suffolk Deeds* 3:70–71.
16. *Sewall Letter Book* 2:9–10.
17. Robert Sanderson signature on articles of agreement, 15 July 1655, Photostat Collection, MHS.
18. "Hull Diaries," 148.
19. RC 7:14.
20. Pierce 1961, lvi, 60.
21. *NEHGR* 31:272.
22. SCCR, file 1430.
23. *Suffolk Deeds* 4:80–82.
24. *Suffolk Deeds* 7:22.
25. *Suffolk Deeds* 8:443–45; 9:71–72, 228–29; 11:109–11.
26. RC 1:62.
27. *Suffolk Deeds* 12:125–26; SCPR 5:225–26; 6:128–33.
28. RC 9:212.
29. SCPR, docket 2082.
30. SCPR, docket 2279.
31. See Crosby 1875 and Noe 1943, Noe 1947, and Noe 1952.
32. For discussion of these works, see Clarke 1940 and Kane 1987.

Thomas Savage, Sr.
1664–1749

A

B

Thomas Savage, Sr., was born in Boston on 19 October 1664 to Habijah Savage (1638–69) and Hannah Tyng (1640–88).[1] His paternal grandparents were Thomas Savage (ca. 1608–82) and Faith Hutchinson (d. 1652); his maternal grandparents were Edward Tyng (ca. 1610–81) and Mary Sears.[2] Savage's father died when he was only five years old, and he was probably raised in Cambridge, Massachusetts, by his mother's second husband, Daniel Gookin. When Savage's grandfather Thomas wrote his will in 1675 he left £150 to his grandson Thomas.[3]

Savage would have begun his training about 1678, and because his uncle Ephraim married a sister of Daniel Quincy (q.v.) and Savage himself married a cousin of Timothy Dwight (q.v.) it has been said that Savage trained together with Quincy and Dwight under John Hull and Robert Sanderson, Sr. (qq.v.).[4] No evidence supports this contention, and it is just as possible that he trained with Jeremiah Dummer, John Coney, or William Rouse (qq.v.), all of whom were then operating their own shops. Thomas Savage was a bearer at the funeral of Timothy Dwight in 1692 and compiled the inventory of Dwight's estate with William Rouse.

Savage would have completed his training about 1685. In 1687 he quitclaimed land in Boston inherited from his grandfather.[5] He was admitted a freeman on 22 March 1689/90.[6] On 6 November 1690 he accepted Samuel Haugh (q.v.) as an apprentice for a term of seven years and six months.[7] The following 5 February he married Mehitable (Phillips) Harwood (1667–1737), widow of Benjamin Harwood and daughter of Henry Phillips (d. 1685), a butcher, and Mary Dwight (b. 1635). Savage and his wife were among the heirs of Henry Phillips who quitclaimed interest in a house and land in Boston in 1698 in a deed witnessed before Jeremiah Dummer in his capacity as justice of the peace by Daniel Gookin and John Dixwell (qq.v.).[8] Savage served in various civic capacities, becoming a member of the Ancient and Honorable Artillery Company in 1693 and serving as clerk of the market in 1694 and constable in 1697.[9]

Savage and his family lived in Bermuda from about 1706 until about 1714. He is identified as being of Bermuda when he and his wife sold land in Boston and Charlestown, Massachusetts, in February and April 1706.[10] Savage's family comprised two daughters from his wife's previous marriage, Rachel and Mehitable, and two daughters and three sons of his own: Thomas (b. 1693/94) (q.v. Appendix B), Habijah (b. 1695), Hannah (b. 1697), Benjamin (b. 1699) (q.v. Appendix B), and Mary.[11] His stepdaughter Mehitable Harwood married John Ince in Boston in 1709, so it is not clear whether his stepdaughters accompanied Savage and his wife to Bermuda.[12] Savage was still in Bermuda when he sold land in Charlestown in May 1713, but he was living in Boston again by July 1714, when he petitioned the selectmen of Boston for a license to sell strong drink. That request was denied, but the next month a similar petition was approved.[13] He was also described as being "of Boston, late of Bermuda," in a deed of October 1714, when he sold land his wife had inherited from her father.[14] His son Thomas, Jr., also a goldsmith, remained in Bermuda when his father returned to Boston; his son Benjamin returned to Boston with him and witnessed a deed for his father in 1717.[15]

The stylistic features of Savage's known pieces of silver, which are marked with two variations of an initials mark, TS with a star below in a heart (A) and TS in a rounded rectangle (B), suggest that they were made in the period before Savage moved to Bermuda or during his stay there. He probably continued his goldsmith business, however, after his return to Boston, supplementing it by selling strong drink and holding minor political offices. He is referred to as "Thomas Savage, Goldsmith," in 1727/28 by the Boston shopkeeper Isaiah Tay (d. 1730), the father-in-law of James Barnes (q.v.), when Tay, in writing his will, describes the tenants of his houses.[16] Savage was chosen a sealer of weights and measures on 14 June 1725, an office he held until 19 March 1736, when, "being grown infirm," he was relieved of his duties.[17] Advancing age probably led Savage to move to Newbury, Massachusetts, where his daughter Mary Crocker dwelled. His wife died there on 6 June 1737, and Savage's membership in the First Church, Boston, was transferred to Newbury on 2 July 1738.[18] He died there on 23 August 1749.[19] No probate survives for him. PEK

SURVIVING OBJECTS

	Mark	Inscription	Patron	Date	Reference	Owner
Caudle cup	A*	Quincy arms, 9 mascles conjoined 3, 2, 3, 1; BC/1699 (+)	Edmund Quincy and/ or First Congregational Society (Unitarian), Quincy, Mass.	1699	Jones 1913, 394	
Porringer	A	C/WD E (later)		ca. 1695	English-Speaking Union 1960, no. 16	
Porringer	B†	I/IM		ca. 1705	Buhler/Hood 1970, no. 40	YUAG
Salver	B*	H/NM (?; erased) EB (later)		ca. 1700	Buhler/Hood 1970, no. 41	YUAG
Salver	B	Taylor arms, a chevron gules between 3 escallops, and crest, an arm embowed holding a spear	Taylor family	ca. 1700	Hyde 1971, 180–81	Bermuda Historical Monuments Trust
Salver	B	Dickinson arms, or a bend gules engrailed between 2 lions rampant, and unidentified crest, a gamb erased; HHH (later)	Dickinson family	ca. 1700	*Antiques* (August 1942): frontis, 66	
Snuffbox	B	MS		ca. 1720	YUAG files	
Tankard	A	I/FM		ca. 1710	Hyde 1971, 178–79	
Tankard	A†	initials erased		ca. 1690		MMA
Tankard	A	E; Oma La Grange (later)		ca. 1705	*Antiques* 27 (March 1935): 109	
Tankard	A	B/BE		ca. 1710	Hyde 1971, 178–79	
Tankard	A	T/ID		ca. 1710	Hyde 1971, 178–79	
Tankard	A*	P/IL		ca. 1710	YUAG files	
Tankard	B	Paynter arms, a chevron gules	Paul Paynter (?)	ca. 1705	Hammerslough/	WA

Mark	Inscription	Patron	Date	Reference	Owner
	between 3 griffins' heads erased, in chief a helmet between 2 rondels; PP			Feigenbaum 1958–73, 1:24–25	

1. RC 9:6, 10, 81, 93; *Cambridge VR* 2:575.
2. Savage 1860–62, 4:26–27, 356–57; *Dunstable VR*, 234.
3. SCPR 6:592.
4. Bigelow 1917, 115; Ensko 1927, 56; Currier 1938, 126; Flynt/Fales 1968, 320.
5. *Suffolk Deeds* 14:144–45.
6. RC 29:161.
7. *Sewall Diary* 1:269.
8. RC 9:192; *Newbury VR* 2:714; Hill/Tuttle 1886–1936, 1:1; SCPR 9:259–60, docket 1450.
9. RC 7:217, 225; Roberts 1895, 1:300. The latter source mistakenly records a second marriage to an Elizabeth and a wrong death date for the goldsmith. The Thomas Savage married to Elizabeth was the goldsmith's son. The Thomas Savage who died in 1721 was his cousin.
10. SCD 22:445–48; MCD 14:59, indexed in the Registry of Deeds as p. 59, actually appears on p. 61.
11. RC 9:208, 220, 223, 234, 253.
12. RC 28:23.
13. MCD 16:295; RC 11:212, 215.
14. MCD 17:337.
15. SCD 32:184.
16. SCPR 28:71–74.
17. Seybolt 1939, 167, 196.
18. Pierce 1961, 143.
19. *Newbury VR* 2:714.

James Sherman
b. 1746/47

James Sherman was born in Boston on 16 January 1746/47, the son of James Sherman (1717–1801), a painter-stainer, and Rebecca Starkey (1722–99), who married in Boston on 18 November 1742.[1] His paternal grandparents were James (ca. 1691–1729) and Margaret Sherman (ca. 1690–1758).[2] His maternal grandparents were Robert Starkey (d. 1722), a bookseller, and Walter (Ross) Starkey.[3] Sherman's apprenticeship would have begun about 1761 and been completed about 1768. Therefore the jeweler James Sherman (q.v.) who arrived in Boston aboard James Dickey's sloop *Lucy* from Halifax on 25 April 1763 is not this goldsmith.[4]

James Sherman, "Silversmith, of Boston," married Mary Holyoke (1741–1809) on 11 July 1769.[5] She was the daughter of the merchant Jacob Holyoke (1697–1767) and Susannah Martin (1697–1784).[6] The Massachusetts tax list of 1771 indicates that after his marriage Sherman lived as a tenant with his father.[7] Sherman is not on the Boston tax list of 1780. He may have worked as a journeyman for Benjamin Burt (q.v.) because a James Sherman, along with the silversmith Edward Revere (1768–1820), witnessed a deed for Burt on 1 December 1788.[8] In *The Genealogies and Estates of Charlestown*, Thomas B. Wyman, Jr., places "Mr. Sherman, Goldsmith," in the West Indies, from where news of his "dying of fever arrived March 15, 1796." This reference may pertain to the silversmith in question because Sherman is not mentioned in his father's will, dated 28 January 1800 and probated on 14 April 1801; presumably he was dead by that time.[9] The references to James Sherman in the Boston town records for the period 1768 to 1796 are probably to his father.[10]

No silver by James Sherman is known. PEK

1. *NEHGR* 31:215; *Index of Obituaries, 1704–1800*, 1:270; *Index of Obituaries, 1784–1840*, 4:4056; RC 24:157, 261; RC 28:261; Thwing.

2. Wyman 1879, 2:862.

3. SCPR, docket 4529; RC 28:78.

4. RC 29:246.

5. RC 30:62; RC 24:243; *Holyoke Diaries*, xv.

6. Thwing; RC 9:233; RC 28:154; *Index of Obituaries, 1704–1800*, 2:532.

7. Pruitt 1978, 10–11.

8. MCD 101:10–11.

9. SCPR 99:171, 197, 210. It is also possible that the individual discussed in Wyman was Sherman Goldsmith, who lived in Charlestown in this period; see Wyman 1879, 2:863.

10. RC 26:36, 113, 175.

James Sherman
w. ca. 1763

A list of port arrivals in Boston includes a jeweler named James Sherman, who arrived in Boston aboard James Dickey's sloop *Lucy* from Halifax, Nova Scotia, on 25 April 1763.[1] Nothing more is known about this craftsman. A goldsmith also named James Sherman (q.v.) began to work in Boston about 1768. PEK

1. RC 29:246.

Timothy Sibley, Jr.
1754–1829

Timothy Sibley, Jr., was born on 19 June 1754 in Sutton, Massachusetts.[1] He was the son of Timothy Sibley, Sr. (1727–1818), a joiner and yeoman of Sutton (q.v. Appendix B), who previously has been misidentified as a silversmith, and Anne Waite (1733–94) of Ipswich, Massachusetts, whom he married in Sutton on 16 October 1753.[2] His paternal grandparents were John Sibley, who was born in Salem, Massachusetts, in 1687 and died in Sutton in 1782, and Zeriah Gould (b. 1694).[3] His maternal grandparents were Benjamin Waite (d. 1739) and Elizabeth Holland (1712–44) of Ipswich.[4] Timothy Sibley, Jr., married Mary Barstow (1756–1833) of Brimfield, Massachusetts, on 5 November 1778.[5] Her parents were Jeremiah (b. 1712) and Elizabeth Barstow.[6]

Sibley's master is unknown, but by the age of twenty-four, Sibley announced his trade in an advertisement in the *Massachusetts Spy* (1778). This advertisement is the primary evidence that Timothy Sibley, Jr., rather than his father, practiced the craft. The advertisement reads, "CLOCKWORK Clock, Watch and Goldsmiths Work of all kinds made, repaired, and sold by TIMOTHY SIBLEY jun. at his Shop in SUTTON, near the Rev. Dr. Hall's Meeting-House. N.B. Cash given by said Sibley, for old Silver Plate."[7] Because Sibley chose to highlight his clockmaking skills in this advertisement, he may have trained in the home town of the Willard clockmaking family, Grafton, which ran along the southeastern boundary of Sutton. Sibley may have gained some of his clockmaking experience with one of the Willard brothers, most likely Benjamin Willard (q.v. Appendix A), because Sibley named his firstborn son Timothy Willard Sibley.[8] Sibley may have trained his younger brother, Stephen (1759–1829), who became a silversmith and clockmaker.

Eight of a total of nine children were born to Sibley in Sutton, which suggests that he lived there for most of his life, perhaps moving briefly to Connecticut to join his brother Asa (1764–1829), who was working in Woodstock as a silversmith and clockmaker.[9] His last child, Origen, was born in nearby Thompson, Connecticut, in 1798.[10] However, Sibley may have been absent from Sutton from the time of Origen's birth through 1812 because his father's will of 1811 provides forgiveness of a debt Timothy owed his father "if my Son Timothy Should Ever Come into these Partes again."[11] Sibley eventually did return to Sutton: his death in 1829 is recorded there.[12]

No silver by Sibley is known, although a wall clock by him survives.[13] JJF

1. *Sutton VR*, 158.
2. *Sutton VR*, 354; WCPR, docket 53609; Sibley 1982, 1:21; *Ipswich VR* 1:379; J. S. Sibley, letter to author, 12 August 1989; Flynt/Fales 1968, 322–23.
3. *Salem VR* 1:379; Sibley 1982, 1:14; Benedict/Tracy 1878, 722; J. S. Sibley, letter to author, 12 August 1989.
4. *Ipswich VR* 1:192; 2:440, 702.
5. *Brimfield VR*, 17; Sibley 1982, 1:21, 46; J. S. Sibley, letter to author, 12 August 1989; *Sutton VR*, 354.
6. *Marlborough VR*, 25.
7. *Massachusetts Spy*, 17 September 1778. Repeated 24 September, 8, 15, 22 October 1778; 28 January, 4, 11, 18, 25 February, 4, 8, 11 March 1779.
8. *Sutton VR*, 158.
9. Sibley 1982, 1:21, 46; *Sutton VR*, 152–53, 156–58.
10. Thompson VR, 231.
11. WCPR, docket 53609.
12. *Sutton VR*, 461.
13. Rodriguez Roque 1984, 90–91.

Thomas Barton Simpkins
1728–1804

Thomas Barton Simpkins, the son of the goldsmith William Simpkins (q.v.) and Elizabeth Symmes (1706/07–94), was born on 4 November 1728.[1] Simpkins undoubtedly served his apprenticeship with his father from 1742 until 1749 and was listed in the Massachusetts tax valuation list of 1771 as William Simpkins's lodger. Simpkins probably was working in a partnership with his father in the shop that was included among William Simpkins's properties in the 1771 tax survey.[2] Thomas Barton Simpkins, along with John Coburn (q.v.), may have appraised the estate of Samuel Edwards in 1762. The copy of the appraisal in the estate papers lists Thomas Simpkins as an appraiser, although the probate court record book identifies William Simpkins as an appraiser.[3]

Following his father's death in 1780, Thomas Barton Simpkins established a solo career as a silversmith that lasted for more than twenty-three years. He continued to occupy the same residence that he had shared with his father, probably on Fore Street. The tax assessment conducted in 1780 listed Thomas B. Simpkins immediately following the entry for his father, who was designated as "Dead."[4] He appeared in the Boston directory of 1789 as Thomas Barton Simpkins, Goldsmith, on Fish Street; however, in the directory for 1796, his location had moved to Ann Street.[5] An account of the administration of William Simpkins's estate records the payment on 30 August 1797 of £50 by Thomas B. Simpkins as rent for his shop. It also states that £66.13.4, or its equivalent of $222.22, was paid to Simpkins from the estate.[6]

The silversmith appears as a grantor in several deeds to dispose of his father's property. The thirteen heirs of William Simpkins, including "Thomas Barton, goldsmith," and Elizabeth Rogers, the daughter of Thomas Barton's sister, Elizabeth, and her husband, Daniel Rogers (q.v.), sold some land on Fore Street in November 1783 to Richard Skillings for £120.[7] Simpkins and some of his relatives also sold three lots on Ann Street between June and August 1798, with Thomas Barton Simpkins contributing one-quarter of the total.[8] "Thomas Barton Simpkins, goldsmith," provided a deposition for a property controversy between Gibbon Sharp, Elizabeth Hichborn, and Jonathan Balch on 7 July 1803, suggesting that Simpkins remained active in his profession until his death in 1804, at the age of seventy-six.[9] Simpkins apparently never married. His obituary appeared in the *Columbian Centinel* on 18 January of that year.[10]

In spite of his lengthy career, very few objects can be attributed to Simpkins. During his thirty-one-year partnership with his father, the elder man's mark probably was used on the silver produced in the shop. In his memoirs, Samuel Davis (1765–1829) describes Simpkins of "Forestreet" as "beadmaker to all the craft—patient and humble, of spotless integrity, unknown, he led the noiseless tenor of his way."[11] If he specialized in the production of gold and silver jewelry, it is not surprising that so little of Simpkins's work is known because jewelry was seldom marked by its maker and few examples have survived. Two marks have been associated with this silversmith: Currier recorded a T SIMPKINS mark of partly conjoined capital letters in a rectangle, and Ensko illustrated a T. B. Simpkins mark in a conforming surround.[12] Objects bearing these marks have not been located, however. DAF

1. RC 24:189.
2. Pruitt 1978, 20–21.
3. Inventory and accounts of the estate of Samuel Edwards, June 1762–78, Smith-Carter Papers, MHS; SCPR 63:37.
4. "Assessors' 'Taking-Books,'" 27.
5. *Boston Directory* 1789, 41; 1796, 92.
6. SCPR 96:479–81.
7. SCD 179:94–96.
8. SCD 190:50–51, 90–91, 139–40.
9. SCD 206:255.
10. *Index of Obituaries, 1784–1840*, 4:4085. No marriage records or probate records have been found for this silversmith.
11. Steinway 1960, 8.
12. Currier 1970, 131; Ensko 1948, 238; see also Flynt/Fales 1968, 323.

William Simpkins
1704–80

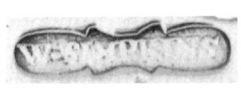

A

B

C

D

William Simpkins, the son of Thomas (1671–1706) and Margery (Barton) Simpkins (d. 1756), was baptized in the Second (or North) Church, Boston, on 22 October 1704. Thomas, a mariner, was the son of Pilgrim Simpkins (1639–1720), also a mariner, and his second wife, Katharine Richardson (ca. 1635–1721). Margery (Barton) Simpkins was the daughter of James (d. 1729), a ropemaker, and Margaret Barton.[1] Margery's sister, Margaret (Barton) Calef, had a daughter, Margaret, who married Jaspar Starr (q.v.).

On 16 May 1726 William Simpkins married Elizabeth Symmes (1706/07–94), the daughter of William (b. 1679) and Elizabeth (Langdon) Symmes (b. 1686).[2] They had eight children: Elizabeth (1726/27–65), who married Daniel Rogers (q.v.) of Ipswich, Massachusetts, in 1760; Thomas Barton (q.v.); Margery (1730–before 1783), who married Thomas Blanchard in 1753; Joanna (1732–before 1783); William (1734–before 1783); Katharine (b. 1736), who married Joshua Davis, a yeoman of Chelmsford, Massachusetts; John (b. 1740), who became a merchant and married (i) Elizabeth Grant and (ii) Mehitabel Torrey; and Mary (b. 1744), who married Robert Rand, gentleman, in 1773.[3]

William Simpkins was probably apprenticed to one of his cousins, Andrew Tyler or William Cowell, Sr., or to John Burt (qq.v.). The latter possibility is suggested by evidence of Simpkins's associations with silversmiths trained by Burt. In 1732, Simpkins, along with Basil Dixwell (q.v.), witnessed a deed

E

F

for Burt's former apprentice Samuel Gray (1710/11–48) (q.v.).[4] Simpkins witnessed a deed for Burt in 1737 with another former Burt apprentice, Edmund Mountfort (q.v.), and Mountfort also witnessed a deed for Simpkins in 1744.[5] In 1745 and 1747 Simpkins and John Doane (q.v.), a probable Burt apprentice, witnessed deeds for James Butler.[6] During his career Simpkins associated with a number of other Boston silversmiths. He may have had a professional relationship with Thomas Townsend (q.v.) because Townsend and Simpkins witnessed a division of real estate in Simpkins's maternal grandfather's estate in 1755.[7] Simpkins granted a mortgage to the parents of the jeweler John Codner (q.v.) in 1766.[8] Simpkins also appraised the estates of a number of silversmiths: John Burt in 1745/46; Jacob Hurd in 1758; William Cowell, Jr., in 1761; and (along with John Coburn) Samuel Edwards (qq.v.) in 1762.[9]

Simpkins's shop was located near the drawbridge in Boston. In 1728, he advertised the sale there of the library of his brother-in-law, the late Reverend Robert Stanton of Salem, Massachusetts.[10] In 1744 Simpkins evidently bought the house and land where his shop was located, along with an adjacent wharf, fronting on Ann Street in Boston "near the . . . Bridge formerly called the Draw Bridge," from his mother, Margery Simpkins, and his aunt, Margaret Calef.[11] In 1746, he advertised the loss from his shop of a piece of silver "3 Inches broad and a quarter of an Inch thick, weighing about 14 Ounces."[12] In 1770, he was involved in transactions concerning a house and land fronting in Fish Street in Boston that had been part of the estate of the tallowchandler Edward Langdon, who was undoubtedly a kinsman of his wife's mother.[13] On the Massachusetts tax list of 1771 Simpkins appears with one poll, one house, one shop (tanhouse, etc.), sixteen pounds' annual value of real estate, and four pounds in merchandise.[14]

Simpkins no doubt trained his son Thomas Barton Simpkins, and he may have trained his future son-in-law Daniel Rogers as well as Samuel Minott (q.v.). Simpkins may have worked in partnership with Minott for several years because their marks appear together on tankards made for the First Church in Milton, Massachusetts, and for the First Congregational Society in Quincy, Massachusetts. However, the marks may also indicate that Minott acquired some of Simpkins's unfinished stock. The advertisement that Minott placed in the *Boston News-Letter* on 1 October 1772 suggests that Minott may have continued his business in the shop formerly used by Simpkins. On that date Minott advertised that he had tea, spices, groceries, and pottery for sale, along with jewelry and plate, at his shop opposite William's Court, and that he carried on the goldsmith's business at his "other shop, North-ward of the Draw-Bridge."[15] Whether Simpkins merely rented the shop to Minott or was a non-working partner in business with him is unclear. Simpkins's estate inventory suggests that his business activities extended well beyond goldsmithing before the outbreak of the Revolution and indicates that he retained ownership of this particular shop until his death in 1780. At that time Simpkins owned warehouses on a wharf and the land behind them as well as a small dwelling house adjoining the warehouse.[16] The administration accounts from Simpkins's estate indicate that his son, Thomas Barton Simpkins, occupied one of these shops while his father's estate was being settled; Minott is not mentioned in the accounts.[17]

Like his father and grandfather, William Simpkins was a member of the Ancient and Honorable Artillery Company, joining in 1739. He was third sergeant of the company in 1743 and ensign in 1757.[18] The town meeting elected him to the office of constable in 1743, but he paid the fine rather than serve in the office. He was a member of the New North Church.[19] He was involved in lawsuits as plaintiff in two cases in 1741, one against the carter James Fairservice and one against the blockmaker Samuel Russell. In 1745, the rope-maker James Barton and William Simpkins together brought suit against the wharfinger Bartholomew Gedney and against the cooper Joseph Dyer in two separate cases.[20]

William Simpkins died intestate in 1780; the inventory of his estate was presented to the court by his administrators, his sons Thomas Barton Simpkins and John Simpkins, on 26 May 1780. The appraisers were Josiah Waters, Benjamin Burt (q.v.), and John Stanton. The values of items listed in the estate are deceiving because they are all given in highly inflated wartime currency. The plate listed appears to be domestic rather than store stock. The inventory also includes a large number of goldsmithing tools:

91^{lb} Iron @ 3/4 Books £50 9 Burnishers 36 Punches 36}	137	3	4
Rais^g Anvil £74 Spoon Teast £46 Stake for Can £30 2 Stakes $^£$16}	166	—	—
3 Round Bottom Stakes £72 2 p^r Flaks £80 18 Hamm^{rs} & Handles £74}	226	—	—
10 p^r Knee & Shoe Chapes 13 6/8 w^t foil £4 Box & Pcell Iron Articles 50}	67 .6..	8	
Stake wth a Shell 20 7 Spoon bunches 62 a Soop d^o £16}	98	—	—
A Numb^r Small Stakes & Bunches £30 a Draw^g Bench & Chizel $^£$56}	86	—	—
Pcell files & boxes £7 borrax boxes blowpipe lamb &c £8}	15	—	—
Boyl^g pan £24 Skillet 32. 3 p^r Iron tongs 16 Ingut and draw^g irons £44}	116	—	—
34^{lb} Lead & Pewt^r 45..6/8 Weights &c £6Block &c £10 2 Glass doors 25}	86 .6.	8	
Pcell Patterns 30 Sett Drawes & Horse £10	40		
a Small Rais^g Anvil, Salt Stake Cream potts d^o, Castor Bunch ⎫			
a Bottom Stake & Buge Hammer ⎭	144	—	—
Wareing apparel divided, a Case wth Bottles	30		
1 Tankard, a Teapott, porringer, a caster ⎫			
Large & Tea Spoons w^t 69^{oz} 10^{dt} @ 13. 6/8 ⎭	920[21]		

The administration of Simpkins's estate took many years; the last of the administrator's accounts was not filed until 1798. Some accounts are rendered in inflated currency, others in specie, so comparisons are difficult to make. The administration account dated 31 October 1797 includes the following items under the date December or January 1780–81: "sundry Articles as ℔ Acc^t taken out by the Widow, who was one of the Admor's [Administrators] most of which remains unpaid" and "To part of the Tools left in T. Simpkins' hand, that would not sell there £425.03.04." An account filed 23 October 1798 includes £50 "Rent of Thos B. Simpkins for Shop," and the "sundries Ch^d to the Several Heirs by there Father" included £66.13.4 to Thomas Barton Simpkins. Other accounts, however, suggest that Thomas Barton Simpkins did not pay rent on the shop during 1783 (after this point he may have inherited it), but that between 1784 and 1796 the executors received shop rent simultaneously from as many as three other individuals. One long account rendered in specie included money paid to Thomas Christy for work done on the shops, to William White for digging a trench at the shops, and to Robert Rand "for Stuff for d^o." Also included were £3.3.7 "To Cash paid Thomas Simpkins for Shop windows & doors at said Shop," (21, 25 July 1783); £2.1.2 "To Cash paid Thomas B. Simpkins, being what he over p^d of ye Stock £2.01.02" (1 July 1785); £1.2 "To Jno Howe's for Plate"; £23 "To 69^{oz} 10^{dwt} Silver which was taken by the Widow"; and £3 for the "Remainder of Tools in Thomas Simpkins' hands" (4 February 1794).[22]

Simpkins is known by several marks, including W. SIMPKINS in a shaped rectangle (A), W Simpkins in a rounded rectangle (B), W·SIMPKINS in a rectangle (C), Simpkins in a rectangle (D), and W·S (E) and WS (F), both in rectangles. Spurious examples of mark (A) exist.[23] A cast handle terminal with an incuse WS on a tankard by Paul Revere, Sr. (q.v.), also may have been made by Simpkins.[24] Simpkins produced a wide variety of holloware forms as well as flatware. Some pieces are ornamented with chased decoration in the fully developed rococo style. Congregational churches in Massachusetts and Connecticut numbered among his patrons. BMW

SURVIVING OBJECTS

	Mark	Inscription	Patron	Date	Reference	Owner
Two beakers	F	The Gift of Mr/ Preserved Hall/to y^c first Church of/ Christ in Hingham	First Parish, Hingham, Mass., for Preserved Hall	ca. 1740	Jones 1913, 215	
Two beakers	F	The Gift of Mrs Hannah Thaxter (Relict of the Hon-^{ble} Sam^{ll} Thaxter) for the first Church of Christ in Hingham/ 1756	First Parish, Hingham, Mass., for Hannah Thaxter	1756	Jones 1913, 215–16	
Beaker (with mark of Samuel Minott)	F	The Gift of Mrs. Susannah Dean/to the Church of Christ in Bedford	Susanna Dean and/or the First Parish, Bedford, Mass.	ca. 1770	YUAG files	
Blackjack	C*	T Stretch/To/S Brenton/1778	T. Stretch	1778		RISD
Bowl	B†	H/SE (+)	Stephen and Elizabeth (Sanders) Hall	ca. 1740	Buhler 1972, no. 196	MFAB
Buckle	F	RG		ca. 1740	Hammerslough/ Feigenbaum 1958–73, 3:134–35	
Cann	A*	Second/ Presbyterian/ Church/in/ Newburyport	Second Presbyterian Church, Newburyport, Mass.	ca. 1750		SI
Cann	A	?		ca. 1760	YUAG files	
Cann	A	none	Nicholas and Sarah (Warren) (Little) Sever (?)	ca. 1750	Hale 1931, n.p.	
Cann	B*	B/DA		ca. 1760		USDS
Cann	B	?		ca. 1750	Sotheby Parke Bernet, 29 January 1975, lot 82	
Cann	B*	none		ca. 1740	YUAG files	

	Mark	Inscription	Patron	Date	Reference	Owner
Cann	D	none		ca. 1745	*Moore Collection* 1980, no. 121	
Cann	E*	HL		ca. 1745	Buhler 1972, no. 198	MFAB
Caster	E*	Lydia/Russel (later)		ca. 1760	Gourley 1965, no. 179	RISD
Cream pail	E*	EC (altered to EG)		ca. 1755	Hammerslough/ Feigenbaum 1958–73, 4:29	WA
Creampot	B*	G/DS		ca. 1750	Johnston 1994, 144	CMA
Creampot	B/F	?		ca. 1750	MFA 1911, no. 942	
Creampot	E (?)	?		ca. 1750	*Antiques* 114 (November 1978): 923	
Creampot	E *or* F	NCE		ca. 1760	MFA 1911, no. 946	
Cup	C	P/ZR (+)		ca. 1735	Buhler 1956, no. 132	
Mug	A	Alleyne arms; Semper Fedelis; MA	Alleyne family	ca. 1735	Parke-Bernet, 4 January 1940, lot 68	
Mug	B/E	unidentified arms; EW; S/SI	Warren family	ca. 1760	MFA 1911, no. 943	
Pepper box	B*	initials erased; R (later)		ca. 1735	DAPC 72.2209	
Pepper box	B	B/RH		ca. 1735	*Antiques* 115 (June 1979): 1102	
Pepper box	?	?		ca. 1735	*Antiques* 119 (January 1981): 118	
Porringer	A	G/RH		ca. 1750	*Antiques* 49 (February 1946): 120, 122	SLAM
Porringer	A	MF	Margaret Fayerweather	ca. 1745	MFA 1911, no. 939	
Porringer	A†/F	P/TH		ca. 1745		HMA
Porringer	B	L/ES	Edward and Susanna (Wadsworth) Langdon	ca. 1745	Buhler 1972, no. 197	MFAB
Porringer	B*	MP		ca. 1750	*The Museum* n.s. 5 (Summer–Fall 1953): 27	NM
Porringer	B	Mary (later)		ca. 1750	Sotheby Parke Bernet, 30 January– 2 February 1980, lot 529	

	Mark	Inscription	Patron	Date	Reference	Owner
Porringer	B*	B/ND		ca. 1750	YUAG files	
Porringer	B	A/ND		ca. 1750	American Art Association–Anderson Galleries, 22–23 January 1937, lot 299	
Porringer	D	C/TE	Thomas and Elizabeth (Scamman) Cutts	ca. 1765	Sprague 1987, no. 46	YIM
Porringer	E	C/TP		ca. 1750	*Antiques* 122 (October 1982): 652	
Porringer (with mark of Samuel Minott)	E*	IP/to/PC		ca. 1765	DAPC 65.4298	Rosenbach Foundation
Two salts	B	THP; TPB (later)		ca. 1755	YUAG files	
Salt	E*	F/EM	Enoch and Mary Freeman	ca. 1745	DAPC 84.3220	
Salver	C	Lechmere arms impaling Phipps (later)		ca. 1760	Sotheby's, 24 October 1987, lot 389	
Sauceboat (mate below)	B	B/IM		ca. 1765	Hammerslough/Feigenbaum 1958–73, 1:134	
Sauceboat (mate above)	D	B/IM		ca. 1765	Hammerslough/Feigenbaum 1958–73, 1:134	
One pair sleeve buttons (gold)	F†	none		ca. 1750		MMA
Two strainers	A	?		ca. 1750	YUAG files	
Strainer	B*	P/TH		ca. 1745		AIC
Sugar bowl (missing cover)	?	H/ES		ca. 1735	Parke-Bernet, 17 May 1968, lot 140	
Tablespoon	A*	SB		ca. 1730	DAPC 77.2586	Presbyterian Historical Society
Tablespoon	A*	G/SP		ca. 1750	DAPC 71.2627	WM
Tablespoon	A*	NL (later)		ca. 1755	Eitner 1976, no. 41	
Tablespoon	B*	D/IR		ca. 1735	Fales 1958, nos. 75–76	WM
Tablespoon	B	F/GS		ca. 1740	DAPC 79.3121	
Tablespoon	B*	LB		ca. 1740	YUAG files	
Tablespoon	D†	SW/1777		1777	DAPC 71.2632	WM
Tablespoon	D*	ES/Dec.ʳ 10/1765 (+)		ca. 1765	DAPC 73.1517	WM
Tablespoon	D*	B/SD (+)		ca. 1760		PEM

	Mark	Inscription	Patron	Date	Reference	Owner
Tankard	A*	Belonging/to the second Church/of/Christ in Roxbury/1761	First Parish, West Roxbury, Mass.	1761	Jones 1913, 489–90	
Tankard	A	W/ES; John Holmes (later)		ca. 1760	Sotheby's, 21 June 1989, lot 138	
Tankard	B	unidentified arms; M/NE		ca. 1760	Colby 1967, E49	
Tankard	B	crest, a bird with olive branch; JSP		ca. 1750	Washington 1925, no. 129	
Tankard	B	SC to HF		ca. 1750	Washington 1925, no. 130	
Tankard	B	MHR/1760	Moses and Rachel Hays	1760	*American Art of the Colonies and Early Republic*, no. 104	
Tankard	B/F	T/GM		ca. 1750		CF
Tankard	c*/D*	The Gift of/Mʳˢ Ann White/to the Church in/Brooklyn	Ann White and/or First Parish, Brookline, Mass.	ca. 1750	Jones 1913, 101	
Tankard	D	C/TE	Thomas and Elizabeth Cutts	ca. 1765	*Moore Collection* 1980, no. 123	
Tankard	F	H/NM		ca. 1735	*Moore Collection* 1980, no. 122	
Two tankards (with mark of Samuel Minott)	F	This tankard is the Property/of the Church of Christ in Milton/and was purchased with part/of its Stock February 15ᵗʰ 1770.	First Congregational Parish, Milton, Mass.	1770	Jones 1913, 292	
Tankard (with mark of Samuel Minott)	F	The Gift of/Mʳˢ Sarah Adams; (Relict/of Mʳ Edward Adams late of/Milton) to the first Church in Braintree.	Sarah (Brackett) Adams and/or First Congregational Society (Unitarian), Quincy, Mass.	ca. 1760	Jones 1913, 397	
Tankard	?	?		ca. 1750	Winchester 1952, 221–22	
Teapot	c†	MS; E.S. & S. Rand . . . (later)		ca. 1755	*Antiques* 116 (July 1979): 91	
Teapot	c	THP	Peyton family	ca. 1760	Christie's, 20–21 January 1989, lot 299	
Teaspoon	E (?)	AT		ca. 1745		YUAG
Teaspoon	E*	T/DM		ca. 1760		PEM
Teaspoon	E (?)	MP		ca. 1745		YUAG

	Mark	Inscription	Patron	Date	Reference	Owner
Teaspoon	E*	EM		ca. 1745	Johnston 1994, 145	CMA
Teaspoon	E†	RM (altered to RD)		ca. 1765	DAPC 73.1205	WM
Teaspoon	E	HM		ca. 1740	DAPC 73.1196	WM
Two-handled cup	B	The Gift of/Cap.ᵗ. Isaac Johnson/to yᵉ Church of/Amity/ The fifth Society/ 1743	Isaac Johnson and/or Congregational Church, Woodbridge, Conn.	1743	Jones 1913, 505	

1. RC 9:75, 82, 120; SCPR 22:60–61; RC 28:349; MCPR 18:311, 616–18; SCPR 15:371–73 new series; 16:169; 22:60–61, 141–42, 633–34, 718.
2. Robbins 1852, 277; RC 9:170; RC 28:16, 135; RC 24:45; *Index of Obituaries, 1784–1840*, 4:4076; *Bradford VR*, 149.
3. RC 24:178, 189, 199, 209, 219, 227, 241, 254; RC 30:9, 372, 433; SCD 179:94–96; SCPR, docket 17187.
4. SCD 47:14–15.
5. YCD 19:232; SCD 68:137–38.
6. SCD 71:146–47; 73:161–62.
7. SCPR, docket 11079.
8. SCD 111:166.
9. SCPR 39:160–61, dockets 11826, 12763, 12962. According to the version of Edwards's inventory filed with the probate court, the appraisers of the estate were William Simpkins, Joseph Bradford, and John Coburn; according to the manuscript version of Edwards's inventory in the Smith-Carter Papers, MHS, the appraisers of the estate were Thomas Simpkins, Joseph Bradford, and John Coburn.
10. Dow 1927, 55; the advertisement was repeated in the 27 June–4 July issue.
11. SCD 68:137–38.
12. *Boston Evening-Post*, 27 January 1746.
13. SCD 117:111–13.
14. Pruitt 1978, 20–21.
15. Dow 1927, 49.
16. SCPR, docket 17187.
17. SCPR 96:479–81.
18. Roberts 1895, 2:11.
19. Seybolt 1939, 230; Robbins 1852, 277; Bigelow-Phillips files, 990.
20. SCCR, Court of Common Pleas Record Book 1741, 216; 1744–46, 150; John M. Fitzgerald to F. H. Bigelow, Boston Court Record References to Goldsmiths, Bigelow-Phillips files.
21. SCPR, docket 17187.
22. SCPR, docket 17187.
23. See a tablespoon and fork (383581, 383582) at SI, 4 beakers (1940.62 A–D) at HU, and another tablespoon (DAPC 71.2629).
24. Skerry 1988, 45.

Charles Simpson
1713–ca. 1749

Charles Simpson was born in Boston on 4 September 1713, the son of Benjamin Simpson (1678–1738), a blacksmith, and Elizabeth Phippenny (d. before 1730), the widow of Daniel Phippenny, who were married in Boston in 1704.[1] Benjamin Simpson married a second time in 1730, wedding Hannah Cowell (b. 1709), the daughter of William Cowell, Sr. (q.v.).[2] Charles Simpson's paternal grandparents were John Simpson (1638–94/95), a joiner, and Abigail Smith (d. after 1707) of Charlestown, Massachusetts.[3] His maternal grandparents are unknown.

Simpson's apprenticeship would have begun about 1727 and finished about 1734. He most likely was trained in the Cowell shop because not only was his father married to one of Cowell's daughters, but Simpson himself married another, Mary Cowell (1717–97), in 1747.[4] Evidence of Charles Simpson's gold-smithing comes from the ledger of Benjamin Greene (q.v.), in which Simpson is identified as a Boston goldsmith in 1737.[5] The following year Simpson purchased a number of items from Greene:

1738

July 17.	To 1 pair womans Buckells &	1 . . 4 . . 6
August	To Mak a Silver Bottom to a box	1 . . 6 . . . .
Septe.r	To 1 pair Large Shue Buckells	5 . . 16 . . 6
	To 1 Large Spoon	2 . . 17 . . 10
	To 1 p.r [illeg.] Buckells	1 . . 11 . . . .
	To 1 Thimble &	9 . . 7 . . 6
	To 1 p.r Stone Studds	0 . . 18 . . . .

Most of the transactions between Simpson and Greene deal in general merchandise and such goods as tallow, hides, and pitch, not with goldsmith's wares. By August 1740 Greene's ledger identifies Simpson as "Carolina, Merct." When administration of Simpson's estate was granted to his widow on 6 April 1749, he was identified as a merchant "of Bath Town in the Province of North Carolina."[6] The goldsmith's brother-in-law, William Cowell, Jr. (q.v.), signed the bond. Entries for Simpson appear in Greene's account book as late as June 1753, when Greene's accounts were carried to another folio that does not survive.

On 3 August 1754 the Superior Court of Judicature at Boston empowered Simpson's widow, Mary, to sell his house and land in Newbury Street, Boston, to pay his debts.[7] Mary Simpson probably then went to live with her brother William Cowell, Jr., because in 1761 she petitioned the Boston selectmen to become a retailer of liquor on the grounds that "the House in which she now dwelleth & where her late Brother William Cowell died has been a licensed House for Tavern & public Victualling for above thirty years past viz.t In the lifetime of her father [William Cowell, Sr.], during her mother's widowhood & the life of her late Brother." The selectmen granted her permission to continue this practice.[8]

No work by Charles Simpson is known to survive, but the following advertisement appeared in the *Boston Gazette* on 7 November 1752: "Taken out of a House in Boston, a Silver Pepper Box, mark'd W.M.C. The maker's name SYMPSON. Whoever will stop or take up said Box, so that the Owner may have it again, shall be well rewarded." The advertisement may refer to a piece made by Charles Simpson. PEK

1. RC 24:95; Roberts 1895, 1:346; *Charlestown VR* 1:102; SCPR, docket 7126; RC 28:15.
2. RC 24:60; RC 28:157.
3. Wyman 1879, 2:867; *Watertown Records* 1894, vol. 1, "Births, Marriages, and Deaths," 6; *Charlestown VR* 1:22, 163.
4. RC 24:126; RC 28:263; *Index of Obituaries, 1784–1840*, 4:4087.
5. Benjamin Greene Ledger, 1734–56, 49, 85, 104, 130, MHS.
6. SCPR, docket 9239.
7. SCD 88:194–95.
8. RC 19:165.

Thomas Skinner
1712/13–61

Born and probably trained as a silversmith in Boston, Thomas Skinner moved to Marblehead, Massachusetts, in the mid-1730s. Marblehead was without a goldsmith after the death of William Jones (q.v.) in 1730, and Skinner may

A

B

C

have moved to take advantage of what he saw as an opportunity. He would not have any local competition until Thomas Grant, Samuel Glover, and William Bubier (qq.v.) came of age in the 1750s.

Skinner was born in Boston on 8 March 1712/13, the son of William (ca. 1666–1726) and Deborah (Long) (Phillips) Skinner (b. 1670). His mother was the daughter of Zachariah (1630–88) and Sarah (Tidd) Long (ca. 1636–74) of Charlestown, Massachusetts. Skinner married first Sarah Caswell (b. 1716) of Charlestown, the daughter of Joseph (1689–1715) and Sarah (Hill) Caswell (1681–1732), on 22 August 1734. The family genealogy indicates that Sarah, their first child, was baptized in Boston on 15 June 1735, and their second child, Deborah, was baptized in Marblehead on 27 March 1737, neatly bracketing the period during which the family moved to Essex County. Their third and last child, named for his father, was baptized in Marblehead on 6 May 1739.[1] Also, Skinner was identified as a goldsmith of Boston in 1734/35 and 1735 and then as a goldsmith of Marblehead in 1739, 1741, and 1744 in deeds when he and his wife sold land she had inherited in Charlestown.[2] He was also identified as a silversmith of Marblehead when he and his siblings sold land in Charlestown in 1740.[3] After the death of his first wife, Skinner married Hannah (Kembell or Kimball) Felton of Marblehead on 21 December 1758. They had two children, Joseph and William. She was appointed administrator of his estate.[4]

Skinner died intestate, and his inventory, taken on 20 April 1761, by Thomas Grant, George Newmarch, and William Goodwin, included no real estate and £114.17.8 of personal estate. His tools included:

Sundry tools & Utensils for the Silver Smith's trade	15.. 7.. 2
35^{oz}.. 16^{dwt} wro^t Silver in buckles Spoons &c: & ye making	16.. 6.. 8
6^{pw} 21^{gr} Gold in buttons rings &c & making	2.. 2.. 2
Old wro^t silver 3^{oz}.. 3^{dwt} at 6/8 p. oz 21/D^o Gold 9^{dwt}. 6^{grs}. 44/5	3.. 5.. 5
Stone Buttons Set in Silver 15/	.. 15.
Glass Case 10/ shop Sash windows 28/8	1.. 18.. 8
Shapes & tongs for buckles 9/. Cash in ye house £6..12	7.. 1.[5]

After Skinner's death, Nathaniel Stacy became the guardian of Skinner's children and represented their interests when Skinner's relatives appointed Nathaniel Phillips as their power of attorney concerning Charlestown real estate.[6]

As the relatively modest amount of goods in this estate indicates, Skinner was not a major producer of holloware. A cann in the Metropolitan Museum of Art is a rare example of his work.[7] The earliest dated object by Skinner is a gold mourning ring made for the funeral of I. Leg, who died on 9 February 1750, aged twenty-five. Several marks are associated with this silversmith: Skinner in a rectangle (A); SKINNER in a rectangle (B); and TS in a rectangle with rounded corners (C). GWRW

SURVIVING OBJECTS

	Mark	Inscription	Patron	Date	Reference	Owner
Cann	C	crest, an eagle; MS		ca. 1745	DAPC 69.1586	MMA
Caster	C*	A/WT		ca. 1750	Parke-Bernet, 14–15 May 1948, lot 188	

	Mark	Inscription	Patron	Date	Reference	Owner
Mourning ring (gold)	c*	I·Leg = ob^t 9 $\frac{\pm}{}$ Feb $\frac{\gamma}{}$ 1750-AE^t 25-	I. Leg	1750	Buhler 1972, no. 224	MFAB
Sugar tongs	c	JH		ca. 1755	Christie's, 23 January 1982, lot 87	
Sugar tongs	c*	RI		ca. 1755		MMA
Tablespoon	A*	B/IL		ca. 1750	Bigelow 1917, 270	
Tablespoon	B†	MS/?B		ca. 1745	DAPC 69.4130	WM
Two tablespoons	c	SM		ca. 1750	Avery 1920, nos. 146–47	MMA
Teaspoon	A†	R/JR		ca. 1750	DAPC 73.1524	WM
Teaspoon	c†	ER		ca. 1750	DAPC 75.2933	WM
Teaspoon	c	LL		ca. 1750		SPNEA

1. RC 24:93; RC 28:15; *Charlestown VR* 1:20, 245, 328; Wyman 1879, 1:194; 2:627, 869; Dana 1900, 413–22.
2. MCD 36:120–22; 40:273–74, 401–02; 42:614–16; 49:169–70.
3. MCD 42:728–29.
4. ECPR 338:103, 106–07, 161–62.
5. ECPR 338:103, 106–07, 161–62.
6. MCD 69:460–61.
7. Lord/Gamage 1972, 291.

Benjamin Smith
w. ca. 1758

Benjamin Smith, a jeweler, is known only from an advertisement that appeared in the *Boston News-Letter* on 4 May 1758:

> A Very great Curiosity to be shewn by *Benja-*
> *Smith*, Jeweller, at the Sign of the Gold Ring, near Dr. *Clark's* in-
> Fish Street, being a Mocow Stone, with a large Tree at its full Extent
> growing in it, being esteemed the most curious Piece of nature of the Kind
> ever seen at *Ten shillings*, old Tenor, each Person for seeing the same.
> The said *Smith* will wait upon any Gentlemen or Ladies inclining to see
> the same, giving seasonable Notice.

Smith's curiosity might have been mocha stone, a variety of chalcedony containing infiltrated dendritic oxides of manganese and iron, which give it the appearance of containing vegetable remains. Smith's origins and identity remain uncertain, and no silver by him has been found. PEK

Jeremiah Snow, Jr.
ca. 1705–after 1788

A

In the past literature on American silversmiths, the three generations of silversmiths named Jeremiah Snow (Jr., III, and IV) have not been differentiated clearly. Jeremiah Snow, Jr., was the son of Jeremiah Snow, Sr. (d. before 1724), a mariner of Philadelphia, and either his first wife, Wealthen Watters (Walters) (d. 1704), whom he wed in Charlestown, Massachusetts, on 10 July 1701, or, more likely, his second wife, Mary Welsh (1688–1746), the daughter of Thomas Welsh (1655–1701), a stonecutter, and Hannah Mousall (1662–1713).[1] If Mary Welsh was the mother of Jeremiah, Jr., then he would have been a first cousin of the Boston jeweler John Welsh (q.v.).

If Snow was born about 1705, he would have completed his training by the

B

C

late 1720s. A Jeremiah Snow of Charlestown, probably the goldsmith, appears in the public record in 1730 when he protested the publication of the banns of marriage of Stephen Foard and Mary Rows (Rouse) on 26 November; his objections were judged to be insufficient on 3 December.[2] On 27 June 1734, Snow himself was married in Boston to Mary Byles (d. before 1786), the daughter of John Byles, formerly of Winchester, Hants, England, and his wife, Elisabeth (d. 1710).[3] John Byles had been allowed to settle in Boston in 1702, using his brother Josiah as surety.[4] Two children were born to Jeremiah and Mary Snow in Boston: Jeremiah III (q.v.), born in 1735, and Mary, born in 1738.[5]

Jeremiah Snow, Jr., is identified as a goldsmith in the records of the Suffolk Court of Common Pleas. In the court session of 2 November 1736, the goldsmith Jeremiah Snow of Boston defaulted in a suit brought against him by the housewright John Parry for an unpaid debt of £10.0.17.[6] In the court session of 5 April 1737 Jeremiah Snow of Boston again defaulted in a suit involving unpaid rent brought by the administrators of Elizabeth Simpson's estate. The court ordered Snow to pay £60 in rent for a tenement located on Orange Street in Boston that had been leased to him on 2 July 1735.[7] Snow next appears in written records on 29 May 1739, when he was charged £1.2 "To 1 pair Shoes & melting Pott" in the account book of the silversmith Benjamin Greene (q.v.).[8]

A long hiatus exists before Snow appears in Boston records again. In January 1780/81 the merchant Gabriel Johonnot of Boston sued Jeremiah Snow of Boston, who was identified as a gentleman, for not paying for two hogsheads of sugar delivered separately to Snow on 2 November 1775 at a cost of £27.4.8 each. Johonnot demanded £60 in damages. Snow defaulted and was ordered by the court to pay damages of £27.4.8 in lawful money.[9] His sale of property in 1781 may have offset these expenses: in April 1781, Snow, identified as a Boston goldsmith, sold one-seventh of the front half of a Boston dwelling house. In 1786 when his son, Jeremiah, sold a quarter interest in this property, he identified it as property he inherited from his uncle, Sutton Byles (d. 1776), after the death of his mother. The elder Snow appeared and acknowledged the deed of 1781 when it was recorded in 1788.[10] The transaction is the last reference to Snow in public records, and no evidence of his death date has been found.

Three initial and surname marks, I·Snow. in rectangle (A), J·Snow in cartouche (B), and I·Snow in rectangle (C), may have been used by this silversmith, although they may also have been used by Snow's son Jeremiah III, and (A) perhaps even by Snow's grandson, Jeremiah IV. Additional marks, I.Snow and I.Snow in rectangles, have also been recorded but have not been located for illustration.[11] JJF

SURVIVING OBJECTS

	Mark	Inscription	Patron	Date	Reference	Owner
Sugar tongs §	B*	TMD		ca. 1780		HD
Tablespoon §	A†	L/IM		ca. 1750	DAPC 71.2828	WM
Tablespoon §	B*	IA/to/RM		ca. 1765		HD
Tablespoon §	B†	ID/NKH (+)		ca. 1765		SI
Tablespoon §	C†	LD		ca. 1770	DAPC 81.3805	
Tablespoon §	C	EA		ca. 1780		HD

Mark	Inscription	Patron	Date	Reference	Owner
A*	unidentified arms; Hannah Arnold	Hannah Arnold	ca. 1760	YUAG files	

Tankard §

§ Possibly by Jeremiah Snow III.

1. Wyman 1879, 2:881, 993, 1006; *Charlestown VR* 1:15, 40, 107, 138, 186, 256; Codman 1918, 209; MCPR, docket 24020. Following the death of Jeremiah Snow, Sr., Mary (Welsh) Snow married, second, about 1724, William Davis (d. ca. 1730) and, third, Joshua Scottow; see Wyman 1879, 1:282. Following Thomas Welsh's death in 1701 his widow married Joseph Lamson.
2. *Charlestown VR* 1:455–56.
3. RC 28:188; SCD 163:185–86; Eaton 1915, 101.
4. RC 11:1; Eaton 1915, 101.
5. RC 24:223, 234.
6. SCCR, Court of Common Pleas Record Book 1736–37, 79.
7. SCCR, Court of Common Pleas Record Book 1736–37, 483.
8. Benjamin Greene Ledger, 1734–56, 31, MHS.
9. SCCR, Court of Common Pleas Record Book 1780, 104, box 1781, file 14.
10. SCD 163:185–86; SCPR, docket 16027.
11. Graham 1936, 67; Thorn 1949, 190; Ensko 1948, 198; Kovel 1961, 253.

Jeremiah Snow III
1735–1803

A

B

C

Jeremiah Snow III was born in Boston on 20 April 1735, the son of Jeremiah Snow, Jr. (q.v.), and Mary Byles.[1] The younger Snow probably was a cousin of the Boston jeweler John Welsh (q.v.), and the goldsmith Daniel Parker (q.v.) probably was a distant relative. Snow probably apprenticed with his father about 1749 and then moved west to Springfield, Massachusetts, after completing his training, purchasing land there in January 1759.[2] On 29 November 1759, he married Mary Brewer (1737–1809), the daughter of Isaac Brewer (1713–ca. 1785) and Mary Bliss (1715/16–59) of nearby Wilbraham, a parish of Springfield until 1763, who were married on 22 April 1736.[3]

In 1762, Snow borrowed £40.12 from the Boston silversmith Benjamin Goodwin (q.v.); in 1764, Goodwin advanced Snow an additional £16.9.3, with written agreements that both debts were to be repaid with interest. On 5 March 1765, Goodwin successfully sued Snow for nonpayment of this debt and was awarded £59.2.2 in damages plus £2.16.10 for the suit's costs. Snow probably raised the funds to repay Goodwin by mortgaging his Springfield home in April to the Boston jeweler Benjamin Pierpont (q.v.). In June 1765, the balance of Snow's debt to Goodwin was paid by the seizure of one acre and sixty rods of property that adjoined his Springfield home. Snow seems to have paid off his mortgage to Pierpont but probably remortgaged his property in 1773.[4]

Snow appears to have remained in Springfield for most of his life, consistently identifying himself as a goldsmith in deeds from 1759 to 1786.[5] The Massachusetts tax valuation list of 1771 recorded his modest ownership of one head of cattle, an acre of upland mowing land, and one house with an adjoining shop.[6] He may have returned to the Boston area briefly beginning in 1774, when for three years he rented an acre of land with dwelling house, shop, barn, and buildings in Charlestown, Massachusetts, from Ebenezer Thwing, at the rate of thirty pounds per annum.[7] In 1786, Snow received forty pounds for one-quarter of the easterly half of a Boston house that he had inherited at his mother's death through the will of his uncle Sutton Byles.[8]

Snow died on 24 February 1803 and was buried in Springfield.[9] Two of his sons followed his career: Jeremiah IV (1764–about 1821–23) became a clockmaker and goldsmith, working in Palmer, Wilbraham, Amherst, and Springfield, Massachusetts, and Ralph Snow (1769–1839) probably became a metalsmith in Springfield and Williamsburg, Massachusetts, and later moved to Troy, New York.[10]

The marks I·SNOW. in rectangle (A), J·SNOW in cartouche (B), and I·SNOW in rectangle (C), which were used by Jeremiah Snow, Jr., may also have been used by Jeremiah Snow III. Mark (A) probably continued to be used by the third generation, Jeremiah IV. Jeremiah III also produced brass-hilted horseman's sabres, probably for use in the revolutionary war. At least two swords with the (A) mark survive.[11] JJF

SURVIVING OBJECTS

	Mark	Inscription	Patron	Date	Reference	Owner
Mustard spoon	A	MH		ca. 1800		CHS
Sword (brass and steel)	A	none		ca. 1775	Mowbray 1979, 27	
Sword (brass and steel)	A	none		ca. 1775	Mowbray 1979, 27	
Sugar tongs §	B*	TMD		ca. 1780		HD
Tablespoon	A†	TD		ca. 1800		HD
Tablespoon	A*	HD		ca. 1800		HD
Tablespoon	A*	CB		ca. 1800		YUAG
Tablespoon §	B*	IA/to/RM		ca. 1765		HD
Tablespoon §	B†	ID/NKH		ca. 1765		SI
Tablespoon §	C†	LD		ca. 1770	DAPC 81.3805	
Tablespoon §	C*	EA		ca. 1780		HD
Tankard §	A*	unidentified arms; Hannah Arnold	Hannah Arnold	ca. 1760	YUAG files	
Teaspoon	A*	PMW		ca. 1800		YUAG
Teaspoon	A	PH		ca. 1790	DAPC 73.1530	WM
Teaspoon	A	MT		ca. 1800	DAPC 73.1528	WM

§ Possibly by Jeremiah Snow, Jr.

1. RC 24:223.
2. HCD 3:73.
3. Warren 1934–35, 1:90–91; 3:630.
4. SCCR, Court of Common Pleas, docket book 24, 142, docket 244; HCD 3:349; 12:824–25; 13:168; Book A, 449–53.
5. HCD 3:73, 349; 12:824–25; 13:168, 361; SCD 163:185–86.
6. Pruitt 1978, 422–23.
7. MCD 75:407–08.
8. SCD 163:185–86; SCPR 75:410–13, docket 16027.
9. Lewis 1938, 58.
10. Mowbray 1979, 30; Flynt/Fales 1968, 326–27.
11. Mowbray 1979, 26–30. Mowbray claimed that Snow produced swords both before and after the Revolution and estimated that several hundred were made.

Joseph Soames
1680/81–1705

Joseph Soames's birth is not recorded, but according to his epitaph in the Copp's Hill Burying Ground he was twenty-four years and six months old when he died on 2 August 1705.[1] Joseph Soames was the son of John Soames (1648–1700), a cooper, and Hannah (Shattuck) Soames (1651–d. by 1714). Hannah was the daughter of Samuel (ca. 1620–ca. 1689), a feltmaker, and Grace Shattuck of Salem, Massachusetts. John Soames was the son of Morris Soames (d. 1689) and Elizabeth (Kendall) Soames of Gloucester, Massachusetts. A Quaker who was banished from the colony in 1669, John Soames returned to Boston in 1670, when Charles II ordered that the Acts of Toleration be accepted in Massachusetts, and became one of the trustees of the first Quaker meetinghouse in Boston. John Soames wrote his will in 1687, when he was bound to sea; it mentions his sons John, Samuel, Joseph, and Benjamin. Although John Soames died on 16 November 1700, his estate took many years to be settled. An inventory taken in 1713 includes 181 ounces of plate, two "great Tables," eighteen "turkey workt" chairs, fifteen leather chairs, and two slaves.[2]

In 1703/04 Joseph Soames, son of John Soames, deceased, sued René Grignon (q.v.) for £150 for failing to live up to his agreement to "teach and Instruct or cause the sd apprentice [Joseph Soames] to be taught and Instructed in the arts trades and Callings of Goldsmith and Jeweller." Joseph Soames, his father, and René Grignon had entered into the apprenticeship agreement on 1 November 1697 for a term of five years. Although it is not clear why Grignon, "altho often . . . Requested" to do so, "refused and still refuseth" to teach Soames the goldsmith's trade, it may have been because Grignon decided to return to Oxford, or New Oxford, Massachusetts, to the fledgling Huguenot settlement that had been established there. Soames must have found another master, for he is referred to as Joseph Soames of Boston, goldsmith, in the suit.[3]

Joseph Soames's work is not known through surviving objects. He died only a few years after completing his apprenticeship and probably made very little silver or jewelry. There is no record that he ever married, and his estate was not probated. BMW

1. His brother John was born in Boston in 1680, and his sister Hannah was born in Boston in 1682; although Joseph's birth is not recorded, he too was undoubtedly born in Boston; RC 9:153, 158. The information on the epitaph is recorded in the Bigelow-Phillips files, 570.
2. *Sewall Diary* 1:437; SCPR 14:247–48; 18:126–27; Bridgman 1851, 95; *Salem VR* 2:277; 6:217; ECPR, docket 25127; *Gloucester VR* 1:667; Whitmore 1878, 49, no. 927; Selleck 1976, 31–32.
3. SCCR, file 6035.

Ebenezer Staniford
1754–82

An obscure goldsmith of Ipswich, Massachusetts, Ebenezer Staniford was baptized there on 17 March 1754, the son of Capt. Thomas (ca. 1710–78), a sea captain and merchant, and Sarah (Burnum) Staniford (ca. 1715–78), who were married in 1732. His mother was the daughter of James (1691–1736) and Sarah (Rogers) Burnum (d. 1727) of Ipswich. His paternal grandfather was Thomas Staniford, who may also have been the maternal grandfather of Thomas Grant (q.v.), a Marblehead, Massachusetts, goldsmith. Ebenezer Staniford married Lucy Fowler (1757?–90) in Ipswich on 26 July 1780, and they had two daughters. Staniford is identified as a goldsmith in his will, written on 9 June 1781. He left his entire estate to his wife, to be divided with their daughter Sarah when she turned eighteen. Ebenezer may have written his will before going to sea as a mariner because he is reported to have died of dysentery in the West

Indies in February 1782. The will was presented by Lucy on 5 March 1782, with Jeremiah Day, Jr., and Ebenezer Safford serving as witnesses. The inventory of his estate apparently has been lost. His widow is said to have been remarried in 1787 to John Curtice Blachford.[1]

A modern family history does not recognize that Staniford was a silversmith. It states that Ebenezer first entered the ministry, subsequently served in the Revolution in Capt. Nathaniel Wade's company in the regiment of Col. William Hodgkins, and then went to sea to meet his fate in the West Indies.[2] No silver by him is known to survive. GWRW

1. *Ipswich VR* 1:64, 71, 150, 350; 2:81, 374, 406, 511, 512, 684; 3:49; ECPR, docket 26178; see also Staniford 1960, 23.
2. Staniford 1960, 23.

Jaspar Starr
1709/10–92

Born in New London, Connecticut, on 21 March 1709/10, Jaspar Starr was the son of Benjamin Starr (1679–1753) and Lydia (Latham) Starr (ca. 1686–1747), daughter of Joseph Latham of New London. Benjamin was the son of Comfort Starr (1644–93) of Scituate, Massachusetts, and Marah (Weld) Starr (b. 1646) of Roxbury, Massachusetts. Their first child, Mary, was born in 1671 in Boston, but they soon moved to New London and later to Middletown, Connecticut, where Benjamin was born. Benjamin Starr began his career as a mariner but soon became a merchant. He made a fortune in the West India trade and was active in town and colony affairs, becoming a member of the Connecticut Governor's Council in 1720.[1]

Jaspar Starr probably went to Boston to serve his apprenticeship. About 1729 he married Margaret Calef (1710–1802), daughter of Robert (d. 1722 or 1723) and Margaret (Barton) Calef (d. 1744) of Boston.[2] Margaret was the cousin of William Simpkins (q.v.). The couple probably moved to New London about 1731. Their first child, Jaspar, was baptized in New London on 31 October 1731.[3] In 1731 Starr also was referred to as being "of New London, Goldsmith," when he and his wife quitclaimed their right in the estate of Robert Calef to Margaret's mother for two hundred pounds and "divers other good causes."[4]

It is not clear how long Jaspar Starr continued to work at his trade, but by 1745 he had become a mariner. That year he led an expedition against Cape Breton as master of the sloop *Defence*.[5] He was back in Boston by 23 May 1767, when he purchased a house and land in Newbury Street from Robert Pierpont for £93.6.8. In that deed and in the deed of 1771 in which he and his wife, Margaret, sold the same property to Benjamin Church, Jr., for £400, he is identified as "Jaspar Starr of Boston, Mariner." At the same time Church sold his farm and sixty acres of land in South Bridgewater, Massachusetts, to Starr.[6] It is not clear whether Starr ever again practiced the silversmithing trade but the Massachusetts tax list of 1771 includes Starr in Bridgewater with one poll, a house and shop adjoining, £10.16 annual value of real estate, pasturage, and animals.[7] Starr lived there until his death in 1792; he and his wife are buried in the Scotland graveyard in South Bridgewater.[8] He left no will, and the estate was not probated.

No silver by Jaspar Starr is known to survive. BMW

1. *Starr Family*, nos. 7, 353; RC 9:120; *Roxbury VR* 1:360; *Scituate VR* 1:328; New London VR 1:15; Middletown VR, vol. LRI, 16.
2. SCPR 37:243–44, docket 4691; RC 9:250; RC 24:67.

3. *Starr Family*, no. 354; Boardman 1938, 375–76.
4. SCPR 31:357–58.
5. *Starr Family*, no. 354; Boardman 1938, 375–76.
6. SCD 110:184–85; 118:200–01.
7. Pruitt 1978, 628–29.
8. *Starr Family*, no. 354.

Daniel Steward
1734–1802

Daniel Steward's roots were in Essex County, Massachusetts. He was born on 21 November 1734 in Salem, the son of Solomon Steward (1698–1758) of Rowley and Martha Farrington (1702–77) of Andover, who were married in Andover on 28 June 1727.[1] Steward's father Solomon was a yeoman, and his mother was admitted to the Bradford church in 1727.[2] His paternal grandparents were James Steward (b. 1664) of Newbury and his wife, Elisabeth (d. 1732).[3] His maternal grandparents were Edward Farrington (1662–1746/47) of Lynn and Martha Brown (1667–1738) of Newbury.[4]

Daniel Steward probably moved from Salem to Lunenberg, Massachusetts, with his parents, who had settled there by 1738, the year they were admitted to the Lunenberg church.[5] His father was prominent in Lunenberg affairs, serving as constable, tithingman, deer reeves, fireman, surveyor of the highway, selectman, and assessor between 1742/43 and 1753/54.[6]

Daniel Steward married Mary (Molly) Ireland (1739–1818) of Cambridge, Massachusetts, in Lunenberg on 14 March 1757, and the couple had eight children, all born in Lunenberg.[7] Mary Ireland was the daughter of Abraham Ireland (b. 1713) of Cambridge and Ann Bird (b. 1714) of Boston, who married in Dorchester, Massachusetts, on 8 April 1736 and became landowners in Lunenberg.[8]

The first land transaction conducted by Steward was his purchase of about twenty-seven acres in Lunenberg in 1773 for £115.2.6 from his father-in-law, Abraham Ireland. Steward, identified as a "clockmaker of Lunenberg," with Philip Goodridge, "gentleman," then sold this land in two parcels for £66.13.4 and £105.13.4, in 1774 and 1777, respectively. Of the five deeds known to have been transacted by Daniel Steward in Worcester County, three name him as a clockmaker, one as a yeoman, and one as a goldsmith. In spite of this singular reference to Steward's being a goldsmith, no silver by him survives, and his master is not known.[9]

Steward served as a private of Lunenberg during the Revolution, returning there after the war and remaining until 1779 or later.[10] He moved to Fitchburg, Massachusetts, in later life, serving as pound keeper there in 1796 and in 1800 signing a deed as clockmaker of Fitchburg.[11] The diary of James Parker of Shirley, Massachusetts, notes that "Mr. Steward fixed my clock" on 22 January 1791, and in August of the same year Parker noted, "Got my watch at Stuarts paid him in cash."[12]

An inventory taken of his estate in 1802 makes clear that Steward, although insolvent at his death, was a practicing clockmaker until he died at the age of sixty-eight. Steward's gravestone is in the South Street Cemetery in Fitchburg.[13] The probate records are particularly rich with details of Steward's tools. Articles "sold at vendue" included such large pieces as an eight-day clock and a "clock machine" as well as screws, nails, and bits; gauges, lathes, and watch and wooden wheels; and screwplates, watch tools, and a crucible. Other items and clocks in Steward's possession at his death included:

tools for making Clocks $13.12 box of old iron $1	14.12
iron Stake 80 cents Blacksmiths vice $3	3.80
one Brass clock in part made with a case	30.0
one ditto in part made $10. one ditto $10	20.0
one wooden clock $5.80 one ditto $6. one ditto $8.	19.80.[14]

The weight of the evidence thus points toward Steward's primarily being a clockmaker, rather than a goldsmith, although like many clockmakers in rural areas, he occasionally may have made silver. JJF

1. *Salem VR* 2:322; *Rowley VR*, 207, 405; Bigelow-Phillips files, 1541, 1544; *Andover VR* 1:142.
2. Admission to Bradford Church noted in Bigelow-Phillips files, 1541.
3. Bigelow-Phillips files, 1541; *Rowley VR*, 524.
4. *Lynn VR* 1:143; *Andover VR* 2:115, 428.
5. Rollins, n.d., n.p.
6. Davis 1896, 117, 122, 125, 130, 133, 139, 140, 141, 162.
7. *Cambridge VR* 1:389; Mrs. Benjamin Taylor to Francis Hill Bigelow, 2 March 1933, Bigelow-Phillips files, 1541–44. According to this correspondence, Mary Ireland Steward died in Bloomfield, Maine, in 1818 "aged 79 yrs," as recorded on her gravestone, Blood Cemetery, old Bloomfield, but this death date has not been proved. Births of Steward children in Davis 1896, 323, as cited in Bigelow-Phillips files, n.p.
8. *Cambridge VR* 1:388; RC 24:102; RC 21:117.
9. WCD 71:117–18; 86:7–8; 89:9; 105:593; 140:26–28.
10. *Mass. Soldiers and Sailors* 14:992; WCD 86:7.
11. Davis 1898–1913, 2:195; WCD 140:26–28.
12. *NEHGR* 70:9–10.
13. Bigelow-Phillips files, 1544.
14. WCPR, docket 56057.

Richard Storer
ca. 1615–57+

Little information is known about Richard Storer's origins, but the records of the Goldsmiths' Company in London reveal that on 21 July 1629 he was apprenticed for ten years to the London goldsmith James Fearne.[1] Storer, who probably was born about 1615, was the son of Paul (d. before 1627), a barber, of Market Hareborough, Leicestershire, England, and Elizabeth Storer (d. 1646).[2] Following his father's death Storer's mother married Robert Hull, father of John Hull (q.v.), around 1627.[3] Storer's apprenticeship was to have ended on the feast day of the Nativity of John the Baptist, 24 June 1639, but it has been generally presumed that Storer cut short his apprenticeship to immigrate to America with his mother and stepfather in 1635. No documentary evidence of his being in New England exists, however, until 25 November 1639, when he was granted land in Braintree, Massachusetts: "Richard Storer, the sonne of Elizabeth Hull, the Wife of our brother Roberte Hull, is Allowed to be an Inhabitant and to have a great lotte at the Mount for three heads."[4] Most likely Storer remained in London and completed his apprenticeship early in 1639 and then immigrated to New England, at which point he was allowed to be an inhabitant and was granted the land in Braintree.

John Hull recorded in his diary how he learned the craft of silversmithing from Storer, but Storer did not remain in New England for very long.[5] By 1646 he probably had returned to London. In December 1646 Robert Hull gave John Hull the twenty-one acres of land that Storer had been given by the town of Boston, which Robert Hull presumably had purchased from Storer upon the latter's return to England.[6] When Robert Hull made out his will in 1657 he bequeathed nine pounds to Storer, but Storer must have died by 1666 when the will was executed, for John Hull was called "the eldest and now only son" when named administrator.[7]

No silver by Storer is known. PEK

1. Apprentice Book 1, fol. 292r, Worshipful Company of Goldsmiths, London.
2. Richard Storer's approximate birth date has been calculated from the date of his apprenticeship.
3. No record of this marriage has been found.
4. RC 2:43.
5. "Hull Diaries," 142.
6. SCPR 1:511.
7. SCPR 1:511.

Samuel Sturgis
1737–62

Samuel Sturgis recently was identified as a goldsmith through his probate papers filed in 1762.[1] He was the son of Solomon (q.v.) and Abigail (Lewis) Sturgis (b. 1711) and was born in Barnstable, Massachusetts, on 7 September 1737.[2] Samuel probably trained with his father and would have begun his apprenticeship about 1751 and completed it about 1758. Samuel's career was very brief. His wife, Abigail (Crocker), the daughter of Cornelius Crocker (b. 1704) and Lydia Jenkins, and her father were appointed in 1762 as administrators of Samuel's estate, which was declared insolvent.[3] Although his probate inventory contained no silversmith's tools, it did include a substantial number of pieces of silver, including two silver-hilted swords valued at £4.10, a tankard and pepper box valued at £10.6, a spout cup, twelve teaspoons, and six large spoons at £6.10.[4] This plate may have been for household use as opposed to stock. No silver by Samuel Sturgis has been identified. JJF and PEK

1. Cullity 1994, 163, citing BCPR 10:108.
2. "Barnstable, Mass. Vital Records," *Mayflower Descendant* 33 (October 1935): 163.
3. *Barnstable and Sandwich VR*, 17, 34, 104.
4. Cullity 1994, 163.

Solomon Sturgis
1703–64

Recent research on the silversmiths of Plymouth, Cape Cod, and Nantucket has uncovered the existence of an additional maker working in Barnstable, Massachusetts, during the colonial period: Solomon Sturgis, who was identified as a goldsmith through his probate papers.[1] Solomon Sturgis, born in Barnstable on 25 September 1703, was the son of Samuel Sturgis and his wife, Mary, the widow of Nathaniel Oris.[2] Solomon would have trained between about 1717 and 1724, perhaps with Moody Russell (q.v.), who returned to Barnstable about 1716 after completing an apprenticeship in Boston. The marriage intentions of Solomon Sturgis and Abigail Lewis (b. 1711) were published in July 1732, and the couple married in August.[3] Abigail was the daughter of Ebenezer Lewis (b. 1666) and Anna Lothrop (b. 1673), who married in Barnstable in 1691.[4] Solomon and Abigail had a son, Samuel (q.v.), who also became a silversmith.

No silver by Solomon Sturgis has been identified. JJF and PEK

1. Cullity 1994, 163; BCPR 10:142².
2. *Barnstable and Sandwich VR*, 45; Savage 1860–62, 3:316, 4:229.
3. *Barnstable and Sandwich VR*, 37, 118.
4. *Barnstable and Sandwich VR* 35, 37.

Caleb Swan
1754–1816

Caleb Swan was born in Charlestown, Massachusetts, on 6 July 1754, the son of Samuel Swan (1725?–1808), a barber, and Joanna Richardson (1724–96), who were married in 1745.[1] His paternal grandparents were Timothy Swan (d. 1746) and Mehitable Austin (1696–1754) of Charlestown.[2] His maternal grandparents were Daniel Richardson (1691–1734) and Joanna Miller (ca. 1692–1749) of Woburn, Massachusetts.[3]

Swan probably trained in Boston with Benjamin Burt (q.v.) from about 1768 to the eve of the Revolution. Swan married Burt's niece Sally [Sarah] Semple (ca. 1756–1821) in Boston on 14 April 1777 and maintained other close connections to Burt.[4] When Swan and his wife bought a house on the west side of Hanover Street, near Friend Street, in 1780, the deed listed his occupation as goldsmith.[5] In 1781, Burt was named administrator of the estate of his brother-in-law Joseph Glidden, and Zachariah Brigden (q.v.) and Swan signed the bond.[6] One of Swan's three children was named Benjamin Burt Swan.[7]

Following the Revolution, Swan and his wife moved from Boston to Charlestown. In 1783 the couple sold land in Boston to Thomas Wallis and mortgaged their house in Hanover Street, transactions that probably predated their move.[8] A deed of 7 August 1784 identifies Swan as being of Charlestown, formerly of Boston.[9] In Middlesex County deeds mentioning him, of which there are many, he is identified as being a merchant of Charlestown as late as 15 April 1796, but beginning 25 June 1798 he is described as being a merchant of Woburn.[10] In July 1802 Sarah Swan reported that her husband was a distracted person, incapable of taking care of his affairs, and asked that a guardian be appointed. Swan was declared non compos, and Swan's brother Samuel became guardian for him on 22 September 1802, a responsibility he carried out until November 1807, when the probate court, upon complaint of Caleb Swan, his wife, and children, dismissed Samuel from his role as guardian for failing to present an accounting.[11] In his will, dated 28 December 1814, Swan is said to be "of Woburn yeoman." Following his death on 30 March 1816, the inventory taken of his estate showed that it amounted to $10,810 in real estate, including the homestead on 222 acres in Woburn and $2,874.81 in personal estate. Charges against the estate amounted to $818.66.[12]

Although some authorities have attributed an initials mark to him, the evidence for the attribution is exceedingly thin.[13] No silver bearing his mark has been positively identified; presumably he worked principally as a retailer of silversmiths' goods rather than as a working goldsmith. PEK

1. *NEHGR* 31:328; *Index of Obituaries, 1784–1840*, 5:4361; Wyman 1879, 2:918; *Charlestown VR* 1:408, 471; *Woburn VR* 1:213; Hunnewell 1888, 258.
2. Usher 1886, 558; *Charlestown VR* 1:246; *NEHGR* 28:448; Griffen 1952, 109.
3. *Woburn VR* 1:211.
4. RC 30:374; in the marriage records the name is recorded as Temple and Sample. Sally Semple's birth date was calculated from her age at death; see *Index of Obituaries, 1784–1840*, 5:4361, and *Woburn VR* 2:186.
5. SCD 132:41–42. Swan mortgaged land in Charlestown to Burt in 1799; see MCD 134:231–34, 487–89; 190:197–98.
6. SCPR 80:199.
7. Wyman 1879, 2:920.
8. SCD 138:229–32; 139:182–83, 199–200.
9. SCD 144:115.
10. MCD 84:595; 95:349; 98:510; 104:452–56; 105:99–100; 112:93–94, 368–70; 113:58–59, 241, 273–74; 115:364–66, 401–02; 116:428–30, 481–82, 498–99, 500–01, 519–21; 118:468; 120:302–03, 313–14, 433–34; 127:440–42; 131:304–05; 134:230–36, 280–81.

11. MCPR, docket 21947.

12. MCPR 127:235, docket 21948.

13. Flynt/Fales 1968, 334.

Robert Swan
1749–1832

Robert Swan was born in Methuen, Massachusetts, on 19 January 1749 to the yeoman Robert Swan (1711–52) and Elizabeth Farnum (1711–80).[1] The younger Robert's father died in October 1752, and in 1760 his mother married Deacon James How.[2] In 1762 Ebenezer Barker, Esq., was appointed to be the guardian of Robert, Jr.[3] Swan's paternal grandparents were the yeoman Robert Swan (1686–1770) and Hannah Stevens (b. 1685) of Andover, Massachusetts.[4] His maternal grandparents were Jonathan Farnum (1684–1761) and Elizabeth Barker (d. 1732) of Andover.[5]

Swan's apprenticeship would have begun about 1765, but the identity of his master is not known. Swan would have been working by about 1772 and probably carried on the occupations of yeoman and silversmith simultaneously. On 26 March 1772 he was identified as a yeoman when he purchased land in Andover from the cooper Benjamin Johnson. The land consisted of one tract of more than twenty-three acres with land and buildings and a second piece with tillage, pasturage, and woodland.[6] He was identified as a yeoman when he purchased additional land in Andover in 1773, 1774, 1778, 1783, and 1784.[7] He was identified as a silversmith, however, in a deed of 1779, when he purchased from Samuel Martin a "half part moiety" in Andover land of which Swan owned the other half.[8] He was identified as a "bucklemaker" in a deed of 1784 that involved the sale of the same land.[9] He also engaged in minor business transactions with the Salem, Massachusetts, silversmith John Hathorne (q.v.).[10]

On 29 April 1773 Swan married Aphia (Affa) Farrington (1756–88), the daughter of John Farrington and Sarah Houghton.[11] Aphia died in 1788, and in 1789 Swan married Susanna (Emery) Abbott (d. 1842), the widow of Nehemiah Abbott.[12] After his second marriage, Swan engaged in a number of additional land transactions, in all of which he was identified as a yeoman.[13] He died in Andover on 25 December 1832 at the age of eighty-four.[14] The inventory of his personal estate amounted to $171.75 and contained no goldsmiths' tools.[15] A third of the real estate was set off for his widow in 1834.[16]

No work by Swan's hand has been identified. Swan has been confused with the silversmith by the same name of Philadelphia, who may have sailed to this country in 1774 aboard the *Sally* from Kilmalalee, Scotland.[17] JJF

1. *Methuen VR*, 122; *Haverhill VR* 1:291; *Andover VR* 1:134; 2:117; ECD 117:19–20.

2. *Methuen VR*, 275, 340, 318; ECPR, docket 26898.

3. ECPR, docket 26878.

4. *Haverhill VR* 1:291; 2:305; ECPR 346:325; *Andover VR* 1:340.

5. *Andover VR* 1:138; 2:119, 429, 432.

6. ECD 134:244–45; 132:201–02.

7. ECD 132:201–02; 134:245; 143:93; 176:12; 175:222–23; 165:197–98; 151:211–12; 176:11v.

8. ECD 176:11v.

9. ECD 136:25–26.

10. English-Touzel-Hathorne Papers, PEM.

11. *Andover VR* 1:131; 2:121, 433.

12. *Andover VR* 2:113, 322, 555.

13. ECD 180:297–98; 151:238; 154:90–91; 176:12; 175:222–23; 162:229–30; 175:223; 187:135–36.

14. *Andover VR* 2:555.

15. ECPR 82:327.

16. ECPR 409:95–96.

17. Cameron 1980, 50; Dobson 1984–86, 1:251.

William Swan
1715–74

A

B

C

William Swan was born in Charlestown, Massachusetts, on 14 August 1715 to Ebenezer Swan (1686–1716), a mariner, of Roxbury, Massachusetts, and Prudence Foster (b. 1684) of Boston, who married on 23 December 1707 in Charlestown.[1] After Ebenezer Swan's early death at sea in 1716, Prudence (Foster) Swan was married a second time to the Reverend John Prentice. Swan's paternal grandparents were Dr. Thomas Swan (d. 1687/88) and Mary Lamb (b. 1644) of Roxbury.[2] His maternal grandparents were Timothy Foster (1638–88) of Dorchester, Massachusetts, and Relief (Holland) Douse (ca. 1649–1743).[3]

Swan probably was trained in Boston, and as a cousin of Edward Foster (q.v.), who was about his age, the two would have apprenticed at about the same time, beginning in 1729, perhaps with the same master. In 1731 Swan's father Ebenezer's estate was partly settled, resulting in young William's receipt of £53.14.8.[4] William Swan married Levinah Keyes on 5 January 1744 in King's Chapel, Boston.[5] She was probably the daughter of Jacob Key or Keyes and Rachel Ross, who were married in Boston on 27 November 1701.[6]

Within two years of his marriage, Swan served with the company of Capt. Jonathan Smith in the Louisbourg Expedition.[7] One likely result of this experience was his commission in 1749 by the Province of Massachusetts Bay for a grace cup. The most ambitious work of Swan's career, the cup was made in honor of Col. Benjamin Pickman for his service in the expedition.[8] The only other evidence of Swan's work in Boston is a bill of £135.1.6 for mourning rings, paid in 1751 by the estate of Samuel Black, merchant of Boston.[9]

Swan's residence in Boston during the early years of his marriage is documented by the births there of his children William, Levinah, and Thomas between 1745 and 1751.[10] Swan moved west by 1754 because the birth of his son Edward is recorded in Marlborough, Massachusetts.[11] By 1756, he had relocated to Worcester, Massachusetts, where seven additional children were born.[12] Swan's good standing in the community can be gleaned from several religious and secular positions he held in Worcester. In 1770 the First Parish Church in Worcester (Old South Church) "voted that Mr. William Swan Set in ye same seat [elder seat] to assist . . . in singing."[13] From 1772 to 1773 Swan was clerk of the market, and in 1774 he was sealer of weights and measures.[14] Swan was also on the Massachusetts tax valuation list of 1771; although he appeared to own little real estate (it was valued at ten shillings, and no other deeds have been found), he did own merchandise valued at twelve pounds and had lent sixteen pounds at interest.[15]

In 1773, shortly before his death, Swan's home was robbed. The following list of stolen goods indicates that Swan actively continued to practice his craft, making smaller objects such as spoons, buttons, and jewelry. His notice in the *Boston News-Letter* recorded the loss of

5 Pair Stone Earing Rings,
1/2 Doz. Tea Spoons partly finished,
5 Pair Stone Sleeve Buttons,
1 Gold Necklace,
Sundry Pair Silver Shoe Buckles; one Pair partly
finished; together with about Twelve Pounds in Cash viz. I Johanna, 1 Guinea,
6 Crowns, the Remainder in Dollars.

    All well disposed Persons are desired to apprehend
the Thief, for which a Reward of SIX DOLLARS
will be given. If the Articles are offered to Sale, its desired they may be stopped.
Worcester, 25th *May*, 1773. WM. SWAN.[16]

Swan most likely worked as a silversmith and jeweler until the end of his life because in his will of 1774 he called himself a goldsmith, rather than the "gentleman" commonly used by older men.[17] His professional status is confirmed by his obituary, which described the fifty-nine-year-old Swan as "Goldsmith, formerly of Boston, a Man of a very respectable Character."[18]

Swan is primarily known for his surname mark, Swan in script in a shaped cartouche (A), but other marks attributed to him include Swan in script in a rectangle (B), and WSWAN in a shaped cartouche (C). SWAN in a rectangle has been recorded in the literature, but no example was found for illustration.[19] Two initials marks have also been assigned to him, although pieces bearing these marks could not be located to assess the validity of the attributions.[20] Swan made a wide variety of forms, ranging from spoons to canns, sauceboats, porringers, and two-handled cups for domestic, ecclesiastical, and commemorative purposes. JJF

SURVIVING OBJECTS

	Mark	Inscription	Patron	Date	Reference	Owner
Two beakers	A	The Property/ Of the Church of Christ/In Northborough/1797 (later)		ca. 1770	Jones 1913, 351	
Cann (mate below)	A*	KC	Katharine [Catherine] (Chandler) Willard	ca. 1755	Conger/ Rollins 1991, no. 195	USDS
Cann (mate above)	A†	KC	Katharine [Catherine] (Chandler) Willard	ca. 1755	Buhler 1972, no. 229	MFAB
Cann	A*	B/DZ		ca. 1740	YUAG files	
Cann	A	HG; EC		ca. 1755	DAPC 73.2256	
Cann	A/C	HT/to HT 3rd (later?)		ca. 1745	Buhler 1979, no. 24	WAM
Cann	B†	F/RS		ca. 1765	Buhler 1965, 66–67	HMA
Cann	C	M[F, I, or S?] D		ca. 1750	Avery 1920, no. 148	MMA
Caster	A	Greenleaf crest, a bird with a sprig in its beak; unidentified initials (later)	Greenleaf family	ca. 1770	Sotheby's, 23–24 June 1994, lot 106	
Caster	?	?		ca. 1770	Christie's, 19 September 1981, lot 81	
Creampot	A	WE	William Ellery (?)	ca. 1740	*Antiques* 122 (July 1982): 43	
Creampot	A	HC	Hannah Chauncy	ca. 1750	Buhler 1965, 64–65	HMA
Creampot	A	KC; JW (later)	Katharine [Catherine] (Chandler) Willard	ca. 1755	Buhler 1972, no. 227	MFAB
Cup	?	?	Thomas Sawyer and/or	ca. 1762	Dresser 1935–	

	Mark	Inscription	Patron	Date	Reference	Owner
			First Church of Christ, Lancaster, Mass.		36, 50	
Cup (attrib.)	none	KC	Katharine [Catherine] (Chandler) Willard	ca. 1755	Buhler 1972, no. 228	MFAB
Grace cup	A*	Pickman arms, gules 2 battle-axes in sal-tire between 4 mart-lets, and crest, a martlet; THE/Gift of the Province of the/ MASSACHUSETTS BAY/To/Benjamin Pickman Esqʳ/1749	Province of Massachu-setts Bay for Benjamin Pickman	1749	Fales 1983, 18–19	PEM
Ladle	A	none		ca. 1760		MFAB
Porringer (mate? below)	A	Greenleaf crest, a bird with a sprig in its beak	Greenleaf family	ca. 1760	Ham-merslough/ Feigenbaum 1958–73, 3:43	
Porringer (mate? above)	A*	Greenleaf crest, a bird with a sprig in its beak	Greenleaf family	ca. 1760	YUAG files	
Porringer	A	T/WF		ca. 1750	Avery 1920, no. 149	MMA
Porringer	A*	V/EL; OL to PL (later)		ca. 1750	DAPC 77.2829	WM
Three porringers	A	KC	Katharine [Catherine] (Chandler) Willard	1750–55	Buhler 1972, no. 226	MFAB
Porringer	C	C/IM; 1744 (+)		1744	YUAG files	
Porringer	?	B/DB		ca. 1770	Antiques 99 (April 1971): 507	
Salver	A	ITL (later)		ca. 1750	YUAG files	
Two sauceboats	A	KC	Katharine [Catherine] (Chandler) Willard	ca. 1755	Ham-merslough/ Feigenbaum 1958–73, 2:58	
Sauceboat	A	none		ca. 1750	Buhler 1979, no. 25	WAM
Serving spoon	C†	A/RM		ca. 1760		WHS
Strainer	A*	FARR TOLLMAN 1745	Farr Tollman	ca. 1745	Gourley 1965, no. 199	RISD
Strainer spoon	A*	none		ca. 1750	Ham-merslough/ Feigenbaum 1958–73, 4:122	WA
Tablespoon	A	S	Salisbury family	ca. 1760	Buhler 1979, no. 26	WAM
Tablespoon	A*	C/IM		ca. 1744		YUAG
Two tablespoons	B*	MY		ca. 1760		YUAG
Two tablespoons	C*	T/FH (+)		ca. 1750	MFA 1911, no. 949	
Tablespoon	C	T/FH (+)		ca. 1750	DAPC 74.2129	WM

	Mark	Inscription	Patron	Date	Reference	Owner
Two tablespoons	?	S/MC		ca. 1770	YUAG files	
Tablespoon	?	R/WM		ca. 1760	YUAG files	
Two tankards	A	The Gift of Mr. Sebastian Smith to the Second Church of Christ in Lancaster, 1765	Sebastian Smith for the Second Church, Lancaster, Mass.	1765	Dresser 1935–36, 50	
Tankard	?	Thomas arms	Thomas family	ca. 1750		AAS
Teaspoon	A	SP		ca. 1765	Buhler 1979, no. 27	WAM
Teaspoon	A	MS		ca. 1770	DAPC 74.2001	WM
Teaspoon	B*	HC		ca. 1760		YUAG
Teaspoon	B	none		ca. 1770	DAPC 82.3360	
Teaspoon	?	BB		ca. 1760	YUAG files	

1. *Charlestown VR* 1:214, 240; *Roxbury VR* 1:335; Wyman 1879, 2:918; RC 21:31; MCPR, docket 21951.
2. *Roxbury VR* 1:208; 2:647; *Roxbury Epitaphs*, n.d., 128; Torrey 1990, 722.
3. *Scituate VR* 1:157; RC 21:24, 121, 139. Relief Foster married (1) John Douse on 31 October 1672; see *Charlestown VR* 1:82. She married (2) Henry Leadbetter; RC 21:101. Marriage of Prudence Foster to Rev. J. Prentice; see Wyman 1879, 1:365; 2:918.
4. SCPR 29:190–91, 293–94.
5. RC 28:276, 334.
6. RC 28:4.
7. "Louisbourg Soldiers," *NEHGR* 25:266.
8. Fales 1983, 18–19.
9. SCPR 45:120–24.
10. RC 24:258, 271, 278.
11. *Marlborough VR*, 178.
12. *Worcester VR*, 249.
13. Rice 1879–95, 4:173.
14. Rice 1879–95, 4:188, 196, 199.
15. Pruitt 1978, 376–77.
16. *Boston Weekly News-Letter*, 27 May, 3 and 10 June 1773.
17. WCPR, docket 57595. Only Swan's will survives.
18. *Boston Weekly News-Letter*, 5 May 1774; "Burial Grounds in Worcester," 61.
19. Ensko 1927, 194; Ensko 1937, 70; Ensko 1948, 237; Graham 1936, 69; Thorn 1949, 196; Kovel 1961, 263.
20. Ensko 1948, 250; Kovel 1961, 263; French (1917) 1967, 111; Graham 1936, 69; Thorn 1949, 196. WS in cartouche, formerly attributed to Swan, is on a cann probably made in the late nineteenth or early twentieth century; see Johnston 1994, 138.

Henry Phillips Sweetser
1742–92

Henry Phillips Sweetser was born in Charlestown, Massachusetts, on 8 November 1742 to Seth Sweetser (1703/04–78), a schoolmaster, and Hannah Bradish (1705–1800).[1] His paternal grandparents were Seth Sweetser (1668–1731) and Sarah (Lynde) Clark (b. 1666).[2] His maternal grandparents were John Bradish (ca. 1678–1741) and Hepzibah Billings (1685–1735).[3]

Sweetser probably began his apprenticeship about 1756 and would have completed it about 1763. The identity of his master is not known. On 16 May 1765 he married Sarah Kettell (1743/44–86), the daughter of James Kettell (1720–93), a baker and innkeeper, and Sarah Call (1725–64), who married in Charlestown in 1743.[4] Henry Flynt and Martha Gandy Fales state that Sweetser was working in Worcester about 1768, but no evidence has been found to back this assertion.[5] In 1770 Sweetser witnessed the will of Francis Diser of Charlestown, who was the father of Richard Trumbull's (q.v.) wife.[6] The Massachusetts tax list of 1771 includes Sweetser in Charlestown with two polls, one-half of a house, an additional building (possibly a shop), £4 annual worth of real estate, and £40 value of merchandise.[7] The two polls indicate that two males over the age of sixteen lived in the household, Sweetser and possibly an older apprentice or journeyman. Sweetser lost his shop and tools during the British bombardment of Charlestown, for which he put in a claim of £42.12.[8] His first wife died in 1786, and the next year Sweetser married Phoebe (Sprague) Hatch (1747–1801), the widow of Asa Hatch and the daughter of Benjamin Sprague (1717–91) and Phoebe Lynde (b. 1726/27) of Malden, Massachusetts.[9]

Sweetser died of hepatitis in December 1792.[10] He was buried on Old Burial Hill in Charlestown.[11] The inventory of his estate, taken on 7 May 1793 by David Goodwin, Benjamin Goodwin, and Ebenezer Breed, amounted to £439.14.7 and included the following silversmith's tools:

2 Glass Cases 9/ 6 window frames 30/	1.19—
288 Squares of Sashes @ 2	2. 8—
1 Iron Crow 5/ 1 ditto Vise 7/6	12.6
4 Anvils 36/ 1 Creasing Iron 5/	2. 1—
1 Small birkIron & 2 teaspoon punchs	6—
1 Nest Brass weights	6—
. . .	
1 box draws with Sund[y] flasks ⎫ & Silvermiths tools ⎭	1.16—
. . .	
1 Ax 1/6 1 p[r] Goldsmiths bellows 12/	13.6

The estate was insolvent, and on 15 April 1794 Sweetser's widow gave notice of the sale at public auction of one dwelling house, seven acres of land, and a barn.[12] The inventory suggests that Sweetser was an active, working goldsmith, but no silver with his mark is known to survive. PEK

1. Wyman 1879, 2:922; *Charlestown VR* 1:199, 354; *Cambridge VR* 1:82; *Index of Obituaries, 1704–1800*, 3:436; *Index of Obituaries, 1784–1840*, 5:4366.
2. Wyman 1879, 2:921; *Charlestown VR* 1:55, 68, 151; Griffen 1952, 109.
3. *Cambridge VR* 2:481.
4. *Charlestown VR* 1:289, 357, 366–67, 415; *Index of Obituaries, 1784–1840*, 5:4368; Griffen 1952, 67–68.
5. Flynt/Fales 1968, 335.
6. MCPR, docket 6326.
7. Pruitt 1978, 178–79.
8. Hunnewell 1888, 155, 164.
9. *Charlestown VR* 1:440; *Malden VR*, 52, 81–82, 298, 379; *Index of Obituaries, 1784–1840*, 5:4368.
10. Hunnewell 1888, 257.
11. Griffen 1952, 109.
12. MCPR, docket 22011.

John Symmes
1740–92

John Symmes was born in Charlestown, Massachusetts, on 13 October 1740 to Zachariah Symmes (1712–before 1776), a hatter who also ran the Cape Breton tavern, and Grace Parker (1716–46), the sister of the silversmith Daniel Parker (q.v.) and of Mary Parker who married John Welsh (q.v.).[1] The jeweler Isaac Parker (q.v.) was Symmes's first cousin. Symmes's paternal grandparents

A

were the Reverend Thomas Symmes (1678–1725) of Bradford, Massachusetts, and Elizabeth Blowers (1675–1714) of Cambridge, Massachusetts.[2] His maternal grandparents were Isaac Parker (1692–1742) and Grace Hall (1696–1754).[3] In 1748/49, when Symmes was a minor, his father joined with Daniel and other heirs of Isaac Parker on his son's behalf to sue Francis Wyman for his illegal possession of their land in Maine.[4]

Symmes's apprenticeship would have begun about 1754, and he probably trained in Boston with his uncle, Daniel Parker, finishing his apprenticeship about 1761. Symmes may have taken over one of the two shops operated by his uncle Parker, who ceased advertising his shop between the Golden Ball and the Sign of Admiral Vernon in 1763. Symmes advertised that his shop was near the Golden Ball in the *Boston Gazette* of 10, 17, and 24 February 1766:

> Imported from LONDON, and to be Sold by
> John Symmes, *Goldsmith*;
> Near the Golden Ball, BOSTON, Viz.
> Best neat new-fashion Shoe and
> Knee Chapes, round Brillient Cypher Button Stones,
> Brillient and Cypher Earing Stones, Brilliant & Cypher
> Ring ditto. Ring Sparks, Ruby and white Foyle,
> Buckle Brushes, rough and smooth Files, &c. &c. &c.

Similar advertisements appeared in the same newspaper on 20 April and 4 May 1767, indicating that Symmes conducted his business in the same manner as his uncle: as a retail silversmith who sold imported wares and silversmiths' and jewelers' supplies. Silver bearing Symmes's mark, an initial and surname (A), is extremely rare.

On 2 June 1766 Symmes married Hepzibah Barrett (b. 1748/49), the daughter of Samuel Barrett (1722–98), a sailmaker, and Mary Shed (1723–90), who married in 1743.[5] The John Symmes who was constable of the South Watch in the 1760s was probably the goldsmith.[6] The Massachusetts tax list of 1771 includes John Symmes in Boston with two polls, a house, twenty pounds' annual value of real estate, fifty pounds' worth of merchandise, and thirty pounds' value of commissions.[7] The two polls indicated that two males over the age of sixteen lived in the household, possibly a journeyman or older apprentice in addition to Symmes. Symmes also appears on the Boston tax list of 1780 in ward 5.[8] Symmes was a Freemason. On 26 December 1777 he, Paul Revere, Jr. (q.v.), and three other men purchased a house and land that was held in trust for St. Andrew's Lodge.[9] Symmes was a plaintiff in a case against John Manley in 1784, but the nature of the suit is unknown.[10]

In the years following the Revolution Symmes may have turned his business interests to auctioneering. In 1787 he informed the Boston selectmen that he had hired a room over Mr. Bradley's store on the dock for the purpose of holding auctions, and he was approved as an auctioneer by the selectmen in 1790 and 1791.[11] An obituary notice in the *Independent Chronicle* reported that Symmes died in 1792 at the age of fifty-two.[12] No probate records survive for him. PEK

SURVIVING OBJECTS

	Mark	Inscription	Patron	Date	Reference	Owner
Cann	A (?)	E/RM; SMW		ca. 1770	Hammerslough/ Feigenbaum 1958–73, 3:14–15	
Tablespoon	A†	SM^c/June/24 1771		1771	DAPC 69.4132	WM

1. *Bradford VR*, 154; Wyman 1879, 2:929; *Charlestown VR* 1:350, 461; *NEHGR* 31:214; Griffen 1952, 110.
2. *Sibley's Harvard Graduates* 4:411–17; *Bradford VR*, 149, 363; *Boston News-Letter* 7–14 October 1725; *Cambridge VR* 1:69; 2:383.
3. *NEHGR* 28:121; Griffen 1952, 86; *Charlestown VR* 1:238; *Medford VR*, 72; MCPR, docket 16584.
4. YCCR, box 106, file 3.
5. RC 24:154, 265; RC 28:274; RC 30:62; SCPR 96:526–30, 659, 678; *Index of Obituaries, 1784–1840*, 1:257; Thwing.
6. RC 20:100, 124, 288.
7. Pruitt 1978, 24–25.
8. "Assessors' 'Taking-Books,'" 27.
9. SCD 128:180.
10. SCCR, Court of Common Pleas Record Book 1784, 58.
11. RC 27:31, 118–19, 148–50.
12. *Index of Obituaries, 1704–1800*, 1:292.

T

Benjamin Tappan, Jr.
1747–1831

Gilbert Stuart, Benjamin Tappan, *oil on wood, 1814. National Gallery of Art, Washington, gift of Lady Vereker.*

A

B

Benjamin Tappan, Jr., the eldest son of Rev. Benjamin Tappan (1720–90) of Newbury, Massachusetts, and Elizabeth Marsh (1723–1807) of Haverhill, Massachusetts, was baptized on 25 October 1747, probably at the First Congregational Church of Manchester, Massachusetts.[1] The silversmith's parents published their intentions to marry on 17 October 1746 in Manchester, where Benjamin had established his ministry after graduating from Harvard College in 1742.[2] The elder Tappan had met his future wife while teaching in Newbury and Haverhill and boarding with his future in-laws, Deacon David Marsh (1698–1777) of Haverhill and Mary Moody (1703–94) of Newbury.[3] The younger Benjamin's paternal grandparents were Samuel Toppan (later changed to Tappan) (1670–1750), a farmer who had settled in Newbury, and Abigail Wigglesworth (1681–1770).[4]

In 1768, Benjamin Tappan, Jr., moved to Northampton, Massachusetts, where the following year he bought property for the first time. This land, which he purchased for twenty-five shillings from Seth Lyman, was opposite the town meetinghouse and probably included his first shop. Tappan sold this lot in August 1770 for two pounds, and in October returned east to marry Sarah Homes (1748–1826) at Boston's Brattle Street Church.[5] This marriage suggests that Tappan may have apprenticed with his wife's father, the Boston silversmith William Homes, Sr. (q.v.). Through this marriage Tappan became the brother-in-law of William Homes, Jr., and of Barnabas Webb (qq.v.). In September 1771 Tappan bought 2½ acres of land in Northampton, and by November he had also purchased a brazier's shop opposite the meetinghouse from Hezekiah Russell.[6] According to Henry Gere's *Reminiscences of Old Northampton*, Tappan had begun working in a small wooden building on Shop Row as early as 1770, a year before his purchase of Russell's brazier shop.[7]

Tappan's career was interrupted by the Revolution, in which as a private in Col. Ezra May's regiment he marched from Northampton to Stillwater, Ticonderoga, and Saratoga in 1777.[8] After the war, Tappan returned once again to Northampton. He was identified as a goldsmith in a deed when he bought land there in 1782.[9] He continued his work as a goldsmith until at least 1785, when he entered into a series of land transactions with Nathaniel Fowle (q.v. Appendix B), a tailor, merchant, and yeoman of Northampton. These deeds suggest that the men shared work space.[10] A reference to a Tappan and Fowle dry goods business, although undated, suggests that the two may have expanded their wares to realize better profits in the growing town of Northampton, but their relationship probably ended in 1806, when they divided their property.[11] What little remained of Tappan's activities as a silversmith probably ceased in 1807, when he sold "eighteen feet in front and rear of my old goldsmith shop and the ground on which it stands."[12] In 1809 he built a brick store on the row, from which he sold dry goods, hardware, shoes, and crockery.[13] This land is probably the same property that Tappan sold that year to his son John, a Boston merchant.[14] Because he was then sixty-two years of age, the elder Tappan probably transferred ownership to his son while continuing to run the business himself. By 1827 the shop was known as Tappan and Whitney.[15]

Tappan consistently identified himself as a goldsmith in nine deeds dated 1769 to 1786, and in a tenth, dated 1794; yet he is remembered in Northampton histories as a well-known merchant.[16] In a series of deeds dating from 1795 to 1808 Tappan is identified as a merchant or trader.[17] Because only a small number of works in silver have been attributed to him, Tappan most likely carried on a successful dry goods business for some years while maintaining his silversmith shop, and in later years abandoned his craft altogether. The portraits made of Tappan and his wife in 1814 by Gilbert Stuart indicate how prosperous he had become in his later years (illus.).[18] Tappan died on 29 January 1831 in Northampton at the age of eighty-three.[19]

Tappan is known to have used two marks: BT in Roman capitals in a rectangle (A) and BT with four pellets between in a serrated rectangle (B). A third mark, BT in script capitals in a shaped cartouche, has been attributed to him, but the attribution is doubtful.[20] JJF

SURVIVING OBJECTS

	Mark	Inscription	Patron	Date	Reference	Owner
Tablespoon	B*	CD		ca. 1770	DAPC 75.4505	WM
Tablespoon	B	SE		ca. 1770	YUAG files	
Tablespoon	B	SS		ca. 1770	Eitner 1976, no. 410 (as BT)	
Tablespoon	B (?)	none		ca. 1765		MFAB
Tablespoon	B*	SF; 1780 (later)		ca. 1770		HD
Tablespoon	B†	SP		ca. 1770	YUAG files	
Tablespoon	B*	EE		ca. 1775		HD
Teaspoon	A	SG		ca. 1770	DAPC 86.2203	
Teaspoon	A	AC		ca. 1770	Avery 1920, no. 153	MMA
Teaspoon	A†	CD		ca. 1775	DAPC 74.2126	WM
Teaspoon	A*	RW		ca. 1770	YUAG files	
Teaspoon	A	MC		ca. 1770	DAPC 73.1125	WM
Two teaspoons	A*	none		ca. 1775		HD
Teaspoon	A*	AF		ca. 1765		HD
Teaspoon	A*	MP		ca. 1770		HD
Teaspoon	B	SE		ca. 1775		CHS

1. *Manchester VR*, 119, 291; *Newbury VR* 1:527; *Sibley's Harvard Graduates* 11:169–72; *Haverhill VR* 1:214; *Index of Obituaries, 1784–1840*, 5:4393.

2. *Haverhill VR* 2:214, 307; *Sibley's Harvard Graduates* 11:170.

3. *Haverhill VR* 1:214; 2:213, 441, 443.

4. *Newbury VR* 1:504; 2:737, 742; *Malden VR*, 103, 322.

5. Trumbull 1898–1902, 2:11, 544; HaCD 8:267; 11:371; Bridgman 1850, 68; *Index of Obituaries, 1784–1840*, 5:4394; RC 30:330.

6. HCD 10:527–28; 11:374.

7. Gere 1902, 40, 628.

8. *Mass. Soldiers and Sailors* 14:384.

9. HCD 20:120.

10. HaCD 8:314; 24:204–05; 26:30–31; 17:132; HCD 27:133; 26:718–19; Flynt/Fales 1968, 221. All deeds transacted by Fowle with Tappan indicate that by the late eighteenth century Fowle was working as a tailor or a merchant.

11. Tappan 1870, 13–15; HaCD 24:204–05; 26:30–31.

12. HaCD 27:74.

13. Gere 1902, 40.

14. HaCD 28:566.

15. Advertisement, 5 December 1828, *Hampshire Gazette*, 5 December 1827 and 1833, cited in Flynt/Fales 1968, 336.

16. HaCD 8:267, 314, 260; HCD 10:527–28; 11:371, 374; 13:736; 19:333–34; 24:333; 26:718–19; Tappan 1915, 24–25, recounts that "to be considered among the first families [of Northampton], one must own a piece of meadow land, must have a pew in the broad aisle of the old church, and must deal at Mr. Benjamin Tappan's store."

17. HaCD 10:179; 11:136, 137; 20:872; 22:372; 25:133; 26:463–64; 27:182.

18. Park 1926, 2:737–39, catalogue numbers 820–21.

19. Bridgman 1850, 68; *Index of Obituaries, 1784–1840*, 5:4392; HaCPR 38:350–51; box 145, no. 6.

20. The mark BT in script capitals in a shaped cartouche, which appears on a creampot and sugar bowl (Buhler 1972, no. 430; *Antiques* 110 [July 1976]: 36), is unlike the craftsman's other punches and is uncharacteristic of Massachusetts marks of this period. The script mark has not been found on flatware comparable to flatware bearing Tappan's marks (A) or (B). Furthermore, none of the silver bearing Tappan's marks is holloware.

John Touzell
ca. 1727–85

A

John Touzell (or Tousell, Towzell) was born into the small French community in Salem, Massachusetts, about 1727. He was particularly well connected within this enclave. His parents were the merchant Capt. John Touzell (ca. 1687–1737) and his wife, Susannah (English) Touzell (1686–1739).[1] On his mother's side, he was the grandson of Philip English (1651–1736) and Mary (Hollingsworth) English (ca. 1652–94), both of whom were accused in the Salem witchcraft episode of 1692. His father perished in a smallpox epidemic in 1737, his mother died two years later, and John and his two sisters were raised by guardians.[2] Following the death of the elder Touzell, the family continued to receive income from his estate on the island of Jersey.[3]

Touzell's master is not known. Benno M. Forman suggested that he was apprenticed to one of the French goldsmiths in Boston or to Jeffrey Lang (q.v.) in Salem.[4] Touzell appears to have been in business for himself by 1749, when he purchased £26.9.10 worth of goldsmith's tools and supplies from Samuel Edwards (q.v.) of Boston, including pliers, tongs, shears, scales and weights, crucibles, and polishing materials.[5] Numerous bills and receipts document Touzell's career during the next three decades as a maker and seller of gold and silver jewelry, silver spoons and tongs, and other small objects and as a repairman.[6] He had minor business dealings with many of his Salem contemporaries, including Richard Lang, Joseph Gardner (qq.v.), Archelaus Rea, Jr. (q.v. Appendix A), and Thorndike Procter (1759–90). Touzell bought jewelry and supplies regularly from Daniel Parker, John Welsh, Benjamin Pierpont (qq.v.), and other Boston silversmiths and jewelers.[7] He paid John Raymond (q.v.) to make jewelry and also purchased merchandise from the

Danvers bucklemaker Henry Buxton (q.v.). Touzell appraised the estates of Jeffrey Lang and Nathaniel Lang (q.v.) and corresponded with the Nantucket silversmiths Samuel Barrett and John Jackson (qq.v.). John Hathorne (q.v.), Touzell's nephew, was his apprentice, and Joseph Hathorne (q.v.), another nephew, may have served his time with Touzell as well. The Marblehead silversmith Thomas Grant (q.v.) may have trained with Touzell or worked for him as a journeyman. Although Touzell rented shop space early in his career (in 1753 he paid nine shillings six pence for one year's rent), by 1771 he owned his own house with at least two adjacent outbuildings.[8]

Touzell is best known today for the following advertisement he placed in the *Boston News-Letter* for 5 November 1767:

> THE *Subscriber's Shop in* Salem *was* BROKE *Open the First of this Instant, in the Night, and the following Articles were Stolen from him, viz.*
>
> ONE pair square Stone Buckles, 4 pair Stone Earings set in gold, 6 or 7 Gold Rings, 5 or 6 pair of Cypher Stone Buttons set in Silver, 50 or 60 pair Silver shoe and knee Buckles, 6 strings of Coral Beeds, Part of a gold Necklace, $1^1/_2$ Dozen Tea-Spoons mark'd *I·T* one large Spoon, Maker's Name *J. Towzel*, 7 pair silver Sleeve Buttons, together with Neck-Buckles, &c, &c, &c.
>
> ANY Person that will discover the Thief or the Goods, that the Owner may recover them again, shall have TEN DOLLARS Reward and all necessary Charges paid by me. *John Towzel*, Goldsmith.[9]

This notice provides a good record of Touzell's stock in trade and also serves to suggest his two maker's marks.

Never married, Touzell died on 14 August 1785, aged fifty-eight years.[10] He termed himself a yeoman in his will, written just a few weeks before his death.[11] His sister Susannah Hathorne, in addition to receiving half his house and garden, was bequeathed "One Silver Porringer, Six large Silver Spoons, one pair of Silver Salts, one Silver Spout Cup, all of them marked I[T]S [and] Six Sweetmeat spoons with forks marked L-G." His other sister, Mary Hathorne, received "one Silver Porringer marked M.E. five large Silver Spoons marked W[B]M also one pair of silver salts" as well as land and other household goods. John Hathorne received the other half of the house and garden, and numerous small bequests were made to other relations. Shortly before he died, Touzell presented to St. Peter's Church a silver cup, possibly of his own making.[12]

Two marks normally are assigned to Touzell: J. TOUZELL in a rectangle (A) and I·T in a rectangle (an example of an object bearing this mark could not be located).[13] One source also gives the mark J. TOUZELL in a rectangle with rounded ends.[14] Spoons by Touzell are known, and a porringer, a rare survival, is in a private collection. GWRW

SURVIVING OBJECTS

	Mark	Inscription	Patron	Date	Reference	Owner
Porringer	A	MA		ca. 1760	Kroening 1982, no. 19	
Tablespoon	A*	EG		ca. 1770		SI
Tablespoon	A†	S/BE		ca. 1755	Buhler/Hood 1970, no. 208	YUAG
Tablespoon	A*	C/SM		ca. 1755	DAPC 71.2451	WM
Tablespoon	A*	N/DH (?)		ca. 1765		PEM
Tablespoon	A*	R/IF		ca. 1765		PEM

1. Belknap 1927, 116; Flynt/Fales 1968, 340–41; Forman 1971, 71–72.
2. Forman 1971, 71.
3. John Touzell to Peter Fall, letter, 4 October 1753, photostat, Bigelow-Phillips files.
4. Forman 1971, 72.
5. A photocopy of the original document is in the Bigelow-Phillips files.
6. Most of these can be found in the following collections at the PEM: John Touzell Miscellaneous Papers, 1710–85; and Hathorne Family Papers, vols. 2–4. See also Waters Family Manuscripts, box 1, folder 2, PEM.
7. Among the other Boston craftsmen were Thomas Townsend, Thomas Clark, James Turner, Joseph Hiller, Sr., and Barnabas Webb (qq.v.).
8. Hathorne Family Papers, vol. 3, fol. 92, PEM; Pruitt 1978, 136–37.
9. Also reprinted in Dow 1927, 56.
10. *Salem VR* 6:277; see also Bentley 1905–62, 1:22.
11. A copy of his will is in the John Touzell Miscellaneous Papers, PEM.
12. John Touzell Miscellaneous Papers, PEM. The cup was converted into a basin in the late nineteenth century; see Jones 1913, 429.
13. Belden 1980, 410.
14. Thorn 1949, 202.

Thomas Townsend
1703/04–57+

A

B

C

Several silver authorities have published Thomas Townsend's birth date as 1701 and his death date as 1777.[1] Although there are many Thomas Townsends in the records, it is most likely that Thomas Townsend the goldsmith was the son of Thomas and Sarah (Brown) Townsend (1664–1750), born in Boston on 9 January 1703/04 and baptized in the Second, or North, Church on the same day.[2] His paternal grandfather may have been Peter Townsend (1642–96), housewright, who married (i) Lydia, (ii) Margaret, and (iii) Anne. The goldsmith Thomas Townsend probably married Sarah Brewster (b. 1715), daughter of John Brewster (ca. 1674–1766), grocer, and Deliverance (Cotta) Brewster (1680–1738/39), in 1735. John, son of Thomas and Sarah Townsend, was baptized in the Second Church in 1738, and another son, Thomas, was born in 1739.[3]

Thomas Townsend was sued twenty-two times by his creditors in the Court of Common Pleas for Suffolk County. Most of the suits involved debts to shopkeepers and artisans. One involved his failure to pay rent on a tenement; another involved payment on a bond from the watchmaker Elijah Collins (q.v. Appendix A) held jointly by Townsend, the sailmaker Thornton Barrett, and the merchant Charles Hobby; and six involved his dealings with other silversmiths and goldsmiths.[4] The suit brought against him by the shopkeeper Joseph Bradford involved 19½ ounces of silver that Townsend had promised to deliver to Bradford "or His Order in Good Silver Spoons & a Silver Cupp or in Good Silver not workt" within three weeks of his agreement with Bradford.[5] The phrase "or His Order" may indicate that Bradford intended to sell the objects rather than to use them himself; this suggests that he received orders and passed them on to Townsend or other silversmiths.

The suits involving transactions with other silversmiths tell us a great deal more about Townsend and his work. John Blowers (q.v.) brought suit against Townsend twice, once in 1736 and once in 1737. The second case involved £4 that Townsend had agreed to pay Blowers within five months. Although the details of the arrangements are not included in the document, Townsend may have been buying items from Blowers or Blowers may have been working for Townsend.[6] Townsend and Knight Leverett (q.v.) were codefendants in a suit brought by Sampson Salter, John Blowers's father-in-law, in 1735/36. Leverett and Townsend defaulted and Salter was awarded £74.8.8.[7] In 1739, John Parkman (q.v.) sued Townsend for £16.4.10 for "value rec'd."[8] In the same year George Hanners, Sr. (q.v.), recovered judgment against Thomas Townsend in a case involving £10.16.2 that Townsend owed to Hanners "for value received."[9] An account of the items that Townsend obtained from Hanners contains the following:

Boston 1733		Det		
Thomas Townsend to George Hanners		£	s	d
May	to one gold ring	1–	6–	7
15	2 Nests of potes	0–	2–	4
	2 pound of allam	0–	2–	4
	1 pound deto	0–	1–	2
1734	to a Sillver Tankerd w^t 23^{oz}			
Novm^{br}	5 peney w^t att 24^s [ripped] p^r ounce	27–	18–	0
8	the fashen	4–	10–	0
	to five peney w^t and 9 grains			
	of gold att 18 pounds p^r ouns	4–	13–	9
		38 = 14 = 2		
		27–	18	
		10 = 16 = 2^{10}		

Townsend was plaintiff in only one case: he brought charges against Thomas Edwards (q.v.) in 1750 for Edwards's failure to pay Townsend what he was owed on account. The dispute appears to have revolved around a question about the relative values of Old and New Tenor. At the court held on 1 January 1750/51, Townsend and Edwards both appeared and agreed to abide by the decision of Rufus Greene, Jacob Hurd, and William Cowell, Jr. (qq.v.), "or any two of them," who were appointed referees by the court to examine the "proofs & Acco^{ts}" of both parties. The referees found a balance due to Townsend of £7.11 "Lawfull Money," plus 45 shillings and 4 pence costs of court.[11] The account filed with the case was as follows:

1748 Dr Mr Thomas Edwards To Thomas Townsend C^r

		Old Tenor	Silver			Old Tenor
Octr 22^d	To fashioning 2 p^r salts	12.		Nov^r	By Cash	£3
				Dec^r	By Irons	4
	To ditto for a strainer	5.6.8			By Cash	3
					By D^o	15
	To D^o a Can Body	4.			By D^o	8
5th	To D^o a porringer	3.10.	7^{oz}17.0		By D^o	3
Decr 8th	To D^o p^r Butter Cups & p^r Salts	36.—	39.10—		By a Hallowing Stamp	13.10
	To D^o a p^r Square Salts	8.—	8.15—		By a Sword blade	5.10
March	To D^o 2 Tea Potts	34–	36.17		By a belt	6.10
	To Cash P^d Mr Bridge	2.10..			By Potts	1.10
	To fashioning of a Ladle	4—	2.5		By a Stone Ring	4—
					By Cash	5
22^d	To D^o for Milk Pott	4—	3–1		By Cash	3–10
					By Shears	1– 4
	To D^o for D^o	4	3.4		By Wier	—10—

April 1749	To D.º a Tea Pott	17.10	16.1.12^{gr}	By Sugar	3:15—	
	To D.º 2 Milk Potts	8	6–4	By Gold	3.13.6	
May 3^d	To D.º a p.^{r} Salts	6	4.11.12	By Cash	20———	
20	To D.º a Strainer	5.6.8	4.16.12	By Irons	3	
	To D.º a Strainer	5.6.8	4. 3.12	By D.º	3–10	
				By D.º	3.10	
June 17	To finishing 2 Tankard	18—	28.13.	By D.º	10	
	Bodies					
				By D.º	5	
July	To fashioning 2 Quart	33.—	29.18—	By D.º	10	
	Tankards			By D.º	6.	
	To D.º a Tankard	16.10.	23.12	By D^o	7.	
Augt 8th	To D^o a Tea Pott	17.10.	18.10—	By 3 nests^{of} Potts & 2^{ll}		
	To D^o a Milk Pott	4.	3.	Allom	1.— 3	
	To 3 oz Silver	10.10 —				
	Old Tenor	£259.		By Cash	5.	
	Bal.^{ce} in Old Tenor	167: 5: 6		By D^o	3.	
		91:14: 6		By 1 Large Nests Potts	— 8	
				By 2 Black Potts	—12	
					162. 5. 6	
				Omitted a piece of Eight and a		
				Drawing Iron £5	5.—	
				old Tenor	167. 5. 6	
	Lawfull Money				£22. 6.1^{12}	

This account shows that Edwards supplied Townsend with silver, and Townsend produced objects according to Edwards's order. Edwards paid Townsend for his services in cash, drawing irons, wire, shears, crucibles, allum, and an occasional ring or small amount of gold or silver. The account indicates that Townsend earned approximately £22.11 sterling per year as a pieceworker for Edwards, receiving approximately 40 percent of his payment in cash and the remainder in goods, primarily goldsmithing tools. Of the £22 sterling that Townsend earned, he had less than £9 to spend in actual currency. Court records show that Townsend was doing work for at least three other silversmiths, and there undoubtedly were more. Townsend would have needed at least £35 per year in cash or credits on shops in order to make enough money to maintain a minimum standard of living for his wife and child.[13]

Although the surviving account with Edwards demonstrates that Townsend was a productive artisan, very little silver bearing Townsend's marks, T·T crowned (A), T·T in a rectangle (B), and TT in a rectangle (C), has survived. He made a quart tankard in the Second Church, Boston, that apparently was purchased by the church before an inventory of the church's plate was taken on 2 March 1730.[14] Townsend was a member of the Second Church, and it therefore makes sense that the church would have asked him to produce a piece of silver for them. As was true of most jobbing silversmiths, the bulk of Townsend's work was marked by the goldsmiths who hired him. One porringer bears both Townsend's mark and that of Samuel Minott (q.v.), a leading retailer.

The last definite reference to Thomas Townsend, goldsmith or silversmith, appears in a Boston court record for 1752. Townsend witnessed a division of real estate with William Simpkins (q.v.) in 1755.[15] A receipt signed by a Thomas Townsend and dated 30 August 1757 at Salem, Massachusetts, indicates that he "Recc.^d of John Touzel [q.v.] a Pair of Gold wires on account of m.^r William Jonson of Lynn."[16] Whether this was Thomas Townsend the silversmith is not absolutely clear from the receipt, but it seems likely. There is no record of his death in either Boston or Salem. BMW

SURVIVING OBJECTS

	Mark	Inscription	Patron	Date	Reference	Owner
Cann	A, B, or C	MH; THT (later)	Mary Hubbard	ca. 1760	Flynt/Fales 1968, 342	
Caster	c†	B/RS; SJT/RHT (later)	Blake family	ca. 1750	Moore Collection 1980, no. 115	
Pepper box	A*	SB (S over earlier initials)		ca. 1740	YUAG files	
Porringer	A	JJ/to/JJW		ca. 1750	Hammerslough/ Feigenbaum 1958–73, 3:44	
Porringer	A	T/BA		ca. 1750		SB
Porringer (with mark of Samuel Minott)	A	The gift of/Jotham Gay/to/Mary Gay	Jotham Gay and/or Mary Gay	ca. 1730	Buhler 1965, 49–51	HMA
Porringer	A	HJ/to/HJT (+)		ca. 1750	Quimby 1995, no. 124	WM
Porringer	B*	MH	Mary Hubbard	ca. 1750	Flynt/Fales 1968, 342 (mark only)	
Strainer spoon	B*	BW		ca. 1740	Johnston 1994, 155	CMA
Tablespoon	A*	Poole crest, a lion's gamb erased; SP (later)	Poole family	ca. 1750	Quimby 1995, no. 125	WM
Tablespoon	B†	MF		ca. 1730	Buhler/Hood 1970, no. 164	YUAG
Tankard	A†	T/WA	William and Anna (Cottle) Titcomb, Jr.	ca. 1725		BCMA
Tankard	B	none		ca. 1740	Jones 1913, 38 (as Thomas Trott)	

1. See, for instance, Flynt/Fales 1968, 342.
2. RC 24:24; Robbins 1852, 283; RC 28:6. There were several Thomas Townsends born in Boston early enough to have been the silversmith. Bigelow and Phillips believed that Townsend was the son of Thomas and Sarah. This is substantiated, albeit circumstantially, by the fact that in January 1737/38, Thomas Townsend, goldsmith, and Sarah Townsend, widow, were joint defendants in a suit filed by David Jenkins in a case of trespass and ejectment; SCCR, Court of Common Pleas Record Book 1737/38, 149. Sarah (Brown) Townsend's vital dates are from her gravestone in the Copp's Hill Burying Ground, which bears the epitaph "Here lyes buried the body of Mrs. Sarah Townsend wife to Mr. Thomas Townsend aged 86 years, died Dec. 1, 1750"; Whitmore 1878, 61, no. 1142.

3. SCPR 11:178, 215, 307; 14:126; Robbins 1852, 232; *Index of Obituaries, 1704–1800*, 1:39; RC 9:151; RC 28:7; Bridgman 1851, 56. The Thomas Townsend who married Ann Shipman, we know from SCD references, was a cordwainer. The other Thomas Townsend who married about this time wed Elizabeth Stone in King's Chapel. The goldsmith Thomas Townsend was a member of the Second Church, and it is therefore likely that John, son of Thomas and Sarah Townsend, who was baptized in that church on 14 May 1738, was his son; RC 24:234. The birth of Thomas to Thomas and Sarah is recorded in RC 24:238. This further suggests that it was the goldsmith who married Sarah Brewster on 24 July 1735; Robbins 1852, 283; RC 28:194.

4. John M. Fitzgerald to F. H. Bigelow, Boston Court Record References to Silversmiths, Bigelow-Phillips files, YUAG. SCCR, Court of Common Pleas Record Book 1732, 286; 1735, 121; 1735–36, 616; 1736–37, 343, 498, 589; 1737–38, 140, 148, 149; 1738, 261, 286; 1739–40, 139, 204; 1740, 32; 1741, 129, 212; 1742–43, 219; 1743–44, 22, 205; 1748–49, 89, 234; 1749–51, 49, 220–22; 1751–52, 102, 219, 225.

5. SCCR, Records of the Superior Court of Judicature 1737, 541. A photostat of the receipt is in the Bigelow-Phillips files.

6. SCCR, Court of Common Pleas Record Book 1735–36, 616; 1736–37, 498.

7. SCCR, Court of Common Pleas Record Book 1735–36, 340.

8. SCCR, Court of Common Pleas Record Book 1738, 261.

9. SCCR, Court of Common Pleas Record Book 1738, 286; SCCR, file 50260. Townsend evidently still did not pay the sum, for he was sued again, by Hanners's widow, in 1740; SCCR, Court of Common Pleas Record Book 1740, 32.

10. This account was probably the one filed in the case because the amount is the same as that mentioned in the record book. A photostat of the document is in the Bigelow-Phillips files, YUAG.

11. SCCR, Court of Common Pleas Record Book 1749–51, 220–22.

12. SCCR, file papers of the Court of Common Pleas, Court held 1 January 1750/51, no. 128.

13. Ward 1983. Billy G. Smith has estimated that in 1762 Philadelphia laborers spent approximately six pounds sterling per person per year on a minimal diet. If Townsend had to feed a wife and one child, his costs for food would have been no less than fifteen pounds per year. Lodging would have cost him another six pounds per year, and firewood at least six pounds per year. Clothing costs for a laborer were about three pounds sterling per year; an artisan probably spent slightly more, women's clothes were probably more, and children's clothes probably cost less, meaning that Townsend's yearly expenditure on clothing would have been about seven pounds; Smith 1981, 167–81.

14. Jones 1913, 38, 43.

15. SCPR, docket 11079.

16. English-Touzel-Hathorne Papers, box 4, folder 5, PEM.

George Trott
1741–1810

George Trott was born in Boston in 1741, the son of the blacksmith Thomas Trott (1705–77) and his wife, Waitstill Payson (1705/06–44), who had been married on 10 January 1727 in Dedham, Massachusetts, by Nehemiah Walker.[1] The jeweler's paternal grandparents were Samuel Trott (1660–1724) and Mercy Beal (1670–1761) of Dorchester, Massachusetts.[2] Trott's brother Jonathan (q.v.) was also a jeweler.

On 30 January 1766, the Reverend Mather Byles married George Trott and Ann Boylston Cunningham (1745–1810), the daughter of James Cunningham, Esq. (1721–95), and Elizabeth Boylston (1717–69).[3] James Cunningham was very active in civic and military organizations. He served as Boston constable in 1746, captain of the South Engine Company from 1756 to 1761, fire ward from 1765 to 1769, member of the Artillery Company from 1758 to 1759 and again from 1761 to 1763, major in the Boston regiment from 1767 to 1772, and a member of the Sons of Liberty.[4] His wife, Elizabeth, was the daughter of the Brookline, Massachusetts, shopkeeper Peter Boylston (d. 1743) and Ann White (d. 1772).[5]

If George Trott apprenticed in the customary fashion, he would have completed his training in 1762. The identity of his master is unknown. The records of the Ancient and Honorable Artillery Company provide the first indication that Trott was a jeweler. George Trott, jeweler, joined the Artillery Company on 6 May 1765, Capt. Alius Paddock and William Josiah Waters serving as sureties for his membership, and he was elected 4th sergeant of the company in 1767.[6] Trott was promoted to lieutenant in November 1771, and on 21 September 1772, Lieutenant Trott led a detachment of the Artillery Company in a mock battle.[7] Trott may have met his wife, Ann Cunningham, through his association with this group: her brother, William Cunningham, joined the same year as Trott, and her father had been an active member for several years.[8] Trott was also active in the revolutionary cause as a member of the Sons of Liberty.[9] John Adams, Trott's cousin by marriage, noted the presence of George Trott, jeweler, at a meeting of the Sons of Liberty in his diary for 15 January 1766.[10] Boston town records for 1770 note that George Trott was chosen as a petit juror for the August court that year, further evidence of his active participation in town government.[11]

Trott appears four times in the daybook of Paul Revere, Jr., between 1783 and 1784.[12] He commissioned six teaspoons on 11 August 1783, a creampot on 29 May 1784, and six large spoons with engraved ciphers on 14 September 1784. Revere also mended a cann for him. Trott paid for these transactions in silver and cash.

According to the Cunningham family genealogy, Trott called himself a tobacconist, a trussmaker, and a merchant at various times, which suggests that he pursued a number of trades in addition to being a jeweler.[13] George Trott, tobacconist, mortgaged his South Bennett Street property to his brother-in-law William Cunningham for $215.41 on 6 June 1796.[14] The loan was to have been repaid within a year, but the deed records that Cunningham was repaid by Trott's estate in May 1810 following the jeweler's death. The *Boston Directory* listed Trott as a tobacconist and trussmaker on South Bennett Street in 1796 and again as a trussmaker at the same address in 1798.[15] A resolution of the Brethren of the Old South Society on 6 September 1795 that "the Treasurer Deacon Jonathan Mason, be requested, untill further directions, to pay Mr. George Trott annually the sum of Fifty Dollars for his weekly services in conducting the Musick of the Society" demonstrates the jeweler's versatility beyond his craft.[16]

In September 1786, George Trott, jeweler, paid his brother Jonathan ten pounds to secure complete ownership of the house and land in the South End of Boston that they had jointly inherited from their father.[17] The deed states that the jeweler was already in residence, undoubtedly referring to the South Bennett Street property mentioned in the Cunningham genealogy and city directories. Trott and his family probably had been living there since Thomas Trott's death in 1777, but the birth of two of the couple's eight children in Braintree, Massachusetts, indicates that the family had moved out of Boston for a few years.[18] There is no indication, however, of the birth order of the children born outside Boston. The census of 1790 listed Trott as the head of a family that included his wife, one boy over sixteen, and three boys under sixteen.[19] By 1798, Trott was living in a wooden house on Bennett Street described in the tax assessment of that year as "Land, 3,240 square feet; house, 1,001 square feet; 3 stories, 29 windows; Value, $1,000."[20] His son Peter, a clockmaker and watchmaker, was listed as sharing the house.[21]

"George Trott, Gentleman, living in good health and perfect memory," wrote his will on 17 September 1799.[22] He died on 2 January 1810 and was buried at King's Chapel.[23] His will was presented for probate on 19 February 1810 by his wife Ann Boylston (Cunningham) Trott, the designated executor, and by the witnesses of the will, Standfast Smith, David Ingalls, and Andrew Cunningham, Ann's youngest brother. Except for specific bequests of one hundred cents to each of his sons, Peter, Jonathan, George, and Andrew Cunningham, Trott left his entire estate to his widow for her use during her lifetime.[24] Ann Trott died shortly after her husband on 28 March 1810.[25] The following April, two of the jeweler's sons, George and Andrew C. Trott, requested that the court appoint Jonathan Trott as administrator for their father's estate.[26] An inventory of the estate of George Trott, jeweler, taken on 23 April 1810 values his house and land on Bennett Street at $4,266 and his personal belongings and household furnishings at an additional $260.66.[27] No jeweler's tools or shop contents are listed. Since Trott was sixty when he died, he could have already dispersed his business to his sons, Andrew Cunningham and Peter, to his brother Jonathan, or to his nephews, Jonathan, Jr. (1771–1813), and John Procter Trott (1769–1852), all of whom were silversmiths, jewelers, or watchmakers. Andrew C. Trott and Peter Trott appear in Boston records as watchmakers; they were probably continuing their father's business.[28] On 2 November 1799, Peter Trott advertised his services in clock and watch repair as well as the sale of imported English watches in his shop at 28 Marlborough Street.[29]

No objects made by George Trott have been identified. There are several initials marks (G·T in a rectangle) that may have been used by Trott or by George Tyler (q.v. Appendix B).[30] DAF

1. Harris 1889, 79–80; RC 21:50; RC 28:323; Codman 1918, 232; SCPR 77:2–4; Waistill Trott became a member of the Old South Church on 19 January 1728; see *Old South Church* 1883, 35; Bridgman 1856, 301.
2. Harris 1889, 79–80; RC 21:132, 255.
3. RC 24:150; RC 30:59; Cunningham 1901, 417; *Brookline VR*, 11; *Index of Obituaries, 1784–1840*, 5:4553; *Index of Obituaries, 1704–1800*, 1:78; 2:267.
4. Cunningham 1901, 416–17.
5. Cunningham 1901, 417; Wyman 1853, 146, 149.
6. Roberts 1895, 2:136.
7. Roberts 1895, 2:136, 172.
8. Roberts 1895, 2:125.
9. Roberts 1895, 2:136.
10. Cunningham 1901, 417; Roberts 1895, 2:126–27; Butterfield 1964, 1:294.
11. RC 18:36.
12. 11 August, 10 September 1783, 29 May, 14 September 1784, vol. 2, Waste Book, 1783–97, 1, 3, 15, 18, Revere Family Papers, MHS.
13. Cunningham 1901, 417.
14. SCD 183:152–53.
15. *Boston Directory* 1796, 101; 1798, 114.
16. Hill 1890, 2:261.
17. SCD 183:151–52.
18. Cunningham 1901, 417.
19. RC 22:493.
20. RC 22:436.
21. Distin/Bishop 1976, 341.
22. SCPR 108:93–94.
23. Bridgman 1853, 95; Cunningham 1901, 417.
24. SCPR 108:93–94.
25. Cunningham 1901, 417.

26. SCPR 108:182.

27. SCPR 108:203–04.

28. Distin/Bishop 1976, 341.

29. *Columbian Centinel*, 2 November 1799. The advertisement was repeated in *Russell's Gazette* on 4 November 1799.

30. There are at least four initials marks: (1) a spoon at CMA (Johnston 1994, 152) and another at WM (DAPC 73.1135); (2) a porringer at RWNAG (*American Silver* 1967, no. 15); (3) a spoon at HD (69.1660); and (4) a spoon at YUAG (1985.84.666).

Jonathan Trott
1730–1815

A

B

Jonathan Trott was born in 1730 in Boston and was the elder brother of George Trott (q.v.).[1] (See the entry on George Trott for biographical information on his parents and grandparents.) Jonathan was born into a strong family tradition of metalsmithing: his father, Thomas, uncle Benjamin, and brother Samuel were all blacksmiths.[2] The marriage intentions of Jonathan Trott and Lydia Procter (b. 1735) were published in 1756.[3] Lydia was the daughter of the Boston schoolmaster and minister John Procter (ca. 1704–57) and his first wife, Lydia Richards (ca. 1704–50), of New London, Connecticut.[4] Trott and his wife had at least four children. Trott joined the Old South Church on 23 October 1757 with a baptismal covenant, which, in contrast to a "full communion," was a qualified type of membership.[5]

The identity of Trott's master is unknown. Trott's professional activities were first indicated in the *Boston Gazette* of 6 November 1758, when Trott reported that his shop had been robbed of a number of items, including a gold necklace and earrings and silver shoe buckles. On 18 October 1765, Jonathan was identified as a jeweler when he and his wife, Lydia Trott, sold their one-quarter interest in the brick house on Queen Street that they had inherited from her father to John Procter, Lydia's brother, for £66.13.4.[6] The deed was witnessed by the watchmaker John Rolestone (q.v. Appendix A). Two years later, Trott purchased a house as well as a goldsmith shop nearby on Newbury Street for £266.13.4 from Elizabeth Beaudrie, a transaction witnessed by the watchmaker Elijah Collins (q.v. Appendix A).[7] Trott arranged a mortgage for this property with his father and brother-in-law, the schoolmaster John Procter, on 21 August 1772 for £200 silver money. The mortgage amount plus six shillings and eight pence interest per ounce was to be repaid to Thomas Hubbard, treasurer of Harvard College, or his successors within a year; the money was repaid by June 1783. The jeweler and his wife sold their interest in her late father's house in north Boston to her brother for £100 in August 1773. In both of these deeds, Trott was referred to as a jeweler living in Boston.[8]

Trott had changed both his residence and his occupation by 1781. In May of that year, Jonathan Trott, innholder of Norwich, Connecticut, and his wife, Lydia, sold their house and the shop nearby on Newbury Street to Josiah Fowle, a Boston barber, for £600.[9] Fowle may have been occupying the property prior to the sale because the deed describes the shop as a barber's shop, rather than a goldsmith's shop. Trott operated the Peck Tavern on the Norwich green and was one of the signers of the town charter. He was still living in Norwich in 1784, when cannon were fired in front of his tavern to proclaim peace.[10] Trott last appears in Suffolk County records on 8 June 1786, when he sold the South End property in Boston inherited from his father to his brother George Trott.[11] By then, Trott had moved to New

London, Connecticut, where he resumed his profession of jeweler. He died in New London in 1815.[12]

Trott trained his two sons, Jonathan, Jr. (1771–1813), and John Procter (1769–1852), as jewelers. Both men worked in New London, Connecticut; John Procter Trott married Lois Chapman of New London.[13]

Most of the surviving objects by Jonathan Trott are spoons. He may have specialized in making small objects and flatware and jobbed out his larger orders to colleagues. For example, Trott commissioned Paul Revere, Jr. (q.v.), to make six tankards to fulfill a large order for the Third Church of Brookfield, Massachusetts, and the charges were recorded by Revere on 9 January 1772:

Mr Jonathan Trott	D^r
	oz
To a Silver Wine Qt Tank^d	24:13
To on Dito weight	25: 1:12
To one Dito	25: 3
To one Dito	24: 5:12
To one Dito	25: 1: 0
To One Dito	24:19: 0
	149: 3: 0[14]

Two marks are associated with this jeweler. Mark (A), an initial and surname separated by a pellet in a shaped cartouche, is found on spoons in the Museum of Fine Arts, Boston, and the Ineson-Bissell Collection, Winterthur Museum.[15] The engraving on these spoons is made with multiple light cuts; the oval bowls are ornamented with a distinctive elongated eleven-lobe shell. Mark (B), I T in a rectangle with lobed ends, appears on a teaspoon with a similar shell, oval bowl, and shaded block letter engraving. Another mark traditionally attributed to Trott, initials and a pellet in a rectangle, appears on several other spoons.[16] These, however, are engraved with deep, bold lines and feature shells of a very different character. This mark may have been used by I. or T. Tyler (q.v.), whose engraving style resembles the work on these spoons (see I. or T. Tyler mark [c]). DAF

SURVIVING OBJECTS

	Mark	Inscription	Patron	Date	Reference	Owner
Beaker	A*	The gift of Remember Preston,/To the Church of Dorchester	First Church, Dorchester, Mass., for Remember Preston	ca. 1760	Jones 1930, 145–46	
Papboat	A	Arnold Welles	Arnold Welles	ca. 1760	Goldsborough 1969, no. 103	MWPI
Porringer spoon	A	SM/to/HD (+)	Samuel May	1769	Buhler 1972, appendix no. 77	MFAB
Tablespoon	A*	MH/To/IW	Hill family	ca. 1760	Buhler 1972, no. 546	MFAB
Tablespoon	A*	G/TR		ca. 1790		YUAG
Tablespoon	A†	C/IE		ca. 1770	DAPC 71.2447	WM
Tablespoon	A*	HF		ca. 1760	YUAG files	

	Mark	Inscription	Patron	Date	Reference	Owner
Tablespoon	B†	F/IS	Josiah Fowle (?)	ca. 1770	DAPC 89.3076	
Six tankards (*with mark of Paul Revere, Jr.*)	none	The Gift of,/Mary Bartlett.Widow of Eph.^m. Bartlett,/to the third Church in Brookfield./1768	Jedidiah Foster, executor of Mary Bartlett's estate, for First Congregational (Unitarian) Society, Brookfield, Mass.	1772	Quimby 1995, no. IIIa–f	WM
Teaspoon	B*	HD		ca. 1760	YUAG files	

1. Harris 1889, 79–80.
2. Harris 1889, 79–80.
3. Thwing; RC 24:223; RC 30:20.
4. Phinney 1943, 145; Caulkins 1857, 28; *Index of Obituaries, 1704–1800*, 3:270; Bridgman 1853, 52; New London VR 2:82.
5. *Old South Church* 1883, 131.
6. SCD 106:109.
7. SCD 111:239–40.
8. SCD 124:138–40.
9. SCD 133:31–33.
10. Flynt/Fales 1968, 343.
11. SCD 183:151–52.
12. Flynt/Fales 1968, 343; Bodenwein 1943, 57.
13. Bodenwein 1943, 57; Thwing; Phinney 1943, 145; Distin/Bishop 1976, 341.
14. 9 January 1772, vol. 1, Waste and Memoranda Book, 1761–83, [39], Revere Family Papers, MHS.
15. Kovel 1961, 271, also shows drawings of J.TROTT in a serrated rectangle, I.TROTT in a rectangle, and J.TROTT in an oval, but examples of these marks have not been located.
16. Ensko 1948, 212; Belden 1980, 413 (mark a); Flynt/Fales 1968, 343.

Richard Trumbull
1744–1815

Richard Trumbull was born in Charlestown, Massachusetts, in August 1744 to Timothy Trumbull (1720–54), an innholder and distiller, and Mary Sutton (b. 1722), who married in 1741.[1] His paternal grandparents were Samuel Trumbull (1683–1759) of Charlestown and Hannah Fowle (b. 1684) of Woburn, Massachusetts.[2] His maternal grandparents were Richard Sutton (1696/97–ca. 1765), a leatherdresser of Charlestown, and Mary Fosdick (1699–1757) of New London, Connecticut.[3] Trumbull's father died when Trumbull was only ten years old, leaving an insolvent estate that burdened his family with considerable debt.[4]

Trumbull would have begun his apprenticeship about 1758 and would have finished his training about 1765. The identity of his master is unknown. In 1771 he married Anne (Diser) Trumbull (d. 1771), the widow of James Trumbull and the daughter of Francis Diser (ca. 1706–70), a mariner, and Mary Bodge (1710–63).[5] In his will, witnessed by Henry Phillips Sweetser (q.v.), Francis Diser bequeathed his daughter a lot at Morton's Point in Charlestown.[6] Shortly after their marriage, Trumbull and his wife mortgaged some property she had inherited; in that deed he was identified as "of Charlestown, Goldsmith."[7] Anne Trumbull died later that year. The Massachusetts tax list of 1771 includes Trumbull in Charlestown with one poll, one-half of a house, an additional building, and £5.10 annual worth of real estate.[8]

In 1775 Trumbull married as his second wife Hannah Bunker (1745–1802), the widow of (1) David Frothingham and (2) Benjamin C. Bunker and the daughter of William Gibson (d. 1763) and Rebecca Simmonds (1718/19–64).[9] Trumbull is said to have occupied a shop on the town's ferry wharf. In the

British bombardment of Charlestown during the Revolution he claimed a loss on buildings and personal estate of £159.18. In 1779 he purchased real estate at the corner of Main and Water streets from William Stanton.[10]

Following the Revolution, Trumbull may have engaged in trades other than goldsmithing. In a deed of 1786 he was identified as "of Charlestown, Innholder."[11] He was sued by Stephen Parker for debt in 1783, and in 1795 Ebenezer Breed foreclosed on the piece of property that Trumbull had mortgaged in 1771.[12] At the time of his death in 1815 he was called a chaisemaker. His inventory amounted to $5,059.27.[13] He was buried in Charlestown's Old Burial Ground.[14]

No silver with his mark is known to survive. PEK

1. *Charlestown VR* 1:269, 363, 468; MCPR, docket 22869; Wyman 1879, 2:955; *NEHGR* 32:61.
2. *Charlestown VR* 1:118; *Woburn VR* 1:97; 3:285; MCPR, docket 22868.
3. Wyman 1879, 2:916; New London VR 1:25; *Ipswich VR* 1:362; ECPR, docket 26858.
4. MCPR, docket 22869.
5. *Charlestown VR* 1:224, 328, 422; Wyman 1879, 1:297.
6. MCPR, docket 6326.
7. MCD 72:63–64.
8. Pruitt 1978, 184–85.
9. *Charlestown VR* 1:252, 331, 376, 493; *Index of Obituaries, 1784–1840*, 5:4560; Wyman 1879, 1:407.
10. Hunnewell 1888, 122, 157.
11. MCD 96:447–48.
12. SCCR, Court of Common Pleas Extended Record Book 1783, 248; MCD 72:63–64.
13. MCPR, docket 22867.
14. Griffen 1952, 113.

James Turner
1721/22–59

A

A noted engraver of silver and prints, James Turner was from Essex County but worked in Boston for about a decade in the 1740s and early 1750s, before moving to Philadelphia. He was probably born in Marblehead, Massachusetts, on 18 March 1721/22, the son of Isaac (ca. 1692–1754) and Mary (Pratt) Turner (b. 1698), who were married in 1719. Details about his early life, schooling, and training remain unknown, although his adult career is well documented and has been chronicled recently by Martha Gandy Fales.[1]

By the early 1740s, probably after his apprenticeship was completed, Turner moved to Boston and embarked on an active career as an engraver there. In the *Boston Evening Post* for 24 June 1745 he announced,

> *James Turner*, Silversmith & Engraver,
>   Near the Town-House in Cornhill, *Boston*,
> *Engraves all sorts of Copper Plates for the Rolling Press, all sorts of Stamps in Brass or Pewter for the common Printing Press, Coats of Arms, Crests, Cyphers, &c. on Gold, Silver, Steel, Copper, Brass or Pewter.*
>   *He likewise makes Watch Faces, makes and cuts Seals, in Gold, Silver or Steel; or makes Steel Faces for Seals, and sets them handsomly in Gold or Silver. He cuts all sorts of Steel Stamps, Brass Rolls and Stamps for Sadlers and Bookbinders, and does all other sorts of Work in Gold or Silver. All after the best and neatest Manner, and at the most reasonable Rates.*

His first documented work is a woodcut of Boston on the cover of the *American Magazine* published in 1743 and 1744 by Rogers and Fowle. The same publishers also issued Turner's first map in 1745, a *Plan of the Town and Harbour of Louisburgh* in woodcut. On 14 March 1748, Turner placed the following notice in the *Boston Evening Post*: "Just Published, a Treatise, proving (*a Posteriori*) that most of the Disorders incident to the *Fair Sex*, are owing to Flatulencies not seasonably vented. Wrote originally in Spanish, by Don Fart-inhando Puff-indost. Sold by J. Bushell, Printer in Newbury-Street. Price Two Shillings, single. Also a Frontispiece to the same, from a Copper Plate, with the Author's Effigies, &c. Sold by J. Turner, Engraver, in Cornhill. N.B., The Book and Prints may be had together or a part of said Bushel or Turner, or of J. Buck, Print Seller in Cornhill." This same year, Turner signed the trade card of the Boston merchants Joseph and Daniel Waldo. In 1750, he embellished his "Chart of the Coasts of Nova-Scotia" with the arms of Gov. Edward Cornwallis. Many of the woodcuts in an edition of *The History of the Holy Jesus*, published in Boston by B. Gray (1746), are attributed to his hand, and he may have made the illustrations for an edition of Aesop's Fables as well.[2]

Some silver with Turner's mark (A) has survived from the early 1740s. The most elaborate example is the Derby family tankard of 1746, marked and documented in a surviving bill:

D Capt Rich.<d> Derby to James Turner C.<r>
By Silver 49<oz>-19<dwt>-0

To a Tankard	28: 10: 12			
To a p.<r> of Cans	26 14: —			
	55: 4: 12			
	49: 19: 0			
To overplus Silver	5: 5: 12 at 40/	£10: 11: 0	
To the Makeing & Engraving y.<e> Tank.<d>		15: 0 —0	
To Making & Engraving y.<e> Cans —		15: 0 —0	
		£40: 11 0	

Boston Oct.<r> 22.<d> 1746 Errors Excepted
p.<r> James Turner[3]

Other holloware with his mark is known, including a pepper box and creampot. Engraving seems to have been his greatest interest or at least his most profitable line of work. As he wrote to Benjamin Franklin on 6 July 1747, "It has been my Ill fortune ever Since I have been for my Self to be Involved in a great deal of large Unprofitable Silver Smiths work which was particularly my Case when your Brother Mr. J[ohn] Franklyn procured me a large Job of Engraveing."[4] The large job may have included the bookplate engraved by Turner for John Franklin.[5]

The engraving on silver marked by other craftsmen has been attributed to Turner's hand, based on its stylistic similarity to the coat of arms on the Derby tankard and other objects. These objects include two flagons made for the First Church of Marblehead by Samuel Burt (q.v.) of Boston in 1748–49 and the presentation cup of 1749 made by William Swan (q.v.).[6]

Fales suggests that Turner left Boston for Philadelphia in 1752 or 1753.[7] A bill from the executors of the estate of William Lynde of Marblehead dated 2 September 1752 suggests that Turner was still in the Boston area at that time:

The hon.<ble> Benj: Lynde Esq.<r> Sam.<ll> Curwin, Esq.<r> and
M.<r> Henry Gibbs Executors to the last Will & Testament

1752   of M.<r> W.<m> Lynde.<d> To James Turner   D.<r>
May 14.   To 8 Escutcheons for y.<e> Funeral of s.<d>   £6.— 8 —[torn]
               Dec.<d>

at 8/. ap^s.

	To an Inscription on y^e Breastplate of the Coffin	8 — 0
June 6th.	To 9 Enamell'd Rings for D^o. w^t. 13^{dwt}. 23^{gr}.	
	To fashoning D^o. at 9/4 ap^s.	4 — 4 — 0
9th.	To adding a Crescent for Difference to each of the Escutcheons at 2/. ap^s.	16 — 0

£ 11 = 16 = 0

Turner gave the executors credit for overplus gold, three books of gold leaf, and "3 ^{1}/$_8$ y^{ds} black A' la mode taken up by S. Curwin Esqr at Mr John Nutting's." The "Ballance due to James Turner" was £9.10.6 ^{3}/$_4$. The executors later received a second bill indicating that Turner also performed engraving. Harold Bowditch has suggested that Turner painted an armorial commemorating the marriage on 28 May 1752 of Andrew Oliver, Jr., and Mary Lynde, William Lynde's niece.[8] Turner also acknowledged receipt of ten shillings from John Touzell (q.v.) on 24 November 1752.[9]

Turner had developed connections with Philadelphia prior to his move there, as his letter to Benjamin Franklin demonstrates. In 1744, Franklin, who was the Philadelphia distributor of the *American Magazine*, commissioned Turner to engrave the plates for Lewis Evans's *An Account of the New Improved Pennsylvania Fireplaces*, and additional commissions for maps, seals, bookplates, and other projects followed. This stream of work may have encouraged his removal to Philadelphia.[10]

After his arrival there, he engraved the plates for the three "most important maps of Pennsylvania to appear in eighteenth-century Philadelphia," including those published by Lewis Evans, Joshua Fisher, and Nicholas Scull, in addition to many other works beyond the purview of this volume. His shop was on Arch Street, and Henry Dawkins worked for him for a time.[11] Turner married Elizabeth MacKay in Philadelphia on 19 December 1756.[12] In 1758, he wrote to Mrs. Franklin seeking permission to borrow a portrait miniature of Franklin to use as a model in preparing a mezzotint. His lengthy and persuasive letter also sheds light on his abilities: "I should long since have asked of Mr. Franklin himself his permission, to carry such a design into execution, had it not been for a difficulty which I foresaw would occur, of obtaining a good likeness: for though I profess myself capable of imitating a good draught, ready made to my hands, yet I have no pretensions to drawing after the life."[13]

It was reported in the *Boston Evening Post* for 10 December 1759 that "we hear from Philadelphia, that Mr. James Turner, engraver, formerly of this town, lately died there of the small pox."[14] Three days later, a notice in the *Pennsylvania Gazette* advertised the sale "at the late Dwelling house of James Turner, Engraver, deceased, in Arch street, sundry sorts of Household Furniture, engraving Tools, a number of Copper plates and Pictures." Fifty years later, Isaiah Thomas described Turner as a "remarkably good workman . . . the best engraver which appeared in the colonies before the revolution, especially on type metal."[15] GWRW

SURVIVING OBJECTS

	Mark	Inscription	Patron	Date	Reference	Owner
Cann	none	HAT (cipher)		ca. 1745	Buhler/Hood 1970, 1:211	
Creampot	A	Macartey arms, a stag tripping; MM	Macartey family	ca. 1750	Sotheby's, 28, 29, 31 January 1987, lot 303	HMA
Pepper box	A†	HAT (cipher); H/TA		ca. 1745	Buhler/Hood 1970, no. 281	YUAG
Tankard	A	Derby arms, on a bend 3 stags' heads, and crest, an eagle preying on an infant	Richard Derby	1746	Fales 1991, 8–9	

1. *Marblehead VR* 1:526; *Salem VR* 2:192; 4:406; 6:287. For some years, it was thought that there were two James Turners, one from Marblehead and one from Philadelphia; see, for example, Groce/Wallace 1957, 639. It is now known that there was only one such individual. Turner's career has been treated in depth in Fales 1991, 1–20, to which the reader is referred for more information.
2. *Philadelphia: Three Centuries of American Art*, 64; Dow 1927, 14; Fales 1973a, 205; Thomas [1810] 1970, 256n. See also Hitchings 1970, 98.
3. Derby Family Papers, box 15, folder 2, PEM; printed in *EIHC* 76, no. 4 (October 1940): 313.
4. *Papers of Benjamin Franklin* 3:144–46.
5. Fales 1973a, 206, fig. 93.
6. Fales 1973a, 207–10, fig. 95; Jones 1913, 261–62, pl. 86.1.
7. Fales 1973a, 206.
8. Curwen Family Papers, box 5, folder 8, PEM. A variant of the bill is published in Bowditch 1944, 179, wherein reference is made to the second bill, not seen by the writer. Bowditch illustrates the painted armorial as fig. 2.
9. English-Touzel-Hathorne Papers, box 4, folder 5, PEM.
10. *Philadelphia: Three Centuries of American Art*, 64.
11. *Philadelphia: Three Centuries of American Art*, 65; *Pennsylvania Journal and Weekly Advertiser*, 18 October 1759, 19 January 1758, as printed in Prime 1969, 1:29, 18. For Turner's maps, see Wheat/Brun 1985.
12. Flynt/Fales 1968, 344.
13. *Works of Benjamin Franklin* 6:30–33.
14. Dow 1927, 14.
15. Thomas [1810] 1970, 256n.

Andrew Tyler
ca. 1692/93–1741

A

Andrew Tyler was the son of Thomas (d. 1703) and Miriam (Simpkins) Tyler (ca. 1659–1730/31). Thomas Tyler was a sea captain who came to Massachusetts from Budleigh, Devonshire, England. He and Miriam Simpkins, daughter of Pilgrim (1639–1720) and Miriam Simpkins (d. 1660), were married about 1684. They resided primarily in Boston but were living in Weymouth, Massachusetts, at least briefly, when their daughter Miriam was born in 1698. Thomas Tyler died at sea in 1703.[1]

Andrew Tyler's birth is not recorded, but he was baptized in the Third (or Old South) Church, Boston, on 29 January 1692/93.[2] He married Miriam Pepperrell (ca. 1694–1766) of Kittery (now in Maine), daughter of William Pepperrell (1648–1733/34), a fisherman, and Margery (Bray) Pepperrell (d. 1741).[3] Their intention was published in Boston on 12 January 1714/15, and they were married in Kittery. Miriam's brother William became the first American baronet after the forces under his command captured the fortress at Louisbourg

B

C

D

E

in 1745. Her sister Margery married Peletiah Whittemore, who were the parents of William Whittemore (q.v.).

Andrew Tyler became a member of the Brattle Street Church on 1 March 1724, and Miriam Tyler joined on 5 April 1724. All sixteen of their children, twelve of whom survived to adulthood, were baptized in the church. The children were Miriam (bap. 1716/17–d. before 1763), who married Judge William Williams in 1733; Andrew (bap. 1717/18–died in infancy); Andrew (1719–75), who attended Harvard College, graduating in the class of 1738, and became a minister (his son, George, became a silversmith [q.v. Appendix B]); William (bap. 1720/21–died in infancy); William (bap. 1722–d. before 1758), who became a ship chandler; Margery (bap. 1723/24–d. before 1740); John (bap. 1725–d. before 1732); Katharine (1726–d. before 1728); Mary (bap. 1727–d. before 1735); Katharine (bap. 1728), who married (i) David Ochterlony in 1757 and (ii) Sir Isaac Heard in 1778; Thomas (bap. 1730–d. before 1763), who became a merchant; Pepperrell (bap. 1731–49), a mariner, who died at sea; John (bap. 1732), a mariner, who married (i) Sarah Compton and (ii) Sally Wales of Roxbury, Massachusetts; Christopher (bap. 1733–d. before 1763), a mariner; Mary (bap. 1735–76), who married Charles Pelham of Newton, Massachusetts; and Jane (bap. 1736–d. before 1763), who married Joseph Gilman of Exeter, New Hampshire.[4]

Andrew Tyler was active in town affairs throughout his life. He served as clerk of the market (1718/19–1719/20), scavenger (1720/21–1722/23, 1724/25–1725/26, 1728/29–1729/30, 1734/35–1735/36), assessor (1725–28), purchaser of grain (1726–29), selectman (1729/30–1731/32), and fireward (1732–33, 1740/41). He was elected constable in March 1723/24 but refused to serve.[5]

We do not know for certain with whom Tyler trained. He was one of the appraisers of the estate of John Coney (q.v.), and Kathryn Buhler believed that he may have been one of Coney's apprentices.[6] Tyler had a very successful goldsmithing business that seems to have been flourishing by 1721. By two deeds dated 9 January 1721/22 and 6 August 1722 Tyler purchased a "brick Messuage or Tenement and Tenements in the present tenure or occupation of the s^d Andrew Tyler and Rachel Winsor Situate in Anne Street," with an adjacent bakehouse and land, from the widow Sarah Martyn and the heirs of the merchant Edward Thomas for a total of £875.12.[7] He probably trained Knight Leverett and Samuel Burrill (qq.v.), as the two were witnesses to a deed of 30 July 1722 by which Tyler sold a parcel of land in Green Street to the housewright Joseph Ricks.[8] Burrill witnessed another deed for Tyler on 17 May 1724 along with Theophilus Burrill (q.v.).[9] Theophilus Burrill may have been working for Tyler as a journeyman because he witnessed another deed for Tyler in 1727.[10] John Banks (q.v.) also may have been working for Tyler as a journeyman at approximately the same time because on 14 August 1724, Tyler purchased a triangle of land west of his garden from the distiller James Gooch and sold another strip of land to the northeast of his garden to Gooch, and both deeds were witnessed by John Banks and Mary Alden.[11] Tyler probably also trained his nephew William Whittemore, and possibly his cousin William Simpkins (q.v.).[12] In addition, George Hanners, Sr. (q.v.), witnessed Tyler's mother's will in 1716/17, which suggests he trained with Tyler.[13] The silversmith I. or T. Tyler (q.v.) may have been related to Andrew Tyler.

Tyler is known to have used several different marks: two versions of AT crowned above a device (variously referred to as a cat or a bird) in a shield (A, B), A·TYLER in an ellipse (C), AT in a rectangle (D), and AT over a device in a heart (E). A prolific silversmith, he boasted clients from throughout New

England, as demonstrated by his church commissions. He made a beaker for the church in Exeter, New Hampshire, about 1715; a tankard, two straight-sided beakers, two cup-shaped beakers, and one mug for the First Church in Lynn, Massachusetts, in 1721; a mug for the First Church in Beverly, Massachusetts, in 1731; a two-handled cup for the church in Hatfield, Massachusetts, about 1732; and a beaker for the church in East Haven, Connecticut, about 1739. He also made an undated beaker in the First Church, Groton, Massachusetts, and a spoon in the First Church, Marblehead, Massachusetts. The estate of Thomas Clarke (d. 1732) paid Andrew Tyler and John Edwards (q.v.) for funeral rings.[14]

Andrew Tyler appears in the ledger of the stationer Daniel Henchman as the purchaser of an account book, paper, foolscap, a copy of "Dr Mathers works," a "Slate in a frame," a psalmbook, bills of lading, "1 Contemplat^{on}," "1 Dayly Como^n," and "1 Ovid Trist"; he paid for his purchases with a gold ring and a Bible. Some of these supplies—the slate, the Ovid, and probably some of the paper—were likely acquired for his children's education. He bought the account book in 1713, just as he began his goldsmithing business; his purchase of the bills of lading in the early 1720s may mark the beginning of his extensive mercantile activities. We know from a letter in the Pepperrell papers that Tyler had been shipping goods to his mother in Kittery for several years.[15]

Although most of Andrew Tyler's early land transactions involved Tyler's house lot, other deeds indicated that he was beginning to invest in land. In March 1719 he purchased a quarter part of a tract of land on Wiscasset Bay in the province of Maine.[16] He sold half of this land to William Pepperrell, Jr., in 1727.[17] In April 1724 he purchased two parcels of land totaling 3,001 acres in Sherborn, Massachusetts, in partnership with the physician William Douglass, Benjamin Bronsdon, Habijah Savage, Esq., the merchant John Binning, and his brother the brazier William Tyler. In November 1724 he and William Douglass purchased 350 acres of land "adjoining to the Town of Oxford" for £83. In 1725 Andrew Tyler purchased half a house on the corner of Anne Street and Paddy's Alley for £542.10.[18] In 1729 Tyler purchased part of a tract of land in Biddeford, in the province of Maine, from William Pepperrell, Jr.[19] In December 1732 he and others sold a small tract of land in Biddeford.[20]

As one of the overseers of the estate of the shopkeeper Isaiah Tay (the father-in-law of James Barnes, Jr. [q.v.]), Tyler was involved in a lawsuit in 1730 and in the sale of a tenement in Shrimpton's Lane occupied by Thomas Savage, Sr. (q.v.), in 1735.[21] In 1734 he was identified as Andrew Tyler, gentleman, when he joined with others in suing the goldsmith John Pitts (q.v.) of Boston for a debt dating from April 1728. But when the watchmaker Elijah Collins (q.v. Appendix A) sued Tyler in January 1737/38, he was again referred to as Andrew Tyler, goldsmith.[22]

Andrew Tyler died in Boston on 12 August 1741. His will, written on 28 May 1740, was probated on 21 August. Tyler left five pounds to each of his ten living children, his books to his son Andrew, thirty pounds to the workhouse in Boston, and a gold ring to each of the overseers of his will, his brothers William Pepperrell, William Tyler, and Peleg Wiswall. He left the rest of his estate to his wife during her "Natural Life," "in order to her good Educating & bringing up" the children; he ordered further that she give each of them "at their Marrying or coming to Lawfull Age such Sum or Sums of Money or other thing or things as she pleases, & charge them with it which shall be apart of their Portion in my Estate after my said Wife her decease." He gave his wife liberty to sell any part of his real estate, on condition that she attain the consent of his overseers, as long as one were still alive. He ordered that after his wife's death his estate be divided into ten equal parts, with each of his sons and daughters receiving an equal share. He made a special arrangement for his married daughter, Miriam, stipulating that her share be put out at interest for her during her husband's lifetime and be paid to her after her husband's death. He appointed his wife, Miriam, sole executor. There was no inventory of his personal estate, but his real estate in Worcester County was appraised after his wife's death at £211.4.8.[23]

Miriam remained a widow for the rest of her life. In her will, written on 6 April 1763, she mentioned her surviving children—Andrew, John, Mary, and Katharine Ochterlony—and her granddaughter Miriam, daughter of her deceased son Thomas. Her will was probated on 4 March 1766. She was buried with her husband in tomb 58 in the Granary Burying Ground.[24] BMW

SURVIVING OBJECTS

	Mark	Inscription	Patron	Date	Reference	Owner
Beaker	A*	The Gift of Jonas Prescot Esq.ʳ to yᵉ Church of Groton	First Parish, Groton, Mass., for Jonas Prescott	ca. 1723	Jones 1913, 190	
Beaker	A or B	The gift of the Honᵇˡᵉ Peter Coffin Esqʳ to the Church at Exeter	Peter Coffin and/or First Congregational Church, Exeter, N.H.	ca. 1715	Jones 1913, 171	
Beaker	A or B	The Gift of The Revᵈ Mʳ Jacob/ Hemmingway and Sarah His Wife To/ The Church of Christ/In East Haven	Rev. Jacob and Sarah Hemmingway and/or Congregational Church, East Haven, Conn.	ca. 1740	Jones 1913, 255	
Beaker	E	The Gift of the Honourable/John Burrell Esq.ʳ,/to the first Church in Lynn/Dec 10 1721	First Church of Christ, Lynn, Mass., for John Burrill	1721	Jones 1913, 160	
Beaker	E	The Gift of John Henry Burchsted Physitian/to the first Church in Lynn/Sept 25 1721	First Church of Christ, Lynn, Mass., for John Henry Burchsted	1721	Jones 1913, 255	
Caster	A	none		ca. 1720	*Antiques* 115 (May 1979): 887	
Caster	B†	none		ca. 1735		AIC
Caster	B	P/WM; P (later)		ca. 1715	Sotheby Parke Bernet, 16–18 November 1978, lot 400	BBC
Caster	C	EW		ca. 1740	YUAG files	
Cup	A or B	?	?	ca. 1720	DAPC 75.5224	

	Mark	Inscription	Patron	Date	Reference	Owner
Cup	E	P/IS		ca. 1720	DAPC 68.6162	MMA
Cup	E	The Gift of the Honourable/John Burrell Esqr-/to the first Church in Lynn/December ye 10th 1721.	First Church of Christ, Lynn, Mass., for John Burrill	1721	Jones 1913, 255	
Cup	E	The Gift of John Henry Burchsted Physitian/to the first Church in Lynn/Sepr. the 25th 1721	First Church of Christ, Lynn, Mass., for John Henry Burchsted	1721	Jones 1913, 255	
Cup	E*	MR; SH	Mary Rand	1728	YUAG files	
Cup	E*	C/GK (+)	Coffin family (?)	ca. 1725	*Antiques* 99 (April 1971): 531	
Cup	E	LC		ca. 1725	YUAG files	
Cup	?	?		ca. 1720		ChM
Mourning ring (gold)	D†	A Brown ob 16 April 1729 AE^t 9	A. Brown	1729	Buhler 1972, no. 117	MFAB
Mug	A *or* B	The Gift of John Henry Burchsted Physitian/to the first Church in Lynn/Septr the 25th 1721	First Church of Christ, Lynn, Mass., for John Henry Burchsted	1721	Jones 1913, 255	
Mug	A *or* B	The Gift of the Honourable John Burrill Esqr-/to the first Church in Lynn/December ye 10th, 1721	First Church of Christ, Lynn, Mass., for John Burrill	1721	Jones 1913, 255	
Mug	C*	The Gift of Hannah Stone to the first Church of Beverly 1731	Hannah Stone and/or First Parish Church, Beverly, Mass.	1731	Jones 1913, 16	
Mug	E*	F/IR		ca. 1725	Shelley 1958, 175	HFM
Pepperbox	B*	S/IE	Josiah and Elizabeth Skillon	ca. 1715	*Antiques* 98 (July 1970): 25	
Pepperbox	C	MF; MW	Martha Williams (?)	ca. 1735	MFA 1911, no. 982	
Pepperbox	C*	M/DL; AM (later)		ca. 1730	Johnston 1994, 155	CMA
Pepperbox	C	S/IM; HM/to/SS (later)		ca. 1730	*American Silver* 1967, no. 3	RWNAG
Pepperbox	E*	C/EM		ca. 1725	Sander 1982, no. 8	SPNEA
Porringer	A*	MC		ca. 1725	Johnston 1994, 156	CMA

	Mark	Inscription	Patron	Date	Reference	Owner
Porringer (with marks of William Homes, Sr.)	A*	D/WL		ca. 1740	Johnston 1994, 73	CMA
Porringer	A	L/BE		ca. 1730	Sotheby's, 30 January– 2 February 1991, lot 141	
Porringer	A *or* B	Ex Dono/T. El- bridge/to/MS	Thomas Elbridge and/ or Martha (Saunders) Salisbury	ca. 1725	Buhler 1979, no. 13	WAM
Porringer	A *or* B	H/BM; Benjamin Pemberton	Benjamin and Mary Hammatt	ca. 1735	Bigelow 1917, 311–12	
Porringer	A *or* B	LB; WB (later)	Bowler family	ca. 1715	Bigelow 1917, 311–12	
Porringer	A†/ C†	H/IM		ca. 1730	Buhler 1972, no. 116	MFAB
Porringer	E	H/ES; 1784 (later)		ca. 1725	MFA 1911, no. 970	
Two porringer spoons	A *or* B	unidentified crest, a lion rampant		ca. 1730	YUAG files	
Porringer spoon	E*	unidentified crest, a lion rampant		ca. 1730		YUAG
Salver	C	T/ES		ca. 1730	YUAG files	
Serving spoon	C	SLW (later)		ca. 1735		MFAB
Snuffbox	E*	HD; H DAVIS/1718	H. Davis	1718		RISD
Spout cup	B*	S/IE (over earlier initials) (+)		ca. 1715	Buhler 1972, no. 115	MFAB
Spout cup	E	B/DA; NW (later)		ca. 1725	YUAG files	
Tablespoon	B	EG; 1632 (later) (+)		ca. 1720	DAPC 71.2445	WM
Tablespoon	C	DS		ca. 1735		CHS
Tablespoon	C	SW		ca. 1735	Buhler 1979, no. 14	WAM
Tablespoon	C*	S/SS/1730		ca. 1730	DAPC 69.4142	WM
Tablespoon	D	S/HE (partially erased); B/HA (later)		ca. 1730	Buhler 1972, appendix no. 78	MFAB
Two tablespoons	D	EW		ca. 1730	*Bulletin DIA* 14 (May 1935): 109–10	DIA
Tablespoon	E*	EF		ca. 1730		YUAG
Tablespoon	E†	D/RS		ca. 1735	DAPC 71.2443	WM
Tablespoon	E*	unidentified crest, a lion rampant		ca. 1735	DAPC 74.1632	
Tankard	A	unidentified initials		ca. 1720	*Antiques* 131 (June 1987): 1169	
Tankard	A	E/IB		ca. 1720	American Art Associa- tion–Ander- son Galler- ies, 2–3 April 1937, lot 258	

	Mark	Inscription	Patron	Date	Reference	Owner
Tankard	A *or* B	M/SB (+)	Samuel and Bethia Moseley	ca. 1735	Buhler 1956, no. 134	
Tankard	A *or* B	C/IH		1741	Sotheby's, 23–25 January 1992, lot 194	
Tankard	A/E	The Gift of the Honourable/John Burrill Esqʳ/to the first Church in Lynn/Decʳ the 10ᵗʰ 1721	First Church of Christ, Lynn, Mass., for John Burrill	1721	Jones 1913, 253	
Tankard	A/E	The gift of John Henry Burchsted Physitian/to the first Church in Lynn/Sepʳ the 25ᵗʰ 1721	First Church of Christ, Lynn, Mass., for John Henry Burchsted	ca. 1721	Jones 1913, 253	
Tankard	A*/E*	V/GE (+)	George and Elizabeth (Eliot) Vaughan	ca. 1725	*Silver Supplement* 1973, no. 75	BMA
Tankard	A*/E*	W/IE		ca. 1730	YUAG files	
Tankard	B*	?		ca. 1715	YUAG files	
Tankard	C	1729/ID/to/ED		1729	*CGA Bulletin*, no. 1 (1971): fig. 4	CGA
Tankard	C*	This Belongs to/ The Church in/ Brattle Street/1732	Brattle Street Church, Boston	1732	YUAG files	
Tankard	?	Scott (?) arms (later)	Scott family (?)	ca. 1725	DAPC 68.3339	
Tankard	?	?		1732	Norman-Wilcox 1954, 48	
Tankard	?	?		ca. 1720	*Antiques* 99 (February 1971): 202	
Teaspoon	D*	AB		ca. 1740	YUAG files	
Teaspoon	D	none	First Congregational Church, Marblehead, Mass.	ca. 1730	Jones 1913, 264	
Two-handled cup	B*	D/MAE (altered to D/MA); L/WS/to/TH (later)		ca. 1715	Buhler/Hood 1970, no. 106	YUAG
Two-handled cup	E*	The Gift of/Henry Dwight Esqʳ/To The Church/of Hatfield	Henry Dwight and/or First Congregational Church, Hatfield, Mass.	ca. 1732	Buhler/Hood 1970, no. 105	YUAG

1. Savage 1860–62, 4:356; SCPR 16:9–10.
2. Records of the Old South Church, Boston, Bigelow-Phillips files, 758. The inscription on Andrew Tyler's tomb says that when he died on 12 August 1741 he was in the forty-ninth year of his age; Bridgman 1856, 178.
3. According to the inscription on her tomb, Miriam Tyler was seventy-two years old when she died in 1766; Bigelow-Phillips files, 758; RC 28:94; *Index of Obituaries, 1704–1800*, 3:486.

4. *Sibley's Harvard Graduates* 10:329–34; *Church in Brattle Square*, 98, 100, 106, 137, 140, 142, 143, 145, 146, 148, 149, 150, 152, 153, 155, 156, 158, 159, 243, 249, 250, 251; RC 28:189; RC 30:22, 59, 106; SCPR 35:467–69; 65:93–94, 266–69. Interestingly, Miriam Tyler's Negro servant, Amoretta, joined the church in 1713; Amoretta died in 1721 (*Church in Brattle Square*, 103).

5. Seybolt 1939, 150, 155, 157, 160, 163, 166, 167, 168, 170, 171, 172, 174, 176, 178, 179, 181, 184, 186, 198, 214, 219*n*.

6. SCPR 22:813–16; Buhler 1956, 31.

7. SCD 35:240; 36:90. In the second deed the property is also referred to as a "Double Dwelling house Bake house & land thereto belonging."

8. Leverett was nineteen at the time and Burrill eighteen; SCD 37:1.

9. SCD 38:49.

10. *York Deeds* 12:331.

11. SCD 38:49; 40:206.

12. Whittemore witnessed a deed for Tyler on 10 February 1727 and on 27 September 1728, when he was, respectively, seventeen and eighteen years old; *York Deeds* 13:43; 12:331. The 1727 deed was also witnessed by Theophilus Burrill.

13. George Hanners was twenty years old at the time; Andrew Tyler was twenty-three; SCPR 29:386–88, 464.

14. Jones 1913, 16, 160, 171, 190, 211, 253, 255, 264; SCPR 30:307–09.

15. Daniel Henchman Ledger, 1712–ca. 1731, fol. 83, NEHGS. The dates are unclear because of water damage to the ledger, but the entry for the bills of lading appears one line before an entry dated May 1723. Andrew Tyler to William Pepperrell, Esq., 2 January 1715/16, NEHGS.

16. *York Deeds* 9:189.

17. *York Deeds* 12:331.

18. SCD 36:262–63; 38:52; 39:106.

19. *York Deeds* 14:54–55.

20. *York Deeds* 15:151–52. After Tyler's death his widow sold other tracts of land in Biddeford; see YCD 23:278v and r.

21. SCCR, Court of Common Pleas Record Book 1730, 384–86; SCD 50:210–12.

22. SCCR, Court of Common Pleas Record Book 1733–34, 612; 1737, 124.

23. SCPR 35:467–69; 66:74, 77–80, docket 7642.

24. SCPR 65:93, 266–69; Bridgman 1856, 178; Bigelow-Phillips files, 758.

I. or T. Tyler
w. ca. 1775

A

B

C

An initial and surname mark (A), either I or T TYLER separated by a pellet, appears on a spoon with a feather edge, a shell drop with alternating convex and concave lobes on the egg-shaped bowl, and the engraved initials "SG" in the Ineson-Bissell Collection at the Winterthur Museum. A sauceboat engraved "M·P," and owned by Historic Deerfield, also bears this mark. The details of the workmanship on both suggest that they were made in Massachusetts. A silversmith named Tyler whose first name began with I or T has not been identified.

This silversmith may have been a member of the Tyler family of Boston, in which metalsmithing seems to have been a tradition. This family included the brazier and pewterer John Tyler (1695–1757) and his brothers the pewterer William Tyler and the goldsmith Andrew Tyler (q.v.). Andrew Tyler's grandson, George Tyler (q.v. Appendix B), also was a silversmith. Possible candidates include James Tyler, one of the ten children of John Tyler (1695–1757) and Sarah Bream (b. 1699), who was born in Boston on 20 April 1734 and was baptized at the New Brick Church on 21 April 1734.[1] Although an account published in the *Boston Gazette* in 1766 seems to suggest that James Tyler was a silversmith, this may not have been the case. The *Gazette* for 2 June 1766 reported that a "James Tyler, Goldsmith," had been injured in an explosion in a Hartford, Connecticut, schoolhouse on 20 May 1766. However, the *Connecticut Courant*, which reported the story on 26 May 1766, listed "James Tiley, Goldsmith," as having suffered a dislocated shoulder and bruises. Since the Connecticut silversmith James Tiley

(1740–92) was working in Hartford between 1765 and 1785, it is evident that the notice in the Boston-based *Gazette* is a misspelled reference to Tiley.

Two additional marks may have been used by I. or T. Tyler. A surname in a serrated rectangle, mark (B), is found on a spoon with feather edge, engraved "S=B," similar to the one with the initial and surname mark (A), also in the Ineson-Bissell Collection. The bowl is decorated with an elaborate shell of eleven lobes in three tiers with a scroll base. The late style of these spoons indicates that this silversmith worked until the end of the eighteenth century. This mark could also have been used by the Boston silversmiths David Tyler (ca. 1760–1804) or George Tyler. Although previously ascribed to Jonathan Trott (q.v.), an initials mark (C), J·T in a rectangle, may be the mark used by I. Tyler in the early years of his career. Two spoons with this mark have downturned handles, midribs, and engraved initials composed of a minimal number of deeply cut lines with emphatically projecting serifs. The egg-shaped bowls are ornamented with shells, one a nine-lobed scallop shell and the other a distinctive eleven-lobed shell. Spoons made by George Tyler exhibit similar engraving and eleven-lobed shells.[2] DAF

SURVIVING OBJECTS

	Mark	Inscription	Patron	Date	Reference	Owner
Sauceboat	A*	MP		ca. 1770	Flynt/Fales 1968, 120–21	HD
Spoon	A	LL		ca. 1775	DAPC 73.1132	WM
Teaspoon	A	AD/1762		1762	DAPC 81.3638	
Teaspoon	A†	SG		ca. 1775	DAPC 73.1549	WM
Teaspoon	B†	SB		ca. 1780	DAPC 83.2631 (as David Tyler)	WM
Teaspoon	B*	EB		ca. 1780	YUAG files	
Teaspoon	C*	IF		ca. 1770		HD
Teaspoon	C*	KA		ca. 1760	Bohan/ Hammerslough 1970, 271 (as Jonathan Trott)	YUAG
Teaspoon	C†			ca. 1765		WM

1. Laughlin (1940, 1970) 1981, 64; Wyman 1864–65, 323; RC 9:223, 246; RC 28:90; RC 24:219; SCPR 52:277. James Tyler's maternal grandparents were Benjamin Bream (d. 1731), a brewer, and his second wife, Elizabeth Clemy (d. 1709); see Thwing; RC 9:217; SCPR 29:199–202; a note in the Bigelow-Phillips files reads "Eliz. wife Benj Brame dyed 30 Novr 1709"; no source is given. His paternal grandparents were Thomas Tyler (d. 1703), a mariner, and Miriam Simpkins (d. 1730/31); see Bridgman 1853, 289; SCPR 16:9–10. James Tyler was designated a legatee in John Tyler's will, which was written on 1 May 1753 and probated on 29 April 1757; SCPR 52:277. He received a considerable inheritance; a bequest of £66.13.4 and a one-quarter share of the undistributed portion of the estate was to be paid him when he reached the age of twenty-one.

2. These spoons are in the CMA and the Ineson-Bissell Collection, WM.

Samuel Usher
w. ca. 1743–48

The ledger of Benjamin Greene (q.v.) lists Samuel Usher of Boston, goldsmith, as a debtor on 10 January 1743. Greene had supplied Usher with "200 Gold Beads & Gold Ab.ᵗ 15 mˢ ago £8.0.0," and Usher paid his debt to Greene on 12 December 1748.[1]

Little else is known about Usher. He probably was descended from the Boston bookseller Hezekiah Usher (d. 1676) and his sons Hezekiah (d. 1697) and John (d. 1726), although his exact relationship to this eminent merchant family is unclear.[2] Beyond the single reference to Usher in Greene's account book, no trace of him has been found in Massachusetts records.

No silver by him is known. PEK

1. Benjamin Greene Ledger, 1734–56, 31, MHS.
2. Savage 1860–62, 4:362–63; Wyman 1879, 2:980.

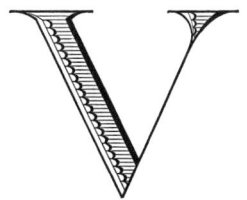

Kiliaen van Rensselaer
1663–1719

A

Kiliaen van Rensselaer, the son of Jeremias van Rensselaer (d. ca. 1675) and Maria van Cortlandt (1645–89), was born in 1663. His mother was the daughter of Oloff and sister of Stephanus van Cortlandt.[1] Kiliaen's grandfather Kiliaen van Rensselaer was a diamond and pearl merchant and the founder of the manor of Rensselaerswyck.[2] A letter written by Maria (van Cortlandt) van Rensselaer to her brother-in-law Richard van Rensselaer in mid-1678 suggests that Maria planned to send her son to Amsterdam to be apprenticed to a silversmith, but because of the war in Europe she arranged an apprenticeship for him in New York City instead. She wrote, "I had planned to send over Kiliaen, but as the war still rages so severely, I have on the advice of friends, apprenticed him here in this country to a silversmith to learn that trade, and meanwhile to see what God may grant in regard to the war."[3] A few years later that family made arrangements for Kiliaen to continue his training in Boston, and he ultimately was apprenticed to Jeremiah Dummer (q.v.) from 1682 to 1683. A letter from Kiliaen's uncle Stephanus van Cortlandt to his sister Maria van Rensselaer in 1682 states, "The man to whom I recommended your son Kiliaen at Boston hanged himself, so that Mr. Patichall and Mr. Usher have apprenticed him to one Mr. Jeremy Dummer. It seems that Kiliaen is not used to living as plainly as they do there."[4] Also documenting his Boston sojourn is a letter from Mrs. Catrina Darrall to Maria van Rensselaer, 31 August 1682: "We received a letter from Kiliaen . . . he is not sorry he went away. He is with a good master, but earns no money at present . . . he sees a fine opportunity for the trade in silversmith's work."[5] Kiliaen may have spent only one year in Boston. His mother let Kiliaen set up his silversmith's shop in the country, probably near her house at Watervliet, New York, in 1683. From 1685 on Kiliaen's energies probably were absorbed in the administration of his family's large landed estate.[6] Two pieces of silver bearing the mark of a demi-horse (A) have tentatively been attributed to van Rensselaer.[7] PEK

SURVIVING OBJECTS

	Mark	Inscription	Patron	Date	Reference	Owner
Porringer	A	demihorse crest; VH (later)	Samuel and Margaret (van Cortlandt) Bayard	ca. 1700	Kernan 1960, 349	MWPI

947

	Mark	Inscription	Patron	Date	Reference	Owner
Teapot	A†	Schuyler arms; JES (cipher)	Johannes and Elizabeth (Staats) Schuyler	ca. 1700	Kernan 1960, 348–49	N-YHS

1. Blackburn/Piwonka 1988, 74–76, 297–98.
2. Rice 1964, 1–2.
3. A. J. F. van Laer to John Marshall Phillips, letter, 23 March 1933, Bigelow-Phillips files.
4. Stephanus van Cortlandt to Maria van Rensselaer, letter, 1682, box 7, folder 394, Van Rensselaer Manor Papers, New York State Archives, Albany, New York.
5. Catrina Darrall to Maria van Rensselaer, letter, 31 August 1682, box 7, folder 396, Van Rensselaer Manor Papers, New York State Archives, Albany, New York.
6. A. J. F. van Laer to C. Louise Avery, letter, 30 March 1932, Bigelow-Phillips files.
7. Kernan 1960, 348–49.

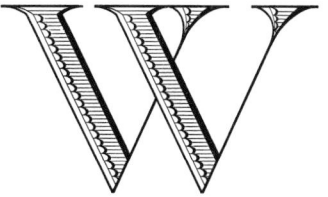

Joseph Watkins
w. ca. 1727

To date, only one document identifying Joseph Watkins as a goldsmith from Marblehead, Massachusetts, in the 1720s has been located; in the same document he is alleged to be a counterfeiter. At a session of the Superior Court of Judicature held in Ipswich, Massachusetts, on 16 May 1727,

> the Jurors . . . Present That Joseph Watkins late of Marblehead . . . Goldsmith and Benjamin Fry of Marblehead aforesaid Cordwainer not having the fear of God before their Eyes but moved by the Instigation of the Devil, Did on or about the first Day of July in the Tenth year of the Reign of our Said Lord the King at Marblehead aforesaid with force and arms feloniously Engrave a Certain Plate to be used for making of false and Counterfeit Bills of the Tenor and in imitation of the fifteen Shilling Bills of Credit on the Province of New Hampshire by Law Established with the Said Government against the Law in that case Provided and against the Peace of our Said Lord the King his Crown and Dignity, The Said Joseph Watkins and Benjamin Fry being brought to the Barr and arraigned upon the Said Indictment upon their arraignment Severally Pleaded Not Guilty.[1]

The jury found Watkins and Fry not guilty, and they were discharged. The reference to Watkins as being "late of Marblehead" may mean that Watkins was in jail elsewhere when brought up for arraignment. Watkins's financial difficulties may have led him to sell his working tools in 1729 to John Northey, a Marblehead glazier, whose son, David (q.v.), was then about to enter the goldsmith's trade.[2] Watkins may have been the Joseph Watkins born to Thomas and Elizabeth Watkins of Boston on 15 January 1670 or the son of John and Mary Watkins (or Wadkins) christened in Charlestown, Massachusetts, on 29 September 1700.[3] GWRW

1. Superior Court of Judicature, Massachusetts, 1725–29:131.
2. See the biography of David Northey for a transcription of the list of tools; photostat in the Bigelow-Phillips files.
3. RC 9:116; *Charlestown VR* 1:188.

Barnabas Webb
ca. 1729–95

A

B

Barnabas Webb was born about 1729, the son of Benjamin Webb (1695–1746), a minister of the First Parish in Eastham, Massachusetts, and Mehitable Williams (ca. 1694–1789), who married in 1720.[1] His paternal grandparents were Benjamin Webb (1667/68–1739) and Susannah Ballantine of Boston and Braintree, Massachusetts.[2] His maternal grandparents were Thomas Williams and Mary Macy of Bridgewater, Massachusetts.

The goldsmith's intentions to marry Mary Homes (1740/41–1833), daughter of William Homes, Sr. (q.v.), were published on 10 May 1759, which suggests that Homes trained Webb.[3] Through this marriage he became the brother-in-law of William Homes, Jr., and Benjamin Tappan (qq.v.), who married Mary's sister in 1770. On 10 May 1761, Webb and his wife became members of the Old South Church.[4]

Barnabas Webb is first identified as a goldsmith in the *Boston Gazette* of 15 November 1756. He advertised that he had found a gold ring in Cambridge, Massachusetts, which could be inquired about at his shop "near the Market" in Boston.[5] In the *Gazette* for 19 January 1761 Webb announced that since his shop near the market had burned, he had opened another one on Back Street in a location formerly occupied by Edward Whittemore (q.v.). Webb did not stay there long, for on 25 March 1762 he advertised in the *Boston News-Letter* that he had moved his shop to Ann Street, near the market.[6] Advertising again in the *Boston Gazette* of 5 and 12 August 1765, he declared that he had "a large Silver Spoon Stopt on Suspicion of its being stolen."[7] In 1767 he sold the Salem, Massachusetts, goldsmith John Touzell (q.v.) £18 worth of merchandise, including two dozen large and small shoe chapes, one dozen knee chapes, a pair of pliers, and a half-dozen crucibles.[8]

Webb was also identified as a goldsmith in a Boston deed dated 12 December 1769 when he granted a mortgage to Benjamin Eustis for a dwelling house and land on Sudbury Street.[9] The mortgage was discharged in 1777. The Massachusetts tax list of 1771 included Webb in Boston with a poll of one, a house, £26.13.4 annual worth of real estate, a slave, and merchandise worth £266.13.4.[10] Only three other goldsmiths—Benjamin Greene, Daniel Parker, and Samuel Minott (qq.v.)—were listed with greater assets, which indicates the degree of Webb's prosperity.

Webb and his family may have left Boston during the Revolution because his son Thomas was baptized on 23 April 1775 in Norton, Massachusetts, where Webb's father-in-law was then living.[11] By 1780 Webb was included in the Boston tax list again, residing in ward 10, with a poll of one and rents 140.[12]

Webb continued to keep a shop on Ann Street after the Revolution, and he was licensed as a retailer there in 1786.[13] About that time he also purchased land in Thomaston, Maine.[14] The first Boston city directory in 1789 listed Webb working as a retailer on Ann Street.[15] According to the *Columbian Centinel* of 30 December 1795, Webb died in Boston at the age of sixty-six, although no probate records are extant for him in Suffolk County.[16]

Fewer than a dozen pieces bearing Webb's marks survive. Two initials marks have been attributed to him—both with pellets (A, B). A BW mark without pellet or period has also been attributed to Webb, but no example could be found for illustration.[17] PEK

SURVIVING OBJECTS

	Mark	Inscription	Patron	Date	Reference	Owner
Porringer	B*	IC/to/AC		ca. 1770	YUAG files	
Sugar tongs	B†	D/TH		ca. 1760	Buhler 1972, no. 296	MFAB
Tablespoon	A *or* B	A		ca. 1790	YUAG files	
Two tablespoons	B*	DS/to/SC		ca. 1750	Buhler 1972, appendix no. 80	MFAB
Teaspoon	A*	HS/to/CB (over earlier initials)		ca. 1770		HD
Teaspoon	A*	PR		ca. 1775	DAPC 75.2756	WM
Teaspoon	A†	EH		ca. 1780		YUAG
Teaspoon	A*	HS		ca. 1770	DAPC 73.1687	WM
Teaspoon	A *or* B	LB; 1769 (+)	Lydia Bowman	1769	YUAG files	
Teaspoon	B*	ES		ca. 1775	DAPC 75.4922	
Teaspoon	B	PC	Philippa Call	ca. 1750	Buhler 1972, appendix no. 81	MFAB

1. *Sibley's Harvard Graduates* 6:112; *Index of Obituaries, 1784–1840*, 5:4756; the silversmith's birth date has been calculated from the death notice that gave his age in 1795 as sixty-six; *Braintree VR*, 673; *Mayflower Descendant* 8:4; 28:110.
2. *Braintree VR*, 646, 732.
3. RC 24:240; her death is recorded in Eaton 1865, 2:455; RC 30:32.
4. *Old South Church* 1883, 48.
5. This advertisement has been identified incorrectly as appearing in the issue of 19 January 1756; see Flynt/Fales 1968, 352.
6. This advertisement also appeared in the 1 April and 8 April issues.
7. Dow 1927, 57, incorrectly states that this advertisement appeared in the issue of 29 July 1765.
8. English-Touzel-Hathorne Papers, PEM.
9. SCD 116:16–18; 128:162–63.
10. Pruitt 1978, 32–33.
11. SCD 131:199–200; *Norton VR*, 146.
12. "Assessors' 'Taking-Books,'" 44.
13. RC 25:320.
14. Knox County, Maine, deeds exist for 17 August 1785 and 4 February 1786; Eaton 1865, 2:455.
15. RC 10:203.
16. *Index of Obituaries, 1784–1840*, 5:4756.
17. Ensko 1948, 160; Kovel 1961, 283; French (1917) 1967, 123; Graham 1936, 77; Thorn 1949, 216.

Edward Webb
ca. 1666–1718

A

Edward Webb, if the attribution to him of the mark EW in a rectangle is correct, was the most prolific of the immigrant goldsmiths who entered Boston during the late seventeenth and early eighteenth centuries. He was the son of Edward Webb, a yeoman, of Wokingham, Berks, England, and served his apprenticeship with William Denny of London from 1680 to 1687; he became a freeman of the Goldsmiths' Company in 1687/88.[1] Royal commissions were often filled in Denny's prominent workshop, and in this environment Webb became familiar with the most sophisticated English silverwork in the prevailing early baroque style.

Webb may have arrived in Boston before 1704. In November of that year

Edward Webb, along with Andrew Gaines, served as security when Peter Patey was admitted as an inhabitant of Boston.[2] A letter dated 30 September 1706 from Walter Newbury to the goldsmith Francis Richardson of Philadelphia, who visited Boston to acquire tools in the early years of the eighteenth century, may also refer to Edward Webb the goldsmith: "One p[s] of news I would not willingly omit y[t] is Ed: Webb's being about to mary wth one Mary Chamberlin, a maid of about 20 years of Age . . . [of] Cituate—I hope it may do well. 'tis a sudden thing. began & Ended y[e] Courtship in a Weeks time. Suppose they'l Consummate in a few Months time—."[3] No marriage between Mary Chamberlain and Edward Webb is recorded. If the marriage did take place, Mary must have died before 1718, when Edward Webb wrote his will. Both Newbury and Richardson were Quakers, as were the Chamberlains. If this letter does refer to the silversmith Edward Webb, then it is likely that he too was a member of the Society of Friends.

In 1709 Edward Webb was one of the appraisers of the estate of Richard Conyers (q.v.) along with Jeremiah Dummer (q.v.), and in 1711 he appraised a "Gold beed necklace" for the estate of the shopkeeper John Hayward of Roxbury, Massachusetts.[4] This suggests that Webb was well respected by his neighbors and may also indicate that Conyers's shop included some items that were best appraised by another London-trained goldsmith. The similarity between the monteith made for John Colman about 1705 in the shop of John Coney (q.v.) and monteiths marked by William Denny suggests that Webb may have worked as a journeyman for Coney during his first few years in Boston.[5]

In spite of Edward Webb's training in one of London's most sophisticated shops, all but one example of the silver that bears his mark is plain, with no engraving other than block initials or simple script and no embossing or elaborate cast and applied ornament. Webb's only known mark is EW in a rectangle (A). The *Boston News-Letter* for 30 August–6 September 1739 includes an advertisement for a stolen spoon marked WEBB, possibly another mark of Edward Webb's.[6] If so, it would make him one of the first silversmiths in Massachusetts to use a full-name mark. The other silversmiths named Webb known to have worked in Boston and eastern Massachusetts—Samuel Webb (1762–1839), and Barnabas Webb (q.v.)—were not yet working at this time.

Edward Webb died in Boston in October 1718, and his will, written on 13 October 1718, was probated on the twenty-seventh. His will includes an eloquent statement of his beliefs and gives us some sense of what he was like as a person:

> First and Principally I Commit my Soul into the Hands of God the Father of Spirits in hopes of Eternal life thro Christ Jesus, who Saves his People from their Sins & is the Author & finisher of my Faith; and my Body I desire may be decently Interred according to the discretion of my Executor; And as touching the Temporal Estate which God hath made me the Steward of I Dispose thereof as follows to say. . . . Item I Give to William Mumford of Boston Stone Cutter (if he survive me) Twenty Pounds. Item I Give to my kind friend Thomas Miller [q.v.] of Boston Goldsmith twenty pounds. Item I Give twenty pounds to Barrat Dyer of Boston Cooper and his Wife. Viz[t] ten pounds to each of them. Item I Give One hundred pounds to my Housekeeper M[rs] Hannah Kelinack of Boston afores[d] Widow; and all my Wearing Apparel both Woolen and linnen & all my Household Stuff & Goods; my working Tools Excepted. Item I give Two hundred pounds to the Poor of the Town of Boston, to be distributed by my Executor according to his good Discretion. And also all the residue of my Estate both real & personal if any shall remain.[7]

The *Boston News-Letter* for 17–24 November 1718 reported that "having no poor friends in England that wanted, and getting his money here, he bequeathed Two Hundred Pounds . . . for the use of the Poor of Boston."[8]

John Edwards and John Dixwell (qq.v.) appraised the estate on 1 November 1718. The inventory included no real estate, and Webb's household goods consisted of three feather beds and bedding, a "Skreen," ten chairs, an oval table, a chest of drawers, "a high Candlestick," pewter plates, dishes, and porringers, iron and brass kitchenware, two pair of andirons, and a "Parcel of Books." The inventory is almost entirely made up of tools and goods in the shop:

A forging Anvil, a Planishing Test, 2 Tests with plaine and flower'd Spoon Swages, 13 Raising Anvills and other Anvills w$^{t\ lb}$ 5:1:12 at 9^d	22: 10. —
59 Hammers at 6^d	1: —9: —6
A board Vice, a Skillett and a p^r Sheers w$^{t\ lb}$ 0:3:25 at 5^d	2: —5: —5
20 Stakes, 8 Spoon punches, 4 Tribletts, 6 Swages, 2 Small Tests, 5 small Anvills, 2 small bekerns & 1 Chissell w$^{t\ lb}$ 1:2:2 at 8^d	5: 13: —4
1 Small Ingott, 1 p^r small Stock Sheeres, 4 p^r hand Sheers	—: 14: —
4 hand Vices, 6 p^r Plyers, 4 p^r Compasses, 3 p^r Cording tongs	—: 15: —
A Mill and Swages	—: 10: —
2 p^r of Organ Bellowes	—: 10: —
1 Lawn Searce, 1 p^r dividers, 6 burnishers	—: 16: —
1 blowpipe, 1 borax pipe, 9 Strainers	—: —4: —
A parcel of Old files & other odd things in a box	—: 10: —
1 Screw plate, 3 Taps, 1 Turning bench Iron	—: —5: —
3 Touch Stones, 2 p^r forging tongs	—: 10: —
4 Leads to Hollow Spoons in Iron Rings	1: —: —
4 p^r Scales, 2 belt weights 15£ 2 piles of weights of 127^{oz}3/4 & 31^{oz}	2: —: —
1 Larg Lamp 2 Copper boyling pans	1: —5: —
2 p^r Iron Screws, 8 p^r flasks	1: 10: —
3^1/$_2$ Doz: bl: potts about 8 Nests crucibles	1: —5: —
A Glass Case	—: 10: —
A Bottle with a little Aqua Fortis	—: 3: —
9 drawing Irons	—: 18: —
1 p^r fine Scales and Glass Case	—: 10: —
3^1/$_2$ £ Iron Ware	—: —8: —
2 old brass boyling pans, and other old brass	1: 19: —
A parcel of Old Iron	—: 13: —8
A parcell of Patterns	—: —8: —
32 Cuting and Dropping punches at 6^d	—: 16: —
A brass Sodering pan$^{&c}$ w^t 21£	1. 11. —6
. . . .	
38 plain Rings, 1 heart in hand Ring, 1 Engraved Ring, 2 p^r plain earrings, 10 p^r gold buttons w^t 4^{oz} = 4^{dwt} at £8 ℔ oz	33: 12: —
Unwrought Gold w^t 16:—6:6 g^r at £7:10 ℔ oz	122: —6: 10
Gold Soder 10^{dwt} bare at	2: 10: —
Gold filings 3^{dwt} 8^{gr} at	—: 16: 8

Sundry Stones set in Gold the Gold w^t 3^{oz} 12^{gr} at   1: —6: —3
Silver filings w^t 5^{oz} 12^{dwt} at 8   2: —4: —9
394^{oz} of wrought and Unwrought Silver at 10/6   206: 17: —
2:6^{dwt} Silver Soder at   —: 23: —8
875: of Sundry Sorts of Coined money at 11/   481: —5: —
2 peices Corral   — 2: —
In Province bills   6: —1: —6

£857. 15: 8[9]

This highly detailed inventory gives us a wealth of information about Webb and his work. He was prepared to produce a full range of goldsmiths' goods, from engraved and stone rings to large pieces of holloware. The fact that he had a very large amount of silver and gold in his possession when he died indicates that he had a flourishing business. Physical evidence from surviving objects suggests that Webb marked his casting patterns; the Museum of Fine Arts, Boston, owns a porringer with Webb's mark in the handle casting.[10] The inventory includes touchstones that were used for assaying metal.

Edward Webb is the only immigrant goldsmith to enter Boston after 1700 who established a successful shop. His inventory demonstrates that he put all of his resources into his business, and he had the good fortune to live and work during years that were economically prosperous for the town of Boston. Webb's influence on the goldsmithing trade must have been significant. BMW

SURVIVING OBJECTS

	Mark	Inscription	Patron	Date	Reference	Owner
Chocolate pot	A*	P/TA		ca. 1710	Christie's, 22–23 January 1993, lot 241	MFAB
Cup	A*	PS; SS		ca. 1710	Buhler/Hood 1970, no. 42	YUAG
Cup (lacks handle)	A	?	Peregrine White family	ca. 1710	Geller 1970, 13	PS
Cup	A*	N/IS; EP (later)		ca. 1710		AIC
Mug	A	B/IG	Blake family	ca. 1710	Doty 1979, no. 100c	CGA
Mug	A	Abigail Hussey	Abigail Hussey	ca. 1707	*Antiques* 141 (June 1992): 930	
Patch box	A*	MB Ex dono to EB/ Eliza Brame (+)	Elizabeth Brame	ca. 1710	Buhler/Hood 1970, no. 44	YUAG
Pepper box	A	N/BL		ca. 1710	Johnston 1994, 173	CMA
Porringer	A	G/RK (later)		ca. 1710	English-Speaking Union 1960, no. 17	MFAB
Porringer	A	IW or MI	Jacob Wendell or Mary Jackson	ca. 1710	Buhler 1972, no. 29	MFAB
Porringer	A	IN	J. Nicolson	ca. 1710	Phillips 1939, no. 185	
Porringer	A	IS/to/RS	Josiah Salisbury	ca. 1710	Buhler 1979, no. 5	WAM

	Mark	Inscription	Patron	Date	Reference	Owner
Porringer	A*	NI (+)		ca. 1710	DAPC 85.2097	
Porringer	A	B/to/EA/Jany 1, 1846 (later)		ca. 1710	Quimby 1995, no. 132	WM
Porringer	A	P/IS (?) (altered to B/AM)		ca. 1710	*Antiques* 93 (May 1968): 619	
Porringer	A	AN (+)	Ann Newberry	ca. 1710	Sotheby's, 13 June 1992, lot 93	
Porringer	A*	Fayerweather (?) crest, a beaver with a fish in its mouth	Paine, Everard, or Fayerweather family	ca. 1710	Puig et al. 1989, no. 181	MIA
Porringer	A*	IB (over earlier initials); Johanna Butler ye: 16th: 9 mo: 1708. (later)	Johanna Butler	ca. 1710	Buhler 1972, no. 28	MFAB
Porringer	A	Abigail Hussey/ Born 10mo 22^d 1679	Abigail Hussey	ca. 1710	MFA 1911, no. 1024 (as Edward Winslow)	
Porringer	?	?		ca. 1715	Norman-Wilcox 1962, no. 55	
Salver	A	SP		ca. 1710	Sotheby's, 23–24 June 1994, lot 118	
Salver	A (?)	W/RA	Wentworth family	ca. 1710	*Bulletin DIA* 18 (May 1939): 4	DIA
Serving spoon	A*	none		ca. 1710	YUAG files	
Tablespoon	A	IP		ca. 1710	*Antiques* 51 (January 1947): 49	New York Society Library
Tablespoon	A*	EI	Elisha Jacobs	ca. 1710	Buhler 1956, no. 138	
Tablespoon	A*	Hephzibah Gardner born 5th of 1mo *1718*		1718	YUAG files	
Tablespoon	A*	G/IM		ca. 1715	DAPC 70.3586	
Tablespoon	A	GI/1717/18	George Jaffrey	1717/18	MFA 1911, no. 1027	
Tablespoon	A*	unidentified arms, fess gules in chief 3 spear heads points down, and crest, a horse's head emerging from a crown; H/LM		ca. 1710	Flynt/Fales 1968, 110	HD
Tablespoon	A*	unidentified arms, per fess a mascle in chief ermine, and crest, a saracen's head wreathed with		ca. 1700	Buhler/Hood 1970, no. 45	YUAG

	Mark	Inscription	Patron	Date	Reference	Owner
		a ribbon and couped at the shoulders; H/LMH				
Tablespoon (mates below)	A	H/LM		ca. 1710	Avery 1920, no. 13 (as Edward Winslow)	MMA
Two tablespoons (mates above and below)	A	H/LM		ca. 1710	*Silver Supplement* 1973, nos. 76a–b	
Tablespoon (mates above and below)	A†	H/LM		ca. 1710	Buhler/Hood 1970, no. 46	YUAG
Tablespoon (mates above)	A	H/LM		ca. 1710	DAPC 86.2608	
Tablespoon	A*	M/IA		ca. 1710	Quimby 1995, no. 133	WM
Tankard	A	The gift of her honored Grand-mother Eliz: Cowin . . . (later)		ca. 1710	Buhler 1956, no. 139	MFAB
Tankard	A	IW/to/RW (+)	John Waldo	ca. 1710	Buhler 1979, no. 6	WAM
Tankard	A*	G/RS (+)		ca. 1710	Buhler/Hood 1970, no. 43	YUAG
Tankard	A*	C/IM		ca. 1710	Bartlett 1984, 7	SLAM
Tankard	A	?/IM; IMW (later)		ca. 1715	Buhler 1972, no. 31	MFAB
Tankard	A*	T/IE; S. Carter (later)		ca. 1715	Buhler 1972, no. 30	MFAB
Tankard	A*	ST; The Gift of M.ʳˢ Sarah Thayer	Sarah (Townsend) Thayer	ca. 1713	Jones 1913, 489	
Tankard	A	unidentified initials		ca. 1710	Parke-Bernet, 14–15 October 1955, lot 288	
Tankard	A	D/SA		ca. 1710	DAPC 77.2217	WM

1. Walter Prideaux of Goldsmiths' Hall to Francis Bradbury (in answer to an inquiry from Francis Hill Bigelow), 27 January 1925, Bigelow-Phillips files. Apprentice Book 3, fol. 92v; Court Book 9, fol 243v. Worshipful Company of Goldsmiths, Goldsmiths' Hall, London. Robert B. Barker letter to Patricia E. Kane, 9 February 1993.
2. RC 11:2.
3. Walter Newbury to Francis Richardson, dated Boston, 30 September 1706, Richardson papers, Downs Manuscript Library, WM. Mary Chamberlain (b. 1685/86) was the daughter of Nathaniel and Abigail Chamberlain of Hull; Savage 1860–62, 1:354.
4. SCPR, docket 3139; SCPR 17:257.
5. See also Ward 1983, 173–74.
6. Dow 1927, 58.
7. SCPR 21:141–42, docket 4086. William Mumford, stonecutter, mentioned in the will, was a prominent member of the Boston Society of Friends; Forbes 1927, 28–34. Mumford was a servant to Henry Shrimpton, a brazier, from whom he inherited five pounds in 1666. Forbes

speculated that Mumford learned how to engrave on copper and brass while working with Shrimpton, and that this provided him with the background he needed to become a stonecutter.

8. Dow 1927, 57–58.
9. SCPR 21:261–62, docket 4086.
10. Buhler 1972, 1:34.

John Welsh
1730–1812

John Welsh (Welch, Walsh) began his career as a jeweler with extensive familial and social connections to his trade. Like his brother-in-law Daniel Parker (q.v.), he capitalized on those contacts to become a successful merchant whose mercantile pursuits eventually overshadowed his goldsmithing activities.

Welsh was the nephew of Jacob Hurd (q.v.), whose sister Elisabeth (1699–ca. 1771) was married to Thomas Welsh (1695/96–1755), a joiner. The couple's son John was born on 24 May 1730 in Charlestown, Massachusetts.[1] His paternal grandparents were the Charlestown stonecutter Thomas Welsh (1655–1701) and Hannah Mousall (Mechell) (1662–1713); after Thomas died Hannah married Joseph Lamson.[2]

Welsh probably trained in Boston beginning about 1744, possibly with his sister Hannah's husband, the jeweler Joseph Hiller, Sr. (q.v.). Welsh married another Charlestown native, Mary Parker (1733–1803), the sister of Daniel Parker, on 1 July 1754, in Charlestown.[3] Upon their marriage the couple resided in Boston, where they were members of the New North Church; nine of their children were baptized there.[4]

Welsh is first identified as a jeweler in a deed of 1755/56. After Mary Welsh inherited land on Beacon Hill from her relative William Willis, the couple at that time sold the land, in tandem with Willis's other heirs, among them Daniel Parker.[5] By 1758, advertisements like the one that appeared in the 16 and 23 October issue of the *Boston Gazette* reveal that Welsh had a shop in Fish Street in the North End of Boston:

> *John Welsh*, Jeweller, in Fish—
> Street, near Dr. *Clark's*, Hereby informs his Customers and others, That he has removed his Shop the opposite Side of the Way; where may be had all Sorts of Jeweller's Works, and all Kinds of loose Stones, at the lowest Rate. ALSO, Red and white Foil, Coral Beads, Borax, Salt-Petre, Pummice-Stone, Rotten-Stone, Steel Shoe and Knee Chapes and Tongs, Files, Bending Wire, and sundry other Articles, very cheap.

Six years later, advertisements in the *Boston Gazette* of 21 May and 4 June 1764 show that Welsh continued to offer his customers a wide range of imported goods:

> Imported, and to be Sold by
> John Welsh,
> JEWELLER,
> *At his Shop in Fish Street, near Dr.* Clark's, Boston;
> All Sorts of loose Stones,— as,
> Diamonds, Emeralds, Amethysts,
> Topaz, Garnetts, best Brilliant Earing Stones, Cypher
> ditto with Cyphers, large eight square and round Cy-
> pher Button Stones with Cyphers, SpareCyphers, round
> and eight square Brilliant Button Stones, Brilliant and Cypher Ring Stones,
> Motto and Coffin ditto, Ring
> Sparks, round, oval and eight square Buckle Stones;
> large and small Locket Stones and Cyphers, Watch

Chrystials, Glazier's Diamonds, Steel top Thimbles,
Stick Coral for Childrens Whistles, Coral Beeds;
Emerald, Amethyst, Topaz, Ruby and white Foyl;
large and small Crucibles, Black-lead Pots, Casting
Sand, Skillets and Ingots, Anvils, large and small round
half round and flat Drawing Plates, ClockScrew Plates,
Ring Swages with Death's Head and Heart in Hand,
Brass Stamps, best and common Sort of WatchPliers,
Clock ditto, Hand Vices, large and small Shears, Sliding Tongs, large and small Beck-Irons, Brass Blow-
Pipes, best Dividers and Cutting Nippers, Thimble
Stamps, Gravers and Scopers, Oyl Stones, MoneyScales
and Weights, Spare Ounce Weights Penny-weights
and Grains, Ring and Buckle Brushes, neal'd fine and
coarse Iron Binding Wire, Sand Paper; a large Assortment of rough and smooth Files both large and
small, Piercing and Needle Files; a large Assortment
of square and round Shoe Chapes, small Knee ditto,
Borax, Salt Petre, Pummice Stone, Flour of ditto,
Rotton Stone, Sandever, Emery, Putty, and sundry
other Articles, all very cheap.

GOLDSMITHS *may be supplied with all Sorts
of* Jeweller'*s Work, at a reasonable Rate.*

Later in 1764 Welsh moved his shop northward on Fish Street "next to Mr.
John Pigeon's Insurance-Office," as his advertisements in the 17 and 31 December
1764 and 14 January 1765 issues of the *Gazette* indicate. The description of this
new location is remarkably like that in an advertisement of 1757 by his associate
John Dexter (q.v.), and it is possible that Welsh took over Dexter's place of
business when Dexter left Boston at about this time.

Welsh's earlier advertisements imply that he primarily sold imported supplies
and wares to goldsmiths, jewelers, and watchmakers. By 1766, however, Welsh
was also selling goods made in New England, as his advertisement in the
Boston Gazette and Country Journal for 30 June 1766 and 7 July states: "Most
sorts of Jewellers Work to be had at said Shop; also several Diamond Rings,
all made here."[6] Welsh continued selling imported wares too, for he advertised
their availability at his shop in the *Gazette* for 27 October 1766.

In 1763 Welsh bought half of a brick house on Middle Street from Josiah
White.[7] In 1765 a fire broke out at Welsh's house "near Mr. Mather's Church,"
a reference to the Old North Church.[8] In 1767 Welsh bought a house and
other buildings on a half acre of land in Roxbury.[9] Welsh may also have owned
another house in the section of Boston known as New Boston, which he
maintained as a rental property. A John Welsh reported to the town selectmen
the leasing of this house to immigrants.[10]

The name John Welsh appears in a number of municipal and national
records in the second half of the eighteenth century, but since a carver named
John Welsh also lived in Boston at the time, it is not always clear when
references in the records are to the jeweler. A John Welsh, possibly the jeweler,
was selected to the following Boston town offices: clerk of the market in 1761
and 1763, scavenger in 1764, 1766, 1780, and 1781, and constable in 1781.[11] Two
men named John Welsh are listed on the Boston tax valuation list of 1771.
One, with a poll of one, a "tanhouse," or workshop, and merchandise worth

£250, was listed as being a lodger with Benjamin While; the other, with a poll of one and £20 annual worth of real estate, had a house.[12] Because the jeweler had purchased a house on Middle Street in 1763, the latter listing is probably for him. Nine years later his holdings had grown substantially: the "Taking-Book" for 1780 for Boston assessed Welsh at a rate of £150.[13] Two of his sons, Jacob and John, Jr., appear next to him, each one assessed at £30. The John Welsh who was among the group that in 1768 commissioned the Liberty Bowl from Paul Revere, Jr. (q.v.), was probably the jeweler because the group also included Welsh's brother-in-law Daniel Parker.

During the Revolution Welsh was drafted but apparently paid a fine instead of serving.[14] In 1776 he was chosen as one of twelve jurymen for "a court to be held at Boston 5 September 1776 by Judge Timothy Pickering, Judge for the Trial & Condemnation of Vessells & c." That year he was also appointed as a Boston warden.[15]

Welsh's family and social connections placed him solidly within the Boston goldsmithing network. Welsh maintained a long professional relation with his brother-in-law, Daniel Parker.[16] After Parker's death, Welsh was one of his creditors, being owed £39.4.^{1}/$_2$ by the estate in 1789.[17] His aunt Mary married Jeremiah Snow, Jr. (q.v.), making Welsh a cousin of that goldsmith and his son, Jeremiah Snow III (q.v.). The John Welsh who ordered a silver squirrel chain for ten shillings from Paul Revere, Jr., on 21 November 1772 may be the jeweler but could have been the carver.[18] Because Welsh, being a jeweler, could have produced the chain himself, other factors—perhaps an overextension of his shop's resources or family conflicts—must have led him to make the purchase, if indeed he did. Welsh probably trained a number of apprentices, among whom may have been his nephew by marriage Isaac Parker (q.v.). Benjamin Loring (q.v.) and John Dexter worked in association with Welsh, as is shown by a receipt they both witnessed in 1757 from Welsh to his brother-in-law, Zachariah Symmes, father of the silversmith John Symmes (q.v.).[19]

Welsh actively sought to broaden his consumer base beyond Boston as early as 1759. The Salem, Massachusetts, silversmith John Touzell (q.v.) was a steady customer from 1759 into the 1770s, purchasing goldsmiths' tools and jewelers' supplies from Welsh. One account, dated 16 September 1760 reads:

Boston Sep ye 16th 1760
Mr Touzel Bought of John Welsh

2 Doz Nee Chapes att 50^s/	£5:0:0
2 Doz & 2 Small files att 2^s/	2.12.0
1 three Squar smoth file 5^s/	0. 5.0
1 hank of Binding wier	0. 4 6
1 pound of Salpetre	1 5 0
1 pound of Sandiver	0 5 0
Rec^d the above John Welsh	£9 11 6[20]

From correspondence with Touzell it is clear that Welsh made business trips to Salem.

Si^r Boston Sep^t 19th 1774
I called of m^r Hillers after I came from your house
and haveing taried there so long that I had not
time to call at your Shop Plese to Send me a coppy
of the articules which you say my sone overcharged
I have sent a cask of Crusibles and Directed it to

be Left at your Shop, it contaînes 11 Dozen at one Dole[r]
a Doz. Plese to Inform me what Quantity you & m[r]
Harthen chuse to Take, from you Estemed friend
John Welsh[21]

Additional correspondence between Welsh and Touzell confirms the familiar nature of their dealings. In August 1768 Welsh wrote Touzell requesting his assistance in collecting two notes from Capt. Benjamin Lemmont that totaled £12.10.8.[22] Welsh wrote a second letter about the Lemmont notes on 17 December 1768 urging Touzell to seek payment from Lemmont and advising Touzell to let him know the results by Monday morning because if he had to sue Lemmont, Tuesday was the last day on which writs were served in the court session.[23] Between 1770 and 1776 Touzell's nephew John Hathorne (q.v.) bought tools, foil, a polishing stone, and stones from Welsh. One of the receipts for payment for these goods was signed on Welsh's behalf by Isaac Parker.[24] In 1769 the Salem silversmith David Northey (q.v.) purchased watchmaking tools from Welsh.[25]

Relatives or associates of Welsh's who moved to towns outside Boston probably provided him with the means of reaching a broader market. John Dexter moved from Boston to Marlborough, Massachusetts, about 1765. Welsh's cousin's son, Jeremiah Snow III, moved to Springfield, Massachusetts, about 1759, which may have provided Welsh with valuable contacts in a Connecticut Valley town, as would Isaac Parker when he moved to Deerfield, Massachusetts, about 1776. By 1784, Welsh was using newspaper advertisements to seek customers outside the Boston area. Every week between 15 July and 19 August that year he advertised "CYPHER Button Stones, and Cyphers, and a good Assortment of Articles for GOLDSMITHS, JEWELERS, CLOCK and WATCH MAKERS, and others" in the Worcester, Massachusetts, newspaper, the *Massachusetts Spy*.

Welsh probably specialized in making flatware and small personal items such as buckles, buttons, rings, brooches, and bead necklaces. Following the Revolution he expanded his business to include a wide range of hardware, in addition to silversmiths' tools. Although he occasionally still referred to himself as a jeweler in the early 1790s, he was mostly known as a merchant. The *Boston Directory* of 1789 reflects this, identifying Welsh as an ironmonger working on Union Street.[26] About this time, Samuel Davis (1765–1829) was apprenticing to the silversmith's trade in Boston. In his memoirs, published in 1811, the Plymouth goldsmith stresses John Welsh's role as a provider of tools and materials for his colleagues and suggests that Welsh had ceased to be an active jeweler by the early nineteenth century: "I ought perhaps to record Mr. Jno. Welsh among the Silversmiths—it had been his profession—who then imported every article or tool used by them—of him, in Union Street: we procured Files, crucibles, Bristol stone, foils wire, Rotten Stone, Pumice, sand, etc., etc., etc."[27] The *Boston Directory* of 1796 confirms Welsh's change of occupation, recording him as a dealer in pewterware, and directories between 1800 and 1803 list him as a hardware retailer.[28]

Welsh was described as a jeweler in public documents until 1791, but Suffolk County deeds substantiate his gradual evolution from craftsman to merchant as well as his increasing prosperity. In a deed of 2 April 1781 Welsh relinquished his claim on several warehouses (more evidence of his mercantile activities) to Giles Alexander.[29] The national census of 1790 lists Welsh as the head of a household consisting of himself and eight women.[30] During 1790 and 1791,

Welsh sold other Boston real estate, including the house on Middle Street that he had purchased in 1763. He moved to the "mansion house" on Union Street that he would occupy until his death in 1812, a commodious abode that the direct tax listing of 1798 valued at $3,500 and described as belonging to "JOHN WELSH, owner and occupier; wood and brick dwelling . . . Land, 2,474 square feet; house, 1,770 square feet; 3 stories, 35 windows."[31] In 1809 Welsh bought land on Scott's Court adjoining his Union Street property as well as land in Prince Street, conveying the latter to his daughters the next year for a nominal sum.[32] The jeweler's wife was not mentioned in these later deeds, for she had died in October 1803.[33]

On 25 October 1812, Welsh died at the age of eighty-two.[34] He had written his will four years earlier, on 10 November 1808, providing in it for the maintenance of his sister Sarah Welsh and distributing real estate and cash to his children—Jacob Welsh, Grace Payson, Mary Welsh, and Sarah Welsh—and to his fifteen grandchildren.[35] Welsh's daughters received the "household goods and furniture of every kind together with all goods in Shop or Store, and all my books in equal shares"; his son was left all his wearing apparel.[36] His son and sons-in law, Jacob Welsh, Samuel Payson, and Daniel Butler, were designated as the estate's executors, and Samuel Harris, Joseph Austin, and the Boston silversmith Joseph Foster (1760–1839) witnessed the will.

The Welsh estate was presented to the probate court on 15 February 1813 appraised at a value of $15,715.35. It included more than $13,000 of real estate, including the Union Street house, the adjoining land on Scott's Court, land on Joiner Street in Charlestown, and 6,880 acres in Ohio. Welsh owned investments in the Union Bank, the Fire & Marine Insurance Office, and the United States Bank, together valued at $1,989. His "House furniture" indicates that he lived comfortably, surrounded by such luxury items as a clock, several mirrors, a carpet, and an upholstered easy chair. Welsh also possessed fifty-eight ounces of silver.[37]

John Welsh has been included in listings of American silversmiths as early as C. Jordan Thorn's *Handbook of American Silver and Pewter Marks* (1949).[38] However, no mark has ever been identified for Welsh, and no jewelry or silver by him is known to survive. Although several unattributed J.W. initial marks exist on buckles, flatware, and some other small silver objects, none can be definitely associated with Welsh. DAF and PEK

1. *Charlestown VR* 1:169, 178, 309; Wyman 1879, 2:1006; MCPR, docket 24024.
2. *Charlestown VR* 1:15, 40, 107, 256; Wyman 1879, 2:1006; MCPR, docket 24020.
3. *Charlestown VR* 1:321, 400.
4. *NEHGR* 6:375; New North Church, 155.
5. SCD 87:273–74. William Willis's heirs included Jane Hall, Samuel and Mary Simonds, Nathan and Esther Howard, Stephen Hall, Willard Hall, Thomas and Martha Parker, Nathan and Grace Spear, John Parker, Daniel Parker, Thomas and Sarah Austin, John and Mary Welsh, and Peter and Esther Edes.
6. The advertisement appeared again on 7 July.
7. SCD 99:253–54. Evidently, White and Welsh continued their association because a few months later White offered his land in Weymouth, Massachusetts, as collateral for a twenty-pound debt to Welsh; SCD 100:88–89.
8. RC 20:163.
9. SCD 110:193–94.
10. RC 20:170, 232.
11. RC 16:49, 82, 110, 165; RC 26:113, 175, 184–85.
12. Pruitt 1978, 10–11, 24–25.
13. "Assessors' 'Taking-Books,'" 27.

14. RC 25:21.

15. RC 18:243, 246.

16. Wyman 1879, 1:504.

17. SCPR 88:172.

18. 21 November 1772, vol. 1, Waste and Memoranda Book, 1761–83, [42], Revere Family Papers, MHS.

19. MCPR, docket 16584.

20. English-Touzel-Hathorne Papers, 25 April 1759 and 16 September 1760 receipts, box 4, folder 5; John Welsh to John Touzell letter, 23 April 1773, box 4, folder 1, PEM.

21. John Welsh to John Touzell letter, 19 September 1774, English-Touzel-Hathorne Papers, PEM.

22. English-Touzel-Hathorne Papers, box 4, folder 1, PEM.

23. English-Touzel-Hathorne Papers, box 4, folder 1, PEM.

24. English-Touzel-Hathorne Papers, receipts of 2 March 1770, 9 August 1770, 2 November 1770, 5 April 1770, 5 February 1772, and 28 June 1776, box 6, folder 12, PEM.

25. Northey Family Papers, PEM.

26. RC 10:204.

27. Steinway 1960, 8–9.

28. RC 10:291; *Boston Directory* 1800, 113; 1803, 129.

29. SCD 134:171.

30. RC 22:448.

31. SCD 168:147, 161, 176, 252; 171:142–43, 150–51; RC 22:248.

32. SCD 131:144; 231:97–98; 235:191–92.

33. *Index of Obituaries, 1784–1840*, 5:4775.

34. *Index of Obituaries, 1784–1840*, 5:4792.

35. SCPR 111:43–46, 291–92. Welsh's grandchildren were John Welsh, Jacob Welsh, Jr., John Welsh Payson, Edward Payson, Sarah R. Payson, Abigail Payson, Ann Payson, Mary P. Payson, Jane Kilby Welsh, Elizabeth Welsh, Mary Welsh, Caroline Eliza Hancock, Christiana Barrett, Abigail Butler, and Ann Butler. Only Jane Kilby Welsh and Caroline Eliza Hancock were mentioned specifically in the will; his other nine granddaughters, who were underage and unmarried at the time of the will's writing, are identified in the executor's account.

36. SCPR 111:43–46.

37. SCPR 111:69–70.

38. Thorn 1949, 216.

Ebenezer White
w. 1780–1800

Nothing is known of Ebenezer White's early years, his master, or the dates of his apprenticeship. The first clue to his trade as a silversmith appears when he purchased land in Northfield, Massachusetts, on 19 December 1780, listing himself in the deed as a goldsmith.[1] According to J. H. Temple and George Sheldon's *History of Northfield*, White built a house on this land.[2] His first child, Nancy, was born in Northfield to White and his wife, Olive, eleven months after he purchased the lot; their remaining six children were born in Northfield between 1782 and 1799.[3]

White announced his trade as a watch-repairer and silversmith with an advertisement in the Springfield *Massachusetts Gazette* on 22 October 1782: "Any gentleman who wants his watch repaired may apply to Ebenezer White of Northfield . . . Also Gold & Silver Smith's work done by Said White." A second advertisement, placed more than a decade later in the *Greenfield Gazette*, omitted reference to goldsmithing and instead concentrated on White's watch-repairing skills:

E. White,
NORTHFIELD,
REPAIRS WATCHES, and
keeps them in repair as follows:
FIRST,—All warranted Watches
shall not vary fifteen minutes in seven

days, for one year, accidents excepted.
SECOND,—All other Watches put
in repair, and warranted to go, and
keep time within fifteen minutes, for
three days, to continue for one year.
THIRD,—After one year, kept in repair for three shillings the year, and
warranted, accidents excepted.[4]

Temple and Sheldon's *History of Northfield* also recalls White as a jeweler, goldsmith, and merchant.[5]

White probably experienced financial difficulties by the late 1780s and may have negotiated a mortgage of the land he purchased in 1780. In 1788, as goldsmith of Northfield, he probably mortgaged this lot to Josiah White, millwright of Northfield, for three hundred pounds, buying it back in December of the same year for the same amount.[6] In 1799, White identified his change of work from goldsmith to trader in a deed mortgaging the property once again to Josiah White.[7] Ebenezer White probably regained this property (although no deed to that effect has been located) because he was to lose this land for a final time in the suit in 1800.

White's unstable finances and his change of trade, both implied by the above-mentioned deeds, seem clearer in light of two separate suits filed against him in 1800 by Ebenezer Lewis and Stephen Higginson, both Boston merchants. The court judged Ebenezer White in debt to Lewis and Higginson and may have imprisoned him in Northampton for nonpayment. White's home lot and shop were ordered appraised and sold to pay this debt.[8] Nothing more is known of him. JJF

1. FCD 3:336–37.
2. Temple/Sheldon 1875, 179.
3. First Church of Northfield Church Records, 1750–94, 69–70, 189, 342, in Corbin Ms. Coll., Reel 82–35, NEHGS.
4. *Greenfield Gazette*, 31 January 1793; repeated 7, 14 February.
5. Temple/Sheldon 1875, 179, 352, 563.
6. FCD 3:335–36; 6:177–78.
7. FCD 13:328.
8. FCD Executions 2:56–61.

Edward Whittemore
1718–72

Edward Whittemore was born on 17 August 1718 and baptized four days later in the Second Church, Boston.[1] His father, the mariner and innholder John Whittemore (1684/85–1748), son of John Whittemore (1662–94), turner, and Elizabeth Anabel (d. 1686), was married to Elizabeth Lloyd (1688–1746) on 8 November 1711 by the Reverend Benjamin Wadsworth.[2] Elizabeth Lloyd was the daughter of Edward (d. 1704), a mariner, and Hannah (Griffen) Lloyd (1657–99) of Charlestown, Massachusetts.[3]

The marriage intentions of Edward Whittemore and Sarah Gridley (1718–74), daughter of John Gridley (1695–1761), a currier, and Johanna Dodge (1696–before 1761), were published on 23 June 1743.[4] The couple were married in the New South Church on 7 July 1743.[5] Edward Whittemore received £150 and one "quarter part of & in all my Moveables" except the liquors as legatee of his father's estate in May 1748.[6] Whittemore's father-in-law, John Gridley, mentions his daughter Sarah, wife of Edward Whittemore, jeweler, in his will, written on 29 May 1761 and presented for probate on 11 December 1761.[7] Sarah received one-fifth of his total estate. Edward and Sarah Whittemore had two children, Edward Lloyd, born on 13 November 1746, and Elizabeth, born on 7 April 1749.[8] Edward Lloyd Whittemore was mentioned in his paternal grandfather's will as the recipient of £33.[9]

Both Whittemore's older brother John and a cousin, William Whittemore (qq.v.), were silversmiths. If he followed the customary practice, Edward Whittemore would have served an apprenticeship between 1732 and 1739 with a jeweler, as yet unidentified. The Edward Whittemore who was owed money by the estate of George Hanners, Jr. (q.v.), in 1760 may have been the jeweler.[10] The earliest indication that Whittemore had established his own shop is an advertisement in the *Boston News-Letter* on 19 January 1761 that states that Barnabas Webb (q.v.) had moved to a shop formerly occupied by Edward Whittemore. By 1763, Whittemore was located on Back Street.

Edward Whittemore was chosen as the "Viewer of Boards, Shingles &c" for the town of Boston during 1749.[11] In response to a public complaint, a committee of Boston selectmen inspected the chimneys of Whittemore's house on Back Street in January 1763 and determined that they were "insufficient and dangerous." The selectmen sent Whittemore the following letter:

> Sir Upon Complaint made by a number of the Inhabitants of the Town of defects in the Chimnies in the House Occupied by you, we issued our Warrants for a Survey, a Copy of the return on Said Warrant you have above Agreable to the directions of the Law in that Case made and provided, we hereby warn you not to make any Fires in said Chimnies, till the defects are cured either by amending repairing or Rebuilding said Chimnies, as you would avoid the Penalty of said Law.
>
> By Order of the Selectmen William Cooper Town Clerk[12]

The *Massachusetts Gazette* reported on 27 February 1772 the death of "Edward Whittemore jeweller formerly of Boston" on the road to Taunton. No mention of Whittemore's death appears in the Taunton vital records, however. On 13 October 1774 the *Massachusetts Gazette* also recorded the death of Sarah Whittemore, "Widow of Mr. Whittemore, Goldsmith."

No mark has been associated with Edward Whittemore. DAF

1. RC 24:133; Robbins 1862, 288.
2. Wyman 1879, 2:1022–23; RC 28:37; *Charlestown VR* 1:123, 126, 135, 142.
3. Wyman 1879, 2:622; Thwing; *Charlestown VR* 1:18, 182.
4. RC 9:222; RC 28:275; *Manchester VR*, 54; *Beverly VR* 2:140; *Wenham VR*, 25; SCPR 59:465–67.
5. RC 28:345.
6. SCPR 41:116–18.
7. SCPR 59:465–67.
8. RC 24:261, 272.
9. SCPR 41:116–18.
10. SCPR 59:190.
11. RC 14:171.
12. RC 19:243.

John Whittemore b. 1714

John Whittemore was born in Boston on 8 May 1714 and was baptized on 16 May 1714 in the Second Church, Boston.[1] (See the entry on Edward Whittemore [q.v.] for biographical information on his parents and grandparents.) He was the elder brother of Edward Whittemore and a cousin of William Whittemore (q.v.).[2] John Whittemore and Lydia Clough (1719–50), daughter of Benjamin (ca. 1691–1744), a blacksmith, and Faith (Hart) Clough (ca. 1688–1762), were married by Rev. Joshua Gee on 3 June 1742 in the Second Church, Boston.[3]

The couple were well provided for by their families. Benjamin Clough's will, probated on 31 July 1744, left sums of money to his daughter Lydia Whittemore and to his two grandsons, John and William Whittemore.[4] In addition, Lydia Whittemore received one-quarter of the household goods upon her mother's death. The silversmith and his family received additional financial assistance four years later as legatees in his father's will, which was presented for probate on 3 May 1748.[5] Whittemore received "one hundred pounds old Tenor & one quarter part of & in all my Moveables Except the Liquors"; his sons John and William received thirty-three pounds each.

Whittemore was identified as a goldsmith in the Court of Common Pleas in January 1747/48, when the executor for William Downe, a Boston shop-keeper, sued him for a debt of £4.6.[6] Whittemore was active as a town official during the 1740s, serving as a constable in 1742 and as the constable for ward 1 in Boston the following year.[7]

Lydia Whittemore died on 5 January 1750 and was buried on Copp's Hill.[8] Whittemore disappears from the Boston records following the death of his wife, so it is likely that he relocated at that time. Although the census of 1790 lists several John Whittemores in other sections of Massachusetts, the silversmith's whereabouts in the second half of the eighteenth century remain undetermined.[9]

No objects made by Whittemore have been identified.   DAF

1. Robbins 1852, 288; RC 24:101.
2. Whitmore 1878, 44, 45; Thwing. John Whittemore's grandfather, the turner John Whittemore, was William Whittemore's uncle.
3. RC 24:135; RC 28:50, 266; Wyman 1879, 2:1023; Thwing; Benjamin Clough's birth date was calculated from his age at the time of death; see Bridgman 1853, 60.
4. SCPR 62:102–03. Clough's total estate was valued at £309.17.6.
5. SCPR 41:116–18.
6. SCCR, Court of Common Pleas Record Book 1746–48, 191–92.
7. RC 14:5; RC 17:50.
8. Bridgman 1851, 86; Wyman 1879, 2:1023; Whitmore 1878, 44, no. 835, gives 15 January 1750 as the death date of Lydia Whittemore.
9. The census of 1790 lists John Whittemores in Royalston, Newburyport, Needham, Westfield, and Spencer, Massachusetts. *U.S. Census, Heads of Families 1790: Massachusetts*, 233, 88, 205, 129, 235.

William Whittemore 1709/10–75 +

A

B

William Whittemore was the son of Pelatiah (1680–1724), a mariner, and Margery (Pepperrell) Whittemore (1689–1769) of Kittery, in York County, now Maine. Pelatiah was the son of John Whittemore (1639–94), a wheelwright from Hitchin in Hertford County, England, who settled in Charlestown, Massachusetts, about 1650, and John's second wife, Mary (Miller) Whittemore, daughter of the Reverend John Miller. Margery Pepperrell was the daughter of William (1648–1733/34) and Margery (Bray) Pepperrell and sister of Sir William Pepperrell and of Miriam Pepperrell, who married Andrew Tyler (q.v.) of Boston.[1]

Thomas B. Wyman records that William Whittemore was born on 10 March 1709/10 and baptized in the North Church in Portsmouth, New Hampshire, on 1 April 1711. Pelatiah Whittemore and his wife, Margery, arrived in Boston with three children in December 1714 or January 1715. Their fourth child,

Margery, died in Boston in July 1715, and another child, Joel, was born in Boston in 1716. Pelatiah Whittemore was lost at sea at the Isles of Shoals in 1724, and his widow married Judge Elihu Gunnison, a prominent shipbuilder of Kittery, Maine, in 1730.[2]

William Whittemore likely served his apprenticeship under his uncle Andrew Tyler in Boston. He witnessed deeds for his uncle on 10 February 1727 and 27 September 1728.[3] Whittemore was admitted as a member of the New North Church in Boston on 24 March 1727 and baptized there on 31 March 1728. The Reverend John Webb of the New North Church officiated at his marriage to Mary Tolman on 3 March 1730/31. They had three children, Hannah, born in 1731/32, William, born in 1734, and Mary, baptized in the New North Church in 1740.[4]

William Whittemore was in Portsmouth, New Hampshire, by 1745, when he is identified as being a goldsmith of Portsmouth and named principal heir in the will of the mariner William Maybury of Kittery.[5] He was also identified as being a goldsmith of Portsmouth when he sued David Patrick and Francis Jackson in York County Court in 1749.[6] He bought half a pew in the North Meetinghouse in Portsmouth in 1749, mortgaged it in 1764 to John Penhallow, and sold it in 1765 to Thomas Hatch.[7] He moved to Kittery Point in 1754, where he lived in a house on land that was part of his late stepfather's estate.[8] He received a small bequest from his grandfather, the elder William Pepperrell, in 1733, and by his will dated 4 July 1759, Whittemore's uncle Sir William Pepperrell left him "all the money that he oweth me." On 14 August 1769 he was made administrator of the estate of his mother, Margery Gunnison, widow.[9] His uncle John Whittemore was the grandfather of two other silversmiths: John Whittemore and Edward Whittemore (qq.v.).

There is evidence that Whittemore was still living in Kittery as late as 1775, but there is no record of his death.[10]

William Whittemore is the best known of Portsmouth's early silversmiths. He made cups for the church in Kittery about 1733, a chalice for St. John's Church, Portsmouth, about 1736, and a beaker for the church in Newington, New Hampshire, that is undated.[11] He is known by two marks, Whittemore in script in a rectangle with indented ends (A) and WW in a rectangle (B).[12]   BMW

SURVIVING OBJECTS

	Mark	Inscription	Patron	Date	Reference	Owner
Beaker	A*	The Gift of John·Downing Junr Esqr/to the Church/ att Newinton	John Downing, Jr., and/or Congregational Church, Newington, N.H.	ca. 1740	Puig et al. 1989, no. 199	MIA
Marrow spoon	A*	TA; WM		ca. 1745		YUAG
Mourning ring (gold)	B	Hon. John frost Esq Obt 25 feb 1732/3 AE 51	John Frost	1733	Ward/ Rowland 1992, 91	SB
Mug	A*	BAM (?)		ca. 1740	YUAG files	
Patch box	B†	AK/This is Thine and/Thou art mine 1734		1734	Gourley 1965, no. 219	RISD
Snuffbox	A†	S Smith	S. Smith	ca. 1735	Quimby 1995, no. 134	WM
Tablespoon	A	W/IM		ca. 1750		SB

	Mark	Inscription	Patron	Date	Reference	Owner
Tablespoon	A	W/TA		ca. 1750	Parsons 1983, 36	NHHS
Two tablespoons	A*	D/EL (+)		ca. 1750	Quimby 1995, no. 135b	WM
Tablespoon	A*	SL/Louis/bourg/1745		1745	*Decorative Arts of New Hampshire,* no. 97	HU
Tablespoon	B	RG		ca. 1775	Eitner 1976, no. 32 (as William Whetcroft)	
Teaspoon	A*	ID/to/SL	John Downing, Jr.	ca. 1740	Quimby 1995, no. 135a	WM
Teaspoon	A	SW		ca. 1750	Parsons 1983, 36	NHHS
Three two-handled cups	A	The Gift of the Hon.ble Wm.Pepperell Esqr/to the First Church of Christ In Kittery/1733.	William Pepperrell, Jr., and First Congregational Church, Kittery, Maine	ca. 1734	Jones 1913, 236	
Wine cup	A	The Gift of Capt/ Christopher Rymes/ 1736. (+)	St. John's Church, Portsmouth, N.H., for Christopher Rymes	1736	Jones 1913, 381–82	

1. Wyman 1879, 2:1021–26; Parsons 1983, 127; *Charlestown VR* 1:101, 110.
2. Wyman 1879, 2:1021–26.
3. *York Deeds* 13:43; 12:331.
4. Whittemore 1893, 45; Parsons 1983, 127, 18–19, 21, 36, 46; RC 28:158; RC 24:205, 219.
5. Batchellor 1907, 1:323.
6. YCCR, box 107, file 27.
7. Etha L. Sargent to E. Alfred Jones, letter, 3 April 1912; RCD 81:303–05.
8. Decatur 1936, 3, 15.
9. Wyman 1879, 2:1026; Sargent 1887, 344, 346, 848–49; Frost 1991, 1:645, 658, 669, 683.
10. Hennessy 1955, 35–38.
11. Jones 1913, 236, 310, 382; Parsons 1983, 18–19; Puig et al. 1989, 243.
12. Whittemore in a plain rectangle has also been published, but such a mark has not been located and is probably an incorrect recording of the (A) mark; see Kovel 1961, 289; French (1917) 1967, 125; Graham 1936, 79; and Thorn 1949, 221. The w·w mark published in Flynt/ Fales 1968, 358, and in Parsons 1983, 127, is on a coffin-end spoon that probably dates from about 1805 and is therefore too late to be Whittemore's work.

Edward Winslow
1669–1753

Edward Winslow was born in Boston on 1 November 1669 to Edward Winslow (ca. 1634–82), a mariner, and his second wife, Elizabeth Hutchinson (1639–1728).[1] His maternal grandparents were Edward Hutchinson (ca. 1613–75) and Catherine Hamby (d. before 1652); Anne Hutchinson was his great grandmother.[2] Through his mother's family Winslow was related to other New England silversmiths: the Rhode Island silversmiths Samuel Vernon (1683–1737) and John Coddington (q.v.) were his first cousins, and Thomas Savage, Sr. (q.v.), was a second cousin.[3] His paternal grandparents were John Winslow (ca. 1597–1674) and Mary Chilton (d. 1679) of Plymouth, Massachusetts, who settled in Boston about 1665.[4]

About 1683 Winslow was apprenticed, probably to Jeremiah Dummer (q.v.),

John Smibert, Edward Winslow, *oil on canvas, 1730. Yale University Art Gallery, Mabel Brady Garvan Collection, 1935.153.*

A

B

C

because along with John Cole (q.v.) he witnessed a deed for Dummer on 18 January 1689, when he was nineteen years old.[5] He came of age on 10 November 1690 and may have married shortly thereafter. Although no marriage record exists, other evidence indicates that his wife was Hannah Moody (ca. 1671–1711), the daughter of Rev. Joshua Moody (d. 1697) and Martha Collins (1639–d. before 1674).[6] After his father-in-law died, Winslow helped handle his mother-in-law's affairs.[7] He also did business for Martha Collins (d. 1699/1700), who was probably his wife's grandmother.[8] Winslow and his wife joined the Old South Church on 5 March 1692. In the same year he appeared on the Boston tax list in division 5 with a tax of £1.2.[9] The couple had ten children, of whom seven survived to adulthood: Edward (1693–d. before 1704); Joshua (1694/95–1769) who married Elizabeth Savage (1704–78), daughter of Thomas Savage and Elizabeth (Lynde) Savage; Hannah (b.1697/98), who married surgeon William Davis (1688–1746); John (1698–99); John (1700–88) who married Mary Vryland; William (1701/02–d. before 1708); Edward (1703/04–33) who married Hannah Savage (1708–55), the daughter of Habijah and Hannah Savage; Samuel (1705–45) who married Rebecca Clarke (b. 1708), daughter of William and Rebecca Clarke; William (1707/08–45) who married Elizabeth Clarke (b. 1716), daughter of William and Hannah Clarke; and Isaac (1709–77) who married Lucy Waldo (1725–69).[10]

Winslow continued to live in the central part of Boston in the first decade of his career, as he still is recorded in division 5 in the list of inhabitants in 1695.[11] He was also listed in Captain Allen's Boston militia company in 1698.[12] But Winslow apparently did not own any real estate prior to his joint purchase with Benjamin Fitch of a tenement and shops near the Town Dock in 1702.[13] He may have lived there or in the brick messuage that he and Thomas Savage (1668–1721) were described as possessing in May 1708, when John and Sarah Phillips and Mary Lynde sold it to Savage.[14]

On 21 October 1708 Winslow purchased a mansion house on King Street from the heirs of Gov. John Leverett; Winslow would live there for the rest of his life.[15] Seeking to enlarge this dwelling, on 31 March 1709 he petitioned the Boston selectmen for permission to erect a timber building for a kitchen at the southwest corner.[16] Additional chimneys were added to the house in 1714 when Lemuel Gowen built an adjacent house, which shared a partition wall to the east of Winslow's. He and Winslow reached an agreement that Gowen would "Carry up Two Funnells for the use of said Winslow, One from the Cellar and the other from his third Story."[17] Winslow's workshop was also in this house because when his inventory was compiled in 1754 a room of the King Street house was designated as the "Working Room."[18] An advertisement for the return of stolen silver in the *Boston News-Letter* for 1–8 October 1711 further indicated that Winslow lived and worked at the same location:

Taken out of the House of Mr. *Edward Winslow* Gold-Smith on the South side of Kings-Street Boston in the time of the Fire on Tuesday night last. *Viz.* A Silver Box in the Fashion of an Heart, Grav'd on the Lid and Bottom, With Branches and Several Posies; Two Stone Rings, several Plain Rings, A Necklace of small Gold Beeds. Sundry Pieces of Outlanddish Gold and Silver Money, Sundry Cornelian and Aggat Stones put for Signets. Whoever will return them to Mr. *Winslow*, the true Owner, or give any true Intelligence of them, or any part or parcel of them, so as he may have them again shall be rewarded to content.

Winslow acquired another house in Boston on 2 March 1709/10 when his mother deeded him her dwelling house on Boston's Milk Street to compensate him for the sums he had paid for her support and livelihood and for the education of her younger children.[19] On 8 March 1710/11 Winslow mortgaged this property to Jonathan Dowse, and maintained it as a rental property until his death.[20] In 1711 Winslow granted a mortgage for a house and land in Hanover Street to Mary Green, Nathaniel Green, and Samuel Moody; the mortgage was discharged in 1716.[21] Winslow conducted additional real estate transactions in Boston in the 1720s. In 1720 he granted a mortgage to the tinplateworker Joseph Hiller for a tenement in Cornhill Street in a deed witnessed by Hiller's son, Benjamin Hiller (q.v.), and in February 1720/21 he sold the same land to Thomas Clarke.[22] In 1721 Winslow purchased a lot in a ten-thousand-acre plot being subdivided in the vicinity of the towns of Oxford, Leicester, and Brookfield, Massachusetts.[23]

As was customary, Winslow probably assumed responsibility for one or two apprentices as soon as he began to work on his own. The list of inhabitants of 1698 includes Winslow with two servants, apprentices whose identities remain unknown. About 1704 Winslow's cousin John Coddington probably began to train in the Winslow shop. He witnessed a deed for Winslow in 1709, when he would have been nineteen years old.[24] William Pollard (q.v.) may also have been an apprentice between 1704 and 1711. Isaac Anthony (q.v.) may have been an apprentice at this time as well. Wendy Cooper has suggested that Winslow may have trained Anthony because a porringer by Anthony has a handle cast from a mold with an impression of an English mark that was also used by Winslow.[25] Winslow's nephew, Moody Russell (q.v.), apparently began his apprenticeship about 1708 because he witnessed a deed for Winslow in 1710/11.[26] Samuel Minott (q.v.), who married one of Winslow's granddaughters and purchased tools from the estate, possibly trained in the shop between about 1746 and 1753.

After his first wife died on 25 April 1711, Winslow married Elizabeth (Dixie) Pemberton (1669–1740) on 22 May 1712; she was the daughter of John and Elizabeth (Allen) Dixie and widow of the brewer Benjamin Pemberton.[27] Edward and Elizabeth had a daughter Elizabeth (b. 1712/13).[28] Soon after his marriage Winslow appeared in the Suffolk County Court of Common Pleas in cases involving the settlement of the estate of his new wife's former husband.[29]

Prominent in civil and military affairs, Winslow joined the Ancient and Honorable Artillery Company in 1700; he became sergeant of the company in 1702, lieutenant in 1711, and captain in 1714 and 1729. He was also a captain of the militia and became a major in April 1729. He was made colonel of the Boston regiment in 1733. Winslow is often referred to in various records by his military titles.[30] He was chosen as one of Boston's constables in 1698/99, the first of many such civic posts he would hold.[31] He was also elected to other posts including tithingman (1702/03), surveyor of highways (1704/05), overseer of the poor (1708/09 [refused], 1711, 1712/13), fireward (1711/12), and selectman (1713/14, 1714/15 [refused]).[32] Along with John Coney and John Noyes (qq.v.) he was asked by the justices of the Superior Court in 1706 to inspect a parcel of money to determine if any of the coins had been clipped, and in 1738 the court asked him to provide information on the value of silver from 1728 to 1738.[33] He also served on several committees of the Old South, or Third, Church between 1722 and 1749, one of which made provision for, and oversaw the building of, a new meetinghouse. In 1747/48 Winslow was one of seven "seaters" chosen by the church members.[34]

Edward Winslow became sheriff of Suffolk County in late 1716 or early 1717.[35] In order to obtain such a position, Winslow had to manipulate his connections with the governor and his Council. Winslow probably was named to the post by Gov. Samuel Shute. As as royal appointee, Winslow had to be confirmed in his position each time a new monarch ascended to the throne, and each time a new govenor was appointed. After George I's death in 1727, William Burnet became governor of Massachusetts and confirmed Winslow as sheriff late in 1728. After Burnet's death, Jonathan Belcher became governor and he confirmed Winslow's appointment in 1732. Although these reappointments were generally routine in nature, it seems that Gov. Belcher was under some pressure to make a change because his son Andrew wanted the job. A letter Belcher wrote to Francis Wilks on 6 January 1732/33 contains evidence of Winslow's efforts to retain his job: "In complyance with your repeated requests I have lately establist Maj[r] Winslow in the Sheriffe's place of the County of Suffolk (worth at least 6 to 700£ a year), altho' my son was very desirous to have it." In a letter written on 30 April 1733, Belcher explained to Richard Partridge why he decided to reappoint Winslow: "I confirm'd Sheriffe Winslow in his post 6 months ago; but had I not, it is a place of great trust & danger, and I shou'd not therefore have been willing to have given it to any child of mine. Remember how Sam Dummer is ruin'd. If And[r] will be diligen & mind his business, his compting house will be much more profitable than any paltry office in this government; and why can't he live by business as I have done before him?"[36]

As sheriff of Suffolk County and one of the leaders of the town's militia, Edward Winslow was constantly at the center of colony affairs. His duties included issuing warrants and tax bills from the county treasurer to the constables; posting warrants calling town meetings; serving writs of execution and attaching goods of debtors to ensure payment of judgments in civil suits; committing individuals who failed to comply with such writs, and also those convicted of crimes, to jail; collecting various fines; attending at the various county courts and at joint meetings of the justices of the peace and the selectmen; and even purchasing furniture for the use of the county court and paying the "Whipper for sundry services" on an annual basis. Winslow also attended sessions of the Governor's Council and of the Assembly and saw to it that the laws passed in each legislative session were published.[37] He was also charged with finding "Dyet and lodging" for three Indian messengers who came to Boston to meet with the governor in 1727.[38] And on 19 October 1732, Benjamin Walker mentions in his diary that Edward Winslow, sheriff, officiated at the hanging of Richard Wilson.[39]

Winslow's duties also required him to participate in ceremonial processions for the governor and to issue and enforce the governor's proclamations. Benjamin Walker records in his diary that when Gov. Burnet moved the 1728 session of the assembly to Salem, Sheriff Edward Winslow, was "before y[e] Chais" with Burnet's "steward & black footman behind [the coach]."[40] When Burnet died suddenly only a year later, Winslow was one of his pallbearers.[41] In addition to these routine duties, Winslow also accompanied Gov. Jonathan Belcher on a trip to the mouth of the Sheepscut River in Maine between 15 and 31 July 1734 to negotiate with the Indians of Machias Harbor, Pemaquid, and Damariscotta.[42]

Sometimes the perils of being sheriff could be physical, but as a leader of the town's militia, Winslow probably felt ready to accept that challenge. As the chief enforcement officer of the royal governor the sheriff was in a precarious position when local controversies arose that pitted the townspeople against established authority. In 1737, after the attack on the market house by a mob that opposed the establishment of a permanent market in Boston, supporters of the rioters sent a threatening letter to Sheriff Winslow that was published in the *Boston Weekly News-Letter* on 21 April. In it they warned Winslow not to search for the rioters, or to attempt to commit them to jail.[43] In 1741, Winslow was attacked by a mob for assisting Capt. James Scott, commander of the H.M.S. *Portland* as Scott attempted to impress local men into the royal navy.[44]

As Gov. Belcher noted, the perils of the position were also economic. In spite of the governor's assessment of the monetary value of the job, he also noted that a sheriff could be financially ruined by the job. Winslow mentions in an account of 1726 that his annual salary was £30. The monetary rewards of the job may have included certain legitimate perquisites, but it is difficult to determine what these might have been.[45] The sheriff could be held personally liable for debts, fines, and taxes that he collected as part of his job. Winslow was in court numerous times to answer to civil suits brought against him by citizens who believed that he had either unfairly fulfilled, or failed to fulfill, his duties as sheriff. For instance, on 25 May 1719, Andrew Faneuil of Boston sued Winslow for not arresting Joseph Hiller against whom Faneuil had recovered a judgment of £107.16.8 in a civil suit. The court found in Faneuil's favor, but Winslow appealed the decision in July 1720, on the grounds that there was a problem with the writ of execution, and that serving it would have resulted in an improper arrest; Winslow apparently won his case.[46]

Winslow served in the post of sheriff until 20 October 1743, and during his tenure in the post had this portrait painted by John Smibert (illus.) as was befitting a man in high public office. On 21 October 1743 Gov. William Shirley appointed Winslow judge of the Inferior Court of Common Pleas, a position he held until his death.[47] He may also have held another appointive post, for in 1753, his son Joshua, executor of his estate, claimed that his father had served in the position of county treasurer "for divers years" and asked to serve in the position himself long enough to close out his father's accounts; Gov. Shirley granted his request.[48]

With the time demands that his positions as sheriff and judge for Suffolk County imposed, Winslow reduced his activities as a craftsman but maintained at least one journeyman to carry out his shop's day-to-day operation. Even before he assumed the post of sheriff, Winslow's shop depended heavily on journeymen. In 1702 Henry Hurst (q.v.) may have been working for him as a journeyman because Winslow and James Barnes, Jr. (q.v.), put up Hurst's bond money when Hurst was sued by the London goldsmith John House.[49] By 1709 Winslow had started a long-term relationship with Thomas Mullins (q.v.), whom he probably also employed as a journeyman. Mullins witnessed deeds for Winslow in 1709/10, 1710/11, and again in 1716.[50] John Banks (q.v.), who may have finished up his apprenticeship with Winslow, also probably worked as a journeyman for him because he witnessed the deed with Mullins in 1716.[51] From about 1730 on, Thomas McCullough (q.v.) apparently oversaw the Winslow shop. An entry for 1742/43 in Benjamin Walker's diary refers to him as "Tom Cully, his [Winslow's] Journayman."[52] In his will Winslow treated the income generated by this journeyman, identified in the will as Thomas Maccollo, as an asset to be used to support his grandchild Rebecca Winslow or, in the case of her death, to be divided among his heirs. He made his wife responsible for supervising Maccollo, and if she were unwilling or unable to do so, the task fell to the executors. The cost of maintaining Maccollo came to slightly more than £74 pounds a year (£1 per week wages, £3 quarterly for rent, and £10 toward wood, with provisions for clothes and medical expenses as necessary). Maccollo's worth was to be derived partly from making his services available to other craftsmen, with a Mr. Hurd, undoubtedly Jacob Hurd (q.v.), cited as the example.[53] Winslow probably had similar arrangements with his other journeymen.

The surviving plate marked by Winslow substantiates these changes in his shop once he had assumed high governmental posts. The majority of pieces with Winslow's mark were probably made before 1720 and were marked with his initials above a fleur-de-lis in a shaped shield (A). A variation without the fleur-de-lis also exists (B). Probably about 1720 he also began using initials in conjoined circles (c).[54] Although the shop remained active after 1720, Winslow probably limited the retail aspect of his business, and hence few pieces made after 1720 bear his mark. In 1722/23 he was called upon to testify with Nathaniel Morse (q.v.) about the quantity and value of the tools of Daniel Légaré (q.v.).[55] Next to John Coney, Winslow produced some of the most ambitious silver made in Boston in the first quarter of the eighteenth century. Among the outstanding pieces are his sugar boxes, chocolate pots, and candlesticks.

Samuel Sewall was an early patron of Winslow's and bought a number of objects from him over the years. On 15 June 1702 he purchased a silver spoon engraved "NR.1701" for £1, a spoon intended for N. Rogers, an individual whose identity is unknown.[56] On 15 May 1708 Sewall bought a gold necklace for his daughter Mary for £1.1.9 for which he found the gold.[57] Acting as an agent for Samuel Gerrish in 1710, Sewall obtained two porringers from Winslow that weighed fifteen ounces and thirteen pennyweight and cost £7.5.2.[58] Sewall bought his son gold buttons costing £1.7 on 28 October 1713.[59] In 1713/14 Sewall bought six spoons for his son and daughter that cost about twenty-one shillings each.[60] In 1721/22 Sewall presented a ring to Gov. Samuel Shute that weighed three pennyweights and three grains and cost 35 shillings 3 pence, and was engraved with the motto "Post tenebras Lucem. Jany 1721/22."[61] The payment of £36 made to Winslow for the funeral of Sewall's daughter-in-law, Mrs. Hannah Sewall, in 1724, was probably for funeral rings.[62] Sewall bought a single ring for £2.8 from Winslow on 9 January 1726/27.[63] When Samuel Hirst died, Sewall recorded sending William Pepperrell and his wife Mary two of Winslow's rings on 25 January 1726/27.[64] Sewall also conducted other kinds of transactions with Winslow. In 1706 Winslow seems to have refined silver for Sewall.[65] In February 1707/08 Winslow repaid Sewall £3 that Sewall "lent him for cousin Moodey."[66] In 1719 Sewall sold Winslow a silver tankard.[67]

Other notable Bostonians owned silver by Edward Winslow. More than sixteen references can be found in estates probated between 1711 and 1743 to funeral or mourning rings purchased from Winslow.[68] The Harvard tutor Henry Flynt recorded that Winslow had made two porringers for him:

1724/5
Mem-January 13th Received the following account from Sherif Winslow
   M^r- Flynt Debt^r Nov. 3^d 1724   Contra Cr

2 Silver Porringers w^d 15^1/$_2$ by a Silver Salt w^d 14^{oz} 15^{dwt} Sept.1724
is added more than a Silver Salt   by Cash received in ful 2-12-6
  15^d wt   Nov. 9th 1724
at 16^{sh} & 6^d ℔ oz—0.12.6
making them 20^{sh} each
          Jan 11th 1724 EE ℔ Edwd Winslow[69]

Winslow also made silver for the stationer Daniel Henchman. Between 1712 and 1721 Winslow was credited for his purchases from Henchman with "Sundries out of his Shop," a pair of clasps, and a note for five gold rings. Winslow continued to be a regular customer of Henchman's until 1742.[70] Winslow paid for his son Isaac's first term at Harvard with two silver spoons, and he paid for the second term with a necklace of gold beads.[71]

In the 1730s and 1740s Winslow's name turns up a few times in public records. He conducted a number of real estate transactions.[72] With John Edwards (q.v.), George Minott, and Timothy Prout, he was a trustee of the estate of Stephen Minot, who died in 1732.[73] In 1740 Winslow was once again widowed and did not marry again until 27 March 1744, when he took as his wife Susanna (Farnum) Lyman (b. 1687), daughter of David and Dorothy Farnum and widow of Capt. Caleb Lyman.[74] After the goldsmith's death, his widow married Nicholas Sever of Kingston, Rhode Island, the former Harvard tutor, in 1757.[75]

Ten letters that Edward Winslow wrote to his son Jacob between 1719 and 1722, and one letter that he wrote to his son Isaac in 1747, give us a sense of the goldsmith and sheriff's interests and concerns.[76] Several of the letters were preserved by Edward Winslow's grandson Isaac (1774–1856), who, at a time when the Puritans were in disfavor, wanted to keep them as evidence of the piety and sincerity of the Pilgrim's descendants. Although many of the letters are therefore ones that touch on religious concerns, the remaining letters suggest that the majority of Winslow's letters to his sons were secular in tone. The letters reveal that Winslow took a strong interest in Joshua's efforts to develop a mercantile business and that he may have actively urged his son to travel to Barbados, Newfoundland, and London to make business contacts. They also reveal the father's anxiety over the future of his younger sons, and over what he should do to make certain that they found suitable careers. On 19 January 1719/20 Winslow wrote to Joshua in Barbados about his younger brothers Edward (Ned), and John then sixteen and nineteen years old:

> I had some incouragm^t that [Captain] Ellery would have taken your Bro Ned— but it,s over[.] m^r A Lyndal[?] Seem,^{d} to desire it, but we could not bring it to pass. I hope some one or other[^{s}?] will. he is Lerning ye Art. I think to gett him to ozburn if I cem [can?]—and John to meet you at the Land [Newfoundland?], if I Can't hear of your arival timely enuf to send him to Barbados. I pray God to bless and prosper you all and fill you with his grace and direct me in what belongs to my part in order to your future Comfort and Settlement in this world.

By 1720, both Joshua and John were in business in Newfoundland. On 13 July 1720, Edward Winslow wrote to Joshua to tell him that he was sending a barrel of flour to "John to incourag him in his beginng" and asked Joshua to "give him your assistance in all things." His reasons for being concerned about John's future are more clearly delineated in a letter he wrote to Joshua the following week (20 July 1720):

I hope John is well wth you and will take up and mind his business very well[.] I have given him such advise w^t ever you do keep him from evil comp: and Drinking to Excess you know my opinion of that worst of all evils.

He went on to express his concern over how Joshua would employ John in the winter, and to caution Joshua not to put too much confidence in his brother "before you have proved & observ^d." In spite of Winslow's hopes for John's reformation, the young man's problems apparently continued, and on 30 June 1722 Winslow mentioned his concerns regarding John again:

> Dr Son I beg your Cair of John keep him from ill Comp^a Charge him frequently to avoid his own sin his gameing humour his Carelessness for his own intrest, if you deserne any swaying of w^t nature so ever Let it not lye hid but advertise him of it—and if you acquaint me of it perhaps my wrighting may be a help to him[.]

Winslow's letter to Joshua on 15 August 1722, indicates that although Ned had found a berth as a mariner on a ship bound for England under the command of a Captain Morriss, his father had not heard from him in months. John was still gambling, and William, now fourteen, was not yet settled in an apprenticeship. This letter is perhaps Edward Winslow's most eloquent statement of concern over his children's career education, and clearest indication of the extent of his own involvement in it.

> I am greatly preplexed in mind concerning your D^rBro Edward, I understand that the Ship & m^rMorriss are arived in england this 4 or 5 months past y^t y^r quaranteen was fulfilld Long before our last Ships Saild from London, y^t Morriss was in Lond° m^r Apthorp tells me he Saw him, yet not a Letter conferming your brother nor from him—m^r Lyde to you makes no mention of his passing your order to morriss which if Ned'y was well I think he would need—all which makes me in great Consern for him and almost sorrey y^t he went so Long & hazardus Voyage but y^t is past & I know don for the best—divine providenc is to be adored allways and on all occations. . . . I have your Brother John's Promis in his Last y^t he will not any more game again Soposing he shall be left ye winter. I begg you if he Stay that you desire m^r Gowin to deal Sharply wth him on y^t affair. if he miscarrey now he is at so his N. Land Credit undon[e]. I know not what to desire conserning your self. Wheather to go farther or return, I Leve y^t wholy to Providenc. resolving to indeavor to be content (Neds long absenc makes me almost affraid)[.] I cant perswad Billy to live wth his Bro Davis [a surgeon]—I think it very well if he would: I want to know your intentions, if for Shopkeeping or otherwise. You thought fit to take him in Case tho I must confess it was never my Judgment to put Children to relations but rather to Strangers—yet at present I cant tell where better to Bestow him[.]

Edward Winslow also emerges from these letters as a man who took his role as religious leader of his household seriously, and who probably led his family in daily devotions. In his letter of 30 June 1722 to Jacob, he expressed his desire to see his children

> growing in grace & Religion in so peculiar a manner I long to See y^t the end of our forefathers coming into this Wilderness maynt be lost which was to Serve god by a pure worship free from human invention & Superstition[.] I hope if ever God give you an other oportunity you[']l improve it by comeing up to all the orders & ordinances of the Gospel and that wth a Sincere heart I reason the neglect of it a very great evil & the Longer the delay the grater ye Contempt and harder to return[.] I thought to have Spoken of it to you before you went off but was diverted, pray dont contem nor neglect it if you

Love your own Soul our time in this world is but very Short & how short we know not, and the main consern of it should be, to provide for a future for an eternity y^t very word if duly thought on is enuf to amais and astonish, O that we may Live here so y^t when we die we may meet in an happy & Glorious Eternity.

In November 1747 he wrote to Isaac, who was about to be married, to give him his thoughts on a man's religious duty.

I think it my duty to put you in mind, nay to charge you as a father, that you begin your new family relation with religious family duties, for I am very confident it will be more easy abundantly to begin at first, than after any Delay. . . . Dear son this theme of religion as to my children has laid heavy on my mind a long time, to see they don't make confession of it before men, and I have not been without fears lest you be drawn from that way of worship which you have been taught from a child. I must say I fear Mr Hooper may draw you away to his church [Isaac eventually joined the liberal West Church]. I would not by any means hinder any of my children from their own serious conscientious persuasions about the way to worship God in, and if upon a strict search, and humble address it appear to you, that this or that way is more edifying, I would recommend it, but to me it seems rather this change may give more latitude to carnality, and looseness in religion, and a seeming easiness, tending to the casting off a strict observation of holy duties and days, so much practised. . . . My fears arise from your acquaintance who I think are not so regardful of the honor of God as to be fashionable there being I perceive a looseness in them who have lately deserted or gone from us. . . . Dear son it would rejoice my heart to see you walk in the steps of your ancestors, so far only as they followed Christ, PS 92.1.2. Dear son these thoughts are the effect of serious consideration after earnest seeking direction and I hope and request earnestly, that they may be seriously regarded, not only for a short view but laid by you to look on and consider hereafter when I cannot repeat them. I think that family duty is too generally thrust out to give way to business, but more so by them that are led aside by new notions in religion, as I have observed in many families who I think have no family worship or very seldom. . . . I hope you will keep it [this letter] by you as the earnest and hearty request of your affectionate father who earnest longs to see his children walk in the paths which lead to happiness, which is obedience to the law of God. . . . You know I am no grammarian so will overlook method in the above and cast a mantle over your fathers infirmities, and pick out his meaning and accept in love what is intended, and give him pleasure before he is called hence, by observing the cautions above which proceed from the most affectionate regard he bears his Dear son, to who it is directed." [77]

These letters confirm that Winslow, although he received royal appointments and would probably have been considered to be a member of the "court" party, nonetheless remained steadfast in his adherence to the religious beliefs of his Puritan ancestors, and that he was not interested in taking part in the social frivolities that he associated with the elite. His words and his handwriting both reveal him as a man who remained firmly rooted in seventeenth-century values to the end of his life.

The *Boston Post Boy* of 3 December 1753 carried the following notice: "Last Saturday night died here in the 85 year of his age the Hon. Edward Winslow, Esq, one of his majesty's justices of the Court of Common Pleas for the County of Suffolk; he was also for many years sheriff of the said county and colonel of the regiment of foot of this town." The inventory of the estate amounted to £1,083.18.5 and included a "parcel" of goldsmith's tools valued at £4.[63] PEK and BMW

SURVIVING OBJECTS

	Mark	Inscription	Patron	Date	Reference	Owner
Baptismal basin	A	Winthrop arms, 3 chevrons gules over all a lion rampant, and crest, a hare courant; Hoc Lavacrum Septentrionati in Bostonio Ecclesiae adusum ss. Baptismi dedicatum est per Adamum Winthrop adortum primi sui Filii qui baptiratus est 18 Aug: 1706	Adam Winthrop for Second Church, Boston	1706	Jones 1913, 40–41	
Beaker	A	The gift of S. Phillips/To yᵉ Chh of Rowly/1714	First Congregational Church, Rowley, Mass., for Rev. Samuel Phillips	1714	Jones 1913, 406	
Beaker	A	The gift of Ez: Rogers to/yᵉ Chh of Rowley/1715	First Congregational Church, Rowley, Mass., for Rev. Ezekiel Rogers	1715	Jones 1913, 405–06	
Beaker	A†	The gift of Colᵒ· Francis Wainwright/To the Church of Ipswich	First Congregational Church, Ipswich, Mass., for Francis Wainwright	1711	Buhler/Hood 1970, no. 56	YUAG
Beaker	A	The Gift of Thomas Bishop to the Second Church of Christ in Roxbury 1721	Thomas Bishop and/or First Parish, West Roxbury, Mass.	1721	Jones 1913, 491	
Beaker	A	The Gift of Mary Haughton/to B·C	Congregational Church, West Parish of Barnstable, West Barnstable, Mass., for Mary (Hinckley) Haughton	ca. 1695	Jones 1913, 483	
Beaker	A	EBC	East Parish Congregational Church, Barnstable, Mass.	ca. 1700	Jones 1913, 9	
Two candlesticks	A*	unidentified crest, a winged unicorn	Porter or Thomas family (?)	ca. 1715	DAPC 73.3130	CW
Two candlesticks	A	none		ca. 1720		MFAB
Two candlesticks	C	Hutchinson arms, a lion rampant over a field of crosses crosslet	Edward Hutchinson	ca. 1720	Safford 1983, 34	MMA
Cann	A	LEVERETT . . . (later)	John Leverett	ca. 1725	*Harvard Alumni Bulletin* (23 June 1933): 999	HU
Cann	C	Hutchinson arms, a lion rampant over a field of crosses	Edward Hutchinson	ca. 1715	Buhler 1972, no. 72	MFAB

	Mark	Inscription	Patron	Date	Reference	Owner
		crosslet, and crest, a cockatrice				
Cann	c	DP (+)		ca. 1730	YUAG files	
Caster	A*	none		ca. 1715	Buhler/Hood 1970, no. 53	YUAG
Caster	c	none		ca. 1720	Buhler 1956, no. 149	
Caudle cup	A	Milford Church 1707	First Congregational Church, Milford, Conn.	ca. 1707	Jones 1913, 286	
Caudle cup	A	M·C	First Congregational Church, Milford, Conn.	ca. 1700	Jones 1913, 286	
Chafing dish	A	G/TR (+)	Goodwill family (?)	ca. 1730		MFAB
Chafing dish	c*	C/WD + E (later)		ca. 1715	English-Speaking Union 1960, no. 23	
Chocolate pot	A	Saltonstall arms	Saltonstall family	ca. 1725	YUAG files	
Chocolate pot	A*	Auchmuty (?) arms, argent a spear between 2 mullets; Auchmuty crest, a mailed dexter arm embowed holding a broken lance shaft; M/TE	Auchmuty family	ca. 1705	Buhler/Hood 1970, no. 49	YUAG
Chocolate pot	A*	Hutchinson arms, per pale a lion rampant over a field of crosses crosslet, and crest, a cockatrice emerging from a ducal crown	Thomas Hutchinson (?)	ca. 1705	Safford 1983, 22–23	MMA
Cup	A	P.L.Jr./1884 (later)		ca. 1705	Puig et al. 1989, no. 179	MIA
Cup	?	N/IS		ca. 1715	YUAG files	
Dram cup	A	?		ca. 1695	MFA 1911, no. 1016	
Flagon	A	This belongs to/the Church in/Brattle Street/1713	Brattle Street Church, Boston	1713	Buhler 1972, no. 71	MFAB
Grace cup	A	Lowell quartering Leversedge arms (later) (+)		ca. 1705	Buhler/Hood 1970, no. 57	YUAG
Mourning ring (gold)	c*	I Dudley late Govr. of NE ob 2 Apr 1720 AE 73	Joseph Dudley	1720	Buhler/Hood 1970, no. 59	YUAG
Mourning ring (gold; attrib.)	none	ELIZH WINSLOW OB . 16 SEP 1740 AE 71	Elizabeth Winslow	1740	Buhler/Hood 1970, no. 60	YUAG

	Mark	Inscription	Patron	Date	Reference	Owner
Mug	A *or* B	AB/to/CEB (later)		ca. 1730	Christie's, 23 January 1982, lot 94	
Mug	c†	E (+)	Edward Hutchinson	ca. 1710	Buhler 1972, no. 70	MFAB
Patch box	c*	none		ca. 1715	*Antiques* 108 (October 1975): 594	
Pepper box	A*	none		ca. 1715	DAPC 78.4065	VMFA
Pepper box	A	EP		ca. 1725	Washington 1925, no. 142	
Pepper box	A	G/MR (later)		ca. 1720	Buhler 1972, no. 73	MFAB
Pepper box	A*	IE P	Jane (Eliot) Pepperrell	ca. 1707	Buhler/Hood 1970, no. 54	YUAG
Pepper box	A*/C*	B/CP		ca. 1725	Buhler/Hood 1970, no. 55	YUAG
Pepper box	A/C	unidentified crest; C/WA		ca. 1720	YUAG files	
Plate (mate below)	A	Hutchinson arms, per pale a lion rampant over a field of crosses crosslet; The Gift of/Thomas Hutchinson/To the Second Church in Boston May 1711	Thomas Hutchinson and/or Second Church, Boston	1711	Quimby 1995, no. 139	WM
Plate (mate above)	A	Hutchinson arms, per pale a lion rampant over a field of crosses crosslet; The Gift of/Edward Hutchinson/To the Second Church in Boston May 1711.	Edward Hutchinson and/or Second Church, Boston	1711	Quimby 1995, no. 138	WM
Plate	A	Palmes arms, 3 fleur-de-lis, a chief varié, a crescent in fess point	Edward Palmes	ca. 1700	Buhler 1972, no. 65	MFAB
Plate (mates below)	A	Foster arms, a chevron or between 3 hunting horns	John Foster	ca. 1705	Avery 1920, no. 12	MMA
Plate (mates above and below)	A	Foster arms, a chevron or between 3 hunting horns (+)	John Foster	ca. 1705	*American Silver* 1967, no. 1	RWNAG
Plate (mates above)	A	Foster arms, a chevron or between 3 hunting horns (+)	John Foster	ca. 1705	Sotheby's, 26 June 1986, lot 53	
Plate	A	Foster arms, a chevron vert between 3 hunting horns (+)	John Foster and/or Second Church, Boston	ca. 1705	Jones 1913, 41–42	
Porringer	A	IT/to/MRT (later)		ca. 1730	Buhler 1979, no. 8	WAM

	Mark	Inscription	Patron	Date	Reference	Owner
Porringer	A*	M/WM		ca. 1730	*Antiques* 126 (October 1984): 788	HD
Porringer	A	T/BS		ca. 1725	YUAG files	
Porringer	A	B/TS	Boylston family	ca. 1725		MFAB
Porringer (with English mark WR*)*	A*	Mary Lowell.1833/ Mary Lowell Coolidge/1891 (later)		ca. 1700	Cooper 1978, 107–09	MFAB
Porringer	A	EH; S. R. Robbins 1813 (later)	Edward Hutchinson	ca. 1720	YUAG files	
Porringer	A	erased		ca. 1705	Fales 1983, 12–13	PEM
Porringer	A	B/LS	Louis and Sarah (Middlecott) Boucher	ca. 1705	Bigelow 1917, 308–09	
Porringer	A	M/SE	Samuel and Esther Mulford	ca. 1705	Sotheby's, 29 April– 1 May 1981, lot 393	
Porringer	A	Winslow arms, on a bend gules 6 loz- enges conjoined, and crest, a tree trunk with new branches, a strap with buckle; W/IS	Winslow family	ca. 1720	Phillips 1939, no. 197	
Porringer (with cover)	C	FI/to/SI; Winthrop Pyemont/from his Aunt Augusta . . . (later)	Johonnot family	ca. 1720	Quimby 1995, no. 142	WM
Porringer	C	RH		ca. 1725		MWPI
Porringer	C*	B/WE	Boylston family	ca. 1725	*Antiques* 108 (October 1975): 594	
Porringer	?	W/DR; 1760 (later)		ca. 1715	*Antiques* 94 (October 1968): 455	
Porringer	?	SG; 1750 (later)	Stephen Gorham	ca. 1730	Bigelow 1917, 314	
Salt	A	Edes crest, a lion's face; E/IM	John and Mary (Tufts) Edes	ca. 1690	Buhler 1972, no. 67	MFAB
Salt	A*	SM	Sarah (Winslow) (Standish) (Payne) Middlecott	ca. 1695	Buhler 1956, no. 144	
Salver	A	A Legacy of Nathaniel Kay . . . (later)		ca. 1705	Jones 1913, 97	
Salver	A	RB to MV		ca. 1700	Buhler 1972, no. 68	MFAB
Salver	A*	C/WS		ca. 1700	Flynt/Fales 1968, 115–16	HD
Salver	A	?	Edward Tyng	ca. 1720	*Sack Collec- tion* 3:825	

	Mark	Inscription	Patron	Date	Reference	Owner
Two salvers	A	E/IG (+)	John and Grizzel (Lloyd) Eastwick	ca. 1715	Jones 1913, 64–65	
Salver	A	Ex EH to MH	Elizabeth (Clarke) Hancock	ca. 1698	*Antiques* 100 (August 1971): 210	BBC
Salver	A*	Belcher arms, or 3 pales azure, a chief vairé vert, argent purpure; AB	Andrew Belcher	ca. 1715	Buhler/Hood 1970, no. 52	YUAG
Salver	A	?		ca. 1720	Sotheby Parke Bernet, 26–28 January 1984, lot 414	
Salver	A	unidentified crest, a unicorn's head		ca. 1715	Buhler 1960, no. 139	AIC
Serving spoon	A	Francis Wardwell	Frances (Cook) Wardwell	ca. 1720	Quimby 1995, no. 142	WM
Serving spoon	A	C/EI		ca. 1715	*CGA Bulletin*, no. 1 (1971): fig. 5	CGA
Serving spoon	C*	none	John Derby	ca. 1710		YUAG
Spout cup	A*	H/SA; R (later)		ca. 1710	English-Speaking Union 1960, no. 22	
Strainer spoon	C*	none		ca. 1720	Gourley 1965, no. 205	LAM
Sugar box	A	Winslow arms, on a bend 7 lozenges conjoined, and crest, a tree trunk with new branches, a strap with buckle; Ex dono/Sarah Middlecott/N England/ to MM/1702	Sarah (Winslow) (Standish) (Payne) Middlecott	1702	Nygren 1971, 38–52	
Sugar box	A	AB to L (later)		ca. 1705		PMA
Sugar box	A*	none	Edward Winslow	ca. 1705	Buhler/Hood 1970, no. 51	YUAG
Sugar box	A	S/GM (later)		ca. 1700	Buhler 1972, no. 69	MFAB
Sugar box	A*/ B†	O/DE/Donum WP 1702	William Partridge for Daniel and Elizabeth (Belcher) Oliver	1702	Quimby 1995, no. 140	WM
Sword	C	none	Benning Wentworth	ca. 1720	Avery 1920, no. 52	MMA
Sword	C	Ex Dono I.M. ad. F.B.	Francis Baudoin	ca. 1725	Safford 1983, 42	MMA
Tablespoon	A	EB		ca. 1710	YUAG files	
Tablespoon	A	D/TS		ca. 1700	Quimby 1995, no. 145	WM

	Mark	Inscription	Patron	Date	Reference	Owner
Tablespoon (mate? below)	A	LB		ca. 1720	*Silver Supplement* 1973, no. 77	
Tablespoon (mate? above)	A*	LB		ca. 1720	Quimby 1995, no. 144	WM
Two tablespoons	A	SI		ca. 1715	Buhler 1956, no. 147	
Tablespoon	A*	AB		ca. 1700	Quimby 1995, no. 146	WM
Tablespoon	A*	M/RS	Richard and Sarah (Winslow) (Standish) (Payne) Middlecott	ca. 1690	Buhler 1972, no. 66	MFAB
Tablespoon	A*	R/SA		ca. 1700	Buhler/Hood 1970, no. 48	YUAG
Tablespoon	C*	Dudley crest, a lion's head erased	Dudley family	ca. 1725	Buhler/Hood 1970, no. 58	YUAG
Tankard	A	Winslow arms	Winslow family	ca. 1720	English-Speaking Union 1960, no. 20	AG
Tankard	A*	R/ID	Rogers family (?)	ca. 1730	Johnston 1994, 175	CMA
Tankard	A*	Hutchinson arms, per pale a lion rampant over a field of crosses crosslet	Hutchinson family	ca. 1730	Phillips 1939, no. 202	
Tankard	A	Hutchinson arms, a lion rampant over a field of crosses crosslet, and crest, a cockatrice emerging from a ducal crown	Thomas Hutchinson (?)	ca. 1710	Avery 1920, no. 51	MMA
Tankard (missing cover)	A*	EIV Junier/Sep.^{t} 24. 1711		1711	Avery 1920, no. 50	MMA
Two tankards	A*	Chester arms, ermine on a chief a griffin passant, and crest, a griffin passant (+)	Chester family	ca. 1700	Quimby 1995, nos. 136–37	WM
Tankard	A*	R/TM; 1728 (later) (+)		ca. 1700	Buhler 1956, no. 146	
Tankard	A*	L/IM		ca. 1705	Buhler 1979, no. 7	WAM
Tankard	A*	Payne (?) arms, on a bend 3 arrows between a leopard's head and an eagle's leg couped, and crest, a demi-cherub holding an arrow; CFD (later)	Thomas and Mary Payne	ca. 1700	Warren 1975, no. 285	BBC
Tankard	A	Paine arms; PT/M	Thomas and Mary Paine family	ca. 1700		MFAB

	Mark	Inscription	Patron	Date	Reference	Owner
Tankard	A	IM		ca. 1700	Wardwell 1966, 80–81	
Tankard	A*	Pickering arms, ermine a lion rampant crowned; P/WH	William and Hannah (Browne) Pickering	ca. 1700	Fales 1983, 10–11	PEM
Tankard	A*	none		ca. 1705	Johnston 1994, 174	CMA
Tankard	A*	C/WH		ca. 1705	Buhler 1956, no. 145	
Tankard	A	F/RP; F/IE/to/WFC (later)	Richard and Parnell (Winslow) Foster	ca. 1705	CGA Bulletin, no. 1 (1971): fig. 2	CGA
Tankard	A	none		ca. 1695	Bulletin DIA 55 (1977): 109–11	DIA
Tankard	A	none		ca. 1730	Quimby 1995, no. 141	WM
Tankard	A	Harvard College (later)		ca. 1705	MFA 1906, no. 324	HU
Tankard	A/C	Foster arms, a chevron vert between 3 hunting horns, and crest, a dexter arm, armed and embowed, grasping a broken tilting spear; B/MA	Foster family	ca. 1725	Christie's, 19 September 1981, lot 88	
Tankard	C	ED		ca. 1730	The Winslows 1974, no. 48	MFAB
Tankard	C*	EJ; 1750 (later)		ca. 1725	DAPC 73.3135	HMA
Tankard	C	B/TM		ca. 1730	Bulletin DIA 12 (March 1931): 70–72	DIA
Tankard	?	unidentified initials		ca. 1700	Jones 1936, 84, 88	

1. RC 9:8, 112; *Mayflower Descendant* 12 (July 1910): 129; SCPR 6:674–76.
2. SCPR 5:287–89; 6:159–63.
3. His mother's sister Ann became the mother of Samuel Vernon, and her sister Susanna was the mother of John Coddington. Another sister, Faith, married Maj. Thomas Savage, grandfather of the goldsmith.
4. Savage 1860–62, 4:601; SCPR, docket 688.
5. SCD 15:148.
6. RC 9:237; *Cambridge VR* 1:150.
7. Samuel Sewall Account Book and Ledger, NEHGS, records transactions under "Mr. Joshua Moody Dr" in 1695, 1697, 1698, and 1699 wherein money is exchanged with Edward Winslow.
8. Samuel Sewall Account Book and Ledger, fol. 77v, NEHGS. The account for Mrs. Martha Collins shows cash lent to her by Edward Winslow in 1698. Winslow also bought a Negro girl named Sarah from Martha Collins in 1695; see MCD 10:416. Martha Collins died on 22 March 1699/1700; see Bigelow-Phillips files, 404b.
9. RC 10:133.
10. RC 9:208, 216, 234, 242; RC 24:4, 12, 24, 38, 52, 64; RC 28:57, 90, 147, 152, 158, 181, 194; *Sibley's Harvard Graduates* 8:333–39.

11. RC 1:170.

12. RC 29:228.

13. SCD 21:101–04. Winslow sold his share of the property to Fitch in 1709; SCD 24:218–21.

14. SCD 24:10.

15. SCD 24:160–62. A subsequent deed in 1722 deals with the ownership of a passage adjacent to the land the house occupied; see SCD 36:125–26.

16. RC 29:191.

17. SCD 28:51.

18. SCPR, docket 10609.

19. SCD 25:11–12.

20. SCD 26:173–74.

21. SCD 26:27–28; 33:154.

22. SCD 35:75–76, 100.

23. SCD 38:21–22.

24. SCD 24:218–21.

25. Cooper 1978, 107–09.

26. SCD 26:173–74.

27. *Swansea VR*, 5; RC 28:43.

28. RC 24:87. Elizabeth (b. 1712/13) married Richard Clarke, one of the consignees of the tea destroyed at the Boston Tea Party; their daughter Susanna married John Singleton Copley (q.v. Appendix A).

29. SCCR, Court of Common Pleas Record Book 1710–13, 226; 1714–15, 68, 89.

30. Roberts 1895, 1:326–27.

31. Seybolt 1939, 97.

32. Seybolt 1939, 106, 111, 120, 122n, 129, 130, 132, 135, 138.

33. Mass. Archives 40:847, 856, 857; SCCR, file 46659.

34. Hill 1890, 1:409, 422, 430, 487, 490, 583, 600.

35. The date on which Winslow was appointed sheriff has been recorded in various ways in the scholarly literature. In a petition of 1743 to Gov. William Shirley, Winslow asked that the payment of his account for services as sheriff not be abated as it had been in the past, noting that he had held the post for twenty-seven years, which indicates he assumed the post in 1716; see Mass. Archives 102:333. He appears as sheriff on writs dated 1717; see Downs Manuscript Collection, nos. 66×154.2 and 74×155. A note in the Bigelow-Phillips files, n.p., from records of the Court of General Sessions for 4 December 1719 shows that authorized payment of £72.14.6 was made to "William Dudley and Edward Winslow Esqr, Sheriffs of the County for one year's salary ending July last."

36. Belcher Papers, Part I, *Massachusetts Historical Collections*, 6ᵗʰ series, vol. 6, 494, 275.

37. The accounts Winslow submitted for reimbursement or pay included expenses incurred in 1721 and 1722 (SCCR, file 16228); dinners during the sessions from July 1724 to July 1725 (SCCR, file 164082); fines collected June 1724 to June 1725; services from July 1725 to July 1726; fines from July 1727 to October 1728 (SCCR, file 164609); expenses for transporting prisoners to Salem, 1734 (SCCR, file 166327); services rendered from March 1734 to March 1735; disbursement for expenses, 1737 (SCCR, file 167266); expenses presented to the justices of the Court of General Sessions, 1740–43 (Bostonian Society, document 352.2); and suits brought in the York County Court of Common Pleas by Thomas Pickering against Winslow in his capacity as sheriff; see YCCR, Court of Common Pleas Record Book 9:52, 173; 10:97, 219, 280; box 42, file 45; box 45, file 80; box 54, file 38; box 58, file 44; box 60, file 54; sessions of April 1731, April 1732, April 1734, April 1735, and January 1736.

38. Mass. Archives 31:161.

39. Benjamin Walker, Jr., Diaries, entry for 19 October 1732, MHS.

40. Benjamin Walker, Jr., Diaries, entry for 30 October 1728, MHS.

41. Benjamin Walker, Jr., Diaries, entry for 11 September 1729, MHS.

42. *Boston Weekly News-Letter*, 11–18 July 1734, 2; speech delivered by Governor Belcher to the House of Representatives as printed in the *Boston Weekly News-Letter*, 19–26 December 1734, 1.

43. Warden 1970, 133.

44. Warden 1970, 221.

45. On the sources of income that justices of the peace may have enjoyed as part of their office, see Osgood 1984, 107–51.

46. SCCR, files 14201, 14647.

47. A photostat of his appointment is in the Bigelow-Phillips files.

48. Mass. Archives 19:51–52.

49. SCCR, file 5565.

50. SCD 25:11–12; 26:173–74; 33:154.

51. SCD 33:154.

52. Benjamin Walker, Jr., Diaries, entry for 11 January 1742/43, MHS.

53. SCPR, docket 10609.

54. An EW mark in a serrated rectangle on a spoon has been misattributed to Winslow; see Eitner 1976, no. 36. The characteristics of the spoon do not relate to Massachusetts work.

55. SCCR, file 16553.

56. Sewall Account Book and Ledger, fols. 87v, 197v, NEHGS.

57. Sewall Account Book and Ledger, fol. 195v, NEHGS.

58. Sewall Account Book and Ledger, fol. 128v, NEHGS.

59. Sewall Account Book and Ledger, fol. 193v, NEHGS.

60. *Sewall Diary* 2:741.

61. *Sewall Diary* 2:989. The motto can be translated, "After darkness light."

62. Sewall Account Book and Ledger, fol. 176v, NEHGS.

63. Sewall Account Book and Ledger, fol. 187r, NEHGS.

64. *Sewall Letter Book* 2:221.

65. Sewall Account Book and Ledger, fols. 120v, 121r, NEHGS.

66. Sewall Account Book and Ledger, fol. 195v, NEHGS.

67. Sewall Account Book and Ledger, fols. 161v, 162r, NEHGS.

68. For the funeral of Francis Wainwright in 1711 Edward Winslow provided eighteen rings weighing one ounce, thirteen pennyweights, and twelve grains each with the making and waste at two shillings six pence per ring. Some of these rings needed to be remade, so the total bill amounted to £13.5.10; see ECPR, docket 28673. When Peter Sargent died in 1713/14 his estate purchased rings from William Cowell, Sr. (q.v.) (£9.12.6), Edward Winslow (£12.3), and Thomas Mullins (£11); see SCPR 22:328. Rings for Jonathan Pollard's funeral in 1725 cost £17.11.9; see SCPR 25:442. The estate of Jonathan Waldo paid Winslow £72.6 for thirty-five rings in 1731; see SCPR 29:412. The estate administration of Mary Saltonstall presented in 1732 shows that Edward Winslow was paid £46.7.6 for rings; see SCPR, docket 5901. In 1733 Ann Penelope Parker's estate recorded payment to Winslow of £21.18.6 for eleven "Comon Gold Rings" presented to the bearers, the ministers, the doctor, and the two women who laid out the corpse as opposed to the six "Mourning Rings" left as legacies to the principal mourners purchased from James Boyer (q.v.) for nearly the same amount; see SCPR 31:510. Thomas Fayerweather's executors' account shows that Winslow was paid £51.17.9 for making twenty-four rings; see SCPR 30:268. Edward Bromfield's estate administration, submitted in 1735, shows that Winslow was paid £38.9, presumably for rings; see SCPR 32:364. Mary Mico's estate administration of 1736/37 records that Winslow was paid £37.8 for eighteen rings; see SCPR 33:90. The estate of Capt. John Gerrish paid Winslow £29.5 for seventeen gold rings in 1743; see SCPR 37:32. The administrator's account of 1743/44 for the estate of William Payne shows that Winslow was paid £29.18 for rings for the funeral; see SCPR 37:47.

69. Henry Flynt Memorandum Book, HU.

70. Daniel Henchman Ledger, 1712–ca. 1735, fols. 39v-r, 128v-r, NEHGS.

71. *Sibley's Harvard Graduates* 8:333–39.

72. In 1734 Winslow granted a mortgage for land in the north of Boston; SCD 48:231. In 1739 Winslow and his wife bought and sold buildings and land on Common Street; SCD 58:129–30; 67:163–64. In 1743 Winslow sold a tenement and land on Marlborough Street; SCD 58:130–31; 67:147–49. He also granted a mortgage to William Nichols in 1744; SCD 69:132–33.

73. SCD 50:93–97; 81:264–68.

74. Benjamin Walker, Jr., Diaries, entry for 18 September 1740, MHS, notes that Mrs. Winslow was buried. RC 9:173; RC 28:267.

75. RC 30:26.

76. The letters are owned by YUAG.

77. This letter exists only as a transcription in the Bigelow-Phillips files. Winslow's original language no doubt was polished by the transcriber.

78. SCPR 49:341–45.

Stephen Winter
ca. 1714 or 1715–47

Stephen Winter was probably born in Boston about 1714 or 1715 to Benjamin and Mary Winter. He married Hannah Hewes (1715–74), daughter of Samuel (d. 1720), a cooper, and Hannah (Johnson) Hewes (d. 1734), in Boston on 31 March 1736 in a ceremony performed by Rev. Samuel Checkley.[1] Five children were born to Stephen and Hannah Winter between 1737 and 1745.[2]

Winter was actively pursuing his career as a jeweler by 1736. On 31 July of that year, Stephen Winter, jeweler, and his wife, Hannah, sold their one-quarter interest in a house on Water Street to her brother, the merchant Samuel Hewes, for £150.[3] One of the witnesses to the deed was Mary Winter, which suggests that the jeweler's widowed mother or perhaps an unmarried sister was residing with him. Winter and his brother Edward, a blacksmith, joined with their sister, Margaret Nash, to post the £500 bond required to administer the estate of her late husband, the silversmith James Nash, Jr. (q.v.), on 30 June 1737.[4] The familial ties between Nash and Winter suggest that the two craftsmen may have apprenticed in the same shop, although the identity of their master is unknown.

The jeweler was an active participant in town government. On 19 March 1738/39, he was elected clerk of the market; on 8 April 1740, he was sworn in as a constable.[5] In July 1740, Winter was one of twelve men responsible for informing the freeholders of Boston of a meeting to consider the offer of Peter Faneuil to fund the construction of a market house on Dock Square.[6] The *New-England Weekly Journal* for 20 January 1740/41 reported that three stolen spoons had been seized by Stephen Winter "Jeweller, at the South End, Boston."[7]

Stephen Winter died in 1747, and an inventory of his estate was taken on 25 November 1747. Winter did not own any real estate; his inventory lists the contents of a parlor, kitchen, chamber, and shop and suggests a comfortable life-style. He owned such luxury items as four looking glasses, two sets of window curtains and valances, and an upholstered easy chair in the chamber; mezzotints, maps, and pictures in the parlor; and a mulatto slave boy. Winter's shop included tools and supplies for all sorts of silver and jewelry work; the silver tankard, porringer, cup, buttons, sword, and eleven spoons included among the shop contents could have been work in progress for customers or stock merchandise displayed in Winter's three shop windows. The shop was equipped with both "shop" and "Jeweller's" signs, emphasizing the variety of objects and services provided by Winter.

Shop A Parcel of Stones, Foil & Brass Box	3.
3 smooth Files 10/ 1 p^r. Large Bellows 30/	2.
a Parcel of small Files in a Draw	. 5
a pair of Shears, Corn Tongs & Compasses	1. 10
a plate Ring Sizes 30/ 1 Hand Vise 8/	1. 18
7 pair of Plyers 20/ 1 p^r. Shears 8/	1. 8
1 Burrus Box, Drill Stock & Drills	1. 15
1 Sparhawk & Swage 20/ 1 Brass Stamp 50/	3. 10
1 pair of Nealing Tongs & a Tin pan 10/ 1 oyl Stone 10/	1.
1 drawing Bench Tongs & 4 old drawing plates	4.
4 Limmell Boxes 5/ 2 blow pipes & a Lamp 10/	. 15
1 Wooden Hand Vise 2 Mallets & 2 Hammers	. 10
4 Dopping punches & Triblet 5/ 2 Leads 8/	. 13

2 Draws of Cement Sticks & Sundrys	1.
1 Iron Mill 20/ Scale & Beam 20/	2.
1 Brass Funnel 5/ old Brass 10/	. 15
Sundry pollishing Stones	. 5
1 Silver Tankard. 1 porringer. 1 Silver Cup 6 Tea spoons } & 5 others w^t 48 Oz @ 58/	139. 4
Silver and Gold Filings	£3. 5
1 p^r. odd stone Buttons	. 10
2 p^r. small Scales & Weights	1.
1 Old Dripping Pan & 6 Candle Molds	. 10
3 Shop Windows £7.10/ a Jeweller's Sign 5/	7. 15
a Shop Sign 4/ a Brass Hilted Sword & Belt 50/	2. 14
a Bench & Skin 10/ an old Brass Cock, an Ingott } & Fire Iron 30/ & a Case of Shop Draws 25/	3. 5[8]

Following Winter's death, his widow, Hannah, established herself as a school-mistress on Winter Street. The *News-Letter* reported the death of Hannah Winter in December 1774.[9]

No mark has been attributed to this jeweler. DAF

1. Thwing; RC 24:105; RC 28:2, 199; SCPR 21:775; 22:88; 30:453; 32:196–97.
2. RC 24:227, 235, 244.
3. SCD 53:200–01.
4. SCPR 19:411–12 new ser.
5. Seybolt 1939, 213, 217.
6. *NEHGR* 30:368.
7. This ad was repeated on 27 January 1740/41. According to Henry Flynt and Martha Gandy Fales, Winter appeared in a Boston directory of 1740 as a jeweler; however, the earliest city directories were not published until 1789, so the source of this information is not clear; Flynt/Fales 1968, 362.
8. SCPR 41:233–35.
9. *Index of Obituaries, 1704–1800*, 3:582.

Eleazer Wyer, Sr.
1752–1800

Eleazer Wyer, Sr., was born in Charlestown, Massachusetts, on 2 January 1752 to William Wyer (1707–86), a sailmaker, and Ann Newell (1713–74), who married in 1731.[1] His paternal grandparents were Robert Wyer (1663/64–1709) and Ruth Johnson (1669–1742).[2] His maternal grandparents were Joseph Newell (1687–1735), a mariner, and Ann Phillips (1689–1768).[3] After the death of her first husband, Ann (Phillips) Newell married Stephen Hall.

Wyer would have begun his apprenticeship about 1766 and completed it about 1773, when he paid taxes in Charlestown.[4] His master probably was Josiah Austin (q.v.) because Wyer is said to have married Austin's daughter Lydia (1750–1821) in 1778.[5] Wyer claimed losses of personal property of £7.10 following the British bombardment of Charlestown in 1775.[6] He served as a constable in Charlestown in 1789.[7] Wyer died in 1800 at the age of forty-eight, but no will or estate administration is recorded for him.[8] His son Eleazer Wyer, Jr. (1786–1848), also followed the goldsmith's trade in Portland, Maine. Some scholars have speculated that the E. Wyer marks could have been used by both father and son, but their style suggests that they are too late to have been used by the father.[9] PEK

1. *Charlestown VR* 1:212, 314, 386; Griffen 1952, 126; Wyman 1879, 2:1055; *NEHGR* 31:79.
2. *Charlestown VR* 1:46; Griffen 1952, 126.

3. *Charlestown VR* 1:135, 235; *NEHGR* 27:278; Griffen 1952, 53; MCPR, docket 15832.

4. Wyman 1879, 2:1055.

5. Hunnewell 1880, 147; *Index of Obituaries, 1784–1840*, 5:5073.

6. Hunnewell 1888, 170.

7. Hunnewell 1888, 21–22.

8. *Index of Obituaries, 1784–1840*, 5:5073.

9. Belden 1980, 456–57.

Thomas Wyllys
w. ca. 1680–94,
d. before 1720

It has not been possible to ascertain with any certainty who Thomas Wyllys's parents were. A number of men named Thomas Wyllys were born in Boston and Charlestown, Massachusetts, in the late seventeenth century, and the Wyllys family of Connecticut was also very prominent. It is also possible that he was an immigrant from England because there is a Thomas Wallis entered as an apprentice to Henry Stafford, goldsmith of London, for seven years at Goldsmiths' Hall, London, in 1658. He was the "son of Robert Wallis late of St. Giles in the Fields, Middlesex, Husbandman deceased" and became a freeman of the company on 14 October 1668.[1]

Thomas Wyllys evidently worked with William Rouse (q.v.), possibly as a journeyman, because on 3 May 1681, William Rouse sued Thomas Hanshes for two pounds and other damages because Hanshes, about six weeks before, had beaten Rouse's servant, Thomas Wyllys, so badly that he had broken Wyllys's leg. The money that Rouse sued for equaled the expense that he had incurred in getting treatment for Wyllys, and the money he had lost while Wyllys was unable to work. The language used in the case suggests that Wyllys was an indentured servant, perhaps working under an agreement similar to the one that survives between Richard Conyers and Henry Hurst (qq.v.).[2]

Thomas Wyllys, goldsmith, married the widow Elizabeth Lemmon (d. ca. 1720) on 24 August 1688. Two weeks earlier, on 7 August, Elizabeth Lemmon, calling herself a spinster, entered into an agreement with the merchant Anthony Haywood of Boston whereby he would hold £120 plus interest in trust for her daughter, Elizabeth Lemmon, who was then a minor, until the girl reached the age of twenty-one. The agreement was witnessed by William Rouse and Thomas Kemble. Apparently Elizabeth Lemmon was trying to ensure that her own independent wealth went to her daughter and that it did not become part of her husband's property as the result of their marriage.[3]

On 1 November 1690, Nicholas Beard and Nathaniel Legg, mariners of the ketch *James* of Salem, Massachusetts, granted power of attorney to "our Trusty & well beloved Friend Thomas Wyllys of Boston . . . Goldsmith."[4] In 1692 Thomas Wyllys, goldsmith, sued William Cross (q.v.), goldsmith, "in an action of the Case for not paying to ye Plt the sume of ffourteen pounds seven shillings & one penny in mony due by Booke for severals he had of ye pl^t since the 18th day of April 1692 at w^{ch} [time?] all acco^{tts} betwixt them were then ballanced then there remaining due to ye pl^t one pounds fourteen shillings 3^d."[5] The jury decided in Wyllys's favor, granting him £7.15.1 and costs of court. In July 1694 the taverner George Monck of Boston sued Wyllys for not paying him "money due for money lent & for vituals he hath had of ye pl^t from the beginning of January 1690/1."[6]

In January 1691/92, Thomas and Elizabeth Wyllys sued Anthony Haywood's executors for interest on the £120 that Elizabeth had given him to keep in trust for her daughter Elizabeth Lemmon. Thomas and Elizabeth Wyllys indicated that before he died, in August 1689, Haywood had paid Thomas

Wyllys £7.4 interest on the money, but that his executors had failed to continue the payments, and the Wyllyses asked damages of £240.[7] The outcome of their suit is not mentioned in the record, but in July 1720, Elizabeth Carder, widow, daughter of Elizabeth Lemmon "who intermarried with Thomas Willis of Boston Goldsmith both deceased," petitioned the Superior Court in an attempt to regain £240 from Anthony Haywood's estate. Elizabeth Carder said that "Thomas Willis and Eliz[a] his wife in the Year one thousand six hundred and ninety four in their Passage to Jamaica were taken by a french privateer and the s[d] Original Bond with divers other Papers were then destroyed and lost."[8] Fortunately, a copy of the agreement was included with other file papers in the 1691/92 case. Although the petition implies that Thomas and Elizabeth Wyllys survived their ordeal at sea, there is no record of a goldsmith Thomas Wyllys working in Jamaica.[9] A brief mention of a man by the same name in Boston records may refer to the silversmith. On 28 October 1717 "Thomas Willis, a lame man for Carolina who had y[n] here ab[t] a mo was warn[d] to depart 14 Aug Last."[10] Thomas Wyllys, the silversmith, suffered a broken leg when he was beaten in 1680 and may well have been lame as a result. He may have gone to one of the southern colonies after his ship to Jamaica was captured in 1694. Returning to Boston in 1717, he could have been warned to depart because he was no longer well known in the town.

No silver by Thomas Wyllys is known to survive. BMW

1. The goldsmith may have been the Thomas born to Thomas Willis (1641–1725) and Grace (Tay) Willis (1645–1716) on 15 August 1666; *Billerica VR*, 202, 332; *Medford VR*, 460; RC 9:20; Wyman 1879, 2:1035. In that case, his paternal grandparents would have been George Willis (ca. 1600–90) and Jane (Palfrey) Willis; Savage 1860–62, 4:574; *Medford VR*, 460. His maternal grandparents, then, would have been William Tay (ca. 1611–83) and Grace (Newell) Tay (ca. 1612–1712); Savage 1860–62, 4:258–59; *Roxbury VR* 2:651. The Thwing catalogue at MHS includes at least three people by the name Thomas Willis living in Boston in the late seventeenth century: one was a mason, one was a housewright, and one other is listed without an occupation. Walter Prideaux of Goldsmiths' Hall to Francis Bradbury, 27 January 1925, includes a transcription of Thomas Wallis's apprenticeship agreement from records at Goldsmiths' Hall, London.
2. SCCR, Supreme Civil Court, 1680–92, 49.
3. Mass. Archives 37:229–30, 232, 233. In this case Elizabeth Lemmon probably was using the term "spinster" as an occupational label since she clearly had a child and may have been a widow. The record of the agreement between Lemmon and Haywood includes a deposition as to the date of Elizabeth Lemmon's marriage to Thomas Wyllys. The marriage is not recorded in RC 9. SCPR 22:23–24.
4. SCCR, file 2645.
5. SCCR, Court of Common Pleas Record Book 1692–98, 8.
6. SCCR, Court of Common Pleas Record Book 1692–98, 66.
7. Mass. Archives 37:231.
8. SCCR, file 14331.
9. Conversations with Robert Barker, London, England, a leading authority on Jamaican silversmiths.
10. RC 13:29.

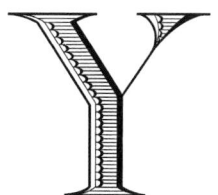

Elijah Yeomans
1751–94

A

B

The peripatetic Connecticut River Valley clockmaker and silversmith Elijah Yeomans was born in Stonington, Connecticut, on 20 September 1751.[1] His parents, Amos Yeomans (1722–ca. 1771) of Stonington and Susanna Downer (1725–ca. 1771) of Franklin, Connecticut, were married either in Lebanon or Stonington on 21 November 1750.[2] His paternal grandparents were Samuel Yeomans (b. 1688) of Stonington and Mary Ingraham.[3] His maternal grandparents were Deacon Joseph Downer (ca. 1692–1756) and Mary Sawyer (ca. 1704–58) of Norwich, Connecticut.[4]

Yeomans's Norwich grandparents may have provided him with the opportunity to apprentice with a clockmaker in the region.[5] In 1771, however, when he was twenty, guardianship papers that described him as "a minor above fourteen years old son of Amos Yeomans late of Stonington" were filed in Hampshire County, Massachusetts, by Simeon Strong, Esq., of Amherst, Massachusetts, and William Williams, Esq., of Hatfield, Massachusetts, who paid two hundred pounds in this binding agreement.[6] Therefore, Yeomans may have finished his training in Hampshire County, where some scholars claim he worked as both a goldsmith and clockmaker in Hadley, Massachusetts, from 1771 to 1783.[7] The *Connecticut Courant* of 21 April 1777 reported that "one John Morris [q.v. Appendix A], a clock maker . . . well known in Hartford, Middletown, and Norwich" stole a quantity of silver bullion, some cash, and several other articles from Elijah Yeomans of Hadley.[8] Evidence suggests, however, that Yeomans returned to Connecticut for at least a few years. In 1778 Yeomans married Lydia Simons (b. 1757), who was probably the daughter of Nathan Simons (b. 1715) and Sarah Balcom of Windham, Connecticut.[9] In 1779, shortly after his marriage in Mansfield, Connecticut, Yeomans served that colony in the Revolution.[10]

Sometime before 1781, however, he was working in Hadley, Massachusetts, because on 28 August 1781, he sold "a Certain Shop being in Hadley aforesaid at the north part of the Town Street" to Japhet Chapin (1762–1833) and John Hodge (1760–1840), goldsmiths of Hadley.[11] Yeomans remained in the area for at least a year after that transaction because on 10 March 1782 the Hadley resident Elizabeth Phelps recorded in her diary, "Fryday Mr. Yeomans here to fix the clock."[12] From 1786 to 1788 Yeomans worked as a clockmaker for the town of Petersham, Massachusetts, and then, about 1792, for Samuel Canfield

(w. 1780–1801+) in Middletown, Connecticut.[13] Yeomans eventually moved to Hartford, Connecticut, where he may have worked for the silversmith David Greenleaf, Jr. (1765–1835).[14] The 17 November 1794 issue of the *Connecticut Courant* announced the death of "Mr. Elijah Yeomans, Silversmith."

Greenleaf and Miles Beach (1742–1828) served as executors of Yeomans's paltry estate, which included a large number of clockmaking parts, along with metalsmithing tools and supplies:

1 pair Bellows 45/ 1 large Anvil or Stake 60/	5	5	0
1 Plating Mill not finished 60/	3	0	0
1 watch Spring Tool 14/one do 7/6	1	1	6
1 Small lathe 10/ 1 watch screw plate & taps 2/6	0	12	6
1 hair Spring plattor 3/ 1 Bitstock & bit 7/	0	10	0
1 Set of Bead Tools 12/ 1 brest plate 1/6	0	13	6
1 Pair Plated Buckles 6/ 1 pr old do /4ᵈ	0	6	4
1 gun or fire lock 30/ 14 Coat buttons/6	1	10	6
1 old watch all to pieces 6/ 1 box of Hair springs 1/6	0	7	6
3 doz watch Crystals 6/ 2 dial plates 4/	0	10	0
3 Main Springs 4/ 6 a number of old do/4ᵈ	0	4	10
a bunch of Pinion & Brass wire 3/6	0	3	6
1 large Screw plate & Tap 2/	0	2	0
1 Garnet Ring 6/ 2 Snuf boxes/6	0	6	6
31 files old & new, Handls & all 8/6	0	8	6
5 Burnishers 6/ 1 Bottle Cro[illeg.] 6ᵈ 1 do oyl/6	0	7	0
4 large Hammers 12/ 2 Small do 3/	0	15	0
2 Tea Spoon Stamps 5/ 1 ingot or skillet 6/	0	11	0
1 ax 3/ 2 pʳ Tongs 4/ 1 Blowpipe 1/	0	8	0
1 pʳ watch Pliars/9 1 pr Cutting do/4ᵈ	0	1	1
1 pʳ Bullit Dividers 1/6 4 Brushes 1/8	0	3	2
9 Gravers Scrapers & Saw 6/	0	6	0
1 paper Containing many Small watch tools	0	6	9
1 drawer full of Buckel & other Tools	[torn]		
1 do Nº 2 full of Buff Sticks & other things	0	3	0
Old Silver, Buttons Tea spoon & wire 6/	0	6	0
Old Gold 1/3 Cash /4ᵈ	0	1	7

The inventory was compiled by Miles Beach and George Smith and amounted to £36.16.2.[15]

Yeomans may have used one of the "2 Tea Spoon Stamps" listed in his inventory to produce silver when he was not employed as a clockmaker. Examples of his work bear the mark YEOMANS in a rectangle (A). Another mark, E Y in a rectangle (B), may possibly be his. JJF

SURVIVING OBJECTS

	Mark	Inscription	Patron	Date	Reference	Owner
Tablespoon (mate below)	A†	MW		ca. 1765	DAPC 69.4140	WM
Tablespoon (mate above)	A*	MW		ca. 1765	YUAG files	
Teaspoon	B*	C/IR		ca. 1775	DAPC 75.2347	HD
Teaspoon	B†	none		ca. 1775		YUAG

1. Stonington VR, 293; Wheeler 1875, 227.
2. Stonington VR, 293; Wheeler 1875, 214; HaCPR box 165, no. 56, notes guardianship in 1771 of Elijah Yeomans, minor, son of Amos Yeomans, late of Stonington; Norwich VR 2:135.
3. Stonington VR, 293; Wheeler 1875, 215.
4. Norwich VR 2:357; Joseph and Mary Downer's birth dates were calculated from their ages at death.
5. Ward/Hosley 1985, 355–56, cat. 236, wherein Chris H. Bailey suggests that "like Jacob Sargeant, a Mansfield native, he [Yeomans] may have been trained by John Avery (1732–1794) or one of the other Norwich-area clockmakers."
6. HaCPR box 165, no. 56.
7. Judd 1976, 380.
8. As cited in Zea/Cheney 1992, 30.
9. Dimock 1898, 382, 420.
10. *Collections of the Connecticut Historical Society* 8:193.
11. HCD 18:131–32. The deed recording Yeomans's initial purchase is missing; Flynt/Fales 1968, 180, 249.
12. Andrews 1965, 128.
13. Clocks made in Petersham by Yeomans are cited by Chris H. Bailey in Ward/Hosley 1985, 356. For mention of Yeomans and Canfield, see Flynt/Fales 1968, 176. See also Palmer 1950, 315. See the Town Records of Petersham 1757–93, wherein it was "Also voted to sink Elijah Yeoman's tax of 2.23.3 in Spooner's bill, 5 March 1786" (p. 344), and it was "voted to sink Elijah Yeoman's tax in all the rate bills . . . 11.4.8" in 1788 (p. 394). This record implies that the town cut Yeomans's taxes in lieu of services. Chris H. Bailey, letter to author, 17 February 1990.
14. Flynt/Fales 1968, 234. Curtis 1913, 115, claimed that Yeomans advertised in Hartford in 1794, but the advertisement has not been found.
15. Hartford, Connecticut, County Probate District 1794, docket 6308, CSL. After debts, including one for £12.4.2 to Samuel Canfield, only £7.8.4 remained. No mention of his wife, Lydia, appeared in the probate records.

Appendixes

Craftsmen in Allied Trades: Clockmakers, Watchmakers, and Engravers

THIS APPENDIX contains brief biographies of craftsmen with skills similar to those of silversmiths and jewelers. Clockmakers and watchmakers who also made silver are included in the main dictionary, but this appendix records those clockmakers and watchmakers for whom no evidence has been found that they identified themselves as silversmiths or made any silver. Similarly, engravers who were silversmiths are recorded in the main dictionary, whereas craftsmen who specialized in engraving, or artists who occasionally turned their hands to engraving, are recorded here. Some silversmiths also produced pewter (William Northey), brass (Jeffrey Lang), and swords (Jeremiah Snow III); however, biographies of pewterers, braziers, gunsmiths, or instrument makers have not been included here.

James Allen
w. ca. 1684

On 29 September 1684 Arthur Mason posted a surety bond to the town of Boston for James Allen, a clockmaker, and his family.[1] Where this clockmaker came from and how long he remained in Boston have yet to be established. PEK

1. RC 10:76.

Joseph Allen
w. ca. 1691–1728

On 27 May 1691 Samuel Sewall noted the following in his account book:

> To Joseph Allen in full 6s
> To begin ye first of May ano
> ther year. ps of $\frac{8}{8}$ was for
> cleansing ye clock & making
> it work.
>
> 0-6-0[1]

C. K. Bolton stated that Allen was recommended to Increase Mather by Nathaniel Mather as a limner, engraver, and watchmaker and that he probably came from Dublin, Ireland.[2] When his wife, Mary, presented his inventory following his death in 1728, he was identified as an ironmonger.[3] PEK

1. Samuel Sewall Account Book, n.p., MHS.
2. Bolton 1900–39, 1:17.
3. SCPR 27:256–57.

James Asby
b. 1739

James Asby was born in 1739 in Penrith, Cumberland, England, and came to America during the French and Indian War. He is said to have established himself as a watchmaker in Boston in 1769, and his advertisements appeared in Boston newspapers in 1771, 1772, and 1773. The one in the *Boston News-Letter* for 16 May 1771 reads,

ASBY,
WATCH MAKER & FINISHER from LONDON,
Opposite Mess. *Cox* & *Berry's* Store in King-Street,
BOSTON,
Having Imported in the last Ships from London,
a large Quantity of Clocks, with curious Paintings and Motions in the Arches. Likewise a compleat
Assortment of Gold, Silver, Pinchbeck and Metal
Watches, of different Prices; particularly one Gold
Watch, calculated to keep Longitude at Sea, it having
every advantageous Improvement from Watches of a
common Construction, not only having a Steel Horizontal Wheel and a ruby Cyllender, tho' being very advantageous against Friction, the main Spring also Keeps
the same elastic Force while the Watch is winding up,
which is a particular Improvement that no common
Watch has, and therefore must lose Time when winding up; it has an Expansion Slide, which must be allowed by all Judges of Mechanism, is the greatest Improvement ever made on Watch Work, which Use is to
make the Watch keep regular Time in both extreme
Heat and Cold, which occasioned the great Mr. Harrison a long Study before compleated. Likewise a compleat Assortment of Watch Chains, Sword Swivels, Seals, &c.
The Subscriber cleans and repairs repeating, horizontal and plain Watches, at the most reasonable Rates.
JAMES ASBY.
N. B. The above Articles to be Sold at the lowest
Prices for Cash only.[1]

The Massachusetts tax list of 1771 confirms that Asby maintained a large stock of merchandise with a value of £60; in addition he had a poll of one, a house with shop adjoining, and £13.6.8 annual value of real estate.[2] At the outbreak of the Revolution, he served with the British forces in Boston and went to Halifax, Nova Scotia, when the British troops evacuated. After serving in the British army in New York in 1777, he returned to England.[3] PEK

1. Dow 1927, 132–33.
2. Pruitt 1978, 20–21.
3. Jones 1930, 9–10; Palmer 1950, 138; Bailey 1975, 46.

Lawrence Ash
w. ca. 1766

On 22 October 1766 Gawen Brown (q.v. Appendix A) reported to the selectmen of Boston that he had in his house as a workman Lawrence Ash from Philadel-phia.[1] This is probably the same individual who advertised in the *Pennsylvania Gazette* of 25 March 1762 as "Clock & Watchmaker, (Late from Mr. Edward Duffields) Having set up his Business in Front-street, six Doors above Market-street, would be greatly obliged to all Gentlemen and Ladies for their Custom, and Recommendation; as it will be his chief Care to finish their Work with the utmost Dispatch. Engraving Likewise performed in all its Branches, in the neatest Manner, by John Sleeper."[2] How long Ash remained in Boston after emigrating from Philadelphia has not been established. PEK

1. RC 20:234.
2. Prime 1969, 227.

James Atkinson
w. ca. 1744–56

The Boston town records report that on 2 January 1744/45, "James Atkinson Watchmaker from London Appeared & desired to be Admitted an Inhabitant & to open a Shop in this Town, which is here by granted, he having brought with him upwards of Five Hundred Pounds Sterling & being a Gentleman of Good Character."[1] He advertised in the Boston newspapers in 1745 and 1748. The earlier advertisement reads,

James Atkinson,
Watch-Maker, in Cornhill, near the Market
in *Boston*, from the North-Side of *Royal Exchange*
in London.
Makes and sells all Sorts of Watches and Clocks made
in a compleat Manner of his own Name warranted,
a variety of both he has now by him: Also repairs all
sorts of Watches in a careful and expeditious Manner;
finishes the Dial Plate, &c. and fits them up in all Respects
compleat and as reasonable as in *London*; sells Ladies
Chains for Watches, and all sorts of Mens Chains, Seals,
Gold and Silver and plain Watch Strings, Ear-Rings, Dia
mond Rings, &c. N. B. Buys Second Hand Plate, and all
sorts of Gold and Silver.
  Has likewise sundry Goods to dispose of imported in the
last Ships from London, *viz.* Fine Beveret Hats, compleat
Setts of Merchant Accompt Books: All sorts of Silver and
plain Ribbon, rich silver Girdles, Bugle Hat-
bands, silk Gloves, silk Laces, silk Garters, the best French
necklaces, letter Gartering, Ferret Laces, stay Galloon,
and scarlet short cloth Cloaks, Hoops, Stays, coarse & fine
Thread Wire, Buttons, fine Horn and twist Horn, Pins and
Needles, Womens and Mens shoe Buckles, sleeve Buttons,
Penknives, Snuff-boxes &c.[2]

Between 1748 and 1752 Atkinson was involved in a number of suits in the Suffolk County Court of Common Pleas. He sued Andrew Hall (1748) and William Murray (1752); he was sued by the jeweler George Foster (q.v.) (1750) and by Simon Rhodes, William Coffin, Benjamin Faneuil, and Thomas Goldthwait (all in 1752).[3] The increased number of suits against him in 1752 may indicate that he was experiencing financial difficulties—difficulties that may have encouraged him to relocate. By August 1753 he had moved to Halifax, Nova Scotia, where he advertised in the *Royal Gazette* that he was open for business: "Watchmaker, from London, opposite the Governor's House, near the Secretary's office, repairs, and cleans all sorts of watches, sells all sorts of material for watches, viz. mainsprings, glasses, pendants, keys, seals, chains, . . . enamel dial plates, etc. buys old silver, gold, gold lace, etc."[4] He died there in 1756, and his estate was administered by Philip Freeman of Boston. His inventory included watchmakers' tools valued at £13.18.[5] PEK

1. Palmer 1950, 139–40; RC 17:92; Bailey 1975, 46.
2. *Boston Gazette*, 8 January 1745; Dow 1927, 133.
3. SCCR, Court of Common Pleas Record Book 1748–49, 61; 1749–51, 120; 1751–52, 118, 213, 249, 274, 306, 314.
4. Mackay 1973, 38.
5. SCPR 51:587–88, 607–08.

John Avery
w. ca. 1726

John Avery has been identified as a clockmaker in Boston about 1726 and is said to have made the clock in the Old North Church.[1] A John Avery, possibly the clockmaker, married Mary Deming in Boston on 13 June 1734.[2] Children were born to John and Mary Avery in Boston in the next decade: Mary (1735); Ruth (1737); John (1739); Hannah (1742); and Samuel (1746).[3] John Avery was elected clerk of the market in 1736/37 and constable in 1737 but refused to serve in either office.[4] PEK

1. Palmer 1950, 140; Distin/Bishop 1976, 285.
2. RC 28:181.
3. RC 24:220, 231, 235, 247, 259.
4. Seybolt 1939, 205, 209.

Richard Avery
w. ca. 1726–40

The Suffolk County Court of Common Pleas records contain references to Richard Avery, a watchmaker or clockmaker, who appeared as a defendant in cases between 1726 and 1728.[1] Avery also appeared as a plaintiff in the court sessions of April 1736, April 1737, and January 1739/40, and again as a defendant in 1739.[2] PEK

1. SCCR, Court of Common Pleas Record Book 1726, 7, 62, 345; 1727–28, 203, 468, 486; 1728, 71, 344, 395.
2. SCCR, Court of Common Pleas Record Book 1735–36, 291; 1736–37, 412; 1739, 8, 140.

Thomas Badley
w. ca. 1712–19/20

Joseph Essex's (q.v. Appendix A) advertisement in the *Boston News-Letter* of 3–10 November 1712 indicates that he and Thomas Badley performed clock and watchmakers' work in Essex's shop.[1] Badley was probably a recent immigrant, for no record of his birth exists in Boston. In 1713 he married Abigail Bill (b. 1691), sister of Mary Bill, wife of Henry Hurst (q.v.).[2] Abigail Bill was also the cousin of Abigail Cheever, the wife of John Burt (q.v.). Joseph Essex married another Bill sister, Hannah. Badley, along with Essex, was the plaintiff in a suit against the clockmaker John Brand (q.v. Appendix A) and also appears in the court records as a defendant.[3] Badley's estate administration, wherein he was identified as a watchmaker, was granted to his wife, Abigail, on 14 March 1719/20. His estate was declared insolvent in April 1720. Nathaniel Morse (q.v.) was appointed by the probate court as one of the commissioners to oversee payments to Badley's creditors.[4] When the jeweler Daniel Légaré (q.v.) petitioned for release from prison where he was being held for debt, the list of his debtors, dated 27 March 1723, included "Boddily late of Boston Watchmaker Run Away."[5] Since Thomas Badley had then been dead for three years, the reference may have been to a son who followed the same trade. PEK

1. Dow 1927, 140–41.
2. RC 28:49. The marriage record lists Badley's name as John.

3. SCCR, Court of Common Pleas Record Book 1710–13, 311, 325.
4. SCPR 21:646–47, 655, 710, 782–83; 22:196–98; Dow 1927, 133.
5. SCCR, file 16553.

Benjamin Bagnall, Jr.
1714/15–73+

Benjamin Bagnall, Jr., the eldest son of Benjamin Bagnall, Sr. (q.v. Appendix A), was born in Boston on 17 March 1714/15.[1] He is believed to have trained with his father and would have finished his apprenticeship about 1736. In 1737 the *New-England Weekly Journal* carried an announcement about his marriage.[2] A transaction recorded by Benjamin Greene (q.v.) in his ledger between 1738/39 and 1740 describes Benjamin Bagnall, Jr., as a watchmaker who paid for the goods received "By Cleaning a Clock & Watches."[3] Bagnall also was identified as a watchmaker when he was sued in 1745 by John Adams of York, Maine, in a case that involved a silver watch that Adams claimed Bagnall had seized illegally.[4] The Benjamin Bagnall who was a defendant in many suits in the Suffolk County Court of Common Pleas in the 1740s may have been the younger Bagnall.[5] The Massachusetts tax list of 1771 describes him as living with his father, and his date of death is unknown.[6] His brother, Samuel (q.v. Appendix A), was also a clockmaker. PEK

1. RC 24:110.
2. Heckscher 1985, 290.
3. Benjamin Greene Ledger, 1734–56, 18, MHS.
4. YCCR, box 100, file 10, Maine State Archives.
5. SCCR, Court of Common Pleas Record Book 1743–44, 334; 1744–46, 98, 130, 137, 153, 158–60, 202, 205–06, 239, 243, 247, 249; 1744–46, 256, 286, 302, 326, 355, 359, 362–63; 1746–48, 9, 27, 87, 91, 95, 112, 125, 163–64; 1749–51, 176.
6. Pruitt 1978, 30–31.

Benjamin Bagnall, Sr.
ca. 1689–1773

According to his obituary, published on 11 July 1773, Benjamin Bagnall was a Quaker and a native of England, where he probably trained as a watchmaker and clockmaker.[1] The earliest evidence of his being in Boston is his marriage to Elizabeth Shove of Charlestown, Massachusetts, in 1713.[2] Seven children were born to the couple between 1715 and 1728: Benjamin (1714/15) (q.v. Appendix A), Elizabeth (1716), Samuel (1718) (q.v. Appendix A), Martha (1720), Sarah (1723), John (1726), and Thomas (1728).[3]

Bagnall had business dealings with a number of craftsmen in the clockmaking and silversmith's trade. His name is on a bill of 1715 between the Boston goldsmith Thomas Mullins (q.v.) and a Mr. Stoddard.[4] In 1719 he was a creditor of the estate of the clockmaker Joseph Essex (q.v. Appendix A). An account survives recording his transactions with the Boston goldsmith Thomas Edwards (q.v.) between 1725 and 1739.[5] He also employed the immigrant watch finisher Odrian Dupee (q.v. Appendix A) beginning in 1739.

Bagnall's name appears frequently in Boston records. In 1723 he was excused from serving as constable, and in 1724 he paid a fine rather than serve.[6] In 1723 the selectmen gave him permission to install a drain from his house to the common sewer in Union Street.[7] Bagnall appeared once as a defendant and many times as a plaintiff in the Suffolk County Court of Common Pleas.[8] The Massachusetts tax list of 1771 includes Bagnall with a poll of one, £20 annual value of real estate, and merchandise worth £520. Benjamin, Jr., lived with his father.[9] Following his death in 1773, Bagnall's estate was declared insolvent.[10]

The earliest surviving Boston tall case clocks are those made by Bagnall, including an example at the Metropolitan Museum of Art.[11] His skill as a clockmaker was reflected in the Boston selectmen's commission for a town clock in 1717. Bagnall completed the work in a year and submitted his bill.[12] In 1735 the selectmen agreed to pay him £10 for one year to take care of this clock "at the old meeting house."[13] PEK

1. *Index of Obituaries, 1704–1800,* 1:13.
2. RC 28:92.
3. RC 24:110, 112, 133, 142, 159, 174, 185.
4. Thomas Mullins to Mr. Stoddard, bill, 7 October 1715, David S. Greenough Papers, MHS.
5. Thomas Edwards Account, Brigden Papers, YU.
6. RC 8:181, 186. .
7. RC 13:116.
8. SCCR, Court of Common Pleas Record Book 1710–13, 218, 243; 1715–18, 88; 1722, 23; 1731, 182; 1733, 129; 1738, 315; 1741, 313; 1744–46, 330. Because Bagnall's son, Benjamin, was working after about 1736, it is possible that the later cases refer to him.
9. Pruitt 1978, 30–31.
10. Dow 1927, 133; SCPR 73:112–15.
11. Heckscher 1985, 290–91; see also Partridge 1935, 26–31, for a discussion of Bagnall and other tall case clocks by him.
12. RC 13:25, 44.
13. RC 13:271.

Samuel Bagnall
1718–after 1773

Samuel Bagnall, the second son of Benjamin Bagnall, Sr. (q.v. Appendix A), was born in Boston on 16 December 1718.[1] Like his older brother Benjamin, Jr. (q.v. Appendix A), he is thought to have trained with his father and would have finished his apprenticeship about 1739. A tall case clock by him is at the Metropolitan Museum of Art, and a few additional examples of his work are known.[2] He is provided for in his father's will of 1772, probated in 1773, which makes clear that Samuel suffered from mental illness. The will instructs that a roomful of furniture be allotted to Samuel and that Benjamin's dwelling house, lands, and residue of personal estate be sold and the income invested to provide for Samuel's support "during the term of his Natural Life or until his Reason be Restored." No record of his death has been found.[3] PEK

1. RC 24:133.
2. Heckscher 1985, 291–92.
3. SCPR 73:112–15.

John Bailey, Jr.
1751–1823

John Bailey, Jr., the son of John Bailey, Sr. (q.v. Appendix A), and Ruth Randall, was born in Hanover, Massachusetts, on 6 May 1751.[1] He probably trained with his father, finishing his apprenticeship about 1772. He is said to have worked first in Hanover—a dwarf tall case clock and a shelf clock made by him in Hanover are known—and then in Lynn, Massachusetts.[2] Probate papers do not survive for him in Essex County. PEK

1. *Hanover VR,* 24.
2. Bailey 1975, 48; Distin/Bishop 1976, fig. 153; Zea/Cheney 1992, 102, 166, fig. 4–10.

John Bailey, Sr.
1730–1810

John Bailey, Sr., the son of John and Elizabeth Bailey, was born in Hanover, Massachusetts, on 30 October 1730.[1] He married Ruth Randall of that town in 1750.[2] Bailey made clocks with wooden works as well as clocks with brass movements.[3] He served in the revolutionary war as a colonel and died in Hanover at the age of eighty in 1810.[4] His sons John, Jr. (q.v. Appendix A), Calvin (1761–1835), and Lebbeus (1763–1827) were also clockmakers. PEK

1. *Hanover VR*, 7.
2. *Hanover VR*, 116.
3. Bailey 1975, 48–52, fig. 46; Zea/Cheney 1992, 22–23, 162–63, 169, figs. 1–15, 1–16, 1–17.
4. *Index of Obituaries, 1784–1840*, 1:180; *Hanover VR*, 201.

Daniel Balch, Sr.
1734/35–90

Daniel Balch, Sr., probably began his clockmaking and watchmaking career about 1755, having been born to the Reverend William Balch and Rebecca Stone of Bradford, Massachusetts, on March 14, 1734/35.[1] Balch probably moved from Bradford to Newburyport, Massachusetts, soon after finishing his apprenticeship; he married Hannah Clement of Newburyport in 1756.[2] He died in Newburyport in November 1790 at age fifty-six and was identified as a watchmaker and clockmaker when his estate was presented for probate in 1791.[3] Both shelf clocks and tall clocks by him are known.[4] PEK

1. *Bradford VR*, 18, 181.
2. *Newbury VR* 2:28.
3. *Newburyport VR* 2:545; *Essex County Probate Index* 1:49.
4. Distin/Bishop 1976, 24, fig. 30a; 92, fig. 187; Zea/Cheney 1992, 17–19, 159, 169, figs. 1–8, 1–9, 1–10.

Colborn Barrell
1735–88+

The son of John Barrell and Ruth Green, Colborn Barrell was born in Boston on 6 November 1735. In the *Boston News-Letter* of 28 May 1772, Colborn Barrell offered for sale "a fine Eight Day Spring Clock with Alarum, good Silver Watches with Chains and Seals.—A fine Watch for a Physician, with Second Hand."[1] Because these wares were included in a list of other merchandise, Barrell was probably a general merchant who sometimes sold watch and clockmakers' wares, rather than a specialized craftsman. The Massachusetts tax list of 1771 shows that he had two polls and extensive holdings, including a house with shop adjoining, a warehouse, £33.6.8 annual worth of real estate, £1,150 in merchandise, £1,150 in commissions, and £3,630 money lent at interest.[2] Barrell fled Boston just prior to the Revolution and declared himself bankrupt after the hostilities.[3] PEK

1. Dow 1927, 133.
2. Pruitt 1978, 38–39.
3. Jones 1930, 22–23.

James Batteson
(Batterson)
w. ca. 1707–15

The minutes of a meeting of the Boston selectmen on 29 September 1707 record the following: "James Batteson, Clockmaker being present Says he came from Pensilvania into this Town Ab[t] a moneth Since, & desires to dwell here, the Select men do now warn him to depart out of Town or to finde Suretyes to Save the Town from Charge by the Last monday in Octob[r] next."[1] By 9 December 1707 Batteson had been able to find John Smith and Thomas Thornton to be surety for him.[2] In the meantime he advertised in the *Boston News-Letter* of 6–13 October 1707, spelling his name Batterson, the way his name has been recorded in the secondary literature:[3]

This is to give Notice to all Gentlemen and others, that
there is lately arrived in Boston from London, by the
way of Pennsilvania, a Clock Maker: If any person or persons
hath any occasion for New Clocks, or to have Old Ones turn'd
into Pendelums; or any other thing either in making or mending: Let them repair to the Sign of the Clock Dial of the South
side of the Town-House in Boston, where they may have them
done at reasonable Rates. Per James Batterson.[4]

The marriage of James Batteson to Mary Coverly on 19 December 1707 is
also recorded in Boston.[5] His name was spelled "Batterson" when he was
identified as a defendant in the Suffolk County Court of Common Pleas
records in 1714 and 1715.[6] No other references exist in Boston records. Chris
Bailey says he later worked in New York City and Charleston, South Carolina.[7] PEK

1. RC 11:64.
2. RC 11:2.
3. Bailey 1975, 45; Palmer 1950, 146.
4. Dow 1927, 134.
5. RC 28:8.
6. SCCR, Court of Common Pleas Record Book 1714–15, 123, 295.
7. Bailey 1975, 45.

James Bichaut
w. ca. 1729

In the *Boston Gazette* of 21–28 July 1729, James Bichaut advertised, "lately
Arrived from London, Makes and Mends all sorts of Clocks and Watches."[1]
No further evidence of Bichaut exists in Boston records. PEK

1. Dow 1927, 134.

David Blaisdell, Jr.
1735/36–94

David Blaisdell, Jr., the son of David Blaisdell, Sr. (q.v. Appendix A), and
Abigail Colby, was born in Amesbury, Massachusetts, on 21 February 1735/36.[1]
He is said to have been trained by his father, who died just before his son
reached his majority. David, Jr., may have trained his brother, Nicholas (q.v.
Appendix A). According to Brooks Palmer, the younger David Blaisdell made
all the metalwork for the *Alliance* and other boats built at Amesbury for
the American navy.[2] In his estate papers, filed in 1794, he is identified as a
blacksmith.[3] PEK

1. *Amesbury VR*, 35; Zea/Cheney 1992, 16.
2. Palmer 1950, 151.
3. *Essex County Probate Index* 1:83.

David Blaisdell, Sr.
1711/12–56

David Blaisdell, Sr., was born in Amesbury, Massachusetts, on 5 February 1711/
12 to John and Hannah Blaisdell. He would have finished his training about
1733, the year his marriage intentions to Abigail Colby were published in
Amesbury.[1] Chris Bailey observes that since Blaisdell produced thirty-hour
posted-design clock movements similar to those of Richard Manning (q.v.
Appendix A), the two men, who were about the same age, may have had
similar training. One Blaisdell clock is dated 1735, and others are rather crudely
engraved.[2] Blaisdell was killed in 1756 near Lake George while serving in the
French and Indian War.[3] When his probate was filed in 1757 he was identified

as a gentleman.[4] His sons Isaac, Nicholas, and David, Jr., and his brother Jonathan (qq.v. Appendix A) were also clockmakers. PEK

1. *Amesbury VR*, 39, 288.
2. Bailey 1975, 47; Distin/Bishop 1976, 13, figs. 15, 15a.
3. Zea/Cheney 1992, 16.
4. *Essex County Probate Index* 1:83.

Isaac Blaisdell
1738–91

Isaac Blaisdell, the son of David Blaisdell, Sr. (q.v. Appendix A), and Abigail Colby, was born in Amesbury, Massachusetts, on 27 March 1738.[1] He may have begun his training with his father, but because his father died when he was eighteen, he finished his apprenticeship with another craftsman about 1759. He is said to have been living in Chester, New Hampshire, by 1762. Tall clocks by him are at Old Sturbridge Village and the New Hampshire Historical Society.[2] PEK

1. *Amesbury VR*, 37.
2. Parsons 1976, 64–65; Zea/Cheney 1992, 16–17, 166, figs. 1–6, 1–7.

Jonathan Blaisdell
1709–82

The older brother of David Blaisdell, Sr. (q.v. Appendix A), Jonathan Blaisdell was born in Amesbury, Massachusetts, on 15 August 1709.[1] At some point he migrated to East Kingston, New Hampshire, where he died. Two tall case clocks by him are known.[2] PEK

1. *Amesbury VR*, 39; Zea/Cheney 1992, 16.
2. Parsons 1976, 18.

Nicholas Blaisdell
1743–ca. 1800

Nicholas Blaisdell was born in Amesbury, Massachusetts, on 27 August 1743, the son of David Blaisdell, Sr. (q.v. Appendix A), and Abigail Colby.[1] Because his father died when Nicholas was thirteen years old, he could not have been trained by him but may have been trained by his older brother David, Jr. (q.v. Appendix A). Nicholas is said to have moved on to Newmarket, New Hampshire, by 1774 and settled in Portland, Maine, after the Revolution. A clock by him is at the New Hampshire Historical Society.[2] PEK

1. *Amesbury VR*, 38.
2. Palmer 1950, 152; Parsons 1976, 299; Bailey 1975, 47; Zea/Cheney 1992, 16.

John Brand
w. ca. 1711/12–15

John Brand, a watchmaker from London, was in Boston by 28 February 1711/12, when the selectmen of Boston admitted him as an inhabitant, Oliver Noyes and Samuel Belknap serving as security for him.[1] A month earlier Brand had placed an advertisement in the *Boston News-Letter* of 21–28 January 1711/12: "John Brand, Watch-Maker, from London, Maketh and Mendeth all Sorts of Clocks and Watches, at very easie Rates, and is to be found at the Sign of the Spring Clock & Watches, near the Draw-Bridge in Anne-Street, Boston."[2] On 27 October 1712 John Brand married Mercy Ovington in Boston.[3] In August 1713 Brand advertised "that his German Servant Man, John Copler [q.v. Appendix A], aged about 26 years, had run away." Brand sued the clockmaker Joseph Essex (q.v. Appendix A) in the Suffolk County Court of Common Pleas. The court records suggest, however, that Brand probably had difficulty establishing his business in Boston because he in turn was sued by a number of individuals including Essex and the clockmaker Thomas Badley (q.v. Appendix A).[4] In May 1714 Brand appears in Boston town records as attorney to George Cabbot.[5] An advertisement in October 1714 indicates that he sold imported watches.[6] Shortly after that advertisement appeared Brand announced that he "designs for a Time to go for England and therefore desires all Persons that have any concerns or dealings with him, forthwith without delay to come and make up Accounts with him."[7] He settled accounts with the Boston stationer Daniel Henchman in January 1714/15, in part by mending a watch for him.[8] No evidence exists that Brand ever returned to Boston. PEK

1. RC 11:139.
2. Dow 1927, 134.
3. RC 28:39.
4. SCCR, Court of Common Pleas Record Book 1710–13, 182, 187, 239, 289, 311, 331; 1714–15, 11, 282–83.
5. RC 11:205–06.
6. Dow 1927, 134.
7. *Boston News-Letter*, 25 October–1 November 1714.
8. Daniel Henchman Ledger, 1712–ca. 1735, fol. 40, NEHGS.

Gawen Brown
ca. 1719–1801

Gawen Brown probably emigrated from London to Boston late in 1748, for in the *Boston Evening-Post* of 16 January 1749 he placed the following advertisement:

> This is to give Notice to the Public, that Gawen Brown, Clock and Watchmaker lately from London, keeps his shop at Mr. Johnson's Japanner, in Brattle-Street, Boston, near Mr. Cooper's Meeting House, where he makes and sells all sorts of plain, repeating, and astronomical Clocks, with Cases, plain, black walnut, mahogany, or Japann'd, or without; likewise does all Sorts of Watch Work in best Manner and sells all sorts of Clock Strings, London Lacker, and white Varnish for Clocks, a great Variety of Files for Clock Works, Glasses or Crystalls, Keys, Strings, Pendants for Watches, &c.[1]

Brown must have found it advantageous to share shop space with Thomas Johnston (q.v. Appendix A), a craftsman whose skills as an engraver, painter, and japanner were useful in the clockmaking and watchmaking trade. A newspaper advertisement of June 1752 indicates that by that date Brown had moved his shop to King Street.[2]

Brown quickly settled into establishing a successful life for himself in Boston. On 5 April 1750 he married Mary Flagg.[3] The preceding month, he and his wife-to-be bought a house on Union Street. In deeds for the transaction he is identified as a clockmaker, although he is called a watchmaker when he mortgaged this property in 1755.[4] His name appeared four times during this period in the Court of Common Pleas records. He sued Sarah Venner, a widow, and Joseph Rogers, a tailor, in 1751 and Joseph Carbutt, a chaisemaker, in 1751 and 1752.[5] Following the death of his first wife, he married Elizabeth Byles in 1760, the daughter of the Reverend Mather Byles, and was admitted into the Hollis Street Church the same year. After her death three years later, he married Elizabeth Adams in 1764.[6]

Brown's name appears frequently in Boston records, including land and court records. On 28 March 1761 Rufus Greene (q.v.) paid Brown 9 shillings and 4 pence for cleaning a clock.[7] The silver watch with "Brown, Boston" on the face that the silversmith Nathaniel Hurd (q.v.) bequeathed to the printer Thomas Fleet in 1777 probably was made by Brown.[8] Beginning in 1761 and continuing until the end of the century, Brown conducted numerous real estate transactions.[9] He was also involved in many suits in the Court of Common Pleas beginning during the Revolution and following it. In most of these cases he was the plaintiff, although occasionally he was cited as the defendant.[10]

Boston town records reveal some information about Brown's activities as a clockmaker. In 1758 he informed the selectmen that he had employed John Cross Smith (q.v. Appendix A), a watchmaker from London.[11] In 1766 Brown further informed the selectmen that he had taken into his house as workmen Lawrence Ash (q.v. Appendix A) from Philadelphia and Thomas Jackson (q.v.) from Canada.[12] The following year he was hired by the town to clean the clock at the New Brick Church.[13] In 1768 he built a clock that was installed in the Old South Church in 1769 and that he finally got the selectmen to purchase from him in 1774.[14] Tall case clocks by Brown are also known.[15]

Brown died in Boston in 1801 at the age of eighty-two.[16]   DAF and PEK

1. Bailey 1975, 46.
2. Dow 1927, 134.
3. RC 28:239.
4. SCD 79:172, 771; 86:260.
5. SCCR, Court of Common Pleas Record Book 1751–52, 22, 95, 210.
6. RC 30:36, 380; *Index of Obituaries, 1704–1800*, 1:43.
7. Rufus Greene Account Book, 1748–74, n.p. under date indicated, Karolik-Codman Papers, MHS.
8. SCPR 77:12–13.
9. SCD 95:235; 96:261; 97:16, 21; 110:260; 116:85; 117:69; 121:232, 258; 129:15, 105; 137:148; 145:281; 189:197.
10. SCCR, Court of Common Pleas Record Book 1780–81, 33; 1783, 31–32, 245–50; 1784, 1, 69; 1786, 45, 87–88, 273; 1789, 6, 12; 1797, 9, 76–77.
11. RC 19:83.
12. RC 20:234.
13. RC 20:270.
14. RC 18:71, 76, 119, 158, 162.
15. Bailey 1975, 46; Distin/Bishop 1976, 30, fig. 45; Zea/Cheney 1992, 12–13, 167, figs. 1–1, 1–2.
16. *Index of Obituaries, 1784–1840*, 1:634; SCPR 99:451–53, 464, 608–09.

John Browne
w. ca. 1725

The Suffolk County Court of Common Pleas records identify John Browne as an engraver who was a defendant in a case in 1725. Nothing more is known of him.[1]   PEK

1. SCCR, Court of Common Pleas Record Book 1725, 383.

William Burgis
w. ca. 1722–31

Richard Holman has written the most complete account of William Burgis and concludes that although Burgis was a sometime engraver, a more accurate description of him is an "instigator" of prints. An Englishman, Burgis is said to have come from New York to Boston in 1722, where he advertised as follows:

Whereas there has been an Advertisement lately publish'd, of a Design to print a View of this Town of Boston, taken from Noddles Island. This is to certify, the Undertaker William Burgis, desires all Gentlemen to be speedy in their Subscription, in order to send the Drawing to England this Fall, that he may conform to the Proposal to that end lately published. N. B. Sufficient Security is given to conform to the Conditions of the said Proposals, or to return the Advance Money.[1]

On 1 October 1728 Burgis married Mehitable (Bill) Selby, who had been a sister-in-law of Henry Hurst (q.v.) and who was a cousin of Abigail (Cheever) Burt, the wife of John Burt (q.v.). Mehitable was the widow of the proprietor of Boston's Crown Coffee House. Following the marriage, Burgis probably carried on that business because in 1729 and 1730 the Boston selectmen's records show that Burgis petitioned to conduct business as a taverner.[2] His petition in 1730 was not approved. Holman claims that Burgis deserted Boston and his wife in 1731. The only print on which Burgis's name appears as the engraver is the mezzotint *To the Merchants of Boston this View of the Light House* (1729), although he was the delineator of some topographical views and has been associated with others.[3] Burgis may have trained the engraver Thomas Johnston (q.v. Appendix A) because the map *Boston in New England* that Burgis published in 1728 was engraved for him by Johnston just at the time that Johnston would have been finishing his apprenticeship.[4] No evidence exists that Burgis engraved silver. PEK

1. Dow 1927, 15–16.
2. RC 13:188–89, 198.
3. Holman 1973, 57–81.
4. For a discussion and illustration of this map, see Reps 1973, 14–15, fig. 6.

William Claggett, Jr.
ca. 1695–1749

William Claggett, Jr., is said to have been an immigrant from Wales who was in Boston as early as 1708; however, the earliest evidence of his being in the town is the record of his marriage to Mary Armstrong on 21 October 1714.[1] A son was born to the couple the following June.[2] William Claggett's epitaph states that he died on 18 October 1749 at age fifty-four, and hence it can be deduced that he was born about 1695. If Claggett was in Boston by 1708 he would have been young enough to train there. Claggett remained in Boston for a brief time after his marriage because he advertised in the *Boston News-Letter* of 26 December to 2 January 1715/16, "To be Sold a new Fashion'd Monethly Clock & Case lately arrived from London, also a new Fashion'd Camblet Bed lin'd with Satten, to be seen at Mr. William Clagget, jun. Clock-Maker, near the Town-House." He was living in Newport, Rhode Island, by the end of 1716. He had a successful career there as a clockmaker, engraver, and merchant.[3] PEK

1. Champlin 1974, 157; RC 28:50.
2. RC 24:104.
3. Zea/Cheney 1992, 13–14.

Preserved Clapp
b. 1731

The clockmaker Preserved Clapp, the son of Preserved and Sarah (West) Clapp, was born in Amherst, Massachusetts, on 6 May 1731.[1] He may be the Preserved Clapp who married Eunice Atherton in Bolton, Massachusetts, on 20 May 1756, which suggests that he was trained in the Bolton area.[2] He presumably settled in Amherst because the Massachusetts tax list of 1771 includes a Preserved Clapp with a poll of one, a horse, cattle, and pasture.[3] Brooks Palmer recorded that Clapp served in the French and Indian War and invented a gun carriage used in the American Revolution.[4] Thomas Johnston (q.v. Appendix A) engraved a copperplate for printing clock dials for Preserved Clapp that is owned by the Peabody Essex Museum.[5] PEK

1. "Amherst Genealogical Record Book," 1:126, Corbin Ms. Coll., microfilm, reel 1, NEHGS.
2. *Bolton VR*, 119.
3. Pruitt 1978, 384–85.
4. Palmer 1950, 169.
5. Palmer 1950, fig. 26; Hitchings 1973, 115, fig. 61.

Thomas Clark
w. ca. 1764

"Thos Clarke Watchmaker" is reported to have arrived in Boston on 15 October 1764 aboard the *Deep Bay* from London.[1] A few weeks later he advertised his wares and services in the *Boston Gazette*:

Thomas Clark,
Clock and Watch-Maker from LONDON,
Takes this Method to inform all Gentlemen and Ladies
in Town and Country, that he has to sell at his Shop
the South Side of the Court-House;
A Fine Assortment of the neatest made CLOCKS and WATCHES, of all
Prices; he will also warrant the same, as they are of
his own Make, and will be sold cheaper than any ever
imported in the Country; the Clocks he will sell with
or without the Case, as it shall suit the Purchaser. He
also mends and cleans either in the best Manner.
   ENGLISH GOODS sold at the same Place by
wholesale or Retail, at the lowest Prizes.[2]

A number of silver scholars have confused this watchmaker with another Thomas Clark (q.v.), the Marblehead-born silversmith who worked in Boston from the late 1740s until his death in 1781.[3] PEK

1. RC 29:261.
2. Issue of 5 November 1764.
3. Ensko 1948, 37; Flynt/Fales 1968, 184; Belden 1980, 111.

John Clarke
w. ca. 1779

The following advertisement appeared in the *Independent Chronicle* for 2 September 1779: "Engraving performed in the neatest manner on Gold, Silver, Copper, Steel, Syphors, Coats of Arms, etc. John Clarke at the Factory House, Boston." Clarke was among the commonest names in New England at that time, hence the identity of this individual has been impossible to establish. No other evidence of an engraver named John Clarke has been found in Boston records. PEK

Isaac Clements
(Clemens)
w. ca. 1774–1806 +

According to E. Alfred Jones's research on loyalist claims following the American Revolution, Isaac Clements called himself a silversmith and an engraver. The literature is not consistent on Clements's birthplace: Jones claimed Boston, while John E. Langdon stated London. No birth record for Isaac Clements has been found in Massachusetts vital records. The two scholars agreed that

Clements was in Boston by 1774, Langdon claiming that he rented part of the shop of Paul Revere, Jr. (q.v.). Following the British troops' evacuation of Boston, Clements settled in New York, where he advertised in the *New-York Gazette and Weekly Mercury* on 21 October 1776 that he had "lately arrived with His Majesty's Fleet from Boston in New-England" and that "he now carries on the engraving business at his Shop near the French Church, in King street New-York." Jones states that during his stay in America Clements was on constant military duty. He apparently served for about four years without pay or rations and counterfeited colonial paper money to inflate the currency. He moved to Quebec about 1780 and in 1786 was in Shelburne, Nova Scotia, where the last record concerning him is dated 1806.[1] PEK

1. Jones 1930, 93; Langdon 1970, 44–46.

Elijah Collins
1706–ca. 1785

Elijah Collins, a watchmaker who worked in Boston from 1727 to about 1785, may be the Elijah Collins born to Samuel and Rebecca Collins of Lynn, Massachusetts, in 1706.[1] Collins advertised in the *Boston Gazette* of 21–28 August 1727 as a "Watchmaker, over against the dwelling House of the late Samuel Lynde, Esq."[2] He was identified as a watchmaker when he bought land in Boston in 1730, and he conducted a number of real estate transactions in Boston between that time and 1772.[3] He witnessed a deed for the jeweler Jonathan Trott (q.v.) in 1767, and with Trott he witnessed a deed for the watchmaker John Rolestone (q.v. Appendix A) in 1768.[4] He may be the "Elisa Collins" included in a list of citizens levied for repair of a pump on town land in Cornhill in 1733.[5]

Collins was identified as a plaintiff with some frequency in the Suffolk County Court of Common Pleas records beginning in 1728.[6] Some of those suits were against silversmiths including Paul Revere, Sr., Thomas Townsend, and Andrew Tyler (qq.v.).[7] Collins was dead by 1785, when the court records describe him as deceased in suits presented on his behalf by John Collins of Newport, Rhode Island.[8] No record of his death has been located. PEK

1. *Lynn VR* 1:115.
2. Dow 1927, 137–38.
3. SCD 45:20; 46:146, 299; 59:51; 120:205–06.
4. SCD 111:239–40; 121:173.
5. RC 13:228–29.
6. SCCR, Court of Common Pleas Record Book 1727–28, 470–71; 1729, 57; 1732, 203; 1733, 337, 516; 1734, 46, 620, 622; 1735, 518–19; 1735–36, 201–03, 432, 435–36; 1736–37, 206, 268–69, 272–74, 278, 281, 580–89, 591–94, 596–98, 602, 605–06; 1738, 186; 1743–44, 263; 1744–46, 287; 1746–48, 276; 1749–51, 55; 1751–52, 164, 250; 1755–56, 212.
7. SCCR, Court of Common Pleas Record Book 1736, 592 (Paul Revere, Sr.), 589 (Thomas Townsend); 1737, 124 (Andrew Tyler).
8. SCCR, Court of Common Pleas Record Book 1785, 18, 212; 1786, 3, 58–59.

John Copler
w. ca. 1714

In 1713 the watchmaker John Brand (q.v. Appendix A) advertised that his German servant, John Copler, had run away. No further trace of Copler has been found in Boston records, and he probably left the area when he deserted his master.[1] PEK

1. Dow 1927, 134.

John Singleton Copley
1738–1815

John Singleton Copley, colonial America's best portrait painter, probably was born in Boston on 3 July 1738. His parents, Richard Copley and Mary Singleton, immigrated to Boston from Ireland in the mid-1730s and ran a tobacco shop on Boston's Long Wharf. In May 1748, when Copley was almost ten years old, his widowed mother married the engraver Peter Pelham (q.v. Appendix A). The following March, Copley's half-brother Henry Pelham (q.v. Appendix A) was born. Peter Pelham died when Copley was only thirteen years old, but from him Copley presumably learned the art of mezzotint engraving. In 1753 Copley issued his only known print, the mezzotint portrait of the Reverend William Welsteed, reusing the plate from which his stepfather produced the portrait of the Reverend William Cooper. Whether Copley ever engraved silver during his formative years is uncertain. By the mid 1750s he was launched on his career as a portrait painter.[1] PEK

1. Prown 1966, 1:7–10; Rebora/Staiti et al. 1995, 25–30, no. 1.

Richard Cranch
ca. 1726–1811

Brooks Palmer stated that Richard Cranch was a watchmaker from England who worked in Salem, Massachusetts, between 1754 and 1767.[1] Cranch purchased plate from the estate of the Boston silversmith Samuel Edwards (q.v.).[2] Cranch is known to have been in Boston by 1767, when he began to advertise watches and watchmakers' tools for sale from his shop on Hanover Street south of the Mill Bridge.[3] In the advertisement that appeared in the *Boston Evening-Post* on 23 November 1767, Cranch informed customers in Salem, Marblehead, and neighboring towns that they could have their watches transported to him free of charge by Mr. Boardman whose stage went between Salem and Boston three times a week. The Massachusetts tax list of 1771 includes Cranch in Boston with a poll of one, a house and shop adjoining, twenty pounds' annual worth of real estate, and forty-six pounds' annual worth of merchandise.[4] By 1775 he decided to relocate in Braintree, Massachusetts, for he advertised in the *Boston News-Letter* for 13 April,

> RICHARD CRANCH,
> WATCH-MAKER,
> Hereby informs his Customers, That he has re-
> moved from his House near the Mill-Bridge,
> Boston, to a House in Braintree, nearly opposite the
> Rev. Mr. Winslow's Church, a few Rods South of Mr.
> Brackett's Tavern; where he proposes carrying on the
> Watch-Maker's Business as usual, And as he has a
> number of Watches in his Hands, belonging to his
> Customers, he desires such as cannot conveniently call
> for them at his House in Braintree, to leave a Line for
> him at the Shop of Messieurs *Nathaniel* and *Joseph Cranch*,
> nearly opposite the Sign of the Lamb, at the South-
> End of Boston, who will convey the same, and receive
> the Watches for the Owners as soon as they are finished.[5]

Cranch died at Quincy, Massachusetts, on 16 October 1811 aged eighty-five.[6] PEK

1. Palmer 1950, 174.
2. Inventory and accounts of the estate of Samuel Edwards, June, 1762–78, Smith-Carter Papers, MHS.
3. Dow 1927, 138.
4. Pruitt 1978, 24–25.
5. Dow 1927, 138–39.
6. *Index of Obituaries, 1784–1840*, 2:1103.

William Davis
w. ca. 1683

On 30 July 1683, David Edwards, a mariner, became surety to the town of Boston for William Davis, a clockmaker, and his family.[1] Because another William Davis, a mariner, also lived in Boston at the time, references to William Davis in records could be to either individual.[2] PEK

1. RC 10:73.
2. Savage 1860–62, 2:23–24; RC 9:162, 165, 189 record children born to William and Mary and William and Martha.

Francis Dewing
w. Boston
ca. 1716–25

Francis Dewing has long been recognized as the first important copper engraver in America.[1] He arrived in Boston from London on 12 July 1716, and his residency was recorded in the minutes of a Boston selectmen's meeting on 30 July 1716: "Lately arrived from London. Francis Dewing who Engraveth and Printeth Copper Plates, Likewise Coats of Arms and Cyphers on Silver Plate. He Likewise Cuts Neatly in wood and Printeth Callicoes, etc. Lodging at Mrs Hawksworths against the Bunch of Grapes in King Street arrivd in the Jollif Galley capt Aram Commander the beginning of July 1716."[2] In July 1718 Dewing was arrested for allegedly counterfeiting bills of credit. He probably was cleared of the charges because he married Katherine Hart on 8 December 1719.[3] He appeared three times as a defendant in the Suffolk County Court of Common Pleas.[4]

In addition to his copperplate engravings, such as Capt. Cyprian Southack's chart, *Sea Coast of English America and the French New Settlements* (1716), Dewing undoubtedly engraved silver for Boston goldsmiths, though none of his work has been identified. His engraving of John Bonner's *The Town of Boston* (1722) is his last known work done in New England. Dewing probably returned to England shortly after 1725 when he appeared again as a defendant in the Suffolk County Court of Common Pleas.[5] He was working in England as late as 1745, when he engraved *The East Front of the New Organ in Salisbury Cathedral*. PEK

1. *DAB*'s excellent overview of this engraver provides references for the early scholarship on him. See also Fielding 1917; Groce/Wallace 1957; and *Boston Prints and Printmakers*.
2. RC 29:237. This information has incorrectly been stated in the literature as appearing in a Boston newspaper.
3. RC 28:98.
4. SCCR, Court of Common Pleas Record Book 1718, 149, 262; 1720, 31.
5. SCCR, Court of Common Pleas Record Book 1725, 201.

John Doane
1733/34–1801

The clockmaker John Doane was born to John Doane, Esq. (1664–1755), of Boston, and his third wife, Jane (Collier) Baxter, on 17 March 1733/34. John Doane, Esq., was the grandfather of the silversmiths John and Joshua Doane (qq.v.) and had an older son named John, the silversmiths' father, who died in 1723.[1] John Doane, Esq., has been misidentified as a clockmaker.[2] The clockmaker published his intentions to marry Lucy Davenport on 27 March 1754.[3]

In the *New-Hampshire Gazette* on 13 May 1757 John Doane, identified as a clockmaker and watchmaker from Boston, advertised that he was at David Griffeth's shop at the sign of the Goldsmith's Arms in Portsmouth, New Hampshire, where he had gold watches and seals for sale. His sojourn in Portsmouth may have been short because in 1760 he was identified as a clockmaker and watchmaker of Boston when he sold property on Mackeral Lane that he had inherited from his father.[4] His mother and her next husband, Capt. Atherton Haugh (b. 1708), son of Samuel Haugh (q.v.), lived next door.[5] Doane and his wife, Lucy, also signed a deed in 1760.[6] From his father Doane also inherited a farm at Scituate, Massachusetts. Doane may have lived in Scituate part of the time. He is identified as a clockmaker of Scituate in a deed, and a clock movement of his is inscribed "Scituate."[7] He was identified as of Cohasset, Massachusetts, in the obituary for his wife, Lucy, in 1788, and when he married his second wife, Rebecca Clark, on 29 April 1790.[8] Doane appeared as a clockmaker in Boston deeds until 1794.[9] He was identified as a watchmaker "late of said Boston" when his estate administration was filed in 1801.[10] DAF

1. Doane 1902, 34–35, 63–64. Jane (Collier) Baxter was the daughter of Lt. Gershom Collier of Hull and the widow of Paul Baxter.
2. Zea/Cheney 1992, 26, n. 16, citing Sotheby's, 26–27 June 1991, lot 354. No documentary evidence exists to identify this John Doane as a clockmaker.
3. RC 30:10.
4. SCD 95:67; SCPR 50:700–05; Drake 1856, 652.
5. RC 30:20; Doane 1902, 34; Drake 1856, 652.
6. SCD 96:98.
7. SCD 122:16; Sotheby's, 26–27 June 1991, lot 354.
8. RC 30:461; *Index of Obituaries, 1784–1840*, 2:1342.
9. SCD 178:159.
10. SCPR 99:408.

Odrian Dupee
w. ca. 1739

Odrian Dupee is said to have worked as a watch finisher in Philadelphia and then worked in New York before coming to Boston.[1] At a meeting of the Boston selectmen on 11 April 1739, "Odrian Dupee, Appearing, Informs that he came to dwell in this Town in February last, from New York where he had dwelt Two years, That he took Lodging at m.[r] James Packnets, That he is by Trade a Watch Maker and Works at present with m.[r] Bagnall, and designs to embrace the first Opportunity of going to St. Thomas's."[2] The selectmen's minutes of 7 November 1739 record further, "Whereas Odrian Dupee came into this Town in April last from New York, and being before the Select men, he was directed to procure sufficient Bondsmen to Indemnity the Town as the law directs—which he has neglected to do, since which his Wife and her mother, and his Daughter, have been Imported by Capt. Albertus Bosch. Ordered That m.[r] Savell take care that Security be given, before Capt. Bosch departs the Town, in the Sum of Three Hundred Pounds."[3] By 26 May 1740: "Florentia the Wife of Odrian Dupee, Dorothy Butler and Agnes Fettes, lately Imported into this Town from New York by Albertus Bosch in the Sloop Wheel of Fortune—Are admitted Inhabitants, m.[r] Benjamin Bagnall having given Bond to the Town Treasurer in the Sum of Three Hundred Pounds to Indemnify the Town, as the Law directs."[4] Presumably Dupee was working for Benjamin Bagnall, Sr. (q.v. Appendix A), who must have valued Dupee's skills to put up such a large sum of money. Dupee does not turn up in any other Boston records, so the length of his stay in the town is uncertain. PEK

1. Palmer 1950, 184.
2. RC 15:172.
3. RC 15:212.
4. RC 15:240.

Thomas Emmes
ca. 1701

Thomas Emmes was an engraver who produced the first copperplate portrait in the colonies, the portrait of Rev. Increase Mather that is the frontispiece of *The Blessed Hope* published in Boston in 1701. Emmes may have belonged to the Emmes, or Eames, family of Boston stonecutters that included Nathaniel Eames (ca. 1690–1750), father-in-law of the silversmith John Parkman (q.v.). Thus far Thomas's parentage has not been established.[1] PEK

1. Saunders/Miles 1987, 80–81.

Edward Tillit Emmett
ca. 1740–98

Edward Tillit Emmett, clockmaker, advertised in the *Boston Gazette* on 16 July 1764 that he "has just opened Shop upon the South Side of the Town-House, in King Street, in the Mansion House of Gillam Phillips, Esq.; where Clocks and Watches are repaired with Fidelity and Dispatch."[1] The Massachusetts tax list of 1771 includes Emmett in Boston with a poll of one, a house and shop adjoining, and fourteen pounds' annual worth of real estate.[2] In 1774, when Emmett married Elizabeth Mitchell of Sherborn in Nantucket, the marriage record stated that he was the son of John, deceased, and Hannah of Boston.[3] Emmett died on Nantucket in 1798.[4] PEK

1. Dow 1927, 139.
2. Pruitt 1978, 10–11.
3. *Nantucket VR* 3:417.
4. *Nantucket VR* 5:244.

Joseph Essex
w. ca. 1712–19

Joseph Essex announced his arrival in Boston with the following advertisement, which appeared in the *Boston News-Letter* for 3–10 November 1712:

These are to give Notice to all Gentlemen, Merchants and Others, That there is lately arriv'd from Great Britain to this Place, Mr. Joseph Essex, who now keeps Shop in Butler's Buildings in King Street, Boston, and performs all sorts of New Clocks and Watch works, viz. 30 hour Clocks, Week Clocks, Month Clocks, Spring Table Clocks, Chime Clocks, quarter Clocks, quarter Chime Clocks, Church Clocks, Terret Clocks, and new Pocket Watches, new repeating Watches; Likewise doth give any Gentlemen, &c. Tryal before Payment or either Clock or Watches, and after Payment for 12 Months will oblige himself to Change either Clock or Watch, if not liked, or else return his Money again: These Articles to be performed by the abovesaid Joseph Essex *and* Thomas Badley.

On 30 March 1713 Essex married Hannah Bill.[1] Through this marriage he became a brother-in-law of Henry Hurst (q.v.), who was married to Hannah's sister Mary. Thomas Badley (q.v. Appendix A), who is mentioned in the advertisement as sharing Essex's shop, married Abigail Bill in 1713, another sister of Hannah's. Essex's marriage also provided him with a kinship tie to John Burt (q.v.) because Burt's wife, Abigail (Cheever) Burt, was a cousin of Hannah, Mary, and Abigail Bill.

Essex may have had difficulty establishing himself in Boston. He was sued by the clockmaker John Brand (q.v. Appendix A); in turn, Essex, along with Thomas Badley, sued Brand.[2] Essex was sued by the jeweler Daniel Légaré (q.v.) in 1714, and in 1723, Essex "of Boston Watchmaker Dec^d" was listed among Légaré's debtors.[3] Administration of Essex's estate, wherein he is identified as a jackmaker, was granted to his widow on 12 October 1719. The estate was insolvent, and Benjamin Bagnall, Sr. (q.v. Appendix A), was among the creditors.[4] On 27 April 1720 his widow married Fardinando Bowd.[5] PEK

1. RC 28:44.
2. SCCR, Court of Common Pleas Record Book 1710–13, 317; 1714–15, 67.
3. SCCR, Court of Common Pleas Record Book 1714–15, 129.
4. SCPR 21:488–89, 505–06, 664–66.
5. RC 28:86.

Peter Etter, Jr.
ca. 1742–98

Peter Etter, a watchmaker who retailed silver holloware and jewelry, is said to have been born in Braintree, Massachusetts, in 1742, although his birth record has not been found.[1] He was the son of Peter Etter (1715–86+), a Swiss-born weaver, who immigrated to America in 1737 and settled in Braintree in 1752; the Peter Etter who married Elizabeth Vesey in Braintree on 27 August 1755 may have been this man.[2] The younger Etter's master is not known, but Etter probably began practicing his trade in Braintree about 1763.

Etter was a loyalist who went to Halifax, Nova Scotia, with the British army in 1776, where according to John Langdon he enlisted in the Royal Fencible American Regiment and served at Fort Cumberland.[3] He may have been working as a watchmaker in Halifax by 1778, possibly with John Finney from Charlestown, Maryland. He advertised as a watchmaker in the *Nova Scotia Gazette and Weekly Chronicle* on 25 July 1780.[4] In his advertisement in that paper on 3 December 1782 Etter again calls himself a watchmaker and clockmaker, with jewelry, hardware, and glass for sale. In an advertisement of 21 June 1785 he refers to himself as a watchmaker and clockmaker, but his goods had expanded to include a wide assortment of silver holloware and flatware.

Etter worked in Halifax until shortly after 1786, when he moved to Westmoreland, then in Nova Scotia, the hometown of his wife, Leticia (Mary) Patton (ca. 1753–97), the daughter of Mark Patton of Westmoreland, whom he wed that year.[5] Apparently he did not stay in Westmoreland long because a death notice for "Mrs. Mary Etter, age 44," who died in Halifax, appeared in Boston's *Columbian Centinel* on 12 April 1797.[6] Shortly thereafter Etter married a second time, to Sarah Huston Wethered (b. 1763), daughter of Samuel Wethered, adjutant of Fort Cumberland, and Dorothy Eager.[7] Etter drowned in the Bay of Fundy while returning from Boston in May 1798, and Sarah Etter and William Allen, his executors, advertised concerning the administration of his estate in June 1798.[8] His estate inventory contained numerous tools and supplies for the watchmaking business.[9] The inventory also contained three dozen and ten pairs of knee buckles and a "Bundle of Anchors and tongues for Buckles," which suggests that Etter may have been making these jewelry items or at least retailing buckles and supplies for making them. No silver by Peter Etter is known. PEK

1. Mackay 1973, 54–55.
2. *Braintree VR*, 815; Jones 1930, 133–34; Langdon 1970, 49.
3. Langdon 1970, 49.
4. Mackay 1973, 54–55.
5. Trueman 1975, 226–28.
6. *Index of Obituaries, 1784–1840*, 2:1516.
7. Trueman 1975, 226–28.
8. *Nova Scotia Gazette*, 19 June 1798.
9. RS 74, Westmoreland County Probate Records, Provincial Archives, Fredericton, New Brunswick, Canada.

Jonas Fitch
1740/41–1808

Jonas Fitch, the son of Zachariah and Elizabeth Fitch, was born in Bedford, Massachusetts, on 5 February 1740/41.[1] He was living in Pepperrell, Massachusetts, by 1771, when the Massachusetts tax list indicated that he had a poll of one (not rateable), a shop, an ironworks, £3.1.10 annual value of real estate, cattle, and pastureland.[2] In 1775 he married Annis Shattuck in Pepperrell.[3] He was an early maker of wooden-work clocks.[4] PEK

1. *Bedford VR*, 24.
2. Pruitt 1978, 246–47.
3. *Pepperrell VR*, 163.
4. Bailey 1975, 52; Zea/Cheney 1992, 20–22, 169–70, figs. 1–13, 1–14.

John Foster
1648–81

John Foster generally is acknowledged as America's first printmaker. He was baptized in Dorchester, Massachusetts, on 10 December 1648 the son of Hopestill and Mary (Bates) Foster and graduated from Harvard College in 1667. As early as 1671 he took up engraving as an avocation. Ten woodcuts are attributed to him, including a three-quarter length portrait of Rev. Richard Mather. He is not know to have engraved in metal and whether he engraved silver is uncertain. His will is dated 18 July 1681 and he probably died shortly thereafter.[1] PEK

1. *DAB*; Shadwell 1969, 16–17; Reaves 1991, 40–41.

James Franklin
1696/97–1735

James Franklin, the son of Josiah (1655–1744) and Abiah Franklin (1667–1752), was born in Boston on 4 February 1696/97.[1] James was the elder brother of Benjamin Franklin and a cousin of the silversmith William Homes, Sr. (q.v.). James Franklin produced a print of the regicide Hugh Peter (1588–1660) to illustrate a new edition of Peter's tract, *A Dying Father's Last Legacy, to an Only Child: Mr. Hugh Peter's Advice to His Daughter*, published in Boston in 1717.[2] Although this print shows that Franklin had skill as an engraver, he primarily is known as a printer who began the *New-England Courant* in 1721. By 1732 he had moved to Rhode Island and founded the *Rhode-Island Gazette*. PEK

1. RC 9:226.
2. Saunders/Miles 1987, 90–91; Reaves 1991, 42–43.

Obadiah Frary
1717–1804

According to Chris Bailey, Obadiah Frary was the first clockmaker in the Massachusetts section of the Connecticut Valley[1]. He was born in Deerfield, Massachusetts, on 20 May 1717 to Nathaniel and Mehitable Frary and hence would have begun his training about 1731.[2] The identity of his master is unknown. He married Eunice Edwards in Northampton, Massachusetts, in 1743.[3] In 1765 he built a tower clock for the Deerfield meetinghouse. The Massachusetts tax list of 1771 includes him among the residents of Southampton, Massachusetts, with a poll of two, a house and shop adjoining, ironworks, £2.11.6 annual worth of real estate, as well as animals and agricultural lands.[4] He died in 1804 at age eighty-seven.[5] Tall case clocks by him survive.[6]   PEK

1. Ward/Hosley 1985, 348–49.
2. *Deerfield VR*, 62.
3. "Northampton Genealogies," Corbin Ms. Coll., microfilm, reel 14, 432, 486, NEHGS.
4. Pruitt 1978, 406–07; the name is spelled Frory.
5. "Northampton Genealogies," Corbin Ms. Coll., microfilm, reel 14, 486, NEHGS.
6. Ward/Hosley 1985, 348–49, no. 232.

Francis Garden
w. ca. 1745–52

The *Boston Evening-Post* of 4 March 1745 contained the following advertisement:

> *Francis Garden*, Engraver,
> from *LONDON*,
> Engraves in the newest manner and at the cheapest rates, Coates
> of Arms, Crests & Cyphers on Gold, Silver, Pewter or Copper.
> To be heard of at Mr. *Caverly's* Distillery at the South End of Boston.
> N.B. He will wait on any person in Town or Country, to do their
> Work at their own Houses, if desired; also Copper-plate printing perform'd
> by him.

Francis Garden was the elder brother of Philips Garden, a London silversmith and retailer. The brothers were the orphan sons of John Garden, a jeweler by trade who was a freeman of the Drapers' Company. Francis was apprenticed in 1724; the Goldsmiths' Company records show that "ffrancis Gardin son of John Gardin Citizen and Draper of London Deced" was apprenticed to "Wm. Tringham Citizen & Goldsmith of London" for seven years for a £10 premium, of which £8.10 was "a publick charity."

Garden became a freeman of the Goldsmiths' Company in 1738 and shortly thereafter came to America. He advertised in the *South-Carolina Gazette* on 19 March 1741, moving on to Boston by 1745. He had returned to London by 1752, for the Goldsmiths' Company records show that he took on an apprentice that year.[1] Henry Flynt and Martha Gandy Fales published an initials mark for Garden, but its source has not been traced.[2]   PEK

1. Prime 1969, 1:19; Robert B. Barker letter, 21 June 1992, to the author provided the information on Garden from the Goldsmiths' Company records; see Apprentice Book 6, 3 December 1724, and Freedom Book 1, 3 October 1738.
2. Flynt/Fales 1968, 223.

**Charles Geddes
ca. 1751–1807**

Charles Geddes, the son of the Edinburgh clockmaker James Geddes, immigrated to Boston in 1773. In the *Boston News-Letter* of 14 October 1773 he advertised,

Charles Geddes,
Clock and Watch Maker, and Finisher, from LONDON,
At his Shop below the Sign of Admiral Vernon,
in King-street, BOSTON,
Makes, mends, cleans, repairs, and
finishes all Sorts of Clocks and Watches, in the best
and neatest Manner, and upon the most reasonable
Terms.[1]

On 2 December 1773 he married Ann Bleigh in Boston.[2] At the outbreak of the Revolution, he joined the loyalist forces and left Boston for New York in 1776. A bracket clock made in New York by him is at the Henry Ford Museum.[3] He ultimately settled in Halifax, where he died on 27 November 1807.[4] PEK

1. Dow 1927, 141.
2. RC 30:434.
3. Distin/Bishop 1976, 90.
4. *Index of Obituaries, 1784–1840*, 2:1799; Langdon 1970, 50–53.

**John Greenwood
1727–92**

John Greenwood, known primarily as a portrait painter, was baptized in Boston on 7 December 1727, the son of Samuel Greenwood (1690–1741/42), a merchant, and his second wife, Mary Charnock.[1] Upon his father's death in 1741/42, John was apprenticed to the Boston engraver Thomas Johnston (q.v. Appendix A). Among the first works Greenwood produced under Johnston's tutelage was the coat of arms for William Clark's funeral in 1742, for which Johnston was paid £57.[2] A court deposition of 16 March 1749 reveals that when Greenwood was an apprentice he also produced a coat of arms to fill an order placed by Bartholomew Cheever. The finished arms were returned to Johnston probably for some alteration.[3] Greenwood is said to have been painting portraits by 1747. He was working on his own by 20 December 1748 when he advertised in the *Boston Gazette* a "Portrait of Ann Arnold—Mezetinto, Just published in mezetinto, and to be sold by J. Buck, at the Spectacles in Queen Street, the effigies of Ann Arnold, who generally goes by the name of Jersey Nanny." Greenwood painted many Boston-area residents before leaving for Paramaribo, the capital of Surinam in 1752. No evidence exists that Greenwood engraved silver during his years in Boston. Greenwood went from Surinam to Amsterdam and spent the remainder of his career in Europe and England.[4] PEK

1. RC 24:181; *Sibley's Harvard Graduates* 5:481–83.
2. Hitchings 1973, 104–05.
3. Hitchings 1973, 103, quotes the deposition in full from SCCR, file 66384.
4. Prown 1966, 1:14–15; Saunders/Miles 1987, 171–75.

**John Hall
w. ca. 1716–21**

In 1716 John Bell conveyed the following to the selectmen of Boston:

These are to Acquaint the Select men of Boston, that I John Bell living in King Street Boston, have lett out a small part of my Shop to John Hall watchmaker; who came from London about 5 months agoe as I am informed; a single person and of a sober life & conversation and follows his business very dilligently; I took him into my Shop upon Thursday the 29th day of March last past: 1716.[1]

John Hall was identified as a watchmaker in two suits in the Suffolk County Court of Common Pleas records in 1720 and 1721.[2] A number of John Halls lived in Boston at this time, and the identity of the watchmaker has yet to be firmly established. PEK

1. RC 29:237.
2. SCCR, Court of Common Pleas Record Book 1720, 383; 1721, 401.

Henry Harmson
w. ca. 1720–37

According to Chris Bailey, Henry Harmson probably came to Marblehead, Massachusetts, from Newport, Rhode Island, where a watchmaker with that name worked about 1725. Harmson was probably in Marblehead by 1730, when a child named Henry Harmson was baptized there. Another child named John was born to Henry Harmson and wife, Margaret, in 1734.[1] Harmson appeared as the plaintiff in the January 1731/32 session of the Suffolk Court of Common Pleas.[2] Bailey stated that Harmson bought a dwelling house in Marblehead in 1733 and died there in 1737. His estate was probated on 13 December 1737, and his inventory included a "clock with seven bells, a time piece, and a set of works." A clock by him is at the Peabody Essex Museum.[3] PEK

1. *Marblehead VR* 1:239.
2. SCCR, Court of Common Pleas Record Book 1731, 518.
3. Bailey 1975, 48; *Essex County Probate Index* 1:410.

John Hatton
w. ca. 1663

In Samuel Sewall's ledger book for the date 1663 "Jn° Hatton, a watchmaker," is listed as a debtor for £9.14.6.[1] No further trace of this individual has been found in Boston records. PEK

1. Samuel Sewall Account Book and Ledger, fol. 8v, NEHGS.

Joseph Hiller, Jr.
1748–1814

Although perhaps a silversmith in early life, Joseph Hiller, Jr., was primarily a watchmaker, clockmaker, and engraver.[1] He was born in Boston on 24 March 1748, the grandson of Benjamin Hiller (q.v.) and the son of Joseph (q.v.) and Hannah (Welsh) Hiller. He may have trained with his father, although no record of his master exists.[2] After the completion of his training, he moved to Salem, Massachusetts, in early 1770 and married Margaret Cleveland (1748–1804) there on 31 October of that year. His advertisement in the *Essex Gazette* for 8–15 May 1770 notes that,

> Joseph Hiller, *Clock and Watch Maker*, INFORMS the Public and his Customers in general, and those of them in the County of ESSEX in particular, that he has removed from King-Street, BOSTON, to a Shop opposite the Court-House, on the Exchange, in SALEM; where he hopes to execute all sorts of CLOCK and WATCH WORK with such Accuracy, Fidelity and Dispatch, as to merit the Approbation of his Employers. N.B. Said HILLER has to sell, a Variety of Watch Chains, Strings, Keys, Seals, &c.

Nearly two and a half years later (1–8 December 1772), he placed another advertisement in the newspaper that further elucidated his craft activities:

> he continues to carry on the CLOCK and WATCH-MAKER'S Business as usual, at his Shop opposite the Court-House in SALEM, where he has to sell, A Variety of Watch Strings, Chains, Seals, Keys, &c.—Said HILLER also carries on the ENGRAVING and SEAL-CUTTING Businesses, in their various Branches. He also makes Stamps, Ink, &c, for marking Gentlemen and Ladies Linen.

While in Salem, Hiller lived on Essex Street and was active in the Essex Lodge of Masons. He was a friend of the Reverend William Bentley, who records several instances of interaction with Hiller in his diary.[3] The Massachusetts tax list of 1771 includes Hiller in Salem with one poll, a quarter of a house with shop adjoining, an additional shop, and five pounds' annual worth of real estate.[4]

A bill dated 14 June 1777 records work Hiller performed for Dr. Edward Augustus Holyoke of Salem between 27 April 1772 and 14 January 1777 and probably accurately conveys the type of work Hiller routinely performed:

1772		
Aprl 27th	To engraveing coat of arms 28/ and 50 impressions 3/	1. 11. 0
June 22nd	To repairing timepiece	0. 4. 8
1773		
Augt 24th	To new main Spring in his Watch	0. 8. 0
1776		
May	To 50 copper plate impressions of his arms	0. 3. 0
Decr 13	To cleaning his Watch	0. 4. 0
1777	To 100 impressions of his armes	7
Jan 14th		2. 10. 8
		2. 17. 8[5]

Hiller was active during the Revolution, leading a company of men to Lexington and participating in the Rhode Island campaign in 1781. He retired with the rank of major. Using connections made during the war with George Washington and others, he obtained the position of naval officer and collector of customs for the ports of Salem and Beverly, a post he held from 1789 to 1802.

After the death of his wife he left Salem for Lancaster and was active for the next ten years in town affairs while living with his children at the so-called Wilder farm. He died there of apoplexy at age sixty-six on 9 February 1814.[6]

No mark has been assigned to Hiller, although he is listed as a silversmith by Ernest Currier, Hollis French, and others. He is included in most lists of clockmakers and watchmakers, but signed examples of his work are not known. The Peabody Essex Museum owns an unmarked English silver nutmeg grater of circa 1790 said to have been given by Hiller to his wife.[7] An oil copy of a St. Memin portrait of Hiller is owned by the Salem Custom House.[8] A mezzotint of John Hancock is signed "Jos. Hiller fecit.," and mezzotints of George and Martha Washington have been attributed to him.[9] An etched portrait of Washington from 1794 is also probably Hiller's work.[10] GWRW

1. Biographical sketches of Hiller include Leavitt 1861, 123–24; Browne 1862, 11; Belknap 1927, 101; and *EIHC* 75, no. 2 (April 1939): 161–62.
2. In this volume, this Joseph Hiller is identified as Jr. to distinguish him from his father, who was a jeweler. Other scholars identify the younger Hiller as Sr. because he had a son, Joseph (1777–95), who was also an engraver; see Shadwell 1969, 37–38; Groce/Wallace 1957, 317.

3. Bentley 1905–62, 1:33, 237, 272.
4. Pruitt 1978, 150–51.
5. Holyoke Family Collection, box 12, folder 3, PEM.
6. Nourse 1890, 182, 358.
7. Fales 1983, 27, fig 18; accession no. 102, 483.
8. *EIHC* 75, no. 2 (April 1939): 161–62.
9. Shadwell 1969a, 240–41.
10. Hart 1907, 1–6. Hart attributes this drypoint etching to Hiller's son Joseph (1777–95), but it seems more likely that it is by Major Hiller himself.

Richard Jennys, Jr.
ca. 1730–92 +

Richard Jennys, Jr., was probably born in Boston about 1730 to Richard Jennys. He attended the Boston Public Latin School graduating in 1744. In the *Boston News-Letter* on 17 July 1766, the following advertisement appeared, "PORTRAIT OF REV. JONATHAN MAYHEW.—Prints of the late Rev. Jonathan Mayhew, D. D. done in Mezotinto by Richard Jennys, jun. are sold by Nathaniel Hurd, Engraver, near the Exchange." This association with Nathaniel Hurd (q.v.) suggests that Jennys learned his engraving skills from him. A son, Richard, was born in Boston to Richard and Sarah Jennys on 28 December 1771.[1] In the Massachusetts tax list of 1771, Richard Jennys was included with one poll, one house with shop adjoining, real estate valued at twenty pounds annually, and £700 worth of merchandise.[2] Between 1777 and 1783 Jennys advertised in Boston as a dry goods merchant. He then worked as a portrait painter in Charleston, South Carolina; Savannah, Georgia; the West Indies; and Connecticut.[3] PEK

1. RC 24:322.
2. Pruitt 1978, 36–37.
3. Saunders/Miles 1987, 275–76.

David Johnson
w. ca. 1681–1707

The watchmaker David Johnson probably arrived in Boston in 1681 because on 13 September that year Samuel Parris, a merchant, became surety for Johnson and his family.[1] Johnson is identified as a watchmaker on the Boston tax list of 1687, which includes him in ward (or division) 6.[2] His name appeared on subsequent tax lists in 1688 and 1691 as well as in the list of Boston inhabitants for 1695 and in a list of individuals in Capt. Allen's Company in 1698.[3] The births of children to David and Priscilla Johnson are recorded in Boston: Mary (1689 and again in 1690), David (1695), Priscilla (1698), and Jennet (1702).[4]

In addition to watchmaking, Johnson ran a tavern called the Rose and Crown, which Thomas Child described as Mr. David Johnson's place in a deposition of 1694/95.[5] In connection with that establishment Johnson's name turns up frequently in the records. Samuel Sewall recorded in his diary on 24 July 1693, "One of the Fleet-Women dies this day . . . at David Johnson's over against the Town-house."[6] Johnson is also mentioned as running a tavern in a suit over nonpayment of a bill in 1695/96, and Sewall records that "David Johnson who entertained Roberts" was fined fifteen shillings in 1699.[7] Johnson's name also occurs in other court cases: he served as a juror in James Herbert's trial for stealing silver from John Coney (q.v.), and he witnessed a list of disputed goods in a case from 1694.[8] He was identified as a taverner when his estate administration was granted to his widow on 15 July 1707.[9] PEK

1. RC 10:70.
2. RC 1:89, 115.
3. RC 1:141, 151–52, 164; RC 29:227.
4. RC 9:185, 190, 222, 241; RC 24:18.
5. SCCR, file 3109.
6. *Sewall Diary* 1:311.
7. SCCR, file 3250; Samuel Sewall Account Book and Ledger, fol. 48r, NEHGS.
8. SCCR, files 2487, 2904.
9. SCPR 16:305–06.

Benjamin Johnston
ca. 1740–1818

Benjamin Johnston, the son of the Boston japanner and engraver Thomas Johnston (q.v. Appendix A), was born in Boston about 1740. Benjamin probably trained with his father, but soon after reaching his majority he settled in Salem, Massachusetts. In a writ of attachment of 1763 Benjamin is described as being a painter-stainer of Salem.[1] He later moved to Newbury where he married Ann Stickney (1742–1827) in 1770.[2] The earliest surviving view of Newburyport was engraved by Benjamin in 1774 and was advertised in the *Essex Journal or, New-Hampshire Packet* on 19 January 1775.[3] He also produced watercolor coats of arms.[4] Johnston died in Newburyport on 30 August 1818 at the age of seventy-six.[5] PEK.

1. Hitchings 1973, 120 citing SCCR, file 83965.
2. *Newbury VR* 1:492.
3. Hitchings 1973, 120–21; Currier (1909) 1978, 1:79–80.
4. Benes 1986, 106–07.
5. *Newburyport VR* 2:686.

Thomas Johnston
ca. 1708–67

Sinclair Hitchings provides the most complete account of Thomas Johnston, the Boston painter, japanner, and engraver.[1] Because no record of his birth exists, the year of his birth has been deduced from his age at death. His apprenticeship would have begun about 1722 and would have been completed about 1727. The identity of his master also is not known, although since Johnston's first signed piece of handiwork is the map of Boston by William Burgis (q.v. Appendix A) (1728), this association opens the possibility that Johnston learned engraving from Burgis. Burgis arrived in Boston at the time Johnston would have been ready to begin his apprenticeship. Furthermore, the spiky style of the leafage on cartouches associated with Burgis—namely, those seen in *A Prospect of the Colledges in Cambridge* and *View of the New Dutch Church*—would become a hallmark of Johnston's engraving style, lending credence to a master-apprentice relationship between the two men.[2]

A comparison of engravings bearing his name and engraved designs on Boston silver suggests that his shop did work for Boston silversmiths, although there is no documentary evidence for it.[3] Johnston trained John Greenwood (q.v. Appendix A) in the art of engraving and heraldic painting in the 1740s. When the London-trained clockmaker and watchmaker Gawen Brown (q.v. Appendix A) first arrived in Boston, his business was located at Johnston's shop between 1749 and 1752. Johnston engraved a copperplate for printing clock dials for the clockmaker Preserved Clapp (q.v. Appendix A). Johnston died in Boston in 1767, and his shop was taken over by his son-in-law Daniel Rea, Jr., and run in association with John Johnston, one of Johnston's children.

Another son, Benjamin (q.v. Appendix A), worked as a painter and engraver in Essex County. PEK

1. Hitchings 1973, 83–132.
2. Holman 1973, 66, 73, figs. 30, 34.
3. For a discussion of Johnston as an engraver of silver, see pp. 80, 81, 83, 90–92.

Edmund Lewis
w. ca. 1748

Edmund Lewis was identified as a watchmaker in the records of the Suffolk County Court of Common Pleas. He was sued by the shopkeeper Henry Laughton in 1748, the widow Mary Warden, the merchant William Randall, and Benjamin Goldthwait in January 1749/50, and by the merchants Edward B. Oliver and Briggs Hallowell in April 1750.[1] The watchmaker may be the Edward Lewis whose intentions to marry Mary Young were published in Boston on 25 June 1739.[2] PEK

1. SCCR, Court of Common Pleas Record Book 1748–49, 106; 1749–51, 29, 44, 62, 82, 93.
2. RC 28:231.

Samuel Luscomb, Jr.
d. 1790

Samuel Luscomb, Jr., was the son of the Salem, Massachusetts, clockmaker, Samuel Luscomb, Sr., and was probably trained by his father. The younger Luscomb appears in the Massachusetts tax list of 1771 with two polls, half a house and shop adjoining, an additional shop, and six pounds' annual worth of real estate.[1] The younger Luscomb died in Salem in 1790.[2] PEK

1. Pruitt 1978, 144–45.
2. Ward 1984a, 402.

Samuel Luscomb, Sr.
d. 1781

Samuel Luscomb was identified as a whitesmith and clockmaker in a list of Salem, Massachusetts, craftsmen compiled about 1762.[1] He appeared in the Massachusetts tax list of 1771 with two polls, two-thirds of a house and shop adjoining, and five pounds' annual worth of real estate.[2] His son, Samuel, Jr., (q.v. Appendix A) was also a clockmaker. Brooks Palmer lists Samuel Luscomb as the clockmaker responsible for the town clock in the East Meetinghouse in 1773. Whether this individual was the father or the son is uncertain.[3] The estate of Samuel, Sr., was presented for probate in 1781.[4] PEK

1. Forman 1971, 64.
2. Pruitt 1978, 144–45.
3. Palmer 1950, 235.
4. ECPR, docket 17446, as cited in Ward 1984a, 402.

Richard Manning
ca. 1701–74

The clockmaker Richard Manning, son of the Ipswich, Massachusetts, gunsmith Thomas Manning, was born about 1701.[1] His career spanned many years and clocks by him dated 1741, 1767, and 1773 are known. The movements of clocks by Manning are similar to those of David Blaisdell, Sr. (q.v. Appendix A), which suggests the two men may have had similar training.[2] The Massachusetts tax list of 1771 includes a Richard Manning in Salem, Massachusetts, with a poll of one, half a warehouse, £4 annual value of real estate, £1,500 lent at interest, 112 tons of vessels, and merchandise valued at £1,450.[3] These assets suggest that Manning was heavily engaged in trade. At the time his estate was probated in 1774 he was identified as a gentleman.[4] His inventory included two unfinished clocks, an engine to cut clock wheels, and other tools related to the clockmaker's trade.[5] James and Thomas Dane (qq.v.) were his nephews. PEK

1. No record of his birth exists in *Ipswich VR*; his age was given as seventy-three when he died in Ipswich in 1774; *Ipswich VR* 2:630.
2. Bailey 1975, 46–47.
3. Pruitt 1978, 134–35.
4. *Essex County Probate Index* 2:586.
5. Bailey 1975, 46.

Thomas Matson
1633–90

Thomas Matson, identified in the will of his daughter Hannah Hanners as a gunsmith, was employed by the town of Boston to keep the town clock in order.[1] At a meeting on 27 February 1670, the town "Agreed with Thomas Matson sen[r] to look after the towne clocke and keepe it in good repaire from the first of March next for one year next ensueinge, & to have 10[s] for his paines about it."[2] This task previously had been done by Richard Taylor (q.v. Appendix A). Matson's daughter was the mother of George Hanners, Sr. (q.v.). PEK

1. SCPR 29:369–70.
2. RC 7:58.

John McLean
w. ca. 1773

An advertisement in the *Boston News-Letter* for 7 January 1773 states, "At Mr. McLean's, Watch-Maker, near the Town Hall, is a Negro man whose extraordinary Genius has been assisted by one of the best Masters in London; he takes Faces at the lowest Rates. Specimens of his Performance may be seen at said Place."[1] This advertisement probably was placed by John McLean who is said to have lived in Boston at that time.[2] PEK

1. Dow 1927, 6.
2. Zea/Cheney 1992, 25, n. 9.

John Morris
w. ca. 1770

In his biography of Simon Willard (q.v. Appendix A), John Ware Willard discusses the assertion made by earlier scholars that an Englishman named Morris was Simon Willard's master. He states that he was unable to trace this individual in Worcester County records.[1] Pendulum bobs cast with the names John Morris and S. Willard and the dates 1770 and 1771 may further identify Morris and lend credence to the statement that he was Willard's master, although Willard claimed he learned little from him.[2] A newspaper advertisement in 1777 stated that Morris stole silver, bullion, cash, and other goods from the silversmith and clockmaker Elijah Yeomans (q.v.).[3] PEK

1. Willard (1911) 1968, 2–3.
2. Bailey 1975, 54; Zea/Cheney 1992, 29–30.
3. Zea/Cheney 1992, 30.

Thomas Moyran (alias Morton, alias Odell)
w. ca. 1704

In the summer of 1704, Massachusetts officials became aware that the twenty-shilling bills of credit were being counterfeited. On 25 July four of the counterfeiters were arrested and the plate and press were seized, but the principal perpetrator, and presumably the engraver, Thomas Moyran, alias Morton, alias Odell, escaped capture.[1] He made his way to Connecticut and then to Philadelphia as this advertisement in the *Boston News-Letter* for 5–12 November 1705 suggests:

> Thomas Odell, who counterfeited a Twenty shilling Bill of Credit of the Province of Massachusetts Bay, was apprehended in Pennsylvania, and taken to Rhode Island, where he escaped, was recaptured and brought to Boston, where he was fined £300, and ordered imprisoned for one year.[2]

In March 1710/11, in a petition for release from prison, Odell stated that he had been imprisoned for six years. The General Court, describing Odell as a very dangerous person, denied the request.[3] PEK

1. Scott 1957, 28–30.
2. Dow 1927, 9.
3. Mass. Archives 71:761–62.

Jonathan Mulliken
w. ca. 1735

The clockmaker Jonathan Mulliken was the brother of the Bradford, Massachusetts, blacksmith John Mulliken. Jonathan was also the uncle of the clockmakers Nathaniel Mulliken, Sr., and Samuel Mulliken (qq.v. Appendix A) and was possibly the individual who trained his nephews. A record of his birth to Robert and Rebecca Mulliken does not exist in Bradford vital records. He is said to have married Martha Marsh, but no record of that marriage has been found. He is believed to have moved to Falmouth, Maine, and Brooks Palmer cited tall clocks with "Jonathan Mulliken, Falmouth" on the dial.[1] PEK

1. Palmer 1950, 246; Zea/Cheney 1992, 19.

Jonathan Mulliken
1746–82

Jonathan Mulliken, son of the clockmaker Samuel Mulliken (q.v. Appendix A), was born in Bradford, Massachusetts, on 7 September 1746.[1] Because his father died when he was ten years old, he must have learned his trade with another craftsman, possibly his uncle Nathaniel Mulliken, Sr. (q.v. Appendix A), of Lexington, Massachusetts. He would have completed his apprenticeship about 1767, the year his uncle died. In addition to clockmaking, Jonathan Mulliken had skills as an engraver. He issued a line engraving, *The Bloody Massacre*, based on the print Paul Revere, Jr. (q.v.), appropriated from Henry Pelham (q.v. Appendix A). Mulliken's engraving, signed "Jon.ᵃ Mulliken New-bury-Port," was most likely issued in 1770.[2] Brooks Palmer stated that Jonathan was in Newburyport, Massachusetts, by 1772.[3] He died there on 19 June 1782 in his thirty-sixth year. His obituary notice called him a clockmaker, but in his estate papers he was identified as a merchant.[4] A tall case clock by him is at Yale.[5] PEK

1. *Bradford VR*, 121.
2. Shadwell 1969, 28–29, no. 36.
3. Palmer 1950, 246.

4. *Newburyport VR* 2:727; *Index of Obituaries, 1704–1800*, 3:161; *Essex County Probate Index* 2:639.
5. Battison/Kane 1973, 58–60, no. 10.

Nathaniel Mulliken, Jr. 1752–76

The son of the Lexington, Massachusetts, clockmaker Nathaniel Mulliken, Sr. (q.v. Appendix A), and his wife, Lydia Stone, Nathaniel Mulliken, Jr., was born on 30 March 1752.[1] Although he followed his father's trade, he must have trained with another craftsman because his father died when Nathaniel was fifteen years old. His career was short-lived, for Nathaniel died in Lexington on 6 February 1776 at age twenty-four.[2] PEK

1. *Lexington VR*, 50.
2. *Lexington VR*, 188; *Index of Obituaries, 1704–1800*, 3:161.

Nathaniel Mulliken, Sr. 1722–67

Nathaniel Mulliken, Sr., son of John Mulliken, a Bradford, Massachusetts, blacksmith, and his wife, Mary Poore, of Newburyport, Massachusetts, was born in Bradford on 8 August 1722.[1] Mulliken probably was trained by his uncle, Jonathan Mulliken (w. ca. 1735) (q.v. Appendix A). Mulliken was living in Lexington, Massachusetts, by 1751, when he married Lydia Stone on 6 June.[2] News of his sudden death on 23 November 1767 at age forty-five was reported in the Boston newspapers: "Monday Mr. Nathaniel Mulliken, of Lexington, Clock-Maker, (who to all Appearance had been as well that Day as at any Time) as he was coming in at the Door of his House, instantly fell, and, notwithstanding all possible Endeavours for Relief, expired in a few moments, to the great Grief of his disconsolate Widow and seven Children."[3] A tall case clock by him is in the collection of Old Sturbridge Village.[4] His brother Samuel (q.v. Appendix A) and sons Joseph (1765–1802) and Nathaniel (q.v. Appendix A) were also clockmakers.[5] Mulliken may have trained his nephew, Jonathan Mulliken (1746–82) and is said to have trained Benjamin Willard (qq.v. Appendix A).[6] PEK

1. *Bradford VR*, 121.
2. *Lexington VR*, 133.
3. Dow 1927, 142; *Index of Obituaries, 1704–1800*, 3:161; *Lexington VR*, 188.
4. Zea/Cheney 1992, 19–20, 160, figs. 1-11, 1-12.
5. Bailey 1975, 47–48.
6. Zea/Cheney 1992, 19–20.

Samuel Mulliken 1720–56

Samuel Mulliken, the older brother of Nathaniel Mulliken, Sr. (q.v. Appendix A), was baptized in Bradford, Massachusetts, on 12 June 1720.[1] Samuel probably was trained by his uncle, Jonathan Mulliken (w. ca. 1735) (q.v. Appendix A). Samuel is said to have moved to Newburyport, Massachusetts, after 1740, but because his son Jonathan (q.v. Appendix A) was born in Bradford in 1746, most likely he did not leave Bradford until after that time. Samuel Mulliken died in Newburyport in 1756 at age thirty-six, and his inventory included clockmaking tools and unfinished clocks.[2] His residence was listed as Newbury, Massachusetts, when his estate was presented for probate on 21 June 1756.[3] His son Jonathan became a clockmaker in Newburyport. PEK

1. *Bradford VR*, 120.
2. Bailey 1975, 47; Zea/Cheney 1992, 17.
3. *Essex County Probate Index* 2:639.

John Newman
w. ca. 1764

In the *Boston Gazette* of 23 July 1764, the following advertisement appeared:

> *John Newman,*
> Clock and Watch-Maker;
> HEREBY informs the Town and Country, That
> he has lately opened his Shop opposite the
> North Door of the Court-House in King-Street, *Boston*;
> where he makes and mends all Sorts of Gold & Silver
> Horozontal striking and repeating Watches, in the best
> and neatest Manner; and extreme reasonable in his
> Demands, Seals, Keys, Glasses, &c. &c. &c.[1]

This individual may be the same John Newman who was admitted to the Almshouse in 1765, being described as "a Stranger who is not an Inhabitant of any Town in this Province, and has not where withall to subsist himself."[2] PEK

1. Dow 1927, 142–43.
2. RC 20:178.

John Odlin
ca. 1602–85

A deed of 11 February 1667 identifies John Odlin (Audlin) as an armorer when he sold land to John Hull (q.v.).[1] Odlin immigrated to New England early, and the births of children to him and his wife, Margaret, are recorded in Boston between 1635 and 1646. He died there in 1685.[2] PEK

1. *Suffolk Deeds* 10:4–5.
2. Savage 1860–62, 3:305; RC 9:3, 5, 9, 11, 23; SCPR 6:834–36.

Robert Peasely
w. ca. 1734–35

Robert Peasely was identified as a watchmaker when he sued the wigmaker Nathaniel Austin in the Suffolk County Court of Common Pleas session of April 1734.[1] Peasely was also a defendant in the same court in October 1734, January 1735, and three times in July 1735. One of the July suits was brought by Rufus Greene (q.v.).[2] The *Boston Gazette* of 11–18 August 1735 contained the following advertisement:

> Whereas Twelve Watches are left in the
> *hands of* James Busby *Wine-Cooper, at the Sign of the Duke of*
> *Marlborough's Arms in King-street* Boston, *by* Robert Peasely,
> *Watchmaker: This is to give Notice to all Persons to whom said*
> *Watches may belong, that they may have them paying Charges,*
> *a Memorandum whereof left by the said* Peasely *is as follows.*
>   No. 1 *Mr.* Hutchinson. 2. Arthur Savage. 3. *Mr.* Par-
> ker of *Andover.* 4. *Mr.* Goffe. 5. Tho. Savage. 6. Ruth
> Read. 7. Henry Wetherhead. 8. Tho. Lechmere. 9. Peter
> Prescot. 10. A Currier. 11. Michael Dalton of *Newbury.*
> 12. A Watch unknown belonging to one in the Country.

These documents suggest that Peasely attempted to set up trade in Boston, ran into financial difficulties, and moved on to a new location. PEK

1. SCCR, Court of Common Pleas Record Book 1733–34, 558.
2. SCCR, Court of Common Pleas Record Book 1734, 344, 665; 1735, 313, 327 (suit brought by Rufus Greene), 359.

Elijah Peck
1752–1801 +

The son of the Boston watchmaker Moses Peck (q.v. Appendix A) and his first wife, Elizabeth Williston, Elijah Peck was born on 24 November 1752.[1] In the Boston tax list of 1780 he is identified as a watchmaker and is included in ward 1 with one poll and real estate with an annual worth of ten pounds.[2] The *Boston Directory* of 1789 lists him as a watchmaker at Williams's Court.[3] In 1791 he married Hannah Childs in Boston.[4] He is mentioned in his father's will (1801), although no record of his death has been found.[5] The Newburyport, Massachusetts, silversmith Jonathan Stickney (q.v. Appendix B) was his brother-in-law. PEK

1. RC 24:280.
2. "Assessors' 'Taking-Books,'" 16.
3. RC 10:196.
4. RC 30:343.
5. SCPR 99:158–60.

Moses Peck
ca. 1718–1801

Moses Peck may not have been a Massachusetts native because no record of his birth has been found in the vital records. He was in Boston by 1743, when he married Elizabeth Williston.[1] The couple had a son, Elijah (q.v. Appendix A), who became a watchmaker. Moses's shop was near Boston's Town House, where he advertised Philadelphia lottery tickets on sale in 1753.[2] An advertisement in the *Boston Gazette* illuminates the nature of his trade: "To be Sold, a Number of good Silver Watches; also an Assortment of Men's Watch Chains, Women's best ditto Gold Pattern, Cornelian and Chrystal Seals, Compass ditto with enamel'd Plates, Steel Keys with Hooks, Silk Strings, Lockets, Main Springs, fine Pendulum Wire, white Clock Lines, &c. &c.—Likewise has new and second hand Eight Day Clocks."[3] Brooks Palmer claimed that Peck continued to advertise until 1789.[4]

Peck wed a second time in 1758, marrying Elizabeth Townsend of Charlestown, Massachusetts.[5] The Massachusetts tax list of 1771 included him with two polls, a house and shop adjoining, a tanhouse (a general term which could refer to another shop), twenty pounds' annual value of real estate, eighty pounds money lent at interest, and one head of cattle.[6] Together with the Boston tax list of 1780, which included him in ward 9 with a poll of one and rents valued at two hundred pounds, these citations indicate that he had moderately substantial means.[7] The Boston directories of 1789 and 1796 listed him as a watchmaker at no. 63 Cornhill.[8] He died in 1801 at age eighty-three.[9] His will mentions among other heirs his son, Elijah Peck, and his daughter, Hannah Stickney, wife of the Newburyport, Massachusetts, silversmith Jonathan Stickney (q.v. Appendix B).[10] PEK

1. RC 28:258.
2. Dow 1927, 143.
3. Dow 1927, 143.
4. Palmer 1950, 256.
5. RC 30:27, 289.
6. Pruitt 1978, 36–37.
7. "Assessors' 'Taking-Books,'" 40.
8. RC 10:195, 273.
9. *Index of Obituaries, 1784–1840*, 4:3483.
10. SCPR 99:158–60, 169, 177–81, 197.

Henry Pelham
1748/49–1806

The son of Peter Pelham (q.v. Appendix A) and Mary Copley, Henry Pelham was born in Boston on 14 March 1748/49.[1] Because his father died when he was only two, Pelham probably studied painting and engraving with his half-brother, John Singleton Copley (q.v. Appendix A). Pelham engraved a plate of the Boston Massacre that he lent to Paul Revere, Jr. (q.v.), and Revere copied it, much to Pelham's chagrin. No evidence exists that Pelham did engraving for silversmiths. A loyalist, Pelham left Boston with the British troops in 1776. He is known for his miniature portraits and engraved maps. He exhibited a painting at the Royal Academy in 1777 and miniatures in 1778. He died in Ireland in 1806.[2] PEK

1. RC 24:267.
2. Jones 1930, 231–32; Groce/Wallace 1957, 496–97; Saunders/Miles 1987, 307–08.

Peter Pelham
ca. 1697–1751

Andrew Oliver provides the most complete account of Peter Pelham.[1] Pelham was born in London and was apprenticed there in 1713 to John Simon, a leading mezzotint engraver. In 1727 he immigrated to Boston. Following the death of his first wife in 1734, he remarried and went to Newport, Rhode Island, returning to Boston by 1737. He did the first mezzotint in British North America. His career combined making mezzotint portraits of New England worthies and teaching school. An advertisement in the *Boston Gazette* of 16–23 January 1738 stated that he taught young ladies and gentlemen "Dancing, Writing, Reading, Painting on Glass, and all sorts of Needle Work."[2] No evidence exists that he ever did engraved work for silversmiths, although his surviving prints attest to his skills as a mezzotint engraver. Upon his marriage to Mary Copley in 1748, he became the stepfather of the artist John Singleton Copley (q.v. Appendix A).[3] His son Henry Pelham (q.v. Appendix A) also was an engraver. Pelham died in Boston in 1751.[4] PEK

1. Oliver 1973, 133–73.
2. Dow 1927, 12.
3. RC 28:288.
4. Groce/Wallace 1957, 497.

James Perrigo
1737–1808

According to Brooks Palmer, James Perrigo was a clockmaker who worked in Wrentham, Massachusetts. He married Elizabeth Pettee there on 28 September 1769 and is included among the residents of that town in the Massachusetts tax list of 1771 with one poll, a house and shop adjoining, one pound annual value of real estate, land, and animals.[1] PEK

1. *Wrentham VR* 2:352; Pruitt 1978, 536–37; Palmer 1950, 257.

Joseph Pope
ca. 1754–1826

The clockmaker Joseph Pope was identified as a watchmaker when he married Ruthy Thayer, daughter of "Mr. Thayer, Tallow-Chandler," in Boston on 6 March 1773.[1] Minutes of a meeting of the Boston selectmen on 4 October 1773 record that a Joseph Pope who arrived in Boston harbor on board Capt. Dolliver's schooner was quarantined for three weeks as a precaution against smallpox.[2] Whether this individual is the clockmaker is unclear. Pope is said to have begun work on an orrery in 1776 and unveiled his creation a decade later. In 1789 it was purchased by Harvard College.[3]

The Boston tax list of 1780 identifies Pope as a clockmaker in ward 12 with one poll and real estate valued at sixty pounds annually.[4] In 1787 he married Elizabeth Pierpont (1761–1838), daughter of the Boston jeweler Benjamin Pierpont (q.v.).[5] The *Boston Directory* of 1789 identified Pope as a watchmaker in Newbury Street with a house in Essex Street.[6] In 1790 Pope advertised that he had lately returned from London and now carried on the clockmaking and watchmaking business at no. 49 Marlborough Street.[7] Pope died in Augusta, Maine, at age seventy-two in 1826, and his widow died in Hallowell, Maine, in 1838.[8] A tall case clock by him is at Old Sturbridge Village.[9] PEK

1. RC 30:433; "Boyle's Journal of Occurrences in Boston," *NEHGR* 84:364.
2. RC 23:193.
3. *Antiques* 31 (March 1931): 112–15; Whitehill et al. 1975, 73.
4. "Assessors' 'Taking-Books,'" 54.
5. RC 30:458.
6. RC 10:194.
7. Palmer 1950, 260.
8. *Index of Obituaries, 1784–1840*, 4:3617–18.
9. Zea/Cheney 1992, 165.

Robert Punt
w. ca. 1670

In the Suffolk County Court in 1670 Freegrace Bendall sued Robert Punt for failing to return a watch that Punt was repairing. Details of the case reveal that Bendall gave the watch to Punt at Jeremiah Dummer's (q.v.) shop and that the watch had originally been purchased from John Hull (q.v.).[1] Further evidence of a watchmaker named Robert Punt has not been found in Boston records. PEK

1. SCCR, files 1043.

Archelaus Rea, Jr.
1754–92

Brooks Palmer lists Archelaus Rea, Jr., as a watchmaker and clockmaker in Salem and Danvers, Massachusetts. He was born in Topsfield, Massachusetts, to Archelaus Rea and Mary Batchelder on 6 November 1754.[1] Rea married Mary Cook of Danvers in 1777.[2] A receipt dated 20 April 1784 shows that he charged John Touzell (q.v.) seven shillings and six pence for repairing and cleaning a watch.[3] The Reverend William Bentley recorded in his diary that Rea died in Danvers in 1792 after being inoculated for smallpox. Estate papers filed for him on 7 January 1793 identify him as a watchmaker.[4] PEK

1. *Topsfield VR*, 91.
2. *Salem VR* 4:242.
3. English-Touzel-Hathorne Papers, box 4, folder 3, PEM.
4. Palmer 1950, 264; *Essex County Probate Index* 2:771.

William Ridgill
w. ca. 1726

William Ridgill was identified as a clockmaker in Suffolk County Court of Common Pleas records in 1726.[1] He may be the William Ridgill (Ridgel) who married Sarah Weeden in Boston in 1713.[2] PEK

1. SCCR, Court of Common Pleas Record Book 1726, 235, 382.
2. RC 28:47.

John Rolestone
ca. 1740–1803

The clockmaker and watchmaker John Rolestone, the son of John Rolestone (1712–76), a sexton, and Ruth Everden (d. 1781), was probably born in Boston about 1740.[1] He would have completed his training about 1761 and may then have worked for the Boston jeweler Jonathan Trott (q.v.) because he witnessed a deed for Trott in 1765.[2] On 27 March 1768 Rolestone married Mary Greenleaf (1742/43–98), and the month following his marriage, John Rolestone, Jr., watchmaker, purchased from Thomas Greenleaf and his wife a dwelling house and buildings in Newbury Street.[3] The deed was witnessed by Elijah Collins (q.v. Appendix A) and Jonathan Trott. In May 1768 Rolestone advertised as follows in the *Boston News-Letter*:

> John Roulstone, Clock and Watch-Maker, Takes this Opportunity to inform those Gentlemen who favour him with their Custom;—That he has removed from the Shop he lately improv'd to a Shop three Doors Southward of that, and the third Door Northward of the White Horse Tavern; Where he does all sorts of Clock and Watch-Work as usual,—has all sorts of Watch Chains, Strings, Seals and Keys, &c. &c.[4]

A daughter Mary was born to John and Mary Rolestone on 13 January 1769, and a daughter Elizabeth Greenleaf was born on 14 October 1770.[5] The Boston records also reveal that John Roulstone, Jr., served as an engine man for fire engine nine, but that by March 1774 he had resigned that post.[6]

Rolestone may have fled Boston during the Revolution, for Abigail Adams wrote to her husband, John Adams, on 16 July 1775 about news of events there, "from Boston tis but very seldom we are able to collect any thing that may be relied upon, . . . I heard yesterday by one Mr. Rolestone a Goldsmith who got out in a fishing Schooner, that there distress encreased upon them fast."[7] His flight from Boston, if that is what it was, was short-lived. The Mr. Roulston with whom the town made an arrangement in 1778 to ring his bell at eleven, one, and nine o'clock may be the watchmaker and goldsmith continuing an employment tradition carried on earlier by his father.[8] Rolestone is also included on the Boston tax list of 1780 in ward 12 and is shown with a poll of one and rents valued at seventy pounds annually.[9]

Following the Revolution, Rolestone and his wife were involved in a number of real estate transactions. On 9 October 1784 they mortgaged the Newbury Street property; the mortgage was discharged in 1805.[10] Eunice Franklin, as executor of the estate of her husband, Samuel Franklin, sold to Rolestone in 1784 the part of her husband's real estate that he had purchased of John and Stephen Greenleaf, that is, interests in the Newbury Street property.[11] In 1792 Rolestone and his wife sold half a tenement near Wing's Lane in Boston.[12] Between 1796 and 1798 Rolestone was also involved in the partitioning of land in Purchase Street.[13] Rolestone is listed as a watchmaker at no. 16 or 18 Newbury Street in the Boston directories from 1789 to 1803, the year of his death.[14] PEK

1. RC 24:85; RC 28:208; SCPR 75:353; 76:68–69; 80:389. No record of the birth of John Rolestone, Jr., has been found.
2. SCD 106:109.
3. SCD 121:173; RC 30:57; RC 24:246; *Index of Obituaries, 1784–1840*, 4:3892.
4. Dow 1927, 144.

5. RC 24:319, 321.
6. RC 23:212.
7. Butterfield/Friedlaender/Kline 1975, 101.
8. RC 25:80.
9. "Assessors' 'Taking-Books,'" 52.
10. SCD 145:112–13.
11. SCD 151:157–58.
12. SCD 174:86–87.
13. SCD 184:273–74; 186:155–57; 189:217.
14. *Index of Obituaries, 1784–1840,* 4:3892; RC 10:196, 279; *Boston Directory* 1798, 98; 1800, 94; 1803, 107.

John Cross Smith
w. ca. 1758

On 3 May 1758 Gawen Brown (q.v. Appendix A) informed the selectmen of Boston that "he has taken into his service John Cross Smith, a young man a watchmaker who came as a passenger with Capt. Partridge from London."[1] No further trace of Smith has been found in Boston records. PEK

1. Palmer 1950, 160; RC 19:83.

Abel Stowell, Sr.
1752–1818

The clockmaker Abel Stowell, Sr., was born on 12 June 1752 in Worcester, Massachusetts.[1] He was the son of Cornelius Stowell (1725/26–1804) and Zurvillar Goulding (1730–1812) of Worcester, who were married on 22 March 1749/50.[2] Stowell's master is unknown, but he would have completed his apprenticeship about 1773. No record of his service during the American Revolution survives, probably because Stowell belonged to a staunchly loyalist family, many of whose members were among those named in the Worcester Protest of 1774 as persons thought to sympathize with England.[3] In spite of his loyalist sympathies, Abel became an upstanding citizen of Worcester after the war, assuming a number of town duties during his lifetime.[4]

Stowell married Relief Jenison (1754–1817) on 22 November 1781.[5] She was the daughter of Capt. Israel (1713–82) and Mary Jenison (1718–75).[6] Four children were born to Abel and Relief Stowell between 1786 and 1793. One of them, Betsy (born 1786), later married the silversmith John Ridgway (1780–1851) of Boston.[7]

Abel's father was a successful weaver who transferred property to Abel in 1784 "in consideration of the love, goodwill and affection which I have and bear toward my son Abel Stowell of Worcester aforesaid Clockmaker and for his settlement in the world. Also in consideration of Services done by the said Abel after he was twenty one years old."[8] This is probably the same site described by Abel Stowell in four advertisements he placed in the *Massachusetts Spy* between 1783 and 1789 as being near the South Meetinghouse, whose clock Stowell made in 1800.[9] Stowell was involved in a number of real estate transactions in Worcester.[10]

Stowell achieved a modicum of success in Worcester as a clockmaker. William Lincoln's *History of Worcester* describes him as having "carried on a very extensive manufacture of tower and church clocks, . . . many [of which] remain to attest the value of his handiwork."[11] From the beginning of his career, Stowell worked strictly as a clockmaker, and his business must have been large enough to require assistance because on two occasions, once in 1785 and once in 1792, Stowell advertised for a "likely Lad, about 14 or 15 years of age as an Apprentice in the Clock Making business."[12] Abel Stowell, Sr., probably worked until his death on 3 August 1818 because his inventory included a sizable collection of clockmaking tools, bells, and parts, along with machinery and patterns.[13]

Stowell's sons Abel, Jr. (b. 1789), and John (b. 1793) followed their father's trade. Abel, Jr., worked as a clockmaker in Medford between 1818 and 1819, continued his craft in Charlestown and Boston until about 1823, and later worked as a watchmaker and jeweler in Boston in 1824 before returning to Medford. John J. Stowell, presumably the son of Abel, Sr., is recorded with Abel, Jr., as a clockmaker in Boston and jeweler of Boston between 1823 and 1825.[14] JJF

1. *Worcester VR*, 244.
2. "Burial Grounds in Worcester," 60, no. 277, 61, no. 282; *Worcester VR*, 114, 427.
3. Jones 1930, 310. Abel Stowell, his father, Cornelius, and father-in-law, Israel Jenison, were on the list.
4. Stowell received payment in 1786 for conveying individuals on behalf of the town of Worcester; in 1793 he was paid for assisting with the maintenance of the grammar school, qualified as a juror, and was selected constable; *Worcester Society of Antiquity* 8:42, 65, 81, 165, 238, 240.
5. *Worcester VR*, 147, 427; "Burial Grounds in Worcester," 61, no. 280.
6. "Burial Grounds in Worcester," 43, nos. 171, 173.
7. Births of Betsy (1786), Abel (1789), John (1793), and Alexander (1795), as well as Cornelius (1784), Faith (1782), and Gustavus-Adolphus (1798), are listed in *Worcester VR*, 244–46. Betsy Stowell and her husband, the silversmith John Ridgway "of Boston," were married in Worcester on 31 December 1807, according to *Worcester VR*, 427. They appear in a deed dated 5 August 1818 (WCD 207:500), transacted three days after Abel Stowell's death, wherein she and her husband, listed as a silversmith of Boston, gave up rights to her father's estate to her brother Abel, Jr., for $250.16. John Ridgway was probably brother to the silversmith James (w. ca. 1809–25), who married Betsy's sister, Faith, in 1802.
8. WCD 122:455–56. This land was described as having "said Abel work Shop Standing on the premises."
9. *Massachusetts Spy*, 5 June 1783, repeated 12, 19, 26 June; 13 January 1785, repeated 20, 27 January; 20 November 1799, repeated 27 November, 11 December; 4 December 1799, repeated 11, 18 December. The First Parish Meetinghouse and Old South Meetinghouse of Worcester described in these advertisements are the same Congregational church established in 1719; see Worthley 1970, 706–07.
10. WCD 104:186; 108:138; 122:578; 127:199; 128:69; 136:149; 142:114; 145:596; 152:591; 156:35; 163:485–86; 203:316; 209:459; 225:361; 262:430.
11. Lincoln 1862, 269, 289.
12. *Massachusetts Spy*, 13 January 1785, repeated 20, 27 January; 22 November 1792, repeated 6 December.
13. WCPR, docket 57123. Stowell died intestate. "Burial Grounds in Worcester," 60, no. 275.
14. WCD 218:29; 221:512; 224:600; 226:522, 650; 228:396; 231:324; 240:501; 245:556. A Cornelius Stowell, either an uncle or unrecorded sibling, appears as a clockmaker of Worcester in deeds with Abel, Jr., between 1819 and 1820 in WCD 218:29; 221:512; 226:522, 650.

Owen Sullivan
d. 1756

According to Kenneth Scott, Owen Sullivan came to Boston either in 1748 or early in 1749. Toward the end of August 1749 he and John Tyas of Roxbury, Massachusetts, were arrested for counterfeiting. While he was in jail, Sullivan is said to have cut a plate for counterfeiting forty-shilling New Hampshire bills. He and Tyas were indicted at a court of assize held in Boston on 7 September 1750 and were sentenced to corporal punishment. After this experience in Boston, Sullivan moved to Providence, Rhode Island, where his ears were cropped in 1752 for counterfeiting bills of credit of that colony. This incident was reported in the *Boston Evening-Post* on 9 October 1752. Sullivan was hanged in New York in 1756 for his continued counterfeiting activities.[1] PEK

1. Dow 1927, 13; Scott 1957, 186–209.

Richard Taylor
d. 1673

Richard Taylor was probably the earliest clockmaker working in New England. The Boston town records of 25 January 1657 state that "Richard Taylor is allowed thirty shillings for repairing the clock for his direction to ring by, and is to have five pounds per annum for the future, provided hee bee att charges to keepe a clocke and to repayre itt."[1] In 1661 he was also given permission to set up a shop, presumably where he could make clock repairs, under the stairs in the west end of the Town House.[2] In 1668 the town records again specify that he is to have five pounds a year for taking care of the town clock.[3] In 1670 this task was taken over by Thomas Matson (q.v. Appendix A). Richard Taylor was in Boston as early as 1642, when he was made a freeman and joined the church, at which time he was called "a single man and a tailor." He died in Boston in 1673.[4] PEK

1. RC 2:141.
2. RC 7:4.
3. RC 7:44.
4. SCPR 7:317–18, docket 657; Savage 1860–62, 4:262–63.

Isaac Webb
w. ca. 1705–09

The following notice appeared in the *Boston News-Letter* of 29 March to 5 April 1708:

> This is to give Notice that Isaac Webb, Watch-Maker and Clock-Maker, that formerly Liv'd next Door to the Royal-Exchange Tavern near to the East End of the Town-House in Boston, is now Removed over-against the West-End of the said Town-House in the High Street two Doors from Prison Lane, at the Sign of the Clock Dial that goes against the Side of the House; So that if any Person or Persons wants any Clock to be made, or any Old Clocks to be turned into Pendelums, or Watches and Clocks to be Mended, or Glasses, Keys, Springs or Chains of the best Sort; Let them repair to the said Webb, where they may be served on reasonable Terms.[1]

In February 1709 the Boston selectmen engaged Webb to work on the town clock in the Old Meeting House, "make the same into an eight-day Clock, he to find all Materials for ye doing thereof, and cause the Same to go well to the Satisfaction of the Select men for which he is to be paid the Sume of Thirteen pounds And after the same is so done he is duly to Attend wind up and keep clean the same yearly, to the Select men's satisfaction and for his s^d service he is to be Allowed & paid fifty two shillings p. Annum."[2] In the selectmen's minutes for August 1709 a further mention occurs about the salary having commenced in May.[3] Webb was identified as a watchmaker in a suit in the Suffolk County Court of Common Pleas.[4] The Isaac Webb who married Abigail Clark on 20 November 1705 was probably the clockmaker.[5] A son Daniel was born to the couple in 1707, and a son Michael Smith was born in 1708.[6] PEK

1. Dow 1927, 145.
2. RC 11:85.

3. RC 11:95.
4. SCCR, Court of Common Pleas Record Book 1706–10, 21.
5. RC 28:17.
6. RC 24:52, 58.

Thomas S. White
w. ca. 1736–38

A notice in the *New-England Weekly Journal* of 9 March 1735/36 stated, "Thomas White, of Boston, engraver, had two young children burned to death in his house, Mar. 6, 1735–36."[1] This individual probably is the Thomas S. White, engraver, who was a plaintiff in the Suffolk County Court of Common Pleas in April and July 1738.[2] The identity of this craftsman has yet to be established. A Thomas White and his wife, Ann, had a daughter Ann born to them on 10 January 1733.[3] However, a marriage record for this couple and the births of any more children have not been found. PEK

1. Dow 1927, 14.
2. SCCR, Court of Common Pleas Record Book 1737, 224, 258.
3. RC 24:214.

Benjamin Willard
1743–1803

Benjamin Willard, the eldest member of the renowned family of Massachusetts clockmakers, was born in Grafton, Massachusetts, to Benjamin and Sarah Brooks Willard on 19 March 1743.[1] He would have finished his apprenticeship about 1764. He is said to have trained with the East Hartford, Connecticut, clockmaker Benjamin Cheney (1725–1815). In 1764 Willard purchased a house and land in Grafton from his father and in the 3 December 1764 issue of the *Connecticut Courant* he advertised that he was setting up a "last making" business in East Hartford, at the home of Benjamin Cheney. In 1766 he went to work for the Lexington, Massachusetts, clockmaker Nathaniel Mulliken, Sr. (q.v. Appendix A), and took over his shop when Mulliken died in 1767.[2] Willard probably began training his brother Simon (q.v. Appendix A) at about that time. In December 1771 Benjamin advertised that he had moved from Lexington to Roxbury, Massachusetts. The advertisement indicates that he also operated a shop in Grafton. During the Revolution he was in York, Pennsylvania. Following the Revolution he lived in Worcester, Massachusetts, and died on a trip to Baltimore, Maryland, in 1803.[3] Many examples of his workmanship survive including a musical clock of his manufacture at Yale.[4] PEK

1. *Grafton VR*, 147.
2. Zea/Cheney 1992, 19–20.
3. Bailey 1975, 54.
4. Battison/Kane 1973, 54–57, no. 9; Zea/Cheney 1992, 29–32, 163–64, fig. 2–1.

Simon Willard
1753–1848

The most famous member of the Willard family of clockmakers, Simon Willard, a younger brother of Benjamin Willard (q.v. Appendix A), was born in Grafton, Massachusetts, on 3 April 1753.[1] Willard's apprenticeship would have begun in 1767, and even though Willard himself claimed he was trained by his brother Benjamin, some authorities believe that his master was an Englishman named Mr. Morris. This individual may have been the John

Morris (q.v. Appendix A) whose name appears with that of S. Willard on cast-lead pendulum bobs dated 1770 and 1771. Willard would have finished his training in 1774. He worked first in Grafton and moved to Roxbury in 1780. His illustrious career has been chronicled by his great-grandson John Ware Willard and others.[2] PEK

1. *Grafton VR*, 149.
2. Willard (1911) 1968; Zea/Cheney 1992, 29–59.

**Robert Williams
w. ca. 1690**

At the Boston town meeting of 17 March 1689/90, an agreement was reached between Robert Williams and the town that "he shall continue as formerlie to warne the Town Meetings upon occasion, to ringe the bell at Five of the Clocke in ye morninge, Exchange Bell at eleaven of ye clocke, and at nine in the night, & carefully looke after & keepe the Town clocke in the old Meetinge house."[1] His employment for these tasks suggests that Robert Williams had some training repairing clocks. This individual is probably the "R.W. the grave-digger, bell-ringer" Sewall refers to in his diary entry of 25 August 1695. He may also have been the Robert who was the husband of Margery and who was dead by 1723, when Margery's epitaph, composed at her death on 31 August 1723 at age seventy-five, records her as the widow of Robert.[2] PEK

1. RC 7:201.
2. Savage 1860–62, 4:566–67; Codman 1918, 249.

Appendix B

Persons Previously Misidentified as Colonial Massachusetts Silversmiths or Jewelers

THE NAMES included in this appendix are of persons previously misidentified as colonial Massachusetts silversmiths or jewelers. Some are of silversmiths who in the past were identified as working in the colonial period, but who were born after 1754, the cut-off date in this study for craftsmen working before the Revolution. Some have been identified as silversmiths, but no proof has been found to substantiate this claim. Some are silversmiths said to have worked in Massachusetts, but proof is lacking that they ever worked as silversmiths in the colony.

Charles Allen

In 1928 Howard Okie listed a C. Allen working at an unknown location about 1760, and James Graham repeated this information in his publication of 1936.[1] In 1948 Stephen Ensko published a mark C·ALLEN in a rectangle for a Charles Allen working about 1760 in Boston, but he cited no evidence as to why the "C" stood for "Charles."[2] Ensko may have concluded that this mark belonged to a Boston maker because the design of the object was similar to other Boston silver. Louise Belden illustrates the mark ALLEN in a rectangle from a spoon with a webbed shell drop and suggests that it might have been used by one of the silversmiths named Allen—John (q.v.), Thomas (q.v. Appendix B), or Charles—working in the Boston area, where webbed shells were used.[3] Henry Flynt and Martha Gandy Fales speculated that Charles Allen might be the son of Samuel Allen of Deerfield, Massachusetts, but noted that no record of a Charles Allen working as a silversmith in Boston about 1760 was found in public documents.[4] Recent research confirms Flynt and Fales' findings: neither a Charles Allen nor a C. Allen worked as a silversmith in Boston in the mid eighteenth century. PEK

1. Okie 1928, 239; Graham 1936, 2.
2. Ensko 1948, 12, 161; subsequent publications included this information: see Thorn 1949, 10; Kovel 1961, 12.
3. Belden 1980, 30.
4. Flynt/Fales 1968, 144.

Thomas Allen

The catalogue of the exhibition "American Church Silver" (1911) included the information that a silversmith named Thomas Allen was in Boston in 1758.[1]

1035

This information has appeared subsequently in most of the standard references. Louise Belden suggested that the mark ALLEN in a rectangle might have been used by this maker or by Charles Allen (q.v. Appendix B) or John Allen (q.v.).[2] A tantalizing bit of evidence appears in a list of people who were erecting buildings damaged in the Boston fire of 1760: "Mr. Allen Smiths shop on Col Wendells Land."[3] It is not clear, however, that Allen's first name was Thomas or that his occupation was that of goldsmith. The shop being rebuilt could have been for a blacksmith or a tinsmith. A comprehensive survey of the public records has turned up no evidence that a goldsmith named Thomas Allen worked in Boston at the time. PEK

1. MFA 1911, 127; the information was based on notes in the Berger file that is part of the Bigelow-Phillips files.
2. Belden 1980, 30.
3. RC 29:113.

Thomas Aylwin
ca. 1738–91

Thomas Aylwin, the son of Thomas Aylwin, a clothworker of Romsey, Hampshire, England, was apprenticed to a member of the London Goldsmith's Company, Richard Sharp, for seven years beginning 4 June 1752 and finishing in 1759.[1] Yet nothing indicates that either Aylwin or Sharp actually were involved in the goldsmith's trade. Just as goldsmiths were sometimes members of other livery companies, so other tradesmen probably were in the Goldsmiths' Company. Aylwin apparently was apprenticed into a trade similar to his father's because he was described as "America Hatter" when he became free of the Goldsmiths' Company on 6 March 1782.[2] Bringing merchandise with him, Aylwin settled in Quebec in 1763 as a merchant. In the *Quebec Gazette* for 25 July 1765 he advertised dry goods for sale and announced the necessity of settling his affairs after the death of his partner, Charles Kerr.[3] In 1770 Aylwin left Quebec for Boston and there married, on 11 September 1771, Lucy Cushing (b. 1745), the daughter of John Cushing, Jr. (1695–1778), judge of the Massachusetts Superior Court from 1747 to 1771, and Mary Cotton (1710–69) of Scituate, Massachusetts.[4] In 1772 Aylwin served on a selectmen's committee to visit the free schools in Boston.[5] A few days after the battle of Lexington and Concord, Aylwin and his family left Boston for Quebec, where he continued his mercantile career until his death in 1791.[6] PEK

1. Apprentice Book 7, 178, Worshipful Company of Goldsmiths, London.
2. Freedom Book 3, Worshipful Company of Goldsmiths, London. Robert Barker provided information on the probability of Aylwin's following the clothworker/haberdasher/hatter trade in a letter to the author, 9 February 1993.
3. Langdon 1970, 32–33.
4. RC 30:43; *Scituate VR* 1:119; 2:77, 378.
5. RC 23:133.
6. Jones 1930, 18.

Joseph Barrett

Joseph Barrett was first mentioned as a silversmith in 1940, when Everett U. Crosby, in *Books and Baskets: Signs and Silver of Old-Time Nantucket*, attributed a spoon bearing the mark J·BARRETT to him. Crosby also identified Barrett as the author of a three-page document, dated 1753, that illustrated spoon designs and gave instructions for their fabrication.[1] Although the spoon may be an early eighteenth-century piece, the document could not have been written in

1753; its spelling idiosyncracies incorrectly approximate language of the 1750s, and its drawings of spoons resemble those made during the early nineteenth century.[2]

In 1968, Henry Flynt and Martha Gandy Fales published a short entry on Barrett, noting that he was "mentioned by some silver authorities as advertising in Nantucket c. 1753. Spoons with marks attributed to him and owned by descendants of an old Nantucket family indicate that he did work in Nantucket around that time." But the mark to which they refer has since been given to John Burger of New York.[3] Moreover, the vital records and deed and probate court registries for Nantucket and mainland Massachusetts counties give no evidence of any Joseph Barrett who might have worked as a silversmith. JJF

1. Crosby 1940, 28–32.
2. Carpenter/Carpenter 1987, 126–27.
3. Flynt/Fales 1968, 153; YUAG files.

C. Brigdens

J. H. Buck included the name C. Brigdens among Boston silversmiths in the 1903 edition of his book *Old Plate*.[1] Although a typographical error for Zachariah Brigden (q.v.), subsequent silver scholars, beginning with Hollis French in 1917, perpetuated this mistake and associated two initials marks and surname marks with the name.[2] No silversmith named C. Brigdens has been identified as working in Massachusetts in the colonial period. PEK

1. Buck 1903, 46, 315.
2. French (1917) 1967, 18; Kovel 1961, 42; Flynt/Fales 1968, 166; Belden 1980, 75.

Ebenezer Brown

Most silver authorities give the goldsmith Ebenezer Brown's life dates as 1773–1816.[1] Henry Flynt and Martha Gandy Fales, however, claim he was born in 1741, conflating the Brown who was a silversmith with an Ebenezer Brown born earlier who was not.[2] The Ebenezer Brown who died in Boston on 6 March 1816 at the age of forty-three was clearly a silversmith: he was identified as a goldsmith in his estate inventory, which contained a substantial number of metalworking tools and raw metals.[3] But this silversmith's birth date of 1773, deduced from the age listed in his obituary notice, falls too late for him to be included here.[4] No evidence exists to document that the Ebenezer Brown born in 1741 ever was a silversmith. DAF

1. French (1917) 1967, 19; Kovel 1961, 44; MFA 1911, 131.
2. Flynt/Fales 1968, 167.
3. SCPR 114:216, 218, 223–24; 115:138–39.
4. *Index of Obituaries, 1784–1840*, 1:629.

John Butler
w. ca. 1775

In 1861, a history of the Essex Lodge of Masons noted that John Butler was "by occupation a silversmith, and as such made the jewels of the lodge."[1] The compiler noted several other details concerning Butler's life, including the comments that he was admitted as a member of the lodge on 14 March 1779 and was its first senior warden; that he was a lieutenant in 1776 in the artillery company commanded by Capt. John Felt; and that Mehitable, his wife, died on 8 October 1787. A later history of the lodge repeats these facts, gives his birth date as 1740 and date of death as 1808, notes that his wife's maiden name was Osgood, and traces his involvement with the lodge at various times, beginning with his early involvement in the founding of the lodge in 1779.[2]

In spite of his seemingly prominent role in the lodge, to date no other information concerning this John Butler has surfaced, and his career as a silversmith remains to be confirmed. Research in a variety of Butler family genealogies, in the vital records of various Essex County towns, and in the Essex County deed and probate records has not yet revealed any information about a John Butler, goldsmith or silversmith, who might be the man investigated here.[3]

It is possible that the lodge's jewels were made by John Butler (q.v.) of Boston and Portland, Maine, who was a jeweler and silversmith, and that the two men's lives were confused. GWRW

1. Leavitt 1861, 91.
2. Hadley 1979, 1–2, 6, 37–38, 43–44, 80.
3. See, for example, Butler 1886; Butler 1888; Butler 1944; and Butler 1919.

? Chasley
w. ca. 1765

Boston records reveal that on 20 November 1765 "Mr. Chasley [?], a Goldsmith," arrived on Abel Badger's sloop *America* from Philadelphia.[1] No further evidence of this individual has been found in Boston records. The possibility exists that the name is an incorrect transcription of Chaffey. A goldsmith named James Chaffey came from London to Philadelphia in 1760 and ultimately settled on Indian Island off the New Brunswick coast.[2] Perhaps he stopped in Boston as he traveled northward. PEK

1. RC 29:262.
2. Mackay 1973, 95.

Henry Cogswell

Based on a pair of beakers in the First Congregational Church at Marblehead, Massachusetts, marked H. Cogswell and engraved with the date 1748, some early scholars presumed that H[enry] Cogswell worked in the eighteenth century. However, the beakers probably were marked by the mid nineteenth-century Salem silversmith Henry Cogswell (1824–65) when he remade them in 1852.[1] No evidence exists that an H. or Henry Cogswell worked as a goldsmith in Massachusetts in the mid eighteenth century. PEK

1. Jones 1913, 260; French (1917) 1967, 29; Ensko 1927, 43; Ensko 1937, 39; Okie 1936, 250; Graham 1936, 17.

Edward Davis

A silversmith by this name is said by some scholars to have been working in Newburyport, Massachusetts, from about 1775 until his death in 1781.[1] The tradition began with Ernest Currier, who mistakenly identified the Newburyport silversmith who used a mark with the initials ED as Edward Davis. No trace of a silversmith named Edward Davis has been found in the records, however, and it is suggested here that the silversmith in question is actually Elias Davis (q.v.). GWRW

1. Currier 1938, 40; Ensko 1948, 45; Thorn 1949, 63; Flynt/Fales 1968, 197; Benes 1986, 182; Belden 1980, 131.

William Dawes
1719–1802

Family genealogies and other sources have identified William Dawes as having joined his nephew William Homes, Jr., in the goldsmith's business on Ann Street in Boston about 1764.[1] On the basis of these historical accounts, Dawes has been included in the standard lists of American silversmiths.[2] No contemporary documentation indicates that Dawes was a silversmith. Beginning in 1742 and continuing to 1788 he was identified as a tailor in Suffolk County deeds.[3] Deeds transacted in 1789 and 1794 identify him as a trader as did his estate administration probated in 1802.[4] DAF

1. Holland 1878, 72–82; Roberts 1895, 2:100–01.
2. French (1917) 1967, 35; Thorn 1949, 64; Flynt/Fales 1968, 200; Kovel 1961, 78.
3. SCD 64:254–55; 66:46–48; 81:185–86; 83:256–57; 88:237–38; 89:107–08; 93:201–02, 255–56; 94:80–82; 103:241; 129:114–15, 226; 130:194–95; 132:21–22; 139:230; 151:256–59; 163:155–56.
4. SCD 167:6–7; 177:16–17; SCPR 100:537–40.

Shem Drowne
1683–1774

In 1920 Louise Avery tentatively attributed a beaker marked SD to Shem Drowne.[1] As early as 1925, however, Francis Hill Bigelow questioned the attribution: "The beaker is doubtless of New England origin, as it was found there; though the attribution to Shem Drowne of Boston is probably erroneous. There seems to be no evidence that Drowne was a silversmith."[2] Suffolk County deeds recorded between 1720 and 1771 give Shem Drowne's occupation as tinplate worker.[3] Nonetheless, most silver authorities continued to include Shem Drowne in their lists of makers, although it is highly unlikely he was a silversmith.[4] Drowne was the brother-in-law of the silversmith Timothy Parrott (q.v.). PEK

1. Avery 1920, 13–14. Prior to Avery's publication, Hollis French included Shem Drowne in his list of American silversmiths.
2. Bigelow 1925, 156.
3. SCD 34:205, 208; 47:311; 48:1; 50:207–08; 99:163–64; 118:215–16.
4. Ensko 1927, 44; Graham 1936, 23; Okie 1936, 254; Thorn 1949, 71; Kovel 1961, 86.

Nathaniel Fowle
1748–1817

In the recent literature Nathaniel Fowle, who was a silversmith in Northampton, Massachusetts, working circa 1816–33, has been confused with another Nathaniel Fowle, whose life dates are 1748–1817.[1] The latter Nathaniel Fowle is usually identified as a tailor in the Hampden County land records in the 1770s and 1780s.[2] He and Benjamin Tappan (q.v.) probably shared workspace in Northampton between 1785 and 1806. The birth date for the Nathaniel Fowle who was the silversmith has yet to be established. The relationship between the two Nathaniel Fowles in the Connecticut Valley and the Nathaniel Fowle who advertised as a jeweler and watchmaker with John Fowle in Boston about 1809 is not known.[3] PEK

1. Flynt/Fales 1968, 221; Belden 1980, 177; Cutten 1939, 2.
2. HCD 14:660; 25:167; 26:227, 546; 27:133; 28:2, 116. A deed of 1777 calls him a yeoman; HCD 14:661.
3. *Boston Directory* 1809, 58; HaCD 28:226.

Benjamin Greenleaf III 1756–80

The Bigelow-Phillips files include a reference to Benjamin Greenleaf, born on 25 June 1745, the son of Joseph and Mary Greenleaf. However, the Benjamin Greenleaf who would go on to be a silversmith was born in Newbury, Massachusetts, on 6 November 1756, the son of Timothy and Susannah Greenleaf, and the younger brother of Timothy Greenleaf (q.v. Appendix B).[1] An obscure maker, Benjamin seems to have practiced in Newburyport, Massachusetts, for only a few years before his death there on 20 December 1780, at age twenty-four. His relationship with Simon Greenleaf (q.v. Appendix B) has yet to be determined.

The inventory of Benjamin Greenleaf's estate was taken on 28 March 1781 by Joseph Moulton (q.v.), Elias Davis (q.v.), and Jonathan Marsh. Greenleaf died intestate, and his estate was valued at £809.12.7. It included "his mansion in an undivided piece of land near the ferry place in Newburyport lying betwen Mr. Watkins and Mrs. Roberts Land" valued at £90, fifty acres of land in Haverhill valued at £330, and other pastureland, meadow, and woodlands in Newbury and Salisbury. His goldsmith's shop in Newburyport was valued at £67.10.

The material in his shop included old silver and gold filings, wrought gold and silver, jewelry, jeweler's supplies, and goldsmith's tools, in all amounting to £143.4.10.[2] GWRW

1. *Newbury VR* 1:193; 2:208. It has been said that he was married in 1766 to Tameson Davis of Gloucester, which seems unlikely; see, for example, Flynt/Fales 1968, 234.
2. ECPR, docket 11729.

Simon Greenleaf 1752–76

According to a family genealogy, Simon Greenleaf was born in Newbury, Massachusetts, in 1752, the son of Hon. Jonathan Greenleaf (1723–1807), a ship carpenter, and Mary (Presbury) Greenleaf (b. 1723), who were married in 1744. (The Newbury vital records, however, give his date of baptism as 21 June 1747.) He was the grandson of Daniel and Sarah (Moody) Greenleaf of Newbury, who were married in 1710, and of Edmund (or Edward) and Catherine (Pierce) Presbury, also of Newbury, who were married in 1713. About 1773, he married Hannah Osgood (1754–1827) of Andover, Massachusetts, who later married Capt. John Lee. Simon and Hannah had one child, a son named Jonathan (1774–98).[1]

The genealogy states that he "had learned the trade of a goldsmith but was never able to engage in much active business" on account of poor health and disabilities. The author paints a vivid and rare description of a unique individual:

> In very early life [he] was afflicted with rheumatism; insomuch that he became somewhat deformed in body, being hunchbacked, and was always a pet in the family, probably from his physical disability. He is said to have been a young man of some genius and wit, having a handsome face and agreeable manners. He was extravagantly fond of dress, in which he greatly indulged, probably to conceal his personal defects, and was rather a gay young man.[2]

In his probate documents, Greenleaf is referred to as a merchant of Newburyport. He died intestate and insolvent. Nothing in his probate docket indicates that he was a silversmith.[3] William Coffin Little (q.v.) was one of his creditors.[4] His relationship to Benjamin Greenleaf III and Timothy Greenleaf (qq.v. Appendix B) is not yet clear. GWRW

1. Greenleaf 1896, 132–33, 408; *Newbury VR* 1:195, 196, 198, 388; 2:205, 206, 410; *Andover VR* 1:284; *Index of Obituaries, 1784–1840*, 3:2755.
2. Greenleaf 1896, 133.
3. The Massachusetts tax list of 1771 includes Greenleaf with a considerable amount of merchandise (£356) and some real estate, helping to confirm his identity as a merchant; see Pruitt 1978, 116–17.
4. ECPR, docket 11803.

Timothy Greenleaf
ca. 1753–86

A man by this name has been identified in an archaeological report as a blacksmith and a goldsmith with a store on Water Street in Newburyport, Massachusetts, until 1786, when he died on 1 February at age thirty-three.[1] It is thus likely that he was born about 1753 and possible that he was active in the colonial period. He was the son of Timothy (1719?–64) and Susanna (1725–71) Greenleaf, who were married in Newbury in 1743.[2] He married Joanna Obear on 30 May 1776 and was the older brother of Benjamin Greenleaf III (q.v. Appendix B).[3] His relationship, if any, with Simon Greenleaf (q.v. Appendix B) has yet to be determined.

However, in his estate papers Greenleaf is referred to as a mariner, with the exception of one reference to him as a blacksmith.[4] In the Essex County land records, he is identified solely as a blacksmith.[5] Like many nonurban craftsmen, Greenleaf may have worked in precious as well as base metals, but confirmation of such activity has not been discovered as yet. GWRW

1. ECPR, docket 11816, cited in Alaric Faulkner et al., *Port and Market: Archaeology of the Central Waterfront, Newburyport, Massachusetts*, A Report Submitted to the National Park Service, Interagency Archeological Services-Atlanta, of work performed under contract CX 5880-7-0084 (typescript, March 1978), 111.
2. *Newbury VR* 1:198, 199; 2:604, 208.
3. *Newburyport VR* 2:200.
4. ECPR, docket 11816.
5. ECD 122:278; 141:138; 145:178.

Samuel Hill, Jr.
ca. 1766–1804

The engraver Samuel Hill, Jr., has been misidentified as the son of Alexander and Thankful Hill who was born in Boston on 27 July 1750 and who joined the Ancient and Honorable Artillery Company in 1794.[1] Hill was identified as junior and an engraver when he and his grandmother Bethiah Call and his wife, Gracey, sold land in Charlestown, Massachusetts, in 1793. His father, Samuel Webb Hill (1740/41–94), witnessed the deed.[2] Samuel's birth is not recorded in Massachusetts vital records, but he was born the year after the marriage of his father and Hannah Curtis, which took place on 14 May 1765.[3] Samuel, Jr., was the nephew of the Charlestown jeweler James Hill (q.v.). The *Boston Directory* of 1789 lists Samuel Hill as an engraver at no. 74 Cornhill, and that same year he began to produce engravings for the *Massachusetts Magazine*.[4] The *Boston Directory* of 1796 listed Hill on Rawson's (or Bromfield's) Lane.[5] He was included in the Boston directories until 1803.[6] His other work includes a billhead dated 1795 for the Boston paper-stainer Ebenezer Clough and the *Map of Massachusetts Proper* in 1801.[7] Hill died in April 1804, and his widow died in 1826.[8] PEK

1. Roberts 1895, 2:276.
2. *Charlestown VR* 1:350; Index of Obituaries, 1784–1840, 3:2237; MCD 118:301–02.

3. RC 30:324.
4. RC 10:186; Fielding 1917, 170.
5. RC 10:255.
6. *Boston Directory* 1798, 63; 1800, 58; 1803, 66.
7. McClelland 1924, 138–39; for the map see pp. 2–3 in this volume.
8. *Index of Obituaries, 1784–1840*, 3:2230, 2236.

Amos Kay

As Henry Flynt and Martha Gandy Fales stated in 1968, "Earlier silver authorities credited silver in St. Paul's Episcopal Church in Edenton, N.C., marked AK, to this man from Boston; others believe Am Kay is a fictitious name. . . . Research in vital records, area histories and newspapers has failed to turn up any information to prove a silversmith of this name worked in N. E."[1] Research for the current publication found nothing to refute the conclusion of Flynt and Fales about Amos Kay. PEK

1. Flynt/Fales 1968, 260.

William Little
w. ca. 1725–75

A silversmith by this name is listed in several sources and given working dates of 1725 to 1775, which suggests that "he may have been Newbury's first active silversmith" a quarter-century before Joseph and William Moulton (qq.v.).[1] It has been suggested as well that he was the father of William Coffin Little (q.v.).[2] Separating the lives and work of the two men (if indeed there were two men) is difficult, especially because each appears to have used a two-initial mark of WL, and no mark WCL is known. However, it is possible that there were not two men before 1770: the early William Little and William Coffin Little may be one and the same, and William Coffin Little may have begun to use his middle name after his son William, born in 1771, was apprenticed to the trade. The younger William Little became a silversmith and practiced his trade in Philadelphia in the early nineteenth century before his death in 1836. A Massachusetts court document of 16 June 1794 concerning the counterfeiting activities of William Little of Newburyport and William C. Little of Amesbury, Massachusetts, each cited as a goldsmith, probably refers to William Little the son and William Coffin Little the father.[3]

The early date range for William Little is based primarily, if not exclusively, on Harold L. Peterson's attribution to him in 1955 of an unmarked small sword in the style of about 1725. Peterson gave no reason for attributing this sword, then in the collection of Kendrick Scofield, to Little.[4] The present location of the sword is not known to the writer. Aside from the sword, no document or object before about 1770 associated with a silversmith William Little has yet been found.[5]

The earliest document relating to a silversmith named William Little is a notice in the Newburyport *Essex Journal* of 18 August 1775 (see William Coffin Little biography). It is possible that this notice was placed by the man who would later call himself William Coffin Little, as in a "Stop Thief!" notice in the *Essex Journal* for 20 February 1788. (By 1788, William Little the younger was seventeen and already an apprentice silversmith.) Otherwise, the documentary record for William Little before 1775 is slim, if not nonexistent.

Spoons and other small objects attributed to William Little have been published; they are discussed in the entry for William Coffin Little. Aside from the small sword cited above, these objects date from about 1765 into the 1790s. GWRW

1. Benes 1986, no. 53; Flynt/Fales 1968, 267; Belden 1980, 273.
2. Flynt/Fales 1968, 267.
3. SCCR, file 134596.
4. Peterson (1955) 1991, no. 3.
5. The mark W:L in a shield is also attributed to William Little, but no object bearing that mark has been located to date; see Belden 1980, 273.

Elijah Loring
1744–82

The mark used by the Barnstable silversmith Elpalet Loring (q.v.) has often been misattributed to his brothers Elijah and Eliphalet Loring (q.v. Appendix B). Authorities attributing the mark to Elijah, who was a blacksmith and not a silversmith, include Stephen Ensko and C. Jordan Thorn.[1] PEK

1. Thorn 1949, 133; Ensko 1989, 130; see also Kovel 1961, 172.

Eliphalet Loring
b. 1736

Some authorities have misattributed the mark used by the Barnstable silversmith Elpalet Loring (q.v.) to his brother Eliphalet Loring. Scholars attributing the mark to Eliphalet, who is not known to have been a silversmith, include Hollis French.[1] PEK

1. French (1917) 1967, 76; see also Kovel 1961, 172.

John McClinch

Although some silver scholars list John McClinch as a silversmith, he appears in Suffolk County deed and probate records in the 1780s and 1803 as a whitesmith.[1] No evidence documents his activity as a silversmith. DAF

1. French (1917) 1967, 79; Kovel 1961, 180; Flynt/Fales 1968, 273; SCD 145:116; SCPR, docket 21936.

Joseph Moulton
1694–1756

Grandson of William, Sr., son of William, Jr. (qq.v. Appendix B), and father of William and Joseph (1724–95) (qq.v.), Joseph Moulton was born in Newbury, Massachusetts, on 25 November 1694. Like his two forebears, Joseph has been regarded as a silversmith, although he was a blacksmith by occupation. The family tradition, according to Henry William Moulton in 1906, indicated that Joseph was "the first goldsmith of New England whose successors have continued this business down to the present time. . . . From 1700 to 1740 a new town rapidly sprang into existence; it was later known as Newburyport. To this growing place Joseph and his son William removed their whitesmithing shop, and at about this time introduced the manufacture of gold beads."[1] As with the earlier William Moultons, several early sources accepted Joseph as a silversmith.[2]

In 1941, however, Stephen Decatur suggested that "probably it was the existence of silver articles marked I.MOULTON, either inscribed with dates in the decade 1750–1760 or else reasonably well traced to those years, which led to the belief that he was a silversmith, since his grandson, Joseph, the next known Moulton with this given name to be a member of the craft, was then too young to have made them and since tradition produced no one else to whom they could be assigned. But the appearance of this same mark on spoons which normally would be considered to date between 1760–1770, after the death of Joseph, finally threw doubt on the correctness of the attribution." Decatur continued, "The complete absence of any recorded pieces of Moulton silver which can be dated prior to *circa* 1750, and the fact that Joseph styled himself 'gentleman' in his will, while each of the other members of the family referred to himself as 'goldsmith,' support the view that he was not a worker in silver, even if he did sometimes make gold beads." "We may accept as a certainty that Joseph was not a silversmith," Decatur concluded, "and should not be so listed until some definite evidence to the contrary is discovered."[3]

Recent research has not revealed any information to challenge Decatur's conclusion. The evidence of such craftsmen as the Northeys and Langs of Salem, Massachusetts, however, does indicate that metalworking artisans in small towns did make, buy, and sell objects fashioned from various materials, including pewter, silver, gold, brass, and iron. Thus, it is possible that Joseph Moulton too occasionally turned his hand to crafting small objects of precious metal. GWRW

1. Moulton 1906, 263, 331 (quotation).
2. Bigelow 1917, 158; French (1917) 1967, 84; Graham 1936, 51; Okie 1936, 273; Thorn 1949, 150.
3. Decatur 1941a, 14.

William Moulton, Jr.
1664–1732

The youngest son of William, Sr. (q.v. Appendix B), and Margaret (Page) Moulton, this William also was thought to have been a silversmith by some early sources. The tradition began in the early twentieth century, when the family genealogist, Henry William Moulton, noted that "the primitive Colonial silversmith of New England was William Moulton whose first silver shoe buckles appeared about 1690," fashioned in his shop on Moulton Hill in Newbury, Massachusetts.[1] This reference led to William's listing in several early lists of American silversmiths.[2]

However, archival research quickly reveals that this William, as Stephen Decatur noted in 1941, was "not a silversmith in any true sense of the term and should not be listed as such." Decatur noted that "the records refer to him as a weaver, 'innholder,' trader, and merchant, and it is plainly evident that he started as a weaver, later branching out into general business activities." Decatur continued, "No piece of silver has ever been found which can be ascribed to him, and his inventory makes no mention of silversmith's tools. In his will he calls himself 'trader,'" and probate records give no evidence that he was a practicing goldsmith.[3] A recent check of the documents confirms Decatur's research. GWRW

1. Moulton 1906, 258–59, 328 (quotation), 329, 331.
2. French (1917) 1967, 84; Ensko 1927, 61; Okie 1936, 273. Modern sources, for example Flynt/Fales 1968, 283, generally discount the early family tradition.
3. Decatur 1941a, 14.

William Moulton, Sr.
ca. 1617–64

The founder of the American branch of the Moulton family that would later gain recognition as silversmiths, William Moulton, Sr., was listed as a silversmith by Hollis French.[1] Born about 1617 in Ormsby, Norfolk, England, he left England in 1637, coming to America as the servant of Robert Page. After landing in Boston, he settled in Winnacunnett (now Hampton), New Hampshire, in 1639, where he married Margaret (d. 1699), the daughter of Robert and Lucia Page. He died there on 18 April 1664. His will and other probate documents indicate that he was a husbandman, or farmer.[2] He was the father of William, Jr. (q.v. Appendix B), mentioned in his will as his "Child which is yet unBorne," and grandfather of Joseph (q.v. Appendix B), both of whom were also erroneously thought to have been silversmiths, as well as the great-grandfather of William and Joseph (qq.v.), the first actual silversmiths in the Moulton family. GWRW

1. French (1917) 1967, 84.
2. ECPR, docket 19049. See also Moulton 1906, 254, 257, 329. Most of William's will is also reprinted here. See also Dow 1893; reprint, 1970; 39, 362, 475, 861–63, 889–90.

Dudley Newhall

Early scholars cite a Dudley Newhall working as a silversmith in Salem, Massachusetts, about 1730; however, as Henry Flynt and Martha Gandy Fales note, no records of this man's activity as a silversmith at this time have been found.[1] A Dudley (S.?) Newhall was listed in Salem as a jeweler in 1821, and a Dudley S. Newhall purchased small amounts of jewelry from the firm of Baldwin and Baker in the early nineteenth century and was a creditor of Jabez Baldwin (1778–1819).[2] He therefore seems to have worked too late for inclusion here. GWRW

1. Belknap 1927, 108; MFA 1911, 150; French (1917) 1967, 86; Thorn 1949, 153; Flynt/Fales 1968, 287.
2. Flynt/Fales 1968, 287; Baldwin and Baker Account Book, 1817–19, PEM.

John Otis
w. ca. 1706

The first edition of Stephen Ensko's *American Silversmiths and Their Marks* stated that John Otis "advertised, March 17, 1706, *Boston News-Letter* as silversmith in Barnstable."[1] The 1948 edition of this work omitted Otis, probably because John Marshall Phillips had brought to Ensko's attention the fact that this advertisement (for a runaway servant girl) did not mention Otis's occupation. Although other silver authorities have also listed Otis, no evidence indicates that he was a silversmith.[2] JJF and PEK

1. Ensko 1927, 64.
2. Okie 1936, 275; Thorn 1949, 157; Kovel 1961, 203; Flynt/Fales 1968, 292.

James Perkins

That a James Perkins who was a silversmith worked in eighteenth-century Massachusetts is relatively certain, although little can be learned about him. The only document about him is a notice he placed in the *Massachusetts Spy* for 1 December 1785, in which he informed the public that he had "lately sat up the silversmith's business at Patch's Tavern; Sign of the American Arms, in Worcester, where he does every kind of Silversmith's work . . . Worcester,

November 28th, 1785."[1] As Perkins had not set up shop on his own property, he may have been too young or too poor to establish himself on his own.

Henry Flynt and Martha Gandy Fales link the silversmith to the James Perkins who died in Boston in 1838 at the age of seventy-eight, giving him a birth date of 1752, although that connection cannot be proven. A number of men with this name lived in Massachusetts in the mid eighteenth century. Massachusetts vital records show no James Perkins born in 1752, but list six men named James Perkins who were born between 1736 and 1763 and eight marriages of men by that name between 1744 and 1783, none of which took place in Worcester County.[2] No fewer than nine James Perkinses served in the Revolution.[3] The census of 1800 identifies a James Perkins with two sons, one daughter, and a wife residing in Worcester County.[4] But thus far it has been impossible to establish which, if any, of these men might be the silversmith and if he worked during the colonial period. JJF

1. For additional information on the Sign of the American Arms, also known as the United States Arms and later as the Exchange Hotel, see Lincoln 1862, 425, and Camp/Camp 1979, 10–17.
2. IGI 1984, p. 28,032–033.
3. *Mass. Soldiers and Sailors* 12:156.
4. 1800 Census, 301.

Ebenezer Pitts, Jr.
d. 1814

The *Boston Evening-Post* of 26 April 1762 announced that on 8 April Ebenezer Pitts, Jr., of Taunton, goldsmith and watchmaker, had married Lydia Cudworth, "a shapely young Lady, graceful in her Carriage, agreeable in her Conversation, and endowed with every necessary Qualification to render the Marriage State agreeable being crown'd with a considerable Fortune." This is the sole mention of Pitts as a goldsmith and watchmaker. In all other records he is identified as a joiner or yeoman and very likely his occupation was given incorrectly in the newspaper. No birth record exists for him in vital records, but he probably was the son of Ebenezer Pitts, a yeoman of Taunton, Massachusetts, and the grandson of Samuel Pitts (d. 1701) of Taunton.[1]

Ebenezer Pitts, Jr., was identified as a joiner numerous times: in a deed from his father for land in Taunton in 1755 on which the younger Pitts was building a house; in probate records in 1758; and in a deed in 1764 when his father conveyed additional land in Taunton to him.[2] Ebenezer Pitts, identified as a yeoman, and his wife, Lydia, sold the land recorded in the 1755 and 1764 deeds in 1779, perhaps at the time they were relocating to the town of Ward in Worcester County.[3]

Pitts's wife, Lydia Cudworth (b. 1744), the daughter of James (1696/97–ca. 1757) and Sibel (Chase) Cudworth (d. ca. 1761), inherited land in Freetown, Massachusetts, when her father's estate was divided.[4] As a yeoman, Pitts and his wife sold land in Freetown in 1779.[5] Pitts had moved to the town of Ward in Worcester County by 1791, when he and his wife, Lydia, identified as being from Ward, sold additional land in Freetown.[6] They sold more land in Freetown in 1794.[7] Ebenezer Pitts identified himself as a yeoman of Ward when he wrote his will on 12 March 1813. The probate court ruled that he was not of sound mind when he wrote the will, and on 4 October 1814 directed that one-third part of the value of the real estate be designated for the widow. The real estate was appraised at $1,295.50.[8] PEK

1. *Bristol County Massachusetts Probate Records* 1987, 1:27.
2. BrCD (Taunton) 42:104; 50:147–48; *Bristol County Massachusetts Probate Records* 1987, 2:229–30.
3. BrCD (Taunton) 59:126.
4. *Bristol County Massachusetts Probate Records* 1987, 2:280; *Freetown VR* n.p.
5. BrCD (Taunton) 59:125–26; BrCD (Fall River) 11:377.
6. BrCD (Taunton) 69:456–57; BrCD (Fall River) 13:420.
7. BrCD (Taunton) 72:363; BrCD (Fall River) 14:175.
8. WCPR 43:296–97; 44:471; 46:259–60, docket 47022.

Jonathan Pollard
1749–1802

Jonathan Pollard was identified as a goldsmith in a biography of his son Benjamin (1780–1836) published in 1855 and has been included in several lists of American silversmiths, although contemporary documentation of Pollard's trade is lacking.[1] Pollard, a great-grandson of the prominent Boston silversmith Edward Winslow (q.v.) and a distant cousin of William Pollard (q.v.), was the second of six children born to Benjamin Pollard (1696–1756) and Margaret Winslow (1724–1814).[2] Benjamin Pollard, a brazier, then Esquire, was the son of Jonathan Pollard (1666–1725) and Mary Winslow.[3] Pollard's maternal grandparents were Joshua Winslow (1694–1769) and Elizabeth Savage (1704–78).[4] Pollard married Mary Johnson (1748–1823) of Dedham, Massachusetts, probably in late 1779 or early 1780, since their son Benjamin was born in 1780.[5] Mary was the daughter of Henry (d. 1751) and Mary Johnson.[6]

Although in August 1771 Pollard and John Winniet rented "a Store near the Golden Ball Tavern at the Rate of Twenty three pounds six shillings and eight pence lawful money p. Annum to be paid at four quarterly payments, as also to pay the Tax on said Store," the use of the store was not specified.[7] Pollard quickly achieved respect in the community; by 1775 he had been selected clerk of the market.[8] He served as aide-de-camp to General William Heath from January 1777 to September 1778.[9] The following year, "Col. Jonathan Pollard" was part of a committee formed to "inspect quality of Flour & the other Necessaries of Life" for ward 8 of Boston.[10]

In Suffolk County deeds Pollard is identified only as Esquire. These transactions include deeds in which the heirs of Benjamin Pollard, including "Jonathan Pollard, Esqr," Margaret Pollard, widow, Joshua Blanchard, Jr., merchant, and his wife, Peggy Savage, sold part of their inherited property on Staniford Street to the Boston merchant Job Prince for five hundred pounds on 24 April 1779.[11] They sold another parcel of land on Common Street in April 1782 to George Hamblin for three hundred pounds.[12] In October 1782, Pollard and his wife sold yet another part of their inheritance, a one-fifth part of two brick houses in Brattle Square, to Blanchard.[13]

Pollard was a member of King's Chapel; he was "seated by the Wardens" in pew 13 in 1789, an association for which he paid £14.19.4.[14]

Jonathan Pollard died in Dedham in 1802.[15] His son Benjamin appointed Isaac Winslow and Joshua Blanchard to administer his inheritance from his father, and from his grandparents Margaret and Benjamin Pollard.[16] DAF

1. Loring 1855, 365–67; Thwing; Flynt/Fales 1968, 302.
2. Thwing; SCD 247:285; RC 9:228; RC 24:168, 271; RC 28:258; *Index of Obituaries, 1704–1800*, 1:241; *Index of Obituaries, 1784–1840*, 4:3603.
3. Thwing; Flynt/Fales 1968, 302; RC 9:101, 210; *Index of Obituaries, 1704–1800*, 1:241.
4. RC 9:216; RC 24:32; RC 28:90; SCPR 68:305–08.
5. Thwing; Flynt/Fales 1968, 302; RC 24:267; *Index of Obituaries, 1784–1840*, 4:3603.
6. SCPR, docket 9700.

7. RC 23:96.
8. RC 18:219.
9. Flynt/Fales 1968, 302.
10. RC 26:36–37.
11. SCD 132:173.
12. SCD 142:193–94.
13. SCD 136:97.
14. Foote 1882, 2:325.
15. *Index of Obituaries, 1784–1840*, 4:3602.
16. SCD 247:285.

James Poupard
w. ca. 1772–1814

Although Howard Okie, C. Jordan Thorn, and other silver authorities place James Poupard in Boston in the eighteenth century, an in-depth examination of the public record finds no evidence to support the assertion.[1] This craftsman did advertise in Philadelphia and Quebec at this time, but not in Massachusetts.[2] PEK

1. Okie 1936, 278; Thorn 1949, 168; Kovel 1961, 221; Flynt/Fales 1968, 304.
2. Brix 1920, 83; Langdon 1960, 81; Langdon 1966, 116.

Thomas Revere, Jr.
ca. 1766–1817

The life dates for the silversmith Thomas Revere, Jr., have been conflated with the life dates of his father, Thomas Revere, Sr. (q.v. Appendix B). The silversmith died in September 1817, and his obituary notice gave his age as fifty-one.[1] Hence, he was born about 1766 and would have been too young to begin working before the Revolution. He may have trained with his uncle, Paul Revere, Jr. (q.v.).[2] DAF and PEK

1. *Index of Obituaries, 1784–1840*, 4:3765.
2. Nielsen 1991, 302, 315–16.

Thomas Revere, Sr.
b. 1738

The standard references give the life dates for the silversmith Thomas Revere as 1738–1817, but these dates are a conflation of life dates for father and son. Thomas Revere, Sr., was a son of Paul Revere, Sr., and brother of Paul Revere, Jr. (qq.v.). No evidence exists that Thomas, Sr., was a silversmith. The elder Thomas Revere served in the Revolution and is probably the Thomas Revere whose application for a license to sell liquor in 1788 noted that his lame arm prevented him from following his trade.[1] His son, Thomas, Jr. (q.v. Appendix B), was a silversmith, but was born too late to be included here. DAF and PEK

1. Forbes 1942, 400.

? Rule
w. ca. 1780

Hollis French, James Graham, Jr., and C. Jordan Thorn recorded a silversmith with the surname Rule as working in Massachusetts about 1780.[1] Although no silversmith with this name has been found in Massachusetts records, a John Rule opened a silversmith's shop in St. John, New Brunswick, in 1798.[2] PEK

1. French (1917) 1967, 101; Graham 1936, 63; Thorn 1949, 177.
2. Langdon 1966, 121.

Benjamin Savage
1699–1750

Benjamin Savage, the son of Thomas Savage, Sr. (q.v.), probably returned to Boston from Bermuda with his parents in 1714, because he witnessed a deed for his father in 1717.[1] Francis Hill Bigelow drafted a biography of Benjamin but noted that no proof existed that he followed his father's trade. Nonetheless, Benjamin Savage has been included in a number of standard reference works.[2] He was in Charleston, South Carolina, by 1732 when he bought a pew in the independent church there. References to him in Charleston records call him a merchant. He married the widow Martha Pickering in 1738 and died in 1750. PEK

1. SCD 32:184.
2. Burton/Ripley 1991, 88; Kovel 1961, 239; Flynt/Fales 1968, 320.

Thomas Savage, Jr.
1693/94–1767

Although a number of scholars have included Thomas Savage, Jr., in lists of craftsmen who worked in Boston, this silversmith apparently did not return to Boston from Bermuda with his father Thomas Savage, Sr. (q.v.), in 1714. Thomas Savage, Jr., is listed among the jurors for a General Court of Assizes in Bermuda on 1 July 1714.[1] He married Elizabeth Fowle (d. 1764), the daughter of Rev. John Fowle and Love (Gibbons) Prout, probably about 1714. Births of children to Thomas and Elizabeth Savage are recorded in Bermuda between 1715 and 1734. He is also identified as being of Bermuda when he and his wife, Elizabeth, sold land in Charlestown in 1717.[2] He died in Bermuda in 1767.[3] PEK

1. Bigelow-Phillips files, 767.
2. MCD 18:364–65.
3. Smith 1945–46, 11–12; Hyde 1971, 178.

Timothy Sibley, Sr.
1727–1818

Timothy Sibley, Sr., was thought to be a silversmith who taught his sons Stephen (1759–1829) and Asa (1764–1829) the trade.[1] A review of the numerous land transactions conducted by the elder Sibley, however, reveals that he worked as a joiner or yeoman.[2] His son Timothy Sibley, Jr. (q.v.), was a silversmith and clockmaker. JJF

1. Flynt/Fales 1968, 322–23.
2. WCD 27:548; 28:51; 30:270; 35:349; 37:60; 249; 45:29; 50:216; 52:500; 53:183; 54:62; 62:31; 67:525; 72:578.

John Sinnet
w. ca. 1769

Although Brooks Palmer listed John Sinnet, a watchmaker, as working in Boston, Sinnet's advertisement in the *Boston News-Letter* of 9 February 1769 indicated that he was actually working in Portsmouth, New Hampshire.[1] No evidence of Sinnet's being in Boston has been found. Palmer states that in 1770–75 he was in New York City.[2] PEK

1. Dow 1927, 144.
2. Palmer 1950, 277.

John Skates

Although Hollis French identified John Skates as a silversmith working in Boston ca. 1668–80, Suffolk County deeds make clear that this individual's occupation was shoemaking.[1] PEK

1. French (1917) 1967, 107; *Suffolk Deeds* 9:181; 10:320; 11:47, 188; SCD 23:165; 25:234; 28:196.

Joseph Smith
w. ca. 1789

Silver authorities generally have assumed that Joseph Smith was working in Boston as early as 1742, because two oval bowls in Boston's Hollis Street Church that bear the mark I·SMITH are inscribed, "The gift of Deacon/Thomas Hubbard/to the/Hollis Street Church/1742."[1] The bowls' oval shapes and neoclassical engraving indicate that they were made around 1800, and the date 1742 may well commemorate an earlier gift (perhaps one melted to make the present bowls) instead of denoting the pieces' date of manufacture. Moreover, no evidence indicates that Smith worked in Boston before the Revolution. The earliest documentation about him is the series of advertisements appearing in the *Massachusetts Gazette* beginning on 29 July 1788 that read,

Joseph Smith,
GOLDSMITH *and* WORKER *in* HAIR
INFORMS his Friends and the Pub-
lick, that he carries on those businesses, in all their
branches, at his shop, No. 48, Newbury-Street, corner of Winter-Street.
   He will be obliged to them if they will call at his
shop, where he will exhibit specimens of the art, and
which, he flatters himself they will pronounce equal
in design and beauty to any of the kind performed in
Europe.
   He will punctually obey the commands, and execute
the orders, of any gentleman or lady who may honour him with their custom.[2]

Smith also appears in the *Boston Directory* of 1789 as "goldsmith and hair-worker, No. 48, Newbury-street."[3] PEK

1. Okie 1936, 283; Ensko 1948, 123; Thorn 1949, 188; Kovel 1961, 252; Flynt/Fales 1968, 325. For information on the bowls, see Jones 1913, 84.
2. This advertisement was repeated on 1, 5, 8, 12, 15, 19, 22, 26 August 1788.
3. RC 10:199.

Nathaniel
Sparhawk, Jr.
b. 1725

Although he was listed as a jeweler by Henry Belknap, numerous advertisements make clear that Nathaniel Sparhawk, Jr., of Salem, Massachusetts, was a general merchant who occasionally retailed jewelry.[1] He may have been born on 24 September 1725, in Lynn, Massachusetts, the son of Nathaniel and Elizabeth Sparhawk.[2] His advertisements in the *Essex Gazette*, such as the one of 23–30 October 1770 and others in 1770 and 1771, indicate that his shop was "next to the Rev. Dr. Whitaker's Meeting-House" and that he sold a wide variety of goods, including on occasion some items of jewelry like the "few Paste PINS, handsome Broches, and Garnet Earings" offered in the issue of the *Gazette* dated 22 January–6 February 1771. GWRW

1. Belknap 1927, 115.
2. *Salem VR* 4:337; Belknap 1927, 115.

Jonathan Stickney
1760–1808

Although some sources list Jonathan Stickney as having been born in 1734 and as having died in either 1800 or 1810, recent research has established his date of birth in Newbury, Massachusetts, as 1760 and his death date as 1808.[1] Thus, he was born too late to be included within the purview of this volume. He worked in Newburyport and was the son-in-law of the Boston watchmaker Moses Peck and brother-in-law of the watchmaker Elijah Peck (qq.v. Appendix A). GWRW

1. French (1917) 1967, 109; Graham 1936, 68; Stickney 1869, 255–56; Benes 1986, 182; Fales 1967a, 199–200; Bentley 1905–62, 2:356; Flynt/Fales 1968, 330–31.

George Tyler
b. 1755

Early scholars confused and conflated two men named George Tyler, only one of whom was a silversmith. Many silver scholars state that the silversmith George Tyler was born in 1740.[1] But that George Tyler, born in Boston on 11 November 1740 to John and Sarah (Bream) Tyler, must have died as a child, because he is not mentioned as a legatee in his father's will, written in 1753.[2] The George Tyler who became a silversmith was the grandson of the silversmith Andrew Tyler (q.v.). George was one of nine sons born to the controversial Dedham, Massachusetts, minister Rev. Andrew Tyler (1719–75) and his wife, Mary Richards (1731–83).[3] But this George Tyler was born in Dedham on 23 September 1755, too late to be included here, although he would have been fully trained by about 1776 and was established as a silversmith in Boston by 1778.[4] DAF

1. MFA 1911, 157; Kovel 1961, 272; Currier 1938, 141; Ensko 1927, 58; Ensko 1937, 38; Ensko 1948, 133; French (1917) 1967, 116; Graham 1936, 72; Thorn 1949, 205; Flynt/Fales 1968, 345.
2. RC 24:241; SCPR 52:277–80.
3. *Dedham VR* 50, 58, 74; *Sibley's Harvard Graduates* 10:329–30; RC 24:125.
4. *Dedham VR*, 88.

B.[enjamin?] West

The name B. West, identified as working in Boston about 1770, has appeared in lists of American silversmiths since 1906, when a spoon with that mark was included in the exhibition "American Silver" at the Museum of Fine Arts, Boston.[1] Francis Hill Bigelow speculated that this maker might be the Benjamin West who was deacon of Boston's Hollis Street Church in 1816 and earlier.[2] No image of the spoon accompanies Bigelow's notes, but he probably derived the date of 1770 from the style of the spoon.

In 1927 Stephen Ensko published the first name of B. West as Benjamin, although when he republished the mark in 1948, he identified the maker simply as B. West, with the date 1830 and the additional fact that West advertised his shop as being one and a half meters from the South Bridge in Boston.[3] Henry Flynt and Martha Gandy Fales illustrated a B·WEST mark on a spoon at Winterthur that also has pseudo-hallmarks and another mark attributed to Richard Ward, who worked in Boston after 1815. Winterhur now says that the pseudo-hallmarks are Irish marks, that Richard Ward is Richard Whitford, and that B. West should be W. West. Thus far no B. West has been identified as a Boston silversmith in the second half of the eighteenth century. PEK

1. MFA 1906, no. 323.
2. Bigelow card file, YUAG.
3. Ensko 1927, 58, 179; Ensko 1948, 139, 160.

Glossary of Tools, Supplies, and Processes Used by Silversmiths and Jewelers

EDGARD MORENO

THE NAMES IN PARENTHESES are parenthetical references to individuals whose biographies appear in this dictionary. The plates are from Denis Diderot, *Encyclopédie, Recueil de Planches*, Vol. 8. Courtesy Beinecke Rare Book and Manuscript Library, Yale University. Plates 1–9 are plates VIII–XVI in "Orfèvre Grossier." Plates 10–12 are plates V–VII in "Orfèvre Bijoutier." Plates 13–16 are plates VIII–XI in "Orfèvre Jouaillier, Metteur en Oeuvre."

Allom (George Hanners, Sr.). See Alum.

Alum A sulfate of aluminum containing potassium and used as a flux.

Annealing The process of heating and cooling metal to make it more workable.

Anvil A forged iron form with one or more case-hardened, polished surfaces upon which a metalsmith can either forge or raise an object. Anvils range in size from large ones weighing in excess of one hundred pounds for forging to smaller examples made for specific purposes such as buttonmaking. Anvils, teasts, punches, and stakes generally function in similar ways and appear to by synonymous in the colonial period. Examples: large forging block and anvil, small bench anvil, money anvil (John Codner); bekern anvil, belly anvil (John Dixwell); tobacco box anvil, broken anvil, forging anvil, locket teast (John Coney); belly pot anvil, great forging anvil, porringer anvil (Samuel Edwards); can anvil (Isaac Perkins); goose neck anvil (Daniel Henchman); raising anvil (Richard Conyers); raising anvils for creampots (Daniel Parker). Plate 3, Fig. 1. See also Beckiron; Punch; Snarling iron; Sparrow hawk; Stake; Teast.

Auger An iron tool with a corkscrew-shaped tip and a wooden handle used to make small holes in metal and wood. (Samuel Edwards).

Balls, iron Cast iron spheres attached to the bottom of the forge bellows that opened the bellows by gravity after manual compression. The size of the bellows determined the diameter of the ball. (John Codner). See Fig. 2, page 8.

Bead tools (Elijah Yeomans). See Dapping; Punch.

Beckiron A forged T-shaped iron anvil having a tall vertical support and a horizontal working surface, often with one conical end and one tapered, rectangular end. A corruption of the French term *bigorne*. Examples: beckiron (John Coney); small bekern (John Dixwell). Plate 13, Fig. 5.

PLATE I.

Fig. 24: Drawing tongs. AA, the bites. BB, the branches. CC, the rings. D, the eye [the space between the bites or jaws].

Fig. 25: Drawing bench with winch. AA, the winches. B, the axle. C, strap. DD, the pegs. EE, the tenons. F, the table. GG, the feet.

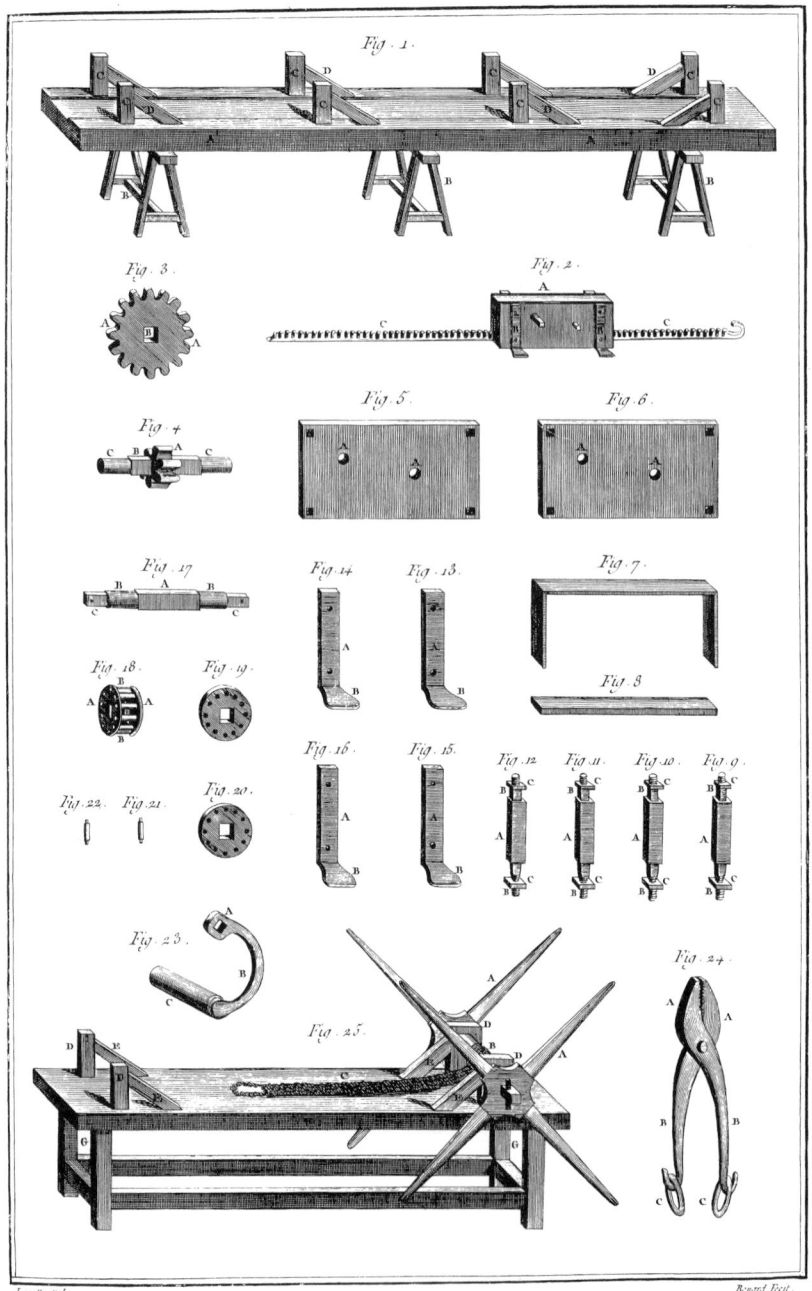

Orfèvre Grossier, Banco à Tirer.

Bellows   A truncated, pyramidal-shaped instrument composed of two wooden sides to which was attached a folding expandable air bladder. Air exited the bladder through a long, tapered metal tube. Bellows were used to supply more air (oxygen) for the processes of melting and soldering. Forge, organ, and possibly large bellows weighing thirty to seventy pounds were fixed at the forge and could be operated by a chain with an iron ring handhold. Smaller hand-held bellows could be used with or instead of a blowpipe for soldering. Examples: forge bellows (John Codner); goldsmiths bellows (Henry Phillip Sweetser); hand bellows (Richard Conyers); large bellows (John Dixwell); p^r organ bellows (James Boyer); pr. bellows (John Coney); iron rings for a forge (Samuel Edwards). See Fig. 2, page 8 and Plate 9, Fig. 16; Plate 16, Fig. 28.

Bench and skin   The workbench, sometimes referred to as a board, and the leather apron attached underneath that caught the waste of fabrication. Examples: bench & skin (Stephen Winter). Plate 13, top.

Bilbow and stock   (Samuel Edwards). See Drill.

Binding wire   Iron wire of approximately heavy sewing thread thickness used to hold separate pieces of metal securely during soldering. Because of its malleability, annealed binding wire allowed close contouring, which was especially useful for soldering complicated forms, for example, a teapot spout to the body. Examples: binding wire (John Coney); neal'd fine and coarse binding wire (John Welsh).

Blocks wheels   Large, circular wooden blocks between which metal objects were supported on the lathe while being skimmed. (John Coney).

Blowpipe   A tapered, metal, L-shaped tube six to nine inches long. When used with a soldering lamp, the blowpipe functioned as a precise and controlled means of increasing air flow and hence temperature for soldering. Brass and silver blowpipes were recorded. The paucity of entries suggests that waterlogged reeds were used for this purpose. Examples: brass blow pipe (Thomas Clark); blowing pipe (John Codner); blowpipes (John Coney). Plate 16, Fig. 31. See also Lamp.

Boiling pan   A metallic vessel filled with a mild acidified solution used to remove borax flux and oxides after soldering by boiling. For this purpose only copper, brass, or lead can be used because iron causes copper deposits or flashing on silver and gold. The paucity of chemicals, especially acids, in the inventories suggests that plain vinegar was the "pickle" of the eighteenth century. Examples: brass pans, copper pans (Richard Conyers); copper boiling pans (John Coney); boiling pans (John Dixwell).

Book, flower   Possibly a design source for engraving and chasing. (Samuel Edwards).

Borax   A silica or glasslike compound used in soldering, melting, and refining as an antioxidant or flux. Borax was sold in cones or blocks and ground for use. For soldering, it was mixed with water to form a paste that was applied to the joints with a brush. Examples: borax (John Coney); borax boxes (John Coney).

Box, jeweling   Possibly a box to contain cut stones. (James Boyer).

Bristol stone   A soft limestone cut into sticks, with ends filed to any form and used with water to remove pits and scratches. Bristol stone was used after filing and before polishing compounds. (James Boyer).

Brush   Bound bunches of fiber, animal hair, or metal bristles, sometimes fitted with wooden handles, made in a wide range of sizes. Brushes with fiber or animal hair bristles were used for applying flux, cleaning joints, and sweeping filings. When coated with abrasives, brushes became polishing tools. Scratch brushes

Pl. IX

PLATE 2.

Fig. 17: Wire die with round and oval holes.
Fig. 19: Drawing block. AA, the box. BB, the screws. CC, the drawing blocks.
Figs. 21, 22; Drawing blocks.
Figs. 36, 37: Drawing blocks.
Fig. 38: Contra block.

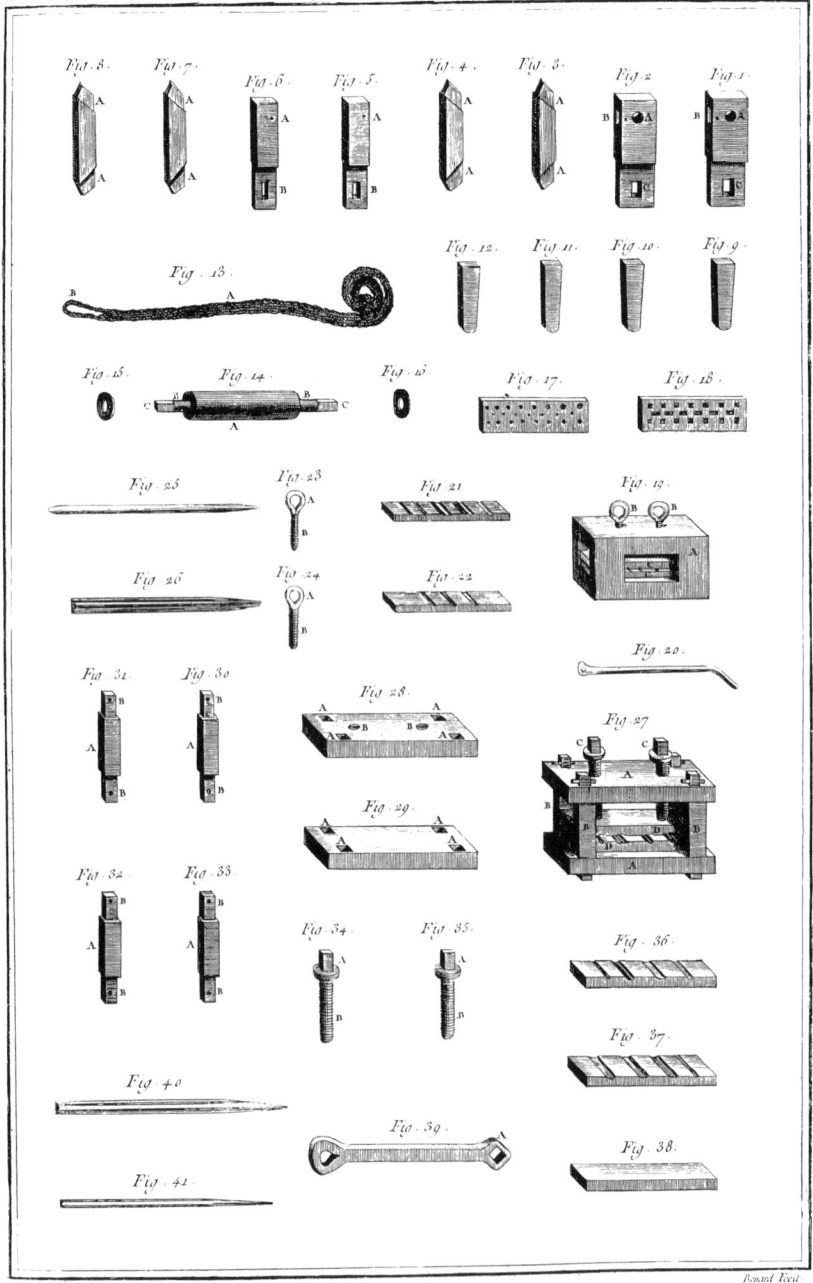

Orfèvre Grossier, *Moulins à tirer*.

had iron, brass, or boar bristles set at a right angle to a wooden or bone handle and were used to clean flux, cement, and other adherents from metal. Scratch brushes were also used to prepare metal surfaces before fire gilding and to polish metal. Examples: scratch brushes (John Coney); 2 brushes (John Codner); brush scrath (John Dixwell); pr bone polishing brushes, pr wood polishing brushes (Zachariah Brigden). Plate 5, Fig. 37; Plate 6, Fig. 18; Plate 12, Figs. 18, 19; Plate 15, Fig. 56; Plate 16, Figs. 18, 20.

Burin An alternative term for graver. See also Graver.

Burnisher A polishing tool, often made with a wooden handle and a blade of polished steel or stone agate. Burnishers were rubbed over the finished object in the final step of polishing to compress and brighten the surface. Examples: stone burnishers (John Coney); small stone burnisher without handle (Benjamin Hurd); 3 burnishers 2 stone 1 steel (Jonathan Reed); burnishing stons (Richard Conyers). Plate 7, Figs. 33–35.

Burnt silver Lemel consolidated through melting. (John Coney). See also Lemel.

Bushboard A tool of unknown purpose. (Joseph Hathorne).

Casting The creation of component parts of objects by pouring molten metal, held in crucibles, into contours impressed in sand contained within flasks or molding boxes. Patterns or models made of wood, wax, or metal were pressed into sand, making hollows that were filled by the flowing metal. Used by most metalsmiths, casting was an efficient technique to make such component parts as finials and small feet. See also Crucible; Flask; Molding box; Pattern.

Cement block A block of pitch, a manufactured product of pine sap, used in chasing as a semiresilient backing. Molten pitch was poured on boards or into trays or bowls and allowed to cool. The metal to be worked was gently heated, then pressed into the pitch for chasing. (John Coney). See Fig. 14, page 13.

Cement stick A tapered wooden spindle four to five inches long with a flattened head capped with pitch, used mostly by jewelers to hold the metal mounts for stones or other small objects that would be crushed if placed in a vise. The heated object was pressed into the pitch, thus holding it fast for filing, engraving, setting, or other work. (Stephen Winter). Plate 15, Figs. 35, 36. See also Cement block.

Chape The metal piece on a buckle that fastens it to the strap.

Charcoal Manufactured carbon from trees used in block form to support small metal pieces while soldering because it provided a heat-retentive and oxygen-reducing surface. It could also be used as fuel in the forge. (John Coney). See Fig. 2, page 8.

Chasing A decorative technique using chasing tools that are hammered into metal, creating various depressions resulting in surface decoration. As opposed to engraving, chasing distends rather than removes metal.

Chasing bag A sand-filled leather bag upon which an object was supported during engraving or chasing. See the portrait of Paul Revere, Jr., on page 795. Examples: chasing bag (Joseph Sanderson); sand bag (Benjamin Hurd); sand cushion (John Coney).

Chasing tool A three- to five-inch long hardened iron rod with one shaped end. The shaped end of a chasing tool can be blunt, linear, or patterned. Example: a set chasing tools (Benjamin Hurd). See also Punch.

Chisel A three- to six-inch long rod or bar of iron with a V-shaped, hardened tip. Chisels held vertically against strips of metal were hammered to produce rough cuts. Chisels were used for coarse cutting of thick metal. Chisels were not

Pl. X.

PLATE 3.
*Fig. 1: Mounted forging
anvil. A, the top steeled [or
hardened]. B, the block.*

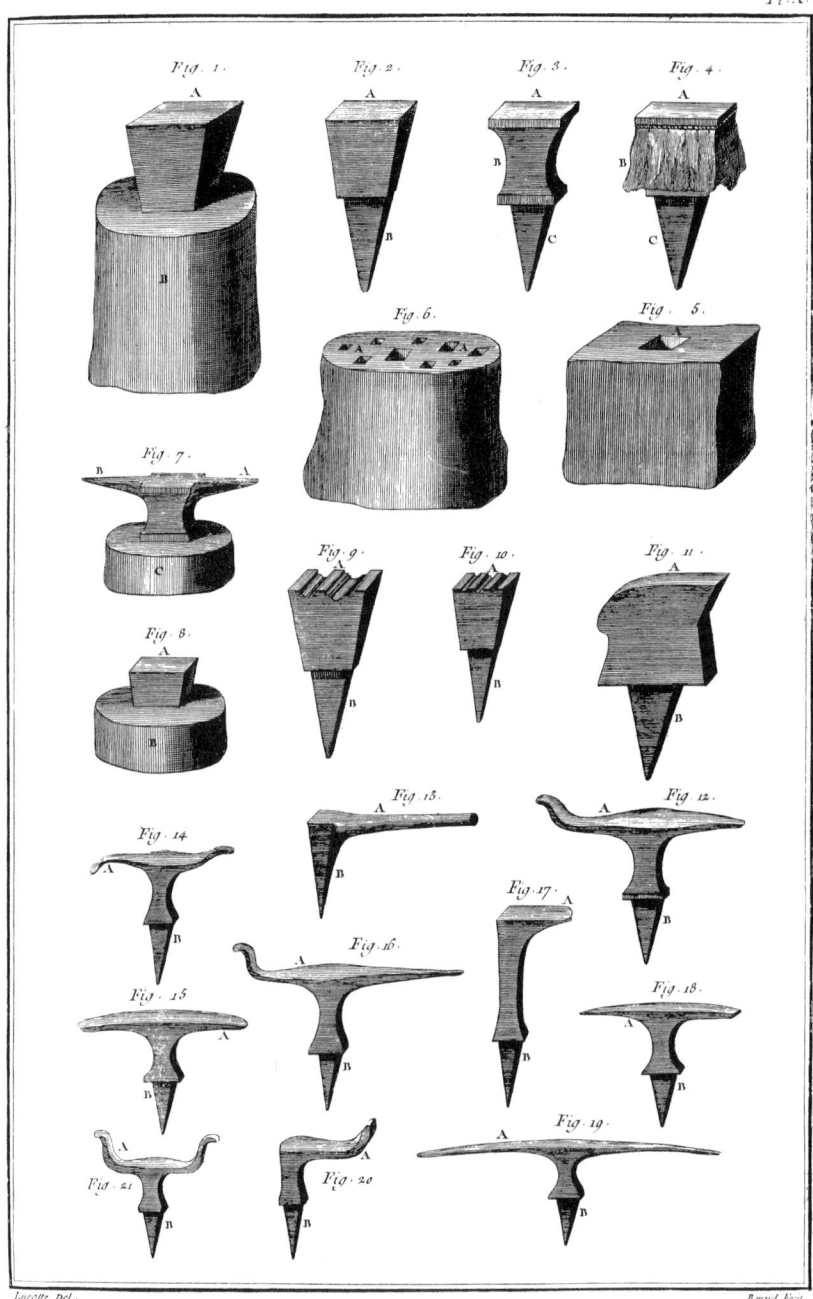

Orfèvre Grossier, Tasseaux et Bigornes.

used on thin sheet; for these cuts, nippers or shears produced less distortion. Examples: cuting chissell (Richard Conyers); cold chizell, boxes of chizells (John Coney). Plate 10, Figs. 13–17; Plate 14, Figs. 22, 24.

Cipher Ciphers were groupings of two or three letters, often interlaced, made from thin twisted gold wire. Ciphers were placed under a faceted quartz crystal as a setting for jewelry. Example: cyphers and letters (James Boyer).

Cistern, lead A large circular container made of lead used to hold acidic solutions needed to remove oxides formed during soldering. (James Boyer). See also Pan, boiling.

Colander A bowl-shaped vessel with perforations used as a strainer. Example: brass cullender (John Coney). See also Strainer.

Compass A metal instrument with two hinged straight arms terminating in points, one of which could hold lead or chalk. A compass was used to mark sheet silver for cutting out disks, and to mark concentric circles as guides for raising. Beam compasses consisted of two separate metal arms that could be attached to either end of a straight edge to scribe large circles. Dividers were similar in appearance to compasses with straight arms always terminating in points. Calipers were distinguished by their curved arms. Dividers and calipers were used to compare measurements, for example, between objects and templates. Compasses, dividers, and calipers were used synonymously in the colonial period. Examples: Compasses, pr silver compasses (John Coney); beam compass, screw compasses (Samuel Edwards). Plate 11, Figs. 20, 21; Plate 14, Figs. 14–17.

Creasing A raising process, also called pilking, using a narrow head hammer, creating radial waves used to make holloware. See also Hammer.

Crucible An elongated, cup-shaped vessel used in the melting, refining, and assaying of precious metals. Crucibles were recorded usually as nests or sets and were commonly referred to as pots. Black or blue crucibles made of charcoal were used to melt metal for casting ingots and parts of objects. White crucibles made of bisque clay absorbed impurities in the molten metal; over time these crucibles became saturated and were discarded. Examples: blw[blue] crucibles of several sizes, nests of white crucibles of several sizes (John Coney); nests small crucibles (John Codner). Plate 8, Figs. 10–13. See also Pot.

Cullender See Colander.

Cutteaw, french Possibly cuttle, a fish bone that could be carved to make molds used in casting. (Benjamin Hurd).

Dapping The hammering of silver or gold sheet into shallow hemispherical depressions hollowed out in wood or iron blocks using iron punches with spherical tips. Most often used to make beads. See also Punch, dapping.

Death's head Components used in making jewelry. Death's heads, used in mourning jewelry, were pieces of white paper approximately one quarter inch in diameter and printed in black ink with the image of a skull. Death's heads were placed under a faceted quartz crystal as a setting for jewelry. (James Boyer).

Die A piece of hardened iron with a filed or engraved cavity used to make decorative elements by hammering silver into the hollow with punches, chasing, or dapping tools. Plate 5, Fig. 21; Plate 10, Fig. 9; Plate 13, Fig. 9.

Dividers (John Dixwell). See Compass.

Drawing bench A wooden frame with metal components used to hold drawing irons, rectangular pieces of steel with tapered, graduated apertures of various shapes through which strips of metal were pulled to make wire. The strips of metal were pulled by large plier-shaped tongs hooked onto a leather strap that became

PLATE 4.

*Fig. 13: Spoon stamp [die]
with its punch. A, the stamp
[die]. B, the punch. C, the
spoon.*

*Figs. 14, 15: Punches to
stamp spoons and forks. BB,
the heads.*

*Figs. 28–31: Mallets of
different sizes. AA, the mallets. BB, the handles.*

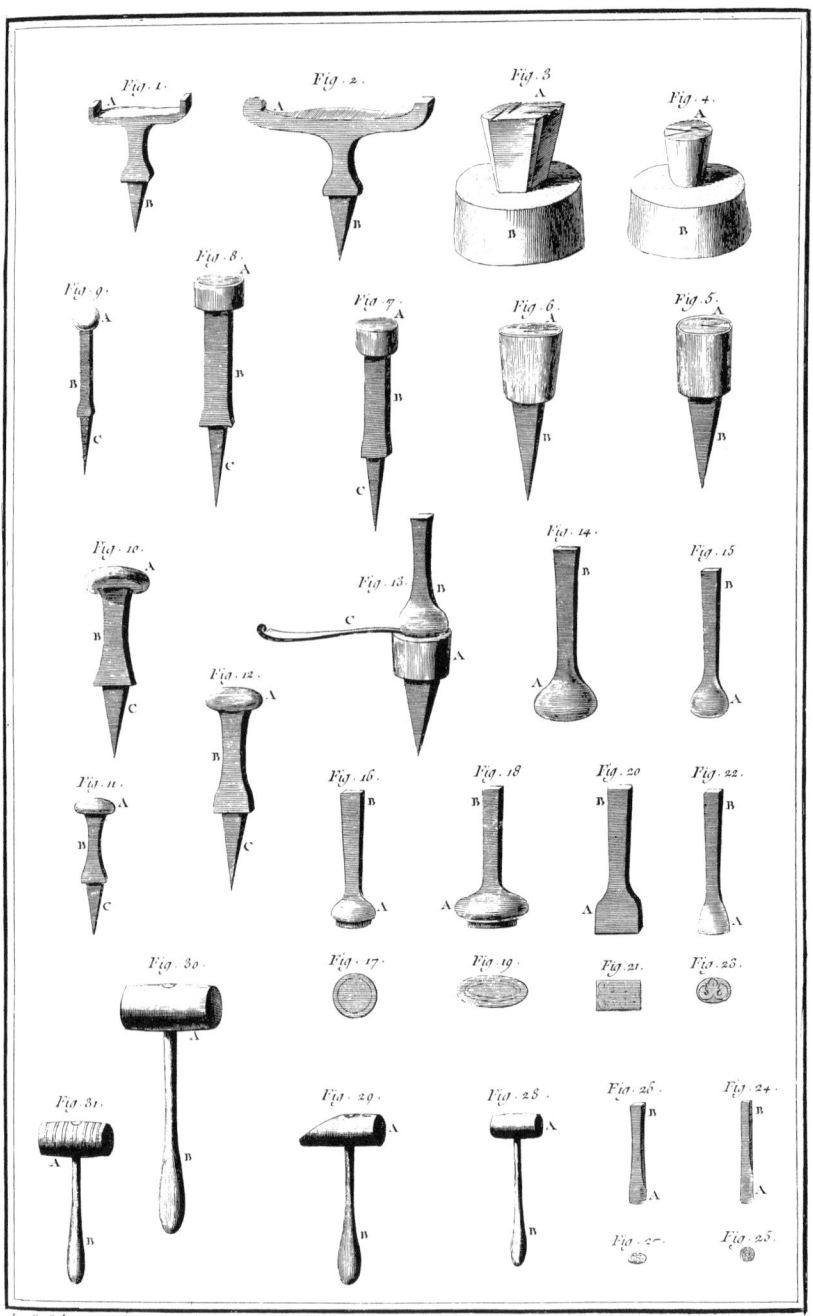

Orfèvre Grossier, outils.

self-locking when pulled. Thin strips of flat metal were first tapered and then pushed through the drawplate held by four pegs opposite the winch. As the winch turned, coiling the strap, the tong pulled the metal strip through the drawplate, thereby producing wire. Examples: drawing bench (John Coney); draw irons (John Dixwell); drawing iron square (Isaac Perkins); half round draw^g irons (Jonathan Reed). Plate 1, Figs. 24, 25; Plate 2, Fig. 17.

Drawing doggs An alternate term for drawing tongs. (David Jesse). See also Drawing bench.

Drawing leather The leather strap used on a drawing bench. (John Coney). See also Drawing bench.

Drawing plates half round and flat (John Welsh). See Drawing swage.

Drawing swage Two rectangular pieces of hardened, polished iron, one of which was cut and filed into a specific profile, the other one left uncut. The swages were clamped together onto a bench or held in a metal frame or box with the cut aperture parallel to the work surface. Metal strips were manually pulled through the swage to produce the intended wire shapes. This type of swage was often produced in a silversmith's shop for stock and custom moldings such as base bands. Drawing swages eliminated the need for costly drawing benches. Plate 2, Figs. 19, 21, 22, 36–38. See also Swage.

Drill A tool with wooden, twine or sinew, and iron components used for making holes. The drill and its stock consisted of a wooden rod that transferred manual motion from the rod to the metal stock or adjustable chuck, which held the threaded iron drill, now known as a drill bit. Two forms of drills were used in the colonial period. The bow drill consisted of a bow string threaded around a stock that, when moved back and forth horizontally, caused the stock to rotate. The upright drill, now called an Archimedes drill, was more efficient than the bow drill because its vertical motion and long crossbar allowed momentum to aid in the drilling. Examples: drill bow & stock, drill stock (Samuel Edwards); drill iron (John Coney); drill stock & drills (Stephen Winter); upright drill stocks (Benjamin Hurd); drilling stock (John Codner); upright drills (James Boyer). Plate 10, Figs. 21–23; Plate 15, Figs. 40–43.

Dropping punch Possibly dapping punch. (Edward Webb). See also Dapping; Punch, dapping.

Emery Powdered Carborundum, a moderately abrasive polishing compound applied in a slurry with a brush or cloth-covered stick. Plate 12, Fig. 10; Plate 15, Fig. 51.

Enamel A silica-based compound with additions of soda, potash, lime, and borax that was melted, cooled, and then finely ground. Color was obtained by adding metallic oxides, for example, lead white, or such elements as cobalt (blue) or manganese (purple). The ground and the colorant were mixed, then applied to the metal surface and heated in a forge until the mixture fused into a solid glass. It was used in the colonial period for jewelry, especially mourning rings. Examples: black enamel, white enamel (Joseph Loring); enamell (Richard Conyers).

Engines for swages A metal frame for holding drawing swages. (Richard Conyers). See also Drawing swage.

File An iron tool, usually with a handle, cut or punched with repetitive patterns, used to remove metal. Files came in numerous lengths and shapes, including round, half-round, flat, and square. Files also were made in two cuts, smooth and rough. Files smaller than six inches in length were known as needle files. Needle files that were bent or crooked are known today as riffler files. Examples:

PL XII.

PLATE 5.
Fig. 2: Two-headed hammer. AA, the heads. B, the handle.
Figs. 6–14: Various raising hammers. AA, the heads. BB, the tails. CC, the handles.
Figs. 15, 16: Small raising hammers. AA, the heads. BB, the tails. CC, the handles.
Figs. 17–19: Steel blocks.
Fig. 21: Dapping die. AAA, the hollows.
Fig. 37: Hide brush. A, the handle.

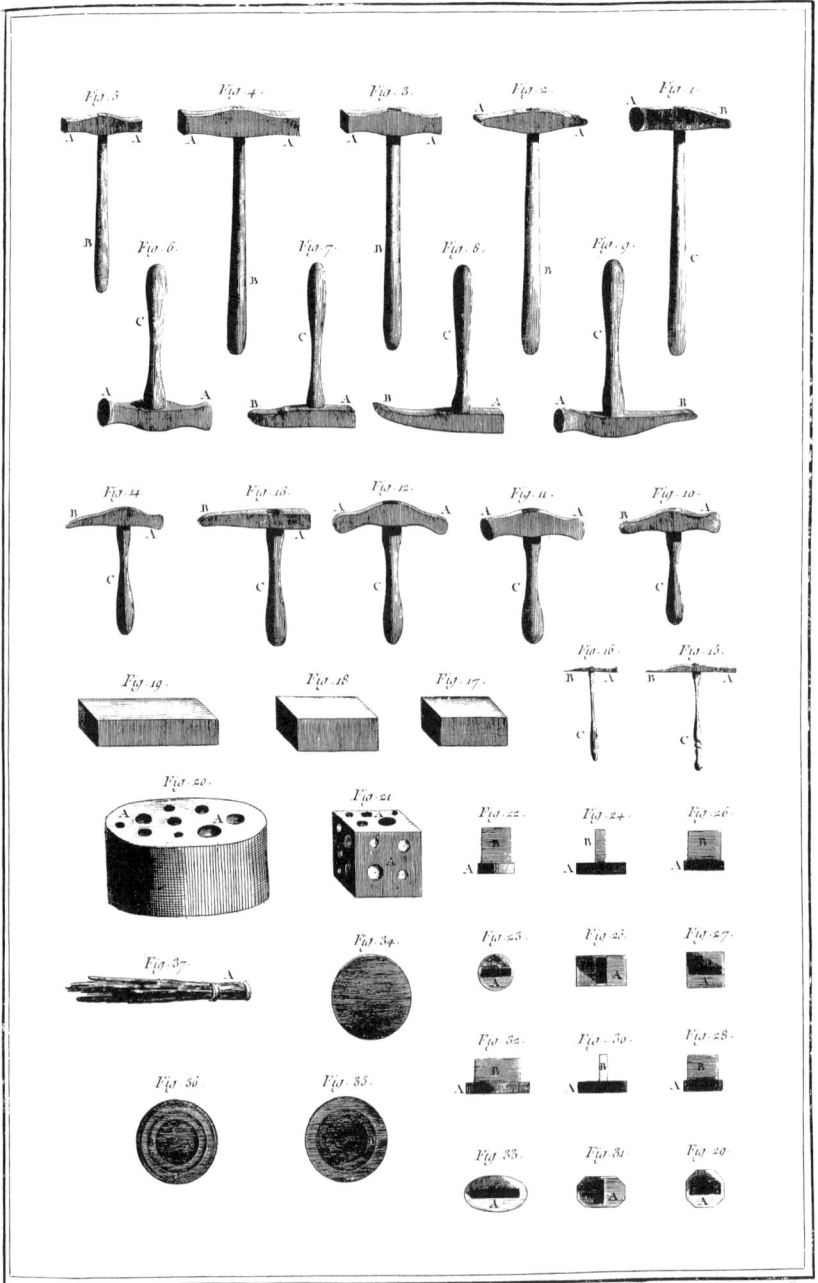

Orfèvre Grossier, *Outils*

crooked files, clock makers files (Samuel Edwards); ¹/₂ round file, ¹/₂ round smooth file, 6 inch flat file, 8 inch flatt file, ¹/₂ round 8 inch files, rough files, smooth files (John Codner); file handels (John Parkman). Plate 7, Figs. 1–4, 9–12, 26; Plate 10, Figs. 30–36; Plate 11, Figs. 1–6; Plate 16, Figs. 9–12.

Flask A two-part, heavy-gauge iron or brass container of varied sizes packed with claylike molding sand for casting. The wooden or metal mold of the object to be cast was impressed half-way into one half of the flask. The top half was then pressed down upon the lower half. The halves were then separated, the model removed and the halves securely bound together with screws. Molten metal from a black crucible was poured into the void created by the model. Examples: large brass casting flasks (Benjamin Hurd); brass flask, iron flasque, flasque screws (John Coney). Plate 9, Figs. 6–12. See also Casting; Molding box; Molding sand.

Flatting mill See Mill.

Fluke The prong part of a buckle that perforates the strap. (John Parkman)

Flux A wide range of compounds and chemical mixtures brushed on metal joints before soldering; these combined with the metal, allowing the solder to melt at a lower, or eutectic, melting point. As an antioxidant, flux also provided a barrier to oxygen, the presence of which inhibited the flow of solder. See also Alum; Borax.

Foil Tin foil, often painted, used behind stones and glass to enhance color and brilliance. Examples: broken sheets of foyle (John Parkman); red and white foyl, amethist and topaz foyl (Daniel Parker); ruby foyl (John Welsh); sheets foyl (John Codner).

Forging A forming technique whereby metal was thinned and moved by repeatedly hammering it on an anvil. The direction and extent of this thinning process could be controlled by the shape of the hammer's face and the force of the blows. Forging hammers were the heaviest hammers used in silversmithing. Forging was done either hot or cold, but in both situations the silver required frequent heatings or annealings to realign its atomic crystalline lattice to prevent stress cracks from forming. Forging was used for the production of sheet silver from ingots, for forming the stems and handles of flatware, and for the production of wire in shops where drawing irons were not available. See Anvil; Hammer.

Funnel A conical object open at both ends and used to facilitate the pouring of powders and liquids. Examples: brass funnel (Stephen Winter); tin funnell (James Hill).

Gimblet An iron rod with a corkscrew-shaped tip and wooden handle used to pierce and enlarge holes in metal. (Samuel Edwards). See also Auger.

Glass case Probably a silversmith's showcase. Examples: glass cases (Richard Conyers); 2 large & 1 small glass cases (John Codner).

Gluepot A container for animal glue. (John Coney).

Gold and silver dust (James Boyer). See also Lemel.

Gouger A small iron rod or bar with a U-shaped cutting edge and a wooden handle usually used for carving wood; the term is used also for a metal engraver. Example: gaugers (John Coney). See also Graver.

Graver A wooden-handled implement, also called a burin, with a two- to three-inch long steel shaft with one sharpened and polished face, used to create lettering or decoration by engraving or cutting and removing metal. Plate 7, Figs. 13–

Pl. XIII

PLATE 6.

Fig. 1: Small hand lathe. AA, the runner. B, the sleeping [fixed] chuck. C, the moving chuck. DD, the points. E, the screw for the points. F, the support [tool rest]. G, the screw for the support. H, the screw for the return [horizontal off-set].

Figs. 2, 3: Sliding vise. AA, the jaws. B, the hinge. C, the branches. D, the slide.

Figs. 4, 5: Hand vise. AA, the jaws. BB, the side beams. C, the hinge. D, the spring. E, the screw. F, the nut.

Fig. 7: Screw vise. AA, the jaws. BB, the legs. C, the hinge. D, the spring. E, the screw. F, the nut.

Fig. 8: Shears. AA, the jaws. B, the hinge. CC, the arms.

Fig. 9: Flat pliers.

Fig. 10: Round pliers.

Fig. 11: Snub nose pliers. AAA, the teeth of the pliers. BBB, the hinges. CCC, the branches.

Figs. 14, 15: Threaders. AA, the screws. BB, the heads.

Figs. 16, 17: Screwplates. AA, the holes.

Fig. 18: Large brush.

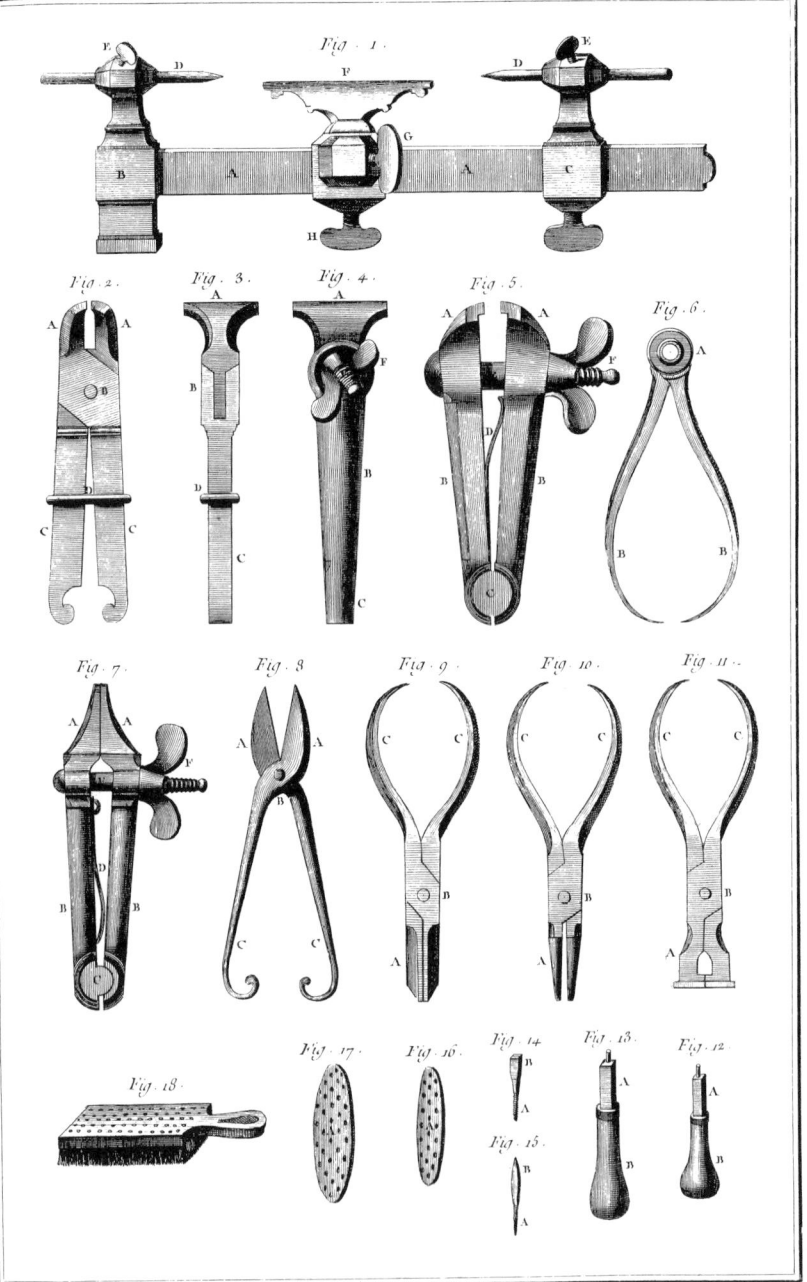

Iacotte Del.

Benard Fecit.

Orfèvre Grossier, Outils.

17, Plate 15, Figs. 26, 27. (John Codner). See the portrait of Paul Revere, Jr., on page 795.

Grindstone, trough, and iron crank
: Grindstones were quarried, wheel-shaped pieces of various abrasive rocks. A forged, L-shaped iron crank provided manual power and held the stone suspended in a wooden trough of water for lubrication. Grindstones were most commonly used to sharpen such edged tools as chisels, but they could also be used in the rough shaping of stakes and chasing tools. (Benjamin Hurd).

Hammer
: A forged iron tool having two hardened polished faces and a wooden handle. Hammers were highly specialized implements that varied in size, weight, and shape depending on their intended function. In general, hammers with flat faces oriented more or less parallel to the length of the handle were used to smooth and planish the metal; those with rounded or curving faces were used for raising, sinking, and forging the metal. The two-handed hammer was the largest forging hammer used. A booge hammer was used in shaping the curved side of porringers and bowls. A riveting hammer was a small, lightweight hammer used to peen or flare the end of wire or a rod, thus fixing in place such component parts as handles and finials. Chasing hammers had broad faces that allowed the metalsmith to concentrate on the shaping end of a chasing punch. Creasing hammers had narrow, rectangular faces and were used to create deep, narrow, radial waves for one technique of raising, also called pilking. Examples: hammers for raising, pilking, swelling, hollowing, creasing, planishing and two-hand hammer, booge hammer (John Coney); forging hammers (Richard Conyers); hollowing hammers, small board hammers (Benjamin Hurd); brass hammer (Samuel Edwards); riveting hammer, long planishing hammer, [planishing hammer] large (Isaac Perkins); large sledge hammer (John Codner); booge hammer (Jonathan Reed). Plate 5, Figs. 2, 12, 15, 16; Plate 10, Figs. 7, 8; Plate 14, Figs. 1, 2.

Hoane
: (Joseph Sanderson). See Oilstone.

Hollowing
: A process by which sheet metal is hammered into successively deeper cavities, usually cut in tree stumps. This first process of raising is similar on a larger scale to dapping.

Ingot mold
: A rectangular iron receptacle used to form molten metal into a bar. The ingot mold was usually greased and sooted to create a parting agent. Iron molds produced smooth-sided ingots that needed less finishing than those produced when metal was poured into molds made of sand. Examples: ingot tool (Isaac Perkins); iron casting ingotts (Daniel Henchman). Plate 8, Figs. 19, 20; Plate 9, Figs. 14, 15.

Iron, turning bench
: (Edward Webb). See Lathe.

Kettle
: A metallic vessel possibly used to heat water to dissolve flux, polishing compounds, and oils that inhibited soldering and bright metal finishing. Examples: old brass kettle (Samuel Edwards); iron kettle (John Codner).

Kettle, soldering
: Receptacle for lead or alloy used for soldering. (Samuel Edwards).

Ladle
: A spoonlike implement with a large bowl. Ladles of water were used to control the fire in the forge. (John Coney).

Lamp
: Possibly a wooden and glass instrument used to focus light. A wooden baluster supported an oil- or water-filled glass globe. A candle placed behind the lamp would cast a narrow beam of light useful for close work. Examples: lamp (Daniel Henchman); larg lamp (Edward Webb). Plate 12, Fig. 3; Plate 15, Fig. 34.

Lamp, tinn & soldering iron
: Soldering lamps made of various base metals had tall, baluster-shaped shafts

PLATE 7.

Figs. 1–4: Rifflers of all kinds.

Fig. 9: Small rectangular English [file].

Fig. 10: Small half round English [file].

Fig. 11: Small triangular English [file].

Fig. 12: Small rat tail English [file]. AA, the cutting edges. BB, the handles.

Figs. 13–17: Gouges and engravers. AA, the edges. BB, the handles.

Fig. 26: Large file.

Fig. 33: Handled burnisher. A, the burnisher. B, the handle.

Also Figs. 34, 35: Other burnishers. AA, the burnishers.

Figs. 45, 46: Large and small snarling irons. A, the cup. B, the point.

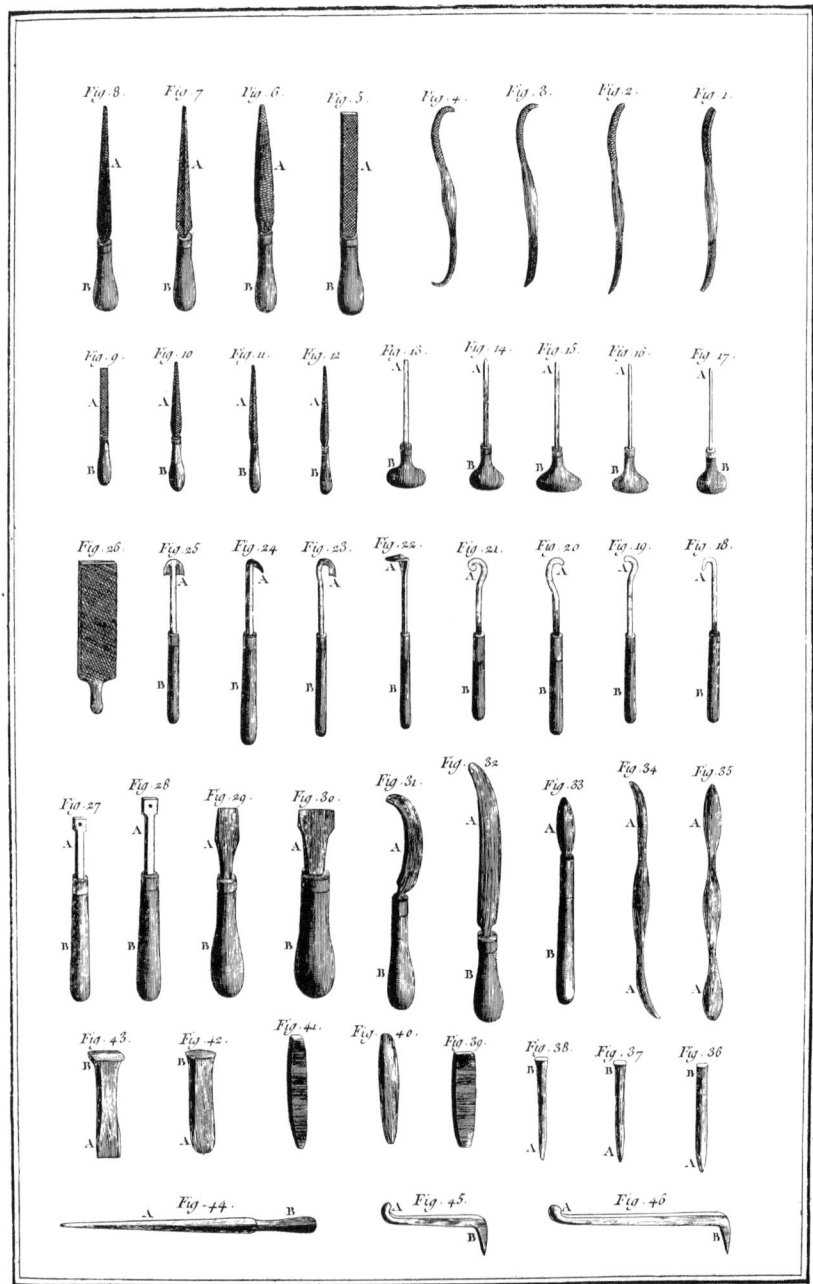

Orfèvre Grossier, Outils.

that supported open receptacles for oil or grease into which a wick was inserted. When lit, a lamp was used to heat soldering irons for lead solders. A lamp could also be used with a blowpipe for silver and gold solders. (John Codner). Plate 9, Fig. 13; Plate 12, Fig. 4; Plate 16, Fig. 30.

Lathe A machine of wood or iron with a horizontal bed, attached to which were one or two movable or stationary chucks to fix rotating objects in place. A sharp instrument was held against the object on the lathe to "skim," or clean, the surface or to incise concentric line decoration. Eighteenth-century lathes used high speeds rather than torque for their operation. They ranged in size from bench-mounted models powered by a hand-held rope to those occupying small rooms, with geared crank or treadle power. Examples: lath, lath iron small (Samuel Edwards); turning lathe (Benjamin Hurd). Plate 6, Fig. 1.

Leads Blocks or swages of lead with carved depressions into which silver was hammered to produce the bowls of spoons. Owing to their softness, lead swages were kept protected, organized, and accessible by being hung away from the workbench. Examples: leads to hollow spoons in (Edward Webb); leads (Stephen Winter).

Lemel The waste metal of fabrication, such as filings, scrapings, skimmings, and other small pieces of metal. Lemel was periodically swept up and collected for refinement in pans or boxes. Examples: tin linsmel pan, brass linsmel box (Benjamin Hurd); limmet, limail pan (John Coney); tin limmel pans (Samuel Edwards); limmy box (John Codner). Plate 13, top.

Loadstone A mineral composed of oxides of iron with magnetic properties. Loadstone was used to separate small iron pieces from silver or gold filings. (John Coney)

Mallet A hammer with a wooden or wrapped rawhide head used to move or bend metal without marring or distorting it. (John Coney). Plate 4, Figs. 28–31.

Measure, copper A container made of various materials, often copper or pewter, that was used to determine dry and liquid amounts. (John Coney).

Mercury An element, also called quicksilver, used for fire gilding. An amalgam of mercury and gold was rubbed on the silver surfaces to be gilded. The piece was then heated, vaporizing the mercury and leaving a thin layer of gold. Mercury was also used in the refining of precious metals, although no evidence is known of this practice in the colonies. Mercury possibly was used to adhere foil to paste stones.

Mill, flatting An iron machine with two rollers used for reducing the thickness of sheet metal through pressure. Although sometimes referred to as plating mills, these tools probably were not used to fuse gold and silver to a base metal. Examples: mill iron (Stephen Winter); flatting mill (John Codner); plating mill (Caleb Beal); mill and swages (Edward Webb); mill to clean silver durt (Samuel Edwards). Plate 11, Fig. 25.

Molding box A rectangular wooden frame with a bottom used to contain claylike casting sand. A pattern or model was impressed into the sand and then carefully removed, leaving a cavity. Molten metal was poured into the impression and allowed to cool. Open molding boxes were used for flat castings, for example, porringer handles. Paired molding boxes also could be used to cast components in the round such as finials and small handles. (John Codner). See also Casting; Flasks; Molding sand.

Molding sand An even, very fine-grain sand with few impurities that compacted very tightly for casting purposes, allowing crisp definition of details and contours. Found

Pl XV

PLATE 8.

Figs. 5, 6: Crucible tongs. AA, the jaws, BB, the eyes, CC, the branches.

Fig. 7: Bent tongs. AA, the jaws. BB, the eye. CC, the branches.

Fig. 8: Straight tongs. AA, the jaws. B, the eye. CC, the arms.

Fig. 9: Tongs.

Figs. 10–13: Crucibles.

Fig. 19: Ingot mold. A, the mold. B, the gateway. CC, the feet. D, the tail.

Fig. 20: Another ingot mold. A, the mold. BB, the feet. C, the tail.

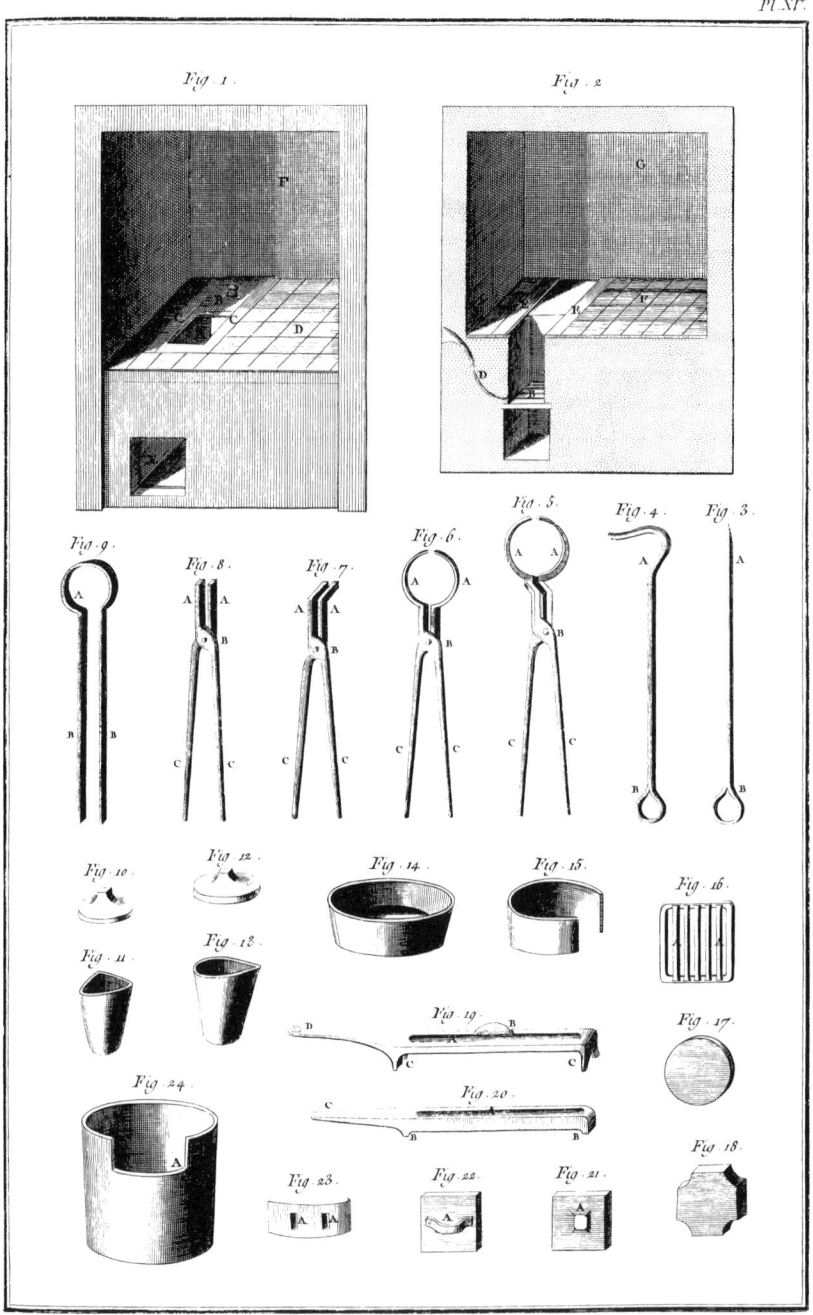

Orfèvre Grossier, Petit Fourneau.

in sediment beds, it also was called French Callis [Calais] sand. (John Dixwell). See also Casting; Flask; Molding box.

Molds In the colonial period molds referred to two different objects: patterns or models of wood and metal that were impressed into sand, forming the casting void; and brass or bronze molds in halves that were used in the production of pewter. The inventories of John Burt, Samuel Edwards, and John Codner list molds that can be construed to be models because of their material. For the most part, goldsmiths did not advertise or record work in base metals. Examples: candlestick moulds (John Coney); pewter & lead moulds (John Burt); copper mold (Thomas Clark); large copper spoon mould (John Codner); brass button mould (Joseph Kneeland); mould for a spoon tin (Samuel Edwards). See also Flask; Pattern.

Mortar and pestle A cylindrical vessel made of iron or brass and used for grinding such substances as enamel and borax with a club-shaped wooden or metal instrument called a pestle. Examples: mortar & pestle brass, mortars & pestles iron (Samuel Edwards); morter (John Coney); pestle (Richard Conyers); pestle & mortar to grind enamel (Joseph Loring). Plate 12, Fig. 17.

Nippers A scissor-shaped iron tool smaller than shears and used for cutting sheet metal. Example: cutting nippers (John Codner). Plate 14, Fig. 12. See also Shears.

Oilstone A flat, hard stone with one or two polished surfaces used with oil as a lubricant in the sharpening of edged iron tools. Examples: oil stone, oyl stone olive (Samuel Edwards); oile things (John Coney). Plate 15, Fig. 57.

Pan, copper handle A circular metallic vessel with a handle used to mix, store, and heat liquids. (Benjamin Hurd).

Pan, dripping Possibly a pan that allowed small quantities of water to fall onto surfaces as they were being polished with powdered abrasives. (Stephen Winter).

Pan, filing (Thomas Clark). See Lemel.

Paper of stones Precious and semiprecious stones were stored in folded packets of paper. It is not clear whether the term refers to a specific number or more likely to the contents of a paper. Examples: paper coffin stones, paper emathist, [paper of] emeralds, paper of garnetts, pap^r buckle sparks (James Boyer).

Paste Brilliant glass used as a substitute for gemstones.

Pattern Patterns cut out of base metal were used as templates either in the initial phase of tracing out a blank or as a reference point during raising. In the first instance the pattern of a teaspoon would have the same contour as the finished spoon but would be larger in the bowl to allow for the dimensional loss when the bowl is hollowed. In raising, a pattern taken from a drawing could be used to compare the work in progress to the desired end product. Examples: patterns (John Coney); brass pattern of spoons, a parcel pewter patterns (Samuel Edwards); brass patterns (Richard Conyers); leaden patterns (Jonathan Reed). See also Molds.

Pestle and mortar See Mortar and pestle.

Pilking See Creasing.

Pipe, borax Perhaps an instrument used instead of a brush to apply flux. This particular inventory had a blowpipe. (Edward Webb).

Planishing A metalsmithing technique whereby the hammer marks left from raising are removed or diminished by light, repetitive conjoined blows with a lightweight hammer that compresses and smooths the metal over stakes or irons. Planishing is the final and least physically demanding of the hammering techniques.

Pl. XVI

PLATE 9.

Fig. 6: Mold. AA, the plates [sides]. BB, the frame. C, the hoop. DD, the iron wedges. E, the mouth [pouring spout].

Fig. 7: Hoop of the mold. AA, the arms. B, the handle.

Fig. 8: The frame of the mold.

Figs. 9, 10: The wedges of the mold.

Figs. 11, 12: The plates of the mold. AA, the mouths.

Fig. 13: Soldering lamp. A, the lamp. B, the stem. C, the lamp carrier.

Figs. 14, 15: Ingots.

Fig. 16: Bellows.

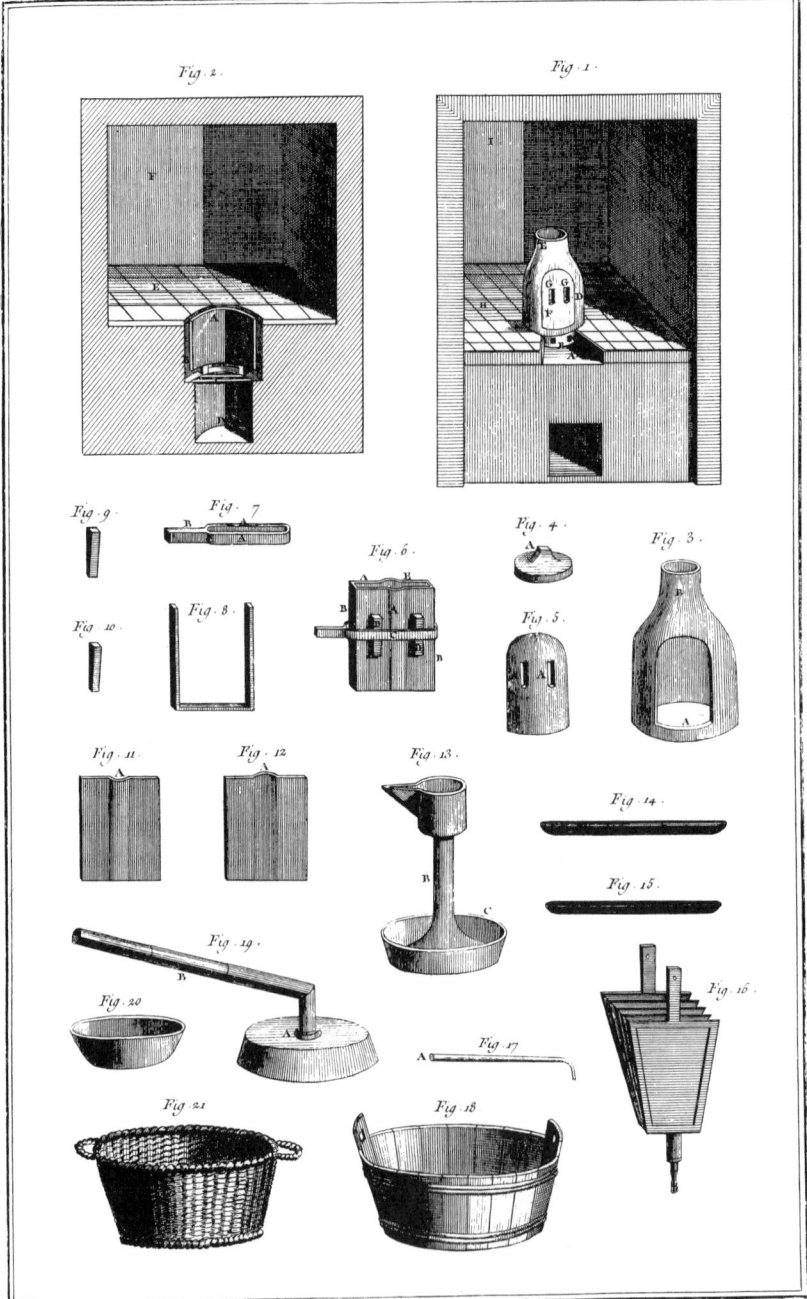

Orfèvre Grossier, Grand Fourneau.

Plates, copper   Highly polished, flat copper sheets $^1/_{16}$ to $^1/_8$ inches in thickness on which designs were cut with gravers. Copper plates were used in the printing of paper currency, bookplates, and illustrations. (John Coney).

Plating mill   See Mill.

Pliers   Hand-held iron tools with two integral handles that are hinged so that the jaws, used to bend metal, can be opened and closed. Spring pliers have a flat steel spring on the handles that forces the jaws into an open position. Specialized pliers are used by watchmakers and clockmakers. Examples: clock [pliers] (John Welsh); plyers (John Coney); flat plyers, small plyers, small round plyers, spring plyers (John Codner); watch plyers, watch plyers best sort, watch plyers better (Samuel Edwards). Plate 6, Figs. 9–11; Plate 14, Fig. 10.

Pot   An alternative name for crucible. Examples: lead glass pot (Samuel Edwards); black melting pots, nest melting potts (Jonathan Reed); iron pots (John Hull); loam pots (John Coney); melting pott (George Hanners, Sr.). See also Crucible.

Powder, plate   Primarily chalk mixed with more abrasive polishing compounds, for example, rouge, tripoli, or sand. Some metalsmiths, such as Paul Revere, Jr., sold plate powder, or silver polish, to the retail market. (Joseph Loring).

Press, drawing   (James Boyer). See Drawing swage.

Pumice   A polishing material made of very porous lava rock, which was high in silica (a strong abrasive), very friable, and easily powdered. Powder or blocks of pumice were used with water to form a slurry of very abrasive material. Also known as rottenstone, pumice was the coarsest of polishing compounds. Examples: pummice stone, flour of [pumice stone] (John Welsh); pumice stone (Samuel Edwards).

Punch   A three- to five-inch iron rod or bar with a shaped and hardened head that was hammered into sheet metal, stamping the metal into a rough form. Punches were often used in conjunction with a lead block that had already been impressed, through hammering, with the profile of the punch or stamp. The sheet metal blank was placed over this hollow and the punch repeatedly hammered down until the sheet conformed to the depression. A punch could be fixed head side up in a vise and used as a stake, which led to a confusion of these two terms. Instead of a lead bottom, a more costly but permanent solution was to make a hollowed-out iron bottom punch. Examples: eight square castor punch, child's [spoon] punch, earing punch, bell punch, punch for whistle, punch for punch ladle, large soop spoon punch, square cannister top punch, tea spoon [punch], bead punches, box of punches, buckles punches, castor punches, clasp punches, bottom punches for castors, freezing punches, marrow spoon punches, large spoon punches (Samuel Edwards); castor punch, button punch (Benjamin Hurd); canister punch, caster punches, boxes of chasing punches, boxes of seal punches, spoon punches, old punches, pepper box punches (John Coney); large iron spoon punch (John Codner); earring punches (Jonathan Reed); brass salt punches (John Burt). Plate 4, Figs. 13–15. See Stamp; Swage.

Punch, cutting   A chisel-shaped punch. (John Coney). Plate 10, Figs. 10–12. See Chisel; Punch.

Punch, dapping   Punches with hemispherically shaped tips in graduated sizes used to make hemispherical shells, two of which were soldered together to form beads. These punches could be used against a lead, wooden, or iron block that had the hollowed impressions. (John Coney). Plate 10, Figs. 18–20. See also Dapping; Die.

Pl. V.

PLATE 10.

Figs. 7, 8: Hammers. AA, the heads. BB, the side. CC, the handles.

Fig. 9: Button die. AA, the hollows.

Figs. 10–12: Burin, chisel, and carp's tongue [rounded]. AAA, the heads. BBB, the edges.

Figs. 13–17: Various chisels. AA, the heads. BB, the points.

Figs. 18–20: The button making tools. AAA, the heads. BBB, the buttons [half-round surface].

Figs. 21, 22: Drill bits. AA, the heads. BB, the tails. CC, the thimble.

Fig. 23: Drill bow. A, the cord. B, the bow.

Fig. 27: Handled mandrel. A, the mandrel. B, the handle.

Figs. 30–36: Flat English file, 31. half-round, 32. squared or tapered, 33. knife edge, 34. triangle, 35. rat tail, 36. oval. AA, the files. BB, the handles.

Fig. 37: Rectangular rasp.

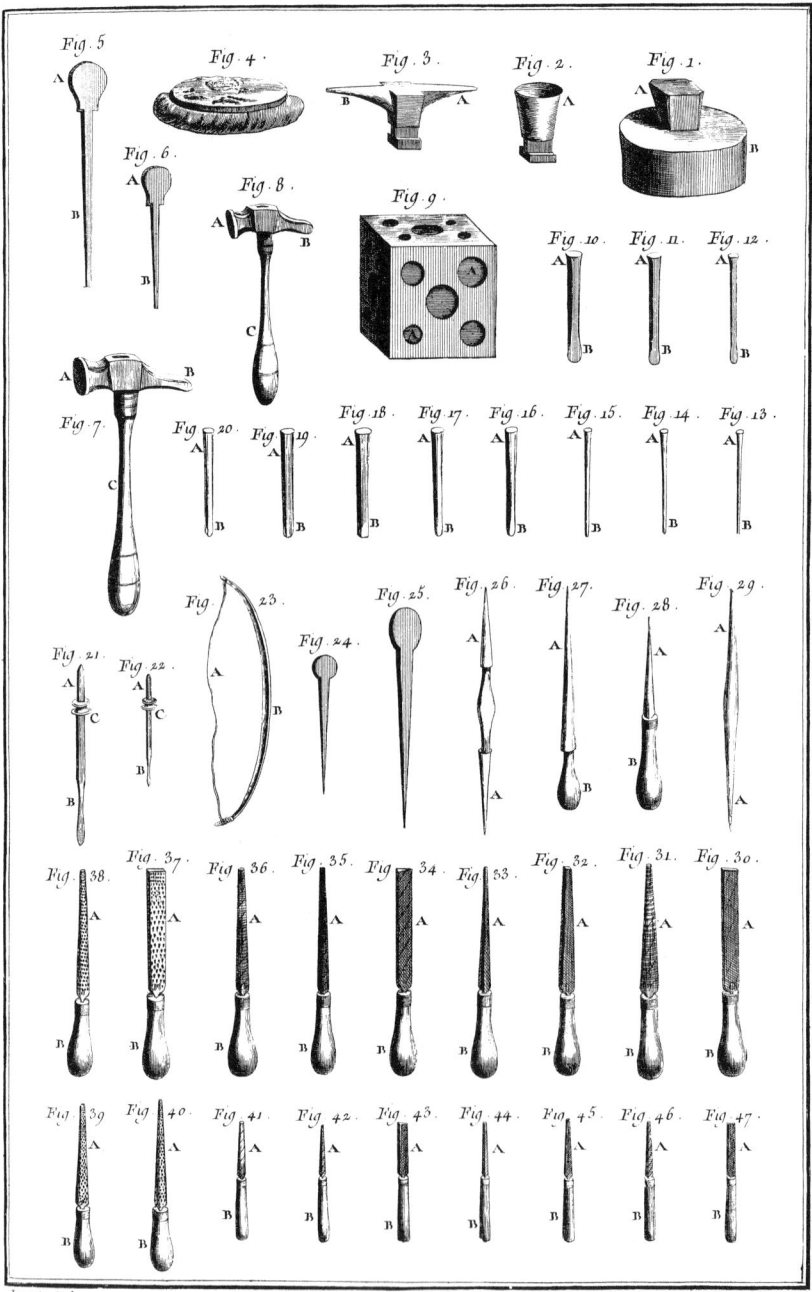

Lacotte Del.   Benard Fecit.

Orfèvre Bijoutier, outils.

Punch, freezing Perhaps punches used to fix pieces together permanently, as in riveting.

Punch, pricket Possibly a punch that produced dots, used for background texturing. (Samuel Edwards). See Punch.

Punch, set A punch with a pointed end used to mark silver for measurements, especially the center of circular sheets before raising. (Samuel Edwards).

Quicksilver (John Hull). See Mercury.

Raising A metalsmithing technique by which sheet metal was hammered over stakes or irons to produce a three-dimensional object; raising is opposed to forging, which moved the metal only in one or at most two dimensions. See also Stake; Iron; Hammer.

Rasp The coarsest cut of files. (John Coney). Plate 10, Fig. 37; Plate 16, Figs. 7, 8. See also File.

Repoussé See Snarling iron.

Ring sizes A graduated set of metal or wooden circles or a plate with graduated holes that was fitted on the client to determine the correct diameter for a ring. Examples: ring sizes (James Boyer); a plate ring sizes (Stephen Winter).

Rouge A red-colored clay that was the finest of the polishing compounds.

Rottenstone (John Welsh, Samuel Edwards). See Pumice.

Rule, brass A brass ruler for measuring. (Samuel Edwards).

Saltpetre Potassium nitrate, a compound used as a flux in casting. (John Coney). See also Flux.

Sand bag (Benjamin Hurd). See Chasing bag.

Sand cushion (John Coney). See Chasing bag.

Sand, wooden thing for Possibly a molding tool. (Samuel Edwards).

Sandever A residue of glass production used as a borax-like flux. (John Coney).

Sandpaper Pieces of paper with one surface coated with different abrasives. Primarily used in the finishing stage of work before polishing. (John Welsh).

Saw A tool with a wooden handle and a toothed, hardened iron blade used for cutting. Frame saws, having an angular metal frame and a five- to eight-inch blade, were used for piercing intricate patterns such as cut card work or, in jewelry, to size rings. Examples: cross cutt saw (William Jones); framd saw (Samuel Edwards); hand saw (David Jesse); small spring saw (John Codner); sawes (Richard Conyers); frame saws (John Coney). Plate 12, Fig. 8; Plate 16, Fig. 1.

Scales Beam scales with two pans and a simple triangular-shaped blade or fulcrum point were used to measure the overall quantity of metal brought in by a client or provided by the silversmith for fashioning an object. Silver and gold were measured in the troy system of weights, which originated in France. The units were pounds, ounces, pennyweights, and grains: 1 lb. equaled 12 oz., which equaled 240 dwt., which equaled 5,760 gr. Most precious metals in the colonies were limited to ounces and pennyweights. One troy ounce equaled 31.1 grams. This system of weight prevailed in the colonies for precious metals, as opposed to avoirdupois weight, in which 16 ounces equaled a pound. Scales were also used in measuring the mixture of metals for solder, in determining the amount of metal needed for casting, and in calculating the client's cost by weight of a finished piece. Jewelers used small scales measured in carat for precious stones: 1 carat equaled 3.1 grains or approximately one-fifth of a gram. Small scales were often made to disassemble into a wooden box that would also

PLATE II.

Figs. 1–6: English riffler files of various types. AA, filing edge.
Fig. 20: Thickness compass. AA, the points. BB, the arms.
Fig. 21: Simple compass. A, the head. BB, the points.
Fig. 22: Scissors. AA, the teeth. BB, the arms.
Fig. 25: Flatting mill. AA, the cylinders. BB, the up-rights of the frame. C, the cross bar of the chassis. D, the hat [top] of the chassis. EE, the screws [these control the gauge]. FF, the pads [floating arbor supports].

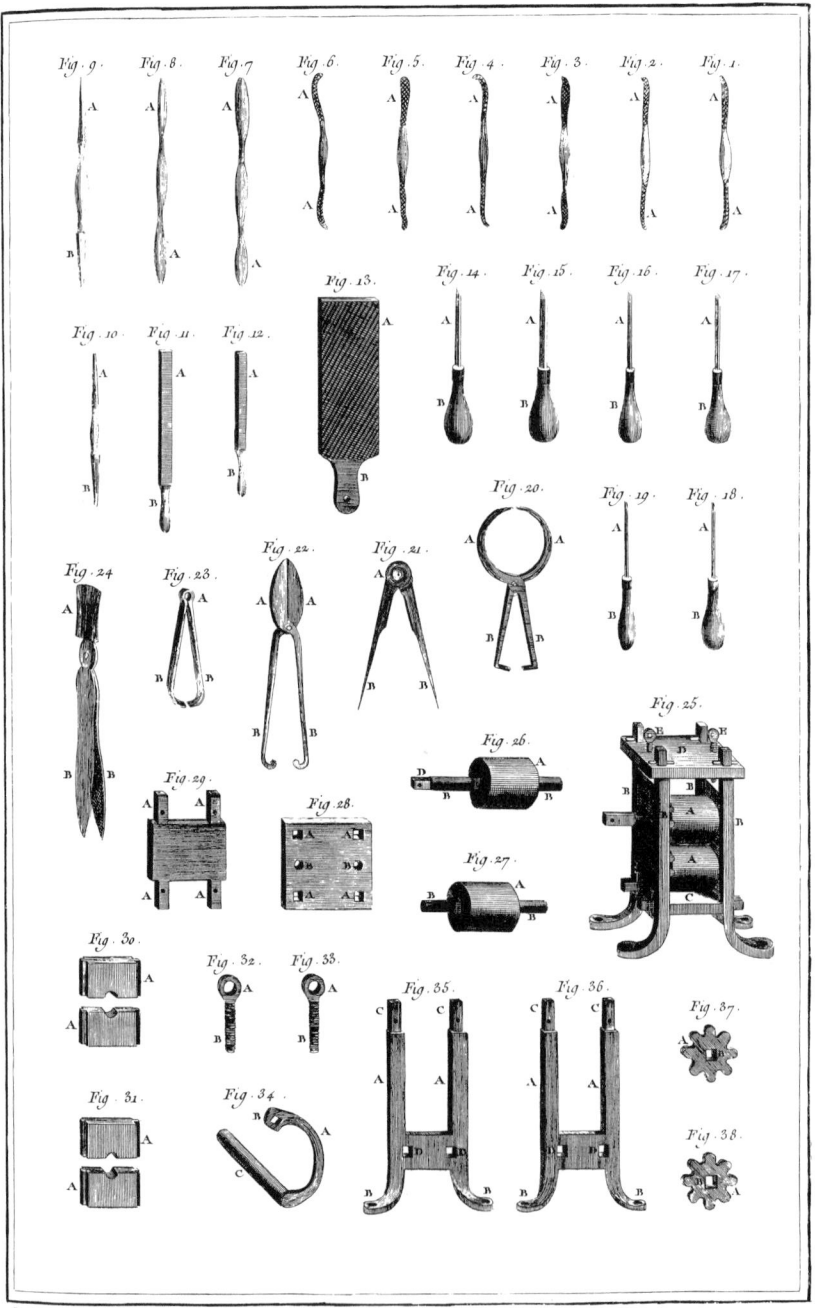

Orfèvre Bijoutier, Outils.

house the nest of weights. Examples: scales (Richard Conyers); box of scales and weights large (John Codner); large beam & scales (John Coney); box beams brass scales, smallest gold scales (Benjamin Hurd); brass scales (Samuel Edwards); diamond scales (James Boyer). See also Weights.

Scissors A cutting tool with two beveled blades used to cut pliable materials such as paper and cloth. (Samuel Edwards). Plate 14, Fig. 11.

Scorper A large engraver usually with a square face, one corner of which acts like a cutting edge. Scorpers were used to remove large amounts of metal quickly, to line sheet metal before creasing, and to enlarge holes for setting stones. (James Boyer). Possibly Plate 15, Fig. 32.

Screw plates and taps The two tools used for making bolts and nuts. A screw plate was a sheet of iron perforated by graduated holes with cut threads. To make a screw or threaded bolt, the plate was forced, through manual turning, onto a metal rod. As the plate was rotated, the softer precious metal rod was cut into by the threaded pattern of the plate. Various sizes or thickness of screws and bolts could be produced from the range of threaded holes on the plate. To make a corresponding nut, a square of sheet metal was drilled a fraction smaller than the diameter of the bolt. A tapered, threaded iron rod, called a tap, was then twisted into the hole, thereby creating the matching thread to receive the bolt. Each diameter of hole in the screw plate would therefore have had a matching tap. These iron tools were used in the fabrication of screws or, more often in precious metals, the making of threaded bolts. Bolts with fine, or closely-spaced, threads were used in attaching finials to lids and grates to chafing dishes. Jewelers used threaded mechanisms for fobs and for the bezels around lockets and miniatures. Examples: screw plates (Richard Conyers); board screw plate (John Parkman); screw plate & pin (Isaac Perkins); screw plate, iron screws (Samuel Edwards); screw plates & taps (John Coney); card screws (John Parkman). Plate 6, Figs. 14–17.

Screws, wooden Possibly thick wooden screws used to tighten the jaws of a vise. (John Codner).

Semitsticks (James Boyer). See Cement stick.

Shears Large, scissor-shaped iron tools for cutting sheet metal. Shears were manufactured in two sizes, the smaller called nippers or hand shears and the larger for thicker metal called stock shears. For straight cuts, the cutting edges were parallel to the arms; for cutting circles, the jaws were slightly curved. Examples: hand shears, stock shears (John Coney); sheers (Richard Conyers). Plate 14, Fig. 13. See also Nippers.

Shop board (David Jesse). See Bench and skin.

Shop sweep (Benjamin Hurd). See Brush.

Shrinker A tool of unknown purpose. (Samuel Edwards).

Silver filings (Edward Webb). See Lemel.

Silver ingot (John Coney). See Ingot mold.

Simmet blocks (Samuel Edwards). See Cement block.

Simmet bullet Possibly a rounded piece of cement held in a vise, or in the hand. (Samuel Edwards). See also Cement stick.

Sinking See Hollowing.

Skillet A utensil of copper, brass, or iron with three or four feet and a long handle. In metalsmithing, skillets were usually made of iron and were used on the forge for melting precious metals. Examples: skillet (Richard Conyers); small

PLATE 12.

Fig. 3: Lamp. A, the glass globe. B, the foot. C, the spout. D, the plateau [candle step]. E, the stem of the plateau. F, the foot of the plateau.

Fig. 4: Soldering lamp. A, the lamp. B, the stem. C, the base.

Fig. 7: Small tongs. A, the head. BB, the arms.

Fig. 8: Handsaw. A, the saw. B, the frame. C, the handle. DD, the screws.

Fig. 10: Emery pot.

Fig. 17: Crushing mortar. A, the mortar. B, the pestle.

Figs. 18, 19: Brushes.

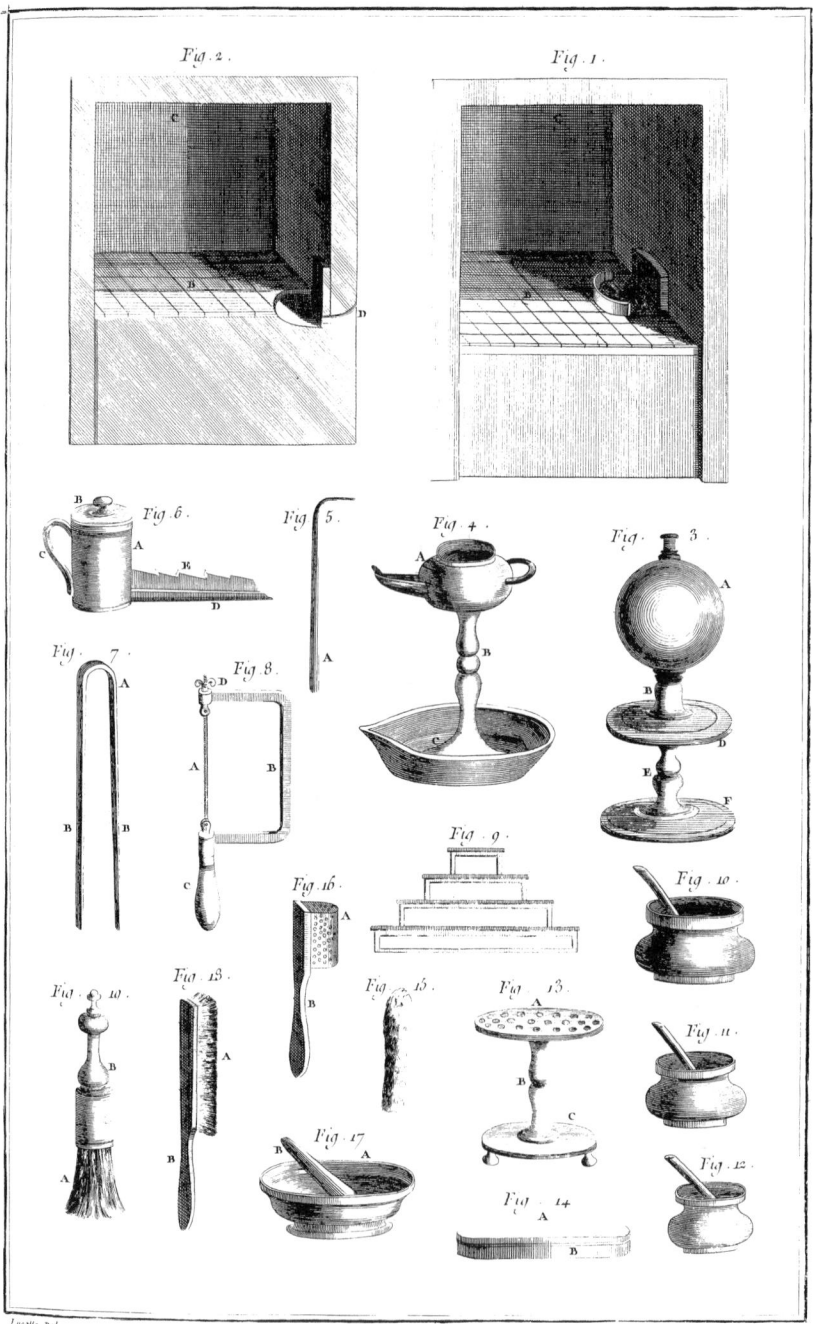

Orfèvre Bijoutier, outils.

casting skillet (Benjamin Hurd); skillet for melting (Isaac Perkins); skillet for silver (George Hanners, Sr.).

Skin, goldbeater's Membrane of the large intestine of cattle used to separate the leaves of metal in goldbeating and to seal lockets in framing portrait miniatures. (Joseph Loring).

Skin and frame (Samuel Edwards). See Bench and skin.

Skinne (Joseph Sanderson). See Chasing bag.

Snarling iron A long iron rod or bar with either a goose-necked or angular short stem terminating in a small, shaped head used for bumping up areas for repoussé. With the inner surface of the object placed over the head of the iron, the opposite end of the iron is hammered nearest its support point, often a vise. The downward force at the hammer point end causes a reciprocal upward blow at the head, producing a series of raised contours that were later defined by chasing. Examples: irons snarling (Samuel Edwards); oune snarling iron (Joseph Sanderson); nurling iron (Richard Conyers); small peecking iron (John Codner). Plate 7, Figs. 45, 46.

Solder An alloy or mixture of metals that, when heated, was used to join two pieces of metal. Solders were formulated to create a range of temperatures that facilitated multiple solderings on a specific object. Generally, silversmiths made and used silver or gold solders, but references indicate some use of soft, or lead/tin, solders as well. The making of solders of different melting points was an essential aspect of the craft and involved mathematics. (John Dixwell).

Soldering iron An iron rod with a copper tip used for low temperature, or lead alloy, solders. In lead/tin soldering the iron was heated on the forge, in a brazier or with a soldering lamp; it was then coated with a flux such as sal ammoniac and applied to the joint with the lead solder applied at the same time to the seam. The low temperatures achieved in this process could not be used for gold or silver solderings. (Samuel Edwards).

Soldering pan A metallic container holding soft, or lead, solder. (John Coney).

Sparrow hawk A small T-shaped anvil, now known as a T-stake, named after a diminutive soaring bird of prey whose outstretched wings resemble this tool. Examples: sparhawks (Samuel Edwards); sparrowhawks (John Coney). See also Anvil.

Spoon tins (Samuel Edwards). See Leads.

Square An L-shaped tool used to check vertical and horizontal trueness. (John Coney).

Stake A forged piece of iron with various contours and one or more polished surfaces primarily used in raising. Although the relationship between stakes and anvils is unclear, it is probable that anvils were larger and were used mostly for forging. Examples: button stake, [stake] for a milk [pot], round bottom stake, gibbet stake, stake to planish a cann, flat bottom stake, role stakes (Samuel Edwards); flatt stake (Isaac Perkins); fork stake (George Hanners, Sr.); bottom stake punches (John Burt). See also Anvil; Beckiron.

Stamp An alternate term for a punch. Some stamps were for specific uses; the spangle stamp, for example, was possibly a tool to make small metallic sequins, called spangles in the period, and money stamps were possibly a die for coins or tokens. Examples: button stamp (Richard Conyers); brass stamp for castor tops, thimble stamp, money stamps (Samuel Edwards); clasp stamp (David Jesse); brass caster stamps, cross stamp (Benjamin Hurd); deaths head stamp, brass hole ring stamp (George Hanners, Sr.); brass hollowing stamp (John Codner); brass salt stamp, spangle stamp (John Coney). See also Die; Punch.

Steel, block of A piece of square or rectangular steel, one-half to two inches in thickness and

Pl. VIII.

PLATE 13.

The top of this plate repre-
sents the jeweler's board. A,
the bench. BB, the arms.
CC, the feet. DD, the wood-
blocks (bench pins). EE, the
drawers. FF, the aprons.
GG, the floor trellis.
Fig. 5: Beckiron. A, the
round beckiron. B, the square
beckiron. C, the stem. D, the
block.
Fig. 9: Dapping block. AA,
the button hollows.

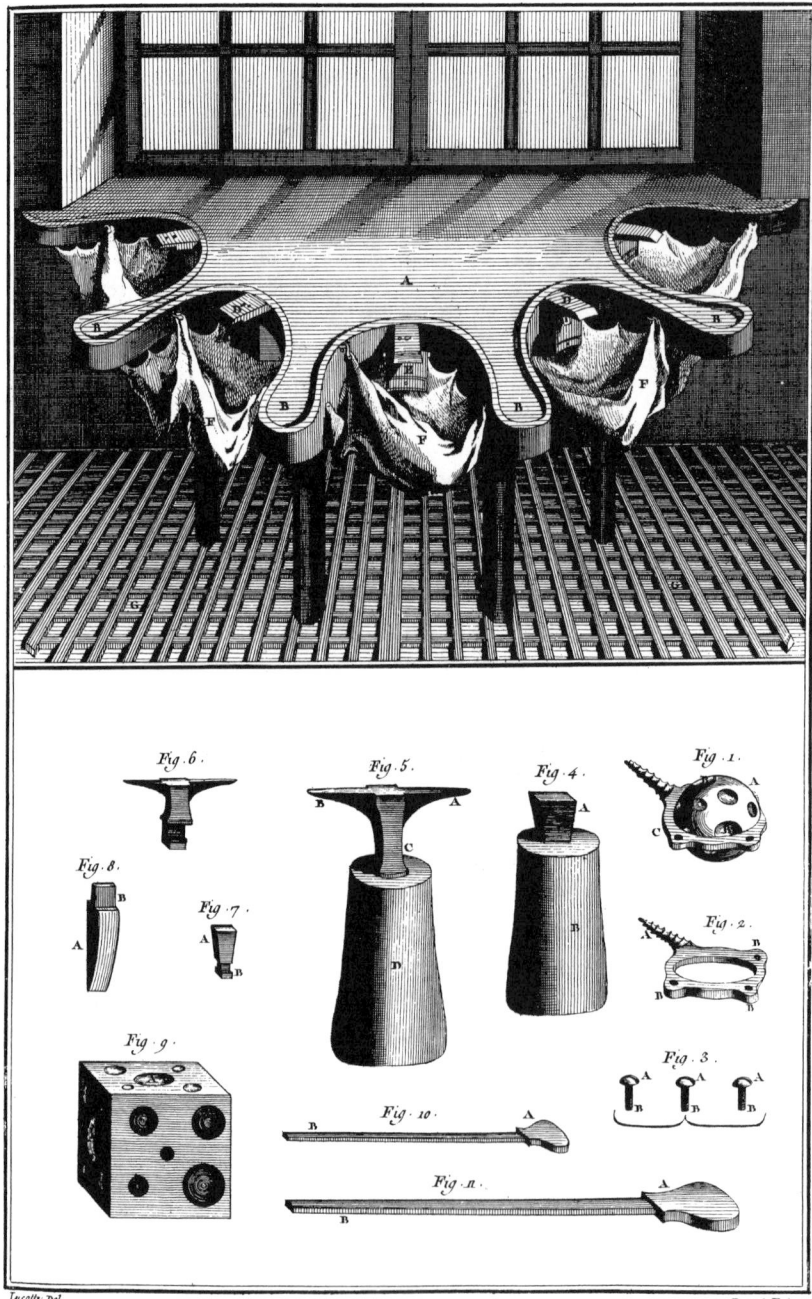

Lucotte Del.   *Benard Fecit.*

Orfèvre Jouaillier, Metteur en Œuvre, Outils.

of various sizes, with one or two polished surfaces used as a hammering surface for straightening sheet or wire. (John Coney). Plate 5, Figs. 17–19. See also Anvil.

Stock shears (Isaac Perkins). See Shears.

Strainer Probably a wire mesh or screen, sometimes hemispherical, with a handle that could be used to sift such materials as gold filings for amalgam gilding, enamels, fluxes such as borax, or other particulate separations. Examples: strainers (John Coney); sett king strainers (Joseph Kneeland); strainges with frames (John Dixwell). See also Colander.

Swage An alternative term for die. A block of iron with incised decoration into which metal was hammered, thereby producing the identical pattern, only reversed. Swages were used instead of drawing irons to produce wire, including beaded wire, and half-round wire used for rings. They could also be highly ornamental, such as those used to make deaths head rings. Swages and bottom punches are synonymous, and the listed spoon swage possibly had an accompanying punch. Examples: deaths head swage, heart & hand ring swage, small spoon swage, tankard swage (Samuel Edwards); flower'd spoon swages (Edward Webb); ring swage, tankard and swage (Richard Conyers); death head ring swage (John Welsh). See also Die; Punch; Stamp.

Swelling A raising process using stakes and hammers that extended the metal to create more volume. Rococo, double-bellied teapots and coffeepots often needed this technique.

Teast Another term for a stake or an anvil. Examples: teast for spoons (George Hanners, Sr.); large planishing teast, spoon teast (Richard Conyers); round teast (John Coney); large spoon teast (Benjamin Hurd); planishing test, swage test (Isaac Perkins); planishing test (Edward Webb). See also Anvil; Stake.

Tongs Forged iron tools with jaws, a hinge, or a bow and six- to thirty-six inch-long arms that were used to hold hot or cold metal objects. Tongs were used to hold sheet for forging or component parts for soldering. Some tongs were made for specific tasks: casting or charging tongs, for example, were bow-shaped tongs used to hold hot crucibles while pouring molten metal. Cornered tongs had jaws at right angles. Flat tongs had jaws that were almost parallel. The width of the jaw was determined by the size of the piece to be held. Nealing [annealing] tongs were used to hold metal being annealed in the forge or brazier. Sliding tongs had an integral bow spring at the grip and a sliding ring that could be moved up the arms to compress them, thus allowing the sliding tongs to function as an elongated hand-held vise. Examples: casting tongs, charge^g tongs, spring tongs (Samuel Edwards); cording tongs (Edward Webb); corn tongs (Stephen Winter); corning tongs (James Boyer); large fire spring tongs (John Codner); flat tongs (John Dixwell); tongs holding (Joseph Sanderson); nealing [tongs] (John Coney); nurling tongs (Richard Conyers); pr. goldsmiths tongs (Thomas Clark); sliding tongs (John Dixwell); tongues belong^g to the forge (John Parkman). Plate 8, Figs. 5–9; Plate 12, Fig. 7; Plate 16, Figs. 24, 27.

Tongues See Fluke.

Touchstone A dark colored agate slab onto which metal of an unknown purity is rubbed in a line. Next to this line a piece of known fineness is rubbed. The comparison of color would lead to an estimate of silver or gold content. Metalsmiths could either make or purchase sets of "needles" that were tipped with graduated finenesses of both gold and silver. (John Coney).

Pl. IX.

PLATE 14.

Figs. 1, 2: Hammers. AA, the heads. BB, the tails. CC, the handles.

Fig. 10: Round pliers. AA, the jaws. BB, the arms.

Fig. 11: Scissors. AA, the jaws. BB, the rings.

Fig. 12: Small shears. AA, the jaws. BB, the branches.

Fig. 13: Large shears. AA, the jaws. BB, the branches.

Fig. 14: Proportional compass. A, the hinge. BB, the curved points. CC, the branches.

Fig. 15: Thickness compass. A, the head. BB, the curved points.

Fig. 16: Straight compass. A, the head. BB, the straight points.

Fig. 17: Screw compass. A, the springhead. BB, the points. C, the hinge. D, the nut.

Fig. 22: Large chisel. A, the head. B, the cutting edge.

Fig. 24: Small chisel. A, the head. B, the cutting edge.

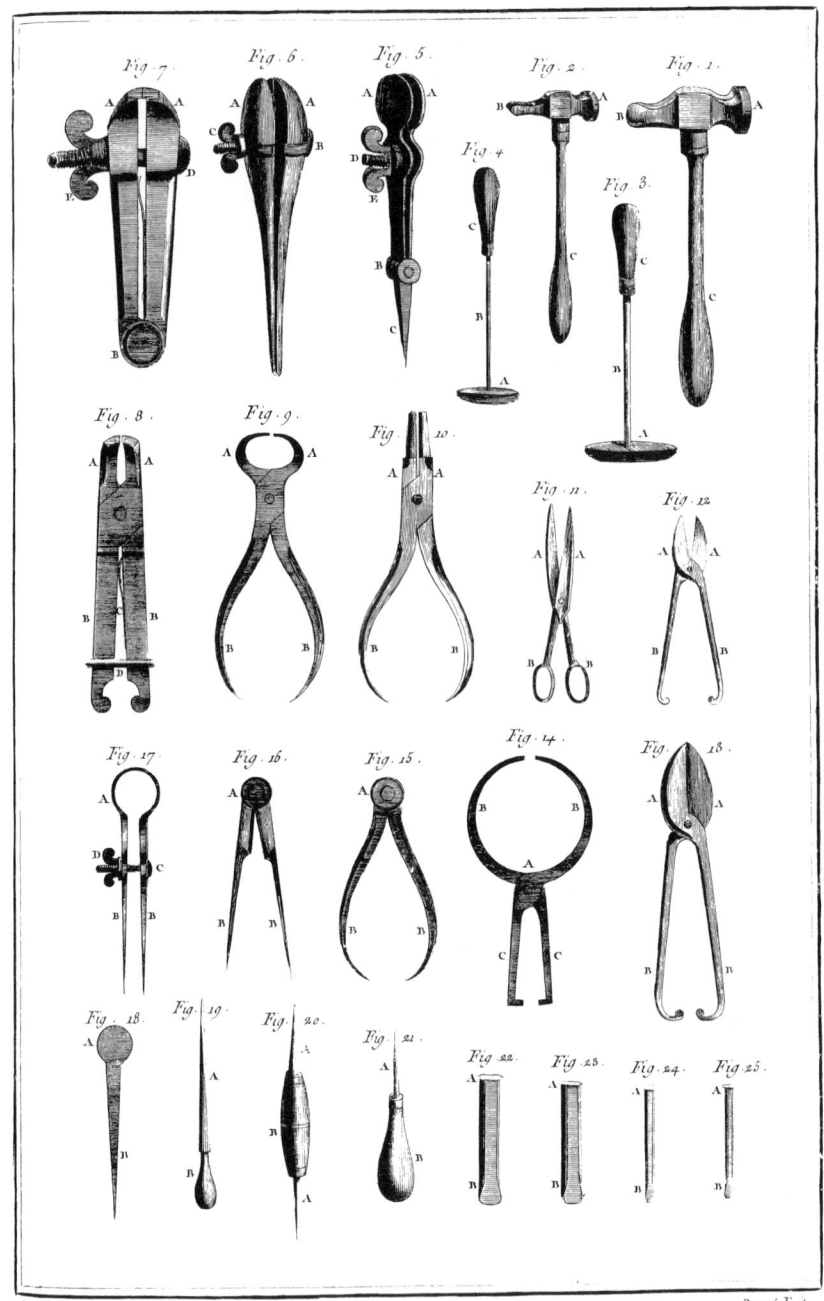

Lacotte Del.

Benard fecit.

Orfèvre Jouaillier, Metteur en Œuvre, Outils.

Triblet Any small iron forming tool, although in French the term *tribouillet* refers specifically to a small, shaped mandrel. Examples: triblet (John Coney); square trib (John Dixwell); eight square tribblet, round tribblet (Samuel Edwards). Plate 10, Fig. 27.

Tripoli A buff-colored clay used immediately before rouge in polishing. (Samuel Edwards).

Turning bench iron (Edward Webb). See Lathe.

Turning tools (John Coney). See Lathe.

Vise A tool made of iron or wood or both, with movable jaws used to hold objects. Vises ranged in size from hand-held to standing wall-mounted or stump-mounted examples for large work. Vises described as board vises probably were vises attached to the board, or bench. Examples: vice (George Hanners, Sr.); vice clamps, drill [vise], turn [vise] (John Coney); old board vice (David Jesse); hand vices (Richard Conyers); wooden vices (James Boyer); charger smll vise, stna.^{d} vise, box vises, vises not so good (Samuel Edwards); large stand^{g} bench vise, bench vise (Benjamin Hurd); wooden hand vise (Stephen Winter). Plate 6, Figs. 2–5, 7.

Weights Cup-shaped or rectangular pieces of metal, usually made of brass, sold in piles or nesting sets and used in conjunction with scales. Weights were usually calibrated in troy ounces, as opposed to avoirdupois, the standard weight scale for nonprecious objects. Examples: setts apothecary [weights], setts grain weights, setts penny weights (Samuel Edwards); [weights] avoirdupoire, [weights] troy (John Dixwell); brass weights, sett of small weights, training weights (Richard Conyers); pile of weights (John Coney). See also Scale.

PLATE 15.

Figs. 26, 27: Small gaugers to cut[?] and to stop[?]. AA, the gauges. BB, the handles.

Fig. 32: Handled scorper. A, the scorper. B, the handle.

Fig. 34: Lamp. A, the glass globe. B, the foot. C, the opening. D, the tray. E, the stem of the tray. F, the foot of the tray.

Figs. 35, 36: Large and small cement gripes. A, the gripe. B, the cement. C, the point.

Fig. 40: Small drill. A, the arc. B, the cord.

Figs. 41, 42: Drills. AA, the head of the drills. BB, the ends. CC, the boxes (i.e., spools).

Fig. 43: Large drill. A, the stem. B, the counter weight. C, the barrel. D, the drill. E, the transversal. FF, the cord.

Fig. 51: Polisher. A, the fabric. B, the wood. C, the handle.

Fig. 56: Small wicker brush.

Fig. 57: Oilstone. A, the stone. B, the box.

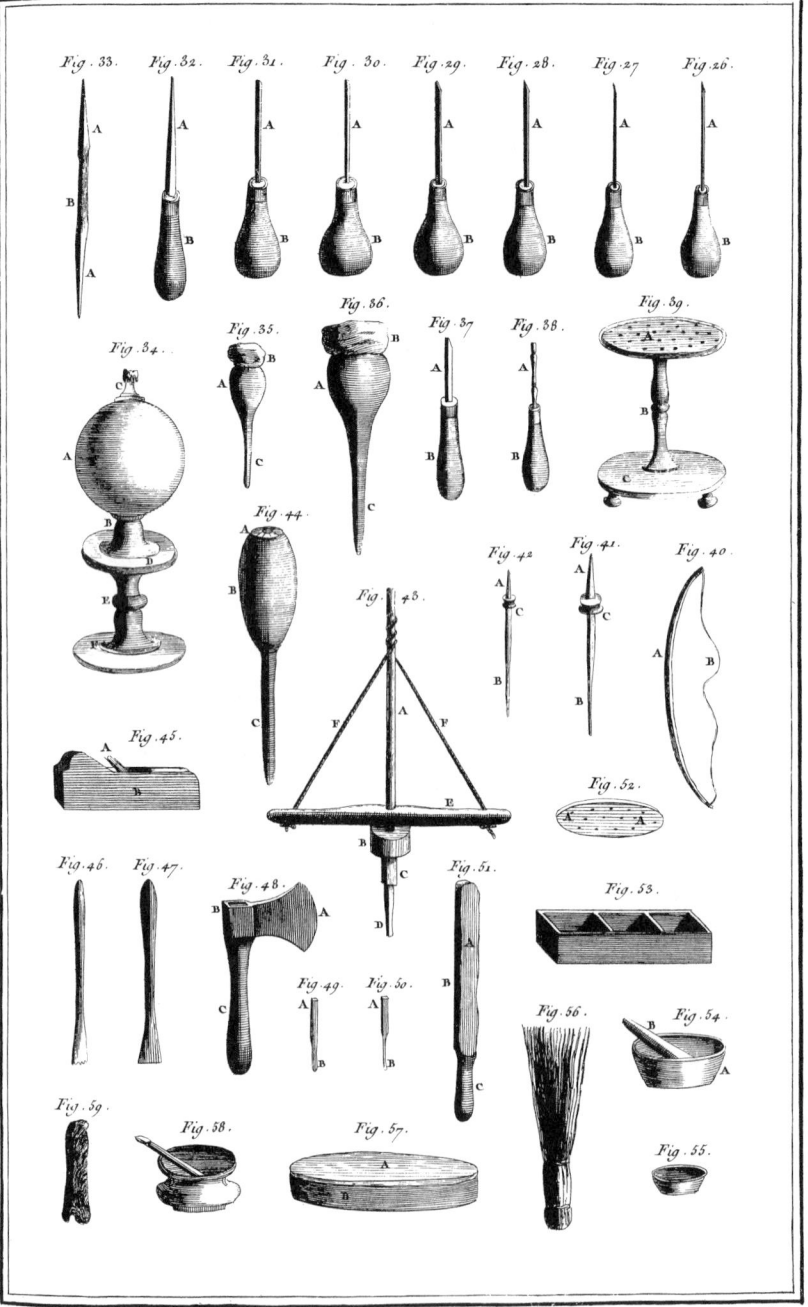

Orfèvre Jouaillier, Metteur en Œuvre , Outils .

Pl. XI.

PLATE 16.

Fig. 1: Handsaw. A, the saw. B, the frame. C, the screw. D, the nut. E, the pivot. F, the handle.

Fig. 7: Squared rasp. A, the rasp. B, the handle.

Fig. 8: Half-round rasp. A, the rasp. B, the handle.

Fig. 9–12: Rifflers of many types. AA, the rifflers. BB, the shanks.

Fig. 18: Brush to clean diamonds. A, the brush. B, the handle.

Fig. 20: Another cleaning brush. A, the brush. B, the handle.

Fig. 24: Tongs. A, the head. BB, the arms.

Fig. 27: Forge tongs. AA, the pincers. BB, the arms.

Fig. 28: Forge bellows.

Fig. 30: Soldering lamp. A, the lamp. B, the stem. C, the foot.

Fig. 31: Blowpipe to solder. A, the mouthpiece. B, the hook.

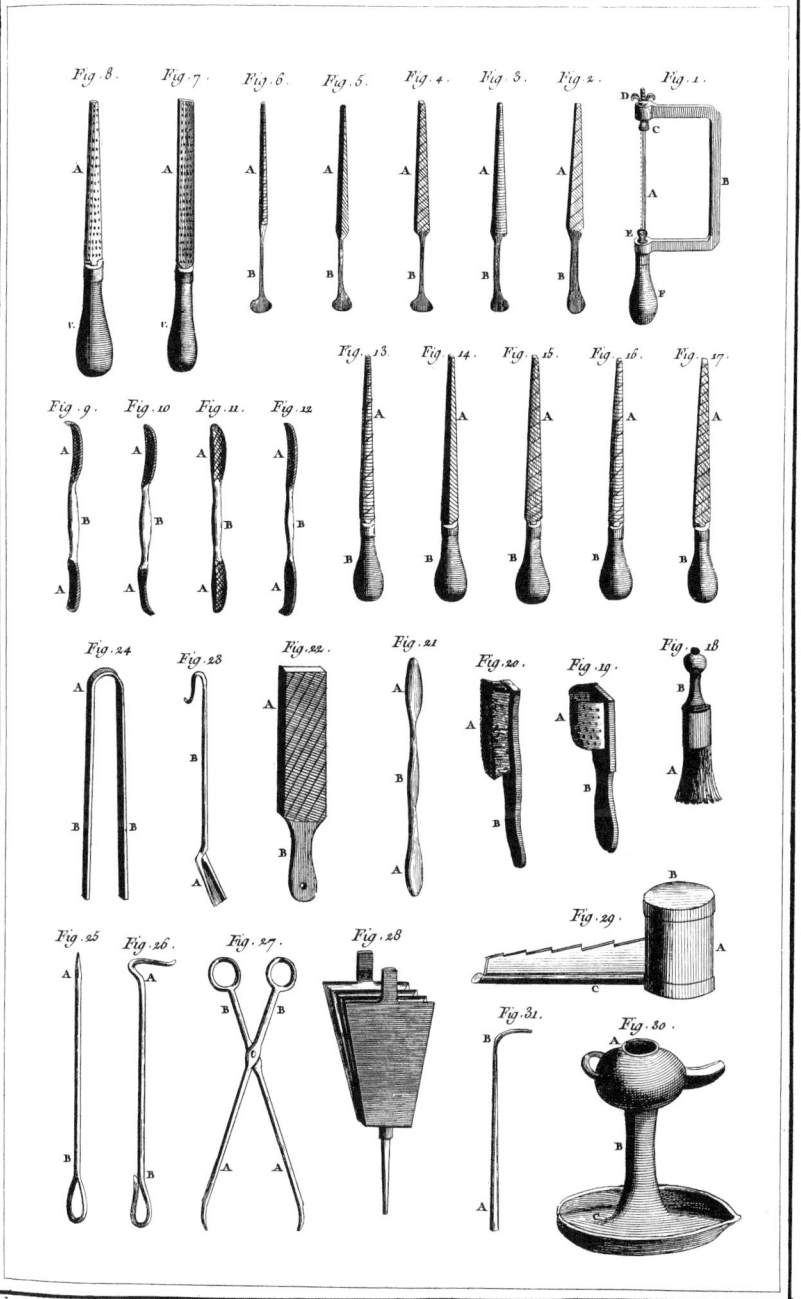

Orfèvre Jouaillier, Metteur en Œuvre, Outils.

Appendix D

References

Abbott 1979 Abbott, Susan Woodruff, comp. *Families of Early Milford, Connecticut.* Baltimore: Genealogical Publishing Company, 1979.

Adams 1910 Adams, William Frederick. *Genealogical and Personal Memoirs Relating to the Families of the State of Massachusetts.* New York: Lewis Historical Publishing Co., 1910.

Agnew 1871 Agnew, David C. A. *Protestant Exiles from France in the Reign of Louis XIV.* 2 vols. London: Reever & Turner; Edinburgh: William Paterson, 1871.

Allen 1894 Allen, Charles Dexter. *American Bookplates.* New York: Macmillan, 1894.

Allen 1900 Allen, Francis Olcott. *The History of Enfield, Connecticut.* 3 vols. Lancaster, Pa.: Wickersham, 1900.

American and English Silver *Exhibition of Old American and English Silver.* Philadelphia: Pennsylvania Museum, 1917.

American Art Association– American Art Association, Anderson Galleries, New York
Anderson Galleries

American Art of the Colonies *American Art of the Colonies and Early Republic.* Chicago: Art Institute of
and Early Republic Chicago, 1971.

American Silver 1967 *American Silver and Pressed Glass: A Collection in the R. W. Norton Art Gallery.* Shreveport: R. W. Norton Art Foundation, 1967.

Amesbury VR *Vital Records of Amesbury, Massachusetts, to the End of the Year 1849.* Topsfield, Mass.: Topsfield Historical Society, 1913.

Anderson Gallery Anderson Gallery, New York

Anderson 1896 Anderson, Joseph, ed. *The Town and City of Waterbury, Connecticut, from the Aboriginal Period to the Year Eighteen Ninety-five.* New Haven: Price and Lee, 1896.

Andover VR *Vital Records of Andover, Massachusetts, to the End of the Year 1849.* 2 vols. Topsfield, Mass.: Topsfield Historical Society, 1912.

Andrews 1965 Andrews, Thomas Eliot, ed. "The Diary of Elizabeth (Porter) Phelps." *New England Historic Genealogical Register* 119 (April 1965): 127–40.

Andrus 1955 Andrus, Vincent D. *Early American Silver, A Picture Book.* New York: The Metropolitan Museum of Art, 1955.

Anthony Family *Genealogy of the Anthony Family from 1495 to 1904.* Sterling, Ill.: Charles L. Anthony, 1904.

Arnold 1911   Arnold, James N. *Vital Records of Rhode Island, 1636–1850.* 21 vols. Providence: Narragansett Historical Publishing Company, 1911.

"Assessors' 'Taking-Books'"   "Assessors' 'Taking-Books' of the Town of Boston, 1780." *Bostonian Society Publications* 9 (1912): 9–59.

Austin 1887   Austin, John Osborne. *Genealogical Dictionary of Rhode Island.* Albany: J. Munsell's Sons, 1887.

Avery 1920   Avery, C. Louise. *American Silver of the Seventeenth and Eighteenth Centuries: A Study Based on the Clearwater Collection.* New York: The Metropolitan Museum of Art, 1920.

Avery (1930) 1968   Avery, C. Louise. *Early American Silver.* 1930. Reprint. New York: Russell & Russell, 1968.

Avery 1930a   Avery, C. Louise. "The Beginnings of American Silver." *Antiques* 18 (August 1930): 122–25.

Babcock 1947   Babcock, Mary Kent Davey. *Christ Church, Salem Street Boston: The Old North Church of Paul Revere Fame.* Boston: Thomas Todd Company, 1947.

Backlin-Landman 1969   Backlin-Landman, Hedy. "Boudinot Furnishings in the Art Museum of Princeton University." *Antiques* 96 (September 1969): 366–71.

Badcock 1677   Badcock, William. *A New Touchstone for Gold and Silver Wares.* London, 1677.

Bailey 1975   Bailey, Chris H. *Two Hundred Years of American Clocks and Watches.* Englewood Cliffs, N.J.: Prentice-Hall, 1975.

Bailyn/Bailyn 1959   Bailyn, Bernard, and Lotte Bailyn. *Massachusetts Shipping, 1697–1714: A Statistical Study.* Cambridge: Harvard University Press, 1959.

Baird 1885   Baird, Charles W. *History of the Huguenot Emigration to America.* 2 vols. New York: Dodd, Mead, 1885.

Balch 1897   Balch, Galusha Burchard. *Genealogy of the Balch Families in America.* Salem, Mass.: E. Putnam, 1897.

Balch Leaflets 1896   "The Diary of Ebenezer Balch." *Balch Leaflets Volume 1. January–April 1896.* Salem, Mass.: Eben Putnam, 1896–97.

Ballard 1955   Ballard, Canon Lockett Ford. *Trinity Church in Newport.* Newport, R.I.: Wilkinson Press, 1955.

Ballard 1981   Ballard, Margaret. "Early Silver in Trinity Church, Newport, Rhode Island." *Antiques* 120 (October 1981): 922–25.

Barber 1838   Barber, John Warner. *Connecticut Historical Collection.* New Haven: Durrie and Peck and J. W. Barber, 1838.

Barker 1986   Barker, Robert. "Jamaican Goldsmiths, Assayers and Their Marks from 1665 to 1765." *Proceedings of the Silver Society* 3 (Spring 1986): 133–37.

Barnstable VR   *Records of the West Parish of Barnstable, Massachusetts, 1668–1807.* Boston: Massachusetts Historical Society, 1924.

Barnstable and Sandwich VR   Smith, Col. Leonard H., Jr., and Nora Smith, comps. *Vital Records of the Towns of Barnstable and Sandwich.* Baltimore: Genealogical Publishing Company, 1982.

Bartlett 1879   Bartlett, John Russell. *Genealogy of that Branch of the Russell Family Which Comprises the Descendants of John Russell.* Providence: Privately printed, 1879.

Bartlett 1984   Bartlett, Louisa. "American Silver." *The Bulletin of the Saint Louis Art Museum.* n.s. 17 (Winter 1984).

Batchellor 1907   Batchellor, Albert Stillman, ed. *Probate Records of the Province of New Hampshire.* Concord: Rumford, 1907.

Batchellor 1910   Batchellor, Albert Stillman, ed. *Miscellaneous Revolutionary Documents of New*

Hampshire. State Papers Series, vol. 30. Manchester, N.H.: Printed for the State by the John B. Clarke Co., 1910.

Bates 1886   Bates, Samuel A., ed. *Records of the Town of Braintree 1640 to 1793.* Randolph, Mass.: D. H. Huxford, 1886.

Battelle 1889   Battelle, Lillian S. *Battelle Genealogical Record.* Cincinnati: Robert Clarke, 1889.

Battison/Kane 1973   Battison, Edwin A., and Patricia E. Kane. *The American Clock, 1725–1865: The Mabel Brady Garvan and Other Collections at Yale University.* Greenwich, Conn.: New York Graphic Society Limited, 1973.

Baumann 1976   Baumann, Richard G. "Peppering the Bostonian Palate: Two Sugar Casters by Paul Revere II." *Muse* 10 (1976): 37–47.

Beaman 1985   Beaman, Alden Gamaliel, comp. *Rhode Island Vital Records, New Series, vol. II; Births 1590–1930 from Newport Common Burial Ground Inscriptions.* East Princeton, Mass.: Rhode Island Families Association, 1985.

Bedford VR   *Vital Records of Bedford, Massachusetts, to the Year 1850.* Boston: New England Historic Genealogical Society, 1903.

Belden 1980   Belden, Louise Conway. *Marks of American Silversmiths in the Ineson–Bissell Collection.* Charlottesville: University Press of Virginia for the H. F. du Pont Winterthur Museum, 1980.

Belknap 1927   Belknap, Henry Wyckoff. *Artists and Craftsmen of Essex County, Massachusetts.* Salem, Mass.: Essex Institute, 1927.

Benedict/Tracy 1878   Benedict, William A., and Hiram A. Tracy. *History of the Town of Sutton, Massachusetts, from 1704 to 1876 Including Grafton until 1735, Millbury until 1813, and parts of Northbridge, Upton, and Auburn.* Worcester, Mass.: Sanford, 1878.

Benes 1986   Benes, Peter. *Old–Town and the Waterside: Two Hundred Years of Tradition and Change in Newbury, Newburyport, and West Newbury, 1635–1835.* Newburyport, Mass.: Historical Society of Old Newbury, 1986.

Bentley 1905–62   Bentley, William. *The Diary of William Bentley, D.D., Pastor of the East Church Salem, Massachusetts.* 4 vols. Salem, Mass.: Essex Institute, 1905–62.

Berry 1909   Berry, Henry F., ed. *The Registers of the Church of St. Michan, Dublin, 1686–1700.* Dublin, Ireland: Alex Thom, 1909.

Beverly VR   *Vital Records of Beverly, Massachusetts, to the End of the Year 1849.* 2 vols. Topsfield, Mass.: Topsfield Historical Society, 1906–07.

Biddle 1963   Biddle, James. *American Art from American Collections.* New York: The Metropolitan Museum of Art, 1963.

Bigelow 1917   Bigelow, Francis Hill. *Historic Silver of the Colonies and Its Makers.* New York: Macmillan, 1917.

Bigelow 1925   Bigelow, Francis Hill. "Early New England Silver." *Antiques* 8 (September 1925): 156–59.

Billerica VR   *Vital Records of Billerica, Massachusetts, to the End of the Year 1850.* Boston: New England Historic Genealogical Society, 1908.

Birk 1967   Birk, Eileen P. "Current and Coming." *Antiques* 92 (September 1967): 258, 268, 294, 296, 298, 302, 304.

Blackburn/Piwonka 1988   Blackburn, Roderic H., and Ruth Piwonka. *Remembrance of Patria: Dutch Arts and Culture in Colonial America, 1609–1776.* Albany: Albany Institute of History and Art, 1988.

Boardman 1906   Boardman, William F. J. *The Ancestry of Jane Maria Greenleaf.* Hartford: Privately printed, 1906.

Boardman 1938   Boardman, Anne Calef. "Robert Calef and Some of His Descendants." *Essex Institute Historical Collections* 74 (October 1938): 373–96.

Bodenwein 1943   Bodenwein, Gordon. "New London, Connecticut, Silversmiths." *Old–Time New England* 33 (April 1943): 57–60.

Bohan 1963   Bohan, Peter J. *American Gold 1700–1860.* New Haven: Yale University Art Gallery, 1963.

Bohan/Hammerslough 1970   Bohan, Peter, and Philip Hammerslough. *Early Connecticut Silver, 1700–1840.* Middletown, Conn.: Wesleyan University Press, 1970.

Bolton 1900–39   Bolton, Charles Knowles. "Workers with Line and Color in New England, 1620–1870." Typescript, Boston Athenaeum, Boston, 1900–39.

Bolton (1927) 1964   Bolton, Charles Knowles. *Bolton's American Armory.* 1927. Reprint. Baltimore: Heraldic Book Company, 1964.

Bolton VR   *Vital Records of Bolton, Massachusetts, to the End of the Year 1849.* Worcester, Mass.: F. P. Rice, 1910.

Boltwood 1862   Boltwood, L. M. *Genealogies of Hadley Families Embracing the Early Settlers of the Towns of Hatfield, South Hadley, Amherst and Granby.* Northampton, Mass.: Metcalf, 1862.

Bond 1860   Bond, Henry. *Genealogies of the Families and Descendants of the Early Settlers of Watertown, Massachusetts.* Boston: New England Historic Genealogical Society, 1860.

Bonhams   Bonhams Auction Galleries, London

Borsay 1977   Borsay, Peter. "The English Urban Renaissance: The Development of Provincial Urban Culture, c. 1680–c. 1760." *Social History* 5 (May 1977): 581–603.

Bortman 1952   Bortman, Mark. *Simon Willard's Letters to Paul Revere 1782–1786.* Privately printed, 1952.

Bortman 1954   Bortman, Jane. "Moses Hayes and His Revere Silver." *Antiques* 66 (October 1954): 304–05.

Boston Deaths, 1630–1699   Record Books, Boston City Archives, Room 201, City Hall, Boston

Boston Deaths, 1700–1800   Record Books, Boston City Archives, Room 201, City Hall, Boston

Boston Deaths, 1800–1810   Record Books, Boston City Archives, Room 201, City Hall, Boston

Boston Deaths, 1810–1848   Record Books, Boston City Archives, Room 201, City Hall, Boston

Boston Directory   Bibliographic information for specific directories cited is given in Spear 1961, 45–57.

Boston Prints and Printmakers   *Boston Prints and Printmakers 1670–1775.* Boston: Colonial Society of Massachusetts, 1973.

Boston Registry Dept. 1893   Boston Registry Department. *Bills of Mortality, 1810–1849, City of Boston with an Essay on the Vital Statistics of Boston from 1810 to 1841.* Boston: Printed for the Registry Department, 1893.

Bowditch 1944   Bowditch, Harold. "Early Water–Color Paintings of New England Coats of Arms." *Publications of the Colonial Society of Massachusetts* 35 (December 1944): 172–210.

Boxford VR   *Vital Records of Boxford, Massachusetts, to the End of the Year 1849.* Topsfield, Mass.: Topsfield Historical Society, 1905.

Boyer/Nissenbaum 1974   Boyer, Paul, and Stephen Nissenbaum. *Salem Possessed: The Social Origins of Witchcraft.* Cambridge and London: Harvard University Press, 1974.

"Boyle's Journal of Occurrences in Boston"   "Boyle's Journal of Occurrences in Boston." *New England Historical and Genealogical Register* 84 (April 1930): 142–71; (July 1930): 248–72; (October 1930): 357–82; 85 (January 1931): 5–28; (April 1931): 117–33.

Bradford VR   *Vital Records of Bradford, Massachusetts, to the End of the Year 1849.* Topsfield, Mass.: Topsfield Historical Society, 1907.

Braintree VR   Bates, Samuel A., ed. *Records of the Town of Braintree, 1640 to 1793.* Randolph, Mass.: D. H. Huxford, 1886.

Branford VR   Barbour Collection, Connecticut State Library, Hartford

Bridgman 1850   Bridgman, Thomas. *Inscriptions on the Gravestones in the Grave Yards of Northampton.* Northampton, Mass.: Hopkins, Bridgman, 1850.

Bridgman 1851   Bridgman, Thomas. *Epitaphs from Copp's Hill Burial Ground.* Boston: J. Munroe, 1851.

Bridgman 1853   Bridgman, Thomas. *Memorials of the Dead in Boston; Containing Exact Transcripts of Inscriptions on the Sepulchral Monuments in the King's Chapel Burial Ground.* Boston: Benjamin B. Mussey, 1853.

Bridgman 1856   Bridgman, Thomas. *The Pilgrims of Boston and Their Descendants.* Boston: Phillips, Sampson, 1856.

Brigham 1954   Brigham, Clarence S. *Paul Revere's Engravings.* Worcester, Mass.: American Antiquarian Society, 1954.

Brimfield VR   *Vital Records of Brimfield, Massachusetts, to the Year 1850.* Boston: New England Historic Genealogical Society at the Charge of the Eddy Town Record Fund, 1931.

Brix 1920   Brix, Maurice. *List of Philadelphia Silversmiths and Allied Artificers from 1682 to 1850.* Philadelphia: Privately printed, 1920.

Brooke 1989   Brooke, John L. *The Heart of the Commonwealth: Society and Political Culture in Worcester County, Massachusetts, 1713–1861.* Cambridge and New York: Cambridge University Press, 1989.

Brooke/Hallen 1886   Brooke, J. M. S., and A. W. C. Hallen, eds. *The Transcript of the Registers of the United Parishes of S. Mary Woolnoth and S. Mary Woolchurch Haw in the City of London.* London: Bowles & Sons, 1886.

Brookline VR   *Vital Records of Brookline, Massachusetts, to the End of the Year 1849.* Salem, Mass.: Essex Institute, 1929.

Brooks 1932   Brooks, James Emery. *My Great Grandfather's House in Exeter, New Hampshire.* Privately printed, 1932.

Browne 1862   Browne, Benjamin F. "An Account of Salem Common, and the Levelling of the Same in 1802." *Essex Institute Historical Collections* 4 (April 1862): 76–88.

Browne 1913   Browne, Benjamin F. "Youthful Recollections of Salem." *Essex Institute Historical Collections* 49 (July 1913): 193–209.

Bubier 1959   Bubier, Madeleine Mason. *Bubier Family Notes.* Providence: By the author, 1959.

Buck 1888   Buck, J. H. *Old Plate, Ecclesiastical, Decorative, and Domestic.* New York: Gorham Manufacturing Company, 1888.

Buck 1903   Buck, J. H. *Old Plate, Ecclesiastical, Decorative, and Domestic.* Rev. ed. New York: Gorham Manufacturing Company, 1903.

Buhler 1950   Buhler, Kathryn C. *American Silver.* Cleveland and New York: World, 1950.

Buhler 1951   Buhler, Kathryn C. "John Edwards, Goldsmith, and His Progeny." *Antiques* 59 (April 1951): 288–92.

Buhler 1955   Buhler, Kathryn C. "Harvard College Plate." *The Connoisseur Year Book* 52 (1955): 49–57.

Buhler 1956   Buhler, Kathryn C. *Colonial Silversmiths, Masters and Apprentices.* Boston: Museum of Fine Arts, Boston, 1956.

Buhler 1957   Buhler, Kathryn C. "The Philip Leffingwell Spalding Collection of Early American Silver." *Walpole Society Notebook*. Portland, Me.: Printed by the Anthoensen Press for the Walpole Society, 1957.

Buhler 1957a   Buhler, Kathryn C. "Introduction." *New Hampshire Silver, 1775–1825*. Manchester, N.H.: Currier Gallery of Art, 1957.

Buhler 1960   Buhler, Kathryn C. *Masterpieces of American Silver*. Richmond: Virginia Museum of Fine Arts, 1960.

Buhler 1960a   Buhler, Kathryn C. "Masterpieces of American Silver." *Antiques* 77 (January 1960): 84–86.

Buhler 1964   Buhler, Kathryn C. "The Nine Colonial Sugar Boxes." *Antiques* 85 (January 1964): 88–91.

Buhler 1965   Buhler, Kathryn C. *Massachusetts Silver in the Frank L. and Louise C. Harrington Collection*. Worcester, Mass.: Barre, 1965.

Buhler 1972   Buhler, Kathryn C. *American Silver, 1655–1825, in the Museum of Fine Arts, Boston*. 2 vols. Boston: Museum of Fine Arts, Boston, 1972.

Buhler 1976   Buhler, Kathryn C. "Colonial Silver in the Museum Collection." *Arts in Virginia* 16 (Winter/Spring 1976): 2–13.

Buhler 1979   Buhler, Kathryn C. *American Silver from the Colonial Period through the Early Republic in the Worcester Art Museum*. Worcester, Mass.: Worcester Art Museum, 1979.

Buhler 1987   Buhler, Kathryn C. "Seth Storer Coburn: Boston Silversmith." *Silver* 20 (January–February 1987): 8–9.

Buhler/Hood 1970   Buhler, Kathryn C., and Graham Hood. *American Silver: Garvan and Other Collections in the Yale University Art Gallery*. 2 vols. New Haven and London: Yale University Press, 1970.

"Burial Grounds in Worcester"   "Inscriptions from the Old Burial Grounds in Worcester, Massachusetts, from 1727 to 1859; with Biographical and Historical Notes." *Collections of the Worcester Society of Antiquity* 1 (1881): 1–160.

Burlington 1901   Burlington Fine Arts Club. *Exhibition of a Collection of Silversmiths' Work of European Origin*. London, 1901.

Burton/Ripley 1991   Burton, E. Milby. *South Carolina Silversmiths, 1690–1860*. Revised and edited by Warren Ripley. Charleston, S.C.: The Charleston Museum, 1991.

Butler 1886   Butler, George H. *Thomas Butler and His Descendants*. New York: no pub., 1886.

Butler 1888   Butler, James Davie. *Butleriana, Genealogica et Biographica; or, Genealogical Notes Concerning Mary Butler and Her Descendants*. Albany: Joel Munsell's Sons, 1888.

Butler 1919   Butler, Henry Langdon. *Tales of Our Kinsfolk, Past and Present: The Story of Our Butler Ancestors*. New York: H. L. Langdon, 1919.

Butler 1944   Butler, Elmer Ellsworth, comp. *Butlers and Kinsfolk*. Milford, N.H.: Cabinet Press, 1944.

Butterfield 1964   Butterfield, L. H., ed. *Diary and Autobiography of John Adams*. 4 vols. New York: Atheneum, 1964.

Butterfield/Friedlaender/Kline 1975   Butterfield, L. H., Marc Friedlaender, and Mary-Jo Kline. *The Book of Abigail and John: Selected Letters of the Adams Family, 1762–1784*. Cambridge: Harvard University Press, 1975.

Buxton 1955   Buxton, Bessie Raymond. "The Day Book of Henry Buxton, the Buckle Maker." *Essex Institute Historical Collections* 91 (January 1955): 80–91.

Cambridge VR   Baldwin, Thomas W., comp. *Vital Records of Cambridge, Massachusetts, to the Year 1850.* 2 vols. Boston: New England Historic Genealogical Society, 1914–15.

Cameron 1980   Cameron, Viola Root. *Emigrants from Scotland to America, 1774–1775.* Baltimore: Genealogical Publishing Co., 1980.

Camp/Camp 1979   Camp, John Robert and Emily Patch Camp. *Four Families in America: Patch, Payne, Camp, McNabb.* Berkshire, N.Y.: H. Fuller Press, 1979.

Campbell (1747) 1969   Campbell, R. *The London Tradesman.* 1747. Reprint. Newton Abbot, Devon: David and Charles Reprints, 1969.

Campbell Museum Collection   *Selections from the Campbell Museum Collection.* Camden, N.J.: Campbell Museum, 1983.

Card 1979   Card, Eva Garnsey, comp. *The Garnsey–Guernsey Genealogy.* Revised by Judith L. Young Thayer. Baltimore: Gateway, 1979.

Carpenter 1954   Carpenter, Ralph E., Jr. *The Arts and Crafts of Newport, Rhode Island, 1640–1820.* Newport: Preservation Society of Newport County, 1954.

Carpenter 1955   Carpenter, Ralph E., Jr. "Discoveries in Newport Furniture and Silver." *Antiques* 68 (July 1955): 44–49.

Carpenter/Carpenter 1987   Carpenter, Charles H., Jr., and Mary Grace Carpenter. *The Decorative Arts and Crafts of Nantucket.* New York: Dodd, Mead, 1987.

Casey 1940   Casey, Dorothy Needham. "Rhode Island Silversmiths." *Rhode Island Historical Society Collections* 33 (July 1940): 49–64.

Caulkins 1857   Caulkins, Frances Manwaring. "Ancient Burial Ground at New London." *New England Historic Genealogical Register* 11 (January 1857): 21–30.

Census 1790   Department of Commerce and Labor, Bureau of the Census. *Heads of Families at the First Census of the United States Taken in the Year 1790, Massachusetts.* Washington, D.C.: Government Printing Office, 1908.

CGA Bulletin 1971   "American Silver at the Currier Gallery of Art." *Currier Gallery of Art Bulletin* (1971).

Champlin 1974   Champlin, Richard L. "'William Claggett and His Clockmaking Family.'" *Newport History* 47 (Summer 1974): 157–90.

Charlestown VR   Joslyn, Roger D., ed. *Vital Records of Charlestown, Massachusetts, to the Year 1850.* Vol. 1. Boston: New England Historic Genealogical Society, 1984.

Chase 1861   Chase, George Wingate. *The History of Haverhill.* Haverhill, Mass.: By the author, 1861.

Chase 1938   Chase, Ada R. "René Grignon, Silversmith." *Antiques* 34 (July 1938): 26–27.

Chelsea VR   Baldwin, Thomas W., comp. *Vital Records of Chelsea, Massachusetts, to the Year 1850.* Boston: Wright & Potter, 1916.

Chilmark VR   *Vital Records of Chilmark, Massachusetts, to the Year 1850.* Boston: New England Historic Genealogical Society at the Charge of the Eddy Town Record Fund, 1904.

Christie's   Christie, Manson & Woods International, Inc., New York

"Church at Westfield"   "The Public Records of the Church of Christ at Westfield of all unto whom the holy ordinance of Baptism that [hath] been administered therein from the beginning of 1679–1836." Typescript, New England Historic Genealogical Society Boston.

Church in Brattle Square   *The Manifesto Church: Records of the Church in Brattle Square Boston with*

Lists of Communicants, Baptisms, Marriages, and Funerals, 1699–1872. Boston: Benevolent Fraternity of Churches, 1902.

Clark 1981   Clark, Kenneth. *Moments of Vision and Other Essays*. New York: Harper and Row, 1981.

Clarke 1932   Clarke, Hermann F. *John Coney, Silversmith, 1655–1722*. Boston: Houghton Mifflin, 1932.

Clarke 1940   Clarke, Hermann F. *John Hull: A Builder of the Bay Colony*. Portland, Me.: Southworth–Anthoensen Press, 1940.

Clarke/Foote 1935   Clarke, Hermann F., and Henry Wilder Foote. *Jeremiah Dummer, Colonial Craftsman & Merchant 1645–1718*. Boston: Houghton Mifflin, 1935.

Clayton 1971   Clayton, Michael. *The Collector's Dictionary of the Silver and Gold of Great Britain and North America*. New York and Cleveland: World, 1971.

Clunie 1977   Clunie, Margaret Burke. "Joseph True and the Piecework System in Salem." *Antiques* 111 (May 1977): 1006–13.

Cobb 1907   Cobb, Philip L. *A History of the Cobb Family*. Cleveland: no pub., 1907.

Codman 1918   Codman, Ogden. *Gravestone Inscriptions and Records of Tomb Burials in the Granary Burying Ground, Boston, Mass.* Salem, Mass.: Essex Institute, 1918.

Cogswell (1878) 1972   Cogswell, Elliott C. *History of Nottingham, Deerfield, and Northwood*. 1878. Reprint. Somersworth, N.H.: New Hampshire Publishing, 1972.

Colby 1967   *American Arts of the Eighteenth–Century Being a Major Loan Exhibition*. Waterville, Me.: Colby College Art Museum, 1967.

Collections of the Connecticut Historical Society   *Collections of the Connecticut Historical Society*. Hartford: Published by the Society, 1901.

Colonial Society 1933   *Records of the Suffolk County Court 1671–1689*. Publications of the Colonial Society of Massachusetts, vols. 29 and 30. Boston: Colonial Society of Massachusetts, 1933.

Comstock 1958   Comstock, Helen. "American Silver at Deerfield." *Antiques* 74 (December 1958): 528–31.

Concord VR   *Concord, Massachusetts, Births, Marriages, and Deaths, 1635–1850*. Boston: T. Todd, 1894.

Conger/Rollins 1991   Conger, Clement E., and Alexandra W. Rollins, eds. *Treasures of State: Fine and Decorative Arts in the Diplomatic Reception Rooms of the U. S. Department of State*. New York: Harry N. Abrams, 1991.

Cooper 1978   Cooper, Wendy A. "New Findings on Colonial New England Goldsmiths and English Sources." *American Art Journal* 10 (November 1978): 107–09.

Corbin Ms. Coll.   Corbin Manuscript Collection, New England Historic Genealogical Society, Boston

Coventry VR   Barbour Collection, Connecticut State Library, Hartford

Crafts/Crafts 1893   Crafts, James M., and William F. Crafts, comps. *A Genealogical and Biographical History of the Descendants of Griffin and Alice Craft of Roxbury, Mass., 1630–1890*. Northampton, Mass.: Gazette Printing Company, 1893.

Crane 1907   Crane, Ellery Bicknell, ed. *Historic Homes and Institutions and Genealogical and Personal Memoirs of Worcester County, Massachusetts*. 4 vols. New York and Chicago: Lewis Publishing Co., 1907.

Cressy 1987   Cressy, David. *Coming Over: Migration and Communication between England and New England in the Seventeenth Century*. Cambridge: Cambridge University Press, 1987.

Crocker 1827   Crocker, Hannah Mather. *Reminiscences and Traditions of Boston*. Boston, 1827.

Crosby 1875   Crosby, Sylvester S. *Early Coins of America and the Laws Governing Their Issue*. Boston: By the author, 1875.

Crosby 1940   Crosby, Everett U. *Books and Baskets, Signs and Silver of Old–Time Nantucket*. Privately printed, 1940.

Crosby 1953   Crosby, Everett U. *Ninety Five Per Cent Perfect*. 3d ed. Nantucket Island, Mass.: Tetaukimmo Press, 1953.

Cullity 1989   Cullity, Brian. *Arts of the Federal Period*. Sandwich, Mass.: Heritage Plantation, 1989.

Cullity 1994   Cullity, Brian. *A Cubberd, Four Joyne Stools and Other Smalle Thinges: The Material Culture of Plymouth Colony; and Silver and Silversmiths of Plymouth, Cape Cod & Nantucket*. Sandwich, Mass.: Heritage Plantation, 1994.

Cunningham 1901   Cunningham, Henry Winchester C. "Andrew Cunningham of Boston and Some of His Descendants." *New England Historic Genealogical Register* 55 (July, October 1901): 304–09, 416–24.

Currier 1938   Currier, Ernest M. *Marks of Early American Silversmiths*. Portland, Me.: Southworth–Anthoensen Press; London: Bernard Quaritch, 1938.

Currier (1909) 1978   Currier, John J. *The History of Newburyport, Massachusetts, 1764–1905*. 2 vols. 1909. Reprint. Somersworth, N.H.: New Hampshire Publishing, 1978.

Currier Gallery 1957   Currier Gallery of Art. *New Hampshire Silver, 1775–1825*. Manchester, N.H.: Currier Gallery of Art, 1957.

Curtis 1913   Curtis, George Munson. *Early Silver of Connecticut and its Makers*. Meriden, Conn.: International Silver Company, 1913.

Cutten 1939   Cutten, George B. "Silversmiths of Northampton, Mass., and Vicinity to 1850." Photocopy of a typescript, Cleveland Museum of Art, 1939.

Cutten 1946   Cutten, George B. "American Silver Sugar Tongs." *Antiques* 49 (February 1946): 112–15.

Cutten 1950   Cutten, George Barton. "Sucket Forks." *Antiques* 57 (June 1950): 440–41.

Cuzner 1965   Cuzner, Bernard. *A Silversmith's Manual*. 2d ed. London: N.A.G. Press, 1965.

DAB   *Dictionary of American Biography*. 21 vols. New York: Charles Scribner's Sons, 1943.

Dale 1931   Dale, T. C., ed. *The Inhabitants of London in 1638*. 2 vols. London: Society of Genealogists, 1931.

Dana 1900   Dana, Elizabeth Ellery. "Richard Skinner of Marblehead and His Bible: Some Materials for a Skinner Genealogy." *New England Historic Genealogical Register* 54 (October 1900): 413–22.

Daniels 1892   Daniels, George F. *History of the Town of Oxford, Massachusetts*. Oxford, Mass.: Privately printed, 1892.

Danvers VR   *Vital Records of Danvers, Massachusetts, to the End of the Year 1849*. 2 vols. Salem, Mass.: Essex Institute, 1909–10.

DAR Patriot Index   *DAR Patriot Index*. 3 vols. Washington, D.C.: National Society, Daughters of the American Revolution, 1966.

Dauterman 1968   Dauterman, Carl Christian, comp. *Checklist of American Silversmiths' Work, 1650–1850, in Museums in the New York Metropolitan Area*. New York: The Metropolitan Museum of Art, 1968.

Davenport 1879   Davenport, Bennett F. "The Davenport Family." *New England Historic Genealogical Register* 33 (January 1879): 25–34.

Davidson 1941   Davidson, Marshall. "A Selection of Early New England Silver in the Metropolitan Museum of Art." *Metropolitan Museum of Art Bulletin* 36 (November 1941): 233–35.

Davidson 1971   Davidson, Ruth. "Museum Accessions: American Paintings, Silver, and Furniture." *Antiques* 99 (March 1971): 344–45, 348, 352, 356, 360.

Davidson 1971a   Davidson, Ruth. "Museum Accessions: Silver, Ceramics, and Glass." *Antiques* 100 (December 1971): 840–41, 844, 848.

Davis 1883   Davis, William T. *Ancient Landmarks of Plymouth. Part I. Historical Sketch and Titles of Estates. Part II. Genealogical Register of Plymouth Families.* Boston: A. Williams, 1883.

Davis 1896   Davis, Walter A., comp. *The Early Records of the Town of Lunenberg, Massachusetts including that Part which is Now Fitchburg 1719–1764.* Fitchburg, Mass.: City Council, 1896.

Davis 1898   Davis, Andrew McFarland. "The Massachusetts Bay Currency, 1690–1750. The Plates." *Proceedings of the American Antiquarian Society*, n.s. 12 (October 1898): 410–24.

Davis 1898–1913   Davis, Walter A., comp. *The Old Records of the Town of Fitchburg, Massachusetts.* 8 vols. Fitchburg, Mass.: Sentinel Printing, 1898–1913.

Davis 1901   Davis, Andrew McFarland. *Currency and Banking in the Province of the Massachusetts–Bay.* 2 vols. New York: Macmillan for the American Economic Association, 1901.

Davis 1972   Davis, Felice. "The American Connoisseur. A 'Young' Collector and American Antiques." *The Connoisseur* 179 (March 1972): 192–99.

Davis 1976   Davis, John D. *English Silver at Colonial Williamsburg.* Williamsburg, Va.: Colonial Williamsburg Foundation, 1976.

Davis 1991   Davis, John D. "Silver Punch Strainers in the John A. Hyman Collection at Colonial Williamsburg." *Antiques* 140 (August 1991): 198–205.

Davisson 1967a   Davisson, William I. "Essex County Price Trends: Money and Markets in 17th Century Massachusetts." *Essex Institute Historical Collections* 103 (April 1967): 144–85.

Davisson 1967b   Davisson, William I. "Essex County Wealth Trends: Wealth and Economic Growth in 17th Century Massachusetts." *Essex Institute Historical Collections* 103 (October 1967): 291–342.

Davisson/Dugan 1971   Davisson, William I., and Dennis J. Dugan. "Commerce in Seventeenth–Century Essex County, Massachusetts." *Essex Institute Historical Collections* 107 (April 1971): 113–42.

Dearborn 1890   Dearborn, John J. *The History of Salisbury, New Hampshire.* Edited by James O. Adams and Henry P. Rolfe. Manchester, N.H.: William E. Moore, 1890.

Decatur 1936   Decatur, Stephen. "The Early Church Silver of Kittery, Maine." *American Collector* 5 (November 1936): 3, 15.

Decatur 1941   Decatur, Stephen. "William Cario, Father and Son, Silversmiths." *American Collector* 10 (September 1941): 6–7, 20.

Decatur 1941a   Decatur, Stephen. "The Moulton Silversmiths." *Antiques* 39 (January 1941): 14–17.

Decatur 1965   Decatur, Stephen. "William Cario, Silversmith." *Old–Time New England* 55 (January–March 1965): 81–83.

Decorative Arts of New Hampshire   Currier Gallery of Art. *Decorative Arts of New Hampshire, 1725–1825.* Manchester, N.H.: Currier Gallery of Art, 1964.

Dedham VR   *The Records of Births, Marriages, and Deaths and intentions of Marriage in the Town of Dedham 1635–1845.* Dedham, Mass.: Dedham Transcript, 1886.

Deerfield VR   Baldwin, Thomas W., comp. *Vital Records of Deerfield, Massachusetts, to the Year 1850.* Boston: Wright & Potter, 1920.

De Matteo 1956   De Matteo, William. *The Silversmith in Eighteenth-Century Williamsburg.* Williamsburg, Va.: Colonial Williamsburg, 1956.

Denny 1894   Denny, C. C. "An Ancient Road, and Reminiscences of Some Worcester Families Who Dwelt on It." *Collections of the Worcester Society of Antiquity* 13 (1894): 368–83.

Dept. of Commerce 1907   Department of Commerce and Labor, Bureau of the Census. *Heads of Families at the First Census of the United States Taken in the Year 1790, New Hampshire.* Washington, D.C.: Government Printing Office, 1907.

Dept. of Commerce 1908   Department of Commerce and Labor, Bureau of the Census. *Heads of Families at the First Census of the United States Taken in the Year 1790, Maine.* Washington, D.C.: Government Printing Office, 1908.

Descendants of Robert Day 1848   Day, George E. *A Genealogical Register of the Descendants in the Male Line of Robert Day of Hartford, Conn. Who Died in the Year 1648.* Northampton, Mass.: J. & L. Metcalf, 1848.

Dexter 1885   Dexter, Franklin Bowditch. *Biographical Sketches of the Graduates of Yale College with Annals of the College History October, 1701–May, 1745.* Vol. 1. New York: Henry Holt, 1885.

"Diary of Ezekiel Price"   "Diary of Ezekiel Price, 1775–1776." *Massachusetts Historical Society Proceedings* 1st ser. 7 (1863): 185–262.

Diary of Joshua Hempstead   *Diary of Joshua Hempstead of New London, Connecticut, Covering a Period of Forty-seven Years from September 1711 to November 1758.* New London, Conn.: New London County Historical Society, 1901.

"Diary of Rev. William Homes"   "Diary of Rev. William Homes of Chilmark, Martha's Vineyard, 1689–1746." *New England Historical and Genealogical Register* 48 (October 1894): 446–53; 49 (October 1895): 413–16; 50 (April 1896): 155–66.

Diderot 1751–65   Diderot, Denis. *Encyclopédie, ou Dictionnaire Raisonné des Sciences, des Arts et de Métiers: Recueil de Planches, sur les Sciences, les Arts Libereaux et les Arts Méchaniques avec leur Explication.* Vol. 8, Sections on the "Orfèvre Grossier," "Orfèvre Bijoutier," and "Orfèvre Jouaillier, Metteur en Oeuvre." Paris: Briasson, David, Le Breton, Durand, 1751–65.

Dimock 1897   Dimock, Susan Whitney, comp. *Births, Marriages, Baptisms and Deaths, from the Records of the Town and Churches in Coventry, Connecticut, 1711–1844.* New York: Baker and Taylor, 1897.

Dimock 1898   Dimock, Susan W. *Births, Baptisms, Marriages and Deaths from the Records of the Town and Churches in Mansfield, Connecticut, 1703–1850.* New York: Baker and Taylor, 1898.

Distin/Bishop 1976   Distin, William H., and Robert Bishop. *The American Clock: A Comprehensive Pictorial Survey.* New York: E. P. Dutton, Inc., 1976.

DNB   *Dictionary of National Biography*

Doane 1902   Doane, Alfred Alder. *The Doane Family: I. Deacon John Doane, of Plymouth: II. Doctor John Doane, of Maryland; and Their Descendants.* Boston: A. A. Doane, 1902.

Dobson 1984–86   Dobson, David. *Directory of Scottish Settlers in North America, 1624–1885.* 6 vols. Baltimore: Genealogical Publishing Co., 1984–86.

Doty 1979   Doty, Robert M., ed. *The Currier Gallery of Art: Handbook of the Collection.* Manchester, N.H.: Currier Gallery of Art, 1979.

Dow 1893   Dow, Joseph. *History of the Town of Hampton, New Hampshire, from its Settlement in 1638 to the Autumn of 1892.* 2 vols. 1893. Reprint. Somersworth, N.H.: Peter E. Randall, 1970.

Dow 1927   Dow, George Francis. *The Arts and Crafts in New England, 1704–1775.* Topsfield, Mass.: Wayside Press, 1927.

Dow 1936   Dow, George Francis. "Trade Cards." *Old–Time New England* 27 (July 1936): 10–22.

Downs 1948   Downs, Joseph. "Recent Additions to the American Wing." *Metropolitan Museum of Art Bulletin* 7 (November 1948): 79–85.

Drake 1856   Drake, Samuel G. *The History and Antiquities of Boston.* Boston: Luther Stevens, 1856.

Drake 1870   Drake, Samuel G. *A Particular History of the Five Years' French and Indian War.* Boston: S. G. Drake, 1870.

Dresser 1935–36   Dresser, Louisa. "Worcester Silversmiths and the Examples of Their Work in the Collections of the Museum." *Worcester Art Museum Annual* 1 (1935–36): 49–57.

Dunstable VR   *Vital Records of Dunstable, Massachusetts, to the End of the Year 1849.* Salem, Mass.: Essex Institute, 1913.

Earle 1888   Earle, Pliny. *The Earle Family: Ralph Earle and His Descendants.* Worcester, Mass.: Press of Charles Hamilton, 1888.

Early Conn. Marriages   Bailey, Frederic W. *Early Connecticut Marriages as Found in Ancient Church Records Prior to 1800.* 7 vols. New Haven: Bureau of American Ancestry, 1896–1906.

Eaton 1865   Eaton, Cyrus. *History of Thomaston, Rockland, and South Thomaston, Maine.* 2 vols. Hallowell, Me.: Masters, Smith, 1865.

Eaton 1915   Eaton, Rev. Arthur Wentworth. "The Byles Family." *New England Historic Genealogical Register* 69 (1915): 101–16.

Edgartown VR   *Vital Records of Edgartown, Massachusetts, to the Year 1850.* Boston: New England Historic Genealogical Society, 1906.

EIHC   *Essex Institute Historical Collections*

Eitner 1976   Eitner, Lorenz. *The Mrs. John Emerson Marble Collection of Early American Silver.* Palo Alto, Calif.: Stanford University Museum, 1976.

Ellesin 1971   Ellesin, Dorothy. "Antiques at Auction." *Antiques* 100 (October 1971): 532–40.

Ellis 1970   Ellis, Ray Lowther, ed. *A Genealogical Register of Edmund Rice Descendants Compiled by the Edmund Rice (1638) Association Inc.* Rutland, Vt.: Charles E. Tuttle, 1970.

Emery 1890   Emery, Rufus. *Genealogical Records of Descendants of John and Anthony Emery of Newbury, Mass.* Salem, Mass.: Emery Cleaves, 1890.

Emlen 1984   Emlen, Robert P. "Wedding Silver for the Browns: A Rhode Island Family Patronizes a Boston Goldsmith." *American Art Journal* 16 (Spring 1984): 39–50.

English-Speaking Union 1960   *American Silver and Art Treasures: An Exhibition Sponsored by the English-Speaking Union and Held at Christie's Great Rooms, London.* London: English-Speaking Union, 1960.

Ensko 1927　Ensko, Stephen G. C. *American Silversmiths and Their Marks.* New York: Privately printed, 1927.

Ensko 1937　Ensko, Stephen G. C. *American Silversmiths and Their Marks, II.* New York: Robert Ensko Inc., 1937.

Ensko 1948　Ensko, Stephen G. C. *American Silversmiths and Their Marks, III.* New York: Robert Ensko, Inc., 1948.

Ensko 1989　Ensko, Stephen G. C. *American Silversmiths and Their Marks, IV.* Boston: David R. Godine, 1989.

Essex County Court Records　*Records and Files of the Quarterly Courts of Essex, Massachusetts.* 9 vols. Salem, Mass.: Essex Institute, 1911–75.

Essex County Probate Index　*Essex County, Massachusetts, Probate Index, 1638–1870.* Transcribed by Melinde Lutz Sanborn from the original by W. P. Upham. 2 vols. Boston: M. L. Sanborn, 1987.

Essex County Probate Records　*The Probate Records of Essex County, Massachusetts, 1635–1681.* 3 vols. Salem, Mass.: Essex Institute, 1916–20.

Evans 1906　Evans, John Thomas. *The Church Plate of Gloucestershire.* Stow–on–the–Wold, England: Bristol and Gloucestershire Archaeological Society, 1906.

Fairbanks 1985　Fairbanks, Jonathan L. "Fakes and Rakers." In *Walpole Society Note Book.* Printed for the Society, 1985.

Fairbanks/Trent 1982　Fairbanks, Jonathan L., and Robert F. Trent. *New England Begins: The Seventeenth Century.* 3 vols. Boston: Museum of Fine Arts, Boston, 1982.

Fairfield VR　Barbour Collection, Connecticut State Library, Hartford

Fales 1957　Fales, Martha Gandy. "Early American Silver at Winterthur." *Antiques* 72 (December 1957): 546–49.

Fales 1958　Fales, Martha Gandy. *American Silver in the Henry Francis du Pont Winterthur Museum.* Winterthur, Del.: H. F. du Pont Winterthur Museum, 1958.

Fales 1959　Fales, Martha Gandy. "Samuel Gilbert's Paul Revere Pitcher." *Antiques* 75 (May 1959): 476–77.

Fales 1965　Fales, Martha Gandy. "Daniel Rogers, Ipswich Goldsmith (The Case of the Double Identity)." *Essex Institute Historical Collections* 101 (January 1965): 40–49.

Fales 1967　Fales, Martha Gandy. "Daniel Rogers, Silversmiths." *Antiques* 91 (April 1967): 487–91.

Fales 1967a　Fales, Martha Gandy. "Notes on Essex County Goldsmiths' Cases." *Essex Institute Historical Collections* 103 (July 1967): 199–200.

Fales 1968　Fales, Martha Gandy. "New England Silver and Silversmiths: The Heritage Foundation Collection." *Antiques* 93 (April 1968): 518–23.

Fales 1970　Fales, Martha Gandy. *Early American Silver.* New York: Funk and Wagnalls, 1970.

Fales 1970a　Fales, Martha Gandy. "Early American Official Silver." *Antiques* 97 (January 1970): 96–99.

Fales 1973　Fales, Martha Gandy. *Early American Silver.* Rev. ed. New York: E. P. Dutton, 1973.

Fales 1973a　Fales, Martha Gandy. "Heraldic and Emblematic Engravers of Colonial Boston." In *Boston Prints and Printmakers, 1670–1775,* 185–220. Boston: Colonial Society of Massachusetts, 1973.

Fales 1974　Fales, Martha Gandy. *Joseph Richardson and Family, Philadelphia Silversmiths.*

Middletown, Conn.: Wesleyan University Press, 1974.

Fales 1983 Fales, Martha Gandy. *Silver at the Essex Institute.* Salem, Mass.: Essex Institute, 1983.

Fales 1983a Fales, Martha Gandy. "Silver at the Essex Institute." *Antiques* 124 (December 1983): 1192–99.

Fales 1985 Fales, Martha Gandy. "Early Maine Silver." *Maine Historical Society Quarterly* 24 (Winter 1985): 338–43.

Fales 1991 Fales, Martha Gandy. "James Turner, Silversmith–Engraver." In *Prints of New England*, edited by Georgia Brady Barnhill, 1–20. Worcester, Mass.: American Antiquarian Society, 1991.

Faulkner 1978 Faulkner, Mary. *Port and Market: Archeology of the Central Waterfront, Newburyport, Mass.: A Report Submitted to the National Park Service.* Newburyport, Mass.: Newburyport Press, 1978.

Federhen 1985 Federhen, Deborah Anne. "Paul Revere, Silversmith: A Study of His Shop Practices and His Objects." M.A. thesis, University of Delaware, 1985.

Federhen 1988 Federhen, Deborah A. "From Artisan to Entrepreneur: Paul Revere's Silver Shop Operation." In *Paul Revere—Artisan, Businessman, and Patriot: The Man Behind the Myth*, 64–93. Boston: Paul Revere Memorial Association, 1988.

Fennimore 1984 Fennimore, Donald L. *Silver and Pewter.* New York: Alfred A. Knopf, 1984.

Fessenden 1850 Fessenden, G. M. "A Genealogy of the Bradford Family." *New England Historic Genealogical Register* 4 (January 1850): 39–50, and (July 1850): 233–45.

Fielding 1917 Fielding, Mantle. *American Engravers upon Copper and Steel.* Philadelphia: no pub., 1917.

First Church, *Records of the First Church in Charlestown, Massachusetts, 1632–1789.* Boston:
Charlestown 1880 Printed for J. F. Hunnewell by D. Clapp and Son, 1880.

First Church, Dorchester 1880 *Records of the First Church at Dorchester in New England, 1636–1734.* Boston: George H. Ellis, 1891.

Fisher 1868 Fisher, E. T., trans. *Report of a French Protestant Refugee in Boston 1687.* Brooklyn, N. Y.: Privately printed, 1868.

Fitts 1912 Fitts, Rev. James Hill. *The History of Newfields, New Hampshire, 1638–1911.* Concord, N.H.: Rumford Press, 1912.

Flagg 1907 Flagg, Norman Gershom, and Lucius C. S. Flagg. *Family Records of the Descendants of Gershom Flagg.* Quincy, Ill.: Privately printed, 1907.

"Flynt Diary" Dunn, Edward T., ed. "The Diary of Tutor Henry Flynt of Harvard College." 2 vols. Typescript, Harvard University Archives, Cambridge, Mass.

Flynt/Fales 1968 Flynt, Henry N., and Martha Gandy Fales. *The Heritage Foundation Collection of Silver.* Old Deerfield, Mass.: Heritage Foundation, 1968.

Fobes 1894 Fobes, Charles S. "The Story of the Presumpscot." *Collections and Proceedings of the Maine Historical Society.* 2d ser. 5 (1894): 361–86.

Fogg 1972 Bolton, Kenyon C., III, Peter G. Huenink, Earl A. Powell III, Harry Z. Rand, and Nanette Sexton. *American Art at Harvard.* Cambridge: Fogg Art Museum, Harvard University, 1972.

Foner 1976 Foner, Eric. *Tom Paine and Revolutionary America.* London: Oxford University Press, 1976.

Foote 1882 Foote, Henry Wilder. *Annals of King's Chapel.* 2 vols. Boston: Little, Brown, 1882.

Foote 1942 Foote, Henry Wilder. *Annals of King's Chapel.* 3 vols. Boston: Houghton Mifflin, 1942.

Forbes 1927   Forbes, Harriette Marrifield. *Gravestones of Early New England and the Men Who Made Them.* Boston: Houghton Mifflin, 1927.

Forbes 1942   Forbes, Esther. *Paul Revere and the World He Lived In.* Boston: Houghton Mifflin, 1942.

Forman 1970   Forman, Benno M. "Urban Aspects of Massachusetts Furniture in the Late Seventeenth Century." In *Country Cabinetwork and Simple City Furniture,* edited by John D. Morse, 1–33. Charlottesville: University Press of Virginia, 1970.

Forman 1971   Forman, Benno M. "Salem Tradesmen and Craftsmen circa 1762: A Contemporary Document." *Essex Institute Historical Collections* 107 (January 1971): 62–81.

Forster 1871   Forster, Edward J., and W. S. Appleton. "Foster of Charlestown, Mass." *New England Historic Genealogical Register* 25 (January 1871): 67–71.

Framingham VR   Baldwin, Thomas, comp. *Vital Records of Framingham, Massachusetts, to the Year 1850.* Boston: Wright & Potter, 1911.

Fredyma 1975   Fredyma, Paul J., and Marie–Louise Fredyma. *A Directory of Boston Silversmiths and Watch and Clock Makers.* Hanover, N.H.: By the author, 1975.

Freeland 1894   Freeland, Mary de Witt. *The Records of Oxford, Massachusetts.* Albany: Joel Munsell's Sons, 1894.

Freeman   Samuel T. Freeman and Co., Philadelphia

Freetown VR   Thomas, Helen Gurney, comp. *Vital Records of the Town of Freetown, Massachusetts, 1686 through 1890.* Bowie, Md.: Heritage Books, 1988.

French 1939   French, Hollis. *Jacob Hurd and His Sons Nathaniel and Benjamin, Silversmiths, 1702–1781.* Cambridge, Mass.: Riverside Press, 1939.

French 1941   *Addenda: Jacob Hurd and His Sons Nathaniel and Benjamin, Silversmiths, 1702–1781.* Cambridge, Mass.: Riverside Press, 1941.

French 1961   "Addenda: Jacob Hurd and His Sons Nathaniel and Benjamin, Silversmiths, 1702–1781." Typescript, Yale University Art Gallery, 1961.

French (1917) 1967   French, Hollis. *A Silver Collectors' Glossary and List of Early American Silversmiths and Their Marks.* 1917. Reprint. New York: Da Capo Press, 1967.

Frost 1991   Frost, John Eldridge. *Maine Probate Abstracts. Volume 1, 1687–1775; Volume 2, 1775–1800.* Camden, Me.: Picton Press, 1991.

Gardner 1907   Gardner, Frank A. *Thomas Gardner, Planter, and Some of His Descendants.* Salem, Mass.: Essex Institute, 1907.

Garrett 1985   Garrett, Elisabeth Donaghy. *The Arts of Independence: The DAR Museum Collection.* Washington, D.C.: The National Society, Daughters of the American Revolution, 1985.

Gaynor/Hagedorn 1994   Gaynor, James M., and Nancy L. Hagedorn. *Tools: Working Wood in Eighteenth–Century America.* Charlottesville: University Press of Virginia, 1994.

Gee 1885   Gee, George E. *The Silversmith's Handbook.* 2d ed. London: Crosby Lockwood, 1885.

Gee 1886   Gee, George E. *The Goldsmith's Handbook.* 3d ed. London: Crosby Lockwood, 1886.

Geller 1970   Geller, L. D. *The Pilgrim Hall Museum after 350 Years.* Plymouth, Mass.: Pilgrim Society, 1970.

Genealogies of Rhode Island Families   *Genealogies of Rhode Island Families from the New England Historical and Genealogical Register.* 2 vols. Baltimore: Genealogical Publishing Co., 1989.

George Vertue "Notebooks"   *George Vertue "Notebooks."* 6 vols. London: Walpole Society, 1930–55.

Gere 1902   Gere, Henry S. *Reminiscences of Old Northampton*. Northampton, Mass.: Hampshire Gazette, 1902.

Gerstell 1972   Gerstell, Vivian S. *Silversmiths of Lancaster, Pennsylvania, 1730–1850*. Lancaster, Pa.: Lancaster County Historical Society, 1972.

Gildrie 1975   Gildrie, Richard P. *Salem, Massachusetts, 1626–1683: A Covenant Community*. Charlottesville: University Press of Virginia, 1975.

Gloucester VR   *Vital Records of Gloucester, Massachusetts, to the End of the Year 1849*. 3 vols. Topsfield, Mass.: Topsfield Historical Society, 1917–24.

Goddard 1871   Goddard, Martha H. LeBaron. "The Le Baron Family." *New England Historic Genealogical Register* 25 (April 1871): 180–81.

Goldenberg 1976   Goldenberg, Joseph A. *Shipbuilding in Colonial America*. Charlottesville: University Press of Virginia, 1976.

Goldsborough 1969   Goldsborough, Jennifer F. *An Exhibition of New London Silver, 1700–1835*. New London, Conn.: Lyman Allyn Museum, 1969.

Goldsborough 1975   Goldsborough, Jennifer F. *Eighteenth and Nineteenth Century Maryland Silver in the Collection of the Baltimore Museum of Art*. Baltimore: Baltimore Museum of Art, 1975.

Goldthwaite 1895   Goldthwaite, Charlotte. *Boardman Genealogy, 1525–1895*. Hartford: Case, Lockwood and Brainard, 1895.

Gooding 1927–30   Gooding, Alfred. "Records of the South Church of Portsmouth, N.H." *New England Historic and Genealogical Register* 81 (1927): 419–53; 82 (1928): 25–53, 138–46, 281–302, 410–26; 83 (1929): 21–39, 168–98, 295–311, 421–38; 84 (1930): 17–34, 439–40.

Gordon/Coburn 1913   Gordon, George A., and Silas R. Coburn. *Genealogy of the Descendants of Edward Colburn/Coburn*. Lowell, Mass.: Walter Coburn, 1913.

Goss 1891   Goss, Elbridge Henry. *The Life of Colonel Paul Revere*. 2 vols. Boston: J. G. Cupples, 1891.

Goss/Zarowin 1985   Goss, K. David, and David Zarowin, eds. *Massachusetts Officers and Soldiers in the French and Indian Wars, 1755–1756*. Boston: New England Historic Genealogical Society and the Society of Colonial Wars in the Commonwealth of Massachusetts, 1985.

Gourley 1965   Gourley, Hugh J., III. *The New England Silversmith: An Exhibition of New England Silver from the Mid–Seventeenth Century to the Present, Selected from New England Collections*. Providence: Museum of Art, Rhode Island School of Design, 1965.

Grafton VR   *Vital Records of Grafton, Massachusetts, to the End of the Year 1849*. Worcester, Mass.: Franklin P. Rice, 1906.

Graham 1936   Graham, James, Jr., comp. *Early American Silver Marks*. New York: James Graham, Jr., 1936.

Grant 1977   Grant, Frederic, Jr. "The Court–Martial of Paul Revere." *Boston Bar Journal* (May 1977): 5–11.

Green/Holland 1973   Green, Frank L., and Milton Holland. *The Odlin–Eliot Collection of Early American Silver*. Tacoma: Washington State American Revolution Bicentennial Commission, 1973.

Greenleaf 1854   Greenleaf, Jonathan. *A Genealogy of the Greenleaf Family*. New York: Edward O. Jenkins, 1854.

Greenleaf 1896   Greenleaf, James Edward. *Genealogy of the Greenleaf Family*. Boston: Frank Wood, 1896.

Griffen 1952   Griffen, William R. J., comp. "Epitaphs on Old Burial Hill (Phipps Street Burial Ground) Charlestown, 1622–1952." Typescript, New England Historic Genealogical Society, Boston, 1952.

Grimwade 1976   Grimwade, Arthur G. *London Goldsmiths, 1697–1837: Their Marks and Lives.* London: Faber and Faber, 1976.

Groce/Wallace 1957   Groce, George C., and David H. Wallace. *New-York Historical Society's Dictionary of Artists in America, 1564–1860.* New Haven and London: Yale University Press, 1957.

Groton VR   *Vital Records of Groton, Massachusetts, to the End of the Year 1849.* 2 vols. Salem, Mass.: Essex Institute, 1927.

Gustafson 1979   Gustafson, Eleanor H. "Museum Accessions." *Antiques* 115 (February 1979): 312, 316.

Gustafson 1982   Gustafson, Eleanor H. "Museum Accessions." *Antiques* 122 (September 1982): 436, 438, 448, 450.

Guthman 1993   Guthman, William H. *Drums A'beating, Trumpets Sounding: Artistically Carved Powder Horns in the Provincial Manner, 1746–1781.* Hartford: Connecticut Historical Society, 1993.

Hadley 1979   Hadley, Harold Pierce. *200 Years of Masonry in Essex Lodge, 1779–1979.* No pub., 1979.

Hale 1931   Hale, Richard Walden. *Catalogue of Silver Owned by Nicholas Sever, A.B. 1701 in 1728; Now Owned by his Descendants and Exhibited at the Fogg Art Museum of Harvard University, 1931.* Boston: no pub., 1931.

Hall 1951   Hall, Ruth Gardiner. *Descendants of Governor William Bradford.* Ann Arbor: no pub., 1951.

Hallen 1889–95   Hallen, A. W. Cornelius. *The Registers of St. Botolph, Bishopsgate, London.* 3 vols. Edinburgh: T. A. Constable, 1889–95.

Hamblin 1852   Hamblin, David. "The First Settlers of Eastham, Mass." *New England Historic Genealogical Register* 6 (January 1852): 41–46.

Hammatt 1850   Hammatt, A. "Physicians of Ipswich." *New England Historic Genealogical Register* 4 (January 1850): 11–16.

Hammatt 1980   Hammatt, Abraham. *The Hammatt Papers: Early Inhabitants of Ipswich, Massachusetts, 1633–1700.* Baltimore: Genealogical Publishing Co., 1980.

Hammerslough/   Hammerslough, Philip H., and Rita F. Feigenbaum. *American Silver Collected*
Feigenbaum 1958–73   *by Philip H. Hammerslough.* 4 vols. Hartford: Privately printed, 1958–73.

Hammond 1887   Hammond, Isaac W., ed. *Rolls and Documents Relating to Soldiers in the Revolutionary War.* 3 vols. Manchester, N.H.: John B. Clark, 1887.

Hammond 1984   Hammond, Dorothy. *Pictorial Price Guide to American Antiques, 1984–85, and Objects Made for the American Market.* New York: E. P. Dutton, 1984.

Hampstead VR   Hammond, Priscilla. "Vital Records of Hampstead, New Hampshire, Compiled from the Town's Original Record Books." Typescript, New England Historic Genealogical Society, Boston, 1938.

Hanks 1970   Hanks, David A. "American Silver at the Art Institute of Chicago." *Antiques* 98 (September 1970): 418–22.

Hanover VR   *A Copy of the Records of Births, Marriages, and Deaths and of the Intentions of Marriage of the Town of Hanover, Mass., 1727–1857.* Rockland, Mass.: Press of the Rockland Standard, 1898.

Harris 1889   Harris, Edward Doubleday. "The Trotts of Dorchester and Boston." *New England Historic Genealogical Register* 43 (January 1889): 79–80.

Hart 1907   Hart, Charles Henry. "An Etched Profile Portrait of Washington by Joseph Hiller, Jr., 1794." *Essex Institute Historical Collections* 43 (January 1907): 1–6.

Harwich VR   Kelley, Louise H., and Dorothy Straw, comps. *Vital Records Town of Harwich, Massachusetts, 1694–1850*. Harwich, Mass.: Harwich Historical Society, 1982.

Hatcher 1988   Hatcher, Patricia Law. *Abstracts of Graves of Revolutionary Patriots*. 4 vols. Dallas: Pioneer Heritage Press, 1988.

Hatcher/Barker 1974   Hatcher, John, and T. C. Barker. *A History of British Pewter*. London: Longman, 1974.

Haverhill VR   *Vital Records of Haverhill, Massachusetts, to the End of the Year 1849*. 2 vols. Topsfield, Mass.: Topsfield Historical Society, 1911.

Hawthorne/Smith 1979   Hawthorne, John G., and Cyril Stanley Smith, eds. *Theophilus on Divers Arts: The Foremost Medieval Treatise on Painting, Glassmaking and Metalwork*. New York: Dover, 1979.

Hayward 1976   Hayward, J. F. *Virtuoso Goldsmiths and the Triumph of Mannerism, 1540–1620*. New York: Rizzoli International; London: Sotheby Parke Bernet, 1976.

Hazen (1837) 1970   Hazen, Edward. *The Panorama of Professions and Trades*. 1837. Reprint. Watkins Glen, N.Y.: Century House, 1970.

Heal (1935) 1972   Heal, Ambrose. *The London Goldsmiths, 1200–1800*. 1935. Reprint. Newton Abbot, Devon: David and Charles Printer, 1972.

Heckscher 1985   Heckscher, Morrison H. *American Furniture in The Metropolitan Museum of Art. II. Late Colonial Period: The Queen Anne and Chippendale Styles*. New York: The Metropolitan Museum of Art and Random House, 1985.

Heckscher/Bowman 1992   Heckscher, Morrison H., and Leslie Greene Bowman. *American Rococo, 1750–1775: Elegance in Ornament*. New York: Distributed by Harry N. Abrams for The Metropolitan Museum of Art and Los Angeles County Museum of Art, 1992.

Hennessy 1955   Hennessy, William G. "The Silversmiths of Portsmouth." *New Hampshire Profiles* 4 (February 1955): 35–38.

Heraldic Journal   *The Heraldic Journal Recording the Armorial Bearings and Genealogies of American Families*. 4 vols. Boston: Wiggin & Lunt, 1856–68.

Higgins 1918   Higgins, Katherine Chapin. *Richard Higgins and His Descendants*. Worcester, Mass.: Privately printed, 1918.

Higginson 1910   Higginson, Thomas Wentworth. *Descendants of the Reverend Francis Higginson*. Privately printed, 1910.

Hill 1890   Hill, Hamilton Andrews. *History of the Old South Church (Third Church) Boston, 1669–1884*. 2 vols. Boston and New York: Houghton, Mifflin; Cambridge, Mass.: Riverside Press, 1890.

Hill/Tuttle 1886–1936   Hill, Don Gleason, and Julius H. Tuttle, eds. *The Record of Births, Marriages and Deaths in the Town of Dedham and Early Dedham Records*. 6 vols. Dedham, Mass.: Dedham Transcript, 1886–1936.

Hinman 1861–62   Hinman, R. R. "Records of Wethersfield, Connecticut." *New England Historic Genealogical Register* 15 (July 1861): 241–46; (October 1861): 295–98; 16 (January 1862): 17–22; (April 1862): 135–42; (July 1862): 263–68.

Hipkiss 1942   Hipkiss, Edwin J. "Boston's Earliest Silversmiths: The Philip Leffingwell Spalding Collection." *Bulletin Museum of Fine Arts, Boston* 40 (October 1942): 81–86.

Hipkiss 1943   Hipkiss, Edwin J. *The Philip Leffingwell Spalding Collection of Early American Silver*. Cambridge: Harvard University Press, 1943.

Hitchings 1970   Hitchings, Sinclair H. "The Graphic Arts in Colonial New England." In

Prints in and of America to 1850, edited by John D. Morse, 83–132. Charlottesville: University Press of Virginia; for the Henry Francis du Pont Winterthur Museum, 1970.

Hitchings 1973   Hitchings, Sinclair. "Thomas Johnston." In *Boston Prints and Printmakers 1670–1775*, 83–132. Boston: Colonial Society of Massachusetts, 1973.

Holland 1878   Holland, Henry W. *William Dawes and His Ride with Paul Revere*. Boston: Privately printed by John Wilson and Son, 1878.

Holman Papers   Holman, Winifred Lovering. Papers, 1928–61. New England Historic Genealogical Society, Boston

Holman 1973   Holman, Richard B. "William Burgis." In *Boston Prints and Printmakers 1670–1775*, 57–81. Boston: Colonial Society of Massachusetts, 1973.

Holyoke Diaries   *Holyoke Diaries, 1709–1856*. Salem, Mass.: Essex Institute, 1911.

Hood 1968   Hood, Graham. "A New Form in American Seventeenth–Century Silver." *Antiques* 94 (December 1968): 879–81.

Hood 1971   Hood, Graham. *American Silver: A History of Style, 1650–1900*. New York, Washington, and London: Praeger, 1971.

Hotten 1874   Hotten, John C., ed. *The Original Lists of Persons of Quality; Emigrants; Religious Exiles; Political Rebels; Serving Men Sold for a Term of Years; Apprentices; Children Stolen; Maidens Pressed; and Others Who Went from Great Britain to the American Plantations, 1600–1700*. London: Chatto and Windus, 1874.

Hovey 1913   Hovey, Daniel. *The Hovey Book Describing the English Ancestry and American Descendants of Daniel Hovey of Ipswich, Massachusetts*. Haverhill, Mass.: Lewis R. Hovey, 1913.

How 1971   How, Mrs. G. E. P. "Robert Sanderson in England." *Antiques* 99 (May 1971): 718–19.

Hoyt 1981   Hoyt, David W. *The Old Families of Salisbury and Amesbury, Massachusetts*. Somersworth, N.H.: New England History Press, 1981.

Hubbard 1935   Hubbard, Howard S. "A Complete Checklist of Household Lights Patented in the United States, 1792–1862." Typescript, South Hadley, Mass., 1935.

Hudson 1871   Hudson, Charles. "Louisbourg Soldiers." *New England Historic Genealogical Register* 24 (October 1870): 367–80; 25 (July 1871): 249–69.

"Hull Diaries"   "The Diaries of John Hull, Mint–Master and Treasurer of the Colony of Massachusetts Bay." In *Transactions and Collections of the American Antiquarian Society* 3: 109–316. Boston: John Wilson and Son, 1857.

Hull VR   Baldwin, Thomas W., comp. *Vital Records of Hull, Massachusetts, to the Year 1850*. Boston: Wright and Potter, 1911.

Humphery–Smith 1984   Humphery–Smith, Cecil R., ed. *The Phillimore Atlas and Index of Parish Registers*. Chicester, Sussex, England: Phillimore, Ltd., 1984.

Hunnewell 1880   Hunnewell, James F., ed. *Records of the First Church in Charlestown, Massachusetts, 1632–1789*. Boston: David Clapp & Son, 1880.

Hunnewell 1888   Hunnewell, James F. *A Century of Town Life: A History of Charlestown, Massachusetts, 1775–1887*. Boston: Little, Brown, 1888.

Hyde 1971   Hyde, Bryden Bordley. *Bermuda's Antique Furniture & Silver*. Hamilton, Bermuda: Bermuda National Trust, 1971.

IGI   *International Genealogical Index*. Microfiche. Salt Lake City: The Church of Jesus Christ of Latter–day Saints.

Index Library   Glencross, Reginald M., ed. *A Calendar of the Marriage License Allegations in the Registry of the Bishop of London, Vol. 1, 1597 to 1648.* Index Library, vol. 62. London: British Record Society, 1937.

Index of Marriages, American Antiquarian Society. *Index of Marriages in the Massachusetts Centinel*
1784–1840 and Columbian Centinel, 1784 to 1840. 4 vols. Boston: G. K. Hall, 1961.

Index of Obituaries, *Index of Obituaries in Boston Newspapers, 1704–1800. Vol. 1. Deaths within*
1704–1800 Boston, Vols. 2–3. Deaths Outside Boston. Boston: G. K. Hall, 1968.

Index of Obituaries, American Antiquarian Society, comp. *Index of Obituaries in Massachusetts Cen-*
1784–1840 tinel and Columbian Centinel, 1784–1840. 5 vols. Boston: G. K. Hall, 1961.

Ipswich VR *Vital Records of Ipswich, Massachusetts.* 2 vols. Salem, Mass.: Essex Institute, 1910.

Jackson (1911) 1969   Jackson, Sir Charles James. *An Illustrated History of English Plate, Ecclesiastical and Secular.* 2 vols. 1911. Reprint. New York: Dover Publications, 1969.

Jackson (1921) 1964   Jackson, Sir Charles James. *English Goldsmiths and Their Marks.* 1921. Reprint. New York: Dover, 1964.

Jackson/Teeples/   Jackson, Ronald Vern, Gary Ronald Teeples, and David Schaefermeyer, eds.
Schaefermeyer 1974   *Census Index, New Hampshire, 1800.* Bountiful, Utah: Accelerated Indexing Systems, Inc., 1974.

Jackson/Teeples/   Jackson, Ronald Vern, Gary Ronald Teeples, and David Schaefermeyer, eds.
Schaefermeyer 1976   *Massachusetts 1820 Index.* Bountiful, Utah: Accelerated Indexing Systems, Inc., 1976.

Jobe 1974   Jobe, Brock. "The Boston Furniture Industry, 1720–1740." In *Boston Furniture of the Eighteenth Century,* edited by Walter Muir Whitehill, Jonathan L. Fairbanks, and Brock Jobe, 3–48. Boston: Colonial Society of Massachusetts, 1974.

Johnson 1984   Johnson, Donald Blake. *Upton's Heritage, The History of a Massachusetts Town.* Canaan, N.H.: Phoenix Publishers, 1984.

Johnston 1994   Johnston, Phillip M. *Catalogue of American Silver: The Cleveland Museum of Art.* Cleveland: Cleveland Museum of Art in Cooperation with Indiana University Press, 1994.

Jonas 1960   Jonas, Manfred. "The Wills of the Early Settlers of Essex County, Massachusetts." *Essex Institute Historical Collections* 96 (July 1960): 228–35.

Jones 1913   Jones, E. Alfred. *The Old Silver of American Churches.* Letchworth, England: National Society of Colonial Dames of America, 1913.

Jones 1928   Jones, E. Alfred. *Old Silver of Europe and America from Early Times to the Nineteenth Century.* Philadelphia: J. B. Lippincott, 1928.

Jones 1930   Jones, E. Alfred. *The Loyalists of Massachusetts, Their Memorials, Petitions, and Claims.* London: Saint Catherine Press, 1930.

Jones 1936   Jones, E. Alfred. "The Collection of Old English Silver of Mr. Edsel B. Ford of Detroit." *Apollo* 24 (August 1936): 83–89.

Jones 1936a   Jones, E. Alfred. "American Silver Porringers in England." *Antiques* 29 (May 1936): 195.

Jones 1943   Jones, E. Alfred, "The English Master of Robert Sanderson." *Antiques* 43 (May 1943): 223–24.

Jones 1974   Jones, Karen M. "Museum Accessions." *Antiques* 106 (September 1974): 382, 386, 478.

Judd 1976   Judd, Sylvester. *The History of Hadley, Massachusetts.* 1905. Reprint. Somersworth, N.H.: New Hampshire Publishing Company, 1976.

Kane 1987   Kane, Patricia E. "John Hull and Robert Sanderson: First Masters of New England Silver." Ph.D. diss., Yale University, 1987.

Kauffman 1969   Kauffman, Henry J. *The Colonial Silversmith: His Techniques and His Products.* New York: Galahad Books, 1969.

Kellogg 1902   Kellogg, Lucy Cutler. *History of the Town of Bernardston, Franklin County, Massachusetts, 1736–1900.* Greenfield, Mass.: Press of E. A. Hall, 1902.

Kent/Levy 1909   Kent, Henry Watson, and Florence N. Levy. *The Hudson–Fulton Celebration.* Vol. 2. New York: The Metropolitan Museum of Art, 1909.

Kernan 1960   Kernan, John D., Jr. "The Demihorse: Mark of a Silversmithing Van Rensselaer?" *Antiques* 78 (October 1960): 348–49.

Kernan 1961   Kernan, John D., Jr. "Detective Work on Some American Silver." *Antiques* 79 (January 1961): 106–07.

Kernan 1961a   Kernan, John D., Jr. "Further Notes on Albany Silversmiths." *Antiques* 80 (July 1961): 60–61.

Kernan 1961b   Kernan, John D. "American Miniature Silver." *Antiques* 80 (December 1961): 567–69.

Kerfoot 1924   Kerfoot, J. B. *American Pewter.* New York: Bonanza Books, 1924.

Kingman 1892   Kingman, Bradford. *Epitaphs from Burial Hill, Plymouth, Massachusetts, from 1657–1892.* Brookline, Mass.: New England Illustrated Historical Publishing Company, 1892.

Knight 1976   Knight, Russell W., ed. "General John Glover's Letterbook." *Essex Institute Historical Collections* 112 (January 1976): i–53.

Koch 1969   Koch, David Warner. "Income Distribution and Political Structure in Seventeenth–Century Salem, Massachusetts." *Essex Institute Historical Collections* 105 (January 1969): 50–71.

Kovel 1961   Kovel, Ralph M., and Terry H. Kovel. *A Directory of American Silver, Pewter and Silver Plate.* New York: Crown Publishers, 1961.

Kroening 1982   Kroening, Marily. *American and European Silver from the Gilson Collection.* Milwaukee: Milwaukee Art Museum, 1982.

Lamson 1895   Lamson, D. F. *History of the Town of Manchester.* Manchester, Mass.: By the Town, 1895.

Lancaster VR   Nourse, Henry S., ed. *The Birth, Marriage, and Death Register, Church Records, and Epitaphs of Lancaster, Massachusetts, 1643–1850.* Lancaster and Clinton, Mass.: W. J. Coulton, 1890.

Langdon 1960   Langdon, John Emerson. *Canadian Silversmiths and Their Marks, 1667–1867.* Lunenburg, Vt.: Stinehour Press, 1960.

Langdon 1966   Langdon, John E. *Canadian Silversmiths, 1700–1900.* Toronto: Privately printed, 1966.

Langdon 1970   Langdon, John Emerson. *American Silversmiths in British North America.* Toronto: Privately printed, 1970.

Laughlin (1940, 1970) 1981   Laughlin, Ledlie Irwin. *Pewter in America: Its Makers and Their Marks.* 3 vols. 1940, 1970. Reprint. New York: American Legacy Press, 1981.

Leavitt 1861   Leavitt, William. "History of the Essex Lodge of FreeMasons." *Essex Institute Historical Collections* 3 (June 1861): 121–33.

Leehey 1988   Leehey, Patrick M. "Reconstructing Paul Revere: An Overview of His Ancestry, Life, and Work." In *Paul Revere—Artisan, Businessman and Patriot: The Man Behind the Myth*, 14–39. Boston: Paul Revere Memorial Association, 1988.

Leicester VR   *Vital Records of Leicester, Massachusetts, to the End of the Year 1849*. Worcester, Mass.: F. P. Rice, 1903.

Levy 5   Levy, Bernard & S. Dean, Inc. *Catalogue V*. New York: Bernard & S. Dean Levy, Inc., 1986.

Lewis 1938   Lewis, Ella May, copier. "Baptisms, Marriages, and Deaths, 1736–1809, First Church, Springfield, Massachusetts." Typescript, New England Historic Genealogical Society, Boston, 1938.

Lexington VR   *Lexington, Massachusetts, Record of Births, Marriages, and Deaths to January 1, 1898*. Boston: Wright and Potter, 1898.

Lichtenstein 1886a   Lichtenstein, Richard C. "Brief Notices of the Early American Engravers." *New England Historic Genealogical Register* 40 (April 1886): 204–05.

Lichtenstein 1886b   Lichtenstein, Richard C. "Early New England and New York Heraldic Book Plates." *New England Historic Genealogical Register* 40 (July 1886): 295–99.

Lichtenstein 1887   Lichtenstein, Richard C. "Early Southern Heraldic Book Plates." *New England Historic Genealogical Register* 41 (July 1887): 296–97.

Lincoln 1862   Lincoln, William. *History of Worcester, Massachusetts, from Its Earliest Settlement to September 1836*. Worcester, Mass.: Charles Hersey, 1862.

Lincoln (1893) 1982   Lincoln, George. *History of the Town of Hingham, Massachusetts*. 3 vols. *Hingham: The Town of Hingham*. 1893. Reprint. Somersworth, N.H.: New England History Press, 1982.

Lippert 1982   Lippert, Catherine. "Silver by Paul Revere." *Perceptions* 2 (1982): 38–44.

Literary Diary of Ezra Stiles   Dexter, Franklin Bowditch, ed. *The Literary Diary of Ezra Stiles*. 3 vols. New York: Charles Scribner's Sons, 1901.

Little 1882   Little, George Thomas. *The Descendants of George Little*. Auburn, Me.: By the author, 1882.

Lord/Gamage 1972   Lord, Priscilla Sawyer, and Virginia Clegg Gamage. *Marblehead: The Spirit of '76 Lives Here*. Philadelphia, New York, London: Chilton Book Company, 1972.

Loring 1855   Loring, James Spear. *Hundred Boston Orators Appointed by the Municipal Authorities and Other Public Bodies from 1770 to 1852*. Boston: John P. Jewett and Company; Cleveland: Jewett, Proctor & Worthington, 1855.

Loyen 1980   Loyen, Frances. *The Thames and Hudson Manual of Silversmithing*. London: Thames and Hudson, 1980.

Lunenberg VR   Davis, Walter A., comp. *The Early Records of the Town of Lunenberg, Massachusetts, Including that part which is now Fitchburg; 1719–1764*. Fitchburg, Mass.: Published by Authority of the City Council, 1896.

Lyme VR   Barbour Collection, Connecticut State Library, Hartford

Lyme VR   Hall, Verne M., and Elizabeth B. Plimpton. *Vital Records of Lyme, Connecticut, to the Year 1850*. Lyme: American Revolution Bicentennial Commission, 1976.

Lynn VR   *Vital Records of Lynn, Massachusetts, to the End of the Year 1849*. 2 vols. Salem, Mass.: Essex Institute, 1905–06.

McClelland 1924   McClelland, Nancy. "The Washington Memorial Paper: An Elegant Device in Paper-Hangings." *Antiques* 6 (September 1924): 138–39.

McCulloch/Beale 1963   McCulloch, Robert, and Alice Beale. "Silversmiths of Barnstable, Massachusetts." *Antiques* 84 (July 1963): 72–74.

McCusker 1978   McCusker, John J. *Money and Exchange in Europe and America, 1600–1775: A Handbook.* Chapel Hill: University of North Carolina Press, 1978.

McFadden/Clark 1989   McFadden, David Revere, and Mark A. Clark. *Treasures for the Table: Silver from the Chrysler Museum.* New York: Hudson Hills Press, 1989.

McKinsey 1984   McKinsey, Kristan Helen. "New York City Silversmiths and Their Patrons, 1687–1750." M.A. thesis, University of Delaware, 1984.

McLanathan 1956   McLanathan, Richard B. K. "American Silver: A Fiftieth Anniversary." *Bulletin Museum of Fine Arts, Boston* 54 (Autumn 1956): 49–66.

McMurray 1925   McMurray, W., ed. *St. Anne and St. Agnes with St. John Zachary: Records of Two City Parishes.* London: Hunter & Longhurst, 1925.

Mackay 1973   Mackay, Donald C. *Silversmiths and Related Craftsmen of the Atlantic Provinces.* Halifax: Petheric Press, 1973.

MacKay 1978   MacKay, Robert E. *Massachusetts Soldiers in the French and Indian Wars, 1744–55.* Boston: Society of Colonial Wars in the Commonwealth of Massachusetts and The New England Historic Genealogical Society, 1978.

Main 1965   Main, Jackson Turner. *The Social Structure of Revolutionary America.* Princeton: Princeton University Press, 1965.

Malden VR   Corey, DeLoraine P., comp. *Births, Marriages, and Deaths in the Town of Malden, Massachusetts, 1645–1850.* Cambridge, Mass.: University Press, 1903.

Manchester VR   *Vital Records of Manchester, Massachusetts, to the End of the Year 1849.* Salem, Mass.: Essex Institute, 1903.

Manwaring 1904   Manwaring, Charles W. *A Digest of the Early Connecticut Probate Records: Vol. 1 Hartford District, 1635–1700.* Hartford: R. S. Peck, 1904.

Marblehead VR   *Vital Records of Marblehead, Massachusetts, to the End of the Year 1849.* 3 vols. Salem, Mass.: Essex Institute, 1903–08.

Marlborough VR   *Vital Records of Marlborough, Massachusetts, to the End of the Year 1849.* Worcester, Mass.: F. P. Rice, 1908.

Marshfield VR   Bowman, George Ernest, trans. "Marshfield, Mass., Vital Records." *Mayflower Descendant* 30 (October 1932): 146–56.

Mass. Soldiers and Sailors   *Massachusetts Soldiers and Sailors of the Revolutionary War.* 17 vols. Boston: Wright & Potter, 1896–1908.

"Materials for a Genealogy of the Lang Family"   "Materials for a Genealogy of the Lang Family communicated by David Perkins." *Essex Institute Historical Collections* 6 (December 1864): 257.

Mayflower Descendant   *Mayflower Descendant: A Quarterly Magazine of Pilgrim History and Genealogy*

Mayne 1969   Mayne, Richard H. *Old Channel Islands Silver.* Jersey, Channel Islands: Print Holdings & Investments Ltd., 1969.

Mazur/Daniels 1969   Mazur, D. Bennett, and Wayne M. Daniels. *A Report of the Board of Chosen Freeholders, Bergen County, New Jersey: The Massacre of Baylor's Dragoons, Excavation of Burial Site.* Rev. ed. River Edge, N. J.: Bergen County Historical Society, 1969.

Medfield VR   *Vital Records of Medfield, Massachusetts, to the Year 1850.* Boston: New England Historic Genealogical Society at the Charge of the Eddy Town Record Fund, 1903.

Medford VR   *Vital Records of Medford, Massachusetts, to the Year 1850.* Boston: New England Historic Genealogical Society at the Charge of the Eddy Town Record Fund, 1907.

Medicus 1944   Medicus, Philip. "American Silver–Hilted Swords: Part II." *Antiques* 46 (December 1944): 342–44.

Medway VR   *Vital Records of Medway, Massachusetts, to the Year 1850.* Boston: New England Historic Genealogical Society at the Charge of the Eddy Town Record Fund, 1905.

Mendon VR   Baldwin, Thomas W., comp. *Vital Records of Mendon, Massachusetts, to the Year 1850.* Boston: Wright & Potter, 1920.

Merriman 1976   Merriman, Jean R. *The Mystery of John Jackson, Eighteenth–Century Silversmith: One Man or Two?* Nantucket, Mass.: Poets Corner Press, 1976.

Methuen VR   *Vital Records of Methuen, Massachusetts, to the End of the Year 1849.* Topsfield, Mass.: Topsfield Historical Society, 1909.

MFA 1906   *American Silver, The Work of Seventeenth– and Eighteenth–Century Silversmiths.* Boston: Museum of Fine Arts, Boston, 1906.

MFA 1911   *American Church Silver of the Seventeenth and Eighteenth Centuries with a Few Pieces of Domestic Plate.* Boston: Museum of Fine Arts, Boston, 1911.

MFA 1920   E.J.H. [Edwin James Hipkiss]. "Minor Arts in New England, 1620." *Bulletin Museum of Fine Arts, Boston* 18 (October 1920): 47–48.

MFA 1991   Fairbanks, Jonathan L., et al. *Collecting American Decorative Arts and Sculpture, 1971–1991.* Boston: Museum of Fine Arts, Boston, 1991.

MHS Proceedings   *Massachusetts Historical Society Proceedings*

Middletown VR   Barbour Collection, Connecticut State Library, Hartford

Miles 1976   Miles, Elizabeth B. *Elizabeth B. Miles Collection of English Silver.* Hartford: Wadsworth Atheneum, 1976.

Milford VR   Barbour Collection, Connecticut State Library, Hartford

Milton VR   *Milton Records: Births, Marriages, and Deaths, 1662–1843, Alphabetically and Chronologically Arranged.* Boston: Alfred Mudge & Son, 1900.

Minneapolis 1956   *French, English and American Silver: A Loan Exhibition in Honor of Russell A. Plimpton.* Minneapolis: Minneapolis Institute of Arts, 1956.

Minor 1946   Minor, Edward E. "Notes on Early American Silver." *Antiques* 49 (April 1946): 238–40.

Moffat 1913   Moffat, R. Burnham. *Pierrepont Genealogies from Norman Times to 1913.* New York: Privately printed, 1913.

Montgomery 1966   Montgomery, Charles F. *American Furniture: The Federal Period in the Henry Francis du Pont Winterthur Museum.* New York: Viking Press, 1966.

Moore 1935   Moore, Howard Parker. *A Genealogy of the First Five Generations in America of the Lang Family.* Rutland, Vt.: Charles E. Tuttle, 1935.

Moore Collection 1980   *American Silver, 1670–1830: The Cornelius C. Moore Collection at Providence College.* Introduction by Alice H. R. Hauck. Providence: Rhode Island Bicentennial Foundation and Providence College, 1980.

Moreno 1988   Moreno, Edgard. "Patriotism and Profit: The Copper Mills at Canton." In *Paul Revere—Artisan, Businessman, and Patriot: The Man Behind the Myth,* 94–115. Boston: Paul Revere Memorial Association, 1988.

Morison 1930   Morison, Samuel Eliot. *Builders of the Bay Colony.* Boston and New York: Houghton Mifflin, 1930.

Morse 1970   Morse, John D., ed. *Country Cabinetwork and Simple City Furniture.* Charlottesville: University Press of Virginia, 1970.

Morse/Leavitt 1903   Morse, J. Howard, and Emily Leavitt. *Morse Genealogy*. New York: Morse Society, 1903.

Moulton 1906   Moulton, Henry William. *Moulton Annals*, edited by Claribel Moulton. Chicago: Edward A. Claypool, 1906.

Mowbray 1979   Mowbray, E. Andrew. "In Search of Jeremiah Snow—Revolutionary War Sword Cutler." *Man at Arms* 1 and 2 (March/April 1979): 27–30.

Naeve/Roberts 1986   Naeve, Milo M., and Lynn Springer Roberts. *A Decade of Decorative Arts: The Antiquarian Society of the Art Institute of Chicago*. Chicago: Art Institute of Chicago, 1986.

Nantucket VR   *Vital Records of Nantucket, Massachusetts, to the Year 1850*. 5 vols. Boston: New England Historic Genealogical Society at the Robert Henry Eddy Memorial Rooms at the Charge of the Eddy Town Record Fund, 1925.

Nash 1979   Nash, Gary B. *The Urban Crucible: Social Change, Political Consciousness and the Origins of the American Revolution*. Cambridge: Harvard University Press, 1979.

National Art Galleries   National Art Galleries, Inc., Hotel Plaza, New York

NEHGR   *New England Historic Genealogical Register*

NEHGR 1855   "Memoir of Peter Chardon Brooks." *New England Historic Genealogical Register* 9 (January 1855): 13–23.

"New Brick Church, Boston"   "New Brick Church, Boston: List of Persons Connected Therewith from 1722 to 1775 Compiled from the Records." *New England Historic and Genealogical Register* 18 (July 1864): 237–40; (October 1864): 337–44; 19 (July 1865): 230–35; (October 1865): 320–24.

Newbury VR   *Vital Records of Newbury, Massachusetts, to the End of the Year 1849*. 2 vols. Salem, Mass.: Essex Institute, 1911.

Newburyport Maritime Society Antiques Show 1981   *Newburyport Maritime Society Antiques Show*. Newburyport, Mass.: Custom House Maritime Museum, 1981.

Newburyport VR   *Vital Records of Newburyport, Massachusetts, to the End of the Year 1849*. 2 vols. Salem, Mass.: Essex Institute, 1911.

New Hampshire Genealogical Record   *New Hampshire Genealogical Record*

New Haven Probate Records   New Haven County Probate Records. Microfilm. New Haven Colony Historical Society, New Haven

New Haven Silversmiths   *An Exhibition of Early Silver by New Haven Silversmiths*. New Haven: New Haven Colony Historical Society, 1967.

New Haven Town Records   Powers, Zara Jones, ed. *New Haven Town Records, 1684–1769*. New Haven Colony Historical Society Ancient Town Records, vol. 3. New Haven: New Haven Colony Historical Society, 1962.

New Haven VR   *Vital Records of New Haven, 1649–1850, Part I*. Hartford, Conn.: Connecticut Society of the Order of the Founders and Patrons of America, 1917.

New London VR   Barbour Collection, microfilm, Connecticut State Library, Hartford

Newman 1967   Newman, Eric P. *The Early Paper Money of America*. Racine, Wis.: Whitman, 1967.

Newport Historical Magazine   *Newport Historical Magazine* 2 (1881–82).

Newton VR   *Vital Records of Newton, Massachusetts, to the Year 1850*. Boston: New England Historic Genealogical Society at the Charge of the Eddy Town Record Fund, 1905.

New York Marriages   *New York Marriages Previous to 1784: A Reprint of the Original Edition of 1800 with Additions and Corrections.* Baltimore: Genealogical Publishing Co., 1968.

NHHS 1973   New Hampshire Historical Society. *The Decorative Arts of New Hampshire: A Sesquicentennial Exhibition.* Concord: New Hampshire Historical Society, 1973.

Nielsen 1991   Nielsen, Donald M. "The Revere Family." *New England Historical and Genealogical Register* 145 (October 1991): 291–316.

Nightingale 1891   Nightingale, J. E. *The Church Plate of the County of Wilts.* Salisbury, England: Bennett Brothers, 1891.

Noble/Cronin 1901–28   *Records of the Court of Assistants of the Colony of the Massachusetts Bay, 1630–1692.* Printed under the supervision of John Noble and John F. Cronin. 3 vols. Boston: County of Suffolk, 1901–28.

Noe 1943   Noe, Sydney P. *The New England and Willow Tree Coinage of Mass.* 1943. Reprint. Lawrence, Mass.: Quarterman Publications, 1973.

Noe 1947   Noe, Sydney P. *The Oak Tree Coinage of Massachusetts.* 1947. Reprint. Lawrence, Mass.: Quarterman Publications, 1973.

Noe 1952   Noe, Sydney P. *The Pine Tree Coinage of Massachusetts.* 1952. Reprint. Lawrence, Mass.: Quarterman Publications, 1973.

Northeast Auctions   Northeast Auctions, Hampton, New Hampshire

Norman–Wilcox 1937   Norman–Wilcox, Gregor. "Some Unpublished American Silver." *Antiques* 31 (March 1937): 126–29.

Norman–Wilcox 1940   Norman–Wilcox, Gregor. "A Collector's Silver." *Antiques* 37 (May 1940): 236–39.

Norman–Wilcox 1944   Norman–Wilcox, Gregor. "American Silver Spice Dredgers, Part II." *Antiques* 45 (February 1944): 80–84.

Norman–Wilcox 1954   Norman–Wilcox, Gregor. "American Silver, 1690–1810, in California Collections." *Antiques* 65 (January 1954): 48–51.

Norman–Wilcox 1962   Norman–Wilcox, Gregor. *Early Silver in California Collections: Old English and Early American Silverwork.* Los Angeles: Los Angeles County Museum of Art, 1962.

Norton VR   *Vital Records of Norton, Massachusetts, to the Year 1850.* Boston: New England Historic Genealogical Society at the Charge of the Eddy Town Record Fund, 1906.

Norwich VR   Barbour Collection, Connecticut State Library, Hartford

Nourse 1890   Nourse, Harry S., ed. *The Birth, Marriage, and Death Register, Church Records and Epitaphs of Lancaster, Massachusetts.* Lancaster, Mass.: W. J. Coulter, 1890.

Noyes 1903   Noyes, Harriette Eliza. *A Memorial History of Hampstead, New Hampshire.* 2 vols. Boston: George B. Reed, 1903.

Noyes/Libby/Davis (1928–39) 1976   Noyes, Sybil, Charles Thornton Libby, and Walter Goodwin Davis. *Genealogical Dictionary of Maine and New Hampshire.* 1928–39. Reprint. Baltimore: Genealogical Publishing Company, 1976.

Nygren 1971   Nygren, Edward J. "Edward Winslow's Sugar Boxes: Colonial Echoes of Courtly Love." *Yale University Art Gallery Bulletin* 35 (Autumn 1971): 38–52.

N–YHS Collections 1891   "New York Provincial Muster Rolls." *Collections of the New–York Historical Society* 24 (1891): 248–51.

Okie 1928   Okie, Howard Pitcher. *Old Silver and Old Sheffield Plate.* Garden City, N.Y.: Doubleday, Doran, 1928.

Okie 1936   Okie, Howard Pitcher. *Old Silver and Old Sheffield Plate.* Garden City, N.Y.: Doubleday, Doran, 1936.

Old South Church 1883   *An Historical Catalogue of the Old South Church (Third Church, Boston).* Boston: Printed for Private Distribution, 1883.

Oliver 1973   Oliver, Andrew. "Peter Pelham (c. 1697–1751): Sometime Printmaker of Boston." In *Boston Prints and Printmakers, 1670–1775,* 133–73. Boston: Colonial Society of Massachusetts, 1973.

Olton 1975   Olton, Charles S. *Artisans for Independence: Philadelphia Mechanics and the American Revolution.* Syracuse: Syracuse University Press, 1975.

Oman 1962   Oman, Charles. *English Domestic Silver.* 5th ed. London: Adam and Charles Black, 1962.

Oman 1970   Oman, Charles. *Caroline Silver, 1625–1688.* London: Faber and Faber, 1970.

Ormsbee 1940   Ormsbee, Thomas Hamilton. "The Burts, Boston Silversmiths." *American Collector* 9 (August 1940): 6–7, 14, 20.

Osgood 1984   Osgood, Russell K. "John Clark, Esq., Justice of the Peace, 1667–1728." In *The Law in Colonial Massachusetts,* edited by Frederick S. Allis, Jr., 107–51. Boston: Colonial Society of Massachusetts, 1984.

Otto 1992   Otto, Julie Helen. "Lydia and Her Daughters: A Boston Matrilineal Case Study." *NEXUS: The Bimonthly Newsletter of the New England Historic Genealogical Society* 9 (February–March 1992): 25–29; (April–May): 57–60.

Paige 1877   Paige, Lucius Robinson. *History of Cambridge, Massachusetts, 1630–1877.* Boston: H. O. Houghton; New York: Hurd and Houghton, 1877.

Paine 1878   Paine, Nathaniel. *Genealogical Notes on the Paine Family of Worcester, Mass.* Albany: Privately printed, 1878.

Paine 1971   Paine, Josiah. *A History of Harwich, Barnstable County, Massachusetts, 1620–1800, including the Early History of That Part Now Brewster.* 1937. Reprint. Yarmouthport, Mass.: Parnassus Imprints, 1971.

Palmer 1950   Palmer, Brooks. *The Book of American Clocks.* New York: Macmillan, 1950.

Papers of Benjamin Franklin   Labaree, Leonard W., ed. *The Papers of Benjamin Franklin.* New Haven: Yale University Press, 1961–.

Park 1921   Park, Lawrence. "Early American Silver." *Bulletin of the Cleveland Museum of Art* 8 (November 1921): 130–32.

Park 1926   Park, Lawrence, comp. *Gilbert Stuart: An Illustrated Descriptive List of His Works Compiled by Lawrence Park with an Account of His Life by John Hill Morgan and an Appreciation by Royal Cortissoz.* 4 vols. New York: William Edwin Rudge, 1926.

Parke–Bernet   Parke–Bernet Galleries, Inc., New York

Parks 1958   Parks, Robert O. *Early New England Silver Lent from the Mark Bortman Collection.* Northampton, Mass.: Smith College Museum of Art, 1958.

Parsons 1976   Parsons, Charles S. *New Hampshire Clocks and Clockmakers.* Exeter, N.H.: Adams Brown Co., 1976.

Parsons 1983   Parsons, Charles S. *New Hampshire Silver.* Adams Brown, 1983.

Partridge 1935   Partridge, Albert E. "Benjamin Bagnall of Boston, Clockmaker." *Old–Time New England* 26 (July 1935): 26–31.

Patterson 1895   Patterson, William D., ed. *The Probate Records of Lincoln County, Maine, 1760 to 1800.* Portland: Maine Genealogical Society, 1895.

Paul Revere 1988   *Paul Revere—Artisan, Businessman, and Patriot: The Man Behind the Myth.* Boston: Paul Revere Memorial Association, 1988.

Paul Revere's Ride   *Paul Revere's Three Accounts of His Famous Ride.* Introduction by Edmund S.

Morgan. Boston: Massachusetts Historical Society, 1961.

Pearson 1904 Pearson, Henry Greenleaf. *The Life of John Andrew, Governor of Massachusetts, 1861–1865*. 2 vols. Boston: Houghton Mifflin, 1904.

Pepperrell VR Rice, George A., comp. and ed. *Vital Records of Pepperrell, Massachusetts, to the Year 1850*. Boston: New England Historic Genealogical Society, 1985.

Perkins 1889 Perkins, George A. *The Family of John Perkins of Ipswich, Massachusetts*. Salem, Mass.: Salem Press, 1889.

Perkins 1895 Perkins, Mary E. *Old Houses of the Ancient Town of Norwich, 1660–1800*. Norwich, Conn.: Bulletin Company, 1895.

Peterson (1954) 1991 Peterson, Harold L. *The American Sword, 1775–1945*. 1954. Reprint. Philadelphia: Ray Riling Arms Books, 1991.

Peterson (1955) 1991 Peterson, Harold L. *American Silver Mounted Swords, 1700–1815*. 1955. Reprint. Philadelphia: Ray Riling Arms Books, 1991.

Philadelphia: Three Centuries Philadelphia Museum of Art. *Philadelphia: Three Centuries of American Art*. *of American Art* Philadelphia: Philadelphia Museum of Art, 1976.

Phillips Phillips, New York

Phillips 1933 Phillips, James Duncan. *Salem in the Seventeenth Century*. Boston and New York: Houghton Mifflin, 1933.

Phillips 1935 Phillips, John Marshall. *Early Connecticut Silver, 1700–1830*. New Haven: Gallery of Fine Arts, Yale University, 1935.

Phillips 1937 Phillips, John Marshall. "Additions to the Garvan Collection of Silver." *Bulletin of the Associates in Fine Arts at Yale University* 8 (June 1937): 3–13.

Phillips 1937a Phillips, James Duncan. *Salem in the Eighteenth Century*. Boston: Houghton Mifflin, 1937.

Phillips 1939 Phillips, John Marshall. *Masterpieces of New England Silver, 1650–1800*. New Haven: Gallery of Fine Arts, Yale University, 1939.

Phillips 1948 Phillips, John Marshall. "Masterpieces in American Silver: Part I, Seventeenth-Century Traditions." *Antiques* 54 (December 1948): 412–16.

Phillips 1949 Phillips, John Marshall. *American Silver*. New York: Chanticleer Press, 1949.

Phillips 1949a Phillips, John Marshall. "A Silver Dram Cup." *Bulletin of the Associates in Fine Arts at Yale University* 17 (July 1949), n.p.

Phillips 1949b Phillips, John Marshall. "Masterpieces in American Silver in Public Collections: Part III, Ecclesiastical Silver." *Antiques* 55 (April 1949): 281–85.

Phillips 1949c Phillips, John Marshall. "Masterpieces in American Silver in Public Collections: Part IV, Rococo and Federal Periods." *Antiques* 56 (July 1949): 41–45.

Phillips 1960 Phillips, John Marshall. *Early American Silver Selected from the Mabel Brady Garvan Collection*. Edited, with introduction and notes, by Meyric R. Rogers. New Haven: Yale University Art Gallery, 1960.

Phinney 1943 Phinney, Mary Allen. *Jirah Isham of New London, Connecticut, and His Descendants*. Rutland, Vt.: Tuttle Publishing Company, 1943.

Pierce 1961 Pierce, Richard D., ed. *Records of the First Church in Boston, 1630–1868*. Publications of the Colonial Society of Massachusetts, vols. 39–41. Boston: Colonial Society of Massachusetts, 1961.

Pierce 1974 Pierce, Richard D., ed. *The Records of the First Church in Salem, Massachusetts, 1629–1736*. Salem, Mass.: Essex Institute, 1974.

Platt 1895 Platt, Franklin. *Notes upon the Ancestry of Ebenezer Greenough*. Philadelphia: no pub., 1895.

Pleasants/Sill 1930   Pleasants, J. Hall, and Howard Sill. *Maryland Silversmiths, 1715–1830*. Baltimore: Lord Baltimore Press, 1930.

Plymouth Church Records   *Plymouth Church Records, 1620–1859*. 3 vols. New York and Cambridge, Mass.: University Press, John Wilson & Son, 1920.

Plymouth VR   "Plymouth, Mass., Vital Records." *Mayflower Descendant* 5 (January 1903): 53–56; (April 1903): 99–100.

Pomeroy 1912   Pomeroy, Albert A. *History and Genealogy of the Pomeroy Family*. Toledo: The Franklin Printing and Engraving Co., 1912.

Pope 1917   Pope, Charles Henry. *Loring Genealogy*. Cambridge, Mass.: Murray and Emery, 1917.

Potter 1835   Potter, Elisha R., Jr. *The Early History of Narragansett*. Rhode Island Historical Society Collections, vol. 3. Providence: Marshall, Brown, 1835.

Potwine 1935   Potwine, Elizabeth B. "John Potwine, Silversmith of Massachusetts and Connecticut." *Antiques* 28 (September 1935): 106–09.

Prime 1969   Prime, Alfred Coxe. *The Arts and Crafts in Philadelphia, Maryland, and South Carolina. Part 1, 1721–1785; Part 2, 1786–1800*. 2 vols. 1929 and 1932. Reprint. New York: Da Capo Press, 1969.

Proper 1965   Proper, David R. "Edmund Currier, Clockmaker." *Essex Institute Historical Collections* 101 (October 1965): 281–88.

Prown 1966   Prown, Jules David. *John Singleton Copley*. 2 vols. Cambridge: Harvard University Press for the National Galley of Art, 1966.

Pruitt 1978   Pruitt, Bettye Hobbs, ed. *The Massachusetts Tax Valuation List of 1771*. Boston: G. K. Hall, 1978.

Puig et al. 1989   Puig, Francis J., Judith Banister, Gerald W. R. Ward, and David McFadden. *English and American Silver in the Collection of the Minneapolis Institute of Arts*. Minneapolis: Minneapolis Institute of Arts, 1989.

Purple 1890   Purple, Samuel S., ed. "Baptisms from 1639 to 1730 in the Reformed Dutch Church, New York, vol. 1." *Collections of the New-York Genealogical and Biographical Society*. Vol. 2. New York: New-York Genealogical and Biographical Society, 1890.

Quimby 1995   Quimby, Ian M. G., with Dianne Johnson. *American Silver at Winterthur*. Winterthur, Del.: Henry Francis du Pont Winterthur Museum, 1995.

Radasch 1966   Radasch, Arthur Hitchcock. *The William Barstow Family, Genealogy of the Descendants of William Barstow, 1635–1965*. Privately printed, 1966.

Raymond 1887   Raymond, M. D. *Gray Genealogy, Being a Genealogical Record and History of the Descendants of John Gray of Beverly, Massachusetts*. Tarrytown, N.Y.: M. D. Raymond, 1887.

RC 1   *First Report of the Record Commissioners of the City of Boston, 1876*. Boston: Rockwell and Churchill, 1881.

RC 2   *Second Report of the Record Commissioners of the City of Boston Containing the Boston Records, 1634–1660, and the Book of Possessions*. Boston: Rockwell and Churchill, 1881.

RC 3   *A Report of the Record Commissioners of the City of Boston Containing Charlestown Land Records, 1638–1802*. Boston: Rockwell and Churchill, 1883.

RC 4   *Fourth Report of the Record Commissioners, of the City of Boston, 1880: Dorchester Town Records*. 2d ed. Boston: Rockwell and Churchill, 1883.

RC 6   *A Report of the Record Commissioners, Containing the Roxbury Land and Church*

Records. Boston: Rockwell and Churchill, 1884.

RC 7 *A Report of the Record Commissioners of the City of Boston, Containing the Boston Records from 1660 to 1701*. Boston: Rockwell and Churchill, 1881.

RC 8 *A Report of the Record Commissioners of the City of Boston, Containing the Boston Records from 1700 to 1728*. Boston: Rockwell and Churchill, 1883.

RC 9 *A Report of the Record Commissioners Containing Boston Births, Baptisms, Marriages, and Deaths, 1630–1699*. Boston: Rockwell and Churchill, 1883.

RC 10 *A Report of the Record Commissioners of the City of Boston, Containing Miscellaneous Papers*. Boston: Rockwell and Churchill, 1886.

RC 11 *A Report of the Record Commissioners of the City of Boston, Containing the Records of Boston Selectmen, 1701 to 1715*. Boston: Rockwell and Churchill, 1884.

RC 12 *A Report of the Record Commissioners of the City of Boston, Containing the Boston Records, 1729 to 1742*. Boston: Rockwell and Churchill, 1885.

RC 13 *A Report of the Record Commissioners of the City of Boston, Containing the Records of Boston Selectmen, 1716 to 1736*. Boston: Rockwell and Churchill, 1885.

RC 14 *A Report of the Record Commissioners of the City of Boston Containing the Boston Town Records, 1742 to 1757*. Boston: Rockwell and Churchill, 1885.

RC 15 *A Report of the Record Commissioners of the City of Boston, Containing the Records of Boston Selectmen, 1736 to 1742*. Boston: Rockwell and Churchill, 1886.

RC 16 *A Report of the Record Commissioners of the City of Boston, Containing the Boston Town Records, 1758 to 1769*. Boston: Rockwell and Churchill, 1886.

RC 17 *A Report of the Record Commissioners of the City of Boston, Containing the Selectmen's Minutes from 1742–43 to 1753*. Boston: Rockwell and Churchill, 1887.

RC 18 *A Report of the Record Commissioners of the City of Boston, Containing the Boston Town Records, 1770 through 1777*. Boston: Rockwell and Churchill, 1887.

RC 19 *A Report of the Record Commissioners of the City of Boston Containing the Selectmen's Minutes from 1754 through 1763*. Boston: Rockwell and Churchill, 1885.

RC 20 *A Report of the Record Commissioners of the City of Boston, Containing the Selectmen's Minutes from 1764 through 1768*. Boston: Rockwell and Churchill, 1889.

RC 21 *A Report of the Record Commissioners of the City of Boston Containing Dorchester Births, Marriages, and Deaths to the End of 1825*. Boston: Rockwell and Churchill, 1890.

RC 22 *A Report of the Record Commissioners of the City of Boston, Containing the Statistics of the United States District Tax of 1798 as Assessed on Boston; and The Names of the Inhabitants of Boston in 1790, as Collected for the First National Census*. Boston: Rockwell and Churchill, 1890.

RC 23 *A Report of the Record Commissioners of the City of Boston, Containing the Selectmen's Minutes from 1769 through April, 1775*. Boston: Rockwell and Churchill, 1890.

RC 24 *A Report of the Record Commissioners of the City of Boston, Containing Boston Births from A.D. 1700 to A.D. 1800*. Boston: Rockwell & Churchill, 1894.

RC 25 *A Report of the Record Commissioners of the City of Boston, Containing the Selectmen's Minutes from 1776 through 1786*. Boston: Rockwell & Churchill, 1894.

RC 26 *A Report of the Record Commissioners of the City of Boston, Containing the Boston Town Records, 1778 to 1783*. Boston: Rockwell & Churchill, 1895.

RC 27   *A Report of the Record Commissioners of the City of Boston, Containing the Selectmen's Minutes from 1787 through 1798.* Boston: Rockwell & Churchill, 1896.

RC 28   *A Report of the Record Commissioners of the City of Boston, Containing the Boston Marriages from 1700 to 1751.* Boston: Municipal Printing Office, 1898.

RC 29   *A Volume of Records Relating to the Early History of Boston, Containing Miscellaneous Papers.* Boston: Municipal Printing Office, 1900.

RC 30   *A Volume of Records Relating to the Early History of Boston, Containing Boston Marriages from 1752 to 1809.* Boston: Municipal Printing Office, 1903.

RC 31   *A Volume of Records Relating to the Early History of Boston Containing Boston Town Records, 1784 to 96.* Boston: Municipal Printing Office, 1903.

RC 32   *A Volume Relating to the Early History of Boston Containing the Aspinwall Notorial Records.* Boston: Municipal Printing Office, 1903.

RC 33   *A Volume of Records Relating to the Early History of Boston Containing Minutes of the Selectmen's Meetings, 1799 to and including 1810.* Boston: Municipal Printing Office, 1904.

RC 34   Drake, Francis S., ed. *The Town of Roxbury. Registry Department of the City of Boston, Records Relating to the Early History of Boston.* Boston: Municipal Printing Office, 1905.

RC 35   *A Volume of Records Containing Boston Town Records, 1796 to 1813.* Boston: Municipal Printing Office, 1905.

RC 36   *Vital Records of the Town of Dorchester from 1826 to 1849.* Boston: Municipal Printing Office, 1905.

RC 37   *A Volume of Records Relating to the Early History of Boston Containing Town Records, 1814 to 1822.* Boston: Municipal Printing Office, 1906.

RC 38   *A Volume of Records Relating to the Early History of Boston Containing Minutes of Selectmen's Meetings, 1811–1817, and Part of 1818.* Boston: Municipal Printing Office, 1908.

RC 39   *A Volume of Records Relating to the Early History of Boston Containing Minutes of the Selectmen's Meetings from September 1, 1818, to April 24, 1822.* Boston: Printing Department, 1909.

Reading VR   Baldwin, Thomas W., comp. *Vital Records of Reading, Massachusetts, to the Year 1850.* Boston: New England Historic Genealogical Society, 1912.

Reaves 1991   Reaves, Wendy Wick. "Effigie Curiously Engraven: Eighteenth-Century American Portrait Prints." In *Prints of New England,* edited by Georgia Brady Barnhill, 39–67. Worcester, Mass.: American Antiquarian Society, 1991.

Rebora/Staiti et al. 1995   Rebora, Carrie, Paul Staiti, Erica Hirshler, Theodore E. Stebbins, Jr., and Carol Troyen. *John Singleton Copley in America.* New York: The Metropolitan Museum of Art, 1995.

Records of the Colony of Rhode Island   Bartlett, John Russell, ed. *Records of the Colony of Rhode Island and Providence Plantations in New England.* 10 vols. Providence: A. C. Greene and Brothers, 1856–65.

Reps 1973   Reps, John W. "Boston by Bostonians: The Printed Plans and Views of the Colonial City by Its Artists, Cartographers, Engravers, and Publishers." In *Boston Prints and Printmakers, 1670–1776,* 3–56. Boston: Colonial Society of Massachusetts, 1973.

Revolutionary War Pensions   *Index of Revolutionary War Pension Applications in the National Archives: Bicentennial Edition.* Washington, D.C.: National Genealogical Society, 1976.

Rice 1879–95   Rice, Franklin P., ed. *Worcester Town Records.* 7 vols. Worcester, Mass.: Worcester Society of Antiquity, 1879–95.

Rice 1964   Rice, Norman S. *Albany Silver, 1652–1825.* Albany: Albany Institute of History and Art, 1964.

Robbins 1852   Robbins, Chandler. *A History of the Second Church, or Old North in Boston.* Boston: John Wilson & Son, 1852.

Robbins 1862   Robbins, James Murray. *Address Delivered before the Inhabitants of the Town of Milton, on the 200th Anniversary of the Incorporation of the Town, June 11th, 1862.* Boston: D. Clapp, 1862.

Robbins 1921   Robbins, William A. "A Muster Roll of Capt. Daniel Cozen's Company." *New York Genealogical and Biographical Record* 52 (July 1921): 256–57.

Roberts 1895   Roberts, Oliver Ayer. *History of the Military Company of the Massachusetts now Called The Ancient and Honorable Artillery Company of Massachusetts, 1637–1888.* 2 vols. Boston: Alfred Mudger Son, 1895.

Rock 1979   Rock, Howard B. *Artisans of the New Republic: The Tradesmen of New York City in the Age of Jefferson.* New York: New York University Press, 1979.

Rodriguez Roque 1984   Rodriguez Roque, Oswaldo. *American Furniture at Chipstone.* Madison: The University of Wisconsin Press, 1984.

Roe 1977   Roe, Albert S. "Robert Sanderson's Silver Caudle Cup in the Winterthur Collection: The Turkey Motif in Seventeenth Century Design." *American Art Journal* 9 (May 1977): 61–77.

Roe/Trent 1982   Roe, Albert S., and Robert F. Trent. "Robert Sanderson and the Founding of the Boston Silversmith's Trade." In *New England Begins: The Seventeenth Century,* edited by Jonathan L. Fairbanks and Robert F. Trent, 3:480–89. Boston: Museum of Fine Arts, 1982.

Rollins n.d.   Rollins, J. R. "Marriages in Lunenberg Prior to 1750 and Admissions to Church in Lunenberg for 1733–1750." Handwritten, unpaginated, New England Historic Genealogical Society, Boston.

Rosenbaum 1954   Rosenbaum, Jeanette W. *Myer Myers, Goldsmith, 1723–1795.* Philadelphia: Jewish Publication Society of America, 1954.

Rowley VR   *Vital Records of Rowley, Massachusetts, to the End of the Year 1849.* Salem, Mass.: Essex Institute, 1928.

Roxbury Epitaphs   *Historical Sketch of the First Burying Place in Roxbury (Eustice St. Burying Ground) and Records of Deaths and Burials from First Church Records and First Town Records from 1630 to 1689.* No pub.

Roxbury VR   *Vital Records of Roxbury, Massachusetts, to the End of the Year 1848.* Salem, Mass.: Essex Institute, 1925–26.

Sabine 1864   Sabine, Lorenzo. *Biographical Sketches of Loyalists of the American Revolution, with an Historical Essay.* Boston: Little, Brown, 1864.

Sack Collection   *American Antiques from the Israel Sack Collection.* 8 vols. Washington, D.C.: Highland House Publishers, 1969–86.

Safford 1983   Safford, Frances Gruber. "Colonial Silver in the American Wing." *The Metropolitan Museum of Art Bulletin* 41 (Summer 1983).

Salem VR   *Vital Records of Salem, Massachusetts, to the End of the Year 1849.* 6 vols. Salem, Mass.: Essex Institute, 1916–25.

Salisbury VR   *Vital Records of Salisbury, Massachusetts, to the End of the Year 1849.* Topsfield, Mass.: Topsfield Historical Society, 1915.

Sanborn 1903   Sanborn, Nathan P. *Gen. John Glover and His Marblehead Regiment in the Revolutionary War*. Marblehead, Mass.: Marblehead Historical Society, 1903.

Sanborn 1917   Sanborn, V. C. "The Grantees and Settlement of Hampton, New Hampshire." *Historical Collections of the Essex Institute* 53 (1917): 228–49.

Sander 1982   Sander, Penny J., ed. *Elegant Embellishments: Furnishings from New England Homes, 1660–1860*. Boston: Society for the Preservation of New England Antiquities, 1982.

Sander 1986   Sander, Penny J. "Collections of the Society." *Antiques* 129 (March 1986): 596–605.

Sargent 1887   Sargent, William M., comp. and ed. *Maine Wills, 1640–1760*. Portland, Me.: Thurston, 1887.

Saunders/Miles 1987   Saunders, Richard H., and Ellen G. Miles. *American Colonial Portraits, 1700–1776*. Washington: Smithsonian Institution Press for the National Portrait Gallery, 1987.

Savage 1860–62   Savage, James. *A Genealogical Dictionary of the First Settlers of New England*. 4 vols. Boston: Little, Brown and Co., 1860–62.

SCCR 1940   *Abstract and Index of the Records of the Inferior Court of Pleas, Suffolk County Court Held at Boston 1680–1698*. Boston, 1940.

Schiffer 1978   Schiffer, Peter, Nancy Schiffer, and Herbert Schiffer. *The Brass Book*. Exton, Pa.: Schiffer Publishing, 1978.

Schofield 1899   Schofield, George A., ed. *The Ancient Records of the Town of Ipswich, vol. 1 from 1634 to 1650*. Ipswich, Mass.: Chronicle Motor Press, 1899.

Scituate VR   *Vital Records of Scituate, Massachusetts, to the Year 1850*. 2 vols. Boston: New England Historic Genealogical Society at the Charge of the Eddy Town Record Fund, 1909.

Scott 1957   Scott, Kenneth. *Counterfeiting in Colonial America*. New York: Oxford University Press, 1957.

Scott 1958   Scott, Kenneth. "Eight Silversmiths of Portsmouth, New Hampshire." *Antiques* 74 (August 1958): 144–45.

Scott 1960   Scott, Kenneth. "Daniel Greenough, Colonial Silversmith of Portsmouth." *Historical New Hampshire* 15 (November 1960): 26–31.

Selleck 1976   Selleck, George A. *Quakers in Boston, 1656–1964: Three Centuries of Friends in Boston and Cambridge*. Cambridge, Mass.: Friends Meeting at Cambridge, 1976.

Sewall Diary   Thomas, M. Halsey, ed. *The Diary of Samuel Sewall, 1674–1729*. 2 vols. New York: Farrar, Straus and Giroux, 1973.

Sewall Letter Book   Sewall, Samuel. *Letter Book*. Collections of the Massachusetts Historical Society, 6th ser., vols. 1 and 2. Boston, 1886.

Seybolt 1939   Seybolt, Robert F. *Town Officials of Colonial Boston*. Cambridge: Harvard University Press, 1939.

Shadwell 1969   Shadwell, Wendy J. *American Printmaking: The First 150 Years*. New York: Museum of Graphic Art, 1969.

Shadwell 1969a   Shadwell, Wendy J. "An Attribution of His Excellency and Lady Washington." *Antiques* 95 (February 1969): 240–41.

Sharples 1906   Sharples, Stephen P., ed. *Records of the Church of Christ at Cambridge in New England, 1632–1830*. Boston: Eben Putnam, 1906.

Sheldon 1895–96   Sheldon, George. *History of Deerfield, Massachusetts*. 2 vols. Deerfield, Mass.: Pocumtuck Valley Memorial Association, 1895–96.

Shelley 1958   Shelley, Donald A. "Henry Ford and the Museum: The Silver." *Antiques* 73 (February 1958): 174–77.

Shepard 1978   Shepard, Lewis A. *American Art at Amherst: A Summary Catalogue of the Collection at the Mead Art Gallery Amherst College.* Middletown, Conn.: Wesleyan University Press, 1978.

Sherborn VR   Baldwin, Thomas W., comp. *Vital Records of Sherborn, Massachusetts, to the Year 1850.* Boston: New England Historic Genealogical Society, 1911.

Sherman 1974   Sherman, Roy V. *The New England Shermans.* No pub., 1974.

Shurtleff 1853   Shurtleff, Nathaniel B., ed. *Records of the Governor and Company of the Massachusetts Bay in New England.* 6 vols. 1853. Reprint. New York: AMS Press, 1968.

Sibley 1982   Sibley, James Scarborough. *The Sibley Family in America, 1629–1972.* 2 vols. Midlothian, Tex.: Privately printed, 1982.

Sibley's Harvard Graduates 1   Sibley, John Langdon. *Biographical Sketches of Graduates of Harvard University.* Vol. 1, 1642–1658. Cambridge, Mass.: Charles William Sever, 1873.

Sibley's Harvard Graduates 2   Sibley, John Langdon. *Biographical Sketches of Graduates of Harvard University.* Vol. 2, 1659–1677. Cambridge, Mass.: Charles William Sever, 1881.

Sibley's Harvard Graduates 3   Sibley, John Langdon. *Biographical Sketches of Graduates of Harvard University in Cambridge, Massachusetts.* Vol. 3, 1678–1689. Cambridge, Mass.: Charles William Sever, 1885.

Sibley's Harvard Graduates 4   Shipton, Clifford K. *Biographical Sketches of Those Who Attended Harvard College in the Classes 1690–1700.* Vol 4. Cambridge: Harvard University Press, 1933.

Sibley's Harvard Graduates 5   Shipton, Clifford K. *Biographical Sketches of Those Who Attended Harvard College in the Classes 1701–1712.* Vol. 5. Boston: Massachusetts Historical Society, 1937.

Sibley's Harvard Graduates 6   Shipton, Clifford K. *Biographical Sketches of Those Who Attended Harvard College in the Classes 1713–1721.* Boston: Massachusetts Historical Society, 1942.

Sibley's Harvard Graduates 7   Shipton, Clifford K. *Biographical Sketches of Those Who Attended Harvard College in the Classes 1722–1725.* Boston: Massachusetts Historical Society, 1945.

Sibley's Harvard Graduates 8   Shipton, Clifford K. *Biographical Sketches of Those Who Attended Harvard University in the Classes 1726–1730.* Boston: Massachusetts Historical Society, 1951.

Sibley's Harvard Graduates 9   Shipton, Clifford K. *Biographical Sketches of Those Who Attended Harvard University in the Classes 1731–1735.* Boston: Massachusetts Historical Society, 1956.

Sibley's Harvard Graduates 10   Shipton, Clifford K. *Biographical Sketches of Those Who Attended Harvard University in the Classes 1736–1740.* Boston: Massachusetts Historical Society, 1958.

Sibley's Harvard Graduates 11   Shipton, Clifford K. *Biographical Sketches of Those Who Attended Harvard University in the Classes 1741–1745.* Boston: Massachusetts Historical Society, 1960.

Sibley's Harvard Graduates 12   Shipton, Clifford K. *Biographical Sketches of Those Who Attended Harvard University in the Classes 1746–1750.* Boston: Massachusetts Historical Society, 1962.

Sibley's Harvard Graduates 13   Shipton, Clifford K. *Biographical Sketches of Those Who Attended Harvard University in the Classes 1751–1755.* Boston: Massachusetts Historical Society, 1965.

Sibley's Harvard Graduates 14   Shipton, Clifford K. *Biographical Sketches of Those Who Attended Harvard University in the Classes 1756–1760.* Boston: Massachusetts Historical Society, 1968.

Sibley's Harvard Graduates 15   Shipton, Clifford K. *Biographical Sketches of Those Who Attended Harvard University in the Classes 1761–1763.* Boston: Massachusetts Historical Society, 1970.

Sibley's Harvard Graduates 16   Shipton, Clifford K. *Biographical Sketches of Those Who Attended Harvard University in the Classes 1764–1767.* Boston: Massachusetts Historical Society, 1972.

Sibley's Harvard Graduates 17   Shipton, Clifford K. *Biographical Sketches of Those Who Attended Harvard University in the Classes 1768–1771.* Boston: Massachusetts Historical Society, 1975.

Sigourney 1857   Sigourney, Henry H. W. *Genealogy of the Sigourney Family.* Boston and Cambridge: James Munroe, 1857.

Silver Supplement 1973   *Silver Supplement to the Guidebook to the Diplomatic Reception Rooms.* Washington, D.C.: Department of State, 1973.

Skerry 1983   Skerry, Janine E. *Made by Design: American Silver from the 17th to the 20th Century.* Exhibition catalogue. Fitchburg, Mass.: Fitchburg Art Museum, 1983.

Skerry 1984   Skerry, Janine E. "The Philip H. Hammerslough Collection of American Silver at the Wadsworth Atheneum, Hartford, Connecticut." *Antiques* 126 (October 1984): 852–59.

Skerry 1988   Skerry, Janine E. "The Revolutionary Revere: A Critical Assessment of the Silver of Paul Revere." In *Paul Revere—Artisan, Businessman, and Patriot: The Man Behind the Myth,* 40–63. Boston: Paul Revere Memorial Association, 1988.

Skinner   Skinner, Inc., Bolton, Massachusetts

Smith 1849   Willis, William, ed. *Journals of the Rev. Thomas Smith, and the Rev. Samuel Deane, Pastors of the First Church in Portland.* 2d ed. Portland, Me.: Joseph S. Bailey, 1849.

Smith 1939   Smith, Helen Burr. "Wm. Cario's Life History Less Vague." *New York Sun* (29 July 1939): 6.

Smith 1945–46   Smith, Mrs. Allan F. "Bermuda Silversmiths and Their Silver." *Bermuda Historical Quarterly* 2 (October–December 1945): 170–80; 3 (January–March 1946): 5–14.

Smith 1981   Smith, Billy G. "Material Lives of Laboring Philadelphians: 1750–1800." *William and Mary Quarterly.* 3d ser. 38 (1981): 163–202.

Snodin 1990   Snodin, Michael. "Paul de Lamerie's Rococo." In *Paul de Lamerie At the Sign of the Golden Ball,* edited by Susan Hare, 16–23. London: Goldsmiths' Hall, 1990.

Snow 1962   Snow, Barbara. "Corporate Collecting." *Antiques* 81 (March 1962): 300–03.

Social Circle in Concord 1882   *The Centennial of the Social Circle in Concord.* Cambridge, Mass.: Riverside Press, 1882.

Sotheby's   Sotheby's, New York

Sotheby Parke Bernet   Sotheby Parke Bernet, Inc., New York

Spang 1962   Spang, Joseph Peter, III. "The Parker and Russell Silver Shop in Old Deerfield." *Antiques* 81 (June 1962): 638–41.

Spear 1961   Spear, Dorothea N. *Bibliography of American Directories through 1860.* Worcester, Mass.: American Antiquarian Society, 1961.

Spencer 1994   Spencer, Hope. "The Identification Is in the Piece: A Process To Try." *Silver* 26 (July–August 1994): 21–23.

Spies 1931   Spies, Francis F. "Stockbridge, Mass., Earliest Town Records 1739–1800 with Genealogical Notes and a List of Revolutionary Soldiers." Typescript, 1931.

Spinney 1942   Spinney, Frank O. "Daniel Greenough: Early New Hampshire Silversmith." *Antiques* 41 (June 1942): 371–73.

Sprague 1987   Sprague, Laura Fecych, ed. *Agreeable Situations: Society, Commerce, and Art in Southern Maine, 1780–1830.* Kennebunk, Me.: Brick Store Museum, 1987.

Stachiw 1979   Stachiw, Myron O. *Massachusetts Officers and Soldiers, 1723–1743. Dummer's War to the War of Jenkin's Ear.* Boston: Society of Colonial Wars in the Commonwealth of Massachusetts and New England Historic Genealogical Society, 1979.

Staniford 1960   Staniford, Edward F. *The Staniford Family History.* Sacramento: Published by the author, 1960.

Stanton 1891   Stanton, William A. *A Record Genealogical, Biographical, Statistical of Thomas Stanton of Connecticut.* Albany: Joel Munsell's Sons, 1891.

Starr Family   Starr, Burgis Pratt. *A History of the Starr Family of New England.* Hartford: Case, Lockwood and Brainard, 1879.

Stauffer 1907   Stauffer, David McNeely. *American Engravers upon Copper and Steel.* 2 vols. New York: Grolier Club of the City of New York, 1907.

Steblecki 1988   Steblecki, Edith J. "Fraternity, Philanthropy, and Revolution: Paul Revere and Freemasonry." In *Paul Revere—Artisan, Businessman, and Patriot: The Man Behind the Myth,* 116–47. Boston: Paul Revere Memorial Association, 1988.

Steiner 1897   Steiner, Bernard Christian. *A History of the Plantation of Menunkatuck and the Original Town of Guilford, Connecticut.* Baltimore: By the author, 1897.

Steinway 1960   Steinway, Ruth Gardner. *Memoirs of Samuel Davis of Plymouth, Massachusetts, 1765–1829.* Plymouth, Mass.: Rogers Print, 1960.

Stickney 1869   Stickney, Matthew Adams. *The Stickney Family: A Genealogical Memoir.* Salem, Mass.: Published by the author, 1869.

Stickney/Stickney 1976   Stickney, Edward, and Evelyn Stickney. *The Bells of Paul Revere, His Sons and Grandsons.* Privately printed, 1976.

Stiles 1794   Stiles, Ezra. *A History of the Three Judges of King Charles I: Major-General Whalley, Major-General Goffe, and Colonel Dixwell.* Hartford: Elisha Babcock, 1794.

Stiles 1904   Stiles, Henry R. *The History of Ancient Wethersfield, Connecticut.* 2 vols. New York: Grafton Press, 1904.

Stillinger 1990   Stillinger, Elizabeth. *American Antiques, The Hennage Collection.* Williamsburg, Va.: Colonial Williamsburg Foundation, 1990.

Stockwell 1904   Stockwell, Mary LeBaron. *Descendants of Francis LeBaron of Plymouth, Massachusetts.* Boston: T. R. Marvin & Son, 1904.

Stone 1843   Stone, Edwin M. *History of Beverly, Civil and Ecclesiastical, from Its Settlement in 1642 to 1842.* Boston: James Munroe, 1843.

Stone 1882   Stone, Waterman. "Descendants of Daniel Stone, of Dorchester, Mass." *New England Historic Genealogical Register* 36 (October 1882): 366–68.

Stonington VR   Barbour Collection, Connecticut State Library, Hartford

Stoughton VR   Endicott, Frederic, ed. *The Records of Births, Marriages and Deaths and Intentions of Marriage in the Town of Stoughton from 1797–1845, Preceded by the Records of the South Precinct of Dorchester from 1715 to 1727.* 7 vols. Canton, Mass.: W. Bease, 1896.

Stratford VR   Barbour Collection, Connecticut State Library, Hartford

Sudbury VR   Woods, H. E., ed. *Vital Records of Sudbury, Massachusetts, to the Year 1850.*

Boston: New England Historic Genealogical Society at the Charge of the Eddy Town Record Fund, 1903.

Suffolk Deeds   *Suffolk Deeds, 1640–1688.* Vols. 1–14. Boston: Rockwell and Churchill, 1880–1906.

Sutton VR   *Vital Records of Sutton, Massachusetts, to the End of the Year 1849.* Worcester, Mass.: F. P. Rice, 1907.

Swansea VR   Fiske, Jane Fletcher, and Margaret F. Costello, eds., transcribed by H. L. Peter Rounds. *Vital Records of Swansea, Massachusetts, to 1850.* Boston: New England Historic Genealogical Society, 1992.

Swift 1888   Swift, C. F. *Genealogical Notes of Barnstable Families Being a Reprint of the Amos Otis Papers Originally Published in the Barnstable Patriot.* Barnstable, Mass.: F. B. and F. P. Gross, 1888.

Swift 1910   Swift, C. W., ed. *Barnstable Town Records.* Yarmouthport, Mass.: C. W. Swift, 1910.

Tapley 1927   Tapley, Harriet Silvester. *Salem Imprints, 1768–1825.* Salem, Mass.: Essex Institute, 1927.

Tapley 1930   Tapley, Harriet S. "The Ledger of Edward Lang, Silversmith of Salem." *Essex Institute Historical Collections* 66 (July 1930): 325–29.

Tappan 1834   "Memoir of Mrs. Sarah Tappan: Family Record." Typescript, Bigelow–Phillips files, 1187–92.

Tappan 1870   Tappan, Lewis. *The Life of Arthur Tappan.* New York: Hurd and Houghton, 1870.

Tappan 1915   Tappan, Daniel Langdon. *Tappan–Toppan Genealogy: Ancestors and Descendants of Abraham Toppan of Newbury, Massachusetts, 1606–1672.* Arlington, Mass.: Privately printed, 1915.

Teele 1887   Teele, Albert Kendall, ed. *The History of Milton, Massachusetts, 1640–1887.* Boston: Rockwell and Churchill, 1887.

Temple/Sheldon 1875   Temple, J. H., and George Sheldon. *History of the Town of Northfield, Massachusetts, for 150 Years, with an Account of the Prior Occupation of the Territory by the Squakheags, and with Family Genealogies.* Albany: Joel Munsell, 1875.

Thayer 1884   Thayer, Oliver. "Early Recollections of the Upper Portion of Essex Street." *Essex Institute Historical Collections* 21 (July, August, September 1884): 211–24.

Thomas [1810] 1970   Thomas, Isaiah. *The History of Printing in America.* 1810. Reprint. New York: Weathervane Books, 1970.

Thomas 1988   Thomas, Mary Lou. "Name Research on Silver." *Silver* 21 (March–April 1988): 16–17.

Thompson VR   Barbour Collection, Connecticut State Library, Hartford

Thorn 1949   Thorn, C. Jordan. *Handbook of American Silver and Pewter Marks.* New York: Tudor, 1949.

Thwing   Thwing Catalogue, Massachusetts Historical Society, Boston

Thwing 1920   Thwing, Annie Haven. *The Crooked and Narrow Streets of the Town of Boston, 1630–1822.* Boston: Marshall Jones, 1920.

Tillotson 1899   Tillotson, Edward Sweetser. *Wethersfield Inscriptions.* Hartford: William F. J. Boardman, 1899.

Topsfield VR   *Vital Records of Topsfield, Massachusetts, to the End of the Year 1849.* Topsfield, Mass.: Topsfield Historical Society, 1903.

Torrey 1990   Torrey, Clarence Almon. *New England Marriages Prior to 1700.* Baltimore:

Genealogical Publishing Co., 1990.

Town Records of Salem *Town Records of Salem, Massachusetts, 1634–1691.* 3 vols. Salem, Mass.: Essex Institute, 1934.

Trask 1869 Trask, William Blake. "Milton Church Records, 1678–1754." *New England Historic Genealogical Register* 23 (October 1869): 445–50.

Trent 1980 Trent, Robert F. "Two Seventeenth–Century Salem Upholstered Chairs." *Essex Institute Historical Collections* 116 (January 1980): 34–40.

Trueman 1975 Trueman, Howard. *The Chignecto Isthmus and Its First Settlers.* Belleville, Ontario: Mika, 1975.

Trumbull 1898–1902 Trumbull, James Russell. *History of Northampton, Massachusetts, from Its Settlement in 1654.* 2 vols. Northampton, Mass.: Press of Gazette Printing Co., 1898–1902. A supplemental typescript volume at the New England Historic Geneological Society, Boston, contains "Northampton Genealogies."

Truro VR Bowman, George Ernest, transcriber. *Vital Records of the Town of Truro, Massachusetts, to the End of the Year 1849.* Boston: Massachusetts Society of Mayflower Descendants, 1933.

Tudor 1896 Tudor, William, ed. *Deacon Tudor's Diary.* Boston: W. Spooner Press, 1896.

Tvrdik 1977 Tvrdik, Valerie, ed. *The Antiquarian Society of the Art Institute of Chicago: The First One Hundred Years.* Chicago: Art Institute of Chicago, 1977.

Untracht 1975 Untracht, Oppi. *Metal Techniques for Craftsmen.* Garden City, N.Y.: Doubleday, 1975.

Upham 1905 Upham, William P. *Records of the First Church in Beverly, Massachusetts, 1667–1772.* Salem, Mass.: Essex Institute, 1905.

Upton VR *Vital Records of Upton, Massachusetts, to the End of the Year 1849.* Worcester, Mass.: F. P. Rice, 1904.

Usher 1886 Usher, James. *History of the Town of Medford.* Boston: Rand Avery, 1886.

Uxbridge VR Baldwin, Thomas W., comp. *Vital Records of Uxbridge, Massachusetts, to the Year 1850.* Boston: Wright & Potter, 1916.

Von Khrum 1978 Von Khrum, Paul. *Silversmiths of New York City 1684–1850.* New York: Privately printed, 1978.

Voye 1975 Voye, Nancy S., ed. *Massachusetts Officers in the French and Indian Wars, 1748–1763.* Boston: Society of Colonial Wars in the Commonwealth of Massachusetts and New England Historic Genealogical Society, 1975.

Wakefield VR Baldwin, Thomas W., comp. *Vital Records of Wakefield, Massachusetts, to the Year 1850.* Boston: Wright & Potter, 1912.

Walsh 1959 Walsh, Richard. *Charleston's Sons of Liberty: A Study of the Artisans, 1763–1789.* Columbia: University of South Carolina Press, 1959.

WAM 1913 *Old Silver Owned in Worcester County.* Worcester, Mass.: Worcester Art Museum, 1913.

WAM 1965 *Paul Revere (1735–1818): The Events of His Life Painted by A. Lassell Ripley and Some Examples of His Silver and Prints.* Worcester, Mass.: Worcester Art Museum, 1965.

Ward 1858 Ward, Andrew Henshaw. *A Genealogical History of the Rice Family: Descendants of Deacon Edmund Rice.* Boston: C. Benjamin Richardson, 1858.

Ward 1980 Ward, Barbara McLean. "American Silver and Gold in the Yale University Art Gallery." *Antiques* 117 (June 1980): 1300–03.

Ward 1983 Ward, Barbara McLean. "The Craftsman in a Changing Society: Boston

Goldsmiths, 1690–1730." Ph.D. diss., Boston University, 1983.

Ward 1984   Ward, Barbara McLean. "Boston Goldsmiths, 1690–1730." In *The Craftsman in Early America*, edited by Ian M. G. Quimby, 126–57. New York and London: W. W. Norton, 1984.

Ward 1984a   Ward, Gerald W. R. "Silver and Society in Salem, Massachusetts, 1630–1820: A Case Study of the Consumer and the Craft." Ph.D. diss., Boston University, 1984.

Ward 1989   Ward, Barbara McLean. "The Edwards Family and the Silversmithing Trade in Boston, 1692–1762." In *The American Craftsman and the European Tradition, 1620–1820*, edited by Francis J. Puig and Michael Conforti, 66–91. Minneapolis: Minneapolis Institute of Arts, 1989.

Ward 1990   Ward, Barbara McLean. "Hierarchy and Wealth Distribution in the Boston Goldsmithing Trade, 1690–1760." *Essex Institute Historical Collections* 126 (July 1990): 129–47.

Ward/Hosley 1985   Ward, Gerald W. R., and William N. Hosley, Jr., eds. *The Great River: Art and Society of the Connecticut Valley, 1635–1820*. Hartford: Wadsworth Atheneum, 1985.

Ward/Rowland 1992   Ward, Gerald W. R., and Rodney D. Rowland. "Strawbery Banke Museum: The Metals." *Antiques* 142 (July 1992): 90–93.

Ward/Ward 1979   Ward, Barbara McLean, and Gerald W. R. Ward, eds. *Silver in American Life*. New York and New Haven: American Federation of Arts and Yale University Art Gallery, 1979.

Warden 1970   Warden, G. B. *Boston, 1689–1776*. Boston: Little, Brown, 1970.

Wardwell 1966   Wardwell, Allen. "One Hundred Years of American Tankards." *Antiques* 90 (July 1966): 80–83.

Warren 1859   Warren, W. E. "The Belknap Family." *New England Historic and Genealogical Register* 13 (January 1859): 17–18.

Warren 1934–35   Warren, Thomas B. "Springfield Families." 2 vols. Typescript copied by Mercy Warren Chapter, Springfield, Mass., 1934–35.

Warren 1973   Warren, David B. "The Hooper Family Coffeepot by Paul Revere." *Antiques* 104 (December 1973): 1046–49.

Warren 1975   Warren, David B. *Bayou Bend: American Furniture, Paintings, and Silver from the Bayou Bend Collection*. Houston: Museum of Fine Arts, Houston, 1975.

Warren/Howe/Brown 1987   Warren, David B., Katherine S. Howe, Michael K. Brown. *Marks of Achievement: Four Centuries of American Presentation Silver*. Houston: Museum of Fine Arts, Houston, in association with Harry N. Abrams, New York, 1987.

Washington 1925   Washington Loan Exhibition Committee. *Exhibition of Early American Paintings, Miniatures and Silver*. Washington, D.C.: National Gallery of Art, National Museum, 1925.

Waterbury VR   Barbour Collection, Connecticut State Library, Hartford

Waters 1893   Waters, Henry F. "Genealogical Gleanings in England." *New England Historic Genealogical Register* 47 (January 1893): 104–40.

Waters 1893a   Waters, Henry F. "Genealogical Gleanings in England." *New England Historic Genealogical Register* 47 (April 1893): 244–92.

Waters 1893b   Waters, Henry F. "Genealogical Gleanings in England." *New England Historic Genealogical Register* 47 (October 1893): 497–532.

Waters 1901   Waters, Henry F. *Genealogical Gleanings in England*. 2 vols. Boston: New

England Historic Genealogical Society, 1901.

Waters 1917   Waters, Thomas Franklin. *Ipswich in the Massachusetts Bay Colony. Volume II. A History of the Town from 1700 to 1917.* Ipswich, Mass.: Ipswich Historical Society, 1917.

Watertown Records 1894   *Watertown Records.* 8 vols. Watertown, Mass.: Historical Society of Watertown, Massachusetts, 1894.

Watertown VR   Barbour Collection, Connecticut State Library, Hartford

Watkins 1957   Watkins, C. Malcolm. "The American Past in the Modern Spirit: The Smithsonian's New Hall." *Antiques* 71 (February 1957): 140–45.

Wayland VR   *Vital Records of Wayland, Massachusetts, to the Year 1850.* Boston: New England Historic Genealogical Society, 1910.

Weis (1936) 1977   Weis, Frederick Lewis. *The Colonial Clergy and the Colonial Churches of New England.* 1936. Reprint. Baltimore: Genealogical Publishing Co., 1977.

Weis 1958   Weis, Frederick Lewis. *Early Generations of the Family of Robert Harrington of Watertown, Massachusetts, 1634, and Some of His Descendants.* Worcester, Mass.: Privately published, 1958.

Weisberger 1977   Weisberger, Bernard A. "Paul Revere: The Man, the Myth, and the Midnight Ride." *American Heritage* 28 (April 1977): 24–37.

Wells/Wells 1910   Wells, Daniel White, and Reuben Field Wells. *A History of Hatfield, Massachusetts.* Springfield, Mass.: F. C. H. Gibbons, 1910.

Wenham VR   *Vital Records of Wenham, Massachusetts, to the End of the Year 1849.* Salem, Mass.: Essex Institute, 1904.

Wenham 1931   Wenham, Edward. "The Silversmiths of Early Boston: Being the Third of a Series Surveying the General Activities of the Silversmith's Craft in the Metropolitan Centers of Early America." *The Antiquarian* 17 (July 1931): 31–34, 60.

"Westfield Deaths"   "An Account or Register of the Deaths of Those Deceased in Westfield, 1728–1836, from the Record of the First Church of Westfield." Typescript, New England Historic Genealogical Society, Boston, 1936.

"Westfield Marriages"   "Westfield Marriage Records as Obtained from the Files at City Hall, Westfield." Typescript, New England Historic Geneological Society, Boston, 1937.

Weston VR   Town of Weston: Births, Deaths, and Marriages, 1707–1850; 1703—Gravestones—1900; Church Records, 1709–1825. Boston: McIndoe Bros., 1901.

Wethersfield VR   Barbour Collection, Connecticut State Library, Hartford

Weymouth VR   *Vital Records of Weymouth, Massachusetts, to the Year 1850.* Boston: New England, Historic Genealogical Society at the Charge of the Eddy Town Record Fund, 1910.

Wheat/Brun 1985   Wheat, James Clement, and Christian F. Brun. *Maps and Charts Published in America before 1800: A Bibliography.* 2d rev. ed. London: Holland Press, 1985.

Wheatland 1863   Wheatland, Henry. "Materials for a Genealogy of the Higginson Family." *Essex Institute Historical Collections* 5 (February 1863): 33–42.

Wheeler 1875   Wheeler, Richard A. *History of the First Congregational Church, Stonington, Connecticut, 1674–1874.* Norwich, Conn.: T. H. Davis, 1875.

Whitcomb/Mayo 1985   Whitcomb, Esther, and Dorothy Mayo. *Bolton Soldiers and Sailors of the American Revolution.* Bowie, Md.: Heritage Books, 1985.

Whitcomb 1938   Whitcomb, Esther K. *History of Bolton, 1738–1938.* Bolton, Mass.: Privately printed, 1938.

Whitehill et al. 1975   Whitehill, Walter Muir, et al. *Paul Revere's Boston: 1735–1818.* Boston: Museum of Fine Arts, Boston, 1975.

Whitman 1842   Whitman, Zachariah G. *The History of the Ancient and Honorable Artillery Company.* Boston: John H. Eastburn, Printer, 1842.

Whitmore 1878   Whitmore, William H. *The Graveyards of Boston. First Volume, Copp's Hill Epitaphs.* Albany: Joel Munsell, 1878.

Whitmore 1969   Whitmore, William H. *The Massachusetts Civil List for the Provincial Periods 1630–1774.* Reprint. Baltimore: Genealogical Publishing Co., 1969.

Whittemore 1893   Whittemore, B. B. *Whittemore Genealogy: A Genealogy of Several Branches of the Whittemore Family.* Nashua, N.H.: Francis P. Whittemore, 1893.

Willard (1911) 1968   Willard, John Ware. *Simon Willard and His Clocks.* 1911. Reprint. New York: Dover, 1968.

Willis 1831–33   Willis, William. *History of Portland.* 2 vols. Portland, Me.: Day, Fraser, 1831–33.

Willis 1849   Willis, William, ed. *Journals of the Rev. Thomas Smith and the Rev. Samuel Deane, Pastors of the First Church in Portland with Notes and Biographical Notices and a Summary History of Portland.* 2d ed. Portland, Me.: Joseph S. Bailey, 1849.

Willis 1865   Willis, William. *The History of Portland from 1632 to 1864: With a Notice of Previous Settlements, Colonial Grants, and Changes of Government in Maine.* Portland: Bailey and Noyes, 1865.

Wilson 1968   Wilson, Philip. "Art at Auction 1967–68." *Antiques* 94 (October 1968): 558–61.

Winchendon VR   *Vital Records of Winchendon, Massachusetts, to the End of the Year 1849.* Worcester, Mass.: F. P. Rice, 1909.

Winchester 1952   Winchester, Alice. "The London Antiques Fair." *Antiques* 62 (September 1952): 220–23.

Winchester 1956   Winchester, Alice. "Colonial Silversmiths—Masters and Apprentices." *Antiques* 70 (December 1956): 552–55.

The Winslows 1974   *The Winslows—Pilgrims, Patrons & Portraits.* Boston: Museum of Fine Arts, Boston, 1974.

Winsor 1880–81   Winsor, Justin, ed. *The Memorial History of Boston.* 4 vols. Boston: James R. Osgood and Co. and Ticknor and Co., 1880–81.

Witness to America's Past   Staff of the Massachusetts Historical Society. *Witness to America's Past: Two Centuries of Collecting by the Massachusetts Historical Society.* Boston: Massachusetts Historical Society and Museum of Fine Arts, Boston, 1991.

Wittmeyer 1886   Wittmeyer, Alfred V., ed. "Register of the Births, Marriages, and Deaths of the 'Eglise François à la Nouvelle York,' from 1688 to 1804," *Collections of the Huguenot Society of America.* Vol 1. New York: Published by the Society, 1886.

Woburn VR   Johnson, Edward F. *Woburn Record of Births, Marriages and Deaths from 1640 to 1873.* Woburn, Mass.: Andrews, Cutler, 1890.

Wood 1965   Wood, Ralph V., Jr. *Herkimer County, New York State: Federal Population Census Schedules 1800, 1810, 1820.* Cambridge, Mass.: no pub., 1965.

Woodstock VR   Barbour Collection, Connecticut State Library, Hartford

Woodworth–Barnes 1990–91   Woodworth–Barnes, Esther Littleford. "Descendants of Ellis Callender of Boston." *New England Historic Genealogical Register* 144 (July 1990): 195–210; (October 1990): 319–30; 145 (January 1991): 31–43.

Worcester Society of Antiquity   *Collection of the Worcester Society of Antiquity.* Vol. 8. Worcester, Mass.: Worcester Society of Antiquity, 1890.

Worcester VR Rice, Franklin P., comp. *Worcester Births, Marriages, and Deaths.* Worcester, Mass.: Worcester Society of Antiquity, 1894.

Works of Benjamin Franklin *The Works of Benjamin Franklin.* 6 vols. Philadelphia: William Duane, 1809.

Worthley 1970 Worthley, Harold Field. *Harvard Theological Studies XXV: An Inventory of the Records of the Particular (Congregational) Churches of Massachusetts Gathered 1620–1805).* Cambridge: Harvard University Press; London: Oxford University Press, 1970.

Wrentham VR Baldwin, Thomas W., comp. *Vital Records of Wrentham, Massachusetts, to the Year 1850.* 2 vols. Boston: Stanhope Press, 1910.

Wright 1917 Wright, O. O. *History of Swansea.* Swansea, Mass.: The Town, 1917.

Wright 1966 Wright, Philip. *Monumental Inscriptions of Jamaica.* London: Society of Genealogists, 1966.

Wroth 1926 Wroth, Lawrence C. *Abel Buell of Connecticut, Silversmith, Type Founder, and Engraver.* 1926. 2d ed. Middletown, Conn.: Wesleyan University Press, 1958.

Wyman 1853 Wyman, Thomas B., Jr. "Pedigree of the Family of Boylston." *New England Historic Genealogical Register* 7 (April 1853): 145–50.

Wyman 1862–63 Wyman, T. B., Jr., comp. *Genealogy of the Name and Family of Hunt.* Boston: Printed by John Wilson and Son, 1862–63.

Wyman 1864–65 Wyman, Thomas B., Jr. "New Brick Church, Boston: List of Persons Connected therewith from 1722 to 1775." *New England Historic Genealogical Register* 18 (July 1864): 237–40; 18 (October 1864): 337–44; 19 (July 1865): 230–35; 19 (October 1864): 320–24.

Wyman 1879 Wyman, Thomas Bellows. *The Genealogies and Estates of Charlestown.* 2 vols. Boston: David Clapp and Son, 1879.

Yarmouth VR Sherman, Robert M., and Ruth Wilder Sherman. *Vital Records of Yarmouth, Massachusetts, to the Year 1850.* Warwick, R.I.: Society of Mayflower Descendants in the State of Rhode Island, 1975.

Ye Ancient Buriall Place of New London, Conn. *Ye Ancient Buriall Place of New London, Conn.* New London, Conn.: Day, 1917.

York Deeds *York Deeds.* 18 vols. Portland, Me.: J. T. Hull et al., 1887–1910.

York VR Bragdon, Lester MacKenzie, and John Eldridge Frost, transcribers. *Vital Records of York, Maine.* Camden, Me.: Picton Press, 1992.

Zea/Cheney Zea, Philip, and Robert C. Cheney. *Clock Making in New England, 1725–1825: An Interpretation of the Old Sturbridge Village Collection.* Sturbridge, Mass.: Old Sturbridge Village, 1992.

Abbreviations

AAS	American Antiquarian Society, Worcester, Massachusetts
AG	Addison Gallery of American Art, Phillips Academy, Andover, Massachusetts
AIC	The Art Institute of Chicago
AIHA	Albany Institute of History and Art
AMB	American Museum in Britain, Bath, England
BBC	Bayou Bend Collection, Museum of Fine Arts, Houston
BCCR	Barnstable County Court Records, Barnstable County Courthouse, Barnstable, Massachusetts. Surviving records include those from the Court of General Sessions of the Peace, the Court of Common Pleas, and the Superior Court.
BCD	Barnstable County Deeds, Barnstable County Courthouse, Barnstable, Massachusetts
BCMA	Bowdoin College Museum of Art, Brunswick, Maine
BCPR	Barnstable County Probate Records, Barnstable County Courthouse, Barnstable, Massachusetts
Berger photograph file	Florence Paull Berger card and photograph file on American silversmiths, Bigelow-Phillips files, Yale University Art Gallery, New Haven
BerkCD	Berkshire County Deeds, Berkshire County Courthouse, Pittsfield, Massachusetts
Bigelow-Phillips files	Research notes of Francis Hill Bigelow and John Marshall Phillips, 13 vols. and oversized photostats, American Arts Office, Yale University Art Gallery, New Haven
BM	The Brooklyn Museum
BMA	The Baltimore Museum of Art
BPL	Boston Public Library
BrCD	Bristol County Deeds, Bristol County Courthouse, Taunton, Massachusetts
BrCPR	Bristol County Probate Records, Bristol County Courthouse, Taunton, Massachusetts
CAM	Cincinnati Art Museum
CaMA	The Carnegie Museum of Art, Pittsburgh
Campbell Museum	Campbell Museum, Camden, New Jersey
CCD	Cumberland County Deeds, Cumberland County Courthouse, Portland, Maine

CD Coventry Deeds, Town Clerk's Office, Coventry, Connecticut

CF Chipstone Foundation, Milwaukee

CGA The Currier Gallery of Art, Manchester, New Hampshire

ChM The Chrysler Museum, Norfolk

CHS Connecticut Historical Society, Hartford

CM Concord Museum, Concord, Massachusetts

CMA The Cleveland Museum of Art

CSL Connecticut State Library, Hartford

CVHM Connecticut Valley Historical Museum, Springfield, Massachusetts

CW Colonial Williamsburg, Williamsburg, Virginia

DAI Dayton Art Institute, Dayton, Ohio

DAPC Decorative Arts Photographic Collection, The Henry Francis du Pont Winter-thur Museum, Winterthur, Delaware

DAR Museum Daughters of the American Revolution Museum, Washington, D.C.

DeYoung The Fine Arts Museums of San Francisco, M. H. DeYoung Memorial Museum

DIA The Detroit Institute of Arts

DMA Dallas Museum of Art

ECD Essex County Deeds, Essex County Courthouse, Salem, Massachusetts

ECCR Essex County Court Records, Court of Common Pleas, the Court of General Sessions of the Peace, and the Superior Court, Essex County Courthouse, Salem, Massachusetts

ECPR Essex County Probate Records, Registry of Probate, Essex County Courthouse, Salem, Massachusetts

FCCR Franklin County Court Records, Franklin County Courthouse, Greenfield, Massachusetts. The surviving records include those from the Court of General Sessions of the Peace, the Court of Common Pleas, and the Superior Court.

FCD Franklin County Deeds, Franklin County Courthouse, Greenfield, Massachu-setts

FCPR Franklin County Probate Records, Franklin County Courthouse, Green-field, Massachusetts

HaCD Hampshire County Deeds, Hampshire County Courthouse, Northampton, Massachusetts

HaCPR Hampshire County Probate Records, Hampshire County Courthouse, North-ampton, Massachusetts

HCCR Hampden County Court Records, Hampden County Courthouse, Springfield, Massachusetts. The surviving records include the Court of General Sessions of the Peace, the Court of Common Pleas, and the Superior Court.

HCD Hampden County Deeds, Hampden County Courthouse, Springfield, Massa-chusetts

HCPR Hampden County Probate Records, Hampden County Courthouse, Spring-field, Massachusetts

HD Historic Deerfield, Inc., Deerfield, Massachusetts

HFM Henry Ford Museum & Greenfield Village, Dearborn, Michigan

HMA Hood Museum of Art, Darmouth College, Hanover, New Hampshire

HP Heritage Plantation of Sandwich, Sandwich, Massachusetts

HSP Historical Society of Pennsylvania, Philadelphia

HU Harvard University, Cambridge, Massachusetts

IMA　Indianapolis Museum of Art

LACMA　Los Angeles County Museum of Art, Los Angeles

LAM　Lyman Allyn Art Museum, New London, Connecticut

MAM　Mead Art Museum, Amherst, Massachusetts

Mass. Archives　Massachusetts Archives, Columbia Point, Boston

MCCR　Middlesex County Court Records, Middlesex County Courthouse, Cambridge, Massachusetts

MCD　Middlesex County Deeds, Registry of Deeds, Middlesex County Courthouse, Cambridge, Massachusetts

MCHA　Monmouth County Historical Association, Freehold, New Jersey

MCNY　Museum of the City of New York

MCPR　Middlesex County Probate Records, Middlesex County Registry of Probate, Middlesex County Courthouse, Cambridge, Massachusetts

MeHS　Maine Historical Society, Portland

MFAB　Museum of Fine Arts, Boston

MFA, Houston　Museum of Fine Arts, Houston

MHS　Massachusetts Historical Society, Boston

MIA　The Minneapolis Institute of Arts

MMA　The Metropolitan Museum of Art, New York

MWPI　Munson-Williams-Proctor Institute Museum, Utica

Navy Museum　The Navy Museum, Department of the Navy, Navy Historical Center, Washington, D.C.

NCCR　Nantucket County Court Records, Nantucket County Courthouse, Nantucket, Massachusetts. The surviving records include the Court of General Sessions of the Peace, the Court of Common Pleas, and the Superior Court.

NCD　Nantucket County Deeds, Nantucket County Courthouse, Nantucket, Massachusetts

NCPR　Nantucket County Probate Records, Nantucket County Courthouse, Nantucket, Massachusetts

ND　Norwich Deeds, Town Clerk's Office, Norwich, Connecticut

NEHGS　New England Historic Genealogical Society, Boston

NHA　Nantucket Historical Association, Nantucket, Massachusetts

NHCHS　New Haven Colony Historical Society, New Haven

NHHS　New Hampshire Historical Society, Concord

NM　The Newark Museum

N-YHS　The New-York Historical Society, New York

OCHS　Old Colony Historical Society, Taunton, Massachusetts

ODHS　Old Dartmouth Historical Society, New Bedford, Massachusetts

OSV　Old Sturbridge Village, Sturbridge, Massachusetts

OYHS　Old York Historical Society, York, Maine

PCCR　Plymouth County Court Records, Plymouth County Courthouse, Plymouth, Massachusetts. Surviving records include the Court of General Sessions of the Peace and the Court of Common Pleas.

PCD　Plymouth County Deeds, Plymouth County Courthouse, Plymouth, Massachusetts

PCPR Plymouth County Probate Records, Plymouth County Courthouse, Plymouth, Massachusetts

PEM Peabody Essex Museum, Salem, Massachusetts

PHM Pilgrim Hall Museum, Plymouth, Massachusetts

PHS Portsmouth Historical Society, Portsmouth, Rhode Island

PMA Philadelphia Museum of Art

PRMA Paul Revere Memorial Association, Boston

PS Pilgrim Society, Plymouth, Massachusetts

PVMA Pocumtuck Valley Memorial Association, Deerfield, Massachusetts

RCD Rockingham County Deeds, Rockingham County Courthouse, Exeter, New Hampshire

RCPR Rockingham County Probate Records, Rockingham County Courthouse, Exeter, New Hampshire

RIHS Rhode Island Historical Society, Providence

RISD Museum of Art, Rhode Island School of Design, Providence

RWNAG R. W. Norton Art Gallery, Shreveport

SB Strawbery Banke, Inc., Portsmouth, New Hampshire

SCCR Suffolk County Court Records are housed in numerous locations. Records of the Court of Common Pleas and the Supreme Judicial Court are at the Massachusetts Archives, Columbia Point, Boston. Some records have also been published. See Colonial Society 1933, Noble/Cronin 1901-28, and SCCR 1940 in *References*.

SCD Suffolk County Deeds, Registry of Deeds, Suffolk County Courthouse, Boston. The first fourteen volumes are published. See *Suffolk Deeds* in *References*.

SCPR Suffolk County Probate Records, Probate Registry, Suffolk County Courthouse, Boston

SFCAI Sterling and Francine Clark Art Institute, Williamstown, Massachusetts

SI Smithsonian Institution, Washington, D.C.

SLAM The Saint Louis Art Museum

SPNEA The Society for the Preservation of New England Antiquities, Boston

USDS Diplomatic Reception Rooms, United States Department of State, Washington, D.C.

VMFA Virginia Museum of Fine Arts, Richmond

WA Wadsworth Atheneum, Hartford

WAM Worcester Art Museum, Worcester, Massachusetts

WCCR Worcester County Court Records, Worcester County Courthouse, Worcester, Massachusetts. The surviving records include the Court of General Sessions of the Peace and the Court of Common Pleas.

WCD Worcester County Deeds, Worcester County Courthouse, Worcester, Massachusetts

WCPR Worcester County Probate Records, Worcester County Courthouse, Worcester, Massachusetts

WHS Woodstock Historical Society, Woodstock, Vermont

WM The Henry Francis du Pont Winterthur Museum, Winterthur, Delaware

YCCR York County Court Records, Maine State Archives, Augusta

YCD   York County Deeds, Registry of Deeds, York County Courthouse, Alfred, Maine. The first eighteen volumes are published. See *York Deeds* in *References*.

YIM   York Institute Museum, Saco, Maine

YU   Yale University, New Haven

YUAG   Yale University Art Gallery, New Haven

Photograph Credits

John Allen A Beaker: Yale University Art Gallery, Mabel Brady Garvan Collection, 1930.1248.

B Tablespoon: The Henry Francis du Pont Winterthur Museum, gift of Mr. and Mrs. Alfred E. Bissell, Ineson-Bissell Silver Collection, 62.240.867.

John Andrew A Ladle: Yale University Art Gallery, gift of Carl R. Kossack, B.S. 1931, M.A. 1933, 1986.103.29.

Isaac Anthony A Tablespoon: Yale University Art Gallery, Mabel Brady Garvan Collection, 1936.10.

B Tablespoon: National Museum of American History, Smithsonian Institution, gift of Arthur Michael, 383460.

Ebenezer Austin A Teaspoon: Yale University Art Gallery, Mabel Brady Garvan Collection, 1930.1471.

B Salt spoon: Yale University Art Gallery, gift of Philip K. Kossack, 1985.87.65.1.

Josiah Austin A Tablespoon: Yale University Art Gallery, Mabel Brady Garvan Collection, 1930.1265a.

B Beaker: Yale University Art Gallery, Bigelow-Phillips files, Berger photograph file.

C Creampot: Museum of Fine Arts, Boston, bequest of Henry W. Cunningham, 31.416.

D Teapot: Courtesy, The Henry Francis du Pont Winterthur Museum, 67.1906.

E Salt: The Metropolitan Museum of Art, bequest of A.T. Clearwater, 1933, 33.120.363. Photograph by Patricia E. Kane.

F Strainer: Yale University Art Gallery, Mabel Brady Garvan Collection, 1930.976.

Nathaniel Austin A Tablespoon: The Henry Francis du Pont Winterthur Museum, gift of Mr. and Mrs. Alfred E. Bissell, Ineson-Bissell Silver Collection, 62.0240.873.

B Tablespoon: The Henry Francis du Pont Winterthur Museum, gift of Mr. and Mrs. Alfred E. Bissell, Ineson-Bissell Silver Collection, 62.0240.874.

C Teaspoon: Historic Deerfield, Inc. Photograph by Patricia E. Kane.

D Teaspoon: Concord Museum. Photograph by Patricia E. Kane.

E Teapot: Concord Museum. Photograph by Patricia E. Kane.

       F Teaspoon: Yale University Art Gallery, gift of Josephine Setze in memory of John Marshall Phillips, 1965.26a.

Loring Bailey A Tablespoon: Museum of Fine Arts, Boston, gift of Thomas L. Sprague, 18.325.

Ebenezer Balch A Tablespoon: Connecticut Historical Society, A-472-4.

John Ball A Tankard: Yale University Art Gallery, Mabel Brady Garvan Collection, 1930.1231.

       B Tankard: Yale University Art Gallery, Mabel Brady Garvan Collection, 1930.1231.

       C Ring (gold): Yale University Art Gallery, Mabel Brady Garvan Collection, 1935.247.

Samuel Barrett A Tablespoon: The Henry Francis du Pont Winterthur Museum, gift of Mr. and Mrs. Alfred E. Bissell, Ineson-Bissell Silver Collection, 62.0240.905.001.

N. Bartlet A Tablespoon: The Henry Francis du Pont Winterthur Museum, gift of Mr. and Mrs. Alfred E. Bissell, Ineson-Bissell Silver Collection, 62.0240.910.

       B Teaspoon: Yale University Art Gallery, Mabel Brady Garvan Collection, 1936.238.

Israel Bartlett A Tablespoon: The Henry Francis du Pont Winterthur Museum, gift of Mr. and Mrs. Gail C. Belden, 72.0193.

       B Tablespoon: Yale University Art Gallery, Mabel Brady Garvan Collection, 1942.11.

Samuel Bartlett A Flagon: First Church, Boston. Photograph courtesy, Museum of Fine Arts, Boston, 168.40.

       B Creampot: Yale University Art Gallery, Mabel Brady Garvan Collection, 1930.1176.

       C Teapot (miniature): Yale University Art Gallery, Mabel Brady Garvan Collection, 1934.375.

Caleb Beal A Tablespoon: Yale University Art Gallery, gift of Frederick C. Kossack, 1985.86.64.

       B Tablespoon: The Henry Francis du Pont Winterthur Museum, gift of Mr. and Mrs. Alfred E. Bissell, Ineson-Bissell Silver Collection, 62.0240.913.

       C Teaspoon: Yale University Art Gallery, Mabel Brady Garvan Collection, 1935.589.

John Blowers A Tankard: Museum of Fine Arts, Boston, gift of Francis S. Eaton, 47.1487.

Daniel Boyer A Porringer: Yale University Art Gallery, gift of Mrs. Alexander Cushing Brown, 1949.227.

       B Sleeve buttons (gold): Yale University Art Gallery research files.

       C Spoon: Yale University Art Gallery, Bigelow-Phillips files, Berger photograph file.

       D Teaspoon: Yale University Art Gallery, gift of Carl R. Kossack, B.S. 1931, M.A. 1933, 1985.84.359.

       E Tablespoon: The Henry Francis du Pont Winterthur Museum, gift of Mr. and Mrs. Alfred E. Bissell, Ineson-Bissell Silver Collection, 62.0240.922.

       F Tablespoon: Yale University Art Gallery, gift of Frederick C. Kossack, 1985.86.84.

William Breed A Pepper box: The Metropolitan Museum of Art, bequest of Margaret N. Breck Stone, 1933, in memory of the Hall-Mansfield Families of New Haven, 33.71.3. Photograph by Patricia E. Kane.

B Porringer: Museum of Fine Arts, Boston, bequest of William Beltran de las Casas, 30.732.

C Porringer: Museum of Fine Arts, Boston, bequest of William Beltran de las Casas, 30.732.

John Bridge A Strainer: Museum of Fine Arts, Boston, gift of the Paul Revere Life Insurance Company, 64.497.

B Flagon: King's Chapel. Photograph courtesy, Museum of Fine Arts, Boston, 60.37.

C Flagon: King's Chapel. Photography courtesy, Museum of Fine Arts, Boston, 60.37.

Zachariah Brigden A Sugar bowl: Yale University Art Gallery, Mabel Brady Garvan Collection, 1930.1228.

B Chocolate pot: Museum of Fine Arts, Boston, gift of the Misses Rose and Elizabeth Townsend, 56.676.

C Tablespoon: The Henry Francis du Pont Winterthur Museum, gift of Mr. and Mrs. Alfred E. Bissell, Ineson-Bissell Silver Collection, 62.0240.985.

D Teaspoon: Yale University Art Gallery, gift of Carl R. Kossack, B.S. 1931, M.A. 1933, 1985.84.369.

E Teaspoon: The Mrs. John Emerson Marble Collection of Early American Silver. Photograph by Hope Spencer.

Benjamin Bunker A Tablespoon: Yale University Art Gallery, gift of Frederick C. Kossack, 1985.86.100.

B Tablespoon: Yale University Art Gallery, gift of Frederick C. Kossack, 1985.86.100.

Samuel Burrill A Flagon: First and Second Church, Boston. Photograph courtesy, Museum of Fine Arts, Boston, 30.67.

B Flagon: First and Second Church, Boston. Photograph courtesy, Museum of Fine Arts, Boston, 30.67.

Benjamin Burt A Cann: Yale University Art Gallery, Mabel Brady Garvan Collection, 1930.951b.

B Tablespoon: Historic Deerfield, Inc. Photograph by Patricia E. Kane.

C Strainer: Yale University Art Gallery, Mabel Brady Garvan Collection, 1930.1150.

John Burt A Tablespoon: The Henry Francis du Pont Winterthur Museum, gift of Mr. and Mrs. Alfred E. Bissell, Ineson-Bissell Silver Collection, 62.0240.973.

B Tablespoon: The Henry Francis du Pont Winterthur Museum, gift of Henry Francis du Pont, 1965, 59.3358.

C Strainer spoon: Museum of Fine Arts, Boston, gift of Arthur D. Foss, 39.14.

D Caster: Yale University Art Gallery, Mabel Brady Garvan Collection, 1930.1230.

E Teaspoon: The Henry Francis du Pont Winterthur Museum, gift of Mr. and Mrs. Alfred E. Bissell, Ineson-Bissell Silver Collection, 62.0240.130.

F Sleeve buttons (gold): Yale University Art Gallery, Mabel Brady Garvan Collection, 1947.194a-b.

G Sleeve buttons (gold): Yale University Art Gallery, Mabel Brady Garvan Collection, 1936.167.

Samuel Burt A Strainer: Historic Deerfield, Inc. Photograph by Patricia E. Kane.

B Teapot: Museum of Fine Arts, Boston, gift of Dr. and Mrs. Somers H. Sturgis, 1982.651.

William Burt A Flagon: Old South Church, Boston. Photograph courtesy, Museum of Fine Arts, Boston, 85.39.

James Butler A Tablespoon: The Minneapolis Institute of Arts, gift, 1966: Society of Mayflower Descendants through Mr. Wright W. Brooks.

John Butler A Porringer: Yale University Art Gallery, Josephine Setze Fund for the John Marshall Phillips Collection, 1990.49.1.

Joseph Callender A Seal of the Massachusetts Bank: Bank of Boston Corporation.

William Cario, Jr. A Tablespoon: Yale University Art Gallery, Mabel Brady Garvan Collection, 1936.277.

Joseph Clark(e), Jr. A Tablespoon: The Henry Francis du Pont Winterthur Museum, gift of Mr. and Mrs. Alfred E. Bissell, Ineson-Bissell Silver Collection, 62.0240.1014.

Thomas Clark(e) A Tablespoon: The Henry Francis du Pont Winterthur Museum, gift of Mr. and Mrs. Alfred E. Bissell, Ineson-Bissell Silver Collection, 62.0240.1017.

B Teaspoon: The Henry Francis du Pont Winterthur Museum, gift of Mr. and Mrs. Alfred E. Bissell, Ineson-Bissell Silver Collection, 62.0240.150.

Ephraim Cobb A Salver: Yale University Art Gallery, Mabel Brady Garvan Collection, 1930.1172.

John Coburn A Cann: Museum of Fine Arts, Boston, gift of the Estates of the Misses Eunice McLellan and Frances Cordis Cruft, 42.382.

B Tablespoon: The Cleveland Museum of Art, gift of Hollis French, 40.380.

C Sugar tongs: Museum of Fine Arts, Boston, gift of the Misses Catharine Langdon Rogers and Clara Bates Rogers, 14.895.

D Salt spoon: The Henry Francis du Pont Winterthur Museum, gift of Mr. and Mrs. Alfred E. Bissell, Ineson-Bissell Silver Collection, 62.0240.738.002.

Seth Storer Coburn A Nutmeg grater: Museum of Fine Arts, Boston, gift of Miss Elizabeth Morford in Memory of her late partner, Lucy Massenburg, 1973.123.

John Coddington A Tankard: Yale University Art Gallery, Mabel Brady Garvan Collection, 1930.1164.

B Tablespoon: Yale University Art Gallery, Mabel Brady Garvan Collection, 1938.308.

John Coney A Tablespoon: Yale University Art Gallery, gift of the children of Mr. and Mrs. Francis P. Garvan, 1935.154.

B Tobacco box: Yale University Art Gallery, Mabel Brady Garvan Collection, 1935.235.

C Chocolate pot: Museum of Fine Arts, Boston, gift of Dr. Lamar Soutter, Marion E. Davis Fund, and Theodora Wilbour Fund in memory of Charlotte Beebe Wilbour, 1976.771.

D Mourning ring (gold): Peabody Essex Museum. Photograph by Patricia E. Kane.

E Snuffbox: Yale University Art Gallery, Mabel Brady Garvan Collection, 1945.124.

F Spout cup: Museum of Fine Arts, Boston, gift of Cortlandt and James Parker in memory of Major General and Mrs. Cortlandt Parker, 1991.687.

Richard Conyers A Tankard: The Henry Francis du Pont Winterthur Museum, gift of Henry Francis du Pont, 65.1355.

John Coverly A Tankard: The Cleveland Museum of Art, gift of Mrs. Thomas S. Grasselli, 43.187.

B Cann: The Metropolitan Museum of Art, bequest of Alphonso T. Clearwater, 1933, 33.120.264. Photograph by Patricia E. Kane.

Thomas Coverly A Porringer: Hood Museum of Art, Dartmouth College, gift of Louise C. and Frank L. Harrington, Class of 1924, M.984.14.3.

B Pepper pot: Photograph courtesy, William Core Duffy.

C Tablespoon: Yale University Art Gallery, gift of Susan W. Abbott and Lois C. Warner in memory of Marion S. Coffill, 1990.30.3.

D Porringer: Hood Museum of Art, Dartmouth College, gift of Louise C. and Frank L. Harrington, Class of 1924, M.984.14.3.

John Cowell A Cann: Historic Deerfield, Inc., 66-456.

William Cowell, Jr. A Porringer: Yale University Art Gallery, Mabel Brady Garvan Collection, 1930.1253.

B Spout cup: Yale University Art Gallery, Mabel Brady Garvan Collection, 1935.233.

William Cowell, Sr. A Tablespoon: The Henry Francis du Pont Winterthur Museum, gift of Mr. and Mrs. Alfred E. Bissell, Ineson-Bissell Silver Collection, 62.0240.1006.

B Porringer: Yale University Art Gallery, Mabel Brady Garvan Collection, 1932.67.

C Porringer: Yale University Art Gallery, Mabel Brady Garvan Collection, 1930.1253.

D Dram cup: Historic Deerfield, Inc. Photograph by Patricia E. Kane.

E Patch box: The Metropolitan Museum of Art, bequest of Alphonso T. Clearwater, 1933, 33.120.140. Photograph by Patricia E. Kane.

Jonathan Crosby A Cann: Museum of Fine Arts, Boston, Anonymous Loan, 245.41.

Alexander Crouckshanks A Strainer: Museum of Fine Arts, Boston, gift of Miss Caroline E. Cabot, 64.1992.

Thomas Dane A Cream pail: Yale University Art Gallery, Mabel Brady Garvan Collection, 1930.1373.

B Tankard: Maine Historical Society.

Lemuel Davenport A Teaspoon: Photograph courtesy, The Henry Francis du Pont Winterthur Museum, Decorative Arts Photographic Collection, 84.3521.

Elias Davis A Teaspoon: Historic Deerfield, Inc., 61-489.

B Cann: Yale University Art Gallery, Bigelow-Phillips files, Berger photograph file.

C Strainer: Yale University Art Gallery, Bigelow-Phillips files, Berger photograph file.

John Dixwell A Beaker: Museum of Fine Arts, Boston, gift of the First Parish (Unitarian), Brewster, Massachusetts, 13.583.

B Beaker: Museum of Fine Arts, Boston, The Philip Leffingwell Spalding Collection. Given in his memory by Katherine Ames Spalding and Philip Spalding, Oakes Ames Spalding, Hobart Ames Spalding, 42.214.

C Spout cup: The Minneapolis Institute of Arts, gift of James F. and Louise H. Bell, 41.15.

D Snuffbox: Yale University Art Gallery, Mabel Brady Garvan Collection, 1936.1323.

E Ring (gold): Yale University Art Gallery, Mabel Brady Garvan Collection, 1947.193.

John Doane A Tankard: Yale University Art Gallery, Mabel Brady Garvan Collection, 1930.1139.

Joshua Doane A Tablespoon: Museum of Art, Rhode Island School of Design, Mary B. Jackson Fund, 40.171. Photograph by Michael Jorge.

Jeremiah Dummer A Cup: First Baptist Church, Boston. Photograph courtesy, Museum of Fine Arts, Boston.

B Caudle cup: The Henry Francis du Pont Winterthur Museum, gift of Henry Francis du Pont, 65.1349.

Timothy Dwight A Salver: Museum of Fine Arts, Boston, gift of Mr. and Mrs. Dudley Leavitt Pickman, 31.227.

John Edwards A Beaker: Yale University Art Gallery, Mabel Brady Garvan Collection, 1930.1245.

B Two-handled cup: Yale University Art Gallery, Mabel Brady Garvan Collection, 1930.1336.

C Beaker: Yale University Art Gallery, Mabel Brady Garvan Collection, 1930.1244.

D Pepper box: Worcester Art Museum, bequest of Mrs. Frances Merrick Lincoln in memory of Daniel Waldo Lincoln, 1928.31.

Joseph Edwards, Jr. A Tablespoon: Museum of Fine Arts, Boston, gift of the Benevolent Fraternity of Churches, 13.401.

B Creampot: The Cleveland Museum of Art, gift of Hollis French, 40.193.

Samuel Edwards A Mug: Museum of Fine Arts, Boston, gift of the Estates of the Misses Eunice McLellan and Frances Cordis Cruft, 42.384.

B Strainer: Museum of Fine Arts, Boston, gift of the Misses Rose and Elizabeth Townsend, 56.671.

C Tablespoon: Yale University Art Gallery, Mabel Brady Garvan Collection, 1930.3369.

D Tablespoon: Museum of Fine Arts, Boston, bequest of Dr. Samuel A. Green, 19.1387.

E Teaspoon: Museum of Fine Arts, Boston, gift of William Storer Eaton, 37.266.

F Teaspoon: Yale University Art Gallery, gift of Philip K. Kossack, 1985.87.367.

G Teaspoon: The Henry Francis du Pont Winterthur Museum, gift of Mr. and Mrs. Alfred E. Bissell, Ineson-Bissell Silver Collection, 62.0240.705.

Thomas Edwards A Porringer: Yale University Art Gallery research files. Photograph by Patricia E. Kane.

B Chafing dish: Museum of Fine Arts, Boston, gift of the Misses Rose and Elizabeth Townsend, 56.670.

C Teaspoon: The Henry Francis du Pont Winterthur Museum, gift of Mr. and Mrs. Alfred E. Bissell, Ineson-Bissell Silver Collection, 62.0240.226.

D Caster: Museum of Fine Arts, Boston, gift of Anna Quincy Churchill, 61.947.

Stephen Emery A Tablespoon: Museum of Fine Arts, Boston, gift of Mr. and Mrs. Henry Herbert Edes, 36.55.

B Creampot: Museum of Fine Arts, Boston, bequest of Miss Mary F. Kimball, 27.229.

C Teaspoon: Yale University Art Gallery, gift of Philip K. Kossack, 1988.92.17.

D Teaspoon: Museum of Fine Arts, Boston, gift of Miss Gertrude Townsend, 37.616.

E Teaspoon: The Henry Francis du Pont Winterthur Museum, gift of Mr. and Mrs. Alfred E. Bissell, Ineson-Bissell Silver Collection, 62.0240.752.1.

F Salt spoon: Museum of Fine Arts, Boston, bequest of Maxim Karolik, 64.923.

Peter Feurt A Grace cup: Yale University Art Gallery, Mabel Brady Garvan Collection, 1932.91.

Joseph Goldthwait A Tankard: Museum of Fine Arts, Boston, bequest of Charles Hitchcock Tyler, 32.373.

Benjamin Goodwin A Cann: Museum of Fine Arts, Boston, gift of Charles D. Gowing, in memory of Anne Locke Gowing, 1974.455.

William Gowen A Teaspoon: Yale University Art Gallery, gift of Carl R. Kossack, B.S. 1931, M.A. 1933, 1985.84.497.

B Tablespoon: Yale University Art Gallery, gift of Carl R. Kossack, B.S. 1931, M.A. 1933, 1985.86.223.

Thomas Grant A Creampot: Museum of Fine Arts, Boston, gift of Mr. and Mrs. William Beltran de las Casas, 30.733.

John Gray A Teaspoon: Lyman Allyn Art Museum, 1982.21. Photograph by Patricia E. Kane.

Samuel Gray (1684-1713) A Porringer: Yale University Art Gallery, Mabel Brady Garvan Collection, 1930.1147.

Samuel Gray (1710/11-48) A Creampot: Museum of Fine Arts, Boston, gift of George P. Nason in Memory of Lucretia Fall Whitney, 61.114.

B Tankard: Courtesy, S. J. Shrubsole Corporation.

C Tankard: Courtesy, Jonathan Trace.

Bartholomew Green A Spout cup: Museum of Fine Arts, Boston, gift of Miss Sarah Sullivan Perkins and Mrs. Elizabeth Perkins Cabot, 20.1844.

Benjamin Greene A Caster: Yale University Art Gallery, Mabel Brady Garvan Collection, 1941.246.

Rufus Greene A Pepper box: Museum of Fine Arts, Boston, M. and M. Karolik Collection, 39.195.

B Porringer: Yale University Art Gallery, Mabel Brady Garvan Collection, 1930.947.

C Teaspoon: Museum of Fine Arts, Boston, gift of Mr. and Mrs. Henry Herbert Edes, 36.59.

David Greenleaf, Sr. A Tablespoon: The Henry Francis du Pont Winterthur Museum, gift of Mr. and Mrs. Alfred E. Bissell, Ineson-Bissell Silver Collection, 62.0240.1137.002.

Daniel Greenough A Sugar box: The Metropolitan Museum of Art, Rogers Fund, 46.61. Photograph by Patricia E. Kane.

René Grignon A Porringer: Yale University Art Gallery, Mabel Brady Garvan Collection, 1931.754.

Samuel Haley or Healey A Teaspoon: Museum of Fine Arts, Boston, gift of Miss Harriet A. Hill, 15.914.

John Hancock A Tankard: The Metropolitan Museum of Art, bequest of Alphonso T. Clearwater, 1933, 33.120.504. Photograph by Patricia E. Kane.

George Hanners, Jr. A Pepper box: Yale University Art Gallery, Mabel Brady Garvan Collection, 1930.1169.

B Mug: The Metropolitan Museum of Art, bequest of Alphonso T. Clearwater, 1933, 33.120.269. Photograph by Patricia E. Kane.

George Hanners, Sr.   A Tankard: Museum of Fine Arts, Boston, gift of Mrs. Elliot P. Cogswell, 1991.661.

B Cup: Yale University Art Gallery, Mabel Brady Garvan Collection, 1932.64.

C Pepper box: Yale University Art Gallery, Mabel Brady Garvan Collection, 1930.1169.

D Two-handled cup: Second Church, Boston. Photograph courtesy, Museum of Fine Arts, Boston, 28.67.

Samuel Haugh   A Tablespoon: The Mrs. John Emerson Marble Collection of Early American Silver. Photograph by Hope Spencer.

Daniel Henchman   A Coffeepot: Yale University Art Gallery, Mabel Brady Garvan Collection, 1935.236.

B Coffeepot: Yale University Art Gallery, Mabel Brady Garvan Collection, 1935.236.

Benjamin Hiller   A Cup: Yale University Art Gallery, Mabel Brady Garvan Collection, 1930.1318.

William Homes, Jr.   A Teaspoon: Private Collection. Photograph by Patricia E. Kane.

B Tablespoon: The Henry Francis du Pont Winterthur Museum, gift of Mr. and Mrs. Alfred E. Bissell, Ineson-Bissell Silver Collection, 62.0240.1196.

C Teaspoon: Yale University Art Gallery, gift of Carl R. Kossack, B.S. 1931, M.A. 1933, 1985.84.518.

D Tablespoon: Yale University Art Gallery, gift of Carl R. Kossack, B.S. 1931, M.A. 1933, 1986.86.257.

E Porringer: Museum of Fine Arts, Boston, bequest of Charles Hitchcock Tyler, 32.384.

F Teaspoon: Historic Deerfield, Inc., 67.112b. Photograph by Patricia E. Kane.

G Tablespoon: The Henry Francis du Pont Winterthur Museum, gift of Mr. and Mrs. Alfred E. Bissell, Ineson-Bissell Silver Collection, 62.0240.1197.

H Teaspoon: Yale University Art Gallery, gift of Carl R. Kossack, B.S. 1931, M.A. 1933, 1985.84.520.2.

I Porringer: Wadsworth Atheneum, gift from the Estate of Mr. and Mrs. Erving Pruyn.

J Ladle: The Mrs. John Emerson Marble Collection of Early American Silver. Photograph by Patricia E. Kane.

K Teaspoon: Yale University Art Gallery, gift of Carl R. Kossack, B.S. 1931, M.A. 1933, 1985.84.525.1.

L Teaspoon: Yale University Art Gallery, Mabel Brady Garvan Collection, 1935.619.1b.

M Teaspoon: The Mrs. John Emerson Marble Collection of Early American Silver. Photograph by Patricia E. Kane.

N Teaspoon: The Mrs. John Emerson Marble Collection of Early American Silver. Photograph by Hope Spencer.

O Ladle: Yale University Art Gallery, Mabel Brady Garvan Collection, 1931.334.

William Homes, Sr.   A Teaspoon: Private Collection. Photograph by Patricia E. Kane.

B Tablespoon: The Henry Francis du Pont Winterthur Museum, gift of Mr. and Mrs. Alfred E. Bissell, Ineson-Bissell Silver Collection, 62.0240.1196.

C Teaspoon: Yale University Art Gallery, gift of Carl R. Kossack, B.S. 1931, M.A. 1933, 1985.84.518.

D Tablespoon: Yale University Art Gallery, gift of Carl R. Kossack, B.S. 1931, M.A. 1933, 1986.86.257.

E Porringer: Museum of Fine Arts, Boston, bequest of Charles Hitchcock Tyler, 32.384.

F Mourning ring (gold): The Mrs. John Emerson Marble Collection of Early American Silver. Photograph by Hope Spencer.

G Tablespoon: The Henry Francis du Pont Winterthur Museum, gift of Mr. and Mrs. Alfred E. Bissell, Ineson-Bissell Silver Collection, 62.0240.1197.

H Teaspoon: Yale University Art Gallery, gift of Carl R. Kossack, B.S. 1931, M.A. 1933, 1985.84.520.2.

I Porringer: Wadsworth Atheneum, gift from the Estate of Mr. and Mrs. Erving Pruyn.

John Hull A Beaker: First and Second Church, Cambridge, Massachusetts. Photograph courtesy, Museum of Fine Arts, Boston, 161.40.

B Beaker: First Church, Boston. Photograph courtesy, Museum of Fine Arts, Boston, 162.40.

C Beaker: Yale University Art Gallery, Mabel Brady Garvan Collection, 1936.139.

Benjamin Hurd A Tablespoon: Yale University Art Gallery, gift of Frederick C. Kossack, 1985.86.273.

B Tablespoon: Yale University Art Gallery, gift of Frederick C. Kossack, 1985.86.274.1.

C Baptismal basin: Collections of the Public Archives of Nova Scotia, Halifax, Artifact 55.13.

Jacob Hurd A Grace cup: Yale University Art Gallery, Mabel Brady Garvan Collection, 1932.48.

B Teapot: Yale University Art Gallery, Mabel Brady Garvan Collection, 1930.1350.

C Tankard: First Church, Dorchester, Massachusetts. Photograph courtesy, Museum of Fine Arts, Boston.

D Teaspoon: The Henry Francis du Pont Winterthur Museum, gift of Mr. and Mrs. Alfred E. Bissell, Ineson-Bissell Silver Collection, 62.0240.344.

E Tankard: First Church of Deerfield, Deerfield, Massachusetts. Photograph by Amanda Merullo.

F Creampot: The Cleveland Museum of Art, gift of Hollis French, 40.222a.

G Tablespoon: Yale University Art Gallery, Mabel Brady Garvan Collection, 1930.3356.

Nathaniel Hurd A Teapot: Museum of Fine Arts, Boston, gift of Miss Margaret Hall, 63.1044.

B Tablespoon: The Henry Francis du Pont Winterthur Museum, gift of Mr. and Mrs. Alfred E. Bissell, Ineson-Bissell Silver Collection, 62.0240.1205.

Henry Hurst A Tankard: Museum of Fine Arts, Boston, gift of Mr. and Mrs. Dudley Leavitt Pickman, 31.228.

John Jackson A Tablespoon: The Henry Francis du Pont Winterthur Museum, gift of Mr. and Mrs. Alfred E. Bissell, Ineson-Bissell Silver Collection, 62.0240.1219.

John Jagger A Tankard: Museum of Fine Arts, Boston, gift in Memory of T. Jefferson Newbold, 53.382.

David Jesse A Tankard: Museum of Fine Arts, Boston, M. and M. Karolik Collection, 39.185.

William Jones A Porringer: Museum of Fine Arts, Boston, The Philip Leffingwell Spalding

Collection. Given in his memory by Katherine Ames Spalding, and Philip Spalding, Oakes Ames Spalding, Hobart Ames Spalding, 42.219.

B Tablespoon: Yale University Art Gallery, gift of Frederick C. Kossack, 1985.86.282.

C Book clasp: Yale University Art Gallery, Mabel Brady Garvan Collection, 1935.231.

Joseph Kneeland A Nutmeg grater: Museum of Fine Arts, Boston, gift of Mrs. Leslie R. More, 55.114.

Edward Lang A Tablespoon: Yale University Art Gallery, gift of Frederick C. Kossack, 1985.86.293.

B Teaspoon: The Henry Francis du Pont Winterthur Museum, gift of Mr. and Mrs. Alfred E. Bissell, Ineson-Bissell Silver Collection, 62.0240.375.

Jeffrey Lang A Tablespoon: Museum of Fine Arts, Boston, gift of Mr. and Mrs. Dudley Leavitt Pickman, 31.235.

B Mourning ring (gold): Yale University Art Gallery, Mabel Brady Garvan Collection, 1934.344.

C Knee buckle: Yale University Art Gallery, Mabel Brady Garvan Collection, 1948.222.

Nathaniel Lang A Teaspoon: Yale University Art Gallery, gift of Philip K. Kossack, 1985.87.464.

Richard Lang A Tablespoon: The Henry Francis du Pont Winterthur Museum, gift of Mr. and Mrs. Alfred E. Bissell, Ineson-Bissell Silver Collection, 62.0240.1249.

B Teaspoon: The Henry Francis du Pont Winterthur Museum, gift of Mr. and Mrs. Alfred E. Bissell, Ineson-Bissell Silver Collection, 62.0240.386.

Knight Leverett A Caster: The Metropolitan Museum of Art, Rogers Fund, 1948, 48.152a,b.

B Caster: The Metropolitan Museum of Art, Rogers Fund, 1948, 48.152a,b.

Paul Little A Teaspoon: The Mrs. John Emerson Marble Collection of Early American Art. Photograph by Hope Spencer.

B Tablespoon: The Henry Francis du Pont Winterthur Museum, gift of Mr. and Mrs. Alfred E. Bissell, Ineson-Bissell Silver Collection, 62.0240.1247.

William Coffin Little A Tablespoon: The Henry Francis du Pont Winterthur Museum, gift of Mr. and Mrs. Alfred E. Bissell, Ineson-Bissell Silver Collection, 62.0240.1245.

B Teaspoon: The Henry Francis du Pont Winterthur Museum, gift of Mr. and Mrs. Alfred E. Bissell, Ineson-Bissell Silver Collection, 62.0240.357.

C Teaspoon: The Henry Francis du Pont Winterthur Museum, 70.0246.

D Salt spoon: Historic Deerfield, Inc., 62.105. Photograph by Patricia E. Kane.

Elpalet Loring, Sr. A Cann: Yale University Art Gallery, Bigelow-Phillips files, Berger photograph file.

Joseph Loring A Tablespoon: Yale University Art Gallery, Mabel Brady Garvan Collection, 1930.3368.

B Sugar bowl: Museum of Fine Arts, Boston, bequest of Miss Mary L. Eliot, 27.194.

C Tablespoon (altered to feeding spoon): Yale University Art Gallery, Mabel Brady Garvan Collection, 1935.614.

D Cann: Yale University Art Gallery, Mabel Brady Garvan Collection, 1930.1316.

E Tablespoon: Yale University Art Gallery, gift of Frederick C. Kossack, 1985.86.306.

F Tablespoon: Museum of Fine Arts, Boston, gift of Mrs. Mary H. Hayes, 31.20.

G   Spoon (miniature): Yale University Art Gallery, gift of Carl R. Kossack, B.S. 1931, M.A. 1933, 1985.84.325.

H   Salt spoon: Yale University Art Gallery, gift of Philip K. Kossack, 1985.87.140.

I   Porringer: Concord Museum.

J   Tablespoon: The Henry Francis du Pont Winterthur Museum, gift of Mr. and Mrs. Alfred E. Bissell, Ineson-Bissell Silver Collection, 62.0240.1236.

Thomas Lynde   A   Sugar bowl: The Cleveland Museum of Art, gift of Hollis French, 40.233.

B   Tablespoon: Worcester Art Museum, purchased from Marion Coffin, 1940.3.

Thomas Milner (or Miller)   A   Mug: Yale University Art Gallery, given in memory of Carroll Cavanagh, B.A. 1936, by Arthur Winslow II, B.A. 1936.

B   Tankard: The Metropolitan Museum of Art, bequest of Alphonso T. Clearwater, 33.120.505.

C   Tankard: Church of Chelmsford, Chelmsford, Massachusetts. Photograph courtesy, Yale University Art Gallery, Bigelow-Phillips files, Berger photograph file.

Samuel Minott   A   Coffeepot: Yale University Art Gallery, Mabel Brady Garvan Collection, 1930.1354.

B   Coffeepot: Yale University Art Gallery, Mabel Brady Garvan Collection, 1930.1354.

C   Tablespoon: Yale University Art Gallery, gift of Miss Mary B. Smith, 1942.10.

D   Tankard: Museum of Art, Rhode Island School of Design, 23.345. Photograph by Patricia E. Kane.

E   Teaspoon: Historic Deerfield, Inc.

F   Tablespoon: The Henry Francis du Pont Winterthur Museum, gift of Mr. and Mrs. Alfred E. Bissell, Ineson-Bissell Silver Collection, 62.0240.1323.

Nathaniel Morse   A   Chafing dish: Yale University Art Gallery, Mabel Brady Garvan Collection, 1930.1133.

B   Tankard: First Church of Christ in Andover, Andover, Massachusetts. Photograph courtesy, Yale University Art Gallery, Bigelow-Phillips files, Berger photograph file.

C   Teaspoon: The Henry Francis du Pont Winterthur Museum, gift of Mr. and Mrs. Alfred E. Bissell, Ineson-Bissell Silver Collection, 62.0240.446.

D   Spout cup: Yale University Art Gallery, Mabel Brady Garvan Collection, 1930.1288.

E   Teaspoon: Historic Deerfield, Inc.

F   Cup: Historic Deerfield, Inc., 1288. Photograph by Amanda Merullo.

G   Candlestick: Historic Deerfield, Inc., 66-454. Photograph by Amanda Merullo.

Obadiah Morse   A   Teaspoon: Yale University Art Gallery, gift of Philip K. Kossack, 1985.87.506.

David Colson Moseley   A   Cann: Museum of Fine Arts, Boston, Charles T. and Susan P. Baker, by bequest of the latter, 21.1257.

B   Beaker: The Metropolitan Museum of Art, bequest of Alphonso T. Clearwater, 33.120.116.

C   Ladle: Bowdoin College Museum of Art, 1912.4.2.

D   Serving spoon: Private collection. Photograph by Carl Kaufman.

E   Spoon: Photograph courtesy, The Henry Francis du Pont Winterthur Museum, Decorative Arts Photographic Collection, 69.7078.

Joseph Moulton (1724-95) A Teaspoon: The Henry Francis du Pont Winterthur Museum, gift of Mr. and Mrs. Alfred E. Bissell, Ineson-Bissell Silver Collection, 62.0240.427.

B Teaspoon: The Henry Francis du Pont Winterthur Museum, gift of Mr. and Mrs. Alfred E. Bissell, Ineson-Bissell Silver Collection, 62.0240.406.

C Teaspoon: Photograph courtesy, The Henry Francis du Pont Winterthur Museum, Decorative Arts Photographic Collection, 88.3489.

D Tablespoon: The Henry Francis du Pont Winterthur Museum, gift of Mr. and Mrs. Alfred E. Bissell, Ineson-Bissell Silver Collection, 62.0240.1305.

Joseph Moulton A Teaspoon: The Henry Francis du Pont Winterthur Museum, gift of Mr. and
(1744-1816) Mrs. Alfred E. Bissell, Ineson-Bissell Silver Collection, 62.0240.427.

B Salt spoon: Yale University Art Gallery, Mabel Brady Garvan Collection, 1936.241a.

C Tablespoon: The Henry Francis du Pont Winterthur Museum, gift of Mr. and Mrs. Alfred E. Bissell, Ineson-Bissell Silver Collection, 62.0240.1268.

D Tablespoon: The Henry Francis du Pont Winterthur Museum, gift of Mr. and Mrs. Alfred E. Bissell, Ineson-Bissell Silver Collection, 62.0240.1305.

E Teaspoon: The Henry Francis du Pont Winterthur Museum, gift of Mr. and Mrs. Alfred E. Bissell, Ineson-Bissell Silver Collection, 62.0240.406.

F Tablespoon: The Henry Francis du Pont Winterthur Museum, 72.0157.

William Moulton A Tablespoon: Yale University Art Gallery, Mabel Brady Garvan Collection, 1938.302.

B Teaspoon: Photograph courtesy, The Henry Francis du Pont Winterthur Museum, Decorative Arts Photographic Collection, 79.4493.

C Teaspoon: Yale University Art Gallery, gift of Mrs. Glen Wright, 1952.22.1.

Gideon Myrick A Tablespoon: Museum of Fine Arts, Boston, gift in Memory of Ruth P. and Pauline Dennis, 1990.349.

Abijah Northey A Teaspoon: The Henry Francis du Pont Winterthur Museum, gift of Mr. and Mrs. Alfred E. Bissell, Ineson-Bissell Silver Collection, 62.0240.441.

B Tablespoon: Peabody Essex Museum. Photograph by Patricia E. Kane.

David Northey A Mourning ring (gold): Museum of Fine Arts, Boston, The Philip Leffingwell Spalding Collection. Given in his memory by Katherine Ames Spalding and Philip Spalding, Oakes Ames Spalding, Hobart Ames Spalding, 42.250.

B Teaspoon: Museum of Fine Arts, Boston, bequest of Maxim Karolik, 64.922.

C Cup: Yale University Art Gallery, Mabel Brady Garvan Collection, 1930.1317.

William Northey A Tablespoon: Peabody Essex Museum, 132,991.2. Photograph by Patricia E. Kane.

B Teaspoon: Peabody Essex Museum, 108,430. Photograph by Patricia E. Kane.

John Noyes A Candlestick: Museum of Fine Arts, Boston, gift of Miss Clara Bowdoin Winthrop, 54.595.

B Flagon: Museum of Fine Arts, Boston, gift of the Benevolent Fraternity of Churches, Silver of the Church in Brattle Square, 13.404.

Andrew Oliver A Tablespoon: The Henry Francis du Pont Winterthur Museum, gift of Mr. and Mrs. Alfred E. Bissell, Ineson-Bissell Silver Collection, 62.0240.1348.

B Teaspoon: Museum of Fine Arts, Boston, gift of Mrs. Eugene C. Hultman, 48.235.

C Ring (gold): Yale University Art Gallery, Mabel Brady Garvan Collection, 1936.173.

Peter Oliver   A   Flagon: The Henry Francis du Pont Winterthur Museum, bequest of Henry Francis du Pont, 66.1052.

  B   Tankard (miniature): Worcester Art Museum, gift of Mr. and Mrs. Samuel T. Hobbs, 1957.38.

Jonathan Otis   A   Tablespoon: Yale University Art Gallery, Mabel Brady Garvan Collection, 1935.237.

  B   Beaker: Yale University Art Gallery, Mabel Brady Garvan Collection, 1930.140.

  C   Beaker: Yale University Art Gallery, Mabel Brady Garvan Collection, 1931.354.

  D   Beaker: Yale University Art Gallery, Mabel Brady Garvan Collection, 1936.140.

  E   Caster: Museum of Art, Rhode Island School of Design, Mary B. Jackson Fund, 36.002.

IP   A   Cup: Yale University Art Gallery, Mabel Brady Garvan Collection, 1932.65.

  B   Tablespoon: The Henry Francis du Pont Winterthur Museum, gift of Mr. and Mrs. Alfred E. Bissell, Ineson-Bissell Silver Collection, 62.0240.1359.

Daniel Parker   A   Tablespoon: Yale University Art Gallery, gift of J. Duke Smith, 1942.12A.

  B   Teaspoon: The Cleveland Museum of Art, gift of Hollis French, 40.245.

  C   Strainer: Private Collection. Photograph by John Stauffer.

Isaac Parker   A   Tablespoon: Yale University Art Gallery, Mabel Brady Garvan Collection, 1930.1263.

  B   Tablespoon: Pocumtuck Valley Memorial Association, Memorial Hall Museum.

John Parkman   A   Tablespoon: National Museum of American History, Smithsonian Institution, 383557.

Timothy Parrott   A   Porringer: Yale University Art Gallery, Bigelow-Phillips files, Berger photograph file.

Parsons   A   Teaspoon: Yale University Art Gallery, Bigelow-Phillips files, Berger photograph file.

Houghton Perkins   A   Teaspoon: The Henry Francis du Pont Winterthur Museum, gift of Mr. and Mrs. Alfred E. Bissell, Ineson-Bissell Silver Collection, 62.0240.524.

  B   Teaspoon: Museum of Fine Arts, Boston, gift of Miss Laura Furness, 43.1349.

Benjamin Pierpont   A   Tablespoon: Yale University Art Gallery, gift of Frederick C. Kossack, 1985.86.368.

  B   Teaspoon: Historic Deerfield, Inc. Photograph by Amanda Merullo.

  C   Strainer spoon: Yale University Art Gallery, Mabel Brady Garvan Collection, 1941.306.

John Pitts   A   Tablespoon: Photograph courtesy, The Henry Francis du Pont Winterthur Museum, Decorative Arts Photographic Collection, 80.3958.

William Pollard   A   Cann: Yale University Art Gallery, John Marshall Phillips Collection, 1954.10.1.

John Potwine   A   Tablespoon: The Henry Francis du Pont Winterthur Museum, gift of Mr. and Mrs. Alfred E. Bissell, Ineson-Bissell Silver Collection, 62.0240.1361.

  B   Teapot: Yale University Art Gallery, John Marshall Phillips Collection, 1955.10.3.

  C   Tablespoon: Yale University Art Gallery, Mabel Brady Garvan Collection, 1930.3305.

  D   Mourning ring (gold): Historic Deerfield, Inc. Photograph by Amanda Merullo.

Jonathan Reed A Two-handled cup: Second Church, Boston. Photograph courtesy, Museum of Fine Arts, Boston, 256.53.

B Tablespoon: The Metropolitan Museum of Art, bequest of Charles Allen Munn, 1924, 24.109.62. Photograph by Patricia E. Kane.

Paul Revere, Jr. A Salt: Yale University Art Gallery, Mabel Brady Garvan Collection, 1930.1393.

B Tankard: The Henry Francis du Pont Winterthur Museum, gift of Henry Francis du Pont, 57.0859.001.

C Mustard pot: Yale University Art Gallery, Mabel Brady Garvan Collection, 1930.956.

D Tablespoon: Yale University Art Gallery, William Inglis Morse Collection, gift of his daughter, Mrs. Frederick W. Hilles, 1959.17.4.

E Tankard: Yale University Art Gallery, Mabel Brady Garvan Collection, 1930.1196.

F Teaspoon: Yale University Art Gallery, William Inglis Morse Collection, gift of his daughter, Mrs. Frederick W. Hilles, 1959.17.6.

G Creampot: The Cleveland Museum of Art, gift of J.H. Wade, 21.88.

H Sugar tongs: Yale University Art Gallery, Mabel Brady Garvan Collection, 1930.1444.

Paul Revere, Sr. A Tankard: Yale University Art Gallery, Mabel Brady Garvan Collection, 1930.962.

B Sleeve buttons (gold): Yale University Art Gallery, William Inglis Morse Collection, gift of his daughter, Mrs. Frederick W. Hilles, 1959.17.2.

C Caster: Private Collection. Photograph by Patricia E. Kane.

D Teapot: Museum of Fine Arts, Boston, bequest of Miss Lois Lilley Howe, 64.2048.

E Porringer: Yale University Art Gallery, William Inglis Morse Collection, gift of his daughter, Mrs. Frederick W. Hilles, 1959.17.1.

F Chafing dish: Museum of Fine Arts, Boston, Pauline Revere Thayer Collection, 35.1756.

G Tablespoon: Museum of Fine Arts, Boston, Pauline Revere Thayer Collection, 35.1818.

Silas Rice A Tablespoon: Photograph courtesy, The Henry Francis du Pont Winterthur Museum, Decorative Arts Photographic Collection, 70.1926.

Daniel Rogers A Tablespoon: The Henry Francis du Pont Winterthur Museum, gift of Mr. and Mrs. Alfred E. Bissell, Ineson-Bissell Silver Collection, 62.0240.1421.

B Tablespoon: The Henry Francis du Pont Winterthur Museum, gift of Mr. and Mrs. Alfred E. Bissell, Ineson-Bissell Silver Collection, 67.0101.

C Tablespoon: The Henry Francis du Pont Winterthur Museum, gift of Mr. and Mrs. Alfred E. Bissell, Ineson-Bissell Silver Collection, 62.0240.1418.

D Tablespoon: The Henry Francis du Pont Winterthur Museum, gift of Mr. and Mrs. Alfred E. Bissell, Ineson-Bissell Silver Collection, 62.0240.1417.

E Tablespoon: The Henry Francis du Pont Winterthur Museum, gift of Mr. and Mrs. Alfred E. Bissell, Ineson-Bissell Silver Collection, 62.0240.1421.

F Tablespoon: The Henry Francis du Pont Winterthur Museum, gift of Mr. and Mrs. Alfred E. Bissell, Ineson-Bissell Silver Collection, 62.0240.1417.

G Tablespoon: The Henry Francis du Pont Winterthur Museum, gift of Mr. and Mrs. Alfred E. Bissell, Ineson-Bissell Silver Collection, 62.0240.1418.

H Salt spoon: The Henry Francis du Pont Winterthur Museum, gift of Mr. and Mrs. Alfred E. Bissell, Ineson-Bissell Silver Collection, 62.0240.817.

I Teaspoon: Yale University Art Gallery, Mabel Brady Garvan Collection, 1935.591.

J Locket (gold): Museum of Fine Arts, Boston, The Philip Leffingwell Spalding Collection. Given in his memory by Katherine Ames Spalding and Philip Spalding, Oakes Ames Spalding, Hobart Ames Spalding, 42.248.

William Rouse A Beaker: First Congregational Church, Guilford, Connecticut. Photograph by Michael Agee.

B Skillet: Yale University Art Gallery, gift of Mr. and Mrs. Donald W. Henry, B.A. 1939, 1976.127.

C Patch box: Yale University Art Gallery, John Marshall Phillips Collection, gift of his nephews, Donald and Marshall Phillips, 1955.10.2.

Daniel Russell, Sr. A Porringer: Yale University Art Gallery, Mabel Brady Garvan Collection, 1931.352a.

B Teaspoon: The Henry Francis du Pont Winterthur Museum, gift of Mr. and Mrs. Alfred E. Bissell, Ineson-Bissell Silver Collection, 62.0240.530.

C Locket (gold): Museum of Fine Arts, Boston, The Philip Leffingwell Spalding Collection. Given in his memory by Katherine Ames Spalding and Philip Spalding, Oakes Ames Spalding, Hobart Ames Spalding, 42.249.

Joseph Russell A Beaker: The Metropolitan Museum of Art, bequest of Alphonso T. Clearwater, 1933, 33.120.119.

Moody Russell A Tablespoon: The Henry Francis du Pont Winterthur Museum, gift of Mr. and Mrs. Alfred E. Bissell, Ineson-Bissell Silver Collection, 62.0240.1426.

B Tablespoon: The Henry Francis du Pont Winterthur Museum, gift of Mr. and Mrs. Alfred E. Bissell, Ineson-Bissell Silver Collection, 62.0240.1427.

C Tankard: Yale University Art Gallery, Mabel Brady Garvan Collection, 1934.359.

D Porringer: Yale University Art Gallery, Mabel Brady Garvan Collection, 1930.1161.

Benjamin Sanderson A Dram cup: Yale University Art Gallery, Mabel Brady Garvan Collection, 1930.1372.

Robert Sanderson, Jr. A Caudle cup: The Henry Francis du Pont Winterthur Museum, gift of Henry Francis du Pont, 61.504.

Robert Sanderson, Sr. A Beaker: First Church, Boston. Photograph courtesy, Museum of Fine Arts, Boston, 162.40.

B Tankard: Private Collection. Photograph by Michael Agee.

C Porringer: Museum of Fine Arts, Boston, The Philip Leffingwell Spalding Collection. Given in his memory by Katherine Ames Spalding and Philip Spalding, Oakes Ames Spalding, Hobart Ames Spalding, 42.252.

Thomas Savage, Sr. A Tankard: The Metropolitan Museum of Art, gift of Frances E. Markoe and Stephen C. Markoe, 1943, 43.83.3. Photograph by Patricia E. Kane.

B Porringer: Yale University Art Gallery, Mabel Brady Garvan Collection, 1930.1254.

William Simpkins A Porringer: Hood Museum of Art, Dartmouth College, gift of Louise C. and Frank L. Harrington, Class of 1924, M.972.81.

B Bowl: Museum of Fine Arts, Boston, gift of Miss Ruth K. Richardson in Memory of T. Fales Gray and Mrs. Gedney K. Richardson, 63.2767.

C Teapot: Private Collection. Photograph courtesy, The Henry Francis du Pont Winterthur Museum, 84.260a.

D Tablespoon: The Henry Francis du Pont Winterthur Museum, gift of Mr. and Mrs. Alfred E. Bissell, Ineson-Bissell Silver Collection, 62.0240.1470.

E Teaspoon: The Henry Francis du Pont Winterthur Museum, gift of Mr. and Mrs. Alfred E. Bissell, Ineson-Bissell Silver Collection, 62.0240.665.

F Sleeve buttons (gold): The Metropolitan Museum of Art, 67.82.1. Photograph by Patricia E. Kane.

Thomas Skinner A Teaspoon: The Henry Francis du Pont Winterthur Museum, gift of Mr. and Mrs. Alfred E. Bissell, Ineson-Bissell Silver Collection, 62.0240.691.

B Tablespoon: The Henry Francis du Pont Winterthur Museum, gift of Mr. and Mrs. Alfred E. Bissell, Ineson-Bissell Silver Collection, 62.0240.1477.

C Teaspoon: The Henry Francis du Pont Winterthur Museum, gift of Mr. and Mrs. Alfred E. Bissell, Ineson-Bissell Silver Collection, 62.0240.662.

Jeremiah Snow, Jr. A Tablespoon: The Henry Francis du Pont Winterthur Museum, gift of Mr. and Mrs. Alfred E. Bissell, Ineson-Bissell Silver Collection, 62.0240.1478.

B Tablespoon: National Museum of American History, Smithsonian Institution, 383583.

C Tablespoon: Photograph Courtesy, The Henry Francis du Pont Winterthur Museum, Decorative Arts Photographic Collection, 81.3805.

Jeremiah Snow III A Tablespoon: Historic Deerfield, Inc.

B Tablespoon: National Museum of American History, Smithsonian Institution, 383583.

C Tablespoon: Photograph Courtesy, The Henry Francis du Pont Winterthur Museum, Decorative Arts Photographic Collection, 81.3805.

William Swan A Cann: Museum of Fine Arts, Boston, M. and M. Karolik Collection, 39.187.

B Cann: Private Collection. Photograph by Samuels Studio.

C Serving spoon: Woodstock Historical Society, Woodstock, Vermont, gift of Mrs. Byron Dexter, 61.2.11.

John Symmes A Tablespoon: The Henry Francis du Pont Winterthur Museum, gift of Mr. and Mrs. Alfred E. Bissell, Ineson-Bissell Silver Collection, 62.0240.1474.

Benjamin Tappan A Teaspoon: The Henry Francis du Pont Winterthur Museum, gift of Mr. and Mrs. Alfred E. Bissell, Ineson-Bissell Silver Collection, 62.0240.696.

B Tablespoon: Private Collection. Photograph by Patricia E. Kane.

John Touzell A Tablespoon: Yale University Art Gallery, Mabel Brady Garvan Collection, 1939.680.

Thomas Townsend A Tankard: Bowdoin College Museum of Art, gift of Henry Brewer Quinby, 1923.108.

B Tablespoon: Yale University Art Gallery, Mabel Brady Garvan Collection, 1936.279.

C Caster: Collection of Kevin Faughman.

Jonathan Trott A Tablespoon: Photograph courtesy, The Henry Francis du Pont Winterthur Museum, Decorative Arts Photographic Collection, 21.2447.

B Tablespoon: Photograph courtesy, The Henry Francis du Pont Winterthur Museum, Decorative Arts Photographic Collection, 89.3076.

James Turner A Pepper box: Yale University Art Galley, Mabel Brady Garvan Collection, 1948.280.

Andrew Tyler A Porringer: Museum of Fine Arts, Boston, The Philip Leffingwell Spalding Collection. Given in his memory by Katherine Ames Spalding and Philip Spalding, Oakes Ames Spalding, Hobart Ames Spalding, 42.258.

B Caster: The Art Institute of Chicago, Mr. and Mrs. William Y. Hutchinson Fund, 1988.194.

C Porringer: Museum of Fine Arts, Boston, The Philip Leffingwell Spalding Collection. Given in his memory by Katherine Ames Spalding and Philip Spalding, Oakes Ames Spalding, Hobart Ames Spalding, 42.258.

D Mourning ring (gold): Museum of Fine Arts, Boston, bequest of Maxim Karolik, 64.855.

E Tablespoon: The Henry Francis du Pont Winterthur Museum, gift of Mr. and Mrs. Alfred E. Bissell, Ineson-Bissell Silver Collection, 62.0240.1489.

I. or T. Tyler A Teaspoon: The Henry Francis du Pont Winterthur Museum, gift of Mr. and Mrs. Alfred E. Bissell, Ineson-Bissell Silver Collection, 62.0240.720.

B Teaspoon: The Henry Francis du Pont Winterthur Museum, Funds for purchase gift of the Ineson-Bissell Fund, 76.0219.

C Teaspoon: The Henry Francis du Pont Winterthur Museum, gift of Mr. and Mrs. Alfred E. Bissell, Ineson-Bissell Silver Collection, 62.0240.700.

Kiliaen van Rensselaer A Teapot: Collection of The New-York Historical Society, 1915.20.

Barnabas Webb A Teaspoon: Yale University Art Gallery, gift of Carl R. Kossack, B.S. 1931, M.A. 1933, 1985.84.685.

B Sugar tongs: Museum of Fine Arts, Boston, gift of J. Vaughan Dennett, 38.981.

Edward Webb A Tablespoon: Yale University Art Gallery, Mabel Brady Garvan Collection, 1930.3345.

William Whittemore A Snuffbox: The Henry Francis du Pont Winterthur Museum, gift of Henry Francis du Pont, 65.1364A,B.

B Patch box: Museum of Art, Rhode Island School of Design, gift of Mrs. Murray S. Danforth, 63.015.

Edward Winslow A Beaker: Yale University Art Gallery, Mabel Brady Garvan Collection, 1930.1246.

B Sugar box: The Henry Francis du Pont Winterthur Museum, gift of Henry Francis du Pont, 59.3363.

C Mug: Museum of Fine Arts, Boston, bequest of Miss Lois Lilley Howe, 64.2046.

Elijah Yeomans A Tablespoon: Courtesy, The Henry Francis du Pont Winterthur Museum, gift of Mr. and Mrs. Alfred E. Bissell, Ineson-Bissell Silver Collection, 62.0240.1600.

B Teaspoon: Yale University Art Gallery, gift of Carl R. Kossack, B.S. 1931, M.A. 1933, 1985.84.702.

Appendix G

Chronology of Colonial Massachusetts Silversmiths and Jewelers

Explanatory Notes

Names in roman caps & lowercase (John Mansfield) are those of silversmiths.

Names in small caps (RICHARD STORER) are those of silversmiths who had at least one apprentice.

Names in sans-serif caps and lowercase (Francis Solomon Légaré) are those of jewelers.

Names in sans-serif small caps (RENÉ GRIGNON) are those of jewelers who had at least one apprentice.

Each craftsman's name that is not within parentheses appears opposite the year as of which he began working at the given location.

The year following each craftsman's name that is within parentheses denotes the approximate year in which he completed his apprenticeship.

An italicized location (*London*) preceding a craftsman's name denotes the location from which he came.

An italicized location following a craftsman's name (*Jamaica*) denotes the location to which he went.

A dagger (†) signifies that the location from which a craftsman came is uncertain.

An asterisk (∗) signifies that the identity of a craftsman's master is uncertain.

	Silversmiths and Jewelers Who Trained Elsewhere and Immigrated to Boston	Silversmiths and Jewelers Who Worked in Boston: Hull & Sanderson Lineage	Silversmiths and Jewelers Who Worked in Boston: Henry Hurst Lineage
1635	1635 *London* John Mansfield		
1636			
1637			
1638			
1639	*London* RICHARD STORER	RICHARD STORER (John Hull, 1646)	
1640			
1641			
1642			
1643			
1644			
1645			
1646		JOHN HULL and 1652 ROBERT SANDERSON, SR. (John Sanderson, *died* 1658; John Hall, 1662; Joseph Sanderson, 1663; JEREMIAH DUMMER, 1667; Samuel Paddy, 1667, *Jamaica*; Benjamin Sanderson, 1671; Daniel Quincy, 1672; Robert Sanderson, Jr., 1673; Timothy Dwight, 1675; Samuel Clarke, 1681)	
1647			
1648			
1649			

Silversmiths and Jewelers Who Worked in Boston: William Cowell, Sr., Lineage	Silversmiths and Jewelers Who Worked in Boston: Unidentified Lineage	Silversmiths and Jewelers Who Worked in Outlying Towns
1635		
1636		
1637		
1638		
1639		
1640		
1641		
1642		
1643		
1644		
1645		
1646		
1647		
1648		
1649		

Silversmiths and Jewelers Who Trained Elsewhere and Immigrated to Boston	Silversmiths and Jewelers Who Worked in Boston: Hull & Sanderson Lineage	Silversmiths and Jewelers Who Worked in Boston: Henry Hurst Lineage
1650		
1651		
1652 *London, Hampton New Hampshire, Watertown* ROBERT SANDERSON, SR.		
1653		
1654		
1655		
1656		
1657		
1658		
1659		
1660		
1661		
1662		
1663		
1664		

Silversmiths and Jewelers Who Worked in Boston: William Cowell, Sr., Lineage	Silversmiths and Jewelers Who Worked in Boston: Unidentified Lineage	Silversmiths and Jewelers Who Worked in Outlying Towns
1650		
1651		
1652		
1653		
1654		
1655		
1656		
1657		
1658		
1659		
1660		
1661		
1662		
1663		
1664		

	Silversmiths and Jewelers Who Trained Elsewhere and Immigrated to Boston	Silversmiths and Jewelers Who Worked in Boston: Hull & Sanderson Lineage	Silversmiths and Jewelers Who Worked in Boston: Henry Hurst Lineage
1665			
1666			
1667		JEREMIAH DUMMER (JOHN CONEY, 1677; SAMUEL PHILLIPS*, 1679, *Salem*; Kiliaen van Rensselaer, 1683, *Watervliet New York*; Eleazer Russell, 1684; EDWARD WINSLOW, 1690; JOHN EDWARDS*, 1692; John Allen*, 1693; John Noyes, 1695; JOHN DIXWELL, 1701; Daniel Gookin, 1704; Shubael Dummer, 1707)	
1668			
1669			
1670			
1671			
1672			
1673			
1674	Richard Nevill†		
1675	*Wesel* WILLIAM ROUSE		
1676			
1677	*London* Thomas Higginson	JOHN CONEY (Benjamin Coney, 1694, *Stratford Connecticut*; Peter Oliver, 1703; Benjamin Hiller, 1709; NATHANIEL MORSE, 1709; ANDREW TYLER, 1714; Thomas Bradford, 1718; PAUL REVERE, SR., 1723)	
1678	*London?* John Bingham		
1679	*London* Nathaniel Gay		

Silversmiths and Jewelers Who Worked in Boston: William Cowell, Sr., Lineage	Silversmiths and Jewelers Who Worked in Boston: Unidentified Lineage	Silversmiths and Jewelers Who Worked in Outlying Towns
1665		
1666		
1667		
1668		
1669		
1670		
1671		
1672		
1673		
1674		
1675	WILLIAM ROUSE (Thomas Wyllys, 1686, *Jamaica*; Michael Rouse, *finished with Henry Hurst*)	
1676		
1677	Thomas Higginson, 1686, *Salem*	
1678		
1679		

	Silversmiths and Jewelers Who Trained Elsewhere and Immigrated to Boston	Silversmiths and Jewelers Who Worked in Boston: Hull & Sanderson Lineage	Silversmiths and Jewelers Who Worked in Boston: Henry Hurst Lineage
1680			
1681			
1682			
1683			
1684	*London* Matthew Mabely		
1685	*South Carolina* Benjamin Grignon		
1686	*London?* John Cole		
1687	*France, England* FRANCIS LÉGARÉ *France, England* RENÉ GRIGNON		
1688			
1689			
1690	*London* William Cross	EDWARD WINSLOW (Isaac Anthony, 1711, *Newport Rhode Island*; John Coddington, 1711, *Newport Rhode Island*; William Pollard, 1711; MOODY RUSSELL, 1715, *Barnstable*; John Banks*, 1717)	
1691			
1692	*London* David Jesse	JOHN EDWARDS (THOMAS EDWARDS, 1722; SAMUEL EDWARDS, 1726)	
1693			
1694			

Silversmiths and Jewelers Who Worked in Boston: William Cowell, Sr., Lineage	Silversmiths and Jewelers Who Worked in Boston: Unidentified Lineage	Silversmiths and Jewelers Who Worked in Outlying Towns
1680		
1681		
1682	Jonathan Belcher	
1683		
1684		
1685	THOMAS SAVAGE, SR. (Samuel Haugh, 1698)	
1686		
1687	RENÉ GRIGNON *Norwich Connecticut* (Thomas Earthy, 1701?; Joseph Soames, 1702)	SAMUEL PHILLIPS *Salem* (Daniel Greenough*, 1707, *New Castle New Hampshire*); Thomas Higginson *Salem, Guilford Connecticut*
1688		FRANCIS LÉGARÉ *Braintree* (Francis Solomon Légaré, 1688, *Boston, Charleston South Carolina*; Daniel Légaré, 1710, *Braintree, Boston*)
1689		
1690		
1691		
1692		
1693		
1694		

	Silversmiths and Jewelers Who Trained Elsewhere and Immigrated to Boston	Silversmiths and Jewelers Who Worked in Boston: Hull & Sanderson Lineage	Silversmiths and Jewelers Who Worked in Boston: Henry Hurst Lineage
1695			
1696			
1697	*London* Richard Conyers *London?* Thomas Milner		
1698			
1699	*Sweden, London* HENRY HURST		HENRY HURST (Michael Rouse,* 1708, *Maryland*; JOHN BURT,* 1714)
1700			
1701	*France?* Moses Prevereau	JOHN DIXWELL (WILLIAM JONES, 1716, *Marblehead*; Daniel Russell, Sr., 1719, *Newport Rhode Island*; Joseph Kneeland, 1721; Joseph Goldthwait, 1727)	
1702			
1703			
1704	*London* Edward Webb		
1705			
1706			
1707			
1708	Thomas Mullins†		
1709		NATHANIEL MORSE (John Banks, *finished with* Edward Winslow; Obadiah Morse, 1733)	

	Silversmiths and Jewelers Who Worked in Boston: William Cowell, Sr., Lineage	Silversmiths and Jewelers Who Worked in Boston: Unidentified Lineage	Silversmiths and Jewelers Who Worked in Outlying Towns
1695			
1696			
1697		Samuel Foster	
1698			
1699		Job Prince, *Milford Connecticut*	Francis Bassett *Charlestown*
1700			
1701			
1702			
1703			
1704	WILLIAM COWELL, SR. (John Potwine, 1719, *Hartford Connecticut*; John Cowell, 1728; RUFUS GREENE, 1728; Benjamin Greene, 1734; William Cowell, Jr., 1734; Charles Simpson, 1734, *North Carolina*)		
1705		SAMUEL GRAY, *New London Connecticut* (JOHN GRAY, 1713)	
1706			
1707			
1708			
1709			

	Silversmiths and Jewelers Who Trained Elsewhere and Immigrated to Boston	Silversmiths and Jewelers Who Worked in Boston: Hull & Sanderson Lineage	Silversmiths and Jewelers Who Worked in Boston: Henry Hurst Lineage
1710	*England* Peter Denman		
1711			
1712			
1713			
1714		ANDREW TYLER (GEORGE HANNERS, SR., 1717; Theophilus Burrill, 1721, *New London Connecticut*; Knight Leverett, 1724; William Whittemore, 1731, *Portsmouth New Hampshire*)	JOHN BURT (JACOB HURD,* 1724; WILLIAM SIMPKINS,* 1725; Samuel Gray, 1731; John Blowers, 1732; JOHN PARKMAN, 1737; Joshua Doane, 1738, *Providence Rhode Island*; Edmund Mountfort, 1738; John Doane, 1741; SAMUEL BURT, 1745; William Burt, 1747; BENJAMIN BURT, 1750)
1715	*London* Peter Boutett		
1716	*Ireland* Daniel Gibbs *Ireland* Abraham Barnes		
1717		GEORGE HANNERS, SR. (George Hanners, Jr., 1742)	
1718			
1719			
1720			
1721	*London* JAMES BOYER		
1722	Matthew Delaney†	THOMAS EDWARDS (Thomas Coverly, 1727; Benjamin Edwards, Jr., 1752, *Woburn*; Zachariah Brigden, 1755)	
1723		PAUL REVERE, SR. (PAUL REVERE, JR., 1755)	
1724	*New York* John LeRoux		JACOB HURD (Isaac Perkins, 1731; JOSIAH AUSTIN,* 1741, *Charlestown*; John Ball, 1745, *Concord*; DANIEL HENCHMAN, 1751; Benjamin Goodwin, 1752; NATHANIEL HURD, 1752; Houghton Perkins, 1756, *Taunton*; Benjamin Hurd, 1760)

Silversmiths and Jewelers Who Worked in Boston: William Cowell, Sr., Lineage	Silversmiths and Jewelers Who Worked in Boston: Unidentified Lineage	Silversmiths and Jewelers Who Worked in Outlying Towns
1710		
1711		
1712		
1713	JOHN GRAY *New London Connecticut* (Daniel Deshon, 1720, *New London Connecticut*)	
1714		
1715		MOODY RUSSELL *Barnstable* (Joseph Russell, 1723 *Barnstable, Bristol*; SOLOMON STURGIS, 1724, *Barnstable*; EPHRAIM COBB,* 1729, *Plymouth, Barnstable*; Jonathan Otis,* 1744, *Newport*; Abraham Higgins, 1759, *Barnstable*; Elpalet Loring, 1761, *Barnstable*)
1716	Jonathan Reed	
1717	Bartholomew Green	
1718		
1719		
1720		
1721	JAMES BOYER (Andrew Oliver, 1745; Daniel Boyer, 1746)	WILLIAM JONES *Marblehead* (John Jagger, 1734, *Marblehead, Boston*)
1722		
1723		
1724		SOLOMON STURGIS *Barnstable* (Samuel Sturgis, 1758, *Barnstable*)

	Silversmiths and Jewelers Who Trained Elsewhere and Immigrated to Boston	Silversmiths and Jewelers Who Worked in Boston: Hull & Sanderson Lineage	Silversmiths and Jewelers Who Worked in Boston: Henry Hurst Lineage
1725			1725 WILLIAM SIMPKINS (Jaspar Starr, 1731, *New London Connecticut*; Basil Dixwell, 1732, *Providence Rhode Island*; Thomas Barton Simpkins, 1749; Daniel Rogers, 1756, *Ipswich*; John Codner,* 1775)
1726	*Dublin* William Caddow	SAMUEL EDWARDS (JOHN COBURN, 1745; DANIEL PARKER, 1747; Ebenezer Austin, 1754, *Hartford Connecticut*; Joseph Edwards, Jr.,* 1758)	
1727	*New York* Peter Feurt		
1728			
1729			
1730			
1731			
1732			
1733			
1734			
1735	*London* Asahel Mason WILLIAM CARIO, SR.†		
1736			
1737			JOHN PARKMAN (Benjamin Goodwin, *finished with Jacob Hurd*)
1738			
1739			

	Silversmiths and Jewelers Who Worked in Boston: William Cowell, Sr., Lineage	Silversmiths and Jewelers Who Worked in Boston: Unidentified Lineage	Silversmiths and Jewelers Who Worked in Outlying Towns
1725		Thomas Townsend	
1726			
1727			Joseph Watkins *Marblehead*
1728	RUFUS GREENE (WILLIAM HOMES, SR., 1737)	JEREMIAH SNOW, JR. (Jeremiah Snow III, 1756, *Springfield*)	JEFFREY LANG *Salem* (Richard Lang, 1754, *Salem*; Nathaniel Lang, 1757, *Salem*)
1729			EPHRAIM COBB *Plymouth, Barnstable* (Nathaniel Barstow*, 1758, *Sunderland*)
1730		Thomas McCullough	DAVID NORTHEY *Salem* (William Northey, 1756, *Salem*; Edward Northey, 1758, *Salem, Gloucester, Manchester*; Abijah Northey, 1761, *Salem*)
1731			
1732		James Nash, Jr.	
1733			
1734		John Pitts; Joseph Pitts; James Butler *Halifax Nova Scotia*; Thomas Skinner *Marblehead*; John Coverly	
1735		Josiah Flagg, Sr.; John Whittemore; WILLIAM CARIO, SR. (William Cario, Jr., 1757)	
1736		William Swan, *Worcester*; Stephen Winter	Thomas Skinner *Marblehead*
1737	WILLIAM HOMES, SR. (Barnabas Webb, 1750; SAMUEL MINOTT*, 1753; William Homes, Jr., 1763; Benjamin Tappan, Jr., 1768, *Northampton*)		
1738		Joseph Candish; Edward Foster; Thomas Eastwick	
1739		Edward Whittemore	Joseph Gardner *Salem*

Silversmiths and Jewelers Who Trained Elsewhere and Immigrated to Boston	Silversmiths and Jewelers Who Worked in Boston: Hull & Sanderson Lineage	Silversmiths and Jewelers Who Worked in Boston: Henry Hurst Lineage
1740		
1741		
1742		
1743		
1744		
1745	JOHN COBURN (David Greenleaf, Sr., 1758, *Lancaster*; Seth Storer Coburn, 1765, *Springfield*; James Ridgway, 1774)	SAMUEL BURT (Caleb Parker, 1753)
1746		
1747	DANIEL PARKER (John Symmes, 1761; Stephen Morse,* 1765, *Gloucester*; Stephen Emery, 1772)	
1748		
1749		
1750		BENJAMIN BURT (Samuel Pedrick, 1764, *Marblehead*; John Andrew, 1768, *Salem*; Edward Dane, 1771; Caleb Swan, 1775, *Charlestown*)
1751		DANIEL HENCHMAN (Benjamin Callender, 1771)
1752		NATHANIEL HURD (Joseph Callender, 1773)
1753		
1754		

	Silversmiths and Jewelers Who Worked in Boston: William Cowell, Sr., Lineage	Silversmiths and Jewelers Who Worked in Boston: Unidentified Lineage	Silversmiths and Jewelers Who Worked in Outlying Towns
1740		Joshua Eames	
1741		Samuel Haley; Stephen Callas; Timothy Parrott	JOSIAH AUSTIN *Charlestown* (Nathaniel Austin,* 1755, *Charlestown, Boston*; Thomas Lynde,* 1766, *Charlestown, Worcester*; James Austin,* 1771, *Boston, Watertown*; Eleazer Wyer, 1773, *Charlestown*); SAMUEL DAVENPORT, *Milton* (Lemuel Davenport, 1761, *Stoughton*); WILLIAM MOULTON, *Newbury,*
1742		William Breed; JOSEPH HILLER, SR. (JOHN WELSH,* 1751)	*Hampstead New Hampshire* (Joseph Moulton, 1765, *Newburyport*); Jacob Morse,* 1772, *Westfield*
1743		James Turner, *Philadelphia*; Samuel Usher	
1744		Ebenezer Balch, *Hartford*; Luke Greenough Pierce; John Bridge	Richard Richardson *Charlestown*
1745			JOSEPH MOULTON *Newbury* (Israel Bartlett, 1769, *Newbury, Haverhill*)
1746		Thomas Clark	
1747		THOMAS DANE (James Dane, 1756, *Falmouth Maine*)	
1748			JOHN TOUZELL *Salem* (Thomas Grant,* 1752, *Marblehead*; Joseph Hathorne, 1766, *Salem*; John Hathorne, 1770, *Salem*)
1749		George Foster	
1750		John Jackson *Nantucket*	
1751		Benjamin Pierpont; Jonathan Trott *New London Connecticut*; JOHN WELSH (John Dexter, 1756, *Marlborough*; Isaac Parker, 1770, *Deerfield*)	John Ball *Concord*
1752		BENJAMIN LORING (Loring Bailey,* 1761, *Hingham*; Joseph Loring,* 1764; Caleb Beal*, 1767)	Benjamin Edwards, Jr. *Woburn, Framingham*; Samuel Glover *Marblehead*
1753	SAMUEL MINOTT (Samuel Bartlett, 1775, *Concord*)		John Jackson *Nantucket*; John Hancock *Charlestown, Providence, Maryland*
1754			William Swan *Marlborough, Worcester*

	Silversmiths and Jewelers Who Trained Elsewhere and Immigrated to Boston	*Silversmiths and Jewelers Who Worked in Boston: Hull & Sanderson Lineage*	*Silversmiths and Jewelers Who Worked in Boston: Henry Hurst Lineage*
1755		PAUL REVERE, JR. (David Colson Moseley, 1773; Samuel Hichborn, 1773)	
1756			
1757			
1758			
1759			
1760			
1761			
1762			
1763			
1764			
1765	*Philadelphia* Daniel Doler		
1766			
1767			
1768	*London* Alexander Crouckshanks		
1769			

	Silversmiths and Jewelers Who Worked in Boston: William Cowell, Sr., Lineage	Silversmiths and Jewelers Who Worked in Boston: Unidentified Lineage	Silversmiths and Jewelers Who Worked in Outlying Towns
1755		JOHN BUTLER *Falmouth Maine* (Paul Little, 1761)	
1756		Samuel Barrett *Nantucket*	Daniel Steward *Lunenberg*; Daniel Rogers *Ipswich*
1757			
1758		Andrew Croswell *Plymouth*; Benjamin Smith	David Greenleaf, Sr. *Lancaster, Norwich*
1759		Josiah Flagg, Jr.	Jeremiah Snow III *Springfield*
1760			
1761		William Delarue	Henry Buxton *Danvers*; Isaac Guernsey *Northampton*
1762		George Trott	
1763		James Sherman	Andrew Croswell *Plymouth*; Samuel Barrett *Nantucket*; Henry Phillips Sweetser *Charlestown*
1764			Edward Lang *Salem*
1765			Elisha Gray *Barnstable*; Richard Trumbull *Charlestown*; N. Bartlet; John Dexter *Marlborough*; Stephen Morse *Gloucester*
1766		Jonathan Crosby	William C. Little *Newburyport*
1767			John Raymond *Salem*; Elias Davis *Newburyport*; William Bubier *Marblehead*; Samuel Pedrick *Marblehead*
1768		James Sherman	John Andrew *Salem*; James Hill *Charlestown*; Reuben Earle *Lancaster*; Benjamin Tappan, Jr. *Northampton*
1769			Nathaniel Barrett *Nantucket*

	Silversmiths and Jewelers Who Trained Elsewhere and Immigrated to Boston	Silversmiths and Jewelers Who Worked in Boston: Hull & Sanderson Lineage	Silversmiths and Jewelers Who Worked in Boston: Henry Hurst Lineage
1770			
1771			
1772			
1773			
1774			
1775			

Silversmiths and Jewelers Who Worked in Boston: William Cowell, Sr., Lineage	Silversmiths and Jewelers Who Worked in Boston: Unidentified Lineage	Silversmiths and Jewelers Who Worked in Outlying Towns
1770		William Gowen *Medford*; Seth Ring *Salem*; Silas Rice *Lancaster*
1771		
1772	Samuel Belknap	Houghton Perkins *Taunton*; Robert Swan *Andover*; Benjamin Bunker *Nantucket*; Elijah Yeomans *Hadley*
1773		Thomas Hunt *Northampton*; Seth Sadler *Upton*
1774		Jonas Bruce *Bolton*
1775	Nathaniel Croswell; T. or I. Tyler.	Timothy Sibley, Jr. *Sutton*; Ebenezer Staniford *Ipswich*; Seth Storer Coburn *Springfield*; Daniel Brown *Ipswich*; Ebenezer White *Northfield*

Index

Bagnall, John, 999
Bagnall, Martha, 999
Bagnall, Samuel (clockmaker) (1718– after 1773), 107n.58, 999, **1000**
Bagnall, Sarah, 999
Bagnall, Thomas, 999
Bailey, Anna, 163
Bailey, Anna Loring (b. 1706), 163
Bailey, Calvin, 1001
Bailey, Chris, 1002, 1015, 1017
Bailey, Elizabeth, 1000
Bailey, John, 721
Bailey, John (John Sr.'s father), 1000
Bailey, John, Jr. (clockmaker) (1751– 1823), **1000**, 1001
Bailey, John, Sr. (clockmaker) (1730– 1810), **1000–01**
Bailey, Lebbeus, 1001
Bailey, Loring (silversmith) (1740–ca. 1814), **163–64**, 184, 185, 663
 works by, **164**
Bailey, Mary, 163
Bailey, Ruth (Randall), 1000
Bailey, Thomas (patron), 868
Bailey, Thomas, Jr., 163
Bailey, Thomas, Sr., 163
Baker, Elizabeth, 785
Baker, Ephraim, 170
Baker, George, 335, 785
Baker, Jabez, 229
Baker, John, 206, 318, 776
Baker, Dr. John, 802
Baker, John (patron), 381
Baker, Sarah (Hurd) (Perkins), 766, 768, 769
Baker, Silence, 391
Baker, Stephen, 133, 532
Baker, William, 406, 769
Baker family, 235, 598
Balch, Daniel, Jr., 711
Balch, Daniel, Sr. (clockmaker) (1734/35–90), **1001**
Balch, Ebenezer (1766–1846), 165
Balch, Ebenezer (silversmith and clockmaker) (1723–1808), 106n.56, 107n.59, **164–66**
 works by, **165–66**
Balch, Hannah (Clement), 1001
Balch, J., Jr., 185
Balch, Jonathan, 165, 892
Balch, Joseph (1760–1855), 165
Balch, Joseph (d. 1733), 164
Balch, Lois (Belden), 165
Balch, Martha (Newmarsh), 164
Balch, Mary (b. 1752), 165
Balch, Mary (Osgood) (1689/90– 1752), 164, 165
Balch, Rebecca (Stone), 1001
Balch, Samuel, 164
Balch, Sarah (Belden), 165
Balch, Timothy, 165
Balch, William, 1001
Baldwin, Eunice (Jenison), 576

Baldwin, Ezra, 743
Baldwin, Isaac, 576
Baldwin, Jabez, 1045
Baldwin and Baker (firm), 1045
Balestier, Maria (Revere), 795, 803
Ball, Abigail (Child), 167
Ball, Briggs, 169n.9
Ball, Elizabeth, 166, 167, 169n.9
Ball, Hannah (Clark), 166–67
Ball, John (1660–1703), 166
Ball, John (d. 1768) (scrivener), 166
Ball, John (silversmith) (1723/24– 81+), **166–69**, 180, 508
 apprenticeship of, 108n.72, 133, 166, 580
 marks of, 80
 relocating of, 109n.76, 117, 166
 works by, **167–68**
 workshop of, 31, 166–67
Ball, John, Jr., 166
Ball, Jonathan (b. 1691), 166–67, 560
Ball, Jonathan (b. 1755), 167, 169n.9
Ball, Marcy, 169n.9
Ball, Rachel (Clark), 166
Ball, Sarah (Brooks) (1723/24–80), 166, 167
Ball, Sarah (John Ball's daughter), 166
Ball, Thomas Brooks, 169n.9
Ballard, John, 227, 773
Ballentine, John, 637–38
balls (tools), **1053**
Balston, Hannah (Hirst), 418
Balston, Nathaniel, 418
Baltimore (Maryland), 95
Bancroft, Daniel, 647
Bangs, Hannah, 395
Bangs, Joshua, 395
Banister, Samuel, 700
Banks, Elizabeth (Gill), 170n.6
Banks, John (d. 1698), 169
Banks, John (husband of Elizabeth Gill), 170n.6
Banks, John (silversmith) (ca. 1696– 1737+), 105n.48, **169–70**, 320, 700, 701, 938, 971
Banks, John, Jr. (b. 1722), 169
Banks, Mehitable (Mattocks), 169
Banks, Sarah (Gwin), 169, 170
Banks family, 836
Bannister, Thomas, 780
Bant, William, 294
baptismal basins
 by B. Burt, 228
 by J. Burt, 249
 by J. Coburn, 298
 by J. Coney, 321
 by W. Cowell, Sr., 350
 by J. Dixwell, 379
 by John Edwards, 411
 by Joseph Edwards, Jr., 424
 by S. Edwards, 446

baptismal basins (*continued*)
 by T. Edwards, 461
 by S. Emery, 471
 by B. Hurd, 576
 by J. Hurd, 584–85
 by J. Kneeland, 638, 639
 by J. Loring, 668
 by S. Minott, 689
 by J. Potwine, 781
 by P. Revere, Jr., 806
 by D. Russell, 868
 by E. Winslow, 976
Barber, Maria, 813, 850
Barbour, Peter, 357
Barker, Benjamin, 693
Barker, Ebenezer, 912
Barley, Thomas, 856
Barnard, John, 262
Barnard, Joseph, 835
Barnard, Rachel, 463
Barnard, Samuel, 196, 411, 835
Barnes, Abraham (silversmith) (w. ca. 1716), 106n.49, **170**
Barnes, Benjamin, 171, 172n.8
Barnes, Elizabeth, 292
Barnes, Huldah, 171
Barnes, Isaiah, 171
Barnes, James (b. 1703), 172n.14
Barnes, James (b. 1711/12), 171
Barnes, James, Jr. (silversmith) (1680– 1721?), 64, **171–72**, 316, 623, 888, 939, 971
 apprenticeship of, 386
 other business interests of, 104n.25, 105n.47
 as silversmith, 104n.25, 105n.47, 171
Barnes, James, Sr. (d. 1711), 171
Barnes, John, 171, 172n.8
Barnes, Jonathan, 292
Barnes, Lydia, 172n.14
Barnes, Mary (b. 1725/26), 171
Barnes, Mary (Gross), 171
Barnes, Mary (Tay) (d. before 1727), 171
Barnes, Mercy, 359
Barnes, Peter, 171, 172n.8
Barnes, Temperance, 171
Barnes, Thomas (husband of Lydia), 172n.14
Barnes, Thomas (silversmith's brother), 171
Barnstable (Massachusetts), 111, 112, *115*, 122
 Congregational Churches (East and West Parishes), 665, 874, 976
 See also Cobb, Ephraim; Gray, Elisha; Higgins, Abraham; Loring, Elpalet; Russell, Joseph and Moody; Sturgis, Samuel and Solomon
baroque style, 77
Barr, Elaine, 38n.2
Barr, I., 343

C

T

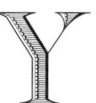

Composed in Adobe Caslon and Monotype Bulmer
by the Monotype Composition Company, Inc., Baltimore, Maryland.

Printed on 50-lb Finch Opaque Text
by the William J. Mack Company, North Haven, Connecticut.

Bound by the Acme Bookbinding Company, Inc., Charlestown, Massachusetts.

Production supervision by Yale University Printing and Graphic Services.

Designed by Roland A. Hoover.